D1370360

AMERICAN WRITERS

AMERICAN WRITERS

JAY PARINI
Editor

SUPPLEMENT XXVII

CHARLES SCRIBNER'S SONS
A part of Gale, Cengage Learning

GALE
CENGAGE Learning·

Farmington Hills, Mich • San Francisco • New York • Waterville, Maine
Meriden, Conn • Mason, Ohio • Chicago

GALE
CENGAGE Learning®

American Writers Supplement XXVII

Editor in Chief: Jay Parini

Project Editor: Lisa Kumar

Permissions: Carissa Poweleit

Composition and Electronic Capture: Gary Leach

Manufacturing: Rita Wimberley

© 2017 Charles Scribner's Sons, a part of Gale, Cengage Learning

ALL RIGHTS RESERVED. No part of this work covered by the copyright herein may be reproduced, transmitted, stored, or used in any form or by any means graphic, electronic, or mechanical, including but not limited to photocopying, recording, scanning, digitizing, taping, Web distribution, information networks, or information storage and retrieval systems, except as permitted under Section 107 or 108 of the 1976 United States Copyright Act, without the prior written permission of the publisher.

This publication is a creative work fully protected by all applicable copyright laws, as well as by misappropriation, trade secret, unfair competition, and other applicable laws. The authors and editors of this work have added value to the underlying factual material herein through one or more of the following: unique and original selection, coordination, expression, arrangement, and classification of the information.

For product information and technology assistance, contact us at
Gale Customer Support, 1-800-877-4253.
For permission to use material from this text or product,
submit all requests online at
www.cengage.com/permissions
Further permissions questions can be emailed to
permissionrequest@cengage.com

While every effort has been made to ensure the reliability of the information presented in this publication, Gale, a part of Cengage Learning, does not guarantee the accuracy of the data contained herein. Gale accepts no payment for listing; and inclusion in the publication of any organization, agency, institution, publication, service, or individual does not imply endorsement of the editors or publisher. Errors brought to the attention of the publisher and verified to the satisfaction of the publisher will be corrected in future editions.

EDITORIAL DATA PRIVACY POLICY. Does this publication contain information about you as an individual? If so, for more information about our editorial data privacy policies, please see our Privacy Statement at www.gale.cengage.com

LIBRARY OF CONGRESS CATALOGING-IN-PUBLICATION DATA

American writers: a collection of literary biographies / Leonard Unger, editor in chief.
   p. cm.
   The 4-vol. main set consists of 97 of the pamphlets originally published as the University of Minnesota pamphlets on American writers; some have been rev. and updated. The supplements cover writers not included in the original series.
   Supplement 2, has editor in chief, A. Walton Litz; Retrospective suppl. 1, c. 1998, was edited by A. Walton Litz & Molly Weigel; Suppl. 5–26 have as editor-in-chief, Jay Parini.
   Includes bibliographies and index.
   Contents: v. 1. Henry Adams to T.S. Eliot — v. 2. Ralph Waldo Emerson to Carson McCullers — v. 3. Archibald MacLeish to George Santayana — v. 4. Isaac Bashevis Singer to Richard Wright — Supplement\[s\]: 1, pt. 1. Jane Addams to Sidney Lanier. 1, pt. 2. Vachel Lindsay to Elinor Wylie. 2, pt. 1. W.H. Auden to O. Henry. 2, pt. 2. Robinson Jeffers to Yvor Winters. — 4, pt. 1. Maya Angelou to Linda Hogan. 4, pt. 2. Susan Howe to Gore Vidal — Suppl. 5. Russell Banks to Charles Wright — Suppl. 6. Don DeLillo to W. D. Snodgrass — Suppl. 7. Julia Alvarez to Tobias Wolff — Suppl. 8. T.C. Boyle to August Wilson. — Suppl. 11 Toni Cade Bambara to Richard Yates.
   ISBN 978-0-684-32512-5
   1. American literature—History and criticism. 2. American literature—Bio-bibliography. 3. Authors, American—Biography. I. Unger, Leonard. II. Litz, A. Walton. III. Weigel, Molly. IV. Parini, Jay. V. University of Minnesota pamphlets on American writers.

PS129 .A55
810'.9
\[B\]
                         73-001759

ISBN-13: 978-0-684-32512-5

This title is also available as an e-book.
ISBN-13: 978-0-684-32513-2
Contact your Gale, Cengage Learning sales representative for ordering information.

Charles Scribner's Sons an imprint of Gale, Cengage Learning
27500 Drake Rd.
Farmington Hills, MI 48331-3535

Printed in Mexico
1 2 3 4 5 6 7 20 19 18 17 16

Acknowledgments

The editors wish to thank the copyright holders of the excerpted criticism included in this volume and the permissions managers of many book and magazine publishing companies for assisting us in securing reproduction rights. Following is a list of the copyright holders who have granted us permission to reproduce material in this volume of *American Writers*. Every effort has been made to trace copyright, but if omissions have been made, please let us know

.

COPYRIGHTED EXCERPTS IN *AMERICAN WRITERS*, VOLUME 27, WERE REPRODUCED FROM THE FOLLOWING SOURCES:

BARNHARDT, WILTON. *Gospel* foreword, St. Martin's Press, 1993. Palgrave Macmillan. / "Mrs. Dimbleby" in *The Story Behind the Story: 26 Writers and How They Work,* W.W. Norton and Company, 2004, pp. 194. © W.W. Norton & Company, Inc. DNU. / Bronwyn Miller, "Bookreporter.com Interview," The Book Report Inc., 2013. © The Book Report. / Bill Krueger, "Wilton Barnhardt: I'm nervous about being in any camp," *Red & White for Life.* © NC State Alumni Association, 2013. © NC State Alumni Association. / Dennis McLellan, "Barnhardt's *Gospel*: A Loose Canon," *Los Angeles Times,* 1993. © Los Angeles Times. / Review of *Gospel, Kirkus Reviews.* © Kirkus Media LLC, 1993. / Bill Krueger, "NC State professor's novel optioned for HBO comedy series," *Red & White for Life.* © NC State Associataion, 2014.

BRAINARD, JOE. *Self Portrait,* Siamese Banana Press, 1972. © The Library of America and thanks to The Hatcher Graduate Library, University of Michigan, Archive of Anne Waldman.

CHRISTGAU, ROBERT. "Beth Ann and Macrobioticism," *The New Journalism,* Tom Wolfe and E.W. Johnson, eds. Harper and Row, 1973, pp. 333-337. HarperCollins Children's Books. / "Writing About Music Is Writing First," *Popular Music.* © Cambridge Journals, 2005. / Hampton Stevens, "Rock Hall of Fame Snubs Red-State Favorites," © Washington Times LLC, 2011. / Jim Farber, "Kiss' Improbably Entry into the Rock and Roll Hall of Fame Is the Final Slide down a Slippery Slope," *NY Daily News,* 2014. © New York Daily News.

COHEN, LEONARD. "Hallelujah," *Leonard Cohen: Poems and Songs,* Everyman's Library/ Alfred A. Knopf, 2011, pp. 167, 168. Leonard Cohen. / "As the Mist Leaves No Scar," *Leonard Cohen: Poems and Songs,* Everyman's Library/ Alfred A. Knopf, 2011, p. 22. / "Fingerprints," *Leonard Cohen: Poems and Songs,* Everyman's Library/Alfred A. Knopf, 2011, p. 62. / "Death of a Ladies Man," *Leonard Cohen: Poems and Songs,* Everyman's Library/Alfred A. Knopf, 2011, pp. 126-128. / "You Know Who I Am," *Leonard Cohen: Poems and Songs,* Everyman's

ACKNOWLEDGEMENTS

Library/Alfred A. Knopf, 2011, p. 88. / "Bird On a Wire," *Leonard Cohen: Poems and Songs,* Everyman's Library/Alfred A. Knopf, 2011, p. 89. / "Suzanne," *Leonard Cohen: Poems and Songs,* Everyman's Library/Alfred A. Knopf, 2011, pp. 64-65. / "Joan of Arc," *Leonard Cohen: Poems and Songs,* Everyman's Library/Alfred A. Knopf, 2011, pp. 92-83. / "Love Is a Fire," *Leonard Cohen: Poems and Songs,* Everyman's Library/Alfred A. Knopf, 2011, p. 10. / "This Is for You," *Leonard Cohen: Poems and Songs,* Everyman's Library/Alfred A. Knopf, 2011, p. 80. / "You Live Like a God," *Leonard Cohen: Poems and Songs,* Everyman's Library/Alfred A. Knopf, 2011, p. 81. / "Came So Far for Beauty," *Leonard Cohen: Poems and Songs,* Everyman's Library/Alfred A. Knopf, 2011, p. 146. / "Diamonds in the Mine," *Leonard Cohen: Poems and Songs,* Everyman's Library/Alfred A. Knopf, 2011, p. 96. / "If It Be Your Will," *Leonard Cohen: Poems and Songs,* Everyman's Library/Alfred A. Knopf, 2011, p. 166. / "Dance Me to the End of Love," *Leonard Cohen: Poems and Songs,* Everyman's Library/Alfred A. Knopf, 2011, p. 162. / "Love Itself," *Leonard Cohen: Poems and Songs,* Everyman's Library/Alfred A. Knopf, 2011, p. 216. / "The Tower of Song," *Leonard Cohen: Poems and Songs,* Everyman's Library/Alfred A. Knopf, 2011, p. 180. / "I'm Your Man," *Leonard Cohen: Poems and Songs,* Everyman's Library/Alfred A. Knopf, 2011, pp. 174-174. / "The Future," *Leonard Cohen: Poems and Songs,* Everyman's Library/Alfred A. Knopf, 2011, pp. 185-186. / "Everybody Knows," *Leonard Cohen: Poems and Songs,* Everyman's Library/Alfred A. Knopf, 2011, p. 178. / "Anthem," *Leonard Cohen: Poems and Songs,* Everyman's Library/Alfred A. Knopf, 2011, p. 189. / "Amen," *Leonard Cohen: Poems and Songs,* Everyman's Library/Alfred A. Knopf, 2011, p. 226. / "Feels So Good," *Leonard Cohen: Poems and Songs,* Everyman's Library/Alfred A. Knopf, 2011, p. 232. / "You Got Me Singing," *Popular Problems,* Sony, 2014.

ELLIS, BRET EASTON. Medium.com, 2013. © Medium.com

HICKAM, HOMER. Jack Bales, "*October Sky*: From Coalwood to Hollywood," *Free Lance-Star,* Fredricksburg.com, 2002. © Fredricksburg.com. / Interview with Imagiverse interview, Imagiverse Educational Consortium, 2003. © Imagiverse Educational Consortium.

HOWARD, ROBERT E. "A Warning," *Robert E. Howard: Selected Poems,* Mind's Eye/HyperPublishing, 2012, p. 18. © 2012 Paradox Entertainment. All rights reserved. Reproduced with permission. / "A Word from the Outer Dark," *Robert E. Howard: Selected Poems,* Mind's Eye/HyperPublishing, 2012, p. 19. © 2012 Paradox Entertainment. All rights reserved. Reproduced with permission. / "Forbidden Magic," *Robert E. Howard: Selected Poems,* Mind's Eye/HyperPublishing, 2012, p. 309. © 2012 Paradox Entertainment. / "This Is a Young World," *Robert E. Howard: Selected Poems,* Mind's Eye/HyperPublishing, 2012, p. 215. © 2012 Paradox Entertainment. All rights reserved. Reproduced with permission. / "A Sonnet of Good Cheer," *Robert E. Howard: Selected Poems,* Mind's Eye/HyperPublishing, 2012, p. 128. © 2012 Paradox Entertainment. All rights reserved. Reproduced with permission.

MACKEY, NATHANIEL. "Capricorn Rising," *Eroding Witness,* University of Illinois Press, 1985, p. 83. © University of Illinois Press. / "Song of the Andoumboulou: 1," *Eroding Witness,* University of Illinois Press, 1985, pp. 33, 35. © University of Illinois Press. / "Poem for Don Cherry," *Eroding Witness,* University of Illinois Press, 1985, pp. 60. © University of Illinois Press. / "Song of the Andoumboulou: 7," *Eroding Witness,* University of Illinois Press, 1985, p. 54. © University of Illinois Press. / "Song of the Andoumboulou: 6," *Eroding Witness,* University of Illinois Press, 1985, p. 50. © University of Illinois Press. / "Song of the Andoumboulou: 8," *School of Udhra,* City Lights Books, 1993, p. 3. © City Lights Publishers. / "Melin," *School of Udhra,* City Lights Books, 1993, p. 23. © City Lights Publishers. / "Out Island," *School of Udhra,* City Lights Books, 1993, pp. 49-53. © City Lights Publishers. / "Epigraph to Song of the Andnoumboulou: 16," *Whatsaid Serif,* City Lights Books, 1998, p. 3.

ACKNOWLEDGEMENTS

© City Lights Publishers. / "Song of the Andoumboulou: 16," *Whatsaid Serif,* City Lights Books, 1998, pp. 3, 4. © City Lights Publishers. / "Song of the Andoumboulou: 26," *Whatsaid Serif,* City Lights Books, 1998, p. 54. © City Lights Publishers. / "Last poem," *Whatsaid Serif,* City Lights Books, 1998, p. 111. © City Lights Publishers. / "Preface," *Splay Anthem,* New Directions, 2006, p. ix. © New Directions Publishing Corporation. / "Andoumboulous Brush," *Splay Anthem,* New Directions, 2006, pp. 3, 5. © New Directions Publishing Corporation. / "On Antiphon Island," *Splay Anthem,* New Directions, 2006, pp. 64, 65. © New Directions Publishing Corporation. / "Day After Day of the Dead," *Nod House,* New Directions, 2011, pp. 48-50. © New Directions Publishing Corporation.

MULLEN, HARRYETTE. "Telegraphs from a Distracted Sibyl," *The Cracks Between What We Are and What We Are Supposed to Be: Essays and Interviews,* University of Alabama Press, 2012, p. 19. / "A profusion of oleanders ???? to beautify," *Urban Tumbleweed: Notes from a Tanka Diary.* © 2013 by Harryette Mullen. / "Thinking thought to be a body...", "marry at a hotel, annul 'em", and "tomboy girl with cowboy boots" from *Recyclopedia.* © 1991, 1995 by Harryette Mullen. All reprinted with the permission of The Permissions Company, Inc., on behalf of Graywolf Press, www.graywolfpress.org / Excerpt from *Sleeping with the Dictionary,* University of California Press, 2002, p. 67. © 2002 University of California Press. All rights reserved. Reproduced with permission.

MUNRO, ALICE. "The Office," *Dance of the Happy Shades,* Penguin Books, 1983, p. 60. © Penguin Books Ltd.

MYERS, WALTER DEAN. "Where Are the People of Color in Children's Books?" *New York Times,* © The New York Times Company, 2014. / "Best of Banned Books Week: Interview with Walter Dean Myers; Story Snoops blog," StorySnoops.com, *Children's Book Review,* 2012. Story Snoops. / Hazel Rochman, "The Booklist Interview," Booklist Publications, 2000, p. 1101. © Booklist Online. / Michael Cart, review of *Darius and Twig,* Booklist Publications, 2013. © Booklist Online. / Jeffrey Brown, "Author Walter Dean Myers Says 'Reading Is Not Optional' for Kids," PBS NewsHour, NewsHour Productions LLC, 2012. © Online NewsHour (PBS). / Michael Cart, review of *Invasion,* Booklist Publications, 2013, p. 42. © Booklist Online. / "Fast Sam, Cool Clyde and Stuff," *Kirkus Reviews.* © Kirkus Media LLC, 1975. / Michael Cart, review of *Harlem,* Booklist Publications, 1997, p. 1021. © Booklist Online. / Ian Chipman, review of *The Cruisers,* Booklist Publications, 2010, p. 96. © Booklist Online. / Felicia R. Lee, "Walter Dean Myers Dies at 76; Wrote of Black Youth for the Young," *New York Times,* 2014, p. B16. © The New York Times Company.

RASH, RON. "Invocation," *Eureka Mill,* Hub City Press, 1998, pp. xv-xvi. Copyright © 1998 Hub City Press. All rights reserved. Reproduced with permission. / "Tobacco," *Eureka Mill,* Hub City Press, 1998, p. 6. Copyright © 1998 Hub City Press. All rights reserved. Reproduced with permission. / "Hand-bill Distributed in Buncombe County, North Carolina: 1915," *Eureka Mill,* Hub City Press, 1998, p. 8. Copyright © 1998 Hub City Press. All rights reserved. Reproduced with permission. / "Last Interview," *Eureka Mill,* Hub City Press, 1998, p. 52. Copyright © 1998 Hub City Press. All rights reserved. Reproduced with permission. / "Sunday Evening at Middlefork Creek Pentecostal Church," *Among the Believers,* Iris Press, 2013, p. 22. Iris Press. / "A Preacher Who Takes up Serpents Laments the Presence of Skeptics in His Church," *Among the Believers,* Iris Press, 2013, pp. 19-20. Iris Press. / "The Preacher Is Called to Testify for the Accused," *Among the Believers,* Iris Press, 2013, p. 28. Iris Press. / "Signs," *Among the Believers,* Iris Press, 2013, p. 33. Iris Press. / "Good Friday, 1995, Driving Westward," *Among the Believers,* Iris Press, 2013, p. 71. Iris Press. / "The Men Who Raised the Dead," *Raising the Dead,* Iris Press, 2002, p. 71. Iris Press. / "The Vanquished," *Raising*

ACKNOWLEDGEMENTS

the Dead, Iris Press, 2002, p. 6. Iris Press. / "The Wolves in the Ashville Zoo," *Raising the Dead,* Iris Press, 2002, p. 56. Iris Press. / "Shelton Laurel," *Raising the Dead,* Iris Press, 2002, pp. 23-24. Iris Press. / "Resolution," *Waking,* Hub City Press, 2011, p. xi. Copyright © 2011 Hub City Press. All rights reserved. Reproduced with permission. / "Water Quilt," *Waking,* Hub City Press, 2011, p. 70. Copyright © 2011 Hub City Press. All rights reserved. Reproduced with permission. / W.B. Yeats, "Lapis Lazuli," *W.B Yeats: The Poems,* Macmillan, 1983, p. 295. Palgrave Macmillan. / Robert Frost, "Design," *The Poetry of Robert Frost: The Collected Poems,* St. Martin's Griffin, 1969, p. 302. Palgrave Macmillan. / Elizabeth Bishop, "The Fish," *Poems,* Farrar, Straus & Giroux., 2011, p. 44. © Farrar, Straus & Giroux.

STONE, RUTH. "Rhythm," *Cheap: New Poems and Ballads,* Harcourt Brace Jovanovich, 1975, pp. 51-52. © Harcourt Brace. / "Shotgun Wedding," *Cheap: New Poems and Ballads,* Harcourt Brace Jovanovich, 1975, p. 55. © Harcourt Brace. / "Dedication," *Cheap: New Poems and Ballads,* Harcourt Brace Jovanovich, 1975. © Harcourt Brace. / "The Season," *In an Iridescent Time,* Harcourt, Brace and Company, 1959. © Harcourt Brace. / "Union," *In an Iridescent Time,* Harcourt, Brace and Company, 1959. © Harcourt Brace. / "One-Reel Tragedy," *In an Iridescent Time,* Harcourt, Brace and Company, 1959. © Harcourt Brace. / "Dedication," *In an Iridescent Time,* Harcourt, Brace and Company, 1959. © Harcourt Brace. / "On the Way," *Simplicity,* Paris Press, 1995, p. 61. © Paris Press. / "Dedication," *Simplicity,* Paris Press, 1995. © Paris Press. / "Being Human," *What Love Comes To: New & Selected Poems,* Copper Canyon Press, 2008, p. 117. © Copper Canyon Press. / "Lighter Than Air," *What Love Comes To: New & Selected Poems,* Copper Canyon Press, 2008, p. 85. © Copper Canyon Press. / "Eta Carinae," *What Love Comes To: New & Selected Poems,* Copper Canyon Press, 2008, p. 24. © Copper Canyon Press. / "Dedication," *What Love Comes To: New & Selected Poems,* Copper Canyon Press, 2008. © Copper Canyon Press. / "Reading the Russians," *In the Next Galaxy,* Copper Canyon Press, 2004, p. 53. © Copper Canyon Press. / "Don't Miss It," *In the Next Galaxy,* Copper Canyon Press, 2004, p. 48. © Copper Canyon Press. / "Dedication," *In the Next Galaxy,* Copper Canyon Press, 2004. © Copper Canyon Press. / "Happiness," *Second-Hand Coat: Poems New and Selected,* Yellow Moon Press, 1991, p. 46. Copyright © 1991 Yellow Moon Press. All rights reserved. Reproduced with permission. / "Dedication," *Second-Hand Coat: Poems New and Selected,* Yellow Moon Press, 1992. Copyright © 1992 Yellow Moon Press. All rights reserved. Reproduced with permission. / "Dedication," *Ordinary Words,* Paris Press, 1999. © Paris Press. / "Breaking the Tired Mold of American Poetry," *Titanic Operas: A Poets' Corner of Contemporary Responses to Dickinson's Legacy,* 1999. © Titanic Operas. / "Dedication," *In the Dark,* Copper Canyon Press, 2004. © Copper Canyon Press. / Acceptance speech, National Book Awards, National Book Foundation, 2002. © National Book Foundation. / Walter Stone, "Woman," *Poets of Today: Volume VI,* Charles Scribner's Sons, 1959, p. 168. © Simon & Schuster. / Walter Stone, "Logos," *Poets of Today: Volume VI,* Charles Scribner's Sons, 1959, p. 153. © Simon & Schuster. / Walter Stone, "Chronicle," *Poets of Today: Volume VI,* Charles Scribner's Sons, 1959, p. 157. © Simon & Schuster. / Walter Stone, "Brothers," *Poets of Today: Volume VI,* Charles Scribner's Sons, 1959, p. 150. © Simon & Schuster. / Walter Stone, "The Man of Property to His Muse," *Poets of Today: Volume VI,* Charles Scribner's Sons, 1959, p. 152. © Simon & Schuster. / J.F. Battaglia, "A Conversation with Ruth Stone," *Boulevard,* University of Illinois, 1996. © University of Illinois Press.

TARTT, DONNA. Elizabeth Lenhard, "Rookie Author Has the Secret," *Orlando Sentinel,* Tribune Publishing, 1992. © The Orlando Sentinel. / Kevin Nance, "*Goldfinch* Could Be Tartt's Great American Novel," *USA Today,* a division of Gannett Publishing, 2013. © USA Today. / Jane Schilling, "Light in a Gothic Darkness," *Sunday Telegraph,* Telegraph Media Group Limited, 2002. © Telegraph Media Group. / Julie Myerson, "*The Goldfinch* by

ACKNOWLEDGEMENTS

Donna Tartt - review," Guardian News and Media Limited, 2013. © Guardian News Service Ltd.

TEASDALE, SARA. "After Parting," *The Collected Poems of Sara Teasdale*, Collier Books, 1966, p. 56. Courtesy of Palgrave Macmillan. / "What Do I Care," *The Collected Poems of Sara Teasdale*, Collier Books, 1966, p. 116. Courtesy of Palgrave Macmillan. / "The Crystal Gazer," *The Collected Poems of Sara Teasdale*, Collier Books, 1966, p. 179. Courtesy of Palgrave Macmillan. / "To a Picture of Eleonora Duse in 'The Dead City,'" *The Collected Poems of Sara Teasdale*, Collier Books, 1966, p. 3,4. Courtesy of Palgrave Macmillan. / "Day's Ending (Tucson)," *The Collected Poems of Sara Teasdale*, Collier Books, 1966, p. 180. Courtesy of Palgrave Macmillan. / "Union Square," *The Collected Poems of Sara Teasdale*, Collier Books, 1966, pp. 31, 32. Courtesy of Palgrave Macmillan. / "Barter," *The Collected Poems of Sara Teasdale*, Collier Books, 1966, p. 97. Courtesy of Palgrave Macmillan. / "Jewels," *The Collected Poems of Sara Teasdale*, Collier Books, 1966, p. 100. Courtesy of Palgrave Macmillan. / "The Kiss," *The Collected Poems of Sara Teasdale*, Collier Books, 1966, p. 28. Courtesy of Palgrave Macmillan. / "Wisdom," *The Collected Poems of Sara Teasdale*, Collier Books, 1966, p. 102. Courtesy of Palgrave Macmillan. / "Refuge," *The Collected Poems of Sara Teasdale*, Collier Books, 1966, p. 104. Courtesy of Palgrave Macmillan. / "Doubt," *The Collected Poems of Sara Teasdale*, Collier Books, 1966, p. 108. Courtesy of Palgrave Macmillan. / "Houses of Dreams," *The Collected Poems of Sara Teasdale*, Collier Books, 1966, pp. 107-108. Courtesy of Palgrave Macmillan. / "I Would Live in Your Love," *The Collected Poems of Sara Teasdale*, Collier Books, 1966, p. 26. Courtesy of Palgrave Macmillan. / "Day and Night," *The Collected Poems of Sara Teasdale*, Collier Books, 1966, p. 125. Courtesy of Palgrave Macmillan. / "Compensation," *The Collected Poems of Sara Teasdale*, Collier Books, 1966, p. 125. Courtesy of Pal-grave Macmillan. / "The Mystery," *The Collected Poems of Sara Teasdale*, Collier Books, 1966, p. 127. Courtesy of Palgrave Macmillan. / "The Nights Remember," *The Collected Poems of Sara Teasdale*, Collier Books, 1966, p. 134. Courtesy of Palgrave Macmillan. / "Spring Torrents," *The Collected Poems of Sara Teasdale*, Collier Books, 1966, p. 132. Courtesy of Palgrave Macmillan. / "I Know the Stars," *The Collected Poems of Sara Teasdale*, Collier Books, 1966, p. 132. Courtesy of Palgrave Macmillan. / "If Death Is Kind," *The Collected Poems of Sara Teasdale*, Collier Books, 1966, p. 148. Courtesy of Palgrave Macmillan. / "The Sanctuary," *The Collected Poems of Sara Teasdale*, Collier Books, 1966, p. 151. Courtesy of Palgrave Macmillan. / "The Broken Field," *The Collected Poems of Sara Teasdale*, Collier Books, 1966, p. 130. Courtesy of Palgrave Macmillan. / "There Will Come Soft Rains," *The Collected Poems of Sara Teasdale*, Collier Books, 1966, p. 143. Courtesy of Palgrave Macmillan. / "Those Who Love," *The Collected Poems of Sara Teasdale*, Collier Books, 1966, p. 173. Courtesy of Palgrave Macmillan. / "Effigy of a Nun," *The Collected Poems of Sara Teasdale*, Collier Books, 1966, p. 172. Courtesy of Palgrave Macmillan. / "I Shall Live to Be Old," *The Collected Poems of Sara Teasdale*, Collier Books, 1966, p. 181. Courtesy of Palgrave Macmillan. / "The Old Enemy," *The Collected Poems of Sara Teasdale*, Collier Books, 1966, p. 182. Courtesy of Palgrave Macmillan. / "To M.," *The Collected Poems of Sara Teasdale*, Collier Books, 1966, p. 209. Courtesy of Palgrave Macmillan. / "In Memory of Vachel Lindsay," *The Collected Poems of Sara Teasdale*, Collier Books, 1966, p. 210. Courtesy of Palgrave Macmillan. / "Since Death Brushed Past Me," *The Collected Poems of Sara Teasdale*, Collier Books, 1966, p. 213. Courtesy of Palgrave Macmillan. / "Foreword," *The Answering Voice: Love Lyrics by Women*, The Macmillan Company, 1930, pp. x, xii. Courtesy of Palgrave Macmillan.

List of Subjects

Introduction   xii

List of Contributors   xv

WILTON BARNHARDT   1
John A. McDermott

JOE BRAINARD   17
Aaron Goldsman

ROBERT CHRISTGAU   33
Jeffrey Bickerstaff

LEONARD COHEN   49
Joseph Dewey

BRET EASTON ELLIS   67
Piers Pennington

BEN HECHT   83
Tom Cerasulo

HOMER HICKAM   99
S. Bailey Shurbutt

ROBERT E. HOWARD   115
Jonas Prida

MEYER LEVIN   133
Jack Fischel

NATHANIEL MACKEY   151
Joseph Pizza

HARRYETTE MULLEN   163
Caleb Puckett

ALICE MUNRO   179
Elizabeth Freudenthal

WALTER DEAN MYERS   199
Amy Alessio

RON RASH   215
Louis H. Palmer III

MONA SIMPSON   233
Laurie Champion

RUTH STONE   249
Jane Beal

DONNA TARTT   267
Deborah Kay Ferrell

SARA TEASDALE   283
Melissa Girard

Cumulative Index   289

Introduction

"Literature adds to reality, it doesn't simply describe it," said C.S. Lewis. That is, literature increases reality, building on what is there, extending and modifying what we see and experience. Poems, novels, plays, and other texts that have achieved a position in the historical imagination— works that have both resonance and resilience— become part of the furniture of our minds. So it makes sense to study these works closely, and to try to understand as best we can the writers who lie behind these works, who bring them into being.

In this twenty-seventh supplement of *American Writers,* we present articles on authors from a variety of genres, many of them working across the genres quite happily, writing poems as well as novels or plays or screenplays. All are well-known figures, and yet none has thus far been featured in this series. Readers with a desire to engage more thoroughly with the work of these writers should find these articles useful. They contain biographical and historical information, and offer numerous close readings of major texts. Their goal, consistent with previous volumes in the series, is to bring forward the works by reading them in their proper biographical and historical context.

This series began with critical and biographical monographs that appeared between 1959 and 1972. The *Minnesota Pamphlets on American Writers* achieved fame in their time; they were incisively written and informative, treating ninety-seven American writers in a format and style that attracted a devoted following of readers. The series proved invaluable to a generation of students and teachers, who could depend on these reliable and interesting critiques of major figures. The idea of reprinting these essays occurred to Charles Scribner, Jr. (1921-1995). The series appeared in four volumes titled *American Writers: A Collection of Literary Biographies* (1974).

Since then, twenty-seven supplements (including this one) have appeared, treating hundreds of well-known and less known American writers: poets, novelists, playwrights, travel writers, memoirists, critics, screenwriters, essayists, and authors of books for children. The idea behind these contemporary volumes is consistent with the original series: to provide informative essays aimed at the general reader. These essays frequently rise to a high level of craft, drawing on deep reserves of scholarship; but they are meant to introduce a body of work of some importance in the history of American literature, and to provide a sense of the scope and nature of the career under review. Each article puts the author at hand in the context of his or her time.

Supplement twenty-seven treats a range of authors from this century and the last. Many of them are novelists, ranging from the pulp fiction of Robert E. Howard through more contemporary writers, including Wilton Barnhardt, Bret Easton Ellis, Meyer Levin, Alice Munro, Mona Simpson, and Donna Tartt. Some of these, of course, have attracted huge followings and won many awards, others less so; but each has accomplished a great deal, and the work itself deserves close study. The same can be said for those who are mainly poets, including Ron Rash, Harryette Mullen, Nathaniel Mackey, Ruth Stone and Sara Teasdale.

It's interesting that a fair number of the authors here defy easy categorization, such as Ron Rash, who writes poetry and fiction with equal facility, or Joe Brainard, Robert Christgau, and Ben Hecht, who make a virtue of their

INTRODUCTION

openness to a variety of forms. Leonard Cohen may be more famous as a singer; but he's also a poet and songwriter, so his work is addressed here for the first time in this series. Homer Hickam is mainly a memoirist, and we discuss his work in this volume as well, along with the popular writer of books for children, Walter Dean Myers.

While each of these writers has been widely discussed in journals and the review pages of newspapers and magazines, few of them—Sara Teasdale and Alice Munro might be exceptions—have had the kind of sustained critical attention they deserve, and we hope to provide a beginning here, as the work in each writer's case certainly deserves close reading.

As ever, we have insisted that each article included in this series should be accessible to the general reader; that is, we never invite or encourage the kind of critical or theoretical jargon that is prevalent today, especially within universities. One could argue that the creation of culture involves the continuous reassessment of major texts, and my belief is that this collection of articles performs a useful task in this regard, offering shrewd and sophisticated yet straightforward introductions to writers who have found a wide readership because of the high quality of their work in various genres, writers who have added something to our realities as readers, as human beings.

—*JAY PARINI*

Contributors

Amy Alessio. Amy Alessio is an award winning teen librarian with a black belt in karate. Her latest co-authored reference titles: *A Year of Programs for Millennials* and *A Year of Club Programs for Teens,* were published by American Library Association Editions in 2015. She has presented over three hundred webinars and live workshops on library services. She served on the Young Adult Library Services Association Board of Directors as well as on selection award committees. She reviews mysteries and romances for *Booklist.* WALTER DEAN MYERS

Jane Beal. Jane Beal received her doctorate in English literature from UC Davis and has taught as a professor of English at Wheaton College and Colorado Christian University. She is the author of *John Trevisa and the English Polychronicon,* editor of *Illuminating Moses: A History of Reception from Exodus to the Renaissance,* and co-editor of *Translating the Past: Essays on Medieval Literature*; she has published essays on the medieval dream vision poem, *Pearl,* and early women writers such as Marie de France, Julian of Norwich, and Queen Elizabeth I as well as numerous works of poetry, fiction, and creative non-fiction. RUTH STONE

Jeffrey Bickerstaff. Jeffrey Bickerstaff received his Ph.D. from Miami University of Ohio. He currently teaches writing and literature at Johnson State College and the Community College of Vermont. His research interests include representations of American politics in literature and film. ROBERT CHRISTGAU

Tom Cerasulo. Tom Cerasulo is Professor of English and Division Chair of Humanities and Fine Arts at Elms College in Chicopee, Massachusetts. He has published on film adaptations, on ethnicity, and on the cultural history of American authorship. Recent work appears in *Arizona Quarterly, MELUS, Studies in American Culture, Twentieth-Century Literature, American Writers, The Blackwell Encyclopedia of Twentieth Century Fiction,* and *Critical Companion to Eugene O ???? Neill.* He is the author of the book *Authors Out Here: Fitzgerald, West, Parker, and Schulberg in Hollywood* (University of South Carolina Press, 2010) and is currently researching a project on writers and the television industry. BEN HECHT

Laurie Champion. A native Texan, Laurie Champion received her Ph.D. from University of North Texas, then taught at Sul Ross State University, in Alpine, Texas, before moving to San Diego, where she currently teaches English at San Diego State University. She has edited or co-edited ten books, including *Texas 5 X 5: Twenty-Five Stories by Five Texas Writers, Texas Told ???? em: Gambling Stories, American Women Writers, 1900-1945: A Bio-Bibliographical Critical Sourcebook, Texas Short Stories II,* and *Contemporary American Women Fiction Writers: An A to-Z Guide.* Additionally, she has published numerous scholarly essays and short stories in distinguished magazines, literary journals, and anthologies. MONA SIMPSON

Joseph Dewey. Joseph Dewey, Assistant Professor of Literature and Composition at Broward College, is the author of five studies of contemporary American literature that have looked at the relationship between literature and religion: *In a Dark Time: The Apocalyptic Temper of the American Novel in the Nuclear Age* (1990);

xv

CONTRIBUTORS

Novels from Reagan's America: A New Realism (1997); *Understanding Richard Powers* (2001); *Beyond Grief and Nothing: A Reading of Don DeLillo* (2006); and *Understanding Michael Chabon* (2014). In addition, Dr. Dewey has co-edited three casebooks, *"The Finer Thread, The Tighter Weave": The Short Fiction of Henry James* (1995); *Under/Words: A Casebook on Underworld* (2003); and *Critical Insights: J. D. Salinger's The Catcher in the Rye* (2011). LEONARD COHEN

Deborah Kay Ferrell. Deborah Kay Ferrell is a professor of English at Finger Lakes Community College. This is her fourth essay for the *American Writers* Series. DONNA TARTT

Jack Fischel. Jack Fischel is Emeritus Professor of History at Millersville University and a Visiting Professor of the Humanities at Messiah College where he teaches a course titled The Holocaust. Fischel is the author of three books on the Holocaust and has edited six others. Dr. Fischel has also written hundreds of articles and reviews for periodicals such *The Weekly Standard, Forward, Midstream, Holocaust and Genocide Studies, Jewish Book World, Hadassah,* and a number of other publications. He has also contributed essays to the *American Writers* series on William Gibson, Leon Uris, Herman Wouk, and Sholem Asch. MEYER LEVIN

Elizabeth Freudenthal. Elizabeth Freudenthal received a doctorate in English from University of California, Santa Barbara, where she conducted interdisciplinary research on the medicalization of personality in contemporary fiction and culture. She has published essays in *New Literary History, Postmodern Culture,* and *Moving On: Essays on the Aftermath of Leaving Academia.* Her current research interests include fiction by contemporary women writers and intersections of disability, trauma, and poverty in health care policy. ALICE MUNRO

Melissa Girard. Melissa Girard is an Assistant Professor of English at Loyola University Maryland, where she teaches courses in modern poetry and poetics, American literature, and gender studies. Her publications on women's poetry have appeared in *JML, Oxford Handbook of Modern and Contemporary American Poetry,* and *Poet Lore* and are forthcoming in *PMLA* and the *Cambridge History of Twentieth-Century Women Poets.* She is the recipient of an NEH Faculty Fellowship for 2015-16 for her current book project on modernist women's poetry and the problem of sentimentality. SARA TEASDALE

Aaron Goldsman. Aaron Goldsman is a Ph.D. candidate in the Department of English at Emory University. His research focuses on gender, sexuality, and the erotics of writing and reading in a range of post-WWII American poetries, with an emphasis on the New York School and its environs. JOE BRAINARD

John A. McDermott. John A. McDermott teaches contemporary American literature and creative writing at Stephen F. Austin State University in Nacogdoches, Texas. His criticism has appeared in *American Book Review, Journal of Popular Culture, Raymond Carver Review,* and elsewhere. He is also the author of a volume of poetry, *The Idea of God in Tennessee* (Aldrich Press 2015). WILTON BARNHARDT

Louis H. Palmer III. Louis H. Palmer III (Tersh) is a Professor in the English Department at Castleton State College in Castleton, Vermont. He teaches courses in American literature, public speaking, and composition. Research interests include regional literatures, the Gothic, nature and outdoor writing and vampires. He serves as Gothic Chair for the Popular Culture Association. He has published articles on William Faulkner, Flannery O'Connor, Cormac McCarthy and others. He recently completed a book, *Vampires in the New World* (ABC-CLIO, 2013), a historical survey of the vampire figure in American literature and film. RON RASH

Piers Pennington. Piers Pennington is co-editor of *Geoffrey Hill and his Contexts* (2011) and a contributor to *The Oxford Handbook of Contem-*

CONTRIBUTORS

porary British & Irish Poetry (2013). His essay on James Lasdun appeared in *British Writers* (2014). BRET EASTON ELLIS

Joseph Pizza. Joseph Pizza completed his D.Phil. in English Language and Literature from the University of Oxford in 2012. Since then, he has been Assistant Professor of English and Director of the Honors program at Belmont Abbey College, in Belmont, North Carolina. In addition to work on modern poetry and African American studies, he has also taught and written widely on jazz, hip hop, and digital rhetoric. NATHANIEL MACKEY

Jonas Prida. Jonas Prida is the interim Vice President for Academic Affairs and Associate Professor of English at the College of St. Joseph in Rutland, Vermont. He has a Ph.D. in English from Tulane University, specializing in antebellum American Literature. In addition to his work on H.P. Lovecraft, Conan the Barbarian, and antebellum popular writer George Lippard, he is interested in 1920s and 30s pulp horror magazines. ROBERT E. HOWARD

Caleb Puckett. Caleb Puckett is a writer, editor, and research consultant based out of Lawrence, Kansas. Puckett has published critical writing over a number of significant move-ments, works, and figures in American literature and history, including pieces on ecopoetics, *Lolita,* and Edgar Allan Poe. HARRYETTE MULLEN

S. Bailey Shurbutt. S. Bailey Shurbutt is professor of English, Project Director of the Appalachian Heritage Writers Project, and Coordinator of the Shepherd University Appalachian Studies program. She has published books, chapters, and essays on a variety of 19th- and 20th-century writers, as well as a series of short biographies of Zelda Fitzgerald, Margaret Atwood, Charlotte Perkins Gilman, Flannery O'Connor and others for Scribner's and journal essays and conference presentations on Christina Rossetti, Fred Chappell, Marilou Awiakta, Denise Giardina, Robert Morgan, and others. Her essays have been published in *Victorian Poetry, Women's Studies,* the *Journal of Appalachian Studies, Women and Language,* the *Southern Literary Journal, Essays in Literature,* and other scholarly publications. Her criticism has been anthologized in *Feminism in Literature* and has appeared in online publications. She was 2006 West Virginia Professor of the Year, 2014 President of the National Appalachian Studies Association, and currently serves as Legislative Coordinator for the WV Advisory Council of Faculty and Director of the 2016 NEH Summer Seminar for Teachers, Voices from the Misty Mountains. HOMER HICKAM

AMERICAN WRITERS

WILTON BARNHARDT

(1960—)

John A. McDermott

WILTON BARNHARDT IS an American fiction writer with several highly acclaimed novels published by the time he was in his early fifties. He is primarily known for a quartet of comedic novels that offer sharp insight into social mores, and the authenticity of his work is often based on deep research. His first novel, *Emma Who Saved My Life,* published in 1989 when he was still in his late twenties, is a coming-of-age story set in the New York City theater world of the 1970s. In 1993 he published *Gospel,* a sprawling novel about the quest for a lost gospel written by a Christian disciple, an epic travelogue of raucous comedy, impressive research, and profound intelligence. Ten years after his first book, Barnhardt published his third novel, *Show World* (1998), a tragic portrayal of a woman's search for her identity, from the elite halls of Smith College to the hypocritical corridors of the U.S. Congress to the carnivorous realm of the entertainment business of Los Angeles. Filled with his expected humor and keen ear for American character, it may be the bleakest of Barnhardt's works.

A fourteen-year gap in his novel publishing ensued, during which Barnhardt established his academic career, teaching at the University of California at Irvine, the University of Alabama at Tuscaloosa, and the California Institute of Technology. He has had a long-term teaching appointment with Warren Wilson College's low-residency M.F.A. program in creative writing (one of the premier programs of its kind). He later returned to his native North Carolina and acted as the founding director of North Carolina State University's M.F.A. program in creative writing. He still holds a professorship at North Carolina State and is active in graduate mentorship and study-abroad opportunities. Proud to have found an academic home at a school valued for its technical expertise in such practical fields as agriculture and engineering—and a school at which his family has deep roots—Barnhardt's approach to teaching fiction is that of a "maker," a hands-on guide who expects apprentice-writers to produce polished work.

His hiatus from publishing novels ended in 2013 with the publication of his fourth book, *Lookaway, Lookaway,* a witty and generous, albeit unsparing, domestic comic drama about the "New South," in particular a well-to-do Charlotte family, the Johnstons. Barnhardt had waited years for his "Southern novel" to brew and it was released to much praise in the American press, his most acclaimed work yet. Barnhardt's combination of erudition, wit, and humility is present in both his writing and his interviews. "I tend to write to amuse, educate, and entertain myself," he admitted in a 2013 interview with *Bookreporter,* "and I have been blessed and pleasantly bemused that anyone else wanted to read alongside me."

BECOMING A WRITER

Wilton Barnhardt was born in Winston-Salem, North Carolina, on July 25, 1960, to William and Mary Barnhardt. In his own words, he was "just your basic middle-class Southern kid" (*Deep South Magazine*). His mother was a schoolteacher and his father worked as a chemist in a cigarette company. In an essay from the anthology *The Story Behind the Story,* Barnhardt describes his youthful reading habits.

> I grew up on Ray Bradbury, sci-fi mags, and comic books by the dozens, a ratty volume of O. Henry, *Alfred Hitchcock's Mystery Magazine* and *Boy's Life,*

not to mention my grandparents' one short story anthology *World's Great Tales!* featuring yellowing pages of Maupassant, Poe, Bierce, Lardner, Shirley Jackson, all of which contributed to my twelve-year-old sensibility that the short story wasn't much good unless it had a surprise ending, a sneaky twist at the end, like a *Twilight Zone* episode. Whereas my taste in novels is broad and tolerant.... any sort of Jamesian dawdle and Proustian, self-indulgence is all right by me.

(p. 194)

He left the South to attend Michigan State University, where he studied journalism and wrote for the student paper, and graduated with a B.A. degree in 1982. He moved to New York City and was hired, through what he calls a series of unlikely factors, by the major weekly sports magazine *Sports Illustrated* to cover stock car racing. Diane Roberts, in her introduction to a public reading by Barnhardt at Florida State University, jokingly said he was hired to cover NASCAR because he was the only Southerner the New York–based magazine knew. Despite the unlikelihood of that career, he wrote sports journalism for several years before he left for graduate studies in literature.

On a lark he had applied to the University of Oxford in England. He was accepted and studied at Brasenose College, where he completed his master's exams on James Joyce's *Finnegans Wake* (1939) and intended to compose a dissertation on Henry James. He never finished that doctorate, but he did begin shaping the manuscript that would become his first novel, inspired by reading Gustave Flaubert's *Sentimental Education* (1869) back when he was in New York. "It struck me as this was how you wrote," he said of the reading experience, in an interview with Bill Krueger. "It started something in me, and I started reading the classics of the 19th Century novel. It started my love and my sense that I was going to write very grandly" (Wilton Barnhardt, 2013).

Perhaps it was the combination of this love for classic novels and his experience with quirky sports journalism that shaped Barnhardt's style. The columns on wide-ranging topics he wrote for *Sports Illustrated* (and continued to write, even after his career as a novelist took off) reveal his penchant for idiosyncratic characters. One profile was on Tom Dempsey, a National Football League kicker who had held the record for longest field goal for decades. Barnhardt's journalism, as with his fiction, begins with character and is powered by plot. It's easy to see why Barnhardt would write about Dempsey, the unlikely football hero—a boy born without toes on his kicking foot, the unassuming family man who has his memorabilia in storage, who'd rather have his children's awards on display, was the same man who made the last-second long-distance kick that no one could top. (Barnhardt's profile was published in 1990; the record was not broken for another twenty-three years.)

Barnhardt is fond of that sort of anomaly. Another profile, published in 1991, followed a middle-aged man who had perfected an underutilized basketball technique, the underhand free throw. As the world-record holder for most consecutive shots made, he traveled the country as a journeyman of the granny shot, crisscrossing America with his wife in an RV. Barnhardt begins that profile by highlighting the unexpected:

Ted St. Martin of Jacksonville is in the *Guinness Book of World Records* and a ball he once used is in the Basketball Hall of Fame. Yet he never made the NBA, never played college ball. Although he used to shoot around as a kid, he wasn't the star of his high school team.

("He Throws Free Throws")

While superficially these short pieces are about achievement in athletics, his prose centers on portraiture—character studies of the quirky, even eccentric. Barnhardt's fiction is similar, always centered on realistic, rounded characters who do the unexpected. Though he excelled at journalism, capturing the character quickly in the event, he is more comfortable having moved on to the larger canvas: "Both journalism and novel-writing tell stories, but the novelist is more megalomaniacal, creating a whole universe in which he is an imperfect deity over the lives of his creation" (*Bookreporter*).

"Imperfect" isn't simply humility but is a clue to the sort of characters Barnhardt adores: the imperfect protagonist, the character for whom we cheer and at whom we wince with equal frequency. Perhaps it takes an imperfect deity to create such compelling imperfect people.

WILTON BARNHARDT

A NOVELIST EMERGES: EMMA WHO SAVED MY LIFE

While ensconced in magazine journalism and covering events such as NASCAR and the 1984 Olympics, then moving on to Oxford to study serious literature, Barnhardt still had time to write what would become his first published novel. Though it took him a year and a half to find an agent willing to risk it, *Emma Who Saved My Life* (1989) was published by St. Martin's Press in the same year he was awarded his M.Phil from Oxford, when he was only twenty-eight.

The novel is a coming-of-age story told in the first person by Gil Freeman. Bitten by the acting bug as a child in Oak Park, Illinois, Gil drops out of college in order to move to New York City to pursue a career in theater. As the novel begins, five years after his return to the Midwest, Gil is ready to write a memoir about his years, 1974 to 1983, in that faraway place, a city that stills seems to hold allure for the sadder-but-wiser man. Though he tells us he would never go back—he's happy, he reminds us in the end, and we believe him—his autobiography is a sort of paean to his lost youth, his lost city, far more than it is a letter to a lost love, Emma Gennaro.

When Gil arrives from Illinois he has already made plans to share an apartment with Lisa, a friend from college, for whom he's nursing an unrequited crush. She's a little older, beautiful in a 1970s feathered-hair way, a *Charlie's Angels* type, everything humble, awkward Gil would admire from afar. Lisa is a Milwaukee girl who wants to be a visual artist but spends her days in a cubicle in the corporate world. Yet with Lisa's months-long head start on becoming a New Yorker, Gil accepts her as more worldly wise, and it is Lisa who introduces him to Emma Gennaro, a third roommate. Emma soon becomes the center of Gil's romantic desires, though this tough, sharp Italian American girl will have none of it.

Emma too is a Midwestern transplant, a middle-class kid from Ohio. Though she fashions herself a poet, she never writes, and though she fashions herself an iconoclast, she is largely reduced to watching television and making sarcastic comments to a small group of friends.

Neurotic, judgmental, acerbic, smart, unkind, funny, terrified (or horrified) by sexuality and its inherent physical (and emotional) messiness, Emma makes herself aloof through most of the book.

As the emotional center of the novel, she is the impossible dream for Gil, the girl who can never be his. By the end of the novel, she is so damaged by her own neuroses, Gil realizes she was never the Emma whom he imagined. To use modern parlance, she's a toxic "manic pixie dream girl." Readers now may find the trope familiar, and there has long been Daisy Buchanan, the early twentieth century's most famous lost dream girl, as a model. Yet Daisy, toxic in her own fashion, seems pale in comparison to dark, dramatic Emma, and Gil is a poor man's Gatsby, if we judge by the ability to re-create one's identity. Because he is both the narrator and protagonist, he is more like Nick Carroway and Jay Gatsby blended into one modest Midwestern boy, too milquetoast to really get the girl—and the girl is really too unstable to fully desire anyway. It's a busted romantic comedy for a disillusioned time, a story determined to make its original readers miss the seventies as the eighties drew to a close. Contemporary readers may find the settings (and the sexual politics) of the era either curious or dated, but the novel has not turned into just a set piece. The writing is raucous at times, tragic at others, a blend Barnhardt continues to take through all his subsequent books.

One disastrous outing for the roommates is a weekend away from the city in the summer of 1976. The Bicentennial celebration roars, and the arrival of the "tall ships" sailing into Manhattan's harbor fills the city with tourists. The trip includes a small band of the roommates' most avant-garde friends, goaded to wild behavior by Emma, intent on annoying Lisa's new conservative beau, Tom, a Wall Street type. Emma is not satisfied with isolating only herself; she wants Lisa and Gil lonely too, all of them trapped in symbiotic misery. Gil and Lisa rebel, and that is part of the drama.

This section demonstrates how Barnhardt uses a vast, rollicking cast of side characters to

populate this first novel and all of his subsequent books. Early on, readers meet Susan, an obese, sex-obsessed vulgarian with both a physical and emotional exhibitionist streak, a grand social connector. Susan is the link between Lisa and Emma and a more bohemian crowd of young New Yorkers; she is also one of the broadest comic characters in the story line and the fulcrum of that Fourth of July gathering. To contemporary readers, she may seem a bit of a dated stock character, the flamboyant woman playing sur-rogate mother and/or lover to a host of young gay men, but she's an effective low-comedy creation and a reminder of the sort of Bette Midler/Fire Island gay culture prominent in the New York of that era. Typical of Barnhardt's eye for realistic human complexity, she's simultane-ously obnoxious and sympathetic, a caricature of what Emma could become.

Gil's various jobs in the theater—as a gofer of sorts at a B-level company, as a bit player, as second fiddle to horrifyingly vain or drunk has-beens—are also sources for supplying comedic side characters. Gil's growing disenchantment with the theater rests on bad bosses and bad agents; his growing personal disenchantment rests on bad dates and bad apartments, the stuff of many people's twenties. Gil's trials would have been familiar to the novel's original audience and still feels recognizable. As his trajectory across the lights of Broadway ebbs and flows, his continued tenuous relationship with Emma—as a friend, just a friend—lends a sort of horrific qual-ity to youthful singledom in the licentious seventies.

Emma's growing animosity toward anything sexual is a strong thread in the novel and paral-lels the subsequent limitations on Gil's dating life after he contracts herpes from one of his series of not particularly promising girlfriends. Gil's predicament shows readers the realities of dating in the disco-saturated seventies, but the book also has a bit of innocence about it, in its pre-AIDS era. Death does not hover around the book the way it might if Gil had stayed another decade. The innocence is also captured, perhaps counter to our expectations, in the representation of pre-gentrified Brooklyn and pre-Giuliani

Manhattan, back when Times Square still had dirty movies and muggers, before it was a family tourist destination. Gil's living quarters are squalid, cramped, and dangerous, yet not quite bohemian and certainly not romantic. Jonathan Larson's musical *Rent* (2005) is still a decade off, and Barnhardt's Alphabet City is not quite as ripe or ribald as Larson's. For all the troubles—muggings, suicides, and social diseases—it still feels quaint. And Gil could always go home, though his family is not really the allure, just the safety of the familiar.

When he does return home, Gil might see it as defeat, but it doesn't seem as much like defeat as pragmatism. About a third of the way into the novel, Gil has a flash of recognition regarding his still-early relationship with Emma and how she is perhaps a stand-in for New York City. In some ways, Gil sums up the twin desires of the book (for girl and glamour) and his final decision to leave the city:

> There were times with Emma where it came to me clearly: NO MORE EMMA, you don't need this, you don't behave right around her, it's not so much being in love as just being in a big mess, an interest-ing mess, but a mess. On the other hand, sometimes … What We Had Was Love.…

> (p. 135)

Gil's relationship with Emma is "an interesting mess" but not a love story in the Romeo and Juliet vein of star-crossed lovers, despite his desire for a big love. This is just one average, modestly talented young man attracted to an al-luring, emotionally fragmented young woman. Gil and Emma have a deep friendship, but they are never really a couple, and her inability to deal with her intimacy issues and Gil's naïveté doom them for any long-term goal. Readers know early on that Gil and Emma can't possibly end up together, yet the desire to see them together remains for most readers right up to the end.

Through Barnhardt's realism—young love is often best left unrequited, or at least imperma-nent—we see a happier, healthier Gil in the end. Yet he is not without his quiet desires to relive it all, to embrace his younger self and go "do New York," as Edith Wharton once counseled Henry James, all over again. In the end, the novel is not

a love letter to Emma nearly as much as it is a love letter to Gil's youth and, most of all, to Gil's New York. The real love in the novel is New York City in the 1970s: dirty, cheap, polluted, unbearable. The real temptation is only in his memory, now that he's settled back in Chicago, married to Sophie (a girl we know much, much less about than damaged Emma). He's about to become a father for the first time, in a plot line that has minor echoes of John Hughes's film of the same era, *She's Having a Baby* (1988). It's Sophie, the pregnant wife (in the course of the book she goes from barely two months pregnant to eight months pregnant—a neat little bit of info, as it takes Gil six months to tell us his story), who encourages Gil to write it all down. It's Sophie who says he may still be in love with Emma. But we know she's wrong.

The New York story ends in Far Rockaway with a failed tryst between Gil and Emma, set up at her behest, not out of love for Gil but for procreative necessity. Their attempt at intimacy is so wretched, it brings Emma's rage out in full force. The last time Gil sees Emma, she is howling at him from a subway platform. Soon after, he leaves the city after his decade of trying to make it and we return to the frame of the novel, the creation of the novel as "autobiography" by a calmer, removed-from-New-York Gil. The novel ends on a wistful note, a bit of searching for Gatsby's green light, but readers aren't really worried he'll end up dead in a swimming pool. Gil's better off where he is and he knows it.

AN EPIC SOPHOMORE EFFORT: GOSPEL

In an interview with Dennis McLellan of the *Los Angeles Times,* Barnhardt said this about the genesis of his second novel, *Gospel* (1993): "I had suspicions I was going to write this book even while I was writing *Emma.*... I hadn't done the traveling for it, I hadn't done the research for it, but I had in my mind a sense of something set in a sort of academic black market of illegal antiquities and it sort of developed from there."

Gospel demanded research and travel. At nearly eight hundred pages, including an index,

it's a sprawling, erudite theological comic adventure. "Epic" is the word for a story that spans continents, for a book with intellectual and spiritual concerns that cover millennia and with a sprawling cast—though at its core, simply a pair of academics—of hundreds. It is also a risky book. *Emma Who Saved My Life* spanned a decade, but limited itself to the concerns of one small band of friends and mainly just the needs of its narrator; the chronology of *Gospel* is shorter, a matter of months, but its concerns are global and historical. As with all of Barnhardt's fiction, the story is grounded in the reader's growing knowledge of its characters as multifaceted humans, characters we might not immediately like but grow to care about.

Similar to its fictional cousin, the far more commercial (and commercially successful) novel *The Da Vinci Code* (2003), published by Dan Brown ten years after *Gospel,* Barnhardt's book is, on its surface, a mystery: the hunt for a lost gospel of the New Testament. Barnhardt wanted to write a "fun book … a page turner: There is an adventure. For those who never want to read a single footnote, there is still a book there for them" (McLellan). But Barnhardt's work is far more resonant than Brown's best seller in its research, in its scope, and in its theological considerations. (It also has many more comedic elements.) Barnhardt raises profound questions about the origins of the Christian faith, about the trajectory of its growth and changes over the centuries, about ancient societies' relationship to Christian teaching and the world of that era and our own. He negotiates the troubles in modern Ireland, the unrest in the Middle East, and, finally, the rise of Christian conservatism and its burgeoning financial and political power in the United States in the early 1990s.

More than twenty years after its publication, the novel was as relevant as ever, and maybe more so, with the rise in fiction that deals with Christian themes. In the intervening decades, the *Left Behind* series of sixteen best-selling Christian novels (1995–2007) by Tim LaHaye and Jerry B. Jenkins (dealing with the "end times" as humanity faces the Apocalypse prophesied in the Bible) had come and gone, Tom Perrotta published his

comic novel *The Leftovers* in 2011, and contemporary American storytelling seems fixated on end-of-the-world dystopianism. Barnhardt, while not writing a dystopian fantasy, reminds readers of how "end times" visions infected the early Church and plays on those ideas as he examines the world of 1990, the year in which the action of the novel takes place.

In its simplest plot outline, *Gospel* is the hunt for the lost Gospel of Matthias, the thirteenth disciple, as pursued by a University of Chicago theologian, Dr. Patrick O'Hanrahan, along with his sometimes-reluctant graduate student assistant, Lucy Dantan, a Southside Chicago Irish American girl. O'Hanrahan, a gifted storyteller whose career has never produced the quality of written scholarship predicted for it, is also the proverbial loose cannon: alcoholic, fun-loving, and irresponsible. O'Hanrahan may be based on some of Barnhardt's teachers during his time at Oxford. In an interview with *Bookreporter,* he said:

> I had a magnificent Irish storytelling scholar for an advisor at Oxford who may well have made up half of what he recited, but it didn't matter. He, like many in the British tutorial system, believed in (1) intimidation of the student through sheer volume of knowledge and expertise, and(2) providing good entertainment value.

O'Hanrahan demonstrates these two values in his every scene, and while he is a difficult character—irresponsible, bitter, chauvinistic, prone to self-aggrandizement and self-reproach—he is also lovable. O'Hanrahan's name should be shorthand for the grand professor, the way Shakespeare's Falstaff is recognized as the grand, not entirely unlikable, buffoon.

As the novel begins, it is Lucy Dantan's job, flying to the United Kingdom from her hometown of Chicago, to lure O'Hanrahan back to Chicago, to corral him from further misadventures, and to keep him from running up the Theology Department's tab. Lucy soon discovers that containing O'Hanrahan is impossible, and she wheedles her way into his project, unknown to the rest of the University of Chicago faculty. O'Hanrahan's old friend Rabbi Mordecai "Morey" Hersch, from Hebrew University in Jerusalem, has control over the lost gospel, and wants O'Hanrahan's help in translating the document, as it is written in an as-yet-undecoded ancient tongue. When the scroll is stolen, the adventure begins.

The book's structure is ambitious, split into fifteen sections, with Lucy and O'Hanrahan's travels across the globe broken up by sections of the translated gospel, complete with 156 informative and funny footnotes. This postmodern move predates David Foster Wallace's 1996 novel *Infinite Jest* and certainly makes *Gospel* an example of the "encyclopedic novel," related to other dense works such as *Ulysses* by James Joyce and more contemporary novels such as Don DeLillo's *Underworld* (1997). Barnhardt even includes a caveat at the beginning, different from the standard disclaimers in a novel: "This is a work of fiction. All of the events, characters, and institutions depicted in this novel are entirely fictitious or are used fictitiously. However, all ancient sources, Biblical citings, apocryphal gospels, and historical information contained in the footnotes of the Gospel are true and accurate."

The footnotes range from the hilarious to the gruesome, from straightforward linguistic explanations of ancient languages or culture to minihagiographies. This density of information is coupled with O'Hanrahan's verbiage—a constant flow of storytelling about the ancient church, about myths and legends associated with early Christianity and the locales that he and Lucy visit. There are seven sections of the translated gospel, divided into chapter and verse just like canonical gospels. The seventh chapter of the gospel is broken into two parts, divided by the last of the Lucy/O'Hanrahan chapters. The mystery follows a picaresque path from Britain to Ireland to Italy, then from Greece to Jerusalem and Africa. It culminates in Louisiana, at a conservative American Christian college and corporate campus called the Promised Land Ministries, run by the Reverend Farley Bullins, a satiric take on televangelists such as Jim Baker and Jimmy Swaggart. The story line runs from early June to late August 1990, alongside the

historical tensions of Iraq's invasion of Kuwait and the beginning of the First Gulf War on August 2, 1990.

On top of all that richness, there is one other grand addition: a character who interjects in voice alone—not the narrator and not merely a voice inside Lucy or O'Hanrahan's head (though it speaks to both), but a larger entity. It seems She is the Holy Spirit as embodied by Sophia, Holy Wisdom, as envisioned by the early Church. Whoever the entity is—and Barnhardt toys with readers throughout—She is a sensible and often amusing traveling companion for the two adventurers, despite how much they want to ignore Her or even feel persecuted by Her, especially in the case of O'Hanrahan.

Not every reviewer enjoyed the novel. *Kirkus Reviews* gave it a terrible write-up, with the reviewer calling the novel a "long winded and lame excuse for an epic adventure." The same writer did not enjoy the footnotes or the *Around the World in Eighty Days* aspect either: "Sadly, the prominence of travelogue commentaries and endless ephemera from centuries of Church history strip the saga of any momentum, turning the characters into mere markers on a map of the ancient world as it is today, who are moved only to be left beached like whales on the next exotic shore."

Barnhardt has said that the novel, to this day, receives mixed reviews—letters from those who loved it, letters from those worried about the state of his soul, letters from scholars who both praise and belittle his scholarship. *Gospel* is, much like the actual gospels, good ground for disagreement. If readers have the stamina of a pilgrim, if they have a sense of humor for the foibles of humans and our sometimes beloved institutions, if they have a thirst for the seemingly trivial that adds up to a satisfying revelation, then it's a trek worth taking. It's not for the distracted. It's a novel in the tradition of many ambitious and brave books. It takes big chances for big rewards, but it will not work for every reader. As James Idema wrote in the *Chicago Tribune*'s original review, "This big, exuberant book succeeds on so many levels one tends to forgive the occasional excess."

SUMMING UP THE 1990S: SHOW WORLD

Barnhardt's third novel, published in 1998, is in many ways a combination of the themes of the first two books. In *Show World* we have Samantha Flint, a small-town girl who goes off to an elite college, then to the big city, this time Washington, D.C., and subsequently Los Angeles, to make her mark, the book's structure much like the bildungsroman of *Emma Who Saved My Life*. As with Gil, Samantha loses her faith (although in a more dramatic downward spiral)—faith in her friends, faith in her ability to muster her talent, faith in both the political culture and the entertainment culture of the United States. The struggle to retain faith is a consistent theme in Barnhardt's work. It's no accident that *Gospel* begins with Matthias lamenting to his brother, "I had lost my faith, Josephus" (p. 1), or that Gil loses faith in Emma and theater. Yet Matthias and Gil are not left entirely bereft. *Show World* is a bleak novel without the emotional uplift of either of the first two. It doesn't have the tour-de-force quality of *Gospel,* but in its more modest scope it hits the bull's eye: readers walk away from *Show World* bruised, wiser to the ways of the world, more tarnished for the knowledge.

Nearly twenty years after its publication, the book was still relevant. Not much changed in the nation's capital or in Hollywood in those subsequent years—sex scandals and hypocrisy and drug problems and all-consuming greed. Barnhardt is both prescient in his take on American pop culture and a gifted reporter with his gaze on the cultural front. The book did not sell as well as it could (or should) have, but one explanation may be that the reading public was burned out on scandals at that particular time. *Show World* was published in the era of the Monica Lewinsky scandal and the O. J. Simpson trial. The plight of Barnhardt's fictional Samantha Flint fits right in with those current events, but perhaps it was all too real for the reading public at the time.

The novel follows Barnhardt's familiar structural adventurousness. This time the book's brief prologue is a letter taken from "The Collected Works of Samantha Flint," a posthumous collection of her journals and memorabilia. The letter is addressed to Samantha's best friend,

mentor, and sometime nemesis, Mimi Mohr. From there the novel is split into three sections: "A Woman of Promise: Northampton and New York, 1978–1983," "The Better Part: Washington, 1989–1993," and "Ruin: Los Angeles, 1997–1998." Each section is separated by another document from "The Collected Works." Prior to "The Better Part" is a fund-raising letter from a conservative politician, Frank Shanker, for whom Samantha reluctantly worked. Prior to "Ruin" is a press release from Mimi Mohr's talent agency regarding a charitable event with a B-list celebrity, Amber Wentworth. The parallel between the two worlds—politics and entertainment—is relentless and pointed in *Show World*. The book's title comes from a garish Los Angeles strip club, and the analogy seems appropriate in Samantha's world; there is not much difference between the demands of pornography and the demands of politics, between wanton sexual appetites and the seedy appetites of the mass media that cover both cities. Both worlds are out to make money, to use people for nefarious purposes, and the only way to escape unscathed is to escape fully. If Sam stays in either place she is bound to fall.

Sam's trajectory is familiar Barnhardt territory, too, in that family plays a part in her development and decline. In *Gospel*, readers learn much about Lucy Dantan's childhood in South Chicago, and even more about O'Hanrahan's youth, his days as a Jesuit, and then his years in a sour marriage and as a less-than-stellar parent. In *Show World*, Barnhardt gives us ample backstory on Samantha's youth. She was raised in Missouri in the struggling middle class. Her father had grand plans to make it with a boat dealership in Boatland (a nice echo of Show World's cadence), a town created to attract tourists to man-made lakes outside of Springfield. Her father slowly goes bust and suffers the humiliation poorly; her parents' divorce and her siblings, two sisters, are doomed, in Samantha's eyes, to live small-town lives, chasing boorish men and raising ungrateful children. Sam sees the dark side of the American Dream: home ownership means debt; family ties are nooses. Gil Freeman and Lucy Dantan had similar fears of family commitment and middle-class

nightmares. Whereas Gil seems to settle, cautiously, for a version of the American Dream, Lucy revolts and, perhaps, dedicates her life to global service. Samantha never finds a happy medium or a healthy alternative.

When Samantha arrives at Smith College she is determined to forge a new identity for herself, to leave Missouri behind. No hick girl from a flyover state, she is going to be a writer, glib and fashionable. When she writes a lyric essay about her youth at Boatland for her first creative writing class, Samantha decides against turning it in and revealing her roots to what she perceives as her more worldly classmates (there are shades of Gatsby here too, echoes of Fitzgerald's poor-boy-at-Princeton youth, the desire to become greater than the privileged kids because the ease with which they flow through the world of money and culture is exasperating). When Sam meets Miriam, the glamorous "Mimi" who disdains college drama and prefers older men, who already knows New York fashion and is comfortable in her isolation—a Jewish girl in the WASP world of Smith—Samantha is smitten. Her girl crush on Mimi evolves into a sort of guild apprenticeship. But Mimi is always more at ease in the world. They make promises to each other, to travel, to help each other achieve their goals—Sam wants to be a novelist—but the world after graduation is more complicated than the young women imagine.

Sam goes off to the District of Columbia and works for a distinguished U.S. senator, Warren Proctor (an echo of the actual distinguished senator from Wisconsin at the time, William Proxmire). Sam is his chief of staff and enjoys her high-pressure job and the power that comes with it. When Proctor retires out of the blue, she is left to scramble and ends up working for a man she loathes, "Family" Frank Shanker, a conservative politician who runs on a social platform that Sam finds revolting. She loses herself in the work and loses her way, drinking too much alcohol, gaining weight, battling insomnia, and sleeping with a married man, another political operative, Cameron Platt. When Shanker's son dies in a sexually comprised situation—and Shanker seems unwilling to mourn but

more than happy to use the situation for his political gain—Sam turns traitor and ends up fired.

It is Mimi's moment to save Sam—she urges her to come out to California, leave Cameron, and work for her. Los Angeles is Mimi's town, where she has become a successful, if ruthless, entertainment agent. Sam's time in D.C. comes to a close but is summed up when she sees her old boss, Proctor, on television, and fears he will tarnish his proud record by returning to D.C. and becoming a lobbyist, a now-familiar career path for retired politicians.

> As he talked, something gave way inside Samantha. Oh, they'd pay him six figures all right. Lunches, galas, parties … all he had to do was shill for somebody. And he'd be ornery at first, hard to match with suitable projects. But soon it would be the old carny routine. Beloved ol' Warren Proctor and this year's snake oil … Not you, thought Samantha. Anyone else in this town can go whore themselves, but please, sir, not you too.… I'm corrupt, thought Samantha sadly, wholly and thoroughly.… but let me keep you in my mind's eye as the man of the people, Senator. Please.
>
> (p. 219)

Samantha's plea goes unresolved. We never learn what becomes of Proctor, but we do go on to see her descent, in Los Angeles, and it isn't pretty. She goes to work for Mimi and marries a young pop singer at Mimi's urging, a troubled young man who is part of a boy band. The marriage is a sham, a ruse to hide his homosexuality and seedy youth as a street prostitute. Sam understands she's being used in order to make sure the preteen girls across America will buy the music. She also becomes hooked on pills, and is knee-deep in emotional disguises. Mimi is busy, too busy with business, to notice Sam's struggles, and when the husband is killed in a seedy hotel known for gay orgies and rampant drug use, Sam is thrust into the spotlight. The California section ends when Sam's involvement comes fully to light—the sort of fears she warned Mimi of in the book's opening letter become a reality, in various ways: Samantha's journey comes to its lowest point on the sunny boardwalk of the Venice Promenade. But Barnhardt does not conclude the novel with Sam's nadir. He backs up and leaves us with that lyrical essay she wrote about Boatland, years

earlier as a freshman at Smith. Once upon a time Sam had talent, and moments of a sometimes idyllic childhood, before it all went sour. As *The Great Gatsby* ended with that beckoning green light, the memory of optimism, and we are all seen as "boats against the current, borne back ceaselessly into the past," *Show World* ends on a long-ago summer day.

> Samantha ran to the top of the trail and turned for the pier, her limbs loose and free, a joy inside escaping with each laughing stride, hurtling herself fast down the child-trampled hill, the spiky grass prickling her bare feet, clasping the beautiful boy's hand before they flew through the air, out ever so far, out above the warm black water, for an airborne moment part of the night and stars and the summer heavens, indulgent and immane.
>
> (p. 342)

Samantha may lose more than her faith; she no longer trusts in friendship or in her country's culture; but we are not left in total nihilism. Readers, to counter Fitzgerald's famous dictum about Americans not being allowed second acts, have more time. We are not Samantha, any more than we are Gatsby. Gil and Lucy and O'Hanrahan all move on. Emma may be a void, and Samantha a disaster, but Barnhardt seems to urge us to put the book down and choose the joyful, not the faithless.

THE RETURN AND THE DEPARTURE: LOOK-AWAY, LOOKAWAY

In an interview with *Deep South Magazine,* Barnhardt knew his ambitions for his one and only Southern novel were large and dynamic. "If I was going to write a Southern novel," he said, "I wanted to talk about class and I wanted to talk about race and I wanted to talk about money and I wanted to talk about the new South vs. the old South, so the characters had to put those thing in play." It's not surprising that it would take a big cast.

The novel revolves around Duke and Jerene Johnston, a well-to-do Charlotte couple, and their four children. While Duke is a prominent lawyer (though no longer practicing, despite being only middle-aged), a distant relative of a famous

Confederate general, and a passionate Civil War historian and reenactor, it is Jerene Jarvis Johnston who has the power of the novel. She is a Southern matriarch in the tradition of Tennessee Williams, *Steel Magnolias,* Scarlett O'Hara, yet she is not tragically melodramatic, ridiculously cornpone, or glossed over with beauty. She is the book's force of nature, and Barnhardt treats her with respect, even as she manipulates and terrorizes, perhaps for sometimes noble purposes. Though she gets only one of the eleven chapters of the novel—each chapter focuses on a different protagonist and no character is given more than one—it is Jerene who holds this world together, the sun around which the action revolves.

Along with the eleven chapters, the novel is divided in into three books. "Book 1: Scandal Averted 2003" begins with a chapter on Duke and Jerene's younger daughter, Jerilyn, who is assaulted at a fraternity party after defying her mother's command not to "rush" a sorority. It is the violation against Jerilyn that swings Jerene into action, actions which come to light years later. Consequences of the past are a recurring motif in the novel. As the South still struggles with its Confederate past, the Johnstons have to wrestle with both distant and recent family histories.

The second chapter introduces Gaston Jarvis, Jerene's brother, a fabulously successful romance novelist whose bitterness is aggravated by a tremendous drinking problem and a long-simmering feud with Duke. Gaston has made piles of money with stories about a Confederate heroine, Cordelia Florabloom, and his hatred for his cash cow, for his dashed dreams of being a "serious" writer, are comic and compelling. After Gaston's chapter, we get the chapter on Jerene: strong-willed, gracious, a woman with whom no one trifles.

"Book 2: Scandal Regained 2007–2008" introduces Annie, the Johnston's eldest daughter, a successful real estate broker. She's smart and obese, the opposite of her younger sister, slender and dull. Annie carries more than weight; she carries a deep unhappiness, perhaps the result of a romantic track record of failure, and a long-term disgust with the religion and politics of her home state and her family. Her involvement with the subprime housing market grows and helps ground the book in its era.

The next chapter focuses on Bo, the elder son, a pastor, a bit of nebbish and married to the more dynamic Kate. Bo's spinelessness in some way mirrors that of his father, a man who should be a powerhouse, a major player in the Charlotte country club scene, but instead is satisfied with staying home and playing with his collection of Confederate memorabilia. Bo is not entirely dislikable—his faith seems genuine—but he's hapless. Bo's chapter is followed by a chapter on Jeannette Jarvis (the elderly mother of Jerilyn, Gaston, and Dillard) who was, for decades, the enabling wife of an alcoholic who abused Gaston terribly while she stood by and did little. It's the cost of her care that has strained Gaston and Jerene's relationship. She is also the keeper of some of the larger secrets of the novel.

Joshua, the younger Johnston brother, is next: a computer geek, a gay man whose best friend is Dorrie Jourdain, a black lesbian. Joshua has a type when it comes to lovers, and it's black men. His sexuality is not acknowledged openly in the family, yet his friendship with Dorrie is accepted.

The next chapter of this section is Dillard's, the sad elderly sister to Jerene and Gaston, the still-grieving mother to Christopher, a boy who died after a sordid life of drug addiction. She is lonely and nearly agoraphobic. Her chapter is followed by Duke's, the fallen patriarch whose passion for Civil War reenactments is deadly serious. Once well-off, now struggling, he becomes obsessed with establishing a reenactment and festival celebrating Charlotte's sole Civil War battle, "the Skirmish at the Trestle," yet unwittingly partners with men more intent on making money than on preserving the city's heritage.

In the siblings' youth, Gaston idolized Duke, a celebrated college football hero, and may have nursed a fondness for the campus hero beyond admiration. *Lookaway, Dixieland*—once the imagined title of a book that Duke and Gaston dreamed of writing back in those heady days—becomes the proposed name for a gated com-

munity planned by those out-of-town investors eager to use Duke's name to give the project legitimacy. That treason eats at Gaston in profound ways. Yet, late in the book, despite their feud, when Duke is reduced even further, it is on Gaston he must rely; Gaston who is holed up in his bizarre, mostly empty, overgrown mansion, a man ravaged by his alcoholism.

The last chapter of the second section is Kate Johnston's. Bo's energetic and popular spouse is frustrated with her role as pastor's wife and longs to do more with her faith than soothe the ruffled feathers of her husband's cranky conservative congregants. She is a spiritual kin to Lucy Dantan from *Gospel* and follows a similar path to her happiness. Both women discover that acting on their faith may mean thinking bigger than the confines of home and hearth and may mean a different role than the one they had imagined for themselves when they were young.

"Book 3: Scandal Redux 2012" belongs to a sole voice, the final speaker of the novel: Dorcas "Dorrie" Jourdain, Joshua's best friend. She's black and lesbian, smart and funny and perhaps a harbinger of the New South's future, fully aware of the violent past of whites rioting and lynching, and yet not without hope. This may be Barnhardt's nod to the end of William Faulkner's *The Sound and the Fury* (1929), a novel of varied voices that closes with a chapter focused on Dilsey, the competent black servant to the increasingly erratic and doomed white family, the Compsons. Much like the Compsons were to Dilsey, "the Johnstons were Dorrie's Designated Crazy Whitefolks—for a while there, she was virtually in the family. And having been away from their orbit, she couldn't help missing them, worrying on their behalf" (*Lookaway*, p. 341). We believe this on all accounts: the Johnstons are crazy, she was virtually family, and she cares about them. If Dorrie, whose family history and present life continues to be scarred by white people every day, can care about those people, there might be hope for reconciliation in the New South. Dorrie's empathy does not excuse the past, but she might be a sign of a new tomorrow. But Barnhardt's vision is not about black sympathy for white insanity. It's about a shifting of power,

and that tremor of change comes from an unlikely source: Jerene.

It's Jerene who recognizes Dorrie's leadership and intelligence. She goes as far as implying that Dorrie would be the rightful heir of Jerene's social status. Yet even in this abdication, Jerene takes center stage. Here, in the last pages of Dorrie's chapter, Barnhardt lets Jerene have, literally, the last words of the novel. "My land," she says, which at first seems to be a exclamation. Or is it more of an observation? A confession? A claim? The phrase becomes a thoughtful play on the South's past, present, and future. It's an invitation to consider the question, whose land is it, this New South? Just as Margaret Mitchell's Scarlett O'Hara was obsessed with keeping her land, Tara, Jerene has been impassioned in preserving her family's heritage, but the reality is the land is no longer hers. The South has broadened, and as the novel closes, "my land," which once applied to Duke, Gaston, or Jerene, now includes a new kind of Southerner, exemplified by Josh and Dorrie.

Barnhardt too is that new Southerner, though as he told *Bookreporter*, he does not believe he is an entirely rare breed:

> I have had to admit that I am, in many ways, culturally Southern. But I'm one of the Southerners who does not sit easily with the flow of the politics or the church or the calcification of white privilege that rarely gives an inch. But there are plenty of us troublemaking redneck liberals; I have plenty of company and, I suspect, through the centuries, always would have had fellow travelers.

Lookaway, Lookaway may be the sole fictional creation where he directly speaks of his cultural heritage, but the book should ensure his place among the essential novelists of the American South. The literary "land," once the domain of William Faulkner and Flannery O'Connor, those fellow travelers of a sort, now too belongs to Barnhardt.

THE MISCELLANY: SHORT STORIES, INTRODUCTIONS, AND BOOK REVIEWS

Barnhardt has only sporadically published short fiction during his long career, but he has stated

that he plans on producing a collection of stories in the future. A clue to the tenor of that collection may be found in one notable published work, the anthology *The Story Behind the Story* (2004), edited by Peter Turchi and Andrea Barrett.

"Mrs. Dimbleby" concerns Alice Shields, harried mother to the spoiled and cold six-year-old Katie Shields, whose behavior makes Alice doubt her every parental choice. The story's immediate action takes place in a single afternoon, during a commute from school to the home of a classmate of Katie's. While chauffeuring Katie, the surprisingly angelic Anna, and Anna's frivolous and a little tipsy mother, Beverly—a woman blessed with a wonderful child despite, from every indication, being a lousy parent—Alice is goaded into recounting the details of a local tragedy.

Mrs. Dimbleby, an entirely offstage character, has killed one of her daughters in an accident. The normally staid and rule-bound mother had, on a whim, driven into a curbside pile of leaves, thinking she was going to amuse her daughter, and unwittingly kills her other girl, who had been playing hide-and-seek in the leaf pile. The death devastates the woman, and Alice is one of the few to extend sympathy to her, even going so far as to visit with her and bring her food after the accident.

The girls, initially amused by the gossip surrounding the child's death, are horrified when Alice tells them the truth. Mrs. Dimbleby isn't a monster, just a woman who made a terrible decision in one fleeting moment, a decision which will haunt her forever. After the tale, which leaves Anna in tears, Beverly informs Alice that the carpooling won't be necessary in the future. This severance might have earlier sent Alice into a spiral of self-doubt, as judged as she feels in the beginning of the story, but she uses it as an opportunity to reclaim her authority as a parent and the story ends with her committed to raising Katie with a firmer, more loving hand.

Unlike Barnhardt's novels, "Mrs. Dimbleby" has a compressed time frame, a small cast, and, most unusually, a narrow lens. Barnhardt explains:

Shamefully, I am a latecomer to the very sort of story I've written here, the place where most writers sensibly start: the small slice-of-life scene, an incident or a moment explored, considered or maybe just brushed against. More importantly for my growth as a writer, I suppose, is that it is "small" in subject matter, family stuff, parents and kids, carpooling neighbors—small, that is, compared to the putative ambitions of a novel. Increasingly, I've come to see that all the high drama in the world rests in our day-to-day chores, our routines with our loved ones, if we're conscious, if we're observant.

(Turchi, ed., p. 194)

Another work of short fiction, this one collected in the anthology *Long Story Short*, was published in 2009. Barnhardt's contribution to this North Carolina–focused book of flash fiction is titled "Stoma." It tells, in just three pages, the story of O'Connell, an emergency room nurse, who tends Angel, a disease-ridden gay prostitute who is ridiculed among the staff because of his particularly horrific infections. A rumination on love and its inevitable disasters, "Stoma," even more than "Mrs. Dimbleby," highlights Barnhardt's skill with compression. It's interesting to see Barnhardt, known for his large-scale projects, wrestle within the confines of a different mode.

As with *Long Story Short*, the anthology *27 Views of Raleigh* (2013) is a regional work. Barnhardt's contribution is the introduction, an amusing history of the North Carolina capital and a defense of its artistic character. Barnhardt's voice here is breezy, educated, and comic; consistent with his fiction, he makes serious points with a light touch. With his typical breadth of knowledge, he amuses readers with anecdotes of the state government and capitol building and surprises with a revelation about William Tecumseh Sherman.

When Sherman was in town … news reached him that President Lincoln had been assassinated. Predictably, his officers and soldiers yearned to raze Raleigh to ashes, just as they'd expertly done to Atlanta and Columbia. Sherman issued orders that nothing should be done to any property or any person and disobedience would meet with the strictest punishments … and Raleigh was spared. Sherman knew that North Carolina was the most reluctant of the Rebel States.

(p. 19)

It's that sort of historical knowledge—reminiscent of Patrick O'Hanrahan's scope in *Gospel*—that makes reading Barnhardt so much fun. Plus, he's not shy about bringing his own opinions to the fore. Walking through Raleigh's cemeteries, filled as they are with Confederate dead and politicians sympathetic to secessionist and segregationist causes, Barnhardt boldly states: "I never wander through Oakwood without being mightily glad that some of these men and their ruinous philosophies are six feet under the dirt where they belong" (p. 20).

Barnhardt also occasionally publishes book reviews. One review—more of a retrospective of an author's work than a mere review—appeared in 2014 in *Slate* magazine. This portrait of the novelist and short-story writer Elizabeth Spencer, whose work has spanned decades and whose collection *Starting Over* appeared when she was ninety-two, is written in Barnhardt's lucid and intelligent style of journalism, traceable all the way back to his reviews for the Michigan State student paper and then polished at *Sports Illustrated*. Yet here too is the mature voice of one accomplished author analyzing another author's distinguished career. Barnhardt admires Spencer, more for her craft and intelligence than her longevity, but he's impressed by the span of her career as well.

> Just think of it—65 years, and counting, of superb writing. From the 20th-century South of sharecroppers and mules … to the 21st-century South of *Starting Over* … it's a New South more New than South. Who among our great living writers has been such a witness to our historical changes and follies? Spencer's life and fiction span an era that comprised the great American questions of equality, justice, human dignity, while never ignoring the great individual questions as well—how do we be true to ourselves in bad circumstances? How do we survive the battles of family obligation, of time passing us by? Spencer's body of work … is a lasting contribution of the permanent national shelf.
>
> ("The Master," *Slate*)

Barnhardt is a generous and astute critic. When he argues that Spencer's 1957 novel *The Voice at the Back Door* was unfairly shunned by the Pulitzer Prize Board and probably deserved the award more than Harper Lee's celebrated novel *To Kill a Mockingbird*, which won in 1961,

he does so knowing it's an unfamiliar, and potentially unpopular, argument and backs it up with a keenly chosen sample from Spencer's writing. Later, when he describes Spencer's disdain for her most famous work, the short story (turned film turned Broadway musical) "The Light in the Piazza," he bucks Spencer's own opinion. "Let's annoy her further," he writes, "by agreeing with what a half-century of readers have decided: 'The Light in the Piazza' is a masterpiece, providing every bit the enjoyment of *Daisy Miller.*"

His dissection of Spencer's European years, and his linking her with Henry James, harkens to Barnhardt's own itinerant youth and his love of James's work, as well as to his literary future. He has said in a number of interviews that a "European" novel, set during the recent economic downturn, is next up on his agenda. Barnhardt's take on the American in Europe, perhaps inspired first by James, then by Spencer, should be witty and observant, a companion to his first four novels and yet, given his love of variety, probably as divergent from them as each was to its predecessor.

ELUDING CATEGORIES: WORKS IN PROGRESS

There have been no film versions of Barnhardt's work as of 2015, but the television network HBO optioned *Lookaway, Lookaway* in 2014 for a comedy series, with Barnhardt coproducing, but not writing, the proposed show. As he told Bill Krueger, "This is meant to be a series about New South as it really is. I don't believe the New South has been adequately portrayed on television. It's always the cartoon south—competitive catty women or an update of *The Beverly Hillbillies* or *The Dukes of Hazzard*. It might be entertaining but its not how we live" (NC State Professor's Novel Optioned, 2014). On the publishing front, he has stated he is working on a collection of stories and two additional novels. Prior to writing *Lookaway, Lookaway,* he had begun heavy research and preliminary writing on a western, though work on the aforementioned European novel is his current project.

Surprisingly, there is no academic criticism of his work. He has yet to be discovered by

scholars, unlike such contemporaries as Jeffrey Eugenides, Jhumpa Lahiri, Jonathan Franzen, and Zadie Smith. He is under the radar for a writer with four ambitious novels to his credit. Barnhardt deserves to be better known and more widely read. His work is challenging but funny; he takes risks in both content and structure, but he is not obtuse or deliberately arcane. His topics are wide ranging, yet his storytelling always comes down to compelling characters acting in believable, if not always admirable, ways. He captures the mindset of late twentieth- and early twenty-first-century America in such detail, in all its bombast and ridiculousness, yet never lets go of empathy. After the publication of *Lookaway, Lookaway,* Barnhardt admitted to a varied career that defies familiar literary labels.

> I've eluded categories. I'm not a naturalist, I'm not a romantic, I'm not a realist. I would probably say that I'm a classicist. I hope I'm writing sort of the classic novels of the 19th century. I'm nervous about being in any camp. I have a New York novel. I have a religious novel. I have a Hollywood novel. This is the Southern novel.
>
> (Krueger, 2013)

Barnhardt's eclectic canon, building strength for twenty years, will hopefully grow to receive the public recognition and scholarly attention it deserves in the next twenty. He has joked that writing fiction is a psychosis of sorts, one that society tolerates only so long as we value the product. Speaking to a university audience in 2013, he kidded,

> You know, it's a good thing that they value novels because we live for four or five years or longer with these characters in our head, walking around—we think they're real. We are doing dialogue in the car, driving along, wondering what they'd say … and if they didn't value novel writing they would hospitalize us, they would think this is a ridiculous thing to do, to create this alternative universe and then live in it for a while and write about it. It's a very strange thing sometimes, I think, writing novels.
>
> (*Southeast Review* podcast)

Strange, indeed, for the nonwriter to contemplate the ridiculousness of crafting pretend people into pretend situations. Yet despite the decades from Flaubert to Barnhardt and all the derivations of storytelling since the nineteenth century, there are many readers more than willing to tolerate the absurdity of fiction writing if that intellectual circus act results in works like the engrossing novels of Wilton Barnhardt.

Selected Bibliography

WORKS OF WILTON BARNHARDT

NOVELS
Emma Who Saved My Life. New York: St. Martin's Press, 1989.
Gospel. New York: St. Martin's Press, 1993.
Show World. New York: St. Martin's Press, 1998.
Lookaway, Lookaway. New York: St. Martin's Press, 2013.

SHORT STORIES
"Mrs. Dimbleby." In *The Story Behind the Story: 26 Writers and How They Work.* Edited by Peter Turchi and Andrea Barrett. New York: Norton, 2004. Pp. 181–193. (With an afterword, "Behind the Story," pp. 194–196.)
"Stoma." In *Long Story Short: Flash Fiction by Sixty-Five of North Carolina's Finest Writers.* Edited by Marianne Gingher. Chapel Hill: University of North Carolina Press, 2009. Pp. 14–16.

MISCELLANY
"How's This for a Real Kick." *Sports Illustrated,* December 24, 1990. (Profile of NFL kicker Tom Dempsey.) http://www.si.com/vault/1990/12/24/123315/hows-this-for-a-real-kick-tom-dempseys-63-yarder-took-flight-20-years-ago
"He Throws Free Throws by the Score." *Sports Illustrated,* January 28, 1991. http://www.si.com/vault/1991/01/28/123518/he-throws-free-throws-by-the-score-floridian-ted-st-martin-has-parlayed-an-astonishing-talent-into-a-unique-career(Profile of Ted St. Martin.)
"Introduction." *27 Views of Raleigh: The City of Oaks in Prose and Poetry.* Edited by Barnhardt. Hillsborough, N.C.: Eno, 2013.
"The Master." *Slate Book Review,* February 4, 2014. http://www.slate.com/articles/arts/books/2014/02/eliza beth_spencer_s_collection_of_short_stories_starting_over _reviewed.html
Wilton Barnhardt author website. http://www.wiltonbarnhardt.com

REVIEWS

"*Gospel,* by Wilton Barnhardt." *Kirkus Reviews,* April 16, 1993. https://www.kirkusreviews.com/book-reviews/wilton-barnhardt/gospel-2/

Idema, James. "The Spell of the Gospel." *Chicago Tribune,* May 9, 1993. (Review of *Gospel*). http://articles.chicagotribune.com/1993-05-09/entertainment/9305090301_1_matthias-jesus-mary-magdalene

Jones, Malcolm. "Southern Discomfort." *New York Times Book Review,* August 30, 2013, p. 9. (Review of *Lookaway, Lookaway.*) http://www.nytimes.com/2013/09/01/books/review/wilton-barnhardts-lookaway-lookaway.html?_r=0

INTERVIEWS

Bass, Erin. "Wilton Barnhardt on Writing His One and Only Southern Novel." *Deep South Magazine,* August 22, 2013. http://deepsouthmag.com/2013/08/wilton-barnhardt-on-writing-his-one-and-only-southern-novel/

"Interview with Wilton Barnhardt." *Bookreporter,* August 21, 2013. http://www.bookreporter.com/authors/wilton-barnhardt/news/interview-082113

Krueger, Bill. "Wilton Barnhardt: I'm Nervous About Being in Any Camp." As interviewed by Cherry Crayton. *Red & White for Life: Blog of the NC State Alumni Association,* July 23, 2013. https://www.alumniblog.ncsu.edu/2013/07/23/wilton-barnhardt-im-nervous-about-being-in-any-camp/

————. "NC State Professor's Novel Optioned for HBO Comedy Series." As interviewed by Sylvia Adcock. *Red & White for Life: Blog of the NC State Alumni Association,* February 10, 2014. https://www.alumniblog.ncsu.edu/2014/02/10/nc-state-professors-novel-optioned-for-hbo-comedy-series/

McLellan, Dennis. "Barnhardt's 'Gospel': A Loose Cannon." *Los Angeles Times,* May 20, 1993. http://articles.latimes.com/1993-05-20/news/vw-37661_1_holy-spirit

TELEVISION INTERVIEW AND PODCAST

"Wilton Barnhardt." Public reading, with an introduction by Diane Roberts. *Southeast Review*/Florida State University, February 4, 2014. http://southeastreview.org/wilton-barnhardt/

"Wilton Barnhardt, *Lookaway, Lookaway.*" *North Carolina Bookwatch,* February 7, 2014. http://video.unctv.org/video/2365174016/

JOE BRAINARD

(1941—1994)

Aaron Goldsman

A CELEBRATED ARTIST, illustrator, and author, Joe Brainard was a central figure of the second generation of the New York School of poets. Recognized primarily as a visual artist and as an illustrator of his poet friends' work, Brainard was also an accomplished writer, publishing over a dozen books in his lifetime as well as numerous poems, prose pieces, and diaries in New York's flourishing little magazine scene of the 1960s and 1970s. As a writer, he is best known for his innovative series of idiosyncratic memoir, *I Remember,* which invented a form that has been reproduced by thousands of students in writing workshops and classrooms around the world. With the publication of his *Collected Writings* by the Library of America in 2012, readers now have access to hundreds of pages of Brainard material, much of which was previously unpublished or only available in the pages of rare books and ephemera limited to the special collections of university libraries and private collectors. Though as of this writing the scholarly reappraisal of Brainard's importance for twentieth-century American literary history has only just begun, his work was an undeniable influence on and interlocutor with that of better-known contemporaries like Ted Berrigan, Ron Padgett, and Anne Waldman.

Over the course of his career, what comes through most strongly in Brainard's work is the force of a unique personality with a singular voice. As the poet John Ashbery famously put it in an essay on Brainard, "Joe Brainard was one of the nicest artists I have ever known. Nice as a person and nice as an artist" (Ashbery, p. 1). Bundled into that one innocuous adjective is a range of impacted meanings and perceptions, Ashbery pointing us to a quality present everywhere in Brainard's oeuvre but difficult to define:

a generosity toward the objects and materials of both his art and his writing; a wondering admiration for and pleasure in the neglected details and detritus of everyday life; and perhaps most of all, an unflinching honesty and openness toward himself and toward his audience. Brainard found ways to be candid without abrasion, sincere without mawkishness, and earnest without embarrassment, a significant accomplishment in a period that prized irony and self-reflexivity over ardent expression. While no naïf himself, Brainard risked appearing so in his work, which often led even his most admiring critics to relegate him to the status of an endearing but minor figure. However, with the perspective afforded by time and access to a much larger sample of his work, twenty-first-century readers may approach Brainard newly as a fascinating artist and writer who worked at the center of some of the most exciting developments of American culture in the second half of the twentieth century.

LIFE

Joe Howard Brainard was born on March 11, 1942, at home in Salem, Arkansas, to Howard Brainard and Alice Marie Brainard (née Burrow). The second of four children, Joe was preceded by older brother Jim by a year and a half. The family moved to Tulsa in the fall of 1943, and Joe and his brother were joined by sister Becky in 1951 and brother John in 1954. The Brainards had moved to Tulsa for work in the industries jump-started by World War II. Although Howard was eventually promoted from an assembly line in the Oklahoma oil fields to a desk job in town, the family of six led a modest life in a working-class neighborhood on the north side of Tulsa. As Brainard's lifelong friend and fellow Tulsa native

Ron Padgett recalls in his book *Joe: A Memoir of Joe Brainard* (2004), "The Brainards were the very image of a respectable, hard-working family" (p. 7).

With the exception of art, Joe's grades in school were average. Inhibited by a natural shyness as well as a stutter, Joe remained a well-liked but quiet presence in his classes. It wasn't until he enrolled in Central High School that he found his niche, befriending Padgett and the aspiring poet Dick Gallup. The pair invited him to work as art director on their new little magazine, the *White Dove Review,* which published its first issue in February 1959. Although the boys were only in high school, they managed to recruit an impressive list of contributors, including Ted Berrigan, Robert Creeley, Allen Ginsberg, LeRoi Jones (later Amiri Baraka), Jack Kerouac, and Gilbert Sorrentino. Berrigan, who had relocated to Oklahoma to pursue a master's degree at the University of Tulsa, became a particular friend. Eight years their senior, Berrigan played mentor to the young group, engaging them in serious discussions about literature and art. In a few years' time, the four would find themselves together in New York City, comprising what John Ashbery once called the "soi-disant Tulsa School of Poetry" (Padgett, p 50).

Brainard's talent as an artist was clear from a very young age. He won numerous awards at school and was the subject of several articles in the local press. His first ambition was to be a fashion designer. By the age of eight, he was designing outfits for his mother, which she would execute herself and wear. In high school, his drawings appeared in advertisements for local department stores and clothiers, his work at a par with that of professional draftsmen. Although his plan had been to pursue a degree in fashion design and illustration after graduation, his exposure to the artistic ambitions of his poet friends seems to have altered his course. In the fall of 1960 he moved to Dayton, Ohio, where he enrolled at the Dayton Art Institute on a full-tuition scholarship. Before the semester began, he accompanied Padgett to New York, where the latter was beginning college at Columbia University. The city left an indelible impression on Brainard, and before the end of his first semester at Dayton he withdrew from his studies and relocated to New York. Although the glamour and opportunity of the metropolis were likely a major pull for the young artist, the instigating factor seems to have been the censorship of some paintings at a student exhibition. As he recalls in *I Remember,* "I remember in Dayton, Ohio, the art fair in the park where they made me take down all my naked self-portraits" (*Collected Writings,* hereafter *CW,* p. 42). His next encounter with formal art education would be as a teacher at Cooper Union seven years later.

Brainard's first New York apartment was a tiny storefront on East Sixth Street near the Bowery. Establishing a spartan sense of interior decor that he would reproduce in a number of apartments in the years that followed, Brainard used the front room of the space as a studio, sleeping on a small bed sequestered in a tiny back room. Money was scarce, and Brainard supported himself doing odd jobs painting signs and menus for local businesses, working shifts in a nearby antique and curio shop, and occasionally selling his blood at five dollars a pint. Berrigan arrived in New York in early 1961, and the trio from Tulsa soon resumed their intimacy. That summer, they were joined by Berrigan's University of Tulsa girlfriend, Pat Mitchell. After the relationship with Berrigan ended, Mitchell and Padgett eventually married, the couple remaining a permanent fixture in Brainard's life.

Struggling in an emotional and artistic rut, Brainard moved to Boston in January 1963. With neither money nor friends close to hand, these were difficult months for Brainard, but they achieved the desired result. By the summer, he'd had his first major breakthrough, experimenting in the collage and assemblage forms that would define his early style. Around this time, he also began writing seriously at the encouragement of his poet friends. Early pieces including "A Play" and "Diary Aug. 4–Aug. 15" were published in Berrigan's new little magazine *C: A Journal of Poetry,* which launched in April 1963. The third issue of *C* (July–August 1963) featured the first of Brainard's many cover designs for the publication. In the decades to come, Brainard

would complete hundreds of illustrations and jacket designs for the work of his friends and acquaintances, as well as for major publications such as *ARTnews*.

Brainard returned to New York in the fall, and soon began making connections in the city's intertwined worlds of art and literature. He also met his first boyfriend, Joe LeSueur, the longtime roommate of the first-generation New York School poet Frank O'Hara, the latter of whom Brainard would later describe as his "hero" (*CW*, p. 236). While Brainard had not exactly hidden his sexuality prior to the affair—he had avoided the draft by disclosing his homosexuality to an army official earlier in 1963—the relationship with LeSueur was his real entrée into city's gay scene, and in particular, the downtown milieu of artists, writers, critics, composers, choreographers, and hangers-on that flourished in the postwar years. Although it would be some time before the gay liberation movement contested the closet and the persecution of the homosexual minority in the United States, Brainard was able to live a relatively open gay life in his New York enclave. As he would later write in a 1971 self-portrait, "The only thing that ever bothered me about being queer was that I thought maybe people wouldn't like me if they knew" (*CW*, p. 359). In his relatively sheltered corner of Manhattan, Brainard was able to thrive as an openly gay artist and writer in ways that may not have been possible elsewhere at that time.

By the spring of 1964 Brainard's relationship with LeSueur had cooled, and he met the poet and librettist Kenward Elmslie. Some ten years older than Brainard and independently wealthy—the publisher Joseph Pulitzer was Elmslie's grandfather—the poet was a crucial source of emotional and (particularly in these early years) financial support for the young artist. Although their complex relationship would evolve over the decades, they remained close companions until Brainard's death in 1994. Beginning in 1965, Brainard would spend nearly every summer at Elmslie's vacation home in Calais, Vermont, playing host to artist and writer friends from the city and completing many of his collaborative works. A great number of these were done with

Elmslie himself, and the latter's Z Press, based in Calais, published several Brainard volumes.

Back in the city, Brainard's career as an artist began to take off. He joined the Charles Alan Gallery in 1964, the site of his first solo show in New York the following year. That show, primarily of collage works and assemblages, was followed by two more at the rechristened Landau-Alan Gallery in 1967 and 1969. Following the closure of the Landau-Alan in 1970, Brainard moved to the Fischbach Gallery, which would mount four solo shows of his work from 1971 to 1975. The last of these, which led to a feature about Brainard in *People* magazine, boasted fifteen hundred small collage works, many no large than two inches by two inches. His immense productivity in the early seventies was at least partially abetted by amphetamines, which—following an intervention led by Ron and Pat Padgett—Brainard gave up in 1976. Although his work was generally well received by critics, each show was followed by a period of gloom in which Brainard questioned his artistic talent. Brainard had counted his commitment to pursuing work across a variety of forms—from collage and assemblage to pen and ink portraits to traditional landscapes in oils—as a strength in earlier years, but by the mid-seventies he began to feel as though his eclecticism was preventing him from achieving the skill and confidence of the painters he admired. Increasingly disappointed with his output, by 1979 he had decided to stop showing new work.

The late sixties and seventies were also a period of great productivity for Brainard as a writer. By the late sixties, he was a regular reader at the St. Mark's Poetry Project in New York, and in 1969 he had a major breakthrough, landing on the *I Remember* form for which he would become most famous as an author. The first volume of his signature remembrances appeared in 1970, followed by *I Remember More* in 1972, *More I Remember More* and *I Remember Christmas* (published by the Museum of Modern Art) in 1973, and, finally, a collected edition titled *I Remember* in 1975. In 1971 Brainard spent two months in Bolinas, California, connecting with West Coast poets like Bill Berkson, Tom Clark,

Allen Ginsberg, and Diane di Prima. He published an account of his stay—an idiosyncratic mix of text and image—as *Bolinas Journal* in 1971. In addition to a number of collaborative books with poets, the first years of the seventies saw the publication of a host of Brainard volumes, including *Some Drawings of Some Notes to Myself* (1971), *The Banana Book* (1972), *The Cigarette Book* (1972), and *The Friendly Way* (1972). In 1971 the Kulchur Foundation brought out a *Selected Writings,* which confirmed Brainard's status as a writer and made a broader swath of his work available to a wider audience for the first time. In 1981 Little Caesar Press in Los Angeles published his final collection of writing, *Nothing to Write Home About.* As its title indicates, by the early eighties Brainard's confidence and interest in his writing was waning alongside that of his art.

In the last fifteen years of his life, Brainard devoted himself to his friendships as well as to an enormous amount of reading, particularly novels. While he was coaxed into doing some occasional work with friends—illustrating, for example, Elmslie's *Sung Sex* in the late eighties—he generally stuck to his resolution to stop making new work. As Ron Padgett records in his memoir, however, these were generally happy years for Brainard. In 1979 he began a relationship with the actor Keith McDermott that lasted into the late eighties, the pair parting as friends. He remained close with Elmslie, continuing their annual tradition of summering together in Vermont. He played the role of diffident mentor to a generation of artists and writers coming up through the New York scene. While no definitive answer ever emerged as to why Brainard gave up his art practice, Padgett speculates that, in addition to his frustration with the quality of his output, Brainard's life itself became the focus of his creative energies. Drawing on a 1973 letter from Brainard, Padgett suggests that, "for him, art was 'simply a way of life' that enabled him to fulfill his need to give people 'a present' and perhaps be loved in return. Gradually, in the mid-1980s, Joe's need to make art diminished as his own life became his art" (p. 310). After receiving an HIV-positive diagnosis in the fall of 1990, Joe

Brainard died of AIDS-related pneumonia on May 25, 1994. As per his request, he was cremated, his ashes divided among his close friends to be scattered in a favorite meadow on Elmslie's property in Vermont.

BRAINARD THE ARTIST

Throughout his life, Brainard thought of himself first and foremost as an artist. As such, an understanding of his achievements as a writer would be incomplete without some attention to his parallel achievements in collage, assemblage, drawing, and painting. Put another way, Brainard's writing is best viewed as one part of a heterogeneous and dynamic aesthetic practice that includes his work in the visual arts. The hallmarks of both his art and his writing—the joyful observation of the quotidian materials of American life; the "camp" mixing of high and low cultural registers; the embrace of a serious kind of silliness; an impulse toward the personal, the coterie, and the autobiographical; and a restless and varied productivity—are all associated with the tendencies of the New York School aesthetic more generally. A key part of this milieu, Brainard's writing, his collaborations with poets, and his art all stand in a porous relationship to each other and to the work of those close to him. Readers interested in a more comprehensive introduction to Brainard's art practice and to his place within critical narratives of twentieth-century American art history may refer to the exhibition catalog for the 2001 major traveling retrospective of his work, and in particular, the well-researched and insightful curatorial essay by Constance M. Lewallen.

As mentioned in the biographical sketch above, Brainard's first major exhibited works were experiments in collage and assemblage he completed in the early to mid-sixties. These pieces tended to be lush, almost baroque collections of objects and images that appealed to Brainard's magpie sensibility. The everyday detritus of life in New York City figured largely, as well as treasures found in local junk shops and Catholic iconography, especially images of the Madonna. His first solo show at the Alan Gal-

lery in 1965 was composed principally of assemblages reminiscent of Catholic altarpieces. In a 1967 article on Brainard published in *ARTnews,* the artist's friend and first-generation New York School poet James Schuyler described one of Brainard's most impressive shrines from the exhibition, *Prell* (1965), as follows:

> A dozen bottles of Prell—that insidious green—terrible green roses and grapes, glass dangles like emeralds, long stings of green glass beads, a couple of strands looped up. Under glass, in the center, a blue-green pietà, sweating an acid yellow. The whole thing cascades from an upraised hand at top: drops and stops like an express elevator. It is a cultivated essence of shop-window shrines and Pentecostal Chapels.... Its own particular harsh pure green is raised and re-inforced until it becomes an architecture. It is to green what a snowball is to white, an impactment.
>
> (p. 74)

In a letter to Schuyler printed in the review, Brainard is careful to explain that *Prell* and the other altarpieces were not made with the intention of insulting or belittling religious belief. Rather, Brainard was interested in the kinds of elevations the religious sensibility of the pieces made possible: "Sometimes what I do is to purify objects" (Schuyler, p. 75). Drawing on the iconographic tradition of Catholicism, Brainard's assemblages raise the dross of everyday life into objects of aesthetic contemplation and pleasure.

Around this time, Brainard also began producing his signature appropriations of Ernie Bushmiller's iconic comic strip character Nancy. An admirer of Bushmiller's bold, clean lines—and, perhaps, drawn to the sexually charged pun made available by the character's name—Brainard delighted in putting the hapless Nancy in surreal and bawdy situations. Examples of his irreverent Nancy drawings include "If Nancy Was an Ashtray" (1972), which features Nancy in profile with an oversized cigarette stubbed out in her mouth, and "If Nancy Was a Boy," which places "her" in the middle distance lifting her red skirt to reveal cartoon male genitalia. In a number of other Nancy pieces, the comic strip character collides with the titans of Western art history. In Brainard's 1971 collage cover for *ARTnews,* for example, Nancy appears in classic paintings by masters such as Francisco Goya and Leonardo da Vinci as well as heroes of the avant-garde like Marcel Duchamp, Piet Mondrian, and Willem de Kooning. Importantly, while his interest in popular culture and the comic strip may invite comparisons with Roy Lichtenstein and Andy Warhol (whom Brainard admired), Brainard was no pop artist. As Constance M. Lewallen has it, "Brainard's relationship to the material world of popular culture was one of affection or amusement or both. Moreover, he was too protean to be stuck with Pop or any other label" (p. 10). Approaching his objects with a genuine ardor, Brainard lacked Pop's sense of ironic distance and cool.

Following the altarpiece shows at the Alan Gallery (later called the Landau-Alan Gallery), Brainard's work shifted to a new form: complex and labor intensive collages of flowers and plant life he called "Gardens," as well as flower paintings in gauche and oils. To complete the gardens, Brainard would paint various plants individually, cut them out, and paste them together to form vibrant, almost surreal allover collages. This form would later evolve into his cutouts, in which similar paintings and drawings would be layered between Plexiglas to form three-dimensional shadow boxes reminiscent of the work of Joseph Cornell. In these as well as his more traditional flower paintings, Brainard was at odds with the prevailing tastes of his time, which tended toward the self-consciously unlovely aesthetics of minimalism and conceptual art. His fascination with the beautiful and the decorative likely contributed to critics' assessment of him as a delightful and talented minor figure, a reputation that he would struggle with throughout his life as an artist.

Despite his eclecticism, from the beginnings of his career Brainard had an ambition to achieve excellence in painting's most prestigious and difficult medium: oils. He particularly admired the figurative work of his friends Fairfield Porter and Alex Katz. Beginning in the early seventies, Brainard began his first serious experiments in oils, painting traditional still lifes and landscapes in Vermont as well as some striking portraits of Elmslie's whippet, Whippoorwill. Brainard was particularly pleased with the latter, writing to

Porter in 1973 that he considered them "a breakthrough" (Padgett, p. 211). The oils were exhibited in a show at the Fischbach gallery in 1974 and were met with critical acclaim. Despite these successes, Brainard never quite felt that he measured up to the skill in the medium of his more focused friends. In a letter to the Padgetts, Brainard confesses that he may lack the "patience" to stick to one form long enough to master it: "I guess that is one reason I like Alex Katz so much," he writes, referring to Katz's commitment to a particular medium and subject. "When I think about him I sometimes think I am just making a bunch of art, which is fine, but I am wondering if that is as good for me as if I were doing something else" (Lewallen, p. 107). This worry may have been a major factor in his decision to stop exhibiting work around 1979.

Brainard's final show at the Fischbach Gallery, which opened in December 1975, was perhaps his most ambitious. Featuring more than fifteen hundred small works in collage, ink, and watercolors, the show was an almost obsessive celebration of the quotidian details of Brainard's everyday life. As John Russell observed in a review for the *New York Times,* "Brainard is a born diarist. No moment of the day is dead to him.... . We sense throughout the show an ongoing energy which insists that images are there to tease, provoke, and give pleasure" (qtd. in Padgett, p. 222). Here as in his writing—much of which takes the form of diaries and journals—Brainard's attention is directed at the vibrancy of ordinary events and objects, and their capacity to please. It also gestures to Brainard's association with the minor, cleverly ramped up to a monumental scale. In an interview with *People* magazine that followed the show, Brainard was explicit about his commitment to the small: "The art scene has gotten too big, too serious, too self-important, and too expensive" (qtd. in Padgett, p. 223). Although an intelligent response to the commodification of the art market, Brainard's stand nonetheless confirmed his ghettoization by critics to the realm of the inspired but minor. More positively, his practice of giving away works to friends who visited the show prefigures his turn to personal relationships in the last fifteen

years of his life. As Padgett suggests, Brainard's art was a present to those he loved, a gift that, in later years, became his attentive presence itself.

BRAINARD THE DESIGNER, ILLUSTRATOR, AND COLLABORATOR

In the early sixties Brainard began doing illustrations and jacket designs for a wide range of his poet friends in addition to collaborative works blending text and image. In his memoir of Brainard, Padgett recalls the earliest example of these collaborations, completed sometime in 1959 or 1960 when the two were seniors in high school. It featured a woodcut of a plaintive girl above a brief poem, the combination of image and caption echoing an original work by Brainard's father and grandfather that hung in the family home (p. 77). In the decades to come, Brainard's designs and illustrations would accompany the work of a wide range of poets, from close friends and New York School stalwarts like John Ashbery, Berrigan, Dick Gallup, Padgett, and Anne Waldman to poets working farther afield, such as Bill Berkson, Robert Creeley, and Lee Harwood. He also did cover designs for the published scores of composers like Ned Rorem and Jack Beeson, as well as set decor for stage productions, most famously a double bill of plays by Frank O'Hara and LeRoi Jones at the Writer's Stage Theater in 1964.

Though Brainard is generally credited as an illustrator in much of his work with poets, he resisted the idea that his drawings stood in any simple relation to the texts of his collaborators. In a diary entry from the summer of 1969, Brainard writes, "I respect poetry very much. (More than I understand it.) And I think that, actually, poetry (in terms of illustrating it) needs respect more than it needs understanding. I don't like that word 'illustrating'" (*CW,* p. 249). Brainard's drawings keep a respectful distance from the poems they accompany, leaving space for free play in the reader's interpretation. In his best collaborative work, there is a sense of give and take in the relation between poet and artist. In an earlier entry from that same diary, Brainard describes the collaborative relationship in terms

of "tension": "Perhaps what is interesting about collaborating is simply the act of *trying* to collaborate. The tension. The tension of trying" (*CW,* p. 245). Hence Brainard's preference for on-the-spot collaborations with his friends: working in tandem, poet and artist are able to make work in which the combination of word and image produces a whole that exceeds the sum of its parts.

Brainard's collaborative ethos is best demonstrated in the comic strips completed with poets published in *C Comics,* two issues of which appeared in 1964 and 1965. Brainard began doing comic strips with Berrigan and Padgett in 1963 and was soon inviting other poet friends to work with him in the form. In addition to Berrigan and Padgett, the two issues of *C Comics* featured collaborations with John Ashbery, Bill Berkson, Robert Dash, Edwin Denby, Kenward Elmslie, Dick Gallup, Barbara Guest, Kenneth Koch, Frank Lima, Frank O'Hara, Peter Schjeldahl, James Schuyler, and Tony Towle. For Brainard, the appeal of the comic strip lay in the relationship between text and image established by the form itself. "I have never been able to accept 'words on drawing' unless there is somehow a reason for them being there," he writes earlier in the first diary entry quoted above. "That is why I like the cartoon form. A cartoon *is* a cartoon. A cartoon is made up of words and pictures" (*CW,* p. 248). The form provides both a rationale and a point of departure, establishing a logic connecting text and image that the playful collaborations torque to great effect.

The first issue of *C Comics* was a simple stack of mimeographed sheets bound with three staples down the left side of the pages. Although the substance and style of the comics change from collaborator to collaborator, they all share a certain madcap quality and surrealist humor. One highlight from the issue is "Red Rydler and His Dog," completed with Frank O'Hara. A spoof of the *Red Ryder* comic books involving a cowboy, his dog, and a shootout over a stolen pair of pants, the zany two-page story uses the conventional trappings of the Western genre to draw out its homoerotic undertones. The scrawled-out face of the dog throughout is also an example of

Brainard's commitment to incorporating mistakes into his work, going so far as to point out errors in several comics with small arrows.

With *C Comics* 2, Brainard and his collaborators made more sophisticated use of the genre. Staple-bound in folio like a trade comic book, the second issue features longer stories and hand-drawn advertisements. While some of the latter were real notices for new releases from presses associated with the New York School like Boke Press, C Press, and Tibor de Nagy Editions, many were joke advertisements done in collaboration with James Schuyler. Perhaps the wittiest of these is a series of public service announcements from a mysterious figure called "The Swan." One titled "I Got My Job on the *New York Times*!" lampoons a recent omnibus review by *Times* art critic Hilton Kramer. The PSA excerpts some especially condescending moments from Kramer's review, such as the critic's description of Jane Freilicher's work as having "a certain lady like charm." Pride of place is given to Kramer's dismissal of paintings by Alex Katz—many of which feature the likenesses of the artist's friends—as trivial occasions for gossipy members of the New York art world to recognize one another in oils. Not only did Schuyler and Brainard appear in Katz's paintings, Kramer's humorless insistence on seriousness of subject and the importance of artistic decorum runs precisely counter to the playful and sociable spirit of the collaborative comics. The pompous language of Kramer's review is ripe for satire, the advertisement serving as a riposte to those who would resist the issue's experiments with a popular form in the name of artistic purity.

Although Brainard's collaborative process mainly involved him supplying images and his partners text, he occasionally coauthored written works as well. Among the most intriguing of these is a 1972 volume completed with Anne Waldman titled *Self-Portrait.* The mimeographed book opens with two self-portraits drawn by its two authors. Waldman's is a childlike smiley face and Brainard's a brisk but striking profile from a perspective slightly behind the artist's left shoulder. The rest of the book comprises parallel entries on the same prompt written by hand,

Brainard taking the top half of the page, Waldman the bottom. Examples include:

One Dumb Thing

One dumb thing that always makes me want to cry is "some day my prince will come" without words.

One Dumb Thing

"You made your bed, now lie in it."

...

Art

Art to me is like walking down the street with someone and saying "don't you love that building?" (too)

Art

Art is a way of talking to yourself, + hopefully to someone else *out there.*

...

Why I Am a Painter

One reason I'm a painter is because I'm not a movie star.

Why I Am a Poet

One reason I'm a poet is because I am not a painter.

Part confession, part conversation, the self-portraits sketched by the book underline how, for Brainard and his milieu, speaking about oneself is always speaking to and with others. As Waldman's entry on "Art" makes clear, even the most solipsistic speech implies "someone else *out there,*" and for Brainard, those others were often very near at hand. Further, the dynamic call-and-response of the form underscores the commitment to equal participation evident across Brainard's collaborations. His illustrations were rarely an appendage to the writing of others. Rather, working with his friends opened a creative space between the ideas and intentions of each participant in which something new and exciting could emerge.

EARLY WRITINGS

In a 1977 interview with the poet Tim Dlugos, Brainard indicates that he began writing in the early sixties, around the time when Ted Berrigan began to publish *C: A Journal of Poetry.* "I had no intentions of being a writer," he tells Dlugos. "Everything was against me. I had no vocabulary, I can't spell, I'm inarticulate. I have sort of learned how to use that. But this happened because all my friends were writers. I wrote a short story, the first thing I remember writing, and I showed it to Ted and he said, 'It's very good.' So I kept at it" (*CW,* p. 498). With characteristic modesty, Brainard downplays his own abilities while giving credit to his friends for their encouragement of his writing practice. Most revealing in his remarks is the emphasis on his immediate friends as the primary audience of his texts, and the ways in which their presence works as a central motivation and inspiration for his writing. As he says later in the interview, referring to James Schuyler, "He was an instant audience; I would do it [write] all day and show it to him, and he would tell me how terrific it was, which was all I needed for the next day" (*CW,* p. 499). Like his art, Brainard's writing is a gift directed to those closest to him. What is perhaps most remarkable about his oeuvre is that, despite its coterie orientation, it still speaks to those outside the charmed circle of Brainard's life and work.

The earliest published example of Brainard's writing was completed somewhat before the date he offers in the interview. (The first issue of *C: A Journal of Poetry* appeared in 1963.) Titled "Self-Portrait on a Christmas Night," the piece was written in December 1961 in the Greenwich Village apartment shared by Ted Berrigan, Ron Padgett, and Pat Mitchell (later Pat Padgett). Although Brainard was only nineteen at the time, the text engages a form and themes that would remain a central part of his writing practice in the years to come: the verbal self-portrait, meditations on art and friendship, and the difficulty of honesty and openness in one's relationship with oneself and others. Of particular importance is the gap between how others see Brainard and the person he both is and would like to become. Brainard handles this classic problem of ambitious adolescence with a mix of youthful melo-

drama and precocious insight. Writing about his friends and family back home in Tulsa, Brainard declares, "nobody really knows me but ... everyone thinks they have my spirit in a bottle and a mathematical equation explaining my art and life, and not art and not life" (*CW,* p. 145). Chafing against the expectations of others, Brainard commits himself to his freedom, and especially his freedom to grow as a person and as an artist. "Must develop and learn more," he writes in the final sentences of the piece, "must understand myself so we can produce together with sureness, confidence, and beauty" (*CW,* p. 146). Invoking George Washington, who appears throughout the self-portrait as a figure for the distance between a public persona and a private self, Brainard closes on a rather grand note: "And I, just like George Washington, am only a 'thing' to the world, but a god to myself" (*CW,* p. 146). As a self-portrait, the piece works the gap between the world and the self, between being a "thing" and a "god," to reveal a probing, earnest, and self-critical sensibility. Although Brainard's later self-portraiture, diaries, and memoir would develop along with his mature voice, the concerns laid out in this early piece would remain with him for decades to come.

Though the diary form is well represented in Brainard's early work, other pieces strike a different pose than the urgent introspection of the Christmas self-portrait. "Back in Tulsa Again," an account of a road trip to Oklahoma taken with Pat, Ron, and Ron's father in May 1962, presents the returning heroes as "three stooges" careening across the country in an "indescribable farce." The story combines madcap humor and mock seriousness with Steinian repetitions, including an allusion to the legendary modernist's famous sentence, "A rose is a rose is a rose." While the piece is shaded by Brainard's anxiety around returning to Tulsa—where everyone, in the words of the Christmas self-portrait, thinks they have his "spirit in a bottle"—the manic hilarity of the narrative is what propels the writing along. Written to amuse Brainard and his friends, "Back in Tulsa Again" demonstrates Brainard's keen eye for a humorous scenario, his facility with direct, declarative language, and his intuitive sense of what will most please his audience.

In addition to diaries and autobiographical narratives, Brainard composed a number of short prose pieces and poems in the early and mid-sixties. Some of these, like "Marge," "Johnny," and the "Nancy" vignettes, are entertaining blends of autobiography and fictional character sketches. Two poems, both titled "I Like," experiment with one of Brainard's favorite forms: the list. Resembling James Schuyler's "Freely Espousing," published in Donald Allen's landmark 1960 anthology *The New American Poetry,* Brainard's poems playfully enumerate their author's likes and dislikes with the occasional surreal interlude. Like the prose pieces, the poems combine candid self-disclosures with unexpected twists and turns, the line breaks lending themselves to both the orderly sequence of the list and the sudden disjunctions of Brainard's asides.

In this period, Brainard also composed a number of prose portraits of his friends, including Ron and Pat Padgett, as well as critical snapshots of artists he admired. "Andy Warhol: Andy Do It," for example, sees Brainard profess his love for Warhol in terms of which the artist would likely have approved. Catching the spirit of Warhol's assembly-line approach to art, Brainard writes, "Andy Warhol I think has creative ideas. Andy Warhol doesn't I don't think do creative paintings. Andy Warhol might not even do paintings at all! ... Andy Warhol perhaps paints ideas, but if so, I sure do like the way his ideas look. Andy Warhol's ideas look great! Andy Warhol paints Andy Warhols. And I like that" (*CW,* p. 178). Perceptively playing on the tension between depth and surface (good-looking ideas) and between originality and appropriation in Warhol's art, Brainard's faux-naïf appreciation fits itself to its object with particular skill. Here as well as across his early writing, Brainard demonstrates his developing ability to perceive clearly what is in front of him, to catch hold of his personal response, and to express both in a manner calculated to please, provoke, and entertain.

I REMEMBER

Though Brainard's work appeared occasionally in various little magazines throughout the 1960s, he began to receive wider acclaim as an author with the publication of *I Remember* in 1970. Anne Waldman's Angel Hair Books brought out the first installment and went on to publish two follow-up volumes in 1972 and 1973. Begun in the summer of 1969 during Brainard's annual stay with Kenward Elmslie in Vermont, the project was helped along in its early stages by the encouragement of James Schuyler, who visited the pair for several weeks that summer. The collected edition of *I Remember,* published by Full Court Press in 1975, boasts more than fifteen hundred entries of varying lengths, each of which begin with the phrase "I remember." Covering a range of topics from childhood memories of family, food, and clothes to more adult ruminations on the body, fantasies, and sex, *I Remember* is a vivid portrait of a remarkable person's experience as well as an almanac of growing up in Middle America in the 1940s and 1950s. As Brainard put it in a letter to Waldman, "I … feel that it is about everybody else as much as it is about me. And that pleases me. I mean, I feel like I am everybody. And it's a nice feeling" (Padgett, p. 146). The peculiar power of the book lies in its balancing act between the general and the particular, the reader drawn in by a voice that is at once singular and immensely relatable.

As Ron Padgett notes, the form of *I Remember* demonstrates the ongoing influence of Gertrude Stein on Brainard's writing, as well as Warhol's serial collages of the 1960s (p. 146). Following the books' success, the form itself soon began to travel on its own, taken up by a range of amateur and professional writers, the latter list including Elmslie, Berrigan, and Harry Mathews. Kenneth Koch used the *I Remember* form in his groundbreaking work with children, including it in his 1970 textbook *Wishes, Lies, and Dreams: Teaching Children to Write Poetry.* Through Koch, the form reached an audience of thousands of poets, teachers, and students, many of whom did not know where it had first originated. To this day, it remains a mainstay of writing curricula. Its popularity, particularly in the classroom, has to do with ease of imitation and the uncanny way simply beginning a sentence with "I remember" can unlock long-forgotten impressions and experiences. In the words of the novelist and essayist Siri Hustvedt, "Joe Brainard discovered a memory machine" (*The Shaking Woman; or, A History of My Nerves,* p. 64, qtd. in *CW,* p. xviii).

While the form is easily duplicated, the wit and warmth of Brainard's version would prove difficult to repeat. Following its own logic of sequence and apposition, the entries leap across decades and disparate locales, the tone shifting from the confessional ("I remember taking an I.Q. test and coming out below average. [I've never told anyone that before]") to the wryly comic ("I remember getting all dressed up to go buy clothes") to the profound: "I remember that life was just as serious then as it is now" (*CW,* pp. 50, 88, 23). Paul Auster nominates that last entry as possibly "the most important sentence in the book, the reason why the fifteen hundred fragments of *I Remember* ultimately cohere to form a solid and integrated work" (*CW,* p. xxii). By approaching even his distant childhood past with generous understanding, Brainard presents his memories with a striking clarity and immediacy. Brainard would continue to write in the voice he'd honed in *I Remember*—casual, charming, and intimate—for the remainder of his career.

DIARIES AND JOURNALS

Of the hundred-some pieces published in the *Collected Writings,* roughly a quarter take the form of journals and diaries. Like the comic strip and *I Remember,* the diary plays to Brainard's preference for serial compositions: repetitive collections of discrete units that nonetheless form a unified whole. However, while Brainard's most famous work focuses on memories of the past, the diaries allow him to direct his attention to the immediate present as it unfolds in real time. They also make available experiments in narrative. The sequences of entries track the progression of events in Brainard's life as well as his shifting responses to the world around him. Readers can follow Brainard's emotional tone as it shifts

among anticipation, anxiety, elation, confusion, satisfaction, and disappointment. The central themes of the diaries remain consistent with Brainard's earliest concerns: art, love, friendship, and the ambition to live the life one desires to lead. In a sense, the diaries are part of a broader practice of self-discipline, Brainard recording the goals he has set for himself and assessing his progress in meeting them. Like his habitual daily schedule—a recurring topic across his writing—and his annual pattern of seasonal migration, the diaries lend structure and order to a life with few conventional obligations and expectations to give it shape.

The diaries and journals can be sorted into roughly two categories. Those in the first and larger group track the day-to-day events of Brainard's life in New York and Vermont. Written as one-off entries as well as in series, these tend to begin and end seemingly at random, Brainard returning to the diary when the spirit moves him. In some cases, such as *Vermont Journal: 1971,* these diaries shape themselves to the rhythm of the summer season, capturing Brainard's sense of long, open days that nonetheless pass too quickly at the house in Calais. The latter group is made up of travel journals organized around particular trips to various locations outside his typical annual itinerary. The earliest of these is *Jamaica 1968,* which records Brainard's vacation on the island with the painters Joe Hazan and Jane Freilicher, their daughter Elizabeth, and Kenward Elmslie. These were followed by *Bolinas Journal* in 1971 and "Washington, D.C. Journal" in 1972. In the travel diaries, Brainard adds a perceptive eye for new locales to his skill as a storyteller, giving the reader an idiosyncratic snapshot of the setting in addition to an account of the trip itself.

The most striking feature of all of Brainard's diaries is the relationship between private reflection and public confession negotiated by his use of the form. The diaries are often addressed to a "you," and the status of that second person remains indeterminate across his writing. In some cases, it seems to be the conventional addressee of the "dear diary" format, but in others, Brainard appears to have a particular second person in mind. Further, Brainard tended to share his diary writing in almost real time, rushing to complete entries in advance of public readings. This could lead to pieces that are highly self-reflexive about the status of their composition and circulation, as in the following entry from 1969:

> I feel good today, but a bit nervous. I'm going to read tonight with Bill Berkson at the St. Mark's Church. In fact, to tell you the truth, that is why I am writing today. To have more that is new to read tonight. I want this reading to be good because, just because I do, and because I feel a bit bad about my show, and this reading, I hope, will make up for that.
>
> (*CW,* p. 238)

Presenting new work immediately to his audience, Brainard invites his listeners at St. Mark's into the emotional weather of his day as he lives it. In addition to the comic effect achieved, no doubt, through his admission that he's writing simply "to have more that is new to read," Brainard signals that he needs something from his audience. The writing thus becomes part of an ongoing relationship, indicative of the communal impulse of his work as well as that of many of his New York School contemporaries. In the diary form, Brainard found a way to write for himself and others simultaneously, achieving the honesty and openness he most wanted in his work as well as his life.

THE SIAMESE BANANA BOOKS

In addition to his innovations in the memoir and diary forms, Brainard also invented a difficult-to-categorize genre of book, examples of which were published by Siamese Banana Press in the early seventies. Part scrapbook, part poetry collection, and part mock encyclopedia, these texts were typically simple mimeographed booklets printed in very small numbers and circulated to a limited audience in New York. Each tends to be organized around a single theme—bananas, cigarettes, household notes—which Brainard attacks from a variety of angles. *The Banana Book* (1972) includes hilarious non sequitur cartoons and one-liners by Brainard about bananas;

handwritten lists of notes on banana-related topics; comic strips, articles, and recipes featuring bananas clipped from newspapers and magazines; compendia of banana-related quotations; poetry and prose on a banana theme written by Brainard's friends; and images lifted from gay porn magazines with bananas drawn over the models' genitalia.

If the diaries and journals were an outlet for Brainard's more sober and reflective meditations on life and art, the Siamese Banana books display his sense of fun and desire to entertain his audience. They are also Brainard's signal contribution to the genre of the artist's book, a form that began to reemerge among the U.S. avant-garde in the years following World War II and that became central to the practice of conceptual artists in the sixties and seventies. Further, in their loose and irreverent style, Brainard's Siamese Banana books anticipated the zine culture that arrived with the punk scene later in the decade. Though aimed toward different ends than the self-consciously serious artist's books of his contemporaries—Brainard's texts bear a stronger resemblance, perhaps, to family scrapbooks and other homemade objects—the Siamese Banana books were nonetheless an innovative and influential experiment in the combination of word, image, and found materials in book form.

LATE WRITINGS

Brainard continued to write and publish regularly into the early eighties, his final major collection, *Nothing to Write Home About,* appearing in 1981. His late work remained as formally diverse and varied as his earlier writings, although his output began to taper off by the mid-seventies. Highlights from this period include his *29 Mini-Essays*—one-line statements on a range of topics beautifully printed by Elmslie's Z Press in 1978—and what he called his "Imaginary Still Lifes," short pieces of descriptive prose Brainard began writing around 1973. According to Padgett, Brainard's process for composing the pieces was fairly straightforward. "To write one," Padgett tells us, "he closed his eyes and wrote a brief description of the still life that appeared in his

mind's eye—for him an easy and enjoyable process" (p. 197). The results range from the simple and direct to the more complex, abstract colors and shapes resolving into particular objects which in turn suggest an emotional complexion or narrative for the imaginary scene. In one, for example, splashes of pink, green, and gold become a kimono discarded on a dressing table in front of a paneled screen. "In this particular Japanese still life," Brainard closes the piece, "one gets the impression that something is going on that cannot be seen" (*CW,* p. 454). Like *I Remember,* Brainard's imaginary still lifes offer a simple structure that invites imitation, the pieces tied to a practice that nearly any writer can easily try out him- or herself. However, also like his earlier project, Brainard brings an inimitable facility to the form that would be hard to match.

Brainard's last piece of published writing is a posthumous verbal portrait of James Schuyler composed several months after the poet's death in April 1991. Reminiscent of the imaginary still lifes, the portrait is a moving tribute to Brainard's recently departed friend:

> Let me be a painter, and close my eyes. I see brown. (Tweed.) And blue. (Shirt.) And—surprise—yellow socks. The body sits in a chair, a king on a throne, feet glued to the floor. The face is hard to picture, until—(click!)—I hear a chuckle. And the voice of distant thunder.
>
> (*CW,* p. 484)

Still a painter more than a decade into his retirement, Brainard captures Schuyler's presence in a few deft strokes. Like so much of Brainard's writing, it is an exercise in memory, in intimacy, and in arresting the immediacy of an impression in vivid form. Though marked by a preference for brevity and simplicity of expression, Brainard's writing should not be considered merely an addendum to his achievements in the visual arts. Rather, his heterogeneous oeuvre should be regarded as a single remarkable project, one that exhorts us to look, and to take pleasure in what we see. As Brainard puts it in a late diary entry from 1978, "it's as simple as this, what I want to tell you about: if perhaps not much, everything. Painting the moment for you tonight" (*CW,* p. 485).

CONCLUSION

Following Brainard's death in 1994, friends, colleagues, and admirers labored to ensure his immense body of work would continue to reach a wider audience. A number of shows were mounted across the United States, with exhibitions at the Tibor de Nagy Gallery as well as a major traveling retrospective organized in 2001 by the University of California, Berkeley Art Museum, which exposed his work to museumgoers in California, Nevada, Colorado, and New York. A new edition of *I Remember* was published by Granary Books in 2001, and in 2012 a film based on the book was released. Two journals—the *James White Review* and *Pressed Wafer*—published special issues devoted to Brainard's life, art, and writing in 2001, and the Poetry Project has hosted numerous evenings in Brainard's memory featuring readings of his work. The publication of the *Collected Writings* in 2012 represents the culmination of a long editorial labor—undertaken chiefly by Ron Padgett, the executor of Brainard's literary estate—to make a host of unpublished Brainard material available for the first time. As if to celebrate the occasion, the first book-length study of Brainard's writing appeared that year as well (*Pop Poetics: Reframing Joe Brainard*, by Andy Fitch), a sign of growing scholarly interest in his literary accomplishments. Brainard will no doubt continue to attract a growing audience as readers rediscover this key figure of twentieth-century American culture.

Selected Bibliography

WORKS OF JOE BRAINARD

WRITINGS

I Remember. New York: Angel Hair Books, 1970.

Bolinas Journal. Bolinas, Calif.: Big Sky Books, 1971.

Some Drawings of Some Notes to Myself. New York: Siamese Banana Press, 1971.

The Banana Book. New York: Siamese Banana Press, 1972.

The Cigarette Book. New York: Siamese Banana Press, 1972.

The Friendly Way. New York: Siamese Banana Press, 1972.

I Remember More. New York: Angel Hair Books, 1972.

I Remember Christmas. New York: Museum of Modern Art, 1973.

More I Remember More. New York: Angel Hair Books, 1973.

New Work. Los Angeles: Black Sparrow Press, 1973.

12 Postcards. Calais, Vt.: Z Press, 1975.

29 Mini-Essays. Calais, Vt.: Z Press, 1978.

24 Pictures & Some Words. Hemet, Calif.: BLT, 1980.

Nothing to Write Home About. Los Angeles: Little Caesar Press, 1981.

Ten Imaginary Still Lifes. New York: Boke Press, 1997.

COLLECTED WORKS AND READINGS

Selected Writings, 1962–1971. New York: Kulchur Foundation, 1971.

I Remember. First collected edition, New York: Full Court Press, 1975. Two additional collected editions, New York: Penguin Books, 1995; New York: Granary Books, 2001.

The Collected Writings of Joe Brainard. Edited by Ron Padgett. New York: Library of America, 2012.

"Joe Brainard." (Audio Recordings.) *PennSound,* n.d. http://writing.upenn.edu/pennsound/x/Brainard.php

COLLABORATIONS

Some Things. [New York]: privately printed, 1963. With Ted Berrigan and Ron Padgett.

C Comics 1. New York: C Press, 1964. With Bill Berkson, Ted Berrigan, Robert Dash, Edwin Denby, Kenward Elmslie, Barbara Guest, Kenneth Koch, Gerard Malanga, Frank O'Hara, Ron Padgett, James Schuyler, Johnny Stanton, Tony Towle, and Tom Veitch.

The Baby Book. New York: Boke Press, 1965. With Kenward Elmslie.

C Comics 2. New York: Boke Press, 1965. With John Ashbery, Bill Berkson, Ted Berrigan, Kenward Elmslie, Dick Gallup, Barbara Guest, Kenneth Koch, Frank Lima, Frank O'Hara, Ron Padgett, Peter Schjeldahl, James Schuyler, and Tony Towle.

100,000 Fleeing Hilda. Tulsa, Okla.: Boke Press, 1967. With Ron Padgett.

The 1967 Game Book Calendar. New York: Boke Press, 1967. With Kenward Elmslie.

The Champ. Santa Barbara, Calif.: Black Sparrow Press, 1968. With Kenward Elmslie.

The Flesh Game. N.p., 1969. With Bill Berkson.

Recent Visitors. Bolinas, Calif.: Best & Co./Boke Press, 1971. With Bill Berkson.

Sufferin' Succotash/Kiss My Ass. New York: Adventures in Poetry, 1971. With Ron Padgett and Michael Brownstein.

Self Portrait. New York: Siamese Banana Press, 1972. With Anne Waldman.

Shiny Ride. New York: Boke Press, 1972. With Kenward Elmslie.

The Class of '47. New York: Bouwerie Editions, 1973. With Robert Creeley.

The Vermont Notebook. Los Angeles: Black Sparrow Press, 1975. With John Ashbery.

1984 Comics. Frankfurt, Germany: März Velag, 1983. With Bill Berkson, Ted Berrigan, Michael Brownstein, Kenward Elmslie, Larry Fagin, Barbara Guest, Kenneth Koch, Harry Matthews, Frank O'Hara, Ron Padgett, Peter Schjeldahl, James Schuyler, and Tony Towle.

Sung Sex. New York: Kulchur Foundation, 1989. With Kenward Elmslie.

Pay Dirt. Flint, Mich.: Bamberger Books, 1992. With Kenward Elmslie.

PAPERS

Joe Brainard Archive, 1960–1992. Archive for New Poetry, Special Collections and Archives, University of California, San Diego.

CRITICAL AND BIOGRAPHICAL STUDIES

Ashbery, John. "Joe Brainard." In *Joe Brainard: Retrospective.* New York: Tibor de Nagy Gallery, 1997. Reprinted in *Joe Brainard: A Retrospective.* Edited by Constance M. Lewallen. Berkeley and New York: University of California, Berkeley Art Museum/Granary Books, 2001. Pp. 1–2.

Dlugos, Tim. "Starting with Nothing and Surprising Himself: The Joe Brainard Interview." *Little Caesar* 10 (1980). Reprinted in *The Collected Writings of Joe Brainard.* Edited by Ron Padgett. New York: Library of America, 2012. Pp. 489–508.

Equi, Elaine, and David Trinidad, eds. *Hello Joe: A Tribute to Joe Brainard. Pressed Wafer* 2 (March 2001).

Estate of Joe Brainard. www.joebrainard.org.

Fitch, Andy. *Pop Poetics: Reframing Joe Brainard.* Champaign, Ill: Dalkey Archive Press, 2012.

Gooch, Brad. "Nancy Ideas." *Artforum International* 39, no. 6:124–128 (February 2001).

James White Review 18, no. 1 (winter 2001). Special Joe Brainard issue.

Lehman, David. *The Last Avant-Garde: The Making of the New York School of Poets.* New York: Doubleday, 1998.

LeSueur, Joe. *Digressions on Some Poems by Frank O'Hara.* New York: Farrar, Straus and Giroux, 2003.

Lewallen, Constance M. *Joe Brainard: A Retrospective.* Berkeley and New York: University of California, Berkeley Art Museum/Granary Books, 2001.

McDermott, Keith. "Homage to Joe." In *Loss Within Loss:*

Artists in the Age of AIDS. Edited by Edmund White. Madison: University of Wisconsin Press, 2001.

Padgett, Ron. *Joe: A Memoir of Joe Brainard.* Minneapolis: Coffee House Press, 2004.

Schuyler, James. "Joe Brainard: Notes and Quotes." *ARTnews* (April 1967). Reprinted in *Selected Art Writings.* Edited by Simon Pettet. Santa Rosa, Calif.: Black Sparrow Press, 1998.

Waldman, Anne. "An Interview with Joe Brainard." *Rocky Ledge* 3 (November–December 1979). Reprinted in *The Collected Writings of Joe Brainard.* Edited by Ron Padgett. New York: Library of America, 2012. Pp. 509–517.

We Remember Joe Brainard. Special issue. *The Poetry Project* 155 (December–January 1994–1995).

Wolf, Matt. *I Remember: A Film About Joe Brainard.* 2012. http://www.joebrainardfilm.com/

Wolf, Reva. *Andy Warhol, Poetry, and Gossip in the 1960s.* Chicago: University of Chicago Press, 1997.

Worden, Daniel. "Joe Brainard's Grid; or, The Matter of Comics." *Nonsite* 15 (January 2015). http://nonsite.org/article/joe-brainards-grid-or-the-matter-of-comics

EXHIBITION HISTORY

SOLO EXHIBITIONS

1965: Alan Gallery, New York.

1967: Landau-Alan Gallery, New York.

1968: Jerold-Morris Gallery, Toronto; Gotham Book Mart and Gallery, New York.

1969: Landau-Alan Gallery, New York.

1970: Phyllis Kind Gallery, Chicago; Benson Gallery, Bridgehampton, N.Y.

1971: Fischbach Gallery, New York; Gotham Book Mart and Gallery, New York.

1972: New York Cultural Center, New York; School of the Visual Arts, New York; Fischbach Gallery, New York.

1973: *102 Works on Paper, 1966–1972,* Utah Museum of Fine Arts, Salt Lake City.

1974: Fischbach Gallery, New York.

1975: Fischbach Gallery, New York.

1976: FIAC, Paris; Coventry Gallery, Paddington, Australia; Suzette Schochett Gallery, Newport, R.I.; E. G. Gallery, Kansas City.

1978: *Joe Brainard: Fête d'Hiver,* Root Art Center, Hamilton College, Clinton, N.Y.; Elaine Benson Gallery, Bridgehampton, N.Y.

1980: Long Beach Museum of Art, Long Beach, Calif.

1987: Mandeville Gallery, University of California, San Diego.

1997: *Joe Brainard: Retrospective,* Tibor de Nagy Gallery,

New York; *Joe Brainard: Small Collages,* Tibor de Nagy Gallery, New York.

2001: *Joe Brainard: A Retrospective,* University of California, Berkeley Art Museum.

2007: *If Nancy Was,* Fischbach Gallery, New York; University of Buffalo Art Gallery.

2008: *Painting the Way I Wish I Could Talk,* Tibor de Nagy Gallery, New York.

GROUP EXHIBITIONS

1962: *Oklahoma Artists: Twenty-First Annual Exhibition,* Tulsa.

1963: *Oklahoma Artists: Twenty-Second Annual Exhibition,* Tulsa.

1965: Alan Gallery, New York; Finch College Museum, New York.

1966: Alan Gallery, New York.

1967: Museum of Modern Art, for the Brussels Embassy, New York.

1968: *Young Artists,* American Federation of Art Circulating Exhibition; Exhibition of drawings for *In Memory of My Feelings,* by Frank O'Hara, Museum of Modern Art, New York.

1969: Arts Council of Great Britain, London; Contemporary Art Society of Indianapolis; Landau-Alan Gallery, New York; University of Illinois, Champaign; Cranbook Academy of Art, Bloomfield Hills, Mich.; *Pop Art,* Hayward Gallery, London.

1970: Virginia Museum of Fine Arts, Richmond.

1972: Webb and Parson's Art Gallery, Bedford Village, N.Y.; *Works on Paper,* Weatherspoon Gallery, Greensboro, N.C.; *Seven Young Artists,* Corcoran Gallery of Art, Washington, D.C.; Parrish Art Museum, Southampton, N.Y.; *White on White,* Chicago Museum of Contemporary Art; *Work with Poets,* Gotham Bookmart and Gallery, New York.

1973: *Guild Hall,* East Hampton, N.Y.; *American Drawings,* Tyler School of Art, Temple University, Philadelphia; *American Drawings, 1970–1973,* Yale University Art Gallery, New Haven, Conn.; *New American Graphic Art,* Fogg Art Museum, Harvard University, Cambridge, Mass.; Summit Art Center, Summit, N.J.; *Drawings,* Margo Leavin Gallery, Los Angeles; *Artist's Books,* Moore College of Art, Philadelphia; University Art Musem, Berkeley, Calif.; Michael Berber Gallery, Pittsburgh; *Summer Exhibition,* Fischbach Gallery, New York; *Collector's Choice,* Philbrook Art Center, Tulsa, Okla.

1974: *Drawings for Books,* Carlton Gallery, New York.

1975: *25 Stills,* Whitney Museum of American Art, New York; *Contemporary Drawings,* William Paterson College, N.J.; *Richard Brown Baker Collects,* Yale University Art Gallery, New Haven, Conn.; *16 Realists,* Fischbach Gallery, New York.

1976: *Collector's Gallery x,* McNay Art Institute, San Antonio, Tex.; *Contemporary Images in Watercolor,* Akron Institute, Akron, Ohio.

1978: *100 Drawings of the 1970s: From the Richard Brown Baker Collection,* Stamford Museum, Stamford, Conn.

1979: *Poets & Painters,* Denver Art Museum.

1995: *American Collage,* ACA Galleries, New York.

1998: *Bathroom,* Thomas Healy Gallery, New York; *I Love This Life,* Transmission Gallery, Glasgow.

1999: *In Memory of My Feelings: Frank O'Hara and American Art,* Museum of Contemporary Art, Los Angeles.

2011: *Painters & Poets: Celebrating Sixty Years,* Tibor de Nagy Gallery, New York.

ROBERT CHRISTGAU

(1942—)

Jeffrey Bickerstaff

ROBERT CHRISTGAU FOUND success early in his career as a practitioner of New Journalism before settling into his self-appointed role as "dean of the American rock critics." In addition to literally thousands of record reviews, he is also the author of three books: *Any Old Way You Choose It* (1973), a collection of his early writings drawn from *Esquire,* the *Village Voice,* and *Newsday*; *Grown Up All Wrong* (1998), critical essays on seventy-five rock and pop artists; and a memoir, *Going into the City: Portrait of a Critic as a Young Man* (2015). Christgau's approach to criticism emphasizes the cultural context of music, and as such his work provides a unique and significant perspective of a tumultuous era.

EARLY YEARS AND WORLDVIEW FORMATION

Robert Christgau was born on April 18, 1942, to Virginia Snyder Christgau, a homemaker, and George Henry Christgau, a firefighter. As he details in his memoir *Going into the City,* he grew up in Queens, New York, where his family belonged to the "theologically conservative" First Presbyterian Church of Flushing (p. 32). A bright, analytical child who loved to read, Christgau endured a worldview-shattering crisis of faith during high school that upset his parents; while his father took his son's nascent atheism as "an affront to his authority," his mother felt sincere concern for his soul (p. 84). For a while thereafter, though, the structure of his worldview remained intact. The death of Christgau's Christian God, this deicide by critical thinking, left a void at the foundation of his conceptual framework. During his intellectually formative college years, Christgau sought to fill this divine empty space with what he calls "an ism," as in empiricism, idealism, naturalism, pragmatism, or any other system of thought he could adopt as a means of interpreting life (p. 98).

As a sixteen-year-old Dartmouth freshman (he would graduate with a B.A. in English in 1962), Christgau identified with a particularly French existentialist articulation of his quandary, which he summarized as man being "in a state of constant anguish because he is continually forced to make moral choices in a world of chaos where no moral code is adequate" (p. 101). In other words, there's no belief system comparable to one rooted in God, no sufficient foundation for a catchall moral system. William James's *Pragmatism* (1907) provided Christgau a kind of solace, but not by providing another godlike unchanging core that brings order to a chaotic universe.

James posits pragmatism as empiricist in attitude, meaning it privileges observed experience over revelation (*Pragmatism,* p. 19). James's theory has roots in his study of the psychology of religion, as evidenced by this passage:

> So the universe has always appeared to the natural mind as a kind of enigma, of which the key must be sought in the shape of some illuminating or power-bringing word or name. That word names the universe's *principle,* and to possess it is, after a fashion, to possess the universe itself.
>
> (p. 19)

The universe is mysterious to its very core, its meaning hovering always enticingly out of grasp. To interpret reality, which is to say, to give it meaning, human beings create belief systems. These systems are ideologies based on a key, a word representing a principle that functions as a foundation, or essence, of the code. "'God,' 'Matter,' 'Reason,' 'the Absolute,' 'Energy,' are," James argues, "so many solving names" (p. 19).

The pragmatist, by contrast, turns away from "verbal solutions, from bad a priori reasons, from

fixed principles, closed systems, and pretended absolutes and origins." In contrast to the closed and the fixed, pragmatism "means the open air and possibilities of nature." Pragmatism "does not stand for any special results" because it has no preconceived notions to defend; it stands against "dogma, artificiality and the pretense of finality in truth." Whereas an absolutist looks upon his belief system as the end of a metaphysical quest, the completion of a journey of discovery, the pragmatist takes a view of theories as "*instruments, not answers to enigmas, in which we can rest*" (p. 19). Theories are tools, "mental modes of *adaption* to reality" (p. 65). The job doesn't end with the creation of the tool; that's when it actually begins.

Pragmatism reads as a philosophy created in the wake of Darwin's paradigm-shattering *Origin of Species* (1859), a study of biological evolution that seemed to have turned the intellectual world back to that of Heraclitus' perpetual flux. Pragmatism seems to embrace Friedrich Nietzsche's idea of a "mobile army of metaphors," and keeps in mind that a theory, metaphor, or any representation is an intellectual construction, a tool that's only true as long as it remains, as James puts it, "a useful one to plunge forward with into the stream of our experience" (p. 89). Since the stream of experience changes incessantly, metaphors must be not only mobile but adaptable. The truth exists in action, so pragmatism focuses on the impact of truth on people's actual lives; it wants to know "the truth's cash-value in experiential terms" (p. 67). It's no wonder that Christgau, as one who "felt like an American, with many of the materialistic vulgarities that implied," and who "liked the brand names and neologisms of American speech," embraced this distinctly American philosophy that alluded to money as it lauded practicality (*Any Old Way You Choose It*, p. 3).

Christgau particularly embraced James's belief that the universe is "unfinished, growing in all sorts of places, especially in the places where thinking beings are at work" (James qtd. in *Going into the City*, p. 101). By conceptualizing the universe as becoming rather than being, Christgau simultaneously embraced what he calls

French pessimism and American optimism, which enabled him to abandon the certainty of any code and bask in "contingency."

Christgau actually took his initial steps toward contingency at his church, "an indoctrination center" that inadvertently steered him toward left-wing politics and intellectualism (*City*, p. 39). Christgau credits 1 Corinthians 13:13 for inspiring his political shift ("And now abideth faith, hope, charity, these three; but the greatest of these is charity"), and weekly scriptural exegeses for his affinity for abstractions. During Sunday school Christgau would joust with the teacher, an open-minded southern lawyer named Bill Sargent who welcomed his student's challenges. Christgau describes himself as "poking at biblical inerrancy," and he recounts his teacher's willingness to confront his doubts, to argue him toward life as a "convinced Christian" (p. 84). Such phrasing indicates Sargent embraced his pupil as one who would respond to the rational rather than the revelatory, and he recognized reasoned debate as his best chance of leading Christgau to a life of faith.

This is not to suggest that Christgau's struggle was purely abstract and impersonal. The beginning of the end of his Christian faith came with his refusal (or inability) to accept that Miriam Meyer, his Jewish girlfriend, would burn for eternity in hell for refusing to accept Jesus Christ as her lord and savior (*City*, p. 93). Apparently love conquers all, including terrifying dogma. Later, sometime after realizing his atheism but before identifying "that isms themselves were the problem," Christgau experienced existential dread so severe that he developed an emptiness in the pit of his stomach that actually hindered his breathing (p. 99). With his solution to the problem of death having vanished with his fundamentalist Christianity, Christgau had to overcome angst, to wrestle with the fact of his mortality, which he appears to have done through force of will. Before turning nineteen, Christgau finally outlasted his despair and "breathed deep." Although the affliction occasionally recurs, "the relief I experienced that day had the weight of revelation" (p. 100).

"Revelation" is a noteworthy term for a couple of reasons. First, it has obvious religious connotations, as each Abrahamic religion is based on the revealed word of God. Revelation, in these contexts, indicates an instantaneous top-down transfer of divine wisdom that contrasts with empiricism, a bottom-up system of knowledge built upon observation and experiment. Christgau has a kind of atheistic revelation, a bodily realization that he can find peace living a finite life in a world without God. Second, it recalls the reaction in 1954 of Mr. Segal, his junior high English teacher, to the Supreme Court's unanimous *Brown v. Board of Education* decision declaring school segregation unconstitutional. Christgau describes Segal's excitement as "a revelation," particularly the idea that he could have personal feelings and empathy for southern Negro students he didn't even know.

Referencing the pivotal Corinthians verse, Christgau asserts that more charity emanated from Mr. Segal's politics than the First Presbyterian pulpit, where the focus tended toward witnessing Christ's word to the unsaved of New York (*City,* pp. 52–53). Corinthians helped lead Christgau toward progressive politics because that's where he witnessed its spirit in action. Besides recalling Corinthians, the Segal moment anticipates Christgau's embrace of pragmatism's construction of the universe as unfinished, a place growing where thinking beings are at work. Through people imbued with the spirit of charity and compassion, the universe could grow better, more just and gentle. Although still a long way from radicalism, the seeds of a social conscience were sown. In essence, Christgau was building a secular foundation for positive Christian values, particularly care for the poor and oppressed. It is not surprising, then, that he "internalized a commitment to racial justice" as his teacher explained the greater significance of the decision (p. 53).

Writers like Christgau who explored racial themes in the mid to late twentieth century had good intentions, likely due to an internal commitment to racial justice, but sometimes produced embarrassingly awkward results. This might be because of a youthful naïveté toward race and, particularly in Christgau's case, a dearth in his formative years of firsthand interaction with African Americans. Christgau admits that even though his junior and senior high schools were integrated, "I made not a single black acquaintance at either location" (*City,* p. 54). He describes the time that he was partnered with an African American girl in a dancing class as "my most embarrassing moment at 16," although the fact that she towered six inches over him seems to have been part of the problem. But from "a safe distance," that is to say the distance created by television and radio, "Negroes" were of interest to Christgau. African American sitcom stars had negligible impact, but he developed emotional connections (however mediated) to black baseball players such as Sam Jethroe, Satchel Paige, and Willie Mays. More than anything, black music resonated with the teenaged Christgau, and he credits the white disc jockey and payola enthusiast Alan Freed for his dedication to the originals: "'Originals' was a big concept for him, and like Mr. Segal he got downright preachy about it. He would only play 'originals.'" Christgau recalls knowing that the originals were by black artists and the covers were by whites. Despite being preachy, Freed "was right—they were better" (p. 55).

Christgau doesn't go into detail about why he preferred the originals. Could he offer an explication without sounding like an absolutist preoccupied with authenticity? Probably. But this preference for the principle recording, one could say his preference for the real, might complicate Christgau's approach, if it weren't already riddled in contradictions. In *Any Old Way You Choose It,* he describes his analysis as dealing "obsessively in paradox" because it seeks to resolve his own polemic (p. 4). Christgau actually describes his temperament as polemical, adding, "Show me an idea and I'll show you what's wrong with it, and six months later I'll show you what's wrong with my objections" (p. 3). His perspective evolves, as his written output indicates.

In his memoir, Christgau explains that the truth of Freed taking payola to play these originals didn't bother him (p. 55). The view of Freed's payola schemes widens a bit in *Grown Up All Wrong,* specifically the way Freed "myste-

riously acquired a substantial portion of the writer's credit" for Chuck Berry's "Maybellene," which he played a lot and turned into a lucrative national hit (p. 43). Christgau makes a lot of the fact that Berry had arrived at Chess Records with an additional song, a blues called "Wee Wee Hours," that he initially presents as Berry's true self-expression. Of course it's the commercial "Maybellene" that Leonard Chess successfully sells, leaving the artist to choose between a life of modest artistic integrity and one of pandering commercial success in this, the art-versus-commerce drama that Christgau constructs seemingly for the sole purpose of turning it on its ear. In essence, he argues that market forces compel Berry away from blues and toward rock and roll, which turns out to be the realm most conducive to his true genius: "Berry had achieved a grip on the white audience and the solid future it could promise, and, remarkably, he had in no way diluted his genius to do so. On the contrary, that was his genius." In other words, the white audience was where the real money was, and Berry's art would not have blossomed "if he hadn't explored his relationship to the white audience" (p. 44). This is a novel resolution to the art-versus-commerce dialectic: commercialism prods the artist toward, not away from, the expression of his unique genius. Christgau's analysis is complicated by the overlap between the market and whiteness, especially the suggestion that whites propelled a black artist to an artistic zenith. And of course no one will ever know how Berry's art would have developed had he aimed his talent toward the less-remunerative blues. It is a theory consistent with contingency, though, as it considers Berry's work not as an isolated thing in itself, but a part of popular culture out in the commerce of the world. The essay also highlights Christgau's sociological approach, as he astutely points out that Berry, "an urban black man who was attracted to mechanization and modernization and had never known brutal poverty," had a much different relationship to his white audience than someone like Muddy Waters would have had (p. 44).

Obviously race is a thorny and continually evolving subject, and Christgau admirably pointed his polemical temperament toward his own articles that touched on it. He writes that, when he got his first job as a music columnist, at *Esquire* magazine in 1967, he carried with him the goal of combating "the most egregious shortcoming of the primitive rock criticism of the time, its inattention to black music" (*Any Old Way,* p. 4). He admits that he probably failed; he never "brings together" the black-white theme running through *Any Old Way,* "and my writing about black music aimed at the black audience, music I hold dear, seems partial, contradictory, sometimes racist." His brutal honesty is commendable, and probably the best way to deal with his review of the 1967 Monterey Pop Festival. In a discussion of Otis Redding's successful performance before a predominately white, hippie crowd, Christgau offers the observation that "Superspade was flying high" (p. 13). He also ridiculed Jimi Hendrix by calling him "a psychedelic Uncle Tom," citing fellow critic Sam Silver's line "Jimi did a beautiful Spade routine" for support (p. 31). Christgau's regret is palpable in his memoir, but he does cut it with the so-sad-it's-funny anecdote about the *Esquire* lawyer who insisted he drop the "psychedelic" because the implication of drug use was potentially libelous. Christgau changed it to "the disastrous 'just another Uncle Tom,'" but restored the original phrasing to reprints. Despite the piece's shortcomings, Christgau argues that it did shed light on "the intersection of black artists and white audience at Monterey, a major theme of my piece" (p. 180). Christgau appears to have attempted to explore ways that African American artists perform race for white audiences. Performance studies, specifically the study of how race, gender, and class are performed by ideological subjects, had not yet gained a foothold in academia. Arguably, Christgau took up the topic before a conceptual framework and vocabulary were in place, which goes some way toward explaining why certain passages read so poorly.

"BETH ANN AND MACROBIOTICISM"

In 1965, just three years out of college and working for the Dorf Feature Service in Newark,

Christgau looked into the story of Beth Ann Simon. Simon was a young bohemian woman who had apparently starved to death while on Diet No. 7, an eating regimen found in Georges Ohsawa's *Zen Macrobiotics*. As the title suggests, the diet had a spiritual component to it, and Simon's death resulted in part from her own zealotry. The twenty-three-year-old Christgau, just past his own anguished search for an "ism," recognized the victim as a "girl dying of the need for the absolute" (*City*, p. 156). The young writer harbored a belief "that this was my story," a phrase that could be taken as an indication of journalistic chutzpa or the recognition of the victim as a kindred spirit, and the New York *Herald Tribune* assigned him the story on spec. Christgau named his piece "Beth Ann and Macrobioticism," with "the deliberately awkward 'ism'" referencing the young woman's "true-believer tendencies" (p. 157).

In *Any Old Way You Choose It*, Christgau describes his early 1960s life as "a life most Americans would describe as bohemian," with an unconventional appearance, irregular employment, and artiness. He had a pop mentality, though, and in a reaction "to the insularity and elitism of radical avant-gardism," Christgau became "an antibohemian bohemian" (p. 3). As the word "elitism" suggests, this estrangement stems from Christgau's pride in his working-class background (he reminds his reader that his father wore a uniform), which differentiated him from politicos who romanticized poverty as well as hippies who ignored money. He bristled at the counterculture's use of the term "pig" in reference to police officers, and was further alienated by the way war protesters abused soldiers: "Nothing in the stoic eyes and acne-shadowed faces of these young noncollegiates said baby killer to us. Absent specific evidence to the contrary, we just saw young guys with limited choices risking their lives inside an oppressive institution" (*City*, p. 188). The passage clearly articulates Christgau's frustration with the movement for failing to recognize that soldiers—and probably, to a lesser extent, police officers—were victims of the very culture they were countering, a blind spot that

the terms "noncollegiate" and "limited choices" suggest had its origin in privilege.

Beth Ann's story seems to have touched Christgau's bohemian and antibohemian sides. He "was outraged by the way the story was mangled in the straight press, but I was also outraged by the uselessness of the death itself" (*Any Old Way*, p. 4). Christgau's unusual relationship to the "young seekers roughly like me," the alienated youth comprising the then-bourgeoning bohemian scene, provided him with both the access and distance necessary for the article's success (*City*, p. 158). While the qualifier "roughly" points to Christgau's inability to fully embrace, or be embraced by, this urban subculture, even his status as a "fringe bohemian" was enough for Beth Ann's husband, Charlie, and their circle of friends to speak openly to him during interviews. On the other hand, his "alienation from the prevailing alienation" gave Christgau enough distance to develop a tone that gibed with the more mainstream readership of the *Herald Tribune* (p. 159).

More than anything, the "anti-religious animus" that had been festering in Christgau animates the piece. He homes in on "the mystical tenor" of the Simons' premacrobiotic use of drugs, and he describes the couple as "the enthusiasts, the extremists, the evangelists" of their scene ("Beth Ann," pp. 333–334). They were the ones who would wholly embrace a new movement, explore it to its outer reaches, then return to "spread the word" (p. 334). This time the Simons drummed the gospel of Ohsawa, a "self-described philosopher-scientist" with a tendency to conflate Zen and Taoism (p. 333). Ohsawa appropriates the concepts of yin and yang to categorize basic types of food, balance being the foundation of his nutritional doctrine. Humble adherence transcends mere physical well-being "to spiritual health and enlightenment," a life in harmony with, as Christgau quotes Ohsawa, "the absolute justice and infinite wisdom of the Order of the Universe" (p. 334).

Ohsawa's notion of absolute justice, flowing as it does from the principle of an uppercase Order of the Universe, stands in stark contrast to Christgau's long struggle with learning how to

make moral decisions in a chaotic universe. The outcome of Beth Ann's story, dying as she did for an absolute, represents for Christgau one way his own spiritual saga might have ended had he not embraced contingency and pragmatism. Noteworthy in this context is Christgau's depiction of Sess Wiener, Beth Ann's father, as "a vigorous pragmatist" beseeching his daughter to recognize the reality of her situation and seek mainstream medical help (p. 335). This dramatization of the clash between absolutism and pragmatism is perhaps the piece's most prominent literary feature. Christgau's goal as a young writer had been to "create nonfiction with the impact of fiction" (*City,* p. 158), and he accomplishes this by situating the ideological battleground within the piece's central figure in much the same way great short-story writers such as Flannery O'Connor did with their protagonists. The application of techniques usually reserved for fiction led Thomas Wolfe to include the story in his 1973 compilation *The New Journalism.* In his brief introduction to the piece, Wolfe praises "the tightness of its structure, which has a classic American short-story quality" (p. 331).

Three visits from Sess Wiener, spaced weeks apart, structure Christgau's depiction of Beth Ann's decline. At first Wiener finds his daughter in the early phase of the diet, a euphoric period of spontaneous enlightenment and freedom from the shackles of pain and lethargy. As a skeptic with a mind for cross-examination, Wiener saw his daughter as too skinny and dismissed any salutary effects as "a combination of self-hypnosis and folk medicine," not the "absolute justice and infinite wisdom of the Order of the Universe" (p. 335). The next visit finds Beth Ann covered with red spots and plagued by back and hip pain so severe that she had difficulty walking. Beth Ann and Charlie were put off by her father's bad vibrations and cut the visit short. When Wiener saw his daughter for the final time, she weighed about eighty pounds and could hardly sit up. He bluntly told her that she was going to die, but Beth Ann slowly explained again, "Daddy, I am not going to die. I am going to get well, and when I get rid of all these poisons in my body I will be well for the rest of my life" (p. 337).

From a pragmatic point of view, any claims to health made by a diet purporting to be in sync with the pattern of the universe is only as true as the results it produces. Christgau presents a father watching his daughter die because of blind faith in a metaphor. He also presents a daughter so desperate for an absolute that she interprets starvation as purification. Christgau does not pass judgment, and there is not a trace of snark in the piece. He illustrates the emotional role absolutes play in people's lives, and the danger of treating a tool used to understand reality as reality itself.

This scene also suggests that Beth Ann's and her father's respective worldviews were formed by their earliest experiences. Sess struggled through a childhood of poverty and tuberculosis to a successful career in law, his pragmatism a measured response to a chaotic and indifferent universe. He ultimately thrived and built a life of secure comfort for his daughter, who as a young child would have experienced existence as ordered and compassionate. Thus Beth Ann grew up unable to understand "her father's values, grounded in the everyday world he had overcome with such difficulty. The everyday world had never been a problem for her, and now she felt herself on the verge of conquering a much greater world, the world within" (p. 337). The article privileges Sess Wiener's values, but despite the apparent cross-generational kinship Christgau felt with his subject's father, a connection based in class and philosophy, Wiener accused the writer of sensationalizing his daughter's death (*City,* p. 158). It seems that feeling "alienation from the prevailing alienation" leads inevitably to more alienation. Nevertheless, Christgau's story articulates an archetypal generational clash bound to play out repeatedly during the sixties. Young bohemians, and later, hippies, raised in postwar affluence, could not come to terms with their parents' point of view, forged as it was during the successive calamities of the Great Depression and World War II. With this analysis, Christgau strongly suggests the privileged roots of bohemianism, which contributed to his estrangement

from the movement and indicated that "mass bohemianism" would be a better fit for him.

IT'S GETTING BETTER ALL THE TIME

In *Any Old Way You Choose It,* Christgau distinguishes between "rock and roll" and "rock." He describes rock and roll as big-beat youth music spanning the years 1955 to 1964. It was a "pop-happy" sound loved by the kids and scorned by just about everyone else (p. 1). Rock descended from rock and roll and actually absorbed its progenitor, meaning rock and roll became a sub-genre of rock. Emanating from the Beatles and Bob Dylan, whose role in the birth of the genre is qualified without explanation by a "maybe," rock has pretensions and is taken seriously enough to have criticism written about it (p. 1). In his memoir *Going into the City* four decades later, Christgau argues that the term "rock," consciously distinguished from the terms "pop" and "rock and roll," represents a counterculture that touted "folkie notions of authenticity" and vilified commerciality (p. 9). This means that rock and roll evolved to the point that its own version of the age-old distinction between high art and mass culture took shape within the genre itself. For his part, Christgau didn't regard "commercial" as an insult, and although his subject in *Any Old Way* is indeed rock, he makes it clear that he remains committed to rock and roll.

Throughout his life Christgau has consistently stood on the pop side of the cultural divide. After college he got a night job filing at a Wall Street brokerage firm, where his boss was the painter Bob Stanley. Christgau notes that Stanley worked assiduously on his abstract expressionist pieces, but "they seldom satisfied him and never sold" (*City,* p. 135). As a mentor, Stanley's influence led the young Christgau toward a fascination with pop art, which began in earnest when he saw a one-man show by Tom Wesselmann at the Green Gallery in late 1962. Christgau recalls himself walking through the high culture shrine and hearing a pop song by Connie Francis. He explains that, fifty years later, the remarkable incongruence of mass culture and high art doesn't have the impact it did then, which in itself suggests

the extent to which pop art and mass culture transformed the world in its own image. His description reads like an account of a heretic infiltrating a temple: he wonders (with a smile) "where this intrusion is coming from," and he stresses that a radio tuned to WABC in the Green Gallery "was impious in the extreme" (p. 137). The radio was actually part of a painting, as Wesselmann incorporated household items and brand-name products into his work.

Christgau strongly takes issue with "the obtuse notion that the Pop artists were parodying the oppressive clichés of mass culture," a theory that "still underlies many accounts of their moment." Christgau suggests that these critics were missing the point of the works to protect their own points of view: "I always thought what satirical intent there was went the other way—that its target was effete aesthetes so disquieted by such imagery they had to rationalize it away" (p. 137). These aesthetes had trouble with the idea that these artists actually "dug the garish ubiquity of advertising and roadside architecture, the labor-saving convenience of home appliances, the lip-smacking zap of fast food" (p. 138). That's not to say that the pieces represent an uncritical celebration of American consumerism; citing Lucy Lippard, Christgau stresses that "enjoyment" isn't the same as "wholesale endorsement." There are layers of meaning, and Christgau has no problem with irony creeping into his analysis, because "irony has not only its uses but its moral and aesthetic strengths, remaining fundamental to the fundamental human business of holding two or more clashing ideas in your head at the same time" (p. 139). The Wesselmann painting challenged Christgau to absorb its "apparent incongruities while giving immediate pleasure to my unformed, willing eye" (pp. 138–139).

Christgau never goes as far as calling high art "bullshit," but he does reject the idea that popular art is its inferior, and he refuses, as his account of the Green Gallery experience illustrates, to ignore the role of pleasure in aesthetic experiences (*Any Old Way,* p. 3). Christgau notes in his memoir that he has engaged in a "lifelong cage match with the Frankfort School" (*City,* p. 143), a group of postwar critical theorists

who critiqued the culture industry as an ideological tool applied by the ruling class to prevent people from appreciating the reality of their material conditions, pleasure and instant gratification being two means of lulling the unsuspecting masses into a state of quiescence. While admitting that popular culture sometimes manipulated public opinion, Christgau asserts that popular music, movies, and journalism "reflected and sometimes spurred public unease" (p. 183). In other words, there is an actual give and take between producers of mass culture and their consumers. Indeed, Christgau praises popular art for its relationship with "the great audience," particularly the way it articulates the realities and fantasies of the audience in a way that provides it "immediate pleasure" (*Any Old Way,* p. 3). He embraced the hippies wholly—he wasn't an anti-hippie hippie, "but in fact I was part of it"—because he conceived of them as "pop bohemians." He identified with them because they were younger and "into the pleasure of flash immediacy. They were not antimachine or antimedia. And most important, they liked mass culture" (p. 5).

Christgau proudly touts himself "a democrat in all things" and states that "an informed celebration of popular culture" has been his mission (*City,* pp. 2–3). He asserts that one of his basic assumptions, namely the political and aesthetic equality of "abject 'mass' culture," now informs academia's cultural studies movement more than it does rock criticism (p. 8). This movement, of course, came years after Christgau's early-sixties stint as a young Dartmouth undergraduate, where the theory on mass culture "assumed an elitism" that he had outright rejected by his senior year. Although he credits his alma mater with making him the writer he is, he insists that most of what he learned was wrong (pp. 97–98). He learned the terms of the debate, though, which he applied to discussions of elitism in rock. For Christgau, rock was actually pop, and as befitted a proponent of an American-born, cash-value-as-truth philosophy, his theory was "pro-'commercial'" (p. 9). In *Any Old Way You Choose It,* he simply calls rock "popular culture created by the counterculture" (p. 5).

The Rolling Stones, probably more than any other band, epitomizes Christgau's theory of countercultural pop music. In the midst of their 1972 North American tour, Christgau declared that "the Rolling Stones epitomized the thing I loved most in the world, rock and roll" (p. 219). In the same piece he pronounces the band "the greatest rock and rollers ever." Bohemian, but unlike the "more privileged" American folkies, antiutopian, the Stones "never idealized, and they never expected to be pure. As a consequence, they were never put off by the commerciality of rock and roll" (p. 222).

Indeed, in his autobiography, *Life,* guitarist Keith Richards' description of the blues and jazz scene in early 1960s London echoes Christgau's take on the American folk scene. Richards recounts seeing a big blues revue on the Manchester stop of a European tour. Muddy Waters' acoustic set was enthusiastically received, but when he returned to do the second half with an electric band, he was virtually booed off the stage. Richards mockingly notes that "none of these blues purists could play anything," but they insisted that "blues was only blues if somebody got up there in a pair of old blue dungarees and sang about how his old lady left him" (p. 83). Electric blues was denounced as rock and roll—"a whole bohemian subculture was threatened by the leather mob." Richards traces the political undercurrent of this school of thought to the folk song collectors Alan Lomax and Ewan MacColl, "patriarchs, or ideologues, of the folk boom" who "took a Marxist line that this music belonged to the people and must be protected from the corruption of capitalism. That's why 'commercial' was such a dirty word in those days." Richards recalls "ludicrous discussions about authenticity" and phrases such as "tripe mongers" and "selling out" slung throughout the music press of the day.

In *Grown Up All Wrong,* Christgau calls the Rolling Stones "our first bohemians" (p. 69). Class-conscious Christgau notes that none of the individual Stones grew up rich, but the perception of them as a working-class band "is a major distortion" (p. 70). They were essentially suburban bohemians, with musical tastes somewhere

toward the middle of the spectrum between pop and arcane. Richards and bandmates Mick Jagger and Brian Jones "were passionate about hard-to-find black records that were as crude and esoteric by the standards of English pop and beat fans as they were crude and commercial by the standards of old-bohemian English blues and jazz cultists" (pp. 70–71). Christgau portrays the Stones as purveyors of "commercially fermented blues-based songs" to whom "compromise" meant only the adoption of a "pop aesthetic" (p. 72). The idea of pop was key to mass bohemianism; the Rolling Stones bridged the gaping chasm between doctrinaire blues aficionados and the pop-inclined white teenagers who were growing into hippies.

Christgau stresses the Stones' role as "heroes of mass bohemianism" (p. 79). The Stones, like the bohemian movements that came before them, revolted against "middle-class morality and genteel culture" (p. 78). On trial in 1967 after a drug raid on his home, Keith Richards was berated by the judge and prosecutor for allowing cannabis to be smoked in his home, and for the spectacle of a young woman wearing only a rug in the presence of eight men. Richards took the bait and declared on the stand that "we are not old men. We are not worried about petty morals" (*Life*, p. 226). The crack got Richards a one-year prison sentence (that was eventually overturned) and turned him into a countercultural hero. Christgau suggests that the Stones could speak for their youthful audience because they too "had never known a nonelectric culture" and "were no more wary of the modern media bath than of their own amps." In other words, the band members grew up ensconced in a mass culture delivered via electricity. Their pop sensibility came naturally, and it "led them to a decidedly nonslumming bohemianism, more unpretentious and déclassé than that of the twenties" (*Grown Up*, p. 76).

Christgau's analysis of this cultural moment reflects his sociological approach to writing about music. He argues that the bohemianism of the Rolling Stones was the culmination of mass culture, compulsory education, and consumer capitalism, for its members were of a social stratum unlikely to have been drawn to a life in the arts in the 1920s. Popular culture, combined with the relative affluence of the postwar years, democratized art and made it available "not just to well-raised well-offs but to the broad range of less statusy war babies who made the hippie movement the relatively cross-class phenomenon it was." For these kids pop culture was synonymous with rock and roll, which in turn was synonymous with the Rolling Stones (*Grown Up*, p. 77).

Of course the political aspects of this cultural moment extend beyond the commercial to the racial, as the Stones "did appropriate many of the essential trappings of their music, like hooks and solos, from black sources" (*Grown Up*, p. 72). Christgau asserts that unlike blues obsessives such as the Animals' Eric Burdon, lead singer Mick Jagger "betrayed no embarrassment about being white" (p. 74). Having rejected any notion of artistic purity, the Stones couldn't be bothered to worry over authenticity. A "compulsive ironist," Jagger's relationship to black music was determined in large part by demographic reality and personal inclination. The music's aggressiveness and sexuality were within his ken, "but the sincerity was beyond him—partly because he was white and English, and especially because he was Mick Jagger" (pp. 72, 73). Jagger never sought to become a true bluesman; "he simply customized certain details of blues phrasing and enunciation for a vocal style of protean originality" (p. 72). Blues and pop were merely two ingredients among many others the mutable Jagger has absorbed over the band's long career. In the late 1970s, long after "these quintessential rock and roll bohemians evolved into quintessential rock and roll professionals," the Stones managed to incorporate elements of both punk and disco, the latest incarnations of the radical and the pop, into their album *Some Girls*. Christgau calls the record "professionalism at its best" and, in an allusion to their song "You Can't Always Get What You Want," he adds that the music may not be exactly what he and other fans want, but, in a pragmatic twist, it's music "we can use" (pp. 81–82).

Christgau's depiction of himself as a pragmatic cultural populist recurs throughout his memoir. When he was eight years old, his family

acquired their first record album, the cast recording of the Broadway musical *South Pacific*. The album was actually a case of 78 rpm records, this being just before the reign of the 33 1/3 rpm long-play format. In his landmark work *American Popular Song,* the composer and music scribe Alec Wilder derided *South Pacific* for lacking, among other things, impact, purity, friendliness, and wit. With the exception of purity, Christgau overwhelmingly recognizes abundance where Wilder perceived only deficiency. Never one to regard commerciality as an insult, Christgau casually notes that purity "didn't move him any more then than it does now" (*City,* p. 43). Five years later, thirteen-year-old Christgau presented a five-minute oral argument called "Why 'Casey at the Bat' Is a Better Poem than 'The Rime of the Ancient Mariner'" to his ninth-grade English class. Privileging as he did a lowbrow, popular poem over such a paragon of literary high art, Christgau states that he's "still slightly flabbergasted that as I turned thirteen I could see my lifework shining before my eyes" (p. 63).

Christgau's view of pop and purity remains more or less consistent throughout his reviews and columns. In 1967 he reservedly recommended records by the Doors, Love, and Jefferson Airplane, his reservations stemming from the groups' lack of pop and abundance of solemnity. Once again taking aim at purity, Christgau laments that "most hippie rock and roll musicians exhibit the same in-group pretentiousness that characterized the folk and jazz purists who were their predecessors" (*Any Old Way,* p. 40). He praises the Doors' "Break On Through" as "a great hard-rock original" while dismissing "The End" with a quip and an "Ugh." He doesn't go into detail about the latter, but pretentiousness must be an accurate description of an eleven-plus-minute epic dramatizing a particularly acute Oedipus complex performed by a band whose name alludes to William Blake via Aldous Huxley. This is certainly a long way from "Sh-Boom" and "Tutti Frutti." And although Christgau often likes such highfalutin' rock despite its allegiance to authenticity and solemn dedication to the creation of momentous art, the attitude, he says, "bugs me. I still remember when rock and roll was mostly fun" (p. 41). With the Beatles' *Sgt. Pepper's Lonely Hearts Club Band,* possibly the world's first concept album, 1967 would prove to be a watershed year for artistically ambitious rock. One gets the sense that Christgau had trouble sorting out how he felt about the record, a grandiose statement infused with vaudevillian buoyancy, for he still seemed to be digesting it six long months after its release. This column, published in *Esquire* in December 1967, exemplifies much of his approach to criticism.

Christgau takes a subtle aim at New Criticism, a school of thought he rejected while at Dartmouth, by dismissing academic approaches that pretend a work of art is an absolute existing in a vacuum. Whereas New Criticism approaches a text as a thing in itself, not its biographical background or status as an emblem of the era that produced it, Christgau argues that "criticism should invoke total aesthetic response" because works had to survive "not in some isolated specimen bottle but out in the commerce of the world" (*Any Old Way,* p. 7). In essence his focus is the cash-value of a work, its truth explored via its impact on the market.

Following the philosophical path he forged for himself after he rejected absolutism and ultimately transcended his need for any "ism," Christgau emphasizes the contingency of art and suggests a pragmatic method of criticism: "the richest and most useful kind of criticism respected the work as it was actually perceived, by people in general." His criticism "bordered on journalism and sociology" because he included everything people reacted to about a piece of music, including "the context in which they heard it and whatever they knew about the artist's life" (p. 7). Christgau admits in his memoir that his style was born of a practical need to compensate for his ignorance of any formal musical theory, "which set me to rationalizing the primacy of sociology in self-defense" (*City,* p. 201). But as his *Sgt. Pepper* column shows, this technique effectively recognizes an album as more than music; it is an artifact of the culture that produced it, an expanding text that includes information about the artists and its reception by fans and the press.

Christgau begins by chronicling the press that accompanied the record's release. Capitol Records sent out a feature using such highbrow terms as "modals" and "atonality"; *Newsweek* positively compared the Beatles to such cultural luminaries as Edith Sitwell, T. S. Eliot, and Alfred, Lord Tennyson; and the trades generated short, enthusiastic articles containing the word "artistic" (*Any Old Way,* pp. 41–42). The press ran stories in which the three non-drumming members of the band revealed that they had tried lysergic acid diethylamide (LSD), adding to the notion that *Sgt. Pepper* is of, and inseparable from, its late-sixties psychedelic context. The actual focus of the column is the vitriolic reaction to Richard Goldstein's negative review in the *New York Times.* Christgau, for his part, was initially disappointed by the record, but then experienced an exaltation that eventually subsided a bit. This distanced sympathy with Goldstein's position, combined with Christgau's overt admiration for his body of work, makes Christgau's take on the matter an interesting one.

Rebuttals to Goldstein came from such hipster outlets as the *Village Voice* and *Crawdaddy,* which accused Goldstein of judging what he failed to understand, and a flood of letters from adolescents and young adults that frequently charged Goldstein with being old. Christgau, then twenty-five, points out that Goldstein himself was only twenty-three when he wrote his review. Ever the populist, Christgau turns the focus of his piece to these letters and thus puts the thoughts and feelings of young fans on a par with the musings and opinions of seasoned critics.

A Brooklyn fan named Sherry Brody asserted that "Lucy in the Sky with Diamonds" is different from "other songs by stupid groups that say I love you and junk like that" (p. 44). Christgau takes pains to insist that he doesn't want to sound condescending, his point being that such a letter can be both charming and "every bit as perceptive as many of its more ambitious competitors." A Juilliard student contended that with *Sgt. Pepper* the Beatles "have refused to prostitute themselves for their fans," while others insisted that the album was "for the people" (p. 45).

Christgau asserts that both of these statements are true, which shows the genius of the Beatles.

How could the Beatles simultaneously be viewed as high art purists and common culture populists? Christgau transitions into analyses of specific songs to pursue the point further. To him, the track "Being for the Benefit of Mr. Kite" is a one-dimensional song about a traveling circus. One fifteen-year-old girl, by contrast, was so moved by the song that she read it as presenting "life as an eerie perverted circus." Although this insight doesn't change Christgau's perception of "Mr. Kite" as an essentially meaningless song, he happily cedes that "if a fifteen-year-old finds life 'an eerie perverted circus'—and for a fifteen-year-old that is an important perception—then that's what 'Being for the Benefit of Mr. Kite' can just as well be about." Good Lennon-McCartney songs are "sufficiently cryptic to speak to the needs of whoever listens," in this case a rock critic who appreciates how the song fits into the vaudeville atmosphere of the record and an adolescent coming to terms with the sinister and debased aspects of life, just as the Beatles themselves are cryptic enough to speak to people on both sides of the high and low cultural divide.

This column epitomizes Christgau's philosophy of rock criticism for many reasons, the most obvious being its consideration of the entire aesthetic response to a record. He not only decenters critical authority by contemplating the opinions of fans with equal gravity, he delves into the commerce of the world by noting *Sgt. Pepper*'s phenomenal sales and chart dominance. He establishes some of the important context of the record's release by exploring pertinent elements of the artists' lives, specifically their ingestion of psychedelics and, by implication, *Sgt. Pepper*'s totemic status within the drug culture. Although by no means a prude, Christgau seems to have been nobody's idea of a druggie, his love for the Beatles stemming in part from their ability to "charge commonplace English with meaning" (p. 45). In his memoir Christgau states that he is "invested in the idea of the ordinary. What's always given me something to write about is a gift for finding the putatively ordinary complex,

fascinating, and inspirational" (*City,* p. 18). Thus the connection he feels with the Beatles and their gift for infusing with meaning such simple phrases as "I want to hold your hand," "Yeah, yeah, yeah," and "It's getting better all the time," the title phrase of one of a *Sgt. Pepper* track. Christgau interprets another *Pepper* tune, "Fixing a Hole," as "a gnomic reminder of the limitations of criticism" (*Any Old Way,* p. 46). Neither he nor any other critic can assign absolute meaning to the record, for its meaning is contingent on the background of the perceiver. Christgau proudly admits "I have my own Beatles," and as such he interprets "Fixing a Hole" as stating that "those who insist upon the absolute rectitude of their opinions will never attain my state of enlightenment." And with that Christgau joins the *Sgt. Pepper* milieu; his column becomes part of the contextual totality that is the work of art. That's according to his philosophy of criticism, anyway, which brings this discussion to the role of the critic, particularly the role of the critic in rock music.

THE ROLE OF THE CRITIC

Christgau concedes that criticism is "second-hand," but makes a good case for its existence, if not its necessity. He describes the source of art as "the deep-seated human need to conjure something out of nothing, to add order and beauty to the inchoate world that radiates out from each of us." Human culture gets increasingly complex, though, and it produces art that "starts seeming pretty inchoate itself. So criticism conjures order and beauty from that" (*City,* p. 6). This implies a view of the critic as serving an almost ecclesiastical function, an interpreter of the creator's work, an intermediary between gods and mortals. But he also points out that judgment lurks in the background, which can result in the critic coming across more like a teacher than a priest. Christgau actually did dub himself "the dean of American rock critics" in the early 1970s. He had been a faculty member in the critical studies program at the California Institute of the Arts, where he taught popular culture and pop history before taking a job teaching at Richmond College on Staten Island in 1971. He also had his semimonthly column in the *Village Voice,* to which he added the "Consumer Guide," brief, letter-graded album reviews. The title and the format stemmed from his desire "to razz a counterculture that considered consumption counterrevolutionary and didn't like grades either" (p. 198). As a critic, he would get invited to promotional parties thrown by record companies, and at one such affair, when somebody asked who he was, "I quipped 'I'm the Dean of American Rock Critics,' everyone laughed, and thus it became so" (pp. 221–222). Christgau insists he was kidding, but he embraced the title and enjoyed the benefits of his inadvertent but effective self-promotion.

There appears to be a contradiction in Christgau's criticism. On the one hand, his work is accessible, the prose jargon-free, the references relatable. He flattens hierarchies, putting teenage fans, critics, and artists on the same level in that they contribute to the totality of the text and the evolution of its meaning. He consciously blurred the distinction between critic and fan, arguing in *Any Old Way You Choose It* that any critic who was no longer a fan, or at least wrote as if they were no longer a fan, was missing out on the fun of the job. He made his work opinionated because consumers "didn't simply evaluate, they liked it or disliked it." His method was "almost willfully inexact" and ultimately "functioned as popular culture itself" (p. 8).

On the other hand, labeling himself "the dean" has a bourgeois connotation that clashes with his populism, and the act of giving grades can put off readers and aggravate artists (at least the ones who pay any attention to critics). The most famous—and entertaining—example of the latter might be Lou Reed's protracted fulmination against rock critics in general and Christgau in particular on the singer's 1978 live album, *Take No Prisoners.* Reed veers from the narrative of "Walk on the Wild Side" to speculate on Christgau's sexual proclivities, twice diagnose him as anal-retentive, and mock his Consumer Guide series, all while the band plays on: "Critics. What does Robert Christgau do in bed? You know, is he a toe-fucker? Man, anal-retentive. The Consumer's Guide to Rock? What

a moron!" He follows that with an excoriation of the *New York Times* rock critic John Rockwell, who according to Reed was a Harvard-educated "opera guy," before cycling back to Christgau: "A Consumer's Guide to Rock, man! And Christgau is like an anal-retentive. Nice little boxes. B-plus. Can you imagine working for a fucking year and you get a B-plus from an asshole in the *Village Voice*?"

Setting aside toes and Freud, Reed does raise a valid point about critics sitting in judgment of an artist's work. Writing about music, exploring the culture that produced it, understanding the personalities behind the work, and considering its impact on the public is one thing, but grading it is another thing altogether. The act of grading puts the reviewer in the position of a teacher (or dean), an evaluator situated above the artist; it also implies that the consumer needs to be guided. In the early twenty-first century, when social media has gone a long way toward democratizing whose opinion gets heard and file-sharing has changed what it means to consume music, one might not remember or realize the impact a select group of critics could have on a new record, or the chasm that often existed between public and elite tastes. David Lee Roth, the lead singer of Van Halen, reportedly once said that rock journalists prefer Elvis Costello to bands such as his because rock journalists look like Elvis Costello. Although the Rolling Stones have for the most part been lauded by critics, Keith Richards did have his problems with cultural elitism, specifically a "wised-up enclave" of self-appointed blues experts, "nerds with glasses deciding what's really blues and what ain't. I mean, these cats *know?*" (*Life,* pp. 82–83). Perhaps nothing illuminates rock's version of the tension between elites and everyday people than the annual kerfuffle accompanying the Rock and Roll Hall of Fame's list of inductees. Populism in American politics took a rightward turn in the run-up to Richard M. Nixon's election in 1968, and that vocabulary to a large extent structures the debate about who should be enshrined in the Cleveland museum.

In 2011 the writer Hampton Stevens argued in the *Washington Times* that the division in rock is "cultural, with artists that appeal to a red-state audience getting shoved aside time and time again in favor of more blue-state-friendly acts." Stevens charged that there's "a prejudice against the mainstream rock of the American heartland," in particular "music that appeals to straight, white, working-class men." Stevens pits this rock-and-roll silent majority against "urbanite" Hall of Fame voters, a "high court of rock snobs, a star chamber of blue state, bluenose elitism" who have, in their "cooler-than-thou pomposity," filled the Hall with "bookish, urbanite musicians." In contrast to the singer-songwriters favored by the bluenoses stands Kiss, which "has sold 100 million records—and whose biggest single celebrates the phrase 'rock and roll' in its title." That Laura Nyro is in while Kiss remains out "is the very definition of cultural elitism," a gesture of arrogant didacticism "meant to instruct the rock audience on what music it 'should' listen to, instead of the stuff people actually like."

When Kiss finally made it into the Hall of Fame in 2014, the *New York Daily News* music critic Jim Farber saw the induction of "the world's cheesiest rock band" and perhaps "the clumsiest musicians ever to make a professional record" as "a populist peak" for the institution. This was not a compliment. Farber blamed the "Internet age, a time when the opinion of anyone can be instantly transmitted by blog and social media to millions." The democratization of opinions, he argued, boosted "the belief that no creative work should be measured by even the loosest critical standards," the sole criteria "being if you happen to really, really like it." According to Farber, the Internet has also threatened the relevance and integrity of critics, forcing them—especially young critics—"to make the case for any artist, lest some nonpro do it first and make the crit look old, jealous or, God forbid, elitist," because "these days, anyone who dares suggest that Kiss isn't of the exact quality or influence of Hall holies like Aretha, Dylan or Chuck Berry risks looking like a snob, a grouch or even an esthetic fascist." Farber obviously reviles this brand of populism and believes in a hierarchy of taste, but the clearest indication of his stance may be his declaration that "even the greatest

seer couldn't envision a day when the band Kiss and the word 'credible' could conceivably appear in the same sentence," which indicates that he assumes rock critics and the Hall of Fame really are a "high court" with the power to bestow artistic value upon a musician's work. This is the attitude that Lou Reed rails against in the aforementioned diatribe. John Rockwell had apparently written an article in which he mentioned the singer's intelligence, to which Reed replied, "Fuck you! I don't need you to tell me that I'm good."

Of course Lou Reed—consummate New Yorker; former lead singer of a band founded by Andy Warhol (the Velvet Underground); writer of songs about sadomasochism ("Venus in Furs"), a heroin overdose ("Heroin"), and transvestism ("Walk on the Wild Side"); and member of the Rock and Roll Hall of Fame both as a part of VU and (posthumously) as a solo artist—would never have been mistaken for a red-state, heartland cultural populist. And of course Christgau—also a New Yorker, plus a graduate of an Ivy League school, and a proud secular-humanist progressive—wouldn't, either. Categories overlap because popular music is complicated, and it is possible that Christgau ultimately reflects this music so well because he is too. He is a populist and a dean, an obliterator of hierarchies and issuer of grades, a defender of common culture and esoteric thinker. But more than anything, Robert Christgau is a writer. He is a writer who has been displaced by media consolidation in the Internet age, but a writer nevertheless.

After a two-year stint with *Newsday,* Christgau returned to the *Village Voice* in 1974 and remained there until 2006, when he was sacked after the paper was bought out by New Times Media, a Phoenix-based company that had been buying up alternative weeklies across the country. Christgau moved on to *Rolling Stone* in 2007, where he lasted less than a year, and then to *Blender,* which folded in early 2009. He also had short stints writing for *Billboard* online and the now-defunct MSN Music. In a panegyric published in *Slate* the week after the *Voice* let him go, the music critic Jody Rosen lamented the loss, if even temporarily, of "the eloquent, often

maddening, always thought-provoking words of Robert Christgau." Rosen recognized the skill and tenacity it took for Christgau to produce over thirteen thousand capsule reviews for his Consumer Guide feature. To Rosen, "Christgau's craft is all about compression," his blurbs "dense with ideas and allusions, first-person confessions and invective, highbrow references and slang." Rosen also argues that Christgau's short pieces were esoteric, difficult even for "the biggest music geek" to decipher. Christgau's greatest strengths were his humor and his "old-fashioned lefty-secular-humanist warmth. He overflows with love for music and a *joie de vivre* that makes his fits of critical pique more principled than mere hipsterish provocations."

CONCLUSION

Rosen, perhaps better than anybody, captures the essence of what makes Christgau's work compelling: his prose overflows with knowledge, love for music, and joyful exuberance. It also reflects the careful attention he pays to his craft, his profession. Indeed, Christgau argues that what sells criticism is "sensibility—a brew of genre knowledge, general knowledge, aesthetic insight, moral passion, palpable delight, prose style, more prose style, and what-have-you" (*City,* p. 6). He knew early on that his life's work would be writing, but he struggled to find the genre that fit him best; he seemed haunted by the idea of criticism being secondary, and not really creative. As a high school student, he challenged himself by choosing Fyodor Dostoyevsky's *Crime and Punishment* (1866) for a book report, which forced him to approach his Christianity from a critical perspective. Decades later, his pride in the work is palpable, and he confidently asserts that what he wrote was indeed creative (pp. 78–79). He worked on short stories and even spent a couple of years flirting with a novel, until he met up with a mentor from his Dartmouth days, Jack Hirschman, one of the lone bohemians on Dartmouth's faculty. Hirschman told him that his talent for writing was criticism, not fiction, and it hurt Christgau so badly he didn't write it down. Soon thereafter, though, he discovered A. J. Liebling's *The Sweet Science,* (a 1949 collection

of essays about boxing that so moved the young Christgau that he began to consider a career in journalism (pp. 144–145). After his success with his article about the tragic death of Beth Ann Simon, Christgau decided to combine his love for writing with his passion for music.

In a 2005 article for the journal *Popular Music,* Christgau makes the simple point that "writing about music is writing first." But it gets a bit more complicated, especially when he argues that "nothing can be reduced to words, not even words" (p. 416). Most of the essay is dedicated to Lester Bangs, who "wrote like rock and roll. He believed it was OK to make mistakes because in rock and roll mistakes are often beautiful" (p. 418). This isn't to say that Christgau gave a pass to reckless writing that got by on passion. He advocated a kind of balance between the unique voice of an author and the structure of the profession: "your voice does have to be your own. But that doesn't leave you free to ignore the mechanics of a craft whose guild automatically enrolls anyone who communicates in written words" (p. 421). Writing well about music does "music an incalculable service." Of course writers can't use words to capture magic moments, "but we can surround them, approximate them, evoke them, open a window on them, open a window for them—and if we get lucky, maybe even fire them a shot of abracadabra" (p. 421). In other words, writing about music has inherent limitations, but when done well it brings the reader up to the very limits of language, to the sublime, and points to the ecstatic magic beyond. It seems, then, that to write well about music is to perform an ecclesiastical function after all, to use words to guide the reader to the ineffable bliss of that rock-and-roll music.

Selected Bibliography

WORKS OF ROBERT CHRISTGAU

CRITICISM AND MEMOIR

Any Old Way You Choose It: Rock and Other Pop Music, 1967–1973. Baltimore, Md.: Penguin, 1973.

Grown Up All Wrong: 75 Great Rock and Pop Artists from Vaudeville to Techno. Cambridge, Mass: Harvard University Press, 1998.

Going into the City: Portrait of a Critic as a Young Man. New York: Dey St., 2015.

Robert Christgau, author website. http://www.robertchristgau.com/ (Christgau's website contains links to many of his essays and reviews.)

RECORD GUIDES

Christgau's Record Guide: Rock Albums of the Seventies. New Haven, Conn.: Ticknor & Fields, 1981.

Christgau's Record Guide: The '80s. New York: Pantheon, 1990.

Christgau's Consumer Guide: Albums of the '90s. New York: St. Martin's Griffin, 2000.

ESSAYS

"Beth Ann and Microbioticism." In *The New Journalism.* Edited by Tom Wolfe and E. W. Johnson. New York: Harper & Row, 1973. Pp. 331–339.

"Writing About Music Is Writing First." *Popular Music* 24, no. 3:415–421 (2005).

CRITICAL STUDIES

Carson, Tom, Kit Rachlis, and Jeff Salamon, eds. *Don't Stop 'til You Get Enough: Essays in Honor of Robert Christgau.* 2nd ed. Austin, Tex.: Nortex Press, 2002.

Rosen, Jody. "The *Village Voice* Fires a Famous Music Critic." September 5, 2006. http://www.slate.com/articles/arts/music_box/2006/09/xed_out.html

OTHER SOURCES

Farber, Jim. "Kiss Makes Rock and Roll Hall of Fame: World Ends." *New York Daily News,* April 6, 2014. http://www.nydailynews.com/entertainment/music-arts/kiss-rock-roll-hall-fame-world-ends-article-1.1743190

James, William. *Pragmatism.* Edited by Thomas Crofts and Philip Smith. New York: Dover, 1995. Kindle edition, Dover, 2012 (all quotations in essay from this edition).

Reed, Lou. *Take No Prisoners.* Lou Reed, 1978. CD.

Richards, Keith, and James Fox. *Life.* New York: Back Bay, 2010.

Stevens, Hampton. "Rock Hall of Fame Snubs Red-State Favorites." *Washington Times,* December 12, 2011. http://www.washingtontimes.com/news/2011/dec/12/wheres-the-rock/

LEONARD COHEN

(1934—)

Joseph Dewey

IT BEGINS, IMPROBABLY enough, with "Turkey in the Straw." In a long and very public career, first as a provocative poet and avant-garde novelist, then as the quintessential gloomy, introspective singer-songwriter, and ultimately as a peripatetic troubadour delivering mesmerizing marathon recitative/concerts that he conceives as "gatherings," the life—and work—of Canadian-born Leonard Cohen has been defined by its resistance to definition. His is a life shaped by the intriguing logic of "nevertheless," the entangling collisions of paradox: he is, after all, both a practicing Jew and an ordained Buddhist monk; an impeccably tailored *chansonnier* whose signature verse nevertheless chronicles the wastrel lifestyle of coffeehouse bohemians, a messy hangover-world of promiscuity, alcohol, and recreational pharmaceuticals; a singer-songwriter who came to the profession awkwardly late, past thirty, but who rose to iconic stature, second only to Bob Dylan in influence, productivity, and longevity; and a 2008 inductee into the Rock and Roll Hall of Fame (along with the likes of the Dave Clark Five and Madonna), who nevertheless by his own admission mastered only six guitar chords, who has never enjoyed even that One Hit to be derided as a One Hit Wonder, whose lyrics are at once layered and enigmatic, conceived as formidable poems rather than as consumer-friendly tunes, and whose voice, burnished by alcohol and cigarettes, is, to put it kindly, hardly radio friendly. More intriguingly, from the beginning, Cohen has been a leering, carnal wolf who nevertheless donned the angel wings of a mystic, a self-conceived pilgrim-soul and an earnest student of world religions who defined his life as a spiritual quest, forthrightly chronicled in his writings and in hundreds of interviews, that often found its most fervent ecstasies wearing skirts. And finally, although he is a disciplined ascetic much taken by the sanctuary silence of retreat, he nevertheless thrives most vibrantly within the sprawling kinetic energy field of performance.

Yet, in a life sustained within contradictions, few are more improbable, or more telling, than Lenny Cohen, Teenage Cowboy. Years before he discovered the robust vibrancy of the Greenwich Village underground and first registered the tectonic liberation of the crazy improvisations of Beat poetry; long before he tapped into the complicated sustenance of sensuality that both delighted the senses and manifested the spiritual; long before he first heard the sonic architectures and unfettered cool of hard bop jazz that redefined for him the function of words; long before he found the elastic dynamic of Buddhist thought with its rigorous discipline and its hard-core faith in defining the self by emptying it of its integrity—long before all of it, there was Lenny Cohen, a sophomore at Montreal's McGill University, his heart suffused by the dark poetry of Federico García Lorca, testing the sudden freedoms of college by, improbably enough, fronting a country-western trio. With two friends, the trio, known as the Buckskin Boys, sported goofy matching buckskin outfits and tirelessly worked a thankless neighborhood circuit of tiny gatherings: church basements, school auditoriums, street fairs, bar mitzvahs. But Lenny Cohen, Teenage Cowboy, would engage his audience, whatever its size, with the very first tune he had ever mastered on the guitar—the country staple "Turkey in the Straw." Even at seventeen, Cohen understood that, despite its nonsense lyrics, its toe-tapping melody structured around two simple chords, this was music that everyone seemed born knowing, music that could bring a room of strangers together. The response was always electric. He would play the silly song

with zest and unaffected brio—and it would, in turn, create a most remarkable communion, new to Cohen, then a fledgling poet who struggled nightly within the necessary isolation of the craft. Communion was immediately addictive, a call-and-response dynamic that was, for him, religious in intensity, like the rich energy he had always felt at temple, ever-changing, robust, abiding, and intrinsically meaningful.

Cohen never forgot that intensity. In the post-modern era into which he emerged, his generation's most accomplished poets too nimbly settled into the margins, where, carefully nurturing a studied disdain for market appeal and relishing the idea of their own obscurity, happily retreating to the hothouse of the university, content to be admired rather than read, they went about the serious business of writing self-consciously obscure verse designed only to engage other poets who also equated "audience" with soul death or artistic compromise. Across more than six decades of writings—fiction, poetry, lyrics—Cohen reconceived words themselves as affirming the centrifugal reach of language; with unapologetic earnestness, he sought to return language, whether expressed into narratives, sculpted into lyric poems, or sung as verses, to its most ancient consolation—the creation of a community. A poet, he reasoned, was a voice, and a voice needed to be heard. Restless when his early work was as enthusiastically feted by the Canadian literary establishment as it was happily ignored by general readers (his most "important" novel sold fewer than fifteen hundred copies), Cohen was drawn by the energy of performance inherent in the emerging world of singer-songwriters. It was at first an awkward fit. But Cohen came ultimately to embrace a kind of sustained performance piece, inhabiting with charm and elegance the avatar of " modern troubadour," using his poetry to sustain a complicated intimacy, not the messy frictions of body on body that he had so earnestly chronicled in his early verse but rather the subtle bindings of heart onto heart that has always been the special province of the poet. Night after night in cavernous venues (between 2008 and 2015 Cohen delivered more than four hundred shows worldwide), his poetry rendered in a sumptuous plainsong, Cohen could somehow simultaneously speak to and for each audience member individually, igniting a kind of collective frisson. His poetry forged a bond that left the poet himself there up on the stage suspended in yet another contradiction: a part of, certainly, but nevertheless apart from the very community his words had called into being, a lesson Lenny Cohen, Teenage Cowboy, first learned playing "Turkey in the Straw" for perfect strangers in near-empty church halls.

OVERVIEW

Through his fictional characters, his verse, his lyrics, indeed through the performance piece that became his life, Cohen became the embodiment of the *anima sola*, the figure of the lonely soul that haunts numerous world religions, most prominently Catholicism. The anima sola is usually pictured as a tormented, deeply feeling isolate, most often rendered as a sensual woman, chained amid the cleansing fires of purgatory, that halfway prison that is neither damnation nor salvation. The woman's wide, soulful eyes seem at once to be deeply penitent yet unrepentantly carnal. For six decades, Leonard Cohen has asked what the soulful eyes of the anima sola had asked for millennia in all but words—I have this heart, what am I to do with it? At first, Cohen's answer was direct, even obvious—the simple, sweet violation of others. Initially, as an emerging poet in Montreal's robust postwar underground literary movement, Cohen recognized that his heart, at once immature and hungry, at once arrogant and needful, too impatient to feel deeply, had to be content with the uncomplicated slam and grab of touch. His early work—two novels and four volumes of poetry—tangled boldly, unflinchingly, with carnality, investigating the frictions of uncouth touch, elevating the pangs of the flesh into spiritual urgencies propelled, ironically, by the itch of the senses and the freewheeling indulgence of drugs and alcohol, thus spiraling, inevitably, into insecurity, loneliness, and spiritual vacuity. The primary characters of his two novels are Cohen's perpetually randy doppelgänger

Lawrence Breavman in *The Favourite Game* (1963); and the nameless anthropologist in *Beautiful Losers* (1966), a widower who, centuries after the death of Saint Kateri Tekakwitha, lusts after this beautiful seventeenth-century Algonquin woman who, her features pocked by smallpox, converted to Catholicism at the age of nineteen and consecrated her purity to Christ, dying at the age of twenty-four. The narrating voices of his early poetry too are characters who hunger for what cannot satisfy. They are creatures born into insufficiency, reminders that long ago humanity had been expelled from the Garden and thus was forever expatriated from contentment. Cohen's early works struggle, ungallantly, against and amid the riptides of need. In them, more is inevitably less, the profane too coolly masquerading as the sacred.

If the heart cannot be sustained by being bartered or animated by coarse friction, if such endeavors only leave it wounded, then perhaps the heart needs to be protected. When Cohen first contemplated the possibility of being a singer of his poems, when he first negotiated the tonic freedoms of the night world of New York's Greenwich Village underground in the mid-1960s, he created verses that read more like diary entries, scalding, honest, intensely egocentric, passionately committed to the arduous work of anatomizing his heart's own agonies and ecstasies. After the long struggle to unburden the heart to another, Cohen retreated with what was left of his heart. For two decades, long before it became a staple of pop culture, Cohen embodied the reclusive singer-songwriter, the Prince of Downers. He became known for morbidly obsessive introspection, gnarring lyrics, even admiring critics agreed, perfect for slitting your wrists to. His signature works of the period—"Bird on a Wire," "Suzanne," "So Long, Marianne," "Diamonds in the Mine"—were intense, claustrophobic with an uncompromising earnestness, a spirit of authentic excavation that signaled in Cohen's lyrics a formidable centripetal energy. Cohen retreated, tending to his bandaged heart, recounting the dissatisfactions, emotional ennui, and apartness of the anima sola. Even when he toured, his stage presence reflected this insularity—he

tenuously engaged small, if devoted, audiences, a man and his guitar isolated in the scooped glare of a single hard white spotlight in a stage otherwise deep in shadow, his performances often unsettled by Cohen's unshakeable stage fright, anxieties that only alcohol and antidepressants could ease. His music, his lyrics, so carefully crafted sometimes over years, served only to isolate him even more in an era when pop songs would be manufactured in minutes in studios. Cohen was a minority enthusiasm; his songs, subtle and understated, required effort, response, thought. Small audiences came to watch Cohen on Cohen. He would recount years later how, when he first worked in a studio, to overcome his insecurities about his meager musical background, surrounded as he was by accomplished career musicians, he could bring himself to record only by looking at his own reflection in a life-size mirror his producer had lugged into the studio: Cohen on Cohen, the anima sola finding comfort in its own agonized reflection.

Ultimately, however, Cohen extricated himself from such thickening quicksand. The jarring juxtaposition of two event-narratives when he was past sixty would help catapult him out of the gravitational pull of such a centripetal spiral. Neither event would seem to promise such a bold and invigorating turn outward: in the one case, the discovery of the serene retreat of a Buddhist sanctuary more than four thousand feet above Los Angeles and, during the same time, the discovery that his much-trusted agent and financial consultant had bilked Cohen out of his considerable life savings (estimates ran into the millions), leaving Cohen essentially broke at the age when most relax into retirement. Either event might easily have sanctioned bitter seclusion, even recuperative exile. Yet by the early 1990s, Cohen's verse began to tap a profound movement outward, a return to the lessons of the Buckskin Boys: a vision of poetry rendered as community event. Buddhism and financial catastrophe introduced into his verse a layered vulnerability. Humbled, taught by both experiences the waste of possessions and the risk of trust, he sought in first his verse and then on stage what he had felt as a child listening to the

cantor in the neighborhood synagogue of Montreal and what he had felt playing his secondhand six-string in those church basements as part of the Buckskin Boys: the compensation of community, how words could turn a room into gold.

The aloof singer-songwriter, the ever-anxious performer, the gloomy emo-laureate tapped into the sheer reach of verse itself: past seventy, he embraced arduous concert tours; he engaged rounds of interviews with cheerful approachability; he discovered the aesthetic viability of music videos; he integrated synthesizers and world music rhythms for backbeat; supremely, he embraced being Leonard Cohen—delighting in tribute concerts, accepting lifetime achievement awards, encouraging new artists to cover his songs. Cohen, now at peace with himself, skipped on stage, beaming, animating three-hour shows with quips and anecdotes, unironically grateful for the presence of others, given to dropping to his knees in humble acknowledgment of the redemptive boost of the audience, the anima sola at last discovering the consolation of others bound to the predicaments his songs rendered. And for the first time, the music itself became an element of Cohen's verse, a kind of counterargument to his vision: that vision remained irredeemably sorrowful, certainly, but now the music—sing-along choruses with breezy rhythms (playful waltzes, gospel, jazz shuffles, syncopated tangos, even ragtime)—swept up audiences, letting them feel that, yes, life is a cruel cycle of anticipation and disappointment; yes, we tender our hearts only to those most capable of shredding them; yes, the world, adrift in a dark time of its own creation, blindly stumbles toward self-inflicted apocalypse; and yes, we each edge every moment closer to the forbidding absolute of death; but we are in this together. Tilt your head back and testify with a full-throated "Hallelujah." In the representative verses of this era—"I'm Your Man," "Everybody Knows," "Tower of Song," "Anthem," and supremely the gospel-infused "Hallelujah"—Cohen relaxed into his art, offering audience members, each bound to the other, the gift of exuberance, the difficult energy of awareness, the trick of an affirmation-despite.

It has become something of a parlor game to locate Leonard Cohen's birth year on a pop culture x-y axis, hoping to define him if only by association: for instance, Cohen was born a year before both Jerry Lee Lewis and Elvis Presley, a year after Philip Roth, almost three years before Thomas Pynchon, two years after Sylvia Plath, nearly the same month as Charles Manson, nearly the same day as Brigitte Bardot. Born September 21, 1934, the son of Russian Jewish immigrants, Leonard Norman Cohen, along with an older sister, Esther (b. 1930), enjoyed a stable and privileged childhood in the upper-middle-class environs of the leafy Westmount neighborhood of Montreal. His father, Nathan, a semi-invalid wounded while serving as an engineer with the Canadian Expeditionary Force during World War I, ran a successful men's clothing company. Nathan Cohen carried himself with elegance, sporting, even about the house, high-button Edwardian spats, a monocle, and a carved, silver-tipped cane. Haunted by his war experiences, Nathan married late. Nearly forty, he married Masha (Marsha) Klonitzky, sixteen years his junior, trained as a nurse, the daughter of a prominent Lithuanian rabbi and Talmudic scholar. Given to melancholia, Masha would assuage it with music. She doted on her only son, nurturing in him the belief that he was destined for great things. She introduced her son to music: first the pennywhistle, then the clarinet, ultimately the piano. But as a child, Cohen was far more enthralled by the sonorous voices of the synagogue cantors that transcended words, doctrine, even the rituals themselves.

That comfortable world of Cohen's childhood, however, was abruptly shattered with the sudden death of his father just after New Year's Day 1944. Although the family was comfortable financially, Cohen reeled from the loss. He compensated by turning outward. A modestly talented student, Cohen began to excel in extracurricular activities, including cheerleading, debating, and hockey, and was voted "most ambitious." He dabbled in hypnotism, fascinated by how pure voice could engage others, actually alter them, shattering barriers of identity. Unerr-

ingly, Cohen found his way to poetry. A teacher introduced him at age fifteen to the brooding verse of the Spaniard Federico García Lorca, who, before being executed by the Fascist government of Francisco Franco just two years after Cohen was born, had created brash romantic poetry that frankly explored very adult themes of sexuality and spiritual isolation. The impact on Cohen was tectonic—he began writing poetry, certain now that he was destined to be a serious writer of enormous influence.

Under the potent sway of Lorca's exemplum, Cohen also began to take guitar lessons from a young Spanish-born flamenco guitarist in his Westmount neighborhood. However, Cohen had taken only three lessons, learning only six chords, before the melancholic teacher took his own life. But Cohen kept at it; he played guitar as a summer camp counselor—his introduction to American folk music—and spent long evenings working through the chords of songs he heard on WWVA, a fifty-thousand-watt country music giant beaming from Wheeling, West Virginia (the station's playlist would provide the repertoire for the Buckskin Boys). In September 1951, indifferent to running his family business, Cohen enrolled at Montreal's prestigious McGill University. An undistinguished student, free-floating among majors (political science, law, criminal justice, literature, education, math), Cohen took a general B.A. degree in 1955. At McGill, however, Cohen discovered Montreal's burgeoning underground literary world of seedy dives where fledgling poets Cohen's age argued passionately about their art and boldly tested radically new avenues of poetic expression, consciously attempting to create a modern Canadian poetry, to break it free of the nearly century-long tradition of staid wisdom verses about nature, singsongy ballads recounting adventure stories of the great outdoors, and tidy, neatly metered historical epics. Cohen first published his verse in the college's mimeographed literary magazine. Romantic and sensual, the poems spoke with an apparent directness that belied Cohen's meticulous crafting of lines for their sonic impact. Unlike his comrades in the arts enthralled by the impersonal metrical experiments of Ezra Pound

and other modernists, Cohen fashioned poems that relished, even indulged, language and explored the dark energy of desire, the insatiable obsessions of love, and the emotional terrorism of betrayal, such autobiographical intimacies transcribed into religious vocabulary and layered with mythological imagery.

In 1956, Cohen—much as a young Lorca had—tried law school. He enrolled in McGill's law school but after a single term left with the self-financed publication of his first book of verse, *Let Us Compare Mythologies,* a slender compendium of forty-four poems. His reputation started to grow (he was hailed as Canada's Arthur Rimbaud, hardly endearing him to Canada's conservative literary establishment, which was searching more for the new Bliss Carman). Sales were slight. Cohen spent a year in New York at Columbia University, however, and gravitated to the Greenwich Village scene, discovering the heady freedoms of Beat poetry and the intoxicating rhythms of bop jazz, as well as a liberating lifestyle in which promiscuity, alcohol, and recreational drugs, most prominently hashish and marijuana, were celebrated as portals into self-discovery. Cohen embraced the experience. After returning briefly to Montreal to try to find his place within his family business (initially he operated a lathe, but when that proved problematic, he draped finished suits onto hangers), he left Montreal in 1959 on a government arts grant. He headed for London, determined in a culture so rich with literary heritage to write his first novel, certain that fiction would provide entrance to a far wider audience than his poetry had. Relishing the lifestyle of an expatriate, Cohen worked on his novel, a thinly veiled autobiography that began with his father's death and ended with his time in New York. But he lacked an ending. Cohen further struggled in the harsh London climate—one dreary afternoon in April 1960, his jaw swollen from a messy wisdom tooth extraction, Cohen stopped at a branch of the Bank of Greece and, while waiting in line, happened to see a teller wearing sunglasses, despite the rain, and sporting a lustrous Mediterranean tan. Within weeks, Cohen had moved to Greece.

Cohen settled on the narrow island of Hydra, an artists' colony with few modern amenities. Cohen was swept up by the rugged landscape, the elegant primitiveness, the luminous magic of the Aegean sun. Cohen thrived—he threw himself into a hedonistic life of women, hashish, and sedatives while rewriting his novel, initially rejected as tediously self-indulgent. His long involvement with the Norwegian model Marianne Ihlen would give the novel its close; the hero at last affirms the truth of beauty and the beauty of truth in the arms (and legs) of an enticing muse figure. Published in 1963, *The Favourite Game* received guarded praise, critics cautious over a first novel that was yet another clichéd *Künstlerroman*. But the critical reception of Cohen's poetry—collected in *The Spice-Box of Earth* (1961) and *Flowers for Hitler* (1964)—had positioned Cohen as the leading poetic voice of Canada's Young Turks. Cohen returned to Montreal to embrace his status. He relished the serpentine lines at book signings and the large audiences, mostly college students, who crowded halls for his readings; with his charisma and his Hollywood good looks (picture the wounded yearning of a young Dustin Hoffman), Cohen became the darling of the arts press, working both radio and the new medium of television, giving interviews and even agreeing to be the subject of a Canadian Broadcasting Company documentary.

That love affair with the Canadian arts community would be sorely tested in 1966 with the publication of Cohen's second novel, *Beautiful Losers*. Cohen, known for spending weeks chiseling a single line of poetry, wrote the book back on Hydra in a two-month burst fueled by amphetamines. An uncompromising exploration of the formal freedoms of postmodernism, an audaciously crafted novel that fused fictional narrative with history, poetry, theology, bits of drama, and even mock newspaper ads, *Beautiful Losers* upended linearity, causality, and the logic of suspense. Its eccentric story line recounts a Prufrockian academic obsessed with an obscure Native American woman more than three centuries dead, a professed virgin, venerated by the Catholic Church to which she had converted; the

book was derided by critics as unreadable, obscene, tasteless. But even that firestorm generated only modest sales at the time—fewer than fifteen hundred copies. It would be Cohen's last novel. In 1966, at age thirty-two, Cohen found himself at a crossroads. He was living on increasingly thinning royalty checks, meager stipends from readings, a modest trust fund, and infrequent government grant money. He had never really had a job. He disdained the notion of retreating to academia; he resisted the idea of returning to his family business. Given the renaissance in folk music on American radio, he thought he might try singing his poems—he had never stopped playing guitar informally for friends. Given his roots in country music and that field's wide popularity, he decided to head to Nashville, then as now the epicenter of country music—but first he would stop in New York City.

He returned to Greenwich Village, specifically the artist commune around the Hotel Chelsea, and there was introduced to the young denizens of the burgeoning folk music scene. Of course, Cohen was older than most of the Village artists, and he was grounded not in three-chord rock and roll or the Delta blues or the populist folk music of the Great Depression but rather in modernist poetry. He was painfully aware of his limitations as a musician and as a vocalist. But his lyrics were hailed for their density, their precise imagery, and their subtle wordplay. He attracted the attention of Judy Collins, who recorded two of Cohen's songs, most famously "Suzanne." Cohen's performance at the Newport Jazz Festival in 1967 impressed the iconic maverick Columbia record producer John Hammond, who had signed Bob Dylan, among scores of other artists. With little coaxing, Hammond signed Cohen. Within months, Cohen, who still could not read music, found himself in the studio recording his first collection of songs. Despite his insecurities, Cohen was certain now that performing his verse would be the avenue to the audience he so deeply desired.

Over the next five years, Cohen released a trilogy of sorts—*Songs of Leonard Cohen* (1967), *Songs from a Room* (1969), and *Songs of Love and Hate* (1971). Critics were unsure how to

respond; the songs were enigmatic, dark, introspective; the melodies spare, brittle, repetitive; the instrumental accompaniment austere, low-keyed; the vocal delivery limited, even abrasive. Critics tried initially to pigeonhole Cohen with other "serious" singer-songwriters and performers—Collins, Joni Mitchell, Paul Simon, Phil Ochs, Dave Van Ronk, Tim Buckley, Roger McGuinn, Joan Baez, and most often Dylan. But it was an awkward fit. Whereas with other songwriters, the words needed the dimension of the music, Cohen's lyrics had come first. They were poems, complex and textured, the music more an afterthought, Cohen's singing a gravelly recitative. Sales were predictably modest. Cohen toured, but his stage performances were uneven—buttressed by LSD and antianxiety drugs, he struggled with his sense of inadequacy, conscious of his age and his decidedly unflamboyant persona as an entertainer. Although he was remarkably prolific—five albums of new material in the 1970s alone—by the end of the decade music itself had shifted into new directions—toward hummable melodies, processed sound, inane lyrics, and theatrical spectacle. Cohen's style of introspective angst bordered on parody (culminating with the debacle of his 1977 Phil Spector collaboration, the aptly titled *Death of a Ladies' Man,* a bombastic, overproduced mess in which Cohen's lyrics were all but lost against oppressive layers of Spector's signature percussive arrangements). Cohen's audience thinned, and, approaching fifty, he faced the chilling stigma of irrelevancy. Amid a succession of much-publicized romances, Cohen had had two children, son Adam (1972–) and daughter Lorca (1974–), with Suzanne Elrod, but he had never married. As his celebrity waned, as he began to question his own talent, Cohen found a new avenue of spiritual exploration: the formality, rituals, and discipline of Zen Buddhism. He was drawn by its sense of the mystical implications of suffering, its imperative to burn clean the accumulations of manufactured identities, and its renunciation of the entangling complications of contemporary life. Rumors swirled that Cohen had retired. In 1984 he returned to verse, publishing *Book of Mercy,* a harrowing collection of fifty austere verses, patterned on the syntax and rhythms of Old Testament psalms, which traced his desperation to lose the self as a way to fulfill its deepest possibility.

It is tempting to say that Cohen's catapult movement outward, his ascendancy into the avatar of Modern Troubadour, began when he first pressed the keys of an electronic table synthesizer. That sound, so vivid, so immediate, conjured a wider, broader vision both for his verse and the music he created for it. *Various Positions* (1984) didn't sound like a Leonard Cohen album—the lyrics, yes, were still introspective, dark and dense, but the music assumed a prominent element, added a cleaner color. Cohen experimented with a brighter, more accessible sound, with sophisticated world music rhythms, lively backup singers, cagey syncopations, engaging hooks, and a boogie backbeat, not quite pop, not quite jazz, not quite commercial, but melodies that were elastic and giving, arrangements that were living, even playful. Lyrics and music, for the first time, cooperated, a celebration at last, whatever the subject, of writing itself, the sonic seduction of lyrics and music. Over the next decade, in a succession of well-reviewed "comeback" albums—most notably *I'm Your Man* (1988) and *The Future* (1992)—Cohen's poetry/lyrics opened into a new, broader audience. His stage presence grew more confident, more at ease, less dependent on drugs and alcohol. In 1993 a retrospective collection of his poems, lyrics, and autobiographical writings, *Stranger Music,* became an international best seller. Under the powerful influence of a wizened California Zen master, Joshu Sasaki Roshi, Leonard Cohen retreated for more than four years in the early 1990s to Mount Baldy, a Zen monastery in the San Gabriel Mountains east of Los Angeles. Cohen relished the quiet, the reassuring daily narrative of manual labor, the necessary renunciation of material excess, the solitude, the embrace of the subtle urgencies of now. He was ordained a monk in 1996. To anyone who asked, he testified that he had, at last, found calm.

That calm would be quickly tested. Cohen found himself the victim of a duplicitous manager who over many years had stolen millions from

him. That commenced years of acrimonious litigation. But Cohen himself responded with a pragmatic resolve. After all, he reasoned, the cracks in the world let in the light. Now approaching seventy, he turned to the consolation of music and to the subtle intimacy of an audience. He mastered the new genre of the music video; he released three albums of new material as well as four concert albums to critical acclaim and wide international sales; he toured nearly continuously for more than a decade. His concerts grew legendary: performances that ran to three hours, Cohen playing to the crowd with genuine modesty, jauntily chatting, tipping his signature black fedora, welcoming them into his songs, recognizing their crucial place within their fragile dynamic. In 2006 Cohen published his first book of new poetry in more than two decades, *Book of Longing,* poems of contentment and spiritual ease, not resignation so much as the willed cheerfulness of a man at the crossroads of where what he knows and cannot get meets what is left of what he can stand without despair. It became an international best seller. Past eighty, Cohen received a shelf of lifetime achievement awards in both music and literature, and he was the subject of a series of tribute concerts featuring a generation of singer-songwriters deeply indebted to Cohen, many born when Cohen was in his fifties. But it was on stage that the octogenarian Cohen at last tapped his deepest consolations. Cohen didn't merely perform; he conjured, creating an exuberant congregation that celebrated music—lyrics and melodies—as a joint enterprise with the audience. It was Cohen as mesmerist, Cohen as cantor, Cohen, at last, as troubadour.

THE DISTANCE OF NEARNESS

We begin with desire because, as Cohen admitted wistfully years later in "Hallelujah," "I did my best, it wasn't much / I couldn't feel, so I learned to touch" (*Poems and Songs,* p. 167). Touch itself proved a problematic dynamic. As Cohen observed in one of his earliest and most anthologized poems, "As the mist leaves no scar / On the dark green hill, / So my body leaves no scar /

On you, nor ever will" ("As the Mist Leaves No Scar," p. 22). Those closing three words shatter—desire, the carefree and careless frictions of passion, can never sustain, can never endure. Indeed, touch merely renders ironic the physical nearness of lovers and ultimately destroys the identity of the lovers themselves, as his narrator laments with deadpan seriousness in "Fingerprints": "I touched you once too often / & I don't know who I am," shocked to find his fingerprints suddenly wiped clean; the last time he recalls seeing them they were "leafing thru your hair" (p. 62).

That reality renders a fetching, spacious innocence to Cohen's first novel, *The Favourite Game,* with its romantic yearning, at once endearing and annoying, to grant a desperate magic to lust, a dimension that the reader knows does not, indeed cannot, exist. Speaking in a lyrical intensity uninformed by modesty, Lawrence Breavman, twenty-something and already world-weary, a would-be artist self-consciously coming of age in postwar Montreal and convinced of his own privilege, is on a quest both to find out who he is and to get laid, preferably in the same urgent experience. For readers of Cohen, Breavman works as an opening gambit, a necessary initial proposition. How, Cohen asks, do we first learn the mysteries of intimacy? Clumsily, as it turns out, and obviously. Breavman emerges into adolescence convinced of two core realities: first, that he is destined to be a Poet, a misfit who cannot engage the world around him without irony (he sleeps late, professes boredom at every turn, cannot commit to schooling, favors the clever epigraph to express unearned cynicism, dismisses adults over twenty-five as hypocrites, and finds the prospect of purposeful employment endlessly amusing); and second, that, like a crafted line of verse itself, physical love is a grand protest against a careless world of "luck and circumstances" (*Favourite Game,* p. 84). Coming into adolescence perpetually horny, he stages pseudo-sexual role-playing games with prepubescent neighborhood girls (his favorites, influenced by the recently concluded world war, include the Soldier and the Gorgeous Whore and, more darkly, the Nazi Interrogator and the Captive

Peasant Girl). Breavman is drawn to the game play of seduction. At thirteen, he tries his scratch talent for hypnotism on the family's husky maid. He fuels his carnal appetite by watching pirated French pornographic shorts. But mostly he hungers for the simplest impress of touch. (His father, emotionally distant, had died when he was nine; his mother had become melancholic, smothering, doting.) In high school, despite his age (he stuffs his shoes with tissue to create the illusion of being an adult), he haunts the night world of Montreal dance halls, standing in stag lines, nursing (appropriately) an Orange Crush, staring meaningfully at exotic French girls who never dance with him. Without conscience, he attends spirited Communist rallies on the assumption that leftist girls are easy. Desire is a game, certainly his favorite game, but a game nevertheless.

As the game's grand-master-in-training, Breavman glorifies the longing after physical love. Indeed, deprivation is the mother of poetry, he grandly laments during one of his frequent bouts of pimply angst (a.k.a. "blue balls"). Gifted with the uncompromising artistic intensities of a Stephen Dedalus but contending as well with the crosswind hormonal urgencies of a Holden Caulfield, Lawrence Breavman epitomizes Cohen's earliest conceptions of the irony of desire, the distance of nearness. For Breavman, physical need simply must have dimension, depth, shadow, meaning. He does not comprehend the implications of disappointment or the implicit selfishness of his quest, nor does he fathom the concept of commitment or the pain of betrayal—two of his lovers are, in fact, married and have children. As he matures into adolescence, he finds insuperable the idea that that gnawing itch may be simply that—yet another shabby manifestation of a depthless world unavailable to spiritual redemption, the bland postwar suburban world of soulnumbing routine and careless amorality (at one point, Breavman observes a homeless man grab a starving street cat, swing it hard down onto the sidewalk, and carry off the carcass, Breavman assumes, to eat it). Amid such commonplace obscenities, physical love, Breavman argues in gorgeously lavender prose, sustains, lifts. His is

not love as it is but rather love as we would want it to be. Consider his indulgent description of one of his lovers: "She stands in my mind alone, unconnected to [my] petty narrative. The colour of the skin was startling, like the white of a young branch when the green is thumb-nailed away. Nipples the colour of bare lips. Wet hair a battalion of glistening spears laid on her shoulders. She was made of flesh and eyelashes"(pp. 52–53).

It is the dilemma in *The Favourite Game,* however, that flesh, no matter how richly described, cannot redeem and that sex itself remains little more than a game of curiosity, compelled by boredom, satisfied by orgasms, and sustained, when it is sustained at all, solely by the fear of the complex ache of loneliness. But even as Breavman pursues his sexual conquests, he keeps confronting a puzzling reality: adoration of the thighs is not enough, need is not what he needs; in disheveled bedrooms in hard dawns, beds morph into prisons. Breavman discovers that his need actually destroys each lover—each becomes his own creation, a kind of tyrannical colonialism, an exhausting game of self-projection. And in the closing pages when a panicky Breavman reaches out to a former lover, Shell, after a particularly precocious boy he had met as a counselor at summer camp is killed in a freak accident (squashed by a bulldozer), Breavman's logic is painfully clear: "I'm afraid of loneliness" (p. 154), he confides melodramatically in a letter. Her eventual answer is telling. Over the phone (Shell has gone to New York), she rejects his neediness—no one, she says, could ever be what he needs. As her name suggests, love offers at best a most tentative and frail sanctuary.

But little in the poetic romanticism of *The Favourite Game* prepared Cohen's readers for the vertiginous drop into the harrowing night world of lust, betrayal, obsession, and perversion he would depict just three years later in *Beautiful Losers,* the twisted tale of a lonesome anthropologist known as "I.," an expert on vanishing North American tribes, trying to come to terms with the bizarre suicide of his Native American wife (she patiently waited to be crushed by the descent of an elevator car she is certain her husband is

riding) and the subsequent revelation of her frequent and prodigious infidelities with his only friend, known as F., a radical political activist championing the separation of the Quebec province from British-controlled Canada. The timid academic sustains a complex infatuation with a long-dead Catholic saint, Kateri Tekakwitha, a beautiful Mohawk, a cheerful and obedient virgin who consecrated her body to the will of Christ after it was ravaged by smallpox contracted from European missionaries. Indeed, to darken the emerging perception of desire itself as imprisonment, Cohen works the metaphor of the impossibility of authentic liberation—the Native Americans from the European colonialists and, in turn, the French from the entrenched British government (F. is committed to an asylum after he blows up a statue of Queen Victoria, a gesture as poetic as it is pointless). Here desire is a game with only losers. *Beautiful Losers* is relentlessly physical—we are given unfiltered accounts of sexual encounters (squirts of funky semen, strands of rust-colored pubic hairs, freakishly wide mud-brown nipples, scatterings of moles, the stench of the anus, dry "cunts" and flagging "pricks," smears of menstrual blood). Desire cannot elevate. Characters masturbate impulsively; they read graphic accounts of Catholic martyrdoms to spur them into orgasm; they contend with symptoms of venereal diseases; they use massive plastic vibrators that they actually name. Here is a world defined entirely by the body—I. peruses Charles Atlas bodybuilding regimens and hoards vials of healing waters from Lourdes; it is a world of orgasms and bowel movements; crabs and lice; spit and shit; grotesque acts of torture, cannibalism, and rape; disturbing accounts of devastating plagues and, ultimately, of the cellular holocaust of decomposition itself.

Unlike the enticing lyricism of Cohen's first novel, *Beautiful Losers* irritates, confuses, annoys; language repels the reader. Both Cohen protagonists, however, struggle to connect in the only vehicle that Cohen can credit—language— and both fail: Breavman in his heartrending letter to Shell, the nameless anthropologist in unreadable pages of often unpunctuated screeds, rambling stories, chunks of research, vulgar diatribes, scatological jokes, hallucinations, and even desperate prayers, all to torture himself (indeed, it is possible that F. himself is some kind of projection of the narrator). I. relentlessly anatomizes what Breavman refuses to acknowledge: the impossibility of purity in a brutal world of casual obscenities. As the novel closes, the narrator himself deconstructs into hallucinations. After hunkering down for a spell in his favorite treehouse (he has a disfigured hand, perhaps from blowing up the statue?), he joins the object of his obsession: he imagines heading out to the open road, accompanied by a mysterious Native American woman identified only as Isis, a mythic figure who, like Kateri Tekakwitha, fuses profound power and intense sensuality; but it is faux-salvation through a shabby hallucination.

THE DISTANCE OF DISTANCE

That sense of spacious loneliness would hang about Cohen's work over the next two decades. In what might stand as the summa of Cohen's middle years, the harrowing poem "Death of a Lady's Man" (spelled "Ladies' Man" on the album of that title), a woman is driven by the raw need to satisfy a man she is sure is the lover for whom she has searched her entire life. She is that familiar Cohen figure, the irrepressible romantic quester, that elegant tangle of matter and ghost, her heart full of moonshine and grace. She makes her pitch, but the man resists. She offers finally, "I'll make a space between my legs / I'll teach you solitude" (*Poems and Songs,* p. 126). It is a stark moment, an unsettling recanting of Cohen's youthful faith in the potency and magic of physical love: lovers apart, separated by the distance of distance. She sighs, "The art of longing's over / And it's never coming back" (p. 127). As the poet voiceover wearily concludes, that whole search for love thing, well, "I guess you go for nothing / If you really want to go that far" (p. 128).

For Cohen, now at midlife, love perplexes. "I cannot follow you my love / You cannot follow me / I am the distance you put between / All of the moments that we will be" ("You Know Who

I Am," p. 88). Yearning without hope of consummation, need without expectation of respite—the works of Cohen's prolific middle passage, seven remarkable albums of original verse he would set to music during the two decades after his arrival in New York's tumultuous folk scene, is indeed a forbidding oeuvre, verses of carefully crafted despair, melancholic introspection, and unshakeable regret. If *The Favourite Game* seduces, coaxes, teases his audience; if *Beautiful Losers* irritates, frustrates, appalls his audience, the work of Cohen's middle passage does not factor in the audience at all. After a remarkable, even meteoric, rise as Canadian poetry's Next Big Thing, at thirty-three Cohen was without a following to satisfy his deep need for an audience. He approached the implications of converting his poetry to song with shaky confidence. He was hardly a musician, had only entertained intimate gatherings, strumming a guitar while reciting new verses; within the robust creative environment of Greenwich Village, he was all too aware of his abundant liabilities as a performer, indeed as a songwriter. He had only one subject—himself, the anima sola, his own fractured and famished heart. "Like a baby stillborn / Like a beast with his horn / I have torn everyone who reached out to me" ("Bird on the Wire," p. 89). That unsettling vision of love's bankruptcies fit most uncomfortably within the era's carefree pop-culture sensibility—indeed, the week Columbia Records released Cohen's first album of eloquent, if tormented introspection, the Beatles' buoyant "All You Need Is Love" was enjoying its month-long ride atop the Billboard charts. Imagine, then, dropping your hi-fi needle on the first track of *The Songs of Leonard Cohen* circa late autumn 1967 and hearing the pulsing ache of the broken E-major chords of "Suzanne," listening to the darkly luminous recollection of this Suzanne with the "perfect body," hearing the mournful laceration of the poet's frustration as he comprehends her sheer inaccessibility. "And you want to travel with her / you want to travel blind" (p. 64). Suzanne is at once so there, so finely detailed—she is wearing "rags and feathers / from Salvation Army counters" and feeds him "tea and oranges / that come all the way from China"—

and yet so elusive, so not there (pp. 64–65). The lovers, just close enough to feel apart, move along the riverfront together as the "sun pours down like honey"; they never touch, can never touch, theirs a love as exquisite as it is empty. You would ask, naturally, what is this? Where is the hook? Where is the finger-popping metered momentum toward some ear-friendly chorus? In a single three-minute piece ("song" does not seem to fit), Cohen deftly shifts from 6/4 time, to 4/4 time, to 2/4 time. Where are the happy, snappy rhymes to help sing along? You couldn't dance to it; you certainly couldn't make out to it; you didn't want to get high to it; you couldn't turn it up loud in the car and just drive crazy; and it surely didn't incite you to go occupy the campus administration building. So, what exactly were you supposed to do? Well, listen to it, eavesdrop on a poet's excavation into his dark heart's recollections of the perfect love that both was and wasn't.

In this difficult middle passage, Cohen offers in "Joan of Arc" a most unsettling vision of perfect love: the flames, hot and ready, beckoning to the lonesome and doomed Joan of Arc, bound to the stake, weary of the battlefields, ready now to surrender. "I'm glad to hear you talk this way / I've watched you riding every day," the seductive flames purr, "and something in me yearns to win / such a cold and very lonesome heroine" (p. 92). Their consummation is as striking as it is terrifying—"deep into his fiery heart" the flames engulf "the dust of Joan of Arc." Clearly Cohen, older than many of the other singer-songwriters of the New York folk scene, separated as well as by nationality and even by musical background, did not share their idealistic anger, could not identify with their lyrics at once so caustic and so public, so compelled by righteous, if quixotic, indignation and uncompromising discontent with the cultural, political, and economic status quo. Those artists were fractious, Cohen was fractured; they were angry, Cohen was hurt; they were redoubtable, Cohen was vulnerable; they were irritated, Cohen was devastated; they were impassioned, indignant; Cohen was confused, uncertain. For other singer-songwriters of the era, words were missiles,

targeted and deliberate, designed to raze, to clear the way to build new, better worlds; for Cohen, words were the last desperate countermeasure to what seemed an inevitable spiral into silence. What am I to do, the anima sola pines, when love does not work, when the heart itself cannot stun, when the nerves go numb, when the body finally collapses of its own irony. "Love is a fire," Cohen intones, it "burns," it "disfigures"—it immolates those most sincerely convinced of its urgencies ("Love Is a Fire," p. 101).

So, for nearly twenty years, Cohen retreated. He pulled up roots; he traveled, he toured, never more alone than when he was pinned in the hard glare of a stage spotlight; he slipped into the narcoleptic nonspace of alcohol and drugs; he bedded, quite publicly, a wide variety of women who were mesmerized by the edgy charisma of his tragic-lover persona; he began experimenting in spiritual solitudes, beginning with a brief flirtation with Scientology but then developing broader interests in European and Middle Eastern mythologies and Eastern meditative religions, ultimately finding his way to Zen Buddhism. For more than two decades, he negotiated, crafted, studied solitude itself, a centripetal retreat into the sanctuary of prolonged emotional recovery, his heart now as unforgiving as a "new razor blade" ("So Long, Marianne," p. 71). There, safely apart, he would scrutinize the perplexing dynamics of desire now that it was interred in the past tense, to sort through memories of that elusive "you" now "kneeling / like a bouquet / in a cave of bone / behind [his] forehead" ("This Is for You," p. 80). Love is now measured by distance, approached only in retrospect. "You live like a god," he tells his lover, "somewhere behind the names / I have for you, / your body made of nets / my shadow's tangled in" ("You Live Like a God," p. 81). Against and amid the landmark achievements of the folk revolution, ardent anthem-songs crafted with unnerving daring and fragile optimism, Cohen's verses come across more like a decades-long *saudade,* melancholy tormented by a longing that he cannot entirely extinguish. "I came so far for beauty," he laments in desolation, "I left so much behind" ("Came So Far for Beauty," p. 146). Suffering,

Cohen knew, was hardly art—suffering was messy, incoherent, pedestrian; suffering had no narrative line; suffering brought no expectation of insight. That was the poet's work, to craft suffering into singular moments of awareness, the difficult embrace of lonely introspection. But it proved a most forlorn vision. There are, he admits, "No chocolates / in your boxes," "no diamonds / in the mine" ("Diamonds in the Mine," p. 96).

THE NEARNESS OF DISTANCE

It became a most prohibitive vision—and its own dead end. By the mid-1980s, Cohen had become something of a caricature, the Woody Allen of emo music, the awkward, eloquent, perpetually sad-faced buzzkill. Encouraged by the difficult wisdom of Zen Buddhism that perceived suffering itself as both ennobling and clarifying and that perceived physical separation itself as too simplistic, Cohen began to grow restless in his role as poet laureate of his own dark corner, tiring of tending the moat he had so diligently guarded between himself and his audience, the anima sola weary of singing to and for itself. Now in his sixties, Cohen reconceived the implications of communication itself as a gesture of consolation, of relaxing into distress and there finding unexpectedly his small, dark corner suddenly populated by others. "Draw us near," he implores a generous universe, "and bind us tight, / all your children here / in their rags of light … / and end this night, / if it be your will" ("If It Be Your Will"). It was time, Cohen affirmed, to end his own long night. Here begins Cohen's radiant closing phase, his catapult vision of the invigorating energy of words themselves, his unironic invitation tendered to his audience to join him in a kind of horizontal immediacy; it marks the beginnings of what he will come to affirm as the intimate, immemorial dance conducted between a poet and an audience, the nearness of apparent distance, the dynamics of which he had first engaged years earlier in those sparsely crowded church basements while fronting the Buckskin Boys or even farther back when he would be enchanted by the synagogue cantor who

could forge a gathering with a single voice. Nearing seventy, Cohen returned to his beginnings. The artist without the audience, Cohen now acknowledged, is an insufferable egoist, a self-perpetuating and self-sustaining pity party. The "you" he invoked now was no longer some lost and distant phantom lover of his but rather his audience, unnameable but real, there beyond the tangling fetters of love, just beyond the edge of the stage. Within the smoldering ache of "Dance Me to the End of Love," Cohen longs only for the saving touch of that reassuring aesthetic bond—an audience at once so near and so distant. Touch me, he pines, "with your naked hand / touch me with your glove" just never, never, slip away ("Dance Me to the End of Love," p. 162).

We are far from the calculating seductions of Lawrence Breavman. Here, Cohen celebrates love not between hearts—that is, still jagged with risk and doomed to shadows—but rather the love between poet and audience, the intimacy shaped by words. "Love," he says, will go on and on until at last it reaches "an open door— / Then Love itself [will be] gone" ("Love Itself," p. 215). Yes, finally. The world itself, not the narrow life of the artist, is a manifestation of loss. We— Cohen intones—we are all in this together. It is then a giddy celebration of the reach of words themselves, verses at once exuberant and wryly understated: "And I'm crazy for love, but I'm not coming on. / I'm just paying my rent every day in the tower of song" ("The Tower of Song," p. 180).

In short, Cohen changed. That evolution was both remarkable and singular. At a time when the other singer-songwriters of his era (those of course who had survived) were content to abide in the familiar, Cohen changed. While Bob Dylan, Joni Mitchell, and Patti Smith maintained the aura of Mystic Poet, while Paul Simon, Neil Young, and Lou Reed simply recast into a variety of backbeats their persona of the soul-damaged urban romantic cursed/blessed with a heart burned by irony, while Tom Waits, Randy Newman, and Bruce Springsteen conducted increasingly complex explorations of increasingly more damaged alter egos, Cohen—with breathtaking confidence—changed, embraced a radical concept

as old as poetry itself: the poet as ventriloquist, speaking both to and for an audience that only hungered not to be apart, not to be alone. "If you want a lover / I'll do anything you ask me to": so begins Cohen's 1988 verse "I'm Your Man" (p. 173). And we assume we are back in the tired familiar—the covetous lover baldly negotiating seduction, willfully playing whatever angle to secure the thin conquest of tacky desire (indeed the beat is playfully suggestive of a burlesque-show drum cadence). But by the close of the verse, Cohen considerably opens the dimension of that "you"—he is addressing not some lover-quarry but rather the broad reach of his audience. The verse turns not carnal and duplicitous but spiritual and magnanimous, at once unaffectedly gentle and inviting. I will be your shadow companion, your benevolent father, your trustworthy guide, your soul protector in the most forbidding and intimidating terrains—just walk with me, he offers, even "across the sand," because, he pauses and adds with humility, "I'm your man." This is no superhero braggadocio; rather, it is the simple reaching-out from one fallible human to as many others as will listen ("I'm Your Man," p. 174). Invariably in concerts Cohen and his "congregation" would all sing that closing refrain in a robust collective. This is a most heartfelt definition of a poet: when life happens to you—and it will—the poet will be what you need.

Few Cohen verses better define this catapult vision than the song that began this era, the luminous "Hallelujah." Initially Columbia had little interest in the song or the album (*Various Positions*). It was 1984. Given the pop culture's easy embrace of the slick, image-driven simplifications of MTV and the mind-anesthetics of processed syntho-electronic dance music, Columbia, without listening to the tracks, initially declined to release yet another self-serving introspective buzzkill from Leonard Cohen. That "Hallelujah" has become Cohen's most recognized work, covered by more than three hundred artists; that it has been rendered in every conceivable setting from solo ukulele to full-throated pipe organ, from bagpipe quartet to string orchestra; that it has been scored in more than

sixty television and film settings ranging from goth sci-fi to children's animation; that it is by itself the subject of a book-length exegesis; that Cohen himself conceived of it as an organic thing, accumulating more than seventy-five assorted verses for it; that it has been used as a meditative piece at memorial services as well as a Christmas carol, a synagogue reflection piece, a wedding march, a folk song, an anniversary waltz, an empowerment power ballad, a schmaltzy oversung showstopper on a variety of television talent competitions, a powerhouse gospel anthem, and even as a gentle lullaby for hip millennial parents, all speak to its universality, an adjective never applied to the intensely autobiographical works of Cohen's dark middle passage. "Hallelujah" is unfettered by irony. It is a song of we, not I. Completed in 1984 as Cohen himself turned fifty amid rumors of his involuntary retirement, the song is a joyous affirmation of the muddle and confusion of we hapless creatures so apparently destined for greatness yet so vulnerable to the clumsy fall into carnality and crossed desires. The poem's original premise triangulated the stories of Old Testament heavyweights David, the gifted singer-king brought low by the seductive Bathsheba, and Samson, the mighty warrior destroyed by the temptress Delilah, with the poet himself, betrayed and abandoned, kicking about the ashes of his own spent romance. It is not extravagant egoism— rather, it is the humbling affirmation that we are all in this together. "And it's no complaint you hear tonight, / and it's not some pilgrim who's seen the light— / it's a cold and it's a broken Hallelujah!" (p. 168). Confronting the perplexing urgencies of the flesh in a creature that so aspires to spiritual dignity, Cohen celebrates with unexpected resilience (and an exclamation point, no less). We do not, cannot understand it all so (pause) Hallelujah! And that optimism, Cohen points out, can come only from the expression of that confusion into the craft of a song; indeed, the opening verse actually charts the creation of the song itself. "It goes like this: the fourth, the fifth / the minor fall, the major lift; / the baffled king composing Hallelujah!" (p. 167). This was not a poem set to guitar chords; "Hallelujah" was a song.

And so Cohen would commence a nearly twenty-year reconsideration of the mission of verse itself; rather than relentlessly interrogating the tipping-point moments of his own emotional life, he extended his voice, reclaimed the privilege of troubadours since the Middle Ages, world-weary pilgrims who would speak in an intensely private voice that nevertheless transcended the boundaries of identity itself, to forge with venues full of strangers an unforced camaraderie, a sly and vital conspiracy between poet and audience. A poem is a space for Us (indeed, Cohen for the first time collaborated with others to create his music). "Things are going to slide in all directions / Won't be nothing / Nothing you can measure any more / The blizzard of the world / has crossed the threshold / and it has overturned / the order of the soul," he intones in "The Future" (pp. 185–186), that unnerving apocalyptic tone, however, upended by the musical setting, a smoking backbeat with an irrepressible rhythmic momentum sustained by crisp trills from an Farfisa organ and a sassy backup vocal trio. Even the video—a dignified Cohen standing indoors, in a driving rain, deadpanning to the camera, all set against snippets of entangled lovers swimming in churning water—maintains the wink-of-the-eye daring that defines Cohen's reclamation of an affirmation-despite. In "Everybody Knows," Cohen, as always positioning himself in the gloaming, acknowledges that the dire straits of the contemporary world are no secret, everybody knows, he rages, that the "dice are loaded." Unavailable to the tempting illusions of more traditional apocalypticism that long promised to millennia of the beleaguered that in the final reel the good guys will win, Cohen knows better. "That's how it goes," he glowers, "Everybody knows" (p. 178). And yet, Cohen testifies, well, there is always a yet. He cautions a world then at the height of the saber-rattling of the Reagan era: you have grown too fond of the tacky melodrama of apocalypse; things are grim enough without such shivery games. So Cohen slyly sets the apocalypse to an irrepressible rhythm, gifts it with an irresistible singalong tagline, and accompanies it with soaring backup vocals. The apocalypse never felt so good—after

all, Cohen reminds us, we are in this together. If plumbing the narrow confines of his own heart had bankrupted Cohen's optimism and had abandoned his verse to self-lacerating discontent and a cloaking depression, his broadened vision now reclaimed a defiant resiliency: "Ring the bells that still can ring / Forget your perfect offering / There is a crack in everything / That's how the light gets in" ("Anthem," p. 188).

The testimony of the impress of Cohen as troubadour, however, comes not from reading these verses or from their recitation or even from the charm of listening to Cohen's recordings—rather, the closing phase of Cohen's career moved effortlessly, easily, even logically to the charged energy field of the stage. That ad-libbed dynamic, evidenced by hours' worth of YouTube archives, fully defines Cohen at last as poet, teasing and being teased by an audience of individuals who, somehow, whatever their native language (and Cohen sold out concerts around the world) Cohen comes to speak to and for. "You got me singing," he celebrates in his 2014 release, *Popular Problems*, "Even though the world is gone / You got me thinking / I'd like to carry on" ("You Got Me Singing"). Let the poet transcribe (y)our anxieties into verse, he coaxes, and let us together sing ourselves to consolation: "Tell me that you love me then / Amen, Amen, Amen.... Amen" ("Amen," p. 225). Cohen's ellipsis renders a sweeping finality to that closing affirmation. His audience, at last, became his congregation, his verse forging an unforced intimacy that he had first felt charming spare crowds while fronting the Buckskin Boys. These concerts, these gatherings, then, became a measure of the nearness of apparent distance, the audience and the poet, at last, one, both acknowledging and refuting the chasm he understood must perforce exist between poet and audience by using a Zen parable he first learned in the monastery. Hard, rough stones, the story goes, when carried about in the same bag will by their very friction, their very interaction, polish each other into a resilient shine. "Feels so good not to wonder who you'll get / Who you love, who you touch and who you kiss / Oh baby, who'd ever guess that there's a side of loneliness

as sweet as this" ("Feels So Good," p. 232). Hallelujah!

Among the dozens of awards garnered by Cohen in the new millennium—most notably a 2010 Grammy Lifetime Achievement; the $15,000 Glenn Gould Prize in 2011, presented every three years to the international artist who essentially transforms their art; his induction in 2010 into the Songwriters Hall of Fame; the prestigious Prince of Asturias Award for Literature in 2011 (other recipients have included Nobelists Mario Vargas Llosa, Camilo José Cela, Günther Grass, and Doris Lessing), none better reflects—and celebrates—Leonard Cohen's singular position between serious art and pop culture than his sharing in 2012 of the inaugural PEN New England Award for Song Lyrics of Literary Excellence, held at the John F. Kennedy Presidential Library Foundation in Boston. The biannual award, really the first of its kind, sought to remind a contemporary pop-culture generation enamored by lyric sheets and music videos, suspicious of the schoolhouse world of "serious" poetry, that serious poetry, long before it was anthologized into textbooks, indeed before it was ever published, long before it ever found its way to transcription, was sung. The award medallion itself featured a silver lyre, the stringed instrument that had been the poet's accompaniment since antiquity. The finest contemporary lyrics, the award reminds, aspire unapologetically to command, to console, to elevate, in short, to matter—the very mission of poetry since *Gilgamesh*. That Cohen shared the award (and the dais) with the ageless rock and roller Chuck Berry made for a kind of too-easy juxtaposition, a literal black-and-white comparison: Berry's songs are sweaty, slyly vulgar, excessive, incessantly rhythmic; Cohen's, by comparison, literate, cool, measured, detached. Indeed the award ceremony itself appeared to underscore that dichotomy: Cohen was presented with his award by a prolix and haughty Salman Rushdie, after which Cohen delivered a modest (if elegant) thank you; Berry, by comparison, after admitting irreverently, midway through Paul Simon's salutary remarks, that he had switched off his hearing aid, declined the offer of the lectern and, signaling for a guitar, strummed

through a spirited ad-libbed rendition of "Johnny B. Goode."

But the two, far from polar opposites, make for a much more intriguing pair. Both in their eighties, both well beyond the age most poets (or musicians, for that matter) are willing to abide the rigors of engaging the audience, both still tirelessly sought that unforced and most complex embrace, the affirmation of an audience, the invigorating energy that reassures the poet that his or her words, which have happened to find their way to melodies, matter only because they are heard. What Berry came to understand working long shifts at an automobile assembly plant outside St. Louis while inventing rockabilly guitar in dives along the Kansas and Missouri border world, Cohen came to understand working the thankless circuit of church basements and bar mitzvahs with the Buckskin Boys and later in the coffeehouses of Greenwich Village: words yearn to be heard. Indeed, words possess a synergistic force with religious intensities. And, in the end, troubadours such as Chuck Berry and Leonard Cohen (call them poets, if you want) write their verse (call them songs, if you will) not because they have mouths but only because others have ears.

Selected Bibliography

WORKS OF LEONARD COHEN

POETRY
Let Us Compare Mythologies. Toronto: Contact Press, 1956.

The Spice-Box of Earth. Toronto: McClelland & Stewart, 1961.

Flowers for Hitler. Toronto: McClelland & Stewart, 1964.

Parasites of Heaven. Toronto: McClelland & Stewart, 1966.

Selected Poems: 1956–1968. Toronto: McClelland & Stewart, 1968.

The Energy of Slaves. Toronto: McClelland & Stewart, 1972.

Death of a Lady's Man. Toronto: McClelland & Stewart, 1978.

Book of Mercy. Toronto: McClelland & Stewart, 1984.

Stranger Music: Selected Poems and Songs. Toronto: Mc-

Clelland & Stewart, 1993.

Book of Longing. Toronto: McClelland & Stewart, 2006.

The Lyrics of Leonard Cohen. London: Omnibus Press, 2009.

Leonard Cohen: Poems and Songs. Edited by Robert Faggen. Everyman's Library Pocket Poets. New York: Random House/Everyman's Library, 2011. (Unless otherwise indicated, all page references in the essay refer to this volume.)

Fifteen Poems. (E-book.) New York: Everyman's Library/ Random House, 2012.

NOVELS
The Favourite Game, London: Secker & Warburg, 1963.

Beautiful Losers. Toronto: McClelland & Stewart, 1966.

STUDIO ALBUMS
Songs of Leonard Cohen, 1967.

Songs from a Room, 1969.

Songs of Love and Hate, 1971.

New Skin for the Old Ceremony, 1974.

Death of a Ladies' Man, 1977.

Recent Songs, 1979.

Various Positions, 1984.

I'm Your Man, 1988.

The Future, 1992.

Ten New Songs, 2001.

Dear Heather, 2004.

Old Ideas, 2012.

Popular Problems, 2014.

COMPILATION ALBUMS
The Best of Leonard Cohen, 1975.

More Best of Leonard Cohen, 1997.

The Essential Leonard Cohen, 2002.

LIVE ALBUMS
Live Songs, 1973.

Cohen Live: Leonard Cohen in Concert, 1994.

Field Commander Cohen: Tour of 1979, 2001.

Live in London, 2009.

Songs from the Road, 2010.

Live in Dublin, 2014.

Can't Forget: A Souvenir of the Grand Tour, 2015.

DOCUMENTARIES
Ladies and Gentlemen ... Mr. Leonard Cohen. Directed by Donald Brittain and Don Owen. National Film Board of Canada, 1965.

Bird on a Wire. Directed by Tony Palmer. Machat Company,

1974. (Film of Cohen's 1972 European tour.)

The Song of Leonard Cohen. Directed by Harry Rasky. CBC, 1980. (Captures the 1979 world tour. The most underrated of the Cohen documentaries includes copious discussions with Cohen about his lyrics.)

I Am a Hotel. Directed by Allan F. Nicholls. Blue Memorial Video, 1983. (Stylized concept film cowritten by and featuring Cohen based on a cycle of five of his songs about loneliness, lost love, alcohol, and the slow burn of lust.)

Songs from the Life of Leonard Cohen. Directed by Bob Portway. BBC, 1988. (Documentary features 1988 concert footage and interviews with Cohen, largely biographical.)

I'm Your Man. Directed by Lian Lunson. Lionsgate/Sundance Channel, 2005. (Film of the January 2005 Sydney Opera House tribute concert featuring Cohen and covers by, among others, Rufus Wainwright, Nick Cave, and U2.)

Leonard Cohen: The Early Years. Produced by Andy Cleland and Rob Johnstone. Chrome Dreams, 2011. (Probing look into Cohen's songwriting influences and studio work from debut album to his problematic collaboration with Phil Spector, told through commentary entirely provided by musicians, critics, and producers.)

INTERVIEWS

Burger, Jeff, ed. *Leonard Cohen on Leonard Cohen: Interviews and Encounters.* Chicago: Chicago Review Press, 2014.

CRITICAL AND BIOGRAPHICAL STUDIES

Gnarowski, Michael. *Leonard Cohen: The Artist and His Critics.* Whitby, Ont.: McGraw-Hill Ryerson, 1976.

Hofmann, Philipp. *Corporeal Cartographies: The Body in the Novels of Leonard Cohen.* Berlin: LIT Verlag, 2010.

Kubernik, Harvey. *Leonard Cohen: Everybody Knows.* Montclair, N.J.: Backbeat Books, 2014.

Leibovitz, Liel. *A Broken Hallelujah, Rock and Roll, Redemption, and the Life of Leonard Cohen.* New York: Norton, 2014.

Leonard Cohen Files. www.leonard.cohenfiles.com

Light, Alan. *The Holy or the Broken: Leonard Cohen, Jeff Buckley, and the Unlikely Ascent of "Hallelujah."* New York: Atria Books, 2012.

Nadel, Ira B. *Various Positions: A Life of Leonard Cohen.* Toronto: Random House, 1996.

Official Leonard Cohen website. www.leonardcohen.com

Ondaatje, Michael. *Leonard Cohen.* Toronto: McClelland & Stewart, 1970.

Scobie, Stephen. *Intricate Preparations: Writing Leonard Cohen.* Toronto: ECW, 2000.

Siemerling, Winfried. *Discoveries of the Other: Alterity in the Work of Leonard Cohen, Hubert Aquin, Michael Ondaatje, and Nicole Brossard.* Toronto: University of Toronto Press, 1994.

Simmons, Sylvie. *I'm Your Man: The Life of Leonard Cohen.* New York: Ecco/HarperCollins, 2012.

BRET EASTON ELLIS

(1964—)

Piers Pennington

NEAR THE END of *American Psycho,* the hugely successful and equally controversial novel that Bret Easton Ellis published in 1991, a mysterious shift in the narrative occurs. Like many of the sections in the novel—which range from brief meditations just a paragraph long to more substantial passages extending over a number of pages—"Chase, Manhattan" is not directly related to the section that comes immediately before it. But, in contrast to the preceding episodes, "Chase, Manhattan" shifts from the first to the third person, rather than remaining in the first person throughout, as Ellis briefly describes the novel's antihero, Patrick Bateman, from an external rather than an internal point of view. The deliberate gaps between the book's individual sections, together with the suggestion of Bateman's unreliable narration, mean that much of the novel's plot remains implicit. Even so, the shift in "Chase, Manhattan" finds Ellis taking the approach one stage further, since it occurs at the level of form rather than content, posing a far more fundamental problem of interpretation: if Bateman is speaking the words in the preceding episodes, then who is speaking the words in this passage? Because the shift occurs at the level of form, rather than content, there is no way of answering the question once and for all. On the one hand, the words might still be spoken by Bateman, in a powerful instance of the depersonalization that he frequently experiences. On the other, the words might be spoken instead by the narrative voice—which has been subtly present throughout, in the naming of the individual sections—as Ellis brings the author's shaping hand to the fore, to indicate the protagonist's desperate loss of control. In any case, the ambiguity of "Chase, Manhattan" poses a specifically literary problem of interpretation, revealing Ellis to be a highly sophisticated writer of prose, as well as

the cult figure whose characters and stories and more general pronouncements upon the modern world and its art continue to cause a stir.

Bret Easton Ellis was born in Los Angeles on March 7, 1964, the only son of Robert and Dale Dennis Ellis—a property developer and a homemaker, who divorced in 1982—and the brother of two younger sisters. The family lived in Sherman Oaks, California, not far away from the studios of Hollywood, and Ellis received his high school education at the private Buckley School, where he contributed music reviews to the school newspaper and published early stories in the literary magazine, as well as writing songs for and playing keyboards in a musical group. Wanting to escape the influence of his father, an alcoholic who was at times abusive, Ellis moved across the country to attend Bennington College, a small liberal arts college in Vermont that encourages its students to follow their own interests rather than to pursue a more limiting range of predefined courses. The choice of Bennington turned out to be especially fortuitous: not only did Ellis number among his contemporaries future authors Jonathan Lethem and Donna Tartt, but his early meeting with Joe McGinniss, a famed prose writer, ultimately launched his literary career. Having taken a journalism course with McGinniss in his first year, Ellis subsequently proposed a sophomore course on writing novels with the same tutor. After suggesting that Ellis shift the narrative of his debut novel from the third person to the first person, McGinniss shared the final draft with an agent as well as an editor at Simon & Schuster. *Less Than Zero* duly appeared in 1985, when Ellis was just twenty-one years old, and it ended up becoming a best seller, despite receiving a number of criticisms for the bleakness of the world that it depicted. Since

then, the author has published five more novels and a collection of loosely connected short stories, as well as numerous pieces of occasional prose. But even though Ellis has been a highly successful author for all of his adult life, constituting a foundational member of the "Literary Brat Pack" with the novelists Jay McInerney and Tama Janowitz, he has also remained at odds with the mainstream literary world, to the extent that he questions whether he is really a "literary" or a "serious" novelist in a revealing 2012 interview with Jon-Jon Goulian of the *Paris Review*. "All I know is that I write the books I want to write," Ellis affirms, having intimated the individuality of his approach to be a partial consequence of the way in which he learned to "deflect" the negative comments that his work received in the writing classes that he attended at Bennington. "You need that kind of armor to survive as a writer." What is more, the author remembers in the same interview how the fame that followed the success of *Less Than Zero* prompted a crisis of identity, as he struggled to reconcile appearance with reality: "I tried my best to play the serious young writer," since "I had a preconceived notion of how a writer should present himself," but he ultimately had to accept that "every major male American writer seemed to come off in a way that … I realized I just couldn't relate to." Ellis continued to encounter comparable problems, however, until a trip from New York to Los Angeles turned into a permanent move following the death in 2004 of his longtime boyfriend, the sculptor Michael Wade Kaplan. Not only did the author still think of himself as an outsider in the capital—"I was always the kid from L.A., the kid from the Valley, the kid who wrote those weird books"—but he was finally tiring of the New York literary world's accompanying demands, as "the publishing scene got too claustrophobic, too cliquey, too irritating for me" (Goulian).

Given the many references in his books to the visual media of film and television, it is not surprising that many of the author's literary works have been adapted for the screen, both with and without his involvement. Ellis wrote a screenplay for *The Informers* (1994)—his only collection of short stories to date—with Nicholas Jarecki, but he was unhappy with the film that appeared in 2008, taking issue with director Gregor Jordan's interpretation of the script. The adaptations of his other novels by other writers have been more successful, however. Ellis was also unhappy with the film version of *Less Than Zero* when it appeared in 1987, yet he subsequently praised the way in which it captured the styles of the period, and he was moved from the start by the cinematic understanding of *The Rules of Attraction*, which appeared in 2002, fourteen years after the book's original publication. Roger Avary, who directed *The Rules of Attraction*, has also written scripts that adapt the novels *Glamorama* (1998) and *Lunar Park* (2005), both of which Ellis has publicly lauded, although doubts remain as to whether the former will ever be realized. Nonetheless, the best known of the adaptations is *American Psycho*, directed by Mary Harron and starring Christian Bale, which appeared to critical plaudits in 2000. The novel attracted early interest from Hollywood when it first appeared in print in 1991, yet Roger Ebert's review of the film revealed that it had "gone through screenplays, directors and stars for years," since it was at one stage "snatched up for Oliver Stone, who planned to star Leonardo DiCaprio." Despite the many twists and turns of its production, however, Harron and fellow screenwriter Guinevere Turner ultimately created a deeply subtle adaptation, by emphasizing the feminism that is latent in the original story. Two years later, there followed a straight-to-video sequel, *American Psycho 2*, which bears only a superficial connection to Ellis' book and Harron's adaptation—and none of their nuance. Just over a decade after Harron's original adaptation first appeared, a remake of the film was rumored to be in the works, but in 2013 the production company in question announced that it was exploring the possibility of developing a TV series as a sequel to the film instead. Meanwhile, a stage adaptation based on Ellis' book and Harron's film, *American Psycho: The Musical*, premiered in London in 2013 and opened on Broadway in spring 2016. Such continued interest in *American*

Psycho comes as no surprise, however, since it has become a touchstone of contemporary culture: Bale's portrayal of Patrick Bateman is now a popular choice of character for Halloween costumes, for instance, while a number of the set pieces in the adaptation—such as the comparison of business cards and the descriptions of contemporary music—have started to assume canonical status.

Even though the adaptations of the books appear to bring the speaking voices of his characters to life, the author's description of the process of composition touches upon what is lost in the transition from page to screen—and, in doing so, confirms his sophisticated understanding of the narrative approach. Ellis is unusually frank in acknowledging the inescapability of subjectivity: "Every one of my books ... is an exercise in voice and character, an exploration, through a male narrator who is always the same age I am at the time, of the pain I'm dealing with in my life"—to the extent that "when *American Psycho* came out, people assumed I was Patrick Bateman" (Goulian). At first glance, Ellis appears to emphasize the understanding that all writing is inherently autobiographical, by collapsing the distance between author and narrator—yet by discussing "voice" and "character" in terms of "exercise" he also calls attention to the fundamental impersonality of literary form, by hinting at the essential separation between author and narrator. Indeed, it is this understanding that prompts Ellis to seize upon the unpredictability of spoken language at the expense of the proprieties of written language. "I like the way my narrators talk," he asserts, noting that "it's not proper syntax or grammar," before pointing out that "it's not supposed to be," for reasons that have to do with maintaining the impression of realism: "My narrators aren't English professors, and I don't want them to sound like they are" (*Paris Review*). To be sure, the mysterious "alchemy" that Ellis ultimately desires is only able to be established in a specifically literary way: "The novelist is aware that the narrator might not speak this way in 'real' life, but they reimagine it in a way that works for the novel."

EARLY WORKS

Ellis' debut novel bears a number of general comparisons with his teenage years. *Less Than Zero* comprises a number of brief sections that document the life of Clay, who has returned home to Los Angeles for the winter break, having recently completed his first term of study at Camden College—a small liberal arts college in New Hampshire, which is modeled on Bennington College and makes a number of further appearances in the author's later works. In the *Paris Review* interview, Ellis acknowledges the presence of "autobiographical elements" in the book, yet he proceeds to suggest that "there is very little in *Less Than Zero* that's based on my real life"—an understanding that appears to be borne out by his memory of the novel's composition: "I had been working on that book, in one form or another, for five years, ever since I was a sophomore in high school," and while the early drafts were like "teen diaries or journal entries," the revisions of the author's shaping hand ultimately presented their content in a more imaginative way, to the extent that "I look back at that book and think of the plot as having imposed itself on the material" (Goulian). Indeed, even though Ellis depicts a world of wealthy people living wealthy lives, similar to the one in which he grew up, *Less Than Zero* also contains a number of scenes that suggest the most extreme violence, including the screening of a snuff movie and the beginnings of a brutal act of exploitation against a very young girl. Not only do the sections intensify the many other instances of impersonal behavior—the fundamental theme of *Less Than Zero*—but the shock of the violence is compounded by the affectless tone that Ellis uses throughout the novel, in what appears to be a deliberate echo of the comparatively neutral presentation of events in visual media. As such, the novel's opening line prepares for the flatness that follows in more ways than one: "People are afraid to merge on freeways in Los Angeles."

Less Than Zero also finds the author experimenting with the narrative approach in another way, however, as the many sections that are written in roman type and present tense are interspersed with a number of more occasional sec-

tions that are written in italic type and past tense, enabling Clay to reflect upon various incidents from earlier in his life, before he moved away for college. Ellis appears to write the sections as asides in which Clay speaks directly to the reader, yet they fail to deliver the revelations of personal insight that the confidential tone suggests. The first of the sections, for instance, in which the protagonist remembers skipping a day of high school in order to visit his childhood home, comes to its close by circling around the significance of the event: "I didn't go out to Palm Springs that day to look around or see the house and I didn't go because I wanted to miss school or anything. I guess I went out there to remember the way things were. I don't know" (p. 44). The final section details a comparable disappointment, but this time the event's significance is ultimately shared between the characters, however underwhelmingly: "I asked her if she remembered that night at Disneyland and she asked, 'What night at Disneyland?' and we hung up," only for Blair to return the call later in the evening and acknowledge that "she did remember that night at Disneyland" (p. 201). Both instances find the author exploiting the separation between character and reader—and, revealingly, the novel comes to its close by emphasizing the subjectivity of its first-person narration, as Clay attempts to make sense of the lyrics to a pop song that has been playing in his head, in a final nod to the novel's title, which is taken from a song by Elvis Costello. "The images, I later found out, were personal and no one I knew shared them," the protagonist reveals, when he begins an interpretation of the lyric that not only recalls the earlier invocation of the supernatural—through the threat of "werewolfs" (p. 78)—but anticipates the violence that comes to the fore in the author's later work: "Images of parents who were so hungry and unfulfilled that they ate their own children" (p. 207).

Ellis published his second novel, *The Rules of Attraction,* in 1987, having started to work on it before *Less Than Zero* appeared in print. In many respects, the book appears to be a direct sequel to the debut novel, since it presents the similar actions of a similar group of (slightly older) people who, like Clay, are studying at Camden College. Even so, the opening section, titled "Fall 1985," finds the author continuing to experiment with the narrative approach, as the opening sentence begins in medias res:

> and it's a story that might bore you but you don't have to listen, she told me, because she always knew it was going to be like that, and it was, she thinks, her first year, or, actually weekend, really a Friday, in September, at Camden, and this was three or four years ago, and she got so drunk that she ended up in bed, lost her virginity (late, she was eighteen) in Lorna Slavin's room, because she was a Freshman and had a roommate and Lorna was, she remembers, a Senior or a Junior and usually sometimes at her boyfriend's place off-campus, to who she thought was a Sophomore Ceramics major but who was actually either some guy from N.Y.U., a film student, and up to New Hampshire just for The Dressed To Get Screwed Party, or a townie.

Not only does Ellis use the opening conjunction to create the impression of an overheard conversation, but he continues to invoke the characteristics of spoken language through the absence of specific detail and the many qualifications to the memory, both of which suggest the mind in the act of thinking. It is artfully done, however: even though the memory is related by a narrator, and even though the length of the sentence calls attention to itself, Ellis maintains a single line of thought—yet, in doing so, he also reveals the underlying complexity of the clauses and their ultimate dependence upon written language. What is more, the possibility of mistaken identity anticipates the more fundamental way in which the author experiments with the narrative approach. The title of the opening section names a time, before the section itself names a place ("Camden"), but the following sections begin differently, by naming the name of the character whose perspective they proceed to present—a development of the technique that James Joyce pioneered in *Ulysses* (1922), which Ellis was studying when he started to work on the story. Indeed, the author's use of various points of view to relate the events—which circle around a love triangle involving the main characters of Sean, Paul, and Lauren—means that readers of the book have no recourse to a finally authoritative perspective, as Ellis complicates the subjectivity

of first-person narration while raising a number of related questions about its reliability and unreliability. The author further experiments with the form of the novel when he includes one section that is written entirely in French and another—after one of the characters has an abortion—that is completely blank. Ellis also begins to explore the possibilities of reflexivity, since one of the later sections is spoken by Clay, the protagonist of *Less Than Zero.* "I go to an Elvis Costello concert in New York but get lost on the way back to Camden College" (p. 205), Clay reveals, in a further nod to the debut novel's title, before mentioning a number of the book's other characters, who are framed in familiar terms: "Rip actually calls me from L.A. a couple of times," yet "I am unsure if it's really him since in a tape Blair sent me she was positive that he had been murdered" (p. 205). The reference ultimately comes full circle when Ellis brings the section to a close by echoing the debut novel's opening line: "People are afraid to merge on campus after midnight" (p. 206).

But, as well as returning to the author's existing characters, *The Rules of Attraction* introduces a number of new characters—who, in turn, appear to provide initial points of departure for Ellis' later works. Victor Johnson, for instance, becomes the protagonist of *Glamorama* (in which he takes the name Victor Ward), while Mitchell Allen makes a cameo in *Lunar Park.* The most fascinating instance, however, is when Sean Bateman remembers a "somber birthday dinner" with his father and "Patrick and his girlfriend Evelyn, who was a junior executive at American Express" (p. 266). Ellis subsequently allows Patrick to speak a section of the novel, in terms that both anticipate and complicate his later appearance as the protagonist of *American Psycho.* On the one hand, the references to the "limousine" and the "Lear" jet (p. 271) resonate with the earlier mentions of "Trump Tower" and "my father's place at the Carlyle" (p. 266) to suggest Bateman's superbly wealthy background. On the other, Patrick also displays a surprising concern, as he complains about the way in which his brother is "so mindless about responsibility and about keeping people waiting" (p. 272).

AMERICAN PSYCHO

American Psycho, the book for which Ellis is best known, was finally published in 1991—yet, at the beginning of the decade, it remained unclear whether the novel was ever going to appear in print. Contemporary newspaper reports suggest that Simon & Schuster, the firm that published both *Less Than Zero* and *The Rules of Attraction,* paid Ellis a substantial advance to write his third story. But when some of the book's most violent passages were leaked to the media in 1990, the scale of the resulting controversy prompted the publisher to withdraw from the project, only weeks before the novel was due to hit the shelves. Even though Ellis freely acknowledged the disturbing nature of a number of the scenes in *American Psycho,* the author was understandably taken aback by the decision, believing the scenes in question to be necessary to the book's overall composition. The saga came to its close a few days later, however, as Vintage Books, part of Random House, announced that it was going to print the book as a paperback the following year. Inevitably, further controversy accompanied the novel's appearance, as many readers struggled to come to terms with the author's portrayal of Patrick Bateman, a young and successful investment banker who initially appears to be the perfect embodiment of the yuppie stereotype that emerged throughout the 1980s—only for that first impression to be complicated by the story's gradual revelation of his secret life as a psychopath, in which he spends much of his free time mutilating and murdering innocent others while committing sundry other crimes. *American Psycho* continues to be notorious today, and such is the graphic nature of the violence that it is still classified as "R 18+" in Australia, where the novel is sold in shrink wrap. Despite its many troubling passages, however, the book has remained in the popular imagination for a reason: by exaggerating the excesses of Wall Street in the 1980s, the author touched upon a number of nascent tendencies that have become widespread in the twenty-first century. Most fundamentally, *American Psycho* constitutes a study of the intensification of capitalism—and the corollary intensification of

materialism—throughout the eighties, as the opening disclaimer appears to acknowledge: "All of the characters, incidents, and dialogue, except for incidental references to public figures, products, or services, are imaginary and are not intended to refer to any living persons or to disparage any company's products or services"— where the unusual inclusion of "products or services" alongside the usual "characters" and "incidents" not only anticipates the protagonist's use of brand names as a means of describing individuals and judging their status, but acknowledges the way in which they constitute the center of the novel's world, by intimating such "products or services" to be as important as the characters in the book.

Indeed, many of the characters in the book frequently appear to be secondary to the products and styles that constitute their outward appearance. Early in the opening section, for instance, Bateman observes that "a guy who looks a lot like Luis Carruthers waves over at Timothy and when Timothy doesn't return the wave the guy—slicked-back hair, suspenders, horn-rimmed glasses—realizes that it's not who he thought it was" (p. 5), an encounter that anticipates the misunderstanding that occurs a couple of pages later: "A figure with slicked-back hair and horn-rimmed glasses approaches in the distance … carrying the same Tumi leather attaché case from D. F. Sanders that Price has," before "he glances at Price as if they were acquainted but just as quickly realizes that he doesn't know Price and just as quickly Price realizes that it's not Victor Powell" (pp. 7–8). Not only does the repetition of "slicked-back hair" and "horn-rimmed glasses" suggest the absence of any distinguishing characteristics of outward appearance, but the recognition that the stranger in the street is "carrying the same Tumi leather attaché case … that Price has" subtly emphasizes the futility of attempting to express individuality through the purchase of consumer products. What is more, Ellis intimates that the absence of essential identity is as internal as it is external, through the language spoken by many of the characters in the book. In the *Paris Review* interview, Ellis takes issue with the "*Gentlemen's*

Quarterly way of living," suggesting that "*American Psycho* is a book about becoming the man you feel you have to be, the man who is cool, slick, handsome, effortlessly moving through the world" (Goulian). In the first of a number of sections to be set at "Harry's" bar, Timothy Price responds to a question about the etiquette of wearing "rounded collars" with an answer that appropriates the language of such magazines: "If it's worn with a blazer then the collar should look soft and it can be worn either pinned or unpinned. Since it's a traditional, preppy look it's best if balanced by a relatively small four-in-hand knot" (p. 32). Later in the novel, when Bateman is having lunch with a colleague, Christopher Armstrong, who has just returned from a holiday in the Bahamas, Ellis repeats the procedure, but this time he turns to the subject of luxury tourism, rather than luxury fashion, in order to bring the contrast between spoken and written language to the fore. Bateman opens the conversation by asking Armstrong about his recent trip abroad. "Well, Travis," his colleague replies, confusing the protagonist with someone else, "travelers looking for that perfect vacation this summer may do well to look south, as far south as the Bahamas and the Caribbean islands. There are at least five smart reasons for visiting the Caribbean including the weather and the festivals and the events, the less crowded hotels and attractions, the price and the unique cultures" (p. 137). The rest of the conversation proceeds in a similarly impersonal manner, even when Bateman attempts to move Armstrong on to the subject of food: "As for dining out, the Caribbean has become more attractive as the island cuisine has mixed well with the European culture. Many of the restaurants are owned and managed by Americans, British, French, Italian, even Dutch expatriates" (pp. 139–140).

Bateman, however, is by no means exempt from the culture. The brief section titled "Rat," for instance, is almost exclusively given over to the protagonist's elaboration of his purchases for the month: each item receives its own paragraph of description, as Bateman lists its unique selling points, his language approximating the language of the sales assistant and the product catalog,

once again—while the protagonist's subsequent care for the animal of the title contrasts with the way in which he treats many of the humans in the book. In this respect, Bateman's many acts of violence appear to constitute his means of expressing his individuality in a world of inescapable conformity. The first hint of the protagonist's secret life is to be found in the novel's opening sentence, which intimates a connection between high finance and violence: "ABANDON ALL HOPE YE WHO ENTER HERE is scrawled in blood red lettering on the side of the Chemical Bank near the corner of Eleventh and First" (p. 3). A further suggestion appears on the following page, when the narrative mentions a newspaper story about a mysterious disappearance, picking out the detail of "a residue of spattered blood" as one of the "only clues" (p. 5). Bateman takes issue with his girlfriend's description of him as "the boy next door" at the dinner party that dominates the rest of the opening section: "'No I'm not,' I whisper to myself. 'I'm a psychopath'" (p. 20). But the first indication that the protagonist actually is a psychopath appears near the end of the second section, when he leaves his apartment with a raincoat that is "covered with what looks liked dried chocolate syrup crisscrossed over the front, darkening the lapels" (p. 30). Even so, it remains unclear whether Bateman's many acts of violence actually happen at all. Literary critics are divided as to whether the protagonist is a reliable or an unreliable narrator, but there are numerous suggestions throughout the novel that his version of events is to be questioned, at the very least, and these suggestions come to the fore in the many scenes that include characters who exist in the real world. When, for instance, Bateman runs into the actor Tom Cruise, who lives in the penthouse of the same apartment building, he makes a mistake that is hard to reconcile with his seemingly obsessive habit of watching videotapes. "To break the noticeably uncomfortable silence, I clear my throat and say, 'I thought you were very fine in *Bartender*'"— only for the actor to correct a fundamental detail: "*Cocktail*. Not *Bartender*. The film was called *Cocktail*" (p. 71). What is more, the protagonist's subsequent attendance at a concert enables him to perceive a moment of highly narcissistic connection with another of the more famous men on the planet: "Bono has now moved across the stage, following me to my seat, and he's staring into my eyes," to the extent that "it's not impossible to believe that an invisible cord attached to Bono has now encircled me" (p. 146). Ellis continues to exploit the subjectivity of the novel's first-person narration when Bateman murders Paul Owen—the colleague who, throughout the book, persistently confuses the protagonist with another Pierce & Pierce colleague, Marcus Halberstam—then proceeds to murder two escorts in Owen's vacant apartment. "There has been no word of bodies discovered in any of the city's four newspapers or on the local news," Bateman reports. "I've gone so far as to ask people—dates, business acquaintances—over dinners, in the halls of Pierce & Pierce," yet "no one has heard anything, has any idea of what I'm talking about" (p. 366). Indeed, when the protagonist visits the vacant apartment for the final time, he finds that it has been put up for sale, in a development that appears to contradict his version of events and—more fundamentally—appears to have serious consequences for his sense of identity: "All frontiers, if there had ever been any, seem suddenly detachable and have been removed, a feeling that others are creating my fate will not leave me for the rest of the day" (p. 370). The section comes to a suggestive close, yet it remains finally unclear whether the real estate agent knows anything about the dead bodies or not. Even so, the most substantial questioning of the protagonist's version of events takes place near the novel's end. Desiring to confess some of his sins, Bateman leaves a long voice message for his colleague Harold Carnes, in which he admits to killing Paul Owen as well as one of the escorts. But when the two run into one another at the opening of a new club, Carnes—who, once again, mistakes the protagonist for someone else—remains perplexed by what he considers to be an elaborate prank, refusing to believe that Bateman left the message, before casting doubt upon the preceding narrative by producing a piece of evidence that appears to undermine the protagonist's major claim: "He stares at me as if

we are both underwater and shouts back, very clearly over the din of the club, 'Because ... I had ... dinner ... with Paul Owen ... twice ... in London ... just ten days ago'" (p. 388). At this point in the novel, though, the numerous instances of mistaken identity mean that the reader cannot be finally sure that Carnes has actually had dinner with Owen, rather than someone else.

Nonetheless, the book comes to a close by intimating that Bateman's ruse is wearing thin, as the final section finds Ellis parodying the procedures that he has used throughout the novel, in order to create the impression of a change in the protagonist's attitude, from confidence to resignation. Even though the opening paragraph continues to provide another catalog of clothes, the gradual lapsing of Bateman's usually meticulous attention to detail suggests that he is tiring of keeping such a close eye upon his colleagues: "What are people wearing? McDermott has on a cashmere sport coat, wool trousers, a silk tie, Hermès. Farrell is wearing a cashmere vest, leather shoes, wool cavalry twill trousers, Garrick Anderson. I'm wearing a wool suit by Armani, shoes by Allen-Edmonds, pocket square by Brooks Brothers" (pp. 394–395). Not only does the opening question suggest a rare moment of personal—yet specifically literary—insight, as the protagonist appears to acknowledge the way in which he has been trying the reader's patience throughout the book, but the perfunctory descriptions of McDermott and Farrell anticipate the vagueness of the following sentences, which return to another of the novel's fundamental themes: "Someone else has on a suit tailored by Anderson and Sheppard. Someone who looks like Todd Lauder, and may in fact be, gives thumbs-up from across the room, etc., etc." (p. 395). The repetitions of "someone" intimate Bateman's acquiescence to the inevitability of mistaken identity, before the repetitions of "etc." find the author going one stage further, by implying a new lack of interest from the protagonist in his surroundings. What is more, the final section continues to find Ellis experimenting with reflexivity, by hinting at the narrative approach, when Bateman suggests there to be "no real structure or topic or internal logic or feeling" to

the conversation in Harry's bar, except for "its own hidden, conspiratorial one. Just words, and like in a movie, but one that has been transcribed improperly, most of it overlaps" (p. 395). The closing sentences proceed to raise the possibility of an explanatory motive, as the protagonist "automatically" and "for no reason" answers the question—"Why?"—that is mysteriously sounded: "Well, though I know I should have done *that* instead of not doing it, I'm twenty-seven for Christ sakes and this is, uh, how life presents itself in a bar or in a club in New York, maybe *anywhere,* at the end of the century and how people, you know, *me,* behave, and this is what being *Patrick* means to me, I guess, so, well, yup, uh ..." (p. 399). Not only does the author emphasize spoken language through the many interjections, but, in going against the grain of Bateman's earlier—highly polished—self, he reveals the fundamental emptiness at the heart of the protagonist, anticipating the novel's closing gesture of a sigh.

LATER WORKS

Ellis followed *American Psycho* by publishing *The Informers,* his first and only collection of short stories, in 1994. The author first started to work on the thirteen pieces, which are mainly split between the landscapes of Los Angeles and Camden College, in 1983, before the publication of his debut novel. But even though the reliance upon the first person resonates with the procedure of *Less Than Zero,* the stories also find Ellis beginning to experiment with the narrative approach, since he presents the perspectives of a number of different characters, while maintaining various strands of coherence, in order to create the impression of a distantly interconnected whole—an approach that anticipates the various points of view in *The Rules of Attraction.* What is more, further evidence of the author's interest in ambiguity is to be found in the realization that a number of the stories in the collection are spoken by characters who remain unidentified by name—a technique that Ellis continued to develop in his later books, with one especially powerful instance being the mysterious voice that

asks "Why?" in the final paragraph of *American Psycho*. The protagonists in the earlier books are frequently incapable of personal insight, and the pieces in *The Informers* make the reader feel a comparable absence, as the title knowingly, because reflexively, suggests. Yet, despite the presence of the supernatural—as the threat of the "werewolves" in *Less Than Zero* becomes the reality of "vampires" in the tenth story, "The Secrets of Summer"—the fact that the thirteen pieces document the usual behavior (exploitative and impersonal) of the usual people (wealthy) at the usual time (the 1980s) means that the narrative approach ultimately provides the main point of interest.

The same is true of *Glamorama,* the novel of more than five hundred pages that Ellis published in 1998, almost a decade after *American Psycho* was originally due to appear. In contrast to his previous works, however, *Glamorama* finds the author moving forward in time, as he casts a critical eye upon the emergence of the celebrity culture at the beginning of the 1990s by intensifying a number of the procedures that he used in *American Psycho*: not only does the novel's setting in the world of high fashion result in the listing of many more brand names, but it similarly includes many more references to many more people from the real world. Even so, there is a fundamental difference between *Glamorama* and Ellis' previous works, since the novel is highly structured, being written in numbered parts and numbered chapters—which, unusually, count down and not up—rather than comprising a freer series of sections. In this respect, it comes as no surprise to find the author hinting at the presence of a plot as early as the opening paragraph of the opening chapter—"33"—when the narrator, Victor Ward, asserts that "I don't want a lot of description, just the story, streamlined, no frills, the lowdown: who, what, where, when and don't leave out why," before repeating his demand, in a more urgent tone: "come on, goddamnit, what's the *story*?" (p. 5). Ward is overseeing the opening of a new club in New York and attempting to account for the mysterious appearance of a number of specks on the wall, but no simple answer to his question is forthcoming, since the many voices that sound in response only confuse the situation—and Ellis proceeds to emphasize the tension between truth and fiction by calling attention to the extent of the media interest in the project. The subsequent description of the magazine journalist gestures toward the inescapability of subjectivity: "The 'reporter' from *Details* stands with us. Assignment: follow me around for a week. Headline: THE MAKING OF A CLUB" (p. 6). Ellis proceeds to make a comparable suggestion about visual media, through the subsequent revelation that the events by the bar are also being recorded in images: "Behind her, some guy … follows us, camcording the scene" (p. 6). What is more, the author continues to emphasize the predominance of visual media by singling out the floor of the club that is lined with video monitors, then returning to the specks on the wall, in order to approach the tension between appearance and reality: "'Reality *is* an illusion, baby,' JD says soothingly. 'Reality *is* an illusion, Victor'" (p. 10). As such, the novel's opening scene anticipates the later complications of the narrative approach. Even though Ward's desire for the "story" contrasts with the many twists and turns of the plot— which finds the protagonist being offered money to track down a stranger's former classmate, before getting caught up with a group of terrorists who disguise themselves as models—Ellis attempts to problematize the relation between words and images by invoking the visual media of film and television. Chapter "2," in the third part of the novel, for instance, begins with the suggestion that Ward's life is still being filmed. "Wakened suddenly out of a brief dreamless nap by someone calling 'Action' softly (though when I open my eyes and look around the living room there's no one here), I get off the couch, noticing vacantly that the script I fell asleep reading has disappeared" (p. 321), the narrator reveals, as the author explores the tension between knowing and not knowing: "There is, I'm noticing, no camera crew around." And yet, inexplicably, their work continues to be done: "Somebody cuts the lights" (p. 324). Later on, Ellis makes the reader feel a comparable uncertainty, as chapter "48" in the fourth section takes the procedure one stage

further. "The film crew follows Tammy into the dining area, where she has a tense breakfast with Bruce. She sips lukewarm hot chocolate, pretending to read *Le Monde*" (p. 333), it begins, only for Ellis to reveal that "Bruce" is pretending as much as Tammy, but in a far more fundamental way: "The actor playing Bruce had a promising career as a basketball player at Duke" (p. 334). Indeed, when the author finally brings the book to its close, he does so by returning to the tension between appearance and reality—"I faded away and my image overlapped and dissolved into an image of myself years later sitting in a hotel bar in Milan where I was staring at a mural" (p. 546)—before the final chapter remembers the specks of the opening scene: "soon it's night and stars hang in the sky above the mountain, revolving as they burn" (p. 546).

Ellis turned further away from his characteristic style for the writing of his fifth novel, *Lunar Park,* which he published with Knopf in 2005. Once again, though, there are a number of continuities with the earlier books. To begin with, the suggestion of the supernatural finds a fuller expression, as Ellis—who is also the story's protagonist—appears to see a footstone at the end of the garden, then appears to stumble upon a trail of slime, before noticing some more substantial damage: "Surrounding the large windows of the master bedroom … were huge patches where the lily white paint was peeling off the side of the house, revealing a pink stucco underneath" (p. 101)—an image that continues to explore the tension between appearance and reality. More fundamentally, however, *Lunar Park* finds the author starting to experiment with a new reflexivity. Not only does the novel begin with a brief line that raises a number of questions about identity—"You do an awfully good impression of yourself" (p. 3)—but the following sentence reflects upon the specifically literary qualities of the line, from Ellis' perspective as author: "This is the first line of *Lunar Park* and in its brevity and simplicity it was supposed to be a return to form, an echo, of the opening line from my debut novel, *Less Than Zero*" (p. 3). The desire for a "return to form" appears to cast light upon Ellis' situation by intimating that he

has been going through a period of creative struggle, and, having quoted the first line of the debut novel, the author proceeds to put his finger upon the source of the later failures: "Since then the opening sentences of my novels—no matter how artfully composed—have become overly complicated and ornate, loaded down with a heavy, useless emphasis on minutiae" (p. 3), he writes, citing as evidence the first lines of *The Rules of Attraction* and *American Psycho* and, finally, *Glamorama*. The following section begins to problematize the relation between autobiography and fiction, by upholding Ellis' early habit of referring to Bennington College as Camden College. But the first major instance of the way in which the author exploits the potential for tension between the two is arises at the beginning of the novel's fourth section, which sets an obvious invention alongside a likely truth: "The two main events during the next phase of my life were the hurried publication of a second novel, *The Rules of Attraction,* and my affair with actress Jayne Dennis … a young model who had seamlessly made the transition to serious actress and had been steadily gaining recognition for her roles in a number of A-list projects" (pp. 10–11)—where "Jayne Dennis" is a character, rather than a person from real life.

In the earlier novels, the absence of personal insight raises a number of questions of specifically literary knowledge, as Ellis constructs his narratives in such a way that the understanding that is denied to his narrators gradually accumulates for his readers. *Lunar Park,* by contrast, finds the author exploiting the inescapable subjectivity of the first person in order to raise a number of different but related questions of knowing and not knowing. By writing (or speaking) the novel *in propria persona,* Ellis constructs his representation of himself by means of his own shaping hand, opening up the possibility of a more playful tension between form and content: any absence of personal insight is now a knowing absence of personal insight, and the author frequently capitalizes upon the resulting freedom by extending the tension to absurd dimensions. One especially powerful instance of such doubleness is to be found in the sentence

that brings the opening chapter to its close, by hinting at the book's impossibly supernatural plot. "Regardless of how horrible the events described here might seem, there's one thing you must remember as you hold this book in your hands: all of it really happened, every word is true" (p. 30), the author writes, when he knows that the reader knows the opposite to be the case. Another instance occurs in the sentence that begins the second chapter—and that also appears to begin the novel afresh, by repeating the line that starts the first chapter, without the quotation marks. The points of punctuation soon reappear, though, as Ellis proceeds to experiment with the new reflexivity in a related way. Not only does the discussion with Jayne about their fancy dress at the Halloween party continue to touch upon the tension between the reliable and the unreliable narrator, but it does so in terms that suggest the impossibility of presenting a completely authentic self to the world: "I told her I'd decided simply to go as 'me.' … 'I've decided against wearing masks,' I said proudly. 'I want to be real, honey. This is what's known as the Official Face'" (p. 32). The quotation marks around "me" anticipate the artifice of "the Official Face" and its implication that it is merely one face among others. Indeed, it soon becomes clear that Ellis presents himself throughout the book as a caricature, rather than a lifelike character or person from real life. The author's understanding of the fundamental impersonality of literary form enabled him to include figures such as Tom Cruise and Bono in *American Psycho,* as well as the many famous people who appear throughout *Glamorama,* and it is similarly the condition for the frequently controversial way in which he portrays his own life and the lives of his friends and family, as he freely acknowledges when he remembers the possibility of writing a piece of true autobiography: "even when I simply *thought* about the memoir it wouldn't go anywhere (I could never be as honest about myself in a piece of nonfiction as I could in any of my novels) and so I gave up" (p. 24). To be sure, the continuous tension between autobiography and fiction means that the reader can never be finally sure—at a number of points—what is invention and what is

truth, especially when it comes to the revelation of private details. On the one hand, the deliberately overblown world of the story appears to preclude the possibility of sincerity, but, on the other, many of the individual sentences about Ellis and his life have the potential to ring true. Even so, the author continues to emphasize the novel's fiction by saturating the book with numerous references to other literary works: Jayne and Ellis are hosting the party at their house on Elsinore Drive—an address that alludes to Shakespeare's most famous play, *Hamlet*—while the admiring student who visits the author in order to get his copy of *Less Than Zero* signed bears more than a passing resemblance to the debut novel's protagonist. "So, Clayton … I assume all your friends call you Clay" (p. 77), the fictional Ellis wonders, before asking him whether he has signed up for his course on novels—only to remember that he has seen the student before, when he dressed as another character from another novel: "Someone I didn't recognize came as Patrick Bateman" and "watching this tall, handsome guy in the bloodstained (and dated) Armani suit lurk around the corners of the party, inspecting the guests as if they were prey, freaked me out" (p. 37).

Ellis continued to experiment with similar questions of reflexivity in his next novel, *Imperial Bedrooms,* a belated sequel to *Less Than Zero,* which was published by Knopf in 2010 and which returns to Los Angeles in order to revisit the original cast of characters later in their lives. Developing the narrative approach of *Lunar Park,* the novel begins with a number of sections in which Ellis refers to himself, only this time he does so through the voice of the adult Clay, who, like his younger self in the debut novel, has come back to the West Coast at the turn of the year. But despite the broader parallels, *Imperial Bedrooms* is by no means a straightforward continuation of *Less Than Zero*: not only does the appearance of Clayton in *Lunar Park* anticipate the reappearance of Clay, but the autobiography at the beginning of *Lunar Park* is retrospectively complicated by Clay's different version of events, which also touches upon the film adaptation of *Less Than Zero.* What is more, Clay now works

in the film industry—in a further twist of reflexivity, he has come back to the city to help with the casting for a screenplay that he has adapted from a novel—and even though he suggests *Less Than Zero* to be "for the most part an accurate portrayal," since "only a few details had been altered and our names weren't changed and there was nothing in it that hadn't happened" (p. 3), he proceeds to cast doubt upon the truth of a number of details, before summarizing the author's relation to his characters:

> He was simply someone who floated through our lives and didn't seem to care how flatly he perceived everyone or that he'd shared our secret failures with the world, showcasing the youthful indifference, the gleaming nihilism, glamorizing the horror of it all.
>
> (pp. 4–5)

Once again, though, Ellis' representation of himself disappears from the story when the main plot begins. Having run into Trent and Blair—who are now married and who now work in the film industry—at their house in Bel Air, the protagonist is gradually reintroduced to the other characters from *Less Than Zero* when he attempts to make sense of a number of related intrigues, which resonate with the suggestions of surveillance that appear throughout *Glamorama.* Not only is Clay followed from the airport to his apartment at the Doheny Plaza (where Ellis actually lives), but he receives a mysterious call from a private number as he arrives there—and when he returns from the party later in the day, he is convinced that someone has broken into the apartment while he has been away. More fundamentally, Ellis finds another way of working the tension between the reliable and the unreliable narrator into the events of the story, since Clay attempts to seduce the young actress Rain Turner by suggesting that she will be able to play a part in the film that he is developing in return for sexual favors. As such, the protagonist is revealed to be far more active than his presentation as the passive observer in *Less Than Zero* initially suggested—and dangerous, too, since his obsession ultimately results in violent consequences, once again.

CONCLUSION

As of early 2016, Ellis had not published any fiction since *Imperial Bedrooms.* Having repeatedly denied the possibility of another story being in the works, however, the author posted a short piece titled "On a New Novel" on the *Medium* website in February 2013, which reads like an attempt to spur himself into writerly action. Not only does Ellis describe the background to the book in terms that remember the opening line of *Less Than Zero*—"The idea to begin a new novel started sometime in January while I was stuck in traffic on the I-10 merging into Hollywood"—but he proceeds to acknowledge that he has indeed been going through a period of creative struggle, which appears to have its roots in the shifting cultural situation: "the thought that I might never write a novel again began to announce itself more loudly than it had in years," with the result that "I started feeling the need to work my way through that transition," from "the world in which I used to write and publish" to "the world we live in now." But despite a number of subsequent rumors—including a potential title of *Tranquil Reflections*—no concrete details about the story's development and publication were available in early 2016. Even so, the author's other writing has continued to hit the headlines. "Generation Wuss," for instance, an essay that appeared in *Vanity Fair* in September 2014, received widespread coverage for its discussion of the difference between appearance and reality in millennial culture. Ellis defines the group of the essay's title as "a generation that appears to be super confident and positive about things but when the least bit of darkness enters into their realm they become paralyzed and unable to process it," before touching upon the difficulties that accompany the contemporary necessity of a "social media presence," especially "keeping the brand in play" and "striving to be liked, to be liked, to be liked"—a process that, the author proceeds to suggest, ultimately creates "its own kind of ceaseless anxiety."

To be sure, Ellis is all too aware of the difficulties that accompany a "social media presence," having joined the microblogging service Twitter in April 2009 and amassed more than a

half-million followers. Indeed, the author has received a great deal of criticism from the media for airing his controversial yet independent views about numerous figures and their works in the modern world, with his thoughts about the film director Kathryn Bigelow (to whom he subsequently apologized), the television show *Glee,* and the writer David Foster Wallace attracting particular opprobrium. Twitter is not the only way in which Ellis has been communicating directly with his audience, though. Developing his interest in the speaking voice, the author launched "The Bret Easton Ellis Podcast" in association with PodcastOne in November 2013. The first guest on the show was the recording artist Kanye West, who earlier in 2013 reimagined a scene from *American Psycho* in order to promote his new album *Yeezus.* Ellis' conversation with West was split over two episodes: the first discussion focused upon issues relating to creativity and popular culture, while the second picked up where the first left off, before the author discussed the media's generally positive reaction to the first installment of his new venture. Since then, Ellis has interviewed numerous guests from the worlds of art and entertainment, whose revelations of personal insight have provided a ready stream of news—a consequence of the author's continuing desire to question the relation between appearance and reality. Ellis also launched his own website in 2015. As well as providing details of his books and other works—a page of photographs takes the place of a conventional biography—breteastonellis.com includes a number of exclusive features, such as recommendations for books, music, films, and television, plus a blog that includes short pieces such as "Living in the Cult of Likability," which appeared in the *New York Times* in December 2015 and extends the argument of the *Vanity Fair* article, "Generation Wuss," in terms that resonate with the presentation of the self in *Lunar Park.* "There are limits to showcasing our most flattering assets because no matter how genuine and authentic we think we are, we're still just manufacturing a construct, no matter how accurate it may be," Ellis writes in the closing paragraph, before emphasizing his belief in individuality—and calling attention to the dangers of expressing it: "Those of us who reveal flaws and inconsistencies become terrifying to others."

Ellis' main creative interest, however, appears to be the visual media of film and television. The author wrote a screenplay for *American Psycho* in the 1990s, and his name has been linked with numerous projects since then—many of which, sadly, appear to have suffered the same fate of never being made. Ellis, for instance, was at one stage in contention to write the script for the adaptation of E. L. James's highly successful novel *Fifty Shades of Grey,* only to lose out to Kelly Marcel—who subsequently appeared with Ellis on the podcast, confessing that she had yet to see the film that was released because the director's interpretation of the screenplay was so different from her original script. The author encountered similar problems with his screenplay for *The Informers,* and the desire to retain complete creative control motivated the independent approach to *The Canyons* (2013), which Ellis suggests in "Generation Wuss" to be "an experimental, guerilla DIY affair that cost $150,000 dollars to shoot ($90,000 out of our own pockets) and that we filmed over twenty days in L.A. during the summer of 2012." Written by Ellis, directed by Paul Schrader, and produced by Braxton Pope, all of whom contributed their own money to the project, *The Canyons* received the remainder of its funding from a successful Kickstarter campaign, which ultimately raised a total of $159,015. In the video accompanying the campaign, Ellis talked about the freedom of being able to realize the film "without any industry people, without the studio, without executives," as the combination of low-cost digital technology and the money from the crowdfunding platform offered the prospect of a "new way of making content" that, once again, promised to enable direct contact with the audience. Indeed, the backers of *The Canyons* were able to have their say in the casting of the film, which starred Lindsay Lohan and was released in August 2013. Despite receiving a number of negative reviews, *The Canyons* ultimately made a profit and is notable for the way in which it finds the author returning to a

number of his fundamental themes. Some of the author's side projects have also seen the light of day. In a continuation of his earlier musical activity, Ellis has been involved in the making of a number of music videos. The author provides the voiceovers for two films that Saman Kesh directed for the band Placebo—"Too Many Friends" (2013) and "Loud Like Love" (2014)—and in doing so, he invokes the sections describing contemporary popular music in *American Psycho* as well as the unreliable narration of Patrick Bateman. Both videos follow the same procedure: Ellis introduces the "event" of the video by calling attention to a number of details, before the "event" plays out with the song—and then, at the end of the video, he provides a number of possible interpretations for the viewer to choose from, preserving the fundamental ambiguity of the scenario. Ellis also wrote the extended video for "Are You Okay?" by the band the Dum Dum Girls in 2013. Clocking in at just over ten minutes, the short film—described as a "psychological thriller"—begins with a scene that hints at the composition of fiction, before the author continues to explore the difference between knowing and not knowing. In 2015 the author wrote and directed another short film of just under ten minutes, *Orpheus,* to support the launch of a new model of sunglasses. As its title indicates, Ellis' film reimagines the classical myth—but in a twist upon the ancient story, the absence of speaking voices throughout the film is broken only by a brief scene in which Eurydice sings the lyrics to a contemporary song in a recording studio. The film *The Curse of Downers Grove,* which Ellis adapted from Michael Hornburg's novel *Downers Grove,* also appeared in 2015. Like *The Canyons,* however, this high-school thriller received a number of negative reviews, since its adherence to the conventions of its genre comes at the expense of any substantial experimentation with the narrative approach.

It remains unclear whether Ellis' next major project will be a book or a film or a television show or something else altogether. What seems certain, however, is that the author's belief in individuality, together with his knack for seizing upon the issues of the day, will produce a fascinating—and controversial—result.

Selected Bibliography

WORKS OF BRET EASTON ELLIS

NOVELS AND SHORT STORIES
Less Than Zero. New York: Simon & Schuster, 1985. New York: Vintage Contemporaries, 1998.

The Rules of Attraction. New York: Simon & Schuster, 1987. New York: Vintage Contemporaries, 1998.

American Psycho. New York: Vintage Books, 1991.

The Informers. New York: Knopf, 1994. New York: Vintage Contemporaries, 1995.

Glamorama. New York: Knopf, 1998. New York: Vintage Contemporaries, 2000.

Lunar Park. New York: Knopf, 2005. New York: Vintage Contemporaries, 2006.

Imperial Bedrooms. New York: Knopf, 2010. New York: Vintage Contemporaries, 2011.

ESSAYS
"On a New Novel." *Medium,* February 27, 2013. https://medium.com/on-a-new-novel

"Generation Wuss." *Vanity Fair,* September 26, 2014. www.vanityfair.fr/culture/livre/articles/generation-wuss-by-bret-easton-ellis/15837

"Bret Easton Ellis on Living in the Cult of Likability." *New York Times,* December 8, 2015. http://www.nytimes.com/2015/12/08/opinion/bret-easton-ellis-on-living-in-the-cult-of-likability.html

SCREENPLAYS
The Canyons. Directed by Paul Schrader. Prettybird Pictures et al., 2013.

The Curse of Downers Grove. Directed by Derick Martini. AliBella Pictures et al., 2015.

SHORT FILMS AND MUSIC VIDEOS
Placebo, "Too Many Friends," 2013. (Narrator.)
Dum Dum Girls, "Are You Okay?," 2014. (Writer.)
Placebo, "Loud Like Love," 2014. (Writer and narrator.)
Orpheus, 2015. (Writer and director.)

ONLINE
Podcast: www.podcastone.com/Bret-Easton-Ellis-Podcast
Twitter: @BretEastonEllis

BRET EASTON ELLIS

Website and blog: www.breteastonellis.com

CRITICAL AND BIOGRAPHICAL STUDIES

Annesley, James. *Blank Fictions: Consumerism, Culture, and the Contemporary American Novel.* London: Pluto Press, 1998.

Baelo-Allué, Sonia. *Bret Easton Ellis's Controversial Fiction: Writing Between High and Low Culture.* London: Continuum, 2011.

Colby, Georgina. *Bret Easton Ellis: Underwriting the Contemporary.* Basingstoke, U.K., and New York: Palgrave Macmillan, 2011.

Ebert, Roger. Film review of *American Psycho. Chicago Sun-Times,* April 14, 2000. http://www.rogerebert.com/reviews/american-psycho-2000

Kjerkegaard, Stefan. "The Medium Is Also the Message: Narrating Media in Bret Easton Ellis's *Glamorama.*" *Style* 45, no. 4:619–637 (winter 2011).

Mandel, Naomi, ed. *Bret Easton Ellis: "American Psycho," "Glamorama," "Lunar Park."* London and New York: Continuum, 2011. (Critical essays.)

Murphet, Julian. *Bret Easton Ellis's "American Psycho": A Reader's Guide.* London and New York: Continuum, 2002.

Tighe, Carl. "Sex, Satire, and Sadism: Bret Easton Ellis, *American Psycho.*" In his *Writing and Responsibility.* London: Routledge, 2005. Pp. 103–115.

Weinreich, Martin. " 'Into the Void': The Hyperrealism of Simulation in Bret Easton Ellis's *American Psycho.*" *Amerikastudien* 49, no. 1:65–78 (2004).

INTERVIEWS

Clarke, Jaime. "Interview with Bret Easton Ellis." *Mississippi Review* 27, no. 3:61–102 (spring–summer 1999).

Goulian, Jon-Jon. "Bret Easton Ellis, The Art of Fiction, No. 216." *Paris Review* 200:168–196 (spring 2012). www.theparisreview.org/interviews/6127/the-art-of-fiction-no-216-bret-easton-ellis

FILM AND STAGE ADAPTATIONS OF THE WORKS OF BRET EASTON ELLIS

Less Than Zero. Screenplay by Harley Peyton. Directed by Marek Kanievska. 20th Century Fox, 1987.

American Psycho. Screenplay by Mary Harron and Guinevere Turner. Directed by Mary Harron. Lionsgate, 2000.

The Rules of Attraction. Screenplay and direction by Roger Avary. Kingsgate Films, 2002.

The Informers. Screenplay by Bret Easton Ellis and Nicholas Jarecki. Directed by Gregor Jordan. Senator Entertainment, 2008.

American Psycho: The Musical. Music and lyrics by Duncan Sheik. Book by Roberto Aguirre-Sacasa. London: Almeida Theatre, 2013. New York: Gerald Schoenfeld Theatre, 2016.

BEN HECHT

(1894—1964)

Tom Cerasulo

NOT ONLY WAS Ben Hecht the most successful American screenwriter of the studio era, working on such classic movies as *Scarface* (1932), *Nothing Sacred* (1937), *Gone with the Wind* (1939), *Gunga Din* (1939), and *Notorious* (1946), he also directed seven films and even briefly had his own television show. But Hecht was also an accomplished novelist, playwright, journalist, and autobiographer, and he often complained that writing for motion pictures had zapped his creative energy for these other, more noble genres. This bellyaching came as no surprise. A die-hard iconoclast and curmudgeon, a man at war with his epoch, Ben Hecht complained about everything.

Hecht will best be remembered in popular culture for his witty, wisecracking journalism and his equally lively writing for stage and screen. With fellow reporter Charles MacArthur he created the newspaper play *The Front Page* (1928), still celebrated today for its rapid-fire dialogue and energetic pace. As a young man working for a city daily, Hecht learned to write quickly and on a deadline, attributes that later served him well as an employee on the clock in Hollywood. Journalism also provided him with subject matter and tone for his film writing. His book *1001 Afternoons in Chicago* (1922), a collection of his slice-of-life columns for the *Chicago Daily News*, displays his emerging talent as a chronicler of flawed heroes in the urban jungle, a skill he would later use for crime films like *Underworld* (1927) and *Scarface*.

Ben Hecht hoped to become a great novelist, and he began his fiction-writing career with highbrow ambitions. He found some early success publishing within the circles of what came to be known as the Chicago Renaissance, the flourishing of literary activity in the city from about 1912 to 1925, whose major figures included Theodore Dreiser, Sherwood Anderson, and Carl Sandburg. Hecht placed his short stories in influential modernist magazines like the *Little Review* and *Smart Set*. He also released several novels, most notably *Erik Dorn* (1921), and edited the *Chicago Literary Times,* a bohemian newspaper.

But Hecht's more consciously artistic output attracted little critical attention in the years that followed, and he has become a mere footnote in literary history. This is a fate that would not have surprised him. In his 1954 autobiography, *A Child of the Century,* he writes: "I can understand the literary critic's shyness toward me. It is difficult to keep praising a novelist or thinker who keeps popping up as the author of innumerable movie melodramas. It is like writing about the virtues of a preacher who keeps carelessly getting himself arrested in bordellos" (p. 2).

As *1001 Afternoons in Chicago* illustrates, Hecht certainly knew his way around a bordello raid, a pool hall fight, or an illegal poker game. But he simply might not have had what it takes to be a great novelist. Even his contemporaries believed this to be true. In 1928 his colleague David Karsner wrote:

> In my opinion Ben Hecht wrote literature in his newspaper pieces if he ever wrote it anywhere. Perhaps he won't like that, for anyone who has written novels prefers the epaulets of a novelist to the chevrons of a columnist. But after all, that preference is only one of the craft's many vanities. Good writing, it seems to me, is the sole criterion, regardless of its form.

Like the members of the Algonquin Round Table, another literary circle he would (grudgingly) be associated with after moving from Chicago to New York, Hecht was better known for his sharp

mind and nimble pen rather than for his deep thoughts or principles. In his later years he embraced his religious heritage and was a committed supporter of the establishment of a Jewish state, but for the better part of his life he was simply a contrarian with a pronounced anarchist streak. If most people were for it—whatever it was—he was against it.

EARLY LIFE AND 1001 AFTERNOONS IN CHICAGO

Ben Hecht will forever be regarded as a favorite son of Chicago. But he was actually born on the Lower East Side of New York City, on February 28, 1894. He was the firstborn son of Jewish immigrants from Belarus. His father, Joseph Hecht, worked as a cutter in the Manhattan garment district. Seeking better opportunities, Joseph moved the family to Chicago when Ben was six years old. Four years later, they moved to Racine, Wisconsin, where Hecht's mother, Sarah Swernofski Hecht, ran Paris Fashions, a downtown shop that sold the dresses her husband designed and manufactured. The business was not a success. In *A Child of the Century* (1954), Ben Hecht writes of his father: "The chief and busiest department of his factory was always an air castle. He had never any profits to share with his family, except the happy smile of his daydreams" (p. 65).

As a child and young adult, Ben was talented and restless. He was considered a violin prodigy at the age of ten and as a young teenager traveled in a circus as an acrobat and magician. He was also a voracious reader, especially drawn to the works of Horatio Alger, Mark Twain, and Edgar Allan Poe. After graduating from high school in 1910, at age sixteen, Hecht attended the University of Wisconsin for three days before deciding he had already read most of the books taught in college. So he dropped out and headed for Chicago. Following a brief stint as a theater manager, Hecht found work as a reporter, first for the *Chicago Daily Journal* and later as a columnist with the *Chicago Daily News*.

Hecht's first role on the *Journal* was as a picture chaser. A picture chaser's job was to obtain a photograph of the victim or perpetrator of a murder, scandal, suicide, or rape. Sometimes Hecht would break into a home to find a picture; one time he even sealed off a chimney to smoke the family out before sneaking inside for his quarry. Hecht writes of his employers:

> They never inquired into the methods by which my contributions to the day's journalism had been obtained. But their grins were broad when I stood before them with my loot. Only once do I remember Mr. Dunne regarding me with nervousness. That was when I appeared at his desk lugging a gilt frame, four feet square, that contained the hand-tinted photo enlargement of a mustachioed Pole, mysteriously shot to death in his bed on Aberdeen Street. It had been the only likeness of the deceased in the basement flat.
>
> (*A Child of the Century*, p. 124)

Soon after, Ben was promoted to reporter. He scoured the streets, saloons, alleys, basements, bordellos, and courtrooms of Chicago in search of stories. He writes, "I ran everywhere in the city like a fly buzzing in the works of a clock, tasted more than any fly belly could hold ... and buried myself in a tick-tock of whirling hours that still echo in me" (p. 113).

When the young reporter could not find a story, he invented one: "Tales of prodigals returned, hoboes come into fortunes, families driven mad by ghosts, vendettas that ended in love feasts, and all of them full of exotic plot turns involving parrots, chickens, goldfish, serpents, epigrams and second act curtains. I made them all up" (p. 133). William MacAdams, Hecht's biographer, writes of Hecht: "He was only too aware that he could create news with impunity, but he hadn't yet learned not to tamper with his publisher's image. One day he filed a heartrending story about an impoverished Bulgarian princess slinging hash on Wabash Avenue, and chose a well-known prostitute to pose for the photo of the princess" (p. 16). Hecht's curiosity about characters both real and imagined, his attraction to the morbid and lurid, his energy, and his ability to create interesting metaphors and turns of phrase come through in his news stories.

Equal parts tough guy and radical bohemian, he took special pleasure in exposing political

corruption and in trying to shock his bourgeois readers out of what he perceived to be their complacency. After moving to the *Daily News* in 1914, Hecht was given a daily column that focused on human-interest stories and portraits of urban grotesques, the people to whom the bustling city often pays no attention at all. Sixty-two of these sketches would be collected in 1922's *1001 Afternoons in Chicago.* While many of these portraits are clichés—hookers with hearts of gold and gamblers confident their bad luck is about to change—they possess an empathy missing from Hecht's later writing. Not only do they capture the friction and hum of industrial city life, they also reveal the hopes, yearnings, and disappointments of the masses living there. Loneliness is a persistent theme. "Grass Figures" has the reporter contemplating the phenomenon of men lying in Grant Park and looking up the sky. In doing so, Hecht hits upon something universal about the human condition. "Waiting. Yes, the whole pack of them are waiting all the time. That's why we all look alike" (pp. 170–171). Some of these pieces, like "Grass Figures," are wistful and tender; others are comedic and parodic. All find Hecht very much an authorial presence and a character in the stories he tells. Despite trying to remain an objective reporter, he often gets pulled in.

1001 Afternoons in Chicago contains some of Hecht's finest writing. It showcases his brand of literary modernism, a style characterized by the use of expressionistic, figurative language to describe the urban environment. In "Michigan Avenue," a street of luxury holds false promise: "The sun bursts a shower of little golden balloons from the high windows" (p. 27) and "the sky stretches itself in a holiday awning over our heads. A breeze coming from the lake brings an odorous spice into our noses. Adventure and romance! Yes—and observe how unnecessary are plots" (p. 29). In the dreamlike "Fog Patterns," the city skyline is obscured: "High up, where the mists thin into a dark sulphurous glow, roof bubbles float. The great cat's work is done. It stands balancing itself on the heads of people and arches its back against the vanished buildings" (p. 11). But soon the fog disappears, and

Chicago and its celebrated architecture come roaring back to life:

> Then its sturdy walls and business windows begin to mock the memory of the fog in my mind. "Fogs do not devour us," they say. "We are the ones who do the devouring. We devour fogs and people and days." Marvelous buildings.

> Overhead the sky floats like a gray and white balloon, as if it were a toy belonging to the city.
>
> (p. 14)

Hecht's extended metaphors and combination of terse sentences interspersed with lyrical passages capture the sights and smells and sounds of the metropolis.

In his preface to *1001 Afternoons in Chicago,* Henry Justin Smith, Hecht's editor on the *Daily News,* describes the young reporter's pitch for the column and its ambitions: "the idea that just under the edge of the news as commonly understood, the news often flatly unimaginatively told, lay life; that in this urban life there dwelt the stuff of literature, not hidden in remote places, either, but walking the downtown streets, peering from the windows of sky scrapers, sunning itself in parks and boulevards" (pp. 5–6). Despite his early enthusiasm, Hecht would always consider these pieces inferior to his "real" work as a literary author. But Smith disagrees. He goes on to say of Hecht: "In the novels he is one of his selves, in the sketches he is many of them. Perhaps that is why he officially spoke slightingly of them at times" (p. 7). Another contemporary of Hecht's, Harry Hansen, who dubbed Hecht "the Pagliacci of the fire escape," posited that the sketches of *1001 Afternoons in Chicago* were superior to the author's novels, since these longer works suffered from a certain sameness, as well as a caustic aimlessness. Hansen writes of Hecht, "In spite of his strictures on the world, he has no program for remodeling the world. He would like to destroy a great many conventions, but he has made no effort to formulate an ideal program of living to take their place."

THE CHICAGO RENAISSANCE AND EARLY NOVELS

Except for a brief stint in Germany covering the aftermath of World War I, Hecht called Chicago

home from 1910 to around 1924. It was a time and place ripe for writerly activity. Not only was Chicago a great newspaper town, but during the early twentieth century it was arguably, as H. L. Mencken claimed, the literary capital of the United States. The huge growth of the city, including an influx of new manufacturing money and a resulting spike in new artistic patrons coming to town, a flowering of world-class museums and exhibition spaces, the sounds of jazz and blues, and the cultural pulse that came from a panoply of immigrants, drew painters and writers to Chicago from the provinces.

American literature of the 1910s and 1920s carries an aesthetic shaped by encounters with Chicago's railroads, skyscrapers, and stockyards. The authors of the city, under the influence of European avant-garde movements, were attempting to craft an American Midwestern modernism. Hecht had several stories published in Mencken's *Smart Set*. Mencken, no friend of the folks he called the "booboisie," was likely attracted to Hecht's attacks on the hypocrisy of the average American. Although *Smart Set* did not pay very well, around fifty dollars, and with the departure of Mencken and coeditor George Jean Nathan in 1923 would soon become a middlebrow magazine filled with the type of formulaic "success stories" that it had been created to oppose, appearing in it was a prestigious feather in Hecht's cap.

Hecht's stories for Mencken drew from his journalism experience and were plot driven. The sketches and stories he published in Margaret Anderson's influential "little magazine" *Little Review*, on the other hand, were more impressionistic and experimental, influenced by the work of French symbolists like Charles Baudelaire, Paul Verlaine, and Stéphane Mallarmé. The most notable of these is 1915's "Life," which was selected for the Small, Maynard company's *Best Short Stories* volume for that year. The story follows a young, snobbish aesthete as he walks down a Chicago street and encounters a lice-ridden beggar who causes him to reevaluate his cynical worldview. Another 1915 Hecht story published in the *Little Review*, "The Sermon in the Depths," also bears the imprint of the French decadents on the young author. It is worth pointing out that the "little" when referring to "little magazines" of the modernist period, publications like the *Little Review* or *Contact* or the *Dial*, does not refer to payment or paper size. It refers to the number of readers being targeted. Such magazines often enjoyed a literate and sophisticated reading audience, but it was usually one that consisted almost solely of other struggling writers.

Appropriately, there was an intense spirit of collaboration among the writers of the Chicago Renaissance. Hecht worked on an aborted play with Sherwood Anderson and composed joint works with the poet Maxwell Bodenheim. Hecht and Bodenheim were simultaneously best friends and bitter enemies. Their biggest falling out occurred when the always-broke Bodenheim wrote to Hecht asking for a loan. Hecht wrote back that he was happy to do it and was enclosing a check. There was no check. When Bodenheim asked if a mistake had been made, Hecht roared with laughter. The two publicly reconciled in 1922, but they would lampoon each other in print for the rest of their lives.

On the surface, Ben Hecht had impressive literary bona fides. He was the founding editor (plus managing editor and copy editor and publisher and distributor) of the *Chicago Literary Times* in 1923–1924. Although "literary" has connotations of the elite, the respectable, the refined, the noble, the sophisticated, the inspiring, the best that has ever been thought and said, and so on, the term actually has no essential qualities and is not an objective category. Yet writing labeled "literary" has worth beyond the commercial, however that worth is defined, which sets it apart from its opposite, "trash," which is not worth keeping. Writers who aspire to write literature hope to stick around.

But in the final analysis, the literary ambitions of Hecht's group were largely for show and for dough. The *Chicago Literary Times* attacked other papers and the pretensions of the literati, but advanced no causes of its own. Of the Chicago Renaissance, Hecht himself later wrote: "The 'Chicago School' produced a number of books of varying merit. Would that our writing had been as fine as our lunches" (*A Child of the*

Century, p. 345). Hecht once accepted an invitation to debate Bodenheim on the topic "People Who Attend Literary Debates Are Imbeciles." The event took place at the Dill Pickle Club, the center of Chicago bohemia. Hecht began the night by looking over the crowd and declaring that the affirmative side rested. Bodenheim simply said, "You win," and the two men walked off with the evening's proceeds.

This jaded view of the literary life is reflected in Hecht's first novel, *Erik Dorn* (1921). Like many first novels, *Erik Dorn* is highly autobiographical. As Nelson Algren writes in his introduction to a 1960s reprint of the book, "in no other American novel is the relationship between the book's hero and the novelist revealed so lucidly" (p. ix). Not only does it draw from Hecht's experiences as a journalist, especially his time on the city beat and his trip to Germany on assignment for the *Chicago Daily News,* but it also contains his philosophical cynicism. The title character of *Erik Dorn* is a restless Chicago newspaperman, a disaffected intellectual, and a dissatisfied husband. Hecht writes: "Into this emptiness of spirit, life had poured its excitements as into a thing bottomless as a mirror. He gave it back an image of words. He was proud of his words. They were his experiences and sophistications" (p. 10). *Erik Dorn* certainly displays Hecht's knack for capturing the physicality of urban life in modernist language: "The city alive with signs, smoke, posters, windows; falling, rising, flinging its chimneys and its streets against the sun … Faces like a flight of paper scraps scattered about him. Bodies poured suddenly across his eyes as if emptied out of funnels" (p. 7). Yet for all its vibrant passages, the novel never really satisfactorily finds its groove either intellectually or emotionally. In fact, Hecht even appears to comment on his own limitations as a writer in *Erik Dorn.* Unlike the novel's character Warren Lockwood, based on Sherwood Anderson, Dorn—like his creator Hecht—will never be a serious artist. Lockwood has a belief system, and he has empathy. Dorn, by his own admission, is too epigrammatic, too coldly clever, and he does not believe in anything.

Erik Dorn is bored with his marriage to the safe Anna and falls in love with a sensitive, troubled woman named Rachel Laskin. She makes him feel alive again. A year after Erik leaves his wife for Rachel and moves to New York, Rachel cruelly leaves him, claiming that only in abandoning him can she be sure he will always love her. Heartbroken, Erik decides to move to Europe to cover the aftermath of the war. There he encounters an old flame of Rachel's, the puritanical lawyer George Hazlitt, who tries to shoot him. In the struggle, George is killed, and an aristocratic European friend of Dorn's takes the blame. Returning to America, Erik decides he still loves Anna and wants her back. But she is now engaged to another man. The book begins and ends with scenes of Dorn's elderly, confused father mumbling to himself. Dorn's search for beauty and meaning—for "the rogue of life" (p. 21)—has led nowhere. He is the same character at the end of the novel as he was at the beginning.

While *Erik Dorn* may feel dated and self-indulgent to many contemporary readers, in its time it was considered a noteworthy novel by a promising new writer, uniting European modernism and a character at odds with the boosterism of American society. Like Ernest Hemingway's *The Sun Also Rises* (1926), *Erik Dorn* reflects the search for meaning of a disillusioned American journalist abroad. Yet unlike Hemingway, Hecht does not give us much of a window into the nature of his protagonist's suffering. For all his facility with words and phrases, Hecht falls short on insight and ideas. Algren writes of Hecht: "He came, too young, to a time when, like Dorn, he had to ask himself, 'What the hell am I talking about?' And heard no answer at all" (p. xvii).

Erik Dorn may fall short on answers to life's questions. It does, however, seem to offer autobiographical insight into Hecht's own life, especially his career as a journalist and more specifically the time he spent in Germany. Without an ability to speak the language, Hecht was sent to postwar Berlin as correspondent for the *Chicago Daily News* from December 1918 until early 1920. Hecht dove headfirst into the nightlife and cultural zeitgeist of Berlin, just as

he had in Chicago years before. Early in his stay he became friends with George Grosz, a key figure in Dadaist "happenings" and other manifestations of the avant-garde. Doug Fetherling writes: "Dear to Hecht was the memory of Grosz's staging of a race between a woman operating a sewing machine and another woman operating a typewriter. The event was preceded by a poetry contest in which an audience which had paid twenty gold marks each listened to twelve compositions shouted simultaneously in one great noise" (p. 27).

In addition to commenting on his professional and artistic life, *Erik Dorn* also appears to comment on Hecht's personal life. The novel foreshadows the crumbling of his 1915–1925 marriage to the reporter Marie Armstrong, the mother of Hecht's daughter Edwina. In 1924 Hecht would leave Chicago and his wife and child and move to New York with his mistress, the writer Rose Caylor. They would marry in 1925 and have a daughter, Jenny.

Autobiography also plays a starring role in Hecht's 1924 novel, *Humpty Dumpty.* Like its predecessor *Erik Dorn,* the theme of the book is the hollow core of American culture in the 1920s. Instead of a journalist, this time the malcontent main character, Kent Savaron, is a novelist. Just as Hecht had done, the well-read teenager Kent leaves his small Wisconsin town for the bright lights of Chicago and the promise of a literary life. But disillusion quickly creeps in. Kent's painfully bourgeois wife is not on his intellectual level and does not get him. The modern world is filled with foolish people and foolish products. As in *Erik Dorn,* the fashions, music, films, and celebrities of the Jazz Age are treated with contempt and derision. Unlike Erik Dorn, and like the Humpty Dumpty of the children's story, Savaron breaks completely and cannot be put back together again. He commits suicide rather than have to continue being a highly evolved, Nietzschean super-brain in a culture of philistines.

If possible, Hecht's 1922 novel *Gargoyles* is even more spiteful and cynical than his autobiographical ones. *Erik Dorn* and *Humpty Dumpty* contain moments of aesthetic beauty, passion, and characters that are somewhat rounded. But *Gargoyles,* perhaps under the influence of literary naturalism and the novels of Theodore Dreiser, contains only types to be dissected with cold, distanced prose. The narrative concerns the political rise of a man named George Basine aiming to be a judge, but much of the book is a series of withering sketches of hypocrites, phonies, sex maniacs, prudes, and predators. In looking for a publisher for *Gargoyles,* Hecht first sent it to G. P. Putnam's Sons. They agreed to publish it—provided Hecht tone down some of the profanity and omit some of the more lurid scenes. The novelist refused on artistic grounds, and the book was published by Boni & Liveright instead.

Another novel Hecht published in 1922 encountered even more opposition and censorship. *Fantazius Mallare: A Mysterious Oath* is the tale of an artist who is driven insane by the hypocrisy of a society filled with liars and cheats. Featuring drawings by the artist Wallace Smith and a long, profanity-filled, jeremiad-like preface by Hecht in which he calls out his imagined enemies, the novel itself takes the form of a journal in which Mallare, a character who previously appeared in a Hecht short story and in *1001 Afternoons in Chicago,* describes his quest to detach himself from the physical world and the realm of the senses. Inspired by the work of the French writer Joris-Karl Huysmans and the decadent movement, the novel is by far Hecht's strangest. Filled with sexual exploits that involve hallucinations, a hunchback dwarf, asphyxiations, and Gypsies, the book tries far too hard to shock its readers. Like much of Hecht's highbrow writing, it is a Jazz Age book that seems stuck in the decadent quicksand of the late nineteenth century, overwritten and too eager to reach for a gaudy phrase.

Fantazius Mallare was to be released in a limited run of two thousand units, and available copies became even fewer when the federal government charged Hecht, Smith, and the publisher with sending obscenity through the U.S. mail. The famous lawyer Clarence Darrow took the case—and lost. Hundreds of copies still in press were confiscated and hundreds more printed copies were seized. Hecht and Smith were fined $1,000 each and briefly became heroes within

their Chicago circle. But the controversy didn't go over so well with his employers at the *Daily News.* He was canned.

Financially and creatively, Hecht could not live up his to early promise as a novelist. *Count Bruga* (1926) is a fictionalized biography of Maxwell Bodenheim, but aspects of it apply to Ben Hecht as well. The narrative follows a small-town boy seeking literary glory who drinks too much, eats too much, and squanders his talent. Another of Hecht's books from this period, the most productive of his career as a novelist, allowed him to collect $2,000 on a bet. *The Florentine Dagger: A Novel for Amateur Detectives* (1923) is a mystery story that began as a wager with a friend that Hecht could write a novel in thirty-six hours that could sell twenty thousand copies and receive critical acclaim. The friend, Charles McArthur's wealthy brother, paid up. But by the late 1920s, Hecht had come to realize that he could not support himself through literary prose alone, and to make a living as a writer he might have to turn to the theater—or worse, the movies—instead.

EARLY THEATER

Ben Hecht is celebrated for his fruitful stage collaborations with Charles MacArthur. But he began his playwriting career, in 1914, with a different writing partner, the lumber industry heir Kenneth Sawyer Goodman. They composed about a dozen one-acts together, collectively published under the title *The Wonder Hat and Other One-Act Plays* (1925). Hecht's first solo play, *The Egotist,* premiered in New York in 1922 and has parallels to his novel *Erik Dorn.* The main character, Felix Tarbell, is a playwright and a daydreamer who fancies himself the model for the dashing male leads in his plays. He enters into an affair with an actress; then he decides to return to his wife. But now the former Mrs. Tarbell has a new boyfriend, and the egoist winds up alone. Another Hecht play with echoes of *Erik Dorn* is 1937's *To Quito and Back.* Like Erik Dorn, the American journalist abroad Alexander Stearns realizes that his world-weariness is just metaphysical emptiness. Mary McCarthy wrote

that the play's hero "for two acts engages in vacillation, amorous and political. He can love neither a woman nor a cause truly, no matter how desperately he desires to do so. In all branches of experience he is irrevocably a tourist" (qtd. in Fetherling, p. 43).

Hecht's cynicism was put to better use in *The Front Page* (1928), a charming, madcap newspaper comedy he cowrote with MacArthur, a fellow reporter. The play has aged well and been revived many times, most notably as the 1940 film version called *His Girl Friday.* MacArthur and Hecht had met in Chicago and reconnected when both were living in New York. They shared a morbid sense of humor and a strong work ethic. Their system of collaboration, which they would also later employ in Hollywood, had MacArthur pacing the room while Hecht scribbled at a lap desk. Each could veto the other's ideas. Their first playwriting effort, "The Moonshooter," Hecht considered "the best work MacArthur and I ever did together" (*A Child of the Century,* p. 414). Unfortunately, it never went anywhere. They lost both copies. Their next play, however, one that drew upon their journalism experience, made it to Broadway in 1928 and would become a classic of the American theater.

The Front Page takes place in the pressroom of the Chicago Criminal Courts Building. The crackerjack reporter Hildy Johnson has decided to quit the newspaper business, get married, and move to Manhattan to work in advertising. He reconsiders his plans when a story literally crawls through the window: Earl Williams, an escaped murderer set for execution for political gain. Unable to resist getting the scoop for his editor Walter Burns, Hildy hides Williams in a desk. Hildy and Burns plot to smuggle the convict out of the building in order to conduct an exclusive interview. But they need to keep the other reporters—as well as the corrupt sheriff and the crooked mayor—from discovering Williams' hiding place, and they lie and scheme and finagle and blackmail to do so. When order is restored, Hildy and his fiancée board a train to New York, seemingly with Walter's blessing. The usually gruff editor even offers a pocket watch as a wedding present. But then he phones the police in

Indiana to have his best reporter sent back, claiming Hildy stole his watch.

In his August 26, 1928, *New York Times* review, Brooks Atkinson wrote of the play's fidelity to realism:

> The skepticism, the callousness, the contempt, the vague dissatisfaction with their lot, the boorishness, the brutal jesting and the omniscience are not invented. Hysterically funny as it may be to hear one of the newsmongers telephone the facts of the birth of a child in a patrol wagon, there is no great perversion of the truth. Hilarious, gruesome and strident by turns, "The Front Page" compresses lively dramatic material into a robust play.
>
> (qtd. in MacAdams, p. 111)

With its frank, profanity-filled dialogue, the play captures the quick tempo of the newspaper trade and the rapid patter of the men who are addicted to it. They are cynical about life. They have dubious morals. But they are romantically sentimental about their devotion to their business. Not only did *The Front Page* shape the public's perceptions of the world of urban journalism, but it also influenced how newspapermen saw themselves and their hard-boiled duty to get the story at all costs.

In *The Front Page,* Hecht and MacArthur use theater to satirize the cutthroat world of the daily paper. In their next play, *Twentieth Century* (1932), they poke fun at the pretension of the theater world itself. The action is set aboard the Twentieth Century express train. Oscar Jaffe, a down-on-his-luck theater producer, runs into an old flame, the actress Lily Garland, who is set to go to Hollywood. Egos clash, emotions flare, and schemes are hatched. Can Jaffe get Garland to sign a contract with him—and fall in love with him again—before the train reaches its final destination? Noting the similarities of the play to *The Front Page,* Doug Fetherling writes: "Both Burns and Jaffe are the type of scoundrel Hecht and MacArthur loved creating, who will commit any crime, perpetrate any outrage, in the name of personal glory and the passion ruling that glory, be it a scoop or a Broadway hit" (p. 100). *Twentieth Century* did not receive the rave reviews of *The Front Page,* but it was a success with audiences. Hecht and MacArthur adapted the play for a movie, starring Carole Lombard and John Barrymore, which was released in 1934 by Columbia Pictures.

Hecht and MacArthur also collaborated on the circus musical *Jumbo* in 1935, the trial drama *Ladies and Gentlemen* in 1939, and the World War II propaganda piece *Fun to Be Free* in 1941. Their final collaboration for the stage was the aptly titled 1946 play *Swan Song.* In it, a failed musician turns insane and murderous. Lacking in suspense, *Swan Song* was a flop. With their later efforts for the theater, Hecht and MacArthur could not recapture the Broadway success of their first two plays together. But to take out some of the sting, they were two of the most in-demand and highly paid screenwriters in Hollywood.

HOLLYWOOD

The first full-length screenplay Ben Hecht and Charles MacArthur wrote together was *Unholy Garden* (1931), starring Ronald Colman as a gentleman thief who falls in love with his beautiful mark. Later in the decade, in 1939, the writing duo adapted *Gunga Din* for the screen and wrote the screenplay for the classic version of Emily Brontë's *Wuthering Heights,* which focuses mainly on the first half of the novel. In between, they formed their own film company and worked on four films which they wrote, produced, and directed at the Paramount Astoria Studios in Queens, New York: *Crime Without Passion* (1934), *Once in a Blue Moon* (1935), *The Scoundrel* (1935), and *Soak the Rich* (1936). *The Scoundrel,* a dark and sophisticated comedy starring Noël Coward as the ghost of a publisher who dies in an airplane crash and cannot be put to rest until he finds someone to mourn for him, won Hecht and MacArthur an Academy Award for Best Original Story.

During his career Hecht was nominated for six Academy Awards and won two of them. The first was for the 1927 silent film *Underworld,* directed by Josef von Sternberg. Hecht's career-long ambivalence about screenwriting was reflected in his attitude toward this first statuette. It was awarded at a ceremony he did not attend and for a film he had disowned.

While living in New York in 1926, Hecht had received a telegram from his friend and fellow writer Herman J. Mankiewicz, who had recently moved to Los Angeles. It read, "Will you accept three hundred per week to work for Paramount Pictures? All expenses paid. The three hundred is peanuts. Millions are to be grabbed out here and your only competition is idiots. Don't let this get around" (*A Child of the Century,* p. 466). In need of money, Hecht packed his bags.

The "idiots" Mankiewicz refers to in his telegram reminds us that the first screenwriters were not really screenwriters at all, at least not in the way playwrights were playwrights. The first "screenwriters" were studio clerks with good imaginations, former newspaper reporters who could work quickly, copywriters who could come up with snappy bits of prose, and people on set who had good ideas in the midst of filming. None of them thought of themselves as creative geniuses who would use the medium to bring their personal visions to the screen.

Underworld, Hecht's first story for Paramount, drew upon his experiences as a Chicago newspaperman on the crime beat. But he believed that his realistic narrative, an eighteen-page treatment based on the exploits of the small-time gangsters Dion O'Banion and Tommy O'Connor, had been turned into a melodramatic mess onscreen. He thought the film would flop and had to be talked out of removing his name from the credits. However, *Underworld* was a hit, and it also set the stage and the style for the expressionistic film noirs of the coming decades. These movies shared literary modernism's fascination with ominous cityscapes, along with its pessimism and hints of misogyny, but they added audience-friendly plots and strands of morality amid a web of sin.

In the end, Hecht was glad he had kept his screen credit. More credits—especially solo credits—meant higher asking prices for his services. Eventually he would make up to $125,000 a script. He received his Academy Award for *Underworld*— in absentia—at the first-ever ceremony, held on May 29 at the Roosevelt Hotel in Los Angeles to honor films made in 1927

and 1928. When it was mailed to his home in New York he used it as a doorstop.

Despite his contempt for Hollywood, Ben Hecht could be called the most successful American screenwriter of the early twentieth century. His biographer William MacAdams dubs him "the most influential writer in the history of American movies, creating a new and exciting language for the screen at the same time that such writers as Dashiell Hammett and Ernest Hemingway were revitalizing the novel" (p. 7). Hecht is credited with writing the screen stories or screenplays for more than fifty films, and he worked without credit on many others. He could produce a screenplay in a matter of days. He was highly paid, amazingly prolific, and well respected within the Hollywood film community. His work for the movies will be his enduring legacy. With his trademark blend of cynicism and sentimentality, he was especially adept at scripting two popular genres: crime or suspense pictures like *Underworld, Scarface,* and *Notorious*; and romantic, screwball comedies like *Nothing Sacred, Twentieth Century,* and the 1952 *Monkey Business.*

But he was only doing it for the money, at least as he claims in *A Child of the Century:*

> For many years Hollywood held this double lure for me, tremendous sums of money for work that required no more effort than a game of pinochle. Of the sixty movies I wrote, more than half were written in two weeks or less. I received for each script, whether written in two or (never more than) eight weeks, from fifty thousand to a hundred and twenty-five thousand dollars. I worked also by the week. My salary ran from five thousand dollars a week up. Metro-Goldwyn-Mayer in 1949 paid me ten thousand a week. David Selznick once paid me thirty-five hundred a day.
>
> (p. 467)

Hecht needed a lot of money because he spent a lot of money. He paid alimony and child support; he had a home in Nyack, New York, an apartment in Manhattan for extramarital indiscretions, and a home in Oceanside, California; he had a staff of servants that included a maid, a driver, a trainer, and a cook.

Although he was one of the few screenwriters with name recognition precisely as a screen-

writer, Hecht never believed the studio movies he worked on were "his." Not even the ones he wrote and directed. It was work for hire. As a novelist Hecht legally owned the material produced by his singular imagination, but as a Hollywood scriptwriter he was usually called upon to work with existing materials owned by someone else and help craft them into a marketable commodity ultimately built by many hands.

Scripts are sketches, parts of a larger whole, invitations to collaborate rather than stand-alone works of art. Most screenwriters learn quickly that there's no such thing as "the script as a whole." Even if one person is responsible for making the entire component, it is still only a part crafted to make the larger machine run more smoothly. The screenplay is not meant to exist on its own, not even to the extent that a dramatic work for the theater, by Ben Hecht for instance, might come alive on the page. The mediocre businessman William Shakespeare may not have realized that he was the great playwright William Shakespeare, but to this day there is still no *Hamlet* of screenplays. The Hollywood script is a written invitation to make art, not a freestanding literary artwork in its own right. A screenplay achieves fruition only through image, dialogue, sound, music, and graphics. A drama text can be repeatedly performed and restaged and reimagined; but once filmed, a screenplay becomes fixed.

There are also other reasons Hecht never considered his screenplays art. Accepting a studio contract placed authors into a structure and hierarchy where time and function were measured, institutionalizing a creative process. Writers, used to being on their own, were asked to assume work roles that served studio needs. They found themselves within an industry that had divided its labor and routinized its work sequences. Each studio was organized around hierarchies of power designed to squeeze maximum value out of employees and the physical plant itself. Writers were often expected to punch clocks and put in a full day. If the typewriter stopped clacking, if a writer took a few moments to think over the next plot point or bit of dialogue, a producer might poke his head into the writer's office and ask why he or she was not working. Jack Warner at Warner Bros. believed his writers were lollygaggers and often used binoculars to spy on them from his office window.

At MGM, where Hecht worked on occasion, the atmosphere was more genteel, but the product was more expensive, and therefore more hands were involved in assembling it. The policy of writers working on a single script—in collaboration, in competition, in pieces—began at MGM in the 1920s and quickly spread to other studios. It was believed that pitting writers against one another caused them to do their best work. Once an individual or a team produced a finished script, that script, in whole or in part, was often sent to other writers to be rewritten. For example, Hecht's story for *Underworld* was given to Robert N. Lee and Charles Furthman to compose a screenplay. The rule of thumb appeared to be that the more people working on a film, and the more money spent on it, the better the finished product.

Producers often took the best from each contributor and put together the shooting script. Here the writer's contribution ended. Once the film went into production, writers were assigned to another project or fired. Following the same pattern, once the movie was shot and moved into postproduction for editing, the director was usually shuffled to another sound stage. The studio system operated like an assembly line. That this system resulted in many wonderful films and a studio lot that was busy 168 hours a week there is no doubt. But behind the practical efficiency lay a will to power. Executives wanted labor divided up in such a way that the guiding vision behind individual films remained their own. Screen credits were sometimes withheld out of spite or granted to secretaries or lovers on a whim. Ben Hecht often worked uncredited on scripts—for instance the 1931 movie adaptation of *The Front Page*—but he never worked unpaid.

A few years after writing the story for *Underworld,* which launched the gangster movie as a popular genre, Hecht wrote the screenplay for the classic *Scarface* (1932). Just as *The Front Page* formed the public's image of the quintessential newspaperman, *Scarface* cemented the prototype

of the modern mobster. Directed by Howard Hawks, who would become a frequent collaborator of Hecht's, and starring Paul Muni as Tony Camonte, the film, loosely adapted from Armitage Trail's 1929 novel, is based on the crime career of Chicago's Al Capone with a little Borgia-type incest innuendo thrown into the mix. After the screenwriters W. R. Burnett and John Lee Mahin turned in a first draft, Howard Hughes paid Hecht $1,000 a day to start from scratch and completely rewrite the script. Hecht's money was delivered, in cash, at 5 p.m. each evening. He finished the script in a swift eleven days. His agent Leyland Hayward, thinking about his 10 percent commission, cursed his client for not writing more slowly.

Hecht worked with director Hawks again on *Viva Villa!* (1934), a biopic of the Mexican revolutionary Pancho Villa. For his screenplay Hecht received an Academy Award nomination. According to William MacAdams, he also received a job offer from Josef Stalin, who loved the film so much he "was prepared to send a battleship to fetch Hecht back to the USSR" (p. 159) to write a script for him. Hecht would receive another nomination for *Angels over Broadway* (1940), a movie he directed, produced, and wrote originally for film. The story concerns a group of people stranded during a rainstorm who form an embezzling plot.

Other notable films Hecht worked on during the studio era were *Nothing Sacred* (1937)—a screwball comedy starring Carole Lombard as a Vermont woman diagnosed with radium poisoning (misdiagnosed, we soon learn), whose supposed affliction is milked by an ambitious Manhattan reporter to increase circulation—and the Alfred Hitchcock thrillers *Spellbound* (1945) and *Notorious* (1946). Hecht would receive his final Academy Award nomination for *Notorious,* the story of a woman (Ingrid Bergman) helping an agent (Cary Grant) dismantle a Nazi spy ring. Hecht had worked uncredited on two earlier Hitchcock films, *Foreign Correspondent* (1940) and *Lifeboat* (1944). Later, he would work without credit on a few more Hitchcock films, *The Paradine Case* (1947), *Rope* (1948), and *Strangers on a Train* (1951).

Hecht also worked uncredited on such film classics as *Queen Christina* (1933), *Gone with the Wind* (1939) (without having read the source novel), *Stagecoach* (1939), *The Shop Around the Corner* (1940), *Gilda* (1946), *The Thing from Another World* (1951), *The Greatest Show on Earth* (1952), *Roman Holiday* (1953), and *Mutiny on the Bounty* (1962). Hecht was perhaps Hollywood's most in-demand script doctor, called in from New York when a project was in serious trouble and time was short. For performing his emergency services in anonymity, he was always well compensated.

Because of the nature of screenwriting, it is difficult in many cases to unearth who came up with what. But screenwriting history has handed down the lion's share of the critical praise to Hecht for the films he worked on. As with many things, it comes down to money. In Hollywood, writers were often judged (even by other writers) on the basis of their weekly salaries, a factor that served to classify them and, more importantly to the anti-union studio management, divide them. Salary in Hollywood meant more than income: it also told its striving denizens—and those around them—where they stood in their profession. In the minds of studio executives, the reason some writers—such as Ben Hecht—made more money than other writers was because they were better writers; the reason they were better writers was because they made more money. Why would a producer hire one $350-a-week writer when he could have three $1,000-a-week writers? To profit from this type of studio thinking, it is said that Hecht employed an office of lesser screenwriters who would work on ideas and come up with lines the boss could use.

One of the reasons Ben Hecht is considered one of the best screenwriters of all time is how quickly he could write a screenplay and how briskly his screenplays read. A script's main requirement is pace: obviously a movie needs to move. Hecht's film dialogue was considered the snappiest in the business. Writing screenplays required little mental effort from him, but that does not mean he was lazy. Hollywood producers knew they could count on him, and he enjoyed that fact. Just as a new recruit who is opposed to

war can sometimes take great pride in becoming the best soldier in the company, Hecht was dismissive of the film industry and those who ran it, but he needed to give the work itself its due respect. "However cynical, overpaid or inept you are, it is impossible to create entertainment without feeling the urges that haunt creative work," he wrote, but then added, "My own discontent with what I was asked to do in Hollywood was so loud that I finally received a hundred and twenty-five thousand dollars for four weeks of script writing" (*A Child of the Century,* p. 474).

Hecht's film career began to cool down in the 1950s. But his name still meant enough that the 1958 sci-fi movie *Queen of Outer Space* paid him to use it, even though he had no part in the story or script. Hecht's last big success as a screenwriter was 1952's *Monkey Business,* a screwball comedy directed by Howard Hawks and coscripted with Lederer and I. A. L. Diamond, about a scientist who creates a youth elixir that makes adults behave like kids. *Actors and Sin* (1952) was Hecht's final film as a director. The movie adapts two of Hecht's short stories. The first part, "Actor's Blood," is about a former actor worried about his daughter's career. She has followed in her father's footsteps, and rather than have her fall into obscurity as he himself has, he shoots and kills her. In the second part, "Concerning a Woman of Sin," a literary agent takes on a nine-year-old child as a client. The little girl is played by Hecht's daughter Jenny. Doug Fetherling writes of the film that "there are too many inside jokes at the expense of a Hollywood he had warred with too often ... he makes fun of the imbecility of producers and the system, but with more of a heavy hand than a quick wrist" (p. 155).

LATER CAREER AND JEWISH ADVOCACY

Ben Hecht's films were banned in England from 1948 until 1951 for his claims in the media that the British were hostile to the creation of a Jewish state. For most of his life, he had been indifferent to Jewish causes and his own Jewishness. But after World War II, Ben Hecht used his considerable energy, as well as his bank account, to become active in the movement to rescue Europe's Jews by any means necessary. In an open letter praising Irgun saboteurs in Palestine, he wrote: "Every time you blow up a British arsenal, or wreck a British jail, or send a British railroad sky high, or rob a British bank, or let go with your guns and bombs at the British betrayers and invaders of your homeland, the Jews of America make a little holiday in their hearts" (qtd. in MacAdams, p. 246).

Hecht's conversion may come as a surprise to readers of his anti-Semitic 1931 novel *A Jew in Love,* the last major novel of his career. The main character, Jo Boshere, modeled after the publisher Horace Liveright with heavy doses of Ben Hecht baked in, is a rapacious, egotistical intellectual with an ugly, hook-nosed face and an insatiable sexual appetite. The dissections of self-deception, hypocrisy, and cynicism that mark Hecht's earlier novels are all present. So too is their tendency toward plotlessness and bitterness. Thanks to an all-out marketing campaign by the publisher Covici Friede, *A Jew in Love* sold well, but in light of his literary transformation from an equal opportunity debunker into an idealistic propagandist, Hecht later regretted writing the book.

In *A Guide for the Bedevilled* (1944), Hecht examines anti-Semitism, arguing against the premise that Jews are somehow responsible for hatred directed toward them. As the war in Europe makes plain, Hecht points out, anti-Semitism is not a harmless social attitude; it is an invitation to murder. The degree to which Hecht knew what he was talking about when he was talking about politics has been questioned by critics, and so has his tendency to reduce complex issues into straw men and vitriolic talking points. But his passion is undeniable.

Hecht's work on behalf of Jewish causes is also reflected in two of his later stage productions. His 1943 pageant *We Will Never Die,* with music by Kurt Weill and staging by Moss Hart, celebrates the Jewish contribution to Western civilization. It was performed in Madison Square Garden to a packed house for two nights before traveling to other cities. The 1946 play *A Flag Is*

Born, starring Paul Muni and a young Marlon Brando, concerns a married couple, both Holocaust survivors, who dream of one day living in a Jewish state in Palestine. They receive visions of five scenes from Jewish history, from the Old Testament to an anticipated future in the homeland. Although critics found the play simplistic, it raised $400,000 for the American League for a Free Palestine. With the proceeds, a ship was bought, named the S.S. *Ben Hecht,* to carry refugees to Palestine. However, the British navy captured it and sent its passengers to a detention camp in Cyprus. Later on, the S.S. *Ben Hecht* was absorbed into the Israeli navy.

One-hundred-plus pages of *A Child of the Century* detail Hecht's efforts on behalf of Jewish causes. He had worked on the autobiography for more than a decade, and it was finally released in 1954. Not surprisingly, much of the book details his heyday in Chicago, and very little of it is about Hollywood. Critical reception to the autobiography was mixed. Many commentators found it long-winded and self-indulgent, yet in the *New York Times Book Review,* Saul Bellow called it "admirable and significant … he roars like an old fashioned lion." Three years later, Hecht published *Charlie: The Improbable Life and Times of Charles MacArthur.* Despite being labeled a biography, most of the material is about MacArthur's experiences in relation to Hecht's. Similarly, *Letters from Bohemia* (1964) reprints letters from deceased friends like Mencken and Bodenheim introduced with short reminiscences about them.

In the last decades of his life, Hecht's writing focused more and more on memoir. Further autobiographical material found its way into *Gaily, Gaily* (1963), a collection of nine fictionalized tales of Hecht's wild youth. The first piece, "Clara," begins: "It took me a month to convince Clara that she was too beautiful and too fine a girl to work in Queen Lil's whorehouse. Thus, on a night in May, Clara came to live in my attic room whose lone window overlooked the Chicago River and the bridge lights swimming in it like Coleridge's fiery snakes" (p. 1).

The book crackles with an energy missing from much of the prose of Hecht's later period.

In "Lunatic," he boasts of the *Little Review* crowd:

> Our philosophy, "Beware the public!" Our battle cry, "No Sales!" Our victory, the mantle of loneliness which our enemies called "egomania."

> Were we good artists, fine geniuses, intellectual world shakers? Go ask the spring lamb whom the sky belongs to. I'll make only one boast of us when we were unknown in Chicago—no one has taken our place.

(pp. 163–164)

In these tall tales, many of which were first published in *Playboy,* he captures the excitement and optimism of his youth. The 1969 movie adaptation *Gaily, Gaily,* directed by Norman Jewison and starring Beau Bridges as "Ben Harvey," dramatizes this halcyon period of Hecht's life.

Hecht also occasionally wrote about other people in the last years of his career. In 1954 Hecht worked with Marilyn Monroe as a ghostwriter for her memoir "My Story," versions of which, with some revision by others, were published in the *London Empire News* later that year and in book form in 1974. *Perfidy* (1961) is the story of the postwar trial of Rudolf Kastner, who negotiated with the Nazis for the lives of Hungarian Jews. The book takes David Ben-Gurion and other leaders of Israel to task for not doing more to save European Jews. It was criticized in the international press for engaging in propagandistic bombast rather than in historical facts, the same charge directed at *A Guide for the Bedevilled.*

Ben Hecht's final work for the theater was *Winkelberg,* produced off-Broadway in 1958. The title character is based on Maxwell Bodenheim. Winkelberg is a literary artist fighting to retain his individuality in a world of complacency. Already dead when the play begins, he is sent by God in search of a pleasant memory from his past so that he may create his own heaven. Winkleberg replays scenes from his life, but they all disappoint him.

In 1958–1959 Hecht had his own TV show. He intended to please as few people as possible. Always the gadfly, he once had a group of

Bowery winos brought into the studio for an unscripted live discussion. Management blacked out the segment. Another night, the gangster Mickey Cohen admitted that he had killed many people but offered in his own defense that all of them had deserved it. After an episode in which the painter Salvador Dali declared he had discovered a new type of orgasm, the show was canceled.

Hecht's final novel, *The Sensualists,* was published in 1959 to poor reviews. Citing its similarity to all the rest of the author's literary output, William MacAdams describes it as "the old story of a man, his wife, and his mistress" (p. 281). Hecht's last screenplay work was for a project that became the James Bond spoof *Casino Royale* (1967). Shortly after completing his script for that film, for which he received no screen credit, Ben Hecht died of a heart attack, on April 18, 1964, at age seventy-one. The Israeli politician Menachem Begin delivered the eulogy.

ASSESSMENT

Ben Hecht never reached the potential that colleagues like Harry Hansen had seen in him as a young man in the early 1920s. Hansen predicted: "Once he gets away from his journalistic ballyhoo, from his superficial estimates of people, from his desire to walk the tight rope and do acrobatic tricks in mid-air to the delight of a gaping mob, he will be able to dig deep and search for the really lasting treasures of literature." But it was not to be. Hecht blamed Hollywood for it.

Although the dimming of his reputation as a novelist coincided with his rise as a screenwriter, it was not the cause. Hollywood was not a glitzy siren luring artists to commit intellectual, aesthetic, and spiritual suicide in Los Angeles swimming pools. Furthermore, it is largely because of Hecht's movie work that we remember his writing today. Richard Corliss writes, "Hecht personifies Hollywood itself: a jumble of talent, cynical and overpaid; most successful when he was least ambitious; often failing when he mistook sentimentality for seriousness, racy, superficial, vital and *American*" (p. 5).

Hecht's remarks about the film industry are bitter in *A Child of the Century.* But he also praises producers like David O. Selznick and Sam Goldwyn, and he has good things to say about the many talented people working in Hollywood. On the other hand, he omits the fact that he was one of them. There is no mention of his Academy Awards in *A Child of the Century.* Not only does Hecht bite the hand that feeds him, he bites the hand of the community that celebrates him.

Part of Hecht's hatred toward Hollywood can be chalked up to disappointment in himself for not protecting himself from the call of the marketplace. He believed his aesthetic capital suffered when he received commercial capital. To sell out, to acknowledge you are selling anything, is to enter into a devil's bargain and to be cast out of the Eden of pure literary production. In such formulations as Hecht's, Hollywood takes the fall as a symbol of all that is wrong with an uneducated, fickle, homogenizing mass culture of consumption. Trying to work both sides of the art and commerce divide, desiring both money and prestige, will turn the noble, special author into a common, workaday hack. In this illusory zero-sum game, which divides up cultural regions the way the movie studios divided up theater territories, an acknowledgment of the successes authors achieved in Hollywood might risk a devaluation of their literary reputations.

But Hecht's literary reputation rests on his journalism and scripts for the screen and stage, not his novels. His newspaper play, *The Front Page,* has never gone out of print. The films he worked on are available on multiple platforms and receive new audiences constantly. His novels have been forgotten. With their navel-gazing pessimism and a style that labors to sound poetic and artsy, perhaps this is as it should be. When Hecht wrote with an eye cocked on high culture, the quality of his prose seemed to wither. But much of his newspaper writing sizzles with modernist sparks. Covering gangsters and tricksters as a beat reporter in Chicago led to crafting indelible stories about them for film. The heroes of Hecht's novels are intellectuals bored into inaction; the heroes of his better scripts are street-smart guys hungry for action. In his screen comedies, Hecht's showy iconoclasm and his outlandish desire to shock the bourgeoisie—while

being a member of the bourgeoisie—was a more comfortable and entertaining match for mass culture than he probably wanted it to be. His mind worked quickly, but not very deeply. He liked melodrama and he was drawn to the sensational. In this way Ben Hecht would always be a self-centered newspaperman, on the make and looking for a scoop.

Selected Bibliography

WORKS OF BEN HECHT

Novels and Short Fiction

Erik Dorn. New York: Putnam, 1921. Chicago: University of Chicago Press, 1963.

Gargoyles. New York: Boni & Liveright, 1922.

Fantazius Mallare: A Mysterious Oath. Chicago: Covici-McGee, 1922.

The Florentine Dagger: A Novel for Amateur Detectives. New York: Boni & Liveright, 1923.

Broken Necks and Other Stories. Girard, Kan.: Haldeman-Julius, 1924.

Humpty Dumpty. New York: Boni & Liveright, 1924.

Count Bruga. New York: Boni & Liveright, 1926.

A Jew in Love. New York: Covici Friede, 1931.

Actor's Blood. New York: Covici Friede, 1936.

A Guide for the Bedevilled. New York: Scribners, 1944.

The Sensualists. New York: Messner, 1959.

Nonfiction

1001 Afternoons in Chicago. Chicago: Covici-McGee, 1922. ReadaClassic.com, 2010.

A Child of the Century. New York: Simon & Schuster, 1954. New York: Primus, 1985.

Charlie: The Improbable Life and Times of Charles MacArthur. New York: Harper, 1957.

Perfidy. New York: Messner, 1961.

Gaily, Gaily. Garden City, N.Y.: Doubleday, 1963.

Letters from Bohemia. Garden City, N.Y.: Doubleday, 1964.

Collections

The Wonder Hat and Other One-Act Plays. With Kenneth Sawyer Goodman. New York: D. Appleton, 1925.

The Collected Stories of Ben Hecht. New York: Crown, 1945.

A Treasury of Ben Hecht: Collected Stories and Other Writings. New York: Crown, 1959.

Plays

The Wonder Hat. With Kenneth S. Goodman. Detroit: Arts and Crafts Theatre, 1916.

The Hero of Santa Maria. With Kenneth S. Goodman. New York: Comedy Theatre, 1917.

The Egotist. New York: Thirty-Ninth Street Theatre, 1922.

The Front Page. With Charles MacArthur. New York: Times Square Theatre, 1928.

The Great Magoo. With Gene Fowler. New York: Selwyn Theatre, 1932.

Twentieth Century. With Charles MacArthur. New York: Broadhurst Theatre, 1932.

Jumbo. With Charles MacArthur. New York: Hippodrome, 1935.

To Quito and Back. New York: Guild Theatre, 1937.

Ladies and Gentlemen. With Charles MacArthur. New York: Martin Beck Theatre, 1939.

Christmas Eve. New York: Henry Miller's Theatre, 1939.

Fun to Be Free: Patriotic Pageant. With Charles MacArthur. New York: Madison Square Garden, 1941.

Lily of the Valley. New York: Windsor Theatre, 1942.

We Will Never Die. New York: Madison Square Garden, 1943.

Swan Song. With Charles MacArthur. New York: Booth Theatre, 1946.

A Flag Is Born. New York: Alvin Theatre, 1946.

Hazel Flagg. New York: Mark Hellinger Theatre, 1953.

Winkelberg. New York: Renata Theatre, 1958.

Films

Underworld. Paramount, 1927. (Story.)

Unholy Garden. With Charles MacArthur. United Artists, 1931. (Screenplay.)

Scarface. United Artists, 1932. (Adaptation.)

Design for Living. Paramount, 1933. (Screenplay.)

Twentieth Century. With Charles MacArthur. Columbia, 1934. (Adaptation from their play.)

Crime Without Passion. With Charles MacArthur. Paramount, 1934. (Adaptation from Hecht's short story.)

Viva Villa! MGM, 1934. (Screenplay.)

Once in a Blue Moon. With Charles MacArthur. Paramount, 1935. (Screenplay.)

The Scoundrel. with Charles MacArthur. Paramount, 1935. (Screenplay.)

Barbary Coast. With Charles MacArthur United Artists, 1935. (Screenplay.)

Soak the Rich. With Charles MacArthur Paramount, 1936. (Screenplay.)

Nothing Sacred. United Artists, 1938. (Screenplay.)

Let Freedom Ring. MGM, 1939. (Screen story and screenplay.)

Gunga Din. With Charles MacArthur. RKO, 1939. (Screen story.)

Wuthering Heights. With Charles MacArthur. United Artists, 1939. (Screenplay.)

Angels over Broadway. Columbia, 1940. (Screen story and screenplay.)

Comrade X. With Charles Lederer. MGM, 1940. (Screenplay.)

Spellbound. United Artists, 1945. (Screenplay.)

Specter of the Rose. Republic, 1946. (Story and screenplay.)

Notorious. RKO, 1946. (Screen story and screenplay.)

Her Husband's Affairs. With Charles Lederer. Columbia, 1947. (Screen story and screenplay.)

Kiss of Death. with Charles Lederer. Twentieth Century-Fox, 1947. (Screenplay.)

Where the Sidewalk Ends. Twentieth Century-Fox, 1950. (Screenplay.)

Actors and Sin. United Artists, 1952. (Story and screenplay.)

Monkey Business. with Charles Lederer and I. A. L. Diamond. Twentieth Century-Fox, 1952. (Screenplay.)

PAPERS

The Newberry Library in Chicago houses the major collection of Hecht's papers, including manuscripts, outlines, notebooks, letters, and clippings. It also has his Academy Award for *Underworld.*

CRITICAL AND BIOGRAPHICAL STUDIES

Algren, Nelson. Introduction to *Erik Dorn.* Chicago: University of Chicago Press, 1963. Pp. vii–xvii.

Bellow, Saul. "The 1,001 Afternoons of Ben Hecht." *New York Times Book Review,* June 13, 1954. http://query.ny times.com/gst/abstract.html?res=9C0DE4D81E3CE43 ABC4B52DFB066838F649EDE

Corliss, Richard. *Talking Pictures: Screenwriters in the American Cinema, 1927–1973.* Woodstock, N.Y.: Overlook Press, 1974.

Fetherling, Doug. *The Five Lives of Ben Hecht.* Toronto: Lester and Orpen, 1977.

Felheim, Marvin. "Tom Sawyer Grows Up: Ben Hecht as a Writer." *Journal of Popular Culture* 9, no. 4:908–915 (spring 1976).

Hansen, Harry. "Ben Hecht: Pagliacci of the Fire Escape." In *Midwest Portraits: A Book of Memories and Friendships.* New York: Harcourt Brace, 1923. Pp. 305–357. Reprinted in *Twentieth-Century Literary Criticism,* vol. 101. Edited by Jennifer Baise and Linda Pavlovski. Detroit: Gale, 2001. *Literature Resource Center.*

Karsner, David. "Ben Hecht." In *Sixteen Authors to One: Intimate Sketches of Leading American Story Tellers.* New York: Lewis Cleveland, 1928. Pp. 235–245. Reprinted in *Twentieth Century Literary Criticism,* vol. 101. Edited by Jennifer Baise and Linda Pavlovski. Detroit: Gale, 2001. *Literature Resource Center.*

MacAdams, William. *Ben Hecht: A Biography.* New York: Barricade Books, 1990.

Martin, Jeffrey Brown. *Ben Hecht, Hollywood Screenwriter.* Ann Arbor, Mich.: UMI Research Press, 1985.

Perry, Albert. "The Dill Pickle and the End of Chicago." In his *Garrets and Pretenders: A History of Bohemianism in America.* New York: Covici Friede, 1933. Pp. 200–211.

Troy, Gil. "From Literary Gadfly to Jewish Activist: The Political Transformation of Ben Hecht." *Journal of Ecumenical Studies* 40, no. 4:431–449 (fall 2003).

HOMER HICKAM

(1943—)

S. Bailey Shurbutt

WHEN ONE THINKS about the many lives of Homer Hickam, whose personal odyssey perhaps rivals that of another "Homer" of considerable note, it is not surprising to learn that when Mrs. Laird, his third-grade teacher, told young Hickam he would someday make his living as a writer, he took her words literally and very much to heart. As he told an Imagiverse Educational Consortium interviewer: "I wanted to be a NASA engineer but I had to be a writer." Looking at the diverse publications of Homer Hickam, it is clear that his experience in storytelling ranges far and wide, from the coming-of-age stories of the Coalwood trilogy (*Rocket Boys,* 1998; *The Coalwood Way,* 2001; and *Sky of Stone,* 2001), to the science fiction stories of the Helium-3 trilogy (*Crater,* 2012; *Crescent,* 2013; and *Crater Trueblood and the Lunar Rescue Company,* 2014), to the Josh Thurlow historical novels (*The Keeper's Son,* 2003; *The Ambassador's Son,* 2005; *The Far Reaches,* 2007), and volumes such as *Red Helmet* (2007), *Back to the Moon* (1999), *Torpedo Junction* (1989), *The Dinosaur Hunter,* (2010), and his 2015 family tale *Carrying Albert Home.*

Hickam has lived many lives in order to be able to write such varied volumes, and that range of experiences all began humbly enough in the West Virginia coal company town of Coalwood. Born Homer Hadley Hickam, Jr., on February 19, 1943, he was the second son of Homer Hickam, Sr., who worked as a mining engineer and administrator, and Elsie Gardener Hickam, who struggled to keep the coal dust out and her family in tune with values she held dear. Like the mountains that offered both sublime vistas and claustrophobic spaces that could smother, the company town of Coalwood was both comfortingly close-knit and fraught with the perils of everyone's knowing everybody else's business.

"Sonny," as Hickam was called in those days, recalls a boyhood filled with the tensions that understandably would have come from a mother who wanted something different for her sons and a father who honored the mines to which he had devoted his life (and indeed, to which he would eventually forfeit his life, as a result of black lung disease).

GROWING UP IN A COMPANY COAL TOWN

Hickam recalls vividly his boyhood home in *We Are Not Afraid,* written as a response to the events of September 11, 2001:

> I knew every inch of the place, every smoky hollow and musical creek. I would have laughed and said I knew every miner who lived there, too, and his missus and their children, and even all the dogs and cats. I would have been certain that I had the place completely figured out in my mind, every curved road that led through the town as well as the crooked paths covered with pine needles that went up and over its forested hills.
>
> (p. 203)

Hickam continues, "Like the beating of my own heart, I knew Coalwood's rhythms, punctuated by the low grumble of the shuffling hardtoe boots as the shifts of miners treaded past my house to and from the tipple ... of Olga Number One" (p. 203).

A company town like Coalwood was a place unique in America, with the exception perhaps of the southern logging towns of a slightly earlier time period, both vanishing dinosaurs of the cultural past. Every person living in the town owed allegiance to the company, an allegiance that came directly through the miner who went down each day into the mine and picked up his

paycheck at week's end. If he were killed in an accident, his family would have less than two weeks to vacate the company-owned home and the town. With the wages he earned, he paid for all the family's day-to-day physical needs as well as his mining equipment, all of which came from the company store. The miner's social life, church life, the schools, health care—every facet of daily living was provided by the company. For all the hardships of this way of life, Hickam's father was proud of the mining community and the care that the company provided for its workers, who, whether events were catastrophic, menial, or heroic, always came together as a community to help each other.

While Hickam's admiration for his father is certain, the tension between the mining superintendent and his family was equally clear, including the conflict, generated in large part by Homer, Sr., between sons Jim and "Sonny" (Homer, Jr.), so very different in their talents, inclinations, and their father's outward appreciation. Yet Hickam also remembers his father, who died in 1989, with immense pride: "In mining circles, he was widely recognized for his mine ventilation innovations" (Julian interview). Homer, Sr., was largely a self-taught engineer, who cared deeply about the workers under his supervision; and though as supervisor he didn't actually have to do so, he "went inside the mine every day" (Julian). His desire that his second son follow him into the mines as a mining engineer, however, was one that never caught the boy's imagination, although young Hickam spent summers during college working in the Coalwood mine of his father. To most of the young men in Coalwood, Hickam remembers, the thought of "having to make a career down in the mines … [was a] nightmare" (Julian).

Growing up in a company town in the late 1950s, in the era directly after *Sputnik* had rocked American education, was like growing up anywhere else in America at that time, a challenging and dynamic experience. The sense of belonging and, at the same time, alienation, from both neighbors and often his own family, inspired young Hickam and his fellow Big Creek High School science nerds, who called themselves the

"Big Creek Missile Agency," or BCMA, to a quest for the perfect rocket propulsion fuel, a mission that would win the support of a football-absorbed Coalwood community and eventually a National Science Fair award in 1960. There was likewise an extraordinary sense of tranquility that the West Virginia boy found growing up in the mountain setting. Hickam writes in *We Are Not Afraid*: "When I was a boy, one of my favorite places to go was a hollow high on the mountain behind my house. [The spot] was filled with tall pine trees and its floor was a plush carpet of dropped needles." Hickam remembers, "I would often go there alone and sit on a dead log and listen to nothing except the beating of my own heart and the thoughts racing through my head.… I was alone in the deep wood, but I was absolutely, utterly at peace" (p. 209).

However, when young Homer looked up at the stars from the mountaintop behind his home, something else caught his attention: the first satellite to streak across the night sky, *Sputnik I*. His imagination was fired. Jack Bales writes about Hickam concerning this event, one that would change both the country and the community of Coalwood. Young Homer Hickam knew now, Bales says, "that his future was not limited to the confines of Coalwood and that the outside world with all its possibilities was indeed within his reach" (p. 3). From this point on, Hickam focused on achieving a dream: meeting Dr. Wernher von Braun and going to NASA as a space engineer (he would indeed accomplish the latter). With such a goal, his world had for Hickam new meaning, and the quest for the perfect rocket propulsion fuel became the goal of the Big Creek Missile Agency as well as Coalwood's. When the local news took up the cause and began to tout the Rocket Boys' accomplishments, the mine machine shop helped construct the rockets the boys designed, and Big Creek High School did its best to provide the academic resources to inspire the six Rocket Boys: Quentin Wilson, Roy Lee Cooke, O'Dell Carroll, Billy Rose, Sherman Siers, and Sonny Hickam. Hickam recalls in an interview looking back at this period: "It was in the 10th grade after I'd seen *Sputnik* fly over Coalwood. Five other boys and I decided to build

our own rockets. That was harder than we realized. We had to learn a lot of things, engineering, drawing, strengths of materials, welding, machine work, and lots of math. I had to learn calculus and differential equations when I was having trouble with algebra!" (Imagiverse). Hickam goes on to tell how the whole town of Coalwood got caught up in rocket fever: "The coalmine machinists volunteered their time to build our rockets when they started to get really complex and required expert machine work. Explosives experts from the mine made suggestions on our propellants, and other mine company employees gave us materials. My dad, the mine superintendent, helped by looking the other way while this was all going on. My mother supplied pots and pans and mixing utensils to make our propellants" (Imagiverse).

This Coalwood "community science project" occurred about the time the football team had been sidelined because of overzealous parental pursuit of a state championship. Everyone was surprised by Coalwood's turning its attention to the quest of six high school science nerds. "At first," Hickam remembers in his Imagiverse interview,

the people of Coalwood opposed what we were doing because we made a lot of noise and smoke but after awhile, most Coalwoodians began to help us. The preacher in town preached a sermon that got us a launch range, which we called Cape Coalwood. Miss Freida Riley, our chemistry and physics teacher got us a book, *Principles of Guided Missile Design,* and also suggested we enter local science fairs to bring honor to our school and town. After three years of experimentation, we were able to fly a rocket over four miles high.

It was this story, thirty years later, that Hickam put into an article for Smithsonian's *Air & Space* magazine that eventually evolved into the award-winning novel *Rocket Boys* (1998) and the movie *October Sky* (1999).

THE WORLD BEYOND COALWOOD, WEST VIRGINIA

When John F. Kennedy campaigned in West Virginia while running for president, he inspired a generation of students who in their own individual ways also wanted to reach for the stars. Hickam explained in his interview with Norman Julian: "I don't know what he thought in private, but I thought what he said in public would have led the country to greatness.... [Kennedy had articulated a] vision of America." Brimming with boundless enthusiasm and a desire to build a better world, Hickam followed his older brother Jim to Virginia Polytechnic Institute (today known as Virginia Tech) to study industrial engineering, graduating in 1965. During his undergraduate studies, he would return each summer to Coalwood to work in his father's mine, never giving up his dream to become a rocket scientist. He writes in the epilogue of *Sky of Stone*: "I became sort of an honorary junior engineer. My father put me through his bootcamp, and Jake Mosby taught me much about mining, too.... I learned more practical engineering under their tutelage than a thousand classrooms could ever hope to provide" (p. 398).

It was about this time that the country was ratcheting up the conflict in Vietnam. As many young West Virginians did, Hickam enlisted in the army after graduation. In 1965 he attended Combat Engineer Officer Candidate School and was commissioned as an officer in the Ordnance Corps. His life was then dramatically altered, when in 1967 he began serving as a first lieutenant in the Fourth Infantry Division in Vietnam. His job was to provide technical and mechanical assistance in the jungle for armored units, keeping their tanks and personnel carriers operating. The jungle mountains of Vietnam were not altogether unlike the hills and "hollers" of West Virginia, except that, as he writes, we "got shot at by all sides. I was present for the Battle of Dak To, where I saw a line of American infantrymen bravely claw up a mountain against the murderous onslaught of an entrenched main-force North Vietnamese Army regiment" (pp. 398–399). Hickam remembers that after their hard-fought victory, he "watched those same grunts march back down again. Within days, the North Vietnamese moved back into their positions on the mountain" (p. 399). The experience was a

metaphor for the frustration and discontent associated with this war.

Hickam was in Vietnam during some of the most savage years of the war, 1967–1968. He writes: "I was at the Oasis, a tiny, exposed firebase near the Cambodian border, when the Tet Offensive was launched. I fought the first day's battle with my boots on the wrong feet, don't ask me why, and was rescued by F-100 Super Sabre jet bombers flown in, via Thailand, from Myrtle Beach Air Force Base." He adds with a touch of Hickam irony, "I figured my mom had sent them" (*Sky of Stone,* p. 399). When his Vietnam tour was up in 1968, Hickam remembers that he was "very tired." He had left an army "torn apart, not by the enemy, but by itself." Indeed, when he returned to the United States in October of that year, Hickam recalls, "many Americans, mostly my own age, went out of their way to insult me. Before I learned not to wear my uniform in public, I was threatened and spat upon." He adds, "I have forgiven them, but it wasn't easy" (p. 399). From his tour of duty in Vietnam, he won both the Army Commendation and Bronze Star medals.

For a short time after his war tour, Hickam worked in Utah for Thiokol, an industrial chemical company that made solid propellant rocket motors. He was assigned to both the Minuteman and Poseidon programs and began to write a novel about his war experiences, but the war was still too close and much too painful, so he gave up the project. Rejoining the army, he was stationed in Puerto Rico, at the Roosevelt Roads Naval Base, where he learned to scuba dive and began a lifelong love affair with the sea, inherited from his mother. Hickam left the army in 1973 to pursue his goal of becoming a rocket engineer, hiring on as a civilian with the Army Missile Command in Huntsville, Alabama (*Sky of Stone,* pp. 399–400). The National Aeronautics and Space Administration was not a possibility at this time, as NASA was letting engineers go rather than hiring, so his Coalwood desire to work in the place made famous by his hero Werhner von Braun was still a pipe dream (Imagiverse). However, becoming a scuba instructor wasn't just a dream, nor was developing his passion for

prose. All during these years, Hickam wrote for a variety of science, history, and scuba magazines, mostly about his scuba-diving adventures. In 1975 he was invited to join a team of divers in North Carolina exploring the wreck of a U-boat near Cape Hatteras (*Sky of Stone,* p. 401). Hickam's water skills were put to use in a different way in 1984, when he was awarded the Alabama Distinguished Service Award for Heroism because of his efforts to rescue the crew and passengers of an overturned paddleboat in the Tennessee River. As a result of this award, he was selected as one of the bearers of the Olympic Torch on its way to Atlanta for the 1996 Olympics. These and other adventures were grist for the literary mill churning in his mind, manifesting years later in his Josh Thurlow adventure series.

Hickam has said that his early writing for magazines and science journals was a great training ground for the creative writing that would follow. Writing was a skill that usually came easily and quickly, which was well and good, as his work with the army missile command was fairly intense. He recalled: "I worked after hours and on weekends. I free-lanced to many magazines on a variety of topics.... I began writing for publication in 1973 and worked hard to hone my writing skills. I studied magazines and wrote articles that I felt would fit. I never failed to place an article that I wrote even though I was at first often rejected. I just stuck with it, something I'd learned how to do in my Rocket Boys days" (Imagiverse). Hickam talks about rejection as "the writer's lot": "When I started out writing for publication, I tried to learn something from each rejection. Ultimately, I began to understand that it was necessary to tailor my articles to the magazines. I read the magazines, noting the style and the emphasis, came up with an idea, wrote a dynamite query letter, and most of the time made a sale" (Imagiverse).

Writing now had become part of his daily routine; so taking a job in Germany, Hickam pursued his interest in U-boat research, and during the three years he lived in the Bavarian town of Grafenwöhr, he continued to write and research articles, while still dreaming of joining the NASA

team back home (*Sky of Stone*, p. 401). He was thirty-eight when NASA expressed an interest in hiring him, and he moved back to Huntsville to work as an engineer on the Spacelab program. Using his diving experience, he began working on NASA's Neutral Buoyancy project to teach astronauts how to manage space weightlessness by functioning in a forty-foot-deep water tank. In 1989 he became training manager of Spacelab-J, a joint project between NASA and the National Space Development Agency of Japan. The manned research module would be launched aboard the shuttle *Endeavor* in 1992. While at NASA, he would also work on Hubble Space Telescope deployment missions and Hubble repair missions. This was also the year Hickam published *Torpedo Junction* (1989), a military history published by the Naval Institute Press about the U.S. war against German U-boats. That year too, Homer, Sr., having retired some years before and moved with Elsie from Coalwood to Myrtle Beach, South Carolina, finally succumbed to black-lung disease, but not before he read with approval his son's first book. During this period Hickam's work took him often to Japan, where he trained Japanese astronauts; and as was the case when he lived in Germany, he fell in love with Japan and the Japanese people, even as love of another sort seemed to evade him (*Sky of Stone*, pp. 401–404).

Hickam tells the story of first meeting Linda Terry in the early years of his work with NASA in 1986. An earlier marriage had failed, and he was understandably wary of another such commitment. Linda was from a well-established Huntsville family, ten years his junior, an artist, and a diver like himself. They were friends for almost thirteen years before he finally asked her to marry him. Hickam relates that their friendship had blossomed into a deep sense of loyalty and affection, so when Linda received word that Hickam had developed decompression sickness while diving off the island of Guanaja in Honduras, she promptly went into action to save him, going "out on a limb for fifteen thousand more dollars than she had" to have him transported home to the NASA decompression chamber (p. 404). "I emerged, somewhat physically damaged

but determined to return to diving.… I also realized I loved Linda and that we were meant to be together." Linda Terry and Homer Hickam were married in 1998, and Hickam is quick to give Linda full credit in their partnership. Today Linda serves as his first editor and personal assistant, she manages mail and their online bookstore, and she shares his love of diving and dinosaur hunting in Montana.

A BILDUNGSROMAN TRILOGY: ROCKET BOYS, THE COALWOOD WAY, *AND* SKY OF STONE

Almost a decade after *Torpedo Junction,* Hickam published the phenomenal best seller *Rocket Boys* (1998), also made into the film *October Sky,* starring Jake Gyllenhaal, Chris Cooper, and Laura Dern. The book put Hickam into the literary spotlight, receiving a National Book Critics Circle nomination for Best Biography, a *New York Times* Great Books award, and Book-of-the-Month honors, in addition to quickly finding its way to the top of the *New York Times* best-seller list, remaining in that spot for several weeks. Surprisingly, the book and the movie had an almost serendipitously peculiar beginning. The book actually began with a request from a Smithsonian *Air & Space* editor for a quick human interest piece, which Hickam produced in just a few hours. The article, about his Rocket Boy days in Coalwood, was such a huge success and the idea so appealing that an agent picked it up immediately. In a 2012 interview, Hickam explained to Amy Beth Inverness that "the book was optioned before I'd finished writing it!" The unfinished novel then transitioned into a movie and finally into a musical: "Universal Studios bought it [the story-rights] based on an outline I did … and filming started well before publication. That's one of the reasons why the film is so different from the book in many important respects. I tried to revise the screenplay to more closely track the memoir and succeeded somewhat but not entirely." *Rocket Boys,* the musical, which Hickam did help to write as a stage play, had three annual runs in Beckley, West Virginia, between 2011 and 2013 and ran from April 17 to May 10, 2015, at the Legacy Theatre in Atlanta.

Rocket Boys—indeed the whole of the Coalwood trilogy—is a remarkable book, solidly ranked among the best coming-of-age stories in the canon; and like all great coming-of-age stories, whether contemporary novels like Terry Kay's *The Year the Lights Came On* (1976) or classics like Mark Twain's *Huckleberry Finn* (1884), contains moving and poignant issues that establish its profundity and significance as a *bildungsroman*. Much more than a memoir about growing up in Appalachia, *Rocket Boys* grapples with many of the important issues of the day, as seen and experienced by a child journeying from boyhood to adulthood, during a unique transitional period in American life—a time that Terry Kay calls "giving way," a period of change when one layer of the social fabric gives way to another, often its antithesis. What makes *Rocket Boys* so interesting is that the microcosm (the community of Coalwood, West Virginia) that Hickam focuses upon is unique even as it is universal.

From the opening pages of *Rocket Boys,* Hickam makes clear there are battles to be waged and conflicts to be resolved on many levels: between parents, siblings, races, classes, and union workers and mine owners (who mostly live somewhere other than the mountains that enrich them). As a three-year-old, Hickam is placed onto the legless lap of his grandfather, Poppy, who had lost both limbs in a mining accident. "Homer, he's just like you!" calls the grandfather to his miner son. Hickam's mother, Elsie, anxiously takes the frightened baby who clutches her tightly, his "heart beating wildly from an unidentified terror" (p. 15). "No, you're not. No, you're not," she softly croons to her son (p. 15). And so the tension is set between traditions of the past and a new world that can only be imagined for the future.

The period into which Hickam drops his story sits squarely upon the political underpinning of the cold war, with the image of *Sputnik I* looming as an emblem representing all the competition and idealism of the generation inspired by John F. Kennedy. On a night when Jake Mosby enlivens the evening by bringing his telescope to the roof of the Coalwood Club House, showing the boys an array of stars "spread out like diamonds on a vast blanket of black velvet," Sonny Hickam, now a teenager, has an epiphany, a vision about his life (*Rocket Boys,* p. 137). He tries to focus the telescope downward toward the town, only to find his viewing field blurred, but pointing the telescope upward, at the infinite and boundless night sky, gives him "a clear vision" of what he sees to be his future. Just as the tiny Russian satellite that rocks the country has set the larger world on a different trajectory, the smaller world of Coalwood has been eclipsed as well: "Sherman gasped so loud it made me look up in time to see the streak of a big blue meteor, yellow sparks flying from its head, coming out of the north. It flew silently across the sky and then fell behind a mountain." All the boys can say is "*Wow*" (p. 137), and from that point on, Sonny Hickam imagines a life different from that of his father.

There are two events in the fall of 1958 that shake up the community of Coalwood: the football team has been suspended for the season (a response to the machinations of a group of Coalwood football fathers who challenge the West Virginia high school athletic commission); and a new and rigorous curriculum has been instituted at Big Creek High School (a response to *Sputnik I*). Everything seems on edge, the world they know careening off into space on a trajectory as wobbly as one of the failed Auk missiles launched by the Rocket Boys of the Big Creek Missal Agency. These two events precipitate a range of issues for the sleepy town of Coalwood. For one, the town's attention turns from Friday night football to the six Rocket Boys and their seemingly impossible ambition to make a rocket that will aim for the stars. With no football to occupy their conversation, the town moves from following the jocks to encouraging the nerds. While Sonny's brother, Jim, is furious with this turn of events and with Homer, Sr., who was one of the overly zealous fathers that had brought down the wrath of the football commission, Sonny is gratified and encouraged. After the local paper begins to tout their progress and the company preacher Reverend Lanier preaches his prodigal son sermon (p. 105), Homer, Sr., relents

and gives the boys a launch site that is less in the line of fire for the community, and he contributes the resources and the miners' skills to make the perfect rocket. Encouraged by their Big Creek High School science teacher, Miss Riley, the Rocket Boys are off and running, their every success and failure cheered or lamented by the town. Sonny thinks to himself, "I had discovered that learning something, no matter how complex, wasn't hard when I had a reason to want to know it" (p. 143). Miss Riley defends them when authorities complain about the supposed fire hazard of their Auk missiles, lobbies for higher math and science classes, and finds them the book that will send them to the National Science Fair, *Principles of Guided Missile Design*. For Sonny, this quest to build the perfect rocket opens his eyes to a range of realities about the town and the country that he had never before considered, and many of these realities provide insight into the "fearful symmetry" that he discovers at the heart of the human experience.

This darker side of the seemingly innocuous world around him forms the substance of the small but significant epiphanies that come to Sonny Hickam over the course of the story. For example, when he learns about separate beaches for African Americans down South, he thinks for the first time about the inherent unfairness of the segregated schools in Coalwood, while his wise friend Reverend Richard, preacher at the African American Church across the mountain who remains a confidant throughout the trilogy, shows Sonny a value system that transcends the segregated world still operating across most of America. When Geneva Eggers, the local lady of ill repute, takes Sonny in on a cold and snowy night when he might have frozen to death, Sonny, unaware of her reputation, judges her more humanely than most in Coalwood. Homer, Sr., explains to his son, "Her husband got killed in the Gary mine five years ago. The police over there chased her this way. I gave her that old shack and I told Tag [the local constable] to leave her alone. Let her do what she wants…. [but] don't go see her again" (p. 219).

This learning to judge without the degrees of prejudice that inform the community is part of Sonny's coming-of-age. The mine rosters reveal surprising diversity in this company town, with Italians, Hungarians, Russians, and Poles living beside the Irish and English families, while the African Americans lived at the opposite end of town. When Sonny asks for Mr. Bykovski's help with the welding and design of his rockets, their talk turns to Sonny's hero, the legendary Dr. von Braun, who Bykovski reminds Sonny had also worked for the Nazis: "Your Dr. von Braun … helped monsters, and for that he should be blamed." However, at the same time, Bykovski tells Sonny, "There are concepts of forgiveness and redemption" that we should also be mindful of (p. 182). Later, Mr. Bykovski is transferred from the welding shop back to the mines, in some part for helping the Rocket Boys too liberally but also for the better pay that goes with working below the surface. Shortly thereafter, he is killed in a mining accident, and his wife must vacate their home. Sonny is saddled with guilt. The inequities, the unfairness, the institutions of prejudice are revealed like a Fourth of July parade to Sonny Hickam, marching before young eyes that used to take the way things were for granted. One day a schoolmate is called out of class to learn that her father "had been beheaded by a sharp piece of slate when the tunnel he was working in collapsed…. the company required the dead miner's family to move within two weeks of the accident" (p. 127). Sonny observes that "there were almost no widows in Coalwood," and the girl never returns to their class (pp. 127–128). When the company is sold off to an out-of-state steel corporation and the houses and utilities of Coalwood go up for sale, Mr. Dubonnet, the union leader and a friendly nemesis to Homer, Sr., goes on the offensive. However, the forces of change are stronger than the miners' protest, and even Reverend Lanier loses his job when the Methodists take up the mortgage on the church, and he, salaried by the company, is let go. These dark times are cyclical, and when a bullet narrowly misses the chair where Homer, Sr., relaxes at home one night, Elsie decides she has had enough and becomes determined to achieve her dream of moving to Myrtle Beach. Sonny sees

the kind of chaos that accompanies social change as the darker side of "giving way."

Still, there are other epiphanies for Sonny Hickam, who is transformed from nominal student to a kid who can teach himself calculus. Hickam writes, "I started to think a lot about infinity.... Sometimes ... I actually felt like I was flying, soaring into the night sky over Coalwood and through the dark valleys and mountain hollows that marched away in the moonlight" (p. 144). These moments of becoming lost in his study of the universe bring to him extraordinary insights. "One night," Hickam muses, "when I was having one of these visions, I had the startling revelation that plane geometry was, in fact, a message from God" (p. 144). By the end of the book, the whole town of Coalwood rallies around the Rocket Boys, who attend the National Science Fair in Chicago and win by the skin of their teeth—and only when the Coalwood community solidly has their back. Life's tragedies, such as losing Miss Riley to lymphoma and Rocket Boy Sherman to heart disease at twenty-six as well as the disasters that befall the mining town of Coalwood, are balanced by the sense of belonging and a universe that, despite its tendency toward chaos, or what Homer, Sr., calls "entropy" (p. 155), still provides moments of light to illuminate the essential darkness. And perhaps most important, Coalwood itself, despite its faults and frailty, provides a place that grounds and connects its people to a tangible reality that is "home." At the end of the book, Hickam recalls a conversation he had with the union boss Mr. Dubonnet: "Mr. Dubonnet had been right that day years ago by the railroad track when he said I had been born in the mountains and that's where I belonged, no matter what I did or where I went" (p. 329). Hickam achieves a fundamental truth and the point of this first book in the trilogy when he has Sonny remember this scene. "I didn't understand him then, but now I did," Sonny muses. "Coalwood, its people, and the mountains were a part of me and I was a part of them and always would be" (p. 329).

For a book written at the same time that the movie script and filming were in progress, there is remarkable coherence in the tone and senti-ment of both genres; however, Hickam has lamented in several interviews and in print his disdain of aspects of the process, though he says he appreciates the final product. The film director Joe Johnston warned Hickam about the irreverence of Hollywood's fingers in his artistic pie: "Homer, selling a book to Hollywood is like selling your baby to the slave traders" (Bales, p. 4). Among those artistic liberties that galled Hickam most was the title change from *Rocket Boys* to *October Sky* (an anagram of the original title), which still rankles him—as does the naming of Homer, Sr., "John" in the film. However, despite other changes, he was able to salvage the flavor of the story. For example, an early script called for the Rocket Boys to be hard-talking local toughs, and Hickam argued for the elimination of the cursing and delinquent tendencies, telling interviewer Jack Bales: "There may have been swearing among the miners, but we boys didn't talk that way" (p. 7). Happily, the profanity was cut from the film. Another sequence in the film had Sonny quitting school to work in the mines. Hickam argued that his parents would have "lived in a tree before they would have let" him quit his education (p. 7). But these issues were minor in the larger scheme of the film, which was a huge commercial success and generally well made, as one would expect from producer Chuck Gordon, who also produced *Field of Dreams* (1989). Hickam told Bales, "I can't argue with the fact that people watch this movie and they're very inspired by it. That's rare these days" (p. 7).

Attempting to follow such a remarkable success with two companion volumes might have seemed daunting to many, but Hickam really had not brought the story to closure, and many of the motifs and ideas introduced in *Rocket Boys* were fleshed out in *The Coalwood Way* and *Sky of Stone*. For example, the family dynamic is clarified in *The Coalwood Way*, which tempers the teenage angst of the first volume and conflict between father and son; and in the final book, *Sky of Stone*, this motif is laid to rest when Sonny literally comes to the rescue of Homer, Sr., who is implicated as supervisor in a mining accident. His mother, Elsie, moves more to the sidelines in the second book and is virtually erased from the

last volume, though her presence in each volume is symbolically important in the conflict between the father's dream and expectations of his son's following him as a mining engineer and the son's dreams of his own autonomy and becoming an aerospace engineer. Throughout both volumes, Coalwood is significant as a symbol for a way of life that is vanishing with each turning page and today is virtually gone.

When *The Coalwood Way* (2001) begins, it is fall 1959. Coalwood has transitioned, after a corporate buyout, from a company town run with a sense of benign paternalism to a mining subsidiary of a large steel corporation, and Sonny Hickam is plagued by a nameless sense of ennui and vague sadness that he doesn't understand. Sonny's grandfather Poppy has suffered a long illness and is dying in the hospital, and Homer, Sr., and Sonny are present on the night he passes—the father in the hospital room and Sonny finding any excuse to be out of the room. "Your Poppy loved you more than anything in the world, Sonny," Homer, Sr., tells his son, "and you couldn't even stay in the same room with him" (p. 33). The guilt laid on the son's shoulders is palpable, and the shadow of this event looms until the final pages of the book.

When Sonny attempts to articulate his name-less sadness, he first talks with his imminently logical Rocket Boy colleague Quentin, who tells him that if his mind "cannot construct the proper scenarios based on the physical and mathematical realities of the material world, then it is hardly worthy" of concern (p. 35). This advice not fully satisfying, Sonny rides his bike over to Mudhole Hollow, where he shares his feelings with Reverend Richard, pastor of the Mudhole Church of Distinct Christianity, where the "colored" congregation worships. After telling Sonny the story of the potter's wheel in Jeremiah, Reverend Richard, who serves in each of the books as Sonny's spiritual adviser and moral mentor, encourages patience and then asks Sonny to do a little encouraging himself of Homer, Sr., the mine superintendent, to provide some glass and lumber to repair the church. Sonny fulfills the request and determines to make a list of those things that cause him grief, in an effort to pinpoint the

ultimate source for his sadness. This quest for the source of the nameless sadness is the mechanism that drives the plot in *The Coalwood Way,* while the metaphor of the potter's wheel steadily evolves to suggest the person Sonny will become is a controlling image.

It is clear that there are both positive and negative aspects to those traditions and habits of mind that inform the "Coalwood way" of doing things, from the sense of community that comes with preparing for the Christmas pageant to the hurtful gossip across the fence line or the cold-shouldering by the Coalwood ladies of Dreama, the girl from across the tracks who lives with the abusive Cuke Snoddy but longs to be part of Coalwood's community. Add to these events the continued fall of coal production in the mine, which both distracts and worries Homer, Sr., and prods him to explore a risky plan to expose a new coal seam in 11 East, and Hickam has provided a range of possibilities for the unnamed sadness that haunts Sonny. Additionally, there is another haunting image that won't dissolve in Sonny Hickam's mind: "a snow goose that had accidentally landed on Cape Coalwood so many months before." In his memory, the lonely bird had landed, surveyed the landscape, then spread its wings "and taken off for a better clime. Overwhelmed and oddly disheartened," Sonny thinks to himself, "I wished with all my heart I could do the same" (p. 251).

The conflicts reach an explosion point when Elsie refuses to suffer another winter of discontent with her cantankerous family, the mine, the community, and the careless loss of her pet squirrel Chipper by the boys; in response, she heads for her sanctuary at Myrtle Beach—leaving the responsibility for the Christmas pageant to Sonny. However, the real tragedy of the unnamed sadness comes when a domestic abuse event involving the ill-fated Dreama turns to murder. As Sonny processes this extraordinary incident in Coalwood, he begins to connect the dots in his meticulous list of sources for the nameless sadness, and they all lead to what he perceives as his father's disdain for him. Sonny thinks to himself: "I knew now what had *really* been bothering me all those months. I had built my

rockets, learned calculus and differential equations, made good grades, gained the respect, even admiration, of my fellow students, my teachers, and even people from all over McDowell County. But my father … still thought I was stupid!" (p. 302). With this insight, he makes a declaration: "I give up." He decides that he hates Christmas because he hates "ugly, blighted, mean, and dirty Coalwood, the whole place and everybody in it" (p. 302). Yes, he thinks to himself: "That list had always needed just one word on it. I'd finally figured out what it was: *Dad*" (p. 303). Elsie's insistence that his father does not, in fact, disdain him is of little avail. Sonny tells her, "Dad was right to be mad.… I acted like a coward [when Poppy died]. I just couldn't stay in that room" (p. 268). But Elsie tells her son, "Sonny, I wouldn't have stayed in that room with those two Hickams for a million dollars.… Nobody's blaming you" (pp. 268–269). When she makes a reference to his list, which Sonny had never shared with her, he is incensed that she must have rummaged through the things in his room. And she tells him, "Sonny, as long as you live in my house, anything you bring into it is fair game.… Parents can do any dang thing they want if it's to make sure their kids get brought up right. That's the way God set things up [and the Coalwood way]" (pp. 269–270). In a moment of surprising revelation, Sonny actually agrees with Elsie: "Considering what else I got out of the deal, I'd take my folks, thank you very much, nosey mother and all" (p. 270).

It is, however, actually the ultra-rational Quentin who begins the process of clearing the emotional air for Sonny, who is simply overwhelmed with the flawed structure and nature of the "universe" around him. Quentin tells him, "You know, Sonny boy, … there's an evolutionary principle for what happens when an animal reaches perfection." When Sonny sarcastically wants to know what that is, Quentin responds, "It perishes" (p. 286). When Sonny discovers a set of engineering draftsman tools, a Christmas gift from his father, he begins to accept that perhaps the family dynamic is not quite as oppressive and black-and-white as he had supposed, and maybe Elsie was right when she said, "Only thing about

your dad is he forgets to tell you what he feels, especially when he's been wrong" (p. 269). At the end of the book, when the miners have successfully exposed the coal seam in the dangerous 11 East and the Christmas pageant goes off unexpectedly well, even without the flawless direction of Elsie Hickam, some of the grayness that had descended on Sonny begins to clear. When Reverend Richard's African American congregation joins in a finale that Sonny devises, much of the conflict seems put to rest. Likewise, Dreama's murderer is brought to justice, and she at last finds a quiet resting place in the Coalwood that she had so earnestly wished to be part of. This domestic violence theme complements the theme of social tolerance, and the nameless sadness that Sonny has attempted to understand throughout the story is dissipated. This theme also connects to the story line of the final novel in the trilogy.

If *The Coalwood Way* is act 2 of the Rocket Boys saga, *Sky of Stone* (2001) is both a fitting finale and the raising of the curtain for what lies beyond Coalwood for Sonny Hickam—the spreading of the wings of the "snow goose." This book takes us far afield from Sonny Hickam's dream to become an aerospace engineer, into a setting where the only stars are the mica glints in a coal-black cavern. Hickam writes: "I've been looking up at the sky ever since *Sputnik* got launched four years ago. Now my sky is five feet high and made of stone.… A sky of stone with stars of mica" (p. 161). Two important events both move the plot and drive the themes of this book, and both are directly connected to motifs established in the first two books, principally the themes of the moral complexity of this flawed universe in which we live and Hickam's uncompromising disparagement of prejudice. Those two events include the attempt by the steel company conglomerate to fire Homer, Sr., from his position as mine superintendent, based on trumped-up charges of mine-safety negligence; and the hiring of the first female training engineer to work in the Coalwood mine, Rita Walicki, who brings out every conceivable degree of shameless chauvinism possible from the un-charming world of deep mining. Of all Hickam's books, this volume is a

treasure trove of the lore, language, and mechanics of coal mining.

It is 1960, and Sonny Hickam has just finished his first year at Virginia Polytechnic Institute in Blacksburg, working on his industrial engineering degree. He has looked forward to spending the summer at the beach with Elsie and helping his mother finish her beach cottage, but an unexpected meeting between a boulder in the road and his father's car (and a firm message from his mother to stay in Coalwood to keep an eye on Homer, Sr.) interrupts Sonny's beach plans. To pay for the damaged vehicle, Sonny gets a summer job in his father's mine, and he very soon learns that Homer, Sr., is being besieged by serious charges of negligence, and his old friend Jake Mosby is disappointingly one of the company investigators. When it becomes clear that there is some mystery keeping his father from defending himself, Sonny's protective defenses and family loyalty inspire him to try to solve the mystery, and in the process he becomes involved with Rita's attempt to win her place among the miners, not just as a "girl" engineer (or "enginette" as she is condescendingly called) but the best mining engineer that his dad has ever trained. Soon Sonny knows he has to transcend his own personal chauvinism to help Rita: "I also remembered her comment that Coalwood had a history of mistreating its women. Maybe Rita was hurtling down the mine shaft this crazy night, with me dragged along behind her, because she was intent on righting all those wrongs she saw" (p. 254). Then in typical Hickam fashion, Sonny has an epiphany: "It came to me in a flash, the way things so often did. Rita was not only out to prove false the superstition about women in a coal mine; she was also out to show she was as good as any man, and maybe better. It was such an alien concept it was nearly past my ability to grasp it" (p. 254). A turning point in the story for Sonny's evolving feminist consciousness occurs when he attends a mine presentation that Homer, Sr., has arranged for Rita. Homer, Sr., tells her: "This is your project, Rita. You ride herd on it" (p. 192). When Rita begins to set up the presentation, she stumbles, and Sonny observes: "Rita, her eyes still on Dad, reached quickly for her posters and knocked them all to the floor. When everybody started to laugh, I pushed inside and helped her gather them up. I didn't say anything, just stacked them on her easel, and went back to my place" (pp. 192–193). When Sonny looks back on the scene, he notes: "I found her eyes on me, saying thanks" (p. 193). The moment is an awakening more for him than for Rita.

Sonny learns during the summer of 1960 not only a mountain of information about mining coal but also how to judge others by the content of their character, intellect, and natural ability rather than their skin color or gender—something he watches his father do as naturally as breathing. He begins to understand for the first time this quiet and undemonstrative man, his father; and he makes the connection between Homer, Sr., and the Atticus Finch of *To Kill a Mockingbird,* thinking "they shared at their core a certain decency, and honesty, too" (p. 319). The tension that Hickam builds as Sonny searches for all the pieces to the puzzle explaining the death of an experienced miner, Tuck Dillon, in the mine explosion that Homer, Sr., is being blamed for is beautifully constructed from a narrative point of view, with Hickam portraying the book's climax in the "negligence hearing" chapters. As the mystery is resolved through Sonny's efforts to defend his father, and with the assistance of Jake, whom he mistakenly thought to be on the other side, many of the other conflicts that have surfaced over the progress of the three volumes are resolved as well, including resolution of the conflict between the two brothers, Sonny and Jim. When Jim comes back to Coalwood to bury Dandy, their dog, having left summer school unexpectedly to drive home, he confesses: "I wonder how I knew to come home" (p. 313). Sonny answers, "Jim, I've come to believe there are things in life we'll never figure out. I mean, just being alive is a miracle when you stop to think about it" (p. 313).

When the mystery concerning Tuck's death is fully understood and the denouement revealed, it is Captain Laird, who returns to Coalwood to defend his protégé, Homer, Sr., who is the voice of reason. Speaking at the accident hearing and

referencing the new steel corporation that now owns the Coalwood mine, Olga Coal, Laird gets to the heart of the issue involving the trumped-up charges against Homer, Sr.: "They want their own man so he can run the mine into the ground. High profits low overhead. That's the name of the game these days" (p. 365). Turning directly to Homer, Sr., Laird explains, "Homer, Amos came down here to use poor Tuck Dillon as an excuse to see you fired—for cause, just the way my handshake agreement stipulated was the only way you could be let go. With you out of the way, Olga Coal could be sold, the steel company could get itself a pile of money without even making an ounce of steel, and the angels would play their trumpets in heaven" (pp. 365–366). When the story comes to an end, there is a sense of a new day rising and an understanding that "Coalwood" is really just a state of mind, one that will remain even when the actual place is gone. Sonny emerges from his summer "sky of stone" to discover a different sky and a different life from that of his father, with whom he now seems reconciled: "I knew then, as I faced the sky, that Coalwood would go on. Its buildings might be torn down, its mine closed, its people might event die, but Coalwood would persevere" (p. 395). Hickam leaves us with the idea that the Coalwood of his books is a place in the heart and in the mind, and if we persevere, we may be able to keep it after it has disappeared.

A BODY OF WORK: WRITING FOR POPULAR CULTURE

Though not in the publication sequence, the book that best follows the Coalwood trilogy narrative is a remarkable novel titled *Red Helmet* (2007). Hickam returns to the mechanics of coal mining as well as to his gender theme of the strong woman who invades the sacred environment of the deep mining community and, through her talent and wit, prevails. Like *Sky of Stone, Red Helmet* employs an element of mystery, and it pursues the themes that Hickam is noted for: tolerance and fairness. Song Hawkins is an Amerasian businesswoman living in New York City. She runs the high-profile conglomerate that

her father created. When she falls in love with a West Virginia mine superintendent, Cable Jordan, she throws all her common-sense business instincts to the wind and marries him, going with him to the company town of Highcoal, West Virginia. There, she is about as comfortable as salmon in the Sahara. She confesses to Doctor K, the company physician, her difficulty adjusting to life in Highcoal: "All of a sudden, I feel like I'm under a microscope." Doctor K agrees that indeed she is: "Being married to Cable, you're like Caesar's wife. He's the most important man in this town and that means you have to be perfect in every way or gossip is going to ensue" (p. 53). When Song, a hard-nosed New Yorker through and through, balks at the inherent unfairness of the situation, the doctor responds: "Gossip is never fair, or it wouldn't be gossip" (p. 53). Of course, Song and Cable, despite their love for each other, are in a doomed relationship and quickly clash, becoming almost estranged, but when Song learns that her father's corporation has purchased the company that owns Cable's mine and intends to get rid of him in order to run the mine more expediently and profitably, she decides to do something both to protect her father's investment and her husband's reputation. She can accomplish nothing without knowing the business through and through, so she joins the Red Helmet trainees in order to do that, and despite Cable's objection, she becomes a miner. However, the challenge of becoming a Red Helmet trainee, who must learn all the intricate jobs in the mine, from operating large equipment to shoveling gob (mine debris), Song finds formidable. *"I guess,"* she thinks to herself, *"I'm my mother's daughter.* That was the answer. The red cap class was her K2 [the technology challenge her mother confronted and prevailed over], a challenge that she needed to overcome, not for anyone or anything but herself" (p. 144).

The plot gives Hickam the opportunity to explore not only the day-to-day dangers of the miner's life but the mechanisms involved in a major rescue operation, particularly when there is a mining disaster that involves a gas explosion and fire, which occurs in this instance. Hickam also is able to do the kind of writing at which he

excels: detailing a complex narrative that portrays a mystery that must be solved by peeling away layers of plot and character. In this case, Song discovers that someone has been skimming from the profits by selling the most expensive coal grade for personal gain and then cooking the books. As she proves herself to be a first-rate miner, she enlists the help of some of Cable's best workers—men with such unlikely names as Square Block, Squirrel, Chevrolet, and Einstein—but the best of these are eliminated in unexpected accidents, and it is clear to Song that she is up against a practiced and ruthless foe. When the field of villains narrows and she determines exactly who her nemesis is, a tug of war ensues that pits her wits against a powerful villain, who, despite every efficient effort on her part, simply will not die. When she, Cable, and their antagonist Bum Wilkes are trapped in a mine explosion, two tensions are at work: the rescue effort to get them out and Bum's attempts to kill Song and Cable. The book is a tour de force in mystery suspense writing and a brilliant reference on mining disasters and their political ramifications, with allusions to the 2006 West Virginia Sago disaster and the 2001 Brookwood disaster in Alabama (p. 283). The book also celebrates what has become a staple in Hickam's oeuvre: the strong female protagonist.

Hickam's fiction also includes *The Dinosaur Hunter* (2010), the Helium-3 books (*Crater*, 2012; *Crescent*, 2013; and *Crater Trueblood and the Lunar Rescue Company*, 2014), the Josh Thurlow World War II series (*The Keeper's Son*, 2003; *The Ambassador's Son*, 2005; and *The Far Reaches*, 2007), and the novel *Carrying Albert Home* (2015), described in the subtitle as a "somewhat true" story of his mother, Elsie, and her early days as the young wife of a coal miner. All express common themes, among them the dangers of intolerance, the importance of family and home, the stupidity of war, and the solidarity that comes when capable men and women work together to create a better world. Hickam's fiction works are by and large high-interest adventure books, often categorized as "young adult" literature, that either take readers back in time or forward into the not-too-distant future—both set-

tings Hickam finds literarily fruitful and fascinating. Perhaps the most interesting of these is the first Josh Thurlow book, *The Keeper's Son*. The historical framework for this story (and all of Hickam's books) is well researched and stems from Hickam's own interests—in the case of *The Keeper's Son* from the scuba work Hickam did in the 1970s off the coast of North Carolina. His diving and exploration of a sunken U-boat and his later research in Germany played an important role in creating the verisimilitude of the tale and giving it a believable historical context. Hickam is interested in a portion of World War II history about which few Americans are aware: "Over four hundred Allied ships, both merchantmen and warships, were sunk by rampaging U-boats along the American east coast from January to August 1942" (*The Keeper's Son*, p. 223). Hickam's interest in this segment of World War II history can also be seen in his first published book, *Torpedo Junction* (1989), which is intimately connected to the Thurlow novels. The first novel in the series, however, finds its historical antecedents long before the war, in the tales of eighteenth- and nineteenth-century Carolina "wreckers" who scavenged the coast looking for wreckage. Josh Thurlow speaks about his own family and most everyone else who lived on the island of Killakeet when he says, "We've been on this island for two hundred years and maybe more. We were wreckers at first … and were considered outlaws. But when the Lighthouse Service came, it changed us. It made us into better people by offering us a chance to serve" (p. 223).

What makes this story particularly interesting is a characteristic of style that Hickam has employed elsewhere in his war stories—that is, giving credibility to both sides in such a conflict and attempting to show the human face of war and humans trying to function in war. Josh Thurlow is the son of the lighthouse keeper and has lived, already at thirty-one, a full and in many ways tragedy-filled life. As a fourteen-year-old, he lost his two-year-old brother, Jacob, while trying to salvage an abandoned boat. Jacob's little moth boat simply floated away in the current, disappearing forever, at least so it would appear.

This incident follows Josh throughout his life in the merchant marines, and when he finds himself back home in the summer of 1942, charged with protecting the coast from marauding U-boats, he experiences a strange convergence of the twain—in this case Josh's patrol boat the *Maudie Jane* and the *U-560* U-boat commanded by Captain Krebs, who carries with him a young "German" boy with a mysterious past. The conflict allows us to get inside the consciousness of two adversaries—Krebs and Thurlow—who under different circumstances would have been comrades, and the surprise ending takes Josh back to the incident seventeen years prior when he lost his brother Jacob.

Krebs, a German orphan who metamorphoses into the most celebrated and ruthless U-boat captain in Germany, understands that it is the anonymity that makes killing easy, while something far greater, the concept of family, transcends the darkness of war (p. 244). Hickam uses the symbol of the lighthouse to represent Truth, which is obscured in the darkness and chaos of war. Keeper Jack, Josh's father, tells him: "Truth, Josh, that's what this lens is all about. It takes the light, all scattered, and focuses it into a single beam, the way the events of our life, all strewn about," turn into a coherent picture with the proper focus. "Most people," Keeper Jack continues, "are afraid of the truth so we just let things stay scattered in our mind" (p. 96).

All the tales of Homer Hickam celebrate the uncommon amid the common in this vast universe—whether readers travel through his works back to the past, to a coal town in West Virginia, or into the far reaches of space sometime in the near future. In a quiet moment before Captain Krebs finds himself off the Carolina coast in a war of wits against Josh Thurlow, at a time directly before his own greatest personal tragedy, Krebs walks along a beach in France with the woman whom he believes is the one true love of his life, the woman whom he thinks he will marry. Miriam picks up a common cockleshell, which appears identical to every other shell on the beach to Krebs, and she tells him: "Try as you might, you can scour this beach and all the beaches of the world and you will not find a single cockleshell that looks the same as this one" (p. 116). War-weary but fascinated by the gentle woman with him, Krebs smiles and asks, "And your point is …?" Miriam smiles back and says, "My point is, Captain Krebs, that there is so much in life that we take as common, yet when we think about it, we realize it isn't common at all. This day, for instance. We shall never know another like it. No matter what we may do, even though we might retrace our steps exactly" (p. 116). Shortly after this conversation, Miriam is killed in an Allied bombing raid.

There is certainly nothing commonplace about the work and life of Homer Hickam—from his Vietnam days to working on Hubble and the Spacelab for NASA, to his diving and sea adventures, to his interest in dinosaur hunting in Montana and forays into paleontology. Homer Hickam is not a man who has sought to be heroic, but something in his upbringing or in his DNA has prompted him, from time to time, to heroic actions. And yet Hickam's best work as an author has been, more often than not, a celebration of the common and the unheroic. The remarkable storytelling of Homer Hickam helps us appreciate the common, and to the degree that we do so, we gain a clearer understanding of all in this vast universe that is so grandly uncommon.

Selected Bibliography

WORKS OF HOMER HICKAM

MEMOIR/NONFICTION

Torpedo Junction: U-Boat War off America's East Coast, 1942. Annapolis, Md.: Naval Institute Press, 1989. Reprinted, 1996.

Rocket Boys. New York: Delacourt Press, 1998.

The Coalwood Way. New York: Delacourt Press, 2001.

Sky of Stone. New York: Delacourt Press, 2001. New York: Random House, 2002.

We Are Not Afraid. Deerfield Beach, Fla.: Health Communications, 2002.

My Dream of Stars: From Daughter of Iran to Space Pioneer. With Anousheh Ansari. New York: Palgrave Macmillan, 2010.

From Rocket Boys to October Sky. Huntsville, Ala.: Homer Hickam Books, 2013. Kindle edition, 2013.

FICTION

Back to the Moon. New York: Delacourt Press, 1999.

The Keeper's Son. New York: Thomas Dunne Books/St. Martin's Press, 2003.

The Ambassador's Son. New York: Thomas Dunne Books/ St. Martin's Press, 2005.

The Far Reaches. New York: Thomas Dunne Books/St. Martin's Press, 2007.

Red Helmet. Nashville, Tenn.: Thomas Nelson, 2007.

The Dinosaur Hunter. New York: Thomas Dunn Books/St. Martin's Press, 2010.

Crater. Nashville, Tenn.: Thomas Nelson, 2012.

Paco, the Cat Who Meowed in Space. Huntsville, Ala.: Homer Hickam Books, 2012.

Crescent. Nashville, Tenn.: Thomas Nelson, 2013.

Crater Trueblood and the Lunar Rescue Company. Nashville, Tenn.: Thomas Nelson, 2014.

Carrying Albert Home: A Novel; The Somewhat True Story of a Man, His Wife, and Her Alligator. New York: William Morrow, 2015.

CRITICAL AND BIOGRAPHICAL STUDIES

"Homer H. Hickam, Jr. (Aerospace Engineer and Writer)." *Current Biography* 61, no. 10:35 (2000).

Morgan, Robert. "Notes from Underground." *New York Times Book Review,* October 21, 2001, p. 22. (Review of *Sky of Stone.*)

Owens, William T. "Country Roads, Hollers, Coal Towns, and Much More: A Teacher's Guide to Teaching About Appalachia." *Social Studies* 91, no. 4:178–186 (2000).

INTERVIEWS

"About Homer." Homer Hickam website. http://homer hickam.com/about-homer/

Bales, Jack. "Sending Spirits Soaring," and "*October Sky*: From Coalwood to Hollywood." *Free Lance-Star* (Fredericksburg, Va.), March 16, 2002, pp. 3–4, 7. https://news.google.com/newspapers?nid=1298&dat=20020316&id=BzEzAAA AIBAJ&sjid=dwgGAAAAIBAJ&pg=4507,4083530&hl=en

"An Interview with Homer Hickam, Jr." Imagiverse Education Consortium, October 10, 2003. http://www.imagi verse.org/interviews/homerhickam/homer_hickam_10_09_03.htm

Inverness, Amy Beth. "Interview with Homer Hickham." May 25, 2012. http://amybethinverness.com/2012/05/25/interview-with-homer-hickam/

Norman, Julian. "Homer H. Hickam Jr. Interview." *Morgantown Dominion Post,* 1999. http://www.mountainlit.com/essays3.htm

FILM BASED ON THE WORK OF HOMER HICKHAM

October Sky. Screenplay by Lewis Colick. Directed by Joe Johnson. Universal Studios, 1999.

ROBERT E. HOWARD

(1906—1936)

Jonas Prida

ROBERT ERVIN HOWARD, creator of Conan the Barbarian and arguably the first writer to explore the genre known as heroic fantasy, lived his entire life in the scrub plains of central Texas. His fantastical gleaming towers are in stark contrast to his rough and tumble youth and life in Cross Plains, Texas. But one helped create the other, and Howard's extraordinary imagination was fed by a mixture of cultural isolation, cowboy tall tales, his father's eclectic library, and wide-ranging correspondence.

Seeing Howard only as the writer behind "the mightiest warrior of the Hyborian Age" ignores large parts of his work. Although Conan remains Howard's most famous character, he also turned his love of Scottish and Irish history into Bran Mak Morn, the last Pictish king, willing to dabble in black magic to defeat the Roman Empire. Taking cues from Talbot Mundy's Middle Eastern adventurers, Howard constructed El Borak, an American adventurer living on the border of modern-day Afghanistan. Mining seventeenth-century English popular history, Howard summoned Solomon Kane, a grim-faced Puritan whose skills with a broadsword were equaled by his wanderlust. His last literary creation, Breckenridge Elkins, was in the tradition of Southwest humor, mixing slapstick violence, cartoonish dialect, and western settings. He wrote boxing stories, horror pieces, poems, and "spicy stories." In his effort to become a professional writer, Howard tried any market, turning his rapid-fire narratives on whatever had a chance of making a sale.

Howard's wide-ranging literary style is directly connected to the rise of pulp magazines in the 1920s and 1930s. Like his frequent correspondent H. P. Lovecraft, Howard published extensively in *Weird Tales,* "The Unique Magazine." His boxing stories were in pulp magazines with titles such as *Fight Stories* and *Action Stories,* while El Borak was published in *Top-Notch* and *Thrilling Adventures.* Pulps were a natural fit for Howard's writing, with their emphasis on action, lean descriptions, and exotic locales. As his fighting sailor Steve Costigan claims, "Action is what I crave," and so did the audiences for pulps. At the same time, the pulps helped shape Howard's style and content; he was willing to shift what he wrote to make a living as a writer, and the pulps favored nonstop action, which Howard was more than willing to provide.

Howard's life and suicide at the age of thirty became subject to a variety of misconceptions and rumors. Stemming largely from the well-meaning but flawed biography *Dark Valley Destiny* (1983), written by fellow fantasy writer L. Sprague de Camp, as well as a confusing posthumous legacy, the actual Robert Howard was eclipsed by the caricature of a neurotic writer, deeply in the grips of an unresolved Oedipal crisis, in love with a woman he couldn't have because of a meddling mother. But more recent research and revitalization in Howard studies in general are helping bring the actual Howard to light.

BIOGRAPHY

Robert Howard was born on January 22, 1906, in Peaster, Texas, west of Fort Worth, the only child of Hester Jane Ervin and Isaac Mordecai Howard, a physician. The small family led the itinerant existence of a country doctor: by the time Howard was nine, the family had moved from Peaster to Seminole to Bronte to Oran to Bagwell, Texas. Isaac Howard liked to engage in financial speculation, and it is likely that the

combination of his professional duties and his desire to get rich led to his movements all over Texas. His wife, who battled sickness for most of her adult life, enjoyed the status that her physician husband offered but disliked his constant travel and her family's frequent moves. However, in 1915 the Howards moved to Cross Cut, and they would live in one of three towns southeast of Abilene—Cross Cut, Burkett, and Cross Plains—for the rest of Robert and Hester's lives.

One of the few upsides to Howard's life during this period of constant travel was access to his father's library and his mother's interest in poetry and storytelling. Dr. Howard's library included medical textbooks, popular histories, and, influentially, texts on mysticism and reincarnation. A reader from an early age, Robert Howard enjoyed popular authors such as Harold Lamb, Rudyard Kipling, Edgar Allan Poe, and Arthur Conan Doyle. Hester frequently recited long passages of poetry from memory. Additionally, Howard's extended family was full of stories: Howard would never forget a relative's cook, "Aunt" Mary Bohannan, who grew up during slavery and horrified and delighted a young Robert Howard with tales of life before emancipation. One of her stories featuring a particularly fiendish house mistress is the likely basis for Howard's masterful "Pigeons from Hell." It was also at an early age that Howard decided on his future occupation, apparently telling the local postmistress, "Some day I am going to be an author and write stories about pirates and maybe cannibals" (Finn, p. 43). He was more right than he knew.

By 1919 the Howards had moved permanently to Cross Plains, a town of roughly two thousand people. Here Howard finished his required schooling, but his parents wanted him to continue his education despite his dislike for it, once commenting, "What I hated was the confinement—the clock-like regularity of everything; the regulation of my speech and actions; most of all the idea that someone considered himself or herself in authority over me" (Finn, p. 89). He and his mother moved to Brownwood, a larger city about thirty-five miles from Cross Plains, and home to Howard Payne College. It was in

Brownwood High School's student paper, the *Tattler*, that Howard published his first work in 1922. Howard continued to publish poems, stories, and humorous anecdotes in the *Tattler* until his graduation in 1923.

Though he humored his father by staying in Brownwood to take business classes, what Robert Howard was really doing was writing. He was already familiar with pulps: he purchased a copy of *Adventure* when he was fifteen and claimed he still had it in 1933. He was submitting material to *Adventure*, but it was *Weird Tales* that gave Howard his first break, publishing his Cro-Magnon versus Neanderthal story "Spear and Fang" in 1924. Howard was paid fifteen dollars and was now an author at the age of eighteen, little knowing that he had lived more than half his life.

Moving back and forth between Cross Plains and Brownwood to take classes occasionally, Howard continued to hold odd jobs—soda jerk, trash hauler, geologist helper. Unsurprisingly, writing was his chosen profession. In 1926 *Weird Tales* wanted to put his story "Wolfshead" on the cover of its April issue. But someone in the office had lost the original, and the magazine requested a carbon copy. Howard, still a novice writer, had not used one. The story goes that he spent the next day and night retyping "Wolfshead" from memory.

Over the course of the next two years Howard graduated from Payne's Business School; met Harold Preece, who would become a longtime friend; wrote large amounts of poetry and his semiautobiographical novel *Post Oaks and Sand Roughs*; and saw the acceptance of his first Kull of Atlantis story in 1927 and his first Solomon Kane tale in 1928. Because of the income generated through sales to *Weird Tales,* Howard was able to stop working his hated odd jobs and dedicate himself full time to writing. Howard later commented, "The idea of a man making his living by writing seemed, in that hardy environment, so fantastic that even today I am sometimes myself assailed by a feeling of unreality."

With the exuberance of the 1920s turning into the desperation of the 1930s, Howard was publishing more stories than ever. In addition to

his material in *Weird Tales,* he entered into the world of boxing magazines. A longtime aficionado of the sport, Howard found it easy to mix his fight knowledge with his developing skills as a writer. In July 1929 his first Steve Costigan story was published in *Fight Stories,* and since payment from *Weird Tales* was frequently interrupted, a second source of income was welcomed. Howard also published a ghostly boxing story in *Argosy* the same year, earning himself one hundred dollars. Although Howard was making more money than ever, his family life was less successful. His father spent the first part of the year visiting Spur, Texas, a town about 150 miles from Cross Plains, leaving Howard and his mother behind.

The year 1930 saw the beginning of the strange literary correspondence and friendship between two seemingly opposite characters. Howard wrote a letter to *Weird Tales* editor Farnsworth Wright, praising the work of the writer H. P. Lovecraft from Providence, Rhode Island. Lovecraft wrote back, and so began a letter-writing relationship that continued until Howard's death. In addition to discussing cosmology, philosophy, and history, these letters most famously include an ongoing dialogue about civilization and barbarism. Howard took the side of barbarism, frequently decrying the excesses and decadence of advanced civilizations, while Lovecraft defended civilization, citing art and culture as its obvious benefits. In increasingly lengthy missives, the two mixed pointed jabs with discussion of football games and travel. These letters also introduced Howard to other members of Lovecraft's circle and fellow *Weird Tales* writers August Derleth, Frank Belknap Long, and Clark Ashton Smith.

Howard continued to sell stories into 1931, but a bank failure wiped out his savings. However, late-arriving checks from earlier *Weird Tales* publications kept Howard from true destitution. By 1932 he had hired Otis Adelbert Kline, a pulp author turned literary agent. In Kline, Howard had access to untapped markets, and through his relationship with Kline, Howard would see his greatest commercial and literary success. By 1933 Howard was well into his Conan cycle; with the

publication of "The Phoenix on the Sword" (1932) and "The Tower of the Elephant" (1933), *Weird Tales* would continue to be the exclusive source for Conan material. But following Kline's advice, he also branched out, placing more boxing stories, historical adventures, and even a detective piece.

In 1934 Novalyne Price, to whom Howard had earlier been introduced, moved to Cross Plains. She was a schoolteacher with literary ambitions, and, as importantly, she was interested in meeting Robert Howard again. Despite his mother Hester's best efforts at keeping them apart, including intercepting phone calls, Robert and Novalyne began their on-again, off-again relationship. Spending all day driving in Howard's newly purchased car or sharing dinner and ice cream, the couple could be on the best of terms one day and fighting the next. Much of this tension was caused by Hester's declining health; in the spring of 1935 she underwent gallbladder surgery and was hospitalized for a month. Tired of Howard's inability to break free of his mother, Novalyne began to end the relationship, finally accepting a graduate position at Louisiana State University in early 1936, the last year of Howard's life. Her memoir of their friendship, *One Who Walked Alone,* was published in 1986 and eventually turned into the film *The Whole Wide World* (1996).

Throughout 1935, Howard was consistently selling boxing stories, desert adventures, and his newly penned westerns. He was finished with Conan, although *Weird Tales* still owed him money for several of the stories. His new character, the buffoonish cowboy Breckenridge Elkins, found a ready audience in *Action Stories,* and Howard was asked to create similar figures for *Argosy* and *Cowboy Stories.* Howard strung together his Elkins stories to create *A Gent from Bear Creek,* published posthumously in 1937, which remains one of the rarest Howard first editions.

By 1936 it became obvious that Hester Howard was dying, and her illness was wearing on her son. In one of his last letters to Lovecraft, Howard wrote: "She is subject to distressing and continual sweats, and naturally has to have

constant attention, so I find little if any time to write" (Finn, p. 290). Although his writing was in demand from a variety of publications, Howard lacked the energy to do much of anything. On June 8, Hester Howard fell into a coma, and on the 11th, after discussing with a nurse his mother's chances to regain consciousness, Robert Howard walked from the house he had lived in with his mother and father for the last eight years and into his car, where he shot himself in the head, dying later that day. His mother died the next day, and the two were buried in Brownwood's Greenleaf Cemetery.

As befits a storyteller of Howard's magnitude, even his death became a story of its own. In Howard's wallet was found the verse, "All fled, all done; so lift me on the pyre; / The feast is over and the lamps expire" (Finn, p. 295). Although later scholarship confirmed that the couplet was typed before Howard's actual suicide, the legend quickly grew that it was Howard's last writing before walking to his car. In fact, the lines are a paraphrase from "The House of Caesar" by the English poet Viola Garvin. Later, Otis Kline would add his own spin to Howard's last moments, claiming that after typing the note, Robert Howard went to his mother and said "It's done" before walking out of the house.

Robert Howard's death at age thirty robbed American letters of a strong regional voice, a writer who could blend the dusty landscapes of Texas with the comic adventures of cowpokes, pettifoggers, and mountain men. A man with so much energy he would yell out his stories as he wrote them, Howard published more than a hundred stories from his first tale in 1924, created an entire genre, and birthed a character still in circulation.

POETRY

Robert Howard was a verse writer as much as he was a prose writer. However, poetry, then as now, did not pay well, and most of Howard's poems either appeared as page filler in *Weird Tales* or remained in his notebooks until after his death.

But his verse gives another glimpse into the topics Howard found intriguing and the intellectual struggle in which he was engaged. His poetry, as collected in *Robert E. Howard: Selected Poems* (2012), edited by Frank Coffman, runs from the adventurous to the sexual, from ballads about beer to songs about werewolves. Throughout his poetry, one finds an author playing with language and using the conventional forms of the early twentieth century to construct energetic, highly readable work.

Befitting a writer who looked at his world as the struggle between barbarism and civilization, Howard's work is filled with lines about the deceitful, hypocritical demands of modernity contrasting with nature's ferocity. For example, in "A Warning," Howard writes of "a world of paper and wood / Culture and cult and lies" (p. 18) and captures a similar sentiment "A Word from the Outer Dark," which gave rise to the title of a seminal collection of Howard essays titled *The Dark Barbarian*.

Howard also wrote horrific poems for *Weird Tales*, and many of these poems reference Lovecraft's expanding Cthulhu Mythos. In a 1932 issue, a reader might have glanced at Howard's piece "Arkham," which uses the name of Lovecraft's fictional Massachusetts town where "inhuman figures leer and slink," a nod to Lovecraft's fascination with degeneration (p. 298). Howard also wrote about another favorite theme of *Weird Tales*: the thing humanity was not meant to know. His sonnet "Forbidden Magic," published in July 1929, includes the lines, "He whispered hints of weird, unhallowed sight; / I followed—" (p. 309).

Not all of Howard's poetry is pessimistic horror. In letters to his friend Tevis Clyde Smith, Howard writes a poem to his typewriter, comically reciting the terrors of a broken key, a hung space bar, and a worn-out ribbon. In his piece "This Is a Young World," Howard takes an almost Whitman-like approach to existence, celebrating the "wildness" and "laughing recklessness" of nature "That shows a kindred for my soul" (p. 215).

In almost all of Howard's poetry, one aspect is apparent: his love for life itself. His "A Sonnet

of Good Cheer" perfectly encapsulates this idea: "Let me arise, a-lust for love and strife" (p. 128). Following these passions through more than eight hundred poems, Howard's verse distills his love and strife down to its primal essence.

HORROR STORIES

As a frequent contributor to *Weird Tales,* Howard wrote a variety of horror stories, including the frequently anthologized "Pigeons from Hell," later an episode on Boris Karloff's *Thriller* television show. He joined fellow *Weird Tales* writers H. P. Lovecraft, Robert Bloch, and August Derleth in contributing to the Cthulhu myth cycle—Howard's fictional grimoire, *Unaussprechlichen Kulten* (roughly translated *Nameless Cults*), along with its fictional writer, Friedrich Wilhelm Von Junzt, have joined the *Necronomicon* and Abdul Alhazred in the canon of fictional texts and authors frequently asked about in rare book stores. Starting with "Wolfshead," Howard's first cover story for *Weird Tales,* written when he was twenty, and continuing throughout his career, his horror fiction weaves history with imagination, and this combination gives texts like "Children of the Night," "The Black Stone," and "Pigeons from Hell" their power.

"The Black Stone," appearing in the November 1931 *Weird Tales,* introduced readers to Von Junzt's book, where "there are statements and hints to freeze the blood of a thinking man" (*Horror Stories,* p. 160). The story's narrator, having accessed one of the few unexpurgated copies, travels to the Hungarian village of Stregoicavar, in hopes of discovering the titular monolith. While there, he learns of the village's bloody history: the original inhabitants, who had a reputation for witchcraft and kidnapping, were slaughtered during a sixteenth-century Turkish invasion. On Midsummer's Night, the narrator finds the monolith. Unfortunately, he also finds himself hypnotized and, while dozing, witnesses an infant being ritually sacrificed and the appearance of a toadlike monster who reflects "all the lust, abysmal greed, obscene cruelty and monstrous evil that has stalked the sons of men since their ancestors mowed blind and hairless in the

tree-tops" (p. 171). Waking with this unearthly knowledge, the narrator returns to the site three days later and recovers a parchment explaining the town's obliteration: the Turks had discovered the secret of the stone, slayed an earthly incarnation of the toad god, and erased all evidence of its existence. Only on Midsummer's Night do the stone and its worshippers flicker back into existence. The story ends with the traditional Howard pessimism: "Man was not always master of the earth—and is he now?" (p. 175).

Like other Howard texts, "The Black Stone" incorporates historical events such as the Turkish invasion of Hungary with the scientific racism of the 1920s and 1930s: the toad worshippers, for example, have "Slavic and Magyar features, but those features were degraded" (p. 169). Howard's history of the area is cobbled together from whatever textbooks he or his father had around their house, but the scant details of Stregoicavar work for the tale, providing Howard with enough evidence to work with but without the weight of specifics to burden the narrative. Von Junzt's *Nameless Cults* adds to the patina of authenticity, with Howard listing dates and publishers for the versions of the text. The story opens with a quatrain from Justin Geoffrey, the mad poet of *People of the Monolith,* another Howard invention, and includes references to other fictional texts, *Remnants of Lost Empires* and *Magyar Folklore.*

"Pigeons" gains its power from Howard's engagement with questions of slavery and its aftermath. The pigeons of the title are holdovers from African American folklore about the souls of the Blassenvilles let out of Hell at sunset. Old Jacob's story of the *zuvembie* comes from Haiti and, before that, the Slave Coast of West Africa. Miss Celia, who becomes the bloodthirsty monster, is from the West Indies and is rumored to have danced in "one of their horrible ceremonies" (p. 444). Joan, Celia's servant, is described as a "mulatto," cultural code for the product of white masters and black slaves. The house itself saw its glory before the Civil War and now is in ruins. Joan's revenge for the abuse at her mistress's hands is a Southern version of the sins of the past manifesting in the present. Jacob's

line "Time means naught to the *zuvembie*; an hour, a day, a year, all is one" (p. 440) is as true for the horrors of slavery in "Pigeons" as it is for the undead Celia. "Pigeons" made its mark on no less than Stephen King, who claimed it was one of the finest horror stories of our century.

HISTORICAL ADVENTURES

Historical pulps like *Oriental Stories, Thrilling Adventure,* and *Golden Fleece* were another outlet for Howard. These descendants of Frank Munsey's *Argosy,* arguably the first pulp, focused on exotic locales and historical events, mixing true-life characters such as Richard the Lionhearted with fictional adventurers. Given Howard's long-standing interest in history, he enthusiastically entered the market when Farnsworth Wright started *Oriental Tales* in 1930. Wright wrote to Howard and told him that he wanted "tales of the Crusades, of Genghis Khan, of Tamerlane, and the wars between Islam and Hindooism," and Howard wasted no time producing a series of historical tales that blend the usual Howard swordplay with the clash of empires (Finn, p. 179).

His first story, "Hawks of Outremer," published in 1931 in *Oriental Tales,* follows Cormac FitzGeoffrey, a renegade half-Norman, half-Gael adventurer who has a grinning skull emblazoned on his shield and wields a sword taken from a slain Norse sea king. FitzGeoffrey seeks vengeance against Nureddin, an Arab chief who has captured a fortress on the disputed border between the Christian Crusaders and the army of the Muslim sultan (and real historical figure) Saladin. FitzGeoffrey finds his way into the fortress at the same time that Saladin does; in the duel that follows, FitzGeoffrey slays Nureddin, realizing that his enemy is also plotting against Saladin. Fully expecting to be killed by Saladin, FitzGeoffrey instead is forced to recognize that "this attitude of fairness, justice and kindliness, even to foes, was not a craft pose of Saladin … but a natural nobility of the Kurd's nature" (*Sword Woman,* p. 195). The tale ends with Saladin freeing FitzGeoffrey and proclaiming, "Your road to the west is clear" (p. 195). In a story where almost everyone is deceitful, including FitzGeoffrey, the one honorable character is Saladin, and it is to Howard's credit that he occasionally avoided the casual racism and stereotyping found in many pulp stories.

A less traditional Howard adventure is "The Shadow of the Vulture," from January 1934 issue of the *Magic Carpet Magazine.* "Shadow" uses the historical siege of Vienna by Suleyman I as the background for the pairing of the drunken swordsman Gottfried von Kalmbach and the flamboyant Red Sonya. Faced with overwhelming odds, Sonya and Kalmbach lead a variety of tactical missions to delay the fall of Vienna and, implicitly, the fall of the West. Vienna's walls hold, and, in a final act of defiance, Sonya and Gottfried decapitate and send the severed head of Suleyman's military commander to him at his palace in Constantinople.

"Vulture" features many standard Howard devices: graphic violence ("Kalmbach watched a Transylvanian gunner being carried off the wall, his brains oozing from a hole in his head"); endurance in the face of death ("The aged commander, fired with superhuman energy, trod the walls, braced the faltering, aided the wounded, fought in the breaches side by side with the common soldiers"); and ironic descriptions of flawed protagonists ("lusty snores resounded where a figure reclined in state in a ragged cloak… It was the paladin Gottfried von Kalmbach who slept the sleep of innocence and ale" (*Sword Woman,* pp. 401–402, 410, 394). But what makes "Vulture" an outlier in Howard's sword-swinging adventure tales is Red Sonya. She is one of the few female characters in Howard—Bêlit and Valeria in the Conan cycle are the others—whose position is not simply ornamental. While there is no doubt of her femininity, with Kalmbach "eying in open admiration the splendid swell of her bosom beneath the pliant mail, the curves of her ample hips and rounded limbs," she is a terrible foe: "Her strokes followed each other too quickly for the eye to follow; her blade was a blur of white fire, and men went down like ripe grain before a reaper" (pp. 402, 404). Sonya several times saves Kalmbach's life, inverting the usual male-savior/female-in-distress dynamic. Sonya's

tactics and personality help save Vienna, with Kalmbach frequently caught up the circumstances of battle instead of dictating them.

Influenced by Talbot Mundy's Eastern adventures such as *King of the Khyber Rifles* (1916), as well as other Mundy works he read in the early 1920s, Howard used Afghanistan and Central Asia as settings for his El Borak tales. El Borak, whose English name is Francis Xavier Gordon, played his part in the Great Game, the clash between the British and Russian empires over these lands in the late nineteenth and early twentieth centuries. Filled with Russian spies, German agents, and British imperialists as well as Kurds, Arabs, and other groups, stories with titles such as "The Daughter of Erlik Khan," published in *Top-Notch* in 1934, and "Son of the White Wolf" in *Thrilling Adventures* (1936) were another welcome source of income. Gordon, the Texan at the center of the stories, is skilled with a gun and a horse, but his most important attribute is the loyalty he commands in his men. Possessed of an almost superhuman confidence in himself, Gordon slips his way into and out of spots that even the Afghans fear. At their best, the El Borak stories are filled with plot, counterplot, and alliances that last only as long as the most recent threat. The El Borak stories also are as relevant now as when they were written; current events in Afghanistan and the Kurdish regions of Syria and Iraq provide distant echoes of the adventures of Francis Gordon.

Howard, like other pulp writers of the 1930s, also tried his hand at writing for the "spicies," pulp magazines that emphasized sex and violence, usually with extremely lurid covers. With titles such as *Spicy Detective Stories* or *Spicy Mystery*, these pulps were generally seen as straining even the line of good taste that *Weird Tales* presented. Howard published five stories in *Spicy-Adventure Stories*, each featuring Wild Bill Clanton, who reads almost as a parody of Howard's overtly masculine heroes. Described in "She Devil" as a "broad-shouldered, clean-waisted, heavy-armed man with wetly plastered black hair," Clanton is Steve Costigan or Conan without their moral compunctions (*The She Devil,* p. 5). He leads the captain and the first mate into a cannibal ambush,

beats another sailor almost to death, and drunkenly seduces Raquel, the titular she-devil, while supposedly steering the ship.

In "Murderer's Grog" (1936), Clanton finds himself near what was then the Afghan border with India, facing incorruptible members of the British Empire on the one hand and gun smugglers on the other. Like El Borak, Clanton tries to play the sides against each other, but fails after he is rebuffed by a duplicitous woman and then drugged with wine laced with hashish, which sends him into a rage. Early in the story, Howard writes about Clanton, "The uncertainty of life—as he led it—had taught him to take what he wanted when it was offered—and frequently when it wasn't" (*The She Devil,* p. 88). Howard's spicy stories offer many of the same features as his work in *Top-Notch* or *Weird Tales*—action, exotic locations, intrigue—but with a sordidness that marks them as something different altogether.

Howard's historical adventures show the range of his reading, as well as the scope of his imagination. From Viking invasions to imperial entanglements, these stories feature antiheroes, entertaining villains, exotic settings, and the action sequences for which Howard is famous. Although overshadowed by his more famous stories, his historical tales display the various forms that Howard's writing took in order to make a living.

PRE-CONAN FANTASY ADVENTURE

Before there was Conan, Howard constructed three other characters that later coalesced into his most famous creation. Solomon Kane, Kull of Atlantis, and Bran Mak Morn embody Howard's usual preoccupations of physical stamina and endurance, violent temperament, and pessimistic outlook. But none of these characters is a replica of the others, and each fills a niche in his development as a writer. In the Kull stories, Howard develops the earth's prehistory, placing Kull as the king of precataclysm Valusia, providing the backdrop for Conan's Hyborian Age. The seventeenth-century Puritan Solomon Kane wanders Europe and Africa, fighting a variety of

mortal and supernatural evils from the dawn of time. Bran Mak Morn, last of Pict kings, traces his lineage back to one of Kull's companions and is in constant battle with imperial Roman forces. Howard worked on the characters nearly simultaneously between the years 1928 and 1932, publishing a few of each character's stories before moving to the next one.

Solomon Kane was the first in print, with "Red Shadows" as the cover story for the August 1928 issue of *Weird Tales*. Kane, wandering the French countryside, finds a dying girl who recounts a raid on her village by Le Loup, a local brigand. Kane, displaying his characteristic monomania for vengeance, follows Le Loup across Europe and into Africa. It is when Kane and Le Loup land in Africa that "Shadows" changes from a standard tale of vengeance to something more interesting. As Kane follows Le Loup, he hears, "The soul of Africa (said the drums); the spirit of the jungle; the chant of the gods of outer darkness … the gods men knew when dawns were young, … the Black Gods (sang the drums)" (*Savage Tales*, p. 43). In the next paragraph, the dynamic of the jungle changes, and with it, Kane's character changes: "You too are of the night (sang the drums); there is the strength of darkness, the strength of the primitive in you; come back down the ages; let us teach you, let us teach you (chanted the drums)" (p. 44). Kane's internal conflict between righteous Puritan and primitive, joyous adventurer leads to introspective moments rarely seen in pulp figures.

One of the darkest Solomon Kane stories is 1932's "Wings in the Night," the last Kane published in Howard's lifetime. In it, Kane battles the akaana, winged creatures sporting fanged teeth, hooked beaks, and talons. After being seriously injured in an aerial battle with one of these monsters, Kane is nursed back to health by villagers who find him in the jungle. While there, he learns of the village's grisly position: surrounded by cannibals, they are also used as food by the akaana. A surprise raid leads to a slaughter of the village Kane had sworn to protect, leaving him "a symbol of Man, staggering among the tooth-marked bones and severed grinning heads of humans, brandishing a futile ax, and scream-

ing incoherent hate at the grisly, winged shapes of Night" (p. 312). His plan for vengeance unfolds under the severed head of the tribal chief, Goru, which Kane keeps in place to remind him of his failures. After trapping all the akaana in a hut filled with food, he burns them alive, thankfully still insane enough not to notice "that the scent was of that nauseating and indescribable odor that only human flesh emits when burning" (pp. 319–320).

"Wings" is a fitting coda to the figure of Solomon Kane. It contains some of Howard's bleakest writings, from Kane's Shakespearian-tinged blasphemy—"for if the brazen-hoofed gods made Man for their sport and plaything, they also gave him a brain that holds craft and cruelty greater than any other living thing" (p. 315)—to his delusional conversations with Goru's rotting head. Kane's act of kindness toward the village leads to their destruction, and his blood-rage leads to the eradication of a race more ancient than humanity. The tale ends with Kane again feeling the call to adventure, the call that started in his first encounter with the jungle drums.

As Howard was writing Solomon Kane, he was working on Kull, an exile from precataclysm Atlantis and soon-to-be king of Valusia, the age's most powerful kingdom. Kull outwardly shares many characteristics with Conan. He is a barbarian who, through his own physical power, ends up ruling a more sophisticated kingdom. But Kull is an introspective figure, given to philosophical musings about the existence of reality and illusion, as likely to brood on his throne as wield his ax. Although only three Kull stories were published during Howard's lifetime, they are important ingredients in his formulation of Conan.

The first Kull story, "The Shadow Kingdom" (1929), incorporates both Kull's barbarian nature and Howard's philosophical question "What … were the realities of life? Ambition, power, pride?" The story begins with Kull as king of Valusia, but his kingdom is surrounded by treachery. Many of Kull's subjects see him as a lawless adventurer who stole a throne. After meeting with the Pict warrior Brule, the Spear-slayer, he is shown the truth behind the treachery:

serpent men who can look like humans have infiltrated the castle and are waiting to strike. The rest of "The Shadow Kingdom" plays out as a paranoid dream, with Kull and Brule killing guardsmen and advisers who look like friends, as well as learning of the darker truth behind the conspiracy. The serpent men are holdovers from an earlier Earth, slowly infiltrating positions of power, replacing kings and queens with their own kind. Surrounded by enemies at what they think is a courtly feast, Brule recites an ancient phrase that unveils all the serpents, and in proper Howard fashion, the "rest was a scarlet maze" of killing (*Kull: Exile of Atlantis,* p. 45). Kull and Brule then realize that they have been tricked again, and a replica Kull is now replacing him in the actual court. Kull kills the serpent king, and declares himself true king of Valusia.

Questions about reality and illusion are even more apparent in "The Mirrors of Tuzun Thune" (1929), which follows a weary Kull, who has found that "the speech of men is as the empty rattle of a jester's bell and the feel comes of things unreal" as he searches to break his ennui (p. 55). Hearing the rumor that the wizard Tuzun Thune has answers to questions of life and death, Kull and Brule voyage to his house. Here Kull looks deeply into the various mirrors of Thune, finding reflections of his past, present, and future in their surfaces. He finds himself spending more time staring into the mirrors, searching for answers about the reflections they contain: "Am I no more than a shadow, a reflection of himself—to him, as he to me? And if I am the ghost, what sort of a world lives upon the other side of this mirror?" (p. 59). It is only when Brule kills Thune that the illusion in the mirror breaks, and Kull learns of the plot to trap him within the reflections. But the text ends with Kull being even less sure of what counts as reality after seeing the other side of the mirror.

Howard's Pict king Bran Mak Morn appeared in a series of *Weird Tales* from 1930 to 1932. Although only appearing in four stories, Mak Morn is another memorable Howard creation, with the tale "The Dark Man" (1931) giving its name to a Howard journal and "Worms of the Earth" (1932) consistently ranked as one of the best Howard texts by readers. In Bran Mak Morn, the philosophical pessimism of Solomon Kane is mixed with Howard's love of Scottish and Irish folklore about the Picts and the little people who battle a range of imperial conquerors.

"Worms of the Earth," published in *Weird Tales,* follows Mak Morn on his supernatural quest to stop Roman legions from conquering the remnants of the Caledonian Pict kingdom. Bran, "a pure-bred Pict of the Old Race," has heard rumors of a door that will access the worms of the earth, a race older than humanity that has been forced underground by unending warfare with Picts, Britons, and other tribes. Mak Morn thinks he can use these creatures to destroy the Romans and restore the Picts' former glory. After exchanging a night of love with Atla, a half-snake woman, in order to find the door, he finds an elaborate tunnel complex where he steals a Black Stone that is held sacred by those beneath the ground. After offering the return of the stone for a promise of bringing Titus Sulla, the Roman leader, to Mak Morn, Mak Morn learns of the underdwellers' vengeance on the Romans. He arrives at the ruins of the Tower of Trajan and finds one survivor, who tells him of the constant burrowing the soldiers heard before the collapse of the tower. He later discovers that the worms of the earth have also kept their vow to bring him Sulla: "In the ghastly light, Bran, soul-shaken, saw the blank glassy eyes, the bloodless features, the loose, writhing, froth-covered lips of sheer lunacy" (*Bran Mak Morn,* pp. 123–124). After killing Sulla in disgust, Mak Morn returns the Stone to the worms and rides away with the final words of Atla in his ears, "But you are stained with the taint—you have called them forth and they will remember!" (p. 127).

In "Worms," all the Howard components are at play. There is the horrific element of the underground creatures, once human but now regressed by being forced to live beneath the surface. Atla invokes the name of R'lyeh, popularized by Lovecraft in his "Call of Cthulhu" and circulated by many *Weird Tales* writers. There is the doomed quest of Bran himself, hoping to revive an empire that has not been unified in five hundred years. There is swordplay and

human endurance in the face of torture. There is Howard's disgust for Romans and civilization, "these Romans, masking their contempt and scorn only under polished satire" (p. 91). Last, there is the acknowledgment that there are forms of vengeance too dark for anyone to contemplate, that certain types of revenge will only perpetuate a cycle too vicious to escape.

BOXING STORIES

At the same time that Howard was filling *Weird Tales* with stories of Solomon Kane and Bran Mak Morn, he was publishing boxing stories in pulps such as *Fight Stories, Action Stories,* and *Jack Dempsey's Fight Magazine* that catered to fans of the sweet science. Howard was intrigued by boxing, both as a fan and as a participant, frequently sparring with friends and roughnecks at the local icehouse during the oil boom in Cross Plains. One reason he published many stories in fight pulps was that, unlike *Weird Tales,* they paid on time. In all, seventeen fighting stories were published during Howard's brief career, most of them featuring the memorable character Steve Costigan.

Steve Costigan, an AB (able-bodied) seaman on the sailing vessel *Sea Girl,* is similar to many other Howard protagonists: a willing combatant with an almost superhuman ability to take punishment. Howard's favorite type of boxer was an "iron man," a fighter whose defenses are "a granite jaw and iron ribs," and Costigan fits the role (*Waterfront Fists,* pp. 95, 104). He routinely is beaten senseless, suffers broken ribs or a nose, has his ears bitten, and gets flattened on the canvas, only to rise at the count of nine. He freely admits, as in "Champ of the Forecastle," that "like most sluggers, I never lose my punch, no matter how badly beaten I am" (p. 165). With titles like "General Ironfist," "Sluggers on the Beach," and "Alleys of Peril," and fighting in such diverse places as Singapore, Stockholm, Texas, the South Sea islands, and Hong Kong, Costigan, accompanied by his white bulldog, Mike, finds himself mixed up in trouble with gangsters, gamblers, and fast women.

Exclusively told in the first person, the Costigan stories feature a comic edge not seen frequently in Howard. Costigan frequently misreads situations, such as in "Sailor's Grudge," when he overhears a conversation between a couple, little knowing that the "couple" are actually brother and sister. He then crashes a film shoot in hopes of beating the male, Bert, to a pulp. Fisticuffs ensue, with Costigan knocking Bert out. Instead of the female reward he assumes is coming, Costigan is slapped, and Howard ends the text with Costigan ruminating, "I learned you can never tell when women is holdin' something on you" (p. 76). Full of pseudo-profanities such as "Hey, you blankey dash-dot-blank," and ironic deflation describing how he "caressed Schimmerling's chin with a right uppercut which stood him on his head" (pp. 26, 292), Howard's boxing stories offer many of the same conventions as his better known works—masculine violence, page-turning action, exotic locales—but with a humorous touch and most of the combatants getting out alive.

CONAN OF CIMMERIA

Despite the quality of Howard's other creations, it is Conan for whom Howard is justifiably best remembered. It has been argued that the Conan cycle started the genre of "sword and sorcery" or "heroic fantasy," depending on nomenclature, and that this branch of fantasy writing represents one of America's original contributions to any literary genre. First published in 1932 as a rewrite of an abandoned Kull story, the Conan story "The Phoenix on the Sword" predates J. R. R. Tolkien's publication of *The Hobbit* (1937) by almost five years and set the template for more than seventy years of heroes, sorcerers, monsters, and treasure.

Howard claimed that the idea for Conan "simply grew up in my mind a few years ago when I was stopping in a little border town on the lower Rio Grande.... He simply stalked full grown out of oblivion and set me at work recording the saga of his adventures" (Finn, p. 205). But the actual formation of the character was a much longer process. As seen in Solomon Kane and Kull, Howard was already working through the narrative and character mechanics that would

develop into Conan. Kull's relative success in *Weird Tales* demonstrated that there was a market for tales of adventure set in a familiar, but non-historical, setting. Taking the plot outline of the rejected Kull story "By This Axe I Rule!," removing the romance subplot, and adding the supernatural, Howard sent the revised text to Farnsworth Wright. Wright found the story intriguing, offered editorial revisions, and published the result, "The Phoenix on the Sword," in December 1932. So began the career of Conan, which would span seventeen stories, one aborted novel, and a slew of contemporary and present-day imitators.

"Between the years when the oceans drank Atlantis and the gleaming cities, and the years of the rise of the Sons of Aryas" is the Hyborian Age, a pseudo-historical period Howard described in a letter to Lovecraft as one "which men have forgotten but which remains in classical names and distorted myths" (*Coming of Conan*, p. 7; Finn, p. 208). Mixing the conceits of Middle Age France and Spain with classical Greece and Stone Age savagery, the Hyborian Age provides the setting for Conan's adventures. Filled with abandoned cities, glittering palaces, dark crypts, and teeming slums are kingdoms with names like Aquilonia, Shem, Zingara, and Stygia. Propelled by Howard's fertile imagination, Conan, "black-haired, sullen-eyed, sword in hand, a thief, a reaver, a slayer, with gigantic melancholies and gigantic mirth," looks to "tread the jeweled thrones of the Earth under his sandalled feet" (*Coming of Conan*, p. 7). Somewhat contradictorily, Howard also considered Conan "the most realistic character I ever evolved" (Finn, p. 235). It is this melding of the fantastic and the realistic that grounds Conan's adventures, making the Hyborian kingdoms a site where mundane survival intersects with supernatural violence.

"Phoenix" starts with Conan already the king of Aquilonia, the most powerful country in Hyboria. Faced with revolt in the streets, palace intrigue, and supernatural enemies, Conan turns to what he knows best: direct action. In the last chapter of the short story, Conan kills all the revolutionaries, a being from the Outer Dark, and, in proper barbarian fashion, asks for wine

because "slaying is cursed dry work" (*Coming of Conan*, p. 26). The text is also peppered with clues to Conan's past adventures. When talking to Prospero, a trusted adviser, Conan runs through a list of countries that exist only as sketches on a map: his homeland of Cimmeria and the northern countries of Asgard and Vanaheim. Howard also shows the reader the barbaric pessimism that underpins Conan's character. Encircled by his enemies, "Conan himself did not hope to survive, but he did ferociously wish to inflict as much damage as he could before he fell" (p. 21).

After the publication of "Phoenix" and "The Scarlet Citadel" (January 1933) came "The Tower of the Elephant" in March 1933. Set in Zamoria and focusing on Conan's efforts to break into the tower and steal a priceless jewel, "Tower" features a young, inexperienced barbarian, a giant poisonous spider, and a spacefaring elephant creature that Conan kills in a mercy slaying. Howard later wrote that he didn't want to put Conan's stories in chronological order: "In writing these yarns I've always felt less as creating them than as if I were simply chronicling his adventures as he told them to me. That's why they skip about so much, without following a regular order" (Herron, p. 168). Whether conscious or not, the movement from king to penniless thief to mercenary is one of the hallmarks of Howard's Conan and one of the sites of later controversy.

Over the course of the next three years, Howard would fill *Weird Tales* with Conan's bloody adventures. Some of these stories are seen as classic Conan: "Queen of the Black Coast," published in May 1934, includes Conan's most developed love interest, the pirate Bêlit, and Howard's deepest exploration of Conan's existential philosophy. Sailing in quest of a forgotten city, Conan is asked if he fears death. After giving the Cimmerian version of the afterlife— "souls enter a gray misty realm of clouds and icy winds, to wander cheerlessly throughout eternity"—he finishes with "I live, I burn with life, I love, I slay, and am content" (*Coming of Conan*, p.133). Some of these texts are less successful: "Shadows in Zamboula," published in November 1935, features the casual racism and stereotyping

rife in pulp fiction. But for Howard these texts sold, and when the payment came in, he was frequently one of the richest men in Cross Plains.

In 1934 Howard was in correspondence with an English publisher, Dennis Archer, about a full-length Conan novel. Before the novel, *The Hour of the Dragon,* could be published, the publishing house went bankrupt, and *Dragon* was instead sold to *Weird Tales,* where it ran as a serial from late 1935 to April 1936. *Hour of the Dragon* follows the abduction, escape, and eventual triumphant return of King Conan to Aquilonia. Once again facing sorcery, this time in the figure of Xaltotun, a wizard from three thousand years in the past and a mortal foe, Conan travels throughout much of civilized Hyboria. By far the longest Conan tale, *Hour of the Dragon* holds a central place in Conan's adventures, tying up loose ends from other stories and expanding on the culture and history of multiple Hyborian kingdoms.

The last Conan text published, and one that Howard called his "grimmest, bloodiest and most merciless story of the series so far" (Herron, p. 121), was "Red Nails," published in *Weird Tales* from July to October 1936. Telling the story of Conan and his companion, Valeria, a pirate of the Red Brotherhood, who find themselves entangled in a decaying city's ancient feud, "Red Nails" lives up to Howard's description. The title's red nails are used to mark the killings of one feuding faction by the other on the pillar of vengeance; Valeria is kidnapped, nearly raped, and slated for death by Talesca, who stays young through ritual sacrifice; torture and mutilation are common. In the conclusion of "Red Nails," weird sorcery and science collide with a long-forgotten magic user operating a primitive electrical weapon.

In the Conan series, Howard found ways to explore his ideas on civilization and barbarism, ideas influenced by his literary mentor Jack London, whom Howard cites as his favorite author, as well as his understanding of Charles Darwin and Thomas Huxley. Darwinian survival at its most basic appears in "The Scarlet Citadel," with lines such as "it was the blind black instinct of self-preservation that held him rigid as a statue" (*Coming of Conan,* p. 95). London's pessimistic determinism is given a barbaric twist in

"Black Colossus," when Howard writes, "Life was a continual battle, or a series of battles" (p. 170). The thinking of Herbert Spencer—who, along with Huxley, helped popularize Darwinian concepts of the decline of societies who become civilized—underpins Howard's frontier Conan story, "Beyond the Black River" (1935), which includes one of Howard's famous quotes: "Civilization is unnatural. It is a whim of circumstance. And barbarism must always ultimately triumph" (*Conquering Sword,* p. 100). "Red Nails" reflects similar sentiments, with the feuding groups turning to decadence, where "any sort of perversity might be expected to be encountered among them" (p. 253). Conan's barbarism is constantly being compared to the civilized actions of nobility, and barbarism comes out the better every time. In "Xuthal of the Dusk," Conan complains, "In my country, no starving man is denied food, but you civilized people must have your recompense" (*Coming of Conan,* p. 227). Far from being only escapist fodder, the best of the Conan stories mix Howard's nonstop action with ruminations on the fate of civilizations, the meaning of existence, and humanity's place in the universe.

WESTERN TALES

Befitting a native Texan who seldom left the state and who was immersed in Texas history, Howard wrote a variety of westerns, ranging from the comic tales of Breckinridge Elkins to the grim realism of "Vultures of Wahpeton." If the number of publications is a measure of success, then Howard's dim-witted but good-natured Elkins is his most successful creation, appearing in every issue of *Action* stories between March 1934 and October 1936, after Howard's death. The collection of Elkins stories, along with additional material linking the episodes together, was published in England as *A Gent from Bear Creek* (1937), making it the first complete Howard novel. Howard's westerns feature his characteristic violence and struggle, but the later stories especially exhibit an ear for dialogue and situational comedy that makes them some of Howard's best writing.

Of his straight westerns, "Vultures of Wahpeton," published in *Smashing Novels Magazine*

(1936), is the most interesting. The story offers no unmitigated hero but many villains. As already seen in Howard, his protagonists are usually motivated by a personal code more than traditional ideas of right and wrong. Corcoran, the gunslinger who becomes a deputy for hire in Wahpeton, kills without regret, is willing to cheat the entire town out of its gold, and double crosses almost every character. At the same time, he "lived by his own code, and it was wild and rough and hard, violent and incongruous" (*End of the Trail,* p. 258). This code also leads him to protect the woman who previously revealed his deception to Middleton, town sheriff and head of a criminal gang, the Vultures.

"Vultures" also displays Howard's populist sympathies and the sense of paranoia that the Kull story "The Shadow Kingdom" employs. Written in 1936 when the unemployment rate for America was greater than 16 percent, the text is scattered with comments about what happens when those enforcing the rules are themselves criminals, a sentiment common during the Great Depression. Middleton, the town's richest citizen as well as its sheriff, says, "As long as a man isn't molested himself, he doesn't care much what happens to his neighbors. We are organized; they are not. We know who to trust; they don't" (p. 215). This lack of trust is endemic in Wahpeton: since anyone could be a Vulture, no one is safe. But the Vultures themselves are being played by Middleton and Corcoran, who plan on pitting the remaining Vultures against town vigilantes while they sneak off with the millions in gold. Farmers, miners, and simple ranchers are powerless against the organized crime of the Vultures, much as Americans felt they were powerless against bankers and Wall Street.

The final twist on "Vultures" is that it was published with two endings: a bleaker, more Howardian ending where Glory Bland, the dance hall woman who betrayed Corcoran, is killed by Middleton, who is subsequently shot dead by Corcoran. The alternate ending has Glory only being grazed by the bullet and recovering after Corcoran kills Middleton. She and Corcoran ride off, ready to marry at the next town. Howard submitted both endings to *Smashing Novels,* and

according to the editor's note that accompanies the story, "The author left it to the editor which ending to use, but the editor passes the buck to the reader. The first is undoubtedly more powerful, dramatically, but it involves frustration. The second will undoubtedly be more pleasing, as it eliminates the tragedy of the girl's death" (p. 261).

Breckinridge Elkins, of Bear Creek, Nevada, appears in twenty-six stories, the most of any recurring character. Elkins fights, rides, and drinks his way around the Mountain West, accompanied by his horse Cap'n Kidd, who is worse tempered than Elkins. Mixing elements of the western with the tall tale, the Elkins stories, much like the Steve Costigan stories, are humorously violent, with the butt of the joke frequently being Elkins himself. With titles such as "The Conquerin' Hero of the Humboldts" (1936), "Mountain Man" (1934), and "The Riot at Cougar Paw" (1935), the Elkins stories are some of the best, but least-explored, material in the Howard canon.

Told in the first person, which they share with the Costigan stories, and taking place in fictional Nevada towns such as War Paint and Grizzly Paw, Elkins' misadventures usually begin, as in "A Gent from Bear Creek," with him coming into a fight:

> The folks on Bear Creek ain't what you'd call peaceable by nature, but I was kind of surprised to come onto Erath Elkins and his brother-in-law Joel Gordon locked in mortal combat on the bank of the creek.... Seeing they was too blind mad to have any sense, I bashed their heads together till they was too dizzy to do anything but holler.
>
> (*Heroes of Bear Creek,* p. 58)

The rest of "Gent" follows Elkins as he deals with a gold rush, a lynching, crooked law enforcement, and a full-scale riot where Elkins throws a roulette wheel and billiard table into his enemies. All of this action is narrated in Elkins' hillbilly dialect, where he lays "hands on as many as I could hug at onst" during the fights and escapes from the wreckage of a jail he has destroyed "like a b'ar out of a deadfall" (pp. 72, 71).

Howard's usual atmosphere of masculine violence is present in Elkins, but it is tempered with the tall tale's cartoonish element. Elkins is shot, stabbed, and beaten with regularity but never suffers any permanent damage. His enemies are equally mistreated, losing ears and skin, thrown through walls, and mowed down by a bench. But at the end of the story, most dust themselves off, get stitched up, and carry on mining and ranching. The pretensions of civilization are also burlesqued, as in "Pistol Politics" (1936), where a spelling bee is held to help sway a local election. Unfortunately, the only people who can spell shoot each other over how "Constantinople" begins, and it is up to the semiliterate Elkins to officiate the contest. Part Pecos Bill, part Steve Costigan, and part Conan, Elkins is a continuation of the Southwest humor tradition and, had Howard not killed himself, would have evolved into a specific Texas literary voice.

CRITICAL TRADITION

Much like H. P. Lovecraft's relationship with August Derleth, Howard's posthumous fame is partially the result of his relationship with a controversial figure in Howard studies, L. Sprague de Camp. A successful fantasy and science fiction writer in his own right, de Camp was hired by Gnome Press in the middle 1950s to edit the Conan stories for a hardback reissue. But de Camp did more than copyedit; he began to change language, invent characters, and insert events. Also, de Camp organized the order of the stories chronologically, differing from Howard's original conception of an adventurer telling the stories as they came to mind. While there are understandable economic arguments for this decision, it set the stage for continued reworking and rewriting of Howard's work.

By the middle 1960s a fantasy boom was on, fueled by the growing counterculture and access to Tolkien's *Lord of the Rings* series, which had appeared in 1954 and 1955. The publishing company Lancer began to reprint Howard, along with revisions done by de Camp, as well as Conan stories that de Camp and fellow writers Lin Carter and Björn Nyberg constructed to fill in the blanks of Conan's career. Lancer went out of business before completing the series, and it sold the rights to Ace Books. The resulting series is known as the Lancer/Ace editions, which, in part owing to cover art by Frank Frazetta, solidified the reputation of Conan and of Robert Howard as the creator of heroic fantasy. These twelve books followed Conan's career from his teenage years in *Conan* to his final adventure in *Conan of the Isles*. Unfortunately, the Lancer/Ace collection did not clearly identify which stories were Howard's, which ones were completed by de Camp, and which ones were created for the series. The confusion around these textual changes continued until the mid-1970s, when Karl Wagner and Berkley Books released the unedited versions of several Conan tales. No complete unedited versions of Howard's Conan were published until the Wandering Star/Del Rey editions in the early 2000s. Complete with drafts, Howard's own plot synopses, and editorial introductions by the noted Howard scholars Rusty Burke and Patrice Louinet, these editions have been a welcome addition to Howard studies, as have later editions that include his work on Solomon Kane, Bran Mak Morn, and others.

De Camp is also responsible for the first full-length biography of Howard, *Dark Valley Destiny,* published in 1983. Like much of de Camp's other work on Howard, it was seen as a mixed blessing. De Camp, although untrained as a psychologist, read Howard's life and writing through a distinctively Freudian lens, coloring much of the popular discussion of Howard. In 1984 *The Dark Barbarian,* edited by Don Herron, was published. This collection of essays was the first serious exploration of Howard's writing, looking at the range of his material, not simply Conan. Critical appraisal of Howard continued into the early years of the twenty-first century, with the centennial release of *Two-Gun Bob* (2006) by Benjamin Szumskyj, a collection of essays, and Mark Finn's *Blood and Thunder* (2014), which provides a more nuanced Howard biography. *A Means to Freedom*: *The Letters of H. P. Lovecraft and Robert Howard* (2011), edited by Rusty Burke and Lovecraft scholars S. T. Joshi and David E. Schultz, is also part of the renewed interest in

both writers and pulp magazines in general. Howard's home of Cross Plains, Texas, hosts Robert Howard Days annually, and the Robert E. Howard Foundation continues to promote serious and popular discussions of Howard's writing.

Several of Howard's characters have been featured in full-length films, with Arnold Schwarzenegger's portrayal in *Conan the Barbarian* (1982) largely responsible for launching his acting career. From the 1970s until the 1990s, two Conan comics ran simultaneously: *The Savage Sword of Conan* and *Conan the Barbarian*. Many heavy metal bands have used material from Howard, and Tor Publishing released more than forty Conan titles between 1982 and 2004. While much of this material is a shadow of Howard's own skill as a writer, it is indicative of his character's enduring popularity.

Few writers can claim to have written a character that still exists in popular culture seventy-five years after appearing. However, the popularity of Conan should not overshadow Howard's other writings. Robert Howard may only have been writing for a living, but his works are far more than paychecks. They incorporate Howard's prodigious imagination, his pessimistic philosophy, and his life in boom-and-bust Texas to construct an authentic American voice.

Selected Bibliography

WORKS OF ROBERT E. HOWARD

POETRY

"This Is a Young World." *The Right Hook* 1, no. 3. Chapbook, 1926. Reprinted in *Robert E. Howard: Selected Poems*. Edited by Frank Coffman. Elgin, Ill.: Mind's Eye HyperPublishing, 2012.

"Forbidden Magic." *Weird Tales,* July 1929. Reprinted in *Robert E. Howard: Selected Poems*. Edited by Frank Coffman. Elgin, Ill.: Mind's Eye HyperPublishing, 2012.

"Arkham." *Weird Tales,* August 1932. Reprinted in *Robert E. Howard: Selected Poems*. Edited by Frank Coffman. Elgin, Ill.: Mind's Eye HyperPublishing, 2012.

"A Warning." In *Echoes from an Iron Harp*. West Kingston, R.I.: D. M. Grant, 1972. Reprinted in *Robert E. Howard: Selected Poems*. Edited by Frank Coffman. Elgin, Ill.: Mind's Eye HyperPublishing, 2012.

"A Sonnet of Good Cheer." In *Robert E. Howard: Selected Poems*. Edited by Frank Coffman. Elgin, Ill.: Mind's Eye HyperPublishing, 2012.

"A Word from the Outer Dark." In *Robert E. Howard: Selected Poems*. Edited by Frank Coffman. Elgin, Ill.: Mind's Eye HyperPublishing, 2012.

HORROR

"Wolfshead." *Weird Tales,* April 1926. Reprinted in *The Horror Stories of Robert Howard*. New York: Del Rey Press, 2008.

"The Children of the Night." *Weird Tales,* April–May 1931. Reprinted in *The Horror Stories of Robert Howard*. New York: Del Rey Press, 2008.

"The Black Stone." *Weird Tales,* November 1931. Reprinted in *The Horror Stories of Robert Howard*. New York: Del Rey Press, 2008.

"Pigeons from Hell." *Weird Tales,* May 1938. Reprinted in *The Horror Stories of Robert Howard*. New York: Del Rey Press, 2008.

HISTORICAL ADVENTURES

"Hawks of Outremer." *Oriental Stories,* spring 1931. Reprinted in *Sword Woman and Other Historical Adventures*. New York: Del Rey Press, 2011.

"The Shadow of the Vulture." *Magic Carpet Magazine,* January 1934. Reprinted in *Sword Woman and Other Historical Adventures*. New York: Del Rey Press, 2011.

"Daughter of Erlik Khan." *Top-Notch,* December 1934. Reprinted in *El Borak and Other Desert Adventures*. New York: Del Rey Press, 2010.

"She Devil." *Spicy-Adventure Stories,* April 1936. Republished in *The She Devil*. New York: Ace Fantasy Books, 1983. (Howard published "She Devil" under the pseudonym Sam Walser.)

"Son of the White Wolf." *Thrilling Adventures,* December 1936. Reprinted in *El Borak and Other Desert Adventures*. New York: Del Rey Press, 2010.

"Murderer's Grog." In *Spicy-Adventure Stories,* 1937. Republished in *The She Devil*. New York: Ace Fantasy Books, 1983. (Howard published "Murderer's Grog" under the pseudonym Sam Walser.)

BOXING STORIES

"Sailor's Grudge." *Fight Stories,* March 1930. Reprinted in *Waterfront Fists and Others: The Collected Fight Stories of Robert E. Howard*. Edited by Paul Herman. Rockville, Md.: Wildside Press, 2004.

"Champ of the Forecastle." *Fight Stories,* November 1930. Reprinted in *Waterfront Fists and Others: The Collected Fight Stories of Robert E. Howard*. Edited by Paul

Herman. Rockville, Md.: Wildside Press, 2004.

"Alleys of Peril." *Fight Stories*, January 1931. Reprinted in *Waterfront Fists and Others: The Collected Fight Stories of Robert E. Howard*. Edited by Paul Herman. Rockville, Md.: Wildside Press, 2004.

HEROIC FANTASY

"Red Shadows." *Weird Tales*, August 1928. Reprinted in *The Savage Tales of Solomon Kane*. New York: Del Rey Books. 2006.

"The Shadow Kingdom." *Weird Tales*, August 1929. Reprinted in *Kull: Exile of Atlantis*. New York: Del Rey Books. 2006.

"The Mirrors of Tuzun Thune." *Weird Tales*, September 1929. Reprinted in *Kull: Exile of Atlantis*. New York: Del Rey Books. 2006.

"The Dark Man." *Weird Tales*, December 1931. Reprinted in *Bran Mak Morn: The Last King*. New York: Del Rey Books. 2005.

"Wings in the Night." *Weird Tales*, July 1932. Reprinted in *The Savage Tales of Solomon Kane*. New York: Del Rey Books. 2006.

"Worms of the Earth." *Weird Tales*, November 1932. Reprinted in *Bran Mak Morn: The Last King*. New York: Del Rey Books. 2005.

CONAN OF CIMMERIA

As discussed, the textual editing and rewriting of many Conan stories by L. Sprague de Camp was not corrected until the release of the Wandering Star/Del Rey editions.

"The Phoenix on the Sword." *Weird Tales*, December 1932. Reprinted in *The Coming of Conan the Cimmerian*. Edited by Patrice Louinet. New York: Del Rey Books. 2003. (Like many Conan stories, "Phoenix" has been reprinted in other places, including Gnome Press's *King Conan* in 1953 and as part of the Lancer/Ace series in *Conan the Usurper*, 1967.)

"The Scarlet Citadel." *Weird Tales*, January 1933. Reprinted in *The Coming of Conan the Cimmerian*. Edited by Patrice Louinet. New York: Del Rey Books. 2003. (Reprinted earlier in Gnome Press's *King Conan* in 1953 and again as part of the Lancer/Ace series in *Conan the Usurper*, 1967.)

"The Tower of the Elephant." *Weird Tales*, March 1933. Reprinted in *The Coming of Conan the Cimmerian*. Edited by Patrice Louinet. New York: Del Rey Books. 2003. (Reprinted earlier in Gnome Press's *The Coming of Conan* in 1953 and as part of the Lancer/Ace series in *Conan*, 1967.)

"Black Colossus." *Weird Tales*, March 1933. Reprinted in *The Coming of Conan the Cimmerian*. Edited by Patrice Louinet. New York: Del Rey Books. 2003. (Reprinted earlier in an edited form in Gnome Press's *Conan the Barbarian* in 1954 and as part of the Lancer/Ace series in

Conan the Freebooter, 1968.)

"Xuthal of the Dusk." *Weird Tales*, September 1933. Reprinted in *The Coming of Conan the Cimmerian*. Edited by Patrice Louinet. New York: Del Rey Books. 2003. (Titled "The Slithering Shadow" in the original *Weird Tales* publication. Republished as "Xuthal" in Gnome Press's 1953 *The Sword of Conan* and again in Lancer/Ace series in *Conan the Adventurer*, 1966.)

"Queen of the Black Coast." *Weird Tales*, May 1934. Reprinted in *The Coming of Conan the Cimmerian*. Edited by Patrice Louinet. New York: Del Rey Books. 2003. (Reprinted earlier in Gnome Press's *The Coming of Conan* in 1953 and as part of the Lancer/Ace series in *Conan of Cimmeria* in 1969.)

"Beyond the Black River." *Weird Tales*, May–June 1935. Reprinted in *The Conquering Sword of Conan*. Edited by Patrice Louinet. New York: Del Rey Books. 2005. (Reprinted earlier in Gnome Press's *King Conan* in 1953 and as part of the Lancer/Ace series in *Conan the Warrior*, 1967; an unedited original version appeared in Berkley Press's *Red Nails*, edited by Karl Wagner, 1977.)

"Shadows in Zamboula." *Weird Tales*, November 1935. Reprinted under its original title of "Man-Eaters of Zamboula" in *The Conquering Sword of Conan*. Edited by Patrice Louinet. New York: Del Rey Books. 2005. (Reprinted earlier in Gnome Press's *Conan the Barbarian* in 1954 and as part of the Lancer/Ace series in *Conan the Wanderer*, 1968; an unedited original version appeared in Berkley Press's *Red Nails*, edited by Karl Wagner, 1977.)

Hour of the Dragon. Serialized in *Weird Tales*, December 1935–April 1936. Reprinted in *The Bloody Crown of Conan*. Edited by Patrice Louinet. New York: Del Rey Books. 2005. (Reprinted earlier by Gnome Press as *Conan the Conqueror* in 1950, as part of the Lancer/Ace series using the same title in 1967, and then under its original title in the 1977 Berkley Press version edited by Karl Wagner.)

"Red Nails." *Weird Tales*, July–August 1936. Reprinted in *The Conquering Sword of Conan*. Edited by Patrice Louinet. New York: Del Rey Books. 2005. (Reprinted earlier in Gnome Press's *The Sword of Conan* in 1952 and as part of the Lancer/Ace series in *Conan the Warrior*, 1967; an unedited original version appeared in Berkley Press's *Red Nails*, edited by Karl Wagner, 1977.)

WESTERNS

"Mountain Man." *Action Stories*, April 1934. Reprinted in *The Riot at Bucksnort and Other Western Stories*. Edited by David Gentzel. Lincoln: University of Nebraska Press, 2005.

"A Gent from Bear Creek." *Action Stories*, October 1934. Reprinted in *Heroes of Bear Creek*. New York: Ace Fantasy Books, 1978. (*Heroes* is a collection that includes the novel *A Gent from Bear Creek*, along with several

posthumously published western tales).

"The Riot at Cougar Paw." *Action Stories,* October 1935. Reprinted in *The Riot at Bucksnort and Other Western Stories.* Edited by David Gentzel. Lincoln: University of Nebraska Press, 2005.

"Pistol Politics." *Action Stories,* April 1936. Reprinted in *The Riot at Bucksnort and Other Western Stories.* Edited by David Gentzel. Lincoln: University of Nebraska Press, 2005.

"The Conquerin' Hero of the Humboldts." *Action Stories,* October 1936. Reprinted in *The Riot at Bucksnort and Other Western Stories.* Edited by David Gentzel. Lincoln: University of Nebraska Press, 2005.

"Vultures of Wahpeton." *Smashing Novels Magazine,* December 1936. Reprinted in *The End of the Trail: Western Stories.* Edited by Rusty Burke. Lincoln: University of Nebraska Press, 2005.

Correspondence and Other Writings

The Collected Letters of Robert E. Howard. 3 vols. Edited by Rob Roehm and Rusty Burke. Plano, Tex.: Robert E. Howard Press, 2007–2008.

A Means to Freedom: The Letters of H. P. Lovecraft and Robert E. Howard. 2 vols. Edited by Rusty Burke, David E. Schultz, and S. T. Joshi. New York: Hippocampus Press, 2011.

Post Oaks and Sand Roughs. West Kingston, R.I.: D. M. Grant, 1989. (A printing of Howard's semiautobiographical novel that covers his time in Cross Plains and Brownwood from 1924 to 1928.)

Papers

After Howard's death, his letters, manuscripts, drafts, and other papers were passed from his father to his agent to fan and eventual editor Glenn Lord, who ultimately collected more than fifteen thousand pages of material. Two years after Lord's death in 2011, the Harry Ransom Center at the University of Texas at Austin announced it had received the Lord estate's donation of this collection. Additionally, a small but valuable collection of manuscripts and ephemera are held at the Robert E. Howard museum in Cross Plains, Texas, as well as at the Cross Plains Library.

CRITICAL AND BIOGRAPHICAL STUDIES

de Camp, L. Sprague. *Dark Valley Destiny: The Life of Robert E. Howard.* New York: Bluejay Books, 1983.

Finn, Mark. *Blood and Thunder: The Life and Art of Robert E. Howard.* 2nd ed. Plano, Tex.: Robert E. Howard Press, 2014. (The critical biography corrects many of the suppositions of *Dark Valley Destiny.*)

Herron, Don. *The Dark Barbarian: The Writings of Robert E. Howard: A Critical Anthology.* Gillette, N.J.: Wildside Press, 2000.

Lord, Glenn. *The Last Celt: A Bio-Bibliography of Robert Ervin Howard.* West Kingston, R.I.: D. M. Grant, 1976.

Price, Novalyne Ellis. *One Who Walked Alone: Robert E. Howard, the Final Years.* West Kingston, R.I.: D. M. Grant, 1986.

Szumskyj, Benjamin. *Two-Gun Bob: A Centennial Study of Robert E. Howard.* New York: Hippocampus Press, 2006.

MEYER LEVIN

(1905—1981)

Jack Fischel

WHEN MEYER LEVIN died in 1981, he left behind a large body of work that includes sixteen novels, two memoirs, essays in publications such as *Commentary, Menorah Journal, Jewish Currents,* and *Congress Bi-Monthly,* and a film, *The Illegals,* which tells the story of the Haganah's efforts to smuggle Jewish survivors of the Holocaust into British-controlled Palestine prior to the establishment of the State of Israel in 1948. Much of Levin's literary output deals with Jewish issues: assimilation (*The Old Bunch,* 1937), the Holocaust (*Eva,* 1959; *The Stronghold,* 1965), the Palestine Yishuv (*The Settlers,* 1972), and Israel (*The Harvest,* 1978). Levin also authored a compilation of Hasidic tales and various series of educational works about Judaism, Jewish history, and philosophy. He is, however, best remembered for his best-selling novel *Compulsion* (1956), based on the murder trial of Nathan Leopold and Richard Loeb, which was adapted as a stage play and subsequently made into a film featuring Orson Welles. Earlier, however, Levin had become involved in a controversy over the stage adaptation of the *Diary of Anne Frank.* In a dispute with Anne's father, Otto Frank, and the producers of the play, Levin charged that the Jewish aspects of the diary, which had been highlighted in his own writing of the play, had been omitted for commercial reasons, if not to satisfy the Jewish self-hating, Stalinist bent of Lillian Hellman and others involved in derailing his efforts. The controversy, which led to a flurry of lawsuits and unfavorable publicity, took its toll on Levin, forcing him into psychotherapy and almost destroying his marriage.

Jewish issues aside, Levin's fiction also includes works of social realism, including *The New Bridge* (1933), which deals with unemployed construction workers at the beginning of the

Depression, and the critically acclaimed *Citizens* (1940), about the 1937 Memorial Day steel strike in Chicago, when the Chicago police shot and killed ten unarmed demonstrators. His only attempt at writing a humorous novel was *Gore and Igor* (1968), a work of fiction poorly received by the critics. His final novel, *The Architect* (1981), is a fictionalized treatment of the life of Frank Lloyd Wright. Levin also authored two autobiographical works: the unsparingly self-searching and evocative *In Search* (1950) and the self-analytical *The Obsession* (1973), which tells the story of his twenty-year battle over the rejection and suppression of his version of *The Diary of Anne Frank.*

DEVELOPMENT AS AN AMERICAN JEWISH WRITER

Although not generally included by critics among the top tier of American Jewish writers, such as Saul Bellow, Bernard Malamud, Norman Mailer, and Philip Roth, Levin did have reviewers who lauded his work. Gary Bossin, in his indispensable doctoral dissertation, "The Literary Achievement of Meyer Levin" (1980), cites a number of Levin's contemporaries who ranked him high among Jewish writers of his time. These included Leslie Fiedler, who wrote that Levin was among the "fewer than ten American Jews" writing fiction prior to 1940 who are "worthy of remembering." Harold Ribalow found several of Levin's novels "seminal works of Jewish creative writing" and goes on to describe Levin's autobiography, *In Search,* as "one of the most moving and eloquent statements ever written by an American Jew." Marie Syrkin noted that "in fiction, drama and essay, Meyer Levin became one of the few American writers wholly dedicated to

the portrayal of the central experience of the Jewish people in the twentieth century: the Nazi Holocaust and its consequences," and Robert Kirsch, the literary editor of the *Los Angeles Times,* wrote that Levin was "perhaps the foremost American-Jewish writer of the twentieth century" (Bossin, pp. 4–5).The list of critics who believed that Levin was a serious and a consequential writer also included Ernest Hemingway, James T. Farrell, Max Lerner, Nelson Algren, Dorothy Rabinowitz, and Allen Guttman (p. 8). Others, however, expressed their doubts about Levin's work, among them Alfred Kazin, Philip Rahv, Granville Hicks, and Pearl K. Bell (p. 8). Kazin, for example, found *The Old Bunch* "more than a little perishable," and Rahv found it "somewhat monotonous" (p. 10).

American Jewish writers who were Meyer Levin's contemporaries included Henry Roth, Michael Gold, Daniel Fuchs, and Clifford Odets, to name a few. Benjamin Balint writes that these writers were isolated figures, and "there seemed something contrived in the ways they strained to make Jewish experience relevant to America" (Balint, p. 54). Balint goes on to note that this was because the fiction of the time was expected to concern itself with the general, the universal, and the result was that some writers in order to be published would mask the Jewishness of their characters. This was a major concern for Levin in the early years of his writing. Balint cites Levin, who wrote in *Commentary,* "I told readers I had early discovered that the big-paying magazines were not interested in stories about Jews.... So I wrote about 'American' youngsters by giving non-Jewish names to the characters I knew in my heart were Jewish kids" (p. 54). His early novel *Frankie and Johnnie* (1930) reflects this commercial reality: here Levin wrote about "American" youngsters by giving non-Jewish names to the characters he knew to be Jewish, and moved them from Chicago's West Side, where Jews predominately lived, to the Irish South Side. In his autobiography *In Search,* Levin reveals that on the eve of publishing *Citizens,* his publisher broached the idea that one of his characters, Mitch Wilner, a Jewish doctor who helps the strikers, be removed because he felt that "the story would be much more typically American if this doctor were not a Jew" (p. 145). This was not the only instance where the Jewishness of his characters was called into question. Levin notes that a publisher reading the proofs of *The Old Bunch* felt that the novel would be "more typical if it consisted of a mélange of nationalities rather than a group of Jews" (p. 146). Levin refused the publishers' suggestions in both instances. The character Wilner remained in *Citizens* and, in fact, reappears in several of his other works of fiction. *The Old Bunch,* for example, remained a novel about Jewish teenagers growing up in Chicago—including Mitch Wilner.

Levin was also critical of his fellow Jews when he wrote, "the Jews won't accept you until the Gentiles have made a fuss about you." Discussing "The Writer and the Jewish Community" in *Commentary* in 1947, he contended that "you could not emerge as an American writer if you write about Jews in the way that you might if you wrote about Armenians or Irish." *The Old Bunch,* stated Levin, was never understood as a story of America, though a similar work about the Irish in Chicago was considered to be directly in the tradition. He also urged that the American Jewish writer should enrich himself from his Jewish past both in the diaspora and in Palestine. Levin traveled in the early 1920s to the Holy Land to witness the daily life of the *halutzim* who were attempting to build a Jewish homeland in Palestine. In fact, Levin lived for a short time on a kibbutz and would draw on his experiences there for his novel *The Settlers.* Unlike Herman Wouk, Levin was not an observant Jew in the traditional sense of attending synagogue on a regular basis. Rather, Levin identified himself as a cultural Jew who revered Jewish history, literature, law, philosophy, and ethical conduct and was particularly drawn to Hasidic lore, which he compiled in 1932 in *The Golden Mountain: Marvellous Tales of Rabbi Israel Baal Shem and of His Great-Grandson, Rabbi Nachman, Retold from Hebrew, Yiddish, and German Sources.*

In the immediate aftermath of the liberation of the concentration camps in 1945, Levin, who served in the Office of War Information (OWI), requested and received a release from the Psycho-

logical Warfare division of the OWI to report on the war as an accredited correspondent for the Overseas News Agency. Levin was determined to tell the story of the fate of the Jews of Europe and disclose the facts behind the gruesome rumors of mass slaughter. In this capacity, Levin visited the recently liberated concentration camps in Germany and in the process interviewed survivors who were placed in displaced persons (DP) camps. One of his many interviews would become the basis for *Eva*, the story of a young Jewish woman who managed to pass as an Aryan until she was discovered to be a Jew and subsequently sent to Auschwitz. Planning on a trip to France, Levin was asked by a rabbi for a favor. The rabbi had found a Jewish survivor from Cologne who directed him to the ruins of a synagogue where a Torah had been buried beneath the floor. Months later, the rabbi received a letter requesting that the Torah be returned to the Cologne synagogue. The rabbi asked Levin if he would carry it back to Cologne. During the long ride to Cologne the trip was uneventful but, as Levin recalls in his autobiography, the Torah, packed in a wooden crate, created a peculiar tension and intensity. It was "as though eternal judgment rode along with me," he writes (*In Search*, p. 285). As Levin drove through the German countryside, his thoughts about the Torah raised questions in his mind about his relationship to Judaism:

> I asked myself, what was the *Torah,* literally, and what was the *Torah* to me? I asked myself, was it because we attempted to plant the Torah in strange lands that persecution arose? ... Then I reflected upon the mystification that the world attached to this document. The ritual evolved by the Jews around a written parchment had been interpreted by some as sorcery, by some as mystical power, and Jews had been slain for the "secrets" of their sacred *Torah,* yet there were no secrets ever, the *Torah* was known and open to the world in every printed testament.
>
> (p. 286)

Reflecting on the importance of Judaism for himself and for mankind, Levin notes that the Torah was a code for moral and physical behavior:

> Our *Torah* then was a governmental code employing the strongest known motive, the religious sanction as sanction. From the beginning its aim was to regulate the life of men in community, toward justice and peace. When we worshipped the *Torah* we worshipped the idea of law itself, the idea of a covenant among men that they might live together.
>
> (pp. 286–287)

The commandment that was most personal to him, and the one that sheds some light on his response to the later controversy over the staging of the *Diary of Anne Frank,* was "Thou shalt not bear false witness." Levin contended that "the bearing of false witness, the lie, was a crime against the very basis of society, for men could never construct a way of living together unless there was a single plan in which they were in agreed communication. This was truth.... This then was my inmost behest. This was *Torah* for me.... Of all the commandments ... for me, this was the essence of our faith" (p. 290).

THE ANNE FRANK CONTROVERSY

In Paris in 1950, Levin was introduced to the French translation of the diary of Anne Frank, which had first been published in Dutch in 1947. He was immediately taken by the diary. He proceeded to contact Anne's father, Otto Frank, the only one of the family to survive the Holocaust, with a proposal to translate the diary into English. Instead, a translation into English by B. M. Mooyart-Doubleday was published in an American edition by the Doubleday company. *The Diary of a Young Girl* (1952) became a best seller, no doubt helped by Levin's rave review on page 1 of the *New York Times Book Review* on June 15, 1952. As a war correspondent who had witnessed the liberation of survivors from camps such as Ohrdruf and Buchenwald, Levin saw himself as an advocate for the survivors of the Shoah and Anne Frank's voice "as the voice of six million vanished Jewish souls" ("The Child Behind the Secret Door," p. 1). What followed has become historically murky. Levin, who had developed a personal relationship with Otto Frank, believed that he had Anne's father's permission to dramatize the play. Cheryl Craw-

ford, who was selected as the producer of the anticipated Broadway play, initially approved Levin's ongoing draft but soon changed her mind about dramatizing his version for a mostly non-Jewish audience. Ultimately it was the married writing team of Frances Goodrich and Albert Hackett, both gentiles, who were chosen to adapt the *Diary,* with input from the famed playwright Lillian Hellman. Levin responded with the accusation that Otto Frank, Crawford, and others, including Doubleday editor Barbara Zimmerman (later Epstein) were under the influence of a cabal of Broadway leftists led by Hellman, who maintained that Levin's version of the play was "too Jewish." Lawrence Graver, the author of *An Obsession with Anne Frank,* points out that it was actually the play's director, Garson Kanin, who told Goodrich and Hackett to take out lines in the script in which Anne speaks about the constancy of the historical persecution of Jews. These lines, according to Kanin, represented "an embarrassing piece of special pleading." Kanin further stated, "The fact that in this play the symbols of persecution and oppression are Jews is incidental and Anne, in stating the argument so, reduces her magnificent stature" (Graver, p. 89). Actually, the changes in the script from the content of the *Diary* were in accord with Otto Frank's desire that the play should emphasize the universality of Anne's diary rather than her Jewishness.

In his memoir *The Obsession* (1973), Levin writes of his response when he attended the pre-Broadway opening in Philadelphia of Goodrich and Hackett's *The Diary of Anne Frank* in 1955, which would not only become a smash hit on Broadway but also be awarded the Pulitzer Prize:

> Sitting there came to be like watching my play prove itself on the stage.... Of course there were differences, too. The slickness and coyness, as in a Hollywood script-polishing job.... In what I was seeing, there was no relationship between the sisters; Margot was a nonentity.... And where was the scene ... in which ... Margot, as in the Diary, said she wanted to become a nurse in Palestine.... These people on the stage never seemed to think about, to question, the meaning of what was happening to them as Jews. In the Diary, and in all I knew of the Holocaust, the question was constantly in the forefront. As I remembered it, Anne's fundamental

outcry, her cry of faith was "It is God who has made us as we are.... We are Jews and we want to be ... and perhaps it is through our suffering that the world will learn the good...." Could this have been omitted?

(p. 121)

Levin next turned to the Hanukkah scene, where Kanin persuaded the play's adapters to substitute the traditional solemn religious hymn for God's salvation, "Ma' oz Tzur" ("Rock of Ages") with the playful " Hanukkah, Oh Hanukkah!" Levin charged that the play made the Hanukkah scene—with the distribution of little gifts and song included—more like Christmas. He notes, "The audience was touched, and all the audience knew these were Jews, and enormous pity was aroused. Pity, yes—but what of understanding? Illumination?" Levin asks, "Where was the final, bitter scene in which Peter declared that if he lived he would change his name and deny his identity as a Jew? And Anne virtually screaming at him, as she had written in her Diary, 'But Peter! That's not honest!' " (p. 122). Concluding his review of the Goodrich-Hackett play, Levin sadly writes in regard to the absence of Jewish consciousness in the play, "Perhaps all this simply didn't have any meaning for the Hellmans and the Hacketts. Or perhaps it did, and therefore had to be omitted" (p. 122).

It didn't help that the budding controversy occurred at the very time that Josef Stalin, prior to his death in 1953, promulgated his anti-Zionist policy, wherein he ordered the purging from public life of hundreds of prominent Soviet Jewish writers, doctors, and academics, who were arrested or executed on trumped up charges. At the same time, this period saw the rise of the House Un-American Activities Committee in the United States. So Levin, fearful that he might be accused of McCarthyism by charging Hellman and the play's new producer Kermit Bloomgarden of following the Moscow party line, initially confined himself to pleading with Frank and his law firm, Paul, Weiss, to at least allow his version of the play to be staged and judged by an impartial group of reviewers. But they refused even to consider this.

After Frank's attorneys rejected Levin's plea, lawsuits followed as Levin charged plagiarism,

insisting that much of his original script was used by the Hacketts. Clashes between Levin and Frank intensified as Levin charged Frank with being untruthful in his promises to give Levin the right to adapt the *Diary,* and Frank's attorneys reciprocated by continuing to refuse Levin permission to produce his play—be it in the United States or Israel. All of this was played out in the press and argued in the leading intellectual publications of the time, dividing the Jewish community. The publicity certainly hurt Levin's subsequent career—how dare Meyer Levin challenge the veracity of an iconic survivor of the Holocaust such as Otto Frank, let alone bring him to court?—but it did not prevent Levin from publishing a novel, *The Fanatic* (1964), which, in not particularly veiled fictional terms, told the story of the controversy and his obsession with the play from his point of view.

Levin's belief that his adaptation of the play had been sidetracked by a Communist conspiracy was reinforced for him by an article in the *New York Times Magazine* by the Hacketts ("Diary of 'The Diary of Anne Frank'"), wherein they note that Hellman gave them advice and suggestions for what he saw as their "de-Judaized" adaptation of the *Diary.* But was the motivation he imputed to them true? Or was Levin's adaptation simply too parochial for Broadway, where commercial success, rather than artistic integrity, was the criterion used in soliciting investors? Rather than a Communist conspiracy being behind the selection of the Hacketts' adaptation instead of the too-Jewish Levin's, perhaps it was the universalist ethos of assimilated Jews, including Otto Frank, whose mantra can be found in the *Diary,* wherein Anne writes, "It's really a wonder that I haven't dropped all my ideals, ... because in spite of everything I still believe that people are really good at heart" (*Anne Frank: The Diary of a Young Girl,* p. 237).

The complexity of the dispute is best described in two academic studies which, unsurprisingly, provide different interpretations of the controversy that created such consternation both inside and outside the Jewish community.

In his *An Obsession with Anne Frank: Meyer Levin and the Diary* (1995), Lawrence Graver, who taught English at Williams College, argued that the sudden rejection and subsequent rebuffs that Levin received in the fall of 1952 with regard to his adaptation of the *Diary* fed in him an anger and refusal to accept Cheryl Crawford and Kermit Bloomgarden's judgment that his script was "unplayable." At first Levin attributed the rejection to "shortsightedness, timidity, box-office anxiety, bad advice, and worries over his disagreements with Otto Frank" (Graver, p. 230). Later, his disappointment morphed into rationalizing his rejection as part of a Communist plot to "de-Judaize" the *Diary.* Graver concludes that it was not a cabal of Stalinists that waylaid Levin's script but rather that "the wound was caused by unresolvable tensions between his romantic desire for self-fulfillment as a Jew and a writer, his personal limitations as a man and writer, and the material, political and cultural conditions of the world in which he lived" (p. 238).

Ralph Melnick, a professor of Judaic studies at the University of Massachusetts, Amherst, in his *The Stolen Legacy of Anne Frank: Meyer Levin, Lillian Hellman, and the Staging of the Diary* (1997), disagrees with Graver's conclusion, "Levin was not the victim of a conspiracy,... nor was Hellman... involved in an elaborate ideologically motivated effort to sabotage Levin's version." (p. 228). Melnick cites examples of how Hellman and others involved in the adaption of the play altered the *Diary* notes to pursue their own agenda. For instance, he states that, in her 1973 memoir *Pentimento* and in television appearances, Hellman contended that "Jews were not the only ones who suffered" from the Nazis, the very words that were put into the mouth of Anne Frank on the stage though they never appeared in the *Diary* (p. 211). Melnick further notes that when Eleanor Roosevelt wrote the introduction to the American edition of *The Diary of a Young Girl,* as edited by Otto Frank, she never mentions the suffering of the Jews who had been singled out for extermination. Roosevelt's introduction was clearly in accord with Otto Frank's wish that Anne be seen as a symbol not of Jewish suffering but against world suffering.

Melnick concludes that he hopes for a reassessment of the falsely crafted ideological image of an adolescent "stripped of her Jewish identity, naively proclaiming on stage and screen a simplistic and unwavering belief in the goodness of people, that remains the fixed and unchallenged image that denies the reality of the Holocaust" (p. 229). How sad and frightening, states Melnick, that Anne's voice has been so indelibly glossed, and the horror of her last years, representative of the agonizing end suffered by millions of Jews, so terribly cleansed. This reassessment of the *Diary*, Melnick declares, will vindicate Levin's decades-long efforts to Judaize the *Diary* of Anne Frank.

In some artistic circles, Levin became a pariah because of his unceasing efforts to use the courts to rectify his grievance against Otto Frank and his attorneys. Yet during this period he used writing as a diversion from the hurt that would remain with him until his death in 1981. Some of Levin's best work emerged in the aftermath of the Anne Frank controversy, and he did get the opportunity to air his side of the dispute in his memoir *The Obsession* (1973). Levin also got to see a staging of his version of the *Diary* of Anne Frank performed by an amateur group in Israel in the mid-1960s, contrary to the legal agreement he had agreed to in the "resolution" of the controversy with Otto Frank's lawyers. And though he did not live to see it, his *Diary* finally had its first professional, American production in 1983 at the Lyric Stage of Boston and was revived there in 1991.

EARLY LIFE AND CAREER

Meyer Levin was born on in Chicago on October 8, 1905, to Joseph and Goldie Levin, immigrants from Lithuania who, in addition to Meyer, had two daughters, Bertha and Bess, both of whom later became teachers. Levin's father was a tailor who worked twelve hours a day and invested his savings in real estate. As Levin relates of his childhood in *In Search,* even though his father overextended himself in buying a three-story brick house on Racine Avenue, he took pride in being a landlord. The neighborhood on Racine

Ave, however, was predominately Italian, and Levin's childhood memories include being called a "sheenie" and being beaten up by Italian street gangs, which resulted in his "fear and shame at being a Jew" (*In Search,* p. 13).

Although his parents wanted him to become a lawyer or physician, Meyer wanted to be a writer. In high school, Meyer was a brilliant student who wrote stories for the school magazine. During these years he sought out a publication that had no taboos and no quota for Jewish stories, and discovered a small magazine published in Chicago called the *Ten Story Book.* The story he sent was accepted and provides insight into Meyer's feelings about himself as a Jew. It tells of a Jewish boy who was ashamed to have his gentile sweetheart encounter his Maxwell Street family. One day his girlfriend insists that they go slumming along the pushcart ghetto street, and when she stops at his father's stand, he pretends not to know his own father (p. 21).

Despite his affection for his parents, Levin had conflicting feelings about their coming from ordinary village folks (*proster Yidden,* plain Jews). He was also embarrassed by some of the ways his mother and father behaved. They spoke Yiddish at home and seemed not to make an effort to become Americanized. Writes Levin, "I sensed and resented this terrible shame and inferiority in my elders; they considered themselves as nothing, greenhorns, Jews" (p. 15).

It is possible that Levin's lifelong compulsion to retrace the steps of his people in exile and his love of Israel was penance for the early conflict outlined in his story, which he later described as "an unconscious bit of autobiography" (*In Search,* p. 21). It appears that Levin shared the guilt that plagued so many Jewish children of immigrants who suffered an inner struggle because of their sense of owing duty and respect to their parents even while they sensed a kind of superiority through their status as natives instead of "greenhorns" (p. 19).

At age sixteen Levin entered the University of Chicago and quickly became part of its literary circle. His writing also earned him a part-time job at the *Chicago Daily News,* a newspaper that was the center of the Chicago literary set.

Levin discovered that at the university, Jews were not accepted into gentile fraternities. Jewish students, however, created their own fraternities, but Levin observed that among the Jewish fraternities, there were "better" ones, and that "the distance between a southside German Jew and a westside Russian Jew was as a distance between the society page of the *Chicago Tribune* and the *Daily Jewish Forward*" (p. 22).

During his years at the university—he would graduate at age nineteen—Levin wrote short stories that were put together in a book called *Septagon* and brought to the attention of Ben Hecht and Maxwell Bodenheim, who were publishing the *Chicago Literary Times.* Hecht's response to Levin was not very encouraging, asking him, "What do you want to get published for?" and trying to disillusion him from becoming a writer. While Levin was writing for the *Chicago Daily News,* the Leopold-Loeb case broke. Levin did not get the assignment to cover the case, but when his novel *Compulsion* was published years later, people thought he did: as he told Ira Berkow, "there is confusion in which people think I was involved with the case in a way I was not. The use of a reporter as a story-telling device … made people identify it with me" (Berkow, p. 274). Levin did, however, cover the arraignment.

As Levin increasingly found himself writing for literary magazines, he followed the axiom to write about what he knew. As his identification with his Jewish identity grew, he became a frequent contributor to the Jewish national literary magazine *Menorah Journal.* In 1929 he published his first novel, *The Reporter,* which was not too well received. In 1933 Levin became an assistant editor and film critic at the newly created *Esquire* magazine, a position he held until 1939. Although his novel *The Old Bunch,* a novel about Jewish friends growing up in a Chicago neighborhood, was published during this period, Levin never lost sight of his concern for social justice. He stated that part of the writer's responsibility is to influence human behavior, and for this he must reach the widest audience. His means of achieving this end was the novel, which resulted in *Citizens,* his classic work tell-

ing the story of how Chicago police shot down ten steel-mill strikers on Memorial Day 1937.

In 1925 Levin visited the Jewish Yishuv (settlement) in Palestine. At the suggestion of his editor at the *Menorah Journal,* he was asked to write about the opening of the Hebrew University. In his autobiography, Levin recalls that for a young American to go to Palestine in 1925 was itself strange. In those days Zionism was something that was discussed in the Jewish press, but it was a question that had not yet entered the psyche of American-born Jews, and he reveals that his own family had no interest in the movement. Nevertheless, Levin found the experience in Palestine electrifying: "I felt like a discoverer. Here were Jews like early Americans, riding guard at night in vigilance against hostile natives, pioneering in the malarial marshes, and living in communal groups" (*In Search,* p. 33). Following the rejection of *Frankie and Johnnie* and before *The Reporter* was published in 1929, Levin returned to Palestine and joined Kibbutz Yagur with the hope of eventually writing about Jewish life among the farm communes, but he returned to the United States when he received word that both *The Reporter* and *Frankie and Johnnie* would be published. In Palestine, however, he not only felt a connection between his Jewishness and the historic land of his people, but he also gathered material for his novel *Yehuda* (1931), the first modern novel about Palestine. The novel, however, was not well received in Jewish circles. Levine writes of his bitterness that "Jews never take up anything of their own until the gentiles have made a fuss over it" (p. 71). But there were other criticisms of his novel, particularly among Zionists, who accused Levin of being something of a traitor. They charged that his book was filled with examples of Jewish mistreatment of Arabs, that Jews were responsible for all the troubles in Palestine, and that he focused unnecessarily on a subplot in which a girl who suffered from kleptomania stole little sums of money from the kibbutz for the purchase of items to attract her lover. This was denounced as casting aspersions on the moral conduct of the kibbutzim. Levin responded to this criticism by pointing out that

his story showed "the comrades dealing with the girl's weakness intelligently. But to my astonishment I was now accused not only of contributing to the legend of sexual license in the settlements, but painting our pioneers as thieves!" (p. 71). Levin fell into depression, and his much-needed feelings of connection with his people were badly dissipated. As his depression worsened, he turned his concern mostly to earning a living.

It was during this period of dejection that Levin completed his book about the Hasidim, *The Golden Mountain* (1932), illustrated by Marek Szwarc. Szwarc was a painter and sculptor who was a Polish Jew but had migrated to Paris in 1910 with his wife and daughter, Tereska. Marek and his wife, Eugenia Markowa, secretly converted to Catholicism in 1920, but when his conversion became known, it shocked his friends and he was ostracized by his family. Nevertheless, Szwarc always considered himself a Jew but also very close to Christianity. During this period of his life, Szwarc's work was dominated by bas-reliefs depicting biblical scenes, especially Old Testament subjects.

Traveling in Europe after graduating from college, Levin encountered Szwarc in Paris and they quickly became friends. It was through the influence of Szwarc that Levin first began to sense the depth of Jewish tradition, and "to realize that it was appropriate for a Jewish artist to occupy himself with the material of Jewish life, that he need not feel ashamed of it, need not feel it was limiting, need not feel that it was of minor value" (p. 31). Szwarc's work also included pictures of Polish Jews in their long coats, with their earlocks and beards, and these Jews impressed Levin as the people of his "immediate past, now viewed as worthy ancestors rather than as ridiculous long-beards" (p. 33).

In 1934 Levin married Mable Schamp Foy, a twenty-year-old widow and a non-Jew. Graver states that Levin's parents tearfully accepted his marriage to the "shiksa"; but when they learned that she had entered the University of Chicago at fifteen, his mother said, "Like you!" and expressed relief that "our prodigy affinity somehow balanced the shikseh part: a brilliant girl" (qtd. in Graver, p. 61). By the early forties they were estranged, and they divorced in 1944. Mable Foy soon remarried after her divorce and committed suicide in 1951. Levin, who was increasingly absorbed with matters concerning the Jewish people, raises the question of intermarriage in his autobiography: "Was it [his marriage to a gentile] an act of spite against this very factor that had given me so much trouble?" The answer challenged one of the most emotionally charged taboos of Jewish religious life: "a Jew can feel free to marry a gentile only when he has fully worked out the role of Jewishness in his life, when he feels secure in his Jewish self. Then he no longer needs the support of restrictions" (*In Search*, pp. 78–79).

In 1948 Levin married Tereska Torrès, the daughter of Marek Szarc, and the couple reared four children, one of whom, Dominique, was from Tereska's first marriage to Georges Torrès, a French Jew serving with the Free French, who was killed in Lorraine fighting with the French Second Armored Division when Tereska was five months pregnant. She and Levin would raise three sons, Eli, Gabriel, and Mikael. Tereska would also write fourteen novels, including *Women's Barracks* (1950), which sold 4 million copies in the United States. Based on her experience serving with the Free French forces in London in the Second World War, the novel was controversial because of its torrid sex scenes and her candid depiction of lesbianism. Prior to their marriage, Tereska accompanied Levin to Poland, where he filmed *The Illegals* (1948), which told the story of the smuggling operation of Jews from the interior of Poland across Europe to the Palestinian coast. Tereska starred in the film. And it was Tereska who, not long after their marriage, first drew Levin's attention to the French translation of Anne Frank's diary.

Prior to the imbroglio over the diary, Tereska had become friends with Otto Frank and was extremely upset when Levin launched a public campaign and legal action against Frank and the producers of the 1955 play. Tereska pleaded with her husband to make his peace over the controversy, but Levin was insistent on seeking justice against those who denied him his rightful place as the author of the stage play or at least allow

his version of the play to be staged. They continually fought over his decades-long obsession, and Tereska considered leaving him on several occasions, even contemplating suicide. Tereska's difficulties with Levin's obsession is detailed in his novel *The Fanatic*.

The Illegals was not the only film Levin made about the efforts of the Haganah ("The Defense"), a mainstream paramilitary organization that was the precursor to the Israel Defense Forces, which organized the effort to smuggle Jews from DP camps in Europe into Palestine. In 1947, strictly adhering to the British White Paper of 1939, the British limited Jewish immigration into Palestine even after the war, when survivors of the concentration camps had nowhere else to turn. The film *My Father's House* (1947), based on Levin's novel, tells the story of a little boy smuggled into Palestine who was obsessed with the belief that he would find his father alive in Palestine. Levin based the book and film on his memory of a boy who would not leave Buchenwald after liberation because his father had said, "Wait here for me until I come back." In the film, the boy's father says, " I will meet you in *Eretz* Israel" (*In Search,* pp. 332–333).

Novelist, filmmaker, reporter: these were many of Levin's accomplishments. But there was also Levin the war correspondent. Although he covered the liberation of the camps, his first experience in war reporting was during the Spanish Civil War (1936–1939). Assigned by *Inside* magazine to go to Spain to cover the conflict, Levin experienced firsthand what war was like. But he also made lasting friendships, including Ernest Hemingway and his future wife, the novelist Martha Gellhorn. Reporting on the role of the correspondent covering war, Levin wrote, "the routine is always embarrassing because the visitor knows that the men who are stationed there cannot help but feel resentful of his privilege of coming—and going away.... in modern warfare ... he has to smell, to see a little, and he has to go away to testify. Even if he doubts himself for not being a participant, he cannot dent the argument in his own mind that public opinion can be of greater importance than the presence of one more man in the army" (*In Search,* p. 113).

During his weeks in Spain writing articles from the Loyalist perspective, Levin encountered the presence of American boys—including many young Jewish men, some of whom were writers—who had come to Spain to fight against fascism. In encountering these volunteers, Levin felt guilty that he had not joined in the fight. This emotion was intensified by the death of James Lardner, who also came as a correspondent and who remained to fight and die for democracy.

Perhaps the lasting impression made by his experience in Spain was observing the conflict between the Communists, the anarchists, and Trotskyites. Levin encountered talk of assassinations and atrocities, and wrote: "But we who weren't communist felt ... that we might be enlisting in a battle that was other than we thought it to be. It was a feeling partly grained with dishonor at having such a feeling, for the big fact remained immutable: this was the battle against fascism, nothing else mattered" (p. 114). It may be that Levin's close-up view of the infighting among the various leftist groups fighting fascism in Spain, especially his distrust of the Communists following orders from Moscow, reverberated during the Anne Frank controversy, when he believed that a Stalinist conspiracy was behind the effort to exorcise his stage version of the *Diary.*

Before he left Spain, Levin was given permission to join the International Brigade for a limited period. Levin wanted to become part of the brigade long enough to take part in the action so that he might write a short book that would be published in time to have some effect in the United States, which had an embargo on arms being sent to the Loyalist government. In his autobiography, Levin wrote, "Wasn't it a way to salve my conscience, while prearranging an honorable desertion?" (p. 115). The book on Spain was never published.

At the end of 1937 he left Spain for Palestine, where he witnessed the struggle between the Arabs and Jews as well as that between the Jews and the British. Levin would continue to visit the Yishuv, and on the eve of Jewish Palestine becoming Israel, Levin approached the Overseas News Agency to send him there to report on this

momentous period of Jewish history. The response Levin received surprised him: they could not use him in Israel because of his Jewish name. As Levin relates the response, they told him that they felt a gentile byline would receive wider acceptance in the American press (p. 471). In fact, despite his reputation as a correspondent, it was more than a year before he could find employment, reporting for the Jewish Telegraph Agency, that would take him to Israel.

The founding of Israel was a momentous event for Levin. He visited Israel a number of times, deepening his connection to his Jewish heritage. In his memoir *In Search,* Levin analyzed the relationship he found between the newly created Jewish state and American Jews. Levin noted the scorn many Israelis had for American Jews: Jews from America who came to Israel and visited the kibbutzim were either patronizing or overly humble, and Levin learned that "the gap in experience, the gap in viewpoint was widening" (p. 495). Levin believed it was his mission as a writer to narrow the gap and was appalled with what little means there were for the two Jewish populations to come to know each other. He noted that the average Israeli had only the most distorted idea of American Jewish life, and the American Jew had an inaccurate view of Israel. Levin was dismayed that the dynamic new country of the Jewish state was absent from the psyche of most Jews in America—the growing Hebrew literature, the new festivals transforming Jewish religious holy days, the economic life bred in both capitalistic and socialist institutions. Little of this, argued Levin, was being transmitted to America. Finally, he despairingly noted that "The Jew of Biblical times … that had so enveloped him in legend had been consigned to remoteness. But conversely, the human, living Jew of Israel could serve to humanize all of our past, to make us feel at home with our ancestors. Through him they became less legendary, and people like ourselves" (pp. 500–501).

On the question of whether the creation of Israel meant the beginning of the end of anti-Semitism, Levin wrote that no one need "believe that anti-Semitism can be dissolved with one historic action; but it cannot be denied that the image of the young Jew of Israel is already replacing the image of the legendary Jew, the hook-nosed bearded Fagin" (p. 510).

Levin also argued that the Jew outside of Israel must engage the Jewish state. All Jews, like the Israelis, must welcome the nourishment of the Jewish past. Israelis understand that their goal as Jews is something more than the creation of a state like other states. Rather, their raison d'être with regard to the creation of Israel was not the ultimate goal of Judaism, but the objective of engaging with Jews the world over in the pursuit of universal justice, based on the morality and ethics of the Torah (pp. 510–511).

WORKS: MAJOR THEMES

Meyer Levin's writings fall into several categories linked by his personal experiences. From his early years growing up in the Jewish community in Chicago, his fiction goes on to span much of the Jewish experience in the twentieth century, including anti-Semitism, the kibbutzim in pre-state Palestine, the founding of Israel, and the Holocaust, as well as his decades-long obsession with the controversy over the staging of *The Diary of Anne Frank.* He also wrote of his journey from the embarrassment he felt for being a Jew to his celebration of Jewish culture and tradition.

But Levin was also concerned with social justice and manifested that concern in his classic fictional account of the Chicago steel strike of 1937, *Citizens.* In his best known work, *Compulsion,* he sought to understand the psychological underpinnings for the gruesome murder of a child. Levin's pride in his ethnicity is also an influence in his fiction. Unlike the negative portraits of Jewish characters in Jerome Weidman's *I Can Get It for You Wholesale* (1937), Budd Schulberg's *What Makes Sammy Run* (1941), or Philip Roth's *Portnoy's Complaint* (1969). Levin portrays positive Jewish characters, be it members of the kibbutzim or the Jewish physician Mitch Wilner, who appears in his novels as the voice of the Jewish tradition of *tikkun olam* (repairing the world).

In reading the body of Levin's work, we must remember that he was an eyewitness to much

that he wrote about. As a correspondent for news agencies, such as the Jewish Telegraphic Agency, he witnessed the aftereffects of the brutality of the Nazi "Final Solution" on the survivors of the concentration camps, whom he interviewed, and which became the basis for *Eva*. He also sought to understand the mentality of the Nazi perpetrators in *The Stronghold,* and in *The Fanatic* the plot turns on the story of a Jewish writer who was murdered by the Nazis. His experiences with survivors could help explain his obsession with telling the story of Anne Frank correctly as a victim of the Holocaust.

Furthermore, Levin briefly joined the Haganah underground and helped smuggle Jews from the interior of Poland to the Palestine shore. He captured this operation in his film *The Illegals*. Levin's fiction on prestate Jewish Palestine and after is based on having lived on the kibbutzim and later elsewhere in Israel, noting the daily life, routine, and hopes of those pioneers and sharing in their experiences to create a Jewish state. His experiences became the basis for his two major works on prestate Palestine and the founding of the State of Israel: *The Settlers* and *The Harvest*. These life experiences are also recounted in his two autobiographical works, *In Search* and *The Obsession.*

NOVELS OF PREWAR CHICAGO: THE OLD BUNCH, CITIZENS, *AND* COMPULSION

The Old Bunch (1937) is perhaps Levin's most important work of fiction. Coming in at 964 pages, it is long but never boring. The book traces the lives of nineteen Jewish teenagers living on Chicago's West Side, but as they age into adulthood, Levin traces his characters' lives as they travel to New York, Paris, and prestate Palestine.

The characters include two physicians—including Mitch Wilner—along with a hatmaker, a furniture manufacturer, a fellow-traveling lawyer, a small-time criminal lawyer, a corrupt lawyer, a high school teacher, a sculptor, an unsuccessful inventor, and a man who walks the tracks during the Depression. The women reflect an era when women were expected to marry early

and have children. Levin artfully traces the interaction of his characters so that the reader cares for the fortunes of each one.

The novel anticipates the social realism that would characterize Levin's future works of fiction. Its characters are confronted with issues familiar to Levin from his years growing up among the Jews of the West Side of Chicago: assimilation, generational conflict between Jewish immigrants and their American-born children, the interaction of wealthy Jews with those who were poor, and how the Depression impacted all of them. Not all of his characters are noble: some are corrupt, others are crooked fixers, and still others are greedy at the expense of their families' happiness. Gary Bossin notes that the immediate reaction to the novel came from leaders of the Jewish community who found it degrading to Jews (Bossin, p. 110). Levin in his autobiography saw this criticism "as that of a people who were assimilationist at heart" and somehow "felt threatened by it, as though [he] were saying that they were not Americans, instead of simply reminding them that they were still Jews" (*In Search,* pp. 93–94). Levin did not view *The Old Bunch* as a socially destructive book. Rather, he believed that he sought to illuminate "a whole organism, much of it repulsive, parts of it in decay, but within which there remained a great capacity for self-renewal.... While novelists emphasized the individual in the family unit as the determining human relationship, I saw the surrounding group, the bunch, as perhaps even more important than the family in the formative years" (pp. 75–76). Levin believed that the children of immigrants learned their values as Americans largely through these group relationships, and making this point was one of Levin's main objectives in writing *The Old Bunch*. His other objective, it would appear, was to explore the meaning of being an American-born Jew of his generation.

Citizens, published in 1940, is a classic work of the social realism. Levin played a role in the Memorial Day steel strike of May 30, 1937, when ten strikers were shot by Chicago police in what has since been described as a massacre. Although the strike was sanctioned by the Congress of

Industrial Organizations, the newspapers and the police viewed it as being led by the "reds," when in fact it attracted non-Communist progressives such as Levin. Then a freelance reporter, Levin acted as a volunteer aide and accompanied the striking steelworkers and their families to the gates of the Republic Steel Company plant. Subsequently, when the violence erupted, Levin retreated with the marchers when the police started to shoot and beat the protestors. As a witness to all these occurrences—the speeches, the shootings, and the chaos that followed—he recorded his interviews and notes for *Citizens*. In the novel, the physician Mitch Wilner becomes Levin's fictional voice. Sympathetic to the plight of the workers, he tends to the wounded and visits the hospitals where the wounded were taken and the homes of the workers who were shot. Levin himself had gone to the hospital, where he saw and photographed the ten dead and seventy-five wounded men, women, and children. More history than fiction, *Citizens* is always riveting and reveals how Levin used fiction to promote his pursuit of social justice.

Written during Levin's ongoing battle over the Hacketts' stage adaptation of the *Diary of Anne Frank,* his novel *Compulsion* (1956) would become a best seller. Based on the sensational Leopold and Loeb murder of the fourteen-year-old Bobby Franks in 1924, Levin's work as a reporter in Chicago at the time provided him with a familiarity with the personalities and social climate surrounding the crime. The novel is told through the eyes of a young reporter, Sid Silver, who is an acquaintance of both Judd Steiner (Nathan Leopold) and Artie Straus (Richard Loeb), and Silver's understanding of the murder leads him to compare the crime to that of Raskolnikov in Fyodor Dostoyevsky's 1866 novel *Crime and Punishment.* Judd's response is to argue that Raskolnikov's crime was simply a "petty attempt at theft, motivated by abysmal poverty," whereas the murder of Paulie Kessler (Bobby Franks) was "a crime … without need, without any of the emotional human drives of lust, hatred, greed.… it became a pure action, the action of an absolute free being—a superman" (pp. 17–18). Levin argues that the murder committed by the two

brilliant, wealthy Jewish university students was influenced by their reading of Friedrich Nietzsche. He describes both Artie and Judd as having it all: wealth, intelligence, and the world at their feet as part of the German Jewish elite of the upper-crust Jewish community of 1920s Chicago. Artie is handsome, athletic, and popular, but he possesses a hidden, powerful sadistic streak and a desire to dominate. Judd is a homosexual and an introvert, a genius who longs for a companion whom he can idolize and worship.

The privilege of wealth and the sense of not being bound by conventional morality led the two to attempt to commit a "perfect crime," carried out as a purely intellectual exercise. Levin argues that the Nietzchean ideas that led to the crime was a precursor of things to come. He views the murder as foretelling the ideas that led to the Holocaust when he writes, "these same years we have seen an outbreak of paranoia and a Nietzschean mania connected with the death of millions" (p. 409). Adam Kirsch, reviewing a 2015 reissue of *Compulsion,* echoes Levin when he states, "In a strange way, their single crime encapsulates the moral anarchy that was responsible for so many millions of deaths, in war and revolution and Holocaust, during the 20th century. As in a laboratory experiment, they demonstrated on a small scale the forces that, unleashed, could destroy the world."

In addition to writing a riveting account of how the two murderers were eventually caught, Levin also deals with Judd's homosexuality, the tension between the families of upper-class German Jews (Judd and Artie) and what were seen as the lower-class families of Russian Jews (Sid Silver), as well as Jewish self-hatred (an attitude Levin wrestled with growing up in Chicago). *Compulsion* was made into a successful stage play and a film. Kirsch suggests, however, that Levin's ultimate objective was to view "a familiar story through a new imaginative lens, provided by Freudian psychoanalysis. Freudian ideas, which were just becoming fashionable in 1924 when the crime was committed, had become widely familiar and well-established by 1956, when *Compulsion* was written."

Compulsion was the last book Levin wrote about the American scene as he turned away from the struggle with his identity as a Jew in America. His experiences as a reporter in World War II Europe, and as an early eyewitness to the horrors of the Holocaust death camps, changed the direction of his life and fiction. He began writing on distinctly Jewish themes with a Zionist outlook, and made his home in Israel.

HOLOCAUST TRILOGY: EVA, THE FANATIC, AND THE STRONGHOLD

When Levin and his family arrived in Israel in 1958 he received a letter from Mrs. Ida Lev, a resident of Tel Aviv and an Auschwitz survivor. She briefly outlined her struggle for survival and asked to meet Levin to determine if he would be interested in her story. After a number of meetings with Mrs. Lev, Levin decided to write *Eva,* based on her experiences. The novel is a fictionalized but fundamentally factual account of how Ida Levy survived the Holocaust. Bossin notes that Levin may have invented some incidents or added to the narrative experiences related to him by other survivors, but he concludes that "whether the story of a single or composite survivor, Eva is unquestionably authentic" (p. 213).

The novel relates how Lev's fictional counterpart, Eva Korngold, is urged by her mother to escape the growing danger of the Nazi roundups by assuming the identity of a recently deceased Ukrainian peasant girl. Now known as Katerina, or Katy, she endures many hazardous escapes from nearly being identified as a Jew until the day it is discovered that she is one, and she is sent to Auschwitz. She escapes when the camp is evacuated and the prisoners are sent on the infamous death march. The novel concludes when she reaches Palestine. Throughout the story Levin gives emphasis to her determination to live, her haunting fears, and her emotions of love and hate.

Even though Levin had achieved success as a novelist, especially after the best-selling *Compulsion,* he could not overcome his bitterness that the "de-Judaized" version of the *Diary* had become a theater classic. The result was *The*

Fanatic (1964), a novel about the Holocaust that also mirrored the events of his then decade-long fight for the staging of his version of the play. Levin's conceit in *The Fanatic* is to tell his story through the travails of a writer, whom he names Leo Kahn, who died in Bergen-Belsen from typhus. Kahn's writings, which survive the Holocaust, include a book titled *Good and Evil,* a meditation on how a just God could allow the suffering and death of millions of Jews. A rabbi, Maury Finkelstein, who is a chaplain serving Jewish survivors in the DP camps and also an aspiring playwright, is given the book by Anika, a survivor who was also the deceased writer's sweetheart but subsequently marries Maury. The rabbi, who had written pageants to raise money for Jewish survivors, concludes not only that *Good and Evil* would be an important play that would convey to the American public the depth of Jewish suffering during the Holocaust, but that he would find a producer who would allow him to adapt the book for the stage. In the course of finding a producer, Maury runs into responses such as "who wants to pay money at the box office to see Jews going to their death" (p. 80). A producer tells Maury, "the play seems to cry out too much with special pleading for the Jews...." Levin has the voice of the deceased author Leo Kahn state that another producer, incorrectly, is sure his book is a universal outcry against human brutality, with the Jew as the example of the sufferer. Still another producer tells Maury, "I must say I find this adaptation in its approach quite chauvinistic" (pp. 164–165).

Like Levin in his attempt to adapt his version of the *Diary* for the commercial stage, Maury finds only frustration that nearly costs him his marriage and his sanity as he fails to bring to the general public the full story of Hitler's objective to rid the planet of every Jewish man, woman, and child.

The title of *The Stronghold* (1965), the third novel in Levin's Holocaust trilogy, refers to a baronial castle that has become a fortress in Nazi territory. It is the last days of the war, and inside the castle are a dozen political prisoners, including collaborationist former officials of a Nazi-occupied country. (After the liberation of Paris in

1944, leaders of the Vichy government in France were imprisoned in a castle in Germany.) Among the prisoners are cabinet ministers, an army marshal, and one woman, the mistress of one of the ex-premiers. As the rescuing American army approaches, a final prisoner arrives, Vered, a former premier and a Jew. (It would seem that Vered is based on Léon Blum, a French prime minister in the 1930s who was sent to a concentration camp during the war.) The Nazi leader Kraus (Adolf Eichmann?), the executor of the Final Solution, hopes to use the hostages as pawns in his efforts to barter them for his own safety.

Although this is the plot outline, the novel really is about Levin's efforts to examine the manner in which former political leaders like these, here challenged by Vered, justified their own acquiescence in the Nazi extermination campaign against the Jews. In particular, one of the hostages, a worker-priest, is forced to reappraise the historical position of the Church toward the Jews. Kraus rationalizes his role in the Final Solution when he states, "I have never been a good Christian … but I have never forgotten that the Jews killed the Savior" (p. 169). Levin's novel asks moral and political questions about the manner in which civilized, educated leaders turned their backs to the Jews in their moment of survival.

SECOND ALIYAH AND THE BIRTH OF ISRAEL: THE SETTLERS AND THE HARVEST

Levin's early visits to Palestine, where he lived on a kibbutz and later wrote of his experiences in his novel *Yehuda* (1931), culminated in his writing the history of the Second Aliyah in *The Settlers* (1972). The Second Aliyah refers to the massive influx of European Jews into Palestine during the years 1904–1914. Between these years approximately thirty-five thousand Jews arrived, mainly from Russia and Poland. Like the first migration from Russia, the Second Aliyah was motivated by a combination of Zionist ideology coupled with anti-Jewish violence and pogroms. It was brought to a halt by the outbreak of the First World War in 1914.

The story of these events, as told by Levin, centers around Yankel Chaimovitch and his family, who flee from the pogroms of czarist Russia and settle in Palestine. In Levin's epic account, he follows the lives of the Chaimovitch children as they work the barren land of Palestine, describing their reaction to the tyranny of their Turkish overlords and their relations with their Arab neighbors (which in many ways anticipates the present conflict), as well as World War I, the Balfour Declaration, and the creation of the Zion Mule Corps, which fought on the British side at Gallipoli in 1915.

The Harvest (1978) continues the story of the Chaimovitch family from 1927 to 1948, wherein the story's focus is on Mati, the family's youngest son, who becomes a pilot and helps build the Israeli air force. Levin describes the secret preparations made by the Haganah to respond to Arab attacks on the kibbutzim as well as the increasing hostility of the British to the Jewish presence in Palestine. He brings the story up to 1948, when Mati is sent by the Yishuv to the United States to raise money, arms, and volunteers to protect the newly created state of Israel against the Arab armies that have attacked the Jewish state.

The 1970s novels bring together Levin's later fiction, wherein he probes the connections between the Holocaust, its aftermath climaxing in the birth of Israel, and the interdependence between the diaspora community and the Jewish state.

AUTOBIOGRAPHICAL WORKS: IN SEARCH AND THE OBSESSION

In Search (1950) is Meyer Levin's memoir of his efforts to exorcise his self-hatred as a Jew. His ghetto childhood, where he was terrified by Italian kids, led him to the point that he felt an unjustified guilt about being Jewish. During the early part of his writing career, he found that publishers had little interest in stories about Jews and, as noted elsewhere in this essay, he disguised Jewish characters as gentiles (*Frankie and*

Johnnie) in order to be published. His evolution as a writer, for the most part, was to prove that his people "did not deserve to be despised but were noble" (p. 520).

The memoir reveals how Levin moved from his own animosity toward being a Jew to his status as one of the most important chroniclers of twentieth-century Jewish history. It chronicles his experiences from his time on a kibbutz in pr- estate Israel, to his work as a war correspondent who witnessed the liberation of Nazi concentration camps, to his efforts to work with the Haganah to bring Holocaust survivors to Palestine by illegally running the British blockade.

Written when he was a frequent visitor to the recently created State of Israel but had not yet made it his home, Levin's autobiography includes his meditation on the issue of Jewish values as it pertains to the relationship between American Jews and Israel as well as his thoughts on intermarriage and educating Jewish children in America about their heritage. Levin's solution to anti-Semitism "is not to be overcome by getting people to forget us, but to know us" (p. 520). He believed that a positive view of Jews was already in the making by the reaction of many in the Christian world to the new Jew of Israel.

Levin begins his second memoir, *The Obsession* (1973), by writing that "in the middle of my life I fell into trouble that was to grip, occupy, haunt and all but devour me these 20 years" (p. 7). The center of this memoir, clearly, is his twenty-year battle over the rejection of his dramatization of the *Diary* of Anne Frank. But it also includes the complications and subsequent litigation that preceded the staging of *Compulsion,* his best-selling novel about the "crime of the century," the Leopold and Loeb murder trial. Levin also gives his account of the difficulties he had in preparing for publication *The Fanatic* (1964), his fictional account of the Anne Frank controversy as told by the ghost of a deceased Holocaust writer. Otto Frank's law firm claimed the novel was libelous and demanded (unsuccessfully) that the book be canceled. *The Obsession* is compelling reading, detailing his

long struggle for vindication in regard to his adaptation of the *Diary.*

CONCLUSION

Above all, Meyer Levin was a storyteller. Like Herman Wouk (1915–) and Leon Uris (1924– 2003), Levin's interest in the later stages of his career was to use fiction to convey the major events that shaped the Jewish experience in the twentieth century. In his autobiography *In Search,* Levin says that his particular task as a writer was to be a link between the Israeli and American Jews, since they were the principal populations for Jewish continuity. Not a religious Jew in its traditional meaning, Levin was, nevertheless, a committed Jew whose understanding of the Torah demanded the promotion of social justice, wherein Israel would fulfill the ethical and moral values of Judaism and become the model for Jewish identity the world over.

Early in his career he had doubts, because of the prevalence of anti-Semitism, about whether he could become a successful American writer using Jewish characters and themes in his fiction. After the Holocaust and the creation of Israel, however, when anti-Semitism in America became "unfashionable," he came to feel that he could write freely as a Jew and as an American.

As in the case of Wouk and Uris, Levin was never considered among the upper tier of American Jewish writers, although there were those who thought that he was the major chronicler of the Jewish experience in his time. Because of his more than twenty-year struggle over the *Diary* of Anne Frank, and his reputation as being litigious (including the suit over the staging of *Compulsion*), Levin was filled with a paranoia that his fiction had systematically been ignored by the literary establishment. He claimed that his critics, consisting of "anti-Jewish-Jews" to whom Zionism and Jewish particularism were anathema, ignored his literary work. Regardless of the fairness of Levin's accusations, his fiction continues to be worth reading, and he deserves to be recognized as an important writer of serious popular fiction.

Levin died July 9, 1981, in Jerusalem, Israel. The cause of his death was unspecified.

Selected Bibliography

WORKS OF MEYER LEVIN

NOVELS

The Reporter. New York: John Day, 1929.

Frankie and Johnnie: A Love Story. New York: John Day, 1930.

Yehuda. New York: J. Cape & H. Smith, 1931.

The New Bridge. New York: Covici Friede, 1933.

The Old Bunch. New York: Citadel Press, 1937.

Citizens. New York: Viking, 1940.

My Father's House. New York: Viking, 1947.

Compulsion. New York: Simon & Schuster, 1956.

Eva. New York: Simon & Schuster, 1959.

The Fanatic. New York: Simon & Schuster, 1964.

The Stronghold. New York: Simon & Schuster, 1965.

Gore and Igor: An Extravaganza. New York: Simon & Schuster, 1968.

The Settlers. New York: Simon & Schuster, 1972.

The Spell of Time. New York: Praeger, 1974.

The Harvest. New York: Simon & Schuster, 1978.

The Architect. New York: Simon & Schuster, 1981.

NONFICTION/MEMOIR

The Golden Mountain: Marvellous Tales of Rabbi Israel Baal Shem, and of His Great-Grandson, Rabbi Nachman, Retold from Hebrew, Yiddish, and German Sources. New York: Behrman House, 1932. Reprinted, 1951.

In Search: An Autobiography. New York: Horizon, 1950.

The Obsession. New York: Simon & Schuster, 1973.

ARTICLES

"What's Left of the Jews." *Nation,* July 28, 1945, p. 74. Republished online, http://www.thenation.com/article/holocaust-whats-left-jews/

"The Child Behind the Secret Door: An Adolescent Girl's Own Story of How She Hid for Two Years During the Nazi Terror." *New York Times Book Review,* June 15, 1952, pp. 1, 22. (Review of *Anne Frank: The Diary of a Young Girl.*)

"The East Side Gangsters of the Paper-Backs: The 'Jewish' Novels that Millions Buy." *Commentary,* October 1953, pp. 334–342. https://www.commentarymagazine.com/articles/the-east-side-gangsters-of-the-paper-backsthe-jewish-novels-that-millions-buy/

"The Writer and the Jewish Community: Case History of a Culture-Maker," *Commentary,* June 1947, pp. 528–530. https://www.commentarymagazine.com/articles/the-writer-and-the-jewish-communitycase-history-of-a-culture-maker/

"What Is an American Jewish Writer?" *Congress Bi-Weekly,* May 19, 1972, p. 22.

"J'Accuse." *Israel Magazine,* January 1976, pp. 19–21.

AS EDITOR

With Charles Angoff. *The Rise of American Jewish Literature: An Anthology of Selections from the Major Novels.* New York: Simon & Schuster, 1970.

PAPERS

The Meyer Levin Collection at the Howard Gotlieb Archival Research Center, Boston, consists of manuscripts, letters, photographs, scrapbooks, printed material, and other items. Manuscripts by Levin in the collection include numerous plays, novels, scripts, short stories, dispatches written while Levin was a correspondent, many short pieces, and other typescripts, carbon copies, and notes for Levin's extensive writings.

CRITICAL AND BIOGRAPHICAL STUDIES

Angoff, Charles. "The Jewishness of Meyer Levin." *Congress Bi-Weekly,* December 27, 1965, pp. 13–14.

Balint, Benjamin. *Running Commentary: The Contentious Magazine That Transformed the Jewish Left into the Neoconservative Right.* New York: Public Affairs, 2010.

Berkow, Ira. "Meyer Levin." In his *Maxwell Street: Survival in a Bazaar.* New York: Knopf Doubleday, 1977. Pp. 269–277.

Bossin, Gary. "The Literary Achievement of Meyer Levin." Ph.D. dissertation, Kent State University, 1980.

Franklin, Ruth. "Did Anne Frank Really Have An 'Infinite Human Spirit'?" *New Republic,* March 8, 2011. https://newrepublic.com/article/84919/meyer-levin-anne-frank-compulsion

Graver, Lawrence. *An Obsession with Anne Frank: Meyer Levin and the Diary.* Berkeley: University of California Press, 1995.

Guttmann, Allen. *The Jewish Writer in America: Assimilation and the Crisis of Identity.* New York: Oxford University Press, 1971.

Hackett, Frances, and Albert Hackett. "Diary of *The Diary of Anne Frank.*" *New York Times Magazine,* September 30, 1956, pp. 1, 3. https://www.nytimes.com/books/97/10/26/home/anne-hackett.html

Hellman, Lillian. *Pentimento.* Boston: Little, Brown, 1973.

Leiter, Robert. "The Obsession." *New York Times,* October 26, 1997. https://www.nytimes.com/books/97/10/26/reviews/971026.26leitert.html (Review of Melnick's *The Stolen Legacy of Anne Frank: Meyer Levin, Lillian Hellman, and the Staging of the Diary.*)

Melnick, Ralph. *The Stolen Legacy of Anne Frank: Meyer Levin, Lillian Hellman, and the Staging of the Diary.* New Haven, Conn.: Yale University Press, 1997.

Moore, Harry T. "Ah Paranoia!" *New Republic,* February 2, 1974, p. 21.

Varon, Benno Weiser. "The Haunting of Meyer Levin," *Midstream,* August–September 1976, pp. 7–23.

REVIEWS

Bell, Pearl K. "Meyer Levin's Obsessions." *Commentary,* June 1, 1978. https://www.commentarymagazine.com/articles/meyer-levins-obsessions/

Bernstein, Richard. "Fixated on a More Jewish Anne Frank." *New York Times,* September 27, 1995. http://www.nytimes.com/1995/09/27/books/books-of-the-times-fixated-on-a-more-jewish-anne-frank.html (Review of Graver's *An Obsession with Anne Frank: Meyer Levin and the Diary.*)

Hertzberg, Arthur. "You Can Come Home Again." *Commentary,* February 1951. https://www.commentarymagazine.com/articles/in-search-by-meyer-levin/ (Review of *In Search.*)

Kazin, Alfred. Review of *The Old Bunch. New York Herald Tribune Book Review,* March 14, 1937, p. 5.

Kirsch, Adam. "The Murder of the Century." *Tablet,* April 16, 2015. http://chicago3966.rssing.com/browser.php?indx=41710303&item=58(Review of *Compulsion.*)

Navasky, Victor S. "The Ordeal of Meyer Levin." *New York Times Book Review,* February 3, 1974. http://query.nytimes.com/mem/archive/pdf?res=9E03E2DB1E3EEE37A25750C0A9649C946590D6CF (Review of *The Obsession.*)

Rosenfeld, Alvin H. "An Obsession with Anne Frank: Meyer Levin and the Diary." *Biography* 20, no. 2:210–214 (spring 1997).

ANNE FRANK DRAMATIZATIONS AND BOOKS

Goodrich, Frances, and Albert Hackett. *The Diary of Anne Frank.* Cheltenham, U.K.: Thomas Nelson, 1998.

Frank, Anne. *Anne Frank: The Diary of a Young Girl.* Translated from the Dutch by B. M. Mooyaart–Doubleday. Garden City, N.Y.: Doubleday, 1952.

Levin, Meyer. *Anne Frank: A Play by Meyer Levin Adapted from the Diary of Anne Frank.* Privately published by the author for literary discussion, 1972.

FILMS BASED ON THE WORKS OF MEYER LEVIN

My Father's House. Screenplay by Meyer Levin. Directed by Herbert Kline. Palestine: Jewish National Fund, 1947.

The Illegals. Written and directed by Meyer Levin, 1948.

Compulsion. Screenplay by Richard Murphy. Directed by Richard Fleischer. Darryl F. Zanuck/Twentieth Century-Fox, 1959.

NATHANIEL MACKEY

(1947—)

Joseph Pizza

IN THE OPENING letter of Nathaniel Mackey's epistolary novel *From a Broken Bottle Traces of Perfume Still Emanate* (2010), the semiautobiographical protagonist, "N.," asserts that "there are musics which haunt us like a phantom limb" (p. 3). Such phantoms populate Mackey's fiction as well as his poetry in diverse ways, becoming, in the process, both muse and method. For instance, one can understand the protagonist of his novel as the amputated form of his forename, "Nathaniel." As such, he is, in some sense, the author, while also attaining the freedom of a cipher, of a character whose lack of concrete, historical identity allows for the emergence of other voices—the gods and goddesses of ancient Egypt, the Dogon people of West Africa, the Loa of Haitian Vodou, exemplars of avant-garde jazz, experimental novelists and poets—voices that constitute a chorus whose song runs not only through the novel but throughout the entirety of Mackey's work. In this way, the texture of his writing is polyvocal, descending from the late-modernist and experimental traditions of Black Mountain and language poetry, where the lyric "I" becomes a complex "we." Indeed, Mackey's interest in what Federico García Lorca termed "duende," the soulful authenticity apparent in, say, the passionately rent voice of the flamenco singer or the bent note of the guitarist, is, in this regard, apposite. In the rending of the poet's voice a kind of doubling occurs, one where other voices—the vox populi—seem to join in a haunting chorus or duet. Like the limping Legba of Haitian Vodou, then, Mackey's "N." and the speakers of his poetry perform in tongues as diverse as the voices they conjure. The result is a body of work that is remarkable for its ability not merely to commemorate, but to re-member the phantom limbs of the American, and especially the African American, experience.

As the major themes of Mackey's work should suggest, he is a thoroughly American writer whose poetry and fiction in many ways seek to occupy the space shared by literature and music. Born on October 27, 1947, in Miami, Florida, and raised in Southern California, he received his B.A. from Princeton University in 1969 and his Ph.D. from Stanford University in 1975. As a teacher he continued to crisscross the country, from the University of Wisconsin (1974–1976), to the University of Southern California (1976–1979) and University of California at Santa Cruz (1979–2010), to Duke University, where since 2010 he has been the Reynolds Price Professor of Creative Writing. For many of these years Mackey worked as a disc jockey, eventually creating his own Sunday program, *Tanganyika Strut,* named after the famous John Coltrane recording sessions, for the independent radio station KUSP in Santa Cruz. In a 1991 interview with Christopher Funkhouser, Mackey explains the uniqueness of the program: "The kind of cross-cultural mix that a radio program like *Tanganyika Strut* offers diverges from a prepackaged sense of what appropriate content for a radio program is, where one is usually offered a homogeneous program" (*Paracritical Hinge,* p. 254). Here, the heterogeneity of his program offers a parallel to the mix of voices apparent in his writing. As he goes on to say, "There's a challenge in heterogeneity, whether it's radio programming, editing a magazine, one's own work, putting together a syllabus for a class, or whatever" (p. 254). The effect of such heterogeneity, what makes it so "challenging," whether in Mackey's radio, editorial, literary, or educational work, is the way it questions identity and forces the audience to reconsider what "a radio program is." This proves to be one of his enduring strategies, making any reference to autobiog-

raphy complicated at best. As he notes in a later interview, the personal in his writing is "refracted" through various personae (p. 321). Indeed, autobiographical connections are, for Mackey, beside the point: "A lot of biographical material comes in there, but neither there nor in my poetry am I writing autobiography. I'm using biographical material as elements of a composition" (p. 322). The result of such refraction and heterogeneity, then, is an oeuvre that is demanding on many levels.

Its complexity notwithstanding, Mackey's work has been celebrated with many honors and awards. Among them, he has received the Whiting Award (1993), the National Book Award for his poetry collection *Splay Anthem* (2006), the Roy Harvey Pearce–Archive for New Poetry Prize (2007), the Stephen Henderson Award (2008), a Guggenheim Fellowship (2010), the Ruth Lilly Poetry Prize (2014), and Yale's Bollingen Prize for Poetry (2015). From 2001 to 2007 he served on the Board of Chancellors of the American Academy of Poets. Despite such recognition, Mackey's writing has received relatively limited attention from scholars. In part, this may be a result of the challenging, experimental nature of his work. As he notes in the manifesto "Destination Out," innovative writing tends to be confined to the fringes: "It will, of course, suffer marginalization, temporary in some cases, unremitting in most" (*Paracritical Hinge,* p. 239). Such marginalization, however, also comes from that fact that Mackey is an African American author. As he notes in the same piece, "Black centrifugal writing has been and continues to be multiply marginalized. Why would it be otherwise?" (p. 239). Marginalized in more ways than one, then, Mackey's writing deserves, as the many awards he has won should suggest, greater attention from scholars. In fact, the difficult nature of his work invites critical reflection. But while it is true that his writing is not widely accessible in the usual sense, it does offer the invitation to participate in a reconsideration of the American experience that is passionately complex and hauntingly moving. As Don Share has noted in celebrating Mackey's achievement, his "rare combinations create an astonishing and resounding effect: his words go where music goes" (*Poetry* magazine, June 2014).

POETRY

Mackey's first collection of poetry, *Eroding Witness,* establishes many of his major themes. The collection contains versions of work published earlier in chapbook form as well as new poetry. It was selected by Michael S. Harper as one of the five volumes published in 1985 in the National Poetry Series and features a mingling of the author's voice with that of Egyptian gods and goddesses, the Andoumboulou, John Coltrane, and Jimi Hendrix, among others. Of the early work, the inclusion of material from the chapbook *Septet for the End of Time* (1983) stands out. The title plays on Olivier Messiaen's famous chamber music work *Quatuor pour la fin du temps* (*Quartet for the End of Time*), which was written and performed by the composer in a Nazi prisoner-of-war camp in 1941. Like Messiaen's work, which is composed of eight movements, the sequence comprises eight poems. However, as Mackey's title indicates, his reimagining of Messiaen's work swerves in the direction of the jazz septet. Indeed, the first piece in what is essentially a sequence of poems is dedicated to the saxophonist and John Coltrane collaborator Pharoah Sanders. In this way, Messiaen's apocalyptic concern with time is translated into the language of jazz. Indeed, whereas Messiaen's quartet concludes with a celebration of the freedom from time ushered in by Christ's Second Coming, Mackey's work explores, in perhaps a parallel sense, the elasticity of time apparent in the polyrhythmic and improvisatorial nature of jazz performance. In this way, it is not so much jazz musicians who influence his work—though they do, and they appear often—but the influence of jazz form that marks his work here and throughout his career. *Septet for the End of Time* invites readers to awaken to this sense of time with the speaker. Each poem begins, "I wake up," ringing changes on a theme, similar to, say, Coltrane's version of "My Favorite Things." In fact, it's worth noting that the reworking of pop standards by jazz musicians—such as, say, Art

Tatum's "Over the Rainbow"—emerges as a structural parallel to Mackey's early work. His first chapbook, *Four for Trane* (1978), borrows the title of Archie Shepp's famous 1964 album of Coltrane covers. In this way, Mackey's poetic work can be understood as originating in the space where the aesthetics of the cover song dovetails with the art of the bricoleur.

The first poem in the sequence, "Capricorn Rising," is a good place to observe this. The poem's irregular line lengths and shifting margins provide a textual equivalent to the polyrhythms of jazz. In this sense, the poem's dedicatee, Pharoah Sanders, can also be considered. A proponent of Coltrane's early "sheets of sound" approach to the saxophone, Sanders' arpeggios are often played so fast that they can be heard as glissandos. This duplicity in the performance can also be found in the poem. First, there is the question of lineation. The passages that begin far to the right of the traditional left margin create an ambiguity: Are they to be understood as new lines with a new margin, or, instead, are they continuations, perhaps completions, given their syntactical sense, of the previous line? The reader, of course, is challenged to wrestle with the prospect of a both/and. Content poses similar ambiguities. The speaker in this poem "wake[s] up mumbling, 'I'm / not at the music's / mercy,'" only to think "damned / if I'm not" (*Eroding Witness*, p. 83). Here, the ambiguity of the opening leaves the reader to ponder how the speaker is, yet is not, constrained by the music. This conflict is then developed in terms of time, of the endlessly recurrent, yet endlessly incomplete—this movement has much in common with the improvised solos of Sanders, Coltrane, and others, which are a hallmark of jazz music. There is, for instance, the repetitive play on a theme which, though theoretically endless and susceptible to expansion or contraction on any given night, remains nevertheless incomplete, merely a part of a larger composition, one performance among hundreds. In that sense, *the* definitive performance of a jazz solo is always "already there"—perhaps in the studio recording—while it is also "yet / to arrive," in the sense that Sanders might play it differently at different times, or, as in the case of

Coltrane, that someone else may later cover it—or even, as with the work of Billie Holiday, do it better. By integrating this multifaceted sense of time into his poetry, then, Mackey opens the verse to a kind of jazz apocalypse, as the title suggests. As David Hajdu has observed in reviewing Mackey's fiction, the author is "not simply writing about jazz, but writing as jazz."

In addition to the early work on display in *Eroding Witness*, the two serial poems that will occupy Mackey's poetic output going forward make their first appearance here. "Song of the Andoumboulou" takes its name from François Di Dio's 1956 recording of Dogon music titled *Les Dogon*, in which a song dedicated to "the spirits," the "Andoumboulou," is described in the liner notes (*Eroding Witness*, p. 31). As Mackey describes them in his 1998 interview with Brent Cunningham, the Andoumboulou are "a form of failed, flawed human being" (*Paracritical Hinge*, p. 317). By extending the Dogon sense of the Andoumboulou, Mackey once again can be seen to use sources in ways akin to the jazz musician, expanding upon a given theme or body of knowledge, or, at times, even deconstructing that body so as to reconstruct, or re-member, it anew. Though this has similarities with T. S. Eliot's deployment of allusion, Mackey's interest in non-Western and avant-garde influences is not programmatically ironic, nor is it an attempt to (re)assert *the* tradition in any comprehensive, all-encompassing way. Instead, the Andoumboulou, and their place in the Dogon cosmology, is approached as yet another haunted music, like that of Pharoah Sanders, one that, from the archaeologist's or the historian's perspective, may appear complete, but which, from the poet's perspective, remains incomplete and so capable of being sutured to any moment through the creative act of re-membering. As "Song of the Andoumboulou: 1" has it, these spirits "will not / ascend without song," the song performed in "our throats … our mouths"—performed, in other words, through the voices of the living (*Eroding Witness*, p. 33). Like the duende of the flamenco singer, then, the voice of this poem becomes plural, splicing speaker with spirits. In fact, as this serial poem develops over the course of suc-

ceeding collections, Mackey will explore further the ways in which the Andoumboulou want to "be sung," to have the "meat" of their bodies "sounded" (p. 35).

The second serial poem that will comprise the majority of Mackey's poetic output going forward is the "Poem for Don Cherry." Subtitled, and hereafter titled, "mu," the poem takes its inspiration from the jazz musician's albums of the same name. Having been a member of the New York Contemporary Five with Archie Shepp and participated in several of Ornette Coleman's free jazz recordings by the time of *Mu* (1969), Cherry was an accomplished proponent of harmolodics and the atonality that it brought to the jazz idiom. More generally, though, the title, of course, stands for the twelfth letter in the Greek alphabet. In Cherry's use, however, it may also be understood as the term for a jazz chord and, more strikingly, as the root for "music," with the etymological sense of *mousike,* "the art of the muses," accompanying it. This latter sense is clearly at the heart of Mackey's employment of the term in his serial poem, where the succeeding parts of "mu" pursue the "art of the muses" through a circuitous journey that continuously returns to the relationship between origin and ending. This can be observed in "'mu' first part," where the speaker wakes on "the day before the / year begins" (p. 60). The woman in the poem similarly appears "Lotusheaded," crowned with lotus flowers, like the Egyptian god of the underworld Osiris or the goddess Isis, whose associations with death, birth, and resurrection add a mythical layer to the poem's circular meditation on waking and sleeping, beginning and ending. The poem ends with the couple watching the sun set, to "see / how far the way we'd / come / went back" (p. 60). Again, recurrence is foregrounded: the end of the last day of the year signals the beginning of the new year; the way or path they've progressed upon simply leads back to the beginning; the earlier association with Egyptian gods of birth and death develops into the parallel posed by the couple's journey, implicit in the speaker's erotic phrasing. The conjunction of these varied influences and their conflation with the intimate experience of the

speaker is a common element in Mackey's poetry. In a related way, the harmony made possible by atonality is essential to Coleman's notion of harmolodics, and, similarly, to Cherry's extension of the practice to the world music, or "fusion," that he pioneered. The tracks of influence will continue to meet and cross as Mackey develops the poem over subsequent volumes.

School of Udhra, Mackey's second full-length collection of poetry, followed in 1993. It consists mainly of the continuation of "Song of the Andoumboulou" together with "Outlantish," first published as a chapbook in 1992, which develops the "mu" poems begun earlier. The collection's title refers to the seventh-century Islamic school of poetry that Mackey connects with the medieval troubadours of Europe (*Paracritical Hinge,* pp. 290–291). Fittingly, the collection begins with a love poem, "Song of the Andoumboulou: 8." The poem is subtitled "maitresse erzulie," who is the spirit of love in Haitian Vodou. Already, then, the continuation of the serial poem from *Eroding Witness* bears the same aspect of composite re-membering, the women of the piece figuring as the romantic object of Udhrite/troubadour poetry, as well as the object of syncretic, Vodou/Christian worship. Reading the poem, then, means hearing each of these varied speakers voiced through Mackey. Once again, the speaker finds himself in a liminal state, "Not yet asleep I'm no longer / awake" (*School of Udhra,* p. 3). In this state, the speaker listens for "Our Mistress's whispers," which hum with the sound of "a crosscut saw" (p. 3). Here, it is the violence of the juxtaposition of the various voices, and the danger of attempting to hear her through them, that comes to the fore. The poem then concludes with the speaker openmouthed, hearing "them / say, / By whatever bit of her I touch / I take / hold" (p. 3). By allowing the voices to speak through him, a perception of the partial, of the incomplete, emerges. As befits a serial work, it is this provisional understanding rather than any complete knowledge of the subject that is grasped in the poem and projected across the sequence.

"Outlantish" continues "mu" in a similar way. Covering the fourth through the eleventh parts of

the poem, the speaker begins again a search for origins: "Close by but / so remote, / drawn off / to this or that ungraspable 'it'" (*School of Udhra,* p. 23). "Ungraspable," it is nonetheless a "loss" or "lack" that is hungered after throughout (p. 23). Although the attempt to sound this loss is never abandoned, the closing poem reveals the journey to have been, once again, circuitous: "As we arrive the ground / again goes under" (p. 49). Having the rug pulled out from under them, the speakers of the poem limp along, resigning themselves to the fact of some "'someone' we / awaited long since lost," some "absent other we embrace" (pp. 50–51). Instead, it is the "mu," the ghostly, amputated form of "muse" or "music," that they are left with. It is, a few stanzas later, the unnamed someone who "Forgives us our / botched observances" (p. 52). Here, the lack of a subject conveys well the absence of the wished-for object. In this way, "Outlantish" continues the choral, circuitous gambit of "mu," while adding a romantic element of longing, and of elegiac loss. As the closing part of this section of the poem has it, the longed-for world is to be understood as "an erotic / inch / out of reach" (p. 53).

Whatsaid Serif (1998) follows *School of Udhra* and consists wholly of new sections of "Song of the Andoumboulou." The title references the call-and-response tradition, with the book imagining a kind of polyvocal, collective "responder or 'what-sayer'" who steers the content of the song into imaginative detours (*Whatsaid Serif,* n.p.). The epigraph for the first poem, "Song of the Andoumboulou: 16," presents a passage from a letter to García Lorca that reads, "What you must search for, and find, is the black torso of the Pharaoh" (p. 3). As Mackey explains, the letter conveys "a statement made by a flamenco singer, Manuel Torre, to García Lorca in the 1920s. He was talking about the quality called *duende* that flamenco singers strive for" (*Paracritical Hinge,* p. 311). The letter's imaginative detour urges the poet to see the root of the Spanish duende in the African image of the Pharaoh, who here becomes another instance of the "phantom limb" that Mackey consistently returns to in explaining the inspiration of his

work. In this way, "Song of the Andoumboulou: 16" can be read as yet another act of remembering through what its subtitle calls *cante moro,* meaning "Moorish song." The poem thus seeks out a meeting place between, or suturing of, Spanish and African culture. The poem begins this with the image of dredgers whose song goes "unsung, lost," and which ultimately amounts to the "same cry taken up in Cairo, Córdoba" (*Whatsaid Serif,* p. 3). The song of the poem, therefore, becomes voiced "between lips, resuscitant" (p. 4). Accordingly, the dredger's lips appear to perform the "letterless" book of memory (p. 4). In an even more marked way than *Eroding Witness* and *School of Udhra,* then, the sections of "Song of the Andoumboulou" that appear in this collection take up the task of giving voice to phantom musics. Once again, however, the sought-after remembrance is only partial. As "Song of the Adoumboulou: 26" has it, "they / had no book, memory dead but for / one recollection, stripped limbs" (p. 54). Bones are all that remain of the "distant kin called after," forgotten, except for such spare "recollections" (p. 54). The book closes, then, not with a new perspective on wholeness, but with new forms of amputation. "Whatsaid" is reduced to "semisaid," straining, with the speaker, "blind," the echo of "an earlier echo" (p. 111). In this way, it advances themes presented in *School of Udhra,* and looks ahead to Mackey's award-winning treatment of these themes in his following book.

Splay Anthem (2006) is by far Mackey's most celebrated collection of poetry. Winner of the 2006 National Book Award for Poetry, it extends both "Song of the Andoumboulou" and "mu," mingling them throughout in a reciprocity not manifest in earlier collections. As Mackey notes in the preface to the book, "*Splay Anthem* takes up and takes farther two ongoing serial poems, *Song of the Andoumboulou* and "*Mu,*" the two now understood as two and the same, each the other's understudy. Each is the other, each is both, announcedly so in this book" (*Splay Anthem,* p. ix). As their many similarities suggest— both take their energies from the improvisational nature of jazz, from the art of the bricoleur, from

Lorca's sense of duende, from the "art of the muse," and from the act of re-membering—this is not really a departure from previous collections. And the poems will continue to develop under their own titles. Now, however, they are explicitly understood to be intertwined, as the response, the "Whatsaid," of the other's call. This is clear in the first "mu" poem's title, "Andoumboulous Brush." Here, the sense of a broken or failed people is applied to the disassembled speaker: "He turned his head, / spoke to my clavicle, … Sprung bone / the / obtuse flute he'd / long wanted" (p. 3). Here, the recollected bone that concludes the sequence in *Whatsaid Serif* sounds its own amputated song, the "croaking / song / to end all song" (p. 3). Of course, as before, the song here remains incomplete, if no longer elegiac: "Thought of his / grandmother, mother, / uncle, brother, aunt, / anyone's guess but / his / what world it was" (p. 5). The sought-after ancestors are now listed with nonchalance, imagined companions, perhaps, on a journey, with "'Drifter's Blues' on the box," transfiguring loss (p. 5). Of course, such transfigurations have been suggested all along. In *Splay Anthem*, however, Mackey converts that loss to gain time and, again, explicitly chooses to make music out of the creaking, broken, occluded perspectives of his speakers.

Another piece in the collection, "On Antiphon Island," subtitled "'mu' twenty-eighth part," broaches the subject of limbo. As the speaker explains, "It / wasn't limbo we were in albeit / we limbo'd" (p. 64). The poem reimagines the Middle Passage, ironized through the suggestion that slaves entering the galleys of a ship engaged in an early version of the popularized dance contest called the limbo. Popular histories of the dance often connect it with African rituals symbolizing the cycle of death and birth through the movement of passing under the bar. The "we" of the poem similarly don "andoumboulouous birth-shirts," while realizing bitterly that "where we / were was the hold of ship we were / caught / in" (p. 64). This bit of realism, however, is countered quickly in a moment that catches, more than previous pieces, the historical weight of the serial poem's title: "Where we / were was what

we meant by 'mu'" (p. 64). Here, "mu" stands for the original loss the poem has in many ways been questing after: the lost homeland and native traditions of a people whose historical identities have been amputated. This ghost of a memory is in many ways the muse of the poem, just as the song of re-memberence is its music. Ultimately, it is a limbo, in the Roman Catholic sense of a no-place, an experience of the afterlife that admits neither Heaven nor Hell. As the speaker concedes mournfully, yet fearlessly, at the close of the poem, "The world was ever after, else-where, / no / way where we were / was there" (p. 65).

Mackey's next collection, *Nod House* (2011), continues to develop these themes in "Song of the Andoumboulou" and "mu" through the perspectives of various exiles and survivors. For instance, "Day After Day of the Dead," subtitled "'mu' forty-eighth part," turns on the desperation of survival. Once again, the speaker is a plural "we," living through day after day of death: "'While we're alive,' we kept / repeating" (*Nod House,* p. 48). The anxiety of repeating the clipped sentence speaks both to the sense of amputation running through work—that is, these people are cut off from past and future by their need to focus on maintaining the tenuous life they still have from moment to moment—and to the overall panic of the poem. In this state, they are "happy to / see / shadow, know touch," happy, in other words, for their material existence, "no longer wanting to know / what soul was" (p. 48). In this intense state of desperation, the notion of soul is farthest from them. Indeed, all reference to meaning or explanation is unwanted: "What / were we doing there the exegete / kept asking, adamant, uninvited, / morose" (p. 50). As in "On Antiphon Island," the attempt to make sense of a suffering that seems hopeless or endless (day after day) appears "morose," partly because it is "uninvited" but partly also because it can bring no comfort. Cut off from home and history, the "we" of the poem is left with only the momentary struggle for survival, "mouthing the blues" (p. 50), much like the various speakers who sound the themes of Mackey's serial poems.

FICTION

Though Mackey's reputation rests squarely with his poetry, his fiction is equally accomplished. His critically praised serial novel, *From a Broken Bottle Traces of Perfume Still Emanate,* comprised four volumes by 2015. Somewhat unusually, the novel has its origins in prose poetry published in *Eroding Witness.* There, "Song of the Andoumboulou: 6" and "Song of the Andoumboulou: 7" present letters addressed to the fictional "Angel of Dust" (*Eroding Witness,* pp. 50, 54). Both anticipate the novel in their self-referentiality, terms of address, and extension of themes evident in Mackey's serial poems. The first, for instance, begins in the mode of response, replying to a comment the Angel of Dust made in "Song of the Andoumboulou: 3," where the poet is accused of mining for an absent, rather than a present, authentic tradition, one which, in terms similar to Eliot's, the past is not merely a source but "a re-source rather than something evasive, elusive, sought after" (p. 50). The speaker/protagonist, N., however, prizes just such elusiveness in the alternative traditions he conjures: "We not only can but should speak of 'loss' or, to avoid, quotation marks notwithstanding, any such inkling of self-pity, speak of *absence* as unavoidably an inherence in the texture of things" (p. 50). Speaking of such *absence* is central to "Song of the Andoumboulou," and it will continue in many ways in *From a Broken Bottle,* as will the concern with miming a phantom limb. (As "Song of the Andoumboulou: 7" asks, "Aren't we all, however absurdly, amputees?" [p. 54]). In these ways and more, the poetical origins of the novel generate overlapping themes and concerns. As Mackey's fiction branches out on its own, the novel's four volumes trace N.'s participation in an evolving avant-garde jazz band, first named the Deconstructive Woodwind Chorus, then the East Bay Dread Ensemble, then the Mystic Horn Society, and, most recently, Molimo m'Atet, during the years 1978–1983.

The novel's first volume, *Bedouin Hornbook* (1986), features the formation and early development of the group. In the author's preface to the 2010 New Directions edition of *From a Broken Bottle,* which includes *Bedouin Handbook* and

the next two volumes of this ongoing work, Mackey talks about the genesis of the novel in the experience of attending a jazz concert in which, surprisingly, he was the only member of the audience (p. ix). Thoughts of a phantom band quickly emerged, and he recounts wondering, "what being in such a band—an L.A. band touched by Trane, the Art Ensemble of Chicago, Sun Ra and such—might be like" (p. ix). In choosing the episodic, epistolary style of the novel, Mackey simply states that "the letters respond to the music's ongoing call" (p. ix). While these remarks have clear connections with his poetry—the close kinship between literature and music, the desire to make phantoms speak, the centrality of jazz—they also shed light on the band's musical aspirations, its locale, and the extremely small audience for it. Indeed, in many ways, the novel addresses the decline of jazz more directly than does the poetry, though in prose, too, Mackey's writing is always dense and allusive. The narrative begins with N. writing to the Angel of Dust about a strange dream he had concerning the writer and the saxophonist Archie Shepp. In it, N. attempts to play bass clarinet on Coltrane's "Naima," only to discover that he is actually holding a pipe and playing Shepp's version of Coltrane's "Cousin Mary" (p. 3). What wakes him up is the disturbing realization that "what I was playing already existed on record" (p. 3). Here, Mackey presents a comical image of the jazz musician as bricoleur. He doesn't just call his instrument a "pipe"; he literally plays one. Similarly, the composition he plays is a cover of a cover, and one that, even at such a remove, still lacks any discernable sense of originality. These concerns certainly came to the fore in Mackey's serial poetry. In the opening of the novel, they serve to set the terms for the protagonist's exploration. Early on, after the band's first few shows, N. appropriates a passage from Victor Zuckerkandl's 1956 book *Sound and Symbol,* "We are always *between* the tones, *on the way* from tone to tone; our hearing does not remain with the tone, it reaches through it and beyond it," using it as a gloss on his understanding of musical pathos as a "longing" for absent kin, for the "brotherly arm" that turns out to be a

"phantom limb" (pp. 15–16) In this way, the passage also illuminates the band's quest to seek out such absences by abiding in the blue notes of experience, where the spaces between the standard notes of the scale point to someone or something more. This mystical realization for N. can be seen in the band's interactions throughout, pushing them forward in their musical explorations while also distinguishing the novel from the project of Mackey's poetry. Though both wrestle with phantoms, the many influences voiced in his serial poems remain in the background of the novel, never more than glosses on the band's own attempts to chase down a musical ghost with mystical overtones.

Volume 2, *Djbot Baghostus's Run* (1993), finds the band exhibiting the sense of duende broached by Mackey in his poetry. After Djamilaa and Aunt Nancy, the female members of the group, stage a form of performance/protest to lobby against the inclusion of a male drummer, the band finds a female drummer, Drennette. Soon after joining the band, Penguin, one of the men in the band, takes to her and composes a piece titled "Drennethology" (p. 328). N. recounts Drennette's unimpressed response, noting that she "changed the rhythm he suggested to something more difficult, more complex, polyrhythmic. 'It's about splitting yourself in two,' she said" (p. 329). Here, the sense of rending oneself, like Lorca's flamenco singer, is apposite. For Drennette, however, it is not only about opening the music to let other people in but also about complicating Penguin's casting of her as a romantic object. In denying one, stable identity, she can resituate herself in the polyrhythmic gaps of her drumming. Identity questions like these continue. Later, the band's phantom member, Jarred Bottle, becomes Djbot Baghostus, the volume's title character. Strangely, the grasshopper under his pillow instructs him:

Tell them you're not from here. Tell them your father is a wealthy man, that he sang with the Ink Spots before they made it big but that nevertheless he's a very wealthy man. Tell them that's why he named you Djbot. Spell it out for them if you have to: d as in dot, j as in jot, b-o-t as in bottle. Tell them it relates to ink, eponymous ink, namesake ink. Tell them you're not from here, even that

you're not really here. Tell them it relates to ink, invisible ink. You can never make too much of it. Tell them you're a ghost.

(p. 362)

Jared's identity here is rent and bent like Drennette's, and like the very music the band plays, but he is also, moreover, the ghostly embodiment of the band. As his name indicates, he is the disappearing ink of Ba-ghost-us, of what could be read as the "ghost" of "us." Fleeing the scene of his would-be murder, the volume ends with the surreal scene of the band members running with him, their phantom limb, into the night.

The third volume of the novel, *Atet A.D.*, opens with the news of Thelonious Monk's death and closes with the band recording an album on John Coltrane's birthday. The implications for the plot, with its recurrent meditations on birth and death, origin and ending, are clear from the beginning. With the news concerning Monk also comes news that Penguin too has retreated from the world. N. equates this with Monk's coma, and when the band is invited to play a memorial gig for him, they assume that they'll be performing without Penguin. Yet he appears midway through their set and, in the midst of playing Monk's "In Walked Bud," engages N. in a musical back and forth that leads the band to a new song, "In Walked Pen." The "duel/duet" that makes the song is described as "a limbo match, a test of who could go lower" (p. 385). In this sense, it is once again an instance in Mackey's oeuvre of a bending back to glimpse a lost past, a bending made possible by rending or doubling one's identity—Penguin/Monk, Penguin/Bud. The end of the volume also plays on such doubles. Drennette, frustrated with the rehearsals for the band's recording, disappears. In retrospect, N. understands her leaving as an attempt to get the band to "let go of our wish to work everything out in advance" (p. 526). On her answering machine, she leaves a recording of John Coltrane instructing other musicians on the *Sun Ship* album to "keep, you, keep a *thing* happening all thru it" (p. 526). By allowing the ghostly voice of Coltrane to speak through her absence on his birthday, Drennette effectively reminds the band of what N., in adapting Zuckerkandl, termed the

need to keep "*on the way* from tone to tone," and by doing so, in this case, avoid any attempt at a perfection or completion that would be false.

Volume 4, *Bass Cathedral,* opens with a track listing for the songs that will appear on the band's album, *Orphic Bend* (pp. 1–2). The title, indeed, bends in many ways, back to the avant-garde jazz musicians of the late 1950s and 1960s who continue to inspire them, especially John Coltrane, as well as to the Egyptian, Dogon, and Haitian cosmologies that appear throughout Mackey's work. In addition to these, though, the adjective "Orphic" suggests a Western impulse, that of Orpheus, the legendary Greek musician and prophet, and so adds another voice or persona to the already heady mix. Like Orpheus, who looked back too soon and so lost his wife Eurydice, the band members of Molimo m'Atet may fear that recording could result in the similar loss of their love, of the atonal and improvisational nature of their music which, in many ways, has proven to be their muse. This, after all, is at the heart of their disagreements during the rehearsals that feature in the closing of volume 3. In a related sense, though, it may also suggest a kinship with the Orpheus who could charm the underworld, as they too, through their various influences, seek a form of musical communion with the dead. In this light, as the band listens to a test pressing of the record, something strange happens: thought balloons, like those in comics, appear to emerge from the point where the needle meets the record (pp. 3–5). This had happened in volume 3, during performance, but here it happens the moment Aunt Nancy's bass begins to play, pausing when her instrument is silent, and then resuming with each note the bass plays on the record. With foreboding, each thought balloon begins with the words "*I dreamt you were gone*" (p. 5). This rises to something like a climax almost a year later, when N. has a dream parallel to the one that began the novel in volume 1: "I dreamt a balloon snuck up on me while I slept. It crept up in back of me and whispered, 'Boo'" (p. 129). "Part inflated ball, part friendly ghost," the message brings "long-sought liberation's new disguise" (p. 129). The grim humor here, as always in Mackey, moves in several directions at

once. The joking "Boo" may indeed be a reflection on the band's sought-after kinship with various dead—as though the haunting had now turned to a new, intimately humorous dimension. In this way, the joking "Boo" would offer a form of liberation. However, as merely "liberation's new disguise," the joke suggests a darker form of humor, one in which the dead still hold a firm grip on the band, tightening it by making even liberation appear as bondage. As N. reflects, by appearing in a dream the reality of the event is forever uncertain, and yet it is just this uncertainty that leads him to repeat the dream, if only to understand it better (p. 130). In this way, the dream insinuates itself into his waking life as "a ventriloquial thought," one "put in my mind as well as a word it put in my mouth, 'boo'" (p. 130). This offers, at the very least, new perspectives on Mackey's use of the concepts of duende and phantom limbs. Here, it appears that the rending of the voice may be less authentic than Lorca assumed, that it may, in fact, be merely a ventriloquism of liberation. In a related sense, the feeling for the various phantom limbs of Mackey's work may be less an attempt—however futile—to re-member forgotten pasts than a form of revenge, a kind of post-bebop invasion of the body snatchers. His poetry, at least from *Splay Anthem* onward, realizes this possibility and so negotiates it among others. His fiction glimpses it in previous volumes but comes face-to-face—or balloon-to-face—with it here. A fifth volume was said to be complete and near publication as of 2016; readers can expect these themes and concerns to be elaborated as the novel continues.

CRITICISM

Mackey's critical work extends over two volumes, *Discrepant Engagement* (1993) and *Paracritical Hinge* (2005). Both collect articles that appeared previously in academic and creative journals, while the latter also includes what would best be termed manifestos, as well as lectures, interviews, and a discography. Overall, Mackey's critical approach is marked by its affinities with trends in African American and postcolonial studies. Even at that, though, his

writing is once again eclectic and unique, incorporating extended studies of Lorca, Walt Whitman, H.D. (Hilda Doolittle), Robert Duncan, Robert Creeley, and Charles Olson. Major modernist figures like T. S. Eliot, William Carlos Williams, and Ralph Ellison also find space in his work. For the most part, though, he focuses on late-twentieth-century African American and Anglophone writers, such as Amiri Baraka, Wilson Harris, and Edward Kamau Braithwaite, to whom he returns frequently. As a result, his critical practice could be said to share his creative writing's affinity for phantom limbs, but rather than engage in archaeology he observes his closest contemporaries' parallel affinities. Consequently, much of his critical writing, especially in the first volume, sheds light on similarities and contrasts between his practices and those of writers who have influenced his approach in some way. Both collections, then, offer glosses on his career as a novelist and poet while also presenting unique perspectives on major and contemporary authors.

Discrepant Engagement opens with a kind of statement of intent that could be said to cover all of Mackey's writing. In elaborating on the title of his work, Mackey explains that his critical essays trace practices that "accent fissure, fracture, incongruity," in the face of "closed orders of identity and signification" (p. 19). For him, such practices "inhabit," "engage" the discrepant, "rather than seek to ignore it" (p. 19). While this ambition is clear in both the work he studies and the approach he takes to such work, it is worth noting that such "engagement" is also, in many ways, at the heart of Mackey's poetry and fiction. From this perspective, his critical practice can be seen as at one with his creative work. The early essay on Amiri Baraka serves as a case in point. Though there are key differences, Baraka's enthusiasm for African American music marks a kinship with Mackey. In exploring Baraka's interest in music, Mackey reads the obliqueness of many of Baraka's poems in light of the latter's interest in the angularity and "circumlocution" of African American music (pp. 41–43). Mackey observes that both Baraka and the music he admires effectively challenge "the epistemic order

… by insisting upon the partial, provisional" (p. 43). As a result, he argues that "Baraka hears a spirit of interrogation and discontent in the most moving of black music" (p. 43). This, similarly, could be said of Mackey's work, as could the sense of dismemberment that he apprizes in Wilson Harris' fiction. As Mackey shows, Harris sees the horrors of the Middle Passage as breaking the "insularity of the various African peoples brought to the New World" (p. 170). However, Harris understands this to have been beneficial, viewing "this breakage, this amputation, as fortunate, an opportune disinheritance or partial eclipse or tribal memory that called creative forces and imaginative freedoms into play" (p. 170). Again, this same sentence could be written in regard to Mackey's own work and so shows both his indebtedness to earlier writers and his ability to take their findings farther, to expand upon them in his own late-twentieth- and twenty-first-century context.

Paracritical Hinge: Essays, Talks, Notes, Interviews contains, as its title indicates, a more eclectic body of work. Alongside essays on Whitman, phrenology, and H.D.'s Egypt are lectures on *cante moro,* literature, improvisation, and notes on black art and innovation, along with a handful of interviews conducted between 1991 and 2000. As in *Discrepant Engagement,* these shed light on Mackey's creative practice while also revealing his critical insight. For instance, in "Gassire's Lute: Robert Duncan's Vietnam War Poems," Mackey tracks the development of the African epic in modernist poetry, from Pound to Duncan, while seizing an essential conflict in the latter's employment of it. Gassire reappears often in Mackey's own poetry and fiction, and so the essay in many ways improvises a tradition and frames a question that his own work will take up. Insightfully, he argues that Duncan uses the lost city at the heart of the epic, Wagadu, as a representation of what Duncan terms "the commune of Poetry" (p. 77). Pointing out that Duncan follows Pound in his understanding of Wagadu, Mackey writes that Duncan's poem "Orders" embodies an unacknowledged tension: "We are at least suspicious of the poetic conceit that wants to attribute a communal impulse … to

Gassire, since we have heard him tell Wagadu to go to hell, watched him sacrifice his sons … and seen him kicked out of Wagadu" (*Paracritical Hinge,* p. 78). The problem, then, for Mackey is that Gassire's pursuit of glory seems to put him at odds with the good of the community. This pursuit, however, is precisely what Pound, and Duncan after him, find admirable. Consequently, Mackey finds the trouble with Pound and Duncan's Gassire to be symptomatic of a larger tension in modernist poetry between the desire to aggrandize the "folk," in all of its many contexts, and the impulse to assert an artistic elite. In Pound, this kind of thinking leads to fascism. In Duncan and others, it leads to conflicts not yet fully addressed. Other pieces in the collection shed more direct light on Mackey's creative practice—the lecture on Lorca, the manifesto of sorts on black art and innovation, and the interviews. Having drawn on several of these throughout this essay, there is little need to say more here. What they present, along with the essays and critical work in *Discrepant Engagement,* is a link between the critical and creative and a gloss on the achievement that is Mackey's writing.

CONCLUSION

As a survey of his writing should show, Nathaniel Mackey is an American writer whose work extends across genres and geographical boundaries. While writing out of the African American experience, he draws on sources as varied as Black Mountain, Dogon cosmology, Haitian Vodou, Egpytian gods and goddesses, and post-bop, avant-garde jazz. Like Amiri Baraka, Mackey draws heavily on African American musical influences, not only citing jazz musicians and compositions, but also composing in a manner that is parallel to jazz. Moreover, unlike much of Baraka's later work, Mackey's poetry and prose pose formal challenges that render them less readily accessible and more akin to the experimentation of Wilson Harris or to the innovation associated with so-called language poets. Indeed, for these very reasons, graphing Mackey's place among contemporary American writers can be more difficult than it may seem.

As an African American writer who engages in formal experimentation, Mackey's work can fall between two camps: innovative poetry and African American poetry. As he terms it in his lecture "Expanding the Repertoire," there has been established a "distinction between a formally innovative willingness to incur difficulty, on the white hand, and a simple disclosure of innovative content, on the black" (*Paracritical Hinge,* p. 241). As he notes earlier in the lecture, "The innovation that's granted to African American writing, where there's any granted at all, tends to be one of content, perspective, or attitude.… its report on the one thing African Americans are regarded as experts on—racial victimization" (p. 240). Caught between both hands, he writes of his experience of having to insist that the category "black experimental writing" isn't inherently problematic (p. 241). While such frustration may be alleviated by the emergence of other writers who could similarly be grouped under that category—Will Alexander and Harryette Mullen, to name two—the conflict may not be easily resolved. Responding to a question about "separate black literary tradition," Mackey explains that "the black literary tradition has been intertwined with the white literary tradition in ways which don't tend to be acknowledged because of the ghetto that black literature has been consigned to in academic and institutional practices" (*Paracritical Hinge,* p. 271). For him, the separation of these otherwise intertwined traditions has less to do with literary practice than with social realities: "The separateness of the black literary tradition has to do with the segregation of black people, the subtle and not-so-subtle apartheid which is the history of this country and continues to be part of the social fabric and the assumptions that govern a great deal of social life" (pp. 271–272). Mackey is skeptical that literary practice, and poetry in particular, can escape or transcend these realities; however, he suggests that the best literature neither dismisses "the social determinants of our being" nor capitulates or caves in to a "rigidly historicist view" of identity (p. 273). Fittingly, this is just what his writing does: through its myriad sources and polyvocality, it resists any easy classification.

In fact, this resistance may be the best way of summing up Mackey's accomplishment. By opening the voice and attempting to re-member phantom limbs, it sounds a music that ranges across continents while yet remaining distinctively American. Steeped in historical memory, yet equally responsive to its historical moment, his writings bear witness to musics that continue to haunt us. Indeed, from Gassire and the Andoumboulou to Robert Duncan and Don Cherry, the many voices and soundings of Nathaniel Mackey's work improvise a rare achievement in American letters.

Selected Bibliography

WORKS OF NATHANIEL MACKEY

POETRY

Four for Trane: Poems. Los Angeles: Golemics, 1978.

Septet for the End of Time. Santa Cruz, Calif.: Boneset, 1983.

Eroding Witness. Urbana and Chicago: University of Illinois Press, 1985.

Outlantish: "Mu" Fourth Part–Eleventh Part. Tucson, Ariz.: Chax Press, 1992.

School of Udhra. San Francisco: City Lights Books, 1993.

Song of the Andoumboulou, 18–20. Santa Cruz, Calif.: Moving Parts Press, 1994.

Whatsaid Serif. San Francisco: City Lights Books, 1998.

Splay Anthem. New York: New Directions, 2006.

Nod House. New York: New Directions, 2011.

Outer Pradesh. Boston: Anomalous Press, 2014.

Blue Fasa. New York: New Directions, 2015.

FICTION

Bedouin Hornbook. Lexington: University of Kentucky Press, 1986.

Djbot Baghostus's Run. Los Angeles: Sun & Moon Press, 1993.

Atet A.D. San Francisco: City Lights Books, 2001.

Bass Cathedral. New York: New Directions, 2008.

From a Broken Bottle Traces of Perfume Still Emanate: Volumes 1–3. New York: New Directions, 2010.

CRITICISM

Discrepant Engagement: Dissonance, Cross-Culturality, and Experimental Writing. Cambridge, U.K., and New York: Cambridge University Press, 1993. Reprint, Tuscaloosa: University of Alabama Press, 2000.

Paracritical Hinge: Essays, Talks, Notes, Interviews. Madison: University of Wisconsin Press, 2005.

AS EDITOR

Hambone. 1982–. (Literary journal.)

Moment's Notice: Jazz in Poetry & Prose. With Art Lange. Minneapolis, Minn.: Coffee House Press, 1993.

American Poetry: The Twentieth Century. With Carolyn Kizer, John Hollander, Robert Haas, and Marjorie Perloff. New York: Literary Classics of the United States, 2000.

REVIEWS, ARTICLES, AND SPECIAL ISSUES

Hajdu, David. "Jazz Man." *New York Times Book Review,* February 24, 2008. http://www.nytimes.com/2008/02/24/books/review/Hajdu-t.html?pagewanted=all&_r=0 (Review of *Bass Cathedral.*)

Leong, Michael. "Root Work." *Boston Review,* August 4, 2015. http://bostonreview.net/poetry/michael-leong-nathaniel-mackey-blue-fasa (Review of *Blue Fasa.*)

"Nathaniel Mackey: A Special Issue." Edited by Paul Naylor. *Callaloo* 23, no. 2 (spring 2000).

"Nathaniel Mackey." Special issue, edited by Joseph Donahue. *Talisman: A Journal of Contemporary Poetry and Poetics* 43 (2015).

Share, Don. "Lines of Affinity." *Poetry,* June 2014. http://www.poetryfoundation.org/poetrymagazine/article/247742

HARRYETTE MULLEN

(1953—)

Caleb Puckett

HARRYETTE MULLEN HAS made a name for herself by defying readers' expectations regarding what constitutes poetry and challenging their assumptions about what it means to be a black experimental poet in contemporary America. As a poet deeply concerned with identity and representation throughout her career, Mullen has always displayed an incisive ability to root out the politics involved with the formation of societal norms and boundaries of selfhood as they apply to gender, race, and cultural affiliation. Mullen's poetry throughout the years has proven to be an oftentimes wry and unfailingly musical amalgamation of various schools, genres, and influences. At any point in one of her poems, readers might detect strains of Sappho and Gertrude Stein or notice curiously transmuted lines pinched from the world of advertising and the Delta blues coming together for revelatory and revolutionary purposes. As a postmodernist, Mullen has regularly displayed a tendency toward dense allusiveness, hybridity, and irony in her work. She has also revealed a deft hand when it comes to creating linguistic innovations and a type of text that favors generative play over closed meaning. Along with poets such as Nathaniel Mackey, Will Alexander, and Erica Hunt, Mullen has tapped into an often overlooked tradition of black experimental poetry and made something very necessary, dynamic, and new of it.

COMING INTO CONSCIOUSNESS: 1953–1975

Harryette Mullen was born to James and Avis Mullen in Florence, Alabama, on July 1, 1953. Mullen's parents, who met and were educated at Talladega College in Alabama, moved to Fort Worth, Texas, three years later to pursue professional opportunities. Like numerous swaths of the South and Southwest, the Fort Worth of Mullen's day was an ethnically diverse but divided city, particularly along the lines of race. Indeed, drinking fountains, buses, and neighborhoods had long been separated along racial lines, and racial tension was an inescapable daily reality for those who ventured outside of their designated areas. In fact, the year the Mullen family moved to Fort Worth, a local black couple who had attempted to move into a white neighborhood was met with great resistance at the hands of protestors who objected to any semblance of mixing or integration. The Mullens would later have a similar experience as the first black family in an all-white neighborhood. Mullen recalls her neighbors leaving the neighborhood because of the unwanted presence of her family and the maliciousness of one neighbor who sent his German shepherd out to harass the Mullen girls when they were biking down the street (Bedient, p. 185). The Mullens and other middle-class black families in Fort Worth were not alone with such experiences. Suffice it to say, a substantial portion of the white population in Texas throughout the 1950s and 1960s expected black citizens, regardless of their educational or economic attainments, to operate out of sight or on the margins of society.

Along with the larger social tensions at play, Mullen experienced discord at home during those early years. By the time she was four, her parents had divorced, with her father relocating to Chicago and her mother staying in Fort Worth to teach at a segregated school. This distress in Mullen's family life, coupled with her father's prolonged distance, would have a lasting effect on her psyche and manifest itself years later in her poetry. Mullen's mother made the best of this change by showing a unwavering commitment to

educating and shaping the characters of her daughters. Like many teachers the world over, Avis Mullen emphasized the importance of literacy and the cultivation of knowledge among her children. She also involved them in a range of artistic and cultural pursuits, including memorizing and reciting poetry by Paul Laurence Dunbar and Langston Hughes in order shape their sensibilities and give them an appreciation of tradition (Mullen, "'When He Is Least Himself,'" p. 277). Looking back on this period, Mullen reflected that she and her sister became writers "because of the separation from [their] father, and also because of the foundation of literacy in a family of teachers, ministers, office workers, printers, and others whose employment required reading and writing" (Pereira, p. 115).

Along with reading and writing, Mullen's mother took a clear interest in equipping her children with critical thinking skills. As Mullen would later recall, her mother would even use an evening watching television as an occasion to analyze consumerism's relationship to the construction of identity and critique representations of race in the media (Griffin et al.). The encouragement, positive reinforcement, and learning opportunities Mullen received would prompt her lasting love of literature and inform her idea of blackness and drive for social justice as she matured. Interestingly, some of the very discussions she had with her mother as a child—including those regarding consumerism and identity—would serve as the impetus for her future books.

Despite their Southern roots and Mullen's identification with the South, the Mullen family occupied an uncomfortable position as perpetual outsiders in the black community of Fort Worth (Dargan, p. 1014). This estrangement was partly the result of living in one neighborhood, working or going to school in another, and attending church in a third (Frost, p. 402). They were never really a committed part of a single area or group of people. Another, more disturbing, reason for this estrangement was that some members of the community viewed the family as outsiders with Northern ways and white affectations. Such members of the community questioned the

family's blackness and castigated them for their perceived airs and racial disloyalty. Years later, Mullen would say that such treatment segregated them from the black community (Hogue, p. 236). While provincialism was certainly at play in such judgments, the Mullens' financial status, educational attainments, and use of the English language did set them apart from others in the community. Mullen has pinpointed language as an especially problematic aspect of forming a stable sense of belonging as a child, noting how she spoke different forms of English—standard English, black standard English, and street vernacular—depending on her company and the situation at hand. Such instances, in her view, pulled her into an "atmosphere of coercion" where she was induced to "conform to a particular way or speaking, writing and so forth" in order to function as a member of the immediate discourse community (Griffin et al.).

However, rather than exclusively adopting one set of speech habits and affixing her identity to a single segment of the community, Mullen learned to embrace a manifold sense of self. From a linguistic standpoint, those early experiences with ambiguity, multilingualism, and code-switching would eventually become one of her chief concerns as a poet and a signature feature of her poetic expression. As she noted in an interview published in *Callaloo,* such experiences inspired her to pursue "the possibility of pushing the boundaries of identity to create a more inclusive, heterogeneous, and interactive text"— one that would allow her to simultaneously acknowledge, explore, and critique the cultures and languages that had affected her sense of identity (Dargan, p. 1016). This approach would also extend to Mullen's eventual and completely conscious effort to bridge cultures by cultivating a reading audience that was varied in both its racial composition and its aesthetic preferences.

By the time Mullen had finished elementary school, Fort Worth was in a state of social transition, with the divisive Jim Crow laws on their way out and integration—however fitful and fraught with difficulty—on the way in. In 1967 the city saw its first black politician elected to city council—an undeniable sign of change.

However, growing up in an environment shot through with exclusion and bigotry had a definite and lasting effect on Mullen's worldview. By the time she entered the University of Texas at Austin in 1971, she had become politically conscious and had a desire to deepen her understanding of the black experience in America. Mullen's choice of English as a major, deepening commitment to writing, and plan to take up teaching as a career seemed inevitable. She had been a devoted reader and writer since childhood, owing in large part to the encouragement of her parents. Mullen's high school English teacher had also nurtured her love of writing and prompted her to submit a group of poems to a contest sponsored by the local newspaper. Mullen won the contest, saw her first poem appear in print, and received an opportunity to read in front of an audience (Williams, p. 702). She was primed to analyze her personal experiences and culture and take up writing in earnest.

The University of Texas proved to be a productive setting for Mullen. As an English major, she was introduced to a range of literary theories and interpretative strategies by her professors and asked to respond to what she read in a critical fashion. However, like most English departments of the time, the curriculum primarily focused on the works of those dead white authors who made up the respective canons of classic British and American literature. Mullen wished to broaden her exposure to other cultures, traditions, and canons—to discover authors of color, both living and dead—so she also took classes in the Ethnic Studies department on a regular basis. Those courses proved instrumental in helping her explore an array of literatures, including ones from the Caribbean and Africa, and frame her sense of history and identity in a new way. The classes she took from the folklorist and ethnographer Roger D. Abrahams were particularly significant when it came to developing her knowledge of African American culture (Hogue, p. 235). Along with attending to her coursework, Mullen formed friendships with like-minded students and began to frequent readings and other literary events around Austin. Those social interactions and cultural performances were an education in and of themselves, particularly when

it came to defining her burgeoning political views and immersing herself in a community of writers, editors, and publishers. As her awareness expanded, her skills as a writer sharpened. She had discovered the pathways to change she required to become an agent of change herself.

Despite her love of writing and early success, Mullen had yet to overcome her reticence with regard to sharing her poetry with the public. Mullen wrote poetry throughout her undergraduate years but did little with it in the way of reading and publishing. Once, at the insistence of a friend, Mullen did agree to read her poetry at a local open mic night, but on the whole she shied away from sharing her work with anyone outside of her immediate circle of friends (Hogue, pp. 233–234). Mullen did, however, devote much of her time to print journalism—a medium well suited to airing her concerns regarding social problems and change. Mullen wrote opinion pieces and worked as an editor for the university's newspaper, the *Daily Texan,* and its monthly supplement, *Black Print. Black Print* was an activist publication devoted to subjects of race and gender equality. Its articles captured the points of tension and transformations taking place across the state of Texas and the nation as a whole. Along with editorials, the supplement featured creative content by black and feminist poets, including Haki Madhubuti, Nikki Giovanni, and Adrienne Rich. Each of those poets, along with a host of others, expanded Mullen's awareness of contemporary poetry and served as exemplars for her early work.

During Mullen's time in Austin, students of color and those espousing progressive politics had a voice on campus, but it is obvious that the university was by no means a bastion of equity and tolerance. Indeed, while the university hired black lecturers and officially sponsored readings by black writers through the English and African Languages departments, Mullen and her allies were in the vanguard of social transformation and had to advocate constantly for representation. They dealt with indifference or outright hostility in some quarters, particularly at an administrative level. Mullen has described the university's regents at the time as "extremely right-wing" and

patently opposed to the ostensible incursion of ideas and figures associated with the Black Arts movement and feminism (Hogue, pp. 237–238). Mullen simultaneously pushed back against such oppression and found ways to navigate a system still largely shaped by white male privilege. This experience would prove pivotal for Mullen, as it would further shape her political consciousness and show her how to contend with the biases and inequities built into the institutions she would one day inhabit as a professional. Mullen graduated from the University of Texas with a B.A. in English in 1975 and continued to pursue her writing in service of social justice from that point forward.

VOICES FAMILIAR AND STRANGE: 1975–1989

The years following Mullen's graduation were marked by restlessness and itinerancy. Mullen worked at Austin Community College from 1975 to 1977, took up a series of temporary office worker positions through Manpower between 1977 and 1979, and was in residence in Galveston as part of the artists-in-schools program of the Texas Commission on the Arts from 1978 to 1981, all the while working on her poetry and immersing herself in the arts community. Mullen began organizing or attending a variety of poetry readings and other literary events in South Texas and soon joined a growing network of writers and artists who circulated in and through the area. Two of the most significant people Mullen met during that time were Lorenzo Thomas and Ahmos Zu-Bolton. Thomas was a transplanted poet and critic from New York City who had been part of the Umbra Workshop, a radical black literary collective operating out of the larger Black Arts movement. Not only did Thomas serve as a vital connection to the Black Arts movement, he also introduced Mullen to a new approach to writing that would eventually alter her poetics in profound ways: language poetry.

Zu-Bolton was an activist, educator, publisher, and poet who was also new to the area. He had been among a group of students who had integrated into Louisiana State University in 1965, and he had served in the U.S. Army during the Vietnam War. He was a well-traveled, worldwise, and tirelessly creative individual. By the time he moved his publishing company to South Texas, he was also a respected figure in the Black Arts movement. Along with writers such as Naomi Shihab Nye, Zu-Bolton was among the writers Mullen invited to be guest speakers and readers at the events she put on at local schools during her tenure as artist in residence. Zu-Bolton also organized his own readings and festivals, many of which Mullen either helped see to fruition or participated in as a reader. In addition, Zu-Bolton published the little magazines *Hoo-Doo* and *Synergy*. *Hoo-Doo* featured a veritable who's who of black, feminist, and experimental writers from across the country, including Amiri Baraka, Yusef Komunyakaa, and Richard Kostelanetz. Many of Mullen's early pieces appeared in its issues and she eventually took on a role as its coeditor.

Influence and collaboration were most certainly in the air around Galveston, as evidenced by Mullen's emerging poetic style, choice of subject matter, and performance and publication record of the time. They all pointed to the Black Arts movement, Zu-Bolton's presence, and her concerted efforts to give voice to what she would later term a "regional" expression of black culture (Hogue, p. 234). Mullen's skills and confidence as a writer developed through these experiences, and her relationship with Zu-Bolton went from collegial to romantic in short order, effectively setting the course for her art and life for the next few years. Zu-Bolton divorced his then-wife in November 1978 and married Mullen less than a month later. The two became an inseparable unit within the larger group of artists operating along the Gulf Coast and began serving a residency together at the Galveston Art Center.

In 1981 Zu-Bolton published Mullen's first book, *Tree Tall Woman,* through his press, Energy Earth Communications. In a number of respects, *Tree Tall Woman* is Mullen's most personal work, for it directly speaks to elements of her upbringing, including her relationship with her parents. The work as a whole, as Mullen writes in her essay "Telegraphs from a Distracted Sibyl," is "a derivation and celebration of [her] mother's

(spoken) voice" and, as such, presents itself as the continuation of very specific oral tradition (*The Cracks Between,* p. 19). Despite the masks and personas Mullen sometimes adopts in her poems, much of the work in *Tree Tall Woman* is autobiographical in nature. Her poem "Father (Part I)," for example, is notable for its poignant weaving together of the private trauma she felt in her father's absence and the social issues she contended with during her girlhood. In this poem and many others, Mullen expands the scope of her vision to examine the traditions, relationship dynamics, and cultural realities she sees as central to the black experience in America. *Tree Tall Woman,* though, is no treatise on social justice matters. Rather, it is an exploration of what it means to be human—to desire, connect with others, and face rejection. Appropriately, then, Mullen also spends a significant portion of the book addressing the joys and vicissitudes of romantic love. Her blues-infused love poems swell with a palpable sense of eroticism, giving readers a preview of the earthy undercurrents that would appear in all her subsequent poetry.

Tree Tall Woman encapsulates many of Mullen's early stylistic influences, with the clearest and most pervasive influences at play being those emanating from the Black Arts movement: poets such as Ishmael Reed, Lorenzo Thomas, and Sonia Sanchez. Mullen consciously situated the book within that movement by focusing on matters involving cultural awareness, tradition, and community. Mullen has, in fact, noted that her express purpose during that period was to write about interactions among black people for an audience of black people (Hogue, p. 239). To connect with this audience, Mullen employed signifying and various elements of black vernacular. She also strove to maintain an authenticity of voice—one idiomatically Southern in its presentation. The book exhibits several now characteristic features of Mullen's writing, including an overarching concern with identity, provocative wordplay, and a palpable sense of musicality. However, the approach and predominant feel of the work suggests Mullen was more oriented toward a certain form of orthodoxy than iconoclastic rule breaking. In that sense, the work

created a situation where Mullen was "placed rather neatly within the category of 'representative blackness' (as well as in the categories of 'feminist' and 'regional' poet)"—categories which would eventually frustrate the recognition and reception of her more radical and less easily labeled works ("Poetry and Identity," *The Cracks Between,* p. 10).

Tree Tall Woman was well received by many in the black poetry community and helped Mullen establish a presence as a poet; however, the book was also indelibly marked by the limitations of her perspective and skills at the time. Mullen has since criticized her totalizing tendencies in the book, particularly as they apply to presenting a single "black voice" in lieu of a more diverse and complicated series of tongues, and she has gone so far as to say she "didn't even really know what [she] was doing" when she created *Tree Tall Woman* (Hogue, pp. 234–235). Mullen would subsequently alter the way she presented the various dimensions of black culture by pulling away from the philosophical sureties and the more predictable uses of linguistic traditions, dialects, and registers she had assumed in *Tree Tall Woman*. In short, her plan moving forward from *Tree Tall Woman* was to take a more nuanced approach to examining black culture and personal identity, as well as to problematize language and represent the various strains that inform any one act of speech or writing in a less one-dimensional fashion. She would hybridize and heighten the density of her work in an attempt to realize a more integrated and open poetics—one capable of capturing the postmodern black experience.

Mullen's ambition and reputation as a poet grew as she continued to publish and perform public readings around Texas. She received a Dobie-Paisano fellowship from the Texas Institute of Letters in recognition of her work and promise as a poet. The fellowship provided her with an opportunity to work on her art without interruption for the next six months—a true boon for a motivated writer. Following this fellowship, Mullen garnered even more recognition, this time in the form of an artist-in-residence grant from the Helene Wurlitzer Foundation. In taking the grant,

she left Texas for Taos, New Mexico. Despite or perhaps because of these successes, Mullen appears to have become quite restless. Her movements during the period suggest a definite desire for change in terms of the poetry, geography, and company she wished to call her own. Mullen and Zu-Bolton chose to part ways, with Zu-Bolton eventually heading to New Orleans, where he would teach and open up a community book center. For her part, Mullen set her eyes on graduate school in the seaside city of Santa Cruz, California. A close partnership and sphere of immediate influence had dissolved for Mullen, but she was resolved to make her life and art new.

In 1985 Mullen enrolled in the History of Consciousness program at the University of California–Santa Cruz (UCSC). UCSC had no English department per se, and the interdisciplinary History of Consciousness program effectively pulled together areas from the humanities, such as literary studies, with areas from the sciences and social sciences, including cultural studies and psychology. The program was known for its theoretical rigor and atmosphere of innovation and progressivism. Unsurprisingly, it was also a hotbed for students drawn to activism and topics in social justice, including a host of future academics and Black Panther cofounder Huey P. Newton. Suffice it to say, Mullen fit into the program and surrounding scene quite well. She soon found a new circle of artists to join, including her roommate at the provost's house, the Chicana poet Lorna Dee Cervantes.

Mullen did not enter the program as an unproven artist. Indeed, she had already started to establish a reputation as a poet, editor, and organizer of arts programming. While Mullen undoubtedly enjoyed some of the advantages associated with her prior accomplishments, she did not simply continue to pursue her art in the same way she had for so many years. Mullen challenged her own attitudes and conceptions and pushed against the status quo. Mullen was unmistakably dissatisfied with the isolationist attitudes and shopworn conventions she saw cropping up in the Black Arts movement and approached her experience at the university with a willingness to be transformed (Griffin et al.). As

she would later say of her decision to seek out a new direction, "I would rather face an uncertain future than go back anywhere in the past.... There is not a set of black behaviors that I must adhere to in order to be who I truly am" (Frost, p. 416). This attitude led her to cast off the philosophical and aesthetic limitations she had adopted as a fledgling poet in Texas and opened her mind to fresh modes of thinking and responding to the world in which she lived: a postsegregation—but not postracial—America.

Mullen focused much of her studies on black literature, with a special emphasis on the slave narratives of writers such as Harriet Jacobs and Frederick Douglass. She also delved into deconstructionism, poststructuralism, and Marxism, among other theories then circulating in her program. The intersections among those areas of thought prompted her to face the gaps in her own knowledge of the black experience and led her to critique her own understanding of what constituted black culture. She soon determined that her understanding of the subject was both naive and problematic. In her own words, she came to recognize that "identity is much more complex and much more negotiated and constructed" than she had previously imagined (Hogue, p. 239). Mullen has characterized this realization as life-altering and has credited it with providing her with a far-reaching yet nuanced view of identity and, by extension, community. Such ideas would inform the content and style of her next three books and would manifest themselves in her critical writing for years to come (Hogue, pp. 239, 252). Such knowledge would also complicate her relationship with black readers and those serving as gatekeepers in avant-garde poetry circles.

Along with this infusion of critical theory, the contemporary avant-garde poetry scene operating out of the San Francisco Bay Area had an immense effect on Mullen's writing. One of Mullen's professors, the black experimental poet Nathaniel Mackey, further exposed her to language poetry. Mullen quickly developed an affinity for the poets associated with the school and began to adopt aspects of their writing to suit her own needs. Mullen identified with their leftist politics and recognized in their art a better way

to address some of her own aesthetic concerns, particularly when it came to creating a generative poetic language and a highly participatory meaning-making environment for her readers. Looking back at this time, Mullen observed that the language poets would become as influential to her work as the poets from the Harlem Renaissance and Black Arts movement, which is to say they proved utterly foundational to her mature poetics (Kane, p. 206). The primary approach and dominant characteristics seen in Mullen's work from this point forward, along with her classification as a language poet, bears out the abiding significance of this discovery. Suffice it to say, Mullen developed into a strong scholar and solidified her mission and skills as a poet during her tenure at the University of California. Her years in graduate school were well spent.

INNOVATIONS AND IDEAS OF SELF: 1989–1995

After leaving Santa Cruz, Mullen enjoyed several years of unalloyed success as an academic and a poet. She received her Ph.D. (1990) and accepted a position teaching literature and history at Cornell University. During those years Mullen developed a reputation as a poet to watch by publishing poems in well-regarded literary journals and readings at places such as New York City's famed Nuyorican Poets Café. She also worked on putting together new poetry collections, publishing *Trimmings* (1991) and *S*PeRM**K*T* (1992) in short succession. (These two collections, together with her next, *Muse & Drudge* in 1995, would be republished together by Graywolf Press in 2006 as the volume *Recyclopedia*.) *Trimmings* and *S*PeRM**K*T* proved to be inevitable but nonetheless bracing expressions of Mullen's newfound approach to poetics, which favored formal experimentation over immediate accessibility. The works were well received by the critical community and garnered Mullen a Gertrude Stein Award for Innovative Poetry and a Rockefeller fellowship in 1994. Such recognition would continue to follow Mullen—despite her near-constant shapeshifting—for the next two decades of her writing career.

The questions concerning black female identity in *Trimmings* and *S*PeRM**K*T* are clearly related to some of the central questions Mullen addresses in *Tree Tall Woman*. Indeed, Mullen has noted that the works ultimately serve to "identify black and feminist consciousness with cultural critique" (Dargan, p. 1015). However, unlike her approach in *Tree Tall Woman*, Mullen had reached a point in her career where she had begun avoiding "overtly confessional or didactic writing" and had found a more sophisticated way to "focus on identity in a critical way to highlight the contradictions of [her] existence in this time and place" (Ghosh, p. 258). Mullen accomplished this change through a series of radical departures from her former manner of writing. *Trimmings* and *S*PeRM**K*T* represent major theoretical and stylistic changes for Mullen and demonstrate why she became of one the most prominent experimental poets of the age. In *Trimmings*, readers are treated to a supercharged version of the signifying, punning, and sound-sense seen in Mullen's earlier poetry, while experiencing new trajectories in terms of her treatment of language and use of form. Mullen dispenses with more traditionally conceived verse poems and instead produces dense prose and list poems. These forms suit the book's subject of commodification and reinforce Mullen's key themes in significant ways. They also continuously nod to the inspirations behind the poetry: the marketplace and Gertrude Stein's *Tender Buttons* (1914).

As an homage and imaginative takeoff on Stein's *Tender Buttons*, *Trimmings* is a challenging conceptual work that takes on the world of domestication and women's fashion in order to examine cultural notions of selfhood. As Mullen has explained, "the whole book is really built around this: both my active and my somewhat critical engagement with Stein, my problematic relation to the Western icon of beauty and the black woman's relationship to that, and my interest in representation itself" (Hogue, p. 246). *Trimmings* analyzes society's ability to use those objects to shape the perceptions and expressions of black women and, ultimately, structure their reality. Read in this way, Mullen's book is a pointed appraisal of the marketplace's in-built

racism and sexism, as well as a denunciation of its manipulative tactics. It is a critique of the effects of commodity fetishism on marginalized populations. In the book, Mullen asks fundamental questions about the nature of that relationship: "Thinking thought to be a body wearing language as clothing or language a body of thought which is a soul or body the clothing of a soul, she is veiled in silence. A veiled, unavailable body makes an available space" ("Thinking thought to be a body," *Recyclopedia,* p. 62). Here, as elsewhere in the book, Mullen posits that language functions like clothing: it is a form of protection, adornment, and identification. This idea may be traced back to the poet's experience speaking various forms of English in her youth in order to operate within different groups and her later realization as a graduate student that language—and, by relation, the very notion of self—is socially constructed.

However much the book takes on the larger social and political forces at work in the United States, it also takes on the social and political dynamics at play in the poetry world, particularly as those dynamics apply to poets of color choosing to operate outside the parameters of more conventional and readily marketable definitions of ethnic literatures. As Amy Moorman Robbins notes, Mullen's work reaches "the very crux of this categorical impasse surrounding the reception of innovative writing that is also overtly identified as African American, writing that insists upon the coexistence of these terms" (p. 353). In poem after poem, Mullen's work pushes against the literary world's categorical controls, simultaneously exposing and breaking free of the status quo. Robbins further notes that "Mullen's Language writing reveals the ways in which the white imagination, and at times white Language writing as well, unconsciously promotes stereotypes and specifically anti-African American racism also through programmatic, received language" (p. 356). Throughout *Trimmings,* Mullen dismantles the barriers set by those arbiters of culture by modeling a desegregated, open-ended poetics.

In her next work, the suggestively named *S*PeRM**K*T,* Mullen once again turns her eye toward consumerism as shaper and signifier of self. *S*PeRM**K*T* serves in several respects as a companion piece to *Trimmings* by offering an extended treatment of that work's principal concerns, albeit done up in a unique fashion. Mullen explains the relationship between *Trimmings* and *S*PeRM**K*T* by saying that "on the one hand, it's the woman with the wardrobe and on the other, it's the woman with her shopping list in the supermarket" (Hogue, p. 242). *S*PeRM**K*T* explores notions of choice and personal autonomy in an environment replete with mass-produced manipulations: the American supermarket. Mullen adopts, repurposes, and riffs on the language of the marketer and politician by placing their words into the mouths of black women. This approach allows her to sardonically expose the manifold implications of their words and images as they apply to race, gender, and class. "So this is generic life, feeding from a dented cant. Devoid of colored labels, the discounted irregulars," writes Mullen, her puns and innuendos cutting through the gloss of consumerist life to reveal the unsettling inequities, oppressions, and predations it enacts ("Pyramids are eroding monuments," *Recyclopedia,* p. 67).

S*PeRM**K*T is a provocative work, both in its critique of materialism's insidious power over the mind and its insistence on taking great linguistic leaps to push readers to think beyond the slogans, clichés, and other intellectual shortcuts that keep institutional oppression in business. As Mullen would later explain in an interview, she has "often [made] an effort to recognize and resist the bias that is built into language through a history of accumulated associations" (Henning). If *S*PeRM**K*T* accomplishes nothing else, it functions as a tool of resistance and criticism, compelling readers to pay closer attention to culture's productions, to what they have consumed and how their consumption may define them. Clues to that central theme appear in the book's title itself, for as Mullen has notes, *S*PeRM**K*T* "comes from the word 'supermarket' with some letters missing ... The missing letters just happen to be U-A-R-E,

so it's like 'you are what you eat'" (Griffin et al.).

While Mullen's boundary pushing in *Trimmings* and *S*PeRM**K*T* represented a true artistic evolution, it did end her tenure as a poet with "mass appeal" (Hogue, p. 252). Such experimentation also altered the composition of her audience in a substantial way. Most alarmingly, Mullen found that her audience had changed from predominantly black to white over the course of those two books. This change disturbed Mullen because she was committed both to connecting with the black community and to bringing disparate groups of readers together—at having an integrated audience. She wanted her art to be progressive in nature, open to all readers and ultimately unifying. Mullen was also disquieted by the fact that her change in audience yet again demonstrated the power of a false dichotomy that had become a very real barrier in the poetry community: "the idea that you can be black *or* innovative" but never both at once (Griffin et al.). Mullen's writing, as she has long maintained, "comes out of a conviction that innovation is intrinsic to black cultural consciousness" (Dargan, p. 1015). Seeing this conviction made manifest in her published works was one thing, but seeing it appreciated by a culturally diverse audience was something altogether different. While Mullen would not retreat from innovation, she would make a conscious effort in her next work, *Muse & Drudge* (1995), to create a poetic dynamic that was capable of breaking free of her largely homogenous readership (Hogue, p. 240).

Mullen's strategy for assembling that readership was to tap into an array of cultural allusions, make ample use of quotations, and continue to open up realms of meaning for whoever entered the text. Like previous works, *Muse & Drudge* primarily deals with the construction of identity. In this case, Mullen uses the oppositional elements of the romanticized female muse and her oft neglected sister, the workaday drudge, to explore a range of issues related to the social and cultural frameworks black women are confronted with in America. *Muse & Drudge* is a curious work in that it is at once disembodied and earthy,

distant and intensely present. Elisabeth Frost describes *Muse & Drudge* as "a long poem in lyric fragments that amalgamate Sappho and the blues, Steinian games with Black Arts radicalism" in a bid to deconstruct identity and examine its tensions (p. 399). Mullen explains that *Muse & Drudge* is "a book of echoes," a work assembled in the manner of a collage by "recycling fragments of language" (Frost, p. 405). What is central to both appraisals is the fluid nature of the work and its implicit assertion that identity remains in flux. Indeed, the poems in *Muse & Drudge* are consistently variable in their construction and connections, and multifarious in their sources and expressions. They span centuries, cultures, and personal histories, providing readers with a vitalizing textural immersion into selfhood.

In the preface to *Recyclopedia,* Mullen explains that while writing *Muse & Drudge,* she "imagined a chorus of women singing verses that are sad and hilarious at the same time" ("Recycle This Book," p. xi). The book does indeed have a strange tragicomic quality to it, much of which is brought about by Mullen's heady mixture of disparate registers, cultural references, and shifting points of identification. Part of the work's appeal also stems from the manic collisions of rhymes and images, as evidenced in the following lines from "marry at a hotel, annul 'em," which push musicality and associative logic to extremes:

divine sunrises
Osiris's irises
his splendid mistress
is his sis Isis

creole cocoa loca
crayon gumbo boca
crayfish Crayola
jumbo mocha-cola

(Recyclopedia, p. 162)

Taking cues from the feminist eroticism of Sappho and the sexual innuendos and social consciousness of blues artists, the poems in *Muse & Drudge* are concurrently sensual and political. Indeed, they spring from and revel in the black female body, all the while offering up sharp metaphors regarding the body's desires, creative

capabilities, and loci of control. As with much of Mullen's work, the body and its identity stand on contested ground:

lifeguard at apartheid park
rough, dirty, a little bit hard
broken blossom, poke a possum
park your quark in a hard aardvark

("tomboy girl with cowboy boots," p. 150)

Despite the hyperkinetic associations and manifold disjunctions in *Muse & Drudge,* Mullen has taken care to ensure that the poems adhere to a few stable conventions which would be familiar to most poetry readers, namely the use of quatrains and end rhymes (Hogue, p. 253). Mullen's use of such conventions lures readers into the poems while also critiquing the seductive comforts of long-established poetic traditions. Along the way, she uses the gestures of those traditions to upend the traditions themselves. She thus creates an ironic legibility, suggesting those long-held conventions serve as a way to structure, contain, or explain away otherness. Readers can thus use those islands of familiarity and other points of shared experience—be they phrases, images, or rhythms drawn from popular culture—to puzzle together a range of interesting interpretations about identity formation throughout the book.

Because the poems in *Muse & Drudge* remain open to so many possible readings, they present themselves as inherently democratic in nature. There is no one authoritative way to approach, appreciate, and benefit from them. It is clear that Mullen remained mindful of readers throughout the creation of *Muse & Drudge* and gauged the relative levels of inclusiveness and exclusiveness at play in the work in hopes of finding a productive balance (Hogue, p. 253). In large part, she succeeded by creating a freewheeling heterogeneity capable of speaking in specifics to the personal experiences of many readers. As such, the work has the capability to trigger a sense of intimacy among those readers. Mullen also succeeded in creating that ever-elusive sense of unity in diversity she had sought in her work after *Tree Tall Woman,* for the book finds a way to encapsulate an eclectic array of communal

experiences—to function as a literary melting pot.

Along with the publication and positive reception of *Muse & Drudge,* 1995 was an important year for Mullen's career in academia, as she accepted a position teaching literature and writing at the University of California–Los Angeles (UCLA). While UCLA boasted a strong reputation as an academic institution and doubtless provided Mullen with an environment amenable to the arts, a palpable sense of tension hung over the city of Los Angeles as a whole—a tension that had, in some form or fashion, long informed Mullen's work and would continue to affect it for the foreseeable future. In a very real sense, Mullen's move to the city embedded her in one of the country's epicenters for racial conflict and further underscored the importance of her message as a poet.

For those living in black and Hispanic neighborhoods of Los Angeles in the early to mid-1990s, poverty, the crack cocaine epidemic, the threat of HIV and AIDS, gang activities, and institutional racism were daily realities. These realities were made manifest to the rest of the country through a new subgenre of hip hop music, gangsta rap, and a series of events that made the national news, including police corruption and brutality trials and the Los Angeles riots of 1992. The latter event proved especially telling, with rioters in the neighborhoods of South Central Los Angeles taking to the streets to protest the acquittal of four police officers who had been tried for beating a unarmed black man, Rodney King, to within an inch of his life. The fires and looting that resulted from the riots led to approximately $1 billion in property damage and gutted entire neighborhoods in the city. The riots also resulted in two thousand injuries and fifty-three deaths, making it the worst rioting the country had experienced since 1967. The post-riot Los Angeles Mullen inhabited was, in some respects, analogous to the Fort Worth of her youth. It was a dynamic, diversely populated space teeming with the tensions born of growth and the competing ideologies of its peoples. Los Angeles was a space of social transition, populated by individuals looking to redress a long his-

tory of inequity and right the direction of their future. Through it all, Los Angeles also proved—much like the rap music of the era—to be a space where sampling, hybridization, and innovation were beginning to coalesce across cultures. For a poet with Mullen's proclivities, taking up residence in such an environment seems fitting.

RECOGNITIONS AND RETURNS: 1996–2015

Mullen quickly established herself as a scholar at UCLA and won a Katherine Newman Award for Best Essay from the Society for the Study of Multi-Ethnic Literatures of the United States (MELUS) in 1996. By 1999 she was on the move again, taking up an artist residency at the Virginia Center for the Creative Arts. Mullen used this residency and the next couple of years to develop her fifth book, *Sleeping with the Dictionary* (2002). Published by the University of California Press, *Sleeping with the Dictionary* ensured Mullen a larger audience than she had been accustomed to as a poet working within the independent small-press scene. Gone were the days of publishing out of an editor's house and hustling to get her work into the hands of readers. Her poetry now appeared alongside classic works by world-renowned poets such as Rainer Maria Rilke and Robert Creeley. Her poetry also began appearing in more reviews, libraries, bookstores, and classrooms than it had in the past.

Unlike some poets who move from the margins to more conventional and well-known publishing venues, Mullen had not altered and did not alter her poetics in order to appeal to the tastes and expectations of a wider or more mainstream readership nor did she position herself as a poet with safe academic designs. Instead, Mullen chose to push her poetry and readers to extraordinary and sometimes difficult places. In *Sleeping with the Dictionary,* Mullen deliberately "manipulat[es] not only the subject matter of her writing so as to re-pose it in a newly figured manner but also the process the reader undertakes in a attempting to read that defamiliarized language"(Beall, p. 125). Mullen deconstructs and reassembles, riffing and punning all along, asking her audience to see the world and

their framing of that world's terms and conditions with new eyes. Given Mullen's high-stakes conceptualism and linguistic dynamics, *Sleeping with the Dictionary* ends up feeling like a work of insurgency—a poetic reckoning—and arguably stands as her most radical and definitive poetic statement to date. Indeed, Jessica Lewis Luck has noted that "*Sleeping with the Dictionary* is Mullen's avant-garde ars poetica, offering a poetics of both/and: both experimental and black, to be sure, but also both procedural and inspired, both linguistic and embodied" (p. 359). In the book, Mullen uses her understanding of linguistics and techniques drawn from Oulipo, the French literary workshop of potential literature, to drive the development of her poems. She packs the work with gnomic puzzles, dense juxtapositions, free-flowing allusions, spirited ironies, and earthy divagations, all the while pushing the limits of meaning-making.

Sleeping with the Dictionary never panders to easy paraphrase, requiring instead a slow, active, and creative engagement from its audience. As with her three previous works, the book presents readers with a rare freedom to think differently and piece together distinctive interpretations of her poetry. Many of the poems, including the work's title piece, acknowledge this peculiar state of being and play with self-reflexivity:

I beg to dicker with my silver-tongued companion, whose lips are ready to read my shining gloss. A versatile partner, conversant and well-versed in the verbal art, the dictionary is not averse to the solitary habits of the curiously wide-awake reader. In the dark night's insomnia, the book is a stimulating sedative, awakening my tired imagination to the hypnagogic trance of language.... Aroused by myriad possibilities, we try out the most perverse positions in the practice of our nightly act, the penetration of the denotative body of the work. Any exit from the logic of language might be an entry in a symptomatic dictionary. The alphabetical order of this ample block of knowledge might render a dense lexicon of lucid hallucinations. Beside the bed, a pad lies open to record the meandering of migratory words. In the rapid eye movement of the poet's night vision, this dictum can be decoded, like the secret acrostic of a lover's name.

("Sleeping with the Dictionary," p. 67)

In true postmodern fashion, Mullen directly addresses her audience, calling attention to the constructedness of her poetry. Mullen acts as both the seduced and the seducer, using the trope of seduction throughout the book as a means to explore the role of language in affecting our experiences and informing our identity. Even mistakes and apparent misconceptions—scrambled, misjudged, and unorthodox utterances—play a part in this formation. They are, in large part, the results of Mullen's serendipitous mode of discovery and strategic approach to presentation. Mullen explains in her interview with Barbara Henning that when she "write[s] something literal and straightforward," she will "alter it so that it is a little blurred, as if you somehow misread or misheard the line." Mullen notes elsewhere in the interview that such an approach is a "way of interrupting and moving language around to open space up for conflicting thoughts," to usher readers beyond the confines of their cultural paradigms and subjectivities. Mullen's approach, then, is interventionist in nature, for one of its chief functions is to steer readers away from habitual and incapacitating thought processes.

In *Sleeping with the Dictionary,* Mullen manages to take a fresh approach to her subject matter by tapping into a range of traditions or schools. Along the way, Mullen pushes back against what she terms the "aesthetic apartheid" at play in literary criticism and history, thus finding a way to both censure the modes of thinking and debunk the myths that she says have allowed scholars and poets for ages to "compartmental-[ize] literary works on the basis of either formal innovation or racial/ethnic representation, but rarely both at once" (qtd. in Robbins, p. 351). Understood in this context, it is clear that "Mullen's work in *Sleeping with the Dictionary* is not simply a piece of evidence that there is a black avant-garde; rather, her work makes manifest and directly engages with the racial politics of the American avant-garde's whiteness as it operates in literary history" (Robbins, p. 367). The book, then, poses a direct challenge to members of the literary establishment by calling out their biases and forcing them to consider a

poetics that cannot be contained within the confines of the dominant critical frameworks. Despite or perhaps because of Mullen's unabashed avant-gardism in *Sleeping with the Dictionary,* she garnered national recognition and wider critical respect for her work. *Sleeping with the Dictionary* earned her spots among the finalists for the 2002 National Book Award and the 2003 Los Angeles Times Book Prize and National Book Critics Circle Award. Mullen was a poet who had arrived largely on her own terms.

Given Mullen's forward-thinking approach to poetry and breakthroughs as a poet, it is curious that she chose to follow *Sleeping with Dictionary* by publishing *Blues Baby: Early Poems* (2002), a markedly autobiographical poetry collection comprising poems from the earliest phase of her career. While *Blues Baby* compiled previously uncollected poems from that period, the heart of the book is, in fact, a republication of *Tree Tall Woman*—the very work from which Mullen had consciously distanced herself over the past decade. Mullen's motivation for publishing what might be characterized as a retrograde work at the zenith of her experimentation remains unclear. However, what is clear is that Mullen had come full circle in terms of how she wished to represent herself and contextualize her work for readers. In many ways, *Blues Baby* provided readers with insight into Mullen's roots and helped them understand her trajectory as an artist. It is also clear that Mullen had reached a point in her writing career where she was able to capitalize on her name and the successes of her mature collections when it came to promoting and selling her lesser-known back catalog.

Over the next couple of years, Mullen sought out and acquired institutional support for her work, including fellowships from the Foundation for Contemporary Arts (2004) and the Guggenheim Foundation (2005). Mullen used the support to work on her scholarship and the book *Recyclopedia: Trimmings, S*PeRM**K*T, and Muse & Drudge* (2006). Much like *Blues Baby, Recyclopedia* did not offer readers any new material, but it did compile previously published works and encapsulate an era of development for the poet in one handy volume. *Recyclopedia* fared

well with critics, eventually earning Mullen a prestigious PEN Beyond Margins award in 2007. Mullen also received the 2006 Elizabeth Agee Prize for Outstanding Scholarship for a collection of her critical essays and interviews, *The Cracks Between What We Are and What We Are Supposed to Be*. While this volume deals with many of Mullen's core concerns—namely, race, gender, and representation in literature—it does so in a primarily self-directed fashion, serving as an apologia for Mullen's own philosophical tendencies, aesthetic preferences, and body of poetry.

Mullen would continue to receive recognition from influential literary organizations over the next few years, including a fellowship from the Academy of American Poets (2009) and a $50,000 Jackson Poetry Prize (2010). While Mullen had doubtless found success as a writer, she had also reached a point where she appeared to be doing more self-anthologizing and explaining of her work than actually creating new poetry. She had reached a point where she appeared to be gazing backward more than forward. However, in 2013, Mullen once again surprised readers with the publication of a new poetry collection, *Urban Tumbleweed: Notes from a Tanka Diary*. *Urban Tumbleweed* proved to be a departure from Mullen's previous works in a number of ways, most notably in terms of her use of a very traditional form, the Japanese tanka, as well as her subject matter, humanity's relationship with its physical environment. While Mullen bends or dismisses certain rules involved with writing traditional tankas, her work in *Urban Tumbleweed* follows many of its conventions, especially with regard to lucidity of image, concision of phrasing, adherence to syllable count, and observational focus on elements of the natural world.

In several respects, *Urban Tumbleweed* could be seen as Mullen's bid to better understand her adopted city and surrounding areas by situating herself in the urban ecosystem. Numerous poems in the book treat the small and simple miracles of everyday life, such as the delight of busy honeybee or the scent of a fresh orange, but just as many point to the disquieting realities of the city. Living in contemporary Los Angeles—land of Hollywood artifice, multicultural collisions

and infusions, and dislocating sprawl—lends Mullen's poetics of place a curious slant and critical impetus. A substantial number of the pieces unambiguously foreground humanity's cupidity, shortsightedness, and adverse impact on the environment. Such poems are, in effect, confrontations meant to make readers more mindful of the world around them and more aware of how their life choices ripple well beyond the individual sphere. When Mullen writes of one of the city's most conspicuous physical features—the congested freeway—the irony of humanity's solution to the problem it has created emerges in a compressed and immediately affecting way:

A profusion of oleanders—to beautify
the freeway and filter the air, though
leaf, stem, and blossom are all poison.

(p. 24)

Lines like these sing as they critique and employ a turn that moves readers from image to idea in a quick, revelatory fashion. At its best, *Urban Tumbleweed* offers such sharp epiphanies, making excellent use of the kinetic power afforded by the tanka.

While *Urban Tumbleweed* distinguishes itself from the bulk of Mullen's other work through its straightforward conceptualism and tendency toward plainspokenness, it does continue her lifelong exploration of identity and the social constructs influencing it. Taken as a whole, the book represents Mullen's attempt to understand the character of a diverse and spirited city—a seeming analogue for her own person. Mullen's observations regarding the minutiae of day-to-day living and the larger political concerns operating in and around Los Angeles paint the portrait of a place-as-character whose actions are by turns stifling, energizing, and oftentimes absurd. Here Mullen reveals herself to be a stranger in a strange land. Like the titular urban tumbleweed—a colloquial term for a plastic bag blowing across the city—the book reveals that Mullen's role as a resident in Los Angeles is artificial and accidental, yet as integral and appropriate to the city's overall identity as a displaced mountain lion searching for sustenance among neat rows of bungalows. Mullen occupies

a liminal space in the book, being simultaneously spectator and participant, audience and actor, in a land where the play is the thing.

Interestingly, despite being a world away from Texas, *Urban Tumbleweed* harkens back to aspects of Mullen's earliest poetry. Like *Tree Tall Woman, Urban Tumbleweed* is steeped in the culture of a particular place and speaks of that culture in an everyday language that its residents would recognize. Despite the occasional journeys to other locales, and Los Angeles' inherent nebulousness, one could argue that the work has a regionalist quality to it. It is—unlike *Muse & Drudge* or *Sleeping with the Dictionary*—marked very much by the spaces and peoples surrounding its conception. Given these familiar qualities, as well as the philosophical inflections readers can trace back to Mullen's more experimental texts, *Urban Tumbleweed* can be seen as being both a new expression and exhibition catalog of select elements of her previous books: a representation of her many representations over the years. In that respect, Mullen's diary serves as a testament to her present-day attentiveness and a reference to the articulations of her past.

CONCLUSION

Harryette Mullen has spent most of her career eschewing the limitations others would impose upon her and defying easy categorization as a poet. Mullen is no unquestioning sentimentalist: her poetic imagination and formal innovations have been born in large part from her abiding desire to move black poetry to a place far beyond the outmoded cultural paradigms and critical frameworks that have so long attempted to contain it and explain it away. While there is little doubt that Mullen remains concerned with amending the present, it is evident that much of her motivation to initiate change comes from her desire to affect the trajectory of future writers and critics. Mullen has said that, when writing her poems and developing her works, she is "usually thinking more about the unborn than those people who are [her] contemporaries" (Hogue, p. 257). This future-oriented attitude and approach have periodically put her at odds with the

dominant modes of the present, but they have made her poetry all the richer. As Mullen reflects in "Telegraphs from a Distracted Sibyl," her "literary background and practice as a writer, in short, has been something of a traditional, eclectic, folksy, trashy, classical, avant-garde, worldly, naive, unorthodox, spiritual, polymorphously perverse, mammy-made, jig-rig, and Rube Goldberg operation" (p. 19). It has been at once a genuine recognition of the past and a wildly fascinating foray into the realm of possibility—a poetics capable of assembling history's myriad lives into a dynamic collage. In the final analysis, it would seem that Mullen has managed to find a way to honor the struggles and strides of her forebears while simultaneously propelling conversations regarding race, gender, and the politics of poetry forward in an inimitable and necessary way. It is this balancing act, along with her work's pleasing virtuosity and multivocality, that makes Mullen such a singular poet and ensures her a place among the most influential literary stylists of the age.

Selected Bibliography

WORKS OF HARRYETTE MULLEN

POETRY
Tree Tall Woman: Poems. Galveston, Tex.: Energy Earth Communications, 1981.

Trimmings. New York: Tender Buttons Press, 1991.

S*PeRM**K*T. Philadelphia: Singing Horse Press, 1992.

Muse & Drudge. Philadelphia: Singing Horse Press, 1995.

Sleeping with the Dictionary. Berkeley: University of California Press, 2002.

Urban Tumbleweed: Notes from a Tanka Diary. St. Paul, Minn.: Graywolf Press, 2013.

COLLECTED WORKS
Blues Baby: Early Poems. Lewisburg, Pa.: Bucknell University Press, 2002.

Recyclopedia: Trimmings, S*PeRM**K*T, and Muse & Drudge. St. Paul, Minn.: Graywolf Press, 2006.

ESSAYS
"'When He Is Least Himself': Dunbar and Double Consciousness in African American Poetry." *African American*

Review 41, no. 2:277–282 (2007).

The Cracks Between What We Are and What We Are Supposed to Be: Essays and Interviews. Tuscaloosa: University of Alabama Press, 2012. (Includes "Telegraphs from a Distracted Sibyl," pp. 18–19.)

CRITICAL STUDIES

Beall, Emily P. "'As Reading As If': Harryette Mullen's 'Cognitive Similes.'" *Journal of Literary Semantics* 34, no. 2:125–137 (2005).

Luck, Jessica Lewis. "Entries on a Post-Language Poetics in Harryette Mullen's *Dictionary.*" *Contemporary Literature* 49, no. 3:357–382 (2008).

Robbins, Amy Moorman. "Harryette Mullen's *Sleeping with the Dictionary* and Race in Language/Writing." *Contemporary Literature* 51, no. 2:341–370 (2010).

INTERVIEWS

Bedient, Calvin. "The Solo Mysterioso Blues: An Interview with Harryette Mullen." In *The Cracks Between What We Are and What We Are Supposed to Be: Essays and Interviews.* Tuscaloosa: University of Alabama Press, 2012. Pp. 185–203.

Dargan, Kyle G. "Everything We Can Imagine: An Interview with Harryette Mullen." *Callaloo* 30, no. 4:1014–1016 (2007).

Frost, Elisabeth A. "An Interview with Harryette Mullen." *Contemporary Literature* 41, no. 3:397–421 (2000).

Ghosh, Nibir K. "I Dream a World: A Conversation with Harryette Mullen." In *The Cracks Between What We Are and What We Are Supposed to Be.* Tuscaloosa: University of Alabama Press, 2012. Pp. 258–273.

Griffin, Farah, Michael Magee, and Kristin Gallagher. "A Conversation with Harryette Mullen." Electronic Poetry Center, 1997. http://wings.buffalo.edu/epc/authors/mullen/interview-new.html

Henning, Barbara. "Conversation with Harryette Mullen: From A to B." *Not Enough Night* (Naropa University), spring 2010. http://www.naropa.edu/academics/jks/publications/notenoughnight/spring-10/conversation-with-harryette-mullen.php

Hogue, Cynthia. "An Interview with Harryette Mullen." In *The Cracks Between What We Are and What We Are Supposed to Be: Essays and Interviews.* Tuscaloosa: University of Alabama Press, 2012. Pp. 233–257.

Kane, Daniel. "An Interview with Harryette Mullen." In *The Cracks Between What We Are and What We Are Supposed to Be: Essays and Interviews.* Tuscaloosa: University of Alabama Press, 2012. Pp. 204–212.

Pereira, Malin. "Harryette Mullen." In *Into a Light Both Brilliant and Unseen: Conversations with Contemporary Black Poets.* Athens: University of Georgia Press, 2010.

Williams, Emily Allen. "Harryette Mullen, 'The Queen of Hip Hyperbole': An Interview." *African American Review* 34, no. 4:701–707 (2000).

ALICE MUNRO

(1931—)

Elizabeth Freudenthal

ALICE MUNRO HAS been one of the greatest chroniclers of social change in the twentieth century. Long appreciated for her formal mastery and innovation of the short-story form, she is also a fierce social critic: principally in regard to women as an economic and social class, but additionally, and no less importantly, of the massive social and environmental changes wrought by late capitalism.

The author of sixteen works of fiction, nearly all short-story collections, Munro has been writing very similar stories—about white women, mostly from small towns in rural Ontario, mostly born around 1930, mostly unhappily married and/or divorced, mostly attempting with mitigated success to break through class barriers—since 1968. Her characters paint makeup onto sagging cheeks, squeeze into old pants, develop passionate, unrequited crushes, and endure sexual assaults. They experience marital infidelity—both as wives of straying husbands and as wives who do the straying. They choose between the hard-won promise of financial independence in a career and the more comfortable but chafing confinement of daily motherhood and wifehood. They tell stories of their childhood experiences of rural poverty to audiences of cultural elites for whom bohemian poverty is fashion. They return to their childhood hometowns to find shacks along gravel roads transformed into sleek suburban tracts.

Munro focuses attention on marginal lives: women born into rural Canadian poverty, four intersection subject positions outside mainstream North American culture. And this attention is careful, respectful, and insightful. She writes of the quotidian experience of living in a woman's body in a particular time and place, from a particular background, with particular experiences of the social norms of femininity.

In addition to consistent thematic content, her stories share a characteristic style of psychological realism fused with ostentatiously formalist technique. In particular, critics laud her for pushing the boundaries of representations of time. An ornately detailed depiction of a dinner party in the 1950s may, in the next sentence, jump forty years into a single character's future memory of another character at that party. And the story might stay there, forty years later, with whole new characters and a transformed narrative conflict inflected by the past but no longer bound to it. These distinctive breathless leaps in a character's time line give her work, paradoxically, both a mythic quality as well as a heightened fidelity to the ways individuals experience time and memory.

In addition to these formal innovations in representation of our experience of time, Munro's work has become increasingly interested in the postmodern emphasis on metafiction. Since at least the 1980s, her work has fixated on our reliance on storytelling to make sense of the world—and the implicit impossibility of our stories to adequately or accurately represent experience.

This combination of attention to the smelly, bruised lives of marginalized women and carefully wrought formal sophistication has won Munro a successively more impressive list of prizes, including far more than these highlights: the Canadian Governor General's Literary Award in 1968, 1978, and 1986, the PEN/Malamud Award for Excellence in Short Fiction in 1997, the National Book Critics Circle Award in 1998, the Man Booker Prize in 2009, and the Nobel Prize for Literature in 2013. The Nobel announcement

tersely summarized Munro as "master of the contemporary short story." Indeed.

LIFE

Alice Ann Laidlaw was born on July 10, 1931, on the outskirts of the small town of Wingham, in Huron County, Ontario. Her father, Robert Eric Laidlaw, operated a commercial fox and mink farm. Her mother, Anne Clarke Chamney Laidlaw, was a former teacher whose hidden talent for entrepreneurship was foiled by her housewife obligations, by the changing twentieth-century economy, and by her long illness and disability.

Munro's life was divided between muddy, musky farming in the country and her marginally tidier, starchier world attending the Wingham town school and visiting her grandmother and aunt. She crossed that divide daily, walking to school and back home through the various class strata embedded in her semirural landscape. She describes her childhood neighborhood to Beverly Rasporich as outside the boundaries of town norms:

> A rural slum wouldn't quite describe it. It wasn't part of the town and there were a lot of bootleggers. And also this was the tail end of the Depression. So there were a lot of people who were just out of work, but a lot of pretty marginal type people tended to live in this area—so that it was a very different community from the town or the surrounding farming community.
>
> (p. 4)

She has worked over the poverty, violence, and stultifying conventions of small-town Ontario in countless stories. The gothic elements of her stories—sexual and physical violence directed at children, symbolic alignments between humans and livestock, melodramatic marriages and separations—are largely drawn from her childhood observations and experiences. Robert Thacker's biographical research uncovered newspaper headlines from the 1930s and 1940s that verify the more gothic undercurrents of Munro's hometown during that time: a lamb born with seven legs and two tails, a hand almost severed, and, perhaps an influence on her early story "A Time of Death," a baby fatally scalded (Thacker 2005, p. 45). Munro's experience of the small-town, rural gothic echoes what she notes in an interview with Jeanne McCulloch and Mona Simpson published in the *Paris Review*: that one of her early literary loves was fiction from the U.S. South, itself a rural gothic tradition. In this literary heritage she found two important influences: The first crucial legacy of that tradition was to show Munro how to write about rural people and country life, which was her own background and which set the stories she wanted to tell. But just as important was a legacy of women's writing. Through southern women's fiction, Munro understood that women were writing about marginal people, about the grotesque, and about disability and illness. As she told McCulloch and Simpson:

> The thing about the Southern writers that interested me, without my being really aware of it, was that all the Southern writers whom I really loved were women. I didn't really like Faulkner that much. I loved Eudora Welty, Flannery O'Connor, Katherine Anne Porter, Carson McCullers. There was a feeling that women could write about the freakish, the marginal.... I came to feel that was our territory, whereas the mainstream big novel about real life was men's territory. I don't know how I got that feeling of being on the margins, it wasn't that I was *pushed* there. Maybe it was because I grew up on a margin. I knew there was something about the great writers I felt shut out from, ... It was: how I can be a writer when I'm the object of other writers?

Munro isn't the only one who senses that the "mainstream big novel about real life" is men's territory. This sense functions as a truism of literary culture, now as much as ever. Women, by contrast, can write about the freakish and marginal because women—especially women who step out of the role of object—are freakish and marginal. To be a woman who writes, when for centuries women were what was written about, is a position so marginal that it approaches the realm of the grotesque. In addition, the fact that Munro had to keep her obsessive reading and writing secret from her strictly pragmatic community reinforced her sense that, as unjust as it may be, a woman who reads and writes is an anomaly.

But disability, or in the pre-disability-activism parlance, "freakishness," is more than a symbol of women's marginalization in Munro's work. She spent the bulk of her adolescence dealing directly with the realities of a chronic, fatal disability. Her mother was diagnosed with Parkinson's disease in 1943. The diagnosis transformed Munro's life. As the family's oldest child—Munro had two younger siblings, Bill and Sheila—she was obligated to take over her mother's domestic role, doing all the housework for the family. In the late 1940s the family's fur business began to decline, and her mother was too ill to help support the family. Munro's father started working night shifts at a factory to cover family expenses. Munro took summer jobs, but calculated that she would need scholarships to pay for college. While managing her household and tending to her sick mother, she buried herself in her studies. She was class valedictorian in 1949. And she indeed won a two-year scholarship to the University of Western Ontario, her ticket into a life that better suited her interests and ambitions. At university she supplemented her scholarship by working two library jobs and selling her blood. Despite this brutal schedule of studies and part-time jobs, she considers her time there as one of her best: an opportunity to devote herself to literary study and, more remarkably for her, a delightful two-year vacation from housework.

Her first published work appeared in her university's literary journal *Folio* in 1950. Her university community encouraged her to begin corresponding with Robert Weaver, host of the Canadian Broadcasting Corporation radio show *Canadian Short Stories*. This connection became crucial to her early success. With his support, she was able to publish stories in Canadian literary magazines throughout the 1950s and 1960s.

When her scholarship ran out in 1951, she left the university and married Jim Munro, another serious reader. The couple moved immediately to Vancouver, British Columbia, where Jim got a job in a department store and the couple rapidly set up a middle-class, suburban life. In the *Paris Review* interview, Munro describes the internalized social pressures on her to get married:

> I was like a Victorian daughter—the pressure to marry was so great, one felt it was something to get out of the way: Well, I'll get that done, and they can't bug me about it, and then I'll be a real person and my life will begin. I think I married to be able to write, to settle down and give my attention back to the important thing.

Her alter ego Rose, in *Who Do You Think You Are?*, makes the same decision for similar reasons. The stories in that collection depict Rose reflecting at various ages afterward on this decision and give the moment far more richness and complexity than Munro allows here. Many other stories of unhappily married and divorced women further dramatize the consequences of so much pressure on young women to marry.

True to her intentions, as a young housewife and mother Munro focused on her writing as much as possible, writing during nap times, school hours, and play times, as often as she could. Between 1953 and 1966 she gave birth to four children, though her second child died at birth. In 1963 Jim quit the department store and the couple opened a bookstore, where they both worked devotedly to maintain a decent living through a business they both loved. She wrote stories in her first collection over fifteen years, including this time of young marriage, early motherhood, and working at Munro's Books. She futilely sent stories to the *New Yorker* throughout the 1950s, along with her successful submissions to Canadian journals and radio programs. Her first collection, *Dance of the Happy Shades*, contained material written during this time. She was thirty-six years old when it was published in 1968. That year her debut won one of Canadian letters' highest honors, the Governor-General's Award.

In 1971 she published her second collection, *Lives of Girls and Women*, a set of stories focusing on a version of Munro's adolescent self, named Del Jordan. While the book was winning rave reviews, Munro's marriage was falling apart. Despite Jim's unwavering support of Munro's then-nascent writing career, the couple's basic incompatibility became hard to ignore. Some of

the pressures on her marriage are explored in many stories from that period: irreconcilable class differences, infidelity, and mutual acrimony. Furthermore, many stories dramatize these conflicts as direct results of women's economic dependence on men. Women can't leave unhappy marriages until they can support themselves and their children, and this was certainly a concern of Munro. According to Thacker's biography of Munro, Jim Munro's purchase of a large, show-piece house in 1966 catalyzed the couple's separation. The house symbolized the couple's incompatible class identifications, with literally no place for Munro's family gifts of plates and bowls that were cheaper-looking than Jim's family china and crystal. The couple separated in 1971, after nearly twenty years of marriage, sharing child-rearing duties and establishing ways to live apart more permanently.

At that point, Munro had been working at the bookstore, taking care of four children—her own and a friend's daughter—and writing. She was averaging about four hours a night of sleep. Her marriage had been falling apart. And, after the separation and these years of difficulty and physical strain, she had to figure out a way to make a living. She took increasingly more lucrative teaching jobs for the next few years, moving back to Ontario in 1973. Then in 1974, she reconnected with Gerald Fremlin, a man she had known when he was a few years ahead of her at Western Ontario University in 1950. A year later, she moved back to rural Ontario with Fremlin. In 1976 she formally divorced Jim Munro and married Fremlin. In the *Paris Review* interview, Munro described how she and Fremlin had reconnected when he heard her give a radio interview:

> I must have said where I was living and given the impression that I was not married anymore, because he then came to see me.… He just called me up and said, This is Gerry Fremlin. I'm in Clinton, and I was wondering if we could have lunch together sometime.… We went to the faculty club and had three martinis each, at lunch. I think we were nervous. But we rapidly became very well acquainted. I think we were talking about living together by the end of the afternoon. It was very quick.

Love in Munro's stories rarely occurs so precipitously and successfully. Munro's second marriage lasted happily until Fremlin's death in April 2013, almost forty years after reconnecting.

She published her third collection, *Something I've Been Meaning to Tell You,* the year she reconnected with Fremlin. She moved to Clinton, Ontario, with him in 1976, twenty miles from her childhood home. She has described in multiple interviews that her move back to the Ottowa Valley was dictated at first by Fremlin's need to take care of his ill mother. By the time she died, Fremlin's attachment to country life kept the couple in his childhood home. As Munro told Rasporich in the 1980s, "I do it because my husband likes this kind of life, and I probably feel it's good for me and like it if someone else gives me a push.… As long as people will let me write, I'm pretty adaptable" (p. 11). Eventually, though, Munro developed as strong a bond to the region as her husband had. Because of the couple's shared interest in the land, they loved traveling together, studying the geological features of their region. This love is increasingly manifest in her work. Fremlin, a geographer, was retired by the time the couple married. However, their shared interest in his research is evident in her middle and late-period work. In these works, geological time and scale provides vivid imagery and metaphor, and geographic features of the landscape figure prominently in multiple stories' settings. The majority of Munro's work was written during this middle and later period of life, with Fremlin, in rural Ontario. Munro remained in Clinton, and in June 2013, approaching her eighty-second birthday, announced her retirement from writing.

EARLY-PERIOD WORK

Munro's early period spans her first five volumes: *Dance of the Happy Shades* (1968), *Lives of Girls and Women* (1971), *Something I've Been Meaning to Tell You* (1974), *Who Do You Think You Are?* (1978; published in the United States in 1979 as *The Beggar Maid*), and *The Moons of Jupiter* (1982). These works are characterized by a more exclusive focus on themes from Munro's

childhood and early adult life: poverty in rural Ontario, failing and failed marriages; the sexual revolution's reinscription of patriarchal privilege; and the challenges facing straight, white women seeking professional, sexual, and romantic fulfillment in a society largely ignorant of women's needs for any of those things. While these themes remain dominant throughout Munro's oeuvre, these earlier volumes feature relatively less formal complexity than later works, although each collection gains in assurance and sophistication. Nonetheless, perhaps as a consequence of relatively less formal complexity, this early work features a relatively more targeted focus on social critique.

Munro's early work features a hallmark of that formal contradiction referenced earlier in this essay: a fixation with postmodern critiques of representation conveyed through ostensibly mimetic depiction of conventional domestic and small-town experience. As Ajay Heble articulates in her trenchant analysis of Munro's early and middle-period work, Munro's stories have always constructed meaning from words not spoken, actions not taken, and events outside of the narrative. Meaning is dependent on storytelling, but stories are always many layers removed from lived experience. Heble discusses multiple instances of characters telling stories about their pasts—stories that leave out key details. More to the point in Munro's work, characters' stories remain untold, letters unwritten, possible future paths foreclosed before characters have a chance to make a choice.

Munro has discussed in multiple interviews her belief that life lacks coherence, connection, and linear stability. Her attraction to the short-story form is explicitly in response to this belief about the fragmented nature of reality. And this sense of fragmentation of experience begins in her earliest work. So it's startling that while her contemporaries' drive toward the same post-structuralist ideas led to more explicitly experimental work in the 1960s—Donald Barthelme, Thomas Pynchon, and John Barth are some examples—her narratives have a surface sheen of conventional realism: characters with motivations, crises, and trajectories. Stable geographical and cultural settings. Heterosexual marriage and its dissolution due to historically lived experiences of social and economic change.

The true hallmark of Munro's early work is her almost preachy depiction of women's and girls' experiences as substantively different than men's and boys'. In this thematic emphasis, her work enacts another key element of postmodernism: privileging previously marginalized voices and perspectives. Munro's early work covers a wide range of experiences specific to girls' and women's lives, with plots that are strongly autobiographical. For example, "The Office," in her first collection, is about a housewife who tries to rent an office space so that she can write in privacy, away from her children. The story pulses with ideas from the era's feminist ferment, about the gendered dichotomy of public and private space and about women's voices and experiences as essentially different from men's. The protagonist/narrator describes her need to find a "room of her own," in a loosely updated retread of Virginia Woolf's famous analysis of the need for a woman writer to carve out independent physical and intellectual space:

> A house is all right for a man to work in. He brings his work into the house, a place is cleared for it; the house rearranges itself as best it can around him. Everybody recognizes that his work *exists....* He can shut his door. Imagine (I said) a mother shutting her door, and the children knowing she is behind it; why, the very thought of it is outrageous to them. A woman who sits staring into space, into a country that is not her husband's or her children's is likewise known to be an offense against nature. So a house is not the same for a woman. She is not someone who walks into the house, to make use of it, and will walk out again. She *is* the house; there is no separation possible.
>
> (p. 60)

In this update to Woolf, a woman needs a room of her own, separate from her house, because she is ontologically bound to domestic space in a way that forecloses any other possibilities of being except that of the freakish "offense against nature." The story goes on to track with comic rage the office landlord continually disrupting the narrator's writing time with increasingly ridiculous concocted pretexts. The landlord's intrusions

eventually become intolerable, and the narrator quits her rented office. The story dramatizes an impossible bind for women: while women are equated with the domestic space, they have no agency within that space. And further, when women attempt to create a space of subjectivity—of actively controlling their own voices and experiences, of the traditionally male-construed public space of rent, business, and writing—men continue to connote that space as domestic and therefore subject to the whims of male dominance.

Another story from that first collection, "Boys and Girls," documents with sensitivity and nuance the way that, too often, a girl's adolescence changes her relationship with her father. The story is about a preteen girl with a little brother, growing up on a silver-fox farm much like that of Munro's own childhood. The children's father and his farmhand are getting ready to shoot two old horses whose utility is no longer worth the price of their upkeep. When the men plan to shoot the first horse, the daughter drags her little brother to watch secretly, demonstrating her mastery of the male space. However, by the time they plan to shoot the second horse, her sense of control and agency has been threatened by the sudden imposition onto her of gendered identity. The narrator/protagonist articulates this threat as one associated with adolescence and notes how her family has begun treating her not only differently, but ominously:

> This winter … I no longer felt safe. It seemed that in the minds of the people around me there was a steady undercurrent of thought, not to be deflected, on this one subject. The word *girl* had formerly seemed to me innocent and unburdened, like the word *child*; now it appeared that it was no such thing. A girl was not, as I had supposed, simply what I was; it was what I had to become. It was a definition, always touched with emphasis, with reproach and disappointment. Also it was a joke on me.

> (p. 119)

This passage presages what we now call the social construction of gender: the idea that masculinity and femininity are created by social expectations, not by any kind of inevitable expression of biological sex characteristics.

But rather than articulating a theory of gender, the story dramatizes the daughter's sorrow over her changed relationship with her father and her failed attempts to adjust the norms of gendered behavior. When the men plan to shoot the second horse, she quails from establishing her own mastery over her family and the family's business, as she did when the first horse was shot. Instead, she sees the horse getting away and has a chance to shut the gate against it. She makes a split decision of consciously futile rebellion: she lets the horse run free. She knows that the rebellion would not save the horse. It would only prolong its death and require her father's extra work to hunt the horse down. When her father finds out what she did, though, he does not get mad. He instead dismisses her action with, "She's only a girl." Her father's refusal to grant her action even a smidgen of deliberation and intention only reinforces her uselessness.

Munro's early work abounds with such fresh, unambiguously feminist depictions of everyday life. For example, she just goes ahead and titles her second collection *Lives of Girls and Women* (1971). This is one of two volumes focusing on a single character through multiple stories. This book focuses on a single bildungsroman time line in the character's life (the other such work, *Who Do You Think You Are?,* tracks the main character through key events throughout her whole life). *Lives* is a cycle of stories depicting Del Jordan's coming-of-age in rural Ontario in the 1940s and 1950s. Del is trying to figure out how to grow up by closely observing the women in her life—a trait that reappears throughout Munro's work. Her mother writes pro-birth-control letters to the newspaper but preaches chastity and single-minded ambition to her daughter. Del unabashedly loves sex and develops a philosophical stance embracing pleasure as a way to reject (or revise) her mother's chaste feminism. In its depiction of multiple ways of being feminist, and the variety of "lives" of the book's title, *Lives of Girls and Women* captured the hearts of feminists of the time.

Munro's next work, *Something I've Been Meaning to Tell You* (1974), retains the feminist perspective and thinly reworked autobiography

of her first two books but begins to expand her formal concerns. A few standout stories truck in metafiction, using the technique to articulate something like a theory of women's writerhood. One example is "Material," a rant about an ex-husband, who is a writer, narrated by his ex-wife, who is also a writer without the fame of her former spouse. Ostensibly the story is an early example of Munro's fixation with the ways the sexual revolution reinforced patriarchal privilege. The ex-husband, Hugo, has used the social phenomenon as an excuse to leave his first wife and children. But the plot also allows the narrator to rip apart academic literary mores, the privilege of successful male authors, and the process of writing itself as a way to transform real people's lives into an abstraction, a tool for the author's continued fame. Angry and fresh, the story articulates a complex ethics of writing that is explicitly female. A few other stories in this collection develop this ethical ambiguity of fiction-making by impugning the narrator herself as morally compromised through her writing. "Winter Wind," about the narrator's grandparents, includes a passage about the narrator using her family, transforming them, manipulating them to suit her own artistic purposes. She adds apologetically that she doesn't do it as much anymore, implying that the technique of drawing stories from an author's life is morally suspect.

The collection's final story, "The Ottowa Valley," turns famously metafictional at the end. In this story, the narrator reflects on a visit she and her mother made to visit her mother's brother and cousins in the eponymous region of Canada, when the narrator was a young adolescent. The mother's arm has begun to tremor, marking the onset of a long, degenerative illness that will turn out to be Parkinson's disease. In the key narrative event, the family is dressing to go to church. The mother has dressed in her nicest outfit, a gray flowered dress, which she carefully planned and packed for the occasion. Right before they are about to enter church, the elastic on the girl's underpants has snapped. She refuses to take them off, given her young adolescent modesty, intensified by the mores of her society. But the mother, whose undergarments are equally worn, has a

safety pin holding her slip together. Munro has ramped up the emotional drama leading to this moment: the family's experience of rural poverty; the defamiliarizing visit to distant relatives, the girl and her mother removed from the quotidian comfort of immediate family; the narrator's complicating recollection and reinterpretation of her own adolescent feelings about her mother's disability; and the girl's observations of her mother with her adult brother and cousin—their relationship alienating the girl from her own experience of the same woman. After these layers have been so carefully assembled, the next action, though ostensibly unimpressive, breaks the story open. The mom gives the girl her safety pin to hold up her underwear. And as they walk into church, the daughter watches her mother boldly walk to the front pew as her slip sags below the hem of her delicate gray flowered dress. Such a precise image of the mother's attempt at dignity and beauty, at the church in the center of her hometown, before facing increasingly difficult disability. Her mother's handing over the safety pin functions as a transfer of dignity and comfort. As well, the safety pin represents an acknowledgment of the material reality of rural poverty: everyone's clothes are worn, every woman is threatened by the onset of age, irrelevance, and infirmity, every woman must attempt to fight this inertia anyway, with dignity, despite lacking the most basic resources for the fight.

After this, Munro's narrator quickly fills space with a denouement of reporting: They leave the church, the adults chatter, joke, and sing a ballad about death. And the story closes with a short flash of metafiction: The narrator notes that the whole episode exists in her memory as snapshots, but that nearly all the characters emerge clearly. All the characters but one:

> The problem, the only problem, is my mother. And she is the one of course that I am trying to get; it is to reach her that this whole journey has been undertaken. With what purpose? To mark her off, to describe, to illumine, to celebrate, to *get rid,* of her; and it did not work, for she looms too close, just as she always did. She is heavy as always, she weighs everything down, and yet she is indistinct, her edges melt and flow. Which means she has stuck to me as

close as ever and refused to fall away, and I could go on, and on, applying what skills I have, using what tricks I know, and it would always be the same.

(p. 246)

The episode in church belies this statement about the impossibility of adequately capturing her mother. The narrator has in fact illuminated her in celebration, as a woman separate from her identity as mother whose dedication to her children costs her a sense of dignity that no one else seems to notice. The episode also captures the narrator's retrospective regret, anger, and shame. Yet the metafictional passage implies that the prior depiction of the safety pin crisis is woefully incomplete. That this colorful, doomed episode in church and at Aunt Dodie's house gets nowhere near the reality of living with this mother/sister/cousin/daughter. This final paragraph of the collection also reads as Munro's thesis statement on much of her writing career: most of her stories have been about her mother, taking various poses of admiration, pity, humiliation, anger, regret, sorrow, grief. And recognizing that this attempt to know her by representing her is inherently futile.

As if taking this volume-ending metafictional passage as a valediction to a certain way of writing, subsequent work seems to have overcorrected this perceived difficulty of representing Munro's mother. Instead, these works channel Munro's experience of her mother into a much broader range of depictions of women and mothers, of disability, of sexuality, and of regret. Women characters are mothers, but their primary relationships are with their husbands, ex-husbands, lovers, or other grown women. Once Munro stops using a child's perspective as a story's focal point, children are rarely more than plot devices in stories that explore adult women's lives. In Munro's next work, in fact, the mother has died during her daughter's infancy. Rose, that daughter and the main character of *Who Do You Think You Are?* (1979; published in the United States and United Kingdom as *The Beggar Maid: Stories of Flo and Rose*), has a father and a stepmother, a series of lovers, and a husband, but no mother—except as understood through others' stories of her. In *Who Do You Think You Are?*—

Munro's only other book of connected short stories after *Lives of Girls and Women*—women characters are bound by these familial relationships but stretching those bonds to their limits.

Rose, the main character of all the stories in this collection, grows up poor in rural Ontario, develops a career as an actress, attempts to assimilate into bourgeois culture, marries, divorces, has lovers, and finally ends up back in her hometown to take care of her ailing stepmother, Flo. The whole book is extremely insightful about Rose's struggle to assimilate into both middle-class culture and norms of femininity. As the stories follow Rose's artistic career in the 1960s and 1970s, Munro offers incisive commentary on the social transformations of the era. For example, Rose tries to leave behind remnants of her childhood culture of rural poverty, while her academic circles are performing bohemian poverty as a fad. Rose can't fit in either way. In making Rose an actress in this milieu, and in making every story about this character, *Who Do You Think You Are?* foregrounds more than most of Munro's work her preoccupation with both class and gender as performance.

The stories continually link gender and class, depicting both as hollow performances with no substance underneath besides an often grim material experience. The tangible reality of rural poverty continually reemerges in this book and elsewhere in Munro's fiction as a counterpoint to any tendency to wax theoretical—her characters' tendencies, or a critic's tendencies. For example, "Privilege" opens with the adult Rose reflecting on her fallback party anecdote: a graphic description of the Girls' Toilet and the Boys' Toilet at her school. Too many people would miss the hole in these outhouses, and layers of snow would preserve the human waste. To Rose, growing up poor meant growing up with frozen shit on the school outhouse floor. To her adult acquaintances, poverty is a fashionable interior decor and her stories are alternately amusing or alarming. But this tension among her own narratives of her life, the material reality of her experience, and the social reception of both is almost flagrantly persistent throughout the volume. In another example, "Half a Grapefruit" begins with each

child in class reporting on his or her breakfast. A list of stark country breakfasts—tea and porridge, tea and bread, bread with corn syrup—signals neighborhood and status. Rose invents an exotic breakfast of "half a grapefruit" to avoid the unmistakable class designations of her actual breakfast of tea and porridge. However, her invented aspirational breakfast does not save her from mockery. In fact, her flight of imagination has invited it: she is called "half a grapefruit" for years.

In the substantive plot of "Privilege," Rose encounters two girls ostensibly symbolizing polar ends of a class spectrum: Franny is a disabled girl, abused by her father and serially gang raped by multiple boys, including her brother. Franny represents to Rose the entire culture of poverty as violation, as abuse, as collective knowledge about individual intimacies, and as pain. Also, Franny represents to Rose the entire endeavor of adolescent girlhood: from Franny's example Rose learns what boys to ignore, what basements or parts of school to avoid, what people to favor in fights. She learns how not to be Franny. But for every attempt to render Franny symbolic, the narrative reminds us that she is real: her muddy bare toes on the outhouse floor, her phlegmy breathing. While rejecting Franny, Rose's adolescent yearnings alight on Cora, an older girl whose womanly body and clothes attract a confusion of lust and aspiration in young Rose. The narrative focuses on Rose's crushy behavior and on Cora's hair, clothes, skin, and makeup—the smell of her nail polish, the droop of her rolled hair. Her grandfather is "the honey-dumper," the man who empties toilets in town. This reference to toilets echoes Franny's story, revealing Cora and Franny as more aligned in class than the story's ostensible polarization suggests. And references to the adult Rose retelling these stories pervade the story—foregrounding the tension between representation and experience, between a symbolic character and her muddy, sweaty toes or damp, talcumed underarms. In this way, the performance of class and the performance of gender are twinned with each other, and with the notion that gender is both a bodily experience and a social, classed construction.

Later stories drive this point home, as Rose gets married for both the concrete reality of economic security and an abstract fantasy of married love. Her identity as a woman is contingent on her husband's projection of her as "The Beggar Maid," a painting that reminds him of Rose. And their idealizations turn out, inevitably, to be impossible to fulfill. Still, Rose cannot divorce him until she can support herself in her own career. And she gives up custody of her children so she can pursue that career, in an early assertion that women cannot "have it all," in the modern plaintive feminist discourse. This plot device allows Munro to explore the psychological, social, and economic realities of an adult woman who is not married and not living with her own children. This type of modern woman, unencumbered but conflicted about it, becomes a common character throughout her later work as well, with divorce a major theme of Munro's work from this book onward.

Munro's use of divorce as a theme is a political rebuke to the primacy of marriage in women's literature—most famously in Jane Austen's novels. Munro's fixation on women and the failure of marriage is part of a long tradition of women's literature as well as a political exploration of the psychic consequences of gender norms. The marriage plot in Western literature is a symptom of the broader patriarchal social structure: women are subordinate to and dependent on men, and their ability to bear and raise children is the sum total of their contribution to society. When Rose rejects the marriage plot structure, she attempts to forge an identity outside these norms. Her failures at this project are ironically associated with her profession as an actress; her livelihood is based on her ability to convincingly perform various modes of femininity for paying audiences, an act she could not keep up as a daughter or as a spouse. And in this respect, Rose is the forebear of multiple unhappily married and divorced women characters throughout Munro's subsequent work.

The Moons of Jupiter (1982) furthers this exploration of women who get divorced in the 1960s and 1970s, as part of the fallout of the sexual revolution and the liberalization of divorce

laws in the 1970s. This generational moment manifests in contemporary culture as discourse of the "Generation X" children of divorce. By contrast, Munro is one of the few contemporary writers—perhaps the only prominent one—conducting a sustained investigation of the emotional experience of women who got divorced in this era. In general, Munro's depictions of heterosexual divorce can be read as political statements about the psychological costs of the sexual revolution. Rather than liberating bourgeois consciousness, the movement gave permission to men to spread the patriarchy around multiple homes, not just their own. And while women are also sexually liberated, their general lack of economic security and independence results in a profoundly asymmetrical experience of the movement. For example, the very short story "Prue" is about a divorced woman whose boyfriend is cavalier in telling her that he fell in love with a younger woman but still plans to eventually marry Prue, who is his age. Another story, "Labor Day Dinner," exemplifies the way Munro explores the psychological impact of the sexual revolution as a way to reinscribe patriarchal norms. The focal plot is a dinner party of post-divorce, reconfigured couples. The protagonist is a divorced woman whose current, live-in lover is a man who makes it clear how much he dislikes her body's signs of aging. The story pries apart this narrative moment—a couple is driving to a dinner party, the woman reflecting on her failures to live up to her lover's youthful ideal. One part of this reflection takes the form of a graphic listing of the kinds of interventions she attempts to halt age's actions on her body: face cream that causes acne, dieting that makes her facial skin sag, armpits that have turned flabby—about which there can be no intervention. She contemplates the futility of trying to fit these absurd beauty norms:

> What is to be done? Now the payment is due, and what for? For vanity. Hardly even for that. Just for having those pleasing surfaces once, and letting them speak for you; just for allowing an arrangement of hair and shoulders and breasts to have its effect. You don't stop in time, don't know what to do instead; you lay yourself open to humiliation.
>
> (p. 137)

When the sexual revolution happens without a full restructuring of the patriarchal structures underpinning society, male norms and ideals persist. Women are stuck in Roberta's bind: constantly assessing her lover's mood, anticipating what impact this or that trivial event may have on him, and struggling to meet his ideals of femininity. All these actions are necessary to keep secure her position in his house as his lover. The story is exhaustive in its depiction of Roberta's emotional work in the relationship, with no attempt to represent her lover's experience. Munro's attention and care is directed toward women and the litany of physical and mental labors required of them by the brave new liberated society, even more tenuous for them than the old, repressed one.

In general, this collection moves Munro further away from the direct autobiographical content of her previous work. There's a far broader diversity of characters and stories: "The Turkey Season," about a cluster of workers preparing turkeys for sale at Christmas season; "Mrs. Cross and Mrs. Kidd," about two women in a retirement home; "Dulse," about a single woman poet fleeing the end of a bad relationship and encountering some workers at an island inn; "Accident," about schoolteacher lovers whose eventual marriage is facilitated by a gruesome event. But these stories maintain Munro's consistent fascination with class and gender, along with the tension between representation and lived experience of those social positions. For example, "The Turkey Season" includes a gruesome description of gutting turkeys as part of Munro's commitment to representing the material culture of poverty, as well as of the toll of women's work on women's bodies. And the title story is about an adult daughter, divorced, with two young adult daughters, visiting her father in the hospital. During the course of the visits, the protagonist/narrator's estrangement from both her father and her daughters is clear; one of her daughters rejects all contact with her. Her position is ostensibly contradictory: free from a bad marriage but locked into alienating and painful relationships with her father and with her children. And the stories that the daughter and

father tell each other—a favorite theme for them is the mythical character namesakes of the moons of Jupiter—reinscribe the same patriarchal norms the narrator is struggling within. That generation of divorced women are left with very little outside of their ability to tell and retell stories.

Munro's next collection, *The Progress of Love* (1986) develops what will become one of Munro's most important themes: the essential fictiveness of human experience. We rely on narrative to make sense of our experience, but these narratives almost never match a known or knowable lived experience. In nearly all of these stories, characters tell stories whose represented truth can never be known. The meaning of narrative is indeterminate and undeterminable. Munro has digested the lessons of academic poststructuralism, but girded this intellectual position with constant reminders, again, of the material reality of living as a woman from a poor, rural background. For example, the title story recounts competing versions of family lore. One contested event features the narrator's grandmother attempting suicide—or pretending to. In another contested event, the narrator's mother has burned up a sizable inheritance out of hatred for her dead father. At the heart of all these contested retellings is the narrator's own experience of marriage, divorce, and subsequent relationships as she wrestles with her mother's stories' relevance to her own life: Houses have changed, romantic configurations have changed, memories themselves have changed. Has love changed? How could one know?

The story "Fits" makes even more clear the stakes of this level of metafiction. The story is one of Munro's very few told from the perspective of a man—this one is a husband whose wife has discovered an ostensible murder-suicide of the couple living next door to them. The narrative constantly references the stories passing around town about the event—who told whom, who was doing what when he or she heard, and who knows what, or doesn't, about the couple. In the main plot of the story, the husband reconstructs, through conversations with his wife and acquaintances, his wife's experience of finding the couple. By the end of the story, the husband's process of trying to understand his wife's role in the murder-suicide becomes a confrontation with the essence of their relationship—and its basis in vaguely threatening mystery that he needs to figure out how to live with.

Munro's stories grew increasingly complex throughout this first phase of her career, with stories leveraging her personal experience in ever more sophisticated ways to depict life—women's lives in particular—as shrouded in difficulty made marginally less painful by the act of storytelling. Munro explores the minutiae of poor women's lives in a way that belies easy political scoring. And the short-story form allows for a fixation on the minutiae of the many materialities of women's lives: The particular way the story of a scandal spreads through town. The squabbles a couple may have about curtains or vases or silverware. A wife's attempts to negotiate potential affairs. What foods people eat, what fabrics they wear, how they use the bathroom. Munro's thematic concerns with marriage and her common reliance on these details of embodied life have incurred some criticism from a literary establishment that sees such choices as shallow or dull. However, there are serious political consequences in portraying poverty in this way: these are ways that she resists reductionist symbolism common in bourgeois discussions of working-class people. And these choices reinforce her commitment to portraying the real, lived experiences of women and the strictures constraining their choices.

MIDDLE-PERIOD WORK

As Munro matured as a writer, she developed increasingly sophisticated formal techniques for representing human experience and, as Charles May in particular has argued, stretching the bounds of the short-story form. The collections named here as middle-period work maintain her dedication to exploring with depth and nuance the lives of women from poor and working-class backgrounds while expanding her thematic and formal scope. The stories written in this period tend to be longer, impelling critics' praise of her short stories as "novel-like," as if the comparison raises the literary value of her chosen form. By

this period, her stories have fully broken free of her direct autobiographical influence to explore women's lives with more nuance, formal innovation, and narrative complexity. *Friend of My Youth* (1990), *Open Secrets* (1994), *The Love of a Good Woman* (1998), *Hateship, Friendship, Courtship, Loveship, Marriage* (2001), and *Runaway* (2004) in many ways represent the pinnacle of Munro's craft.

Friend of My Youth (1990) picks up on Munro's previous collection's exploration of the fictiveness of human experience with stories that are more richly layered, more temporally complex, and rooted in deeper mystery than those that came before. The fact that we know only stories is so deeply engrained in our social lives and our very identities; and our stories are only ever partly true. The title story, one of the best in the collection, is explicitly about how a woman's life becomes transformed by the stories others tell of her, and about how a mother and daughter use these stories of another woman to construct their own relationship. The narrator defines herself by telling that woman's story differently than her mother would. That woman's story is itself drawn from Munro's experience, as she notes in the *Paris Review* interview. A young woman, Flora, is engaged to a young man when her sister gets pregnant. The young man marries the sister, and the trio live together in a house. The baby dies and the married sister develops a fatal illness. When she dies, the man marries the nurse, and not Flora, his original fiancée, though they continue to live together. The husband and sisters belong to a strict Christian order, Cameronians, or Reformed Protestants, migrated from Scotland, which is itself a topic of speculative narrative. The first-person narration about this family once more trucks in the metafictional. Soon enough the frame narrative returns to the foreground, with the narrator's mother stricken with Parkinson's disease. The narrator tries to use stories to fill in the forbiddingly large number of gaps in her knowledge of her mother. Such gaps include a house littered with letters begun and never finished, as the mother's illness made handwriting impossible. So the layers accumulate: a strictly religious community producing what

seems to be an emotionally untenable arrangement; failed childbirth, failed coupling, a religious order that may or may not impose peace and satisfaction in its adherents; two disabled, deceased mothers; and multiple attempts to recover something knowable and meaningful about these women through narrative. The women themselves reject such narrative attempts directly, as Flora does in a letter to the narrator's mother, or indirectly, as the mother does by never finishing any of her own letters. The metafictional postmodern stance on representation, that all is story and story is inadequate, becomes a complex meditation on the impossibility of knowing those closest to us, no matter how hard we try. This story is just one example of the density and intellectual sophistication of Munro's middle-period work.

In one of Munro's more famous stories, "Meneseteung," she stretches metafiction out into historical fiction, a trick she occasionally turns throughout her career. A contemporary researcher reconstructs the experience of Almeda Roth, a Victorian-era poet who lives near the lawless edge of town, where prostitutes and alcoholics live, work, and fight. While Roth has a somewhat gothic encounter with a beaten prostitute lying outside her window, she is making grape jelly. A cheesecloth of grape pulp is draining into a bucket in the kitchen—an image strongly reminiscent of menstrual blood. The story's obsessive detail with bodily functions—sweat, food, menstruation, insomnia—echoes Angela Carter's revisions of fairy tales from this era. Both authors use these representations of the bodily experience of Victorian womanhood as political statements reclaiming women's history and women's experience. However, the story's obsessive metafiction counters the politics of embodiment with a reminder that embodied experience remains known only through representation, which is necessarily inadequate. For example, the narrative reconstructs Roth's including some aspects of her town's landscape in her poem (the natural beauty) and leaving many out (signs of human intervention in the landscape—cleared brush, manure, barns). And the whole story is encased in a frame narrative of a contemporary figure

reading Victorian-era newspapers to research Roth's life. Once more we have attempts to recover knowledge about dead women; women whose function as wife and mother has been foiled by both their own choices and their inherent tendencies; the futile use of multiple types of written narrative—poetry, historical record, and tombstones—to construct meaning about the past and about women's lives; and a metafictional admission of the failure to capture any of the foregoing story correctly. As these stories exemplify, *Friend of My Youth* layers politics (deep commitment to valuing marginalized women's experience) and formalism (intensely sophisticated narrative complexity and concern about the simultaneous powers and failures of representation) onto each other in ways that few other writers achieve.

Munro's next collection, *Open Secrets* (1994), differs from other works in its coherent thematic focus on one particular aspect of women's and girls' experience: the threat and experience of sexual violence. The whole book is haunted by this knowledge about the vulnerability of women's bodies, with more explicit references to violence than we usually find in Munro's work. Stories take place in and around the same rural Canadian town, Carstairs, with stories ranging from pioneer days, through industrial transformations, to the postindustrial contemporary. The book follows women in various types of families as they either experience sexual violence or face or ignore the evidence all around them of its presence. In this way, the book seems to be a history of the ways that our societies are built upon such threats; that violence itself, not sex and decidedly not love, is the foundation of everything humans build. In *Open Secrets,* social and economic reproduction demands the blood sacrifice of women and girls.

The violence in these stories is frequently mediated by conflicting narratives about it, narratives which obfuscate and transform events such that they become their own type of violence. In the title story, which takes up directly the volume's frequent reference to vanished girls, townspeople trade various theories about the causes of one twelve-year-old's disappearance.

Throughout the collection, theories about girls who vanish are more or less divided between the slut/virgin poles, with some people believing that these girls have run away to have sex with older men in other towns, while others believe that the girls have been abducted and murdered by older men in other towns. Because of the sexual repression embedded in the town's Scottish Protestant roots, and because of the standard patriarchy, there are troubling threads of characters sexualizing victimhood throughout the collection. For example, in "Spaceships Have Landed," a young woman is visiting an in-home bar with her alcoholic, gropey boyfriend, the son of the wealthy Doud family that has run the town's piano factory for a good part of the town's history. Rhea, the woman, is observing the wife who runs the bar and contemplating the rumors that she is also a prostitute. She imagines the woman's experience:

> Then, on a waiting bed, she arranges herself without the least hesitation or enthusiasm. This indifferent readiness, this cool accommodation, the notion of such a quick and driven and bought and paid-for encounter, was to Rhea shamefully exciting.
>
> To be so flattened and used and hardly to know who was doing it to you, to take it all in with that secret capability, over and over again.
>
> (p. 232)

The passage sexualizes a fantasy of women's subordinate position, glamorizes the lack of intimacy, and makes objectification arousing. This complex representation of women's sexuality refutes simplistic interpretations of women as victims of sexual violence or even simply of objectification. Women can also find agency and desire in passivity.

However, a few other stories confront the actual experience of violent objectification, which is far from arousing. "A Wilderness Station," about the founding of Carstairs, is about an indentured bride who escapes two abusive brothers in a story that is reconstructed by various characters' letters to each other, some of which were never mailed. "Open Secrets" weaves the story of a girl's disappearance with that of an older woman whose sick husband has become

sexually brutal. "Vandals" is about a woman who, as a girl, was repeatedly raped, along with her brother, by a neighbor. Throughout these stories, the economic life of the town progresses. A few pioneer families build the town's first buildings. A journeying saleswoman settles as the town's librarian. A piano factory is built, operates for decades as the lifeblood of the town and its main conduit of class divisions, and then closes due to the changed economy and poor management of the man who inherited the business. Rural, dirt-road neighborhoods are scraped and rebuilt into tidy suburbs. But rather than romanticizing the past, as many tales of this transformed landscape do, *Open Secrets* lays open the brutality at the heart of these transformations.

The Love of a Good Woman (1998) continues these themes with even more complex, layered, expansive stories of women and girls attempting to negotiate the conflicts between their own desires and the strictures of gender norms and expectations. Stories in this collection hone Munro's time-leap technique, layering asynchronous episodes, flashes forward and back, and bait-and-switch plots. The title story is particularly magisterial in its telescopic exploration of an entire town captured in a patchwork of episodes surrounding a local man's death. It begins with a detailed description of a local museum exhibit of a set of optometry instruments from the 1950s. The set was donated by an anonymous donor, and the optometrist has died. The instruments look like a snowman, an elf head, and a dark mirror; the black paint has rubbed off them. This short passage launches the entire collection with central Munro themes: the instruments used to check one's vision are out of use. Our ability to see the past (or present) cannot be evaluated, let alone improved; our tools are better understood as their own layered metaphors and symbol rather than as functional instruments of progress; and the people serving as our links to recovering our vision have died. The story then branches out to use the optometrist's death as a path through the social life of the entire town. A gang of boys discovers the man's car and body. As they travel through town, assessing whom to tell, how, and when,

they encounter their families of varying class positions. The reader meets the law enforcement officials who eventually hear the report. And then the narrative leaps to a seemingly unconnected invalid woman's house, where the focal point of the narrative is the nurse hired to take care of her. The story builds elaborately realistic psychological complexity in the relationships among the ill wife, her husband, and her nurse. And eventually, without feeling contrived or forced, the plot links back to the dead optometrist: soon before she dies, the wife tells the nurse that he was assaulting her, and that her husband killed him in vengeance. Then the nurse must decide what to do with this knowledge. The story does not definitively state whether or not the wife's story is accurate—she could have been lying to the nurse. The nurse, through whose perspective most of this part of the story is narrated, is hostile to the wife and angling to replace her after she dies. The nurse's interpretation of the wife as a cruel liar may or may not be accurate. And the story leaves open whether or not the wife's story about the husband is accurate, and what kind of life the nurse manages to make with the husband, given the possibility that he is a murderer. Munro's framing this story in a story of the town—with multiple family intimacies, the geography of the boys' walk through it, the civic institution of the town museum—all strongly suggest that the story's central mystery structures the town itself. Once more, echoing *Open Secrets,* social life is built upon deceit, assault, and the unknowability of the most major truths about other people.

The stories in this and the next volume, *Hateship, Friendship, Courtship, Loveship, Marriage* (2001), truck in the same methods and conceptual content. These stories are longer than Munro's earlier stories, more richly and densely layered, more generationally and temporally expansive, and more committed to representing the failures of representation. The formal complexity of these works makes her political project relatively less apparent than in her early period works. However, her commitment to representing the vagaries and complexities of women's experience is stronger than ever. In fact, embedding a representation of women's experience in such dizzyingly sophisti-

cated formal techniques is more true to the political project of making marginalized experience central to our consciousness. Women's lives are not reducible to the simpler explorations of victimization by patriarchal culture. Women are full participants in culture, with complex reactions to it, desires and experiences that defy easy categorization. Furthermore, as Isla Duncan argues in her narratological analysis of Munro's work, these volumes are more emphatic in their exploration of the failures of memory—crucial life events are forgotten, misremembered, or replaced by fictions.

Hateship includes the story "The Bear Came Over the Mountain," which was made into a movie, *Away from Her,* in 2006. This story treats marriage, disability, aging, social change, and class with deep nuance and psychological complexity. Another of Munro's rare stories told from a male character's perspective, it treats a man's marriage to a woman, Fiona, who has developed dementia and begun a relationship with another man, Aubrey, in her retirement home. The husband, Grant, reflects on his own past infidelities, in a more complex treatment of the impact of the sexual revolution than Munro's earlier work displays. Grant then allies with Aubrey's wife to negotiate Fiona and Aubrey's relationship. Aubrey and his wife are lower class than Grant and Fiona, and Grant was below Fiona when they got married. Grant's experience of social power throughout his life, including his feeling of alienation within Fiona's family, has informed his sense of entitlement at one of his otherwise most vulnerable moments, witnessing his wife's budding relationship with another man. "The Bear Came Over the Mountain" is a masterwork of fiction exploring the ways that social power drives sex and marriage, and the way that disability destabilizes previously held positions of entitlement and power. Counterintuitively, Fiona's disability restores to her an agency she lost long before to her unfaithful spouse.

Stories in *Runaway* (2004), in many ways the pinnacle of Munro's work, are loosely bound, as perhaps expected, by a leitmotif of runaways—a runaway goat, a runaway daughter, a runaway wife, a runaway fiancée. These stories

cross generational and historical lines, about women born throughout the twentieth century. And the eponymous leitmotif enables Munro to deepen her career-long exploration of absence. For example, one of Munro's crowning achievements is her triptych of stories about Juliet, a woman who, by the final story, has experienced the death of her husband, parents, and friends and the permanent estrangement of her daughter. In the first story, "Chance," young Juliet has abandoned her teaching job, itself taken on a break from working toward a Ph.D. in classics, to visit Eric, a man she had met on a previous train ride—a train ride where a man who tried to befriend her kills himself soon after she rebuffed his friendship. In "Soon," Juliet has had a baby with Eric and is visiting her parents while her mother is dying. And in "Silence," Eric has died, and Juliet finds a way to cope with the permanent estrangement of their grown daughter Penelope. In this sequence of stories, Munro, who has rarely dealt with organized religion in a sustained, significant way, explores faith and religion in the context of loss. In "Soon," the rationalist Juliet has ongoing arguments with her parents over the value of faith. In "Silence" these arguments, presumably with Penelope, are entirely outside the narrative but have determined the plot. Moments in the series suggest her being more open to nonrational experience than her words suggest. For example, she purchases a Chagall print for her parents that strongly implies a sensitivity to spiritual modes of understanding, as does her lifelong study of ancient Greek culture. Nonetheless, Penelope has joined an alternative religious community and permanently rejected Juliet as a mother or even an acquaintance. Prior to this work, Munro's direct reference to religion has been more focused on the alternative religious movements of the 1960s, or on sideways uses of religious affiliation as class markers in her small-town milieus. With this sequence, Munro is able to incorporate one of the major social movements of twentieth-century North America, the alternative spirituality explosion, into her long-standing thematic concerns with the ability of women of her generation to become economically independent from men and build identities outside gender

norms. Juliet was raised in a nonreligious home, but her mother, Sara, develops a relationship with a minister, Don, in her dying months and develops a faith she cannot articulate. In opposition, Juliet, in "Soon," articulates a fierce atheism. But the discourse of faith for both her mother and her daughter is represented by their clergy rather than by themselves. Don and the woman Juliet bitterly nicknames "Mother Shipton" are the mouthpieces for Juliet's mother and daughter. However, Sara is unable to explain herself to Juliet, and Penelope is almost entirely absent from the narrative. Meanwhile, Sara and Juliet have each, in their own ways, rejected the feminine norms of housework, marriage, and motherhood. And Juliet's attempts to forge an identity outside those strictures lead to more absence. She becomes a woman of ever-shrinking presence in the world until finally she arrives at something like a sardonic, self-conscious, but deeply felt hope:

> She keeps on hoping for a word from Penelope, but not in any strenuous way. She hopes as people who know better hope for undeserved blessings, spontaneous remissions, things of that sort.
>
> (p. 158)

For Juliet, faith is nothing but absence. But she cobbles together a version of it to cope with the sorrow of absence. In *Runaway,* this is about the most that women can hope for: significantly constrained possibilities, compromised settling into a life that will have to somehow be enough.

LATE-PERIOD WORK

Munro's final three books are distinct enough in their preoccupations to warrant their own category, despite being otherwise continuous with her later work in themes and form. Beginning with *The View from Castle Rock* (2006), Munro includes a significant amount of explicitly acknowledged autobiographical material in her collections. Her material is more pared down, more expressionistic, with more mystery and feeling layered onto the word itself rather than the complex narrative structures of her middle-period work. And her material is significantly darker than ever before, with stories of infidelity alongside blackmail, invasion, murder, and the specter of death.

The View from Castle Rock publishes work that Munro had been developing for many years, drawn more directly from her own life as well as from her own genealogical research. The first half of the collection is lightly fictionalized family history; the second half is lightly fictionalized autobiography. She states in a foreword that this latter material was too close to her own life to be collected in other volumes, though it's not tightly accurate to the detail. One difference between this work and other more directly autobiographical material from her early stage is that this later work omits the metafictional asides about the inadequacy and compromised ethics of "using people up" in stories. Nonetheless, many hallmarks of her more explicitly fictional stories are present: her interest in historical fiction, in temporal fragmentation and discontinuity, in women's social and economic positions, and in the transformation of rural landscape and culture. For example, "Hired Girl" closely resembles an early story, "Sunday Afternoon," from *Dance of the Happy Shades.* A working-class girl gets a summer job as a maid for a wealthy family with wealthy friends and frequent afternoon parties. In "Sunday Afternoon," the girl gets assaulted by a tipsy cousin of the family—though she appears to regard the encounter with a mix of arousal and humiliation. In "Hired Girl," which is much longer and more detailed, the assault is part of a fantasy constructed by the girl in a letter to a friend at home. But the mixture of sexual adventurousness, keen and embittered class consciousness, and vulnerability to exploitation and violation remains. In the later work it is much more pointed, though the assault is a fantasy. Similarly, a brief episode in that story echoes some of Rose's experience in *Who Do You Think You Are?* In the later story, the young Munro-like figure exaggerates stories of the poverty in her hometown to exact some kind of vague social power over the daughter of the wealthy household. Rose fails when she attempts this at parties. Young "Alice" seems to succeed. That and other attempts to maintain her dignity in the household are surprisingly effective, given that

she is working for a woman who trucks in frequent petty humiliations. Once more in Munro the domestic woman's space of aprons, hors d'oeuvres, and dish washing is riven with conflict, while completely denuded of any romanticism or sentiment. Munro's work has always deconstructed the public/private gendered binary this way. Her final books are no different, despite the dramatically different status of women by 2006.

Too Much Happiness (2009) and *Dear Life* (2012), Munro's final collections, lay bare the grim underpinnings of her vision. Characters in *Too Much Happiness* include a widow with late-stage cancer talking her way out of assault by a thief who has invaded her home; a wife visiting her husband, in jail for murdering their kids; and a woman who, along with her friend, was responsible for the death of another girl at their summer camp years before the story begins. The title story closes the volume and can be read as a valedictory meditation on three of Munro's fixations: women's experience, aging and death, and historical fiction. The story follows the thoughts of the great nineteenth-century mathematician Sophia Kovalevsky, as she nears death. Like Shakespeare's Prospero, this Kovalevsky provides a metafictional foil for Munro toward the end of her own career: a woman who exceeded the expectations of women in her time and place, a woman whose experiences of romantic love and professional achievement do not conform, a woman close to death pondering the nature of meaningful success in a milieu denying all but the most narrow definitions of it to women.

But, like the Shakespeare who created Prospero, Munro was not quite finished with literature. Her final book, *Dear Life,* unites fiction, again, with explicitly named autobiography. In this volume, unlike *Castle Rock,* the fictional and autobiographical sections take different forms. The fiction is tight and precise, with every word almost allegorical in its intense lyrical economy. The autobiographical sketches, however, are truly sketchy: loosely drawn, impressionistic, and pervaded by a *sense* of the fog of memory, a fog that never clouds her previous autobiographically or historiographically drawn pieces.

Still, uniting both sections is a conviction in the inevitability of indeterminacy and ambiguity. For example, "To Reach Japan" pulls a somewhat typical Munro infidelity past ordinary sorrow to a truly existential breaking point. The protagonist, Greta, is a poet who has married a dully pragmatic engineer; they have a young daughter. The mother and daughter travel by train to meet Greta's lover. While en route, Greta has another fling and, while she is occupied, her daughter gets lost looking for her. A panicked Greta finds the girl in the loud space between train cars. Later, they arrive at their destination, and the story closes with this passage:

> First a shock, then a tumbling in Greta's insides, an immense settling. She was trying to hang on to Katy but at this moment the child pulled away and got her hand free. She didn't try to escape. She just stood waiting for whatever had to come next.
>
> (p. 30)

The narrative coyly uses an ambiguous "she" to reference either the mother or the daughter. Both have escaped a few times over during the course of the story. Both are stalled in between, en route. And both acquiesce to an inevitably unknown, uncontrollable future. Their attempts at freedom last only the distance of the train trip.

With more emotional intensity than in previous collections, these stories cobble together a present moment composed of partly recalled past moments, endless questions about those past moments, difficulty reshaping these fragments into a linear narrative that might lend structure and stability to our present selves. Munro's autobiographical sketches bring this most clearly to the fore, full of her attempts to puzzle out her parents' motivations for various actions that don't make sense in retrospect, questions she will never be able to ask them, fragments of her childhood—of her self—that even the all-powerful Munro can't make cohere.

CONCLUSION

In 2013 Christian Lorentzen's *London Review of Books* essay reviewing *Dear Life* was a lone, controversial voice protesting Munro's lioniza-

tion among the literati. After noting that any dissent would be interpreted as misogyny instead of evaluated on its merits, he developed an argument that could, in fact, be interpreted as misogyny; or at least as the kind of indirect misogyny that devalues what is associated with women—sentiment, melodrama, parochialism—rather than explicitly devaluing women themselves. Her work is maudlin, he argues, with an emotional authenticity compromised by a formulaic reliance on "epiphany." She reworks the same narrow material and technique over decades while incongruously being hailed as original. And her old-fashioned subject matter and genteel diction tap into our baser longings for a past era of stable, if chafing, gender norms and (though Lorentzen does not mention race, his argument suggests it) pre-civil-rights white-only society. His argument is delightfully written, livened with the particular relish we enjoy while roasting a sacred cow. Philip Marchand develops a milder, more staid version of this complaint, arguing that the constraints imposed upon Munro's characters become constraints on the fiction itself.

Lorentzen and Marchand's arguments indeed hold water. Over several decades, Munro has reworked a handful of stock plots: the Adultery Story, the Coming-of-Age Story, the Dissolving Marriage story, the Aging Story. And all these stories are the Problem with Memory Story. Also, Munro's incorporation of the gothic material of her childhood approaches a level of absurdity to a readership accustomed to a level of social services and civic infrastructure unimaginable in the Hanratty or Carstairs of Munro's characters' Depression-era childhoods. However, one man's sensationalist, formulaic gothic is another woman's actual lived experience. The murder-suicide story "Fits," described by Lorentzen as pulp fiction without the genre's pleasure, was directly based on an older couple who died the same way in Munro's town. So was the story of the man who married his fiancée's sister, and then that woman's nurse, with the ex-fiancée in the same house. In both the fictional and real-life versions of that household, the ex-fiancée's side of the house did not get painted. Criticisms of

her work as sentimental and formulaic should be tempered by two notions: "sentimental" writing takes seriously the emotional labor that women are charged with performing; and the "formulaic" story of gender inequality still needs writing, preferably by someone sensitive to the depth and complexity of women's experience of our still-patriarchal social, economic, and political structures.

The myriad critics who praise Munro's short stories for resembling novels are enacting a similar interpretive politics, applied to genre. As Charles May in particular has argued about Munro, this praise implies a literary hierarchy, with big novels up top and short stories somewhere below. These critical perspectives drive home the political risks and strengths of her work. Munro's work and its reception question what genres and forms matter in our culture and whose lives count as appropriately literary. Munro herself, in an interview quoted earlier, notes the literary establishment's consensus that the "mainstream big novel about real life" is what men write. By this accepted logic, small works by and about women do not constitute real life. That leaves four decades of stories about pseudo-rural Canadian women out of the real life of literature.

Munro's career began before the canon wars of the 1980s and 1990s, which, drawing on the impact of 1960s and 1970s social movements, re-scripted the narrative about mainstream and marginal literature. Munro's rise in critical and popular esteem corresponds with the rise of other literary voices outside the mainstream novel of "real [white man's] life." And from the perspective of women writers of color, Munro's position as a white woman whose contract granting the *New Yorker* the right of first refusal of all her stories dates from 1977, Munro's voice is one of undeniable privilege. Nonetheless, it took forty years and myriad awards for Munro to begin publishing work explicitly about her own life. And that mainstream big novel still grabs headlines and magazine covers.

While her work does not represent the voice of all North American or even Canadian women, her work and her closely correlated life depict the tremendous changes in the "lives of girls and

women" since the 1930s. From being defined only as a wife and mother and ridiculed for any other ambitions, to the ability to be wife, mother, professional, and divorcée all at once. From near-universal economic dependence on men to widespread opportunities for self-sufficiency. From being celebrated by 1970s feminists for writing the goddess back into literature to being celebrated by 2000s academic men for capturing universal human experience. From outcast girl outrunning bullies past the frozen outhouse to Nobel Prize–winning doyenne of letters.

Selected Bibliography

WORKS OF ALICE MUNRO

First Editions

Dance of the Happy Shades and Other Stories. Toronto: Ryerson, 1968.

Lives of Girls and Women. Toronto: McGraw-Hill Ryerson, 1971.

Something I've Been Meaning to Tell You: *Thirteen Stories*. Toronto: McGraw-Hill Ryerson, 1974.

Who Do You Think You Are?: *Stories*. Toronto: Macmillan of Canada, 1978. Also published as *The Beggar Maid*: *Stories of Flo and Rose*. New York: Knopf, 1979.

The Moons of Jupiter: *Stories*. Toronto: Macmillan of Canada, 1982.

The Progress of Love. Toronto: McClelland & Stewart, 1986.

Friend of My Youth: *Stories*. Toronto: McClelland & Stewart, 1990.

Open Secrets: *Stories*. Toronto: McClelland & Stewart, 1994.

The Love of a Good Woman: *Stories*. Toronto: McClelland & Stewart, 1998.

Hateship, Friendship, Courtship, Loveship, Marriage: *Stories*. Toronto: McClelland & Stewart, 2001.

Runaway: *Stories*. Toronto: McClelland & Stewart, 2004.

The View from Castle Rock: *Stories*. Toronto: McClelland & Stewart, 2006.

Too Much Happiness: *Stories*. Toronto: McClelland & Stewart, 2009.

Dear Life: *Stories*. Toronto: McClelland & Stewart, 2012.

Anthologies, Collections, and Reprints

Selected Stories. Toronto: McClelland & Stewart, 1996.

Queenie: *A Story*. London: Profile Books/London Review of Books, 1998, 1999.

Away from Her. Toronto: Penguin Canada, 2001. New York: Vintage, 2007.

No Love Lost. Toronto: McClelland & Stewart, 2003.

Vintage Munro. New York: Vintage, 2004.

Alice Munro's Best: Selected Stories. Toronto: McClelland & Stewart, 2006, 2008.

Carried Away: *A Selection of Stories*. New York: Knopf, 2006.

New Selected Stories. London: Chatto & Windus, 2011.

CRITICAL AND BIOGRAPHICAL STUDIES

Aubrey, Kim. "How to Write like Alice Munro." *Writer's Chronicle* 38, no. 1:12–15 (2005).

Blodgett, E. D. *Alice Munro*. Boston: Twayne, 1988.

Bloom, Harold, ed. *Alice Munro*. New York: Chelsea House, 2009.

Carrington, Ildikó de Papp. *Controlling the Uncontrollable*. Dekalb: Northern Illinois University Press, 1989.

Carscallen, James. *The Other Country: Patterns in the Writing of Alice Munro*. Toronto: ECW Press, 1993.

Cox, Ailsa. *Alice Munro*. Tavistock, U.K.: Northcote House/British Council, 2004.

Duncan, Isla. *Alice Munro's Narrative Art*. London: Palgrave Macmillan, 2011.

Franzen, Jonathan. "Alice's Wonderland." *New York Times Book Review,* November 14, 2004. http://www.nytimes.com/2004/11/14/books/review/runaway-alices-wonderland.html (Review of *Runaway*.)

Heble, Ajay. *The Tumble of Reason: Alice Munro's Discourse of Absence*. Toronto, London and Buffalo: University of Toronto Press, 1994.

Heller, Deborah. *Daughters and Mothers in Alice Munro's Later Stories*. Seattle: Workwomans Press, 2009.

Howells, Coral Ann. *Alice Munro*. Manchester, U.K.: Manchester University Press, 1998.

Hoy, Helen. "Alice Munro: 'Unforgettable, Indigestible Messages.'" *Journal of Canadian Studies* 26, no. 1:5–21 (1991).

Lorentzen, Christian. "Poor Rose." *London Review of Books* 35, no. 11:11–12 (2013). (Review of *Dear Life*.)

MacKendrick, Louis King, ed. *Probable Fictions: Alice Munro's Narrative Acts*. Downsview, Ont.: ECW Press, 1983.

————. *Some Other Reality: Alice Munro's " Something I've Been Meaning to Tell You."* Toronto, ECW Press, 1993.

Martin, W. R. *Alice Munro: Paradox and Parallel*. Edmonton: University of Alberta Press, 1987.

Marchand, Philip. "The Problem with Alice Munro." *Canadian Notes & Queries* 72:10–12 (fall–winter 2007).

May, Charles E., ed. *Alice Munro: Critical Insights*. Ipswich, Mass.: Salem Press, 2013.

McCaig, JoAnn, *Reading In: Alice Munro's Archives,* Waterloo, Ont.: Wilfrid Laurier University Press, 2002.

McCullough, Jeanne, and Mona Simpson. "Alice Munro, The Art of Fiction No. 137." *Paris Review* 131 (summer 1994). http://www.theparisreview.org/interviews/1791/the-art-of-fiction-no-137-alice-munro

Miller, Judith, ed. *The Art of Alice Munro: Saying the Unsayable; Papers from the Waterloo Conference.* Waterloo, Ont.: University of Waterloo Press, 1984.

Munro, Sheila. *Lives of Mothers & Daughters: Growing Up with Alice Munro.* New York: Union Square Press, 2008.

Pfaus, B. *Alice Munro.* Ottowa, Ont.: Golden Dog, 1984.

Rasporich, Beverly Jean. *Dance of the Sexes: Art and Gender in the Fiction of Alice Munro.* Edmonton: University of Alberta Press, 1990.

Redekop, Magdelene. *Mothers and Other Clowns: The Stories of Alice Munro.* London and New York: Routledge, 1992.

Ross, Catherine Sheldrick. *Alice Munro: A Double Life.* Toronto: ECW Press, 1992.

Strayed, Cheryl. "Munro Country." *Missouri Review* 32, no. 2:96–108 (2009).

Thacker, Robert, ed. *The Rest of the Story: Critical Essays on Alice Munro.* Toronto: ECW Press, 1999.

———. *Alice Munro: Writing Her Lives; A Biography.* Toronto: McClelland & Stewart, 2005.

WALTER DEAN MYERS

(1937—2014)

Amy Alessio

MOST AUTHORS AIM to create memorable, meaningful books. A rare few of those authors become both critically successful and popular with readers. Fewer still leave a legacy of awards, a deep connection with readers of all ages, and more than one hundred books that have sold some 15 million copies. While Walter Dean Myers did all those things, he was concerned most with creating representation for African American youth in literature.

A body of work so illustrious would seem to make considerable impact in this area, yet Myers expressed doubt that he was able to effect much change. In his 2014 *New York Times* essay "Where Are the People of Color?" written a few months before his death, Myers reflected on his past, when he was unable to find characters like himself.

> I've reached an age at which I find myself not only examining and weighing my life's work, but thinking about how I will pass the baton so that those things I find important will continue. In 1969, when I first entered the world of writing children's literature, the field was nearly empty. Children of color were not represented, nor were children from the lower economic classes. Today, when about 40 percent of public school students nationwide are black and Latino, the disparity of representation is even more egregious. In the middle of the night I ask myself if anyone really cares.

Artists with great bodies of work can often group their creations into periods or subjects, such as Pablo Picasso's blue period or Claude Monet's haystacks. Overarching themes or types of skills can be discerned across those subjects. Myers' work is no exception, yet it covers fiction, nonfiction, humor, mystery, gritty urban realism, fantasy, and even science fiction. The breadth of his work is reflected on the Walter Dean Myers website, which invites parents and teachers to click on lists by appropriate grade level, reading age, or topic. He wrote novels, poetry, short stories, picture books, retellings of fairy tales, biographies, an interactive book for discussion of teen pregnancy, and collaborations with family and others; even a graphic novel of one of his most influential works, *Monster,* has been published. Few genres seem to be omitted. Myers' works are often grouped into categories: hard-hitting realistic young adult books, war stories, sports titles, nonfiction books, essays, and humorous fare or works featuring the life and culture of Harlem. The overarching theme of Myers' desire to find himself and other African Americans portrayed realistically in books is evidenced throughout his pages, but no theme or message takes away from his skill in making good writing accessible and appealing to young readers.

In a 2012 online interview with *Story Snoops,* Myers spelled out his purpose as a writer. "If there is a universal theme in my work," he said, "it deals with man's need to identify and celebrate, within a given culture, his own humanity. This is the ultimate goal of my characters."

Although Myers began writing stories in fifth grade, it was only after years of trouble in high school, then a period in the army and as a civil service worker, that he published his first book, *Where Does the Day Go?* (1969). His foster parents, Florence and Herbert Dean, did not understand reading and writing books as a viable career path. While his mother supported his love of books, Myers learned after Herbert Dean's death that the man could not read. Yet he drew from their loving household to portray positive African American father figures, families, and peer groups previously unseen in books featuring people of color.

After being hired as an editor for a large publishing house, Myers was able to champion African American authors such as Nikki Giovanni in addition to continuing his own writing. He was temporarily heartened by the increase of books by African American authors in the 1960s. By the 1970s, though, he lamented that libraries, the main markets for those books at that time, stopped buying them as soon as budgets were cut. In his 1986 essay "I Actually Thought We Would Revolutionize the Industry," Myers described this rise and fall for the *New York Times*:

> We can be sure, however, of one thing: if we continue to make black children nonpersons by excluding them from books and by degrading the black experience, and if we continue to neglect white children by not exposing them to any aspect of other racial and ethnic experiences in a meaningful way, we will have a next racial crisis.

He also wrote about the racism he encountered as an author. In a 1979 essay for the *Interracial Books for Children Bulletin* titled "The Black Experience in Children's Books: One Step Forward, Two Steps Back," he recounts that a white dancer was drawn in the pictures of his early book *Dancer,* though there were none in the story. His daughter's school librarian told him that his picture book *Where Does the Day Go?* was not appropriate for that library. In this angry essay, Myers shows how ground had been lost again in the battle to have diverse books after gains in the 1960s. Publishers, he said, engaged in a kind of circular reasoning, wherein they expressed no interest in seeking a market for diverse books and then turned around and said that those books did not sell well.

It is painful that, thirty years later, he would write an article on similar themes for the *New York Times*. Myers did more than write books, promote other African American authors, and write about the lack of diverse books. He also visited schools and made a point of connecting with thousands of teens in detention centers. He wanted them to read and to see reading as a key to their future. During his time serving as National Ambassador for Young People's Literature (2012–2013), Myers made sure that deten-tion centers were included among the educational visits that position entailed. His motto was "Reading is not optional." He described his reasons for including young detainees in an interview with Amy Nathan for PEN America:

> I've seen a decline in detention centers reading skills over the last 20 years. There is a need to explain to these young people (there are about one hundred thousand kids in jail on any given day!) that for them to take advantage of any opportunity that comes along they will have to become excellent readers. We need to put it bluntly enough to stop the defensive derision some of them use to cover up their poor skills.

Each of his many works can be connected to a personal interest, skill, passion, or experience of his own. It is not unusual for authors to invest themselves in their work in this way. As an advocate for young people, Myers demonstrated his willingness to fight for a positive future for young people, especially those raised in hard situations or those in trouble. Myers took that fight an additional step and invested in the future of young people.

BIOGRAPHY

Walter Milton Myers was born into a poor family in Martinsburg, West Virginia, on August 12, 1937, in the same area where his ancestors had been slaves. When he was two years old his mother Mary died, and his father, George Myers, was left with seven children and no way to support them. The area was still recovering from the Great Depression, and in a segregated society African Americans were the first to lose jobs.

Two of Walter's siblings, Geraldine and Viola, were George's daughters with his first wife, Florence Brown. After she and George divorced, Florence, who was ostracized by her German relatives for marrying an African American, moved to Baltimore, leaving her daughters with their father in Martinsburg. By 1939 she had married Herbert Dean and moved with him from Baltimore to Harlem. A year later the couple went to Martinsburg to bring her daughters back to Harlem, and they brought Walter with them.

Myers retained little contact with George Myers in later years, though he did stay in touch with his siblings.

Florence taught him to read when he was four years old. He remembers sitting on her lap and following along the pages of her *True Romance* magazines "as she half read, half acted out the stories of lost loves and sudden passions" (*Bad Boy,* p. 15). In interviews later in life, Myers recalled his bafflement at the "heaving bosoms" that featured so regularly in those *True Romance* stories and said that while he did not understand everything, he nevertheless enjoyed listening to Florence read and learning the words. Later on Florence gave him Classic Comics to read.

Myers was dogged by problems in elementary school as he got into mischief and struggled with a speech impediment, making class participation painful. His fifth-grade teacher, Mrs. Conway, recognized the reader in Myers as he sneaked looks at comics while sitting in the back of the room as punishment for some infraction or other. She gave him a selection of good books, then allowed him to write out selections instead of being required to read aloud, which eased his discomfort.

His early reading choices, both the pulp fiction and the better stories he was given by Mrs. Conway, already showed the budding author that, as an African American, he was not represented in those stories. In a 2006 interview, Myers told Peggy O'Crowley about the view he formed growing up in a poor area reading books about mainly white characters. "I saw the world divided between people who had value and those that did not. Black people did not have value."

He started developing other interests through activities at the corner church. Myers spent a lot of time there, learning modern dance and playing basketball. Those activities would play important roles in books such as *Hoops* (1981), *Slam!* (1998), and *Juba!* (2015).

After being placed in an accelerated middle school, Myers went to Stuyvesant High School, where his English teacher Bonnie Liebow made an individualized reading list for him that formed the basis of his only real connection to high school. She also encouraged him to write. As he was sitting outside the guidance counselor's office for truancy one day, Mrs. Liebow saw him and whispered, "Whatever happens, don't stop writing" (*Bad Boy,* p. 153).

He attended high school so seldom he once showed up only to find that school had let out for the summer. Walter worked at odd jobs to save money for a typewriter. Herbert Dean bought him a Royal machine, recognizing his son's strongest desire even if he himself did not understand the value in reading and writing.

After high school it became clear to Myers that his choices in his current situation were limited. Following some dangerous run-ins with neighborhood gangs, he had to protect himself with a stiletto and knew it was time for a change. He joined the army on his seventeenth birthday.

He returned to New York at age twenty and eventually took the civil service exam and got a job at the post office, all the while trying to keep up with his writing. He married Joyce Smith in 1960, and they would have two children, Karen and Michael. During that busy time, Myers got a lot of rejections but published some poems and short stories for adults in small literary magazines.

He refers to a "turning point in my writing" (*Bad Boy,* p. 203) when he read James Baldwin's "Sonny's Blues." The story vividly depicts African American urban life. Upon reading that, Myers felt writing about his experience had legitimacy and merit. He had discovered his voice and his mission, to show the importance of the voice of African American youth. His next story, about basketball, was accepted "the first time [he] sent it out" (*Bad Boy,* p. 203). When his half-brother Wayne was killed in Vietnam, his story about that grief was accepted by *Essence* magazine. Myers continued honing his writing skills by taking writing classes and also tried to keep up with studies at City College. It was hard, as he and Joyce each worked two jobs to try to make ends meet. The marriage did not survive the strain, and they would divorce in 1970.

In 1968 he entered a contest sponsored by the Council on Interracial Books for Children that would lead to the publication by Parents'

Magazine Press of his picture book *Where Does the Day Go?,* about an African American boy, Steven, and his father walking in the park with an interracial group of friends. Myers also took a writing class with the author John Oliver Killens, who in 1970 encouraged him to apply for an editorial position at Bobbs-Merrill, a publishing house that was trying to recruit diverse editors. Despite having at that time no high school or college diploma, he was hired. The first book he edited was a prose title by the poet Nikki Giovanni.

In 1974 Myers married Constance Brendel, and they had a son, Christopher, who would grow into a gifted artist whose collaboration with his father as illustrator would produce many award-winning books. In 1975 Myers published his first young adult novel, *Fast Sam, Cool Clyde, and Stuff,* about scenes in a Harlem neighborhood. The editorial job at Bobbs-Merrill ended in 1977, and Myers made the decision to become a full-time writer. Even after achieving success in his writing career he returned to school, earning his B.A. degree in 1984 from Empire State College, where his classwork included research on people in prisons that would lead many years later to one of his most read works, *Monster* (1999).

All of these experiences helped to make him the prolific writer and advocate for young people that remains his legacy. His long list of awards and honors includes a National Book Award nomination, two Newbery Honor titles, the inaugural Michael L. Printz Award, and many Coretta Scott King Author Awards and Honors. Lifetime achievement awards were given decades before his death and before many of his books were published, including the Young Adult Library Services Association's Margaret A. Edwards award in 1994 for impact of a body of work and the first Coretta Scott King–Virginia Hamilton Award for Lifetime Achievement in 2010. In 2012 he earned the inaugural New York City Literary Honor for Children's Literature for writing about New York life and for the body of his work.

Myers' life was devoted to research and writing, his family, and connecting with and being an advocate for young readers, though he also made

time for the three musical instruments he played and to perform in readers' theater with fellow authors such as Avi. He died on July 1, 2014, at age seventy-six, and *Juba!,* his last young adult novel, was published posthumously in 2015 along with the graphic-novel version of *Monster.*

In addition to his son Christopher, many authors and literary professionals point to Myers as helping to inspire the We Need Diverse Books movement. His 2014 *New York Times* essay deploring the dearth of characters of color is cited prominently on the movement's website (http://weneeddiversebooks.org/faq/) and by those promoting the cause.

In a 2015 tribute, the author Kelechi Urama describes the inspiration she drew as a writer from reading Myers' *Slam!* after encountering mainly white characters in books she read when she was in middle school. *Slam!,* she writes, "told me that I could write about characters that looked like me—that a young black girl with barrettes at the end of her braids could be the hero of her own story."

CHANCES AND CHOICES

Though his historical titles, poetry, nonfiction, and picture books have all been awarded accolades, Myers is best known for his resonant, deeply realistic young adult fiction. Young people in desperate circumstances fill these pages, facing the consequences of their actions and trying to find their way out. Myers forces readers to see all facets of characters, even those who have committed terrible crimes, to understand the journey that led to those choices.

The first of his serious young adult novels was *It Ain't All for Nothin'* (1978). In her review for the *Bulletin for the Center of Children's Books,* Zena Sutherland notes that one of the strengths of Myers' writing is that "none of the characters is superficially drawn as all good or all bad." Tippy was raised by his grandmother and is forced to live with a father he barely knows after she goes into a nursing home. Lonnie beats his son, neglects him, and forces him to participate in robberies. When a member of

Lonnie's crew is shot, Tippy calls the police on his father to save both the crew member and himself. Tippy is offered a hopeful ending when he is placed with a man in his community who has shown him kindness. Not all of Myers' characters, however, are offered hope or definitive outcomes.

The *Young Landlords,* published the following year, was a Coretta Scott King Honor title. Myers got the idea for the novel after hearing about decrepit buildings being sold for tiny amounts of money, and he wondered what it would be like if teens took one over. In the book, six teens calling themselves the Action Group decide to buy a building to do some good. They encounter many humorous problems, such as hiring a maintenance man who builds an exploding still in the basement and a tenant who uses karate to try to avoid paying rent. Two members of the group who are becoming more than friends get locked in a bathroom while trying to fix the plumbing and get accused of hanky-panky by the tenant. The humor does not diminish the serious issues addressed in the book or the respect Myers shows the savvy group of teens. When a young single mother cannot pay the rent, one teen wants to evict her while another urges compassion, reminding them all that they wanted to do good. While lighter in tone than *It Ain't All for Nothin',* the difficulties faced by members of the teen group and their tenants are no laughing matter, as they all try to use the building as a chance for a better life.

In the 1984 novel *Motown and Didi,* a Coretta Scott King Author Award recipient, Myers shows that love can survive the harshest situations. Motown was a minor character who befriended Tippy in *It Ain't All for Nothin'* and gave him advice about surviving. Didi tells the police about Touchy, the man who sells her brother the drugs which eventually kill him. Touchy and his gang beat and rape her in retaliation. Motown hears the beating happening from his "home" in an abandoned building and helps Didi. The two begin to lean on each other and fall in love in a memorable adventure. In *Motown and Didi,* Myers employs a technique that was new to him, the omniscient point of view, which allows him to show sympathy even for the worst characters to even greater effect. This point of view will return in *Monster* and *Shooter* (2004), among other of his notable works. In her 1991 book *Presenting Walter Dean Myers,* Rudine Sims Bishop details how this point of view works to show compassion even for Touchy. "We see Touchy, the drug dealer, being psychologically abused as a child by his wife-beating father, and we begin to understand why he is so cold and unfeeling that he doesn't want to be touched" (p. 54).

The Newbery Honor title *Scorpions* impressed the 1989 committee, reviewers, and readers with its honesty and profound realism. The main character, twelve-year-old Jamal, must decide if he wants to lead his brother Randy's gang, the Scorpions, after Randy goes to prison for murder. Jamal is disturbed to discover that, even though he gains respect, he has terrible new responsibilities after he is given a gun. His best friend, Tito, becomes as important a character as Jamal as he tries to pull his old friend from the abyss in front of him. Though he does not want his dangerous new role, Jamal sees no other path because he needs to get money for his brother's appeal. The omniscient narrator returns here, heightening the suspense surrounding the gun. Bishop finds *Scorpions* "a powerful statement about the destructive potential of drugs and guns placed in the hands of poor and directionless young men" (p. 64).

The Newbery Honor title *Somewhere in the Darkness* (1992) reflects another painful family relationship that pulls the hero away from where he wants to be. In this case, it is another father-son relationship. Crab escapes prison to convince his fourteen-year-old son Jimmy that he did not murder anyone. They meet people from Crab's past in Chicago and Arkansas before one of those former associates turns Crab in to the authorities. He dies after an encounter with police. Jimmy is returned to his beloved foster mother in the same way Tippy is left in the care of a loving adult after a painful break with his father. In her review for *Horn Book,* Ellen Fader remarked that "there is not an unnecessary word or phrase; the scenes

are vivid and emotionally powerful; and the characters are heartbreakingly realistic" (p. 344).

In 2000 the Young Adult Library Services Association's inaugural Michael L. Printz Award for an outstanding book for young adults was awarded to Myers for *Monster*. This was six years after the same organization awarded Myers the lifetime achievement Margaret Edwards Award for *Hoops, Motown and Didi, Fallen Angels* (1988), and *Scorpions*. First published in 1999, *Monster* was also a National Book Award finalist. In 2015 the title was still a best seller, number one in Amazon's rankings of "Teen and Young Adult Prejudice and Racism Fiction."

The stylistically bold *Monster* is written in the form of a screenplay by Steve Harmon, a sixteen-year-old witnessing his trial after he served as lookout in a robbery that resulted in murder. Written in current, accessible language, the story of a teen with the wrong friends at the wrong time in the wrong place, with dire consequences, transcends the year it was published with its powerful questions about racism and culpability. The book has landed on many challenged-books lists for raw, racially charged language and subject matter. In his 2012 interview with *Story Snoops*, Myers reflected on the reaction of readers to Steve's plight. "I still get dozens of letters from young people (and some teachers) saying that Steve should never have been brought to trial because he didn't actually pull the trigger. The lack of understanding of the law here is tragic."

In a 2000 interview with Hazel Rochman for *Booklist*, Myers described how his research on prison inmates for a class at Empire State College led to *Monster*:

> I did 600 pages of interviews with prisoners in New York and New Jersey. And patterns began to emerge. They all knew why they were in jail; they knew what crimes they had committed or had been accused of committing, but they never seemed to be really sure of the path that had got them there.

Another pattern that emerged from his interviews was that the prisoners tried to separate their crimes from themselves as people, and it also became evident to Myers that no one starts out life as a murderer. In *Monster*, Myers' use of the screenplay style takes the effect of his omniscient point of view one step further. As Steve's story begins to take shape, the technique of writing it as a screenplay helps to show how Steve distances himself from his actions in the same way the subjects of Myers' interviews did.

Shooter (2004) moves to the aftermath of a painful, violent story. This time the situation has gone beyond help and teens have died. Carla, Cameron, and Len are high school friends with an interest in guns. They are bullied at school, and Len decides to end it all by shooting classmates, then himself. Like *Monster*, it is written through interviews conducted in the wake of the violence and from different points of view, ending with the grim and gruesome yet memorable medical examiner's report. Each skillfully written interview gives hints about both the subject and interviewer to help readers get a broader picture of the people and situation that led up to the tragic act. Myers was inspired to write *Shooter* after the 1999 Columbine High School massacre and his earlier prison interviews. He noticed that the bitter young people he encountered in prisons frequently had been bullied before they became bullies themselves. Following Columbine, he went to Colorado and talked with people there. In an interview with Donna Carillo for *Scholastic News Online*, he recalled that "what I saw was kids being bullied, pushed around, sometimes by fellow students, sometimes by family members. These kids would get so angry and upset."

In a parallel article, "Stopping the Bullies," also with Carillo for *Scholastic News Online*, Myers described how bullying knows no racial or economic lines—it is universal. He posited that because athletes are now "cultural icons," the physical is given more weight in our society, and that may be a factor in the bullying. While *Shooter* does not offer hope in the way that his 2010 novel *Lockdown* does, he hoped that the story would open discussions about bullying. "I want to send the message that the people who are being bullied are not unique."

The National Book Awards finalist *Autobiography of My Dead Brother* (2006) shares a stark narrative about urban realities with black-and-white illustrations by Myers' son Christopher. As

in *Scorpions,* the painful reality of what happens next after entering into criminal activities is laid bare. The story begins and ends with funerals of young men from drive-by shootings. Fifteen-year-old Jesse, a talented artist, thinks of his seventeen-year-old friend Rise as his brother, though Rise runs with a faster crowd. The two belong to a club, the Counts, that has been around for many years. It isn't a gang, but Rise's new drug-dealing ways move it into new territory with a painful conclusion.

The desperate question of how to get out of an increasingly bad and dangerous situation is also a strong theme in the National Book Awards finalist *Lockdown* (2010), featuring fourteen-year-old Reese, who is in prison for stealing prescription pads. He wants to behave and get out, but he gets into trouble defending a weaker, bullied inmate. When he is assigned to work at a senior center, he meets Mr. Hooft, whose stories of surviving an American Japanese internment camp inspire Reese to focus on a more positive future. Historical reflections play a prominent role in Myers' work, and he uses the Japanese incarceration analogy to highlight the African American urban plight to good effect here. Reese's future may hold more hope than that of *Monster*'s Steve, but the hope here prevails in a realistically drawn, difficult situation about the downward spiral of the wrong path.

Darius & Twig (2013), another Coretta Scott King Honor book, promises more hope than other Myers titles but also reflects his themes of getting out of desperate circumstances and away from adults making bad choices. Friends since childhood, Darius and Twig are hoping to use their talents to move beyond their neighborhood after high school. Two teen thugs bully them, but Darius works on his writing for a chance at a college scholarship. As an athlete, Twig's gift for running puts him in danger of exploitation by adults. Reviewing the novel for *Booklist,* Michael Cart wrote that *Darius & Twig* is "another gritty, suspenseful, street-smart novel with a viscerally real setting in which young men must struggle to overcome obstacles by finding the best within themselves."

Several of Myers' works have been banned for language, harsh subject matter, and violent situations. In a 2012 PBS interview with Jeffrey Brown, Myers said that writing these types of titles was his way of offering readers respect by showing them hope and understanding:

> Well, the most positive thing I can give them is their own presence, acknowledging them, you know, if I say to a kid, you are a human being that I understand, that I'm not going to excuse your—if you have done a crime, I'm not going to excuse your crime, but I know where you are coming from. I know that you feel and that you're thinking. And that's—I need to do that. I need to write that.

SPORTS

Many of Myers's fiction and nonfiction books feature basketball, baseball, and boxing, among other sports. While these stories also continue to focus on the harsh realities of the urban experience for young people, the game details and themes give them a broader appeal and readership. His own interest in basketball likely helped infuse stories with his own passion. In an interview with kids for *Scholastic Online,* Myers reflected that his six-foot frame added to his love of basketball. "If I had my choice I would be a star player in the NBA (who wrote in the off season)."

Hoops (1981) and *The Outside Shot* (1984) feature Lonnie Jackson in his senior year of high school and then in his freshman year of college. *Hoops,* an Edgar Allan Poe Award nominee for its fast pacing and taut, suspenseful plot, shows the danger of seeing a future in professional sports as the only ticket out of a poor, crime-ridden neighborhood. While it does become Lonnie's connection to college, his relationship with Coach Cal shows the darker possibilities of sports. Lonnie does not trust Cal, because he knows about his drinking problems and also that the former professional player was removed from the sport for point shaving and gambling with game outcomes. However, Cal's past mistakes do not prevent him from encouraging Lonnie. Cal ends up sacrificing his own life to ensure that the illegal gamblers and team sponsors who are try-

ing to keep Lonnie out of a championship game do not win. While Myers stays with Lonnie as the narrator, conversations with other people bring out Cal's past and the background on the situation. In both *Hoops* and *The Outside Shot*, Myers uses teen language for Lonnie's narration, which provides an endearing, funny veil. Rudine Sims Bishop agrees that "this voice also allows Myers to return to the humor that is missing from most of the urban reality novels" (p. 61).

The Outside Shot follows Lonnie through his freshman year at Montclare State College in Indiana. Here he encounters the realities that he is not a star player and that the classwork is harder than he imagined. He encounters racism and is suspected of being involved with another point-shaving situation. Some of Cal's friends who stayed in professional ball come to his aid. Lonnie's best friend at college is his roommate and teammate, Colin, who comes from a small farm town in Illinois. When Lonnie visits him at home, he sees that poverty and the desire to find a better life through sports is not limited to African American urban boys like himself.

The Mop and Moondance books are notable as Myers' first tween books, for readers younger than twelve. They feature a Little League team rather than basketball. Three orphans try to find happy endings in the humorous *Me, Mop, and the Moondance Kid* (1988) and its sequel, *Mop, Moondance, and the Nagasaki Knights* (1992). TJ and his brother Moondance have recently been adopted from an orphanage, and they are trying to prevent the friend called Miss Olivia Parrish, or Mop, from being moved to a faraway facility. They all work toward encouraging their Little League coach to adopt her. Everyone is working together to make their team win. Myers manages to show how supportive relationships can become family, as he does in some of the harder realistic books, in the midst of the humorous tone and younger focus.

"Basketball is my thing. I can hoop. Case closed." The opening lines of one of Myers' most popular works, the Coretta Scott King Award title *Slam!*, do not close the case on the story of Greg "Slam" Harris, who tries to cope with his anger, failing grades, and prospects for the future. The seventeen-year-old Greg transferred to a mostly white magnet school and feels comfortable only on the court as everything around him changes. His grandmother is ill, his father is drinking, and he discovers that his friend and court opponent Ice is dealing drugs. He fantasizes about being a wealthy professional player, but reality keeps pulling him back. Myers switches from fast-paced game sequences to short, powerful scenes in Greg's teen vernacular. While Greg does not directly express his feelings, the words convey them on every page. He knows the future will take hard work and hard choices. It ends with Greg's determination. "Maybe if I could get my game right, all my game, on and off the court, I could get over."

Kick (2011) is a soccer story written in collaboration with Myers fan Ross Workman, who had written to the author to compliment his writing. Kevin is looking forward to helping his team win the state cup in soccer when he is arrested after helping a female friend. He can't reveal why he was driving her father's car without giving away her family's troubles, and he does not want to do that even though the arrest jeopardizes his soccer. Kevin's father was a police officer killed in the line of duty, so a judge asks Sergeant Brown to investigate. He becomes Kevin's mentor after they circle each other a bit and delve beneath appearances. Myers wrote the first-person narrative for Sergeant Brown, and Workman the voice of Kevin, for a successful partnership.

Whether or not they play a given sport, readers of Myers' books will likely already know about the basics of several popular sports and be able to relate to and empathize with the characters without playing basketball or soccer themselves.. Especially with these sports titles, Myers creates action-filled scenes and emotionally packed books, a winning combination.

WAR

While Myers is well known for his urban stories, his war stories are especially promoted by educators because they portray the African American experience in several U.S. conflicts, a point of

view that is almost nowhere else to be found in young adult literature. He also looks at the morality of conflicts where relatively little information is related in textbooks, including the Vietnam War and the Iraq War. He pulls no punches and offers no stereotypes to move readers away from the gritty, morally and physically painful situations in which soldiers find themselves. For that reason, Myers' *Fallen Angels* (1988) is his most challenged title, with obscene language given most often as the reason for pulling the book from schools and libraries.

Inspired both by Myers' three years in the army and by the death of his half-brother in Vietnam, the story of seventeen-year-old Richie Perry comes to vivid life in this multiple-award-winning title. Richie, like Myers as a young man, sees no way off the harsh streets and no way to afford college. The army seems like the answer. In the jungles of Vietnam he meets Peewee, Lobel, Johnson, and Brunner. In the vein of Joseph Heller's *Catch-22* (1961), Myers utilizes humor in the interactions among the infantrymen as they try to avoid thinking about the terrible things they have to do each day while fighting the Viet Cong. A new friend is killed on Richie's first mission. Their leader is racist, which ultimately bonds the group together against him. Their lieutenant is killed, and Richie realizes that the African American soldiers seem to be sent on the most dangerous missions. He and the other men also do not understand why the United States is involved in this conflict at all. After being wounded in a later skirmish, Richie longs to return home, though he does not know what his prospects hold there either. Another wound sends Richie and Peewee home on the same plane that is carrying caskets filled with dead soldiers.

Fallen Angels has been compared to Stephen Crane's 1895 classic, *The Red Badge of Courage*, with the theme of lost innocence amid wartime death. Richie's initial bravery, as well as his fears and dread, are relatable to teen readers who may not be as familiar with the Vietnam War as those who lived during that time. Winner of another Coretta Scott King Award, *Fallen Angels* continues to offer historical and racial perspective for younger readers who may not

understand why the United States continues to get involved in new conflicts such as the Iraq War, which provides the background for the follow-up to *Fallen Angels: Sunrise over Fallujah* (2008).

Readers wanting to know what happens next for Richie get some answers in *Sunrise over Fallujah*, when his nephew, Robin Perry, is moved to join the army after the events of September 11, 2001. Robin becomes part of the Civilian Affairs Battalion, which provides medicine, water, and assistance to the Iraqi people attempting to set up a new society after Saddam Hussein is gone. Robin quickly learns that several Iraqi groups hate each other or Americans, and that he has to be vigilant and cautious. Robin refers to the famous real-life kidnapped soldier Jessica Lynch as he realizes some soldiers he knows have been kidnapped. His group is attacked by people in an ambulance, and he witnesses other deaths by improvised explosive devices. Robin's unit is asked to go on a highly dangerous assignment, and none of the soldiers return the same. In a parallel to *Fallen Angels*, questions about why the army is there when the people in the country do not want them come across clearly, as does Myers' familiar theme of characters finding themselves in desperate situations. As a teenager Robin had more choices than Richie, and he finds himself wondering why he made this choice as he is asked to do things he would never have dreamed of doing at home in Harlem.

Another Perry goes to war in *Invasion* (2013). This time it is Marcus Perry, Richie Perry's father, one of the soldiers storming Omaha Beach in World War II. The story centers around Josiah "Woody" Wedgewood, who is only vaguely aware of what his group is supposed to do when they land on the beach. Woody runs into Marcus on the beach and recognizes him as someone from his hometown. Myers uses that connection to show the segregation of the troops and the total, brutal confusion of the scene at the beach. He switches writing tense from past to present for the deadly invasion, drawing readers right into the deadly, slow, terrible battle, revealing the soldiers' horror in the same way that casting his

narrative in the form of a screenplay shows readers of *Monster* the detachment Steve has from the person he was when he was the lookout for the robbery. While the reasons for fighting World War II may be clearer to modern readers than those behind the wars in Vietnam or Iraq, Myers evokes in all three books the terrible losses these young men face. In his review for *Booklist,* Cart described how "Myers has done peace an inestimable service by showing so vividly what a truly terrible idea war is."

Writing about World War II was not new for Myers, as evidenced by his 1999 historical novel for the My Name Is America Series, *We Were Heroes: The Journal of Scott Pendleton Collins, a World War II Soldier, Normandy, France, 1944.* This book tells the story of another young, bewildered soldier's horrifying experience during the Normandy invasion. Through this title and others, Myers made war stories more accessible for readers ages ten to fourteen, rather than the books, like the three Perry family war stories, aimed at firmly young adult readers. The 2002 picture book *Patrol* allows readers age eight and above to comprehend a little about the jungles the soldiers encountered in the Vietnam War. The nonfiction titles *USS Constellation: Pride of the American Navy* (2004) and *The Harlem Hellfighters: When Pride Met Courage* (2009), bring facts to middle school readers about U.S. military history and, especially, in *The Harlem Hellfighters,* the role played by African Americans.

The subject of race is inherent in any discussion of the U.S. Civil War, so that conflict was perhaps a natural subject for Myers. He writes of the slave experience in *The Glory Field* (1994), a work of historical fiction covering 250 years of one African American family and its descendants through the aftermath of slavery to the struggle to own land and become equal citizens. Myers addresses a different aspect of the Civil War in the 2009 novel *Riot,* outlining how the 1863 military draft pitted Irish Immigrants against African Americans in New York City. As Lincoln beseeched immigrants to enlist to fight with the North, they resented the African Americans and feared that they would take away jobs. Myers returns to the screenplay format to show the different facets of the escalating conflict to profound effect. The biracial Claire, for example, is told point blank by another character who believes Claire is white that "coloreds" would take their jobs. In an essay on how Myers' screenplay style in *Monster* and *Riot* works well with young adult readers, Dean Schneider in *Booklist* compares how the books' main characters have more than a screenplay style in common: "As Steve Harmon's arrest propels him into an identity crisis and a search for answers as to why he ended up on trial for murder, Claire's peripheral association with the Draft Riots causes her to question herself" (p. S20.)

The range of subjects and Myers' ability to write both fiction and nonfiction brings power and passion to both types of his works. Writing about wars was a way for Myers to draw analogies to modern issues while bringing readers into a world they might not otherwise see.

A RANGE OF NONFICTION

Ever-curious and inspired to research different topics, Myers' nonfiction titles were not limited to war or battleship accounts. Biographies and inspirational guides helped him on his mission to show that people in desperate circumstances can find within themselves a pathway out of their dilemma. His compassion and empathy for characters both good and bad also works in his nonfiction to help readers truly understand the subjects and feel Myers' encouragement for their own futures.

Even in nonfiction Myers experimented with format. While traditional biographies appear in his bibliography, it also includes works with an unusual focus, photography, poetry, picture books, and even interactive formats.

One example of the latter is *Sweet Illusions* (1986), published by the New York Teachers and Writers Collaborative. Myers wrote episodes about teenage pregnancy, each narrated by a different character, reflecting several different cultures and situations. At the end of each chapter, readers are invited to write a song, list, or different ending to that section. The workbook

received positive reviews. Bishop remarked that "it is an unusual book that succeeds because it draws on Myers' highly developed craftsmanship" (p. 101).

Now Is Your Time! The African American Struggle for Freedom (1991) is another collection of stories, though this time they are true stories with biographical anecdotes mixed in. In this Coretta Scott King Honor title, readers are taken through the lives of several families through recognizable events such as the Dred Scott case. Reviewers found this format both readable and confusing, though they agreed that this book filled a void in portrayals of the African American role in famous historical events.

In 1993 Myers published several important and unusual works. The first, the biography *Malcolm X: By Any Means Necessary,* "traces the major events of Malcolm's life in the context of the broader history of the civil rights movement in America" (*Contemporary Authors Online*). Rather than providing a straight recounting of his life and actions, the book tries to show young adult readers why Malcolm was so powerful in that time of needed change. (In 2000 Myers would revisit the subject of Malcolm X in a title for younger readers, *Malcolm X: A Fire Burning Brightly.*) In the preface Myers lays out his position: "Malcolm and the Nation of Islam drove the civil rights movement, gave it the dark side that many feared it might have. It was Malcolm who said to black Americans that they did not always have to hide their pain, or their outrage" (p. xi).

In the same year, Myers published a book about Martin Luther King, Jr. While many biographies of King have been published for young readers, Myers was one of the first to write one for younger grade school readers and also for picture-book readers. *Young Martin's Promise* (1993), for the earliest self-readers in kindergarten and up, covers events from King's childhood that show the inequality of segregation. Written more as an accessible narrative than as a historical account, it was meant to make inexplicable stories that may have inspired King's work understandable for young children. The 2004 title *I've Seen the Promised Land,* for grades one through three,

with vivid illustrations, covers territory that *Young Martin's Promise* does not, by relating the facts and harsh realities of King's movement and his assassination.

The third important nonfiction book from 1993 was *Brown Angels,* the first of his collections of photographs and poetry featuring African American children and families. In her biography of Myers, Denise Jordan describes how the Angels books came to be: "Myers was looking for a picture of a black child to use in a piece he was working on. After a bit of searching, he found what he was looking for and much more. The mischievous looks, sly grins or serious expressions on the children's faces captivated him" (Jordan, p. 70). Soon he had a collection of hundreds of photographs, and the publications grew from there.

At Her Majesty's Request: An African Princess in Victorian England (1999) tells the true story of Sarah, an Egbado princess who was rescued from execution by an English soldier and ends up under the protection of Queen Victoria. She enjoys an exalted status in some ways but limitations due to her race in other aspects. Myers began his research in a packet of letters but added to it, including pictures and other interesting documentation, to create a story for middle and high school readers that turns the traditional white princess story on its head. In this way the book is reminiscent of Myers' early twist on the traditional fairy tale, his picture book *The Dragon Takes a Wife* (1972). It is about Henry, who must fight a knight in order to win a wife. He meets Mabel Mae Jones, an African American fairy, who greets him with "What's bugging you, Baby?" Mabel's hip jargon follows her as she pretends to be a dragon so Henry can get practice fighting. He falls for her, gets a job at the post office, and they live happily ever after. When the book came out in the early 1970s, Myers received a lot of hate mail for his recasting of the fairy-tale genre.

Myers offers encouragement to teens, especially those interested in literary pursuits, in both his 2001 autobiography *Bad Boy: A Memoir* and *Just Write! Here's How* (2012). *Just Write* includes an afterword from his teen *Kick* col-

laborator, Ross Workman. Myers gives readers his "Six Box Model for Fiction" where writers can map out key pieces of their work, including conflict, characters, solutions, growth, action and resolution (p. 50). His practical advice and approaches for novels are designed to help young writers overcome their fears and hang-ups and just get their books done. The notable *Bad Boy* offers inspiration in a different way. Myers, with his trademark humor, recounts scenes from his childhood, in the same vein as *Fast Sam,* from classmates who bully him to escapades where he tries to break a family watch with a shoe or admits that Florence Dean needed to get out and away from his antics at times. Detailed too are his issues with school along with the history of his family. The last chapter addresses the beginning of his career as a writer and his parent's reactions. Landing on many notable lists, this poignant set of chapters and scenes is meant to show his turnaround and the way choices can impact the rest of one's life, much as it does for many of Myers' fictional heroes.

MUSIC, DANCE, AND, AS ALWAYS, HARLEM

As a musician who played flute, among other instruments, Myers incorporated his love of music, dance, jazz, and other aspects of African American culture as a main theme in several works. Though lacking the desperate choices of the harsher city stories, characters in the young adult music- or dance-themed stories have had plenty of struggles. Picture books featuring music show positive African American cultural elements in the way that Myers' nonfiction picture books on war or on Martin Luther King preach eloquently with illustrations.

Most of Myers' books are set in Harlem, and among them are several collections of short stories of life in the neighborhood. While these employ Myers' nostalgia for the good memories of his childhood, they also show the racial undercurrents that come to the forefront in his edgier works. *Fast Sam, Cool Clyde, and Stuff* was Myers' first young adult novel, written in flashbacks from eighteen-year-old Frances (a.k.a. Stuff) about moving to 116th Street at age twelve.

He fondly remembers the first adventures he had with his new friends. Life in Harlem is the theme here, with adult realities creeping in on Stuff's humorous memories. The boys in the group are falsely accused of stealing a purse when the owner, whom they were trying to help, thought they looked like the culprits. Clyde's father is killed in an industrial accident. Gloria, one of the girls in his new neighborhood group, brings some female friends to have a talk about sex with all of them. Reviewers remarked on Myers' humor, normal teen dialogue, and irony. The *Kirkus* reviewer found that "in general his colloquial first-person narrative projects a sense of enviable group rapport with an easy mix of nostalgia and humor" (*Kirkus Reviews,* 1975). *Fast Sam* became the first of Myers' many Coretta Scott King Honor books.

The volumes *145th Street: Short Stories* (2000) and *What They Found: Love on 145th Street* (2007) both show the positive elements of a supportive community. Myers infuses plenty of despair in these characters' situations, but hope, humor, and love dominate as they help each other survive.

> "Don't give me no okay," Kitty said. "I want to know if you love me."
>
> "Something like that." Mack said.
>
> That's what he said to Kitty, but to everybody else he was planning his whole life.
>
> *(145th Street: Short Stories,* p. 91)

In the last story of the first collection, some friends of J. T., who doesn't want them to know what his home life is like, insist on entering his apartment, knowing that he and his mother are barely surviving.

> "I couldn't even do nothing for my own mother," J. T. said. He had tears running down his cheeks....
>
> "This is 145th Street," Peaches said. "Hurt happens here just like everywhere else. Sometimes you can deal with it, sometimes you just got to get some help."
>
> *(145th Street: Short Stories,* p. 149)

Some characters are seen again in the follow-up collection, but *What They Found* centers more on

the people surrounding a beauty salon. These stories too deal out life's realities to characters, including drug use, jail, and other prevalent problems. Both collections were placed on notable children's literature lists, though *What They Found* drew considerably more accolades. With each new collection, Myers seemed to hone his short-story craft, growing in a similar way as many of his characters.

Myers' *Here in Harlem: Poems in Many Voices* (2009) explores similar territory in poetic form. In the introduction, Myers explains how he was inspired by Edgar Lee Masters' *Spoon River Anthology* (1915) to have people in a town tell their stories in verse. While Masters' town was fictional, Myers set these poems in his beloved neighborhood. More than fifty poems are interspersed among period photos from his collection, which provide ambiance more than connections to the tales. Placed on multiple notable lists for both children's literature and poetry, this collection shows the continuation of Myers' development of voice collections into increasingly superior projects.

His love of Harlem was expressed in delightful picture books through which Myers garnered ever more accolades. The 1997 collaboration *Harlem* with his illustrator son, Christopher, combines their different perspectives on their experiences. Designed for young adult readers, this Caldecott Honor and Coretta Scott King Illustrator Honor title evokes both points of view. In his review for *Booklist,* Cart described this combination. "The author views Harlem—where he grew up—as a symbol of African American aspiration; the artist shares a more concrete city composed of 'colors loud enough to be heard.'"

Two other notable collaborations between father and son, *Blues Journey* (2003) and *Jazz* (2006), celebrate music through lyrical poetry and vivid illustrations. Both books landed on several lists for children's literature, poetry, and illustrations, including a Coretta Scott King Illustrator Honor award for *Jazz*. Christopher Myers expressed the duality of vision he experienced working with his "pop" in an interview with TeachingBooks: "When he does his work, I don't feel that my job is simply to support his text. I

feel that my job is to tell a different story that intertwines with his. Our stories overlap, contrast and compare in very interesting ways."

Learning dance in the church on the corner perhaps inspired Myers to write about it. His second picture book, *The Dancers* (1972), is about a boy who goes with his father, who works at the theater, and becomes intrigued by ballet. *Juba!,* Myers' last novel, published posthumously in 2015, follows the story of a real-life African American dancer who became famous as a teen in the 1840s after moving to London. After this rise, his life took a series of tragic turns and he died in a Liverpool workhouse in 1854. Notes from Constance Myers on Walter's research fills out the engrossing, but tragic, tale.

SERIES

Myers' ability to make his characters and stories real and recognizable for his readers accounted for his work being as popular as it was critically lauded. While some of his books landed more on the popular appeal side rather than on the literary side, they still represent his mission to show African Americans in positive, equal situations to white characters.

Between 1992 and 1994 Myers developed a series called 18 Pine Street, in which he mainly created the outlines for others to write. As he describes it in his interview with Amanda Smith, "These are little moral tales that I do, with enough romance to be interesting." The series featured African American girls in the same way that Sweet Valley High was designed to do, though the stories reflect a more difficult reality than the upper-middle-class Wakefield sisters usually encounter. Myers illustrated his skill and respect for creating smart, brave, appealing female characters in *Motown and Didi*, the *145th Street* short story collections, and many more, where positive female characters foster and parent other characters. The 18 Pine Street series includes stories such as *Intensive Care,* in which Jennifer borrows her mother's car and is hit by a drunk driver. One of Jennifer's passengers is injured, and she faces the consequences.

Myers's 1985–1986 Arrow mystery series follows white teens Ken and Chris Arrow around the world as they travel with their anthropologist mother and solve cases involving local cultures and people. Another series, the Cruisers, renamed the News Crew, was published from 2010 to 2014 (a coauthor finished the last volume). The series features four teens who are known in their gifted Harlem middle school for cruising along, not caring if they get Cs. They deal with issues such as racism after a school mock Civil War, theater politics, and more, all with Myers' trademark current teen dialogue and page-turning pace. In Ian Chipman's review of the opening book, *The Cruisers* (2010), for *Booklist,* he sums up these short but well-crafted volumes: "Although this book isn't the kind of towering shot he sometimes delivers, he legs it out by doing all the little things right: fleet pacing, a spot-on voice, good characters, great dialogue, smart ideas, and an unusual story that can maneuver whip-quick from light to heavy and right back again." Delivering what readers needed in a format they would understand and want summarizes not only his series, but Myers' writing career.

LAYERS OF LEGACIES

Though the majority of his young readers would likely not know or care about the fact that he won every available major prize in children's literature, Myers inspired them to continue reading. In the *New York Times* obituary for Myers, another award-winning author, Avi, remembers how he once gained the respect of a young audience simply by mentioning Myers' name:

Avi … recalled visiting young people in a Virginia prison a decade ago. He received a tepid reception. Then the young prisoners asked him if he knew anyone famous.

Avi mentioned Mr. Myers. "They sat straight up and shouted, 'You know him! What is he like?' " Avi recalled. "They were readers."

(Lee, p. B16)

Myers' passion for connecting with young readers was equaled only by his tireless advocacy for changes in the publishing industry. Interviewed by the editor Roger Sutton after winning the Margaret A. Edwards Award, Myers told a story to illustrate how publishers wanted African American authors to write only about certain subjects:

There was a time when [Langston Hughes] was desperate for money and he went to a publication saying "Listen, I'll write under a different name." They said no, they weren't interested. You do black stuff so well, continue doing that.

("An Interview in School Library Journal," p. 27)

A publishing legacy of more than a hundred books in addition to stories, poems, and essays in every genre and format proves that there is relevancy in all these areas for African American characters, portrayals, and advocacy. These are more than "black subjects." Myers also inspired an award-winning creator son and other authors who continue writing for a diverse young adult audience. These achievements surpass awards and will continue to encourage and connect with other creators and readers.

Selected Bibliography

WORKS OF WALTER DEAN MYERS

YOUNG ADULT NOVELS

Fast Sam, Cool Clyde, and Stuff. New York: Viking, 1975.

It Ain't All for Nothin'. New York: Viking, 1978.

The Young Landlords. New York: Viking, 1979.

Hoops. New York: Delacorte, 1981.

Motown and Didi: A Love Story. New York: Viking Kestrel, 1984.

The Outside Shot. New York: Delacorte, 1984.

Fallen Angels. New York: Scholastic, 1988.

Me, Mop, and the Moondance Kid. Delacorte, 1988.

Scorpions. New York: Harper & Row, 1989.

Mop, Moondance, and the Nagasaki Knights. New York: Delacorte, 1992.

Somewhere in the Darkness. New York: Scholastic, 1992.

The Glory Field. New York: Scholastic, 1994.

Slam! New York: Scholastic, 1998.

We Were Heroes: The Journal of Scott Pendleton Collins, a World War II Soldier, Normandy, France, 1944. New York: Scholastic, 1999.

Monster. New York: HarperCollins, 1999.

Shooter. Amistad/HarperTempest, 2004.

Autobiography of My Dead Brother. Amistad/HarperTempest, 2006.

Sunrise over Fallujah. New York: Scholastic, 2008.

Riot. New York: Egmont USA, 2009.

The Cruisers. New York: Scholastic, 2010.

Lockdown. New York: HarperTeen/Amistad, 2010.

Kick. New York: HarperTeen, 2011.

Darius & Twig. New York: Amistad/HarperCollins, 2013.

Invasion. New York: Scholastic, 2013.

Juba! New York: Amistad/HarperCollins, 2015.

SHORT STORIES

145th Street: Short Stories. New York: Delacorte, 2000.

What They Found: Love on 145th Street. New York: Wendy Lamb Books/Random House, 2007.

PICTURE BOOKS

Where Does the Day Go? New York: Parents Magazine Press, 1969.

The Dancers. New York: Parents Magazine Press, 1972.

The Dragon Takes a Wife. Indianapolis: Bobbs-Merrill, 1972.

POETRY

Brown Angels: An Album of Pictures and Verse. New York: HarperCollins, 1993.

Harlem: A Poem. New York: Scholastic, 1997.

Malcolm X: A Fire Burning Brightly.. New York: Harper-Collins, 2000.

Blues Journey. New York: Holiday House, 2003.

Jazz. New York: Holiday House, 2006.

Here in Harlem: Poems in Many Voices. New York: Holiday House, 2009.

NONFICTION

Sweet Illusions. New York: New York Teachers & Writers Collaborative, 1986.

Now Is Your Time! The African-American Struggle for Freedom. New York: HarperCollins, 1991.

Malcolm X: By Any Means Necessary. New York: Scholastic, 1993.

Young Martin's Promise. Austin, Tex.: Raintree/Steck-Vaughn, 1993.

At Her Majesty's Request: An African Princess in Victorian England. New York: Scholastic, 1999.

Bad Boy: A Memoir. New York: HarperCollins, 2001.

Patrol. New York: HarperCollins, 2002.

I've Seen the Promised Land: The Life of Dr. Martin Luther King, Jr. New York: HarperCollins, 2004.

USS Constellation: Pride of the American Navy. New York: Holiday House, 2004.

The Harlem Hellfighters: When Pride Met Courage. New York: HarperCollins, 2009.

Just Write! Here's How. New York: HarperCollins, 2012.

ESSAYS

"I Actually Thought We Would Revolutionize the Industry." *New York Times.* November 9, 1986. http://www.nytimes.com/1986/11/09/books/children-s-books-i-actually-thought-we-would-revolutionize-the-industry.html?pagewanted=all

"The Black Experience in Children's Books: One Step Forward, Two Steps Back." *Interracial Books for Children Bulletin* 10, no. 6:15 (1979).

"Where Are the People of Color in Children's Books?" *New York Times,* March 15, 2014. http://www.nytimes.com/2014/03/16/opinion/sunday/where-are-the-people-of-color-in-childrens-books.html?_r=0

PAPERS

A selection of Myers' manuscripts are held at the Kerlan Collection, University of Minnesota. https://www.lib.umn.edu/clrc/kerlan-collection

CRITICAL AND BIOGRAPHICAL STUDIES

Bishop, Rudine Sims. *Presenting Walter Dean Myers.* Boston: Twayne, 1991.

"Christopher Myers: Author Program In-Depth Interviews." TeachingBooks, 2006. http://www.teachingbooks.net/content/interviews/MyersC_qu.pdf

Jordan, Denise. *Walter Dean Myers: A Biography of an Award-Winning Urban Fiction Author.* Berkeley Heights, N.J.: Enslow, 2013.

Lee, Felicia R. "Walter Dean Myers Dies at 76; Wrote of Black Youth for the Young." *New York Times.* July 3, 2014, p. B16. http://www.nytimes.com/2014/07/04/arts/walter-dean-myers-childrens-author-dies-at-76.html

Urama, Kelechi. "How the Critically Acclaimed Author of *Monster,* Walter Dean Myers, Impacted Me as a Black Writer." *Xojane,* February 23, 2015. http://www.xojane.com/entertainment/author-monster-walter-dean-myers

"Walter Dean Myers." *Contemporary Authors Online.* Detroit: Gale, 2015.

"Walter Dean Myers." Author website, http://www.walterdeanmyers.net

REVIEWS

Cart, Michael. Review of *Harlem. Booklist,* February 15,

1997, p. 1021.

———. Review of *Darius & Twig*. *Booklist*, March 15, 2013, p. 76.

———. Review of *Invasion*. *Booklist*, December 15, 2013, p. 42.

Chipman, Ian. Review of *The Cruisers*. *Booklist*, September 1, 2010, p. 96.

Fader, Ellen. "A Review of *Somewhere in the Darkness*." *Horn Book Magazine* 68, no. 3:344–345 (May–June 1992).

"Fast Sam, Cool Clyde, and Stuff." *Kirkus Reviews*, April 1, 1975.

Schneider, Dan. "The Novel as Screenplay: *Monster* and *Riot* by Walter Dean Myers." *Booklist*, January 1, 2010, p. S20.

Sutherland, Zena. Review of *It Ain't All for Nothin'*. *Bulletin for the Center of Children's Books* 32, no. 5:84–85 (January 1979).

INTERVIEWS

"Best of Banned Books Week: Interview with Walter Dean Myers." *Story Snoops*, October 4, 2012. http://www.storysnoops.com/blog/?p=3971

Brown, Jeffrey. "Author Walter Dean Myers Says 'Reading Is Not Optional' for Kids." *PBS NewsHour*, July 31, 2012. http://www.pbs.org/newshour/bb/entertainment-july-dec 12-myers_07-31/

Carillo, Donna. "Walter Dean Myers Talks to Scholastic News Online." *Scholastic News Online*, n.d. http://teacher.scholastic.com/scholasticnews/indepth/bullying/bullying_news/index.asp?article=waterdeanmyers2&topic=0

———. "Walter Dean Myers on Stopping the Bullies." *Scholastic NewsOnline*, n.d. http://teacher.scholastic.com/scholasticnews/indepth/bullying/bullying_news/index.asp?article=WalterDeanMyers&topic=0

Nathan, Amy. "Reading Is Not Optional: An Interview with Walter Dean Myers." PEN America, 2012. http://www.pen.org/reading-not-optional-interview-walter-dean-myers#sthash.eAzk0Mjq.dpuf

O'Crowley, Peggy. "Walter Dean Myers: Telling Stories, Writer 'Elevates the Language in Fiction for Minority Youth.'" *Star Ledger*, NJ.com, December 31, 2006. http://blog.nj.com/iamnj/2006/12/hamady_ndaiye.html

Rochman, Hazel. "The Booklist Interview." *Booklist*, February 15, 2000, p. 1101.

Scholastic students. "Walter Dean Myers Interview." Scholastic, n.d. http://www.scholastic.com/teachers/article/walter-dean-myers-interview-transcript

Smith, Amanda. "Walter Dean Myers: This Award-Winning Author Tells It Like It Is." *Publishers Weekly*, July 20, 1992, p. 217.

Sutton, Roger. "An Interview in School Library Journal: Walter Dean Myers." *School Library Journal* 40, no. 6:24–28 (June 1994).

RON RASH

(1953—)

Louis H. Palmer III

"WATER HAS ITS own archaeology, not a layering but a leveling, and thus is truer to our sense of the past, because what is memory but near and far events spread and smoothed beneath the present's surface." So begins Ron Rash's short story "The Woman at the Pond" from his 2013 collection, *Nothing Gold Can Stay,* one of the many books that have established him not only as a long-esteemed regional voice but as an important American writer with an international reputation. That reputation was affirmed in 2014 with John Lang's *Understanding Ron Rash,* the first book-length study of his work, along with *The Ron Rash Reader,* edited by Randall Wilhelm. As both these works illustrate, Ron Rash is unique in many ways. He is adept in three separate genres—poetry, short stories, and the novel—and often uses the same material in each one, allowing readers a fascinating window into how an accomplished master of each form can rethink and remold similar subject matter to suit each one. He is a conscious participant in two distinct literary traditions, that of Appalachia and that of the greater South, again allowing unique insight into the similarities, contrasts, and points of comparison between the two. Since his first published collection of short stories in 1994, he has become one of the most prolific of his contemporaries, producing, in addition to the *Reader,* five collections of stories, four poetry collections, and six novels, along with numerous other publications in periodicals, journals, and anthologies as of 2016. He is the recipient of many awards, including the Frank O'Connor International Short Story Award, the James Still Award from the Fellowship of Southern Writers, the Sherwood Anderson Prize, two O. Henry Prizes, and the Novello Literary Award.

Ron Rash was born on September 25, 1953, in Chester, South Carolina, a small mill town. His parents, Sue and James, had met while working at the mill and went on to earn college degrees, with James earning his master's at Clemson University and becoming professor of art at Gardner-Webb College in the small town of Boiling Springs, North Carolina (near Charlotte, and now within the suburban radius of that city). Ron grew up in Boiling Springs, with frequent visits to his maternal grandmother's farm in the Appalachian Mountains of the western part of the state. He graduated from Gardner-Webb with a B.A. in English and then, like his father, received an M.A. from Clemson. He taught high school in Oconee County, South Carolina, then went on to teach at the postsecondary level at Tri-County Technical College in Pendleton, South Carolina, at Clemson, and at Western Carolina University in Cullhowee, North Carolina, where he now holds the John Parris Chair in Appalachian Studies. Starting in the late 1970s, he began to publish poetry and short stories in small, mostly regional, magazines. His first book was not published until the mid-1990s, but since then he has published at a prodigious pace.

Rash's work as a whole has not received a lot of scholarly attention, the most substantial comprehensive studies being Randall Wilhelm's introduction to *The Ron Rash Reader* and John Lang's *Understanding Ron Rash.* The *Reader* offers a good introduction to the author, with samples from most of his works, including the opening chapters from the first five novels. Wilhelm's essay does an excellent job in giving an overview, detailing Rash's themes and surveying his oeuvre. Lang's *Understanding Ron Rash* is a meticulous reading of Rash's work through 2014 and is immensely helpful in tracing the

complex patterns of cross-fertilization and development within the Rash opus. Lang, professor of English emeritus at Emory & Henry College in Virginia, was the editor of the *Iron Mountain Review* for more than twenty years. He provides a detailed bibliography of secondary sources and reviews. This is the definitive study of Rash, the starting place for all new work to come and the central secondary source for this essay.

Many of the articles on Rash's work are source studies or comparative essays. Examples of the first include John Lane's "The Girl in the River: The Wild and Scenic Chattooga, Ron Rash's *Saints at the River,* and the Drowning of Rachel Trois" (2008) and Kara Baldwin's "'Incredible Eloquence': How Ron Rash's Novels Keep the Celtic Literary Tradition Alive" (2006). Comparative studies include Matthew Boyelston's "Wild Boar in These Woods: The Influence of Seamus Heaney on the Poetry of Ron Rash" (2009) and Jesse Graves' "Lattice Work: Formal Tendencies in the Poetry of Robert Morgan and Ron Rash" (2007). Other essays of note include Christopher Morrow's "Acknowledgment, Adaptation, and Shakespeare in Ron Rash's *Serena*" and Rachel Willis' "Masculinities and Murder: George Pemberton in Ron Rash's *Serena,*" both in 2013. There is much more to be done in the field of Rash scholarship.

EARLY STORIES AND POETRY

Rash's first book was a collection of short stories titled *The Night the New Jesus Fell to Earth,* published in 1994 and set in Cliffside, North Carolina, a fictional college town named after a (real) small town near Boiling Springs. Cliffside, as its name suggests, is a piedmont location, set in that part of the Carolinas at the foot of the mountains along the "fall line," a geographical drop in elevation that was originally settled because of the availability of water power for timber processing, transportation, and later for textile mills. This foothills area is also a dividing line between the mountain south and the coastal plain, which developed distinct cultures, so it became a cultural mixing zone, where the lumber

mills and textile plants drew on both regions for labor. This dynamic, of an interstitial or border zone "in between," is one that seems to fascinate Rash, and one that powers and characterizes much of his work.

The interconnected short stories in *The Night the New Jesus Fell to Earth* are narrated by three young adults who are brought together in the middle of the night after the demise by fire of Greene's Café, the local diner and community gathering place. Randy is recently divorced and runs a chicken farm, Tracy is a builder and volunteer firefighter, and Vincent is the son of an art professor. Their stories revolve around the eccentric and peculiar behaviors of the residents of Cliffside, including themselves. Each perspective is unique. Vincent's stories are about his childhood struggles to come to terms with growing up as the son of an eccentric, absentminded father under the eyes of a small town's interested populace. Randy experiences a crushing divorce that leaves him living in his truck and desperate enough to try possum ranching. Tracy, already an outsider because of her unfeminine profession, negotiates the rough seas of Baptist religion. Rash's influences here are clearly Eudora Welty and Flannery O'Connor, with some of the more comic works of William Faulkner thrown in. The strength of these stories is in their portrayal of place as a determinant of and irritant to character. As in much of Rash's subsequent work, environment—in the broadest sense—is integral to every other aspect of the fiction. Especially in comparison to some of Rash's later, darker work, these stories are leavened by a bemused sense of humor.

One story, "Badeye," told from Vincent's perspective, involves a character who provides snow cones to the children of the village and moonshine to their elders out of an old pickup truck. His nickname comes from his missing eye, covered by an eyepatch. Vincent is eight, and his mother has Badeye marked as "an intruder, a bringer of tooth decay, bad eating habits, and other things" (p. 8). This proves to be true when Vincent begins obsessively collecting snakes with the help of his father, an abstracted college art professor. The mother, who has a biblically

influenced fear of snakes, refuses to have them in her house, so the males set up cages in the garage. It turns out that Badeye has access to the snake Vincent wants more than others, the beautiful and deadly coral snake. In exchange for Vincent making a nighttime delivery of a quart of moonshine to a neighbor, he gives him the snake. Vincent's curiosity leads him to sample the moonshine, then try to pick up the snake. He is bitten, and his parents rush him to the hospital. This is the end of both snow cones and snake collecting for Vincent. Badeye disappears, and Vincent remembers his mother's joy at the approach of autumn: no more snakes. The story is an ironic take on a temptation and loss-of-innocence tale, with tongue-in-cheek biblical references. It is nicely paced and sincerely narrated by the older Vincent.

Rash's first book of poetry, *Eureka Mill,* published in 1998, has a similar focus on place and a remarkable thematic unity. The book's title comes from the textile mill where the book's central character, based on Rash's grandfather, works. It includes the stories of other mill workers and is set mainly during the early decades of the twentieth century into the 1950s, a time when many Southern mountain farmers became textile workers due to a series of historic destabilizations, of which the Great Depression, the agricultural crises of the 1920s, and the two world wars are the best known to the nation as a whole. The poems are divided into six sections, beginning with a separate italicized "*Invocation.*" This poem describes a careful ceremony, where the speaker spreads out a "*fraying Springmaid bedsheet*" as a tablecloth, then pours moonshine into a mason jar lid and lights it to "*a blue trembling,*" an offering to summon "*a tobacco-breathed haint, shadowless shadow, / bloodless blood-kin,*" addressed as his grandfather who worked at the Eureka Mill where he is treaded like a part of a machine. The poem ends, "*and let me not forget / your lives were more than that*" (pp. xv–xvi>). This example brings together many of the features of Rash's poetry. The language is simple and direct, primarily single-syllable words. He does not shy away from colloquial terms and subjects associated with Appalachian stereotypes,

such as "haint" and "kin" or the reference to moonshine. In like manner, the political message is not obscured. Instead, Rash foregrounds the speaker's concern that such a message should not reduce the lives of the mill hands to the political dimension only. Rash manages to convey the values of Appalachian speech through rhythm rather than through misspellings and grammatical shenanigans, preserving linguistic idiosyncrasies while investing the language with a kind of gravitas. In this way he is identifying with writers like James Still and Chris Offutt, who demonstrate that language as spoken in the region is distinct from what people still call standard American English and yet presents a richness and complexity of its own.

Rash's close attention to speech rhythms, his use of enjambment, and his attention to alliteration and internal rhyme give the poems a narrative force or drive that pulls the reader forward to the end, where Rash often will provide a payoff in the form of a volta or an additional insight. Because of the simple language and narrative energy, it is easy for the reader to miss (or overlook) the amount of depth and complexity that the poems present. On rereading, such riches become apparent. In the quoted passages above, for example, one might overlook that the worn-out tablecloth sheet is "Springmaid" and that the owner of the mill is Springs, or the metaphor of the writer's hand weaving a thread of truth, which serves to draw a parallel between the work of writing and the work of reading while reminding us of the ever-present threat of losing hands or fingers that the job of weaving in an industrial mill entailed. Because of his focus on specific eras and settings and on immediate details, Rash is often treated as a realist. *Eureka Mill*'s focus would seem to bear this out. But "*Invocation*" is, after all, a poem about magic, about a ritual attempt to summon a dead spirit, one that, at least by implication, succeeds. Like the works of Robert Frost, a poet to whom Rash occasionally makes reference, Rash's poetry conceals hidden thematic depths under a surface of realistic, occasionally folksy, portrayal. The poems in the volume run roughly in a chronological order, beginning with descriptions of agricultural

drought and debt, then moving on to the tribulations of factory work and mill-town life. In "Tobacco," the speaker describes the brutal process of trying to grow tobacco as a cash crop, "the kind of toil we'd never known before, / plowing, chopping, suckering and topping" (p. 6), only to become further indebted because prices fall in years of successful crops. "Handbill Distributed in Buncombe County, North Carolina: 1915" purports to be a found poem, a pamphlet promising the advantages of mill work: "In that mill my fourteen-year-old girl / earns more than a grown man in the hills" (p. 8). In "Bearings," the grandfather, unable to read, attempts to find his place in the mill village where all the houses look the same. Lost, he asks for his own name and is directed to the house of a man who was fired the week before. Rash turns this into a metaphor for finding himself in this new, alien world. He throws his old boots on the roof so that he can find his house in the future. The poem dramatizes the disorientation of the new life as well as the camaraderie of the mill village. In other poems, the workers deal with labor strife, loyalties conflicted because "Colonel" Springs claims he is losing money by keeping the mill open when others have closed ("1934," p. 39). Poems are also told from the organizers' perspectives and those of the women seeing their spouses deal with the stresses of mill work by getting drunk. "Breaking the Whistle" tells of a drunken act of sabotage where the workers disable the whistle to give themselves a few more hours of sleep. One dramatic monologue, "Last Interview," is from the perspective of Colonel Springs himself. It begins, "That's an early portrait on the wall" (p. 52), referring to himself, but also, chillingly, to Robert Browning's "My Last Duchess." Like that 1842 poem, this one turns into a screed, mocking the workers' agrarian hopes and the reporter's prolabor perspective. If all men are created equal, he says, "see how soon we sort the top ones out" (p. 52). Like Browning's Duke of Ferrara, Springs cannot see outside his own perspective, and unlike Browning's character, he doesn't even have the excuse of appreciating art. The workers' support of the mill and rejection of the union are demon-

strated to be a short-sighted decision that has only increased his contempt for them. Unlike many politically committed artists, Rash shows this to us rather than telling us about it.

The final poems deal with the grandfather's declining health and the next generation's move into the mill. In "First Shift," from a child's perspective, his parents join his grandfather at the mill, where he cannot follow. He expresses his gratitude and guilt. "July 1949" details the speaker's mother's move from a farm to become a mill worker, leaving a hoe to rust in a field, history repeating with a different outcome, once again a debt unpayable.

If the focus of *Eureka Mill* was work, Rash's second book of poems, *Among the Believers,* focuses on religion in the broadest sense. Published in 2000, it includes an introduction by Anthony Hecht, who says that Rash's work provides a "stunning experience" for the reader, an "achievement" that "inheres in ... remarkable skill, partly from the richness of his regional past, largely from his dramatic instincts, stoic voice and deep humanity" (p. xi). Hecht compares the reading of the volume as a whole to the experience of reading a "perfectly completed novella," mentioning William Faulkner, Flannery O'Connor, Eudora Welty, Anton Chekov, and Thomas Hardy as antecedents, as well as Robert Frost and Mark Twain. Acknowledging the overabundance of fiction writers in his list, he cites the "pervading and presiding atmosphere ... embodied in a landscape expressive of the destiny of all his characters" (p. xi). The consistency of setting found in *Eureka Mill* is somewhat broader here, encompassing Watauga, Madison, and Buncombe Counties, all in the mountains of western North Carolina, as well as the predominantly piedmont setting found in the previous volume.

The title suggests that these poems might be about religious subjects, a recurring pattern of reference in Rash's work. In an interview with Thomas Bjerre in *Appalachian Journal*, Rash characterized himself as a believer: "I grew up in a culture where belief was just a given; not having it was almost beyond imagination" (pp. 222–223). However, only one of the four sections is

explicitly concerned with Christian beliefs and practices, with a few of the poems in the other sections joining them. About half the poems deal with religion in this strict sense. This encourages the reader to look at the title in a broader context.

The specifically religious poems reflect Rash's engagement with his own Christian beliefs, which he has characterized as "more in Kierkegaard's camp than in Jerry Falwell's" (Bjerre, p. 223), which presumably means characterized by doubt and skepticism rather than by dogmatic certainties. In "Sunday Evening at Middlefork Creek Pentecostal Church" (p. 22), he draws a parallel between poetry and speaking in tongues: "Like poets, they know a fallen world's / words fail a true vision." Two poems are dramatic monologues from the perspective of an unknown "preacher," suggesting the doubting narrator of the Old Testament's Ecclesiastes.

In "A Preacher Who Takes Up Serpents Laments the Presence of Skeptics in His Church," the narrator links the unbelievers who "gawk like I'm something / in a tent at a county fair" with "manure maggots" who "wallow in the filth of man's creation," which a reader might see as a typical condemnation, except that he goes on to further link them with "the stench of sulphur" from the nearby heavily polluted Pigeon River. We realize that he is contrasting man's creation with God's creation, represented by the quiescent snakes he handles. He also criticizes "my own people" (p. 19), his congregants, who see him as acting out of pride. "Only the serpents sense the truth" as a coral snake adorns his wrist, "a harmless bright bracelet" (p. 20). In this poem, Rash casts a sympathetic eye on one of the most hot-button stereotypes about Appalachian religion. Of the many sects of evangelical Christians, outsiders do not look, for example, at the "no-hellers," who believe in a benevolent universe with no hell and a heaven that resembles an unspoiled Appalachia—it is always the snake handlers. These sects are invariably portrayed as suicidal fanatics who hate the fallen, sinful world and are doing all they can to leave it. In contrast, Rash's preacher sees the snakes as representing creation and the skeptics as representing the polluters. In "The Preacher Is Called to Testify

for the Accused," Rash riffs on Frost's "Design" and the supposed fatalism of Appalachians. The preacher explains that everything is meant to be, according to God's plan, and that is why his son Isaac, who had won a pistol playing poker, happened to meet his best friend, Ezra, on a warm riverbank, and why they proceeded to get drunk and argue, resulting in Isaac shooting Ezra. According to the preacher, this was no more of a crime than Judas's—also part of God's plan, resulting in the salvation of mankind. "If my son hangs," he concludes, his death is a betrayal. His death is like that of Judas, but he is condemned by self-righteous men like those who condemned Jesus. The poem is a rhetorical tour de force, either a brilliant piece of sophistry or the perspective of a brilliant but scary mind. If the judge or jury addressed in the poem should convict, they are aligning themselves with Pontius Pilate, suggesting that human justice and divine justice are at odds. It rewrites Frost's speculation about "design of darkness to appall," without the undercutting commentary, "If design govern in a thing so small" (Frost, p. 302).

Many of the poems refer to other kinds of belief, what could be called superstitions, such as the belief that an owl calling outside your window three nights in a row betokens death ("The Corpse Bird"), or that salamanders placed in a spring house purify the water ("Spring Lizards"). Others look back to Welsh and Scottish myths and legends for material ("On the Border," "From the Mabinogion"). To get a handle on Rash's theme in this volume, perhaps "Signs," which begins section 3, offers some clues. It explains that the speaker's kin were backward-looking in the sense that they believed in signs that explained the world. Their example has led him to believe that experience is only understood in retrospect, "when first translated by / signs first forgotten or misread" (p. 33). Whether we take the theocentric view of the preacher, or this view, which suggests that the cosmos operates through a kind of cosmic dramatic irony, Rash's believers are neither monolithic nor proscriptive in their beliefs.

The volume concludes with "Good Friday, 1995, Driving Westward," a title that references

John Donne's "Good Friday, 1613, Riding Westward." But whereas for Donne his westward motion is toward death rather than resurrection where "my Soules forme bends toward the East" (p. 454), as he imagines witnessing Christ's crucifixion, the speaker in this poem goes west to find comfort in an ancestral graveyard. He imagines his predecessors, "hardshell Baptists, farmers" emerging during their expected resurrection, "shaking dirt off strange new forms" to "take their first dazed steps toward heaven" (p. 71). He uses heliotropic imagery to emphasize that he is describing their belief that "the soul is another seed" and that "all things planted rise toward the sun" (p. 71), collapsing God into nature. Whereas Donne's poem is a tortured examination of the speaker's faith, Rash's is a calm affirmation of the ancestors' beliefs, an appropriate way to end a volume about believers.

Among the Believers was followed by *Raising the Dead* (2002) and more recently by *Waking* (2011). *Raising the Dead* is unified by location and theme, although the theme is less broadly sociocultural than the first two books. Most of the poems in this elegiac collection concern the creation of Lake Jocassee in western South Carolina, with some reference to nearby Lake Keowee. Both reservoirs were created by flooding valleys in the early 1970s, and together they represent almost 26,000 acres (41 square miles) of land covered. The flooding of these valleys displaced farms, roads, and communities in a pattern that has been repeated all over the South, mainly for reservoirs and hydropower development but also for projects like the Blue Ridge Parkway and Great Smoky Mountains National Park. Of the five sections in *Raising the Dead,* sections 1 and 5 deal directly with the flooded valley beneath Lake Jocassee; the other sections concern death and mourning in broader senses, with section 3 centering around the death of Rash's older cousin as a teenager in a highway accident. Section 2 is primarily historical, often about ancestors or ancestral figures, whereas section 4 concerns more contemporary events and settings. Each section concludes with a poem in italics that serves as a kind of coda. One of these, the volume's last poem, "*The Men Who Raised the Dead,*" is about moving the corpses from a soon-to-be-flooded graveyard. The gravediggers are characterized as older men chosen because they were familiar with loss. They work deliberately in hot May weather, resting often, bringing up coffins or small artifacts that had been part of the dead person's clothing. The poem ends with the quiet death of one of the workers, who is placed with the older remains: *"all the others to be saved / if not from death, from water"* (p. 71).

The poem both celebrates and ironizes the work of gravedigging. It is a small enough gesture from the faceless institutions that are separating people from ancestral land, but at the same time it is presented as a sort of dignifying ritual as performed by these local elders, complete with a sacrifice. Rash doesn't let us forget that these ancestral lands were appropriated once before, either. In "The Vanquished," we are reminded that "even two centuries gone / their absence lingered" in genes and names and in artifacts and bones disturbed by the plow. The speaker compares these traces of aboriginal peoples to "a once-presence / keen as the light of dead stars" (p. 6).

Flooding a settled valley is an apt metaphor for both ecological and cultural change, and this volume develops the first and extends the latter. Nature in Rash's earlier work took second place to the cultural landscape, but here seems to be emerging into a more central position, especially in short lyrics such as "Shee-Show" and "Carolina Parakeet," which celebrate an endangered flower and an extinct bird. In "The Wolves in the Asheville Zoo," the speaker thinks about an ancestor fresh from the British Isles hearing the cry of the wolf in this new land, after leaving a country where wolves "vanished far back as firedrakes" (p. 56). Nature and culture are not presented in a binary opposition here, but as interlinked forces that affect us through "blood-memory," a concept introduced in "First Shift" in *Eureka Mill* as a debt to the work of his forebears, but broadened here to serve as a mystical link between progenitor and ancestor.

Rash had written a couple of Civil War poems in *Among the Believers,* but his interest in the era begins to come into sharper focus in this

volume. "Antietam" tells the story of a man scaring vultures from a fox's corpse during a present-day visit to the Civil War battlefield, but connects it to the folklore belief in a mass return of the scavengers each year on the anniversary of this bloody battle. "Shelton Laurel" is a monologue in the form of a letter from a brother to a sister after the war. The brother admits to his participation in the 1863 Shelton Laurel massacre, where thirteen unarmed Unionists were shot by a Confederate brigade, including a boy of thirteen. Both groups consisted of members of the same community. Rash claims that "a lot of my own family fought for the Union" (Bjerre, p. 219), and that conflicting loyalties made for hard feelings after the war, even down to the present day. Shelton Laurel will continue to appear as a point of focus in Rash's poetry and fiction. In this poem, the brother has deserted following the massacre and is living in a cave. "Last week, / I watched our neighbors die like snakes. Gut-shot / then hacked with hoes until their moaning ceased.... I was there, dear sister, I was there, / and still feel I am there although I hide / miles away." He feels his life is "stilled like the hands of a broken pocket-watch" and he hopes to be able to emerge again. He cannot face a world that "will have its way with us despite / what we might wish, or once believed" (p. 23). The poem could be a suicide note, but the speaker's fascination with the blind fish he finds in the cave suggests otherwise. He seems to be setting himself up as a kind of hermit and, having given up on being a fighter, seems to be seeking some kind of absolution.

Waking, Rash's next poetry collection, follows many of the same threads that the other collections have traced. It contains five sections, containing ten, eleven, or twelve poems each. The volume as a whole has a kind of dual focus, concentric and eccentric, on the one hand focusing on artifacts and what William Blake called "minute particulars," while on the other hand looking outward at nature in a larger, although never a grand, scale. This dual view anticipates the contrasting points of view in his novel *Above the Waterfall* (2015), where two narrators, a jaded retiring sheriff and a park ranger who is also a naturalist/poet, give us very different images of the same events. Rash wears away relentlessly at the nature/culture divide, a quality he shares with other poets from the region, in John Lang's opinion: "For Rash, as for many Appalachian poets, nature is generally presented not apart from human activity but as part of a dynamic interaction based on an agrarian lifestyle (or on memories of that lifestyle)" (p. 51). The move to connect nature with religion that concludes *Among the Believers* becomes more apparent in the poems of *Waking*. The volume opens with an italicized poem, *"Resolution,"* that serves as a kind of ars poetica: it describes the varying conditions in a river, from whitewater to stillness, asserting that *"it's all beyond your reach,"* even though it seems to be *"as near and known as your outstretched hand"* (p. xi). This poem might also help us begin to understand Rash's obsessive interest with water, one of the first things a reader notices when looking at his work as a whole. The contrasting interplay between surface and depth forms the basic structure of the poem, beginning with the seemingly counterintuitive observation that the fastest-moving water is often the shallowest, the current being pushed to the surface. The speaker leads our attention away from the fast-moving shallows to *"here,"* deeper water where we can see the life of the river—crayfish and sculpin—as well as its foundation in rock, mica, and sand. As an introduction to a volume of poems, the statement *"It's all beyond your reach"* seems off-putting; we are used to invitations like Frost's "You come too." The last line shifts our attention from the unreachable depths to our own presence. An outstretched hand may be *"near and known"* to its owner, but it is also reaching toward those mysteries, or for help, perhaps. The river here, with its fast-moving surfaces and unreachable depths, can be a Hericlitean metaphor for existence as a continuous flow, or a critique of our modern life of dazzling surfaces that distract us with their *"surge and clatter"* but are *"quickly gone."* In providing us an image of the poem as a window through which we can see a world beyond, Rash gives us a version of the finger and the moon, reminding us that a nature poem serves as the finger pointing

to the moon, not the moon itself. The nature poet wants us to get out into nature, not only to read about it.

Many of the poems in this volume describe objects that provide links to or windows into nature or the past. Titles include "The Wallet," "Pocketknives," "Car Tags," "Mirror," "Hearth," "Bloodroot," "Raspberries," and "The Barn-Fox." In "Water Quilt," a grandmother insists on washing her quilts in a creek each spring, so that "some part /of water stayed in the cloth" (p. 70), providing a higher purity only found in the flowing stream. Here a yearly task becomes a ritual of cleansing but also a continuous link between nature and everyday life.

In "Spillcorn," a kinsman who logs in the forest carries a book to read. His profession and its product merge into the environment, the paper of the book acknowledged as leaves, and the power of reading seen as smoothing the roughness caused by logging. Although some of the poems are narrative, there seems to be a move toward lyrics that rely more on image than plot. Rash seems most comfortable with the short six- or seven-syllable lines that pull the reader on to a conclusion.

In interviews, Rash often points to Welsh models for his poetry and refers to Dylan Thomas and Gerard Manley Hopkins, English-language poets who mined Welsh poetics for forms and patterns. He has referred to *cynghanedd,* usually translated as "harmony," a technique that uses stress, alliteration, and rhyme within a line, as one of his poetic techniques borrowed from the Welsh, as well as the short seven-syllable line.

NOVELS

Rash's six novels, especially *Serena* (2008), have brought him recognition from beyond the Appalachian region. This is partly because of the change, with *Saints at the River* (2004), to national (as opposed to regional) publishing houses, but also simply because novels command a much broader audience. Film versions of two novels, *The World Made Straight* in 2015 and *Serena* in 2014, have been released, the second

starring Bradley Cooper and Jennifer Lawrence, to little positive notice. A film of his first novel, *One Foot in Eden,* was apparently in the works as well. Rash's expressed attitude toward film versions of his work is that

> I would defer to Harry Crews on that point.... He said, "They're not going to do anything to my book." He said it much more colorful language, but he said that the book is a thing itself. Having said that, I'm human, and if they did some awful thing with space aliens coming down to rescue Billy or Amy or something like that I would probably be horrified, but that's the devil's bargain you make if you allow someone to option the movie.
>
> (Bjerre, p. 227)

Of the two films, *The World Made Straight* is the stronger, despite *Serena*'s star power. It sticks closely to the 2006 novel and offers above-average performances. Noah Wyle does a solid job as Candler and singer Steve Earle is an amazingly creepy villain as the drug lord Carlton Toomey. *Serena*'s major problem is that the director tries to humanize the title character, taking away some of the mythic power that readers find in her in the novel. The film also eliminates the "chorus" of mountaineers who comment, sometimes humorously, on the events in the novel. At least one of the devil's bargains has paid off.

Rash's first novel, *One Foot in Eden* (2002), is concerned with the flooding of the Jocassee Valley, taking place in the 1950s, as the countryside that will be flooded to form the Jocassee reservoir is being prepared. Rash is revisiting material he wrote about in *Raising the Dead* and in the story "Speckled Trout" from *Chemistry and Other Stories* (2007). This novel focuses on a love triangle that results in the death of one character. Holland Winchester is a local troublemaker and Korean War veteran who suddenly disappears. Sheriff Will Alexander investigates, leading him to suspect Holland's neighbor, Billy Holcombe, who has ample motive in that his wife, Amy, has had an affair with Holland. But no body can be found. The story is told from the perspectives of, respectively, the sheriff, Billy, Amy, a deputy, and finally, Isaac, the son of Amy and Billy and the biological son of the murdered man. A plot that could easily become a melo-

drama turns in Rash's treatment into a study of the tensions brought to a specific locale by the forces of a larger history. The story, like others by Rash, is labeled "Southern gothic" by readers, perhaps because of its matter-of-fact treatment of the details of dealing with a dead body—Billy manages to outwit the sheriff by concealing the body in a tree above a horse's corpse, thereby explaining the presence of vultures. The title emphasizes one of Rash's recurring themes, perhaps taken from his study of British folklores—the idea of betweenness, of liminality. To have "one foot in Eden" is, presumably, to have one foot in the fallen world as well. The setting of the soon-to be-flooded valley emphasizes this, as do the sheriff's musings about the Cherokees, a previously displaced population from the same area. Sheriff Alexander is one of a long line of Rash characters who are locals but also intellectuals, aware of the movement of larger forces around them. As observer-participant in the larger drama, he is balanced by Holland's mother, a widow who is purported to be a witch, who dispenses folk remedies and advice to Amy and her son, Isaac. Isaac eventually discovers the secret of his parentage.

Saints at the River, Rash's second novel, also deals with conflicts over land use. This one has a contemporary South Carolina setting and concerns a Midwestern teenager who is visiting the area as a tourist with her family. Wading in the Tamassee, a local whitewater river, she slips into the water and is washed over a waterfall and drowned. Her body is trapped in an underwater cave behind a powerful hydraulic, an eddy that holds objects in place, and the question of how to retrieve her remains becomes a focal point for debate between various interests within the community, as well as a focus for national media attention.

The novel is narrated by Maggie Glenn, a photographer sent up from Columbia to cover the story. Because she is an Oconee County native, her editor expects her to be able to mediate between the mountain folk and the reporter he is sending upstate with her. The drowned girl's father, Herb Kowalsky, wants to have a portable dam placed in the river to divert the current

enough to retrieve the body. Local environmentalist Luke Miller, the leader of a group of river guides and Maggie's former lover, insists that the Wild and Scenic Rivers Act, which provides legal protection for the river, would be violated by the anchor points that building the dam would place in the riverbed. Local pulpwooders and developers support Kowalsky's position because such a precedent might allow for a more open-ended interpretation of the law that they could turn to their benefit. Kowalsky makes the mistake of criticizing the local search-and-rescue team who have been risking their lives, calling them hillbillies. The federal Forest Service representatives see their role as mediating between constituents rather than enforcing the law.

It turns out that Allen Hemphill, the reporter working with Maggie, has lost his wife and daughter in an accident, making him feel more sympathetic to Kowalsky. Maggie, on the other hand, although she is no longer enamored with Luke, sides with the preservationists. Ironically, one of her pictures accompanying Allen's article helps to bring political pressure to bear on the Forest Service to permit the dam. The photo shows Kowalsky with the river in the background, captioned "A father's grief" (p. 154). A combination of political muscle and the eloquent testimony of the drowned girl's mother allow the dam to be built, but it fails, and a local diver is drowned. The local ranger and sheriff refuse to allow the dam to be rebuilt, resulting in a standoff until the drowned diver's brother chooses to use an illegal and time-honored method to release the bodies. He throws three sticks of dynamite into the rapid, which brings up the bodies.

The novel also follows Maggie's personal struggle to come to terms with her father, who is dying of cancer. Although they share an intense love for the region, they too belong to clashing cultures. Her college education allows her to act superior, while his pride causes him to keep his distance. She finally does the right thing, according to the mores of her community—she chooses to come home and care for him.

This novel provides an example of the ways in which Rash recycles the same material in his three genres. "Something Rich and Strange," a

short story originally published in 2004 and collected in *Nothing Gold Can Stay* (2013) begins with the story of the girl's drowning with some details changed—she is from Nebraska, not Minnesota. The story takes a different direction in its account of the search and rescue. A diver who is also a high school teacher finds the girl, but is yanked away when he tries to move her. He claims to have felt life in her and heard her whispering, but refuses to go back in. Later he changes his mind, but they have to wait for weeks until the river goes down. During the second dive, he sees her, "less of what she had been, the blue rubbed from her eyes, flesh freed from the chandelier of bone" (p. 49), but he reports that she is no longer there, so the search is called off. A poem from *Waking* (2011) titled "The Girl in the River" describes a drowning, followed by a search by divers who can see her but not reach her; one of the divers approaches near enough to touch her hair but then almost drowns. The girl is left in the river, and the divers are tormented by dreams where she calls them to her with her eyes.

Each of the three treatments starts with the same events but leads us to a different conclusion. This demonstrates Rash's acute awareness of the differences between the genres, as well as a certain playfulness—a tendency to treat his own creations as fluid and flexible rather than fixed.

Rash's third novel, *The World Made Straight,* is a coming-of-age story about a young man in the 1970s, struggling to decide on a future that involves either drug dealing or college. Travis Shelton's dilemma is complicated by a mentor figure, who started out by going to college and leaving town but who returned to town to deal drugs. A curious young man, he is led into reading about his family by Leonard Shuler, the mentor, whom he moves in with after a disagreement with his father. Leonard encourages Travis to study for the GED high school equivalency exam, and the two seem to have positive mutual influence on each other. Shuler decides to stop dealing and takes Travis to visit the site of the Shelton Laurel massacre during the Civil War. Travis is descended from the family of a group of Unionist sympathizers who were killed by a Confederate unit made up of their neighbors. Leonard's ancestor, it turns out, was the surgeon for the Confederate unit and might have been present at the massacre.

Carlton Toomey, the local drug kingpin, enslaves Leonard's sometime girlfriend, Dena, over a drug debt. Travis releases her, setting the group up for a final confrontation that plays out like a Jacobean drama. At the novel's end, Travis heads out of town, but is it toward a new life, or will he end up coming back? We don't know.

Serena, Rash's fourth novel, was published in 2008 and was a finalist for the PEN/Faulkner Award for Fiction. According to Randall Wilhelm, "Rash's masterpiece to date is unquestionably the epic and ambitious *Serena,* a sweeping novel of Olympian proportions" (p. 17). It certainly represents a change in scope from the earlier novels, which tended to be fairly small in scale, especially considering the number of characters. Serena is longer, almost four hundred pages, and broader in scope that anything Rash has written to date. It tells the story of the title character, wife and business partner to the Boston timber baron George Pemberton, during the early years of the Great Depression. They are in North Carolina, trying to extract as much timber as possible before other interests, including the real-life naturalist and writer Horace Kephart, can establish a national park in the Smokies. Rash opens the book with a quotation from Christopher Marlowe: "*A hand, that with a grasp may grip the worlde,*" and the allusion is appropriate for a story with the kind of heroine that could be one of Marlowe's overreachers. Serena is less a developed character than an embodiment of will, dedicated to the colonial exploitation of North Carolina and then the Brazilian mahogany forests, where there is, she says, "no law but nature's law" (p. 29).

The novel begins with Pemberton bringing his bride, Serena, home to his camp after a whirlwind courtship and marriage. They are met at the station by a young woman, pregnant with Pemberton's child, and her father, who pulls a knife on Pemberton. Pemberton gets out his wedding gift from Serena, an elkhorn hunting knife. He easily disembowels the father, who dies on

the spot. Serena returns his knife to the daughter and advises her to sell it because "It's all you'll ever get from my husband and me" (p. 10). Already conversant with the details and personalities of the camp, Serena immediately takes charge, riding out on her white Arabian horse to supervise the lumbermen. She wins a bet with one of the workers about the amount of board feet in a tree, and orders a Mongolian golden eagle to hunt the rattlesnakes that plague the clear-cuts, staying up late for days to break and train the wild bird. The story is told from a limited third-person perspective that follows Pemberton, except for short passages that concern Rachel, the mother of Pemberton's son, and a group of loggers who provide commentary on the action, often humorous, much like the commentary of a Greek chorus.

Serena saves the life of a local man who loses his hand in a logging accident, and he becomes her loyal factotum, following her everywhere and doing her bidding. When she miscarries and the doctor says she won't be able to have any more children, she decides to have Pemberton's illegitimate son, now a young child, and his mother killed. Rachael narrowly escapes, but Serena finds out that Pemberton has sent Rachael money. At Pemberton's birthday celebration, she brings in her henchman's mother, a blind woman who is rumored to be clairvoyant. When asked how Pemberton will die, she replies, "They ain't one thing can kill a man like you" (p. 344), to the guests' amusement. Serena encourages Pemberton to go hunting for his most desired trophy, a rumored mountain lion, now exceedingly rare, and she provides him with a special rifle.

When Pemberton goes off on his hunt, he eats a sandwich that Serena has poisoned, then is led into a nest of rattlesnakes by her man, appropriately named Galloway. Snakebit, he falls and breaks his ankle. Galloway helps him into a clearing, leaving him for the panther to finish off. As the panther approaches, Pemberton recalls his first meeting with Serena. In this way several things kill him, not one thing.

Several reviewers noted the plot's similarity to *Macbeth* and the Jacobean revenge dramas. An essay by Christopher Morrow investigates the

Macbeth connection, examining whether it is close enough to be called an adaptation despite Rash's reluctance to describe it as such (Morrow, p. 154). Pemberton's downfall, like Macbeth's, comes despite an apparent prognostication of invulnerability. Serena, even more so than Lady Macbeth, exemplifies an indomitable force. As such she seems never to have moments of doubt or regret, and the drama is played out in an unambiguous moral context. From the opening scene, it is clear that this is a story of good versus evil: good represented by the mountain folk and evil by the forces of voracious capitalism, personified by the Pembertons. It is in the next generation, as the brief epilogue demonstrates, that Serena does get her just desserts.

As in the case of *Saints at the River*, Rash published a short story, "Pemberton's Bride," in his 2007 collection *Chemistry and Other Stories*, which follows the basic plot of the first part of the novel with some name changes. The short story ends with the sheriff confronting Pemberton about Sarah's (Rachael's counterpart in the story) drowning and the murder of her child, with Serena and her henchman, here named Chaney, implicated by the evidence. In both cases, the wedge between Pemberton and Serena becomes the child after she has lost the ability to have children, but the short story provides a simpler and more brutal resolution, one that lacks the leavening presence of the chorus of mountaineers. Again, readers get an opportunity to explore the differences between what the two types of fiction can accomplish, beginning with the same materials.

In his next two novels, Rash returned to the more intimate scale of his earlier works. Both *The Cove* (2011) and *Above the Waterfall* (2015) have a similar focus on a few characters. *The Cove* takes place during World War I and revolves around a farm and homestead tucked into a mountain cove, one that is believed to be cursed or haunted. There Laurel Shelton lives with her brother Hank, who has returned from the war missing an arm. In the nearby college town, a local military recruiter, Chauncey, is carrying out a campaign of intolerance and persecution against all things German, especially a German professor

at the college. A young man, Walter, a flutist who claims to be mute, comes to the cove and becomes ill from being stung by a swarm of yellow jackets. Laurel nurses him back to health, and she eventually learns that he is a German national who has escaped from a nearby internment camp. Walter and Laurel fall in love, but eventually Chauncey finds out that they have been harboring what he considers to be an enemy, and he allows himself to be bullied into leading a lynch mob against Walter. Things go bad quickly, and Chauncey ends up shooting Laurel by mistake, then killing Hank on purpose to keep him quiet. He stumbles into a newly dug well and is never heard from again. Meanwhile, armistice is declared and Walter is able to walk away in the confusion of the celebration.

Chauncey is a bit of a cartoonish character, and Rash, sensitive to criticism about this, actually revised the book between the hardcover and paperback editions to downplay his part in the narrative. The book emphasizes the differences between privilege based on social class (Chauncey's jingoism is based on ignorance and insecurity) and the ways in which art (Walter's musical talent) and education (Laurel is an avid reader and amateur naturalist) can bring richness to the most isolated lives. It leaves open the question of environmental determinism—is the cove really cursed?

Above the Waterfall, like *Saints at the River,* focuses on environmental conflicts caused, in this case, by class conflicts. The story is narrated, like *One Foot in Eden,* using first-person perspectives but with only two narrators. One is Les, the local sheriff, and the other is Becky Shytle, a Forest Service ranger and environmental educator. Their perspectives are radically different, allowing Rash to include poetry within his fiction—Becky's perspective includes poems and notes from her nature journals.

The story involves an upscale resort with a stocked trout stream, which borders both a state park and the farmstead of Gerald, an elderly local who is Becky's friend and mentor and a thorn in the side of the resort owner, Tucker, who doesn't appreciate Gerald's trespassing and spooking his well-heeled clients. Les is a few weeks away from retiring as sheriff and is dealing with a crystal meth epidemic. He is a mediator who just wants everybody to get along, a pragmatist who takes bribes from local marijuana growers while planning regular meth busts. Les and Becky are cautiously pursuing a potential romantic relationship that Les imagines as a post on a dating website: "Man who encouraged clinically depressed wife to kill herself seeks woman, traumatized by school shooting, who later lived with ecoterrorist bomber" (p. 10). Both see themselves as damaged goods. Becky takes solace in her spartan lifestyle and reverential devotion to nature and nature writing. Whereas Les's first response seems to be to fix the world, Becky's is to withdraw from it. If nature is a church, Les is a missionary and Becky is a hermit.

So when someone pours kerosene into the trout stream and the resort's security camera shows Gerald was there, Les is forced to put him under house arrest while he picks his way through a political minefield to find the real culprit. This he does, following a trail that leads from the pawnbroker by way of the meth-user community to some of the town's more upright citizens. The novel's two voices are so divergent that it reads like a crime novel that had an unlikely encounter with a book of nature poetry. Les sorts things out, further bending an already bent law and sacrificing his marijuana fund in exchange for what he regards as a karmic debt. At the conclusion, he and Becky embrace on a bridge over the stream. Their relationship is left an open question.

Like *Saints at the River* and *Serena,* this plot focuses on the environmental conflicts and contradictions that shape present-day concerns, but it muddies the waters, so to speak. For Rash, the conflict is never as simple as humanity versus nature or the economy versus the environment. He gives readers a window into the southern Appalachians and the nature and cultures that make it such a compelling place. Becky has been present at a school shooting, which could represent the closest thing to pure evil that exists in contemporary American life, but she has also been involved with an ecoterrorist, someone willing to kill humans in order to prevent damage to nature. The crime described here, killing

hatchery-grown trout that are provided for rich folk to catch in a very comfortable, artificial version of "nature," hardly rises to the level of the Pemberton's wholesale clear-cutting, which took a constant, deadly toll on both humans and the environment. Les's messy solution does not make him seem heroic, and Becky's withdrawal into nature writing and leading groups of schoolchildren around a preserve is not world changing. Rash brackets the book with references to the cave paintings at Lascaux, perhaps to suggest that, in the thirty-thousand-year span of human creation, our perspectives can only be limited, our solutions contingent.

LATER SHORT FICTION

The bulk of this essay has focused on poetry and longer fiction, so it must fail to do comprehensive justice to what many consider Rash's strongest genre, the short story. In all, Rash has published fifty stories in his various collections, as well several more that have not been collected. After *The Night the New Jesus Fell to Earth* (1997), Rash published *Casualties* (2000), a collection that is now out of print. Many of the same stories (eight out of fourteen) were included in his next collection, *Chemistry and Other Stories* (2007), with some revisions, which Lang describes as "not substantive but stylistic" (p. 23). The title of *Casualties* suggests both the results of war and Rash's continuing theme of emotional or spiritual damage. In these two collections, while abandoning the close focus on one location, Rash keeps to a small group of locations, including Oconee County in South Carolina, where Lake Jocassee is located, and Watauga and Madison Counties in North Carolina, keeping to the piedmont and mountain areas of the state.

"Chemistry" takes place in both Cliffside and Oconee County and involves a high school chemistry teacher who abandons the Presbyterian Church to return to his Pentecostal roots after dealing with a severe depression. He also takes up scuba diving. The story is told from the point of view of his son, who is puzzled by his father's peculiar behavior but tries to be supportive. Both the Presbyterianism and the lake house where he

goes diving are representations of the climb in social class that his education has made possible, but the days when he "could understand everything from a single atom to the whole universe with a blackboard and a piece of chalk, and it was as beautiful as any hymn the way it all came together," are gone, and he feels the need "to look somewhere else" (*Chemistry,* p. 36). His hobby leads to his drowning, caused by what the coroner describes as "nitrogen narcosis, sometimes called rapture of the deep" (p. 38), and the son takes comfort in the fact that he had taken off his mask in his last moments. "But sometimes as I sit on the porch with darkness settling around me, it is easy for me to imagine that my father pulling off the mask was something more—a gesture of astonishment at what he drifted toward" (p. 39). The obvious conflict here is between the scientific view that sees depression as "a chemical imbalance … with an easy solution, so many milligrams of Elavil, so many volts of electricity," and the religious perspective that sees it as not "that simple" (p. 35). The story contains a more subtle conflict, between a father who grew up in one world and his family that lives in another. Neither the mother nor the son has the tools to understand the father's beliefs or his suffering, but the son is trying to do so.

One of the new stories in *Chemistry and Other Stories* takes its title from a poem by another writer who kept revising his work, William Butler Yeats. "Their Ancient, Glittering Eyes" stands out because of its humorous treatment. Three old-timers at Riverside Gas and Grocery begin a quest to capture a huge fish that a boy has seen in a pool outside the store. The old men catch a glimpse of the fish and are hooked. The game warden, from Wisconsin and therefore a Yankee, treats the sighting with condescension and declares the fish a trout or a carp, suggesting to the old men that their eyesight might not be very good. The sighting brings on a frenzy of fishing and speculation in the small community. A rainbow of colors and flavors of rubber worms, lures, flies, and live baits are deployed, all in vain. After some time with no success, the town's enthusiasm declines, and the three are left by themselves. They mount a

campaign against the fish, procuring a heavy-duty ocean fishing rod, a hay hook, and a live water snake as bait. Rash describes the preparations with mock heroic language that emphasizes the elders' age and infirmities. When they finally do manage to hook the monster fish, they play it up to a sandbar where they can see it clearly.

> "Lord amercy," Campbell exclaimed, for what they saw was over six feet long and enclosed in a brown suit of prehistoric armor, the immense tail curved like a scythe.
>
> (p. 18)

Using a library reference book, they identify it as a sturgeon. On impulse, they release it, but manage to break off one of its armored scales with the hook. They confront Meekins, the game warden, with this evidence:

> "*Acipenser fulvescens,*" Rudisell said, the Latin uttered slowly as if an incantation. He put the scute back in his pocket and, without further acknowledgement of Meekins's existence, stepped around the truck and onto the hardtop. Campbell followed with the fishing equipment and Creech came last with the book. It was a slow, dignified procession. They walked westward toward the store, the late-afternoon sun burnishing their cracked and wasted faces. Coming out of the shadows, the blinked their eyes as if dazzled, much in the manner of old-world saints who have witnessed the blinding brilliance of the one true vision.
>
> (p. 22)

Rash is working within a web of allusions here. The closing lines above suggest the three wise men present at Jesus' birth. Yeats's poem quoted in the title describes the eyes of Chinese sages carved into a landscape made of the blue semiprecious stone, lapis lazuli. The poem concludes "their eyes, / their ancient, glittering eyes, are gay" (p. 295). The fish, who is seen briefly to have "an array of rusting hooks and lures that hung from the lips like medals" (p. 19), recalls the Elizabeth Bishop poem "The Fish," where the speaker catches and releases a battered, monstrous fish whose mouth shows five old lines "like medals with their ribbons." The speaker in Bishop's poem says, "victory filled up / the little rented boat" (p. 44), much in the way that the three men are victors in their contest with the

supercilious warden. They are ridiculous and dignified at the same time, their quest absurd yet somehow sacramental.

Burning Bright (2010), Rash's fourth collection, speaks to his success in that all twelve of the stories were first published in periodicals, some of which, like *Tin House* and *Oxford American,* are more national than regional publications. It won the prestigious Frank O'Connor International Short Story Award. In terms of variety of settings, Rash's trajectory from Cliffside seems to be widening. Although most of the stories take place in the southern mountains, two, "The Corpse Bird," set in Raleigh, and "The Woman Who Believed in Jaguars," set in Columbia, South Carolina, extend beyond into the flatland South. Like the poetry, Rash's newer stories take place in a variety of time periods, from the Civil War to the present. One story, "Into the Gorge," won Rash his second O. Henry Prize.

"The Ascent" was included in *Best American Short Stories 2010.* Like a growing number of Rash's works, including *The World Made Straight* and *Above the Waterfall,* this story deals with drug addiction, specifically methamphetamines. Jared, the main character, is a fifth-grade boy who is spending the first day of his Christmas vacation away from a home "where everything, the rickety chairs and sagging couch, the gaps where the TV and microwave had been, felt sad" (p. 76). He is hiking up into Great Smoky Mountains National Park, pretending to fight bears with his pocketknife to impress a girl at school who had told him that his clothes smelled bad. He comes upon a wrecked plane that contains two frozen corpses, a man and a woman. He finds a ring on the woman's finger and brings it back to his parents, who are busy arranging beer cans, tin foil, fishing bobbers, and sticks in the fireplace to make "a Christmas tree, … just one that's chopped up, is all" (p. 82). His father leaves with the ring, and Jared helps his mother light the Christmas tree, "the foil and cans withered and blackened, the fishing bobbers melting" (p. 82). A couple of days later he returns to the plane and brings his parents the man's watch, a Rolex. They head for town and he returns to the plane, which he pretends to fix, then sits in

the back as the lethal cold settles in, imagining that they are taking off.

Rash's ironic use of the Christmas tree and the hearth, symbols of family togetherness and holiday celebration, and the inversion by which an eleven-year-old becomes the caregiver for his parents, brings into focus the devastation wrought by addiction. Jared's suicidal abandonment of his parents mirrors their abandonment of him.

"Lincolnites" is set during the Civil War, and according to Lang, is based on an incident from Rash's family stories (p. 114). Lincolnites were Union sympathizers like the ones killed in the Shelton Laurel massacre that informs *The World Made Straight* and several of Rash's poems. In this story, Lily, a pregnant young woman with an infant child who is left to run a farm by herself, has to deal with a Confederate soldier who wants to "requisition" her chickens and her plow horse. She offers to trade—"You know my meaning" (p. 199)—so that she can keep the horse. She takes him to her root cellar and pins him to the floor with a knitting needle through his stomach, locking him in the cellar until she is sure he's dead. The she goes back, nurses her child, and prepares supper. She anticipates burying the body, hoping "she could get it done by noon" (p. 205).

Many of Rash's stories are concerned with correcting or complicating stereotypes about Appalachian culture. In the Civil War stories, he often refutes the "solid South" idea that everyone in the South supported slavery and secession. Another important stereotype that he takes issue with is that of hillbilly ignorance. Many stories take place in or near Boone or Mars Hill, college towns in the mountains, and many of his characters have advanced degrees and hold education as a core value.

In *Nothing Gold Can Stay* (2013), some reviewers saw a new harshness or lack of sympathy in Rash's work. This can be seen in some of his more satirical pieces, such as "A Servant of History," which looks back to the early twentieth-century ballad collectors, when folklorists such as Cecil Sharp and Olive Dame Campbell searched the Appalachian region for songs and ballads. In this story, the servant of history is James Wilson, a newly graduated Brit who sees

himself as "venturing among the new world's Calibans" (p. 83) to retrieve authentic ballads. He arrives in Sylva and is rather disappointed to find no log cabins and teepees, but "actual houses, most prosperous looking" (p. 84). He finds an informant, who tells him "I a go ba rafe" (p. 86), when asked his name (I go by Rafe), which Wilson misunderstands as Iago Barafe, which he thinks is properly Elizabethan. A somewhat greater misunderstanding results when Rafe takes him to visit the McDonalds, where the ancient grandmother sings him a traditional ballad. When he asks for more, and tries to ingratiate himself by mentioning a family tartan, Clan Campbell, the mood changes. The old woman sings "The Snows of Glencoe," a description of the massacre of the hospitable McDonalds by the treacherous Campbells who were their guests. Wilson is treated to a hot poker applied to his tongue before he escapes. He returns in silent triumph to England, all of his notions about new world savagery confirmed.

The satire is obvious here, aimed at the outsiders who see Appalachians as a strange and isolated people with unique cultural features, the same culture managers who encouraged dulcimer playing because it was more "authentic" to their idealized idea of Appalachia than the more raucous banjo.

Another story, "The Trusty," Rash's first story to be published in the *New Yorker,* also deals with misunderstanding and stereotyping. The story's title character is a trusty for a chain gang working on a road. He carries water from an isolated cabin, where he meets a young woman married to an older man. Over the course of several days, he flirts with her and tells her he has enough money to get them both away if she will help him to escape. She agrees to take him to Asheville over the mountain. He leaves his water buckets and meets her behind her house, where she has him put on her husband's shoes. Once in the woods, he changes into the clothes she gives him and follows her on a long journey up and down, across streams and through laurel slicks. It is getting dark when he recognizes his own handprint where he had stopped to drink before. He hears the click of a rifle and realizes

that he has been duped. His scorn for these country folk has been obvious, and now he realizes that they have outsmarted him, and that no one will ever find his body.

A somewhat gentler story is "The Woman at the Pond," where a young man fishing meets a woman with a bruised cheek stranded by her lover. She assures him that she will be fine, and he leaves her there, but returns years later as the pond is drained to make sure her body is not found. As he leaves, the narrator says, "I can look back and I can no longer tell what was and what is" (p. 208).

CONCLUSION

Rash's work has certain unifying themes and images. Culture, both dynamic and static, looms large. Much of the thrust of his work is against common stereotypes, which is appropriate because Appalachia continues to be rife with stereotypical representations. He has a keen eye for problems emerging out of class conflict, again a major issue in a region that has been constantly exploited for its resources by outside interests. Thematically, generational conflict, war trauma and other types of psychological damage, religious doubt and belief, economic hardship, the push and pull of rural life, educational achievement, the power of heritage, the burdens of the past, escaping home and returning to it, all appear in his writings. The imagery that he keeps returning to is that of water—brooks, streams, whitewater rivers, waterfalls, lakes, and reservoirs suffuse his work—water as a metaphor for time, for change, for the past, for baptism, even as a portal to the next world. At the same time, fire imagery also frequently appears, usually in conjunction with the home fire. Nature underlies and animates everything, serving less as a backdrop than as illumination for the stage of Rash's writing. Rash's world, like that of his muse Flannery O'Connor, is not always a kind place, but it is an intense one, fused with mystery and power. Finally Rash is an unabashedly literary writer, as the titles of his books demonstrate: Frost, Blake, O'Connor, Yeats, hymns, the Bible, Shakespeare, and Marlowe might begin the list,

but one would have to refer to the whole of the Western tradition, especially in its Southern U.S. and Appalachian branches, to begin to find all of the echoes and influences here. We can expect him to continue to bring us novels, poems, and stories that emerge from a region but speak to a world's concerns and that give us powerful insights into the unique and dynamic features of the natural world.

Selected Bibliography

WORKS OF RON RASH

NOVELS
One Foot in Eden. Charlotte, N.C.: Novello Festival Press, 2002.
The World Made Straight. New York: Holt, 2006.
Saints at the River. New York: Holt, 2004.
Serena. New York: Ecco/HarperCollins, 2008.
The Cove. New York: Ecco/HarperCollins, 2011.
Above the Waterfall. New York: Ecco/HarperCollins, 2015.

SHORT STORY COLLECTIONS
The Night the New Jesus Fell to Earth and Other Stories from Cliffside, North Carolina. Columbia, S.C.: Bench Press, 1994.
Casualties. Beaufort, S.C.: Bench Press, 2000.
Chemistry and Other Stories. New York: Picador, 2007.
Burning Bright. New York: Ecco/HarperCollins, 2010.
Nothing Gold Can Stay. New York: Ecco/HarperCollins, 2013.

POETRY COLLECTIONS
Eureka Mill. Corvallis, Ore.: Bench Press, 1998.
Among the Believers. Oak Ridge, Tenn.: Iris, 2000.
Raising the Dead. Oak Ridge, Tenn.: Iris, 2002.
Waking. Spartanburg, S.C.: Hub City, 2011.

COLLECTED WORKS
Wilhelm, Randall, ed. *The Ron Rash Reader.* Columbia: University of South Carolina Press, 2014.

CRITICAL AND BIOGRAPHICAL STUDIES
Baldwin, Kara. "'Incredible Eloquence': How Ron Rash's

Novels Keep the Celtic Literary Tradition Alive." *South Carolina Review* 39, no. 1:37–46 (fall 2006).

Boyelston, Matthew. "Wild Boar in These Woods: The Influence of Seamus Heaney on the Poetry of Ron Rash." *South Carolina Review* 41, no. 2:11–17 (spring 2009).

Brinkmeyer, Robert H., Jr. "Discovering Gold in the Back of Beyond: The Fiction of Ron Rash." *Virginia Quarterly Review* 89, no. 3:219–223 (summer 2013).

Brown, Joyce Compton. "The Dark and Clear Vision of Ron Rash." *Appalachian Heritage* 30, no. 4:15–24 (fall 2002).

Brown, Joyce Compton, and Mark Powell. "Ron Rash's *Serena* and the 'Blank and Pitiless Gaze' of Exploitation in Appalachia." *North Carolina Literary Review* 19:70–89 (2010).

Clabough, Casey. "An Appalachian Man of Letters." Review of *The Ron Rash Reader* and *Understanding Ron Rash*. *Sewanee Review* 123, no. 2:345–350 (spring 2015).

Graves, Jesse. "Lattice Work: Formal Tendencies in the Poetry of Robert Morgan and Ron Rash." *Southern Quarterly* 45, no. 1:78–86 (fall 2007).

Higgins, Anna Dunlap. "'Anything but Surrender': Preserving Southern Appalachia in the Works of Ron Rash." *North Carolina Literary Review* 13:49–58 (2004).

House, Silas. "Making Himself Heard." *Appalachian Heritage* 30, no. 4:11–14 (fall 2002).

———. "A Matter of Life and Death: Old and New Appalachia Meet in *One Foot in Eden*." *Iron Mountain Review* 20:21–25 (spring 2004).

Lane, John. "The Girl in the River: The Wild and Scenic Chattooga, Ron Rash's *Saints at the River*, and the Drowning of Rachel Trois." *South Carolina Review* 41, no. 1:162–167 (fall 2008).

Lang, John. *Understanding Ron Rash*. Columbia: University of South Carolina Press, 2014. (The bibliography at the back of the book is the most recent and comprehensive one available.)

Lee, Maureen, and John Lee. "Ron Rash Bibliography." *South Carolina Review* 39, no. 1:46–56 (fall 2006).

Lefler, Susan M. "Inside the Prism: Themes That Flow Throughout Ron Rash's Works." *Appalachian Heritage* 32, no. 4:72–77 (fall 2004).

Miller, Mindy Beth. "Long Remember, Long Recall: The Preservation of Appalachian Regional Heritage in Ron Rash's *One Foot in Eden*." *Journal of Kentucky Studies* 26:198–209 (September 2009).

Morrow, Christopher L. "Acknowledgment, Adaptation, and Shakespeare in Ron Rash's *Serena*." *South Central Review* 30, no. 2:131–161 (summer 2013).

Peeler, Tim. "Resting on the Gift of Their Labors: The Poetry of Ron Rash." *Iron Mountain Review* 20:7–12 (spring 2004).

"Ron Rash Issue." Edited and with an introduction by John Lang. *Iron Mountain Review* 20:2–36 (spring 2004).

Smith, Jimmy Dean. "Spirit Country: The Voice of the Earth and Ron Rash's Southern Appalachia." *North Carolina Literary Review* 20:111–120 (2011).

Smith, Newton. "Words to Raise the Dead: The Poetry of Ron Rash." *Iron Mountain Review* 20:13–20 (spring 2004).

Vernon, Zachary. "The Role of Witness: Ron Rash's Peculiarly Historical Consciousness." *South Carolina Review* 42, no. 2:19–21 (2010).

Willis, Rachel. "Masculinities and Murder: George Pemberton in Ron Rash's *Serena*." *James Dickey Review* 24, no. 2:13–34 (spring–summer 2013).

INTERVIEWS

Bjerre, Thomas, "'The Natural World Is the Most Universal of Languages': An Interview with Ron Rash." *Appalachian Journal* 34, no. 2:216–214 (winter 2007).

Brown, Joyce Compton. "Ron Rash: The Power of Blood-Memory." In *Appalachia and Beyond: Conversations with Writers from the Mountain South*. Edited by John Lang. Knoxville: University of Tennessee Press, 2006. Pp. 335–353.

Kingsbury, Pam. "Language Can Be Magical: An Interview with Ron Rash." http://www.southernscribe.com/zine/authors/Rash_Ron.htm

Shuler, Jack. "Interview with Ron Rash." *South Carolina Review* 33, no. 1:11–16 (fall 2000).

OTHER SOURCES

Bishop, Elizabeth. *Poems*. New York: Farrar, Straus and Giroux, 2011.

Donne, John. *The Complete English Poems of John Donne*. Edited by C. A. Patrides. London: J. M. Dent and Sons, 1985.

Frost, Robert. *The Poetry of Robert Frost*. Edited by Edward Connery Lathem. New York, Henry Holt/St. Martin's, 1969.

Yeats, William Butler. *The Poems: A New Edition*. Edited by Richard J. Finneran. New York: Macmillan, 1983.

FILMS BASED ON THE WORKS OF RON RASH

Serena. Screenplay by Christopher Kyle. Directed by Suzanne Bier. Magnolia Pictures, 2014.

The World Made Straight. Screenplay by Shane Danielson. Directed by David Burris. Millennium Entertainment, 2015.

MONA SIMPSON

(1957—)

Laurie Champion

MONA SIMPSON'S SIX novels represent contemporary American life. She focuses primarily on families, portraying nontraditional lifestyles. Many of her works depict single-parent households and concentrate on children's relationships with their mothers. Often, the classic search-for-the-father motif is enacted by children or young adolescents. Frequently the characters undergo a coming-of-age experience, and in this way the novels represent the bildungsroman tradition. In addition to looking for their fathers, her characters search for intangibles such as love, home, friendship, and parenthood. Throughout her fictional works, many of which draw from her own intriguing life experiences, characters both literally and symbolically embark on journeys. Although Simpson gives vivid details of the landscape and describes the geography as her characters travel about, she remains focused on character development. As in the classic journey motif, it is not the destination but the journey that becomes important in Simpson's works. Whether they find their fathers, discover what their mothers' boyfriends are hiding, or discover whatever else they seek to know is not nearly as significant as how the characters change as a result of their searches.

BIOGRAPHY

Mona (Elizabeth) Simpson was born Mona Jandali on June 14, 1957, to Joanne Carole Schieble, who grew up on a Wisconsin farm, and Abdulfattah Jandali, an immigrant from Homs, Syria. Mona spent her youth in Green Bay, Wisconsin. When she was a young child her father left the family, and her parents divorced in 1962. Joanne then married George Simpson, an ice-skating teacher, and Mona took her stepfather's name. When Mona was twelve years old, her mother and George Simpson divorced, and she and her mother moved to Los Angeles. Years later, when Mona was in her twenties, she learned that her mother and Jandali had given birth to a son before she was born. That brother turned out to be Apple cofounder Steve Jobs (1955–2011), who had been adopted as an infant. Once the siblings were united, they remained friends for the rest of Jobs's life.

Simpson graduated from Beverly Hills High School, and in 1979 she received a B.A. degree from the University of California, Berkeley. She worked for various newspapers as a journalist in the San Francisco Bay area, then moved to New York, where she was a student in the graduate writing program at Columbia University. She received an M.F.A. in 1983 and later worked as an editor at the *Paris Review*.

In 1993 Simpson married Richard Appel, who wrote for the television series *The Simpsons*. The character "Mona Simpson," Homer's mother in that series, is named for her, as Appel used her name for one episode and it clicked. Beginning in 1988 she was a Bard Center fellow, teacher, and then Sadie Samuelson Levy Professor of Languages and Literature at Bard College. In late 1993, when Appel got a job writing for television, Simpson moved back to Southern California. She traveled back and forth from New York to Los Angeles to continue teaching at Bard for one semester a year. She and Appel had two children, Gabriel and Grace. She and Appel divorced, and she has continued to live in Los Angeles, where she is a professor at the University of California, Los Angeles. She also travels to New York, where she holds a distinguished position as writer in residence at Bard.

Simpson's writing has garnered extensive critical acclaim, including many awards, grants,

and fellowships. She was accepted to Yaddo, a prestigious writers' colony in Saratoga Springs, New York, where she finished her first novel, *Anywhere but Here* (1986). In 1995 she spent several weeks at the MacDowell Colony, a writers' retreat in New Hampshire. In 1986 she was awarded the Whiting Award and a National Endowment for the Arts grant. Two years later she was awarded a Guggenheim Fellowship and a Hodder Fellowship. In 1995 she received the Lila Wallace–Reader's Digest Writers' Award, then in 2001 the *Chicago Tribune*'s Heartland Prize. More recently, in 2008, she was given the Literature Award from the American Academy of Arts and Letters and was awarded Bard College's 2013 Mary McCarthy Prize.

Simpson began her literary career during the 1980s, while employed as an editor for the *Paris Review*. She began publishing short stories in distinguished literary magazines such as *Ploughshares, Harper's, North American Review,* and *Iowa Review.* Her short stories have been included in prestigious collections such as *Best American Short Stories, Pushcart Prize, Best of the Small Presses* and *20 Under 30.* Although she began her career as a short-story writer, Simpson is best known for her novels, beginning with the 1986 publication of *Anywhere but Here* and continuing through several more volumes including *Casebook,* which appeared in 2014.

ANYWHERE BUT HERE

Simpson's first novel, *Anywhere but Here* (1986), explores the dynamic relationship between Adele August and her adolescent daughter, Ann. After she was abandoned by Ann's father, Adele married Ted Diamond, an ice skating teacher, and as the novel begins Ann and Adele are now leaving him, driving from their home in Bay City, Wisconsin, to Southern California, where Adele hopes her daughter will become a movie star. The novel has a nontraditional structure, weaving back and forth between past and present (occasionally veering into the future) and switching points of view. Narratives begin virtually in the middle of scenes and end abruptly, resuming

later in the novel or sometimes alternating between time frames. The epigraph to the novel quotes Ralph Waldo Emerson, who says that three of our desires are never satisfied: the rich craving more, the sick wanting something different, and the traveler's desire to be "anywhere but here." The epigraph sums up the mother and daughter's journey, for as they move from one geographic locale to another and from one state of mind to another, it becomes apparent that it is not physical locations they are trying to escape but their lots in life. Ann even says that she "want[s] anything else" than living with her stepfather on Carriage Court (p. 39).

Throughout the novel, both mother and daughter worry about money, and the distinction between social classes is a major subject in the book. On their road trip they sometimes splurge by lodging at more expensive hotels and eating out almost every night, but they constantly wonder whether they can afford these amenities. Although only a child, Ann frequently mentions the cost of things. In a role reversal, she chides her mother if she spends too much, reminding her that they can't afford luxuries. When they reach Scottsdale, Arizona, and Adele pulls into the Luau Hotel, which she had seen listed in a magazine, Ann tells her to find a cheaper place to stay, suggesting they look for a Travel Lodge. "I worried about money," she says. "And I knew it was a bigger system that I understood. I tried to pick the cheaper thing, like a superstition" (p. 7). En route to the Travel Lodge, they have a minor car accident and leave the car in the repair shop. Adele asks the policeman to drive them to the Luau, where they stay a week. Adele scolds Ann: "You try and save a few pennies and you end up spending thousands" (p. 8). Ann notes that they "didn't talk about money" while waiting for the car to be repaired (p. 9). While staying at the Luau, they browse the local shops, and Adele orders $150 worth of custom-made perfume and leaves it to be wrapped and packed. "We can't afford *that,*" Ann tells her immediately after they leave the shop (p. 18). Later, Ann notes that she could wash the car herself instead of paying someone, and when her mother checks into the ritzy Bel Air Hotel, she asks, "Can we afford this

place?" (p. 31). Then she orders an expensive steak for dinner to spite her mother for indulging in the hotel: "If we could afford to stay here then we could afford to eat, and I was going to eat" (p. 33). Much later, Adele throws away a cake they just bought at a bake sale because she's afraid crumbs might get in the car. Ann tells her she'll hold it, then reminds her they paid seven dollars for it. These sorts of arguments about money continue throughout the novel.

Both during their travels and while staying in one place, the characters often feel lost in time and space. They sometimes quite literally can't seem to keep both feet on the ground. While living in Bay City with Ted, Ann argues with Adele; afterward, Adele acts as if things are back to normal, while Ann thinks, "I didn't want anything. I'd lost my attraction for gravity and I couldn't get it back by myself. I knew it would always be there again in the morning, after sleep. But for that night, I didn't care, I didn't want a thing" (p. 101). When her mother makes her get out of the car near the roadside on the way to a benefit dinner, Ann trembles and can't control her shaking hands. She considers her options, then runs through the woods and emerges along another highway. She stands on the steps of a bridge so her mother can see her when she comes back to pick her up, believing that when she stops the car and beckons her "the world would stop in light" (p. 103).

Ann recalls one day when Adele and Carol, Ann's aunt, were searching for her and her cousin Benny, and Ann felt as if she were virtually spinning off the planet: "Then it was black and Benny was hugging me and we were dizzy, turning, standing up. That was something about Benny, always. He could hug you so hard, hanging on as if he were dying, falling off the spinning planet, out of the earth's fall, and his fingernails bit into you and you were there, black for a second" (p. 129). Similarly, Carol remembers Ann and Benny jumping through the air and reminds Ann of the time she was suspended in space. She tells Ann that when Benny was a small child, he

tried to jump off the garage roof. He wanted to fly like Peter Pan. He had you up there too, but we

didn't know. I'd found him, curled and bloody, and raced him off to the hospital in the car.

You had been afraid to jump. You kept so quiet up there that even after we came home in the station wagon, nobody knew to get you down. I fixed cinnamon toast and Benny was watching cartoons in the breezeway, and it was Benny who remembered you all of a sudden.

(p. 456)

Again, while playing with Benny, she refers to the earth spinning. She notes that as she lay in a pile of leaves in her grandmother's yard, she hears "the earth spin," as she digs her "hands into the ground" and holds on (p. 321). Later on, when Benny dies, Ann retreats to her grandmother's backyard after the funeral and notes that the Popsicle-stick crosses she and Benny used to mark pets' graves are gone. She holds a fistful of dirt and watches it fall from her fingers. She notes that "things didn't stay and for no good reason.... I thought about our crosses; wood wouldn't dissolve into the ground, not in five or ten years. No one would take them, but they were gone. Things just disappeared and we weren't even surprised. We didn't expect them to last" (p. 369). In this scene, gravity makes the dirt fall from her fingers, and objects disappear into space with no explanation. Another, more subtle reference to time and space occurs when a teacher asks Ann a question, and she answers, "I lost my place" (p. 178). Indeed, throughout the novel the characters both literally and figuratively lose their places in the universe.

Underscoring the notion of gravity, references to clocks and time occur throughout the novel. At the beginning of the novel, Ann recalls her mother's habit of demanding that she get out of the car during their trip from Wisconsin to California. Ann contemplates, "I lost time then; I don't know if it was minutes or if it was more. There was nothing to think because there was nothing to do" (p. 3). When her mother would return for her, she would look "back once in a quick good-bye to the fields" (p. 4). Later, she recalls that as she grew older, she slid under the covers at night and evaded sleep, as if she were "stealing time and comfort" that she is not entitled to (p. 70). Throughout the novel, alarm

clocks ring too early, too loudly, and too often, as if to disrupt the characters' already uncomfortable sense of timelessness. Waiting outside as her mother speaks to a realtor, Ann measures time with an obsessive behavior, convincing herself that only after she had stepped on every stone and recited the name of every flower behind the realtor's officer will her mother leave the office. Carol notes that Ann's grandmother, her own mother, died at "five thirteen" on Ann's seventh birthday (p. 166). This reporting of a very specific time suggests that Carol tries to ground herself, situate herself in time and space, after the shock of her mother dying.

Perhaps because the characters don't feel emotionally stable and can't find comfort despite shifting geographical locals, they develop obsessive-compulsive habits to help provide routine and stability. These behaviors recur throughout the novel: Ann develops an eating disorder, and the characters constantly count, organize, clean, and collect objects. Many of the rules at Ted's house result from his penchant for cleanliness. He insists they open the refrigerator with their elbows, not their hands, to prevent leaving smudges on the chrome; that everyone polish sinks and faucets with a towel after each use; and that the lawn be mowed one even row at a time. Adele angrily demands that the floor be cleaned and instructs Ann to vacuum each square of linoleum five times. While cleaning the floor, Ann counts the tiles, first adding, then multiplying the squares. Adele acknowledges that while she is cleaning the house, her concentration on the task at hand enables her to forget everything else. Clearly, the behaviors centered on keeping the house clean go beyond a concern for cleanliness and reflect more about the characters' obsessiveness than they do about keeping a tidy house.

Other forms of obsessive-compulsive behaviors include arranging objects in patterns and collecting objects. Ann's grandmother, Lillian, arranges toast cut into four squares neatly around an egg. She also collects rocks and displays them in a ritualized manner. She carefully inscribes where she got each rock on a piece of paper taped to the bottom of the rock. Then she meticulously wraps each rock in colored tissue paper. Carol's

son Hal collects silver dollars, and other characters save theirs for him. Ann mentions three pairs of shoes, her grandmother's, her mother's, and hers, and notes that they are all white. Ann lines up the shoes in her mind and places the white ones in a mental category. Later, Ann sees her boots "lined up" in the closet, with the points positioned toward the front (p. 145). Apparently, Ann has placed the boots in the closet in a categorized row; now she notices they are positioned as such. Placing them a particular way and noticing that placement both reflect obsessive traits.

Ann and Adele exhibit obsessive-compulsive habits when they relentlessly attempt to collect all the stamps needed for a contest held by the local grocery store chain. They get all but one of the consecutive numbers needed and continue to buy groceries they don't need in hopes of getting the winning stamp. They even go to stores out of town, thinking that the grocery store chain has a system that involves shopping at different stores. Additionally, when they purchase the items, they choose them "carefully, superstitiously, as if the difference between a package of ovenproof tin foil and a box of animal crackers would make the difference in our lives" (p. 113). Their obsessive-compulsive natures are reflected both in the overall challenge of collecting all of the stamps and in the way they attempt to get the stamps.

Whether the characters are obsessive-compulsive or whether they get lost in time and space, *Anywhere but Here* is ultimately a story about mother-daughter bonds. Ann and Adele's relationship evolves throughout the novel. They fight but defend each other, they disagree only to agree later, they hurt each other yet try to keep each other from getting hurt. By the end of the novel the strength of their relationship is illustrated and shown to be solid. The way their relationship evolves and develops throughout the novel is best illustrated by comparing two scenes, one at the beginning of the novel and one at the end, both instances in which Ann and her mother have been going somewhere and Ann gets out of the car. At the beginning of the novel, Ann recalls that during their trip to California, her mother

often would shout for her to "Get out," open Ann's car door, and push her (p. 3). Ann recalls that she would stand on the side of the road after her mother forced her from the car, noting that as "the wheels of the familiar white Continental turned, a spot of gravel hit my shoes and my mother's car drove away. When it was nothing but a dot in the distance, I started to cry" (p. 4). At the end of the novel, Ann, now an adult, returns home after a visit, and her mother drives her to the airport when she leaves. They arrive early, so her mother suggests they sit together in the car: "Sit a second, we'll just talk, we'll wait here," she says (p. 502). Ann notes that her mother "looks perfect.... I feel like she is leaving, not me." They sit and talk, and as she is leaving, Ann simply says, "Mom," then kisses her and runs from the car (p. 503). At the beginning of the novel, Ann leaves the car while they drive; at the end, they sit in the idling car only to talk. At the beginning, they don't want to be together; at the end they can't stand the thought of living apart.

THE LOST FATHER

A sequel to *Anywhere but Here, The Lost Father* (1992) focuses on Ann's search for the father who had abandoned the family when she was a child, a situation alluded to in the first book but not its central subject. Although the names have changed, some of the characters in *The Lost Father* are the same as those in *Anywhere but Here*. Adele (August) Diamond becomes Adele Stevenson, and Ann August becomes Ann Stevenson, who changes her name several times in the novel, devising variants on the name she was given at birth, Mayan Atassi, a legacy from her Egyptian immigrant father, John Atassi. Whereas *Anywhere but Here* centers on the relationship between Adele and Ann, mother and daughter, *The Lost Father* emphasizes a nonexistent relationship between a father and daughter.

As the novel opens, Ann, now in her late twenties, has changed her name back to Mayan Atassi and is a medical student in New York City. Since childhood, she has been obsessed with find-

ing her father. She talks incessantly about her quest with friends, coworkers, anyone who will listen. Whenever she gets the opportunity, whether sneaking upstairs to a pay phone she stumbles upon inside a restaurant or deliberately looking inside a library, Mayan searches phone books for her father's name. She makes it a point to find the local phone book when she travels to a new city. She dials the telephone operator at all hours to inquire about a listing for her father, hires a private detective, tries to involve the FBI, and takes several road trips, ultimately traveling abroad to Egypt. Her need to find her father grows and grows, until even she realizes her search has become an obsession.

After her futile trip to Egypt, she realizes that searching for her father has consumed her life; however, she also recognizes that she is unable to stop looking. She keeps taking note of this or that person to talk to about her father, acknowledging that this search has become her life: "I kept promising myself just this one more thing, this was the last.... I knew I'd never be satisfied until I met every person who'd been touched by my father, every student who'd heard him lecture, any secretary or mailman who had a rub with his life. It felt like I'd never be able to sit still again" (p. 431). Finally she admits: "I was becoming a crazy person.... I let so many things go. Now I'd stopped even opening my bills. I avoided people. I was so ashamed. This had gone on too long, farther than it should have and I knew better" (p. 431). As is typical of obsessive behaviors, she can't stop her actions even though she finds no real comfort in them. In fact, her obsessive search brings her shame and defeat, yet she continues, all the while recognizing the pattern of behaviors, thoughts, and emotions she perpetuates.

The search brings about other obsessive characteristics, such as her propensity to makes lists. She wakes up late and makes so many lists that they seem to grow on paper in her hand. Not only does she make lists of information she has found and of places to look and people to see regarding her father, she also compulsively makes lists of actions she has already taken. As a child, on her grade-school sheet of ruled notebook

paper she makes a vertical list of all the cities where she has searched in telephone books for her father's name during school-sponsored field trips. Later, she makes the same sort of list of all her friends, so her obsessive traits are not limited to her search for her father.

The Lost Father is a coming-of-age story in the bildungsroman tradition, where one of the major elements is the search for identity. Mayan thinks that if she finds her father she will find herself. She recalls that his last words to her when she was a young child were instructions to remember that he was her father and that nobody else can be a father to her. And she does not forget. As she matures, she realizes that since he left, she has had no father. As she matures, she understands the significance of this absence:

> I finished my childhood without a father. I remember the consternation: I used to stand outside, my arms crossed, tennis shoes scraping the porch lip just for the feel of it, counting cars from the highway. It was still light out and my grandmother was asleep, already done for the day. This was the year before my mother and I left. I could see cars in the distance but from our porch I couldn't tell what make they were or if there was one person inside or two. I'd follow them to see if they'd turn at our off-ramp. They almost never did. I still believed my father would come back. But would he make it *in time.*
>
> If you asked me if I thought he was alive, I would have said, yes, and I'd have meant it. Sometimes I wondered, would I ever just see him again in my life without my doing anything. If someone else, something, would arrange it. Now, I figured, if I found him I would never know.
>
> (pp. 341–342)

Mayan's search for identity and her maturation are linked to her struggle to find the correct name for herself. Over time she calls herself Mayan Atassi, Mayan Amneh Stevenson, and Ann Stevenson. Whereas at one point she states in a matter-of-fact way that she "just started using the name Ann" (p. 339), she boldly announces, "My name is Mayan Atassi" when she gets to Egypt (p. 410).

Her search for identity involves not only finding her father but defining her gender. Thus the novel also explores the lives of three generations of women: Mayan, her mother, and her maternal grandmother, Lillian, who is no longer alive when the novel opens but who appears in Mayan's recollections. Her grandmother and her mother teach her traditional women's roles and convince her that she needs a man in order to survive. Her mother tells her she needs to look pretty to attract the attention of males. However, Mayan is able to overcome these lessons and discovers that she can support herself emotionally and financially. At one point, she announces that she "never wanted to be a girl" (p. 121). She and her two friends, Mai linn and Emily, promise each other never to become mothers, never to let being girls stop them from high achievements. They vow not to spend time on "dumb girl things in life" (p. 123) and warn each other against wearing makeup or fretting over clothes, boys, and social events.

As in most novels that portray a search, it is not whether she finds her father that is central to her growth, but what happens to her as she looks. Her own explanation of searching for something reflects this notion:

> All investigation is the same. You call a lot of different people. You ask questions, one leads to another, they form a chain. Science is like that....
>
> And investigation was not all discovery. It was mostly not. It was mostly the mundane next ten things. Sending the three dollars for the copy from the county clerk's office. Calling back after somebody-you-don't-know's lunch.
>
> (p. 431)

Yet, after all the searching, when she finally finds her father, she feels let down. Meeting him does not impact her life. In fact, she seems more disappointed that the search itself was unsuccessful than she does in discovering that her father is far from the man she had envisioned.

When she finds him, she approaches him and simply says, "I'm looking for John Atassi" (p. 451). And when she asks if he is that man, he simply says, "Yes" (p. 451). Upon meeting him, she finds herself quickly wanting to go home. She comes to realize that "he was still a man who had left his family and not tried to find us. I learned that people cannot be more or better than their lives" (p. 475). So she realizes she has built

him up to be something he's not, and when she meets him she sees that she has created in her mind, in her search, a father who does not exist. Ironically, once Mayan finally finds her father, he is more lost to her than he was during all those years she spent searching for him. Once she sees who he really is, the father she yearns for disappears forever.

A REGULAR GUY

As in *The Lost Father* and *Anywhere but Here*, *A Regular Guy* (1996) depicts a mother who is raising her daughter without a father; however, unlike Ann (Mayan), Jane di Natali, the ten-year-old girl in *A Regular Guy,* does not seek out her father. Rather, her mother, Mary, a free-spirited hippie living in an Oregon commune in the mountains, teaches her to drive an old truck and sends her off to drive by herself to California to live with her father because she can no longer afford to take care of her.

A Regular Guy is told from various points of view and introduces a variety of characters, most of whom do not develop the plot. Much of the style is descriptive, as readers are often told what the characters do or are given objective, report-like accounts of their traits, which read like a series of character sketches. Although the novel weaves back and forth between past and present, it focuses on a ten-year time span that centers on Tom Owens and Jane di Natali.

Tom Owens, referred to as Owens throughout the novel, shares striking similarities with Simpson's brother, Steve Jobs, cofounder of Apple. Both dropped out of college, started a business in their parents' garage, and became very wealthy at an early age. Both left the companies they helped create, forced out due to power struggles. Both dabbled in politics. And both wear self-imposed uniforms: Steve Jobs's signature jeans and black turtleneck; Owens' jeans and T-shirt. Most relevant to the plot of *A Regular Guy,* both Steve Jobs and Tom Owens fathered daughters from whom they were estranged during the girls' early childhoods. Perhaps coincidentally, or perhaps as a wink to her brother, Simpson makes several references to

fruit in general and to apples in particular throughout the novel. For example, prior to moving to California, Mary resides on an apple farm commune in Oregon, where every meal includes apples. Later, a reference to a bushel of apples Owens' father brings when he comes to visit immediately precedes a flashback explaining how Owens and his cofounder, Frank, began Genesis, the company that parallels Apple in the novel.

A young, self-made tycoon, Tom Owens is described as anything but ordinary. He is too busy to flush the toilet and does not feel the need to wear deodorant because he thinks a proper diet prevents perspiration or body odor. He is handsome, wealthy, and appreciates both science and art. He often repeats stories he's told people and watches movies he's already seen. A vegetarian, he adheres to faddish food frenzies. He considers life's options from a detached perspective and does not indulge the needs or wants of others. He is almost always late to appointments, meetings, and social events, or he skips them altogether. Genesis, the biotech company he cofounded, is described somewhat vaguely, with talk of stem cells, proteins, and compounds; at one point Owens says that he thinks Genesis has discovered "a neurotrophin that can regenerate brains" (p. 41).

Owens' longtime friend Noah Kaskie, an academic scientist who publishes articles in journals, is a hands-on scientist at heart and seeks knowledge for the sake of advancing knowledge. He makes discoveries, whereas Owens utilizes discoveries. Thrilled to experiment and make scientific breakthroughs, Noah turns down a job offer from Owens that includes a million-dollar bonus. Born unable to walk, Noah is wheelchair bound, but he never dwells on his disability. He pines for his student, Louise, throughout the novel and marries her near the end of the book.

Occasionally, *A Regular Guy* has elements of magical realism. Owens mysteriously comes to visit Mary and Jane one night in Oregon, and Jane remembers the visit "as in a silver dream" (p. 14). Owens and Mary lift her from a "curled position" and "spread her across [Owens'] outstretched legs" (p. 14). The next morning "the floor was swept and there was no trace of him"

(p. 15). In the mountains, where she lives in a cabin, Jane cracks nuts with her teeth and sucks the ends of weeds. While driving to California, she sees a man she recognizes from a picture who seems to fade away as quickly as he appears. At another point, storms remind Jane of the days when she lived in a region that was not quite a forest but not a home, either:

> Then she would find herself—no coat, no umbrella, soaked shoes—running across roads, darting and slanting, daring cars, gauging the density and smear of headlights. She yearned to live unsheltered again and to recognize: This rain is the voice of the world. When teeth chatter and body shivers beyond control, this is the real cold, the real hunger.
>
> In the mountains, she had eaten her scabs. It was a habit she could never quit.
>
> (pp. 29–30)

Switching points of view, moving back and forth in time, and interjecting various styles throughout the novel, *A Regular Guy* is less concerned with plot than with character and style. The basic plot begins when Jane leaves for California and finds her father, Owens. Owens asks Mary to join them, and although May and Jane don't live with him, he supports them. He has a girlfriend, Olivia, and after they break up near the end of the novel, he marries another woman. The plights of a self-made tycoon, who has experienced life's ups and downs, and a young woman, whose future lies ahead of her, are illustrated through Owens' acknowledgment at the end of the novel of three regrets: he regrets not working harder on his relationship with Olivia; he regrets the way his career with Genesis ended; and he regrets that he hadn't spent more time with his mother. As he pauses between telling Jane the second and last regret, she anticipates that the last regret will be that he didn't spend time with her during her childhood. His comment about his mother seems trite to Jane, but the first two regrets, along with Jane's desire for her father to want her, sum up several of the novel's themes.

OFF KECK ROAD

Simpson's fourth novel, *Off Keck Road*, appeared in 2000. Unlike *Anywhere but Here, The Lost Father,* and *A Regular Guy,* which explore relationships between family members, portray broken family bonds, and depict nontraditional families, *Off Keck Road* explores the characters of three single women. Covering almost a half-century, the plot highlights these women, who all live somewhat ordinary lives in Green Bay, Wisconsin. The title refers to Keck Road, the proverbial other side of the tracks (or in this case, the river), where a cluster of houses sits on the outskirts of Green Bay. Although filled with descriptions of landscapes in and around the city, Green Bay is depicted more as a state of mind than as a geographical locale. It possesses the traits of a small town: everyone knows everyone, people carry high school memories far past their graduation dates, and petty gossip abounds, especially early in the novel when characters eavesdrop with rotary-phone party lines. However, throughout the course of the novel, ways of life shift as fast-food restaurants and strip malls replace homegrown restaurants and familiar shops owned by local merchants. New generations bring newcomers, who buy property, tear it down, and rebuild, thus creating both new structures and new communities.

As the title suggests, the novel comments on social classes and depicts gaps between the working, middle, and upper-middle classes. A dead-end street, Keck Road has only eight small houses: "On one corner, there was a white farmhouse, and on the other, a small tavern, pink and gray, that looked like an ordinary house during the day. Children's boots drooped on the porch. A little farther up, the plowed middle of the road narrowed, and on top of the icy snow were springs of hay" (p. 6). On Keck Road children run down to the railroad tracks and shoot skeets. They fight over money, climb "over creeks on rocks and cement drainpipes," and build forts in trees (p. 37). They play games outside, throw snowballs, and ride sleds. Readers are given an outsider's perspective of Keck Road at the beginning of the novel, when, in 1956, Bea Maxwell drives there to pick up her friend June Umberhum. She notices that the children seem "scantily dressed and altogether unattended, some downright wild, such as the one swinging from a

bare hickory branch, which looked like it could break any minute, some fifteen feet above the snow. That child, like many others, was not wearing mittens" (p. 7). She is shocked to see that a woman carrying an infant is already pregnant again.

Later, Bea finds out the woman she had seen is Shelley, one of five children who grew up on Keck Road and has spent most her life caring for her grandmother and working odd jobs such as cutting grass and plowing snow for the neighbors. Shelley has been denied jobs because of her limp, which people label a visual disfigurement. In contrast to Shelley's background, Bea grew up in Green Bay on Mason Drive. Everyone knew her. She had "attended De Pere High. Her father was the revered Dr. Maxwell. Everyone had known her parents and the house they lived in" (p. 156). Even later, as a senior citizen, her social esteem brings her privileges such as the option to work odd hours at her job. Somewhere between Shelley's and Bea's social classes, June was born on Keck Road but left to attend University of Wisconsin, where she became a sorority sweetheart.

While the novel shows that social class determines differences in lifestyles, it also demonstrates the much greater impacts class differences can have on people's lives when Shelley is struck with polio. Whereas the less-privileged children stand in line in the high-school gym to receive the polio vaccination, those "on the other side of the river" go to Dr. Herbert Maxwell, Bea's father, who administers the vaccine by appointment (p. 15). Seemingly it wouldn't make a difference, but those in the gym are subjects in a polio vaccine experiment, while Dr. Maxwell's patients are not. When administered at the gym, children form a line and are given either the vaccine or a placebo. Shelley is exposed to the disease because she is given the placebo; she does not receive the vaccine at all. Waiting in line at the gym, June cuts ahead of Shelley and gives her daughter the dose Shelley is next in line to receive. Although a seemingly random event exposes Shelley to polio, had she lived "on the other side of the river" she wouldn't be a candidate for the placebo, whether it was administered arbitrarily or not.

In some ways, *Off Keck Road* is a character study much like *A Regular Guy*. Readers get realistic accounts of the central three characters, Bea, June, and Shelley, who is a generation younger than the other two. When the novel opens, Bea, who grew up as the prominent doctor's daughter, has left her advertising career in Chicago to return home to take care of her mother. She gets a job working for a real estate agent and becomes a successful saleswoman herself. She spends a great deal of time knitting, and donates knitted blankets, shawls, leg warmers, and other items to the needy. Shelley, by contrast, is still challenged by the limp the polio has left her with and also distraught from her grandmother's death, as her grandmother was one she loved "the way you love only one person, the person who had put your life over anything else" (p. 17). Less privileged than Bea, June has also left Green Bay, only to have returned after a divorce. Although they weren't friends before they left Green Bay, Bea and June become very good friends upon their return. They talk endlessly about love and worry whether a woman should call a man. Bea and Shelley meet only because both of them become romantically involved with Bill Alberts.

Although the three women spend a lot of time and energy on romantic relationships, *Off Keck Road* might be considered an anti–love story. Not in the sense that the people get emotionally hurt because of romantic entanglements, but because the novel depicts, on the one hand, the sort of love that seems more practical than romantic, and on the other, a disinterest in romance. Bea's mother observes about her daughter that there isn't much "going on in the dating department" (p. 31). And Bea seems to agree, for even decades later, she recalls the high school romance she had with Alexander Pray and is still embarrassed to discuss it, not because she had sex with him, during a time when women were denied sexual pleasure, but because of how little had happened between the two of them. Throughout her life, Bea has relationships with men that go nowhere. Nevertheless, she remains "happy, cheerful, busy,

occupied, oblivious to the whole underworld of flirtation, as if she were missing the receiving wires" (p. 27). Her boss, Bill Alberts, although married, flirts with her endlessly, and they even go to restaurants together; however, the potential romance never gets any further than a dance together in the office, where "there was a kiss or almost, something between a bump and a kiss" (p. 50).

Bea also has a deep friendship with a priest, and although possibilities abound, in the end she accepts that he is a priest and always will be, and he concedes that as long as he gets hugs, he is all right. Bea's attitude reflects that she doesn't need a male partner to feel complete, an attitude that deepens as the novel progresses. Near the end of the story, she no longer even tries to get the attention of a man. She knows she will continue to go to Chicago twice a year to buy expensive clothes, but her motive has shifted. When she was younger, she "cultivated a dramatic style" to get men's attention (p. 156); now she enjoys compliments from women who often notice the new styles she sports. Bea remains content in Green Bay, where she subscribes to *New York* magazine, serves on the board of the historical society, continues to work part-time selling real estate, and spends her spare time knitting.

Until the end of the novel, Shelley lacks the confidence to secure a successful romantic relationship. During adolescence, she doesn't think she's pretty and she believes she has to work to get the attention of boys. Also, her mother lectures her, making her think boys will use her for sex: "Don't you let anyone fool with you," she tells Shelley. She warns her, "Some boy may try, but it'll only be to laugh at you for it later" (p. 35). Because of her insecurities, Shelley believes that sex for the girls who wore nice clothes and seemed squeaky clean would be "quaint like a valentine," with "precise touches" (p. 35); but for her, she thinks sex would be a boy chasing her, then "getting her down to hurt her, dust in her mouth and dry heat, a rubbing" (p. 35). She begins an affair with George, a married man, and remains in it for thirteen years. She does not really consider her relationship with George romantic because they already knew each other too well. She considers her affair "the opposite of romance" (p. 74). He lives across the street, and one day, unknown to her, he and his family move to Florida. However, by the end of the novel, after she becomes a nurse for Bill Alberts, the two strike up a romance.

June has experienced a failed marriage, but remarries after she has left Green Bay again. She then tells Bea, "So you're it" (p. 133), teasing Bea for her status as still unmarried. In the end, it seems all the women's lives are the same with or without men in their lives. Men are the exception to their lifestyles, not the rule. Their destinies are realized, and they live most of their lives alone yet fulfilled.

MY HOLLYWOOD

Whereas Simpson's other novels explore nontraditional families, single-parent households, and women who remain unmarried and childless for life, *My Hollywood* (2010) portrays traditional nuclear families: those with a mother, father, and children. However, it is clear that the family members are not fulfilled in these roles. In fact, family roles often oppress the characters, creating feelings of inadequacy and overwhelming them. Nuclear family roles become a burden instead of a comfort.

The novel shifts points of view, alternating between Claire's and Lola's. Claire, a composer, has moved to Los Angeles from New York because her husband, Paul, has been given an assignment to write for a comedy show. They have a seventeen-week-old baby, William, and after a massive search for a nanny, including formal interviews, they hire one who works only a day before they fire her for inappropriately touching Will's penis. Later, at a bus stop, Claire meets Lola, a nanny who has raised five children of her own back in the Philippines, and hires her on the spot.

The chapters alternate between Claire's and Lola's stories, both told from the first-person point of view. These alternating points of view highlight the contrast between Claire and Lola, and sometimes the contrast is pointed out more

directly in the narrative. Whereas taking care of children seems natural for Lola, Claire feels overwhelmed by motherhood. When Claire and Paul take Will for a stroll and decide to stop at the park, Claire tells Will, "*five more minutes,*" a warning she mimics from other mothers (p. 28). When Will pushes another child, Clair is dumbfounded. She knows that Lola would know how to handle the situation. Lola, says Claire, "prided herself on her instincts. I didn't seem to have any" (p. 29). When feeling frustrated, Claire consults a friend who has read child-rearing books, whereas Lola seeks council from a group of domestic workers who stay at the House of Ruth, a house for immigrant domestic workers. Claire mimics and uses textbook methods to care for Will; Lola instead uses instinct and advice from mentors.

The novel shows how domestic labor is unappreciated even when it's paid for. The husbands don't understand how difficult it is to take care of children and manage a household, and when domestic duties are hired out, the mothers seem to lack empathy as well. On their first date, Claire and Paul had agreed that domestic duties should be split fifty-fifty between a married couple. However, the subject is never brought up again, until they have Will. Paul chants the mantra "He'll be all right" any time there's a concern about Will, and later, Claire realizes that many mothers feel motherhood is the "hardest job [they've] ever had" (p. 195). And later, after she fires Lola, she quickly finds herself exhausted after Will goes to bed, so she has no time to study music. She sees that she has taken care of Will all day and wonders how they had come to this agreement. She quickly becomes aware how hard Lola had worked while Paul seems oblivious. Paul doesn't think being a parent is a job, nor does he think being a mother is difficult. He doesn't see the need to hire another nanny after Lola is fired.

My Hollywood highlights the support the immigrant domestic workers provide each other. Staying together at the House of Ruth, a place in West Los Angeles, they offer everyday, face-to-face help and support. They mentor each other by helping to secure jobs, giving practical advice to each other, and creating better working conditions. They write a standard contract to be signed by both the nanny and the hiring family to document job duties and benefits. The women practice mentoring in the classic sense. Ruth's teacher was a picture bride, who then worked domestic jobs. Ruth went on to mentor Lola, who now mentors Lucy, and so on. Thus, mentoring is passed down from one woman to another, and all sorts of advice and tips are passed down orally through this system. For example, Lola recalls Ruth's advice: "Always the parents first.... A kid cannot fire you. Even here" (p. 43). Although they work too many hours, these women find ways to spend quality time together. They help each other with chores, play practical jokes on each other, and share their lives outside work with each other. The bond created in this system of mentoring is extremely important to the women, both individually and as a social group. At the end of the novel, Lola sums up her life quite simply. In addition to her role as mother and surrogate mother, she is proud of her role as one of the immigrant women who banded together. She speaks of her time working in America: "And I made some women laugh along the way," she says. "America was my adventure. With the other babysitters" (p. 358).

Women of the past and present who stay at the House of Ruth all contribute to and consult *The Book of Ruth,* a sort of how-to manual for domestic workers, especially nannies, written by the women themselves over decades. "HOW TO WORK FOR THE WHITE" is typed on the first page and the volumes consist of a plethora of practical advice for immigrant domestic workers (p. 45). The book is also a guest book, a journal for the women, a memorial book, and an etiquette book. Everyone who stays at the House of Ruth signs the book, women write poems and stories in the book, and they document events such as baptisms, weddings, and deaths as a way to pay tribute to their loved ones overseas since they cannot attend the ceremonies. The book tells of traits of the hiring families, such as reporting that "*They do not like their own smell. Their waste. Their own used things. Americans, they are very dirty. They used to be clean. The grandparents*

are clean. And the habits they lost are what they crave from us" (p. 45). The book contains recipes and tips such as how to set a table or choose oranges for a dessert. It gives insights such as noting that if the family's dog likes you, you're hired, and tells readers to avoid working for families who won't use paper towels.

By far the most apparent contrast between the nannies and the mothers who hire nannies is the economic disparity between them. While the immigrant workers worry about their jobs and about saving money to send home, the women who hire nannies boast of new cars, expensive jewelry, and their nannies. They even create a hierarchy of nannies, noting that some are "trophy" nannies and that rich people have a different sort of nanny than the upper middle class. While the nannies turn spare change into rolled coins to save, the upper class throws change in the garbage. The immigrant workers can't afford to engage in work, or hobbies referred to as work, for free. Lola is confused when she discovers that when Claire performs in a concert in New York, she spends more to pay Lola's expenses to care for Will than she earns for the performance. Lola says, "Me, I work for money" (p. 21).

Lola is loyal both to the children she cares for and to her identity as a nanny. She turns down a job making almost twice as much as Claire and Paul pay her because she has grown attached to "Williamo." However, Claire and Paul are not nearly so loyal. Lola is fired, or "chopped," as the women at Ruth's House say, because a preschool teacher tells Claire she thinks Lola's cultural differences make it impossible for her to discipline Will properly. Lola ultimately goes to work for Judith, a single parent, and develops a bond with her daughter, Laura. She writes in *The Book of Ruth* that she won't leave Laura until after she is five, then scratches that out and puts eight. But Judith too chops Lola when Lola returns to the Philippines to attend her daughter's wedding.

Lola arrives home only to discover that her husband is having an affair, so when Claire begs her to return to America to work for both her and Judith, Lola agrees. And when she gets back to California, it's clear Laura has missed her terribly and that she has missed Laura. Whereas most of the mothers in the novel lack the confidence to be a mother or resist that role, Lola embraces the role, both as a birth mother to her own children and as a surrogate mother to those she cares for. At the end of the novel, she proudly explains her purpose in life: "When I signed up to be a mother, it was already decided. And I was a success," she says (p. 357). She adds, "I went to America and took care kids. By loving them, I was able to pay the tuitions of my own, so they are now professional class. My children, they will not have to go anywhere. They can stay home. That is what I did for my life" (p. 358).

CASEBOOK

Mona Simpson's writing took a new direction with *Casebook,* which appeared in 2014. The novel centers on Miles Adler-Hart, who is nine years old when the book opens. The novel has aspects of a coming-of-age story and is told from a first-person, adolescent point of view, characteristics that might classify it as young adult fiction. However, *Casebook* crosses boundaries of young adult fiction with its complex narrative structure and other complicated writing techniques.

The basic plot of *Casebook* involves the attempt of Miles and his best friend, Hector, to find out about Eli Lee, Miles's (still-married) mother's boyfriend. But beyond this simple premise, *Casebook* reflects elements of postmodern literature. The novel opens with a "Note to Customer" written by a comic book store owner who says the book was handed to him by one of the authors of *Two Sleuths,* a national best seller. He says this is more like a prequel to the other book, with authorial footnotes added. He tells readers that the author may revise the book, so this may be the first version of future drafts. The "Note to Customer" is signed by Hershel Geschwind, who owns Neverland Comics in Santa Monica, California. Later in the novel, Miles gets a summer job at Neverland Comics, where he works for Hershel Geschwind. Hershel helps Miles and Hector get *Two Sleuths* published and promises to help promote it. Also, one of three short epigraphs that appear before the title page

of *Casebook* says, "Yours, always, always," and is attributed to Eli J. Lee. This is a direct quote from one of the notes Eli writes to Miles's mother within the novel proper of *Casebook*. Additionally, a major clue to Eli's personal history is discovered when Miles and Hector find out that Eli's wife writes romance novels, one she states in an interview as being written to retaliate against Eli's infidelity. A note to customers, an epigraph that quotes the very text it introduces, and the portrayal of a novel-within-a-novel are all elements that highlight the notion that *Casebook* is a text.

Casebook becomes even more self-reflexive by pointing out within the text of the novel (*Casebook* itself) that the characters write the very book (*Two Sleuths*) mentioned in the "Note to Customer" and by the placement of footnotes throughout the book. The footnotes represent commentary that Hector inserts into the text after Miles gives it to him for review. Like references to *Two Sleuths*, the footnotes serve to remind readers that they are reading the book Miles and Hector are writing. By scattering the footnotes throughout the novel, the reminder remains a constant thread.

Another postmodern technique used in *Casebook*, one that also draws attention to the book as literature, are the many, many references to all sorts of media, including books, television shows, movies, plays, poems, and songs, sprinkled throughout the novel. Other textual references allude more specifically to *Casebook*. For example, in *Casebook* adolescents solve a mystery much like the characters in the classic Hardy Boys and Nancy Drew series. Both the Hardy Boys and Nancy Drew are mentioned in *Casebook* as if to highlight the comparison for readers. These references also relate back to *Two Sleuths*, the book Miles and Hector write. This literary technique gives the book a layering quality, adding depth to what might be an otherwise mundane plot.

Throughout *Casebook* references are made to characters who read books and watch movies and who quote from authors, including novelists, playwrights, and poets. Characters in the novel either mention or quote from classics such as *The Great Gatsby* and *Moby-Dick* and from literary greats such as William Shakespeare and W. B. Yeats. Almost as if to trace literature from its classic roots to the contemporary best seller, Simpson also alludes to more contemporary literature such as the Harry Potter series and Nick Hornby's *About a Boy* (1998). Abundant allusions to literary works remind readers that *Casebook* itself is a text and invite comparisons of it to other literary texts. References to other literary texts blend with a plot that involves the writing of a novel to add yet another layer to the structure of the book.

Complex literary devices aside, the novel is propelled by Miles and Hector's investigation of Miles's mother's boyfriend, Eli Lee. At the beginning of the novel, Miles's homegrown detective work consists primarily of various forms of eavesdropping. He eavesdrops on his mother's therapy sessions through a heating vent, sits in a tree and hears conversations through a window, and climbs on rooftops and listens to people converse below him. He uses crudely assembled homemade devices or amateur tools such as walkie-talkies or gadgets to bug telephones. Later, he reads other people's e-mails and uses Internet search engines to investigate people. He also snoops through the mail, reads notes intended for other people, and looks through his mother's dresser drawers, as well as sifting through other people's private storage places.

One problem Miles and Hector's eavesdropping and snooping brings about is exposure to conversations and ideas not intended for them or for adolescents in general; therefore, situations arise in which they cannot comprehend the conversations they hear or events they witness. For example, while lying under his parents' bed and listening to them talk, Miles hears his father say that he doesn't think of his mother "*that way* anymore" (p. 5), but Miles doesn't understand what "that way" means. Later, he sits in a tree and hears his mother and Eli talking. He notices that from his perspective, it takes longer for the words to come together and for him to make sense of the conversation: "Possible meanings assembled, like a puzzle that could be put together different ways but that still left extra pieces until the real form used every one of them" (p. 14).

He listens to his parents as they discuss their failing relationship, hears his mother talking to Eli, and hears the personal problems his mother tells her therapist. However, he does not quite grasp the complexity of what he hears. When Hector's own mother moves out, both boys' worldviews shift a bit, as neither are prepared for a world in which marriages this close to home break up.

Their eavesdropping, spying, and other tactics to find out information do not prepare them for life's challenges. Miles continually seems surprised at situations such as his father moving out of the house. It seems that both Miles and Hector listen to adult conversations from detached perspectives and aren't able to process what they should know is coming when it finally emerges. They lack the emotional skills to assimilate what they understand cognitively. This is somewhat ironic, because they are the ones responsible for the surfacing of the very truths that they do not fully understand. And as Miles points out, he seems to discover things even when he isn't looking for them: "Espionage had a life of its own. Secrets opened to me when I wasn't even looking" (p. 60).

In addition to Miles and Hector's inability to accept what they hear, the novel expounds all sorts of truisms, while questioning other sorts of truth. It does so directly through quotes that Miles's mother writes on the chalkboard, many of them from Albert Einstein. These quotes, often proverbs and axioms, raise questions about life and offer guidance. Less directly, the novel shows how Miles and Hector discover that people are not truthful. For example, when Miles goes to New York to visit his father's family, he says, "you bent through a small door and entered a world where all of a sudden you were better" (p. 24). His father tells his family that his children are straight-A students even though his school doesn't use the grading system. Miles says that, essentially, they function "inside a snow globe" (p. 24). Another subtle way of alluding the truth is the use of nicknames. It is never explained why Miles's mother is called "Mims" or "the Mims," and his sisters are referred to as "Boop One" and "Boop Two." Miles calls Eli "the dork guy," and another character "Surferdude," both of which are somewhat self-explanatory. The two nicknames Miles creates reveal more truth-telling than their real names because they describe them, whereas a given name is usually a nondescript label.

The reference to bending through a door and entering another realm mentioned above could be a nod to Lewis Carroll's *Alice in Wonderland* (1865), where, like the world in which Miles and Hector have found themselves, things are not what they appear. Similarly, Miles later acknowledges that, like Humpty Dumpty, "whatever held people was fragile and, once broken, couldn't be put together again" (pp. 26–27). The essential lessons Miles learns through his search entail being able to distinguish between appearance and reality. After he and Hector come closer to unraveling Eli's lies, Miles contemplates the significance of his deception:

> I thought our life was over, though I couldn't have said why.... Something I'd believed in more than I knew was over. My mother's hope. Our good future. The happy ending, but to what? ...
>
> It seemed our family had been lying. We'd been trying to be this great divorced family when really our lives, like the lives of any kids who were the products of failure, were coming out worse....
>
> I tried to conjure my dad as an antidote.... Maybe he would get remarried, I thought, and have a whole nother family. An unbroken one.
>
> (pp. 172–173)

Selected Bibliography

WORKS OF MONA SIMPSON

NOVELS

Anywhere but Here. New York: Knopf, 1986.
The Lost Father. New York: Knopf, 1992.
A Regular Guy. New York: Knopf, 1996.
Off Keck Road. New York: Knopf, 2000.
My Hollywood. New York: Knopf, 2010.

Casebook. New York: Knopf, 2014.

CRITICAL STUDIES AND REVIEWS

Abissi, Colette. "Novel Explores Love's Ambiguities." *New Directions for Women* 16, no. 3:14 (May–June 1987). (Review of *Anywhere but Here.*)

Anshaw, Carol. "The Book of Jobs." *Village Voice,* October 15, 1996, pp. 45–46. (Review of *A Regular Guy.*)

D'Erasmo, Stacey. "Life Is What Happens to Other People." *New York Times Book Review,* November 12, 2000, p. 14. (Review of *Off Keck Road.*)

Eder, Richard. "A Daddy Fixation." *Los Angeles Times Book Review,* February 9, 1992, p. 3. (Review of *The Lost Father.*)

Heller, Dana A. "Shifting Gears: Transmission and Flight in Mona Simpson's *Anywhere but Here.*" *University of Hartford Studies in Literature* 21:37–44 (1989).

Kakutani, Michiko. "A Rich (and Nasty) Father, Defined by His Ties." *New York Times,* October 15, 1996, p. C15. (Review of *The Lost Father.*)

Mitgang, Herbert. "Mona Simpson, Writing of Peripatetic Dreamers." *New York Times,* January 24, 1987, p. 13. (Review of *Anywhere but Here.*)

Schillinger, Liesl. "For Love and Money." *New York Times Book Review,* August 8, 2010, p. A15. (Review of *My Hollywood.*)

Seligman, Craig. "Oblivious Father." *New York Times Book Review,* October 27, 1996, p. 16. (Review of *A Regular Guy.*)

Shepard, Jim. "Just One Thing to End All Wanting." *New York Times Book Review,* February 9, 1992, p. 10. (Review of *The Lost Father.*)

Smyth, Jacqui. "Getaway Cars and Broken Homes: Searching for the American Dream 'Anywhere but Here.'" *Frontiers* 20, no. 2:115–132 (1999).

Ward, Elizabeth. "Two Women in Search of the American Dream." *Washington Post Book World,* February 1, 1987, p. 7. (Review of *Anywhere but Here.*)

Williams, John. "Snooping Around." *New York Times Book Review,* June 1, 2014, p. 42. (Review of *Casebook.*)

FILM BASED ON THE WORK OF MONA SIMPSON

Anywhere but Here. Screenplay by Alvin Sargent. Directed by Wayne Wang. 20th Century Fox, 1999.

RUTH STONE

(1915—2011)

Jane Beal

RUTH STONE WAS an American poet and teacher of poetry. Born in Virginia and raised in Indiana, she married chemist John Clapp, Jr., in 1935, when she was twenty, and later gave birth to a daughter, Marcia. She first studied at the collegiate level, without formally enrolling, at the University of Illinois, Urbana-Champagne; she later audited courses at Harvard University. After obtaining a divorce from her first husband, she married the writer Walter Stone in 1944, and he became the father of her two younger daughters, Phoebe and Abigail. Her work as a poet began to gain recognition, including *Poetry*'s Bess Hokin Prize (1953) and a Kenyon Review Fellowship in poetry (1956), while her husband was a professor of English at Vassar College. But tragedy struck Stone's life when her husband committed suicide while on sabbatical leave in London.

With three daughters to raise on her own, Stone began a series of poetry residencies and visiting teaching positions at a number of colleges and universities across the United States, beginning with a two-year poetry fellowship from the Radcliffe Institute for Independent Study of Harvard University in Cambridge, Massachusetts. When she was not teaching, she would return with her family to a farmhouse she had purchased in Goshen, Vermont. Her itinerant life ended after twenty-five years when she was awarded tenure at the State University of New York at Binghamton in her seventies. After her retirement, she received an honorary doctorate from Middlebury College in Vermont. She published thirteen print collections of poetry in her lifetime and received many awards, including a Pushcart Prize and the National Book Award; her book *What Love Comes To: New & Selected Poems* (2008) was a finalist for the Pulitzer Prize.

Her verses express, with often acerbic wit, what has been called her "tragicomic vision": an unrelenting and incisive commentary on poverty, loss, the human body, relationships between men and women, odd characters on the edges of American communities, old age, the universe, and poetry itself. At times bawdy, at times profound, her poems never fail to make a sharp point.

CHILDHOOD

Ruth Swan Perkins Stone was born in the home of her maternal grandparents in Roanoke, Virginia, on June 8, 1915. She was the firstborn child of Roger McDowell Perkins and Ruth Ferguson Perkins, from whom she received her first name. Her middle name, Swan, was her paternal grandmother's maiden name, and it features significantly in poems alluding to her identity (as does her married name, Stone). Ruth had two younger siblings, Edgar and Elsie.

Ruth's father was trained as a printer, but he lived for his music, for he was a drummer. Ruth wrote of him in her poem, "Rhythm," which appears in her collection *Cheap* (1975):

I am the drummer's daughter.
He beat time out of me.
Rat-a-tat-tat
Rat-a-tat-tat
In Norfolk on the sea.
Young he was and handsome.
A gambler, by G.
I was his first-born daughter.
He rolled the dice for me.
And down I dropped ripe as a plum
Out of my mama's belly.

(p. 51)

In these lines, Stone expands and slightly varies the five-line limerick form, which is often used

249

to express silly, funny, or even bawdy sentiments. But in "Rhythm," Stone inverts convention, using a typically humorous form to convey serious matter—a characteristic of her poetry generally.

Her rhythm and rhyme make a sexual pun on her own birth story and suggest, not unlike Theodore Roethke's poem "My Papa's Waltz," that she experienced the careless violence of her drunken father as a young girl. Later in "Rhythm" she writes of the birth of her brother and sister, the poverty of their family, and her father, asleep in her mother's bed, who "smelled of strong whiskey" (p. 51). In the last stanza, she speaks of her deceased parents and her own identity:

My daddy's dust is scattered.
My mama's salt as the sea.
And when I'm ready to lay me down
Here's what they'll say of me.
She is a drummer's daughter.
She learned what her daddy taught her …
She'll have to beat time, by G.

(pp. 51–52)

The music of drumbeats marches through Stone's work. Many of her early poems have strong, readily discernable metric patterns and cadences that are evident in oral performance; if read silently, they echo rhythmically in the reader's inner ear. This tendency in Stone's poetry came not only from her father's drumming but also from the classical music on phonograph records that her father played for his children on a windup Victrola and the reading he did aloud from the King James Bible as well as comical pieces by Bill Nye (the pen name of the nineteenth-century humorist and journalist Edgar Wilson Nye).

Like her father, Stone's mother gave her the gift of music, for her mother was a singer. As Stone said, "When I think back, I had a mother who sang all the time. She just sang old songs around the house.... I was just used to hearing her singing, entertaining herself.... Can you imagine? There I was with a mother who sang and a father who played percussion. What could I do?" (deNiord, 2010, p. 49). She had to become a poet. In addition to singing, her mother introduced her to English poetry, helping her to develop her mind and ear for the future.

My mother read poetry—Tennyson—to me from the time, apparently, she started suckling me at her breasts. She loved Tennyson deeply. The *Idylls of the King* and all that. And she read them aloud to herself as she was nursing me. She had this big leather bound book of Tennyson. And it probably had a deep influence on me.

(Gilbert 1973, pp. 53–54)

Stone said that her mother loved her poetry, and when she herself became a mother, she would write down the poems her daughter Abigail, nicknamed "Blue Jay," made up when she was in the bathtub. "This is the thing that has made me feel all children are poets and the parent who loves the poetry is the one who preserves the poet. It's the parent who isn't perceptive who kills it. Otherwise, we'd all be singing birds" (p. 55). So Stone knew music and poetry from infancy.

Through her parents' Bible reading, Stone was also introduced to the elements of Christianity in childhood. Her father's family attended the Presbyterian Church, and so she attended Sunday school as a child as well. There, she said, "I was listening, and I was thinking—I said, *this is not true*. This is not true, and I don't believe it, you know. From then on, I had no religion.... I could see easily enough that everyone came to death and was put in the ground" (deNiord, 2010, p. 53). In her later years, it seems she neither had nor practiced any formal religious faith.

Yet her poem "The Tree," published in her collection *Cheap* (1975) and republished in *Second-Hand Coat* (1987), suggests that the poet at times perceived a profound connection between herself and Jesus. In it, she writes of the death of her husband Walter in words and images that strongly evoke the suffering Christ on the Cross. Indeed, she expresses herself in "The Tree" like a medieval contemplative mystic imagining a spiritual marriage to Christ.

Stone alluded to ideas and passages from scripture in poems throughout her life. In her first book, *In an Iridescent Time* (1959), she was preoccupied at times with the problem of evil. She writes in "The Season" (poem 16), "I know what calls the Devil from the pits / With a thief's fingers there he slouches and sits," and she ad-

dresses "Satan" directly in her poem "Experience" (poem 50). Later, in "On the Way," she calls herself an "Aryan skeptic" (*Simplicity*, 1995, p. 61)—contrasting both her ethnic heritage and doubt with her husband Walter's Jewishness and faith. Yet she often uses biblical source material to critique the problems of patriarchal theology on the one hand and the problems of the broken world on the other (as in her poems "A Male Tale" and "Prophets"). Elsewhere, she also echoes the words of Jesus (Luke 1:37) and, at the same time, affirms her belief in the possibility of an afterlife: "I do not doubt that all things are possible, / even that wildest hope that we may meet beyond the grave" ("Being Human," *Topography*, 1971, p. 12). In an interview she gave in her nineties, she characterized that "wildest hope" as essentially no hope (deNiord, 2010, p. 54), but it seems her thoughts and feelings about eternal hope vacillated in her lifetime.

It is relatively easy to understand Stone's ambivalence toward Christianity, given the cruelties of her father, who was Christianity's first representative in her life, and the suffering she experienced after her husband's suicide as well as her feminist rejection of patriarchy as she grew older. However, to miss the influence of Christian thought on Stone's poetry is to miss out on a deeper understanding of how her doubts, throughout her life, were tempered by childhood faith.

Stone's religious, social, and poetic sensibilities were further fostered in the home of her paternal grandparents, Edgar and Nora Perkins, in Indianapolis, Indiana, where she was raised, from age six onward, after her family returned there from Virginia. Her grandfather was a state senator, and her grandmother, the mother of seven children, was a writer and a painter. Stone long remembered that her grandmother's easel was always set up in the kitchen. The well-established, upper-middle-class household provided new encouragement for her as a young girl surrounded by creative great-aunts and great-uncles who wrote poetry, played music, and painted. The storytelling at the family dinner table was full of laughter, which contrasted somewhat with the formal tea parties where Stone learned to pour

tea and act like a lady—things she later said that she "had to learn to forget" (Barker, p. 34).

Stone loved to remember the friendship she found in the house, where her grandmother's youngest child, Harriet Perkins, was close to her in age. She wrote about her young aunt, who was nine when Stone was six and first arrived in Indiana, in poems like "Lighter than Air" and "How to Catch Aunt Harriet." In addition to recalling eating ice cream and going swimming together, a seemingly stray pair of lines in "Lighter than Air" suggests that the two girls were allies when Indiana thunderstorms poured over the landscape: "The lightning flashed / and we hid in the closet; the thunder crashed" (*What Love Comes To*, p. 85). Perhaps the storms Stone remembered were not exclusively literal and climatic but metaphoric for darker experiences.

Stone was sexually abused as a young girl, and like many children who experience such abuse, she tried to escape the memory of it. A cousin, a boy, molested her on at least one occasion (Stone qtd. in Wheler). The extent of the abuse Stone experienced is unclear, but other poems, written both early and late in her publishing career, as in "Love's Relative" (*In an Iridescent Time*, poem 52) or "All in Time," particularly stanza 12 (*What Love Comes To*, p. 21), suggest that her father's interactions with her were tainted. Stone's early experiences of human sexuality influenced Stone's formation as a woman, a poet, and later, a self-identified political and feminist writer (though, in her nineties, she apparently rejected the feminist moniker [deNiord, 2010, p. 51]). As a child, these experiences may have played their part in motivating her to read because reading let her out of the ordinary world, with its different forms of misery, and into the extraordinary world of the imagination.

Stone was an avid reader from the age of three. She recalled that after her mother turned off the light and went to bed, she would turn the light back on and read all night—and then get up and go to school the next day (Bradley, p. 73). As she grew older, she read great prose writers of the English, American, and Russian literary traditions. In her poem "Reading the Russians,"

she remembers "all those Victorian translations / where I was transfixed: / lying stomach down on my bed / that summer of my fourteenth year, / a library book flat under my right thumb" (*In the Next Galaxy*, 2002, p. 53). She would read seven or eight books a week, but in school, she said, "I was bored!" (Bradley, p. 56).

In her poem "Grade School," Stone pays homage to two of her elementary school teachers, Mrs. Ellery and Mr. Vollar, and notes, "Aesop, Shakespeare, Tennyson: at the start / of every day some poem we learned by heart" (*In the Next Galaxy*, p. 85). In Indiana in the 1920s, the memorization of poetry was a key part of elementary education, and this emphasis had a significant impact on Stone. She gained further motivation to pursue poetry on her own, apart from formal instruction, when she won a citywide poetry contest. The prize consisted of two books: an anthology of modern poetry and a book by Louis Untermeyer about the craft of poetry. Stone felt like it was a "great game" and a "total joy" (Bradley, p. 70) to write in all of the poetic forms she found in the book. Later in her life, in her Vermont farmhouse, she often would invite guests to play "the poetry game," which involved writing poems on various subjects in different forms and reading these aloud.

Two of Stone's most vivid memories from childhood were the time she looked up at the stars at night, in wonder and awe, and the time she went into the house of a stranger and saw his little daughter laid out in a coffin (Bradley, pp. 76–77). Stone spoke of these moments in interviews and alluded to them in her poems.

> Parallel to my literary development was my interest in the natural sciences. When I was a kid, I used to lie on the grass in the summer and look up at the stars. And then I'd read. I'd get books from the library about the stars. I remember when I saw my first photograph of a galaxy. I can still see it in front of my eyes. It was astounding and beautiful. I completely accepted the whole thing.... I never lost that hunger, that need to know more and more and more. I accept the universe. I don't fight against it. I know people who won't look at the stars because they don't want to. They are frightened and they don't want to know.... it makes them fear their own death.
>
> (Bradley, pp. 76–77)

As a mature poet, Stone would often seem to be caught between amazement at the beauty of the universe and the reality of death.

When she was a teenager Stone attended Shortridge High School. There she had the odd experience of feeling as if, for three months, the writerly part of her self went away: "I suddenly woke up to the fact that it was gone. I was devastated. And then it came back without my noticing it, and it went on" (Bradley, p. 71). This vulnerability to losing part of herself, her identity as a poet, would be exacerbated later in her life.

Stone's high school years coincided with the Great Depression, a time period that she wrote about in her poem "Eden, Then and Now," which begins in 1929, when Stone was fourteen years old. Years later, she memorialized in her poem the keen observations she made when her country changed after the stock market crashed, the "folks out of context, ... / This phenomenon investors said / would pass away" (*In the Next Galaxy*, p. 45). The biting double entendre of the final line in this quotation is typical Ruth Stone. She goes on in the poem to note that her father was then working for a daily paper (the *Indianapolis Star*) as a union printer and to admit that because he gave her mother a dollar a day they could consider themselves wealthy. But immediately after this revelation, the poet observes the harsh treatment the new poor faced. Though written long after the fact, these verses reveal when Stone first began to focus a hard eye on social injustice.

MARRIAGE, MOTHERHOOD, AND LOSS

As a young woman Stone experienced another life-changing event: she met John Clapp, Jr. He became her husband on June 23, 1935, when they married in Marion, Indiana. She had turned twenty just two weeks earlier. Her father, Stone later said, was too poor to send her to college (Gilbert, p. 58). About her first husband, she said: "I didn't want to marry him, and he was pressuring me, and everybody seemed to think he was right.... Obviously, I feared and hated him.... I tried to love my first husband the way I loved my family, and I was submissive to him, but he was very

domineering" (Gilbert, pp. 58–59). Her poem "Shotgun Wedding" gives voice in verse to related feelings: "They approach the zenith / Rowing the air like a pair of swans / With blood-red eyes" (*Cheap,* p. 55).

The couple lived for a few years in Indiana, where John worked as chemist. When he was accepted to the University of Illinois, Urbana-Champagne, to study for his doctorate in physics, Stone studied informally at the university. After seven years of marriage Stone gave birth to a daughter, whom she named Marcia (b. 1942). But her marriage was "extremely unhappy and very unfortunate" (Stone qtd. in Gilbert, p. 57). In fact, there was domestic abuse in it, as there had been in Stone's childhood. Stone said of her marriage to John that "I used to wake up every day and have *forgotten* all the terrible traumas of the day before, of living with a creature who was so alien, who assaulted me in some strange way and I had no defenses. And every day I'd forget all the happenings of the day before and start out again" (p. 57). Eventually, this situation was no longer tolerable, and Stone began to look for a way out. Her poem "1941" suggests she had a brief sexual relationship with an African American man in Indianapolis, which may have been her first step away from her unhappy marriage.

Later, at the University of Illinois, where her husband was a graduate student, Ruth Stone met Walter Stone, another writer. He was Jewish, the son of a "devout cantor" and an "Orthodox housekeeper," as she says in her poem, "On the Way" (*Simplicity,* p. 61). They began an affair, when Stone was in her late twenties, based on mutual physical and intellectual attraction. In Stone's words, "The reason Walter fell in love with me, I'm sure, is not only because of our physical attraction to one another but because of the writing" (Gilbert, p. 60). She wrote about their illicit trysts, the tenderness of them contrasted with the threat of death as the events of World War II exploded around the world, in "Coffee and Sweet Rolls," recalling "dingy hotels / … where we lay like embryos … / to be issued out into the terrible world" (*Simplicity,* pp. 106–107). The shadow of World War II darkened the early years of the relationship between Ruth and Walter, a shadow Stone memorialized in various poems including "In the Next Galaxy," "That Winter," and "Resonance."

After Stone had been married for nearly a decade, her father helped her to obtain a divorce. On July 10, 1944, in San Francisco, California, she married Walter, who had been serving in the navy during World War II, during a three-day leave he had received from his navy base, Port Chicago, which was thirty miles north of the city by the bay. Walter left on what Stone later called a "leaky Liberty ship" for Kiska, an island in the Rat Islands group of the Aleutian Islands in Alaska. The couple eventually had two daughters, Phoebe (born in 1949) and Abigail ("Blue Jay," born in 1953). As adults, both daughters would become published writers.

At the end of World War II, Walter left the navy and was reunited with Stone. He attended graduate school at Harvard University. After first teaching in Illinois, he accepted the position of assistant professor of English at Vassar College in Poughkeepsie, New York, in 1952. Stone's training in her grandmother's household proved useful as she played the role of a faculty member's wife. But she felt that she was also recognized by the college community as different and accomplished in her own right (Gilbert, p. 62). Her husband promoted her poetry by typing it up and sending it out for publication, and she won *Poetry*'s Bess Hokin Prize in 1953 and the Kenyon Review Fellowship in Poetry in 1956, which was awarded by John Crowe Ransom, the first editor of the *Kenyon Review.* With the money from the fellowship, Stone bought the farmhouse in Goshen, Vermont, that she would make her lifelong home. Ruth and Walter both had books ready to be printed in 1959: her first poetry collection, *In an Iridescent Time, Poems, 1953–58,* which was bound together with first books by Donald Finkel and Gene Baro and published as part of the volume *Poets of Today,* volume 6 (1959), edited by John Hall. Walter was already enjoying some additional financial success with a grant from the American Philosophical Society.

The couple appeared to be thriving, personally and professionally. Certainly when Stone

spoke of the marriage in later years, she usually did so in glowing terms, for it was clearly happier than her first. Stone said that was Walter a "genius" who was very "supportive" of her poetry (Gilbert, p. 60). In *Poems, 1953–58,* Walter also spoke well of Ruth, describing her sensually ("Ten P.M.," in Hall, ed., *Poets of Today,* p. 163), sexually ("The Web," p. 164, and "Compelled to Love," p. 166), and naturally:

> She thinks like earth.
> She ebbs and flows with private seasons.
> Fall is her fruit,
> and spring is her birth.
> In winter she makes rhymes of reasons
> and plays them on her flute.
>
> ("Woman," p. 168)

Clearly Ruth and Walter inspired one another as both lovers and writers. Yet like any marriage, theirs also experienced times of stress. This is suggested in Stone's poem "Union," in *In an Iridescent Time,* where she writes, "Her highness, smooth as egg, concealed as much.... He never cracked her shell or saw the bird / Undeveloped, piteous, absurd" (poem 41), and in Walter's poems alluding to himself in the role of King Lear, who in Shakespeare's classic play is an old man, with three daughters, who slowly loses his mind (see "Modern Poetry and the Tradition," p. 151, and "Lear," p. 173, in Hall, ed., *Poets of Today*). Much later, Stone would wonder if Walter, a smoker, had contracted throat cancer at this time, and if that had been affecting him as well (deNiord, 2010, p. 52). She certainly believed that secondhand smoke affected her for many years afterward.

Another source of strain may have come from nude photographs that Walter took of Stone and apparently shared with other navy sailors with whom he served during World War II. Walter alludes to these pictures in his poem, "Brothers": "Sixteen first imagined her, setting her hair in a mirror. / The image remains with the sailors; she mirrors their sea" (p. 149). Ruth Stone refers to the images negatively in "One Reel Tragedy," where she remembers:

> About his neck he wears a camera
> He has three eyes; one with insomnia.

> ...
> Picture his Sundays in a darkened room
> Where he prints and develops the prizes of the groom.
> Give and take, shutter and snap, her flesh
> lies in the acid fixer, and the threshhold of mirrors subdivides her soul.
>
> ...
> He sells her piece by piece and pose by pose.
> Her selves go stealing forth, a trade that grows
>
> ...
> So her symbolic anonymity
> Is shared in tortured prisons, and with free
> Hoarse-throated boys with dirty hands; or deep
> In the sea's diatoms she may sleep
> Beside a sailor's beautiful picked bones
> Safe in his sea chest while the planet groans.
>
> (*In an Iridescent Time,* poem 54)

This poem can be compared to "When I Was Thirty-Five, You Took My Photograph" (*In the Next Galaxy,* p. 61), in which Stone expresses more detached feelings.

The idea conveyed by "Brothers" and "One Reel Tragedy," namely that these photographs went down to a watery grave with navy servicemen during World War II, may reflect events from not only maritime battles but also from the Port Chicago disaster of July 17, 1944. The navy servicemen working at Port Chicago, located thirty miles north of San Francisco, endured a horrifying tragedy when 4,600 tons of munitions exploded. It happened as cargo handlers, all of whom were African American enlisted men, were packing bombs, depth charges, and ammunition into the SS *Quinault Victory* and SS *E. A. Bryan,* two merchant ships that were bound for the Pacific theater of the war. The explosion killed 320 men on the pier, including all of the cargo handlers, and injured nearly 400 more.

Ruth Stone writes about this disaster in her poem "Happiness," which recalls the first days of her marriage:

> The first night in our rented basement room,
> as we came together ...
> Port Chicago exploded!
> Several thousand pounds of human flesh
> shot like hamburger through the air;
> making military funerals, even with wax,
> even with closed caskets, bizarre.

As well as certain facts: there were no white males loading ammunition on that ship.

(*Second-Hand Coat*, p. 46)

Every building at the Port Chicago base was damaged; several were flattened. Remaining servicemen were reassigned to Mare Island Naval Shipyard in Vallejo, California. Meanwhile, Walter embarked for Kiska after this disaster with the memory of it, no doubt, vividly in his mind.

Walter's memories, along with whatever level of stress or strain he may have felt in his marriage (in relation to his wife, as a result of his paternal responsibility for his daughters, or because of an increasing sense of physical ill health), may have triggered a deeper sense of despair over time. As a Jewish American navy serviceman during World War II, he may have been affected by memories of trauma, including the later knowledge of the murder of 6 million Jews in the Holocaust. His poems from 1953 to 1958, however, suggest that he was wrestling with demons from his younger years. While his writing is versatile, inspired by metaphysical and Romantic poetry, on the one hand, and by Ruth, to whom he dedicated the book, on the other, it is also influenced by his own dark frame of mind. In several poems, he is clearly meditating on death.

In "Logos," Walter Stone speaks of the death of the singing bird, which seems emblematic of the poet himself:

the rot is in the root,
the tree of pleasure kills the singing bird,
the birds die and their dying kills the trees.
The furies turn flesh backward into Word
the mind runs mad and eats itself like fruit.
Dream me distractions more terrible than these!

(Hall, ed., p. 153)

In "Chronicle," he says, "I heard the doors of music close, / and felt my heart go wild, wild, / and I was ready then for death" (p. 157). In "Brothers," an elaborate poem in which he imagines himself as a succession of selves that he names by ages ("Five," "Sixteen," "Twenty-Two," and so on), and whom he calls "brothers," he writes about his final self dying:

in the long processions of seasons the house will decay,
the brothers will fade, with no one left to keep
the tall, old skeleton which declines with its owner:
in a rotting hallway the final brother will sleep.

(p. 150)

In "The Man of Property to His Muse," he writes, "I am warden / of a fine prison, and I die among my things" (p. 152). These poems reveal a progression in thought from fantasies of death ("distractions") to readiness for death ("I was ready then for death"), from death anticipated in a future time ("the final brother will sleep") to death experienced as a present reality: "I die among my things." These poems were a prelude to Walter Stone's last act.

In 1959 the family moved to London for Walter's sabbatical leave from Vassar. There, in a rented room, Walter Stone committed suicide at the age of forty-two. Stone received a phone call from a landlady who wanted to inform her of finding the body hung from a hook on the back of a door. But Stone handed the phone to her teenage daughter, Marcia, who was the first to hear the news clearly and then tell her mother. Stone then woke and told her young daughter, Phoebe, who fell to the floor, crying, "Not my daddy! Not my daddy!" So Stone did not wake the youngest child, Abigail, to tell her. Many years later, Stone expressed deep regret for this decision, which she apparently made in order to protect her youngest child—however briefly—from the terrible sorrow. That night, the bereaved family slept together in the same bed to try to comfort one another after receiving such terrible news (Stone qtd. in Block). The shock of this event irreparably altered Stone's world, and she would write about it in numerous poems over the course of the rest of her life.

At the time of his death, Stone had been with Walter for at least fifteen years and married to him for much of that time, during which they had shared life together: writing, parenting, and working in the academic community at Vassar College. As Stone said: "Sometime in the year after he died, I remember saying aloud or saying to myself, 'The bird has died.' It's exactly what happened. I really felt that the bird in me had

died" (Gilbert, p. 64). In the immediate aftermath her husband's death, Stone had to make arrangements to return home with her children. Then she went to work to support her family. In the long season of grief that followed, she felt that she lost her ability to remember: "I couldn't remember anything. I just forgot more and more and more things. I couldn't sleep; I didn't sleep for a year except in little snatches" (p. 65). Stone was grieving, and she became severely depressed.

But she continued to write. In her poems, she does remember many things. Fighting against forgetfulness, her poems become like little lights in the dark. Stone herself became competent in new aspects of living. She continued to raise her daughters and run her house, but she also "began gardening, making fires, cutting wood, hauling oil" (p. 65). She grew through her loss even as she recorded its impact on her life in her poems.

WIDOWHOOD, TEACHING, AND WRITING

Ruth Stone was forty-four years old when she became a widow. Her first book of poetry was published, but she later said that neither it nor her husband's poems published in *Poets of Today VI* meant anything to her: "They meant nothing to me. Absolutely nothing. All the reason for doing them had died with him" (Gilbert, p. 58). She had dedicated her book to Walter, and added, "With this book the author pays tribute to Vassar College on the occasion of its Centennial" (epigraph in *In an Iridescent Time*). Yet she had lost her husband, and with him, not only the college community where they had written and worked together but part of her identity, including, for a time, the "writerly part" of her self.

She began to recover her identity as a poet four years later. From 1963 to 1965 she held a two-year fellowship at the Radcliffe Institute for Independent Study, where she both wrote and taught. While there, she formed close ties with other fellows, especially the poet Maxine Kumin and novelist Tillie Olson. She began to write the poems that would form the basis for her next poetry collection, *Topography and Other Poems*, which would be published in 1971. All three

women—Kumin, Olson, and Stone—would later be recognized and appreciated as significant feminist writers. However, at this time, Stone was already being recognized, specifically by the Poetry Society of America, which awarded her the Shelley Memorial Award for 1964–1965.

The Radcliffe fellowship opened up new opportunities for Stone to teach creative writing at colleges and universities across the country. For the next twenty-five years, she lived the life of an itinerant professor and poet in residence, teaching at Wellesley College in Massachusetts (fall 1965); Brandeis University in Massachusetts (1965–1966, 1975); the University of Wisconsin, Madison (1967–1969); the University of Illinois, Urbana-Champagne (1971–1973); Centre College in Kentucky (winter 1975); University of Virginia, Charlottesville (1977–1978); University of California, Davis (spring 1978, fall 1978, spring 1981); New York University (fall 1984, fall 1985, spring 1986); Cooper Union in New York City (1986); and Old Dominion University in Norfolk, Virginia (1989–1990). As a result of this constant journeying, she met many young poets across the nation and influenced their development, so much so that she became known as "Mother Poet" (Freeman, p. 10) and "America's Akhmatova" (Willis Barnstone, on the back cover of *Simplicity*).

Although it seems that what she called the "poetry factory" ("Some Things You Need to Know Before You Join the Union") treated Stone unfairly in providing only short-term appointments over more than two decades, Stone was conscious of the value of teaching only part-time because it gave her greater freedom to write. She did finally accept a full-time teaching position, and when she had been teaching for five years in a row, she commented, at the age of eighty-one, to J. F. Battaglia:

> I think that probably the only way to really remain a writer in the best sense of the word is not to go into teaching and certainly not to go into scholarship. Not to go into the academic thing. I've only been steadily teaching for these five years because other times I've taught at the most two years and had a lot of space in between. Financially it may have been difficult, but artistically it was probably the only way I could do it. But now, I

don't think it's as hard. I think I can manage it—I do manage it—I sort of don't allow my teaching and my writing to overlap in my mind.... I don't think that scholarship needs to hurt you. I think what hurts is the competitive pressure to write criticism and to do scholarship without it being meaningful to you.

Stone's commitment to earn enough money to give herself the freedom to write, if not a lifestyle of luxury, resulted in the production of vivid, astonishing, and wonderful collections of poems—and in verses that were lyrical, poignant, and shocking—that were recognized with significant awards from the very same "poetry factory" that she critiqued.

During her many years of traveling throughout the United States, Stone published *Unknown Messages* (1973), *Cheap* (1975), *American Milk* (1986), *Second-Hand Coat: Poems New and Selected* (1987), and *The Solution* (1989), and she received many awards in this period for her creative work. In addition to the Shelley Memorial Award, she received two Guggenheim Fellowships (1972–1973 and 1975–1976), and she used the money from one of them to roof her house in Vermont—a fact she mentions in her poem "It Follows" (in which she ironically considers using the money to get a facelift instead). In 1983 she received the Delmore Swartz Award. In 1986 she received a Whiting Award. This time, she used the money to buy plumbing for her house. Stone was a practical poet.

In 1988 Stone received the Paterson Poetry Prize—and she reached a significant turning point in her teaching career. She held a visiting position in the English department at the State University of New York at Binghamton and then in 1989 accepted a tenure-track position, which she began in the spring term of 1990 in the year she turned seventy-five. She received tenure at the age of seventy-seven. She had already had a distinguished, if unusual, career as an American poet, but now she began to achieve recognition at a new level. From 1990 to 2000 she published three major poetry collections: *Who Is the Widow's Muse?* (Yellow Moon Press, 1991), *Simplicity* (Paris Press, 1996), and *Ordinary Words* (Paris Press, 2000), as well as the chapbook *Nursery Rhymes from Mother Stone*. *Simplicity* won the Pushcart Prize, after being published with the support of an Eric Mathieu King Award from the Academy of American Poets, and *Ordinary Words* won the National Book Critics Circle Award. The (ironically titled) *Simplicity* was justly acknowledged as a tour de force in American poetry, containing one of Stone's most significant poems, "Scheherazade Is Nailed and Mailed in Five Days," which Jan Freeman has called "a major American poem. A landmark" (p. 9).

In the subsequent decade, Ruth Stone published three more major collections of poetry, all with Copper Canyon Press: *In the Next Galaxy* (2002), which won the National Book Award in the same year that Stone received the Wallace Stevens Award "for proven mastery in the art of poetry"; *In the Dark* (2004), which won the Patterson Award for Sustained Literary Achievement; and *What Love Comes To: New & Selected Poems* (2008), which won the Milt Kessler Poetry Book Award and was a finalist for the Pulitzer Prize. Stone was named the poet laureate of Vermont in 2007; the state of Vermont also acknowledged her with the Walter Cerf Award for Lifetime Achievement in the Arts.

POETRY AND INSPIRATION

Ruth Stone often spoke of her poems coming to her in a rush, as if from outside of her, and how she would run to get a pen or pencil to write them down before they escaped.

> It's a funny thing. Even as a child, I would hear a poem coming toward me from way off in the universe. I wouldn't hear it. I would feel it, and it would come right toward me. If I didn't catch it, if I didn't run in the house and write it down, it would go right through me and back into the universe. So I'd never see it again. I'd never hear it again. I've lost about ninety-nine percent of my poems this way. Sometimes I would catch the last line and write it through the bottom up. I have to say, I never thought they were mine. They weren't mine. They belonged somewhere else.
>
> (deNiord, 2010, p. 50)

In addition to retelling this story many times to different people who asked about the source of her inspiration, Stone also wrote verses about

how poems came to her. Elizabeth Gilbert, the author of the 2006 best seller *Eat, Pray, Love*, remembered Stone telling her about her experience of writing, and she paid homage to Ruth Stone in a TED talk (February 2009) on nurturing creativity. However, Stone also said that only about half of her poems came to her spontaneously. On others, she worked very hard, writing and rewriting, even up to sixteen pages for the draft of a single poem, especially when she was refining her craft at the Radcliffe Institute (deNiord, 2010, p. 50).

Stone viewed poems in two complementary ways: as emotional responses to the wounds the poet experiences in this life and as dramatic stories. She told J. F. Battaglia:

> I think poems are closer to your mad reactions to life. Also to the self, the wounded. I think a lot of poetry comes out of wounds. I'm sure stories do too, but actually fiction for me is objective because I think that fiction automatically became for me the observed Other. Poetry, as your own emotional outcries, is more personal. Poetry comes more out of the self; fiction is the self observing....

> I realize that I'm probably also a prose writer, because that's what I've been reading for over seventy years: You can see it in the poetry—that I'm a storyteller. And I see that I'm constantly collecting people as characters and seeing situations that are happening in an art form, or dialogue and so forth that just fascinates me. You know, I constantly see people that way. I see everything dramatically.

This perspective on her identity as poet and storyteller can explain the impulse toward lyrical and narrative forms so often seen in Stone's poems. It also provides context for an otherwise shocking statement that she made late in life: "I've never thought of myself as a poet. Never" (deNiord, 2010, p. 50). For though Stone became well-regarded for her accomplishments in poetry, two of her earliest publications were short stories: "The Secret Profession," published in *Commentary* in 1955, and "The Hedgerows in England," published in the *New Yorker* in 1962.

FICTION AND AUTOBIOGRAPHY

In Stone's short story "The Secret Profession," her protagonist, Margery, is a woman married to a novelist and professor of Eastern College, Dr. Henry Freed. They have two daughters, one of whom is named Elizabeth. Margery writes privately, with a small group of five others, but wishes for a wider audience. One day, while working in her garden, she is interrupted by a thirty-year-old German Jewish man named Mr. Harrison Finebein. He is looking for a job as a teacher or a librarian. He says he writes and shows Margery a long list of his works. He mentions he gets by on his savings, as a single man, but that he is also working on a grant. He had tried to get into graduate school at the University of Chicago, but he was not successful. He repeats the same things over and over again, and his mannerisms are disturbing. When Margery politely inquires about his parents, he says they are dead and adds, "They cooked them"—a clear allusion to the Holocaust. Margery gasps in surprise, but Mr. Finebein changes the subject to her garden.

Margery offers him flowers, accidentally failing to remove a white one that has died from the bouquet, which offends her visitor. She then phones her husband to arrange coffee for the three of them. Henry is irritated that she has called and interrupted his work at the college, but she insists that she needs his help to get rid of the visitor. She warns her husband that Mr. Finebein seems to be paranoid and insane—and that he is a writer.

Margery drives to the college with Mr. Finebein, but when the two of them arrive, Henry takes the driver's seat. The Freeds and Mr. Finebein proceed to the coffee shop, where their interactions are awkward. Margery complains of a headache, and Mr. Finebein interprets her illness as dislike of his company, which Margery denies (but the reader suspects he may have overheard her harsh estimation of his character when she was speaking about him on the phone to her husband). Margery asks Mr. Finebein what Germany was like under Hitler. He replies, "Pure hell" and closes his eyes. Mr. Finebein mentions a Professor Goldmark, a Renaissance scholar, whose help he sought but did not obtain. He speculates that Goldmark, an Episcopalian, converted. "You're wrong," Henry says, "he's not a Jew." Mr. Finebein wonders aloud if he

should convert, as if doing so might help him to obtain work. The Freeds do not answer him.

Instead, Henry reviews a list of Mr. Finebein's writings, and asks, "Any published?" Mr. Finebein does not answer the question, though earlier he had boasted to Margery that they were and that he had received awards for them. The Freeds watch their guest eat his strawberry ice cream, noticing that he laps up even the last pink drop of it. Margery begins to suspect that Mr. Finebein's list of publications is entirely made up.

After the Freeds drive Mr. Finebein to his rented place, the meeting ends on a cold note, as Henry says he will not be able to meet again for a few weeks. "Or next semester? Or next year?" Mr. Finebein asks sarcastically. The Freeds drive away, and Margery tells her husband that Mr. Finebein is angry, even furious—and that she does not believe he has written a line, "not a line." When her husband makes a sharp turn, and she is thrown against the passenger side of the car, she asks, "Why don't you learn how to drive?" That is the end of the story.

In the course of the narrative, it becomes apparent that the "secret profession" of the title is not writing, which all three main characters do to various extents, but lying. Mr. Finebein, a Holocaust survivor in America, lies to the Freeds because he desperately needs work. When Mr. Finebein says Margery dislikes his company, Margery disagrees: a polite lie. Henry also lies to Mr. Finebein when he says he cannot meet him again for a few weeks: a polite but clearly self-serving lie meant to help him avoid another uncomfortable encounter. Mr. Finebein is understandably angry. Meanwhile Margery, Stone tells us, "felt contaminated" and "a sense of universal failure welled up in her." The backdrop for these lies is, of course, the lies of Hitler and the tragedy of the Holocaust, which continue to play out in the postwar world of which the Freeds and Mr. Finebein are a part.

Like "The Secret Profession," Stone's story "The Hedgerows in England" explores the dynamics of lying. In "Hedgerows," Mrs. Stanley has accompanied her husband, Dr. Stanley, an assistant professor of English literature, to Cam-

bridge, England, for his sabbatical from Eastern College, which is located in New York. They have brought with them their three daughters, Edith, Fanny, and Annabel. The action of the story begins when Mrs. Stanley meets an old woman crossing the street who tells her that her aunt broke her hip stepping off a bus and died in bed; the old woman, who had been a young woman at the time and engaged to be married, had not cared for her aunt despite the aunt's expectation that she would. This confession clearly makes Mrs. Stanley uncomfortable, and she disengages herself from the old woman so she can continue to the silver stall in the local market.

There she is persuaded to buy a teakettle warmer, being told it is made of melted bell metal (though she suspects it is brass), and two spoons supposedly from the time of Queen Anne. She spends more for these items than she can really afford, even though she suspects she is being overcharged because she is an American. She wants these antiques; she wants part of the history of England to keep.

Later she goes for a walk with her husband in the gardens at Christ's College, though she feels cold and does not want to go. She pays attention to the gardeners at work and then to a robin, but her husband talks about Milton and later takes her picture in front of a 350-year-old mulberry tree not far from the bust of the seventeenth-century poet. They separate: he to the library, she to the butcher's. They plan to reunite for tea later.

At home, Mrs. Stanley meets her daughters with her silver treasures in tow: the youngest, Annabel, is jealous that her mother bought something for herself but not for her; the eldest, Edith, likes the tea warmer, but when the middle child, Fanny, says she does not, Edith advises her to go back to her artwork. Her husband arrives and complains about the tea and the peanut butter sandwiches his wife is serving. The daughters complain about difficulties they are having with teachers and friends at school. It seems they miss their life in New York just as their mother does. Mrs. Stanley decides to share the victory of the spoons with her family. As they admire them, she

checks their markings against her book on English silver—only to discover that they are most certainly not from Queen Anne's era. "That isn't the seventeenth century," her husband remarks (p. 141). Instead, the spoons appear to date to 1903. The silver, Mrs. Stanley notices, is scratched.

Her husband mentions how the library at Cambridge has all the books he had been wanting for his research. As he talks, Mrs. Stanley thinks about her garden and remembers lines from Henry Wadsworth Longfellow's 1858 poem "The Courtship of Miles Standish": "I have been thinking all day, dreaming all night and thinking all day, of the hedgerows of England—they are in blossom now, and the country is all like a garden." To her husband, Mrs. Stanley says aloud, "Yes, I know, and I'm glad we came" (p. 141). Her words are clearly untrue, for she has been cold all day and wishing for her own garden at home in New York. She is lying to her husband just as the silver-sellers at the market lied to her. The irony of her response, however, is much deeper.

Both of Ruth Stone's published short stories are forms of thinly veiled autobiography. Stone is the inspiration for the protagonists, Margery Freed and Mrs. Stanley, both of whom are gardeners, professors' wives, and mothers; notably, Margery Freed is a writer, and Mrs. Stanley has her picture taken by her husband. Walter Stone is clearly the inspiration for the protagonists' husbands, Dr. Henry Freed and Dr. Stanley, who are both professors at "Eastern College" (i.e., Vassar College) who write and/or study literature. Stone's daughters are inspirational too: Marcia is the model for Edith (and possibly Elizabeth in "The Secret Profession"); Phoebe for Fanny; and Abigail for Annabel. The settings, New York and England, roughly correspond to Ruth Stone's lived experience; the plots may as well. The stories may be compared fruitfully with the transcripts and recordings of the many interviews Stone gave over the years. Together, the stories and the interviews form Ruth Stone's autobiography and reveal her thoughts and feelings about her life at different points in time.

In 1999 Stone published a third story, which could be considered either a prose poem or flash fiction: "In the Arboretum" (*Ordinary Words*, pp. 44–45). The protagonist is once again Ruth Stone, speaking *in propria persona*, and she is taking a walk on the redwood-forested grounds where she is living as an artist in residence when she hears a male owl, then she sees a fledgling hawk down: "Totally vulnerable, with its terrible innocence, it cannot feed itself. It cannot fly yet. It has this brief corridor to cross" (p. 44). As she walks and collects a few eucalyptus leaves, Stone remembers an eight-year-old girl in Vermont who was raped and strangled, her body abandoned in the fields until the members of her impoverished community went out to find it. When she retraces her steps, Stone says, "I look for the hawk child. She is gone" (p. 45). "In the Arboretum" is a short, powerful narrative that combines Stone's attentiveness to the viciousness of predator and prey in the natural world with a critique of social injustice.

SOURCES AND INFLUENCES

Stone's poetry, like her prose, is deeply influenced by her perceptions of nature. Stone was a gardener all her life, and perhaps in part for that practical reason, nature, in Stone's poems, is rarely idealized. Instead, she examines it with a poetic microscope, writing of the unification of egg and sperm, and with a poetic telescope, writing of planets, stars, and cosmic events across the whole of the scientifically studied galaxy. Her reflections on events in the natural world can be ironic, or turn to social commentary, or even turn away from nature to human impositions on landscape, as when she writes in "Don't Miss It": "If you're looking for a heron on one leg, / for a white egret in this water-logged parcel, / you may be blind to boarded-up gas pumps" (*In the Next Galaxy*, p. 48). Her critical eye evaluates decay in nature, considering its harshness, as in her meditation on a dead female mole infested with maggots ("The System," *What Love Comes To*, p. 252). Occasionally, she describes nature in spiritually transcendent terms, as in "Eta Carinae," in which she writes of giant stars in a

nearby galaxy: "The supernovae, like Christ / come to illuminate the ignorant" (*What Love Comes To,* p. 24).

Stone's poetry is full of responses to nature, but not in a Romantic vein; her work does not seem to be strongly influenced by either the English or the American poetic tradition. She said that she avoided reading the work of other poets because she did not wish to be influenced by them. Instead, she wanted to develop her own style and focus on her own content. Reading her poetry, anyone can see that she achieved her goal, for her allusions to other poets and poems are few and far between. Yet at various times throughout her life, Stone mentioned her early knowledge of the poetry of Alfred Tennyson, her natural sense of empathy with Emily Dickinson (Gilbert, p. 56), and her admiration of Gerard Manley Hopkins and "his ideas about stretching the line" (Bradley, p. 74). Emily Dickinson in particular was an important foremother-poet for Ruth Stone.

In 1998 Stone participated in a project of the Dickinson Electronic Archives (hosted by Amherst College) called *Titanic Operas.* The project gathers the prose and poetic responses of twenty-six American women poets to the legacy of Emily Dickinson. Stone wrote a brief statement paying tribute to Dickinson for the project:

When I read Emily Dickinson's poems, these original hard as steel poems, and I feel the intensity in every word, words used in new ways, beat to her will, then I think she was self-sufficient, an artist whose mind was never asleep, whose concentration recreated, made fresh, all that she saw and felt, as though she saw through the ordinary barriers not as a visionary but as a laser beam. But when I think of how little recognition she received in her lifetime, and how devastated she must have felt, though her fierce pride concealed it, then I am angry and sad. Yes, a great artist knows and can work in almost total isolation, but it is a terrible thing to have to do. The original mind seems eccentric, even crazy sometimes. In her cryptic inventions, she broke the tiresome mold of American poetry. We still stand among those shards and splinters.

("Breaking the Tired Mold of American Poetry")

In the electronic archive, this statement is followed by a few poems by Emily Dickinson, which Stone considers one by one, and then by twelve of Stone's own poems. There is an audio file of the whole as well as an electronic transcript. Stone's contribution constitutes an electronic chapbook of her own work, even as it pays homage to Emily Dickinson. Stone admired some twentieth-century poets as well.

In discussing her own vital use of the image (Bradley, p. 75), Stone has suggested her philosophical connections to certain Imagist poets, including those whom she mentions by name: Wallace Stevens ("Words," *Ordinary Words,* p. 3), e. e. cummings, and Edna St. Vincent Millay (the latter two both in "Fragrance," *What Love Comes To,* p. 45). She complained about Ezra Pound and his negative impact on H.D. (Hilda Doolittle) (Battaglia, 1996), emphasizing the importance of having freedom to write poetry however it comes, irrespective of rules. Stone also indicated her affinity for the work of Alicia Ostriker.

When asked, Alicia Ostriker reflected on the similarities her poetry has with that of Ruth Stone:

I am tickled that Ruth sees me as aligned with her. Here's what I think we have in common. We are both unabashed lovers of life, which includes sex and children. We both have a sense of humor. We both have a strain of rationalism and science in our work. We are realistic about relationships—which forms a big topic for us—we are feminists but not separatists; we both like a conversational style (though I sometimes write more lyrically). I think there is a straight-forwardness about us both (interview 4/00).

(qtd. in Wheler)

Ostriker is one of many American poets who has read Stone's work with respect and sensitivity to her themes.

In addition to Alicia Ostriker, the poet and literary critic Sandra Gilbert has long expressed admiration for the work of Ruth Stone; indeed, Gilbert has been one of Stone's champions. She actively promoted Stone's career by interviewing her, facilitating her employment as a visiting poet at the University of California, Davis, and co-editing (with Wendy Barker) a book of critical essays on her poetry as well as choosing her for

the National Book Award for her poetry collection *Ordinary Words*. The importance of Sandra Gilbert in Stone's career has been vital, and Stone acknowledged this: she dedicated one of her poetry collections, *Second-Hand Coat*, to, among others, Sandra Gilbert and her husband Elliot, whom she called "my brilliant, enduring friends."

Stone's dedications of her poetry collections give insight into those who formed her inner circle and inspired her the most. Her first collection, *In an Iridescent Time*, was dedicated to her husband Walter and paid tribute to the collegiate community that they shared at Vassar College. Her second collection, *Topography and Other Poems*, was dedicated to seven people, many of whom had acted as patrons and promoters of Stone's poetry: Constance Smith, director of the Radcliffe Institute for Independent Study; Jean and Frank White, Margaret and Leslie Fiedler, and Alice McIntyre; and Dr. Maxie Maultsby, Jr. Stone dedicated *Cheap: New Poems and Ballads*, her third full poetry collection, to "the countless women I respect and admire, and especially Marcia Stone Croll, Phoebe Stone, and Blue Jay Stone, my incomparable daughters." She dedicated subsequent collections to her daughters as well. Stone's beloved daughters clearly inspired her.

Second-Hand Coat: Poems New and Selected was dedicated not only to the Elliots but to her grandchildren, Nora Swan Croll, Ehsan Jessie Croll, Ethan David Carlson, Hillery Ruth Stone, Bianca Rose Stone, and Walter Joseph Stone. In naming her grandchildren in her dedication, Stone pointed to her dual legacy as both a poet and as a mother and grandmother, the matriarch of a growing family. She also dedicated the book to William B. Goodman, "editor and friend."

Stone's daughter Phoebe played a special role in illustrating, with her own artwork, *Who Is the Widow's Muse?*, which is an extraordinary series of poems. Stone dedicated *Who Is the Widow's Muse?* to "Kandace Lombard, who asked the question," for as a student, Kandace Brill Lombard met Stone once when Stone was giving a poetry reading at a conference in Buffalo, New York, and she asked her the question that titles the collection. Lombard subsequently wrote the

first doctoral dissertation about Stone (2002), under the direction of Leslie Fiedler at the State University of New York at Buffalo. Lombard had already published an essay about Stone, titled "Under the Seal of My Widowhood," in the critical volume edited by Gilbert and Barker (1996).

Stone dedicated her Pushcart Prize–winning volume *Simplicity* (1995) to Ingrid Arnesen, Deborah Campbell, and Jan Freeman, whom she called "my poetry daughters." One of these women, Jan Freeman, wrote a critical essay on Stone, which was published in 1996. Stone dedicated *Ordinary Words* to "my beautiful daughters, Marcia, Phoebe, and Abigail." As Stone's sight began to fade and she struggled with partial blindness from a botched surgery, her daughters helped her prepare new poetry manuscripts for publication with Copper Canyon Press, and she acknowledged their help in dedications to the books. She dedicated *In the Next Galaxy* (2004) to Abigail, saying, "During my recent loss of vision, she has provided the light," and *In the Dark* (2004) to Marcia and her granddaughter, the poet Nora Swan Croll, "who were my eyes for many months, reading aloud, transcribing from my notebooks, discussing, organizing, typing, and proofreading."

Stone dedicated *What Love Comes To: New & Selected Poems* (2008) to the memory of her son-in-law Don Croll, who passed away in the same year she published this book. This death impressed upon her once again the sorrow of loss. Stone wrote in the dedication: "To Don Croll, August 19, 1939 to January 11, 2008: Beloved father of my grandchildren Nora Swan, Jesse Ehsan, and Sahara Najat; world traveler, lover of the Persian language, and my dear friend for over fifty years.' She added an epitaph, four lines of poetry from Edward Fitzgerald"s late-nineteenth-century translation *The Rubáiyát of Omar Khayyám*: "For some we loved, the loveliest and the best / That from his Vintage rolling Time hath prest / Have drunk their Cup a Round or two before, / And one by one crept silently to rest." This dedication, like the others, reveals how important Stone's inner circle was to her life as a person as well as a poet.

In her poems, it is apparent that Stone talks to herself, her younger self, or her body; Walter and her daughters; and members of her extended family, including her mother, father, aunts, uncles, and grandparents. But she also talks as if she were a ventriloquist, using dramatic monologue to give voice to the voiceless. In these poems, she speaks from the perspective of women who have struggled on the edges of American community (the most notable of which is certainly "The Song of Absinthe Granny"), but also from the perspectives of those who have judged these women unfairly ("How They Got Her to Quiet Down" and "Sleeping Beauty IV"). Stone consistently notices outsiders—at bus stops, on the street, in institutions—and she memorializes them in her poems. She compels readers to identify with these outsiders and thus to gain a deeper empathy with the poet's vision.

Stone's poetic vision of the world has been called "tragi-comic," for her ironic sense of humor in the face of the brokenness of the world shines through her work. In her work, she treats many themes, including love and loss, poverty, the human body, relationships between men and women, the marginalized members of American communities, old age, the universe, and poetry itself. Her vision and themes perhaps can be best understood in the context of her view of the purpose of poetry: to bring about healing. In her interview with J. F. Battaglia, she said:

> Having children be encouraged to write how they feel and how they respond to the world, that's a wonderful thing, and it's also giving them an idea that poetry is not all something that they are taught—this is a poem and this is what it means, et cetera—which was a dreadful way of teaching poetry—but that it's the right of every human being. Poetry, in many ways, is an expression of the psyche. Maybe it's the wounded [psyche] inside us, as well as the joyous. I remember little children in—maybe it was here in Middlebury, or down in Maryland—but I asked them to write about something that they miss. Well, several of them wrote about loss, the loss of grandparents, of friends, or animals, and so forth—you know, all kinds of painful loss—and they were little kindergarten ones. Wonderful things they wrote. Expressions of art in all forms, but especially language, is healing.

As these words suggest, Stone believed that poetry could bring healing to poets, including children, and she was concerned with passing on a poetic legacy to the next generation. But to Stone, poetry not only brought about healing. As she used to say, sometimes in the middle of department meetings, "Poetry saves lives!" (as noted by Liz Rosenberg, qtd. in "Professor Emerita Ruth Stone").

LEGACY

Ruth Stone died on November 18, 2011, and she was given a green burial by her family: buried behind her house in Goshen, Vermont, under raspberry canes, with no grave marker. Versions of her obituary appeared in major newspapers across the United States, including the *New York Times, Los Angeles Times,* and *Guardian,* among many others. Her daughter Phoebe wrote a beautiful and moving tribute to her several months after her death that recalled Stone not only as a poet but also as a mother and a gardener.

Stone's legacy lives on in many ways: in her daughters and granddaughters, some of whom have become writers themselves, and in her students and colleagues, many of whom have been inspired by her. The essay collection *The House Is Made of Poetry* (1996), edited by Wendy Barker and Sandra M. Gilbert, celebrates Stone's poetic achievement, as does volume 27 of *Paintbrush: A Journal of Poetry and Translation,* which was entirely dedicated to her work. The Vermont College of Fine Arts has established an annual award in her name, the Ruth Stone Poetry Prize, and the Ruth Stone Foundation exists to protect and promote her work as well as her farmhouse home in Vermont.

In her lifetime, Stone published her poems in over fifty anthologies. Stone also recorded her poems on many separate occasions, so her voice can be heard in recorded interviews and YouTube video clips as well as in the film *USA the Movie* (2005), reading her poem, "Be Serious." Her voice will live on for future generations because her poetry has an extraordinary quality to it, which demands our attention, especially in dif-

ficult times. As Stone herself said in her acceptance speech for the National Book Award:

> I think that poetry rises especially in times of oppression, like in Yugoslavia, where it became a great thing for the oppressed recently and what seems recently to me. Of course, all of the arts, everything that the wonderful human mind does is, is important. I do want to say that, printing and the publishers are utterly important. I mean, sometimes you may think they do it for money, but they don't make that much money. So I also want to say, bless the publishers, bless the people who read and who push their children to read, because reading, it seems to me, I know it's a recent thing, that we didn't used to read, but it was a concrete event, it really was, and I also want to say a blessing to Gutenberg. That's who we owe it to, don't we? Thank you.

Selected Bibliography

WORKS OF RUTH STONE

POETRY

In an Iridescent Time. New York: Harcourt, Brace, 1959.

Topography, and Other Poems. New York: Harcourt Brace Jovanovich, 1971.

Unknown Messages. Hindsboro, Ill.: Nemesis Press, 1973.

Cheap: New Poems and Ballads. New York: Harcourt Brace Jovanovich, 1975.

American Milk. Paterson, N.J.: From Here Press, 1986.

Second-Hand Coat: Poems New and Selected. Boston: D. R. Godine, 1987. Cambridge, Mass.: Yellow Moon Press, 1991.

The Solution. Baltimore: Alembic Press, 1989.

Who Is the Widow's Muse? Illustrated by Phoebe Stone. Cambridge, Mass.: Yellow Moon Press, 1991.

Nursery Rhymes from Mother Stone. (Chapbook.) Binghamton, N.Y.: Mbira Press, 1992.

Simplicity. Ashfield, Mass.: Paris Press, 1995. (Winner of the Pushcart Prize.)

Ordinary Words. Ashfield, Mass: Paris Press, 2000. (Winner of the National Book Critics Circle Award.)

In the Next Galaxy. Port Townsend, Wash.: Copper Canyon Press. 2002. (Winner of the National Book Award.)

In the Dark. Port Townsend, Wash.: Copper Canyon Press, 2004, 2007.

What Love Comes To: New & Selected Poems. Port Townsend, Wash.: Copper Canyon Press, 2008. Hexham, U.K.: Bloodaxe Books, 2009. (Finalist for the Pulitzer Prize.)

SHORT STORIES AND COMMENTARY

"The Secret Profession." *Commentary* 20:328–334 (1955). https://www.commentarymagazine.com/article/the-secret-professiona-story/

"The Hedgerows in England." *New Yorker,* March 17, 1962, pp. 127–128. http://www.newyorker.com/magazine/1962/03/17/the-hedgerows-in-england

"Breaking the Tired Mold of American Poetry." In *Titanic Operas: A Poets' Corner of Contemporary Responses to Dickinson's Legacy.* (N.d., but after 1995). http://archive.emilydickinson.org/titanic/stone.html

"In the Arboretum." In her *Ordinary Words.* Ashfield, Mass. Paris Press, 2000.

RECORDINGS

Look to the Future. Audio recording. Introduced by Bianca Stone. Ashfield, Mass.: Paris Press, 2012.

Ruth Stone. Video recording. Filmed by Pamela Robertson-Pearce; edited by Neil Astley. https://www.youtube.com/watch?v=kyzXn3rAGQM

CRITICAL AND BIOGRAPHICAL STUDIES

Barker, Wendy. "Mapping Ruth Stone's Life and Art." In *The House Is Made of Poetry: The Art of Ruth Stone.* Edited by Wendy Barker and Sandra M. Gilbert. Carbondale: Southern Illinois University Press, 1996.

Barker, Wendy, and Sandra M. Gilbert, eds. *The House Is Made of Poetry: The Art of Ruth Stone.* Carbondale: Southern Illinois University Press, 1996.

Freeman, Jan. "Stone, Ruth." In *The Oxford Companion to Women's Writing in the United States.* Edited by Cathy N. Davidson and Linda Wagner-Martin. New York: Oxford University Press, 1995. P. 854.

———. "Poetry and Life, Poetry and Ruth." In *The House Is Made of Poetry: The Art of Ruth Stone.* Edited by Wendy Barker and Sandra M. Gilbert. Carbondale: Southern Illinois University Press, 1996. Pp. 9–16.

Lombart, Kandace Brill. "'Under the Seal of My Widowhood': The Motif of the Widow in Literature from Petronius's Matron of Ephesus to Ruth Stone's *Who Is the Widow's Muse?*" Ph.D. dissertation, State University of New York, 2002.

Wheler, Mary Ann. "Ruth Stone: Voice from Society's Margins." Modern American Poetry, 2000. http://www.english.illinois.edu/maps/poets/s_z/stone/wehler.htm

INTERVIEWS

Battaglia, J. F. "A Conversation with Ruth Stone." *Boulevard* 12, nos. 1–2 (1996). Excerpt at http://www.english.illi

nois.edu/maps/poets/s_z/stone/onlineints.htm

Block, Melissa. "The Imagined Galaxies of Ruth Stone," National Public Radio, July 19, 2004. Audio. http://www.npr.org/2004/07/19/3600925/the-imagined-galaxies-of-ruth-stone

Bradley, Robert. "An Interview with Ruth Stone: 1990." In *The House Is Made of Poetry: The Art of Ruth Stone.* Edited by Wendy Barker and Sandra M. Gilbert. Carbondale: Southern Illinois University Press, 1996. Pp. 67–77.

deNiord, Chard. "Ruth Stone: An Interview." *American Poetry Review,* July–August 2010, pp. 49–54.

———. "Ruth Stone." In his *Sad Friends, Drowned Lovers, Stapled Songs: Conversations and Reflections on Twentieth-Century American Poets.* Grosse Point Farms, Mich.: Marick Press, 2011.

Gilbert, Sandra M. "An Interview with Ruth Stone: 1973." In *The House Is Made of Poetry: The Art of Ruth Stone.* Edited by Wendy Barker and Sandra M. Gilbert. Carbondale: Southern Illinois University Press, 1996. Pp. 52–66.

Wheler, Mary Ann. "An Interview with Ruth Stone." *Paterson Literary Review* 30 (2002). Excerpt at http://www.english.illinois.edu/maps/poets/s_z/stone/interview.htm

BIOGRAPHICAL NOTES, OBITUARIES, MEMORIALS, AND OTHER SOURCES

Astley, Neil. "Ruth Stone." Bloodaxe Blogs, November 27, 2011. http://bloodaxeblogs.blogspot.com/2011/11/ruth-stone-1915-2011.html (With pictures of Ruth at different ages.)

Block, Melissa. "Remembering Poet Ruth Stone." National Public Radio, November 28, 2011. http://www.npr.org/2011/11/28/142864291/remembering-poet-ruth-stone

deNiord, Chard. "Ruth Stone Obituary." *Guardian,* November 27, 2011. http://www.theguardian.com/books/2011/nov/27/ruth-stone

———. "Ruth Stone's 1st Interview, Lucille Clifton's Last: A Conversation with Jericho Brown and Chard deNiord." Blog, *The Best American Poetry,* December 11, 2011. http://blog.bestamericanpoetry.com/the_best_american_poetry/2011/12/ruth-stones-1st-interview-lucille-cliftons-last-a-conversation-with-jericho-brown-chard-diniord.html

Grimes, William. "Ruth Stone, a Poet Celebrated Late in Life, Dies at 96." *New York Times,* November 24, 2011. http://www.nytimes.com/2011/11/24/arts/ruth-stone-national-book-award-winner-dies-at-96.html?_r=0

Hall, John, ed. *Poets of Today.* Vol. 6. New York: Charles Scribner's Sons, 1959. (Includes Walter Stone's *Poems 1953–58.*)

Kildegaard, Athena. "Ruth Stone: Poet of Wonder and Grief." *Bloom,* March 31, 2014. http://bloom-site.com/2014/03/31/ruth-stone-poet-of-wonder-and-grief/

Lombart, Kandace Brill. "Ruth Stone: Poet Who Chronicled Love and Loss." *Independent,* December 3, 2011. http://www.independent.co.uk/news/obituaries/ruth-stone-poet-who-chronicled-love-and-loss-6271514.html

Paintbrush 27 (2000–2001). (Special edition devoted to the work of Ruth Stone.)

"Professor Emerita Ruth Stone." *Binghamton University Magazine,* fall 2011. http://www.binghamton.edu/magazine/index.php/in-memoriam/show/professor-emerita-ruth-stone

"Ruth Stone." Academy of American Poets, n.d. http://www.poets.org/poetsorg/poet/ruth-stone

"Ruth Stone." Poetry Foundation, n.d. http://www.poetryfoundation.org/bio/ruth-stone

Stone, Phoebe. "Vermont Poet Ruth Stone Remembered by Her Daughter." *Burlington Free Press,* May 11, 2014. http://www.burlingtonfreepress.com/story/life/arts/2014/05/11/vermont-poet-ruth-stone-remembered-daughter/8902405/

Stone, Ruth. Acceptance speech for the National Book Award, 2002. http://www.nationalbook.org/nbaacceptspeech_rstone.html#.UzM9HtzYalI

Thorton, Lori. "Is Recently Deceased Poet Ruth Stone Related?" *Smoky Mountain Family Historian,* November 26, 2011. http://familyhistorian.blogspot.com/2011/11/is-recently-deceased-poet-ruth-stone.html

DONNA TARTT

(1963—)

Deborah Kay Ferrell

DONNA TARTT IS at once a best-selling novelist, a Pulitzer Prize winner, and an enigmatic figure with a cultlike following. She emerged on the literary scene in 1992 with her much-hyped best seller *The Secret History*. It received a $450,000 advance and was published by Knopf after a bidding war with Random House. Originally titled "The God of Illusions," even as it was being publicized at the American Booksellers Association convention in June of 1991 the name was mysteriously changed. *The Secret History* was officially launched more than a year later, and according to Patricia Holtz of the *Globe and Mail* it was "heralded as the major debut novel of the fall of 1992." Some critics speculated that much of the ado concerning the success of *The Secret History* could be attributed to its prerelease publicity. Great attention was given to the design of the book. Its jacket type appeared "on a thin acetate cover rather than a paper jacket" (Curry). In response to the criticism that *The Secret History* was being given more attention than books that were then considered more literary, Carl Lennertz, Knopf's vice president for marketing, stated, "You can do all the gimmicks, from the book production to sending out reader's editions, but if the book doesn't have it, it won't sell" (Curry).

Ten years passed before Tartt's much anticipated second novel, *The Little Friend* (2002), made its debut. During that time, she became a bit of a recluse, hanging out with trusted friends and diligently working on her second novel, which she had begun before finishing *The Secret History*. Of her initial fame, Tartt said, "It's very strange, almost impossible to relate to.... It's unlike anything that's happened to you before.... You don't know how you will react until it happens. I've been sitting in a room with a

typewriter for nine years. Not even a typewriter, a notebook and pencil" (Mabe). There was great speculation about Tartt producing a second novel. Many feared that she was a one-hit wonder; however, Tartt responded to the speculators in an article in the *Independent*: "I can't write quickly.... If I could write a book a year and maintain the same quality, I'd be happy.... But I don't think I'd have any fans" (Coles). Fans waited for a decade and communicated with each other on websites such as the Donna Tartt Shrine. *The Little Friend* was originally titled " Tribulation," a fact some critics suggested bore a semblance to her composition style. However, in an interview with Elizabeth Lenhard, Tartt explained:

> I love big stacks of white paper, and I'm very superstitious about the pens I use.... A writing teacher of mine once said it was good to write in longhand. You feel the book coming through your hand. It takes a long time to write out the word. It makes you think carefully about the relationship of the words, like drawing someone.

While Tartt toured for a year to promote *The Secret History,* she was more reclusive and exclusive in her appearances and interviews for *The Little Friend*. She was under tight security. Her interviews were conducted primarily through e-mails because she said that she communicated best through writing. What emerged was a book that some hailed as coming from the rich tradition of William Faulkner, Flannery O'Conner, and Eudora Welty. Tartt, a Mississippi native, is perhaps truest to herself in this Southern gothic tome, which focuses on a young girl's attempt to solve the mystery of the murder of her brother twelve years earlier. The book is lush in its landscape and peppered with characters that have come to often be associated with Southern eccentrics: a mother who has taken to her bed, backwoods snake handlers, and white trailer

trash. Add to that a murder mystery and the looming Southern Baptist church, and what ensues is a potboiler of a novel. Tartt knows her territory well, and she writes with great authenticity. The reader is taken back to the Mississippi of the 1970s, for better and for worse, and Tartt's complex tragedy of a Southern family who has seen better days rings as true as the story's character development, setting, and dialogue. In comparing *The Little Friend* to *The Secret History,* Kathryn Holmquist writes that the former "has a broader sweep as a novel, with an omniscient narrator dipping in and out of the consciousnesses of its characters. The influence of Henry James, who neutrally chronicled the moral failings of his characters, is obvious. This is a novel intended to be a classic, rather than a literary event."

Almost twenty-one years from the phenomenon that was *The Secret History,* Tartt debuted *The Goldfinch.* It won the Pulitzer Prize in 2014. After the publication of *The Little Friend,* Tartt had retreated once again. She had not given an interview in ten years, and she rarely appeared in print. *The Goldfinch* first emerged in 2008, but for enigmatic reasons was not published until September 2013. It is a dark bildungsroman that follows the protagonist, Theo Decker, through ten years of his tumultuous life. The novel moves from New York City to the suburban wastelands of Nevada to the Netherlands, where the novel culminates in a nail-biting climax. Likened to Charles Dickens' *Great Expectations,* both in scope and character development, *The Goldfinch* focuses on Theo's friendship with Boris, his drug-using, daring, criminal friend who hails from Russia, the Ukraine, and most recently Australia. All along, Theo is in possession of a priceless painting that he was urged to take from an elderly gentleman during a bombing at the Metropolitan Museum of Art. Theo survives this terrorist attack, but his beloved mother is killed. In the ensuing decade, much of the plot revolves around his keeping the painting, *The Goldfinch,* while his life becomes a reckless adventure as he grows from an adolescent to a young man. In his review of the book, Kevin Nance wrote:

Haunted, guilt-ridden, and prone to self-endangerment—much of it centered around the painting, to which he clings as a symbol of his lost, beloved parent—Theo takes the reader on a fantastic journey. It's full of moral confusion, hairpin plot turns, and best of all, a vivid, raucous cast of characters drawn with the fond yet gimlet-eyed insight of Charles Dickens, whose spirit hovers over this book like a guardian angel.

PERSONAL LIFE

Despite her fame and literary success, Donna Louise Tartt remains as mysterious as the novels she writes. She has been called a "highly elusive creature," and since her first publicity tour for *The Secret History,* Tartt has been reluctant to give interviews (Adams). In 2013 Tartt told Mick Brown, "When people ask you why you did this or that you're sort of compelled to make up the reasons, but the real reason is, I don't know why."

Born on December 23, 1963, in Greenwood, Mississippi, to Don and Taylor Tartt, Donna was so small as a baby that she wore doll clothes. She comes from an old Southern family (her mother's maiden name is Boushe), and she was raised in the gently decaying family mansion in Grenada, Mississippi. Tartt remembers spending her childhood around fussy old aunts and a great-grandfather who concocted home remedies of whiskey with lemon and sugar to combat tonsillitis and other illnesses that were vague and prolonged. The same grandfather also gave her codeine-laced cough syrup. Tartt says of that time, "I spent nearly two years of my childhood submerged in a pretty powerfully altered state of consciousness.... I was convinced that I would die soon" (Wyndham). She became an insomniac in a house of insomniacs. Her sister would be awake at three o'clock in the morning, lying on the couch, laconic, in a daze. In her family home, there was always someone to talk to in the middle of the night. Tartt's ideas often come to her during this time, and she writes them down in one of the many notebooks that she keeps.

Tartt began writing and illustrating her own books when she was five years old. She would cut out pictures of an animal in *National Geographic* and write a story about it. Tartt's early love of storytelling can be traced to her family.

Her childhood was filled with thrilling narratives. "The Dixie patriarch [her great grandfather] would chill the girl to the marrow with medical horror stories of the Confederacy—'One bottle of rubbing alcohol could have saved hundreds of those boys!'" (Tonkin).

Her love of reading can be primarily credited to her mother and grandmother. When Tartt was growing up, her mother, a secretary, read her Kenneth Grahame's *The Wind in the Willows* (1908) and Robert Louis Stevenson. Her grandmother read her a chapter of Charles Dickens' *Oliver Twist* (1838) after school every day. As a treat, she would read Donna a chapter of a Nancy Drew book, but Tartt found the real excitement in Dickens. Her family was bookish and eccentric. Tartt's mother read novels while driving the car. Tartt describes her family as a "'different' family ... the family that talked to their cats" (Coffey).

Her parents' marriage was an unhappy one. Although she is close to her mother and speaks to her every day, during an interview in November 1992 she said she had not spoken to her father in more than twenty years. Tartt describes her mother as an "elegant but comical Ava Gardner who can tell a good story" (Holmquist), but she is much more reticent about her father, who owned a gas station and was a small-town politician. When compared to Dix, the womanizing father in *The Little Friend,* Tartt says he was ten times worse. Tim Adams, writing for the *Guardian* in 2013, noted, "Nothing of her past, you imagine, has escaped her attention."

Tartt began her official literary career at the age of thirteen when she published a poem in the *Mississippi Literary Review*. When she was fourteen she began working at the local library, where she devoured books, especially those by Dickens. Unlike other writers from Mississippi who aspired to go to the state capital, Jackson, Tartt made it as far as Oxford, hometown of William Faulkner and the University of Mississippi (Ole Miss), a campus that has a large Greek community of sororities and fraternities. As a freshman, she joined Kappa Kappa Gamma. Of this time Tartt remarked, "I wasn't a very successful Kappa.... My mother wanted me to do it. (She)

thought I wasn't socializing well with people, and this would force me to be out and about" (Lenhard).

While at Ole Miss, Tartt took creative writing classes with graduate students whom she outshone. One of her mentors, Willie Morris, a writer in residence and a former editor of *Harper's,* declared her a genius. She also worked with the novelist and short-story writer Barry Hannah, who became the director of the M.F.A. program at Ole Miss. Recalling her days as a writer at the college, Hannah said, "She was quite the prodigy here.... I remember Donna's tremendous felicity with a sentence. Her prose was so sweet and clear, near perfect. Sometimes it was so good, I would just clap" (Curry). Both mentors urged her to transfer to the creative writing program at Bennington College in Vermont.

In the 1980s Bennington became known as a hotbed of young writing talent, especially after Bret Easton Ellis published his debut novel *Less Than Zero* (1985) while still a student at the college. Ellis became known as a member of the so-called literary brat pack, a moniker that was a nod to the Hollywood "brat pack," a group of young actors whose careers peaked at the same time as Ellis and other celebrated young writers like Tama Janowitz and Jay McInerney were beginning theirs. Ellis became a friend of Tartt's, reviewing chapters of *The Secret History* during the writing process. Recalling their days as students, Ellis said, "we all sort of looked up to Donna ... not only as the best writer, but also the smartest, toughest writer in the class" (qtd. in Lenhard, October 4, 1992). Tartt is sometimes erroneously grouped with the literary brat pack; however, her work has little in common with theirs. Her prose differs from what was regarded as brat pack writers' groundbreaking minimalism, influenced by Raymond Carver and Ann Beattie, and their clear, dispassionate depictions of urban angst and suburban anxiety. Tartt's writing style, by contrast, belongs more in the nineteenth century than the twenty-first. She is famous for her use of long, complex sentences that are ornate, rich in texture and details. She prefers literature from an earlier time period and can quote at great length passages from the classics.

Tartt is considered a Southern gothic writer, although most of her subject matter does not take place in the South. Tartt has objected to this classification. In her tour for *The Little Friend,* she said, "It's not pleasant to be lumped into a group of black writers or women writers or gay writers. Why be a part of a group simply because of the circumstances of your birth?" (Moore).

Before *The Secret History* was completed, Brett Easton Ellis introduced Tartt to the powerful literary agent Amanda "Binky" Urban. Two years later, she circulated the manuscript to publishers, and the bidding war and the legend began. Since the publication of her first novel, Tartt has become a mythological figure. Much attention has been paid to her appearance, and little has changed throughout the decades. She is petite at barely five feet tall, and she wears her hair in a chin-length black bob. Tartt's eyes have been described as being green or golden, like a cat's eyes. She is known for wearing tailored clothing and was once likened to a Victorian doll because of a ruffled shirt she wore with a suit during one interview. In the early days, she smoked Marlboro Golds and was known at Bennington as being able to drink men under the table. It has been written that she converted to Catholicism, and once she proclaimed in French that she would never marry. In a 2013 interview with Mick Brown of the *Vancouver Sun,* she stated: "My idea of hell is a crowded and oppressive domestic life. Some people love that. It's absolutely my worst nightmare." Tartt will happily push around a comma for hours, and it is in writing that she gets most of her joy. In an interview with Charlie Rose she defined the good life as her "two great salvations, love and work," and she said that she had found both.

THE SECRET HISTORY

The Secret History is a mystery, but it is unusual for that genre. In the first paragraph of the prologue, the reader knows what it is about: the death of Bunny Corcoran at the hands of his five best friends. Ben Macintyre, writing for the London *Times,* calls it a "whodunit in reverse."

Rich in texture and compelled by a spellbinding plot, the novel is a page-turner, moving at a rapid clip.

Tartt's prose is almost flawless, and her characters are fascinating. Despite the premise of the novel being given away, the prologue still has an intriguing ending. Reflecting on the murder, the narrator, Richard Papen, writes: "I suppose at one time in my life I might have had any number of stories, but now there is no other. This is the only story I will ever be able to tell" (p. 4).

The novel's setting is Hampden College, a picture-perfect place for the well-to-do amidst the natural splendor of Vermont. It is reminiscent of Bennington College, Tartt's alma mater. Catherine Fitzpatrick remarks of the similarities, "Tartt writes precisely about what she knows best: a clique of arrogant students pursuing Greek studies at a posh Vermont college."

Richard Papen, the newcomer to the group, is a transfer student from Plano, California. He is unhappy and directionless, with close ties to no one. He is the only child of a gas station owner and a "mother who didn't pay much attention to me" (p. 8). A history of family violence is revealed as Papen recalls the time his father hit his mother simply because she mentioned that the neighbors were putting an addition onto their house. Papen is a loner filled with ennui. He's not particularly interested in his pre-med major, and he finds California boring and nondescript. His life is going nowhere until he stumbles upon a flyer for Hampden College. He applies on a whim, and after he is accepted, and told in no uncertain terms by his father that he cannot pay for the college, he becomes a scholarship student. He takes off to Vermont on a Greyhound bus with nothing but his suitcase. As the reviewer Boyd Tonkin puts it, "oikish parvenu of a narrator, Richard Papen, falls in love with the social grace and occult lore of a conspiratorial in-group." Papen himself says, "I do not now nor did I ever have anything in common with any of them, nothing except a knowledge of Greek and the year of my life I spent in their company" (p. 9).

The leader of the group is Henry Winter, an erudite scholar who spends his free time translat-

ing John Milton's *Paradise Lost* into Latin. He looms over the novel larger than life, not only because of his physical presence but also because of the power he holds over his group of friends. Upon seeing him, Papen observes that he is well over six feet tall with dark hair and

> a square jaw and course, pale skin. He might have been handsome had his features been less set, or his eyes, behind the glasses, less expressionless and blank. He wore dark English suits and carried an umbrella (a bizarre sight in Hampden) and he walked stiffly through the throngs of hippies and beatniks and preppies and punks with the self-conscious formality of an old ballerina, surprising in one so large as he.
>
> (p. 18)

As Henry's character is revealed, the reader learns that he is a dilettante who never graduated from high school. He is accepted at Hampden College because of his great wealth. Since he does not need a college degree, Henry is not confined to the academic requirements to earn one. It is revealed that he has taken nineteen classes with Julian Morrow, the classics professor, who is the Svengali-like leader of the five students Richard observes from a distance before he is admitted into the group.

Twins, a boy and a girl from Virginia who are inseparable from one another, are two other members of the exclusive sect. Charles and Camilla are almost wraithlike, pale and blond and slight, with a penchant for wearing white. They are in stark contrast to the student body of Hampden, who, like Henry, is normally swathed in black. When Richard first observes them from a distance, he thinks they are boyfriend and girlfriend, an eerie bit of foreshadowing, until he gets a closer look at them and realizes that they are not only siblings but twins. In the first part of the novel, they do not even appear as separate entities. They live together in an old apartment that is shabby chic, much like their background. They are orphans whose home, when away from college, is with their Nana in the family mansion that is falling into a state of disrepair. The twins finish one another's sentences, and, inevitably, when Charles is seated in a chair, Camilla is perched on its armrest. They are constantly smok-ing cigarettes, and on Sundays they are hosts to a salon where all six members gather to drink whiskey and eat dinner.

Francis Abernathy is, as Richard calls him, "the most exotic of the set" (p. 18). He is incredibly wealthy and dresses the part with stiffly starched shirts and French cuffs. He is so pale that Richard likens him to an albino except for the fact that he has bright red hair. He makes quite the appearance with his ever-present flowing black coat and an old-fashioned pince-nez. Francis is central to the progress of the novel in that the group spends their weekends in an old mansion that his aunt owns on a lake not far from the college. It is there that the group retreats as they enjoy one another's camaraderie in the halcyon days as fall fades into winter. Richard narrates:

> The idea of living there, of not having to go back ever again to asphalt and shopping malls and modular furniture; ... of no one every marrying or going home or getting a job in a town a thousand miles away or doing any of the traitorous things friends do after college; of everything remaining exactly as it was, that instant—the idea was so truly heavenly that I'm not sure I thought, even then, it could ever really happen, but I like to believe I did.
>
> (p. 103)

Edmund "Bunny" Corcoran, the murder victim, is a hapless, oafish young man, who at twenty-four is the oldest member of the group. He failed two grades when he was a young student. Bunny has dyslexia and what Richard describes as the attention span of a child. He copies his fellow students' work, and when he has to write a paper on John Donne, Bunny panics and invents a term, "Metahemeralism," that he desperately tries to support and develop despite his friends telling him that it is not even a word. Papen describes him as "a sloppy blond boy, rosy-cheeked and gum-chewing, with a relentlessly cheery demeanor and his fists thrust deep in the pockets of his knee-sprung trousers" (p. 18). He is the son of a banker and has four brothers, all of whom resemble each other. Papen likens the Corcorans to the Kennedys but notes that, unlike his brothers, Bunny looks like Teddy more than the other sons. Bunny is far less intelligent than his fellow classics students, and he is

a moocher. He takes people out to eat but expects them to pay the bill. When Papen first lunches with him at the Brasserie, a restaurant that the characters frequent, Bunny orders enormous amounts of food and gets drunk. They stay until night falls. The reader comes to know that Bunny's wealth is a facade. He and his venerable family are pretentious. Henry says of them, "The Corcorans have delusions of grandeur. The problem is, they lack the money to back them up. No doubt they think it is very aristocratic and grand, farming their sons off on other people" (p. 195). At lunch, Bunny establishes a pattern where he conveniently has an excuse not to pay for anything. Richard and he must wait until Henry comes to bail them out, a motif that becomes established throughout the novel.

Julian Morrow, the group's classics professor, is an erudite man who lives in the world of the past and occupies his own building, the Lyceum. At the beginning of the novel, Richard hears contradictory descriptions of Morrow: that "he was a brilliant man; that he was a fraud; that he had no college degree; that he had been a great intellectual in the forties, and a friend to Ezra Pound and T. S. Eliot" (p. 17). Julian is especially close to Henry and encourages his group of students to participate in the Dionysian frenzy, the *bakcheia*. The group becomes obsessed with performing this bacchanal, a ceremony where they invoke the god of ritual madness. They hope to experience a state of altered consciousness.

It is here that things begin to go terribly wrong. As the novel progresses, the reader learns that Henry, Charles, Camilla, and Francis have succeeded in taking part in a bacchanal and killed a man. Chillingly, Henry tells Richard that it was "a minor thing, really. An accident" (p. 163). They had done everything they could to invoke the bacchanal—fasting, drinking, chanting, even taking small bits of poison, but they were unsuccessful. Bunny was a distraction—he would not bathe or fast, so that he could be pure for the ceremony—and Henry tells Richard he would have ruined the whole thing. Just as they are about to give up, and winter is approaching, they

succeed. The experience is mystical. Henry describes it as:

> heart-shaking. Glorious. Torches, dizziness, singing. Wolves howling all around us and a bull bellowing in the dark. The river ran white. It was like a film in fast motion, the moon waxing and waning, clouds rushing across the sky. Vines grew from the ground so fast they twined up the trees like snakes; seasons passing in the wink of an eye, entire years for all I knew.
>
> (p. 167)

It is during this ritual that they happen upon a chicken farmer and kill him in a terrible, violent way. The dead man's neck is broken, and his brain is all over his face. They have ripped out his stomach. Camilla recalls his entrails steaming. The group has no remorse for the murder, but Bunny reads about it in Henry's diary and begins to behave erratically, blaming Henry for leaving him out of the bacchanal.

Bunny's unraveling becomes the focus of the novel. As Henry and Francis tell Richard about the murder, Henry says of Bunny: "The problem is he's just a fool, and sooner or later he's going to say the wrong thing to the wrong person" (p. 177). Bunny starts drinking uncontrollably. He holds the group at bay. He becomes insatiable. Henry and Francis funnel thousands of dollars his way. Francis remarks that he has spent so much of his money that his mother thinks he has a drug problem. At the cottage, Bunny throws fits, primarily at Henry. Richard enters the room where an argument has occurred. He observes:

> I was unprepared for what I saw: books were scattered in a frenzy across the floor; the night table was knocked over; against the wall lay the splay-legged remains of a black Malacca chair. The shade of the pole lamp was askew and cast a crazy irregular light over the room. In the middle of it was Bunny, his face resting on the tweed elbows of his jacket and one foot, still in its wing-tipped shoe, dangling off the edge of the bed.
>
> (p. 214)

It is when Bunny tells Richard that the group has killed the chicken farmer that Henry resolves they must kill him. The plan to murder him is rather easy. Spring has come to the college, and the group knows that Bunny loves to take long

hikes on Sunday afternoons. Henry proposes the perfect plan: they will meet Bunny at the top of Mount Cataract and push him over, making it look as if Bunny simply lost his footing and fell. While they are successful in their plan, things become complicated when a great snowfall comes suddenly and covers up the evidence of Bunny's death.

The ensuing weeks are spent in mass hysteria. Bunny's family has posted a $50,000 reward, and everyone turns up from the local townspeople to the FBI in the search for him. The Corcorans stay in what Henry calls a "terrible place. One of those big flat motels with a neon sign and no room service" (p. 334). The group of friends, besides Henry and Richard, are beside themselves. Richard looks on as an observer as Charles begins to drink more than he ever has, and the group starts unraveling. When Bunny's body is found and it is returned to Connecticut, the drama escalates as even Henry is affected because he has been invited to stay with the family. He suffers from sleeplessness and terrible headaches. The Corcorans' life is revealed in all of its absurdity as Bunny's father, Mac, vacillates between being delighted with his grandchildren to outbursts of grief over his dead son. Once the funeral takes place, it seems as if all will return to normal, but the damage is irrevocable.

The group of friends is no longer close. Charles is arrested for driving drunk, and Francis is in a dark mood. Richard finds solace in mindless parties and narcotics that he has stolen from Mrs. Corcoran. Camilla and Charles have been separated by Henry, and Francis tells Richard that the twins have, at times, had an incestuous relationship. He notes that Bunny claimed he even walked in on them once. While the group has been successful in covering up the murder of Bunny, everything has been torn asunder, never more so than, when building to the climax of the novel, Julian discovers a typewritten letter that Bunny wrote him. At first Julian believes the letter is a terrible crank, but Richard knows that it is real because it is rambling, incoherent, and childish at times. The letter is a plea for help, Richard notes with a pang. "Please Help me, this is why I wrote you, you are the only person that

can" (p. 498). Francis turns over the letter, and he and Richard recognize an irregular piece of "hotel stationery, engraved at the top, with the address and letterhead of the Excelsior: the hotel where Bunny and Henry had stayed in Rome" (p. 499). The duo search for Henry, hoping that he can steal the letter away, but he is not at home. They discover that Camilla is now living with him at the Albemarle. They return to Julian's office to find Henry there. Suspense is heightened as Richard tries to warn Henry of the letter that Julian is holding in his hand. Richard looks at Henry, who finally understands, but it is a second too late, "and in that split second, Julian looked down—casually, just as an afterthought, but a second too soon" (p. 507). Julian is oddly cool, and when Henry asks him to let him explain, he listens before abruptly cutting Henry off. With this knowledge that the group of friends really killed Bunny, Julian vanishes from the college.

The novel's denouement occurs with a wildly jealous Charles showing up at the Albemarle with a gun. Richard is grazed by a bullet. There is a struggle for the weapon, and then Henry, after telling Camilla that he loves her, shoots himself twice in the head.

In a brief epilogue, Richard tells of the death of Henry and the lives of the friends. They have been forever ruined after the murder of Bunny. Richard is the only one who graduates from Hampden, and he moves to California. Francis tries to kill himself after his grandfather discovers his sexuality. Richard and Camilla go to his bedside in a Boston hospital. Francis tells his friends that he must marry a woman or lose his inheritance. Charles has run off to Texas with a woman he met in a detox center, and Camilla has become the caretaker of Nana in Virginia. Richard proposes marriage to Camilla, but she responds that she still loves Henry. The weather has been dreary in Boston, and Richard realizes that a departure by plane from the East Coast is too abrupt. He drives back to California dejected, the rain his constant companion.

Deemed implausible at times and excoriated by many for being propelled by the plot, the novel challenged critics to decide whether it had literary merit. *Kirkus Reviews* dismissed it as

"The Brat Pack meets The Bacchae in this precious, way-too-long, and utterly unsuspenseful town-and-gown murder tale." The *Secret History* also became a commercial best seller, which is often incongruous with literary fiction. Tartt and the novel enthralled the general public. She became a literary star with profiles in *People* and *Vanity Fair.* As mentioned earlier, critics believed the book was getting more fanfare than it deserved at the expense of more literary texts. Even while praising it, the famously difficult-to-please literary critic of the *New York Times,* Michiko Kakutani, noted that the novel was "ferociously well-paced entertainment … 'The Secret History' succeeds magnificently. Forceful, cerebral and impeccably controlled, [it] achieves just what Ms. Tartt seems to have set out to do: it marches with cool, classical inevitability toward its terrible conclusion."

THE LITTLE FRIEND

On September 15, 2002, 150,000 copies of *The Little Friend* were released during its first printing. Its debut was in Dutch rather than English. Tartt was treated as a superstar in the Netherlands, where one in twenty people had bought *The Secret History.* There was even a three-minute segment that featured Tartt on Dutch national television. Of her reception Tartt noted, "I'm still stunned by what happened in Holland.… After it was all over, I really felt like Cinderella home from the ball" (Weaver).

As with *The Secret History, The Little Friend* starts off with a prologue that details a murder: "For the rest of her life, Charlotte Cleve would blame herself for her son's death because she had decided to have the Mother's Day dinner at six in the evening instead of noon, after church, which is when the Cleves usually had it" (p. 3). With that captivating first line, the reader is introduced to a family whose lives have forever been changed because of the death of Robin, the beloved child of an old Southern clan whose grandeur is a thing of the past, living in a genteel old manse appropriately named Tribulation. Now what is left is a matriarchy with Edie, the grandmother, at its helm, and her three sisters, who function as a chorus and nurture the remaining children, Harriet, the protagonist of the novel, and her older sister, Allison. Charlotte, who is the girls' mother and Edie's daughter, has remained all but comatose since the murder. She lives in a world where day and night meld together, in a tranquilized delirium. She is a ghostlike figure, floating in and out of the book in a nightgown. The main caretaker of the girls is Ida Rhew, their black maid who was with the family on that tragic day, forgoing her own celebration to attend to the Cleves' needs. The death is a horrible one, rendered in all of its sorrow by the rich details of the setting. A storm is brewing; there is dry thunder rumbling in the background. The backyard is deserted. Clothes are whipping on the line. A busybody neighbor is the first to see the horror, letting out a scream, and then Charlotte stumbles upon her dead son: "He was hanging by the neck from a piece of rope, slung over a low branch of the black-tupelo that stood near the overgrown privet.… The toes of his limp tennis shoes dangled six inches above the grass" (p. 14).

What follows is a family left in ruins. The girls' father, Dix, a banker, has retreated to Nashville. His sole role in the novel is from a distance. He sends the family checks and visits on holidays, and he makes Harriet miserable. He fights with Charlotte and tries to impose order, and when not doing that, he spends his time hunting. The plot of the novel takes place twelve years later, during the summer, when Harriet resolves she will find her brother's killer even though so much time has passed. Harriet, a baby at the time of Robin's death, is left haunted by the family lore that has only grown more intricate during the passing years. She and her best friend, a boy about her age named Hely, embark upon an adventure based on the fact that Ida Rhew ran off Danny Ratliff, a poor white friend of Robin's, on the day of the murder. It is here that the novel becomes a story of two families: the Cleves, with almost nothing left but their nobility, and the Ratliffs, ruffians who live on barren land, in a trailer park, with their grandmother Gum, a wizened, stick-thin, cancer-plagued woman who

discourages any upward mobility her grandsons may think of. She often quotes her father, who was suspicious of a man who liked books. Dennis Moore, writing for *USA Today,* states: "The story broadens to examine Southern racial and social strata, religious and generational eccentricities, and the passion of youth that gives way to the ambivalence of age."

Harriet, with the unwavering green-eyed gaze of her grandmother Edie, is a somber child with a bowl cut of thick black hair. She favors the literary works of Rudyard Kipling, Robert Louis Stevenson, and Arthur Conan Doyle. Largely inspired by their adventures, Harriet is determined to punish Danny Ratliff for the murder of her brother. Natasha Walter writes in the *Guardian:*

> As Harriet trudges through one lonely summer, encountering misunderstanding, bereavement, solitude and straightforward cruelty, she drifts further and further into her obsessions. Eventually other, tougher, meaner characters are dragged into her warped world and she is almost destroyed by her attempt to exact pointless revenge on individuals who bear illogical grudges against her.

The Ratliffs prove formidable foes, as three of the brothers must deal with their own personal demons. Farish, the oldest son, is a mean, paranoid, meth-fueled man who spent most of his service during the Vietnam War in a mental ward. The victim of a self-inflicted gunshot wound to the head during a police standoff, he has been psychotic ever since. He runs a taxidermy business that is a front for his meth lab. Danny, Harriet's murder suspect, is the most tragic of the brothers, as he presents a more human side, wronged by life and his upbringing. He is aware of his familial circumstances and how they have stymied any hopes and dreams he may have wished to embark on. Curtis, the third brother, has Down syndrome and provides an innocent sweetness to this otherwise crazed family. Eugene, the fourth brother, is inspired to take up the gift of snake handling to prove his worthiness as a born-again Christian. Each of the brothers, except Curtis, plays a role that is critical in Harriet's quest to avenge the murder of her brother.

The novel is a tour de force as Harriet and Hely ride around their small Mississippi home-town on their bicycles. Their backwoods Southern village serves effectively as the setting, and everything seems reminiscent of another time. The novel takes place in the seventies, an era of great change, yet the old order still exists with the white folks and their black servants. Ida Rhew, in particular, plays an important role in that she is the mother figure Harriet and Alison lack. Tartt is never oversentimental in her creation of this forced relationship. Although the children love her, it is clear that for Ida her job is a job. Once Harriett sees Ida Rhew's home, she is startled by the contrast between their lives, as Ida stands in the front door of her shack, in an old sweater made for a man. In fact, the travesty of the Cleves' supposedly fair and affectionate treatment of Ida is revealed as she sacrifices her own familial obligations to satisfy her employers. She works for twenty dollars a week, a gross underpayment for running a household, and she is frustrated in her attempts at housekeeping by Charlotte's hoarding, particularly of old newspapers and magazines that she stacks against the walls.

The air is humid and thick, the house in a state of gentle disrepair as Edie comes forth as the only white grown-up who acts like one. She is tough and brisk, supervising the children of her daughter as they grow into their teenage years. The novel is not without its humor, dark though it may sometimes be. At times it is even laugh-out-loud funny as Tartt presents her characters, almost verging on stereotypes but not quite. When Harriet resolves that the only safe place for her is at Baptist summer camp, it is Edie who drives her there. Tartt's writing is wittily clever as she describes the trip. Edie, who has always done what she wants, is at the helm of her ancient Oldsmobile and waxing nostalgic about bygone days:

> "Hospitality was the keynote of life in those days," said Edie. Her voice—clear, declamatory—rose effortlessly over the hot wind roaring through the car windows; grandly, without bothering to signal, she swept into the left lane and cut in front of a log truck.

(p. 383)

There is also the scene where Gum, driving the Trans Am home from jury duty, is attacked by the king cobra Harriet had intended for Danny. As Harriet and Hely manage to accomplish the impossible by dropping the snake into the speeding car from a highway overpass, Gum squeals to a stop and leaves the car, the snake hanging off her shoulder:

> out tumbled not Danny Ratliff but an emaciated mummy of a creature: frail, sexless, clad in a repellent mustard-yellow pantsuit. Feebly it clawed at itself, tottered onto the highway then halted, and it wobbled a few feet in the opposite direction. Aii-ieeeeeee, it wailed.
>
> (p. 371)

The two grandmothers could not be more different, and Tartt renders one as an eccentric aristocrat while the other is as hard on her luck in every way. Both are deftly and consistently drawn, and each is unforgettable in her own way.

Parts of the novel read like a thriller. In twenty breathless pages, Harriet is in a showdown with Danny in the town's water tower. It is rank and bug infested. The only escape ladder is rusting and falling apart as Danny tries to catch Harriet. It has been established that Danny cannot swim, but that Harriet, following in the footsteps of Harry Houdini, is a master at holding her breath. Danny must constantly jump out of the water to breathe as he tries to catch Harriet and kill her. Harriet rests atop the water, eluding his grasp, in a dead man's float. The tension is palpable as Danny becomes exhausted and Harriet finally escapes, the rusting ladder crumbling beneath her feet.

Many reviewers have criticized the ending of the novel, claiming that it has no resolution. This may be somewhat true. At the end of *The Little Friend,* Charlotte has a hushed conversation on the telephone with Dix. It is late summer, and the children are returning to school. Hely has been accepted into the band clique at school, and he has less time left for Harriet, who now seems alone. Danny Ratliff is jailed for the murder of his brother, and Harriet is plagued by doubts of whether or not he was Robin's killer. And then there is the question of the title of the book. Who is the little friend? Some have speculated that it

is Hely, Harriet's sleuthing partner, but it seems more obvious that the little friend is Danny Ratliff, that poor, hopeless loser who had all odds against him, even as a child when his attempts to bring a birthday present to Robin's party are futile. In the end, he comes off as plain sad. He had liked Robin, admired the family's old mansion despite its decay, and as a grown man, he tried to escape his family's hard luck, but it was not to be. In the end, *The Little Friend* is about loss—Harriet's and Danny's loss of hope as well as Robin's death, which permeates the pages of the novel like old perfume.

Jane Shilling writes that "the brilliance of *The Little Friend* resides in Tartt's ability to observe with the skewed clarity of a child—or a drug addict.... Though her prose is finely wrought, it is also highly readable. Once gripped, one gallops through this novel as through a volume of Dickens or Tolstoy, drawn towards the great final set-piece as though by a magnet." Tartt was hailed for being able to handle so many points of view and her ability to capture the nuanced Southern gothic world she created. Those who were expecting a novel like *The Secret History* were surprised that *The Little Friend* was so different. It harked back to the works of William Faulkner, Harper Lee, and Flannery O'Conner. Katherine Viner, writing for the *Guardian,* remarked that *The Little Friend* shared with *The Secret History* "the theme of a dark incident shaping a life but which in execution is southern and languorous and female and wholly different from its taut, masculine, east coast predecessor."

THE GOLDFINCH

Tartt's third novel debuted in 2013 to mixed reviews. It was eleven years in the making. Coincidentally, Carel Fabritius' 1654 painting, from which Tartt's novel got its name, opened at the Frick Collection the same week in October that the novel was released. Likening Tartt to Dickens, Stephen King, in his review for the *New York Times,* wrote that "*The Goldfinch* is a rarity that comes along perhaps half a dozen times per decade, a smartly written literary novel that connects with the heart as well as the mind."

However, critics deemed to be more highbrow than the *New York Times* reviewers, specifically those from the *New Yorker, New York Review of Books,* and *Paris Review,* were not so quick to praise this polarizing novel. The *New Yorker* critic James Woods found the book "stuffed with relentless, far-fetched plotting; cloying stock characters; and an overwrought message tacked on at the end as a plea for seriousness" (qtd. in Peretz). In a *Vanity Fair* article titled "It's Tartt— But Is It Art?" the question of what makes great literature is discussed. *The Goldfinch* was criticized for its unrealistic plot, its implausibility, its lazy clichés. Still the novel went on to win the Pulitzer Prize despite the fact that *The Goldfinch* "had gotten some of the severest pans in memory from the country's most important critics and sparked a full-on debate in which the naysayers believe that nothing less is at stake than the future of reading itself" (Peretz).

The Goldfinch begins with its protagonist, Theo Decker, in the Netherlands. Holed up in a hotel room for over a week, he has been hiding from the world since he shot a man dead in his ill-fated attempt to get *The Goldfinch* back after it has been used for more than a decade as collateral for drug kingpins. Wrought by guilt and anguish, ill with a fever that will not go away, Decker himself can do nothing more than read the papers, order room service, and ruminate about the events that have gotten him to this point in his life.

In this in-between nowhere land, where night melds into day, during the week that leads up to Christmas, Theo contemplates his past and how he got to this moment in time after reuniting with his boyhood friend. Boris, his childhood chum turned international drug dealer, has always lived outside of the law. Raising himself as his violent, abusive father went from one mining job to another, all over the world, Boris verges upon caricature. He is a Russian, via Ukraine, via Australia. He is as skinny as a whip, with his dark hair always falling in his eyes. Boris always appears to be dirty with a grime he cannot wash away. He speaks in heavily accented English, and he is fluent in several other languages. Boris is gaudy and vulgar in his behavior and appearance.

Boris is nowhere to be found after the shooting, and Theo, alone, has visions of his dead mother in the hotel mirror. She becomes his saving grace as he contemplates suicide after realizing that his life has meant nothing since her death, that he has been forever traumatized since they were in a terrorist bombing at the Metropolitan Museum of Art, where his mother died, and thirteen-year-old Theo was one of the few survivors after the attack. The scenes are not unrealistic in a post–September 11 world where a significant portion of the American public still continues to live in a collective state of paranoia.

In the rubble that remains of the gallery where the explosion hit hardest, Theo wakens to smoke and debris and is urged by a critically injured, elderly man by the name of Blackwell to take the painting titled *The Goldfinch.* The man also gives Theo his ring and urges him to go to a store named Hobart and Blackwell and buzz the green bell. Prior to the blast, Theo, who was on his way to school with his mother to talk about his being suspended, noticed Blackwell with a charming young girl about his age, as they perused the gallery titled "PORTRAITURE AND NATURE MORTE: NORTHERN MASTER-WORKS OF THE GOLDEN AGE" (p. 22). It is here that the novel's implausible plot line develops as Theo's life becomes entangled with the man's ring, the girl, and Blackwell's surviving partner, Hobart. Everything in *The Goldfinch* becomes a matter of happenstance as characters are separated and reunited, and the stolen painting becomes a symbol, larger than life, as all points lead back to it and Theo's quest to keep it. The painting is the first one his mother ever loved when she saw it in an art book that was given to her as a child. She tells Theo: "He [Fabritius] was Rembrandt's pupil, Vermeer's teacher, ... And this one little painting is really the missing link between the two of them—that clear pure daylight, you can see where Vermeer got his quality of light from" (pp. 26–27).

Without his beloved mother, Theo is believed to be an orphan—his father left the family some time ago and is nowhere to be found. He is taken

in by the Barbours, an illustrious New York family, because of his tenuous friendship with their son, Andy, a boy who is ghostly pale and whose only commonality with Theo is that they were both bullied in school by the same people. When asked if he has anyone to stay with, Theo's first thought is Andy, a boy who hates sailing even though it is a hobby his father is fanatical about. This fact becomes pivotal later in the novel. Tartt is careful with her plotting, and no detail is extraneous.

Although Mrs. Barbour is a socialite who is rarely home for dinner, and her husband, Chase, suffers from bipolar disorder, the family provides stability for Theo. He becomes used to their charmed existence, and Mrs. Barbour protects him from the army of social workers, psychiatrists, counselors, and investigators who try to find out from Theo what happened on that ill-fated day. Theo also develops a friendship with Hobie, Blackwell's partner. Just as Theo is becoming comfortable, and the family has invited him to stay with them as they ready for their summer trip to their home in Maine, Theo's father shows up, and the young boy's hopes of normalcy are dashed. Criticizing the novel for bearing a resemblance to the Harry Potter series, Julie Myerson writes:

> Hobie is the business partner of the dead man who, it turns out, was the uncle of the red-haired girl who, like Theo, has survived the attack. Finding sanctuary in his increasingly regular visits to the kindly wizard—sorry, antiques dealer—Theo befriends her. He is therefore aghast when his alcoholic, drug-and-gambling-addict father turns up with a Juicy Couture–wearing, cocaine-snorting girlfriend and whisks him off to live with them in Vegas.

Approximately a quarter of the novel takes place in Nevada, where Theo goes to live with his father and his father's girlfriend, Xandra, who is tanned and toned and works as a manager in a bar. Theo's father is out of control. He is an alcoholic who thinks he has recovered because he now drinks beer instead of hard liquor, and he takes drugs from OxyContin to Vicodin to calm himself down. The couple leaves Theo to take care of himself. They live in a desolate subdivision in the desert, so far from anything that

Domino's does not even deliver pizzas there. Until he meets Boris at school, Theo's lone companion is Xandra's dog, Popper. Although the desert does have its beauty—Theo has never seen stars in the sky like he has there—his school is a place of transients: hotel and casino workers and the children of military personnel. Theo meets Boris in an AP English class, and Boris nicknames him Potter, after the children's book hero, because of the horn-rimmed glasses that Mrs. Barbour chose for him. Theo is a misfit in his school and notes that this was not the first time he had been called by this name:

> It was not the first time, in Vegas, I'd heard the Harry Potter comment. My New York clothes—khakis, white oxford shirts, the tortoiseshell glasses which I unfortunately needed to see—made me look like a freak at a school where most people dressed in tank tops and flip flops.
>
> (p. 236)

Despite the rough beginning of their friendship, Theo and Boris become the closest of friends. With no supervision at home, they become thieves who are constantly drunk or high.

The Goldfinch is ever present as Theo has managed to take his stolen picture all the way to Nevada, and he is obsessed with keeping it in pristine condition. He has wrapped it in cloth and bundled it up in newspaper, the coolness of the twenty-four-hour air conditioning simulating the climate-controlled temperature of museums. From time to time he gets it out to look at it, marveling at what a miracle it is, noticing everything from the brushstrokes to the frame of the painting that has the indentation of nail holes. *The Goldfinch* takes him back to happier times with his mother as he remembers the small things about her, from the stories she told him about her childhood in Kansas to their everyday outings in New York City. The painting comes to embody his mother, her love of it the only tangible object that remains of her.

Just as Theo is adjusting to his life in Nevada, gangsters come after his father for a gambling debt. In desperation, his father demands that Theo call up his attorney back east, a Mr. Bracegirdle, so that he can get money from Theo's inheritance. The money is tied up in a trust for Theo's educa-

tion, and when his father finds out that it is untouchable, he cries out in baleful wails, one of the most harrowing scenes in the novel. It is not long after that his father is killed in a fiery car crash believed to be a suicide. Theo, afraid he will become a ward of the state, takes Popper and heads to New York on a bus. He says goodbye to Boris, who begs him to wait just another day before he leaves. Theo is terrified and refuses to stay. This act will come to play a crucial part in the novel as it nears its climax. Theo takes the painting from his closet and puts it in a suitcase. His plan is to find Hobie, the man he befriended after the terrorist attack, and who was the caretaker of Pippa, the girl he was infatuated with in the museum.

It is in New York City that all the strands of the plot begin to come together. Theo is now sixteen, and he can legally choose to live with Hobie. Because of his drug-and-drink-fueled days in Nevada, he must study very hard to make up what he has missed in his education. He is admitted to an impressive early college program. Depressed over the events in his life, especially the loss of his mother that haunts him throughout the novel, Theo is an underachiever, both socially and academically. He sees Pippa on her infrequent visits to Hobie. Through the years, his infatuation has grown to what he believes is love. Although not conventionally attractive—Pippa has a limp and bears the scars from the terrorist attack—Theo sees her as "the golden thread running through everything, a lens that magnified beauty so that the whole world stood transfigured in relation to her, and her alone" (p. 464).

As an adult, Theo takes over the business end of Hobie's antiques shop. Things are a mess. Rather than keeping the shop open, Hobie spends his time downstairs in his workshop nursing old furniture and repairing broken pieces of Americana so that to the uninitiated they appear genuine. There are back notices from the IRS. The business is cash negative. Theo takes matters into his own hands. He opens up the shop and begins to sell Hobie's mix-matched pieces as real. Theo admits that he does this not only to save Hobie's business but because he likes the game of it. In many ways, he is his father's son, and he

is reminiscent of the boy who, with Boris, stole from the grocery store and the mall, gleefully outrunning cops as they got away with their ill-gotten goods. Theo ponders the morality of his actions:

> It was the secret no one told you, the thing you had to learn for yourself: viz. that in the antiques trade there was really no such thing as a "correct" price. Objective value—list value—was meaningless. If a customer came in clueless with money in hand (as most of them did), it didn't matter what the books said, what the experts said, what similar items at Christie's had recently gone for. An object—*any* object—was worth whatever you could get somebody to pay for it.
>
> (p. 457)

Of course what no one realizes is that the work Hobie produces is as valuable as the true antiques Theo sells. With Hobie's fine attention to every intricacy of his repairs, he has created an art of his own. Theo's ruse has saved the business, but he remains a troubled man. He is addicted to pain pills and occasionally snorts heroin. He is haunted by his mother's memory and suffers trauma when he is in closed spaces or large crowds. He has tinnitus that at times overpowers outside noises and conversations. His only solace is the painting that he has stored in a climate-controlled warehouse. However, he has become paranoid and guilt-ridden for keeping *The Goldfinch*. He pays for the warehouse in cash and never goes to visit it.

As with Tartt's previous books, she returns to pick up a thread that she has left in an earlier part of the novel. Like Dickens, Tartt is able to keep a highly intricate novel with many characters suspenseful, and she never drops the plotline. Theo runs into Andy's older brother, Platt, on a street in Manhattan. Platt is much changed from the bully he was when Theo was living with the Barbours. He is now paunchy around the middle and ruddy-faced. He has a job working at an academic publisher. When Theo asks about Andy, he learns that his childhood friend died in a sailing accident. Mr. Barbour, in a state of mania, set sail on a windy, choppy day. Andy was on the boat with him. Always a reluctant and poor sailor—Andy hated the sea—he tried to keep the boat afloat but was knocked into the water by a

sail; the only thing remaining was his jacket tied to a mast. Platt invites Theo to dinner with the family.

To Theo's shock, Mrs. Barbour is no longer the socialite she once was. Since the death of her husband and Andy, she has become a recluse, preferring to lie around in a nightgown and a bed jacket with a giant diamond brooch pinned to it. Theo is also reunited with Kitsey, the only girl in the Barbour family. She has become a cool beauty, like her mother had been before her, and the two begin dating. Things seem to be perfect in Theo's world, yet he remains haunted by his past and his love for Pippa. He also does not know what to do with the painting. A part of him wishes that he had turned it over to the proper authorities when he was younger, but he knows that as a grown man he will be prosecuted for art theft. The last artifact from Theo's time with his mother, the symbol of her sparkling memory, *The Goldfinch* lies in a cold storage unit. The one object that has given Theo stability in his young life is unattainable. It might as well be hanging in a museum. He remains a drug addict, buying his pills in thousand-dollar batches.

Real trouble begins when Lucius Reeve enters Theo's life. He is a shady character who befriends rich, old, and lonely women, especially preying on widows, in the hopes of gaining their trust and access to their private heirlooms. Lucius confronts Theo; he knows that he has been selling Hobie's work as originals, and he threatens to blackmail him. Theo's world is spinning out of control as he and Kitsey become engaged and he is trapped in the world of high society. Theo needs time alone, he needs his drugs, but he is caught up in a whirlwind, especially as the novel progresses and Lucius reveals his real reason for blackmailing Theo. There are rumors that *The Goldfinch* has turned up in the drug underworld, and Lucius Reeve, who has connections to the art underworld, knows that *The Goldfinch* has been used in collateral for drug deals. He believes Theo has the painting. It is at this point that Boris shows up on the doorstep of the antiques shop. Boris has turned into a handsome young man, but he is involved in a world of crime. He tells Theo that he had taken *The Goldfinch* from him

in Nevada, before Theo got on the bus to return to the East Coast. His explanation for doing so was to protect the painting from a Mr. Silver, a gangster who came to collect a debt from Theo's father. Boris tells Theo that he took the painting for safekeeping, but he has used it over the years as collateral for his narcotics trade. The novel builds to its climax. Theo has no hopes of ever having a life with Pippa, it is discovered that Kitsey has a lover the Barbours do not approve of, and the painting is lost. Boris vows to return it to Theo.

The climax of the novel takes place in the Netherlands. Theo and Boris meet and go in search of the painting. Theo kills a man in a shootout. Blood-spattered, he makes his way back to his hotel only to find himself sick with fever. The following days and nights meld together as Theo thinks about his mother, his past, the painting, and everything that has led up to this moment in time. Boris has disappeared only to return on Christmas Day. He tells Theo about the search to find *The Goldfinch*. After remembering a drug den where masterworks were kept as collateral, Boris gives the police an anonymous tip that *The Goldfinch* is there. He collects the reward money and gives part of it to Theo. Theo returns to New York only to meet a beleaguered Hobie. Lucius Reeves has told him of his suspicions, and it is then that Theo tells Hobie the truth about everything. Theo then spends his time buying back the forged pieces of furniture. Although he still sees the Barbours, it is revealed that he is not going to marry Kitsey. The book ends with his musings about the nature of art. The same might be said about many critics' reactions to the book.

CONCLUSION

While critics debate the literary merit of Tartt's novels, just as they did with Dickens, there is no doubt as to her popularity. She is a skillful writer who can spin a sentence with her long, elegant prose. Her plotlines are spellbinding, and she can tell a riveting story. Tartt once stated that she has five novels in her. When her fourth arrives, there is no doubt that it will be greeted with great

fanfare. Tartt has retreated from the public eye, probably to her desk with her notebooks and pen. She has become a figure on the landscape of the literary imagination. Through her writing and persona, Tartt has created an indelible image as writer-as-celebrity.

Selected Bibliography

WORKS OF DONNA TARTT

The Secret History. New York: Knopf, 1992.
The Little Friend. New York: Knopf, 2002.
The Goldfinch. New York: Little, Brown, 2013.

INTERVIEWS AND FEATURE ARTICLES

Adams, Tim. "Donna Tartt: The Slow-Burn Literary Giant." *Guardian,* October 12, 2013. http://www.theguardian.com/theobserver/2013/oct/13/donna-tartt-quiet-american-profile

Brown, Mick. "'If I'm Not Working, I'm Not Happy.'" *Vancouver Sun,* December 21, 2013, p. C6.

Coffey, Edel. "The Very, Very Private Life of Ms. Donna Tartt." *Irish Independent,* November 25, 2013, p. 32.

Coles, Mark. *BBC: Today.* "The Secret History of Donna Tartt." http://www.bbc.co.uk/radio4/today/reports/archive/arts/tartt.shtml

Curry, George E. "A First Novelist Skips to the End." *Chicago Tribune,* October 7, 1992. http://articles.chicagotribune.com/1992-10-07/features/9203310736_1_donna-tartt-elle-and-mirabella-magazines-secret-history

Fitzpatrick, Catherine. "With Publicity Like This, Donna Tartt's No Secret." *Milwaukee Sentinel,* September 26, 1992, p. C2.

Holmquist, Kathryn. "A Taste of Tartt." *Irish Times,* November 9, 2002, p. 56.

Lenhard, Elizabeth. "Rookie Author Has the Secret." *Orlando Sentinel,* October 4, 1992, p. F1. http://articles.orlandosentinel.com/1992-10-04/entertainment/9210020942_1_donna-tartt-secret-history-murderous-passions

Mabe, Chauncey. "Tartt's Content." *Sun Sentinel,* September 27, 1992. http://articles.sun-sentinel.com/1992-09-27/features/9201240163_1_donna-tartt-twin-peaks-novel

Macintyre, Ben. "Tartt Bites the Big Apple." *Times* (London), September 2, 1992.

Moore, Dennis. "A Decade Later, Another 'Illusion' Crafted." *USA Today,* October 15, 2002. http://usatoday30.usatoday.com/life/books/reviews/2002-10-14-tartt-little-friend_x.htm

Peretz, Evgenia. "It's Tartt—But Is It Art?" *Vanity Fair,* June 30, 2014. *http://www.vanityfair.com/culture/2014/07/goldfinch-donna-tartt-literary-criticism*

Rose, Charlie. "Donna Tartt on Her Novel *The Goldfinch.* rdquo; Charlierose.com, February 6, 2014. http://www.charlierose.com/watch/60339993

Tonkin, Boyd. "The Vanishing." *Independent* (U.K.), May 21, 2002. Archived at http://www.languageisavirus.com/donna_tartt/interviews-whatever-happend-to.php#.V4A3OzW5JLU

Viner, Katharine. "A Talent to Tantalise." *Guardian,* October 18, 2002. http://www.theguardian.com/books/2002/oct/19/fiction.features

Weaver, Teresa K. "The Re-emergence of Donna Tartt." *Atlanta Journal-Constitution,* October 20, 2002.

Wyndham, Susan. "Secret History of Donna Tartt." *Sunday Star-Times* (Wellington, New Zealand), November 10, 2002, p. C3.

REVIEWS

Holtz, Patricia. "Promising, but Not What Was Promised." *Globe and Mail,* September 26, 1992.

Kakutani, Michiko. "Books of the Times: Students Indulging in Course of Destruction." *New York Times,* September 4, 1992. http://www.nytimes.com/1992/09/04/books/books-of-the-times-students-indulging-in-course-of-destruction.html (Review of *The Secret History.*)

Kirkus Reviews. Review of *The Secret History.* September 16, 1992.

King, Stephen. "Flights of Fancy: Donna Tartt's *Goldfinch.*" *New York Times Book Review,* October 10, 2013. http://www.nytimes.com/2013/10/13/books/review/donna-tartts-goldfinch.html

Myerson, Julie. "*The Goldfinch* by Donna Tartt." *Guardian,* October 19, 2013. http://www.theguardian.com/books/2013/oct/19/goldfinch-donna-tartt-review

Nance, Kevin. "*Goldfinch* May Be Tartt's Great American Novel." Gannet News Service, October 21, 2013. http://usatoday30.usatoday.com/LIFE/usaedition/2013-10-22-Review-of-The-Goldfinchs_ST_U.htm

Shilling, Jane. "Light in a Gothic Darkness." *Sunday Telegraph,* October 27, 2002. http://www.telegraph.co.uk/culture/books/3584826/Light-in-a-Gothic-darkness.html

Walter, Natasha. "Soaringly, Incredulously, Gorgeously Cruel." *Guardian,* October 26, 2002. http://www.theguardian.com/books/2002/oct/26/featuresreviews.guardianreview1

SARA TEASDALE

(1884—1933)

Melissa Girard

SARA TEASDALE WAS one of the most popular and critically acclaimed poets of the World War I era. A contemporary of T. S. Eliot, Ezra Pound, and H.D. (Hilda Doolittle), she burst onto the American poetry scene at the beginning of its greatest renaissance. Teasdale had no quarrel with the "new" poetry, but she wrote using the traditional forms and techniques of a previous age. Yet, while Teasdale largely eschewed the new vogue in free verse, critics and popular readers alike recognized something timeless in her lyrics. Teasdale drew inspiration from Sappho and Emily Dickinson—two classic poets whose stars were also rising in the first decades of the twentieth century. Like Robert Frost, Edwin Arlington Robinson, and Edgar Lee Masters, Teasdale seemed to combine the best of the old and the new. Because of the rhetorical simplicity and emotional sincerity of her poetry, Teasdale's reputation grew among proponents of the new poetry. Critics such as Harriet Monroe, the influential founder and editor of *Poetry* magazine, helped Teasdale become one of the leading voices of her generation.

The modernist era was a time of tremendous social and political upheaval, and women of Teasdale's generation had access to unprecedented freedoms. With the onset of World War I and the subsequent expansion of the women's suffrage movement, relationships between men and women altered fundamentally. In her popular collections *Helen of Troy and Other Poems* (1911), *Rivers to the Sea* (1915), and *Love Songs* (1917), Teasdale chronicled the changing conventions of modern love. Although she wrote using traditional rhyme schemes and meters, Teasdale brought the sensibility of the New Woman into American poetry. Her female speakers display a new form of confidence and independence: they express their desire for love in their own words and on their own terms. Poems such as "After Parting" were considered to be remarkably explicit for their time:

I set my shadow in his sight,
And I have winged it with desire,
That it may be a cloud by day
And in the night a shaft of fire.

(Collected Poems, p. 56)

In addition to her popular books of poetry, Teasdale also edited an anthology, *The Answering Voice*: *One Hundred Love Lyrics by Women* (1917), which collected some of the period's most important love poems. In the preface Teasdale notes, with pleasure, the recent explosion of women's writing. "It is undeniable," she says, "that a new impetus has been given to women to express themselves in poetry" (p. x). Furthermore, she continues, these modernist era poems differ "radically in feeling" from the poems of the previous generation:

One finds little now of that ingratiating dependence upon the beloved, those vows of eternal and unwavering adoration, which filled the poems of even the sincerest of women of the times before our own. One finds little, too, of the pathetic despair so often present in the earlier work.

(p. xii)

Thanks in large part to Teasdale's success, bold, realistic love poems written by women for women became one of the modernist era's dominant poetic trends. Following just a few years after Teasdale, poets such as Edna St. Vincent Millay, Dorothy Parker, Louise Bogan, and Elinor Wylie would pick up where she left off. A generation later, Sylvia Plath and Anne Sexton would also cite Teasdale as a primary influence on their poetic development.

Although Teasdale did not consider herself to be a feminist—finding all such labels unnecessarily constricting—she wrote about women's lives and emotions with remarkable candor and insight. Modern scholarship on Teasdale has emphasized the political significance of her personal reflections. Scholars such as William Drake and Cheryl Walker have shown how Teasdale's autobiographical poems, which deepened and matured as she grew older, provide a valuable window on the modern problem of feminine identity formation. Like many early twentieth-century women, Teasdale struggled to balance her professional ambitions with society's expectation that she should become a wife and mother. In her later volumes of poetry—*Flame and Shadow* (1920), *Dark of the Moon* (1926), and the posthumously published *Strange Victory* (1933)—she writes openly of her attempts to maintain a sense of self and to find self-fulfillment within the confines of marriage.

As critical tastes changed, Teasdale's traditional lyrics fell out of fashion. Compared to her more sophisticated modernist contemporaries, Teasdale's instinctive approach to poetry began to seem naive. While Eliot, Pound, and William Carlos Williams grounded their poetry in new formal theories and techniques, Teasdale insisted that poetic form was of no real significance at all. After being awarded the Columbia Prize for Poetry in 1918, Teasdale said, "The only vital thing about a poem is its content. If a poem is of any value it must spring directly from the experience of the writer" ("Sara Teasdale Wins Columbia $500 Prize"). "The writing of poems should be considered as natural and simple as the writing of letters," Teasdale continued. "Children should make up poems without the slightest embarrassment" (p. 3). This insistence on poetry's innate simplicity and accessibility put Teasdale at odds with a literary academy that placed increasing value on poetic difficulty and professionalization.

To her early-twentieth-century readers, Teasdale's statements were a familiar part of the "poetess" tradition. Female poets like Teasdale frequently claimed that writing poetry was "natural" in order to conceal the role they played in authoring their own careers. As Teasdale writes in her poem "What Do I Care?": "It is my heart that makes my songs, not I" (*CP*, p. 116). Teasdale's feigned modesty is modeled directly on the feminine personae of nineteenth-century poets like Christina Rossetti and Elizabeth Barrett Browning, both of whom she greatly admired. Because of her cautious temperament and traditional background, it never occurred to Teasdale, as it would to poets such as Millay, Parker, and Wylie a few years later, to dispense with this public performance of femininity. Teasdale fiercely guarded her reputation for respectability: although her divorce in 1929 and suicide in 1933 threatened to expose her marital problems and severe depression, in her will, Teasdale had directed her close friend and literary executor, Margaret Conklin, to withhold from publication all material that she considered to be too revealing.

As the twentieth century progressed, critics judged Teasdale harshly for the remnants of a genteel tradition that remained in her poetry. By midcentury, her poems no longer seemed quite so bold or realistic. Today, Teasdale's poetry is rarely included on syllabi of modernist poetry, and all of her popular books have fallen out of print. To Teasdale's harshest critics, her poetry is indistinguishable from the broader field of poetess poetry that dominated the popular magazines and newspapers of the twilight era. However, to Teasdale's defenders, her reputation for simplicity and demure femininity are merely a facade, masking innumerable depths and complexities that lay just beneath the surface of her perfectly polished lyrics.

BIOGRAPHY

Sara Trevor Teasdale was born on August 8, 1884, in St. Louis, Missouri, the youngest child of an old and respected St. Louis family. At the time of her birth, her eldest brother, George Willard, was almost twenty, and her other brother, John Warren, Jr., was fourteen. Teasdale's only sister, Mary Willard, referred to affectionately as "Mamie," was seventeen. Mamie instantly adored her baby sister and doted upon her growing up.

For most of Teasdale's young life, her parents, Mary Elizabeth Willard and John Warren Teasdale, made their family home at 3668 Lindell Boulevard. In 1904 the Teasdales moved to 38 Kingsbury Place, a large home in a fashionable neighborhood, which is still standing today.

Teasdale's father, who was in his mid-forties when she was born, ran J. W. Teasdale & Co., a prosperous wholesale business in dried fruits, beans, and nuts. His income provided Teasdale with a life of considerable comfort. She attended the city's finest schools and began traveling the world at a young age. In 1898 she attended Mary Institute, one of the most prestigious girls' schools in St. Louis, which had been founded by T. S. Eliot's grandfather. At the time Teasdale attended the school, Eliot resided in the house next door. However, because Teasdale disliked commuting by train to Mary Institute, the following year she transferred to Hosmer Hall, another girls' school of high academic standing that stressed college preparation for women. At Hosmer Hall, Teasdale was introduced to an influential network of well-educated, artistically minded young women, who shaped her literary development significantly. Zoë Akins, who won a Pulitzer Prize in 1935 for her dramatization of Edith Wharton's *The Old Maid,* and Caroline Risque, a noted painter and sculptor, were among Teasdale's friends in the graduating class of 1903.

From a young age, Teasdale reportedly suffered from debilitating health problems, which were so severe that they frequently required hospitalization and the help of a trained live-in nurse. Teasdale's parents worried continually about their daughter's frail health and, as a result, limited activities that they considered to be overly strenuous or stimulating, including both reading and writing. In retrospect, their concerns seem to have been unjustified. According to her biographer William Drake, there is no medical evidence that Teasdale suffered from any physical illness or injury (p. 9). Instead, she tended to be diagnosed with vague and improbable diseases, such as nervousness and neurasthenia, diagnoses that were extremely common at the time. One of Teasdale's closest childhood friends, Williamina Parrish, remembered the young Teasdale as "a

Princess in her Tower ... Nothing was lacking to her except vigorous health" (qtd. in Carpenter, p. 110). According to Parrish, Teasdale suspected that her health problems were related to her parents' overprotectiveness. Teasdale once told Parrish, "I often wonder if I had been born into a family with no means, if I would have better health" (qtd. in Carpenter, p. 110). However, although Teasdale's diagnoses may have been unfounded, they caused her very real anxiety and fear. She would be plagued by illness and preoccupied with her health for the rest of her life.

Although Teasdale's parents were loving and generous, their lives were governed by a strict sense of Victorian propriety. Like many middle-class Victorian women, Teasdale's mother believed that girls should be delicate, deferential, and subservient. She attempted to cultivate these traditional feminine qualities in Teasdale. When friends such as the poet Orrick Johns would visit, Mrs. Teasdale frequently remarked that her daughter should learn to bake a good cake to serve to young men, rather than trying to entertain them with poetry (Carpenter, p. 16). However, feminine submissiveness was at odds with Teasdale's literary ambitions. As a young woman, she struggled to reconcile her desire for a professional career with her parents' traditional beliefs and values, which she had also internalized. In her early letters and journals, Teasdale repeatedly refers to this inner conflict as a war between "Puritanism" and "Paganism." American society was changing rapidly in the early twentieth century, and Teasdale embraced her era's new freedoms with caution.

In December 1910 Teasdale's career began to take off. *Helen of Troy and Other Poems* was accepted for publication by G. P. Putnam's Sons, after circulating for nearly a year in both England and America. That same month, Teasdale was invited to join the Poetry Society of America, a newly formed professional organization with strict membership requirements. In the winter of 1911 Teasdale visited New York City for seven weeks to attend the Poetry Society's monthly meetings and to rendezvous with the poet John Myers O'Hara. Teasdale and O'Hara had carried on a long and intimate correspondence since

1908, which had recently turned romantic. However, when they finally met face to face, Teasdale was sadly disappointed. In person, she found O'Hara to be coolly distant, shy, and vain—not the passionate lover she had expected from his letters. Nonetheless, Teasdale's exhilaration over being in New York resulted in a flood of new love poems, mostly named after the city's famous landmarks. In poems such as "The Metropolitan Tower," "Union Square," and "Central Park at Dusk," Teasdale chronicled her romantic disillusionment with remarkable honesty and directness. These poems, which she published in *Helen of Troy* later that year, helped to launch her national career.

For the next few years, prior to her marriage in 1914, Teasdale spent much of her time in New York, becoming part of an influential coterie of writers and editors affiliated with the Poetry Society. Her closest friends during this time included Jessie Belle Rittenhouse, Louis and Jean Starr Untermeyer, John Hall Wheelock, Eunice Tietjens, and Harriet Monroe. Although Teasdale did not entirely share the *Poetry* editor's enthusiasm for the "new" poetry—she criticized, for instance, Monroe's "unfortunate adoration of Ezra [Pound]"—she considered Monroe to be "one of the deepest, tenderest women [she] ever knew" (qtd. in Drake, p. 110). Monroe was also a staunch supporter of Teasdale's career; she began publishing Teasdale's poems regularly in *Poetry* magazine beginning with the March 1914 issue.

Tietjens and Monroe also played matchmaker for Teasdale, introducing her to two very different suitors—the poet Vachel Lindsay and the businessman Ernst Filsinger—both of whom proposed marriage to Teasdale in 1914. Lindsay, a native of Springfield, Illinois, had built a national reputation on the basis of his innovative performance poems, such as "The Congo," and a populist, folk poetics that he termed the "Gospel of Beauty." Lindsay was a modern-day troubadour, traveling the country, evangelizing on behalf of poetry. He fell deeply in love with Teasdale and attempted to convince her to join him in an unconventional life built around their shared passion for poetry. Teasdale was drawn to

Lindsay and came close to accepting his proposal. Ultimately, however, her Puritan side won out; she decided that she was not willing to risk the financial and social uncertainties of Lindsay's bohemian life. On December 19, 1914, she married Filsinger, a hardworking businessman and enthusiastic supporter of the arts, who provided her with the security and respectability of a conventional middle-class marriage. Teasdale regretted her choice almost immediately. As the years progressed, she struggled to balance her own career with her husband's and grew increasingly ambivalent about her role as a wife. Teasdale and Filsinger divorced in August 1929, having spent much of the previous decade apart, as a result of their competing work schedules and Teasdale's many illnesses.

Although marriage did not bring Teasdale the happiness she had hoped, her career continued to flourish. In the teens, Teasdale published two influential books of poetry—*Rivers to the Sea* (1915) and *Love Songs* (1917)—as well as an edited anthology, *The Answering Voice: One Hundred Love Lyrics by Women* (1917). In 1918, on the strength of these combined works, she was awarded the Columbia Prize for Poetry, the precursor to the Pulitzer Prize and the field's highest honor. Over the next decade Teasdale reached the height of her fame, with critics hailing each of her new volumes of poetry as her best work yet. *Flame and Shadow* (1920) proved as popular as her earlier work, and *Dark of the Moon* (1926) landed Teasdale on the best-seller list for the first time.

Yet, while Teasdale became one of the most popular and critically acclaimed poets in the United States, her mental and physical health continued to deteriorate. Her chronic depression seems to have been exacerbated, first, by the devastation of World War I, which affected her deeply, and then by a series of personal losses that followed the war, including the strain of her failing marriage, the death of her parents, and the death of Vachel Lindsay by suicide in 1931, which took a particular toll on Teasdale. She spent the final few years of her life suffering from extreme paranoia regarding her physical health and withdrawing increasingly from society. On

January 29, 1933, while recovering from pneumonia, Teasdale committed suicide by taking an overdose of sleeping pills. Her later poems provide an important chronicle of her struggle to achieve psychological health and to find peace in poetry. As she writes in "The Crystal Gazer," "I shall gather myself into myself again, / I shall take my scattered selves and make them one" (*CP,* p. 179).

EARLY POETRY

After graduating from Hosmer Hall, Teasdale joined a small group of artistically minded friends to form the Potters, a women's club dedicated to the serious study of literature and the arts. Her earliest publications were in the *Potter's Wheel,* the handmade, multimedia magazine that the club produced from 1904 to 1907. Women's clubs like the Potters were extremely popular at the turn of the twentieth century, especially in progressive cities such as St. Louis. At a time when few women had the opportunity to attend college, women's clubs provided both mutual support and constructive criticism that aided women's professional development. The Potters club was especially noteworthy because so many of its members went on to professional careers in literature and the arts. In addition to Teasdale, Williamina Parrish, the editor of the *Potter's Wheel,* became a successful photographer, as did her sister, Grace Parrish; Caroline Risque became a noted painter and sculptor; Vine Colby became a journalist; and Petronelle Sombart performed on Broadway. As a member of the Potters, Teasdale began to hone her craft and to take herself seriously as a writer.

The *Potter's Wheel* circulated widely within St. Louis literary circles, and in 1906 it was reviewed favorably by William Reedy, the influential editor of the *Mirror.* Over the next year, Reedy introduced Teasdale's writing to the world by reprinting her short prose sketch "The Crystal Cup" and her long poem "Guenevere" from the *Potter's Wheel.* Unique among literary periodicals of its time, the *Mirror* offered St. Louis readers an international perspective on literature and the arts. For instance, Reedy

promoted the French symbolist and decadent poetry of Charles Baudelaire, Stéphane Mallarmé, Paul Verlaine, and Arthur Rimbaud, whose bold experiments would influence the young T. S. Eliot as well as Teasdale. With Reedy's assistance, Teasdale published one of her sonnets, written to the Italian actress Eleonora Duse, in the journal *Poet Lore.* These sonnets would soon form the basis of Teasdale's first book of poetry, *Sonnets to Duse and Other Poems,* published by the Poet Lore Company in 1907. Teasdale paid $250 to subsidize the printing of one thousand copies of the book, hoping that this investment would help launch her professional career.

Teasdale later dismissed *Sonnets to Duse* as an immature work, and, stylistically, it is largely derivative of the poetry of this period. However, the writer Arthur Symons, a leading proponent of decadent and symbolist poetry, reviewed the book favorably in the October 5, 1907, issue of the *Saturday Review of Literature.* Symons seemed to recognize something fresh in Teasdale's idealization of Duse. Indeed, Teasdale's portrait of Duse is neither accurate nor realistic. Despite her passion for the popular actress, Teasdale never saw Duse perform. She based her poems entirely on photographs, reviews, and written accounts of the actress, which she had studied intensely. Perhaps because of this remove from the actual woman, Teasdale's sonnets transform Duse into an ancient Greek muse: "As within a glass / I see your face when Homer's tales were sung" (*Sonnets,* p. 12). In "To a Picture of Eleonora Duse," which Teasdale later included in her *Collected Poems,* she blurs Duse with Tiresias, the blind prophet who would also feature prominently in Eliot's *Waste Land* (1922):

Yea, like a flower within a desert place,
Whose petals fold and fade for lack of rain,
Are these, your eyes, where joy of sight was slain,
And in the silence of your lifted face,
The cloud is rent that hides a sleeping face,
And vanished Grecian beauty lives again.

(*CP,* p. 3)

Teasdale's fascination with "Grecian beauty" aligns her with high modernists such as Eliot, Ezra Pound, and H.D., who were also mining

ancient myths and culture at this same moment. In 1916, H.D.'s *Sea Garden,* which was modeled in part on Sappho's fragmentary verse, would give rise to the newly sparse style of imagism. Teasdale was also strongly influenced by Sappho and, like H.D., was drawn to the beauty and power of mythic female figures such as Cassandra and Helen of Troy. Through these ancient muses, modernist women poets channeled a new form of poetic authority. As Teasdale writes of Duse, "Yea, speak to her, and at your lightest tone, / Her lips will part and words will come at last" (*CP,* p. 4).

Duse also played an important role in the development of the poet Amy Lowell. In 1902, at the age of twenty-eight, Lowell authored her first adult poem in praise of one of Duse's performances in Boston. Years later, when the two poets became friends, Teasdale and Lowell discovered their mutual attraction to the actress and exchanged poems. More than just a schoolgirl crush, Duse served as an important artistic inspiration for these two women poets, both attempting to make their poetry "new" in the first decade of the twentieth century.

A NEW WOMAN

In 1908 Teasdale developed an important friendship with Marion Cummings Stanley, which helped her break free from her parents' influence and begin to find her own voice as a writer. Stanley, who was eight years older than Teasdale, was also a poet and, later, a philosophy instructor at the University of Arizona. She rightly recognized that Teasdale's traditional upbringing and her conservative social milieu were paralyzing the young poet and preventing her from advancing her professional career. Stanley invited Teasdale to Arizona for an extended stay in the winter of 1908. At the age of twenty-four, Teasdale had never traveled anywhere without her parents' supervision. In Tucson, Teasdale was free for the first time to organize her own schedule, select her own company, and pursue her own interests. With Stanley's guidance and encouragement, Teasdale established the daily writing routine that she would maintain with few interruptions

for the rest of her career. In 1921 Teasdale reflected back on her friendship with Stanley and the importance of the time they had spent together in Arizona in her poem "Day's Ending (Tucson)," writing, "I became a woman / Under those vehement stars" (*CP,* p. 180).

The poems Teasdale began writing in Arizona would become part of *Helen of Troy and Other Poems.* As its title indicates, the collection contains a variety of historical poems grounded in Western feminine mythology—in particular, six blank verse monologues that give voice to Helen of Troy, Sappho, Erinna, Guenevere, Beatrice, and Mariana Alcoforado, the seventeenth-century "Portuguese Nun." Although these poems provide evidence of Teasdale's growing technical skill, they are largely influenced by the popular themes and styles of the fin de siècle. As in *Sonnets to Duse,* Teasdale's portraits of these great women can seem overly theatrical and artificial when measured by today's standards. However, alongside these historical poems, *Helen of Troy* also includes a selection of love lyrics, which were noteworthy for their simplicity of expression and the boldness of their sentiment. These were the poems most remarked upon by reviewers, and, based on their success, Teasdale's closest friends, such as the critic Jessie Rittenhouse, advised her to specialize in the lyric and abandon the formal rhetoric of the receding age.

Teasdale's New York poems are the most significant of these new lyrics. She authored this sequence of seven love poems staged on the city's streets during a seven-week visit in the winter of 1911. In January, Teasdale attended one of the first meetings of the Poetry Society of America, a newly formed "Poets Union," which is still in existence today. At the meeting, Teasdale heard Witter Bynner read and met Ezra Pound, on his first and only visit to the society, just as he was about to leave the United States for England. Although Teasdale reportedly disliked Pound, she embraced the sense of artistic freedom and creative innovation on display that evening.

Within her New York poems, Teasdale's female speaker assumes the role of a tourist, traveling from the quiet warmth of her hotel room

on "A Winter Night" through the city's signature destinations named in her titles, including "The Metropolitan Tower," "Gramercy Park," "In the Metropolitan Museum," and "Coney Island." All the while, her male companion remains oblivious to her love. By the end of the poetic sequence, in "Union Square" and "Central Park at Dusk," their unrequited affair has drawn to a disappointing close. Teasdale likely based this portrait of romantic disillusionment on her own unrequited love affair with John Myers O'Hara. However, throughout these poems, the speaker displays a form of boldness that Teasdale herself seems only yet to have imagined.

Teasdale's new freedoms are most evident in "Union Square," the poem that gained her instant notoriety when it was published in October 1911. In the poem's scandalous final lines, Teasdale's speaker seems to sympathize with—perhaps, even to envy—the prostitutes working in Union Square:

Past the fiery lights of the picture shows—
Where the girls with thirsty eyes go by
On the errand each man knows.

And on we walked and on we walked,
At the door at last we said good-bye;
I knew by his smile he had not heard
My heart's unuttered cry.

With the man I love who loves me not
I walked in the street-lamps flare—
But oh, the girls who ask for love
In the lights of Union Square.

(*CP,* pp. 31–32)

Throughout her urban trek, Teasdale's speaker had waited patiently, demurely, for her companion to declare himself, since she lacked the courage to "ask for love" outright. Ironically, he never heard her "heart's unuttered cry." In the poem's final exclamation—"But, oh"—she yearns for a new form of freedom (Girard, p. 42).

It was remarkably daring for a woman to speak so openly about sexual desire in 1911, and even more so for a woman of Teasdale's high social standing and genteel background. Some of Teasdale's male friends, including O'Hara and Louis Untermeyer, advised her not to publish the poem, worrying that it would destroy her reputation. But Jessie Rittenhouse admired "Union Square" and encouraged Teasdale to make it public. A month after the poem appeared, Teasdale wrote to Rittenhouse, "But for your assuring me that it wasn't so wicked after all, I should have let it stay in the seclusion of my tiny red note-book" (qtd. in Drake, pp. 69–70). Following "Union Square," Teasdale was branded a New Woman. Although she claimed to be uncomfortable with this reputation for boldness, she continued to challenge the staid conventions of the love lyric tradition.

MODERN LOVE SONGS

Teasdale capitalized on the success of *Helen of Troy and Other Poems* by publishing two additional volumes of poetry and an edited anthology in quick succession. *Rivers to the Sea* appeared to wide acclaim in 1915, selling out its initial print run of 1,640 copies within three months and earning Teasdale hefty royalties. Because of the book's success, Teasdale's publisher, Macmillan, pressured her to release another volume quickly. In 1917 Teasdale published a popular anthology, *The Answering Voice: One Hundred Love Lyrics by Women,* and a collection of poetry, *Love Songs,* which combined new and previously published poems. Although book sales had fallen off sharply during World War I, *Love Songs* reportedly sold more than 2,000 copies in its first six months. Over the next two years *Love Songs* was reprinted five times, and, over the next decade, it went through fifteen editions. In 1918 Teasdale was awarded the Columbia Prize for Poetry in honor of these combined works.

Many in the poetry world were surprised when the popular and accessible Teasdale was selected for this prestigious award. In *Poetry* magazine, Harriet Monroe, Teasdale's close friend and a leading advocate of the new poetry, went so far as to question the credibility of the judges. Monroe named other, more innovative modernist works such as T. S. Eliot's *Prufrock and Other Observations* (1917), H.D.'s *Sea Gar-*

den (1916), and Ezra Pound's *Lustra* (1916), which she felt were more deserving of the honor. Although Monroe did congratulate Teasdale on her award, she praised *Love Songs* solely for its "refreshing simplicity" (pp. 267–268). This kind of superficial appreciation was typical of Teasdale's modernist critics. Around the same time, the *New York Times* similarly applauded Teasdale for providing a "light" relief from more "serious" modernist poetry. "To chance upon a book by Sara Teasdale," wrote the *Times,* "is to feel the thrill of one who, pushing through the heavy branches in a wood, stops suddenly to hear the song of a bird" (p. 51). Although positive, such reviews avoided substantive engagement with *Love Songs'* dominant themes and methods. In the eyes of her critics, Teasdale was a popular but insubstantial poet.

Teasdale's stated aims in *Rivers to the Sea* and *Love Songs* were more complex. In a publicity interview that appeared in newspapers nationwide following her receipt of the award, Teasdale discussed her poetic philosophy in detail. The interview, which she provided at the behest of her publisher, Macmillan, provides rare insight into her poetic method. Unlike many of her modernist contemporaries, Teasdale was reluctant to espouse any formal theories. She also shied away from public talks and interviews. Here, Teasdale claims that her modern love songs are part of a new movement in American poetry toward greater realism and emotional sincerity. She goes on to suggest that "deep emotion"— what she describes as a "primitive and brutal feeling"—could push modern poetry in a new direction. In particular, she cites Edgar Lee Masters' *Spoon River Anthology* (1915) and Robert Frost's unflinching portraits of New England life as influences on her own mode of poetic realism. "Poetry is valuable in proportion as it deepens our sense of living," Teasdale explains. "The best poets in America today are encouraging us to face life, rather than showing us an escape from it" ("Sara Teasdale Wins Columbia $500 Prize").

Love Songs' opening poem, "Barter," highlights the subtlety and sophistication of Teasdale's new poetic realism. The collection famously begins:

> Life has loveliness to sell,
> All beautiful and splendid things,
> Blue waves whitened on a cliff,
> Soaring fire that sways and sings,
> And children's faces looking up
> Holding wonder like a cup.
>
> (*CP,* p. 97)

At first glance, the poem's regular rhythms and comforting images seem to confirm Teasdale's reputation as a "light" poet. However, upon closer examination, it becomes clear that all of this "loveliness" is for sale. In Teasdale's ironic rendering, all of life's "beautiful and splendid things," the natural world, even "children's faces," have been transformed almost imperceptibly into commodities. An earlier manuscript version of the poem lends support to this politicized reading. "Barter" was originally titled "Buying Loveliness," and the opening line initially read, "Life will not give, but she will sell" (qtd. in Drake, p. 160).

Many of the poems contained within *Love Songs* express similarly dark insights into the nature of modern life and love. For instance, the poems "Debt," "Jewels," and "Riches" also take up the relationship between economic and emotional value. "Jewels" closes with a particularly striking image:

> But I will turn my eyes away from you
> As women turn to put away
> The jewels they have worn at night
> And cannot wear in sober day.
>
> (*CP,* p. 100)

By putting away her jewels, grown gaudy in the sober light of day, the speaker is renouncing her memories of youthful romance, described earlier in the poem as "sapphire," "amethyst," and "diamond." She rejects this superficial beauty, just as she turns away from her lover at the end of the poem. In her pursuit of a "brutally" honest emotional realism, Teasdale was attempting to create a modern love poetry stripped of all jewelry. Her modern speakers continually point out the emptiness and superficiality of classic romantic gestures.

Even seemingly romantic poems like "The Kiss" assert a new independence in the face of love:

> I hoped that he would love me,
> And he has kissed my mouth,
> But I am like a stricken bird
> That cannot reach the south.
>
> For though I know he loves me,
> Tonight my heart is sad;
> His kiss was not so wonderful
> As all the dreams I had.
>
> (*CP,* p. 28)

Teasdale is at the height of her powers in deceptively simple lyrics like "The Kiss." The poem is a significant historical artifact, attesting to the modernist era's rapidly changing gender codes. In "The Kiss," love is no longer a drama between a man and a woman but, now, between a woman and herself. Although American women gained new freedoms in the early part of the twentieth century, including the unprecedented freedom to choose their own romantic partners, Teasdale suggests that they remained constrained by the same inherited romantic scripts. This psychological struggle between romantic "dreams" and the realities of modern love represents one of *Love Songs*' unifying themes.

SONGS OUT OF SORROW

Although a sense of romantic disillusionment remains constant throughout *Love Songs,* it is difficult to discuss the collection as a cohesive volume because it contains both new and selected poems. More than 60 percent of *Love Songs*' selections are reprinted from *Helen of Troy and Other Poems* and *Rivers to the Sea,* and there are noteworthy differences between earlier poems, like "The Kiss," and new ones, such as "Barter" and "Jewels." In her later poems, Teasdale's autobiographical speakers acquire a greater degree of maturity. In "Wisdom," which is part of a new sequence of poems titled "Songs out of Sorrow," this maturity arrives at a painful cost:

> When I have ceased to break my wings
> Against the faultiness of things,
> And learned that compromises wait
> Behind each hardly opened gate,
> When I can look Life in the eyes,
> Grown calm and very coldly wise,
> Life will have given me the Truth,
> And taken in exchange—my youth.
>
> (*CP,* p. 102)

Despite an acute awareness of "the faultiness of things," there is no despair to be found in *Love Songs.* In "Refuge," which concludes "Songs out of Sorrow," the speaker has instead learned to draw on a new source of strength: "If I can sing, I still am free" (*CP,* p. 104). Other new poems included in *Love Songs* display a similar sense of self-reliance and an unyielding faith in the power of poetry.

By 1917 Teasdale had been married to the businessman Ernst Filsinger for three years. Although Filsinger was by all accounts an attentive and loving spouse, Teasdale was unhappy in their marriage. On the eve of their wedding, Teasdale had convinced herself that she wanted to be a wife and mother. In reality, she found the bonds of conventional marriage painful to bear. William Drake reports that Teasdale also obtained an abortion in August 1917. She confided in her close friend John Hall Wheelock that she felt she had to choose between motherhood and a career, because caring for a child would consume her limited energy (p. 172). Filsinger and Teasdale remained married until 1929 but did not have children. Her poems written during this period provide considerable insights into her psychological conflict with marriage.

Throughout *Love Songs,* Teasdale's mature poetic speakers have found love but found it to be lacking. In "Doubt," the speaker struggles to conserve a portion of autonomy within the confines of marriage:

> My soul lives in my body's house,
> And you have both the house and her—
> But sometimes she is less your own
> Than a wild, gay adventurer;
> A restless and an eager wraith,
> How can I tell what she will do—

Oh, I am sure of my body's faith,
But what if my soul broke faith with you?

(*CP*, p. 108)

Casting herself as a "restless and eager wraith," a ghost haunting her own marriage, Teasdale's speaker asserts an unruly form of independence, asking, "How can I tell what she will do"? The poem is concerned not only with infidelity but also with how a woman's very "soul" might lose "faith" with marriage.

"Houses of Dreams" is similarly critical of the metaphysical bonds of love and marriage:

You took my empty dreams
And filled them every one
With tenderness and nobleness,
April and the sun.

The old empty dreams
Where my thoughts would throng
Are far too full of happiness
To even hold a song.

Oh, the empty dreams were dim
And the empty dreams were wide,
They were sweet and shadowy houses
Where my thoughts could hide.

But you took my dreams away
And you made them all come true—
My thoughts have no place now to play,
And nothing now to do.

(*CP*, p. 107)

Perhaps the most leveling critique contained within the volume, "Houses of Dreams" portrays a successful marriage—"full of happiness," "tenderness and nobleness." Yet, it is this happiness that threatens to undo the speaker. "You took my dreams away," she accuses, "And you made them all come true." The speaker suggests that love and marriage have "filled" the previously "empty" spaces where desire and yearning once roamed freely. Now, instead of satisfaction—dreams come true—the speaker has been left with no thoughts of her own, nowhere to hide, "nothing now to do." More than simple disillusionment, the poem points toward a structural critique of domesticity, an institution that it represents as all-powerful, all-consuming, and identity-effacing.

When placed alongside *Love Songs'* more classically romantic lyrics, these sharply critical poems create an uneasy juxtaposition. "Houses of Dreams," for instance, provocatively undercuts the widely anthologized "I Would Live in Your Love":

I would live in your love as the sea-grasses live in the sea,
Borne up by each wave as it passes, drawn down by each wave that recedes;
I would empty my soul of the dreams that have gathered in me,
I would beat with your heart as it beats, I would follow your soul as it leads.

(*CP*, p. 26)

Like William Blake and Emily Dickinson, Teasdale wrote predominantly in quatrains and was unafraid of the nursery-rhyme rhythms of common measure (alternating lines of iambic tetrameter and trimeter). However, as here, she sometimes varies this traditional meter. "I Would Live in Your Love" is written predominantly in anapests, which are interrupted by caesurae in lines 1, 2, and 3 and spondees on "sea-grasses" and "drawn down." The anapests, combined with a sea motif, mimic the ebb and flow of the speaker's desire. She is "borne up" and "drawn down," but never entirely washed away by love. Nonetheless, the speaker tells us how far she "would" be willing to go. Followed so closely by the emptiness of "Houses of Dreams," this youthful abandon comes across as naive, misguided, or, perhaps, insincere.

THE UNCHANGING ACHE OF THINGS

The heartbreak of "Songs out of Sorrow" foreshadowed the darker mood of Teasdale's next volume of poetry, *Flame and Shadow* (1920), a haunting collection marked by the profound losses of the period. The title refers to the flame of beauty and the shadow of death, which were inextricably linked for Teasdale. Critics noted the new direction in her writing, with Marguerite

Wilkinson declaring that Teasdale had forged a new philosophy of life and Babette Deutsch, among other critics, noting that Teasdale's mature wisdom was precisely what a postwar audience required.

While completing the manuscript in the summer of 1920, Teasdale wrote to her husband, "'Flame and Shadow' *is* a good book, if a somewhat sad one. If you stay away any longer, any poems will have to be written with tears instead of a pencil" (qtd. in Drake, p. 195). Soon after the armistice ended the fighting of World War I in November 1918, Filsinger went to Europe on an extended business trip to secure new trade agreements for his company and to help rebuild the European economy. It was the first of many separations for the couple. Over the next decade, Filsinger's career would take him around the world. Because of the demands of her own career and her increasingly frail health, Teasdale did not accompany him on his many travels. She was lonely in her husband's absence and also missed his expertise and careful attention in managing the day-to-day aspects of her career. It was Filsinger, not Teasdale, who responded to the increasing number of professional invitations and letters from fans that Teasdale received on a daily basis. However, in Filsinger's absence, Teasdale also felt more estranged from him than ever before.

In section 3 of *Flame and Shadow,* Teasdale writes openly of the loneliness she is experiencing with her partner of four years, a direct reference to her time with Filsinger. In "Day and Night," the first poem in this section, Teasdale mourns their separation: "Warsaw in Poland / Is half the world away" (*CP,* p. 125). But, as the sequence continues, it becomes clear that the distance between them is emotional as well as physical. In the next poem, "Compensation," Teasdale characterizes her condition as "A thirsty body, a tired heart / And the unchanging ache of things" (*CP,* p. 125). The speaker longs for more from this unfulfilling relationship. In "The Mystery," Teasdale writes,

The spirit eludes us,
Timid and free—

Can I ever know you
Or you know me?

(*CP,* p. 127)

When Teasdale filed for divorce in 1929, her friends and family expressed shock at her decision. Filsinger was on a business trip in Cape Town, South Africa, when he received a letter from Teasdale announcing the end of their marriage. She had traveled to Reno, Nevada, in May 1929 with the hopes of securing an expedited divorce, which could be finalized before Filsinger's return in the fall. To guard their privacy, Teasdale burned all of her letters to Filsinger, as well as her notebook and journal entries from this period. In the only letter that has survived, Teasdale makes clear that her decision to leave him is firm and begs Filsinger not to contest the divorce. Although he was distraught over their breakup, he complied with her wishes.

Teasdale's poetry provides the only extant record of her marital dissatisfaction, and it has offered critics some clues about her change of heart. In section 5 of *Flame and Shadow,* she documents a romantic awakening. The love she describes is not new but "wrapped in memories," which haunt the speaker (*CP,* p. 134). In "Spring Torrents," she asks, "Will it always be like this until I am dead, / Every spring must I bear it all again?" (*CP,* p. 132). The next poem in this group, "I Know the Stars," is even more explicit about the tortures of this unrequited love:

I cannot tell if you love me
Or do not love me at all.

I know many things,
But the years come and go,
I shall die not knowing
The thing I long to know.

(*CP,* p. 132)

According to William Drake, Filsinger's departure for Europe had reignited Teasdale's passion for John Hall Wheelock. The poems in section 5 contain many direct references to their long relationship, including their walks together throughout the city in "Nightfall." Teasdale had fallen in love with Wheelock during a visit to

New York in 1914. Before Filsinger and Vachel Lindsay proposed marriage, Teasdale had set her sights on Wheelock, a fellow poet and successful editor at Charles Scribner's Sons. Although the two remained intimate friends throughout their lives, Wheelock did not reciprocate Teasdale's romantic feelings. In section 5 of *Flame and Shadow,* Teasdale appears to lay this hopeless love to rest. However, in section 9, "By the Sea," her feelings return yet again. Drake notes that Teasdale authored these poems of frustrated love in June 1919 during a visit to the Wheelock family home in East Hampton, Long Island (p. 184). In "If Death Is Kind," the final poem in the sequence, Teasdale concludes, "Here for a single hour in the wide starlight / We shall be happy, for the dead are free" (*CP,* p. 148).

Throughout *Flame and Shadow,* Teasdale's heartache over her failed marriage and her unrequited love for Wheelock slip into a more metaphysical grief. In "The Sanctuary," she expresses the futile desire to remain free from the world's pain:

> If I could keep my innermost Me
> Fearless, aloof and free
> Of the least breath of love or hate,
> And not disconsolate
> At the sick load of sorrow laid on men;
>
> …
>
> I could look even at God with grave forgiving eyes.
>
> (*CP,* p. 151)

In addition to its many love poems, *Flame and Shadow* also contains a series of poems focused on World War I. Some of these poems are oblique, like "The Sanctuary," where she mentions only "the sick load of sorrow laid on men," or "The Broken Field," where she writes, "My soul is a broken field / Ploughed by pain" (*CP,* p. 130). These poems make no mention of the trenches of Europe or the violent devastation of the war, but their imagery foreshadows the war poems that follow a few pages later in section 8 of *Flame and Shadow.* Despite her best attempts, Teasdale was unable to create an inner sanctuary sealed off from this collective pain.

NOT ONE WILL KNOW OF THE WAR

With the outbreak of World War I, Teasdale became deeply concerned about political developments in Europe. She began writing poems in response to the war in January 1915 with the poem "Dusk in War Time," which was later collected in *Rivers To the Sea.* In this first war poem, Teasdale expresses sympathy for those suffering abroad: "But oh, the woman over the sea / Waiting at dusk for one who is dead!" (*Rivers,* p. 97). However, as the war progressed, she began to observe its effects much closer to home. In "Spring in the Naugatuck Valley," Teasdale criticizes a New England factory that is producing munitions for the war:

> They are shaping brass and bullets
> That will kill their fellow-men;
> Forging in the April midnight
> Shrapnel fillers, shot and shell,
> And the murderers go scathless
> Though they do the work of Hell.

"Spring in the Naugatuck Valley" appeared in the progressive magazine *Survey* in April 1915, but it was subsequently omitted from all of her popular books of poetry. Between 1915 and 1919 Teasdale authored more than twenty additional poems explicitly focused on the war. These timely lyrics appeared in popular magazines, including *Harper's Monthly Magazine,* the *Century, Everybody's Magazine,* and the *Nation.* However, for reasons about which scholars can only speculate, Teasdale left the vast majority of these war poems out of her subsequent books of poetry. John Hall Wheelock believed that her decision was the result of a keen "political" sense. According to Wheelock, Teasdale enjoyed her prominence as a popular poet and knew when to withhold poems that might confuse or disturb her public image (qtd. in Drake, p. 174).

Six of Teasdale's war poems appeared in the original edition of *Flame and Shadow.* When assembling *The Collected Poems of Sara Teasdale* in 1937, her literary executor, Margaret Conklin, omitted three of them, including "Winter Stars":

> The world's heart breaks beneath its wars,
> All things are changed, save in the east,

The faithful beauty of the stars.

(*Flame and Shadow*, p. 94)

Stars are one of the volume's dominant motifs, and the poem originally helped to connect Teasdale's individual heartache to the collective grief of the war. The world is in mourning in *Flame and Shadow,* and the "faithful beauty" of the stars provides no consolation for these losses. Their persistence in the face of such tremendous heartbreak only highlights their distance from humans.

"There Will Come Soft Rains" also explores the relationship between humans and the natural world. The poem is Teasdale's best-known response to World War I and one of her most influential poems. Three decades after its initial publication, in the wake of World War II, Ray Bradbury featured the poem as the foundation of a postapocalyptic short story, titled "August 2026: There Will Come Soft Rains," in *The Martian Chronicles* (1950). In his adaptation, Bradbury portrays a future world that has been destroyed by mankind's heedless progress: mechanical mice scurry energetically around a house while a dog, covered in radioactive sores, lies down and dies. All the while, Bradbury's "smart house" of the future continues to recite Teasdale's poem, which was one of its previous owners' favorite works of literature. Bradbury's story shares with Teasdale's poem the terrifying insight that mankind is no longer organically connected to the natural world. The only species capable of mass, mechanized self-destruction, humans are utterly alone, detached from a natural world that no longer even notices we are there:

And not one will know of the war, not one
Will care at last when it is done.

Not one would mind, neither bird nor tree,
If mankind perished utterly;

And Spring herself, when she woke at dawn,
Would scarcely know that we were gone.

(*CP,* p. 143)

Unlike the soldier poetry of Wilfred Owen, Isaac Rosenberg, and Siegfried Sassoon, which provided firsthand accounts of the gruesome violence of trench warfare, Teasdale's poetry chronicled the war's effects at home. In poems like "Winter Stars" and "There Will Come Soft Rains," the word "war" is mentioned only briefly. Its eerie presence disrupts the surface calm and beauty of American life.

Well into 1917, Teasdale maintained a strict adherence to pacifism, opposing war in any guise on moral grounds. Although she understood the necessity of America's intervention into World War I, she found it difficult to support the parades, singing, and other patriotic displays that were rallying American enthusiasm for the war effort. In her letters from this period, she comments frequently on the "war-madness" that was sweeping America. Her poem "Sons" also recounts her ambivalent feelings while watching a military parade: "Men in brown with marching feet / Like a great machine moved down the street" (*Everybody's Magazine,* p. 98). Amy Lowell, who was one of Teasdale's closest friends, similarly described the alienating experience of watching the war from the sidelines in her poem "In a Stadium," which appeared in *Pictures of the Floating World* (1919). Lowell's book of poems is an apt companion to *Flame and Shadow.* Both volumes provide a distinctively gendered perspective on the war by combining personal romantic lyrics with political poems in a striking manner. These provocative poems on love and war have yet to receive the critical attention that they deserve.

A HOUSE OF SHINING WORDS

Teasdale's next volume of poetry, *Dark of the Moon* (1926), sold out its initial print run of five thousand copies almost immediately and landed her on the best-seller lists for the first time. The title indicated her desire to explore the areas unlighted by the moon of traditional romantic love. Critics rightly identified a deepening of the introspective qualities that had always distinguished her poetry. They were uniformly in praise of the depth of feeling and musicality that remained in her poetry, and many considered the new volume to be Teasdale's best work. In the years immediately following its publication,

Teasdale's mental and physical health deteriorated so severely that she found it nearly impossible to write poetry. It would be another seven years before she published her last volume of poetry, *Strange Victory* (1933), which appeared posthumously, assembled by Margaret Conklin, following Teasdale's detailed directions.

In her final poems, Teasdale displays a new form of self-consciousness about her gender identity and her changing role in society as a maturing woman. "Day's Ending (Tucson)" is among her most explicit feminist statements. Throughout the poem, she rejects a romantic ideology that defines women's lives in terms of the men they love and marry. "Only yourself can heal you / Only yourself can lead you," Teasdale repeats (*CP*, p. 180). Now past the age of forty, Teasdale embraced the solitude and independence that comes with the middle stage of life. In "The Solitary," she mourns the neediness of her youth, suggesting that she had once been too willing to share herself with others and to allow public expectations to shape her thoughts and words. In the poem's powerful concluding image, Teasdale's speaker claims that she is "self-complete as a flower or a stone" (*CP*, p. 179).

However, despite the strength and resilience suggested by such imagery, Teasdale's independence had been hard-won. Throughout her late poems, she adopts the persona of a virginal woman, sealed off from romantic and sexual desire. The poems suggest that she has had to chasten her desire to love and be loved, in order to achieve a fragile form of power. In "The Crystal Gazer," she is clairvoyant, likening herself to a sibyl, and in "Those Who Love," she channels the mythic restraint of "Francesca, Guinevere, / Deirdre, Iseult, Heloise" (*CP*, p. 173). Although these mythic allusions are reminiscent of her early poetry, Teasdale invokes these figures to a decidedly different effect in *Dark of the Moon*. They are no longer romantic heroines, provoking the idealizations of a young girl, but mature women like Teasdale herself, filled with feminine pride and a stubborn sense of self-respect.

Teasdale's new persona is embodied most fully in "Effigy of a Nun." The poem describes a sculpture of a sixteenth-century nun clasping a crucifix. Looking deeply into this woman's eyes, Teasdale sees "infinite gentleness, infinite irony." Despite the time and distance separating them, Teasdale seems to identify with her predecessor, "She who so loved herself and her own warring thoughts" (*CP*, p. 172). Like many of Teasdale's late poems, "Effigy of a Nun" is musically complex. The poem is written predominantly in dactylic tetrameter, a strict meter that can be difficult to pull off successfully. Teasdale varies the meter in key places and alternates masculine and feminine rhymes at the ending of each line to create a subtle rocking rhythm throughout. This cadence heightens the poem's mystical qualities. By the poem's final stanza, the nun's eyes have closed. The speaker's gaze has magically, almost imperceptibly, shifted inward onto herself. Although Teasdale clearly portrays the nun as a dignified and imposing figure, her speaker is still left with some lingering doubts about the high price she has had to pay for her insight. At the end of the poem, her final impression is one of emptiness.

The critic Cheryl Walker, who provides an important analysis of the gender politics of Teasdale's poetry and career, notes a strong resemblance between "Effigy of a Nun" and Sylvia Plath's "The Moon and the Yew Tree." Both poets explored the meaning of the effigy late in their careers, as they approached their own deaths. Walker compares *Dark of the Moon* and *Strange Victory* to Plath's *Ariel* (1965) and *Winter Trees* (1971), as books that convey a strong sense of the writers' inescapable movement toward death. Because both poets chose to end their own lives, their explorations of self within their poetry have taken on an added significance.

Teasdale's late poems are preoccupied with death. In "I Shall Live to Be Old," she insists, "I shall cling to life as the leaves to the creaking oak" (*CP*, p. 181). Then, in "The Old Enemy," she claims instead, "Rebellion against death, the old rebellion / Is over; I have nothing left to fight" (*CP*, p. 182). In the final years of her life, Teasdale's depression became more severe than ever before. She became consumed by her own

"warring thoughts." She clung to her work and the few friends that remained, but she was never truly well after her divorce in 1929. The one bright spot for Teasdale in these dark days was Margaret Conklin, a college student who had written her an admiring letter in 1926. The two became close friends, and Teasdale later made Conklin her literary executor. She found their friendship to be a source of strength and inspiration when she needed it the most. In one of her final poems "To M.," which appeared in *Strange Victory,* Teasdale writes to Conklin, "I shall find no better thing upon the earth / Than the willful, noble, faulty thing which is you" (*CP,* p. 209).

In December 1931 Teasdale received news that her close friend and onetime suitor Vachel Lindsay had committed suicide. She had been in close correspondence with Lindsay and his wife, Elizabeth Connor Lindsay, during the previous months, and she knew that his mental health had been deteriorating. Nonetheless, Lindsay's death was shattering. In the poem "In Memory of Vachel Lindsay" from *Strange Victory,* Teasdale remembers the poet as "You whom the world could not break, nor the years tame" (*CP,* p. 210). Grieving for her friend, she became increasingly convinced that her own death was near. On December 6, 1931, the day after Lindsay's death, a benzoin inhaler that Teasdale was using to treat a chest cold exploded in her face and caused minor burns. Although her injuries were by all accounts minor, Teasdale believed that she would be permanently disfigured. She wrote the poem "Since Death Brushed Past Me" in response to the accident: "Since Death brushed past me once more to-day, / Let me say quickly what I must say" (*CP,* p. 213).

Teasdale's few remaining friends, including Conklin, Filsinger, Wheelock, Monroe, and Rittenhouse, were unaware that she was living in a near constant state of panic and paranoia about her health. Remarkably, until the final months of her life, she was still able to appear cheerful and amusing in public on the limited occasions when she socialized. In October 1932 Teasdale was diagnosed with pneumonia. By the end of November, X-rays by her doctors confirmed that her lungs were clear. But she remained convinced that her blood vessels were about to rupture and that a massive stroke was imminent. Teasdale's brother, John Warren, Jr., had died at the age of forty-seven from complications due to a stroke, a loss that likely provoked Teasdale's paranoia. In December 1932 she began accumulating sleeping pills, having now descended into a state of uncontrollable terror about her health. In the early morning hours of January 29, 1933, at home in her New York apartment, Teasdale took a heavy dose of sleeping pills and lay down in a warm bath. Her nurse, Rita Brown, discovered her body in the bathroom the following morning around 9 a.m. Because the bathwater was still warm, Teasdale's death must have occurred only a short time before. Some of Teasdale's friends believed that her actions had been a cry for help and that she had intended to be found before her death. Newspapers also initially reported her death as an accident, caused by unresolved complications of pneumonia and submersion in a tub. However, despite these ambiguities, the medical examiner's reports, which were not made public at the time, determined that Teasdale's death had been the result of suicide by drugs, a conclusion that subsequent biographers such as Carol Schoen and William Drake have confirmed. At the end of her life, no longer able to write poetry, Teasdale lost the sense of safety and security that she had once found in her "house of shining words" (*CP,* p. 104).

Selected Bibliography

WORKS OF SARA TEASDALE

POETRY

Sonnets to Duse and Other Poems. Boston: Poet Lore, 1907.

Helen of Troy and Other Poems. New York: Putnam, 1911. Revised and reissued, New York: Macmillan, 1922.

Rivers to the Sea. New York: Macmillan, 1915.

Love Songs. New York: Macmillan, 1917. Reissued in revised format, 1975.

Flame and Shadow. New York: Macmillan, 1920. Revised, London: Jonathan Cape, 1924.

Dark of the Moon. New York: Macmillan, 1926.

A Country House. With drawings by Herbert F. Roese. Borzoi Chap Books, no. 4. New York: Knopf, 1932.

Strange Victory. Edited by Margaret Conklin. New York: Macmillan, 1933. (Posthumous publication.)

UNCOLLECTED POEMS

"Spring in the Naugatuck Valley." *Survey* 34, no. 1:27 (April 1915).

"Sons." *Everybody's Magazine* 38, no. 1:98 (January 1918).

COLLECTED WORKS

The Collected Poems of Sara Teasdale. New York: Macmillan, 1937. (Cited in the text as *CP.*) Reissued in new format, 1945; reissued with introduction by Marya Zaturenska, 1966.

Those Who Love: Love Poems by Sara Teasdale. Edited by Arthur Wortman and Bill Greer. Kansas City, Mo.: Hallmark, 1969.

Mirror of the Heart: Poems of Sara Teasdale. Edited by William Drake. New York: Macmillan, 1984.

EDITED ANTHOLOGIES

The Answering Voice: One Hundred Love Lyrics by Women. Boston: Houghton Mifflin, 1917. Revised, with fifty recent poems added, New York: Macmillan, 1928.

Rainbow Gold: Poems Old and New Selected for Girls and Boys by Sara Teasdale. Illustrated by Dugald Walker. New York: Macmillan, 1922.

Stars To-Night: Verses Old and New for Boys and Girls. Illustrated by Dorothy Pulis Lathrop. New York: Macmillan, 1930.

JOURNALS, CORRESPONDENCE, AND MANUSCRIPTS

The primary archive of Teasdale's papers is the Sara Teasdale Collection at the Beinecke Rare Book and Manuscript Library, Yale University, New Haven, Connecticut. Its extensive holdings include Teasdale's poetry notebooks, comprising six leather-bound volumes dating from April 1, 1911, through October 1, 1932, and containing many manuscript drafts and unpublished poems, including additional World War I poems. Teasdale was a frequent contributor to periodicals, and her notebooks also contain accurate records of her many magazine submissions and acceptances. The collection also contains handmade issues of the *Potter's Wheel* from 1903 to 1907. An additional archive of Teasdale's correspondence resides at the Missouri Historical Society, St. Louis, Missouri. This valuable collection features letters between Teasdale and the Filsinger family, including many letters sent to her husband's sisters, Irma and Wander Filsinger, two of Teasdale's most frequent and intimate correspondents.

CRITICAL AND BIOGRAPHICAL STUDIES

Carpenter, Margaret Haley. *Sara Teasdale: A Biography.* New York: Schulte, 1960.

D'Amico, Diane. "Saintly Singer or Tanagra Figurine? Christina Rossetti Through the Eyes of Katharine Tynan and Sara Teasdale." *Victorian Poetry* 32, nos. 3–4: 387–407 (autumn–winter 1994).

Drake, William. *Sara Teasdale: Woman & Poet.* San Francisco: Harper & Row, 1979.

Girard, Melissa. "'How Autocratic Our Country Is Becoming': The Sentimental Poetess at War." *Journal of Modern Literature* 32, no. 2:41–64 (winter 2009).

Larsen, Jeanne. "Lowell, Teasdale, Wylie, Millay, and Bogan." In *The Columbia History of American Poetry.* Edited by Jay Parini and Brett Candlish Millier. New York: Columbia University Press, 1993. Pp. 203–232.

Mannino, Mariann. "Sara Teasdale: Fitting Tunes to Everything." *Turn of the Century Women* 5, nos. 1–2:37–41 (1990).

Newcomb, John Timberman. "Poetry's Opening Door: Harriet Monroe and American Modernism." *American Periodicals* 15, no. 1:6–22 (2005).

Rittenhouse, Jessie B. *My House of Life.* Boston: Houghton Mifflin, 1934.

Saul, George Brandon. "A Delicate Fabric of Bird Song: The Verse of Sara Teasdale." *Arizona Quarterly* 13, no. 1:62–66 (1957).

Schoen, Carol. *Sara Teasdale.* Boston: Twayne, 1986.

Tietjens, Eunice. *The World at My Shoulder.* New York: Macmillan, 1938.

Walker, Cheryl. *Masks Outrageous and Austere: Culture, Psyche, and Persona in Modern Women Poets.* Bloomington: Indiana University Press, 1991.

REVIEWS

Deutsch, Babette. "Indian Summer." *New Republic,* December 1, 1926, p. 48. (Review of *Dark of the Moon.*)

Review of *Love Songs. Dial* 63:457 (November 8, 1917).

Review of *Love Songs. New York Times Book Review,* October 21, 1917, p. 51. http://timesmachine.nytimes.com/timesmachine/1917/10/21/issue.html

Wilkinson, Marguerite. "Death as a Poet Sees It." *New York Times,* October 31, 1920, p. 10. (Review of *Flame and Shadow.*)

OTHER SOURCES

"Sara Teasdale Wins Columbia $500 Prize for Best Book of Poems Published in 1917." *Brooklyn Daily Eagle,* June 9, 1918, p. 8. http://bklyn.newspapers.com/image/55297918/

Lowell, Amy. "In a Stadium." In *Pictures of the Floating World.* New York: Macmillan, 1919. P. 231.

Monroe, Harriet. "Comment: Sara Teasdale's Prize." *Poetry* 12, no. 1:264–269 (1918).

Cumulative Index

All references include volume numbers in boldface roman numerals followed by page numbers within that volume. Subjects of articles are indicated by boldface type.

A

"A" (Zukofsky), **Supp. III Part 2:** 611, 612, 614, 617, 619, 620, 621, 622, 623, 624, 626, 627, 628, 629, 630, 631; **Supp. IV Part 1:** 154; **Supp. XVI:** 287, *287*

Aal, Katharyn Machan, **Supp. IV Part 1:** 332; **Supp. XXIII:** 54

Aaron, Daniel, **IV:** 429; **Supp. I Part 2:** 647, 650

Aaron's Rod (Lawrence), **Supp. I Part 1:** 255

Abacus (Karr), **Supp. XI: 240–242,** 248, 254

Abádi-Nagy, Zoltán, **Supp. IV Part 1:** 280, 289, 291

"Abandoned Farmhouse" (Kooser), **Supp. XIX:** 117, 119

"Abandoned House, The" (L. Michaels), **Supp. XVI:** 214

"Abandoned Newborn, The" (Olds), **Supp. X:** 207

"Abandoned Stone Schoolhouse in the Nebraska Sandhills, An" (Kooser), **Supp. XIX:** 124–125

"Abba Jacob" (Nelson), **Supp. XVIII:** 177

"Abbé François Picquet"(Kenny), **Supp. XXIII:** 153

Abbey, Edward, **Supp. VIII:** 42; **Supp. X:** 24, 29, 30, 31, 36; **Supp. XIII: 1–18; Supp. XIV:** 179; **Supp. XXV:** 208; **Supp. XXVI:** 31, 37

Abbey's Road (Abbey), **Supp. XIII:** 12

Abbott, Carl, **Supp. XVIII:** 142

Abbott, Clifford F., **Supp. XXVI:** 89

Abbott, Edith, **Supp. I Part 1:** 5

Abbott, Jack Henry, **Retro. Supp. II:** 210

Abbott, Jacob, **Supp. I Part 1:** 38, 39

Abbott, Lyman, **III:** 293

Abbott, Sean, **Retro. Supp. II:** 213

ABC of Color, An: Selections from Over a Half Century of Writings (Du Bois), **Supp. II Part 1:** 186

ABC of Reading (Pound), **III:** 468, 474–475

"Abdication, An" (Merrill), **Supp. III Part 1:** 326

'Abdu'l-Bahá, **Supp. XX: 117, 122**

Abel, Lionel, **Supp. XIII:** 98

Abel, Sam, **Supp. XIII:** 199

Abelard, Peter, **I:** 14, 22

Abeles, Sigmund, **Supp. VIII:** 272

Abeng (Cliff), **Supp. XXII:** 66, 69–71

Abercrombie, Joe, **Supp. XXV:** 74

Abercrombie, Lascelles, **III:** 471; **Retro. Supp. I:** 127, 128

Abernathy, Milton, **Supp. III Part 2:** 616

Abernon, Edgar Vincent, Viscount d', **Supp. XVI:** 191

Aberration of Starlight (Sorrentino), **Supp. XXI:** 234–235

Abhau, Anna. *See* Mencken, Mrs. August (Anna Abhau)

"Abide with Me" (Hoffman), **Supp. XVIII:** 86

Abide with Me (Strout), **Supp. XXIII:** 273, 275, **278–280,** 285

"Ability" (Emerson), **II:** 6

Abingdon, Alexander, **Supp. XVI:** 99

Abish, Walter, **Supp. V:** 44

"Abishag" (Glück), **Supp. V:** 82

"Abnegation, The" (Bronk), **Supp. XXI:** 32

Abney, Lisa, **Supp. XXII:** 9

Abood, Maureen, **Supp. XXII:** 90

"Abortion, The" (Sexton), **Supp. II Part 2:** 682

"Abortions" (Dixon), **Supp. XII:** 153

"About C. D. Wright" (Colburn), **Supp. XV:** 341

"About Effie" (Findley), **Supp. XX: 50**

"About Hospitality" (Jewett), **Retro. Supp. II:** 131

"About Kathryn" (Dubus), **Supp. VII:** 91

"About Language" (Wrigley), **Supp. XVIII:** 300–301

"About Looking Alone at a Place: Arles" (M. F. K. Fisher), **Supp. XVII:** 89, 91

About the House (Auden), **Supp. II Part 1:** 24

About These Stories: Fiction for Fiction Writers and Readers (Huddle, ed.), **Supp. XXVI:** 160

About Town: "The New Yorker" and the World It Made (Yagoda), **Supp. VIII:** 151

"About Zhivago and His Poems"(O'Hara), **Supp. XXIII:** 214

Above Pate Valley (Snyder), **Supp. VIII:** 293

Above the River (Wright), **Supp. III Part 2:** 589, 606

Above the Waterfall (Rash), **Supp. XXVII:** 221, 225, 226–227, 228

"Abraham" (Schwartz), **Supp. II Part 2:** 663

Abraham, Nelson Algren. *See* Algren, Nelson

Abraham, Pearl, **Supp. XVII:** 49; **Supp. XX: 177; Supp. XXIV: 1–15**

"Abraham Davenport" (Whittier), **Supp. I Part 2:** 699

"Abraham Lincoln" (Emerson), **II:** 13

Abraham Lincoln: The Prairie Years (Sandburg), **III:** 580, 587–589, 590

Abraham Lincoln: The Prairie Years and the War Years (Sandburg), **III:** 588, 590

Abraham Lincoln: The War Years (Sandburg), **III:** 588, 589–590; **Supp. XVII:** 105

"Abraham Lincoln Walks at Midnight" (Lindsay), **Supp. I Part 2:** 390–391

"Abram Morrison" (Whittier), **Supp. I Part 2:** 699

Abramovich, Alex, **Supp. X:** 302, 309

Abrams, David, **Supp. XXII:** 61

Abrams, M. H., **Supp. XVI:** 19; **Supp. XXIII:** 42

Abridgment of Universal Geography, An: Together with Sketches of History (Rowson), **Supp. XV:** 243

"Absalom" (Rukeyser), **Supp. VI:** 278–279

Absalom, Absalom! (Faulkner), **II:** 64, 65–67, 72, 223; **IV:** 207; **Retro. Supp. I:** 75, 81, 82, 84, 85, 86, 87, 88, 89, 90, 92, 382; **Supp. V:** 261; **Supp. X:** 51; **Supp. XIV:** 12–13; **Supp. XXVI:** 8, 12

"Absence"(J. Schoolcraft), **Supp. XXIII:** 228, 231

"Absence of Mercy" (Stone), **Supp. V:** 295

"Absentee, The" (Levertov), **Supp. III Part 1:** 284

Absentee Ownership (Veblen), **Supp. I Part 2:** 642

"Absent-Minded Bartender" (X. J. Kennedy), **Supp. XV:** 159

"Absent Thee from Felicity Awhile" (Wylie), **Supp. I Part 2:** 727, 729

Absolutely True Diary of a Part-Time Indian, The (Alexie), **Supp. XXVI:** 108

"Absolution" (Fitzgerald), **Retro. Supp. I:** 108

"Absolution" (Sobin), **Supp. XVI:** 289

"Abuelita's Ache" (Mora), **Supp. XIII:** 218

Abysmal Brute, The (London), **II:** 467

Abyssinia and the Imperialists (C. L. R. James), **Supp. XXI:** 166

Abyss of Human Illusion, The (Sorrentino), **Supp. XXI:** 225, 227, 237–238

"Academic Story, An" (Simpson), **Supp. IX:** 279–280

"Academic Zoo, The: Theory—in Practice" (Epstein), **Supp. XIV:** 107–108, 109

"A Capella" (Wrigley), **Supp. XVIII:** 300

"Accident" (Minot), **Supp. VI: 208–209**

"Accident" (Munro), **Supp. XXVII:** 188

"Accident, The" (Southern), **Supp. XI:** 295

"Accident, The" (Strand), **Supp. IV Part 2:** 624

Accident/A Day's News (Wolf), **Supp. IV Part 1:** 310

Accidental Tourist, The (Tyler), **Supp. IV Part 2:** 657, 668–669; **Supp. V:** 227

Accordion Crimes (Proulx), **Supp. VII:** 259–261

"Accountability" (Dunbar), **Supp. II Part 1:** 197, 204

"Account of the Method of Drawing Birds" (Audubon), **Supp. XVI:** 12

"Accusation, The" (Wright), **Supp. III Part 2:** 595

"Accusation of the Inward Man, The" (Taylor), **IV:** 156

"Accusing Message from Dead Father" (Karr), **Supp. XI:** 244

Ace, Goodman, **Supp. IV Part 2:** 574

Ache of Appetite, The (Hadas), **Supp. XXIII: 120–121**

Achievement in American Poetry (Bogan), **Supp. III Part 1:** 63–64

Acker, Kathy, **Supp. XII:1–20; Supp. XXI:** 236

Ackerley, J. R., **Supp. XX: 237**

Ackerman, Diane, **Supp. XIII:** 154

"Acknowledgment" (Lanier), **Supp. I Part 1:** 364

"Acknowledgment, Adaptation, and Shakespeare in Ron Rash's *Serena*" (Morrow), **Supp. XXVII:** 216

Ackroyd, Peter, **Supp. V:** 233; **Supp. XVII:** 180

"Acquaintance in the Heavens, An" (Dillard), **Supp. VI:** 34

"Acquainted with the Night" (Frost), **II:** 155; **Retro. Supp. I:** 137; **Supp. XXI:** 26

Across Spoon River (Masters), **Supp. I Part 2:** 455, 457, 459, 460, 466, 474–475, 476

Across the Layers: Poems Old and New (Goldbarth), **Supp. XII:** 181, **187–189**

Across the River and into the Trees (Hemingway), **I:** 491; **II:** 255–256, 261; **Retro. Supp. I:** 172, **184–185; Supp. XIX:** 248

"Acteon" (Stallings), **Supp. XXV:** 231–232

"Actfive" (MacLeish), **III:** 18–19, 22

Actfive and Other Poems (MacLeish), **III:** 3, 17–19, 21

Action (Shepard), **Supp. III Part 2:** 446

Active Anthology (Pound, ed.), **Supp. III Part 2:** 617; **Supp. XXVI:** 224

Active Service (Crane), **I:** 409

"Act of Creation and Its Artifact, The" (Sorrentino), **Supp. XXI:** 229, 235

Act of Love (film), **Supp. XXVI:** 136

Act of Love, An (Wolfert), **Supp. XXI:** 270, **275–277**

Act of Love, An: A Completely Retold Version of the Novel (Wolfert), **Supp. XXI:** 276

Acton, Patricia Nassif, **Supp. X:** 233

Actors and Sin (film), **Supp. XXVII:** 94

"Actor's Blood" (Hecht), **Supp. XXVII:** 94

Actor's Nightmare, The (Durang), **Supp. XXIV:** 116, 119

Acts and Monuments of These Latter and Perilous Days (Fox), **Supp. XXII:** 36

Acts of Faith (Caputo), **Supp. XIX: 29–30**

"Acts of the Apostles, The" (Bronk), **Supp. XXI:** 28

Actual, The (Bellow), **Retro. Supp. II:** 33

"Actual Experience, Preferred Narratives" (Julier), **Supp. IV Part 1:** 211

Acuff, Roy, **Supp. V:** 335

Ada (Nabokov), **Retro. Supp. I:** 265, 266, 270, 276–277, 278, 279

"Ada" (Stein), **IV:** 43

"Adagia" (Stevens), **IV:** 78, 80, 88, 92

"Adagio" (Hull), **Supp. XXI:** 136–137

"Adam" (Hecht), **Supp. X:** 62

"Adam" (W. C. Williams), **Retro. Supp. I:** 422, 423

"Adam and Eve" (Eugene), **Supp. X:** 204

"Adam and Eve" (Shapiro), **Supp. II Part 2:** 708, 712

"Adamantine Practice of Poetry, The" (Wright), **Supp. XV:** 341–342, 343–344

Adam Bede (G. Eliot), **II:** 181

Adamé, Leonard, **Supp. XIII:** 316

Adam & Eve & the City (W. C. Williams), **Retro. Supp. I:** 423

Adamic, Louis, **Supp. XXIII:** 166

"Adamic Purity as Double Agent" (Whalen-Bridge), **Retro. Supp. II:** 211–212

"Adam Robinson Acquires Grandparents and a Little Sister" (P. E. Jones), **Supp. XXII:** 151

"Adams" (Saunders), **Supp. XIX:** 232

Adams, Althea. *See* Thurber, Mrs. James (Althea Adams)

Adams, Annie. *See* Fields, Annie Adams

Adams, Brooks, **Supp. I Part 2:** 484

Adams, Charles, **Supp. I Part 2:** 644

Adams, Charles Francis, **I:** 1, 4; **Supp. I Part 2:** 484

Adams, Franklin P., **Supp. I Part 2:** 653; **Supp. IX:** 190; **Supp. XV:** 294, 297

Adams, Henry, **I: 1–24,** 111, 243, 258; **II:** 278, 542; **III:** 396, 504; **IV:** 191, 349; **Retro. Supp. I:** 53, 59; **Retro. Supp. II:** 207; **Supp. I Part 1:** 299–300, 301, 314; **Supp. I Part 2:** 417, 492, 543, 644; **Supp. II Part 1:** 93–94, 105; **Supp. III Part 2:** 613; **Supp. IV Part 1:** 31, 208; **Supp. XXIV:** 224

Adams, Mrs. Henry (Marian Hooper), **I:** 1, 5, 10, 17–18

Adams, Henry B., **Supp. I Part 1:** 369

Adams, James Truslow, **Supp. I Part 2:** 481, 484, 486

Adams, J. Donald, **IV:** 438

Adams, John, **I:** 1; **II:** 103, 301; **III:** 17, 473; **Supp. I Part 2:** 483, 506, 507, 509, 510, 511, 517, 518, 520, 524

Adams, John Luther, **Supp. XII:** 209

Adams, John Quincy, **I:** 1, 3, 16–17; **Supp. I Part 2:** 685, 686

Adams, Léonie, **Supp. I Part 2:** 707; **Supp. IX:** 229; **Supp. V:** 79; **Supp. XVII:** 75

Adams, Luella, **Supp. I Part 2:** 652

Adams, Noah, **Supp. XVII:** 218

Adams, Phineas, **Supp. XXV:** 37

Adams, Phoebe, **Supp. IV Part 1:** 203; **Supp. VIII:** 124

Adams, Samuel, **Supp. I Part 2:** 516, 525

Adams, Tim, **Supp. XXVII:** 269

Adams, Timothy Dow, **Supp. XVI:** 67, 69

Ada; or Ardor (Nabokov), **III:** 247

Adaptation (film), **Supp. XXV:** 160

"Ad Castitatem" (Bogan), **Supp. III Part 1:** 50

Adcock, Betty, **Supp. XVIII:** 181–182, 182

Addams, Jane, **Supp. I Part 1: 1–26; Supp. XI:** 200, 202

Addams, John Huy, **Supp. I Part 1:** 2

"Add Blue to Make White Whiter" (Vaz), **Supp. XXVI:** 263

"Addendum" (Wright), **Supp. V:** 339

Addiego, John, **Supp. XII:** 182

Adding Machine, The (Rice), **I:** 479

Adding Machine, The: Selected Essays (Burroughs), **Supp. III Part 1:** 93, 97

"Adding to the Unhappiness: Those Poems You Are Writing" (Gallagher), **Supp. XXIV:** 172

Addison, Joseph, **I:** 8, 105, 106–107, 108, 114, 131, 300, 304; **III:** 430

"Address Delivered at Lenox, An" (Channing), **Supp. XXIV: 79–80**

"Addressed to a Political Shrimp, or, Fly upon the Wheel" (Freneau), **Supp. II Part 1:** 267

"Address to My Soul" (Wylie), **Supp. I Part 2:** 729

"Address to the Deist, An" (Wheatley), **Supp. XX: 287**

"Address to the Devil" (Jarman), **Supp. XVII:** 114

Address to the Government of the United States on the Cession of Louisiana to the French, An (Brown), **Supp. I Part 1:** 146

"Address to the Scholars of New England" (Ransom), **III:** 491

"Address with Exclamation Points, A" (Simic), **Supp. VIII:** 283

"Adieu to Norman, Bon Jour to Joan and Jean-Paul"(O'Hara), **Supp. XXIII:** 219

Adisa, Opal Palmer, **Supp. XXII:** 66, 74, 78

"Adjutant Bird, The" (Banks), **Supp. V:** 5

Adkins, Nelson F., **II:** 20

Adler, Alfred, **I:** 248

Adler, Betty, **III:** 103

Adler, George J., **III:** 81

Adler, Renata, **Supp. X:** 171

Admiral of the Ocean Sea: A Life of Christopher Columbus (Morison), **Supp. I Part 2:** 486–488

"Admirals" (Chabon), **Supp. XI:** 72

"Admonition, An" (Brodsky), **Supp. VIII:** 33

"Adolescence" (Bidart), **Supp. XV:** 32

"Adolescence" (Dove), **Supp. IV Part 1:** 245

"Adolescence" (Olds), **Supp. X:** 211

"Adolescence II" (Dove), **Supp. IV Part 1:** 242, 244–245

Adolescent's Christmas, An: 1944 (C. Bly), **Supp. XVI:** 31–32

"Adolf Eichmann" (Carruth), **Supp. XVI:** 47

"Adonais" (Shelley), **II:** 516, 540

Adonai: The Pilgrim of Eternity (Lippard), **Supp. XXIII:** 180, 189, 190

Adorno, Theodor, **Supp. I Part 2:** 645, 650; **Supp. IV Part 1:** 301

"Adrienne Rich: The Poetics of Change" (Gelpi), **Supp. I Part 2:** 554

Adrift in Macao (Durang), **Supp. XXIV:** 125

"Adultery" (Banks), **Supp. V:** 15

"Adultery" (Dubus), **Supp. VII:** 85

Adultery and Other Choices (Dubus), **Supp. VII:** 83–85

Adulthood Rites (O. Butler), **Supp. XIII:** 63, **64–65**

Adult Life of Toulouse Lautrec by Henri Toulouse Lautrec, The (Acker), **Supp. XII:** 5, 6, **8–9**

Adventure (London), **II:** 466

Adventures in Ancient Egypt (Goldbarth), **Supp. XII:** 191

Adventures in Value (Cummings), **I:** 430

"Adventures of a Book Reviewer" (Cowley), **Supp. II Part 1:** 137, 142

Adventures of a Novelist (Atherton), **Supp. XXIV:** 17–18, 19–20, 21

Adventures of Augie March, The (Bellow), **I:** 144, 147, 149, 150, 151, 152–153, 154, 155, 157, 158–159, 164; **Retro. Supp. II:** 19, 20, **22–23**, 24, 30; **Supp. VIII:** 234, 236–237; **Supp. XXIV:** 220

Adventures of a Young Man (Dos Passos), **I:** 488, 489, 492

Adventures of Captain Bonneville (Irving), **II:** 312

Adventures of Harry Franco, The: A Tale of the Great Panic (Briggs), **Supp. XVIII:** 1, 2, 5–8

Adventures of Harry Richmond, The (Meredith), **Supp. XX: 234**

Adventures of Huckleberry Finn, The (Twain), **I:** 307, 506; **II:** 26, 72, 262, 266–268, 290, 418, 430; **III:** 101, 112–113, 357, 554, 558, 577; **IV:** 198, 201–204, 207; **Retro. Supp. I:** 188; **Retro. Supp. II:** 121; **Supp. I Part 1:** 247; **Supp. IV Part 1:** 247, 257; **Supp. IV Part 2:** 502; **Supp. V:** 131; **Supp. VIII:** 198; **Supp. X:** 230; **Supp. XII:** 16; **Supp. XVI:** 222; **Supp. XX:**

171; **Supp. XXII:** 81; **Supp. XXVII:** 104

Adventures of Jimmy (Broughton), **Supp. XV:** 146

Adventures of Roderick Random, The (Smollett), **I:** 134

Adventures of the Letter I (Simpson), **Supp. IX:** 266, **273–274**

Adventures of Tom Sawyer, The (Twain), **II:** 26; **III:** 223, 572, 577; **IV:** 199–200, 203, 204; **Supp. I Part 2:** 456, 470; **Supp. XVI:** 66

Adventures While Preaching the Gospel of Beauty (Lindsay), **Supp. I Part 2:** 374, 376, 381, 382–384, 389, 399

Adventures with Ed (Loeffler), **Supp. XIII:** 1

Advertisements for Myself (Mailer), **III:** 27, 35–38, 41–42, 45, 46; **Retro. Supp. II:** 196, 199, 200, 202, 203, 212; **Supp. IV Part 1:** 90, 284; **Supp. XIV:** 157; **Supp. XXIV:** 281

"Advertisements for Myself on the Way Out" (Mailer), **III:** 37

Advice (Bodenheim), **Supp. XXV:** 22

"Advice to a Prophet" (Wilbur), **Supp. III Part 2:** 555–557

Advice to a Prophet and Other Poems (Wilbur), **Supp. III Part 2:** 554–558

"Advice to a Raven in Russia" (Barlow), **Supp. II Part 1:** 65, 74, 80, 83

"Advice to Players" (Bidart), **Supp. XV:** 35

Advice to the Lovelorn (film), **Retro. Supp. II:** 328

Advice to the Privileged Orders, Part I (Barlow), **Supp. II Part 1:** 80

Aegerter, Lindsay Pentolfe, **Supp. XXII:** 69

"Aeneas and Dido" (Brodsky), **Supp. VIII:** 24–25

"Aeneas at Washington" (Tate), **IV:** 129

Aeneid (Virgil), **I:** 396; **II:** 542; **III:** 124; **Supp. XV:** 23; **Supp. XXIV:** 162–163

Aeneus Tacticus, **I:** 136

Aerial View (Barabtarlo), **Retro. Supp. I:** 278

"Aeria the Evanescent" (Sobin), **Supp. XVI:** 292

Aeschylus, **I:** 274, 433; **III:** 398; **IV:** 358, 368, 370; **Retro. Supp. I:** 65; **Supp. I Part 2:** 458, 494

Aesop, **I:** 387; **II:** 154, 169, 302; **III:** 587

Aesthetic (Croce), **III:** 610

"Aesthetics" (Mumford), **Supp. II Part 2:** 476

"Aesthetics of Silence, The" (Sontag), **Supp. III Part 2:** 459

"Aesthetics of the Shah" (Olds), **Supp. X:** 205

"Affair at Coulter's Notch, The" (Bierce), **I:** 202

Affaire de viol, Une (C. Himes). *See Case of Rape, A* (C. Himes)

"Affair of Outposts, An" (Bierce), **I:** 202

Affliction (Banks), **Supp. V:** 15, 16

Affluent Society, The (Galbraith), **Supp. I Part 2:** 648

Afghanistan Picture Show, An: or, How I Saved the World (Vollmann), **Supp. XVII:** 226, **228–229**, 233

"Aficionados, The" (Carver), **Supp. III Part 1:** 137

"Afloat" (Beattie), **Supp. V:** 29

Afloat and Ashore (Cooper), **I:** 351, 355

"Afoot" (P. N. Warren as Kilina), **Supp. XX: 261–262**

Africa, Its Geography, People, and Products (Du Bois), **Supp. II Part 1:** 179

Africa, Its Place in Modern History (Du Bois), **Supp. II Part 1:** 179

"Africa, to My Mother" (D. Diop), **Supp. IV Part 1:** 16

Africana (H. L. Gates, ed.), **Supp. XX: 99**

African American Century, The : How Black Americans Have Shaped Our Country (H. L. Gates), **Supp. XX: 102**

African American Lives (television production), **Supp. XX: 99**

African American Lives 2 (television production), **Supp. XX: 99**

African American National Biography (H. L. Gates, ed.), **Supp. XX: 99**

African American Writers (Smith, ed.), **Supp. XIII:** 115, 127

"African Book" (Hemingway), **II:** 259

"African Chief, The" (Bryant), **Supp. I Part 1:** 168

"African Fragment" (Brooks), **Supp. III Part 1:** 85

African Queen, The (film), **Supp. XI:** 17

"African Roots of War, The" (Du Bois), **Supp. II Part 1:** 174

African Silences (Matthiessen), **Supp. V:** 203

African Treasury, An (Hughes, ed.), **Supp. I Part 1:** 344

"Afrika Revolution" (Baraka), **Supp. II Part 1:** 53

"AFRO-AMERICAN LYRIC" (Baraka), **Supp. II Part 1:** 59

After (Bukiet), **Supp. XVII:** 43, **44–45**

After (Hirshfield), **Supp. XXIII:** 133–135, 139

"After a Greek Proverb" (Stallings), **Supp. XXV:** 225

After All: Last Poems (Matthews), **Supp. IX:** 155, **167–169**

After and Before the Lightning (Ortiz), **Supp. IV Part 2:** 513

"After a Nightmare" (Davison), **Supp. XXVI:** 69

"After a Party" (Salinas), **Supp. XIII:** 327

"After Apple-Picking" (Frost), **Retro. Supp. I:** 126, 128

"After Arguing against the Contention That Art Must Come from Discontent" (Stafford), **Supp. XI:** 327

After Confession: Poetry as Autobiography (Harris), **Supp. XIV:** 269

After Confession: Poetry as Autobiography (K. Sontag and D. Graham), **Supp. XV:** 104

"After Cowboy Chicken Came to Town" (Jin), **Supp. XVIII:** 97–98

"After Disappointment" (Jarman), **Supp. XVII:** 118–119

After Disillusion: Poems (Wolf), **Supp. XXII:** 275

"After Edward Hopper: Somebody in a Bar" (Ferry), **Supp. XXIV:** 162

After Experience (Snodgrass), **Supp. VI:** 314–316, 317

"After great pain, a formal feeling comes" (Dickinson), **Retro. Supp. I:** 37

"After Hearing a Waltz by Bartók" (A. Lowell), **II:** 522

After Henry (Didion), **Supp. IV Part 1:** 195, 196, 199, 207, 208, 211

"After Henry" (Didion), **Supp. IV Part 1:** 211

"After Holbein" (Wharton), **IV:** 325; **Retro. Supp. I:** 382

After House, The (Rinehart), **Supp. XXV:** 193

After Ikkyu and Other Poems (Harrison), **Supp. VIII:** 42

"After-Image" (Bierds), **Supp. XVII:** 31–32

"After-Image" (Caldwell), **I:** 309

After-Images: Autobiographical Sketches (Snodgrass), **Supp. VI:** 314, **319–323,** 324, 326–327

After I's (Zukofsky), **Supp. III Part 2:** 628, 629

Afterlife (Monette), **Supp. X:** 153

Afterlife (Updike), **Retro. Supp. I:** 322

Afterlife, The (Levis), **Supp. XI:** 259, **260–264**

"After Magritte" (McClatchy), **Supp. XII:** 264

"After Making Love" (Dunn), **Supp. XI:** 153

Aftermath (Longfellow), **II:** 490

"Aftermath" (Longfellow), **II:** 498

After New Formalism (A. Finch, ed.), **Supp. XVII:** 74

"Afternoon" (Ellison), **Supp. II Part 1:** 238

"Afternoon at MacDowell" (Kenyon), **Supp. VII:** 159

"Afternoon Miracle, An" (O. Henry), **Supp. II Part 1:** 390

Afternoon of a Faun (Hearon), **Supp. VIII: 63–64**

Afternoon of an Author: A Selection of Uncollected Stories and Essays (Fitzgerald), **II:** 94

"Afternoon of a Playwright" (Thurber), **Supp. I Part 2:** 620

Afternoon of the Unreal (Salinas), **Supp. XIII:** 311, **316–318**

"Afternoon with the Old Man, An" (Dubus), **Supp. VII:** 84

"After Parting" (Teasdale), **Supp. XXVII:** 283

"After Punishment Was Done with Me" (Olds), **Supp. X:** 213

"After Reading *Barely and Widely,*" (Zukofsky), **Supp. III Part 2:** 625, 631

"After Reading 'In the Clearing' for the Author, Robert Frost" (Corso), **Supp. XII:** 130

"After Reading *Mickey in the Night Kitchen* for the Third Time before Bed" (Dove), **Supp. IV Part 1:** 249

"After Reading the Greek Poet"(Kenny), **Supp. XXIII:** 150

"After Reading Tu Fu, I Go Outside to the Dwarf Orchard" (Wright), **Supp. V:** 343

"After Reading Wang Wei, I Go Outside to the Full Moon" (Wright), **Supp. V:** 343

Aftershocks (Stallings), **Supp. XXV:** 222

"Aftershocks" (Stallings), **Supp. XXV:** 222, 231

After Shocks, Near Escapes (Dobyns), **Supp. XIII: 80–82**

"After Song, An" (W. C. Williams), **Retro. Supp. I:** 413

After Strange Gods (T. S. Eliot), **I:** 588

After Such Knowledge: Memory, History, and the Legacy of the Holocaust (E. Hoffman), **Supp. XVI:** 152–153, **158–161**

"After the Alphabets" (Merwin), **Supp. III Part 1:** 356

"After the Argument" (Dunn), **Supp. XI:** 149

"After the Baptism" (C. Bly), **Supp. XVI:** 40

"After the Burial" (J. R. Lowell), **Supp. I Part 2:** 409

"After the Curfew" (Holmes), **Supp. I Part 1:** 308

"After the Death of John Brown" (Thoreau), **IV:** 185

"After the Denim" (Carver), **Supp. III Part 1:** 144

"After the Dentist" (Swenson), **Supp. IV Part 2:** 645

After the Fall (A. Miller), **III:** 148, 149, 156, 161, 162, 163–165, 166

"After the Fire" (Merrill), **Supp. III Part 1:** 328

"After the Flood" (Sanders), **Supp. XVI:** 274–275

After the Fox (film), **Supp. IV Part 2:** 575

After the Genteel Tradition (Cowley), **Supp. II Part 1:** 143

"After the Heart's Interrogation" (Komunyakaa), **Supp. XIII:** 120

After the Lost Generation: A Critical Study of the Writers of Two Wars (Aldridge), **Supp. IV Part 2:** 680; **Supp. XIX:** 250

"After the Night Office—Gethsemani Abbey" (Merton), **Supp. VIII:** 195–196

After the Others (Weigl), **Supp. XIX:** 282, 283–284

"After the Persian" (Bogan), **Supp. III Part 1:** 64

After the Plague (Boyle), **Supp. XX: 20**

"After the Plague" (Boyle), **Supp. XX: 20**

"After the Pleasure Party" (Melville), **III:** 93

"After the Rain" (Halliday), **Supp. XIX:** 91

"After the Resolution" (Dunn), **Supp. XI:** 151

After the Stroke (Sarton), **Supp. VIII:** 264

"After the Surprising Conversions" (R. Lowell), **I:** 544, 545; **II:** 550; **Retro. Supp. II:** 187

"After 37 Years My Mother Apologizes for My Childhood" (Olds), **Supp. X:** 208

After This (McDermott), **Supp. XVIII:** 155, **166–167**

Afterthoughts (L. P. Smith), **Supp. XIV:** 339, 345

"Afterthoughts on the Rosenbergs" (Fiedler), **Supp. XIII:** 99

"After Twenty Years" (Rich), **Supp. I Part 2:** 559–560

"Afterwake, The" (Rich), **Supp. I Part 2:** 553

"Afterward" (Wharton), **Retro. Supp. I:** 372

"Afterword"(Hadas), **Supp. XXIII:** 113

"After Working Long" (Kenyon), **Supp. VII:** 170

"After Yitzl" (Goldbarth), **Supp. XII:** 186

"After You, My Dear Alphonse" (Jackson), **Supp. IX:** 119

"After Your Death" (Trethewey), **Supp. XXI:** 255

"After Your Nap" (B. Kelly), **Supp. XVII:** 124

"Again" (Dixon), **Supp. XII:** 157

"Again, Kapowsin" (Hugo), **Supp. VI:** 141

"Again Just Now" (Budbill), **Supp. XIX:** 11

"Against" (Goldbarth), **Supp. XII:** 193

"Against Decoration" (Karr), **Supp. XI:** 248

"Against Epiphanies" (C. Baxter), **Supp. XVII:** 20

Against Interpretation (Sontag), **Supp. III Part 2:** 451, 455; **Supp. XIV:** 15

"Against Interpretation" (Sontag), **Supp. III Part 2:** 456–458, 463

"Against Modernity" (Ozick), **Supp. V:** 272

"Against Nature" (Karr), **Supp. XI:** 243

Against Nature (Updike), **Retro. Supp. I:** 323

Against Our Vanishing: Winter Conversations with Allen Grossman on the Theory and Practice of Poetry (Halliday), **Supp. XIX: 82–84,** 88

"Against Realism" (Halliday), **Supp. XIX:** 93

Against the Cold (Bynner), **Supp. XV:** 51

"Against the Crusades" (Stern), **Supp. IX:** 300

Against the Current: As I Remember F. Scott Fitzgerald (Kroll Ring), **Supp. IX:** 63

Agamben, Giorgio, **Supp. XVI:** 289

Agapida, Fray Antonio (pseudonym). *See* Irving, Washington

"Agassiz" (J. R. Lowell), **Supp. I Part 2:** 414, 416

Agassiz, Louis, **II:** 343; **Supp. I Part 1:** 312; **Supp. IX:** 180

Âge cassant, L' (Char; Sobin, trans.), **Supp. XVI:** 282

"Aged Wino's Counsel to a Young Man on the Brink of Marriage, The" (X. J. Kennedy), **Supp. XV:** 156

Agee, Emma, **I:** 26

Agee, James, **I: 25–47,** 293; **IV:** 215; **Supp. IX:** 109; **Supp. XIV:** 92; **Supp. XV:** 143

"Agency Without Mastery: Chronic Pain and Posthuman Life Writing" (Gilmore), **Supp. XXVI:** 53

"Agent, The" (Wilbur), **Supp. III Part 2:** 557–561

Age of Anxiety, The (Auden), **Supp. II Part 1:** 2, 19, 21

"Age of Conformity, The" (Howe), **Supp. VI:** 117

Age of Grief, The: A Novella and Stories (Smiley), **Supp. VI:** 292, **299–301**

Age of Innocence, The (Wharton), **IV:** 320–322, 327–328; **Retro. Supp. I:** 372, 374, **380–381; Supp. IV Part 1:** 23

Age of Longing, The (Koestler), **I:** 258

Age of Reason, The (Paine), **Supp. I Part 2:** 503, 515–517, 520

"Age of Strolling, The" (Stern), **Supp. IX:** 297

"Ages, The" (Bryant), **Supp. I Part 1:** 152, 155, 166, 167

"Ages of the Women, The" (Gibran), **Supp. XX:** 115

"Aggrandizement, The" (Bronk), **Supp. XXI:** 32

"Aging" (Jarrell), **II:** 388

Aging and Gender in Literature (George), **Supp. IV Part 2:** 450

"Agio Neró" (Mora), **Supp. XIII:** 224

"Agitato ma non Troppo" (Ransom), **III:** 493

"Agnes of Iowa" (Moore), **Supp. X:** 165, 178

Agnes of Sorrento (Stowe), **Supp. I Part 2:** 592, 595–596

Agnon, S. Y., **Supp. V:** 266; **Supp. XXV:** 267

Agony & the Agony, The (Silver), **Supp. XXIV:** 265, **274–275**

"Agosta the Winged Man and Rasha the Black Dove" (Dove), **Supp. IV Part 1:** 246–247

Agrarian Justice (Paine), **Supp. I Part 2:** 517–518

"Agricultural Show, The" (McKay), **Supp. X:** 139

Agrippa: A Book of the Dead (W. Gibson), **Supp. XVI:** 125

Agua de dos ríos/Water from Two Rivers (Espaillat), **Supp. XXI:** 104, 112–113

Agua Fresca: An Anthology of Raza Poetry (Rodríguez, ed.), **Supp. IV Part 2:** 540

Agua Santa/Holy Water (Mora), **Supp. XIII: 222–225**

Agüero Sisters, The (García), **Supp. XI: 185–190**

Aguiar, Marian, **Supp. XXII:** 68

Aguiar, Sarah Appleton, **Supp. XIII:** 30

Aguilar, Carmen, **Supp. XXIII:** 200

Ah, Wilderness! (O'Neill), **III:** 400–401; **Supp. IV Part 2:** 587

Ah, Wilderness!: The Frontier in American Literature (Humphrey), **Supp. IX:** 104

Ahearn, Barry, **Retro. Supp. I:** 415

Ahearn, Frederick L., Jr., **Supp. XI:** 184

Ahearn, Kerry, **Supp. IV Part 2:** 604

Ahmed Arabi Pasha, **I:** 453

Ahnebrink, Lars, **III:** 328

Ahrens, Sylvia, **Supp. XX: 162**

Ah Sin (Harte), **Supp. II Part 1:** 354–355

"Ah! Sun-flower" (Blake), **III:** 19

Ai, **Supp. XXVI:** 66

Aida (rock musical), **Supp. XXI:** 148

Aidoo, Ama Ato, **Supp. XXII:** 68

AIDS and Its Metaphors (Sontag), **Supp. III Part 2:** 452, 466–468

Aids to Reflection (Coleridge), **II:** 10

Aiieeeee! An Anthology of Asian-American Writers (The Combined Asian Resources Project), **Supp. X:** 292

Aiken, Conrad, **I: 48–70,** 190, 211, 243; **II:** 55, 530, 542; **III:** 458, 460; **Retro. Supp. I:** 55, 56, 57, 58, 60, 62; **Supp. X:** 50, 115; **Supp. XV:** 144, 297, 298, 302, 306, 309; **Supp. XVII:** 135; **Supp. XXIV:** 36; **Supp. XXV:** 19; **Supp. XXVI:** 225

"Aimless Love" (Collins), **Supp. XXI:** 61

"Aim Was Song, The" (Frost), **Retro. Supp. I:** 133

Ainger, Arthur Campbell, **Supp. XX: 230**

Ainsworth, Linda, **Supp. IV Part 1:** 274

Ainsworth, William, **III:** 423

Air-Conditioned Nightmare, The (H. Miller), **III:** 186

Airing Dirty Laundry (Reed), **Supp. X:** 241

"Air Is Full of Little Holes, The" (Brockmeier), **Supp. XXII:** 60

"Airmail from Mother" (Kooser), **Supp. XIX:** 120

"Air Plant, The" (Crane), **I:** 401

Air Raid: A Verse Play for Radio (MacLeish), **III:** 21

"Airs above the Ground" (Sarton), **Supp. VIII:** 261

Air Tight: A Novel of Red Russia. See We the Living (Rand)

Air Up There, The (film, Glaser), **Supp. XVII:** 9

"Airwaves" (Mason), **Supp. VIII:** 146

Airways, Inc. (Dos Passos), **I:** 482

A Is for Anne: Mistress Hutchinson Disturbs the Commonwealth (Schott), **Supp. XXIII:** 240, **246–247**

"A is for Dining Alone" (M. F. K. Fisher), **Supp. XVII:** 86

Aitken, Robert, **Supp. I Part 2:** 504

Aizenberg, Susan, **Supp. XXI:** 131

Akhmadulina, Bella, **Supp. III Part 1:** 268

Akhmatova, Anna, **Supp. III Part 1:** 268, 269; **Supp. VIII:** 20, 21, 25, 27, 30; **Supp. XXI:** 132

Akhmatova Translations, The (Kenyon), **Supp. VII:** 160

"Akhnilo" (Salter), **Supp. IX:** 260

Akins, Zoë, **Supp. XVI:** 187; **Supp. XXVII:** 285

Aksenev, Vasily P., **Retro. Supp. I:** 278

"Al Aaraaf" (Poe), **III:** 426–427

Al Aaraaf, Tamerlane, and Minor Poems (Poe), **III:** 410

"Alabama Jones" (Mosher), **Supp. XXII:** 204, 211

"Alain Locke and Cultural Pluralism" (Kallen), **Supp. XIV:** 197

"Alain Locke: Bahá'í Philosopher" (Buck), **Supp. XIV:** 199

Alain Locke: Faith and Philosophy (Buck), **Supp. XIV:** 200

Alarçon, **Supp. XVII:** 74

Alarcón, Justo, **Supp. IV Part 2:** 538, 539, 540

Alarcón, Norma, **Supp. XXIII:** 194, 204–205

À la Recherche du Temps Perdu (Proust), **IV:** 428

"Alarm" (X. J. Kennedy), **Supp. XV:** 163

"Alastor" (Shelley), **Supp. I Part 2:** 728

"Alatus" (Wilbur), **Supp. III Part 2:** 563

Alaya (Hirshfield), **Supp. XXIII:** 131

"Alba" (Creeley), **Supp. IV Part 1:** 150

Alba, Richard D., **Supp. XX: 43**

Albee, Edward, **I: 71–96,** 113; **II:** 558, 591; **III:** 281, 387; **IV:** 4, 230; **Retro. Supp. II:** 104; **Supp. VIII:** 331; **Supp. XIII:** 196, 197; **Supp. XXIV:** 113, 263, 270

Albers, Joseph, **Supp. IV Part 2:** 621

Alberti, Rafael, **Supp. XV:** 75

Albright, Margery, **Supp. I Part 2:** 613

"Album, The" (Morris), **III:** 220

Album, The (Rinehart), **Supp. XXV:** 197, 200

Alcestiad, The (Wilder), **IV:** 357, 374

"Alchemist, The" (Bogan), **Supp. III Part 1:** 50

"Alchemist in the City, The" (Hopkins), **Supp. IV Part 2:** 639

Alchymist's Journal, The (Connell), **Supp. XIV:** 80

"Alcmena" (Winters), **Supp. II Part 2:** 801

Alcott, Abba. *See* Alcott, Mrs. Amos Bronson (Abigail May)

Alcott, Amos Bronson, **II:** 7, 225; **IV:** 172, 173, 184; **Retro. Supp. I:** 217; **Supp. I Part 1:** 28, 29–32, 35, 39, 41, 45; **Supp. II Part 1:** 290; **Supp. XVI:** 84, 89; **Supp. XXV:** 250

Alcott, Mrs. Amos Bronson (Abigail May), **IV:** 184; **Supp. I Part 1:** 29, 30, 31, 32, 35

Alcott, Anna. *See* Pratt, Anna

Alcott, Louisa May, **IV:** 172; **Supp. I Part 1: 28–46; Supp. IX:** 128; **Supp. XV:** 338; **Supp. XVI:** 84

Alcott, May, **Supp. I Part 1:** 41

Alcuin: A Dialogue (Brown), **Supp. I Part 1:** 126–127, 133

Alden, Hortense. *See* Farrell, Mrs. James T. (Hortense Alden)

Alden, John, **I:** 471; **II:** 502–503

"Alder Fork, The" (Leopold), **Supp. XIV:** 186

Aldington, Perdita, **Supp. I Part 1:** 258

Aldington, Richard, **II:** 517; **III:** 458, 459, 465, 472; **Retro. Supp. I:** 63, 127; **Supp. I Part 1:** 257–262, 270

Aldington, Mrs. Richard. *See* Doolittle, Hilda

Aldo Leopold: His Life and Work (Meine), **Supp. XIV:** 179

"Aldo Leopold's Intellectual Heritage" (Nash), **Supp. XIV:** 191–192

Aldon, Raymond, **Supp. XV:** 297

Aldrich, Thomas Bailey, **II:** 400; **Supp. II Part 1:** 192; **Supp. XIV:** 45; **Supp. XVIII:** 4

Aldrich, Tom, **Supp. I Part 2:** 415

Aldridge, John W., **Supp. I Part 1:** 196; **Supp. IV Part 1:** 286; **Supp. IV Part 2:** 680, 681; **Supp. VIII:** 189; **Supp. XI:** 228; **Supp. XIX:** 250

Aleck Maury Sportsman (Gordon), **II:** 197, 200, 203–204

Alegría, Claribel, **Supp. IV Part 1:** 208

Aleichem, Sholem, **Supp. XXIII:** 4, 7

Aleichem, Sholom, **IV:** 3, 10; **Supp. IV Part 2:** 585

"Alert Lovers, Hidden Sides, and Ice Travelers: Notes on Poetic Form and Energy" (Dunn), **Supp. XI:** 153

"Aleš Debeljak" (Simic), **Supp. VIII:** 279

"Alex" (Oliver), **Supp. VII:** 232

Alexander, Doris, **Supp. XVII:** 99

Alexander, Elizabeth, **Supp. XVIII:** 171, 185, 186; **Supp. XXI:** 246, 257

Alexander, George, **II:** 331

Alexander, Michael, **Retro. Supp. I:** 293

Alexander, Paul, **Supp. XXV:** 84

Alexander, Will, **Supp. XXVII:** 163

"Alexander Crummell Dead" (Dunbar), **Supp. II Part 1:** 207, 208–209

Alexander's Bridge (Cather), **I:** 313, 314, 316–317, 326; **Retro. Supp. I:** 1, 6, 7, 8

Alexander the Great, **IV:** 322

"Alexandra" (Cather), **Retro. Supp. I:** 7, 9, 17

Alexandrov, V. E., **Retro. Supp. I:** 270

Alexie, Sherman, **Supp. XVIII:** 58; **Supp. XXVI:** 103, 108

Alger, Horatio, **Supp. XXVII:** 84

Algic Researches (H. Schoolcraft), **Supp. XXIII:** 227

Algonquin Round Table, **Supp. IX:** 190, 191, 197

Algren, Nelson, **I:** 211; **Supp. IX: 1–18;** **Supp. V:** 4; **Supp. XII:** 126; **Supp. XIII:** 173; **Supp. XIV:** 3; **Supp. XVII:** 161; **Supp. XXI:** 264; **Supp. XXIII:** 165; **Supp. XXV:** 185; **Supp. XXVII:** 87, 134

Alhambra, The (Irving), **II:** 310–311

Ali, Agha Shahid, **Supp. XVII:** 74

Ali, Ayaan Hirsi, **Supp. XXIV:** 15

Alias Grace (Atwood), **Supp. XIII:** 20, **31–32**

Alice (film; Allen), **Supp. XV:** 2, 11

"Alice Doane's Appeal" (Hawthorne), **II:** 227

"Alice Drops Her Cigarette on the Floor ... " (Findley), **Supp. XX: 50–51**

"Alice in the Looking Glass" (Stallings), **Supp. XXV:** 234

Alice in Wonderland (Carroll), **Supp. I Part 2:** 622

Alice Ordered Me to Be Made (Notley), **Supp. XXII:** 224, 227, 228

"Alice Ordered Me to Be Made" (Notley), **Supp. XXII:** 227

Alice's Adventures in Wonderland (Carroll), **Supp. XVI:** 261

"Alicia and I Talking on Edna's Steps" (Cisneros), **Supp. VII:** 64

"Alicia Who Sees Mice" (Cisneros), **Supp. VII:** 60

Alien 3 (screenplay, W. Gibson), **Supp. XVI:** 120, 124

"Ali in Havana" (Talese), **Supp. XVII:** 207, 208

Alison, Archibald, **Supp. I Part 1:** 151, 159

Alison's House (Glaspell), **Supp. III Part 1:** 182, 188, 189

Alive (screenplay, Shanley), **Supp. XIV:** 316

Alive and Writing: Interviews with American Authors of the 1980s (McCaffery and Gregory), **Supp. X:** 260

"Alki Beach" (Hugo), **Supp. VI:** 135

Alla Breve Loving (Wright), **Supp. XV:** 339, 340

"Alla Breve Loving" (Wright), **Supp. XV:** 340

"All Apologies" (Biss), **Supp. XXVI:** 56

"All Around the Town" (Benét), **Supp. XI:** 48, 58

"All Around the Town" (Taggard), **Supp. XXVI:** 144

All at Sea (Lardner), **II:** 427

All Aunt Hagar's Children (E. P. Jones), **Supp. XXII:** 140, 143, **150–153**

"All Aunt Hagar's Children" (E. P. Jones), **Supp. XXII:** 151

"All Boy" (Rawlings), **Supp. X:** 222

Allegiances (Stafford), **Supp. XI: 322–323,** 329

"Allegory of the Cave" (Dunn), **Supp. XI:** 150

"Allegory Unlimited" (Cassill), **Supp. XIX:** 266

Allegro, Johnny (film, Tetzloff), **Supp. XVII:** 62

"Allegro, L' " (Milton), **Supp. XIV:** 8

Allen, Brooke, **Supp. VIII:** 153

Allen, Bruce, **Supp. XXII:** 205, 212; **Supp. XXIII:** 106, 300

Allen, Claudia, **Supp. XXIII:** 79

Allen, Dick, **Supp. IX:** 279

Allen, Donald, **Supp. VIII:** 291; **Supp. XIII:** 112; **Supp. XXIII:** 215, 220; **Supp. XXVI:** 223; **Supp. XXVII:** 25

Allen, Frank, **Supp. XI:** 126; **Supp. XII:** 186; **Supp. XXVI:** 150

Allen, Fred, **Supp. XXV:** 255

Allen, Frederick Lewis, **Supp. I Part 2:** 655

Allen, Gay Wilson, **IV:** 352; **Supp. I Part 2:** 418

Allen, Ivan, **Supp. XXII:** 245

Allen, Paula Gunn. *See* Gunn Allen, Paula

Allen, Robert Moore, **Supp. XX:** 164

Allen, Walter, **I:** 505; **III:** 352; **Supp. IV Part 2:** 685; **Supp. IX:** 231

Allen, Woody, **Supp. I Part 2:** 607, 623; **Supp. IV Part 1:** 205; **Supp. X:** 164; **Supp. XI:** 307; **Supp. XV: 1–18;** **Supp. XVII:** 48

"Aller et Retour" (Barnes), **Supp. III Part 1:** 36

Aller Retour New York (H. Miller), **III:** 178, 182, 183

Allerton, Isaac, **Supp. XXII:** 44

Allessandrini, Goffredo, **Supp. IV Part 2:** 520

Alleys of Eden, The (R. O. Butler), **Supp. XII:** 62, **62–64,** 68

All God's Children Need Traveling Shoes (Angelou), **Supp. IV Part 1:** 2, 9–10, 12–13, 17

All God's Chillun Got Wings (O'Neill), **III:** 387, 391, 393–394

All Gone (Dixon), **Supp. XII:** 148, 149

"All Hallows" (Glück), **Supp. V:** 82

"All I Can Remember" (Jackson), **Supp. IX:** 115

"Alligators, The" (Updike), **IV:** 219

Allingham, John Till, **Supp. XV:** 243

All in the Family (Boyce), **Supp. XXI:** 8

"ALL IN THE STREET" (Baraka), **Supp. II Part 1:** 53

"All in Time" (Stone), **Supp. XXVII:** 251

Allison, Dorothy, **Supp. XVIII:** 195

"All I Want" (Tapahonso), **Supp. IV Part 2:** 508

"All Little Colored Children Should Play the Harmonica" (Patchett), **Supp. XII:** 309

"All Mountains" (Doolittle), **Supp. I Part 1:** 271

All My Friends Are Going to Be Strangers (McMurtry), **Supp. V:** 224, 228, 229

All My Pretty Ones (Sexton), **Supp. II Part 2:** 678, 679–683

"All My Pretty Ones" (Sexton), **Supp. II Part 2:** 681–682

"All My Sad Captains" (Jewett), **Retro. Supp. II:** 134

All My Sons (A. Miller), **III:** 148, 149, 150, 151–153, 154, 155, 156, 158, 159, 160, 164, 166

All New People (Lamott), **Supp. XX: 135–136**

"All Night, All Night" (Schwartz), **Supp. II Part 2:** 665

All Night Long (Caldwell), **I:** 297

"All-Night Melodies" (Nelson), **Supp. XVIII:** 185

All-Night Visitors (Major), **Supp. XXII: 173–174**

"All of Us" (Major), **Supp. XXII:** 185

All of Us: The Collected Poems (Carver), **Supp. XXIV:** 167

All of What We Loved (Bronk), **Supp. XXI:** 32

"All Our Lost Children: Trauma and Testimony in the Performance of Childhood" (Pace), **Supp. XI:** 245

All Our Yesterdays (Parker), **Supp. XIX: 187–188**

"All Out" (Hecht), **Supp. X:** 72

All Over (Albee), **I:** 91–94

"Allowance" (Minot), **Supp. VI:** 206, 207–208

"Alloy" (Rukeyser), **Supp. VI:** 279

"All Parrots Speak" (Bowles), **Supp. IV Part 1:** 89

Allport, Gordon, **II:** 363–364

All Quiet on the Western Front (Remarque), **Supp. IV Part 1:** 380, 381

"ALL REACTION IS DOOMED-!-!-!" (Baraka), **Supp. II Part 1:** 59

"All Revelation" (Frost), **II:** 160–162

"All Riptides Roar with Sand from Opposing Shores" (Vaz), **Supp. XXVI:** 264–265

Allsburg, Christ Van, **Supp. XXV:** 83, 87

"All Shall Love Me and Despair"(Thompson), **Supp. XXIII:** 295

All Shot Up (C. Himes), **Supp. XVI:** 143, 144

"All Souls" (Gioia), **Supp. XV:** 117

"All Souls" (Wharton), **IV:** 315–316; **Retro. Supp. I:** 382

"All Souls' Night" (Yeats), **Supp. X:** 69

All Souls' Rising (Bell), **Supp. X:** 12, **13–16,** 17

"All-Star Literary Vaudeville" (Wilson), **IV:** 434–435

Allston, Washington, **II:** 298

All Stories Are True (Wideman), **Supp. X:** 320

"All That Is" (Wilbur), **Supp. III Part 2:** 563

All That Was Possible (Sturgis), **Supp. XX: 227, 232, 235–237**

"All the Bearded Irises of Life: Confessions of a Homospiritual" (Walker), **Supp. III Part 2:** 527

"All the Beautiful Are Blameless" (Wright), **Supp. III Part 2:** 597

ALL: The Collected Poems, 1956–1964 (Zukofsky), **Supp. III Part 2:** 630

ALL: The Collected Short Poems, 1923–1958 (Zukofsky), **Supp. III Part 2:** 629

All the Conspirators (Isherwood), **Supp. XIV:** 156, 159, 160

All the Dark and Beautiful Warriors (Hansberry), **Supp. IV Part 1:** 360, 374

All the Days and Nights: The Collected Stories (Maxwell), **Supp. VIII:** 151, 158, 169

"All the Dead Dears" (Plath), **Retro. Supp. II:** 246; **Supp. I Part 2:** 537

"All the Dead"(P. Benedict), **Supp. XXIII:** 37

All the Good People I've Left Behind (Oates), **Supp. II Part 2:** 510, 522, 523

"All the Hippos Were Boiled in Their Tanks" (Burroughs and Kerouac), **Supp. III Part 1:** 94

All the King's Men (Warren), **I:** 489; **IV:** 243, 248–249, 252; **Supp. V:** 261;

Supp. VIII: 126; **Supp. X:** 1; **Supp. XVIII:** 77, 79; **Supp. XXIV:** 226

All the Little Live Things (Stegner), **Supp. IV Part 2:** 599, 604, 605, 606, 609–610, 611, 613

All the Pretty Horses (film), **Supp. VIII:** 175

All the Pretty Horses (McCarthy), **Supp. VIII:** 175, **182–183,** 188

All the Sad Young Men (Fitzgerald), **II:** 94; **Retro. Supp. I:** 108

"All the Time in the World" (Dubus), **Supp. VII:** 91

"All the Way to Flagstaff, Arizona" (Bausch), **Supp. VII:** 47, 49

"All This and More" (Karr), **Supp. XI:** 243

All Thy Conquests (Hayes), **Supp. XXVI:** 134,135–136

All Tomorrow's Parties (W. Gibson), **Supp. XVI:** 119, 121, 123, 124, **130**

"All Too Real" (Vendler), **Supp. V:** 189

All Trivia: Triva, More Trivia, Afterthoughts, Last Words (L. P. Smith), **Supp. XIV:** 339

All-True Travels and Adventures of Lidie Newton (Smiley), **Supp. VI:** 292, **305–307**

All We Need of Hell (Crews), **Supp. XI:** **114**

Almack, Edward, **Supp. IV Part 2:** 435

al-Maghut, Muhammad, **Supp. XIII:** 278

"Almanac" (Swenson), **Supp. IV Part 2:** 641

Almanac of the Dead (Silko), **Supp. IV Part 2:** 558–559, 560, 561, 570–571

Alma: or, The Dead Women (Notley), **Supp. XXII:** 223, 224, 231, 236

Almon, Bert, **Supp. IX:** 93

"Almost" (Untermeyer), **Supp. XV:** 304

Almost Learning to Live in This World (Schott), **Supp. XXIII: 247–248**

Almost Revolution, The (Priaulx and Ungar), **Supp. XI:** 228

Alnilam (Dickey), **Supp. IV Part 1:** 176, 186, 188–189

"Alone" (Caputo), **Supp. XIX:** 29

"Alone" (Levine), **Supp. V:** 184, 185, 186

"Alone" (Pickering), **Supp. XXI:** 204

"Alone" (Poe), **Retro. Supp. II:** 266

"Alone" (Singer), **IV:** 15

"Alone" (Winters), **II Part 2:** 786, 811

"Alone and Lonely" (Budbill), **Supp. XIX:** 10

Aloneness (Brooks), **Supp. III Part 1:** 85, 86

Alone with America (Corso), **Supp. XII:** 131

Alone with America (Howard), **Supp. IX:** 326

"Along America's Edges" (Sobin), **Supp. XVI:** 288

"Along the Color Line" (Du Bois), **Supp. II Part 1:** 173

Along the Illinois (Masters), **Supp. I Part 2:** 472

Alouette, L' (Anouilh), Supp. I Part 1: 286–288

"Alphabet" (Nye), **Supp. XIII:** 283

Alphabet, An (Doty), **Supp. XI:** 120

Alphabet for Gourmets, An (M. F. K. Fisher), **Supp. XVII:** 86, 87, 92

Alphabet of Grace, The (Buechner), **Supp. XII:** 52

"Alphabet of My Dead, An" (Pinsky), **Supp. VI:** 235, 250

"Alphabet of Subjects, An" (Zukofsky), **Supp. III Part 2:** 624

"Alpine Christ, The" (Jeffers), **Supp. II Part 2:** 415, 419

Alpine Christ and Other Poems, The (Jeffers), **Supp. II Part 2:** 419

"Alpine Idyll, An" (Hemingway), **II:** 249; **Retro. Supp. I:** 176

Al Que Quiere! (W. C. Williams), **Retro. Supp. I:** 414, 416, **417,** 428

Alraune (Ewers; Endore, trans.), **Supp. XVII:** 54

Alsop, Joseph, **II:** 579

"Altar, The" (Herbert), **Supp. IV Part 2:** 646

"Altar, The" (MacLeish), **III:** 4

"Altar Boy" (Fante), **Supp. XI:** 160, 164

"Altar of the Dead, The" (James), **Retro. Supp. I:** 229

"Altars in the Street, The" (Levertov), **Supp. III Part 1:** 280

Alter, Robert, **Supp. XII:** 167

Altgeld, John Peter, **Supp. I Part 2:** 382, 455

Althea (Masters), **Supp. I Part 2:** 455, 459

Altick, Richard, **Supp. I Part 2:** 423

Altieri, Charles, **Supp. VIII:** 297, 303; **Supp. XXIII:** 220

Altman, Robert, **Supp. IX:** 143; **Supp. XXIV:** 166, 172

"Alto" (C. Frost), **Supp. XV:** 101

"Altra Ego" (Brodsky), **Supp. VIII:** 31–32

Altruists, The (Silver), **Supp. XXIV: 273**

A Lume Spento (Pound), **Retro. Supp. I:** 283, 285

"Aluminum House" (F. Barthelme), **Supp. XI:** 26

Alvares, Mosseh, **Supp. V:** 11

Alvarez, A., **Supp. I Part 2:** 526, 527; **Supp. II Part 1:** 99; **Supp. IX:** 248

Alvarez, Joseph A., **Supp. XXII:** 13–14

Alvarez, Julia, **Supp. VII: 1–21;** **Supp. XI:** 177; **Supp. XVII:** 71, 112; **Supp. XXIV:** 86, 89

"Always a Rose" (L.-Y. Lee), **Supp. XV:** 215, 216

"Always in Good Humor" (Adams), **Supp. XV:** 294

Always Outnumbered, Always Outgunned (Mosley), **Supp. XIII:** 242

"Always the Stories" (Ortiz), **Supp. IV Part 2:** 499, 500, 502, 504, 512

Always the Young Strangers (Sandburg), **III:** 577–578, 579

Always Young and Fair (Richter), **Supp. XVIII: 215–216**

Amadeus (Shaffer), **Supp. XIV:** 330

"Amahl and the Night Visitors: A Guide to the Tenor of Love" (Moore), **Supp. X:** 167

"Am and Am Not" (Olds), **Supp. X:** 212

"Amanita, The" (Francis), **Supp. IX:** 81

Amaranth (Robinson), **III:** 509, 510, 512, 513, 522, 523

"Amateur Iconography: Resurrection" (Stallings), **Supp. XXV:** 233

"Amateurs, The" (Swados), **Supp. XIX:** 256

Amazing Adele, The (Barillet and Grédy; Loos, trans.), **Supp. XVI:** 194

Amazing Adventures of Kavalier and Clay, The (Chabon), **Supp. XI:** 68, 76, **77–80; Supp. XXII:** 49

Amazing Adventures of Leticia Carberry (Rinehart), **Supp. XXV:** 194

Amazing Adventures of the Escapist, The (Chabon, ed.), **Supp. XIX:** 174

Amazing Interlude, The (Rinehart), **Supp. XXV:** 194

Amazing Science Fiction Stories, **Supp. XVI:** 121

Amazons: An Intimate Memoir by the First Woman to Play in the National Hockey League (DeLillo), **Supp. VI:** 2

Ambassador Morgenthau's Story (Morgenthau), **Supp. XXIII:** 21, 22

Ambassador of Peace, An (Abernon), **Supp. XVI:** 191

Ambassadors, The (H. James), **II:** 320, 333–334, 600; **III:** 517; **IV:** 322; **Retro. Supp. I:** 215, 218, 219, 220, 221, **232–233**

Ambassador's Son, The (Hickam), **Supp. XXVII:** 111

Ambelain, Robert, **Supp. I Part 1:** 260, 273, 274

"Amber" (Gansworth), **Supp. XXVI:** 114

"Ambition Bird, The" (Sexton), **Supp. II Part 2:** 693

Ambition: The Secret Passion (Epstein), **Supp. XIV:** 113–114

Ambler, Eric, **III:** 57

Ambrose Holt and Family (Glaspell), **Supp. III Part 1:** 175, 181, 184, 187, 188

"Ambrose Seyffert" (Masters), **Supp. I Part 2:** 464

"Ambush" (Komunyakaa), **Supp. XIII:** 122

Amen Corner, The (Baldwin), **Retro. Supp. II:** 5, 7; **Supp. I Part 1:** 48, 51, 54, 55, 56

America (Benét), **Supp. XI:** 46, 47, 51

"America" (Ginsberg), **Supp. II Part 1:** 58–59, 317

"America" (song), **IV:** 410

"America, America!" (poem) (Schwartz), **Supp. II Part 2:** 665

"America, Commerce, and Freedom" (Rowson and Reinagle), **Supp. XV:** 240

"America, Home of the Red Man" (Zitkala-Ša), **Supp. XXV:** 281

"America, Seen Through Photographs, Darkly" (Sontag), **Supp. III Part 2:** 464

"America! America!" (story) (Schwartz), **Supp. II Part 2:** 640, 658–659, 660

America and Americans (Steinbeck), **IV:** 52

"America and the Vidal Chronicles" (Pease), **Supp. IV Part 2:** 687

America as a Civilization (Lerner), **III:** 60

America Behind the Color Line (H. L. Gates), **Supp. XX:** 102, 105

America Beyond the Color Line (television program), **Supp. XX:** 99

America Hispana: A Portrait and a Prospect (W. Frank), **Supp. XX:** 76

"America Independent" (Freneau), **Supp. II Part 1:** 261

America Is Worth Saving (Dreiser), **Retro. Supp. II:** 96

American, The (James), **I:** 226; **II:** 326–327, 328, 331, 334; **IV:** 318; **Retro. Supp. I:** 220, **221,** 228, 376, 381

Americana (DeLillo), **Supp. VI:** 2, 3, 5, 6, 8, 13, 14

American Adam, The (R. W. B. Lewis), **II:** 457–458; **Supp. XIII:** 93

American Almanac (Leeds), **II:** 110

American Anthem (Doctorow and Suares), **Supp. IV Part 1:** 234

"American Apocalypse" (Gunn Allen), **Supp. IV Part 1:** 325

American Aristocracy (film), **Supp. XVI:** 185–186

American Blood, (Nichols), **Supp. XIII:** 268

American Blues (T. Williams), **IV:** 381, 383

American Buffalo (Mamet), **Supp. XIV:** 239, 241, 242, 244–245, 246, 254, 255

American Caravan: A Yearbook of American Literature (Mumford, ed.), **Supp. II Part 2:** 482

American Cause, The (MacLeish), **III:** 3

American Childhood, An (Dillard), **Supp. VI:** 19–21, 23, 24, 25, 26, 30, 31

"American Childhood in the Dominican Republic, An" (Alvarez), **Supp. VII:** 2, 5

American Child Supreme, An: The Education of a Liberation Ecologist (Nichols), **Supp. XIII:** 256, 257, 258, 264, 265, 266, 267, 268, 269

American Civilization (C. L. R. James), **Supp. XXI:** 169

American Claimant, The (Twain), **IV:** 194, 198–199

American Crisis I (Paine), **Supp. I Part 2:** 508

American Crisis II (Paine), **Supp. I Part 2:** 508

American Crisis XIII (Paine), **Supp. I Part 2:** 509

"American Critic, The" (J. Spingarn), **I:** 266

American Culture, Canons, and the Case of Elizabeth Stoddard (Smith and Weinauer), **Supp. XV:** 270

American Daughter, An (Wasserstein), **Supp. XV: 330–332,** 333

American Democrat, The (Cooper), **I:** 343, 346, 347, 353

American Desert (Everett), **Supp. XVIII: 62–63**

American Diary (Webb), **Supp. I Part 1:** 5

American Drama since World War II (Weales), **IV:** 385

American Dream, An (Mailer), **III:** 27, 33–34, 35, 39, 41, 43, 44; **Retro. Supp. II:** 203, **204–205**

American Dream, The (Albee), **I:** 74–76, 77, 89, 94; **Supp. XXIV:** 113

"American Dreams" (Simpson), **Supp. IX:** 274

American Earth (Caldwell), **I:** 290, 308

"American Emperors" (Poirier), **Supp. IV Part 2:** 690

American English (Marckwardt), **Supp. XXIV:** 255

American Exodus, An (Lange and Taylor), **I:** 293

American Experience, The (Parkes), **Supp. I Part 2:** 617–618

American Express (Corso), **Supp. XII:** 129

"American Express" (Salter), **Supp. IX:** 260–261

"American Fear of Literature, The" (Lewis), **II:** 451

American Female Patriotism (S. Warner as Wetherell), **Supp. XVIII: 260–261,** 262, 263

American Fictions (Hardwick), **Supp. X:** 171

American Fictions, 1940–1980 (Karl), **Supp. IV Part 1:** 384; **Supp. XXI:** 234

"American Financier, The" (Dreiser), **II:** 428

American Folkways (book series), **I:** 290

American Guerilla in the Philippines (Wolfert), **Supp. XXI:** 267

"American Heart of Darkness: The Moral Vision of Five Novels of the Vietnam War" (Palm), **Supp. XXII:** 103

"American Heritage" (Gansworth), **Supp. XXVI:** 114

American Heroine: The Life and Legend of Jane Addams (A. F. Davis), **Supp. I Part 1:** 1

American Historical Novel, The (Leisy), **Supp. II Part 1:** 125

"American Horse" (Erdrich), **Supp. IV Part 1:** 333

American Humor: A Study of the National Character (Rourke), **IV:** 339, 352; **Supp. XIX:** 147

American Hunger (Wright), **Supp. IV Part 1:** 11

"American Husband, The" (Atherton), **Supp. XXIV:** 24

American Indian Anthology, An (Tvedten, ed.), **Supp. IV Part 2:** 505

American Indian Stories (Zitkala-Ša), **Supp. XXV:** 272–273, 282–283, 284–285

"American Indian Women: At the Center of Indigenous Resistance in Contemporary North America" (Jaimes and Halsey), **Supp. IV Part 1:** 331

"American in England, An" (Wylie), **Supp. I Part 2:** 707

Americanize the First American (Zitkala-Ša), **Supp. XXV:** 283

American Jitters, The: A Year of the Slump (Wilson), **IV:** 427, 428

American Journal (Hayden), **Supp. II Part 1:** 367

American Journey: The Times of Robert F. Kennedy (Plimpton, ed.), **Supp. XVI:** 245

"American Land Ethic, An" (Momaday), **Supp. IV Part 2:** 488

American Landscape, The, **Supp. I Part 1:** 157

American Language, The (Mencken), **II:** 289, 430; **III:** 100, 104, 105, 108, 111, 119–120

American Language, The: Supplement One (Mencken), **III:** 111

American Language, The: Supplement Two (Mencken), **III:** 111

"American Letter" (MacLeish), **III:** 13

"American Liberty" (Freneau), **Supp. II Part 1:** 257

"American Life in Poetry" (column, Kooser), **Supp. XIX:** 116, 127

American Linden (Zapruder), **Supp. XXVI:** 54

American Literary History (Harrison), **Supp. VIII:** 37

American Mercury, **Supp. XI:** 163, 164

American Milk (Stone), **Supp. XXVII:** 257

American Mind, The (Commager), **Supp. I Part 2:** 650

American Moderns: Bohemian New York and the Creation of a New Century (Stansell), **Supp. XVII:** 106

American Moderns: From Rebellion to Conformity (Geismar), **Supp. IX:** 15; **Supp. XI:** 223

"American Names" (Benét), **Supp. XI:** 47

American Nature Writers (Elder, ed.), **Supp. IX:** 25

American Nature Writers (Winter), **Supp. X:** 104

American Negro, The (W. H. Thomas), **Supp. II Part 1:** 168

American Notebooks, The (Hawthorne), **II:** 226

American Novel Since World War II, The (Klein, ed.), **Supp. XI:** 233

Americano, The (film), **Supp. XVI:** 185

"American Original, An: Learning from a Literary Master" (Wilkinson), **Supp. VIII:** 164, 165, 168

American Ornithology (Wilson), **Supp. XVI:** 4, 6

American Pastoral (P. Roth), **Retro. Supp. II:** 279, 289, **292–293; Supp. XI:** 68

American Pictures: A Personal Journey Through the American Underclass (Holdt), **Supp. XXVI:** 26

American Places (Porter, Stegner and Stegner), **Supp. IV Part 2:** 599

"American Poet" (Shapiro), **Supp. II Part 2:** 701

"American Poetry" (Simpson), **Supp. IX:** 272

American Poetry, 1922: A Miscellany (Untermeyer, ed.), **Supp. XV:** 306

"American Poetry and American Life" (Pinsky), **Supp. VI:** 239–240

American Poetry from the Beginning to Whitman (Untermeyer, ed.), **Supp. XV:** 310

American Poetry since 1900 (Untermeyer, ed.), **Supp. XV:** 306

American Poetry since 1945: A Critical Survey (Stepanchev), **Supp. XI:** 312

American Poetry since 1960 (Mesic), **Supp. IV Part 1:** 175

American Poets since World War II Dictionary of Literary Biography (Gwynn, ed.), **Supp. XV:** 343

American Popular Song (Wilder), **Supp. XXVII:** 42

American Primer, An (Boorstin), **I:** 253

American Primer, An (Whitman), **IV:** 348

"American Primitive" (W. J. Smith), **Supp. XIII:** 333

American Primitive: Poems (Oliver), **Supp. VII:** 234–237, 238

American Procession, An: The Major American Writers from 1830–1930— the Crucial Century (Kazin), **Supp. VIII: 105–106,** 108

"American Prose Writers" articles (Briggs), **Supp. XVIII:** 11

American Psycho (Ellis), **Supp. XXVII:** 67, 71–74, 75, 76

American Psycho (film), **Supp. XXVII:** 68, 79

American Psycho 2 (film), **Supp. XXVII:** 68

American Psycho: The Musical, **Supp. XXVII:** 68

American Radio Company, The (radio show, Keillor), **Supp. XVI:** 176–177

"American Realist Playwrights, The" (McCarthy), **II:** 562

American Register, or General Repository of History, Politics, and Science, The (Brown, ed.), **Supp. I Part 1:** 146

American Renaissance (Matthiessen), **I:** 259–260; **III:** 310; **Supp. XIII:** 93

"American Rendezvous, An" (Beauvoir), **Supp. IX:** 4

American Scene, The (James), **II:** 336; **III:** 460; **Retro. Supp. I:** 232, 235

American Scenes (Kozlenko, ed.), **IV:** 378

"American Scholar, The" (Emerson), **I:** 239; **II:** 8, 12–13; **Retro. Supp. I:** 62, 74–75, 149, 298; **Retro. Supp. II:** 155; **Supp. I Part 2:** 420; **Supp. IX:** 227, 271; **Supp. XIV:** 104

"American Scholar, The" (Pickering), **Supp. XXI:** 196

Americans in England; or, Lessons for Daughters (Rowson), **Supp. XV:** 240

"American Soldier, The" (Freneau), **Supp. II Part 1:** 269

American Songbag, The (Sandburg), **III:** 583

"American Student in Paris, An" (Farrell), **II:** 45

"American Sublime, The" (Stevens), **IV:** 74

American Taliban (Abraham), **Supp. XXIV:** 2, **12–14**

"American Tar, The; or, The Press Gang Defeated" (Rowson and Taylor), **Supp. XV:** 238

"American Temperament, The" (Locke), **Supp. XIV:** 211

American Tragedy, An (Dreiser), **I:** 497, 498, 499, 501, 502, 503, 511–515, 517, 518, 519; **III:** 251; **IV:** 35, 484; **Retro. Supp. II:** 93, 95, **104–108; Supp. XVII:** 155

"American Triptych" (Kenyon), **Supp. VII:** 165

"American Use for German Ideals" (Bourne), **I:** 228

American Village, The (Freneau), **Supp. II Part 1:** 256, 257

"American Village, The" (Freneau), **Supp. II Part 1:** 256

American Wives and English Husbands (Atherton), **Supp. XXIV:** 18, 22

America's Coming-of-Age (Brooks), **I:** 228, 230, 240, 245, 258; **IV:** 427

America's Humor: From Poor Richard to Doonesbury (Blair and Hill), **Retro. Supp. II:** 286

"America's Indian Problem" (Zitkala-Ša), **Supp. XXV:** 282

"America's Part in World Peace" (Locke), **Supp. XIV:** 208

America's Rome (Vance), **Supp. IV Part 2:** 684

America: The Story of a Free People (Commager and Nevins), **I:** 253

America Was Promises (MacLeish), **III:** 16, 17

"Amerika" (Snyder), **Supp. VIII:** 301

Ames, Christopher, **Supp. XVIII:** 242–243

Ames, Fisher, **Supp. I Part 2:** 486

Ames, Lois, **Supp. I Part 2:** 541, 547

Ames, William, **IV:** 158

Ames Stewart, Beatrice, **Supp. IX:** 200

Amichai, Yehuda, **Supp. XI:** 267

Amick, Steve, **Supp. XXII:** 205, 216

Amidon, Stephen, **Supp. XI:** 333

Amiel, Henri F., **I:** 241, 243, 250

Amis, Kingsley, **IV:** 430; **Supp. IV Part 2:** 688; **Supp. VIII:** 167; **Supp. XIII:** 93; **Supp. XV:** 117

Amis, Martin, **Retro. Supp. I:** 278

"Amish, The"(Thompson), **Supp. XXIII:** 295–296

"Amity Hills" (Skloot), **Supp. XX: 204**

Ammons, A. R., **Supp. III Part 2:** 541; **Supp. IX:** 41, 42, 46; **Supp. VII: 23–38; Supp. XII:** 121; **Supp. XIX:** 83; **Supp. XV:** 115; **Supp. XVII:** 242; **Supp. XXVI:** 67

Ammons, Elizabeth, **Retro. Supp. I:** 364, 369; **Retro. Supp. II:** 140

Amnesia Moon (Lethem), **Supp. XVIII:** 136, **138–139**

"Among Children" (Levine), **Supp. V:** 192

Among Friends (M. F. K. Fisher), **Supp. XVII:** 89, 90–91, 92

Among My Books (J. R. Lowell), **Supp. I Part 2:** 407

"Among School Children" (Yeats), **III:** 249; **Supp. IX:** 52; **Supp. XIV:** 8

Among the Believers (Rash), **Supp. XXVII:** 218–220, 221

"Among the Hills" (Whittier), **Supp. I Part 2:** 703

Among the Isles of Shoals (Thaxter), **Supp. XIII:** 152

"Among Those Present" (Benét), **Supp. XI:** 53

"Amoral Moralist" (White), **Supp. I Part 2:** 648

Amory, Cleveland, **Supp. I Part 1:** 316

Amory, Fred, **Supp. III Part 1:** 2

Amos (biblical book), **II:** 166

Amos and Andy (television program), **Supp. XX: 103**

Amplitude (Gallagher), **Supp. XXIV:** 166, 170

Amran, David, **Supp. XIV:** 150

"Am Strand von Tanger" (Salter), **Supp. IX:** 257

"AMTRAK" (Baraka), **Supp. II Part 1:** 60

"Amulet, The" (Antin), **Supp. XX:** 10

"Amulets" (Hull), **Supp. XXI:** 139

Amy and Isabelle (film), **Supp. XXIII:** 275–276

Amy and Isabelle (Strout), **Supp. X:** 86; **Supp. XXIII:** 273, 274–275, **276–278,** 285

"Amy Lowell of Brookline, Mass." (Scott), **II:** 512

Amy Lowell: Portrait of the Poet in Her Time (Gregory), **II:** 512

"Amy Wentworth" (Whittier), **Supp. I Part 2:** 694, 696

Anabase (Perse), **III:** 12

"Anabasis (I)" (Merwin), **Supp. III Part 1:** 342, 346

"Anabasis (II)" (Merwin), **Supp. III Part 1:** 342, 346

Anagrams: A Novel (Moore), **Supp. X:** 163, 164, 167, **169–171,** 172

Analects (Confucius), **Supp. IV Part 1:** 14

Analects, The (Pound, trans.), **III:** 472

Analogy (J. Butler), **II:** 8

"Analysis of a Theme" (Stevens), **IV:** 81

Anarchiad, The, A Poem on the Restoration of Chaos and Substantial Night, in Twenty Four Books (Barlow), **Supp. II Part 1:** 70

Anarchist Woman, An (Hapgood), **Supp. XVII:** 102–103; **Supp. XXI:** 5

Anatomy Lesson, and Other Stories, The (Connell), **Supp. XIV:** 84, 87, 89

"Anatomy Lesson, The" (Connell), **Supp. XIV:** 84, 86, 87

Anatomy Lesson, The (P. Roth), **Retro. Supp. II:** 286, 290; **Supp. III Part 2:** 422–423, 425

"Anatomy Lesson of Dr. Nicholaas Tulp, Amsterdam, 1632, The" (Bierds), **Supp. XVII:** 27–28

Anatomy of Criticism (Frye), **Supp. XIII:** 19; **Supp. XIV:** 15

Anatomy of Melancholy (Burton), **III:** 78; **Supp. XVII:** 229

Anatomy of Nonsense, The (Winters), **Supp. II Part 2:** 811, 812

Anaya, Rudolfo A., **Supp. IV Part 2:** 502; **Supp. XIII:** 213, 220; **Supp. XIX:** 97

"Ancestor" (A. Finch), **Supp. XVII:** 72

Ancestors (Atherton), **Supp. XXIV:** 23, 25

Ancestors (Maxwell), **Supp. VIII:** 152, 168

"Ancestors, The" (Tate), **IV:** 128

Ancestral Voice: Conversations with N. Scott Momaday (Woodard), **Supp. IV Part 2:** 484, 485, 486, 489, 493

"Anchorage" (Harjo), **Supp. XII:** 220–221

Ancient Child, The: A Novel (Momaday), **Supp. IV Part 2:** 488, 489–491, 492, 493

"Ancient Dog Grave, Unearthed During Construction of the Athens Metro, An" (Stallings), **Supp. XXV:** 232

"Ancient Egypt/Fannie Goldbarth" (Goldbarth), **Supp. XII:** 191–192

Ancient Evenings (Mailer), **Retro. Supp. II:** 206, 210, 213

Ancient Law, The (Glasgow), **II:** 179–180, 192

Ancient Musics (Goldbarth), **Supp. XII:** 191–192

"Ancient Semitic Rituals for the Dead" (Goldbarth), **Supp. XII:** 191–192

Ancient Track, The (Lovecraft), **Supp. XXV:** 120

"Ancient World, The" (Doty), **Supp. XI:** 122

& (And) (Cummings), **I:** 429, 431, 432, 437, 445, 446, 448

Andersen, Hans Christian, **I:** 441; **Supp. I Part 2:** 622

Andersen, Hendrik Christian, **Supp. XX: 232**

Anderson, Charles R., **Supp. I Part 1:** 356, 360, 368, 371, 372

Anderson, Frances, **I:** 231

Anderson, Guy, **Supp. X:** 264, 265

Anderson, Henry J., **Supp. I Part 1:** 156

Anderson, Irwin M., **I:** 98–99

Anderson, Mrs. Irwin M., **I:** 98–99

Anderson, Jon, **Supp. V:** 338

Anderson, Judith, **III:** 399

Anderson, Karl, **I:** 99, 103

Anderson, Lorraine, **Supp. XVIII:** 189

Anderson, Margaret, **I:** 103; **III:** 171, 471; **Supp. XXV:** 18; **Supp. XXVII:** 86

Anderson, Marian, **Supp. XXII:** 283

Anderson, Mary Jane. *See* Lanier, Mrs. Robert Sampson (Mary Jane Anderson)

Anderson, Maxwell, **III:** 159

Anderson, Quentin, **Retro. Supp. I:** 392

Anderson, Robert, **Supp. I Part 1:** 277; **Supp. V:** 108

Anderson, Sally, **Supp. XIII:** 95

Anderson, Sherwood, **I: 97–120,** 211, 374, 375, 384, 405, 423, 445, 480, 487, 495, 506, 518; **II:** 27, 38, 44, 55, 56, 68, 250–251, 263, 271, 289, 451, 456–457; **III:** 220, 224, 382–383, 453, 483, 545, 576, 579; **IV:** 27, 40, 46, 190, 207, 433, 451, 482; **Retro. Supp. I:** 79, 80, 177; **Supp. I Part 2:** 430, 459, 472, 613; **Supp. IV Part 2:** 502; **Supp. IX:** 14, 309; **Supp. V:** 12, 250; **Supp. VIII:** 39, 152; **Supp. XI:** 159, 164; **Supp. XII:** 343; **Supp. XV:** 298; **Supp. XVI:** 17, 20; **Supp. XVII:** 105; **Supp. XX: 69, 75; Supp. XXIII:** 68, 162, 164; **Supp. XXIV:** 136; **Supp. XXV:** 18; **Supp. XXVII:** 83, 86

Anderson, Mrs. Sherwood (Tennessee Mitchell), **I:** 100; **Supp. I Part 2:** 459, 460

Anderson, T. J., **Supp. XIII:** 132

Anderson, Wendy, **Supp. XXI:** 255

Andersson, A., **III:** 252

"And Hickman Arrives" (Ellison), **Retro. Supp. II:** 118, 126; **Supp. II Part 1:** 248

And in the Hanging Gardens (Aiken), **I:** 63

"And It Came to Pass" (Wright), **Supp. XV:** 348

And I Worked at the Writer's Trade (Cowley), **Supp. II Part 1:** 137, 139, 141, 143, 147, 148

"...And Ladies of the Club" (J. W. Miller), **Supp. XX: 161**

And Live Apart (Peacock), **Supp. XIX: 196–197**

Andorra (Cameron), **Supp. XII:** 79, 81, **88–91**

"—and Other Poets" (column; Untermeyer), **Supp. XV:** 294

"—and Other Poets" (Untermeyer), *Supp. XV:* 297

"Andoumboulous Brush" (Mackey), **Supp. XXVII:** 156

Andracki, Thaddeus, **Supp. XXVI:** 108

Andral, Gabriel, **Supp. I Part 1:** 302

Andre, Michael, **Supp. XII:** 117–118, 129, 132, 133–134

"Andrea Is Changing Her Name" (Brockmeier), **Supp. XXII:** 61

Andre's Mother (McNally), **Supp. XIII:** 206

Andress, Ursula, **Supp. XI:** 307

"Andrew Jackson" (Masters), **Supp. I Part 2:** 472

Andrews, Bruce, **Supp. IV Part 2:** 426

Andrews, Peter, **Supp. XX: 87**

Andrews, Raymond, **Supp. XXVI: 1–16**

Andrews, Roy Chapman, **Supp. X:** 172

Andrews, Tom, **Supp. XI:** 317

Andrews, Wayne, **IV:** 310

Andrews, William L., **Supp. IV Part 1:** 13; **Supp. XIX:** 72; **Supp. XXV: 105**

Andrews, William P., **Supp. XXV:** 250

Andreyev, Leonid Nikolaevich, **I:** 53; **II:** 425

Andria (Terence), **IV:** 363

"Androgynous Kiss" (Gallagher), **Supp. XXIV:** 170

"Andromache" (Dubus), **Supp. VII:** 84

"And Summer Will Not Come Again" (Plath), **Retro. Supp. II:** 242

"And That Night Clifford Died" (Levine), **Supp. V:** 195

And the Band Played On (Shilts), **Supp. X:** 145

"And the Moon Be Still as Bright" (Bradbury), **Supp. IV Part 1:** 106

"And the Sea Shall Give up Its Dead" (Wilder), **IV:** 358

And Things That Go Bump in the Night (McNally), **Supp. XIII: 196–197,** 205, 208

And to Think That I Saw It on Mulberry Street (Geisel), **Supp. XVI:** 100, 101, 104

"And *Ut Pictura Poesis* Is Her Name" (Ashbery), **Supp. III Part 1:** 19

And We Are Millions (Ryan), **Supp. XVIII:** 225

"And Winter" (Boyle), **Supp. XXIV:** 63

"Andy Warhol: Andy Do It" (Brainard), **Supp. XXVII:** 25

"Anecdote and Storyteller" (Howe), **Supp. VI:** 127

"Anecdote of the Jar" (Stevens), **IV:** 83–84

"Anemone" (Rukeyser), **Supp. VI:** 281, 285

"Angel, The" (Buck), **Supp. II Part 1:** 127

"Angel and Unicorn and Butterfly" (Everwine), **Supp. XV:** 76

Angela's Ashes (McCourt), **Supp. XII: 271–279,** 283, 285; **Supp. XXII:** 94

"Angel at the Grave, The" (Wharton), **IV:** 310; **Retro. Supp. I:** 365

"Angel Butcher" (Levine), **Supp. V:** 181

Angel City (Shepard), **Supp. III Part 2:** 432, 445

Angelica (Holding), **Supp. XXII: 120–121**

"Angel Is My Watermark!, The" (H. Miller), **III:** 180

Angell, Carol, **Supp. I Part 2:** 655

Angell, Katharine Sergeant. *See* White, Katharine

Angell, Roger, **Supp. I Part 2:** 655; **Supp. V:** 22; **Supp. VIII:** 139

Angel Landing (Hoffman), **Supp. X: 82–83**

"Angel Levine" (Malamud), **Supp. I Part 2:** 431, 432, 433–434, 437

Angel of Bethesda, The (Mather), **Supp. II Part 2:** 464

"Angel of the Bridge, The" (Cheever), **Supp. I Part 1:** 186–187

"Angel of the Odd, The" (Poe), **III:** 425

Angelo Herndon Jones (Hughes), **Retro. Supp. I:** 203

"Angel on the Porch, An" (Wolfe), **IV:** 451

Angelou, Maya, **Supp. IV Part 1: 1–19; Supp. XI:** 20, 245; **Supp. XIII:** 185; **Supp. XVI:** 259; **Supp. XXI:** 172

"Angel Poem, The" (Stern), **Supp. IX:** 292

Angels and Earthly Creatures (Wylie), **Supp. I Part 2:** 709, 713, 724–730

Angels Flight (Connelly), **Supp. XXI:** 72, **72–73,** 75, 80

"Angels for Djuna Barnes" (Boyle), **Supp. XXIV:** 63

Angels in America: A Gay Fantasia on National Themes (Kushner), **Supp.**

IX: 131, 134, **141–146; Supp. XXIV:** 272

"Angels of the Love Affair" (Sexton), **Supp. II Part 2:** 692

Angels over Broadway (screenplay, Hecht), **Supp. XXVII:** 93

"Angel's Trumpet, The"(P. Benedict), **Supp. XXIII:** 48

"Angel Surrounded by Paysans" (Stevens), **IV:** 93

Angel That Troubled the Waters, The (Wilder), **IV:** 356, 357–358

"Anger" (Creeley), **Supp. IV Part 1:** 150–152

Anger (Sarton), **Supp. VIII: 256**

"Anger against Children" (R. Bly), **Supp. IV Part 1:** 73

Angle of Ascent (Hayden), **Supp. II Part 1:** 363, 367, 370

"Angle of Geese" (Momaday), **Supp. IV Part 2:** 485

Angle of Geese and Other Poems (Momaday), **Supp. IV Part 2:** 487, 491

Angle of Repose (Stegner), **Supp. IV Part 2:** 599, 605, 606, 610–611

"*Angle of Repose* and the Writings of Mary Hallock Foote: A Source Study" (Williams-Walsh), **Supp. IV Part 2:** 611

"Anglo-Mongrels and the Rose" (Loy), **Supp. XXII:** 156, 159, 166–167

Anglo-Saxon Century, The (Dos Passos), **I:** 474–475, 483

Angoff, Charles, **III:** 107

"Angola Question Mark" (Hughes), **Supp. I Part 1:** 344

Angry Hills, The (Uris), **Supp. XX: 246, 250**

Angry Wife, The (Sedges), **Supp. II Part 1:** 125

"Angry Women Are Building: Issues and Struggles Facing American Indian Women Today" (Gunn Allen), **Supp. IV Part 1:** 324

"Animal, Vegetable, and Mineral" (Bogan), **Supp. III Part 1:** 66

"Animal Acts" (Simic), **Supp. VIII:** 278

Animal and Vegetable Physiology Considered with Reference to Natural Theology (Roget), **Supp. I Part 1:** 312

"Animal Bodies: Corporeality, Class, and Subject Formation in *The Wide, Wide World*" (Mason), **Supp. XVIII:** 263

Animal Dreams (Kingsolver), **Supp. VII:** 199, 204–207

Animal Magnetism (Prose), **Supp. XVI:** 251, 260

"Animals, The" (Merwin), **Supp. III Part 1:** 348

"Animals Are Passing from Our Lives" (Levine), **Supp. V:** 181, 182

Animals in That Country, The (Atwood), **Supp. XIII:** 20, 33

Animals of the Soul: Sacred Animals of the Oglala Sioux (Brown), **Supp. IV Part 2:** 487

"Animals You Eat, The" (X. J. Kennedy), **Supp. XV:** 169

"Animula" (Eliot), **Retro. Supp. I:** 64

Anita Loos Rediscovered (M. A. Loos), **Supp. XVI:** 196

Ankor Wat (Ginsberg), **Supp. II Part 1:** 323

Ann, Leslee, **Supp. XXIV:** 264

"Annabelle" (Komunyakaa), **Supp. XIII:** 117

"Annabel Lee" (Poe), **Retro. Supp. I:** 273; **Retro. Supp. II:** 266

Anna Christie (O'Neill), **III:** 386, 389, 390; **Supp. XXII:** 24

"Anna Grasa" (Weigl), **Supp. XIX:** 278

"Anna in Mourning" (Weigl), **Supp. XIX:** 288

Anna Karenina (Tolstoy), **I:** 10; **II:** 290; **Retro. Supp. I:** 225; **Supp. V:** 323

"*Anna Karenina*" (Trilling), *Supp. III Part 2:* 508

Annan, Noel, **Supp. XX: 240**

"Anna's Grace" (Weigl), **Supp. XIX:** 282–283

"Anna Who Was Mad" (Sexton), **Supp. II Part 2:** 692

"Ann Burlak" (Rukeyser), **Supp. VI:** 280

"Anne" (Oliver), **Supp. VII:** 232

"Anne" (R. H. Davis), **Supp. XVI:** 91, 92

"Anne at the Symphony" (Shields), **Supp. VII:** 310

"Anne Bradstreet's Poetic Voices" (Requa), **Supp. I Part 1:** 107

Anne of Geierstein: or, The Maiden of the Mist (Scott), **Supp. XX: 234**

Anne Sexton: The Artist and Her Critics (McClatchy), **Supp. XII:** 253

"Ann from the Street" (Dixon), **Supp. XII:** 146–147

"Ann Garner" (Agee), **I:** 27

"Anniad, The" (Brooks), **Supp. III Part 1:** 77, 78

Annie (musical), **Supp. IV Part 2:** 577

Annie Allen (Brooks), **Supp. III Part 1:** 76–79

Annie Dillard Reader, The (Dillard), **Supp. VI:** 23

Annie Hall (film; Allen), **Supp. IV Part 1:** 205; **Supp. XV:** 1, 2, 4, 5, **6–7,** 14

Annie John (Kincaid), **Supp. VII:** 184–186, 193

Annie Kilburn, a Novel (Howells), **II:** 275, 286, 287

"Annihilation" (X. J. Kennedy), **Supp. XV:** 168

"Annihilation of Matter, The" (Bronk), **Supp. XXI:** 30

Anniversary (Shields), **Supp. VII:** 320, 322, 323, 324

"Anniversary Poem" (Oppen), **Supp. XXVI:** 237

"Annunciation" (Nelson), **Supp. XVIII:** 174

"Annunciation, The" (Le Sueur), **Supp. V:** 130

Ann Vickers (Lewis), **II:** 453

"A No-Account Creole, A" (Chopin), **Retro. Supp. II:** 64

"Anodyne" (Komunyakaa), **Supp. XIII:** 130

Another America/Otra America (Kingsolver), **Supp. VII:** 207–209

"Another Animal" (Swenson), **Supp. IV Part 2:** 639

Another Animal: Poems (Swenson), **Supp. IV Part 2:** 639–641, 649

Another Antigone (Gurney), **Supp. V:** 97, 98, 100, 101, 102, 105

"Another August" (Merrill), **Supp. III Part 1:** 326

"Another Beer" (Matthews), **Supp. IX:** 158

Another Country (Baldwin), **Retro. Supp. II:** 9–11, 14; **Supp. I Part 1:** 51, 52, 56–58, 63, 67, 337; **Supp. II Part 1:** 40; **Supp. VIII:** 349

"Another Language" (Jong), **Supp. V:** 131

Another Mother Tongue: Gay Words, Gay Worlds (Grahn), **Supp. IV Part 1:** 330

"Another Night in the Ruins" (Kinnell), **Supp. III Part 1:** 239, 251

"Another Night with Snow" (W. V. Davis), **Supp. XXI:** 90, 91

"Another Old Woman" (W. C. Williams), **Retro. Supp. I:** 423

Another Part of the Forest (Hellman), **Supp. I Part 1:** 282–283, 297

Another Republic: 17 European and South American Writers (Strand, trans.), **Supp. IV Part 2:** 630

Another Roadside Attraction (Robbins), **Supp. X:** 259, 261, 262, 263, 264, 265–266, **267–269,** 274, 275, 277, 284

Another Side of Bob Dylan (album, Dylan), **Supp. XVIII:** 25

"Another Spring Uncovered" (Swenson), **Supp. IV Part 2:** 644

Another Thin Man (film), **Supp. IV Part 1:** 355

Another Time (Auden), **Supp. II Part 1:** 15

Another Turn of the Crank (Berry), **Supp. X:** 25, 35

"Another upon the Same" (Taylor), **IV:** 161

"Another Voice" (Wilbur), **Supp. III Part 2:** 557

"Another Wife" (Anderson), **I:** 114

"Another Winter Night" (Budbill), **Supp. XIX:** 10

Another Woman (film; Allen), **Supp. XV:** 11

Another You (Beattie), **Supp. V:** 29, 31, 33–34

Anouilh, Jean, **Supp. I Part 1:** 286–288, 297

Ansa, Tina McElroy, **Supp. XVIII:** 195

Ansay, A. Manette, **Supp. XXV:** 142

"Anselm" (Berrigan), **Supp. XXIV:** 43

Ansen, Alan, **Supp. XXIII:** 112, 122, 123

Ansky, S., **IV:** 6

Ansky, Shloime, **Supp. IX:** 131, 138

"Answer, The" (Jeffers), **Supp. III Part 2:** 423

Answered Prayers: The Unfinished Novel (Capote), **Supp. III Part 1:** 113, 125, 131–132; **Supp. XVI:** 245

"Answering the Deer: Genocide and Continuance in the Poetry of American Indian Women" (Gunn Allen), **Supp. IV Part 1:** 322, 325

Answering Voice, The: One Hundred Love Lyrics by Women (Teasdale, ed.), **Supp. XXVII:** 283, 286, 289

"Answer of Minerva, The: Pacifism and Resistance in Simone Weil" (Merton), **Supp. VIII:** 204

Antaeus (Wolfe), **IV:** 461

"Ante-Bellum Sermon, An" (Dunbar), **Supp. II Part 1:** 203–204

Antheil, George, **III:** 471, 472; **IV:** 404

"Anthem" (Cohen), **Supp. XXVII:** 52, 63

Anthem (Rand), **Supp. IV Part 2:** 523

Anthology of Holocaust Literature (Glatstein, Knox, and Margoshes, eds.), **Supp. X:** 70

Anthology of Modern American Poetry (Nelson, ed.), **Supp. XXII:** 271

Anthology of Twentieth-Century Brazilian Poetry, An (Bishop and Brasil, eds.), **Retro. Supp. II:** 50; **Supp. I Part 1:** 94

Anthon, Kate, **I:** 452

Anthony, Adelina, **Supp. XXIII:** 197

Anthony, Andrew, **Supp. XVI:** 235, 245, 246

Anthony, Saint, **III:** 395

Anthony, Susan B., **Supp. XI:** 200

"Anthropologist as Hero, The" (Sontag), **Supp. III Part 2:** 451

"Anthropology of Water, The" (Carson), **Supp. XII:** 102–103

Anthropos: The Future of Art (Cummings), **I:** 430

Antichrist (Nietzsche), **III:** 176

"Antietam" (Rash), **Supp. XXVII:** 221

"Anti-Father" (Dove), **Supp. IV Part 1:** 246

"Anti-Feminist Woman, The" (Rich), **Supp. I Part 2:** 550

Antigone (Sophocles), **Supp. I Part 1:** 284; **Supp. X:** 249

"Anti-Memoir"(Dybek), **Supp. XXIII:** 78

Antin, David, **Supp. VIII:** 292; **Supp. XII:** 2, 8

Antin, Mary, **Supp. IX:** 227; **Supp. XVI:** 148, 149; **Supp. XX:** 1–16

Anti-Oedipus: Capitalism and Schizophrenia (Deleuze and Guattari), **Supp. XII:** 4

Antiphon, The (Barnes), **Supp. III Part 1:** 43–44

"Antiquities" (Mather), **Supp. II Part 2:** 452

"Antiquity of Freedom, The" (Bryant), **Supp. I Part 1:** 168

"Antislavery Tocsin, An" (Douglass), **Supp. III Part 1:** 171

Antoine, Andre, **III:** 387

Antony and Cleopatra (Shakespeare), **I:** 285

"Antony on Behalf of the Play" (Burke), **I:** 284

"An trentiesme de mon Eage, L'" (MacLeish), **III:** 9

Antrim, Donald, **Supp. XX:** 90

"Ants" (R. Bly), **Supp. IV Part 1:** 71

Anxiety of Influence, The (Bloom), **Supp. XIII:** 46

"Any City" (Untermeyer), **Supp. XV:** 296

"Any Object" (Swenson), **Supp. IV Part 2:** 640

Any Old Way You Choose It (Christgau), **Supp. XXVII:** 33, 35, 37, 39, 40, 44

Anyplace but Here (Bontemps and Conroy), **Supp. XXII:** 11

"Any Porch" (Parker), **Supp. IX:** 194

Anything Else (film; Allen), **Supp. XV:** 2, 11

Anywhere but Here (Simpson), **Supp. XXVII:** 234–237

"Anywhere Out of This World" (Baudelaire), **II:** 552

Any Woman Can't (Wasserstein), **Supp. XV:** 322

Any Woman's Blues (Jong), **Supp. V:** 115, 123, 126

Anzaldúa, Gloria, **Supp. IV Part 1:** 330; **Supp. XIII:** 223; **Supp. XXIII:** 193, 194, 205

"Apache Tears" (Cliff), **Supp. XXII:** 76

"Aphorisms on Futurism" (Loy), **Supp. XXII:** 159

"Aphorisms on Society" (Stevens), **Retro. Supp. I:** 303

"Apiary IX" (C. Frost), **Supp. XV:** 106

"Apisculptures" (Bierds), **Supp. XVII:** 29

"Apocalypse: What Disaster Reveals" (Díaz), **Supp. XXIV:** 94–95

Apollinaire, Guillaume, **I:** 432; **II:** 529; **III:** 196; **IV:** 80; **Retro. Supp. II:** 326; **Supp. XV:** 182; **Supp. XXIII:** 208

"Apollo Takes Charge of His Muses" (Stallings), **Supp. XXV:** 229

Apologies to the Iroquois (Wilson), **IV:** 429

"Apology" (C. Frost), **Supp. XV:** 103

"Apology, An" (Malamud), **Supp. I Part 2:** 435, 437

"Apology for Bad Dreams" (Jeffers), **Supp. II Part 2:** 427, 438; **Supp. XVII:** 112

"Apology for Crudity, An" (Anderson), **I:** 109

Apology for Poetry (Sidney), **Supp. II Part 1:** 105

Apostle, The (Asch), **Supp. XXIII:** 2, 4, 9, **13–14**

"Apostle of the Tules, An" (Harte), **Supp. II Part 1:** 356

"Apostrophe to a Dead Friend" (Kumin), **Supp. IV Part 2:** 442, 451, 452

"Apostrophe to a Pram Rider" (White), **Supp. I Part 2:** 678

"Apostrophe to Man (on reflecting that the world is ready to go to war again)" (Millay), **III:** 127

"Apostrophe to Vincentine, The" (Stevens), **IV:** 90

"Apotheosis" (Kingsolver), **Supp. VII:** 208

"Apotheosis of Martin Luther King, The" (Hardwick), **Supp. III Part 1:** 203–204

Appalachee Red (Andrews), **Supp. XXVI:** 5–6, 7, 14

Appalachia (Wright), **Supp. V:** 333, 345

Appalachia Inside Out (Miller, Higgs, and Manning, eds.), **Supp. XX: 166**

"Appalachian Book of the Dead III" (Wright), **Supp. V:** 345

"Appalachian Education: A Critique and Suggestions for Reform" (J. W. Miller), **Supp. XX: 165**

"Appalachian Literature: At Home in This World" (J. W. Miller), **Supp. XX: 165**

"Appalachian Values/American Values" (J. W. Miller), **Supp. XX: 165**

Appaloosa (Parker), **Supp. XIX:** 187

"Appeal to H. G. Wells" (Sturgis), **Supp. XX: 233, 240**

"Appeal to Progressives, An" (Wilson), **IV:** 429

Appeal to Reason (Paine), **I:** 490

Appeal to the World, An (Du Bois), **Supp. II Part 1:** 184

Appearance and Reality (Bradley), **I:** 572

Appel, Richard, **Supp. XXVII:** 233

"Appendix to 'The Anniad' " (Brooks), **Supp. III Part 1:** 77

"Applause, Applause"(Thompson), **Supp. XXIII:** 289, 291, 301

Apple, Max, **Supp. VIII:** 14; **Supp. XVII: 1–11,** 49–50

Apple, Sam, **Supp. XVII:** 8

"Apple, The" (Kinnell), **Supp. III Part 1:** 250

Applebaum, Anne, **Supp. XVI:** 153

Applebome, Peter, **Supp. XXI:** 38

Applegarth, Mabel, **II:** 465, 478

"Apple-Maggot Fly, The" (Major), **Supp. XXII:** 182

"Apple of Discord, The" (Humphrey), **Supp. IX:** 109

"Apple Peeler" (Francis), **Supp. IX:** 82

"Apple Rind" (C. Frost), **Supp. XV:** 102

"Apples" (Brockmeier), **Supp. XXII:** 51, 53

"Apples, The" (Di Piero), **Supp. XIX:** 46

Appleseed, Johnny (pseudonym). *See* Chapman, John (Johnny Appleseed)

Apple That Astonished Paris, The (Collins), **Supp. XXI:** 53, 57

Appleton, Nathan, **II:** 488

Appleton, Thomas Gold, **Supp. I Part 1:** 306; **Supp. I Part 2:** 415

"Apple Tree, The" (McCarriston), **Supp. XIV:** 263, 268

"Applicant, The" (Plath), **Retro. Supp. II:** 252; **Supp. I Part 2:** 535, 544, 545

"Application, The" (Neugeboren), **Supp. XVI:** 219, 220, 225

"Applications of the Doctrine" (Hass), **Supp. VI: 100–101**

Appointment, The (film), **Supp. IX:** 253

Appointment in Samarra (O'Hara), **III:** 361, 363–364, 365–367, 371, 374, 375, 383

Appreciation of Sarah Orne Jewett (Cary), **Retro. Supp. II:** 132

"Apprentice, The"(Dybek), **Supp. XXIII:** 71

"Approaches, The" (Merwin), **Supp. III Part 1:** 350

"Approaching Artaud" (Sontag), **Supp. III Part 2:** 470–471

"Approaching Prayer" (Dickey), **Supp. IV Part 1:** 175

"Approaching the Mohawk Village: Jogues' Journal"(Kenny), **Supp. XXIII:** 152

Approach to Literature, An: A Collection of Prose and Verse with Analyses and Discussions (Brooks, Warren, and Purser), **Su pp. XIV:**4

"Approach to Thebes, The" (Kunitz), **Supp. III Part 1:** 265–267

Approach to Vedanta, An (Isherwood), **Supp. XIV:** 157, 163, 164

"Appropriation of Cultures, The" (Everett), **Supp. XVIII:** 66

Approximately Paradise (Skloot), **Supp. XX: 196, 202, 203–204**

"Après-midi d'un faune, L' " (Mallarmé), **III:** 8

"April" (Bierds), **Supp. XVII:** 29

"April" (W. C. Williams), **Retro. Supp. I:** 422

"April" (Winters), **Supp. II Part 2:** 788

April, Steve. *See* Lacy, Ed

April Galleons (Ashbery), **Supp. III Part 1:** 26

"April Galleons" (Ashbery), **Supp. III Part 1:** 26

April Hopes (Howells), **II:** 285, 289

"April Lovers" (Ransom), **III:** 489–490

"April Saturday 1960" (Huddle), **Supp. XXVI:** 150

"April Showers" (Wharton), **Retro. Supp. I:** 361

"April Today Main Street" (Olson), **Supp. II Part 2:** 581

April Twilights (Cather), **I:** 313; **Retro. Supp. I:** 5

"Apt Pupil" (King), **Supp. V:** 152

Arabian Nights, **I:** 204; **II:** 8; **Supp. I Part 2:** 584, 599; **Supp. IV Part 1:** 1

"Arabic Coffee" (Nye), **Supp. XIII:** 276

"Araby" (Joyce), **I:** 174; **Supp. VIII:** 15

Aragon, Louis, **I:** 429; **III:** 471; **Retro. Supp. II:** 85, 321

Arana-Ward, Marie, **Supp. VIII:** 84

Ararat (Glück), **Supp. V:** 79, 86–87

Aratani, Mariko, **Supp. XXIII:** 136

"Arbiter, The" (Toole), **Supp. XXVI:** 243

Arbre du voyageur, L' (W. J. Smith; Haussmann, trans.), **Supp. XIII:** 347

Arbus, Diane, **Supp. XII:** 188

Arbuthnott, John (pseudonym). *See* Henry, O.

"Arc, The" (Bidart), **Supp. XV:** 25–26, 27

Archaeologist of Morning (Olson), **Supp. II Part 2:** 557

Archaeology of the Circle: New and Selected Poems (Weigl), **Supp. XIX:** 282

"Archaic Maker, The" (Merwin), **Supp. III Part 1:** 357

Archaic Smile (Stallings), **Supp. XXV:** 221, 222, 223, 224, 228–231, 233

"Archaic Torso of Apollo" (Rilke), **Supp. XV:** 148

"Archaischer Torso Apollos" (Rilke), **Supp. XVII:** 244

"Archbishop, The" (Gioia), **Supp. XV:** 126, 127

Archer (television show), **Supp. IV Part 2:** 474

Archer, William, **IV:** 131; **Retro. Supp. I:** 228

Archer at Large (Macdonald), **Supp. IV Part 2:** 473

Archer in Hollywood (Macdonald), **Supp. IV Part 2:** 474

"Archetype and Signature: The Relationship of Poet and Poem" (Fiedler), **Supp. XIII:** 101

"Archibald Higbie" (Masters), **Supp. I Part 2:** 461

"Architect, The" (Bourne), **I:** 223

Architect, The (Briggs and Ranlett), **Supp. XVIII:** 3

Architect, The (Levin), **Supp. XXVII:** 133

Archuleta, Elizabeth, **Supp. XXVI:** 106

Arctic Dreams (Lopez), **Supp. V:** 211

Arctic Refuge: A Circle of Testimony (Haines), **Supp. XII:** 205

"Arcturus" (Connell), **Supp. XIV:** 88

À rebours (Huysmans), **Supp. XX: 239**

Arendt, Hannah, **II:** 544; **Retro. Supp. I:** 87; **Retro. Supp. II:** 28, 117; **Supp. I Part 2:** 570; **Supp. IV Part 1:** 386; **Supp. VIII:** 98, 99, 100, 243; **Supp. XII:** 166–167

Arensberg, Louise, **Supp. XXII:** 162

Arensberg, Walter, **IV:** 408; **Retro. Supp. I:** 416; **Supp. XXII:** 162

Aren't You Happy for Me? (Bausch), **Supp. VII:** 42, 51, 54

Areopagitica (Milton), **Supp. I Part 2:** 422

"Are You a Doctor?" (Carver), **Supp. III Part 1:** 139–141

Are You Mr. William Stafford? (Stafford), **Supp. XI:** 317

Are You My Mother? A Comic Drama (Bechdel), **Supp. XXV:** 1, 2, 9–14

"Are You Okay?" (video, Ellis), **Supp. XXVII:** 80

Argall: The True Story of Pocahontas and Captain John Smith (Vollmann), **Supp. XVII:** 225, 226, 231, 232, 233

"Argonauts of 49, California's Golden Age" (Harte), **Supp. II Part 1:** 353, 355

"Arguantando" (Díaz), **Supp. XXIV:** 88–89

"Arguments of Everlasting" (B. Kelly), **Supp. XVII:** 129

"Arguments with the Gestapo Continued: II" (Wright), **Supp. XV:** 344

"Arguments with the Gestapo Continued: Literary Resistance" (Wright), **Supp. XV:** 344

Ari (musical, Uris), **Supp. XX: 247**

Aria da Capo (Millay), **III:** 137–138

"Ariadne and the Rest" (Stallings), **Supp. XXV:** 223, 229

Ariadne's Thread: A Collection of Contemporary Women's Journals (Lifshin, ed.), **Supp. XVI:** 37–38

"Arias, 1971" (Hull), **Supp. XXI:** 135

Ariel (Plath), **Retro. Supp. II:** 250–255; **Supp. I Part 2:** 526, 539, 541; **Supp. V:** 79; **Supp. XXI:** 58; **Supp. XXII:** 93; **Supp. XXVII:** 296

"Ariel" (Plath), **Supp. I Part 2:** 542, 546

"Ariel Poems" (Eliot), **I:** 579

Ariosto, Ludovico, **Supp. XV:** 175

"Arioso: Critical Notice of His Life and Genius" (Hunt), **Supp. XV:** 175

Arise, Arise (Zukofsky), **Supp. III Part 2:** 619, 629

Aristides. *See* Epstein, Joseph

"Aristocracy" (Emerson), **II:** 6

Aristocracy and Justice (More), **I:** 223

Aristocrat, The (Richter), **Supp. XVIII:** 220

Aristophanes, **I:** 436; **II:** 577; **Supp. I Part 2:** 406

Aristotle, **I:** 58, 265, 280, 527; **II:** 9, 12, 198, 536; **III:** 20, 115, 145, 157, 362, 422, 423; **IV:** 10, 18, 74–75, 89; **Supp. I Part 1:** 104, 296; **Supp. I Part 2:** 423; **Supp. IV Part 1:** 391; **Supp. IV Part 2:** 526, 530; **Supp. X:** 78; **Supp. XI:** 249; **Supp. XII:** 106; **Supp. XIV:** 242–243

Aristotle Contemplating the Bust of Homer (Rembrandt), **Supp. IV Part 1:** 390, 391

"Arkansas Traveller" (Wright), **Supp. V:** 334

"Arkham" (Howard), **Supp. XXVII:** 118

Arlen, Harold, **Supp. XXII:** 6

"Arm, The" (X. J. Kennedy), **Supp. XV:** 169

"Armadillo, The" (Bishop), **Supp. I Part 1:** 93

Armadillo in the Grass (Hearon), **Supp. VIII:** 58–59

"Armageddon" (Ransom), **III:** 489, 492

Armageddon (Uris), **Supp. XX:** 243, 247, 248, 252–253

Armah, Aiy Kwei, **Supp. IV Part 1:** 373

Armenian Golgotha: A Memoir of the Armenian Genocide, 1915– 1918 (Grigoris Balakian; trans. Peter Balakian and Sevag), **Supp. XXIII:** 28, **29–32**

Armies of the Night, The (Mailer), **III:** 39–40, 41, 42, 44, 45, 46; **Retro. Supp. II:** 205, 206–207, 208; **Supp. IV Part 1:** 207; **Supp. XIV:** 49, 162

"Arm in Arm" (Simpson), **Supp. IX:** 267–268

Arminius, Jacobus, **I:** 557

Armitage, Shelley, **Supp. IV Part 2:** 439

Arm of Flesh, The (Salter), **Supp. IX:** 251

"Armor" (Dickey), **Supp. IV Part 1:** 179

Armored Attack (film), **Supp. I Part 1:** 281

Arms, George W., **Supp. I Part 2:** 416–417

Armstrong, George, **Supp. I Part 2:** 386

Armstrong, Louis, **Retro. Supp. II:** 114

"'Arm the Paper Arm': Kenneth Koch's Postmodern Comedy" (Chinitz), **Supp. XV:** 180, 185

"Army" (Corso), **Supp. XII:** 117, 127

Army Brat (W. J. Smith), **Supp. XIII:** 331, 347

"Army Recruiting Methods" (Bodenheim), **Supp. XXV:** 19

Arna Bontemps Langston Hughes: Letters 1925–1967 (Nichols), **Retro. Supp. I:** 194

"Arna Bontemps Talks About the Renaissance" (Collins), **Supp. XXII:** 7

Arner, Robert D., **Retro. Supp. II:** 62

"Arnie" (Budbill), **Supp. XIX:** 6

Arnold, Edwin T., **Supp. VIII:** 189

Arnold, George W., **Supp. I Part 2:** 411

Arnold, Marilyn, **Supp. IV Part 1:** 220

Arnold, Matthew, **I:** 222, 228, 275; **II:** 20, 110, 338, 541; **III:** 604; **IV:** 349; **Retro. Supp. I:** 56, 325; **Supp. I Part 2:** 416, 417, 419, 529, 552, 602; **Supp. IX:** 298; **Supp. XIV:** 11, 335; **Supp. XIX:** 41; **Supp. XXI:** 90

Arnold, Thurman, **Supp. I Part 2:** 645

Aronson, Steven M. L., **Supp. V:** 4

Around about America (Caldwell), **I:** 290

"Arrangement in Black and White" (Parker), **Supp. IX:** 198

Arregoces, Christina, **Supp. XXVI:** 148, 158

"Arrival at Santos" (Bishop), **Retro. Supp. II:** 46; **Supp. IX:** 45–46

"Arrival of the Bee Box, The" (Plath), **Retro. Supp. II:** 255

Arrivistes, The: Poem 1940–1949 (Simpson), **Supp. IX:** 265, **267–268**

Arrogance (J. Scott), **Supp. XVII:** 186– **188**, 189, 191, 192, **194**

"Arrow" (Dove), **Supp. IV Part 1:** 250

"Arrowhead Hunting" (Stallings), **Supp. XXV:** 232

Arrow mystery series (Myers), **Supp. XXVII:** 212

Arrowsmith (Lewis), **I:** 362; **II:** 445–446, 449

"Arsenal at Springfield, The" (Longfellow), **Retro. Supp. II:** 168

"Arson at Midnight" (Nelson), **Supp. XVIII:** 186

"Arson Plus" (Hammett), **Supp. IV Part 1:** 343; **Supp. XXI:** 68

"Ars Poetica" (Dove), **Supp. IV Part 1:** 250

"Ars Poetica" (Dunn), **Supp. XI:** 154

"Ars Poetica" (MacLeish), **III:** 9–10

"Ars Poetica" (X. J. Kennedy), **Supp. XV:** 154

"Ars Poetica: A Found Poem" (Kumin), **Supp. IV Part 2:** 455

"Ars Poetica; or, Who Lives in the Ivory Tower" (McGrath), **Supp. X:** 117

"Ars Poetica: Some Recent Criticism" (Wright), **Supp. III Part 2:** 603

"Art" (Emerson), **II:** 13

Art (Reza), **Supp. XXI:** 148

"Art and Architecture of the Double Ending, The"(Painter), **Supp. XXIII:** 295

"Art and Neurosis" (Trilling), **Supp. III Part 2:** 502

Art and Technics (Mumford), **Supp. II Part 2:** 483

Art & Ardor: Essays (Ozick), **Supp. V:** 258, 272

Art as Experience (Dewey), **I:** 266

Art by Subtraction (Reid), **IV:** 41

Art Chronicles 1954–1966 (O'Hara), **Supp. XXIII:** 220

Art de toucher le clavecin, L' (Couperin), *III:* 464

"Artemis" (Davison), **Supp. XXVI:** 69

Artemis to Actaeon and Other Verse (Wharton), **Retro. Supp. I:** 372

Arte of English Poesie (Puttenham), **Supp. I Part 1:** 113

"Art"(Hadas), **Supp. XXIII:** 115–116

"Art History" (Cliff), **Supp. XXII:** 75–76

Arthur, Anthony, **Supp. IV Part 2:** 606

Arthur Mervyn; or, Memoirs of the Year 1793 (Brown), **Supp. I Part 1:** 137–140, 144

"Article of Faith" (Sobin), **Supp. XVI:** 291

Articles of Light & Elation (Sobin), **Supp. XVI:** 291

Articulation of Sound Forms in Time (Howe), **Supp. IV Part 2:** 419, 431–433

"Artificer" (X. J. Kennedy), **Supp. XV:** 160

"Artificial Nigger, The" (O'Connor), **III:** 343, 351, 356, 358; **Retro. Supp. II:** 229, 232

Artist, The: A Drama without Words (Mencken), **III:** 104

Artist as Revolutionary, The (Buhle), **Supp. XXI:** 172

"Artist of the Beautiful, The" (Hawthorne), **Retro. Supp. I:** 149

Artistry of Grief (Torsney), **Retro. Supp. I:** 224

Artists and Concubines (Silver), **Supp. XXIV:** 265

"Artists' and Models' Ball, The" (Brooks), **Supp. III Part 1:** 72

Art of Detective Fiction, The (Swales), **Supp. XIX:** 183

"Art of Disappearing, The" (Nye), **Supp. XIII:** 287

Art of Drowning, The (Collins), **Supp. XXI:** 54, 60, 64

Art of Eating, The (M. F. K. Fisher), **Supp. XVII:** 87, 90, 91

Art of Fiction, The (Gardner), **Supp. VI:** 73

"Art of Fiction, The" (H. James), **Retro. Supp. I:** 226; **Retro. Supp. II:** 223

Art of Hunger, The (Auster), **Supp. XII:** 22

"Art of Keeping Your Mouth Shut, The" (Heller), **Supp. IV Part 1:** 383

"Art of Literature and Commonsense, The" (Nabokov), **Retro. Supp. I:** 271

Art of Living and Other Stories, The (Gardner), **Supp. VI:** 72

Art of Love, The (Koch), **Supp. XV:** 182

"Art of Love, The" (Koch), **Supp. XV:** 182

Art of Poetry, The (Koch), **Supp. XV:** 175–176, 178, 188

"Art of Poetry, The" (Koch), **Supp. XV:** 182

"Art of Poetry, The" (McClatchy), **Supp. XII:** 262

Art of Political Murder, The (Goldman), **Supp. XXV:** 49, 57–59

"Art of Romare Bearden, The" (Ellison), **Retro. Supp. II:** 123

"Art of Storytelling, The" (Simpson), **Supp. IX:** 277

Art of Sylvia Plath, The (Newman), **Supp. I Part 2:** 527

Art of the Moving Picture, The (Lindsay), **Supp. I Part 2:** 376, 391–392, 394; **Supp. XVI:** 185

Art of the Novel (H. James), **Retro. Supp. I:** 227

"Art of Theodore Dreiser, The" (Bourne), **I:** 235

Art of the Personal Essay, The (Lopate, comp.), **Supp. XIII:** 280–281; **Supp. XVI:** 266

Art of the Self, The: Essays a Propos "Steps" (Kosinski), Supp. VII: 222

Art of the Wasted Day, The (Hampl), **Supp. XXII:** 85

Arts and Sciences (Goldbarth), **Supp. XII: 184–186**

Arts and Sciences: A Seventies Seduction (Mallon), **Supp. XIX:** 132, 135

"Art's Bread and Butter" (Benét), **Retro. Supp. I:** 108

Artsybashev, Mikhail, **Supp. XXIII:** 1

Arvin, Newton, **I:** 259; **II:** 508; **Retro. Supp. I:** 19, 137

Asali, Muna, **Supp. XIII:** 121, 126

"As a Little Child" (Taggard), **Supp. XXII:** 272

"As a Young Man" (Hayes), **Supp. XXVI:** 134–135

Asbury, Herbert, **Supp. IV Part 1:** 353

"Ascent, The" (Rash), **Supp. XXVII:** 228–229

Ascent of F6, The (Auden), **Supp. II Part 1:** 11, 13

Ascent to Truth, The (Merton), **Supp. VIII:** 208

Asch, Nathan, **Supp. XV:** 133, 134; **Supp. XXIII:** 4; **Supp. XXVI: 17–29**

Asch, Sholem, **IV:** 1, 9, 11, 14; **Retro. Supp. II:** 299; **Supp. XXIII:** 1–18; **Supp. XXVI:** 18

Ascherson, Neal, **Supp. XII:** 167

Ascher-Walsh, Rebecca, **Supp. XIX:** 54

"As Close as Breathing" (Jarman), **Supp. XVII:** 120

As David Danced (Bronk), **Supp. XXI:** 24

"As David Danced" (Bronk), **Supp. XXI:** 26

As Does New Hampshire and Other Poems (Sarton), **Supp. VIII:** 259

"As Evening Lays Dying" (Salinas), **Supp. XIII:** 319

"As Flowers Are" (Kunitz), **Supp. III Part 1:** 265

"Ash" (Sobin), **Supp. XVI:** 284–285

Ash, Nathan, **Supp. XXII:** 277

Ashbery, John, **Retro. Supp. I:** 313; **Supp. I Part 1:** 96; **Supp. III Part 1: 1–29; Supp. III Part 2:** 541; **Supp. IV Part 2:** 620; **Supp. IX:** 52; **Supp. VIII:** 272; **Supp. XI:** 139; **Supp. XIII:** 85; **Supp. XIX:** 40, 83; **Supp.**

XV: 176, 177, 178, 188, 250; **Supp. XXI:** 227; **Supp. XXIII:** 207, 209, 210, 211, 215, 217, 220; **Supp. XXIV:** 33, 37, 44; **Supp. XXVI:** 70; **Supp. XXVII:** 17, 18, 22, 23

"Ashes" (Lamott), **Supp. XX: 141**

"Ashes" (Levine), **Supp. V:** 188

"Ashes of the Beacon" (Bierce), **I:** 209

Ashes: Poems Old and New (Levine), **Supp. V:** 178, 188–189

Ashford, Margaret Mary (Daisy), **II:** 426

Ashman, Angela, **Supp. XXIV:** 200

"Ash Wednesday" (Garrett), **Supp. VII:** 109–110

"Ash Wednesday" (Merton), **Supp. VIII:** 199

Ash Wednesday (T. S. Eliot), **I:** 570, 574–575, 578–579, 580, 582, 584, 585; **Retro. Supp. I:** 64

"Ash Wednesday" (T. S. Eliot), **Supp. IV Part 2:** 436

Asian American Authors (Hsu and Palubinskas, eds.), **Supp. X:** 292

Asian American Heritage: An Anthology of Prose and Poetry (Wand), **Supp. X:** 292

Asian Figures (Mervin), **Supp. III Part 1:** 341

Asian Journal of Thomas Merton, The (Merton), **Supp. VIII:** 196, 206, 208

"Asian Peace Offers Rejected without Publication" (R. Bly), **Supp. IV Part 1:** 61

"Asides on the Oboe" (Stevens), **Retro. Supp. I:** 305

"As I Ebb'd with the Ocean of Life" (Whitman), **IV:** 342, 345–346; **Retro. Supp. I:** 404, 405

As I Lay Dying (Faulkner), **II:** 60–61, 69, 73, 74; **IV:** 100; **Retro. Supp. I:** 75, 82, 84, 85, 86, 88, 89, 91, 92; **Supp. IV Part 1:** 47; **Supp. IX:** 99, 103, 251; **Supp. VIII:** 37, 178; **Supp. XIV:** 24

"As I Lay with My Head in Your Lap, Camerado" (Whitman), **IV:** 347

Asimov, Isaac, **Supp. IV Part 1:** 116; **Supp. XVI:** 122

Asinof, Eliot, **II:** 424

As I Remember It (PBS documentary), **Supp. XVIII:** 277

Asirvatham, Sandy, **Supp. XVI:** 249

"As Is the Daughter, So Is Her Mother" (Patchett), **Supp. XII:** 310

"As It Was in the Beginning" (Benét), **Supp. XI:** 56

"As I Walked Out One Evening" (Auden), **Supp. II Part 1:** 13; **Supp. XV:** 126; **Supp. XX:** 138

"As I Went Down by Havre de Grace" (Wylie), **Supp. I Part 2:** 723

Ask a Policeman (Hinojosa), **Supp. XIX: 110–111**

"Ask Me" (Stafford), **Supp. XI:** 326–327

Ask Me Tomorrow (Cozzens), **I:** 365–367, 379

Ask the Dust (Fante), **Supp. XI:** 159, 160, 166, **167–169,** 172, 173, 174

"Ask the Optimist!" (Saunders), **Supp. XIX:** 235

Ask Your Mama (Hughes), **Supp. I Part 1:** 339, 341–342

Ask Your Mama: 12 Moods for Jazz (Hughes), **Retro. Supp. I:** 210, 211

As Little Children (R. P. Smith), **Supp. XIV:** 333

"As One Put Drunk into the Packet Boat" (Ashbery), **Supp. III Part 1:** 18

"Asparagus" (Nelson), **Supp. XVIII:** 178

"Aspects of Robinson" (Kees), **Supp. XV:** 134

Aspects of the Novel (Forster), **Retro. Supp. I:** 232; **Supp. VIII:** 155; **Supp. XXI:** 233

"Aspen and the Stream, The" (Wilbur), **Supp. III Part 2:** 555, 556

Aspern Papers, The (James), **Supp. V:** 101, 102

"Aspern Papers, The" (James), **Retro. Supp. I:** 219, 227, 228

Asphalt Georgics (Carruth), **Supp. XVI:** 54

Asphalt Jungle (film, Huston), **Supp. XIII:** 174

"Asphodel" (Welty), **IV:** 265, 271

"Asphodel, That Greeny Flower" (W. C. Williams), **Retro. Supp. I:** 429

"Aspic and Buttermilk" (Olds), **Supp. X:** 213

Asquith, Herbert Henry, **Retro. Supp. I:** 59

"Ass" (Cisneros), **Supp. VII:** 67

Assante, Armand, **Supp. VIII:** 74

Assassin, The: A Play in Three Acts (Shaw), **Supp. XIX:** 248

Assassins, The (Oates), **Supp. II Part 2:** 512, 517–519

"Assault" (Millay), **III:** 130–131

"Assemblage of Husbands and Wives, An" (Lewis), **II:** 455–456

"Assembloir" (Monson), **Supp. XXIV:** 237

Assembly (O'Hara), **III:** 361

As She Climbed Across the Table (Lethem), **Supp. XVIII: 140–141,** 148

Assignment, Wildlife (LaBastille), **Supp. X: 99,** 104

"Assimiliation in Recent American Jewish Autobiographies" (Krupnick), **Supp. XVI:** 153

Assistant, The (Malamud), **Supp. I Part 2:** 427, 428, 429, 431, 435, 441–445, 451; **Supp. XVI:** 220

Assommoir, L' (Zola), **II:** 291; **III:** 318

Assorted Prose (Updike), **IV:** 215–216, 218; **Retro. Supp. I:** 317, 319, 327

Astaire, Adele, **Supp. XVI:** 187

"As the Mist Leaves No Scar" (Cohen), **Supp. XXVII:** 56

As They Were (M. F. K. Fisher), **Supp. XVII:** 88

As They Were (M. F. K. Fisher), **Supp. XVII:** 89, 91

Astor, Mary, **Supp. IV Part 1:** 356; **Supp. XII:** 173

Astoria, or, Anecdotes of an Enterprise beyond the Rocky Mountains (Irving), **II:** 312

"Astounding News by Electric Express via Norfolk! The Atlantic Crossed in

Three Days Signal Triumph of Mr. Monck's Flying-Machine . . ." (Poe), **III:** 413, 420

Astraea (Holmes), **III:** 82

Astro, Richard, **Supp. I Part 2:** 429, 445

"Astrological Fricassee" (H. Miller), **III:** 187

"Astronomer's Wife" (Boyle), **Supp. XXIV:** 58

Astrophil and Stella (Sidney), **Supp. XIV:** 128

Asturias, Miguel Ángel, **Supp. XXIV:** 89

"As Weary Pilgrim" (Bradstreet), **Supp. I Part 1:** 103, 109, 122

As We Know (Ashbery), **Supp. III Part 1:** 9, 21–25

"As We Know" (Ashbery), **Supp. III Part 1:** 21–22

Aswell, Edward C., **IV:** 458, 459, 461

"Asylum, The" (Carruth), **Supp. XVI:** 48–49

"As You Like It" (Chopin), **Supp. I Part 1:** 217

As You Like It (Shakespeare), **Supp. I Part 1:** 308

"At a Bar" (Ferry), **Supp. XXIV:** 162

"At a Bar in Charlotte Amalie" (Updike), **IV:** 214

"At a Lecture" (Brodsky), **Supp. VIII:** 33

"At a Low Bar" (Ferry), **Supp. XXIV:** 149

"At a March against the Vietnam War" (R. Bly), **Supp. IV Part 1:** 61

"At a Reading" (McClatchy), **Supp. XII:** 256–257

"Atavism of John Tom Little Bear, The" (O. Henry), **Supp. II Part 1:** 410

"At Chênière Caminada" (Chopin), **Supp. I Part 1:** 220

"At Chinese Checkers" (Berryman), **I:** 182

Atchity, Kenneth John, **Supp. XI:** 227

"At Death's Window" (Lamott), **Supp. XX:** 144

At Eighty-Two (Sarton), **Supp. VIII:** 264

Atet A.D. (Mackey), **Supp. XXVII:** 158–159

"At Every Gas Station There Are Mechanics" (Dunn), **Supp. XI:** 144

At Fault (Chopin), **Retro. Supp. II:** 57, 60, **62–63; Supp. I Part 1:** 207, 209–211, 220

"At Fifty" (Bronk), **Supp. XXI:** 31

At Heaven's Gate (Warren), **IV:** 243, 247–248, 251

Atheism Refuted: in a Discourse to Prove the Existence of God (Paine), **Supp. I Part 2:** 517

"Athénaïse" (Chopin), **Retro. Supp. II:** 66, 67; **Supp. I Part 1:** 219–220

At Her Majesty's Request: An African Princess in Victorian England (Myers), **Supp. XXVII:** 209

Atherton, Gertrude, **I:** 199, 207–208; **Supp. XXIV:** 17–32; **Supp. XXVI:** 276

Athey, Jean L., **Supp. XI:** 184

At Home: Essays, 1982–1988 (Vidal), **Supp. IV Part 2:** 682, 687, 688

"At Home With" (column; Leland), **Supp. XV:** 69

"At Kino Viejo, Mexico" (Ríos), **Supp. IV Part 2:** 541

Atkinson, Brooks, **IV:** 288; **Supp. IV Part 2:** 683; **Supp. XIX:** 244; **Supp. XXVII:** 90

Atlanta (film, July), **Supp. XXIV:** 201, 209–210

Atlantis (Doty), **Supp. XI:** 121, **126–129**

"Atlantis" (Doty), **Supp. XI:** 127–128

Atlas, James, **Supp. V:** 233; **Supp. XV:** 25; **Supp. XXIV:** 172

Atlas, The (Vollmann), **Supp. XVII:** 226, 227

Atlas Shrugged (Rand), **Supp. IV Part 2:** 517, 521, 523, 524–526, 528, 531

At Liberty (T. Williams), **IV:** 378

"At Melville's Tomb" (H. Crane), **I:** 393; **Retro. Supp. II:** 76, 78, 80, 82

"At Mother Teresa's" (Nye), **Supp. XIII:** 276

"At Nightfall" (Kooser), **Supp. XIX:** 122–123

At Night the Salmon Move (Carver), **Supp. III Part 1:** 142

At Night the States (Notley), **Supp. XXII:** 224, 231–232

"At night the states" (Notley), **Supp. XXII:** 232

"At North Farm" (Ashbery), **Supp. III Part 1:** 1–2

At Paradise Gate (Smiley), **Supp. VI:** 292, **293–294**

"At Paso Rojo" (Bowles), **Supp. IV Part 1:** 87

At Play in the Fields of the Lord (Matthiessen), **Supp. V:** 199, 202, 204–206, 212

"At Play in the Paradise of Bombs" (Sanders), **Supp. XVI:** 272–273, 274, 277

"At Pleasure By" (Pinsky), **Supp. VI:** 245

"A-Train / Ziggurat / Elegy"(Balakian), **Supp. XXIII:** 32

At Risk (Hoffman), **Supp. X:** 87

"At Sea" (Hemingway), **II:** 258

"At Shaft 11" (Dunbar), **Supp. II Part 1:** 212

"At Sixty" (Davison), **Supp. XXVI:** 77

"At Slim's River" (Haines), **Supp. XII:** 208–209

"At St. Croix" (Dubus), **Supp. VII:** 83, 87

At Sundown (Whittier), **Supp. I Part 2:** 704

"At Sunset" (Simic), **Supp. VIII:** 282

At Swim-Two-Birds (O'Brien), **Supp. XXV:** 65

Attaway, William, **Supp. XXI:** 264

Attebery, Brian, **Supp. IV Part 1:** 101

Attendant, The (Bronk), **Supp. XXI:** 24

"Attendant, The" (Bronk), **Supp. XXI:** 26

"Attention"(Hadas), **Supp. XXIII:** 121

"At That Time, or The History of a Joke" (Paley), **Supp. VI:** 229–230

"At the Alhambra"(P. Benedict), **Supp. XXIII:** 40

At the Back of the North Wind (Macdonald), **Supp. XIII:** 75

"At the Birth of an Age" (Jeffers), **Supp. II Part 2:** 432

"At the Bomb Testing Site" (Stafford), **Supp. XI:** 317–318, 321, 323

At the Bottom of the River (Kincaid), **Supp. VII:** 182–184, 185

"At the 'Cadian Ball" (Chopin), **Retro. Supp. II:** 64, 65, 68

"At the Cancer Clinic" (Kooser), **Supp. XIX:** 127

"At the Chelton-Pulver Game" (Auchincloss), **Supp. IV Part 1:** 27

"At the Drugstore" (Taylor), **Supp. V:** 323

At the Edge of the Body (Jong), **Supp. V:** 115, 130

"At the End of the Curse, a Blessing" (Verducci), **Supp. XXII:** 209

At the End of the Open Road (Simpson), **Supp. IX:** 265, 269, **271–273,** 277

At the End of This Summer: Poems 1948–1954 (Levis), **Supp. XII:** 211

"At the End of War" (Eberhart), **I:** 522–523

"At the Executed Murderer's Grave" (Wright), **Supp. III Part 2:** 595, 597

"At the Fishhouses" (Bishop), **Retro. Supp. II:** 45; **Supp. I Part 1:** 90, 92

At the Gates of the Animal Kingdom (Hempel), **Supp. XXI:** 115, **122–124**

"At the Grave of My Guardian Angel: St. Louis Cemetery, New Orleans" (Levis), **Supp. XI:** 268–269

"At the Gym" (Doty), **Supp. XI:** 135

"At the Indian Store" (McCarriston), **Supp. XIV:** 271

"At the Lake" (Oliver), **Supp. VII:** 244

"At the Landing" (Welty), **IV:** 265–266; **Retro. Supp. I:** 348

"At the Last" (Bynner), **Supp. XV:** 44

"At the Last Rites for Two Hot Rodders" (X. J. Kennedy), **Supp. XV:** 166

At the Mountains of Madness (Lovecraft), **Supp. XXII:** 58; **Supp. XXV:** 109, 111, 114

"At the Owl Club, North Gulfport, Mississippi, 1950" (Trethewey), **Supp. XXI:** 249

At the Owl Woman Saloon (Gallagher), **Supp. XXIV:** 166, 172, 173, 174, 175–177

"At the Premiere" (Keillor), **Supp. XVI:** 167

At the Rendezvous of Victory (C. L. R. James), **Supp. XXI:** 172

At the Root of Stars (Barnes), **Supp. III Part 1:** 34

At the Sign of the Sphinx (Wells), **Supp. XXVI:** 274

"At the Site of Last Night's Fire" (Davison), **Supp. XXVI:** 69

"At the Slackening of the Tide" (Wright), **Supp. III Part 2:** 597

"At the Street Corner" (Ferry), **Supp. XXIV:** 162

"At the Tomb of Walt Whitman" (Kunitz), **Supp. III Part 1:** 262

"At the Tourist Centre in Boston" (Atwood), **Supp. XIII:** 33

"At the Town Dump" (Kenyon), **Supp. VII:** 167

"At the Worcester Museum" (Pinsky), **Supp. VI:** 251

"At the Zoo in Spain" (Major), **Supp. XXII:** 182

"Atticus Finch and the Mad Dog: Harper Lee's *To Kill a Mockingbird*" (Jones), **Supp. VIII:** 128

"Atticus Finch—Right and Wrong" (Freedman), **Supp. VIII:** 127–128

"Attic Which Is Desire, The" (W. C. Williams), **Retro. Supp. I:** 422

"At Tikal" (Bronk), **Supp. XXI: 28–29**

"At Times in Flight: A Parable" (H. Roth), **Supp. IX:** 234

Attitudes toward History (Burke), **I:** 274

Atwan, Robert, **Supp. XVI:** 273, 277

At Weddings and Wakes (McDermott), **Supp. XVIII:** 155, **160–162,** 166

"At White River" (Haines), **Supp. XII:** 208–209

Atwood, Margaret, **Supp. IV Part 1:** 252; **Supp. V:** 119; **Supp. XI:** 317; **Supp. XIII: 19–39,** 291, 306; **Supp. XXI:** 39, 42

"Atwood's Gorgon Touch" (Davey), **Supp. XIII:** 33

"Aubade" (McCarriston), **Supp. XIV:** 271

"Aubade: November" (McCarriston), **Supp. XIV:** 261–262

"Aubade of an Early Homo Sapiens" (C. Frost), **Supp. XV:** 97–98

"Aubade: Opal and Silver" (Doty), **Supp. XI:** 129

"Au Bal Musette" (Van Vechten), **Supp. II Part 2:** 735

Auchincloss, Hugh D., **Supp. IV Part 2:** 679

Auchincloss, Louis, **I:** 375; **III:** 66; **Retro. Supp. I:** 370, 373; **Supp. IV Part 1: 21–38**

"Auction" (Simic), **Supp. VIII:** 278

"Auction, The" (Crane), **I:** 411

"Auction Model 1934" (Z. Fitzgerald), **Supp. IX:** 61

Auden, W. H., **I:** 71, 381, 539; **II:** 367, 368, 371, 376, 586; **III:** 17, 134, 269, 271, 292, 476–477, 504, 527, 530, 542, 615; **IV:** 136, 138, 240, 430; **Retro. Supp. I:** 430; **Retro. Supp. II:** 183, 242, 244, 323; **Supp. I Part 1:** 270; **Supp. I Part 2:** 552, 610; **Supp. II Part 1: 1–28; Supp. III Part 1:** 2, 3, 14, 26, 60, 61, 64, 341; **Supp. III Part 2:** 591, 595; **Supp. IV Part 1:** 79, 84, 136, 225, 302, 313; **Supp. IV Part 2:** 440, 465; **Supp. IX:** 94, 287, 288; **Supp. V:** 337; **Supp. VIII:** 19, 21, 22, 23, 30, 32, 155, 190; **Supp. X:** 35, 57, 59, 115–116, 117, 118–119; **Supp. XI:** 243, 244; **Supp. XII:** 253, 264–265, 266, 269–270; **Supp. XIV:** 156, 158, 160, 162, 163; **Supp. XIX:** 147, 151; **Supp. XV:** 74, 117–118, 139, 144, 186; **Supp. XX: 138; Supp. XXI:** 60, 98; **Supp. XXIII:** 117, 207

"Auden's OED" (McClatchy), **Supp. XII:** 264–265

"Audition" (Alvarez), **Supp. VII:** 10

Audubon, John James, **III:** 210; **IV:** 265; **Supp. IX:** 171; **Supp. XVI: 1–14**

Audubon, John Woodhouse, **Supp. XVI:** 10

Audubon, Maria Rebecca, **Supp. XVI:** 11

Audubon, Victor Gifford, **Supp. XVI:** 10

Audubon and His Journals (M. Audubon, ed.), **Supp. XVI:** 11, 12

Audubon Reader, The: The Best Writings of John James Audubon (Sanders, ed.), **Supp. XVI:** 269

Auer, Jane. *See* Bowles, Jane

Auerbach, Eric, **III:** 453

Auerbach, Nina, **Supp. I Part 1:** 40

"August" (Oliver), **Supp. VII:** 235

"August" (Rich), **Supp. I Part 2:** 564

August, Timothy K., **Supp. XXVI:** 210, 211

"August 1968" (Auden), **Supp. II Part 1:** 25

"August 2026: There Will Come Soft Rains" (Bradbury), **Supp. XXVII:** 295

"August Darks, The" (Clampitt), **Supp. IX:** 43, **50–51,** 52

Augustine, Saint, **I:** 279, 290; **II:** 537; **III:** 259, 270, 292, 300; **IV:** 69, 126; **Retro. Supp. I:** 247; **Supp. VIII:** 203; **Supp. XI:** 245; **Supp. XIII:** 89; **Supp. XXI:** 83; **Supp. XXII:** 92–93

August Snow (Price), **Supp. VI:** 264

"Au Jardin" (Pound), **III:** 465–466

Aunt Carmen's Book of Practical Saints (Mora), **Supp. XIII: 227–229**

"Aunt Cynthy Dallett" (Jewett), **II:** 393

"Aunt Gladys" (Karr), **Supp. XI:** 241

"Aunt Granny Lith" (Offutt), **Supp. XIX:** 165, 166

"Aunt Imogen" (Robinson), **III:** 521

"Aunt Jemima of the Ocean Waves" (Hayden), **Supp. II Part 1:** 368, 379

"Aunt Jennifer's Tigers" (Rich), **Supp. XV:** 252

Aunt Jo's Scrapbooks (Alcott), **Supp. I Part 1:** 43

"Aunt Mary" (Oliver), **Supp. VII:** 232

"Aunt Mary" (Stowe), **Supp. I Part 2:** 587

"Aunt Moon's Young Man" (Hogan), **Supp. IV Part 1:** 400

"Aunt Rectita's Good Friday" (X. J. Kennedy), **Supp. XV:** 166

"Aunt Sarah" (R. Lowell), **II:** 554

"Aunt Sue's Stories" (Hughes), **Retro. Supp. I:** 197, 199

"Aunt Violet's Canadian Honeymoon/ 1932" (Shields), **Supp. VII:** 311

"Aunt Violet's Things" (Shields), **Supp. VII:** 311–312

"Aurelia: Moon Jellies" (Mora), **Supp. XIII:** 224

"Aurelio" (Di Piero), **Supp. XIX:** 38

Au revoir les enfants (film, Malle), **Supp. XXIII:** 122

Aurora 7 (Mallon), **Supp. XIX:** 132, **135–136**

Aurora Dawn (Wouk), **Supp. XXV:** 255, 258

Aurora Leigh (E. Browning), **Retro. Supp. I:** 33; **Supp. XI:** 197

Aurora Means Dawn (Sanders), **Supp. XVI:** 268

Auroras of Autumn, The (Stevens), **Retro. Supp. I:** 297, 300, **309–312**

"Auroras of Autumn, The" (Stevens), **Retro. Supp. I:** 311, 312; **Supp. III Part 1:** 12

Auschwitz: the Nazis and the "Final Solution" (television documentary), **Supp. XVII:** 40

Auslander, Joseph, **Supp. XIV:** 120

"Auspex" (Frost), **Retro. Supp. I:** 122

"Auspex" (J. R. Lowell), **Supp. I Part 2:** 424

Austen, Jane, **I:** 130, 339, 375, 378; **II:** 272, 278, 287, 568–569, 577; **IV:** 8; **Retro. Supp. I:** 354; **Supp. I Part 1:** 267; **Supp. I Part 2:** 656, 715; **Supp. IV Part 1:** 300; **Supp. IX:** 128; **Supp. VIII:** 125, 167; **Supp. XII:** 310; **Supp. XV:** 338; **Supp. XX: 108; Supp. XXII:** 206; **Supp. XXVI:** 130; **Supp. XXVII:** 187

Austenfeld, Thomas, **Supp. XXIV:** 64

Auster, Paul, **Supp. XII: 21–39; Supp. XIV:** 292; **Supp. XXI:** 20; **Supp. XXVII:** 26

Austerities (Simic), **Supp. VIII: 276–278,** 283

"Austerities" (Simic), **Supp. VIII:** 277

"Austerity Measures" (Stallings), **Supp. XXV:** 221

"Austerity Measures: A Letter from Greece" (Stallings), **Supp. XXV:** 221, 224, 225

Austin, Mary, **Supp. XXVI:** 31

Austin, Mary Hunter, **Retro. Supp. I:** 7; **Supp. IV Part 2:** 503; **Supp. X:** 29; **Supp. XIII:** 154

"Authentic Unconscious, The" (Trilling), **Supp. III Part 2:** 512

Author and Agent: Eudora Welty and Diarmuid Russell (Kreyling), **Retro. Supp. I:** 342, 345, 347, 349–350

"Author at Sixty, The" (Wilson), **IV:** 426

"Author of 'Beltraffio,' The" (James), **Retro. Supp. I:** 227

"Author's Explanation, The" (Larsen), **Supp. XVIII:** 131

"Author's House" (Fitzgerald), **Retro. Supp. I:** 98

"Author's Reflections, An: Willie Loman, Walter Younger, and He Who Must Live" (Hansberry), **Supp. IV Part 1:** 370

"Author to Her Book, The" (Bradstreet), **Supp. I Part 1:** 119; **Supp. V:** 117–118; **Supp. XV:** 125–126

"Autism Poem #20: The Knot Garden"(Crooker), **Supp. XXIII:** 56–57

"Autobiographical Note" (H. Miller), **III:** 174–175

"Autobiographical Notes" (Baldwin), **Supp. I Part 1:** 54

"Autobiographical Notes" (Holmes), **Supp. I Part 1:** 301

"Autobiographic Chapter, An" (Bourne), **I:** 236

Autobiography (Franklin), **II:** 102, 103, 108, 121–122, 302

Autobiography (James), **I:** 462

"Autobiography" (MacLeish), **III:** 20

Autobiography (Van Buren), **III:** 473

Autobiography (W. C. Williams), **Supp. I Part 1:** 254

Autobiography (Zukofsky), **Supp. III Part 2:** 627

Autobiography by Jesus of Nazareth (Pettis), **Supp. XXIII:** 189

"Autobiography"(Dybek), **Supp. XXIII:** 78

"Autobiography in the Shape of a Book Review" (Bynner), **Supp. XV:** 40

"Autobiography of a Confluence, The" (Gunn Allen), **Supp. IV Part 1:** 321

Autobiography of Alice B. Toklas, The (Stein), **IV:** 26, 30, 35, 43; **Supp. IV Part 1:** 11, 81

Autobiography of an Ex-Colored Man, The (J. W. Johnson), **Supp. II Part 1:** 33, 194; **Supp. XVIII:** 127; **Supp. XXII:** 7

Autobiography of a Schizophrenic Girl (Renée), **Supp. XVI:** 64, 66

Autobiography of a Thief, The (Hapgood), **Supp. XVII:** 96, 101–102

Autobiography of Benjamin Franklin (Franklin), **Supp. IV Part 1:** 5

Autobiography of LeRoi Jones, The (Baraka), **Retro. Supp. I:** 411

Autobiography of Malcolm X (Little), **Supp. I Part 1:** 66; **Supp. X:** 27; **Supp. XIII:** 264; **Supp. XXII:** 95

Autobiography of Mark Twain, The (Twain), **IV:** 209

Autobiography of My Dead Brother (Myers), **Supp. XXVII:** 204–205

Autobiography of My Mother, The (Kincaid), **Supp. VII:** 182, 188–190, 191, 192, 193

Autobiography of Red: A Novel in Verse (Carson), **Supp. XII:** 97, **106–110**

Autobiography of Upton Sinclair, The (Sinclair), **Supp. V:** 276, 282

Autobiography of W. E. B. Du Bois, The (Du Bois), **Supp. II Part 1:** 159, 186

Autobiography of William Carlos Williams, The (W. C. Williams), **Retro. Supp. I:** 51, 428

Autocrat of the Breakfast-Table, The (Holmes), **Supp. I Part 1:** 306–307

"Autographic Disclosures and Genealogies of Desire in Alison Bechdel's *Fun Home*" (Watson), **Supp. XXV:** 8

"Automatic Gate, The" (Southern), **Supp. XI:** 294

"Automotive Passacaglia" (H. Miller), **III:** 186

"Autopsy Room, The" (Carver), **Supp. III Part 1:** 137

"Auto Wreck" (Shapiro), **Supp. II Part 2:** 706

"Autre Temps" (Wharton), **IV:** 320, 324

"Autumn" (Berrigan), **Supp. XXIV:** 37

"Autumn, Mist" (Hull), **Supp. XXI:** 133

"Autumn Afternoon" (Farrell), **II:** 45

"Autumnal" (Eberhart), **I:** 540–541

"Autumn Begins in Martins Ferry, Ohio" (Wright), **Supp. III Part 2:** 599

"Autumn Courtship, An" (Caldwell), **I:** 309

"Autumn Equinox" (Skloot), **Supp. XX:** 202

Autumn Garden, The (Hellman), **Supp. I Part 1:** 285–286, 290

"Autumn Garden, The: Mechanics and Dialectics" (Felheim), **Supp. I Part 1:** 297

"Autumn Holiday, An" (Jewett), **II:** 391; **Retro. Supp. II:** 140–141

"Autumn Musings" (Harte), **Supp. II Part 1:** 336

"Autumn of the Revolutionary, The" (Goldman), **Supp. XXV:** 54–55

"Autumn's Day" (Rilke; Berrigan, trans.), **Supp. XXIV:** 37

Autumn Spring (Pickering), **Supp. XXI:** 204–205, 206

"Autumn Within" (Longfellow), **II:** 499

"Autumn Woods" (Bryant), **Supp. I Part 1:** 164

Autum of the Patriarch, The (García Márquez), **Supp. XXIV:** 89

"Au Vieux Jardin" (Aldington), **Supp. I Part 1:** 257

"Aux Imagistes" (W. C. Williams), **Supp. I Part 1:** 266

Available World, The (Monson), **Supp. XXIV:** 230, **239–240,** 241

Avakian, Aram, **Supp. XI:** 294, 295, 309

Avalanche (Boyle), **Supp. XXIV:** 62

Avalanche, The (Atherton), **Supp. XXIV:** 24–25

"Ave Atque Vale" (Bynner), **Supp. XV:** 49

Avedon, Richard, **Supp. I Part 1:** 58; **Supp. V:** 194; **Supp. X:** 15

Aveling, Edward, **Supp. XVI:** 85

"Avenue" (Pinsky), **Supp. VI:** 248

Avenue Bearing the Initial of Christ into the New World: Poems 1946–1964 (Kinnell), **Supp. III Part 1:** 235, 239–241

"Avenue of the Americas" (Simic), **Supp. VIII:** 278

"Average Torture" (Karr), **Supp. XI:** 243

Avery, George C., **Supp. XX:** **84**

Avery, John, **Supp. I Part 1:** 153

"Avey" (Toomer), **Supp. IX:** 317

Avi, **Supp. XXVII:** 212

Avon's Harvest (Robinson), **III:** 510

Awake and Sing! (Odets), **Supp. II Part 2:** 530, 531, 536–538, 550; **Supp. IV Part 2:** 587

"Awake at Midnight"(Schott), **Supp. XXIII:** 246

Awake in Spain (O'Hara), **Supp. XXIII:** 216

Awakening, The (Chopin), **Retro. Supp. I:** 10; **Retro. Supp. II:** 57, 59, 60, 67, **68–71,** 73; **Supp. I Part 1:** 200, 201, 202, 211, 220–225; **Supp. V:** 304; **Supp. VIII:** 198; **Supp. XII:** 170

Awakening Land, The (Richter), **Supp. XVIII:** 207, 215

Away from Her (film), **Supp. XXVII:** 193

Awful Rowing Toward God, The (Sexton), **Supp. II Part 2:** 694–696

Awiakta, Marilou, **Supp. IV Part 1:** 319, 335

Awkward Age, The (James), **II:** 332; **Retro. Supp. I:** 229, **230–231**

Axe Handles (Snyder), **Supp. VIII:** 303–305

Axel's Castle: A Study in the Imaginative Literature of 1870 to 1930 (Wilson), **I:** 185; **II:** 577; **IV:** 428, 431, 438, 439, 443; **Supp. VIII:** 101

"Ax-Helve, The" (Frost), **Retro. Supp. I:** 133

Azikewe, Nnamdi, **Supp. IV Part 1:** 361

"Aztec Angel" (Salinas), **Supp. XIII:** 314

Aztec Treasure House, The: New and Selected Essays (Connell), **Supp. XIV:** 80, 97

B

"Bab, the Sub-Deb" (Rinehart), **Supp. XXV:** 195

Babbitt (Lewis), **II:** 442, 443–445, 446, 447, 449; **III:** 63–64, 394; **IV:** 326

Babbitt, Irving, **I:** 247; **II:** 456; **III:** 315, 461, 613; **IV:** 439; **Retro. Supp. I:** 55; **Supp. I Part 2:** 423

Babcock, Elisha, **Supp. II Part 1:** 69

Babel, Isaac, **IV:** 1; **Supp. IX:** 260; **Supp. XII:** 308–309; **Supp. XVII:** 41; **Supp. XXIII:** 68

Babel, Isaak, **Supp. XIV:** 83, 84

Babel to Byzantium (Dickey), **Supp. IV Part 1:** 177, 185

Baber, Asa, **Supp. XXIII:** 52

Baber, Bob Henry, **Supp. XXIII:** 39

Babeuf, François, **Supp. I Part 2:** 518

"Babies, The" (Strand), **Supp. IV Part 2:** 625

Babouk (Endore), **Supp. XVII:** 56–57, 61, **64**

Baby, Come on Inside (Wagoner), **Supp. IX:** **335**

"Baby, The" (Barthelme), **Supp. IV Part 1:** 49

Baby Doll (T. Williams), **IV:** 383, 386, 387, 389, 395

"Baby Face" (Sandburg), **III:** 584

"Babylon Revisited" (Fitzgerald), **II:** 95; **Retro. Supp. I:** 109

"Baby or the Botticelli, The" (Gass), **Supp. VI:** 92

"Baby Pictures of Famous Dictators" (Simic), **Supp. VIII:** 276

"Baby's Breath" (Bambara), **Supp. XI:** 15, 16

"Babysitter, The" (Coover), **Supp. V:** 43–44

Baby Sweet's (Andrews), **Supp. XXVI:** 7–9, 12, 14

"Baby Villon" (Levine), **Supp. V:** 182

Baby with the Bathwater (Durang), **Supp. XXIV:** 121–122

Bacall, Lauren, **Supp. IV Part 1:** 130

"Baccalaureate" (MacLeish), **III:** 4

Bacchae, The (Euripides), **Supp. VIII:** 182

Bach, Caleb, **Supp. XXV:** 53

Bach, Johann Sebastian, **Supp. I Part 1:** 363; **Supp. III Part 2:** 611, 612, 619

Bacardy, Don, **Supp. XIV:** 166, 170, 172, 173

Bache, Richard, **Supp. I Part 2:** 504

Bachelard, Gaston, **Supp. XIII:** 225; **Supp. XVI:** 292

"Bachelor Girl, The" (Boyce), **Supp. XXI:** 3

Bachelor Girls (Wasserstein), **Supp. XV:** 327–328, 332

Bachman, John, **Supp. XVI:** 10, 11

Bachmann, Ingeborg, **Supp. IV Part 1:** 310; **Supp. VIII:** 272

Bachofen, J. J., **Supp. I Part 2:** 560, 567

Back Bog Beast Bait (Shepard), **Supp. III Part 2:** 437, 438

Backbone (C. Bly), **Supp. XVI:** 34–36, 37, 40, 41

Back Country, The (Snyder), **Supp. VIII:** 296–299

"Back from the Argentine" (Leopold), **Supp. XIV:** 186

"Background with Revolutionaries" (MacLeish), **III:** 14–15

"Back in the Saddle Again" (Swados), **Supp. XIX:** 259

Back in the World (Wolff), **Supp. VII:** 344, 345

"Back in Tulsa Again" (Brainard), **Supp. XXVII:** 25

Backis, Charles, **Supp. XXI:** 195

"Backlash Blues, The" (Hughes), **Supp. I Part 1:** 343

"Backlash of Kindness, A" (Nye), **Supp. XIII:** 285, 286

"Backslider, The" (R. Fisher), **Supp. XIX:** 70, 71

"Back Street Guy" (Halliday), **Supp. XIX:** 88

Back to China (Fiedler), **Supp. XIII:** 102–103

Back to Methuselah (Shaw), **IV:** 64

"Backwacking: A Plea to the Senator" (Ellison), **Retro. Supp. II:** 126; **Supp. II Part 1:** 248

Backward Glance, A (Wharton), **Retro. Supp. I:** 360, 363, 366, 378, 380, 382; **Supp. XX: 229; Supp. XXVI:** 271

"Backward Glance o'er Travel'd Roads, A" (Whitman), **IV:** 348

Bacon, Francis, **II:** 1, 8, 11, 15–16, 111; **III:** 284; **Retro. Supp. I:** 247; **Supp. I Part 1:** 310; **Supp. I Part 2:** 388; **Supp. IX:** 104; **Supp. XIV:** 22, 210

Bacon, Helen, **Supp. X:** 57

Bacon, Katie, **Supp. XXII:** 207; **Supp. XXIII:** 275

Bacon, Leonard, **II:** 530; **Supp. XXII:** 273

Bacon, Roger, **IV:** 69

"Bacterial War, The" (Nemerov), **III:** 272

Bad and the Beautiful, The (film), **Supp. XVIII:** 250

Bad Boy: A Memoir (Myers), **Supp. XXVII:** 209, 210

Bad Boy Brawly Brown (Mosley), **Supp. XIII:** 237, 239, 240–241

Bad Boys (Cisneros), **Supp. VII:** 58

"Bad Company" (Gallagher), **Supp. XXIV:** 174, 176

"Bad Dream" (Taylor), **Supp. V:** 320

Badè, William Frederic, **Supp. IX:** 178

"Badeye" (Rash), **Supp. XXVII:** 216–217

"Bad Fisherman, The" (Wagoner), **Supp. IX:** 328

Bad for Each Other (film), **Supp. XIII:** 174

"Badger" (Clare), **II:** 387

Badger, A. G., **Supp. I Part 1:** 356

"Badger and the Bear, The" (Zitkala-Ša), **Supp. XXV:** 275

Bad Government and Silly Literature (C. Bly), **Supp. XVI:** 37, 38, 40

Badlands (film; Malick), **Supp. XV:** 351

"Bad Lay" (McCarriston), **Supp. XIV:** 267

Badley, Linda, **Supp. V:** 148

Bad Man, A (Elkin), **Supp. VI: 47**

Bad Man Ballad (Sanders), **Supp. XVI:** 268

Bad Man Blues: A Portable George Garrett (Garrett), **Supp. VII:** 111

"Bad Music, The" (Jarrell), **II:** 369

"Bad People" (Halliday), **Supp. XIX:** 90, 91

"Bad Summer on K2, A" (Krakauer and Child), **Supp. XVIII:** 107, 108

"Bad Woman, A" (Fante), **Supp. XI:** 165

Baeck, Leo, **Supp. V:** 260

Baecker, Diann L., **Supp. VIII:** 128

Baer, William, **Supp. XIII:** 112, 118, 129; **Supp. XXIII:** 124

Baez, Joan, **Supp. IV Part 1:** 200; **Supp. VIII:** 200, 202; **Supp. XVIII:** 24, 25–26, 27

Bag of Bones (King), **Supp. V:** 139, 148, 151

"Bagpipe Music" (MacNeice), **Supp. X:** 117

"Bahá'í Faith: Only Church in World That Does Not Discriminate" (Locke), **Supp. XIV:** 200

Bahá'u'lláh, **Supp. XX: 117, 121, 122**

"Bahá'u'lláh in the Garden of Ridwan" (Hayden), **Supp. II Part 1:** 370, 378

Bahr, David, **Supp. XV:** 66

Bahr, Thomas, **Supp. XXII:** 206, 214

"Bailbondsman, The" (Elkin), **Supp. VI:** 49, **50,** 58

Bailey, Gamaliel, **Supp. I Part 2:** 587, 590

Bailey, Peter, **Supp. XVI:** 69

Bailey, William, **Supp. IV Part 2:** 631, 634

Bailey's Café (Naylor), **Supp. VIII: 226–228**

Bailyn, Bernard, **Supp. I Part 2:** 484, 506

Bair, Deirdre, **Supp. X:** 181, 186, 187, 188, 192, 194, 195, 196, 197

Baird, Linnett, **Supp. XII:** 299

Baird, Peggy, **I:** 385, 401

Baiting the Void (Schott), **Supp. XXIII: 247–248**

Bakan, David, **I:** 59

Baker, Carlos, **II:** 259

Baker, Chet, **Supp. XXI:** 131

Baker, David, **Supp. IX:** 298; **Supp. XI:** 121, 142, 153; **Supp. XII:** 175, 191–192; **Supp. XIX:** 115

Baker, George Pierce, **III:** 387; **IV:** 453, 455

Baker, Gladys, **Supp. XIV:** 121

Baker, Houston, **Supp. XXII:** 6

Baker, Houston A., Jr., **Retro. Supp. II:** 121; **Supp. IV Part 1:** 365; **Supp. X:** 324

Baker, Jeff, **Supp. XXIV:** 166, 178

Baker, Katherine, **Supp. XX: 69**

Baker, Kevin, **Supp. XIV:** 96

Baker, Mabel, **Supp. XVIII:** 259, 263, 266–267, 269

Baker, Nicholson, **Supp. XIII: 41–57**

Baker, Robert, **Supp. XVI:** 288, 290

Bakerman, Jane S., **Supp. IV Part 2:** 468

Bakhtin, Mikhail, **Retro. Supp. II:** 273; **Supp. IV Part 1:** 301; **Supp. X:** 120, 239; **Supp. XXII:** 259

Bakst, Léon, **Supp. IX:** 66

Bakunin, Mikhail Aleksandrovich, **IV:** 429

Balaban, John, **Supp. XIX:** 281

Balakian, Anna, **Supp. XXIII:** 20

Balakian, Diran, **Supp. XXIII:** 28

Balakian, Grigoris, **Supp. XXIII:** 28, 29–32

Balakian, Jan, **Supp. XV:** 327

Balakian, Nona, **Supp. XXIII:** 20

Balakian, Peter, **Supp. XXIII: 19–34**

"Balance" (Bierds), **Supp. XVII:** 31

"Balance" (Nelson), **Supp. XVIII:** 174–175

Balbo, Ned, **Supp. XIX:** 161; **Supp. XVII:** 120

Balbuena, Bernado de, **Supp. V:** 11

Balch, Emily Greene, **Supp. I Part 1:** 25

Balcony, The (Genet), **I:** 84

Bald Soprano, The (Ionesco), **I:** 74

Baldwin, David, **Supp. I Part 1:** 47, 48, 49, 50, 51, 54, 65, 66

Baldwin, James, **Retro. Supp. II: 1–17;** **Supp. I Part 1: 47–71,** 337, 341; **Supp. II Part 1:** 40; **Supp. III Part 1:** 125; **Supp. IV Part 1:** 1, 10, 11, 163, 369; **Supp. V:** 201; **Supp. VIII:** 88, 198, 235, 349; **Supp. X:** 136, 324; **Supp. XI:** 288, 294; **Supp. XIII:** 46, 111, 181, 186, 294; **Supp. XIV:** 54, 71, 73, 306; **Supp. XVI:** 135, 141, 143; **Supp. XVIII:** 25; **Supp. XX: 147; Supp. XXI:** 245; **Supp. XXIV:** 185; **Supp. XXVII:** 201

Baldwin, Kara, **Supp. XXVII:** 216

Baldwin, Samuel, **Supp. I Part 1:** 48

Bales, Jack, **Supp. XXVII:** 100, 106

Balint, Benjamin, **Supp. XXVII:** 134

Balitas, Vincent D., **Supp. XVI:** 222; **Supp. XXVI:** 149

Balkun, Mary McAleer, **Supp. XX: 281**

Ball, Gordon, **Supp. XIV:** 148

Ball, John, **Supp. XV:** 202

"Ballad: Between the Box Cars" (Warren), **IV:** 245

"Ballade" (MacLeish), **III:** 4

"Ballade at Thirty-Five" (Parker), **Supp. IX:** 192

"Ballade for the Duke of Orléans" (Wilbur), **Supp. III Part 2:** 556

"Ballade of Broken Flutes, The" (Robinson), **III:** 505

"Ballade of Meaty Inversions" (White), **Supp. I Part 2:** 676

"Ballad of a Thin Man" (song, Dylan), **Supp. XVIII:** 30, 31

"Ballad of Aunt Geneva, The" (Nelson), **Supp. XVIII:** 175

"Ballad of Billie Potts, The" (Warren), **IV:** 241–242, 243, 253

"Ballad of Carmilhan, The" (Longfellow), **II:** 505

"ballad of chocolate Mabbie, the" (Brooks), **Supp. IV Part 1:** 15

"Ballad of Dead Ladies, The" (Villon), **Retro. Supp. I:** 286

Ballad of Dingus Magee, The (Markson), **Supp. XVII:** 139, 141

"Ballad of East and West, The" (Kipling), **Supp. IX:** 246; **Supp. XX:** 23

"Ballad of Jesse Neighbours, The" (Humphrey), **Supp. IX:** 100

"Ballad of Jesus of Nazareth, A" (Masters), **Supp. I Part 2:** 459

"Ballad of John Cable and Three Gentlemen" (Merwin), **Supp. III Part 1:** 342

"Ballad of Larry and Club" (Jarman), **Supp. XVII:** 115

"Ballad of Nat Turner, The" (Hayden), **Supp. II Part 1:** 378

"Ballad of Pearl May Lee, The" (Brooks), **Supp. III Part 1:** 74, 75

"Ballad of Plastic Fred, The" (Gansworth), **Supp. XXVI:** 104

Ballad of Remembrance, A (Hayden), **Supp. II Part 1:** 367

"Ballad of Remembrance, A" (Hayden), **Supp. II Part 1:** 368, 372, 373

"Ballad of Ruby, The" (Sarton), **Supp. VIII:** 259–260

"Ballad of San Isidro, The" (Espaillat), **Supp. XXI:** 108

"Ballad of Sue Ellen Westerfield, The" (Hayden), **Supp. II Part 1:** 364

Ballad of the Brown Girl, The (Cullen), **Supp. IV Part 1:** 167, 168, 169–170, 173

"Ballad of the Brown Girl, The" (Cullen), **Supp. IV Part 1:** 168

"Ballad of the Children of the Czar, The" (Schwartz), **Supp. II Part 2:** 649

"Ballad of the Girl Whose Name Is Mud" (Hughes), **Retro. Supp. I:** 205

"Ballad of the Goodly Fere", **III:** 458

"Ballad of the Harp-Weaver" (Millay), **III:** 135

"Ballad of the Sad Cafe, The" (McCullers), **II:** 586, 587, 588, 592, 595, 596–600, 604, 605, 606

"Ballad of the Sixties" (Sarton), **Supp. VIII:** 259

"Ballad of Trees and the Master, A" (Lanier), **Supp. I Part 1:** 370

"Ballad of Typical Lovers" (Taggard), **Supp. XXII:** 277

"Ballad of William Sycamore, The" (Benét), **Supp. XI:** 44, 47

Ballads and Other Poems (Longfellow), **II:** 489; **III:** 412, 422; **Retro. Supp. II:** 157, 168

Ballads for Sale (A. Lowell), **II:** 527

"Ballads of Lenin" (Hughes), **Supp. I Part 1:** 331

Ballantyne, Sheila, **Supp. V:** 70

Ballard, J. G., **Supp. XVI:** 123, 124; **Supp. XVIII:** 136

Ballard, Josephine. *See* McMurtry, Josephine

"Ballena" (Mora), **Supp. XIII:** 224

"Ballet in Numbers for Mary Ellen, A" (Karr), **Supp. XI:** 241

"Ballet of a Buffoon, The" (Sexton), **Supp. II Part 2:** 693

"Ballet of Central Park, The" (Boyle), **Supp. XXIV:** 59

"Ballet of the Fifth Year, The" (Schwartz), **Supp. II Part 2:** 650

Ball Four (Bouton), **Supp. XX:** 274

"Ball Game, The" (Creeley), **Supp. IV Part 1:** 140

Ballistics (Collins), **Supp. XXI:** 57, 65

"Ballistics" (Collins), **Supp. XXI:** 65

"Balloon Hoax, The" (Poe), **III:** 413, 420

Balloonists, The (Biss), **Supp. XXVI:** 45, 48–50

"Balm of Recognition, The: Rectifying Wrongs through Generations" (E. Hoffman, lecture), **Supp. XVI:** 155

Balo (Toomer), **Supp. III Part 2:** 484

Balsan, Consuelo, **IV:** 313–314

Balthus, **Supp. IV Part 2:** 623

Balthus Poems, The (Dobyns), **Supp. XIII:** 87

Baltimore, Lord, **I:** 132

Balzac, Honoré de, **I:** 103, 123, 339, 376, 474, 485, 499, 509, 518; **II:** 307, 322, 324, 328, 336, 337; **III:** 61, 174, 184, 320, 382; **IV:** 192; **Retro. Supp. I:** 91, 217, 218, 235; **Retro. Supp. II:** 93; **Supp. I Part 2:** 647; **Supp. XVI:** 72

Bambara, Toni Cade, **Supp. XI:** 1–23

Bam opgrunt (At the abyss) (Asch), **Supp. XXIII:** 6

Banana Book, The (Brainard), **Supp. XXVII:** 20, 27–28

Banana Bottom (McKay), **Supp. X:** 132, **139–140**

Bananas (film; Allen), **Supp. XV:** 3, 4

Bancal, Jean, **Supp. I Part 2:** 514

Bancroft, George, **I:** 544; **Supp. I Part 2:** 479; **Supp. XXII:** 33

Band, Millen, **Supp. XVIII:** 238

Bandaged Nude, The (Ryan as Finnegan), **Supp. XVIII:** 233, **235–236**

"Bandages" (Davison), **Supp. XXVI:** 72

Bandbox (Mallon), **Supp. XIX:** 132, 143

Band of Angels (Warren), **IV:** 245, 254–255

Bandung Files (television series), **Supp. XXI:** 170

Bang the Drum Slowly (Harris), **II:** 424–425

Banjo: A Story without a Plot (McKay), **Supp. X:** 132, **138–139**

"Banjo Song, A" (Dunbar), **Supp. II Part 1:** 197

Bank Director's Son, The: A Real and Intensely Interesting Revelation of City Life (Lippard), **Supp. XXIII:** 184

Bankhead, Tallulah, **IV:** 357; **Supp. IV Part 2:** 574

"Banking Potatoes" (Komunyakaa), **Supp. XIII:** 126

"Bank of England Restriction, The" (Adams), **I:** 4

Banks, Carolyn, **Supp. XXVI:** 9

Banks, Joanne Trautmann, **Supp. XIII:** 297

Banks, Russell, **Supp. IX:** 153; **Supp. V:** 1–19, 227; **Supp. X:** 85; **Supp. XI:** 178; **Supp. XII:** 295, 309, 343; **Supp. XX:** 90; **Supp. XXIV:** 97

"Banned Poem" (Nye), **Supp. XIII:** 282

Bannon, Barbara, **Supp. XI:** 228

"Banyan" (Swenson), **Supp. IV Part 2:** 651, 652

"Baptism" (Olsen). *See* "O Yes" (Olsen)

"Baptism" (Trethewey), **Supp. XXI:** 246

Baptism, The (Baraka), **Supp. II Part 1:** 40, 41–42, 43

Baptism of Desire (Erdrich), **Supp. IV Part 1:** 259

Barabtarlo, Gennady, **Retro. Supp. I:** 278

Baraka, Imamu Amiri (LeRoi Jones), **Retro. Supp. I:** 411; **Retro. Supp. II:** 280; **Supp. I Part 1:** 63; **Supp. II Part 1:** 29–63, 247, 250; **Supp. III Part 1:** 83; **Supp. IV Part 1:** 169, 244, 369; **Supp. VIII:** 295, 329, 330, 332; **Supp. X:** 324, 328; **Supp. XIII:** 94; **Supp. XIV:** 125, 144; **Supp. XXI:** 172, 227, 228; **Supp. XXIII:** 215; **Supp. XXIV:** 34, 183; **Supp. XXVII:** 18, 22, 160, 161, 166

"Bar at the Andover Inn, The" (Matthews), **Supp. IX:** 168

"Barbados" (Marshall), **Supp. XI:** 281

"Barbara Frietchie" (Whittier), **Supp. I Part 2:** 695–696

Barbarella (film), **Supp. XI:** 293, **307–308**

"Barbarian Status of Women, The" (Veblen), **Supp. I Part 2:** 636–637

Barbarous Coast, The (Macdonald), **Supp. IV Part 2:** 472, 474

Barbary Shore (Mailer), **III:** 27, 28, 30–31, 33, 35, 36, 40, 44; **Retro. Supp. II:** 199–200, 207; **Supp. XIV:** 162

Barber, Charles, **Supp. XXIII:** 125

Barber, David, **Supp. IV Part 2:** 550; **Supp. XII:** 188–189

Barber, Rowland, **Supp. IV Part 2:** 581

Barber, Samuel, **Supp. IV Part 1:** 84

"Barber's Unhappiness, The" (Saunders), **Supp. XIX:** 229

"Barclay of Ury" (Whittier), **Supp. I Part 2:** 693

Barcott, Bruce, **Supp. XVII:** 32

Bard of Savagery, The: Thorstein Veblen and Modern Social Theory (Diggins), **Supp. I Part 2:** 650

"Barefoot Boy, The" (Whittier), **Supp. I Part 2:** 691, 699–700

Barefoot in the Park (Simon), **Supp. IV Part 2:** 575, 578–579, 586, 590

Bare Hills, The (Winters), **Supp. II Part 2:** 786, 788
"Bare Hills, The" (Winters), **Supp. II Part 2:** 790
Barely and Widely (Zukofsky), **Supp. III Part 2:** 627, 628, 635
Barenblat, Rachel, **Supp. XIII:** 274
Barfield, Owen, **III:** 274, 279
"Bargain Lost, The" (Poe), **III:** 411
Barillas, William, **Supp. XIV:** 177
Barillet, Pierre, **Supp. XVI:** 194
Barker, Arthur, **Supp. XIII:** 167
Barker, Clive, **Supp. V:** 142
Barker, Wendy, **Supp. XXVII:** 261, 263
Barking Dog (Budbill), **Supp. XIX:** 1, 5
"Barking Man" (Bell), **Supp. X:** 9
Barking Man and Other Stories (Bell), **Supp. X: 9**
Barksdale, Richard, **Retro. Supp. I:** 202, 205; **Supp. I Part 1:** 341, 346
Barlow, Joel, **Supp. I Part 1:** 124; **Supp. I Part 2:** 511, 515, 521; **Supp. II Part 1: 65–86,** 268
Barlow, Judith, **Supp. XXI:** 6
Barlow, R. H., **Supp. XXV:** 122
Barlow, Ruth Baldwin (Mrs. Joel Barlow), **Supp. II Part 1:** 69
"B.A.R. Man, The" (Yates), **Supp. XI:** 341
Barnaby Rudge (Dickens), **III:** 421
Barnacle Soup and Other Stories of the West of Ireland (Gallagher and Gray), **Supp. XXIV:** 166, 172, 178
Barnard, Frederick, **Supp. I Part 2:** 684
Barnard, Rita, **Retro. Supp. II:** 324
Barn Blind (Smiley), **Supp. VI: 292–293**
"Barn Burning" (Faulkner), **II:** 72, 73; **Supp. IV Part 2:** 682; **Supp. XX:** 174
Barnes, Djuna, **Supp. III Part 1: 31–46;** **Supp. IV Part 1:** 79, 80; **Supp. XVI:** 282; **Supp. XXII:** 165, 167
Barnes, Kate, **Supp. XXVI:** 36
Barnes, Kim, **Supp. XVIII:** 293
Barnet, Andrea, **Supp. XXII:** 159, 164
Barnett, Claudia, **Supp. XV:** 323, 330, 334
Barnett, Samuel, **Supp. I Part 1:** 2
Barn Fever (Davison), **Supp. XXVI:** 66, 75–76, 77
"Barn Fever" (Davison), **Supp. XXVI:** 75, 77
"Barn-Fox, The" (Rash), **Supp. XXVII:** 222
Barnhardt, Wilton, **Supp. XXII:** 266; **Supp. XXVII: 1–15**
"Barn Owl" (Kooser), **Supp. XIX:** 123
Barnstone, Tony, **Supp. XIII:** 115, 126
Barnstone, Willis, **Supp. I Part 2:** 458
Barnum, P. T., **Supp. I Part 2:** 703
Baro, Gene, **Supp. XXVII:** 253
Baroja, Pío, **I:** 478
Baron, Zach, **Supp. XVIII:** 150
"Baroque Comment" (Bogan), **Supp. III Part 1:** 56, 58
"Baroque Sunburst, A" (Clampitt), **Supp. IX:** 49
"Baroque Wall-Fountain in the Villa Sciarra, A" (Wilbur), **Supp. III Part 2:** 553
Barr, Robert, **I:** 409, 424

Barracks Thief, The (Wolff), **Supp. VII:** 344–345
"Barred Owl" (Offutt), **Supp. XIX:** 170
Barren Ground (Glasgow), **II:** 174, 175, 178, 179, 184–185, 186, 187, 188, 189, 191, 192, 193, 194; **Supp. X:** 228
Barrés, Auguste M., **I:** 228
Barresi, Dorothy, **Supp. XV:** 100, 102
Barrett, Amy, **Supp. XVIII:** 136
Barrett, E. B., **Supp. XV:** 309
Barrett, Elizabeth, **Supp. IV Part 2:** 430
Barrett, George, **Supp. IX:** 250
Barrett, Ralph, **Supp. I Part 2:** 462
Barrie, J. M., **Supp. XX: 234**
"Barrie Cooke Painting" (Gallagher), **Supp. XXIV:** 171
Barrier, Rober G., **Supp. XXI:** 48–49
Barrier of a Common Language: An American Looks at Contemporary British Poetry (Gioia), **Supp. XV: 112, 116–117**
"Barroco: An Essay" (Sobin), **Supp. XVI:** 291
Barron, Jonathan, **Supp. IX:** 299
Barrow, John, **II:** 18
Barrus, Clara, **I:** 220
"Barry" (Biss), **Supp. XXVI:** 47
Barry, Iris, **Supp. XIII:** 170
Barry, Philip, **Retro. Supp. I:** 104; **Supp. IV Part 1:** 83; **Supp. V:** 95
Barstow, Elizabeth Drew. *See* Stoddard, Elizabeth
Bartas, Seigneur du, **IV:** 157
"Barter" (Teasdale), **Supp. XXVII:** 290, 291
Barth, John, **I: 121–143; Supp. I Part 1:** 100; **Supp. III Part 1:** 217; **Supp. IV Part 1:** 48, 379; **Supp. IX:** 208; **Supp. V:** 39, 40; **Supp. X:** 263, 301, 302, 307; **Supp. XI:** 309; **Supp. XII:** 29, 289, 316; **Supp. XIII:** 41, 101, 104; **Supp. XVII:** 183; **Supp. XVIII:** 136, 140, 141; **Supp. XX: 21; Supp. XXII:** 259, 261; **Supp. XXIII:** 42; **Supp. XXVII:** 183
Barth, Karl, **III:** 40, 258, 291, 303, 309; **IV:** 225; **Retro. Supp. I:** 325, 326, 327
Barth, Robert C., **Supp. XV:** 169
Barthé, Richmond, **Retro. Supp. II:** 115
Barthelme, Donald, **Supp. IV Part 1: 39–58,** 227; **Supp. V:** 2, 39, 44; **Supp. VIII:** 75, 138; **Supp. X:** 263; **Supp. XI:** 25; **Supp. XII:** 29; **Supp. XIII:** 41, 46; **Supp. XIX:** 235; **Supp. XVI:** 206; **Supp. XXVII:** 183
Barthelme, Frederick, **Supp. XI: 25–41; Supp. XXI:** 38
Barthelme, Peter, **Supp. XI:** 25
Barthelme, Steven, **Supp. XI:** 25, 27, 37
Barthes, Roland, **Supp. IV Part 1:** 39, 119, 126; **Supp. XIII:** 83; **Supp. XVI:** 285, 294; **Supp. XVII:** 244
Bartholomew and the Oobleck (Geisel), **Supp. XVI:** 104
"Bar Time" (B. Collins), **Supp. XVIII:** 245
"Bartleby, the Scrivener; A Story of Wall-Street" (Melville), **III:** 88–89; **Retro. Supp. I:** 255

Bartleby in Manhattan and Other Essays (Hardwick), **Supp. III Part 1:** 204, 210
"Bartleby the Scrivener" (Melville), **Supp. XVIII:** 4
Bartlet, Phebe, **I:** 562
Bartlett, Lee, **Supp. VIII:** 291
Bartlett, Mary Dougherty, **Supp. IV Part 1:** 335
Bartlett, William Irving, **Supp. XXV:** 250–251
Barton, Bruce, **III:** 14; **Retro. Supp. I:** 179
Barton, Priscilla. *See* Morison, Mrs. Samuel Eliot (Priscilla Barton)
Barton, Ralph, **Supp. XVI:** 195
Barton, Rev. William E., **Retro. Supp. I:** 179
Bartov, Omer, **Supp. XVI:** 153–154
Bartram, John, **Supp. I Part 1:** 244
Bartram, William, **II:** 313; **Supp. IX:** 171; **Supp. X:** 223
Barzun, Jacques, **Supp. XIV:** 54
"Basement" (Bambara), **Supp. XI:** 5
Basement Tapes, The (album, Dylan), **Supp. XVIII:** 27, 30, 32
"Base of All Metaphysics, The" (Whitman), **IV:** 348
"Base Stealer, The" (Francis), **Supp. IX:** 82
Bashevis, Isaac. *See* Singer, Isaac Bashevis
Bashir, Antonious, **Supp. XX: 116, 120**
Basil Stories, The (Fitzgerald), **Retro. Supp. I:** 109
Basin and Range (McPhee), **Supp. III Part 1:** 309
"Basin of Eggs, A" (Swenson), **Supp. IV Part 2:** 645
"Basket" (Huddle), **Supp. XXVI:** 150
"Basket, The" (A. Lowell), **II:** 522
"Basketball and Beefeaters" (McPhee), **Supp. III Part 1:** 296
"Basketball and Poetry: The Two Richies" (Dunn), **Supp. XI:** 140
"Basketball Player" (L. Michaels), **Supp. XVI:** 209
"Basket of Trips"(Strout), **Supp. XXIII:** 283, 285
Baskin, Leonard, **Supp. X:** 58, 71; **Supp. XV:** 348
Bass, George, **Supp. XXII:** 6
Bass, Rick, **Supp. XIV:** 227; **Supp. XVI: 15–29; Supp. XXI:** 40, 45; **Supp. XXVI:** 31, 187
Bassard, Katherine Clay, **Supp. XXII:** 148
Bass Cathedral (Mackey), **Supp. XXVII:** 159
Basso, Hamilton, **Retro. Supp. I:** 80
Bastard, The (Caldwell), **I:** 291, 292, 308
"Bastille Day" (Lamott), **Supp. XX: 143**
"Bat, The" (Kenyon), **Supp. VII:** 168
Bat, The (Rinehart and Hopwood), **Supp. XXV:** 195, 200
Bataille, Georges, **Supp. VIII:** 4; **Supp. XII:** 1
"Batard" (London), **II:** 468–469
Batchelor, John Calvin, **Supp. XIX:** 142

Bate, Walter Jackson, **II:** 531; **Supp. XXVI:** 63

"Bateau ivre, Le" (Rimbaud; Berrigan, trans.), **Supp. XXIV:** 40

Bates, Arlo, **Retro. Supp. I:** 35

Bates, Blanche, **Supp. XVI:** 182

Bates, Kathy, **Supp. XIII:** 207

Bates, Lee, **Retro. Supp. II:** 46

Bates, Milton J., **Supp. XII:** 62

Bates, Sylvia Chatfield, **II:** 586

Bateson, Gregory, **Supp. XV:** 146

"Bath, The" (Carver), **Supp. III Part 1:** 144, 145

"Bath, The" (Snyder), **Supp. VIII:** 302

Bathwater Wine (Coleman), **Supp. XI:** 83, 90, **91**

Battaglia, J. F., **Supp. XXVII:** 256, 258, 263

"Batter my heart, three person'd God" (Donne), **Supp. I Part 2:** 726; **Supp. XVII:** 119

"Battle, The" (Simpson), **Supp. IX:** 268–269

Battle Cry (film), **Supp. XX: 246**

Battle Cry (Uris), **Supp. XX: 243, 246, 248–250, 255, 256**

Battlefield Where the Moon Says I Love You, The (Stanford), **Supp. XV:** 345

Battle for the Solomons (Wolfert), **Supp. XXI:** 267

Battle-Ground, The (Glasgow), **II:** 175, 176, 177, 178, 193

"Battle Hymn of the Republic" (Sandburg), **III:** 585

"Battle Hymn of the Republic, The" (Howe), **III:** 505

"Battle Hymn of the Republic, The" (Updike), **Retro. Supp. I:** 324

Battle of Angels (T. Williams), **IV:** 380, 381, 383, 385, 386, 387

"Battle of Aspen, The" (Thompson), **Supp. XXIV:** 286–287

"Battle of Lovell's Pond, The" (Longfellow), **II:** 493

Battle of the Atlantic, The (Morison), **Supp. I Part 2:** 490

"Battle of the Baltic, The" (Campbell), **Supp. I Part 1:** 309

"Battle of the Bunker, The" (Snodgrass), **Supp. VI:** 319–320

"***Battle of the Century!!!, The***" (Goldbarth), **Supp. XII:** 193

Battle of the Little Big Horn, The (Sandoz), **Supp. XXIII:** 146

Battle-Pieces and Aspects of the War (Melville), **II:** 538–539; **III:** 92; **IV:** 350; **Retro. Supp. I:** 257

"Battler, The" (Hemingway), **II:** 248; **Retro. Supp. I:** 175

"Battle That Ended the Century, The" (Lovecraft and Barlow), **Supp. XXV:** 122

Baubles (Wells), **Supp. XXVI:** 275

"Baubles after Bombs" (Peacock), **Supp. XIX:** 200

"Baudelaire" (Schwartz), **Supp. II Part 2:** 663

Baudelaire, Charles, **I:** 58, 63, 384, 389, 420, 569; **II:** 543, 544–545, 552; **III:** 137, 141–142, 143, 409, 417, 418,

421, 428, 448, 466, 474; **IV:** 74, 79, 80, 87, 211, 286; **Retro. Supp. I:** 56, 90; **Retro. Supp. II:** 261, 262, 322, 326; **Supp. I Part 1:** 271; **Supp. III Part 1:** 4, 6, 105; **Supp. XIII:** 77, 284; **Supp. XV:** 165; **Supp. XXI:** 228; **Supp. XXIV:** 152; **Supp. XXVI:** 39

Baudrillard, Jean, **Supp. IV Part 1:** 45

Bauer, Dale, **Retro. Supp. I:** 381

Bauer, Douglas, **Supp. XII:** 290

Baum, L. Frank, **Supp. I Part 2:** 621; **Supp. IV Part 1:** 101, 113; **Supp. XII:** 42

Baumann, Walter, **III:** 478

Bausch, Richard, **Supp. VII: 39–56; Supp. XVII:** 21; **Supp. XXVI:** 13

Bawer, Bruce, **Supp. IX:** 135; **Supp. VIII:** 153; **Supp. X:** 187

Baxter, Charles, **Supp. XII:** 22; **Supp. XIV:** 89, 92; **Supp. XVII: 13–24; Supp. XXIII:** 289

Baxter, John, **Supp. XI:** 302

Baxter, Richard, **III:** 199; **IV:** 151, 153; **Supp. I Part 2:** 683

"Baxter's Procrustes" (Chesnutt), **Supp. XIV:** 76

"Bay City Blues" (Chandler), **Supp. IV Part 1:** 129

Baylies, William, **Supp. I Part 1:** 153

Baym, Nina, **Supp. IV Part 2:** 463; **Supp. X:** 229; **Supp. XVI:** 92; **Supp. XVIII:** 258, 259; **Supp. XXIV:** 28

"Bayou" (Di Piero), **Supp. XIX:** 37

Bayou Folk (Chopin), **Retro. Supp. II: 64–65,** 73; **Supp. I Part 1:** 200, 216, 218

Baziotes, William, **Supp. XV:** 144

"B.C." (Taggard), **Supp. XXII:** 278

Beach, Anna Hampstead, **Supp. XVII:** 75

Beach, Joseph Warren, **I:** 309, 500; **II:** 27; **III:** 319

Beach, Sylvia, **IV:** 404; **Retro. Supp. I:** 109, 422; **Supp. XXII:** 165

"Beaches in Winter" (Kriegel), **Supp. XXIV:** 220, 225

"Beach Women, The" (Pinsky), **Supp. VI:** 241

"Beaded Pear, The" (Simpson), **Supp. IX:** 276

Beagle, Peter, **Supp. X:** 24

Beam, Jeffrey, **Supp. XII:** 98

Beaman, E. O., **Supp. IV Part 2:** 604

Bean, Michael, **Supp. V:** 203

Bean, Robert Bennett, **Supp. II Part 1:** 170

Bean Eaters, The (Brooks), **Supp. III Part 1:** 79–81

Be Angry at the Sun (Jeffers), **Supp. II Part 2:** 434

Bean Spasms (Berrigan, Padgett, and Brainard), **Supp. XXIV:** 41–42

"Beanstalk Country, The" (T. Williams), **IV:** 383

Bean Trees, The (Kingsolver), **Supp. VII:** 197, 199–201, 202, 207, 209

"Bear" (Hogan), **Supp. IV Part 1:** 412

Bear, The (Faulkner), **Supp. VIII:** 184

"Bear, The" (Faulkner), **II:** 71–72, 73, 228; **IV:** 203; **Supp. IV Part 2:** 434;

Supp. IX: 95; **Supp. X:** 30; **Supp. XIV:** 32; **Supp. XXI:** 37

"Bear, The" (Kinnell), **Supp. III Part 1:** 244

"Bear, The" (Momaday), **Supp. IV Part 2:** 480, 487

Bear and His Daughter: Stories (Stone), **Supp. V:** 295, 308

"Bear Came Over the Mountain, The" (Munro), **Supp. XXVII:** 193

Beard, Charles, **I:** 214; **IV:** 429; **Supp. I Part 2:** 481, 490, 492, 632, 640, 643, 647

Beard, James, **I:** 341; **Supp. XVII:** 89, 90

Beard, Mary, **Supp. I Part 2:** 481

"Bearded Oaks" (Warren), **IV:** 240

Bearden, Romare, **Retro. Supp. I:** 209; **Supp. VIII:** 337, 342; **Supp. XXI:** 249

"Beard of Bees, A" (X. J. Kennedy), **Supp. XV:** 171

Beardon, Romare, **Supp. XV:** 144

"Beards, The" (Lethem), **Supp. XVIII:** 148

Beardsley, Aubrey, **II:** 56; **IV:** 77

"Bearings" (Rash), **Supp. XXVII:** 218

Beaser, Robert, **Supp. XV:** 259

"Beast" (Swenson), **Supp. IV Part 2:** 639

"Beast & Burden, The: Seven Improvisations" (Komunyakaa), **Supp. XIII:** 120, 121

Beast God Forgot to Invent, The (Harrison), **Supp. VIII:** 37, 46, **51–52**

Beast in Me, The (Thurber), **Supp. I Part 2:** 615

"Beast in the Jungle, The" (H. James), **I:** 570; **II:** 335; **Retro. Supp. I:** 235; **Supp. V:** 103–104; **Supp. XXVI:** 141

Beast in View (Rukeyser), **Supp. VI:** 272, 273, 279, 280

Beasts of Bethlehem, The (X. J. Kennedy), **Supp. XV:** 163

"Beat! Beat! Drums!" (Whitman), **III:** 585

Beat Down to Your Soul: What Was the Beat Generation? (Charters, ed.), **Supp. XIV:** 152

"Beatific Effigies" (Bronk), **Supp. XXI:** 31

Beaton, Cecil, **Supp. XVI:** 191

Beats, The (Krim, ed.), **Supp. XV:** 338

Beattie, Ann, **Supp. V: 21–37; Supp. XI:** 26; **Supp. XII:** 80, 139, 294; **Supp. XXI:** 118; **Supp. XXIII:** 289; **Supp. XXVII:** 269

Beattie, L. Elisabeth, **Supp. XX: 164, 165**

Beatty, General Sam, **I:** 193

Beaty, Jerome, **Supp. IV Part 1:** 331

"Beau Monde of Mrs. Bridge, The" (Connell), **Supp. XIV:** 88, 89

Beaumont, Francis, **Supp. I Part 2:** 422

"Beauties of Santa Cruz, The" (Freneau), **Supp. II Part 1:** 260

Beautiful and Damned, The (Fitzgerald), **II:** 88, 89–91, 93, 263; **Retro. Supp. I: 103–105,** 105, 106, 110; **Supp. IX:** 56, 57

Beautiful Changes, The (Wilbur), **Supp. III Part 2:** 544–550

"Beautiful Changes, The" (Wilbur), **Supp. III Part 2:** 549, 550

Beautiful Child (Silver), **Supp. XXIV: 273–274**

"Beautiful Child, A" (Capote), **Supp. III Part 1:** 113, 125

"Beautiful & Cruel" (Cisneros), **Supp. VII:** 63, 67

"Beautiful Gestures, The" (Huddle), **Supp. XXVI:** 154

Beautiful Losers (Cohen), **Supp. XXVII:** 51, 54, 57–58, 59

"Beautiful Wall, Machu Picchu, The" (Bronk), **Supp. XXI:** 31, 32

"Beautiful Woman Who Sings, The" (Gunn Allen), **Supp. IV Part 1:** 326

"Beauty" (Emerson), **II:** 2, 5

"Beauty" (Sanders), **Supp. XVI:** 277

"Beauty" (Wylie), **Supp. I Part 2:** 710

"Beauty and the Beast" (Dove), **Supp. IV Part 1:** 245

"Beauty and the Beast" (fairy tale), **IV:** 266; **Supp. X:** 88

"Beauty and the Shoe Sluts" (Karr), **Supp. XI:** 250

Beauty of the Husband, The: A Fictional Essay in Twenty-Nine Tangos (Carson), **Supp. XII: 113–114**

Beauty Queen, The (P. N. Warren), **Supp. XX: 268–269**

Beauty's Punishment (Rice), **Supp. VII:** 301

Beauty's Release: The Continued Erotic Adventures of Sleeping Beauty (Rice), **Supp. VII:** 301

Beauvoir, Simone de, **IV:** 477; **Supp. I Part 1:** 51; **Supp. III Part 1:** 200–201, 208; **Supp. IV Part 1:** 360; **Supp. IX:** 4

Beaver Men: Spearheads of Empire (Sandoz), **Supp. XXIV:** 244, **246–247**

"Be Careful" (Zach; Everwine, trans.), **Supp. XV:** 86

Be Careful How You Live (Lacy), **Supp. XV:** 203–204

"Because I could not stop for Death—" (Dickinson), **Retro. Supp. I: 38–40,** 41, 43, 44

"Because It Happened" (Goldbarth), **Supp. XII:** 192

"Because of Libraries We Can Say These Things" (Nye), **Supp. XIII:** 283

"Because of the Waters of the Flood" (Helprin), **Supp. XXV:** 85

"Because the Body Is a Flower"(Crooker), **Supp. XXIII:** 55

"Because You Mentioned the Spiritual Life" (Dunn), **Supp. XI:** 154

Bech: A Book (Updike), **IV:** 214; **Retro. Supp. I:** 329, 335

Bechdel, Alison, **Supp. XXV: 1–15**

Beck, Dave, **I:** 493

Beck, Ervin, **Supp. XXIII:** 94, 95

Beck, Jack, **Supp. IV Part 2:** 560

Beck, Nicholas, **Supp. XVIII:** 252

Beck, Stefan, **Supp. XXII:** 268

Becker, Carl, **Supp. I Part 2:** 492, 493

Becker, Paula. *See* Modersohn, Mrs. Otto (Paula Becker)

Beckett, Samuel, **I:** 71, 91, 142, 298, 461; **III:** 387; **IV:** 95; **Retro. Supp. I:** 206; **Supp. IV Part 1:** 297, 368–369; **Supp. IV Part 2:** 424; **Supp. V:** 23, 53; **Supp. XI:** 104; **Supp. XII:** 21, 150–151; **Supp. XIII:** 74; **Supp. XIV:** 239; **Supp. XVII:** 185; **Supp. XX: 17;** **Supp. XXI:** 18; **Supp. XXII:** 263

Beckett, Tom, **Supp. IV Part 2:** 419

Beckford, William, **I:** 204

Beckonings (Brooks), **Supp. III Part 1:** 85

"Becky" (Toomer), **Supp. III Part 2:** 481, 483; **Supp. IX:** 312

Becky and Her Friends (Hinojosa), **Supp. XIX: 108–109**

Becoming a Man: Half a Life Story (Monette), **Supp. X:** 146, 147, 149, 151, 152, **155–157**

"Becoming a Meadow" (Doty), **Supp. XI:** 124–125

"Becoming and Breaking: Poet and Poem" (Ríos), **Supp. IV Part 2:** 539

Becoming Canonical in American Poetry (Morris), **Retro. Supp. I:** 40

Becoming Light: New and Selected Poems (Jong), **Supp. V:** 115

Bécquer, Gustavo Adolfo, **Supp. XIII:** 312

"Bed, The" (Dixon), **Supp. XII:** 154

Beddoes, Thomas Lovell, **III:** 469; **Retro. Supp. I:** 285

Bedichek, Roy, **Supp. V:** 225

Bedient, Calvin, **Supp. IX:** 298; **Supp. XII:** 98

"Bed in the Sky, The" (Snyder), **Supp. VIII:** 300

Bednarik, Joseph, **Supp. VIII:** 39

Bedouin Hornbook (Mackey), **Supp. XXVII:** 157–158

"Bedrock" (Proulx), **Supp. VII:** 253

"Bed Time" (Davison), **Supp. XXVI:** 72

"Bee, The" (Lanier), **Supp. I Part 1:** 364

Beecher, Catharine, **Supp. I Part 2:** 581, 582–583, 584, 586, 588, 589, 591, 599; **Supp. X:** 103; **Supp. XI:** 193

Beecher, Charles, **Supp. I Part 2:** 588, 589

Beecher, Edward, **Supp. I Part 2:** 581, 582, 583, 584, 588, 591

Beecher, Harriet. *See* Stowe, Harriet Beecher

Beecher, Henry Ward, **II:** 275; **Supp. I Part 2:** 581; **Supp. XI:** 193; **Supp. XVIII:** 4

Beecher, Lyman, **Supp. I Part 2:** 580–581, 582, 583, 587, 588, 599; **Supp. XI:** 193

Beecher, Mrs. Lyman (Roxanna Foote), **Supp. I Part 2:** 580–581, 582, 588, 599

Beeching, Jack, **Supp. X:** 114, 117, 118, 123, 125, 126

"Beehive" (Toomer), **Supp. IX:** 317

"Bee Hunt, The" (Irving), **II:** 313

"Beekeeper's Daughter, The" (Plath), **Retro. Supp. II:** 246–247

"Bee Meeting, The" (Plath), **Retro. Supp. II:** 254–255

Bee Poems (Plath), **Retro. Supp. II:** 254–255

Beer, John, **Supp. XVII:** 239

Beer, Thomas, **I:** 405

Beerbohm, Max, **III:** 472; **IV:** 436; **Supp. I Part 2:** 714

"Beer Bottle" (Kooser), **Supp. XIX:** 117

"Beer in the Sergeant Major's Hat, or The Sun Also Sneezes" (Chandler), **Supp. IV Part 1:** 121

Beers, Henry A., **Supp. XX: 68**

"Bees Bees Bees" (J. Scott), **Supp. XVII:** 188, 190

Beethoven, Ludwig van, **II:** 536; **III:** 118; **IV:** 274, 358; **Supp. I Part 1:** 363; **Supp. VIII:** 103

Beet Queen, The (Erdrich), **Supp. IV Part 1:** 259, 260, 264–265, 266, 273, 274, 275

Befo' de War: Echoes in Negro Dialect (Gordon), **Supp. II Part 1:** 201

"Before" (Goldbarth), **Supp. XII:** 175

"Before" (Snyder), **Supp. VIII:** 301

Before Adam (London), **II:** 466

Before Breakfast (O'Neill), **Supp. XXII:** 22

Before Disaster (Winters), **Supp. II Part 2:** 786, 800

"Before Disaster" (Winters), **Supp. II Part 2:** 801, 815

"Before I Knocked" (D. Thomas), **III:** 534

Beforelife, The (F. Wright), **Supp. XVII:** 240, 245–246

"Before March" (MacLeish), **III:** 15

Before My Life Began (Neugeboren), **Supp. XVI: 224–225**

"Before the Altar" (A. Lowell), **II:** 516

"Before the Birth of one of her children" (Bradstreet), **Supp. I Part 1:** 118

Before the Gringo Came (Atherton), **Supp. XXIV:** 22

"Before the Sky Darkens" (Dunn), **Supp. XI:** 155

"Begat" (Sexton), **Supp. II Part 2: 693**

Beget, Philippe, **Supp. XXIII:** 74

"Beggar Maid, The" (Munro), **Supp. XXVII:** 187

Beggar Maid, The: Stories of Flo and Rose (Munro). *See Who Do You Think You Are?* (Munro)

Beggarman, Thief (Shaw), **Supp. XIX:** 251–252

Beggar on Horseback (Kaufman and Connelly), **III:** 394

"Beggar Said So, The" (Singer), **IV:** 12

Beggars in the House of Plenty (Shanley), **Supp. XIV:** 316, **327–328**

Beggar's Opera, The (Gay), **Supp. I Part 2:** 523

Begiebing, Robert, **Retro. Supp. II:** 210

Begin Again (Paley), **Supp. VI:** 221

Beginners (Carver), **Supp. XXIV:** 177

"Beginning and the End, The" (Jeffers), **Supp. II Part 2:** 420–421, 424

"Beginning of Decadence, The" (Jeffers), **Supp. II Part 2:** 420

"Beginning of Enthusiasm, The" (Salinas), **Supp. XIII:** 327–328

Beginning of Wisdom, The (Benét), **I:** 358; **Supp. XI:** 44

"Beginnings of Sorrow, The"(P. Benedict), **Supp. XXIII:** 48

Be Glad You're Neurotic (Bisch), **Supp. I Part 2:** 608

"Begotten of the Spleen" (Simic), **Supp. VIII:** 277

"Behaving Like a Jew" (Stern), **Supp. IX: 290–291,** 294

Behavior of Titans, The (Merton), **Supp. VIII:** 201

Behind a Mask (Alcott), **Supp. I Part 1:** 36–37, 43–44

"Behind a Wall" (A. Lowell), **II:** 516

Behind the Movie Camera (radio show), **Supp. XV:** 147

"Behold the Key" (Malamud), **Supp. I Part 2:** 437

Behrendt, Stephen, **Supp. X:** 204

Behrman, S. N., **Supp. V:** 95

Beichman, Arnold, **Supp. XXV:** 254, 258, 264

Beidler, Peter G., **Supp. IV Part 2:** 557

Beidler, Philip D., **Supp. XII:** 69

Beige Dolorosa (Harrison), **Supp. VIII:** 40, 51

Beiles, Sinclair, **Supp. XII:** 129

Beiliss, Mendel, **Supp. I Part 2:** 427, 446, 447, 448

"Being a Constellation" (A. Finch), **Supp. XVII:** 72

"Being a Lutheran Boy-God in Minnesota" (R. Bly), **Supp. IV Part 1:** 59, 67

Being and Race (C. Johnson), **Supp. VI:** 193, 199

Being and Time (Heidegger), **Supp. VIII:** 9

Being Busted (Fiedler), **Supp. XIII:** 95, 102, 104

Being Geniuses Together: 1920–1930 (Boyle), **Supp. XXIV:** 63, 64

Being John Malkovich (Kaufman), **Supp. XV:** 16

Being Perfect (Quindlen), **Supp. XVII:** 167, 179

Being There (Kosinski), **Supp. VII:** 215, 216, 222–223

Beiswanger, George, **Retro. Supp. II:** 220

Beka Lamb (Edgell), **Supp. XXIII:** 83, 85, **86–88,** 93–94, 95

Belasco, David, **Supp. XVI:** 182; **Supp. XXI:** 151

Bel Canto (Patchett), **Supp. XII:** 307, 310, **320–322**

Belchamber (Sturgis), **Supp. XX: 227, 233, 238–240**

"Beleaguered City, The" (Longfellow), **II:** 498

Belfry of Bruges, The, and Other Poems (Longfellow), **II:** 489; **Retro. Supp. II:** 157, 168

"Belief" (Levine), **Supp. V:** 186, 190

"Belief in the Self Abandoned, The" (Bronk), **Supp. XXI:** 30

"Beliefs of Writers, The" (Doctorow), **Supp. IV Part 1:** 235–236

Believeniks! (Lethem and Sorrentino), **Supp. XVIII:** 148–149

Believers (C. Baxter), **Supp. XVII:** 20–21, 22

"Believers" (C. Baxter), **Supp. XVII:** 21

"Believers, The/Los Creyentes" (Kingsolver), **Supp. VII:** 208

Belinda (Rice), **Supp. VII:** 301–302

"Belinda's Petition" (Dove), **Supp. IV Part 1:** 245

"Belita" (Ríos), **Supp. IV Part 2:** 541

Belitt, Ben, **Supp. XII:** 260

Bell, Archibald, **Supp. XX: 284, 285**

Bell, Bernard, **Supp. XXII:** 182

Bell, Clive, **IV:** 87

Bell, Daniel, **Supp. I Part 2:** 648

Bell, George Kennedy Allen, **Retro. Supp. I:** 65

Bell, Madison Smartt, **Supp. X: 1–20; Supp. XIX:** 58–59, 60–61; **Supp. XVII:** 236; **Supp. XXI:** 48; **Supp. XXIII:** 43

Bell, Marvin, **Supp. IX:** 152; **Supp. V:** 337, 339; **Supp. XI:** 316; **Supp. XXIV:** 165

Bell, Michael, **Retro. Supp. II:** 139

Bell, Pearl K., **Supp. XI:** 233; **Supp. XXV:** 253; **Supp. XXVII:** 134

Bell, Quentin, **Supp. I Part 2:** 636

Bell, Whitfield J., Jr., **II:** 123

Bellafante, Gina, **Supp. VIII:** 85

Bellamy, Edward, **II:** 276; **Supp. I Part 2:** 641; **Supp. XI:** 200, 203

Bellarosa Connection, The (Bellow), **Retro. Supp. II:** 31, 32

"Belle Dollinger" (Masters), **Supp. I Part 2:** 463

Belleforest, François de, **IV:** 370

"Belle Zoraïde, La" (Chopin), **Supp. I Part 1:** 215–216

Bell in the Fog and Other Stories, The (Atherton), **Supp. XXIV:** 23

Bell Jar, The (Plath), **Retro. Supp. II:** 242, **249–250; Supp. I Part 2:** 526, 527, 529, 531–536, 539, 540, 541, 542, 544

Belloc, Hilary, **III:** 176; **IV:** 432

"Bellocq" (Trethewey), **Supp. XXI:** 253

Bellocq, E. J., **Supp. XXI:** 246, 251

Bellocq's Ophelia (Trethewey), **Supp. XXI:** 243, 246, **251–254**

"Bellocq's Ophelia" (Trethewey), **Supp. XXI:** 254

Bellow, Saul, **I:** 113, 138–139, **144–166,** 375, 517; **II:** 579; **III:** 40; **IV:** 3, 19, 217, 340; **Retro. Supp. II: 19–36,** 118, 279, 307, 324; **Supp. I Part 2:** 428, 451; **Supp. II Part 1:** 109; **Supp. IV Part 1:** 30; **Supp. IX:** 212, 227; **Supp. V:** 258; **Supp. VIII:** 98, 176, 234, 236–237, 245; **Supp. XI:** 64, 233; **Supp. XII:** 159, 165, 170, 310; **Supp. XIII:** 106; **Supp. XIX:** 157, 158, 261; **Supp. XV:** 143; **Supp. XVI:** 208; **Supp. XVIII:** 90; **Supp. XX: 244; Supp. XXII:** 268; **Supp. XXIII:** 166; **Supp. XXV:** 79; **Supp. XXVII:** 95

Bellows, George, **Supp. XV:** 295

"Bells, The" (Poe), **III:** 593; **Retro. Supp. II:** 266; **Supp. I Part 2:** 388

"Bells, The" (Sexton), **Supp. II Part 2:** 673

"Bells for John Whiteside's Daughter" (Ransom), **III:** 490

"Bells of Lynn, The" (Longfellow), **II:** 498

"Bells of San Blas, The" (Longfellow), **II:** 490–491, 493, 498

"Bell Tower, The" (Melville), **III:** 91

"Belly, The" (Dobyns), **Supp. XIII:** 87

'Bel of Prairie Eden (Lippard), **Supp. XXIII:** 178, 186

"Belonging" (Pickering), **Supp. XXI:** 202

"Belonging Kind, The" (W. Gibson and J. Shirley), **Supp. XVI:** 123

Beloved (Morrison), **Supp. III Part 1:** 364, 372–379; **Supp. IV Part 1:** 13–14; **Supp. V:** 259; **Supp. VIII:** 343; **Supp. XIII:** 60; **Supp. XXII:** 78, 109; **Supp. XXIV:** 186

Beloved, The (Gibran), **Supp. XX: 125**

"Beloved, The" (Halliday), **Supp. XIX:** 92

Beloved Lady: A History of Jane Addams' Ideas on Reform and Peace (Farrell), **Supp. I Part 1:** 24

Beloved Stranger, The (Bynner), **Supp. XV:** 44, 50

Bemorse, John, **Supp. XX: 62**

Benchley, Robert, **I:** 48, 482; **II:** 435; **III:** 53; **Supp. IX:** 190, 195, 204

Benda, W. T., **Retro. Supp. I:** 13

Bender, Aimee, **Supp. XXII:** 49

Bending of a Twig, The (Coke), **Supp. XX: 235**

Bend Sinister (Nabokov), **III:** 253–254; **Retro. Supp. I:** 265, 266, 270

"Beneath the Sidewalk" (Dunn), **Supp. XI:** 145

"Beneath the Smooth Skin of America" (Sanders), **Supp. XVI:** 275

Benedict, Elizabeth, **Supp. XVIII:** 289

Benedict, Laura, **Supp. XXIII:** 35, 36, 49

Benedict, Pinckney, **Supp. XXIII: 35–50**

Benedict, Ruth, **Supp. IX:** 229

Benefactor, The (Sontag), **Supp. III Part 2:** 451, 455, 468, 469

"Benefit Performance" (Malamud), **Supp. I Part 2:** 431

Benét, Laura, **Supp. XI:** 44

Benét, Rosemary, **Supp. XI:** 44, 51; **Supp. XXV:** 201

Benét, Stephen Vincent, **I:** 358; **II:** 177; **III:** 22; **IV:** 129; **Supp. XI: 43–61**

Benét, William Rose, **II:** 530; **Retro. Supp. I:** 108; **Supp. I Part 2:** 709; **Supp. XI:** 43, 44; **Supp. XIV:** 119, 122, 129

Ben Franklin's Wit and Wisdom (Franklin), **II:** 111

Ben-Gurion, David, **Supp. XX: 243**

Ben-Hur (film), **Supp. IV Part 2:** 683

Benigna Machiavelli (Gilman), **Supp. XI:** 201, 208

Benitez, R. Michael, **Retro. Supp. II:** 264

"Benito Cereno" (Melville), **III:** 91; **Retro. Supp. I:** 255; **Retro. Supp. II:** 188; **Supp. XVII:** 185

Benito Cereno (R. Lowell), **II:** 546; **Retro. Supp. II:** 181

Benito's Dream Bottle (Nye), **Supp. XIII:** 278

"Bênitou's Slave, The" (Chopin), **Retro. Supp. II:** 64

Benjamin, Walter, **Supp. IX:** 133; **Supp. XVI:** 290, 291; **Supp. XXIII:** 28, 29, 30, 31

Benjamin Franklin (Van Doren), **Supp. I Part 2:** 486

"Benjamin Pantier" (Masters), **Supp. I Part 2:** 461

Bennett, Anne Virginia, **II:** 184

Bennett, Arnold, **I:** 103; **II:** 337; **Supp. XVI:** 190

Bennett, Elizabeth, **Supp. VIII:** 58

Bennett, Patrick, **Supp. V:** 225

Bennett, Paula, **Retro. Supp. I:** 29, 33, 42; **Supp. XX:** 286

Bennett, Reginald, **Supp. XXII:** 218

Bennett, William, **Supp. VIII:** 245

Benson, A. C., **Supp. XX:** 238

Benson, Arthur, **Supp. XX:** 233

Benson, E. F., **Supp. XX:** 229

Benson, Heidi, **Supp. XVIII:** 136

Benson, Jackson J., **Supp. IV Part 2:** 613

Benson, Martin, **Supp. XVIII:** 38

Benstock, Shari, **Retro. Supp. I:** 361, 368, 371, 382; **Supp. XX:** 240

Bentham, Jeremy, **I:** 279; **Supp. I Part 2:** 635

Bentley, Anna, **Supp. XXI:** 5

Bentley, Arthur, **Supp. XXI:** 4, 5

Bentley, Eric R., **IV:** 396

Bentley, Nelson, **Supp. IX:** 324

Bentley, Richard, **III:** 79, 86

Benton, Robert, **Supp. IV Part 1:** 236

"Bent Tones" (Wright), **Supp. XV:** 346

Benveniste, Emile, **Supp. XVI:** 292

Benzel, Jan, **Supp. XVI:** 112

Beowulf, **Supp. II Part 1:** 6; **Supp. XVII:** 70, 73

Beran, Carol, **Supp. XIII:** 25

"Berck-Plage" (Plath), **Retro. Supp. II:** 253–254

Bercovitch, Sacvan, **Retro. Supp. I:** 408; **Retro. Supp. II:** 325, 330; **Supp. I Part 1:** 99; **Supp. I Part 2:** 659

Berdyaev, Nikolai, **I:** 494; **III:** 292

"Bereaved Apartments" (Kingsolver), **Supp. VII:** 203

"Bereavement in their death to feel" (Dickinson), **Retro. Supp. I:** 43, 44

"Berenice" (Poe), **III:** 415, 416, 425; **Retro. Supp. II:** 270

Bérénice (Racine), **II:** 573

Berenson, Bernard, **Retro. Supp. I:** 381; **Supp. IV Part 1:** 314; **Supp. XIV:** 335, 336, 337; **Supp. XVII:** 99; **Supp. XXI:** 5

Berenson, Mary Smith, **Supp. XXI:** 4, 5, 6

Berg, James, **Supp. XIV:** 157, 159

Berg, Stephen, **Supp. IV Part 1:** 60

Berger, Alan, **Supp. XVII:** 39

Berger, Charles, **Retro. Supp. I:** 311

Berger, John, **Supp. XVI:** 284; **Supp. XXIII:** 167, 168–169; **Supp. XXIV:** 94

Berger, Roger, **Supp. XIII:** 237

Berger, Thomas, **III:** 258; **Supp. XII:** 171

Berghash, Rachel, **Supp. XXIV:** 172

Bergman, Ingmar, **I:** 291; **Supp. XV:** 7, 8, 12

Bergson, Henri, **I:** 224; **II:** 163, 165, 166, 359; **III:** 8, 9, 488, 619; **IV:** 86, 122, 466, 467; **Retro. Supp. I:** 55, 57, 80; **Supp. IV Part 1:** 42; **Supp. XXII:** 158

Berkeley, Anthony, **Supp. IV Part 1:** 341

Berkeley, George, **II:** 10, 349, 357, 480, 554

Berkman, Alexander, **Supp. XXIII:** 161; **Supp. XXV:** 19

Berkman, Leonard, **Supp. XV:** 321

Berkow, Ira, **Supp. XXVII:** 139

Berkowitz, Gerald, **Supp. IV Part 2:** 590

Berkson, Bill, **Supp. XXIII:** 217, 218; **Supp. XXVII:** 22, 23

Berlin, Isaiah, **Supp. XXII:** 258

Berlin Alexanderplatz (Döblin), **Supp. XV:** 137

Berlin Stories (Isherwood), **Supp. IV Part 1:** 82; **Supp. XIV:** 155, 156, 161, 162, 164, 165

Berlioz, Hector, **Supp. XV:** 33

Berlyne, Daniel E., **Supp. I Part 2:** 672

Berman, Alexander, **Supp. XVII:** 103

Berman, Carolyn Vellenga, **Supp. XXII:** 147

Bernard Clare (Farrell), **II:** 38, 39

Bernardin, Susan, **Supp. XXVI:** 111

Bernard of Clairvaux, Saint, **I:** 22; **II:** 538

Bernays, Thekla, **Retro. Supp. II:** 65

Berne, Suzanne, **Supp. XII:** 320

Berne, Victoria (pseudonym). *See* Fisher, M. F. K.

Berneis, Peter, **IV:** 383

Bernhard, Brendan, **Supp. XIV:** 163

Bernhard, Thomas, **Supp. XX:** 91

Bernhardt, Sarah, **I:** 484; **Retro. Supp. I:** 377

Bernice (Glaspell), **Supp. III Part 1:** 179

"Bernice Bobs Her Hair" (Fitzgerald), **II:** 88; **Retro. Supp. I:** 103

Bernstein, Aline, **IV:** 455, 456

Bernstein, Andrea, **Supp. IX:** 146

Bernstein, Carl, **Supp. XXIV:** 293

Bernstein, Charles, **Supp. IV Part 2:** 421, 426; **Supp. XXIV:** 40, 41, 45–46

Bernstein, Elizabeth, **Supp. XII:** 318

Bernstein, Leonard, **I:** 28; **Supp. I Part 1:** 288, 289; **Supp. IV Part 1:** 83, 84

Bernstein, Melvin, **Supp. XIV:** 41, 46

Bernstein, Michael André, **Retro. Supp. I:** 427

Bernstein, Richard, **Supp. IX:** 253, 262; **Supp. XII:** 113; **Supp. XIV:** 33; **Supp. XXII:** 261

Berrett, Jesse, **Supp. XIII:** 241, 242

Berrigan, Ted, **Supp. XIV:** 150; **Supp. XXII:** 224, 225, 228, 231; **Supp. XXIII:** 218, 221; **Supp. XXIV:** 33–47; **Supp. XXVII:** 18, 22, 24

Berroa y Canelo, Quiterio, **Supp. XXI:** 104

"Berry" (Hughes), **Supp. I Part 1:** 329, 330

Berry, Eleanor, **Supp. XXIII:** 246

Berry, Faith, **Retro. Supp. I:** 194, 201

Berry, Walter, **IV:** 313–314, 326

Berry, Wendell, **Supp. VIII:** 304; **Supp. X:** 21–39; **Supp. XII:** 202; **Supp. XIII:** 1–2; **Supp. XIV:** 179; **Supp. XVI:** 39, 56; **Supp. XVIII:** 192; **Supp. XXI:** 90

"Berry Feast, A" (Snyder), **Supp. VIII:** 289, 297

Berryman, John, **I:** 167–189, 405, 441–442, 521; **II:** 554; **III:** 273; **IV:** 138, 430; **Retro. Supp. I:** 430; **Retro. Supp. II:** 175, 178; **Supp. I Part 2:** 546; **Supp. II Part 1:** 109; **Supp. III Part 2:** 541, 561, 595, 596, 603; **Supp. IV Part 2:** 620, 639; **Supp. IX:** 152; **Supp. V:** 179–180, 337; **Supp. XI:** 240; **Supp. XV:** 93; **Supp. XVII:** 111; **Supp. XXII:** 83

Berryman, Mrs. John, **I:** 168–169

Berryman's Sonnets (Berryman), **I:** 168, 175–178

"Berry Territory" (Snyder), **Supp. VIII:** 304

Berthoff, Warner, **Supp. I Part 1:** 133

Berthoff, Werner, **Supp. XXVI:** 23

Bertolucci, Bernardo, **Supp. IV Part 1:** 94

"Bertrand Hume" (Masters), **Supp. I Part 2:** 463–464

Besco, Glenn, **Supp. XXIII:** 125

"Be Serious" (Stone), **Supp. XXVII:** 263

Bessie, Alvah C., **Supp. XXVI:** 28

"Best, the Most, The" (Carruth), **Supp. XVI:** 59

Best American Essays 1987, The (G. Talese and R. Atwan, eds.), **Supp. XVI:** 273

Best American Essays 1988, The (Dillard, ed.), **Supp. VIII:** 272

Best American Essays 1989, The (Wolff, ed.), **Supp. XVII:** 208

Best American Essays 1993, The (J. Epstein, ed.), **Supp. XVI:** 275

Best American Essays 1997, The (Frazier, ed.), **Supp. VIII:** 272; **Supp. XVII:** 207

Best American Essays 1999, The (E. Hoagland and R. Atwan, eds.), **Supp. XVI:** 277

Best American Essays 2008, The, **Supp. XXIV:** 230

Best American Essays 2009, The, **Supp. XXIV:** 230

Best American Essays for College Students, The (R. Atwan, ed.), **Supp. XVI:** 273

Best American Fantasy, 2010 (Brockmeier, ed.), **Supp. XXII:** 49–50

Best American New Voices 2001 (C. Baxter, ed.), **Supp. XVII:** 22

Best American Poetry, The: 1988 (Ashbery, ed.), **Supp. III Part 1:** 26

Best American Poetry 2000, The (Dove and Lehman, eds.), **Supp. XXI:** 246

Best American Poetry 2006, The (Collins, ed.), **Supp. XXI:** 54

Best American Short Stories, **I:**174; **II:** 587; **III:** 443; **Supp. IV Part 1:** 102, 315; **Supp. IX:** 114; **Supp. X:** 301

Best American Short Stories, 1915–1050, The, **Supp. IX:** 4

Best American Short Stories 1965, The (Foley, ed.), **Supp. XVI:** 225

Best American Short Stories 1979, The, **Supp. XXIII:** 290

Best American Short Stories 1982, The (Gardner, ed.), **Supp. XVII:** 16

Best American Short Stories 1983, The (A. Tyler, ed.), **Supp. XVI:** 37

Best American Short Stories 1986, The (Carver, ed.), **Supp. XVII:** 17

Best American Short Stories 1988, The (Helprin, ed.), **Supp. XVI:** 16

Best American Short Stories 1989, The (Atwood, ed.), **Supp. XVII:** 18; **Supp. XXI:** 39, 42

Best American Short Stories 1991, The (Adams and Kenison, eds.), **Supp. XVI:** 256

Best American Short Stories 1996, The, **Supp. XXIII:** 295

Best American Short Stories 1997, **Supp. XXII:** 75

Best American Short Stories 2001, The (Kenison and Kingsover, eds.), **Supp. XVI:** 24

Best American Short Stories 2007, The, **Supp. XXIII:** 290

Best American Short Stories 2010, The (Russo and Pitlor, eds.), **Supp. XXVII:** 228

Best American Short Stories of 1942, The, **Supp. V:** 316

Best American Short Stories of 1944, The, **Supp. IX:** 119

Best American Short Stories of the Century (Updike, ed.), **Supp. X:** 163

Best American Short Stories of the Eighties, The (Ravenal, ed.), **Supp. IV Part 1:** 93

Best American Sports Writing of the Century, The (Halberstam, ed.), **Supp. XVII:** 204

"Best China Saucer, The" (Jewett), **Retro. Supp. II:** 145–146

Best Creative Nonfiction, Vol. 1, The (Gutkind, ed.), **Supp. XXVI:** 53

Best Creative Nonfiction, Vol. 2, The (Gutkind, ed.), **Supp. XXIV:** 230

Bester, Alfred, **Supp. XVI:** 123

Best Hour of the Night, The (Simpson), **Supp. IX: 277–279**

Bestiaire, Le (Apollinaire), **IV:** 80

Bestiary, A (Wilbur), **Supp. III Part 2:** 552

"Bestiary for the Fingers of My Right Hand" (Simic), **Supp. VIII:** 274, 275

Best Man, The: A Play About Politics (Vidal), **Supp. IV Part 2:** 683

Best Mystery Stories (Wells, ed.), **Supp. XXVI:** 277

"Best of Everything, The" (Yates), **Supp. XI:** 341

Best of Pickering, The (Pickering), **Supp. XXI:** 192, 198

Best of Plimpton (Plimpton), **Supp. XVI:** 238, 239, 240

Beston, Henry, **Supp. XXVI: 31–44**

Best Short Plays, The (Mayorga), **IV:** 381

Best Short Stories, The (O'Brien, ed.), **I:** 289

Best Short Stories by Negro Writers, The (Hughes, ed.), **Supp. I Part 1:** 345

Best Short Stories of 1926, The (O'Brien, ed.), **Supp. XVIII:** 279

Best Short Stories of 1934 (O'Brien, ed.), **Supp. XVIII:** 227

Best Short Stories of 1938 (O'Brien, ed.), **Supp. XIX:** 256; **Supp. XX:** 34

Best That Ever Did It, The (Lacy), **Supp. XV:** 201–202

Best Times, The: An Informal Memoir (Dos Passos), **I:** 475, 482

Best Words, Best Order: Essays on Poetry (Dobyns), **Supp. XIII:** 74, **76–78,** 87

Best Years of Our Lives, The (film; Wyler), **Supp. XV:** 195

"BETANCOURT" (Baraka), **Supp. II Part 1:** 33, 34

Bête humaine, La (Zola), **III:** 316, 318

"Beth Ann and Macrobioticism" (Christgau), **Supp. XXVII:** 37–39

"Bethe" (Hellman), **Supp. I Part 1:** 293

Bethea, David, **Supp. VIII:** 27

Bethel Merriday (Lewis), **II:** 455

Bethke, Bruce, **Supp. XVI:** 121

Bethlehem in Broad Daylight (Doty), **Supp. XI:** 121, **122–123**

Bethune, Jane, **Supp. XXVI:** 240, 245

Bethune, Mary McLeod, **Retro. Supp. I:** 197; **Supp. I Part 1:** 333

Bethurum, Dorothy, **IV:** 121

"Betrayal" (Lanier), **Supp. I Part 1:** 364

"Betrothed" (Bogan), **Supp. III Part 1:** 49–51

Bettelheim, Bruno, **Supp. I Part 2:** 622; **Supp. X:** 77, 84; **Supp. XIV:** 126; **Supp. XVI:** 33

Better Days (Price), **Supp. VI:** 264

Better Sort, The (James), **II:** 335

Better Than Sex (Thompson), **Supp. XXIV:** 283

"Better Things in Life, The" (Loos), **Supp. XVI:** 194

Betty Leicester (Jewett), **II:** 406

Betty Leicester's Christmas (Jewett), **II:** 406; **Retro. Supp. II:** 145

Betty's Summer Vacation (Durang), **Supp. XXIV: 125–126**

Between Angels (Dunn), **Supp. XI: 149–159**

"Between Angels" (Dunn), **Supp. XI:** 150

Between Fantoine and Agapa (Pinget), **Supp. V:** 39

"Between Memory and History: A Writer's Voice" (Kreisler), **Supp. XVI:** 155

"Between Queer Performances" (Hardin), **Supp. XXVI:** 242

Between Silences: A Voice from China (Jin), **Supp. XVIII:** 91, 92, 93

"Between the Porch and the Altar" (R. Lowell), **II:** 540–541

"Between the World and Me" (Wright), **Supp. II Part 1:** 228

Between Time and Timbuktu (Vonnegut), **Supp. II Part 2:** 753, 759

Between Two Rivers (Kenny), **Supp. XXIII:** 143

Beuka, Robert A., **Supp. XIX:** 263; **Supp. XXI:** 47

"Be Very Afraid—Of Loss of Liberty at Home" (P. N. Warren), **Supp. XX: 272–273**

Bevis, Howard L., **Supp. I Part 2:** 611

Bevis, John, **Supp. I Part 2:** 503

Bewilderment: New Poems and Translations (Ferry), **Supp. XXIV: 160–161**

"Bewitched" (Wharton), **IV:** 316

Bewley, Marius, **I:** 336

Beyer, Werner, **Supp. XXIII:** 145

Beyle, Marie Henri. *See* Stendhal

Beyond (Goldbarth), **Supp. XII:** 192

Beyond a Boundary (C. L. R. James), **Supp. XXI:** 159, 170–171

Beyond Black Bear Lake (LaBastille), **Supp. X:** 95, **99–102,** 108

"Beyond Charles River to the Acheron" (R. Lowell), **II:** 541

Beyond Criticism (Shapiro), **Supp. II Part 2:** 703, 711

Beyond Culture (Trilling), **Supp. III Part 2:** 508–512

Beyond Desire (Anderson), **I:** 111

Beyond Document: The Art of Nonfiction Film (Warren, ed.), **Supp. IV Part 2:** 434

Beyond Forgetting (Hughes, ed.; foreword by Gallagher), **Supp. XXIV:** 167, 171

Beyond Good and Evil (Nietzsche), **Supp. IV Part 2:** 519

"Beyond Harm" (Olds), **Supp. X:** 210

Beyond Katrina: A Meditation on the Mississippi Gulf Coast (Trethewey), **Supp. XXI:** 248

"Beyond My Solitude" (Gibran), **Supp. XX:** 119

"Beyond the Alps" (R. Lowell), **II:** 547, 550

"Beyond the Bayou" (Chopin), **Supp. I Part 1:** 215

"Beyond the Black River" (Howard), **Supp. XXVII:** 126

Beyond the Boom: New Voices on American Life, Culture and Politics (Teachout), **Supp. XIX:** 137

Beyond the Horizon (O'Neill), **III:** 389; **Supp. XXI:** 13; **Supp. XXII:** 22

Beyond the Hundredth Meridian: John Wesley Powell and the Second Opening of the West (Stegner), **Supp. IV Part 2:** 599, 603–604, 611

"Beyond the Kittery Bridge" (Hatlen), **Supp. V:** 138

Beyond the Law (film) (Mailer), **Retro. Supp. II:** 205

Beyond Therapy (Durang), **Supp. XXIV: 119–120**

"Beyond the Sea (at the sanatorium)" (Salinas), **Supp. XIII:** 325

Beyond the Wall: Essays from the Outside (Abbey), **Supp. XIII:** 13

Beyond the Wall of Sleep (Lovecraft), **Supp. XXV:** 113

Beyond the Writers' Workshop: New Ways to Write Creative Nonfiction (C. Bly), **Supp. XVI:** 41

Beyond Tragedy (Niebuhr), **III:** 300–303

Bezner, Kevin, **Supp. XII:** 202

B. F.'s Daughter (Marquand), **III:** 59, 65, 68, 69

Bhagavad Gita, **III:** 566; **IV:** 183

"Biafra: A People Betrayed" (Vonnegut), **Supp. II Part 2:** 760

Bianchi, Martha Dickinson, **I:** 470; **Retro. Supp. I:** 35, 37, 38

Bible, **I:** 191, 280, 414, 421, 490, 506; **II:** 6, 12, 15, 17, 108, 231, 237, 238, 252, 267, 302; **III:** 28, 199, 308–309, 341, 343, 350, 356, 402, 492, 519, 565, 577; **IV:** 11, 13, 42, 57, 60, 67, 152, 153, 154, 155, 164, 165, 296, 337, 341, 367, 369, 370, 371, 438; **Retro. Supp. I:** 91; **Supp. I Part 1:** 4, 6, 63, 101, 104, 105, 113, 193, 369; **Supp. I Part 2:** 388, 433, 494, 515, 516, 517, 583, 584, 587, 589, 653, 689, 690, 691; **Supp. IV Part 1:** 284; **Supp. IX:** 246; **Supp. VIII:** 20; **Supp. XIV:** 225. *See also* names of biblical books; New Testament; Old Testament

Biblia Americana (Mather), **Supp. II Part 2:** 442

Biblical Dialogues between a Father and His Family (Rowson), **Supp. XV:** 245–246

"Bibliography of the King's Book, A, or, Eikon Basilike" (Howe), **Supp. IV Part 2:** 435

Bibliography of the King's Book, A; or, Eikon Basilike (Almack), **Supp. IV Part 2:** 435

"Bicentennial" (Davison), **Supp. XXVI:** 73, 77

Bickel, Freddy. *See* March, Fredric

Bicycle Thieves (film, De Sica), **Supp. XXVI:** 134

Bidart, Frank, **Retro. Supp. II:** 48, 50, 52, 182, 183, 184; **Supp. XIX:** 82; **Supp. XV:** 19–37; **Supp. XVIII:** 91,92

Bid Me to Live (Doolittle), **Supp. I Part 1:** 258, 260, 268, 269, 270

"Bien Pretty" (Cisneros), **Supp. VII:** 70

"Bienvenidos" (Mora), **Supp. XIII:** 220

Bierce, Albert, **I:** 191, 209

Bierce, Ambrose, **I:** 190–213, 419; **II:** 74, 264, 271; **IV:** 350; **Retro. Supp. II:** 72; **Supp. XXV:** 26

Bierce, Mrs. Ambrose, **I:** 194–195, 199

Bierce, Day, **I:** 195, 199

Bierce, Helen, **I:** 210

Bierce, Leigh, **I:** 195, 198, 208

Bierce, General Lucius Verus, **I:** 191

Bierce, Marcus, **I:** 190, 191

Bierce, Mrs. Marcus, **I:** 190, 191

Bierds, Linda, **Supp. XVII:** 25–37

Biffle, Kent, **Supp. V:** 225

"Bi-Focal" (Stafford), **Supp. XI:** 318, 321

Bigamist's Daughter, A (McDermott), **Supp. XVIII:** 155, **156–158,** 160, 166

Big as Life (Doctorow), **Supp. IV Part 1:** 231, 234

Big Bad Love (film, Howard), **Supp. XXI:** 39

Big Bad Love (L. Brown), **Supp. XXI:** 40, 42, **44–45**

"Big Bite" (Mailer), **Retro. Supp. II:** 204

"Big Blonde" (Parker), **Supp. IX:** 189, 192, 193, 195, 196, 203

Big Bozo, The (Glaspell), **Supp. III Part 1:** 182

Bigelow, Gordon, **Supp. X:** 222, 227, 229

Bigelow, Jacob, **Supp. I Part 1:** 302

Bigelow Papers, Second Series, The (J. R. Lowell), **Supp. I Part 2:** 406, 415–416

Bigelow Papers, The (J. R. Lowell), **Supp. I Part 2:** 406, 407, 408, 410, 411–412, 415, 417, 424

"Big Fiddle" (Boyle), **Supp. XXIV:** 54

Big Fix, The (Lacy), **Supp. XV:** 204–205

Bigfoot Dreams (Prose), **Supp. XVI:** 253–254

Big Funk, The: A Casual Play (Shanley), **Supp. XIV:** 316, **327**

"Big Game" (Boyle), **Supp. XX: 20**

Big Game, The (film), **Supp. XIX:** 244

Big Gold Dream, The (C. Himes), **Supp. XVI:** 143, 144

"Bight, The" (Bishop), **Retro. Supp. II:** 38, 45

Big Hunger: Stories 1932–1959 (Fante), **Supp. XI:** 160

Big Knife, The (Odets), **Supp. II Part 2:** 546, 547, 548

Big Knockover, The (Hammett), **Supp. I Part 1:** 292; **Supp. IV Part 1:** 344, 345, 356

Big Laugh, The (O'Hara), **III:** 362, 373–375

Big Man (Neugeboren), **Supp. XVI:** 219, **220,** 221, 225

Big Money, The (Dos Passos), **I:** 482, 483, 486–487, 489; **Supp. I Part 2:** 646, 647

Big Picture (Everett), **Supp. XVIII:** 54, 66

"Big Picture" (Everett), **Supp. XVIII:** 66

"Big Picture" (Halliday), **Supp. XIX:** 93

"Big Rock Candy Figgy Pudding Pitfall, The" (Didion), **Supp. IV Part 1:** 195

Big Rock Candy Mountain, The (Stegner), **Supp. IV Part 2:** 596, 597, 598, 599, 600, 603, 604, 605, 606–607, 608, 610–611

Bigsby, C. W. E. (Christopher), **Supp. IX:** 137, 140; **Supp. XV:** 332

Big Sea, The (Hughes), **Retro. Supp. I:** 195, 197, 199, 201, 204; **Supp. I Part 1:** 322, 332, 333; **Supp. II Part 1:** 233–234; **Supp. XIX:** 77; **Supp. XXII:** 3

Big Sky, The (Mora), **Supp. XIII:** 221

Big Sleep, The (Chandler), **Supp. IV Part 1:** 122–125, 127, 128, 134

Big Sleep, The (film), **Supp. IV Part 1:** 130; **Supp. XVIII:** 148

Big Strike, The (Ryan as Quin), **Supp. XVIII:** 226,**232–233**

Big Sur (Kerouac), **Supp. III Part 1:** 230

Big Sur and the Oranges of Hieronymous Bosch (H. Miller), **III:** 189–190

Big Time, The (Hayes), **Supp. XXVI:** 144

Big Town, The (Lardner), **II:** 426, 429

"Big Two-Hearted River" (Hemingway), **II:** 249; **Retro. Supp. I:** 170–171; **Supp. IX:** 106; **Supp. XIV:** 227, 235

"Big Wind" (Roethke), **III:** 531

"Big Winner Rises Late, The" (Dunn), **Supp. XI:** 146

"Bilingual/*Bilingüe*" (essay; Espaillat), *Supp. XXI:* 103

"Bilingual/*Bilingüe*" (poem; Espaillat), *Supp. XXI:* 104

"Bilingual Christmas" (Mora), **Supp. XIII:** 216–217

"Bilingual Sestina" (Alvarez), **Supp. VII:** 10

"Bill" (Winters), **Supp. II Part 2:** 792

"Bill, The" (Malamud), **Supp. I Part 2:** 427, 430, 434

"Bill Collector's Vacation, The" (Hampl), **Supp. XXII:** 83

"Billie Holiday" (Carruth), **Supp. XVI:** 50

Billings, Gladys. *See* Brooks, Mrs. Van Wyck

Billings, Josh, **Supp. XVIII:** 1, 4

Bill of Rites, a Bill of Wrongs, a Bill of Goods, A (Morris), **III:** 237

"Bill's Beans" (Nye), **Supp. XIII:** 283

"Billy" (Gordon), **Supp. IV Part 1:** 306

"Billy" (McCarriston), **Supp. XIV:** 265

Billy Bathgate (Doctorow), **Supp. IV Part 1:** 217, 219, 222, 224, 227, 229–231, 231, 232, 233, 238

Billy Bathgate (film), **Supp. IV Part 1:** 236

Billy Budd, Sailor (Melville), **III:** 40, 93–95; **IV:** 105; **Retro. Supp. I:** 249, **258–260**

Billy Collins Live: A Performance at the Peter Norton Symphony Space April 20, 2005 (CD, Collins), **Supp. XXI:** 51

"Billy Gardner's Ground Out" (Skloot), **Supp. XX: 205, 207**

Billy Phelan's Greatest Game (W. Kennedy), **Supp. VII:** 131, 132, 134, 135, 142–147, 149, 151, 153, 155

Billy Ray's Farm: Essays from a Place Called Tula (L. Brown), **Supp. XXI:** 48, 49

Billy's Boy (P. N. Warren), **Supp. XX: 261, 265–267**

Billy the Kid, **Supp. IV Part 2:** 489, 490, 492

Biloxi Blues (Simon), **Supp. IV Part 2:** 576, 577, 584, 586–587, 590

"Bimini" (Hemingway), **II:** 258

Bingham, Anne, **Supp. XV:** 239

Bingham, Millicent Todd, **I:** 470; **Retro. Supp. I:** 36

Bingham, Remica L., **Supp. XXI:** 256

Bingo Palace, The (Erdrich), **Supp. IV Part 1:** 259, 260, 261, 263–264, 265, 266–267, 268–269, 270, 271–273, 274, 275

"Binsey Poplars" (Hopkins), **Supp. I Part 1:** 94; **Supp. IV Part 2:** 639

Binswanger, Ludwig, **Supp. XV:** 26
Biographia Literaria (Coleridge), **II:** 10;
  Retro. Supp. I: 308
"Biography" (Francis), **Supp. IX:** 77
"Biography" (Pinsky), **Supp. VI:** 235,
  236, 239, 241, **243,** 249, 250
*Biography and Poetical Remains of the
  Late Margaret Miller Davidson*
  (Irving), **II:** 314
"Biography in the First Person" (Dunn),
  Supp. XI: 144
"Biography of an Armenian Schoolgirl"
  (Nye), **Supp. XIII:** 275, 280
"Biography of a Story" (Jackson), **Supp.
  IX:** 113
Biondi, Joann, **Supp. XI:** 103
"Biopoetics Sketch for *Greenfield Re-
  view*" (Harjo), **Supp. XII:** 216
"Biotherm"(O'Hara), **Supp. XXIII:** 208,
  218–219
"Birchbrook Mill" (Whittier), **Supp. I
  Part 2:** 699
"Birches" (Frost), **II:** 154; **Retro. Supp.
  I:** 132; **Supp. XIII:** 147
Bird, Alan, **Supp. I Part 1:** 260
Bird, Gloria, **Supp. XII:** 216
Bird, Isabella, **Supp. X:** 103
Bird, Robert M., **III:** 423
"Bird, The" (Simpson), **Supp. IX:** 269–
  270
"Bird, the Bird, the Bird, The" (Creeley),
  Supp. IV Part 1: 149
"Bird, The"(Le Sueur), **Supp. XXIII:** 167
"Bird Banding with the Biologists" (Ray),
  Supp. XVIII: 194
*Bird by Bird: Some Instructions on Writ-
  ing and Life* (Lamott), **Supp. XX: 132,
  137–138**
"Bird came down the Walk, A"
  (Dickinson), **Retro. Supp. I:** 37
"Bird Frau, The" (Dove), **Supp. IV Part
  1:** 245
"Bird in Hand" (screen story) (West and
  Ingster), **Retro. Supp. II:** 330
Bird Kingdom of the Mayas (LaBastille),
  Supp. X: 96
"Bird on a Wire" (Cohen), **Supp. XXVII:**
  51
Birds and Beasts (W. J. Smith), **Supp.
  XIII:** 346
"Birds for Christmas, The" (Richard),
  Supp. XIX: 221
Bird's Nest, The (Jackson), **Supp. IX:
  124–125**
Birds of America (McCarthy), **II:** 579–
  583; **Supp. X:** 177
Birds of America (Moore), **Supp. X:** 163,
  165, 167, 168, 171, **177–179**
Birds of America, The (Audubon), **Supp.
  XVI: 5–6,** 7, 9, 10, 12, 13
"Birds of Killingsworth, The"
  (Longfellow), **Retro. Supp. II:** 164
Birds of North America (Audubon
  Society), **Supp. X:** 177
"Birds of Vietnam, The" (Carruth), **Supp.
  XVI:** 55
"Bird-Window-Flying" (Gallagher),
  Supp. XXIV: 169
"Bird-Witted" (Moore), **III:** 214
Birkelo, Cheryl, **Supp. XX: 220–221**

Birkerts, Sven, **Supp. IV Part 2:** 650;
  Supp. V: 212; **Supp. VIII:** 85; **Supp.
  X:** 311; **Supp. XX:** 92
Birkhead, L. M., **III:** 116
"Birmingham Sunday" (Hughes), **Supp. I
  Part 1:** 343
Birnbaum, Henry, **Supp. XII:** 128
Birnbaum, Robert, **Supp. X:** 13; **Supp.
  XVI:** 75; **Supp. XXIII:** 73, 75, 275
Birney, James G., **Supp. I Part 2:** 587,
  588
Birstein, Ann, **Supp. VIII:** 100
"Birthday, A" (Untermeyer), **Supp. XV:**
  296
Birthday Basket for Tía, A (Mora), **Supp.
  XIII:** 221
"Birthday Cake" (Carruth), **Supp. XVI:**
  59
"Birthday Cake for Lionel, A" (Wylie),
  Supp. I Part 2: 721
"Birthday Girl: 1950" (McCarriston),
  Supp. XIV: 261
"Birthday of Mrs. Pineda, The" (Ríos),
  Supp. IV Part 2: 542, 546
"Birthday Poem, A" (Hecht), **Supp. X:**
  64
"Birthday Present, A" (Plath), **Supp. I
  Part 2:** 531
"Birthmark" (July), **Supp. XXIV:** 206
"Birthmark, The" (Ellison), **Retro. Supp.
  II:** 116; **Supp. II Part 1:** 237–238
"Birth-mark, The" (Hawthorne), **Retro.
  Supp. I:** 152
*Birth-mark, The: Unsettling the Wilder-
  ness in American Literary History*
  (Howe), **Supp. IV Part 2:** 422, 431,
  434
Birth of a Nation, The (film), **Supp. I
  Part 1:** 66
*Birth of a World: Bolívar in Terms of His
  Peoples* (W. Frank), **Supp. XX:** 80
Birth of the Poet, The (Gordon), **Supp.
  XII:** 7
Birth of Tragedy, The (Nietzsche), **Supp.
  IV Part 1:** 105, 110; **Supp. IV Part
  2:** 519; **Supp. VIII:** 182
"Birth of Venus, The" (Botticelli), **IV:**
  410
"Birth of Venus, The" (Rukeyser), **Supp.
  VI:** 281
"Birth of Water Stories, The" (Vaz),
  Supp. XXVI: 260
"Birthplace: New Rochelle" (Oppen),
  Supp. XXVI: 231
"Birthplace Revisited" (Corso), **Supp.
  XII:** 123
"Birthright" (McKay), **Supp. X:** 136
Bisch, Louis E., **Supp. I Part 2:** 608
Bisco, John, **Supp. XVIII:** 11
"B is for Bachelors" (M. F. K. Fisher),
  Supp. XVII: 86
Bishop, Elizabeth, **Retro. Supp. I:** 140,
  296, 303; **Retro. Supp. II: 37–56,**
  175, 178, 189, 233, 234, 235; **Supp. I
  Part 1: 72–97,** 239, 320, 326; **Supp.
  III Part 1:** 6, 7, 10, 18, 64, 239, 320,
  326; **Supp. III Part 2:** 541, 561;
  Supp. IV Part 1: 249, 257; **Supp. IV
  Part 2:** 439, 626, 639, 641, 644, 647,
  651, 653; **Supp. IX:** 40, 41, 45, 47,

  48; **Supp. V:** 337; **Supp. X:** 58; **Supp.
  XI:** 123, 136; **Supp. XIII:** 115, 348;
  Supp. XV: 20–21, 100, 101, 112, 119,
  249, 251; **Supp. XVII:** 36, 76; **Supp.
  XXI:** 58, 84, 131; **Supp. XXIII:** 117;
  Supp. XXV: 222; **Supp. XXVI:** 67,
  78; **Supp. XXVII:** 228
Bishop, James, Jr., **Supp. XIII:** 1, 5, 6,
  7, 9, 11, 15
Bishop, John Peale, **I:** 432, 440; **II:** 81,
  85, 86–87, 91, 209; **IV:** 35, 140, 427;
  Retro. Supp. I: 109; **Supp. I Part 2:**
  709
Bishop, John W., **Supp. I Part 1:** 83
Bishop, Judith, **Supp. XVI:** 295
Bishop, Morris, **Supp. I Part 2:** 676
Bishop, Rudine Sims, **Supp. XXVII:** 203
Bishop, William Thomas, **Supp. I Part
  1:** 83
"Bishop Orders His Tomb at St. Praxed's
  Church, The" (R. Browning), **Supp.
  XV:** 127
"Bishop's Beggar, The" (Benét), **Supp.
  XI:** 56
"Bismarck" (Chapman), **Supp. XIV:** 52,
  53
Bismark, Otto von, **Supp. I Part 2:** 643
Biss, Eula, **Supp. XXVI: 45–60**
"Bistro Styx, The" (Dove), **Supp. IV
  Part 1:** 250–251
Bitov, Andrei, **Retro. Supp. I:** 278
Bits of Gossip (R. H. Davis), **Supp. XVI:**
  82–83, 84, 85, 89
"Bitte Nehmen Sie Die Blumen" (Boyle),
  Supp. XXIV: 57
"Bitter Drink, The" (Dos Passos), **Supp.
  I Part 2:** 647
"Bitter Farce, A" (Schwartz), **Supp. II
  Part 2:** 640, 657–658
Bitter Medicine (Paretsky), **Supp. XXV:**
  174, 179, 183
"Bitter Pills for the Dark Ladies" (Jong),
  Supp. V: 118
Bitterroot (Burke), **Supp. XIV:** 34, 35
"Bittersweet Nightshade" (Skloot), **Supp.
  XX:** 202
Bitter Victory (Hardy; Kinnell, trans.),
  Supp. III Part 1: 235
Bittner, William, **Supp. XX: 74,Supp.
  XX:** 77, 76, 78, 80
Bitzer, G. W. "Billy", **Supp. XVI:** 183
Bixby, Horace, **IV:** 194
Bjerre, Thomas Aervold, **Supp. XXI:** 41,
  47; **Supp. XXVII:** 218
Bjorkman, Frances Maule, **Supp. V:** 285
Bjorkman, Stig, **Supp. XV:** 6
Björnson, Björnstjerne, **II:** 275
Black, Cheryl, **Supp. XXI:** 6
Black 100, The (Salley), **Supp. XIV:** 195
Blackamerican Literature, 1760-Present
  (R. Miller), **Supp. X:** 324
Black American Literature Forum, **Supp.
  XI:** 86, 92, 93
Black and Blue (Quindlen), **Supp. XVII:**
  166, **176–178**
"Black and Tan" (Bell), **Supp. X:** 9
Black and White (Sorrentino), **Supp.
  XXI:** 228
Black Armour (Wylie), **Supp. I Part 2:**
  708, 709, 712–714, 729

"Black Art" (Baraka), **Supp. II Part 1:** 49, 50–51, 59, 60

"Black Art, The" (Sexton), **Supp. II Part 2:** 682

"Black Aspen, The" (Davison), **Supp. XXVI:** 78

"Black Ball, The" (Ellison), **Retro. Supp. II:** 124

Black Bart and the Sacred Hills (Wilson), **Supp. VIII:** 330, 331

Black Beetles in Amber (Bierce), **I:** 204, 209

"Blackberries" (Komunyakaa), **Supp. XIII:** 126

"Blackberry Eating" (Kinnell), **Supp. III Part 1:** 250

"Blackberrying" (D. West), **Supp. XVIII:** 283

Blackberry Winter (Warren), **IV:** 243, 251, 252

Black Betty (Mosley), **Supp. XIII:** 237, **Supp. XIII:** 240, 243

"Black Birch in Winter, A" (Wilbur), **Supp. III Part 2:** 561

"Black Boy" (Boyle), **Supp. XXIV:** 59

Black Boy (Wright), **IV:** 477, 478, 479, 480–482, 488, 489, 494; **Retro. Supp. II:** 117; **Supp. II Part 1:** 235–236; **Supp. IV Part 1:** 11; **Supp. XVIII:** 286

"Black Boys and Native Sons" (Howe), **Retro. Supp. II:** 112

Blackburn, Alex, **Supp. XIII:** 112

Blackburn, Paul, **Supp. XXII:** 164, 169; **Supp. XXIV:** 34, 37

Blackburn, William, **IV:** 100

"Black Buttercups" (Clampitt), **Supp. IX:** 42

Black Cargo, The (Marquand), **III:** 55, 60

Black Cargoes: A History of the Atlantic Slave Trade (Cowley), **Supp. II Part 1:** 140

"Black Cat, The" (Poe), **III:** 413, 414, 415; **Retro. Supp. II:** 264, 267, 269, 270; **Supp. XXV:** 112

Black Cherry Blues (Burke), **Supp. XIV:** 30

"Black Christ, The" (Cullen), **Supp. IV Part 1:** 170, 171–172

Black Christ and Other Poems, The (Cullen), **Supp. IV Part 1:** 166, 170

"Black Clay Fish from Oaxaca, A" (Bronk), **Supp. XXI:** 31

"Black Colossus" (Howard), **Supp. XXVII:** 126

"Black Cottage, The" (Frost), **Retro. Supp. I:** 128

"BLACK DADA NIHILISMUS" (Baraka), **Supp. II Part 1:** 39, 41

"Black Death" (Hurston), **Supp. VI:** 153

Black Dog, Red Dog (Dobyns), **Supp. XIII:** 87, **88–89**

"Black Dog, Red Dog" (Dobyns), **Supp. XIII:** 89

Black Dog of Fate: A Memoir (Balakian), **Supp. XXIII:** 19, **20–24,** 24, 25

"Black Earth" (Moore), **III:** 197, 212

Black Echo, The (Connelly), **Supp. XXI:** 67, 68, 75, 80

"Black Experience in Children's Books, The: One Step Forward, Two Steps Back" (Myers), **Supp. XXVII:** 200

Black Fire (Jones and Neal, eds.), **Supp. X:** 324, 328

Black Fire: An Anthology of Afro American Writing (Baraka, ed.), **Supp. II Part 1:** 53

Black Flame, The (Du Bois), **Supp. II Part 1:** 159, 185–186

Black Folk, Then and Now: An Essay in the History and Sociology of the Negro Race (Du Bois), **Supp. II Part 1:** 159, 178, 183, 185

Blackford, Holly, **Supp. XXII:** 300

"Black Fox, The" (Whittier), **Supp. I Part 2:** 692

Black Freckles (Levis), **Supp. XI:** 257, 271

"Black Gang", **IV:** 406, 407

Black Genius (Mosley, ed.), **Supp. XIII:** 246

Blackguard (Bodenheim), **Supp. XXV:** 17, 18, 22, 23–24

"Black Hood, The" (Francis), **Supp. IX:** 83, 91

Black House, The (Theroux), **Supp. VIII:** 319

Black Humor (C. Johnson), **Supp. VI:** 187, 199

Black Ice, The (Connelly), **Supp. XXI:** **70,** 75

Black Image in the White Mind, The (Fredrickson), **Supp. I Part 2:** 589

"Black Is My Favorite Color" (Malamud), **Supp. I Part 2:** 437

Black Jacobins, The (C. L. R. James), **Supp. XXI:** 159, 166–167

"Black Jewel, The" (Merwin), **Supp. III Part 1:** 355

Black Lamb and Grey Falcon (R. West), **Supp. XVI:** 152

"Black Laughter" (Taggard), **Supp. XXII:** 274

"Blacklegs" (B. Kelly), **Supp. XVII:** 131

Black Light (Kinnell), **Supp. III Part 1:** 235, 243

Black Like Me (Griffin), **Supp. XXV:** 51

Blacklist (Paretsky), **Supp. XXV:** 182, 184

"Blacklist and the Cold War, The" (Kramer), **Supp. I Part 1:** 295

Black Literature in America (Baker), **Supp. X:** 324

Black Magic, A Pictorial History of the Negro in American Entertainment (Hughes), **Supp. I Part 1:** 345

Black Magic: Collected Poetry 1961– 1967 (Baraka), **Supp. II Part 1:** 45, 49–50

"Blackmailers Don't Shoot" (Chandler), **Supp. IV Part 1:** 121–122

Black Manhattan (J. W. Johnson), **Supp. IV Part 1:** 169

Black Mass, A (Baraka), **Supp. II Part 1:** 46, 48–49, 56, 57

"Black Mesa, The" (Merrill), **Supp. III Part 1:** 328

Black Metropolis (Cayton and Drake), **IV:** 475, 486, 488

Black Misery (Hughes), **Supp. I Part 1:** 336

Blackmur, Helen Dickson (Mrs. R. P. Blackmur), **Supp. II Part 1:** 90

Blackmur, Richard P., **I:** 50, 63, 67, 280, 282, 386, 455, 472; **II:** 320, 537; **III:** 194, 208, 462, 478, 497; **Supp. II Part 1:** 87–112, 136; **Supp. II Part 2:** 543, 643; **Supp. XII:** 45

Black Music (Baraka), **Supp. II Part 1:** 47, 51

Black Nativity (Hughes), **Retro. Supp. I:** 196

"Black News" (Biss), **Supp. XXVI:** 56

Black No More (Schuyler), **Supp. XIX:** 73; **Supp. XVI:** 142

Black on Black: "Baby Sister" and Selected Writings (C. Himes), **Supp. XVI:** 145

"Black or White" (Major), **Supp. XXII:** 185

"Blackout" (Hay), **Supp. XIV:** 121

Black Oxen (Atherton), **Supp. XXIV:** 25–26

Black Oxen (Atherton, Dawson, ed.), **Supp. XXIV:** 31

"Black Panther" (Hughes), **Retro. Supp. I:** 211

"Black Petal" (L.-Y. Lee), **Supp. XV:** 224–225

Black Power (Wright), **IV:** 478, 488, 494

"Black Rainbow, A: Modern Afro-American Poetry" (Dove and Waniek), **Supp. IV Part 1:** 244

Black Reconstruction (Du Bois), **Supp. II Part 1:** 159, 162, 171, 182

Black Riders and Other Lines, The (Crane), **I:** 406, 419

Black Riviera, The (Jarman), **Supp. XVII:** 109, 110, **115–116**

Blackrobe: Isaac Jogues (Kenny), **Supp. XXIII:** 143, 147, **151–152,** 153, 154

"Black Rook in Rainy Weather" (Plath), **Supp. I Part 2:** 543, 544; **Supp. XXIII:** 63

Blacks (Brooks), **Supp. III Part 1:** 69, 72, 86, 87

Blacks, The (Genet), **Supp. IV Part 1:** 8

Black Skin, White Masks (Fanon), **Retro. Supp. II:** 118

Black Sleuth, The (J. Bruce), **Supp. XVI:** 143

Blacksnake at the Family Reunion (Huddle), **Supp. XXVI:** 147, 151

Black Spear, The (Hayden), **Supp. II Part 1:** 375

Black Spring (H. Miller), **III:** 170, 175, 178, 180–182, 183, 184; **Supp. X:** 187

"Black Stone, The" (Howard), **Supp. XXVII:** 119

"Black Stone Lying on a White Stone" (Vallejo), **Supp. XIII:** 324

Black Sun (Abbey), **Supp. XIII:** 4, **8–9,** 17

"Black Swan" (B. Kelly), **Supp. XVII:** 130–131

"Black Swan, The" (Jarrell), **II:** 382

Black Swan, The (Merrill), **Supp. III Part 1:** 319, 320

"Black Tambourine" (Crane), **I:** 387–388; **II:** 371

Black Thunder (Bontemps), **Supp. XXII:** 4, 9

"Black Tuesday" (Swenson), **Supp. IV Part 2:** 646

Black Virgin Mountain (Heinemann), **Supp. XXII:** 103, **114–116**

Black Voices (Chapman), **IV:** 485

"Blackwater Mountain" (Wright), **Supp. V:** 335, 340

"Black Wedding, The" (Singer), **IV:** 12–13

Blackwell, Alice Stone, **Supp. XI:** 195, 197

Blackwell, Elizabeth, **Retro. Supp. II:** 146

Black Woman, The (Bambara, ed.), **Supp. XI:** 1

"Black Workers" (Hughes), **Retro. Supp. I:** 202

"Black Writer and the Southern Experience, The" (Walker), **Supp. III Part 2:** 521

Black Zodiac (Wright), **Supp. V:** 333, 344, 345

Blade Runner (film), **Supp. XI:** 84

Blades, John, **Supp. XX:** 87

"Blades of Steel" (R. Fisher), **Supp. XIX:** 72

Blaine, Anita McCormick, **Supp. I Part 1:** 5

Blaine, Nell, **Supp. XV:** 179; **Supp. XXIII:** 217

Blair, Hugh, **II:** 8, 17; **Supp. I Part 2:** 422

Blair, Robert, **Supp. I Part 1:** 150

Blair, Walter, **II:** 20; **Retro. Supp. II:** 286

Blaisdell, Gus, **Supp. XIV:** 87

Blake, Casey Nelson, **Supp. XX:** 69, 70, **78**

Blake, William, **I:** 381, 383, 389, 390, 398, 447, 476, 525, 526, 533; **II:** 321; **III:** 5, 19, 22, 195, 196, 197, 205, 485, 528, 540, 544–545, 567, 572; **IV:** 129; **Retro. Supp. I:** 76, 300; **Supp. I Part 1:** 80; **Supp. I Part 2:** 385, 514, 517, 539, 552, 708; **Supp. V:** 208, 257, 258; **Supp. VIII:** 26, 99, 103; **Supp. X:** 120; **Supp. XII:** 45; **Supp. XIV:** 344; **Supp. XVI:** 282; **Supp. XVII:** 119; **Supp. XX:** 115, 116; **Supp. XXII:** 225, 257; **Supp. XXIV:** 159; **Supp. XXV:** 248; **Supp. XXVI:** 235; **Supp. XXVII:** 292

Blakely, Barbara, **Supp. XIII:** 32

Blanc, Marie Thérèse, **Retro. Supp. II:** 135

Blanc-Bentzon, Mme. Thérèse, **II:** 405

Blanche, Jacques-Émile, **Supp. XX:** 232

Blanche of Brandywine (Lippard), **Supp. XXIII:** 178, 185

Blanchot, Maurice, **Supp. XVI:** 288; **Supp. XXIV:** 40

Blancs, Les (Hansberry), **Supp. IV Part 1:** 359, 364, 365, 369, 372–374

Blancs, Les: The Collected Last Plays of Lorraine Hansberry (Nemiroff, ed.), **Supp. IV Part 1:** 365, 368, 374

"'Blandula, Tenulla, Vagula'" (Pound), **III:** 463; **Supp. V:** 336, 337, 345

Blankenship, Tom, **IV:** 193

"Blank Paper" (Peacock), **Supp. XIX:** 198–199

Blank Wall, The (Holding), **Supp. XXII:** 119, 120, 121, 130, **131–133,** 134

Blanshard, Rufus A., **I:** 67

Blassingame, John, **Supp. XX:** 106

Blauvelt, William Satake, **Supp. V:** 171, 173

Blavatsky, Elena Petrovna, **III:** 176

"Blazing in Gold and Quenching in Purple" (Dickinson), **Retro. Supp. I:** 30

Bleak House (Dickens), **II:** 291; **Supp. IV Part 1:** 293

Blechman, Burt, **Supp. I Part 1:** 290

"Bleeder" (Dobyns), **Supp. XIII:** 88

"Bleeding" (Swenson), **Supp. IV Part 2:** 646–647

Bleeding Kansas (Paretsky), **Supp. XXV:** 183

"Blessed Is the Man" (Moore), **III:** 215

"Blessed Man of Boston, My Grandmother's Thimble, and Fanning Island, The" (Updike), **IV:** 219

"Blessing, A" (Wright), **Supp. III Part 2:** 600, 606

Blessing on the Moon, A (Skibell), **Supp. XVII:** 48

Blessings (Quindlen), **Supp. XVII:** 167, **178–179**

"Blessing the Animals" (Komunyakaa), **Supp. XIII:** 129–130

"Blessing the Children" (Hogan), **Supp. IV Part 1:** 401

Bless Me, Ultima (Anya), **Supp. XIII:** 220

Blew, Mary Clearman, **Supp. XIV:** 227

Bligh, S. M., **I:** 226

"Blight" (Dybek), **Supp. XXIII:** 72

Blind Alleys (film), **Supp. XXI:** 146

Blind Assassin, The (Atwood), **Supp. XIII:** 20, **32**

Blind Bow-Boy, The (Van Vechten), **Supp. II Part 2:** 737, 740–742

"Blind Date" (Halliday), **Supp. XIX:** 85

Blind Date (Kosinski), **Supp. VII:** 215, 224–225

"Blinded by the Light" (Boyle), **Supp. XX:** 20

Blind Lion, The (Gunn Allen), **Supp. IV Part 1:** 324

"Blind Man's Holiday" (O. Henry), **Supp. II Part 1:** 401

Blind Man with a Pistol (C. Himes), **Supp. XVI:** 143, 144

Blindness and Insight (de Man), **Retro. Supp. I:** 67

"Blind Poet, The: Sidney Lanier" (Warren), **Supp. I Part 1:** 371, 373

"Blindsided" (E. P. Jones), **Supp. XXII:** 151–152

"Blind Tom" (R. H. Davis), **Supp. XVI:** 89, 90

Blithedale Romance, The (Hawthorne), **II:** 225, 231, 239, 241–242, 271, 282, 290; **IV:** 194; **Retro. Supp. I:** 63, 149, 152, 156–157, **162–163; Supp. I Part 2:** 579; **Supp. II Part 1:** 280; **Supp. VIII:** 153, 201

Blitzstein, Marc, **Supp. I Part 1:** 277

Blix (Norris), **III:** 314, 322, 327, 328, 333

Blixen, Karen Denisen Baroness. *See* Dinesen, Isak

"Blizzard in Cambridge" (R. Lowell), **II:** 554

Blizzard Voices, The (Kooser), **Supp. XIX:** 123

Bloch, Ernest, **Supp. XX:** 75

Bloch, Robert, **Supp. XXV:** 111, 145; **Supp. XXVII:** 119

Block, Lawrence, **Supp. XXI:** 67

"Blocks" (O'Hara), **Supp. XXIII:** 214

Blok, Aleksandr Aleksandrovich, **IV:** 443; **Supp. XXVI:** 144

"Blond" (Trethewey), **Supp. XXI:** 244

Blonde Bait (Lacy), **Supp. XV:** 204

Blonde on Blonde (album, Dylan), **Supp. XVIII:** 20, 27, 30

Blondin, Antoine, **Supp. XVI:** 230

"Blood" (Hoffman), **Supp. XVIII:** 86

"Blood" (Singer), **IV:** 15, 19

Blood, Tin, Straw (Olds), **Supp. X:** 212–**215**

Blood and Guile (Hoffman), **Supp. XVIII: 83–84**

Blood and Guts in High School (Acker), **Supp. XII:** 5, 6, **11–12**

Blood and Thunder (Finn), **Supp. XXVII:** 128

"Blood Bay, The" (Proulx), **Supp. VII:** 262–263

"Blood-Burning Moon" (Toomer), **Supp. III Part 2:** 483; **Supp. IX:** 314–315

"Bloodchild" (O. Butler), **Supp. XIII:** 61, **69–70**

Bloodchild and Other Stories (O. Butler), **Supp. XIII:** 69

"Blood Donor" (Hay), **Supp. XIV:** 121

Blood for a Stranger (Jarrell), **II:** 367, 368–369, 370–371, 375, 377

"Blood from the Stone" (Oppen), **Supp. XXVI:** 230–231

Blood Issue (Crews), **Supp. XI:** 103

Bloodlines (Wright), **Supp. V:** 332, 335, 340

Blood Meridian (McCarthy), **Supp. XXIII:** 42

Blood Meridian; or, The Evening Redness in the West (McCarthy), **Supp. VIII:** 175, 177, **180–182,** 188, 190

Blood of My Blood (Gambino), **Supp. XX:** 35

"Blood of the Conquistadores, The" (Alvarez), **Supp. VII:** 7

"Blood of the Lamb, The" (hymn), **Supp. I Part 2:** 385

Blood of the Martyr (Crane), **I:** 422

"Blood of the Martyrs, The" (Benét), **Supp. XI:** 56, 58

Blood of the Prophets, The (Masters), **Supp. I Part 2:** 458, 459, 461

Blood on the Forge (Attaway), **Supp. II Part 1:** 234–235

Blood on the Tracks (album, Dylan), **Supp. XVIII:** 20, 27, 30

"Blood Relatives" (Apple), **Supp. XVII:** 6

"Blood Returns, The" (Kingsolver), **Supp. VII:** 209

"Bloodroot" (Rash), **Supp. XXVII:** 222

"Bloodshed" (C. Ozick), **Supp. XVII:** 43

Bloodshed and Three Novellas (Ozick), **Supp. V:** 259–260, 261, 266–268

"Blood Soup"(Dybek), **Supp. XXIII:** 71

"Blood Stains" (Francis), **Supp. IX:** 86

Blood Work (Connelly), **Supp. XXI:** 72

Blood Work (film, Eastwood), **Supp. XXI:** 74

Bloody Crossroads, The: Where Literature and Politics Meet (Podhoretz), **Supp. VIII: 241–242**

Bloody News from My Friend (Samianto, trans. Balakian), **Supp. XXIII:** 28

Bloom, Alice, **Supp. IV Part 1:** 308

Bloom, Allan, **Retro. Supp. II:** 19, 30, 31, 33–34

Bloom, Claire, **Retro. Supp. II:** 281; **Supp. IX:** 125

Bloom, Harold, **Retro. Supp. I:** 67, 193, 299; **Retro. Supp. II:** 81, 210, 262; **Supp. IV Part 2:** 620, 689; **Supp. IX:** 146, 259; **Supp. V:** 178, 272; **Supp. VIII:** 180; **Supp. XII:** 261; **Supp. XIII:** 46, 47; **Supp. XIV:** 14; **Supp. XV:** 134; **Supp. XVII:** 70, 141; **Supp. XXIII:** 42; **Supp. XXV:** 251

Bloom, Larry, **Supp. XIII:** 133

Bloom, Leopold, **I:** 27, 150; **III:** 10

Bloom, Lynn Z., **Supp. IV Part 1:** 6

Bloomfield, Leonard, **I:** 64

Bloomingdale Papers, The (Carruth), **Supp. XVI:** 48–50

"Blossom and Fruit" (Benét), **Supp. XI:** 52–53

Blotner, Joseph, **Retro. Supp. I:** 88

Blouin, Lenora, **Supp. VIII:** 266

"Blouse, The"(Rudman), **Supp. XXIII:** 124

"Blowing Soap Bubbles"(Crooker), **Supp. XXIII:** 56

"Blowin' in the Wind" (song, Dylan), **Supp. XVIII:** 24, 25, 26, 29

Bluckled Bag, The (Rinehart), **Supp. XXV:** 197

Blue Angel (Prose), **Supp. XVI:** 249, 259–260

Blue Angel, The (film), **Supp. XVIII:** 243

Blue Arabesque: A Search for the Sublime (Hampl), **Supp. XXII:** 86, 98–99

"Blue Battalions, The" (Crane), **I:** 419–420

"Blue Bead, The"(Hadas), **Supp. XXIII:** 118, 119

"Bluebeard" (Barthelme), **Supp. IV Part 1:** 47

"Bluebeard" (Millay), **III:** 130

"Blueberries" (Frost), **Retro. Supp. I:** 121, 128

"Blue Boy"(Dybek), **Supp. XXIII:** 76

Blue Calhoun (Price), **Supp. VI:** 265–266

Blue Caterpillar, The (Pickering), **Supp. XXI:** 202–203

Blue City (Macdonald, as Millar), **Supp. IV Part 2:** 466–467

Blue Devils of Nada, The: A Contemporary American Approach to Aesthetics (Murray), **Supp. XIX: 159–160**

Blue Estuaries, The: Poems, 1923–1968 (Bogan), **Supp. III Part 1:** 48, 57, 66

Blue Hammer, The (Macdonald), **Supp. IV Part 2:** 462

"Blue Hotel, The" (Crane), **I:** 34, 415–416, 423

"Blue Hour, The" (Komunyakaa), **Supp. XIII:** 130

Blue in the Face (Auster), **Supp. XII:** 21

Blue Jay's Dance, The: A Birth Year (Erdrich), **Supp. IV Part 1:** 259–260, 265, 270, 272

"Blue Juniata" (Cowley), **Supp. II Part 1:** 144

Blue Juniata: Collected Poems (Cowley), **Supp. II Part 1:** 140

"Blue Lick" (Offutt), **Supp. XIX:** 164, 165

Blue Light (Mosley), **Supp. XIII: 245–247**, 248, 249

"Blue Light Lounge Sutra for the Performance Poets at Harold Park Hotel" (Komunyakaa), **Supp. XIII:** 125

"Blue Meridian" (Toomer), **Supp. III Part 2:** 476, 487; **Supp. IX:** 320

"Blue Moles" (Plath), **Supp. I Part 2:** 539

Blue Mountain Ballads (music) (Bowles), **Supp. IV Part 1:** 84

Blue Movie (Southern), **Supp. XI:** 309

"Blue Notes" (Matthews), **Supp. IX:** 169

Blue Pastoral (Sorrentino), **Supp. XXI:** 226, 235–236

Blue Pastures (Oliver), **Supp. VII:** 229–230, 245

"Blueprint for Negro Writing" (Wright), **Supp. XVIII: 282–283**

"Blueprints" (Kingsolver), **Supp. VII:** 203

Blue Religion, The (Connelly, ed.), **Supp. XXI:** 74–75, 79

Blue Rhine, Black Forest (Untermeyer), **Supp. XV:** 310

"Blue Ribbon at Amesbury, A" (Frost), **Retro. Supp. I:** 138

"Blues Ain't No Mockin Bird" (Bambara), **Supp. XI:** 3

"Blues and the Fable in the Flesh, The" (lecture, Murray), **Supp. XIX:** 153

Blues Baby: Early Poems (Mullen), **Supp. XXVII:** 174

"Blues Chant Hoodoo Rival" (Komunyakaa), **Supp. XIII:** 117, 118

Blue Screen (Parker), **Supp. XIX:** 186

"Blues for Another Time" (Dunn), **Supp. XI:** 148

"Blues for Jimmy" (McGrath), **Supp. X:** 116

"Blues for John Coltraine, Dead at 41" (Matthews), **Supp. IX:** 157

Blues for Mister Charlie (Baldwin), **Retro. Supp. II:** 8; **Supp. I Part 1:** 48, 61–62, 63

"Blues for Warren" (McGrath), **Supp. X:** 116

Blue Shoe (Lamott), **Supp. XX: 138–140**

Blues If You Want (Matthews), **Supp. IX:** 155, **163–165**

"Blues I'm Playing, The" (Hughes), **Retro. Supp. I:** 204; **Supp. XIX:** 75

Blues Journey (Myers), **Supp. XXVII:** 211

"Blue Sky, The" (Snyder), **Supp. VIII:** 306

Blues Legacies and Black Feminism (A. Davis), **Supp. XXVI:** 50

Bluesman (Dubus III), **Supp. XXIV: 102–104**

"Blues on a Box" (Hughes), **Retro. Supp. I:** 208

"Blues People" (Ellison), **Retro. Supp. II:** 124

Blues People: Negro Music in White America (Baraka), **Retro. Supp. II:** 124; **Supp. II Part 1:** 30, 31, 33–35, 37, 41, 42, 53

"Blue Spruces in Pairs, a Bird Bath Between": (Bronk), **Supp. XXI:** 30

Bluest Eye, The (Morrison), **Supp. III Part 1:** 362, 363–367, 379; **Supp. IV Part 1:** 2, 253; **Supp. VIII:** 213, 214, 227; **Supp. XI:** 4, 91

Bluestone, George, **Supp. IX:** 7, 15

Blue Swallows, The (Nemerov), **III:** 269, 270, 271, 274–275, 278, 284, 286–288

"Blue Tattoo" (Nelson and Espeland), **Supp. XVIII:** 181

Blue Voyage (Aiken), **I:** 53, 56

Bluhm, Norman, **Supp. XXIII:** 217

Blum, Gustav, **Supp. XV:** 194

Blum, Morgan, **I:** 169

Blum, W. C (pseudonym). *See* Watson, James Sibley, Jr.

Blumenthal, Nathaniel. *See* Branden, Nathaniel

Blumenthal, Sidney, **Supp. VIII:** 241

Blunden, Edmund, **Supp. XIX:** 133

Blunt, Wilfrid Scawen, **III:** 459

Bly, Carol, **Supp. XVI: 31–43**

Bly, Robert, **I:** 291; **Supp. III Part 2:** 599; **Supp. IV Part 1: 59–77,** 177; **Supp. IV Part 2:** 623; **Supp. IX:** 152, 155, 265, 271, 290; **Supp. V:** 332; **Supp. VIII:** 279; **Supp. X:** 127; **Supp. XI:** 142; **Supp. XIII:** 284; **Supp. XV:** 74, 176; **Supp. XVI:** 32, 36, 39, 177, 212, 230; **Supp. XVII:** 243, 244; **Supp. XXI:** 83, 84–86, 87, 91, 93, 94, 95; **Supp. XXII:** 83; **Supp. XXIII:** 136; **Supp. XXIV:** 219

"B Negative" (X. J. Kennedy), **Supp. XV: 156–157**

"Boarder, The" (Simpson), **Supp. IX:** 269

Boarding House Blues (Farrell), **II:** 30, 43, 45

Boarding School, The (Foster), **Supp. XXV:** 35, 36, 37, 45–47

Boas, Franz, **I:** 214; **Supp. I Part 2:** 641; **Supp. IX:** 329; **Supp. VIII:** 295; **Supp. XIV:** 199, 209, 210

"Boat, The" (Oliver), **Supp. VII:** 247

"Boat, The" (Sexton), **Supp. II Part 2:** 692

Boating Party, The (Renoir), **Supp. XII:** 188

"Boat Is Tethered to the Floor,' The: After the Harlem Renaissance" (H. Johnson), **Supp. XXVI:** 175

Boat of Quiet Hours, The (Kenyon), **Supp. VII:** 167–169, 171

"Boat of Quiet Hours, The" (Kenyon), **Supp. VII:** 168

"Boat Ride" (Gallagher), **Supp. XXIV:** 169

"Bob and Spike" (Wolfe), **Supp. III Part 2:** 580

Bobbed Hair (Wells, et al), **Supp. XXVI:** 275

"Bobby Shafter's Gone to Sea" (Swados), **Supp. XIX:** 267

"Bob Dylan's 115th Dream" (song, Dylan), **Supp. XVIII:** 25

Bobrowski, Johannes, **Supp. XV:** 78

Bob the Gambler (F. Barthelme), **Supp. XI:** 30, 31, 32, 34–35, 36–37

Boccaccio, Giovanni, **III:** 283, 411; **IV:** 230

"Bocca della Verità, La" (Davison), **Supp. XXVI:** 74

Bocock, Maclin, **Supp. X:** 79

Boddy, Kasia, **Supp. XXII:** 261

Bodelson, Anders, **Supp. XVI:** 33

Bodenheim, Maxwell, **II:** 42, 530; **Retro. Supp. I:** 417; **Supp. I Part 1:** 257; **Supp. XXV:** 17–33; **Supp. XXVII:** 86, 87, 139

"Bodies" (Oates), **Supp. II Part 2:** 520

"Bodies and Souls: The Haitian Revolution and Madison Smartt Bell's *All Souls' Rising*" (Trouillot), **Supp. X:** 14

Bodies of Water (Cliff), **Supp. XXII:** 66–67, 74–75

Bodies of Work: Essays (Acker), **Supp. XII:** 7

Bodily Harm (Atwood), **Supp. XIII:** 25–27

Bodley Head Jack London (London), **II:** 483

Body (Crews), **Supp. XI:** 108–109

"Body, The" (Heldreth), **Supp. V:** 151

Body and Soul (Conroy), **Supp. XVI:** 63, 72–74, 77

"Body and Soul: A Meditation" (Kumin), **Supp. IV Part 2:** 442, 452

Body and Soul: Essays on Poetry (Jarman), **Supp. XVII:** 110, 111–112

"Body and Soul: Parts of a Life" (Jarman), **Supp. XVII:** 112, 113

Body and the Song, The (Bishop), **Retro. Supp. II:** 40

"Body Bright" (Sanders), **Supp. XVI:** 276

Body of Martin Aquilera, The (Everett), **Supp. XVIII:** 57

Body of Poetry, The: Essays on Women, Form, and the Poetic Self (A. Finch), **Supp. XVII:** 69–70, 77–78

Body of This Death: Poems (Bogan), **Supp. III Part 1:** 47, 49–52, 58

Body of Waking (Rukeyser), **Supp. VI:** 274, 281

"Body of Waking" (Rukeyser), **Supp. VI:** 279

"Body on Fire, the Soul in Flight, The" (Jarman), **Supp. XVII:** 111, 112

Body Rags (Kinnell), **Supp. III Part 1:** 235, 236, 243–245, 250, 253, 254

"Body's Curse, The" (Dobyns), **Supp. XIII:** 87

"Body's Weight" (Espaillat), **Supp. XXI:** 111

"Body's Weight, The" (Dobyns), **Supp. XIII:** 89

Body Traffic (Dobyns), **Supp. XIII:** 87, 89

"'Body with the Lamp Lit Inside, The'" (Mills), **Supp. IV Part 1:** 64

Body Work (Paretsky), **Supp. XXV:** 177, 178, 179, 181, 184–185

Boehm, David, **Supp. XVIII:** 58

Boehme, Jakob, **I:** 10

Bogan, Louise, **I:** 169, 185; **Retro. Supp. I:** 36; **Supp. I Part 2:** 707, 726; **Supp. III Part 1:** 47–68; **Supp. IX:** 229; **Supp. VIII:** 171, 265; **Supp. X:** 58, 102; **Supp. XIII:** 347; **Supp. XIV:** 129; **Supp. XVII:** 75; **Supp. XXIII:** 145; **Supp. XXVII:** 261

Bogan, Major Benjamin Lewis, **IV:** 120

Bogart, Humphrey, **Supp. I Part 2:** 623; **Supp. IV Part 1:** 130, 356

Bogdanovich, Peter, **Supp. V:** 226

Bogey Man, The (Plimpton), **Supp. XVI:** 241

Boggs, Francis W., **Supp. XVI:** 182

"Bogs" (Pickering), **Supp. XXI:** 198

"Bohemian, The" (Hapgood), **Supp. XVII:** 103

"Bohemian, The" (Harte), **Supp. II Part 1:** 339

"Bohemian Girl, The" (Cather), **Retro. Supp. I:** 7

"Bohemian Hymn, The" (Emerson), **II:** 19

"Bohemians" (Saunders), **Supp. XIX:** 234

"Boids and Beasties" (Geisel), **Supp. XVI:** 100

Boissevain, Eugen, **III:** 124

Boissière, Ralph de, **Supp. XXI:** 160

Boit, Edward, **Retro. Supp. II:** 366

Bojorquez, Jennifer, **Supp. XII:** 318

"Boke, A" (Berrigan), **Supp. XXIV:** 42

Boker, George, **Supp. XV:** 269

Bolaño, Roberto, **Supp. XXV:** 49

"Bold Words at the Bridge" (Jewett), **II:** 394

Boleslavsky, Richard, **Supp. XIV:** 240, 243

Boleyn, Anne, **Supp. I Part 2:** 461

Bolick, Katie, **Supp. XVI:** 167; **Supp. XXIII:** 135, 137, 138; **Supp. XXIV:** 167, 173, 177

Bolinas Journal (Brainard), **Supp. XXVII:** 20, 27

Bolivar, Simon, **Supp. I Part 1:** 283, 284, 285

Bolonik, Kera, **Supp. XVIII:** 60

Bolton, Guy, **Supp. I Part 1:** 281

Bolts of Melody: New Poems of Emily Dickinson (Todd and Bingham, eds.), **I:** 470; **Retro. Supp. I:** 36

"Bomb" (Corso), **Supp. XII:** 117, 124, 125–126, 127

Bombeck, Erma, **Supp. XVII:** 168

Bombs Away (Steinbeck), **IV:** 51–52

"Bona and Paul" (Toomer), **Supp. IX:** 307, 318–319

Bonaparte, Darren, **Supp. XXVI:** 88

Bonaparte, Marie, **III:** 418; **Retro. Supp. II:** 264, 266

"Bon-Bon" (Poe), **III:** 425

Bond, The (Boyce), **Supp. XXI:** 5, 11–12

Bond, The (N. Boyce), **Supp. XVII:** 99, 100

Bondage (Hwang), **Supp. XXI:** 147

Bondsman, The (Massinger), **Supp. XV:** 238

Bondwoman's Narrative, by Hannah Crafts, a Fugitive Slave, Recently Escaped from North Carolina, The, **Supp. XX:** 105

Bone, Martyn, **Supp. XXII:** 247

Bone, Robert, **Supp. IX:** 318–319; **Supp. XI:** 283; **Supp. XVIII:** 285

Bone by Bone (Matthiessen), **Supp. V:** 199, 212, 213, 214

"Bone Deposit" (Ray), **Supp. XVIII:** 194

Boners (Abingdon). *See Schoolboy Howlers* (Abingdon)

"Bones" (Goldbarth), **Supp. XII:** 173–174

"Bones and Jewels" (Monette), **Supp. X:** 159

"Bones and Shells" (Sanders), **Supp. XVI:** 271–272

"Bones of a House" (Cowley). *See* "Blue Juniata"

Bones on Black Spruce Mountain, The (Budbill), **Supp. XIX:** 11–12

Bonetti, Kay, **Supp. VIII:** 47, 152, 159, 160, 165, 168, 170, 223; **Supp. XII:** 61; **Supp. XIV:** 232, 234; **Supp. XXI:** 36

"Bonfire" (Gallagher), **Supp. XXIV:** 170

Bonfire of the Vanities, The (Wolfe), **Supp. III Part 2:** 584–586

Bonheur, Rosa, **Supp. XV:** 276

Bonhoeffer, Dietrich, **Supp. VIII:** 198

Boni, Charles, **Supp. XIV:** 288

Boni and Liveright, **Retro. Supp. I:** 59, 80, 178

Bonicelli, Vittorio, **Supp. XI:** 307

Bonifacius (Mather), **Supp. II Part 2:** 461, 464

Bonnefoy, Yves, **Supp. III Part 1:** 235, 243

Bonner, Robert, **Retro. Supp. I:** 246

Bonneville, Mme. Marguerite, **Supp. I Part 2:** 520, 521

Bonneville, Nicolas de, **Supp. I Part 2:** 511, 518, 519

Bonney, William. *See* Billy the Kid

Bontemps, Arna, **Retro. Supp. I:** 194, 196, 203; **Supp. I Part 1:** 325; **Supp. IV Part 1:** 170; **Supp. IX:** 306, 309; **Supp. XVIII:** 282; **Supp. XXII:** 1–16

Book, A (Barnes), **Supp. III Part 1:** 36, 39, 44

Book about Myself, A (Dreiser), **I:** 515; **Retro. Supp. II:** 104

"Book as a Container of Consciousness, The" (Gass), **Supp. VI:** 92

Booker, Keith, **Supp. XV:** 197

"Bookies, Beware!" (Heller), **Supp. IV Part 1:** 383

"Book Notes and News" (column, Boyce), **Supp. XXI:** 2

Book of American Negro Poetry, The (J. W. Johnson, ed.), **Supp. IV Part 1:** 165, 166; **Supp. XXII:** 11; **Supp. XXVI:** 165

Book of Americans, A (Benét), **Supp. XI:** 46, 47, 51

Book of Beb, The (Buechner), **Supp. XII:** 53

Book of Breeething, The (Burroughs), **Supp. III Part 1:** 97, 103

Book of Burlesques, A (Mencken), **III:** 104

Book of Common Prayer, A (Didion), **Supp. IV Part 1:** 196, 198, 203–205, 207, 208

Book of Daniel, The (Doctorow), **Supp. IV Part 1:** 218, 219, 220–222, 227, 231, 237–238, 238; **Supp. V:** 45

Book of Dreams (Kerouac), **Supp. III Part 1:** 225

"Book of Ephraim, The" (Merrill), **Supp. III Part 1:** 330–334

Book of Folly, The (Sexton), **Supp. II Part 2:** 691, 692–694

Book of Gallant Vagabonds, The (Beston), **Supp. XXVI:** 33

Book of Gods and Devils, The (Simic), **Supp. VIII: 281**

Book of Guys, The (Keillor), **Supp. XVI:** 177

"Book of Hours of Sister Clotilde, The" (A. Lowell), **II:** 522

Book of Jamaica, The (Banks), **Supp. V:** 11, 12, 16

"Book of Life" (Bidart), **Supp. XV:** 23

Book of Living Verse, The; English and American Poetry from the Thirteenth Century to the Present Day (Untermeyer, ed.), **Supp. XV:** 310

Book of Longing (Cohen), **Supp. XXVII:** 56

Book of Love, A (Vildrac; Bynner, trans.), **Supp. XV:** 50

Book of Lyrics (Bynner), **Supp. XV:** 51

Book of Martyrs (Fox). *See Acts and Monuments of These Latter and Perilous Days* (Fox)

Book of Medicines, The (Hogan), **Supp. IV Part 1:** 397, 410, 411–414

"Book of Medicines, The" (Hogan), **Supp. IV Part 1:** 412, 413

"Book of Memory, The" (Auster), **Supp. XII:** 21–22

Book of Mercy (Cohen), **Supp. XXVII:** 54

Book of My Nights (L.-Y. Lee), **Supp. XV:** 215, **223–226**

Book of Negro Folklore, The (Hughes, ed.), **Supp. I Part 1:** 345; **Supp. XXII:** 11–12

Book of Nightmares, The (Kinnell), **Supp. III Part 1:** 235, 236, 243, 244, 246–254

Book of One's Own, A: People and Their Diaries (Mallon), **Supp. XIX:** 134

Book of Prefaces, A (Mencken), **III:** 99–100, 105

Book of Repulsive Women, The (Barnes), **Supp. III Part 1:** 33

Book of Revelation, **Supp. XXIII:** 44

Book of Roses, The (Parkman), **Supp. II Part 2:** 597, 598

Book of the Body, The (Bidart), **Supp. XV:** 21, **25–27**

"Book of the Dead, The" (Rukeyser), **Supp. VI:** 272, 278, 279; **Supp. XV:** 349

"Book of the Grotesque, The" (Anderson), **I:** 106

Book of the Homeless, The (Wharton), **Retro. Supp. I:** 377

Book of the Hopi (Waters), **Supp. X:** 124

Book of Tobit (Bible), **Supp. XII:** 54

Book of Verses, A (Masters), **Supp. I Part 2:** 458

Book of Wonder (Dunsany), **Supp. XXV:** 113

Book of Yaak, The (Bass), **Supp. XVI: 18–19**

"Book of Yolek, The" (Hecht), **Supp. X:** 69, **70–71**

"Books" (Collins), **Supp. XXI:** 55

"Books Considered" (Bloom), **Supp. I Part 1:** 96

"Books I Left Behind, The" (Pickering), **Supp. XXI:** 196

Books in My Life, The (H. Miller), **II:** 176, 189

"Books/P,L,E, The" (Goldbarth), **Supp. XII:** 190

Bookviews, **Supp. XI:** 216

"Book World Live", **Supp. XVIII:** 143–144

"Boolean Algebra: X2=X" (Bronk), **Supp. XXI:** 30

"Boom" (Nemerov), **III:** 278

Boom! (T. Williams), **IV:** 383

Boomer Girls: Poems by Women of the Baby Boom Generation (Gemin and Sergi, eds.), **Supp. XXI:** 246

Boom Town (Wolfe), **IV:** 456

"Boom Town" (Wolfe), **IV:** 469

Boone, Daniel, **II:** 207; **III:** 444; **IV:** 192, 193

Boorstin, Daniel, **I:** 253

Booth, Charles, **Supp. I Part 1:** 13

Booth, John Wilkes, **III:** 588

Booth, Philip, **I:** 522; **Supp. IX:** 269; **Supp. XI:** 141; **Supp. XIII:** 277; **Supp. XV:** 92; **Supp. XXVI:** 68

Booth, General William, **Supp. I Part 2:** 384, 386

"Booze"(P. Benedict), **Supp. XXIII:** 36

Borah, William, **III:** 475

Borden, Lizzie, **II:** 5

Border and the Buffalo, The (J. Cook), **Supp. XXIV:** 248

"Border Crossings: An Interview with Eric Gansworth" (de la Paz and Purdy), **Supp. XXVI:** 101

Borderlands/La Frontera: The New Mestiza (Anzaldúa), **Supp. XIII:** 223

Border Matters (Saldívar), **Supp. XIX:** 112–113

Borders (Mora), **Supp. XIII:** 213, **215–217**

Border Trilogy (McCarthy), **Supp. VIII:** 175, 182

"Border View, Hot Springs, Texas" (W. V. Davis), **Supp. XXI:** 95

Borel, Pétrus, **III:** 320

Borges, Jorge Luis, **I:** 123, 135, 138, 140, 142; **Supp. III Part 2:** 560; **Supp. IV Part 2:** 623, 626, 630; **Supp. V:** 238; **Supp. VIII:** 15, 348, 349; **Supp. XII:** 21, 147; **Supp. XIX:** 131; **Supp. XV:** 34; **Supp. XVI:** 201, 206; **Supp. XVII:** 47; **Supp. XXIII:** 68; **Supp. XXV:** 50, 69

"Borges and I" (Bidart), **Supp. XV:** 34, 35

"Borinken Blues" (Komunyakaa), **Supp. XIII:** 117

"Born, The" (Lamott), **Supp. XX: 143–144**

"Born a Square: The Westerner's Dilemma" (Stegner), **Supp. IV Part 2:** 595; **Supp. V:** 224

"Born Bad" (Cisneros), **Supp. VII:** 62

Born on the Fourth of July (Kovic), **Supp. XIX:** 17

"Borough of Cemeteries" (Shaw), **Supp. XIX:** 246

Borrowed Time: An AIDS Memoir (Monette), **Supp. X:** 145, 146, 147, 152, 154, 155

Bose, Sudip, **Supp. XXII:** 205, 206, 214

Bosmajian, Hamida, **Supp. XXII:** 290

"Bosque del Apache Wildlife Refuge" (Mora), **Supp. XIII:** 218

Boss Dog, The: A Story of Provence (M. F. K. Fisher), **Supp. XVII:** 91

Bossin, Gary, **Supp. XXVII:** 133, 143, 145

Bost, Suzanne, **Supp. XXII:** 66, 70, 75, 78

"Boston" (Hardwick), **Supp. III Part 1:** 201

Boston (Sinclair), **Supp. V:** 282, 288–289

Boston, B. H., **Supp. XIII:** 312

Boston Adventure (Stafford), **Retro. Supp. II:** 177, 178

"Boston Common" (Berryman), **I:** 172

"Boston Hymn" (Emerson), **II:** 13, 19

Bostonians, The (H. James), **I:** 9; **II:** 282; **IV:** 202; **Retro. Supp. I:** 216, 225

Boston Marriage (Mamet), **Supp. XIV:** 247

"Boston Nativity, The" (R. Lowell), **II:** 538

Boswell, James, **IV:** 431; **Supp. I Part 2:** 656

Boswell: A Modern Comedy (Elkin), **Supp. VI:** 42, **44–45,** 57

Bosworth, Patricia, **Supp. IV Part 2:** 573, 591

"Bothersome Sex and O'Brien, The" (Ryan as Quin), **Supp. XVIII:** 238

Botticelli (McNally), **Supp. XIII:** 197

Botticelli, Sandro, **IV:** 410; **Retro. Supp. I:** 422

"Botticellian Trees, The" (W. C. Williams), **Retro. Supp. I:** 422

"Bottled" (H. Johnson), **Supp. XXVI:** 164, 165

"Bottle of Milk for Mother, A" (Algren), **Supp. IX:** 3

"Bottle of Perrier, A" (Wharton), **IV:** 316

"Bottles" (Kenyon), **Supp. VII:** 171

"Bottom Line, The" (Elkin), **Supp. VI:** 52, **53**

Bottom: On Shakespeare (Zukofsky), **Supp. III Part 2:** 622, 624, 625, 626, 627, 629

Boublil, Alain, **Supp. XXI:** 155

Boucher, Anthony, **Supp. IV Part 2:** 473; **Supp. XV:** 203, 205

Boucicault, Dion, **Supp. XXII:** 70

Boughton, Henrietta Breckenridge. *See* Young, Barbara

Boukreev, Anatoli, **Supp. XVIII:** 112

Boulanger, Nadia, **Supp. IV Part 1:** 81

"Boulot and Boulette" (Chopin), **Supp. I Part 1:** 211

Boulton, Agnes, **III:** 403; **Supp. XXII:** **17–31**

Bound East for Cardiff (O'Neill), **III:** 388

Bound for Glory (Guthrie), **Supp. XVIII:** 23

"Bounty" (Saunders), **Supp. XIX:** 226, 227

"Bounty" (P. Benedict), **Supp. XXIII:** 41

"Bouquet, The" (Stevens), **IV:** 90

"Bouquet of Dark Red Mums, The" (Notley), **Supp. XXII:** 230

"Bouquet of Roses in Sunlight" (Stevens), **IV:** 93

Bourdin, Henri L., **Supp. I Part 1:** 251

Bourgeois, Monique, **Supp. XXII:** 99–100

Bourgeois Poet, The (Shapiro), **Supp. II Part 2:** 701, 703, 704, 713, 714–716

Bourget, James, **IV:** 319

Bourget, Paul, **II:** 325, 338; **IV:** 311, 315; **Retro. Supp. I:** 224, 359, 373; **Supp. XX:** 232; **Supp. XXIV:** 23

Bourjaily, Vance, **III:** 43; **Supp. IX:** 260; **Supp. XXIV:** 225

Bourke-White, Margaret, **I:** 290, 293, 295, 297

Bourne, Charles Rogers, **I:** 215

Bourne, Mrs. Charles Rogers, **I:** 215

Bourne, Randolph, **I:** **214–238**, 243, 245, 246–247, 251, 259; **Supp. I Part 2:** 524; **Supp. XV:** 141, 298, 301

Boursicot, Bernard, **Supp. XXI:** 152, 153, 154

Bouton, Jim "Bulldog", **Supp. XX:** 274

Bouton, John Bell, **Supp. XXIII:** 188, 189

Bowden, Charles, **Supp. XIII:** 17

Bowditch, Nathaniel, **Supp. I Part 2:** 482

Bowen, Barbara, **Supp. IX:** 311

Bowen, Elizabeth, **Retro. Supp. I:** 351; **Supp. IV Part 1:** 299; **Supp. IX:** 128; **Supp. VIII:** 65, 165, 251, 265

Bowen, Francis, **Supp. I Part 2:** 413

Bowen, Henry, **Supp. XVIII:** 4

Bowen, Louise de Koven, **Supp. I Part 1:** 5

Bowen, Michael, **Supp. VIII:** 73

Bowers, John, **Supp. XI:** 217–218

"Bowlers Anonymous" (Dobyns), **Supp. XIII:** 86

Bowles, Emily, **Supp. XVIII:** 200, 202

Bowles, Jane (Jane Auer), **II:** 586; **Supp. IV Part 1:** 89, 92

Bowles, Paul, **I:** 211; **II:** 586; **Supp. II Part 1:** 17; **Supp. IV Part 1:** **79–99**

Bowles, Samuel, **I:** 454, 457; **Retro. Supp. I:** 30, 32, 33

"Bowl of Blood, The" (Jeffers), **Supp. II Part 2:** 434

"Bowls" (Moore), **III:** 196

Bowman, James, **I:** 193

"Bows to Drouth" (Snyder), **Supp. VIII:** 303

Box, Edgar (pseudonym). *See* Vidal, Gore

Box and Quotations from Chairman Mao Tse-tung (Albee), **I:** 89–91, 94

Boxer and the Spy, The (Parker), **Supp. XIX:** 190

Box Garden, The (Shields), **Supp. VII:** 314–315, 320

"Box of Pastels, A" (Kooser), **Supp. XIX:** 128

"Box of Rocks, A" (Gallagher), **Supp. XXIV:** 175

"Box Seat" (Toomer), **Supp. III Part 2:** 484; **Supp. IX:** 316, 318

Boy, A (Ashbery), **Supp. III Part 1:** 5

"Boy and Dog" (L. Brown), **Supp. XXI:** 38, 42, **43–44**

Boyce, Horace, **II:** 136

Boyce, Neith, **Supp. XVII:** 96, 97, 98–99, 100, 106; **Supp. XXI:** **1–16**

Boyd, Brian, **Retro. Supp. I:** 270, 275

Boyd, Janet L., **Supp. X:** 229

Boyd, Kristen, **Supp. XXIII:** 246

Boyd, Nancy (pseudonym). *See* Millay, Edna St. Vincent

Boyd, Thomas, **I:** 99; **IV:** 427

Boyelston, Matthew, **Supp. XXVII:** 216

Boyesen, H. H., **II:** 289

"Boy from Lam Kien, The" (July), **Supp. XXIV:** 200, 204

"Boyhood" (Collins), **Supp. XXI:** 64

"Boyhood" (Farrell), **II:** 28

"Boy in France, A" (Salinger), **III:** 552–553

"Boy in the Basement, The" (Inge), **Supp. XXV:** 105, 106

Boy in the Water (Dobyns), **Supp. XIII:** 75, **84**

Boyle, Kay, **IV:** 404; **Supp. XXIV:** **49–66**

Boyle, T. Coraghessan, **Supp. VIII:** **1–17; Supp. XX:** **17–32; Supp. XXI:** 226; **Supp. XXII:** 262

Boyle, Thomas John. *See* Boyle, T. C.

Boynton, H. W., **Supp. IX:** 7

Boynton, Percy Holmes, **Supp. I Part 2:** 415

Boynton, Robert, **Supp. XVII:** 209; **Supp. XVIII:** 105, 107, 116

Boynton, Robert S., **Supp. XXV:** 158

"Boy on a Train" (Ellison), **Retro. Supp. II:** 124

"Boy Riding Forward Backward" (Francis), **Supp. IX:** 82

"Boys and Girls" (Cisneros), **Supp. VII:** 59–60

"Boys and Girls" (Munro), **Supp. XXVII:** 184

"Boy's Dream Ballad, The" (Very), **Supp. XXV:** 244

Boy's Froissart, The (Lanier), **Supp. I Part 1:** 361

"Boys" (Kenny), **Supp. XXIII:** 149

Boy's King Arthur, The (Lanier), **Supp. I Part 1:** 361

Boy's Mabinogion, The (Lanier), **Supp. I Part 1:** 361

"Boys of '29, The" (Holmes), **Supp. I Part 1:** 308

Boys of '76, The (Coffin), **III:** 577

Boy's Percy, The (Lanier), **Supp. I Part 1:** 361

"Boy Story" (Huddle), **Supp. XXVI:** 151

Boy's Town (Howells), **I:** 418

Boy's Will, A (Frost), **II:** 152, 153, 155–156, 159, 164, 166; **Retro. Supp. I:** 124, 127, 128, 131; **Retro. Supp. II:** 168

"Boy Up a Tree" (Hoffman), **Supp. XVIII:** 86

"Boy Who Wrestled with Angels, The" (Hoffman), **Supp. X:** 90

"Boy with One Shoe, The" (Jewett), **Retro. Supp. II:** 132

"Brace, The" (Bausch), **Supp. VII:** 48

Bracebridge Hall, or, The Humorists (Irving), **I:** 339, 341; **II:** 308–309, 313

Bracher, Frederick, **I:** 378, 380; **Supp. I Part 1:** 185

Brackenridge, Hugh Henry, **Supp. I Part 1:** 124, 127, 145; **Supp. II Part 1:** 65

Brackett, Leigh, **Supp. IV Part 1:** 130

Bradbury, John M., **I:** 288–289; **IV:** 130, 135

Bradbury, Malcolm, **Supp. VIII:** 124; **Supp. XVIII:** 140

Bradbury, Ray, **Supp. I Part 2:** 621–622; **Supp. IV Part 1:** **101–118; Supp. XVI:** 122; **Supp. XVII:** 41; **Supp. XXIII:** 290; **Supp. XXV:** 141; **Supp. XXVII:** 295

"Brad Carrigan, American" (Saunders), **Supp. XIX:** 233

Braddon, Mary E., **Supp. I Part 1:** 35, 36

Bradfield, Scott, **Supp. VIII:** 88

Bradford, Gamaliel, **I:** 248, 250

Bradford, Roark, **Retro. Supp. I:** 80

Bradford, William, **Retro. Supp. II:** 161, 162; **Supp. I Part 1:** 110, 112; **Supp. I Part 2:** 486, 494; **Supp. XXII:** **33–47**

Bradlee, Ben, **Supp. V:** 201

Bradley, Bill, **Supp. VIII:** 47

Bradley, F. H., **Retro. Supp. I:** 57, 58

Bradley, Francis Herbert, **I:** 59, 567–568, 572, 573

Bradshaw, Barbara, **Supp. XIII:** 313

Bradstreet, Anne, **I:** 178–179, 180, 181, 182, 184; **III:** 505; **Retro. Supp. I:** 40; **Supp. I Part 1:** **98–123**, 300; **Supp. I Part 2:** 484, 485, 496, 546, 705; **Supp. V:** 113, 117–118; **Supp. XIII:** 152; **Supp. XIV:** 128; **Supp. XVIII:** 304; **Supp. XXII:** 46

Bradstreet, Elizabeth, **Supp. I Part 1:** 108, 122

Bradstreet, Simon, **I:** 178; **Supp. I Part 1:** 103, 110, 116

Bradstreet, Mrs. Simon. *See* Bradstreet, Anne

Brady, Alice, **III:** 399

Brady, Catherine, **Supp. XXIII:** 301

Brady, Matthew, **Supp. XVIII:** 4

Bragdon, Claude, **Supp. XX: 117**

"Bragdowdy and the Busybody, The" (Thurber), **Supp. I Part 2:** 617

Bragg, Rick, **Supp. XVIII:** 195

"Brahma" (Emerson), **II:** 19, 20

Brahms, Johannes, **III:** 118, 448

"Brahms in Delirium" (Skloot), **Supp. XX: 203**

Braided Creek (Kooser and Harrison), **Supp. XIX:** 126

"Braiding" (L.-Y. Lee), **Supp. XV:** 214

"Brain and the Mind, The" (James), **II:** 346

Brainard, Joe, **Supp. XV:** 33; **Supp. XXIII:** 217; **Supp. XXIV:** 33, 34, 35, 39, 41, 42, 43; **Supp. XXVII: 17–31**

"Brain Damage" (Barthelme), **Supp. IV Part 1:** 44

"Braindead Megaphone, The" (Saunders), **Supp. XIX:** 235

Braindead Megaphone, The: Essays (Saunders), **Supp. XIX: 234–236**

"Brain Scan" (Skloot), **Supp. XX: 200**

"Brain to the Heart, The" (Komunyakaa), **Supp. XIII:** 120

Braithwaite, Chris, **Supp. XXII:** 212

Braithwaite, Edward Kamau, **Supp. XXVII:** 160

Braithwaite, William Stanley, **Retro. Supp. I:** 131; **Supp. IX:** 309; **Supp. XV:** 296–297, 301–302, 305, 306

Brakhage, Stan, **Supp. XII:** 2

Braly, Malcolm, **Supp. XVIII:** 147

"Bramble, The" (Wrigley), **Supp. XVIII:** 301

Brame, Gloria, **Supp. XV:** 113; **Supp. XXIII:** 122

Bramen, Carrie Tirado, **Supp. XXIV:** 192

Bramer, Monte, **Supp. X:** 152

Branch Will Not Break, The (Wright), **Supp. III Part 2:** 596, 598–601; **Supp. IV Part 1:** 60; **Supp. IX:** 159

Brancusi, Constantin, **III:** 201; **Retro. Supp. I:** 292

Brancusi, Constantine, **Supp. XXVI:** 224

Brande, Dorothea, **Supp. I Part 2:** 608

Brandel, Marc, **Supp. XXI:** 276

Branden, Nathaniel, **Supp. IV Part 2:** 526, 528

"Branding Cities" (Greenberg), **Supp. XXII:** 244

"Brand-Name Blues" (Kaufmann), **Supp. XI:** 39

Brand New Life, A (Farrell), **II:** 46, 48

Brando, Marlon, **II:** 588; **Supp. IV Part 2:** 560; **Supp. XVIII:** 251

Brandon, Henry, **Supp. I Part 2:** 604, 612, 618

Brandt, Alice, **Supp. I Part 1:** 92

Brandt, Carl, **Supp. XI:** 45

Brant, Sebastian, **III:** 447, 448

Brantley, Ben, **Supp. XXIV:** 268, 269–270, 271, 272, 274

Braque, Georges, **III:** 197; **Supp. IX:** 66; **Supp. XXVI:** 259

Brashford, Jake, **Supp. X:** 252

Brasil, Emanuel, **Supp. I Part 1:** 94

"Brasília" (Plath), **Supp. I Part 2:** 544, 545

"Brass Buttons" (McCoy), **Supp. XIII:** 161

"Brass Candlestick, The" (Francis), **Supp. IX:** 89

Brass Check, The (Sinclair), **Supp. V:** 276, 281, 282, 284–285

Brass Knuckles (Dybek), **Supp. XXIII: 68–69**

"Brass Ring, The" (Carver), **Supp. III Part 1:** 137

"Brass Spittoons" (Hughes), **Supp. I Part 1:** 326–327

Brass Verdict, The (Connelly), **Supp. XXI: 78–79**

Brats (X. J. Kennedy), **Supp. XV:** 163

Brautigan, Richard, **III:** 174; **Supp. VIII:** 42, 43; **Supp. XII:** 139; **Supp. XVI:** 172; **Supp. XXI:** 53

Brave Cowboy, The (Abbey), **Supp. XIII:** 4–5

Brave Men (Pyle), **Supp. XVII:** 61

Brave New World (Huxley), **II:** 454; **Supp. XIII:** 29; **Supp. XVIII:** 137

"Brave New World" (MacLeish), **III:** 18

Bravery of Earth, A (Eberhart), **I:** 522, 524, 525, 526, 530

"Brave Tailors of Maida, The" (Talese), **Supp. XVII:** 208

"Brave Words for a Startling Occasion" (Ellison), **Retro. Supp. II:** 118

Braving the Elements (Merrill), **Supp. III Part 1:** 320, 323, 325–327, 329

Bravo, The (Cooper), **I:** 345–346, 348

"Bravura" (Francis), **Supp. IX:** 90

Brawley, Benjamin, **Supp. I Part 1:** 327, 332

Brawl in a Tavern, A (Shaw), **Supp. XIX:** 241

Brawne, Fanny, **I:** 284; **II:** 531

Braxton, Joanne, **Supp. IV Part 1:** 12, 15

Brazil (Bishop), **Retro. Supp. II:** 45; **Supp. I Part 1:** 92

"Brazil" (Marshall), **Supp. XI:** 281

Brazil (Updike), **Retro. Supp. I:** 329, 330, 334

"Brazil, January 1, 1502" (Bishop), **Retro. Supp. II:** 47

Braziller, George, **Supp. X:** 24; **Supp. XXIII:** 214

Brazzi, Rossano, **Supp. IV Part 2:** 520

"Bread" (Dickey), **Supp. IV Part 1:** 182

"Bread" (Olds), **Supp. X:** 206

"Bread Alone" (Wylie), **Supp. I Part 2:** 727

Bread in the Wilderness (Merton), **Supp. VIII:** 197, 208

"Bread of Desire, The" (Nelson), **Supp. XVIII:** 177

Bread of Idleness, The (Masters), **Supp. I Part 2:** 460

"Bread of This World, The" (McGrath), **Supp. X:** 119, 127

Bread of Time, The (Levine), **Supp. V:** 180

Bread without Sugar (Stern), **Supp. IX: 297–298**

"Break, The" (Sexton), **Supp. II Part 2:** 689

"Breakaways, The" (Siddons), **Supp. XXII:** 244

Breakdown (Paretsky), **Supp. XXV:** 185

Breakfast at Tiffany's (Capote), **Supp. III Part 1:** 113, 117, 119–121, 124, 126

Breakfast of Champions (Vonnegut), **Supp. II Part 2:** 755, 759, 769, 770, 777–778

Breaking and a Death, A (Kees), **Supp. XV:** 145

Breaking and Entering (X. J. Kennedy), **Supp. XV:** 153, **160–162**

Breaking Hard Ground (D. Hunter), **Supp. XVI:** 38

Breaking Ice (McMillan, ed.), **Supp. XIII:** 182–183

Breaking of the Day, The (Davison), **Supp. XXVI:** 65, 68–70

"Breaking of the Day, The" (Davison), **Supp. XXVI:** 68, 69

Breaking Open (Rukeyser), **Supp. VI:** 274, 281

"Breaking Open" (Rukeyser), **Supp. VI:** 286

Breaking Point, The (Rinehart), **Supp. XXV:** 196

Breaking Ranks: A Political Memoir (Podhoretz), **Supp. VIII: 239–241,** 245

"Breaking the Code of Silence: Ideology and Women's Confessional Poetry" (Harris), **Supp. XIV:** 269

"Breaking the Whistle" (Rash), **Supp. XXVII:** 218

"Breaking Up of the Winships, The" (Thurber), **Supp. I Part 2:** 616

Brearton, Fran, **Supp. XXIV:** 167

Breast, The (P. Roth), **Retro. Supp. II:** 287–288; **Supp. III Part 2:** 416, 418

"Breast, The" (Sexton), **Supp. II Part 2:** 687

"Breasts" (Gallagher), **Supp. XXIV:** 168, 174

"Breasts" (Simic), **Supp. VIII:** 275

"Breasts"(Dybek), **Supp. XXIII:** 77

"Breath" (Espaillat), **Supp. XXI:** 109

"Breath" (Levine), **Supp. V:** 185

Breathe No More, My Lady (Lacy), **Supp. XV:** 203

Breathing Lessons (Tyler), **Supp. IV Part 2:** 669–670

Breathing Room (Davison), **Supp. XXVI:** 66, 78–79

"Breathing Room" (Davison), **Supp. XXVI:** 79

Breathing the Monster Alive (Gansworth), **Supp. XXVI:** 112–113

Breathing the Water (Levertov), **Supp. III Part 1:** 274, 283, 284

"Breath of Life, The" (C. Baxter), **Supp. XVII:** 23

Breath's Burials (Sobin), **Supp. XVI:** **288–289**

Breaux, Zelia, **Retro. Supp. II:** 114

Brecht, Bertolt, **I:** 60, 301; **III:** 161, 162; **IV:** 394; **Supp. I Part 1:** 292; **Supp. II Part 1:** 10, 26, 56; **Supp. IV Part 1:** 359; **Supp. IX:** 131, 133, 140; **Supp. X:** 112; **Supp. XIII:** 206, 286; **Supp. XIV:** 162; **Supp. XVIII:** 33; **Supp. XXIV:** 267

Breen, Jon L., **Supp. XXVI:** 277, 281

Breen, Joseph I., **IV:** 390

Breines, Ron, **Supp. XVIII:** 97

Breit, Harvey, **I:** 433; **III:** 575; **Retro. Supp. II:** 230; **Supp. XVIII:** 254; **Supp. XXI:** 277

Breman, Paul, **Supp. XXII:** 8

Bremer, Anne, **Supp. XXII:** 277

Bremer, Fredrika, **Supp. I Part 1:** 407

Bremer, Richard, **Supp. XXIII:** 236

Brendan: A Novel (Buechner), **Supp. XII:** 53

Brennan, Matthew C., **Supp. XIX:** 121; **Supp. XV:** 113, 125

Brent, David, **Supp. XXII:** 259

Brent, Linda, **Supp. IV Part 1:** 12, 13

Brentano, Franz, **II:** 350; **Supp. XIV:** 198, 199

Brer Rabbit (tales), **Supp. IV Part 1:** 11, 13; **Supp. XIV:** 88

Breslin, James E. B., **Retro. Supp. I:** 430

Breslin, John B., **Supp. IV Part 1:** 308

Breslin, Paul, **Supp. VIII:** 283

Bresson, Robert, **Supp. IV Part 1:** 156

"Bresson's Movies" (Creeley), **Supp. IV Part 1:** 156–157

"Bret Easton Ellis Podcast, The", **Supp. XXVII:** 79

Breton, André, **III:** 425; **Supp. XIII:** 114; **Supp. XVII:** 244

Brett, George, **II:** 466; **Supp. V:** 286

Brett, Reginald Baliol, **Supp. XX:** **230**

Brevoort, Henry, **II:** 298

Brew, Kwesi, **Supp. IV Part 1:** 10, 16

Brewer, Gaylord, **Supp. XV:** 330

"Brewing of Soma, The" (Whittier), **Supp. I Part 2:** 704

Brewsie and Willie (Stein), **IV:** 27

Brewster, Martha, **Supp. I Part 1:** 114

"Brewsterville Croesus, A" (Briggs), **Supp. XVIII:** 16

Brewsterville letters (Briggs), **Supp. XVIII:** 1, **5**, **15–16**

"Brian Age 7" (Doty), **Supp. XI:** 136

Briand, Paul, **Supp. XVIII:** 155

"Briar Patch, The" (Warren), **IV:** 237

Briar Rose (Coover), **Supp. V:** 52

"Briar Rose (Sleeping Beauty)" (Sexton), **Supp. II Part 2:** 690

Brice, Fanny, **II:** 427

"Brick, The" (Nye), **Supp. XIII:** 276

"Bricklayer in the Snow" (Fante), **Supp. XI:** 164–165

"Brick Layer's Lunch Hour, The" (Ginsberg), **Supp. II Part 1:** 318

Brickman, Marshall, **Supp. XV:** 5

"Bricks, The" (Hogan), **Supp. IV Part 1:** 413

"Bridal Ballad, The" (Poe), **III:** 428

"Bridal Bed, The" (Gibran), **Supp. XX:** **124**

Bridal Dinner, The (Gurney), **Supp. V:** 109, 110

Bridal Hunt (Silver), **Supp. XXIV:** 264

"Bride Comes to Yellow Sky, The" (Crane), **I:** 34, 415, 416, 423

Bridegroom, The (Jin), **Supp. XVIII:** **97–98**

"Bridegroom, The" (Jin), **Supp. XVIII:** 98

Bridegroom Cometh, The (W. Frank), **Supp. XX:** **77**

"Bridegroom's Body, The" (Boyle), **Supp. XXIV:** 54, **55–56**

"Bride in the 30's, A" (Auden), **Supp. II Part 1:** 9

Bride of Lammermoor (Scott), **II:** 291

Bride of Samoa (film), **Supp. IV Part 1:** 82

"Bride of the Innisfallen, The" (Welty), **IV:** 278–279; **Retro. Supp. I:** 353

Bride of the Innisfallen, The, and Other Stories (Welty), **IV:** 261, 275–279; **Retro. Supp. I:** 352–353, 355

Brides of the South Wind: Poems 1917–1922 (Jeffers), **Supp. II Part 2:** 419

Bridge, Horatio, **II:** 226

"BRIDGE, THE" (Baraka), **Supp. II Part 1:** 32, 36

Bridge, The (H. Crane), **I:** 62, 109, 266, 385, 386, 387, 395–399, 400, 402; **IV:** 123, 341, 418, 419, 420; **Retro. Supp. I:** 427; **Retro. Supp. II:** 76, 77, 81, 83, **84–87**; **Supp. IX:** 306; **Supp. V:** 342; **Supp. XXIII:** 146; **Supp. XXVI:** 21, 25, 28

Bridge, The (Talese), **Supp. XVII:** 202, 203, 208

Bridge at Remagen, The (film), **Supp. XI:** 343

"Bridge Burners, The" (Van Vechten), **Supp. II Part 2:** 733

Bridgehead: The Drama of Israel (W. Frank), **Supp. XX:** **80**

Bridge of San Luis Rey, The (Wilder), **I:** 360; **IV:** 356, 357, 360–363, 365, 366

"Bridge of Sighs" (P. Benedict), **Supp. XXIII:** 47–48

Bridge of Years, The (Sarton), **Supp. VIII:** 253

"Bridges" (Kingsolver), **Supp. VII:** 208

Bridges, Harry, **I:** 493; **Supp. XIX:** 264; **Supp. XVIII:** 238

Bridges, Lloyd, **Supp. XV:** 202

Bridges, Robert, **II:** 537; **III:** 527; **Supp. I Part 2:** 721; **Supp. II Part 1:** 21; **Supp. XIV:** 336, 341, 342, 343

"Bridging" (Apple), **Supp. XVII:** 5

Bridgman, P. W., **I:** 278

"Bridle, The" (Carver), **Supp. III Part 1:** 138

"Brief and Blameless Outline of the Ontogeny of Crow, A" (Wright), **Supp. XV:** 347

Brief and Frightening Reign of Phil, The (Saunders), **Supp. XIX:** **230–231**, 233

"Brief Début of Tildy, The" (O. Henry), **Supp. II Part 1:** 408

"Brief Encounters on the Inland Waterway" (Vonnegut), **Supp. II Part 2:** 760

"Brief History of My Mother's Temper, A" (Huddle), **Supp. XXVI:** 150

Brief History of the Dead, The (Brockmeier), **Supp. XXII: 57–59,** 61

Briefings (Ammons), **Supp. VII:** 29

Brief Interviews with Hideous Men (Wallace), **Supp. X: 308–310**

"Brief Interviews with Hideous Men" (Wallace), **Supp. X:** 309

"Briefly It Enters, and Briefly Speaks" (Kenyon), **Supp. VII:** 174

"Brief Study of the British, A" (Saunders), **Supp. XIX:** 235

Brief Wondrous Life of Oscar Wao, The (Díaz), **Supp. XXIV:** 83, 84, 85, 87, **89–92,** 93

Brier, His Book (J. W. Miller), **Supp. XX: 165, 168, 170**

"Brier Grows Wild, The" (J. W. Miller), **Supp. XX:** 170

"Brier Losing Touch with His Traditions, The" (J. W. Miller), **Supp. XX:** 165, 169

Brier Poems, The (J. W. Miller), **Supp. XX: 168**

"Brier Sermon, The—You Must Be Born Again" (J. W. Miller), **Supp. XX:** 165, **169–170**

Briffault, Robert, **Supp. I Part 2:** 560, 567

"Brigade de Cuisine" (McPhee), **Supp. III Part 1:** 307–308

Brigadier and the Golf Widow, The (Cheever), **Supp. I Part 1:** 184–185, 192

Briggs, Charles Frederick, **Supp. I Part 2:** 411; **Supp. XVIII: 1–18**

brigham, besmilr, **Supp. XV:** 349

"Bright and Morning Star" (Wright), **IV:** 488

Bright Book of Life: American Novelists and Storytellers from Hemingway to Mailer (Kazin), **Supp. VIII:** 102, 104

Bright Center of Heaven (Maxwell), **Supp. VIII: 153–155,** 164

"Brightness from the North" (B. Kelly), **Supp. XVII:** 131

Brighton Beach Memoirs (Simon), **Supp. IV Part 2:** 576, 577, 584, 586–587, 590

Bright Procession (Sedges), **Supp. II Part 1:** 125

Bright Room Called Day, A (Kushner), **Supp. IX:** 133, **138–141,** 142

Brillat-Savarin, Jean Anthelme, **Supp. XVII:** 82, 86, 87

"Brilliance" (Doty), **Supp. XI:** 124, 128

"Brilliant California Novelist, A" (Forman), **Supp. XXIV:** 30

"Brilliant Leaves" (Gordon), **II:** 199

"Brilliant Sad Sun" (W. C. Williams), **Retro. Supp. I:** 422

"Bring Brang Brung" (Muñoz), **Supp. XXV:** 135–136

"Bringing Back the Trumpeter Swan" (Kumin), **Supp. IV Part 2:** 454

Bringing It All Back Home (album, Dylan), **Supp. XVIII:** 20, 25, 26, 30
Bringing It All Back Home (McNally), **Supp. XIII:** 197–198
Bringing the Devil to His Knees (C. Baxter), **Supp. XVII:** 22
"Bringing the Strange Home" (Dunn), **Supp. XI:** 141
"Bring the Day!" (Roethke), **III:** 536
Brinkley, Douglas, **Supp. XIII:** 9; **Supp. XXIV:** 281, 293
Brinkmeyer, Robert H., Jr., **Supp. XI:** 38
Brinnin, John Malcolm, **IV:** 26, 27, 28, 42, 46; **Supp. XV:** 139
Brissot, Jacques Pierre, **Supp. I Part 2:** 511
"Britain's Negro Problem in Sierra Leone" (Du Bois), **Supp. I Part 1:** 176
"British Guiana" (Marshall), **Supp. XI:** 281–282
"British Poets, The" (Holmes), **Supp. I Part 1:** 306
"British Prison Ship, The" (Freneau), **Supp. II Part 1:** 261
Brittan, Gordon G., Jr., **Supp. XIV:** 234
Britten, Benjamin, **II:** 586; **Supp. II Part 1:** 17; **Supp. IV Part 1:** 84
Broadwater, Bowden, **II:** 562
Broadway, Broadway (McNally). *See It's Only a Play* (McNally)
Broadway, J. William, **Supp. V:** 316
Broadway Bound (Simon), **Supp. IV Part 2:** 576, 577, 584, 586–587, 590
Broadway Danny Rose (film; Allen), **Supp. XV:** 9
"Broadway Sights" (Whitman), **IV:** 350
Broccoli, Albert R. "Cubby", **Supp. XI:** 307
Brock
Bröck, Sabine, **Supp. XI:** 275, 277, 278
Brockmeier, Kevin, **Supp. XXII:** 49–63
Brodeur, Brian, **Supp. XXVI:** 150
Brodhead, Richard, **Retro. Supp. II:** 139; **Supp. XIV:** 61
Brodkey, Harold, **Supp. VIII:** 151; **Supp. X:** 160
Brodkin, Joel, **Supp. XXV:** 261
Brodskii, Iosif Alexsandrovich. *See* Brodsky, Joseph
Brodsky, Joseph, **Supp. VIII:** 19–35; **Supp. X:** 65, 73; **Supp. XV:** 134, 135, 256; **Supp. XXIII:** 122
Brody, Alter, **Supp. XV:** 302, 307
Brodyar, Anatole, **Supp. XIV:** 106
Brokeback Mountain (film), **Supp. XX:** 273
"Brokeback Mountain" (Proulx), **Supp. VII:** 264–265
"Broken Balance, The" (Jeffers), **Supp. II Part 2:** 426
"Broken Field, The" (Teasdale), **Supp. XXVII:** 294
"Broken Field Running" (Bambara), **Supp. XI:** 10, 11
Broken Frieze, The (Everwine), **Supp. XV:** 74, 75, 89
Broken Ground, The (Berry), **Supp. X:** 30
"Broken Home, The" (Merrill), **Supp. III Part 1:** 319, 325

"Broken Oar, The" (Longfellow), **Retro. Supp. II:** 169
"Broken Promise" (MacLeish), **III:** 15
Broken Span, The (W. C. Williams), **IV:** 419; **Retro. Supp. I:** 424
"Broken Tower, The" (H. Crane), **I:** 385, 386, 400, 401–402; **Retro. Supp. II:** 89, 90
Broken Vessels (Dubus), **Supp. VII:** 90–91; **Supp. XI:** 347
"Broken Vessels" (Dubus), **Supp. VII:** 90
Broken Wings, The (al-Ajni&hudot;a al-Mutakassirah) (Gibran), **Supp. XX:** 115, 124, 125
"Broker" (H. Roth), **Supp. IX:** 234
Bromfield, Louis, **IV:** 380
"Brompton Cocktail" (Mamet), **Supp. XIV:** 252
Bromwich, David, **Retro. Supp. I:** 305; **Supp. XII:** 162
"Broncho That Would Not Be Broken, The" (Lindsay), **Supp. I Part 2:** 383
Bronk, William, **Supp. XV:** 115; **Supp. XXI:** 17–34; **Supp. XXVI:** 237
Brontë, Anne, **Supp. IV Part 2:** 430
Brontë, Branwell, **I:** 462
Brontë, Charlotte, **I:** 458; **II:** 175; **Supp. IV Part 2:** 430; **Supp. IX:** 128; **Supp. XII:** 104, 303; **Supp. XV:** 338; **Supp. XVI:** 158; **Supp. XX:** 108
Brontë, Emily, **I:** 458; **Retro. Supp. I:** 43; **Supp. IV Part 2:** 430; **Supp. IX:** 128; **Supp. X:** 78, 89; **Supp. XV:** 338
"Bronze" (Francis), **Supp. IX:** 76
"Bronze" (Merrill), **Supp. III Part 1:** 336
Bronze Booklets on the History, Problems, and Cultural Contributions of the Negro series, **Supp. XIV:** 202
"Bronze Buckaroo, The" (Baraka), **Supp. II Part 1:** 49
"Bronze Horses, The" (A. Lowell), **II:** 524
"Bronze Tablets" (A. Lowell), **II:** 523
Bronzeville Boys and Girls (Brooks), **Supp. III Part 1:** 79
"Bronzeville Mother Loiters in Mississippi, A. Meanwhile, a Mississippi Mother Burns Bacon" (Brooks), **Supp. III Part 1:** 80
"Brooch, The" (Singer), **IV:** 20
Brook, Peter, **Retro. Supp. II:** 182
Brooke, Rupert, **II:** 82; **III:** 3
Brook Evans (Glaspell), **Supp. III Part 1:** 182–185
"Brooking Likeness" (Glück), **Supp. V:** 85
"Brooklyn" (Marshall), **Supp. XI:** 281, 282
"Brooklyn" (Shaw), **Supp. XIX:** 239, 240
Brooklyn Noir (McLoughlin, ed.), **Supp. XXIV:** 14
Brooks, Albert (Al Pew), **Supp. XXI:** 22
Brooks, Carrellin, **Supp. XXV:** 8
Brooks, Cleanth, **I:** 280, 282; **III:** 517; **IV:** 236, 279; **Retro. Supp. I:** 40, 41, 90; **Retro. Supp. II:** 235; **Supp. I Part 2:** 423; **Supp. III Part 2:** 542; **Supp. IX:** 153, 155; **Supp. V:** 316; **Supp. X:** 115, 123; **Supp. XIV:** 1–20;

Supp. XIX: 246
Brooks, David, **Supp. IV Part 2:** 623, 626, 630; **Supp. VIII:** 232
Brooks, Gwendolyn, **Retro. Supp. I:** 208; **Supp. III Part 1:** 69–90; **Supp. IV Part 1:** 2, 15, 244, 251, 257; **Supp. XI:** 1, 278; **Supp. XIII:** 111, 112, 296; **Supp. XIV:** 73; **Supp. XVIII:** 175, 181, 185; **Supp. XXI:** 230
Brooks, Mel, **Supp. IV Part 1:** 390; **Supp. IV Part 2:** 591
Brooks, Paul, **Supp. IX:** 26, 31, 32
Brooks, Phillips, **II:** 542; **Retro. Supp. II:** 134; **Supp. XIII:** 142
Brooks, Van Wyck, **I:** 106, 117, 215, 222, 228, 230, 231, 233, 236, 239–263, 266, 480; **II:** 30, 271, 285, 309, 337, 482; **III:** 394, 606; **IV:** 171, 312, 427, 433; **Retro. Supp. II:** 46, 137; **Supp. I Part 2:** 423, 424, 650; **Supp. II Part 1:** 137; **Supp. VIII:** 98, 101; **Supp. XIV:** 11; **Supp. XV:** 298, 301; **Supp. XX:** 68
Brooks, Mrs. Van Wyck (Eleanor Kenyon Stimson), **I:** 240, 245, 250, 252
Brooks, Mrs. Van Wyck (Gladys Billings), **I:** 258
Broom of the System, The (Wallace), **Supp. X:** 301, 302–305, 310
"Brooms" (Simic), **Supp. VIII:** 275
Brosi, George, **Supp. XX:** 166; **Supp. XXIII:** 39
Brosnan, Jim, **II:** 424–425; **Supp. XX:** 195
Brossard, Chandler, **Supp. XXII:** 258
Brother Carl (Sontag), **Supp. III Part 2:** 452
"Brother Death" (Anderson), **I:** 114
Brother Fire (Di Piero), **Supp. XIX:** 35, 38, 45–47
Brotherhood of the Grape, The (Fante), **Supp. XI:** 160, 171–172
Brother in Elysium, The: Ideas of Friendship and Society in the United States (Bronk), **Supp. XXI:** 21, 22, 25, 31
"Brothers" (Anderson), **I:** 114
"Brothers" (Huddle), **Supp. XXVI:** 154
"Brothers" (Stone), **Supp. XXVII:** 254
"Brothers" (W. Stone), **Supp. XXVII:** 255
Brothers, The (F. Barthelme), **Supp. XI:** 25, 28, 29, 30, 32–33
Brothers and Keepers (Wideman), **Supp. X:** 320, 321–322, 323, 325–327, 328, 329–330, 331, 332
Brothers Ashkenazi, The (Singer), **IV:** 2
Brothers Karamazov, The (Dostoevsky), **II:** 60; **III:** 146, 150, 283; **Supp. IX:** 102, 106; **Supp. XI:** 172; **Supp. XII:** 322
Brothers of No Kin (Richter), **Supp. XVIII:** 209
"Brothers of No Kin" (Richter), **Supp. XVIII:** 208
Brother to Dragons: A Tale in Verse and Voices (Warren), **IV:** 243–244, 245, 246, 251, 252, 254, 257
Broughton, James, **Supp. XV:** 146
Broughton, Rhoda, **II:** 174; **IV:** 309, 310; **Supp. XX:** 232

Broun, Heywood, **I:** 478; **II:** 417; **IV:** 432; **Supp. IX:** 190; **Supp. XXII:** 277
Broussais, François, **Supp. I Part 1:** 302
Brouwer, Joel, **Supp. XXII:** 223, 237
Browder, Earl, **I:** 515; **Supp. XX: 76, 77**
Brower, David, **Supp. X:** 29
Brower, Reuben, **Supp. XV:** 20
Brown, Alice, **II:** 523; **Retro. Supp. II:** 136
Brown, Andrew, **Supp. XVI:** 150
Brown, Ashley, **Retro. Supp. II:** 48; **Supp. I Part 1:** 79, 80, 82, 84, 92
Brown, Charles Brockden, **I:** 54, 211, 335; **II:** 74, 267, 298; **III:** 415; **Supp. I Part 1: 124–149; Supp. II Part 1:** 65, 292; **Supp. XXIII:** 178
Brown, Mrs. Charles Brockden (Elizabeth Linn), **Supp. I Part 1:** 145, 146
Brown, Clifford, **Supp. V:** 195
Brown, Dan, **Supp. XXVII:** 5
Brown, Deborah, **Supp. XVII:** 75
Brown, Dee, **Supp. IV Part 2:** 504
Brown, Elijah, **Supp. I Part 1:** 125
Brown, Fleda, **Supp. XXIII:** 59
Brown, George Douglas, **III:** 473
Brown, Harry, **Supp. IV Part 2:** 560
Brown, Harvey, **Supp. XIV:** 148
Brown, Himan, **Supp. XIX:** 241, 242
Brown, H. Rap, **Supp. XXI:** 171
Brown, Jeffrey, **Supp. XXVII:** 205
Brown, John, **II:** 13; **IV:** 125, 126, 172, 237, 249, 254; **Supp. I Part 1:** 345; **Supp. VIII:** 204
Brown, Joseph Epes, **Supp. IV Part 2:** 487
Brown, Larry, **Supp. XVIII:** 195; **Supp. XXI: 35–50**
Brown, Leonard, **Supp. IX:** 117
Brown, Mary Armitt, **Supp. I Part 1:** 125
Brown, Mick, **Supp. XXVII:** 268, 270
Brown, Nell Porter, **Supp. XXV:** 130, 131, 138
Brown, Percy, **II:** 20
Brown, Robert (Anahalihs), **Supp. XXVI:** 89, 95
Brown, Robert E., **Supp. X:** 12
Brown, Scott, **Supp. XI:** 178
Brown, Slater, **IV:** 123; **Retro. Supp. II:** 79
Brown, Solyman, **Supp. I Part 1:** 156
Brown, Sterling, **Retro. Supp. I:** 198; **Supp. IV Part 1:** 169; **Supp. XIV:** 202; **Supp. XXII:** 1, 8, 12
Brown, Tina, **Supp. XVI:** 176–177
Brown, Wesley, **Supp. V:** 6
Brown, William Hill, **Supp. XXV:** 38
Brown, William Wells, **Supp. XXIII:** 184
Brown Angels (Myers), **Supp. XXVII:** 209
Brown Decades, The (Mumford), **Supp. II Part 2:** 475, 478, 491–492
Brown Dog (Harrison), **Supp. VIII:** 51
Brown Dog of the Yaak: Essays on Art and Activism (Bass), **Supp. XVI:** 22
"Brown Dwarf of Rügen, The" (Whittier), **Supp. I Part 2:** 696
Browne, Charles Farrar, **II:** 289; **IV:** 193, 196; **Supp. XVIII:** 1, 4
Browne, Roscoe Lee, **Supp. VIII:** 345

Browne, Thomas, **II:** 15–16, 304; **III:** 77, 78, 198, 487; **IV:** 147; **Supp. IX:** 136; **Supp. XII:** 45; **Supp. XVI:** 292
Browne, William, **Supp. I Part 1:** 98
Brownell, W. C., **II:** 14
Brownell, William Crary, **Retro. Supp. I:** 365, 366
Browner, Stephanie P., **Supp. XVIII:** 17
Brown Girl, Brownstones (Marshall), **Supp. XI:** 275, 276, **278–280,** 282
Brownies' Book, The (Hughes), **Supp. I Part 1:** 321
Browning, Dominique, **Supp. XXVI:** 131
Browning, Elizabeth Barrett, **I:** 458, 459; **Retro. Supp. I:** 33, 43; **Supp. XVIII:** 175–176; **Supp. XX: 108; Supp. XXVII:** 284
Browning, Oscar, **Supp. XX: 231**
Browning, Robert, **I:** 50, 66, 103, 458, 460, 468; **II:** 338, 478, 522; **III:** 5, 8, 467, 469, 484, 511, 521, 524, 606, 609; **IV:** 135, 245, 366, 416; **Retro. Supp. I:** 43, 55, 217; **Retro. Supp. II:** 188, 190; **Supp. I Part 1:** 2, 6, 79, 311; **Supp. I Part 2:** 416, 468, 622; **Supp. III Part 1:** 5, 6; **Supp. IV Part 2:** 430; **Supp. X:** 65; **Supp. XV:** 92, 250, 275
Brownmiller, Susan, **Supp. X:** 252
Brownrigg, Sylvia, **Supp. XXV:** 59–60
"Brown River, Smile" (Toomer), **Supp. IV Part 1:** 16
Brownstone Eclogues and Other Poems (Aiken), **I:** 65, 67
Brown: The Last Discovery of America (Rodriguez), **Supp. XIV:** 297, 298, 300, **305–309,** 310, 311–312
Broyard, Anatole, **Supp. IV Part 1:** 39; **Supp. VIII:** 140; **Supp. X:** 186; **Supp. XI:** 348; **Supp. XVI:** 213
Broyles, Yolanda Julia, **Supp. XIX:** 112
Bruccoli, Matthew, **Retro. Supp. I:** 98, 102, 105, 114, 115, 359; **Supp. IV Part 2:** 468, 470
Bruce, John Edward, **Supp. XVI:** 143
Bruce, Lenny, **Supp. VIII:** 198
Bruce, Virginia, **Supp. XII:** 173
Bruce-Novoa, Juan, **Supp. VIII:** 73, 74
Bruchac, Joseph, **Supp. IV Part 1:** 261, 319, 320, 321, 322, 323, 325, 328, 398, 399, 403, 408, 414; **Supp. IV Part 2:** 502, 506
Brueghel, Pieter, **I:** 174; **Supp. I Part 2:** 475
Brueghel, Pieter, the Elder, **Retro. Supp. I:** 430
Bruell, Edwin, **Supp. VIII:** 126
Brugh, Spangler Arlington. *See* Taylor, Robert
"Bruja: Witch" (Mora), **Supp. XIII:** 214, 220, 221, **Supp. XIII:** 222
Brulé, Claude, **Supp. XI:** 307
Brumer, Andy, **Supp. XIII:** 88
Brummels, J. V., **Supp. XIX:** 119
Brunner, Emil, **III:** 291, 303
"Brush Fire" (J. Wright), **Supp. XVII:** 241
Brustein, Robert, **Supp. VIII:** 331; **Supp. XXIV:** 116

Brutus, **IV:** 373, 374; **Supp. I Part 2:** 471
"Brutus and Antony" (Masters), **Supp. I Part 2:** 472
"Bryan, Bryan, Bryan, Bryan" (Lindsay), **Supp. I Part 2:** 394, 395, 398
Bryan, George, **Retro. Supp. II:** 76
Bryan, Sharon, **Supp. IX:** 154
Bryan, William Jennings, **I:** 483; **IV:** 124; **Supp. I Part 2:** 385, 395–396, 455, 456
Bryant, Austin, **Supp. I Part 1:** 152, 153
Bryant, Frances, **Supp. I Part 1:** 153
Bryant, Louise, **Supp. X:** 136
Bryant, Peter, **Supp. I Part 1:** 150, 151, 152, 153. *See also* George, Peter
Bryant, William Cullen, **I:** 335, 458; **II:** 311; **III:** 81; **IV:** 309; **Retro. Supp. I:** 217; **Retro. Supp. II:** 155; **Supp. I Part 1: 150–173,** 312, 362; **Supp. I Part 2:** 413, 416, 420; **Supp. IV Part 1:** 165; **Supp. XIII:** 145; **Supp. XIX:** 4; **Supp. XXV:** 250
Bryant, Mrs. William Cullen (Frances Fairchild), **Supp. I Part 1:** 153, 169
Bryer, Jackson R., **Supp. IV Part 2:** 575, 583, 585, 586, 589, 591; **Supp. XIII:** 200, **Supp. XIII:** 205
Bryher, Jackson R. (pseudonym). *See* Ellerman, Winifred
Brynner, Witter, **Supp. XXII:** 273
Bubber Goes to Heaven (Bontemps), **Supp. XXII:** 4
"Bubbs Creek Haircut" (Snyder), **Supp. VIII:** 306
Buber, Martin, **II:** 228; **III:** 45, 308, 528; **IV:** 11; **Supp. I Part 1:** 83, 88; **Supp. XVI:** 291
Buccaneers, The (Wharton), **IV:** 327; **Retro. Supp. I:** 382
Buchanan Dying (Updike), **Retro. Supp. I:** 331, 335
Buchbinder, David, **Supp. XIII:** 32
Buchwald, Art, **Supp. XII:** 124–125; **Supp. XVI:** 110–111
Buchwald, Emilie, **Supp. XVI:** 35, 36
Buck, Dudley, **Supp. I Part 1:** 362
Buck, Gene, **II:** 427
Buck, John, Sr., **Supp. XXVI:** 89
Buck, Pearl S., **Supp. II Part 1: 113–134; Supp. XIV:** 274
Buckdancer's Choice (Dickey), **Supp. IV Part 1:** 176, 177, 178, 180
"Buckdancer's Choice" (Dickey), **Supp. IV Part 1:** 191
Bucke, Richard Maurice, **Retro. Supp. I:** 407
"Buckeyes" (P. Benedict), **Supp. XXIII:** 46
"Buck Fever" (Humphrey), **Supp. IX:** 109
"Buck in the Snow, The" (Millay), **III:** 135
Buckley, Christopher, **Supp. IX:** 169; **Supp. XI:** 257, 329; **Supp. XV:** 76–77, 86
Buckley, James, Jr., **Supp. XVII:** 220
Buckminster, Joseph, **Supp. II Part 1:** 66–67, 69
Bucknell, Katherine, **Supp. XIV:** 170

Bucolics (Auden), **Supp. II Part 1:** 21, 24
Budbill, David, **Supp. XIX:** 1–16
Budd, Louis J., **IV:** 210
Buddha, **I:** 136; **II:** 1; **III:** 173, 179, 239, 567; **Supp. I Part 1:** 363; **Supp. I Part 2:** 397
Buddha, The: The Story of Siddhartha (film, Grubin), **Supp. XXIII:** 138, 140
"Buddha Boy" (Saunders), **Supp. XIX:** 235
"Buddha's Last Instruction, The" (Oliver), **Supp. VII:** 239
"Buddies"(Kenny), **Supp. XXIII:** 150
Budding Prospects (Boyle), **Supp. VIII:** 8–9; **Supp. XX:** 27–28
Buechner, Frederick, **III:** 310; **Supp. XII:** 41–59
Buell, Lawrence, **Supp. IX:** 29; **Supp. V:** 209; **Supp. XV:** 269, 282
"Buffalo" (Peacock), **Supp. XIX:** 198
"Buffalo, The" (Moore), **III:** 215
"Buffalo Bill". *See* Cody, William
Buffalo Girls (McMurtry), **Supp. V:** 229
Buffalo Girls (screenplay) (McMurtry), **Supp. V:** 232
Buffalo Hunters, The: The Story of the Hide Men (Sandoz), **Supp. XXIV:** 244, 247–249, 256
Buffett, Jimmy, **Supp. VIII:** 42
Buffon, Comte de, **II:** 101
Buford, Fanny McConnell, **Retro. Supp. II:** 117
Bugeja, Michael, **Supp. X:** 201
Bugged for Murder (Lacy), **Supp. XV:** 205
"Buglesong" (Stegner), **Supp. IV Part 2:** 606
Buhle, Paul, **Supp. XXI:** 172
"Buick" (Shapiro), **Supp. II Part 2:** 705
"Builders" (Yates), **Supp. XI:** 342–343
Builders, The (Glasgow), **II:** 183–184, 193
"Builders, The" (Hay), **Supp. XIV:** 125
Builders in Sand (W. Frank), **Supp. XX:** 68
Builders of the Bay Colony (Morison), **Supp. I Part 2:** 484–485
"Builders of the Bridge, The" (Mumford), **Supp. II Part 2:** 475
"Building" (Snyder), **Supp. VIII:** 305
"Building, Dwelling, Thinking" (Heidegger), **Retro. Supp. II:** 87
Building a Character (Stanislavsky), **Supp. XIV:** 243
" 'Building' Larry Brown(s) at Algonquin Books of Chapel Hill" (Perry), **Supp. XXI:** 42
"Building of the Ship, The" (Longfellow), **II:** 498; **Retro. Supp. II:** 159, 167, 168
"Build Soil" (Frost), **Retro. Supp. I:** 138, 139
"Build Soil" (Snyder), **Supp. VIII:** 304
Build-Up, The (W. C. Williams), **Retro. Supp. I:** 423
Bukiet, Melvin Jules, **Supp. XVII: 39–51**
Bukowski, Charles, **Supp. III Part 1:** 147; **Supp. XI:** 159, 161, 172, 173; **Supp. XVII:** 245

Bulgakov, Mikhail, **Supp. XIV:** 97
"Bulgarian Poetess, The" (Updike), **IV:** 215, 227; **Retro. Supp. I:** 329
Bull, Ole, **II:** 504
"Bulldozer, The" (Francis), **Supp. IX:** 87
"Bullet in the Brain" (Wolff), **Supp. VII:** 342–343
Bullet Park (Cheever), **Supp. I Part 1:** 185, 187–193, 194, 195
Bullets over Broadway (film; Allen), **Supp. XV:** 12, 12–13
Bullfight, The (Mailer), **Retro. Supp. II:** 205
Bullfighter Checks Her Makeup, The: My Encounters with Extraordinary People (Orlean), **Supp. XXV:** 159, 163–164
Bullins, Ed, **Supp. II Part 1:** 34, 42
Bullock, Sandra, **Supp. X:** 80
"Bull-Roarer, The" (Stern), **Supp. IX:** 297
"Bully, The" (Dubus), **Supp. VII:** 84
"Bulsh" (X. J. Kennedy), **Supp. XV:** 161
Bultmann, Rudolf, **III:** 309
Bulwark, The (Dreiser), **I:** 497, 506, 516–517; **Retro. Supp. II:** 95, 96, 105, 108
Bulwer-Lytton, Edward George, **IV:** 350
"Bums in the Attic" (Cisneros), **Supp. VII:** 62
Bunche, Ralph, **Supp. I Part 1:** 343; **Supp. XIV:** 202; **Supp. XXII:** 12
"Bunchgrass Edge of the World, The" (Proulx), **Supp. VII:** 263
Bunge, Nancy, **Supp. XVII:** 218; **Supp. XXII:** 175, 177, 178, 180, 183; **Supp. XXVI:** 257
"Bunner Sisters, The" (Wharton), **IV:** 317
Bunting, Basil, **Retro. Supp. I:** 422; **Supp. III Part 2:** 616, 620, 624; **Supp. XIV:** 286
Buntline, Ned, **Supp. XXIII:** 182
Buñuel, Luis, **III:** 184; **Retro. Supp. II:** 337
Bunyan, John, **I:** 445; **II:** 15, 104, 228; **IV:** 80, 84, 156, 437; **Supp. I Part 1:** 32
Bunyan, Paul, **Supp. XXII:** 203
Burana, Lily, **Supp. XI:** 253
Burbank, Luther, **I:** 483
Burbank, Rex, **IV:** 363
Burch, Michael, **Supp. XXI:** 99
Burchfield, Alice, **Supp. I Part 2:** 652, 660
Burden of Proof, The (Turow), **Supp. XVII: 216–217,** 218
Burden of Southern History, The (Woodward), **Retro. Supp. I:** 75
Burdens of Formality, The (Lea, ed.), **Supp. X:** 58
Burger, Gottfried August, **II:** 306
Burgess, Anthony, **Supp. IV Part 1:** 227; **Supp. IV Part 2:** 685; **Supp. V:** 128; **Supp. XXIII:** 42
Burgh, James, **Supp. I Part 2:** 522
"Burglar of Babylon, The" (Bishop), **Retro. Supp. II:** 47; **Supp. I Part 1:** 93
Burgum, E. B., **IV:** 469, 470
Burham, Philip, **Supp. XX:** 44
"Burial of Jonathan Brown, The"(Hadas), **Supp. XXIII:** 115

Buried Child (Shepard), **Supp. III Part 2:** 433, 447, 448; **Supp. XIV:** 327
"Buried Lake, The" (Tate), **IV:** 136
Burkard, Michael, **Supp. XXIV:** 165
Burke, Carolyn, **Supp. XXII:** 156, 158, 162, 165, 167, 168
Burke, Edmund, **I:** 9; **III:** 310; **Supp. I Part 2:** 496, 511, 512, 513, 523; **Supp. II Part 1:** 80; **Supp. XVII:** 236
Burke, James Lee, **Supp. XIV: 21–38;** **Supp. XXI:** 67, 72, 80
Burke, Kenneth, **I:** 264–287, 291; **III:** 497, 499, 546; **IV:** 123, 408; **Retro. Supp. I:** 297; **Retro. Supp. II:** 117, 120; **Supp. I Part 2:** 630; **Supp. II Part 1:** 136; **Supp. IX:** 229; **Supp. VIII:** 105; **Supp. XIV:** 3; **Supp. XXI:** 89
Burke, Rusty, **Supp. XXVII:** 128
Burke, William, **Supp. XXI:** 215
"Burl" (Mosher), **Supp. XXII:** 204, 211
Burley, Justin, **Supp. XVI:** 158
"Burly Fading One, The" (Hayden), **Supp. II Part 1:** 366
Burn, Stephen J., **Supp. XX: 85; Supp. XXII:** 266, 268
"Burned" (Levine), **Supp. V:** 186, 192
"Burned" (Stallings), **Supp. XXV:** 233
"Burned Diary, The" (Olds), **Supp. X:** 215
"Burned Man" (Huddle), **Supp. XXVI:** 148, 151
Burne-Jones, Edward, **Supp. XXII:** 156
Burnett, Allison, **Supp. XVII:** 22
Burnett, David, **Supp. XI:** 299
Burnett, Frances Hodgson, **Supp. I Part 1:** 44
Burnett, Whit, **III:** 551; **Supp. XI:** 294
Burnett, W. R., **Supp. XXVII:** 93
Burney, Fanny, **Supp. XV:** 232; **Supp. XX: 108**
Burnham, James, **Supp. I Part 2:** 648
Burnham, John Chynoweth, **I:** 59
"Burning, The" (Welty), **IV:** 277–278; **Retro. Supp. I:** 353
Burning Angel (Burke), **Supp. XIV:** 30, 32
Burning Bright (Rash), **Supp. XXVII:** 228–229
Burning Bright (Steinbeck), **IV:** 51, 61–62
Burning Bright: An Anthology of Sacred Poetry (Hampl, ed.), **Supp. XXII:** 87
"Burning Bush" (Cliff), **Supp. XXII:** 75
Burning Bush (Untermeyer), **Supp. XV: 309**
"Burning Bush" (Untermeyer), **Supp. XV:** 309
Burning Bush, The (Asch), **Supp. XXIII:** 7
Burning Bush, The (H. and G. Herczeg), **Supp. XVII:** 62
Burning Chrome (W. Gibson), **Supp. XVI:** 118, 122, **128**
"Burning Chrome" (W. Gibson), **Supp. XVI:** 117, 120, 123, 124, 128
Burning City (Benét), **Supp. XI:** 46, 58
Burning Daylight (London), **II:** 474, 481

Burning Down the House: Essays on Fiction (C. Baxter), **Supp. XVII:** 13, 20, 21

"Burning Down the Little House on the Prairie: Asian Pioneers in Contemporary North America" (Martín-Lucas), **Supp. XXVI:** 218

Burning House, The (Beattie), **Supp. V:** 29

"Burning Ladder, The" (Gioia), **Supp. XV:** 118

Burning Mystery of Anna in 1951, The (Koch), **Supp. XV:** 182–183

"Burning of Paper Instead of Children, The" (Rich), **Supp. I Part 2:** 558

"Burning Shit at An Khe" (Weigl), **Supp. XIX:** 279–280

Burning the Days (Salter), **Supp. XIX:** 252

Burning the Days: Recollections (Salter), **Supp. IX:** 245, 246, 248, 260, **261–262**

"Burning the Small Dead" (Snyder), **Supp. VIII:** 298

Burning Tigris, The: The Armenian Genocide and America's Response (Balakian), **Supp. XXIII:** 19, 21, 22, **25–28**, 30

"Burning Tobacco Beds" (J. W. Miller), **Supp. XX:** 167

Burn Marks (Paretsky), **Supp. XXV:** 174–175, 178, 180

Burns, Carol, **Supp. XVIII:** 162

Burns, David, **III:** 165–166

Burns, Ken, **Supp. XIV:** 14

Burns, Michael, **Supp. XV:** 339

Burns, Robert, **II:** 150, 306; **III:** 592; **IV:** 453; **Supp. I Part 1:** 158; **Supp. I Part 2:** 410, 455, 683, 685, 691, 692; **Supp. IX:** 173; **Supp. XII:** 171; **Supp. XIII:** 3; **Supp. XVIII:** 82

Burnshaw, Stanley, **Retro. Supp. I:** 298, 303; **Supp. III Part 2:** 615

"Burn the Cities" (West), **Retro. Supp. II:** 338

Burnt Mountain (Siddons), **Supp. XXII:** 253

Burnt Norton (T. S. Eliot), **I:** 575, 580–581, 582, 584, 585; **III:** 10

"Burnt Norton" (T. S. Eliot), **Retro. Supp. I:** 66; **Supp. XV:** 216

Burnt-Out Case, A (Greene), **Supp. VIII:** 4

"Burnt-out Spa, The" (Plath), **Retro. Supp. II:** 246

Burn Witch Burn (A. Merritt), **Supp. XVII:** 58

Burr, Aaron, **I:** 7, 549, 550; **II:** 300; **IV:** 264; **Supp. I Part 2:** 461, 483

Burr: A Novel (Vidal), **Supp. IV Part 2:** 677, 682, 684, 685, 687, 688, 689, 691

Burr Oaks (Eberhart), **I:** 533, 535

Burroughs, Edgar Rice, **Supp. IV Part 1:** 101

Burroughs, John, **I:** 220, 236, 506; **IV:** 346; **Supp. IX:** 171; **Supp. XXVI:** 37

Burroughs, William S., **III:** 45, 174, 258; **Supp. II Part 1:** 320, 328; **Supp. III Part 1:** 91–110, 217, 226; **Supp. IV Part 1:** 79, 87, 90; **Supp. XI:** 297,

308; **Supp. XII:** 1, 3, 118, 121, 124, 129, 131, 136; **Supp. XIV:** 137, 140–141, 143–144, 150; **Supp. XVI:** 135; **Supp. XVII:** 225; **Supp. XVIII:** 137; **Supp. XXIII:** 213; **Supp. XXIV:** 42

Burrow, Trigant, **Supp. II Part 1:** 6

Burrows, Ken, **Supp. V:** 115

Bursey, Jeff, **Supp. XXII:** 257

Burson, Claudia, **Supp. XV:** 343

Burstein, Janet, **Supp. XVII:** 41, 44, 48

"Bursts of Light" (Bronk), **Supp. XXI:** 33

Burt, Stephen, **Supp. XV:** 341, 342, 345, 347, 351; **Supp. XVII:** 18, 246

Burt, Steve, **Supp. V:** 83

Burtis, Thomson, **Supp. XIII:** 163

Burton, Robert, **II:** 535; **III:** 77, 78; **Supp. I Part 1:** 349

Burton, Sue D., **Supp. XIX:** 90

Burton, William Evans, **III:** 412

"Burying Ground by the Ties" (MacLeish), **III:** 14

Bury My Heart at Wounded Knee (Brown), **Supp. IV Part 2:** 504

Bury the Dead (Shaw), **IV:** 381; **Supp. XIX:** **242–244**, 249, 252

"Bus Along St. Clair: December, A" (Atwood), **Supp. XIII:** 33

Busch, Frederick, **Supp. X:** 78; **Supp. XII:** 343; **Supp. XVII:** 175; **Supp. XXVI:** 9

Bush, Barney, **Supp. XII:** 218, 222

Bush, Douglas, **Supp. I Part 1:** 268; **Supp. XIV:** 10

"Busher Comes Back, The" (Lardner), **II:** 422

"Busher's Letters Home, A" (Lardner), **II:** 418–419, 421

Bushmiller, Ernie, **Supp. XXVII:** 21

Bushrui, Suheil, **Supp. XX:** **113, 117, 120, 122, 126–127**

"Business and Poetry" (Gioia), **Supp. XV:** 113, 115

"Business Deal" (West), **IV:** 287

"Business Man, A" (Jewett), **Retro. Supp. II:** 132

Business of Memory, The: The Art of Remembering in an Age of Forgetting (C. Baxter, ed.), **Supp. XVII:** 21

"Business Trip" (Hoffman), **Supp. XVIII:** 86

"Bus Riley's Back in Town" (Inge), **Supp. XXV:** 95

Buss, Helen M., **Supp. IV Part 1:** 12

Bus Stop (Inge), **Supp. XXV:** 93, 99–100

Butcher, Fanny, **Supp. XXV:** 199

Butcher, Margaret Just, **Supp. XIV:** 203

"Butcher, The" (Southern), **Supp. XI:** 294

"Butcher Cock, The"(P. Benedict), **Supp. XXIII:** 46–47

"Butcher Shop" (Simic), **Supp. VIII:** 273

But Gentlemen Marry Brunettes (Loos), **Supp. XVI:** 190–191

"But He Says I Misunderstood" (Notley), **Supp. XXII:** 227

Butler, Benjamin, **I:** 457

Butler, Dorothy. *See* Farrell, Mrs. James T. (Dorothy Butler)

Butler, Elizabeth, **Supp. I Part 1:** 260

Butler, Ethel, **Supp. XIV:** 125

Butler, Hugo, **Supp. XVII:** 63

Butler, James D., **Supp. IX:** 175

Butler, Joseph, **II:** 8, 9

Butler, Judith, **Supp. XII:** 6

Butler, Maud. *See* Falkner, Mrs. Murray C. (Maud Butler)

Butler, Nicholas Murray, **I:** 223; **Supp. I Part 1:** 23; **Supp. III Part 2:** 499

Butler, Octavia, **Supp. XIII:** **59–72**

Butler, Robert Olen, **Supp. XII:** **61–78,** 319

Butler, Samuel, **II:** 82, 86; **IV:** 121, 440; **Supp. VIII:** 171

Butler-Evans, Elliot, **Retro. Supp. II:** 121

"But Only Mine" (Wright), **Supp. III Part 2:** 595

Butscher, Edward, **Supp. I Part 2:** 526

Butter Battle Book, The (Geisel), **Supp. XVI:** 110

"Buttercups" (R. Lowell), **Retro. Supp. II:** 187

Butterfield, R. W., **I:** 386

Butterfield, Stephen, **Supp. IV Part 1:** 3, 11

Butterfield 8 (O'Hara), **III:** 361

"Butterflies Under Persimmon" (Jarman), **Supp. XVII:** 120

Butterfly (Harvey), **Supp. XIII:** 184

"Butterfly, The" (Brodksy), **Supp. VIII:** 26

"Butterfly and the Traffic Light, The" (Ozick), **Supp. V:** 263, 265

Butterfly in the Typewriter (MacLaughlin), **Supp. XXVI:** 241, 243, 252

Butterfly Plague, The (Findley), **Supp. XX:** **50, 52, 53**

Butterfly Stories (Vollmann), **Supp. XVII:** 226

"Butterfly-toed Shoes" (Komunyakaa), **Supp. XIII:** 126

Butter Hill and Other Poems (Francis), **Supp. IX:** 88, 89

"Button-Down Builders, The" (Siddons), **Supp. XXII:** 243–244

Buttons, Red, **Supp. IV Part 2:** 574

Buttrick, George, **III:** 301; **Supp. XII:** 47–48

"But What Is the Reader to Make of This?" (Ashbery), **Supp. III Part 1:** 25

Butz, Earl, **Supp. X:** 35

"Buz" (Alcott), **Supp. I Part 1:** 43

Buzinski, Jim, **Supp. XX:** 273

"By an *Objibwa Female* Pen: Invitation to sisters to a walk in the Garden, after a shower"(J. Schoolcraft), **Supp. XXIII:** 230

Byatt, A. S., **Supp. XXI:** 147

By Avon River (Doolittle), **Supp. I Part 1:** 272

"By Blue Ontario's Shore" (Whitman), **Retro. Supp. I:** 399, 400

"By Candlelight" (Major), **Supp. XXII:** 185

"By Disposition of Angels" (Moore), **III:** 214

"By Earth" (Olds), **Supp. X:** 214

"Bye for Now, Broadway, My New Friend" (Silver), **Supp. XXIV:** 276
"By Fire" (Olds), **Supp. X:** 214
Bygones (Untermeyer), **Supp. XV:** 304, **308–309,** 312, 313
By Land, By Sea (Hoffman), **Supp. XVIII:** 86
By Land and by Sea (Morison), **Supp. I Part 2:** 492
Byles, Mather, **Supp. XX: 279, 282**
By-Line: Ernest Hemingway (Hemingway), **II:** 257–258
By Love Possessed (Cozens), **I:** 358, 365, 372–374, 375, 376, 377, 378, 379
"By Morning" (Swenson), **Supp. IV Part 2:** 642
"By Night" (Francis), **Supp. IX:** 76
Bynner, Witter, **II:** 513, 527; **Supp. XIII:** 347; **Supp. XV: 39–54**
Byrd, William, **Supp. IV Part 2:** 425; **Supp. XXI:** 35; **Supp. XXII:** 193
Byrne, Donn, **IV:** 67
Byrne, Edward, **Supp. XXV:** 226, 227
Byron, George Gordon, Lord, **I:** 343, 568, 577; **II:** 135, 193, 296, 301, 303, 310, 315, 331, 566; **III:** 82, 137, 170, 409, 410, 412, 469; **IV:** 245, 435; **Supp. I Part 1:** 150, 312, 349; **Supp. I Part 2:** 580, 591, 683, 685, 719; **Supp. XIII:** 139; **Supp. XVI:** 188, 203, 206, 210
"Byron's Cain" (L. Michaels), **Supp. XVI:** 203
"Bystanders" (Matthews), **Supp. IX:** 160
By the Bias of Sound (Sobin), **Supp. XVI:** 281
By the North Gate (Oates), **Supp. II Part 2:** 504
"By the People" (Stratton-Porter), **Supp. XX: 221**
"By the Sea" (Teasdale), **Supp. XXVII:** 294
By the Shores of Silver Lake (L. I. Wilder), **Supp. XXII:** 294, 295, 299
"By the Time You Get There, by the Time You Get Back" (Muñoz), **Supp. XXV:** 134
"By the Waters of Babylon" (Benét), **Supp. XI:** 56, 58
By the Waters of Manhattan (Reznikoff), **Supp. XIV:** 288, 293, 294
By the Waters of Manhattan: An Annual (Reznikoff), **Supp. XIV:** 277, 280, 289
By the Waters of Manhattan: Selected Verse (Reznikoff), **Supp. XIV:** 281, 291
By the Well of Living and Seeing and the Fifth Book of the Maccabees (Reznikoff), **Supp. XIV:** 281
By the Well of Living and Seeing: New and Selected Poems 1918–1973 (Reznikoff), **Supp. XIV:** 281, 287–288, 295
By Way of Orbit (O'Neill), **III:** 405
Byzantine Parables (Notley), **Supp. XXII:** 235, 237

C

"C 33" (H. Crane), **I:** 384; **Retro. Supp. II:** 76

Cabala, The (Wilder), **IV:** 356, 358–360, 369, 374
"Cabaret" (Boyle), **Supp. XXIV:** 61
Cabaret (film), **Supp. XIV:** 155, 162
Cabaret (play), **Supp. XIV:** 162; **Supp. XVII:** 45
Cabbages and Kings (O. Henry), **Supp. II Part 1:** 394, 409
Cabell, James Branch, **II:** 42; **III:** 394; **IV:** 67, 359, 360; **Retro. Supp. I:** 80; **Supp. I Part 2:** 613, 714, 718, 721; **Supp. X:** 223
"Cabin, The" (Carver), **Supp. III Part 1:** 137, 146
Cabin, The: Reminiscence and Diversions (Mamet), **Supp. XIV:** 240
Cabinet of Dr. Caligari, The (film), **Retro. Supp. I:** 268
Cable, George Washington, **II:** 289; **Retro. Supp. II:** 65; **Supp. I Part 1:** 200; **Supp. II Part 1:** 198; **Supp. XIV:** 63
Cables to the Ace; or, Familiar Liturgies of Misunderstanding (Merton), **Supp. VIII:** 208
Cabot, James, **II:** 14; **IV:** 173
Cabot, John, **Supp. I Part 2:** 496, 497
Cachoeira Tales and Other Poems, The (Nelson), **Supp. XVIII: 178–179**
"Cachoiera Tales, The" (Nelson), **Supp. XVIII:** 179
Cactus Flower (Barillet and Grédy), **Supp. XVI:** 194
"Caddy's Diary, A" (Lardner), **II:** 421–422
"Cadence" (Dubus), **Supp. VII:** 84–85
Cadieux, Isabelle, **Supp. XIII:** 127
"Cadillac Flambé" (Ellison), **Retro. Supp. II:** 119, 126; **Supp. II Part 1:** 248
Cadillac Jack (McMurtry), **Supp. V:** 225
Cadillac Jukebox (Burke), **Supp. XIV:** 32
Cadle, Dean, **Supp. I Part 2:** 429
Cady, Edwin H., **II:** 272
"Caedmon" (Garrett), **Supp. VII:** 96–97
Caesar, Julius, **II:** 12, 502, 561–562; **IV:** 372, 373
Caesar, Sid, **Supp. IV Part 2:** 574, 591
"Cafeteria, The" (Singer), **Retro. Supp. II:** 316
Cage, John, **Supp. IV Part 1:** 84; **Supp. V:** 337, 341; **Supp. XXIII:** 211
"Cage and the Prairie: Two Notes on Symbolism, The" (Bewley), **Supp. I Part 1:** 251
Cage Keeper, The (Dubus III), **Supp. XXIV: 99–102**
"Cage Keeper, The" (Dubus III), **Supp. XXIV:** 101–102, 104
Cage of Age, The (Bronk), **Supp. XXI:** 32
Cage of Spines, A (Swenson), **Supp. IV Part 2:** 641–642, 647
"Cage of the Body, The"(Schott), **Supp. XXIII:** 243–244
Cagney, James, **Supp. IV Part 1:** 236; **Supp. XIII:** 174
Cagney, William, **Supp. XIII:** 174

Cahalan, James, **Supp. XIII:** 1, 2, 3, 4, 12
Cahan, Abraham, **Supp. IX:** 227; **Supp. XIII:** 106; **Supp. XXI:** 3, 14; **Supp. XXIII:** 1, 2, 9, 16; **Supp. XXVI:** 123
Cahill, Tim, **Supp. XIII:** 13
Cain, James M., **III:** 99; **Supp. IV Part 1:** 130; **Supp. XI:** 160; **Supp. XIII:** 159, 165
Cain, Kathleen Shine, **Supp. XX: 247, 248**
Caine Mutiny, The (film), **Supp. XXV:** 260, 261
Caine Mutiny, The (Wouk), **Supp. XXV:** 253, 255, 256, 259–261
Caine Mutiny Court-Martial, The (Wouk), **Supp. XXV:** 253, 256
Caird, G. B., **Supp. XXI:** 91–92
Cairns, Huntington, **III:** 103, 108, 114, 119
Cairo! Shanghai! Bombay! (Williams and Shapiro), **IV:** 380
C: A Journal of Poetry, **Supp. XXVII:** 18, 24
Cake (Bynner), **Supp. XV:** 50
Cakes and Ale (Maugham), **III:** 64
Calabria, Frank, **Supp. XIII:** 164
Calamity Jane (Martha Jane Canary), **Supp. V:** 229–230; **Supp. X:** 103
"Calamus" (Whitman), **IV:** 342–343; **Retro. Supp. I:** 52, 403, 404, 407
Calasso, Roberto, **Supp. IV Part 1:** 301
Calavito, Jason, **Supp. XXV:** 123
Calder, William M., III, **Supp. XXIII:** 112
Calderón, Hector, **Supp. IV Part 2:** 544
Caldwell, Christopher, **Supp. IV Part 1:** 211
Caldwell, Erskine, **I:** 97, 211, **288–311; IV:** 286; **Supp. IV Part 2:** 601; **Supp. XXI:** 35; **Supp. XXII:** 196
Caldwell, Mrs. Erskine (Helen Lannegan), **I:** 289
Caldwell, Mrs. Erskine (Margaret Bourke-White), **I:** 290, 293–295, 297
Caldwell, Mrs. Erskine (Virginia Fletcher), **I:** 290
Caldwell, Gail, **Supp. XXVI:** 158
Caldwell, Reverend Ira Sylvester, **I:** 289, 305
Caldwell, Zoe, **Supp. XIII:** 207
Caleb Williams (Godwin), **III:** 415
"Calendar" (Creeley), **Supp. IV Part 1:** 158
Calendar of Saints for Unbelievers, A (Wescott), **Supp. XIV:** 342
Calendars (A. Finch), **Supp. XVII: 76–77**
Calhoun, John C., **I:** 8; **III:** 309
"Caliban in the Coal Mines" (Untermeyer), **Supp. XV:** 296
"California" (Carruth), **Supp. XVI:** 56
"California" (Didion), **Supp. IV Part 1:** 195
"California, This Is Minnesota Speaking" (Dunn), **Supp. XI:** 146
California and Oregon Trail, The (Parkman), **Supp. I Part 2:** 486

California: An Intimate History (Atherton), **Supp. XXIV:** 27

California Daughter (Leider), **Supp. XXIV:** 30

"California Hills in August" (Gioia), **Supp. XV:** 118–119

"California Indians of Today, The" (Zitkala-Ša), **Supp. XXV:** 284

"California Indian Trails and Prayer Trees" (Zitkala-Ša), **Supp. XXV:** 284

Californians (Jeffers), **Supp. II Part 2:** 415, 418, 420

Californians, The (Atherton), **Supp. XXIV:** 18, 21, 22

"California Oaks, The" (Winters), **Supp. II Part 2:** 798

"California Plush" (Bidart), **Supp. XV:** 23

"California Republic" (Didion), **Supp. IV Part 1:** 205

"California Requiem, A" (Gioia), **Supp. XV:** 126

California Suite (film), **Supp. IV Part 2:** 589

California Suite (Simon), **Supp. IV Part 2:** 581, 582

"Caligula" (R. Lowell), **II:** 554

Callahan, John F., **Retro. Supp. II:** 119, 126, 127

"Call at Corazón" (Bowles), **Supp. IV Part 1:** 82, 87

Calle, Sophia, **Supp. XII:** 22

"Called Back" (Kazin), **Supp. VIII:** 104

Calley, Captain William, **II:** 579

Calley, John, **Supp. XI:** 305

Callicott, J. Baird, **Supp. XIV:** 184

Calligrammes (Apollinaire), **I:** 432

"Calling Jesus" (Toomer), **Supp. III Part 2:** 484

Calling Myself Home (Hogan), **Supp. IV Part 1:** 397, 399, 400, 401, 413

Calling the Wind: Twentieth Century African-American Short Stories (Major, ed.), **Supp. XXII:** 172

Calling Western Union (Taggard), **Supp. XXII:** 271–272, **281–283**

Call It Experience (Caldwell), **I:** 290–291, 297

"Call It Fear" (Harjo), **Supp. XII:** 220

Call It Sleep (H. Roth), **Supp. IX:** 227, 228, **229–231; Supp. VIII:** 233; **Supp. XIII:** 106

"Call Letters: Mrs. V. B." (Angelou), **Supp. IV Part 1:** 15

Call Me Ishmael (Olson), **Supp. II Part 2:** 556; **Supp. XXI:** 21

Call Me Shakespeare (Endore), **Supp. XVII:** 65

"Call of Cthulhu, The" (Lovecraft), **Supp. XXV:** 109, 114, 116–117, 118; **Supp. XXVII:** 123

Call of the Gospel, The (Mather), **Supp. II Part 2:** 448

Call of the Wild, The (London), **II:** 466, 470–471, 472, 481

"Call of the Wild, The" (Snyder), **Supp. VIII:** 301

"Calloway's Code" (O. Henry), **Supp. II Part 1:** 404

"Call to Arms" (Mumford), **Supp. II Part 2:** 479

Call to Arms, The (film), **Retro. Supp. I:** 325

Calmer, Ned, **Supp. XI:** 219

Calvert, George H., **Supp. I Part 1:** 361

Calverton, V. F., **Supp. VIII:** 96

Calvin, John, **II:** 342; **IV:** 160, 490

Calvino, Italo, **Supp. IV Part 2:** 623, 678; **Supp. XIX:** 34; **Supp. XXI:** 225; **Supp. XXII:** 263

Cambridge Companion to Native American Literature, The (Porter and Roemer, eds.), **Supp. XX: 270**

Cambridge Edition of the Works of F. Scott Fitzgerald, The (Bruccoli, ed.), **Retro. Supp. I:** 115

Cambridge Film Handbook for *On the Waterfront* (Rapf), **Supp. XVIII:** 251

"Cambridge"(O'Hara), **Supp. XXIII:** 219

"Cambridge Thirty Years Ago" (J. R. Lowell), **Supp. I Part 2:** 419

Cambridge University Press, **Retro. Supp. I:** 115

"Camellia Sabina" (Moore), **III:** 208, 215

"Cameo" (Trethewey), **Supp. XXI:** 250

"Cameo Appearance" (Simic), **Supp. VIII:** 283

"Camera Notes" (column, Stratton-Porter), **Supp. XX: 217**

Camera Obscura (Nabokov), **III:** 255

Cameron, Angus, **Supp. XXI:** 268, 269, 275, 278

Cameron, Elizabeth, **I:** 10, 17

Cameron, Kenneth W., **II:** 16

Cameron, Peter, **Supp. XII: 79–95**

Cameron, Sharon, **Retro. Supp. I:** 43; **Retro. Supp. II:** 40

Camerson, Don, **I:** 10, 17

Camino, Léon Felipe, **Retro. Supp. II:** 89

Camino Real (T. Williams), **IV:** 382, 385, 386, 387, 388, 391, 392, 395, 398

Camões, Luiz Vaz de, **II:** 133; **Supp. I Part 1:** 94

"Camouflaging the Chimera" (Komunyakaa), **Supp. XIII: 122–123**

Camp, James, **Supp. XV:** 165

Camp, Walter, **II:** 423

Campana, Dino, **Supp. V:** 337

Campbell, Alan, **Supp. IV Part 1:** 353; **Supp. IX:** 196, 198, 201

Campbell, Alexander, **Supp. I Part 2:** 381, 395

Campbell, Donna, **Retro. Supp. II:** 139

Campbell, E. Simms, **Supp. XXII:** 12

Campbell, Helen, **Supp. XI:** 200, 206

Campbell, James, **Supp. XII:** 127

Campbell, James Edwin, **Supp. II Part 1:** 202

Campbell, Joanna (pseudonym). *See* Bly, Carol

Campbell, Joseph, **I:** 135; **IV:** 369, 370; **Supp. IX:** 245; **Supp. XXV:** 74

Campbell, Lewis, **III:** 476

Campbell, Thomas, **II:** 8, 303, 314; **III:** 410; **Supp. I Part 1:** 309, 310

Campbell, Virginia, **Supp. XIII:** 114

Campbell, Will D., **Supp. XXI:** 247

Campbell (Hale), Janet, **Supp. IV Part 2:** 503

"Campers Leaving: Summer 1981" (Kenyon), **Supp. VII:** 169

"Camp Evergreen" (Kenyon), **Supp. VII:** 168

"Camping in Madera Canyon" (Swenson), **Supp. IV Part 2:** 649

Campion, Jane, **Supp. XXIV:** 172

Campion, Peter, **Supp. XXV:** 227, 233

Campion, Thomas, **I:** 439; **Supp. VIII:** 272

"Campo" (Muñoz), **Supp. XXV:** 130

Campo, Rafael, **Supp. XVII:** 112

Camus, Albert, **I:** 53, 61, 292, 294, 494; **II:** 57, 244; **III:** 292, 306, 453; **IV:** 6, 211, 236, 442, 487; **Retro. Supp. I:** 73; **Retro. Supp. II:** 20; **Supp. I Part 2:** 621; **Supp. VIII:** 11, 195, 241; **Supp. XI:** 96; **Supp. XIII:** 74, 165, 233, 247; **Supp. XVII:** 137

Camuto, Christopher, **Supp. V:** 212–213

"Canada" (Di Piero), **Supp. XIX:** 39

Canada Fragrant with Resin, **Supp. XVI:** 149

Canadé, Eugene, **Supp. XXI:** 22, 23

"Canadian Mosaic, The" (Beran), **Supp. XIII:** 25

"Canadians and Pottawatomies" (Sandburg), **III:** 592–593

Canadian Short Stories (radio show), **Supp. XXVII:** 181

"Can a Good Wife Be a Good Sport?" (T. Williams), **IV:** 380

"Canal, The: A Poem on the Application of Physical Science to Political Economy" (Barlow), **Supp. II Part 1:** 73

Canan, Peter, **Supp. XXV:** 123

Canary, Martha Jane. *See* Calamity Jane (Martha Jane Canary)

"Canary for One, A" (Hemingway), **Retro. Supp. I:** 170, 189

Canary in a Cat House (Vonnegut), **Supp. II Part 2:** 758

"Canary in Bloom" (Dove), **Supp. IV Part 1:** 248

Canby, Henry Seidel, **IV:** 65, 363

"Cancer" (McClatchy), **Supp. XII:** 266

"Cancer Match, The" (Dickey), **Supp. IV Part 1:** 182

"Cancíon y Glosa" (Merwin), **Supp. III Part 1:** 342

Candide (Hellman), **I:** 28; **Supp. I Part 1:** 288–289, 292

Candide (Voltaire), **Supp. I Part 1:** 288–289; **Supp. XI:** 297; **Supp. XVI:** 189

Candide (Voltaire; Wilbur, trans.), **Supp. III Part 2:** 560

"Candle Hat" (Collins), **Supp. XXI:** 60

Candle in the Cabin, The (Lindsay), **Supp. I Part 2:** 398, 400

"Candles" (Plath), **Retro. Supp. II:** 248, 257

Candles in Babylon (Levertov), **Supp. III Part 1:** 283

Candles in the Sun (T. Williams), **IV:** 381

Candles of Your Eyes, The (Purdy), **Supp. VII:** 278

Candy (Southern), **Supp. XI:** 297, **298–299,** 305

"Candy-Man Beechum" (Caldwell), **I:** 309

Cane (Toomer), **Supp. III Part 2:** 475, 481–486, 488; **Supp. IV Part 1:** 164, 168; **Supp. IX:** 305, 306, 307, **308–320; Supp. XIX:** 73; **Supp. XX: 73**

"Cane in the Corridor, The" (Thurber), **Supp. I Part 2:** 616

Canfield, Cass, **Supp. I Part 2:** 668

Canfield, Dorothy, **Retro. Supp. I:** 4, 11, 14, 18; **Supp. XX: 39.** *See also* Fisher, Dorothy Canfield

Canfield, William W., **Supp. XXVI:** 86

Can Grande's Castle (A. Lowell), **II:** 518, 524

"Canicula di Anna" (Carson), **Supp. XII: 101–102**

"Can I Get You Anything?" (Carver and Gallagher), **Supp. XXIV:** 178

"Canis Major" (Frost), **Retro. Supp. I:** 137

"Canned Stuff" (Pickering), **Supp. XXI:** 198

Cannery Row (Steinbeck), **IV:** 50, 51, 64–65, 66, 68

Cannibal Galaxy, The (Ozick), **Supp. V:** 270

Cannibals and Christians (Mailer), **III:** 38–39, 40, 42; **Retro. Supp. II:** 203, 204, 205; **Supp. XXIV:** 281

Canning, George, **I:** 7, 8

Canning, Richard, **Supp. X:** 147

Cannon, Jimmy, **II:** 424

Cannon, Steve, **Retro. Supp. II:** 111

Cannon between My Knees, A (Gunn Allen), **Supp. IV Part 1:** 324

Canolle, Jean, **Supp. XVI:** 194

"Canonization, The" (Donne), **Supp. XIV:** 8

"Can Poetry Matter?" (Gioia), **Supp. XV:** 113, 114

Can Poetry Matter?: Essays on Poetry and American Culture (Gioia), **Supp. XV:** 112, **113–115**

"Canso" (Merwin), **Supp. III Part 1:** 344

Can Such Things Be? (Bierce), **I:** 203, 204, 205, 209

Canterbury Tales (Chaucer), **II:** 504; **III:** 411; **IV:** 65

Canterbury Tales, The (Chaucer), **Supp. XIX:** 4

"Canticle of Her Coming and Going" (Espaillat), **Supp. XXI:** 106

"Canto Amor" (Berryman), **I:** 173

Canto I (Pound), **III:** 469, 470; **Retro. Supp. I:** 286

Canto II (Pound), **III:** 470

Canto III (Pound), **III:** 470

Canto IV (Pound), **III:** 470

Canto VIII (Pound), **III:** 472

Canto IX (Pound), **III:** 472

Canto X (Pound), **III:** 472

Canto XIII (Pound), **III:** 472

Canto XXXIX (Pound), **III:** 468

Canto LXV (Pound), **Retro. Supp. I:** 292

Canto LXXXI (Pound), **III:** 459; **Retro. Supp. I:** 293

Cantor, Lois, **Supp. IV Part 1:** 285

Cantos (Pound), **I:** 482; **III:** 13–14, 17, 457, 462, 463, 466, 467, 469–470, 472–473, 474, 475, 476, 492; **Retro. Supp. I:** 284, 292, **292–293,** 293, 427; **Supp. I Part 1:** 272; **Supp. II Part 1:** 5; **Supp. II Part 2:** 420, 557, 564, 644; **Supp. IV Part 1:** 153; **Supp. V:** 343, 345; **Supp. VIII:** 305; **Supp. XIV:** 55, 96; **Supp. XV:** 349

"Cantus Planis" (Pound), **III:** 466

Cantwell, Robert, **Retro. Supp. I:** 85; **Supp. VIII:** 96; **Supp. XIII:** 292

Can Women Be Gentlemen? (Atherton), **Supp. XXIV:** 20–21, 30

"Canyon de Chelly, Return, 1978"(Kenny), **Supp. XXIII:** 155

Canyons, The (film), **Supp. XXVII:** 79–80

"Can You Carry Me" (O'Hara), **III:** 369

Can You See Me Yet? (Findley), **Supp. XX: 52–53**

Canzoneri, Robert, **IV:** 114, 116

Canzoni (Pound), **Retro. Supp. I:** 286, 288, 413

"Cap" (Shaw), **Supp. IV Part 1:** 345

"Cape Breton" (Bishop), **Supp. I Part 1:** 92; **Supp. IX:** 45

Cape Cod (Thoreau), **II:** 540

"Cape Cod, Rome, and Jerusalem" (Chapman), **Supp. XIV:** 55

Capital City (Sandoz), **Supp. XXIV:** 244, **252–253,** 255

Capitalism: The Unknown Ideal (Rand), **Supp. IV Part 2:** 518, 527, 531, 532

Caponi, Gena Dagel, **Supp. IV Part 1:** 95

Capote, Truman, **Supp. I Part 1:** 291, 292; **Supp. III Part 1: 111–133; Supp. III Part 2:** 574; **Supp. IV Part 1:** 198, 220; **Supp. VIII:** 105; **Supp. XII:** 43, 249; **Supp. XV:** 146; **Supp. XVI:** 245–246; **Supp. XVII:** 236

Capouya, Emile, **Supp. I Part 1:** 50

Cappetti, Carla, **Supp. IX:** 4, 8

Capra, Frank, **Supp. XVI:** 102

Capra, Fritjof, **Supp. X:** 261

"Capricious Gardens" (Eugenides), **Supp. XXIV:** 133–134

"Capricorn Rising" (Mackey), **Supp. XXVII:** 153

Capron, Marion, **Supp. IX:** 193

"Capsule History of Conservation, A" (Stegner), **Supp. IV Part 2:** 600

"Captain Carpenter" (Ransom), **III:** 491

Captain Craig (Robinson), **III:** 508, 523; **Supp. II Part 1:** 192

"Captain Jim's Friend" (Harte), **Supp. II Part 1:** 337

"Captain Jones's Invitation" (Freneau), **Supp. II Part 1:** 261

"Captain's Son, The" (Taylor), **Supp. V:** 314, 325, 327

"Captain's Wife, The" (Salter), **Supp. IX:** 261

"Capt Christopher Levett (of York)" (Olson), **Supp. II Part 2:** 576, 577

Captive Israel (Reznikoff), **Supp. XIV:** 283

"Captivity and Restoration of Mrs. Mary Rowlandson, The" (Howe), **Supp. IV Part 2:** 419, 431, 434

"Captivity of the Fly" (MacLeish), **III:** 19

"Captured Goddess, The" (A. Lowell), **II:** 520

Caputi, Jane, **Supp. IV Part 1:** 334, 335

Caputo, Philip, **Supp. XI:** 234; **Supp. XIX: 17–31; Supp. XXII:** 104; **Supp. XXV:** 153

Capuzzo, Michael, **Supp. XIII:** 254

Car (Crews), **Supp. XI: 110–111**

Carabi, Angels, **Supp. VIII:** 223; **Supp. XII:** 215

"Caramels" (Zinberg), **Supp. XV:** 195

Caravan (Bynner), **Supp. XV:** 50

"Caravaggio: Swirl & Vortex" (Levis), **Supp. XI:** 258, 269

Carby, Hazel B., **Supp. IV Part 1:** 13; **Supp. XXI:** 171

"Carcassonne" (Faulkner), **Retro. Supp. I:** 81

Card, Antha E., **Supp. I Part 2:** 496

Cárdenas, Lupe, **Supp. IV Part 2:** 538, 539, 540

Cardinale, Anthony, **Supp. XVII:** 239

Cardinale, Ernesto, **Supp. XII:** 225

"Cardinal Ideograms" (Swenson), **Supp. IV Part 2:** 645

"Cards" (Beattie), **Supp. V:** 31

"Career Woman" (Hay), **Supp. XIV:** 131

Carefree (film, Sandrich), **Supp. XVII:** 59

"Careful" (Carver), **Supp. III Part 1:** 138

Careful and Strict Enquiry into the Modern Prevailing Notions of That Freedom of Will, Which Is Supposed to be Essential to Moral Agency, Vertue and Vice, Reward and Punishment, Praise and Blame, A (Edwards), **I:** 549, 557, 558, 562

Carel: A Poem and Pilgrimage in the Holy Land (Melville), **III:** 92–93

Careless Love and Its Apostrophes (Bronk), **Supp. XXI:** 32

"Carentan O Carentan" (Simpson), **Supp. IX:** 267

Carew, Thomas, **IV:** 453

Carey, Gary, **Supp. XVI:** 186

Carey, Lynn, **Supp. XXIII:** 273

Carey, Mathew, **Supp. XV:** 238

"Car Games" (Conroy), **Supp. XVI:** 72

Cargill, Oscar, **Supp. II Part 1:** 117

Caribbean as Columbus Saw It (Morison and Obregon), **Supp. I Part 2:** 488

"Caribou Kitchen" (A. Finch), **Supp. XVII:** 76–77

Caribou Rising: Defending the Porcupine Herd, Gwich-'in Culture, and the Arctic National Wildlife Refuge (Bass), **Supp. XVI:** 27–28, 28

Carillo, Donna, **Supp. XXVII:** 204

"Caring for the World"(Schott), **Supp. XXIII:** 249–250

Carl, K. A., **III:** 475

Carleton, George W., **Supp. XVIII:** 4

Carlin, George, **Supp. XXI:** 51

Carlin, Terry, **Supp. XXI:** 4, 5, 14

Carlisle, Harry, **Supp. XVIII:** 223, 233

Carl Krinken: His Christmas Stocking (S. and A. Warner), **Supp. XVIII:** 264

"Carlos Who Died, and Left Only This, The" (Ríos), **Supp. IV Part 2:** 547

Carlotta (empress of Mexico), **Supp. I Part 2:** 457

Carl Sandburg (Golden), **III:** 579

Carlson, Susan L., **Supp. XV:** 323

Carlyle, Thomas, **I:** 103, 279; **II:** 5, 7, 11, 15–16, 17, 20, 145, 315; **III:** 82, 84, 85, 87; **IV:** 169, 182, 338, 350; **Retro. Supp. I:** 360, 408; **Supp. I Part 1:** 2, 349; **Supp. I Part 2:** 410, 422, 482, 485, 552; **Supp. XXV:** 242

"Carma" (Toomer), **Supp. III Part 2:** 481–483; **Supp. IX:** 312–313

"Carmen de Boheme" (Crane), **I:** 384

Carmen Jones (film), **Supp. I Part 1:** 66

Carmina Burana, **Supp. X:** 63

Carmon, Walt, **Supp. XXII:** 277

Carnegie, Andrew, **I:** 483; **IV:** 192; **Supp. I Part 2:** 639, 644; **Supp. V:** 285

Carnegie, Dale, **Supp. I Part 2:** 608

"Carnegie Hall: Rescued" (Moore), **III:** 215

Carne-Ross, Donald S., **Supp. I Part 1:** 268, 269; **Supp. XXIV:** 153

Carnes, Mark C., **Supp. X:** 14

"Carnets" poems (Sobin), **Supp. XVI:** 286–287

Carnovsky, Morris, **III:** 154

"Carol for Carolyn, A" (A. Finch), **Supp. XVII:** 74, 75

"Carolina Parakeet" (Rash), **Supp. XXVII:** 220

Caroling Dusk: An Anthology of Verse by Negro Poets (Cullen, ed.), **Supp. IV Part 1:** 166, 169; **Supp. XXVI:** 165, 170

"Carol of Occupations" (Whitman), **I:** 486

"Carolyn Kizer and the Chain of Women" (A. Finch), **Supp. XVII:** 74–75

Carolyn Kizer: Perspectives on Her Life and Work (A. Finch), **Supp. XVII:** **74–75**

"Carpe Diem" (Frost), **Supp. XII:** 303

"Carpe Noctem, if You Can" (Thurber), **Supp. I Part 2:** 620

Carpenter, Dan, **Supp. V:** 250

Carpenter, David, **Supp. VIII:** 297

Carpenter, Edward, **Supp. XX: 230**

Carpenter, Frederic I., **II:** 20

"Carpenter Bee" (Trethewey), **Supp. XXI:** 250

Carpentered Hen and Other Tame Creatures, The (Updike), **IV:** 214; **Retro. Supp. I:** 320

Carpenter's Gothic (Gaddis), **Supp. IV Part 1:** 288, 289–291, 293, 294

Carr, Dennis W., **Supp. IV Part 2:** 560

Carr, Elias, **Supp. XIV:** 57

Carr, Rosemary. *See* Benét, Rosemary

Carrall, Aaron, **Supp. IV Part 2:** 499

Carrel, Alexis, **IV:** 240

"Carrell/Klee/and Cosmos's Groom" (Goldbarth), **Supp. XII:** 183

"Carriage from Sweden, A" (Moore), **III:** 212

Carrie (King), **Supp. V:** 137

Carried Away (Harrison), **Supp. VIII:** 39

Carrier of Ladders (Merwin), **Supp. III Part 1:** 339, 346, 350–352, 356, 357

"Carriers of the Dream Wheel" (Momaday), **Supp. IV Part 2:** 481

Carriers of the Dream Wheel: Contemporary Native American Poetry (Niatum, ed.), **Supp. IV Part 2:** 484, 505

Carrington, Carroll, **I:** 199

"Carrion Spring" (Stegner), **Supp. IV Part 2:** 604

Carroll, Bart, **Supp. XXV:** 71

Carroll, Charles, **Supp. I Part 2:** 525

Carroll, Lewis, **I:** 432; **II:** 431; **III:** 181; **Supp. I Part 1:** 44; **Supp. I Part 2:** 622, 656; **Supp. XVI:** 103; **Supp. XXV:** 87; **Supp. XXVI:** 274

Carroll, Maureen P., **Supp. XXIV:** 177

"Carrots, Noses, Snow, Rose, Roses" (Gass), **Supp. VI:** 87

Carrouges, Michel, **Supp. IV Part 1:** 104

"Carrousel, The" (Rilke), **III:** 558

Carruth, Hayden, **Supp. IV Part 1:** 66; **Supp. IX:** 291; **Supp. XIII:** 39; **Supp. XIII:** 112; **Supp. XIV:** 273–274; **Supp. XIX:** 1; **Supp. XVI:** **45–61;** **Supp. XXI:** 31; **Supp. XXIV:** 167

Carruth, Joe-Anne McLaughlin, **Supp. XVI:** 47

"Carry" (Hogan), **Supp. IV Part 1:** 412

Carrying Albert Home (Hickam), **Supp. XXVII:** 111

"Carrying On" (Dunn), **Supp. XI:** 145

Cars of Cuba (García), **Supp. XI:** 190

Carson, Anne, **Supp. XII: 97–116;** **Supp. XV:** 252; **Supp. XXV:** 222

Carson, Johnny, **Supp. IV Part 2:** 526

Carson, Rachel, **Supp. IX: 19–36;** **Supp. V:** 202; **Supp. X:** 99; **Supp. XVI:** 36; **Supp. XXVI:** 31

Carson, Tom, **Supp. XI:** 227

Cart, Michael, **Supp. X:** 12; **Supp. XXVII:** 205

"Car Tags" (Rash), **Supp. XXVII:** 222

Carter, Angela, **Supp. XXVII:** 190

Carter, Elliott, **Supp. III Part 1:** 21

Carter, Hodding, **Supp. XIV:** 2

Carter, Jared, **Supp. XVII:** 110

Carter, Jimmy, **Supp. I Part 2:** 638; **Supp. XIV:** 107

Carter, Lin, **Supp. XXVII:** 128

Carter, Marcia, **Supp. V:** 223

Carter, Mary, **Supp. IV Part 2:** 444

Carter, Paul, **Supp. XX: 77, 78**

Carter, Peter, **Supp. XVIII:** 267

Carter, Stephen, **Supp. XI:** 220

Cartesian Sonata and Other Novellas (Gass), **Supp. VI: 92–93**

Cartier, Jacques, **Supp. I Part 2:** 496, 497

Cartier-Bresson, Henri, **Supp. VIII:** 98

"Cartographies of Silence" (Rich), **Supp. I Part 2:** 571–572

"Cartography" (Espaillat), **Supp. XXI:** 107

Cartwright, Louis, **Supp. XIV:** 147, 149, 151

Carver, Raymond, **Supp. III Part 1: 135–151;** **Supp. IV Part 1:** 342; **Supp. V:** 22, 23, 220, 326; **Supp. VIII:** 15; **Supp. X:** 85, 167; **Supp. XI:** 26, 65,

116, 153; **Supp. XII:** 79, 139, 289, 294; **Supp. XIX:** 209; **Supp. XXI:** 36, 115, 116, 118, 119; **Supp. XXIII:** 289, 296; **Supp. XXIV:** 97, 166, 167, 173, 177–178; **Supp. XXVI:** 147, 180; **Supp. XXVII:** 269

Carver: A Life in Poems (Nelson), **Supp. XVIII:** 171, 172, **181–182,** 183

Carville, James, **Supp. XXIV:** 282

Carving Hawk (Kenny), **Supp. XXIII:** 143, 150

Cary, Alice, **Retro. Supp. II:** 145; **Supp. XV:** 273; **Supp. XXII:** 206

Cary, Phoebe, **Supp. XV:** 273

Cary, Richard, **Retro. Supp. II:** 132, 137

"Casabianca" (Bishop), **Retro. Supp. II:** 42; **Supp. I Part 1:** 86

Casablanca (film), **Supp. VIII:** 61; **Supp. XV:** 14

Casanova: His Known and Unknown Life (Endore), **Supp. XVII:** 54

"Casa solariega, La" ("The Family Mansion") (Espaillat), **Supp. XXI:** 107

"Case Against Mist, The" (Halliday), **Supp. XIX:** 91

Casebook (Simpson), **Supp. XXVII:** 234, 244–246

Case for West-Indian Self-Government, The (C. L. R. James), **Supp. XXI:** 159, 161

Case of Jennie Brice, The (Rinehart), **Supp. XXV:** 193, 200

Case of Rape, A (C. Himes), **Supp. XVI:** 143

Case of the Crushed Petunias, The (T. Williams), **IV:** 381

Case of the Officers of Excise (Paine), **Supp. I Part 2:** 503–504

Casey, Helen Marie, **Supp. XXIII:** 246

Casey, John, **Supp. X:** 164

Cash, Arthur, **Supp. IV Part 1:** 299

Cashman, Nellie, **Supp. X:** 103

Casiero, Robert, **Supp. XIV:** 167

Casino Royale (film), **Supp. XI: 306–307; Supp. XXVII:** 96

Caskey, William, **Supp. XIV:** 166

"Cask of Amontillado, The" (Poe), **II:** 475; **III:** 413; **Retro. Supp. II:** 268, 269, 270, 273

Caso, Frank, **Supp. XVIII:** 95

Caspary, Vera, **Supp. XIX:** 78

Casper, Robert N., **Supp. XV:** 339, 347

Casper and His Friends (S. and A. Warner), **Supp. XVIII:** 264

Cassada (Salter), **Supp. IX: 251–252**

Cassada, Jackie, **Supp. XXIII:** 291

Cassady, Carolyn, **Supp. XIV:** 150

Cassady, Neal, **Supp. II Part 1:** 309, 311; **Supp. XIV:** 137, 144

"Cassandra" (Stallings), **Supp. XXV:** 233

"Cassandra Southwick" (Whittier), **Supp. I Part 2:** 693

Cassell, Verlin, **Supp. XI:** 315

Cassill, Ronald Verlin, **Supp. V:** 323; **Supp. XIX:** 266; **Supp. XVIII:** 72

Cassirer, Ernst, **I:** 265; **IV:** 87, 89

Cass Timberlane (Lewis), **II:** 455–456

Cast a Cold Eye (McCarthy), **II:** 566

Castaway (Cozzens), **I:** 363, 370, 374, 375, 379
"Caste in America" (Du Bois), **Supp. II Part 1:** 169
Castiglione, Baldassare, **I:** 279; **III:** 282
"Castilian" (Wylie), **Supp. I Part 2:** 714
Castillo, Ana, **Supp. XI:** 177; **Supp. XXIII:** 194
"Castle in Lynn, A" (McCarriston), **Supp. XIV:** 265, 268
"Castles and Distances" (Wilbur), **Supp. III Part 2:** 550
Castle Sinister (Marquand), **III:** 58
Cast of Thousands (Loos), **Supp. XVI:** 192, 193, 195
Castro, Fidel, **II:** 261, 434; **Supp. XX: 80**
Cast the First Stone (C. Himes), **Supp. XVI:** 135, 137–138
"Casual Incident, A" (Hemingway), **II:** 44
Casualties (Rash), **Supp. XXVII:** 227
"Casualty Report" (Halliday), **Supp. XIX:** 85
Caswell, Michelle, **Supp. XXII:** 262
"Cat, The" (Matthews), **Supp. IX: 157–158**
Cat, You Better Come Home (Keillor), **Supp. XVI:** 177
"Catbird Seat, The" (Thurber), **Supp. I Part 2:** 623
"Catch" (Francis), **Supp. IX:** 82
Catch-22 (Heller), **III:** 558; **Supp. IV Part 1:** 379, 380, 381–382, 383, 384–386, 387, 390, 391, 392, 393, 394; **Supp. V:** 244, 248; **Supp. XII:** 167–168; **Supp. XXIII:** 100; **Supp. XXVII:** 207
Catcher in the Rye, The (Salinger), **I:** 493; **III:** 551, 552, 553–558, 567, 571; **Retro. Supp. I:** 102; **Retro. Supp. II:** 222, 249; **Supp. I Part 2:** 535; **Supp. V:** 119; **Supp. VIII:** 242; **Supp. XI:** 65; **Supp. XVII:** 2; **Supp. XXIII:** 100; **Supp. XXIV:** 133
"Catching Frogs" (Kenyon), **Supp. VII:** 170
Catching the Mermother (A. Finch), **Supp. XVII:** 72
catechism of d neoamerican hoodoo church (Reed), **Supp. X:** 240, 241
Catered Affair, The (film), **Supp. IV Part 2:** 683
"Cathay" (Goldbarth), **Supp. XII:** 185, 186
Cathay (Pound), **II:** 527; **Retro. Supp. I:** 289
Cathedral (Carver), **Supp. III Part 1:** 144–146; **Supp. XII:** 139
"Cathedral" (Carver), **Supp. III Part 1:** 144–145; **Supp. XXIV:** 177
Cathedral, The (J. R. Lowell), **Supp. I Part 2:** 407, 416–417
Cather, Willa, **I: 312–334**, 405; **II:** 51, 96, 177, 404, 412; **III:** 453; **IV:** 190; **Retro. Supp. I: 1–23**, 355, 382; **Retro. Supp. II:** 71, 136; **Supp. I Part 2:** 609, 719; **Supp. IV Part 1:** 31; **Supp. VIII:** 101, 102, 263; **Supp. X:** 103; **Supp. XIII:** 253; **Supp. XIV:**

112; **Supp. XIX:** 131; **Supp. XV:** 40, 51; **Supp. XVI:** 226; **Supp. XVIII:** 207; **Supp. XXIII:** 290; **Supp. XXIV:** 29, 30, 244; **Supp. XXV:** 201
Catherine, Saint, **II:** 211
Catherine II, **Supp. I Part 2:** 433
Catholic Art and Culture (Watkin), **Retro. Supp. II:** 187
"Catholic Novelist in the Protestant South, The" (O'Connor), **Retro. Supp. II:** 223, 224
"Cathy Queen of Cats" (Cisneros), **Supp. VII:** 59
Cat Inside, The (Burroughs), **Supp. III Part 1:** 105
Cat in the Hat, The (Geisel), **Supp. XVI:** 106–107, 112
Cat in the Hat Come Back, The (Geisel), **Supp. XVI:** 107
"Cat in the Hat for President, The" (Coover), **Supp. V:** 44, 46–47
Cat in The Hat Songbook, The (Geisel), **Supp. XVI:** 104
Cato, **II:** 114, 117
Cat on a Hot Tin Roof (T. Williams), **II:** 190; **IV:** 380, 382, 383, 386, 387, 389, 390, 391, 394, 395, 397–398; **Supp. XXV:** 93
"Cat People: What Dr. Seuss Really Taught Us" (Menand), **Supp. XVI:** 106
Cats and Dogs (Silver), **Supp. XXIV:** 265, 274
Cat's Cradle (Vonnegut), **Supp. II Part 2:** 758, 759, 767–768, 770, 771, 772; **Supp. V:** 1
Cat's Eye (Atwood), **Supp. XIII: 29–30**
Catskill Eagle, A (Parker), **Supp. XIX:** 185
"Cat's Meow, A" (Brodsky), **Supp. VIII:** 31
"Cats of Ulthar, The" (Lovecraft), **Supp. XXV:** 114
Cat's Quizzer, The (Geisel), **Supp. XVI:** 111
"Catterskill Falls" (Bryant), **Supp. I Part 1:** 160
"Cattle Car Complex" (T. Rosenbaum), **Supp. XVII:** 48
Cattlemen from the Rio Grande Across the Far Marias (Sandoz), **Supp. XXIV:** 244, **249–251**, 256
Catullus, **Supp. XII:** 2, 13, **112**; **Supp. XV:** 23, 27, 35, 36
Catullus, Gaius Valerius, **I:** 381; **Supp. I Part 1:** 261; **Supp. I Part 2:** 728
Catullus (Gai Catulli Veronensis Liber) (Zukofsky), **Supp. III Part 2:** 625, 627, 628, 629
"Catullus: Carmina" (Carson), **Supp. XII: 112**
"Catullus: Excrucior" (Bidart), **Supp. XV:** 32, 35
"Cat Walked Through the Casserole, The" (Nelson and Espeland), **Supp. XVIII: 181**
Cat Walked Through the Casserole and Other Poems for Children (Nelson and Espeland), **Supp. XVIII:** 181

"Cat Who Aspired to Higher Things, The" (X. J. Kennedy), **Supp. XV:** 163
Cat Who Went to Heaven, The (Coatsworth), **Supp. XXVI:** 33
"Caucasian Storms Harlem, The" (R. Fisher), **Supp. XIX:** 78
Caudwell, Christopher, **Supp. X:** 112; **Supp. XXII:** 284
"Caul, The" (Banks), **Supp. V:** 10–11
Cause for Wonder (Morris), **III:** 232–233
"Causerie" (Tate), **IV:** 129
Causes and Consequences (Chapman), **Supp. XIV:** 41, 49, 51
"Causes of American Discontents before 1768, The" (Franklin), **II:** 120
Causley, Charles, **Supp. XV:** 117
Cavafy, Constantine P., **Supp. IX:** 275; **Supp. XI:** 119, 123; **Supp. XXI:** 131; **Supp. XXIII:** 150; **Supp. XXV:** 225, 233
Cavalcade of America, The (radio program), **III:** 146
Cavalcanti (Pound, opera), **Retro. Supp. I:** 287
Cavalcanti, Guido, **I:** 579; **III:** 467; **Supp. III Part 2:** 620, 621, 622, 623
Cavalieri, Grace, **Supp. IV Part 2:** 630, 631
"Cavalry Crossing the Ford" (Whitman), **IV:** 347
"Cave, The" (Bass), **Supp. XVI:** 23
Cave, The (Warren), **IV:** 255–256
Cavelieri, Grace, **Supp. XXIII:** 135
Cavell, Stanley, **Retro. Supp. I:** 306–307, 309
Cavender's House (Robinson), **III:** 510
Caver, Christine, **Supp. XXI:** 215
Caves of Death, The (Atherton; Joshi, ed.), **Supp. XXIV:** 23
"Caviar" (Boyle), **Supp. XX: 19**
Caviare at the Funeral (Simpson), **Supp. IX:** 266, **276–277**
"Cawdor" (Jeffers), **Supp. II Part 2:** 431
Caxton, William, **III:** 486
Cayton, Horace, **IV:** 475, 488
Cazamian, Louis, **II:** 529
C Comics, **Supp. XXVII:** 23
"Ceiling, The" (Brockmeier), **Supp. XXII:** 52–53
Celan, Paul, **Supp. X:** 149; **Supp. XII:** 21, 110–111; **Supp. XVI:** 284–285, 288; **Supp. XVII:** 241
"Celebrated Jumping Frog of Calaveras County, The" (Twain), **IV:** 196
Celebrated Jumping Frog of Calaveras County, The, and Other Sketches (Twain), **IV:** 197
Celebration (Crews), **Supp. XI:** 103, **108**
Celebration (Swados), **Supp. XIX: 269–270**
Celebration at Dark (W. J. Smith), **Supp. XIII:** 332
"Celebration for June 24th" (McGrath), **Supp. X:** 116
Celebration of the Sound Through (Sobin), **Supp. XVI:** 284–285
Celebrations after the Death of John Brennan (X. J. Kennedy), **Supp. XV:** 165
Celebrity (film; Allen), **Supp. XV:** 11

"Celebrity" (Pickering), **Supp. XXI:** 198

"Celery" (Stein), **IV:** 43

"Celestial Games" (Conroy), **Supp. XVI:** 72

"Celestial Globe" (Nemerov), **III:** 288

Celestial Navigation (Tyler), **Supp. IV Part 2:** 662–663, 671

"Celestial Railroad, The" (Hawthorne), **Retro. Supp. I:** 152; **Supp. I Part 1:** 188

Celibate Season, A (Shields), **Supp. VII:** 323, 324

Cellini (Shanley), **Supp. XIV:** 316, **329–330**

"Cemetery at Academy, California" (Levine), **Supp. V:** 182

Cemetery Nights (Dobyns), **Supp. XIII:** 85, 87, 89

"Cenotaph, The" (Stallings), **Supp. XXV:** 225, 234

"Censors As Critics: *To Kill a Mockingbird* As a Case Study" (May), **Supp. VIII:** 126

"Census-Taker, The" (Frost), **Retro. Supp. I:** 129

"Centaur, The" (Swenson), **Supp. IV Part 2:** 641

Centaur, The (Updike), **IV:** 214, 216, 217, 218, 219–221, 222; **Retro. Supp. I:** 318, 322, 324, 331, 336

"Centennial Meditation of Columbia, The" (Lanier), **Supp. I Part 1:** 362

Centeno, Agusto, **IV:** 375

"Centipede" (Dove), **Supp. IV Part 1:** 246

"Cento: A Note on Philosophy" (Berrigan), **Supp. XXIV:** 42–43

"Central Man, The" (Bloom), **Supp. IV Part 2:** 689

"Central Park" (R. Lowell), **II:** 552

Central Park (Wasserstein and Drattel), **Supp. XV:** 333

"Central Park at Dusk" (Teasdale), **Supp. XXVII:** 286, 289

Central Park West (Allen), **Supp. XV:** 13

Century of Dishonor, A (Jackson), **Retro. Supp. I:** 31

"Cerebral Snapshot, The" (Theroux), **Supp. VIII:** 313

"Ceremonies" (Rukeyser), **Supp. VI:** 279

"Ceremony" (Monson), **Supp. XXIV:** 230

Ceremony (Silko), **Supp. IV Part 1:** 274, 333; **Supp. IV Part 2:** 557–558, 558–559, 559, 561–566, 570; **Supp. XVIII:** 59

Ceremony (Wilbur), **Supp. III Part 2:** 550–551

"Ceremony, The" (Harjo), **Supp. XII:** 230

"Ceremony, The—Anatomy of a Massacre" (E. Hoffman, play), **Supp. XVI:** 160

Ceremony in Lone Tree (Morris), **III:** 229–230, 232, 238, 558

Ceremony of Brotherhood, A (Anaya and Ortiz, eds.), **Supp. IV Part 2:** 502

Cerf, Bennett, **III:** 405; **IV:** 288; **Retro. Supp. II:** 330; **Supp. XIII:** 172; **Supp. XIX:** 244

"Certain Attention to the World, A" (Haines), **Supp. XII:** 201

"Certain Beasts, Like Cats" (Bronk), **Supp. XXI:** 30

Certain Distance, A (Francis), **Supp. IX:** 85

"Certain Music, A" (Rukeyser), **Supp. VI:** 273

Certain Noble Plays of Japan (Pound), **III:** 458

Certain People (Wharton), **Retro. Supp. I:** 382

"Certain Poets" (MacLeish), **III:** 4

Certain Slant of Sunlight, A (Berrigan), **Supp. XXIV:** 43

"Certain Testimony" (Bausch), **Supp. VII:** 48

Certificate, The (Singer), **IV:** 1; **Retro. Supp. II: 314–315**

"Cerulean" (Everett), **Supp. XVIII:** 66

Cervantes, Lorna Dee, **Supp. IV Part 2:** 545

Cervantes, Miguel de, **I:** 130, 134; **II:** 8, 272, 273, 276, 289, 302, 310, 315; **III:** 113, 614; **IV:** 367; **Retro. Supp. I:** 91; **Supp. I Part 2:** 406; **Supp. V:** 277; **Supp. XIII:** 17; **Supp. XXIII:** 4

Cervantes. Lorna Dee, **Supp. XXVII:** 168

Césaire, Aimé, **Supp. X:** 132, 139; **Supp. XIII:** 114

"Cesarean" (Kenyon), **Supp. VII:** 173

Cézanne, Paul, **II:** 576; **III:** 210; **IV:** 26, 31, 407; **Supp. V:** 333, 341–342; **Supp. XIX:** 36

Chabon, Michael, **Supp. XI: 63–81; Supp. XIX:** 135, 138, 174, 223; **Supp. XVI:** 259; **Supp. XX: 177; Supp. XXII:** 49; **Supp. XXIV:** 131

Chaboseau, Jean, **Supp. I Part 1:** 260

Chace, Bill, **Supp. XXI:** 256

Chagall, Marc, **Supp. XXIII:** 6

Chaikin, Joseph, **Supp. III Part 2:** 433, 436–437

"Chain, The" (Kumin), **Supp. IV Part 2:** 452

Chainbearer, The (Cooper), **I:** 351, 352–353

"Chain of Love, A" (Price), **Supp. VI: 258–259,** 260

Chain Saw Dance, The (Budbill), **Supp. XIX: 5–6**

Chains of Dew (Glaspell), **Supp. III Part 1:** 181

Chalk Face (W. Frank), **Supp. XX: 73–74**

Challacombe, Robert Hamilton, **III:** 176

Challenge (Untermeyer), **Supp. XV:** 296, 303

"Challenge" (Untermeyer), **Supp. XV:** 296

"Challenge from Beyond, The" (Lovecraft, Howard, Long, Merritt, and Moore), **Supp. XXV:** 122

Chalmers, George, **Supp. I Part 2:** 514, 521

"Chambered Nautilus, The" (Holmes), **Supp. I Part 1:** 254, 307, 312–313, 314

Chamberlain, John, **Supp. I Part 2:** 647; **Supp. IV Part 2:** 525

Chamberlain, Neville, **II:** 589; **Supp. I Part 2:** 664

Chamber Music (Joyce), **III:** 16

Chambers, Richard, **Supp. III Part 2:** 610, 611, 612

Chambers, Whittaker, **Supp. III Part 2:** 610; **Supp. IV Part 2:** 526; **Supp. XV:** 143

Chameleon (C. Baxter), **Supp. XVII:** 14–15

"Champ, The" (Zinberg), **Supp. XV:** 193

"Champagne Regions" (Ríos), **Supp. IV Part 2:** 553

"Champion" (Lardner), **II:** 420–421, 428, 430

Champion, Laurie, **Supp. VIII:** 128

"Champ of the Forecastle" (Howard), **Supp. XXVII:** 124

Champollion-Figeac, Jean Jacques, **IV:** 426

"Chance" (Doolittle), **Supp. I Part 1:** 271

"Chance" (Munro), **Supp. XXVII:** 193

Chance, Frank, **II:** 418

Chance Acquaintance, A (Howells), **II:** 278

"Chance Encounter, A" (Swados), **Supp. XIX:** 261, 262

"Chanclas" (Cisneros), **Supp. VII:** 61

Chandler, Raymond, **Supp. III Part 1:** 91; **Supp. IV Part 1: 119–138,** 341, 344, 345; **Supp. IV Part 2:** 461, 464, 469, 470, 471, 472, 473; **Supp. XI:** 160, 228; **Supp. XII:** 307; **Supp. XIII:** 159, 233; **Supp. XIV:** 21; **Supp. XIX:** 178, 189; **Supp. XV:** 119; **Supp. XVI:** 122; **Supp. XVII:** 137; **Supp. XVIII:** 136,137, 137–138; **Supp. XXI:** 67; **Supp. XXII:** 119; **Supp. XXIV:** 284; **Supp. XXV:** 180

Chandler, Sherry, **Supp. XXIII:** 247

Chaney, "Professor" W. H., **II:** 463–464

Chang, Leslie C., **Supp. IV Part 1:** 72

"Change, The: Kyoto-Tokyo Express" (Ginsberg), **Supp. II Part 1:** 313, 329

Changed Man, A (Prose), **Supp. XVI:** 261–262

"Changeling" (Espaillat), **Supp. XXI:** 100

Changeling (Middleton), **Retro. Supp. I:** 62

"Changeling, The" (J. R. Lowell), **Supp. I Part 2:** 409

"Changeling, The" (Whittier), **Supp. I Part 2:** 697

Change of World, A (Rich), **Supp. I Part 2:** 551, 552

"Changes of Mind" (Baker), **Supp. XIII:** 52

"Changes of the Soul" (Taggard), **Supp. XXII:** 280

"Change the Joke and Slip the Yoke" (Ellison), **Retro. Supp. II:** 118

Change Your Bedding! (O'Hara), **Supp. XXIII:** 210

Changing Light at Sandover, The (Merrill), **Supp. III Part 1:** 318, 319, 323, 327, 332, 335–336; **Supp. XII:** 269–270; **Supp. XV:** 264

"Changing Same, The" (Baraka), **Supp. II Part 1:** 47, 51, 53

Changing the Bully Who Rules the World: Reading and Thinking about Ethics (C. Bly), **Supp. XVI:** 32, **39–40,** 41

Chanler, Mrs. Winthrop, **I:** 22; **IV:** 325

Channing, Carol, **IV:** 357

Channing, Edward, **Supp. I Part 2:** 479–480

Channing, Edward Tyrrel, **Supp. I Part 1:** 155; **Supp. I Part 2:** 422; **Supp. XXV:** 240

Channing, William Ellery, **I:** 336; **II:** 224, 495; **IV:** 172, 173, 176, 177; **Retro. Supp. I:** 54; **Supp. I Part 1:** 103; **Supp. I Part 2:** 589; **Supp. XXIV:** 67–81; **Supp. XXV:** 250

Channing, William Henry, **IV:** 178; **Supp. II Part 1:** 280, 285; **Supp. XXIV:** 68

Channing: The Reluctant Radical (Mendelsohn), **Supp. XXIV:** 72

Chanson de Roland, La, **I:** 13

"Chanson un Peu Naïve" (Bogan), **Supp. III Part 1:** 50–51

"Chanteuse" (Doty), **Supp. XI:** 119

"Chant for May Day" (Hughes), **Supp. I Part 1:** 331

Chants (Mora), **Supp. XIII: 214–215**

Chaos (Dove), **Supp. IV Part 1:** 243

Chapelle, Howard I., **Supp. XXV:** 217

"Chaperone, The" (Van Vechten), **Supp. II Part 2:** 728

Chaplin, Charles Spencer "Charlie," **I:** 27, 32, 43, 386, 447; **III:** 403; **Supp. I Part 2:** 607; **Supp. IV Part 1:** 146; **Supp. IV Part 2:** 574; **Supp. XX:** 75; **Supp. XXI:** 170; **Supp. XXII:** 25, 26

"Chaplinesque" (H. Crane), **Retro. Supp. II:** 79

"Chapman" (Rukeyser), **Supp. VI:** 273

Chapman, Abraham, **IV:** 485

Chapman, George, **Supp. I Part 2:** 422

Chapman, Ian, **Supp. XXVII:** 212

Chapman, John, **Supp. XXV:** 105

Chapman, John (Johnny Appleseed), **Supp. I Part 2:** 397

Chapman, John Jay, **IV:** 436; **Supp. XIV: 39–56**

Chapman, Stephen, **Supp. XIII:** 12

Chappell, Fred, **Supp. IV Part 1:** 69; **Supp. XI:** 317; **Supp. XVIII:** 87

Chapters in a Mythology: The Poetry of Sylvia Plath (Kroll), **Supp. I Part 2:** 541–543

Chapters on Erie (Adams and Adams), **Supp. I Part 2:** 644

Chapter Two (Simon), **Supp. IV Part 2:** 575, 586

"Chapter VI" (Hemingway), **II:** 252

Char, René, **Supp. XVI:** 282; **Supp. XVII:** 244

"Character" (Emerson), **II:** 6

"Character of Aboriginal Historical Tradition"(J. Schoolcraft), **Supp. XXIII:** 228–229

"Character of Presidents, The" (Doctorow), **Supp. IV Part 1:** 224

"Character of Socrates, The" (Emerson), **II:** 8–9

Character of the Poet, The (Simpson), **Supp. IX:** 273, 275, 278

"Characters in Fiction" (McCarthy), **II:** 562

"Charades" (Moore), **Supp. X:** 178

"Charge It" (Fante), **Supp. XI:** 164–165

"Charioteer, The" (Stallings), **Supp. XXV:** 233

Chariot in the Sky: A Story of the Jubilee Singers (Bontemps), **Supp. XXII:** 6, 13

"Charity" (Peacock), **Supp. XIX:** 221–222

Charity (Richard), **Supp. XIX: 220–222**

Charlatan, The (Singer), **IV:** 1

"Charles" (Jackson), **Supp. IX:** 125

Charles, Abram, **Supp. XXVI:** 87

Charles, Larry, **Supp. XVIII:** 21

"Charles Baxter, August Kleinzahler, Adrienne Rich: Contemporary Stevensians and the Problem of 'Other Lives' " (S. Burt), **Supp. XVII:** 18–19

Charles Goodnight: Cowman and Plainsman (Haley), **Supp. V:** 226

Charles Simic: Essays on the Poetry (Weigl), **Supp. VIII:** 269

Charles the Bold, Duke of Burgundy, **III:** 487

Charleville, Victoria Verdon, **Supp. I Part 1:** 200–201, 205, 206, 210

Charley's Aunt (B. Thomas), **II:** 138

Charlie Chan Is Dead: An Anthology of Contemporary Asian American Fiction (Hagedorn), **Supp. X:** 292

"Charlie Christian Story, The" (Ellison), **Retro. Supp. II:** 121

"Charlie Howard's Descent" (Doty), **Supp. XI:** 122

Charlie: The Improbable Life and Times of Charles MacArthur (Hecht), **Supp. XXVII:** 95

Charlotte: A Tale of Truth (Rowson), **Supp. I Part 1:** 128; **Supp. XV: 234–235,** 238. *See also Charlotte Temple* (Rowson)

Charlotte's Daughter; or, The Three Orphans (Rowson), **Supp. XV:** 246

Charlotte's Web (White), **Supp. I Part 2:** 655, 656, 658, 667, 670

Charlotte Temple (Rowson), **Supp. XV:** 229, **238–239; Supp. XXV:** 35, 36. *See also Charlotte: A Tale of Truth* (Rowson)

Charm, The (Creeley), **Supp. IV Part 1:** 139, 141, 144, 149–150

Charmed Life, A (McCarthy), **II:** 571–574

Charming Billy (McDermott), **Supp. XVIII:** 155, **162–164,** 166

Charms for the Easy Life (Gibbons), **Supp. X:** 45, **47–48**

Charnel Rose, The (Aiken), **I:** 50, 57, 62

Charney, Samuel, **Supp. XXIII:** 6

Charon's Cosmology (Simic), **Supp. VIII: 276–278**

Charterhouse, The (Percy), **Supp. III Part 1:** 388

Chart for Rough Water (W. Frank), **Supp. XX:** 78

Charvat, William, **II:** 244

Charyn, Jerome, **Supp. XVII:** 5

Chase, Mary Ellen, **Retro. Supp. II:** 243, 245; **Supp. XXIV:** 30

Chase, Richard, **IV:** 202, 443; **Retro. Supp. I:** 40, 395

Chase, Salmon P., **Supp. I Part 2:** 584

Chase, Stuart, **Supp. I Part 2:** 609

Chase, The (Foote), **Supp. I Part 1:** 281

Chasing the Dime (Connelly), **Supp. XXI:** 74

"Chaste Land, The" (Tate), **IV:** 122

Château, The (Maxwell), **Supp. VIII:** 152, 160, **165–167,** 168, 169

Chatham, Russell, **Supp. VIII:** 40

"Chattanooga Nights" (L. Brown), **Supp. XXI:** 39

Chatterdon, The Black Death, and Meriwether Lewis (Reznikoff), **Supp. XIV:** 288

Chatterton, Thomas, **Supp. I Part 1:** 349; **Supp. I Part 2:** 410, 716

Chatterton, Wayne, **Supp. IX:** 2, 4, 11–12

"Chatty Letters During a Journey from Aruba to Rio" (Thompson), **Supp. XXIV:** 282

Chatwin, Bruce, **Supp. VIII:** 322

Chaucer, Geoffrey, **I:** 131; **II:** 11, 504, 516, 542, 543; **III:** 283, 411, 473, 492, 521; **Retro. Supp. I:** 135, 426; **Supp. I Part 1:** 356, 363; **Supp. I Part 2:** 422, 617; **Supp. V:** 259; **Supp. XII:** 197; **Supp. XIX:** 4; **Supp. XVII:** 70

Chauncy, Charles, **I:** 546–547; **IV:** 147

Chavez, César, **Supp. V:** 199

Chávez, Denise, **Supp. IV Part 2:** 544; **Supp. XI:** 316

Chavez, Lydia, **Supp. VIII:** 75

Chavkin, Allan, **Supp. IV Part 1:** 259

Chavkin, Nancy Feyl, **Supp. IV Part 1:** 259

Chawla, Louise, **Supp. XXI:** 24

Chayefsky, Paddy, **Supp. XI:** 306

Cheang, Shu Lea, **Supp. XI:** 20

Cheap: New Poems and Ballads (Stone), **Supp. XXVII:** 249, 250, 257, 262

"Cheater's Guide To Love, The" (Díaz), **Supp. XXIV:** 84, 92, 93

"Cheat Takes Over" (Leopold), **Supp. XIV:** 189

"Cheers" (Carver), **Supp. III Part 1:** 138

Cheetham, James, **Supp. I Part 2:** 521

Cheever, Benjamin Hale, **Supp. I Part 1:** 175; **Supp. XXIV:** 97

Cheever, David W., **Supp. I Part 1:** 304

Cheever, Ezekiel, **Supp. I Part 1:** 174, 193

Cheever, Federico, **Supp. I Part 1:** 175

Cheever, Fred, **Supp. I Part 1:** 174

Cheever, Frederick L., **Supp. I Part 1:** 174

Cheever, John, **Retro. Supp. I:** 116, 333, 335; **Supp. I Part 1: 174–199; Supp. IX:** 114, 208; **Supp. V:** 23, 95; **Supp. VIII:** 151; **Supp. XI:** 65, 66, 99; **Supp. XII:** 140; **Supp. XIV:** 93; **Supp. XV:** 119, 142; **Supp. XXIII:** 104, 109, 275; **Supp. XXV:** 79, 142; **Supp. XXVI:** 147

Cheever, Mrs. John (Mary Winternitz), **Supp. I Part 1:** 175

Cheever, Mary Liley, **Supp. I Part 1:** 174

Cheever, Susan. *See* Cowley, Susan Cheever (Susan Cheever)

Cheever Evening, A (Gurney), **Supp. V:** 95

Chekhov, Anton, **I:** 52, 90; **II:** 27, 38, 44, 49, 198, 542; **III:** 362, 467; **IV:** 17, 53, 359, 446; **Retro. Supp. I:** 5, 355; **Retro. Supp. II:** 299; **Supp. I Part 1:** 196; **Supp. II Part 1:** 6; **Supp. IV Part 2:** 585; **Supp. IX:** 260, 265, 274; **Supp. V:** 265; **Supp. VIII:** 153, 332; **Supp. XI:** 66; **Supp. XII:** 94, 307; **Supp. XIII:** 79; **Supp. XIV:** 87, 242; **Supp. XIX:** 172, 241; **Supp. XV:** 320, 329; **Supp. XVIII:** 102; **Supp. XXII:** 60; **Supp. XXIII:** 162, 290; **Supp. XXVII:** 218

"Chekhov's Sense of Writing as Seen Through His Letters" (Dobyns), **Supp. XIII:** 77–78

"Chemin de Fer" (Bishop), **Retro. Supp. II:** 41; **Supp. I Part 1:** 80, 85, 86

"Chemistry" (Rash), **Supp. XXVII:** 227

Chemistry and Other Stories (Rash), **Supp. XXVII:** 222, 225, 227–228

Cheney, Brainard, **Retro. Supp. II:** 229

Cheney, Matthew, **Supp. XXII:** 50

Chenzira, Ayoka, **Supp. XI:** 19

Chéri (Colette; stage adaptation, Loos), **Supp. XVI:** 194

Cherkovski, Neeli, **Supp. XII:** 118, 132, 134

Chernyshevski, Nikolai, **III:** 261, 262, 263; **Retro. Supp. I:** 269

Cherokee Lottery, The: A Sequence of Poems (W. J. Smith), **Supp. XIII:** **340–344**

"Cherríe Moraga's Radical Revision of *Death of a Salesman*"(Wiley), **Supp. XXIII:** 199

Cherry (Karr), **Supp. XI:** 239, **251–254**

"Cherrylog Road" (Dickey), **Supp. XVIII:** 191

Cherry Orchard, The (Chekhov), **IV:** 359, 426; **Supp. VIII:** 153

Cheslock, Louis, **III:** 99, 118, 119

Chesnutt, Charles Waddell, **Supp. II Part 1:** 174, 193, 211; **Supp. IV Part 1:** 257; **Supp. XIV:** **57–78**

"Chess House, The" (Dixon), **Supp. XII:** 139

Chessman, Caryl, **Supp. I Part 2:** 446

Chester, Alfred, **Retro. Supp. II:** 111, 112; **Supp. X:** 192

Chesterfield, Lord, **II:** 36

Chesterton, Gilbert Keith, **I:** 226; **IV:** 432

Cheuse, Alan, **Supp. IV Part 2:** 570

Chevigny, Bell Gale, **Supp. XI:** 283

Cheyenne Autumn (Sandoz), **Supp. XXIII:** 146; **Supp. XXIV:** 244, 248, 256, **258–260**

"Chicago" (Sandburg), **III:** 581, 592, 596; **Supp. III Part 1:** 71

Chicago (Shepard), **Supp. III Part 2:** 439

Chicago: City on the Make (Algren), **Supp. IX:** 1, 3

"*Chicago Defender* Sends a Man to Little Rock, The" (Brooks), **Supp. III Part 1:** 80–81

"Chicago Hamlet, A" (Anderson), **I:** 112

Chicago Loop (Theroux), **Supp. VIII:** 324

"Chicago Picasso, The" (Brooks), **Supp. III Part 1:** 70–71, 84

Chicago Poems (Sandburg), **III:** 579, 581–583, 586

"Chicano/Borderlands Literature and Poetry" (Ríos), **Supp. IV Part 2:** 537, 538, 542, 545

Chicano! The History of the Mexican American Civil Rights Movement (Rosales), **Supp. XXV:** 133

Chick, Nancy, **Supp. IV Part 1:** 1

"Chickamauga" (Bierce), **I:** 201

"Chickamauga" (Wolfe), **IV:** 460

Chickamauga (Wright), **Supp. V:** 333, 343–344

"Chickamauga" (Wright), **Supp. V:** 334

"Chicken Market" (Skloot), **Supp. XX:** **198, 200**

"Chiefly about War Matters" (Hawthorne), **II:** 227; **Retro. Supp. I:** 165

"Chiffon" (Hull), **Supp. XXI:** 138

"Child" (Plath), **Supp. I Part 2:** 544

Child, Greg, **Supp. XVIII:** 107

Child, Julia, **Supp. XVII:** 89, 90

Child, Lydia Maria, **Supp. XIII:** 141; **Supp. XVIII:** 11

"Child, The" (Ríos), **Supp. IV Part 2:** 543

"Child by Tiger, The" (Wolfe), **IV:** 451

"Childhood" (Wright), **Supp. V:** 341

Childhood, A: The Biography of a Place (Crews), **Supp. XI:** 102–103, 245

"Childhood, When You Are in It . . ." (Kenyon), **Supp. VII:** 160, 170

Childhood and Other Neighborhoods (Dybek), **Supp. XXIII:** 68, **69–70**

"Childhood Sketch" (Wright), **Supp. III Part 2:** 589

"Child Is Born, A" (Benét), **Supp. XI:** 46

"Child Is the Meaning of This Life, The" (Schwartz), **Supp. II Part 2:** 659–660

"Childlessness" (Merrill), **Supp. III Part 1:** 323

"Childless Woman" (Plath), **Supp. I Part 2:** 544

Child-Life (Whittier and Larcom, eds.), **Supp. XIII:** 142

Child-Life in Prose (Whittier and Larcom, eds.), **Supp. XIII:** 142

Childlike Life of the Black Tarantula, The (Acker), **Supp. XII:** 4, 6, **7–8**

"Child Margaret" (Sandburg), **III:** 584

"Child of Courts, The" (Jarrell), **II:** 378, 379, 381

Child of God (McCarthy), **Supp. VIII:** **177–178**

Child of My Heart (McDermott), **Supp. XVIII:** 155, **164–166**

Child of the Century, A (Hecht), **Supp. XXV:** 29; **Supp. XXVII:** 83, 84, 91, 95, 96

"CHILD OF THE THIRTIES" (Baraka), **Supp. II Part 1:** 60

"Child on Top of a Greenhouse" (Roethke), **III:** 531

Children (Gurney), **Supp. V:** 95, 96

"Children" (Stowe), **Supp. I Part 2:** 587

"Children, The" (Jarman), **Supp. XVII:** 116

Children, The (Wharton), **IV:** 321, 326; **Retro. Supp. I:** 381

"Children, the Sandbar, That Summer" (Rukeyser), **Supp. VI:** 274

Children and Others (Cozzens), **I:** 374

Children Is All (Purdy), **Supp. VII:** 277, 278, 282

"Children of Adam" (Whitman), **IV:** 342; **Retro. Supp. I:** 403, 405

Children of Job, The: American Second-Generation Witnesses to the Holocaust (A. Berger), **Supp. XVII:** 39

Children of Light (Stone), **Supp. V:** 304–306

Children of Light and the Children of Darkness, The (Niebuhr), **III:** 292, 306, 310

"Children of the Dirty War" (Goldman), **Supp. XXV:** 52

Children of the Frost (London), **II:** 469, 483

Children of the Holocaust (H. Epstein), **Supp. XVII:** 48; **Supp. XXII:** 95

"Children of the Lord's Supper, The" (Tegnér), **Retro. Supp. II:** 155, 157

Children of the Market Place (Masters), **Supp. I Part 2:** 471

"Children on Their Birthdays" (Capote), **Supp. III Part 1:** 114, 115

Children Playing Before a Statue of Hercules (Sedaris, ed.), **Supp. XXIII:** 289

"Children Selecting Books in a Library" (Jarrell), **II:** 371

Children's Hour, The (Hellman), **Supp. I Part 1:** 276–277, 281, 286, 297

"Children's Rhymes" (Hughes), **Supp. I Part 1:** 340

Childress, Mark, **Supp. X:** 89

Child's Garden of Verses, A (Stevenson), **Supp. IV Part 1:** 298, 314; **Supp. XIII:** 75

"Child's Nature, A" (Jin), **Supp. XVIII:** 93

"Child's Reminiscence, A" (Whitman), **IV:** 344

Childwold (Oates), **Supp. II Part 2:** 519–520

Chile Woman (G. Jones), **Supp. XXIV:** 185

Chill, The (Macdonald), **Supp. IV Part 2:** 473

Chills and Fever (Ransom), **III:** 490, 491–492, 493

Chilly Scenes of Winter (Beattie), **Supp. V:** 21, 22, 23, 24, 26, 27

Chime of Words, A: The Letters of Logan Pearsall Smith (Tribble, ed.), **Supp. XIV:** 348–349

Chimera (C. Frost), **Supp. XV:** 94, 95, 100

"Chimes for Yahya" (Merrill), **Supp. III Part 1:** 329

Chin, Frank, **Supp. V:** 164, 172

Chin, Mei, **Supp. XVIII:** 95

"China" (C. Johnson), **Supp. VI:** 193–194

Chinaberry Tree, The (Fauset), **Supp. XIX:** 73

"Chinaman's Hat" (Kingston), **Supp. V:** 169

China Men (Kingston), **Supp. V:** 157, 158, 159, 160, 161, 164–169; **Supp. X:** 292; **Supp. XV:** 220

"China Poet, The" (Sturgis), **Supp. XX:** 233, 240

China Trace (Wright), **Supp. V:** 332, 340, 341, 342

"Chinese Apples" (Di Piero), **Supp. XIX:** 40

Chinese Apples: New and Selected Poems (Di Piero), **Supp. XIX:** 33, 36, 37, 38, 39, 40, 44, 45, 46, 47–48

Chinese Classics (Legge), **III:** 472

Chinese Materia Medica (P. Smith), **III:** 572

"Chinese New Year" (Hull), **Supp. XXI:** 135

"Chinese Nightingale, The" (Lindsay), **Supp. I Part 2:** 392–393, 394

Chinese Nightingale and Other Poems, The (Lindsay), **Supp. I Part 2:** 392

Chinese Siamese Cat, The (Tan), **Supp. X:** 289

Chinese Translations, The (Bynner), **Supp. XV:** 47, 52

Chinitz, David, **Supp. XV:** 180, 185

"Chinoiseries" (A. Lowell), **II:** 524–525

Chip (Untermeyer), **Supp. XV:** 310

"Chipeta, Widow of Chief Ouray with a Word About a Deal in Blankets" (Zitkala-Ša), **Supp. XXV:** 281

Chirico, Giorgio de, **Supp. III Part 1:** 14

Chirico, Miriam M., **Supp. XV:** 323

"Chiron" (Winters), **Supp. II Part 2:** 801

"Chitlins at the Waldorf" (Crouch), **Supp. XIX:** 158

"Chloroform Jags" (J. Scott), **Supp. XVII:** 189

"Chocklit Geography: Raymond Andrews's Mythical South" (Harris), **Supp. XXVI:** 14

Chodorov, Jerome, **IV:** 274

"Choice, The" (Karr), **Supp. XI:** 251

"Choice of Accommodations, A" (Lahiri), **Supp. XXI:** 183

"Choice of Profession, A" (Malamud), **Supp. I Part 2:** 437

Choice of Wars, A (Shaw), **Supp. XIX:** 245

"Choices" (Gallagher), **Supp. XXIV:** 171

Chomei, Kamo No, **IV:** 170, 171, 184

Chomsky, Noam, **Supp. IV Part 2:** 679

Choosing not Choosing (Cameron), **Retro. Supp. I:** 43

Chopin, Felix, **Supp. I Part 1:** 202

Chopin, Frédéric, **Supp. I Part 1:** 363

Chopin, Jean, **Supp. I Part 1:** 206

Chopin, Kate, **II:** 276; **Retro. Supp. I:** 10, 215; **Retro. Supp. II:** 57–74; **Supp. I Part 2:** 200–226; **Supp. V:** 304; **Supp. X:** 227; **Supp. XVIII:** 194

"Chopin in Winter"(Dybek), **Supp. XXIII:** 72

"Choral: The Pink Church" (W. C. Williams), **Retro. Supp. I:** 428

"Chord" (Merwin), **Supp. III Part 1:** 356

"Chord"(Dybek), **Supp. XXIII:** 78

"Chords and Dischords" (column; Untermeyer), **Supp. XV:** 294

"Chorus, The"(Hadas), **Supp. XXIII:** 119–120

Choruses from Iphigenia in Aulis (Doolittle, trans.), **Supp. I Part 1:** 257, 268, 269

Chosen, The (Potok), **Supp. XXVI:** 125

"Chosen Blindness" (Karr), **Supp. XI:** 251

Chosen Country (Dos Passos), **I:** 475, 490–491

Chosen Place, The Timeless People, The (Marshall), **Supp. XI:** 275, 276, **282–284**

Chosön (P. Lowell), **II:** 513

Choukri, Mohamed, **Supp. IV Part 1:** 92

Chovteau, Mane Thérèse, **Supp. I Part 1:** 205

Chris Durang and Dawne (Durang), **Supp. XXIV:** 113, 124

"ChrisEaster" (Peacock), **Supp. XIX:** 198, 199

Chrisman, Robert, **Supp. IV Part 1:** 1

Christabel (Coleridge), **Supp. IV Part 2:** 465

"Christ for Sale" (R. Lowell), **II:** 538

Christgau, Robert, **Supp. XXVII:** 33–47

Christian, Graham, **Supp. XII:** 193

Christian Dictionary, A (Wilson), **IV:** 153

"Christian in World Crisis, The" (Merton), **Supp. VIII:** 203

Christianity and Power Politics (Niebuhr), **III:** 292, 303

"Christianity and the Survival of Creation" (Berry), **Supp. X:** 30

Christianity of Sholem Asch, The: An Appraisal from the Jewish Viewpoint (Lieberman), **Supp. XXIII:** 3, 7

"Christian Minister, The" (Emerson), **II:** 10

Christian Philosopher, The (Mather), **Supp. II Part 2:** 463–464

Christian Realism and Practical Problems (Niebuhr), **III:** 292, 308

"Christian Roommates, The" (Updike), **IV:** 226–227; **Retro. Supp. I:** 319, 323

Christiansen, Carrie, **I:** 210

Christian's Secret of a Happy Life, The (H. W. Smith), **Supp. XIV:** 333–334

Christie, Agatha, **Supp. IV Part 1:** 341; **Supp. IV Part 2:** 469

Christ in Concrete (di Donato), **Supp. XX:** 33, 34–40, 42, 43, 46

"Christ in Concrete" (di Donato), **Supp. XX:** 34

Christine (King), **Supp. V:** 139, 148

"Christ Light, The" (Chopin), **Retro. Supp. II:** 61

"Christmas" (Saunders), **Supp. XIX:** 232

"Christmas, or the Good Fairy" (Stowe), **Supp. I Part 2:** 586

"Christmas 1944" (Levertov), **Supp. III Part 1:** 274

"Christmas Banquet, The" (Hawthorne), **II:** 227

Christmas Card, A (Theroux), **Supp. VIII:** 322

Christmas Carol, A (Dickens), **Retro. Supp. I:** 196; **Supp. I Part 2:** 409–410; **Supp. X:** 252, 253; **Supp. XXV:** 149, 152

Christmas Carollin' (Wells), **Supp. XXVI:** 275

"Christmas Eve at Johnson's Drugs N Goods" (Bambara), **Supp. XI:** 11–12

"Christmas Eve in the Time of War: A Capitalist Meditates by a Civil War Monument" (R. Lowell), **II:** 538

"Christmas Eve under Hooker's Statue" (R. Lowell), **II:** 539–540

"Christmas Gift" (Warren), **IV:** 252–253

"Christmas Greeting, A" (Wright), **Supp. III Part 2:** 601

"Christmas Hymn, A" (Wilbur), **Supp. III Part 2:** 557

Christmas Memory, A (Capote), **Supp. III Part 1:** 118, 119, 129

"Christmass Poem" (West), **Retro. Supp. II:** 338

Christmas Story (Mencken), **III:** 111

"Christmas to Me" (Lee), **Supp. VIII:** 113

Christographia (Taylor), **IV:** 164–165

Christ on a Clothesline (Loy), **Supp. XXII:** 168

"Christ on the Cross/Nuestro Señor Crucificado" (Mora), **Supp. XIII:** 229

Christopher, Mary (pseudonym). *See* West, Dorothy

Christopher and His Kind: 1929–1939 (Isherwood), **Supp. XIV:** 157, 163, 164, 171

"Christopher Cat" (Cullen), **Supp. IV Part 1:** 173

Christopher Columbus, Mariner (Morison), **Supp. I Part 2:** 488

Christopher Isherwood: A Critical Biography (Finney), **Supp. XIV:** 158

Christophersen, Bill, **Supp. IX:** 159, 167; **Supp. XI:** 155; **Supp. XIII:** 87; **Supp. XXI:** 103

"Christ's Passion" (Karr), **Supp. XI:** 251

Christus: A Mystery (Longfellow), **II:** 490, 493, 495, 505–507; **Retro. Supp. II:** 161, 165, 166

Chroma (F. Barthelme), **Supp. XI:** 30, 33, 34

"Chroma" (F. Barthelme), **Supp. XI:** 31

"Chronicle" (W. Stone), **Supp. XXVII:** 255

"Chronicle of Race Relations, A" (Du Bois), **Supp. II Part 1:** 182

Chronicle of the Conquest of Granada (Irving), **II:** 310

Chronicles: Volume One (Dylan), **Supp. XVIII:** 20, 21, 23, 24, 28, **32–33**

"Chronologues" (Goldbarth), **Supp. XII:** 183, 184

"Chrysanthemums, The" (Steinbeck), **IV:** 53

"Chrysaor" (Longfellow), **II:** 498

Chu, Louis, **Supp. X:** 291

Chuang, Hua, **Supp. X:** 291

Chuang-Tzu, **Supp. VIII:** 206

"Chunk of Amethyst, A" (R. Bly), **Supp. IV Part 1:** 72

Church, Margaret, **IV:** 466

"Church and the Fiction Writer, The" (O'Connor), **Retro. Supp. II:** 223, 233; **Supp. XVIII:** 161

"Church Going" (Larkin), **Supp. XXI:** 93

"Churchgoing" (Nelson), **Supp. XVIII:** 173

Churchill, Charles, **Supp. XV:** 232

Churchill, Winston, **I:** 9, 490; **Supp. I Part 2:** 491

Church of Dead Girls, The (Dobyns), **Supp. XIII:** 75, **83–84**

"Church of Omnivorous Light, The" (Wrigley), **Supp. XVIII:** 306–307

"Church of the Latter Day Saints, The" (Mosher), **Supp. XXII:** 208

"Church Porch, The" (Herbert), **IV:** 153

Church Psalmody, Selected from Dr. Watts and Other Authors (Mason and Greene, ed.), **I:** 458

Ciannic, Saint, **II:** 215

Ciano, Edda, **IV:** 249

Ciardi, John, **I:** 169, 179, 535; **III:** 268; **Supp. IV Part 1:** 243; **Supp. IV Part 2:** 639; **Supp. IX:** 269, 324; **Supp. XII:** 119

Cicada (Haines), **Supp. XII: 206–207**

"Cicadas" (Wilbur), **Supp. III Part 2:** 549

Cicero, **I:** 279; **II:** 8, 14–15; **III:** 23; **Supp. I Part 2:** 405

Cider House Rules, The (Irving), **Supp. VI:** 164, **173–175**

"Cigales" (Wilbur), **Supp. III Part 2:** 549

"Cigarette" (L. Michaels), **Supp. XVI:** 214

Cigarette Book, The (Brainard), **Supp. XXVII:** 20

Cimarron, Rose (Burke), **Supp. XIV:** 22, 35

"Cimetière Marin, Le" (Valéry), **IV:** 91–92

Cimino, Michael, **Supp. X:** 126

Cincinnati Kid, The (film), **Supp. XI: 306**

"Cinderella" (Jarrell), **II:** 386

"Cinderella" (Perrault), **IV:** 266, 267

"Cinderella" (Sexton), **Supp. II Part 2:** 691

"Cinema, The" (Salter), **Supp. IX:** 257

Cinema of Tony Richardson, The: Essays and Interviews (Phillips), **Supp. XI:** 306

Cinthio, **IV:** 370

Ciolkowski, Laura, **Supp. XVI:** 24

CIOPW (Cummings), **I:** 429

"Circe" (Welty), **Retro. Supp. I:** 353

Circle Game, The (Atwood), **Supp. XIII:** 20, 33

Circle in the Dirt (Moraga), **Supp. XXIII:** 195, 202

"Circle in the Fire, A" (O'Connor), **III:** 344–345, 349–350, 351, 353, 354; **Retro. Supp. II:** 229, 232

"Circle of Breath" (Stafford), **Supp. XI:** 318, 322

Circle of Hanh, The (Weigl), **Supp. XIX:** 273, 275, 282, **284–286**

"Circles" (Emerson), **I:** 455, 460

"Circles" (R. Lowell), **II:** 554

Circular Staircase, The (Rinehart), **Supp. XXV:** 189, 192, 200

Circumference: Varieties of Metaphysical Verse 1456–1928 (Taggard, ed.), **Supp. XXII:** 279

"Circus" (Huddle), **Supp. XXVI:** 150

"Circus, The" (Porter), **III:** 443, 445

"Circus Animals' Desertion" (Yeats), **I:** 389

Circus Fire, The (O'Nan), **Supp. XXV:** 153

"Circus in the Attic" (Warren), **IV:** 253

Circus in the Attic, The (Warren), **IV:** 243, 251–253

"Circus in Three Rings" (Plath), **Retro. Supp. II:** 243; **Supp. I Part 2:** 536

Circus of Needs, A (Dunn), **Supp. XI: 147–148**

"Cirque d'Hiver" (Bishop), **Supp. I Part 1:** 85

Cisneros, Sandra, **Supp. IV Part 2:** 544; **Supp. VII: 57–73; Supp. XI:** 177; **Supp. XVII:** 71; **Supp. XXII:** 177; **Supp. XXV:** 133

Cities of the Interior (Nin), **Supp. X:** 182

Cities of the Plain (McCarthy), **Supp. VIII:** 175, **186–187**

Cities of the Red Night (Burroughs), **Supp. III Part 1:** 106

"Citizen Cain" (Baraka), **Supp. II Part 1:** 49

Citizen Kane (film), **Retro. Supp. I:** 115; **Supp. V:** 251; **Supp. XI:** 169

"Citizen of the World" (Goldsmith), **II:** 299

Citizens (Levin), **Supp. XXVII:** 133, 134, 139, 142, 143–144

Citro, Joseph, **Supp. XXII:** 208, 218

"City" (Francis), **Supp. IX:** 87

"City, The" (Stallings), **Supp. XXV:** 233

"City and Country"(Hadas), **Supp. XXIII:** 115, 116

City and the Island, The (Davison), **Supp. XXVI:** 65, 70–71

City and the Pillar, The (Vidal), **Supp. IV Part 2:** 677, 680–681; **Supp. XIV:** 170

"*City and the Pillar, The,* as Gay Fiction" (Summers), **Supp. IV Part 2:** 680–681

"City Articles" series (Briggs), **Supp. XVIII:** 12

City Block (W. Frank), **Supp. XX: 71, 72, 76**

City Boy (L. Michaels), **Supp. XVI:** 212

"City Boy" (L. Michaels), **Supp. XVI:** 203–204

City Boy (Thompson), **Supp. XXIII:** 294, **298–299**

City Boy, The (Wouk), **Supp. XXV:** 256, 259

City Dog (Di Piero), **Supp. XIX:** 33–34, 35, 38, 46, 48

"City Dog" (Di Piero), **Supp. XIX:** 47

City in History, The (Mumford), **Supp. II Part 2:** 495

"City in the Sea, The" (Poe), **III:** 411; **Retro. Supp. II:** 274

City in Which I Love You, The (L.-Y. Lee), **Supp. XV:** 212, **215–220**

"City in Which I Love You, The" (L.-Y. Lee), **Supp. XV:** 215, **217–218**

City in Winter, A (Helprin), **Supp. XXV:** 84, 87

City Life (Barthelme), **Supp. IV Part 1:** 44, 47

City of Bones (Connelly), **Supp. XXI: 74–75,** 77

"City of Change, A" (Bynner), **Supp. XV:** 45

City of Dreadful Night (Siegel), **Supp. XXII:** 258

City of Glass (Auster), **Supp. XII:** 22, **24–26**

City of God, The (St. Augustine), **IV:** 126

City of Names (Brockmeier), **Supp. XXII:** 55–56, 57

"City of Refuge, The" (R. Fisher), **Supp. XIX:** 65, 66, **67–68**

City of Refuge, The: The Collected Stories of Rudolph Fisher (McCluskey, ed.), **Supp. XIX:** 68–69

City of the Living and Other Stories, The (Stegner), **Supp. IV Part 2:** 599, 609, 613

City of Words: American Fiction 1950–1970 (T. Tanner), **Supp. XVI:** 69

City of Your Final Destination, The (Cameron), **Supp. XII:** 79, 82, **91–94**

"City on a Hill" (R. Lowell), **II:** 552

City on a Hill: Testing the American Dream at City College (Traub), **Supp. XXIV:** 221

"City Person Encountering Nature, A" (Kingston), **Supp. V:** 170

"City Planners, The" (Atwood), **Supp. XIII:** 33

"City Winter, A"(O'Hara), **Supp. XXIII:** 210

City Winter and Other Poems, A (O'Hara), **Supp. XXIII:** 210, 214

City Without Men (film), **Supp. XVIII:** 247

City Without Walls (Auden), **Supp. II Part 1:** 24

Civil Disobedience (Thoreau), **IV:** 185; **Supp. I Part 2:** 507

Civilization in the United States (Stearns), **I:** 245

"Civil Rights" (Lanier), **Supp. I Part 1:** 357

CivilWarLand in Bad Decline (Saunders), **Supp. XIX: 224–227**

"CivilWarLand in Bad Decline" (Saunders), **Supp. XIX:** 224–225, 227

Civitatis Anthology of African American Slave Narratives, The (H. L. Gates and Andrews, eds.), **Supp. XX: 105**

Cixous, Hélène, **Supp. X:** 102; **Supp. XIII:** 297; **Supp. XV:** 347

Clabough, Casey, **Supp. XXIV:** 194

Claiborne, Craig, **Supp. XVII:** 89

Claiborne, William, **I:** 132

"Claim, The"(Balakian), **Supp. XXIII:** 20

Claiming an Identity They Taught Me to Despise (Cliff), **Supp. XXII:** 66, 67–68, 70

Claiming of Sleeping Beauty, The (Rice), **Supp. VII:** 301

Claman, Emily Rosamund, **Supp. XXVI:** 175

Clampitt, Amy, **Supp. IX: 37–54; Supp. X:** 120; **Supp. XI:** 249; **Supp. XV:** 251, 256

Clancy's Wake, At (Crane), **I:** 422

"Clandeboye" (Leopold), **Supp. XIV:** 189

"Clara" (Hecht), **Supp. XXVII:** 95

Clara Howard; or, The Enthusiasm of Love (Brown), **Supp. I Part 1:** 145

Clara's Ole Man (Bullins), **Supp. II Part 1:** 42

Clara Wharton (Hayden), **Supp. XXV:** 38

Clare, John, **II:** 387; **III:** 528; **Supp. XVI:** 295

Clarel: A Poem and Pilgrimage in the Holy Land (Melville), **Retro. Supp. I:** 257

Clarence Major and His Art (Bell), **Supp. XXII:** 182

Clarissa (Richardson), **II:** 111; **Supp. I Part 2:** 714; **Supp. V:** 127; **Supp. XV:** 231; **Supp. XX: 236**

Clarissa Harlow (Richardson), **Supp. XXV:** 39

Clark, Alex, **Supp. XII:** 307

Clark, Charles, **I:** 470

Clark, Eleanor. *See* Warren, Mrs. Robert Penn (Eleanor Clark)

Clark, Francis Edward, **II:** 9

Clark, Geoffrey, **Supp. XI:** 342

Clark, Harry Hayden, **Supp. I Part 2:** 423

Clark, John Bates, **Supp. I Part 2:** 633

Clark, Kenneth, **Supp. XIV:** 342, 348; **Supp. XIX:** 151

Clark, Lewis Gaylord, **Supp. XVIII:** 4, 7, 8

Clark, Shirley, **Supp. XXI:** 22

Clark, Thomas, **Supp. III Part 2:** 629; **Supp. IV Part 1:** 140, 145, 147

Clark, Tom, **Supp. XXIV:** 36, 37, 41, 44

Clark, Walter, **Supp. XI:** 315

Clark, William, **III:** 14; **IV:** 179, 283

Clark, Willis Gaylord, **Supp. I Part 2:** 684

Clarke, Brock, **Supp. XXIII:** 109

Clarke, James Freeman, **Supp. II Part 1:** 280; **Supp. XXV:** 250

Clarke, John, **Supp. IV Part 1:** 8

Clarke, John J., **III:** 356

Clarke, Samuel, **II:** 108

Clark Lectures, **Retro. Supp. I:** 65

Claros varones de Belken (Hinojosa). *See Fair Gentlemen of Belken County* (Hinojosa)

Clash by Night (film), **Supp. XXVI:** 134

Clash by Night (Odets), **Supp. II Part 2:** 531, 538, 544–546, 550, 551

Classical Tradition, The (Highet), **Supp. I Part 1:** 268

Classic Ballroom Dances (Simic), **Supp. VIII:** 271, **276–278,** 283

Classics (Hadas), **Supp. XXIII:** 124

Classics and Commercials: A Literary Chronicle of the Forties (Wilson), **IV:** 433

"Classics"(Hadas), **Supp. XXIII:** 124

"CLASS STRUGGLE" (Baraka), **Supp. III Part 1:** 55

"Claude Glass, The: 1890" (Bierds), **Supp. XVII:** 27

Claudel, Paul, **I:** 60

Claudelle Inglish (Caldwell), **I:** 304

Clavel, Marcel, **I:** 343

"CLAY" (Baraka), **Supp. II Part 1:** 54

Clay, Henry, **I:** 8; **Supp. I Part 2:** 684, 686

Clay's Ark (O. Butler), **Supp. XIII:** 63

Clayton, John J., **Supp. IV Part 1:** 238

Clayton, Sarah Turner, **Supp. XXV:** 251

"Clean, Well Lighted Place, A" (Hemingway), **Retro. Supp. I:** 181

"Clear, with Light Variable Winds" (A. Lowell), **II:** 522

"Clear Days" (White), **Supp. I Part 2:** 664, 665

Clearing (Berry), **Supp. X:** 22

"Clearing, A" (Simpson), **Supp. IX:** 280

"Clearing, The" (Kenyon), **Supp. VII:** 174

"Clearing the Title" (Merrill), **Supp. III Part 1:** 336

"Clearing Up the Question of Stesichoros' Blinding by Helen" (Carson), **Supp. XII:** 107–108

"Clear Morning" (Glück), **Supp. V:** 88

"Clearness" (Wilbur), **Supp. III Part 2:** 544, 550

"Clear Night" (Wright), **Supp. V:** 341

Clear Pictures: First Loves, First Guides (Price), **Supp. VI:** 253, 254, 255, 256, 265

Clear Springs (Mason), **Supp. VIII:** 134–136, 137–138, 139, 147

Cleary, Rebecca Lauck, **Supp. XVIII:** 195

Cleaver, Eldridge, **Retro. Supp. II:** 12; **Supp. IV Part 1:** 206; **Supp. X:** 249

"Cleaving, The" (L.-Y. Lee), **Supp. XV:** 215, **218–220**

Cleland, John, **Supp. V:** 48, 127

Clemenceau, Georges, **I:** 490

"Clemency" (Wrigley), **Supp. XVIII:** 307–308

Clemens, Jane, **I:** 247

Clemens, Orion, **IV:** 193, 195

Clemens, Samuel Langhorne. *See* Twain, Mark

Clemens, Mrs. Samuel Langhorne (Olivia Langdon), **I:** 197, 208, 247; **Supp. I Part 2:** 457

Clemens, Susie, **IV:** 208

Clementine Recognitions (novel), **Supp. IV Part 1:** 280

Clements, Colin Campbell, **Supp. XVI:** 190

Clemons, Walter, **Supp. IV Part 1:** 305, 307

Cleopatra, **III:** 44; **IV:** 373; **Supp. I Part 1:** 114

"Clepsydra" (Ashbery), **Supp. III Part 1:** 10–15

"Clerks, The" (Robinson), **III:** 517–518

"Cleveland" (Halliday), **Supp. XIX:** 90

Cleveland, Carol, **Supp. IX:** 120, 125

Cleveland, Ceil, **Supp. V:** 222

Cleveland, Grover, **II:** 126, 128, 129, 130, 137, 138; **Supp. I Part 2:** 486

"Clever Magician Carrying My Heart, A" (Salinas), **Supp. XIII:** 323

Cliff, Michelle, **Supp. XXII: 65–80**

"Cliff, The" (C. Baxter), **Supp. XVII:** 16–17

Clifford, Craig, **Supp. IX:** 99

Clift, Montgomery, **III:** 161

Clifton, Lucille, **Supp. XVIII:** 177

Climate of Monastic Prayer, The (Merton), **Supp. VIII:** 205, 207

Climb, The (Boukreev), **Supp. XVIII:** 112

"Climber, The" (Mason), **Supp. VIII:** 140–141

Climbing High: A Woman's Account of Surviving the Everest Tragedy (Gammelgaard), **Supp. XVIII:** 112

"Climbing the Tower" (Crews), **Supp. XI:** 102

Clinton, De Witt, **I:** 338

"Clipped Wings" (H. Miller), **III:** 176–177

Clippinger, David, **Supp. XXI:** 24

Clive, Robert, **Supp. I Part 2:** 505

Clock Winder, The (Tyler), **Supp. IV Part 2:** 661–662, 670

Clock Without Hands (McCullers), **II:** 587–588, 604–606

Clockwork Orange, A (Burgess), **Supp. XIII:** 29

Clorindy (Cook), **Supp. II Part 1:** 199

"Close, The" (Jarman), **Supp. XVII:** 113

"Close Calls" (Wolff), **Supp. VII:** 332–333

"Closed Book, A" (Mosley), **Supp. XIII:** 237

Close Quarters (Heinemann), **Supp. XXII:** 103, **104–109,** 111, 115

Close Range: Wyoming Stories (Proulx), **Supp. VII:** 261–265

"Close Reading: Windows"(Hirshfield), **Supp. XXIII:** 131

Closers, The (Connelly), **Supp. XXI: 76–77**

Closest Possible Union, The (J. Scott), **Supp. XVII: 185–186,** 188, 191

"Closet, The" (Goodman), **Supp. XXVI:** 121

Close the Book (Glaspell), **Supp. III Part 1:** 179

"Close the Book" (R. Lowell), **II:** 554

Close to Me & Closer ... (The Language of Heaven) and Désamère (Notley), **Supp. XXII:** 234

Close to Shore: A True Story of Terror in an Age of Innocence (Capuzzo), **Supp. XIII:** 254

Closet Writing & Gay Reading: The Case of Melville's Pierre (Creech), **Retro. Supp. I:** 254

Closing Circle, The (Commoner), **Supp. XIII:** 264

Closing of the American Mind, The (Bloom), **Retro. Supp. II:** 19, 30, 31

"Closing of the Rodeo, The" (W. J. Smith), **Supp. XIII:** 332

Closing Time (Heller), **Supp. IV Part 1:** 382, 386, 391–394

Closset, Marie, **Supp. VIII:** 251, 265

Clotel (Brown), **Supp. XXIII:** 184

"Cloud, The" (Shelley), **Supp. I Part 2:** 720

"Cloud and Fame" (Berryman), **I:** 173

Cloud Atlas (D. Mitchell), **Supp. XXIV:** 86

Cloud Forest, The: A Chronicle of the South American Wilderness (Matthiessen), **Supp. V:** 202, 204

"Cloud on the Way, The" (Bryant), **Supp. I Part 1:** 171

"Cloud River" (Wright), **Supp. V:** 341

"Clouds" (Levine), **Supp. V:** 184

Cloudsplitter (Banks), **Supp. V:** 16

"Clover" (Lanier), **Supp. I Part 1:** 362–364

Clover and Other Poems (Lanier), **Supp. I Part 1:** 362

"Clown" (Corso), **Supp. XII:** 127

Clown in the Belfry, The: Writings on Faith and Fiction (Buechner), **Supp. XII:** 53

Cluck, Julia, **Supp. I Part 2:** 728

Clue, The (Wells), **Supp. XXVI:** 277

Clue of the Eyelash, The (Wells), **Supp. XXVI:** 280

Clum, John M., **Supp. XIII: 200,** 201, 209

Cluny, Hugo, **IV:** 290

Clurman, Harold, **I:** 93; **IV:** 381, 385

Clytus, Radiclani, **Supp. XIII:** 128, **Supp. XIII:** 129, 132

"C.O." (Wrigley), **Supp. XVIII:** 298

"Coal: Beginning and End" (Winters), **Supp. II Part 2:** 791

Coale, Howard, **Supp. XIII:** 15

"Coals" (Hoffman), **Supp. XVIII:** 86

Coalwood Way, The (Hickam), **Supp. XXVII:** 106, 107–108

"Coast, The" (column), **Supp. IV Part 1:** 198

"Coast Guard's Cottage, The" (Wylie), **Supp. I Part 2:** 723

Coast of Chicago, The (Dybek), **Supp. XXIII:** 72–74, 75

Coast of Trees, A (Ammons), **Supp. VII:** 24, 34

"Coast-Range Christ, The" (Jeffers), **Supp. II Part 2:** 414, 419

"Coast-Road, The" (Jeffers), **Supp. II Part 2:** 425

"Coat, The" (Everwine), **Supp. XV:** 80

Coates, Joseph, **Supp. VIII:** 80; **Supp. XXII:** 205

Coates, Robert, **I:** 54; **IV:** 298

"Coatlicue's Rules: Advice from an Aztec Goddess" (Mora), **Supp. XIII:** 223

"Coats" (Kenyon), **Supp. VII:** 172

Coatsworth, Elizabeth Jane, **Supp. XXVI:** 33

Cobb, Lee J., **III:** 153

Cobb, Ty, **III:** 227, 229

Cobbett, William, **Supp. I Part 2:** 517; **Supp. XV:** 237

"Cobbler Keezar's Vision" (Whittier), **Supp. I Part 2:** 699

"Cobweb, The" (Carver), **Supp. III Part 1:** 148

Cobwebs From an Empty Skull (Bierce), **I:** 195

Coccimiglio, Vic, **Supp. XIII:** 114

"Cock-a-Doodle-Doo!" (Melville), **III:** 89

"Cockayne" (Emerson), **II:** 6

"Cock-Crow" (Gordon), **II:** 219

Cock Pit (Cozzens), **I:** 359, 378, 379

Cockpit (Kosinski), **Supp. XII:** 21

Cockpit: A Novel (Kosinski), **Supp. VII:** 215, 223–224, 225

"Cock Robin Takes Refuge in the Storm House" (Snodgrass), **Supp. VI:** 319

Cocktail Hour, The (Gurney), **Supp. V:** 95, 96, 100, 101, 103, 105, 108

Cocktail Hour and Two Other Plays: Another Antigone and *The Perfect Party* (Gurney), **Supp. V:** 100

Cocktail Party, The (Eliot), **I:** 571, 582–583; **III:** 21; **Retro. Supp. I:** 65; **Supp. V:** 101, 103

Cocteau, Jean, **III:** 471; **Retro. Supp. I:** 82, 378; **Supp. IV Part 1:** 82; **Supp. XVI:** 135; **Supp. XX:** 236

"Coda: Wilderness Letter" (Stegner), **Supp. IV Part 2:** 595

"Code, The" (Frost), **Retro. Supp. I:** 121, 128

Codex (Grossman), **Supp. XXV:** 64, 66–68

Codman, Florence, **Supp. II Part 1:** 92, 93

Codman, Ogden, Jr., **Retro. Supp. I:** 362, 363

Codrescu, Andrei, **Supp. XXII:** 155

Cody, William ("Buffalo Bill"), **I:** 440; **III:** 584; **Supp. V:** 230

"Coffee and Sweet Rolls" (Stone), **Supp. XXVII:** 253

"Coffee Lips" (Ferry), **Supp. XXIV:** 153, 162

Coffey, Michael, **Supp. V:** 243; **Supp. XV:** 65; **Supp. XX:** 88

Coffey, Warren, **III:** 358

Coffin, Charles, **III:** 577

Coffman, Frank, **Supp. XXVII:** 118

Cogan, David J., **Supp. IV Part 1:** 362

Cogan, Joshua, **Supp. XXI:** 247

Cogewea the Half-Blood: A Depiction of the Great Montana Cattle Range (Mourning Dove (Christal Quintasket)), **Supp. XXV:** 285

Coghill, Nevill, **Supp. II Part 1:** 4; **Supp. XIV:** 13

Cohan, George M., **II:** 427; **III:** 401

Cohen, Edward M., **Supp. XVI:** 212

Cohen, Esther, **Supp. XV:** 323

Cohen, Hettie, **Supp. II Part 1:** 30

Cohen, Joshua, **Supp. XXII:** 268

Cohen, Leonard, **Supp. XXVII: 49–65**

Cohen, Marty, **Supp. X:** 112

Cohen, Norman J., **Supp. IX:** 132, 143

Cohen, Rosetta, **Supp. XV:** 257

Cohen, Sarah Blacher, **Supp. V:** 273

Cohen, Victor, **Supp. XVIII:** 235, 236

"Coherent Decentering: Towards a New Model of the Poetic Self" (A. Finch), **Supp. XVII:** 76

Cohn, Jan, **Supp. XXV:** 192, 200

"Coin" (Goldbarth), **Supp. XII:** 187

Coindreau, Maurice, **III:** 339

Coiner, Constance, **Supp. XIII:** 297, 302

Coit, Lille Hitchcock, **Supp. X:** 103

"Coitus" (Pound), **III:** 466

Coke, Desmond, **Supp. XX: 235**

Colburn, Nadia Herman, **Supp. XV:** 339, 341, 347

"Cold, The" (Kenyon), **Supp. VII:** 164

"Cold, The" (Winters), **Supp. II Part 2:** 790–791, 809, 811

"Cold-blooded Creatures" (Wylie), **Supp. I Part 2:** 729

Colden, Cadwallader, **Supp. I Part 1:** 250

"Colder the Air, The" (Bishop), **Supp. I Part 1:** 86

Cold Feet (Harrison), **Supp. VIII:** 39

Cold Frame (C. Frost), **Supp. XV:** 93, 96

Cold Ground Was My Bed Last Night (Garrett), **Supp. VII:** 98

"Cold Ground Was My Bed Last Night" (Garrett), **Supp. VII:** 100

"Cold Hill Side, The"(Hadas), **Supp. XXIII:** 121

"Cold Night, The" (W. C. Williams), **Retro. Supp. I:** 418

"Cold Plunge into Skin Diving, A" (Knowles), **Supp. XII:** 241

Cold Spring, A (Bishop), **Retro. Supp. II:** 45

Cold Springs Harbor (Yates), **Supp. XI:** 348

Cold War American Poetry, **Supp. V:** 182

Cold War and the Income Tax, The (Wilson), **IV:** 430

Cole, Bruce, **Supp. XX: 106**

Cole, Goody, **Supp. I Part 2:** 696–697

Cole, Lester, **Retro. Supp. II:** 329

Cole, Nat King, **Retro. Supp. I:** 334; **Supp. X:** 255

Cole, Thomas, **Supp. I Part 1:** 156, 158, 171

Cole, William, **Supp. XIX:** 120

"Coleman" (Karr), **Supp. XI:** 244

Coleman, Wanda, **Supp. XI: 83–98**

Coleridge, Samuel Taylor, **I:** 283, 284, 447, 522; **II:** 7, 10, 11, 19, 71, 169, 273, 301, 502, 516, 549; **III:** 77, 83–84, 424, 461, 488, 523; **IV:** 74, 173, 250, 349, 453; **Retro. Supp. I:** 65, 308; **Supp. I Part 1:** 31, 311, 349; **Supp. I Part 2:** 376, 393, 422; **Supp. IV Part 2:** 422, 465; **Supp. IX:** 38, 50; **Supp. V:** 258; **Supp. XIII:** 139; **Supp. XIV:** 21–22; **Supp. XV:** 250; **Supp. XXI:** 52, 55; **Supp. XXIII:** 231; **Supp. XXIV:** 74

Coles, Katharine, **Supp. IV Part 2:** 630

Coles, Robert, **Supp. XXIV:** 172, 265; **Supp. XXVI:** 250, 252

Colette, Sidonie-Gabrielle, **Supp. VIII:** 40, 171; **Supp. XVI:** 193–194

"Coliseum, The" (Poe), **III:** 411

Collage of Dreams (Spencer), **Supp. X:** 196

"Collapse of Tomorrow, The" (Mumford), **Supp. II Part 2:** 482

"Collected by a Valetudinarian" (E. Stoddard), **Supp. XV:** 286–287

Collected Earlier Poems (Hecht), **Supp. X:** 58, 59

Collected Earlier Poems (W. C. Williams), **Retro. Supp. I:** 414, 428

Collected Earlier Poems 1940–1960 (Levertov), **Supp. III Part 1:** 273, 275

Collected Essays (Tate), **IV:** 133–134

Collected Essays, Volume 2: Literary Criticism (Lovecraft), **Supp. XXV:** 121

Collected Essays of Ralph Ellison, The (Ellison), **Retro. Supp. II:** 119

Collected Essays of Robert Creeley, The (Creeley), **Supp. IV Part 1:** 153, 154

Collected Later Poems (W. C. Williams), **Retro. Supp. I:** 428

Collected Plays (A. Miller), **III:** 158

Collected Plays, 1974–1983 (Gurney), **Supp. V:** 99

Collected Poems (Aiken), **I:** 50

Collected Poems (Berrigan), **Supp. XXIV:** 39, 45, 46

Collected Poems (Burke), **I:** 269

Collected Poems (Cummings), **I:** 430, 439, 441

Collected Poems (Doolittle), **Supp. I Part 1:** 264–267, 269

Collected Poems (Frost), **Retro. Supp. I:** 136

Collected Poems (Hull), **Supp. XXI:** 141

Collected Poems (Kees; Justice, ed.), **Supp. XV:** 134

Collected Poems (Lindsay), **Supp. I Part 2:** 380, 387, 392, 396–397, 400

Collected Poems (Markson), **Supp. XVII:** 143

Collected Poems (Moore), **III:** 194, 215

Collected Poems (O'Hara), **Supp. XXIII:** 207, 211, 220

Collected Poems (Price), **Supp. VI:** 267

Collected Poems (R. Lowell), **Supp. XV:** 20

Collected Poems (Simpson), **Supp. IX:** 279

Collected Poems (W. C. Williams), **IV:** 415; **Retro. Supp. I:** 430

Collected Poems (Winters), **Supp. II Part 2:** 791, 810

Collected Poems (Wright), **Supp. III Part 2:** 602

Collected Poems (Yeats), **Supp. XV:** 152

Collected Poems, 1918–1938 (Taggard), **Supp. XXII:** 283

Collected Poems, 1923–1953 (Bogan), **Supp. III Part 1:** 64

Collected Poems, 1936–1976 (Francis), **Supp. IX:** 77, 80, **87**

Collected Poems, The (Stevens), **III:** 273; **IV:** 75, 76, 87, 93; **Retro. Supp. I:** 296, 309

Collected Poems 1909–1935 (Eliot), **I:** 580; **Retro. Supp. I:** 66

Collected Poems 1909–1962 (Eliot), **I:** 583

Collected Poems 1917–1952 (MacLeish), **III:** 3, 4, 19

Collected Poems 1921–1931 (W. C. Williams), **Retro. Supp. I:** 422; **Supp. XIV:** 285

Collected Poems 1930–1960 (Eberhart), **I:** 522, 525–526, 540, 541

Collected Poems: 1939–1989 (W. J. Smith), **Supp. XIII:** 332, 340, 343, 345

Collected Poems: 1940–1978 (Shapiro), **Supp. II Part 2:** 703, 717

Collected Poems: 1951–1971 (Ammons), **Supp. VII:** 24, 26–29, 32, 33

Collected Poems: 1956–1976 (Wagoner), **Supp. IX:** 323, **328–329**

Collected Poems of Amy Clampitt, The (Clampitt), **Supp. IX:** 37, 44, 53

Collected Poems of George Garrett (Garrett), **Supp. VII:** 109

Collected Poems of Hart Crane, The (Crane), **I:** 399–402

Collected Poems of James Agee, The (Fitzgerald, ed.), **I:** 27–28

Collected Poems of James T. Farrell, The (Farrell), **II:** 45

Collected Poems of Kay Boyle (Boyle), **Supp. XXIV:** 63

Collected Poems of Langston Hughes, The (Rampersad and Roessel, ed.), **Retro. Supp. I:** 194, 196, 212

Collected Poems of Muriel Rukeyser, The (Rukeyser), **Supp. VI:** 274

Collected Poems of Sara Teasdale, The (Teasdale), **Supp. XXVII:** 287, 294–295

Collected Poems of Thomas Merton, The, **Supp. VIII:** 207, 208

Collected Poetry (Auden), **Supp. II Part 1:** 18

Collected Prose (Wright), **Supp. III Part 2:** 596

Collected Prose, The (Bishop), **Retro. Supp. II:** 51

Collected Recordings (W. C. Williams), **Retro. Supp. I:** 431

Collected Shorter Poems, 1946-1991 (Carruth), **Supp. XVI:** 47

Collected Short Stories, The (Wharton), **Retro. Supp. I:** 362, 363, 366

Collected Sonnets (Millay), **III:** 136–137

Collected Stories (Carver), **Supp. XXIV:** 177

Collected Stories, 1939–1976 (Bowles), **Supp. IV Part 1:** 92

Collected Stories, The (Paley), **Supp. VI:** 218

Collected Stories, The (Price), **Supp. VI:** 266

Collected Stories, The (Theroux), **Supp. VIII:** 318

Collected Stories, The (Wharton), **Retro. Supp. I:** 361

Collected Stories of Amy Hempel, The (Hempel), **Supp. XXI:** 115, 117

Collected Stories of Eudora Welty, The (Welty), **Retro. Supp. I:** 355

Collected Stories of Isaac Bashevis Singer (Singer), **Retro. Supp. II: 307–308**

Collected Stories of Katherine Anne Porter (Porter), **III:** 454

Collected Stories of Peter Taylor (Taylor), **Supp. V:** 314, 320, 323–324, 325, 326

Collected Stories of Richard Yates, The, **Supp. XI:** 349

Collected Stories of Wallace Stegner (Stegner), **Supp. IV Part 2:** 599, 605

Collected Stories of William Faulkner (Faulkner), **II:** 72; **Retro. Supp. I:** 75

Collected Stories of William Humphrey, The (Humphrey), **Supp. IX:** 106

Collected Works (Bierce), **I:** 204, 208–210

Collected Works of Buck Rogers in the 25th Century, The (Bradbury), **Supp. IV Part 1:** 101

Collected Writings (Brainard), **Supp. XXVII:** 17, 26–27, 29

Collected Writings, The (Z. Fitzgerald; Bruccoli, ed.), **Supp. IX:** 65, 68

Collecting the Animals (Everwine), **Supp. XV:** 73, 75, **78–81**, 85, 88

Collection of Epigrams, **II:** 111

Collection of Poems, on American Affairs, and a Variety of Other Subjects . . . (Freneau), **Supp. II Part 1:** 274

Collection of Select Aphorisms and Maxims (Palmer), **II:** 111

"Collectors" (Carver), **Supp. III Part 1:** 141–142

Collette, **Supp. XVII:** 86

Collier, John, **Supp. XXI:** 8

Collier, Lucy Wood, **Supp. XXI:** 8

Collier, Michael, **Supp. XVII:** 23, 110

Collingwood, R. G., **I:** 278

Collins, Billy, **Supp. XI:** 143; **Supp. XIV:** 123; **Supp. XVII:** 245; **Supp. XXI: 51–66; Supp. XXIII:** 138

Collins, Brennan, **Supp. XXVI:** 12, 13

Collins, Doug, **Supp. V:** 5

Collins, Eddie, **II:** 416

Collins, L. M., **Supp. XXII:** 7

Collins, Richard, **Supp. XI:** 171

Collins, Ronald, **Supp. XXI:** 24

Collins, Wilkie, **Supp. I Part 1:** 35, 36; **Supp. IV Part 1:** 341; **Supp. XX: 236**

Collins, William, **Supp. I Part 2:** 714

Collinson, Peter , **II:** 114

Collinson, Peter (pseudonym). See Hammett, Dashiell

"Collision" (Huddle), **Supp. XXVI:** 155

Colloff, Pamela, **Supp. XIII:** 281

Colloque Sentimental (ballet), **Supp. IV Part 1:** 83

"Colloquy" (Kees), **Supp. XV:** 133

"Colloquy in Black Rock" (Lowell), **II:** 535

"Colloquy in Black Rock" (R. Lowell), **Retro. Supp. II:** 178

"Colloquy of Monos and Una, The" (Poe), **III:** 412

"Colloquy on a Bed" (Bronk), **Supp. XXI:** 31

Colonel's Dream, The (Chesnutt), **Supp. XIV:** 63, 75–76

Colônia, Regina, **Retro. Supp. II:** 53

Colony (Siddons), **Supp. XXII:** 239

Color (Cullen), **Supp. IV Part 1:** 164, 166, 167, 168

"Colorado" (Beattie), **Supp. V:** 27

Color and Democracy: Colonies and Peace (Du Bois), **Supp. II Part 1:** 184, 185

"Color-Blind Raspberry Picker, The"(Hadas), **Supp. XXIII:** 113

Color Curtain, The (Wright), **IV:** 478, 488

"Colored Americans" (Dunbar), **Supp. II Part 1:** 197

Colored People (H. L. Gates), **Supp. XX: 101, 103, 104–105, 109, 111**

"Color Line, The" (Douglass), **Supp. III Part 1:** 163–165

Color Line, The (W. B. Smith), **Supp. II Part 1:** 168

Color of a Great City, The (Dreiser), **Retro. Supp. II:** 104

Color of Darkness (Purdy), **Supp. VII:** 271

Color of Water, The (McBride), **Supp. XXVI:** 191

Color Purple, The (Walker), **Supp. III Part 2:** 517, 518, 520, 525–529, 532–537; **Supp. VIII:** 141; **Supp. X:** 252, 330; **Supp. XX: 107**

Color Schemes (Cheang; film), **Supp. XI:** 20

"Colors of Night, The" (Momaday), **Supp. IV Part 2:** 490

"Colors without Objects" (Swenson), **Supp. IV Part 2:** 645

"Color: The Unfinished Business of Democracy" (Locke), **Supp. XIV:** 202, 207

Colossus, The (Plath), **Retro. Supp. II: 245–247; Supp. I Part 2:** 529, 531, 536, 538, 540; **Supp. V:** 79; **Supp. XI:** 317

"Colossus, The" (Plath), **Retro. Supp. II:** 250; **Supp. XXIII:** 113

Colossus of Maroussi, The (H. Miller), **III:** 178, 185–186

"Colour out of Space, The" (Lovecraft), **Supp. XXV:** 109, 111, 114–116, 118, 121

"Colt, The" (Stegner), **Supp. IV Part 2:** 600

Coltelli, Laura, **Supp. IV Part 1:** 323, 330, 335, 409; **Supp. IV Part 2:** 493, 497, 559

Colter: The True Story of the Best Dog I Ever Had (Bass), **Supp. XVI:** 23

Coltrane, John, **Supp. VIII:** 197; **Supp. XXII:** 172

Coltrane, John (pseud.). *See* O'Nan, Stewart

Colum, Mary, **I:** 246, 252, 256; **Supp. I Part 2:** 708, 709

"Columba" (Cliff), **Supp. XXII:** 74, 76

Columbia Anthology of American Poetry (Parini, ed.), **Supp. XXV:** 251

Columbiad, The (Barlow), **Supp. II Part 1:** 67, 72, 73, 74, 75–77, 79

Columbia History of the American Novel, **Supp. XV:** 270

Columbia Literary History of the United States, **Supp. XV:** 270

"Columbia U Poesy Reading—1975" (Corso), **Supp. XII:** 134

"Columbine, The" (Very), **Supp. XXV:** 242, 244

Columbus, Christopher, **I:** 253; **II:** 6, 310; **III:** 8; **Supp. I Part 2:** 397, 479, 480, 483, 486–488, 491, 495, 497, 498

"Columbus to Ferdinand" (Freneau), **Supp. II Part 1:** 255

Comanche Moon (McMurtry), **Supp. V:** 232

"Come, Break With Time" (Bogan), **Supp. III Part 1:** 52

Come, Thief (Hirshfield), **Supp. XXIII:** 134, 138

Come Along with Me (Jackson), **Supp. IX:** 117, 118, 122

Come Back, Charleston Blue (film), **Supp. XVI:** 144

Come Back, Little Sheba (film), **Supp. XXV:** 95

Come Back, Little Sheba (Inge), **Supp. XXV:** 94–95, 96–97

Comeback, The (Gurney), **Supp. V:** 97

"Come Back to the Raft Ag'in, Huck Honey!" (Fiedler), **Supp. XIII:** 93, **96–97,** 101

Come Blow Your Horn (Simon), **Supp. IV Part 2:** 574, 575, 577, 578, 586, 587, 591

Come By Here (Major), **Supp. XXII:** 171, 182

"Come Dance with Me in Ireland" (Jackson), **Supp. IX:** 119

"Comedian as the Letter C, The" (Stevens), **IV:** 84–85, 88; **Retro. Supp. I:** 297, 301, 302

"Comedy Cop" (Farrell), **II:** 45

Comedy of a Country House (J. Sturgis), **Supp. XX: 238**

"Comedy's Greatest Era" (Agee), **I:** 31

"Come In" (Frost), **Retro. Supp. I:** 139

"Come On, Baby" (Zinberg), **Supp. XV:** 195

Come On All You Ghosts (Zapruder), **Supp. XXVI:** 54

"Come on Back" (Gardner), **Supp. VI:** 73

"Come Out into the Sun" (Francis), **Supp. IX:** 82

Come Out into the Sun: Poems New and Selected (Francis), **Supp. IX: 82–83**

"Come out the Wilderness" (Baldwin), **Supp. I Part 1:** 63

Comer, Anjanette, **Supp. XI:** 305

Comer, Cornelia, **I:** 214

"Come Rain or Come Shine" (song), **Supp. XXII:** 6

"Come Shining: The Spiritual South" (exhibition; Luster), **Supp. XV:** 350

Come with Me: Poems for a Journey (Nye), **Supp. XIII:** 279

"Comforts of Home, The" (O'Connor), **III:** 349, 351, 355; **Retro. Supp. II:** 237

Comic Artist, The (Glaspell and Matson), **Supp. III Part 1:** 182

"Comic Imagination of the Young Dickens, The" (Wright), **Supp. III Part 2:** 591

"Comic Textures and Female Communities 1937 and 1977: Clare Boothe and Wendy Wasserstein" (Carlson), **Supp. XV:** 323

Comic Tragedies (Alcott), **Supp. I Part 1:** 33

Coming After (Notley), **Supp. XXII:** 223, 227, 230, 232, 236

"Coming and Going" (Gallagher), **Supp. XXIV:** 175, 176–177

"Coming Close" (Levine), **Supp. V:** 192

Coming Forth by Day of Osiris Jones, The (Aiken), **I:** 59

"Coming Home" (Gordon), **Supp. IV Part 1:** 309

"Coming Home to Vermont" (McCarriston), **Supp. XIV:** 269

"Coming in From the Cold" (Walker), **Supp. III Part 2:** 526

Coming into Eighty (Sarton), **Supp. VIII:** 262

"Coming into Eighty" (Sarton), **Supp. VIII:** 262

Coming into the Country (McPhee), **Supp. III Part 1:** 298, 301–306, 309, 310

Coming Into Writing (Cixous), **Supp. X:** 102

Coming of Age in Mississippi (Moody), **Supp. IV Part 1:** 11

Comings Back (Goldbarth), **Supp. XII:** 180

"Coming to Canada--Age Twenty Two" (Shields), **Supp. VII:** 311

Coming to Canada: Poems (Shields), **Supp. VII:** 311–312

"Coming to Memoir as a Journalist" (Epstein), **Supp. XXII:** 95

"Coming to the Morning" (Merwin), **Supp. III Part 1:** 356

"Coming to This" (Strand), **Supp. IV Part 2:** 627

Comiskey, Charles, **II:** 422

Commager, Henry Steele, **I:** 253; **Supp. I Part 1:** 372; **Supp. I Part 2:** 484, 647, 650

Command the Morning (Buck), **Supp. II Part 1:** 125

"CommComm" (Saunders), **Supp. XIX:** 234

"Commencement Address, A" (Brodsky), **Supp. VIII:** 31

"Commencement Day Address, The" (Schwartz), **Supp. II Part 2:** 660

Commentaries (Caesar), **II:** 502, 561

"Commentary" (Auden), **Supp. II Part 1:** 13

"Comment on Curb" (Hughes), **Supp. I Part 1:** 340

"Comments/Questions" (Nelson), **Supp. XVIII:** 172

"Commerce" (Nye), **Supp. XIII:** 281

Commins, Saxe, **Retro. Supp. I:** 73; **Retro. Supp. II:** 337

Commodity of Dreams & Other Stories, A (Nemerov), **III:** 268–269, 285

Common Carnage (Dobyns), **Supp. XIII:** 87

"Common Ground, A" (Levertov), **Supp. III Part 1:** 277

"Common Life, The" (Auden), **Supp. IV Part 1:** 302, 313

"Common Meter" (R. Fisher), **Supp. XIX:** 71

Common Room, A: Essays 1954–1987 (Price), **Supp. VI:** 264–265, 267

Commons, John, **Supp. I Part 2:** 645

Common Sense (Paine), **II:** 117; **Supp. I Part 1:** 231; **Supp. I Part 2:** 505, 506–508, 509, 513, 516, 517, 521

Communal Cot (Loy), **Supp. XXII:** 168

"Communication" (Dobyns), **Supp. XIII:** 91

"Communion" (Dubus), **Supp. VII:** 91

Communion (Mora), **Supp. XIII: 217–219**

Communist Manifesto, The (Marx and Engels), **II:** 463; **Supp. XXI:** 162–163

"Community Life" (Moore), **Supp. X:** 178

"Community of Glaciers, The" (Bass), **Supp. XVI:** 23

Comnes, Gregory, **Supp. IV Part 1:** 283, 284, 291

"Companions, The" (Nemerov), **III:** 269, 278, 287

Company of Poets, A (Simpson), **Supp. IX:** 265, 275

Company of Women, The (Gordon), **Supp. IV Part 1:** 302–304, 304, 306, 313

Company She Keeps, The (McCarthy), **II:** 562, 563–566

"Comparisons of Wonder" (Jarman), **Supp. XVII:** 114

Compass Flower, The (Merwin), **Supp. III Part 1:** 353, 357

"Compassionate Friendship" (Doolittle), **Supp. I Part 1:** 257, 258, 259, 260, 271

"Compatibility" (C. Frost), **Supp. XV:** 103

"Compendium" (Dove), **Supp. IV Part 1:** 248

"Compensation" (Teasdale), **Supp. XXVII:** 293

"Complaint" (W. C. Williams), **Retro. Supp. I:** 418

"Complete Birth of the Cool, The" (Wright), **Supp. XV:** 343, 344

Complete Collected Poems of William Carlos Williams, 1906–1938, The (W. C. Williams), **Retro. Supp. I:** 424

"Complete Destruction" (W. C. Williams), **IV:** 413

"Complete Life of John Hopkins, The" (O. Henry), **Supp. II Part 1:** 405

Complete Poems (Frost), **II:** 155, 164

Complete Poems (Reznikoff), **Supp. XIV:** 281

Complete Poems (Sandburg), **III:** 590–592, 594, 596

Complete Poems, The (Bishop), **Retro. Supp. II:** 49; **Supp. I Part 1:** 72, 82, 94

Complete Poems, The (Bradbury), **Supp. IV Part 1:** 105

Complete Poems, The: 1927–1979 (Bishop), **Retro. Supp. II:** 51

Complete Poems of Emily Dickinson, The (Bianchi and Hampson, eds.), **Retro. Supp. I:** 35

Complete Poems of Emily Dickinson, The (T. H. Johnson, ed.), **I:** 470

Complete Poems of Frederick Goddard Tuckerman, The (Momaday), **Supp.**

IV Part 2: 480

Complete Poems of Hart Crane, **Retro. Supp. II:** 81

Complete Poems to Solve, The (Swenson), **Supp. IV Part 2:** 652

Complete Poetical Works (A. Lowell), **II:** 512, 516–517

Complete Poetical Works (Hulme), **III:** 464

Complete Poetical Works (Longfellow), **Retro. Supp. II:** 154

Complete Poetical Works of Amy Lowell, The (A. Lowell), **Supp. XV:** 295–296

Complete Stories (O'Connor), **Supp. X:** 1

Complete Tragedies, The: Euripedes II, **Supp. XV:** 50

"Complete with Starry Night and Bourbon Shots" (Goldbarth), **Supp. XII:** 192–193

Complete Works of Kate Chopin, The (Seyersted, ed.), **Supp. I Part 1:** 212, 225

Complete Works of the Gawain-Poet (Gardner), **Supp. VI:** 64, 65

"Complex Histories, Contested Memories: Some Reflections on Remembering Difficult Pasts" (E. Hoffman, lecture), **Supp. XVI:** 155

"Complicated Thoughts About a Small Son" (White), **Supp. I Part 2:** 678

"Compliments of the Season" (O. Henry), **Supp. II Part 1:** 392, 399

"Compline" (Auden), **Supp. II Part 1:** 23

"Composing a Life" (Pickering), **Supp. XXI:** 191, 196

Composition as Explanation (Stein), **IV:** 32, 33, 38

"Composition as Explanation" (Stein), **IV:** 27, 28

"Compound Eye, The" (Davison), **Supp. XXVI:** 74

"Compounding *of* Consciousness" (James), **II:** 358–359

Comprehensive Bibliography (Hanneman), **II:** 259

Compton-Burnett, Ivy, **I:** 93; **II:** 580; **Supp. XXIII:** 209

Compulsion (Levin), **Supp. XXVII:** 133, 139, 142, 144–145, 147

"Comrade Laski, C.P.U.S.A. \[M.L.\]" (Didion), **Supp. IV Part 1:** 200

"Comrade Poets" (Hayes), **Supp. XXVI:** 144

Comstock, Anthony, **Retro. Supp. II:** 95

Comus (Milton), **II:** 12; **Supp. I Part 2:** 622

Conan Doyle, Arthur. *See* Doyle, Arthur Conan

Conan the Barbarian (comic), **Supp. XXVII:** 129

Conan the Barbarian (film), **Supp. XXVII:** 129

Conceptions of Reality in Modern American Poetry (Dembo), **Supp. I Part 1:** 272

"Concept of Character in Fiction, The" (Gass), **Supp. VI:** 85, **86**

Concept of Dread, The (Kierkegaard), **III:** 305

"Concerning a Woman of Sin" (Hecht), **Supp. XXVII:** 94

Concerning Children (Gilman), **Supp. XI:** 206

"Concerning Mold upon the Skin, Etc." (J. Scott), **Supp. XVII:** 188

"Concerning Necessity" (Carruth), **Supp. XVI:** 57

"Concerning Some Recent Criticism of His Work" (Doty), **Supp. XI:** 131

Concerning the End for Which God Created the World (Edwards), **I:** 549, 557, 559

Concerning the League (Woodbury, Henry, and Webster, trans.), **Supp. XXVI:** 81, 82, 87, 90

"Concerning Things That Can Be Doubled"(Crooker), **Supp. XXIII:** 64

Concerto for Two Pianos, Winds, and Percussion (Bowles), **Supp. IV Part 1:** 83

"Concert of Tenses, A" (Gallagher), **Supp. XXIV:** 172

Concert of Tenses, A: Essays on Poetry (Gallagher), **Supp. XXIV:** 166, 167, 171–172

Conchologist's First Book, The (Poe), **III:** 412

Conclusive Evidence (Nabokov), **III:** 247–250, 252

"Concord Hymn" (Emerson), **II:** 19

Concrete Blonde, The (Connelly), **Supp. XXI:** 70–71, 78, 80

"Concrete Universal, The: Observations on the Understanding of Poetry" (Ransom), **III:** 480

Concurring Beasts (Dobyns), **Supp. XIII:** 76

Condé, Maryse, **Supp. XXIII:** 94

Condensed Novels and Other Papers (Harte), **Supp. II Part 1:** 342

"Condition, The" (Karmi; Everwine, trans.), **Supp. XV:** 78

Condition of Man, The (Mumford), **Supp. II Part 2:** 483, 484, 486, 495–496, 498

"Condolence" (Parker), **Supp. IX:** 191

"Condominium, The" (Elkin), **Supp. VI:** 49, **50–51,** 55, 56

Condon, Charles R., **Supp. XIII:** 163

Condor and the Cows, The: A South American Travel Diary (Isherwood and Caskey), **Supp. XIV:** 166

"Condor and the Guests, The" (Connell), **Supp. XIV:** 86

Condorcet, Marquis de, **Supp. I Part 2:** 511

Conduct of Life, The (Emerson), **II:** 1–5, 8

Conduct of Life, The (Mumford), **Supp. II Part 2:** 485, 496–497

"Conductor of Nothing, The" (Levine), **Supp. V:** 189

"Coney Island" (Teasdale), **Supp. XXVII:** 289

Coney Island of the Mind, A (Ferlinghetti), **Supp. XIX:** 4; **Supp. XXI:** 53

Confederacy of Dunces, A (Toole), **Supp. XXVI:** 239, 240, 242, 243–244, 246, 250–253

"Conference Male, The" (Mora), **Supp. XIII:** 218

"Confession" (Peacock), **Supp. XIX:** 206

Confession, The (Rinehart), **Supp. XXV:** 200

"Confessional" (Bidart), **Supp. XV:** 29–30, 31

"Confessional Poem" (Nelson), **Supp. XVIII:** 174

Confession de Claude, La (Zola), **I:** 411

"Confession of a House-Breaker, The" (Jewett), **Retro. Supp. II:** 146–147

Confession of Jereboam O. Beauchamp, The (pamphlet), **IV:** 253

Confessions (Augustine), **I:** 279; **Supp. XVI:** 288; **Supp. XXII:** 93

"Confessions" (Huddle), **Supp. XXVI:** 150

Confessions (Rousseau), **I:** 226

Confessions of a Barbarian: Selections from the Journals of Edward Abbey, 1951–1989 (Abbey; Petersen, ed.), **Supp. XIII:** 2, 4

"Confessions of a Latina Author" (Mora), **Supp. XIII:** 221

"Confessions of a Wannabe Negro" (McKnight), **Supp. XX: 152–153, 158**

Confessions of Nat Turner, The (Styron), **IV:** 98, 99, 105, 113–117; **Supp. X:** 16, 250

Confetti (Mora), **Supp. XIII:** 221

Confidence (James), **II:** 327, 328

Confidence-Man, The (Melville), **III:** 91; **Retro. Supp. I:** 255–256, 257; **Retro. Supp. II:** 121; **Supp. XIV:** 49

Confidence Man, The (Van Vechten), **Supp. II Part 2:** 737

Confidential Clerk, The (Eliot), **I:** 570, 571–572, 583, 584; **Retro. Supp. I:** 65

Confident Years, 1885–1915, The (Brooks), **I:** 257, 259; **Supp. I Part 2:** 650

"Configurations" (Ammons), **Supp. VII:** 28

Configurations: New and Selected Poems, 1958–1998 (Major), **Supp. XXII: 182**

Confronting the Horror: The Novels of Nelson Algren (Giles), **Supp. IX:** 11, 15

Confucius, **II:** 1; **III:** 456, 475; **Supp. IV Part 1:** 14

Confusion (Cozzens), **I:** 358, 359, 377, 378

"Confusion of Planes We Must Wander in Sleep, The" (Weigl), **Supp. XIX:** 283

Congdon, Don, **Supp. XXII:** 204

Congo (film), **Supp. IV Part 1:** 83

Congo (screenplay, Shanley), **Supp. XIV:** 316

"Congo, The" (Lindsay), **Supp. I Part 2:** 388–389, 392, 395

Congo and Other Poems, The (Lindsay), **Supp. I Part 2:** 379, 382, 389, 390, 391; **Supp. XXV:** 18

"Congregation" (Trethewey), **Supp. XXI:** 245, 247

"Congregation of Grackles, A"(Crooker), **Supp. XXIII:** 63

"Congress of the Insomniacs, The" (Simic), **Supp. VIII:** 281–282

Congreve, William, **III:** 195; **Supp. V:** 101; **Supp. XVIII:** 12

Coningsby (Disraeli), **II:** 127

"Conjectural Reading" (Bronk), **Supp. XXI:** 31

Conjectures of a Guilty Bystander (Merton), **Supp. VIII:** 197, 206, 207

Conjugal Bliss: A Comedy of Marital Arts (Nichols), **Supp. XIII:** 269

"Conjugation of the Paramecium, The" (Rukeyser), **Supp. VI:** 271

Conjugations and Reiterations (Murray), **Supp. XIX:** 161

"Conjuration" (Wilbur), **Supp. III Part 2:** 551

Conjure (recording), **Supp. X:** 241

Conjure (Reed), **Supp. X:** 240, 242

Conjure-Man Dies, The: A Mystery Tale of Dark Harlem (R. Fisher), **Supp. XIX:** 65, 71, **77–78**; **Supp. XVI:** 143

Conjure Woman, The (Chesnutt), **Supp. II Part 1:** 193; **Supp. XIV:** 57, **58–61,** 62, 63

Conklin, Grof, **Supp. I Part 2:** 672

Conklin, Peggy, **Supp. XXII:** 27

Conkling, Hilda, **II:** 530

Conkling, Roscoe, **III:** 506

Conley, Robert J., **Supp. V:** 232

Conley, Susan, **Supp. XIII:** 111, 112

Connaroe, Joel, **Supp. IV Part 2:** 690

"Connecticut Lad, A" (White), **Supp. I Part 2:** 677

"Connecticut Valley" (Cowley), **Supp. II Part 1:** 141–142

Connecticut Yankee in King Arthur's Court, A (Twain), **I:** 209; **II:** 276; **IV:** 205

Connell, Evan S., **Supp. XIV: 79–100;** **Supp. XXIII:** 302

Connell, Norreys (pseudonym). *See* O'Riordan, Conal Holmes O'Connell

Connelly, Marc, **III:** 394; **Supp. I Part 2:** 679; **Supp. IX:** 190

Connelly, Michael, **Supp. XXI: 67–82**

Conner, Dan, **Supp. XXIII:** 125

Connery, Thomas B., **Supp. XVII:** 106

Connoisseur, The (Connell), **Supp. XIV:** 87

"Connoisseur of Chaos" (Stevens), **IV:** 89; **Retro. Supp. I:** 306

Connolly, Cyril, **Supp. XIV:** 158, 343, 348

Connors, Elizabeth. *See* Lindsay, Mrs. Vachel (Elizabeth Connors)

Connotations (Kenny), **Supp. XXIII:** 143, 144, 146, 150, 155

Conover, Roger, **Supp. I Part 1:** 95

Conover, Roger L., **Supp. XXII:** 155, 162

Conquering Horse (Manfred), **Supp. X:** 126

Conqueror, The (Atherton), **Supp. XXIV:** 23

"Conqueror Worm, The" (Poe), **Retro. Supp. II:** 261

Conquest of Canaan (Dwight), **Supp. I Part 1:** 124

Conquistador (MacLeish), **III:** 2, 3, 13–14, 15

Conrad, Alfred, **Retro. Supp. II:** 245

Conrad, Alfred H., **Supp. I Part 2:** 552

Conrad, C. A., **Supp. XXII:** 155

Conrad, David, **Supp. I Part 2:** 552

Conrad, Jacob, **Supp. I Part 2:** 552

Conrad, Joseph, **I:** 123, 343, 394, 405, 409, 415, 421, 485, 506, 575–576, 578; **II:** 58, 73, 74, 91, 92, 144, 263, 320, 338, 595; **III:** 28, 102, 106, 328, 464, 467, 491, 512; **IV:** 476; **Retro. Supp. I:** 80, 91, 106, 108, 231, 274, 377; **Retro. Supp. II:** 222; **Supp. I Part 1:** 292; **Supp. I Part 2:** 621, 622; **Supp. IV Part 1:** 197, 341; **Supp. IV Part 2:** 680; **Supp. V:** 249, 251, 262, 298, 307, 311; **Supp. VIII:** 4, 310; **Supp. XIV:** 112; **Supp. XIX:** 27; **Supp. XVI:** 158, 212; **Supp. XVIII:** 98, 102; **Supp. XX: 195;** **Supp. XXIV:** 286; **Supp. XXV:** 208

Conrad, Paul, **Supp. I Part 2:** 552

Conrad, Peter, **Supp. IV Part 2:** 688

"Conrad Aiken: From Savannah to Emerson" (Cowley), **Supp. II Part 1:** 43

Conrad Richter's Ohio Trilogy (Edwards), **Supp. XVIII:** 220

Conroy, Frank, **Supp. VIII:** 145; **Supp. XI:** 245; **Supp. XVI: 63–78;** **Supp. XXII:** 50

Conroy, Jack, **Supp. XXII:** 1, 5, 10

Conroy, Pat, **Supp. XVIII:** 193; **Supp. XXII:** 239

Cons, Scams, and Grifts (Gores), **Supp. XXI:** 70

Conscience with the Power and Cases thereof (Ames), **IV:** 158

"Conscientious Objector, The" (Shapiro), **Supp. II Part 2:** 710

"Consciousness and Dining" (Harrison), **Supp. VIII:** 46

"Conscript, The" (Lovecraft), **Supp. XXV:** 119

"Conscription Camp" (Shapiro), **Supp. II Part 2:** 705

"Consejos de Nuestra Señora de Guadalupe: Counsel from the Brown Virgin" (Mora), **Supp. XIII:** 224

"Conservation Esthetic" (Leopold), **Supp. XIV:** 179, 181, 186, 189–190

"Conserving Natural and Cultural Diversity: The Prose and Poetry of Pat Mora" (Murphy), **Supp. XIII:** 214

Considerable Town, A (M. F. K. Fisher), **Supp. XVII:** 90

"Considerations by the Way" (Emerson), **II:** 2, 5

Consider the Oyster (M. F. K. Fisher), **Supp. XVII:** 84, 87

Considine, Bob, **II:** 424

"Consolation" (Bausch), **Supp. VII:** 48

"Consolation for Tamar" (Stallings), **Supp. XXV:** 228

Consolation of Philosophy, The (Boethius), **Supp. XXVI:** 250

"Consolations" (Stafford), **Supp. XI:** 329

"Conspiracy of History, The: E. L. Doctorow's *The Book of Daniel*" (Levine), **Supp. IV Part 1:** 221

Conspiracy of Kings, The (Barlow), **Supp. II Part 1:** 80

Conspiracy of Pontiac, The (Parkman), **Supp. II Part 2:** 590, 595, 596, 599–600

Constab Ballads (McKay), **Supp. X:** 131, 133

Constance (Kenyon), **Supp. VII:** 170–172

Constancy (Boyce), **Supp. XVII:** 100; **Supp. XXI:** 6, 7, 12

"Constellation Orion, The" (Kooser), **Supp. XIX:** 120

Constitution of the Confederacy by Dekanawidah: Collected and Translated from \[the\] Mohawk Text by Chief Seth Newhouse, **Supp. XXVI:** 90

Constitution of the Five Nations, The (Parker), **Supp. XXVI:** 87

Construction of Boston, The (Koch), **Supp. XV:** 187

"Constructive Work" (Du Bois), **Supp. II Part 1:** 172

"Consumer's Report" (X. J. Kennedy), **Supp. XV:** 161–162

"Consumption" (Bryant), **Supp. I Part 1:** 169–170

Contact Collection of Contemporary Writers (McAlmon), **Supp. XXII:** 166

"Contagiousness of Puerperal Fever, The" (Holmes), **Supp. I Part 1:** 303–304

"Contemplation in a World of Action" (Merton), **Supp. VIII:** 204

"Contemplation of Poussin" (Sarton), **Supp. VIII:** 261

"Contemplations" (Bradstreet), **Supp. I Part 1:** 112, 113, 119–122

Contemporaries (Kazin), **Supp. VIII:** 102, **103–104**

Contemporary American Playwrights (Bigsby), **Supp. XV:** 332

Contemporary American Poetry (Poulin, ed.), **Supp. IX:** 272; **Supp. XI:** 259

Contemporary Authors Autobiography, **Supp. XXII:** 225

Contending Forces (Hopkins), **Supp. XVIII:** 284

"Contentment" (Holmes), **Supp. I Part 1:** 307

"Contents" (Halliday), **Supp. XIX:** 92

"Contest, The" (Paley), **Supp. VI:** 223, 230, 231

"Contest for Aaron Gold, The" (P. Roth), **Supp. III Part 2:** 403

Continental Drift (Banks), **Supp. V:** 13–14, 16, 227

Continental Op, The (Hammett), **Supp. IV Part 1:** 344

Continent's End: An Anthology of Contemporary California Poets (Taggard, Sterling, and Rorty, eds.), **Supp. XXII:** 276

Continuing Education, A (Pickering), **Supp. XXI:** 194, 195–196

Continuity of American Poetry, The (Pearce), **Supp. I Part 1:** 111; **Supp. I Part 2:** 475

Continuous Harmony, A: Essays Cultural and Agricultural (Berry), **Supp. X:** 33

Continuous Life, The (Strand), **Supp. IV Part 2:** 630, 631–633

Contoski, Victor, **Supp. XII:** 181

"Contract" (Lardner), **II:** 432

"Contraption, The" (Swenson), **Supp. IV Part 2:** 643

"Contrariness of the Mad Farmer, The" (Berry), **Supp. X:** 35

"Contrast, a Spenetic Effusion, The" (J. Schoolcraft), **Supp. XXIII:** 231–232

"Contrition" (Dubus), **Supp. VII:** 84

"Control Burn" (Snyder), **Supp. VIII:** 301

"Control Is the Mainspring" (Komunyakaa), **Supp. XIII:** 122, 124

"Controlling the 'Sloppiness of Things' in Frank Conroy's *Stop-Time*" (Strychacz), **Supp. XVI:** 69–70

Control of Nature, The (McPhee), **Supp. III Part 1:** 310–313

Controversial Sholem Asch, The (Siegel), **Supp. XXIII:** 3

"Conventional Wisdom, The" (Elkin), **Supp. VI:** 52–53

"Convergence" (Ammons), **Supp. VII:** 28

"Convergence of the Twain, The" (Hardy), **Supp. VIII:** 31, 32

Conversation (Aiken), **I:** 54

Conversation at Midnight (Millay), **III:** 138

"Conversation of Eiros and Charmion, The" (Poe), **III:** 412

"Conversation on Conversation" (Stowe), **Supp. I Part 2:** 587

"Conversations in Moscow" (Levertov), **Supp. III Part 1:** 282

Conversations on Some of the Old Poets (J. R. Lowell), **Supp. I Part 2:** 405

Conversations with Albert Murray (Maguire, ed.), **Supp. XIX:** 160–161

Conversations with Byron (Blessington), **Retro. Supp. II:** 58

Conversations with Eudora Welty (Prenshaw, ed.), **Retro. Supp. I:** 339, 340, 341, 342, 343, 352, 354

"Conversations with Helmholtz" (Allen), **Supp. XV:** 15

Conversations with Ishmael Reed (Dick and Singh, eds.), **Supp. X:** 244

Conversations with James Baldwin (Standley and Pratt, eds.), **Retro. Supp. II:** 6

Conversations with Richard Wilbur (Wilbur), **Supp. III Part 2:** 542–543

"Conversation with a Fireman from Brooklyn" (Gallagher), **Supp. XXIV:** 169–170

"Conversation with My Father, A" (Paley), **Supp. VI:** 220

"Conversion of the Jews, The" (P. Roth), **Retro. Supp. II:** 281; **Supp. III Part 2:** 404, 406; **Supp. XXVI:** 119

Convict, The: Stories (Burke), **Supp. XIV:** 25

"Convicta et Combusta" (J. Scott), **Supp. XVII:** 189

"Convolvulus" (Schott), **Supp. XXIII:** 248

"Convoy" (Weigl), **Supp. XIX:** 278

Conway, Jill, **Supp. I Part 1:** 19

Coode, John, **I:** 132

Cook, Bruce, **Supp. XII:** 130, 131, 133–134

Cook, Captain James, **I:** 2

Cook, Eleanor, **Retro. Supp. I:** 311

Cook, Elisha, **Supp. IV Part 1:** 356

Cook, Elizabeth Christine, **II:** 106

Cook, George Cram "Jig", **Supp. XXI:** 5, 6

Cook, Jessie W., **Supp. XXV:** 278

Cook, Johnny, **Supp. XXIV:** 248

Cook, Mercer, **Supp. IV Part 1:** 368

Cook, Richard, **Supp. XXII:** 158

Cookbook Collector, The (Goodman), **Supp. XXVI:** 130–131

Cooke, Alistair, **III:** 113, 119, 120

Cooke, Delmar G., **II:** 271

Cooke, Grace MacGowan, **Supp. V:** 285

Cooke, Philip Pendleton, **III:** 420

Cooke, Rose Terry, **II:** 401; **Retro. Supp. II:** 51, 136, 138; **Supp. XIII:** 152

"Cookie" (Taylor), **Supp. V:** 320

"Cookies, The" (Nye), **Supp. XIII:** 281

Cooking of Provincial France, The (M. F. K. Fisher), **Supp. XVII:** 89

Cook-Lynn, Elizabeth, **Supp. IV Part 1:** 325

"Cool Air" (Lovecraft), **Supp. XXV:** 110

Coolbrith, Ina, **I:** 193, 196

"Coole Park" (Yeats), **Supp. VIII:** 155, 159

"Coole Park and Ballylee" (Yeats), **Supp. VIII:** 156

Cooler by the Lake (Heinemann), **Supp. XXII:** 103, **114**

Cooley, John, **Supp. V:** 214

Cooley, Peter, **Supp. XIII:** 76

Coolidge, Calvin, **I:** 498; **II:** 95; **Supp. I Part 2:** 647

Cooling Time: An American Poetry Vigil (Wright), **Supp. XV:** 353

Cool Million, A (West), **III:** 425; **IV:** 287, 288, 297–299, 300; **Retro. Supp. II:** 321, 322–323, 328, **335–337**

"Cool Million, A" (screen story) (West and Ingster), **Retro. Supp. II:** 330

"Cool Tombs" (Sandburg), **III:** 554

Coon, Ross, **IV:** 196

Cooney, Seamus, **Supp. XIV:** 289

"Coon Hunt" (White), **Supp. I Part 2:** 669

Co-op (Sinclair), **Supp. V:** 290

Cooper, Bernard, **Supp. XI:** 129

Cooper, Frederic Taber, **Supp. XX: 219–220; Supp. XXIV:** 28–29

Cooper, Gary, **Supp. IV Part 2:** 524

Cooper, James Fenimore, **I:** 211, 257, **335–357; II:** 74, 277, 295–296, 302, 306, 309, 313, 314; **III:** 51; **IV:** 205, 333; **Retro. Supp. I:** 246; **Retro. Supp. I:** 160; **Supp. I Part 1:** 141, 155, 156, 158, 171, 372; **Supp. I Part 2:** 413, 495, 579, 585, 652, 660; **Supp. IV Part 1:** 80; **Supp. IV Part 2:** 463, 469; **Supp. V:** 209–210; **Supp. VIII:** 189; **Supp. XIV:** 227; **Supp. XVIII:**

4; **Supp. XXIII:** 178

Cooper, Mrs. James Fenimore (Susan A. De Lancey), **I:** 338, 351, 354

Cooper, Jane, **Supp. XV:** 259

Cooper, Rand Richards, **Supp. XVI:** 74

Cooper, Susan Fenimore, **I:** 337, 354

Cooper, William, **I:** 337–338, 351

Cooper, Mrs. William, **I:** 337

Cooperman, Robert, **Supp. XXIII:** 247

Coover, Robert, **Supp. IV Part 1:** 388; **Supp. V:** 39–55; **Supp. XII:** 152; **Supp. XIV:** 96; **Supp. XVII:** 6; **Supp. XXI:** 236; **Supp. XXII:** 259

Copacetic (Komunyakaa), **Supp. XIII:** **116–118,** 126

Cope, Wendy, **Supp. XV:** 117

Copelin, David, **Supp. XXIV:** 264

Copland, Aaron, **II:** 586; **Supp. I Part 1:** 281; **Supp. III Part 2:** 619; **Supp. IV Part 1:** 79, 80–81, 84; **Supp. XXII:** 283; **Supp. XXVI:** 134

Coplas de Don Jorge Manrique (Longfellow, trans.), **II:** 488, 492

Coppée, François Edouard Joachim, **II:** 325

Copperhead, The (Frederic), **II:** 134–135

Copperhead Cane (J. W. Miller), **Supp. XX:** **163, 164, 166–167**

Copper Sun (Cullen), **Supp. IV Part 1:** 167, 168

Coppola, Francis Ford, **Supp. XI:** 171, 172; **Supp. XII:** 75

Coprolites (Goldbarth), **Supp. XII:** **177–178,** 180, 183

Coquette, The (Foster), **Supp. XXV:** 35, 36, 38–45

Coral and Captive Israel (Reznikoff), **Supp. XIV:** 288

"Coral Ring, The" (Stowe), **Supp. I Part 2:** 586

"Cora Unashamed" (Hughes), **Supp. I Part 1:** 329, 330

"Corazón del Corrido" (Mora), **Supp. XIII:** 225

Corban Ephphata (Li Lin Lee), **Supp. XV:** 225

Corbett, Gentlemen Jim, **II:** 416

Corbett, William, **Supp. XI:** 248; **Supp. XVI:** 286, 295; **Supp. XXIV:** 45

Corbière, Jean Antoine, **II:** 354–355, 528

Cordiall Water, A: A garland of Odd & Old Receipts to Assuage the Ills of Man and Beast (M. F. K. Fisher), **Supp. XVII:** 88, 90

Cording, Robert, **Supp. IX:** 328; **Supp. XII:** 184

Core, George, **Supp. XVIII:** 86; **Supp. XXI:** 193

Corelli, Marie, **III:** 579

Corey, Lewis, **Supp. I Part 2:** 645

"Corinna's Going a-Maying" (Herrick), **Supp. XIV:** 8, 9

"Coriolan" (Eliot), **I:** 580

"Coriolanus and His Mother" (Schwartz), **Supp. II Part 2:** 643, 644–645

"Corkscrew" (Hammett), **Supp. IV Part 1:** 345, 347

Corkum, Gerald, **I:** 37

Corky's Brother (Neugeboren), **Supp. XVI:** 225

"Corky's Brother" (Neugeboren), **Supp. XVI:** 225

Corliss, Richard, **Supp. VIII:** 73; **Supp. XXVII:** 96

Corman, Cid, **Supp. III Part 2:** 624, 625, 626, 627, 628; **Supp. IV Part 1:** 144; **Supp. VIII:** 292; **Supp. XV:** 74, 153; **Supp. XXI:** 23, 27

Corman, Roger, **Supp. XXV:** 154

"Corn" (Lanier), **Supp. I Part 1:** 352, 353, 354, 356–361, 364, 366

Corn, Alfred, **Supp. IX:** 156; **Supp. XV:** 250

Corneille, Pierre, **Supp. I Part 2:** 716; **Supp. IX:** 131

Cornelius, Randy, **Supp. XXVI:** 89

Cornell, Esther, **I:** 231

Cornell, Joseph, **Supp. XXI:** 131; **Supp. XXII:** 167, 168

Cornell, Katherine, **IV:** 356

Cornell, Valerie, **Supp. XX:** **94–95**

"Corners" (Dunn), **Supp. XI:** 148

Cornhuskers (Sandburg), **III:** 583–585

"Corn-Planting, The" (Anderson), **I:** 114

"Corn story (or the origin of corn)"(J. Schoolcraft), **Supp. XXIII:** 234–235

Cornucopia: New and Selected Poems, 1975–2002 (Peacock), **Supp. XIX:** **203–204**

Corn Village (Le Sueur), **Supp. XXIII:** 167

Coronation Murder-Mystery, The (O'Hara, Ashbery, and Koch), **Supp. XXIII:** 217

"Coroner's Report" (Wrigley), **Supp. XVIII:** 295

"Corporal of Artillery" (Dubus), **Supp. VII:** 84, 85

"Corpse Bird, The" (Rash), **Supp. XXVII:** 219, 228

"Corpse Plant, The" (Rich), **Supp. I Part 2:** 555

Corpus Christi (McNally), **Supp. XIII:** **205–206,** 209

Corradi, Juan, **Supp. IV Part 1:** 208

Corrections, The (Franzen), **Supp. XIX:** 54; **Supp. XX: 83,** 84, 85, 90, 91, 91–93, 95

Corregidora (G. Jones), **Supp. XXIV:** 183–184, **185–187,** 190, 193, 194, 195

"Correspondences" (Baudelaire), **I:** 63

"Corrido de Gregorio Cortez" (Mora), **Supp. XIII:** 225

"Corrigenda" (Komunyakaa), **Supp. XIII:** 115, 116

Corrosive Sublimate (Sorrentino), **Supp. XXI:** 226, 228

Corruption City (McCoy), **Supp. XIII:** 175

Corso, Gregory, **Supp. II Part 1:** 30; **Supp. IV Part 1:** 90; **Supp. XII:** 117–138; **Supp. XIV:** 150; **Supp. XVI:** 135; **Supp. XXI:** 53; **Supp. XXIII:** 215

Corsons Inlet (Ammons), **Supp. VII:** 25–26, 28–33, 36

"Corsons Inlet" (Ammons), **Supp. VII:** 25–26

Cortázar, Julio, **Retro. Supp. I:** 278; **Supp. XXII:** 265

"Cortège for Rosenbloom" (Stevens), **IV:** 81

Cortez, Hernando, **III:** 2

" 'Coruscating Glamour': Lynda Hull and the Movies" (Goldstein), **Supp. XXI:** 134

Cory, William Johnson, **Supp. XX: 230, 231**

Coser, Lewis, **Supp. I Part 2:** 650

Cosgrave, Patrick, **Retro. Supp. II:** 185

Cosmic Optimism: A Study of the Interpretation of Evolution by American Poets from Emerson to Robinson (Conner), **Supp. I Part 1:** 73

Cosmogony of the Iroquois Confederacy (Newhouse), **Supp. XXVI:** 87

Cosmological Eye, The (H. Miller), **III:** 174, 184

"Cosmological Eye, The" (H. Miller), **III:** 183

"Cosmos" (Beattie), **Supp. V:** 35

"Cost, The" (Hecht), **Supp. X:** 62–63

Costello, Bonnie, **Retro. Supp. II:** 40

Costello, Mark, **Supp. XXIII:** 290

Costner, Kevin, **Supp. VIII:** 45

"Cost of Living, The" (Malamud), **Supp. I Part 2:** 429, 437

"Costume as Metaphor" (Bronk), **Supp. XXI:** 26

Cott, Jonathan, **Supp. XVI:** 104, 106

"Cottagers' Corner" column (D. West), **Supp. XVIII:** 286

"Cottage Street, 1953" (Wilbur), **Supp. III Part 2:** 543, 561

"Cottagette, The" (Gilman), **Supp. XI:** 207

Cotten, Joseph, **Supp. IV Part 2:** 524

Cotter, James Finn, **Supp. X:** 202

Cotton, John, **Supp. I Part 1:** 98, 101, 110, 111, 116

Cotton, Joseph, **Supp. XII:** 160

Cotton, Seaborn, **Supp. I Part 1:** 101

Cotton Club, The (Major), **Supp. XXII:** 174

"Cotton Club Classics" (Halliday), **Supp. XIX:** 92, 93

Cotton Comes to Harlem (C. Himes), **Supp. XVI:** 143, 144

Cotton Comes to Harlem (film, O. Davis), **Supp. XVI:** 144

"Cotton Song" (Toomer), **Supp. IX:** 312

Couch, W. T., **Supp. X:** 46

Coughlin, Ruth Pollack, **Supp. VIII:** 45

Coulette, Henri, **Supp. V:** 180; **Supp. XIII:** 312; **Supp. XV:** 74, 75

Coultrap-McQuin, Susan, **Supp. XVI:** 85, 92

"Council of State, A" (Dunbar), **Supp. II Part 1:** 211, 213

Count Bruga (Hecht), **Supp. XXV:** 27; **Supp. XXVII:** 89

"Count Dracula" (Allen), **Supp. XV:** 15

"Countee Cullen at 'The Heights' " (Tuttleton), **Supp. IV Part 1:** 166

Counterfeiters, The (Gide), **Supp. IV Part 1:** 80; **Supp. IV Part 2:** 681

"Countering" (Ammons), **Supp. VII:** 28

Counterlife, The (P. Roth), **Retro. Supp. II:** 279, 280, 291; **Supp. III Part 2:** 424–426

Counter-Statement (Burke), **I:** 270–272; **IV:** 431

"Countess, The" (Whittier), **Supp. I Part 2:** 691, 694

Count Frontenac and New France Under Louis XIV (Parkman), **Supp. II Part 2:** 607, 609–610

"Counting Small-Boned Bodies" (R. Bly), **Supp. IV Part 1:** 62

"Counting the Body"(Schott), **Supp. XXIII:** 251–252

"Counting the Children" (Gioia), **Supp. XV: 122–123**

"Counting the Mad" (Justice), **Supp. VII:** 117

"Count Lothar's Heart" (Boyle), **Supp. XXIV:** 58

Count of Monte Cristo, The (Dumas), **III:** 386, 396; **Supp. XVII:** 64, 216

"Countries We Live In, The" (Zach; Everwine, trans.), **Supp. XV:** 87

"Country Boy in Boston, The" (Howells), **II:** 255

Country By-Ways (Jewett), **II:** 402

Country Doctor, A (Jewett), **II:** 391, 392, 396, 404–405; **Retro. Supp. II:** 131, 141, 146

"Country Full of Swedes" (Caldwell), **I:** 297, 309

Country Girl, The (Odets), **Supp. II Part 2:** 546, 547, 548–549

"Country House" (Kumin), **Supp. IV Part 2:** 446

"Country Husband, The" (Cheever), **Supp. I Part 1:** 184, 189

"Country Life" (Pickering), **Supp. XXI:** 197

"Country Marriage" (C. Frost), **Supp. XV:** 99

Countrymen of Bones (R. O. Butler), **Supp. XII:** 62, **65–66**

"Country Mouse, The" (Bishop), **Retro. Supp. II:** 37, 38, 51

Country Music: Selected Early Poems (Wright), **Supp. V:** 332, 335, 338, 342

Country of a Thousand Years of Peace, The (Merrill), **Supp. III Part 1:** 321, 322, 331

"Country of Elusion, The" (O. Henry), **Supp. II Part 1:** 407

Country Of Language, The (Sanders), **Supp. XVI:** 277

Country of Marriage, The (Berry), **Supp. X:** 33

Country of Strangers, A (Richter), **Supp. XVIII:** 217

Country of Survivors (Di Piero), **Supp. XIX:** 36

Country of the Pointed Firs, The (Jewett), **II:** 392, 399, 405, 409–411; **Retro. Supp. I:** 6; **Retro. Supp. II:** 134, 136, 139, 140, 141, 145, 146, 147; **Supp. VIII:** 126; **Supp. XIII:** 152; **Supp. XXIII:** 275, 278

"Country Printer, The" (Freneau), **Supp. II Part 1:** 269

"Country Song" (Stallings), **Supp. XXV:** 222, 234

"Country Wife, The" (Gioia), **Supp. XV:** 120

Count Your Bullets (film), **Supp. XVII:** 141

Count Zero (W. Gibson), **Supp. XVI:** 19, **126–127,** 129

Coup, The (Updike), **Retro. Supp. I:** 331, 334, 335

"Coup de Grâce, The" (Bierce), **I:** 202

Couperin, François, **III:** 464

"Couple, The" (Olds), **Supp. X:** 206

"Couple of Hamburgers, A" (Thurber), **Supp. I Part 2:** 616

"Couple of Nuts, A" (Z. Fitzgerald), **Supp. IX:** 58, 71, 72

"Couples" (Halliday), **Supp. XIX:** 89

Couples (Updike), **IV:** 214, 215, 216, 217, 227, 229–230; **Retro. Supp. I:** 320, 327, 330; **Supp. XII:** 296

Cournos, John, **III:** 465; **Supp. I Part 1:** 258

"Course in Creative Writing, A" (Stafford), **Supp. XI:** 327

"Course of a Particular, The" (Stevens), **Retro. Supp. I:** 312

"Coursier de Jeanne d'Arc, Le" (McCarriston), **Supp. XIV:** 267–268

Courtier, The (Castiglione), **III:** 282

" 'Courtin,' The" (J. R. Lowell), **Supp. I Part 2:** 415

"Courting" (Huddle), **Supp. XXVI:** 151

"Courting of Sister Wisby, The" (Jewett), **Retro. Supp. II:** 134, 135, 146

"Courting the Famous Figures at the Grotto of Improbable Thought" (B. Kelly), **Supp. XVII:** 127–128

Courtney, W. L., **Supp. XXIV:** 29

"Courtship" (Dove), **Supp. IV Part 1:** 248

"Courtship, A"(Thompson), **Supp. XXIII:** 293

"Courtship, Diligence" (Dove), **Supp. IV Part 1:** 248

Courtship of Miles Standish, The (Longfellow), **II:** 489, 502–503; **Retro. Supp. II:** 155, **161–162,** 163, 166, 168

"Cousin Aubrey" (Taylor), **Supp. V:** 328

"Cousin Claire" (Andrews), **Supp. XXVI:** 11

Cousine Bette (Balzac), **Retro. Supp. II:** 98

Couturier, Maurice, **Supp. IV Part 1:** 44

Covarrubias, Miguel, **Supp. XVI:** 187

Cove, The (Rash), **Supp. XXVII:** 225–226

"Covered Bridges" (Kingsolver), **Supp. VII:** 203

"Cover Photograph" (Nelson), **Supp. XVIII:** 173

"Cover Stories" (Skloot), **Supp. XX: 195, 207**

"Cover Versions" (Halliday), **Supp. XIX:** 84

Cowan, Lester, **III:** 148

Cowan, Louise, **IV:** 120, 125

Coward, Noel, **Retro. Supp. I:** 65; **Supp. I Part 1:** 332; **Supp. V:** 101; **Supp. XV:** 329; **Supp. XXIV:** 267

"Cowardice" (Theroux), **Supp. VIII:** 313

Cowboy Mouth (Shepard), **Supp. III Part 2:** 441–442

"Cowboys" (Salter). *See* "Dirt" (Salter)

Cowboys (Shepard), **Supp. III Part 2:** 432

Cowboys #2 (Shepard), **Supp. III Part 2:** 437, 438

Cowell, Henry, **Supp. IV Part 1:** 80, 82

Cowen, Philip, **Supp. XX:** 2

Cowen, Wilson Walker, **Supp. IV Part 2:** 435

Cowie, Alexander, **IV:** 70

"Cow in Apple Time, The" (Frost), **II:** 154; **Retro. Supp. I:** 131

Cowl, Jane, **IV:** 357

Cowley, Abraham, **III:** 508; **IV:** 158; **Supp. I Part 1:** 357

Cowley, Malcolm, **I:** 246, 253, 254, 255, 256, 257, 283, 385; **II:** 26, 57, 94, 456; **III:** 606; **IV:** 123; **Retro. Supp. I:** 73, 91, 97; **Retro. Supp. II:** 77, 83, 89, 221, 330; **Supp. I Part 1:** 174; **Supp. I Part 2:** 609, 610, 620, 647, 654, 678; **Supp. II Part 1:** 103, **135–156; Supp. VIII:** 96; **Supp. XV:** 142; **Supp. XX: 76; Supp. XXVI:** 17

Cowley, Marguerite Frances Baird (Mrs. Malcolm Cowley), **Supp. I Part 2:** 615; **Supp. II Part 1:** 138, 139

Cowley, Muriel Maurer (Mrs. Malcolm Cowley), **Supp. II Part 1:** 139

Cowley, Susan Cheever (Susan Cheever), **Supp. I Part 1:** 175; **Supp. IX:** 133; **Supp. XXIV:** 97

Cowper, William, **II:** 17, 304; **III:** 508, 511; **Supp. I Part 1:** 150, 151, 152; **Supp. I Part 2:** 539

"Cow Wandering in the Bare Field, The" (Jarrell), **II:** 371, 388

Cox, Martha Heasley, **Supp. IX:** 2, 4, 11–12

Cox, Sidney, **Retro. Supp. I:** 131; **Supp. XXI:** 19, 21

Cox, Stephen, **Supp. IV Part 2:** 523, 524

Cox, Steve, **Supp. XIX:** 116, 128

Coxey, Jacob, **I:** 464

"Coxon Fund, The" (James), **Retro. Supp. I:** 228

"Coy Mistress" (A. Finch), **Supp. XVII:** 72

Coyne, Patricia, **Supp. V:** 123

"Coyote Ortiz: *Canis latrans latrans* in the Poetry of Simon Ortiz" (P. C. Smith), **Supp. IV Part 2:** 509

Coyote's Daylight Trip (Gunn Allen), **Supp. IV Part 1:** 320, 324

Coyote Was Here (Ortiz), **Supp. IV Part 2:** 499

Cozzens, James Gould, **I: 358–380; II:** 459

Crabbe, George, **II:** 304; **III:** 469, 508, 511, 521; **Supp. XXIV:** 159

"Crab-Boil" (Dove), **Supp. IV Part 1:** 249

"Cracked Looking-Glass, The" (Porter), **III:** 434, 435, 446

"Cracker Chidlings" (Rawlings), **Supp. X:** 224, 228

Cracks (Purdy), **Supp. VII:** 277–278

Cracks Between What We Are and What We Are Supposed to Be, The (Mullen), **Supp. XXVII:** 175

"Cracks in the Universe" (Davison), **Supp. XXVI:** 78

Crack-Up, The (Fitzgerald), **II:** 80; **III:** 35, 45; **Retro. Supp. I:** 113, 115; **Supp. IX:** 61; **Supp. V:** 276

"Crack-Up, The" (Fitzgerald), **I:** 509; **Retro. Supp. I:** 113, 114

"Crack-up of American Optimism, The: Vachel Lindsay, the Dante of the Fundamentalists" (Viereck), **Supp. I Part 2:** 403

"Cradle and the Bookcase, The"(Hadas), **Supp. XXIII:** 122

"Cradle Me" (Biss), **Supp. XXVI:** 48

Cradle Will Rock, The (Blitzstein), **Supp. I Part 1:** 277, 278

Craft of Fiction, The (Lubbock), **I:** 504; **Supp. VIII:** 165

Craft of Peter Taylor, The (McAlexander, ed.), **Supp. V:** 314

Craig, David M., **Supp. XXII:** 187, 191, 192

Craig, Gordon, **III:** 394; **Supp. XXI:** 6

Crain, Jane Larkin, **Supp. V:** 123; **Supp. XII:** 167, 168

Crais, Robert, **Supp. XXI:** 70

Cram, Ralph Adams, **I:** 19

Cramer, Steven, **Supp. XI:** 139; **Supp. XV:** 26

"Cramped Quarters" (Davison), **Supp. XXVI:** 77

"Cranbrook Schools: Adventures in Bourgeois Topologies" (Monson), **Supp. XXIV:** 235

Crandall, Reuben, **Supp. I Part 2:** 686

Crane, Agnes, **I:** 406

Crane, Edmund, **I:** 407

Crane, Hart, **I:** 61, 62, 97, 109, 116, 266, **381–404; II:** 133, 215, 306, 368, 371, 536, 542; **III:** 260, 276, 453, 485, 521; **IV:** 122, 123–124, 127, 128, 129, 135, 139, 140, 141, 341, 380, 418, 419; **Retro. Supp. I:** 427; **Retro. Supp. II:** 75–91; **Supp. I Part 1:** 86; **Supp. II Part 1:** 89, 152; **Supp. III Part 1:** 20, 63, 350; **Supp. IX:** 38, 229, 320; **Supp. V:** 342; **Supp. VIII:** 39; **Supp. X:** 115, 116, 120; **Supp. XI:** 123, 131; **Supp. XII:** 198; **Supp. XIX:** 35; **Supp. XV:** 138; **Supp. XX: 80; Supp. XXI:** 131, 132, 136, 230; **Supp. XXII:** 274; **Supp. XXIII:** 146, 174, 207; **Supp. XXV:** 19; **Supp. XXVI:** 21, 23–24, 25, 28, 143

Crane, Jonathan, Jr., **I:** 407

Crane, Jonathan Townley, **I:** 406

Crane, Mrs. Jonathan Townley, **I:** 406

Crane, Luther, **I:** 406

Crane, Milton, **Supp. XV:** 144

Crane, Nellie, **I:** 407

Crane, R. S., **Supp. I Part 2:** 423

Crane, Stephen, **I:** 34, 169–170, 201, 207, 211, **405–427,** 477, 506, 519; **II:** 58, 144, 198, 262, 263, 264, 276, 289, 290, 291; **III:** 314, 317, 334, 335, 454, 505, 585; **IV:** 207, 208, 256, 350, 475; **Retro. Supp. I:** 231, 325; **Retro. Supp. II:** 97, 123; **Supp. I Part 1:** 314; **Supp. III Part 2:** 412; **Supp. IV Part 1:** 350, 380; **Supp. IV Part 2:**

680, 689, 692; **Supp. IX:** 1, 14; **Supp. VIII:** 98, 105; **Supp. X:** 223; **Supp. XI:** 95; **Supp. XII:** 50; **Supp. XIV:** 21, 50, 51, 227; **Supp. XVII:** 71, 228; **Supp. XVIII:** 74, 75; **Supp. XXIII:** 26

Crane, William, **I:** 407

Cranford (Gaskell), **Supp. IX:** 79

Crash (film, Cronenberg), **Supp. XXVI:** 28

"Crash Report" (McGrath), **Supp. X:** 116

Crater (Hickam), **Supp. XXVII:** 111

Crater, The (Cooper), **I:** 354, 355

Crater Trueblood and the Lunar Rescue Company (Hickam), **Supp. XXVII:** 111

Cratylus (Plato), **II:** 10

Cravan, Arthur, **Supp. XXII:** 164, 169

"Craven Street Gazette" (Franklin), **II:** 119

"Crawdad, The" (F. Wright), **Supp. XVII:** 244

Crawdad Creek (Sanders), **Supp. XVI:** 269

Crawford, Brad, **Supp. XI:** 133

Crawford, Eva, **I:** 199

Crawford, F. Marion, **III:** 320

Crawford, Joan, **Supp. I Part 1:** 67

Crawford, John E., **Supp. XXIII:** 165

Crawford, Kathleen, **I:** 289

Crawford, Neta C., **Supp. XXVI:** 85

"Crayon House" (Rukeyser), **Supp. VI:** 273

Crayon Miscellany, The (Irving), **II:** 312–313

Crazed, The (Jin), **Supp. XVIII: 99–100**

"Crazy about her Shrimp" (Simic), **Supp. VIII:** 282

"Crazy Cock" (H. Miller), **III:** 177

Crazy Gypsy (Salinas), **Supp. XIII:** 311, **313–315,** 316

"Crazy Gypsy" (Salinas), **Supp. XIII:** 313–314

Crazy Horse, **Supp. IV Part 2:** 488, 489

Crazy Horse (McMurtry), **Supp. V:** 233

Crazy Horse in Stillness (Heyen), **Supp. XIII:** 344

Crazy Horse: The Strange Man of the Oglaglas (Sandoz), **Supp. XXIV:** 244, 256, **257–258**

"Crazy Hunter, The" (Boyle), **Supp. XXIV: 54–55**

Crazy Hunter, The: Three Short Novels (Boyle), **Supp. XXIV: 54–56**

"Crazy in the Stir" (C. Himes), **Supp. XVI:** 137

Crazy Kill, The (C. Himes), **Supp. XVI:** 143

Crazy Man (Bodenheim), **Supp. XXV:** 22, 24

Creating a Role (Stanislavsky), **Supp. XIV:** 243

"Creation, According to Coyote, The" (Ortiz), **Supp. IV Part 2:** 505

Creation: A Novel (Vidal), **Supp. IV Part 2:** 677, 685, 688

"Creation of Anguish" (Nemerov), **III:** 269

"Creation Story" (Gunn Allen), **Supp. IV Part 1:** 325

"Creative and Cultural Lag" (Ellison), **Retro. Supp. II:** 116; **Supp. II Part 1:** 229; **Supp. XVIII:** 283

Creative Criticism (Spingarn), **I:** 266

"Creative Democracy" (Locke), **Supp. XIV:** 208

Creative Present, The (Balkian and Simmons, eds.), **Supp. XI:** 230

"Creatures" (Gallagher), **Supp. XXIV:** 176, 177

Creatures in an Alphabet (illus. Barnes), **Supp. III Part 1:** 43

"Creatures of the Genitive" (Davison), **Supp. XXVI:** 74

"Credences of Summer" (Stevens), **IV:** 93–94

"Credentials" (Halliday), **Supp. XIX:** 90

"Credo" (Bynner), **Supp. XV:** 50

"Credo" (Du Bois), **Supp. II Part 1:** 169

"Credo" (Jeffers), **Supp. II Part 2:** 424

"Credos and Curios" (Thurber), **Supp. I Part 2:** 606, 613

Creech, James, **Retro. Supp. I:** 254

"Creed for Americans, A" (Benét), **Supp. XI:** 52

"Creed of a Beggar, The" (Lindsay), **Supp. I Part 2:** 379

Creegan, Andy, **Supp. XIX:** 205

Creekmore, Hubert, **II:** 586

Creeley, Robert, **Retro. Supp. I:** 411; **Supp. II Part 1:** 30; **Supp. III Part 1:** 2; **Supp. III Part 2:** 622, 626, 629; **Supp. IV Part 1: 139–161,** 322, 325; **Supp. XI:** 317; **Supp. XIII:** 104, 112; **Supp. XIV:** 150; **Supp. XVI:** 283; **Supp. XXI:** 23, 27, 227, 230; **Supp. XXII:** 227; **Supp. XXIV:** 35, 37; **Supp. XXVII:** 18, 22, 160

Creelman, James Ashmore, **Supp. XVI:** 186–187

"Cremona Violin, The" (A. Lowell), **II:** 523

"Crêpe de Chine" (Doty), **Supp. XI:** 128

"Crêpes Flambeau" (Gallagher), **Supp. XXIV:** 170

Crescent (Hickam), **Supp. XXVII:** 111

"Cressy" (Harte), **Supp. II Part 1:** 354, 356

"Cretan Woman, The" (Jeffers), **Supp. II Part 2:** 435

Crèvecoeur, Michel-Guillaume Jean de, **I:** 229; **Supp. I Part 1: 227–252**

Crèvecoeur's Eighteenth-Century Travels in Pennsylvania and New York (Adams), **Supp. I Part 1:** 251

Crevel, René, **Supp. XIV:** 343

Crewe-Jones, Florence, **Supp. XVII:** 58

Crewe Train (Macaulay), **Supp. XII:** 88

Crews, Harry, **Supp. X:** 11, 12; **Supp. XI: 99–117,** 245; **Supp. XVIII:** 195; **Supp. XXI:** 35, 38, 40, 44

Crews, James, **Supp. XXIII:** 134–135

Crichton, Michael, **Supp. XIV:** 316

Crick, Philip, **Supp. XVI:** 289

Cricket (C. L. R. James; Grimshaw, ed.), **Supp. XXI:** 172

"Cricket" (C. Miller), **Supp. XXII:** 199

"Crickets" (R. O. Butler), **Supp. XII:** 71

Criers and Kibitzers, Kibitzers and Criers (Elkin), **Supp. VI: 45–46,** 57

Crime and Punishment (Dostoevsky), **II:** 60, 130; **IV:** 484; **Supp. IV Part 2:** 525; **Supp. VIII:** 282; **Supp. XII:** 281; **Supp. XIX:** 276; **Supp. XVII:** 155; **Supp. XVIII:** 278

Crime at Scottsboro, The (Endore), **Supp. XVII:** 59

Crime Beat (Connelly), **Supp. XXI:** 67, 79

Crimes and Misdemeanors (film; Allen), **Supp. XV: 1, 2, 11,** 12

Crime Without Passion (film), **Supp. XXVII:** 90

"Criminal"(Strout), **Supp. XXIII:** 283, 285

Crisis papers (Paine), **Supp. I Part 2:** 508–509, 510

"Criteria of Negro Art" (Du Bois), **Supp. II Part 1:** 181; **Supp. XIX:** 66–67

"Critiad, The" (Winters), **Supp. II Part 2:** 794, 799

Critical Anthology A (Untermeyer), **Supp. XV:** 310

Critical Essays on Charlotte Perkins Gilman (Karpinski, ed.), **Supp. XI:** 201

Critical Essays on Kay Boyle (Elkins, ed.), **Supp. XXIV:** 64

Critical Essays on Peter Taylor (McAlexander), **Supp. V:** 319, 320, 323–324

Critical Essays on Robert Bly (W. V. Davis), **Supp. IV Part 1:** 64, 69

Critical Essays on Wallace Stegner (Arthur), **Supp. IV Part 2:** 606

Critical Fable, A (A. Lowell), **II:** 511–512, 527, 529–530

Critical Guide to Leaves of Grass, A (J. Miller), **IV:** 352

Critical Mass (Paretsky), **Supp. XXV:** 185

Critical Response to Joan Didion, The (Felton), **Supp. IV Part 1:** 210

Critical Temper of Alain Locke, The: A Selection of His Essays on Art and Culture (Stewart, ed.), **Supp. XIV:** 196, **210–211,** 213

"Critic as Artist, The" (Wilde), **Supp. X:** 189

Criticism and Fiction (Howells), **II:** 288

Criticism and Ideology (Eagleton), **Retro. Supp. I:** 67

Criticism in the Borderlands (Calderón and Saldívar, eds.), **Supp. IV Part 2:** 544

"Critics, The" (Jong), **Supp. V:** 119

"Critics and Connoisseurs" (Moore), **III:** 209

Critic's Notebook, A (Howe), **Supp. VI:** 126–128

"Critic's Task, The" (Kazin), **Supp. VIII:** 103

"Critic Who Does Not Exist, The" (Wilson), **IV:** 431

"Critique de la Vie Quotidienne" (Barthelme), **Supp. IV Part 1:** 50

Critique of Pure Reason (Kant), **Supp. XVI:** 184

Croce, Benedetto, **I:** 58, 255, 265, 273, 281; **III:** 610

Crockett, Davy, **II:** 307; **III:** 227; **IV:** 266; **Supp. I Part 2:** 411

"Crocodilopolis" (Cliff), **Supp. XXII:** 76

Crofter and the Laird, The (McPhee), **Supp. III Part 1:** 301–302, 307

Croll, Nora Swan, **Supp. XXVII:** 262

Croly, Herbert, **I:** 229, 231, 235; **IV:** 436; **Supp. I Part 1:** 111

Cromwell, Oliver, **IV:** 145, 146, 156; **Supp. I Part 1:** 111

Cronenberg, David, **Supp. XXI:** 152, 154

Cronin, A. J., **Supp. XVII:** 59

Cronin, Dr. Archibald, **III:** 578

Cronin, Gloria, **Supp. XXVI:** 123

Cronin, Justin, **Supp. X:** 10

Crooke, Dr. Helkiah, **Supp. I Part 1:** 98, 104

Crooked Little Heart (Lamott), **Supp. XX:** 138

Crooker, Barbara, **Supp. XXIII: 51–66,** 245, **246,** 251

Crooks, Alan, **Supp. V:** 226

Crooks, Robert, **Supp. XIII:** 237

"Crop, The" (O'Connor), **Retro. Supp. II:** 223–225

Crosby, Caresse, **I:** 385; **III:** 473; **Retro. Supp. II:** 85; **Supp. XII:** 198

Crosby, Harry, **I:** 385; **Retro. Supp. II:** 85

"Cross" (Hughes), **Supp. I Part 1:** 325; **Supp. XVIII:** 124

Cross, Charles, **Supp. XXIV:** 173

Crossan, John Dominic, **Supp. V:** 251

"Cross Country Snow" (Hemingway), **II:** 249

Cross Creek (Rawlings), **Supp. X:** 223, 226, 228, **231–232,** 233, 234, 235

Cross Creek Cookery (Rawlings), **Supp. X:** 233

"Cross Cut" (Davison), **Supp. XXVI:** 74

"Crossing, The" (Huddle), **Supp. XXVI:** 154

Crossing, The (McCarthy), **Supp. VIII:** 175, **184–186**

"Crossing, The" (Swenson), **Supp. IV Part 2:** 644

"Crossing Brooklyn Ferry" (Whitman), **IV:** 333, 340, 341; **Retro. Supp. I:** 389, 396, 397, 400–401; **Supp. XXIII:** 109

"Crossing into Poland" (Babel), **Supp. XIV:** 84

"Crossing New River" (Huddle), **Supp. XXVI:** 148, 150

Crossings (Chuang), **Supp. X:** 291

"Crossings" (Hogan), **Supp. IV Part 1:** 412

"Crossing the Void" (Davison), **Supp. XXVI:** 76

Crossing the Water (Plath), **Retro. Supp. II:** 248; **Supp. I Part 2:** 526, 538

Crossing to Safety (Stegner), **Supp. IV Part 2:** 599, 606, 612, 613–614

"Cross of Snow, The" (Longfellow), **II:** 490; **Retro. Supp. II:** 169–170

"Crossover" (O. Butler), **Supp. XIII:** 61

"Cross-PolliNation" (Gansworth), **Supp. XXVI:** 111

"Cross-Roads, The" (A. Lowell), **II:** 523

"Crossroads of the World Etc." (Merwin), **Supp. III Part 1:** 347, 348

Cross-Section (Seaver), **IV:** 485

Cross the Border, Close the Gap (Fiedler), **Supp. XIII:** 104

Cross Ties (X. J. Kennedy), **Supp. XV:** 165, **166–167**

"Cross Ties" (X. J. Kennedy), **Supp. XV:** 158

Crouch, Stanley, **Supp. XIX:** 158

"Croup" (Karr), **Supp. XI:** 243

Crouse, Russel, **III:** 284

"Crow" (Hogan), **Supp. IV Part 1:** 405

Crow (Hughes), **Supp. XV:** 347, 348

"Crow, The" (Creeley), **Supp. IV Part 1:** 148–149

Crow and the Heart,The (Carruth), **Supp. XVI:** 47–48

"Crowded Countries of the Bomb, The" (Oppen), **Supp. XXVI:** 232

"Crowded Street, The" (Bryant), **Supp. I Part 1:** 168

Crowder, A. B., **Supp. XI:** 107

"Crow Jane" (Baraka), **Supp. II Part 1:** 38

Crow Mercies (Schott), **Supp. XXIII: 252–254**

"Crow Mercies" (Schott), **Supp. XXIII:** 253

Crowninshield, Frank, **III:** 123; **Supp. IX:** 201

Crown of Columbus (Erdrich and Dorris), **Supp. IV Part 1:** 260

"Crows, The" (Bogan), **Supp. III Part 1:** 50, 51

Crucial Instances (Wharton), **Retro. Supp. I:** 365, 367

Crucible, The (A. Miller), **III:** 147, 148, 155, 156–158, 159, 166; **Supp. XIII:** 206; **Supp. XXV:** 93

"Crucified" (Gibran), **Supp. XX: 119**

"Crucifix in the Filing Cabinet" (Shapiro), **Supp. II Part 2:** 712

"Crude Foyer" (Stevens), **Retro. Supp. I:** 310

"Cruel and Barbarous Treatment" (McCarthy), **II:** 562, 563

"Cruel Mother, The" (B. Kelly), **Supp. XVII:** 126

Cruise of the Dazzler, The (London), **II:** 465

Cruise of the Snark, The (London), **II:** 476–477; **Supp. XXV:** 217

Cruisers, The (Myers), **Supp. XXVII:** 212

"Cruising with the Beach Boys" (Gioia), **Supp. XV:** 118

" 'Crumbling Idols' by Hamlin Garland" (Chopin), **Supp. I Part 1:** 217

"Crusade of the Excelsior, The" (Harte), **Supp. II Part 1:** 336, 354

"Crusoe in England" (Bishop), **Retro. Supp. II:** 50; **Supp. I Part 1:** 93, 95, 96; **Supp. III Part 1:** 10, 18

Cruz, Angie, **Supp. XXVI:** 263–264

Cruz-Hacker, Alba, **Supp. XXI:** 107

Cry, the Beloved Country (Paton), **Supp. VIII:** 126

Cryer, Dan, **Supp. VIII:** 86, 88; **Supp. XII:** 164

Crying of Lot 49, The (Pynchon), **Supp. II Part 2:** 618, 619, 621, 630–633

"Crying Sisters, The" (Rand), **Supp. IV Part 2:** 524

"Crying Wolf" (C. Frost), **Supp. XV:** 101

"Cry of the Graves, The" (Gibran), **Supp. XX: 124**

Cryptogram, The (Mamet), **Supp. XIV:** 240, 247, 255

"Crystal, The" (Aiken), **I:** 60

"Crystal, The" (Lanier), **Supp. I Part 1:** 364, 370

"Crystal Cage, The" (Kunitz), **Supp. III Part 1:** 258

Crystal Cup, The (Atherton), **Supp. XXIV:** 26

"Crystal Cup, The" (Teasdale), **Supp. XXVII:** 287

"Crystal Gazer, The" (Teasdale), **Supp. XXVII:** 287, 296

Crystal Vision (Sorrentino), **Supp. XXI:** 235, 236

"Crytal" (Sobin), **Supp. XVI:** 283

Cry to Heaven (Rice), **Supp. VII:** 300–301

"Cuba" (Hemingway), **II:** 258

"Cuba Libre" (Baraka), **Supp. II Part 1:** 33

Cuba: Prophetic Island (W. Frank), **Supp. XX: 80, 81**

"Cubism, Barcelona" (Hull), **Supp. XXI:** 137

Cudjoe, Selwyn, **Supp. IV Part 1:** 6

"Cudjo's Own Story of the Last American Slaver" (Hurston), **Supp. VI:** 153

Cudlipp, Thelma, **I:** 501

Cudworth, Ralph, **II:** 9, 10

"Cuentista" (Mora), **Supp. XIII:** 224

"Cuento de agua santa, Un" (Mora), **Supp. XIII:** 224

"Cui Bono" (H. Johnson), **Supp. XXVI:** 167, 173

Cujo (King), **Supp. V:** 138–139, 143, 149, 152

Cukor, George, **Supp. XVI:** 192

Cullen, Countee, **Retro. Supp. I:** 207; **Retro. Supp. II:** 114; **Supp. I Part 1:** 49, 325; **Supp. III Part 1:** 73, 75, 76; **Supp. IV Part 1: 163–174; Supp. IX:** 306, 309; **Supp. X:** 136, 140; **Supp. XIII:** 186; **Supp. XIX:** 78; **Supp. XVIII:** 122,131, 185, 279, 280, 282, 284; **Supp. XXII:** 3, 6, 7, 8

"Cultivation of Christmas Trees, The" (Eliot), **I:** 579

Cult of Alien Gods, The: H. P. Lovecraft and Extraterrestrial Pop Culture (Calavito), **Supp. XXV:** 123

"Cult of Personality in American Letters, The" (Swados), **Supp. XIX:** 265

"Cult of the Best, The" (Arnold), **I:** 223

"Cultural Exchange" (Hughes), **Supp. I Part 1:** 341

"Cultural Pluralism: A New Americanism" (Locke), **Supp. XIV:** 195

"Cultural Relativism and Ideological Peace" (Locke), **Supp. XIV:** 202, 212

"Culture" (Emerson), **III:** 2, 4

"Culture, Self, and Style" (Gass), **Supp. VI:** 88

"Culture and Religion" (Olds), **Supp. X:** 214

Culture of Cities, The (Mumford), **Supp. II Part 2:** 492, 494–495

Cummings, E. E., **I:** 44, 48, 64, 105, 176, **428–450,** 475, 477, 482, 526; **III:** 20, 196, 476; **IV:** 384, 402, 415, 427, 433; **Retro. Supp. II:** 178, 328; **Supp. I Part 2:** 622, 678; **Supp. III Part 1:** 73; **Supp. IV Part 2:** 637, 641; **Supp. IX:** 20; **Supp. XV:** 312, 338; **Supp. XXVI:** 32; **Supp. XXVII:** 261

Cummings, Robert, **Supp. IV Part 2:** 524

Cummins, Ann, **Supp. XXIII:** 280

Cummins, James, **Supp. XVII:** 74

Cunard, Lady, **III:** 459

Cunningham, Brent, **Supp. XXVII:** 153

Cunningham, J. V., **Supp. XV:** 169

Cunningham, Merce, **Supp. IV Part 1:** 83; **Supp. XV:** 187

Cunningham, Michael, **Supp. XII:** 80; **Supp. XV: 55–71**

Cunningham, Rodger, **Supp. XXIII:** 38–39

Cup of Gold (Steinbeck), **IV:** 51, 53, 61–64, 67

"Cupola, The" (Bogan), **Supp. III Part 1:** 53

"Curandera" (Mora), **Supp. XIII:** 214, 222

Curé de Tours, Le (Balzac), **I:** 509

Cure for Dreams, A: A Novel (Gibbons), **Supp. X: 45–47,** 48, 50

Curie, Marie, **IV:** 420, 421; **Supp. I Part 2:** 569

Curie, Pierre, **IV:** 420

Curiosa Americana (Mather), **Supp. II Part 2:** 463

Curiosities (Matthews), **Supp. IX:** 151, 152

"Curious Case of Sidd Finch, The" (Plimpton), **Supp. XVI:** 244

"Curious Shifts of the Poor" (Dreiser), **Retro. Supp. II:** 97

"Current" (Espaillat), **Supp. XXI:** 106

"Currents and Counter-Currents in Medical Science" (Holmes), **Supp. I Part 1:** 305

"Curried Cow" (Bierce), **I:** 200

Curry, Professor W. C., **IV:** 122

Curse of Downers Grove, The (film), **Supp. XXVII:** 80

Curse of the Jade Scorpion, The (film; Allen), **Supp. XV:** 11

Curse of the Starving Class (Shepard), **Supp. III Part 2:** 433, 447–448

Curse of the Werewolf, The (film), **Supp. XVII:** 56

"Curse of Yig, The" (Lovecraft and Bishop), **Supp. XXV:** 122

"Curse on a Thief, A" (X. J. Kennedy), **Supp. XV:** 171

"Curtain, The" (Chandler), **Supp. IV Part 1:** 122

Curtain Calls: British and American Women and the Theater, 1660–1820 (Saar), **Supp. XV:** 237

Curtain of Green, A (Welty), **IV:** 261–264, 268, 283

"Curtain of Green, A" (Welty), **IV:** 263–264

Curtain of Green and Other Stories, A (Welty), **Retro. Supp. I:** 343, 344, 345, 346, 347, 355

Curtain of Trees (opera), **Supp. IV Part 2:** 552

"Curtain Raiser, A" (Stein), **IV:** 43, 44

"Curtains" (Cisneros), **Supp. VII:** 66

Curtin, John, **Supp. IX:** 184

Curtis, George William, **Supp. I Part 1:** 307; **Supp. XVIII:** 3, 14

Curve (Goldbarth), **Supp. XII:** 181

Curve of Binding Energy, The (McPhee), **Supp. III Part 1:** 301

Curzon, Mary, **III:** 52

Cushing, Caleb, **Supp. I Part 2:** 684, 686

Cushman, Howard, **Supp. I Part 2:** 652

Cushman, Stephen, **Retro. Supp. I:** 430

Cusick, Albert, **Supp. XXVI:** 87

"Custard Heart, The" (Parker), **Supp. IX:** 201

Custer, General George, **I:** 489, 491

Custer Died for Your Sins (Deloria), **Supp. IV Part 1:** 323; **Supp. IV Part 2:** 504

"Custody"(Schott), **Supp. XXIII:** 241

"Custom House, The" (Hawthorne), **II:** 223; **Retro. Supp. I:** 147–148, 157; **Supp. XXI:** 181

Custom of the Country, The (Wharton), **IV:** 318; **Retro. Supp. I:** 374, **375–376; Supp. XXIV:** 23

"Cut" (Plath), **Retro. Supp. II:** 253

"Cut-Glass Bowl, The" (Fitzgerald), **II:** 88

Cutting, Bronson, **III:** 600

Cutting Lisa (Everett), **Supp. XVIII: 56**

"Cuttings, *later*" (Roethke), **III:** 532

"Cyberpunk" (Bethke), **Supp. XVI:** 121

Cyberspace trilogy (W. Gibson). *See* Sprawl trilogy (W. Gibson)

"Cycles, The" (Pinsky), **Supp. VI:** 250–252

Cyclopedia of American Literature (Duyckinck and Duyckinck), **Supp. XXV:** 250

Cynic's Word Book, The (Bierce), **I:** 197, 205, 208, 209, 210

Cynthia Ozick (Lowin), **Supp. V:** 273

Cynthia Ozick's Comic Art (Cohen), **Supp. V:** 273

Cynthia Ozick's Fiction (Kauvar), **Supp. V:** 273

"Czeslaw Milosz and Memory" (Hampl), **Supp. XXII:** 92

D

Da Capo: Best Music Writing 2002 (Lethem, ed.), **Supp. XVIII:** 148

Dacey, Philip, **Supp. IV Part 1:** 70

Dacier, André, **II:** 10

"Dad" (Cullen), **Supp. IV Part 1:** 167

"Daddy" (Plath), **Retro. Supp. II:** 250–251; **Supp. I Part 2:** 529, 542, 545, 546; **Supp. II Part 2:** 688; **Supp. XXII:** 30; **Supp. XXIII:** 112, 113

"Daddy"(Hadas), **Supp. XXIII:** 112, 113

Daddy's Little Boy (Collins), **Supp. XXI:** 54

"Daemon, The" (Bogan), **Supp. III Part 1:** 58, 61

"Daemon Lover, The" (Jackson), **Supp. IX:** 116–117

"Daffodils" (Nelson and Espeland), **Supp. XVIII:** 181

"Daffodils" (Wordsworth), **Supp. XIII:** 284

"Daffy Duck in Hollywood" (Ashbery), **Supp. III Part 1:** 18

D'Agata, John, **Supp. XII:** 97, 98

"Dagon" (Lovecraft), **Supp. XXV:** 111, 121

Dago Red (Fante), **Supp. XI:** 160, 169

Dahl, Roald, **Supp. IX:** 114

Dahlberg, Edward, **I:** 231; **Retro. Supp. I:** 426; **Supp. III Part 2:** 624; **Supp. XIV:** 148; **Supp. XVIII:** 148; **Supp. XXII:** 257

Dahlberg, R'lene, **Supp. XIV:** 148

Daiches, David, **Retro. Supp. II:** 243; **Supp. I Part 2:** 536

Daily Horoscope (Gioia), **Supp. XV:** 112, **118–121,** 126

"Daily Horoscope" (Gioia), **Supp. XV:** 119

Daily Modernism (Podnieks), **Supp. X:** 189

Dain Curse, The (Hammett), **Supp. IV Part 1:** 348

"Daisies" (Glück), **Supp. V:** 88

"Daisy" (Oates), **Supp. II Part 2:** 523

Daisy (S. and A. Warner), **Supp. XVIII:** 268

Daisy-Head Mayzie (Geisel), **Supp. XVI:** 112

Daisy Miller (H. James), **Retro. Supp. I:** 216, 220, 222, 223, 228, 231; **Supp. XVIII:** 165; **Supp. XXIV:** 23

"Daisy Miller" (H. James), **II:** 325, 326, 327, 329; **IV:** 316

"Dakota (IV)" (Gansworth), **Supp. XXVI:** 111

Dale, Charlie, **Supp. IV Part 2:** 584

Daley, Yvonne, **Supp. XXII:** 216

Dali, Salvador, **II:** 586; **Supp. IV Part 1:** 83; **Supp. XIII:** 317

Dalibard, Thomas-François, **II:** 117

"Dallas-Fort Worth: Redband and Mistletoe" (Clampitt), **Supp. IX:** 45

"Dalliance of Eagles, The" (Whitman), **IV:** 348

Dalva (Harrison), **Supp. VIII:** 37, 45, 46, **48–49**

Daly, Carroll John, **Supp. IV Part 1:** 343, 345

Daly, John, **II:** 25, 26

Daly, Julia Brown, **II:** 25, 26

"Dalyrimple Goes Wrong" (Fitzgerald), **II:** 88

"Dam, The" (Rukeyser), **Supp. VI:** 283

Damas, Leon, **Supp. X:** 139

Damascus Gate (Stone), **Supp. V:** 308–311

Damballah (Wideman), **Supp. X:** 319, 320, 321, 322, 323, 326, 327, 331, 333–334

Dameshek, Brandon, **Supp. XIX:** 273, 277, 287

Damnation of Theron Ware, The (Frederic), **II:** 140–143, 144, 146, 147; **Retro. Supp. I:** 325

Damned If I Do (Everett), **Supp. XVIII:** 66

"Damned Thing, The" (Bierce), **I:** 206

Damon, Matt, **Supp. VIII:** 175

Damon, S. Foster, **I:** 26; **II:** 512, 514, 515

"Damon and Vandalia" (Dove), **Supp. IV Part 1:** 252

Dana, H. W. L., **I:** 225

Dana, Richard Henry, Jr., **III:** 81; **Supp. XX: 227; Supp. XXV:** 208

Dana, Richard Henry, Sr., **I:** 339, 351; **Supp. I Part 1:** 103, 154, 155; **Supp. I Part 2:** 414, 420; **Supp. XXV:** 250

Dana, Robert, **Supp. V:** 178, 180

"Dana Gioia and Fine Press Printing" (Peich), **Supp. XV:** 117

"Dance" (Kenny), **Supp. XXIII:** 148

"Dance, The" (Crane), **I:** 109

"Dance, The" (Roethke), **III:** 541

"Dance, The" (W. C. Williams), **Supp. XVII:** 113

Dance and the Railroad, The (Hwang), **Supp. XXI:** 145, 146

"Dance in a Buffalo Skull" (Zitkala-Ša), **Supp. XXV:** 276

"Dance Me to the End of Love" (Cohen), **Supp. XXVII:** 61

Dance of Death, The (Auden), **Supp. II Part 1:** 10

Dance of Death, The (Bierce and Harcourt), **I:** 196

Dance of Life, The (Ellis), **Supp. XX: 117**

Dance of the Happy Shades (Munro), **Supp. XXVII:** 181, 182, 194

Dance of the Sleepwalkers (Calabria), **Supp. XIII:** 164

"Dance of the Solids, The" (Updike), **Retro. Supp. I:** 323

"Dancer" (Hoffman), **Supp. XVIII:** 86

Dancer (Myers), **Supp. XXVII:** 200

"Dancer, The" (Swados), **Supp. XIX:** 261, 263–264

Dancers, The (Myers), **Supp. XXVII:** 211

"Dancers Work by Forgetting" (Espaillat), **Supp. XXI:** 102

"Dances of Madness" (Schott), **Supp. XXIII:** 245

Dances with Wolves (film), **Supp. X:** 124

Dance to the Music of Time, A (Powell), **Supp. XVIII:** 146

Dancing After Hours (Dubus), **Supp. VII:** 91

Dancing Back Strong the Nation (Kenny), **Supp. XXIII:** 144, **148**

Dancing Bears, The (Merwin), **Supp. III Part 1:** 343–344

Dancing on the Stones (Nichols), **Supp. XIII:** 256, 257, 259, 267, 269

"Dancing the Jig" (Sexton), **Supp. II Part 2:** 692

Dandelion Wine (Bradbury), **Supp. IV Part 1:** 101, 109–110

Dandurand, Karen, **Retro. Supp. I:** 30

"Dandy Frightening the Squatters, The" (Twain), **IV:** 193–194

Dangel, Mary Jo, **Supp. XVIII:** 156

Dangerous Crossroads (film), **Supp. XIII:** 163

Dangerous Day (Rinehart), **Supp. XXV:** 195

Dangerous Moonlight (Purdy), **Supp. VII:** 278

"Dangerous Road Before Martin Luther King" (Baldwin), **Supp. I Part 1:** 52

Dangerous Summer, The (Hemingway), **II:** 261

Dangerous Thoughts (Ryan as Quin), **Supp. XVIII:** 226

"Dangers of Authorship, The" (Blackmur), **Supp. II Part 1:** 147

Dangling Man (Bellow), **I:** 144, 145, 147, 148, 150–151, 153–154, 158, 160, 161, 162, 163; **Retro. Supp. II:** 19, 20–21, 22, 23; **Supp. VIII:** 234; **Supp. XIX:** 157

"Dang Little Squirt" (Bontemps), **Supp. XXII:** 4

Daniel (biblical book), **Supp. I Part 1:** 105

Daniel (film), **Supp. IV Part 1:** 236

Daniel, Arnaut, **III:** 467

Daniel, Robert W., **III:** 76

Daniel, Samuel, **Supp. I Part 1:** 369

Daniel Deronda (G. Eliot), **I:** 458

Daniels, Frank, **Supp. XXII:** 196

Daniels, Kate, **Supp. XVII:** 112

Danielson, Linda, **Supp. IV Part 2:** 569

D'Annunzio, Gabriele, **II:** 515

Danny and the Deep Blue Sea: An Apache Dance (Shanley), **Supp. XIV:** 315, **318–319,** 320, 321, 323, 324

Danny O'Neill pentalogy (Farrell), **II:** 35–41

Danse Macabre (King), **Supp. IV Part 1:** 102; **Supp. V:** 144; **Supp. XXV:** 123

"Danse Russe" (W. C. Williams), **IV:** 412–413

"Dans le Restaurant" (Eliot), **I:** 554, 578

Dans l'ombre des cathédrales (Ambelain), **Supp. I Part 1:** 273

Dante Alighieri, **I:** 103, 136, 138, 250, 384, 433, 445; **II:** 8, 274, 278, 289, 490, 492, 493, 494, 495, 504, 508, 524, 552; **III:** 13, 77, 124, 182, 259, 278, 448, 453, 467, 533, 607, 609, 610–612, 613; **IV:** 50, 134, 137, 138, 139, 247, 437, 438; **Retro. Supp. I:** 62, 63, 64, 66, 360; **Retro. Supp. II:** 330; **Supp. I Part 1:** 256, 363; **Supp. I Part 2:** 422, 454; **Supp. III Part 2:** 611, 618, 621; **Supp. IV Part 2:** 634; **Supp. V:** 277, 283, 331, 338, 345; **Supp. VIII:** 27, 219–221; **Supp. X:** 120, 121, 125; **Supp. XII:** 98; **Supp. XV:** 254; **Supp. XVII:** 227, 241

Danvis Tales: Selected Stories (Robinson; Budbill, ed.), **Supp. XIX:** 6

Danziger, Adolphe, **I:** 199–200

Danziger, Jeff, **Supp. XXII:** 208

Dar (Nabokov), **III:** 246, 255

D'Arcy, Randall, **Supp. XVII:** 76

Dardis, Tom, **Supp. XVIII:** 249

"Dare's Gift" (Glasgow), **II:** 190

Darius & Twig (Myers), **Supp. XXVII:** 205

Dark and Feeling, The: Black American Writers and Their Work (Major), **Supp. XXII:** 180

Dark Angel, The (Bolton), **Supp. I Part 1:** 281

"Dark Angel Travels With Us to Canada and Blesses Our Vacation, The" (Dunn), **Supp. XI:** 146

Dark at the Top of the Stairs, The (film), **Supp. XXV:** 102

Dark at the Top of the Stairs, The (Inge), **Supp. XXV:** 93, 95, 100–102

Dark Barbarian, The (Howard, Herron ed.), **Supp. XXVII:** 118, 128

Dark Carnival (Bradbury), **Supp. IV Part 1:** 102

Darker (Strand), **Supp. IV Part 2:** 619, 626–628

Darker Face of the Earth, The (Dove), **Supp. IV Part 1:** 255–257

"Dark Fire" (Hadas), **Supp. XXIII:** 126

Dark Green, Bright Red (Vidal), **Supp. IV Part 2:** 677

Dark Half, The (King), **Supp. V:** 141

Dark Harbor: A Poem (Strand), **Supp. IV Part 2:** 633–634

"Dark Hills, The" (Robinson), **III:** 523

Dark Horses (X. J. Kennedy), **Supp. XV:** 167–170

Dark Hours, The (W. V. Davis), **Supp. XXI:** 91–92, 93

"Dark Houses" (Davison), **Supp. XXVI:** 72

Dark Laughter (Anderson), **I:** 111, 116; **II:** 250–251

"Darkling Alphabet, A" (Snodgrass), **Supp. VI:** 323

Darkling Child (Merwin and Milroy), **Supp. III Part 1:** 346

"Darkling Summer, Ominous Dusk, Rumorous Rain" (Schwartz), **Supp. II Part 2:** 661

"Darkling Thrush" (Hardy), **Supp. IX:** 40

"Dark Man, The" (Howard), **Supp. XXVII:** 123

"Dark Men, The" (Dubus), **Supp. VII:** 86

Dark Mirrors (Sobin), **Supp. XVI:** 295

Dark Mother, The (W. Frank), **Supp. XX:** 70–71

Dark Mountains, The (Hoffman), **Supp. XVIII:** 76–77

Darkness and the Light, The (Hecht), **Supp. X:** 58

Darkness at Noon (Koestler), **Supp. XXIII:** 1

Darkness More Than Night, A (Connelly), **Supp. XXI:** 73–74, 80

"Darkness on the Edge of Town" (O'Brien), **Supp. V:** 246

Darkness Surrounding Us, The (Sorrentino), **Supp. XXI:** 227, 228

Darkness under the Trees/Walking behind the Spanish (Salinas), **Supp. XIII:** 311, 319–324

"Dark Night" (St. John of the Cross), **Supp. XV:** 30

Dark Night of the Soul, The (St. John of the Cross), **I:** 1, 585

Dark of the Moon (Teasdale), **Supp. XXVII:** 284, 286, 295–296

"Dark Ones" (Dickey), **Supp. IV Part 1:** 182

Dark Power (Holding), **Supp. XXII:** 122–123, 124

Dark Princess: A Romance (Du Bois), **Supp. II Part 1:** 179, 181–182

Dark Room, The (T. Williams), **IV:** 381

Dark Sacred Night (CD), **Supp. XXI:** 75

Dark Shadows (television show), **Supp. XIX:** 57

"Dark Summer" (Bogan), **Supp. III Part 1:** 51, 53

Dark Summer: Poems (Bogan), **Supp. III Part 1:** 52–53, 57

"Dark Tower, The" (column), **Supp. IV Part 1:** 168, 170

Dark Tower, The: The Gunslinger (King), **Supp. V:** 152

Dark Tower IV, The: Wizard and Glass (King), **Supp. V:** 139

Dark Tunnel, The (Macdonald as Millar), **Supp. IV Part 2:** 465, 466

"Dark TV Screen" (Simic), **Supp. VIII:** 282

Dark Valley Destiny (Sprague de Camp), **Supp. XXVII:** 115, 128

"Dark Voyage, The" (McLay), **Supp. XIII:** 21

"Dark Walk, The" (Taylor), **Supp. V:** 320–321, 322, 326

Darkwater: Voices from Within the Veil (Du Bois), **Supp. II Part 1:** 178, 180, 183

Dark Waves and Light Matter (Goldbarth), **Supp. XII:** 176, 193

Dark World (Carruth), **Supp. XVI:** 55

"Darling" (Nye), **Supp. XIII:** 283–284

"Darling, The" (Chekhov), **Supp. IX:** 202

Darling-Darling (Barillet and Grédy; Loos, trans.), **Supp. XVI:** 194

Darnell, Linda, **Supp. XII:** 173

Darragh, Tina, **Supp. IV Part 2:** 427

Darreu, Robert Donaldson, **Supp. II Part 1:** 89, 98, 102

Darrow, Clarence, **Supp. I Part 1:** 5; **Supp. I Part 2:** 455; **Supp. XXVII:** 88

Dartmouth, Earl of, **Supp. XX:** 284

Darwin, Charles, **I:** 457; **II:** 323, 462, 481; **III:** 226, 231; **IV:** 69, 304; **Retro. Supp. I:** 254; **Retro. Supp. II:** 60, 65; **Supp. I Part 1:** 368; **Supp. IX:** 180; **Supp. XI:** 203; **Supp. XVI:** 13; **Supp. XX:** 18; **Supp. XXVII:** 34, 126

"Darwin in 1881" (Schnackenberg), **Supp. XV:** 253, 254, 258

Daryush, Elizabeth, **Supp. V:** 180

Dasburg, Andrew, **Supp. XXI:** 6

Dash, Julie, **Supp. XI:** 17, 18, 20

Dash, Robert, **Supp. XXVII:** 23

Dashell, Alfred, **Supp. X:** 224

"DAS KAPITAL" (Baraka), **Supp. II Part 1:** 55

Datlow, Ellen, **Supp. XVI:** 123

"Datum Centurio" (Wallace), **Supp. X:** 309

Daudet, Alphonse, **II:** 325, 338

"Daughter" (Caldwell), **I:** 309

"Daughter in the House" (X. J. Kennedy), **Supp. XV:** 160

Daughter of Earth (Smedly), **Supp. XIII:** 295

"Daughter of Erlik Khan, The" (Howard), **Supp. XXVII:** 121

Daughter of the Land, A (Stratton-Porter), **Supp. XX:** 222

Daughter of the Snows, A (London), **II:** 465, 469–470

Daughter of the Vine, A (Atherton), **Supp. XXIV:** 18, 22

"Daughters" (Anderson), **I:** 114

Daughters (Marshall), **Supp. XI:** 275, 276, 277, 286–288, 289, 290

"Daughters, 1900" (Nelson), **Supp. XVIII:** 175

Daughters, I Love You (Hogan), **Supp. IV Part 1:** 397, 399, 401

"Daughters of Invention" (Alvarez), **Supp. VII:** 9

Daughters of the Dust (Dash; film), **Supp. XI:** 17, 18; **Supp. XX:** 154

Daughters of Valor: Contemporary Jewish American Women Writers (Halio and Siegel, eds.), **Supp. XXVI:** 123

Daumier, Honoré, **IV:** 412

Dave, R. A., **Supp. VIII:** 126

Davenport, Abraham, **Supp. I Part 2:** 699

Davenport, Basil, **Supp. XXV:** 27

Davenport, Gary, **Supp. IX:** 98

Davenport, Guy, **Supp. XIV:** 96; **Supp. XXI:** 235

Davenport, Herbert J., **Supp. I Part 2:** 642

Davenport, James, **I:** 546

Daves, E. G., **Supp. I Part 1:** 369

Davey, Frank, **Supp. XIII:** 33

"David" (Garrett), **Supp. VII:** 109–110

"David" (Gordon), **Supp. IV Part 1:** 298–299

David, Gray, **Supp. XX:** 260

"David and Agnes, a Romance" (Keillor), **Supp. XVI:** 175

David Blaize (Benson), **Supp. XX:** 234

David Copperfield (Dickens), **I:** 458; **II:** 290; **Retro. Supp. I:** 33; **Supp. XVI:** 65, 72; **Supp. XX:** 234

"David Crockett's Other Life" (Nye), **Supp. XIII:** 282

Davideis (Cowley), **IV:** 158

David Harum (Westcott), **I:** 216

David Huddle Reader, A: Selected Prose and Poetry (Huddle), **Supp. XXVI:** 160

"David Lynch Keeps His Head" (Wallace), **Supp. X:** 314

David Show, The (Gurney), **Supp. V:** 97

Davidson, Cathy, **Supp. XV:** 238

Davidson, Donald, **I:** 294; **III:** 495, 496; **IV:** 121, 122, 124, 125, 236; **Supp. II Part 1:** 139; **Supp. XIV:** 2; **Supp. XX:** 164

Davidson, James West, **Supp. XXII:** 218

Davidson, Jo, **Supp. XXI:** 7

Davidson, John, **Retro. Supp. I:** 55

Davidson, Michael, **Supp. VIII:** 290, 293, 294, 302–303; **Supp. XXVI:** 224

Davidson, Phebe, **Supp. XXIII:** 252

Davidson, Sara, **Supp. IV Part 1:** 196, 198, 203

Davidson, Sue, **Supp. XIX:** 260

Davidsz de Heem, Jan, **Supp. XI:** 133

Davie, Donald, **III:** 478; **Supp. IV Part 2:** 474; **Supp. V:** 331; **Supp. X:** 55, 59; **Supp. XVII:** 111, 112, 121

Davies, Arthur, **III:** 273

Davies, Sir John, **III:** 541

Davies, Marion, **Supp. XVI:** 186

Da Vinci, Leonardo, **I:** 274; **II:** 536; **III:** 210

Da Vinci Code, The (Brown), **Supp. XXVII:** 5

Davis, Allen F., **Supp. I Part 1:** 1, 7

Davis, Allison, **Supp. I Part 1:** 327

Davis, Angela, **Supp. I Part 1:** 66; **Supp. X:** 249; **Supp. XXVI:** 50

Davis, Arthur B., **Supp. XVIII:** 119

Davis, Bette, **I:** 78; **Supp. I Part 1:** 67

Davis, Bill, **Supp. XIII:** 267

Davis, Christina, **Supp. XV:** 264

Davis, Cynthia, **Supp. XVIII:** 281, 286

Davis, Donald, **Supp. XIII:** 93

Davis, Elizabeth Gould, **Supp. I Part 2:** 567

Davis, George, **II:** 586

Davis, Glover, **Supp. V:** 180, 182, 186

Davis, Jefferson, **II:** 206; **IV:** 122, 125, 126

Davis, Jordan, **Supp. XV:** 178, 181, 186, 188

Davis, Katie, **Supp. VIII:** 83

Davis, L. J., **Supp. XI:** 234

Davis, Lydia, **Supp. XII:** 24; **Supp. XVII:** 21

Davis, Marcia, **Supp. XVIII:** 91, 100

Davis, Mary H., **Supp. XVIII:** 77

Davis, Miles, **Supp. XV:** 346; **Supp. XXII:** 172

Davis, Ossie, Jr., **Supp. IV Part 1:** 362; **Supp. XVI:** 144

Davis, Rebecca Harding, **Supp. I Part 1:** 45; **Supp. XIII:** 292, 295, 305; **Supp. XVI: 79–96**

Davis, Richard Harding, **III:** 328; **Supp. II Part 1:** 393; **Supp. XVI:** 85

Davis, Robert Gorham, **II:** 51; **IV:** 108

Davis, Stuart, **IV:** 409; **Supp. XV:** 295; **Supp. XXI:** 6

Davis, Thadious, **Supp. XVIII:** 120, 121, 123, 127, 129

Davis, Thulani, **Supp. XI:** 179; **Supp. XIII:** 233, 234, 239

Davis, William Virgil, **Supp. IV Part 1:** 63, 64, 68, 69, 70; **Supp. XXI: 83–96**

Davison, Jane, **Supp. XXVI:** 64, 65

Davison, Peter, **Supp. XXI:** 91; **Supp. XXVI: 61–80**

Davy's Lake (M. Finch), **Supp. XVII:** 69

Dawn (Dreiser), **I:** 498, 499, 503, 509, 515, 519

Dawn (O. Butler), **Supp. XIII:** 63, **64**

"Dawnbreaker" (Hayden), **Supp. II Part 1:** 370

Dawn in Russia (W. Frank), **Supp. XX: 76**

Dawn Patrol, The (film), **Supp. XIV:** 81

"Dawn Patrol: A Review of the Literature of the Negro for 1948" (Locke), **Supp. XIV:** 211

Dawson, Edward, **IV:** 151

Dawson, Emma, **I:** 199

Dawson, Melanie, **Supp. XXIV:** 25, 31

Dawson, Ruth, **Supp. XI:** 120

Day, Dorothy, **II:** 215; **Supp. I Part 2:** 524; **Supp. X:** 142; **Supp. XXV:** 19, 30

Day, Fred Holland, **Supp. XX: 114, 115**

Day, Georgiana, **Supp. I Part 2:** 585

Day, Richard, **Supp. XVIII:** 251

"Day After Day of the Dead" (Mackey), **Supp. XXVII:** 156

Dayan, Joan, **Retro. Supp. II:** 270

"Day and Night" (Teasdale), **Supp. XXVII:** 293

"Day Book" (Notley), **Supp. XXII:** 230

Day Book, A (Creeley), **Supp. IV Part 1:** 155

"Daybreak" (Kinnell), **Supp. III Part 1:** 250

"Daybreak Blues" (Kees), **Supp. XV:** 133

"Day-Breakers, The" (Bontemps), **Supp. XXII:** 8

"Daybreak in Alabama" (Hughes), **Retro. Supp. I:** 211; **Supp. I Part 1:** 344

Day by Day (R. Lowell), **Retro. Supp. II:** 184, 186, 191

"Day-Care Field Trip: Aquarium" (Karr), **Supp. XI:** 243

"Day-Dream, A" (Bryant), **Supp. I Part 1:** 160

"Day-Dream of a Grocer, The" (Twain), **Supp. XVIII:** 9

"Day for Poetry and Song, A" (Douglass), **Supp. III Part 1:** 172

"Day in the Life of Half of Rumpelstiltskin, A" (Brockmeier), **Supp. XXII:** 50, 52, 53

"Day Lady Died, The" (O'Hara), **Supp. XIX:** 85; **Supp. XXIII:** 216, 219

Day Late and a Dollar Short, A (McMillan), **Supp. XIII:** 184, **Supp. XIII:** 185, **191–192**

"Day longs for the evening, The" (Levertov), **Supp. III Part 1:** 274

Daynard, Jodi, **Supp. XVIII:** 97

Day of a Stranger (Merton), **Supp. VIII:** 203

"Day of Days, A" (James), **II:** 322

Day of Doom (Wigglesworth), **IV:** 147, 155, 156

Day of the Body (C. Frost), **Supp. XV:** 93, **98–100,** 106

Day of the Locust, The (West), **I:** 298; **IV:** 288, 299–306; **Retro. Supp. II:** 321, 323, 324, 329, **337–338; Supp. II Part 2:** 626; **Supp. XI:** 296; **Supp. XII:** 173; **Supp. XIII:** 170; **Supp. XIV:** 328; **Supp. XVIII:** 246

"Day of Wrath" (Davison), **Supp. XXVI:** 74

"Day on the Big Branch, A" (Nemerov), **III:** 275–276

"Day on the Connecticut River, A" (Merrill), **Supp. III Part 1:** 336

Day Room, The (DeLillo), **Supp. VI:** 4

"Days" (Emerson), **II:** 19, 20

"Days and Nights" (Koch), **Supp. XV:** 179, 180

"Days and Nights: A Journal" (Price), **Supp. VI:** 265

Days Before, The (Porter), **III:** 433, 453

"Day's Ending (Tucson)" (Teasdale), **Supp. XXVII:** 288, 296

Days in the Yellow Leaf (Hoffman), **Supp. XVIII:** 75

"Days of 1935" (Merrill), **Supp. III Part 1:** 325, 328

"Days of 1941 and '44" (Merrill), **Supp. III Part 1:** 336

"Days of 1964" (Merrill), **Supp. III Part 1:** 328, 352

"Days of 1971" (Merrill), **Supp. III Part 1:** 328

"Days of 1981" (Doty), **Supp. XI:** 123

"Days of Awe: The Birth of Lucy Jane" (Wasserstein), **Supp. XV:** 332

"Days of Edward Hopper" (Haines), **Supp. XII:** 210

"Days of Heaven" (Bass), **Supp. XVI:** 20

Days of Obligation: An Argument with My Mexican Father (Rodriguez), **Supp. XIV:** 298, 300, **302–305,** 307, 310

Days of Our Lives (soap opera), **Supp. XI:** 83

Days of Our Lives Lie in Fragments: New and Old Poems (Garrett), **Supp. VII:** 109–110, 111

Days of the Phoenix (Brooks), **I:** 266

Days of Wine and Roses (J. P. Miller), **Supp. XIII:** 262

Days: Tangier Journal, 1987–1989 (Bowles), **Supp. IV Part 1:** 94

Days to Come (Hellman), **Supp. I Part 1:** 276, 277–278

Days without End (O'Neill), **III:** 385, 391, 397

"Day's Work, A" (Capote), **Supp. III Part 1:** 120

"Day's Work, A" (Porter), **III:** 443, 446

"Day the Presidential Candidate Came to Ciudad Tamaulipas, The" (Caldwell), **I:** 309

"Day the Singer Fell, The" (Swados), **Supp. XIX:** 258

Day the World ended, The (Coover), **Supp. V:** 1

"Day with Conrad Green, A" (Lardner), **II:** 428–429, 430

"Deacon, The" (Huddle), **Supp. XXVI:** 151, 153–154, 158

"Deacon's Masterpiece, The" (Holmes), **Supp. I Part 1:** 302, 307

"Dead, The" (Collins), **Supp. XXI:** 64

"Dead, The" (Joyce), **I:** 285; **III:** 343; **Supp. XXIII:** 71

"Dead, The" (Very), **Supp. XXV:** 249

Dead and the Living, The (Olds), **Supp. X:** 201, **204–206,** 207

"Dead Body, The" (Olds), **Supp. X:** 210

"Dead by the Side of the Road, The" (Snyder), **Supp. VIII:** 301

"Dead Doe" (B. Kelly), **Supp. XVII:** 128–129

Dead End (Kingsley), **Supp. I Part 1:** 277, 281

Dead Father, The (Barthelme), **Supp. IV Part 1:** 43, 47, 50–51

"Dead Fiddler, The" (Singer), **IV:** 20

Dead Fingers Talk (Burroughs), **Supp. III Part 1:** 103

"Dead Hand" series (Sinclair), **Supp. V:** 276, 277, 281

"Dead Language Lessons" (Stallings), **Supp. XXV:** 233

"Dead Languages, The" (Humphrey), **Supp. IX:** 109

Dead Lecturer, The (Baraka), **Supp. II Part 1:** 31, 33, 35–37, 49

Dead Letters Sent (Kenny), **Supp. XXIII:** 143, 145

"Dead Letters Sent (By the Ontario Shores)"(Kenny), **Supp. XXIII:** 145

Deadline at Dawn (Odets), **Supp. II Part 2:** 546

Deadlock (Paretsky), **Supp. XXV:** 173, 176, 178–179

"Dead-Lock and Its Key, A" (E. Stoddard), **Supp. XV:** 286

"Dead Loon, The" (Bynner), **Supp. XV: 44–45**

Deadly Affair, A (Lacy), **Supp. XV:** 205–206

Deadly is the Female (film), **Supp. XVII:** 62

Dead Man's Walk (McMurtry), **Supp. V:** 231, 232

Dead Man's Walk (screenplay; McMurtry and Ossana), **Supp. V:** 231

Dead Man Walking (opera libretto, McNally), **Supp. XIII:** 207

Dead Poets Society (film), **Supp. XXI:** 192, 193, 194, 199

"Dead Reckoning" (Jarman), **Supp. XVII:** 113

"Dead Soldier's Talk, The" (Jin), **Supp. XVIII:** 92

Dead Souls (Gogol), **I:** 296

"Dead Souls on Campus" (Kosinski), **Supp. VII:** 222

"Dead Wingman, The" (Jarrell), **II:** 374

"Dead Wood, Green Wood" (Hadas), **Supp. XXIII:** 120

"Dead Yellow Women" (Hammett), **Supp. IV Part 1:** 345

Dead Zone, The (King), **Supp. V:** 139, 143, 144, 148, 152

Dean, James, **I:** 493

Dean, Man Mountain, **II:** 589

Deane, Silas, **Supp. I Part 2:** 509, 524

"Dean of Men" (Taylor), **Supp. V:** 314, 323

Dean's December, The (Bellow), **Retro. Supp. II:** 30–31

"Dear Adolph" (Benét), **Supp. XI:** 46

"Dear America" (Ortiz), **Supp. IV Part 2:** 503

"Dear Dark Continent" (Notley), **Supp. XXII:** 223

"Dearest M—" (Carruth), **Supp. XVI:** 59

Dear Ghosts (Gallagher), **Supp. XXIV:** 166, 167, 170–171, 176

"Dear Judas" (Jeffers), **Supp. II Part 2:** 431–432, 433

Dear Juliette (Sarton), **Supp. VIII:** 265

Dear Life (Munro), **Supp. XXVII:** 195

Dear Lovely Death (Hughes), **Retro. Supp. I:** 203; **Supp. I Part 1:** 328

"Dear Mr. Walrus" (Boyle), **Supp. XXIV:** 58–59

Dear Rafe (Hinojosa), **Supp. XIX:** 98, 105–106

"Dear Smoker" (Biss), **Supp. XXVI:** 51

"Dear Villon" (Corso), **Supp. XII:** 135

"Dear World" (Gunn Allen), **Supp. IV Part 1:** 321

Deasy, Philip, **Supp. XX: 42**

Death (Allen), **Supp. XV:** 3

"Death" (Corso), **Supp. XII:** 127

"Death" (Mailer), **III:** 38

"Death" (R. Lowell), **II:** 536

"Death" (W. C. Williams), **Retro. Supp. I:** 422

"Death" (West), **IV:** 286

"Death, Decay and Change" (Very), **Supp. XXV:** 243

"Death and Absence" (Glück), **Supp. V:** 82

Death and Birth of David Markand, The (W. Frank), **Supp. XX: 76–77**

Death and Taxes (Parker), **Supp. IX:** 192

"Death and the Child" (Crane), **I:** 414

"Death as a Society Lady" (Hecht), **Supp. X:** 71–72

Death before Bedtime (Vidal as Box), **Supp. IV Part 2:** 682

"Death Be Not Proud" (Donne), **Supp. XVI:** 158

"Death by Water" (Eliot), **I:** 395, 578

Death Comes for the Archbishop (Cather), **I:** 314, 327, 328–330; **Retro. Supp. I:** 16–18, 21; **Supp. XIII:** 253; **Supp. XXIV:** 253

Death in Paradise (Parker), **Supp. XIX:** 186

Death in the Afternoon (Hemingway), **II:** 253; **IV:** 35; **Retro. Supp. I:** 182; **Supp. VIII:** 182; **Supp. XIX:** 246; **Supp. XVI:** 205; **Supp. XX:** 76

"Death in the Country, A" (Benét), **Supp. XI:** 53–54

Death in the Family, A (Agee), **I:** 25, 29, 42, 45

Death in the Fifth Position (Vidal as Box), **Supp. IV Part 2:** 682

"Death in the Woods" (Anderson), **I:** 114, 115; **Supp. XXIV:** 136

Death in the Woods and Other Stories (Anderson), **I:** 112, 114, 115

Death in Venice (Mann), **III:** 231; **Supp. IV Part 1:** 392; **Supp. V:** 51

"Death in Viet Nam" (Salinas), **Supp. XIII:** 315

"Death in Winter" (C. Frost), **Supp. XV:** 98

Death Is a Lonely Business (Bradbury), **Supp. IV Part 1:** 102, 103, 111–112, 115

"Death Is Not the End" (Wallace), **Supp. X:** 309

Death Is the Place (Bronk), **Supp. XXI:** 32

Death Kit (Sontag), **Supp. III Part 2:** 451, 468–469

"Deathlight" (Huddle), **Supp. XXVI:** 150

Death Likes It Hot (Vidal as Box), **Supp. IV Part 2:** 682

"*Death*/Muerta" (Mora), **Supp. XIII:** 228

Death Notebooks, The (Sexton), **Supp. II Part 2:** 691, 694, 695

"Death of a Columnist" (Siddons), **Supp. XXII:** 241–242

Death of Adam, The: Essays on Modern Thought (Robinson), **Supp. XXI:** 212

"Death of a Jazz Musician" (W. J. Smith), **Supp. XIII:** 334

Death of a Kinsman, The (Taylor), **Supp. V:** 324, 326

"Death of a Lady's Man" (Cohen), **Supp. XXVII:** 58

Death of a Man (Boyle), **Supp. XXIV:** 60

"Death of an Old Seaman" (Hughes), **Retro. Supp. I:** 199

"Death of a Pig" (White), **Supp. I Part 2:** 665–668

Death of a Salesman (A. Miller), **I:** 81; **III:** 148, 149, 150, 153–154, 156, 157, 158, 159, 160, 163, 164, 166; **IV:** 389; **Supp. IV Part 1:** 359; **Supp. XIV:** 102, 239, 254, 255; **Supp. XV:** 205; **Supp. XX: 27; Supp. XXIII:** 199

"Death of a Soldier, The" (Stevens), **Retro. Supp. I:** 299, 312. *see also* "Lettres d'un Soldat" (Stevens)

"Death of a Soldier, The" (Wilson), **IV:** 427, 445

"Death of a Toad" (Wilbur), **Supp. III Part 2:** 550

"Death of a Traveling Salesman" (Welty), **IV:** 261; **Retro. Supp. I:** 344

"Death of a Young Son by Drowning" (Atwood), **Supp. XIII:** 33

Death of Bessie Smith, The (Albee), **I:** 76–77, 92

Death of Billy the Kid, The (Vidal), **Supp. IV Part 2:** 683

Death of Cock Robin, The (Snodgrass), **Supp. VI:** 315, 317–319, 324

Death of Dreams, A (Hoffman), **Supp. XVIII:** 79

"Death of General Wolfe, The" (Paine), **Supp. I Part 2:** 504

"Death of Halpin Frayser, The" (Bierce), **I:** 205

"Death of Justina, The" (Cheever), **Supp. I Part 1:** 184–185

Death of Life, The (Barnes), **Supp. III Part 1:** 34

Death of Malcolm X, The (Baraka), **Supp. II Part 1:** 47

"Death of Marilyn Monroe, The" (Olds), **Supp. X:** 205

"Death of Me, The" (Malamud), **Supp. I Part 2:** 437

"Death of Slavery, The" (Bryant), **Supp. I Part 1:** 168–169

"Death of St. Narcissus, The" (Eliot), **Retro. Supp. I:** 291

"Death of the Ball Turret Gunner, The" (Jarrell), **II:** 369–370, 372, 374, 375, 376, 378

"Death of the Fathers, The" (Sexton), **Supp. II Part 2:** 692

"Death of the Flowers, The" (Bryant), **Supp. I Part 1:** 170

Death of the Fox (Garrett), **Supp. VII:** 99, 101–104, 108

"Death of the Hat, The" (Collins), **Supp. XXI:** 59

"Death of the Hired Man, The" (Frost), **III:** 523; **Retro. Supp. I:** 121, 128; **Supp. IX:** 261

Death of the Kapowsin Tavern (Hugo), **Supp. VI:** 133–135

"Death of the Kapowsin Tavern" (Hugo), **Supp. VI:** 137, 141

"Death of the Lyric, The: The Achievement of Louis Simpson" (Jarman and McDowell), **Supp. IX:** 266, 270, 276

"Death of the Virgin, The (Rembrandt)" (Davison), **Supp. XXVI:** 70

"Death of Venus, The" (Creeley), **Supp. IV Part 1:** 143, 144–145

"Death on All Fronts" (Ginsberg), **Supp. II Part 1:** 326

"Deaths" (Dunn), **Supp. XI:** 147

"Death Sauntering About" (Hecht), **Supp. X:** 72

Deaths for the Ladies (and Other Disasters) (Mailer), **Retro. Supp. II:** 203

Death's Jest-Book (Beddoes), **Retro. Supp. I:** 285

Death Song (McGrath), **Supp. X:** 127

"Death the Carnival Barker" (Hecht), **Supp. X:** 72

"Death the Film Director" (Hecht), **Supp. X:** 72

"Death the Judge" (Hecht), **Supp. X:** 72

"Death the Mexican Revolutionary" (Hecht), **Supp. X:** 72

"Death the Oxford Don" (Hecht), **Supp. X:** 72

"Death the Painter" (Hecht), **Supp. X:** 72

Death the Proud Brother (Wolfe), **IV:** 456

"Death to Van Gogh's Ear!" (Ginsberg), **Supp. II Part 1:** 320, 322, 323

"Death Warmed Over!" (Bradbury), **Supp. IV Part 1:** 104–105, 112

Death Wish, The (Holding), **Supp. XXII:** 120, **123,** 134, 135

Deaver, Philip F., **Supp. XXVI:** 151, 160–161

Débâcle, La (Zola), **III:** 316

"Debate with the Rabbi" (Nemerov), **III:** 272

Debeljak, Aleš, **Supp. VIII:** 272

De Bellis, Jack, **Supp. I Part 1:** 366, 368, 372

Debo, Annette, **Supp. XXI:** 254

DeBoer-Langworthy, Carol, **Supp. XVII:** 98, 99, 100

DeBold, Kathleen, **Supp. XXV:** 4

De Bosis, Lauro, **IV:** 372

"Debriefing" (Sontag), **Supp. III Part 2:** 468–470

Debs, Eugene, **I:** 483, 493; **III:** 580, 581; **Supp. I Part 2:** 524; **Supp. IX:** 1, 15; **Supp. XXIII:** 161, 162

"Debt" (Teasdale), **Supp. XXVII:** 290

Debt to Pleasure, The (Lanchester), **Retro. Supp. I:** 278

Debussy, Claude, **Retro. Supp. II:** 266; **Supp. XIII:** 44

"Decades" (Sorrentino), **Supp. XXI:** 229

Decameron (Boccaccio), **III:** 283, 411; **Supp. IX:** 215

de Camp, L. Sprague, **Supp. XXVII:** 115, 128

"Deceased" (Hughes), **Retro. Supp. I:** 208

"December" (Oliver), **Supp. VII:** 245

"December 1, 1994" (Stern), **Supp. IX:** 299

December 7 (film, Ford), **Supp. XVIII:** 247

"December 24" (Di Piero), **Supp. XIX:** 39

"December 28: Returning to Chicago" (Di Piero), **Supp. XIX:** 39

"December Dawn" (Skloot), **Supp. XX:** **202**

"December Eclogue" (Winters), **Supp. II Part 2:** 794

"Decent Woman, A" (Boulton), **Supp. XXII:** 22–23

De Cenzo, Giorgia, **Supp. XXI:** 256

Deception (P. Roth), **Retro. Supp. II:** 291; **Supp. III Part 2:** 426–427

"Deceptions" (Dobyns), **Supp. XIII:** 77

De Chiara, Ann. *See* Malamud, Mrs. Bernard (Ann de Chiara)

De Chirico, Giorgio, **Supp. XIII:** 317

"Decided Loss, A" (Poe), **II:** 411

"Decision" (Boyle), **Supp. XXIV:** 54

"Decisions to Disappear" (Dunn), **Supp. XI:** 144

"Decisive Moment, The" (Auster), **Supp. XIV:** 292

Decker, James A., **Supp. III Part 2:** 621

Declaration of Gentlemen and Merchants and Inhabitants of Boston, and the Country Adjacent, A (Mather), **Supp. II Part 2:** 450

Declaration of Paris, The (Adams), **I:** 4

Declaration of the Rights of Man and the Citizen, **Supp. I Part 2:** 513, 519

Declaration of Universal Peace and Liberty (Paine), **Supp. I Part 2:** 512

Declension in the Village of Chung Luong (Weigl), **Supp. XIX:** 287, 288

Decline and Fall (Waugh), **Supp. I Part 2:** 607; **Supp. XV:** 142

Decline and Fall of the English System of Finance, The (Paine), **Supp. I Part 2:** 518

Decline and Fall of the Roman Empire, The (Gibbons), **Supp. III Part 2:** 629

"Decline of Book Reviewing, The" (Hardwick), **Supp. III Part 1:** 201–202

Decline of the West, The (Spengler), **I:** 270; **IV:** 125

"Decolonizing the Tongue: Reading Speech and Aphasia in the Work of Michelle Cliff" (Aguiar), **Supp. XXII:** 68

Deconstructing Harry (film; Allen), **Supp. XV:** 12, **13**

"Décor" (X. J. Kennedy), **Supp. XV:** 171

"Decoration Day" (Jewett), **II:** 412; **Retro. Supp. II:** 138

Decoration of Houses, The (Wharton and Codman), **IV:** 308; **Retro. Supp. I:** 362, 363–364, 366

"Decoy" (Ashbery), **Supp. III Part 1:** 13–14

Decter, Midge, **Supp. XX: 248**

Dedalus, Stephen, **Supp. XIX:** 47

"De Daumier-Smith's Blue Period" (Salinger), **III:** 560–561

"Dedication" (Nelson), **Supp. XVIII:** 173, 180

"Dedication and Household Map" (Erdrich), **Supp. IV Part 1:** 272

"Dedication Day" (Agee), **I:** 34

"Dedication for a Book" (Hay), **Supp. XIV:** 125

"Dedication for a Book of Criticism" (Winters), **Supp. II Part 2:** 801

"Dedication in Postscript, A" (Winters), **Supp. II Part 2:** 801

Dedications and Other Darkhorses (Komunyakaa), **Supp. XIII:** 112, **113–114**

"Dedication to Hunger" (Glück), **Supp. V:** 83

"Dedication to My Wife, A" (Eliot), **I:** 583

Dee, Jonathan, **Supp. XXIII:** 302

Dee, Ruby, **Supp. IV Part 1:** 362

Deeck, William, **Supp. XXVI:** 278

Deeds of Utmost Kindness (Gander), **Supp. XV:** 340

Deegan, Thomas, **Supp. XXIII:** 100, 107–108

"Deep Breath at Dawn, A" (Hecht), **Supp. X:** 58

Deep End, The (film), **Supp. XXII:** 120, 131, 133

Deeper into Movies: The Essential Kael Collection from '69 to '72 (Kael), **Supp. IX:** 253

"Deeper Wisdom, The" (Hay), **Supp. XIV:** 129

Deep Green Sea (R. O. Butler), **Supp. XII:** 62, **74**

Deephaven (Jewett), **II:** 398–399, 400, 401, 410, 411; **Retro. Supp. II:** 133, 134, 135, 136, 137, 138, 140, 141, 143, 144

"Deep Sight and Rescue Missions" (Bambara), **Supp. XI:** 18–19

Deep Sightings and Rescue Missions: Fiction, Essays, and Conversations (Bambara), **Supp. XI:** 1, 3, **14–20**

Deep Sleep, The (Morris), **III:** 224–225

"Deep Song" (G. Jones), **Supp. XXIV:** 194

Deep South (Caldwell), **I:** 305, 309, 310

Deepstep Come Shining (Wright), **Supp. XV:** 337, 341, 344, **349–350,** 351, 353

"Deep Water" (Marquand), **III:** 56

"Deep Woods" (Nemerov), **III:** 272–273, 275

"Deer at Providencia, The" (Dillard), **Supp. VI:** 28, 32

Deer Camp: Last Light in the Northeast Kingdom (Ostrum, ed.), **Supp. XXII:** 218

"Deer Dancer" (Harjo), **Supp. XII:** 224–225

"Deer Ghost" (Harjo), **Supp. XII:** 225

Deer Park, The (Mailer), **I:** 292; **III:** 27, 31–33, 35–36, 37, 39, 40, 42, 43, 44; **Retro. Supp. II: 200–202,** 205, 207, 211

Deer Park, The: A Play (Mailer), **Retro. Supp. II:** 205

Deer Pasture, The (Bass), **Supp. XVI:** 15, 16, 23

Deerslayer, The (Cooper), **I:** 341, 349, 350, 355; **Supp. I Part 1:** 251

Deese, Helen, **Supp. XXV:** 251

"Defeat" (Boyle), **Supp. XXIV: 60–61**

Defence, The (Nabokov), **Supp. XXII:** 263

"Defence of Poesie, The" (Bronk), **Supp. XXI:** 32

"Defence of Poesy, The" (Sidney), **Supp. V:** 250

"Defence of Poetry" (Longfellow), **II:** 493–494

"Defender of the Faith" (P. Roth), **Retro. Supp. II:** 281; **Supp. III Part 2:** 404, 407, 420

"Defending *The Searchers* (Scenes in the Life of an Obsession)" *(Lethem), Supp. XVIII:* 136,141

"Defenestration in Prague" (Matthews), **Supp. IX:** 168

Defenestration of Prague (Howe), **Supp. IV Part 2:** 419, 426, 429–430

Defense, The (Nabokov), **III:** 251–252; **Retro. Supp. I:** 266, 268, **270–272**

"Defense of Poetry" (Francis), **Supp. IX:** 83–84

DeFeo, Ronald, **Supp. XXIII:** 106

Defiant Ones, The (film), **Supp. I Part 1:** 67

"Defining the Age" (W. V. Davis), **Supp. IV Part 1:** 64

"Definition" (Ammons), **Supp. VII:** 28

Defoe, Daniel, **I:** 204; **II:** 104, 105, 159, 304–305; **III:** 113, 423; **IV:** 180; **Supp. I Part 2:** 523; **Supp. V:** 127

De Forest, John William, **II:** 275, 280, 288, 289; **IV:** 350

DeFrees, Madeline, **Supp. XVIII:** 293; **Supp. XXVI:** 180

Deganawida, the Peacemaker, **Supp. XXVI: 81–100**

"Deganawidah: The Peacemaker"(Kenny), **Supp. XXIII:** 151

Degas, Brian, **Supp. XI:** 307

Degler, Carl, **Supp. I Part 2:** 496

"Degrees of Fidelity" (Dunn), **Supp. XI:** 148, 156

Deguy, Michel, **Supp. XV:** 178

De Haven, Tom, **Supp. XI:** 39; **Supp. XII:** 338–339

Deitch, Joseph, **Supp. VIII:** 125

"Dejection" (Coleridge), **II:** 97

DeJong, Constance, **Supp. XII:** 4

DeJong, David Cornel, **I:** 35

Dekker,Thomas, **Supp. XVII:** 232

de Kooning, Elaine de, **Supp. XXIII:** 210, 217

de Kooning, Willem, **Supp. XII:** 198; **Supp. XV:** 177, 178

de Kooning, Willem de, **Supp. XXIII:** 208, 210, 211, 217, 220

Delacroix, Henri, **I:** 227

De La Mare, Walter, **III:** 429; **Supp. II Part 1:** 4; **Supp. XVII:** 69

Delamotte, Eugenia C., **Supp. XI:** 279

De Lancey, James, **I:** 338

De Lancey, Mrs. James (Anne Heathcote), **I:** 338

De Lancey, Susan A. *See* Cooper, Mrs. James Fenimore

De Lancey, William Heathcote, **I:** 338, 353

Delano, Amasa, **III:** 90

De la Paz, Oliver, **Supp. XXVI:** 101, 103, 111

Delattre, Roland A., **I:** 558

De Laurentiis, Dino, **Supp. XI:** 170, 307

De la Valdéne, Guy, **Supp. VIII:** 40, 42

Delbanco, Andrew, **Supp. XXIV:** 69

Delbanco, Nicholas, **Supp. XXII:** 204

Del Cabral, Manuel, **Supp. XXI:** 104

DelCorso's Gallery (Caputo), **Supp. XIX:** 22–23

Delectorskaya, Lydia, **Supp. XXII:** 99

De l'éducation d'un homme sauvage (Itard), **Supp. I Part 2:** 564

Deleuze, Gilles, **Supp. XXV:** 123

"Delft" (Goldbarth), **Supp. XII:** 189

Delft: An Essay-Poem (Goldbarth), **Supp. XII:** 187

Delicate Balance, A (Albee), **I:** 86–89, 91, 93, 94

Delicate Balance, The (Hay), **Supp. XIV:** 121, 122, 124, 129, 133–134

"Delicate Balance, The" (Hay), **Supp. XIV:** 122

"Delicate Prey, The" (Bowles), **Supp. IV Part 1:** 86

Delicate Prey and Other Stories, The (Bowles), **Supp. IV Part 1:** 86–87

Délie (Scève), **Supp. III Part 1:** 11

Delights & Shadows (Kooser), **Supp. XIX:** 115, 116, 117, 121, **127–128**

DeLillo, Don, **Retro. Supp. I:** 278; **Retro. Supp. II:** 279; **Supp. IX:** 212; **Supp. VI: 1–18; Supp. XI:** 68; **Supp. XII:** 21, 152; **Supp. XIX:** 54; **Supp. XVII:** 183; **Supp. XVIII:** 136, 140; **Supp. XX: 83, 87, 91; Supp. XXIII:** 109; **Supp. XXVII:** 6

De Lint, Charles, **Supp. XXII:** 59

DeLisle, Anne, **Supp. VIII:** 175

Deliverance (Dickey), **Supp. IV Part 1:** 176, 186–188, 190; **Supp. X:** 30; **Supp. XX: 173–174; Supp. XXIII:** 43, 50

Deliverance, The (Glasgow), **II:** 175, 176, 177–178, 181

"Delivering" (Dubus), **Supp. VII:** 87

Dell, Floyd, **I:** 103, 105; **Supp. I Part 2:** 379; **Supp. XV:** 295; **Supp. XVII:** 96; **Supp. XXI:** 6; **Supp. XXII:** 275; **Supp. XXV:** 18

Della Francesca, Piero, **Supp. XV:** 262

"Della Primavera Trasportata al Morale" (W. C. Williams), **Retro. Supp. I:** 419, 422

DeLoria, Philip J., **Supp. XIV:** 306

Deloria, Vine, Jr., **Supp. IV Part 1:** 323; **Supp. IV Part 2:** 504; **Supp. XXVI:** 98

"Delta Autumn" (Faulkner), **II:** 71

"Delta Factor, The" (Percy), **Supp. III Part 1:** 386

Delta of Venus: Erotica (Nin), **Supp. X:** 192, 195

Delta Wedding (Welty), **IV:** 261, 268–271, 273, 281; **Retro. Supp. I:** 349–350, 351

Delusions (Berryman), **I:** 170

De Man, Paul, **Retro. Supp. I:** 67; **Supp. XVII:** 70

DeMarinis, Rick, **Supp. XIV:** 22

DeMars, James, **Supp. IV Part 2:** 552

Dembo, L. S., **I:** 386, 391, 396, 397, 398, 402; **III:** 478; **Supp. I Part 1:** 272; **Supp. XIV:** 277, 282, 288, 290; **Supp. XXVI:** 226–227, 235

"Dementia Translucida" (Bierds), **Supp. XVII:** 33

"Demeter"(Crooker), **Supp. XXIII:** 61

"Demeters"(Hadas), **Supp. XXIII:** 113

Demetrakopoulous, Stephanie A., **Supp. IV Part 1:** 12

De Mille, Agnes, **Supp. XXVI:** 66

DeMille, Cecil B., **Supp. IV Part 2:** 520; **Supp. XV:** 42

Demme, Jonathan, **Supp. V:** 14

Democracy (Adams), **I:** 9–10, 20; **Supp. IV Part 1:** 208; **Supp. XIX:** 139

Democracy (Didion), **Supp. IV Part 1:** 198, 208–210

"Democracy" (J. R. Lowell), **Supp. I Part 2:** 419

Democracy and Education (Dewey), **I:** 232

Democracy and Other Addresses (J. R. Lowell), **Supp. I Part 2:** 407

Democracy and Social Ethics (Addams), **Supp. I Part 1:** 8–11

Democracy in America (Tocqueville), **Retro. Supp. I:** 235; **Supp. XIV:** 306

Democratic Vistas (Whitman), **IV:** 333, 336, 348–349, 351, 469; **Retro. Supp. I:** 408; **Supp. I Part 2:** 456

Democritus, **I:** 480–481; **II:** 157; **III:** 606; **Retro. Supp. I:** 247

"Demon Lover, The" (Rich), **Supp. I Part 2:** 556

"Demonstrators, The" (Welty), **IV:** 280; **Retro. Supp. I:** 355

DeMott, Benjamin, **Supp. IV Part 1:** 35; **Supp. V:** 123; **Supp. XIII:** 95; **Supp. XIV: 106; Supp. XXV:** 86

DeMott, Robert, **Supp. VIII:** 40, 41

Demuth, Charles, **IV:** 404; **Retro. Supp. I:** 412, 430; **Supp. XXI:** 6

"Demystified Zone" (Paley), **Supp. VI:** 227

Denby, Edwin, **Supp. XXIV:** 36, 45; **Supp. XXVII:** 23

Denmark Vesey (opera) (Bowles), **Supp. IV Part 1:** 83

Dennett, Daniel, **Supp. XXII:** 265

Denney, Joseph Villiers, **Supp. I Part 2:** 605

Denney, Reuel, **Supp. XII:** 121; **Supp. XXI:** 19

Dennie, Joseph, **II:** 298; **Supp. I Part 1:** 125

Denning, Michael, **Supp. XXVI:** 28

Denniston, Dorothy Hamer, **Supp. XI:** 276, 277

"Den of Lions" (Plath), **Retro. Supp. II:** 242

"Dental Assistant, The" (Simpson), **Supp. IX:** 280

Den Uyl, Douglas, **Supp. IV Part 2:** 528, 530

"Deodand, The" (Hecht), **Supp. X:** 65

"Departing" (Cameron), **Supp. XII:** 81

"Departure" (Glück), **Supp. V:** 89

"Departure" (Plath), **Supp. I Part 2:** 537

"Departure, The" (Freneau), **Supp. II Part 1:** 264

"Departure from Hydra, The" (Koch), **Supp. XV:** 180–181

Departures (Justice), **Supp. VII:** 124–127

Departures and Arrivals (Shields), **Supp. VII:** 320, 322

"Depressed by a Book of Bad Poetry, I Walk Toward an Unused Pasture and Invite the Insects to Join Me" (Wright), **Supp. III Part 2:** 600

"Depressed Person, The" (Wallace), **Supp. X:** 309

"Depression Days" (Mora), **Supp. XIII:** 224–225

"Deprived of Unhappiness" (Pickering), **Supp. XXI:** 203

De Puy, John, **Supp. XIII:** 12

De Quincey, Thomas, **Supp. XXVI:** 283

D'Erasmo, Stacey, **Supp. IX:** 121

Derby, J. C., **Supp. XVIII:** 4

De Reilhe, Catherine, **Supp. I Part 1:** 202

De Rerum Natura (Lucretius), **II:** 162

"De Rerum Virtute" (Jeffers), **Supp. II Part 2:** 424

De Rioja, Francisco, **Supp. I Part 1:** 166

"Derivative Sport in Tornado Alley" (Wallace), **Supp. X:** 314

Derleth, August, **Supp. I Part 2:** 465, 472; **Supp. XXV:** 111, 122; **Supp. XXVII:** 117, 119, 128

Deronda, Daniel, **II:** 179

Derricotte, Toi, **Supp. XVIII:** 177

Derrida, Jacques, **Supp. IV Part 1:** 45; **Supp. XV:** 215, 224; **Supp. XVI:** 285, 288

Deruddere, Dominique, **Supp. XI:** 173

Der Wilde Jäger (Bürger), **II:** 306

Derzhavin, Gavrila Romanovich, **Supp. VIII:** 27

Desai, Anita, **Supp. XVI:** 156, 157, 158

Désamère (Notley), **Supp. XXII:** 226

De Santis, Christopher, **Retro. Supp. I:** 194

Descartes, René, **I:** 255; **III:** 618–619; **IV:** 133

"Descendant of Solomon and the Queen of Sheba" (Major), **Supp. XXII:** 182

Descendents, The (Glasgow), **II:** 173, 174–175, 176

Descending Figure (Glück), **Supp. V:** 83–84

"Descending Theology: Christ Human" (Karr), **Supp. XI:** 251

"Descending Theology: The Garden" (Karr), **Supp. XI:** 251

"Descent, The" (W. C. Williams), **Retro. Supp. I:** 428, 429

"Descent from the Cross" (Eliot), **Retro. Supp. I:** 57, 58

"Descent in the Maelström, A" (Poe), **Retro. Supp. II:** 274

"Descent into Proselito" (Knowles), **Supp. XII:** 237

"Descent into the Maelström, A" (Poe), **III:** 411, 414, 416, 424

Descent of Alette, The (Notley), **Supp. XXII:** 223, 224, 226, 227, 233–234

Descent of Man (Boyle), **Supp. VIII:** 1, 12–13; **Supp. XX:** 17, 18, 20

"Descent of Man" (Boyle), **Supp. VIII:** 14; **Supp. XX:** 18

Descent of Man, The (Darwin), **Supp. XIV:** 192

Descent of Man, The (Wharton), **IV:** 311; **Retro. Supp. I:** 367

Descent of Man and Other Stories, The (Wharton), **Retro. Supp. I:** 367

Descent of Winter, The (W. C. Williams), **Retro. Supp. I:** 419, 428

De Schloezer, Doris, **III:** 474

"Describers" (Halliday), **Supp. XIX:** 85

"Description" (Doty), **Supp. XI:** 126

"Description of the great Bones dug up at Clavarack on the Banks of Hudsons River A.D. 1705, The" (Taylor), **IV:** 163, 164

"Description without Place" (Stevens), **Retro. Supp. I:** 422

"Desert" (Hughes), **Retro. Supp. I:** 207

"Deserted Cabin" (Haines), **Supp. XII:** 203

Deserted Village, The (Goldsmith), **II:** 304

Desert Is My Mother, The/El desierto es mi madre (Mora), **Supp. XIII:** 214, 221

Desert Music, The (W. C. Williams), **IV:** 422; **Retro. Supp. I:** 428, 429

"Desert Music, The" (W. C. Williams), **Retro. Supp. I:** 428, 429

"Desert Places" (Frost), **II:** 159; **Retro. Supp. I:** 121, 123, 129, 138, 299; **Supp. XIV:** 229

Desert Rose, The (McMurtry), **Supp. V:** 225, 231

Desert Solitaire (Abbey), **Supp. X:** 30; **Supp. XIII:** 7–8, 12; **Supp. XIV:** 177, 179

Desert Solitaire: A Season in the Wilderness (Abbey), **Supp. XXV:** 208

"Design" (Frost), **II:** 158, 163; **Retro. Supp. I:** 121, 126, 138, 139; **Supp. IX:** 81; **Supp. XVII:** 132; **Supp. XVIII:** 298

"Designated National Park, A" (Ortiz), **Supp. IV Part 2:** 509

"Designs on a Point of View" (Everwine), **Supp. XV:** 76

DeSilva, Bruce, **Supp. XXII:** 205, 206, 217

Des Imagistes (Pound), **II:** 513; **Supp. I Part 1:** 257, 261, 262

Desire (album, Dylan), **Supp. XVIII:** 28

"Desire" (Beattie), **Supp. V:** 29

Desire (Bidart), **Supp. XV:** 32–34, 35

"Desire" (Everwine), **Supp. XV:** 85

Desire, Desire, Desire (Durang), **Supp. XXIV:** 113

"Desire and Denial" (Bronk), **Supp. XXI:** 26

"Désirée's Baby" (Chopin), **Retro. Supp. II:** 64, 65; **Supp. I Part 1:** 213–215

"Desire"(Hadas), **Supp. XXIII:** 117

Desire under the Elms (O'Neill), **III:** 387, 390

"Desolate Field, The" (W. C. Williams), **Retro. Supp. I:** 418

"Desolation, A" (Ginsberg), **Supp. II Part 1:** 313

Desolation Angels (Kerouac), **Supp. III Part 1:** 218, 225, 230

"Desolation Is a Delicate Thing" (Wylie), **Supp. I Part 2:** 729

"Desolation Row" (song, Dylan), **Supp. XVIII:** 30

Despair (Nabokov), **Retro. Supp. I:** 270, 274

Desperate Characters (Fox), **Supp. XX:** 91

"Despisals" (Rukeyser), **Supp. VI:** 282

Des Pres, Terrence, **Supp. X:** 113, 120, 124

"Destination Out" (Mackey), **Supp. XXVII:** 152

"Destiny and the Lieutenant" (McCoy), **Supp. XIII:** 171

"Destroyer, The" (Davison), **Supp. XXVI:** 71

"Destruction of Kreshev, The" (Singer), **IV:** 13; **Retro. Supp. II:** 307

Destruction of the European Jews, The (Hilberg), **Supp. V:** 267

"Destruction of the Goetheanum, The" (Salter), **Supp. IX:** 257

"Destruction of the Long Branch, The" (Pinsky), **Supp. VI:** 239, 240, 243–244, 245, 247, 250

Destructive Element, The (Spender), **Retro. Supp. I:** 216

"Detail & Parody for the poem 'Paterson'" (W. C. Williams), **Retro. Supp. I:** 424

Detmold, John, **Supp. I Part 2:** 670

De Tolnay, Charles, **Supp. XXII:** 255

Detour at Night (Endore), **Supp. XVII:** 64

Deuce, The (R. O. Butler), **Supp. XII:** 62, 69–70, 72

Deus Lo Volt! (Connell), **Supp. XIV:** 80, 81, 95

Deuteronomy (biblical book), **II:** 166

Deutsch, Andre, **Supp. XI:** 297, 301

Deutsch, Babette, **Supp. I Part 1:** 328, 341; **Supp. XV:** 305; **Supp. XXV:** 21; **Supp. XXVII:** 293

Deutsch, Michel, **Supp. IV Part 1:** 104

"Devaluation Blues: Ruminations on Black Families in Crisis" (Coleman), **Supp. XI:** 87

Devane, William, **Supp. XI:** 234

Devasahayam, Madona, **Supp. XXII:** 260
"Development of My Mind and Character, The" (Notley), **Supp. XXII:** 227
"Development of the Literary West" (Chopin), **Retro. Supp. II:** 72
"Development of the Modern English Novel, The" (Lanier), **Supp. I Part 1:** 370–371
DeVeriante (Herbert of Cherbury), **II:** 108
"Devil and Daniel Webster, The" (Benét), **III:** 22; **Supp. XI:** 45–46, 47, 50–51, 52
Devil and Daniel Webster and Other Writings, The (Benét), **Supp. XI:** 48
"Devil and Tom Walker, The" (Irving), **II:** 309–310
Devil At Large, The: Erica Jong on Henry Miller (Jong), **Supp. V:** 115, 131
Devil-Doll, The (film, Browning), **Supp. XVII:** 58–59
Devil Finds Work, The (Baldwin), **Retro. Supp. II:** 14; **Supp. I Part 1:** 48, 52, 66–67
Devil in a Blue Dress (Mosley), **Supp. XIII:** 237, 239
"Devil in Manuscript, The" (Hawthorne), **II:** 226; **Retro. Supp. I:** 150–151
Devil in Paradise, A (H. Miller), **III:** 190
"Devil in the Belfry, The" (Poe), **III:** 425; **Retro. Supp. II:** 273
"Devil Is a Busy Man, The" (Wallace), **Supp. X:** 309
Devil's Dictionary, The (Bierce), **I:** 196, 197, 205, 208, 209, 210
Devil's Stocking, The (Algren), **Supp. IX:** 5, 16
"Devil's Thumb, The" (Krakauer), **Supp. XVIII:** 107
Devil's Tour, The (Karr), **Supp. XI:** 240, **242–244**
Devil Tree, The (Kosinski), **Supp. VII:** 215, 222, 223
"Devising" (Ammons), **Supp. VII:** 28
Devlin, Paul, **Supp. XIX:** 159
De Voe, Edward Thomas, **Supp. XXV:** 23, 29
De Voto, Bernard, **I:** 247, 248; **II:** 446; **Supp. IV Part 2:** 599, 601
"Devout Meditation in Memory of Adolph Eichmann, A" (Merton), **Supp. VIII:** 198, 203
De Vries, Peter, **Supp. I Part 2:** 604
Dewberry, Elizabeth, **Supp. XII:** 62, 72
Dewey, John, **I:** 214, 224, 228, 232, 233, 266, 267; **II:** 20, 27, 34, 229, 361; **III:** 112, 294–295, 296, 303, 309–310, 599, 605; **IV:** 27, 429; **Supp. I Part 1:** 3, 5, 7, 10, 11, 12, 24; **Supp. I Part 2:** 493, 641, 647, 677; **Supp. IX:** 179; **Supp. V:** 290; **Supp. XIV:** 3; **Supp. XV:** 41
Dewey, Joseph, **Supp. IX:** 210
Dewey, Thomas, **IV:** 161
Dewey Defeats Truman (Mallon), **Supp. XIX:** 132, 137, **138**
Dexter, Peter, **Supp. XIV:** 221
De Young, Charles, **I:** 194
Dhairyam, Sagari, **Supp. IV Part 1:** 329, 330

Dharma Bums, The (Kerouac), **Supp. III Part 1:** 230, 231; **Supp. VIII:** 289, 305
"D. H. Lawrence" (Bynner), **Supp. XV:** 46
D. H. Lawrence: An Unprofessional Study (Nin), **Supp. X:** 182–183
D. H. Lawrence: The World of the Major Novels (Sanders), **Supp. XVI:** 267
D'Houdetot, Madame, **Supp. I Part 1:** 250
"Diabetes" (Dickey), **Supp. IV Part 1:** 182
Diaghilev, Sergei, **Supp. I Part 1:** 257
Dial (publication), **I:** 58, 109, 115, 116, 215, 231, 233, 245, 261, 384, 429; **II:** 8, 430; **III:** 194, 470, 471, 485; **IV:** 122, 171, 427; **Retro. Supp. I:** 58; **Retro. Supp. II:** 78; **Supp. I Part 2:** 642, 643, 647; **Supp. II Part 1:** 168, 279, 291; **Supp. II Part 2:** 474; **Supp. III Part 2:** 611
"Dialectical Materialism" (Weigl), **Supp. XIX:** 281
Dialectical Materialism and the Fate of Humanity (C. L. R. James), **Supp. XXI:** 169
"Dialectics of Love, The" (McGrath), **Supp. X:** 116
"Dialogue" (Rich), **Supp. I Part 2:** 560
Dialogue, A (Baldwin and Giovanni), **Supp. I Part 1:** 66
"Dialogue Between Franklin and the Gout" (Franklin), **II:** 121
"Dialogue Between General Wolfe and General Gage in a Wood near Boston, A" (Paine), **Supp. I Part 2:** 504
"Dialogue between Old England and New" (Bradstreet), **Supp. I Part 1:** 105–106, 110–111, 116
"Dialogue between the Writer and a Maypole Dresser, A" (Taylor), **IV:** 155
Dialogues (Bush, ed.), **III:** 4
Dialogues in Limbo (Santayana), **III:** 606
"Dialogue: William Harvey; Joan of Arc" (Goldbarth), **Supp. XII:** 178
Dialogue with a Dead Man (J. W. Miller), **Supp. XX: 163, 164, 167**
"Diamond as Big as the Ritz, The" (Fitzgerald), **II:** 88–89
Diamond Cutters and Other Poems, The (Rich), **Supp. I Part 2:** 551, 552, 553
"Diamond Guitar, A" (Capote), **Supp. III Part 1:** 124
Diamond Necklace, A (Notley), **Supp. XXII:** 228
"Diamonds in the Mine" (Cohen), **Supp. XXVII:** 51, 60
"Diana and Persis" (Alcott), **Supp. I Part 1:** 32, 41
"Diaper Brigade, The" (Ryan as Quin), **Supp. XVIII:** 230
Diaries of Charlotte Perkins Gilman (Knight, ed.), **Supp. XI:** 201
"Diary–1903" (Boyce), **Supp. XXI:** 8
"Diary Aug. 4–Aug. 5" (Brainard), **Supp. XXVII:** 18
Diary of a Chambermaid, The (film; Renoir), **Supp. XVI:** 193

Diary of Anaïs Nin, The (1931–1974), **Supp. X:** 181, 185–189, 191, 192, 193, 195
Diary of Anne Frank, The, **Supp. XXI:** 245
Diary of a Rapist, The: A Novel (Connell), **Supp. XIV:** 80, 82, 94
Diary of a Young Girl, The (Frank, tr. Mooyart-Doubleday), **Supp. XXVII:** 135, 137
Diary of a Yuppie (Auchincloss), **Supp. IV Part 1:** 31, 32–33
Diary of "Helena Morley", The (Bishop, trans.), **Retro. Supp. II:** 45, 51; **Supp. I Part 1:** 92
Dias, Robert Vas, **Supp. XXII:** 164, 169
Diay of Anne Frank, The (Goodrich and Hackett), **Supp. XXVII:** 136
Díaz, Junot, **Supp. XXIV: 83–95; Supp. XXV:** 49, 61
Díaz del Castillo, Bernál, **III:** 13, 14
Dick, Philip K., **Supp. XVI:** 123; **Supp. XVIII:** 136, 137, 138, 139, 142; **Supp. XXII:** 49
Dickens, Charles, **I:** 152, 198, 505; **II:** 98, 179, 186, 192, 271, 273–274, 288, 290, 297, 301, 307, 316, 322, 559, 561, 563, 577, 582; **III:** 146, 247, 325, 368, 411, 421, 426, 572, 577, 613–614, 616; **IV:** 21, 192, 194, 211, 429; **Retro. Supp. I:** 33, 91, 218; **Retro. Supp. II:** 204; **Supp. I Part 1:** 13, 34, 35, 36, 41, 49; **Supp. I Part 2:** 409, 523, 579, 590, 622, 675; **Supp. IV Part 1:** 293, 300, 341; **Supp. IV Part 2:** 464; **Supp. IX:** 246; **Supp. VIII:** 180; **Supp. XI:** 277; **Supp. XII:** 335, 337; **Supp. XIII:** 233; **Supp. XV:** 62; **Supp. XVI:** 63, 65–66, 72–73, 202; **Supp. XVIII:** 7, 136, 146; **Supp. XX: 21, 87, 195; Supp. XXII:** 206; **Supp. XXIII:** 4, 85, 290; **Supp. XXIV:** 87; **Supp. XXV:** 258; **Supp. XXVII:** 269
Dickey, James, **I:** 29, 535; **III:** 268; **Retro. Supp. II:** 233; **Supp. III Part 1:** 354; **Supp. III Part 2:** 541, 597; **Supp. IV Part 1: 175–194; Supp. V:** 333; **Supp. X:** 30; **Supp. XI:** 312, 317; **Supp. XIX:** 282; **Supp. XV:** 115, 348; **Supp. XVIII:** 191, 299; **Supp. XXI:** 35; **Supp. XXIII:** 43, 50; **Supp. XXIV:** 42; **Supp. XXVI:** 67
Dick Gibson Show, The (Elkin), **Supp. VI:** 42, **48–49**
Dickie, Margaret, **Retro. Supp. II:** 53, 84
Dickinson, Donald, **Retro. Supp. I:** 206, 212
Dickinson, Edward, **I:** 451–452, 453
Dickinson, Mrs. Edward, **I:** 451, 453
Dickinson, Emily, **I:** 384, 419, 433, **451–473; II:** 272, 276, 277, 530; **III:** 19, 194, 196, 214, 493, 505, 508, 556, 572, 576; **IV:** 134, 135, 331, 444; **Retro. Supp. I: 25–50; Retro. Supp. II:** 39, 40, 43, 45, 50, 76, 134, 155, 170; **Supp. I Part 1:** 29, 79, 188, 372; **Supp. I Part 2:** 375, 546, 609, 682, 691; **Supp. II Part 1:** 4; **Supp. III**

Part 1: 63; **Supp. III Part 2:** 600, 622; **Supp. IV Part 1:** 31, 257; **Supp. IV Part 2:** 434, 637, 641, 643; **Supp. IX:** 37, 38, 53, 87, 90; **Supp. V:** 79, 140, 332, 335; **Supp. VIII:** 95, 104, 106, 108, 198, 205, 272; **Supp. XII:** 226; **Supp. XIII:** 153, 339; **Supp. XIV:** 45, 127–128, 133, 261, 284; **Supp. XIX:** 86; **Supp. XV:** 287, 303, 309; **Supp. XVII:** 288; **Supp. XVII:** 71, 73, 74, 75, 132; **Supp. XVIII:** 301; **Supp. XX: 106, 108; Supp. XXI:** 52, 61, 64, 132, 214; **Supp. XXII:** 81, 82, 225, 277–278; **Supp. XXIII:** 19, 165; **Supp. XXVII:** 261, 283, 292

Dickinson, Gilbert, **I:** 469

Dickinson, Goldsworthy Lowes, **Supp. XIV:** 336

Dickinson, Lavinia Norcross, **I:** 451, 453, 462, 470

Dickinson, Stephanie, **Supp. XXIII:** 250

Dickinson, Mrs. William A. (Susan Gilbert), **I:** 452, 453, 456, 469, 470

Dickinson, William Austin, **I:** 451, 453, 469

Dickinson and the Strategies of Reticence (Dobson), **Retro. Supp. I:** 29, 42

Dickson, Helen. *See* Blackmur, Helen Dickson

Dickstein, Morris, **Supp. XIII:** 106; **Supp. XXIV:** 222, 223

"Dick Whittington and His Cat", **Supp. I Part 2:** 656

"DICTATORSHIP OF THE PROLE-TARIAT, THE" (Baraka), **Supp. II Part 1:** 54

Dictionary of Afro-American Slang (Major), **Supp. XXII:** 172, 174, 180

Dictionary of Literary Biography (Barron and Meyer, eds.), **Supp. XIX:** 195; **Supp. XVIII:** 173

Dictionary of Literary Biography (Gwynn, ed.), **Supp. XIX:** 121; **Supp. XVIII:** 173

Dictionary of Literary Biography (Kibler, ed.), **Supp. IX:** 94, 109; **Supp. XI:** 297

Dictionary of Literary Biography (Knight, ed.), **Supp. XIV:** 144

Dictionary of Literary Biography (Martine, ed.), **Supp. XXII:** 187

Dictionary of Literary Biography (Sicher, ed.), **Supp. XVII:** 41

Dictionary of Literary Biography (Twentieth-Century American Nature Poets, Bryson and Thompson, eds.), **Supp. XXIII:** 129

Dictionary of Modern English Usage, A (Fowler), **Supp. I Part 2:** 660

Dictionary of the Mohawk Language, A (Pyrlaeus), **Supp. XXVI:** 86

"Dictum: For a Masque of Deluge" (Merwin), **Supp. III Part 1:** 342–343

"Didactic Poem" (Levertov), **Supp. III Part 1:** 280

Diderot, Denis, **II:** 535; **IV:** 440; **Supp. XVI:** 293; **Supp. XVII:** 145

Did I Ever Tell You How Lucky You Are? (Geisel), **Supp. XVI:** 109

Di Dio, François, **Supp. XXVII:** 153

Didion, Joan, **Retro. Supp. I:** 116; **Retro. Supp. II:** 209; **Supp. I Part 1:** 196, 197; **Supp. III Part 1:** 302; **Supp. IV Part 1: 195–216; Supp. XI:** 221; **Supp. XII:** 307; **Supp. XXV:** 208; **Supp. XXVI:** 45, 49, 53

Dido, **I:** 81

Dido, Queen of Hearts (Atherton), **Supp. XXIV:** 26

Di Donato, Peter, **Supp. XX: 34**

Di Donato, Pietro, **Supp. XX: 33–47**

"Did 'Paco's Story' Deserve Its Award" (Kakutani), **Supp. XXII:** 109

"Did You Ever Dream Lucky?" (Ellison), **Supp. II Part 1:** 246

Dieckmann, Katherine, **Supp. XXIII:** 295, 296

"Die-Hard, The" (Benét), **Supp. XI:** 54–55, 56

Diehl, Digby, **Supp. IV Part 1:** 204

Dien Cai Dau (Komunyakaa), **Supp. XIII:** 121, **122–124,** 125, 131, 132

Dies, Martin, **Supp. XVIII:** 229

"Dies Irae" (R. Lowell), **II:** 553

Die Zeit Ohne Beispiel, (Goebbels), **III:** 560

Difference Engine, The (W. Gibson and B. Sterling), **Supp. XVI:** 121, 124, **128–129**

Different Drummer, A (Larkin; film), **Supp. XI:** 20

Different Fleshes (Goldbarth), **Supp. XII:** 181–182, 188

Different Hours (Dunn), **Supp. XI:** 139, 142, 143, 155

"Different Road, A" (Strout), **Supp. XXIII:** 282–283

Different Seasons (King), **Supp. V:** 148, 152

Different Ways to Pray (Nye), **Supp. XIII:** 274, 275, 277, 285, 287

"Different Ways to Pray" (Nye), **Supp. XIII:** 275

"Difficulties of a Statesman" (Eliot), **I:** 580

"Difficulties of Modernism and the Modernism of Difficulty" (Poirier), **Supp. II Part 1:** 136

Diff'rent (O'Neill), **III:** 389; **Supp. XXII:** 22

Di Filippo, Paul, **Supp. XXII:** 260, 261

DiGaetani, John L., **Supp. XIII:** 200

Digges, Deborah, **Supp. XXIII:** 57

"Digging" (Sanders), **Supp. XVI:** 272

"Digging in the Garden of Age I Uncover a Live Root" (Swenson), **Supp. IV Part 2:** 649

Digging Up the Dirt (Moraga), **Supp. XXIII:** 197

Diggins, John P., **Supp. I Part 2:** 650

Digital Barbarism: A Writer's Manifesto (Helprin), **Supp. XXV:** 81, 84, 88–89

"Dignity of Life, The" (C. Bly), **Supp. XVI:** 34, 36–37

Digregorio, Charles, **Supp. XI:** 326

"Digression on *Number I,* 1948" (O'Hara), **Supp. XXIII:** 214

"Dilemma" (Budbill), **Supp. XIX:** 2

"Dilemma of Determinism, The" (James), **II:** 347–348, 352

"Dilemma of the Negro Writer, The" (speech, C. Himes), **Supp. XVI:** 140

"Dilettante, The" (Wharton), **IV:** 311, 313

"Dilettante, The: A Modern Type" (Dunbar), **Supp. II Part 1:** 199

Dillard, Annie, **Supp. VI: 19–39; Supp. VIII:** 272; **Supp. X:** 31; **Supp. XIII:** 154; **Supp. XXVI:** 31, 37

Dillard, R. H. W., **Supp. XII:** 16

Dillman, Bradford, **III:** 403; **Supp. XII:** 241

Dillon, Brian, **Supp. X:** 209

Dillon, George, **III:** 141; **Supp. III Part 2:** 621

Dillon, Millicent, **Supp. IV Part 1:** 95

Dilsaver, Paul, **Supp. XIII:** 112

Dilthey, Wilhelm, **I:** 58

Dime-Store Alchemy: The Art of Joseph Cornell, **Supp. VIII:** 272

"Diminuendo" (Dunn), **Supp. XI:** 152–153

"Dimout in Harlem" (Hughes), **Supp. I Part 1:** 333

"Dinah's Lament" (Nelson), **Supp. XVIII:** 183

Dinesen, Isak, **IV:** 279; **Supp. VIII:** 171; **Supp. XVI:** 250

Dining Room, The (Gurney), **Supp. V:** 105–106

"Dinner at ------, A" (O. Henry), **Supp. II Part 1:** 402

"Dinner at Sir Nigel's" (Bowles), **Supp. IV Part 1:** 94

Dinner at the Homesick Restaurant (Tyler), **Supp. IV Part 2:** 657, 667–668

"Dinner at Uncle Borris's" (Simic), **Supp. VIII:** 272

Dinner Bridge (Lardner), **II:** 435

Dinosaur Hunter, The (Hickam), **Supp. XXVII:** 111

Dinosaur Tales (Bradbury), **Supp. IV Part 1:** 103

"Diogenes Invents a Game" (Karr), **Supp. XI:** 240–241

"Diogenes Tries to Forget" (Karr), **Supp. XI:** 241

Diomede, Matthew, **Supp. XX: 46**

Dionysis in Doubt (Robinson), **III:** 510

Dionysus in 69 (Schechner), **Supp. XXIV:** 116

Diop, Birago, **Supp. IV Part 1:** 16

Diop, David, **Supp. IV Part 1:** 16

Di Piero, W. S., **Supp. XIX: 33–48; Supp. XVII:** 241

Di Prima, Diane, **Supp. III Part 1:** 30; **Supp. XIV:** 125, 144, 148, 150

Dirda, Michael, **Supp. XXI:** 233

Direction of Poetry, The: An Anthology of Rhymed and Metered Verse Written in the English Language since 1975 (Richman, ed.), **Supp. XV:** 250, 251

Direction of Poetry, The: Rhymed and Metered Verse Written in the English Language since 1975 (Richman), **Supp. XI:** 249

"Directive" (Bishop), **Retro. Supp. II:** 42

"Directive" (Frost), **III:** 287; **Retro. Supp. I:** 140; **Supp. VIII:** 32, 33;

Supp. XXVI: 77

"Dire Cure" (Matthews), **Supp. IX:** 168

"Dirge" (Dunbar), **Supp. II Part 1:** 199

"Dirge Notes" (Huddle), **Supp. XXVI:** 148, 153

"Dirge without Music" (Millay), **III:** 126

"Dirt" (Salter), **Supp. IX:** 257, 260, 261

"Dirt and Desire: Essay on the Phenomenology of Female Pollution in Antiquity" (Carson), **Supp. XII:** 111

Dirty Bird Blues (Major), **Supp. XXII:** **180–181**

Dirty Dingus Magee (film), **Supp. XVII:** 139

"Dirty English Potatoes" (X. J. Kennedy), **Supp. XV:** 165

"Dirty Memories" (Olds), **Supp. X:** 211

Dirty Story (Shanley), **Supp. XIV:** 316, 331

"Dirty Word, The" (Shapiro), **Supp. II Part 2:** 710

Dirty Work (L. Brown), **Supp. XXI:** 37, 39, 40, 42, **45**

"'Disabled Imagination' and the Masculine Metaphor in the Works of Leonard Kriegel, The" (Haugen), **Supp. XXIV:** 215

Disappearance of the Jews, The (Mamet), **Supp. XIV:** 249–250, 250–251, 252, 254

Disappearances (Auster), **Supp. XII:** 23

"Disappearances" (Hogan), **Supp. IV Part 1:** 401

Disappearances (Mosher), **Supp. XXII:** 204, 205, 206, 207, 208, 209, **210**

"Disappeared, The " (C. Baxter), **Supp. XVII:** 19

Disappearing Acts (McMillan), **Supp. XIII:** 182, 183, **188–189**, 192

Disappearing Ink: Poetry at the End of Print Culture (Gioia), **Supp. XV:** 112

"Disappointment, The" (Creeley), **Supp. IV Part 1:** 143

"Disappointment and Desire" (R. Bly), **Supp. IV Part 1:** 71

Disappointment Artist, The (Lethem), **Supp. XVIII:** 135, 141, **148**

"Discards" (Baker), **Supp. XIII:** 53, 55–56

Discerning the Signs of the Times (Niebuhr), **III:** 300–301, 307–308

Disch, Thomas M., **Supp. XIX:** 1

"Disciple of Bacon, The" (Epstein), **Supp. XII:** 163–164

"Discipline" (L. Brown), **Supp. XXI:** 44

Discomfort, Zone, The: A Personal History (Franzen), **Supp. XX: 83, 84, 95**

"Discordants" (Aiken), **I:** 65

Discourse on Method (Descartes), **I:** 255

"Discourtesies" (Kirsch), **Supp. XV:** 341

"Discovering Theme and Structure in the Novel" (Schuster), **Supp. VIII:** 126

"Discovery" (Freneau), **Supp. II Part 1:** 258

"Discovery of the Madeiras, The" (Frost), **Retro. Supp. I:** 139

"Discovery of What It Means to Be an American, The" (Baldwin), **Supp. I Part 1:** 54–55

Discovery! The Search for Arabian Oil (Stegner), **Supp. IV Part 2:** 599

Discrepant Engagement (Mackey), **Supp. XXVII:** 159, 160, 161

Discrete Series (Oppen), **Supp. XXVI:** 224, 226–227, 230, 235

"Discrete Series" (Zukofsky), **Supp. III Part 2:** 616

"Discretions of Alcibiades" (Pinsky), **Supp. VI:** 241

"Disease, The" (Rukeyser), **Supp. VI:** 279

Disenchanted, The (play, Schulberg and Breit), **Supp. XVIII:** 254

Disenchanted, The (Schulberg), **II:** 98; **Retro. Supp. I:** 113; **Supp. XVIII: 247–250**, 253

Disenchantments: An Anthology of Modern Fairy Tale Poetry (Mieder), **Supp. XIV:** 126

"Dish of Green Pears, A" (Ríos), **Supp. IV Part 2:** 552

"Disillusion and Dogma" (Untermeyer), **Supp. XV:** 306

Dismantling the Silence (Simic), **Supp. VIII: 273–274**, 275, 276

Disney, Walt, **III:** 275, 426

"Disney of My Mind" (Chabon), **Supp. XI:** 63

Disobedience (Notley), **Supp. XXII:** 235, 236

Dispatches (Herr), **Supp. XI:** 245; **Supp. XIX:** 17

"Displaced Person, The" (O'Connor), **III:** 343–344, 350, 352, 356; **Retro. Supp. II:** 229, 232, 236

"Disposal" (Snodgrass), **Supp. VI:** 314

Dispossessed, The (Berryman), **I:** 170, 172, 173, 174, 175, 176, 178

"Disquieting Muses, The" (Plath), **Supp. I Part 2:** 538

Disraeli, Benjamin, **II:** 127

Dissent (Didion), **Supp. IV Part 1:** 208

"Dissent in Ashcroft's America" (P. N. Warren), **Supp. XX: 273**

"Dissenting Opinion on Kafka, A" (Wilson), **IV:** 437–438

Dissent in Three American Wars (Morison, Merk, and Freidel), **Supp. I Part 2:** 495

Dissertation on Liberty and Necessity, Pleasure and Pain, A (Franklin), **II:** 108

Dissertations on Government; the Affairs of the Bank: and Paper Money (Paine), **Supp. I Part 2:** 510

"Distance" (Carver), **Supp. III Part 1:** 146

"Distance" (Everwine), **Supp. XV:** 85

"Distance" (Paley), **Supp. VI:** 222

"Distance, The" (Karr), **Supp. XI:** 241

"Distance from the Sea, A" (Kees), **Supp. XV:** 147

"Distance Nowhere" (Hughes), **Retro. Supp. I:** 207

"Distance Up Close, The" (Peacock), **Supp. XIX:** 196–197, 198

"Distant Episode, A" (Bowles), **Supp. IV Part 1:** 84–85, 86, 90

Distant Episode, A: The Selected Stories (Bowles), **Supp. IV Part 1:** 79

Distant Rain: A Conversation Between Jakuch\[omacron\] Setouchi & Tess Gallagher (Setouchi and Gallagher), **Supp. XXIV:** 166, 178

Distinguished Guest, The (Miller), **Supp. XII: 299–301**

Distortions (Beattie), **Supp. V:** 21, 23, 24, 25, 27

"Distrest Shepherdess, The" (Freneau), **Supp. II Part 1:** 258

District of Columbia (Dos Passos), **I:** 478, 489–490, 492

Disturber of the Peace (Manchester), **III:** 103

Disturbing the Peace (Yates), **Supp. XI:** 345, 346

"Diver, The" (Hayden), **Supp. II Part 1:** 368, 372, 373

"Divided Life of Jean Toomer, The" (Toomer), **Supp. III Part 2:** 488

Divided Self, The (Laing), **Supp. XX: 95**

Divina Commedia (Longfellow, trans.), **II:** 490, 492, 493

"Divina Pastora, La" (C. L. R. James), **Supp. XXI:** 160

"Divine, The" (Di Piero), **Supp. XIX:** 41

"Divine Collaborator" (Simic), **Supp. VIII:** 282

Divine Comedies (Merrill), **Supp. III Part 1:** 324, 329–332

Divine Comedy (Dante), **I:** 137, 265, 400, 446; **II:** 215, 335, 490, 492, 493; **III:** 13, 448, 453; **Supp. V:** 283, 331, 338, 345; **Supp. X:** 253; **Supp. XIV:** 6; **Supp. XIX:** 36, 39

Divine Husband, The (Goldman), **Supp. XXV:** 49–50, 55–57

"Divine Image, The" (Blake), **Supp. V:** 257

Divine Pilgrim, The (Aiken), **I:** 50, 55

Divine Right's Trip (Norman), **Supp. XXIII:** 42

Divine Tragedy, The (Longfellow), **II:** 490, 500, 505, 506, 507; **Retro. Supp. II:** 165, 166

Divine Weekes and Workes (Sylvester, trans.), **Supp. I Part 1:** 104

Divine Weeks (Du Bartas), **IV:** 157–158

Diving into the Wreck: Poems 1971–1972 (Rich), **Supp. I Part 2:** 550, 559–565, 569; **Supp. XV:** 252

"Diving Past African Violets" (A. Finch), **Supp. XVII:** 72

Diving Rock on the Hudson, A (H. Roth), **Supp. IX:** 236, **237–238**

"Divinity in Its Fraying Fact, A" (Levis), **Supp. XI:** 271

"Divinity School Address" (Emerson), **II:** 12–13

"Divinity School or Trusting the Act of Writing" (Abraham), **Supp. XXIV:** 1, 3–4

"Divisions upon a Ground" (Hecht), **Supp. X:** 58

"Divorce" (Karr), **Supp. XI:** 244

"Divorced Fathers and Pizza Crusts" (Halliday), **Supp. XIX:** 93

Divorced in America: Marriage in an Age of Possibility (Epstein), **Supp. XIV:** 113

"Divorce Dream" (Halliday), **Supp. XIX:** 90

"Divorce in the United States" (Atherton), **Supp. XXIV:** 24

Dix, Douglas Shields, **Supp. XII:** 14

Dixie City Jam (Burke), **Supp. XIV:** 32

Dixon, Ivan, **Supp. IV Part 1:** 362

Dixon, Stephen, **Supp. XII: 139–158**

Dixon, Terrell F., **Supp. XVI:** 21

Dixon, Thomas, Jr., **Supp. II Part 1:** 169, 171, 177

Djbot Baghostus's Run (Mackey), **Supp. XXVII:** 158

Djinn (Robbe-Grillet), **Supp. V:** 48

D'Lugoff, Burt, **Supp. IV Part 1:** 362, 370

Dlugos, Tim, **Supp. XXVII:** 24

Dmytryk, Edward, **Supp. XX: 41**

Do, Lord, Remember Me (Garrett), **Supp. VII:** 98–100, 110

"Doaksology, The" (Wolfe), **IV:** 459

Do Androids Dream of Electric Sheep? (Dick), **Supp. XVIII:** 137

Dobard, Raymond G., **Supp. XXVI:** 200

Dobie, J. Frank, **Supp. V:** 225; **Supp. XIII:** 227

Döblin, Alfred, **Supp. XV:** 137

Dobriansky, Lev, **Supp. I Part 2:** 648, 650

Dobrin, Sidney I., **Supp. XVIII:** 192, 195

Dobson, Joanne, **Retro. Supp. I:** 29, 31, 42; **Supp. XVIII:** 259

Dobyns, Stephen, **Supp. XIII: 73–92**

"Docking at Palermo" (Hugo), **Supp. VI:** 137–138

"Dock Rats" (Moore), **III:** 213

"Dock-Witch, The" (Ozick), **Supp. V:** 262, 264

"Doc Mellhorn and the Pearly Gates" (Benét), **Supp. XI:** 55

"Doctor, The" (Dubus), **Supp. VII:** 80–81

"Doctor and the Doctor's Wife, The" (Hemingway), **II:** 248; **Retro. Supp. I:** 174, 175

Doctor Breen's Practice, a Novel (Howells), **I:** 282

Doctor Faustus (Mann), **III:** 283

Doctor Jazz (Carruth), **Supp. XVI:** 47, 59

"Doctor Jekyll" (Sontag), **Supp. III Part 2:** 469

"Doctor Leavis and the Moral Tradition" (Trilling), **Supp. III Part 2:** 512–513

Doctor Martino and Other Stories (Faulkner), **II:** 72; **Retro. Supp. I:** 84

"Doctor of the Heart, The" (Sexton), **Supp. II Part 2:** 692

Doctorow, E. L., **Retro. Supp. I:** 97; **Supp. III Part 2:** 590, 591; **Supp. IV Part 1: 217–240; Supp. V:** 45; **Supp. XVI:** 73; **Supp. XVII:** 183; **Supp. XX: 84, 90; Supp. XXI:** 18–19; **Supp. XXII:** 268

Doctor Sax (Kerouac), **Supp. III Part 1:** 220–222, 224–227

Doctor Sleep (Bell), **Supp. X: 9–11**

"Doctors' Row" (Aiken), **I:** 67

Doctor's Son and Other Stories, The (O'Hara), **III:** 361

Doctor Stories, The (W. C. Williams), **Retro. Supp. I:** 424

"Doctor's Wife, The" (Ozick), **Supp. V:** 262, 265

Doctor Zhivago (Pasternak), **IV:** 434, 438, 443

"Documentary" (Simic), **Supp. VIII:** 282

Dodd, Elizabeth, **Supp. V:** 77

Dodd, Susan, **Supp. XXV:** 129

Dodd, Wayne, **Supp. IV Part 2:** 625

Dodge, Mabel, **Supp. XX: 69; Supp. XXI:** 5, 6, 8, 12; **Supp. XXII:** 158, 161. *See also* Luhan, Mabel Dodge

Dodson, Owen, **Supp. I Part 1:** 54

Dodsworth (Lewis), **II:** 442, 449–450, 453, 456

Doenitz, Karl, **Supp. I Part 2:** 491

Does Civilization Need Religion? (Niebuhr), **III:** 293–294

"Does 'Consciousness' Exist?" (James), **II:** 356

"Does Education Pay?" (Du Bois), **Supp. II Part 1:** 159

"Dog" (B. Kelly), **Supp. XVII:** 126

Dog (Shepard), **Supp. III Part 2:** 434

"Dog Act, The" (Komunyakaa), **Supp. XIII:** 114–115

"Dog and the Playlet, The" (O. Henry), **Supp. II Part 1:** 399

Dog Beneath the Skin, The (Auden), **Supp. II Part 1:** 10

"Dog Creek Mainline" (Wright), **Supp. V:** 340

"Dogdom of the Dead, The" (Stallings), **Supp. XXV:** 228

"Dogfight" (W. Gibson and Swanwick), **Supp. XVI:** 128

Dog in the Manger, The (Vega; Merwin, trans.), **Supp. III Part 1:** 341, 347

Dog of the Marriage, The (Hempel), **Supp. XXI:** 115, 116, 117, 118, **126–127**

"Dog"(P. Benedict), **Supp. XXIII:** 36–37, 39

Dogs Bark, but the Caravan Rolls On (Conroy), **Supp. XVI:** 63, 70, 74, **75–76**

Dogs Bark, The: Public People and Private Places (Capote), **Supp. III Part 1:** 120, 132

"Dog's Eye" (J. W. Miller), **Supp. XX: 167**

"Dogs of Bucharest, The" (Gallagher), **Supp. XXIV:** 171

Dogs of God (Benedict), **Supp. XXIII:** 35, **41–45**, 49–50

Dog Soldiers (Stone), **Supp. V:** 298, 299–301

Dog Star, The (Di Piero), **Supp. XIX:** 38, **40–41**, 43

"Dog Stories" (Prose), **Supp. XVI:** 256

Dog & the Fever, The (Quevedo), **Retro. Supp. I:** 423

"Dogtown Letters, The" (Jarman and R. McDowell), **Supp. XVII:** 111

"Dogwood, The" (Levertov), **Supp. III Part 1:** 276

"Dogwood Tree, The: A Boyhood" (Updike), **IV:** 218; **Retro. Supp. I:** 318, 319

Doig, Ivan, **Supp. XIV:** 227

"Doing Battle with the Wolf" (Coleman), **Supp. XI:** 87–88

"Doing Jigsaw Puzzles" (Crooker), **Supp. XXIII:** 56

Doing Literary Business: American Women Writers in the Nineteenth Century (Coultrap-McQuin), **Supp. XVI:** 85

Doings and Undoings (Podhoretz), **Supp. VIII: 236–237**

"Do-It-Yourself" (C. Baxter), **Supp. XVII:** 14–15

Dolan, Jill, **Supp. XV:** 327

Dolben, Digby Mackworth, **Supp. XX: 230**

"Dolce Far' Niente" (Humphrey), **Supp. IX:** 106

Dolci, Carlo, **III:** 474–475

Dollars and Cents (A. Warner), **Supp. XVIII:** 264

"Dollhouse, The" (Haines), **Supp. XII:** 204

"Dollhouse, The" (Stallings), **Supp. XXV:** 231, 232

Dollmaker's Ghost, The (Levis), **Supp. XI:** 259, 260, **264–268**

Doll's House, A (Ibsen), **III:** 523; **IV:** 357; **Supp. XVI:** 182

Dolmetsch, Arnold, **III:** 464

Dolores Claiborne (King), **Supp. V:** 138, 141, 147, 148, 149–150, 152

"Dolph Heyliger" (Irving), **II:** 309

Dolphin, The (R. Lowell), **Retro. Supp. II:** 183, 186, 188, **190–191; Supp. XII:** 253–254

"Dolphins" (Francis), **Supp. IX:** 83

Dome of Many-Coloured Class, A (A. Lowell), **II:** 515, 516–517

Domesday Book (Masters), **Supp. I Part 2:** 465, 466–469, 471, 473, 476

"Domestic Economy" (Gilman), **Supp. XI:** 206

"Domestic Manners" (Hardwick), **Supp. III Part 1:** 211

Domestic Work (Trethewey), **Supp. XXI:** 243, 244, **248–251,** 254

"Domestic Work, 1937" (Trethewey), **Supp. XXI:** 248

"Dominant White, The" (McKay), **Supp. X:** 134

Dominguez, Robert, **Supp. VIII:** 83

Domini, John, **Supp. XIX:** 45; **Supp. XXI:** 235

Dominique, Jean. *See* Closset, Marie

Donahoe, Edward, **Supp. XVIII:** 132

Donahue, Deirdre, **Supp. XXV:** 9

Donahue, Phil, **Supp. IV Part 2:** 526; **Supp. X:** 311

Donaldson, Susan, **Supp. XXII:** 148

Doña Perfecta (Galdós), **II:** 290

Dong, Stella, **Supp. XVI:** 222

Don Juan (Byron), **Supp. XV:** 259

"DON JUAN IN HELL" (Baraka), **Supp. II Part 1:** 33

Donkey of God, The (Untermeyer), **Supp. XV:** 310

"Donna mi Prega" (Cavalcanti), **Supp. III Part 2:** 620, 621, 622

Donn-Byrne, Brian Oswald. *See* Byrne, Donn

Donne, John, **I:** 358–359, 384, 389, 522, 586; **II:** 254; **III:** 493; **IV:** 83, 88, 135, 141, 144, 145, 151, 156, 165, 331, 333; **Retro. Supp. II:** 76; **Supp. I Part 1:** 80, 364, 367; **Supp. I Part 2:** 421, 424, 467, 725, 726; **Supp. III Part 2:** 614, 619; **Supp. IX:** 44; **Supp. VIII:** 26, 33, 164; **Supp. XII:** 45, 159; **Supp. XIII:** 94, 130; **Supp. XIV:** 122; **Supp. XV:** 92, 251; **Supp. XVI:** 158, 204; **Supp. XVIII:** 35, 39, 50–51, 307; **Supp. XXIV:** 167; **Supp. XXVII:** 220

Donne's Sermons: Selected Passages (L. P. Smith, ed.), **Supp. XIV:** 342

Donoghue, Denis, **I:** 537; **Supp. IV Part 1:** 39; **Supp. VIII:** 105, 189

Donohue, H. E. F., **Supp. IX:** 2, 3, 15, 16

Donoso, José, **Supp. XXIV:** 86

Do Not Deny Me (Thompson), **Supp. XXIII:** 300–301

"Do Not Weep Maiden, For War Is Kind" (Crane), **Supp. XVIII:** 75

Donovan, Josephine, **Retro. Supp. II:** 138, 139, 147

Don Quixote (Cervantes), **I:** 134; **II:** 291, 434; **III:** 113, 614; **Supp. I Part 2:** 422; **Supp. IX:** 94; **Supp. XXIV:** 87

Don Quixote: Which Was a Dream (Acker), **Supp. XII:** 5, **12–14**

Don't Ask (Levine), **Supp. V:** 178

Don't Ask Questions (Marquand), **III:** 58

Don't Bet on the Prince: Contemporary Feminist Fairy Tales in North America and England (Zipes), **Supp. XIV:** 126

Don't Drink the Water (Allen), **Supp. XV:** 3, **14**

Don't Look Back (film, Pennebaker), **Supp. XVIII:** 19

"Don't Miss It" (Stone), **Supp. XXVII:** 260

"Don't Neglect Your Wife" (script, Atherton), **Supp. XXIV:** 25

"Don't Shoot the Warthog" (Corso), **Supp. XII:** 123

Don't Stop the Carnival (Wouk), **Supp. XXV:** 257, 263–264

"Don't Tell Mother" (Wasserstein), **Supp. XV:** 319

"Don't Think Twice, It's All Right" (song, Dylan), **Supp. XVIII:** 24

Don't Worry About the Kids (Neugeboren), **Supp. XVI:** 226

"Don't Worry About the Kids" (Neugeboren), **Supp. XVI:** 226

Don't You Want to Be Free? (Hughes), **Retro. Supp. I:** 203; **Supp. I Part 1:** 339

"Doodler, The" (Merrill), **Supp. III Part 1:** 321

Doolan, Moira, **Retro. Supp. II:** 247

Doolittle, Hilda (H. D.), **II:** 517, 520–521; **III:** 194, 195–196, 457, 465; **IV:** 404, 406; **Retro. Supp. I:** 288, 412, 413, 414, 415, 417; **Supp. I Part 1:** 253–275; **Supp. I Part 2:** 707; **Supp. III Part 1:** 48; **Supp. III Part 2:** 610; **Supp. IV Part 1:** 257; **Supp. V:** 79; **Supp. XV:** 43, 249, 301, 302; **Supp. XVII:** 77; **Supp. XXII:** 88; **Supp. XXIV:** 64; **Supp. XXVII:** 160, 261, 287

Doolittle, Thomas, **IV:** 150

"Doomed by Our Blood to Care" (Orfalea), **Supp. XIII:** 278

"Doomsday" (Plath), **Retro. Supp. II:** 242

Doomsters, The (Macdonald), **Supp. IV Part 2:** 462, 463, 472, 473

Doomswoman, The (Atherton), **Supp. XXIV:** 22

Doonesbury (Trudeau), **Supp. XXIV:** 283

"Door, The" (Creeley), **Supp. IV Part 1:** 145, 146, 156–157

Door, The (Rinehart), **Supp. XXV:** 197, 200

"Door, The" (White), **Supp. I Part 2:** 651, 675–676

Door in the Dark, The (Frost), **II:** 156

Door in the Hive, A (Levertov), **Supp. III Part 1:** 283, 284

"Door of the Trap, The" (Anderson), **I:** 112

"Doors" (Dybek), **Supp. XXIII:** 69

Doors (Hoffman), **Supp. XVIII:** 86–87

"Doors" (Hoffman), **Supp. XVIII:** 86–87

"Doors, Doors, Doors" (Sexton), **Supp. II Part 2:** 681

Doors, The, **Supp. X:** 186

"Doorways into the Depths" (Sanders), **Supp. XVI:** 272

Doreski, William, **Retro. Supp. II:** 185

Dorfman, Ariel, **Supp. IX:** 131, 138

Dorfman, Joseph, **Supp. I Part 2:** 631, 647, 650

Doris of Dobbs Ferry (Wells), **Supp. XXVI:** 277

Dorman, Jen, **Supp. XI:** 240

Dorn, Edward, **Supp. IV Part 1:** 154; **Supp. XXIV:** 33, 44

Dorn, Sarah, **Supp. XXI:** 243

"Dorothea Dix, Samaritan" (J. Scott), **Supp. XVII:** 189

Dorr, Julia, **Supp. XV:** 286

Dorrance Doings (Wells), **Supp. XXVI:** 277

Dorrance Domain, The (Wells), **Supp. XXVI:** 277

Dorris, Michael, **Supp. IV Part 1:** 260, 272

Dos Passos, John, **I:** 99, 288, 374, 379, **474–496,** 517, 519; **II:** 74, 77, 89, 98; **III:** 2, 28, 29, 70, 172, 382–383; **IV:** 340, 427, 433; **Retro. Supp. I:** 105, 113, 187; **Retro. Supp. II:** 95, 196; **Supp. I Part 2:** 646; **Supp. III Part 1:** 104, 105; **Supp. V:** 277; **Supp. VIII:** 101, 105; **Supp. XIV:** 24; **Supp. XV:** 135, 137, 182; **Supp. XVII:** 105, 107; **Supp. XXI:** 8; **Supp. XXIII:** 68; **Supp. XXVI:** 17, 32, 133, 135

"Dos Passos: Poet Against the World" (Cowley), **Supp. II Part 1:** 143, 145

Dostoevsky: A Screenplay (Carver and Gallagher), **Supp. XXIV:** 178

Dostoevsky, Fyodor, **I:** 53, 103, 211, 468; **II:** 60, 130, 275, 320, 587; **III:** 37, 61, 155, 174, 176, 188, 189, 267, 272, 283, 286, 354, 357, 358, 359, 467, 571, 572; **IV:** 1, 7, 8, 17, 21, 50, 59, 106, 110, 128, 134, 285, 289, 476, 485, 491; **Retro. Supp. II:** 20, 204, 299; **Supp. I Part 1:** 49; **Supp. I Part 2:** 445, 466; **Supp. IV Part 2:** 519, 525; **Supp. VIII:** 175; **Supp. X:** 4–5; **Supp. XI:** 161; **Supp. XII:** 322; **Supp. XVI:** 63; **Supp. XVII:** 225; **Supp. XVIII:** 278, 280; **Supp. XX: 45; Supp. XXIII:** 4; **Supp. XXIV:** 132

Doty, Mark, **Supp. IX:** 42, 300; **Supp. XI: 119–138; Supp. XXI:** 129, 130, 131, 139, 141; **Supp. XXIII:** 126, 221

Doty, M. R. *See* Dawson, Ruth; Doty, Mark

Double, The (Dostoevsky), **Supp. IX:** 105

"Double, The" (Levis), **Supp. XI:** 260, **261–263**

Double, The (Rank), **Supp. IX:** 105

Double Agent, The (Blackmur), **Supp. II Part 1:** 90, 108, 146

Double Axe, The (Jeffers), **Supp. II Part 2:** 416, 434

"Double Blind" (Skloot), **Supp. XX: 194, 208**

Doubleday, Frank, **I:** 500, 502, 515, 517; **III:** 327

Doubleday, Mrs. Frank, **I:** 500

Double Deuce (Parker), **Supp. XIX:** 183

Double Down (F. and S. Barthelme), **Supp. XI:** 27, 34, 35, 36–38

Double Dream of Spring, The (Ashbery), **Supp. III Part 1:** 11–13

Double Fold: Libraries and the Assault on Paper (Baker), **Supp. XIII:** 52, 56

Double Game (Calle), **Supp. XII:** 22

"Double Gap, The" (Auchincloss), **Supp. IV Part 1:** 33

"Double-Headed Snake of Newbury, The" (Whittier), **Supp. I Part 2:** 698

Double Honeymoon (Connell), **Supp. XIV:** 80, 87

Double Image, The (Levertov), **Supp. III Part 1:** 274, 276

"Double Image, The" (Sexton), **Supp. II Part 2:** 671, 677–678

Double Indemnity (film), **Supp. IV Part 1:** 130

Double Legacy: Reflections on a Pair of Deaths (Hadas), **Supp. XXIII:** 123, **126–127**

"Double Limbo" (Komunyakaa), **Supp. XIII:** 132

Double Man, The (Auden), **Supp. III Part 1:** 16; **Supp. X:** 118

"Double Ode" (Rukeyser), **Supp. VI:** 282–283, 286

Double Persephone (Atwood), **Supp. XIII:** 19

Double Play (Parker), **Supp. XIX: 189– 190**

Doubles in Literary Psychology (Tymms), **Supp. IX:** 105

Double Vision: American Thoughts Abroad (Knowles), **Supp. XII:** 249

"Doubt" (Teasdale), **Supp. XXVII:** 291–292

"Doubt on the Great Divide" (Stafford), **Supp. XI:** 322

Dougherty, Robin, **Supp. XXII:** 205

Dougherty, Steve, **Supp. X:** 262

Douglas, Aaron, **Supp. I Part 1:** 326

Douglas, Alfred, **Supp. X:** 151

Douglas, Ann, **Supp. XII:** 136; **Supp. XVIII:** 258; **Supp. XX: 69**

Douglas, Claire, **III:** 552

Douglas, Ellen, **Supp. XXI:** 38

Douglas, George (pseudonym). *See* Brown, George Douglas

Douglas, Kirk, **Supp. XIII:** 5–6

Douglas, Lloyd, **IV:** 434

Douglas, Marjory Stoneman, **Supp. XVIII:** 195

Douglas, Melvyn, **Supp. V:** 223

Douglas, Michael, **Supp. XI:** 67

Douglas, Paul, **III:** 294

Douglas, Stephen A., **III:** 577, 588–589; **Supp. I Part 2:** 456, 471

Douglas, William O., **III:** 581

Douglass, Frederick, **Supp. I Part 1:** 51, 345; **Supp. I Part 2:** 591; **Supp. II Part 1:** 157, 195, 196, 292, 378; **Supp. III Part 1: 153–174; Supp. IV Part 1:** 1, 2, 13, 15, 256; **Supp. VIII:** 202; **Supp. XVIII:** 16; **Supp. XX: 109, 281; Supp. XXIII:** 167

Douglass, Thomas E., **Supp. XXIII:** 36

Douglass Pilot, The (Baldwin, ed.), **Supp. I Part 1:** 49

Dove, Belle, **I:** 451

Dove, Rita, **Supp. IV Part 1: 241–258; Supp. XVII:** 71, 110; **Supp. XVIII:** 172, 174; **Supp. XXI:** 243, 246, 247, 249, 251

Dove of the East and Other Stories, A (Helprin), **Supp. XXV:** 79, 83, 84–85

"Dover Beach" (Arnold), **Retro. Supp. I:** 325; **Supp. XIX:** 41

Dow, Lorenzo, **IV:** 265

Dowd, Douglas, **Supp. I Part 2:** 645, 650

"Do We Understand Each Other?" (Ginsberg), **Supp. II Part 1:** 311

Dowie, William, **Supp. V:** 199

Do with Me What You Will (Oates), **Supp. II Part 2:** 506, 515–517

Dowling, Eddie, **IV:** 394

Down and Out (Shanley), **Supp. XIV:** 317

"Down at City Hall" (Didion), **Supp. IV Part 1:** 211

"Down at the Cross" (Baldwin), **Retro. Supp. II:** 1, 2, 7, 12, 13, 15; **Supp. I Part 1:** 60, 61

"Down at the Dinghy" (Salinger), **III:** 559, 563

"Down by the Station, Early in the Morning" (Ashbery), **Supp. III Part 1:** 25

Downers Grove (Hornburg), **Supp. XXVII:** 80

Downey, Sharon D., **Supp. XX: 244**

Downhill Racer (film), **Supp. IX:** 253

"Down Home" (J. W. Miller), **Supp. XX: 169**

"Down in Alabam" (Bierce), **I:** 193

Downing, Ben, **Supp. XII:** 175, 189, 190–191

Downing, Major Jack (pseudonym). *See* Smith, Seba

Down in My Heart (Stafford), **Supp. XI:** 313, 315

Down Mailer's Way (Solotaroff), **Retro. Supp. II:** 203

"Down the Highway" (song, Dylan), **Supp. XVIII:** 24

Down the Rabbit Hole: Adventures and Misadventures in the Realm of Children's Literature (Lanes), **Supp. XVI:** 104

Down There on a Visit (Isherwood), **Supp. XIV:** 159, 161, 164, **168–169,** 170, 171

Down the River (Abbey), **Supp. XIII:** 12–13

"Down the River with Henry Thoreau" (Abbey), **Supp. XIII:** 12–13

Down These Mean Streets (P. Thomas), **Supp. XIII:** 264

Down the Starry River (Purdy), **Supp. VII:** 278

Down to the River: Portraits of Iowa Musicians (Dyas), **Supp. XIX:** 174

Downtown (Siddons), **Supp. XXII:** 239, 240, 242, **247–249, 251–252,** 253

"Downtrodden Mary's Failed Campaign of Terror" (Saunders), **Supp. XIX:** 226

"Downward Path to Wisdom, The" (Porter), **III:** 442, 443, 446

"Down Where I Am" (Hughes), **Supp. I Part 1:** 344

Down with Starvation Wages in Southeast Missouri (C. L. R. James), **Supp. XXI:** 169

"Dowsing for Joy" (Skloot), **Supp. XX: 203**

Dowson, Ernest C., **I:** 384

Doyle, Arthur Conan, **Retro. Supp. I:** 270; **Supp. IV Part 1:** 128, 341; **Supp. IV Part 2:** 464, 469; **Supp. XI:** 63; **Supp. XXVI:** 282

Doyle, C. W., **I:** 199

"Draba" (Leopold), **Supp. XIV:** 186

Drabble, Margaret, **Supp. IV Part 1:** 297, 299, 305

Drabelle, Dennis, **Supp. XIII:** 13

Drach, Ivan, **Supp. III Part 1:** 268

Dracula (film), **Supp. IV Part 1:** 104; **Supp. XVII:** 57

Dracula (Stoker), **Supp. XXVI:** 58

"Draft Horse, The" (Frost), **Retro. Supp. I:** 141

"Draft Lyrics for *Candide*" (Agee), **I:** 28

Draft of XVI Cantos, A (Pound), **III:** 472; **Retro. Supp. I:** 292

Draft of XXX Cantos, A (Pound), **III:** 196; **Retro. Supp. I:** 292

Drafts &Fragments (Pound), **Retro. Supp. I:** 293

"Dragon" (Lovecraft), **Supp. XXV:** 111

Dragon Country (T. Williams), **IV:** 383

Dragone, Nichole, **Supp. XXIII:** 157

Dragon Seed (Buck), **Supp. II Part 1:** 124

Dragon's Teeth (Sinclair), **Supp. V:** 290

Dragon Takes a Wife, The (Myers), **Supp. XXVII:** 209

Drake, Benjamin, **Supp. I Part 2:** 584

Drake, Daniel, **Supp. I Part 2:** 584

Drake, Sir Francis, **Supp. I Part 2:** 497

Drake, Robert, **Supp. XX: 274**

Drake, St. Clair, **IV:** 475

Drake, Sylvia, **Supp. XXI:** 155

Drake, William, **Supp. XV:** 295; **Supp. XXVII:** 284, 285, 291, 293, 294, 297

Dramatic Duologues (Masters), **Supp. I Part 2:** 461

"Drapery Factory, Gulfport. Mississippi, 1956" (Trethewey), **Supp. XXI:** 246

Drattel, Deborah, **Supp. XV:** 333

Drat These Brats (X. J. Kennedy), **Supp. XV:** 163

"Draught" (Cowley), **Supp. II Part 1:** 141, 142

Drayton, Michael, **IV:** 135; **Retro. Supp. II:** 76

"Dr. Bergen's Belief" (Schwartz), **Supp. II Part 2:** 650

Dr. Bloodmoney (Dick), **Supp. XVIII:** 138

"Dreadful Has Already Happened, The" (Strand), **Supp. IV Part 2:** 627

Dread Road, The (Le Sueur), **Supp. XXIII:** 168, 169, **169–170,** 173

"Dream, A" (Ginsberg), **Supp. II Part 1:** 312

"Dream, A" (Tate), **IV:** 129

"Dream, The" (Hayden), **Supp. II Part 1:** 368, 377

Dream at the End of the World, The: Paul Bowles and the Literary Renegades in Tangier (Green), **Supp. IV Part 1:** 95

"Dream Avenue" (Simic), **Supp. VIII:** 282

"Dream Boogie" (Hughes), **Retro. Supp. I:** 208; **Supp. I Part 1:** 339–340

"Dreambook Bestiary" (Komunyakaa), **Supp. XIII:** 120

Dreamer (C. Johnson), **Supp. VI:** 186, **196–199**

dreamer examines his pillow, the (Shanley), **Supp. XIV:** 315, **327**

"Dreamer in a Dead Language" (Paley), **Supp. VI:** 217

Dreaming in Cuban (García), **Supp. XI:** 178, **179–185,** 190

"Dreaming of Hair" (L.-Y. Lee), **Supp. XV:** 214

"Dreaming the Breasts" (Sexton), **Supp. II Part 2:** 692

"Dreaming Water" (Espaillat), **Supp. XXI:** 102

"Dream Interpretation" (Hadas), **Supp. XXIII:** 113, 121

"Dream Interpreted, The" (Paine), **Supp. I Part 2:** 505

Dream Jumbo (Longo), **Supp. XVI:** 124

Dream Keeper, The (Hughes), **Supp. I Part 1:** 328, 332, 333, 334

Dream Keeper and Other Poems, The (Hughes), **Retro. Supp. I:** 201, 202

Dreamland (Baker), **Supp. XIV:** 96

"Dream-Land" (Poe), **Retro. Supp. II:** 274

Dream Life of Balso Snell, The (West), **IV:** 286, 287, 288–290, 291, 297; **Retro. Supp. II:** 321, 322, 327, 328, **330–332**

"Dream Machine, The" (Hadas), **Supp. XXIII:** 122–123

Dream Me Home Safely: Writers on Growing up in America (Shreve, ed.), **Supp. XXIII:** 284

Dream of a Common Language, The: Poems, 1974–1977 (Rich), **Supp. I Part 2:** 551, 554, 569–576

Dream of Arcadia: American Writers and Artists in Italy (Brooks), **I:** 254

Dream of Governors, A (Simpson), **Supp. IX:** 265, **269–270**

"Dream of Her Grandfather, A" (Zitkala-Ša), **Supp. XXV:** 282, 283

"Dream of Italy, A" (Masters), **Supp. I Part 2:** 458

"Dream of Mourning, The" (Glück), **Supp. V:** 84

"Dream of the Blacksmith's Room, A" (R. Bly), **Supp. IV Part 1:** 73

"Dream of the Cardboard Lover" (Haines), **Supp. XII:** 204

Dream of the Golden Mountains, The (Cowley), **Supp. II Part 1:** 139, 141, 142, 144

"Dream Pang, A" (Frost), **II:** 153

Dream-Quest of Unkown Kadath, The (Lovecraft), **Supp. XXV:** 113–114

"Dreams About Clothes" (Merrill), **Supp. III Part 1:** 328–329

"Dreams"(Dybek), **Supp. XXIII:** 73

Dreams from Bunker Hill (Fante), **Supp. XI:** 160, 166, **172–173**

"Dreams in the Witch House, The" (Lovecraft), **Supp. XXV:** 111, 123

"Dreams"(Kenny), **Supp. XXIII:** 153

"Dreams of Adulthood" (Ashbery), **Supp. III Part 1:** 26

"Dreams of Glory on the Mound" (Plimpton), **Supp. XVI:** 238–239

"Dreams of Math" (Kenyon), **Supp. VII:** 160–161

"Dreams of the Animals" (Atwood), **Supp. XIII:** 33

"Dream Variations" (Hughes), **Retro. Supp. I:** 198; **Supp. I Part 1:** 323

"Dream Vision" (Olsen), **Supp. XIII:** 295–296

Dream with No Stump Roots in It, A (Huddle), **Supp. XXVI:** 152

"Dream with No Stumps in It, A" (Huddle), **Supp. XXVI:** 152

Dream Work (Oliver), **Supp. VII:** 234–235, 236–238, 240

Dred: A Tale of the Great Dismal Swamp (Stowe), **Supp. I Part 2:** 592

Dreiser, Theodore, **I:** 59, 97, 109, 116, 355, 374, 375, 475, 482, **497–520; II:** 26, 27, 29, 34, 38, 44, 74, 89, 93, 180, 276, 283, 428, 444, 451, 456–457, 467–468; **III:** 40, 103, 106, 251, 314, 319, 327, 335, 453, 576, 582; **IV:** 29, 35, 40, 135, 208, 237, 475, 482, 484; **Retro. Supp. I:** 325, 376; **Retro. Supp. II:** 93–110, 114, 322; **Supp. I Part 1:** 320; **Supp. I Part 2:** 461, 468;

Supp. III Part 2: 412; **Supp. IV Part 1:** 31, 236, 350; **Supp. IV Part 2:** 689; **Supp. IX:** 1, 14, 15, 308; **Supp. V:** 113, 120; **Supp. VIII:** 98, 101, 102; **Supp. XI:** 207; **Supp. XIV:** 111; **Supp. XVII:** 95, 96–97, 105, 155; **Supp. XVIII:** 1, 6, 76, 226; **Supp. XXI:** 275; **Supp. XXIII:** 161, 164; **Supp. XXV:** 18; **Supp. XXVI:** 133, 273; **Supp. XXVII:** 83, 88

"Drenched in Light" (Hurston), **Supp. VI:** 150–151

Drennen, Eileen M., **Supp. XXII:** 241, 243

Dresser, Paul, **Retro. Supp. II:** 94, 103

Dress Gray (teleplay), **Supp. IV Part 2:** 683

Dress Gray (Truscott), **Supp. IV Part 2:** 683

"Dressing for Dinner" (Ríos), **Supp. IV Part 2:** 548

Dressing Up for the Carnival (Shields), **Supp. VII:** 328

"Dress of One Occasion" (Stallings), **Supp. XXV:** 233

"Dress Rehearsal" (Skloot), **Supp. XX: 204**

Drew, Bettina, **Supp. IX:** 2, 4

Drew, Elizabeth, **Retro. Supp. II:** 242, 243

Drexler, Eric, **Supp. XVI:** 121

Dreyfus, Alfred, **Supp. I Part 2:** 446

"Dr. Hanray's Second Chance" (Richter), **Supp. XVIII:** 218

Drift and Mastery (Lippmann), **I:** 222–223

"Driftwood" (C. Frost), **Supp. XV:** 106–107

"Drinker, The" (R. Lowell), **II:** 535, 550

"Drinking Cold Water" (Everwine), **Supp. XV:** 80–81

"Drinking from a Helmet" (Dickey), **Supp. IV Part 1:** 180

Drinking Gourd, The (Hansberry), **Supp. IV Part 1:** 359, 365–367, 374

Drinks before Dinner (Doctorow), **Supp. IV Part 1:** 231, 234–235

Driscoll, David, **Supp. XIX:** 241, 242

Driskill, Qwo-Li, **Supp. XXIII:** 147, 148, 149

Drive, He Said (Larner), **Supp. XVI:** 220

"Drive Home, The" (Banks), **Supp. V:** 7

"Driver" (Merrill), **Supp. III Part 1:** 331

"Driving Alone in Winter" (W. V. Davis), **Supp. XXI:** 89, 90, 94

"Driving Through Minnesota During the Hanoi Bombings" (R. Bly), **Supp. IV Part 1:** 61; **Supp. XVII:** 243

"Driving through Oregon" (Haines), **Supp. XII:** 207

"Driving to Oregon"(Thompson), **Supp. XXIII:** 291

"Driving toward the Lac Qui Parle River" (R. Bly), **Supp. IV Part 1:** 61

"Dr. Jack-o'-Lantern" (Yates), **Supp. XI:** 340–341

Dr. Jekyll and Mr. Hyde (film), **Supp. XVII:** 57

"Drone" (Coleman), **Supp. XI:** 85–86

Drop City (Boyle), **Supp. XX: 30–31**

Drown (Díaz), **Supp. XXIV:** 83, 84, 85, 86, **88–89,** 90, 93

"Drowned Man, The: Death between Two Rivers" (McGrath), **Supp. X:** 116

"Drowning" (Boyle), **Supp. XX:** 18

"Drowning 1954" (Keillor), **Supp. XVI:** 172

Drowning Pool, The (film), **Supp. IV Part 2:** 474

Drowning Pool, The (Macdonald), **Supp. IV Part 2:** 470, 471

Drowning Season, The (Hoffman), **Supp. X: 82**

Drowning with Others (Dickey), **Supp. IV Part 1:** 176, 178, 179

"Drowsy Day, A" (Dunbar), **Supp. II Part 1:** 198

Dr. Seuss. *See* Geisel, Theodor Seuss (Dr. Seuss)

Dr. Seuss and Mr. Geisel (J. and N. Morgan), **Supp. XVI:** 103

Dr. Seuss Goes to War: The World War II Editorial Cartoons of Theodor Seuss Geisel (Minear), **Supp. XVI:** 101

Dr. Seuss's ABC (Geisel), **Supp. XVI:** 99

Dr. Strangelove; or, How I Learned to Stop Worrying and Love the Bomb (film), **Supp. XI:** 293, **301–305**

Drugiye Berega (Nabokov), **III:** 247–250, 252

"Drug Shop, The, or Endymion in Edmonstoun" (Benét), **Supp. XI:** 43

"Drug Store" (Shapiro), **Supp. II Part 2:** 705

"Drugstore in Winter, A" (Ozick), **Supp. V:** 272

Drukman, Steven, **Supp. XIII:** 195, 197, 202

"Drum" (Hogan), **Supp. IV Part 1:** 413

"Drum, The" (Alvarez), **Supp. VII:** 7

"Drumlin Woodchuck, A" (Frost), **II:** 159–160; **Retro. Supp. I:** 138

Drummond, William, **Supp. I Part 1:** 369

Drummond de Andrade, Carlos, **Supp. IV Part 2:** 626, 629, 630

Drums at Dusk (Bontemps), **Supp. XXII:** 5, 9–10

Drum-Taps (Whitman), **IV:** 346, 347, 444; **Retro. Supp. I:** 406

"Drunken Fisherman, The" (R. Lowell), **II:** 534, 550

"Drunken Sisters, The" (Wilder), **IV:** 374

Drunk in the Furnace, The (Merwin), **Supp. III Part 1:** 345–346

"Drunk in the Furnace, The" (Merwin), **Supp. III Part 1:** 346

Druten, John van, **Supp. XIV:** 162

"Dr. Williams' Position" (Pound), **Supp. XVII:** 226–227

Dryden, John, **II:** 111, 542, 556; **III:** 15; **IV:** 145; **Retro. Supp. I:** 56; **Supp. I Part 1:** 150; **Supp. I Part 2:** 422; **Supp. IX:** 68; **Supp. XIV:** 5; **Supp. XV:** 258; **Supp. XX: 280; Supp. XXIV:** 158; **Supp. XXV:** 119

Drye, Captain Frank, **Retro. Supp. II:** 115

Dry Salvages, The (Eliot), **I:** 581

"Dry Salvages, The" (Eliot), **Retro. Supp. I:** 66

"Dry September" (Faulkner), **II:** 72, 73
"Dry Spring"(Thompson), **Supp. XXIII:** 291
Dry Sun, Dry Wind (Wagoner), **Supp. IX:** 323, 324
D'Souza, Dinesh, **Supp. X:** 255
"Dual" (Goldbarth), **Supp. XII:** 188
"Dual Curriculum" (Ozick), **Supp. V:** 270
"Dualism" (Reed), **Supp. X:** 242
Duane's Depressed (McMurtry), **Supp. V:** 233
Du Bartas, Guillaume, **Supp. I Part 1:** 98, 104, 111, 118, 119
Duberman, Martin, **Supp. I Part 2:** 408, 409
Dubie, Norman, **Supp. XXIV:** 165
"Dubin's Lives" (Malamud), **Supp. I Part 2:** 451
Dubious Honors (M. F. K. Fisher), **Supp. XVII:** 91
"Dubliners" (J. Joyce), **Supp. XVI:** 41
Dubliners (Joyce), **I:** 130, 480; **III:** 471; **Supp. VIII:** 146
Dublin's Lives (Malamud), **Supp. XIX:** 142
Du Bois, Nina Gomer (Mrs. W. E. B. Du Bois), **Supp. II P art 1:** 158; **Supp. XIV:** 200
Du Bois, Shirley Graham, **Supp. II Part 1:** 186; **Supp. XXI:** 171. *See also* Graham, Shirley
Du Bois, W. E. B., **I:** 260; **Supp. I Part 1:** 5, 345; **Supp. II Part 1:** 33, 56, 61, **157–189,** 195; **Supp. IV Part 1:** 9, 164, 170, 362; **Supp. X:** 133, 134, 137, 139, 242; **Supp. XIII:** 185, **Supp. XIII:** 186, 233, 238, 243, 244, 247; **Supp. XIV:** 54, 69, 72, 201, 202; **Supp. XIX:** 67, 69, 77; **Supp. XVI:** 135; **Supp. XVIII:** 119, 122, 126, 130; **Supp. XX: 102, 105, 106; Supp. XXI:** 166, 277; **Supp. XXII:** 3; **Supp. XXVI:** 88, 168
DuBose, Martha Hailey, **Supp. XXV:** 192, 199, 200
Dubreuil, Jean, **Supp. IV Part 2:** 425
Dubus, Andre, **Supp. VII: 75–93; Supp. XI:** 347,**Supp. XI:** 349; **Supp. XIV:** 21; **Supp. XXIV:** 97
Dubus, Andre, III, **Supp. XXIV: 97–112**
Duchamp, Marcel, **IV:** 408; **Retro. Supp. I:** 416, 417, 418, 430; **Supp. IV Part 2:** 423, 424; **Supp. XII:** 124; **Supp. XV:** 157; **Supp. XXII:** 162, 163, 168
"Duchess at Prayer, The" (Wharton), **Retro. Supp. I:** 365
Duchess of Malfi, The (Webster), **IV:** 131
"Duckling Girl" (Dubus III), **Supp. XXIV:** 100–101, 105
Duck Soup (film), **Supp. IV Part 1:** 384
Duck Variations, The (Mamet), **Supp. XIV:** 239, 240, 249
Ducornet, Rikki, **Supp. XXII:** 261
Dudley, Anne. *See* Bradstreet, Anne
Dudley, Joseph, **III:** 52
Dudley, Thomas, **III:** 52; **Supp. I Part 1:** 98, 99, 110, 116
"Duenna"(Schott), **Supp. XXIII:** 249
"Duet, With Muffled Brake Drums" (Updike), **Retro. Supp. I:** 319

Duet for Cannibals (Sontag), **Supp. III Part 2:** 452, 456
Duffey, Bernard, **Supp. I Part 2:** 458, 471
Duffield, Pitts, **Supp. XXI:** 3
Duffus, R. L., **Supp. I Part 2:** 650
Duffy, Martha, **Supp. IV Part 1:** 207; **Supp. XX: 244**
Duffy, William, **Supp. XVI:** 32
Du Fu (Tu Fu), **Supp. XV:** 217
Dufy, Raoul, **I:** 115; **IV:** 80
Dugan, Alan, **Supp. XIII:** 76
Dugan, James, **Supp. XV:** 197
"Dugout"(Kenny), **Supp. XXIII:** 155
Duhamel, Marcel, **Supp. XVI:** 135, 143
Dujardin, Edouard, **I:** 53
"Duke de l'Omelette, The" (Poe), **III:** 411, 425
Duke Herring (Bodenheim), **Supp. XXV:** 27
"Duke in His Domain, The" (Capote), **Supp. III Part 1:** 113, 126
Duke of Deception, The (G. Wolff), **Supp. II Part 1:** 97; **Supp. XI:** 246
"Duke's Child, The" (Maxwell), **Supp. VIII:** 172
"Dulce et Decorum Est" (Owen), **Supp. XVIII:** 92
"Dulham Ladies, The" (Jewett), **II:** 407, 408; **Retro. Supp. II:** 143
"Dulse" (Munro), **Supp. XXVII:** 188
Duluth (Vidal), **Supp. IV Part 2:** 677, 685, 689, 691–692
Dumas, Alexandre, **III:** 386; **Supp. XVII:** 64
"Dumb Oax, The" (Lewis), **Retro. Supp. I:** 170
"Dummy, The" (Sontag), **Supp. III Part 2:** 469
"Dump Ground, The" (Stegner), **Supp. IV Part 2:** 601
Dunant, Sarah, **Supp. XIX:** 186
Dunayevskaya, Raya, **Supp. XXI:** 169
Dunbar, Alice Moore (Mrs. Paul Laurence Dunbar), **Supp. II Part 1:** 195, 200, 217
Dunbar, Paul Laurence, **Supp. I Part 1:** 320; **Supp. II Part 1:** 174, **191–219; Supp. III Part 1:** 73; **Supp. IV Part 1:** 15, 165, 170; **Supp. X:** 136; **Supp. XI:** 277; **Supp. XIII:** 111; **Supp. XXII:** 11; **Supp. XXVII:** 164
Duncan, Harry, **Supp. XV:** 75
Duncan, Isadora, **I:** 483; **Supp. XV:** 42, 50
Duncan, Isla, **Supp. XXVII:** 193
Duncan, Robert, **Retro. Supp. II:** 49; **Supp. III Part 2:** 625, 626, 630, 631; **Supp. VIII:** 304; **Supp. XVI:** 282–283; **Supp. XXIII:** 213; **Supp. XXVII:** 160
Dunciad, The (Pope), **I:** 204
Dunford, Judith, **Supp. VIII:** 107
Dunlap, William, **Supp. I Part 1:** 126, 130, 137, 141, 145
Dunn, Stephen, **Supp. XI: 139–158; Supp. XIX:** 85
Dunne, Finley Peter, **II:** 432
Dunne, John Gregory, **Supp. IV Part 1:** 197, 198, 201, 203, 207

"Dunnet Shepherdess, A" (Jewett), **II:** 392–393; **Retro. Supp. II:** 139
Dunning, Stephen, **Supp. XIV:** 126
Dunning, William Archibald, **Supp. II Part 1:** 170; **Supp. XIV:** 48
Dunnock, Mildred, **III:** 153
Dunster, Henry, **Supp. I Part 2:** 485
"Dunwich Horror, The" (Lovecraft), **Supp. XXV:** 111, 120
"Duo Tried Killing Man with Bacon" (Goldbarth), **Supp. XII:** 176
Dupee, F. W., **I:** 254; **II:** 548; **Supp. IX:** 93, 96; **Supp. VIII:** 231
DuPlessis, Rachel Blau, **Supp. IV Part 2:** 421, 426, 432; **Supp. XVI:** 284; **Supp. XXVI:** 228, 234, 237–238
Duplicate Keys (Smiley), **Supp. VI:** 292, **294–296**
Duplications, The (Koch), **Supp. XV:** 181, 183, 186
Durable Fire, A (Sarton), **Supp. VIII:** 260
Durand, Asher, B., **Supp. I Part 1:** 156, 157
Durand, Régis, **Supp. IV Part 1:** 44
Durang, Christopher, **Supp. XXIV: 113– 130,** 263
"Durango Suite" (Gunn Allen), **Supp. IV Part 1:** 326
Durant, Kenneth, **Supp. XXII:** 278, 281
"Durations" (Matthews), **Supp. IX:** 152– 153, 154
Dürer, Albrecht, **III:** 212; **Supp. XII:** 44
Durham, David Anthony, **Supp. XVIII:** 100
"During Fever" (R. Lowell), **II:** 547
Durkheim, Émile, **I:** 227; **Retro. Supp. I:** 55, 57; **Supp. I Part 2:** 637, 638
Durrell, Lawrence, **III:** 184, 190; **IV:** 430; **Supp. X:** 108, 187; **Supp. XVI:** 294
Dürrenmatt, Friedrich, **Supp. IV Part 2:** 683
Duse, Eleonora, **II:** 515, 528
Dusk and Other Stories (Salter), **Supp. IX: 260–261**
"Dusk in War Time" (Teasdale), **Supp. XXVII:** 294
Dusk of Dawn: An Essay Toward an Autobiography of a Race Concept (Du Bois), **Supp. II Part 1:** 159, 183, 186
Dusselier, Jane, **Supp. XXVI:** 210
"Dust" (R. Fisher), **Supp. XIX:** 71
"Dusting" (Alvarez), **Supp. VII:** 4
"Dusting" (Dove), **Supp. IV Part 1:** 247, 248
"Dusting" (Schnackenberg), **Supp. XV:** 256
"Dust of Snow" (Frost), **II:** 154
Dust Tracks on a Road (Hurston), **Supp. IV Part 1:** 5, 11; **Supp. VI:** 149, 151, 158–159
"Dusty Braces" (Snyder), **Supp. VIII:** 302
Dutchman (Baraka), **Supp. II Part 1:** 38, 40, 42–44, 54, 55
"Dutch Nick Massacre, The" (Twain), **IV:** 195
"Dutch Picture, A" (Longfellow), **Retro. Supp. II:** 171

Dutton, Charles S., **Supp. VIII:** 332, 342
Dutton, Clarence Earl, **Supp. IV Part 2:** 598
Duvall, Robert, **Supp. V:** 227
"Duwamish" (Hugo), **Supp. VI:** 136
"Duwamish, Skagit, Hoh" (Hugo), **Supp. VI:** 136–137
"Duwamish No. 2" (Hugo), **Supp. VI:** 137
Duyckinck, Evert, **III:** 77, 81, 83, 85; **Retro. Supp. I:** 155, 247, 248; **Supp. I Part 1:** 122, 317; **Supp. XXV:** 250
Duyckinck, George, **Supp. I Part 1:** 122; **Supp. XXV:** 250
"Dvonya" (Simpson), **Supp. IX:** 274
Dwelling Places: Poems and Translations (Ferry), **Supp. XXIV:** 152–153
Dwellings: A Spiritual History of the Living World (Hogan), **Supp. IV Part 1:** 397, 410, 415–416, 417
Dwight, Sereno E., **I:** 547
Dwight, Timothy, **Supp. I Part 1:** 124; **Supp. I Part 2:** 516, 580; **Supp. II Part 1:** 65, 69
Dworkin, Andrea, **Supp. XII:** 6
Dwyer, Jim, **Supp. XVI:** 16, 19
Dyas, Sandra, **Supp. XIX:** 174
Dybbuk, A, or Between Two Worlds: Dramatic Legend in Four Acts (Kushner), **Supp. IX:** 138
Dybbuk, The (Ansky), **IV:** 6
Dybek, Stuart, **Supp. XXIII: 67–81**
Dybuk, The (Ansky), **Supp. XXIII:** 8
Dyer, Geoff, **Supp. X:** 169
Dyer, Joyce, **Supp. XX: 166**
Dyer, R. C., **Supp. XIII:** 162
Dyer, Richard, **Supp. XXII:** 261
Dyer's Thistle (Balakian), **Supp. XXIII:** 25
Dying Animal, The (P. Roth), **Retro. Supp. II:** 288
"Dying Elm, The" (Freneau), **Supp. II Part 1:** 258
"Dying Indian, The" (Freneau), **Supp. II Part 1:** 262
"Dying Man, The" (Roethke), **III:** 540, 542, 543–545
Dykeman, Wilma, **Supp. XX: 163**
Dykes to Watch Out For (Bechdel), **Supp. XXV:** 1, 3–4
Dylan, Bob, **Supp. VIII:** 202; **Supp. XIII:** 114, 119; **Supp. XV:** 349, 350; **Supp. XVIII: 19–34; Supp. XXII:** 83
Dylan's Visions of Sin (Ricks), **Supp. XVIII:** 20
"Dynamics of Heroic Action, The" (lecture, Murray), **Supp. XIX:** 153
Dynamo (O'Neill), **III:** 396
"Dynasties" (Gibran), **Supp. XX: 118**
"Dysfunctional Narratives: Or, 'Mistakes Were Made' " (C. Baxter), **Supp. XVII:** 20
"Dysfunctional Nation" (Karr), **Supp. XI:** 245
Dyson, A. E., **Retro. Supp. II:** 247
Dyson, Freeman, **Supp. XVII:** 42

E

"Each and All" (Emerson), **II:** 19
Each Happiness Ringer by Lions (Hirshfield), **Supp. XXIII:** 135
Each in His Season (Snodgrass), **Supp. VI:** 324, 327
"Each Like a Leaf" (Swenson), **Supp. IV Part 2:** 644
Eads, Martha Greene, **Supp. XVIII:** 49
Eady, Cornelius, **Supp. XXI:** 246
Eager, Allen, **Supp. XI:** 294
"Eagle, The" (Tate), **IV:** 128
"Eagle and the Mole, The" (Wylie), **Supp. I Part 2:** 710, 711, 713, 714, 729
"Eagle and the Skylark, The" (Gibran), **Supp. XX: 124**
Eagle as Wide as the World, The (X. J. Kennedy), **Supp. XV:** 162, 164
"Eagle Poem" (Harjo), **Supp. XII:** 224, 226
"Eagles" (Dickey), **Supp. IV Part 1:** 186
Eagle's Mile, The (Dickey), **Supp. IV Part 1:** 178, 185–186
"Eagle That Is Forgotten, The" (Lindsay), **Supp. I Part 2:** 382, 387
Eagleton, Terry, **Retro. Supp. I:** 67
Eakin, Paul John, **Supp. VIII:** 167, 168; **Supp. XIII:** 225; **Supp. XVI:** 70
Eakins, Thomas, **Supp. XIV:** 338; **Supp. XXII:** 18–19
Eames, Emma, **Supp. XX: 232, 240**
Eames, Roscoe, **II:** 476
"Earl: My Life with a Louse" (Keillor), **Supp. XVI:** 176
"Earl Painter" (Banks), **Supp. V:** 14–15
"Early Adventures of Ralph Ringwood, The" (Irving), **II:** 314
Early Americana (Richter), **Supp. XVIII:** 208, 210, 211, 220
Early Autumn (Parker), **Supp. XIX:** 184–185
Early Ayn Rand, The: A Selection of Her Unpublished Fiction (Rand), **Supp. IV Part 2:** 520
Early Dark (Price), **Supp. VI:** 262
Early Diary of Anaïs Nin, The, **Supp. X:** 184, 192
Early Elkin (Elkin), **Supp. VI: 42–43,** 45
"Early Evenin' Blues" (Hughes), **Retro. Supp. I:** 205
"Early Evening, Frankfort, Kentucky" (Trethewey), **Supp. XXI:** 243, 250
"Early History of a Seamstress" (Reznikoff), **Supp. XIV:** 277, 289
Early History of a Sewing-Machine Operator (Reznikoff), **Supp. XIV:** 289
"Early History of a Sewing-Machine Operator" (Reznikoff), **Supp. XIV:** 277
"Early History of a Writer" (Reznikoff), **Supp. XIV:** 278, 290
"Early in the Morning" (L.-Y. Lee), **Supp. XV:** 214
Early Lectures of Ralph Waldo Emerson, The (Emerson), **II:** 11
Early Light (Di Piero), **Supp. XIX:** 38, **38–40**
Early Lives of Melville, The (Sealts), **Retro. Supp. I:** 257
"Early Marriage" (Richter), **Supp. XVIII:** 209

Early Martyr and Other Poems, An (W. C. Williams), **Retro. Supp. I:** 423
"Early Morning: Cape Cod" (Swenson), **Supp. IV Part 2:** 641
"Early Rooms"(Hirshfield), **Supp. XXIII:** 130
"Early Spring between Madison and Bellingham" (R. Bly), **Supp. IV Part 1:** 71
Early Writing (O'Hara), **Supp. XXIII:** 220
Earnhardt, Dale, **Supp. XII:** 310
Earnshaw, Doris, **Supp. IV Part 1:** 310
"Earth" (Bryant), **Supp. I Part 1:** 157, 164, 167
"Earth, The" (Sexton), **Supp. II Part 2:** 696
Earth Abides (Stewart), **Supp. XVIII:** 138
"Earth and Fire" (Berry), **Supp. X:** 27
Earth as Air, The: An Ars Poetica (Sobin), **Supp. XVI: 285–286**
"Earth Being" (Toomer), **Supp. IX:** 320
Earth Goat (online), **Supp. XXII:** 61
Earth Gods, The (Gibran), **Supp. XX: 116, 123**
"Earth is parched with heat, The" (Very), **Supp. XXV:** 239
"Earthly Care a Heavenly Discipline" (Stowe), **Supp. I Part 2:** 586
"Earthly City of the Jews, The" (Kazin), **Retro. Supp. II:** 286
Earthly Meditations (Wrigley), **Supp. XVIII:** 304–305
"Earthly Meditations" (Wrigley), **Supp. XVIII:** 304–306
Earthly Possessions (Tyler), **Supp. IV Part 2:** 665–666, 671
Earth Power Coming (Ortiz, ed.), **Supp. IV Part 2:** 502
"Earth's Holocaust" (Hawthorne), **II:** 226, 231, 232, 242; **III:** 82; **Retro. Supp. I:** 152
Earth Without You, The (F. Wright), **Supp. XVII:** 243
Eason, Laura, **Supp. XXIII:** 79
East Coker (Eliot), **I:** 580, 581, 582, 585, 587
"East Coker" (Eliot), **Retro. Supp. I:** 66; **Supp. VIII:** 195, 196
"Easter" (Toomer), **Supp. III Part 2:** 486
"Easter, an Ode" (R. Lowell), **II:** 536
"Easter 1916" (Yeats), **Supp. XXI:** 61
"Easter Island: The Statues Speak" (Davison), **Supp. XXVI:** 71
"Easter Morning" (Ammons), **Supp. VII:** 34
"Easter Morning" (Clampitt), **Supp. IX:** 45
"Eastern Standard" (Huddle), **Supp. XXVI:** 149
"Easter Ode, An" (Dunbar), **Supp. II Part 1:** 196
"Easter"(O'Hara), **Supp. XXIII:** 211
Easter Parade, The (Yates), **Supp. XI:** 346, 349
"Easter Sermon, 1866" (Nelson), **Supp. XVIII:** 177
"Easter Service" (Di Piero), **Supp. XIX:** 39–40

"Easter Sunday: Recollection" (Gunn Allen), **Supp. IV Part 1:** 322

"Easter Wings" (Herbert), **Supp. IV Part 2:** 646

"East European Cooking" (Simic), **Supp. VIII:** 277

East Is East (Boyle), **Supp. VIII:** 1–3; **Supp. XX: 23–24, 25, 28**

Eastlake, William, **Supp. XIII:** 12

East Lynne (Wood), **Supp. I Part 1:** 35, 36; **Supp. I Part 2:** 459, 462; **Supp. XVI:** 182

Eastman, Elaine Goodale, **Supp. X:** 103

Eastman, Max, **Supp. III Part 2:** 620; **Supp. X:** 131, 134, 135, 137; **Supp. XV:** 295; **Supp. XVI:** 185; **Supp. XVII:** 96; **Supp. XXI:** 6; **Supp. XXII:** 274, 275, 277

Eastman, P. D., **Supp. XXV:** 1

East of Eden (Steinbeck), **IV:** 51, 56–57, 59

"East of the Sun and West of the Moon" (Merwin), **Supp. III Part 1:** 344

Easton, Alison, **Retro. Supp. II:** 143, 144, 145

Easton, Bret Ellis, **Supp. XI:** 65

Easton, Nina J., **Supp. XIX:** 137

Easton, Robert, **Supp. IV Part 2:** 461, 474

East River (Asch), **Supp. XXIII:** 1, 3, 7, **14–15**

"East-Side: New York" (Bodenheim), **Supp. XXV:** 22

East Wind (A. Lowell), **II:** 527

East Wind: West Wind (Buck), **Supp. II Part 1:** 114–115

Easy Rawlins mysteries, **Supp. XIII:** 236, **237–241,** 242

Easy Rider (film), **Supp. XI:** 293, **308, 309**

Easy Rider (Hopper), **Supp. XXVI:** 26

Eat a Bowl of Tea (Chu), **Supp. X:** 291

"Eating " (Bass), **Supp. XVI:** 23–24

"Eating Alone" (L.-Y. Lee), **Supp. XV:** 214

"Eating Barley Sugar and Waiting to Be Ninety"(Hadas), **Supp. XXIII:** 120–121

Eating Naked (Dobyns), **Supp. XIII: 78–79**

"Eating Out" (L. Michaels), **Supp. XVI:** 209

"Eating Poetry" (Strand), **Supp. IV Part 2:** 626

"Eating the Whole" (C. Frost), **Supp. XV:** 101

"Eating Together" (L.-Y. Lee), **Supp. XV:** 214

"Eating with My Fingers" (C. Frost), **Supp. XV:** 97

Eaton, Edith, **Supp. X:** 291

Eaton, Mark A., **Supp. XXIII:** 129, 130, 136

Eaton, Peggy, **Supp. I Part 2:** 461

Eaton, Winnifred, **Supp. X:** 291

"Eatonville Anthology, The" (Hurston), **Supp. VI:** 152

Eat Pray Love (Gilbert), **Supp. XXII:** 83, 90

Eat the Document (film, Pennebaker), **Supp. XVIII:** 19, 26, 27, 28

"Ebb and Flow, The" (Taylor), **IV:** 161

"Ebenezer Marsh, 1725" (Schnackenberg), **Supp. XV:** 256

Eben Holden (Bacheller), **I:** 216

Eberhardt, Isabelle, **Supp. IV Part 1:** 92

Eberhart, Mrs., **I:** 521–522, 530

Eberhart, Richard, **I: 521–543; II:** 535–536; **III:** 527; **IV:** 416; **Retro. Supp. II:** 176, 178; **Supp. I Part 1:** 83; **Supp. XII:** 119; **Supp. XXVI:** 68

Ebert, Roger, **Supp. XXVII:** 68

Eble, Kenneth E., **Supp. I Part 1:** 201

Ebony and Topaz (C. S. Johnson, ed.), **Supp. XXVI:** 170

"Ecce Homo" (Cliff), **Supp. XXII:** 76

Eccentricities of a Nightingale (T. Williams), **IV:** 382, 385, 397, 398

Ecclesiastica Historia Integram Ecclesiae (Taylor), **IV:** 163

"Echart" (Sobin), **Supp. XVI:** 289

"Echo, The" (Bowles), **Supp. IV Part 1:** 84, 86, 87

Echo, Thomas William, **Supp. XXVI:** 87

Echoes inside the Labyrinth (McGrath), **Supp. X:** 127

Echo Park (Connelly), **Supp. XXI: 77–78**

Eckehart, Meister, **Supp. XV:** 225

Eckhart, Maria, **Supp. V:** 212

Eclipse (Hogan), **Supp. IV Part 1:** 397, 400, 402

Eclipse, a Nightmare (Montalembert), **Supp. XV:** 349

"Eclipse"(Schott), **Supp. XXIII:** 252

"Eclogue" (Oppen), **Supp. XXVI:** 232

Eclogues (Virgil), **Supp. VIII:** 31; **Supp. XXIV:** 156

Eclogues of Virgil, The (Ferry, trans.), **Supp. XXIV: 156–157**

"Ecologue" (Ginsberg), **Supp. II Part 1:** 326

"Ecologues of These States 1969–1971" (Ginsberg), **Supp. II Part 1:** 325

Ecology of a Cracker Childhood (Ray), **Supp. XVIII:** 189, 191, 192, 193, **195–199,** 201, 202, 204

"Economics of Negro Emancipation in the United States, The" (Du Bois), **Supp. II Part 1:** 174

"Economics of the Cracker Landscape: Poverty as an Environmental Issue in Larry Brown's *Joe*" (Watson), *Supp. XXI:* 46

"Economic Theory of Women's Dress, The" (Veblen), **Supp. I Part 2:** 636

Economy of the Unlost: Reading Simonides of Keos with Paul Celan (Carson), **Supp. XII:** 110–111

Ecotactics: The Sierra Club Handbook for Environmental Activists (Mitchell and Stallings, eds.), **Supp. IV Part 2:** 488

"Ecstasy" (Bierds), **Supp. XVII:** 34

"Ecstasy" (Olds), **Supp. X:** 206

"Ecstasy of Influence, The" (Lethem), **Supp. XVIII:** 150

"Ecstatic" (Komunyakaa), **Supp. XIII:** 131

Edda, **Supp. X:** 114

Eddy, Mary Baker, **I:** 583; **III:** 506

Edel, Leon, **I:** 20; **II:** 338–339; **Retro. Supp. I:** 218, 224, 231

Edelberg, Cynthia, **Supp. IV Part 1:** 155

"Eden, Then and Now" (Stone), **Supp. XXVII:** 252

"Eden and My Generation" (Levis), **Supp. XI:** 270

Edenbaum, Robert, **Supp. IV Part 1:** 352

Eden Tree (Bynner), **Supp. XV:** 42, 51

Edenville Owls (Parker), **Supp. XIX:** 190

Eder, Richard, **Supp. XII:** 189; **Supp. XV:** 62, 187, 259, 261

Edgar Huntly; or, Memoirs of a Sleep-Walker (Brown), **Supp. I Part 1:** 140–144, 145

"Edge" (Plath), **Retro. Supp. II:** 256; **Supp. I Part 2:** 527, 547

Edge, Mary E., **II:** 316

Edgell, David, **Supp. XXIV:** 71

Edgell, Zee, **Supp. XXIII: 83–96**

"Edge of Possibility, The: Susan Warner and the World of Sunday School Fiction" (S. Gates), **Supp. XVIII:** 267

"Edge of the Great Rift, The" (Theroux), **Supp. VIII:** 325

Edge of the Sea, The (Carson), **Supp. IX:** 19, **25–31,** 32

Edge of the Woods, The: Iroquoia, 1534–1701 (Parmenter), **Supp. XXVI:** 85

Edgers, Geoff, **Supp. XV:** 113

Edgeworth, Maria, **II:** 8; **Supp. XV:** 231; **Supp. XX: 108**

Edible Woman, The (Atwood), **Supp. XIII:** 19, 20, **20–21**

"Edict by the King of Prussia, An" (Franklin), **II:** 120

Edie: An American Biography (Stein), **Supp. XVI:** 245

Edinburgh Days: or, Doing What I Want to Do (Pickering), **Supp. XXI:** 200–201

Edison, Thomas A., **I:** 483; **Supp. I Part 2:** 392

Edith Wharton (Joslin), **Retro. Supp. I:** 376

Edith Wharton: A Biography (Lewis), **Retro. Supp. I:** 362

Edith Wharton: A Woman in Her Time (Auchincloss), **Retro. Supp. I:** 370

Edith Wharton: Matters of Mind and Spirit (Singley), **Retro. Supp. I:** 373

Edith Wharton's Argument with America (Ammons), **Retro. Supp. I:** 364

Edith Wharton's Brave New Politics (Bauer), **Retro. Supp. I:** 381

Edith Wharton's Letters from the Underworld (Waid), **Retro. Supp. I:** 360

Edith Wharton: Traveller in the Land of Letters (Goodwyn), **Retro. Supp. I:** 370

"Editing and Glosses" (Reznikoff), **Supp. XIV:** 283

Editing of Emily Dickinson, The (Franklin), **Retro. Supp. I:** 41

"Editor and the Schoolma'am, The" (Frederic), **II:** 130

"Editor's Easy Chair" (Howells), **II:** 276

"Editor's Study, The" (Howells), **II:** 275, 276, 285

"Editor Whedon" (Masters), **Supp. I Part 2:** 463

Edlin, Mari, **Supp. X:** 266

Edman, Irwin, **III:** 605; **Supp. XXV:** 255, 258

Edmond (Mamet), **Supp. XIV:** 241, 248, 249, 250

Edmonds, Dale, **Supp. XXIII:** 291

Edmondson, Belinda, **Supp. XXII:** 70

Edmundson, Mark, **Retro. Supp. II:** 262

Edmund Wilson (Kriegel), **Supp. XXIV: 216–217**

Edsel (Shapiro), **Supp. II Part 2:** 703, 704, 717–719

Edson, Margaret, **Supp. XVIII: 35–52**

Edson, Russell, **Supp. VIII:** 279

"Educated American Woman, An" (Cheever), **Supp. I Part 1:** 194

"Education, An" (Ozick), **Supp. V:** 267

Education and Living (Bourne), **I:** 252

"Education by Poetry" (Frost), **Supp. XV:** 215

"Education of a Storyteller, The" (Bambara), **Supp. XI:** 20

Education of Black People, The (Du Bois), **Supp. II Part 1:** 186

Education of Harriet Hatfield, The (Sarton), **Supp. VIII: 257–258**

Education of Henry Adams, The (Adams), **I:** 1, 5, 6, 11, 14, 15–18, 19, 20–21, 111; **II:** 276; **III:** 504; **Retro. Supp. I:** 53, 59; **Supp. IX:** 19; **Supp. XIV:** 299

Education of H*y*m*a*n K*a*p*l*a*n, The (Rosten), **Supp. XVII:** 9

"Education of Mingo, The" (C. Johnson), **Supp. VI:** 193, 194

"Education of Norman Podhoretz, The" (Goldberg), **Supp. VIII:** 238

Education of Oscar Fairfax, The (Auchincloss), **Supp. IV Part 1:** 25, 36

"Education of the Poet" (Glück), **Supp. V:** 78, 80

Education sentimentale (Flaubert), **III:** 315

"Education the Imagination" (Koch), **Supp. XV:** 175–176, 177

Edwards, Clifford, **Supp. XVIII:** 220

Edwards, Eli. *See* McKay, Claude

Edwards, Esther, **I:** 545

Edwards, Harry Stillwell, **Supp. XXII:** 193

Edwards, John, **I:** 478

Edwards, Jonathan, **I: 544–566; II:** 432; **Retro. Supp. II:** 187; **Supp. I Part 1:** 301, 302; **Supp. I Part 2:** 552, 594, 700; **Supp. IV Part 2:** 430; **Supp. VIII:** 205; **Supp. XXIV:** 72

Edwards, Sarah, **I:** 545

Edwards, Thomas, **Supp. XV:** 20

Edwards, Thomas R., **Supp. XVI:** 207

Edwards, Timothy, **I:** 545

Edwards-Yearwood, Grace, **Supp. VIII:** 81; **Supp. XXII:** 213

"Edwin Arlington Robinson" (Cowley), **Supp. II Part 1:** 144

Edwin Arlington Robinson (Winters), **Supp. II Part 2:** 812

Edwin Booth (play), **Supp. IV Part 1:** 89

E. E. Cummings (Marks), **I:** 438

E. E. Cummings: A Miscellany (Cummings), **I:** 429, 441

E. E. Cummings: A Miscellany, Revised (Cummings), **I:** 429

"Effects of Analogy" (Stevens), **Retro. Supp. I:** 297

"Effigy of a Nun" (Teasdale), **Supp. XXVII:** 296

Effluences from the Sacred Caves; More Selected Essays and Reviews (Carruth), **Supp. XVI:** 46

"Effort at Speech between Two People" (Rukeyser), **Supp. VI:** 276, 284

"Efforts of Affection" (Moore), **III:** 214

"Efforts of Affection: A Memoir of Marianne Moore" (Bishop), **Retro. Supp. II:** 52

Egan, Jennifer, **Supp. XIX: 49–63; Supp. XXIII:** 299, 300

Egan, Leona, **Supp. XXI:** 6

"Egg, The" (Anderson), **I:** 113, 114

"Egg, The" (Snyder), **Supp. VIII:** 302

Eggers, David, **Supp. XXIV:** 131, 200

Eggleston, George Cary, **Supp. XVIII:** 15

"Eggplant Epithalamion, The" (Jong), **Supp. V:** 119

"Eggs" (Olds), **Supp. X:** 206

"Eggshell" (Stern), **Supp. IX:** 299

Egoist, The (Meredith), **II:** 186

Egorova, Lubov, **Supp. IX:** 58

"Egotism, or the Bosom Sergent" (Hawthorne), **II:** 227, 239

Egotist, The (Hecht), **Supp. XXVII:** 89

"Egyptian Pulled Glass Bottle in the Shape of a Fish, An" (Moore), **III:** 195, 213

Ehrenfels, Christian von, **Supp. XIV:** 198

Ehrenpreis, Irvin, **Supp. XII:** 128

Ehrenreich, Barbara, **Supp. XVII:** 210

Ehrhart, W. D., **Supp. XIX:** 281

Ehrlich, Gretel, **Supp. XIV:** 227; **Supp. XVIII:** 189; **Supp. XXVI:** 31, 187

"Ehue! fugaces, Posthume, Posthume, Labuntur anni" (Very), **Supp. XXV:** 243, 247

Eichmann, Adolf, **Supp. XII:** 166

Eichmann in Jerusalem (Arendt), **Retro. Supp. II:** 28; **Supp. VIII:** 243; **Supp. XII:** 166

"Eichmann in New York: The New York Intellectuals and the Hannah Arendt Controversy" (Rabinbach), **Supp. XII:** 166

"Eidolon" (Warren), **IV:** 239

"Eiger Dreams" (Krakauer), **Supp. XVIII:** 107

Eiger Dreams: Ventures Among Men and Mountains (Krakauer), **Supp. XVIII:** 105, 106, 107

Eight Cousins (Alcott), **Supp. I Part 1:** 29, 38, 42, 43

18 Pine Street series (Myers), **Supp. XXVII:** 211

18 Poems from the Quechua (Strand, trans.), **Supp. IV Part 2:** 630

"18 West 11th Street" (Merrill), **Supp. III Part 1:** 323, 328

1876: A Novel (Vidal), **Supp. IV Part 2:** 677, 684, 688, 689, 691, 692; **Supp. XIX:** 141

"18,000 CDs" (Halliday), **Supp. XIX:** 92

"Eighth Air Force" (Jarrell), **II:** 373–374, 377

Eight Harvard Poets, **I:** 429, 475

"Eighth Avenue Incident" (Halliday), **Supp. XIX:** 89–90

"Eighth Day, The" (Apple), **Supp. XVII:** 6, 50

"Eighth Ditch, The" (Baraka), **Supp. II Part 1:** 40

"'80s Pastoral: Frederick Barthelme's *Moon Deluxe* Ten Years On" (Peters), **Supp. XI:** 39

Eight Men (Wright), **IV:** 478, 488, 494

80 Flowers (Zukofsky), **Supp. III Part 2:** 631

Eikon Basilike, The, **Supp. IV Part 2:** 435

Eileen (Masters), **Supp. I Part 2:** 460

Eimi (Cummings), **I:** 429, 433, 434, 439–440

"Einstein" (MacLeish), **III:** 5, 8, 10–11, 18–19

Einstein, Albert, **I:** 493; **III:** 8, 10, 21, 161; **IV:** 69, 375, 410, 411, 421; **Retro. Supp. I:** 63; **Supp. I Part 2:** 609, 643; **Supp. III Part 2:** 621; **Supp. V:** 290; **Supp. XII:** 45

Eiseley, Loren, **III:** 227–228

Eisenberg, Deborah, **Supp. XXIII:** 290

Eisenhower, Dwight D., **I:** 136, 376; **II:** 548; **III:** 215; **IV:** 75; **Supp. I Part 1:** 291; **Supp. III Part 2:** 624; **Supp. V:** 45

Eisenstadt, Jill, **Supp. XVIII:** 135

Eisenstein, Sergei, **I:** 481; **Supp. XXI:** 170

Eisinger, Chester E., **I:** 302; **II:** 604; **Supp. IX:** 15

Eisner, Douglas, **Supp. X:** 155

Elam, Angela, **Supp. XI:** 290

El Bernardo (Balbuena), **Supp. V:** 11

Elbert, Sarah, **Supp. I Part 1:** 34, 41

Elder, Donald, **II:** 417, 426, 435, 437; **Supp. XV:** 137

Elder, John, **Supp. IX:** 25; **Supp. XXVI:** 38

Elder, Lonne, III, **Supp. IV Part 1:** 362

Elder, Richard, **Supp. XII:** 172

"Elder Sister, The" (Olds), **Supp. X:** 205–206

Elder Statesman, The (Eliot), **I:** 572, 573, 583; **Retro. Supp. I:** 53, 65

"Eldest Sister to Psyche, The" (Stallings), **Supp. XXV:** 234

E. L. Doctorow (Harter and Thompson), **Supp. IV Part 1:** 217

Eldredge, Kay, **Supp. IX:** 254, 259

Eldridge, Florence, **III:** 154, 403; **IV:** 357

Eleanor of Aquitaine, **III:** 470

Eleanor of Guienne, **I:** 14

Eleanor: or, Slave Catching in the Quaker City (Lippard), **Supp. XXIII:** 180, 185

"Elect, The" (Taylor), **Supp. V:** 323

"Elections, Nicaragua, 1984" (Kingsolver), **Supp. VII:** 208

Elective Affinities (Goethe; Bogan and Mayer, trans.), **Supp. III Part 1:** 63
Electra (Euripides), **III:** 398
Electra (Sophocles), **III:** 398; **IV:** 370; **Supp. IX:** 102
"Electra on Azalea Path" (Plath), **Supp. I Part 2:** 538
"Electrical Storm" (Bishop), **Supp. I Part 1:** 93
"Electrical Storm" (Hayden), **Supp. II Part 1:** 370
"Electric Arrows" (Proulx), **Supp. VII:** 256
"Electric Girl, The" (P. Benedict), **Supp. XXIII:** 40
"Electricity Saviour" (Olds), **Supp. X:** 215
Electric Kool-Aid Acid Test, The (Wolfe), **Supp. III Part 2:** 575–577, 582–584; **Supp. XI:** 239
Electric Lady, The (film), **Supp. XI:** 309
Electronic Book Review, **Supp. XXII:** 256, 257, 261
Elegant Extracts (Knox), **II:** 8
"Elegant Tom Dillar" (Briggs), **Supp. XVIII:** 17
"Elegiac" (Ferry), **Supp. XXIV:** 148–149
Elegiac Feelings American (Corso), **Supp. XII:** 131–134
"Elegiac Fragments" (Everwine), **Supp. XV:** 89
Elegies (Rukeyser), **Supp. VI:** 273
"Elegies" (Rukeyser), **Supp. VI:** 272
"Elegies for Paradise Valley" (Hayden), **Supp. II Part 1:** 363
"Elegy" (Bidart), **Supp. XV:** 25, 29
Elegy (Levis), **Supp. XI:** 257, 259, 261, **271–272**
"Elegy" (Merwin), **Supp. III Part 1:** 351
"Elegy" (Stafford), **Supp. XI:** 322
"Elegy" (Tate), **IV:** 128
"Elegy, for the U.S.N. Dirigible, Macon, An" (Winters), **Supp. II Part 2:** 810
"Elegy Ending in the Sound of a Skipping Rope" (Levis), **Supp. XI:** 271–272
"Elegy for 41 Whales Beached in Florence, Oregon, June 1979" (Bierds), **Supp. XVII:** 27
"Elegy for D. H. Lawrence, An" (W. C. Williams), **Retro. Supp. I:** 421
"Elegy for My Father" (Strand), **Supp. IV Part 2:** 628
"Elegy for My Mother" (Wagoner), **Supp. IX:** 330
"Elegy for Redondo Beach" (Jarman), **Supp. XVII:** 112, 113
Elegy for September, An (Nichols), **Supp. XIII:** 268
"Elegy for Thelonious" (Komunyakaa), **Supp. XIII:** 118
"Elegy for the Lost Umbrella" (Stallings), **Supp. XXIII:** 124; **Supp. XXV:** 231, 232
"Elegy for the Native Guards" (Trethewey), **Supp. XXI:** 255
"Elegy for the U.S.N. Dirigible, Macon, A" (Winters), **Supp. II Part 2:** 810
"Elegy in Dialogue" (Taggard), **Supp. XXII:** 276

"Elegy"(J. Schoolcraft), **Supp. XXIII:** 231
"Elegy of Last Resort" (Nemerov), **III:** 271
"Elegy with a Thimbleful of Water in the Cage" (Levis), **Supp. XI:** 272
Elegy Written in a Country Churchyard (Gray), **I:** 68
"Elegy Written in a Country Churchyard" (Gray), **Supp. XIV:** 8
"Elementary Scene, The" (Jarrell), **II:** 387, 388, 389
"Elements" (M. Frank), **Supp. X:** 213
Elements of Style, The (Strunk), **Supp. I Part 2:** 670
"Elenita, Cards, Palm, Water" (Cisneros), **Supp. VII:** 64
"Eleonora" (Poe), **III:** 412
Eleothriambos (Lee), **IV:** 158
"Elephant & Ocean" (Notley), **Supp. XXII:** 230
"Elephants" (Moore), **III:** 203
"Elephant's Dance, The" (D. West), **Supp. XVIII:** 281
"Elevator, The" (Dixon), **Supp. XII:** 154
"Elevator Boy" (Hughes), **Retro. Supp. I:** 200; **Supp. I Part 1:** 326
"Eleven" (Cisneros), **Supp. VII:** 69
Eleven Essays in the European Novel (Blackmur), **Supp. II Part 1:** 91, 111
Eleven Heavy Things (installation, July), **Supp. XXIV:** 200
Eleven Kinds of Loneliness (Yates), **Supp. XI:** **340–343,** 349
Eleven Poems on the Same Theme (Warren), **IV:** 239–241
"Eleven Times a Poem" (Corso), **Supp. XII:** 132, 133
El Greco (Doménikos Theotokópoulos), **I:** 387; **III:** 212
El-Hage, George N., **Supp. XX: 116**
"El-Hajj Malik El-Shabazz" (Hayden), **Supp. II Part 1:** 379
"Eli, the Fanatic" (P. Roth), **Supp. III Part 2:** 407–408
Elia, Nada, **Supp. XXII:** 73
Eliade, Mircea, **Supp. XVI:** 292
Elie, Paul, **Supp. XXII:** 91–92
Eliot, Charles William, **I:** 5; **II:** 345; **Retro. Supp. I:** 55; **Supp. I Part 2:** 479; **Supp. IX:** 94
Eliot, George, **I:** 375, 458, 459, 461, 467; **II:** 179, 181, 191–192, 275, 319, 324, 338, 577; **IV:** 311, 322; **Retro. Supp. I:** 218, 220, 225; **Supp. I Part 1:** 370; **Supp. I Part 2:** 559, 579; **Supp. IV Part 1:** 31, 297; **Supp. IV Part 2:** 677; **Supp. IX:** 38, 43, 51; **Supp. V:** 258; **Supp. XI:** 68; **Supp. XII:** 335; **Supp. XIV:** 344; **Supp. XX: 108**
Eliot, T. S., **I:** 48, 49, 52, 59, 60, 64, 66, 68, 105, 107, 215–216, 236, 243, 256, 259, 261, 266, 384, 386, 395, 396, 399, 403, 430, 433, 441, 446, 475, 478, 479, 482, 521, 522, 527, **567–591**; **II:** 65, 96, 158, 168, 316, 371, 376, 386, 529, 530, 532, 537, 542, 545; **III:** 1, 4, 5, 6, 7–8, 9, 10, 11, 14, 17, 20, 21, 23, 26, 34, 174, 194, 195–196, 205–206, 220, 236, 239, 269,

270–271, 277–278, 301, 409, 428, 435, 436, 453, 456–457, 459–460, 461–462, 464, 466, 471, 476, 478, 485, 488, 492, 493, 498, 504, 509, 511, 517, 524, 527, 539, 572, 575, 586, 591, 594, 600, 613; **IV:** 27, 74, 82, 83, 95, 122, 123, 127, 129, 134, 138, 140, 141, 191, 201, 237, 331, 379, 402, 403, 418, 419, 420, 430, 431, 439, 442, 491; **Retro. Supp. I:** **51–71,** 74, 80, 89, 91, 171, 198, 210, 283, 289, 290, 292, 296, 298, 299, 311, 324, 359, 411, 413, 414, 416, 417, 420, 428; **Retro. Supp. II:** 79, 178, 189, 262, 326; **Supp. I Part 1:** 257, 264, 268, 270, 274, 299; **Supp. I Part 2:** 387, 423, 455, 536, 554, 624, 659, 721; **Supp. II Part 1:** 1, 4, 8, 20, 30, 91, 98, 103, 136, 314; **Supp. III Part 1:** 9, 10, 26, 31, 37, 41, 43, 44, 48, 62–64, 73, 91, 99–100, 105–106, 273; **Supp. III Part 2:** 541, 611, 612, 617, 624; **Supp. IV Part 1:** 40, 47, 284, 380, 404; **Supp. IV Part 2:** 436; **Supp. IX:** 158–159, 229; **Supp. V:** 79, 97, 101, 338, 343, 344; **Supp. VIII:** 19, 21, 93, 102, 105, 182, 195, 205, 290, 292; **Supp. X:** 59, 115, 119, 124, 187, 324; **Supp. XI:** 242; **Supp. XII:** 45, 159, 198, 308; **Supp. XIII:** 77, 104, 115, 332, 341–342, 344, 346; **Supp. XIV:** 5, 13, 107, 287, 290, 306, 347; **Supp. XIX:** 12; **Supp. XV:** 20, 51, 139, 177, 181, 186, 216, 218, 250, 251, 258, 298, 302, 303, 306, 307; **Supp. XVI:** 158–159, 204, 207, 282; **Supp. XVII:** 36, 71, 75, 111, 240; **Supp. XVIII:** 136; **Supp. XX: 86, 108, 199; Supp. XXIII:** 25, 60, 166; **Supp. XXVI:** 143; **Supp. XXVII:** 153, 284, 287
Eliot's Early Years (Gordon), **Retro. Supp. I:** 55
"Elizabeth" (Longfellow), **I:** 502
"Elizabeth, 1905" (Schnackenberg), **Supp. XV:** 253, 256
Elizabeth Appleton (O'Hara), **III:** 362, 364, 375–377
"Elizabeth Bishop (1911–1979)" (Merrill), **Retro. Supp. II:** 53
"Elizabeth Bishop in Brazil" (Brown), **Supp. I Part 1:** 96
"Elizabeth Bishop's *North & South*" (R. Lowell), **Retro. Supp. II:** 40–41
"Elizabeth Gone" (Sexton), **Supp. II Part 2:** 674, 681
Elizabeth Rex (Findley), **Supp. XX: 62–63**
Elizabeth Stoddard and the Boundaries of Bourgeois Culture (Mahoney), **Supp. XV:** 270
Elk Heads on the Wall (Ríos), **Supp. IV Part 2:** 540
Elkin, Stanley, **Supp. VI: 41–59**
Elkins, Andrew, **Supp. XXIII:** 131, 135
Elkins, Marilyn, **Supp. XXIV:** 64
"Elk Song" (Hogan), **Supp. IV Part 1:** 406
Ella in Bloom (Hearon), **Supp. VIII: 70–71**

Elledge, Jim, **Supp. XIII:** 88

Ellen Foster: A Novel (Gibbons), **Supp. X:** 41, **42–44,** 46, 47, 49, 50

Ellen Montgomery's Bookshelf (S. and A. Warner), **Supp. XVIII:** 264

Ellen Rogers (Farrell), **II:** 42–43

"Ellen's Dream" (Gioia), **Supp. XV:** 128

"Ellen West" (Bidart), **Supp. XV: 26–27**

Eller, Ernest, **Supp. I Part 2:** 497

Ellerman, Winifred, **Supp. I Part 1:** 258–259. *See also* McAlmon, Mrs. Robert (Winifred Ellerman)

"*El libro de la sexualidad*" (Simic), Supp. VIII: 283

Ellington, Duke, **Retro. Supp. II:** 115; **Supp. IV Part 1:** 360; **Supp. IX:** 164

Elliot, Charles, **Supp. V:** 161

Elliot, George P., **Supp. XV:** 92

Elliott, George B., **III:** 478

Elliott, J. W. M., **Supp. XXVI:** 87, 88

Ellipse, The: Selected Poems of Leonardo Sinisgalli (Di Piero, trans.), **Supp. XIX:** 34

"Ellipsis" (C. Frost), **Supp. XV:** 107

Ellis, Albert, **Supp. IV Part 2:** 527

Ellis, Anne, **Supp. XVI:** 38

Ellis, Bret Easton, **Supp. X:** 7; **Supp. XII:** 81; **Supp. XVIII:** 135; **Supp. XXVII: 67–81,** 269

Ellis, Charles, **Supp. I Part 1:** 99

Ellis, Havelock, **II:** 276; **Supp. XX: 117, 235; Supp. XXII:** 198

Ellis, John Harvard, **Supp. I Part 1:** 103

Ellis, Katherine, **IV:** 114

Ellis, Kelly, **Supp. XXI:** 249

Ellis, Ron, **Supp. XXII:** 209

Ellis, Thomas Sayers, **Supp. XXI:** 246

"Ellis Island" (Helprin), **Supp. XXV:** 85

Ellis Island and Other Stories (Helprin), **Supp. XXV:** 82, 83, 85

Ellison, Harlan, **Supp. XIII:** 61

Ellison, Ralph, **IV:** 250, 493; **Retro. Supp. II:** 3, **111–130; Supp. II Part 1:** 33, **221–252; Supp. IV, Part 1:** 374; **Supp. IX:** 114, 316; **Supp. VIII:** 105, 245; **Supp. X:** 324; **Supp. XI:** 18, 92, 275; **Supp. XIII:** 186, 233, 305; **Supp. XIV:** 306; **Supp. XIX:** 148, 149, 155; **Supp. XV:** 194; **Supp. XVI:** 135, 139; **Supp. XVIII:** 59, 61, 62, 277, 283

Ellmann, Maud, **Supp. IV Part 1:** 302

Ellmann, Richard, **Supp. VIII:** 105; **Supp. XV:** 74

Ellroy, James, **Supp. XIV:** 26; **Supp. XXI:** 71

Elm, Damas, **Supp. XXVI:** 89

Elman, Richard, **Supp. V:** 40

"Elmer" (Faulkner), **Retro. Supp. I:** 79, 80

Elmer Gantry (Lewis), **I:** 26, 364; **II:** 447–449, 450, 455

Elmer the Great (Lardner), **II:** 427

"Elms" (Glück), **Supp. V:** 85

"Elms Dying, The—And My Friend, Lew Stillwell, Dead" (Bronk), **Supp. XXI:** 31

Elmslie, Kenward, **Supp. XXVII:** 19, 23, 26

Eloges (Perse), **Supp. XIII:** 344

"Eloquence of Grief, An" (Crane), **I:** 411

"El Paso Del Norte"(Kenny), **Supp. XXIII:** 150

"El Río Grande" (Mora), **Supp. XIII:** 224

"*El* Round up" (Alvarez), **Supp. VII:** 11

"El Salvador: Requiem and Invocation" (Levertov), **Supp. III Part 1:** 284

Elsasser, Henry, **I:** 226

"Elsa Wertman" (Masters), **Supp. I Part 2:** 462–463

Elsie John and Joey Martinez: Two Stories (Huncke), **Supp. XIV:** 148

Elsie Venner (Holmes), **Supp. I Part 1:** 243, 315–316

Elton, Charles, **Supp. XIV:** 192

Éluard, Paul, **III:** 528; **Supp. IV Part 1:** 80; **Supp. XVII:** 244

Elvins, Kells, **Supp. III Part 1:** 93, 101

Ely, Richard T., **Supp. I Part 1:** 5; **Supp. I Part 2:** 640, 645

"Emancipation. A Life Fable" (Chopin), **Retro. Supp. II:** 59; **Supp. I Part 1:** 207–208

"Emancipation in the British West Indies" (Emerson), **II:** 13

"Emancipation Proclamation, The" (Emerson), **II:** 13

Emanuel, James, **Supp. I Part 1:** 346

Embargo, The (Bryant), **Supp. I Part 1:** 152–153

"Embarkation for Cythera, The" (Ferry), **Supp. XXIV:** 149

Embarrassments (James), **Retro. Supp. I:** 229

Embezzler, The (Auchincloss), **Supp. IV Part 1:** 24, 30–31

"Embraces" (Davison), **Supp. XXVI:** 72

"Embroidery, The" (C. Frost), **Supp. XV:** 97

"Emerald" (Doty), **Supp. XI:** 131

"Emerald, The" (Merrill), **Supp. III Part 1:** 328

Emerald City (Egan), **Supp. XIX:** 49, **52–53**

"Emerald City" (Egan), **Supp. XIX:** 52

"Emergence of Flight from Aristotle's Mud, The" (Goldbarth), **Supp. XII:** 190

Emergency Exit (Major), **Supp. XXII:** 174, **175,** 182

"Emergency Haying" (Carruth), **Supp. XVI:** 55

"Emergency Room" (Mora), **Supp. XIII:** 218

"Emerging Voices: The Teaching of Writing" (Mora), **Supp. XIII:** 220

Emerson, and Other Essays (Chapman), **Supp. XIV:** 41–44

Emerson, Ellen, **Supp. I Part 1:** 33

Emerson, John, **Supp. XVI:** 185, 186, 190, 192

Emerson, Ralph Waldo, **I:** 98, 217, 220, 222, 224, 228, 239, 246, 251, 252, 253, 257, 260, 261, 283, 386, 397, 402, 424, 433, 444, 447, 455, 458, 460–461, 463, 464, 485, 561; **II: 1–24,** 49, 92, 127–128, 169, 170, 226, 233, 237, 273–274, 275, 278, 289, 295, 301, 313, 315, 336, 338, 344, 402, 491, 503; **III:** 53, 82, 171, 174, 260, 277, 409, 424, 428, 453, 454, 507, 576–577, 606, 614; **IV:** 60, 167, 169, 170, 171, 172, 173–174, 176, 178, 183, 186, 187, 192, 201, 202, 211, 335, 338, 340, 342, 350; **Retro. Supp. I:** 34, 53, 54, 57, 62, 74–75, 76, 125, 148–149, 152–153, 159, 217, 250, 298, 392, 400, 403; **Retro. Supp. II:** 96, 113, 135, 142, 155, 207, 262; **Supp. I Part 1:** 2, 28–29, 31, 33, 188, 299, 308–309, 317, 358, 365, 366, 368; **Supp. I Part 2:** 374, 383, 393, 407, 413, 416, 420, 422, 474, 482, 580, 582, 602, 659, 679; **Supp. II Part 1:** 280, 288; **Supp. III Part 1:** 387; **Supp. IV Part 2:** 439, 597, 619; **Supp. IX:** 38, 90, 175, 176, 181; **Supp. V:** 118; **Supp. VIII:** 42, 105, 106, 108, 198, 201, 204, 205, 292; **Supp. X:** 42, 45, 121, 223; **Supp. XI:** 203; **Supp. XIII:** 141, 145, 233, 246, **Supp. XIII:** 247; **Supp. XIV:** 41–44, 46, 54, 104, 177; **Supp. XV:** 219, 224; **Supp. XVI:** 84; **Supp. XVII:** 42, 236; **Supp. XX: 115, 116; Supp. XXI:** 217; **Supp. XXIII:** 161, 190; **Supp. XXIV:** 4, 67, 74, 77; **Supp. XXV:** 241, 250; **Supp. XXVI:** 37; **Supp. XXVII:** 234

"Emerson and the Essay" (Gass), **Supp. VI:** 88

"Emerson the Lecturer" (J. R. Lowell), **Supp. I Part 2:** 420, 422

Emerson-Thoreau Award, **Retro. Supp. I:** 67

Emery, Clark, **III:** 478

Emery, Mary Lou, **Supp. XXII:** 73

E. M. Forster (Trilling), **Supp. III Part 2:** 496, 501, 504

"Emigre in Autumn, An" (Gioia), **Supp. XV:** 120

Emily, Alone (O'Nan), **Supp. XXV:** 145, 149, 150–151

"Emily Dickinson and Class" (Erkkila), **Retro. Supp. I:** 42–43

Emily Dickinson Editorial Collective, **Retro. Supp. I:** 47

Emily Dickinson in Southern California (X. J. Kennedy), **Supp. XV: 164–165**

"Emily Dickinson's Defunct" (Nelson), **Supp. XVIII:** 173

Emily Dickinson: Woman Poet (Bennett), **Retro. Supp. I:** 42

Eminent Victorians (Strachey), **Supp. I Part 2:** 485

Emma (Austen), **Supp. XVIII:** 149

"Emma and Eginhard" (Longfellow), **III:** 505

"Emma Enters a Sentence of Elizabeth Bishop's" (Gass), **Supp. VI:** 93

Emmanuel Appodocca: or, A Blighted Life (Philip), **Supp. XXI:** 160

"Emmaus" (Di Piero), **Supp. XIX:** 42, 43

Emma Who Saved My Life (Barnhardt), **Supp. XXVII:** 1, 3–5, 7

Emperor Jones, The (O'Neill), **II:** 278; **III:** 391, 392

Emperor of Haiti (Hughes), **Supp. I Part 1:** 339

"Emperor of Ice Cream, The" (Stevens), **IV:** 76, 80–81

"Emperors" (Dunn), **Supp. XI:** 155

"Emperor's New Clothes, The" (Anderson), **I:** 441

"Empire" (Ford), **Supp. V:** 69

Empire: A Novel (Vidal), **Supp. IV Part 2:** 677, 684, 686, 690; **Supp. XIX:** 132

"Empire Builders" (MacLeish), **III:** 14

Empire City, The: or, New York by Night and Day (Lippard), **Supp. XXIII:** 178, 180, 183, 184, 185

Empire Falls (Russo), **Supp. XII:** 339–343

Empire of Summer, The (Doty), **Supp. XI:** 120

Empire of the Senseless (Acker), **Supp. XII:** 5, **6,** 14–16

"Empires" (Simic), **Supp. VIII:** 282

"Emporium" (Shapiro), **Supp. II Part 2:** 705

Empress of the Splendid Season (Hijuelos), **Supp. VIII: 86–89**

Empson, William, **I:** 522, 533; **II:** 536; **III:** 286, 497, 498, 499; **IV:** 136, 431; **Retro. Supp. I:** 263; **Retro. Supp. II:** 253; **Supp. XVI:** 190

Empty Bed, The (Hadas), **Supp. XXIII:** 117–118

Empty Hands, The (Bronk), **Supp. XXI:** 31

"Empty Hills, The" (Winters), **Supp. II Part 2:** 792, 793, 796

"Empty Icon Frame" (Stallings), **Supp. XXV:** 233

Empty Mirror, Early Poems (Ginsberg), **Supp. II Part 1:** 308, 311, 313–314, 319, 329

"Empty Room" (Hughes), **Supp. I Part 1:** 337

"Empty Threat, An" (Frost), **II:** 159

Emshwiller, Ed, **Supp. XVIII:** 145

"Encantadas, The" (Melville), **III:** 89; **Supp. XVIII:** 4

Enchanter, The (Nabokov), **Retro. Supp. I:** 266

"Enclosed Dreams, Highways and Labyrinths: Jonathan Lethem's *Amnesia Moon*" (Rossi), **Supp. XVIII:** 139

"Encomium Twenty Years Later" (Tate), **I:** 381

"Encounter" (Espaillat), **Supp. XXI:** 107

"Encounter, The" (Pound), **III:** 466

Encounter in April (Sarton), **Supp. VIII:** 259

"Encounter in April" (Sarton), **Supp. VIII:** 259

"Encountering the Sublime" (McClatchy), **Supp. XII:** 261

"Encounter in Vindija Cave, Present-Day Croatia: Late October"(Schott), **Supp. XXIII:** 254

"Encounter on the Seine: Black Meets Brown" (Baldwin), **Retro. Supp. II:** 2

Encounters with Chinese Writers (Dillard), **Supp. VI:** 19, 23, 31

Encounters with the Archdruid (McPhee), **Supp. III Part 1:** 292–294, 301; **Supp. X:** 30

Encyclopedia of Arkansas History and Culture, The (online), **Supp. XXII:** 50

Encyclopedia of Scotland, The (A. Finch), **Supp. XVII: 70–71**

Encyclopedia of World Biography, The, **Supp. XXI:** 74

"End, The" (Olds), **Supp. X:** 205

"Endangered Species" (Mora), **Supp. XIII:** 219–220

Endecott and the Red Cross (R. Lowell), **II:** 545

Endgame (Beckett), **Supp. XIII:** 196; **Supp. XXII:** 263

"Endgame" (Tan), **Supp. X:** 290

"Endicott and the Red Cross" (Hawthorne), **Retro. Supp. II:** 181, 187–188

"End of Books, The" (Coover), **Supp. V:** 53

End of Books, The" (Coover), **Supp. XXII:** 259

End of Dreams, The (Skloot), **Supp. XX: 196, 202–203**

End of Education, The (Postman), **Supp. XI:** 275

"End of FIRPO in the World, The" (Saunders), **Supp. XIX:** 229

End of Me, The (Hayes), **Supp. XXVI:** 142–143

"End of Season" (Warren), **IV:** 239–240

"End of Something, The" (Hemingway), **II:** 248

End of the Affair, The (Greene), **Supp. XI:** 99

End of the Age of Innocence, The (Price), **Retro. Supp. I:** 377

"End of the Line, The" (Helprin), **Supp. XXV:** 81

"End of the Line, The" (Jarrell), **III:** 527

"End of the Rainbow, The" (Jarrell), **II:** 386

End of the Road (film), **Supp. XI:** 309

End of the Road, The (Barth), **I:** 121, 122, 126–131; **Supp. XI:** 309; **Supp. XVIII:** 140, 141

"End of the World, The" (Gioia), **Supp. XV:** 126

"End of the World, The" (MacLeish), **III:** 8

Endor (Nemerov), **III:** 269, 270, 279

Endore, Guy, **Supp. XVII: 53–67**

"Ends" (Dixon), **Supp. XII:** 153

End to Innocence, An: Essays on Culture and Politics (Fiedler), **Supp. XIII: 98–99**

Endure: The Diaries of Charles Walter Stetson (Stetson), **Supp. XI:** 196

"Enduring Chill, The" (O'Connor), **III:** 349, 351, 357; **Retro. Supp. II:** 236

Enduring Vision of Norman Mailer, The (Leeds), **Retro. Supp. II:** 204

Endymion (Keats), **IV:** 405; **Retro. Supp. I:** 412

End Zone (DeLillo), **Supp. VI:** 2, 3, 4, 10, 11, 12

Enemies (Boyce and Hapgood), **Supp. XVII:** 100; **Supp. XXI:** 7, 13

Enemies: A Love Story (Singer), **IV:** 1; **Retro. Supp. II:** 310–311

Enemy, The: Time (T. Williams), **IV:** 391

Enemy of the People, An (adapt. Miller), **III:** 154–156

"Energy Vampire" (Ginsberg), **Supp. II Part 1:** 326

"Enforcement of the Slave Trade Laws, The" (Du Bois), **Supp. II Part 1:** 161

"Engaging the Past" (Bell), **Supp. X:** 17

Engel, Bernard F., **I:** 532

Engels, Friedrich, **IV:** 429, 443–444; **Supp. I Part 1:** 13; **Supp. XXI:** 162

Engels, John, **Supp. XXVI:** 152

Engineer of Beasts, The (Sanders), **Supp. XVI:** 270

Engineer of Moonlight (DeLillo), **Supp. VI:** 4

Engineers and the Price System, The (Veblen), **I:** 475–476; **Supp. I Part 2:** 638, 642, 648

Engines of Creation: the Coming Era of Nanotechnology (Drexler), **Supp. XVI:** 121

"England" (Moore), **III:** 203, 207, 214

Englander, Nathan, **Supp. XX: 177, 179; Supp. XXIV:** 131; **Supp. XXV:** 268

Engle, Paul, **III:** 542; **Retro. Supp. II:** 220, 221; **Supp. V:** 337; **Supp. XI:** 315; **Supp. XIII:** 76; **Supp. XVIII:** 72

English, Zoë, **Supp. XVI:** 293

English Elegy, The: Studies in the Genre from Spenser to Yeats (Sacks), **Supp. IV Part 2:** 450

English Hours (James), **II:** 337; **Retro. Supp. I:** 235

English Language, The (L. P. Smith), **Supp. XIV:** 341

English-Latin Gradus or Verse Dictionary, An (Ainger), **Supp. XX: 230**

"English Lesson"(Strout), **Supp. XXIII:** 273–274, 284

Englishmen of Letters (James), **II:** 327

English Notebooks, The (Hawthorne), **II:** 226, 227–228

English Novel, The (Lanier), **Supp. I Part 1:** 371

English Poets, The: Lessing, Rousseau (J. R. Lowell), **Supp. I Part 2:** 407

English Prosody and Modern Poetry (Shapiro), **Supp. II Part 2:** 710

English Traits (Emerson), **II:** 1, 5, 6–7, 8

"English Writers on America" (Irving), **II:** 308

Engstrand, Stuart, **Supp. I Part 1:** 51

"Enigma Variations" (Nelson), **Supp. XVIII:** 177

"Enoch" (Very), **Supp. XXV:** 246, 247

"Enoch and the Gorilla" (O'Connor), **Retro. Supp. II:** 225

Enormous Changes at the Last Minute (Paley), **Supp. VI:** 218

"Enormous Changes at the Last Minute" (Paley), **Supp. VI:** 226, 232

"Enormous Radio, The" (Cheever), **Supp. I Part 1:** 175–177, 195

Enormous Radio and Other Stories, The (Cheever), **Supp. I Part 1:** 175–177

Enormous Room, The (Cummings), **I:** 429, 434, 440, 445, 477; **Supp. XXI:** 277

"Enough for a Lifetime" (Buck), **Supp. II Part 1:** 127

Enough Rope (Parker), **Supp. IX:** 189, 192

Enquiry Concerning Political Justice (Godwin), **Supp. I Part 1:** 126, 146

"En Route" (Boulton), **Supp. XXII:** 25

Entered From the Sun (Garrett), **Supp. VII:** 105–106, 107–109

"Entering the Building" (Notley), **Supp. XXII:** 237

"Entering the Kingdom" (Oliver), **Supp. VII:** 234

Entertaining Strangers (Gurney), **Supp. V:** 98, 99

Enter without Desire (Lacy), **Supp. XV:** 201

Entranced, The (Lippard), **Supp. XXIII:** 178, 180, 190

Entrance: Four Chicano Poets, **Supp. XIII:** 316

Entrance to Porlock, The (Buechner), **Supp. XII:** 52

Entries (Berry), **Supp. X:** 23

"Entropy" (Pynchon), **Supp. II Part 2:** 619, 621

"Entry" (Huddle), **Supp. XXVI:** 149

Entry in an Unknown Hand (F. Wright), **Supp. XVII:** 240, 244, 245

Environmental Imagination, The (Buell), **Supp. IX:** 29; **Supp. V:** 209

"Envoy" (Collins), **Supp. XXI:** 57

"Envoys, The" (Merrill), **Supp. III Part 1:** 326

"Envy; or, Yiddish in America" (Ozick), **Supp. V:** 263, 265–266

"Eolian Harp, The" (Coleridge), **I:** 284

"Eolian Harp, The"(Coleridge), **Supp. XXIII:** 231

"Eototo" (Sobin), **Supp. XVI:** 283–284

"Ephemera, The" (Franklin), **II:** 121

Ephesians (biblical book), **Supp. I Part 1:** 117

"Epic Poetry" (Very), **Supp. XXV:** 241

Epictetus, **III:** 566

"Epicurean, The" (Auchincloss), **Supp. IV Part 1:** 25

Epicurus, **I:** 59

Epidemic of Genius, An (Wolfert), **Supp. XXI:** 278

"Epigram" (R. Lowell), **II:** 550

"Epilogue" (R. Lowell), **Retro. Supp. II:** 191

"Epimanes" (Poe), **III:** 411

"Epimetheus" (Longfellow), **II:** 494

"Epiphany" (X. J. Kennedy), **Supp. XV:** 166, 167

"Epipsychidion" (Shelley), **Supp. I Part 2:** 718

"Episode, The" (Huddle), **Supp. XXVI:** 150

Episode in Palmetto (Caldwell), **I:** 297, 307

"Episode in the Life of an Ancestor" (Boyle), **Supp. XXIV:** 56

Episode of the Wandering Knife, The (Rinehart), **Supp. XXV:** 198, 200

"Epistle" (L.-Y. Lee), **Supp. XV:** 212

Epistles (Horace), **Supp. XXIV:** 156

Epistles of Horace, The (Ferry, trans.), **Supp. XXIV:** 157–158

Epistle to a Godson (Auden), **Supp. II Part 1:** 24

"Epistle to Be Left in the Earth" (MacLeish), **III:** 13

"Epistle to George William Curtis" (J. R. Lowell), **Supp. I Part 2:** 416

"Epistle to Léon-Paul Fargue" (MacLeish), **III:** 15

"Epitaph Ending in And, The" (Stafford), **Supp. XI:** 321–322

Epitaph for a Dead Beat (Markson), 139; **Supp. XVII: 136–138,** 141

Epitaph for a Desert Anarchist (Bishop), **Supp. XIII:** 1

Epitaph for a Tramp (Markson), **Supp. XVII:** 136, 137, 139 142

"Epitaph for Fire and Flower" (Plath), **Supp. I Part 2:** 537

"Epitaph for S.P." (Davison), **Supp. XXVI:** 71

"Epitaph for the Race of Man" (Millay), **III:** 127–128

"Epithalamium" (Auden), **Supp. II Part 1:** 15

"Epstein" (P. Roth), **Retro. Supp. II:** 281; **Supp. III Part 2:** 404, 406–407, 412, 422

Epstein, Barbara, **Supp. XIX:** 268

Epstein, Helen, **Supp. XVII:** 47; **Supp. XXII:** 95

Epstein, Jacob, **Supp. XXIII:** 6

Epstein, Jason, **Supp. VIII:** 233

Epstein, Joseph, **Supp. IV Part 2:** 692; **Supp. VIII:** 236, 238; **Supp. XIV:** 101–117; **Supp. XVI:** 230, 275

Epstein, Leslie, **Supp. XII: 159–174;** **Supp. XVIII:** 92, 99

Epstein, Philip, **Supp. XII:** 159

"Equal in Paris" (Baldwin), **Retro. Supp. II:** 3; **Supp. I Part 1:** 52

"Equals" (Untermeyer), **Supp. XV:** 304

Equation for Evil (Caputo), **Supp. XIX:** 25–26

"Equations of the Light" (Gioia), **Supp. XV:** 125

"Equilibrists, The" (Ransom), **III:** 490, 494

"Equinox 1980" (Davison), **Supp. XXVI:** 77

"Equinox"(Crooker), **Supp. XXIII:** 55

"Equipment for Pennies" (H. Roth), **Supp. IX:** 233

Erasmus, Desiderius, **Supp. XV:** 258

Erasure (Everett), **Supp. XVIII:** 54, 60, **61–62**

"Erat Hora" (Pound), **III:** 463; **Retro. Supp. I:** 413

Erdrich, Louise, **Supp. IV Part 1: 259–278,** 333, 404; **Supp. X:** 290; **Supp. XVIII:** 189; **Supp. XXIV:** 245; **Supp. XXVI:** 102

"Erectus" (Karr), **Supp. XI:** 243

"Ere Sleep Comes Down to Soothe the Weary Eyes" (Dunbar), **Supp. II Part 1:** 199, 207–208

"Ergo Non Sum. Est." (Bronk), **Supp. XXI:** 31

"Ergotism"(Schott), **Supp. XXIII:** 245

Erik Dorn (Hecht), **Supp. XXVII:** 83, 87–88, 89

Erikson, Erik, **I:** 58, 214, 218

Erisman, Fred, **Supp. VIII:** 126

Erkkila, Betsy, **Retro. Supp. I:** 42; **Supp. XX: 281, 287, 287–288**

Ernest, John, **Supp. XXI:** 24

"Ernest: or Parent for a Day" (Bourne), **I:** 232

Ernst, Max, **Retro. Supp. II:** 321

Eroding Witness (Mackey), **Supp. XXVII:** 152–153, 154, 157

"Eros" (Komunyakaa), **Supp. XIII:** 130

"Eros and Anteros" (E. Stoddard), **Supp. XV:** 283

Eros and Civilization (Marcuse), **Supp. XII:** 2

"Eros at Temple Stream" (Levertov), **Supp. III Part 1:** 278–279

Eros the Bittersweet (Carson), **Supp. XII:** 97, **98–99**

Eros Trilogy, The (Silver), **Supp. XXIV:** 264, 267

"Eros Turannos" (Robinson), **III:** 510, 512, 513–516, 517, 518

"Eroticism in Women" (Nin), **Supp. X:** 195

"Errand" (Carver), **Supp. III Part 1:** 149

Erskine, Albert, **IV:** 261; **Retro. Supp. II:** 117

Erskine, John, **I:** 223; **Supp. X:** 183; **Supp. XIV:** 120

Erstein, Hap, **Supp. IV Part 2:** 589, 590

"Escape" (MacLeish), **III:** 4

Escape Artist, The (Wagoner), **Supp. IX:** 324, **334–335**

"Escape"(Thompson), **Supp. XXIII:** 301

Escher, M. C., **Supp. XII:** 26; **Supp. XVI:** 102

"Escudilla" (Leopold), **Supp. XIV:** 188

Esenwein, J. Berg, **Supp. XXVI:** 281

Eshleman, Clayton, **Supp. XVI:** 284

"Eskimo Love" (Apple), **Supp. XVII:** 5

Espaillat, Rhina P., **Supp. XXI: 97–114**

Esparza, Laura, **Supp. XXIII:** 197

Especially Maine (Beston), **Supp. XXVI:** 32

Espeland, Pamela, **Supp. XVIII:** 180, 181

Espen, Hal, **Supp. X:** 15

Espey, John, **III:** 463, 468, 478

Esposito, Michael, **Supp. XX: 34, 40**

Esposito, Scott, **Supp. XVII:** 234

Esquibel, Catrióna Rueda, **Supp. XXIII:** 202

Essais (Renouvier), **II:** 344–345

Essay Concerning Human Understanding, An (Locke), **I:** 554; **II:** 8, 348–349

Essay on American Poetry (Brown), **Supp. I Part 1:** 156

"Essay on Aristocracy" (Paine), **Supp. I Part 2:** 515

Essay on Criticism, An (Pope), **Supp. XXVI:** 271, 284

"Essay on Friendship, An" (McClatchy), **Supp. XII:** 258–259

"Essay on Love" (Carruth), **Supp. XVI:** 56

Essay on Man (Pope), **II:** 111; **Supp. I Part 2:** 516

"Essay on Marriage" (Carruth), **Supp. XVI:** 48

Essay on Our Changing Order (Veblen), **Supp. I Part 2:** 629, 642

"Essay on Poetics" (Ammons), **Supp. VII:** 29–31

Essay on Projects (Defoe), **II:** 104

"Essay on Psychiatrists" (Pinsky), **Supp. VI:** 237, 238, 241, 242, 249, 250

Essay on Rime (Shapiro), **I:** 430; **Supp. II Part 2:** 702, 703, 708–711

"Essay on Sanity" (Dunn), **Supp. XI:** 147

"Essay on the Character of Robespierre" (Paine), **Supp. I Part 2:** 515

Essay on the Chinese Written Character (Fenollosa), **III:** 474

"Essay on What I Think About Most" (Carson), **Supp. XII: 111–112**

Essays (Emerson), **II:** 1, 7, 8, 12–13, 15, 21

Essays (Montaigne), **Supp. XXVI:** 39

Essays, Speeches, and Public Letters by William Faulkner (Meriweather, ed.), **Retro. Supp. I:** 77

Essays and Poems (Very), **Supp. XXV:** 247, 249–250

Essays in Anglo-Saxon Law (Adams), **I:** 5

Essays in London (James), **II:** 336

Essays in Radical Empiricism (James), **II:** 355, 356–357

Essays on Norman Mailer (Lucid), **Retro. Supp. II:** 195

Essays on the Nature and Principles of Taste (Alison), **Supp. I Part 1:** 151

Essays to Do Good (Mather), **II:** 104; **Supp. II Part 2:** 461, 467

"Essay: The Love of Old Houses" (Doty), **Supp. XI:** 136

"Essay Toward a Point of View, An" (Brooks), **I:** 244

"Essay Vanishes, The" (Monson), **Supp. XXIV:** 238

"Essence, Absence, and Sobin's *Venus Blue*" (English), **Supp. XVI:** 293

Essential Dykes to Watch Out For, The (Bechdel), **Supp. XXV:** 2

Essential Haiku, The (Hass), **Supp. VI:** 102

Essential Keats (Levine, ed.), **Supp. V:** 179

"Essential Oils—are wrung" (Dickinson), **I:** 471; **Retro. Supp. I:** 43, 46

"Essentials" (Toomer), **Supp. III Part 2:** 486

Essentials: A Philosophy of Life in Three Hundred Definitions and Aphorisms (Toomer), **Supp. III Part 2:** 486

Essentials: Definitions and Aphorisms (Toomer), **Supp. IX:** 320

"Essentials of Spontaneous Prose" (Kerouac), **Supp. III Part 1:** 227–228

Essential Works of the Founding Fathers, The (Kriegel, ed.), **Supp. XXIV:** 214

Estampas del valle y otras obras (Hinojosa). See *Valley, The* (Hinojosa)

Esta puente, mi espalda: Voces de mujeres tercermundistas en los Estados Unidos (Moraga, Castillo, and Alarcón, eds.), **Supp. XXIII:** 194

"Estate Sale" (Nye), **Supp. XIII:** 283

Estess, Sybil, **Supp. IV Part 2:** 449, 452

Esther (Adams), **I:** 9–10, 20

"Esther" (Toomer), **Supp. IX:** 313–314

"Esther Kahn" (Symons), **Supp. XX: 239**

"Esthétique du Mal" (Stevens), **IV:** 79; **Retro. Supp. I:** 300, 311, 312

"Estoy-eh-muut and the Kunideeyahs (Arrowboy and the Destroyers)" (film), **Supp. IV Part 2:** 560

Estrada, Genaro, **Retro. Supp. II:** 89

Estray, The (Longfellow, ed.), **Retro. Supp. II:** 155

Esty, William, **III:** 358

"Eta Carinae" (Stone), **Supp. XXVII:** 260–261

"Etching, An" (Masters), **Supp. I Part 2:** 458

Eternal Feminine, The (Wells), **Supp. XXVI:** 275

"Eternal Goodness, The" (Whittier), **Supp. I Part 2:** 704

Eternal Spring, The (Boyce), **Supp. XVII:** 100; **Supp. XXI:** 4, 5, 11

"Eternity, An" (W. C. Williams), **Retro. Supp. I:** 423

"Eternity Is Now" (Roethke), **III:** 544–545

"Ethan Brand" (Hawthorne), **II:** 227

Ethan Frome (Wharton), **IV:** 316–317, 327; **Retro. Supp. I:** 372–373; **Supp. IX:** 108; **Supp. XVIII:** 216; **Supp. XXIII:** 275, 281

"Ethical Turn in Postcolonial Theory and Narrative, The: Michelle Cliff's *No Telephone to Heaven*" (Moynagh), **Supp. XXII:** 73

Ethics (Spinoza), **IV:** 12; **Retro. Supp. II:** 300

"Ethics of Culture, The" (Locke), **Supp. XIV:** 211

"Ethics of Frank Costello, The" (Talese), **Supp. XVII:** 202

Etiquette and Vitriol: The Food Chain and Other Plays (Silver), **Supp. XXIV:** 263, 264

"Étiquettes Jaunes, Les"(O'Hara), **Supp. XXIII:** 214

"Etude" (Kooser), **Supp. XIX:** 115

Etulain, Richard, **Supp. IV Part 2:** 597, 601, 604, 606, 607, 608, 610, 611

"Etymology" (Nelson), **Supp. XVIII:** 185

Euclid, **III:** 6, 620

"Euclid Alone Has Looked on Beauty Bare" (Millay), **III:** 133

"Euclidean Spaces: Linear Time" (Bronk), **Supp. XXI:** 31

Eugene, Frank, **Supp. X:** 204

Eugene Onegin (Pushkin), **III:** 246, 263

Eugene Onegin (Pushkin; Nabokov, trans.), **Retro. Supp. I:** 266, 267, 272

Eugenides, Jeffrey, **Supp. XIX:** 138; **Supp. XXI:** 229; **Supp. XXIV:** 131–146

Eugénie, Empress, **IV:** 309

Eugénie Grandet (Balzac), **II:** 328

"Eugénie Grandet" (Barthelme), **Supp. IV Part 1:** 47

"Eulogy for Richard Hugo (1923–1982)" (Wagoner), **Supp. IX:** 330–331

"Eulogy on the Flapper" (Z. Fitzgerald), **Supp. IX:** 71

Eumenides (Aeschylus), **Retro. Supp. I:** 65

"E Unibus Pluram: Television and U.S. Fiction" (Wallace), **Supp. X:** 315–316

"Euphemisms" (Matthews), **Supp. IX: 167–168**

Eureka (Poe), **III:** 409, 424, 428–429

Eureka Mill (Rash), **Supp. XXVII:** 217–218

Eurekas (Goldbarth), **Supp. XII:** 181

Euripides, **I:** 325; **II:** 8, 282, 543; **III:** 22, 145, 398; **IV:** 370; **Supp. I Part 1:** 268, 269, 270; **Supp. I Part 2:** 482; **Supp. V:** 277

"Euripides and Professor Murray" (Eliot), **Supp. I Part 1:** 268

"Euripides—A Playwright" (West), **IV:** 286; **Retro. Supp. II:** 326

"Europe" (Ashbery), **Supp. III Part 1:** 7–10, 13, 18

European Discovery of America, The: The Northern Voyages (Morison), **Supp. I Part 2:** 496–497

Europeans, The (H. James), **I:** 452; **II:** 327, 328; **Retro. Supp. I:** 216, 220

Europe Central (Vollmann), **Supp. XVII:** 225, 226, 227, 229, 231, **233–235**, 236

"Europe! Europe!" (Ginsberg), **Supp. II Part 1:** 320, 322

Europe of Trusts, The: Selected Poems (Howe), **Supp. IV Part 2:** 420, 422, 426

Europe without Baedeker (Wilson), **IV:** 429

"Eurydice in Darkness" (Davison), **Supp. XXVI:** 71

Eurydice in the Underworld (Acker), **Supp. XII:** 7

"Eurydice Reveals Her Strength" (Stallings), **Supp. XXV:** 230

"Eurydice's Footnote" (Stallings), **Supp. XXV:** 230

Eustace, Saint, **II:** 215

Eustace Chisholm and the Works (Purdy), **Supp. VII:** 273–274, 279–280

"Euthanasia" (Tate), **IV:** 122

Eva (Levin), **Supp. XXVII:** 135, 143, 145

"Evaluation" (Bronk), **Supp. XXI:** 32

Eva-Mary (McCarriston), **Supp. XIV:** 259, 260, **263–268**

"Evangeline" (Dixon), **Supp. XII:** 153

Evangeline (Longfellow), **II:** 489, 501–502; **Retro. Supp. II:** 155, **156–159**, 162, 164; **Supp. I Part 2:** 586

Evanier, David, **Supp. XVI:** 212

Evans, Alice, **Supp. XVII:** 71, 72

Evans, Mary Ann. See Eliot, George

Evans, Oliver, **Supp. IV Part 1:** 85, 91

Evans, Sandy, **Supp. XIII:** 129

Evans, Walker, **I:** 36, 38, 293; **Retro. Supp. II:** 85

Eva's Man (G. Jones), **Supp. XXIV:** 183, 184, 185, **188–190**, 193

Eve (A. Finch), **Supp. XVII: 72–74**

"Eve" (W. C. Williams), **Retro. Supp. I:** 423

Even Cowgirls Get the Blues (Robbins), **Supp. X:** 259, 260, 261, 262–263, 264, 266, **269–271,** 272, 274, 277, 284; **Supp. XIII:** 11

"Evening" (Carver), **Supp. III Part 1:** 148

Evening (Minot), **Supp. VI:** 204–205, 208, **213–215**

"Evening at a Country Inn" (Kenyon), **Supp. VII:** 167

"Evening in Advent, An" (W. V. Davis), **Supp. XXI:** 92

"Evening in a Lumber Yard"(Le Sueur), **Supp. XXIII:** 165

"Evening in a Sugar Orchard" (Frost), **Retro. Supp. I:** 133

"Evening in Nuevo Leon, An" (Caldwell), **I:** 309

"Evening in the Sanitarium" (Bogan), **Supp. III Part 1:** 61

Evening Light, The (Skloot), **Supp. XX:** **196, 201–202**

"Evening Love-of-Self" (Taggard), **Supp. XXII:** 280–281

"Evening of the 4th of July, The" (Kees), **Supp. XV:** 140, 142

"Evening on the Cote d'Azur" (Yates), **Supp. XI:** 349

Evening Performance, An: New and Selected Short Stories (Garrett), **Supp. VII:** 109

"Evenings at Home" (Hardwick), **Supp. III Part 1:** 195–196

"Evening's at Seven, The" (Thurber), **Supp. I Part 2:** 616

"Evening Star" (Bogan), **Supp. III Part 1:** 56

Evening Star, The (McMurtry), **Supp. V:** 230

Evening Star, The (screenplay, McMurtry), **Supp. V:** 232

"Evening Sun" (Kenyon), **Supp. VII:** 168

Evening Sun Turned Crimson, The (Huncke), **Supp. XIV:** 140, 149–150

"Evening Sun Turned Crimson, The" (Huncke), **Supp. XIV:** 137–138, 139

"Evening Wind, The" (Bryant), **Supp. I Part 1:** 164

"Evening without Angels" (Stevens), **Retro. Supp. I:** 302

Evening with Richard Nixon, An (Vidal), **Supp. IV Part 2:** 683

"Even Sea, The" (Swenson), **Supp. IV Part 2:** 641

Even Stephen (Perelman and West), **Retro. Supp. II:** 328

"Event, An" (Wilbur), **Supp. III Part 2:** 547, 554

"Event, The" (Dove), **Supp. IV Part 1:** 242, 247–248

"Even the Vanishing Housed"(Hirshfield), **Supp. XXIII:** 132

"Eventide" (Brooks), **Supp. III Part 1:** 73

"Eventide" (Purdy), **Supp. VII:** 270

"Event Itself, The" (Carruth), **Supp. XVI:** 47

Eve of Saint Agnes, The (Keats), **II:** 82, 531

"Eve of St. Agnes, The" (Clampitt), **Supp. IX:** 40

"Ever a Bridegroom: Reflections on the Failure of Texas Literature" (McMurtry), **Supp. V:** 225

Everett, Alexander Hill, **Supp. I Part 1:** 152

Everett, Percival, **Supp. XVIII: 53–67**

Everlasting Story of Nory, The (Baker), **Supp. XIII:** 52, **Supp. XIII: 53–55**

"Everly Brothers, The" (Skloot), **Supp. XX: 199**

Ever-Present Past, The (Hamilton), **Supp. XVI:** 196

Evers, Medgar, **IV:** 280; **Retro. Supp. II:** 13; **Supp. I Part 1:** 52, 65

Everson, William, **Supp. XXII:** 276

Everwine, Peter, **Supp. V:** 180; **Supp. XIII:** 312; **Supp. XV: 73–90**

"Everybody Knows" (Cohen), **Supp. XXVII:** 52, 62

"Everybody's Protest Novel" (Baldwin), **Retro. Supp. II:** 4; **Supp. I Part 1:** 50, 51

"Everybody's Reading Li Po' Silkscreened on a Purple T-Shirt" (Komunyakaa), **Supp. XIII:** 120

Everybody's Story: Writing by Older Minnesotans (C. Bly, ed.), **Supp. XVI:** 38

"Everybody Was Very Nice" (Benét), **Supp. XI:** 53

"Everyday Alchemy" (Taggard), **Supp. XXII:** 274–275, 276, 279

"Every-Day Girl, A" (Jewett), **Retro. Supp. II:** 132

Everyday People (O'Nan), **Supp. XXV:** 142, 146–147, 150

"Everyday Use" (Walker), **Supp. III Part 2:** 534

"Every-Day Work" (Jewett), **Retro. Supp. II:** 132

Everyman (Ashbery), **Supp. XXIII:** 210

Everyone Says I Love You (film; Allen), **Supp. XV:** 11

Every Pleasure (Goldbarth), **Supp. XII:** 181

Every Soul Is a Circus (Lindsay), **Supp. I Part 2:** 384, 394, 399

"Everything Is a Human Being" (Walker), **Supp. III Part 2:** 527

Everything Is Illuminated (Foer), **Supp. XII:** 169

Everything Is Now (Cliff), **Supp. XXII:** 67, 74, 76

"Everything Stuck to Him" (Carver), **Supp. III Part 1:** 143

Everything That Moves (Schulberg), **Supp. XVIII:** 254

Everything That Rises Must Converge (O'Connor), **III:** 339, 348–349, 350–351; **Retro. Supp. II:** 235, **236–237**

"Everything That Rises Must Converge" (O'Connor), **III:** 349, 352, 357; **Retro. Supp. II:** 236

Everything You Always Wanted to Know about Sex (film; Allen), **Supp. XV:** 4–5, 13

Eve's Diary (Twain), **IV:** 208–209

"Eve Speaks" (Untermeyer), **Supp. XV:** 300

"Eve the Fox" (Gunn Allen), **Supp. IV Part 1:** 331

"Evidence" (Harjo), **Supp. XII:** 219

"Evidence-cum-Witness: Subaltern History, Violence, and the (De)formation of a Nation in Michelle Cliff's *No Telephone to Heaven*" (Sethuraman), **Supp. XXII:** 73

Evidence of the Senses, The (Kelley), **Supp. IV Part 2:** 529

Evidence of Things Not Seen, The (Baldwin), **Retro. Supp. II:** 15

"Evidences of Revealed Religion, The" (Channing), **Supp. XXIV:** 74

"Evil Seekers, The" (Sexton), **Supp. II Part 2:** 696

"Evolution" (Swenson), **Supp. IV Part 2:** 639

Evolving the Idol: The Poetry of Gustaf Sobin (Crick), **Supp. XVI:** 289

Ewing, Jon, **Supp. X:** 253

Ewings, The (O'Hara), **III:** 383

"Examination at the Womb Door" (Hughes), **Supp. XV:** 347

"Examination of the Hero in a Time of War" (Stevens), **Retro. Supp. I:** 305–306, 308

"Excavation of Troy" (MacLeish), **III:** 18

Excellent Becomes the Permanent, The (Addams), **Supp. I Part 1:** 25

"Excelsior" (Longfellow), **Retro. Supp. II:** 169

"Excerpts from Swan Lake" (Cameron), **Supp. XII:** 80, **84**

"Excerpts from the Epistemology Workshops" (Rand), **Supp. IV Part 2:** 529

"Excess of Charity" (Wylie), **Supp. I Part 2:** 720

"Exchange, The" (Swenson), **Supp. IV Part 2:** 644

"Excitement, The " (Jarman), **Supp. XVII:** 120–121

"Exclusive" (Olds), **Supp. X:** 206

"Excrement Poem, The" (Kumin), **Supp. IV Part 2:** 448

"Excursion" (Garrett), **Supp. VII:** 100

Excursions (Thoreau), **IV:** 188

"Excursion to Canada, An" (Thoreau), **Supp. XVIII:** 4

"Excursus of Reassurance in Begonia Time, An" (Carruth), **Supp. XVI:** 58

Executioner (Weigl), **Supp. XIX:** 277

Executioner's Song, The (Mailer), **Retro. Supp. II:** 108, 209

Exekiel, **Supp. XXI:** 91

Exemplar of Liberty: Native America and the Evolution of Democracy (Grinde and Johansen), **Supp. XXVI:** 98

"Exercise and Abstinence" (Swados), **Supp. XIX:** 265

Exercises in History, Chronology, and Biography, in Question and Answer (Rowson), **Supp. XV:** 245

Ex-Friends: Falling Out with Allen Ginsberg, Lionel and Diana Trilling, Lillian Hellman, Hannah Arendt, and Norman Mailer (Podhoretz), **Supp.**

VIII: 239, **242–244**

"Exhausted Bug, The" (R. Bly), **Supp. IV Part 1:** 73

"Exhortation" (Bogan), **Supp. III Part 1:** 58

"Exhortation" (McKay), **Supp. X:** 135

"Ex-husband"(Schott), **Supp. XXIII:** 249

"Exile" (Gass), **Supp. VI:** 92

"Exile" (Oates), **Supp. II Part 2:** 523

Exile, The (Buck), **Supp. II Part 1:** 119, 131

"Exiles, The" (Bradbury), **Supp. IV Part 1:** 113

"Exiles, The" (Whittier), **Supp. I Part 2:** 692–693

Exiles and Fabrications (Scott), **II:** 512

Exile's Daughter, The (Spencer), **Supp. II Part 1:** 121

"Exile's Departure, The" (Whittier), **Supp. I Part 2:** 683

Exiles from Paradise: Zelda and Scott Fitzgerald (Mayfield), **Supp. IX:** 65

"Exile's Letter" (Karr), **Supp. XI:** 241

Exile's Return (Cowley), **Supp. III Part 1:** 136, 138, 140, 141, 144, 147, 148

"Exile's Return, The" (R. Lowell), **II:** 539; **Retro. Supp. II:** 187

Exiles: Three Short Novels (Caputo), **Supp. XIX:** 25, **26–27**

"Existences" (Stafford), **Supp. XI:** 324

Existentialism from Dostoevsky to Sartre (W. Kaufmann), **Supp. XVII:** 137

Exit into History (Hoffman), **Supp. XVI:** 148, 150, **151–153**

Exit to Eden (Rampling), **Supp. VII:** 301–302

Exley (Clarke), **Supp. XXIII:** 109

Exley, Frederick, **Supp. XVI:** 69; **Supp. XVII:** 135; **Supp. XXIII:** 78, **97–110**

Exodus (biblical book), **IV:** 300

Exodus (film), **Supp. XX:** 246

Exodus (Uris), **Supp. IV Part 1:** 379; **Supp. XX:** 243–244, 244, 245, 247, 248, 250–251, 257

Exodus Revisited (Uris), **Supp. XX:** 247

"Exorcism" (Snodgrass), **Supp. VI:** 314

"Exorcism, An" (Malamud), **Supp. I Part 2:** 435

Exorcist, The (film), **Supp. I Part 1:** 66

"Expanded Composition, The" (Major), **Supp. XXII:** 174

"Expanding Rooms" (Notley), **Supp. XXII:** 229

"Expanding the Repertoire" (Mackey), **Supp. XXVII:** 161

"Expanses" (Dickey), **Supp. IV Part 1:** 186

"Ex Parte" (Lardner), **II:** 432

"Expatiation on the Combining of Weathers at Thirty-seventh and Indiana Where the Southern More or Less Crosses the Dog, The" (Carruth), **Supp. XVI:**51–52

"Expectant Father Compares His Wife to a Rabbit, An" (White), **Supp. I Part 2:** 678

"Expedition to the Pole, An" (Dillard), **Supp. VI:** 32, 34

"Expelled" (Cheever), **Supp. I Part 1:** 174, 186

Expense of Greatness, The (Blackmur), **Supp. II Part 1:** 90, 107

Expense of Vision, The (Holland), **Retro. Supp. I:** 216

"Expensive Gifts" (Miller), **Supp. XII:** 294

"Expensive Moment, The" (Paley), **Supp. VI:** 222, **227–228,** 230

Expensive People (Oates), **Supp. II Part 2:** 509, 510–511

"Experience" (Emerson), **Supp. XIV:** 42

"Experience" (Stone), **Supp. XXVII:** 251

"Experience and Fiction" (Jackson), **Supp. IX:** 121

"Experience and the Objects of Knowledge in the Philosophy of F. H. Bradley" (Eliot), **I:** 572; **Retro. Supp. I:** 59

Experience of Literature, The (Trilling), **Supp. III Part 2:** 493

"Experiences and Principles of an Historian" (Morison), **Supp. I Part 2:** 492

Experimental Death Unit # 1 (Baraka), **Supp. II Part 1:** 46

"Experimental Life, The" (Bourne), **I:** 217, 220

"Experiment in Misery, An" (S. Crane), **I:** 411; **Retro. Supp. II:** 97

Experiments and Observations on Electricity (Franklin), **II:** 102, 114–115

Experiments in Survival (Kriegel and Henrich, eds.), **Supp. XXIV:** 214

"Expiation" (Hoffman), **Supp. XVIII:** 86

"Expiation" (Wharton), **Retro. Supp. I:** 367

"Explaining an Affinity for Bats" (Stallings), **Supp. XXV:** 227, 233

"Explaining Evil" (Gordon), **Supp. IV Part 1:** 310

"Explaining Ted Kooser" (Gioia), **Supp. XIX:** 121

"Explanation" (Stevens), **IV:** 79

Explanation of America, An (Pinsky), **Supp. VI:** 237, **241–243**

Exploding Gravy (X. J. Kennedy), **Supp. XV:** 163

"Exploit" (Wharton), **IV:** 324

"Exploration in the Great Tuolumne Cañon" (Muir), **Supp. IX:** 181

"Explorer, The" (Brooks), **Supp. III Part 1:** 79–80

"Exploring the Magalloway" (Parkman), **Supp. II Part 2:** 591

"Exposed Nest, The" (Frost), **Supp. XXVI:** 74

Expositor's Bible, The (G. A. Smith), **III:** 199

Expressions of Sea Level (Ammons), **Supp. VII:** 24, 28, 36

"Exteriority" (Monson), **Supp. XXIV:** 230, 238

"Extinction of Silence, The" (Stallings), **Supp. XXV:** 234

Extract from Captain Stormfeld's Visit to Heaven (Twain), **IV:** 209–210

Extracts from Adam's Diary (Twain), **IV:** 208–209

Extra Indians (Gansworth), **Supp. XXVI:** 104, 107–108

"Extraño, Un" (Gallagher), *Supp. XXIV:* 170

"Exulting, The" (Roethke), **III:** 544

"Eye, The" (Bowles), **Supp. IV Part 1:** 93

Eye, The (Nabokov), **III:** 251

Eye-Beaters, Blood, Victory, Madness, Buckhead and Mercy, The (Dickey), **Supp. IV Part 1:** 178, 182–183

"Eye for an Eye, An" (Humphrey), **Supp. IX:** 108

Eye in the Rock, The (Haines), **Supp. XII:** 208, 209

Eye in the Sky (Dick), **Supp. XVIII:** 138

"Eye-Mote, The" (Plath), **Retro. Supp. II:** 246, 247

"Eye of Paris, The" (H. Miller), **III:** 183–184

Eye of the Poet, The: Six Views of the Art and Craft of Poetry (Citino, ed.), **Supp. XIII:** 115; **Supp. XXI:** 54

"Eye of the Rock, The" (Haines), **Supp. XII:** 208

"Eye of the Story, The" (Porter), **IV:** 279

Eye of the Story, The: Selected Essays and Reviews (Welty), **Retro. Supp. I:** 339, 342, 344, 345, 346, 351, 354, 355, 356

"Eyes, The" (Wharton), **IV:** 315

"Eyes like They Say the Devil Has" (Ríos), **Supp. IV Part 2:** 543, 544

Eyes of the Dragon, The (King), **Supp. V:** 139, 152

Eyes of the Heart: A Memoir of the Lost and Found (Buechner), **Supp. XII:** 53

"Eyes of Zapata" (Cisneros), **Supp. VII:** 70

"Eyes to See" (Cozzens), **I:** 374

Eye-to-Eye (Nye), **Supp. XIII:** 274

Eysturoy, Annie O., **Supp. IV Part 1:** 321, 322, 323, 328

Ezekiel (biblical book), **II:** 541

"Ezekiel" (R. Fisher), **Supp. XIX:** 71

Ezekiel, Mordecai, **Supp. I Part 2:** 645

"Ezekiel Learns" (R. Fisher), **Supp. XIX:** 71

"Ezra Pound" (Bynner), **Supp. XV:** 49

"Ezra Pound: His Cantos" (Zukofsky), **Supp. III Part 2:** 612, 619, 622

Ezra Pound's Mauberley (Espey), **III:** 463

"Ezra Pound's Very Useful Labors" (Schwartz), **Supp. II Part 2:** 644

F

Faas, Ekbert, **Supp. VIII:** 292

"Fabbri Tape, The" (Auchincloss), **Supp. IV Part 1:** 21–22

Fabens, Charles, **Supp. XXV:** 283

Faber, Geoffrey, **Retro. Supp. I:** 63

Faber Book of Movie Verse, The (French and Wlaschin, eds.), **Supp. XVI:** 294

"Fable" (Merwin), **Supp. III Part 1:** 343

"Fable" (Wylie), **Supp. I Part 2:** 714

Fable, A (Faulkner), **II:** 55, 73; **Retro. Supp. I:** 74

"Fable, A" (Glück), **Supp. V:** 86

"Fable, The" (Winters), **Supp. II Part 2:** 792, 793, 796

"Fable Containing a Reflection the Size of a Match Head in Its Pupil, A" (Brockmeier), **Supp. XXII:** 59

"Fable Ending in the Sound of a Thousand Parakeets, A" (Brockmeier), **Supp. XXII:** 59

Fable for Critics, A (J. R. Lowell), **Supp. I Part 2:** 406, 407–408, 409, 412–413, 416, 420, 422

"Fable for Critics, A" (J. R. Lowell), **Supp. XVIII:** 3, 8

"Fable of the War, A" (Nemerov), **III:** 272

Fables (Gay), **II:** 111

Fables and Distances: New and Selected Essays (Haines), **Supp. XII:** 197, 199, 207–208, 211

Fables for Our Time (Thurber), **Supp. I Part 2:** 610

Fables of Identity: Studies in Poetic Mythology (Frye), **Supp. X:** 80

Fables of La Fontaine, The (Moore), **III:** 194, 215

"Fables of Representation: Poetry of the New York School" (Hoover), **Supp. XV:** 179

"Fables of the Fallen Guy" (Rosaldo), **Supp. IV Part 2:** 544

"Fables of the Moscow Subway" (Nemerov), **III:** 271

"Fable with a Photograph of a Glass Mobile on the Wall, A" (Brockmeier), **Supp. XXII:** 59

"Fable with Slips of White Paper Spilling from the Pockets, A" (Brockmeier), **Supp. XXII:** 59

Fabulators, The (Scholes), **Supp. V:** 40

Fabulous Small Jews (Epstein), **Supp. XIV:** 112

Face against the Glass, The (Francis), **Supp. IX:** 80–81

Face in the Crowd, A (film, Kazan), **Supp. XVIII:** 252–253

Face in the Crowd, A (O'Nan and King), **Supp. XXV:** 150, 152

Face of Time, The (Farrell), **II:** 28, 34, 35, 39

Faces of Jesus, The (Buechner), **Supp. XII:** 53

Face to the Wind (film), **Supp. XVII:** 141

Face Value (Hwang), **Supp. XXI:** 148, 154, 155

Fachinger, Petra, **Supp. XVI:** 153

"Facing It" (Komunyakaa), **Supp. XIII:** 117, 124, 125

Facing Shadows (Jin), **Supp. XVIII:** 92, 93

Facing the Music (L. Brown), **Supp. XXI:** 39, 42, 42–44

"Facing the Music" (L. Brown), **Supp. XXI:** 38–39, 41, 42, 43

"*Facing the Music:* What's Wrong with All Those Happy Endings" (Neal), **Supp. XXI:** 41

"Facing West from California's Shores" (Jeffers), **Supp. II Part 2:** 437–438

Fact, Fiction, and Representation: Four Novels by Gilbert Sorrentino (Mackey), **Supp. XXI:** 236

"Fact in Fiction, The" (McCarthy), **II:** 562

"Fact of Blackness, The" (Fanon), **Supp. XX:** 152

"Facts" (Franzen), **Supp. XX:** 85

"Facts" (Levine), **Supp. V:** 193

"Facts" (Oliver), **Supp. VII:** 231–232

"Facts" (Snyder), **Supp. VIII:** 301

"Facts, The" (Lardner), **II:** 431

Facts, The: A Novelist's Autobiography (P. Roth), **Retro. Supp. II:** 280, 291; **Supp. III Part 2:** 401, 405, 417, 426

"Facts and Traditions Respecting the Existence of Indigenous Intermittent Fever in New England" (Holmes), **Supp. I Part 1:** 303

"Facts in the Case of M. Valdemar, The" (Poe), **III:** 416

Fader, Ellen, **Supp. XXVII:** 203–204

Faderman, Lillian, **Retro. Supp. II:** 135; **Supp. XIII:** 313

Fadiman, Clifton, **II:** 430, 431, 443, 591–592; **Supp. IX:** 8; **Supp. XVI:** 100, 106; **Supp. XVII:** 87, 90; **Supp. XXIII:** 2

Fading, My Parmacheene Belle (J. Scott), **Supp. XVII:** 184–185, 188

Fading Smile, The (Davison), **Supp. XXVI:** 61, 66, 68

"Fado" (McClatchy), **Supp. XII:** 265–266

"Fado" (Vaz), **Supp. XXVI:** 261–262

Fado and Other Stories (Vaz), **Supp. XXVI:** 259–264, 268

Faerie Queene, The (Spenser), **III:** 487; **IV:** 253; **Supp. XIV:** 6; **Supp. XV:** 181

Faery, Rebecca Blevins, **Retro. Supp. I:** 374

Fagan, Kathy, **Supp. V:** 180; **Supp. XV:** 73

Fagan, Louise, **Supp. XIX:** 204, 205

Fahrenheit 451 (Bradbury), **Supp. IV Part 1:** 101, 102, 104, 107–109, 110, 113; **Supp. XIII:** 29

"Failure" (Gioia), **Supp. XV:** 125

"Failure" (Zach; Everwine, trans.), **Supp. XV:** 86

"Failure: A Meditation" (Monson), **Supp. XXIV:** 236

"Failure of David Barry, The" (Jewett), **Retro. Supp. II:** 132

Fainlight, Ruth, **Supp. XV:** 261, 264

Faint Perfume (Gale), **Supp. I Part 2:** 613

Fair, Bryan K., **Supp. VIII:** 128

Fairbanks, Douglas, **Supp. XVI:** 185, 186

Fairchild, Frances. *See* Bryant, Mrs. William Cullen (Frances Fairchild)

Fairchild, Hoxie, **Supp. XIV:** 120

Fairfield, Flora (pseudonym). *See* Alcott, Louisa May

Fair Gentlemen of Belken County (Hinojosa), **Supp. XIX:** 105

Fairly Conventional Woman, A (Shields), **Supp. VII:** 312, 316, 318

"Fairly Sad Tale, A" (Parker), **Supp. IX:** 192

Fair Warning (R. O. Butler), **Supp. XII:** 62, 75–76

"Fairy-Tale Logic" (Stallings), **Supp. XXV:** 223, 234

Faith (Goldbarth), **Supp. XII:** 181, 182–183

Faith and History (Niebuhr), **III:** 308

Faith and the Good Thing (C. Johnson), **Supp. VI:** 187, 188–190, 191, 193, 194, 196

Faith for Living (Mumford), **Supp. II Part 2:** 479–480

Faithful Narrative of the Surprising Works of God in the Conversion of Many Hundred Souls in Northampton, and the Neighboring Towns and Villages of New-Hampshire in New-England, A (Edwards), **I:** 545, 562

Faithful: Two Diehard Boston Red Sox Fans Chronicle the Historic 2004 Season (O'Nan and King), **Supp. XXV:** 153

"Faith Healer" (Komunyakaa), **Supp. XIII:** 117

Faith Healer of Olive Avenue, The (Muñoz), **Supp. XXV:** 127, 131, 135–137

"Faith in a Tree" (Paley), **Supp. VI:** 217–218, 224, 230

"Faith in Search of Understanding" (Updike), **Retro. Supp. I:** 327

"Faith of an Historian" (Morison), **Supp. I Part 2:** 492

"Faith of Fishermen, The" (J. W. Miller), **Supp. XX:** 170

Faker's Dozen, A (Bukiet), **Supp. XVII:** 47

Falcoff, Mark, **Supp. VIII:** 88

Falcon (Hammett), **Supp. IV Part 1:** 351

Falconer (Cheever), **Supp. I Part 1:** 176, 193–195, 196

Falconer, A. F., **Supp. XIV:** 2

"Falcon of Ser Federigo, The" (Longfellow), **II:** 505

Falcon: Poems on Soviet Themes (Taggard), **Supp. XXII:** 284

Falk, Peter, **Supp. XI:** 174

Falkner, Dean, **II:** 55

Falkner, John, **II:** 55

Falkner, Murray, **II:** 55

Falkner, Murray C., **II:** 55

Falkner, Mrs. Murray C. (Maud Butler), **II:** 55

Falkner, William C., **II:** 55

"Fall" (Francis), **Supp. IX:** 76

"Fall, The" (Bass), **Supp. XVI:** 25

"Fall 1961" (R. Lowell), **II:** 550

Fallen Angels (Myers), **Supp. XXVII:** 204, 207

"Fallen Western Star: The Decline of San Francisco as a Literary Region" (Gioia), **Supp. XV:** 112, 115–116

"Fallen Western Star" Wars, The: A Debate about Literary California (Foley, ed.), **Supp. XV:** 112, 116

"Fall in Corrales" (Wilbur), **Supp. III Part 2:** 556

Falling (Dickey), **Supp. IV Part 1:** 178, 181–182

"Falling" (Dickey), **Supp. IV Part 1:** 182

"Falling Asleep over the Aeneid" (R. Lowell), **II:** 542; **Retro. Supp. II:** 188

Falling in Place (Beattie), **Supp. V:** 28–29

"Falling into Holes in Our Sentences" (R. Bly), **Supp. IV Part 1:** 71

Falling into Life (Kriegel), **Supp. XXIV: 217–219**

"Falling Water" (Davison), **Supp. XXVI:** 79

"Fall Journey" (Stafford), **Supp. XI:** 322

Fall of a Doll's House, The (J. Davison), **Supp. XXVI:** 65

Fall of America, The: 1965–1971 (Ginsberg), **Supp. II Part 1:** 323, 325, 327; **Supp. XV:** 264

Fall of Eve, The (Loos), **Supp. XVI:** 187

Fall of the City, The: A Verse Play for Radio (MacLeish), **III:** 20

"Fall of the Dolls' House, The" (Davison), **Supp. XXVI:** 73–74

"Fall of the House of Usher, The" (Poe), **III:** 412, 414, 415, 419; **Retro. Supp. II:** 270; **Supp. XXV:** 112

Fall of the Magicians, The (Kees), **Supp. XV:** 144

Fall of the Year, The (Mosher), **Supp. XXII:** 205, 206, 208, 209, **214**

"Fall of Troy, Teh"(Hadas), **Supp. XXIII:** 113

Fallows, James, **Supp. VIII:** 241

Fall Quarter (Kees), **Supp. XV:** 141

Fall & Rise (Dixon), **Supp. XII:** 147–148, 148, 153, 157

Falls, Robert, **Supp. XXI:** 148; **Supp. XXIV:** 270

"Falls, The" (Olds), **Supp. X:** 215

"Falls, The" (Saunders), **Supp. XIX:** 229

"Falls Fight, The" (Howe), **Supp. IV Part 2:** 431–432

Falon, Janet Ruth, **Supp. IV Part 2:** 422

False Coin (Swados), **Supp. XIX: 260–261,** 263

"False Dawn" (Wharton), **Retro. Supp. I:** 381

"False Documents" (Doctorow), **Supp. IV Part 1:** 220, 236

"False Leads" (Komunyakaa), **Supp. XIII:** 116

Falwell, Jerry, **Supp. XX: 273**

Fame and Obscurity: Portraits by Gay Talese (Talese), **Supp. XVII:** 202, 203, 204

Fame & Folly: Essays (Ozick), **Supp. V:** 272

"Familiar Epistle to a Friend, A" (J. R. Lowell), **Supp. I Part 2:** 416

Familiar Territory: Observations on American Life (Epstein), **Supp. XIV: 106**

"Familiar Things" (Pickering), **Supp. XXI:** 204

"Family" (Sanders), **Supp. XVI:** 276

"Family" (Wilson), **IV:** 426

Family, Kinship, and Sympanthy in Nineteenth-Century America (Weinstein), **Supp. XVIII:** 261

"Family, The" (Taggard), **Supp. XXII:** 284

"Family Affair, A" (Chopin), **Retro. Supp. II:** 71

"Family and Socialism, The" (Ryan as Quin), **Supp. XVIII:** 238

Family Arsenal, The (Theroux), **Supp. VIII:** 322

Family Barcus, The"(Thompson), **Supp. XXIII:** 299

Family Chronicle: An Odyssey from Russia to America (Reznikoff), **Supp. XIV:** 277, 288, 289

Family Devotions (Hwang), **Supp. XXI:** 145, 146

"Family History" (Mora), **Supp. XIII:** 217

"Family History, A" (R. H. Davis), **Supp. XVI:** 82

Family Honor (Parker), **Supp. XIX:** 186

Family Life (Banks), **Supp. V:** 7

Family Markowitz, The (Goodman), **Supp. XXVI:** 119, 121–123

"Family Matters" (Alvarez), **Supp. VII:** 10

Family Moskat, The (Singer), **IV:** 1, 17, 20, 46; **Retro. Supp. II:** 304

"Family of Little Feet, The" (Cisneros), **Supp. VII:** 61

Family Party, A (O'Hara), **III:** 362

Family Pictures (Brooks), **Supp. III Part 1:** 69, 85, 86

Family Pictures (Miller), **Supp. XII:** 291, **295–297,** 299

"Family Portrait" (Trethewey), **Supp. XXI:** 250

"Family Reunion" (J. W. Miller), **Supp. XX: 167**

"Family Reunion" (X. J. Kennedy), **Supp. XV:** 169

Family Reunion, The (Eliot), **I:** 570–571, 572, 581, 584, 588; **Retro. Supp. I:** 62, 65

"Family Secrets" (Kingsolver), **Supp. VII:** 208

"Family Sideshow, The" (Karr), **Supp. XI:** 245

"Family Story, The" (Skloot), **Supp. XX: 195**

"Family Ties" (Mora), **Supp. XIII:** 215

"Family Tree" (Komunyakaa), **Supp. XIII:** 117–118, 126

"Family Wasserstein, The" (Hoban), **Supp. XV:** 319, 325

Famous American Negroes (Hughes), **Supp. I Part 1:** 345

"Famous Gilson Bequest, The" (Bierce), **I:** 204

Famous Last Words (Findley), **Supp. XX: 49, 55–56**

Famous Negro Athletes (Bontemps), **Supp. XXII:** 6

Famous Negro Music Makers (Hughes), **Supp. I Part 1:** 345

"Famous New York Trials" (Ellison), **Supp. II Part 1:** 230

Fanatic, The (Levin), **Supp. XXVII:** 137, 141, 143, 145, 147

Fanatics, The (Dunbar), **Supp. II Part 1:** 213–214

Fancher, Edwin, **Retro. Supp. II:** 202

Fancher, Lou, **Supp. XVI:** 177

"Fancy and Imagination" (Poe), **III:** 421

Fancy Dancer, The (P. N. Warren), **Supp. XX: 267–268**

"Fancy Flights" (Beattie), **Supp. V:** 25

"Fancy's Show Box" (Hawthorne), **II:** 238

"Fancy Woman, The" (Taylor), **Supp. V:** 316–317, 319, 323

"Fang" (Goldbarth), **Supp. XII:** 190

Fanny: Being the True History of the Adventures of Fanny Hackabout-Jones (Jong), **Supp. V:** 115, 127

Fanny Hill (Cleland), **Supp. V:** 48, 127

Fan of Swords, The (al-Maghut), **Supp. XIII:** 278

Fanon, Frantz, **Retro. Supp. II:** 118; **Supp. X:** 131, 141; **Supp. XX: 152**

"Fan's Further Notes, A"(Exley), **Supp. XXIII:** 108

Fanshawe (Hawthorne), **II:** 223–224; **Retro. Supp. I:** 149, 151

Fan's Notes, A: A Fictional Memoir (Exley), **Supp. XVI:** 69; **Supp. XXIII:** 78, 97, 98, **99–103,** 106, 109

"Fantasia on 'The Nut-Brown Maid' " (Ashbery), **Supp. III Part 1:** 19

"Fantasia on the Relations between Poetry and Photography" (Strand), **Supp. IV Part 2:** 631

"Fantastic Fables" (Bierce), **I:** 209

"Fantasy"(O'Hara), **Supp. XXIII:** 220

Fante, John, **Supp. XI: 159–176**

Fantzius Mallare: A Mysterious Oath (Hecht), **Supp. XXVII:** 88

Faraday, Michael, **I:** 480–481

Far and Away (Jarman), **Supp. XVII:** 110, 115

"Far and Away" (Jarman), **Supp. XVII:** 115

Farber, Jim, **Supp. XXVII:** 45

"Farewell" (Emerson), **II:** 13

"Farewell" (Ryan as Quin), **Supp. XVIII:** 229

Farewell, My Lovely (Chandler), **Supp. IV Part 1:** 122, 125–126, 127, 128, 130

"Farewell, My Lovely!" (White), **Supp. I Part 2:** 661–663, 665

Farewell, The (Gibran), **Supp. XX: 121**

"Farewell Performance" (Merrill), **Supp. III Part 1:** 336–337

Farewell-Sermon Preached at the First Precinct in Northampton, after the People's Publick Rejection of their Minister, A (Edwards), **I:** 548, 562

"Farewell Sweet Dust" (Wylie), **Supp. I Part 2:** 727–728

"Farewell to America, A" (Wheatley), **Supp. XX: 283**

Farewell to Arms, A (Hemingway), **I:** 212, 421, 476, 477; **II:** 68–69, 248–249, 252–253, 254, 255, 262, 265; **Retro. Supp. I:** 171, 178, **180–182,** 187, 189; **Retro. Supp. II:** 108; **Retro. IV Part 1:** 380–381, 381; **Supp. VIII:** 179; **Supp. XII:** 241–242; **Supp. XXI:** 277

"Farewell to Miles" (Berryman), **I:** 173

"Farewell to My Union Brothers" (Ryan as Quin), **Supp. XVIII:** 238

Farewell to Reform (Chamberlain), **Supp. I Part 2:** 647

Farewell to Sport (Gallico), **Supp. XVI:** 238

"Farewell to the Middle Class" (Updike), **Retro. Supp. I:** 321

Far Field, The (Roethke), **III:** 528, 529, 539, 545, 547–548

"Far Field, The" (Roethke), **III:** 537, 540

Far-Flung (Cameron), **Supp. XII:** 81

Far from the Madding Crowd (Hardy), **II:** 291

Faríd, 'Umar ibn al-, **Supp. XX:** 117

Faris, Athénaíse Charleville, **Supp. I Part 1:** 204

Farley, Abbie, **I:** 458

Farley, Harriet, **Supp. XIII:** 140

"Farm, The" (Creeley), **Supp. IV Part 1:** 155

Farmer (Harrison), **Supp. VIII:** 39, **44–45**

Farmer, Frances, **Supp. XV:** 196–197

Farmer, Richard, **Supp. XIV:** 2

"Farmer and the Fox, The" (Leopold), **Supp. XIV:** 188

Farmer Boy (L. I. Wilder), **Supp. XXII:** 294, 297, 299

"Farmers' Daughters, The" (W. C. Williams), **Retro. Supp. I:** 423

Farmers Hotel, The (O'Hara), **III:** 361

"Farmer's Sorrow, A" (Jewett), **Retro. Supp. II:** 132

"Farmer's Wife, The" (Sexton), **Supp. II Part 2:** 676

"Farmer & Wife" (Davison), **Supp. XXVI:** 79

"Farm Garden" (Nelson), **Supp. XVIII:** 186

"Farm Implements and Rutabagas in a Landscape" (Ashbery), **Supp. III Part 1:** 13

Farming: A Hand Book (Berry), **Supp. X:** 31, 35

"Farmlights in Iowa" (Kooser), **Supp. XIX:** 120

"Farm on the Great Plains, The" (Stafford), **Supp. XI:** 322

Farnol, Jeffrey, **Supp. I Part 2:** 653

Far North (Shepard), **Supp. III Part 2:** 433, 435

"Far Northern Birch, The" (Francis), **Supp. IX:** 90

Farnsworth, Elizabeth, **Supp. XI:** 139

"Farrago" (Kees), **Supp. XV:** 145

Farrand, Max, **II:** 122

Farrar, Geraldine, **Retro. Supp. I:** 10

Farrar, John, **II:** 191; **Supp. XI:** 47

Far Reaches, The (Hickam), **Supp. XXVII:** 111

Farrell, Barry, **Supp. XIV:** 142

Farrell, James Francis, **II:** 25, 26

Farrell, James T., **I:** 97, 288, 475, 508, 517, 519; **II: 25–53,** 416, 424; **III:** 28, 114, 116, 118, 119, 317, 382; **IV:** 211, 286; **Retro. Supp. II:** 196, 327; **Supp. I Part 2:** 679; **Supp. VIII:** 96, 97; **Supp. XIV:** 3; **Supp. XV:** 141; **Supp. XXVI:** 18; **Supp. XXVII:** 134

Farrell, Mrs. James T. (Dorothy Butler), **II:** 26

Farrell, Mrs. James T. (Hortense Alden), **II:** 26, 27, 45, 48

Farrell, John, **II:** 26

Farrell, John C., **Supp. I Part 1:** 24

Farrell, Kate, **Supp. XV:** 187–188,**Supp. XV:** 190

Farrell, Kevin, **II:** 26

Farrell, Mary, **II:** 25

"Far Rockaway" (Schwartz), **Supp. II Part 2:** 649

Farrow, Mia, **Supp. XV:** 8, 10

Far Side of the Dollar, The (Macdonald), **Supp. IV Part 2:** 473

Farther Off from Heaven (Humphrey), **Supp. IX:** 93, 96, 101, **103–104,** 105, 109

Farther Off from Heaven (Inge), **Supp. XXV:** 94, 100

Far Tortuga (Matthiessen), **Supp. V:** 201, 206–207

"Fascinating Fascism" (Sontag), **Supp. III Part 2:** 465

"Fascination of Cities, The" (Hughes), **Supp. I Part 1:** 325

Fashion, Power, Guilt and the Charity of Families (Shields), **Supp. VII:** 323

Fasman, Jonathan, **Supp. V:** 253

Fast, Howard, **Supp. I Part 1:** 295; **Supp. XXI:** 277; **Supp. XXIII:** 165

Fast, Jonathan, **Supp. V:** 115

Fast and Loose (Wharton), **Retro. Supp. I:** 361

"Faster than Light" (Nelson), **Supp. XVIII:** 178–179

"Fastest Runner on Sixty-first Street, The" (Farrell), **II:** 45

Fast Lane on a Dirt Road (Sherman), **Supp. XXII:** 205

Fast Sam, Cool Clyde, and Stuff (Myers), **Supp. XXVII:** 202, 210

Fast Sooner Hound, The (Bontemps and Conroy), **Supp. XXII:** 5, 10–11

"Fat" (Carver), **Supp. III Part 1:** 141

Fatal Interview (Millay), **III:** 128–129, 130

"Fatality" (Bausch), **Supp. VII:** 54

Fatal Lady (film), **Supp. XIII:** 166

"Fate" (Emerson), **II:** 2–3, 4, 16; **Supp. XIV:** 42

"Fate" (Koch), **Supp. XV:** 183

"Fate" (Mailer), **Retro. Supp. II:** 207

"Fate of Pleasure, The" (Trilling), **Supp. III Part 2:** 510

Fate of the Jury, The (Masters), **Supp. I Part 2:** 466, 468, 469

"Fat Girl, The" (Dubus), **Supp. VII:** 84, 85

"Father" (Kooser), **Supp. XIX:** 117, 127

"Father" (Levine), **Supp. V:** 188

"Father" (Sanders), **Supp. XVI:** 277

"Father" (Trethewey), **Supp. XXI:** 253

"Father" (Walker), **Supp. III Part 2:** 522

"Father, The" (Carver), **Supp. III Part 1:** 137, 140

Father, The (Olds), **Supp. X: 209–211**

"Father (Part I)" (Mullen), **Supp. XXVII:** 167

"Father Abraham" (Faulkner), **Retro. Supp. I:** 81, 82

Fatheralong: A Meditation on Fathers and Sons, Race and Society (Wideman), **Supp. X:** 320, 332–333, 334, 335

"Father and Daughter" (Eberhart), **I:** 539

Father and Glorious Descendant (Lowe), **Supp. X:** 291

"Father and Son" (Eberhart), **I:** 539

Father and Son (Farrell), **II:** 34, 35, 290, 291

Father and Son (Gosse), **Supp. VIII:** 157

"Father and Son" (Hughes), **Retro. Supp. I:** 204; **Supp. I Part 1:** 329, 339

"Father and Son" (Kunitz), **Supp. III Part 1:** 262

Father and Son (L. Brown), **Supp. XXI:** 36, 40, 41, **46–47**

"Father and Son" (Schwartz), **Supp. II Part 2:** 650

Father Bombo's Pilgrimage to Mecca (Freneau), **Supp. II Part 1:** 254

Father Fisheye (Balakian), **Supp. XXIII:** 19

"Father Fisheye"(Balakian), **Supp. XXIII:** 19

"Father Fitzgerald" (Nelson and Espeland), **Supp. XVIII:** 181

"Father Guzman" (Stern), **Supp. IX: 293,** 296

"Father John Melby and the Ghost of Amy Elizabeth" (Brockmeier), **Supp. XXII:** 60

Father of the Blues (Bontemps as Handy), **Supp. XXII:** 5

"Father out Walking on the Lawn, A" (Dove), **Supp. IV Part 1:** 246

"Fathers" (Creeley), **Supp. IV Part 1:** 157–158

Fathers, The (Tate), **IV:** 120, 127, 130, 131–133, 134, 141; **Supp. X:** 52

Fathers and Crows (Vollmann), **Supp. XVII:** 226, 231–232

"Fathers and Daughters, Mothers and Sons"(Hadas), **Supp. XXIII:** 119

"Fathers and Sons" (Hemingway), **II:** 249, 265–266; **Retro. Supp. I:** 175

"Father's Body, The" (Dickey), **Supp. IV Part 1:** 176

"Father's Day" (Connelly), **Supp. XXI:** 79–80

"Father's Story, A" (Dubus), **Supp. VII:** 88

"Father's Voice" (Stafford), **Supp. XI:** 322

"Fat Lady, The" (Carruth), **Supp. XVI:** 48

"Fat Man, Floating" (Dunn), **Supp. XI:** 144

Fat Men in Skirts (Silver), **Supp. XXIV: 265–267,** 275

"Fat Tuesday"(P. Benedict), **Supp. XXIII:** 38

Faulkes Chronicle, The (Huddle), **Supp. XXVI:** 148, 158, 159–160

Faulkner, Barry, **Supp. XV:** 41

Faulkner, William, **I:** 54, 97, 99, 105, 106, 115, 117, 118, 123, 190, 204–205, 211, 288, 289, 291, 292, 297, 305, 324, 374, 378, 423, 480, 517; **II:** 28, 51, **54–76,** 131, 174, 194, 217, 223,

228, 230, 259, 301, 306, 431, 458–459, 542, 594, 606; **III:** 45, 70, 108, 164, 218, 220, 222, 236–237, 244, 292, 334, 350, 382, 418, 453, 454, 482, 483; **IV:** 2, 4, 33, 49, 97, 98, 100, 101, 120, 131, 203, 207, 211, 217, 237, 257, 260, 261, 279, 280, 352, 461, 463; **Retro. Supp. I:** 73–95, 215, 339, 347, 356, 379, 382; **Retro. Supp. II:** 19, 221, 326; **Supp. I Part 1:** 196, 197, 242, 372; **Supp. I Part 2:** 450, 621; **Supp. III Part 1:** 384–385, 396; **Supp. IV Part 1:** 47, 130, 257, 342; **Supp. IV Part 2:** 434, 463, 468, 502, 677, 682; **Supp. IX:** 20, 95; **Supp. V:** 58, 59, 138, 210, 226, 237, 261, 262, 334–336; **Supp. VIII:** 37, 39, 40, 104, 105, 108, 175, 176, 180, 181, 183, 184, 188, 189, 215; **Supp. X:** 44, 228; **Supp. XI:** 92, 247; **Supp. XII:** 16, 289, 310, 313; **Supp. XIII:** 100, 169; **Supp. XIV:** 1, 12–13, 21, 24, 93, 306; **Supp. XIX:** 97, 154, 166; **Supp. XV:** 92, 135, 338; **Supp. XVI:** 148, 189; **Supp. XVII:** 225; **Supp. XVIII:** 76, 84, 90, 148, 249; **Supp. XX: 137, 162, 185, 195; Supp. XXI:** 36, 38, 256; **Supp. XXII:** 193, 203, 205; **Supp. XXIII:** 166; **Supp. XXIV:** 54, 64, 132, 136, 215; **Supp. XXV:** 49; **Supp. XXVI:** 1, 9, 45, 144, 147; **Supp. XXVII:** 11, 216, 218, 267, 276

Faulkner: A Collection of Critical Essays (Warren), **Retro. Supp. I:** 73

Faulkner at Nagano (Jelliffe, ed.), **I:** 289; **II:** 63, 65

Faulkner-Cowley File, The: Letters and Memories 1944–1962 (Cowley, ed.), **Retro. Supp. I:** 73, 92; **Supp. II Part 1:** 140, 141

"Faultlines"(Hadas), **Supp. XXIII:** 117–118

"Faun" (Plath), **Supp. I Part 2:** 537

"Fauna" (Jeffers), **Supp. II Part 2:** 415

Fauset, Arthur Huff, **Supp. XVIII:** 126

Fauset, Jessie, **Supp. I Part 1:** 321, 325; **Supp. IV Part 1:** 164

Fauset, Jessie Redmon, **Supp. XIX:** 69, 78; **Supp. XVIII:** 122,127

Faust (Goethe), **I:** 396; **II:** 489; **III:** 395; **Supp. II Part 1:** 16; **Supp. IX:** 141

Faust, Beatrix Hapgood, **Supp. XXI:** 8

Faust, Clarence H., **II:** 20

Faute de l'Abbé Mouret, La (Zola), **III:** 322

"Favor, The" (Carver and Gallagher), **Supp. XXIV:** 178

Favor Island (Merwin), **Supp. III Part 1:** 346, 347

"Favor of Love, A" (Peacock), **Supp. XIX:** 203

Favourite Game, The (Cohen), **Supp. XXVII:** 51, 54, 56–57, 59

"Favrile" (Doty), **Supp. XI:** 131

"Fawn" (Davison), **Supp. XXVI:** 75

"Fawn, with a Bit of Green" (Swados), **Supp. XIX:** 258

Fay (L. Brown), **Supp. XXI:** 40, 41, 47

Fay, Bernard, **IV:** 41

"Fear, The" (Frost), **Retro. Supp. I:** 128

Fear and Loathing in Las Vegas (Thompson), **Supp. XXIV:** 280, 282, 283, 287, **288–292,** 293

Fear and Loathing on the Campaign Trail '72 (Thompson), **Supp. XXIV:** 279, 281, 282, 289, **292–293**

Fear and Trembling (Kierkegaard), **Supp. XX: 132**

"Fear & Fame" (Levine), **Supp. V:** 192

Fearful Child, The (C. Frost), **Supp. XV:** 96, 97, 106

"Fearful Child, The" (C. Frost), **Supp. XV:** 96

Fearing, Kenneth, **Supp. XV:** 138; **Supp. XXVI:** 134, 143

"Fearless" (Mosley), **Supp. XIII:** 241

Fearless Jones (Mosley), **Supp. XIII: 241–242**

"Fear of Concrete" (Halliday), **Supp. XIX:** 91

Fear of Fifty: A Midlife Memoir (Jong), **Supp. V:** 114, 115, 116, 131

Fear of Flying (Jong), **Supp. V:** 113, 115, 116, 119–123, 124, 129

"Feast, The" (Kinnell), **Supp. III Part 1:** 239, 250

Feast of All Saints, The (Rice), **Supp. VII:** 299–301

Feast of Love, The (C. Baxter), **Supp. XVII:** 13, 21–22

Feast of Love, The (film, R. Benton), **Supp. XVII:** 22

Feast of Snakes, A (Crews), **Supp. XI:** 102, **107–108; Supp. XXI:** 40

"Feast of Stephen, The" (Hecht), **Supp. X:** 63–64

Feast of the Goat, The (Llosa), **Supp. XXIV:** 89

"Featherbed for Critics, A" (Blackmur), **Supp. II Part 1:** 93, 151

Feather Crowns (Mason), **Supp. VIII: 146–147**

"Feathers" (Carver), **Supp. III Part 1:** 145

Feathers (Van Vechten), **Supp. II Part 2:** 736, 749

"Feathers, The" (Hogan), **Supp. IV Part 1:** 416

Feathers Left Around (Wells), **Supp. XXVI:** 282

"February" (Ellison), **Supp. II Part 1:** 229

"February 14th" (Levine), **Supp. V:** 194

February in Sydney (Komunyakaa), **Supp. XIII: 124–125,** 129

"February in Sydney" (Komunyakaa), **Supp. XIII:** 125

"February: Thinking of Flowers" (Kenyon), **Supp. VII:** 171

"Feces" (McClatchy), **Supp. XII:** 266, 267–268

Fechner, Gustav, **II:** 344, 355, 358, 359, 363

Feder, Lillian, **IV:** 136; **Supp. XVI:** 49, 50

Federal Arts Project, **Supp. III Part 2:** 618

Federigo, or, The Power of Love (Nemerov), **III:** 268, 276, 282, 283–284, 285

"Fedge, The" (Halliday), **Supp. XIX:** 93

"Fedora" (Chopin), **Supp. I Part 1:** 220

Fedorko, Kathy A., **Retro. Supp. I:** 361, 374

"Feeling and Precision" (Moore), **III:** 206

Feeling Italian: The Art of Ethnicity in America (Ferraro), **Supp. XX: 43**

"Feeling of Effort, The" (James), **II:** 349

Feeling Very Strange: The Slipstream Anthology (Kelly and Kessel, eds.), **Supp. XIX:** 231

"Feel Like a Bird" (Swenson), **Supp. IV Part 2:** 639

"Feel Me" (Swenson), **Supp. IV Part 2:** 647

Feeney, Mary, **Supp. IX:** 152, 154

Feinsilver, Pamela, **Supp. XX: 135**

Feinstein, Herbert, **Supp. XIX:** 260

Feinstein, Sascha, **Supp. XIII:** 125

Feldman, Charles K., **Supp. XI:** 307

Feldman, Morton, **Supp. XXIII:** 211

Fellini, Federico, **Supp. XII:** 172; **Supp. XV:** 8

"Fellini the Cat" (Peacock), **Supp. XIX:** 206

"Fellow Citizens" (Sandburg), **III:** 553

Fellows, John, **Supp. I Part 2:** 520

Fellow Travelers (Mallon), **Supp. XIX:** 132, **143–144**

"Felo de Se" (Wylie), **Supp. I Part 2:** 727, 729

Felton, Sharon, **Supp. IV Part 1:** 210

"Female Author" (Plath), **Retro. Supp. II:** 243

"Female Frailty" (Freneau), **Supp. II Part 1:** 258

"Female Laughter and Comic Possibilities: *Uncommon Women and Others*" (Chirico), **Supp. XV:** 323

Female Patriot, The; or, Nature's Rights (Rowson), **Supp. XV:** 237–238

Female Prose Writers of America (Hart), **Supp. XVIII:** 257, 264

"Female Voice in *To Kill a Mockingbird,* The: Narrative Strategies in Film and Novel" (Shakelford), **Supp. VIII:** 129

" 'Feminine' Epic, The" (Notley), **Supp. XXII:** 232, 234, 236

"Feminine Landscape of Leslie Marmon Silko's *Ceremony,* The" (Gunn Allen), **Supp. IV Part 1:** 324

Feminine Note in Fiction, The (Courtney), **Supp. XXIV:** 29

Feminism and the Politics of Literary Reputation: The Example of Erica Jong (Templin), **Supp. V:** 116

"Feminismo" (Robbins), **Supp. X:** 272

"Feminist Criticism in the Wilderness" (Showalter), **Supp. X:** 97

"Feminist Manifesto" (Loy), **Supp. XXII:** 160

Feminization of American Culture, The (Douglas), **Supp. XVIII:** 258

"Fence, The" (Oliver), **Supp. VII:** 232

"Fence Posts" (Snyder), **Supp. VIII:** 304

Fences (Wilson), **Supp. VIII:** 329, 330, 331, **334–337,** 350

Fenick, Elizabeth, **Retro. Supp. II:** 221

"Fenimore Cooper's Literary Offenses" (Twain), **IV:** 204–205

Fennell, Frank L., **Supp. XVII:** 177–178
Fenollosa, Ernest, **III:** 458, 465, 466, 474, 475, 477; **Retro. Supp. I:** 289; **Supp. IV Part 1:** 154
Fenollosa, Mrs. Ernest, **III:** 458
"Fenstad's Mother" (C. Baxter), **Supp. XVII:** 18
Fenton, Charles, **Supp. XI:** 43
Fenton, James, **Supp. XV:** 117
Fenton, William, **Supp. XXVI:** 96
Ferdinand: Including "It Was" (Zukofsky), *Supp. III Part 2:* 630
"Fergus" (Bourne), **I:** 229
Ferguson, James, **Supp. I Part 2:** 503
Ferguson, Otis, **Supp. IX:** 7
Ferguson, SallyAnn H., **Supp. XXVI:** 166
Ferguson, William, **Supp. XII:** 189
Ferguson Affair, The (Macdonald), **Supp. IV Part 2:** 473
Fergusson, Francis, **I:** 265, 440; **Supp. XV:** 20
Ferlinghetti, Lawrence, **Supp. IV Part 1:** 90; **Supp. VIII:** 290, 292; **Supp. XII:** 121, 125; **Supp. XIII:** 275; **Supp. XIX:** 4; **Supp. XXI:** 53; **Supp. XXIII:** 219
Fermata, The (Baker), **Supp. XIII:** 49–52, 54
"Fern" (Toomer), **Supp. III Part 2:** 481; **Supp. IX:** 313
Fern, Fanny, **Retro. Supp. I:** 246; **Supp. V:** 122
Fernández, Enrique, **Supp. VIII:** 73
Fernandez, Ramon, **Retro. Supp. I:** 302, 303; **Supp. XVI:** 214
"Fern-Beds in Hampshire Country" (Wilbur), **Supp. III Part 2:** 558
"Fern Hill" (D. Thomas), **IV:** 93; **Supp. XX: 204**
"Fern-Life" (Larcom), **Supp. XIII:** 143
Ferragammo, Salvatore, **Supp. XVI:** 192
Ferraro, Thomas J., **Supp. XX: 34, 43**
Ferreo, Guglielmo, **Supp. I Part 2:** 481
Ferris, Anthony, **Supp. XX: 124**
Ferris, Beth, **Supp. XXVI:** 183
Ferry, David, **Supp. XXIV: 147–164; Supp. XXV:** 222
"Ferry, The" (Cliff), **Supp. XXII:** 74
Fessenden, Thomas Green, **II:** 300
Fessier, Michael, **Supp. XIII:** 164
"Festival Aspect, The" (Olson), **Supp. II Part 2:** 585
"Festival of Regrets, The" (Wasserstein), **Supp. XV:** 333
Festival of San Joaquin, The (Edgell), **Supp. XXIII:** 84, 85, **90–91,** 94
Fetching the Dead (Sanders), **Supp. XVI:** 269
Fêtes galantes (Verlaine), **IV:** 79
Fetherling, Doug, **Supp. XXVII:** 88, 90, 94
Fetid Itch (Silver), **Supp. XXIV:** 265
"Fetish" (McClatchy), **Supp. XII:** 256
Fetterley, Judith, **Retro. Supp. II:** 139; **Supp. XXIV:** 28
Fetterly, Judith, **Supp. XXV:** 285
"Feud" (Zinberg), **Supp. XV:** 195
"Fever" (Carver), **Supp. III Part 1:** 145
"Fever 103°" (Plath), **Supp. I Part 2:** 541

Fever Pitch (Hornby), **Supp. XII:** 286; **Supp. XXIII:** 109
Fever: Twelve Stories (Wideman), **Supp. X:** 320
"Few Don'ts by an Imagiste, A" (Pound), **III:** 465; **Retro. Supp. I:** 288; **Supp. I Part 1:** 261–262
"Few Kind Words for Anger, A" (Kriegel), **Supp. XXIV:** 220
"Few Stray Comments on the Cultivation of the Lyric, A" (Sobin), **Supp. XVI:** 285
"Few Words of Introduction, A" (McNally), **Supp. XIII:** 198–199
Feydeau, Georges, **Supp. XXIV:** 271
Feynman, Richard, **Supp. XXV:** 267
Fiamengo, Janice, **Supp. XIII:** 35
"Fiat Lux" (H. Johnson), **Supp. XXVI:** 172
Fiber (Bass), **Supp. XVI:** 22
"Fiber: A Post-Pastoral Georgic" (Gifford), **Supp. XVI:** 22
Ficke, Arthur Davison, **Supp. XIII:** 347; **Supp. XV:** 40, 42, 43, 46, 48, 49
"Fiction" (Stafford), **Supp. XI:** 327
"Fiction: A Lens on Life" (Stegner), **Supp. IV Part 2:** 595, 596, 600
Fictional World of William Hoffman, The (Frank, ed.), **Supp. XVIII:** 74, 79, 80, 87
Fiction and the Figures of Life (Gass), **Supp. VI:** 85
Fiction of Joseph Heller, The (Seed), **Supp. IV Part 1:** 391
Fiction of Paule Marshall, The (Denniston), **Supp. XI:** 276
Fiction of the Forties (Eisinger), **I:** 302; **II:** 604
Fictions in Autobiography: Studies in the Art of Self-Invention (Eakin), **Supp. XVI:** 70
"Fiction Writer and His Country, The" (O'Connor), **III:** 342; **Retro. Supp. II:** 223, 225; **Supp. II Part 1:** 148
Fiddler's Trance, The (Skloot), **Supp. XX: 196, 202**
Fidelity (Glaspell), **Supp. III Part 1:** 177
Fiedler, Leslie A., **II:** 27; **III:** 218; **Retro. Supp. II:** 280, 324; **Supp. II Part 1:** 87; **Supp. IV Part 1:** 42, 86; **Supp. IX:** 3, 227; **Supp. X:** 80; **Supp. XIII: 93–110; Supp. XIV:** 11; **Supp. XIX:** 251; **Supp. XVIII:** 146; **Supp. XXIII:** 42; **Supp. XXV:** 268; **Supp. XXVII:** 133, 262
Fiedler on the Roof: Essays on Literature and Jewish Identity (Fiedler), **Supp. XIII:** 106–107
"Fie! Fie! Fi-Fi!" (Fitzgerald), **Retro. Supp. I:** 100
Field, Eugene, **Supp. II Part 1:** 197
Field, John, **IV:** 179
"Field Events" (Bass), **Supp. XVI:** 19
"Field Full of Black Cats, A" (C. Frost), **Supp. XV:** 101
Field Guide, (Hass), **Supp. VI:** 97–98, **99–101,** 102, 103, 106
Field Guide to Contemporary Poetry and Poetics (Friebert and Young, eds.), **Supp. XI:** 270

"Field Guide to the Western Birds" (Stegner), **Supp. IV Part 2:** 609
Fielding, Henry, **I:** 134; **II:** 302, 304–305; **III:** 61; **Supp. I Part 2:** 421, 422, 656; **Supp. IV Part 2:** 688; **Supp. IX:** 128; **Supp. V:** 127; **Supp. XI:** 277; **Supp. XVIII:** 2, 7; **Supp. XXV:** 258
Fielding, Richard, **Supp. XV:** 232
"Field-larks and Blackbirds" (Lanier), **Supp. I Part 1:** 355
Field of Honor (Hay), **Supp. XIV:** 120–121, 125, 130
"Field of Honor" (Hay), **Supp. XIV:** 120–121, 129–130
Field of Vision, The (Morris), **III:** 226–228, 229, 232, 233, 238
"Field Report" (Corso), **Supp. XII:** 124, **136**
"Fields" (Wright), **Supp. XV:** 342
Fields, Annie Adams, **II:** 401, 402, 403–404, 406, 412; **IV:** 177; **Retro. Supp. II:** 134, 135, 142; **Supp. I Part 1:** 317; **Supp. XVI:** 84, 88
Fields, James T., **II:** 274, 279, 402–403; **Retro. Supp. II:** 135; **Supp. I Part 1:** 317; **Supp. XIII:** 150; **Supp. XVI:** 84, 88
Fields, Mrs. James T., **Supp. XIV:** 44, 46. *See* Fields, Annie Adams
Fields, Jerry, **Supp. XXVI:** 86
Fields, Joseph, **IV:** 274
Fields, The (Richter), **Supp. XVIII: 213–214,** 220
Fields, W. C., **II:** 427; **IV:** 335
"Fields at Dusk, The" (Salter), **Supp. IX:** 260
Fields of Fire (Webb), **Supp. XXII:** 115
Fields of Praise, The (Nelson), **Supp. XVIII:** 171, 173, **177–178**
Fields of Wonder (Hughes), **Retro. Supp. I:** 206, 207; **Supp. I Part 1:** 333–334
Fierce Invalids Home from Hot Climates (Robbins), **Supp. X:** 267, 276–277, **282–285**
Fiery, Marion, **Supp. XXII:** 293
Fiery Chariot, The (Hurston), **Supp. VI:** 155–156
"Fiesta, 1980" (Díaz), **Supp. XXIV:** 88
15 Poems (Banks), **Supp. V:** 5
"Fifteenth Farewell" (Bogan), **Supp. III Part 1:** 51, 58
"Fifth Avenue, Uptown" (Baldwin), **Supp. I Part 1:** 52
"Fifth Avenue—Spring Afternoon" (Untermeyer), **Supp. XV:** 296
Fifth Book of Peace, The (Kingston), **Supp. V:** 173
Fifth Chinese Daughter (Wong), **Supp. X:** 291
Fifth Column, The (Hemingway), **II:** 254, 258; **Retro. Supp. I:** 184
"Fifth Column of the Fencerow" (Leopold), **Supp. XIV:** 185
Fifth Decad of Cantos, The (Pound), **Retro. Supp. I:** 292
"Fifth Movement: *Autobiography*" (Zukofsky), **Supp. III Part 2:** 611
Fifth Sunday (Dove), **Supp. IV Part 1:** 251, 252–253

"Fifth Sunday" (Dove), **Supp. IV Part 1:** 252

50 Poems (Cummings), **I:** 430, 440, 442–443, 444–445, 446

Fifty Best American Short Stories (O'Brien), **III:** 56

"Fifty Dollars" (Elkin), **Supp. VI: 43–44**

"55 Miles to the Gas Pump" (Proulx), **Supp. VII:** 264

55 Poems (Zukofsky), **Supp. III Part 2:** 611, 621

"Fifty Grand" (Hemingway), **II:** 250, 424; **Retro. Supp. I:** 177

Fifty Shades of Grey (James), **Supp. XXVII:** 79

Fifty Stories (Boyle), **Supp. XXIV:** 58

"Fifty Suggestions" (Poe), **Retro. Supp. II:** 266

"52 Oswald Street" (Kinnell), **Supp. III Part 1:** 251

Fifty Years Among Authors, Editors, and Publishers (Derby), **Supp. XVIII:** 4

"Fifty Years Among the Black Folk" (Du Bois), **Supp. II Part 1:** 169

"Fifty Years of American Poetry" (Jarrell), **Retro. Supp. I:** 52

Fig Connection, The (Franzen and Siebert), **Supp. XX: 84**

Fight, The (Mailer), **Retro. Supp. II:** 207, 208

Fight Back: For the Sake of the People, For the Sake of the Land (Ortiz), **Supp. IV Part 2:** 497, 498, 499, 503, 510–512, 514

"Fighters, The" (Zinberg), **Supp. XV:** 193

Fight for Freedom (Hughes), **Supp. I Part 1:** 345

Fighting Angel (Buck), **Supp. II Part 1:** 119, 131

Fighting France; From Dunkerque to Belfort (Wharton), **Retro. Supp. I:** 377, 378

Fightin': New and Collected Stories (Ortiz), **Supp. IV Part 2:** 513

"Figlia che Piange, La" (Eliot), **I:** 570, 584; **III:** 9

Figliola, Samantha, **Supp. V:** 143

"Figure a Poem Makes, The" (Frost), **Retro. Supp. I:** 139

"Figured Wheel, The" (Pinsky), **Supp. VI:** 243, 244, 245, 246

Figured Wheel, The: New and Collected Poems (Pinsky), **Supp. VI:** 247–248

"Figure in the Carpet, The" (James), **Retro. Supp. I:** 228, 229

"Figure in the Doorway, The" (Frost), **Retro. Supp. I:** 138

Figure of Fulfillment, The (Lerperger; Miller, trans.), **Supp. XX: 165, 167–168**

Figures from the Double World (McGrath), **Supp. X: 118–119**

Figures in Black: Words, Signs, and the "Racial" Self (H. L. Gates), **Supp. XX: 99, 100, 106, 107**

"Figures in the Clock, The" (McCarthy), **II:** 561–562

Figures Made Visible in the Sadness of Time (Everwine), **Supp. XV:** 75, 88

Figures of Time (Hayden), **Supp. II Part 1:** 367

Filbin, Thomas, **Supp. XXIII:** 299

"Filling Out a Blank" (Wagoner), **Supp. IX:** 324

Fillmore, Millard, **III:** 101

Film Flam: Essays on Hollywood (McMurtry), **Supp. V:** 228

Films of Ayn Rand, The (Cox), **Supp. IV Part 2:** 524

Filo, John, **Supp. XII:** 211

Filreis, Alan, **Supp. XXI:** 262, 267, 268, 269, 271, 273, 275, 277, 278

Filson, John, **Retro. Supp. I:** 421

Final Beast, The (Buechner), **Supp. XII: 49–51**

"Finale" (Longfellow), **II:** 505, 506–507

"Finale: Presto" (Davison), **Supp. XXVI:** 70

"Final Fear" (Hughes), **Supp. I Part 1:** 338

Final Harvest: Emily Dickinson's Poems (T. H. Johnson, ed.), **I:** 470, 471

"Finally Harriet" (Wolfert), **Supp. XXI: 265–267**

Final Payments (Gordon), **Supp. IV Part 1:** 297, 299, 300–302, 304, 306, 314

"Final Report, A" (Maxwell), **Supp. VIII:** 169

"Final Soliloquy of the Interior Paramour" (Stevens), **Retro. Supp. I:** 312

Final Solution, The (Reitlinger), **Supp. XII:** 161

Financier, The (Dreiser), **I:** 497, 501, 507, 509; **Retro. Supp. II:** 94, 101–102, 105; **Supp. XVIII:** 246

Finch, Annie, **Supp. XVII: 69–79**

Finch, Henry Leroy, **Supp. XVII:** 69

Finch, Margaret Rockwell, **Supp. XVII:** 69

Finch, Robert, **Supp. XIV:** 186–187; **Supp. XXVI:** 38

"Finches, Little Pats of Butter on the Wing"(Crooker), **Supp. XXIII:** 62

Find a Victim (Macdonald), **Supp. IV Part 2:** 467, 472, 473

Fin de Chéri, La (Colette; stage adaptation, Loos), **Supp. XVI:** 194

Finder, Henry, **Supp. XX:** 90

"Fin de Saison Palm Beach" (White), **Supp. I Part 2:** 673

"Finding a Bible in an Abandoned Cabin" (Wrigley), **Supp. XVIII: 293–294,** 296, **297,** 300, **301,** 303

Finding a Form (Gass), **Supp. VI:** 91–92, 93

Finding a Girl in America (Dubus), **Supp. VII:** 85–88

"Finding a Girl in America" (Dubus), **Supp. VII:** 87

"Finding Amy" (O'Nan), **Supp. XXV:** 143, 150

"Finding Beads" (Hogan), **Supp. IV Part 1:** 400

Finding Losses (Bronk), **Supp. XXI:** 31, 32

"Finding of Zach, The" (Dunbar), **Supp. II Part 1:** 212

Findings and Keepings: Analects for an Autobiography (Mumford), **Supp. II Part 2:** 483

Finding the Center: Narrative Poetry of the Zuni Indians (Tedlock), **Supp. IV Part 2:** 509

Finding the Islands (Merwin), **Supp. III Part 1:** 353, 357

"Finding the Place: A Migrant Childhood" (Stegner), **Supp. IV Part 2:** 597

Findley, Timothy, **Supp. XX: 49–65**

"Find the Woman" (Macdonald, as Millar), **Supp. IV Part 2:** 466

Fine, David, **Supp. XI:** 160

Fine, Richard, **Supp. XVIII:** 248

Fine Clothes to the Jew (Hughes), **Retro. Supp. I:** 200, 201, 203, 205; **Supp. I Part 1:** 326–328

"Fine Old Firm, A" (Jackson), **Supp. IX:** 120

Fine Preserving (Plagemann), **Supp. XVII:** 91

Fine Preserving: M. F. K. Fisher's Annotated Edition of Catherine Plagemann's Cookbook (Plagemann; M. F. K. Fisher, ed.), **Supp. XVII:** 91

Finer Grain, The (James), **II:** 335

Fine Writing (L. P. Smith), **Supp. XIV:** 347

"Fingerprints" (Cohen), **Supp. XXVII:** 56

"Finis" (X. J. Kennedy), **Supp. XV:** 169

"Finished Basement" (Di Piero), **Supp. XIX:** 47

Finished Man, The (Garrett), **Supp. VII:** 96, 97–98

Fink, Jonathan, **Supp. XXI:** 244, 245, 248, 255, 256

Fink, Mike, **IV:** 266

Finkel, Donald, **Supp. XXVII:** 253

Finkelstein, Norman, **Supp. XXI:** 24, 33

Finkle, David, **Supp. XXI:** 47

Finley, John H., **II:** 418

Finn, David, **Supp. VIII:** 106–107

Finn, Mark, **Supp. XXVII:** 128

Finnegan, Robert (pseudonym). *See* Ryan, Paul William

Finnegans Wake (Joyce), **III:** 7, 12, 14, 261; **IV:** 182, 369–370, 418, 421; **Supp. I Part 2:** 620; **Supp. II Part 1:** 2; **Supp. XIII:** 191; **Supp. XVIII:** 32

Finney, Brian, **Supp. XIV:** 158, 160, 161, 165, 166, 167, 169

"Finnish Rhapsody" (Ashbery), **Supp. III Part 1:** 26

Finster, Howard, **Supp. XV:** 349

Firbank, Ronald, **IV:** 77, 436; **Supp. XXIII:** 209

"Fire" (Hughes), **Supp. I Part 1:** 327

"Fire and Cloud" (Wright), **IV:** 488

"Fire and Ice" (Frost), **II:** 154; **Retro. Supp. I:** 133; **Supp. XIX:** 122

Fire and Ice (Stegner), **Supp. IV Part 2:** 598, 607–608

"Fire and the Cloud, The" (Hurston), **Supp. VI:** 158

"Fire and the Hearth, The" (Faulkner), **II:** 71

Firebird (Doty), **Supp. XI:** 119–120, 121, **132–133,** 134

"Firebombing, The" (Dickey), **Supp. IV Part 1:** 180–181, 187, 189–190

"Fireborn Are at Home in Fire, The" (Sandburg), **III:** 591

"Fire by Night" (R. Fisher), **Supp. XIX:** 70–71

"Fire Chaconne" (Francis), **Supp. IX:** 87

Firecrackers (Van Vechten), **Supp. II Part 2:** 740, 742–744, 749

"Fire Dreams"(Thompson), **Supp. XXIII:** 296

Fire: From "A Journal of Love," the Unexpurgated Diary of Anaïs Nin, 1934–1937, **Supp. X:** 184, 185, 189, 194, 195

"Fire in the House, The" (Davison), **Supp. XXVI:** 71

Firelight Fairy Book, The (Beston), **Supp. XXVI:** 33

"Fireman, The " (Bass), **Supp. XVI:** 24

Fireman's Wife and Other Stories, The (Bausch), **Supp. VII:** 48, 54

Fire Next Time, The (Baldwin), **Retro. Supp. II:** 5, 8, 9; **Supp. I Part 1:** 48, 49, 52, 60–61

"Fire Next Time, The" (Baldwin). *See* "Down at the Cross" (Baldwin)

"Fire of Driftwood, The" (Longfellow), **II:** 499; **Retro. Supp. II:** 159, 168

"Fire of Life" (McCullers), **II:** 585

Fire on the Mountain (Abbey), **Supp. XIII:** 6

"Fire Poem" (Merrill), **Supp. III Part 1:** 321

"Fires" (Bass), **Supp. XVI:** 20

"Fires" (Carver), **Supp. III Part 1:** 136–139, 147

Fire Sale (Paretsky), **Supp. XXV:** 175–176, 178

Fire Screen, The (Merrill), **Supp. III Part 1:** 319, 325–329

"Fire Season" (Didion), **Supp. IV Part 1:** 199

"Fire Sequence" (Winters), **Supp. II Part 2:** 791, 796, 800

Fire Sermon (Morris), **III:** 238–239

"Fire Sermon, The" (Eliot), **Retro. Supp. I:** 60–61

Fires: Essays, Poems, Stories (Carver), **Supp. III Part 1:** 136, 140, 142, 146–147

Fireside Travels (J. R. Lowell), **Supp. I Part 2:** 407, 419–420

Firestarter (King), **Supp. IX:** 114; **Supp. V:** 140, 141, 144

"fire the bastards" (Green), **Supp. IV Part 1:** 285

"Fire-Truck, A" (Wilbur), **Supp. III Part 2:** 556

"Fireweed" (Clampitt), **Supp. IX:** 44–45

"Firewood" (Banks), **Supp. V:** 15

"Fireworks" (Ford), **Supp. V:** 69

"Fireworks" (Shapiro), **Supp. II Part 2:** 707

Fireworks: A History and Celebration (Plimpton), **Supp. XVI:** 245

Fir-Flower Tablets (A. Lowell), **II:** 512, 526–527

Firger, Jessica, **Supp. XIX:** 51, 58, 59, 62

Firkins, Oscar W., **II:** 271; **Supp. XV:** 297, 309

"Firmament, The" (Bryant), **Supp. I Part 1:** 162

Firmat, Gustavo Pérez, **Supp. VIII:** 76, 77, 79; **Supp. XI:** 184

"First American, The" (Toomer), **Supp. III Part 2:** 480, 487

"First Birth" (Olds), **Supp. X:** 212

First Book of Africa, The (Hughes), **Supp. I Part 1:** 344–345

First Book of Jazz, The (Hughes), **Supp. I Part 1:** 345

First Book of Negroes, The (Hughes), **Supp. I Part 1:** 345

First Book of Rhythms, The (Hughes), **Supp. I Part 1:** 345

First Book of the West Indies, The (Hughes), **Supp. I Part 1:** 345

Firstborn (Glück), **Supp. V:** 80, 81, 82, 84

"Firstborn" (Wright), **Supp. V:** 340

"First Chaldaic Oracle" (Carson), **Supp. XII:** 111

"First Communion" (Fante), **Supp. XI:** 160

"First Confession" (X. J. Kennedy), **Supp. XV: 154–155**

"First Day of School, The" (Gibbons), **Supp. X:** 41, 42

"First Death in Nova Scotia" (Bishop), **Supp. I Part 1:** 73

"First Formal" (Olds), **Supp. X:** 212

First Four Books of Poems, The (Glück), **Supp. V:** 81, 83

First Four Years, The (L. I. Wilder), **Supp. XXII:** 296, 298, 299–300

"First Grade" (Stafford), **Supp. XI:** 328

First Hand (Bierds), **Supp. XVII:** 32, 34–36

"First Hawaiian Bank" (Nye), **Supp. XIII:** 278

"First Heat" (Taylor), **Supp. V:** 323

First Hour, The (Di Piero), **Supp. XIX:** 36–37, 40

"First Hour of the Night, The" (Bidart), **Supp. XV: 30–32**

"First Hunters and the Last, The" (Sobin), **Supp. XVI:** 292

First Indian on the Moon (Alexie), **Supp. XXVI:** 103

"First Job, The" (Cisneros), **Supp. VII:** 62

"1st Letter on Georges" (Olson), **Supp. II Part 2:** 578

First Light (C. Baxter), **Supp. XVII:** 15, **17–18,** 19, 22

First Light (Preston), **Supp. XVII:** 18

First Light (Wagoner), **Supp. IX:** 330

"Firstling, The" (Davison), **Supp. XXVI:** 69

"First Love" (Welty), **IV:** 264; **Retro. Supp. I:** 347

First Love: A Lyric Sequence (Untermeyer), **Supp. XV:** 295

"First Love: A Quiz" (Stallings), **Supp. XXV:** 221, 233

First Lover and Other Stories, The (Boyle), **Supp. XXIV: 57–58**

First Man, The (O'Neill), **III:** 390

First Manifesto (McGrath), **Supp. X:** 115

"First Meditation" (Roethke), **III:** 545–546

"First Noni Daylight, The" (Harjo), **Supp. XII:** 219

"First Passover" (Longfellow), **II:** 500–501

"First Person Female" (Harrison), **Supp. VIII:** 40, 41, 48

"First Place, The" (Wagoner), **Supp. IX:** 328

First Poems (Buechner), **Supp. XII:** 45

First Poems (Merrill), **Supp. III Part 1:** 318–321, 323

First Poems 1946–1954 (Kinnell), **Supp. III Part 1:** 235, 238–239

"First Praise" (W. C. Williams), **Retro. Supp. I:** 413

First Principles (Spencer), **Supp. I Part 1:** 368

"First Reader" (Collins), **Supp. XXI:** 55–56

"First Ride and First Walk" (Goldbarth), **Supp. XII:** 182–183

"First Seeing the St. Lawrence River"(Kenny), **Supp. XXIII:** 152

"First Seven Years, The" (Malamud), **Supp. I Part 2:** 431

"First Sex" (Olds), **Supp. X:** 208

"First Shift" (Rash), **Supp. XXVII:** 218, 220

"First Snow" (Mosher), **Supp. XXII:** 211

"First Snow in Alsace" (Wilbur), **Supp. III Part 2:** 545, 546, 559

"First Song" (Kinnell), **Supp. III Part 1:** 239

"First Spade in the West, The" (Fiedler), **Supp. XIII:** 103

"First Steps" (McClatchy), **Supp. XII:** 256

First There Is the Need (Reznikoff), **Supp. XIV:** 291

"First Things First" (Auden), **Supp. II Part 1:** 13

"First Thought, Best Thought" (Ginsberg), **Supp. II Part 1:** 327

"First Time I Saw Paris, The" (Fante), **Supp. XI:** 174

"First Travels of Max" (Ransom), **III:** 490–491

"First Tycoon of Teen, The" (Wolfe), **Supp. III Part 2:** 572

"First Views of the Enemy" (Oates), **Supp. II Part 2:** 508

"First Wife, The" (Buck), **Supp. II Part 1:** 127

First Words before Spring (Untermeyer), **Supp. XV:** 310

"First World War" (White), **Supp. I Part 2:** 665

"Fish" (F. Barthelme), **Supp. XI:** 26

"Fish" (Levis), **Supp. XI:** 259–260

Fish, Stanley, **Supp. IV Part 1:** 48; **Supp. XIV:** 14, 15

"Fish, The" (Bishop), **Supp. XV:** 100, 102; **Supp. XXVII:** 228

"Fish, The" (Moore), **III:** 195, 197, 209, 211, 213–214; **Supp. XXI:** 26

"Fish, The" (Oliver), **Supp. VII:** 236

"Fish, The/Lago Chapala" (Everwine), **Supp. XV:** 82–83

"Fish and Shadow" (Pound), **III:** 466
"Fishboy" (Richard), **Supp. XIX:** 212–213
Fishboy: A Ghost's Story (Richard), **Supp. XIX:** 209, **213–220,** 221
Fishburne, Laurence, **Supp. VIII:** 345
"Fish Cannery" (Fante), **Supp. XI:** 167
Fisher, Alexander Metcalf, **Supp. I Part 2:** 582
Fisher, Alfred, **Retro. Supp. II:** 243
Fisher, Barbara, **Supp. XXII:** 206
Fisher, Craig, **Supp. V:** 125
Fisher, Dorothy Canfield, **Retro. Supp. I:** 21, 133; **Supp. II Part 1:** 117. *See also* Canfield, Dorothy
Fisher, Mary, **Supp. I Part 2:** 455
Fisher, M. F. K., **Supp. XVII: 81–93**
Fisher, Phillip, **Retro. Supp. I:** 39
Fisher, Rudolph, **Retro. Supp. I:** 200; **Supp. I Part 1:** 325; **Supp. X:** 139; **Supp. XIX: 65–80; Supp. XVI:** 143
Fisher, Vardis, **Supp. IV Part 2:** 598
Fisher King, The (Marshall), **Supp. XI:** 275–276, **288–290**
"Fisherman, The" (Merwin), **Supp. II Part 1:** 346
"Fisherman and His Wife, The" (Welty), **IV:** 266
"Fisherman from Chihuahua, The" (Connell), **Supp. XIV:** 86
"Fishing" (Harjo), **Supp. XII:** 227–228
"Fishing Idyll, A" (Mosher), **Supp. XXII:** 209
"Fish in the Stone, The" (Dove), **Supp. IV Part 1:** 245, 257
"Fish in the unruffled lakes" (Auden), **Supp. II Part 1:** 8–9
"Fish R Us" (Doty), **Supp. XI:** 135
Fisk, James, **I:** 4, 474
Fiske, John, **Supp. I Part 1:** 314; **Supp. I Part 2:** 493
Fisketjon, Gary, **Supp. XXIV:** 178
"Fit Against the Country, A" (Wright), **Supp. III Part 2:** 591–592, 601
Fitch, Clyde, **Supp. IV Part 2:** 573
Fitch, Elizabeth. *See* Taylor, Mrs. Edward (Elizabeth Fitch)
Fitch, James, **IV:** 147
Fitch, Noël Riley, **Supp. X:** 186, 187
"Fits" (Munro), **Supp. XXVII:** 189, 196
"Fitting, The" (Hull), **Supp. XXI:** 134, 135
Fit to Be Tied (Silver), **Supp. XXIV: 271–272**
Fitts, Dudley, **I:** 169, 173; **Supp. I Part 1:** 342, 345; **Supp. XIII:** 346; **Supp. XXII:** 281; **Supp. XXVI:** 65
FitzGerald, Edward, **Supp. I Part 2:** 416; **Supp. III Part 2:** 610
Fitzgerald, Ella, **Supp. XIII:** 132
Fitzgerald, F. Scott, **I:** 107, 117, 118, 123, 188, 221, 288, 289, 358, 367, 374–375, 382, 423, 476, 482, 487, 495, 509, 511; **II: 77–100,** 257, 263, 272, 283, 415, 416, 417–418, 420, 425, 427, 430, 431, 432, 433, 434, 436, 437, 450, 458–459, 482, 560; **III:** 2, 26, 35, 36, 37, 40, 44, 45, 69, 106, 244, 284, 334, 350–351, 453, 454, 471, 551, 552, 572; **IV:** 27, 49, 97,

101, 126, 140, 191, 222, 223, 287, 297, 427, 471; **Retro. Supp. I:** 1, 74, **97–120,** 178, 180, 186, 215, 359, 381; **Retro. Supp. II:** 257, 321, 326, 328; **Supp. I Part 1:** 196, 197; **Supp. I Part 2:** 622; **Supp. III Part 2:** 409, 411, 585; **Supp. IV Part 1:** 123, 197, 200, 203, 341; **Supp. IV Part 2:** 463, 468, 607, 689; **Supp. IX:** 15, 20, 55, 57–63, 199; **Supp. V:** 23, 95, 226, 251, 262, 276, 313; **Supp. VIII:** 101, 103, 106, 137; **Supp. X:** 225; **Supp. XI:** 65, 221, 334; **Supp. XII:** 42, 173, 295; **Supp. XIII:** 170, 263; **Supp. XV:** 135; **Supp. XVI:** 64, 75, 191, 192, 294; **Supp. XVIII:** 148, 246, 248, 251, 254; **Supp. XX: 74; Supp. XXI:** 262; **Supp. XXII:** 82, 92; **Supp. XXIII:** 68, 101, 174
Fitzgerald, Robert, **I:** 27–28; **III:** 338, 348; **Retro. Supp. II:** 179, 221, 222, 223, 228, 229; **Supp. IV Part 2:** 631; **Supp. XV:** 112, 249; **Supp. XXII:** 281; **Supp. XXIII:** 112
Fitzgerald, Zelda (Zelda Sayre), **I:** 482; **II:** 77, 79, 82–85, 88, 90–91, 93, 95; **Supp. IV Part 1:** 310; **Supp. IX: 55–73; Supp. X:** 172. *See also* Sayre, Zelda
"Fitzgerald's Tragic Sense" (Schorer), **Retro. Supp. I:** 115
"Fitzgerald: The Romance of Money" (Cowley), **Supp. II Part 1:** 143
Fitzpatrick, Catherine, **Supp. XXVII:** 270
5 Detroits (Levine), **Supp. V:** 178
Five Came Back (West), **IV:** 287
Five Corners (screenplay, Shanley), **Supp. XIV:** 316
"Five-Dollar Bill, The" (D. West as Mary Christopher), **Supp. XVIII:** 282
"Five Dollar Guy, The" (W. C. Williams), **Retro. Supp. I:** 423
Five Easy Pieces (film), **Supp. V:** 26
"Five Elephants" (Dove), **Supp. IV Part 1:** 244–245
"Five Fucks" (Lethem), **Supp. XVIII:** 139
Five Groups of Verse (Reznikoff), **Supp. XIV:** 279, 282
Five Hundred Hats of Bartholomew Cubbins, The (Geisel), **Supp. XVI:** 100
Five Hundred Scorpions (Hearon), **Supp. VIII:** 57, 65, **66**
Five Indiscretions (Ríos), **Supp. IV Part 2:** 545–547
Five Men and Pompey (Benét), **Supp. XI:** 43, 44
Five Plays (Hughes), **Retro. Supp. I:** 197, 209
"Five Poems About Poetry" (Oppen), **Supp. XXVI:** 233
"Five Psalms" (Jarman), **Supp. XVII:** 120
Five Temperaments (Kalstone), **Retro. Supp. II:** 40
5,000 Fingers of Dr. T, The (film), **Supp. XVI:** 103
Five Young American Poets, **I:** 170; **II:** 367

Fixer, The (Malamud), **Supp. I Part 2:** 428, 435, 445, 446–448, 450, 451
"Fixin' Road" (Boulton), **Supp. XXII:** 23
"Fix It (Winter)"(Hadas), **Supp. XXIII:** 115
Fjellestad, Danuta Zadworna, **Supp. XVI:** 150
Flaccus, Kimball, **Retro. Supp. I:** 136
Flacius, Matthias, **IV:** 163
"Flagellant's Song" (X. J. Kennedy), **Supp. XV:** 165
Flag for Sunrise, A (Stone), **Supp. V:** 301–304
Flagg, Fannie, **Supp. XXII:** 213–214
Flag Is Born, A (Hecht), **Supp. XXVII:** 94–95
Flag of Childhood, The: Poems from the Middle East (Nye, ed.), **Supp. XIII:** 280
"Flag of Summer" (Swenson), **Supp. IV Part 2:** 645
Flagons and Apples (Jeffers), **Supp. II Part 2:** 413, 414, 417–418
Flags in the Dust (Faulkner), **Retro. Supp. I:** 81, 82, 83, 86, 88
Flame and Shadow (Teasdale), **Supp. XXVII:** 284, 286, 292–295
Flamel, Nicolas, **Supp. XII:** 178
Flaming Corsage, The (W. Kennedy), **Supp. VII:** 133, 153–156
Flammarion, Camille, **Supp. I Part 1:** 260
Flanagan, John T., **Supp. I Part 2:** 464, 465, 468
Flanner, Janet, **Supp. XVI:** 195
"Flannery O'Connor: Poet to the Outcast" (Sister Rose Alice), **III:** 348
Flappers and Philosophers (Fitzgerald), **II:** 88; **Retro. Supp. I:** 103; **Supp. IX:** 56
"Flappers Were Her Daughters, The: The Liberated, Literary World of Gertrude Atherton" (Richey), **Supp. XXIV:** 30
Flash and Filigree (Southern), **Supp. XI:** 295, **296–297**
"Flashcards" (Dove), **Supp. IV Part 1:** 250
Flash Fiction: Seventy-two Very Short Stories (J. Thomas, ed.), **Supp. XVI:** 268
"Flash in the Pan" (Shaw), **Supp. XIX:** 245
Flats (Wurlitzer), **Supp. XXVI:** 26
"Flat Sky of Summer"(Balakian), **Supp. XXIII:** 25
Flatt, Lester, **Supp. V:** 335
"Flatted Third, The" (Huddle), **Supp. XXVI:** 153
Flaubert, Gustave, **I:** 66, 123, 130, 272, 312, 314, 315, 477, 504, 506, 513, 514; **II:** 182, 185, 194, 198–199, 205, 209, 230, 289, 311, 316, 319, 325, 337, 392, 401, 577, 594; **III:** 196, 207, 251, 315, 461, 467, 511, 564; **IV:** 4, 29, 31, 37, 40, 134, 285, 428; **Retro. Supp. I:** 5, 215, 218, 222, 225, 235, 287; **Supp. III Part 2:** 411, 412; **Supp. XI:** 334; **Supp. XIV:** 87, 336; **Supp. XXIII:** 254; **Supp. XXVII:** 2

"Flavia and Her Artists" (Cather), **Retro. Supp. I:** 5

Flavoring of New England, The (Brooks), **I:** 253, 256

Flavor of Man, The (Toomer), **Supp. III Part 2:** 487

"Flaw, The" (Peacock), **Supp. XIX:** 206

Flaxman, Josiah, **Supp. I Part 2:** 716

"Flea, The" (Donne), **Supp. XVIII:** 307

"Flèche d'Or" (Merrill), **Supp. III Part 1:** 328

Flecker, James Elroy, **Supp. I Part 1:** 257

"Flee on Your Donkey" (Sexton), **Supp. II Part 2:** 683, 685

Fleming, Ian, **Supp. XI:** 307; **Supp. XX:** 195; **Supp. XXVI:** 126

Fleming, Rene, **Supp. XII:** 321

Fleming, Robert E., **Supp. XVII:** 155; **Supp. XXII:** 184

Flesch, Rudolf, **Supp. XVI:** 105, 106

Flesh and Blood (Cunningham), **Supp. XV:** 63–65

Flesh and Blood (play; Cunnigham and Gaitens), **Supp. XV:** 65

"Fleshbody" (Ammons), **Supp. VII:** 27

Fletcher, H. D., **II:** 517, 529

Fletcher, John, **Supp. IV Part 2:** 621

Fletcher, John Gould, **I:** 243; **II:** 517, 529; **III:** 458; **Supp. I Part 1:** 263; **Supp. I Part 2:** 422; **Supp. XV:** 298, 302, 306, 307, 308

Fletcher, Phineas, **Supp. I Part 1:** 369

Fletcher, Virginia. *See* Caldwell, Mrs. Erskine (Virginia Fletcher)

Fleurs du mal, Les (Beaudelaire; Millay and Dillon, trans.), **III:** 141–142

"Flight" (Bierds), **Supp. XVII:** 36

"Flight" (Updike), **IV:** 218, 222, 224; **Retro. Supp. I:** 318

Flight (White), **Supp. XVIII:** 127

"Flight, The" (Haines), **Supp. XII:** 204–205

"Flight, The" (Roethke), **III:** 537–538

Flight 115; or, Pas de Fumer sur la Piste (O'Hara and Berkson), **Supp. XXIII:** 217, 218

Flight among the Tombs (Hecht), **Supp. X:** 58, 71–74

"Flight for Freedom" (McCoy), **Supp. XIII:** 170

"Flight from Byzantium" (Brodsky), **Supp. VIII:** 30–31

"Flight of Besey Lane, The" (Jewett), **Retro. Supp. II:** 139

Flight of the Rocket, The (Fitzgerald), **II:** 89

Flights of the Harvest-Mare (Bierds), **Supp. XVII:** 26–27

Flight to Canada (Reed), **Supp. X:** 240, 249–252

Flinn, Mary, **Supp. XVII:** 110

Flint, F. S., **II:** 517; **III:** 459, 464, 465; **Retro. Supp. I:** 127; **Supp. I Part 1:** 261, 262

Flint, Helen, **Supp. XXII:** 278

Flint, R. W., **Supp. XVI:** 47, 49, 57

"Flitting Flies" (X. J. Kennedy), **Supp. XV:** 166, **167**

Flivver King, The (Sinclair), **Supp. V:** 290

Floating House, The (Sanders), **Supp. XVI:** 269

Floating Light Bulb, The (Allen), **Supp. XV:** 2, 3, 13

Floating Opera, The (Barth), **I:** 121, 122–126, 127, 129, 130, 131

"Floating Poem, Unnumbered, The" (Rich), **Supp. I Part 2:** 572–573

"Floating Trees" (Wright), **Supp. XV:** 348

Flood (Matthews), **Supp. IX:** 154, **160–161**

Flood (Warren), **IV:** 252, 256–257

"Flood of Years, The" (Bryant), **Supp. I Part 1:** 159, 170, 171; **Supp. I Part 2:** 416

"Floor and the Ceiling, The" (W. J. Smith), **Supp. XIII:** 345, 346

"Floor Plans" (Komunyakaa), **Supp. XIII:** 114

"Floral Conversation" (Peacock), **Supp. XIX:** 200

"Floral Decorations for Bananas" (Stevens), **IV:** 8

Florentine Dagger, The: A Novel for Amateur Detectives (Hecht), **Supp. XXVII:** 89

Florida (Acker), **Supp. XII:** 5

"Florida" (Bishop), **Retro. Supp. II:** 43

"Florida Road Workers" (Hughes), **Retro. Supp. I:** 203

"Florida Sunday, A" (Lanier), **Supp. I Part 1:** 364, 366

Florist's Daughter, The (Hampl), **Supp. XXII:** 84, 85, 94, **95–98**

"Flossie Cabanis" (Masters), **Supp. I Part 2:** 461–462

"Flossy Frills Helps Out" (Wells), **Supp. XXVI:** 276

"Flounder" (Trethewey), **Supp. XXI:** 244, 245, 246, 251

Flow Chart (Ashbery), **Supp. VIII:** 275

"Flowchart" (Ashbery), **Supp. III Part 1:** 26

Flower, Dean, **Supp. XXII:** 205, 212

Flower, Fruit, and Thorn Pieces (Richter), **Supp. XVI:** 182

Flower-de-Luce (Longfellow), **II:** 490

Flower Drum Song (Rodgers and Hammerstein), **Supp. XXI:** 148

Flower Drum Song, The (Lee), **Supp. XXI:** 148

Flower Fables (Alcott), **Supp. I Part 1:** 33

"Flower-Fed Buffaloes, The" (Lindsay), **Supp. I Part 2:** 398

"Flower Garden" (Jackson), **Supp. IX:** 119

"Flower-gathering" (Frost), **II:** 153

Flower Herding on Mount Monadnock (Kinnell), **Supp. III Part 1:** 235, 239, 241–244

"Flower Herding on Mount Monadnock" (Kinnell), **Supp. III Part 1:** 242

"Flowering Death" (Ashbery), **Supp. III Part 1:** 22

"Flowering Dream, The" (McCullers), **II:** 591

"Flowering Judas" (Porter), **III:** 434, 435–436, 438, 441, 445, 446, 450–451

Flowering Judas and Other Stories (Porter), **III:** 433, 434

Flowering of New England, The (Brooks), **IV:** 171–172; **Supp. VIII:** 101

Flowering of the Rod (Doolittle), **Supp. I Part 1:** 272

Flowering Peach, The (Odets), **Supp. II Part 2:** 533, 547, 549–550

"Flowering Plum" (Glück), **Supp. V:** 82

Flowers, The (Gilb), **Supp. XXV:** 138

Flowers for Hitler (Cohen), **Supp. XXVII:** 54

"Flowers for Marjorie" (Welty), **IV:** 262

"Flowers of the Fallow" (Larcom), **Supp. XIII:** 143, 145–146

"Flowers Well if anybody" (Dickinson), **Retro. Supp. I:** 30

"Fluff and Mr. Ripley" (D. West), **Supp. XVIII:** 284

"Fly, The" (Kinnell), **Supp. III Part 1:** 249

"Fly, The" (Shapiro), **Supp. II Part 2:** 705

"Fly, The" (Simic), **Supp. VIII:** 278

Flye, Father James Harold, **I:** 25, 26, 35–36, 37, 42, 46; **IV:** 215

"Fly in Buttermilk, A" (Baldwin), **Retro. Supp. I:** 8

Flying at Night: Poems 1965–1985 (Kooser), **Supp. XIX:** 128

"Flying High" (Levertov), **Supp. III Part 1:** 284

"Flying Home" (Ellison), **Retro. Supp. II:** 117, **125–126; Supp. II Part 1:** 235, 238–239

"Flying Home" (Kinnell), **Supp. III Part 1:** 250

"Flying Home" and Other Stories (Ellison), **Retro. Supp. II:** 119, 124

"Flying Home from Utah" (Swenson), **Supp. IV Part 2:** 645

"Flying over Clouds" (Gioia), **Supp. XV:** 118

Flying Solo (Kriegel), **Supp. XXIV: 219–221**

"Flying to Hanoi" (Rukeyser), **Supp. VI:** 279

Flynn, Elizabeth Gurley, **Supp. XVIII:** 225

Flynn, Richard, **Supp. XVII:** 115; **Supp. XVIII:** 183

Fly-Truffler, The (Sobin), **Supp. XVI:** **294–295,** 296

Foata, Anne, **Supp. XI:** 104

FOB (Hwang), **Supp. XXI:** 143, 144, 145, 146, **148–150**

Focillon, Henri, **IV:** 90

Foer, Jonathan Safran, **Supp. XII:** 169; **Supp. XX: 177; Supp. XXIV:** 131; **Supp. XXV:** 268

Foerster, Norman, **I:** 222; **Supp. I Part 2:** 423, 424; **Supp. IV Part 2:** 598

"Fog" (Sandburg), **III:** 586

"Fog Galleon" (Komunyakaa), **Supp. XIII:** 127

"Foggy and dripping" (Kooser), **Supp. XIX:** 125

"Foggy Lane, The" (Simpson), **Supp. IX:** 274

"Fog Man, The" (Boyle), **Supp. XX:** 20

"Fog Patterns" (Hecht), **Supp. XXVII:** 85

Folded Leaf, The (Maxwell), **Supp. III Part 1:** 62; **Supp. VIII: 159–162**

Folding Star, The (Hollinghurst), **Supp. XIII:** 52

Foley, Barbara, **Supp. XXVI:** 28

Foley, Jack, **Supp. X:** 125; **Supp. XV:** 112, 116; **Supp. XVII:** 77

Foley, Martha, **II:** 587; **Supp. XVI:** 225

Folk-Lore in the Old Testament (Frazer), **Supp. XX:** 116–117

Folks, Jeffrey, **Supp. XXVI:** 15

Folks from Dixie (Dunbar), **Supp. II Part 1:** 211–212

Folkways (Sumner), **III:** 102

Follain, Jean, **Supp. IX:** 152, 154

Follett, Wilson, **I:** 405; **Supp. XIII:** 173

Follower of Dusk (Salinas), **Supp. XIII:** 326

"Following the Bones" (W. V. Davis), **Supp. XXI:** 96

Following the Equator (Twain), **II:** 434; **IV:** 208

Follow Me Home (Hoffman), **Supp. XVIII:** 86

Folly (Minot), **Supp. VI:** 205, 208, **210–213**

Folly in the Forest (Wells), **Supp. XXVI:** 276

Folly of Others, The (Boyce), **Supp. XVII:** 100; **Supp. XXI:** 10

Folsom, Charles, **Supp. I Part 1:** 156

Folsom, Ed, **Retro. Supp. I:** 392

Folson, Marcia McClintock, **Retro. Supp. II:** 139

Fonda, Henry, **Supp. I Part 1:** 67; **Supp. IV Part 1:** 236

Fonda, Jane, **III:** 284; **Supp. XI:** 307

Fonda, Peter, **Supp. VIII:** 42; **Supp. XI:** 293, 308

"Fondled Memories" (Molesworth), **Supp. XIX:** 121–122

"Fond Memories of a Black Childhood" (D. West), **Supp. XVIII:** 289

Foner, Eric, **Supp. I Part 2:** 523

Fong and the Indians (Theroux), **Supp. VIII:** 314, 315, **316–317**

Fontanne, Lynn, **III:** 397

Food and Drink (Untermeyer), **Supp. XV:** 310

Food Chain, The (Silver), **Supp. XXIV:** 265, **270–271,** 274

Fool for Love (Shepard), **Supp. III Part 2:** 433, 447, 448

Fooling with Words (PBS special, Moyers), **Supp. XXIII:** 139

"Foolishness" (Pickering), **Supp. XXI:** 197

Fools (Simon), **Supp. IV Part 2:** 584–585

Fools Crow (Welch), **Supp. XXIV:** 257

Fool's Progress, The: An Honest Novel (Abbey), **Supp. XIII:** 4, **13–15**

"Football Rebellion in Backwoods Georgia, A" (Andrews), **Supp. XXVI:** 3, 4

Foot Book, The (Geisel), **Supp. XVI:** 108

Foote, Bud, **Supp. XXVI:** 5

Foote, Horton, **Supp. I Part 1:** 281; **Supp. VIII:** 128, 129

Foote, Mary Hallock, **Retro. Supp. II:** 72; **Supp. IV Part 2:** 611

Foote, Roxanna. *See* Beecher, Mrs. Lyman (Roxanna Foote)

Foote, Samuel, **Supp. I Part 2:** 584

Foote, Stephanie, **Retro. Supp. II:** 139

"Foot Fault" (pseudonym). *See* Thurber, James

Footing on This Earth, A (Hay), **Supp. XIV:** 125, 126, 130

"Footing up a Total" (A. Lowell), **II:** 528

"Footnote to Howl" (Ginsberg), **Supp. II Part 1:** 316–317

"Footnote to Weather Forecasts, A" (Brodsky), **Supp. VIII:** 32

Footprints (Hearon), **Supp. VIII: 69–70**

Footprints (Levertov), **Supp. III Part 1:** 272, 281

"Footsteps of Angels" (Longfellow), **II:** 496

"For A, at Fourteen" (Weigl), **Supp. XIX:** 287

For a Bitter Season: New and Selected Poems (Garrett), **Supp. VII:** 99–100

"For a Dead Kitten" (Hay), **Supp. XIV:** 119–120

"For a Dead Lady" (Robinson), **III:** 508, 513, 517

"For a Ghost Who Once Placed Bets in the Park" (Levis), **Supp. XI:** 265

"Foraging" (H. Johnson), **Supp. XXVI:** 172

"For a Lamb" (Eberhart), **I:** 523, 530, 531

"For All" (Snyder), **Supp. VIII:** 304

"For All Tuesday Travelers" (Cisneros), **Supp. VII:** 67–68

"For a Lost Child" (Stafford), **Supp. XI:** 329

"For a Marriage" (Bogan), **Supp. III Part 1:** 52

"For an Emigrant" (Jarrell), **II:** 371

"For Anna Akmatova" (R. Lowell), **II:** 544

"For Anna Mae Pictou Aquash, Whose Spirit Is Present Here and in the Dappled Stars" (Harjo), **Supp. XII:** 225

"For Anne, at a Little Distance" (Haines), **Supp. XII:** 207

"For Annie" (Poe), **III:** 427; **Retro. Supp. II:** 263

"For an Old Friend Encountered Unexpectedly" (Espaillat), **Supp. XXI:** 111–112

"For a Southern Man" (Cisneros), **Supp. VII:** 67

"For Bailey" (Angelou), **Supp. IV Part 1:** 15

Forbes, Genevieve, **Supp. XXV:** 196

Forbes, Malcolm, **Supp. IV Part 1:** 94

"Forbidden, The" (Glück), **Supp. XIV:** 269

"Forbidden Magic" (Howard), **Supp. XXVII:** 118

"For Bill Nestrick (1940–96)" (Bidart), **Supp. XV:** 35

For Bread Alone (Choukri), **Supp. IV Part 1:** 92

"Force" (Di Piero), **Supp. XIX:** 35–36, 42, 44

Force of Desire, The (Bronk), **Supp. XXI:** 31, 32

Force of Evil (film, Polonsky), **Supp. XXI:** 261, 272, 275

Force of Spirit, The (Sanders), **Supp. XVI:** 277–278

Forché, Carolyn, **Supp. IV Part 1:** 208; **Supp. XIX:** 193

Ford, Arthur, **Supp. IV Part 1:** 140

Ford, Ford Madox, **I:** 288, 405, 409, 417, 421, 423; **II:** 58, 144, 198, 257, 263, 265, 517, 536; **III:** 458, 464–465, 470–471, 472, 476; **IV:** 27, 126, 261; **Retro. Supp. I:** 127, 177, 178, 186, 231, 286–287, 418; **Supp. II Part 1:** 107; **Supp. III Part 2:** 617; **Supp. VIII:** 107; **Supp. XIV:** 3

Ford, Harrison, **Supp. VIII:** 323

Ford, Harry, **Supp. V:** 179; **Supp. XIII:** 76

Ford, Henry, **I:** 295, 480–481; **III:** 292, 293; **Supp. I Part 1:** 21; **Supp. I Part 2:** 644; **Supp. III Part 2:** 612, 613; **Supp. IV Part 1:** 223; **Supp. V:** 290

Ford, John, **Supp. I Part 2:** 422; **Supp. III Part 2:** 619; **Supp. XVIII:** 247

Ford, Mark, **Supp. XXIII:** 220

Ford, Mary K., **Supp. XX:** 239

Ford, Richard, **Supp. IV Part 1:** 342; **Supp. V:** 22, **57–75; Supp. XXIV:** 97

Ford, Webster (pseudonym). *See* Masters, Edgar Lee

"Fording and Dread" (Harrison), **Supp. VIII:** 41

"Ford Madox Ford" (R. Lowell), **II:** 547; **Retro. Supp. II:** 188

"For Dudley" (Wilbur), **Supp. III Part 2:** 558

Fordyce, David, **II:** 113

For Eager Lovers (Taggard), **Supp. XXII:** 274–275

Foregone Conclusion, A (Howells), **II:** 278–279, 282

"Foreign Affairs" (Kunitz), **Supp. III Part 1:** 265

Foreign Correspondent (screenplay, Hecht), **Supp. XXVII:** 93

"Foreigner, A" (Bynner), **Supp. XV:** 46

"Foreigner, The" (Jewett), **II:** 409–410; **Retro. Supp. II:** 133, 142

"Foreigners" (Jarman), **Supp. XVII:** 113

"Foreign Language, The" (Franzen), **Supp. XX:** 84

"Foreign Shores" (Salter), **Supp. IX:** 260

Forensic and the Navigators (Shepard), **Supp. III Part 2:** 439

Forerunner, The (Boyce), **Supp. XXI:** 2, 4, **10–11**

Forerunner, The: His Parables and Poems (Gibran), **Supp. XX:** 115, 118–119, 119

Foreseeable Future, The (Price), **Supp. VI:** 265

Foreseeable Futures (Matthews), **Supp. IX:** 155, **163,** 169

Foresman, Rebecca, **Supp. XXIV:** 171

"For Esmé with Love and Squalor" (Salinger), **III:** 560

"Forest" (Simic), **Supp. VIII:** 273

Forest, Jean-Claude, **Supp. XI:** 307

Forester's Letters (Paine), **Supp. I Part 2:** 508

"Forest Hymn, A" (Bryant), **Supp. I Part 1:** 156, 162, 163, 164, 165, 170

"Forest in the Seeds, The" (Kingsolver), **Supp. VII:** 203

Forest of the South, The (Gordon), **II:** 197

"Forest of the South, The" (Gordon), **II:** 199, 201

Forest without Leaves (Adams and Haines), **Supp. XII:** 209

"Forever, Said the Duck" (Lethem), **Supp. XVIII:** 139

"Forever and the Earth" (Bradbury), **Supp. IV Part 1:** 102

"Forever in That Year" (Carruth), **Supp. XVI:** 51

"Forever"(Thompson), **Supp. XXIII:** 296

"Forever Young" (Jarman and R. McDowell), **Supp. XVII:** 111

"For Fathers of Girls" (Dunn), **Supp. XI:** 146

For Frank O'Hara's Birthday (Notley), **Supp. XXII:** 224, 227

"For/From Lew" (Snyder), **Supp. VIII:** 303

"For Garrison Keillor, Fantasy Is a Lot More Fun then Reality" (Letofsky), **Supp. XVI:** 167

"For George Santayana" (R. Lowell), **II:** 547

"Forgetfulness" (Collins), **Supp. XXI:** 58

"Forgiveness" (Peacock), **Supp. XIX:** 200

Forgotten Helper, The: A Story for Children (Moore), **Supp. X:** 175

"Forgotten in an Old Notebook" (F. Wright), **Supp. XVII:** 244

Forgotten Village, The (Steinbeck), **IV:** 51

"For Grace, After a party"(O'Hara), **Supp. XXIII:** 214

"For Grizzel McNaught (1709–1792)" (A. Finch), **Supp. XVII:** 72

Forgue, Guy J., **III:** 118, 119

For Her Dark Skin (Everett), **Supp. XVIII:** 56, 60

"FOR HETTIE" (Baraka), **Supp. II Part 1:** 32

"FOR HETTIE IN HER FIFTH MONTH" (Baraka), **Supp. II Part 1:** 32, 38

"For Homer" (Corso), **Supp. XII:** 135

"For I'm the Boy" (Barthelme), **Supp. IV Part 1:** 47

"For James Dean"(O'Hara), **Supp. XXIII:** 214

"For Janice and Kenneth to Voyage"(O'Hara), **Supp. XXIII:** 214

"For Jeff" (Kooser), **Supp. XIX:** 125

"For Jessica, My Daughter" (Strand), **Supp. IV Part 2:** 629

"For John, Who Begs Me not to Enquire Further" (Sexton), **Supp. II Part 2:** 676

"For Johnny Pole on the Forgotten Beach" (Sexton), **Supp. II Part 2:** 675

"For Joy to Leave Upon" (Ortiz), **Supp. IV Part 2:** 508

"For Judy, Whose Husband Is Undergoing Surgery"(Crooker), **Supp. XXIII:** 61

"Fork" (Simic), **Supp. VIII:** 275

"For Karl Shapiro, Having Gone Back to the Sonnet" (Kooser), **Supp. XIX:** 118

"Forked Tongue" (Davison), **Supp. XXVI:** 71

"Forky" (Dubus III), **Supp. XXIV:** 99, 101

"For Lack of a Treaty" (Davison), **Supp. XXVI:** 79

For Lancelot Andrewes (Eliot), **Retro. Supp. I:** 64

For Lizzie and Harriet (R. Lowell), **Retro. Supp. II:** 183, 186, 190

"Forlorn Hope of Sidney Lanier, The" (Leary), **Supp. I Part 1:** 373

For Love (Creeley), **Supp. IV Part 1:** 139, 140, 142–145, 147–149, 150, 154

"For Love" (Creeley), **Supp. IV Part 1:** 145

For Love (Miller), **Supp. XII:** 297–299, 299

For Love of Imabelle (C. Himes), **Supp. XVI:** 135, 143, 144

Form, Cycle, Infinity: Landscape Imagery in the Poetry of Robert Frost and George Seferis (Hadas), **Supp. XXIII:** 121–122

"Formal Elegy" (Berryman), **I:** 170

Formal Feeling Comes, A (A. Finch, ed.), **Supp. XVII:** 71–72

"Formalist Criticism: Its Principles and Limits" (Burke), **I:** 282

Forman, Henry James, **Supp. XXIV:** 29, 30

Forman, Milos, **Supp. IV Part 1:** 236

"Form and Function of the Novel, The" (Goldbarth), **Supp. XII:** 183

"For Marse Chouchoute" (Chopin), **Retro. Supp. II:** 60

"For Mary Ann Youngren" (Bidart), **Supp. XV:** 29

"Format and Form" (A. Rich), **Supp. XVII:** 74

"Formation of a Separatist, I" (Howe), **Supp. IV Part 2:** 427

"Form Is Emptiness" (Baraka), **Supp. II Part 1:** 51

"For Mr. Death Who Stands with His Door Open" (Sexton), **Supp. II Part 2:** 695

Forms of Discovery (Winters), **Supp. II Part 2:** 812, 813

Forms of Fiction, The (Gardner and Dunlap), **Supp. VI:** 64

"Forms of Love, The" (Oppen), **Supp. XXVI:** 225

"For My Children" (Karr), **Supp. XI:** 254

"For My Daughter" (Kees), **Supp. XV:** 141, 147

"For My Daughter" (Olds), **Supp. X:** 206

"For My Former Wife, Watching TV, in the Past" (Kooser), **Supp. XIX:** 120

"For My Lover, Returning to His Wife" (Sexton), **Supp. II Part 2:** 688

Fornés, Maria Irene, **Supp. XXI:** 144; **Supp. XXIII:** 194, 200

"For Night to Come" (Stern), **Supp. IX:** 292

"For Once, Then, Something" (Frost), **II:** 156–157; **Retro. Supp. I:** 126, 133, 134

"For Peg: A Remnant of Song Still Distantly Sounding" (Carruth), **Supp. XVI:** 54

"For Pot-Boiling" (Hay), **Supp. XIV:** 128

"For Radicals" (Bourne), **I:** 221

"For Rainer Gerhardt" (Creeley), **Supp. IV Part 1:** 142–143, 147

Forrestal, James, **I:** 491; **Supp. I Part 2:** 489

Forrester, Fanny, **Supp. XVIII:** 13

Forrey, Carolyn, **Supp. XXIV:** 30

"For Richard After All" (Kingsolver), **Supp. VII:** 208

"For Sacco and Vanzetti" (Kingsolver), **Supp. VII:** 208

"Forsaken Brother, The"(J. Schoolcraft), **Supp. XXIII:** 235

"Forsaken Merman" (Arnold), **Supp. I Part 2:** 529

"Forsaking the Promised Land" (diss. Collins), **Supp. XXVI:** 12

"For S.F.S. 1875–1962" (J. W. Miller), **Supp. XX:** 166

For Spacious Skies (Buck), **Supp. II Part 1:** 131

Forster, E. M., **I:** 292; **IV:** 201; **Retro. Supp. I:** 59, 232; **Supp. III Part 2:** 503; **Supp. IX:** 128; **Supp. V:** 258; **Supp. VIII:** 155, 171; **Supp. XII:** 79, 81; **Supp. XIV:** 159, 160, 163; **Supp. XV:** 62; **Supp. XVI:** 236; **Supp. XVIII:** 143; **Supp. XX:** 229, 235, 239, 240; **Supp. XXI:** 233

Forster, John, **II:** 315

Fort, Paul, **II:** 518, 528, 529; **Retro. Supp. I:** 55

"For the Ahkoond" (Bierce), **I:** 209

For the Body (Nelson), **Supp. VIII:** 173

For the Century's End: Poems 1990–1999 (Haines), **Supp. XII:** 211–213

"For the Chinese New Year and Bill Berkson"(O'Hara), **Supp. XXIII:** 218

"For the Dedication of the New City Library, Boston" (Holmes), **Supp. I Part 1:** 308

"For the Fallen" (Levine), **Supp. V:** 188

For the Health of the Land: Previously Unpublished Essays and Other Writings (Leopold), **Supp. XIV:** 183

"For the Lady in the Black Raincoat Who Slept Through an Entire Poetry Reading" (Espaillat), **Supp. XXI:** 108

"For the Last Wolverine" (Dickey), **Supp. IV Part 1:** 182

"For the Losers of Things" (Stallings), **Supp. XXV:** 222

"For the Lovers of the Absolute" (Simic), **Supp. VIII:** 278–279

"For the Man Cutting the Grass" (Oliver), **Supp. VII:** 235

"For the Marriage of Faustus and Helen" (H. Crane), **I:** 395–396, 399, 402; **Retro. Supp. II:** 78–79, 82

"For the Meeting of the National Sanitary Association, 1860" (Holmes), **Supp. I Part 1:** 307

For the New Intellectual (Rand), **Supp. IV Part 2:** 521, 526–527, 527, 532

"For the New Railway Station in Rome" (Wilbur), **Supp. III Part 2:** 554

"For the Night" (Kenyon), **Supp. VII:** 163

"For Theodore Roethke: 1908–1963" (R. Lowell), **II:** 554

"For the Poem *Patterson*" (W. C. Williams), **Retro. Supp. I:** 424

"For the Poets of Chile" (Levine), **Supp. V:** 188

"FOR THE REVOLUTIONARY OUTBURST BY BLACK PEOPLE" (Baraka), **Supp. II Part 1:** 55

"For the Sleepless" (Dunn), **Supp. XI:** 145

For the Time Being (Auden), **Supp. II Part 1:** 2, 17, 18

For the Time Being (Dillard), **Supp. VI:** 23, 27, 29, 32, **34–35**

"For the Twentieth Century" (Bidart), **Supp. XV:** 35

For the Union Dead (R. Lowell), **II:** 543, 550–551, 554, 555; **Retro. Supp. II:** 181, 182, 186, 189; **Supp. X:** 53

"For the Union Dead" (R. Lowell), **II:** 551; **Retro. Supp. II:** 189

"For the Walking Dead" (Komunyakaa), **Supp. XIII:** 121

"For the West" (Snyder), **Supp. VIII:** 299

"For the Word Is Flesh" (Kunitz), **Supp. III Part 1:** 262–264

"Fortress, The" (Glück), **Supp. V:** 82

"Fortress, The" (Sexton), **Supp. II Part 2:** 682

Fortress of Solitude, The (Lethem), **Supp. XVIII:** 135, 136, **145–148,** 150

"Fort Robinson" (Kooser), **Supp. XIX:** 120

"Fortunate Traveler" (Hull), **Supp. XXI:** 140

Fortune, T. Thomas, **Supp. II Part 1:** 159

Fortune's Bones: The Manumission Requiem (Nelson), **Supp. XVIII:** 171, 172–173, 182–183

Fortune's Daughter (Hoffman), **Supp. X:** 77, 85

"Fortune Spill, The" (Nelson), **Supp. XVIII:** 175

45 Mercy Street (Sexton), **Supp. II Part 2:** 694, 695, 697

Forty Poems Touching on Recent American History (Bly, ed.), **Supp. IV Part 1:** 61

42nd Parallel, The (Dos Passos), **I:** 482, 484–485

Forty Stories (Barthelme), **Supp. IV Part 1:** 47, 49, 53, 54

For Whom the Bell Tolls (Hemingway), **II:** 249, 254–255, 261; **III:** 18, 363; **Retro. Supp. I:** 115, 176–177, 178, **184,** 187; **Supp. XVII:** 229; **Supp. XXV:** 146

For Whom the Southern Belle Tolls (Durang), **Supp. XXIV:** 113, 118, 125

Foscolo, Ugo, **II:** 543

Foss, Sam Walter, **Supp. II Part 1:** 197

"Fossils, The" (Kinnell), **Supp. III Part 1:** 244

Foster, Edward, **Supp. IV Part 2:** 431, 434; **Supp. XVI:** 281, 293; **Supp. XXI:** 33

Foster, Edward Halsey, **Supp. XII:** 120, 129, 130, 135; **Supp. XVIII:** 265, 268

Foster, Emily, **II:** 309

Foster, Frances Smith, **Supp. XX: 287**

Foster, Hannah Webster, **Supp. XV:** 234; **Supp. XXV: 35–48**

Foster, John Wilson, **Supp. XIII:** 32–33

Foster, Michael K., **Supp. XXVI:** 83

Foster, Phil, **Supp. IV Part 2:** 574

Foster, Richard, **Supp. XV:** 269

Foster, Stephen, **Supp. I Part 1:** 100–101; **Supp. I Part 2:** 699

Foucault, Michel, **Supp. VIII:** 5; **Supp. XII:** 98; **Supp. XV:** 344; **Supp. XVI:** 285

Foulke, Robert, **Supp. XXV:** 217

"Founder, The" (Stern), **Supp. IX:** 297

Founding of Harvard College, The (Morison), **Supp. I Part 2:** 485

"Foundry Workers" (Bodenheim), **Supp. XXV:** 22

"Fountain, The" (Bryant), **Supp. I Part 1:** 157, 165, 166, 168

Fountain, The (O'Neill), **III:** 391

Fountain and Other Poems, The (Bryant), **Supp. I Part 1:** 157

Fountainhead, The (film), **Supp. IV Part 2:** 524

Fountainhead, The (Rand), **Supp. IV Part 2:** 517, 521–523, 525, 531; **Supp. XXIV:** 281

Fountainhead, The: A Fiftieth Anniversary Celebration (Cox), **Supp. IV Part 2:** 523

"Fountain Piece" (Swenson), **Supp. IV Part 2:** 641

4-H Club (Shepard), **Supp. III Part 2:** 439

"Four Ages of Man, The" (Bradstreet), **Supp. I Part 1:** 111, 115

Four American Indian Literary Masters (Velie), **Supp. IV Part 2:** 486

"Four Angers"(Hadas), **Supp. XXIII:** 115

"Four Beasts in One; the Homo Cameleopard" (Poe), **III:** 425

Four Black Revolutionary Plays (Baraka), **Supp. II Part 1:** 45; **Supp. VIII:** 330

"Four Brothers" (Di Piero), **Supp. XIX:** 37

"Four Brothers, The" (Sandburg), **III:** 585

"Four Dancers at an Irish Wedding" (Gallagher), **Supp. XXIV:** 168, 170

Four Days (screenplay, P. Benedict), **Supp. XXIII:** 35

Four Dogs and a Bone and the Wild Goose (Shanley), **Supp. XIV:** 316, **328–329**

"Four Evangelists, The" (Komunyakaa), **Supp. XIII:** 131

"Four for Sir John Davies" (Roethke), **III:** 540, 541

Four for Trane (Mackey), **Supp. XXVII:** 153

"Four Girls, The" (Alvarez), **Supp. VII:** 7

"Four Horse Songs" (Harjo), **Supp. XII:** 220

"400-Meter Free Style" (Kumin), **Supp. IV Part 2:** 442

"400-Pound CEO, The" (Saunders), **Supp. XIX:** 225

Fourier, Charles, **II:** 342

"Four in a Family" (Rukeyser), **Supp. VI:** 272

Four in Hand: A Quartet of Novels (Warner), **Supp. VIII:** 164

"Four Lakes' Days" (Eberhart), **I:** 525

"Four Mad Studies" (Di Piero), **Supp. XIX:** 37

"Four Meetings" (James), **II:** 327

Four Million, The (O. Henry), **Supp. II Part 1:** 394, 408

"Four Monarchyes" (Bradstreet), **Supp. I Part 1:** 105, 106, 116

"Four Mountain Wolves" (Silko), **Supp. IV Part 2:** 561

Four of a Kind (Marquand), **III:** 54, 55

"Four of the Horsemen (Hypertense and Stroke, Coronary Occlusion and Cerebral Insult)" (Karr), **Supp. XI:** 250

"Four Poems" (Bishop), **Supp. I Part 1:** 92

"Four Poems at the End of Summer"(Hadas), **Supp. XXIII:** 117

"Four Preludes on Playthings of the Wind" (Sandburg), **III:** 586

Four Quartets (T. S. Eliot), **I:** 570, 576, 580–582, 585, 587; **II:** 537; **III:** 539; **Retro. Supp. I:** 66, 67; **Supp. II Part 1:** 1; **Supp. IV Part 1:** 284; **Supp. V:** 343, 344; **Supp. VIII:** 182, 195; **Supp. XIII:** 344; **Supp. XIV:** 167; **Supp. XV:** 216, 260, 266

Four Saints in Three Acts (Stein), **IV:** 30, 31, 33, 43, 44–45

"Four Seasons" (Bradstreet), **Supp. I Part 1:** 112–113

Four Seasons of Success, The (Schulberg), **Supp. XVIII:** 254

"Four Sides of One Story" (Updike), **Retro. Supp. I:** 328

"Four Skinny Trees" (Cisneros), **Supp. VII:** 64

"14: In A Dark Wood: Wood Thrushes" (Oliver), **Supp. VII:** 244

"14 Men Stage Head Winter 1624/ 25" (Olson), **Supp. II Part 2:** 574

14 Stories (Dixon), **Supp. XII:** 141, **145–147**

Fourteen Hundred Thousand (Shepard), **Supp. III Part 2:** 439

Fourteen Sisters of Emilio Montez O'Brien, The (Hijuelos), **Supp. VIII: 82–85**

Fourteen Stories (Buck), **Supp. II Part 1:** 126

"Fourteenth Ward, The" (H. Miller), **III:** 175

Fourth Book of Peace, The (Kingston), **Supp. V:** 173

"Fourth Down" (Marquand), **III:** 56

Fourth Group of Verse, A (Reznikoff), **Supp. XIV:** 282, 284
"Fourth of July in Maine" (R. Lowell), **II:** 535, 552–553
Fourth Wall, The (Gurney), **Supp. V:** 109–110
Fowler, Douglas, **Supp. IV Part 1:** 226, 227
Fowler, Gene, **Supp. VIII:** 290
Fowler, Henry Watson, **Supp. I Part 2:** 660
Fowler, Karen Joy, **Supp. XXII:** 49
Fowler, Singrid, **Supp. VIII:** 249, 258
Fowler, Virginia C., **Supp. VIII:** 224
Fox, Alan, **Supp. XIII:** 120
Fox, Dixon Ryan, **I:** 337
Fox, Joe, **Supp. IX:** 259, 261
Fox, John, **Supp. XIII:** 166; **Supp. XXII:** 36
Fox, Linda C., **Supp. XIII:** 217–218
Fox, Paula, **Supp. XX:** 91
Fox, Ruth, **Supp. I Part 2:** 619
"Fox, The" (Levine), **Supp. V:** 181, 189
Fox-Genovese, Elizabeth, **Supp. IV Part 1:** 286; **Supp. XXII:** 190, 192, 200
Fox in Socks (Geisel), **Supp. XVI:** 108, 112
"Fox Night" (Jarman), **Supp. XVII:** 120
Fox of Peapack, The (White), **Supp. I Part 2:** 676, 677–678
"Fox of Peapack, The" (White), **Supp. I Part 2:** 677
"Fox Point Health Clinic, 1974" (Halliday), **Supp. XIX:** 89, 93
Fox's Earth (Siddons), **Supp. XXII:** 239
Foye, Raymond, **Supp. XIV:** 150
Fradkin, Lori, **Supp. XIX:** 52
Fraenkel, Michael, **III:** 178, 183
"Fragging" (Komunyakaa), **Supp. XIII:** 123
Fragile Beauty, A: John Nichols' Milagro Country: Text and Photographs from His Life and Work (Nichols), **Supp. XIII:** 268
"Fragility" (Shields), **Supp. VII:** 318
"Fragment" (A. Lowell), **II:** 516
"Fragment" (Ashbery), **Supp. III Part 1:** 11, 13, 14, 19, 20
"Fragment" (Ortiz), **Supp. IV Part 2:** 507
"Fragment of a Meditation" (Tate), **IV:** 129
"Fragment of an Agon" (Eliot), **I:** 579–580
"Fragment of a Prologue" (Eliot), **I:** 579–580
"Fragment of New York, 1929" (Eberhart), **I:** 536–537
"Fragments" (Emerson), **II:** 19
"Fragments for Fall" (Salinas), **Supp. XIII:** 320–321
"Fragments of a Hologram Rose" (W. Gibson), **Supp. XVI:** 122, 123, 128
"Fragments of a Liquidation" (Howe), **Supp. IV Part 2:** 426
"Fragments: On Dentistry" (Monson), **Supp. XXIV:** 236
Fragonard, Jean Honoré, **III:** 275; **IV:** 79
Fraiman, Susan, **Supp. IV Part 1:** 324
"Frame for Poetry, A" (W. J. Smith), **Supp. XIII:** 333

France, Anatole, **IV:** 444; **Supp. I Part 2:** 631; **Supp. XIV:** 79
France and England in North America (Parkman), **Supp. II Part 2:** 596, 600–605, 607, 613–614
Franchere, Hoyt C., **II:** 131
Franchiser, The (Elkin), **Supp. VI:** 51–52, 58
Francini, Antonella, **Supp. XXVI:** 169
Franciosi, Robert, **Supp. XIV:** 283
Francis, Lee, **Supp. IV Part 2:** 499
Francis, Richard, **Supp. XV:** 121
Francis, Robert, **Supp. IX:** 75–92
Francis of Assisi, Saint, **III:** 543; **IV:** 69, 375, 410; **Supp. I Part 2:** 394, 397, 441, 442, 443
Franco, Francisco, **II:** 261
Franco, Harry (pseudonym). *See* Briggs, Charles Frederick
Franconia (Fraser), **Retro. Supp. I:** 136
"Franconia" tales (Abbott), **Supp. I Part 1:** 38
Frank, Anne, **Supp. X:** 149; **Supp. XVII:** 39
Frank, Frederick S., **Retro. Supp. II:** 273
Frank, Harriet, Jr., **Supp. XXV:** 102
Frank, James M., **Supp. XIV:** 1
Frank, Jerome, **Supp. I Part 2:** 645
Frank, Joseph, **II:** 587
Frank, Mary, **Supp. X:** 213
Frank, Robert, **Supp. XI:** 295; **Supp. XII:** 127; **Supp. XIV:** 150
Frank, Sheldon, **Supp. XXII:** 210
Frank, Waldo, **I:** 106, 109, 117, 229, 236, 245, 259, 400; **Retro. Supp. II:** 77, 79, 83; **Supp. IX:** 308, 309, 311, 320; **Supp. XV:** 298; **Supp. XX:** 67–82
Frank, W. L., Jr., **Supp. XVIII:** 77
Frankel, Charles, **III:** 291
Frankel, Haskel, **Supp. I Part 2:** 448
Frankenberg, Lloyd, **I:** 436, 437, 445, 446; **III:** 194
Frankenheimer, John, **Supp. XI:** 343
Frankenstein (film), **Supp. IV Part 1:** 104; **Supp. XVII:** 57
Frankenstein (Gardner), **Supp. VI:** 72
Frankenstein (Shelley), **Supp. XII:** 79
Frankfurter, Felix, **I:** 489
"Frankie" (Keillor), **Supp. XVI:** 167
Frankie and Johnnie (Levin), **Supp. XXVII:** 134, 139
Frankie and Johnny (film), **Supp. XIII:** 206
Frankie and Johnny in the Clair de Lune (McNally), **Supp. XIII:** 200, 201
Franklin, Benjamin, **II:** 6, 8, 92, 101–125, 127, 295, 296, 302, 306; **III:** 74, 90; **IV:** 73, 193; **Supp. I Part 1:** 306; **Supp. I Part 2:** 411, 503, 504, 506, 507, 510, 516, 518, 522, 524, 579, 639; **Supp. VIII:** 202, 205; **Supp. XIII:** 150; **Supp. XIV:** 306; **Supp. XVIII:** 12; **Supp. XX:** 284; **Supp. XXIV:** 224; **Supp. XXVI:** 83, 84
Franklin, Cynthia, **Supp. IV Part 1:** 332
Franklin, Ruth, **Supp. XVI:** 160
Franklin, R. W., **Retro. Supp. I:** 29, 41, 43, 47
Franklin, Sarah, **II:** 122
Franklin, Temple, **II:** 122

Franklin, Walt, **Supp. XXIII:** 54
Franklin, Wayne, **Supp. XXII:** 205
Franklin, William, **II:** 122; **Supp. I Part 2:** 504
Franklin Evans (Whitman), **Retro. Supp. I:** 393
"Frank O'Connor and *The New Yorker*" (Maxwell), **Supp. VIII:** 172
Frank O'Hara: Poet Among Painters (Perloff), **Supp. XXIII:** 210
Franks, Lucinda, **Supp. XIII:** 12
"Frank Sinatra Has a Cold" (Talese), **Supp. XVII:** 203
"Frank Stanford of the Mulberry Family: An Arkansas Epilogue" (Wright), **Supp. XV:** 339–340
"Franny" (Salinger), **III:** 564, 565–566
Franny and Zooey (Salinger), **III:** 552, 564–567; **IV:** 216; **Supp. XIII:** 263
Franscell, Ron, **Supp. XXII:** 206, 216
Franzen, Jonathan, **Retro. Supp. II:** 279; **Supp. XIX:** 54; **Supp. XX:** 83–97; **Supp. XXII:** 255; **Supp. XXIV:** 131
Fraser, G. S., **Supp. XII:** 128; **Supp. XIV:** 162
Fraser, Joe, **III:** 46
Fraser, Marjorie Frost, **Retro. Supp. I:** 136
Frayn, Michael, **Supp. IV Part 2:** 582
Frazee, E. S., **Supp. I Part 2:** 381
Frazee, Esther Catherine. *See* Lindsay, Mrs. Vachel Thomas (Esther Catherine Frazee)
Frazer, Sir James G., **I:** 135; **II:** 204; **III:** 6–7; **IV:** 70; **Retro. Supp. I:** 80; **Supp. I Part 1:** 18; **Supp. I Part 2:** 541; **Supp. XX:** 117
Frazier, Ian, **Supp. VIII:** 272
Frazier, Kathleen, **Supp. XXI:** 22
"Freak Power in the Rockies" (Thompson), **Supp. XXIV:** 286–287, 292, 293
"Freak Show, The" (Sexton), **Supp. II Part 2:** 695
Freaks: Myths and Images of the Secret Self (Fiedler), **Supp. XIII:** 106, 107
Freckles (film), **Supp. XX:** 223
Freckles (Stratton-Porter), **Supp. XX:** 211, 218, 218–219, 222
Fred Allen Show, **Supp. XXV:** 254
Freddy and Fredericka (Helprin), **Supp. XXV:** 81, 84, 87–88
Freddy's Book (Gardner), **Supp. VI:** 72
Frederic, Harold, **I:** 409; **II:** 126–149, 175, 276, 289; **Retro. Supp. I:** 325; **Supp. XXIV:** 30
"Frederick Douglass" (Dunbar), **Supp. II Part 1:** 197, 199
"Frederick Douglass" (Hayden), **Supp. II Part 1:** 363
Frederick Douglass: Slave, Fighter, Freeman (Bontemps), **Supp. XXII:** 13
Frederick the Great, **II:** 103; **Supp. I Part 2:** 433
Fredrickson, George M., **Supp. I Part 2:** 589
"Free" (O'Hara), **III:** 369
Free, and Other Stories (Dreiser), **Retro. Supp. II:** 104
Free Agents (Apple), **Supp. XVII:** 5–6

Free Air (Lewis), **II:** 441

Freedman, David, **Supp. XXV:** 255

Freedman, Monroe H., **Supp. VIII:** 127

Freedman, Richard, **Supp. V:** 244

Freedom (Franzen), **Supp. XXII:** 255

"Freedom" (Larsen), **Supp. XVIII:** 124

"Freedom" (White), **Supp. I Part 2:** 659

"Freedom, New Hampshire" (Kinnell), **Supp. III Part 1:** 238, 239, 251

"Freedom and Discipline" (Carruth), **Supp. XVI:** 50

Freedom Business, The (Nelson), **Supp. XVIII: 186**

Freedom Is the Right to Choose: An Inquiry into the Battle for the American Future (MacLeish), **III:** 3

"Freedom's a Hard-Bought Thing" (Benét), **Supp. XI:** 47, 48

"Freedom's Plow" (Hughes), **Supp. I Part 1:** 346

Free Enterprise (Cliff), **Supp. XXII:** 66–67, **77–78**

"Free Everything" (July), **Supp. XXIV:** 210

"Free Fantasia: Tiger Flowers" (Hayden), **Supp. II Part 1:** 363, 366

Freeing of the Dust, The (Levertov), **Supp. III Part 1:** 281–282

"Free Lance, The" (Mencken), **III:** 104, 105

Free-Lance Pallbearers, The (Reed), **Supp. X:** 240, **242–243,** 244

Freeland (Lane), **Supp. XXII:** 297

Free Life, A (Jin), **Supp. XVIII: 101–102**

Freeloaders, The (Lacy), **Supp. XV:** 204

"Freely Espousing" (Schuyler), **Supp. XXVII:** 25

"Free Man" (Hughes), **Supp. I Part 1:** 333

Freeman, Chris, **Supp. XIV:** 157, 159

Freeman, Douglas Southall, **Supp. I Part 2:** 486, 493

Freeman, Jan, **Supp. XXVII:** 257, 262

Freeman, Jesse, **Supp. XXVI:** 11

Freeman, John, **Supp. XVIII:** 90

Freeman, Joseph, **II:** 26; **Supp. I Part 2:** 610; **Supp. XXII:** 274, 277

Freeman, Mary E. Wilkins, **II:** 401; **Retro. Supp. II:** 51, 136, 138; **Supp. IX:** 79

Freeman, Morgan, **Supp. XII:** 317

Freeman, Suzanne, **Supp. X:** 83

Free Man, The (Richter), **Supp. XVIII:** 215

"Free Man's Worship, A" (Russell), **Supp. I Part 2:** 522

Freewheelin' Bob Dylan, The (album, Dylan), **Supp. XVIII:** 20, 24, 29

Free Will & Wanton Lust (Silver), **Supp. XXIV:** 265, **267–268,** 270

Freier, Mary, **Supp. XXV:** 197

Freilicher, Jane, **Supp. XV:** 178; **Supp. XXIII:** 209, 210, 212, 217

Freinman, Dorothy, **Supp. IX:** 94

Frémont, John Charles, **Supp. I Part 2:** 486

Fremont-Smith, Eliot, **Supp. XIII:** 263

Fremstad, Olive, **I:** 319; **Retro. Supp. I:** 10

French, Warren, **Supp. XII:** 118–119

French Chef, The (television program), **Supp. XVII:** 89

French Connection, The (film), **Supp. V:** 226

"French Informal Report, The"(Kenny), **Supp. XXIII:** 152

French Leave (X. J. Kennedy), **Supp. XV:** 165

Frenchman Must Die, A (Boyle), **Supp. XXIV:** 62

French Poets and Novelists (James), **II:** 336; **Retro. Supp. I:** 220

"French Scarecrow, The" (Maxwell), **Supp. VIII:** 169, 170

French Ways and Their Meaning (Wharton), **IV:** 319; **Retro. Supp. I:** 378

Freneau, Eleanor Forman (Mrs. Philip Freneau), **Supp. II Part 1:** 266

Freneau, Philip M., **I:** 335; **II:** 295; **Supp. I Part 1:** 124, 125, 127, 145; **Supp. II Part 1:** 65, **253–277**

Frenzy (Everett), **Supp. XVIII: 59–60**

Frescoes for Mr. Rockefeller's City (MacLeish), **III:** 14–15

"Fresh Air" (Koch), **Supp. XV:** 181, 185

Fresh Air Fiend: Travel Writings, 1985–2000 (Theroux), **Supp. VIII:** 325

Fresh Brats (X. J. Kennedy), **Supp. XV:** 163

"Freshman" (Sanders), **Supp. XVI:** 277

Freud, Sigmund, **I:** 55, 58, 59, 66, 67, 135, 241, 242, 244, 247, 248, 283; **II:** 27, 370, 546–547; **III:** 134, 390, 400, 418, 488; **IV:** 7, 70, 138, 295; **Retro. Supp. I:** 80, 176, 253; **Retro. Supp. II:** 104; **Supp. I Part 1:** 13, 43, 253, 254, 259, 260, 265, 270, 315; **Supp. I Part 2:** 493, 527, 616, 643, 647, 649; **Supp. IV Part 2:** 450; **Supp. IX:** 102, 155, 161, 308; **Supp. VIII:** 103, 196; **Supp. X:** 193, 194; **Supp. XII:** 14–15; **Supp. XIII:** 75; **Supp. XIV:** 83; **Supp. XV:** 219; **Supp. XVI:** 157–158, 161, 292; **Supp. XXII:** 165, 198

"Freud and Literature" (Trilling), **Supp. III Part 2:** 502–503

Freudenberger, Nell, **Supp. XXV:** 149

Freudian Psychology and Veblen's Social Theory, The (Schneider), **Supp. I Part 2:** 650

Freudian Wish and Its Place in Ethics, The (Holt), **I:** 59

"Freud's Room" (Ozick), **Supp. V:** 268

Freud: The Mind of the Moralist (Sontag and Rieff), **Supp. III Part 2:** 455

"Freud: Within and Beyond Culture" (Trilling), **Supp. III Part 2:** 508

Frey, Charles, **Supp. XXII:** 301

Frey, Hillary, **Supp. XIX:** 55; **Supp. XXII:** 53

Frey, James, **Supp. XXII:** 95; **Supp. XXIII:** 109; **Supp. XXIV:** 230, 236

"Friday Morning Trial of Mrs. Solano, The" (Ríos), **Supp. IV Part 2:** 538, 548

Friebert, Stuart, **Supp. XIX:** 276

Frieburger, William, **Supp. XIII:** 239

Friede, Donald, **Supp. XVII:** 85, 86, 87, 90

Friedenberg, Edgar Z., **Supp. VIII:** 240

Friedman, Bruce Jay, **I:** 161; **Supp. IV Part 1:** 379

Friedman, Lawrence S., **Supp. V:** 273

Friedman, Milton, **Supp. I Part 2:** 648

Friedman, Norman, **I:** 431–432, 435, 439

Friedman, Stan, **Supp. XII:** 186

Friedmann, Georges, **Supp. I Part 2:** 645

"Fried Sausage" (Simic), **Supp. VIII:** 270

Friend, Julius, **Retro. Supp. I:** 80

Friend, The (Coleridge), **II:** 10

"Friend Husband's Latest" (Sayre), **Retro. Supp. I:** 104

"Friendly Debate between a Conformist and a Non-Conformist, A" (Wild), **IV:** 155

"Friendly Neighbor" (Keillor), **Supp. XVI:** 172

Friendly Way, The (Brainard), **Supp. XXVII:** 20

Friend of My Youth (Munro), **Supp. XXVII:** 190–191

"Friend of My Youth" (Munro), **Supp. XXVII:** 190

Friend of the Earth, A (Boyle), **Supp. VIII:** 12, 16; **Supp. XX: 29–30**

"Friend of the Fourth Decade, The" (Merrill), **Supp. III Part 1:** 327

"Friends" (Beattie), **Supp. V:** 23, 27

"Friends" (Paley), **Supp. VI:** 219, 226

"Friends" (Sexton), **Supp. II Part 2:** 693

Friend's Delight, The (Bierce), **I:** 195

"Friends from Philadelphia" (Updike), **Retro. Supp. I:** 319

"Friendship" (Emerson), **Supp. II Part 1:** 290; **Supp. XXV:** 250

Friends: More Will and Magna Stories (Dixon), **Supp. XII:** 148, 149

"Friends of Heraclitus, The" (Simic), **Supp. VIII:** 284

"Friends of Kafka, The" (Singer), **Retro. Supp. II:** 308

"Friends of the Family, The" (McCarthy), **II:** 566

"Friend to Alexander, A" (Thurber), **Supp. I Part 2:** 616

"Frigate Pelican, The" (Moore), **III:** 208, 210–211, 215

Frightened Wife, The (Rinehart), **Supp. XXV:** 198, 200

"Frill, The" (Buck), **Supp. XIV:** 274

"Fringe, The" (Bass), **Supp. XVI:** 19

Frings, Ketti, **Supp. XXV:** 95

Frobenius, Leo, **III:** 475; **Supp. III Part 2:** 620

Froebel, Friedrich, **Supp. XIV:** 52–53

Frog (Dixon), **Supp. XII:** 151

"Frog Dances" (Dixon), **Supp. XII:** 151

"Frog Pond, The" (Kinnell), **Supp. III Part 1:** 254

"Frogs" (Nelson), **Supp. XVIII:** 176

"Frog Takes a Swim" (Dixon), **Supp. XII:** 152

Frohock, W. M., **I:** 34, 42

Frolic of His Own, A (Gaddis), **Supp. IV Part 1:** 279, 291, 292–294; **Supp. XX: 91**

From a Broken Bottle Traces of Perfume Still Emanate (Mackey), **Supp. XXVII:** 151, 157–159

"From a Mournful Village" (Jewett), **Retro. Supp. II:** 146

"From an Alabama Farm" (Nelson), **Supp. XVIII:** 182

"From an Old House in America" (Rich), **Supp. I Part 2:** 551, 565–567

From Another World (Untermeyer), **Supp. XV:** 293, 303, 310–311, 313

"From a Phrase of Simone Weil's and Some Words of Hegel's" (Oppen), **Supp. XXVI:** 236

"From a Roadside Motel" (F. Wright), **Supp. XVII:** 245

"From a Survivor" (Rich), **Supp. I Part 2:** 563

From A to Z (musical review; Allen), **Supp. XV:** 3, 13

From a Work in Progress (Notley), **Supp. XXII:** 232

"From a Work in Progress" (Notley), **Supp. XXII:** 232

From a Writer's Notebook (Brooks), **I:** 254

From Bauhaus to Our House (Wolfe), **Supp. III Part 2:** 580, 581, 584

From Bondage (H. Roth), **Supp. IX:** 236, **238–240**

"From *Chants* to *Borders* to *Communion*" (Fox), *Supp. XIII:* 217, 217–218

"From Chicago" (Anderson), **I:** 108–109

From Colony to Nation: Women Activists and the Gendering of Politics in Belize, 1912–1982 (Macpherson), **Supp. XXIII:** 84

From Death to Morning (Wolfe), **IV:** 450, 456, 458

"From Dick to Lethem: The Dickian Legacy, Postmodernism, and Avant-Pop in Jonathan Lethem's *Amnesia Moon*" (Rossi), *Supp. XVIII:* 137, 138–139

"From Discord, a Wife Makes a Nice New Life—Too Nice" (Linfield), **Supp. XVII:** 177

From Down to the Village (Budbill), **Supp. XIX:** 6–7

"From Feathers to Iron" (Kunitz), **Supp. III Part 1:** 261

"From Fifth Avenue Up" (Barnes), **Supp. III Part 1:** 33, 44

"From Gorbunov and Gorchakov" (Brodsky), **Supp. VIII:** 26

"From Grand Canyon to Burbank" (H. Miller), **III:** 186

"From Hell to Breakfast", **Supp. IX:** 326–327

From Here to Eternity (film), **Supp. XI:** 221

From Here to Eternity (J. Jones), **I:** 477; **Supp. XI:** 215, 216, 217, 218, **219–221**, 223, 224, 226, 229, 230, 231, 232, 234; **Supp. XIX:** 248; **Supp. XX:** 248; **Supp. XXII:** 140

From Here to Eternity (miniseries), **Supp. XI:** 234

From Jordan's Delight (Blackmur), **Supp. II Part 1:** 91

"From Lumaghi Mine" (Wrigley), **Supp. XVIII:** 295

Fromm, Erich, **I:** 58; **Supp. VIII:** 196

From Morn to Midnight (Kaiser), **I:** 479

"From Native Son to Invisible Man" (Locke), **Supp. IX:** 306

"From Pico, the Women: A Life" (Creeley), **Supp. IV Part 1:** 149

From Plotzk to Boston (Antin), **Supp. XX:** 2

From Ritual to Romance (Weston), **II:** 540; **III:** 12; **Supp. I Part 2:** 439

From Room to Room (Kenyon), **Supp. VII:** 163–165, 166, 167

"From Room to Room" (Kenyon), **Supp. VII:** 159, 163–165

From Sand Creek: Rising in this Heart Which Is Our America (Ortiz), **Supp. IV Part 2:** 512–513

"From Sea Cliff, March" (Swenson), **Supp. IV Part 2:** 649

From Stone Orchard: A Collection of Memories (Findley), **Supp. XX:** 57

"From the Antigone" (Yeats), **III:** 459

From the Ashes: Voices of Watts (Schulberg, ed.), **Supp. XVIII:** 254

From the Barrio: A Chicano Anthology (Salinas and Faderman, eds.), **Supp. XIII:** 313

From the Beginning (Notley), **Supp. XXII:** 226, 235–236

From the Briarpatch File: On Context, Procedure, and American Identity (Murray), **Supp. XIX:** 161

"From the Childhood of Jesus" (Pinsky), **Supp. VI:** 244–245, 247

"From the Corpse Woodpiles, From the Ashes" (Hayden), **Supp. II Part 1:** 370

"From the Country to the City" (Bishop), **Supp. I Part 1:** 85, 86

"From the Cupola" (Merrill), **Supp. III Part 1:** 324–325, 331

"From the Dark Side of the Earth" (Oates), **Supp. II Part 2:** 510

"From the Diary of a New York Lady" (Parker), **Supp. IX:** 201

"From the Diary of One Not Born" (Singer), **IV:** 9

"From the Dreams" (Notley), **Supp. XXII:** 224

"From the East, Light" (Carver), **Supp. III Part 1:** 138

From the First Nine: Poems 1946–1976 (Merrill), **Supp. III Part 1:** 336

"From the Flats" (Lanier), **Supp. I Part 1:** 364

From the Flower Courtyard (Everwine), **Supp. XV:** 75

From the Heart of Europe (Matthiessen), **III:** 310

From the Meadow: Selected and New Poems (Everwine), **Supp. XV:** 75, **88–89**

"From the Memoirs of a Private Detective" (Hammett), **Supp. IV Part 1:** 343

"From the Nursery" (Kenyon), **Supp. VII:** 171

"From the Poets in the Kitchen" (Marshall), **Supp. XI:** 277

"From the Reservation to *Dawn of the Dead* to James Dickey and Back Again" (Gansworth), **Supp. XXVI:** 113

From the Terrace (O'Hara), **III:** 362

"From the Thirties: Tillie Olsen and the Radical Tradition" (Rosenfelt), **Supp. XIII:** 296, 304

From the Western Door to the Lower West Side (Gansworth and Rogovin), **Supp. XXVI:** 112

"From Trollope's Journal" (Bishop), **Retro. Supp. II:** 47

"Front, A" (Jarrell), **II:** 374

Front, The (film), **Supp. I Part 1:** 295

Frontain, Raymond-Jean, **Supp. XXVI:** 242

"Front and the Back Parts of the House, The" (Maxwell), **Supp. VIII:** 169

Frontier Eden (Bigelow), **Supp. X:** 227

"Frontiers of Culture" (Locke), **Supp. XIV:** 213

"Front Lines" (Snyder), **Supp. VIII:** 301

Front Page, The (Hecht and MacArthur), **Supp. XXVII:** 83, 89–90, 96

Front Porch (Inge), **Supp. XXV:** 94

Front Runner, The (P. N. Warren), **Supp. XX:** 259, 262–264

Frost, A. B., **Retro. Supp. II:** 72

Frost, Carol, **Supp. XV:** 91–109

Frost, Elisabeth, **Supp. XXVII:** 171

Frost, Isabelle Moodie, **II:** 150, 151

Frost, Jeanie, **II:** 151

Frost, Richard, **Supp. XV:** 92

Frost, Robert, **I:** 26, 27, 60, 63, 64, 171, 229, 303, 326, 418; **II:** 55, 58, **150–172**, 276, 289, 388, 391, 471, 523, 527, 529, 535; **III:** 5, 23, 67, 269, 271, 272, 275, 287, 453, 510, 523, 536, 575, 581, 591; **IV:** 140, 190, 415; **Retro. Supp. I:** 67, **121–144**, 276, 287, 292, 298, 299, 311, 413; **Retro. Supp. II:** 40, 47, 50, 146, 178, 181; **Supp. I Part 1:** 80, 242, 263, 264; **Supp. I Part 2:** 387, 461, 699; **Supp. II Part 1:** 4, 19, 26, 103; **Supp. III Part 1:** 63, 74–75, 239, 253; **Supp. III Part 2:** 546, 592, 593; **Supp. IV Part 1:** 15; **Supp. IV Part 2:** 439, 445, 447, 448, 599, 601; **Supp. IX:** 41, 42, 75, 76, 80, 87, 90, 266, 308; **Supp. VIII:** 20, 30, 32, 98, 100, 104, 259, 292; **Supp. X:** 64, 65, 66, 74, 120, 172; **Supp. XI:** 43, 123, 150, 153, 312; **Supp. XII:** 130, 241, 303, 307; **Supp. XIII:** 143, 147, 334–335; **Supp. XIV:** 42, 122, 222, 229; **Supp. XIX:** 1, 123; **Supp. XV:** 21, 51, 65, 96, 212, 215, 250, 256, 293, 296, 299, 301, 302, 306, 348; **Supp. XVII:** 36, 110, 115–116; **Supp. XVIII:** 298, 300; **Supp. XX: 69, 199; Supp. XXI:** 19, 28, 51, 99, 104, 107, 205; **Supp. XXII:** 206; **Supp. XXIII:** 79, 145; **Supp. XXIV:** 159; **Supp. XXV:** 222; **Supp. XXVI:** 61, 62, 63, 65, 67, 164; **Supp. XXVII:** 217, 218, 219, 283, 290

Frost, William Prescott, **II:** 150–151

"Frost: A Dissenting Opinion" (Cowley), **Supp. II Part 1:** 143

Frost: A Time to Talk (Francis), **Supp. IX:** 76, **85–86**

"Frost at Midnight" (Coleridge), **Supp. X:** 71

"Frost Flowers" (Kenyon), **Supp. VII:** 168

"Frost: He Is Sometimes a Poet and Sometimes a Stump-Speaker" (Newsweek), **Retro. Supp. I:** 137

Frothingham, Nathaniel, **I:** 3

Frothingham, Octavius B., **IV:** 173

"Frozen City, The" (Nemerov), **III:** 270

"Frozen Fields, The" (Bowles), **Supp. IV Part 1:** 80

"Frozen Ship, The" (Very), **Supp. XXV:** 243

Frucht, Abby, **Supp. XXVI:** 156

"Fructifying a Cycle: Homage to Alan Ansen"(Hadas), **Supp. XXIII:** 123

"Fruit Garden Path, The" (A. Lowell), **II:** 516

"Fruit of the Flower" (Cullen), **Supp. IV Part 1:** 167

Fruit of the Tree, The (Wharton), **IV:** 314–315; **Retro. Supp. I:** 367, **370–371,** 373

"Fruit of Travel Long Ago" (Melville), **III:** 93

Fruits and Vegetables (Jong), **Supp. V:** 113, 115, 117, 118, 119

"Fruits of the Sea, The" (Di Piero), **Supp. XIX:** 47

Frumkes, Lewis Burke, **Supp. XII:** 335–336

Fry, Christopher, **Supp. I Part 1:** 270

Fry, Roger, **Supp. XIV:** 336

Fry, Stephen M., **Supp. XIX:** 159

Frye, Joanne, **Supp. XIII:** 292, 296, 298, 302

Frye, Northrop, **Supp. I Part 2:** 530; **Supp. II Part 1:** 101; **Supp. X:** 80; **Supp. XIII:** 19; **Supp. XIV:** 11, 15; **Supp. XVI:** 149, 156; **Supp. XX:** 50; **Supp. XXIII:** 42

Fryer, Judith, **Retro. Supp. I:** 379

F. Scott Fitzgerald: A Critical Portrait (Piper), **Supp. IX:** 65

"F. S. F., 1896–1996, R.I.P." (Doctorow), **Retro. Supp. I:** 97

Fuchs, Daniel, **Supp. XIII:** 106; **Supp. XXVII:** 134

Fuchs, Miriam, **Supp. IV Part 1:** 284

Fuehrer Bunker, The (Snodgrass), **Supp. VI:** 314, 315–317, 319–321

Fuel (Nye), **Supp. XIII:** 277, **282–284**

"Fuel" (Nye), **Supp. XIII:** 283

Fuertes, Gloria, **Supp. V:** 178

Fugard, Athol, **Supp. VIII:** 330; **Supp. XIII:** 205

Fugitive Group, The (Cowan), **IV:** 120

Fugitive Kind, The (T. Williams), **IV:** 381, 383

Fugitives, The (group), **IV:** 122, 124, 125, 131, 237, 238

Fugitives, The: A Critical Account (Bradbury), **IV:** 130

"Fugitive Slave Law, The" (Emerson), **II:** 13

Fugitive's Return (Glaspell), **Supp. III Part 1:** 182–184

"Fulfillment" (H. Johnson), **Supp. XXVI:** 164, 173

Fuller, B. A. G., **III:** 605

Fuller, Edmund, **Supp. XXII:** 211, 212

Fuller, Hiram, **Supp. XVIII:** 12,14

Fuller, Jesse "Lonecat", **Supp. XV:** 147

Fuller, Margaret, **I:** 261; **II:** 7, 276; **IV:** 172; **Retro. Supp. I:** 155–156, 163; **Retro. Supp. II:** 46; **Supp. I Part 2:** 524; **Supp. II Part 1:** 279–306; **Supp. IX:** 37; **Supp. XVIII:** 3, 11, 12, 16; **Supp. XXV:** 249

Fuller, Thomas, **II:** 111, 112

Fullerton, Morton, **Supp. XX:** 231

Fullerton Street (Wilson), **Supp. VIII:** 331

"Full Fathom Five" (Plath), **Supp. I Part 2:** 538

Full Measure: Modern Short Stories on Aging (D. Sennett, ed.), **Supp. XVI:** 37

Full Monty, The (musical, McNally), **Supp. XIII:** 207

"Full Moon" (Hayden), **Supp. II Part 1:** 370

Full Moon and Other Plays (Price), **Supp. VI:** 266

"Full Moon and You're Not Here" (Cisneros), **Supp. VII:** 71–72

"Full Moon: New Guinea" (Shapiro), **Supp. II Part 2:** 707

"Fullness of Life, The" (Wharton), **Retro. Supp. I:** 363

Full of Life (Fante), **Supp. XI:** 160

Full of Life (film), **Supp. XI:** 170

Full of Lust and Good Usage (Dunn), **Supp. XI: 145–147**

Full Speed Ahead: Tales from the Log of a Correspondent with Our Navy (Beston), **Supp. XXVI:** 33

"Full Summer" (Olds), **Supp. X:** 212

Fulton, Ben, **Supp. XXII:** 207

Fulton, Robert, **Supp. I Part 2:** 519; **Supp. II Part 1:** 73

Fun and Games (Major), **Supp. XXII:** 180

Funaroff, Sol, **Supp. XXVI:** 143

"Functional Poem" (Halliday), **Supp. XIX:** 85

Function of Criticism, The (Winters), **Supp. II Part 2:** 812, 813

"Fundamentalism" (Tate), **IV:** 125

"Fundamental Project of Technology, The" (Kinnell), **Supp. III Part 1:** 253

"Funeral of Bobò, The" (Brodsky), **Supp. VIII:** 27, 28

Fungi from Yuggoth (Lovecraft), **Supp. XXV:** 119–120

Fun Home: A Family Tragicomic (Bechdel), **Supp. XXV:** 1, 4–9

Funiculi-Funicula (Wellman), **Supp. XXV:** 20

Funkhouser, Christopher, **Supp. XXVII:** 151

"Funnel" (Sexton), **Supp. II Part 2:** 675

Fun to Be Free (Hecht and MacArthur), **Supp. XXVII:** 90

"Furious Seasons, The" (Carver), **Supp. III Part 1:** 137

Furious Seasons and Other Stories (Carver), **Supp. III Part 1:** 142, 143, 146

"Furious Versions" (L.-Y. Lee), **Supp. XV: 215–217,** 218, 220

"Furnished Room, The" (Hayden), **Supp. II Part 1:** 386–387, 394, 397, 399, 406, 408

"Furor Scribendi" (O. Butler), **Supp. XIII:** 70

Furors Die (Hoffman), **Supp. XVIII: 80–81**

Fur Person, The (Sarton), **Supp. VIII: 264–265**

Further Adventures with You (Wright), **Supp. XV:** 339, 342, **343–345**

Further Fables for Our Time (Thurber), **Supp. I Part 2:** 612

"Further in Summer than the Birds" (Dickinson), **I:** 471

Further Poems of Emily Dickinson (Bianchi and Hampson, ed.), **Retro. Supp. I:** 35

Further Range, A (Frost), **II:** 155; **Retro. Supp. I:** 132, 136, 137, 138, 139

Furthman, Charles, **Supp. XXVII:** 92

"Fury, The (Skloot), **Supp. XX: 197**

"Fury of Aerial Bombardment, The" (Eberhart), **I:** 535–536

"Fury of Flowers and Worms, The" (Sexton), **Supp. II Part 2:** 694

"Fury of Rain Storms, The" (Sexton), **Supp. II Part 2:** 695

Fury of the Jungle (film), **Supp. XIII:** 163

Fussell, Paul, **Supp. V:** 241

Fussell, Paul K., **Supp. XXV:** 253

"Futility" (H. Johnson), **Supp. XXVI:** 167, 172

"Future, if Any, of Comedy, The" (Thurber), **Supp. I Part 2:** 620

Future, The (album, Cohen), **Supp. XXVII:** 54

"Future, The" (Cohen), **Supp. XXVII:** 62

Future, The (film, July), **Supp. XXIV:** 199, 200, 202, **209,** 210

Future in the Present, The (C. L. R. James), **Supp. XXI:** 172

Future is Ours, Comrade, The: Conversations with the Russians (Kosinski), **Supp. VII:** 215

Futureland: Nine Stories of an Imminent World (Mosley), **Supp. XIII: 247–249**

"Future Life, The" (Bryant), **Supp. I Part 1:** 170

Future of Southern Letters, The (J. W. Miller), **Supp. XX: 161**

Future of the Race, The (H. L. Gates), **Supp. XX: 101, 104, 111**

Future Punishment of the Wicked, The (Edwards), **I:** 546

G

"Gabriel" (Rich), **Supp. I Part 2:** 557

Gabriel, Ralph H., **Supp. I Part 1:** 251

Gabriel, Trip, **Supp. V:** 212

Gabriel Conroy (Harte), **Supp. II Part 1:** 354
"Gabriel's Truth" (Kenyon), **Supp. VII:** 166
Gaddis, William, **Supp. IV Part 1: 279–296; Supp. IV Part 2:** 484; **Supp. IX:** 208; **Supp. V:** 52; **Supp. X:** 301, 302; **Supp. XX: 83, 91; Supp. XXI:** 226; **Supp. XXIII:** 107
Gadiot, Pud, **Supp. XI:** 295
Gaily, Gaily (film), **Supp. XXVII:** 95
Gaily, Gaily (Hecht), **Supp. XXVII:** 95
Gain (Powers), **Supp. IX:** 212, **220–221**
Gaines, Ernest J., **Supp. X:** 24, 250
Gaines, James R., **Supp. IX:** 190
Gainor, J. Ellen, **Supp. XXI:** 6
Gaitens, Peter, **Supp. XV:** 65
Gajarsa, Arthur, **Supp. XXVI:** 83
Galamain, Ivan, **Supp. III Part 2:** 624
Galassi, Jonathan, **Supp. XIX:** 34; **Supp. XVIII:** 92; **Supp. XXII:** 177
Galatea 2.2 (Powers), **Supp. IX:** 212, **219–220**
"Galatea Encore" (Brodsky), **Supp. VIII:** 31
Galbraith, John Kenneth, **Supp. I Part 2:** 645, 650
Galdós, Benito Pérez. *See* Pérez Galdós, Benito
Gale, Zona, **Supp. I Part 2:** 613; **Supp. VIII:** 155
Galehouse, Maggie, **Supp. XXI:** 215
"Gale in April" (Jeffers), **Supp. II Part 2:** 423
Galignani, Giovanni Antonio, **II:** 315
Galileo Galilei, **I:** 480–481; **Supp. XII:** 180; **Supp. XIII:** 75
Gallagher, Tess, **Supp. XVI:** 36; **Supp. XVII:** 110; **Supp. XXI:** 246; **Supp. XXIV: 165–181**
Gallant, Mavis, **Supp. VIII:** 151
Gallatin, Albert, **I:** 5
"Gallery" (Goldbarth), **Supp. XII:** 188
"Gallery of Real Creatures, A" (Thurber), **Supp. I Part 2:** 619
Gallico, Paul, **Supp. XVI:** 238
Gallows Songs (Snodgrass), **Supp. VI:** 317
Gallup, Dick, **Supp. XXIV:** 34, 35, 39, 44; **Supp. XXVII:** 18, 22, 23
Gallup, Donald, **III:** 404, 478
"Galop" (Davison), **Supp. XXVI:** 71
Galsworthy, John, **III:** 70, 153, 382
Galton Case, The (Macdonald), **Supp. IV Part 2:** 463, 473, 474
Galvin, Frances, **Supp. XXI:** 5
"Gal Young 'Un" (Rawlings), **Supp. X:** 228
Gambino, Richard, **Supp. XX: 35**
"Gambler, the Nun, and the Radio, The" (Hemingway), **II:** 250
"Gambler's Wife, The" (Dunbar), **Supp. II Part 1:** 196
Gambone, Philip, **Supp. XII:** 81
"Gambrel Roof, A" (Larcom), **Supp. XIII:** 144
"Game at Salzburg, A" (Jarrell), **II:** 384, 389
Game Management (Leopold), **Supp. XIV:** 182

"Game of Catch, A" (Wilbur), **Supp. III Part 2:** 552
Game Players of Titan, The (Dick), **Supp. XVIII:** 138
"Games in Frank Conroy's *Stop-Time*" (T. Adams), **Supp. XVI:** 67
"Games Two" (Wilbur), **Supp. III Part 2:** 550
Gammelgaard, Lene, **Supp. XVIII:** 112
"Gamut, The" (Angelou), **Supp. IV Part 1:** 15
Gander, Forrest, **Supp. XV:** 339, 340, 342
Gandhi, Indira, **Supp. X:** 108
Gandhi, Mahatma, **III:** 179, 296–297; **IV:** 170, 185, 367; **Supp. VIII:** 203, 204; **Supp. X:** 27
Gandhi on Non-Violence (Merton, ed.), **Supp. VIII:** 204–205
Gangemi, Merry, **Supp. XXV:** 6
Gang of Five: Leaders at the Center of the Conservative Crusade (Easton), **Supp. XIX:** 137
"Gang of Mirrors, The" (Simic), **Supp. VIII:** 283
Gannett, Ezra Stiles, **Supp. XXIV:** 74
Gansevoort, Guert, **III:** 94
Gansevoort, Peter, **III:** 92
Gansworth, Eric, **Supp. XXVI: 101–116**
"Gap" (Bierds), **Supp. XVII:** 35–36
Garabedian, Michael, **Supp. XIII:** 115
Garbage (Ammons), **Supp. VII:** 24, 35–36
Garbage (Dixon), **Supp. XII:** 147, 148
Garbage Man, The (Dos Passos), **I:** 478, 479, 481, 493
Garber, Frederick, **Supp. IX:** 294–295
Garbo, Greta, **Supp. I Part 2:** 616
García, Cristina, **Supp. VIII:** 74; **Supp. XI: 177–192**
García Lorca, Federico. *See* Lorca, Federico García
"García Lorca: A Photograph of the Granada Cemetery, 1966" (Levis), **Supp. XI:** 264
García Márquez, Gabriel, **Supp. V:** 244; **Supp. VIII:** 81, 82, 84, 85; **Supp. XII:** 147, 310, 316, 322; **Supp. XIII:** 226; **Supp. XVII:** 45; **Supp. XXIV:** 86, 89, 190; **Supp. XXV:** 49, 69
Gard, Claire, **Supp. XXIII:** 94
Gardaphe, Fred, **Supp. XX: 38, 41**
"Garden" (Marvell), **IV:** 161; **Supp. XVI:** 204
"Garden, The" (Glück), **Supp. V:** 83
"Garden, The" (Strand), **Supp. IV Part 2:** 629
"Garden, The" (Very), **Supp. XXV:** 248
"Garden Among Tombs" (B. Kelly), **Supp. XVII:** 126
"Garden by Moonlight, The" (A. Lowell), **II:** 524
"Gardener Delivers a Fawn, The" (C. Frost), **Supp. XV:** 99
Gardener's Son, The (McCarthy), **Supp. VIII:** 187
Garden God, The: A Tale of Two Boys (Reid), **Supp. XX: 235**
"Gardenias" (Doty), **Supp. XI:** 122
"Gardenias" (Monette), **Supp. X:** 159

"Garden Lodge, The" (Cather), **I:** 316, 317
Garden of Adonis, The (Gordon), **II:** 196, 204–205, 209
Garden of Earthly Delights, A (Oates), **Supp. II Part 2:** 504, 507–509
Garden of Earthly Delights, The (Bosch), **Supp. XXII:** 255, 261
"Garden of Eden" (Hemingway), **II:** 259
Garden of Eden, The (Hemingway), **Retro. Supp. I:** 186, **187–188**
"Garden of Flesh, Garden of Stone" (B. Kelly), **Supp. XVII:** 128
Garden of Last Days, The (Dubus III), **Supp. XXIV:** 101, **107–108**
"Garden of the Moon, The" (Doty), **Supp. XI:** 122
Garden of the Prophet, The (Gibran), **Supp. XX: 119, 122**
"Garden of the Trumpet Tree, The" (B. Kelly), **Supp. XVII:** 131
"Gardens, The" (Oliver), **Supp. VII:** 236
"Gardens of Mont-Saint-Michel, The" (Maxwell), **Supp. VIII:** 169
"Gardens of the Villa D'Este, The" (Hecht), **Supp. X:** 59
"Gardens of Zuñi, The" (Merwin), **Supp. III Part 1:** 351
Garden Thieves, The: Twentieth Century African-American Poetry (Major, ed.), **Supp. XXII:** 172
Gardiner, Judith Kegan, **Supp. IV Part 1:** 205
Gardner, Erle Stanley, **Supp. IV Part 1:** 121, 345
Gardner, Isabella, **IV:** 127
Gardner, John, **Supp. I Part 1:** 193, 195, 196; **Supp. III Part 1:** 136, 142, 146; **Supp. VI: 61–76; Supp. XXV:** 152
Gardner, Thomas, **Supp. XXI:** 214
Gardons, S. S. *See* Snodgrass, W. D.
"Gare de Lyon" (M. F. K. Fisher), **Supp. XVII:** 91
Garfield, John, **Supp. XII:** 160
Gargoyles (Hecht), **Supp. XXVII:** 88
Garibaldi, Giuseppe, **I:** 4; **II:** 284
Garibay, Angel M., **Supp. XV:** 77
Garland, Hamlin, **I:** 407; **II:** 276, 289; **III:** 576; **Retro. Supp. I:** 133; **Retro. Supp. II:** 72; **Supp. I Part 1:** 217; **Supp. IV Part 2:** 502; **Supp. XVIII:** 6
Garland Companion, The (Zverev), **Retro. Supp. I:** 278
"Garments" (Gibran), **Supp. XX: 124**
Garments the Living Wear (Purdy), **Supp. VII:** 278–279, 280–281
Garner, Dwight, **Supp. X:** 202; **Supp. XVIII:** 89; **Supp. XXV:** 9
Garnett, Edward, **I:** 405, 409, 417; **III:** 27
Garrett, George P., **Supp. I Part 1:** 196; **Supp. VII: 95–113; Supp. X:** 3, 7; **Supp. XI:** 218; **Supp. XVIII:** 74, 75; **Supp. XXVI:** 153, 157
Garrigue, Jean, **Supp. XII:** 260
Garrison, Deborah, **Supp. IX:** 299
Garrison, Fielding, **III:** 105
Garrison, William Lloyd, **Supp. I Part 2:** 524, 588, 683, 685, 686, 687; **Supp.**

XIV: 54; **Supp. XXIV:** 77
"Garrison of Cape Ann, The" (Whittier), **Supp. I Part 2:** 691, 694
Garry Moore Show (television show), **Supp. IV Part 2:** 575
"Garter Motif" (White), **Supp. I Part 2:** 673
Gartner, Zsuzsi, **Supp. X:** 276
Garvey, Marcus, **Supp. III Part 1:** 175, 180; **Supp. IV Part 1:** 168; **Supp. X:** 135, 136; **Supp. XXI:** 166, 168; **Supp. XXII:** 7
Garvin, Viola, **Supp. XXVII:** 118
Gas (Kaiser), **I:** 479
Gas-House McGinty (Farrell), **II:** 41–42
Gaskell, Elizabeth, A., **Supp. I Part 2:** 580
Gasoline (Corso), **Supp. XII:** 118, **121–123,** 134
Gasoline Wars, The (Thompson), **Supp. XXIII:** 290
"Gasoline Wars, The"(Thompson), **Supp. XXIII:** 291
Gass, William H., **Supp. IX:** 208; **Supp. V:** 44, 52, 238; **Supp. VI: 77–96;** **Supp. XII:** 152; **Supp. XIV:** 305; **Supp. XVII:** 183
"Gassire's Lute: Robert Duncan's Vietnam War Poems" (Mackey), **Supp. XXVII:** 160
Gassner, John, **IV:** 381; **Supp. I Part 1:** 284, 292
"Gas Stations" (Apple), **Supp. XVII:** 4
Gastronomical Me, The (M. F. K. Fisher), **Supp. XVII:** 84, 85, 87, 91, 92
Gates, David, **Supp. V:** 24; **Supp. XIII:** 93; **Supp. XVI:** 73, 74; **Supp. XX:** 92
Gates, Elmer, **I:** 515–516
Gates, Henry Louis, Jr., **Retro. Supp. I:** 194, 195, 203; **Supp. X:** 242, 243, 245, 247; **Supp. XIX:** 147, 149; **Supp. XVIII:** 287; **Supp. XX: 99–112, 279, 286; Supp. XXIV:** 192; **Supp. XXVI:** 13
Gates, Lewis E., **III:** 315, 330
Gates, Sondra Smith, **Supp. XVIII:** 267, 269
Gates, The (Rukeyser), **Supp. VI:** 271, 274, 281
"Gates, The" (Rukeyser), **Supp. VI:** 286
Gates, Tudor, **Supp. XI:** 307
Gates of Ivory, the Gates of Horn, The (McGrath), **Supp. X:** 118
Gates of Wrath, The; Rhymed Poems (Ginsberg), **Supp. II Part 1:** 311, 319
"Gathering" (Trethewey), **Supp. XXI:** 249
Gathering Forces, The (C. L. R. James), **Supp. XXI:** 171
"Gathering of Dissidents, A" (Applebaum), **Supp. XVI:** 153
Gathering of Fugitives, A (Trilling), **Supp. III Part 2:** 506, 512
Gathering of Zion, The: The Story of the Mormon Trail (Stegner), **Supp. IV Part 2:** 599, 602–603
Gather Together in My Name (Angelou), **Supp. IV Part 1:** 2, 3, 4–6, 11

Gathorne-Hardy, Robert, **Supp. XIV:** 344, 347, 348, 349
Gaudier-Brzeska, Henri, **III:** 459, 464, 465, 477
Gaughran, Richard, **Supp. XXI:** 47–48
Gauguin, Paul, **I:** 34; **IV:** 290; **Supp. IV Part 1:** 81; **Supp. XII:** 128
"Gauguin in Oregon" (Skloot), **Supp. XX: 203**
"Gauley Bridge" (Rukeyser), **Supp. VI:** 278
Gauss, Christian, **II:** 82; **IV:** 427, 439–440, 444
Gauthier, Jacquie, **Supp. XIX:** 204
Gautier, Théophile, **II:** 543; **III:** 466, 467; **Supp. I Part 1:** 277
Gay, John, **II:** 111; **Supp. I Part 2:** 523; **Supp. XIV:** 337
Gay, Peter, **I:** 560
Gay, Sydney Howard, **Supp. I Part 1:** 158; **Supp. XVIII:** 3
Gay, Walter, **IV:** 317
Gayatri Prayer, The, **III:** 572
Gay Canon, The (Drake), **Supp. XX: 274**
"Gay Chaps at the Bar" (Brooks), **Supp. III Part 1:** 74, 75
" 'Gay Culture': Still of the Wild Frontier" (P. N. Warren), **Supp. XX: 272**
Gaylord, Winfield R., **III:** 579–580
Gay Talese Reader, The: Portraits & Encounters (Talese), **Supp. XVII:** 202, 208
"Gaze, The"(Hadas), **Supp. XXIII:** 120
"Gazebo" (Carver), **Supp. III Part 1:** 138, 144, 145
Gazer's Spirit, The (Hollander), **Supp. XIX:** 121
Gazer Within, The, and Other Essays by Larry Levis, **Supp. XI:** 270
Gazzara, Ben, **Supp. VIII:** 319
Gazzo, Michael V., **III:** 155
"Geas" (Monson), **Supp. XXIV:** 238–239
Geddes, Virgil, **Supp. XXV:** 23
"Geese Flying over Hamilton, New York"(Balakian), **Supp. XXIII:** 24
"Geese Gone Beyond" (Snyder), **Supp. VIII:** 304
Geffen, David, **Supp. XXI:** 154
"Gegenwart" (Goethe), **Supp. II Part 1:** 26
Geisel, Theodor Seuss (Dr. Seuss), **Supp. X:** 56; **Supp. XVI: 97–115**
Geismar, Maxwell, **II:** 178, 431; **III:** 71; **Supp. IX:** 15; **Supp. XI:** 223
Geist, Bill, **Supp. XXIII:** 298
Gelb, Arthur, **IV:** 380; **Supp. XXI:** 12
Gelb, Barbara, **Supp. XXI:** 12
Gelbart, Larry, **Supp. IV Part 2:** 591
Gelder, Robert Van, **Supp. XIII:** 166
Gelfant, Blanche H., **II:** 27, 41; **Supp. XVII:** 161
Gelfman, Jean, **Supp. X:** 3
Gellert, Hugo, **Supp. XXII:** 277
Gellhorn, Martha. *See* Hemingway, Mrs. Ernest (Martha Gellhorn)
Gelpi, Albert, **Supp. I Part 2:** 552, 554, 560
Gelpi, Barbara, **Supp. I Part 2:** 560
Gemin, Pamela, **Supp. XXI:** 246
Gemini (Innaurato), **Supp. XXIV:** 117

Gemini: an extended autobiographical statement on my first twenty-five years of being a black poet (Giovanni), **Supp. IV Part 1:** 11
"Gen" (Snyder), **Supp. VIII:** 302
"Gender Norms" (Radinovsky), **Supp. XV:** 285
"Gender of Sound, The" (Carson), **Supp. XII:** 106
"Genealogies"(Hadas), **Supp. XXIII:** 116
"Genealogy" (Komunyakaa), **Supp. XIII:** 129
"General Aims and Theories" (Crane), **I:** 389
General Died at Dawn, The (Odets), **Supp. II Part 2:** 546
"General Gage's Confession" (Freneau), **Supp. II Part 1:** 257
"General Gage's Soliloquy" (Freneau), **Supp. II Part 1:** 257
General History of the Robberies and Murders of the Most Notorious Pyrates from Their First Rise and Settlement in the Island of New Providence to the Present Year, A (C. Johnson), **Supp. V:** 128
General in His Labyrinth, The (García Márquez), **Supp. XXIV:** 89
"General Returns from One Place to Another, The"(O'Hara), **Supp. XXIII:** 216–217
"General William Booth Enters into Heaven" (Lindsay), **Supp. I Part 2:** 374, 382, 384, 385–388, 389, 392, 399
General William Booth Enters into Heaven and Other Poems (Lindsay), **Supp. I Part 2:** 379, 381, 382, 387–388, 391
"Generation of the Dispossessed" (P. N. Warren), **Supp. XX: 272**
"Generations"(Kenny), **Supp. XXIII:** 154
"Generations of Men, The" (Frost), **Retro. Supp. I:** 128; **Supp. XIII:** 147
Generation Without Farewell (Boyle), **Supp. XXIV:** 60, 62
"Generation Wuss" (Ellis), **Supp. XXVII:** 78, 79
Generous Man, A (Price), **Supp. VI:** 259, 260, 261
Genesis (biblical book), **I:** 279; **II:** 540; **Retro. Supp. I:** 250, 256; **Supp. XII:** 54
"Genesis" (Stegner), **Supp. IV Part 2:** 604
Genesis: Book One (Schwartz), **Supp. II Part 2:** 640, 651–655
Gene Stratton-Porter (Richards), **Supp. XX: 217–218**
Gene Stratton-Porter, Naturalist and Novelist (Long), **Supp. XX: 212**
"Gene Stratton-Porter: Women's Advocate" (Obuchowski), **Supp. XX: 222**
Genet, Jean, **I:** 71, 82, 83, 84; **Supp. IV Part 1:** 8; **Supp. XI:** 308; **Supp. XII:** 1; **Supp. XIII:** 74; **Supp. XVII:** 95; **Supp. XXIII:** 213; **Supp. XXIV:** 210
"Genetic Coding" (Sorrentino), **Supp. XXI:** 227
"Genetic Expedition" (Dove), **Supp. IV Part 1:** 249, 257

"Genetics of Justice" (Alvarez), **Supp. VII:** 19

"Genial Host, The" (McCarthy), **II:** 564

"Genie in the Bottle, The" (Davison), **Supp. XXVI:** 74

"Genie in the Bottle, The" (Wilbur), **Supp. III Part 2:** 542

"Genius, The" (MacLeish), **III:** 19

Genius and Lust: A Journey through the Major Writings of Henry Miller (Mailer), **Retro. Supp. II:** 208

"Genius Child" (Hughes), **Retro. Supp. I:** 203

"Genius of Bob Dylan, The" (Lethem), **Supp. XVIII:** 146

"Genius," The (Dreiser), **I:** 497, 501, 509–511, 519; **Retro. Supp. II:** 94–95, **102–103,** 104, 105

Genocide of the Mind: New Native America Writing (Moore, ed.), **Supp. XXVI:** 113

Genova, Lisa, **Supp. XXIII:** 127

"Genteel Tradition in American Philosophy, The" (Santayana), **I:** 222

Gent from Bear Creek, A (Howard), **Supp. XXVII:** 117, 126

"Gent from Bear Creek, A" (Howard), **Supp. XXVII:** 127

"Gentle Communion" (Mora), **Supp. XIII:** 218–219

Gentle Crafter, The (O. Henry), **Supp. II Part 1:** 410

Gentle Furniture-Shop, The (Bodenheim), **Supp. XXV:** 20

"Gentle Lena, The" (Stein), **IV:** 37, 40

Gentleman Caller, The (T. Williams), **IV:** 383

"Gentleman from Cracow, The" (Singer), **IV:** 9

"Gentleman of Bayou Têche, A" (Chopin), **Supp. I Part 1:** 211–212

"Gentleman of Shalott, The" (Bishop), **Supp. I Part 1:** 85, 86

Gentleman's Agreement (Hobson), **III:** 151

"Gentleman's Agreement" (Richard), **Supp. XIX:** 220–221

Gentlemen I Address You Privately (Boyle), **Supp. XXIV: 53–54**

Gentlemen Prefer Blondes (Loos; musical adaptation), **Supp. XVI:** 193

Gentlemen Prefer Blondes: The Illuminating Diary of a Professional Lady (Loos), **Supp. XVI:** 181, 183, 186, **188–189**

Gentlemen Prefer "Books" (J. Yeats), **Supp. XVI:** 190

Gentle People, The: A Brooklyn Fable (Shaw), **Supp. XIX:** 244–245, 249

Gentry, Marshall Bruce, **Supp. IV Part 1:** 236

"Genuine Man, The" (Emerson), **II:** 10

"Genus Narcissus" (Trethewey), **Supp. XXI:** 256

Geo-Bestiary (Harrison), **Supp. VIII:** 53

"Geode" (Frost), **II:** 161

Geographical History of America, The (Stein), **IV:** 31, 45; **Supp. XVIII:** 148

Geography and Plays (Stein), **IV:** 29–30, 32, 43, 44

Geography III (Bishop), **Retro. Supp. II:** 50; **Supp. I Part 1:** 72, 73, 76, 82, 93, 94, 95

Geography of a Horse Dreamer (Shepard), **Supp. III Part 2:** 432

Geography of Home, The: California's Poetry of Place (Bluckey and Young, eds.), **Supp. XIII:** 313

Geography of Lograire, The (Merton), **Supp. VIII:** 208

Geography of the Heart (F. Johnson), **Supp. XI:** 129

"Geometric Poem, The" (Corso), **Supp. XII:** 132, 133–134

George, Diana Hume, **Supp. IV Part 2:** 447, 449, 450

George, Henry, **II:** 276; **Supp. I Part 2:** 518

George, Jan, **Supp. IV Part 1:** 268

George, Lynell, **Supp. XIII:** 234–235, 237, 249

George, Peter, **Supp. XI:** 302, 303, 304

George and the Dragon (Shanley), **Supp. XIV:** 315

George Bernard Shaw: His Plays (Mencken), **III:** 102

George Mills (Elkin), **Supp. VI: 53–54**

George Oppen and the Fate of Modernism (Nicholls), **Supp. XXVI:** 228

George Palmer Putnam: Representative American Publisher (Greenspan), **Supp. XVIII:** 257

"George Robinson: Blues" (Rukeyser), **Supp. VI:** 279

George's Mother (Crane), **I:** 408

"George Thurston" (Bierce), **I:** 202

George Washington Crossing the Delaware (Koch), **Supp. XV:** 186

"George Washington"(Kenny), **Supp. XXIII:** 154

Georgia Boy (Caldwell), **I:** 288, 305–306, 308, 309, 310

"Georgia Dusk" (Toomer), **Supp. IX:** 309

"Georgia: Invisible Empire State" (Du Bois), **Supp. II Part 1:** 179

"Georgia Night" (Toomer), **Supp. III Part 2:** 481

Georgia Scenes (Longstreet), **II:** 70, 313; **Supp. I Part 1:** 352

Georgics (Virgil), **Retro. Supp. I:** 135; **Supp. XVI:** 22; **Supp. XXIV:** 153

Georgics of Virgil, The (Ferry, trans.), **Supp. XXIV: 158–160**

Georgie May (Bodenheim), **Supp. XXV:** 25

Georgoudaki, Ekaterini, **Supp. IV Part 1:** 12

Gerald McBoing-Boing (film), **Supp. XVI:** 102

"Geraldo No Last Name" (Cisneros), **Supp. VII:** 60–61

Gerald's Game (King), **Supp. V:** 141, 148–150, 151, 152

Gerald's Party (Coover), **Supp. V:** 49–50, 51, 52

Gérando, Joseph Marie de, **II:** 10

"Geranium" (O'Connor), **Retro. Supp. II:** 221, 236

Gerard, Jeremy, **Supp. XXI:** 147

Gerber, Dan, **Supp. VIII:** 39

Gerber, Lisa, **Supp. XXVI:** 187

Gerhardt, Rainer, **Supp. IV Part 1:** 142

"German Girls! The German Girls!, The" (MacLeish), **III:** 16

"German Refugee, The" (Malamud), **Supp. I Part 2:** 436, 437

"Germany's Reichswehr" (Agee), **I:** 35

Germinal (Zola), **III:** 318, 322

Gernsback, Hugo, **Supp. IV Part 1:** 101

"Gernsback Continuum, The" (W. Gibson), **Supp. XVI:** 123, 128

"Gerontion" (Eliot), **I:** 569, 574, 577, 578, 585, 588; **III:** 9, 435, 436; **Retro. Supp. I:** 290; **Supp. XV:** 341; **Supp. XVI:** 158–159

Gerry, Elbridge, **Supp. I Part 2:** 486

"Gerry's Jazz" (Komunyakaa), **Supp. XIII:** 125

Gershwin, Ira, **Supp. I Part 1:** 281

"Gert" (Monette), **Supp. X:** 158

"Gertrude Atherton and the New Woman" (Forrey), **Supp. XXIV:** 30

Gertrude of Stony Island Avenue (Purdy), **Supp. VII:** 281–282

Gertrude Stein (Sprigge), **IV:** 31

Gertrude Stein: A Biography of Her Work (Sutherland), **IV:** 38

"Gertrude Stein and the Geography of the Sentence" (Gass), **Supp. VI:** 87

Gesell, Silvio, **III:** 473

"Gestalt at Sixty" (Sarton), **Supp. VIII:** 260

"Gesture of a Woman-in-Process" (Trethewey), **Supp. XXI:** 249–250

"Gesture toward an Unfound Renaissance, A" (Stafford), **Supp. XI:** 323

"Get It Again" (Halliday), **Supp. XIX:** 85

Getlin, Josh, **Supp. V:** 22; **Supp. VIII:** 75, 76, 78, 79

"Getting Along" (Larcom), **Supp. XIII:** 144

"Getting Along with Nature" (Berry), **Supp. X:** 31–32

"Getting Away from Already Pretty Much Being Away from It All" (Wallace), **Supp. X:** 314–315

"Getting Born" (Shields), **Supp. VII:** 311

Getting Even (Allen), **Supp. XV:** 3, 14, 15

"Getting Lucky" (L. Michaels), **Supp. XVI:** 205, 209

"Getting Out of Jail on Monday" (Wagoner), **Supp. IX:** 327

"Getting Over Arnette"(P. Benedict), **Supp. XXIII:** 39

"Getting over Robert Frost" (Davison), **Supp. XXVI:** 79

"Getting There" (Plath), **Supp. I Part 2:** 539, 542

"Getting to the Poem" (Corso), **Supp. XII:** 135

Getty, J. Paul, **Supp. X:** 108

Getty, Norris, **Supp. XV:** 136–137, 138, 139, 142, 143, 145, 146

Gettysburg, Manila, Acoma (Masters), **Supp. I Part 2:** 471

"Gettysburg: July 1, 1863" (Kenyon), **Supp. VII:** 172

Gevers, Nick, **Supp. XXII:** 59

Geyer, Bernadette, **Supp. XXIII:** 251

Ghachem, Malick, **Supp. X:** 17

Ghazálí, al-, **Supp. XX:** 117

"Ghazals: Homage to Ghalib" (Rich), **Supp. I Part 2:** 557

Ghost, The (Crane), **I:** 409, 421

"Ghost, The" (Peacock), **Supp. XIX:** 199

"Ghost Cat" (Peacock), **Supp. XIX:** 206

"Ghost Chant, et alii" (Komunyakaa), **Supp. XIII:** 114

Ghost Country (Paretsky), **Supp. XXV:** 183

Ghost in the Music, A (Nichols), **Supp. XIII:** 267

"Ghost Jam"(Hadas), **Supp. XXIII:** 119

"Ghostlier Demarcations, Keener Sounds" (Vendler), **Supp. I Part 2:** 565

"Ghostly Father, I Confess" (McCarthy), **II:** 565–566

Ghostly Lover, The (Hardwick), **Supp. III Part 1:** 194–196, 208, 209

Ghost Money (Hull), **Supp. XXI:** 129, **132–135,** 136

Ghost of Meter, The (A. Finch), **Supp. XVII:** 71, 73

"Ghost of the Buffaloes, The" (Lindsay), **Supp. I Part 2:** 393

Ghost of Tradition, The (Walzer), **Supp. XVIII:** 174

Ghosts (Auster), **Supp. XII:** 22, **24,** **26–27**

Ghosts (Ibsen), **III:** 152

Ghosts (Wharton), **IV:** 316, 327

Ghosts of Tsavo: Stalking the Mystery Lions of East Africa (Caputo), **Supp. XIX:** 28

Ghost Town (Coover), **Supp. V:** 52–53

Ghost Trio, The (Bierds), **Supp. XVII:** 29, **30**

Ghost Writer, The (P. Roth), **Retro. Supp. II:** 22, 290, 291; **Supp. III Part 2:** 420–421; **Supp. XVII:** 43

Giachetti, Fosco, **Supp. IV Part 2:** 520

"Giacometti" (Wilbur), **Supp. III Part 2:** 551

Giacometti, Alberto, **Supp. VIII:** 168, 169

Giacomo, Padre, **II:** 278–279

Giant's House, The: A Romance (McCracken), **Supp. X:** 86

"Giant Snail" (Bishop), **Retro. Supp. II:** 49

Giant Weapon, The (Winters), **Supp. II Part 2:** 810

"Giant Woman, The" (Oates), **Supp. II Part 2:** 523

Gibbon, Edward, **I:** 4, 378; **IV:** 126; **Supp. I Part 2:** 503; **Supp. III Part 2:** 629; **Supp. XIII:** 75; **Supp. XIV:** 97

Gibbons, James, **Supp. XVII:** 228

Gibbons, Kaye, **Supp. X:** **41–54; Supp. XII:** 311

Gibbons, Reginald, **Supp. X:** 113, 124, 127; **Supp. XIX:** 40, 41–42, 281; **Supp. XV:** 105

Gibbons, Richard, **Supp. I Part 1:** 107

"Gibbs" (Rukeyser), **Supp. VI:** 273

Gibbs, Barbara, **Supp. IV Part 2:** 644

Gibbs, Wolcott, **Supp. I Part 2:** 604, 618; **Supp. VIII:** 151

Gibran, Kahlil, **Supp. XX: 69,** **113–129**

"GIBSON" (Baraka), **Supp. II Part 1:** 54

Gibson, Charles Dana, **Supp. X:** 184

Gibson, Graeme, **Supp. XIII:** 20

Gibson, John Arthur, **Supp. XXVI:** 83, 84, 87, 89

Gibson, Simeon, **Supp. XXVI:** 96

Gibson, Wilfrid W., **Retro. Supp. I:** 128

Gibson, William, **Supp. XVI: 117–133;** **Supp. XXII:** 49

Giddins, Gary, **Supp. XIII:** 245

Gide, André, **I:** 271, 290; **II:** 581; **III:** 210; **IV:** 53, 289; **Supp. I Part 1:** 51; **Supp. IV Part 1:** 80, 284, 347; **Supp. IV Part 2:** 681, 682; **Supp. VIII:** 40; **Supp. X:** 187; **Supp. XIV:** 24, 348; **Supp. XVII:** 242

Gideon Planish (Lewis), **II:** 455

Gielgud, John, **I:** 82; **Supp. XI:** 305

Gierow, Dr. Karl Ragnar, **III:** 404

Gifford, Barry, **Supp. XXV:** 29

Gifford, Bill, **Supp. XI:** 38

Gifford, Terry, **Supp. XVI:** 22

"Gift, The" (Creeley), **Supp. IV Part 1:** 153

"Gift, The" (Doolittle), **Supp. I Part 1:** 267

Gift, The (Hyde), **Supp. XVIII:** 150

"Gift, The" (Jarman), **Supp. XVII:** 116

"Gift, The" (L.-Y. Lee), **Supp. XV:** 213, 214

Gift, The (Nabokov), **III:** 246, 255, 261–263; **Retro. Supp. I:** 264, 266, **268–270,** 273, 274–275, 278

"Gift from the City, A" (Updike), **Retro. Supp. I:** 320

"Gift of God, The" (Robinson), **III:** 512, 517, 518–521, 524

Gift of the Black Folk, The: The Negroes in the Making of America (Du Bois), **Supp. II Part 1:** 179

"Gift of the Magi, The" (O. Henry), **Supp. II Part 1:** 394, 406, 408

"Gift of the *Osuo*, The" (C. Johnson), **Supp. VI:** 194

"Gift of the Prodigal, The" (Taylor), **Supp. V:** 314, 326

"Gift Outright, The" (Frost), **II:** 152; **Supp. IV Part 1:** 15

"Gifts" (Davison), **Supp. XXVI:** 71

"Gifts of Our Fathers, The" (Gansworth), **Supp. XXVI:** 110

Gigi (Colette; stage adaptation, Loos), **Supp. XVI:** 193

"Gigolo" (Plath), **Retro. Supp. II:** 257

"G.I. Graves in Tuscany" (Hugo), **Supp. VI:** 138

"Gila Bend" (Dickey), **Supp. IV Part 1:** 185–186

Gilb, Dagoberto, **Supp. XXV:** 138

Gilbert, Elizabeth, **Supp. XXII:** 83, 90; **Supp. XXVII:** 258

Gilbert, Jack, **Supp. IX:** 287

Gilbert, Peter, **Supp. IX:** 291, 300

Gilbert, Roger, **Supp. XI:** 124

Gilbert, Sandra M., **Retro. Supp. I:** 42; **Retro. Supp. II:** 324; **Supp. IX:** 66; **Supp. XV:** 270; **Supp. XXIV:** 28; **Supp. XXVII:** 261–262, 263

Gilbert, Susan. *See* Dickinson, Mrs. William A.

Gilbert and Sullivan, **Supp. IV Part 1:** 389

"Gilbert Stuart Portrait of Washington, The" (Kooser), **Supp. XIX:** 124

Gil Blas (Le Sage), **II:** 290

Gilded Age, The (Twain), **III:** 504; **IV:** 198

Gilded Lapse of Time, A (Schnackenberg), **Supp. XV:** 258, **260–263**

"Gilded Lapse of Time, A" (Schnackenberg), **Supp. XV:** 257

"Gilded Six-Bits, The" (Hurston), **Supp. VI:** 154–155

Gilder, R. W., **Retro. Supp. II:** 66; **Supp. I Part 2:** 418

Gildersleeve, Basil, **Supp. I Part 1:** 369

Gildner, Gary, **Supp. XXVI:** 4

Gilead (Robinson), **Supp. XXI:** 212, **216–220,** 223

Giles, H. A., **Retro. Supp. I:** 289

Giles, James R., **Supp. IX:** 11, 15; **Supp. XI:** 219, 223–224, 228, 234

"Giles Corey of the Salem Farms" (Longfellow), **II:** 505, 506; **Retro. Supp. II:** 166, 167

Giles Goat-Boy (Barth), **I:** 121, 122–123, 129, 130, 134, 135–138; **Supp. V:** 39

Gilgamesh: A New Rendering in English Verse (Ferry), **Supp. XXIV:** 147, **150–151**

Gill, Brendan, **Supp. I Part 2:** 659, 660

Gillespie, Nick, **Supp. XIV:** 298, 311

Gillette, Chester, **I:** 512

Gillian, Maria Mazziotti, **Supp. XXIII:** 248

Gilligan, Carol, **Supp. XIII:** 216; **Supp. XXII:** 18

Gillis, Jim, **IV:** 196

Gillis, Steve, **IV:** 195

Gilman, Charlotte Perkins, **Supp. I Part 2:** 637; **Supp. V:** 121, 284, 285; **Supp. XI:** **193–211; Supp. XIII:** 295, 306; **Supp. XVI:** 84; **Supp. XXIII:** 26

Gilman, Daniel Coit, **Supp. I Part 1:** 361, 368, 370

Gilman, Owen W., Jr., **Supp. XXVI:** 148

Gilman, Richard, **IV:** 115; **Supp. IV Part 2:** 577; **Supp. XIII:** 100; **Supp. XIX:** 251

Gilmore, Eddy, **Supp. I Part 2:** 618

Gilmore, Leigh, **Supp. XXVI:** 53

Gilmore, Lyman, **Supp. XXI:** 20, 22, 24

Gilmore, Mikal, **Supp. XVI:** 123, 124

Gilpin, Charles, **III:** 392

Gilpin, Dewitt, **Supp. XV:** 197

Gilpin, Laura, **Retro. Supp. I:** 7

Gilpin, Sam, **Supp. V:** 213

Gilpin, William, **Supp. IV Part 2:** 603

"Gil's Furniture Bought & Sold" (Cisneros), **Supp. VII:** 61–62, 64

Gilt Edged Guilt (Wells), **Supp. XXVI:** 281

Gilyard, Keith, **Supp. XXI:** 246

"Gimcrackery" articles (Briggs), **Supp. XVIII:** 8–9

"Gimpel the Fool" (Singer), **IV:** 14; **Retro. Supp. II:** 22, 307

Gimpel the Fool and Other Stories (Singer), **IV:** 1, 7–9, 10, 12

"Gin" (Levine), **Supp. V:** 193

"Gingerbread House, The" (Coover), **Supp. V:** 42–43

Gingerbread Lady, The (Simon), **Supp. IV Part 2:** 580, 583–584, 588

Gingerich, Willard, **Supp. IV Part 2:** 510

Gingertown (McKay), **Supp. X:** 132, 139

Gingold, Hermione, **Supp. XV:** 13

Gingrich, Arnold, **Retro. Supp. I:** 113; **Supp. XVII:** 88; **Supp. XX:** 34

Ginna, Robert, **Supp. IX:** 259

Ginsberg, Allen, **I:** 183; **Retro. Supp. I:** 411, 426, 427; **Retro. Supp. II:** 280; **Supp. II Part 1:** 30, 32, 58, **307–333; Supp. III Part 1:** 2, 91, 96, 98, 100, 222, 226; **Supp. III Part 2:** 541, 627; **Supp. IV Part 1:** 79, 90, 322; **Supp. IV Part 2:** 502; **Supp. IX:** 299; **Supp. V:** 168, 336; **Supp. VIII:** 239, 242–243; **Supp. X:** 120, 204; **Supp. XI:** 135, 297; **Supp. XII:** 118–119, 121–122, 124, 126, 130–131, 136, 182; **Supp. XIV:** 15, 53, 54, 125, 137, 141, 142, 143–144, 148, 150, 269, 280, 283; **Supp. XV:** 134, 177, 263; **Supp. XVI:** 123, 135; **Supp. XVII:** 138, 243; **Supp. XVIII:** 20, 27, 29, 30; **Supp. XXI:** 53; **Supp. XXII:** 172, 225; **Supp. XXIII:** 211, 213, 215; **Supp. XXIV:** 34, 36, 37; **Supp. XXV:** 29; **Supp. XXVI:** 70; **Supp. XXVII:** 18

Gioia, Dana, **Supp. IX:** 279; **Supp. XII:** 209; **Supp. XIII:** 337; **Supp. XIX:** 117, 144; **Supp. XV:** 111–131, 251; **Supp. XVII:** 69, 72, 112; **Supp. XXI:** 99; **Supp. XXIII:** 112; **Supp. XXV:** 222

Giono, Jean, **Supp. XVI:** 135

Giordano, Tony J., **Supp. XXIII:** 125

Giotto di Bondone, **Supp. I Part 2:** 438; **Supp. XI:** 126

Giovani, Regula, **Supp. XV:** 270

Giovanni, Nikki, **Supp. I Part 1:** 66; **Supp. II Part 1:** 54; **Supp. IV Part 1:** 11; **Supp. VIII:** 214; **Supp. XXII:** 11; **Supp. XXVII:** 165, 200, 202

Giovanni's Room (Baldwin), **Retro. Supp. II:** 5, 6, **6–7,** 8, 10; **Supp. I Part 1:** 51, 52, 55–56, 57, 60, 63, 67; **Supp. III Part 1:** 125

Giovannitti, Arturo, **I:** 476; **Supp. XV:** 299, 301, 302, 307

"Giraffe" (Swenson), **Supp. IV Part 2:** 651

Giraldi, Giovanni Battista. *See* Cinthio

"Girl" (Kincaid), **Supp. VII:** 182–183

Girl, The (Le Sueur), **Supp. XXIII:** 172–**174**

"Girl, The" (Olds), **Supp. X:** 207

"Girl Friend Poems" (Wright), **Supp. XV:** 349

"Girl from Lynn Bathes Horse!!" (McCarriston), **Supp. XIV:** 266

"Girl from Red Lion, P.A., A" (Mencken), **III:** 111

Girl in Glass, The: Love Poems (W. J. Smith), **Supp. XIII:** 335

Girl in Landscape (Lethem), **Supp. XVIII:** 136, **141–143**

"Girl in the Grave, The" (McCoy), **Supp. XIII:** 170

"Girl in the River, The" (Rash), **Supp. XXVII:** 224

"Girl in the River, The: The Wild and Scenic Chattooga, Ron Rash's *Saints at the River,* and the Drowning of Rachel Trois" (Lane), **Supp. XXVII:** 216

Girl Like I, A (Loos), **Supp. XVI:** 181, 183, 184, 187, 194, 196

"Girl of the Golden West" (Didion), **Supp. IV Part 1:** 195, 208, 211

Girl of the Golden West, The (Puccini), **III:** 139

Girl of the Limberlost (film), **Supp. XX:** **223**

Girl of the Limberlost (Stratton-Porter), **Supp. XX:** **211, 221–222**

"Girl on a Scaffold" (C. Frost), **Supp. XV:** 98

"Girl on the Baggage Truck, The" (O'Hara), **III:** 371–372

Girl on the Via Flaminia, The (Hayes), **Supp. XXVI:** 135, 136–137, 144

"Girls" (Gallagher), **Supp. XXIV:** 174–175, 177

Girls at Play (Theroux), **Supp. VIII:** 314, 315, 316, **317**

"Girls at the Sphinx, The" (Farrell), **II:** 45

"Girls in Their Summer Dresses, The" (Shaw), **Supp. XIX:** 246

Girl Sleuth, The: A Feminist Guide (Mason), **Supp. VIII:** 133, 135, **139,** 142

"Girl's Story, A" (Bambara), **Supp. XI:** 10–11

"Girl the Prince Liked, The" (Z. Fitzgerald), **Supp. IX:** 71

Girl Who Had to Die, The (Holding), **Supp. XXII:** **126–127**

Girl Who Loved Tom Gordon, The (King), **Supp. V:** 138, 152

"Girl Who Raised Pigeons, The" (E. P. Jones), **Supp. XXII:** 143

Girl with Curious Hair (Wallace), **Supp. X:** 301, **305–308**

"Girl with Curious Hair" (Wallace), **Supp. X:** 306

"Girl with Silver Eyes, The" (Hammett), **Supp. IV Part 1:** 344, 345

"Girl with Talent, The" (Z. Fitzgerald), **Supp. IX:** 71

Girodias, Maurice, **III:** 171; **Supp. XI:** 297

Giroux, Robert, **Retro. Supp. II:** 177, 229, 235; **Supp. IV Part 1:** 280; **Supp. VIII:** 195; **Supp. XV:** 146

Gish, Dorothy, **Retro. Supp. I:** 103

Gish, Lillian, **Supp. XVI:** 184

Gissing, George, **II:** 138, 144

Gitagovinda, **Supp. XXII:** 258

Gita-govínda: Love Songs of Radha and Krishna (Jayadeva; Siegel, trans.), **Supp. XXII:** 258

Gittings, Robert, **II:** 531

Gittleman, Edwin, **Supp. XXV:** 237, 251

"Given" (C. Frost), **Supp. XV:** 96

Given Sugar, Given Salt (Hirshfield), **Supp. XXIII:** 133

"Give Us Back Our Country" (Masters), **Supp. I Part 2:** 472

Give Us This Day (film, Dmytryk), **Supp. XX:** **40–41**

"Give Way, Ye Gates" (Roethke), **III:** 536

"Give Your Heart to the Hawks" (Jeffers), **Supp. II Part 2:** 433

"Giving Blood" (Updike), **IV:** 226; **Retro. Supp. I:** 332

Giving Good Weight (McPhee), **Supp. III Part 1:** 307

"Giving in to You" (X. J. Kennedy), **Supp. XV:** 160

"Giving Myself Up" (Strand), **Supp. IV Part 2:** 627

Giving Up America (Abraham), **Supp. XXIV:** 2, 3, **7–9**

Giving Up the Ghost (Moraga), **Supp. XXIII:** **197–199**

G. K. the DJ (Keillor), **Supp. XVI:** 171

Glackens, William, **Retro. Supp. II:** 103

Gladden, Washington, **III:** 293; **Supp. I Part 1:** 5

Gladstone, William Ewart, **Supp. I Part 2:** 419

"Gladys Poem, The" (Alvarez), **Supp. VII:** 10

Glamorama (Ellis), **Supp. XXVII:** 68, 71, 75–76, 76, 78

"Glance at German 'Kultur,' A" (Bourne), **I:** 228

Glance Away, A (Wideman), **Supp. X:** 320

"Glance from the Bridge, A" (Wilbur), **Supp. III Part 2:** 551

"Glance in the Mirror, A" (Swados), **Supp. XIX:** 261–262

Glance toward Shakespeare, A (Chapman), **Supp. XIV:** 44

Glancy, Diane, **Supp. XXI:** 246

Glanville-Hicks, Peggy, **Supp. IV Part 1:** 84

Glare (Ammons), **Supp. VII:** 35–36

Glasgow, Cary, **II:** 173, 182

Glasgow, Ellen, **II:** **173–195; IV:** 328; **Supp. X:** 228, 234; **Supp. XXIV:** 30; **Supp. XXV:** 201; **Supp. XXVI:** 276

Glasmon, Kubec, **Supp. XIII:** 166

Glaspell, Susan, **Supp. III Part 1:** **175–191; Supp. X:** 46; **Supp. XVII:** 99; **Supp. XXI:** 5

"Glass" (Francis), **Supp. IX:** 80

Glass, Irony, and God (Carson), **Supp. XII:** 97, **104–106**

Glass, Philip, **Supp. XXI:** 146, 147

"Glass Ark, The" (Komunyakaa), **Supp. XIII:** 129

Glass Bees, The (Jünger; Bogan and Mayer, trans.), **Supp. III Part 1:** 63

"Glass Blower of Venice" (Malamud), **Supp. I Part 2:** 450

"Glass Essay, The" (Carson), **Supp. XII:** **104–105**

"Glass Face in the Rain, A: New Poems" (Stafford), **Supp. XI:** 327–328

Glass Key, The (Hammett), **Supp. IV Part 1:** 351–353

"Glass Meadows" (Bausch), **Supp. VII:** 53–54

Glass Menagerie, The (T. Williams), **I:** 81; **IV:** 378, 379, 380, 382, 383, 385, 386, 387, 388, 389, 390, 391, 392, 393–394, 395, 398; **Supp. IV Part 1:** 84; **Supp. XXV:** 101

"Glass Mountain, The" (Barthelme), **Supp. IV Part 1:** 47

"Glass Tent, The" (Everwine), **Supp. XV:** 76

Glatstein, Jacob, **Supp. X:** 70

Glazer, Nathan, **Supp. VIII:** 93, 243

"Gleaners, The" (Merwin), **Supp. III Part 1:** 346

Gleanings in Europe (Cooper), **I:** 346

Gleason, Ralph J., **Supp. IX:** 16

Glenday, Michael, **Retro. Supp. II:** 210

Glengarry Glen Ross (film), **Supp. XIV:** 242

Glengarry Glen Ross (Mamet), **Supp. XIV:** 239, 240, 242, 245, 246, 250, 254, 255

Glimcher, Arne, **Supp. VIII:** 73

"Glimpses" (Jones), **Supp. XI:** 218

Glimpses of the Moon, The (Wharton), **II:** 189–190; **IV:** 322–323; **Retro. Supp. I:** 381

"Glimpses of Vietnamese Life" (Levertov), **Supp. III Part 1:** 282

Glisson, J. T., **Supp. X:** 234

"Glittering Trout" (Davison), **Supp. XXVI:** 79

Gloria Mundi (Frederic), **II:** 144–145

Gloria Naylor (Fowler), **Supp. VIII:** 224

"Glorious Fourth, The" (Ryan as Quin), **Supp. XVIII:** 229

Glorious Ones, The (Prose), **Supp. XVI:** 251

Glory, The (Wouk), **Supp. XXV:** 254, 257, 265–266

Glory Field, The (Myers), **Supp. XXVII:** 208

Glory of Hera, The (Gordon), **II:** 196–197, 198, 199, 217–220

Glory of the Conquered, The (Glaspell), **Supp. III Part 1:** 176

Glory River (Huddle), **Supp. XXVI:** 151

Gloss, Molly, **Supp. XXIII:** 280

Glossary of Literary Terms (Abrams), **Supp. XVI:** 19

Glotfelty, Cheryll, **Supp. IX:** 25

Glover, Joyce Lee, **Supp. XIX:** 112

Glover, Michael, **Supp. XXIV:** 168

Glow, The (Wrigley), **Supp. XVIII:** 295

"Glow, The" (Wrigley), **Supp. XVIII:** 296–297, 307

Gluck, Christoph Willibald, **II:** 210, 211

Glück, Louise, **Supp. V: 77–94; Supp. VIII:** 272; **Supp. X:** 209; **Supp. XIV:** 269; **Supp. XV:** 19, 252; **Supp. XVII:** 241; **Supp. XXV:** 222

"Glutton, The" (Shapiro), **Supp. II Part 2:** 705

"Glutton for Punishment, A" (Yates), **Supp. XI:** 341

Glyph (Everett), **Supp. XVIII: 60–61**

Gnädiges Fräulein, The (T. Williams), **IV:** 382, 395, 398

Gnomes and Occasions (Nemerov), **III:** 269

Gnomologia (Fuller), **II:** 111

"Gnothis Seauton" (Emerson), **II:** 11, 18–19

Go (Holmes), **Supp. XIV:** 144

"Go Ahead; Goodbye; Good Luck; and Watch Out" (Bronk), **Supp. XXI:** 31

"Goal of Intellectual Men, The" (Eberhart), **I:** 529–530

Go-Between, The (Hartley), **Supp. I Part 1:** 293

Gobineau, Joseph Arthur de, **Supp. XIV:** 209

God (Allen), **Supp. XV:** 3

God and the American Writer (Kazin), **Supp. VIII: 108–109**

Godard, Jean-Luc, **Supp. I Part 2:** 558

Godbey (Masters), **Supp. I Part 2:** 472

God Bless You, Mr. Rosewater (Vonnegut), **Supp. II Part 2:** 758, 767, 768–769, 771, 772

Goddess Abides, The (Buck), **Supp. II Part 1:** 129, 131–132

Gödel, Kurt, **Supp. IV Part 1:** 43

Godfather (Puzo), **Supp. IV Part 1:** 390

Godfires (Hoffman), **Supp. XVIII: 81–82**

God in Ruins, A (Uris), **Supp. XX: 247, 256**

"God in the Doorway" (Dillard), **Supp. VI:** 28

"God is a distant-stately Lover" (Dickinson), **I:** 471

Godkin, E. L., **II:** 274

God Knows (Heller), **Supp. IV Part 1:** 386, 388–389

God Made Alaska for the Indians (Reed), **Supp. X:** 241

God of His Fathers, The (London), **II:** 469

God of Vengeance, The (Asch), **IV:** 11; **Supp. XXIII: 5, 8–9**

Go Down, Moses (Faulkner), **Retro. Supp. I:** 75, 82, 85, 86, 88, 89, 90, 92; **Supp. XVIII:** 203

"Go Down, Moses" (Faulkner), **II:** 71–72

Go Down, Moses (Hayden), **Supp. II Part 1:** 365

Go Down, Moses and Other Stories (Faulkner), **II:** 71; **Supp. X:** 52

"Go Down Death A Funeral Sermon" (J. W. Johnson), **Supp. IV Part 1:** 7

"God Rest Ye Merry, Gentlemen" (Hemingway), **IV:** 122

Godric (Buechner), **Supp. XII:** 53

Gods, The (Goldbarth), **Supp. XII:** 189, 190

Gods Arrive, The (Wharton), **IV:** 326–327; **Retro. Supp. I:** 382

God Save the Child (Parker), **Supp. XIX:** 183–184

"God Save the Rights of Man" (Freneau), **Supp. II Part 1:** 268

"Gods|Children" (Swenson), **Supp. IV Part 2:** 645

"God's Christ Theory" (Carson), **Supp. XII:** 106

God's Country (Everett), **Supp. XVIII: 57–58,** 64, 65

God's Country and My People (Morris), **III:** 238

Gods Determinations touching his Elect: and the Elects Combat in their Conversion, and Coming up to God in Christ together with the Comfortable Effects thereof (Taylor), **IV:** 155–160, 165

God-Seeker, The (Lewis), **II:** 456

God Sends Sunday (Bontemps), **Supp. XXII:** 2, 3, 9

God's Favorite (Simon), **Supp. IV Part 2:** 575, 586, 588, 590

"God's Fool" (Gibran), **Supp. XX: 118**

God's Little Acre (Caldwell), **I:** 288, 289, 290, 297, 298–302, 305–306, 309, 310; **Supp. XXII:** 196

God's Man: A Novel in Wood Cuts (Ward), **I:** 31

Gods of Peg¿na, The (Dunsany), **Supp. XXV:** 113

Gods of Winter, The (Gioia), **Supp. XV:** 112, **121–125**

"Gods of Winter, The" (Gioia), **Supp. XV:** 117

"God's Peace in November" (Jeffers), **Supp. II Part 2:** 420

God's Silence (F. Wright), **Supp. XVII:** 240, 246–247

"God Stiff" (Carson), **Supp. XII: 106**

God's Trombones (J. W. Johnson), **Supp. II Part 1:** 201

"God's Youth" (Untermeyer), **Supp. XV:** 296

"God the Father and the Empty House" (McCarriston), **Supp. XIV:** 273

Godwin, William, **II:** 304; **III:** 415; **Supp. I Part 1:** 126, 146; **Supp. I Part 2:** 512, 513–514, 522, 709, 719

God without Thunder (Ransom), **III:** 495–496, 499

Godwulf Manuscript, The (Parker), **Supp. XIX: 178–182**

Goebbels, Josef, **III:** 560

Goebel, Irma, **Supp. X:** 95

Goen, C. C., **I:** 560

Goethe, Johann Wolfgang von, **I:** 181, 396, 587–588; **II:** 5, 6, 320, 344, 488, 489, 492, 502, 556; **III:** 395, 453, 607, 612, 616; **IV:** 50, 64, 173, 326; **Retro. Supp. I:** 360; **Retro. Supp. II:** 94; **Supp. I Part 2:** 423, 457; **Supp. II Part 1:** 26; **Supp. III Part 1:** 63; **Supp. IX:** 131, 308; **Supp. X:** 60; **Supp. XI:** 169; **Supp. XVIII:** 278; **Supp. XX: 84; Supp. XXIV:** 152

Go for the Body (Lacy), **Supp. XV:** 201, 204

Gogan, Robert, **Supp. XXI:** 24

Gogol, Nikolai, **I:** 296; **IV:** 1, 4; **Retro. Supp. I:** 266, 269; **Supp. VIII:** 14; **Supp. XI:** 45; **Supp. XVIII:** 102; **Supp. XXII:** 59

Goia, Dana, **Supp. XIX:** 121

Goines, Donald, **Supp. XXIII:** 174

"Going, Going, Gone" (Skloot), **Supp. XX: 207**

Going, William T., **Supp. VIII:** 126

"Going 1960–1970" (Huddle), **Supp. XXVI:** 148

Going After Cacciato (O'Brien), **Supp. V:** 237, 238, 239, 244–246, 248, 249

Going All the Way (Wakefield), **Supp. VIII:** 43

Going Away (Sigal), **Supp. XXVI:** 26

"Going Critical" (Bambara), **Supp. XI:** 14

Going Down (Markson), **Supp. XVII:** 136, 138, **139–140,** 141, 142–143, 144, 145

Going for the Rain (Ortiz), **Supp. IV Part 2:** 499, 505–508, 509, 514

"Going Home by Last Night" (Kinnell), **Supp. III Part 1:** 244

"Going Home in America" (Hardwick), **Supp. III Part 1:** 205

"Going Home"(Kenny), **Supp. XXIII:** 144, 148

Going into the City: Portrait of a Critic as a Young Man (Christgau), **Supp. XXVII:** 33, 39

"Going North" (Salinas), **Supp. XIII:** 316

Going Places (L. Michaels), **Supp. XVI:** 201, **203–206**

"Going Places" (L. Michaels), **Supp. XVI:** 203

"Going South" (J. W. Miller), **Supp. XX:** 169

Going South (Lardner and Buck), **II:** 427

Going To and Fro and Walking Up and Down (Reznikoff), **Supp. XIV:** 280, 282, 284, 285

Going to Meet the Man (Baldwin), **Supp. I Part 1:** 60, 62–63; **Supp. XX:** 147

"Going to Meet the Man" (Baldwin), **Retro. Supp. II:** 8, 9; **Supp. I Part 1:** 62–63

"Going to Naples" (Welty), **IV:** 278; **Retro. Supp. I:** 352, 353

"Going to Shrewsbury" (Jewett), **II:** 393

"Going to the Bakery" (Bishop), **Supp. I Part 1:** 93

Going-to-the-Stars (Lindsay), **Supp. I Part 2:** 398

Going-to-the-Sun (Lindsay), **Supp. I Part 2:** 397–398

Going to the Territory (Ellison), **Retro. Supp. II:** 119, 123–124

"Going towards Pojoaque, A December Full Moon/72" (Harjo), **Supp. XII:** 218

"Going Under" (Dubus), **Supp. VII:** 83

"Gold" (Francis), **Supp. IX:** 82

Gold (O'Neill), **III:** 391

Gold, Arthur, **Supp. XXIV:** 160, 161

Gold, Charles H., **Supp. XXVI:** 6

Gold, Don, **Supp. XXII:** 258

Gold, Michael, **II:** 26; **IV:** 363, 364, 365; **Retro. Supp. II:** 323; **Supp. I Part 1:** 331; **Supp. I Part 2:** 609; **Supp. XIV:** 288; **Supp. XXII:** 277; **Supp. XXVII:** 134

Goldbarth, Albert, **Supp. XII: 175–195**

Goldbarth's Book of Occult Phenomena (Goldbarth), **Supp. XII:** 181

Goldberg, Carole, **Supp. XXII:** 207

Goldberg, Michael, **Supp. XXIII:** 210, 216, 217

Goldberg, S. L., **Supp. VIII:** 238

"Gold Bug, The" (Poe), **III:** 410, 413, 419, 420

Gold Bug Variations, The (Powers), **Supp. IX:** 210, 212, **216–217,** 219

Gold Cell, The (Olds), **Supp. X: 206–209**

Gold Diggers, The (Monette), **Supp. X:** 153

Golde, Miss (Mencken's Secretary), **III:** 104, 107

Golden, Harry, **III:** 579, 581; **Supp. VIII:** 244

Golden, Mike, **Supp. XI:** 294, 295, 297, 299, 303

Golden Age, The (Gurney), **Supp. V:** 101–103

Golden Apples (Rawlings), **Supp. X: 228–229,** 230, 234

Golden Apples, The (Welty), **IV:** 261, 271–274, 281, 293; **Retro. Supp. I:** 341, 342, 343, **350–351,** 352, 355

Golden Apples of the Sun, The (Bradbury), **Supp. IV Part 1:** 102, 103

Golden Book of Springfield, The (Lindsay), **Supp. I Part 2:** 376, 379, 395, 396

Golden Bough, The (Frazer), **II:** 204, 549; **III:** 6–7; **Supp. I Part 1:** 18; **Supp. IX:** 123; **Supp. X:** 124

Golden Bowl, The (James), **II:** 320, 333, 335; **Retro. Supp. I:** 215, 216, 218–219, 232, **234–235,** 374

Golden Boy (Odets), **Supp. II Part 2:** 538, 539, 540–541, 546, 551

Golden Calves, The (Auchincloss), **Supp. IV Part 1:** 35

Golden Child (Hwang), **Supp. XXI:** 147–148

Golden Day, The (Mumford), **Supp. II Part 2:** 471, 475, 477, 483, 484, 488–489, 493

Golden Fleece, The (Gurney), **Supp. V:** 97

Golden Gate (film, Madden), **Supp. XXI:** 147

Golden Gate, The (Seth), **Supp. XVII:** 117

Golden Gate Country (Atherton), **Supp. XXIV:** 27

Golden Grove, The: Selected Passages from the Sermons and Writings of Jeremy Taylor (L. P. Smith), **Supp. XIV:** 345

"Golden Heifer, The" (Wylie), **Supp. I Part 2:** 707

"Golden Honeymoon, The" (Lardner), **II:** 429–430, 431

Golden Journey, The (W. J. Smith and Bogan, comps.), **Supp. XIII:** 347

Golden Ladder series (S. and A. Warner), **Supp. XVIII:** 267

"Golden Lads" (Marquand), **III:** 56

Golden Legend, The (Longfellow), **II:** 489, 490, 495, 505, 506, 507; **Retro. Supp. II:** 159, 165, 166

Golden Mean and Other Poems, The (Tate and Wills), **IV:** 122

Golden Mountain, The (Levin), **Supp. XXVII:** 134, 140

Golden Peacock (Atherton), **Supp. XXIV:** 26

"Golden Retrievals" (Doty), **Supp. XI:** 132

Golden Shakespeare, The: An Anthology (L. P. Smith), **Supp. XIV:** 349

Golden Slippers: An Anthology of Negro Poetry for Young Readers (Bontemps, ed.), **Supp. XXII:** 5, 11

Goldensohn, Lorrie, **Retro. Supp. II:** 51

Golden State (Bidart), **Supp. XV:** 21, **23–25**

"Golden State" (Bidart), **Supp. XV:** 23, 24, 25

Golden States (Cunningham), **Supp. XV:** 55, **56–59,** 63

Golden Treasury of Best Songs and Lyrical Poems in the English Language (Palgrave), **Retro. Supp. I:** 124

Golden Treasury of the Best Songs and Lyrical Poems in the English Language (Palgrave), **Supp. XIV:** 340

Goldenweiser, Alexander Aleksandrovich, **Supp. XXVI:** 89

Golden Whales of California and Other Rhymes in the American Language, The (Lindsay), **Supp. I Part 2:** 394–395, 396

Goldfinch, The (Tartt), **Supp. XXVII:** 268, 276–280

"Goldfish Bowl, The" (Francis), **Supp. IX:** 78

Gold Fools (Sorrentino), **Supp. XXI:** 237

Goldin Boys, The (Epstein), **Supp. XIV:** 112

Golding, Arthur, **III:** 467, 468

Golding, William, **Supp. IV Part 1:** 297

Goldini, Carlo, **II:** 274

Goldkorn Tales (Epstein), **Supp. XII: 163–164**

Goldman, Albert, **Supp. XI:** 299

Goldman, Arnold, **Supp. XXI:** 13

Goldman, Emma, **III:** 176, 177; **Supp. I Part 2:** 524; **Supp. XVII:** 96, 103, 104; **Supp. XXIII:** 162

Goldman, Francisco, **Supp. XXV: 49–62**

Goldman, William, **Supp. IV Part 2:** 474

"Gold Mountain Stories" project (Kingston), **Supp. V:** 164

Gold of Chickaree, The (S. and A. Warner), **Supp. XVIII:** 267, 268, 269

Goldring, Douglas, **III:** 458

Goldsmith, Oliver, **II:** 273, 282, 299, 304, 308, 314, 315, 514; **Retro. Supp. I:** 335; **Supp. I Part 1:** 310; **Supp. I Part 2:** 503, 714, 716; **Supp. XVIII:** 12

Gold Standard and the Logic of Naturalism, The (W. B. Michaels), **Retro. Supp. I:** 369

Goldstein, Laurence, **Supp. XXI:** 134

Goldstein, Rebecca, **Supp. XVII:** 44

Goldstein, Richard, **Supp. XXVII:** 43

Goldthwaite, Melissa, **Supp. XXVI:** 56

Goldwater, Barry, **I:** 376; **III:** 38

Goldwyn, Samuel, **Retro. Supp. II:** 199; **Supp. I Part 1:** 281; **Supp. XXIV:** 28; **Supp. XXV:** 195

Golem, The (Leivick), **IV:** 6; **Supp. XXIII:** 8

"Golgotha Is a Mountain" (Bontemps), **Supp. XXII:** 3, 8

"Goliardic Song" (Hecht), **Supp. X:** 63

"Go Like This" (Moore), **Supp. X:** 165

Goll, Ivan, **Supp. III Part 1:** 235, 243–244; **Supp. III Part 2:** 621

Gomes, Albert, **Supp. XXI:** 160

Goncharova, Natalya, **Supp. IX:** 66

Goncourt, Edmond de, **II:** 325, 328; **III:** 315, 317–318, 321; **Retro. Supp. I:** 226

Goncourt, Jules de, **II:** 328; **III:** 315, 317–318, 321

Gone Fishin' (Mosley), Supp. XIII: **235–236,** 240

"Gone to Feed the Roses" (Vaz), **Supp. XXVI:** 268

"Gone to War" (E. Stoddard), **Supp. XV:** 282

"Gone West" (Rodriguez), **Supp. XIV:** 308

Gone with the Wind (film), **Retro. Supp. I:** 113; **Supp. XXVII:** 83

Gone with the Wind (Mitchell), **II:** 177; **Retro. Supp. I:** 340; **Supp. XX:** 243; **Supp. XXII:** 190, 195

Gongora y Argote, Luis de, **II:** 552

Gonzalez, David, **Supp. VIII:** 85

González, Jovita, **Supp. XIX:** 99

Gonzo: The Life of Hunter S. Thompson (Wenner and Seymour), **Supp. XXIV:** 280, 281, 282, 288

Gooch, Brad, **Supp. XII:** 121; **Supp. XXIII:** 218, 220

Good, George, **Supp. XI:** 306

"Good, the Plaid, and the Ugly, The" (Wasserstein), **Supp. XV:** 327

"Good and Not So Good, The" (Dunn), **Supp. XI:** 141

"Good Anna, The" (Stein), **IV:** 37, 40, 43

Good As Gold (Heller), **Supp. IV Part 1:** 386, 388, 394

Good as I Been to You (album, Dylan), **Supp. XVIII:** 28

"Good As Yesterday" (Muñoz), **Supp. XXV:** 134, 135

Good Boys and Dead Girls and Other Essays (Gordon), **Supp. IV Part 1:** 309–310

"Good Brother" (Muñoz), **Supp. XXV:** 135

Good Brother, The (Offutt), **Supp. XIX:** 163, **168–169**

"Good-by and Keep Cold" (Frost), **Retro. Supp. I:** 135

"Goodbye" (Davison), **Supp. XXVI:** 69

"Good-bye" (Emerson), **II:** 19

"Goodbye, Christ" (Hughes), **Retro. Supp. I:** 202, 203

Goodbye, Columbus (P. Roth), **Retro. Supp. II:** 280, 281, 290; **Supp. III Part 2:** 403–406; **Supp. XIV:** 112; **Supp. XX:** 177; **Supp. XXVI:** 123

"Goodbye, Columbus" (P. Roth), **Supp. III Part 2:** 401, 404, 408–409, 411

Goodbye, Columbus and Five Short Stories (P. Roth), **Retro. Supp. II:** 279

"Goodbye, Goldeneye" (Swenson), **Supp. IV Part 2:** 651

"Goodbye, Mr. Chipstein" (Epstein), **Supp. XIV:** 103, 108

"Goodbye, My Brother" (Cheever), **Supp. I Part 1:** 175, 177, 193

"Goodbye and Good Luck" (Paley), **Supp. VI:** 219, 223

Goodbye Girl, The (film), **Supp. IV Part 2:** 589

Goodbye Girl, The (musical), **Supp. IV Part 2:** 576, 588

Goodbye Girl, The (Simon), **Supp. IV Part 2:** 575

Goodbye Look, The (Macdonald), **Supp. IV Part 2:** 473, 474

"Good-Bye My Fancy" (Whitman), **IV:** 348

"Goodbye to All That" (Biss), **Supp. XXVI:** 46, 47, 53

"Goodbye to All That" (Didion), **Supp. IV Part 1:** 197

Goodbye to All That (Graves), **I:** 477; **Supp. XXVI:** 53

Goodbye to Berlin (Isherwood), **Supp. XIV:** 159, 161, 162, 169

"Goodbye to My Twinkle Days" (Nguyen), **Supp. XXVI:** 209

"Good-Bye to the Mezzogiorno" (Auden), **Supp. II Part 1:** 19

"Goodbye to the Poetry of Calcium" (Wright), **Supp. III Part 2:** 599

"Good Company" (Matthews), **Supp. IX:** 160

"Good Country People" (O'Connor), **III:** 343, 350, 351, 352, 358; **Retro. Supp. II:** 229, 232

Good Day to Die, A (Harrison), **Supp. VIII:** **42–44,** 45, 47

Good Day to Die, A (O'Nan as James Coltrane), **Supp. XXV:** 146

Good Doctor, The (Simon), **Supp. IV Part 2:** 575, 585

Good Earth, The (Buck), **Supp. I Part 1:** 49; **Supp. II Part 1:** 115–175, 118, 125, 132

Good European, The (Blackmur), **Supp. II Part 1:** 91

Good Evening Mr. & Mrs. America, and All the Ships at Sea (Bausch), **Supp. VII:** 41, 47, 52

"Good Friday" (Jarman), **Supp. XVII:** 116

"Good Friday, 1613, Riding Westward" (Donne), **Supp. XXVII:** 220

"Good Friday, 1995, Driving Westward" (Rash), **Supp. XXVII:** 219–220

"Good Girl" (Peacock), **Supp. XIX:** 199

Good Gray Poet, The (O'Connor), **Retro. Supp. I:** 407

Good Health and How We Won It (Sinclair), **Supp. V:** 285–286

Good Hearts (Price), **Supp. VI:** 259, 265

"Good Job Gone, A" (Hughes), **Retro. Supp. I:** 204

Good Journey, A (Ortiz), **Supp. IV Part 2:** 497, 499, 503, 505, 509–510, 514

Good Life, The (Nearing and Nearing), **Supp. XXVI:** 35

Good Lord Bird, The (McBride), **Supp. XXVI:** 191, 200, 202–204

Good Luck, Miss Wyckoff (Inge), **Supp. XXV:** 93, 95, 106–107

Good Luck in Cracked Italian (Hugo), **Supp. VI:** 133, 137–138

Goodman, Allegra, **Supp. XII:** 159; **Supp. XVI:** 205; **Supp. XX:** 177; **Supp. XXVI:** **117–132**

Goodman, Ellen, **Supp. XVI:** 103

Goodman, Jack, **Supp. XXI:** 277

Goodman, Jenny, **Supp. XV:** 343, 344

Goodman, Kenneth Sawyer, **Supp. XXVII:** 89

Goodman, Paul, **I:** 218, 261; **III:** 39; **Supp. I Part 2:** 524; **Supp. VIII:** 239–240

Goodman, Philip, **III:** 105, 108

Goodman, Walter, **Supp. IV Part 2:** 532

Good Man Is Hard to Find, A (O'Connor), **III:** 339, 343–345

"Good Man Is Hard to Find, A" (O'Connor), **III:** 339, 344, 353; **Retro. Supp. II:** 230–231

Good Man Is Hard to Find and Other Stories, A (O'Connor), **Retro. Supp. II:** 229, **230–232**

Good Morning, America (Sandburg), **III:** 592–593

"Good Morning, Major" (Marquand), **III:** 56

Good Morning, Midnight (Rhys), **Supp. III Part 1:** 43

"Good Morning, Revolution" (Hughes), **Retro. Supp. I:** 201, 203

Good Morning Blues: The Autobiography of Count Basie (Murray), **Supp. XIX:** 159

Good Morning Revolution: Uncollected Writings of Social Protest (Hughes), **Retro. Supp. I:** 194, 201, 202, 209

Good Mother, The (Miller), **Supp. XII:** 289, **290–294,** 299, 301

Good News (Abbey), **Supp. XIII: 11–12**

"Good News from New-England" (E. Johnson), **Supp. I Part 1:** 115

Good News of Death and Other Poems (Simpson), **Supp. IX:** 265, **268–269**

"Goodnight, Saigon" (lecture, Caputo), **Supp. XIX:** 17, 30

Good Night, Willie Lee, I'll See You in the Morning (Walker), **Supp. III Part 2:** 520, 531

"Good Oak" (Leopold), **Supp. XIV:** 185, 187, 191

"Good Old Times, The: New York Fifty Years Ago" (Briggs), **Supp. XVIII:** 15

"Good Pine, A" (Offutt), **Supp. XIX:** 174

Goodrich, Chris, **Supp. XXII:** 206, 214

Goodrich, Frances, **Supp. XXVII:** 136

Goodrich, Samuel G., **Supp. I Part 1:** 38

Good Scent from a Strange Mountain, A (R. O. Butler), **Supp. XII:** 62, **70–72**

Good School, A (Yates), **Supp. XI:** 334, **346–347,** 348, 349

"Good Shepherdess, The/La Buena Pastora" (Mora), **Supp. XIII:** 228–229

Good Wife, The (O'Nan), **Supp. XXV:** 145, 149

Good Will (Smiley), **Supp. VI:** 292, **299–300**

Goodwin, K. L., **III:** 478

Goodwin, Stephen, **Supp. V:** 314, 316, 322, 323, 325

"Good Word for Winter, A" (J. R. Lowell), **Supp. I Part 2:** 420

Goodwyn, Janet, **Retro. Supp. I:** 370

Goody, Alex, **Supp. XXII:** 160

"Goophered Grapevine, The" (Chesnutt), **Supp. XIV:** 57, **58–61**

"Goose Fish, The" (Nemerov), **III:** 272, 284

"Goose Pond" (Kunitz), **Supp. III Part 1:** 262

Goose-Step, The (Sinclair), **Supp. V:** 276

Gordimer, Nadine, **Supp. XV:** 251

Gordon, Ambrose, **Supp. XV:** 144

Gordon, A. R., **III:** 199

Gordon, Caroline, **II: 196–222,** 536, 537; **III:** 454, 482; **IV:** 123, 126–127, 139, 282; **Retro. Supp. II:** 177, 222, 229, 233, 235; **Supp. II Part 1:** 139

Gordon, Charles G., **I:** 454

Gordon, Don, **Supp. X:** 119

Gordon, Eugene, **Supp. II Part 1:** 170; **Supp. XVIII:** 280

Gordon, Fran, **Supp. XIII:** 111

Gordon, James Morris, **II:** 197

Gordon, Lois, **Supp. IV Part 1:** 48; **Supp. V:** 46

Gordon, Lyndall, **Retro. Supp. I:** 55

Gordon, Mary, **Supp. IV Part 1: 297–317**

Gordon, Neil, **Supp. XVI:** 156

Gordon, Peter, **Supp. XII:** 3–4, 4–5, 8

Gordon, Ruth, **IV:** 357; **Supp. XX:** 50

Gore, Thomas Pryor, **Supp. IV Part 2:** 679

Gore and Igor (Levin), **Supp. XXVII:** 133

Gores, Joe, **Supp. XXI:** 70

Gorey, Edward, **IV:** 430, 436; **Supp. XXIII:** 209

"Gorge, The" (Huddle), **Supp. XXVI:** 154

Gorilla, My Love (Bambara), **Supp. XI:** 1, **2–7**

"Gorilla, My Love" (Bambara), **Supp. XI:** 2, 3–4

Gorki, Maxim, **I:** 478; **II:** 49; **III:** 402; **IV:** 299; **Supp. I Part 1:** 5, 51; **Supp. XIX:** 241

Gorky, Maxim, **Supp. XXIII:** 1, 4

Gorman, Herbert, **Supp. XXV:** 25

Gorney, Cynthia, **Supp. XVI:** 112

Gorra, Michael, **Supp. V:** 71

Goslings, The (Sinclair), **Supp. V:** 276, 281

Go South to Sorrow (Rowan), **Supp. XIV:** 306

Gospel (Barnhardt), **Supp. XXVII:** 1, 5–7, 8, 11, 13

Gospel According to Joe, The (Gurney), **Supp. V:** 99

"Gospel According to Saint Mark, The" (Gordon), **Supp. IV Part 1:** 310

Gospel according to the Son (Mailer), **Retro. Supp. II:** 213

"Gospel for the Twentieth Century, The" (Locke), **Supp. XIV:** 206

"Gospel of Beauty, The" (Lindsay), **Supp. I Part 2:** 380, 382, 384, 385, 391, 396

Gospels, The (di Donato), **Supp. XX: 45–46**

Gospel Singer, The (Crews), **Supp. XI:** 102, **109**

Gosse, Edmund, **II:** 538; **IV:** 350; **Supp. VIII:** 157

"Gossip" (Conroy), **Supp. XVI:** 71–72

Gossips, Gorgons, and Crones: The Fates of the Earth (Caputi), **Supp. IV Part 1:** 335

Go Tell It on the Mountain (Baldwin), **Retro. Supp. II:** 1, 2, 3, **4–5,** 7, 14; **Supp. I Part 1:** 48, 49, 50, 51, 52, 53–54, 55, 56, 57, 59, 61, 63, 64, 67; **Supp. II Part 1:** 170

Gotera, Vince, **Supp. XIII:** 115, 116, 119, 121, 127

Gothic Revival, The: An Essay on the History of Taste (Clark), **Supp. XIV:** 348

Gothic Writers (Thomson, Voller, and Frank, eds.), **Retro. Supp. II:** 273

"Go to the Devil and Shake Yourself" (song), **Supp. I Part 2:** 580

"Go to the Shine That's on a Tree" (Eberhart), **I:** 523

Go to the Widow-Maker (Jones), **Supp. XI:** 214, **225–226,** 227, 229, 233

"Gots Is What You Got" (Di Piero), **Supp. XIX:** 35, 36, 38, 41, 42, 45–46

Gottfried, Alex, **Supp. XIX:** 260

Gottfried, Martin, **Supp. IV Part 2:** 584

Gotthelf, Allan, **Supp. IV Part 2:** 528

Gottlieb, Adolph, **Supp. XV:** 144

Gottlieb, Edward, **Supp. XX: 250**

Gottlieb, Leopold, **Supp. XXIII:** 6

Gottlieb, Morton, **Supp. XVI:** 196

Gottlieb, Robert, **Supp. IV Part 2:** 474; **Supp. XXVI:** 244, 246, 250

Gottschalk and the Grande Tarantelle (Brooks), **Supp. III Part 1:** 86

"Gottschalk and the Grande Tarantelle" (Brooks), **Supp. III Part 1:** 86–87

Gould (Dixon), **Supp. XII:** 152, **153**

Gould, Edward Sherman, **I:** 346

Gould, Janice, **Supp. IV Part 1:** 322, 327; **Supp. XII:** 229

Gould, Jay, **I:** 4

Gould, Joe, **Supp. XV:** 143

Goulian, Jon-Jon, **Supp. XXVII:** 68

Gourd Dancer, The (Momaday), **Supp. IV Part 2:** 481, 487, 491, 493

Gourmont, Remy de, **I:** 270, 272; **II:** 528, 529; **III:** 457, 467–468, 477; **Retro. Supp. I:** 55

Gouverneurs de la Rosée (Roumain), **Supp. IV Part 1:** 360, 367

Government Girl (film, Nichols), **Supp. XVIII:** 247

"Governors of Wyoming, The" (Proulx), **Supp. VII:** 264

"Gowane"(Kenny), **Supp. XXIII:** 147–148

Goyen, William, **Supp. V:** 220

Grabhorn, Janet, **Supp. XV:** 142

"Grace" (Budbill), **Supp. XIX:** 2

"Grace" (Dubus), **Supp. VII:** 91

"Grace" (Harjo), **Supp. XII:** 224

Grace Notes (Dove), **Supp. IV Part 1:** 248–250, 252

Grace (Eventually): Thoughts on Faith (Lamott), **Supp. XX: 143–145**

Grade, Chaim, **Supp. XVII:** 41

"Grade School" (Stone), **Supp. XXVII:** 252

"Graduation" (Dubus), **Supp. VII:** 84

Grady, Henry W., **Supp. I Part 1:** 370

Graeber, Laurel, **Supp. V:** 15

Graham, Billy, **I:** 308

Graham, David, **Supp. XIX:** 81; **Supp. XV:** 104

Graham, Don, **Supp. XI:** 252, 254

Graham, Jorie, **Supp. IX:** 38, 52; **Supp. X:** 73; **Supp. XII:** 209; **Supp. XIII:** 85; **Supp. XVII:** 110, 111, 133, 240, 241, 242

Graham, Martha, **Supp. XI:** 152

Graham, Maryemma, **Retro. Supp. I:** 201, 204

Graham, Nan, **Supp. XII:** 272

Graham, Sheilah, **II:** 94; **Retro. Supp. I:** 97, 113–114, 115; **Supp. IX:** 63

Graham, Shirley, **Supp. I Part 1:** 51; **Supp. XXI:** 277. *See also* Du Bois, Shirley Graham

Graham, Stephen, **Supp. I Part 2:** 397

Graham, Tom (pseudonym). *See* Lewis, Sinclair

"Graham House, April '76"(Balakian), **Supp. XXIII:** 24

Grahn, Judy, **Supp. IV Part 1:** 325, 330; **Supp. XXIII:** 195

"Grain Field" (Crapsey), **Supp. XVII:** 77

Grainger, Percy, **Supp. I Part 2:** 386

Grain of Mustard Seed, A (Sarton), **Supp. VIII: 259–260,** 263

Gramar (Lowth), **II:** 8

"Gramercy Park" (Teasdale), **Supp. XXVII:** 289

Grammar of Motives, A (Burke), **I:** 272, 275, 276–278, 283, 284

Gramsci, Antonio, **Supp. XX: 35–36**

Granados, Gabriel Bernal, **Supp. XV:** 350

Granath, Jack, **Supp. XVIII:** 93

Granberry, Edwin, **I:** 288

Grand Canyon, Inc. (Everett), **Supp. XVIII:** 66

Grand Design, The (Dos Passos), **I:** 489–490

"Grande Malade, The" (Barnes), **Supp. III Part 1:** 36

"Grandfather" (Dunn), **Supp. XI:** 147

"Grandfather and Grandson" (Singer), **Retro. Supp. II:** 307

Grandfathers, The (Richter), **Supp. XVIII: 219–220**

"Grandfather's Blessing" (Alvarez), **Supp. VII:** 2

"Grand Forks" (Bierds), **Supp. XVII:** 34

"Grand Forks" (Simpson), **Supp. IX:** 280–281

"Grand Inquisitor" (Dostoevsky), **IV:** 106

Grandissimes (Cable), **II:** 291

"Grand-Master Nabokov" (Updike), **Retro. Supp. I:** 317

"Grand Miracle, The" (Karr), **Supp. XI:** 251

"Grandmother" (Gunn Allen), **Supp. IV Part 1:** 320, 325

"Grandmother in Heaven" (Levine), **Supp. V:** 186

"Grandmother of the Sun: Ritual Gynocracy in Native America" (Gunn Allen), **Supp. IV Part 1:** 328

Grandmothers of the Light: A Medicine Woman's Sourcebook (Gunn Allen, ed.), **Supp. IV Part 1:** 332, 333–334

"Grandmother Songs, The" (Hogan), **Supp. IV Part 1:** 413

"Grandpa and the Statue" (A. Miller), **III:** 147

"Grandparents" (R. Lowell), **II:** 550

"Grandsire Bells, The" (Bierds), **Supp. XVII:** 28–29

"Grandstand Complex, The" (McCoy), **Supp. XIII:** 166

Grange, Red, **II:** 416

Granger's Index to Poetry (anthology), **Retro. Supp. I:** 37, 39

Granite & Cedar (Miller), **Supp. XXII:** 214

Grant, Gavin, **Supp. XIX:** 175

Grant, Lee, **Supp. XIII:** 295

Grant, Madison, **Supp. II Part 1:** 170

Grant, Richard, **Supp. X:** 282

Grant, Ulysses S., **I:** 4, 15; **II:** 542; **III:** 506, 584; **IV:** 348, 446; **Supp. I Part 2:** 418; **Supp. XXIV:** 224

Grantwood, **Retro. Supp. I:** 416, 417

"Grapes, The" (Hecht), **Supp. X:** 65–66

"Grape Sherbet" (Dove), **Supp. IV Part 1:** 246

Grapes of Wrath, The (Steinbeck), **I:** 301; **III:** 589; **IV:** 51, 53–55, 59, 63, 65, 67, 68, 69; **Supp. V:** 290; **Supp. XI:** 169; **Supp. XIV:** 181; **Supp. XV:** 351; **Supp. XX: 28**

"Grapevine, The" (Ashbery), **Supp. III Part 1:** 4

"Grass" (Sandburg), **III:** 584

Grass, Günter, **Supp. VIII:** 40

Grass County (Kooser), **Supp. XIX:** 119

"Grasse: The Olive Trees" (Wilbur), **Supp. III Part 2:** 550

"Grass Figures" (Hecht), **Supp. XXVII:** 85

Grass Harp, The (Capote), **Supp. III Part 1:** 114–117, 123

Grass Still Grows, The (A. Miller), **III:** 146

"Gratified Desire" (Davison), **Supp. XXVI:** 74

"Grating Parmesan"(Crooker), **Supp. XXIII:** 56

Gratitude to Old Teachers (R. Bly), **Supp. IV Part 1:** 73

Grattan, Bill, **Supp. XXIII:** 273, 274, 275, 276, 279, 280

Graupner, Gottlieb, **Supp. XV:** 240, 244

"Grave, A" (Moore), **III:** 195, 202, 208, 213

Grave, The (Blair), **Supp. I Part 1:** 150

"Grave, The" (Porter), **III:** 433, 443, 445–446

"Grave, The" (Winters), **Supp. II Part 2:** 795, 796

"Graven Image" (O'Hara), **III:** 320

Grave of Light: New and Selected Poems, 1970–2005 (Notley), **Supp. XXII:** 226, 235, 236

Grave of the Right Hand, The (Wright), **Supp. V:** 332, 338, 339

"Grave Piece" (Eberhart), **I:** 533

Graver, Lawrence, **Supp. XXVII:** 136, 137, 140

Graves, Billy, **Supp. I Part 2:** 607

Graves, Jesse, **Supp. XXVII:** 216

Graves, John, **Supp. V:** 220

Graves, Morris, **Supp. X:** 264

Graves, Peter, **Supp. IV Part 2:** 474

Graves, Rean, **Supp. I Part 1:** 326

Graves, Robert, **I:** 437, 477, 523; **Supp. I Part 2:** 541; **Supp. IV Part 1:** 280, 348; **Supp. IV Part 2:** 685; **Supp. XXVI:** 53

"Graveyard, The" (Very), **Supp. XXV:** 249

"Graveyard Blues" (Trethewey), **Supp. XXI:** 245, 255, 256

Graveyard for Lunatics, A (Bradbury), **Supp. IV Part 1:** 102, 114–116

Gravity's Rainbow (Pynchon), **Supp. II Part 2:** 617, 618–619, 621–625, 627, 630, 633–636; **Supp. IV Part 1:** 279; **Supp. V:** 44; **Supp. XIV:** 49; **Supp. XVII:** 236; **Supp. XXII:** 255; **Supp. XXIV:** 140

Gray, Cecil, **Supp. I Part 1:** 258

Gray, Francine Du Plessix, **Supp. V:** 169

Gray, James, **III:** 207; **Supp. I Part 2:** 410

Gray, Jeffrey, **Supp. XV:** 27

Gray, Josie, **Supp. XXIV:** 166, 167, 172, 178

Gray, Paul, **Supp. IV Part 1:** 305; **Supp. IV Part 2:** 639; **Supp. XVI:** 74; **Supp. XVIII:** 94

Gray, Thomas, **I:** 68; **Supp. I Part 1:** 150; **Supp. I Part 2:** 422, 716

Gray, Thomas A., **Supp. I Part 2:** 710

"Gray Heron, The" (Kinnell), **Supp. III Part 1:** 250

"Gray Mills of Farley, The" (Jewett), **Retro. Supp. II:** 132, 144

"Gray Poem" (Everwine), **Supp. XV:** 81

Grayscale: Poems (Huddle), **Supp. XXVI:** 150

Grayson, Charles, **Supp. XIII:** 171

"Gray Squirrel" (Francis), **Supp. IX:** 90

"Gray Wolf's H 'ant, The" (Chesnutt), **Supp. XIV:** 60

Grealy, Lucy, **Supp. XII:** 310

Greasy Lake (Boyle), **Supp. VIII: 14–15**

"Greasy Lake" (Boyle), **Supp. VIII:** 15; **Supp. XX: 18–19**

Greasy Lake & Other Stories (Boyle), **Supp. XX: 17, 18–19**

Great Action Stories (Kittredge and Krauzer), **Supp. XXVI:** 182

"Great Adventure of Max Breuck, The" (A. Lowell), **II:** 522

Great American Detective, The (Kittredge and Krauzer), **Supp. XXVI:** 182

Great American Novel, The (P. Roth), **Retro. Supp. II:** 283, 288–289; **Supp. III Part 2:** 414–416

Great American Short Novels (Phillips, ed.), **Supp. VIII:** 156

Great Battles of the World (Crane), **I:** 415

"Great Carousel, The" (Untermeyer), **Supp. XV:** 296

Great Christian Doctrine of Original Sin Defended, The . . . (Edwards), **I:** 549, 557, 559

Great Circle (Aiken), **I:** 53, 55, 57

"Great Class-Reunion Bazaar, The" (Theroux), **Supp. VIII:** 312

Great Day, The (Hurston), **Supp. VI:** 154

Great Days (Barthelme), **Supp. IV Part 1:** 39

Great Days, The (Dos Passos), **I:** 491

Great Digest (Pound, trans.), **III:** 472

"Great Divider, The" (Saunders), **Supp. XIX:** 235

"Great Elegy for John Donne" (Brodsky), **Supp. VIII:** 21, 23

"Greater Good, A" (Di Piero), **Supp. XIX:** 39

Greater Inclination, The (Wharton), **Retro. Supp. I:** 363, **364–365,** 366

Greater Sea, The (Gibran), **Supp. XX: 118**

"Greater Self, The" (Gibran), **Supp. XX: 118**

"Greater Torment, The" (Blackmur), **Supp. II Part 1:** 92

Greatest Hits 1969–1996 (Salinas), **Supp. XIII:** 311

"Greatest of These, The" (C. Miller), **Supp. XXII:** 188, 196

"Greatest Thing in the World, The" (Mailer), **Retro. Supp. II:** 196

Great Expectations (Acker), **Supp. XII:** 5, **9–11**

Great Expectations (Dickens), **III:** 247; **Supp. I Part 1:** 35; **Supp. XVI:** 73; **Supp. XVIII:** 146; **Supp. XXVII:** 268

"Great Expectations, No Satisfaction" (D. Gates), **Supp. XVI:** 73

"Great Figure, The" (W. C. Williams), **IV:** 414

"Great Fillmore Street Buffalo Drive, The" (Momaday), **Supp. IV Part 2:** 493

Great Gatsby, The (Fitzgerald), **I:** 107, 375, 514; **II:** 77, 79, 83, 84, 85, 87, 91–93, 94, 96, 98; **III:** 244, 260, 372, 572; **IV:** 124, 297; **Retro. Supp. I:** 98, 105, **105–108,** 110, 114, 115, 335, 359; **Retro. Supp. II:** 107, 201; **Supp. II Part 2:** 626; **Supp. III Part 2:** 585; **Supp. IV Part 2:** 468, 475; **Supp. IX:** 57, 58; **Supp. X:** 175; **Supp. XI:** 65, 69, 334; **Supp. XVI:** 64, 75; **Supp. XVIII:** 76, 148, 165; **Supp. XX: 59, 60, 61, 72; Supp. XXII:** 81, 82, 88; **Supp. XXIII:** 101; **Supp. XXVII:** 9

Great Gatsby, The (Fitzgerald) (Modern Library), **Retro. Supp. I:** 113

Great God Brown, The (O'Neill), **III:** 165, 391, 394–395

Great Goodness of Life: A Coon Show (Baraka), **Supp. II Part 1:** 47

Great Heart: The History of a Labrador Adventure (Davidson and Rugge), **Supp. XXII:** 218

"Great Idea Lives Forever, A: Shouldn't Its Copyright?" (Helprin), **Supp. XXV:** 84, 88

Great Inclination, The (Wharton), **IV:** 310

"Great Infirmities" (Simic), **Supp. VIII:** 277

Great Jones Street (DeLillo), **Supp. VI:** 2, 3, 8–9, 11, 12

"Great Lawsuit, The: Man *versus* Men: Woman *versus* Women" (Fuller), **Retro. Supp. I:** 156; **Supp. II Part 1:** 292

Great Ledge, The (Davison), **Supp. XXVI:** 66, 77–78

"Great Ledge, The" (Davison), **Supp. XXVI:** 77, 78

"Great Men and Their Environment" (James), **II:** 347

"Great Mississippi Bubble, The" (Irving), **II:** 314

Great Mistake, The (Rinehart), **Supp. XXV:** 198, 200

Great Railway Bazaar, The: By Train through Asia (Theroux), **Supp. VIII:** 318, 319, **320–321,** 322

"Great Scott" (Conroy), **Supp. XVI:** 75, 77

Great Shark Hunt, The (Thompson), **Supp. XXIV:** 286

"Great Sleigh-Ride of Brewsterville, The" (Briggs), **Supp. XVIII:** 16

"Great Spirit, The" (Zitkala-Ša), **Supp. XXV:** 276, 282

Great Stories of Suspense (Millar, ed.), **Supp. IV Part 2:** 474

Great Topics of the World (Goldbarth), **Supp. XII:** 187, 189, 191

Great Valley, The (Masters), **Supp. I Part 2:** 465

Great World and Timothy Colt, The (Auchincloss), **Supp. IV Part 1:** 25, 31, 32

Grédy, Jean-Pierre, **Supp. XVI:** 194

"Greek Boy, The" (Bryant), **Supp. I Part 1:** 168

Greek Mind/Jewish Soul: The Conflicted Art of Cynthia Ozick (Strandberg), **Supp. V:** 273

"Greek Partisan, The" (Bryant), **Supp. I Part 1:** 168

"Greeks, The" (McCarriston), **Supp. XIV:** 271

"Greeks, the Chines, or Say the Mayans, The" (Bronk), **Supp. XXI:** 31

Greeley, Horace, **II:** 7; **IV:** 197, 286–287

Green, Anna Katharine, **Supp. XXV:** 199; **Supp. XXVI:** 277, 282

Green, Archie, **Supp. XXVI:** 134

Green, Ashbel, **Supp. IV Part 2:** 474

Green, David Gordon, **Supp. XXV:** 153

Green, Henry, **IV:** 279; **Retro. Supp. I:** 354; **Supp. III Part 1:** 3; **Supp. XI:** 294–295, 296, 297; **Supp. XII:** 315

Green, Jack, **Supp. IV Part 1:** 284–285

Green, Martin, **Supp. I Part 1:** 299

Green, Michelle, **Supp. IV Part 1:** 95

Green, Rose Basile, **Supp. XX: 33, 41**

"Green Automobile, The" (Ginsberg), **Supp. II Part 1:** 322

Greenberg, Clement, **Supp. XV:** 141, 143, 144, 145

Greenberg, Eliezer, **Supp. I Part 2:** 432; **Supp. XXIII:** 7

Greenberg, Hayim, **Supp. XXIII:** 3

Greenberg, Jonathan, **Supp. XII:** 285

Greenberg, Miriam, **Supp. XXII:** 244

Greenberg, Samuel, **I:** 393

Green Bough, A (Faulkner), **Retro. Supp. I:** 84

"Green Canoe" (Halliday), **Supp. XIX:** 88

Green Centuries (Gordon), **II:** 196, 197–207, 209

"Green Crab's Shell, A" (Doty), **Supp. XI:** 126

"Green Door, The" (O. Henry), **Supp. II Part 1:** 395

Greene, A. C., **Supp. V:** 223, 225

Greene, Graham, **I:** 480; **II:** 62, 320; **III:** 57, 556; **Retro. Supp. I:** 215; **Supp. I Part 1:** 280; **Supp. IV Part 1:** 341; **Supp. IX:** 261; **Supp. V:** 298; **Supp. XI:** 99,**Supp. XI:** 104; **Supp. XIII:** 233; **Supp. XIX:** 29–30; **Supp. XVIII:** 79

Greene, Helga, **Supp. IV Part 1:** 134, 135

Greene, J. Lee, **Retro. Supp. II:** 121

Greene, Nathanael, **Supp. I Part 2:** 508

Greene, Richard Tobias, **III:** 76

Greene, Robert, **Supp. XVII:** 232

Green Eggs and Ham (Geisel), **Supp. XVI:** 108, 109

"Greene-ing of the Portables, The" (Cowley), **Supp. II Part 1:** 140

"Greenest Continent, The" (Stevens), **Retro. Supp. I:** 304

Greenfeld, Josh, **III:** 364

Greenfield, Josh, **Supp. XIX:** 269

"Green Hell" (Boyle), **Supp. XX: 18**

Green Hills of Africa (Hemingway), **II:** 253; **Retro. Supp. I:** 182, 186

Greening of America, The (C. Reich), **Supp. XVII:** 3

"Green Lagoons, The" (Leopold), **Supp. XIV:** 188

"Green Lampshade" (Simic), **Supp. VIII:** 283

Greenlanders, The (Smiley), **Supp. VI:** 292, **296–298,** 299, 305, 307

Greenlaw, Edwin A., **IV:** 453

"Greenleaf" (O'Connor), **III:** 350, 351; **Retro. Supp. II:** 233, 237

Greenman, Walter F., **I:** 217, 222

Green Memories (Mumford), **Supp. II Part 2:** 474, 475, 479, 480–481

Green Mountain Ghosts, Ghouls, and Unsolved Mysteries (Citro), **Supp. XXII:** 208, 218

"Green Pasture, The" (Leopold), **Supp. XIV:** 184

Green Pastures, The (Connelly), **Supp. II Part 1:** 223

"Green Red Brown and White" (Swenson), **Supp. IV Part 2:** 639

"Green River" (Bryant), **Supp. I Part 1:** 155, 164

Green Shadows, White Whale (Bradbury), **Supp. IV Part 1:** 102, 103, 116

"Green Shirt, The" (Olds), **Supp. X:** 209

"Greensleeves" (Jarman), **Supp. XVII:** 113

"Greensleeves" (Notley), **Supp. XXII:** 228

Greenslet, Ferris, **I:** 19; **Retro. Supp. I:** 9, 10, 11, 13; **Retro. Supp. II:** 41

Greenspan, Alan, **Supp. IV Part 2:** 526

Greenspan, Ezra, **Supp. XVIII:** 257

Greenstreet, Sydney, **Supp. IV Part 1:** 356

"Green Thought, A" (L. Michaels), **Supp. XVI:** 204

"Green-Thumb Boy" (Nelson), **Supp. XVIII:** 182

Greenwald, Ted, **Supp. IV Part 2:** 423

Green Wall, The (Wright), **Supp. III Part 2:** 591, 593, 595

Green Wave, The (Rukeyser), **Supp. VI:** 273, 280

"Green Ways" (Kunitz), **Supp. III Part 1:** 265

Green with Beasts (Merwin), **Supp. III Part 1:** 340, 344–346

Greenwood, Grace, **Supp. XIII:** 141

"Greeting Card Verse" (Peacock), **Supp. XIX:** 200

Greetings from Ice Country (Muñoz), **Supp. XXV:** 130

Gregerson, Linda, **Supp. IV Part 2:** 651; **Supp. X:** 204–205; **Supp. XI:** 142

"Gregorio Valdes" (Bishop), **Retro. Supp. II:** 51

Gregory, Alyse, **I:** 221, 226, 227, 231

Gregory, Horace, **II:** 512; **Supp. III Part 2:** 614, 615; **Supp. IX:** 229; **Supp. XV:** 143

Gregory, Lady Isabella Augusta, **III:** 458

Gregory, Sinda, **Supp. X:** 260, 268

Grendel (Gardner), **Supp. VI:** 63, **67, 68,** 74

Grenstone Poems (Bynner), **Supp. XV:** 44

"Gretel in Darkness" (Glück), **Supp. V:** 82

Gretta (Caldwell), **I:** 301, 302

Greuze, Jean Baptiste, **Supp. I Part 2:** 714

Grey, Zane, **Supp. XIII:** 5; **Supp. XXVI:** 186

Greyhounding This America (Kenny), **Supp. XXIII: 155**

Gridley Firing (Hayford), **Supp. XXII:** 204

"Grief Has Stamped" (Pedersen; Nelson, trans.), **Supp. XVIII:** 180

Grieg, Michael, **Supp. XV:** 133, 148

Griffin, Bartholomew, **Supp. I Part 1:** 369

Griffin, John Howard, **Supp. VIII:** 208; **Supp. XXI:** 74; **Supp. XXV:** 51

Griffin, Merv, **Supp. IV Part 2:** 526

Griffith, Albert J., **Supp. V:** 325

Griffith, D. W., **I:** 31, 481–482; **Retro. Supp. I:** 103, 325; **Supp. XI:** 45; **Supp. XVI:** 183, 184; **Supp. XXI:** 170

Griffith, Paul, **Supp. XVIII:** 173, 175

Griffiths, Clyde, **I:** 511

Grile, Dod (pseudonym). *See* Bierce, Ambrose
Grimm, Herman, **II:** 17
Grimm brothers, **II:** 378; **III:** 101, 491, 492; **IV:** 266; **Supp. I Part 2:** 596, 622; **Supp. X:** 78, 84, 86
Grimshaw, Anna, **Supp. XXI:** 172
Grinde, Donald A., Jr, **Supp. XXVI:** 98
Grinnell, George Bird, **Supp. XVI:** 13
Gris, Juan, **I:** 442; **Retro. Supp. I:** 430
Griswold, Rufus Wilmot, **III:** 409, 429; **Retro. Supp. II:** 261, 262; **Supp. XV:** 277, 278; **Supp. XVI:** 8, 10–11; **Supp. XXV:** 250
"Grizzly" (Kittredge), **Supp. XXVI:** 187
Grogg, Sam, Jr., **Supp. IV Part 2:** 468, 471
Gromer, Crystal, **Supp. XII:** 297
Gronlund, Laurence, **II:** 276
Grooms, Red, **Supp. XV:** 178
Grooves: A Kind of Mystery (Brockmeier), **Supp. XXII:** 55, 56, 59
"Groping for Trouts" (Gass), **Supp. VI:** 87
Grosholz, Emily, **Supp. XII:** 185; **Supp. XIX:** 37–38, 278
Grosman un zun (Grosman and Son) (Asch), **Supp. XXIII:** 7
Gross, Robert A., **Supp. XIX:** 151
Gross, Terry, **Supp. XVI:** 167; **Supp. XXI:** 247, 255
"*Grosse Fuge*" (Doty), *Supp. XI:* 126–127
Grossman, Allen, **Retro. Supp. II:** 83; **Supp. XIX:** 82, 86, 94; **Supp. XVIII:** 91
Grossman, Lev, **Supp. XXV:** 4, **63–78**
Grosz, George, **III:** 172; **IV:** 438; **Retro. Supp. II:** 321; **Supp. X:** 137; **Supp. XXVII:** 88
"Grotesque in Modern Fiction, The" (E. Hoffman, Ph.D. dissertation), **Supp. XVI:** 147
"Groundhog, The" (Eberhart), **I:** 523, 530–532, 533
"Ground on Which I Stand, The" (Wilson), **Supp. VIII:** 331
"Ground Swell" (Jarman), **Supp. XVII:** 118
Group, The (McCarthy), **II:** 570, 574–578
"Group of Two, A" (Jarrell), **II:** 368
Group Therapy (Hearon), **Supp. VIII:** 64–65
"Grove" (Goldbarth), **Supp. XII:** 176
Groves of Academe, The (McCarthy), **II:** 568–571
Growing into Love (X. J. Kennedy), **Supp. XV:** 153, **158–160**
Growing Pains (J. S. Untermeyer), **Supp. XV:** 303
"Growing Season, The" (Caldwell), **I:** 309
Growing Up Gay: A Literary Anthology (Singer, ed.), **Supp. IV Part 1:** 330
"Growing Up Good in Maycomb" (Shaffer), **Supp. VIII:** 128
Growing Up Native American (Riley, ed.), **Supp. XXVI:** 104

"Grown-Up" (Jewett), **Retro. Supp. II:** 134
Grown Up All Wrong (Christgau), **Supp. XXVII:** 33, 35–36, 40–41
"Growth" (R. Lowell), **II:** 554
"Growth and Decay in Recent Verse" (Untermeyer), **Supp. XV:** 299
Growth of the American Republic, The (Morison and Commager), **Supp. I Part 2:** 484
"Growtown Buggle, The" (Jewett), **Retro. Supp. II:** 132
Grubin, David, **Supp. XXIII:** 138
Gruenberg, Louis, **III:** 392
Grumbach, Doris, **II:** 560
"Gryphon" (C. Baxter), **Supp. XVII:** 14, 17
"Guacamaja" (Leopold), **Supp. XIV:** 188–189
Guardian Angel (Paretsky), **Supp. XXV:** 178, 179
Guardian Angel, The (Holmes), **Supp. I Part 1:** 315–316
"Guardian of the Law" (R. Fisher), **Supp. XIX:** 71
Guard of Honor (Cozzens), **I:** 370–372, 375, 376–377, 378, 379
Guardsman, The (Molnar), **Supp. XVI:** 187
Guare, John, **Supp. XIII:** 196, 207
Guattari, Félix, **Supp. XXV:** 123
Gubar, Susan, **Retro. Supp. I:** 42; **Retro. Supp. II:** 324; **Supp. IX:** 66; **Supp. XV:** 270; **Supp. XXIV:** 28
"Guenevere" (Teasdale), **Supp. XXVII:** 287
Guerard, Albert, Jr., **Supp. X:** 79; **Supp. XIII:** 172
Guérin, Maurice de, **I:** 241
"Guerrilla Handbook, A" (Baraka), **Supp. II Part 1:** 36
Guess and Spell Coloring Book, The (Swenson), **Supp. IV Part 2:** 648
Guess Who's Coming to Dinner (film), **Supp. I Part 1:** 67
Guest, Barbara, **Supp. XXIII:** 215; **Supp. XXVII:** 23
Guest, Judith, **Supp. XVI:** 36
Guest, Val, **Supp. XI:** 307
Guest Book (Bynner), **Supp. XV:** 51
"Guest Ellen at the Supper for Street People, The" (Ferry), **Supp. XXIV:** 152–153, 162
"Guests of Mrs. Timms, The" (Jewett), **II:** 408; **Retro. Supp. II:** 135
Guevara, Martha, **Supp. VIII:** 74
Guevara, Fray Miguel de, **Supp. XXI:** 104
"Guevara . . .Guevara" (Salinas), **Supp. XIII:** 312–313, 315
Guggenheim, Peggy, **Supp. XXII:** 165
Guided Tours of Hell (Prose), **Supp. XVI:** 257, 261
"Guided Tours of Hell" (Prose), **Supp. XVI:** 257
Guide for the Bedevilled, A (Hecht), **Supp. XXVII:** 94, 95
Guide for the Perplexed (Maimonides), **Supp. XVII:** 46

Guide in the Wilderness, A (Cooper), **I:** 337
"Guidelines" (Espaillat), **Supp. XXI:** 99
"Guide to Dungeness Spit, A" (Wagoner), **Supp. IX:** 325–326, 329
Guide to Ezra Pound's Selected Cantos' (Kearns), *Retro. Supp. I:* 292
Guide to Kulchur (Pound), **III:** 475
Guide to the Ruins (Nemerov), **III:** 269, 270–271, 272
Guillén, Jorge, **Supp. XXIV:** 152
Guillén, Nicolás, **Retro. Supp. I:** 202; **Supp. I Part 1:** 345
Guillevic, Eugene, **Supp. III Part 1:** 283
"Guilt, The" (Peacock), **Supp. XIX:** 200
"Guilty Man, The" (Kunitz), **Supp. II Part 1:** 263
Guilty of Everything: The Autobiography of Herbert Huncke (Huncke), **Supp. XIV:** 138, 140, 141, 150
Guilty Pleasures (Barthelme), **Supp. IV Part 1:** 44, 45, 53
Guimond, James, **Supp. XXI:** 228
Guinness, Alec, **Retro. Supp. I:** 65; **Supp. XX:** 50
Gulag Archipelago, The (Solzhenitsyn), **Supp. XVII:** 229
"Gulf, The" (Dunn), **Supp. XI:** 149
Gulistan (Saadi), **II:** 19
Gullible's Travels (Lardner), **II:** 426, 427
Gulliver, Adelaide Cromwell, **Supp. XVIII:** 286
"Gulliver Found" (Bronk), **Supp. XXI:** 33
Gulliver's Travels (Swift), **I:** 209, 348, 366; **II:** 301; **Supp. I Part 2:** 656; **Supp. XI:** 209; **Supp. XVI:** 110
"Gulls" (Hayden), **Supp. II Part 1:** 367
"Gulls, The" (Nemerov), **III:** 272
"Gulls on Dumps" (Di Piero), **Supp. XIX:** 41
"Gun, The" (Dobyns), **Supp. XIII:** 88
Gun, with Occasional Music (Lethem), **Supp. XVIII: 137–138**
Günderode: A Translation from the German (Fuller), **Supp. II Part 1:** 293
Gunderson, Gwen, **Supp. XXVI:** 134
Gundy, Jeff, **Supp. XI:** 315; **Supp. XVI:** 46, 265, 275
Gunfight at the O.K. Corral (film), **Supp. XX: 246**
Gunga Din (screenplay, Hecht and MacArthur), **Supp. XXVII:** 83, 90
"Gun Hand, The" (Davison), **Supp. XXVI:** 71
Gun in Cheek (Pronzini), **Supp. XXVI:** 278
Gunman's Rhapsody (Parker), **Supp. XIX:** 187
Gunn, Robin Wright, **Supp. XXI:** 243, 244
Gunn, Thom, **Supp. IX:** 269
Gunn, Thomas, **Supp. V:** 178
Gunn Allen, Paula, **Supp. IV Part 1: 319–340,** 404; **Supp. IV Part 2:** 499, 502, 557, 568; **Supp. XII:** 218
"Gunnar's Sword" (C. Bly), **Supp. XVI:** 34, 35, 37, 42
"Guns as Keys; and the Great Gate Swings" (A. Lowell), **II:** 524

Gurdjieff, Georges, **Supp. IX:** 320; **Supp. V:** 199

Gurganus, Allan, **Supp. XII:** 308–309, 310

Gurko, Leo, **III:** 62

Gurney, A. R., **Supp. IX:** 261; **Supp. V: 95–112**

Gurney, Mary (Molly) Goodyear, **Supp. V:** 95

Gussow, Mel, **Supp. IX:** 93; **Supp. XII:** 325, 328, 341

Gustavus Vassa, the African (Vassa), **Supp. IV Part 1:** 11

Gusto, Thy Name Was Mrs. Hopkins: A Prose Rhapsody (Francis), **Supp. IX:** 89

Guston, Philip, **Supp. XXIII:** 210

Gute Mensch von Sezuan, Der (Brecht), **Supp. IX:** 138

Gutenberg, Johann, **Supp. I Part 2:** 392

Guthrie, A. B., **Supp. X:** 103

Guthrie, Woody, **Supp. XVIII:** 23

Gutman, Herbert, **Supp. I Part 1:** 47

Guttenplan, D. D., **Supp. XI:** 38

"Gutting of Couffignal, The" (Hammett), **Supp. IV Part 1:** 345

Guttman, Allen, **Supp. XXVII:** 134

Guy, David, **Supp. XXVI:** 9

Guy Domville (James), **II:** 331; **Retro. Supp. I:** 228

"Gwendolyn" (Bishop), **Retro. Supp. II:** 51

Gwynn, R. S., **Supp. XVIII:** 184

Gypsy Ballads (Hughes, trans.), **Supp. I Part 1:** 345

Gypsy's Curse, The (Crews), **Supp. XI:** 110

"Gyroscope, The" (Rukeyser), **Supp. VI:** 271

Gysin, Brion, **Supp. XII:** 129

H

Ha, Quan Manh, **Supp. XXVI:** 213, 214, 215

Haardt, Sara. *See* Mencken, Mrs. H. L. (Sara Haardt)

Haas, Robert, **Supp. XXII:** 177

Habakkuk (biblical book), **III:** 200, 347

Habibi (Nye), **Supp. XIII:** 273, **279**

"Habit" (James), **II:** 351

Habitations of the Word (Gass), **Supp. VI:** 88

"Hack, The" (Swados), **Supp. XIX:** 267

"Hackberry"(P. Benedict), **Supp. XXIII:** 37–38, 39

Hacker, Marilyn, **Supp. XV:** 250; **Supp. XVII:** 71, 76, 112; **Supp. XVIII:** 177, 178

Hacker, Randi, **Supp. XXVI:** 121

Hacket, Albert, **Supp. XXVII:** 136

Hackett, David, **Supp. XII:** 236

Hadas, Rachel, **Supp. XXIII: 111–128; Supp. XXIV:** 157

Hadda, Janet, **Retro. Supp. II:** 317

Haddád, 'Abd al-Masíh, **Supp. XX: 116**

"Hades Welcomes His Bride" (Stallings), **Supp. XXV:** 229–230

Haeckel, Ernst Heinrich, **II:** 480

Haegert, John, **Supp. XVI:** 69

Hafen, P. Jane, **Supp. XXV:** 280

Hafif, Marcia, **Supp. IV Part 2:** 423

Hagar's Daughter (P. Hopkins), **Supp. XVI:** 143

Hagedorn, Jessica, **Supp. X:** 292

Hagen, Beulah, **Supp. I Part 2:** 679

Hager, Kelly, **Supp. XVIII:** 183

Hagestadt, Emma, **Supp. XXVI:** 212

Haggard, Rider, **III:** 189

Haggas, Carol, **Supp. XXVI:** 159, 160

Hagoromo (play), **III:** 466

Hagstrum, Jean, **Supp. XV:** 74

"Hail Mary" (Fante), **Supp. XI:** 160, 164

Haines, George, IV, **I:** 444

Haines, John, **Supp. XII: 197–214**

"Hair" (Corso), **Supp. XII:** 117, 126, 127

"Hair, The" (Carver), **Supp. III Part 1:** 137

"Haircut" (Lardner), **II:** 430, 436

"Hair Dressing" (Untermeyer), **Supp. XV:** 304, 305

Hairpiece: A Film for Nappy-Headed People (Chenzira; film), **Supp. XI:** 19–20

"Hairs" (Cisneros), **Supp. VII:** 59

Hairs/Pelitos (Cisneros), **Supp. VII:** 58

Hairy Ape, The (O'Neill), **III:** 391, 392, 393

"Haïta the Shepherd" (Bierce), **I:** 203

Haj, The (Uris), **Supp. XX: 244, 245, 247, 255–256**

Hajdu, David, **Supp. XXVII:** 153

Haldeman, Anna, **Supp. I Part 1:** 2

Hale, Edward Everett, **Supp. I Part 2:** 584; **Supp. XI:** 193, 200

Hale, John Parker, **Supp. I Part 2:** 685

Hale, Nancy, **Supp. VIII:** 151, 171

Haley, Alex, **Supp. I Part 1:** 47, 66

Haley, J. Evetts, **Supp. V:** 226

"Half a Century Gone" (R. Lowell), **II:** 554

"Half a Grapefruit" (Munro), **Supp. XXVII:** 186–187

Half-a-Hundred: Tales by Great American Writers (Grayson, ed.), **Supp. XIII:** 171

Half and Half: Writers on Growing Up Biracial and Bicultural (Hearn, ed.), **Supp. XXV:** 51

Half Asleep in Frog Pajamas (Robbins), **Supp. X:** 259, **279–282**

Half Breed, The (film), **Supp. XVI:** 185

Half-Century of Conflict, A (Parkman), **Supp. II Part 2:** 600, 607, 610

"Half Deity" (Moore), **III:** 210, 214, 215

"Half Hour of August" (Ríos), **Supp. IV Part 2:** 552

"Half-Life of Cardio-Pulmonary Function, A" (Gansworth), **Supp. XXVI:** 111

Half-Life of Cardio-Pulmonary Function, A: Poems and Paintings (Gansworth), **Supp. XXVI:** 110–111

Half-Lives (Jong), **Supp. V:** 115, 119

Half Moon Street: Two Short Novels (Theroux), **Supp. VIII:** 322, 323

Half of Paradise (Burke), **Supp. XIV:** 22, 24

Half-Past Nation Time (C. Johnson), **Supp. VI:** 187

Half Remembered (Davison), **Supp. XXVI:** 61, 63, 65, 66–67, 70, 71

"Half-Skinned Steer, The" (Proulx), **Supp. VII:** 261–262

"Half Sonnets" (Jarman), **Supp. XVII:** 115

Half Sun Half Sleep (Swenson), **Supp. IV Part 2:** 645–646

Halfway (Kumin), **Supp. IV Part 2:** 441–442

"Halfway" (Rich), **Supp. I Part 2:** 553

Halfway Down the Hall: New and Selected Poems (Hadas), **Supp. XXIII: 118–119**

Halfway Home (Monette), **Supp. X:** 154

Halfway to Silence (Sarton), **Supp. VIII:** 261

Half You Don't Know, The: Selected Stories (Cameron), **Supp. XII:** 79, 80, 81

Haliburton, Thomas Chandler, **II:** 301; **IV:** 193; **Supp. I Part 2:** 411

Halifax, Lord, **II:** 111

Hall, Daniel, **Supp. XII:** 258

Hall, Donald, **I:** 567; **III:** 194; **Supp. IV Part 1:** 63, 72; **Supp. IV Part 2:** 621; **Supp. IX:** 269; **Supp. XIV:** 82, 126; **Supp. XV:** 21, 153, 176; **Supp. XVI:** 39, 230, 235; **Supp. XX: 194; Supp. XXI:** 86; **Supp. XXIII:** 209; **Supp. XXVI:**

Hall, Hazel, **Supp. XXII:** 275

Hall, James, **II:** 313; **Supp. I Part 2:** 584, 585

Hall, James Baker, **Supp. X:** 24

Hall, John, **Supp. XXVII:** 253

Hall, Rachel, **Supp. XXIII:** 301

Hall, Timothy L., **Supp. VIII:** 127, 128

Halleck, Fitz-Greene, **Supp. I Part 1:** 156, 158

"Hallelujah" (Cohen), **Supp. XXVII:** 52, 56, 61–62

"Hallelujah: A Sestina" (Francis), **Supp. IX:** 82

"Hallelujah on the Bum" (Abbey), **Supp. XIII:** 2

"Haller's Second Home" (Maxwell), **Supp. VIII:** 169

Halliday, Mark, **Supp. XIX: 81–95; Supp. XV:** 19, 20, 21, 23, 25, 27, 30

Hallock, Rev. Moses, **Supp. I Part 1:** 153

Hall of Mirrors, A (Stone), **Supp. V:** 295, 296–299, 300, 301

"Hallowe'en" (Huncke), **Supp. XIV:** 145

"Halloween Party, The" (Chabon), **Supp. XI:** 72

Halloween Tree, The (Bradbury), **Supp. IV Part 1:** 102, 112–113

"Halls, The" (Halliday), **Supp. XIX:** 90

Hallwas, John E., **Supp. I Part 2:** 454

Halpern, Daniel, **Supp. IV Part 1:** 94–95, 95

Halpern, Paul, **Supp. XXV:** 123

Halpern, Sue, **Supp. XXVI:** 128

Halsey, Theresa, **Supp. IV Part 1:** 330, 331

"Halt in the Desert, A" (Brodsky), **Supp. VIII:** 24

"Halves" (Dunn), **Supp. XI:** 149

Hamburg, Victoria, **Supp. XVI:** 126

Hamerik, Asger, **Supp. I Part 1:** 356
Hamill, Pete, **Supp. XX: 244, 255**
Hamill, Sam, **Supp. X:** 112, 125, 126, 127
Hamilton, Alexander, **I:** 485; **Supp. I Part 2:** 456, 483, 509
Hamilton, Alice, **Supp. I Part 1:** 5
Hamilton, David, **Supp. IX:** 296
Hamilton, Edith, **Supp. XVI:** 196
Hamilton, Lady Emma, **II:** 524
Hamilton, Hamish, **Supp. I Part 2:** 617
Hamilton, Walton, **Supp. I Part 2:** 632
Hamilton Stark (Banks), **Supp. V:** 8, 9–10, 11
"Hamlen Brook" (Wilbur), **Supp. III Part 2:** 564
"Hamlet" (Laforgue), **I:** 573; **III:** 11
Hamlet (Miller and Fraenkel), **III:** 178, 183
Hamlet (Shakespeare), **I:** 53, 183, 205, 377, 586–587; **II:** 158, 531; **III:** 7, 11, 12, 183; **IV:** 116, 131, 227; **Supp. I Part 1:** 369; **Supp. I Part 2:** 422, 457, 471; **Supp. IV Part 2:** 612; **Supp. IX:** 14
Hamlet, The (Faulkner), **II:** 69–71, 73, 74; **IV:** 131; **Retro. Supp. I:** 82, 91, 92; **Supp. IX:** 103; **Supp. VIII:** 178; **Supp. XI:** 247
"Hamlet and His Problems" (Eliot), **I:** 586–587
Hamlet of A. MacLeish, The (MacLeish), **III:** 11–12, 14, 15, 18
Hamlin, Eva, **Retro. Supp. II:** 115
"Hammer" (Bidart), **Supp. XV:** 35
Hammer, Adam, **Supp. XIII:** 112
Hammer, Langdon, **Retro. Supp. II:** 45, 53; **Supp. X:** 65
"Hammer Man, The" (Bambara), **Supp. XI:** 4–5
Hammett, Dashiell, **IV:** 286; **Retro. Supp. II:** 327; **Supp. I Part 1:** 286, 289, 291, 292, 293, 294, 295; **Supp. III Part 1:** 91; **Supp. IV Part 1:** 120, 121, **341–357**; **Supp. IV Part 2:** 461, 464, 468, 469, 472, 473; **Supp. IX:** 200; **Supp. XI:** 228; **Supp. XIII:** 159; **Supp. XIV:** 21; **Supp. XIX:** 178; **Supp. XVII:** 137; **Supp. XXI:** 68; **Supp. XXVI:** 277, 282
Hammon, Jupiter, **Supp. XXII:** 11
Hammond, John, **Supp. XVIII:** 24
Hammond, Karla, **Supp. IV Part 2:** 439, 442, 448, 637, 640, 644, 648
Hampl, Patricia, **Supp. IX:** 291; **Supp. XI:** 126; **Supp. XVII:** 21; **Supp. XXII: 81–101**
Hampson, Alfred Leete, **Retro. Supp. I:** 35–36, 38
"Hamrick's Polar Bear" (Caldwell), **I:** 309–310
Hamsun, Knut, **Supp. VIII:** 40; **Supp. XI:** 161, 167; **Supp. XII:** 21, 128
Hancock, John, **Supp. I Part 2:** 524; **Supp. XX: 282**
Hancock, Wade, **Supp. XVI:** 34
"Handbill Distributed in Buncombe County, North Carolina: 1915" (Rash), **Supp. XXVII:** 218

Handbook of North American Indians (Sando), **Supp. IV Part 2:** 510
Handcarved Coffins: A Nonfiction Account of an American Crime (Capote), **Supp. III Part 1:** 131
Handel, Georg Friedrich, **III:** 210; **IV:** 369
"Handfasting" (Wright), **Supp. XV:** 343
"Handfuls" (Sandburg), **III:** 584
"Handle with Care" (Fitzgerald), **Retro. Supp. I:** 114
Handley, William R., **Supp. XVIII:** 58
Handmaid's Tale, The (Atwood), **Supp. XIII:** 19, 20, **27–29**
"Hand of Casino, 1954, A" (Skloot), **Supp. XX: 194, 202**
"Hand of Emmagene, The" (Taylor), **Supp. V:** 314, 325–326
Hand of the Potter, The: A Tragedy in Four Acts (Dreiser), **Retro. Supp. II:** 104; **Supp. XVII:** 96
"Hands" (Anderson), **I:** 106, 107
"Hands" (Mora), **Supp. XIII:** 215
Hands of Orlac, The (M. Renard; Crewe-Jones, trans.), **Supp. XVII:** 58
Hand to Mouth (Auster), **Supp. XII:** 21
"Hand to Mouth" (Auster), **Supp. XII:** 31
Handy, Lowney, **Supp. XI:** 217, 220, 221, 225
Handy, W. C., **Supp. VIII:** 337
Handy Guide for Beggars, A (Lindsay), **Supp. I Part 2:** 376–378, 380, 382, 399
Haney, David, **Supp. XXI:** 253
"Hanged Man, A" (Cliff), **Supp. XXII:** 74
"Hanging Burley" (J. W. Miller), **Supp. XX: 167**
Hanging Garden, The (Wagoner), **Supp. IX: 338–339**
"Hanging Gardens of Tyburn, The" (Hecht), **Supp. X:** 58
"Hanging Man, The" (Davison), **Supp. XXVI:** 74
"Hanging of the Crane, The" (Longfellow), **Retro. Supp. II:** 169, 171
Hanging On (Conroy), **Supp. XVI:** 69
"Hanging Pictures in Nanny's Room" (Kenyon), **Supp. VII:** 164
"Hanging the Wash" (Alvarez), **Supp. VII:** 4
"Hangman, The" (Sexton), **Supp. II Part 2:** 680, 691
Hangover Mass (X. J. Kennedy), **Supp. XV:** 165
Hangsaman (Jackson), **Supp. IX:** 116, 123, **124**
Hanh, Thich Nhat, **Supp. V:** 199
Hanks, Lucy, **III:** 587
Hanks, Nancy. *See* Lincoln, Mrs. Thomas (Nancy Hanks)
Hanley, Lynne T., **Supp. IV Part 1:** 208
"Hanlon Mountain in Mist" (J. W. Miller), **Supp. XX: 164, 166–167**
Hanna, Mark, **Supp. I Part 2:** 395
Hannah, Barry, **Supp. X:** 285; **Supp. XIX:** 209; **Supp. XXI:** 38, 118; **Supp. XXVII:** 269

Hannah and Her Sisters (film; Allen), **Supp. XV:** 9, **10–11**
"Hannah Armstrong" (Masters), **Supp. I Part 2:** 461
"Hannah Binding Shoes" (Larcom), **Supp. XIII:** 141, 143
"Hannah Byde" (D. West), **Supp. XVIII:** 280
Hannah's House (Hearon), **Supp. VIII:** 58, **60–61**
Hanneman, Audre, **II:** 259
Hannibal Lecter, My Father (Acker), **Supp. XII:** 6
Hanoi (McCarthy), **II:** 579
"Hanoi Drifting, January 2003" (Weigl), **Supp. XIX:** 288
Hansberry, Lorraine, **Supp. IV Part 1: 359–377; Supp. VIII:** 329
Hanscom, Leslie, **Supp. XI:** 229
"Hansel and Gretel" (Prose), **Supp. XVI:** 256, 258
Hansen, Erik, **Supp. V:** 241
Hansen, Harry, **IV:** 366; **Supp. XXII:** 194, 277; **Supp. XXVII:** 85, 96
Han-shan, **Supp. VIII:** 292
Hanson, Curtis, **Supp. XI:** 67
Hanson, Elizabeth, **Supp. XXIV:** 220
Hanson, William F., **Supp. XXV:** 279, 280
Han Suyin, **Supp. X:** 291
Hanzlicek, C. G., **Supp. XV:** 73
Hapax (Stallings), **Supp. XXV:** 221, 222, 224, 231–233
Hapgood, Charles H., II, **Supp. XXI:** 6
Hapgood, Hutchins, **Supp. XVII: 95–108; Supp. XXI:** 1, 3, 9, 10
Hapgood, Norman, **Supp. XXI:** 2
Hapgoods, The: Three Earnest Brothers (Marcaccio), **Supp. XVII:** 106
"Happenings: An Art of Radical Juxtaposition" (Sontag), **Supp. III Part 2:** 456
"Happenstance" (Komunyakaa), **Supp. XIII:** 130
Happenstance (Shields), **Supp. VII:** 315–318, 320, 323, 324, 326
Happersberger, Lucien, **Supp. I Part 1:** 51
"Happiest Girl in the Whole U.S.A., The" (Muñoz), **Supp. XXV:** 131, 132
"Happiest I've Been, The" (Updike), **IV:** 219
Happily Ever After (Quindlen), **Supp. XVII:** 167
"Happiness" (Oliver), **Supp. VII:** 236
"Happiness" (Sandburg), **III:** 582–583
"Happiness" (Stone), **Supp. XXVII:** 254–255
"Happiness"(Hadas), **Supp. XXIII:** 117
Happiness of Getting It Down Right, The (Steinman, ed.), **Supp. VIII:** 172
"Happiness of the Garden Variety" (Richard), **Supp. XIX:** 212
"Happy Birthday" (Bambara), **Supp. XI:** 4
Happy Birthday (Loos), **Supp. XVI:** 193
Happy Birthday, Wanda June (Vonnegut), **Supp. II Part 2:** 759, 776–777
Happy Birthday of Death, The (Corso), **Supp. XII: 127–129**

Happy Childhood, A (Matthews), **Supp. IX:** 155, 160, **161–163**

Happy Days (Beckett), **Retro. Supp. I:** 206; **Supp. XXIV:** 123

Happy Days, 1880–1892 (Mencken), **III:** 100, 111, 120

"Happy End" (Simic), **Supp. VIII:** 276–277

"Happy Failure, The" (Melville), **III:** 90

Happy Families Are All Alike (Taylor), **Supp. V:** 322–323, 325

Happy Isles of Oceania, The: Paddling the Pacific (Theroux), **Supp. VIII:** 324

"Happy Journey to Trenton and Camden, The" (Wilder), **IV:** 366

"Happy Man, The" (Lethem), **Supp. XVIII:** 139

"Happy Marriage, The" (MacLeish), **III:** 15–16

Happy Marriage and Other Poems, The (MacLeish), **III:** 4

Happy to Be Here (Keillor), **Supp. XVI:** 165, 171

"Happy To Be Here" (Keillor), **Supp. XVI:** 168

"Hapworth 16, 1924" (Salinger), **III:** 552, 571–572

Haram, Karen, **Supp. XXIII:** 276

"Harbor Dawn, The" (H. Crane), **Supp. XXI:** 132, 136

"Harbor Lights" (Doty), **Supp. XI:** 122

Harcourt, Alfred, **II:** 191, 451–452; **III:** 587; **Retro. Supp. I:** 131; **Supp. XV:** 308

Harcourt, Lewis, **Supp. XX: 232–233**

Harcourt, T. A., **I:** 196

Hardball (Paretsky), **Supp. XXV:** 177, 182, 184

Hard Candy, a Book of Stories (T. Williams), **IV:** 383

"Hardcastle Crags" (Plath), **Supp. I Part 2:** 537

"Hard Daddy" (Hughes), **Retro. Supp. I:** 200

"Hard Drive" (Huddle), **Supp. XXVI:** 151

"Hardened Criminals, The" (Lethem), **Supp. XVIII:** 139

Harder They Fall, The (Schulberg), **Supp. XV:** 194, 201

"Hardest Thing, The" (Huddle), **Supp. XXVI:** 151

Hard Facts (Baraka), **Supp. II Part 1:** 54, 55, 58

Hard Freight (Wright), **Supp. V:** 332, 339–340

Hard Hours, The (Hecht), **Supp. X:** 57, **59–62,** 63, 64

Hardie, Kier, **Supp. I Part 1:** 5

Hardin, Michael, **Supp. XXVI:** 242

Harding, Walter, **IV:** 177, 178

Harding, Warren G., **I:** 486; **II:** 253, 433; **Supp. I Part 1:** 24

"Hard Kind of Courage, The" (Baldwin), **Supp. I Part 1:** 52

Hard Laughter (Lamott), **Supp. XX: 132–133**

Hard Maple (S. and A. Warner), **Supp. XVIII:** 264

"Hard Rain's A-Gonna Fall, A" (song, Dylan), **Supp. XVIII:** 26, 29

Hard Time (Paretsky), **Supp. XXV:** 176, 177, 179, 182, 183

"Hard Time Keeping Up, A" (Ellison), **Retro. Supp. II:** 124

Hard Times (Dickens), **Supp. I Part 2:** 675

"Hard Times in Elfland, The" (Lanier), **Supp. I Part 1:** 365

"Hard Traveling: *Fay*'s Deep South Landscape of Violence" (Beuka), **Supp. XXI:** 47

Hard Way Around, The: The Passages of Joshua Slocum (Wolff), **Supp. XXV:** 217

Hardwick, Elizabeth, **II:** 543, 554, 566; **Retro. Supp. II:** 179, 180, 183, 184, 190, 221, 228–229, 245; **Supp. I Part 1:** 196; **Supp. III Part 1: 193–215; Supp. IV Part 1:** 299; **Supp. V,** 319; **Supp. X,** 171; **Supp. XII:** 209; **Supp. XIV:** 89

"Hard Work 1956" (Dunn), **Supp. XI:** 147

Hardy, Barbara, **Supp. I Part 2:** 527

Hardy, Deborah, **Supp. XXVI:** 241, 242, 246

Hardy, Oliver, **Supp. I Part 2:** 607; **Supp. IV Part 2:** 574

Hardy, René, **Supp. III Part 1:** 235

Hardy, Thomas, **I:** 59, 103, 292, 317, 377; **II:** 181, 184–185, 186, 191–192, 271, 275, 372, 523, 542; **III:** 32, 453, 485, 508, 524; **IV:** 83, 135, 136; **Retro. Supp. I:** 141, 377–378; **Supp. I Part 1:** 217; **Supp. I Part 2:** 429, 512; **Supp. II Part 1:** 4, 26; **Supp. IX:** 40, 78, 85, 108, 211; **Supp. VIII:** 32; **Supp. X:** 228; **Supp. XI:** 311; **Supp. XIII:** 294, Supp. XIII: 130; **Supp. XIV:** 24; **Supp. XIX:** 86, 87; **Supp. XV:** 170; **Supp. XVIII:** 74; **Supp. XX: 195; Supp. XXI:** 109; **Supp. XXVI:** 67, 78; **Supp. XXVII:** 218

Hardy and the Poetry of Truth-Seeking (Halliday), **Supp. XIX:** 82

Harjo, Joy, **Supp. IV Part 1:** 325, 404; **Supp. IV Part 2:** 499, 507; **Supp. XII: 215–234; Supp. XVIII:** 189

Harlan's Race (P. N. Warren), **Supp. XX: 264–265**

"Harlem" (Hughes), **Retro. Supp. I:** 194, 204; **Supp. I Part 1:** 340; **Supp. VIII:** 213

Harlem (Myers), **Supp. XXVII:** 211

Harlem, Mecca of the New Negro (Locke), **Supp. XIV:** 201

"Harlem Dancer, The" (McKay), **Supp. X:** 134

Harlem Gallery (Tolson), **Retro. Supp. I:** 208, 209, 210

Harlem Glory: A Fragment of Aframerican Life (McKay), **Supp. X:** 132, **141–142**

Harlem Hellfighters, The: When Pride Met Courage (Myers), **Supp. XXVII:** 208

Harlem: Negro Metropolis (McKay), **Supp. X:** 132, 141, 142

Harlem Renaissance Remembered, The (Bontemps, ed.), **Supp. XXII:** 7

"Harlem Runs Wild" (McKay), **Supp. X:** 140

Harlem Shadows (McKay), **Supp. X:** 131–132, 136

Harlem Underground (Lacy), **Supp. XV:** 206

"Harlequin of Dreams, The" (Lanier), **Supp. I Part 1:** 365

Harlot's Ghost (Mailer), **Retro. Supp. II:** 211–212

Harlow, Jean, **IV:** 256; **Retro. Supp. I:** 110

"Harm" (C. Frost), **Supp. XV:** 101

Harmon, William, **Retro. Supp. I:** 37; **Supp. XI:** 248

"Harmonic" (F. Barthelme), **Supp. XI:** 26

Harmonium (Stevens), **III:** 196; **IV:** 76, 77, 78, 82, 87, 89, 92; **Retro. Supp. I:** 296, 297, 299, **300–302,** 301, 302

"Harmony of the Gospels" (Taylor), **IV:** 149

Harmony of the World (C. Baxter), **Supp. XVII:** 16–17

"Harmony of the World" (C. Baxter), **Supp. XVII:** 16

Harnett, Vincent, **Supp. XV:** 198

"Harp, The" (Weigl), **Supp. XIX:** 278

Harper (film), **Supp. IV Part 2:** 473

Harper, Donna, **Retro. Supp. I:** 194, 195, 209

Harper, Frances E. Watkins, **Supp. II Part 1:** 201–202; **Supp. XVIII:** 284; **Supp. XXII:** 11

Harper, Gordon Lloyd, **Retro. Supp. II:** 23

Harper, Michael S., **Retro. Supp. II:** 116, 123; **Supp. XV:** 74; **Supp. XXIV:** 184; **Supp. XXVII:** 152

Harper, William Rainey, **Supp. I Part 2:** 631

Harper's Anthology of 20th Century Native American Poetry (Niatum, ed.), **Supp. IV Part 1:** 331

"Harriet" (R. Lowell), **II:** 554

Harrigan, Edward, **II:** 276; **III:** 14

Harriman, Margaret, **Supp. XXIV:** 19

Harrington, Michael, **I:** 306

Harrington, Ollie, **Supp. XVI:** 142–143

Harris, Celia, **Retro. Supp. I:** 9

Harris, Corra, **Supp. XXII:** 190, 193, 196

Harris, George, **II:** 70

Harris, George Washington, **Supp. XXII:** 193

Harris, Joel Chandler, **III:** 338; **Supp. I Part 1:** 352; **Supp. II Part 1:** 192, 201; **Supp. XIV:** 61; **Supp. XX: 103**

Harris, Judith, **Supp. XIV:** 269

Harris, Julie, **II:** 587, 601; **Supp. IX:** 125

Harris, Leonard, **Supp. XIV:** 196, 211–212

Harris, MacDonald, **Supp. XI:** 65

Harris, Marie, **Supp. IX:** 153

Harris, Peter, **Supp. X:** 206, 207

Harris, Susan K., **Supp. XV:** 269

Harris, Thomas, **Supp. XIV:** 26; **Supp. XXI:** 67, 78

Harris, Trudier, **Supp. XXVI:** 13–14

Harris, Victoria Frenkel, **Supp. IV Part 1:** 68, 69
Harris, Violet J., **Supp. XXII:** 10, 13
Harris, William E., **Supp. XXIV:** 26
Harris, Wilson, **Supp. XXI:** 170; **Supp. XXVII:** 160, 161
Harrison, Colin, **Supp. XIV:** 26
Harrison, Hazel, **Retro. Supp. II:** 115
Harrison, Jim, **Supp. VIII:** 37–56; **Supp. XIX:** 125, 126
Harrison, Judy, **Supp. XXIII:** 278
Harrison, Kathryn, **Supp. X:** 191
Harrison, Ken, **Supp. IX:** 101
Harrison, Oliver (pseudonym). *See* Smith, Harrison
Harrod, Lois Marie, **Supp. XXIII:** 131–132
Harron, Mary, **Supp. XXVII:** 68
Harry: A Portrait (Boyce), **Supp. XVII:** 104; **Supp. XXI:** 7, 13–14
Harryhausen, Ray, **Supp. IV Part 1:** 115
Harryman, Carla, **Supp. XV:** 344
"Harry of Nothingham" (Hugo), **Supp. VI:** 146–147
"Harry's Death" (Carver), **Supp. III Part 1:** 146
"Harsh Judgment, The" (Kunitz), **Supp. III Part 1:** 264
Hart, Albert Bushnell, **Supp. I Part 2:** 479, 480, 481
Hart, Bernard, **I:** 241, 242, 248–250, 256
Hart, Henry, **Retro. Supp. II:** 187; **Supp. XIV:** 97
Hart, James D., **Supp. XVIII:** 257
Hart, John Seely, **Supp. XVIII:** 257, 258, 264
Hart, Lorenz, **III:** 361
Hart, Moss, **Supp. IV Part 2:** 574; **Supp. XV:** 329
Hart, Pearl, **Supp. X:** 103
"Hart Crane" (Tate), **I:** 381
"Hart Crane and Poetry: A Consideration of Crane's Intense Poetics with Reference to 'The Return' " (Grossman), **Retro. Supp. II:** 83
Harte, Anna Griswold, **Supp. II Part 1:** 341
Harte, Bret, **I:** 193, 195, 203; **II:** 289; **IV:** 196; **Retro. Supp. II:** 72; **Supp. II Part 1:** 335–359, 399; **Supp. XV:** 115
Harte, Walter Blackburn, **I:** 199
Harter, Carol C., **Supp. IV Part 1:** 217
Hartigan, Grace, **Supp. XXIII:** 210, 212, 217
Hartley, David, **III:** 77
Hartley, Lois, **Supp. I Part 2:** 459, 464–465
Hartley, L. P., **Supp. I Part 1:** 293
Hartley, Marsden, **IV:** 409, 413; **Retro. Supp. I:** 430; **Supp. X:** 137; **Supp. XV:** 298
Hartman, Geoffrey, **Supp. IV Part 1:** 119; **Supp. XII:** 130, 253
Hartman, Saidiya, **Supp. XX:** 154
Harum, David, **II:** 102
"Harvard" (R. Lowell), **II:** 554
Harvard College in the Seventeenth Century (Morison), **Supp. I Part 2:** 485
"Harvest" (E. P. Jones), **Supp. XXII:** 141

"Harvest, The" (Hempel), **Supp. XXI:** 115, **122–123**
Harvest, The (Levin), **Supp. XXVII:** 143, 146
Harvester, The (Stratton-Porter), **Supp. XX: 211, 212, 218, 221**
"*Harvester, The:* The Natural Bounty of Gene Stratton-Porter" (Birkelo), **Supp. XX: 220–221**
"Harvesters of Night and Water" (Hogan), **Supp. IV Part 1:** 412
"Harvest Song" (Toomer), **Supp. III Part 2:** 483
Harvill Book of 20th Century Poetry in English, **Supp. X:** 55
Harvin, Emily, **Supp. XXIII:** 174
"Harv Is Plowing Now" (Updike), **Retro. Supp. I:** 318
Harwood, Lee, **Supp. XXVII:** 22
Haselden, Elizabeth Lee, **Supp. VIII:** 125
"Hasidic Noir" (Abraham), **Supp. XXIV: 14–15**
Haskell, Mary, **Supp. XX: 115, 117**
"Haskell's Mill" (Davison), **Supp. XXVI:** 73, 75, 76
Hass, Robert, **Supp. VI: 97–111; Supp. VIII:** 24, 28; **Supp. XI:** 142, 270; **Supp. XIV:** 83, 84; **Supp. XXI:** 60; **Supp. XXVI:** 61, 68
Hassam, Childe, **Retro. Supp. II:** 136
Hassan, Ihab, **IV:** 99–100, 115; **Supp. XI:** 221
Hasse, Henry, **Supp. IV Part 1:** 102
Hasty-Pudding, The (Barlow), **Supp. II Part 1:** 74, 77–80
"Hater of Mediocrity, The" (Boulton), **Supp. XXII:** 23
Hateship, Friendship, Courtship, Loveship, Marriage (Munro), **Supp. XXVII:** 190, 192–193
Hate That Hate Produced, The (CBS documentary), **Supp. XX: 102**
Hatful of Rain, A (film), **Supp. XXVI:** 134
Hatful of Rain, A (Gazzo), **III:** 155
Hatlen, Burton, **Supp. V:** 138, 139–140; **Supp. XXI:** 24
"Hatred"(O'Hara), **Supp. XXIII:** 212
"Hattie Bloom" (Oliver), **Supp. VII:** 232
Haugen, Hayley Mitchell, **Supp. XXIV:** 215
Haunch, Paunch, and Jowl (Ornitz), **Supp. IX:** 227
Haunted Lady, The (Rinehart), **Supp. XXV:** 198, 200
"Haunted Landscape" (Ashbery), **Supp. III Part 1:** 22
Haunted Merchant, The (Briggs), **Supp. XVIII:** 2, 8
"Haunted Mind" (Simic), **Supp. VIII:** 282
"Haunted Mind, The" (Hawthorne), **II:** 230–231
"Haunted Oak, The" (Dunbar), **Supp. II Part 1:** 207, 208
"Haunted Palace, The" (Poe), **III:** 421
"Haunted Valley, The" (Bierce), **I:** 200
Haunting, The (film), **Supp. IX:** 125
Haunting of Hill House, The (Jackson), **Supp. IX:** 117, 121, 126

Hauptmann, Gerhart, **III:** 472
Haussmann, Sonja, **Supp. XIII:** 331, **Supp. XIII:** 347
"Havanna vanities come to dust in Miami" (Didion), **Supp. IV Part 1:** 210
Havel, Hippolyte, **Supp. XXI:** 4, 6
Haven, Cynthia, **Supp. XV:** 252, 264; **Supp. XXIII:** 134, 138, 139
Haven's End (Marquand), **III:** 55, 56, 63, 68
"Have You Ever Faked an Orgasm" (Peacock), **Supp. XIX:** 199
"Have You Ever Tried to Enter the Long Black Branches" (Oliver), **Supp. VII:** 247
"Having a Coke with You"(O'Hara), **Supp. XXIII:** 219
"Having Been Interstellar" (Ammons), **Supp. VII:** 25
"Having It Out With Melancholy" (Kenyon), **Supp. VII:** 171
"Having Lost My Sons, I Confront the Wreckage of the Moon: Christmas, 1960" (Wright), **Supp. III Part 2:** 600
"Having Saints" (Davison), **Supp. XXVI:** 71
"Having Snow" (Schwartz), **Supp. II Part 2:** 652
"Having Words"(Thompson), **Supp. XXIII:** 293–294
"Hawaii, Washington, Vermont: A Frame for the Verse" (Taggard), **Supp. XXII:** 281–282
Hawaiian Hilltop (Taggard), **Supp. XXII:** 275
Hawai'i One Summer (Kingston), **Supp. V:** 157, 160, 166, 169–170
Haweis, Stephen, **Supp. XXII:** 157, 158, 159, 161, 163, 165
"Hawk, The" (Francis), **Supp. IX:** 81
Hawke, David Freeman, **Supp. I Part 2:** 511, 516
Hawkes, John, **I:** 113; **Retro. Supp. II:** 234; **Supp. III Part 1:** 2; **Supp. IX:** 212; **Supp. V:** 40; **Supp. XVII:** 183; **Supp. XXI:** 210
Hawkins, Gary, **Supp. XXI:** 35, 39
Hawkins, William, **II:** 587
Hawk in the Rain, The (Hughes), **Retro. Supp. II:** 244; **Supp. I Part 2:** 537, 540
Hawk Is Dying, The (Crews), **Supp. XI:** 111
Hawk Moon (Shepard), **Supp. III Part 2:** 445
Hawks, Howard, **Supp. IV Part 1:** 130; **Supp. XVIII:** 148
"Hawk's Cry in Autumn, The" (Brodsky), **Supp. VIII:** 29
"Hawks of Outremer" (Howard), **Supp. XXVII:** 120
"Hawk's Shadow" (Glück), **Supp. V:** 85
Hawk's Well, The (Yeats), **III:** 459–460
Hawley, Adelaide, **Supp. XIV:** 207
Hawley, Joseph, **I:** 546
Hawthorne (James), **II:** 372–378; **Retro. Supp. I:** 220, **223–224**
"Hawthorne" (Longfellow), **Retro. Supp. II:** 169
"Hawthorne" (R. Lowell), **II:** 550

Hawthorne, Julian, **II:** 225; **Supp. I Part 1:** 38; **Supp. XV:** 274
Hawthorne, Nathaniel, **I:** 106, 204, 211, 340, 355, 363, 384, 413, 458, 561–562; **II:** 7, 8, 40, 60, 63, 74, 89, 127–128, 138, 142, 198, **223–246,** 255, 259, 264, 267, 272, 274, 277, 281, 282, 295, 307, 309, 311, 313, 322, 324, 326, 402, 408, 446, 501, 545; **III:** 51, 81–82, 83, 84, 85, 87, 88, 91, 92, 113, 316, 359, 412, 415, 421, 438, 453, 454, 507, 565, 572; **IV:** 2, 4, 167, 172, 179, 194, 333, 345, 453; **Retro. Supp. I:** 1, 53, 59, 62, 63, 91, **145–167,** 215, 218, 220, 223, 248–249, 252, 257, 258, 331, 365; **Retro. Supp. II:** 136, 142, 153, 156–157, 158, 159, 187, 221; **Supp. I Part 1:** 38, 188, 197, 317, 372; **Supp. I Part 2:** 420, 421, 545, 579, 580, 582, 587, 595, 596; **Supp. III Part 2:** 501; **Supp. IV Part 1:** 80, 127, 297; **Supp. IV Part 2:** 463, 596; **Supp. IX:** 114; **Supp. V:** 152; **Supp. VIII:** 103, 105, 108, 153, 201; **Supp. X:** 78; **Supp. XI:** 51, 78; **Supp. XII:** 26; **Supp. XIII:** 102; **Supp. XIV:** 48; **Supp. XV:** 269, 272, 282; **Supp. XVI:** 83, 84, 157; **Supp. XVII:** 42; **Supp. XVIII:** 258, 260; **Supp. XXI:** 201; **Supp. XXIII:** 161, 190, 290; **Supp. XXV:** 242, 249
Hawthorne, Mrs. Nathaniel (Sophia Peabody), **II:** 224, 244; **III:** 75, 86
Hawthorne, Rose, **II:** 225
Hawthorne, Una, **II:** 225
"Hawthorne and His Mosses" (Melville), **Retro. Supp. I:** 254; **Supp. XIV:** 48
"Hawthorne Aspect \[of Henry James\], The" (Eliot), **Retro. Supp. I:** 63
"Hawthorne in Solitude" (Cowley), **Supp. II Part 1:** 143
Hay, John, **I:** 1, 10, 12, 14–15; **Supp. I Part 1:** 352
Hay, Mrs. John, **I:** 14
Hay, Sara Henderson, **Supp. XIV:** 119–135
Hayakawa, S. I., **I:** 448; **Supp. I Part 1:** 315; **Supp. XV:** 176
Haycroft, Howard, **Supp. XXV:** 199; **Supp. XXVI:** 277
Hayden, Robert, **Supp. II Part 1:** 361–383; **Supp. IV Part 1:** 169; **Supp. XIII:** 115, 127; **Supp. XIV:** 119, 123
Hayden, Sterling, **Supp. XI:** 304
Hayden, William R., **Supp. XXV:** 38
Haydn, Hiram, **IV:** 100, 358
Hayduke Lives! (Abbey), **Supp. XIII:** 16
Hayek, Friedrich A. von, **Supp. IV Part 2:** 524
Hayes, Alfred, **Supp. XXVI: 133–146**
Hayes, Helen, **Supp. XVI:** 193, 195
Hayes, Ira, **Supp. IV Part 1:** 326
Hayes, Richard, **Supp. V:** 320
Hayes, Rutherford B., **Supp. I Part 2:** 419
Hayford, James, **Supp. XXII:** 204, 218
Haygood, Wil, **Supp. VIII:** 79
"Haying While the Sun Shines" (L. I. Wilder), **Supp. XXII:** 290

Hayne, Paul Hamilton, **Supp. I Part 1:** 352, 354, 355, 360, 372
Haynes, Todd, **Supp. XVIII:** 23
Haynes-Smith, William, **Supp. XX: 231, 232, 233**
Hayward, Florence, **Retro. Supp. II:** 65
Hayward, John, **Retro. Supp. I:** 67
Hayward, Leland, **Supp. XIX:** 250
Haywood, "Big" Bill, **I:** 483; **Supp. V:** 286; **Supp. XXIII:** 162
Hazan, Joe, **Supp. XXIII:** 212
Hazard, Grace, **II:** 530
Hazard of Fortunes, A (Howells), **Retro. Supp. II:** 288
Hazard of New Fortunes, A (Howells), **II:** 275, 276, 286–297, 290
Hazel, Robert, **Supp. VIII:** 137, 138
Hazen, General W. B., **I:** 192, 193
Hazlitt, Henry, **Supp. IV Part 2:** 524
Hazlitt, William, **I:** 58, 378; **II:** 315; **Supp. XXI:** 205
Hazmat (McClatchy), **Supp. XII: 265–270**
Hazo, Samuel, **I:** 386; **Supp. XIV:** 123, 124
Hazzard, Shirley, **Supp. VIII:** 151
H.D. *See* Doolittle, Hilda
"He" (Porter), **III:** 434, 435
"Head and Shoulders" (Fitzgerald), **Retro. Supp. I:** 101
Headhunter (Findley), **Supp. XX: 57–59, 60, 61**
"Head-Hunter, The" (O. Henry), **Supp. II Part 1:** 403
"Headless Hawk, The" (Capote), **Supp. III Part 1:** 124
Headlines (T. Williams), **IV:** 381
Headlong Hall (Peacock), **Supp. I Part 1:** 307
Headmaster, The (McPhee), **Supp. III Part 1:** 291, 294, 298
"Head of Joaquín Murrieta, The" (Rodriguez), **Supp. XIV:** 122
Headsman, The (Cooper), **I:** 345–346
Heads of Grain (al-Sanábil) (Gibran), **Supp. XX: 124**
"Headwaters" (Momaday), **Supp. IV Part 2:** 486
"Head Wound" (Halliday), **Supp. XIX:** 92
Healing, The (G. Jones), **Supp. XXIV:** 183, 185, **190–192,** 195
Healy, Eloise Klein, **Supp. XI:** 121, 124, 126, 127, 129, 137
Healy, Tim, **II:** 129, 137
Heaney, Sally, **Supp. XVII:** 241
Heaney, Seamus, **Retro. Supp. II:** 245; **Supp. IX:** 41, 42; **Supp. X:** 67, 122; **Supp. XI:** 249; **Supp. XV:** 256; **Supp. XXI:** 54, 243
"Heard through the Walls of the Race-track Glen Motel" (X. J. Kennedy), **Supp. XV:** 170
"Hearing, The" (Huddle), **Supp. XXVI:** 155
Hearn, Lafcadio, **I:** 211; **II:** 311
Hearon, Shelby, **Supp. VIII: 57–72**
Hearst, Patty, **Supp. IV Part 1:** 195
Hearst, William Randolph, **I:** 198, 207, 208; **IV:** 298

Heart and Perimeter (Bierds), **Supp. XVII: 28–29**
"Heart and the Lyre, The" (Bogan), **Supp. III Part 1:** 65
"Heart as Origami, The (Hirshfield), **Supp. XXIII:** 132
"Heartbeat" (Harjo), **Supp. XII:** 221–222
Heartbreak Hotel (Siddons), **Supp. XXII:** 239, 241, 242
Heartbreak Kid, The (film), **Supp. IV Part 2:** 575, 589
"Heart Failure"(Schott), **Supp. XXIII:** 252
"Heart Finds Its Own Conclusion, The" (Muñoz), **Supp. XXV:** 136
Heart for the Gods of Mexico, A (Aiken), **I:** 54
"Hearth" (Rash), **Supp. XXVII:** 222
"Hear the Nightingale Sing" (Gordon), **II:** 200
Hear the Wind Blow (Sanders), **Supp. XVI:** 268
Heart is a Lonely Hunter, The (McCullers), **II:** 586, 588–593, 604, 605
Heartland (film), **Supp. XXVI:** 183–184
Heart of a Woman, The (Angelou), **Supp. IV Part 1:** 2, 5, 7–9, 9, 14, 17
Heart of Darkness (Conrad), **Retro. Supp. II:** 292; **Supp. V:** 249, 311; **Supp. VIII:** 4, 316; **Supp. XIX:** 28; **Supp. XX: 18, 57–58; Supp. XXIV:** 286
"Heart of Darkness" (Conrad), **I:** 575, 578; **II:** 595; **Supp. XVI:** 212
Heart of Darkness (Didion), **Supp. IV Part 1:** 207
Heart of Dixie (film), **Supp. XXII:** 239, 241
Heart of Haiku, The (Hirshfield), **Supp. XXIII:** 137–138
Heart of Happy Hollow, The (Dunbar), **Supp. II Part 1:** 214
Heart of Knowledge, The: American Indians on the Bomb (Gunn Allen and Caputi, eds.), **Supp. IV Part 1:** 334–335
"Heart of Knowledge, The: Nuclear Themes in Native American Thought and Literature" (Caputi), **Supp. IV Part 1:** 335
Heart of the Earth (Moraga), **Supp. XXIII:** 196
"Heart of the Park, The " (O'Connor), **Retro. Supp. II:** 225
Heart of the West (O. Henry), **Supp. II Part 1:** 410
"Hearts, The" (Pinsky), **Supp. VI:** 245–247, 248
"'Hearts and Flowers' " (MacLeish), **III:** 8
"Hearts and Heads" (Ransom), **Supp. I Part 1:** 373
"Heart's Graveyard Shift, The" (Komunyakaa), **Supp. XIII:** 120
Heart-Shape in the Dust (Hayden), **Supp. II Part 1:** 365, 366
Heart's Needle (Snodgrass), **I:** 400
"Heart's Needle" (Snodgrass), **Supp. VI: 311–313,** 320

"Hearts of Oak" (Rowson), **Supp. XV:** 243

"Heart Songs" (Proulx), **Supp. VII:** 254

Heart Songs and Other Stories (Proulx), **Supp. VII:** 252–256, 261

Heart to Artemis, The (Bryher), **Supp. I Part 1:** 259

"Heart to Heart" (Zitkala-Ša), **Supp. XXV:** 284

Heartwood (Burke), **Supp. XIV:** 35

Heath, Shirley, **Supp. XX: 90**

Heath Anthology of American Literature, The, **Supp. IX:** 4; **Supp. XV:** 270, 313

Heathcote, Anne. *See* De Lancey, Mrs. James

"Heathen Chinee, The" (Harte), **Supp. II Part 1:** 350–351, 352

Heathen Days, 1890–1936 (Mencken), **III:** 100, 111

Heath-Stubbs, John, **Supp. XV:** 153

Heaton, David, **Supp. XXVI:** 7

Heat's On, The (C. Himes), **Supp. XVI:** 143, 144

"Heaven" (Dunn), **Supp. XI:** 154

"Heaven" (Levine), **Supp. V:** 182

"Heaven" (Patchett), **Supp. XII:** 309

Heaven and Earth: A Cosmology (Goldbarth), **Supp. XII: 187**

"Heaven and Earth in Jest" (Dillard), **Supp. VI:** 24, 28

"Heaven as Anus" (Kumin), **Supp. IV Part 2:** 448

Heavenly Conversation, The (Mather), **Supp. II Part 2:** 460

"Heavenly Feast, The" (Schnackenberg), **Supp. XV:** 257, 259

Heavens (Untermeyer), **Supp. XV:** 306

Heavens and Earth (Benét), **Supp. XI:** 44

Heaven's Coast (Doty), **Supp. XI:** 119, 121, **129–130,** 134; **Supp. XXIII:** 126

Heaven's Prisoners (Burke), **Supp. XIV:** 23, 29

"Heavy Angel, The" (Everwine), **Supp. XV:** 80

"Heavy Bear Who Goes with Me, The" (Schwartz), **Supp. II Part 2:** 646

"Heavy Trash" (Halliday), **Supp. XIX:** 92, 93

Hebert, Ernest, **Supp. XXII:** 207

Heble, Ajay, **Supp. XXVII:** 183

"He Came Also Still" (Zukofsky), **Supp. III Part 2:** 612

Hecht, Anthony, **IV:** 138; **Supp. III Part 2:** 541, 561; **Supp. X: 55–75; Supp. XII:** 269–270; **Supp. XV:** 251, 256; **Supp. XXVII:** 218

Hecht, Ben, **I:** 103; **II:** 42; **Supp. I Part 2:** 646; **Supp. XI:** 307; **Supp. XIII:** 106; **Supp. XXV:** 18, 19, 22, 27, 29; **Supp. XXVII: 83–98,** 139

Hecht, S. Theodore, **Supp. III Part 2:** 614

Heckewelder, John, **II:** 503

"Hedge Island" (A. Lowell), **II:** 524

"Hedgerows in England, The" (Stone), **Supp. XXVII:** 258, 259–260

Hedges, William I., **II:** 311–312

"He 'Digesteth Harde Yron' " (Moore), **Supp. IV Part 2:** 454

Hedin, Robert, **Supp. XII:** 200, 202

Hedylus (Doolittle), **Supp. I Part 1:** 259, 270

"Heel & Toe To the End" (W. C. Williams), **Retro. Supp. I:** 430

Heffernan, Michael, **Supp. XII:** 177

"HEGEL" (Baraka), **Supp. II Part 1:** 53

Hegel, Georg Wilhelm Friedrich, **I:** 265; **II:** 358; **III:** 262, 308–309, 480, 481, 487, 607; **IV:** 86, 333, 453; **Supp. I Part 2:** 633, 635, 640, 645; **Supp. XVI:** 289; **Supp. XXVI:** 234

"Hegemony of Race, The" (Du Bois), **Supp. II Part 1:** 181

Hegger, Grace Livingston. *See* Lewis, Mrs. Sinclair (Grace Livingston Hegger)

"He Had Spent His Youth Dreaming" (Dobyns), **Supp. XIII:** 90

Heidegger, Martin, **II:** 362, 363; **III:** 292; **IV:** 491; **Retro. Supp. II:** 87; **Supp. V:** 267; **Supp. VIII:** 9; **Supp. XVI:** 283, 288; **Supp. XXVI:** 234

Heidenmauer, The (Cooper), **I:** 345–346

Heidi Chronicles, The (Wasserstein), **Supp. IV Part 1:** 309; **Supp. XV:** 319, 325–327

"Height of the Ridiculous, The" (Holmes), **Supp. I Part 1:** 302

Heilbroner, Robert, **Supp. I Part 2:** 644, 648, 650

Heilbrun, Carolyn G., **Supp. IX:** 66; **Supp. XI:** 208; **Supp. XIV:** 161, 163; **Supp. XX: 108**

Heilman, Robert Bechtold, **Supp. XIV:** 11, 12

Heilpern, John, **Supp. XIV:** 242

Heim, Michael, **Supp. V:** 209

Heine, Heinrich, **II:** 272, 273, 277, 281, 282, 387, 544; **IV:** 5; **Supp. XV:** 293, 299; **Supp. XVI:** 188

Heineman, Frank, **Supp. III Part 2:** 619

Heinemann, Larry, **Supp. XXII: 103–117**

Heinlein, Robert, **Supp. IV Part 1:** 102; **Supp. XVI:** 122; **Supp. XVIII:** 149

Heinz, Helen. *See* Tate, Mrs. Allen (Helen Heinz)

Heiress, The (film), **Retro. Supp. I:** 222

"Heirs" (Nye), **Supp. XIII:** 284

"He Is Not Worth the Trouble" (Rowson), **Supp. XV:** 240

"He Knew" (C. Himes), **Supp. XVI:** 137

"Helas" (Creeley), **Supp. IV Part 1:** 150, 158

Helburn, Theresa, **IV:** 381

Heldreth, Leonard, **Supp. V:** 151

"Helen" (R. Lowell), **II:** 544

"Helen, Thy Beauty Is to Me" (Fante), **Supp. XI:** 169

"Helen: A Courtship" (Faulkner), **Retro. Supp. I:** 81

"Helen I Love You" (Farrell), **II:** 28, 45

Helen in Egypt (Doolittle), **Supp. I Part 1:** 260, 272, 273, 274; **Supp. XV:** 264

Helen Keller: Sketch for a Portrait (Brooks), **I:** 254

Helen of Troy and Other Poems (Teasdale), **Supp. XXVII:** 283, 285–286, 288–289

"Helen of Tyre" (Longfellow), **II:** 496

Heliodora (Doolittle), **Supp. I Part 1:** 266

Helium-3 series (Hickam), **Supp. XXVII:** 111

"He Lives On the Landing" (Espaillat), **Supp. XXI:** 108

"Helix" (Sobin), **Supp. XVI:** 283

Hellbox (O'Hara), **III:** 361

Helle, Anita, **Supp. XXIII:** 117

Heller, Joseph, **III:** 2, 258; **IV:** 98; **Retro. Supp. II:** 324; **Supp. I Part 1:** 196; **Supp. IV Part 1: 379–396; Supp. V:** 244; **Supp. VIII:** 245; **Supp. XI:** 307; **Supp. XII:** 167–168; **Supp. XVII:** 322; **Supp. XVII:** 139; **Supp. XXIII:** 100

"Hell-Heaven" (Lahiri), **Supp. XXI: 181–183,** 183, 184–186, 188

Hellman, Lillian, **I:** 28; **III:** 28; **Supp. I Part 1: 276–298; Supp. IV Part 1:** 1, 12, 83, 353, 355, 356; **Supp. IX:** 196, 198, 200–201, 204; **Supp. VIII:** 243; **Supp. XXVII:** 133, 136

Hellmann, Lillian, **Retro. Supp. II:** 327

Hello (Creeley), **Supp. IV Part 1:** 155, 157

"Hello, Hello Henry" (Kumin), **Supp. IV Part 2:** 446

"Hello, Stranger" (Capote), **Supp. III Part 1:** 120

Hello Dolly! (musical play), **IV:** 357

Hell's Angels: A Strange and Terrible Saga (Thompson), **Supp. XXIV:** 282, 283, 288, 290–291

Hellyer, John, **Supp. I Part 2:** 468

Helm, Bob, **Supp. XV:** 147

Helm, Levon, **Supp. XVIII:** 26

Helmets (Dickey), **Supp. IV Part 1:** 175, 178, 180

"Helmsman, The" (Doolittle), **Supp. I Part 1:** 266

"Help" (Barth), **I:** 139

"Help Her to Believe" (Olsen). *See* "I Stand There Ironing" (Olsen)

Helprin, Mark, **Supp. XIX:** 142; **Supp. XXV: 79–91**

"Helsinki Window" (Creeley), **Supp. IV Part 1:** 158

"Hema and Kaushik" (Lahiri), **Supp. XXI:** 183, 188

Hemenway, Robert E., **Supp. IV Part 1:** 6

Hemingway, Dr. Clarence Edwards, **II:** 248, 259

Hemingway, Ernest, **I:** 28, 64, 97, 99, 105, 107, 117, 150, 162, 190, 211, 221, 288, 289, 295, 367, 374, 378, 421, 423, 445, 476, 477, 478, 482, 484–485, 487, 488, 489, 491, 495, 504, 517; **II:** 27, 44, 51, 58, 68–69, 78, 90, 97, 127, 206, **247–270,** 289, 424, 431, 456, 457, 458–459, 482, 560, 600; **III:** 2, 18, 20, 35, 36, 37, 40, 61, 108, 220, 334, 363, 364, 382, 453, 454, 471–472, 476, 551, 575, 576, 584; **IV:** 27, 28, 33, 34, 35, 42, 49, 97, 108, 122, 126, 138, 190, 191, 201, 216, 217, 257, 297, 363, 404, 427, 433, 451; **Retro. Supp. I:** 74, 98,

108, 111, 112, 113, 115, **169–191,** 215, 292, 359, 418; **Retro. Supp. II:** 19, 24, 30, 68, 115, 123; **Supp. I Part 2:** 621, 658, 678; **Supp. II Part 1:** 221; **Supp. III Part 1:** 146; **Supp. III Part 2:** 617; **Supp. IV Part 1:** 48, 102, 123, 197, 236, 342, 343, 344, 348, 350, 352, 380–381, 383; **Supp. IV Part 2:** 463, 468, 502, 607, 679, 680, 681, 689, 692; **Supp. IX:** 16, 57, 58, 94, 106, 260, 262; **Supp. V:** 237, 240, 244, 250, 336; **Supp. VIII:** 40, 101, 105, 179, 182, 183, 188, 189, 196; **Supp. X:** 137, 167, 223, 225; **Supp. XI:** 214, 221; **Supp. XIII:** 96, 255, 270; **Supp. XIV:** 24, 83; **Supp. XIX:** 131, 154, 157, 246; **Supp. XV:** 69, 135; **Supp. XVI:** 203, 205–206, 208, 210, 233, 236–237, 281–282; **Supp. XVII:** 4, 105, 107, 137, 228, 229; **Supp. XVIII:** 74, 90, 102; **Supp. XX:** **45, 74, 76; Supp. XXI:** 7, 8, 36, 262; **Supp. XXIII:** 4, 68, 166, 174, 275, 299; **Supp. XXIV:** 54, 64, 97, 284; **Supp. XXVI:** 17, 32, 135, 147, 180; **Supp. XXVII:** 134, 141

Hemingway, Mrs. Ernest (Hadley Richardson), **II:** 257, 260, 263

Hemingway, Mrs. Ernest (Martha Gellhorn), **II:** 260

Hemingway, Mrs. Ernest (Mary Welsh), **II:** 257, 260

Hemingway, Mrs. Ernest (Pauline Pfeiffer), **II:** 260

Hemingway, Mrs. Ernest (Martha Gellhorn), **Supp. XXVII:** 141

"Hemingway in Paris" (Cowley), **Supp. II Part 1:** 144

"Hemingway Story, A" (Dubus), **Supp. VII:** 91

"Hemingway: The Old Lion" (Cowley), **Supp. II Part 1:** 143

"Hemp, The" (Benét), **Supp. XI:** 44

Hempel, Amy, **Supp. XIX:** 209; **Supp. XXI:** 115–128

"Henchman, The" (Whittier), **Supp. I Part 2:** 696

Henderson, Alice Corbin, **Supp. I Part 2:** 387; **Supp. XV:** 302–303

Henderson, Darwin L., **Supp. XIII:** 213, 221–222

Henderson, Jane, **Supp. VIII:** 87; **Supp. XX:** 84

Henderson, Katherine, **Supp. IV Part 1:** 203, 207

Henderson, Linda. *See* Hogan, Linda

Henderson, Robert W., **Supp. VIII:** 124

Henderson, Stephen, **Supp. IV Part 1:** 365

Henderson, the Rain King (Bellow), **I:** 144, 147, 148, 152, 153, 154, 155, 158, 160, 161, 162–163; **Retro. Supp. II:** 19, **24–25,** 30

"Hen Flower, The" (Kinnell), **Supp. III Part 1:** 247–248

Henie, Sonja, **Supp. XII:** 165

Henkin, Joshua, **Supp. XXII:** 216

Henle, James, **II:** 26, 30, 38, 41; **Supp. IX:** 2

Henley, Beth, **Supp. XXI:** 145

Hennesy, Dale, **Supp. XV:** 5

Henning, Barbara, **Supp. XXVII:** 174

Henninger, Katherine, **Supp. XXI:** 253

Henri, Robert, **IV:** 411; **Supp. I Part 2:** 376

Henrich, Edith, **Supp. XXIV:** 214

Henry, Arthur, **I:** 515; **Retro. Supp. II:** 97

Henry, DeWitt, **Supp. XI:** 342

Henry, O., **I:** 201; **III:** 5; **Supp. I Part 2:** 390, 462; **Supp. II Part 1: 385–412; Supp. XV:** 40

Henry, Robert, **Retro. Supp. II:** 103

Henry, William A., III, **Supp. IV Part 2:** 574

Henry and Clara (Mallon), **Supp. XIX:** 132, **136–137,** 139, 141

Henry and June (film), **Supp. X:** 186

Henry and June: From the Unexpurgated Diary of Anaïs Nin, **Supp. X:** 184, 185, 187, 194

Henry Holt and Company, **Retro. Supp. I:** 121, 131, 133, 136

Henry IV (Shakespeare), **III:** 166; **Supp. VIII:** 164

"Henry James, Jr." (Howells), **II:** 289; **Retro. Supp. I:** 220

"Henry James and the Art of Teaching" (Rowe), **Retro. Supp. I:** 216

"Henry Lagoon" (Huddle), **Supp. XXVI:** 155

"Henry Manley, Living Alone, Keeps Time" (Kumin), **Supp. IV Part 2:** 451

"Henry Manley Looks Back" (Kumin), **Supp. IV Part 2:** 451

"Henry Manley" poems (Kumin), **Supp. IV Part 2:** 446

Henry Miller Reader, The (Durrell, ed.), **III:** 175, 190

"Henry's Confession" (Berryman), **I:** 186

Henry VIII (Shakespeare), **Supp. IX:** 235

Henslee, **Supp. IV Part 1:** 217

Henson, Josiah, **Supp. I Part 2:** 589

Hentoff, Margot, **Supp. IV Part 1:** 205

Hentz, Caroline Lee, **Supp. I Part 2:** 584

Henze, Hans Werner, **Supp. II Part 1:** 24

"He of the Assembly" (Bowles), **Supp. IV Part 1:** 90

Hepburn, Katharine, **Supp. IX:** 189; **Supp. XI:** 17

Heraclitus, **II:** 1, 163; **IV:** 86

Herakles: A Play in Verse (MacLeish), **III:** 21, 22

Herald of the Autochthonic Spirit (Corso), **Supp. XII:** 134–136

He Ran All the Way (film), **Supp. XVII:** 63

Herberg, Will, **III:** 291

Herbert, Edward, **II:** 11

Herbert, Francis (pseudonym). *See* Bryant, William Cullen

Herbert, George, **II:** 12; **IV:** 141, 145, 146, 151, 153, 156, 165; **Retro. Supp. II:** 40; **Supp. I Part 1:** 80, 107, 108, 122; **Supp. IV Part 2:** 646; **Supp. XV:** 92, 212, 251; **Supp. XXI:** 109

Herbert, Zbigniew, **Supp. VIII:** 20

Herbert Huncke Reader, The (Schafer, ed.), **Supp. XIV:** 137, 138, 139, 140,

145, 147, 150, 151–152

Herbert of Cherbury, Lord, **II:** 108

"Herbert West—Reanimator" (Lovecraft), **Supp. XXV:** 112

"Herbert White" (Bidart), **Supp. XV:** 24, 27

Herbs and the Earth (Beston), **Supp. XXVI:** 35–36

Herbst, Josephine, **Retro. Supp. II:** 325, 328; **Supp. XIII:** 295; **Supp. XXVI:** 18, 26, 28

"Her Choice" (Larcom), **Supp. XIII:** 144

"Her Dead Brother" (R. Lowell), **Retro. Supp. II:** 188

"Her Dream Is of the Sea" (Ríos), **Supp. IV Part 2:** 546

"Here" (Kenyon), **Supp. VII:** 164

Here and Beyond (Wharton), **Retro. Supp. I:** 382

Here and Now (Levertov), **Supp. III Part 1:** 275, 276

"Here and There" (Wallace), **Supp. X:** 305–306

Here Comes the Mystery Man (Sanders), **Supp. XVI:** 269

"Here Comes Winston, Full of the Holy Spirit" (Eugenides), **Supp. XXIV:** 133

Heredia, Juanita, **Supp. XI:** 185, 190

Heredity and Variation (Lock), **Retro. Supp. I:** 375

Heredity: A Psychological Study of Its Phenomena, Laws, Causes, and Consequences (Ribot), **Supp. XX:** 238

Here in Harlem: Poems in Many Voices (Myers), **Supp. XXVII:** 211

"Here Inside My Forehead" (Rasmussen; Nelson and Espeland, trans.), **Supp. XVIII:** 180

Here is Your War (Pyle), **Supp. XVII:** 61

Here Let Us Feast (M. F. K. Fisher), **Supp. XVII:** 86, 87

Here Lies (Parker), **Supp. IX:** 192

Herendeen, Anne, **Supp. XXII:** 275

Here on Earth (Hoffman), **Supp. X:** 77, 89

Heresy and the Ideal: On Contemporary Poetry (Baker), **Supp. XI:** 142

"Here to Learn" (Bowles), **Supp. IV Part 1:** 93

"Here to Yonder" (Hughes), **Retro. Supp. I:** 205

"Her Father's Letters" (Milburn), **Supp. XI:** 242

"Her Favorite Story" (Richard), **Supp. XIX:** 211, 212

Herford, Beatrice, **Supp. XXVI:** 275

Herford, Oliver, **Supp. XXVI:** 275

Herford, Reverend Brooke, **I:** 471

Herford, Will, **Supp. XXII:** 275

"Her Game" (Skloot), **Supp. XX:** 196, **202**

Hergesheimer, Joseph, **Supp. I Part 2:** 620; **Supp. XVI:** 187

"Heritage" (Cullen), **Supp. IV Part 1:** 164–165, 168, 170, 171

"Heritage" (Hogan), **Supp. IV Part 1:** 413

"Her Kind" (Sexton), **Supp. II Part 2:** 687

Herland (Gilman), **Supp. XI:** 208–209

Herman, Florence. *See* Williams, Mrs. William Carlos (Florence Herman)

Herman, Jan, **Supp. XIV:** 150–151

Herman, William (pseudonym). *See* Bierce, Ambrose

"Her Management" (Swenson), **Supp. IV Part 2:** 642

"Herman Melville" (Auden), **Supp. II Part 1:** 14

Herman Melville (Mumford), **Supp. II Part 2:** 471, 476, 489–491

"Hermes of the Ways" (Doolittle), **Supp. I Part 1:** 266

"Hermes: Port Authority: His Song" (Di Piero), **Supp. XIX:** 47

Hermetic Definition (Doolittle), **Supp. I Part 1:** 271, 272, 273, 274

Hermia Suydam (Atherton), **Supp. XXIV:** 21, 28

"Hermitage, The" (Haines), **Supp. XII:** 205–206

Hermit and the Wild Woman, The (Wharton), **IV:** 315; **Retro. Supp. I:** 371

"Hermit and the Wild Woman, The" (Wharton), **Retro. Supp. I:** 372

"Hermit Meets the Skunk, The" (Kumin), **Supp. IV Part 2:** 447

Hermit of 69th Street, The: The Working Papers or Norbert Kosky (Kosinski), **Supp. VII:** 215, 216, 223, 226–227

"Hermit of Saba, The" (Freneau), **Supp. II Part 1:** 259

"Hermit Picks Berries, The" (Kumin), **Supp. IV Part 2:** 447

Hermit's Story, The (Bass), **Supp. XVI:** 23–24

"Hermit Thrush, A" (Clampitt), **Supp. IX:** 40

Hermit-Woman, The (G. Jones), **Supp. XXIV:** 185, 194

Hernández, Miguel, **Supp. V:** 194; **Supp. XIII:** 315, 323; **Supp. XXI:** 104

Herne, James A., **II:** 276; **Supp. II Part 1:** 198

Hernton, Calvin, **Supp. X:** 240

"Hero, The" (Moore), **III:** 200, 211, 212

Hero, The: A Study in Tradition, Myth, and Drama (Raglan), **I:** 135; **Supp. XIX:** 147

Hero and the Blues, The (Murray), **Supp. XIX:** 153, 154

Hérodiade (Mallarmé), **I:** 66

Herodotus, **Supp. I Part 2:** 405

Heroes, The (Ashbery), **Supp. III Part 1:** 3

Heroes and Saints (Moraga), **Supp. XXIII:** 195, 196, 197, **203–204**

Heroes and Saints and Other Plays (Moraga), **Supp. XXIII:** 197

Hero in America, The (Van Doren), **II:** 103

"Heroines of Nature: Four Women Respond to the American Landscape" (Norwood), **Supp. IX:** 24

"Heron, The" (Roethke), **III:** 540–541

"Her One Bad Eye" (Karr), **Supp. XI:** 244

"Her Own People" (Warren), **IV:** 253

Her Place in These Designs (Espaillat), **Supp. XXI:** 99, 104

"Her Quaint Honour" (Gordon), **II:** 196, 199, 200

Herr, Michael, **Supp. XI:** 245; **Supp. XIX:** 17

Herreshoff, David, **Supp. XIX:** 265

Herrick, Robert, **II:** 11, 18, 444; **III:** 463, 592; **IV:** 453; **Retro. Supp. I:** 319; **Retro. Supp. II:** 101; **Supp. I Part 2:** 646; **Supp. XIII:** 334; **Supp. XIV:** 8, 9; **Supp. XV:** 155; **Supp. XXI:** 14

Herrmann, John, **Retro. Supp. II:** 328; **Supp. XXII:** 277

Herron, Don, **Supp. XXVII:** 128

Herron, George, **Supp. I Part 1:** 7

"Hers" (column, Prose), **Supp. XVI:** 254

Herschdorfer, Helen, **Supp. XXI:** 262

Herschel, Sir John, **Supp. I Part 1:** 314

"Her Sense of Timing" (Elkin), **Supp. VI:** 56, 58

Hersey, John, **IV:** 4; **Supp. I Part 1:** 196; **Supp. XVI:** 105–106; **Supp. XX:** 251

"Her Sweet turn to leave the Homestead" (Dickinson), **Retro. Supp. I:** 44

"Her Untold Story"(Thompson), **Supp. XXIII:** 301

Herzog (Bellow), **I:** 144, 147, 149, 150, 152, 153, 154, 155, 156, 157, 158, 159–160; **Retro. Supp. II:** 19, 26–27; **Supp. IV Part 1:** 30; **Supp. XIX:** 157

Herzog, Tobey C., **Supp. XXII:** 116

"He's About 22. I'm 63" (H. Johnson), **Supp. XXVI:** 174

Heschel, Abraham, **Supp. XXI:** 110, 112

Hesford, Walter A., **Supp. XV:** 215, 217, 218

"He/She" (Dunn), **Supp. XI:** 149

"Hesitation Blues" (Hughes), **Retro. Supp. I:** 211

He Sleeps (McKnight), **Supp. XX: 151, 152–155, 158**

"He Sleeps" (McKnight), **Supp. XX: 152, 155**

Hesse, Hermann, **Supp. V:** 208

Hester, Carolyn, **Supp. XVIII:** 24

"Hetch Hetchy Valley" (Muir), **Supp. IX:** 185

He Who Gets Slapped (Andreyev), **II:** 425

"He Who Spits at the Sky" (Stegner), **Supp. IV Part 2:** 605

"He Will Not Leave a Note" (Ríos), **Supp. IV Part 2:** 548

Hewitt, James, **Supp. XV:** 240

Hewitt, J. N. B., **Supp. XXVI:** 81, 89, 90, 96, 97

Hewlett, Maurice, **I:** 359

Heyen, William, **Supp. XIII:** 285, 344; **Supp. XV:** 212

"Hey! Hey!" (Hughes), **Supp. I Part 1:** 327–328

Heyman, Stanley, **Supp. XXV:** 253

Hey Rub-a-Dub-Dub (Dreiser), **I:** 515; **II:** 26; **Retro. Supp. II:** 104, 105, 108

"Hey Sailor, What Ship?" (Olsen), **Supp. XIII:** 293, 294, 298, **299**

Heyward, DuBose, **Supp. XIX:** 78; **Supp. XVIII:** 281

Hiawatha, **Supp. XXVI:** 81, 82, 83, 86

Hiawatha (Longfellow), **Supp. I Part 1:** 79; **Supp. III Part 2:** 609, 610; **Supp. XXI:** 12

"Hibernaculum" (Ammons), **Supp. VII:** 26–27

Hichborn, Philip, **Supp. I Part 2:** 707, 708

Hichborn, Mrs. Philip. *See* Wylie, Elinor

"Hic Jacet" (W. C. Williams), **Retro. Supp. I:** 414

Hickam, Homer, **Supp. XXVII: 99–113**

Hickok, Guy, **Supp. XXI:** 7

Hickok, James Butler ("Wild Bill"), **Supp. V:** 229, 230

Hicks, Granville, **I:** 254, 259, 374; **II:** 26; **III:** 342, 355, 452; **Supp. I Part 1:** 361; **Supp. I Part 2:** 609; **Supp. IV Part 1:** 22; **Supp. IV Part 2:** 526; **Supp. VIII:** 96, 124; **Supp. XII:** 250; **Supp. XIII:** 263; **Supp. XXI:** 276; **Supp. XXII:** 279; **Supp. XXVI:** 144; **Supp. XXVII:** 134

Hicks, Sally, **Supp. XXI:** 255

Hicok, Bethany, **Retro. Supp. II:** 39

"Hidden" (Nye), **Supp. XIII:** 283

"Hidden Gardens" (Capote), **Supp. III Part 1:** 125

Hidden in Plain View (Tobin and Dobard), **Supp. XXVI:** 200

Hidden Law, The (Hecht), **Supp. X:** 58

"Hidden Name and Complex Fate" (Ellison), **Supp. II Part 1:** 245

Hiddenness, Uncertainty, Surprise: Three Generative Energies of Poetry (Hirshfield), **Supp. XXIII:** 137

Hidden Wound, The (Berry), **Supp. X:** 23, 25, 26–27, 29, 34, 35

"Hide-and-Seek" (Francis), **Supp. IX:** 81

"Hiding" (Minot), **Supp. VI:** 203, 206

Hiding Place (Wideman), **Supp. X:** 320, 321, 327, 329, 331–332, 333

"Hidin' Out in Honky Heaven: On Race Relations in Vermont" (Budbill), **Supp. XIX:** 5

Hienger, Jorg, **Supp. IV Part 1:** 106

Hieronymus Bosch (De Tolnay), **Supp. XXII:** 255

Higgins, George, **Supp. IV Part 1:** 356

Higginson, Thomas Wentworth, **I:** 451–452, 453, 454, 456, 458, 459, 463, 464, 465, 470; **Retro. Supp. I:** 26, 31, 33, 35, 39, 40; **Supp. I Part 1:** 307, 371; **Supp. IV Part 2:** 430

Higgs, Robert, **Supp. XX: 166**

"High Bridge above the Tagus River at Toledo, The" (W. C. Williams), **Retro. Supp. I:** 429

"High Dive: A Variant" (Kumin), **Supp. IV Part 2:** 442

"High Diver" (Francis), **Supp. IX:** 82

"Higher Keys, The" (Merrill), **Supp. III Part 1:** 335–336

Higher Learning in America, The (Veblen), **Supp. I Part 2:** 630, 631, 641, 642

Highet, Gilbert, **Supp. I Part 1:** 268

"High Heav'd my breast"(J. Schoolcraft), **Supp. XXIII:** 235

High Noon (film), **Supp. V:** 46

"High on Sadness" (Komunyakaa), **Supp. XIII:** 114

"High School Senior" (Olds), **Supp. X:** 212

Highsmith, Patricia, **Supp. IV Part 1:** 79, 94, 132; **Supp. XXII:** 136

"High Spirits, The" (Huddle), **Supp. XXVI:** 154

High Spirits, The: Stories of Men and Women (Huddle), **Supp. XXVI:** 153–154

"High Tide" (Marquand), **III:** 56

High Tide in Tucson: Essays from Now or Never (Kingsolver), **Supp. VII:** 198, 201, 209

"High-Toned Old Christian Woman, A" (Stevens), **Retro. Supp. I:** 301

"High Water" (Mosher), **Supp. XXII:** 205, 211

"Highway, The" (Merwin), **Supp. III Part 1:** 346

Highway 61 Revisited (album, Dylan), **Supp. XVIII:** 20, 27, 30, 32

"Highway 61 Revisited" (song, Dylan), **Supp. XVIII:** 30

"Highway 99E from Chico" (Carver), **Supp. III Part 1:** 136

"Highway Apple Trees" (Espaillat), **Supp. XXI:** 100–102

High Window, The (Chandler), **Supp. IV Part 1:** 127–129, 130, 131

"High Yaller" (R. Fisher), **Supp. XIX:** 72

Hijuelos, Oscar, **Supp. IV Part 1:** 54; **Supp. VIII:** 73–91

Hike and the Aeroplane (Lewis), **II:** 440–441

Hilberg, Raul, **Supp. V:** 267

Hildebrand, Al, **III:** 118

Hiler, Hilaire, **Retro. Supp. II:** 327; **Supp. III Part 2:** 617

"Hill, A" (Hecht), **Supp. X:** 59–60, 63

Hill, Abram, **Supp. XV:** 194

Hill, Anita, **Supp. XX:** 110

Hill, Geoffrey, **Supp. XXVI:** 67

Hill, Hamlin, **Retro. Supp. II:** 286

Hill, James J., **Supp. I Part 2:** 644

Hill, Joe, **I:** 493; **Supp. XVIII:** 224; **Supp. XXIII:** 162

Hill, Josiah, **Supp. XXVI:** 87, 88

Hill, Lee, **Supp. XI:** 293, 294, 297, 299, 301, 305, 307

Hill, Pamela Smith, **Supp. XXII:** 295

Hill, Patti, **I:** 289

Hill, Peggy, **Supp. XIII:** 163

"Hill, The" (Strand), **Supp. IV Part 2:** 627

"Hill, The" (Toomer), **Supp. III Part 2:** 486

Hill, Vernon, **Supp. I Part 2:** 397

"Hillcrest" (Robinson), **III:** 504

Hill-Lubin, Mildred A., **Supp. IV Part 1:** 13

Hillman, Sidney, **Supp. I Part 1:** 5

Hillringhouse, Mark, **Supp. IX:** 286, 288, 299

Hills Beyond, The (Wolfe), **IV:** 450, 451, 460, 461

"Hills Beyond, The" (Wolfe), **IV:** 460

Hillside and Seaside in Poetry (Larcom, ed.), **Supp. XIII:** 142

"Hillside Thaw, A" (Frost), **Retro. Supp. I:** 133

"Hills Like White Elephants" (Hemingway), **Retro. Supp. I:** 170

Hills of the Shatemuc, The (S. Warner), **Supp. XVIII:** 266

"Hill-Top View, A" (Jeffers), **Supp. II Part 2:** 417

Hill Towns (Siddons), **Supp. XXII:** 239, 253

"Hill Wife, The" (Frost), **II:** 154; **Retro. Supp. I:** 131

Hillyer, Catherine, **Supp. XV:** 244

Hillyer, Robert, **I:** 475; **Supp. IX:** 75; **Supp. XIV:** 11

Hilton, James, **Supp. XIII:** 166

"Hiltons' Holiday, The" (Jewett), **II:** 391; **Retro. Supp. II:** 134

Him (Cummings), **I:** 429, 434–435

Himes, Chester Bomar, **Retro. Supp. II:** 117; **Supp. I Part 1:** 51, 325; **Supp. XIII:** 233; **Supp. XVI:** 135–146

Himes, Norman, **Supp. V:** 128

"Him on a Bicycle" (Weigl), **Supp. XIX:** 276

"Him with His Foot in His Mouth" (Bellow), **Retro. Supp. II:** 34

Him with His Foot in His Mouth and Other Stories (Bellow), **Retro. Supp. II:** 31

Hinchman, Sandra K., **Supp. IV Part 1:** 210

Hinckley, David, **Supp. XXII:** 215

Hindemith, Paul, **IV:** 357; **Supp. IV Part 1:** 81

Hindsell, Oliver, **Supp. XIII:** 162

Hindus, Milton, **Supp. XIV:** 288, 291, 292, 293; **Supp. XXIII:** 16

Hines, Suzanne, **Supp. XIV:** 151

Hinge Picture (Howe), **Supp. IV Part 2:** 423–424

Hinojosa, Rolando, **Supp. XIX:** 97–114

"Hinterlands" (W. Gibson), **Supp. XVI:** 123, 128

"Hippies: Slouching towards Bethlehem" (Didion), **Supp. IV Part 1:** 200

Hippolytus (Euripides), **II:** 543; **Supp. I Part 1:** 270

Hippolytus Temporizes (Doolittle), **Supp. I Part 1:** 270

"Hips" (Cisneros), **Supp. VII:** 61, 62

"Hipster's Hipster" (Ginsberg), **Supp. XIV:** 141

"Hired Girl" (Munro), **Supp. XXVII:** 194

Hirsch, Edward D., **Supp. IX:** 262; **Supp. V:** 177; **Supp. XIV:** 15; **Supp. XIX:** 202; **Supp. XV:** 78, 225; **Supp. XVII:** 23; **Supp. XXIII:** 124

Hirsch, Sidney, **Supp. XIV:** 1. *See* Mttron-Hirsch, Sidney

Hirschfeld, Jane, **Supp. XVII:** 241

Hirschorn, Clive, **Supp. IV Part 2:** 577, 579

Hirshfield, Jane, **Supp. XXIII:** 129–141

Hirson, Roger, **Supp. XI:** 343

"His Bride of the Tomb" (Dunbar), **Supp. II Part 1:** 196

"His Chest of Drawers" (Anderson), **I:** 113, 114

"His Daily Journal" (Kenny), **Supp. XXIII:** 153

"His Father's Whistle" (Wrigley), **Supp. XVIII:** 299

His First, Best Country (J. W. Miller), **Supp. XX: 163, 166, 172–175**

His Fortunate Grace (Atherton), **Supp. XXIV:** 22

His Girl Friday (film), **Supp. XXVII:** 83

His Human Majesty (Boyle), **Supp. XXIV:** 62

"His Last Day" (C. Himes), **Supp. XVI:** 137

"His Lover" (Dubus), **Supp. VII:** 86

"His Music" (Dunn), **Supp. XI:** 149

"His Own Key" (Ríos), **Supp. IV Part 2:** 543

His Picture in the Papers (film; Emerson), **Supp. XVI:** 185

His Religion and Hers (Gilman), **Supp. XI:** 209

Hiss, Alger, **Supp. XV:** 143

"Hiss, Chambers, and the Age of Innocence" (Fiedler), **Supp. XIII:** 99

"His Shield" (Moore), **III:** 211

"His Story" (Cisneros), **Supp. VII:** 67

His Thought Made Pockets & the Plane Buckt (Berryman), **I:** 170

"His Three Women" (Gioia), **Supp. XV:** 119–120

Histoire comparée des systèmes de philosophie (Gérando), **II:** 10

Histoire de la brume, L' (Dybek; trans. Beget), **Supp. XXIII:** 74

Historical and Moral View of the Origin and Progress of the French Revolution (Wollstonecraft), **Supp. I Part 1:** 126

"Historical Conceptualization" (Huizinga), **I:** 255

Historical Evidence and the Reading of Seventeenth-Century Poetry (Brooks), **Supp. XIV:** 11

"Historical Interpretation of Literature, The" (Wilson), **IV:** 431, 433, 445

Historical Jesus, The: The Life of a Mediterranean Jewish Peasant (Crossan), **Supp. V:** 251

Historical Life of Jesus, The (Pettis), **Supp. XXIII:** 189

"Historical Value of Crèvecoeur's *Voyage . . .,*" (Adams), **Supp. I Part 1:** 251

"History" (Emerson), **II:** 13, 15

"History" (Hughes), **Supp. I Part 1:** 344

History (R. Lowell), **Retro. Supp. II:** 183, 190

"History" (Simic), **Supp. VIII:** 279

"History, Myth, and the Western Writer" (Stegner), **Supp. IV Part 2:** 596, 601

"History among the Rocks" (Warren), **IV:** 252

History as a Literary Art (Morison), **Supp. I Part 2:** 493

"History as Fate in E. L. Doctorow's Tale of a Western Town" (Arnold), **Supp. IV Part 1:** 220

"History Is the Memory of Time" (Olson), **Supp. II Part 2:** 574

"History Lesson" (Trethewey), **Supp. XXI:** 248, 249

"History Lessons" (Komunyakaa), **Supp. XIII:** 126

History Man, The (Bradbury), **Supp. XVIII:** 140

"History of a Literary Movement" (Nemerov), **III:** 270

"History of a Literary Radical, The" (Bourne), **I:** 215, 235, 236

History of a Radical: Essays by Randolph Bourne (Brooks), **I:** 245

"History of Armenia, The"(Balakian), **Supp. XXIII:** 23, 24

"History of Buttons, The" (Goldbarth), **Supp. XII:** 187

History of English Literature (Taine), **III:** 323

History of English Prosody (Saintsbury), **Supp. XV:** 181

History of Fortus, The (Emerson), **II:** 8

History of Henry Esmond, The (Thackeray), **II:** 91, 130

History of Modern Poetry, A (Perkins), **Supp. I Part 2:** 475; **Supp. XV:** 185

History of My Heart (Pinsky), **Supp. VI:** 243, 244, 245

History of New York, from the Beginning of the World to the End of the Dutch Dynasty, A (Irving), **II:** 300–303, 304, 310

History of Pendennis, The (Thackeray), **II:** 291

"History of Red, The" (Hogan), **Supp. IV Part 1:** 411

"History of Rodney, The" (Bass), **Supp. XVI:** 20

History of Roxbury Town (Ellis), **Supp. I Part 1:** 99

History of Southern Literature, The (Rubin), **Supp. XX:** 161

History of the African-American People (Proposed) by Strom Thurmond, The (Everett and Kincaid), **Supp. XVIII:** 62, **63–64**

History of the American Film, A (Durang), **Supp. XXIV:** 113, 117, **118–119**

"History of the Blues, A" (Biss), **Supp. XXVI:** 50

History of the Conquest of Mexico (Prescott), **Retro. Supp. I:** 123

History of the Conquest of Peru (Morison, ed.), **Supp. I Part 2:** 494

History of the Dividing Line betwixt Virginia and North Carolina (Byrd), **Supp. IV Part 2:** 425

History of the Life and Voyages of Christopher Columbus, A (Irving), **II:** 310, 314

History of the Navy of the United States of America (Cooper), **I:** 347

History of the Rise and Fall of the Slave-power in America (Wilson), **Supp. XIV:** 48, 49

History of the Russian Revolution, A (Trotsky), **Supp. XXI:** 161

History of the United States (Bancroft), **Supp. XXII:** 33

History of the United States of America during the Administrations of Thomas Jefferson and James Madison (Adams), **I:** 6–9, 10, 20, 21

History of the Work of Redemption, A (Edwards), **I:** 560

History of United States Naval Operations in World War II (Morison), **Supp. I Part 2:** 490–492

History of Womankind in Western Europe, The, **Supp. XI:** 197

"History Teacher, The" (Collins), **Supp. XXI:** 57

"History Through a Beard" (Morison), **Supp. I Part 2:** 490

His Toy, His Dream, His Rest (Berryman), **I:** 169, 170, 183, 184–186

"His Words" (Roethke), **III:** 544

Hitchcock, Ada. *See* MacLeish, Mrs. Archibald (Ada Hitchcock)

Hitchcock, Alfred, **IV:** 357; **Supp. IV Part 1:** 132; **Supp. VIII:** 177; **Supp. XX:** 253; **Supp. XXII:** 119

Hitchcock, George, **Supp. X:** 127; **Supp. XVII:** 110

"Hitch Haiku" (Snyder), **Supp. VIII:** 297

"Hitch-Hikers, The" (Welty), **IV:** 262

"Hitchhiking Is Illegal in Nevada" (Lethem), **Supp. XVIII:** 136

Hitchins, Christopher, **Supp. VIII:** 241

Hitler, Adolf, **I:** 261, 290, 492; **II:** 146, 454, 561, 565, 592; **III:** 2, 3, 110, 115, 140, 156, 246, 298, 446; **IV:** 5, 17, 18, 298, 372; **Supp. I Part 2:** 431, 436, 446, 664; **Supp. V:** 290

Hitler, Wendy, **III:** 404

Hitler Lives ? (film), **Supp. XVI:** 102

Hix, H. L., **Supp. XV:** 114

H. L. Mencken, a Portrait from Memory (Angoff), **III:** 107

"H. L. Mencken Meets a Poet in the West Side Y.M.C.A." (White), **Supp. I Part 2:** 677

H. L. Mencken: The American Scene (Cairns), **III:** 119

H. M. Pulham, Esquire (Marquand), **II:** 482–483; **III:** 58, 59, 65, 68–69

Hnizdovsky, Jacques, **Supp. XIII:** 346

"Hoadley's Test Case in Indiana" (Neugeboren), **Supp. XVI:** 219

Hoagland, Edward, **Supp. XIV:** 80; **Supp. XVI:** 277; **Supp. XXII:** 204, 206

Hoagland, Tony, **Supp. XIX:** 81, 89

"Hoarder, The" (Sexton), **Supp. II Part 2:** 692

"Hoarfrost" (C. Baxter), **Supp. XVII:** 15

Hoban, Phoebe, **Supp. XV:** 319, 325

Hoban, Russell, **Supp. XXIII:** 42

Hobb, Gormley, **I:** 203

Hobbes, Thomas, **I:** 277; **II:** 9, 10, 540; **III:** 306; **IV:** 88; **Supp. XII:** 33; **Supp. XIV:** 5, 7

Hobbit, The (Tolkien), **Supp. XXVII:** 124

Hobson, Geary, **Supp. IV Part 1:** 321; **Supp. IV Part 2:** 502

Hobson, J. A., **I:** 232

Hobson, John A., **Supp. I Part 2:** 650

Hobson, Laura Z., **III:** 151

Hocking, Agnes, **Supp. VIII:** 251

Hocking, William Ernest, **III:** 303

Hodge, Merle, **Supp. XXIII:** 94

Hodges, Campbell B., **Supp. XIV:** 8

Hodgson, Captain Joseph, **III:** 328

Hoffa, Jimmy, **I:** 493

Hoffenberg, Mason, **Supp. XI:** 294, 297, 299, 305

Hoffer, Eric, **Supp. VIII:** 188; **Supp. XIX:** 264

Hoffman, Abbie, **Supp. XIV:** 150

Hoffman, Alice, **Supp. X: 77–94; Supp. XIII:** 13

Hoffman, Allen, **Supp. XVII:** 42, 44

Hoffman, Daniel, **Retro. Supp. II:** 265

Hoffman, Daniel G., **I:** 405; **II:** 307; **Supp. XI:** 152

Hoffman, Dustin, **Supp. IV Part 1:** 236

Hoffman, E. T. A., **Supp. XVI:** 157

Hoffman, Eva, **Supp. XVI: 147–164**

Hoffman, Frederick J., **I:** 60, 67; **II:** 443; **IV:** 113

Hoffman, Josiah Ogden, **II:** 297, 300

Hoffman, Matilda, **II:** 300, 314

Hoffman, Paul, **Supp. XV:** 141–142

Hoffman, Roy, **Supp. XX: 177**

Hoffman, Todd, **Supp. XVIII:** 101

Hoffman, William, **Supp. XVIII: 69–88**

Hoffman, William M., **Supp. X:** 153

Hoffmann, E. T. A., **III:** 415

Hofmann, Hans, **Supp. XV:** 144

Hofmeister, Tim, **Supp. XIX:** 115

Ho for a Hat (W. J. Smith), **Supp. XIII:** 346

Hofstadter, Richard, **Supp. VIII:** 98, 99, 108

Hogan, Linda, **Supp. IV Part 1:** 324, 325, **397–418; Supp. XVIII:** 189

Hogan, Randolph, **Supp. XVI:** 252–253

Hogan, Ron, **Supp. XVIII:** 138, 139

Hogarth, William, **Supp. XII:** 44

Hogg, James, **I:** 53; **Supp. I Part 1:** 349; **Supp. IX:** 275

Hoggart, Richard, **Supp. XIV:** 299

"Hog-Nosed Snake, The" (Kooser), **Supp. XIX:** 128

Hogue, W. Lawrence, **Supp. XXII:** 175–176

Hohne, Karen, **Supp. V:** 147

Hojoki (Chomei), **IV:** 170

Holbrook, David, **Supp. I Part 2:** 526–527, 546

Holcroft, Thomas, **Supp. I Part 2:** 514

Holden, Jonathan, **Supp. XI:** 143

Holden, Raymond, **Supp. XIV:** 121–122

Holden, William, **Supp. XI:** 307

Hölderlin, Friedrich, **Supp. XVI:** 48; **Supp. XXIV:** 152

Holding, Elisabeth Sanxay, **Supp. XXII: 119–137**

"Holding On" (Levine), **Supp. V:** 184

Holding the Line: Women in the Great Arizona Mine Strike of 1983 (Kingsolver), **Supp. VII:** 197, 201–202, 204

"Holding the Mirror Up to Nature" (Nemerov), **III:** 275, 276

"Hold Me" (Levine), **Supp. V:** 186

Holdt, Jacob, **Supp. XXVI:** 26

Hold the Press (film), **Supp. XIII:** 163

Hold with the Hares (Zinberg), **Supp. XV:** 197–198,**Supp. XV:** 203

Hole in Texas, A (Wouk), **Supp. XXV:** 257, 266–267

"Hole in the Floor, A" (Wilbur), **Supp. III Part 2:** 556–557

Hole in the Sky: A Memoir (Kittredge), **Supp. XXVI:** 177, 179, 180–181, 182, 184–185

Holiday (Barry), **Retro. Supp. I:** 104

"Holiday" (Porter), **III:** 454

Holiday (W. Frank), **Supp. XX: 72–73**

Holiday, Billie, **Supp. I Part 1:** 80; **Supp. IV Part 1:** 2, 7; **Supp. XIX:** 147

Holiday Song for Four-Part Chorus of Mixed Voices with Piano Accompaniment (Taggard and Schuman), **Supp. XXII:** 283

Holinshed, Raphael, **IV:** 370

Holladay, Polly, **Supp. XXI:** 6

Holland, Josiah, **Supp. I Part 2:** 420

Holland, Laurence Bedwell, **Retro. Supp. I:** 216

Holland, Theodore, **I:** 453

Holland, Mrs. Theodore, **I:** 453, 455, 465

Holland, William, **IV:** 381

Hollander, John, **Supp. III Part 2:** 541; **Supp. IV Part 2:** 642; **Supp. IX:** 50, 153, 155; **Supp. XII:** 254, 255, 260; **Supp. XIX:** 121; **Supp. XV:** 256; **Supp. XVII:** 112; **Supp. XXIII:** 112

Hollenberg, Donna, **Supp. XXIV:** 64

Holley, Marietta, **Supp. XIII:** 152

Holliday, Billie, **Supp. XXI:** 131

Hollinghurst, Alan, **Supp. XIII:** 52

Hollins Critic (Nelson), **Supp. XIX:** 3

Hollis, Thomas Brand, **Supp. I Part 2:** 514

Hollow Men, The (T. S. Eliot), **I:** 574, 575, 578–579, 580, 585; **III:** 586; **Retro. Supp. I:** 63, 64

"Hollow Tree, A" (R. Bly), **Supp. IV Part 1:** 64, 66

Hollyberrys at the Shore, The, **Supp. X:** 42

"Hollywood!" (Vidal), **Supp. IV Part 2:** 688

Hollywood: American Movie-City (Rand, unauthorized), **Supp. IV Part 2:** 519

Hollywood: A Novel of America in the 1920s (Vidal), **Supp. IV Part 2:** 677, 684, 686, 688, 690, 691

Hollywood Ending (film; Allen), **Supp. XV:** 11

Hollywood on Trial (film), **Supp. I Part 1:** 295

Holmes, Abiel, **Supp. I Part 1:** 300, 301, 302, 310

Holmes, Mrs. Abiel (Sarah Wendell), **Supp. I Part 1:** 300

Holmes, John, **I:** 169; **Supp. II Part 1:** 87; **Supp. IV Part 2:** 440–441; **Supp. XIV:** 119; **Supp. XXVI:** 68

Holmes, John Clellon, **Supp. XII:** 118; **Supp. XIV:** 144, 150

Holmes, Martha Stoddard, **Supp. XX:** 205, 207

Holmes, Oliver Wendell, **I:** 487; **II:** 225, 273–274, 402, 403; **III:** 81–82, 590, 591–592; **IV:** 429, 436; **Retro. Supp.**

II: 155; **Supp. I Part 1:** 103, 243, 254, **299–319;** **Supp. I Part 2:** 405, 414, 415, 420, 593, 704, 705; **Supp. XI:** 194; **Supp. XXIV:** 77

Holmes, Oliver Wendell, Jr., **I:** 3, 19; **Supp. IV Part 2:** 422

Holmes, Mrs. Oliver Wendell (Amelia Jackson), **Supp. I Part 1:** 303

Holmes, Steven J., **Supp. IX:** 172, 177

Holmes, Ted, **Supp. V:** 180

Holmes, William Henry, **Supp. IV Part 2:** 603–604

Holmquist, Kathryn, **Supp. XXVII:** 268

Holocaust (Reznikoff), **Supp. XIV:** 281, **291–293**

Holocaust in American Life, The (Novick), **Supp. XVI:** 154

Holt, Edwin E., **I:** 59

Holt, Felix, **II:** 179

Holt, Henry, **II:** 348; **III:** 587

Holt, Patricia, **Supp. XIV:** 89

Holtby, Winifred, **Supp. I Part 2:** 720

Holy Ghostly, The (Shepard), **Supp. III Part 2:** 437–438, 447

"Holy Innocents, The" (R. Lowell), **II:** 539

Holy Sonnets (Donne), **IV:** 145; **Supp. I Part 1:** 367; **Supp. III Part 2:** 619; **Supp. XIII:** 130–131; **Supp. XVIII:** 50–51

"Holy Terror, A" (Bierce), **I:** 203

"Holy Terror, The" (Maxwell), **Supp. VIII:** 169

Holy the Firm (Dillard), **Supp. VI:** 23, **29,** 30, 31, 32

Holy War, The (Bunyan), **IV:** 156

"Holy Week"(Thompson), **Supp. XXIII:** 300

Holz, Patricia, **Supp. XXVII:** 267

"Homage to Arthur Rimbaud" (Wright), **Supp. V:** 339

Homage to Baudelaire (Duncan, ed.), **Supp. XV:** 75

Homage to Catalonia (Orwell), **Supp. XVII:** 229

"Homage to Che Guevara" (Banks), **Supp. V:** 5

Homage to Clio (Auden), **Supp. II Part 1:** 24

"Homage to Elizabeth Bishop" (Ivask, ed.), **Supp. I Part 1:** 96

"Homage to Ezra Pound" (Wright), **Supp. V:** 339

Homage to Frank O'Hara (Ashbery), **Supp. III Part 1:** 2–3

"Homage to Franz Joseph Haydn" (Hecht), **Supp. X:** 69

"Homage to Hemingway" (Bishop), **IV:** 35

Homage to Mistress Bradstreet (Berryman), **I:** 168, 169, 170–171, 172, 174, 175, 178–183, 184, 186

"Homage to Paul Cézanne" (Wright), **Supp. V:** 341–342

Homage to Sextus Propertius (Pound), **Retro. Supp. I:** 290

"Homage to Sextus Propertius" (Pound), **III:** 462, 476; **Supp. III Part 2:** 622

"Homage to Shakespeare" (Cheever), **Supp. I Part 1:** 180

"Homage to the Empress of the Blues" (Hayden), **Supp. II Part 1:** 379

"Homage to the Memory of Wallace Stevens" (Justice), **Supp. VII:** 126

Homage to Theodore Dreiser (Warren), **I:** 517

Homans, Margaret, **Supp. X:** 229

"Home" (Hughes), **Supp. I Part 1:** 329, 330

"Home" (Mora), **Supp. XIII:** 217

Home (Robinson), **Supp. XXI:** 212, **220–223**

Home (Updike), **Retro. Supp. I:** 320

"Home" (Weigl), **Supp. XIX:** 287

"Home, Home on the Strange" (J. D. Reed), **Supp. XVI:** 174

"Home, Sweet Home" (Fante), **Supp. XI:** 164, 165

Home, The (Gilman), **Supp. XI: 206–207**

"Home, The" (Jarman), **Supp. XVII:** 116

"Home Address" (Bronk), **Supp. XXI:** 27

"Home after Three Months Away" (R. Lowell), **II:** 547

Home and Colonial Library (Murray), **Retro. Supp. I:** 246

"Home and the Open Road: The Nonfiction of Larry Brown" (Barrier), **Supp. XXI:** 48–49

Home as Found (Cooper), **I:** 348, 349, 350, 351

Home at the End of the World, A (Cunningham), **Supp. XV: 59–62,** 63

"Home Away from Home, A" (Humphrey), **Supp. IX:** 101

Home Book of Shakespeare Quotations (Stevenson), **Supp. XIV:** 120

"Home Burial" (Frost), **Retro. Supp. I:** 124, 125, 128, **129–130; Supp. VIII:** 31; **Supp. XIX:** 9; **Supp. XV:** 159

Homecoming (Alvarez), **Supp. VII:** 1, 3–5, 9

"Homecoming" (Carruth), **Supp. XVI:** 55

"Homecoming" (McGrath), **Supp. X:** 116

"Homecoming, The" (Gioia), **Supp. XV:** 123, 124

Homecoming, The (Wilson), **Supp. VIII:** 330

Homecoming Game, The (Nemerov), **III:** 268, 282, 284–285

"Home during a Tropical Snowstorm I Feed My Father Lunch" (Karr), **Supp. XI:** 241–242, 248

Home Economics (Berry), **Supp. X:** 28, 31–32, 35, 36, 37

"Home Economics for Halfbacks" (Skloot), **Supp. XX: 195, 207**

Home Fires and Reservation Roads (Gansworth), **Supp. XXVI:** 114

Home from the Hill (film), **Supp. IX:** 95

Home from the Hill (Humphrey), **Supp. IX:** 93, 95, **96–98,** 104, 106, 109

"Home Grown" (Vital), **Supp. XVI:** 160

"Homeland" (Merwin), **Supp. III Part 1:** 351

Homeland and Other Stories (Kingsolver), **Supp. VII:** 199, 202–204, 207

Home on the Range (Baraka), **Supp. II Part 1:** 47
Homeplace (Siddons), **Supp. XXII:** 253
Home Place, The (Morris), **III:** 221, 222, 232
Homeplace, The (Nelson), **Supp. XVIII: 174–175**
Homer, **I:** 312, 433; **II:** 6, 8, 133, 302, 543, 544, 552; **III:** 14, 21, 278, 453, 457, 473, 567; **IV:** 54, 371; **Retro. Supp. I:** 59; **Supp. I Part 1:** 158, 283; **Supp. I Part 2:** 494; **Supp. X:** 36, 120, 122; **Supp. XIV:** 21; **Supp. XVII:** 70, 227
Homer, Louise, **Retro. Supp. I:** 10
Homer, Winslow, **Supp. XXI:** 243
"Home Range" (Leopold), **Supp. XIV:** 184, 185
"Home Repairs" (Skloot), **Supp. XX: 204**
Homer's Art (Notley), **Supp. XXII:** 232
"Homer's Art" (Notley), **Supp. XXII:** 232–233
"Homesick Blues" (Hughes), **Supp. I Part 1:** 327
Home: Social Essays (Baraka), **Supp. II Part 1:** 45, 61
"Homesteading on the Extraterrestrial Frontier" (Abbott), **Supp. XVIII:** 142
Home to Harlem (McKay), **Supp. X:** 132, 137–138, **138–139; Supp. XVIII:** 127
"Home Videos" (Brockmeier), **Supp. XXII:** 60
Homeward Bound (Cooper), **I:** 348
"Homeward Star, The" (Palmer), **Supp. XV:** 81–82
Homewood trilogy (Wideman), **Supp. X:** 319
"Homework" (Cameron), **Supp. XII:** 80, **83,** 84
"Homily" (Tate), **IV:** 121–122
Homing with the Birds (Stratton-Porter), **Supp. XX: 212, 216, 222**
"Homme Moyen Sensuel, L' " (Pound), **III:** 462
Homme révolté, L' (Camus), III: 306
"Homoeopathy and Its Kindred Delusions" (Holmes), **Supp. I Part 1:** 303–304, 305
Homo Ludens (Huizinga), **II:** 416–417, 425
"Homosexuality: Is It Disgusting, or Is It Delightful?" (Durang), **Supp. XXIV:** 114
"Homosexuality"(O'Hara), **Supp. XXIII:** 212
"Homosexual Villain, The" (Mailer), **III:** 36
"Homo Will Not Inherit" (Doty), **Supp. XI:** 128
"Homunculus, The: A Novel in One Chapter" (McKnight), **Supp. XX: 152**
Hone and Strong Diaries of Old Manhattan, The (Auchincloss, ed.), **Supp. IV Part 1:** 23
"Honey" (Beattie), **Supp. V:** 33
"Honey" (Wright), **Supp. III Part 2:** 589
Honey, Maureen, **Supp. XXVI:** 166
"Honey, We'll Be Brave" (Farrell), **II:** 45
Honey and Salt (Sandburg), **III:** 594–596

"Honey and Salt" (Sandburg), **III:** 594
"Honey Babe" (Hughes), **Supp. I Part 1:** 334
"Honey Tree, The" (Oliver), **Supp. VII:** 236
Hong, Maxine. *See* Kingston, Maxine Hong
Hong, Terry, **Supp. XXVI:** 216
Hongo, Garrett, **Supp. X:** 292; **Supp. XIII:** 114; **Supp. XVII:** 112
"Honkytonk" (Shapiro), **Supp. II Part 2:** 705
"Honky Tonk in Cleveland, Ohio" (Sandburg), **III:** 585
Honorable Men (Auchincloss), **Supp. IV Part 1:** 23
Honor Thy Father (Talese), **Supp. XVII:** 204–205, 210
Hood, Mary, **Supp. XXVI:** 15
Hood, Tom, **I:** 195
"Hoodoo in America" (Hurston), **Supp. VI:** 153–154
"Hook" (Wright), **Supp. III Part 2:** 604
Hook, Sidney, **I:** 265; **Supp. IV Part 2:** 527; **Supp. VIII:** 96, 100; **Supp. XIV:** 3
Hooker, Adelaide. *See* Marquand, Mrs. John P. (Adelaide Hooker)
Hooker, Isabella Beecher, **Supp. XI:** 193
Hooker, Samuel, **IV:** 162, 165
Hooker, Thomas, **II:** 15–16; **IV:** 162
Hooper, Marian. *See* Adams, Mrs. Henry (Marian Hooper)
Hoops (Myers), **Supp. XXVII:** 201, 204, 205–206
Hoosier Holiday, A (Dreiser), **Retro. Supp. II:** 104
Hoover, Herbert, **Supp. I Part 2:** 638
Hoover, J. Edgar, **Supp. XIII:** 170
Hoover, Paul, **Supp. XV:** 179
"Hope" (Bontemps), **Supp. XXII:** 2
"Hope" (Jarrell), **II:** 389
"Hope" (Matthews), **Supp. IX:** 163
Hope, A. D., **Supp. XIII:** 347
Hope, Lynn, **Supp. II Part 1:** 38
Hope, The (Wouk), **Supp. XXV:** 254, 257, 265–266
"Hope Atherton's Wanderings" (Howe), **Supp. IV Part 2:** 432
"Hopeless Kill, The"(Kenny), **Supp. XXIII:** 145
Hope of Heaven (O'Hara), **III:** 361
"Hopes Rise" (Boyle), **Supp. XX: 20**
"Hop-Frog" (Poe), **Retro. Supp. II:** 264, 268, 269
"Hop Frog" (Poe), **Supp. XXV:** 112
Hopkin, Pauline, **Supp. XVI:** 143
Hopkins, Anne Yale, **Supp. I Part 1:** 100, 102, 113
Hopkins, Gerard Manley, **I:** 171, 179, 397, 401, 522, 525, 533; **II:** 537; **III:** 197, 209, 523; **IV:** 129, 135, 141, 421; **Retro. Supp. II:** 40; **Supp. I Part 1:** 79, 81, 94; **Supp. III Part 2:** 551; **Supp. IV Part 1:** 178; **Supp. IV Part 2:** 637, 638, 639, 641, 643; **Supp. IX:** 39, 42; **Supp. V:** 337; **Supp. X:** 61, 115; **Supp. XIII:** 294; **Supp. XIV:** 83; **Supp. XV:** 250, 347; **Supp. XVI:** 282; **Supp. XVII:** 241; **Supp. XVIII:** 78,

79; **Supp. XX: 230; Supp. XXIII:** 121; **Supp. XXVII:** 222
Hopkins, Gerard Walter Sturgis, **Supp. XX: 229, 233, 240**
Hopkins, L. A., **I:** 502
Hopkins, Lemuel, **Supp. II Part 1:** 70
Hopkins, Miriam, **IV:** 381; **Supp. I Part 1:** 281
Hopkins, Pauline, **Supp. XVIII:** 284
Hopkins, Samuel, **I:** 547, 549; **Supp. XXIV:** 68
Hopkins, Vivian, **II:** 20
Hopkinson, Francis, **Supp. I Part 2:** 504
Hopler, Jay, **Supp. XXIII:** 132
Hopper (Strand), **Supp. IV Part 2:** 632
Hopper, Dennis, **Supp. XI:** 293, 308; **Supp. XXVI:** 26
Hopper, Edward, **IV:** 411, 413; **Supp. IV Part 2:** 619, 623, 631, 634; **Supp. XIX:** 117
Hopwood, Avery, **Supp. IV Part 2:** 573; **Supp. XXV:** 195
Horace, **II:** 8, 154, 169, 543, 552, 568; **III:** 15; **IV:** 89; **Supp. I Part 2:** 423; **Supp. IX:** 152; **Supp. X:** 65; **Supp. XII:** 258, 260, 262
Horae Canonicae (Auden), **Supp. II Part 1:** 21
"Horatian Ode" (Marvell), **IV:** 135
"Horatian Ode upon Cromwell's Return from Ireland" (Marvell), **Supp. XIV:** 10
Horgan, Paul, **Supp. XV:** 46, 49, 52
Horkheimer, Max, **Supp. I Part 2:** 645; **Supp. IV Part 1:** 301
Horn, Dara, **Supp. XVII:** 50; **Supp. XX: 177**
Horn, Mother, **Supp. I Part 1:** 49, 54
Hornburg, Michael, **Supp. XXVII:** 80
Hornby, Nick, **Supp. XII:** 286; **Supp. XXIII:** 109
Horn of Africa (Caputo), **Supp. XIX:** 21–23
Horn of Life, The (Atherton), **Supp. XXIV:** 26, 27
"Horn of Plenty" (Hughes), **Retro. Supp. I:** 210; **Supp. I Part 1:** 342
Horovitz, Israel, **Supp. XV:** 321
Horowitz, James. *See* Salter, James
Horowitz, Mark, **Supp. V:** 219, 231
"Horrible" (Halliday), **Supp. XIX:** 91
"Horror at Martin's Beach, The" (Lovecraft and Greene), **Supp. XXV:** 122
"Horror at Red Hook, The" (Lovecraft), **Supp. XXV:** 110
"Horse, The" (Levine), **Supp. V:** 182
"Horse, The" (Wright), **Supp. III Part 2:** 592, 601
"Horse, The"(Le Sueur), **Supp. XXIII:** 168
Horse Eats Hay (play), **Supp. IV Part 1:** 82
Horse Feathers (film), **Supp. IV Part 1:** 384
"Horseflies" (Wrigley), **Supp. XVIII:** 307
Horse Has Six Legs, The (Simic), **Supp. VIII:** 272

"Horselaugh on Dibber Lannon" (Fante), **Supp. XI:** 164

Horseman, Pass By (McMurtry), **Supp. V:** 220–221, 224

"Horses" (Doty), **Supp. XI:** 122

Horses and Men (Anderson), **I:** 112–113, 114

"Horses and Men in Rain" (Sandburg), **III:** 584

"Horse Show, The" (W. C. Williams), **Retro. Supp. I:** 423

Horses Make a Landscape More Beautiful (Walker), **Supp. III Part 2:** 521, 533

"Horse Thief" (Caldwell), **I:** 310

"Horseweed" (Offutt), **Supp. XIX:** 166, 167

Horse With a Green Vinyl Mane (P. N. Warren), **Supp. XX: 261**

"Horsie" (Parker), **Supp. IX:** 193

Horstmann, Steffen, **Supp. XXV:** 226

Horton, George Moses, **Supp. XXII:** 11

Horton, Philip, **I:** 383, 386, 387, 393, 441; **Supp. XV:** 138

Horton Hatches the Egg (Geisel), **Supp. XVI:** 100, 112

Horton Hears a Who! (Geisel), **Supp. XVI:** 102

"Horton's Ape"(P. Benedict), **Supp. XXIII:** 41

Horwitz, Tony, **Supp. XVIII:** 195–196

Hosea (biblical book), **II:** 166

Hospers, John, **Supp. IV Part 2:** 528

"Hospice" (Hull), **Supp. XXI:** 138

Hospital, Janette Turner, **Supp. IV Part 1:** 311–302

Hospital Sketches (Alcott), **Supp. I Part 1:** 34, 35

Hostages to Fortune (Humphrey), **Supp. IX:** 96, **104–106,** 109

Hostess to Murder (Holding), **Supp. XXII:** 126, **127**

"Hot Combs" (Trethewey), **Supp. XXI:** 249

"Hot Cross Bum" (Loy), **Supp. XXII:** 168

"Hot Dog" (Stern), **Supp. IX: 298–299**

"Hotel, The"(Hadas), **Supp. XXIII:** 121

"Hotel Bar" (McClatchy), **Supp. XII:** 269

Hotel Dwellers, The (Lacy), **Supp. XV:** 205

Hotel Insomnia (Simic), **Supp. VIII:** 280, **281–282**

Hotel Lambosa and Other Stories (Koch), **Supp. XV:** 186

Hotel New Hampshire, The (Irving), **Supp. VI:** 163, 164, **172–173,** 177, 179; **Supp. XIX:** 164

"Hot-Foot Hannibal" (Chesnutt), **Supp. XIV:** 60

"Hot Ice"(Dybek), **Supp. XXIII:** 72–73

"Hot Night on Water Street" (Simpson), **Supp. IX:** 269, 270

"Hot Time, A" (Gunn Allen), **Supp. IV Part 1:** 333

Houdini, Harry, **IV:** 437; **Supp. XXV:** 121

"Hound of Heaven" (Thompson), **Retro. Supp. I:** 55

"Hourglass, The" (Kees), **Supp. XV:** 147

"Hour in Chartres, An" (Bourne), **I:** 228

"Hour of Peonies, The"(Crooker), **Supp. XXIII:** 58

Hour of the Dragon, The (Howard), **Supp. XXVII:** 126

Hours, The (Cunningham), **Supp. XII:** 80; **Supp. XV: 65–68**

"Hours before Eternity" (Caldwell), **I:** 291

House, Bridge, Fountain, Gate (Kumin), **Supp. IV Part 2:** 448, 449, 451, 454

House, Edward, **Supp. I Part 2:** 643

"House, The" (Merrill), **Supp. III Part 1:** 323

House at Pooh Corner, The (Milne), **Supp. IX:** 189

"House at the End of the World, The" (Brockmeier), **Supp. XXII:** 52, 53

House Behind the Cedars, The (Chesnutt), **Supp. XIV: 69–71**

Houseboat Days (Ashbery), **Supp. III Part 1:** 18–20

Housebreaker of Shady Hill and Other Stories, The (Cheever), **Supp. I Part 1:** 184

"House by the Sea, The" (E. Stoddard), **Supp. XV:** 277

House by the Sea, The (Sarton), **Supp. VIII:** 264

House Divided, A (Buck), **Supp. II Part 1:** 118

"House Divided, The/La Casa Divida" (Kingsolver), **Supp. VII:** 207

"House Guest" (Bishop), **Retro. Supp. II:** 49; **Supp. I Part 1:** 93

"House Holding" (Davison), **Supp. XXVI:** 73, 74

Household Saints (film), **Supp. XVI:** 256

Household Saints (Prose), **Supp. XVI:** 252–253, 254, 261

"House in Athens, The" (Merrill), **Supp. III Part 1:** 323

House in the Uplands, A (Caldwell), **I:** 297, 301, 306

"House in Turk Street, The" (Hammett), **Supp. IV Part 1:** 344

"House in Winter, The" (Sarton), **Supp. VIII:** 259

"House in Winter, The"(Hirshfield), **Supp. XXIII:** 132

House Is Made of Poetry, The (Baker and Gilbert, eds.), **Supp. XXVII:** 263

"Housekeeping" (Alvarez), **Supp. VII:** 3–5, 10

Housekeeping (Robinson), **Supp. XXI:** 210–211, **212–216,** 218, 223

"Housekeeping" (Trethewey), **Supp. XXI:** 249

"Housekeeping for Men" (Bourne), **I:** 231

House Made of Dawn (Momaday), **Supp. IV Part 1:** 274, 323, 326; **Supp. IV Part 2:** 479, 480, 481–484, 485, 486, 504, 562

Houseman, John, **Supp. IV Part 1:** 173

House Next Door, The (Siddons), **Supp. XXII:** 239

House Next Door, The (television movie), **Supp. XXII:** 239

"House of Caesar, The" (Garvin), **Supp. XXVII:** 118

House of Dust, The: A Symphony (Aiken), **I:** 50

House of Earth trilogy (Buck), **Supp. II Part 1:** 118, 123

House of Five Talents, The (Auchincloss), **Supp. IV Part 1:** 21, 25–27

"House of Flowers" (Capote), **Supp. III Part 1:** 123

House of Games (Mamet), **Supp. XIV:** 243

House of Houses (Mora), **Supp. XIII:** 213, 215, 218, 219, 223–224, **225–227,** 228, 229

House of Incest (Nin), **Supp. III Part 1:** 43; **Supp. X:** 187, 190, 193

House of Lee, The (Atherton), **Supp. XXIV:** 26–27

House of Life, The: Rachel Carson at Work (Brooks), **Supp. IX:** 26

House of Light (Oliver), **Supp. VII:** 238–240

House of Mirth, The (Wharton), **II:** 180, 193; **IV:** 311–313, 314, 316, 318, 323, 327; **Retro. Supp. I:** 360, 366, 367, **367–370,** 373, 380; **Supp. XX: 239, 240**

"House of Mist, The" (Rand), **Supp. IV Part 2:** 524

"House of My Own, A" (Cisneros), **Supp. VII:** 64

"House of Night, The" (Freneau), **Supp. II Part 1:** 259, 260

"House of Representatives and Me, The" (Conroy), **Supp. XVI:** 75

House of Sand and Fog (Dubus III), **Supp. XXIV:** 97, **104–107**

House of Sleeping Beauties, The (Hwang), **Supp. XXI:** 146

House of the Far and Lost, The (Wolfe), **IV:** 456

"House of the Injured, The" (Haines), **Supp. XII:** 203

"House of the One Father" (Antin), **Supp. XX: 3, 13**

House of the Prophet, The (Auchincloss), **Supp. IV Part 1:** 31

House of the Seven Gables (Hawthorne), **I:** 106; **II:** 60, 224, 225, 231, 237, 239, 240–241, 243, 244; **Retro. Supp. I:** 63, 149, **160–162,** 163, 164; **Supp. I Part 2:** 579

House of the Solitary Maggot, The (Purdy), **Supp. VII:** 274–275

"House on 15th S.W., The" (Hugo), **Supp. VI:** 140

"House on Main Street, The" (B. Kelly), **Supp. XVII:** 127

House on Mango Street, The (Cisneros), **Supp. VII:** 58, 59–64, 65, 66, 67, 68, 72; **Supp. XXV:** 133

"House on Mango Street, The" (Cisneros), **Supp. VII:** 59

House on Marshland, The (Glück), **Supp. V:** 81–83, 84

"House on Moscow Street, The" (Nelson), **Supp. XVIII:** 174

"House on the Heights, A" (Capote), **Supp. III Part 1:** 120

"House on the Hill, The" (Robinson), **III:** 505, 524

"House Raising" (Offutt), **Supp. XIX:** 166

"Houses" (Hogan), **Supp. IV Part 1:** 402

"Houses, The" (Merwin), **Supp. III Part 1:** 354

"Houses of Dreams" (Teasdale), **Supp. XXVII:** 292

"Houses of the Spirit" (Karr), **Supp. XI:** 250

"House Sparrows" (Hecht), **Supp. X:** 68

"House That Doesn't House, The" (Bronk), **Supp. XXI:** 34

House That Tai Maing Built, The (Lee), **Supp. X:** 291

"House Unroofed by the Gale" (Tu Fu), **II:** 526

"House Where Mark Twain Was Born, The" (Masters), **Supp. I Part 2:** 472

"Housewife" (Hempel), **Supp. XXI:** 124

"Housewife" (Sexton), **Supp. II Part 2:** 682

"Housewife's Paradise, The" (Davison), **Supp. XXVI:** 76

" 'Housing the Deliberations': New York, War, and Frank O'Hara"(Ward), **Supp. XXIII:** 218

Housman, A. E., **III:** 15, 136, 606; **Supp. II Part 1:** 4; **Supp. IV Part 1:** 165; **Supp. XV:** 40–41

Houston, Robert, **Supp. XXV:** 54

Houston Trilogy (McMurtry), **Supp. V:** 223–225

How" (Ginsberg), **Supp. XIV:** 142, 143

"How" (Moore), **Supp. X:** 167

"How About This?" (Carver), **Supp. III Part 1:** 141

"How America Came to the Mountains" (J. W. Miller), **Supp. XX: 169**

"How Annandale Went Out" (Robinson), **III:** 513

Howard, Arliss, **Supp. XXI:** 39

Howard, Ben, **Supp. XVI:** 54

Howard, Gerald, **Supp. XII:** 21

Howard, Jane, **Retro. Supp. I:** 334

Howard, June, **Retro. Supp. II:** 139

Howard, Leon, **Supp. I Part 2:** 408, 422, 423

Howard, Maureen, **Supp. XII:** 285; **Supp. XVII:** 183

Howard, Richard, **Retro. Supp. II:** 43; **Supp. IV Part 2:** 624, 626, 640; **Supp. IX:** 324, 326; **Supp. VIII:** 273; **Supp. X:** 152; **Supp. XI:** 317; **Supp. XII:** 254; **Supp. XIII:** 76; **Supp. XV:** 23, 24; **Supp. XXIV:** 155

Howard, Robert E., **Supp. XXV:** 122; **Supp. XXVII: 115–131**

Howard, Vilma, **Retro. Supp. II:** 111, 112

Howards, J. Z., **Supp. VIII:** 178

Howards End (Forster), **Supp. XII:** 87

Howarth, Cora, **I:** 408, 409

Howbah Indians (Ortiz), **Supp. IV Part 2:** 513

"How Black Sees Green and Red" (McKay), **Supp. X:** 136

How Britain Rules Africa (Padmore), **Supp. XXI:** 166

"How David Did Not Care" (R. Bly), **Supp. IV Part 1:** 73

"How Did I Love Him?" (Nelson), **Supp. XVIII:** 176

"How Do I Love Thee?" (Browning), **Supp. XVIII:** 176

Howe, Daniel Walker, **Supp. XXIV:** 79

Howe, Darcus, **Supp. XXI:** 170

Howe, E.W., **I:** 106

Howe, Florence, **Supp. XIII:** 295, 306

Howe, Harriet, **Supp. XI:** 200, 201

Howe, Irving, **IV:** 10; **Retro. Supp. I:** 369; **Retro. Supp. II:** 112, 286; **Supp. I Part 2:** 432; **Supp. II Part 1:** 99; **Supp. IX:** 227; **Supp. VI:** 113–129; **Supp. VIII:** 93, 232; **Supp. X:** 203, 245; **Supp. XII:** 160; **Supp. XIII:** 98; **Supp. XIV:** 103–104, 104; **Supp. XIX:** 257, 265; **Supp. XVII:** 50; **Supp. XXIII:** 3, 7; **Supp. XXIV:** 220–221, 222

Howe, James Wong, **Supp. I Part 1:** 281; **Supp. V:** 223

Howe, Julia Ward, **III:** 505; **Retro. Supp. II:** 135

Howe, LeAnne, **Supp. XXVI:** 84, 98

Howe, M. A. DeWolfe, **I:** 258; **II:** 406; **Supp. XIV:** 54

Howe, Mary Manning, **Supp. IV Part 2:** 422

Howe, Samuel, **Supp. I Part 1:** 153

Howe, Susan, **Retro. Supp. I:** 33, 43; **Supp. IV Part 2: 419–438; Supp. XVI:** 284

Howell, Chris, **Supp. XIII:** 112

Howell, James, **II:** 111

Howells, Margaret, **II:** 271

Howells, William C., **II:** 273

Howells, William Dean, **I:** 109, 192, 204, 210, 211, 254, 355, 407, 411, 418, 459, 469; **II:** 127–128, 130, 131, 136, 137, 138, 140, **271–294,** 322, 331–332, 338, 397–398, 400, 415, 444, 451, 556; **III:** 51, 118, 314, 327–328, 461, 576, 607; **IV:** 192, 202, 342, 349; **Retro. Supp. I:** 220, 334, 362, 378; **Retro. Supp. II:** 93, 101, 135, 288; **Supp. I Part 1:** 306, 318, 357, 360, 368; **Supp. I Part 2:** 414, 420, 645–646; **Supp. II Part 1:** 198, 352; **Supp. IV Part 2:** 678; **Supp. VIII:** 98, 101, 102; **Supp. XI:** 198, 200; **Supp. XIV:** 45–46; **Supp. XV:** 269, 274, 285, 287; **Supp. XVIII:** 6; **Supp. XXIV:** 24

Howells, Mrs. William Dean (Elinor Mead), **II:** 273

Howells, Winifred, **II:** 271

"Howells as Anti-Novelist" (Updike), **Retro. Supp. I:** 334

Howells: His Life and World (Brooks), **I:** 254

Hower, Edward, **Supp. XII:** 330, 343

Howes, Barbara, **Supp. XIII:** 331

How Good Is David Mamet, Anyway? (Heilpern), **Supp. XIV:** 242

"How I Became a Shadow" (Purdy), **Supp. VII:** 269

"How I Came to Vedanta" (Isherwood), **Supp. XIV:** 164

"How I Come to You" (Peacock), **Supp. XIX:** 198

"How I Learned to Sweep" (Alvarez), **Supp. VII:** 4

"How I Spent My Forties" (Wasserstein), **Supp. XV:** 325, 330, 332

"How It Began" (Stafford), **Supp. XI:** 327

"How It Feels to Be Colored Me" (Hurston), **Supp. VI:** 152

"How It Is" (Budbill), **Supp. XIX:** 10

"How It Is" (Everwine), **Supp. XV:** 79, 86

"How I Told My Child About Race" (Brooks), **Supp. III Part 1:** 78

"How I Went to the Mines" (Harte), **Supp. II Part 1:** 336

"How I Write" (Franzen), **Supp. XX: 84**

"How I Write" (Welty), **IV:** 279, 280

"How I Wrote *The Promised Land*" (Antin), **Supp. XX: 3**

"How Jonah Did Not Care" (R. Bly), **Supp. IV Part 1:** 73

Howl (Ginsberg), **Retro. Supp. I:** 426; **Supp. III Part 1:** 92; **Supp. IV Part 1:** 90; **Supp. V:** 336; **Supp. VIII:** 290; **Supp. XIV:** 15, 126, 157; **Supp. XVIII:** 20, 29

"How Laddie and the Princess Spelled Down at the Christmas Bee" (Stratton-Porter), **Supp. XX: 216**

Howl and Other Poems (Ginsberg), **Supp. II Part 1:** 308, 317–318, 319; **Supp. X:** 123

Howlett, William, **Retro. Supp. I:** 17

Howl: Original Draft Facsimile, Transcript and Variant Versions (Gimsberg), **Supp. XIV:** 142

"How Many Midnights" (Bowles), **Supp. IV Part 1:** 86–87

"How Many Nights" (Kinnell), **Supp. III Part 1:** 245–246

How Much? (Blechman), **Supp. I Part 1:** 290

"How Much Are You Worth" (Salinas), **Supp. XIII:** 325–326

"How Much Earth" (Levine), **Supp. V:** 184

How Much Earth: The Fresno Poets (Buckley, Oliveira, and Williams, eds.), **Supp. XIII:** 313

"How Not to Forget" (Bartov), **Supp. XVI:** 153–154

"How Poetry Comes to Me" (Corso), **Supp. XII:** 122

"How Poetry Comes to Me" (Snyder), **Supp. VIII:** 305

How Reading Changed My Life (Quindlen), **Supp. XVII:** 167, 179–180

"How She Came By Her Name: An Interview with Louis Massiah" (Bambara), **Supp. XI:** 20

"How Soon Hath Time" (Ransom), **IV:** 123

How Spring Comes (Notley), **Supp. XXII:** 226, 229

How Stella Got Her Groove Back (McMillan), **Supp. XIII:** 185, **190–191**

How the Alligator Missed Breakfast (Kinney), **Supp. III Part 1:** 235, 253

"How the Devil Came Down Division Street" (Algren), **Supp. IX:** 3

How the García Girls Lost Their Accents (Alvarez), **Supp. VII:** 3, 5–9, 11, 15, 17, 18

How the Grinch Stole Christmas! (Geisel), **Supp. XVI:** 102

How the Other Half Lives (Riis), **I:** 293

"How the Saint Did Not Care" (R. Bly), **Supp. IV Part 1:** 73

"How the Women Went from Dover" (Whittier), **Supp. I Part 2:** 694, 696, 697

"How They Got Her to Quiet Down" (Stone), **Supp. XXVII:** 263

"How This Magazine Wronged Herman Wouk" (Lewis), **Supp. XXV:** 253

"How To" (Carruth), **Supp. XVI:** 51

"How-To" (Monson), **Supp. XXIV:** 237

How To Be Alone: Essays (Franzen), **Supp. XX: 83, 90, 93–94**

"How to Be an Other Woman" (Moore), **Supp. X:** 165, 167, 168

"How to Become a Writer" (Moore), **Supp. X:** 167, 168

"How to Be Happy: Another Memo to Myself" (Dunn), **Supp. XI:** 145

"How to Catch Aunt Harriet" (Stone), **Supp. XXVII:** 251

How To Cook a Wolf (M. F. K. Fisher), **Supp. XVII:** 84–85, 87

"How to Date a Browngirl, Blackgirl, Whitegirl, or Halfie" (Díaz), **Supp. XXIV:** 88

How to Develop Your Personality (Shellow), **Supp. I Part 2:** 608

"How to Grow Orchids Without Grounds: A Manual" (Vaz), **Supp. XXVI:** 263

How to Know God: The Yoga Aphorisms of Patanjali (Isherwood and Prabhavananda)), **Supp. XIV:** 164

"How To Like It" (Dobyns), **Supp. XIII: 85–86**

"How to Live on $36,000 a Year" (Fitzgerald), **Retro. Supp. I:** 105

"How to Live. What to Do" (Stevens), **Retro. Supp. I:** 302

"How to Love a Bicycle" (Biss), **Supp. XXVI:** 48

"How Tom is Doin' " (Kees), **Supp. XV:** 143

How to Read (Pound), **Supp. VIII:** 291

How to Read a Novel (Gordon), **II:** 198

How to Read a Poem and Fall in Love with Poetry (Hirsch), **Supp. XIX:** 202

How to Read a Poem: And Fall in Love with Poetry (Hirsch), **Supp. XXIII:** 124

How to Read a Poem . . . and Start a Poetry Circle (Peacock), **Supp. XIX:** 194, 202–203, 205

How to Save Your Own Life (Jong), **Supp. V:** 115, 123–125, 130

"How to Study Poetry" (Pound), **III:** 474

"How to Talk to Your Mother" (Moore), **Supp. X:** 167, 172

"How to Tell Stories to Children" (July), **Supp. XXIV:** 206–207

How to Win Friends and Influence People (Carnegie), **Supp. I Part 2:** 608

How to Worry Successfully (Seabury), **Supp. I Part 2:** 608

How to Write (Stein), **IV:** 32, 34, 35

"How to Write a Blackwood Article" (Poe), **III:** 425; **Retro. Supp. II:** 273

"How to Write a Memoir Like This" (Oates), **Supp. III Part 2:** 509

"How to Write Like Somebody Else" (Roethke), **III:** 540

How to Write Short Stories (Lardner), **II:** 430, 431

"How Vincentine Did Not Care" (R. Bly), **Supp. IV Part 1:** 73

How We Became Human: New and Selected Poems (Harjo), **Supp. XII: 230–232**

"How We Danced" (Sexton), **Supp. II Part 2:** 692

How We Got Insipid (Lethem), **Supp. XVIII:** 149

"How We Got in Town and Out Again" (Lethem), **Supp. XVIII:** 149

"How You Sound??" (Baraka), **Supp. II Part 1:** 30

Hoy, Philip, **Supp. X:** 56, 58

Hoyer, Linda Grace (pseudonym). *See* Updike, Mrs. Wesley

Hoyt, Constance, **Supp. I Part 2:** 707

Hoyt, Elinor Morton. *See* Wylie, Elinor

Hoyt, Helen, **Supp. XXII:** 275

Hoyt, Henry (father), **Supp. I Part 2:** 707

Hoyt, Henry (son), **Supp. I Part 2:** 708

Hoyt, Henry Martyn, **Supp. I Part 2:** 707

H. P. Lovecraft (Canan), **Supp. XXV:** 123

Hsu, Kai-yu, **Supp. X:** 292

Hsu, Ruth Y., **Supp. XV:** 212

Hubba City (Reed), **Supp. X:** 241

Hubbard, Elbert, **I:** 98, 383

Hubbell, Jay B., **Supp. I Part 1:** 372

"Hubbub, The" (Ammons), **Supp. VII:** 35

Huber, François, **II:** 6

Huckins, Olga, **Supp. IX:** 32

Huckleberry Finn (Twain). *See Adventures of Huckleberry Finn, The* (Twain)

Hucksters, The (Wakeman), **Supp. XXV:** 258

Hud (film), **Supp. V:** 223, 226

Huddle, David, **Supp. XXVI: 147–162**

Hudgins, Andrew, **Supp. X:** 206; **Supp. XVII:** 111, 112; **Supp. XVIII:** 176

Hudson, Henry, **I:** 230; **Supp. XXVI:** 86

"Hudsonian Curlew, The" (Snyder), **Supp. VIII:** 302

Hudson River Bracketed (Wharton), **IV:** 326–327; **Retro. Supp. I:** 382

Huebsch, B. W., **III:** 110

Hueffer, Ford Madox, **Supp. I Part 1:** 257, 262. *See also* Ford, Ford Madox

Huene-Greenberg, Dorothee von, **Supp. XX:** 46

Huff (television series), **Supp. XIX:** 222

"Hug, The" (Gallagher), **Supp. XXIV:** 168

Hug Dancing (Hearon), **Supp. VIII: 67–68**

Huge Season, The (Morris), **III:** 225–226, 227, 230, 232, 233, 238

Hugging the Jukebox (Nye), **Supp. XIII: 275–276, 277**

"Hugging the Jukebox" (Nye), **Supp. XIII:** 276

Hughes, Brigid, **Supp. XVI:** 247

Hughes, Carolyn, **Supp. XII:** 272, 285

Hughes, Frieda, **Supp. I Part 2:** 540, 541

Hughes, Glenn, **Supp. I Part 1:** 255

Hughes, H. Stuart, **Supp. VIII:** 240

Hughes, James Nathaniel, **Supp. I Part 1:** 321, 332

Hughes, John, **Supp. XXVII:** 5

Hughes, Ken, **Supp. XI:** 307

Hughes, Langston, **Retro. Supp. I: 193–214; Retro. Supp. II:** 114, 115, 117, 120; **Supp. I Part 1: 320–348; Supp. II Part 1:** 31, 33, 61, 170, 173, 181, 227, 228, 233, 361; **Supp. III Part 1:** 72–77; **Supp. IV Part 1:** 15, 16, 164, 168, 169, 173, 243, 368; **Supp. IX:** 306, 316; **Supp. VIII:** 213; **Supp. X:** 131, 136, 139, 324; **Supp. XI:** 1; **Supp. XIII:** 75, 111, 132, 233; **Supp. XIX:** 72, 75, 77; **Supp. XVI:** 135, 138; **Supp. XVIII:** 90, 277, 279, 280, 281, 282; **Supp. XXI:** 243; **Supp. XXII:** 3, 4, 5, 6, 8, 13–14; **Supp. XXIV:** 183; **Supp. XXVI:** 166; **Supp. XXVII:** 164

Hughes, Nicholas, **Supp. I Part 2:** 541

Hughes, Robert, **Supp. X:** 73

Hughes, Ted, **IV:** 3; **Retro. Supp. II:** 244, 245, 247, 257; **Supp. I Part 2:** 536, 537, 538, 539, 540, 541; **Supp. XV:** 117, 347, 348; **Supp. XXII:** 30

Hughes, Thomas, **Supp. I Part 2:** 406

"Hugh Harper" (Bowles), **Supp. IV Part 1:** 94

Hughie (O'Neill), **III:** 385, 401, 405

Hugh Selwyn Mauberley (Pound), **I:** 66, 476; **III:** 9, 462–463, 465, 468; **Retro. Supp. I: 289–290,** 291, 299; **Supp. XIV:** 272

Hugo, Richard, **Supp. IX:** 296, 323, 324, 330; **Supp. VI: 131–148; Supp. XI:** 315, 317; **Supp. XII:** 178; **Supp. XIII:** 112, 113, 133; **Supp. XVIII:** 293, 299; **Supp. XXI:** 243; **Supp. XXVI:** 180, 187

Hugo, Victor, **II:** 290, 490, 543; **Supp. IV Part 2:** 518; **Supp. IX:** 308

Hui-neng, **III:** 567

Huis Clos (Sartre), **Supp. IV Part 1:** 84

Huizinga, Johan, **I:** 225; **II:** 416–417, 418, 425

Hulbert, Ann, **Supp. XI:** 38–39

Hull, Lynda, **Supp. XI:** 131; **Supp. XXI: 129–142**

Hull, Thomas, **Supp. XXV:** 123

Hulme, Thomas E., **I:** 68, 69, 475; **III:** 196, 209, 463–464, 465; **IV:** 122; **Supp. I Part 1:** 261, 262; **Supp. XV:** 43

Human, All Too Human (Nietzsche), **Supp. X:** 48

"Human Culture" (Emerson), **II:** 11–12

Human Desire (film), **Supp. XXVI:** 134

Human Factor, The (Greene), **Supp. V:** 298

"Human Figures" (Doty), **Supp. XI:** 123–124

"Human Fly, The" (Boyle), **Supp. XX: 19**

"Human Geography" (Jarman), **Supp. XVII:** 116

"Human Immortality" (James), **II:** 353–354

"Human Life" (Emerson), **II:** 11–12

"Human Pig" (Jin), **Supp. XVIII:** 99

Human Rights, Human Wrongs: The Oxford Amnesty Lectures, 2001, **Supp. XVI:** 155

"Human Soul as a Rube Goldberg Device, The: A Choose-Your-Own-Adventure-Story" (Brockmeier), **Supp. XXII:** 60–61

Human Stain, The (P. Roth), **Retro. Supp. II:** 279, 289, 294–295

"Human Things" (Nemerov), **III:** 279

Human Universe (Olson), **Supp. II Part 2:** 571

"Human Universe" (Olson), **Supp. II Part 2:** 565, 567

Human Vibration (Richter), **Supp. XVIII:** 209

Human Wishes (Hass), **Supp. VI:** 105–106, 107

Human Work (Gilman), **Supp. XI:** 206

Humbert, Humbert, **Supp. X:** 283

Humble Inquiry into the Rules of the Word of God, An, Concerning the Qualifications Requisite to a Complete Standing and Full Communion in the Visible Christian Church (Edwards), **I:** 548

Humboldt, Alexander von, **III:** 428

Humboldt's Gift (Bellow), **Retro. Supp. II:** 19, 28–29, 34; **Supp. XIII:** 320

Hume, David, **I:** 125; **II:** 349, 357, 480; **III:** 618

Humes, Harold, **Supp. V:** 201; **Supp. XIV:** 82

Humes, Harry, **Supp. XIX:** 281; **Supp. XXIII:** 54

Humes, H. L. "Doc", **Supp. XI:** 294

"Humility" (Hoffman), **Supp. XVIII:** 86

Hummer, T. R., **Supp. XIX:** 278; **Supp. XXI:** 91

"Hummingbirds, The" (Welty), **IV:** 273

Humors and/or Not So Humorous (Kenny), **Supp. XXIII:** 155

Humphrey, William, **Supp. IX:** 93–112; **Supp. XV:** 353

Humphreys, Christmas, **Supp. V:** 267

Humphreys, David, **Supp. II Part 1:** 65, 69, 70, 268

Humphreys, Josephine, **Supp. XII:** 311

Humphries, Rolfe, **III:** 124; **Retro. Supp. I:** 137

Humpty Dumpty (Hecht), **Supp. XXVII:** 88

Hunchback of Notre Dame, The (film), **Supp. IV Part 1:** 101

Hunches in Bunches (Geisel), **Supp. XVI:** 111

Huncke, Herbert, **Supp. XII:** 118; **Supp. XIV: 137–153**

Huncke's Journal (Huncke), **Supp. XIV:** 139, 144, 145, 146

Hundred Camels in the Courtyard, A (Bowles), **Supp. IV Part 1:** 90

"Hundred Collars, A" (Frost), **Retro. Supp. I:** 128; **Supp. XIII:** 147

Hundred Secret Senses, The (Tan), **Supp. X:** 289, 293, 295, 297, 298, 299

Hundreds of Hens and Other Poems for Children by Halfdan Rasmussen (Nelson and Espeland, trans.), **Supp. XVIII:** 180

Hundred White Daffodils, A: Essays, Interviews, Newspaper Columns, and One Poem (Kenyon), **Supp. VII:** 160–162, 165, 166, 167, 174

Huneker, James, **III:** 102

"Hunger" (Davison), **Supp. XXVI:** 69

Hunger (Hamsun), **Supp. XI:** 167

"Hunger" (Hogan), **Supp. IV Part 1:** 411

"Hunger . . ." (Rich), **Supp. I Part 2:** 571

"Hungerfield" (Jeffers), **Supp. II Part 2:** 416–417, 436

Hungerfield and Other Poems (Jeffers), **Supp. II Part 2:** 422

Hunger of Memory: The Education of Richard Rodriguez (Rodriguez), **Supp. XIV:** 297, 298, **298–302,** 310

Hungry Ghosts, The (Oates), **Supp. II Part 2:** 504, 510

Hungry Hearts (Prose), **Supp. XVI:** 253

"Hungry Intellectual, A" (Le Sueur), **Supp. XXIII:** 164

Hungry Woman, The: A Mexican Medea (Moraga), **Supp. XXIII:** 196

Hunnewell, Susannah, **Supp. VIII:** 83

Hunt, Erica, **Supp. XXVII:** 163

Hunt, Harriot K., **Retro. Supp. II:** 146

Hunt, Leigh, **II:** 515–516; **Supp. XV:** 175

Hunt, Richard Morris, **IV:** 312

Hunt, Robert, **Supp. XV:** 42, 49, 52

Hunt, William, **II:** 343

"Hunter" (Bierds), **Supp. XVII:** 30

Hunter, Dianna, **Supp. XVI:** 38

Hunter, Dr. Joseph, **II:** 217

Hunter, J. Paul, **Supp. IV Part 1:** 332

Hunter, Kim, **Supp. I Part 1:** 286

"Hunter of Doves" (Herbst), **Retro. Supp. II:** 325

"Hunter of the West, The" (Bryant), **Supp. I Part 1:** 155

Hunters, The (film), **Supp. IX:** 250

Hunters, The (Salter), **Supp. IX:** 246, **249–250**

Hunters and Gatherers (Prose), **Supp. XVI:** 257

"Hunters in the Snow" (Brueghel), **I:** 174; **Retro. Supp. I:** 430

"Hunters in the Snow" (Wolff), **Supp. VII:** 339–340

"Hunter's Moon—Eating the Bear" (Oliver), **Supp. VII:** 234

"Hunter's Vision, The" (Bryant), **Supp. I Part 1:** 160

Hunting for Hope: A Father's Journey (Sanders), **Supp. XVI:** 276–277, 278

"Hunting Is Not Those Heads on the Wall" (Baraka), **Supp. II Part 1:** 45

Huntington, Collis P., **I:** 198, 207

"Hunt in the Black Forest, The" (Jarrell), **II:** 379–380

Huntley, Jobe, **Supp. I Part 1:** 339

"Hurrah, Hurrah" (Nelson), **Supp. XVIII:** 175

Hurray Home (Wideman), **Supp. X:** 320

Hurricane (radio play, Boyce), **Supp. XXI:** 13

"Hurricane, The" (Crane), **I:** 401

"Hurricane, The" (Freneau), **Supp. II Part 1:** 262

"Hurricane Belle" (Notley), **Supp. XXII:** 228

"Hurry Kane" (Lardner), **II:** 425, 426, 427

"Hurry up Please It's Time" (Sexton), **Supp. II Part 2:** 694, 695

Hurst, Fannie, **Supp. XVIII:** 278, 279

Hurston, Zora Neale, **Retro. Supp. I:** 194, 198, 200, 201, 203; **Supp. I Part 1:** 325, 326, 332; **Supp. II Part 1:** 33; **Supp. IV Part 1:** 5, 11, 12, 164, 257; **Supp. VI: 149–161;** **Supp. VIII:** 214; **Supp. X:** 131, 139, 232, 242; **Supp. XI:** 85; **Supp. XIII:** 185, 233, 236, 295, 306; **Supp. XIX:** 72, 75; **Supp. XVIII:** 122, 279, 280, 282; **Supp. XX: 107; Supp. XXII:** 12; **Supp. XXVI:** 1, 12, 164, 167

Hurt, John, **Supp. XIII:** 132

"Hurt Hawks" (Jeffers), **Supp. XXIII:** 145

Hurwitt, Robert, **Supp. XXIII:** 281

Husbands and Wives (film; Allen), **Supp. XV:** 12

"Husband's Song, The" (Di Piero), **Supp. XIX:** 39

Husband's Story, The (Shields), **Supp. VII:** 316. See also "Happenstance" (Shields)

"Husband's Tale, The" (Huddle), **Supp. XXVI:** 151

Husserl, Edmund, **II:** 362, 363; **IV:** 491; **Supp. IV Part 1:** 42, 43

Hussey, Jo Ella, **Supp. XII:** 201

Hustler, The (film), **Supp. XI:** 306

Huston, John, **I:** 30, 31, 33, 35; **II:** 588; **III:** 161; **Supp. IV Part 1:** 102, 116, 355; **Supp. XI:** 307; **Supp. XIII:** 174

Hustvedt, Siri, **Supp. XXVII:** 26

"Huswifery" (Taylor), **IV:** 161; **Supp. I Part 2:** 386

"Hut, The" (Sobin), **Supp. XVI:** 284–285

Hutchens, John K., **Supp. IX:** 276

Hutcheson, Francis, **I:** 559

Hutchins, Patricia, **III:** 478

Hutchinson, Abigail, **I:** 562

Hutchinson, Anne, **Supp. I Part 1:** 100, 101, 113; **Supp. IV Part 2:** 434; **Supp. VIII:** 202, 205

Hutchinson, George, **Supp. XVIII:** 119–120, 121, 132

Hutchinson, Lucy, **Supp. XXV:** 224

Hutchinson, Paul E., **Supp. XXVI:** 156

Hutchinson, Thomas, **Supp. XX: 282**

Hutton, James, **Supp. IX:** 180

Huwayyik, Yusuf, **Supp. XX:** 115

Huxley, Aldous, **II:** 454; **III:** 281, 428, 429–430; **IV:** 77, 435; **Supp. I Part 2:** 714; **Supp. XIV:** 3, 164; **Supp. XVI:** 189, 192; **Supp. XVIII:** 137;

"Idea, The" (Carver), **Supp. III Part 1:** 143

"Idea, The" (Strand), **Supp. IV Part 2:** 631

Ideal Husband (Wilde), **II:** 515

Idea of Florida in the American Literary Imagination, The (Rowe), **Supp. X:** 223

"Idea of Form at Spruce Creek, The" (Weigl), **Supp. XIX:** 283–284

"Idea of Ice, The" (C. Baxter), **Supp. XVII:** 15

"Idea of Order, An" (Wiman), **Supp. XVIII:** 173

"Idea of Order at Key West, The" (Stevens), **IV:** 89–90; **Retro. Supp. I:** 302, 303, 313

Ideas of Order (Stevens), **Retro. Supp. I:** 296, 298, **302–303,** 303, 305

Idema, James, **Supp. XXVII:** 7

"Identification Pleas" (Gansworth), **Supp. XXVI:** 114

"Identity Theft: True Memory, False Memory, and the Holocaust" (R. Franklin), **Supp. XVI:** 160

Ideograms in China (Michaux; Sobin, trans.), **Supp. XVI:** 288

"Ideographs" (Olds), **Supp. X:** 205

Ides of March, The (Wilder), **IV:** 357, 372

"I Did Not Learn Their Names" (Ellison), **Retro. Supp. II:** 124

"I Died with the First Blow & Was Reborn Wrong" (Coleman), **Supp. XI:** 91

"Idiom of a Self, The" (Pinsky), **Supp. VI:** 240

"Idiot, The" (Crane), **I:** 401

Idiot, The (Dostoevsky), **I:** 468

"Idiots First" (Malamud), **Supp. I Part 2:** 434–435, 437, 440–441

Idiots Karamazov, The (Durand and Innaurato), **Supp. XXIV:** 113, 116

"Idiot Wind" (song, Dylan), **Supp. XVIII:** 30

Idle Idylls (Wells), **Supp. XXVI:** 275

I Don't Need You Any More (A. Miller), **III:** 165

Idoru (W. Gibson), **Supp. XVI:** 119, 124, **129–130**

"I Dream I'm the Death of Orpheus" (Rich), **Supp. I Part 2:** 557–558

I Dreamt I Became a Nymphomaniac! Imagining (Acker), **Supp. XII:** 4, 6, **8,** 11

"I Dreamt You Young" (Espaillat), **Supp. XXI:** 107

"Idyll" (Shaw), **Supp. XIX:** 241

Idylls of the King (Tennyson), **III:** 487; **Supp. I Part 2:** 410; **Supp. XIII:** 146

Idyl of Work, An (Larcom), **Supp. XIII:** 139, 142, 146–147, 150

"If" (Creeley), **Supp. IV Part 1:** 158

If Beale Street Could Talk (Baldwin), **Retro. Supp. II:** 13–14; **Supp. I Part 1:** 48, 59–60, 67

"If Biblical Law Ruled Modern Society . . ." (P. N. Warren), **Supp. XX:** 272

If Blessing Comes (Bambara), **Supp. XI:** 1

"If Death Is Kind" (Teasdale), **Supp. XXVII:** 294

I Feel a Little Jumpy around You (Nye and Janeczko, eds.), **Supp. XIII:** 280

"I felt a Funeral, in my Brain" (Dickinson), **Retro. Supp. I:** 38

"If Grown-Ups Were Smart" (Nelson and Espeland), **Supp. XVIII:** 181

If He Hollers Let Him Go (C. Himes), **Supp. XVI:** 135, 138–139, 142

"If I Could Be Like Wallace Stevens" (Stafford), **Supp. XI:** 327

"If I Could Do Whatever I Wanted" (Nelson and Espeland), **Supp. XVIII:** 181

"If I Could Only Live at the Pitch That Is Near Madness" (Eberhart), **I:** 523, 526–527

If I Could Write This in Fire (Cliff), **Supp. XXII:** 67, 69

"If I Could Write This in Fire, I Would Write This in Fire" (Cliff), **Supp. XXII:** 65–66, 68–69

If I Die in a Combat Zone (O'Brien), **Supp. V:** 238, 239, 240, 245

If I Ever Get Out of Here (Gansworth), **Supp. XXVI:** 102, 108–109

"If I Had My Way" (Creeley), **Supp. IV Part 1:** 157

"If I Might Be" (Chopin), Retro. Supp. II: 61

"I Find the Real American Tragedy" (Dreiser), **Retro. Supp. II:** 105

If I Ran the Circus (Geisel), **Supp. XVI:** 105

If I Ran the Zoo (Geisel), **Supp. XVI:** 104–105

If It Die (Gide), **I:** 290

"If It Were Not for You" (Carruth), **Supp. XVI:** 57

"If I Were a Man" (Gilman), **Supp. XI:** 207

"If I Were the Wind" (Leopold), **Supp. XIV:** 184

If Morning Ever Comes (Tyler), **Supp. IV Part 2:** 658–659

If Mountains Die: A New Mexico Memoir (Nichols), **Supp. XIII:** 255, 257, 267

"If Nancy Was a Boy" (Brainard), **Supp. XXVII:** 21

"If Nancy Was an Ashtray" (Brainard), **Supp. XXVII:** 21

I Forgot to Go to Spain (Harrison), **Supp. VIII:** 39, **52–53**

"If Poetry Were Not a Morality" (Gallagher), **Supp. XXIV:** 170

If the River Was Whiskey (Boyle), **Supp. VIII:** 15–16; **Supp. XX:** 17, 19

"If They Knew Yvonne" (Dubus), **Supp. VII:** 81

"If We Had Bacon" (H. Roth), **Supp. IX:** 232, 234

"If We Had Known" (Francis), **Supp. IX:** 78

"If We Must Die" (McKay), **Supp. IV Part 1:** 3; **Supp. X:** 132, 134

"If We Take All Gold" (Bogan), **Supp. III Part 1:** 52

If You Call This a Cry Song (Carruth), **Supp. XVI:** 56

If You Want to Write (Ueland), **Supp. XVII:** 13

I Gaspiri (Lardner), **II:** 435

"I Gather the Limbs of Osiris" (Pound), **Retro. Supp. I:** 287

I Get on the Bus (McKnight), **Supp. XX: 148–150, 152**

"I Give You Back" (Harjo), **Supp. XII:** 223

Ignatius of Loyola, **IV:** 151; **Supp. XI:** 162

Ignatius Rising (Nevils and Hardy), **Supp. XXVI:** 241

Ignatow, David, **Supp. XIII:** 275

"Ignis Fatuus" (Tate), **IV:** 128

"Ignorant Lust after Knowledge, The" (Bronk), **Supp. XXI:** 31

"I Go Back to May 1937" (Olds), **Supp. X:** 207

I Go Dreaming Serenades (Salinas), **Supp. XIII:** 316

"I Got a Guy Once" (Gallagher), **Supp. XXIV:** 176

"I Got My Job on the *New York Times!*" (Schuyler and Brainard), **Supp. XXVII:** 23

I Got the Blues (Odets), **Supp. II Part 2:** 530

Iguana Killer, The (Ríos), **Supp. IV Part 2:** 542–544

"I Had Eight Birds Hatcht in One Nest" (Bradstreet), **Supp. I Part 1:** 102, 115, 117, 119

"I had no time to Hate" (Dickinson), **Retro. Supp. I:** 44–45, 46

I Had Trouble in Getting to Solla Sollew (Geisel), **Supp. XVI:** 108, 109

I Hate Miranda July (blog), **Supp. XXIV:** 200

"I Have a Rendezvous with Life" (Cullen), **Supp. IV Part 1:** 168

"I Have Been Thinking About Snow" (Monson), **Supp. XXIV:** 235

"I Have Increased Power" (Ginsberg), **Supp. II Part 1:** 313

"I Have Moved West" (Taggard), **Supp. XXII:** 274

"I Have Seen Black Hands" (Wright), **Supp. II Part 1:** 228

"I Hear an Army" (Joyce), **Supp. I Part 1:** 262

"I heard a Fly buzz when I died" (Dickinson), **Retro. Supp. I:** 38

"I Heard Immanuel Singing" (Lindsay), **Supp. I Part 2:** 379

I Heard It Through the Grapevine (Turner), **Supp. XX: 110**

"I Hear It Was Charged against Me" (Whitman), **IV:** 343

I Hear Men Talking (Le Sueur), **Supp. XXIII:** 162, 167, **171–172**

"I Held a Shelley Manuscript" (Corso), **Supp. XII:** 128

"I Held His Name" (Ríos), **Supp. IV Part 2:** 547

"Ike and Nina" (Boyle), **Supp. XX: 19**

"I Kiss a Door" (July), **Supp. XXIV:** 204

I Knew a Phoenix (Sarton), **Supp. VIII:** 249, 251–252

"I Know a Man" (Creeley), **Supp. IV Part 1:** 147–148, 149

I Know Some Things: Stories about Childhood by Contemporary Writers (Moore, ed.), **Supp. X:** 175

"I Know the Stars" (Teasdale), **Supp. XXVII:** 293

"I Know Why the Caged Bird Cannot Read" (Prose), **Supp. XVI:** 259

I Know Why the Caged Bird Sings (Angelou), **Supp. IV Part 1:** 2–4, 5, 7, 11, 12, 13, 14, 15, 17; **Supp. XVI:** 259

"Ikon: The Harrowing of Hell" (Levertov), **Supp. III Part 1:** 284

"Iktomi and the Ducks" (Zitkala-Ša), **Supp. XXV:** 275–276

Ile (O'Neill), **III:** 388; **Supp. XXV:** 20

"I Led Three Lives" (television program), **Supp. XX:** 195

"I Let Him Take Me" (Cisneros), **Supp. VII:** 71

Iliad (Bryant, trans.), **Supp. I Part 1:** 158

Iliad (Chapman, trans.), **Supp. XXV:** 226

Iliad (Homer), **II:** 470; **Supp. IV Part 2:** 631; **Supp. IX:** 211; **Supp. X:** 114; **Supp. XVII:** 117; **Supp. XXI:** 36

Iliad (Pope, trans.), **Supp. I Part 1:** 152

"I Like" (Brainard), **Supp. XXVII:** 25

"I like to see it lap the Miles" (Dickinson), **Retro. Supp. I:** 37

"I Live Up Here" (Merwin), **Supp. III Part 1:** 349

"I'll Be Doing More of Same" (Franzen), **Supp. XX:** 89

"Illegal Alien" (Mora), **Supp. XIII:** 215

"Illegal Days, The" (Paley), **Supp. VI:** 222

Illegals, The (film), **Supp. XXVII:** 133, 140, 143

"Illegibility" (F. Wright), **Supp. XVII:** 244

Illig, Joyce, **Retro. Supp. II:** 20

"Illinois" (Masters), **Supp. I Part 2:** 458

"Illinois Bus Ride" (Leopold), **Supp. XIV:** 189

Illinois Poems (Masters), **Supp. I Part 2:** 472

"Illinois Village, The" (Lindsay), **Supp. I Part 2:** 381

"Ill-Lit" (F. Wright), **Supp. XVII:** 245

Ill-Lit: Selected & New Poems (F. Wright), **Supp. XVII:** 245

Illness as Metaphor (Sontag), **Supp. III Part 2:** 452, 461, 466

I'll Take My Stand ("Twelve Southerners"), **II:** 196; **III:** 496; **IV:** 125, 237; **Supp. X:** 25, 52–53; **Supp. XIV:** 3

"I'll Take You to Tennessee" (Connell), **Supp. XIV:** 82

Illumination (Frederic), **II:** 141

Illumination, The (Brockmeier), **Supp. XXII:** 61

Illumination Night (Hoffman), **Supp. X:** 85, **86,** 88, 89

Illuminations (Rimbaud), **Supp. XXI:** 233

"Illusion, An" (Wells), **Supp. XXVI:** 275

Illusion and Reality (Caudwell), **Supp. XXII:** 284

Illusion comique, L' (Corneille), **Supp. IX:** 138

"Illusion of Eternity, The" (Eberhart), **I:** 541

"Illusion of Fiction in Frank Conroy's *Stop-Time,* The" (R. Ramsey), **Supp. XVI:** 69

Illusions (Dash; film), **Supp. XI:** 20

"Illusions" (Emerson), **II:** 2, 5, 14, 16

Illustrated Man, The (Bradbury), **Supp. IV Part 1:** 102, 103, 113

Illustrations of China and Its People (Thompson), **Supp. XXI:** 151

Illustrations of Political Economy (Martineau), **Supp. II Part 1:** 288

"I Look at My Hand" (Swenson), **Supp. IV Part 2:** 638, 647

I Love Gootie: My Grandmother's Story (Apple), **Supp. XVII:** 9–10

I Love Myself When I Am Laughing . . . : A Zora Neale Hurston Reader (Walker), **Supp. III Part 2:** 531, 532

"I Love the Way It Goes" (O'Hara), **Supp. XXIII:** 220

"I'm a Fool" (Anderson), **I:** 113, 114, 116; **Supp. I Part 2:** 430

Image and Idea (Rahv), **Supp. II Part 1:** 146

Image and the Law, The (Nemerov), **III:** 268, 269–271, 272

"Image in the Mirror, The" (Swados), **Supp. XIX:** 265

"Images" (Hass), **Supp. VI:** 103

"Images and 'Images'" (Simic), **Supp. VIII:** 274

"Images for Godard" (Rich), **Supp. I Part 2:** 558

"Images of Walt Whitman" (Fiedler), **IV:** 352

"Imaginary Dialogue, An" (Espaillat), **Supp. XXI:** 103

"Imaginary Friendships of Tom McGrath, The" (Cohen), **Supp. X:** 112

"Imaginary Iceberg, The" (Bishop), **Retro. Supp. II:** 42; **Supp. I Part 1:** 86, 88

"Imaginary Jew, The" (Berryman), **I:** 174–175

Imaginary Letters (Pound), **III:** 473–474

Imaginary Paintings (C. Baxter), **Supp. XVII:** 18–19

"Imaginary Prisons" (Schnackenberg), **Supp. XV:** 257, 258

Imagination and Fancy; or, Selections from the English Poets, illustrative of those first requisites of their art; with markings of the best passages, critical notices of the writers, and an essay in answer to the question 'What is Poetry?' (Hunt), **II:** 515–516

"Imagination as Value" (Stevens), **Retro. Supp. I:** 298

"Imagination of Disaster, The" (Gordon), **Supp. IV Part 1:** 306

Imaginative Qualities of Actual Things (Sorrentino), **Supp. XXI:** 226, 230, 231–232, 234

"Imagine a Day at the End of Your Life" (Beattie), **Supp. V:** 33

Imagined London: A Tour of the World's Greatest Fictional City (Quindlen), **Supp. XVII:** 167, 180

Imagineering Atlanta (Rutheiser), **Supp. XXII:** 244

"Imagine Kissing Pete" (O'Hara), **III:** 372; **Supp. VIII:** 156

Imaging Robert: My Brother, Madness, and Survival (Neugeboren), **Supp. XVI:** 225, **226–229**

"Imagining How It Would Be to Be Dead" (Eberhart), **I:** 533

Imagining Los Angeles: A City in Fiction (Fine), **Supp. XI:** 160

"Imagining Their Own Hymns" (B. Kelly), **Supp. XVII:** 126–127

"Imagining the Midwest" (Sanders), **Supp. XVI:** 275–276

Imagining the Worst: Stephen King and the Representations of Women (Lant and Thompson), **Supp. V:** 141

"Imagisme" (Pound), **Retro. Supp. I:** 288

Imagistes, Des: An Anthology of the Imagists (Pound, ed.), **III:** 465, 471; **Retro. Supp. I:** 288

Imago (O. Butler), **Supp. XIII:** 63, **65–66**

"Imago" (Stevens), **IV:** 74, 89

Imagoes (Coleman), **Supp. XI:** 89–90

I Married a Communist (P. Roth), **Retro. Supp. II:** 289, 293–294

I Married an Angel (film), **Supp. XVI:** 193

"I May, I Might, I Must" (Moore), **III:** 215

Imbusch, Kevin, **Supp. XXIII:** 125

"I'm Crazy" (Salinger), **III:** 553

"I'm Here" (Roethke), **III:** 547

Imitations (R. Lowell), **II:** 550

Imitations (R. Lowell), **II:** 543, 544–545, 555; **Retro. Supp. II:** 181, 187

"Imitations of Drowning" (Sexton), **Supp. II Part 2:** 684, 686

"Immaculate Man" (Gordon), **Supp. IV Part 1:** 311

"Immanence of Dostoevsky, The" (Bourne), **I:** 235

"Immigrants" (Mora), **Supp. XIII:** 216

Immigrant Saint: The Life of Mother Cabrini (di Donato), **Supp. XX:** 44

"Immigrant Story, The" (Paley), **Supp. VI:** 230

Immobile Wind, The (Winters), **Supp. II Part 2:** 786

"Immobile Wind, The" (Winters), **Supp. II Part 2:** 788, 811

"Immolatus" (Komunyakaa), **Supp. XIII:** 126

"Immoral Proposition, The" (Creeley), **Supp. IV Part 1:** 144

"Immortal Autumn" (MacLeish), **III:** 13

"Immortality Ode" (Nemerov), **III:** 87

Immortality Ode (Wordsworth), **II:** 17; **Supp. I Part 2:** 673

Immortal Marriage, The (Atherton), **Supp. XXIV:** 26

"Immortal Woman, The" (Tate), **IV:** 130, 131, 137

"I'm Not Ready to Die Yet" (Harjo), **Supp. XII:** 231

I'm Not There (film, Haynes), **Supp. XVIII:** 23

"I'm on My Way" (Salinas), **Supp. XIII:** 320

"Impasse" (Hughes), **Supp. I Part 1:** 343

"Impatient Mary" (Taggard), **Supp. XXII:** 278

Imperative Duty, An, a Novel (Howells), **II:** 286

Imperial Bedrooms (Ellis), **Supp. XXVII:** 77–78

Imperial Eyes: Travel Writing and Transculturation (Pratt), **Retro. Supp. II:** 48

Imperial Germany and the Industrial Revolution (Veblen), **Supp. I Part 2:** 642, 643

Imperial Way, The: By Rail from Peshawar to Chittagong (Theroux), **Supp. VIII:** 323

"Implements from the 'Tomb of the Poet'" (Stallings), **Supp. XXV:** 232

"Implosions" (Rich), **Supp. I Part 2:** 556

"Imp of the Perverse, The" (Poe), **III:** 414–415; **Retro. Supp. II:** 267

Impolite Interviews, **Supp. XI:** 293

"Importance of Artists' Biographies, The" (Goldbarth), **Supp. XII:** 183, 184, 191

Importance of Being Earnest, The (Wilde), **Supp. XIV:** 324, 339

Importance of Gaining and Preserving the Friendship of the Indians to the British Interest Considered (Kennedy and Parker), **Supp. XXVI:** 84

"Important Houses, The" (Gordon), **Supp. IV Part 1:** 315

"Impossible Indispensability of the Ars Poetica, The" (Carruth), **Supp. XVI:** 57

"Impossible to Tell" (Pinsky), **Supp. VI:** 247, 248

"Imposter, The" (West), **Retro. Supp. II:** 322, 327

"Impressionism and Symbolism in *Heart of Darkness*" (Watt), **Supp. VIII:** 4

"Impressionism"(Crooker), **Supp. XXIII:** 57

"Impressions of a European Tour" (Bourne), **I:** 225

"Impressions of an Indian Childhood" (Zitkala-Ša), **Supp. XXV:** 272

"Impressions of a Plumber" (H. Roth), **Supp. IX:** 228, 234

"Impressions of Europe, 1913–1914" (Bourne), **I:** 225

"I Must Have Called and So He Comes" (Notley), **Supp. XXII:** 224

"I'm Walking behind the Spanish" (Salinas), **Supp. XIII:** 323–324

I'm Your Man (album, Cohen), **Supp. XXVII:** 54

"I'm Your Man" (Cohen), **Supp. XXVII:** 52, 61

"I/Myself" (Shields), **Supp. VII:** 311

"In a (Low) Bar" (Ferry), **Supp. XXIV:** 153

"In Absence" (Lanier), **Supp. I Part 1:** 364

"In Absentia" (Bowles), **Supp. IV Part 1:** 94

"In a Cab" (Untermeyer), **Supp. XV:** 296

"In a Coffee Pot" (Hayes), **Supp. XXVI:** 133–134, 144

"In a Country Cemetery" (Kooser), **Supp. XIX:** 120

Inada, Lawson Fusao, **Supp. V:** 180

"In a Dark Room, Furniture" (Nye), **Supp. XIII:** 274

"In a Dark Time" (Roethke), **III:** 539, 547, 548

In a Different Voice (Gilligan), **Supp. XXII:** 18

"In a Disused Graveyard" (Frost), **Retro. Supp. I:** 126, 133

In a Dusty Light (Haines), **Supp. XII:** 207

"In a Garden" (A. Lowell), **II:** 513

"In a Hard Intellectual Light" (Eberhart), **I:** 523

"In a Hollow of the Hills" (Harte), **Supp. II Part 1:** 354

In America (Sontag), **Supp. XIV:** 95–96

"In Amicitia" (Ransom), **IV:** 141

In a Narrow Grave: Essays on Texas (McMurtry), **Supp. V:** 220, 223

In an Iridescent Time, Poems, 1953–58 (Stone), **Supp. XXVII:** 250–251, 253, 262

"Inanna" (A. Finch), **Supp. XVII:** 72

"In Another Country" (Hemingway), **I:** 484–485; **II:** 249

In April Once (Percy), **Retro. Supp. I:** 341

"In a Prominent Bar in Secaucus One Day" (X. J. Kennedy), **Supp. XV:** 154, 155–156

"In Armenia, 1987"(Balakian), **Supp. XXIII:** 25

In A Shallow Grave (Purdy), **Supp. VII:** 272

In a shlekhter tsayt (In a bad time) (Asch), **Supp. XXIII:** 4

"In a Stadium" (A. Lowell), **Supp. XXVII:** 295

"In a Station of the Metro" (Pound), **Retro. Supp. I:** 288; **Supp. I Part 1:** 265; **Supp. XIV:** 284–285

"In a Strange Town" (Anderson), **I:** 114, 115

"In Athens Once" (Rodriguez), **Supp. XIV:** 303

"In a Tub" (Hempel), **Supp. XXI:** 119

In Battle for Peace: The Story of My 83rd Birthday (Du Bois), **Supp. II Part 1:** 185

In Bed One Night & Other Brief Encounters (Coover), **Supp. V:** 49, 50

"In Bertram's Garden" (Justice), **Supp. VII:** 117

"In Blackwater Woods" (Oliver), **Supp. VII:** 244, 246

In Black & Whitey (Lacy), **Supp. XV:** 206–207

"In Broad Daylight" (Jin), **Supp. XVIII:** 94

In Broken Country (Wagoner), **Supp. IX:** 330

"In California" (Simpson), **Supp. IX:** 271

"In Camp" (Stafford), **Supp. XI:** 329

"Incant against Suicide" (Karr), **Supp. XI:** 249

"In Celebration of My Uterus" (Sexton), **Supp. II Part 2:** 689

"Incendiary, The" (Rowson), **Supp. XV:** 234

"In Certain Places and Certain Times There Can Be More of You" (Dunn), **Supp. XI:** 144

Incest: From "A Journal of Love," the Unexpurgated Diary of Anaïs Nin, 1932–1934 (Nin), **Supp. X:** 182, 184, 185, 187, 191

"In Chandler Country" (Gioia), **Supp. XV:** 119

Inchbald, Elizabeth, **II:** 8

"In Cheever Country" (Gioia), **Supp. XV:** 119

Inchiquin, the Jesuit's Letters (Ingersoll), **I:** 344

"Incident" (Cullen), **Supp. IV Part 1:** 165, 166

Incidental Numbers (Wylie), **Supp. I Part 2:** 708

Incidentals (Sandburg), **III:** 579

Incidentals in the Day World (Notley), **Supp. XXII:** 223, 226, 227

Incident at Vichy (A. Miller), **III:** 165, 166

Incidents in the Life of a Slave Girl (Brent), **Supp. IV Part 1:** 13

Incidents in the Life of a Slavegirl (Jacobs), **Supp. XVI:** 85

"Incipience" (Rich), **Supp. I Part 2:** 559

"In Clare" (McCarriston), **Supp. XIV:** 270–271

Including Horace (Untermeyer), **Supp. XV:** 301, 303–304

In Cold Blood: A True Account of a Multiple Murder and Its Consequences (Capote), **Retro. Supp. II:** 107–108; **Supp. I Part 1:** 292; **Supp. III Part 1:** 111, 117, 119, 122, 123, 125–131; **Supp. III Part 2:** 574; **Supp. IV Part 1:** 220; **Supp. XIV:** 162; **Supp. XXV:** 57

In Cold Hell, in Thicket (Olson), **Supp. II Part 2:** 571

"In Cold Hell, in Thicket" (Olson), **Supp. II Part 2:** 558, 563–564, 566, 572, 580

"Incoming Tide"(Strout), **Supp. XXIII:** 282, 285

"Incomparable Light, The" (Eberhart), **I:** 541

Incorporative Consciousness of Robert Bly, The (Harris), **Supp. IV Part 1:** 68

In Country (Mason), **Supp. VIII:** 133, **142–143,** 146

"In Country of Conscience" (J. W. Miller), **Supp. XX: 165**

" 'Incredible Eloquence': How Ron Rash's Novels Keep the Celtic Literary Tradition Alive" (K. Baldwin), **Supp. XXVII:** 216

"Incredible Survival of Coyote, The" (Snyder), **Supp. VIII:** 297

"Increment" (Ammons), **Supp. VII:** 28

In Defense of Ignorance (Shapiro), **Supp. II Part 2:** 703, 704, 713–714

In Defense of Reason (Winters), **Supp. I Part 1:** 268

In Defense of Women (Mencken), **III:** 109

Indelible (Hadas), **Supp. XXIII: 119**

Indelible Alison Bechdel, The (Bechdel), **Supp. XXV:** 4

Indemnity Only (Paretsky), **Supp. XXV:** 172–173, 176, 178

Independence Day (film), **Supp. X:** 80

Independence Day (Ford), **Supp. V:** 57, 62–63, 67–68

"Independent Candidate, The, a Story of Today" (Howells), **II:** 277

"Indestructible Mr. Gore, The" (Vidal), **Supp. IV Part 2:** 679

Index of American Design, **Supp. III Part 2:** 618

"India" (Rodriguez), **Supp. XIV:** 302

"Indian at the Burial-Place of His Fathers, An" (Bryant), **Supp. I Part 1:** 155–156, 167–168

"Indian Burying Ground, The" (Freneau), **Supp. II Part 1:** 264, 266

"Indian Camp" (Hemingway), **II:** 247–248, 263; **Retro. Supp. I:** 174–175, 176, 177, 181; **Supp. XVI:** 208

Indian Country (Caputo), **Supp. XIX:** 22–25

Indian Country (Matthiessen), **Supp. V:** 211

"Indian Country" (McCarriston), **Supp. XIV:** 271

"Indian Country" (Simpson), **Supp. IX:** 274

Indian Earth (Bynner), **Supp. XV:** 46

"Indian Gifts to Civilized Man" (Zitkala-Ša), **Supp. XXV:** 281

"Indian Girls" (McCarriston), **Supp. XIV:** 272–273

"Indian Manifesto" (Deloria), **Supp. IV Part 1:** 323

"Indian Names" (Sigourney), **Retro. Supp. II:** 47

"Indian's Awakening, The" (Zitkala-Ša), **Supp. XXV:** 281

"Indian Student, The" (Freneau), **Supp. II Part 1:** 264

"Indian Student, The" (Simpson), **Supp. IX:** 280

Indian Summer (Howells), **II:** 275, 279–281, 282

Indian Summer (Knowles), **Supp. XII:** 249, 250

Indian Summer: Musings on the Gift of Life (Pickering), **Supp. XXI:** 204

Indian Summers (Gansworth), **Supp. XXVI:** 104

"Indian Teacher Among Indians, An" (Zitkala-Ša), **Supp. XXV:** 272

"Indian Uprising, The" (Barthelme), **Supp. IV Part 1:** 44

"Indian Wooing" (C. Miller), **Supp. XXII:** 197–198

Indifferent Children, The (Auchincloss), **Supp. IV Part 1:** 25

Indirections (Cox), **Supp. XXI:** 21

Indiscretions (Pound), **Retro. Supp. I:** 284

"Indispensability of the Eyes, The" (Olds), **Supp. X:** 202

"In Distrust of Merits" (Moore), **III:** 201, 214

"Individual and the State, The" (Emerson), **II:** 10

Individualism, Old and New (Dewey), **Supp. I Part 2:** 677

"Indolence" (Pickering), **Supp. XXI:** 203

In Dreams Begin Responsibilities (Schwartz), **Supp. II Part 2:** 642, 645–650

"In Dreams Begin Responsibilities" (Schwartz), **Supp. II Part 2:** 641, 649, 654

In Dubious Battle (Steinbeck), **IV:** 51, 55–56, 59, 63

"In Durance" (Pound), **Retro. Supp. I:** 285

"Industry of Hard Kissing, The" (Ríos), **Supp. IV Part 2:** 547

"In Duty Bound" (Gilman), **Supp. XI:** 196–197

"I Need, I Need" (Roethke), **III:** 535–536

"I Need Help" (Stern), **Supp. IX:** 290

"Ineffectual Marriage" (Loy), **Supp. XXII:** 165

"Inés in the Kitchen" (García), **Supp. XI:** 190

"I never saw a Moor" (Dickinson), **Retro. Supp. I:** 37

I Never Told Anybody: Teaching Poetry Writing in a Nursing Home (Koch), **Supp. XV:** 190

"I Never Will Be Married, I'd Rather Be Excus'd" (Rowson), **Supp. XV:** 240

Inevitable Exiles (Kielsky), **Supp. V:** 273

"Inevitable Trial, The" (Holmes), **Supp. I Part 1:** 318

"Inexhaustible Hat, The" (Wagoner), **Supp. IX:** 327

"In Extremis" (Berry), **Supp. X:** 23

Inez, Colette, **Supp. XXIII:** 54, 245

"Infancy" (Wilder), **IV:** 375

"Infant Boy at Midcentury" (Warren), **IV:** 244–245, 252

Infante, Guillermo Cabrera, **Retro. Supp. I:** 278

"Infant Sea Turtles" (F. Wright), **Supp. XVII:** 245

Infants of the Spring (Thurman), **Supp. XIX:** 73; **Supp. XVIII:** 281

Inferno (Dante), **IV:** 139; **Supp. V:** 338; **Supp. VIII:** 219–221

Inferno of Dante, The (Pinsky), **Supp. VI:** 235, 248

Infidel (Ali), **Supp. XXIV:** 15

"Infidelity" (Komunyakaa), **Supp. XIII:** 130

Infidels (album, Dylan), **Supp. XVIII:** 28

"Infiltration of the Universe" (MacLeish), **III:** 19

Infinite Jest: A Novel (Wallace), **Supp. X:** 301, **310–314; Supp. XX:** 91; **Supp. XXVII:** 6

"Infinite Reason, The" (MacLeish), **III:** 19

"Infirmity" (R. Lowell), **II:** 554

"Infirmity" (Roethke), **III:** 548

In Five Years Time (Haines), **Supp. XII:** 206

"In Flower" (Snodgrass), **Supp. VI:** 325

"Influence of Landscape upon the Poet, The" (Eliot), **Retro. Supp. I:** 67

"In Football Season" (Updike), **IV:** 219

Informer, The (film), **Supp. III Part 2:** 619

Informers, The (Ellis), **Supp. XXVII:** 74–75

Informers, The (screenplay, Ellis and Jarecki), **Supp. XXVII:** 68, 79

Inge, William, **Supp. XXV: 93–108**

Ingersoll, Charles J., **I:** 344

Ingersoll, Robert Green, **Supp. II Part 1:** 198

Ingmundson, Kris, **Supp. XXIV:** 230, 234

Ingraham, Lloyd, **Supp. XVI:** 184

"Ingrained Reflexes" (Huddle), **Supp. XXVI:** 154

Ingster, Boris, **Retro. Supp. II:** 330

"In Guatemala, All Is Forgotten" (Goldman), **Supp. XXV:** 58

Inhabitants, The (Morris), **III:** 221–222

"Inheritance and Invention in Li-Young Lee's Poetry" (Xiaojing), **Supp. XV:** 214

"Inheritance"(Kenny), **Supp. XXIII:** 154

"Inheritance of Tools, The" (Sanders), **Supp. XVI:** 273

Inheritors (Glaspell), **Supp. III Part 1:** 175, 179–181, 186, 189

"In him we live, & move, & have our being" (Very), **Supp. XXV:** 246

"In Hollywood with the Zuni God of War" (Major), **Supp. XXII:** 180

"In Honor of David Anderson Brooks, My Father" (Brooks), **Supp. III Part 1:** 79

"Inhumanist, The" (Jeffers), **Supp. II Part 2:** 423, 426

"In Illo Tempore" (Karr), **Supp. XI:** 242

"In Interims: Outlyer" (Harrison), **Supp. VIII:** 38

"Initial" (F. Wright), **Supp. XVII:** 243

"Injudicious Gardening" (Moore), **III:** 198

"Injustice" (Paley), **Supp. VI:** 220

Injustice Collectors, The (Auchincloss), **Supp. IV Part 1:** 25

Ink, Blood, Semen (Goldbarth), **Supp. XII:** 181, 183

Ink Dark Moon, The: Love Poems by Ono no Komachi and Izumi Shikibu (Aratani and Hirshfield, trans.), **Supp. XXIII:** 136

Ink Truck, The (W. Kennedy), **Supp. VII:** 132, 133–138, 140, 141, 149, 152

In Life Sentences: Literary Essays (Epstein), **Supp. XIV:** 112

"In Limbo" (Wilbur), **Supp. III Part 2:** 544, 561

In Limestone Country (Sanders), **Supp. XVI:** 272

"In Line" (Major), **Supp. XXII:** 185

In Love (Hayes), **Supp. XXVI:** 133, 139, 140–141

In Love and Trouble: Stories of Black Women (Walker), **Supp. III Part 2:** 520, 521, 530, 531, 532

In Mad Love and War (Harjo), **Supp. XII: 224–226**

"In Memoriam" (Emerson), **II:** 13

"In Memoriam" (Hay), **Supp. XIV:** 122, 127

"In Memoriam" (Tennyson), **Retro. Supp. I:** 325; **Supp. I Part 2:** 416

In Memoriam: 1933 (Reznikoff), **Supp. XIV:** 280, 285

In Memoriam to Identity (Acker), **Supp. XII:** 5, **16–18**

"In Memory of Arthur Winslow" (R. Lowell), **II:** 541, 547, 550; **Retro. Supp. II:** 187

"In Memory of Congresswoman Barbara Jordan" (Pinsky), **Supp. VI:** 250

"In Memory of Joe Brainard" (Bidart), **Supp. XV:** 33

"In Memory of My Feelings" (O'Hara), **Supp. XV:** 215–216

In Memory of My Feelings (O'Hara; Berkson, ed.), **Supp. XXIII:** 220

"In Memory of My Feelings"(O'Hara), **Supp. XXIII:** 208, 215–216

"In Memory of Vachel Lindsay" (Teasdale), **Supp. XXVII:** 297

"In Memory of W. B. Yeats" (Auden), **Supp. VIII:** 19, 30; **Supp. XI:** 243, 244; **Supp. XIX:** 85

"In Memory of W. H. Auden" (Stern), **Supp. IX:** 288

"In Memory"(Schott), **Supp. XXIII:** 254

"In Mercy on Broadway" (Doty), **Supp. XI:** 132

In Morocco (Wharton), **Retro. Supp. I:** 380; **Supp. IV Part 1:** 81

Inmost Leaf, The: A Selection of Essays (Kazin), **Supp. VIII:** 102, 103

In Motley (Bierce), **I:** 209

In My Father's Court (Singer), **IV:** 16–17; **Retro. Supp. II: 301–302**

"In My Life" (Dubus), **Supp. VII:** 81

"In My Other Life" (Huddle), **Supp. XXVI:** 151

Innaurato, Albert, **Supp. XXIV:** 113, 116, 117

"In Navaho Country" (Bronk), **Supp. XXI:** 30

Inner Circle, The (Boyle), **Supp. XX: 24, 26**

Inner Landscape (Sarton), **Supp. VIII:** 259

Inner Room, The (Merrill), **Supp. III Part 1:** 336

"In Nine Sleep Valley" (Merrill), **Supp. III Part 1:** 328

Innocent Mrs. Duff, The (Holding), **Supp. XXII:** 119, 120, 123, **130–131**, 135, 136

Innocents, The: A Story for Lovers (Lewis), **II:** 441

Innocents Abroad, The; or, The New Pilgrim's Progress (Twain), **II:** 275, 434; **IV:** 191, 196, 197–198

Innocents at Cedro, The: A Memoir of Thorstein Veblen and Some Others (Duffus), **Supp. I Part 2:** 650

"In Off the Cliffs of Moher" (McCarriston), **Supp. XIV:** 270

In Old Plantation Days (Dunbar), **Supp. II Part 1:** 214

In Ole Virginia (Page), **Supp. II Part 1:** 201

In Orbit (Morris), **III:** 236

In Other Words (Swenson), **Supp. IV Part 2:** 650–652

In Other Words: Literature by Latinas of the United States (Fernandez, ed.), **Supp. XXI:** 104

In Our Terribleness (Some elements and meaning in black style) (Baraka), **Supp. II Part 1:** 52, 53

In Our Time (Hemingway), **I:** 117; **II:** 68, 247, 252, 263; **IV:** 42; **Retro. Supp. I:** 170, 173, 174, 178, 180; **Supp. IX:** 106

"In Our Time" (Wolfe), **Supp. III Part 2:** 584

"Inpatient" (Kenyon), **Supp. VII:** 169

In Persuasion Nation (Saunders), **Supp. XIX: 231–234**

"In Persuasion Nation" (Saunders), **Supp. XIX:** 233–234

In Pharaoh's Army: Memories of the Lost War (Wolff), **Supp. VII:** 331–334, 335, 338

"In Plaster" (Plath), **Supp. I Part 2:** 540

"In Prague, in Montmartre" (Bierds), **Supp. XVII:** 27

"In Praise of Johnny Appleseed" (Lindsay), **Supp. I Part 2:** 397

"In Praise of Limestone" (Auden), **Supp. II Part 1:** 20–21; **Supp. VIII:** 23

In Pursuit of a Vanishing Star (Sobin), **Supp. XVI: 294**

"In Quercy, 1993" (Davison), **Supp. XXVI:** 78

In Quest of the Ordinary (Cavell), **Retro. Supp. I:** 307

Inquiry into the Moral and Religious Character of the American Government, An (H. Warner), **Supp. XVIII:** 259

Inquiry into the Nature of Peace, An (Veblen), **Supp. I Part 2:** 642

Inquisitor, The (Rowson), **Supp. XV: 232, 238**

In Radical Pursuit (Snodgrass), **Supp. VI:** 312, 316, 318

In Reckless Ecstasy (Sandburg), **III:** 579

In Recognition of William Gaddis (Kuehl and Moore), **Supp. IV Part 1:** 279

"In Retirement" (Malamud), **Supp. I Part 2:** 437

"In Retrospect" (Angelou), **Supp. IV Part 1:** 15

"In Right" (Wolfert), **Supp. XXI:** 263, 264, 272

"Inroads of Time, The" (D. West), **Supp. XVIII:** 286–287

In Russia (A. Miller), **III:** 165

"In Sabine" (Chopin), **Supp. I Part 1:** 213

"In School-Days" (Whittier), **Supp. I Part 2:** 699–700

"Inscription for the Entrance to a Wood" (Bryant), **Supp. I Part 1:** 154, 155, 161–162

Inscriptions, 1944–1956 (Reznikoff), **Supp. XIV:** 281

In Search (Levin), **Supp. XXVII:** 133, 134, 138, 142, 143, 146–147

In Search of America: The Image of the United States in Travel Writing of the 1980s and 1990s (Rutkowska), **Supp. XXII:** 208

"In Search of a Motif for Expressive Female Figuration" (Major), **Supp. XXII:** 184

In Search of Bisco (Caldwell), **I:** 296

In Search of Lost Time (Proust), **Supp. XXV:** 71

In Search of Nella Larsen: A Biography of the Color Line (Hutchinson), **Supp. XVIII:** 120

"In Search of Our Mothers' Gardens" (Walker), **Supp. III Part 2:** 520–532, 524, 525, 527, 529, 532–533, 535, 536; **Supp. IX:** 306; **Supp. XVIII:** 200, 283

"In Search of Thomas Merton" (Griffin), **Supp. VIII:** 208

"In Search of Yage" (Burroughs), **Supp. III Part 1:** 98

"Insect Life in Florida" (Hull), **Supp. XXI:** 133

Insel (Loy), **Supp. XXII:** 167

"Insertion of Self into a Space of Borderless Possibilities, The" (Fjellestad), **Supp. XVI:** 150

"In Shadow" (Crane), **I:** 386

"In Sickness and in Health" (Auden), **Supp. II Part 1:** 15

"In Sickness and in Health" (Humphrey), **Supp. IX:** 94

Inside, Outside (Wouk), **Supp. XXV:** 254, 255, 257, 265

Inside Diameter: The France Poems (Major), **Supp. XXII:** 182

Inside His Mind (A. Miller), **III:** 154

Inside Memory (Findley), **Supp. XX: 51, 63**

"Inside Norman Mailer" (Apple), **Supp. XVII:** 3, 4

"Insider Baseball" (Didion), **Supp. IV Part 1:** 211

Inside Sports magazine, **Supp. V:** 58, 61

"Insipid Profession of Jonathan Horneboom, The" (Lethem), **Supp. XVIII:** 149

"In So Many Dark Rooms" (Hogan), **Supp. IV Part 1:** 400

"Insomnia" (Bishop), **Supp. I Part 1:** 92

"Insomniac" (Plath), **Supp. I Part 2:** 539

"In Spain, Throwing Carnations" (P. N. Warren), **Supp. XX: 272**

"Inspiration for Greatness" (Caldwell), **I:** 291

"Instability of Race Types, The" (Boas), **Supp. XIV:** 209

"Installation #6" (Beattie), **Supp. V:** 33

"Instead of Dying" (Gallagher), **Supp. XXIV:** 171

"Insterstices" (Berrigan), **Supp. XXIV:** 36

Instinct of Workmanship and the State of the Industrial Arts, The (Veblen), **Supp. I Part 2:** 642

Instincts of the Herd in Peace and War, The (Trotter), **I:** 249

Institute (Calvin), **IV:** 158, 160

"Instruction Manual, The" (Ashbery), **Supp. III Part 1:** 6–7, 10, 12

Instructions, The (Levin), **Supp. XXII:** 268

"Instructions for the Afternoon" (Gioia), **Supp. XV:** 120

Instructions to the Double (Gallagher), **Supp. XXIV:** 165, 167, 168, 169, 174

"Instructions to the Double" (Gallagher), **Supp. XXIV:** 168

"Instruction to Myself" (Brooks), **Supp. III Part 1:** 87

Instrument, The (O'Hara), **III:** 362, 364

"In Such Times, Ties Must Bind" (Nye), **Supp. XIII:** 286

In Sunlight and in Shadow (Helprin), **Supp. XXV:** 81, 88

"Insurance and Social Change" (Stevens), **Retro. Supp. I:** 297

Insurgent Mexico (Reed), **I:** 476

In Suspect Terrain (McPhee), **Supp. III Part 1:** 309, 310

"In Tall Grass" (Sandburg), **III:** 585

"Integer Vitae" (Horace), **Supp. XV:** 304

Intellectual History, An (Senghor), **Supp. X:** 139

"Intellectual Pre-Eminence of Jews in Modern Europe, The" (Veblen), **Supp. I Part 2:** 643–644

Intellectual Things (Kunitz), **Supp. III Part 1:** 260, 262–264

Intellectual versus the City, The (White), **I:** 258

"In Temporary Pain" (Bynner), **Supp. XV:** 41–42

Intensive Care (Myers), **Supp. XXVII:** 211

Intentions (Wilde), **Retro. Supp. I:** 56

"Interest in Life, An" (Paley), **Supp. VI:** 222, 224–225

Interest of Great Britain Considered, with Regard to Her Colonies and the Acquisition of Canada and Guadeloupe, The (Franklin), **II:** 119

Interior Landscapes (Vizenor), **Supp. IV Part 1:** 262

Interiors (film; Allen), **Supp. IV Part 1:** 205; **Supp. XV:** 1, 7, 10

Interlocking Lives (Koch), **Supp. XV:** 185

"Interlude" (A. Lowell), **Retro. Supp. II:** 46

Interlunar (Atwood), **Supp. XIII:** 35

"Intermezzo" (Schnackenberg), **Supp. XV:** 254

"In Terms of the Toenail: Fiction and the Figures of Life" (Gass), **Supp. VI:** 85

"International Episode, An" (James), **II:** 327

International Workers Order, **Retro. Supp. I:** 202

Interpretation of Christian Ethics, An (Niebuhr), **III:** 298–300, 301, 302

"Interpretation of Dreams, The" (Matthews), **Supp. IX:** 162–163

Interpretation of Music of the XVIIth and XVIIIth Centuries, The (Dolmetsch), **III:** 464

Interpretations and Forecasts: 1922–1972 (Mumford), **Supp. II Part 2:** 481

Interpretations of Poetry and Religion (Santayana), **III:** 611

Interpreter of Maladies (Lahiri), **Supp. XXI:** 175–176, **177–180,** 183

"Interpreter of Maladies" (Lahiri), **Supp. XXI:** 183, 184

Interpreters and Interpretations (Van Vechten), **Supp. II Part 2:** 729, 733–734

"Interrogate the Stones" (MacLeish), **III:** 9

"Interrogation of the Prisoner Bung By Mister Hawkins and Sergeant Tree, The" (Huddle), **Supp. XXVI:** 147, 149, 152

Interrogations at Noon (Gioia), **Supp. XV:** 112, **125–127,** 128, 129

"Interrupted Conversation, An" (Van Vechten), **Supp. II Part 2:** 735

"Interrupted Elegy" (Peacock), **Supp. XIX:** 200

Intersect: Poems (Shields), **Supp. VII:** 310–311

Intersexes, The (Prime-Stevenson as Mayne), **Supp. XX:** **235**

Interstate (Dixon), **Supp. XII:** 140, 152–153, 153, 156

"Interview" (Hay), **Supp. XIV:** 132

"Interview, The" (Thurber), **Supp. I Part 2:** 616

"Interview With a Lemming" (Thurber), **Supp. I Part 2:** 603

"Interview with Larry Rivers, An"(O'Hara), **Supp. XXIII:** 214

"Interview with Peter Everwine, An" (Veinberg and Buckley), **Supp. XV:** 76–77

"Interview with the Crab" (Lethem), **Supp. XVIII:** 148

Interview with the Vampire (Rice), **Supp. VII:** 287, 288–291, 297–298, 303

"Interview with the Vampire" (Rice), **Supp. VII:** 288

Interzone (Burroughs), **Supp. IV Part 1:** 90

"In the Absence of Bliss" (Kumin), **Supp. IV Part 2:** 453

"In the Afternoon" (Dunn), **Supp. XI:** 146

"In the Alley" (Elkin), **Supp. VI:** **46–47**

In the American Grain (W. C. Williams), **Retro. Supp. I:** 420–421

In the American Jungle (W. Frank), **Supp. XX:** **76**

In the American Tree (Silliman), **Supp. IV Part 2:** 426

"In the Arboretum" (Stone), **Supp. XXVII:** 260

In the Bank of Beautiful Sins (Wrigley), **Supp. XVIII:** **300–302**

In the Bar of a Tokyo Hotel (T. Williams), **IV:** 382, 386, 387, 391, 393

In the Beauty of the Lilies (Updike), **Retro. Supp. I:** 322, 325, 326, 327, 333

"In the Beeyard" (Bierds), **Supp. XVII:** 29

"In the Beginning" (Quindlen), **Supp. XVII:** 166

"In the Beginning . . ." (Simic), **Supp. VIII:** 270, 271

In the Belly of the Beast: Letters from Prison (Abbott), **Retro. Supp. II:** 210

"In the Black Morning" (Wolfert), **Supp. XXI:** 265

"In the Black Museum" (Nemerov), **III:** 275

"In the Blink of God's Eye" (E. P. Jones), **Supp. XXII:** 150

"In the Bodies of Words" (Swenson), **Supp. IV Part 2:** 651

"In the Boston Children's Hospital" (Huddle), **Supp. XXVI:** 151

"In the Box"(Kenny), **Supp. XXIII:** 155

"In the Cage" (Gass), **Supp. VI:** 85

In the Cage (James), **Retro. Supp. I:** 229

"In the Cage" (James), **II:** 332; **Retro. Supp. I:** 231

"In the Cage" (R. Lowell), **Retro. Supp. II:** 187

"In the Cave at Lone Tree Meadow" (Haines), **Supp. XII:** 212

"In the Cemetery Where Al Jolson Is Buried" (Hempel), **Supp. XXI:** 115, **121–122**

"In the City Ringed with Giants" (Kingsolver), **Supp. VII:** 209

"In the Clearing" (Brodsky), **Supp. VIII:** 32

In the Clearing (Frost), **II:** 153, 155, 164; **Retro. Supp. I:** 121, 122, 141

"In the Closet of the Soul" (Walker), **Supp. III Part 2:** 526

"In the Cold Air Register" (W. V. Davis), **Supp. XXI:** 94

"In the Confidence of a Story-Writer" (Chopin), **Retro. Supp. II:** 66–67; **Supp. I Part 1:** 217

In the Country of Last Things (Auster), **Supp. XII:** 23, **29–30,** 31, 32

"In the Courtyard of the Isleta Missions" (R. Bly), **Supp. IV Part 1:** 71

"In the Dark" (Levine), **Supp. V:** 194

In the Dark (Stone), **Supp. XXVII:** 257

"In the Dark New England Days" (Jewett), **Retro. Supp. II:** 139

"In the Days of Prismatic Colour" (Moore), **III:** 205, 213

In the Days of the Comet (Wells), **Supp. XX:** **233, 240**

In the Electric Mist with Confederate Dead (Burke), **Supp. XIV:** 30, 31–32

"In the Field" (Wilbur), **Supp. III Part 2:** 558

"In the 51st State" (Berrigan), **Supp. XXIV:** 35

"In the First Stanza" (C. Kizer), **Supp. XVII:** 75

"In the Fleeting Hand of Time" (Corso), **Supp. XII:** 122–123

"In the Footsteps of Gutenberg" (Mencken), **III:** 101

"In the Forest" (Simpson), **Supp. IX:** 270

"In the Forest of the Laughing Elephant" (Caputo), **Supp. XIX:** 27

"In the Forties" (R. Lowell), **II:** 554

"In the Garden" (Ferry), **Supp. XXIV:** 153

In the Garden of the North American Martyrs (Wolff), **Supp. VII:** 341–342

In the Garret (Van Vechten), **Supp. II Part 2:** 735

"In the Grove: The Poet at Ten" (Kenyon), **Supp. VII:** 160

"In the Hall of Mirrors" (Merrill), **Supp. III Part 1:** 322

In the Harbor (Longfellow), **II:** 491

In the Heart of the Heart of the Country (Gass), **Supp. VI: 82–83,** 84, 85, 93

In the Heat of the Night (Ball), **Supp. XV:** 202

In the Heat of the Night (film), **Supp. I Part 1:** 67

In the Hollow of His Hand (Purdy), **Supp. VII:** 278–280

In the House of Light (Everwine, trans.), **Supp. XV:** 73, 75, **76–78,** 82

"In the Laboratory of Kisses" (Gallagher), **Supp. XXIV:** 170

In the Lake of the Woods (O'Brien), **Supp. V:** 240, 243, 250–252

In the Land of the White Death: A Epic Story of Survival in the Siberian Arctic (Albanov), **Supp. XVIII:** 114

"In the Last Days" (Everwine), **Supp. XV:** 88, 89

"In the Late Summer Garden"(Crooker), **Supp. XXIII:** 55

In the Loyal Mountains (Bass), **Supp. XVI: 19–20**

"In the Loyal Mountains" (Bass), **Supp. XVI:** 20

"In the Mean Mud Season" (Huddle), **Supp. XXVI:** 154

In the Mecca (Brooks), **Supp. III Part 1:** 74

"In the Mecca" (Brooks), **Supp. III Part 1:** 70, 83–84

"In the Metropolitan Museum" (Teasdale), **Supp. XXVII:** 289

In the Midst of Life (Bierce), **I:** 200–203, 204, 206, 208, 212

"In the Miro District" (Taylor), **Supp. V:** 323

In the Miro District and Other Stories (Taylor), **Supp. V:** 325–326

In the Money (W. C. Williams), **Retro. Supp. I:** 423

"In the Motel" (X. J. Kennedy), **Supp. XV:** 163

"In the Naked Bed, in Plato's Cave" (Schwartz), **Supp. II Part 2:** 646–649

In the Name of the Neither (Sobin), **Supp. XVI:** 291

In the Next Galaxy (Stone), **Supp. XXVII:** 257, 262

"In the Next Galaxy" (Stone), **Supp. XXVII:** 253

"In the Night" (Kincaid), **Supp. VII:** 183

In the Night Season: A Novel (Bausch), **Supp. VII:** 52–53

"In the Old Neighborhood" (Dove), **Supp. IV Part 1:** 241, 257

"In the Old World" (Oates), **Supp. II Part 2:** 503, 504

"In the Park" (Biss), **Supp. XXVI:** 48

"In the Park" (Huncke), **Supp. XIV:** 139

In the Pines (Notley), **Supp. XXII:** 236–237

"In the Pit" (Proulx), **Supp. VII:** 255, 261

In the Pond (Jin), **Supp. XVIII: 95–96**

In the Presence of the Sun (Momaday), **Supp. IV Part 2:** 489, 490, 491–493, 493

"In the Quiet Night" (Li Po), **Supp. XV:** 47

"In the Realm of the Fisher King" (Didion), **Supp. IV Part 1:** 211

"In the Red Room" (Bowles), **Supp. IV Part 1:** 93

"In the Region of Ice" (Oates), **Supp. II Part 2:** 520

In the Room We Share (Simpson), **Supp. IX:** 279

"In These Dissenting Times" (Walker), **Supp. III Part 2:** 522

"In the Shadow of Gabriel, A.D.1550" (Frederic), **II:** 139

In the Shadow of Memory (Skloot), **Supp. XX: 193, 196, 205, 205–206**

"In the Shadow of Memory" (Skloot), **Supp. XX: 206**

In the Shadow of the Morning: Essays on Wild Lands, Wild Waters, and a Few Untamed People (Caputo), **Supp. XIX:** 28–29

In the Spirit of Crazy Horse (Matthiessen), **Supp. V:** 211

"In the Subway" (Untermeyer), **Supp. XV:** 296

In the Summer House (Jane Bowles), **Supp. IV Part 1:** 83, 89

"In the Syntax: Rewriting Joan Didion's 'Goodbye to All That' " (Biss), **Supp. XXVI:** 54

In the Tennessee Country (Taylor), **Supp. V:** 328

"In the Thick of Darkness" (Salinas), **Supp. XIII:** 325

In the Time of Butterflies (Alvarez), **Supp. XXIV:** 89

"In the Time of the Blossoms" (Mervin), **Supp. III Part 1:** 352

In the Time of the Butterflies (Alvarez), **Supp. VII:** 1, 12–15, 18

In the Time of the Present (Kenny), **Supp. XXIII:** 146, **156**

"In the Tube" (Jarman), **Supp. XVII:** 121

"In the Tunnel Bone of Cambridge" (Corso), **Supp. XII:** 120–121

"In the Upper Pastures" (Kumin), **Supp. IV Part 2:** 453

In the Valley (Frederic), **II:** 133–134, 136, 137

"In the Village" (Bishop), **Retro. Supp. II:** 38; **Supp. I Part 1:** 73, 74–75, 76, 77, 78, 88

"In the Waiting Room" (Bishop), **Retro. Supp. II:** 50; **Supp. I Part 1:** 81, 94, 95; **Supp. IV Part 1:** 249

In the Walled City (O'Nan), **Supp. XXV:** 142

"In the Ward: The Sacred Wood" (Jarrell), **II:** 376, 377

In the Western Night: Collected Poems 1965–90 (Bidart), **Supp. XV:** 19, **30–32**

"In the White Night" (Beattie), **Supp. V:** 30–31

"In the Wind My Rescue Is" (Ammons), **Supp. VII:** 25

"In the Winter Dark" (Peacock), **Supp. XIX:** 206

In the Winter of Cities (T. Williams), **IV:** 383

"In the X-Ray of the Sarcophagus of Ta-pero" (Goldbarth), **Supp. XII:** 191

"In the Yard" (Swenson), **Supp. IV Part 2:** 647

In the Zone (O'Neill), **III:** 388

In This, Our Life (film), **Supp. I Part 1:** 67

"In This Country, but in Another Language, My Aunt Refuses to Marry the Men Everyone Wants Her To" (Paley), **Supp. VI:** 225

"In This Dream" (J. W. Miller), **Supp. XX:** 170

In This Hung-up Age (Corso), **Supp. XII: 119–120,** 129

In This Our Life (Glasgow), **II:** 175, 178, 189

In This Our World (Gilman), **Supp. XI:** 196, 200, 202

"In Those Days" (Jarrell), **II:** 387–388

"Intimately Connected to the Zeitgeist" (Franzen), **Supp. XX: 94**

Intimates (Huddle), **Supp. XXVI:** 155–156

"In Time of War" (Auden), **Supp. II Part 1:** 8, 13

In Times Like These (Edgell), **Supp. XXIII:** 84, **89–90,** 94

"Into Egypt" (Benét), **Supp. XI:** 56, 57–58

Intolerance (film; Griffith), **Supp. XVI:** 184

"Into My Own" (Frost), **II:** 153; **Retro. Supp. I:** 127

"Into Night" (McKnight), **Supp. XX: 151–152**

"Into the Gorge" (Rash), **Supp. XXVII:** 228

Into the Interior (Cliff), **Supp. XXII:** 67, 78–79

"Into the Night Life . . ." (H. Miller), **III:** 180, 184

"Into the Nowhere" (Rawlings), **Supp. X:** 220

Into the Stone (Dickey), **Supp. IV Part 1:** 178

"Into the Stone" (Dickey), **Supp. IV Part 1:** 179

Into the Stone and Other Poems (Dickey), **Supp. IV Part 1:** 176

"Into the Streets May First" (Hayes), **Supp. XXVI:** 134, 144

Into the Wild (Krakauer), **Supp. XVIII:** 106, **107–108,** 116, 117

Into Thin Air: A Personal Account of the Mount Everest Disaster (Krakauer), **Supp. XVII:** 210; **Supp. XVIII:** 105, **109–113,** 117

In Touch: The Letters of Paul Bowles (J. Miller, ed.), **Supp. IV Part 1:** 95

"Intoxicated, The" (Jackson), **Supp. IX:** 116

"Intrigue" (Crane), **I:** 419

Introducing Irony: A Book of Poetic Short Stories and Poems (Bodenheim), **Supp. XXV:** 22–23

"Introducing the Fathers" (Kumin), **Supp. IV Part 2:** 452

Introductio ad Prudentiam (Fuller), **II:** 111

"Introduction"(Strout; *Ploughshares* spring 2010), **Supp. XXIII:** 284

"Introduction to a Haggadah" (Paley), **Supp. VI:** 219

Introduction to Objectivist Epistemology (Rand), **Supp. IV Part 2:** 527, 528–529

Introduction to Objectivist Epistemology 2nd ed. (Rand), **Supp. IV Part 2:** 529

"Introduction to Poetry" (Collins), **Supp. XXI:** 57

Introduction to Poetry, An (Gioia and X. J. Kennedy), **Supp. XV:** 113, 153

"Introduction to Some Poems, An" (Stafford), **Supp. XI:** 311, 324

Introduction to the Geography of Iowa, The (Doty), **Supp. XI:** 120

"Introduction to the Hoh" (Hugo), **Supp. VI:** 136–137

"Introduction to *The New Writing in the USA*" (Creeley), **Supp. IV Part 1:** 153–154

"Introduction to William Blake, An" (Kazin), **Supp. VIII:** 103

Introitus (Longfellow), **II:** 505, 506–507

"Intruder, The" (Dubus), **Supp. VII:** 76–78, 91

Intruder, The (Maeterlinck), **I:** 91

Intruder in the Dust (Faulkner), **II:** 71, 72; **Supp. XVI:** 148

Intuition (Goodman), **Supp. XXVI:** 128–130

"Invaders, The" (Haines), **Supp. XII:** 205

Invaders, The (W. Frank), **Supp. XX:** **79–80**

Invasion (Myers), **Supp. XXVII:** 207

Invasion of Privacy: The Cross Creek Trial of Marjorie Kinnan Rawlings (Acton), **Supp. X:** 233

Inventing Memory: A Novel of Mothers and Daughters (Jong), **Supp. V:** 115, 129

Inventing the Abbotts (Miller), **Supp. XII:** **294–295**

"Invention of Autobiography. The" (Hampl), **Supp. XXII:** 93–94

"Invention of God in a Mouthful of Milk, The" (Karr), **Supp. XI:** 250

Invention of Solitude, The (Auster), **Supp. XII:** 21–22

Inventions of the March Hare (Eliot), **Retro. Supp. I:** 55–56, 58

"Inventions of the March Hare" (Eliot), **Retro. Supp. I:** 55

"Inventory" (Parker), **Supp. IX:** 192

Inverness, Amy Beth, **Supp. XXVII:** 103

"Inverted Forest, The" (Salinger), **III:** 552, 572

"Investigation" (Ryan as Quin), **Supp. XVIII:** 227–228

"Investigations of a Dog" (Kafka), **IV:** 438

"Investiture, The" (Banks), **Supp. V:** 7

"Investiture at Cecconi's" (Merrill), **Supp. III Part 1:** 336

"Invicibility"(O'Hara), **Supp. XXIII:** 214

"Invisible" (Pickering), **Supp. XXI:** 201

Invisible Circus, The (Egan), **Supp. XIX:** 49, **50–52**

Invisible Company, The (Sanders), **Supp. XVI:** 270–271

Invisible Man (Ellison), **IV:** 493; **Retro. Supp. II:** 3, 12, 111, 112, 113, 117, 119, **120–123**, 125; **Supp. II Part 1:** 40, 170, 221, 224, 226, 227, 230, 231–232, 235, 236, 241–245; **Supp. IX:** 306; **Supp. X:** 242; **Supp. XI:** 18, 92; **Supp. XIX:** 154, 155; **Supp. XVIII:** 59; **Supp. XXVI:** 215

Invisible: Poems (Nye), **Supp. XIII:** 277

Invisible Spectator, An (Sawyer-Lauçanno), **Supp. IV Part 1:** 95

Invisible Swords (Farrell), **II:** 27, 46, 48–49

Invisible Worm, The (Millar), **Supp. IV Part 2:** 465

Invitation to a Beheading (Nabokov), **III:** 252–253, 254, 257–258; **Retro. Supp. I:** 265, 270, 273

"Invitation to the Country, An" (Bryant), **Supp. I Part 1:** 160

"Invocation" (H. Johnson), **Supp. XXVI:** 166, 174

"Invocation" (McKay), **Supp. X:** 134

Invocation (Rash), **Supp. XXVII:** 217

"Invocation" (Untermeyer), **Supp. XV:** 296

"Invocation to Kali" (Sarton), **Supp. VIII:** 260

"Invocation: *To my Maternal Grand-father on hearing his descent from Chippewa ancestors misrepresented*"(J. Schoolcraft), Supp. *XXIII:* 232

"Invocation to the Social Muse" (MacLeish), **III:** 15

"In Weather" (Hass), **Supp. VI: 102–103**

"In Your Fugitive Dream" (Hugo), **Supp. VI:** 143

"In Your Good Dream" (Hugo), **Supp. VI:** 143–144

"Iola, Kansas" (Clampitt), **Supp. IX:** 45–46

Iola Leroy (Harper), **Supp. XVIII:** 284

Ion (Doolittle, trans.), **Supp. I Part 1:** 269, 274

Ion (Plato), **I:** 523

"Ione" (Dunbar), **Supp. II Part 1:** 199

Ionesco, Eugène, **I:** 71, 74, 75, 84, 295; **II:** 435; **Supp. VIII:** 201; **Supp. XIX:** 131; **Supp. XXIV:** 113

Ionica (Cory), **Supp. XX: 230**

Ionica II (Cory), **Supp. XX: 230**

"I Only Am Escaped Alone to Tell Thee" (Nemerov), **III:** 272, 273–274

"I Opened All the Portals Wide" (Chopin), **Retro. Supp. II:** 71

I Ought to Be in Pictures (Simon), **Supp. IV Part 2:** 584

Iphigenia (Notley), **Supp. XXII:** 226, 235

Iphigenia in Tauris (Euripedes), **Supp. XV:** 42, 50

I Promessi Sposi (Manzoni), **II:** 291

"I Put My Hand on My Son's Head" (Kooser), **Supp. XIX:** 120

Iram, Dhát al-'Imád (Gibran), **Supp. XX:** **116**

"Iraq Drifting, July 2003" (Weigl), **Supp. XIX:** 288

"Irascibles, The" (Kees), **Supp. XV:** 145–146

Ireland: A Terrible Beauty (Uris), **Supp. XX:** 244, 245–246, 246, 254

I Remember (Brainard), **Supp. XXVII:** 17, 18, 26, 29

I Remember (collected edition, Brainard), **Supp. XXVII:** 19

"I Remember" (Sexton), **Supp. II Part 2:** 680

I Remember Christmas (Brainard), **Supp. XXVII:** 19

I Remember More (Brainard), **Supp. XXVII:** 19

"Irenicon" (Shapiro), **Supp. II Part 2:** 704

Irigaray, Luce, **Supp. XII:** 6

Iris (Jarman), **Supp. XVII:** 110, **116–117**

"Iris by Night" (Frost), **Retro. Supp. I:** 132

"Irises" (L.-Y. Lee), **Supp. XV:** 214–215

Irish in America, The (Coffey, ed.), **Supp. XIX:** 133

Irish Stories of Sarah Orne Jewett, The (Jewett), **Retro. Supp. II:** 142

Irish Triangle, An (Barnes), **Supp. III Part 1:** 34

"Iron Characters, The" (Nemerov), **III:** 279, 282

"Iron Hans" (Sexton), **Supp. II Part 2:** 691

Iron Heel, The (London), **II:** 466, 480

Iron John: A Book about Men (R. Bly), **Supp. IV Part 1:** 59, 67; **Supp. XVI:** 177

"Iron Table, The" (Jane Bowles), **Supp. IV Part 1:** 82–83

"Iron Throat, The" (Olsen), **Supp. XIII:** 292, 297, 299

Ironweed (W. Kennedy), **Supp. VII:** 132, 133, 134, 135, 142, 144, 145–147, 148, 150, 153

"Irony as Art: The Short Fiction of William Humphrey" (Tebeaux), **Supp. IX:** 109

"Irony Is Not Enough: Essay on My Life as Catherine Deneuve" (Carson), **Supp. XII: 112–113**

Irony of American History, The (Niebuhr), **III:** 292, 306–307, 308

"Irrational Element in Poetry, The" (Stevens), **Retro. Supp. I:** 298, 301

"Irrevocable Diameter, An" (Paley), **Supp. VI:** 231–232

Irvine, Lorna, **Supp. XIII:** 26

Irving, Ebenezer, **II:** 296

Irving, Sir Henry, **IV:** 350

Irving, John, **Supp. VI: 163–183; Supp. X:** 77, 85

Irving, John Treat, **II:** 296

Irving, Peter, **II:** 296, 297, 298, 299, 300, 303

Irving, Washington, **I:** 211, 335, 336, 339, 343; **II: 295–318,** 488, 495; **III:** 113; **IV:** 309; **Retro. Supp. I:** 246; **Supp. I Part 1:** 155, 157, 158, 317; **Supp. I Part 2:** 377, 487, 585; **Supp. II Part 1:** 335; **Supp. IV Part 1:** 380; **Supp. XVIII:** 12; **Supp. XXIII:** 178

Irving, William, **II:** 296

Irving, William, Jr., **II:** 296, 297, 298, 299, 303

Irwin, Mark, **Supp. XII:** 21, 22, 24, 29

Irwin, Robert, **Supp. XX: 120**

Irwin, William Henry, **Supp. II Part 1:** 192

Is 5 (Cummings), **I:** 429, 430, 434, 435, 440, 445, 446, 447

"Isaac and Abraham" (Brodsky), **Supp. VIII:** 21

"Isaac and Archibald" (Robinson), **III:** 511, 521, 523

Isaacs, Neil D., **Supp. XIX:** 255

"Isabelle" (Saunders), **Supp. XIX:** 225

"Isabel Sparrow" (Oliver), **Supp. VII:** 232

Isaiah (biblical book), **Supp. I Part 1:** 236; **Supp. I Part 2:** 516; **Supp. XXI:** 107

"Isaiah Beethoven" (Masters), **Supp. I Part 2:** 461

I Sailed with Magellan (Dybek), **Supp. XXIII: 75–78,** 79

"I Saw in Louisiana a Live-Oak Growing" (Whitman), **I:** 220

"I Shall Be Released" (Dylan), **Supp. XV:** 349

"I Shall Live to Be Old" (Teasdale), **Supp. XXVII:** 296

I Shall Spit on Your Graves (film), **Supp. I Part 1:** 67

Isháq, Adib, **Supp. XX: 117**

Isherwood, Christopher, **II:** 586; **Supp. II Part 1:** 10, 11, 13; **Supp. IV Part 1:** 79, 82, 102; **Supp. XI:** 305; **Supp. XIV: 155–175; Supp. XVI:** 194

Isherwood Century, The (Berg and Freeman), **Supp. XIV:** 157, 159

Isherwood's Fiction (Schwerdt), **Supp. XIV:** 155

Ishiguro, Kazuo, **Supp. VIII:** 15

Ishi Means Man (Merton), **Supp. VIII:** 208

"Ishmael's Dream" (Stern), **Supp. IX:** 287

I Should Have Stayed Home (McCoy), **Supp. XIII:** 167, **168–170,** 171

"I Should Worry" (Kees), **Supp. XV:** 140

"I Sigh in the Afternoon" (Salinas), **Supp. XIII:** 318

"I Sing the Body Electric" (Whitman), **Retro. Supp. I:** 394, 395

"Isis: Dorothy Eady, 1924" (Doty), **Supp. XI:** 122

"Is It O.K. to Be a Luddite?" (Pynchon), **Supp. XVI:** 128

"Is It True?" (Hughes), **Supp. I Part 1:** 342

I: Six Nonlectures (Cummings), **I:** 430, 433, 434

"Island" (Hughes), **Supp. I Part 1:** 340

"Island Fever" (Vaz), **Supp. XXVI:** 261

Island Garden, An (Thaxter), **Retro. Supp. II:** 136; **Supp. XIII:** 152

Island Holiday, An (Henry), **I:** 515

Island in the Atlantic (W. Frank), **Supp. XX:** 79

Island in the Sun (film), **Supp. XXVI:** 134

"Island of the Fay, The" (Poe), **III:** 412, 417

Islands (Siddons), **Supp. XXII:** 239

"Islands, The" (Hayden), **Supp. II Part 1:** 373

"Island Sheaf, An" (Doty), **Supp. XI:** 136

Islands in the Stream (Hemingway), **II:** 258; **Retro. Supp. I:** 186

Isn't It Romantic (Wasserstein), **Supp. XV: 323–325,** 327

Is Objectivism a Religion? (Ellis), **Supp. IV Part 2:** 527

"Isolation of Modern Poetry, The" (Schwartz), **Supp. II Part 2:** 644

"Israel" (Reznikoff), **Supp. XIV:** 283

Israel Potter, or Fifty Years of Exile (Melville), **III:** 90; **Supp. XVIII:** 4

"Israfel" (Poe), **III:** 411

Is Sex Necessary? (Thurber and White), **Supp. I Part 2:** 607, 612, 614, 653

"Issues, The" (Olds), **Supp. X:** 205

"Istanbul" (Collins), **Supp. XXI:** 60

"I Stand Here Ironing" (Olsen), **Supp. XIII:** 292, 294, 296, 298, 300, 305

I Stole a Million (West), **IV:** 287

"Is Verse a Dying Technique?" (Wilson), **IV:** 431

It (Creeley), **Supp. IV Part 1:** 157, 158

IT (King), **Supp. V:** 139, 140, 141, 146–147, 151, 152

"It" (Olds), **Supp. X:** 208

It Ain't All for Nothin' (Myers), **Supp. XXVII:** 202–203

Italian American Reconciliation: A Folktale (Shanley), **Supp. XIV:** 315, **324–326,** 328, 330

Italian Backgrounds (Wharton), **Retro. Supp. I:** 370

Italian Hours (James), **I:** 12; **II:** 337; **Retro. Supp. I:** 235

Italian Journeys (Howells), **II:** 274

"Italian Morning" (Bogan), **Supp. III Part 1:** 58

Italian Villas and Their Gardens (Wharton), **IV:** 308; **Retro. Supp. I:** 361, 367

Italie, Hillel, **Supp. XV:** 128

It All Adds Up: From the Dim Past to the Uncertain Future (Bellow), **Retro. Supp. II:** 32

"It Always Breaks Out" (Ellison), **Retro. Supp. II:** 126; **Supp. II Part 1:** 248

Itard, Jean-Marc Gaspard, **Supp. I Part 2:** 564

"I taste a liquor never brewed" (Dickinson), **Retro. Supp. I:** 30, 37

It Came from Outer Space (film), **Supp. IV Part 1:** 102

It Can't Happen Here (Lewis), **II:** 454

It Chooses You (July), **Supp. XXIV:** 199, 209, 210

"It Don't Mean a Thing If It Ain't Got That Swing" (Matthews), **Supp. IX: 164–165**

I Tell You Now (Ortiz), **Supp. IV Part 2:** 500

"It Follows" (Stone), **Supp. XXVII:** 257

"It Goes Something Like This" (Gansworth), **Supp. XXVI:** 110

"Ithaca" (Glück), **Supp. V:** 89

It Happened One Night (Capra), **Supp. XV:** 197

It Has Come to Pass (Farrell), **II:** 26

"I think to live May be a Bliss" (Dickinson), **Retro. Supp. I:** 44

"I Thought It Was Harry" (Bronk), **Supp. XXI:** 31

I Thought of Daisy (Wilson), **IV:** 428, 434, 435

"It If Be Your Will" (Cohen), **Supp. XXVII:** 60

"Itinerary of an Obsession" (Kumin), **Supp. IV Part 2:** 450

"It Is a Strange Country" (Ellison), **Supp. II Part 1:** 238

"It Is Dangerous to Read Newspapers" (Atwood), **Supp. XIII:** 33

"It Must Be Abstract" (Stevens), **IV:** 95; **Retro. Supp. I:** 307

"It Must Change" (Stevens), **Retro. Supp. I:** 300, 307, 308

"It Must Give Pleasure" (Stevens), **Retro. Supp. I:** 307, 308, 309

"'It Out-Herods Herod. Pray You, Avoid It'" (Hecht), **Supp. X:** 62, 64

"It's All Over Now, Baby Blue" (song, Dylan), **Supp. XVIII:** 30

It's Loaded, Mr. Bauer (Marquand), **III:** 59

It's Nation Time (Baraka), **Supp. II Part 1:** 52, 53

"It's Nation Time" (Baraka), **Supp. II Part 1:** 53

It's Only a Play (McNally), **Supp. XIII:** 198

"It's Tartt—But Is It Art?" *(Vanity Fair),* **Supp. XXVII:** 277

It Was (Zukofsky), **Supp. III Part 2:** 630

"It Was Romance" (July), **Supp. XXIV:** 202–203

It Was the Nightingale (Ford), **III:** 470–471

"It Was When" (Snyder), **Supp. VIII:** 300

Ivanhoe (Scott), **I:** 216; **Supp. I Part 2:** 410

Ivens, Bryna, **Supp. XV:** 311, 312

Ivens, Joris, **I:** 488; **Retro. Supp. I:** 184

"Iverson Boy, The" (Simpson), **Supp. IX:** 280

"Ives" (Rukeyser), **Supp. VI:** 273, 283

Ives, George H., **Supp. I Part 1:** 153

I've Seen the Promised Land (Myers), **Supp. XXVII:** 209

Ivory Grin, The (Macdonald), **Supp. IV Part 2:** 471, 472

"Ivory Novel, The" (Halliday), **Supp. XIX:** 90

Ivory Tower, The (James), **II:** 337–338

"Ivory Tower, The: Louis Untermeyer as Critic" (Aiken), **Supp. XV:** 298

Ivry, Sara, **Supp. XX:** 179

"Ivy Winding" (Ammons), **Supp. VII:** 33

Iwamatsu, Mako, **Supp. XXI:** 150

"I Wandered Lonely as a Cloud" (Wordsworth), **Retro. Supp. I:** 121–122; **Supp. X:** 73; **Supp. XIV:** 184

"I want, I want" (Plath), **Retro. Supp. II:** 246

"I Wanted to Be There When My Father Died" (Olds), **Supp. X:** 210

"I Want to Be a Father Like the Men" (Cisneros), **Supp. VII:** 71

"I Want to Be Miss America" (Alvarez), **Supp. VII:** 18

"I Want to Know Why" (Anderson), **I:** 114, 115, 116; **II:** 263

"I Want You Women Up North To Know" (Olsen), **Supp. XIII:** 292, 297

"I Was Born in Lucerne" (Levine), **Supp. V:** 181, 189

"I Was Marching"(Le Sueur), **Supp. XXIII:** 167

"I Was Really Very Hungry" (M. F. K. Fisher), **Supp. XVII:** 91

"I Went into the Maverick Bar" (Snyder), **Supp. VIII:** 301

"I Will Lie Down" (Swenson), **Supp. IV Part 2:** 640

I Will Say Beauty (C. Frost), **Supp. XV:** 96, **105–107**

I Wonder As I Wander (Hughes), **Retro. Supp. I:** 196, 203; **Supp. I Part 1:** 329, 332–333

I Would Have Saved Them If I Could (L. Michaels), **Supp. XVI:** 203, 205, **206–210**

"I Would Live in Your Love" (Teasdale), **Supp. XXVII:** 292

"Iya, the Camp-Eater" (Zitkala-Ša), **Supp. XXV:** 276

"Iyani: It goes this Way" (Gunn Allen), **Supp. IV Part 1:** 321

"I years had been from home" (Dickinson), **I:** 471

Iyer, Pico, **Supp. V:** 215

Izzo, David Garrett, **Supp. XIV:** 155, 156, 159, 160, 161, 163, 169, 171

J

Jab (Halliday), **Supp. XIX: 91–94**

"Jachid and Jechidah" (Singer), **IV:** 15

Jack and Jill (Alcott), **Supp. I Part 1:** 42

"Jack and the Beanstalk" (Hay), **Supp. XIV:** 124

"Jack in the Pot" (D. West), **Supp. XVIII:** 283

Jack Kelso (Masters), **Supp. I Part 2:** 456, 471–472

Jacklight (Erdrich), **Supp. IV Part 1:** 259, 270

Jack London, Hemingway, and the Constitution (Doctorow), **Supp. IV Part**

1: 220, 222, 224, 232, 235

Jackman, Harold, **Supp. XVIII:** 131

Jackpot (Caldwell), **I:** 304

"Jack Schmidt, Arts Administrator" (Keillor), **Supp. XVI:** 171

"Jack Schmidt on the Burning Sands" (Keillor), **Supp. XVI:** 171

Jackson, Amelia. *See* Holmes, Mrs. Oliver Wendell (Amelia Jackson)

Jackson, Andrew, **I:** 7, 20; **III:** 473; **IV:** 192, 248, 298, 334, 348; **Supp. I Part 2:** 456, 461, 473, 474, 493, 695

Jackson, Blyden, **Supp. I Part 1:** 337

Jackson, Charles, **Supp. I Part 1:** 303

Jackson, George, **Supp. I Part 1:** 66

Jackson, Helen Hunt, **I:** 459, 470; **Retro. Supp. I:** 26, 27, 30–31, 32, 33

Jackson, James, **Supp. I Part 1:** 302, 303

Jackson, J. O., **III:** 213

Jackson, Joe, **Supp. I Part 2:** 441

Jackson, Katherine Gauss, **Supp. VIII:** 124

Jackson, Lawrence, **Retro. Supp. II:** 113, 115

Jackson, Lawrence P., **Supp. XXII:** 140

Jackson, Melanie, **Supp. X:** 166

Jackson, Michael, **Supp. VIII:** 146

Jackson, Richard, **II:** 119; **Supp. IX:** 165

Jackson, Shelley, **Supp. XVIII:** 136

Jackson, Shirley, **Supp. IX: 113–130**

Jackson, Thomas J. ("Stonewall"), **IV:** 125, 126

"Jackson Hotel" (Hull), **Supp. XXI:** 134, 135

Jackson Pollock (O'Hara), **Supp. XXIII:** 214–215

"Jackson Square" (Levertov), **Supp. III Part 1:** 276

Jackstraws (Simic), **Supp. VIII:** 280, 282–283

"Jackstraws" (Simic), **Supp. VIII: 283**

Jack Tier (Cooper), **I:** 354, 355

"Jacob" (Garrett), **Supp. VII:** 109–110

"Jacob" (Schwartz), **Supp. II Part 2:** 663

Jacob, Max, **Supp. XV:** 178, 182

"Jacob and the Indians" (Benét), **Supp. XI:** 47–48

"Jacob Bayer and the Telephone" (Helprin), **Supp. XXV:** 81

Jacobs, Catherine Haydon, **Supp. XXI:** 98

Jacobs, Harriet, **Supp. XVI:** 85

Jacobs, Jill Suzanne, **Supp. XX: 178, 186**

Jacobs, Rita D., **Supp. XII:** 339

Jacobsen, Josephine, **Supp. XIII:** 346; **Supp. XIV:** 260

"Jacob's Ladder" (Rawlings), **Supp. X:** 224, 228

Jacob's Ladder, The (Levertov), **Supp. III Part 1:** 272, 276–278, 281

"Jacob's Ladder, The" (Levertov), **Supp. III Part 1:** 278

Jacobson, Dale, **Supp. X:** 112

Jacobson, Kristin, **Supp. XVIII:** 113

Jacobson, Leslie, **Supp. XV:** 323

Jacoby, Russell, **Supp. IV Part 2:** 692

"Jacquerie, The" (Lanier), **Supp. I Part 1:** 355, 356, 360, 364, 370

Jacques le fataliste (D. Diderot), **Supp. XVII:** 145

Jade Mountain, The: A Chinese Anthology, Being Three Hundred Poems of the T'ang Dynasty (Bynner, trans.), **II:** 527; **Supp. XV:** 46, 47, 48

Jafsie and John Henry: Essays on Hollywood, Bad Boys, and Six Hours of Perfect Poker (Mamet), **Supp. XIV:** 252

Jaggi, Maya, **Supp. XXV:** 50, 56, 57

Jaguar Totem (LaBastille), **Supp. X:** 99, 106, **107–109**

Jailbird (Vonnegut), **Supp. II Part 2:** 760, 779–780

Jaimes, M. Annette, **Supp. IV Part 1:** 330, 331

Jain, Manju, **Retro. Supp. I:** 53, 58

"Jake Flower, The" (Major), **Supp. XXII:** 182

Jake's Women (Simon), **Supp. IV Part 2:** 576, 588

"Jakie's Mother" (Fante), **Supp. XI:** 164

Jakobson, Roman, **Supp. IV Part 1:** 155

Jamaica 1968 (Brainard), **Supp. XXVII:** 27

"Jamaica Kincaid's New York" (Kincaid), **Supp. VII:** 181

James, Alice, **I:** 454; **Retro. Supp. I:** 228, 235

James, A. Lloyd, **Supp. XIV:** 343

James, Caryn, **Supp. X:** 302, 303

James, C. L. R. (Cyril Lionel Robert), **Supp. XXI: 159–173**

James, Etta, **Supp. X:** 242

James, Henry, **I:** 4, 5, 9, 10, 12, 15, 16, 20, 52, 93, 109, 211, 226, 228, 244, 246, 251, 255, 258, 259, 336, 363, 374, 375, 379, 384, 409, 429, 436, 439, 452, 454, 459, 461–462, 463, 464, 485, 500, 504, 513, 514, 517–518, 571; **II:** 38, 58, 60, 73, 74, 95, 138, 140, 144, 147, 196, 198, 199, 228, 230, 234, 243, 259, 267, 271, 272, 275, 276, 278, 281, 282, 283, 284, 285, 286, 287, 288, 290, 306, 309, 316, **319–341,** 398, 404, 410, 415, 427, 444, 542, 544, 547–548, 556, 600; **III:** 44, 51, 136, 194–195, 199, 206, 208, 218, 228–229, 237, 281, 319, 325, 326, 334, 409, 453, 454, 457, 460, 461, 464, 511, 522, 576, 607; **IV:** 8, 27, 34, 37, 40, 53, 58, 73, 74, 134, 168, 172, 182, 198, 202, 285, 308, 309, 310, 311, 314, 316, 317, 318, 319, 321, 322, 323, 324, 328, 347, 352, 359, 433, 439, 476; **Retro. Supp. I:** 1, 8, 53, 56, 59, 108, 112, **215–242,** 272, 283, 284, 362, 366, 367, 368, 371, 373, 374, 375, 376, 377, 378, 379; **Retro. Supp. II:** 93, 135, 136, 203, 223; **Supp. I Part 1:** 35, 38, 43; **Supp. I Part 2:** 414, 454, 608, 609, 612–613, 618, 620, 646; **Supp. II Part 1:** 94–95; **Supp. III Part 1:** 14, 200; **Supp. III Part 2:** 410, 412; **Supp. IV Part 1:** 31, 35, 80, 127, 197, 349, 353; **Supp. IV Part 2:** 613, 677, 678, 682, 689, 693; **Supp. IX:** 121; **Supp. V:** 97, 101, 103, 258, 261, 263, 313; **Supp. VIII:** 98, 102, 156, 166, 168; **Supp.**

XI: 153; **Supp. XIII:** 102; **Supp. XIV:** 40, 110, 112, 335, 336, 348, 349; **Supp. XV:** 41; **Supp. XVII:** 5, 47; **Supp. XVIII:** 160, 258; **Supp. XX:** **227, 228, 232, 233, 238, 240; Supp. XXI:** 225; **Supp. XXII:** 89; **Supp. XXIV:** 132, 224; **Supp. XXVI:** 141, 145; **Supp. XXVII:** 268

James, Henry (father), **II:** 7, 275, 321, 337, 342–344, 364; **IV:** 174; **Supp. I Part 1:** 300

James, Henry (nephew), **II:** 360

James, Horace, **Supp. XIV:** 57

James, P. D., **Supp. XIX:** 131

James, William, **I:** 104, 220, 224, 227, 228, 255, 454; **II:** 20, 27, 165, 166, 276, 321, 337, **342–366,** 411; **III:** 303, 309, 509, 599, 600, 605, 606, 612; **IV:** 26, 27, 28–29, 31, 32, 34, 36, 37, 43, 46, 291, 486; **Retro. Supp. I:** 57, 216, 227, 228, 235, 295, 300, 306; **Supp. I Part 1:** 3, 7, 11, 20; **Supp. XIV:** 40, 50, 197, 199, 212, 335; **Supp. XVII:** 97; **Supp. XXVII:** 33, 34

James, William (grandfather), **II:** 342

James Baldwin: The Legacy (Troupe, ed.), **Retro. Supp. II:** 15

James Baldwin—The Price of the Ticket (film), **Retro. Supp. II:** 2

James Dickey and the Politics of Canon (Suarez), **Supp. IV Part 1:** 175

"James Dickey on Yeats: An Interview" (Dickey), **Supp. IV Part 1:** 177

James Hogg: A Critical Study (Simpson), **Supp. IX:** 269, 276

"James Is a Girl" (Egan), **Supp. XIX:** 61

James Jones: A Friendship (Morris), **Supp. XI:** 234

James Jones: An American Literary Orientalist Master (Carter), **Supp. XI:** 220

"James Jones and Jack Kerouac: Novelists of Disjunction" (Stevenson), **Supp. XI:** 230

James Jones: Reveille to Taps (television documentary), **Supp. XI:** 234

Jameson, Anna Brownell, **Supp. XXIII:** 225, 226, 232, 235

Jameson, F. R., **Supp. IV Part 1:** 119

Jameson, Sir Leander Starr, **III:** 327

James Shore's Daughter (Benét), **Supp. XI:** 48

"James Thurber" (Pollard), **Supp. I Part 2:** 468

"James Whitcomb Riley (From a Westerner's Point of View)" (Dunbar), **Supp. II Part 1:** 198

Jammes, Francis, **II:** 528; **Retro. Supp. I:** 55

"Jan, the Son of Thomas" (Sandburg), **III:** 593–594

Jan. 31 (Goldbarth), **Supp. XII:** 177, **178–179,** 180

"Jane Awake"(O'Hara), **Supp. XXIII:** 210

Janeczko, Paul, **Supp. XIII:** 280

Jane Eyre (Brontë), **Supp. XVI:** 158; **Supp. XXII:** 120

Janet, Pierre, **I:** 248, 249, 252; **Retro. Supp. I:** 55, 57

Jane Talbot: A Novel (Brown), **Supp. I Part 1:** 145–146

"Janet Waking" (Ransom), **III:** 490, 491

"Janice" (Jackson), **Supp. IX:** 117

Janowitz, Tama, **Supp. X:** 7; **Supp. XXVII:** 68, 269

Jantz, Harold S., **Supp. I Part 1:** 112

"January" (Barthelme), **Supp. IV Part 1:** 54

"January" (W. V. Davis), **Supp. XXI:** 89, 90

January Man, The (screenplay, Shanley), **Supp. XIV:** 316

"January Thaw" (Leopold), **Supp. XIV:** 183–184

"Janus" (Beattie), **Supp. V:** 31

Janzen, Jean, **Supp. V:** 180

"Japan" (Collins), **Supp. XXI:** 56

Japanese Americans: The Formation and Transformations of an Ethnic Group (Spickard), **Supp. XXI:** 149

"Japanese Beetles" (X. J. Kennedy), **Supp. XV:** 161, 165

Japanese by Spring (Reed), **Supp. X:** 241, **253–255**

Japanese Cooking: A Simple Art (Tsuji), **Supp. XVII:** 90

"Japan's Young Dreams" (Geisel), **Supp. XVI:** 102

Jara, Victor, **Supp. IV Part 2:** 549

Jarecki, Dave, **Supp. XXIII:** 239

Jarecki, Nicholas, **Supp. XXVII:** 68

Jarman, Mark, **Supp. IV Part 1:** 68; **Supp. IX:** 266, 270, 276; **Supp. XII:** 209; **Supp. XV:** 251; **Supp. XVIII:** 178; **Supp. XXV:** 221–222

Jarmon, Mark, **Supp. XVII: 109–122**

Jarrell, Randall, **I:** 167, 169, 173, 180; **II: 367–390,** 539–540; **III:** 134, 194, 213, 268, 527; **IV:** 352, 411, 422; **Retro. Supp. I:** 52, 121, 135, 140; **Retro. Supp. II:** 44, 177, 178, 182; **Supp. I Part 1:** 89; **Supp. I Part 2:** 552; **Supp. II Part 1:** 109, 135; **Supp. III Part 1:** 64; **Supp. III Part 2:** 541, 550; **Supp. IV Part 2:** 440; **Supp. IX:** 94, 268; **Supp. V:** 315, 318, 323; **Supp. VIII:** 31, 100, 271; **Supp. XI:** 311, 315; **Supp. XII:** 121, 260, 297; **Supp. XV:** 93, 153; **Supp. XVII:** 111; **Supp. XXVI:** 67

Jarrell, Mrs. Randall (Mary von Schrader), **II:** 368, 385

Jarry, Alfred, **Retro. Supp. II:** 326; **Supp. XV:** 177–178, 182, 188

Jarvis, John Wesley, **Supp. I Part 2:** 501, 520

Jaskoski, Helen, **Supp. IV Part 1:** 325; **Supp. XXII:** 166

"Jasmine" (Komunyakaa), **Supp. XIII:** 132

"Jason" (Hecht), **Supp. X:** 62

"Jason" (MacLeish), **III:** 4

Jason and Medeia (Gardner), **Supp. VI:** 63, **68–69**

"Jasper Notes" (G. Jones), **Supp. XXIV:** 194

Jaspers, Karl, **III:** 292; **IV:** 491

Jauss, David, **Supp. XXI:** 129, 132, 133, 134, 139

Jay, William, **I:** 338

Jayber Crow (Berry), **Supp. X:** 28, 34

"Jaz Fantasia" (Sandburg), **III:** 585

Jazz (Myers), **Supp. XXVII:** 211

"Jazz Age Clerk, A" (Farrell), **II:** 45

Jazz Country: Ralph Ellison in America (Porter), **Retro. Supp. II:** 127

"Jazzonia" (Hughes), **Supp. I Part 1:** 324

Jazz Poetry Anthology, The (Komunyakaa and Feinstein, eds.), **Supp. XIII:** 125

"Jazztet Muted" (Hughes), **Supp. I Part 1:** 342

J. B.: A Play in Verse (MacLeish), **II:** 163, 228; **III:** 3, 21–22, 23; **Supp. IV Part 2:** 586

"Jealous" (Ford), **Supp. V:** 71

Jealous Gods, The (Atherton), **Supp. XXIV:** 26

Jealousies, The: A Faery Tale, by Lucy Vaughan Lloyd of China Walk, Lambeth (Keats), **Supp. XII:** 113

Jean-Christophe (Rolland), **Supp. XX:** 70

"Jean Harlow's Wedding Night" (Wasserstein), **Supp. XV:** 328

Jean Huguenot (Benét), **Supp. XI:** 44

"Jeff Briggs's Love Story" (Harte), **Supp. II Part 1:** 355

Jeffers, Robinson, **I:** 66; **III:** 134; **Retro. Supp. I:** 202; **Supp. II Part 2: 413–440; Supp. IX:** 77; **Supp. VIII:** 33, 292; **Supp. X:** 112; **Supp. XI:** 312; **Supp. XV:** 113, 114, 115; **Supp. XVII:** 111, 112, 117; **Supp. XXI:** 87; **Supp. XXIII:** 145

Jeffers, Una Call Kuster (Mrs. Robinson Jeffers), **Supp. II Part 2:** 414

Jefferson, Blind Lemon, **Supp. VIII:** 349

Jefferson, Margo, **Supp. XX: 87; Supp. XXIV:** 271

Jefferson, Thomas, **I:** 1, 2, 5, 6–8, 14, 485; **II:** 5, 6, 34, 217, 300, 301, 437; **III:** 3, 17, 18, 294–295, 306, 310, 473, 608; **IV:** 133, 243, 249, 334, 348; **Supp. I Part 1:** 146, 152, 153, 229, 230, 234, 235; **Supp. I Part 2:** 389, 399, 456, 474, 475, 482, 507, 509, 510, 511, 516, 518–519, 520, 522; **Supp. X:** 26; **Supp. XIV:** 191; **Supp. XX: 285; Supp. XXIV:** 85, 281

Jefferson and/or Mussolini (Pound), **Retro. Supp. I:** 292

"Jefferson Davis as a Representative American" (Du Bois), **Supp. II Part 1:** 161

J-E-L-L-O (Baraka), **Supp. II Part 1:** 47

"Jelly-Bean, The" (Fitzgerald), **II:** 88

"Jellyfish, A" (Moore), **III:** 215

Jemie, Onwuchekwa, **Supp. I Part 1:** 343

Jenkins, Jerry B., **Supp. XXVII:** 5

Jenkins, J. L., **I:** 456

Jenkins, Joe, **Supp. XX: 117, 120, 122**

Jenkins, Kathleen, **III:** 403

Jenkins, Susan, **IV:** 123

Jenks, Deneen, **Supp. IV Part 2:** 550, 554

Jenks, Tom, **Supp. XIX:** 51

Jenkyns, Richard, **Supp. XXV:** 223

Jennie Gerhardt (Dreiser), **I:** 497, 499, 500, 501, 504–505, 506, 507, 519;

Retro. Supp. II: 94, **99–101**

"Jennie M'Grew" (Masters), **Supp. I Part 2:** 468

Jennifer Lorn (Wylie), **Supp. I Part 2:** 709, 714–717, 718, 721, 724

Jennison, Peter S., **Supp. XIX:** 268

"Jenny Garrow's Lover" (Jewett), **II:** 397

"Jerboa, The" (Moore), **III:** 203, 207, 209, 211–212

Jeremiah, **Supp. X:** 35

Jeremy's Version (Purdy), **Supp. VII:** 274

"Je Reviens"(Dybek), **Supp. XXIII:** 78

"Jericho" (R. Lowell), **II:** 536

Jerome, Judson, **Supp. XXIII:** 54

"Jerry's Garage" (Budbill), **Supp. XIX:** 7

"Jersey City Gendarmerie, Je T'aime" (Lardner), **II:** 433

Jersey Rain (Pinsky), **Supp. VI:** 235, **247–250**

"Jerusalem" (Nye), **Supp. XIII:** 287

Jerusalem: Song of Songs (Uris), **Supp. XX:** 244–245, 246, 255

Jerusalem the Golden (Reznikoff), **Supp. XIV:** 280, 285, 286

"Jessie and Jesus" (Andrews), **Supp. XXVI:** 11

Jessie and Jesus and Cousin Claire (Andrews), **Supp. XXVI:** 2, 10, 11–12

Jessup, Richard, **Supp. XI:** 306

"Je Suis Perdu" (Taylor), Supp. V: 314, 321–322

Jesuits in North America in the Seventeenth Century, The (Parkman), **Supp. II Part 2:** 597, 603–605

Jesus, **I:** 27, 34, 68, 89, 136, 552, 560; **II:** 1, 16, 197, 198, 214, 215, 216, 218, 219, 239, 373, 377, 379, 537, 538, 539, 549, 569, 585, 591, 592; **III:** 39, 173, 179, 270, 291, 296–297, 300, 303, 305, 307, 311, 339, 340, 341, 342, 344, 345, 346, 347, 348, 352, 353, 354, 355, 436, 451, 489, 534, 564, 566, 567, 582; **IV:** 51, 69, 86, 107, 109, 117, 137, 138, 141, 144, 147, 149, 150, 151, 152, 155, 156, 157, 158, 159, 163, 164, 232, 241, 289, 293, 294, 296, 331, 364, 392, 396, 418, 430; **Supp. I Part 1:** 2, 54, 104, 107, 108, 109, 121, 267, 371; **Supp. I Part 2:** 379, 386, 458, 515, 580, 582, 583, 587, 588, 683; **Supp. V:** 280

Jesus, the Son of Man (Gibran), **Supp. XX:** **115–116,** 117, **122–123**

"Jesus Asleep" (Sexton), **Supp. II Part 2:** 693

"Jesus of Nazareth, Then and Now" (Price), **Supp. VI:** 268

"Jesus Papers, The" (Sexton), **Supp. II Part 2:** 693

"Jesus Raises Up the Harlot" (Sexton), **Supp. II Part 2:** 693

"Jesus Shaves" (Davison), **Supp. XXVI:** 74

"Jesus Stories, The" (Brockmeier), **Supp. XXII:** 52

Jetée, La (film), **Supp. IV Part 2:** 436

"Jeune Parque, La" (Valéry), **IV:** 92

"Jew as Writer/The Writer as Jew, The: Reflections on Literature and Identity"

(Apple), **Supp. XVII:** 1, 9

"Jewbird, The" (Malamud), **Supp. I Part 2:** 435

"Jewboy, The" (P. Roth), **Supp. III Part 2:** 412

"Jewels" (Teasdale), **Supp. XXVII:** 290, 291

Jewett, Caroline, **II:** 396

Jewett, Katharine, **Retro. Supp. II:** 46

Jewett, Mary, **II:** 396, 403

Jewett, Rutger, **Retro. Supp. I:** 381

Jewett, Sarah Orne, **I:** 313; **II: 391–414; Retro. Supp. I:** 6, 7, 19; **Retro. Supp. II:** 51, 52, **131–151,** 156; **Supp. I Part 2:** 495; **Supp. IX:** 79; **Supp. VIII:** 126; **Supp. XIII:** 153; **Supp. XXIII:** 275, 278

Jewett, Theodore Furber, **II:** 395

Jewett, Dr. Theodore Herman, **II:** 396–397, 402

"Jew for Export, The" (Mamet), **Supp. XIV:** 251–252

Jew in Love, A (Hecht), **Supp. XXVII:** 94

Jew in Our Day, The (W. Frank), **Supp. XX:** **79**

Jew in the American Novel, The (Fiedler), **Supp. XIII:** 106

"Jewish Graveyards, Italy" (Levine), **Supp. V:** 190

"Jewish Hunter, The" (Moore), **Supp. X:** 163, 165, **174**

Jewison, Norman, **Supp. XI:** 306; **Supp. XIV:** 316

"Jew of Persia, A" (Helprin), **Supp. XXV:** 80, 85

Jews of Shklov (Schneour), **IV:** 11

Jews without Money (Gold), **Supp. XIV:** 288–289

JFK (film), **Supp. XIV:** 48

Jig of Forslin, The: A Symphony (Aiken), **I:** 50, 51, 57, 62, 66

Jigonsaseh, **Supp. XXVI:** 81, 82, 83, 86

"Jig Tune: Not for Love" (McGrath), **Supp. X:** 116

"Jihad" (McClatchy), **Supp. XII:** 266

"Jilting of Granny Weatherall, The" (Porter), **III:** 434, 435, 438

Jim Crow's Last Stand (Hughes), **Retro. Supp. I:** 205

Jiménez, Juan Ramón, **Supp. XIII:** 315, 323

Jimmie Higgins (Sinclair), **Supp. V:** 288

"Jimmy Harlow" (X. J. Kennedy), **Supp. XV:** 170

Jimmy's Blues (Baldwin), **Retro. Supp. II:** 8, 9, 15

Jim's Book: A Collection of Poems and Short Stories (Merrill), **Supp. III Part 1:** 319

Jin, Ha, **Supp. XVIII: 89–104**

Jitney (Wilson), **Supp. VIII:** 330, 331, 351

Jitterbug Perfume (Robbins), **Supp. X:** 273, **274–276,** 279

Joachim, Harold, **Retro. Supp. I:** 58

Joan, Pope, **IV:** 165

Joanna and Ulysses (Sarton), **Supp. VIII: 254–255**

Joan of Arc, **IV:** 241; **Supp. I Part 1:** 286–288; **Supp. I Part 2:** 469

"Joan of Arc" (Cohen), **Supp. XXVII:** 59

Joans, Ted, **Supp. IV Part 1:** 169

Job (biblical book), **II:** 165, 166–167, 168; **III:** 21, 199, 512; **IV:** 13, 158; **Supp. I Part 1:** 125

Job, The (Burroughs and Odier), **Supp. III Part 1:** 97, 103

Job, The: An American Novel (Lewis), **II:** 441

"Job History" (Proulx), **Supp. VII:** 262

Jobim, Antonio Carlos, **Supp. IV Part 2:** 549

Jobim, Antônio Carlos, **Supp. XXI:** 100

"Job of the Plains, A" (Humphrey), **Supp. IX:** 101

Jocks, Christopher, **Supp. XXVI:** 97

"Jody Rolled the Bones" (Yates), **Supp. XI:** 335, 341

"Joe" (Alvarez), **Supp. VII:** 7–8

Joe (Brown), **Supp. XVIII:** 195

Joe (L. Brown), **Supp. XXI:** 41, **45–46,** 47

"Joe, the Vanishing American" (Swados), **Supp. XIX:** 258–259

Joe: A Memoir of Joe Brainard (Padgett), **Supp. XXVII:** 18

"Joe Hill" (Hayes), **Supp. XXVI:** 134

Joe Hill: A Biographical Novel (Stegner), **Supp. IV Part 2:** 599

Joe Jones (Lamott), **Supp. XX: 134–135**

"Joe Louis: The King as a Middle-Aged Man" (Talese), **Supp. XVII:** 202

"Joe Messenger Is Dreaming"(P. Benedict), **Supp. XXIII:** 47

"Joe's Jitters" (Bronk), **Supp. XXI:** 27

Joe Turner's Come and Gone (Wilson), **Supp. VIII:** 334, **337–342,** 345

Joe versus the Volcano (screenplay, Shanley), **Supp. XIV:** 316

"Joey Martiney" (Huncke), **Supp. XIV:** 149

Johannes in Eremo (Mather), **Supp. II Part 2:** 453

Johansen, Bruce E., **Supp. XXVI:** 98

John XXIII, Pope, **Supp. I Part 2:** 492

John (biblical book), **I:** 68; **Supp. XV:** 222, 224

"John" (Shields), **Supp. VII:** 310–311

John, Augustus, **Supp. XXII:** 157

John, Elton, **Supp. XXI:** 148

"John, John Chinaman" (Buck), **Supp. II Part 1:** 128

John, Orrick, **Supp. XXVI:** 134

John Addington Symonds: A Biographical Study (Brooks), **I:** 240, 241

John-a-Dreams: A Tale (J. Sturgis), **Supp. XX:** 233

"John Archer's Nose" (R. Fisher), **Supp. XIX:** 71–72, 78

John Barleycorn (London), **II:** 467, 481

John Brown (Du Bois), **Supp. II Part 1:** 171–172

"John Brown" (Emerson), **II:** 13

"John Brown" (Lindsay), **Supp. I Part 2:** 393

John Brown's Body (Benét), **II:** 177; **Supp. XI:** 45, 46, 47, **56–57**

John Brown: The Making of a Martyr (Warren), **IV:** 236

John Bull in America; or, The New Munchausen (Paulding), **I:** 344

"John Burke" (Olson), **Supp. II Part 2:** 579, 580

"John Burns of Gettysburg" (Harte), **Supp. II Part 1:** 343

"John Carter" (Agee), **I:** 27

John Chancellor Makes Me Cry (Siddons), **Supp. XXII:** 245

"John Coltrane: Where Does Art Come From?" (Baraka), **Supp. II Part 1:** 60

John Deth: A Metaphysical Legend and Other Poems (Aiken), **I:** 61

"John Endicott" (Longfellow), **II:** 505, 506; **Retro. Supp. II:** 165–166, 167

"John Evereldown" (Robinson), **III:** 524

John Fante Reader, The (Cooper, ed.), **Supp. XI:** 174

John Fante: Selected Letters, 1932–1981 (Cooney, ed.), **Supp. XI:** 170

"John Gardner: The Writer As Teacher" (Carver), **Supp. III Part 1:** 136, 146–147

John Gaunt (R. H. Davis), **Supp. XVI:** 89

John Jay Chapman and His Letters (Howe), **Supp. XIV:** 54

John Keats (A. Lowell), **II:** 530–531

John Kennedy Toole: The Omega Point (film, Sandord), **Supp. XXVI:** 240, 241, 243, 246, 253

"John Kinsella's Lament for Mrs. Mary Moore" (Yeats), **Supp. XVII:** 144

"John Lamar" (R. H. Davis), **Supp. XVI:** 89–90

John Lane, **Retro. Supp. I:** 59

"John L. Sullivan" (Lindsay), **Supp. I Part 2:** 394, 395

"John Marr" (Melville), **III:** 93

John Marr and Other Sailors (Melville), **III:** 93; **Retro. Supp. I:** 257

John Muir: A Reading Bibliography (Kimes and Kimes), **Supp. IX:** 178

Johnny Appleseed and Other Poems (Lindsay), **Supp. I Part 2:** 397

"Johnny Bear" (Steinbeck), **IV:** 67

Johnny Got His Gun (Trumbo), **Supp. XXI:** 45

"Johnny Mnemonic" (W. Gibson), **Supp. XVI:** 122, 123–125, 128, 131

"Johnny Panic and the Bible of Dreams" (Plath), **Retro. Supp. II:** 245

"Johnny Ray" (Ríos), **Supp. IV Part 2:** 543

Johnny Tremain (Forbes), **Supp. XIX:** 235

John of the Cross (Saint), **I:** 585; **Supp. IV Part 1:** 284; **Supp. XV:** 223; **Supp. XVII:** 112

John Paul Jones: A Sailor's Biography (Morison), **Supp. I Part 2:** 494–495

"John Redding Goes to Sea" (Hurston), **Supp. VI:** 150

Johns, George Sibley, **Retro. Supp. II:** 65

Johns, Jasper, **Supp. XXIII:** 217

Johns, Orrick, **Retro. Supp. II:** 71; **Supp. XXVII:** 285

John Sloan: A Painter's Life (Brooks), **I:** 254

"John Smith Liberator" (Bierce), **I:** 209

Johnson, Alexandra, **Supp. X:** 86

Johnson, Alvin, **I:** 236; **Supp. XV:** 304

Johnson, Ben, **Retro. Supp. I:** 56

Johnson, Buffie, **Supp. IV Part 1:** 94

Johnson, Caitlin, **Supp. XXIII:** 281

Johnson, Carol Siri, **Supp. XXIII:** 257, 258, 264, 269

Johnson, Charles, **Supp. I Part 1:** 325; **Supp. V:** 128; **Supp. VI: 185–201;** **Supp. X:** 239; **Supp. XIII:** 182; **Supp. XIX:** 160

Johnson, Charles S., **Supp. IX:** 309; **Supp. XXII:** 6, 7

Johnson, Claudia Durst, **Supp. VIII:** 126–127

Johnson, Clifton, **Supp. XXI:** 248, 250

Johnson, Denis, **Supp. XIX:** 209; **Supp. XXI:** 118, 131

Johnson, Diane, **Retro. Supp. I:** 196; **Supp. XIII:** 127

Johnson, Eastman, **IV:** 321

Johnson, Edward, **IV:** 157; **Supp. I Part 1:** 110, 115

Johnson, Fenton, **Supp. XI:** 129

Johnson, Georgia Douglas, **Supp. IV Part 1:** 164

Johnson, Helene, **Supp. XVIII:** 282; **Supp. XXVI: 163–176**

Johnson, James Weldon, **Retro. Supp. II:** 114; **Supp. I Part 1:** 324, 325; **Supp. II Part 1:** 33, 194, 200, 202–203, 206–207; **Supp. III Part 1:** 73; **Supp. IV Part 1:** 7, 11, 15, 16, 164, 165, 166, 169; **Supp. X:** 42, 136, **246;** **Supp. XIX:** 73; **Supp. XVIII:** 122, 127, 282

Johnson, Jeff, **Supp. XXV:** 98

Johnson, Joyce, **Supp. XIV:** 150

Johnson, Kent, **Supp. XV:** 347

Johnson, Lady Bird, **Supp. IV Part 1:** 22

Johnson, Lyndon B., **I:** 254; **II:** 553, 582; **Retro. Supp. II:** 27

Johnson, Marguerite. *See* Angelou, Maya

Johnson, Maurice, **Supp. XV:** 136, 137, 138

Johnson, Michael K., **Supp. XVIII:** 59, 64

Johnson, Mordecai, **Supp. XIV:** 202

Johnson, Nunnally, **Supp. IV Part 1:** 355

Johnson, Pamela Hansford, **IV:** 469

Johnson, Rafer, **Supp. I Part 1:** 271

Johnson, Reed, **Supp. IV Part 2:** 589

Johnson, Richard, **Supp. XIII:** 132

Johnson, Robert, **Supp. IV Part 1:** 146; **Supp. VIII:** 15, 134

Johnson, Robert K., **Supp. IV Part 2:** 573, 584

Johnson, Robert Underwood, **Supp. IX:** 182, 184, 185

Johnson, Samuel, **II:** 295; **III:** 491, 503; **IV:** 452; **Retro. Supp. I:** 56, 65; **Supp. I Part 1:** 33; **Supp. I Part 2:** 422, 498, 503, 523, 656; **Supp. IV Part 1:** 34, 124; **Supp. XI:** 209; **Supp. XII:** 159; **Supp. XIII:** 55, 347; **Supp. XVI:** 204; **Supp. XVII:** 1; **Supp. XXIV:** 152

Johnson, Samuel, Jr., **Supp. XXV:** 241, 250

Johnson, Sarah Anne, **Supp. XIX:** 49, 50, 52, 54, 55, 56, 58, 59, 60, 61; **Supp. XVIII:** 145

Johnson, Steve, **Supp. XVI:** 177

Johnson, Thomas H., **I:** 470–471; **IV:** 144, 158; **Retro. Supp. I:** 26, 28, 36, 39, 40, 41, 43

Johnson, Walter, **II:** 422

Johnson, Willard "Spud", **Supp. XV:** 42, 46

"Johnson Girls, The" (Bambara), **Supp. XI:** 7

Johnsrud, Harold, **II:** 562

Johnston, Basil, **Supp. IV Part 1:** 269

Johnston, Jill, **Supp. XXV:** 5

Johnston, Mary, **II:** 194

Johnston, Robert M., **Supp. I Part 1:** 369

"John Sutter" (Winters), **Supp. II Part 2:** 810

John's Wife (Coover), **Supp. V:** 51–52

John the Baptist, **I:** 389; **II:** 537, 591

John Wesley Harding (album, Dylan), **Supp. XVIII:** 27

Jolas, Eugène, **Retro. Supp. II:** 85, 328; **Supp. IV Part 1:** 80

Jolie Blon's Bounce (Burke), **Supp. XIV:** 26, 33–34

Jolly (Mamet), **Supp. XIV:** 240, 254

"Jolly Corner, The" (James), **I:** 571; **Retro. Supp. I:** 235

Jolly Plays for Holidays (Wells), **Supp. XXVI:** 275

"Jon" (Saunders), **Supp. XIX:** 232, 234

"Jonah" (R. Lowell), **II:** 536

Jonah's Gourd Vine (Hurston), **Supp. VI:** 149, 155

"Jonathan Edwards" (Holmes), **Supp. I Part 1:** 302, 315

"Jonathan Edwards in Western Massachusetts" (R. Lowell), **II:** 550

Jonathan Franzen at the End of Postmodernism (Burns), **Supp. XX: 85**

Jonathan Troy (Abbey), **Supp. XIII:** 4, 13

Jones, Anne, **Supp. X:** 8

Jones, Anne Goodwyn, **Supp. XXII:** 252

Jones, Carolyn M., **Supp. VIII:** 128; **Supp. XIX:** 160

Jones, Chuck, **Supp. XVI:** 102

Jones, David, **Supp. XVII:** 241

Jones, Dennis, **Supp. XXIII:** 228, 233

Jones, Derek Anson, **Supp. XVIII:** 38, 39

Jones, Edith Newbold. *See* Wharton, Edith

Jones, Edward P., **Supp. XXI:** 247; **Supp. XXII: 139–153**

Jones, E. Stanley, **III:** 297

Jones, Everett LeRoi. *See* Baraka, Imamu Amiri

Jones, Gayl, **Supp. XXIV: 183–197**

Jones, George Frederic, **IV:** 309

Jones, Grover, **Supp. XIII:** 166

Jones, Harry, **Supp. I Part 1:** 337

Jones, Harry L., **Supp. XXV:** 251

Jones, Howard Mumford, **I:** 353; **Supp. IV Part 2:** 606; **Supp. XIV:** 11; **Supp. XXVI:** 63

Jones, James, **III:** 40; **IV:** 98; **Supp. XI:** 213–237; **Supp. XIX:** 248, 252; **Supp. XX:** 248; **Supp. XXV:** 145

Jones, James Earl, **Supp. VIII:** 334; **Supp. XI:** 309

Jones, Jennifer, **Supp. IV Part 2:** 524

Jones, John Paul, **II:** 405–406; **Supp. I Part 2:** 479, 480, 494–495

Jones, Kirkland C., **Supp. XVIII:** 173, 174, 175; **Supp. XXII:** 9

Jones, LeRoi. *See* Baraka, Imamu Amiri

Jones, Louis B., **Supp. XVI:** 41

Jones, Loyal, **Supp. XX: 170**

Jones, Lucretia Stevens Rhinelander, **IV:** 309

Jones, Madison, **Retro. Supp. II:** 235; **Supp. X:** 1

Jones, Major (pseudonym). *See* Thompson, William T.

Jones, Malcolm, **Supp. V:** 219; **Supp. XX: 93, 138**

Jones, Mildred, **Supp. XVIII:** 281

Jones, Robert Edmond, **III:** 387, 391, 394, 399; **Supp. XXI:** 6, 12

Jones, Rodney, **Supp. XXVI:** 66

Jones, Sharon L., **Supp. XVIII:** 280, 285, 286

Jones, Tommy Lee, **Supp. V:** 227

"Jones's Private Argyment" (Lanier), **Supp. I Part 1:** 352

"Jones's *The Thin Red Line:* The End of Innocence" (Michel-Michot), **Supp. XI:** 224–225

Jong, Allan, **Supp. V:** 115

Jong, Erica, **Supp. V: 113–135**

Jong-Fast, Molly Miranda, **Supp. V:** 115

Jonson, Ben, **I:** 58, 358; **II:** 11, 16, 17, 18, 436, 556; **III:** 3, 463, 575–576; **IV:** 395, 453; **Retro. Supp. II:** 76; **Supp. I Part 2:** 423; **Supp. IV Part 2:** 585; **Supp. XX:** 197; **Supp. XXIV:** 159

Jonsson, Thorsten, **Retro. Supp. I:** 73

Joplin, Janis, **Supp. IV Part 1:** 206; **Supp. XI:** 239

Joplin, Scott, **Supp. IV Part 1:** 223

Jordan, A. Van, **Supp. XVIII:** 172

Jordan, Barbara, **Supp. VIII:** 63; **Supp. XI:** 249

Jordan, David, **Supp. XIX:** 141

Jordan, Denise, **Supp. XXVII:** 209

Jordan, June, **Supp. XII:** 217; **Supp. XXII:** 172; **Supp. XXIV:** 188

Jordan, Marie, **Supp. XV:** 224

Jo's Boys (Alcott), **Supp. I Part 1:** 32, 35, 40–41, 42

Joseph Heller (Ruderman), **Supp. IV Part 1:** 380

"Josephine Has Her Day" (Thurber), **Supp. I Part 2:** 606

Josephine Stories, The (Fitzgerald), **Retro. Supp. I:** 109

"Joseph Martinez" (Huncke), **Supp. XIV:** 149

"Joseph Pockets" (Stern), **Supp. IX:** 292

Josephson, Matthew, **I:** 259

"José's Country" (Winters), **Supp. II Part 2:** 789, 790

Joshi, S. T., **Supp. XXIV:** 23; **Supp. XXV:** 111, 118, 123; **Supp. XXVII:** 128

Josh Thurlow series (Hickam), **Supp. XXVII:** 111

Joshua (biblical book), **Supp. I Part 2:** 515

"Joshua Clark"(Kenny), **Supp. XXIII:** 154

Joslin, Katherine, **Retro. Supp. I:** 376

Journal (Emerson), **Supp. I Part 1:** 309

"Journal" (L. Michaels), **Supp. XVI:** 213

Journal (Thoreau), **IV:** 175

Journal (Woolman), **Supp. VIII:** 202

"Journal for My Daughter" (Kunitz), **Supp. III Part 1:** 268

"Journal of an Airman" (Auden), **Supp. XIX:** 151

Journal of Arthur Stirling, The (Sinclair), **Supp. V:** 280

"Journal of a Solitary Man, The" (Hawthorne), **II:** 226

Journal of a Solitude (Sarton), **Supp. VIII:** 256, 262–263

Journal of My Other Self (Rilke), **Retro. Supp. II:** 20

Journal of the Fictive Life (Nemerov), **III:** 267, 268, 269, 272, 273, 274, 280–281, 284–285, 286, 287

Journal of the Plague Year, A (Defoe), **III:** 423

"Journal of the Year of the Ox, A" (Wright), **Supp. V:** 343

Journals (Thoreau), **Supp. I Part 1:** 299

Journals and Other Documents on the Life and Voyages of Christopher Columbus (Morison, ed.), **Supp. I Part 2:** 494

Journals of Ralph Waldo Emerson, The (Emerson), **II:** 8, 17, 21

Journals of Susanna Moodie, The: Poems (Atwood), **Supp. XIII:** 33

"Journey, A" (Wharton), **Retro. Supp. I:** 364

"Journey, The" (Winters), **Supp. II Part 2:** 795

"Journey, The" (Wright), **Supp. III Part 2:** 605–606

"Journey, the Arrival and the Dream, The" (Gioia), **Supp. XV:** 120

"Journey, The: For Jane at Thirteen" (Kumin), **Supp. IV Part 2:** 442

Journey and Other Poems, The (Winters), **Supp. II Part 2:** 786, 794, 795, 796, 799, 800, 801

Journey Around My Room: The Autobiography of Louise Bogan—A Mosaic (Bogan), **Supp. III Part 1:** 47, 48, 52, 53

Journey Down, The (Bernstein), **IV:** 455

Journey Home, The (Abbey), **Supp. XIII:** 2, 12

"Journey into Speech, A" (Cliff), **Supp. XXII:** 69

Journeyman (Caldwell), **I:** 297, 302–304, 307, 309; **Supp. XXVI:** 134

Journeyman: Travels of a Writer (Findley), **Supp. XX: 50**

"Journey of an Eyeball, The" (Vaz), **Supp. XXVI:** 261

Journey of Tai-me, The (Momaday), **Supp. IV Part 2:** 485

"Journey of the Magi" (Eliot), **Retro. Supp. I:** 64

Journey to a War (Auden and Isherwood), **Supp. II Part 1:** 13; **Supp. XIV:** 156, 158, 162

Journey to Love (W. C. Williams), **IV:** 422; **Retro. Supp. I:** 429

Journey to My Father; Isaac Bashevis Singer (Zamir), **Retro. Supp. II:** 317

"Journey to Nine Miles" (Walker), **Supp. III Part 2:** 527

"Journey to the Interior" (W. J. Smith), **Supp. XIII:** 339, 340

Journey with Genius: Recollections and Reflections Concerning the D. H. Lawrences (Bynner), **Supp. XV:** 46

Jowett, Benjamin, **Supp. XIV:** 335

"Joy" (Moore), **Supp. X:** 174

"Joy" (Singer), **IV:** 9; **Retro. Supp. II:** 307

Joyce, Cynthia, **Supp. X:** 194, 195, 196

Joyce, James, **I:** 53, 105, 108, 130, 174, 256, 285, 377, 395, 475–476, 478, 480, 483, 576; **II:** 27, 42, 58, 73, 74, 198, 209, 264, 320, 569; **III:** 7, 16, 26–27, 45, 174, 181, 184, 261, 273, 277, 343, 396, 398, 465, 471, 474; **IV:** 32, 73, 85, 95, 103, 171, 182, 211, 286, 370, 412, 418, 419, 428, 434, 456; **Retro. Supp. I:** 59, 63, 75, 80, 89, 91, 108, 109, 127, 287, 290, 292, 334, 335, 420; **Retro. Supp. II:** 221, 326; **Supp. I Part 1:** 257, 262, 270; **Supp. I Part 2:** 437, 546, 613, 620; **Supp. II Part 1:** 136; **Supp. III Part 1:** 35, 36, 65, 225, 229; **Supp. III Part 2:** 611, 617, 618; **Supp. IV Part 1:** 40, 47, 80, 227, 300, 310; **Supp. IV Part 2:** 424, 677; **Supp. IX:** 211, 229, 235, 308; **Supp. V:** 261, 331; **Supp. VIII:** 14, 40, 103; **Supp. X:** 115, 137, 194, 324; **Supp. XI:** 66; **Supp. XII:** 139, 151, 165, 191, 289; **Supp. XIV:** 83; **Supp. XIX:** 151, 172; **Supp. XVI:** 41, 189, 282; **Supp. XVII:** 44; **Supp. XXI:** 7; **Supp. XXII:** 141, 143–144; **Supp. XXIII:** 162; **Supp. XXVI:** 17, 135

Joy Comes in the Morning (J. Rosen), **Supp. XVII:** 50

Joy in the Morning (B. Smith), **Supp. XXIII:** 257, 258, **269–270**

Joy Luck Club, The (Tan), **Supp. X:** 289, 291, 293, 294, 296, 297, 298, 299

"Joy of Sales Resistance, The" (Berry), **Supp. X:** 36

J R (Gaddis), **Supp. IV Part 1:** 279, 280, 285–289, 291, 294; **Supp. IV Part 2:** 484; **Supp. XXI:** 226

Juana Inés de la Cruz, Sor, **Supp. XXI:** 94, 104

Juan de la Cruz (John of the Cross), **Supp. XXI:** 99, 104

"Juan's Song" (Bogan), **Supp. III Part 1:** 50

Juba! (Myers), **Supp. XXVII:** 201, 202, 211

Juba to Jive: A Dictionary of African-American Slang (Major), **Supp. XXII:** 172, 180

Jubilate Agno (Smart), **Supp. IV Part 2:** 626

Judah, Hettie, **Supp. XIII:** 246

Judah the Pious (Prose), **Supp. XVI:** 249, 250, 262

"Judas Maccabaeus" (Longfellow), **II:** 506; **Retro. Supp. II:** 165, 167

Judd, Sylvester, **II:** 290; **Supp. I Part 2:** 420

Judd Rankin's Daughter (Glaspell), **Supp. III Part 1:** 186–188

Jude the Obscure (Hardy), **Supp. I Part 1:** 217

Judevine (Budbill), **Supp. XIX:** 4, **8–9,** 12

Judevine: A Play in Three Acts/Two Acts (Budbill), **Supp. XIX: 12–13**

Judge, Jane, **Supp. XXII:** 191

"Judgement Day" (O'Connor), **III:** 349, 350; **Retro. Supp. II:** 236

Judgment Day (Farrell), **II:** 29, 31, 32, 34, 39

"Judgment of Paris, The" (Merwin), **Supp. III Part 1:** 350

Judgment of Paris, The (Vidal), **Supp. IV Part 2:** 680, 682

"Judgment of the Sage, The" (Crane), **I:** 420

Judith (Farrell), **II:** 46, 48

"Judith" (Garrett), **Supp. VII:** 109–110

"Juggernaut" (Bass), **Supp. XVI:** 16–17

"Jug of Sirup, A" (Bierce), **I:** 206

"Jugurtha" (Longfellow), **II:** 499

"Juice or Gravy" (P. Roth), **Retro. Supp. II:** 279

"Juke Box Love Song" (Hughes), **Retro. Supp. I:** 209

"Julia" (Hellman), **Supp. I Part 1:** 280, 293

Julia France and Her Times (Atherton), **Supp. XXIV:** 24, 27

"Julia Miller" (Masters), **Supp. I Part 2:** 461

Julian (Vidal), **Supp. IV Part 2:** 677, 684–685, 685, 689

Julian, Norman, **Supp. XXVII:** 101

Julian the Apostate, **Retro. Supp. I:** 247

"Julian Vreden" (Bowles), **Supp. IV Part 1:** 94

Julie and Romeo (Ray), **Supp. XII:** 308, 310

Julien, Isaac, **Supp. XI:** 19

Julie; ou, La nouvelle Héloïse (Rousseau), **Supp. XVI:** 184

Julier, Laura, **Supp. IV Part 1:** 211

Julip (Harrison), **Supp. VIII: 51**

Julius Caesar (Shakespeare), **I:** 284; **Supp. XXVI:** 40

July, Miranda, **Supp. XXIV: 199–211**

"July Midnight" (A. Lowell), **II:** 521

"July 1949" (Rash), **Supp. XXVII:** 218

Jumbo (Hecht and MacArthur), **Supp. XXVII:** 90

Jumel, Madame, **Supp. I Part 2:** 461

Jumping Out of Bed (R. Bly), **Supp. IV Part 1:** 71

"Jump-Up Day" (Kingsolver), **Supp. VII:** 203

"Junctions" (Lamott), **Supp. XX: 143**

"June 1940" (Kees), **Supp. XV:** 141

"June Light" (Wilbur), **Supp. III Part 2:** 545

June Moon (Lardner and Kaufman), **II:** 427

"June Recital" (Welty), **IV:** 272–273

Juneteenth (Ellison), **Retro. Supp. II:** 119, 124, **126–128**

"Juneteenth" (Ellison), **Retro. Supp. II:** 119, 126; **Supp. II Part 1:** 248

"June the Third" (Gander), **Supp. XV:** 340

June-Tree: New and Selected Poems, 1974–2000 (Balakian), **Supp. XXIII:** 19, **24–25,** 32

Jung, Carl, **I:** 58, 135, 241, 248, 252, 402; **III:** 400, 534, 543; **Supp. I Part 2:** 439; **Supp. IV Part 1:** 68, 69; **Supp. VIII:** 45; **Supp. X:** 193; **Supp. XV:** 214; **Supp. XX: 63, 117**

Junger, Ernst, **Supp. III Part 1:** 63

Jungle, The (Sinclair), **III:** 580; **Supp. V:** 281–284, 285, 289

Jungle Lovers (Theroux), **Supp. VIII:** 314, 315, 316, **317**

"Junior Addict" (Hughes), **Supp. I Part 1:** 343

"Juniper" (Francis), **Supp. IX:** 79

"Junk" (Wilbur), **Supp. III Part 2:** 556

Junker, Howard, **Supp. XV:** 116

Junkie: Confessions of an Unredeemed Drug Addict (Burroughs), **Supp. III Part 1:** 92, 94–96, 101

Junky (Burroughs), **Supp. XIV:** 143

Juno and the Paycock (O'Casey), **Supp. IV Part 1:** 361

"Jupiter Doke, Brigadier General" (Bierce), **I:** 204

Jupiter Laughs (A. Cronin), **Supp. XVII:** 59

Jurgen (Cabell), **III:** 394; **IV:** 286; **Retro. Supp. I:** 80; **Supp. I Part 2:** 718

Jury of Her Peers, A: American Women Writers from Anne Bradstreet to Annie Proulx (Showalter), **Supp. XX: 274**

Jusserand, Jules, **II:** 338

Just above My Head (Baldwin), **Retro. Supp. II:** 14–15

"Just a Little One" (Parker), **Supp. IX:** 191

Just and the Unjust, The (Cozzens), **I:** 367–370, 372, 375, 377, 378, 379

Just an Ordinary Day (Jackson), **Supp. IX:** 120

Just Before Dark: Collected Nonfiction (Harrison), **Supp. VIII:** 41, 45, 46, 53

Just Before the Divorce (Hayes), **Supp. XXVI:** 144

"Just Before the War with the Eskimos" (Salinger), **III:** 559

"Just Boys" (Farrell), **II:** 45

"Just for the Thrill: An Essay on the Difference Between Women and Men" (Carson), **Supp. XII: 103–104**

"Justice" (Hughes), **Supp. I Part 1:** 331

"Justice, A" (Faulkner), **Retro. Supp. I:** 83

Justice, Donald, **Retro. Supp. I:** 313; **Supp. III Part 2:** 541; **Supp. V:** 180, 337, 338, 341; **Supp. VII: 115–130;** **Supp. XI:** 141, 315; **Supp. XIII:** 76, 312; **Supp. XV:** 74, 93, 118, 119, 134; **Supp. XVII:** 110, 120, 246; **Supp. XX: 199; Supp. XXIV:** 165

Justice and Expediency (Whitter), **Supp. I Part 2:** 686

"Justice Denied in Massachusetts" (Millay), **III:** 140

Justice for Salcido (Endore), **Supp. XVII:** 63

Justice of Gold in the Damnation of Sinners, The (Edwards), **I:** 559

"Justice to Feminism" (Ozick), **Supp. V:** 272

"Just Introduced" (Taggard), **Supp. XXII:** 274

Just Kids (Smith), **Supp. XXII:** 94

"Just Like a Woman" (Dylan), **Supp. XV:** 350

"Just Like Job" (Angelou), **Supp. IV Part 1:** 15

"Just One of the Boys" (Swados), **Supp. XIX:** 259

Just Whistle: A Valentine (Wright), **Supp. XV: 346–348**

Just Wild About Harry (H. Miller), **III:** 190

Just Write! Here's How (Myers), **Supp. XXVII:** 209–210

Juvenal, **II:** 8, 169, 552

K

K (Rinehart), **Supp. XXV:** 193–194, 200

"K, The" (Olson), **Supp. II Part 2:** 558, 563, 569

Kaaterskill Falls (Goodman), **Supp. XXVI:** 123–125

Kabir, **Supp. IV Part 1:** 74

"Kabnis" (Toomer), **Supp. III Part 2:** 481, 484; **Supp. IX:** 309, 310, **319–320**

Kachel, Elsie. *See* Stevens, Mrs. Wallace (Elsie Kachel)

"Kaddish" (Ginsberg), **Supp. II Part 1:** 319, 327

Kaddish and Other Poems, 1958–1960 (Ginsberg), **Supp. II Part 1:** 309, 319–320; **Supp. XIV:** 269

Kael, Pauline, **Supp. IX:** 253; **Supp. XV:** 147, 148

Kafka, Franz, **II:** 244, 565, 569; **III:** 51, 253, 418, 566, 572; **IV:** 2, 113, 218, 437–439, 442; **Retro. Supp. II:** 20, 221, 282; **Supp. I Part 1:** 197; **Supp. III Part 1:** 105; **Supp. III Part 2:** 413; **Supp. IV Part 1:** 379; **Supp. IV Part 2:** 623; **Supp. VIII:** 14, 15, 103; **Supp. XII:** 21, 37, 98, 168; **Supp. XIII:** 305; **Supp. XVI:** 17, 201, 206, 209; **Supp. XVII:** 244; **Supp. XX: 18, 21, 85, 87; Supp. XXII:** 89, 90, 94; **Supp. XXIII:** 68

Kafka Americana (Lethem and Scholtz), **Supp. XVIII:** 144–145

Kaganoff, Penny, **Supp. XI:** 122

Kagan's Superfecta (A. Hoffman), **Supp. XVII:** 42
Kahane, Jack, **III:** 171, 178
Kahn, Otto, **I:** 385; **IV:** 123; **Retro. Supp. II:** 81, 84, 85; **Supp. XX:** 75
Kahn, R. T., **Supp. XI:** 216
"Kai, Today" (Snyder), **Supp. VIII:** 300
Kaiser, Georg, **I:** 479
Kaiser, Henry, **Supp. I Part 2:** 644
Kakutani, Michiko, **Supp. IV Part 1:** 196, 201, 205, 211, 212; **Supp. V:** 63; **Supp. VIII:** 81, 84, 86, 88, 141; **Supp. X:** 171, 301, 302, 310, 314; **Supp. XI:** 38, 179; **Supp. XII:** 165, 171, 172, 299; **Supp. XIX:** 142; **Supp. XVI:** 71; **Supp. XVII:** 6; **Supp. XX: 92, 94; Supp. XXII:** 109; **Supp. XXVI:** 246; **Supp. XXVII:** 274
Kalem, T. E., **Supp. IV Part 2:** 585
Kalevala (Finnish epic), **II:** 503, 504; **Retro. Supp. II:** 155
Kalevala (Lönnrot), **Retro. Supp. II:** 159, 160
Kalfus, Ken, **Supp. XVII:** 50
Kalki: A Novel (Vidal), **Supp. IV Part 2:** 677, 682, 685, 691, 692
Kallan, Richard A., **Supp. XX: 244**
Kallen, Horace, **I:** 229; **Supp. I Part 2:** 643; **Supp. XIV:** 195, 197, 198
Kallman, Chester, **II:** 586; **Supp. II Part 1:** 15, 17, 24, 26
"Kallundborg Church" (Whittier), **Supp. I Part 2:** 696
Kalstone, David, **Retro. Supp. II:** 40
Kamel, Rose, **Supp. XIII:** 306
Kamenev, Lev, **Supp. XXI:** 167
Kamera Obskura (Nabokov), **III:** 255
Kamhi, Michelle Moarder, **Supp. IV Part 2:** 529, 530
Kaminsky, Wally, **Supp. XVIII:** 72
Kamp, David, **Supp. XVIII:** 150
Kandy-Kolored Tangerine-Flake Streamline Baby, The (Wolfe), **Supp. III Part 2:** 569, 573–576, 580, 581
Kane, Daniel, **Supp. XXIV:** 37
Kane, Julie, **Supp. XVII:** 78
Kane, Lesley, **Supp. XIV:** 250
Kanellos, Nicolás, **Supp. VIII:** 82; **Supp. XIII:** 213
Kanin, Garson, **Supp. IV Part 2:** 574
"Kansas City Coyote" (Harjo), **Supp. XII:** 219, 222
"Kansas Emigrants, The" (Whittier), **Supp. I Part 2:** 687
Kant, Immanuel, **I:** 61, 277, 278; **II:** 10–11, 362, 480, 580–581, 582, 583; **III:** 300, 480, 481, 488, 612; **IV:** 90; **Supp. I Part 2:** 640; **Supp. IV Part 2:** 527; **Supp. XIV:** 198, 199; **Supp. XVI:** 184
Kanter, Hal, **IV:** 383
Kapital, Das (Marx), **III:** 580; **Supp. XXI:** 161, 162, 163
Kaplan, Abraham, **I:** 277
Kaplan, Justin, **I:** 247–248; **Retro. Supp. I:** 392
Kaplan, Mary Jo, **Supp. XIX:** 266
Kaplan, Steven, **Supp. V:** 238, 241, 243, 248
Karate Is a Thing of the Spirit (Crews), **Supp. XI: 112–113**

Karbo, Karen, **Supp. X:** 259, 262
"Karintha" (Toomer), **Supp. IX:** 311
Karl, Frederick R., **Supp. IV Part 1:** 384; **Supp. XXI:** 234
Karloff, Boris, **Supp. XXVII:** 119
"Karloff and the Rock" (Di Piero), **Supp. XIX:** 44
Karl Shapiro's America (film), **Supp. II Part 2:** 703
Karmi, T., **Supp. XV:** 78, 88
Karr, Mary, **Supp. XI: 239–256; Supp. XIII:** 285; **Supp. XV:** 223; **Supp. XVI:** 63, 70, 77; **Supp. XVII:** 242
Karsner, David, **Supp. XXVII:** 83
Karyotakis, Konstantine, **Supp. XXIII:** 125
Kasabian, Linda, **Supp. IV Part 1:** 206
Kasper, Catherine, **Supp. XVI:** 294–295
Kate Chopin (Toth), **Retro. Supp. II:** 71
Kate Chopin: A Critical Biography (Seyersted), **Retro. Supp. II:** 65; **Supp. I Part 1:** 225
Kate Chopin and Edith Wharton: An Annotated Bibliographical Guide to Secondary Sources (Springer), **Supp. I Part 1:** 225
Kate Chopin and Her Creole Stories (Rankin), **Retro. Supp. II:** 57; **Supp. I Part 1:** 200, 225
"Kate Chopin's *The Awakening* in the Perspective of Her Literary Career" (Arms), **Supp. I Part 1:** 225
Kate Vaiden (Price), **Supp. VI:** 264, 265
"Käthe Kollwitz" (Rukeyser), **Supp. VI:** 283, 284
Katherine and Jean (Rice), **Supp. VII:** 288
"Kathleen" (Whittier), **Supp. I Part 2:** 693
Kathleen and Frank: The Autobiography of a Family (Isherwood), **Supp. XIV:** 158, 171
Kathy Goes to Haiti (Acker), **Supp. XII:** 5
Katz, Alan, **Supp. XXII:** 177
Katz, Alex, **Supp. XV:** 185; **Supp. XXVII:** 21, 22
Katz, Jonathan, **Supp. XII:** 179
Katz, Steve, **Supp. V:** 44
Katz, Steven T., **Supp. XVI:** 154
Katzenberg, Jffrey, **Supp. XXI:** 154
Kauffman, Carol, **Supp. XI:** 295
Kauffmann, Stanley, **III:** 452; **Supp. I Part 2:** 391; **Supp. XVI:** 74
Kaufman, Boris, **Supp. XVIII:** 251
Kaufman, Charlie, **Supp. XV:** 16
Kaufman, Ellen, **Supp. XXIII:** 132, 133
Kaufman, George S., **II:** 427, 435, 437; **III:** 62, 71–72, 394; **Retro. Supp. II:** 327; **Supp. IV Part 2:** 574; **Supp. IX:** 190; **Supp. XV:** 329
Kaufmann, James, **Supp. XI:** 39
Kaufmann, Walter, **Supp. XVII:** 137
Kauvar, Elaine M., **Supp. V:** 273
Kavanaugh (Longfellow), **I:** 458; **II:** 489, 491; **Retro. Supp. II:** 156; **Supp. I Part 2:** 420
Kaveney, Roz, **Supp. XI:** 39
Kawabata, Yasunari, **Supp. XV:** 186; **Supp. XXI:** 146

Kay, Terry, **Supp. XXVII:** 104
Kay Boyle: Artist and Activist (Spanier), **Supp. XXIV:** 64
Kay Boyle: Author of Herself (Mellen), **Supp. XXIV:** 64
Kay Boyle for the Twenty-First Century (Austenfeld, ed.), **Supp. XXIV:** 64
Kaye-Smith, Sheila, **Supp. XVIII:** 130–131
Kazan, Elia, **III:** 153, 163; **IV:** 383; **Supp. I Part 1:** 66, 295; **Supp. XVI:** 193; **Supp. XVIII:** 250–251, 252; **Supp. XXV:** 95, 102
Kazin, Alfred, **I:** 248, 417, 419, 517; **II:** 177, 459; **IV:** 236; **Retro. Supp. II:** 206, 243, 246, 286; **Supp. I Part 1:** 195, 196, 294, 295, 296; **Supp. I Part 2:** 536, 631, 647, 650, 678, 679, 719; **Supp. II Part 1:** 143; **Supp. IV Part 1:** 200, 382; **Supp. IX:** 3, 227; **Supp. V:** 122; **Supp. VIII: 93–111; Supp. XIII:** 98, 106; **Supp. XIV:** 11; **Supp. XV:** 142; **Supp. XXIII:** 2, 106; **Supp. XXIV:** 222; **Supp. XXVII:** 134
Keach, Stacey, **Supp. XI:** 309
Kean, Danuta, **Supp. XXI:** 80
Keane, Sarah, **Supp. I Part 1:** 100
Kearns, Cleo McNelly, **Retro. Supp. I:** 57
Kearns, George, **Retro. Supp. I:** 292
Keating, AnnLouise, **Supp. IV Part 1:** 330
Keaton, Buster, **I:** 31; **Supp. I Part 2:** 607; **Supp. IV Part 2:** 574
Keaton, Diane, **Supp. XV:** 5
Keats, John, **I:** 34, 103, 284, 314, 317–318, 385, 401, 448; **II:** 82, 88, 97, 214, 368, 512, 516, 530–531, 540, 593; **III:** 4, 10, 45, 122, 133–134, 179, 214, 237, 272, 275, 469, 485, 523; **IV:** 360, 405, 416; **Retro. Supp. I:** 91, 301, 313, 360, 395, 412; **Supp. I Part 1:** 82, 183, 266, 267, 312, 349, 362, 363, 365; **Supp. I Part 2:** 410, 422, 424, 539, 552, 675, 719, 720; **Supp. III Part 1:** 73; **Supp. IV Part 1:** 123, 168, 325; **Supp. IV Part 2:** 455; **Supp. IX:** 38, 39, 45; **Supp. VIII:** 41, 273; **Supp. XI:** 43, 320; **Supp. XII:** 9, 113, 255; **Supp. XIII:** 131, 281; **Supp. XIV:** 274; **Supp. XIX:** 33, 276; **Supp. XV:** 92; **Supp. XVII:** 76, 112; **Supp. XX: 115, 116; Supp. XXI:** 131; **Supp. XXIV:** 159
Keats, John (other), **Supp. IX:** 190, 195, 200
Keegan, Abigail, **Supp. XXIII:** 129, 130, 136
"Keela, the Outcast Indian Maiden" (Welty), **IV:** 263
Keeley, Mary Paxton, **Supp. XV:** 136
"Keen Scalpel on Racial Ills" (Bruell), **Supp. VIII:** 126
Keep, The (Egan), **Supp. XIX:** 49, **56–61**
"Keep A-Inchin' Along" (Van Vechten), *Supp. III Part 2:* 744
Keeper's Son, The (Hickam), **Supp. XXVII:** 111–112
Keeping (Goldbarth), **Supp. XII:** 179–180, 180

"Keeping Accounts" (Davison), **Supp. XXVI:** 77

"Keeping Informed in D.C." (Nemerov), **III:** 287

Keeping Slug Woman Alive: A Holistic Approach to American Indian Texts (Sarris), **Supp. IV Part 1:** 329

"'Keeping Their World Large'" (Moore), **III:** 201–202

Keeping the Night (Everwine), **Supp. XV:** 75, **81–85,** 86

"Keeping Things Whole" (Strand), **Supp. IV Part 2:** 624

Keep It Simple: A Defense of the Earth (Nichols), **Supp. XIII:** 268

"Keep the Saving Habit" (L. I. Wilder), **Supp. XXII:** 290

"Keep Your Pity" (Boyle), **Supp. XXIV:** 58, 59

Kees, Weldon, **Supp. X:** 118; **Supp. XII:** 198; **Supp. XV:** 113, 114, 115, **133–149**

Kehe, Marjorie, **Supp. XXVI:** 209

Keillor, Garrison, **Supp. XII:** 343; **Supp. XIII:** 274; **Supp. XVI: 165–179; Supp. XXI:** 53, 62; **Supp. XXII:** 83; **Supp. XXIII:** 57, 58, 138

Keillor, Gary Edward. *See* Keiller, Garrison

Keith, Brian, **Supp. IV Part 2:** 474

Keith, Minor C., **I:** 483

Kelleghan, Fiona, **Supp. XVIII:** 136, 139, 140

Keller, A. G., **III:** 108

Keller, Christopher J., **Supp. XVIII:** 192, 195

Keller, Helen, **I:** 254, 258; **Supp. XXIII:** 161

Keller, Lynn, **Supp. IV Part 2:** 423; **Supp. V:** 78, 80

Kelley, David, **Supp. IV Part 2:** 528, 529

Kelley, Florence, **Supp. I Part 1:** 5, 7

Kelley, Mary, **Supp. XVIII:** 257, 260

Kelley, Robin, **Supp. XVIII:** 231

Kellogg, Reverend Edwin H., **III:** 200

Kellogg, Paul U., **Supp. I Part 1:** 5, 7, 12

Kelly, **II:** 464

Kelly, Brigit Pegeen, **Supp. XVII: 123–134; Supp. XXIII:** 54

Kelly, Emmett, **Supp. XI:** 99, 106

Kelly, Gene, **Supp. XXI:** 148

Kelly, James Patrick, **Supp. XIX:** 231; **Supp. XVIII:** 145

Kelly, Walt, **Supp. XI:** 105

Kelly, William, **Supp. XV:** 75, 88

Kelsey, Penelope Myrtle, **Supp. XXIII:** 143, 153–164

Kelsh, Nick, **Supp. XVII:** 167, 179

Kemble, Fanny, **Retro. Supp. I:** 228

Kemble, Gouverneur, **II:** 298

Kemble, Peter, **II:** 298

Kempf, Andrea, **Supp. XXVI:** 212

Kempton, Murray, **Supp. VIII:** 104

Kempton-Wace Letters, The (London and Strunsky), **II:** 465

Kendall, Elaine, **Supp. XXVI:** 121

Kennan, George F., **Supp. VIII:** 241

Kennedy, Albert J., **Supp. I Part 1:** 19

Kennedy, Archibald, **Supp. XXVI:** 84

Kennedy, Arthur, **III:** 153

Kennedy, Burt, **Supp. IV Part 1:** 236

Kennedy, Jeffery, **Supp. XXI:** 6; **Supp. XXV:** 20

Kennedy, J. Gerald, **Retro. Supp. II:** 271

Kennedy, John F., **I:** 136, 170; **II:** 49, 152–153; **III:** 38, 41, 42, 234, 411, 415, 581; **IV:** 229; **Supp. I Part 1:** 291; **Supp. I Part 2:** 496; **Supp. VIII:** 98, 104, 203; **Supp. XII:** 132; **Supp. XXVI:** 43

Kennedy, Mrs. John F., **I:** 136

Kennedy, John Pendleton, **II:** 313; **Supp. XXII:** 193

Kennedy, Robert, **Supp. V:** 291

Kennedy, Robert F., **I:** 294; **Supp. I Part 1:** 52; **Supp. XI:** 343

Kennedy, Sarah, **Supp. XVIII:** 293, 299, 301

Kennedy, William, **Supp. VII: 131–157; Supp. XIX:** 141; **Supp. XVII:** 135; **Supp. XX: 90; Supp. XXIV:** 281, 282, 283

Kennedy, X. J., **Supp. V:** 178, 182; **Supp. XV:** 113, **151–173**

Kenner, Hugh, **III:** 475, 478; **IV:** 412; **Supp. I Part 1:** 255; **Supp. IV Part 2:** 474; **Supp. XV:** 147; **Supp. XXI:** 235; **Supp. XXVI:** 228

Kenneth Koch, a Tragedy (O'Hara and Rivers), **Supp. XXIII:** 217

"Kenneth Koch's 'Serious Moment'" (Spurr), **Supp. XV:** 183

Kenneth Millar/Ross Macdonald: A Checklist (Bruccoli), **Supp. IV Part 2:** 464, 469, 471

Kenney, Michael, **Supp. XIX:** 51, 52–53

Kenney, Susan, **Supp. XVIII:** 288, 289

Kenny, Maurice, **Supp. IV Part 2:** 502; **Supp. XXIII: 143–159**

Kent, George, **Supp. IV Part 1:** 11

Kent, Rockwell, **Supp. XV:** 41; **Supp. XXII:** 281

Kenton, Edna, **Supp. XXI:** 6; **Supp. XXV:** 21

Kenton, Maxwell. *See* Burnett, David; Hoffenberg, Mason; Southern, Terry

"Kent State, May 1970" (Haines), **Supp. XII:** 211

"Kentucky Derby Is Decadent and Depraved, The" (Thompson), **Supp. XXIV:** 282, **287–288**

Kentucky Straight (Offutt), **Supp. XIX: 163–167,** 171, 172

Kenya, the Land of Conflict (Kenyatta), **Supp. XXI:** 166

Kenyatta, Jomo, **Supp. X:** 135; **Supp. XXI:** 166

Kenyon, Jane, **Supp. VII: 159–177; Supp. VIII:** 272

Keogh, Tom, **Supp. XVI:** 230

Kepler, Johannes, **III:** 484; **IV:** 18

Keplinger, David, **Supp. XIX:** 273

Keppel, Frederick P., **I:** 214

"Kéramos" (Longfellow), **II:** 494; **Retro. Supp. II:** 167, 169

Kéramos and Other Poems (Longfellow), **II:** 490

Kerber, Linda K., **Supp. XXV:** 44

Kercheval, Jesse Lee, **Supp. XIX:** 51

Kerim, Ussin, **Supp. IX:** 152

Kermode, Frank, **IV:** 133; **Retro. Supp. I:** 301

Kern, Jerome, **II:** 427

Kerouac, Jack, **III:** 174; **Retro. Supp. I:** 102; **Supp. II Part 1:** 31, 307, 309, 318, 328; **Supp. III Part 1:** 91–94, 96, 100, **217–234; Supp. IV Part 1:** 90, 146; **Supp. IX:** 246; **Supp. V:** 336; **Supp. VIII:** 42, 138, 289, 305; **Supp. XII:** 118, 121, 122, 123, 126, 131, 132; **Supp. XIII:** 275, 284; **Supp. XIV:** 137, 138, 141, 142, 143–144; **Supp. XV:** 134, 221; **Supp. XVI:** 123; **Supp. XVII:** 135, 138; **Supp. XX: 17; Supp. XXIII:** 100, 213; **Supp. XXIV:** 34, 44; **Supp. XXV:** 29; **Supp. XXVI:** 252; **Supp. XXVII:** 18

Kerr, Deborah, **Supp. XI:** 307

Kerr, Orpheus C. (pseudonym). *See* Newell, Henry

Kerr, Walter, **Supp. IV Part 2:** 575, 579

Kerridge, Richard, **Supp. XVI:** 26

Kesey, Ken, **III:** 558; **Supp. III Part 1:** 217; **Supp. V:** 220, 295; **Supp. X:** 24, 265; **Supp. XI:** 104; **Supp. XXIII:** 100

Kessel, John, **Supp. XIX:** 231; **Supp. XVIII:** 145

Kessler, Milton, **Supp. XIX:** 195

Kessler, Rod, **Supp. XXVI:** 156

Kesten, Stephen, **Supp. XI:** 309

Ketchum, Liza, **Supp. XIX:** 266

Ketchup (Shanley), **Supp. XIV:** 315

Kevane, Bridget, **Supp. XI:** 185, 190

"Key, The" (Welty), **IV:** 262

"Keys" (Nye), **Supp. XIII:** 281

"Key to the Highway" (Halliday), **Supp. XIX:** 84

Key to Uncle Tom's Cabin, A (Stowe), **Supp. I Part 2:** 580

Key West (H. Crane), **Retro. Supp. II:** 84

"Key West" (H. Crane), **I:** 400

Key West: An Island Sheaf (Crane), **I:** 385, 399–402

"Khalil the Heretic" (Gibran), **Supp. XX: 124**

Khrushchev, Nikita, **I:** 136

Kiang Kang-hu, **Supp. XV:** 45, 47

Kick (Myers and Workman), **Supp. XXVII:** 206

Kick for a Bite, A (Cobbett), **Supp. XV:** 237

"Kicking the Candles Out" (Jarman), **Supp. XVII:** 113

Kid, The (Aiken), **I:** 61

Kid, The (Chaplin), **I:** 386

Kidder, Tracy, **Supp. III Part 1:** 302; **Supp. XVIII:** 106, 114

Kiddush Ha-Shem: An Epic of 1648 (Asch), **Supp. XXIII:** 3, 6, **10,** 11, 12, 16

Kidesh ha-Shem (Sanctification of the name) (Asch), **Supp. XXIII:** 6

Kidman, Nicole, **Supp. X:** 80

"Kidnaper" (Gallagher), **Supp. XXIV:** 168, 174

"Kidnapping in the Family, A" (Fante), **Supp. XI:** 164

"Kid's Guide to Divorce, The" (Moore), **Supp. X:** 167, 172

Kidwell, Clara Sue, **Supp. IV Part 1:** 333

Kielsky, Vera Emuma, **Supp. V:** 273

Kiely, Brendan, **Supp. XVII:** 75

Kieran, John, **II:** 417

Kierkegaard, Søren Aabye, **II:** 229; **III:** 292, 305, 309, 572; **IV:** 438, 491; **Retro. Supp. I:** 326; **Retro. Supp. II:** 222; **Supp. V:** 9; **Supp. VIII:** 7–8; **Supp. XX:** 132

Kiernan, Robert F., **Supp. IV Part 2:** 684

Kieseritsky, L., **III:** 252

Kilgo, Jim, **Supp. XVIII:** 192

"Kilim" (McClatchy), **Supp. XII:** 258

Kilina, Patricia (pseudonym). *See* Warren, Patricia Nell

"Killed at Resaca" (Bierce), **I:** 202

"Killed at the Ford" (Longfellow), **Retro. Supp. II:** 170–171

Killens, John Oliver, **Supp. IV Part 1:** 8, 369; **Supp. XXVII:** 202

"Killer in the Rain" (Chandler), **Supp. IV Part 1:** 122

"Killers, The" (Hemingway), **II:** 249; **Retro. Supp. I:** 188, 189

Killers, The: A Narrative of Real Life in Philadelphia (Lippard), **Supp. XXIII:** 178, 184

Killing Mister Watson (Matthiessen), **Supp. V:** 212, 214

"Killing of a State Cop, The" (Ortiz), **Supp. IV Part 2:** 499

Killing of Sister George, The (Marcus), **Supp. I Part 1:** 277

Killing Orders (Paretsky), **Supp. XXV:** 176, 177, 179, 182–813

"Killings" (Dubus), **Supp. VII:** 85–86

"Killing the Ghost of Ripton" (Carruth), **Supp. XIX:** 1

"Killing the Plants" (Kenyon), **Supp. VII:** 167, 168

Kilmer, Joyce, **Supp. I Part 2:** 387; **Supp. XV:** 294

Kilpatrick, James K., **Supp. X:** 145

Kilvert, Francis, **Supp. VIII:** 172

Kim (Kipling), **Supp. X:** 230

Kim, Alfred, **Supp. XI:** 140

Kim, Sharon, **Supp. XVIII:** 267

Kimball, Frederic, **Supp. XXI:** 146

Kimball, J. Golden, **Supp. IV Part 2:** 602

Kimbrough, Mary Craig. *See* Sinclair, Mary Craig (Mary Craig Kimbrough)

Kimes, Maymie B., **Supp. IX:** 178

Kimes, William F., **Supp. IX:** 178

Kimmelman, Bert, **Supp. XXI:** 24

Kimura, Takeshi, **Supp. XXVI:** 88

"Kin" (Welty), **IV:** 277; **Retro. Supp. I:** 353

Kinard, Agnes Dodds, **Supp. XIV:** 122, 123, 127

Kincaid, Jamaica, **Supp. VII: 179–196**

Kincaid, James, **Supp. XVIII:** 62, 63

"Kindness" (Dunn), **Supp. XI:** 149, 150

"Kindness" (Nye), **Supp. XIII:** 285

"Kindness" (Plath), **Retro. Supp. II:** 256

Kind of Light that Shines on Texas, The (McKnight), **Supp. XX: 151–152**

"Kind of Light that Shines on Texas, The" (McKnight), **Supp. XX:** 151

Kind of Order, A Kind of Folly, A: Essays and Conversations (Kunitz), **Supp. III Part 1:** 262, 268

Kindred (O. Butler), **Supp. XIII: 59–60,** 69

"Kind Sir: These Woods" (Sexton), **Supp. II Part 2:** 673

Kinds of Love (Sarton), **Supp. VIII: 253–254,** 256

Kinfolk (Buck), **Supp. II Part 1:** 126

King, Alexander, **IV:** 287

King, Carole, **Supp. XII:** 308

King, Clarence, **I:** 1

King, Ernest, **Supp. I Part 2:** 491

King, Fisher, **II:** 425

King, Francis, **Supp. XIV:** 155, 156, 166, 169

King, Grace, **Retro. Supp. II:** 136

King, Martin Luther, Jr., **Retro. Supp. II:** 12, 13; **Supp. XVIII:** 24; **Supp. XX:** 281

King, Michael, **Supp. XII:** 182

King, Queen, Knave (Nabokov), **III:** 251; **Retro. Supp. I:** 270

King, Starr, **Supp. II Part 1:** 341, 342

King, Stephen, **Supp. IV Part 1:** 102, 104; **Supp. IV Part 2:** 467; **Supp. IX:** 114; **Supp. V: 137–155;** **Supp. XIII:** 53; **Supp. XXIII:** 290; **Supp. XXV:** 123, 152, 153; **Supp. XXVII:** 276

King, Tabitha (Mrs. Stephen King), **Supp. V:** 137

King, The (Barthelme), **Supp. IV Part 1:** 47, 52

"King, The" (Gibran), **Supp. XX: 123–124**

King Coffin (Aiken), **I:** 53–54, 57

"King David" (Benét), **Supp. XI:** 44

"King David" (Reznikoff), **Supp. XIV:** 283

Kingdom and the Power, The (Talese), **Supp. XVII:** 202, 203, 204, 210

Kingdom by the Sea, The: A Journey around Great Britain (Theroux), **Supp. VIII:** 323

"Kingdom County Come" (Mosher), **Supp. XXII:** 211–212

Kingdom Far and Clear, A: The Complete Swan Lake Trilogy (Helprin), **Supp. XXV:** 87

Kingdom of Earth (T. Williams), **IV:** 382, 386, 387, 388, 391, 393, 398

"Kingdom of Earth, The" (T. Williams), **IV:** 384

Kingdom of Fear (Thompson), **Supp. XXIV:** 283

"Kingdom of God Is Within You, The" (Very), **Supp. XXV:** 249

Kingfisher, The (Clampitt), **Supp. IX:** 38

"Kingfishers, The" (Olson), **Supp. II Part 2:** 557, 558–563, 582

King Jasper (Robinson), **III:** 523

King Kong (film), **Supp. IV Part 1:** 104; **Supp. XVII:** 58

King Lear (Shakespeare), **I:** 538; **II:** 540, 551; **Retro. Supp. I:** 248; **Supp. IV Part 1:** 31, 36; **Supp. IX:** 14; **Supp. XI:** 172; **Supp. XV:** 349

King Leopold's Soliloquy (Twain), **IV:** 208

King My Father's Wreck, The (Simpson), **Supp. IX:** 266, 267, 270, 275, 276

King of Babylon Shall Not Come Against You, The (Garrett), **Supp. VII:** 110–111; **Supp. X:** 3

"King of Beasts" (P. N. Warren), **Supp. XX:** 272

"King of Folly Island, The" (Jewett), **II:** 394; **Retro. Supp. II:** 132, 133

King of Kings (film), **Supp. IV Part 2:** 520

King of Paris (Endore), **Supp. XVII:** 64

King of Spain, The (Bodenheim), **Supp. XXV:** 26

"King of the Bingo Game" (Ellison), **Retro. Supp. II:** 117, 125; **Supp. II Part 1:** 235, 238, 240–241

"King of the Cats, The" (Benét), **Supp. XI:** 49–50

"King of the Clock Tower" (Yeats), **III:** 473

"King of the Desert, The" (O'Hara), **III:** 369

King of the Fields, The (Singer), **Retro. Supp. II:** 317

King of the Jews (Epstein), **Supp. XII:** 161, **166–170,** 172

King of the Mountain (Garrett), **Supp. VII:** 96, 97

"King of the River" (Kunitz), **Supp. III Part 1:** 263, 267–268

"King of the Sea" (Marquand), **III:** 60

"King over the Water" (Blackmur), **Supp. II Part 1:** 107

"King Pandar" (Blackmur), **Supp. II Part 1:** 92, 102

"King Pest" (Poe), **Retro. Supp. II:** 273

Kingsblood Royal (Lewis), **II:** 456

Kingsbury, John, **Supp. I Part 1:** 8

"King's Daughters, Home for Unwed Mothers, 1948" (Stanford), **Supp. XV:** 345

King's Henchman, The (Millay), **III:** 138–139

Kingsley, Sidney, **Supp. I Part 1:** 277, 281

King's Mare, The (Canolle; Loos, trans.), **Supp. XVI:** 194

"King's Missive, The" (Whittier), **Supp. I Part 2:** 694

Kingsolver, Barbara, **Supp. VII: 197–214; Supp. XIII:** 16; **Supp. XVIII:** 189

King's Stilts, The (Geisel), **Supp. XVI:** 100, 104

Kingston, Earll, **Supp. V:** 160

Kingston, Maxine Hong, **Supp. IV Part 1:** 1, 12; **Supp. V: 157–175,** 250; **Supp. X:** 291–292; **Supp. XI:** 18, 245; **Supp. XV:** 220, 223

"King Volmer and Elsie" (Whittier), **Supp. I Part 2:** 696

Kinkaid, Jamaica, **Supp. XXII:** 65

Kinmont, Alexander, **Supp. I Part 2:** 588–589

Kinnaird, John, **Retro. Supp. I:** 399

Kinnell, Galway, **Supp. III Part 1: 235–256; Supp. III Part 2:** 541; **Supp. IV**

Part 2: 623; **Supp. V:** 332; **Supp. VIII:** 39; **Supp. XI:** 139; **Supp. XII:** 241; **Supp. XV:** 212; **Supp. XVI:** 53; **Supp. XXII:** 83; **Supp. XXVI:** 67

Kinsella, Thomas, **Supp. XX: 195–196, 197, 207**

Kinsey, Alfred, **IV:** 230; **Supp. XIV:** 140

Kinzie, Mary, **Supp. XII:** 181; **Supp. XXIII:** 124

"Kipling" (Trilling), **Supp. III Part 2:** 495

Kipling, Rudyard, **I:** 421, 587–588; **II:** 271, 338, 404, 439; **III:** 55, 328, 508, 511, 521, 524, 579; **IV:** 429; **Supp. IV Part 2:** 603; **Supp. X:** 255; **Supp. XX: 23**

Kirby, David, **Supp. XIII:** 89; **Supp. XIX:** 81

Kirkland, Caroline, **Supp. XVIII:** 258

Kirkland, David, **Supp. XVI:** 186

Kirkland, Jack, **I:** 297

Kirkland, John, **Supp. XXIV:** 70

Kirkpatrick, Jeane, **Supp. VIII:** 241

Kirkus, Virginia, **Supp. XV:** 198

Kirkwood, Cynthia A., **Supp. XI:** 177, 178, 179

Kirp, David L., **Supp. XI:** 129

Kirsch, Adam, **Supp. XV:** 251, 260, 264, 266, 341, 347, 350–351; **Supp. XXV:** 222, 233, 253, 262, 268; **Supp. XXVII:** 144

Kirsch, Robert, **Supp. XXVII:** 134

Kirstein, Lincoln, **Supp. II Part 1:** 90, 97; **Supp. IV Part 1:** 82, 83; **Supp. XXII:** 281

Kishef-makherin fun Kastilye, Di (The witch of Castle) (Asch), **Supp. XXIII:** 6

"Kiss, The" (Di Piero), **Supp. XIX:** 45, 47

Kiss, The (Harrison), **Supp. X:** 191

"Kiss, The" (Sexton), **Supp. II Part 2:** 687

"Kiss, The" (Teasdale), **Supp. XXVII:** 291

"Kiss Away" (C. Baxter), **Supp. XVII:** 20

Kissel, Howard, **Supp. IV Part 2:** 580

Kiss Hollywood Good-by (Loos), **Supp. XVI:** 190, 195

Kissinger, Henry, **Supp. IV Part 1:** 388; **Supp. XII:** 9, 14; **Supp. XXV:** 264

Kiss of the Spider Woman, the Musical (McNally), **Supp. XIII:** 207, **Supp. XIII:** 208

Kiss Tomorrow Good-bye (McCoy), **Supp. XIII:** 170, **172–173,** 174

"Kit and Caboodle" (Komunyakaa), **Supp. XIII:** 115

Kit Brandon: A Portrait (Anderson), **I:** 111

Kitchen, Judith, **Supp. IV Part 1:** 242, 245, 252; **Supp. IX:** 163; **Supp. XI:** 312, 313, 315, 317, 319, 320, 326, 329; **Supp. XV:** 215, 219; **Supp. XXVI:** 154–155

"Kitchenette" (Brooks), **Retro. Supp. I:** 208

Kitchen God's Wife, The (Tan), **Supp. X:** 289, 292, 293, 294–295, 296–297, 298–299

"Kitchen Terrarium: 1983" (McCarriston), **Supp. XIV:** 270

Kit O'Brien (Masters), **Supp. I Part 2:** 471

Kittel, Frederick August. *See* Wilson, August

Kittredge, Charmian. *See* London, Mrs. Jack (Charmian Kittredge)

Kittredge, William, **Supp. VIII:** 39; **Supp. XI:** 316; **Supp. XII:** 209; **Supp. XIII:** 16; **Supp. XXVI: 177–190**

"Kitty Hawk" (Frost), **II:** 164; **Retro. Supp. I:** 124, 141

Kizer, Carolyn, **Supp. XVII:** 71, 72, 73, 74

Klaidman, Stephen, **Supp. XIX:** 269

Klail City (Hinojosa), **Supp. XIX:** 97, **101–103**

Klail City Death Trip (Hinojosa). *See Ask a Policeman* (Hinojosa); *Becky and Her Friends* (Hinojosa); *Dear Rafe* (Hinojosa); *Fair Gentlemen of Belken County* (Hinojosa); *Klail City* (Hinojosa); *Korean Love Songs from Klail City Death Trip* (Hinojosa); *Partners in Crime: A Rafe Buenrostro Mystery* (Hinojosa); *Rites and Witnesses: A Comedy* (Hinojosa); *Useless Servants, The* (Hinojosa); *Valley, The* (Hinojosa)

"Klassikal Lymnaeryx" (Stallings), **Supp. XXV:** 233

Klein, Joe, **Supp. XII:** 67–68

Klein, Marcus, **Supp. I Part 2:** 432; **Supp. XI:** 233

Kleist, Heinrich von, **Supp. IV Part 1:** 224

Kline, Franz, **Supp. XII:** 198; **Supp. XXIII:** 210, 211, 217

Kline, George, **Supp. VIII:** 22, 28

Klinghoffer, David, **Supp. XVI:** 74

Klinkowitz, Jerome, **Supp. IV Part 1:** 40; **Supp. X:** 263; **Supp. XI:** 347; **Supp. XXI:** 233

Klise, James, **Supp. XXII:** 53

Kloefkorn, Bill, **Supp. XIX:** 119

Knapp, Adeline, **Supp. XI:** 200

Knapp, Friedrich, **III:** 100

Knapp, Samuel, **I:** 336

Knapp, Samuel Lorenzo, **Supp. XV:** 246

"Kneeling Down to Look into a Culvert" (R. Bly), **Supp. XXI:** 88

Kneel to the Rising Sun (Caldwell), **I:** 304, 309

"Knees/Dura-Europos" (Goldbarth), **Supp. XII:** 185

"Knife" (Simic), **Supp. VIII:** 275

"Knife Longs for the Ruby, The" (Vaz), **Supp. XXVI:** 266–267

Knight, Arthur, **Supp. XIV:** 144

Knight, Etheridge, **Supp. XI:** 239; **Supp. XXIII:** 174

Knight, Lania, **Supp. XXIII:** 273, 274, 275, 276, 279, 280

"Knight in Disguise, The" (Lindsay), **Supp. I Part 2:** 390

Knightly Quest, The (T. Williams), **IV:** 383

Knight's Gambit (Faulkner), **II:** 72

Knish, Anne. *See* Ficke, Arthur Davison

"Knit One, Purl Two" (K. Snodgrass), **Supp. XVI:** 42

"Knock" (Dickey), **Supp. IV Part 1:** 182

Knocked Out Loaded (album, Dylan), **Supp. XVIII:** 28

"Knocking Around" (Ashbery), **Supp. III Part 1:** 22

"Knocking on Heaven's Door" (Lamott), **Supp. XX: 140–141**

"Knocking on Three, Winston" (Epstein), **Supp. XIV:** 109

Knock on Any Door (film, Ray), **Supp. XVII:** 150

Knock on Any Door (W. Motley), 158; **Supp. XVII: 150–155,** 159, 160

Knockout Artist, The (Crews), **Supp. XI: 113–114**

Knoll, Robert E., **Supp. XV:** 118

Knopf, Alfred A., **III:** 99, 105, 106, 107; **Retro. Supp. I:** 13, 19, 317; **Supp. I Part 1:** 324, 325, 327; **Supp. IV Part 1:** 125, 354; **Supp. XIII:** 172

Knopf, Blanche, **Supp. I Part 1:** 324, 325, 327, 328, 332, 341; **Supp. IV Part 1:** 128, 346, 348; **Supp. XIII:** 169

"Knot, The" (Rich), **Supp. I Part 2:** 555

Knot-Holes (Bodenheim and Saphier), **Supp. XXV:** 20

Knotts, Kristina, **Supp. XIII:** 238

"Knowing, The" (Olds), **Supp. X:** 215

"Knowledge Forwards and Backwards" (Stern), **Supp. IX:** 296

"Knowledge of Plates" (Bronk), **Supp. XXI:** 33

Knowles, John, **Supp. IV Part 2:** 679; **Supp. XII: 235–250; Supp. XX: 84**

Known World, The (E. P. Jones), **Supp. XXII:** 139, 140, 142, **146–150,** 150

Knox, Bernard, **Supp. XXIV:** 153

Knox, Frank, **Supp. I Part 2:** 488, 489

Knox, Israel, **Supp. X:** 70

Knox, Vicesimus, **II:** 8

Knoxville: Summer of 1915 (Agee), **I:** 42–46

Knudson, R. Rozanne, **Supp. IV Part 2:** 648

Kober, Arthur, **Supp. I Part 1:** 292

Koch, Frederick, **IV:** 453

Koch, John, **Supp. VIII:** 88

Koch, Kenneth, **Supp. XIX:** 81; **Supp. XV: 175–192; Supp. XXIII:** 124, 207, 209, 210, 211, 215, 217, 220; **Supp. XXIV:** 33, 36, 42, 44; **Supp. XXVII:** 23, 26

Koch, Vivienne, **III:** 194; **IV:** 136, 140; **Retro. Supp. I:** 428, 430

"Kochinnenako in Academe: Three Approaches to Interpreting a Keres Indian Tale" (Gunn Allen), **Supp. IV Part 1:** 329

"Kodachromes of the Island" (Hayden), **Supp. II Part 1:** 367, 380

Koestler, Arthur, **I:** 258; **Supp. I Part 2:** 671; **Supp. XXIII:** 1

Kokkinen, Eila, **Supp. XIV:** 146, 148

"Kola Street"(Asch), **Supp. XXIII:** 7

Kolba, Ellen D., **Supp. XVIII:** 257

Kolbenheyer, Dr. Frederick, **Supp. I Part 1:** 207

Kolodny, Annette, **Supp. X:** 97, 103, 229

Komisarjevsky, W. P., **Supp. XXIII:** 5

"Komodo" (C. Frost), **Supp. XV:** 95

Komunyakaa, Yusef, **Supp. XIII:** 111–136; **Supp. XXI:** 129, 139; **Supp. XXIII:** 254; **Supp. XXVII:** 166

Konigsberg, Allan Stewart. *See* Allen, Woody

Kon-Tiki (Heyerdahl), **II:** 477

Koopman, Harry Lyman, **Retro. Supp. I:** 40

Ko; or, A Season on Earth (Koch), **Supp. XV:** 175, 180, 181, 183, 186

Kooser, Ted, **Supp. XIX:** 115–130; **Supp. XV:** 113, 115; **Supp. XXI:** 243

Kootz, Samuel, **Supp. XV:** 144

Kora and Ka (Doolittle), **Supp. I Part 1:** 270

Kora in Hell (W. C. Williams), **Retro. Supp. I:** 416, **417–418,** 419, 430, 431; **Supp. XXI:** 232

Korb, Rena, **Supp. XI:** 2

Korczak, Janosz, **Supp. X:** 70

Korean Love Songs from Klail City Death Trip (Hinojosa), **Supp. XIX:** 98, **103–104**

Kornblatt, Joyce Reiser, **Supp. XV:** 62

Kornfield, Jack, **Supp. XX:** 142; **Supp. XXIII:** 138

Korrektur (Bernhard), **Supp. XX:** 91

Kort, Amy, **Supp. XIII:** 148

Korwin, Yala, **Supp. XXI:** 99

Kosinski, Jerzy, **Supp. VII:** 215–228; **Supp. XII:** 21

"Kostas Tympakianakis" (Merrill), **Supp. III Part 1:** 326

Kostelanetz, Richard, **Supp. XXVII:** 166

Koteliansky, S. S., **Supp. VIII:** 251, 265

Kouidis, Virginia M., **Supp. XXII:** 161, 162, 166, 167, 169

Kovic, Ron, **Supp. XIX:** 17; **Supp. XXII:** 104

Kowloon Tong (Theroux), **Supp. VIII:** 325

Kozlenko, William, **IV:** 378, 381

Krabbenhoft, Ken, **Supp. XVII:** 112

Kraft, James, **Supp. XV:** 40, 41, 42, 43, 52

Krakauer, Jon, **Supp. XVII:** 210; **Supp. XVIII:** 105–118

Kramer, Dale, **Supp. I Part 2:** 669

Kramer, Glenn Philip, **Supp. XXIII:** 125

Kramer, Hilton, **III:** 537; **Supp. I Part 1:** 295, 296; **Supp. VIII:** 239; **Supp. XIX:** 269; **Supp. XV:** 113; **Supp. XXVII:** 23

Kramer, Lawrence, **Supp. IV Part 1:** 61, 65, 66; **Supp. IX:** 291

Kramer, Peter D., **Supp. XVI:** 229

Kramer, Robert, **Supp. XXVI:** 26

Kramer, Stanley, **II:** 421, 587

Krapp's Last Tape (Beckett), **I:** 71; **III:** 387; **Retro. Supp. I:** 206

Krassner, Paul, **Supp. IV Part 1:** 385; **Supp. XI:** 293

Kraus, Karl, **Supp. XX:** 84

Krauth, Leland, **Supp. XVIII:** 58

Krauzer, Steven M., **Supp. XXVI:** 181, 182, 188

Kreisler, Harry, **Supp. XVI:** 155

Kreitman, Esther, **IV:** 2

Krementz, Jill, **Supp. XXV:** 263

"Kremlin of Smoke" (Schnackenberg), **Supp. XV:** 257–258

Kreyling, Michael, **Supp. XXVI:** 14

Kreymborg, Alfred, **II:** 530; **III:** 465; **IV:** 76; **Retro. Supp. I:** 417; **Supp. XV:** 301, 306; **Supp. XXII:** 161–162; **Supp. XXV:** 18, 19, 21

Kriegel, Leonard, **Supp. XXIV:** **213–228**

Krim, Seymour, **Supp. XV:** 338; **Supp. XVI:** 217; **Supp. XVIII:** 285

Krisak, Len, **Supp. XXI:** 99, 104

Kristeva, Julia, **Supp. XII:** 6

Kristofferson, Kris, **Supp. XIII:** 119

Kristol, Irving, **Supp. VIII:** 93, 244; **Supp. XIII:** 98

Kristwald, Elfriede, **Supp. XXVI:** 4, 7

Krivak, Andrew, **Supp. XVII:** 242

Kroll, Jack, **Supp. IV Part 2:** 590; **Supp. XXIII:** 103

Kroll, Judith, **Supp. I Part 2:** 541–543, 544, 546

Kroll Ring, Frances. *See* Ring, Frances Kroll

Krondorfer, Björn, **Supp. XVI:** 160

Kronenberger, Louis, **Supp. XXII:** 191, 192

Krook, Dorothea, **Retro. Supp. II:** 243

Kropotkin, Peter, **I:** 493; **Supp. I Part 1:** 5; **Supp. IV Part 2:** 521

Krueger, Bill, **Supp. XXVII:** 13

Kruif, Paul de, **II:** 446

Krupat, Arnold, **Supp. IV Part 2:** 500

Krupnick, Mark, **Supp. XVI:** 153

Krutch, Joseph Wood, **II:** 459; **III:** 425; **IV:** 70, 175

Krutikov, Mikhail, **Supp. XXIII:** 11

Kubach, David, **Supp. XXVI:** 243, 245, 246, 248

Kublai Khan, **III:** 395

"Kubla Khan" (Coleridge), **Supp. XIII:** 131, 283

Kubrick, Stanley, **Supp. IV Part 1:** 392; **Supp. XI:** 293, **Supp. XI:** 301, 302–303

"Kubuku Rides (This Is It) " (L. Brown), **Supp. XXI:** 39, 42–43

Kuehl, John, **Supp. IV Part 1:** 279, 284, 285, 287

Kuehl, Linda, **Supp. IV Part 1:** 199

"Kugelmass Episode, The" (Allen), **Supp. XV:** 15, 16

Kukachin, Princess, **III:** 395

"Ku Klux" (Hughes), **Retro. Supp. I:** 205

Kulshrestha, Chirantan, **Retro. Supp. II:** 21

Kumin, Maxine, **Supp. IV Part 2:** **439–457; Supp. XIII:** 294; **Supp. XVII:** 71, 75–76; **Supp. XX: 164; Supp. XXVI:** 68; **Supp. XXVII:** 256

Kundera, Milan, **Supp. VIII:** 241

Kunerth, Jeff, **Supp. XXI:** 47

Kunitz, Stanley, **I:** 179, 180, 181, 182, 521; **II:** 545; **Supp. III Part 1:** 257–270; **Supp. V:** 79; **Supp. XI:** 259;

Supp. XIII: 341; **Supp. XXVI:** 64, 67, 68

Kuo, Helena, **Supp. X:** 291

Kuropatkin, General Aleksei Nikolaevich, **III:** 247–248

Kurth, Peter, **Supp. XVIII:** 145

Kurzy of the Sea (Barnes), **Supp. III Part 1:** 34

Kushner, Tony, **Supp. IX:** 131–149; **Supp. XX:** 177; **Supp. XXI:** 145; **Supp. XXIV:** 263

Kussy, Bella, **IV:** 468

Kutnik, Jerzy, **Supp. XXII:** 177

Kuttner, Henry, **Supp. IV Part 1:** 102

Kuzma, Greg, **Supp. XV:** 118

Kyger, Joanne, **Supp. XXIV:** 37

L

LaBastille, Anne, **Supp. X:** **95–110; Supp. XXVI:** 34

"Labor Day Dinner" (Munro), **Supp. XXVII:** 188

"Labor's Cultural Degradation" (Swados), **Supp. XIX:** 264–265

"Labours of Hercules, The" (Moore), **III:** 201

La Bruyère, Jean de, **I:** 58

La Bufera e Altro (Montale), **Supp. V:** 337

LaBute, Neil, **Supp. XXI:** 147

Labyrinth of Love (Untermeyer), **Supp. XV:** 312

Labyrinth of Solitude, The (Paz), **Supp. XIII:** 223

Lacan, Jacques, **Supp. IV Part 1:** 45; **Supp. VIII:** 5; **Supp. XII:** 98

La Casa en Mango Street (Cisneros), **Supp. VII:** 58–59

Lacayo, Richard, **Supp. XXV:** 4

Lachaise, Gaston, **I:** 434

"Lackawanna" (Merwin), **Supp. III Part 1:** 350

Lackawanna Elegy (Goll; Kinnell, trans.), **Supp. III Part 1:** 235, 243–244

Laclède, Pierre, **Supp. I Part 1:** 205

"Lacquer Prints" (A. Lowell), **II:** 524–525

Lacy, Ed, **Supp. XV:** **193–210**

Ladder, The (Rasmussen; Nelson, trans.), **Supp. XVIII:** 180–181

Ladder of Years (Tyler), **Supp. IV Part 2:** 657, 671–672

Ladders to Fire (Nin), **Supp. X:** 185

Laddie (Stratton-Porter), **Supp. XX:** 211, 213

"Laddie, the Princess and the Pie" (Stratton-Porter), **Supp. XX:** 216

"Ladies" (Coleman), **Supp. XI:** 93

Ladies Almanack (Barnes), **Supp. III Part 1:** 37–39, 42; **Supp. XXII:** 167

Ladies and Gentlemen (Hecht and MacArthur), **Supp. XXVII:** 90

Ladies Auxiliary, The (Mirvis), **Supp. XX: 177, 179–185**

"Ladies in Spring" (Welty), **IV:** 276–277; **Retro. Supp. I:** 353

Lady, The (Richter), **Supp. XVIII:** 211–212, 220

Lady Audley's Secret (Braddon), **Supp. I Part 1:** 35, 36
"Lady Barberina" (James), **Retro. Supp. I:** 227
"Lady Bates" (Jarrell), **II:** 380–381
Lady Chatterley's Lover (Lawrence), **III:** 170; **IV:** 434; **Supp. XVI:** 267
Ladye Annabel (Lippard), **Supp. XXIII:** 178
Lady from Louisiana (film, Vorhaus), **Supp. XVII:** 59
"Lady from Redhorse, A" (Bierce), **I:** 203
Lady in Kicking Horse Reservoir, The (Hugo), **Supp. VI:** 134, **138–139**
Lady in the Lake, The (Chandler), **Supp. IV Part 1:** 127, 129–130
"Lady in the Lake, The" (Chandler), **Supp. IV Part 1:** 129
Lady in the Lake, The (film), **Supp. IV Part 1:** 130
"Lady in the Pink Mustang, The" (Erdrich), **Supp. IV Part 1:** 270
"Lady Is Civilized, The" (Taylor), **Supp. V:** 315
Lady Is Cold, The (White), **Supp. I Part 2:** 653
Lady Killer (Holding), **Supp. XXII:** 126, **127,** 130
"Lady Lazarus" (Plath), **Retro. Supp. II:** 250, 251, 255; **Supp. I Part 2:** 529, 535, 542, 545
Lady of Aroostook, The (Howells), **II:** 280
"Lady of Bayou St. John, A" (Chopin), **Retro. Supp. II:** 58
"Lady of the Lake, The" (Malamud), **Supp. I Part 2:** 437
Lady Oracle (Atwood), **Supp. XIII:** 21, **23–24**
"Lady Poverty" (Notley), **Supp. XXII:** 234–235
Lady Sings the Blues (film), **Supp. I Part 1:** 67
"Lady's Maid's Bell, The" (Wharton), **IV:** 316
"Lady Wentworth" (Longfellow), **II:** 505
"Lady with a Lamp" (Parker), **Supp. IX:** 193
"Lady with the Heron, The" (Merwin), **Supp. III Part 1:** 343
"Lady with the Pet Dog, The" (Chekov), **Supp. XXII:** 60
"Lady with the Pet Tribble, The" (Brockmeier), **Supp. XXII:** 60
La Farge, John, **I:** 1, 2, 20; **II:** 322, 338; **Retro. Supp. I:** 217
La Farge, Oliver, **Supp. IV Part 2:** 503
Lafayette, Marquis de, **I:** 344, 345; **II:** 405–406; **Supp. I Part 2:** 510, 511, 683
"La Figlia che Piange" (Eliot), **Retro. Supp. I:** 63
La Follette, Robert, **I:** 483, 485, 492; **III:** 580
La Fontaine, Jean de, **II:** 154; **III:** 194; **IV:** 80
Laforgue, Jules, **I:** 386, 569, 570, 572–573, 575, 576; **II:** 528; **III:** 8, 11, 466; **IV:** 37, 79, 80, 122; **Retro. Supp. I:** 55, 56; **Supp. XIII:** 332, 335, 346; **Supp. XV:** 165

La Gallienne, Eva, **Supp. VIII:** 251
"Lager Beer" (Dunbar), **Supp. II Part 1:** 193
"La Gringuita: On Losing a Native Language" (Alvarez), **Supp. VII:** 18
Laguna Woman (Silko), **Supp. IV Part 2:** 557, 560–561
LaHaye, Tim, **Supp. XXVII:** 5
Lahiri, Jhumpa, **Supp. XXI: 175–189;** **Supp. XXIII:** 289
Lahr, John, **Supp. XXI:** 18
Laing, R. D., **Supp. I Part 2:** 527; **Supp. XX: 94**
La kabbale pratique (Ambelain), **Supp. I Part 1:** 273
"Lake, The" (Bradbury), **Supp. IV Part 1:** 101
Lake, The (play), **Supp. IX:** 189
Lakeboat (Mamet), **Supp. XIV:** 240–241
"Lake Chelan" (Stafford), **Supp. XI:** 321
Lake Effect Country (Ammons), **Supp. VII:** 34, 35
"Lake Isle of Innisfree, The" (Yeats), **Retro. Supp. I:** 413; **Supp. XIX:** 92
"Lake Return" (Wright), **Supp. XV:** 345
Lake Wobegon Days (Keillor), **Supp. XVI:** 165, 166, **173–174**
Lake Wobegon Summer 1956 (Keillor), **Supp. XVI:** 178
Lalic, Ivan V., **Supp. VIII:** 272
Lamantia, Philip, **Supp. VIII:** 289
Lamb, Brian, **Supp. XIX:** 156; **Supp. XX: 101**
Lamb, Charles, **III:** 111, 207; **Supp. VIII:** 125
Lamb, Wendy, **Supp. IV Part 2:** 658
Lambardi, Marilyn May, **Retro. Supp. II:** 45–46
Lamb in His Bosom (C. Miller), **Supp. XXII:** 187, **189–191,** 193–194, 195, 197, 198, 199, 200
"Lambkill" (Davison), **Supp. XXVI:** 75
"Lame Feet of Salvation, The" (W. V. Davis), **Supp. XXI:** 87–88
"Lament" (Wilbur), **Supp. III Part 2:** 550
Lament and Chastisement (O'Hara), **Supp. XXIII:** 209
"Lamentation in Winter"(Schott), **Supp. XXIII:** 243
"Lamentations" (Glück), **Supp. V:** 83, 84
"Lament for Dark Peoples" (Hughes), **Retro. Supp. I:** 199
"Lament for Saul and Jonathan" (Bradstreet), **Supp. I Part 1:** 111
"Lament-Heaven" (Doty), **Supp. XI:** 125
"Lament of a New England Mother, The" (Eberhart), **I:** 539
Laments for the Living (Parker), **Supp. IX:** 192
"Lame Shall Enter First, The" (O'Connor), **III:** 348, 351, 352, 355, 356–357, 358; **Retro. Supp. II:** 237
"Lamia" (Davison), **Supp. XXVI:** 74
Lamia (Keats), **II:** 512; **III:** 523
Lamming, George, **Supp. XXI:** 170
Lamott, Anne, **Supp. XX: 131–146**
La Motte-Fouqué, Friedrich Heinrich Karl, **III:** 77, 78

L'Amour, Louis, **Supp. XIII:** 5; **Supp. XXVI:** 186
Lamp for Nightfall, A (Caldwell), **I:** 297
Lamplit Answer, The (Schnackenberg), **Supp. XV:** 251, 254, **256–260**
"Lana Turner Has Collapsed!"(O'Hara), **Supp. XXIII:** 220
"Lance" (Nabokov), **Retro. Supp. I:** 266
Lancelot (Percy), **Supp. III Part 1:** 384, 395–396
Lancelot (Robinson), **III:** 513, 522
Lanchester, John, **Retro. Supp. I:** 278
"Land" (Emerson), **II:** 6
"Land Aesthetic, The" (Callicott), **Supp. XIV:** 184
Land and Freedom (film, Loach), **Supp. XXIII:** 163
"Land and Language" (J. W. Miller), **Supp. XX: 170**
Landau, Deborah, **Supp. XI:** 122, 123
"Land beyond the Blow, The" (Bierce), **I:** 209
"Land Ethic, The" (Leopold), **Supp. XIV:** 179, 180, 183, 191, 192
Landfall (Wagoner), **Supp. IX:** 330
"Landing in Luck" (Faulkner), **Retro. Supp. I:** 85
"Landing on the Moon" (Swenson), **Supp. IV Part 2:** 643
"Landings" (Hoffman), **Supp. XVIII:** 86
"Landing Under Water, I See Roots" (A. Finch), **Supp. XVII:** 76
"Land"(Kenny), **Supp. XXIII:** 147
Landlord at Lion's Head, The (Howells), **II:** 276, 287–288
Landmarks of Healing: A Study of House Made of Dawn (Scarberry-García), **Supp. IV Part 2:** 486
Land of Little Rain, The (Dillard), **Supp. VI: 27–28**
Land of Look Behind, The (Cliff), **Supp. XXII:** 65–66, 68–69
Land of the Free U.S.A. (MacLeish), **I:** 293; **III:** 16–17
Land of Unlikeness (R. Lowell), **II:** 537–538, 539, 547; **Retro. Supp. II:** 177, 178, **184–185**
Landor, Walter Savage, **III:** 15, 469; **Supp. I Part 2:** 422
"Landscape" (Sarton), **Supp. VIII:** 259
"Landscape #11" (Halliday), **Supp. XIX:** 93
Landscape and Journey (W. V. Davis), **Supp. XXI:** 83, 88, 90, **92–93,** 95
"Landscape as a Nude" (MacLeish), **III:** 14
Landscape at the End of the Century (Dunn), **Supp. XI:** 139, 143, **150–151**
"Landscape Chamber, The" (Jewett), **II:** 408–409
"Landscape for the Disappeared" (Komunyakaa), **Supp. XIII:** 120, 126
Landscape in American Poetry (Larcom), **Supp. XIII:** 142
"Landscape Painter, A" (James), **II:** 322; **Retro. Supp. I:** 219
"Landscape Symbolism in Kate Chopin's *At Fault*" (Arner), **Retro. Supp. II:** 62

"Landscape: The Eastern Shore" (Barth), **I:** 122

"Landscape with Boat" (Stevens), **Retro. Supp. I:** 306

"Landscape with Bottles"(Schott), **Supp. XXIII:** 242

"Landscape with the Fall of Icarus" (Brueghel), **Retro. Supp. I:** 430

Land's End: A Walk through Province-etown (Cunningham), **Supp. XV:** 69

Land That Drank the Rain, The (Hoffman), **Supp. XVIII:** 76, 80, 81, 82

"Land Where There Is No Death, The" (Benét), **Supp. XI:** 56

Lane, Ann, **Supp. XI:** 195, 208

Lane, Cornelia. *See* Anderson, Mrs. Sherwood

Lane, Homer, **Supp. II Part 1:** 6; **Supp. XIV:** 160

Lane, John, **Supp. XXIV:** 22; **Supp. XXVII:** 216

Lane, Nathan, **Supp. XIII:** 207

Lane, Rose Wilder, **Supp. IV Part 2:** 524; **Supp. XXII:** 293–294, 295, 296, 297, 301

Lanes, Selma G., **Supp. XVI:** 104, 107

Lang, Andrew, **Retro. Supp. I:** 127; **Supp. XXVI:** 33

Lang, John, **Supp. XXVII:** 215, 221, 227, 229

Lang, Violet, **Supp. XII:** 119

Lang, V. R. "Bunny", **Supp. XXIII:** 209

Langdon, Olivia. *See* Clemens, Mrs. Samuel Langhorne (Olivia Langdon)

Lange, Carl Georg, **II:** 350

Lange, Dorothea, **I:** 293; **Supp. XIV:** 181

Langland, Joseph, **III:** 542

Langston Hughes, American Poet (Walker), **Supp. III Part 2:** 530–531

Langston Hughes and the "Chicago Defender": Essays on Race, Politics, and Culture (De Santis, ed.), **Retro. Supp. I:** 194

Langston Hughes: Modern Critical Views (Bloom, ed.), **Retro. Supp. I:** 193

Langston Hughes Reader, The (Hughes), **Retro. Supp. I:** 202; **Supp. I Part 1:** 345

Langston Hughes: The Poet and His Critics (Barksdale), **Retro. Supp. I:** 202

"Language, Visualization and the Inner Library" (Shepard), **Supp. III Part 2:** 436, 438, 449

Language and Imagery of the Bible, The (Caird), **Supp. XXI:** 91–92

"Language and the Writer" (Bambara), **Supp. XI:** 18

Language As Gesture (Blackmur), **Supp. II Part 1:** 108

Language as Symbolic Action (Burke), **I:** 275, 282, 285

Language Book, The (Andrews and Bernstein), **Supp. IV Part 2:** 426

"Language Divine!"(J. Schoolcraft), **Supp. XXIII:** 225

Language God Talks, The: On Science and Religion (Wouk), **Supp. XXV:** 257, 267

Language in Thought and Action (Hayakawa), **I:** 448

"Language of Being and Dying, The" (Gass), **Supp. VI:** 91

"Language of Home, The" (Wideman), **Supp. X:** 320, 323–324

Language of Life, The (Moyers, television series), **Supp. XIII:** 274, 276

Language of the American South, The (Brooks), **Supp. XIV:** 14

"Language of the Brag, The" (Olds), **Supp. X:** 204

"Language We Know, The" (Ortiz), **Supp. IV Part 2:** 500

Lanier, Clifford, **Supp. I Part 1:** 349, 350, 353, 355, 356, 371

Lanier, James F. D., **Supp. I Part 1:** 350

Lanier, Lyle H., **Supp. X:** 25

Lanier, Robert Sampson, **Supp. I Part 1:** 349, 351, 355, 356, 361

Lanier, Mrs. Robert Sampson (Mary Jane Anderson), **Supp. I Part 1:** 349

Lanier, Sidney, **IV:** 444; **Supp. I Part 1:** 349–373; **Supp. I Part 2:** 416; **Supp. IV Part 1:** 165

Lanier, Mrs. Sidney (Mary Day), **Supp. I Part 1:** 351, 355, 357, 361, 362, 364, 370, 371

"Lanier as Poet" (Parks), **Supp. I Part 1:** 373

"Lanier's Reading" (P. Graham), **Supp. I Part 1:** 373

"Lanier's Use of Science for Poetic Imagery" (Beaver), **Supp. I Part 1:** 373

Lankes, J. J., **Supp. XXII:** 275

Lannegan, Helen. *See* Caldwell, Mrs. Erskine

Lannin, Paul, **II:** 427

Lanny Budd novels (Sinclair), **Supp. V:** 290

Lansdale, Joe R., **Supp. XXV:** 145

Lant, Kathleen Margaret, **Supp. V:** 141

Lanterns on the Levee (Percy), **Supp. XXII:** 193

Lanthenas, François, **Supp. I Part 2:** 515

"Lanyard, The" (Collins), **Supp. XXI:** 56, **62–64**

Laotzu, **III:** 173, 189, 567; **Supp. XV:** 39, 46, 48

Lapine, James, **Supp. XXI:** 147–148

"Lapis Lazuli" (Yeats), **I:** 532; **III:** 40

Laplace, Pierre Simon de, **III:** 428

Lapouge, M. G., **Supp. I Part 2:** 633

Lappa, Katherine, **Supp. XV:** 176

Lapsing to Grace (Espaillat), **Supp. XXI:** 99, 100

Lapsley, Gaillard, **Supp. XX: 231**

Laqueur, Thomas, **Supp. XVI:** 154

Larbaud, Valery, **IV:** 404; **Supp. XIII:** 332; **Supp. XIV:** 338

Larcom, Lucy, **Retro. Supp. II:** 145; **Supp. XIII: 137–157**

Larcom's Poetical Works (Larcom), **Supp. XIII:** 142

Lardner, James, **Supp. XXVII:** 141

Lardner, John, **II:** 437

Lardner, Ring, **I:** 487; **II:** 44, 91, 259, 263, **415–438; III:** 566, 572; **IV:** 433; **Retro. Supp. I:** 105; **Retro. Supp. II:**

222; **Supp. I Part 2:** 609; **Supp. IX:** 200; **Supp. XVI:** 189

Lardner, Ring, Jr., **Supp. XI:** 306

"Lardner, Shakespeare and Chekhov" (Matthews), **II:** 430

"Large Bad Picture" (Bishop), **Retro. Supp. II:** 43; **Supp. I Part 1:** 73, 80–82, 85, 86, 89, 90

"Large Coffee" (Lardner), **II:** 437

Large Glass, or The Bride Stripped Bare by Her Bachelors, Even (Duchamp), **Supp. IV Part 2:** 423, 424

Largo (Handel), **IV:** 369

"Lark" (Taggard), **Supp. XXII:** 280

Lark, The (Hellman), **Supp. I Part 1:** 286–288, 297

Lark: Four-Part Chorus for Mixed Voices (A Capella) with Baritone Solo (Taggard and Copland), **Supp. XXII:** 283

Larkin, Philip, **Supp. I Part 2:** 536; **Supp. XI:** 243, 249; **Supp. XIII:** 76, 85; **Supp. XV:** 117, 251; **Supp. XVII:** 110; **Supp. XVIII:** 173; **Supp. XX: 199; Supp. XXI:** 84, 93; **Supp. XXVI:** 67

Larkin, Sharon Alile, **Supp. XI:** 20

Larmore, Phoebe, **Supp. X:** 266

Larner, Jeremy, **Supp. XVI:** 220

La Rochefoucauld, François de, **I:** 279; **II:** 111; **Supp. XIV:** 130

"La Rose des Vents" (Wilbur), **Supp. III Part 2:** 550

"Larry Brown's *Dirty Work:* A Study of Man's Responsibility for Suffering" (Prevost), **Supp. XXI:** 45

"Larry"(O'Hara), **Supp. XXIII:** 212

Larry's Party (Shields), **Supp. VII:** 324, 326–327

Larsen, Nella, **Supp. I Part 1:** 325, 326; **Supp. IV Part 1:** 164; **Supp. XVIII: 119–134**

Larson, Charles, **Supp. IV Part 1:** 331

Larson, Clinton, **Supp. XI:** 328

Larson, Kelli, **Supp. XVIII:** 131

LaRue, Dorie, **Supp. XXI:** 43

"Larval Stage of a Bookworm" (Mencken), **III:** 101

La Salle and the Discovery of the Great West (Parkman), **Supp. II Part 2:** 595, 598, 605–607; **Supp. XVIII:** 114

Las Casas, Bartolomé de, **Supp. XXIV:** 87

Lasch, Christopher, **I:** 259

Lasdun, James, **Supp. XXIV:** 154

Lasher (Rice), **Supp. VII:** 299–300

Lask, Thomas, **III:** 576; **Supp. XVI:** 250

Laski, Harold, **Supp. I Part 2:** 632, 643

Lass, Abraham H., **Supp. XXIV:** 214

Lassalle, Ferdinand, **IV:** 429

Lasser, Louise, **Supp. XV:** 4

"Last Acts" (Olds), **Supp. X:** 210

Last Adam, The (Cozzens), **I:** 362–363, 364, 368, 375, 377, 378, 379

Last Analysis, The (Bellow), **I:** 152, 160, 161; **Retro. Supp. II:** 26

Last and Lost Poems of Delmore Schwartz (Phillips, ed.), **Supp. II Part 2:** 661, 665

Last Avant-Garde, The: The Making of the New York School of Poets (Lehman), **Supp. XV:** 178–179, 187

Last Beautiful Days of Autumn, The (Nichols), **Supp. XIII:** 254, 255, 267, 269

Last Best Place, The: A Montana Anthology (Kittredge and Smith, eds.), **Supp. XXVI:** 188

Last Blue (Stern), **Supp. IX: 299–300**

Last Book, The (Pickering), **Supp. XXI:** 203–204

Last Carousel, The (Algren), **Supp. IX:** 16

Last Centennial, The (P. N. Warren as Kilina), **Supp. XX: 261–262**

"Last Child" (X. J. Kennedy), **Supp. XV:** 162, 165

"Last Class with Roethke" (Gallagher), **Supp. XXIV:** 171

Last Clean Shirt, The (film, Leslie and O'Hara), **Supp. XXIII:** 217

Last Coyote, The (Connelly), **Supp. XXI: 71**

"Last Dance" (Dubus III), **Supp. XXIV:** 100

"Last Day in the Field, The" (Gordon), **II:** 200

"Last Day of the Last Furlough" (Salinger), **III:** 552–553

"Last Days of Alice" (Tate), **IV:** 129

"Last Days of August, The" (Nye), **Supp. XIII:** 284

"Last Days of John Brown, The" (Thoreau), **IV:** 185

Last Days of Louisiana Red, The (Reed), **Supp. X:** 240, **248–249**

Last Decade, The (Trilling), **Supp. III Part 2:** 493, 499

"Last Demon, The" (Singer), **IV:** 15, 21

Last Detective, The (Crais), **Supp. XXI:** 70

Last Exit to Brooklyn (Selby), **Supp. III Part 1:** 125; **Supp. XXI:** 227, 231

Last Flower, The (Thurber), **Supp. I Part 2:** 610

"Last Frontier" (McCarriston), **Supp. XIV:** 272

Last Generation, The (Moraga), **Supp. XXIII:** 201

Last Gentleman, The (Percy), **Supp. III Part 1:** 383–388, 392–393

"Last Good Country, The" (Hemingway), **II:** 258–259

Last Good Time, The (Bausch), **Supp. VII:** 45–46

"Last Great Saloon, The"(Exley), **Supp. XXIII:** 103

"Last Hiding Places of Snow, The" (Kinnell), **Supp. III Part 1:** 252

"Last Hours, The" (Dunn), **Supp. XI:** 141

Last House: Reflections, Dreams, and Observations, 1943–1991 (M. F. K. Fisher), **Supp. XVII:** 92

Last Husband and Other Stories, The (Humphrey), **Supp. IX:** 94

"Last Interview" (Rash), **Supp. XXVII:** 218

Last Jew in America, The (Fiedler), **Supp. XIII:** 103

"Last Jew in America, The" (Fiedler), **Supp. XIII:** 103

Last Laugh, Mr. Moto (Marquand), **III:** 57

"Last Leaf, The" (Holmes), **Supp. I Part 1:** 302, 309

"Last Leaf, The" (Porter), **III:** 444

"Last Lie, The" (Weigl), **Supp. XIX:** 279

"Last Light" (Major), **Supp. XXII:** 185

"Last Look at the Lilacs" (Stevens), **IV:** 74

Last Man, The (Kees), **Supp. XV:** 142, 143, 145

"Last May" (Dixon), **Supp. XII: 143**

"Last Mermother, The" (A. Finch), **Supp. XVII:** 72

"Last Mohican, The" (Malamud), **Supp. I Part 2:** 437–438, 450, 451

"Lastness" (Kinnell), **Supp. III Part 1:** 248–249

"Last Night" (Olds), **Supp. X:** 212

Last Night at the Lobster (O'Nan), **Supp. XXV:** 149–150, 151

"Last Night at Tía's" (Alvarez), **Supp. VII:** 5

Last Night of Summer, The (Caldwell), **I:** 292–293

Last Notes from Home (Exley), **Supp. XXIII:** 97, 98, **106–108**

Last of Mr. Norris, The (Isherwood), **Supp. XIV:** 161

"Last of the Brooding Miserables, The" (Karr), **Supp. XI:** 250

"Last of the Caddoes, The" (Humphrey), **Supp. IX:** 101

Last of the Crazy People, The (Findley), **Supp. XX: 51–52**

"Last of the Gold Star Mothers, The" (C. Bly), **Supp. XVI:** 34, 35, 36

"Last of the Legions, The" (Benét), **Supp. XI:** 56, 57

Last of the Mohicans, The (Cooper), **I:** 341, 342, 349

Last of the Red Hot Lovers (Simon), **Supp. IV Part 2:** 575, 583, 589

"Last of the Valerii, The" (James), **II:** 327; **Retro. Supp. I:** 218

"Last One, The" (Merwin), **Supp. III Part 1:** 355

Last Picture Show, The (film), **Supp. V:** 223, 226

Last Picture Show, The (McMurtry), **Supp. V:** 220, 222–223, 233

Last Place on Earth, The: Scott and Amundsen's Race to the South Pole (Huntford), **Supp. XVIII:** 114

Last Puritan, The (Santayana), **III:** 64, 600, 604, 607, 612, 615–617

Last Radio Baby, The (Andrews), **Supp. XXVI:** 2–3, 7, 10

"Last Ride Together, The" (Browning), **I:** 468

"Last River, The" (Kinnell), **Supp. III Part 1:** 236

Last Song, The (Harjo), **Supp. XII:** 218

"Last Song for the Mend-It Shop" (Nye), **Supp. XIII:** 283

"Last Tango in Fresno" (Salinas), **Supp. XIII:** 318

"Last Trip to Greece"(Hadas), **Supp. XXIII:** 118–119

Last Tycoon, The: An Unfinished Novel (Fitzgerald), **II:** 84, 98; **Retro. Supp. I:** 109, 114, **114–115; Retro. Supp. II:** 337; **Supp. IV Part 1:** 203; **Supp. IX:** 63; **Supp. XII:** 173; **Supp. XIII:** 170; **Supp. XVIII:** 248, 250

"Last WASP in the World, The" (Fiedler), **Supp. XIII:** 103

"Last Watch, The" (Gibran), **Supp. XX: 119**

Last Watch of the Night: Essays Too Personal and Otherwise (Monette), **Supp. X:** 147, 148, 153, **157–159**

"Last Will" (Stallings), **Supp. XXV:** 232

"Last Word, The" (column, Quindlen), **Supp. XVII:** 165, 167, 170

Last Word, The: Letters between Marcia Nardi and William Carlos Williams (O'Neil, ed.), **Retro. Supp. I:** 427

"Last Words" (Levine), **Supp. V:** 190

"Last Words" (Olds), **Supp. X:** 210

Last Worthless Evening, The (Dubus), **Supp. VII:** 87–88

"Las Vegas (What?) Las Vegas (Can't Hear You! Too Noisy) Las Vegas! ! ! !" (Wolfe), **Supp. III Part 2:** 572

"Late" (Bogan), **Supp. III Part 1:** 53

"Late Air" (Bishop), **Supp. I Part 1:** 89

"Late Autumn" (Sarton), **Supp. VIII:** 261

"Late Bronze, Early Iron: A Journey Book" (Sobin), **Supp. XVI:** 290

Late Child, The (McMurtry), **Supp. V:** 231

"Late Conversation" (Doty), **Supp. XI:** 122

"Late Elegy for John Berryman, A" (W. V. Davis), **Supp. XXI:** 91

"Late Encounter with the Enemy, A" (O'Connor), **III:** 345; **Retro. Supp. II:** 232

Late Fire, Late Snow (Francis), **Supp. IX: 89–90**

"Late Fragment" (Gallagher), **Supp. XXIV:** 172

Late George Apley, The (Marquand), **II:** 482–483; **III:** 50, 51, 52, 56–57, 58, 62–64, 65, 66

Late George Apley, The (Marquand and Kaufman), **III:** 62

"Late Hour" (Everwine), **Supp. XV:** 85

Late Hour, The (Strand), **Supp. IV Part 2:** 620, 629–630

"Lately, at Night" (Kumin), **Supp. IV Part 2:** 442

"Late Moon" (Levine), **Supp. V:** 186

"Late Night Ode" (McClatchy), **Supp. XII:** 262–263

Later (Creeley), **Supp. IV Part 1:** 153, 156, 157

Later Life (Gurney), **Supp. V:** 103, 105

La Terre (Zola), **III:** 316, 322

Later the Same Day (Paley), **Supp. VI:** 218

"Late September in Nebraska" (Kooser), **Supp. XIX:** 120

Late Settings (Merrill), **Supp. III Part 1:** 336

"Late Sidney Lanier, The" (Stedman), **Supp. I Part 1:** 373

"Late Snow & Lumber Strike of the Summer of Fifty-Four, The" (Snyder), **Supp. VIII:** 294

"Late Start, A" (L. Brown), **Supp. XXI:** 40–41

"Latest Freed Man, The" (Stevens), **Retro. Supp. I:** 306

"Latest Injury, The" (Olds), **Supp. X:** 209

Latest Literary Essays and Addresses (J. R. Lowell), **Supp. I Part 2:** 407

"Late Subterfuge" (Warren), **IV:** 257

"Late Summer Lilies" (Weigl), **Supp. XIX:** 288

"Late Summer Love Song" (Davison), **Supp. XXVI:** 69

"Late Supper, A" (Jewett), **Retro. Supp. II:** 137

"Late Victorians" (Rodriguez), **Supp. XIV:** 303–304

"Late Walk, A" (Frost), **II:** 153; **Retro. Supp. I:** 127

Latham, Edyth, **I:** 289

Lathrop, George Parsons, **Supp. I Part 1:** 365

Lathrop, H. B., **Supp. III Part 2:** 612

Lathrop, Julia, **Supp. I Part 1:** 5

Latière de Trianon, La (Wekerlin), **II:** 515

"La Tigresse" (Van Vechten), **Supp. II Part 2:** 735, 738

Latimer, Hugh, **II:** 15

Latimer, Margery, **Supp. IX:** 320

La Tour Dreams of the Wolf Girl (Huddle), **Supp. XXVI:** 148, 151, 158, 159

La Traviata (Verdi), **III:** 139

"Latter-Day Warnings" (Holmes), **Supp. I Part 1:** 307

"Latter Rain, The" (Very), **Supp. XXV:** 249

"Lattice Work: Formal Tendencies in the Poetry of Robert Morgan and Ron Rash" (Graves), **Supp. XXVII:** 216

La Turista (Shepard), **Supp. III Part 2:** 440

Lauber, John, **Supp. XIII:** 21

Laud, Archbishop, **II:** 158

"Lauds" (Auden), **Supp. II Part 1:** 23

"Laughing Man, The" (Salinger), **III:** 559

Laughing Matters (Siegel), **Supp. XXII:** 260

Laughing to Keep From Crying (Hughes), **Supp. I Part 1:** 329–330

Laughing Wild (Durang), **Supp. XXIV:** 114, **124**

"Laughing with One Eye" (Schnackenberg), **Supp. XV:** 253

Laughlin, James, **III:** 171; **Retro. Supp. I:** 423, 424, 428, 430, 431; **Supp. VIII:** 195; **Supp. XV:** 140; **Supp. XVI:** 284; **Supp. XXI:** 29

Laughlin, Jay, **Supp. II Part 1:** 94

Laughlin, J. Laurence, **Supp. I Part 2:** 641

Laughter in the Dark (Nabokov), **III:** 255–258; **Retro. Supp. I:** 270

"Laughter of Women, The" (Davison), **Supp. XXVI:** 75

Laughter on the 23rd Floor (Simon), **Supp. IV Part 2:** 575, 576, 588, 591–592

"Launcelot" (Lewis), **II:** 439–440

"Laura Dailey's Story" (Bogan), **Supp. III Part 1:** 52

Laurel, Stan, **Supp. I Part 2:** 607; **Supp. IV Part 2:** 574

Laurel and Hardy Go to Heaven (Auster), **Supp. XII:** 21

Laurence, Alexander, **Supp. XVIII:** 138

Laurence, Dan H., **II:** 338–339

Laurens, John, **Supp. I Part 2:** 509

Lauter, Paul, **Supp. XV:** 313

Lautréamont, Comte de, **III:** 174

Lavender Locker Room, The (P. N. Warren), **Supp. XX:** 261, **273–274**

Law, John, **Supp. XI:** 307

Law and Order (television), **Supp. XVII:** 153

Law and the Testimony, The (S. and A. Warner), **Supp. XVIII:** 264

Lawd Today (Wright), **IV:** 478, 492

Law for the Lion, A (Auchincloss), **Supp. IV Part 1:** 25

Lawgiver, The (Wouk), **Supp. XXV:** 253, 256, 257, 267–268

"Law Lane" (Jewett), **II:** 407

"Lawns of June, The" (Peacock), **Supp. XIX:** 196

"Law of Nature and the Dream of Man, The: Ruminations of the Art of Fiction" (Stegner), **Supp. IV Part 2:** 604

Lawrence, D. H., **I:** 291, 336, 377, 522, 523; **II:** 78, 84, 98, 102, 264, 517, 523, 532, 594, 595; **III:** 27, 33, 40, 44, 46, 172, 173, 174, 178, 184, 229, 261, 423, 429, 458, 546–547; **IV:** 138, 339, 342, 351, 380; **Retro. Supp. I:** 7, 18, 203, 204, 421; **Retro. Supp. II:** 68; **Supp. I Part 1:** 227, 230, 243, 255, 257, 258, 263, 329; **Supp. I Part 2:** 546, 613, 728; **Supp. II Part 1:** 1, 9, 20, 89; **Supp. IV Part 1:** 81; **Supp. VIII:** 237; **Supp. X:** 137, 193, 194; **Supp. XII:** 172; **Supp. XIV:** 310; **Supp. XV:** 45, 46, 158, 254; **Supp. XVI:** 267; **Supp. XX: 69; Supp. XXII:** 198; **Supp. XXIII:** 166, 275; **Supp. XXIV:** 51, 52, 57, 58, 64; **Supp. XXVI:** 144

Lawrence, Elizabeth, **Supp. XXIII:** 259, 264

Lawrence, Frieda, **Supp. XV:** 46

Lawrence, Rhoda, **Supp. I Part 1:** 45

Lawrence, Seymour, **Supp. IX:** 107; **Supp. XI:** 335, 346, 348

Lawrence, T. E., **Supp. XIV:** 159

Lawrence of Arabia (Aldington), **Supp. I Part 1:** 259

Lawrence of Arabia (film), **Supp. I Part 1:** 67

Laws (Hadas), **Supp. XXIII:** 119–120, 124

Laws (Plato), **Supp. IV Part 1:** 391

Laws of Ice, The (Price), **Supp. VI:** 264

Laws of Our Fathers, The (Turow), **Supp. XVII:** 218–219

Lawson, John Howard, **I:** 479, 482

Lawton Girl, The (Frederic), **II:** 132–133, 144

Layachi, Larbi (Driss ben Hamed Charhadi), **Supp. IV Part 1:** 92, 93

Layard, John, **Supp. XIV:** 160

Lay Down My Sword and Shield (Burke), **Supp. XIV:** 22, 25, 34

"Layers, The" (Kunitz), **Supp. III Part 1:** 260, 266–267

"Layers, The: Some Notes on 'The Abduction' " (Kunitz), **Supp. III Part 1:** 266

"Lay-mans Lamentation, The" (Taylor), **IV:** 162–163

Lay of the Land, The: Metaphor as Experience and History in American Life and Letters (Kolodny), **Supp. X:** 97

"Layover" (Hass), **Supp. VI:** 109

"Lay Preacher" (Dennie), **Supp. I Part 1:** 125

Layton, Irving, **Supp. XII:** 121

Lazar, Irving "Swifty", **Supp. XIX:** 250

Lazarillo de Tormes (Mendoza), **III:** 182

Lazar Malkin Enters Heaven (S. Stern), **Supp. XVII:** 42; **Supp. XX: 178**

Lazarus Laughed (O'Neill), **III:** 391, 395–396

Lazer, Hank, **Supp. IX:** 265

Lea, Luke, **IV:** 248

Leachman, Cloris, **Supp. XXI:** 146

Leacock, Stephen, **Supp. IV Part 2:** 464

"LEADBELLY GIVES AN AUTOGRAPH" (Baraka), **Supp. II Part 1:** 49

Leaflets: Poems, 1965–1968 (Rich), **Supp. I Part 2:** 551, 556–557

"League of American Writers, The: Communist Organizational Activity among American Writers 1929–1942" (Wolfe), **Supp. III Part 2:** 568

League of Brightened Philistines and Other Papers, The (Farrell), **II:** 49

Leahy, Anna, **Supp. XXI:** 246

"Leakage" (Skloot), **Supp. XX: 202**

Leal, Luis, **Supp. XIX:** 98, 112

"Leaning" (Webb), **Supp. XX: 56**

Leaning Forward (Paley), **Supp. VI:** 221

"Leaning Tower, The" (Porter), **III:** 442, 443, 446–447

Leaning Tower and Other Stories, The (Porter), **III:** 433, 442, 443–447

"Leap, The" (Dickey), **Supp. IV Part 1:** 182

"Leaping Up into Political Poetry" (R. Bly), **Supp. IV Part 1:** 61, 63

Leap Year (Cameron), **Supp. XII:** 79–80, 81, **85–86**, 88

Lear, Edward, **III:** 428, 536; **Supp. XVI:** 103; **Supp. XXVI:** 274

Lear, Linda, **Supp. IX:** 19, 22, 25, 26

Learned Ladies, The (Molière; Wilbur, trans.), **Supp. III Part 2:** 560

"Learning a Dead Language" (Merwin), **Supp. III Part 1:** 345

Learning a Trade: A Craftsman's Notebooks, 1955–1997 (Price), **Supp. VI:** 254, 255, 267

"Learning Bones" (Espaillat), **Supp. XXI:** 107

Learning to Live in This World (Schott), **Supp. XXIII:** 248

Learning to Love: Exploring Solitude and Freedom (Merton), **Supp. VIII:** 200

Learning to Love You More (website), **Supp. XXIV:** 200

"Learning to Read" (Harper), **Supp. II Part 1:** 201–202

"Learning to Speak" (Everwine), **Supp. XV:** 79

"Learning to Speak" (Gansworth), **Supp. XXVI:** 111

"Learning to Think" (Kittredge), **Supp. XXVI:** 181

"Learning to Work Together" (L. I. Wilder), **Supp. XXII:** 290

Learning Tree, The (Park), **Supp. XIX:** 154

Leary, Lewis, **III:** 478

Leary, Paris, **Supp. IV Part 1:** 176

Leary, Timothy, **Supp. X:** 265; **Supp. XIV:** 150

Lease, Joseph, **Supp. XXI:** 246

Least Heat Moon, William, **Supp. V:** 169

Leather-Stocking Tales, The (Cooper), **I:** 335

Leatherwood God, The (Howells), **II:** 276, 277, 288

Leave It to Beaver (television show), **Supp. XX: 103**

"Leave Me Alone a Little" (Taggard), **Supp. XXII:** 274

"Leaves" (Updike), **Retro. Supp. I:** 323, 329, 335

Leaves and Ashes (Haines), **Supp. XII:** 206

Leaves from the Notebook of a Tamed Cynic (Niebuhr), **III:** 293

Leaves of Grass (Whitman), **II:** 8; **IV:** 331, 332, 333, 334, 335, 336, 340, 341–342, 348, 350, 405, 464; **Retro. Supp. I:** 387, 388, 389, 390, **392–395,** 406, 407, 408; **Retro. Supp. II:** 93; **Supp. I Part 1:** 365; **Supp. I Part 2:** 416, 579; **Supp. III Part 1:** 156; **Supp. IX:** 265; **Supp. V:** 170; **Supp. VIII:** 275; **Supp. X:** 120; **Supp. XIV:** 334; **Supp. XIX:** 276; **Supp. XV:** 218; **Supp. XVIII:** 4; **Supp. XXI:** 205; **Supp. XXII:** 92; **Supp. XXIII:** 165; **Supp. XXIV:** 85

"Leaves of Grass" (Whitman), **IV:** 463

Leaves of Grass (1856) (Whitman), **Retro. Supp. I:** 399–402

Leaves of Grass (1860) (Whitman), **Retro. Supp. I:** 402–405

Leaves of the Tree, The (Masters), **Supp. I Part 2:** 460

"Leaving" (Hogan), **Supp. IV Part 1:** 400

"Leaving" (Wilbur), **Supp. III Part 2:** 563

"Leaving, The" (B. Kelly), **Supp. XVII:** 127, 132

Leaving a Doll's House: A Memoir (C. Bloom), **Retro. Supp. II:** 281

Leaving Another Kingdom: Selected Poems (Stern), **Supp. IX:** 296

"Leaving Bartram's Garden in Southwest Philadelphia" (Di Piero), **Supp. XIX:** 46

"Leaving Brooklyn" (Neugeboren), **Supp. XVI:** 226

Leaving Cheyenne (McMurtry), **Supp. V:** 220, 221–222, 224, 229

Leaving Home (Keillor), **Supp. XVI:** 175

"Leaving One, The" (Offutt), **Supp. XIX:** 165–166

"Leaving the Island" (Olds), **Supp. X:** 214

"Leaving the Yellow House" (Bellow), **Retro. Supp. II:** 27, 32

"Leaving Town" (Kenyon), **Supp. VII:** 163

Leavis, F. R., **I:** 522; **III:** 462–463, 475, 478; **Retro. Supp. I:** 67; **Retro. Supp. II:** 243; **Supp. I Part 2:** 536; **Supp. VIII:** 234, 236, 245

Leavis, Queenie, **Supp. XX: 232**

"Leavis-Snow Controversy, The" (Trilling), **Supp. III Part 2:** 512

Leavitt, Caroline, **Supp. XX: 186**

Leavitt, David, **Supp. VIII:** 88

Lebanon (C. Miller), **Supp. XXII:** 198–199

Le Braz, Anatole, **Supp. XIII:** 253

Le Carre, John, **Supp. XX: 195**

Lecker, Robert, **Supp. XIII:** 21

LeClair, Thomas (Tom), **Supp. IV Part 1:** 286; **Supp. V:** 53; **Supp. XII:** 152; **Supp. XX: 93; Supp. XXII:** 206, 210, 261, 264

Le Conte, Joseph, **II:** 479; **III:** 227–228

"Lecture, The" (Singer), **IV:** 21

"LECTURE PAST DEAD CATS" (Baraka), **Supp. II Part 1:** 52

Lectures in America (Stein), **IV:** 27, 32, 33, 35, 36, 41, 42

"Lectures on Poetry" (Bryant), **Supp. I Part 1:** 159, 161

Lectures on Rhetoric (Blair), **II:** 8

"Leda and the Swan" (Yeats), **III:** 347; **Supp. IX:** 52

Ledger (Fitzgerald), **Retro. Supp. I:** 109, 110

Lee (Masters), **Supp. I Part 2:** 471

Lee, Baayork, **Supp. XXI:** 148

Lee, C. Y., **Supp. XXI:** 148

Lee, Don, **Supp. XII:** 295; **Supp. XVII:** 13, 14, 15, 16

Lee, Don L. *See* Madhubuti, Haki R.

Lee, Gypsy Rose, **II:** 586; **III:** 161; **Supp. IV Part 1:** 84

Lee, Harper, **Supp. VIII: 113–131; Supp. XXVII:** 276

Lee, Harriett, **Supp. XV:** 230

Lee, James Kyun-Jin, **Supp. XV:** 213

Lee, James W., **Supp. IX:** 94, 97, 109

Lee, James Ward, **Supp. VIII:** 57

Lee, Lawrence, **Supp. XXV:** 29

Lee, Li Lin, **Supp. XV:** 211, 212

Lee, Li-Young, **Supp. XV: 211–228; Supp. XVII:** 241

Lee, Richard E., **Supp. XIX:** 226, 227

Lee, Robert E., **II:** 150, 206; **IV:** 126; **Supp. I Part 2:** 471, 486

Lee, Robert N., **Supp. XXVII:** 92

Lee, Samuel, **IV:** 158

Lee, Spike, **Retro. Supp. II:** 12; **Supp. XI:** 19; **Supp. XIII:** 179, 186; **Supp. XVI:** 144; **Supp. XX: 110; Supp. XXVI:** 199

Lee, Virginia Chin-lan, **Supp. X:** 291

Leeds, Barry, **Retro. Supp. II:** 204

Leeds, Daniel, **II:** 110

Leeds, Titan, **II:** 110, 111

Leeming, David, **Retro. Supp. II:** 4, 10

"Lees of Happiness, The" (Fitzgerald), **II:** 88

"Le Filme" (Weigl), **Supp. XIX:** 288

Left Behind series (LaHaye and Jenkins), **Supp. XXVII:** 5

Left Hand of God, The (film), **Supp. XXVI:** 134

Left Out in the Rain: New Poems 1947–1985 (Snyder), **Supp. VIII:** 305

Leftovers, The (Perrota), **Supp. XXVII:** 6

"Legacy" (Dunn), **Supp. XI:** 148

"Legacy" (Komunyakaa), **Supp. XIII:** 132

"Legacy" (W. V. Davis), **Supp. XXI:** 93–94

"Legacy of Aldo Leopold, The" (Stegner), **Supp. XIV:** 193

"Legacy of Channing, The" (Robinson), **Supp. XXIV:** 79

Legacy of Fear, A (Farrell), **II:** 39

"Legacy of the Ancestral Arts, The" (Locke), **Supp. XIV:** 201

Legacy of the Civil War, The: Meditations on the Centennial (Warren), **IV:** 236

"Legal Alien" (Mora), **Supp. XIII:** 215

"Legal Tender Act, The" (Adams), **I:** 5

Légende de la mort, La (Le Braz), **Supp. XIII:** 253

"Legend of Duluoz, The" (Kerouac), **Supp. III Part 1:** 218, 226, 227, 229

"Legend of Lillian Hellman, The" (Kazin), **Supp. I Part 1:** 297

"Legend of Monte del Diablo, The" (Harte), **Supp. II Part 1:** 339

"Legend of Paper Plates, The" (Haines), **Supp. XII:** 204

"Legend of Sammtstadt, A" (Harte), **Supp. II Part 1:** 355

"Legend of Sleepy Hollow, The" (Irving), **II:** 306–308

Legends (A. Lowell), **II:** 525–526

Legends and Dreams (P. N. Warren), **Supp. XX: 261**

Legends of Mexico (Lippard), **Supp. XXIII:** 178, 186

Legends of New England (Whittier), **Supp. I Part 2:** 684, 692

Legends of the Fall (Harrison), **Supp. VIII:** 38, 39, **45–46,** 48

"Legends of the Revolution" (series, Lippard), **Supp. XXIII:** 178

Legends of the West (Hall), **II:** 313

Léger, Fernand, **Retro. Supp. I:** 292

Legge, James, **III:** 472

Leggett, William, **Supp. I Part 1:** 157

"Legion, The" (Karr), **Supp. XI:** 243

"Legs" (Halliday), **Supp. XIX:** 90

Legs (W. Kennedy), **Supp. VII:** 133, 134, 138–142, 143, 151

Le Guin, Ursula K., **Supp. IV Part 1:** 333; **Supp. XXII:** 49

Lehan, Richard, **Retro. Supp. II:** 104

Lehman, David, **Supp. IX:** 161; **Supp. XIII:** 130; **Supp. XV:** 178–179, 180, 187, 190; **Supp. XXI:** 246; **Supp. XXVI:** 50

Lehmann, John, **Retro. Supp. II:** 243; **Supp. XIV:** 158, 159

Lehmann, Paul, **III:** 311

Lehmann-Haupt, Christopher, **Retro. Supp. II:** 291; **Supp. IV Part 1:** 205, 209, 306; **Supp. IX:** 95, 103; **Supp. XVI:** 73, 210, 294, 295; **Supp. XXII:** 205, 213; **Supp. XXIII:** 103

Lehrer, Jim, **Supp. XVIII:** 39

Leiber, Fritz, **Supp. XVI:** 123

Leibling, A. J., **Supp. XIV:** 112

Leibniz, Gottfried Wilhelm von, **II:** 103; **III:** 428

Leibowitz, Herbert A., **I:** 386; **Supp. XV:** 78

Leich, Roland, **Supp. XIV:** 123

Leichum, Laura, **Supp. XIX:** 197

Leider, Emily Wortis, **Supp. XXIV:** 19, 20, 22, 26, 27, 30

Leiding, Reba, **Supp. XXVI:** 159

Leighton, Betty, **Supp. XXI:** 42

Leimbach, Laura, **Supp. XXIII:** 54

Leithauser, Brad, **Retro. Supp. I:** 133; **Supp. XV:** 250; **Supp. XVII:** 112; **Supp. XXII:** 207

Leitz, Robert, **Supp. XIV:** 62

Leivick, H., **IV:** 6

Lekachman, Robert, **Supp. I Part 2:** 648

Leland, Charles, **Supp. II Part 1:** 193

Leland, Charles Godfrey, **I:** 257

Leland, John, **Supp. XIX:** 157; **Supp. XV:** 69

Lem, Stanislaw, **Supp. IV Part 1:** 103

"Le marais du cygne" (Whittier), **Supp. I Part 2:** 687

Lemay, Harding, **Supp. IX:** 98; **Supp. VIII:** 125

Lemercier, Eugène, **Retro. Supp. I:** 299

Lemkin, Raphael, **Supp. XXIII:** 31

"Lemorne *versus* Huell" (E. Stoddard), **Supp. XV:** 270, 273, 283

Le Morte D'Arthur Notes (Gardner), **Supp. VI:** 65, 66

Lenhard, Elizabeth, **Supp. XXVII:** 267

Lenin, V. I., **I:** 366, 439, 440; **III:** 14–15, 262, 475; **IV:** 429, 436, 443–444; **Supp. I Part 2:** 647; **Supp. XXI:** 164

Lennertz, Carl, **Supp. XXVII:** 267

Lennon, J. Robert, **Supp. XXV:** 151

"Lenny Dying, Pacific Standard Time"(Thompson), **Supp. XXIII:** 294

"Lenore" (Poe), **III:** 411

"Lenox Avenue: Midnight" (Hughes), **Retro. Supp. I:** 198

"Lens of Poetry, The" (Bronk). *See Attendant, The* (Bronk)

Leonard, Elmore, **Supp. IV Part 1:** 356; **Supp. X:** 5; **Supp. XIV:** 26

Leonard, John, **Supp. IV Part 1:** 24; **Supp. IV Part 2:** 474; **Supp. V:** 164, 223–224; **Supp. XI:** 13; **Supp. XIX:** 269; **Supp. XVIII:** 147, 148; **Supp. XXI:** 233, 239

Leonardo da Vinci, **Supp. XII:** 44; **Supp. XXII:** 171

León-Portilla, Miguel, **Supp. XV:** 77

Leontiev, Constantine, **Supp. XIV:** 98

Leopard, The (Lampedusa), **Supp. XII:** 13–14

Leopardi, Giacomo, **II:** 543; **Supp. XIX:** 33, 43

"Leopard Man's Story, The" (London), **II:** 475

Leopard's Mouth Is Dry and Cold Inside, The (Levis), **Supp. XI:** 258

Leopold, Aldo, **Supp. V:** 202; **Supp. X:** 108; **Supp. XIV: 177–194; Supp. XXI:** 203; **Supp. XXVI:** 31

"Leper's Bell, the" (Komunyakaa), **Supp. XIII:** 118

Lerman, Leo, **Supp. X:** 188; **Supp. XVI:** 194

Lerner, Ben, **Supp. XXIV:** 45

Lerner, Max, **III:** 60; **Supp. I Part 2:** 629, 630, 631, 647, 650, 654; **Supp. XXVII:** 134

Lerperger, Emil, **Supp. XX: 165, 167**

Lesbian Nation: The Feminist Solution (Johnston), **Supp. XXV:** 5

"Lesbos" (Plath), **Retro. Supp. II:** 254

Lesesne, Teri, **Supp. XIII:** 277

LeSieg, Theo (pseudonym). *See* Geisel, Theodor Seuss (Dr. Seuss)

Leskov, Nikolai, **IV:** 299

Leslie, Alfred, **Supp. XII:** 127; **Supp. XXIII:** 217

"Less and Less Human, O Savage Spirit" (W. Stevens), **Supp. XVI:** 64

Lesser, Wendy, **Supp. IV Part 2:** 453; **Supp. XII:** 297; **Supp. XVI:** 201

Lessing, Gotthold, **Supp. I Part 2:** 422

"Lesson, The" (Bambara), **Supp. XI:** 5–6

"Lesson, The" (Dunbar), **Supp. II Part 1:** 199

"Lesson, The" (Olsen), **Supp. XIII:** 297

"Lesson, The"(Schott), **Supp. XXIII:** 254

"Lesson for the Ill Clothed and Ill Fed, A" (Ryan as Quin), **Supp. XVIII:** 230–231

Lesson of the Master, The (James), **Supp. XVIII:** 248

"Lesson of the Master, The" (James), **Retro. Supp. I:** 227

Lesson of the Masters: An Anthology of the Novel from Cervantes to Hemingway (Cowley-Hugo, ed.), **Supp. II Part 1:** 140

"Lesson on Concealment, A" (Brown), **Supp. I Part 1:** 133

"Lessons" (Epstein), **Supp. XII:** 163

"Lessons from an Older Man"(Thompson), **Supp. XXIII:** 293

"Lessons of the Body" (Simpson), **Supp. IX:** 267

Less than One (Brodsky), **Supp. VIII:** 22, 29–31

Less Than Zero (Ellis), **Supp. XXVII:** 67, 69–70, 71, 74, 75, 77, 78, 269

Less Than Zero (film), **Supp. XXVII:** 68, 77

Lester, Jerry, **Supp. IV Part 2:** 574

Lester, Ketty, **Supp. XV:** 133, 147

Le Style Apollinaire (Zukofsky), **Supp. III Part 2:** 616

Le Sueur, Arthur, **Supp. XXIII:** 161, 162

LeSueur, Joe, **Supp. XXIII:** 212, 216, 218, 220

Le Sueur, Meridel, **Supp. V:** 113, 130; **Supp. XII:** 217; **Supp. XXIII: 161–176; Supp. XXVI:** 28

Lesy, Michael, **Supp. XXV:** 146

"Let America Be America Again" (Hughes), **Retro. Supp. I:** 202; **Supp. I Part 1:** 331

Let Evening Come (Kenyon), **Supp. VII:** 160, 169–171

Lethem, Jonathan, **Supp. IX:** 122; **Supp. XVIII: 135–153; Supp. XXII:** 49; **Supp. XXVII:** 67

Let It Come Down (Bowles), **Supp. IV Part 1:** 87

Let It Ride (Pickering), **Supp. XXI:** 198–199

"Let Me Be" (Levine), **Supp. V:** 181, 189

"Let Me Begin Again" (Levine), **Supp. V:** 181, 189

"Let No Charitable Hope" (Wylie), **Supp. I Part 2:** 713–714, 729

Let No Man Write My Epitaph (film, Leacock), **Supp. XVII:** 150, 158

Let No Man Write My Epitaph (W. Motley), **Supp. XVII:** 150, **158–160**

Let Noon Be Fair (W. Motley), **Supp. XVII:** 161

Letofsky, Irv, **Supp. XVI:** 167

"Let one Eye his watches keep/While the Other Eye doth sleep" (Fletcher), **Supp. IV Part 2:** 621

Let's Balance the Books (radio show; Untermeyer), **Supp. XV:** 311

"Letter . . ." (Whittier), **Supp. I Part 2:** 687

"Letter, A" (Bogan), **Supp. III Part 1:** 54

"Letter, May 2, 1959" (Olson), **Supp. II Part 2:** 579, 580

"Letter, Much Too Late" (Stegner), **Supp. IV Part 2:** 613

"Letter, The" (Boulton), **Supp. XXII:** 22

"Letter, The" (Gioia), **Supp. XV:** 120

"Letter, The" (Malamud), **Supp. I Part 2:** 435–436

"Letter about Money, Love, or Other Comfort, If Any, The" (Warren), **IV:** 245

Letter Addressed to the People of Piedmont, on the Advantages of the French Revolution, and the Necessity of Adopting Its Principles in Italy, A (Barlow), **Supp. II Part 1:** 80, 81

"Letter for Marion, A" (McGrath), **Supp. X:** 116

"Letter from Aldermaston" (Merwin), **Supp. III Part 1:** 347

"Letter from a London Attic" (Pickering), **Supp. XXI:** 194

"Letter from a Region in My Mind" (Baldwin). *See* "Down at the Cross"

"Letter from Aunt Belle, A" (Kooser), **Supp. XIX:** 117

Letter from Li Po, A (Aiken), **I:** 68

"Letter from 'Manhattan' " (Didion), **Supp. IV Part 1:** 205

"Letter from the Country" (column, C. Bly), **Supp. XVI:** 33

Letter from the End of the Twentieth Century (Harjo), **Supp. XII:** 223

"Letter from the End of the Twentieth Century" (Harjo), **Supp. XII:** 227

"Letter Home" (Trethewey), **Supp. XXI:** 254

"Letter on Céline" (Kerouac), **Supp. III Part 1:** 232

Letters (Cato), **II:** 114

Letters (Landor), **Supp. I Part 2:** 422

Letters (White), **Supp. I Part 2:** 651, 653, 675, 680

Letters (Wolfe), **IV:** 462

"Letters, The" (Swados), **Supp. XIX:** 261, 262

Letters and Leadership (Brooks), **I:** 228, 240, 245, 246

"Letters for the Dead" (Levine), **Supp. V:** 186

Letters from an American Farmer (Crèvecoeur), **Supp. I Part 1:** 227–251

Letters from Bohemia (Hecht), **Supp. XXVII:** 95

Letters from Maine (Sarton), **Supp. VIII: 261**

"Letters from Maine" (Sarton), **Supp. VIII:** 261

"Letters from My Father" (R. O. Butler), **Supp. XII:** 71

Letters from the Country (C. Bly), **Supp. XVI: 33–34,** 35, 37

Letters from the Earth (Twain), **IV:** 209

Letters from the East (Bryant), **Supp. I Part 1:** 158

"Letters from the Ming Dynasty" (Brodsky), **Supp. VIII:** 28

"Letters from the *Samantha*" (Helprin), **Supp. XXV:** 85

Letters of Angelicus and Fidelio Fobb (O'Hara and Berkson), **Supp. XXIII:** 218

Letters of a Traveller (Bryant), **Supp. I Part 1:** 158

Letters of a Traveller, Second Series (Bryant), **Supp. I Part 1:** 158

Letters of a Woman Homesteader (Stewart), **Supp. XXVI:** 183

Letters of Emily Dickinson, The (T. H. Johnson and Ward, eds.), **I:** 470; **Retro. Supp. I:** 28

Letters of William James (Henry James, ed.), **II:** 362

Letters on Various Interesting and Important Subjects . . . (Freneau), **Supp. II Part 1:** 272

Letters to a Niece (Adams), **I:** 22

Letters to a Teacher (Pickering), **Supp. XXI:** 195, 201–202

Letters to a Young Poet (Rilke), **Supp. XIII:** 74; **Supp. XV:** 93

"Letters to Dead Imagists" (Sandburg), **I:** 421

"Letters Written on a Ferry While Crossing Long Island Sound" (Sexton), **Supp. II Part 2:** 683

"Letter to Abbé Raynal" (Paine), **Supp. I Part 2:** 510

"Letter to a Kiss That Died for Us" (Gallagher), **Supp. XXIV:** 170

Letter to a Man in the Fire: Does God Exist or Does He Care? (Price), **Supp. VI:** 267–268

"Letter to American Teachers of History, A" (Adams), **I:** 19

Letter to an Imaginary Friend (McGrath), **Supp. X:** 111, 112–113, 116, **119–125**

"Letter to a Reader" (Sanders), **Supp. XVI:** 266, 267, 268, 269, 275

"Letter to a Young Author" (P. N. Warren), **Supp. XX: 272**

"Letter to a Young Contributor" (Higginson), **Retro. Supp. I:** 31

"Letter to a Young Writer" (Price), **Supp. VI:** 267

"Letter to Bell from Missoula" (Hugo), **Supp. VI:** 142–143

"Letter to E. Franklin Frazier" (Baraka), **Supp. II Part 1:** 49

"Letter to Elaine Feinstein" (Olson), **Supp. II Part 2:** 561

"Letter to Francis Picabia, A" (Boyle), **Supp. XXIV:** 63

"Letter to Freddy" (music) (Bowles), **Supp. IV Part 1:** 82

"Letter to Garber from Skye" (Hugo), **Supp. VI:** 146

"Letter to George Washington" (Paine), **Supp. I Part 2:** 517

"Letter to His Brother" (Berryman), **I:** 172, 173

Letter to His Countrymen, A (Cooper), **I:** 346, 347, 349

"Letter to Kizer from Seattle" (Hugo), **Supp. VI:** 142

Letter to Lord Byron (Auden), **Supp. II Part 1:** 11

"Letter to Lord Byron" (Mumford), **Supp. II Part 2:** 494

"Letter to Matthews from Barton Street Flats" (Hugo), **Supp. VI:** 133

"Letter to Mexico" (Biss), **Supp. XXVI:** 48

"Letter to Minnesota" (Dunn), **Supp. XI:** 146

"Letter to Mr." (Poe), **III:** 411

"Letter Too Late to Vallejo" (Salinas), **Supp. XIII:** 313, 324

"Letter to Sister Madeline from Iowa City" (Hugo), **Supp. VI:** 142–143

"Letter to Soto" (Salinas), **Supp. XIII:** 325

"Letter to the Lady of the House" (Bausch), **Supp. VII:** 48

"Letter to the Rising Generation, A" (Comer), **I:** 214

"Letter to Walt Whitman" (Doty), **Supp. XI:** 135–136

"Letter to Wendell Berry, A" (Stegner), **Supp. IV Part 2:** 600

"Letter Writer, The" (Singer), **IV:** 20–21

"Let the Air Circulate" (Clampitt), **Supp. IX:** 45

Let the Hurricane Roar (Lane), **Supp. XXII:** 297

"Letting Down of the Hair, The" (Sexton), **Supp. II Part 2:** 692

Letting Go (P. Roth), **Retro. Supp. II:** 282, 283; **Supp. III Part 2:** 403, 404, 409–412

"Letting the Puma Go" (Dunn), **Supp. XI:** 149

"Lettres d'un Soldat" (Stevens), **Retro. Supp. I:** 299

Let Us Compare Mythologies (Cohen), **Supp. XXVII:** 53

Let Us Go into the Starry Night (Shanley), **Supp. XIV:** 317

Let Us Highly Resolve (Stratton-Porter), **Supp. XX: 223**

Let Us Now Praise Famous Men (Agee and Evans), **I:** 25, 27, 35, 36–39, 42, 45, 293

Let Your Mind Alone! (Thurber), **Supp. I Part 2:** 608

Leutze, Emanuel, **Supp. X:** 307

Levels of the Game (McPhee), **Supp. III Part 1:** 292, 294, 301

Levertov, Denise, **Retro. Supp. I:** 411; **Supp. III Part 1: 271–287; Supp. III Part 2:** 541; **Supp. IV Part 1:** 325; **Supp. VIII:** 38, 39; **Supp. XIX:** 282; **Supp. XVI:** 39, 40; **Supp. XXI:** 228; **Supp. XXII:** 83, 168, 177

Levi, Primo, **Supp. X:** 149; **Supp. XVII:** 48

Leviathan (Auster), **Supp. XII:** 27, **33–34**

"Leviathan" (Merwin), **Supp. III Part 1:** 345

"Leviathan" (R. Lowell), **II:** 537, 538

Levin, Adam, **Supp. XXII:** 268

Levin, Harry, **Supp. I Part 2:** 647

Levin, Jennifer, **Supp. X:** 305

Levin, Meyer, **Supp. XX: 34; Supp. XXVII: 133–149**

Lévinas, Emmanuel, **Supp. XVI:** 290, 291

Levine, Ellen, **Supp. V:** 4; **Supp. XI:** 178

Levine, Paul, **Supp. IV Part 1:** 221, 224

Levine, Philip, **Supp. III Part 2:** 541; **Supp. IX:** 293; **Supp. V: 177–197,** 337; **Supp. XI:** 123, 257, 259, 267, 271, 315; **Supp. XIII:** 312; **Supp. XIX:** 45; **Supp. XV:** 73, 74, 212

Levine, Rosalind, **Supp. XII:** 123

Levine, Sherry, **Supp. XII:** 4

Levis, Larry, **Supp. IX:** 299; **Supp. V:** 180; **Supp. XI: 257–274; Supp. XIII:** 312; **Supp. XV:** 73; **Supp. XVII:** 110

Lévi-Strauss, Claude, **Supp. I Part 2:** 636; **Supp. IV Part 1:** 45; **Supp. IV Part 2:** 490; **Supp. XVIII:** 190

Levitation: Five Fictions (Ozick), **Supp. V:** 268–270

"Levitation with Baby" (Nelson), **Supp. XVIII:** 173

Levitt, Saul, **Supp. XV:** 197

Levy, Alan, **Supp. IV Part 2:** 574, 589

Levy, D. A., **Supp. XXIII:** 174

Levy, G. Rachel, **Supp. I Part 2:** 567

Levy, Julien, **Supp. XXII:** 167, 168

Lévy-Bruhl, Lucien, **Retro. Supp. I:** 57

Levy Mayer and the New Industrial Era (Masters), **Supp. I Part 2:** 473

Lewallen, Constance M., **Supp. XXVII:** 20, 21

Lewes, George Henry, **II:** 569

Lewin, Albert, **Supp. XIV:** 279, 293

Lewis, C. Day, **III:** 527

Lewis, Dr. Claude, **II:** 442

Lewis, C. S., **Supp. XXV:** 73

Lewis, David Levering, **Supp. XIX:** 74, 75; **Supp. XVIII:** 127; **Supp. XXII:** 13

Lewis, Edith, **I:** 313; **Retro. Supp. I:** 19, 21, 22

Lewis, Edwin, J., **II:** 439, 442

Lewis, Jerry, **Supp. IV Part 2:** 575; **Supp. X:** 172

Lewis, John L., **I:** 493

Lewis, Lilburn, **IV:** 243

Lewis, Lorene, **Supp. IV Part 2:** 596, 597

Lewis, Lucy, **IV:** 243

Lewis, Maggie, **Supp. V:** 23

Lewis, Meriwether, **II:** 217; **III:** 14; **IV:** 179, 243, 283

Lewis, Merrill, **Supp. IV Part 2:** 596, 597

Lewis, Michael, **II:** 451, 452; **Supp. XVII:** 210

Lewis, Michael J., **Supp. XXV:** 253

Lewis, Robert Q., **Supp. IV Part 2:** 574

Lewis, R. W. B., **I:** 386, 561; **II:** 457–458; **Retro. Supp. I:** 362, 367; **Supp. I Part 1:** 233; **Supp. XIII:** 93; **Supp. XXIII:** 42

Lewis, Sinclair, **I:** 116, 212, 348, 355, 362, 374, 378, 487, 495; **II:** 27, 34, 74, 79, 271, 277, 306, **439–461,** 474; **III:** 28, 40, 51, 60, 61, 63–64, 66, 70, 71, 106, 394, 462, 572, 606; **IV:** 53, 326, 366, 455, 468, 475, 482; **Retro. Supp. I:** 332; **Retro. Supp. II:** 95, 108, 197, 322; **Supp. I Part 2:** 378, 613, 709; **Supp. IV Part 2:** 678; **Supp. IX:** 308; **Supp. V:** 278; **Supp. X:** 137; **Supp. XVII:** 41; **Supp. XVIII:** 278; **Supp. XXII:** 190; **Supp. XXIII:** 165, 166; **Supp. XXIV:** 29

Lewis, Mrs. Sinclair (Dorothy Thompson), **II:** 449–450, 451, 453

Lewis, Mrs. Sinclair (Grace Livingston Hegger), **II:** 441

Lewis, Wyndham, **III:** 458, 462, 465, 470; **Retro. Supp. I:** 59, 170, 292; **Supp. III Part 2:** 617; **Supp. XXVI:** 144

Lewisohn, Ludwig, **Supp. XXIII:** 1

Lexicon Tetraglotton (Howell), **II:** 111

"Lexington Avenue Musedog" (Peacock), **Supp. XIX:** 204

"Leyenda" (Mora), **Supp. XIII:** 214

Leyner, Mark, **Supp. XIX:** 223

Leyte (Morison), **Supp. I Part 2:** 491

"Liar, The" (Baraka), **Supp. II Part 1:** 36

"Liars, The" (Sandburg), **III:** 586

Liars' Club, The: A Memoir (Karr), **Supp. XI:** 239, 240, 241, 242, **244–248,** 252, 254; **Supp. XVI:** 70

Liar's Dice (C. Frost), **Supp. XV:** 93, 96

"Liar's Dice" (C. Frost), **Supp. XV:** 94, 107

Liars in Love (Yates), **Supp. XI:** 348, 349

Libation Bearers, The (Aeschylus), **III:** 398; **Supp. IX:** 103

Li Bay. *See* Li Po

Libby, Anthony, **Supp. XIII:** 87

Libera, Padre, **II:** 278

Liberal Imagination, The (Trilling), **III:** 308; **Retro. Supp. I:** 97, 216; **Supp. II Part 1:** 146; **Supp. III Part 2:** 495, 498, 501–504

Liberating Voices: Oral Tradition in African American Literature (G. Jones), **Supp. XXIV:** 185

Liberation (J. Scott), **Supp. XVII:** 192, **194–196**

"Liberation" (Winters), **Supp. II Part 2:** 791

Liber Brunenesis (yearbook), **IV:** 286

Liberties, The (Howe), **Supp. IV Part 2:** 426–428, 430, 432

Liberties of America, The (H. Warner), **Supp. XVIII:** 259

Liberty Jones (play), **Supp. IV Part 1:** 83

"Liberty Tree" (Paine), **Supp. I Part 2:** 505

Libra (DeLillo), **Supp. VI:** 2, **4, 5,** 6, **7,** 9, 10, 12, 13, 14, 16

Library for Juana, A (Mora), **Supp. XIII:** 218

Library of America, **Retro. Supp. I:** 2

"Library of Babel, The" (J. Borges), **Supp. XVII:** 47

"Library of Law, A" (MacLeish), **III:** 4

"Library of Moloch, The" (Bukiet), **Supp. XVII:** 47, 49

"Librettos for Eros" (Gander), **Supp. XV:** 340

Lice, The (Merwin), **Supp. III Part 1:** 339, 341–342, 346, 348, 349, 355

"License Plate, The" (Ferry), **Supp. XXIV:** 157

Lichtenberg, Georg Christoph, **Supp. XIV:** 339

Lichtenstein, Roy, **Supp. I Part 2:** 665; **Supp. XV:** 186; **Supp. XXVII:** 21

"Liddy's Orange" (Olds), **Supp. X:** 209

"Lie, The" (Antin), **Supp. XX:** 7, **9–10**

Lieberman, Herman (Chaim), **Supp. XXIII:** 3, 7

Lieberman, Laurence, **Supp. XI:** 323–324

Liebestod (Wagner), **I:** 284, 395

Liebling, A. J., **IV:** 290; **Supp. VIII:** 151; **Supp. XVI:** 167; **Supp. XXVII:** 46–47

Lie Down in Darkness (Styron), **IV:** 98, 99, 100–104, 105, 111; **Supp. XI:** 343

"Lie Down with the Lamb" (Gallagher), **Supp. XXIV:** 171

Lie of the Mind, A (Shepard), **Supp. III Part 2:** 433, 435, 441, 447–449

"Lies" (Haines), **Supp. XII:** 204

Lies (Hoffman), **Supp. XVIII:** **78–79**

"Lies and Consequences" (Pickering), **Supp. XXI:** 204

Lies Like Truth (Clurman), **IV:** 385

Lieutenant, The (Dubus), **Supp. VII:** 78

"Life" (Hecht), **Supp. XXVII:** 86

Life (Richards), **Supp. XXVII:** 40

"Life" (Wharton), **Retro. Supp. I:** 372

Life along the Passaic River (W. C. Williams), **Retro. Supp. I:** 423

Life Among the Savages (Jackson), **Supp. IX:** 115, **125**

Life and Adventures of Charles Anderson Chester, The (Lippard), **Supp. XXIII:** 184

"Life and Death Kisses, The" (Grossman), **Supp. XIX:** 87

Life and Gabriella (Glasgow), **II:** 175, 176, 182–183, 184, 189

"Life and I" (Wharton), **Retro. Supp. I:** 360, 361, 362

"Life and Letters" (Epstein), **Supp. XIV:** 104–105

"Life and Letters in New England" (Emerson), **Supp. XXIV:** 67

Life and Letters of Harrison Gray Otis, Federalist, 1765–1848, The (Morison), **Supp. I Part 2:** 480–481

Life and Letters of Sir Henry Wotton (L. P. Smith), **Supp. XIV:** 340–341

Life and Mind of Emily Dickinson, The (Taggard), **Supp. XXII:** 279

Life and Times of Frederick Douglass, Written by Himself, The (Douglass), **Supp. III Part 1:** 155, 159–163

Life and Writings of Horace McCoy, The (Wolfson), **Supp. XIII:** 172, 174

"Life as a Visionary Spirit" (Eberhart), **I:** 540, 541

"Life at Angelo's, A" (Benét), **Supp. XI:** 53

Life at Happy Knoll (Marquand), **III:** 50, 61

Life Before Man (Atwood), **Supp. XIII:** **24–25**

Lifeboat (screenplay, Hecht), **Supp. XXVII:** 93

"Life Cycle of Common Man" (Nemerov), **III:** 278

"Lifecycle Stairmaster" (Karr), **Supp. XI:** 250

Life Estates (Hearon), **Supp. VIII:** **68–69**

Life for Life's Sake (Aldington), **Supp. I Part 1:** 256

Life Full of Holes, A (Layachi), **Supp. IV Part 1:** 92

"Lifeguard" (Updike), **IV:** 226; **Retro. Supp. I:** 325

"Lifeguard, The" (Dickey), **Supp. IV Part 1:** 179–180

"Life in the 30s" (column, Quindlen), **Supp. XVII:** 165, 167–169

Life in the Clearings (Shields), **Supp. VII:** 313

"Life in the Country: A City Friend Asks, 'Is It Boring?' " (Paley), **Supp. VI:** 231

Life in the Forest (Levertov), **Supp. III Part 1:** 282–283

Life in the Iron Mills (R. H. Davis), **Supp. XIII:** 292, 295, 299, 305; **Supp. XVI:** 79–82, **85–88,** 91

Life in the Iron Mills and Other Stories (T. Olson, ed.), **Supp. XVI:** 83

Life in the Theatre, A (Mamet), **Supp. XIV:** 241, 255

Life in the War Zone (Atherton), **Supp. XXIV:** 24

Life Is a Miracle: An Essay Against Modern Superstition (Berry), **Supp. X:** 35

"Life Is Fine" (Hughes), **Supp. I Part 1:** 334, 338

"Life Is Motion" (Stevens), **IV:** 74

Life & Letters of Gene Stratton-Porter (Meehan), **Supp. XX:** 213

Life of Albert Gallatin, The (Adams), **I:** 6, 14

"Life of a Man of the World, The" (Lippard), **Supp. XXIII:** 189

Life of an Ordinary Woman, The: Anne Ellis (A. Ellis), **Supp. XVI:** 38

Life of Captain Cipriani, The: An Account of British Government in the West Indies (C. L. R. James), **Supp. XXI:** 161

Life of Dryden (S. Johnson), **Retro. Supp. II:** 223

Life of Emily Dickinson, The (Sewall), **Retro. Supp. I:** 25

Life of Forms, The (Focillon), **IV:** 90

Life of Franklin Pierce (Hawthorne), **Retro. Supp. I:** 163

Life of George Cabot Lodge, The (Adams), **I:** 21

Life of George Washington (Irving), **II:** 314, 315–316

Life of Henry James (Edel), **Retro. Supp. I:** 224

"Life of Irony, The" (Bourne), **I:** 219

Life of Jesus (Renan), **Supp. XX:** 122

"Life of Lincoln West, The" (Brooks), **Supp. III Part 1:** 86

Life of Mary, The (Rilke; F. Wright, trans.), **Supp. XVII:** 244

Life of Michelangelo (Grimm), **II:** 17

"Life of Nancy, The" (Jewett), **Retro. Supp. II:** 133, 144

Life of Oliver Goldsmith, The, with Selections from His Writings (Irving), **II:** 315

Life of Phips (Mather), **Supp. II Part 2:** 451, 452, 459

Life of Poetry, The (Rukeyser), **Supp. VI:** 271, 273, 275–276, 282, 283, 286

Life of Samuel Johnson (Boswell), **Supp. I Part 2:** 656

Life of Savage (S. Johnson), **Supp. I Part 2:** 523

Life of the Drama, The (Bentley), **IV:** 396

"Life of the Mind, The" (Kees), **Supp. XV:** 140

Life of the Right Reverend Joseph P. Machebeuf, The (Howlett), **Retro. Supp. I:** 17

Life of Thomas Paine, author of Rights of Men, With a Defence of his Writings (Chalmers), **Supp. I Part 2:** 514

Life of Thomas Paine, The (Cobbett), **Supp. I Part 2:** 517

"Life of Towne, The" (Carson), **Supp. XII:** 102

Life of William Ellery Channing (W. H. Channing), **Supp. XXIV:** 68

"Life on Beekman Place, A" (Naylor), **Supp. VIII:** 214

"Life on the Black List" (Endore), **Supp. XVII:** 63

Life on the Hyphen: The Cuban-American Way (Firmat), **Supp. VIII:** 76; **Supp. XI:** 184

Life on the Mississippi (Twain), **I:** 209; **IV:** 198, 199; **Supp. I Part 2:** 440

"Life on the Rocks: The Galápagos" (Dillard), **Supp. VI:** 32

"Life Stories, East and West" (E. Hoffman), **Supp. XVI:** 157

Life Story (Baker), **II:** 259

Life Studies (R. Lowell), **I:** 400; **II:** 384, 386, 543, 546–550, 551, 555; **Retro. Supp. II:** 180, 185, 186, 188, 189, 191; **Supp. I Part 2:** 543; **Supp. XI:** 240, 244, 250, 317; **Supp. XII:** 255; **Supp. XIV:** 15; **Supp. XV:** 252

"Life Studies" (R. Lowell), **Retro. Supp. II:** 188

"Life Styles in the Golden Land" (Didion), **Supp. IV Part 1:** 200

Life Supports: New and Collected Poems (Bronk), **Supp. XXI:** 19, 31, 32

"Life That Is, The" (Bryant), **Supp. I Part 1:** 169

"Life Work" (Stafford), **Supp. XI:** 329–330

"Life You Save May Be Your Own, The" (O'Connor), **III:** 344, 350, 354; **Retro. Supp. II:** 229, 230, 233

Lifshin, Lyn, **Supp. XVI:** 37

"Lifting, The" (Olds), **Supp. X:** 210

"Ligeia" (Poe), **III:** 412, 414; **Retro. Supp. II:** 261, 270, 271, 275

Liggett, Walter W., **Supp. XIII:** 168

Light, James F., **IV:** 290; **Retro. Supp. II:** 325

Light, Kate, **Supp. XVII:** 109

Light and Dark (Bronk), **Supp. XXI:** 27–29, 31

"Light and the Sufferer" (Lethem), **Supp. XVIII:** 139–140

Light around the Body, The (R. Bly), **Supp. IV Part 1:** 61–62, 62; **Supp. XVII:** 243; **Supp. XXI:** 84–85

"Light Comes Brighter, The" (Roethke), **III:** 529–530

"Lighter than Air" (Stone), **Supp. XXVII:** 251

"Light from Above" (Eberhart), **I:** 541

Light in August (Faulkner), **II:** 63–64, 65, 74; **IV:** 207; **Retro. Supp. I:** 82, 84, 85, 86, 89, 92; **Supp. XIV:** 12

Light in the Forest, The (Richter), **Supp. XVIII:** 216–217

Light in the Morning (Baker), **Supp. XVIII:** 263, 269

"Light in the Piazza, The" (Spencer), **Supp. XXVII:** 13

Light in the Window, A (Rinehart), **Supp. XXV:** 198–199, 202

"Light Man, A" (James), **II:** 322; **Retro. Supp. I:** 219

"Lightning" (Barthelme), **Supp. IV Part 1:** 53

"Lightning" (Bynner), **Supp. XV:** 44

"Lightning" (Oliver), **Supp. VII:** 235

"Lightning, The" (Swenson), **Supp. IV Part 2:** 645

"Lightning Flash, The" (Gibran), **Supp. XX:** 123

"Lightning Rod Man, The" (Melville), **III:** 90; **Supp. XVIII:** 4

"Light of the Body, The" (Davison), **Supp. XXVI:** 71

"Light of the World, The" (Hemingway), **II:** 249

"Lights" (Dybek), **Supp. XXIII:** 72

Lights in the Valley (Bodenheim), **Supp. XXV:** 29

"Lights in the Windows" (Nye), **Supp. XIII:** 280

"Lights Must Never Go Out, The" (Hadas), **Supp. XXIII:** 125

"Light Through the Window, The" (Brockmeier), **Supp. XXII:** 52, 59

Light Verse and Satires (Bynner), **Supp. XV:** 52

Light Years (Salter), **Supp. IX:** 257–259

"LIKE, THIS IS WHAT I MEANT!" (Baraka), **Supp. II Part 1:** 59

"Like All the Other Nations" (Paley), **Supp. VI:** 220

"Like a Rolling Stone" (song, Dylan), **Supp. XVIII:** 20, 30

"Like Decorations in a Nigger Cemetery" (Stevens), **IV:** 74, 79; **Retro. Supp. I:** 305

Like Ghosts of Eagles (Francis), **Supp. IX:** 86

"Like Life" (Moore), **Supp. X:** 163, 165, **172–173**

Like Life: Stories (Moore), **Supp. X:** 163, **171–175,** 177, 178

"Likeness to God" (Channing), **Supp. XXIV:** **75–76,** 77, 78

"Like Talk" (Mills), **Supp. XI:** 311

"Like the New Moon I Will Live My Life" (R. Bly), **Supp. IV Part 1:** 71

Li'l Abner (Capp), **IV:** 198

"Lilacs" (A. Lowell), **II:** 527

"Lilacs, The" (Wilbur), **Supp. III Part 2:** 557–558

"Lilacs for Ginsberg" (Stern), **Supp. IX:** 299

Liliom (Molnar), **Supp. XVI:** 187

Lilith's Brood (O. Butler), **Supp. XIII:** 63

Lillabulero Press, **Supp. V:** 4, 5

Lillian Hellman (Adler), **Supp. I Part 1:** 297

Lillian Hellman (Falk), **Supp. I Part 1:** 297

Lillian Hellman: Playwright (Moody), **Supp. I Part 1:** 280

Lillo, George, **II:** 111, 112

"Lily Daw and the Three Ladies" (Welty), **IV:** 262

Lily for My Love, A (Berrigan), **Supp. XXIV:** 35

Lima, Agnes de, **I:** 231, 232

Lima, Frank, **Supp. XXIII:** 217, 221; **Supp. XXVII:** 23

Lima, Maria Helena, **Supp. XXII:** 73

Lima Beans (Kreymborg), **Supp. XXII:** 163

"Limbo: Altered States" (Karr), **Supp. XI:** 249–250

"Limen" (Trethewey), **Supp. XXI:** 250

Lime Orchard Woman, The (Ríos), **Supp. IV Part 2:** 538, 547–550, 553

"Lime Orchard Woman, The" (Ríos), **Supp. IV Part 2:** 548

Limitations (Turow), **Supp. XVII: 222–223**

"Limits" (Emerson), **II:** 19

Limits of Mortality, The: An Essay on Wordsworth's Major Poems (Ferry), **Supp. XXIV:** 147, 148

Lincoln, Abraham, **I:** 1, 4, 30; **II:** 8, 13, 135, 273, 555, 576; **III:** 576, 577, 580, 584, 587–590, 591; **IV:** 192, 195, 298, 347, 350, 444; **Supp. I Part 1:** 2, 8, 26, 309, 321; **Supp. I Part 2:** 379, 380, 382, 385, 390, 397, 399, 418, 424, 454, 456, 471, 472, 473, 474, 483, 579, 687; **Supp. IX:** 15; **Supp. VIII:** 108; **Supp. XIV:** 73

Lincoln, Kenneth, **Supp. IV Part 1:** 329; **Supp. IV Part 2:** 507

Lincoln, Thomas, **III:** 587

Lincoln, Mrs. Thomas (Nancy Hanks), **III:** 587

Lincoln: A Novel (Vidal), **Supp. IV Part 2:** 677, 684, 685, 688, 689–690, 691, 692

"Lincolnites" (Rash), **Supp. XXVII:** 229

Lincoln Lawyer, The (Connelly), **Supp. XXI: 77,** 78

Lincoln on Race and Slavery (H. L. Gates), **Supp. XX: 108–109**

"Lincoln Relics, The" (Kunitz), **Supp. III Part 1:** 269

Lincoln: The Man (Masters), **Supp. I Part 2:** 471, 473–474

Lindbergh, Charles A., **I:** 482

"Linden Branch, The" (MacLeish), **III:** 19, 20

Linden Hills (Naylor), **Supp. VIII:** 214, 218, **219–223**

Linderman, Lawrence, **Supp. IV Part 2:** 579, 583, 585, 589

Lindner, April, **Supp. XV:** 111, 119

"Lindo y Querido" (Muñoz), **Supp. XXV:** 135

Lindsay, Howard, **III:** 284

Lindsay, John, **Supp. I Part 2:** 374

Lindsay, Olive, **Supp. I Part 2:** 374, 375, 392

Lindsay, Vachel, **I:** 384; **II:** 263, 276, 530; **III:** 5, 505; **Retro. Supp. I:** 133; **Supp. I Part 1:** 324; **Supp. I Part 2: 374–403,** 454, 473, 474; **Supp. III Part 1:** 63, 71; **Supp. XV:** 293, 297, 299, 301, 306; **Supp. XVI:** 184–185; **Supp. XXV:** 18; **Supp. XXVII:** 286, 294, 297

Lindsay, Mrs. Vachel (Elizabeth Connors), **Supp. I Part 2:** 398, 399, 473

Lindsay, Vachel Thomas, **Supp. I Part 2:** 374, 375

Lindsay, Mrs. Vachel Thomas (Esther Catherine Frazee), **Supp. I Part 2:** 374, 375, 384–385, 398

Lindsey, David, **Supp. XIV:** 26

"Line, The" (Olds), **Supp. X:** 206

Lineage of Ragpickers, Songpluckers, Elegiasts, and Jewelers, A (Goldbarth),

Supp. XII: 191

"Line"(Crooker), **Supp. XXIII:** 58

Line Dance (Crooker), **Supp. XXIII:** 56, **58–60**

"Line Dance"(Crooker), **Supp. XXIII:** 59

"Line of Least Resistance, The" (Wharton), **Retro. Supp. I:** 366

Line Out for a Walk, A: Familiar Essays (Epstein), **Supp. XIV:** 107

"Liner Notes for the Poetically Unhep" (Hughes), **Retro. Supp. I:** 210

"Lines, Written on Reading Stuart's Account of the Treatment of Slaves in Charleston" (Very), **Supp. XXV:** 239

"Lines After Rereading T. S. Eliot" (Wright), **Supp. V:** 343

"Lines Composed a Few Miles Above Tintern Abbey" (Wordsworth), **Supp. III Part 1:** 12

"Lines Composed Over Three Thousand Miles from Tintern Abbey" (Collins), **Supp. XXI:** 57–58

"Lines for an Interment" (MacLeish), **III:** 15

"Lines for My Father" (Cullen), **Supp. IV Part 1:** 167

"Lines from Israel" (R. Lowell), **II:** 554

"Lines from Pietro Longhi" (Sobin), **Supp. XVI:** 289

"Lines on Revisiting the Country" (Bryant), **Supp. I Part 1:** 164

"Lines Suggested by a Tennessee Song" (Agee), **I:** 28

"Lines to a Friend Asleep"(J. Schoolcraft), **Supp. XXIII:** 228, 230

"Line-Storm Song, A" (Frost), **Retro. Supp. I:** 127

"Lines written at Castle Island, Lake Superior"(J. Schoolcraft), **Supp. XXIII:** 229, 232, 233

"Lines Written at Port Royal" (Freneau), **Supp. II Part 1:** 264

"Lines Written in an Asylum" (Carruth), **Supp. XVI:** 48

"Lines Written in Manassas", **Supp. XV:** 99–100

Lineup, The (Connelly), **Supp. XXI:** 67, 68–69

"Line Written in the Dark Illegible Next Day" (F. Wright), **Supp. XVII:** 242

Linfield, Susie, **Supp. XVII:** 169, 177

Lingeman, Richard, **Supp. X:** 82; **Supp. XXII:** 104

"Linguistics 101" (Huddle), **Supp. XXVI:** 152

Linn, Elizabeth. *See* Brown, Mrs. Charles Brockden (Elizabeth Linn)

Linn, John Blair, **Supp. I Part 1:** 145

Linnaeus, Carolus, **II:** 6; **Supp. I Part 1:** 245

"Linnets" (Levis), **Supp. XI:** 260, 261

"Linoleum" (Gallagher), **Supp. XXIV:** 170

"Linoleum Roses" (Cisneros), **Supp. VII:** 63, 66

Linotte: 1914–1920 (Nin), **Supp. X:** 193, 196, 197

Linschoten, Hans, **II:** 362, 363, 364

"Lion" (B. Kelly), **Supp. XVII:** 133

"Lion and Honeycomb" (Nemerov), **III:** 275, 278, 280

Lion and the Archer, The (Hayden), **Supp. II Part 1:** 366, 367

Lion and the Honeycomb, The (Blackmur), **Supp. II Part 1:** 91

Lion Country (Buechner), **Supp. XII:** 52, 53

Lionel Lincoln (Cooper), **I:** 339, 342

"Lion for Real, The" (Ginsberg), **Supp. II Part 1:** 320

Lionhearted, The: A Story about the Jews of Medieval England (Reznikoff), **Supp. XIV:** 280, 289

Lion in the Garden (Meriweather and Millgate), **Retro. Supp. I:** 91

"Lionizing" (Poe), **III:** 411, 425

"Lions, Harts, and Leaping Does" (Powers), **III:** 356

Lions and Shadows: An Education in the Twenties (Isherwood), **Supp. XIV:** 158, 159, 160, 162

"Lions in Sweden" (Stevens), **IV:** 79–80

Lipman, William R., **Supp. XIII:** 170

Li Po, **Supp. XI:** 241; **Supp. XII:** 218; **Supp. XV:** 47, 217

Lippard, George, **Supp. XXIII: 177–192**

Lippard, Lucy, **Supp. XXVII:** 39

Lippmann, Walter, **I:** 48, 222–223, 225; **III:** 291, 600; **IV:** 429; **Supp. I Part 2:** 609, 643; **Supp. VIII:** 104

Lipschitz, Moryce, **Supp. XXIII:** 6

Lips Together, Teeth Apart (McNally), **Supp. XIII: 201–202,** 208, 209

Lipsyte, Robert, **Supp. XVI:** 220

Lipton, James, **Supp. IV Part 2:** 576, 577, 579, 583, 586, 588

Lipton, Lawrence, **Supp. IX:** 3

"Lisbon Story" (Vaz), **Supp. XXVI:** 267–268

Lisbon Traviata, The (McNally), **Supp. XIII:** 198, **199–200,** 201, 204, 208

Lish, Gordon, **Supp. XIX:** 209; **Supp. XXI:** 115, 121; **Supp. XXIII:** 274; **Supp. XXIV:** 166, 177

Lisicky,Paul, **Supp. XI:** 120, 131, 135

Lisk, Thomas, **Supp. XXI:** 24

"Lisp, The" (Olds), **Supp. X:** 211

Listen, Ruben Fontanez (Neugeboren), **Supp. XVI: 220–221**

"Listeners, The" (de la Mare), **Supp. XVII:** 69

"Listeners and Readers: The Unforgetting of Vachel Lindsay" (Trombly), **Supp. I Part 2:** 403

"Listening" (J. W. Miller), **Supp. XX: 167**

"Listening" (Paley), **Supp. VI:** 218, 231, 232

"Listening" (Stafford), **Supp. XI:** 321, 322

Listening to Prozac (P. Kramer), **Supp. XVI:** 229

"Listening to the Desert" (Henderson), **Supp. XIII:** 221–222

"Listening to the Mockingbird" (Woodard), **Supp. VIII:** 128

Listening to Your Life: Daily Meditations with Frederick Buechner (Buechner), **Supp. XII:** 53

Listen to the Desert/Oye al desierto (Mora), **Supp. XIII:** 221

"Listen to the People" (Benét), **Supp. XI:** 51–52

Liston, Sonny, **III:** 38, 42

Li T'ai-po, **II:** 526

"Litany" (Ashbery), **Supp. III Part 1:** 21–22, 25, 26

"Litany" (Collins), **Supp. XXI:** 56–57

"Litany" (Sandburg), **III:** 593

"Litany, The" (Gioia), **Supp. XV:** 125, 126

"Litany for Dictatorships" (Benét), **Supp. XI:** 46, 58

"Litany for Survival, A" (Lorde), **Supp. XII:** 220

"Litany of the Dark People, The" (Cullen), **Supp. IV Part 1:** 170, 171

"Litany of the Heroes" (Lindsay), **Supp. I Part 2:** 397

"Litany of Washington Street, The" (Lindsay), **Supp. I Part 2:** 376, 398–399

"Literary Achievement of Meyer Levin, The" (Bossin), **Supp. XXVII:** 133

Literary Anthropology (Trumpener and Nyce), **Retro. Supp. I:** 380

Literary Art and Activism of Rick Bass, The (Weltzien), **Supp. XVI:** 20–21

"Literary Blacks and Jews" (Ozick), **Supp. V:** 272

"Literary Career of Elizabeth Barstow Stoddard, The" (Matlack), **Supp. XV:** 269

Literary Criticism: A Short History (Brooks and Wimsatt), **Supp. XIV:** 12

"Literary Criticism of Georg Lukács, The" (Sontag), **Supp. III Part 2:** 453

"Literary Development or California, The" (Atherton), **Supp. XXIV:** 22

Literary Disruptions (Klinkowitz), **Supp. XXI:** 233

Literary Essays of Thomas Merton, The, **Supp. VIII:** 207

"Literary Folk As They Came and Went with Ourselves" (E. Stoddard), **Supp. XV:** 274

Literary Friends and Acquaintance (Howells), **Supp. I Part 1:** 318; **Supp. XV:** 287

"Literary Heritage of Tennyson, The" (Locke), **Supp. XIV:** 197

Literary History of the United States (Spiller et al., ed.), **Supp. I Part 1:** 104; **Supp. II Part 1:** 95

"Literary Importation" (Freneau), **Supp. II Part 1:** 264

"Literary Life of America, The" (Brooks), **I:** 245

"Literary London" (Atherton), **Supp. XXIV:** 24

Literary Outlaw: The Life and Times of William S. Burroughs (Morgan), **Supp. XIV:** 141

Literary Situation, The (Cowley), **Supp. II Part 1:** 135, 140, 144, 146, 147, 148

"Literary Worker's Polonius, The" (Wilson), **IV:** 431, 432

"Literature" (Emerson), **II:** 6

Literature (X. J. Kennedy), **Supp. XV:** 153

Literature and American Life (Boynton), **Supp. I Part 2:** 415

Literature and Insurgency: Ten Studies in Racial Evolution (Underwood), **Supp. XXIV:** 29

Literature and Life (Howells), **Supp. XIV:** 45–46

Literature and Morality (Farrell), **II:** 49

"Literature and Place: Varieties of Regional Experience" (Erisman), **Supp. VIII:** 126

"Literature as a Symptom" (Warren), **IV:** 237

"Literature in Low Life" (Hapgood), **Supp. XVII:** 103

"Literature of Exhaustion, The" (Barth), **Supp. IV Part 1:** 48

"Lithuanian Nocturne" (Brodsky), **Supp. VIII:** 29

"Lit Instructor" (Stafford), **Supp. XI:** 321

Littauer, Kenneth, **Retro. Supp. I:** 114

Little Acts of Kindness (Budbill), **Supp. XIX:** 3, **14–15**

"Little Bernhardt" (Shaw), **Supp. XIX:** 246

Little Big Man (Berger), **Supp. XII:** 171

Little Big Man (film), **Supp. X:** 124

Littlebird, Harold, **Supp. IV Part 2:** 499

Littlebird, Larry, **Supp. IV Part 2:** 499, 505

Little Birds: Erotica (Nin), **Supp. X:** 192, 195

"Little Brown Baby" (Dunbar), **Supp. II Part 1:** 206

"Little Brown Jug" (Baraka), **Supp. II Part 1:** 51

"Little Burst, A"(Strout), **Supp. XXIII:** 282

"Little by Little"(Hadas), **Supp. XXIII:** 115

Little Casino (Sorrentino), **Supp. XXI:** 237, 238

"Little Clown, My Heart" (Cisneros), **Supp. VII:** 71

"Little Cosmic Dust Poem" (Haines), **Supp. XII:** 209–210

"Little Country Girl, A" (Chopin), **Retro. Supp. II:** 71

"Little Curtis" (Parker), **Supp. IX:** 193

Little Disturbances of Man, The (Paley), **Supp. VI:** 218

"Little Dog" (Hughes), **Supp. I Part 1:** 329

Little Dorrit (Dickens), **Supp. I Part 1:** 35

"Little Edward" (Stowe), **Supp. I Part 2:** 587

"Little Elegy" (X. J. Kennedy), **Supp. XV:** 155

"Little Elegy for Antonio Machado"(O'Hara), **Supp. XXIII:** 220

Little Essays Drawn from the Writings of George Santayana (L. P. Smith), **Supp. XIV:** 342

"Little Expressionless Animals" (Wallace), **Supp. X:** 305

"Little Fable" (Hay), **Supp. XIV:** 131

Little Face and Other Stories (Thompson), **Supp. XXIII: 293–294**

"Little Face"(Thompson), **Supp. XXIII:** 293

Littlefield, Catherine, **Supp. IX:** 58

Little Fling, A (Pickering), **Supp. XXI:** 203

Little Foxes, The (Hellman), **Supp. I Part 1:** 276, 278–279, 281, 283, 297

"Little Fred, the Canal Boy" (Stowe), **Supp. I Part 2:** 587

"Little French Mary" (Jewett), **II:** 400

Little Friend, Little Friend (Jarrell), **II:** 367, 372, 375–376

Little Friend, The (Tartt), **Supp. XXVII:** 267, 269, 270, 274–276

"Little Gidding" (Eliot), **I:** 582, 588; **II:** 539; **Retro. Supp. I:** 66

"Little Girl, My Stringbean, My Lovely Woman" (Sexton), **Supp. II Part 2:** 686

"Little Girl, The" (Paley), **Supp. VI:** 222, **228–229**

"Little Girl Tells a Story to a Lady, A" (Barnes), **Supp. III Part 1:** 36

"Little Goose Girl, The" (Grimm), **IV:** 266

Little Ham (Hughes), **Retro. Supp. I:** 203; **Supp. I Part 1:** 328, 339

Little House in the Big Woods (L. I. Wilder), **Supp. XXII:** 294, 295, 296, 297, 298–299, 300

Little House on the Prairie (L. I. Wilder), **Supp. XXII:** 294, 295–296, 297, 299, 301

Little House on the Prairie (television series), **Supp. XXII:** 289

"Little House" series (L. A. Wilder), **Supp. XXII:** 289

"Little House" series (L. I. Wilder), **Supp. XXVI:** 217–218

Little House Traveler, A (L. I. Wilder), **Supp. XXII:** 301

Little Ignorance, A (Schott), **Supp. XXIII:** 239, 241

Little King, The (Bynner), **Supp. XV:** 42, 50

Little Lady of the Big House, The (London), **II:** 481–482

Little Liar, The (film; Ingraham), **Supp. XVI:** 184–185

"Little Lion Face" (Swenson), **Supp. IV Part 2:** 651

"Little Lobelia's Song" (Bogan), **Supp. III Part 1:** 66

"Little Local Color, A" (Henry), **Supp. II Part 1:** 399

Little Lord Fauntleroy (Burnett), **Retro. Supp. I:** 188; **Supp. XVI:** 182

"Little Love, The" (H. Johnson), **Supp. XXVI:** 173

"Little Lyric" (Hughes), **Supp. I Part 1:** 334

Little Man, Little Man (Baldwin), **Supp. I Part 1:** 67

"Little Man at Chehaw Station, The" (Ellison), **Retro. Supp. II:** 123

Little Me (musical), **Supp. IV Part 2:** 575

Little Men (Alcott), **Supp. I Part 1:** 32, 39, 40

"Little Morning Music, A" (Schwartz), **Supp. II Part 2:** 662–663

Little Ocean (Shepard), **Supp. III Part 2:** 447

"Little Old Girl, A" (Larcom), **Supp. XIII:** 144

"Little Old Spy" (Hughes), **Supp. I Part 1:** 329

Little Orphan Annie (film), **Supp. XVIII:** 244

"Little Owl Who Lives in the Orchard" (Oliver), **Supp. VII:** 239

"Little Peasant, The" (Sexton), **Supp. II Part 2:** 690

"Little People"(Kenny), **Supp. XXIII:** 151

"Little Rapids, The" (Swenson), **Supp. IV Part 2:** 645

Little Red Song Book (Hill), **Supp. XVIII:** 224

Little Regiment and Other Episodes of the American Civil War, The (Crane), **I:** 408

Little River: New and Selected Poems (McCarriston), **Supp. XIV: 269–272**

"Little Road not made of Man , A" (Dickinson), **Retro. Supp. I:** 44

"Little Sawtooth" (Huddle), **Supp. XXVI:** 154, 155

Little Sister, The (Chandler), **Supp. IV Part 1:** 122, 130, 131–132

"Little Sleep's-Head Sprouting Hair in the Moonlight" (Kinnell), **Supp. III Part 1:** 247

"Little Snow White" (Grimm), **IV:** 266

"Little Spirit, or Boy-Man, The: An Odjibwa Tale"(J. Schoolcraft), **Supp. XXIII:** 234

Little Star (Halliday), **Supp. XIX: 82, 84–85,** 87

"Little Star" (Halliday), **Supp. XIX:** 83, 84, 93

"Little Testament of Bernard Martin, Aet. 30" (Mumford), **Supp. II Part 2:** 472, 473, 474

"Little Things" (Olds), **Supp. X:** 208

Little Tour in France (James), **II:** 337

Little Town, The (Asch), **Supp. XXIII:** 4, 5, **7–8**

"Little Travel Diary, A"(O'Hara), **Supp. XXIII:** 220

Little Women (Alcott), **Supp. I Part 1:** 28, 29, 32, 35, 37, 38, 39–40, 41, 43, 44; **Supp. IX:** 128

Little Yellow Dog, A (Mosley), **Supp. XIII:** 237, 241

"Liturgy and Spiritual Personalism" (Merton), **Supp. VIII:** 199

Litz, A. Walton, **Retro. Supp. I:** 306

"Liu Ch'e" (Pound), **III:** 466

"Live" (Sexton), **Supp. II Part 2:** 684, 686

Live from Baghdad (screenplay, Shanley), **Supp. XIV:** 316

Live from Golgotha (Vidal), **Supp. IV Part 2:** 677, 682, 691, 692

Live Now and Pay Later (Garrett), **Supp. VII:** 111

"Live-Oak with Moss" (Whitman), **Retro. Supp. I:** 403

Live or Die (Sexton), **Supp. II Part 2:** 670, 683–687

Liveright, Horace, **Retro. Supp. I:** 80, 81, 83; **Supp. I Part 2:** 464; **Supp. XX: 71, 75; Supp. XXII:** 25; **Supp. XXIV:** 28; **Supp. XXV:** 24

Livermore, Elizabeth, **Supp. XXII:** 70

Lives (Plutarch), **II:** 5, 104

Lives of a Cell, The (L. Thomas), **Retro. Supp. I:** 322, 323

Lives of Distinguished American Naval Officers (Cooper), **I:** 347

Lives of Girls and Women (Munro), **Supp. XXVII:** 181, 182, 184

"Lives of Gulls and Children, The" (Nemerov), **III:** 271, 272

Lives of the Animals (Wrigley), **Supp. XVIII: 306–308**

Lives of the Artists (Vasari), **Supp. I Part 2:** 450

"Lives of the Bohemians" (Lethem), **Supp. XVIII:** 135

Lives of the Heart, The (Hirshfield), **Supp. XXIII:** 132–133, 135

Lives of the Muses, The: Nine Women and the Artists They Inspired (Prose), **Supp. XVI:** 250, 260

"Lives of the Philosophers, The" (Brockmeier), **Supp. XXII:** 59, 61

Lives of the Poets (Doctorow), **Supp. IV Part 1:** 234

"Lives of the Poets" (Doctorow), **Supp. IV Part 1:** 234

"Lives of the—Wha'?, The" (Goldbarth), **Supp. XII:** 191

"Living" (Wright), **Supp. XV:** 345

Living, The (Dillard), **Supp. VI:** 23

"Living at Home" (Gordon), **Supp. IV Part 1:** 311

Living by Fiction (Dillard), **Supp. VI:** 23, 31, **32,** 33

Living by the Word (Walker), **Supp. III Part 2:** 521, 522, 526, 527, 535

Living End, The (Elkin), **Supp. VI: 54,** 58

Living Instead (Bronk), **Supp. XXI:** 32

"Living in the Cult of Likability" (Ellis), **Supp. XXVII:** 79

"Living in the Flatlands" (Carruth), **Supp. XVI:** 54

Living in Time (Hadas), **Supp. XXIII:** 120, **122–123**

Living Is Easy, The (D. West), **Supp. XVIII:** 277, 280, **284–286,** 287

"Living Like Weasels" (Dillard), **Supp. VI:** 26, 33

Living Novel, The (Hicks), **III:** 342

Living of Charlotte Perkins Gilman, The (Gilman), **Supp. XI:** 193, 209

Living off the Country: Essays on Poetry and Place (Haines), **Supp. XII:** 199, 203, 207

"Living on a Giant" (X. J. Kennedy), **Supp. XV:** 163

Living Out Loud (Quindlen), **Supp. XVII:** 166, **167–169**

Living Present, The (Atherton), **Supp. XXIV:** 24

Living Reed, The (Buck), **Supp. II Part 1:** 129–130

Livingston, Myra Cohn, **Supp. XV:** 153, 162

Living Theater, **Retro. Supp. I:** 424

"Living There" (Dickey), **Supp. IV Part 1:** 182–183

Living the Spirit: A Gay American Indian Anthology (Roscoe, ed.), **Supp. IV Part 1:** 330

"Living Together: A Letter" (Biss), **Supp. XXVI:** 51

Living to Prowl (Pickering), **Supp. XXI:** 203

"Living with a Peacock" (O'Connor), **III:** 350

"Living Words and Cartoon Translations" (Jocks), **Supp. XXVI:** 97

"Livvie" (Welty), **IV:** 265; **Retro. Supp. I:** 348–349

"Livvie Is Back" (Welty), **Retro. Supp. I:** 351

Livy, **II:** 8

Lizzie (film), **Supp. IX:** 125

"Llantos de La Llorona: Warnings from the Wailer" (Mora), **Supp. XIII:** 217, 224

"L'Lapse" (Barthelme), **Supp. IV Part 1:** 45–47, 48

Llosa, Mario Vargas, **Supp. XIX:** 131; **Supp. XXIV:** 89

Lloyd, Fabien. *See* Cravan, Arthur

Lloyd, Henry Demarest, **Supp. I Part 1:** 5

Lloyd George, Harold, **I:** 490

"LMFBR" (Snyder), **Supp. VIII:** 302

Loach, Ken, **Supp. XXIII:** 163

"Loaded Inflections" (Halliday), **Supp. XIX:** 90, 91

"Loam" (Sandburg), **III:** 584–585

"Loan, The" (Malamud), **Supp. I Part 2:** 427, 428, 431, 437

Loberer, Eric, **Supp. XV:** 339

"Local" (McCarriston), **Supp. XIV:** 270

Local Color (Capote), **Supp. III Part 1:** 120

"Local Color" (London), **II:** 475

"Local Family Keeps Son Happy" (Keillor), **Supp. XVI:** 168, 169

Local Girls (Hoffman), **Supp. X:** 77, **90–91,** 92

"Local Girls" (Hoffman), **Supp. X:** 90

Local Habitation & A Name, A (Kooser), **Supp. XIX:** 116, 118, **119–120**

Local Men (Whitehead), **Supp. XV:** 339

"Local Metaphysics" (Huddle), **Supp. XXVI:** 149

Local Time (Dunn), **Supp. XI:** 143, **148–149**

Local Wonders: Seasons in the Bohemian Alps (Kooser), **Supp. XIX:** 115, **126**

"Location" (Halliday), **Supp. XIX:** 87

Lock, Helen, **Supp. XIII:** 233, 237–238

Lock, Robert H., **IV:** 319; **Retro. Supp. I:** 375

Lockdown (Myers), **Supp. XXVII:** 204, 205

Locke, Alain, **Retro. Supp. II:** 115; **Supp. I Part 1:** 323, 325, 341; **Supp. II Part 1:** 53, 176, 182, 228, 247;

Supp. IV Part 1: 170; **Supp. IX:** 306, 309; **Supp. X:** 134, 137, 139; **Supp. XIV:** 195–219; **Supp. XIX:** 69, 75; **Supp. XVIII:** 122; **Supp. XXII:** 7, 13

Locke, Duane, **Supp. IX:** 273

Locke, Jane Ermine, **Supp. XXV:** 38

Locke, John, **I:** 554–555, 557; **II:** 15–16, 113–114, 348–349, 480; **III:** 294–295; **IV:** 149; **Supp. I Part 1:** 130, 229, 230; **Supp. I Part 2:** 523

Locke, Sondra, **II:** 588

"Locked House, A" (Snodgrass), **Supp. VI:** 323

Locked Room, The (Auster), **Supp. XII:** 22, 24, **27–28**

Locket, The (Masters), **Supp. I Part 2:** 460

Lockridge, Ross, Jr., **Supp. XIX:** 263

"Locksley Hall" (Tennyson), **Supp. IX:** 19

Lockwood Concern, The (O'Hara), **III:** 362, 364, 377–382

"Locus" (Ammons), **Supp. VII:** 28

"Locus" (Hayden), **Supp. II Part 1:** 361–362, 381

"Locusts, the Plaza, the Room, The" (Kees), **Supp. XV:** 141

Loden, Barbara, **III:** 163

Lodge, Henry Cabot, **I:** 11–12, 21

Lodge, Mrs. Henry Cabot, **I:** 11–12, 19

Lodge, Thomas, **IV:** 370

Loeb, Gerald, **Supp. IV Part 2:** 523

Loeb, Harold, **Supp. XXIV:** 49

Loeb, Jacques, **I:** 513; **Retro. Supp. II:** 104; **Supp. I Part 2:** 641

Loeffler, Jack, **Supp. XIII:** 1, 3, 12, 14, 16

Loft, William D., **Supp. XXVI:** 96

Loftus, Mary J., **Supp. XXI:** 245

Lofty Dogmas (A. Finch, M. Kumin and D. Brown, eds.), **Supp. XVII:** 75–76

"Log" (Merrlll), **Supp. III Part 1:** 328

Logan, Joshua, **Supp. XXV:** 95

Logan, Rayford W., **Supp. II Part 1:** 171, 194; **Supp. XIV:** 73

Logan, William, **Supp. X:** 201, 213; **Supp. XI:** 131, 132; **Supp. XII:** 98, 107, 113, 184; **Supp. XV:** 212, 226, 251, 257, 260–261, 262,**Supp. XV:** 263, 266

Log Book of "The Loved One," The, **Supp. XI:** 306

Logenbach, James, **Supp. XVII:** 183

"Logging and Pimping and 'Your Pal, Jim' " (Maclean), **Supp. XIV:** 229

"Logos" (W. Stone), **Supp. XXVII:** 255

Logue, Christopher, **Supp. XIV:** 82

Lohengrin (Wagner), **I:** 216

Lohrfinck, Rosalind, **III:** 107, 117

Lolita (Nabokov), **III:** 246, 247, 255, 258–261; **Retro. Supp. I:** 263, 264, 265, 266, 269, 270, **272–274**, 275; **Supp. V:** 127, 252; **Supp. VIII:** 133; **Supp. XVI:** 294; **Supp. XXII:** 260

"Lolita" (Parker), **Supp. IX:** 193

Lolly Dinks' Doings (E. Stoddard), **Supp. XV:** 273,**Supp. XV:** 286

Lombard, Kandace, **Supp. XXVII:** 262

Lombardi, Marilyn May, **Retro. Supp. II:** 40

Lomokome Papers, The (Wouk), **Supp. XXV:** 256, 262

London, Eliza, **II:** 465

London, Jack, **I:** 209; **II:** 264, 440, 444, 451, **462–485**; **III:** 314, 580; **Supp. IV Part 1:** 236; **Supp. IX:** 1, 14; **Supp. V:** 281; **Supp. XIII:** 312; **Supp. XIV:** 227; **Supp. XV:** 115; **Supp. XVI:** 181; **Supp. XVIII:** 90; **Supp. XXII:** 203; **Supp. XXVII:** 126

London, Mrs. Jack (Bessie Maddern), **II:** 465, 466, 473, 478

London, Mrs. Jack (Charmian Kittredge), **II:** 466, 468, 473, 476, 478, 481

London, John, **II:** 464, 465

London, Scott, **Supp. XIV:** 301, 307, 311

"London 1972: Silent Zone" (Davison), **Supp. XXVI:** 72

London Embassy, The (Theroux), **Supp. VIII:** 323

London Fields (Amis), **Retro. Supp. I:** 278

"London Letter" (column; Eliot), **Supp. XV:** 306

London Magazine (Plath), **Supp. I Part 2:** 541

London Snow: A Christmas Story (Theroux), **Supp. VIII:** 322

London Suite (Simon), **Supp. IV Part 2:** 576, 581, 582, 588

London: The Biography (Ackroyd), **Supp. XVII:** 180

Loneliness of the Long Distance Runner, The (Sillitoe), **Supp. XX: 195**

Lonely Are the Brave (film), **Supp. XIII:** 6

"Lonely Coast, A" (Proulx), **Supp. VII:** 264

Lonely Crusade (C. Himes), **Supp. XVI:** 135, 139–140

Lonely for the Future (Farrell), **II:** 46, 47

"Lonely Gay Teen Seeking Same" (Egan), **Supp. XIX:** 61

Lonely Impulse of Delight, A (Shanley), **Supp. XIV:** 317–318

"Lonely Street, The" (W. C. Williams), **IV:** 413

"Lonely Worker, A" (Jewett), **Retro. Supp. II:** 132

Lonergan, Wayne, **Supp. I Part 1:** 51

Lonesome Boy (Bontemps), **Supp. XXII:** 6, 13–14

Lonesome Dove (McMurtry), **Supp. V:** 226–228, 231, 232, 233

Lonesome Traveler (Kerouac), **Supp. III Part 1:** 219, 225

"Lonesome Whistle Blowing" (Skow), **Supp. XVI:** 174

"Lone Striker, A" (Frost), **Retro. Supp. I:** 136, 137

Long, Ada, **Supp. V:** 178

Long, Frank Belknap, **Supp. XXV:** 111, 122; **Supp. XXVII:** 117

Long, Haniel, **Supp. XV:** 46, 49

Long, Huey, **I:** 489; **II:** 454; **IV:** 249; **Supp. IV Part 2:** 679; **Supp. XIV:** 14

Long, John Luther, **Supp. XXI:** 150

Long, Judith Reick, **Supp. XX: 212, 215, 217, 223**

Long, Ray, **II:** 430; **III:** 54

Long after Midnight (Bradbury), **Supp. IV Part 1:** 102

Long Ago in France: The Years in Dijon (M. F. K. Fisher), **Supp. XVII:** 91

Long and Happy Life, A (Price), **Supp. VI:** 258, **259–260**, 262, 264, 265

Long Approach, The (Kumin), **Supp. IV Part 2:** 452–453, 453

Longbottom, Robert, **Supp. XXI:** 148

Long Christmas Dinner, The (Wilder), **IV:** 357, 365; **Supp. V:** 105

Long Christmas Dinner and Other Plays (Wilder), **IV:** 365–366

Long Day's Dying, A (Buechner), **Supp. XII: 45–47**

Long Day's Journey into Night (O'Neill), **III:** 385, 401, 403–404; **Supp. IV Part 1:** 359; **Supp. XIV:** 327; **Supp. XXI:** 13; **Supp. XXII:** 27, 29, 30

Long Desire, A (Connell), **Supp. XIV:** 79, 80, 97

"Long Distance" (Stafford), **Supp. XI:** 329

"Long-Distance Runner, The" (Paley), **Supp. VI:** 221–222, 228, 230

Long Dream, The (Wright), **IV:** 478, 488, 494

"Long Embrace, The" (Levine), **Supp. V:** 187

"Long Enough" (Rukeyser), **Supp. VI:** 274

"Longest Night of My Life, The " (Nichols), **Supp. XIII:** 269

Longfellow, Henry Wadsworth, **I:** 458, 471; **II:** 274, 277, 295–296, 310, 313, 402, **486–510**; **III:** 269, 412, 421, 422, 577; **IV:** 309, 371; **Retro. Supp. I:** 54, 123, 150, 155, 362; **Retro. Supp. II: 153–174**; **Supp. I Part 1:** 158, 299, 306, 317, 362, 368; **Supp. I Part 2:** 405, 406, 408, 409, 414, 416, 420, 586, 587, 602, 699, 704; **Supp. II Part 1:** 291, 353; **Supp. III Part 2:** 609; **Supp. IV Part 1:** 165; **Supp. IV Part 2:** 503; **Supp. XII:** 260; **Supp. XIII:** 141; **Supp. XIV:** 120; **Supp. XVIII:** 4; **Supp. XXI:** 51; **Supp. XXIII:** 223

"Long Feud" (Untermeyer), **Supp. XV:** 309

Long Feud: Selected Poems (Untermeyer), **Supp. XV:** 312

"Long Fourth, A" (Taylor), **Supp. V:** 313

Long Fourth and Other Stories, A (Taylor), **Supp. V:** 318–319

Long Gay Book, A (Stein), **IV:** 42

Long Goodbye, The (Chandler), **Supp. IV Part 1:** 120, 122, 132–134, 135

Long Goodbye, The (T. Williams), **IV:** 381

"Long Hair" (Snyder), **Supp. VIII:** 300

Longing for Home, The: Recollections and Reflections (Buechner), **Supp. XII:** 53

Longinus, Dionysius Cassius, **I:** 279

"Long-Legged House, The" (Berry), **Supp. X:** 21, 24–25, 27, 31

Long Live Man (Corso), **Supp. XII:** 129–130, 132

Long Love, The (Sedges), **Supp. II Part 1:** 125

Long Made Short (Dixon), **Supp. XII:** 152

Long March, The (Styron), **IV:** 97, 99, 104–107, 111, 113, 117

"Long Night, The" (Bambara), **Supp. XI:** 9

Long Night of White Chickens, The (Goldman), **Supp. XXV:** 49, 51–53

"Long Novel, A" (Ashbery), **Supp. III Part 1:** 6

Longo, Robert, **Supp. XVI:** 124

Long Patrol, The (Mailer), **III:** 46

"Long Peace Among Iroquois Nations, The" (Crawford), **Supp. XXVI:** 85

"Long Point Light" (Doty), **Supp. XI:** 127

Long Road of Woman's Memory, The (Addams), **Supp. I Part 1:** 17–18

"Long Run, The" (Wharton), **IV:** 314

Long Season, The (Brosnan), **II:** 424, 425; **Supp. XX:** 195

"Long Shadow of Lincoln, The: A Litany" (Sandburg), **III:** 591, 593

Longshot O'Leary (McGrath), **Supp. X:** 117

"Long Shower, The" (Francis), **Supp. IX:** 90

"Long Stemmed Roses" (Jarman), **Supp. XVII:** 115

Long Story Short (Gingher, ed.), **Supp. XXVII:** 12

Longstreet, Augustus B., **II:** 70, 313; **Supp. I Part 1:** 352; **Supp. V:** 44; **Supp. X:** 227

"Long Summer" (R. Lowell), **II:** 553–554

"Long Term" (Dunn), **Supp. XI:** 149

"Long Thoughts, The"(Dybek), **Supp. XXIII:** 71

Longtime Companion (film), **Supp. X:** 146, 152

Long Valley, The (Steinbeck), **IV:** 51

Long View (Taggard), **Supp. XXII: 283–284**

Long Voyage Home, The (O'Neill), **III:** 388

"Long Wail, A" (Crews), **Supp. XI:** 101

"Long Walk, The" (Bogan), **Supp. III Part 1:** 61

Long Walk Home, The (Kriegel), **Supp. XXIV:** 214–216

Long Walks and Intimate Talks (Paley), **Supp. VI:** 221

Long Way from Home, A (McKay), **Supp. X:** 132, 140

Long Winter, The (L. I. Wilder), **Supp. XXII:** 291, 294, 295

Lönnrot, Elias, **Retro. Supp. II:** 159

Looby, Christopher, **Supp. XIII:** 96

Look, Dan, **Supp. XXV:** 123

Look, Stranger! (Auden), **Supp. II Part 1:** 11

"Look, The" (Olds), **Supp. X:** 210

Look at Me (Egan), **Supp. XIX:** 49, 53–56, 60, 61

Look at the Harlequins (Nabokov), **Retro. Supp. I:** 266, 270

Lookaway, Lookaway (Barnhardt), **Supp. XXVII:** 1, 9–11, 13

"Look for My White Self" (Ammons), **Supp. VII:** 25

"Look Fred, You're a Doctor, My Problem Is Something Like This" (Berrigan), **Supp. XXIV:** 37

Look Homeward, Angel (Wolfe), **II:** 457; **IV:** 450, 452, 453, 454, 455–456, 461, 462, 463, 464, 468, 471; **Supp. XI:** 216

"Looking" (Sanders), **Supp. XVI:** 277

"Looking a Mad Dog Dead in the Eyes" (Komunyakaa), **Supp. XIII:** 114

"Looking at Each Other" (Rukeyser), **Supp. VI:** 280, 285–286

"Looking at Kafka" (P. Roth), **Supp. III Part 2:** 402

"Looking at Women" (Sanders), **Supp. XVI:** 274

"Looking Back" (Harjo), **Supp. XII:** 218

"Looking Back" (Merwin), **Supp. III Part 1:** 352

"Looking Back at Girlhood" (Jewett), **Retro. Supp. II:** 131, 133

Looking Backward (Bellamy), **II:** 276; **Supp. I Part 2:** 641; **Supp. XI:** 200

"Looking for a Ship" (McPhee), **Supp. III Part 1:** 312–313

"Looking for Dragon Smoke" (R. Bly), **Supp. IV Part 1:** 60

Looking for Holes in the Ceiling (Dunn), **Supp. XI:** 139, **143–145**

Looking for Langston (Julien; film), **Supp. XI:** 19, 20

Looking for Lincoln (television production), **Supp. XX: 99**

Looking for Luck (Kumin), **Supp. IV Part 2:** 453, 454–455

"Looking for Mr. Green" (Bellow), **Retro. Supp. II:** 27

"Looking for the Buckhead Boys" (Dickey), **Supp. IV Part 1:** 182, 183

"Looking Forward to Age" (Harrison), **Supp. VIII:** 49

"Looking from Inside My Body" (R. Bly), **Supp. IV Part 1:** 71

"Looking Glass, The" (Wharton), **Retro. Supp. I:** 382

"Lookout's Journal" (Snyder), **Supp. VIII:** 291

"Looks Like They'll Never Learn" (McCoy), **Supp. XIII:** 166

"Look to the Woods" (P. N. Warren), **Supp. XX: 272**

"Look to Thy Heart . . ." (Hay), **Supp. XIV:** 130

Loon, Hendrik Willem van, **Supp. XVI:** 185

Loon Lake (Doctorow), **Supp. IV Part 1:** 219, 222, 224–227, 230, 231, 232, 233

"Loon Point" (O'Brien), **Supp. V:** 237

Loos, Adolf, **Supp. XVI:** 187

Loos, Anita, **Supp. XVI: 181–199**

Loos, Mary Anita, **Supp. XVI:** 196

Loose Canons (H. L. Gates), **Supp. XX: 101, 108, 109–110, 111**

Loosestrife (Dunn), **Supp. XI: 152–154**

"Loosestrife" (Dunn), **Supp. XI:** 154

"Loose Woman" (X. J. Kennedy), **Supp. XV:** 159

Loose Woman: Poems (Cisneros), **Supp. VII:** 58, 71–72

Lopate, Edward, **Supp. XVI:** 266

Lopate, Philip, **Supp. XII:** 184; **Supp. XIII:** 280–281; **Supp. XVI:** 230

Lopatnikoff, Nikolai, **Supp. XIV:** 123

Lopez, Barry, **Supp. IV Part 1:** 416; **Supp. V:** 211; **Supp. X:** 29, 31; **Supp. XIII:** 16; **Supp. XIV:** 227

Lopez, Rafael, **Supp. IV Part 2:** 602

Lorax, The (Geisel), **Supp. XVI:** 109–110

Lorca, Federico García, **IV:** 380; **Supp. I Part 1:** 345; **Supp. IV Part 1:** 83; **Supp. VIII:** 38, 39; **Supp. XIII:** 315, 323, 324; **Supp. XV:** 186; **Supp. XXI:** 100; **Supp. XXVII:** 53, 151, 155, 160

Lord, Judge Otis P., **I:** 454, 457, 458, 470

Lorde, Audre, **Supp. I Part 2:** 550, 571; **Supp. IV Part 1:** 325; **Supp. XI:** 20; **Supp. XII:** 217, 220; **Supp. XIII:** 295; **Supp. XVII:** 71; **Supp. XXIII:** 194

Lord Jim (Conrad), **I:** 422; **II:** 26; **Retro. Supp. II:** 292; **Supp. I Part 2:** 623; **Supp. IV Part 2:** 680; **Supp. V:** 251

"Lord of Hosts" (Pinsky), **Supp. VI:** 244

Lord of the Flies (W. Golding), **Supp. XVI:** 65

Lord of the Rings (Tolkien), **Supp. V:** 140; **Supp. XXVII:** 128

Lords of Misrule, The (X. J. Kennedy), **Supp. XV:** 154, **170–171**

Lords of the Housetops (Van Vechten), **Supp. II Part 2:** 736

Lord's Prayer, **I:** 579

Lord Timothy Dexter of Newburyport, Mass. (Marquand), **III:** 55

Lord Weary's Castle (R. Lowell), **II:** 538, 542–551; **Retro. Supp. II:** 178, **186–187**, 188; **Supp. XV:** 252

"Lorelei" (Plath), **Retro. Supp. II:** 246; **Supp. I Part 2:** 538

Lorentzen, Christian, **Supp. XXVII:** 195–196

"Lorenzo" (Bynner), **Supp. XV:** 46, 50

Lorimer, George Horace, **II:** 430; **Retro. Supp. I:** 101, 113

Lorre, Peter, **Supp. IV Part 1:** 356

"Los Alamos" (Momaday), **Supp. IV Part 2:** 482

Los Amigos de Becky (Hinojosa). *See Becky and Her Friends* (Hinojosa)

"Los Angeles, 1980" (Gunn Allen), **Supp. IV Part 1:** 325

"Los Angeles Days" (Didion), **Supp. IV Part 1:** 211

Los Cerritos (Atherton), **Supp. XXIV:** 22

"Lo! School in Poetry, The" (Taggard), **Supp. XXII:** 276

"Loser, The" (Talese), **Supp. XVII:** 202, 208

Loser and Still Champion: Muhammad Ali (Schulberg), **Supp. XVIII:** 254

Losey, Joseph, **IV:** 383

Lose Your Mother: A Journey Along the Atlantic Slave Route (Hartman), **Supp. XX: 154**

"Losing a Language" (Merwin), **Supp. III Part 1: 356**

Losing Battles (Welty), **IV: 261, 281–282; Retro. Supp. I: 341, 352, 353–354**

"Losing the Marbles" (Merrill), **Supp. III Part 1: 337**

"Losing Track of Language" (Clampitt), **Supp. IX: 38, 40**

Losses (Jarrell), **II: 367, 372, 373–375, 376, 377, 380–381**

"Losses" (Jarrell), **II: 375–376**

Lossky, N. O., **Supp. IV Part 2: 519**

"Loss of Breath" (Poe), **III: 425–426**

"Loss of My Arms and Legs, The" (Kingsolver), **Supp. VII: 208**

Loss of Roses, A (Inge), **Supp. XXV: 95, 103–104, 106**

"Loss of the Creature, The" (Percy), **Supp. III Part 1: 387**

"Lost" (Wagoner), **Supp. IX: 328**

"Lost, The" (Boyle), **Supp. XXIV: 59**

"Lost, The/Los Perdidos" (Kingsolver), **Supp. VII: 208**

"Lost and Found" (Levine), **Supp. V: 188**

"Lost and Found" (Nelson), **Supp. XVIII: 176**

"Lost Bodies" (Wright), **Supp. V: 342**

"Lost Boy, The" (Wolfe), **IV: 451, 460, 466–467**

"Lost Children, The"(Crooker), **Supp. XXIII: 54**

"Lost Decade, The" (Fitzgerald), **II: 98**

"Lost Dogs of Phnom Penh, The" (Boyle), **Supp. XXIV: 64**

Lost Ecstasy (Rinehart), **Supp. XXV: 196**

Lost Father, The (Simpson), **Supp. XXVII: 237–239**

"Lost Fugue for Chet" (Hull), **Supp. XXI: 137–138, 141**

Lost Galleon and Other Tales, The (Harte), **Supp. II Part 1: 344**

Lost Get-Back Boogie, The (Burke), **Supp. XIV: 22, 25**

"Lost Girls, The" (Hogan), **Supp. IV Part 1: 406–407**

Lost Grizzlies, The: A Search for Survivors in the Wilderness of Colorado (Bass), **Supp. XVI: 25, 26**

Lost Highway (film), **Supp. X: 314**

Lost Illusions (Balzac), **I: 500**

"Lost in Nostalgia: The Autobiographies of Eva Hoffman and Richard Rodriguez" (Fachinger), **Supp. XVI: 153**

Lost in the Bonewheel Factory (Komunyakaa), **Supp. XIII: 114–115, 116**

Lost in the City (E. P. Jones), **Supp. XXII: 140, 142, 143–146, 148, 149**

Lost in the Cosmos: The Last Self-Help Book (Percy), **Supp. III Part 1: 397**

Lost in the Funhouse (Barth), **I: 122, 135, 139; Supp. X: 307**

"Lost in the Whichy Thicket" (Wolfe), **Supp. III Part 2: 573, 574**

Lost in Translation (E. Hoffman), **Supp. XVI: 147, 148–151, 153, 154, 159**

"Lost in Translation" (Hass), **Supp. VIII: 28**

"Lost in Translation" (Merrill), **Supp. III Part 1: 324, 329–330**

Lost in Yonkers (film), **Supp. IV Part 2: 588**

Lost in Yonkers (Simon), **Supp. IV Part 2: 576, 577, 584, 587–588, 590–591**

"Lost Jerusalem" (Untermeyer), **Supp. XV: 307**

Lost Lady, A (Cather), **I: 323–325, 327; Retro. Supp. I: 15–16, 20, 21, 382**

Lost Light (Connelly), **Supp. XXI: 72, 75–76**

"Lost Lives" (Sorrentino), **Supp. XXI: 226**

"Lost Lover, A" (Jewett), **II: 400–401, 402; Retro. Supp. II: 137**

"Lost Loves" (Kinnell), **Supp. III Part 1: 237, 245**

Lost Man's River (Matthiessen), **Supp. V: 212, 213, 214, 215**

"Lost on September Trail, 1967" (Ríos), **Supp. IV Part 2: 540**

Lost Puritan (Mariani), **Retro. Supp. II: 189**

Lost Roads Project, The: A Walk-In Book of Arkansas (exhibition; Wright and Luster), **Supp. XV: 337, 348**

"Lost Sailor, The" (Freneau), **Supp. II Part 1: 264**

Lost Son, The (Roethke), **III: 529, 530–532, 533**

"Lost Son, The" (Roethke), **III: 536, 537–539, 542**

"Lost Sons" (Salter), **Supp. IX: 260**

Lost Souls (Singer). *See* Meshugah (Singer)

"Lost"(Thompson), **Supp. XXIII: 299, 300**

"Lost Treaties of the California Indians" (Zitkala-Ša), **Supp. XXV: 284**

Lost Weekend, The (Jackson), **Supp. XIII: 262**

"Lost World, A" (Ashbery), **Supp. III Part 1: 9**

"Lost World, The" (Chabon), **Supp. XI: 72–73**

Lost World, The (Jarrell), **II: 367, 368, 371, 379–380, 386, 387**

"Lost World, The" cycle (Chabon), **Supp. XI: 71–73**

"Lost World of Richard Yates, The: How the Great Writer of the Age of Anxiety Disappeared from Print" (O'Nan), **Supp. XI: 348**

"Lost Young Intellectual, The" (Howe), **Supp. VI: 113, 115–116**

Lost Zoo, The: (A Rhyme for the Young, But Not Too Young) (Cullen), **Supp. IV Part 1: 173**

Loti, Pierre, **II: 311, 325; Supp. IV Part 1: 81**

"Lot of People Bathing in a Stream, A" (Stevens), **IV: 93**

Lotringer, Sylvère, **Supp. XII: 4**

"Lot's Wife" (Nemerov), **III: 270**

"Lottery, The" (Jackson), **Supp. IX: 113, 114, 118, 120, 122–123**

Lottery, The; or, The Adventures of James Harris (Jackson), **Supp. IX: 113, 115, 116, 124, 125**

Lotze, Hermann, **III: 600**

Loud and Clear (Quindlen), **Supp. XVII: 167, 170–172**

"Loud Like Love" (video, Ellis), **Supp. XXVII: 80**

Louganis, Greg, **Supp. XX: 264**

"Louie, His Cousin & His Other Cousin" (Cisneros), **Supp. VII: 60**

Louinet, Patrice, **Supp. XXVII: 128**

Louis, Joe, **II: 589; Supp. IV Part 1: 360**

Louis, Pierre Charles Alexandre, **Supp. I Part 1: 302, 303**

"Louisa, Please Come Home" (Jackson), **Supp. IX: 122**

Louis Lambert (Balzac), **I: 499**

"Louis Simpson and Walt Whitman: Destroying the Teacher" (Lazer), **Supp. IX: 265**

"Louis Zukofsky: *All: The Collected Short Poems, 1923–1958*" (Creeley), **Supp. IV Part 1: 154**

"Lounge" (Francis), **Supp. IX: 83**

Lounsberry, Barbara, **Supp. XVII: 208**

Lounsbury, Floyd G., **Supp. XXVI: 89**

Lounsbury, Thomas R., **I: 335**

Louter, Jan, **Supp. XI: 173**

"Love" (Collins), **Supp. XXI: 61**

"Love," (Gibran), **Supp. XX: 119**

"Love" (Olson), **Supp. II Part 2: 571**

"Love" (Paley), **Supp. VI: 219, 222, 230**

Love, Deborah, **Supp. V: 208, 210**

Love Alone: 18 Elegies for Rog (Monette), **Supp. X: 146, 154**

Love Always (Beattie), **Supp. V: 29, 30, 35**

Love among the Cannibals (Morris), **III: 228, 230–231**

"Love Among the Ruins" (Mosley), **Supp. XIII: 247**

"Love and Art" (Huddle), **Supp. XXVI: 150**

Love and Death (film; Allen), **Supp. XV: 2, 5–6, 7, 11**

Love and Death in the American Novel (Fiedler), **Supp. XIII: 93, 96, 99–101, 104**

Love and Exile (Singer), **Retro. Supp. II: 302–304, 315**

Love and Fame (Berryman), **I: 170**

Love and Friendship (Bloom), **Retro. Supp. II: 31, 33–34**

Love and Glory (Parker), **Supp. XIX: 189**

"Love and How to Cure It" (Wilder), **IV: 365**

Love and Other Games of Chance (Siegel), **Supp. XXII: 255, 256, 261–265, 266, 267**

Love and Scorn: New and Selected Poems (C. Frost), **Supp. XV: 95, 96, 100, 103–105, 106**

Love and Theft (album, Dylan), **Supp. XVIII: 28, 31**

"Love and the Hate, The" (Jeffers), **Supp. II Part 2: 434–435**

Love and the Incredibly Old Man (Siegel), **Supp. XXII: 267–268**

Love and Will (Dixon), **Supp. XII:** 148, 149

Love and Work (Price), **Supp. VI:** 261

"Love as a Great Power" (Bronk), **Supp. XXI:** 31

"Love Calls Us to the Things of This World" (Wilbur), **Supp. III Part 2:** 544, 552–553

Love Course, The (Gurney), **Supp. V:** 98

Lovecraft, H. P., **Supp. XXII:** 49; **Supp. XXV: 109–126; Supp. XXVII:** 115, 117, 119, 128

Lovecraft and Influence (R. H. Waugh, ed.), **Supp. XXV:** 123

Loved One, The (film), **Supp. XI: 305–306,** 307

Loved One, The (Waugh), **Supp. XI:** 305

Love Expert, The (film; Kirkland), **Supp. XVI:** 186

Love Feast (Buechner), **Supp. XII:** 52

Love for Love (Congreve), **Supp. XVIII:** 12

"Love Fossil" (Olds), **Supp. X:** 203

"Love"(Hadas), **Supp. XXIII:** 117

Love in a Dead Language (Siegel), **Supp. XXII:** 255, **258–261,** 265–266, 267

Love in Buffalo (Gurney), **Supp. V:** 96

Love in Chartres (Asch), **Supp. XXVI:** 18, 19, 20–21, 25

"Love—In Other Words" (Lee), **Supp. VIII:** 113

"Love in the Air" (Jin), **Supp. XVIII:** 93–94

"Love in the Morning" (Dubus), **Supp. VII:** 91

Love in the Ruins: The Adventures of a Bad Catholic at a Time near the End of the World (Percy), **Supp. III Part 1:** 385, 387, 393–394, 397–398

Love in the Western World (de Rougemont), **Retro. Supp. I:** 328

"Love Is a Deep and a Dark and a Lonely" (Sandburg), **III:** 595

"Love Is a Fire" (Cohen), **Supp. XXVII:** 60

"Love Itself" (Cohen), **Supp. XXVII:** 61

Lovejoy, Elijah P., **Supp. I Part 2:** 588; **Supp. XXIV:** 78

Lovejoy, Owen R., **Supp. I Part 1:** 8

Lovejoy, Thomas, **Supp. X:** 108

"Lovejoy Street" (Stallings), **Supp. XXV:** 224

Lovelace, Richard, **II:** 590

"Love Letter (Schnackenberg), **Supp. XV:** 258–259

Love Letters (film), **Supp. IV Part 2:** 524

Love Letters (Gurney), **Supp. V:** 105, 108–109

Love Letters, The (Massie), **Supp. IV Part 2:** 524

Love Letters and Two Other Plays: The Golden Age and What I Did Last Summer (Gurney), **Supp. V:** 100

"Love Lies Sleeping" (Bishop), **Retro. Supp. II:** 42

Love Life (Mason), **Supp. VIII:** 145–146

"Love Life" (Mason), **Supp. VIII: 145–146**

Lovell, Julia, **Supp. XVIII:** 101

Lovely Bones, The (Sebold), **Supp. XXII:** 55

Lovely Lady, The (Lawrence), **Retro. Supp. I:** 203

"Lovely Lady, The" (Lawrence), **Supp. I Part 1:** 329

Love Me (Keillor), **Supp. XVI:** 178

Love Medicine (Erdrich), **Supp. IV Part 1:** 259, 260, 261, 263, 265, 266, 267–268, 270, 271, 274–275; **Supp. X:** 290

Love Medicine (expanded version) (Erdrich), **Supp. IV Part 1:** 263, 273, 274, 275

"Love Minus Zero/No Limit" (song, Dylan), **Supp. XVIII:** 31

"Love Nest, The" (Lardner), **II:** 427, 429

Love Nest, The, and Other Stories (Lardner), **II:** 430–431, 436

Lovenheim, Barbara, **Supp. X:** 169

Love of a Good Woman, The (Munro), **Supp. XXVII:** 190, 192

"Love of a Good Woman, The" (Munro), **Supp. XXVII:** 192

"Love of Annunziata, The" (di Donato), **Supp. XX: 40**

"Love of Elsie Barton: A Chronicle, The" (Warren), **IV:** 253

Love of Landry, The (Dunbar), **Supp. II Part 1:** 212

"Love of Morning, The" (Levertov), **Supp. III Part 1:** 284

Love of the Last Tycoon, The: A Western. See Last Tycoon, The

"Love on the Bon Dieu" (Chopin), **Supp. I Part 1:** 213

Love on the Hoof (O'Hara and Lima), **Supp. XXIII:** 217

Love Poems (Sexton), **Supp. II Part 2:** 687–689

Love Poems (Tentative Title) (O'Hara), **Supp. XXIII:** 219

Love Poems of May Swenson, The (Swenson), **Supp. IV Part 2:** 652, 653

"Love Poet" (Agee), **I:** 28

"Lover" (Hoffman), **Supp. XVIII:** 87

"Love Ritual" (Mora), **Supp. XIII:** 215

Lover of Horses, The (Gallagher), **Supp. XXIV:** 166, 172, 173–174, 176

"Lover of Horses, The" (Gallagher), **Supp. XXIV:** 173–174, 176

Loveroot (Jong), **Supp. V:** 115, 130

"Lovers, The" (Berryman), **I:** 174

"Lovers, The" (Buck), **Supp. II Part 1:** 128

"Lover's Garden, A" (Ginsberg), **Supp. II Part 1:** 311

"Lovers of the Poor, The" (Brooks), **Supp. III Part 1:** 81, 85

Lovers Should Marry (Martin), **Supp. IV Part 1:** 351

"Lover's Song" (Yeats), **Supp. I Part 1:** 80

"Love Rushes By" (Salinas), **Supp. XIII:** 326–327

"Love's Ghost" (Nelson), **Supp. XVIII:** 176

Lovesick (Stern), **Supp. IX: 295–296**

Love's Labour's Lost (Shakespeare), **III:** 263

Love's Old Sweet Song (Saroyan), **Supp. IV Part 1:** 83

"Love Song During Riot with Many Voices" (Hull), **Supp. XXI:** 136

"Love Song of J. Alfred Prufrock, The" (T. S. Eliot), **I:** 52, 66, 569–570; **III:** 460; **Retro. Supp. I:** 55, 56, 57, 60; **Supp. II Part 1:** 5; **Supp. XIII:** 346; **Supp. XVI:** 150; **Supp. XXV:** 22; **Supp. XXVI:** 237

"Love Song of St. Sebastian" (Eliot), **Retro. Supp. I:** 57

"Love Songs" (Loy), **Supp. XXII:** 161

Love Songs (Teasdale), **Supp. XXVII:** 283, 289, 290–291

"Love Songs to Joannes" (Loy), **Supp. XXII:** 161, 163

Love's Pilgrimage (Sinclair), **Supp. V:** 286

"Love's Relative" (Stone), **Supp. XXVII:** 251

"Love the Wild Swan" (Jeffers), **Supp. VIII:** 33

Love to Mamá: A Tribute to Mothers (Mora, ed.), **Supp. XIII:** 221

Lovett, Robert Morss, **II:** 43

Lovett-Graff, Bennett, **Supp. XXV:** 123

"Love-Unknown" (Herbert), **Supp. I Part 1:** 80

Love! Valor! Compassion! (film), **Supp. XIII:** 206

Love! Valour! Compassion! (McNally), **Supp. XIII:** 199, **203–204,** 208, 209

"Love *versus* Law" (Stowe), **Supp. I Part 2:** 585–586

"Love Wall" (Peacock), **Supp. XIX:** 200

Love with a Few Hairs (Mrabet), **Supp. IV Part 1:** 92

Loving a Woman in Two Worlds (R. Bly), **Supp. IV Part 1:** 66, 67, 68–69, 71, 72

Loving in the War Years: Lo que nunca pasó por sus labios (Moraga), **Supp. XXIII:** 194, 195

"Loving on Borrowed Time" (J. W. Miller), **Supp. XX: 164**

"Loving Shepherdess, The" (Jeffers), **Supp. II Part 2:** 432

"Loving the Killer" (Sexton), **Supp. II Part 2:** 688

"Loving Wife" (C. Miller), **Supp. XXII:** 196–197, 199

Lovin' Molly (film), **Supp. V:** 223, 226

Low Country (Siddons), **Supp. XXII:** 239

Lowe, John, **Supp. XIII:** 238

Lowe, Pardee, **Supp. X:** 291

Lowell, Abbott Lawrence, **I:** 487; **II:** 513; **Supp. I Part 2:** 483

Lowell, Amy, **I:** 231, 384, 405, 475, 487; **II:** 174, **511–533,** 534; **III:** 465, 581, 586; **Retro. Supp. I:** 131, 133, 288; **Retro. Supp. II:** 46, 175; **Supp. I Part 1:** 257–259, 261–263, 265, 266; **Supp. I Part 2:** 465, 466, 707, 714, 729; **Supp. XIV:** 128; **Supp. XV:** 43, 293, 295, 297, 298, 299, 300, 301, 303, 306; **Supp. XX: 69; Supp. XXII:** 161; **Supp. XXVII:** 288, 295

Lowell, Blanche, **Supp. I Part 2:** 409

Lowell, Harriet, **II:** 553, 554

Lowell, James Russell, **I:** 216, 458; **II:** 273, 274, 289, 302, 320, 402, 529, 530, 532, 534, 551; **III:** 409; **IV:** 129, 171, 175, 180, 182–183, 186; **Retro. Supp. I:** 228; **Retro. Supp. II:** 155, 175, 326; **Supp. I Part 1:** 168, 299, 300, 303, 306, 311, 312, 317, 318, 362; **Supp. I Part 2: 404–426; Supp. II Part 1:** 197, 291, 352; **Supp. XV:** 278, 279; **Supp. XVI:** 84; **Supp. XVIII:** 2–3, 4, 8, 12

Lowell, Mrs. James Russell (Maria White), **Supp. I Part 2:** 405, 406, 414, 424

Lowell, Percival, **II:** 513, 525, 534

Lowell, Robert, **I:** 172, 381, 382, 400, 442, 521, 544–545, 550; **II:** 371, 376, 377, 384, 386–387, 532, **534–557; III:** 39, 44, 142, 508, 527, 528–529, 606; **IV:** 120, 138, 402, 430; **Retro. Supp. I:** 67, 140, 411; **Retro. Supp. II:** 27, 40, 44, 46, 48, 50, **175–193,** 221, 228–229, 235, 245; **Supp. I Part 1:** 89; **Supp. I Part 2:** 538, 543, 554; **Supp. III Part 1:** 6, 64, 84, 138, 147, 193, 194, 197–202, 205–208; **Supp. III Part 2:** 541, 543, 555, 561, 599; **Supp. IV Part 2:** 439, 620, 637; **Supp. IX:** 325; **Supp. V:** 81, 179, 180, 315–316, 337, 344; **Supp. VIII:** 27, 100, 271; **Supp. X:** 53, 58; **Supp. XI:** 146, 240, 244, 250, 317; **Supp. XII:** 253–254, 255; **Supp. XIII:** 76; **Supp. XIV:** 15, 126, 269; **Supp. XIX:** 197; **Supp. XV:** 20, 22, 93, 184, 249, 251, 253, 340; **Supp. XVII:** 239; **Supp. XX: 199, 203; Supp. XXI:** 131; **Supp. XXIII:** 211, 220; **Supp. XXIV:** 153; **Supp. XXVI:** 67, 68

Lowell, Rose, **Supp. I Part 2:** 409

"Lowell in the Classroom" (Vendler), **Retro. Supp. II:** 191

Lowenthal, Michael, **Supp. XII:** 82

Lower Depths, The (Gorki), **III:** 402

"Lower the Standard" (Shapiro), **Supp. II Part 2:** 715

Lowes, John Livingston, **II:** 512, 516, 532; **IV:** 453, 455

Lowin, Joseph, **Supp. V:** 273

"Low Lands" (Davison), **Supp. XXVI:** 76

"Low-Lands" (Pynchon), **Supp. II Part 2:** 620, 624

Lowle, Percival, **Supp. I Part 2:** 404

Lownsbrough, John, **Supp. IV Part 1:** 209, 211

Lowry, Beverly, **Supp. XXI:** 48

Lowry, Malcolm, **Supp. XVII:** 135, 136; **Supp. XXVI:** 28

Lowth, Richard, **II:** 8

Loy, Mina, **III:** 194; **Supp. XXII: 155–170**

Loy, Myrna, **Supp. IV Part 1:** 355

"Loyal Woman's No, A" (Larcom), **Supp. XIII:** 142, 143–144

"Luani of the Jungle" (Hughes), **Supp. I Part 1:** 328

Lubbock, Percy, **I:** 504; **II:** 337; **IV:** 308, 314, 319, 322; **Retro. Supp. I:** 366, 367, 373; **Supp. VIII:** 165; **Supp. XX: 231**

Lubin, Isidor, **Supp. I Part 2:** 632

Lubow, Arthur, **Supp. VIII:** 310

Lucas, Craig, **Supp. XXIV:** 263

Lucas, Victoria (pseudonym). *See* Plath, Sylvia

Luce, Dianne C., **Supp. VIII:** 189

Lucid, Robert F., **Retro. Supp. II:** 195, 204

"Lucid Eye in Silver Town, The" (Updike), **IV:** 218

"Lucid Walking" (A. Finch), **Supp. XVII:** 72

"Lucinda Matlock" (Masters), **Supp. I Part 2:** 461, 465

"Luck" (Dunn), **Supp. XI:** 149

Luck, Jessica Lewis, **Supp. XXVII:** 173

Luck of Barry Lyndon, The (Thackeray), **II:** 290

"Luck of Roaring Camp, The" (Harte), **Supp. II Part 1:** 335, 344, 345–347

"Luck of the Bogans, The" (Jewett), **Retro. Supp. II:** 142

Lucky Life (Stern), **Supp. IX: 290–291**

"Lucky Lucy's Daily Dream Book" (Di Piero), **Supp. XIX:** 38–39

Lucretius, **I:** 59; **II:** 162, 163; **III:** 600, 610–611, 612; **Supp. I Part 1:** 363

Lucy (Kincaid), **Supp. VII:** 180, 185, 186, 187–188, 194

Lucy, Saint, **II:** 211

Lucy Crown (Shaw), **Supp. XIX:** 251

Lucy Gayheart (Cather), **I:** 331; **Retro. Supp. I:** 19

"Lucy Tavish's Journey" (E. Stoddard), **Supp. XV:** 286

Lucy Temple (Rowson). *See Charlotte's Daughter; or, The Three Orphans*

Ludlow, Andrea, **Supp. XVIII:** 90

Ludvigson, Susan, **Supp. IV Part 2:** 442, 446, 447, 448, 451

Lueders, Edward, **Supp. XVI:** 265

"Luggage" (Bidart), **Supp. XV:** 35

Luhan, Mabel Dodge, **Retro. Supp. I:** 7; **Supp. XV:** 46, 50; **Supp. XXIV:** 30. *See also* Dodge, Mabel

Lu Ji, **Supp. VIII:** 303

Lukas, Michael, **Supp. XXVI:** 56

Luke (biblical book), **III:** 606

"Luke Havergal" (E. A. Robinson), **Supp. XVII:** 69

"Luke Havergal" (Robinson), **III:** 524

Lukeman, Gary, **Supp. XV:** 221

Luks, George, **IV:** 411; **Retro. Supp. II:** 103

"Lullaby" (Auden), **Supp. II Part 1:** 9

"Lullaby" (Bishop), **Supp. I Part 1:** 85

"Lullaby" (Everwine), **Supp. XV:** 89

"Lullaby" (Silko), **Supp. IV Part 2:** 560, 568–569

"Lullaby for Amy" (Jarman), **Supp. XVII:** 113, 121

"Lullaby of Cape Cod" (Brodsky), **Supp. VIII:** 27–28

Lullaby Raft (Nye), **Supp. XIII:** 278

Lullaby Raft (Nye, album), **Supp. XIII:** 274

Lullaby: The Comforting of Cock Robin (Snodgrass), **Supp. VI:** 324

"Lulls" (Walker), **Supp. III Part 2:** 525

"Lulu" (Wedekind), **Supp. XII:** 14

Lulu on the Bridge (film), **Supp. XII:** 21

Lulu's Library (Alcott), **Supp. I Part 1:** 43

"Lumber" (Baker), **Supp. XIII:** 55, 56

"Lumens, The" (Olds), **Supp. X:** 209

Lume Spento, A (Pound), **III:** 470

Lumet, Sidney, **Supp. IV Part 1:** 236; **Supp. IX:** 253

Luminous Debris: Reflecting on Vestige in Provence and Languedoc (Sobin), **Supp. XVI: 291–293,** 293–294

Luminous Face, The (Wells), **Supp. XXVI:** 280

"Lumumba's Grave" (Hughes), **Supp. I Part 1:** 344

"Luna, Luna" (Mora), **Supp. XIII:** 217

Lunar Baedecker (Loy), **Supp. XXII:** 165, **Supp. XXII:** 167, 166, 168

Lunar Baedecker and Time-Tables (Loy), **Supp. XXII:** 168

Lunar Follies (Sorrentino), **Supp. XXI:** 226, 237, 238–239

Lunar Park (Ellis), **Supp. XXVII:** 68, 71, 76–77

"Lunatic" (Hecht), **Supp. XXVII:** 95

Lunch Poems (O'Hara), **Supp. XXIII:** 219–220, 220

Lunsford, Bascom Lamar, **Supp. XX: 163**

Lupercal (Hughes), **Retro. Supp. II:** 245; **Supp. I Part 2:** 540

Lupton, Mary Jane, **Supp. IV Part 1:** 7

Lure of the Labrador Wild, The (Wallace), **Supp. XXII:** 218

Luria, Isaac, **IV:** 7

Lurie, Alison, **Supp. X:** 166; **Supp. XVI:** 103, 111–112

Lusitania Songspiel, Das (Durang), **Supp. XXIV:** 113, 116

Lust and Other Stories (Minot), **Supp. VI:** 205

Luster, Deborah, **Supp. XV:** 337, **Supp. XV:** 353, 348, 349, 350

Lustgarten, Edith, **III:** 107

Lustra (Pound), **Retro. Supp. I:** 289, 290

"Luther" (Huddle), **Supp. XXVI:** 152

Luther, Martin, **II:** 11–12, 506; **III:** 306, 607; **IV:** 490

"Luther on Sweet Auburn" (Bambara), **Supp. XI:** 16–17

Lux, Thomas, **Supp. XI:** 270; **Supp. XIX:** 276

Luxury Girl, The (McCoy), **Supp. XIII:** 163

Lyall, Sarah, **Supp. XIII:** 247

Lycidas (Milton), **II:** 540; **IV:** 347; **Retro. Supp. I:** 60; **Retro. Supp. II:** 186; **Supp. I Part 1:** 370; **Supp. IX:** 41

Lycographia (Paullini), **Supp. XVII:** 55

"Lydia and Marian" (Rowson), **Supp. XV:** 234

Lydon, Meghan, **Supp. XXVI:** 14–15

Lydon, Susan, **Supp. XII:** 170

Lyell, Charles, **Supp. IX:** 180

Lyell, Frank H., **Supp. VIII:** 125

Lyford, Harry, **Supp. I Part 2:** 679

"Lying" (Wilbur), **Supp. III Part 2:** 547, 562

"Lying and Looking" (Swenson), **Supp. IV Part 2:** 652

"Lying in a Hammock at William Duffy's Farm in Pine Island, Minnesota" (Wright), **Supp. III Part 2:** 589, 599, 600

"Lying in the Pollen and Water" (C. Frost), **Supp. XV:** 96

Lying Ladies, The (Ryan as Finnegan), **Supp. XVIII: 233–235,** 237

"Lying Next to the Knife" (McElwee), **Supp. XXIV:** 167, 173

Lyles, Lois F., **Supp. XI:** 7, 8

Lyly, John, **III:** 536; **Supp. I Part 1:** 369

Lynch, Anne, **Supp. XV:** 273

Lynch, Doris, **Supp. XVI:** 294

Lynchburg (Gander), **Supp. XV:** 340

"Lynched Man, The" (Karr), **Supp. XI:** 241

Lynchers, The (Wideman), **Supp. X:** 320

"Lynching, The" (McKay), **Supp. I Part 1:** 63

"Lynching of Jube Benson, The" (Dunbar), **Supp. II Part 1:** 214

"Lynching Song" (Hughes), **Supp. I Part 1:** 331

Lynd, Staughton, **Supp. VIII:** 240

Lynda Hull: Collected Poems (Hull), **Supp. XXI:** 129

Lynes, Katherine R., **Supp. XXVI:** 166, 170, 171, 175

Lynn, Kenneth, **Supp. XIII:** 96–97

Lynn, Kenneth S., **Supp. XIV:** 103

Lynn, Vera, **Supp. XI:** 304

Lyon, George Ella, **Supp. XX: 161–162**

Lyon, Kate, **I:** 409; **II:** 138, 143, 144

Lyon, Thomas, **Supp. IX:** 175

"Lyonnesse" (Plath), **Supp. I Part 2:** 541

Lyons, Bonnie, **Supp. V:** 58; **Supp. VIII:** 138

Lyons, Donald, **Supp. XXIV:** 274

Lyons, Nathan, **Supp. XXV:** 251

Lyons, The (Silver), **Supp. XXIV:** 263, **276**

Lyotard, Jean-François, **Supp. IV Part 1:** 54

Lyrical Ballads (Wordsworth), **III:** 583; **IV:** 120; **Supp. IX:** 274; **Supp. XI:** 243; **Supp. XIX:** 1; **Supp. XV:** 21

Lyrics of Love and Laughter (Dunbar), **Supp. II Part 1:** 207

Lyrics of Lowly Life (Dunbar), **Supp. II Part 1:** 197, 199, 200, 207

Lyrics of the Hearthside (Dunbar), **Supp. II Part 1:** 206

Lytal, Tammy, **Supp. XI:** 102

Lytle, Andrew, **IV:** 125; **Retro. Supp. II:** 220, 221, 235; **Supp. II Part 1:** 139; **Supp. X:** 1, 25; **Supp. XI:** 101

Lyttelton, Alfred, **Supp. XX: 230**

Lytton of Knebworth. *See* Bulwer-Lytton, Edward George

M

Mabie, Hamilton W., **Supp. XVIII:** 257

MCabe, Susan, **Supp. XXII:** 234

MacAdams, William, **Supp. XXVII:** 84, 91, 93, 96

McAlexander, Hubert H., **Supp. V:** 314, 319, 320, 323

McAlmon, Robert, **IV:** 404; **Retro. Supp. I:** 418, 419, 420; **Retro. Supp. II:** 328; **Supp. I Part 1:** 259; **Supp. III Part 2:** 614; **Supp. XXII:** 166, 215; **Supp. XXIV:** 62, 63

McAlmon, Mrs. Robert (Winifred Ellerman), **III:** 194. *See also* Ellerman, Winifred

McAlpine, Erica, **Supp. XXV:** 222, 233, 234

McAninch, Jerry, **Supp. XI:** 297, 298

MacArthur, Charles, **Supp. XXVII:** 83, 89

Macaulay, Catherine, **Supp. I Part 2:** 522

Macaulay, Rose, **Supp. XII:** 88; **Supp. XIV:** 348

Macaulay, Thomas, **II:** 15–16; **III:** 113, 591–592

Macauley, Robie, **Retro. Supp. II:** 228; **Supp. X:** 56

Macbeth (Shakespeare), **I:** 271; **IV:** 227; **Retro. Supp. I:** 131; **Supp. I Part 1:** 67; **Supp. I Part 2:** 457; **Supp. IV Part 1:** 87; **Supp. XIV:** 8; **Supp. XXVII:** 225

Macbeth (silent film), **Supp. XVI:** 184

MacBeth, George, **Retro. Supp. II:** 250

McBride, James, **Supp. XXVI: 191–205**

MacBride, Roger, **Supp. XXII:** 297, 301

McCabe, Tracy, **Supp. XXVI:** 166

McCafferty, Larry, **Supp. XVII:** 227

McCaffery, Larry, **Supp. IV Part 1:** 217, 227, 234; **Supp. V:** 53, 238; **Supp. VIII:** 13, 14; **Supp. X:** 260, 268, 301, 303, 307; **Supp. XVI:** 117; **Supp. XXII:** 177

McCann, Janet, **Supp. XXIII:** 51, 53, 54, 64

McCann, Jannet, **Supp. XXI:** 92

McCarriston, Linda, **Supp. X:** 204; **Supp. XIV: 259–275**

McCarthy, Charles Joseph, Jr. *See* McCarthy, Cormac

McCarthy, Cormac, **Supp. VIII: 175–192; Supp. XII:** 310; **Supp. XVII:** 185; **Supp. XXI:** 38, 40; **Supp. XXII:** 49; **Supp. XXIII:** 42, 44

McCarthy, Eugene, **Retro. Supp. II:** 182

McCarthy, Joseph, **I:** 31, 492; **II:** 562, 568; **Supp. I Part 1:** 294, 295; **Supp. I Part 2:** 444, 611, 612, 620; **Supp. XV:** 198, 311–312; **Supp. XXIII:** 7

McCarthy, Mary, **II: 558–584; Supp. I Part 1:** 84; **Supp. IV Part 1:** 209, 297, 310; **Supp. VIII:** 96, 99, 100; **Supp. X:** 177; **Supp. XI:** 246; **Supp. XIV:** 3; **Supp. XV:** 142; **Supp. XVI:** 64, 70; **Supp. XVII:** 43; **Supp. XXVII:** 89

McCay, Maura, **Supp. XII:** 271, 276

McClanahan, Ed, **Supp. X:** 24

McClanahan, Thomas, **Supp. XII:** 125–126

McClatchy, J. D., **Supp. XII: 253–270; Supp. XV:** 185, 257, 258

McClaurin, Irma, **Supp. XXIII:** 84, 86, 93, 94

McClellan, John L., **I:** 493

McClung, Isabelle, **Retro. Supp. I:** 5

McClure, Charlotte, **Supp. XXIV:** 29

McClure, John, **Retro. Supp. I:** 80

McClure, Michael, **Supp. II Part 1:** 32; **Supp. VIII:** 289; **Supp. XVI:** 283

McClure, S. S., **I:** 313; **II:** 465; **III:** 327; **Retro. Supp. I:** 5, 6, 9; **Supp. XV:** 40

McCluskey, John, Jr., **Supp. XIX:** 65, 68, 71, 72, 78

McCombs, Judith, **Supp. XIII:** 33

McConagha, Alan, **Supp. XVI:** 166

McConnell, Frank, **Supp. X:** 260, 274

McCorkle, Jill, **Supp. X:** 6; **Supp. XVIII:** 195; **Supp. XXV:** 129, 130

McCourt, Frank, **Supp. XII: 271–287**

McCoy, Horace, **Supp. XIII: 159–177; Supp. XXV:** 26

McCracken, Elizabeth, **Supp. X:** 86; **Supp. XII:** 310, 315–316, 321

McCrae, Fiona, **Supp. XVIII:** 60, 62

McCullers, Carson, **I:** 113, 190, 211; **II: 585–608; IV:** 282, 384, 385, 386; **Retro. Supp. II:** 324; **Supp. II Part 1:** 17; **Supp. IV Part 1:** 31, 84; **Supp. IV Part 2:** 502; **Supp. VIII:** 124; **Supp. XII:** 309; **Supp. XIV:** 120; **Supp. XV:** 338

McCullers, Reeves, **III:** 585, 586, 587

McCulloch, Jeanne, **Supp. XXVII:** 180

McDavid, Raven I., **III:** 120; **Supp. XIV:** 14

McDermott, Alice, **Supp. XII:** 311; **Supp. XVIII: 155–169**

McDermott, John J., **II:** 364

MacDiarmid, Hugh, **Supp. X:** 112

Macdonald, C. G., **Supp. XVII:** 73–74

MacDonald, Dwight, **Supp. XXV:** 266

Macdonald, Dwight, **I:** 233, 372, 379; **III:** 39; **Supp. V:** 265; **Supp. XIV:** 340; **Supp. XV:** 140

McDonald, E. J., **Supp. I Part 2:** 670

Macdonald, George, **Supp. XIII:** 75

MacDonald, Jeanette, **II:** 589

Macdonald, Ross, **Supp. IV Part 1:** 116, 136; **Supp. IV Part 2: 459–477; Supp. XIII:** 233; **Supp. XVIII:** 137, 136; **Supp. XXI:** 67

MacDonald, Ruth K., **Supp. XVI:** 102

McDonnell, Thomas P., **Supp. XX: 45**

MacDougall, Ruth Doan, **Supp. XV:** 58; **Supp. XVI:** 174

MacDowell, Edward, **I:** 228; **III:** 504, 508, 524

McDowell, Frederick P. W., **II:** 194

McDowell, Mary, **Supp. I Part 1:** 5

McDowell, Robert, **Supp. IX:** 266, 270, 276, 279

MacDowell, Robert, **Supp. XI:** 249

McDowell, Robert, **Supp. XVII:** 109, 110, 111

McDowell. Deborah, **Supp. XVIII:** 125, 129

McElderry, Margaret K., **Supp. XV:** 162

McElligot's Pool (Geisel), **Supp. XVI:** 104

McElrath, Joseph, **Supp. XIV:** 62

McElroy, Joseph, **Supp. IV Part 1:** 279, 285

McElwee, Caroline, **Supp. XXIV:** 167, 173

McEuen, Kathryn, **II:** 20
McEwen, Arthur, **I:** 206
McFarland, Ron, **Supp. IX:** 323, 327, 328, 333
McGann, Jerome, **Retro. Supp. I:** 47
McGill, Meredith, **Supp. XVIII:** 17
McGillis, Ian, **Supp. XVIII:** 150
MacGillivray, William, **Supp. XVI:** 8
McGinity, Keren, **Supp. XX:** 9
McGovern, Edythe M., **Supp. IV Part 2:** 573, 582, 585
McGovern, George, **III:** 46
MacGowan, Christopher, **Retro. Supp. I:** 430
MacGowan, Kenneth, **III:** 387, 391
McGrath, Abigail, **Supp. XXVI:** 164, 165, 172
McGrath, Douglas, **Supp. XV:** 12
McGrath, Joseph, **Supp. XI:** 307, 309
McGrath, Patrick, **Supp. IX:** 113; **Supp. XXII:** 58
McGrath, Thomas, **Supp. X: 111–130**
"McGrath on McGrath" (McGrath), **Supp. X:** 119, 120
McGuane, Thomas, **Supp. V:** 53, 220; **Supp. VIII:** 39, 40, 42, 43
MacGuffin, The (Elkin), **Supp. VI: 55–56**
McGuiness, Daniel, **Supp. XV:** 261
McGuinniss, Joe, **Supp. XXVII:** 67
Machado y Ruiz, Antonio, **Supp. XIII:** 315, 323
Machan, Tibor, **Supp. IV Part 2:** 528
McHaney, Pearl, **Supp. XXI:** 244, 255, 256, 257
McHaney, Thomas, **Supp. XVIII:** 199,203
Machen, Arthur, **IV:** 286
McHenry, Tim, **Supp. XXV:** 161
Machiavelli, Niccolò, **I:** 485; **Supp. XIX:** 34
"Machine-Gun, The" (Jarrell), **II:** 371
"Machines Mourn the Passing of People, The" (Stallings), **Supp. XXV:** 228
"Machine Song" (Anderson), **I:** 114
McHugh, Heather, **Supp. XIX:** 84; **Supp. XXIV:** 154
McHugh, Vincent, **Supp. XV:** 147
McInerney, Jay, **Supp. X:** 7, 166; **Supp. XI:** 65; **Supp. XII:** 81; **Supp. XVIII:** 148; **Supp. XXVII:** 68, 269
"Mac in Love" (Dixon), **Supp. XII: 142**
McIntire, Holly, **Supp. V:** 338
McIntosh, Maria, **Retro. Supp. I:** 246
Macintyre, Ben, **Supp. XXVII:** 270
Mack, Maynard, **Supp. XIV:** 12
Mackail, John William, **Supp. I Part 1:** 268; **Supp. I Part 2:** 461
McKay, Claude, **Supp. I Part 1:** 63; **Supp. III Part 1:** 75, 76; **Supp. IV Part 1:** 3, 79, 164; **Supp. IX:** 306; **Supp. X: 131–144; Supp. XI:** 91; **Supp. XIX:** 73; **Supp. XVII:** 74; **Supp. XVIII:** 122, 127, 280, 282; **Supp. XX: 69; Supp. XXII:** 275
McKay, Donald, **Supp. I Part 2:** 482
McKay, Nellie Y., **Supp. XX: 105**
McKee, Elizabeth, **Retro. Supp. II:** 221, 222
McKee, Ellen, **Retro. Supp. II:** 67

McKeen, William, **Supp. XXIV:** 279, 280, 281, 282, 288
McKenney, Eileen, **IV:** 288; **Retro. Supp. II:** 321, 330
McKenney, Ruth, **IV:** 288; **Retro. Supp. II:** 321; **Supp. XVIII:** 238
MacKenzie, Agnes, **I:** 199
Mackenzie, Captain Alexander, **III:** 94
Mackenzie, Compton, **II:** 82; **Retro. Supp. I:** 100, 102
McKenzie, Geraldine, **Supp. XII:** 107
MacKenzie, Margaret, **I:** 199
Mackey, Louis, **Supp. XXI:** 236, 237
Mackey, Nathaniel, **Supp. XXVII: 151–162,** 163, 168
McKibben, Bill, **Supp. XVIII:** 192
McKinley, William, **I:** 474; **III:** 506; **Supp. I Part 2:** 395–396, 707
MacKinnon, Catharine, **Supp. XII:** 6
McKnight, Reginald, **Supp. XX: 147–159**
MacLachlan, Suzanne L., **Supp. XII:** 300,**Supp. XII:** 299
MacLauchlin, Cory, **Supp. XXVI:** 240, 241, 242, 243, 244, 246, 252
McLaverty, Michael, **Supp. X:** 67
McLay, Catherine, **Supp. XIII:** 21
Maclean, Alasdair, **Supp. V:** 244
McLean, Carolyn (pseudonym). *See* Bly, Carol
Maclean, Norman, **Supp. XIV: 221–237; Supp. XVI:** 98; **Supp. XXVI:** 184
MacLeish, Archibald, **I:** 283, 293, 429; **II:** 165, 228; **III: 1–25,** 427; **Supp. I Part 1:** 261; **Supp. I Part 2:** 654; **Supp. IV Part 1:** 359; **Supp. IV Part 2:** 586; **Supp. X:** 120; **Supp. XIV:** 11
MacLeish, Mrs. Archibald (Ada Hitchcock), **III:** 1
MacLeish, Kenneth, **III:** 1
McLellan, Dennis, **Supp. XXVII:** 5
McLellan, Joseph, **Supp. XXIV:** 226
McLennan, Gordon Lawson, **Supp. IX:** 89
McLeod, A. W., **Supp. I Part 1:** 257
MacLeod, Charlotte, **Supp. XXV:** 192
McLuhan, Marshall, **Supp. IV Part 2:** 474
McLure, Michael, **Supp. XIV:** 150
Macmahon, Arthur, **I:** 226
McMahon, Helen, **Supp. IV Part 2:** 579
McMichael, Barbara Lloyd, **Supp. XXII:** 206, 207, 215, 216
McMichael, George, **Supp. VIII:** 124
McMichael, Morton, **Supp. I Part 2:** 707
McMichaels, James, **Supp. XIII:** 114
McMillan, James B., **Supp. VIII:** 124
McMillan, Terry, **Supp. XIII: 179–193**
McMullan, Jim, **Supp. XIV:** 124
McMurtry, Josephine, **Supp. V:** 220
McMurtry, Larry, **Supp. V: 219–235; Supp. X:** 24; **Supp. XI:** 172
McNally, Terrence, **Supp. XIII: 195–211**
McNally, T. M., **Supp. XX:** 92
McNamee, Thomas, **Supp. XXII:** 218
McNamer, Deirdre, **Supp. XI:** 190
McNeese, Gretchen, **Supp. V:** 123
MacNeice, Louis, **II:** 586; **III:** 527; **Supp. II Part 1:** 17, 24; **Supp. IV Part 2:** 440; **Supp. X:** 116; **Supp.**

XIII: 347
McNeil, Claudia, **Supp. IV Part 1:** 360, 362
M-a-c-n-o-l-i-a (Jordan), **Supp. XVIII:** 172
McPhee, John, **Supp. III Part 1: 289–316; Supp. X:** 29, 30; **Supp. XVIII:** 106–107, 114
MacPherson, Aimee Semple, **Supp. V:** 278
Macpherson, Anne, **Supp. XXIII:** 84
McPherson, Dolly, **Supp. IV Part 1:** 2, 3, 4, 6, 8, 11, 12
McPherson, James Alan, **Supp. XXII:** 141
McPherson, James Allen, **Retro. Supp. II:** 126
Macpherson, Jay, **Supp. XIII:** 19
MacPherson, Jennifer, **Supp. XXIII:** 248
MacPherson, Kenneth, **Supp. I Part 1:** 259
McPherson, Sandra, **Supp. XXIII:** 57
McPhillips, Robert, **Supp. XV:** 119, 250, 251, 252, 264, 266; **Supp. XXIII:** 111, 112, 114, 127
McQuade, Molly, **Supp. IX:** 151, 163; **Supp. VIII:** 277, 281; **Supp. XX:** 90
McQueen, Steve, **Supp. XI:** 306
Macrae, John, **I:** 252–253
McRobbie, Angela, **Supp. IV Part 2:** 691
MacShane, Frank, **Supp. IV Part 2:** 557; **Supp. XI:** 214, 216
"MacSwiggen" (Freneau), **Supp. II Part 1:** 259
McTaggart, John, **I:** 59
McTeague (Norris), **III:** 314, 315, 316–320, 322, 325, 327–328, 330, 331, 333, 335; **Retro. Supp. II:** 96; **Supp. IX:** 332
McWhorter, Dianne, **Supp. XXIII:** 38
McWilliams, Carey, **Supp. XI:** 169; **Supp. XXIV:** 282
Madama Butterfly (opera, Puccini), **III:** 139; **Supp. XXI:** 150, 155
"Madam and the Minister" (Hughes), **Supp. I Part 1:** 335
"Madam and the Wrong Visitor" (Hughes), **Supp. I Part 1:** 335
"Madame and Ahmad" (Bowles), **Supp. IV Part 1:** 93
"Madame Bai and the Taking of Stone Mountain" (Bambara), **Supp. XI:** 14–15
Madame Bovary (Flaubert), **II:** 185; **Retro. Supp. I:** 225; **Retro. Supp. II:** 70; **Supp. XI:** 334; **Supp. XX:** 58
"Madame Célestin's Divorce" (Chopin), **Supp. I Part 1:** 213
Madame Curie (film), **Retro. Supp. I:** 113
"Madame de Mauves" (James), **II:** 327; **Retro. Supp. I:** 218, 220
Madame de Treymes (Wharton), **IV:** 314, 323; **Retro. Supp. I:** 376
"Madame Rose Hanie" (Gibran), **Supp. XX:** 124
"Madame Swann at Home"(Hadas), **Supp. XXIII:** 113
"Madam's Calling Cards" (Hughes), **Retro. Supp. I:** 206

Madden, David, **Supp. IV Part 1:** 285

Maddern, Bessie. *See* London, Mrs. Jack (Bessie Maddern)

Mad Dog Black Lady (Coleman), **Supp. XI:** 85–89, 90

Mad Dog Blues (Shepard), **Supp. III Part 2:** 437, 438, 441

Maddox, Lucy, **Supp. IV Part 1:** 323, 325

Mad Ducks and Bears: Football Revisited (Plimpton), **Supp. XVI:** 243

Mademoiselle Coeur-Brisé (Sibon, trans.), **IV:** 288

Mademoiselle de Maupin (Gautier), **Supp. I Part 1:** 277

"Mad Farmer, Flying the Flag of Rough Branch, Secedes from the Union, The" (Berry), **Supp. X:** 35

"Mad Farmer Manifesto, The: The First Amendment" (Berry), **Supp. X:** 35

"Mad Farmer's Love Song, The" (Berry), **Supp. X:** 35

Madheart (Baraka), **Supp. II Part 1:** 47

Madhouse, The (Farrell), **II:** 41

Madhubuti, Haki R. (Don L. Lee), **Supp. II Part 1:** 34, 247; **Supp. IV Part 1:** 244; **Supp. XXVII:** 165

Madison, Charles, **Supp. XXIII:** 6, 13

Madison, Dolley, **II:** 303

Madison, James, **I:** 1, 2, 6–9; **II:** 301; **Supp. I Part 2:** 509, 524

"Madison Smartt Bell: *The Year of Silence*" (Garrett), **Supp. X:** 7

Mad Love (film, Freund), **Supp. XVII:** 58

"Madman, A" (Updike), **Retro. Supp. I:** 320

Madman, The: His Parables and Poems (Gibran), **Supp. XX:** 115, 118, 125

"Madman's Song" (Wylie), **Supp. I Part 2:** 711, 729

Madonick, Michael, **Supp. XVII:** 123

"Madonna" (R. Lowell), **II:** 535–536

"Madonna of the Evening Flowers" (A. Lowell), **II:** 524

"Madonna of the Future, The" (James), **Retro. Supp. I:** 219

"Mad Song" (Gioia), **Supp. XV:** 128

Madwoman in the Attic, The (Gilbert and Gubar), **Retro. Supp. I:** 42; **Supp. IX:** 66

"Maelzel's Chess-Player" (Poe), **III:** 419, 420

"Maestria" (Nemerov), **III:** 275, 278–279

Maeterlinck, Maurice, **I:** 91, 220; **Supp. XX:** 115, 116

"Magalu" (H. Johnson). *See* "Magula" (H. Johnson)

"Magazine-Writing Peter Snook" (Poe), **III:** 421

Magdeburg Centuries (Flacius), **IV:** 163

Magellan, Ferdinand, **Supp. I Part 2:** 497

Maggie: A Girl of the Streets (S. Crane), **I:** 407, 408, 410–411, 416; **IV:** 208; **Retro. Supp. II:** 97, 107; **Supp. XVII:** 228; **Supp. XXIII:** 165

Maggie Cassidy (Kerouac), **Supp. III Part 1:** 220–221, 225, 227, 229, 232

Maggie-Now (B. Smith), **Supp. XXIII:** 258, 267–269

"Maggie of the Green Bottles" (Bambara), **Supp. XI:** 2–3

"Maggie's Farm" (song, Dylan), **Supp. XVIII:** 25, 26

"Magi" (Plath), **Supp. I Part 2:** 544–545

"Magi, The" (Garrett), **Supp. VII:** 97

"Magic" (Pickering), **Supp. XXI:** 202

"Magic" (Porter), **III:** 434, 435

"Magical Thinking" (Hull), **Supp. XXI:** 137, 139

Magic Barrel, The (Malamud), **Supp. I Part 2:** 427, 428, 430–434

"Magic Barrel, The" (Malamud), **Supp. I Part 2:** 427, 428, 431, 432–433

Magic Christian, The (film), **Supp. XI:** 309

Magic Christian, The (Southern), **Supp. XI:** 297, 299–301, 309

Magic City (Komunyakaa), **Supp. XIII:** 125–127, 128, 131

"Magic Flute, The" (Epstein), **Supp. XII:** 165

Magic Flute, The (Mozart), **III:** 164

Magician King, The (Grossman), **Supp. XXV:** 74–77

Magician of Lublin, The (Singer), **IV:** 6, 9–10; **Retro. Supp. II:** 308–309

Magicians, The (Grossman), **Supp. XXV:** 64, 68–74

Magician's Assistant, The (Patchett), **Supp. XII:** 307, 310, 317–320, 322

Magician's Land, The (Grossman), **Supp. XXV:** 77

"Magician's Wife, The" (Gordon), **Supp. IV Part 1:** 306

Magic Journey, The (Nichols), **Supp. XIII:** 266–267

Magic Keys, The (Murray), **Supp. XIX:** 157–158

Magic Kingdom, The (Elkin), **Supp. VI:** 42, 54–55, 56, 58

"Magic Mirror, The: A Study of the Double in Two of Doestoevsky's Novels" (Plath), **Supp. I Part 2:** 536

Magic Mountain, The (Mann), **III:** 281–282; **Supp. IV Part 2:** 522; **Supp. XII:** 321; **Supp. XVII:** 137

Magic Tower, The (Willams), **IV:** 380

Magnaghi, Ambrogio, **Supp. XVI:** 286

Magnalia Christi Americana (Mather), **II:** 302; **Supp. I Part 1:** 102; **Supp. I Part 2:** 584; **Supp. II Part 2:** 441, 442, 452–455, 460, 467, 468; **Supp. IV Part 2:** 434

Magnes, Judah, **Supp. XXIII:** 6

Magnificat (Nelson), **Supp. XVIII:** 176–177

"Magnificent Little Gift" (Salinas), **Supp. XIII:** 318

"Magnifying Mirror" (Karr), **Supp. XI:** 240

Magpie, The (Baldwin, ed.), **Supp. I Part 1:** 49

"Magpie Exhorts"(Schott), **Supp. XXIII:** 250

Magpie's Shadow, The (Winters), **Supp. II Part 2:** 786, 788

"Magpie's Song" (Snyder), **Supp. VIII:** 302

Magritte, René, **Supp. IV Part 2:** 623

Maguire, Roberta S., **Supp. XIX:** 160–161

"Magula" (H. Johnson), **Supp. XXVI:** 164, 166, 170–172, 174

Magus, The (Fowles), **Supp. XIX:** 58

Mahan, Albert Thayer, **Supp. I Part 2:** 491

Mahan, David C., **Supp. XXI:** 86

"Mahatma Joe" (Bass), **Supp. XVI:** 19

Mahin, John Lee, **Supp. XXVII:** 93

Mahlis, Kristen, **Supp. XXIII:** 90, 94

"Mahogany Tree, The" (M. F. K. Fisher), **Supp. XVII:** 88

Mahomet and His Successors (Irving), **II:** 314

Mahoney, Jeremiah, **IV:** 285

Mahoney, Lynn, **Supp. XV:** 270

"Maiden, Maiden" (Boyle), **Supp. XXIV:** 58

"Maiden in a Tower" (Stegner), **Supp. IV Part 2:** 613

Maiden's Prayer, The (Silver), **Supp. XXIV:** 275–276

"Maiden Without Hands" (Sexton), **Supp. II Part 2:** 691

"Maid of St. Philippe, The" (Chopin), **Retro. Supp. II:** 63

"Maid's Shoes, The" (Malamud), **Supp. I Part 2:** 437

Mailer, Fanny, **III:** 28

Mailer, Isaac, **III:** 28

Mailer, Norman, **I:** 261, 292, 477; **III:** 26–49, 174; **IV:** 98, 216; **Retro. Supp. II:** 182, 195–217, 279; **Supp. I Part 1:** 291, 294; **Supp. III Part 1:** 302; **Supp. IV Part 1:** 90, 198, 207, 236, 284, 381; **Supp. IV Part 2:** 689; **Supp. VIII:** 236; **Supp. XI:** 104, 218, 222, 229; **Supp. XIV:** 49, 53, 54, 111, 162; **Supp. XVII:** 225, 228, 236; **Supp. XVIII:** 19–20; **Supp. XX:** 90; **Supp. XXIII:** 105, 106; **Supp. XXIV:** 281; **Supp. XXV:** 145

"Maimed Man, The" (Tate), **IV:** 136

Maimonides, Moses, **Supp. XVII:** 46–47

Main Currents in American Thought: The Colonial Mind, 1625–1800 (Parrington), **I:** 517; **Supp. I Part 2:** 484

"Maine Roustabout, A" (Eberhart), **I:** 539

"Maine Speech" (White), **Supp. I Part 2:** 669–670

Maine Woods, The (Thoreau), **IV:** 188

Mains d'Orlac, Les (M. Renard), **Supp. XVII:** 58

Main Street (Lewis), **I:** 362; **II:** 271, 440, 441–442, 447, 449, 453; **III:** 394; **Supp. XIX:** 142; **Supp. XXII:** 282

"Maintenance" (Pickering), **Supp. XXI:** 204

Maitland, Margaret Todd, **Supp. XVI:** 292

Majdoubeh, Ahmad, **Supp. XX:** 116

"Majesty" (July), **Supp. XXIV:** 201–202, 203

Major, Clarence, **Supp. XXII:** 171–186

"Majorat, Das" (Hoffman), **III:** 415

Major Barbara (Shaw), **III:** 69

"Major Chord, The" (Bourne), **I:** 221

Majors and Minors (Dunbar), **Supp. II Part 1:** 197, 198

"Major's Tale, The" (Bierce), **I:** 205

Make Believe (J. Scott), **Supp. XVII:** **191–192,** 193, 194, 195

Make-Believe Town: Essays and Remembrances (Mamet), **Supp. XIV:** 240, 251

Make It New (Pound), **III:** 470

Makers and Finders (Brooks), **I:** 253, 254, 255, 257, 258

Makers of the Modern World (Untermeyer), **Supp. XV:** 312

"Making a Change" (Gilman), **Supp. XI:** 207

"Making a Living" (Sexton), **Supp. II Part 2:** 695

"Making Changes" (L. Michaels), **Supp. XVI:** 204

"Making Do" (Hogan), **Supp. IV Part 1:** 406

Making Face, Making Soul: Haciendo Caras, Creative and Critical Perspectives by Feminists of Color (Anzaldúa, ed.), **Supp. IV Part 1:** 330

Making It (Podhoretz), **Supp. VIII:** 231, 232, 233, **237–238,** 239, 244

"Making Light of Auntie" (X. J. Kennedy), **Supp. XV:** 163

"Making Love in 2003" (July), **Supp. XXIV:** 204–205, 210

"Making Marks" (Davison), **Supp. XXVI:** 72

"Making Much of Orioles" (Davison), **Supp. XXVI:** 74, 75

"Making of a Marginal Farm, The" (Berry), **Supp. X:** 22

Making of Americans, The (Stein), **IV:** 35, 37, 40–42, 45, 46; **Supp. III Part 1:** 37

"Making of Ashenden, The" (Elkin), **Supp. VI:** 49, 50

"Making of a Soldier USA, The" (Simpson), **Supp. IX:** 270

"Making of Garrison Keillor, The" (McConagha), **Supp. XVI:** 166"

Making of Modern Atlanta, The (documentary), **Supp. XXII:** 251

"Making of Paths, The" (Stegner), **Supp. IV Part 2:** 614

"Making of Poems, The" (W. J. Smith), **Supp. XIII:** 348

Making of the Modern Mind (Randall), **III:** 605

Making the Light Come: The Poetry of Gerald Stern (Somerville), **Supp. IX:** 296–297

"Making Up Stories" (Didion), **Supp. IV Part 1:** 196, 203, 205

Making Your Own Days: The Pleasures of Reading and Writing Poetry (Koch), **Supp. XV:** 188; **Supp. XXIII:** 124

Maladies de la volonté, Les (Ribot), **Supp. XX:** 238

Malady of the Ideal, The: Oberman, Maurice de Guérin, and Amiel (Brooks), **I:** 240, 241, 242

Malamud, Bernard, **I:** 144, 375; **II:** 424, 425; **III:** 40, 272; **IV:** 216; **Retro. Supp. II:** 22, 279, 281; **Supp. I Part**

2: **427–453; Supp. IV Part 1:** 297, 382; **Supp. IX:** 114, 227; **Supp. V:** 257, 266; **Supp. XIII:** 106, 264, 265, 294; **Supp. XVI:** 220; **Supp. XXVI:** 180

Malamud, Mrs. Bernard (Ann de Chiara), **Supp. I Part 2:** 451

Malandrinos, Cheryl C., **Supp. XXVI:** 219

Malanga, Gerard, **Supp. III Part 2:** 629; **Supp. XXIII:** 221

Malaquais, Jean, **Retro. Supp. II:** 199

Malatesta, Sigismondo de, **III:** 472, 473

Malcolm (Purdy), **Supp. VII:** 270–273, 277

"Malcolm Cowley and the American Writer" (Simpson), **Supp. II Part 1:** 147

Malcolm Lowry's "Volcano": Myth Symbol Meaning (Markson), **Supp. XVII:** 142, 144

"MALCOLM REMEMBERED (FEB. 77)" (Baraka), **Supp. II Part 1:** 60

Malcolm X, **Retro. Supp. II:** 12, 13; **Supp. I Part 1:** 52, 63, 65, 66; **Supp. IV Part 1:** 2, 10; **Supp. VIII:** 330, 345; **Supp. X:** 240; **Supp. XIV:** 306

Malcolm X (film), **Retro. Supp. II:** 12

Malcolm X: A Fire Burning Bright (Myers), **Supp. XXVII:** 209

Malcolm X: By Any Means Necessary (Myers), **Supp. XXVII:** 209

"Maldrove" (Jeffers), **Supp. II Part 2:** 418

Male, Roy, **II:** 239

Male Animal, The (Thurber), **Supp. I Part 2:** 605, 606, 610–611

"Malediction upon Myself" (Wylie), **Supp. I Part 2:** 722

Malefactors, The (Gordon), **II:** 186, 199, 213–216; **IV:** 139

"Malest Cornifici Tuo Catullo" (Ginsberg), **Supp. II Part 1:** 315

Malick, Terrence, **Supp. XI:** 234; **Supp. XV:** 351

Malin, Irving, **I:** 147; **Supp. XVI:** 71–72

"Malinche's Tips: Pique from Mexico's Mother" (Mora), **Supp. XIII:** 223

"Malinke's Atonement" (Antin), **Supp. XX:** 10

"Mallard" (C. Frost), **Supp. XV:** 98, 99

Mallarmé, Stéphane, **I:** 66, 569; **II:** 529, 543; **III:** 8, 409, 428; **IV:** 80, 86; **Retro. Supp. I:** 56; **Supp. I Part 1:** 261; **Supp. II Part 1:** 1; **Supp. III Part 1:** 319–320; **Supp. III Part 2:** 630; **Supp. XIII:** 114; **Supp. XV:** 158; **Supp. XVI:** 282, 285

Malle, Louis, **Supp. XXIII:** 122

Mallia, Joseph, **Supp. XII:** 26, 29, 37

Mallon, Anne-Marie, **Supp. XXI:** 215

Mallon, Thomas, **Supp. IV Part 1:** 200, 209; **Supp. XIX:** **131–145**

Maloff, Saul, **Supp. VIII:** 238

Malory, Thomas, **II:** 302; **III:** 486; **IV:** 50, 61; **Supp. IV Part 1:** 47

"Mal Paso Bridge" (Jeffers), **Supp. II Part 2:** 415, 420

Malraux, André, **I:** 33–34, 127, 509; **II:** 57, 376; **III:** 35, 310; **IV:** 236, 247,

434; **Retro. Supp. I:** 73; **Retro. Supp. II:** 115–116, 119; **Supp. II Part 1:** 221, 232; **Supp. XIX:** 157

Maltese Falcon, The (film), **Supp. IV Part 1:** 342, 353, 355

Maltese Falcon, The (Hammett), **IV:** 286; **Supp. IV Part 1:** 345, 348–351

Mama (McMillan), **Supp. XIII:** 182, **187–188**

"Mama and Daughter" (Hughes), **Supp. I Part 1:** 334

Mama Day (Naylor), **Supp. VIII:** **223–226,** 230

"Mama I Remember" (Nelson), **Supp. XVIII:** 173

Mama Poc: An Ecologist's Account of the Extinction of a Species (LaBastille), **Supp. X:** 99, **104–105,** 106

Mama Poems, The (Kenny), **Supp. XXIII:** 143, **154**

Mama's Bank Account (K. Forbes), **Supp. XVII:** 9

Mama's Promises (Nelson), **Supp. XVIII:** **173–174**

"Mama Still Loves You" (Naylor), **Supp. VIII:** 214

Mambo Hips and Make Believe (Coleman), **Supp. XI:** **94–96**

Mambo Kings, The (film), **Supp. VIII:** 73, 74

Mambo Kings Play Songs of Love, The (Hijuelos), **Supp. VIII:** 73–74, **79–82**

"Ma'me Pélagie" (Chopin), **Retro. Supp. II:** 64

Mamet, David, **Supp. XIV:** **239–258,** 315

"Mamie" (Sandburg), **III:** 582

Mammedaty, Novarro Scott. *See* Momaday, N. Scott

"Mammon and the Archer" (O. Henry), **Supp. II Part 1:** 394, 408

Mammonart (Sinclair), **Supp. V:** 276–277

"Mammy" (D. West), **Supp. XVIII:** 283

"Mamouche" (Chopin), **Retro. Supp. II:** 66

Mamoulian, Rouben, **Supp. XVIII:** 281

"Man" (Corso), **Supp. XII:** 130

"Man" (Herbert), **II:** 12

"Man Against the Sky, The" (Robinson), **III:** 509, 523

"Man and a Woman Sit Near Each Other, A" (R. Bly), **Supp. IV Part 1:** 71

Man and Boy (Morris), **III:** 223, 224, 225

"Man and the Snake, The" (Bierce), **I:** 203

"Man and Woman" (Caldwell), **I:** 310

Manassas (Sinclair), **Supp. V:** 280, 281, 285

"Man Bring This Up Road" (T. Williams), **IV:** 383–384

"Man Carrying Thing" (Stevens), **IV:** 90

Manchester, William, **III:** 103

"Man Child, The" (Baldwin), **Supp. I Part 1:** 63

Man Could Stand Up, A (Ford), **I:** 423

"Mandarin's Jade" (Chandler), **Supp. IV Part 1:** 125

Mandel, Charlotte, **Supp. XVI:** 57

Mandelbaum, Maurice, **I:** 61

Mandelbaum, Michael, **Supp. XXV:** 264

Mandelstam, Osip, **Retro. Supp. I:** 278; **Supp. III Part 1:** 268; **Supp. VIII:** 21, 22, 23, 27; **Supp. XIII:** 77; **Supp. XV:** 254, 261, 263

"Mandelstam: The Poem as Event" (Dobyns), **Supp. XIII:** 78

"Mandolin" (Dove), **Supp. IV Part 1:** 247

"Mandoline" (Verlaine), **IV:** 79

"Mandrin Question, The" (Vaz), **Supp. XXVI:** 267

"Man Eating" (Kenyon), **Supp. VII:** 173

"Manet in Late Summer" (Skloot), **Supp. XX: 201**

"Man Feeding Pigeons" (Clampitt), **Supp. IX: 49–50,** 52

Manfred, Frederick, **Supp. X:** 126

Man from Kinvara, The (Gallagher), **Supp. XXIV:** 166, 172, 173

Man From Limbo, The (Endore), **Supp. XVII:** 55

Man fun natseres, Der (Asch), **Supp. XXIII:** 6

Mangione, Jerre, **Supp. XXV:** 28

"Mango Says Goodbye Sometimes" (Cisneros), **Supp. VII:** 64

Manhattan (film; Allen), **Supp. IV Part 1:** 205; **Supp. XV:** 5, **7–8,** 13

"Manhattan Dawn" (Justice), **Supp. VII:** 117

"Manhattan: Luminism" (Doty), **Supp. XI:** 135

Manhattan Murder Mystery (film; Allen), **Supp. XV:** 5, 11

Manhattan Transfer (Dos Passos), **I:** 26, 475, 478, 479, 480, 481, 482–484, 487; **II:** 286; **Supp. I Part 1:** 57; **Supp. XXVI:** 18

"Mania" (R. Lowell), **II:** 554

"Manic in the Moon, The" (Thurber), **Supp. I Part 2:** 620

Manifest; and Furthermore (Bronk), **Supp. XXI:** 32

"Manifesto: A Press Release from PRKA" (Saunders), **Supp. XIX:** 235

Manikin, The (J. Scott), **Supp. XVII: 189–191,** 192**,** 194

"Man in Black" (Plath), **Supp. I Part 2:** 538

Man in Lower Ten, The (Rinehart), **Supp. XXV:** 192, 200

Man in Prehistory (Chard), **Supp. XII:** 177–178

Man in the Black Coat Turns, The (R. Bly), **Supp. IV Part 1:** 66–68, 71, 73

"Man in the Brooks Brothers Shirt, The" (McCarthy), **II:** 563–564

"Man in the Drawer, The" (Malamud), **Supp. I Part 2:** 437

Man in the Flying Lawn Chair and Other Excursions and Observations, The (Plimpton), **Supp. XVI:** 234

Man in the Gray Flannel Suit, The (Wilson), **Supp. IV Part 1:** 387

Man in the High Castle, The (Dick), **Supp. XVIII:** 138

Man in the Middle, The (Wagoner), **Supp. IX:** 324, **332–333**

"Man in the Rain, The" (Ryan as Quin), **Supp. XVIII:** 226

"Man in the Toolhouse, The" (Swados), **Supp. XIX:** 263

Mankiewicz, Frank, **Supp. XXIV:** 279

Mankiewicz, Herman J., **Supp. XVI:** 189; **Supp. XXVII:** 91

Mankiewicz, Joseph, **Retro. Supp. I:** 113

Mankowitz, Wolf, **Supp. XI:** 307

"Man Made of Words, The" (Momaday), **Supp. IV Part 2:** 481, 484–485, 486, 487, 488

Man-Made World, The (Gilman), **Supp. XI:** 207

"Man-Moth, The" (Bishop), **Retro. Supp. II:** 42; **Supp. I Part 1:** 85–87, 88

Mann, Barbara Alice, **Supp. XXVI:** 81, 85, 86, 88, 90, 92, 95

Mann, Charles, **Retro. Supp. II:** 40

Mann, Erika, **Supp. II Part 1:** 11

Mann, Seymour (Samuel Weisman), **Supp. V:** 113

Mann, Thomas, **I:** 271, 490; **II:** 42, 539; **III:** 231, 281–282, 283; **IV:** 70, 73, 85; **Supp. IV Part 1:** 392; **Supp. IV Part 2:** 522; **Supp. IX:** 21; **Supp. V:** 51; **Supp. XI:** 275; **Supp. XII:** 173, 310, 321; **Supp. XIV:** 87; **Supp. XIX:** 147, 151, 157; **Supp. XVII:** 137; **Supp. XX: 85; Supp. XXIII:** 4

Mannequins' Demise: A Play in Eight Scenes (Budbill), **Supp. XIX:** 12

Mannerhouse (Wolfe), **IV:** 460

Manner Music, The (Reznikoff), **Supp. XIV: 293–295**

"Manners" (Bishop), **Supp. I Part 1:** 73

"Manners" (Emerson), **II:** 4, 6

"Manners, Morals, and the Novel" (Trilling), **Supp. III Part 2:** 502, 503

Mannheim, Karl, **I:** 279; **Supp. I Part 2:** 644

Manning, Ambrose, **Supp. XX: 166**

Manning, Frederic, **III:** 459

Manning, Robert, **Supp. IX:** 236

Mannix, Daniel P., **Supp. II Part 1:** 140

Man Nobody Knows, The (B. Barton), **Retro. Supp. I:** 179

Mano, D. Keith, **Supp. XVI:** 250

Mano, Guy Levis, **Supp. XVI:** 282

"Man of Indeterminate Age on a Subway Grate, A" (DI Piero), **Supp. XIX:** 47

"Man of Letters" (Pickering), **Supp. XXI:** 192, 195–196

"Man of Letters as a Man of Business, The" (Howells), **Supp. XIV:** 45–46

"Man of No Account, The" (Harte), **Supp. II Part 1:** 339

"Man of Property to His Muse, The" (W. Stone), **Supp. XXVII:** 255

"Man of the Crowd, The" (Poe), **III:** 412, 417; **Retro. Supp. I:** 154

Man on Spikes (Asinof), **II:** 424

Man on Stage (Dixon), **Supp. XII:** 141, **154–155**

"Man on the Dump, The" (Stevens), **IV:** 74; **Retro. Supp. I:** 306

"Man on the Stairs, The" (July), **Supp. XXIV:** 202

"Man on the Train, The" (Percy), **Supp. III Part 1:** 387

Manor, The (Singer), **IV:** 6, 17–19

Manrique, Jorge, **Retro. Supp. II:** 154

Mansart Builds a School (Du Bois), **Supp. II Part 1:** 185–186

Man's Fate (Malraux), **I:** 127; **Retro. Supp. II:** 121

"Man's Fate A Film Treatment of the Malraux Novel" (Agee), **I:** 33–34

Mansfield, June, **Supp. X:** 183, 194

Mansfield, Katherine, **III:** 362, 453

Mansfield, Stephanie, **Supp. IV Part 1:** 227

Man's Hope (Malraux), **IV:** 247

Mansion, The (Faulkner), **II:** 73; **Retro. Supp. I:** 74, 82

Man's Nature and His Communities (Niebuhr), **III:** 308

Manson, Charles, **Supp. IV Part 1:** 205

"Man Splitting Wood in the Daybreak, The" (Kinnell), **Supp. III Part 1:** 254

"Man's Pride" (Jeffers), **Supp. II Part 2:** 417

"Man's Story, The" (Anderson), **I:** 114

Man's Woman, A (Norris), **III:** 314, 322, 328, 329, 330, 332, 333

Man That Corrupted Hadleyburg, The (Twain), **I:** 204; **IV:** 208

"Man That Was Used Up, The" (Poe), **III:** 412, 425

"Mantis" (Zukofsky), **Supp. III Part 2:** 617

"'Mantis': An Interpretation" (Zukofsky), **Supp. III Part 2:** 617–618

"Man to Know in the Restaurants, The" (Siddons), **Supp. XXII:** 244

Man to Send Rain Clouds, The (Rosen, ed.), **Supp. IV Part 2:** 499, 505, 513

"Man to Send Rain Clouds, The" (Silko), **Supp. IV Part 2:** 559

Mantrap (Lewis), **II:** 447

Manuductio Ad Ministerium (Mather), **Supp. II Part 2:** 465–467

"Manuelzinho" (Bishop), **Retro. Supp. II:** 47–48

Manuscript Books of Emily Dickinson, The (Franklin, ed.), **Retro. Supp. I:** 29, 41

"Man Waiting for It to Stop, A" (Dunn), **Supp. XI:** 144

"Man Who Became a Woman, The" (Anderson), **I:** 114

"Man Who Carries the Desert Around Inside Himself, The: For Wally" (Komunyakaa), **Supp. XIII:** 125

"Man Who Closed Shop, The" (Dunn), **Supp. XI:** 149

Man Who Gave Up His Name, The (Harrison), **Supp. VIII:** 45, 52

Man Who Had All the Luck, The (A. Miller), **III:** 148, 149, 164, 166

"Man Who Knew Belle Star, The" (Bausch), **Supp. VII:** 46

"Man Who Knew Coolidge, The" (Lewis), **II:** 449

Man Who Knew Coolidge, The: Being the Soul of Lowell Schmaltz, Constructive and Nordic Citizen (Lewis), **II:** 450

Man Who Lived Underground, The (Wright), **Supp. II Part 1:** 40

"Man Who Lived Underground, The" (Wright), **IV:** 479, 485–487, 492; **Retro. Supp. II:** 121

"Man Who Made Me Love Him, The" (Weigl), **Supp. XIX:** 278

"Man Who Makes Brooms, The" (Nye), **Supp. XIII:** 276

"Man Who Studied Yoga, The" (Mailer), **III:** 35–36; **Retro. Supp. II:** 200

"Man Who Wanted to Win, The" (McCoy), **Supp. XIII:** 161

"Man Who Was Made of Netting, The" (Vaz), **Supp. XXVI:** 266

Man Who Was There, The (Morris), **III:** 220–221

"Man Who Writes Ants, The" (Merwin), **Supp. III Part 1:** 348

"Man with a Family" (Humphrey), **Supp. IX:** 94

Man without a Country, The (Hale), **I:** 488

"Man with the Blue Guitar, The" (Stevens), **I:** 266; **IV:** 85–87; **Retro. Supp. I:** 303–305, 306, 307, 309

Man with the Blue Guitar and Other Poems, The (Stevens), **IV:** 76; **Retro. Supp. I:** 303, 422

Man with the Golden Arm, The (Algren), **Supp. IX:** 1, 3, 9–11, 14, 15; **Supp. V:** 4

Man with the Golden Arm, The (film), **Supp. IX:** 3

"Man with the Golden Beef, The" (Podhoretz), **Supp. IX:** 3

"Man with the Hoe, The" (Markham), **Supp. XV:** 115

Man with the Mask, The (Lippard), **Supp. XXIII:** 178, 183–184, 188

Many a Monster (Ryan as Finnegan), **Supp. XVIII:** 233, **236–238**

Manyan Letters (Olson), **Supp. II Part 2:** 571

Many Circles (Goldbarth), **Supp. XII:** 193

"Many Handles" (Sandburg), **III:** 594

"Many Happy Returns" (Auden), **Supp. II Part 1:** 15

Many Happy Returns (Berrigan), **Supp. XXII:** 224; **Supp. XXIV:** 37, 41

Many Loves (W. C. Williams), **Retro. Supp. I:** 424

"Many Mansions" (H. Roth), **Supp. IX:** 233, 234

Many Marriages (Anderson), **I:** 104, 111, 113

"Many of Our Waters: Variations on a Poem by a Black Child" (Wright), **Supp. III Part 2:** 602

"Many Swans" (A. Lowell), **II:** 526

"Many Thousands Gone" (Baldwin), **Retro. Supp. II:** 4; **Supp. I Part 1:** 51

"Many Wagons Ago" (Ashbery), **Supp. III Part 1:** 22

Many-Windowed House, A (Cowley), **Supp. II Part 1:** 141, 143

"Many-Windowed House, A" (Cowley), **Supp. II Part 1:** 137

Mao II (DeLillo), **Supp. VI:** 2, 4, **5,** 6, **7,** 8, 9, 14, 16

"Map, The" (Bishop), **Retro. Supp. II:** 41; **Supp. I Part 1:** 72, 82, 85–88, 93

"Map, The" (Strand), **Supp. IV Part 2:** 623–624

"Maple Leaf, The" (Joplin), **Supp. IV Part 1:** 223

"Maple Tree, The" (D. West), **Supp. XVIII:** 284

Map of Another Town: A Memoir of Provence (M. F. K. Fisher), **Supp. XVII:** 88, 89, 92

"Map of Montana in Italy, A" (Hugo), **Supp. VI:** 139

Mapp and Lucia (Benson), **Supp. XX: 229**

Mapping American Culture (Franklin and Steiner), **Supp. XXII:** 205

"Maps" (Hass), **Supp. VI:** 103–104

Mapson, Jo-Ann, **Supp. IV Part 2:** 440, 454

Map to the Next World, A: Poems and Tales (Harjo), **Supp. XII: 228–230**

"Maquillage" (Hull), **Supp. XXI:** 133

"Mara" (Jeffers), **Supp. II Part 2:** 434

Ma Rainey's Black Bottom (Wilson), **Supp. VIII:** 331, **332–334,** 346, 349, 350

Maranen (Asch), **Supp. XXIII:** 10

Marat, Jean Paul, **IV:** 117; **Supp. I Part 2:** 514, 515, 521

"Marathon" (Glück), **Supp. V:** 85

Marble Faun, The (Faulkner), **II:** 55, 56; **Retro. Supp. I:** 79

Marble Faun, The; or, The Romance of Monte Beni (Hawthorne), **II:** 225, 239, 242–243, 290, 324; **IV:** 167; **Retro. Supp. I:** 63, 149, 163, **164–165; Supp. I Part 1:** 38; **Supp. I Part 2:** 421, 596; **Supp. XIII:** 102

Marbles (Brodsky), **Supp. VIII:** 26–27

Marburg, Anita, **Supp. XXII:** 281

Marcaccio, Michael, **Supp. XVII:** 97, 106

Marcel, Kelly, **Supp. XXVII:** 79

"March" (W. C. Williams), **Retro. Supp. I:** 418

March, Alan, **Supp. XVI:** 242

March, Fredric, **III:** 154, 403; **IV:** 357; **Supp. X:** 220

"March, March on Down the Field" (Shaw), **Supp. XIX:** 246

Marchalonis, Shirley, **Supp. XIII:** 138, 140, 141, 143, 147–148

Marchand, Philip, **Supp. XXVII:** 196

"Marché aux Oiseaux" (Wilbur), **Supp. III Part 2:** 550

"Märchen, The" (Jarrell), **II:** 378–379

March Hares (Frederic), **II:** 143–144

Marching Men (Anderson), **I:** 99, 101, 103–105, 111

"Marching Music" (Simic), **Supp. VIII:** 281

"Marcia" (R. H. Davis), **Supp. XVI:** 91–92

Marcks, Greg, **Supp. XVIII:** 150

Marckwardt, Albert H., **Supp. XXIV:** 255

Marco Millions (O'Neill), **III:** 391, 395

Marcosson, Isaac, **III:** 322

Marcus, Greil, **Supp. XVIII:** 30, 53; **Supp. XXVI:** 142

Marcus, Steven, **Retro. Supp. II:** 196, 200

Marcus Aurelius, **II:** 1; **III:** 566; **Supp. XVIII:** 304

Marcuse, Herbert, **Supp. I Part 2:** 645; **Supp. VIII:** 196; **Supp. XII:** 2

Mardi and a Voyage Thither (Melville), **I:** 384; **II:** 281; **III:** 77–79, 84, 87, 89; **Retro. Supp. I:** 247, 254, 256

Margaret (Judd), **II:** 290

Margaret & Dusty (Notley), **Supp. XXII:** 231

"Margaret Fuller, 1847" (Clampitt), **Supp. IX:** 43

"Marginalia" (Wilbur), **Supp. III Part 2:** 544

Margin of Hope, A: An Intellectual Autobiography (Howe), **Supp. VI:** 113–114, 117, 125, 128

"Margins of Maycomb, The: A Rereading of *To Kill a Mockingbird*" (Phelps), **Supp. VIII:** 128

Margoshes, Samuel, **Supp. X:** 70

"Margrave" (Jeffers), **Supp. II Part 2:** 426

Margret Howth (R. H. Davis), **Supp. XVI:** 81, 83, 84, **88–89**

Margret Howth: A Story of Today (J. Yellin, ed.), **Supp. XVI:** 88

Margulies, Donald, **Supp. XXI:** 145

"Maria Concepción" (Porter), **III:** 434–435, 451

Mariana (Vaz), **Supp. XXVI:** 258–259, 263

Mariani, Paul L., **Retro. Supp. I:** 412, 419; **Retro. Supp. II:** 189

Marianne Moore Reader, (Moore), **III:** 199

Marie Antoinette (film), **Retro. Supp. I:** 113

Marie Blythe (Mosher), **Supp. XXII:** 206, 209, **212**

Marie Laveau (Prose), **Supp. XVI:** 251

Mariella Gable, Sister, **III:** 339, 355

"Marijuana and a Pistol" (C. Himes), **Supp. XVI:** 137

"Marijuana Notation" (Ginsberg), **Supp. II Part 1:** 313

Maril, Herman, **Supp. XXI:** 22, 23

Marilyn: A Biography (Mailer), **Retro. Supp. II:** 208

"Marin" (Cisneros), **Supp. VII:** 60, 61

Marin, Jay, **Retro. Supp. II:** 325

"Marina" (Eliot), **I:** 584, 585; **Retro. Supp. I:** 64

Mariners, Renegades, and Castaways (C. L. R. James), **Supp. XXI:** 159, 169–170

"Marine Surface, Low Overcast" (Clampitt), **Supp. IX:** 47–48

Marinetti, F. T., **Supp. XXII:** 159, 160, 161, 163

Marinetti, Tommaso, **Retro. Supp. I:** 59

Marionettes, The (Faulkner), **Retro. Supp. I:** 79

"Mari Sandoz's *Slogum House:* Greed as a Woman" (Riley), **Supp. XXIV:** 252

Maritain, Jacques, **I:** 402; **Supp. XXVI:** 231, 232

Maritime Compact (Paine), **Supp. I Part 2:** 519

Maritime History of Massachusetts, 1783–1860, The (Morison), **Supp. I Part 2:** 481–483

Marjolin, Jean-Nicolas, **Supp. I Part 1:** 302

Marjorie Kinnan Rawlings: Sojourner at Cross Creek (Silverthorne), **Supp. X:** 220, 234

Marjorie Morningstar (film), **Supp. XXV:** 262

Marjorie Morningstar (Wouk), **Supp. XXV:** 253, 254, 256, 258, 261–262, 268

"Mark, The" (Bogan), **Supp. III Part 1:** 52

Marker, Chris, **Supp. IV Part 2:** 434, 436

"Market" (Hayden), **Supp. II Part 1:** 368, 369

Marketplace, The (Frederic), **II:** 145–146

Markham, Edwin, **I:** 199, 207; **Supp. XV:** 115

Markings (Hammarskjold), **Supp. II Part 1:** 26

Mark of the Vampire (film, Browning), **Supp. XVII:** 58

Markopoulos, Gregory, **Supp. XII:** 2

Markowick-Olczakova, Hanna, **Supp. X:** 70

Marks, Alison, **Supp. I Part 2:** 660

Marks, Barry A., **I:** 435, 438, 442, 446

Markson, David, **Supp. XVII: 135–147**

Mark Twain in Eruption (Twain), **IV:** 209

Mark Twain's America (De Voto), **I:** 248

Mark Twain's Autobiography (Twain), **IV:** 209

Marley, Bob, **Supp. IX:** 152

Marlowe, Christopher, **I:** 68, 368, 384; **II:** 590; **III:** 259, 491; **Retro. Supp. I:** 127; **Retro. Supp. II:** 76; **Supp. I Part 2:** 422; **Supp. XXI:** 227

Marlowe, Kimberly B., **Supp. XXII:** 214

"Marlowe Takes on the Syndicate" (Chandler), **Supp. IV Part 1:** 135

Marne, The (Wharton), **IV:** 319, 320; **Retro. Supp. I:** 378

Marquand, John, **Supp. XI:** 301

Marquand, Mrs. John P. (Adelaide Hooker), **III:** 57, 61

Marquand, Mrs. John P. (Christina Sedgwick), **III:** 54, 57

Marquand, J. P., **I:** 362, 375; **II:** 459, 482–483; **III: 50–73,** 383; **Supp. I Part 1:** 196; **Supp. IV Part 1:** 31; **Supp. V:** 95

Marquand, Philip, **III:** 52

Marquis, Don, **Supp. I Part 2:** 668

Marra, Anthony, **Supp. XXVI:** 216

Marrásh, Francis al-, **Supp. XX:** 117

"Marriage" (Corso), **Supp. XII:** 117, 124, **127–128**

Marriage (Moore), **III:** 194

"Marriage" (Moore), **III:** 198–199, 213

"Marriage, A" (Untermeyer), **Supp. XV:** 305

Marriage A-la-Mode (Dryden), **Supp. IX:** 68

Marriage and Other Science Fiction (Goldbarth), **Supp. XII:** 189, 190

"Marriage in the Sixties, A" (Rich), **Supp. I Part 2:** 554

Marriage of Bette and Boo, The (Durang), **Supp. XXIV:** 114, 121, **122–123**

Marriage of Heaven and Hell (Blake), **Supp. XXII:** 257

"Marriage of Heaven and Hell, The" (Blake), **III:** 544–545; **Supp. VIII:** 99

"Marriage of Phaedra, The" (Cather), **Retro. Supp. I:** 5

Marriage Plot, The (Eugenides), **Supp. XXIV:** 135, **143–145**

"Marriage Rhapsody"(Hadas), **Supp. XXIII:** 114

Married (Strindberg), **Supp. XXII:** 23

"Married" (Taggard), **Supp. XXII:** 274

Married Men (Wolfert), **Supp. XXI:** 277

Married People (Rinehart), **Supp. XXV:** 201

Marrow of Tradition, The (Chesnutt), **Supp. XIV:** 63, **71–75,** 76

Marryat, Captain Frederick, **III:** 423

"Marrying Absurd" (Didion), **Supp. IV Part 1:** 200

"Marrying Iseult?" (Updike), **Retro. Supp. I:** 329

Marrying Man (Simon), **Supp. IV Part 2:** 588

"Marrying the Hangman" (Atwood), **Supp. XIII:** 34

Marry Me: A Romance (Updike), **Retro. Supp. I:** 329, 330, 332

"Mars and Hymen" (Freneau), **Supp. II Part 1:** 258

Marsden, Dora, **III:** 471; **Retro. Supp. I:** 416

Marsena (Frederic), **II:** 135, 136–137

Marsh, Edward, **Supp. I Part 1:** 257, 263

Marsh, Frederick T., **Supp. XX: 39, 46**

Marsh, Fred T., **Supp. IX:** 232

Marsh, John R., **Supp. XIX:** 187

Marsh, Mae, **Supp. I Part 2:** 391

Marshall, George, **III:** 3

Marshall, John, **Supp. I Part 2:** 455; **Supp. XIX:** 62; **Supp. XVI:** 117; **Supp. XXIII:** 275, 276

Marshall, Paule, **Supp. IV Part 1:** 8, 14, 369; **Supp. XI:** 18, **275–292;** **Supp. XIII:** 295; **Supp. XX: 154**

Marshall, Tod, **Supp. XV:** 224; **Supp. XVII:** 25, 26, 29, 32

"Marshall Carpenter" (Masters), **Supp. I Part 2:** 463

"Marshes of Glynn, The" (Lanier), **Supp. I Part 1:** 364, 365–368, 370, 373

"'Marshes of Glynn, The': A Study in Symbolic Obscurity" (Ross), **Supp. I Part 1:** 373

Marsh Island, A (Jewett), **II:** 405; **Retro. Supp. II:** 134

"Marshland Elegy" (Leopold), **Supp. XIV:** 187, 189

"Mars Is Heaven!" (Bradbury), **Supp. IV Part 1:** 103, 106

Mars-Jones, Adam, **Supp. XXI:** 116

Marsman, Henrik, **Supp. IV Part 1:** 183

Marston, Ed, **Supp. IV Part 2:** 492

Marston, Elsa, **Supp. XXIII:** 241

Marta y Maria (Valdes), **II:** 290

"Martha's Lady" (Jewett), **Retro. Supp. II:** 140, 143

Marthe, Saint, **II:** 213

Martial, **II:** 1, 169; **Supp. IX:** 152

Martian Chronicles, The (Bradbury), **Supp. IV Part 1:** 102, 103, 106–107

Martian Time-Slip (Dick), **Supp. XVIII:** 142

Martin, Benjamin, **Supp. I Part 2:** 503

Martin, Charles, **Supp. XVII:** 112

Martin, Dick, **Supp. XII:** 44

Martin, Jay, **I:** 55, 58, 60, 61, 67; **III:** 307; **Retro. Supp. II:** 326, 327, 329; **Supp. XI:** 162

Martin, John, **Supp. XI:** 172

Martin, Judith, **Supp. V:** 128

Martin, Nell, **Supp. IV Part 1:** 351, 353

Martin, Reginald, **Supp. X:** 247, 249

Martin, Robert, **Supp. XX: 165**

Martin, Stephen-Paul, **Supp. IV Part 2:** 430

Martin, Tom, **Supp. X:** 79

Martin du Gard, Roger, **Supp. I Part 1:** 51

Martineau, Harriet, **Supp. II Part 1:** 282, 288, 294; **Supp. XVIII:** 7; **Supp. XXIV:** 78

Martin Eden (London), **II:** 466, 477–481

Martinelli, Sheri, **Supp. IV Part 1:** 280

Martínez, Guillermo, **Supp. XIII:** 313

Martinez-Avila, Raul, **Supp. XXIII:** 125

Martini, Adrienne, **Supp. XVIII:** 35

Martín-Lucas, Belén, **Supp. XXVI:** 218

Mart'nez, Rafael, **Retro. Supp. I:** 423

Martone, John, **Supp. V:** 179

Marty (Chayefsky), **Supp. XV:** 205

"Martyr, The" (Porter), **III:** 454

Martz, Louis L., **IV:** 151, 156, 165; **Supp. I Part 1:** 107; **Supp. XIV:** 12; **Supp. XXI:** 85

Marvell, Andrew, **IV:** 135, 151, 156, 161, 253; **Retro. Supp. I:** 62, 127; **Retro. Supp. II:** 186, 189; **Supp. I Part 1:** 80; **Supp. XII:** 159; **Supp. XIV:** 10; **Supp. XVI:** 204; **Supp. XXI:** 227; **Supp. XXIII:** 62

"Marvella, for Borrowing" (Ríos), **Supp. IV Part 2:** 551

"Marvelous Sauce, The", **Supp. XVII:** 189

Marvels and Masterpieces (al-Badá'i' wa'l-Tará'if) (Gibran), **Supp. XX: 116, 124**

Marx, Eleanor, **Supp. XVI:** 85

Marx, Karl, **I:** 60, 267, 279, 283, 588; **II:** 376, 462, 463, 483, 577; **IV:** 429, 436, 443–444, 469; **Retro. Supp. I:** 254; **Supp. I Part 2:** 518, 628, 632, 633, 634, 635, 639, 643, 645, 646; **Supp. III Part 2:** 619; **Supp. IV Part 1:** 355; **Supp. IX:** 133; **Supp. VIII:** 196; **Supp. X:** 119, 134; **Supp. XIII:** 75; **Supp. XXI:** 162, 263

Marx, Leo, **Supp. I Part 1:** 233

"Marxism and Monastic Perpectives" (Merton), **Supp. VIII:** 196

Mary (Asch), **Supp. XXIII:** 2, 7, **14**

Mary (Nabokov), **Retro. Supp. I: 267– 268,** 270, 277

"Mary" (Trethewey), **Supp. XXI:** 246

"Mary in Old Age" (Ferry), **Supp. XXIV:** 162

"Mary Karr, Mary Karr, Mary Karr, Mary Karr" (Harmon), **Supp. XI:** 248

Maryles, Daisy, **Supp. XII:** 271

Mary Magdalene, **I:** 303

"Mary Magdalene at Easter" (Davison), **Supp. XXVI:** 71

Mary; or, The Test of Honour (Rowson), **Supp. XV: 233,** 236

"Mary O'Reilly" (Anderson), **II:** 44

"Mary Osaka , I Love You" (Fante), **Supp. XI:** 169

Mary Roberts Rinehart Crime Book, The (Rinehart), **Supp. XXV:** 199

"Mary Snorak the Cook, Skermo the Gardener, and Jack the Parts Man Provide Dinner for a Wandering Stranger" (Grossman), **Supp. XIX:** 87

"Mary's Song" (Plath), **Supp. I Part 2:** 541

"Mary Winslow" (R. Lowell), **Retro. Supp. II:** 187

Marzynski, Marian, **Supp. XVI:** 153

"Masculinities and Murder: George Pemberton in Ron Rash's *Serena*" (Willis), **Supp. XXVII:** 216

Masefield, John, **II:** 552; **III:** 523

Masked and Anonymous (film, Dylan and Charles), **Supp. XVIII:** 21, 28

Mask for Janus, A (Merwin), **Supp. III Part 1:** 339, 341, 342

Maslin, Janet, **Supp. XVI:** 213; **Supp. XXI:** 79

Maslow, Abraham, **Supp. I Part 2:** 540

Maso, Carole, **Supp. XXII:** 261

Mason, Bobbie Ann, **Supp. VIII: 133–149; Supp. XI:** 26; **Supp. XII:** 294, 298, 311; **Supp. XX: 162; Supp. XXV:** 153

Mason, Charlotte, **Supp. XIV:** 201

Mason, David, **Supp. V:** 344; **Supp. XV:** 116, 251; **Supp. XVII:** 109, 110, 112, 121; **Supp. XVIII:** 182, 183

Mason, Jennifer, **Supp. XVIII:** 263

Mason, Lowell, **I:** 458

Mason, Margaret, **Supp. XXIII:** 209

Mason, Marsha, **Supp. IV Part 2:** 575, 586

Mason, Otis Tufton, **Supp. I Part 1:** 18

Mason, Walt, **Supp. XV:** 298

Mason & Dixon (Pynchon), **Supp. XVII:** 232

"Mason Jars by the Window" (Ríos), **Supp. IV Part 2:** 548

"Masque in Green and Black"(Hadas), **Supp. XXIII:** 121

Masque of Mercy, A (Frost), **II:** 155, 165, 167–168; **Retro. Supp. I:** 131, 140

"Masque of Mummers, The" (MacLeish), **III:** 18

"Masque of Pandora, The" (Longfellow), **Retro. Supp. II:** 167

Masque of Pandora, The, and Other Poems (Longfellow), **II:** 490, 494, 506; **Retro. Supp. II:** 169

Masque of Poets, A (Lathrop, ed.), **Retro. Supp. I:** 31; **Supp. I Part 1:** 365, 368

Masque of Reason, A (Frost), **II:** 155, 162, 165–167; **Retro. Supp. I:** 131, 140; **Retro. Supp. II:** 42

"Masque of the Red Death, The" (Poe), **III:** 412, 419, 424; **Retro. Supp. II:** 262, 268–269

"Masquerade" (Banks), **Supp. V:** 7

Massachusetts, Its Historians and Its History (Adams), **Supp. I Part 2:** 484

"Massachusetts 1932" (Bowles), **Supp. IV Part 1:** 94

"Massachusetts to Virginia" (Whittier), **Supp. I Part 2:** 688–689

"Massacre and the Mastermind, The" (Bausch), **Supp. VII:** 49

"Massacre at Scio, The" (Bryant), **Supp. I Part 1:** 168

"Massacre of the Innocents, The" (Davison), **Supp. XXVI:** 70

"Massacre of the Innocents, The" (Simic), **Supp. VIII:** 282

Masses and Man (Toller), **I:** 479

"Masseur de Ma Soeur, Le" (Hecht), **Supp. X:** 58

Massey, Raymond, **Supp. IV Part 2:** 524

"Mass Eye and Ear: The Ward" (Karr), **Supp. XI:** 244

"Mass for the Day of St. Thomas Didymus" (Levertov), **Supp. III Part 1:** 283

Massie, Chris, **Supp. IV Part 2:** 524

Massing, Michael, **Supp. IV Part 1:** 208

Massinger, Philip, **Supp. I Part 2:** 422; **Supp. XV:** 238

Master Builder, The (Ibsen), **Supp. IV Part 2:** 522

Master Class (McNally), **Supp. XIII: 204–205,** 208

"Masterful" (Matthews), **Supp. IX: 161–162**

Mastering the Art of French Cooking (Child), **Supp. XVII:** 89

"Master Misery" (Capote), **Supp. III Part 1:** 117

Master of Dreams: A Memoir of Isaac Bashevis Singer (Telushkin), **Retro. Supp. II:** 317

"Master of Secret Revenges, The" (Gass), **Supp. VI:** 93

Master of the Crossroads (Bell), **Supp. X: 16–17**

"'Masterpiece of Filth, A': Portrait of Knoxville Forgets to Be Fair" (Howards), **Supp. VIII:** 178

Masterpieces of American Fiction, **Supp. XI:** 198

"Master Player, The" (Dunbar), **Supp. II Part 1:** 200

Masters, Edgar Lee, **I:** 106, 384, 475, 480, 518; **II:** 276, 529; **III:** 505, 576, 579; **IV:** 352; **Retro. Supp. I:** 131; **Supp. I Part 2:** 378, 386, 387, **454–478; Supp. III Part 1:** 63, 71, 73, 75; **Supp. IV Part 2:** 502; **Supp. IX:** 308; **Supp. XIV:** 282–283; **Supp. XV:** 256, 293, 297, 301, 306; **Supp. XXV:** 18; **Supp. XXVII:** 283, 290

Masters, Hardin W., **Supp. I Part 2:** 468

Masters, Hilary, **Supp. IX:** 96

Masters of Sociological Thought (Coser), **Supp. I Part 2:** 650

Masters of the Dew (Roumain), **Supp. IV Part 1:** 367

Masters of the Short Story (Kriegel and Lass, eds.), **Supp. XXIV:** 214

"Masters of War" (song, Dylan), **Supp. XVIII:** 24

"Master's Pieces, The" (H. L. Gates), **Supp. XX: 109**

Matchmaker, The (Wilder), **IV:** 357, 369, 370, 374; **Supp. XX: 50**

Mate of the Daylight, The, and Friends Ashore (Jewett), **II:** 404; **Retro. Supp. II:** 146–147

Materassi, Mario, **Supp. IX:** 233

"Material" (Munro), **Supp. XXVII:** 185

Materials, The (Oppen), **Supp. XXVI:** 229–232

"Math Bending unto Angels" (Vaz), **Supp. XXVI:** 260

Mather, Cotton, **II:** 10, 104, 302, 506, 536; **III:** 442; **IV:** 144, 152–153, 157; **Supp. I Part 1:** 102, 117, 174, 271; **Supp. I Part 2:** 584, 599, 698; **Supp. II Part 2: 441–470; Supp. IV Part 2:** 430, 434

Mather, Increase, **II:** 10; **IV:** 147, 157; **Supp. I Part 1:** 100

Mathews, Cornelius, **III:** 81; **Supp. I Part 1:** 317

Mathews, Shailer, **III:** 293

"Matinees" (Merrill), **Supp. III Part 1:** 319, 327

"Matins" (C. Frost), **Supp. XV:** 105

"Matins" (Glück), **Supp. V:** 88

"Matins" (Nelson), **Supp. XVIII:** 177

Matisse, Henri, **III:** 180; **IV:** 90, 407; **Supp. I Part 2:** 619; **Supp. IX:** 66; **Supp. VIII:** 168; **Supp. X:** 73, 74; **Supp. XXII:** 98, 99; **Supp. XXVI:** 259

"Matisse: Blue Interior with Two Girls–1947" (Hecht), **Supp. X: 73–74**

"Matisse: The Red Studio" (Snodgrass), **Supp. VI:** 316–317

Matlack, James, **Supp. XV:** 269, 271, 286

Matlock, Lucinda, **Supp. I Part 2:** 462

Matos, Juan, **Supp. XXI:** 104

Matrimaniac, The (film), **Supp. XVI:** 185, 186

Matrix Trilogy, The (film), **Supp. XVI:** 271

Matson, Harold, **Supp. XIII:** 164, 166, 167, 169, 172

Matson, Peter, **Supp. IV Part 1:** 299

Matson, Suzanne, **Supp. VIII:** 281

Matters of Fact and Fiction: Essays 1973–1976 (Vidal), **Supp. IV Part 2:** 687

Matters of Life and Death: New American Stories (Wolff, ed.), **Supp. XXIII:** 289

Matthew (biblical book), **IV:** 164; **Supp. XV:** 222

Matthew Arnold (Trilling), **Supp. III Part 2:** 500–501

Matthews, Jackson, **Supp. XVI:** 282

Matthews, T. S., **II:** 430; **Supp. XV:** 142

Matthews, William, **Supp. IX: 151–170; Supp. V:** 4, 5; **Supp. XIII:** 112; **Supp. XXI:** 87; **Supp. XXVI:** 66

Matthiessen, F. O., **I:** 254, 259–260, 517; **II:** 41, 554; **III:** 310, 453; **IV:** 181; **Retro. Supp. I:** 40, 217; **Retro. Supp.**

II: 137; **Supp. IV Part 2:** 422; **Supp. XIII:** 93; **Supp. XIV:** 3; **Supp. XXI:** 277; **Supp. XXV:** 251

Matthiessen, Peter, **Supp. V: 199–217,** 332; **Supp. XI:** 231, 294; **Supp. XIV:** 82; **Supp. XIX:** 268; **Supp. XVI:** 230

Mattingly, Garrett, **Supp. IV Part 2:** 601

Mattos, Anita, **Supp. XXIII:** 197

Mattu, Ravi, **Supp. XVI:** 124

"Maud Island" (Caldwell), **I:** 310

Maud Martha (Brooks), **Supp. III Part 1:** 74, 78–79, 87; **Supp. XI:** 278

"Maud Muller" (Whittier), **Supp. I Part 2:** 698

Maugham, W. Somerset, **III:** 57, 64; **Supp. IV Part 1:** 209; **Supp. X:** 58; **Supp. XIV:** 161

Maule's Curse: Seven Studies in the History of American Obscurantism (Winters), **Supp. II Part 2:** 807–808, 812

"Mau-mauing the Flak Catchers" (Wolfe), **Supp. III Part 2:** 577

Maupassant, Guy de, **I:** 309, 421; **II:** 191–192, 291, 325, 591; **IV:** 17; **Retro. Supp. II:** 65, 66, 67, 299; **Supp. I Part 1:** 207, 217, 223, 320; **Supp. XIV:** 336

"Maurice Barrès and the Youth of France" (Bourne), **I:** 228

Maurice Kenny: Celebrations of a Mohawk Writer (Kelsey, ed.), **Supp. XXIII:** 143

Maurier, George du, **II:** 338

Maurras, Charles, **Retro. Supp. I:** 55

Maus II: And Here My Troubles Began (A. Speigelman), **Supp. XVII:** 48

Mauve Gloves & Madmen, Clutter & Vine (Wolfe), **Supp. III Part 2:** 581

Maverick, Augustus, **Supp. XVIII:** 4

Maverick in Mauve (Auchincloss), **Supp. IV Part 1:** 26

"Mavericks, The" (play) (Auchincloss), **Supp. IV Part 1:** 34

"Mavericks, The" (story) (Auchincloss), **Supp. IV Part 1:** 32

"Max" (H. Miller), **III:** 183

Max, D. T., **Supp. XXI:** 117

Max and the White Phagocytes (H. Miller), **III:** 178, 183–184

Maximilian (emperor of Mexico), **Supp. I Part 2:** 457–458

Maximilian: A Play in Five Acts (Masters), **Supp. I Part 2:** 456, 457–458

"Maximus, to Gloucester" (Olson), **Supp. II Part 2:** 574

"Maximus, to himself" (Olson), **Supp. II Part 2:** 565, 566, 567, 569, 570, 572

Maximus Poems, The (Olson), **Retro. Supp. I:** 209; **Supp. II Part 2:** 555, 556, 563, 564–580, 584; **Supp. VIII:** 305; **Supp. XV:** 170, 264, 349; **Supp. XVI:** 287

Maximus Poems 1–10, The (Olson), **Supp. II Part 2:** 571

Maximus Poems IV, V, VI (Olson), **Supp. II Part 2:** 555, 580, 582–584

Maximus Poems Volume Three, The (Olson), **Supp. II Part 2:** 555, 582, 584–585

"Maximus to Gloucester, Letter 19 (A Pastoral Letter)" (Olson), **Supp. II Part 2:** 567

"Maximus to Gloucester, Sunday July 19" (Olson), **Supp. II Part 2:** 580

"Maximus to himself June 1964" (Olson), **Supp. II Part 2:** 584

Maxwell, Glyn, **Supp. XV:** 252, 253, 260, 261, 263, 264

Maxwell, William, **Supp. I Part 1:** 175; **Supp. III Part 1:** 62; **Supp. VIII: 151–174; Supp. XVII:** 23

May, Abigail (Abba). *See* Alcott, Mrs. Amos Bronson (Abigail May)

May, Charles, **Supp. XXVII:** 189, 196

May, Elaine Tyler, **Supp. XXII:** 81, 95

May, Jill, **Supp. VIII:** 126

"May 24, 1980" (Brodsky), **Supp. VIII:** 28

"May 1968" (Olds), **Supp. X:** 211–212

Mayakovsky, Vladimir, **Supp. XXIII:** 207; **Supp. XXVI:** 144

"Mayakovsky" (O'Hara), **Supp. XXIII:** 212, 214

"Mayan Glyphs Unread, The" (Bronk), **Supp. XXI:** 31

"Mayan Warning" (Mora), **Supp. XIII:** 214

Maybe (Hellman), **Supp. IV Part 1:** 12

"Maybe" (Oliver), **Supp. VII:** 239

"Maybe, Someday" (Ritsos), **Supp. XIII:** 78

May Blossom (Belasco), **Supp. XVI:** 182

"Mayday" (Faulkner), **Retro. Supp. I:** 80

"May Day" (Fitzgerald), **II:** 88–89; **Retro. Supp. I:** 103

"May Day Dancing, The" (Nemerov), **III:** 275

May Days (Pickering), **Supp. XXI:** 197–198

May Days: An Anthology of Verse from Masses-Liberator (Taggard, ed.), **Supp. XXII:** 275–276

"May Day Sermon to the Women of Gilmer County, Georgia, by a Woman Preacher Leaving the Baptist Church" (Dickey), **Supp. IV Part 1:** 182

Mayer, Bernadette, **Supp. XXIV:** 41

Mayer, Elizabeth, **Supp. II Part 1:** 16; **Supp. III Part 1:** 63

Mayer, John, **Retro. Supp. I:** 58

Mayer, Louis B., **Supp. XII:** 160; **Supp. XVIII:** 250

Mayes, Wendell, **Supp. IX:** 250

Mayfield, Sara, **Supp. IX:** 65

"May First" (Hayes), **Supp. XXVI:** 144

Mayflower, The (Stowe), **Supp. I Part 2:** 585, 586

Mayle, Peter, **Supp. XVI:** 295

Maynard, Joyce, **Supp. V:** 23

Maynard, Tony, **Supp. I Part 1:** 65

Mayne, Xavier. *See* Prime-Stevenson, Edward Irenaeus

Mayo, Robert, **III:** 478

Mayor (Allen), **Supp. XXII:** 245

Mayorga, Margaret, **IV:** 381

"Mayor of Glory River, The" (Huddle), **Supp. XXVI:** 151

"May-Pole of Merry Mount, The" (Hawthorne), **Supp. XXII:** 44

"Maypole of Merrymount, The" (Hawthorne), **II:** 229

"May Queen" (Di Piero), **Supp. XIX:** 41

May Sarton: Selected Letters 1916–1954, **Supp. VIII:** 265

"May Sun Sheds an Amber Light, The" (Bryant), **Supp. I Part 1:** 170

"May Swenson: The Art of Perceiving" (Stanford), **Supp. IV Part 2:** 637

May the Generations Die in the Right Order (Schott), **Supp. XXIII: 248–250**

"Maze" (Eberhart), **I:** 523, 525–526, 527

Mazel (R. Goldstein), **Supp. XVII:** 44

Mazower, David, **Supp. XXIII:** 4, 5

Mazur, Gail, **Supp. XVIII:** 92

Mazurkiewicz, Margaret, **Supp. XI:** 2

Mazzeno, Laurence W., **Supp. XXV:** 253, 256, 258, 259, 263

Mazzini, Giuseppe, **Supp. I Part 1:** 2, 8; **Supp. II Part 1:** 299

M. Butterfly (Hwang), **Supp. X:** 292; **Supp. XXI:** 143, 147, **150–154**

Mc. Names starting with Mc are alphabetized as if spelled Mac.

"M. Degas Teaches Art & Science at Durfee Intermediate School, Detroit, 1942" (Levine), **Supp. V:** 181, 193

"Me, Boy Scout" (Lardner), **II:** 433

Me, Mop, and the Moondance Kid (Myers), **Supp. XXVII:** 206

Me, Vashya! (T. Williams), **IV:** 381

Mead, Elinor. *See* Howells, Mrs. William Dean (Elinor Mead)

Mead, George Herbert, **II:** 27, 34; **Supp. I Part 1:** 5; **Supp. I Part 2:** 641

Mead, Margaret, **Supp. I Part 1:** 49, 52, 66; **Supp. IX:** 229

Mead, Taylor, **Supp. XV:** 187

Meade, Frank, **Retro. Supp. II:** 114

Meade, Marion, **Supp. IX:** 191, 193, 194, 195

Meadow, Lynne, **Supp. XIII:** 198

"Meadow House" (Carruth), **Supp. XVI:** 48

Meadowlands (Glück), **Supp. V:** 88–90

"Mean, Mrs." (Gass), **Supp. VI:** 83

"Me and the Mule" (Hughes), **Supp. I Part 1:** 334

Me and You and Everyone We Know (film, July), **Supp. XXIV:** 199, 200, 201, 203, 206, **207–209**

Mean Free Path (Lerner), **Supp. XXIV:** 45

Meaning a Life (M. Oppen), **Supp. XXVI:** 225, 228

"Meaningless Institution, A" (Ginsberg), **Supp. II Part 1:** 313

"Meaning of a Literary Idea, The" (Trilling), **Supp. III Part 2:** 498

"Meaning of Birds, The" (C. Smith), **Supp. X:** 177

"Meaning of Death, The, An After Dinner Speech" (Tate), **IV:** 128, 129

"Meaning of Life, The" (Tate), **IV:** 137

"Meaning of Simplicity, The" (Ritsos), **Supp. XIII:** 78

"Mean Mud Season, The" (Huddle), **Supp. XXVI:** 149

Means of Escape (Caputo), **Supp. XIX:** 18, 21, 25

Mean Spirit (Hogan), **Supp. IV Part 1:** 397, 404, 407–410, 415, 416–417

Means to Freedom, A: The Letters of H. P. Lovecraft and Robert Howard (Burke, Joshi, and Schultz eds.), **Supp. XXVII:** 128

Meantime, The (Bronk), **Supp. XXI:** 31

Mearns, Hughes, **III:** 220

"Measure" (Hass), **Supp. VI: 99–100,** 101

Measure for Measure (Shakespeare), **Supp. XXVI:** 78

"Measuring My Blood" (Vizenor), **Supp. IV Part 1:** 262

Meatyard, Gene, **Supp. X:** 30

Me: By Jimmy (Big Boy) Valente (Keillor), **Supp. XVI:** 177

Mechan, Dennis B., **Supp. XVI:** 267–268

Mechanic, The (Bynner and DeMille), **Supp. XV:** 42, 50

"Mechanism" (Ammons), **Supp. VII:** 28

"Mechanism in Thought and Morals" (Holmes), **Supp. I Part 1:** 314

Mecom, Mrs. Jane, **II:** 122

"Meddlesome Jack" (Caldwell), **I:** 309

Medea (Jeffers), **Supp. II Part 2:** 435

Medea and Some Poems, The (Cullen), **Supp. IV Part 1:** 169, 173

"Me Decade and the Third Great Awakening, The" (Wolfe), **Supp. III Part 2:** 581

"Médecin Malgré Lui, Le" (W. C. Williams), **IV:** 407–408

"Medfield" (Bryant), **Supp. I Part 1:** 157

Medical History of Contraception, A (Himes), **Supp. V:** 128

"Medicine Song" (Gunn Allen), **Supp. IV Part 1:** 326

Médicis, Marie de, **II:** 548

Medina (McCarthy), **II:** 579

"Meditation, A" (Eberhart), **I:** 533–535

"Meditation 1.6" (Taylor), **IV:** 165

"Meditation 1.20" (Taylor), **IV:** 165

"Meditation 2.68A" (Taylor), **IV:** 165

"Meditation 2.102" (Taylor), **IV:** 150

"Meditation 2.112" (Taylor), **IV:** 165

"Meditation 20" (Taylor), **IV:** 154–155

"Meditation 40" (Second Series) (Taylor), **IV:** 147

"Meditation at Lagunitas" (Hass), **Supp. VI:** 104–105; **Supp. XXI:** 60; **Supp. XXVI:** 61

"Meditation at Oyster River" (Roethke), **III:** 537, 549

Meditations (Descartes), **III:** 618

Meditations (Marcus Aurelius), **Supp. XVIII:** 304

"Meditations for a Savage Child" (Rich), **Supp. I Part 2:** 564–565

Meditations from a Movable Chair (Dubus), **Supp. VII:** 91

Meditations in an Emergency (O'Hara), **Supp. XXIII: 213–214,** 219, 220

"Meditations in an Emergency"(O'Hara), **Supp. XXIII:** 212, 214

"Meditations in a Swine Yard" (Komunyakaa), **Supp. XIII:** 131

"Meditations of an Old Woman" (Roethke), **III:** 529, 540, 542, 543, 545–547, 548

"Meditations on Grass"(Crooker), **Supp. XXIII:** 55

Meditations on the Insatiable Soul (R. Bly), **Supp. IV Part 1:** 72–73

Meditative Poems, The (Martz), **IV:** 151

"Mediterranean, The" (Tate), **IV:** 129

"Medium of Fiction, The" (Gass), **Supp. VI:** 85–86

"Medley" (Bambara), **Supp. XI:** 9

"Medusa" (Bogan), **Supp. III Part 1:** 50, 51

Meehan, Jeannette Porter, **Supp. XX: 213, 214, 217, 220, 224**

Meehan, Thomas, **Supp. IV Part 2:** 577–578, 586, 590

Meek, Martha, **Supp. IV Part 2:** 439, 440, 441, 442, 445, 447, 448

Meeker, Richard K., **II:** 190

Meese, Elizabeth, **Supp. XIII:** 297

"Meeting" (J. W. Miller), **Supp. XX: 167**

"Meeting, The" (F. Wright), **Supp. XVII:** 245

"Meeting and Greeting Area, The" (Cameron), **Supp. XII: 84–85**

Meeting by the River, A (Isherwood), **Supp. XIV:** 164, **170–171,** 172

"Meeting-House Hill" (A. Lowell), **II:** 522, 527

"Meeting in the Kitchen, The" (Schnackenberg), **Supp. XV:** 256

"Meeting of the Tisdale Fellows, The" (Huddle), **Supp. XXVI:** 155

"Meeting South, A" (Anderson), **I:** 115

"Meeting the Mountains" (Snyder), **Supp. VIII:** 300

Meeting Trees (Sanders), **Supp. XVI:** 269

Meet Me at the Morgue (Macdonald), **Supp. IV Part 2:** 472

Mehta, Sonny, **Supp. XI:** 178

Mehta, Ved, **Supp. XX: 87**

Meine, Curt, **Supp. XIV:** 179

Meiners, R. K., **IV:** 136, 137, 138, 140

Meinong, Alexius, **Supp. XIV:** 198, 199

Meisner, Sanford, **Supp. XIV:** 240, 242

Meister, Charles W., **II:** 112

Mejia, Jaime, **Supp. XIX:** 97

"Melancholia" (Dunbar), **Supp. II Part 1:** 194

Melancholy Baby (Parker), **Supp. XIX:** 186

"Melanctha" (Stein), **IV:** 30, 34, 35, 37, 38–40, 45

"Melancthon" (Moore), **III:** 212, 215

Melbourne House (S. and A. Warner), **Supp. XVIII:** 268

Meliboeus Hipponax (Lowell). *See Bigelow Papers, The* (Lowell)

Melinda and Melinda (Allen), **Supp. XV:** 16

Mellaart, James, **Supp. I Part 2:** 567

Mellard, James, **Supp. IV Part 1:** 387

Mellen, Joan, **Supp. XXIV:** 51, 52, 56, 64

Mellon, Andrew, **III:** 14

Mellor, W. M., **Supp. XX: 56**

Melnick, Jeffrey, **Supp. X:** 252

Melnick, Ralph, **Supp. XXVII:** 137–138

Melnyczuk, Askold, **Supp. IV Part 1:** 70

Melodrama Play (Shepard), **Supp. III Part 2:** 440–441, 443, 445

Melodramatists, The (Nemerov), **III:** 268, 281–283, 284

Melopoeia (Espaillat and Tavano), **Supp. XXI:** 99–100

Melting-Pot, The (Zangwill), **I:** 229

"Melungeons" (Offutt), **Supp. XIX:** 171

Melville, Allan, **III:** 74, 77

Melville, Gansevoort, **III:** 76

Melville, Herman, **I:** 104, 106, 211, 288, 340, 343, 348, 354, 355, 561–562; **II:** 27, 74, 224–225, 228, 230, 232, 236, 255, 259, 271, 272, 277, 281, 295, 307, 311, 319, 320, 321, 418, 477, 497, 539–540, 545; **III:** 29, 45, 70, **74–98,** 359, 438, 453, 454, 507, 562–563, 572, 576; **IV:** 57, 105, 194, 199, 202, 250, 309, 333, 345, 350, 380, 444, 453; **Retro. Supp. I:** 54, 91, 160, 215, 220, **243–262; Retro. Supp. II:** 76; **Supp. I Part 1:** 147, 238, 242, 249, 309, 317, 372; **Supp. I Part 2:** 383, 495, 579, 580, 582, 602; **Supp. IV Part 2:** 463, 613; **Supp. V:** 279, 281, 298, 308; **Supp. VIII:** 48, 103, 104, 105, 106, 108, 156, 175, 181, 188; **Supp. XI:** 83; **Supp. XII:** 282; **Supp. XIII:** 294, 305; **Supp. XIV:** 48, 227; **Supp. XV:** 287; **Supp. XVII:** 42, 185; **Supp. XVIII:** 1, 4, 6, 7, 9; **Supp. XXI:** 169; **Supp. XXII:** 174, 262; **Supp. XXIII:** 164, 165, 174, 190; **Supp. XXIV:** 88

Melville, Mrs. Herman (Elizabeth Shaw), **III:** 77, 91, 92

Melville, Maria Gansevoort, **III:** 74, 77, 85

Melville, Thomas, **III:** 77, 79, 92; **Supp. I Part 1:** 309

Melville, Whyte, **IV:** 309

Melville Goodwin, USA (Marquand), **III:** 60, 65–66

Melville's Marginalia (Cowen), **Supp. IV Part 2:** 435

"Melville's Marginalia" (Howe), **Supp. IV Part 2:** 435

Member of the Wedding, The (McCullers), **II:** 587, 592, 600–604, 605, 606; **Supp. VIII:** 124

"Meme Ortiz" (Cisneros), **Supp. VII:** 60

Memmon (song cycle) (Bowles), **Supp. IV Part 1:** 82

Memmott, Carol, **Supp. XXVI:** 209

Memnoch the Devil (Rice), **Supp. VII:** 289, 290, 294, 296–299

"Memoir" (Hempel), **Supp. XXI:** 118

"Memoir" (Untermeyer), **II:** 516–517

"Memoir, A" (Koch), **Supp. XV:** 184

Memoir from Antproof Case (Helprin), **Supp. XXV:** 84, 87

"Memoirist's Apology, A" (Karr), **Supp. XI:** 245, 246

Memoir of Mary Ann, A (O'Connor), **III:** 357

Memoir of Thomas McGrath, A (Beeching), **Supp. X:** 114, 118

Memoirs (W. Frank), **Supp. XX: 67, 69, 70, 81**

Memoirs of a Preacher, a Revelation of the Church and the Home, The (Lippard), **Supp. XXIII:** 178, 183–184, 188, 190

Memoirs of Arii Taimai (Adams), **I:** 2–3

"Memoirs of Carwin, the Biloquist" (Brown), **Supp. I Part 1:** 132

Memoirs of Hecate County (Wilson), **IV:** 429

Memoirs of Margaret Fuller Ossoli (Fuller), **Supp. II Part 1:** 280, 283, 285

"Memoirs of Stephen Calvert" (Brown), **Supp. I Part 1:** 133, 144

Memorabilia (Xenophon), **II:** 105

Memorable Providences (Mather), **Supp. II Part 2:** 458

Memorial, The: Portrait of a Family (Isherwood), **Supp. XIV:** 156, 159, 160–161

"Memorial Day" (Cameron), **Supp. XII:** 80, **82–83**

"Memorial for the City" (Auden), **Supp. II Part 1:** 20

"Memorial Rain" (MacLeish), **III:** 15

"Memorial to Ed Bland" (Brooks), **Supp. III Part 1:** 77

"Memorial Tribute" (Wilbur), **Supp. IV Part 2:** 642

"Memories" (Whittier), **Supp. I Part 2:** 699

Memories of a Catholic Girlhood (McCarthy), **II:** 560–561, 566; **Supp. XI:** 246; **Supp. XVI:** 64, 70

"Memories of East Texas" (Karr), **Supp. XI:** 239

"Memories of Uncle Neddy" (Bishop), **Retro. Supp. II:** 38; **Supp. I Part 1:** 73, 93

"Memories of West Street and Lepke" (R. Lowell), **II:** 550

"Memory" (Epstein), **Supp. XII:** 163

"Memory" (Everwine), **Supp. XV:** 82

"Memory, A" (Welty), **IV:** 261–262; **Retro. Supp. I:** 344–345

"Memory, Narrative, and the Discourses of Identity in *Abeng* and *No Telephone to Heaven*" (Smith), **Supp. XXII:** 70

"Memory, The" (Gioia), **Supp. XV:** 119

Memory and Enthusiasm: Essays, 1975–1985 (Di Piero), **Supp. XIX:** 34, 41, 42

"Memory and Imagination" (Hampl), **Supp. XXII:** 94

Memory Gardens (Creeley), **Supp. IV Part 1:** 141, 157

"Memory Harbor" (Skloot), **Supp. XX: 201**

Memory of Murder, A (Bradbury), **Supp. IV Part 1:** 103

Memory of Old Jack, The (Berry), **Supp. X:** 34

Memory of Two Mondays, A (A. Miller), **III:** 153, 156, 158–159, 160, 166

"Memory's Power" (Huddle), **Supp. XXVI:** 160

"Memo to Non-White Peoples" (Hughes), **Retro. Supp. I:** 209

"Men" (Boyle), **Supp. XXIV:** 61

Men, Women and Ghosts (A. Lowell), **II:** 523–524

"Menace of the Peyote, The" (Zitkala-Ša), **Supp. XXV:** 281

Menaker, Charlotte, **Supp. XIX:** 266

Menaker, Daniel, **Supp. VIII:** 151; **Supp. XXIII:** 276

Menand, Louis, **Supp. XIV:** 40, 197; **Supp. XVI:** 106, 107; **Supp. XXIII:** 104–105

Men and Angels (Gordon), **Supp. IV Part 1:** 304–305, 306, 308

Men and Brethen (Cozzens), **I:** 363–365, 368, 375, 378, 379

Men and Cartoons (Lethem), **Supp. XVIII:** 145, **148**

"Men and Women" (R. Bly), **Supp. IV Part 1:** 72

"Men at Forty" (Justice), **Supp. VII:** 126–127

Mencius (Meng-tzu), **IV:** 183

Mencken, August, **III:** 100, 108

Mencken, August, Jr., **III:** 99, 109, 118–119

Mencken, Mrs. August (Anna Abhau), **III:** 100, 109

Mencken, Burkhardt, **III:** 100, 108

Mencken, Charles, **III:** 99

Mencken, Gertrude, **III:** 99

Mencken, H. L., **I:** 199, 210, 212, 235, 245, 261, 405, 514, 515, 517; **II:** 25, 27, 42, 89, 90, 91, 271, 289, 430, 443, 449; **III: 99–121**, 394, 482; **IV:** 76, 432, 440, 475, 482; **Retro. Supp. I:** 1, 101; **Retro. Supp. II:** 97, 98, 102, 265; **Supp. I Part 2:** 484, 629–630, 631, 647, 651, 653, 659, 673; **Supp. II Part 1:** 136; **Supp. IV Part 1:** 201, 314, 343; **Supp. IV Part 2:** 521, 692, 693; **Supp. XI:** 163–164, 166; **Supp. XIII:** 161; **Supp. XIV:** 111; **Supp. XV:** 297, 301, 303; **Supp. XVI:** 187–188, 189; **Supp. XVII:** 106; **Supp. XXII:** 23, 187, 277; **Supp. XXIV:** 26, 281; **Supp. XXVII:** 86

Mencken, Mrs. H. L. (Sara Haardt), **III:** 109, 111

"Men Deified Because of Their Cruelty" (Simic), **Supp. VIII:** 282

Mendelbaum, Paul, **Supp. V:** 159

Mendele, **IV:** 3, 10

Mendelief, Dmitri Ivanovich, **IV:** 421

Mendelsohn, Daniel, **Supp. X:** 153, 154; **Supp. XV:** 257, 258, 261, 266

Mendelsohn, Jack, **Supp. XXIV:** 72, 77

Mendelsohn, Jane, **Supp. XXVI:** 158

Mendelssohn, Moses, **Supp. XXIII:** 4

Mendes, Alfred, **Supp. XXI:** 160

Mending Skins (Gansworth), **Supp. XXVI:** 103, 104, 106

"Mending Wall" (Frost), **II:** 153–154; **Retro. Supp. I:** 128, 130; **Supp. X:** 64

"Meneseteung" (Munro), **Supp. XXVII:** 190–191

Men from the Boys, The (Lacy), **Supp. XV:** 202, 205

"Menielle" (Stallings), **Supp. XXV:** 223

Men in the Off Hours (Carson), **Supp. XII:** 111–113

"Men in the Storm, The" (Crane), **I:** 411

"Men Loved Wholly Beyond Wisdom" (Bogan), **Supp. III Part 1:** 50

"Men Made Out of Words" (Stevens), **IV:** 88

Men Must Act (Mumford), **Supp. II Part 2:** 479

Mennes, John, **II:** 111

Mennoti, Gian Carlo, **Supp. IV Part 1:** 84

Men of Brewster Place, The (Naylor), **Supp. VIII:** 213, **228–230**

"Men of Color, to Arms!" (Douglass), **Supp. III Part 1:** 171

Men of Good Hope: A Story of American Progressives (Aaron), **Supp. I Part 2:** 650

Mens' Club, The (film), **Supp. XVI:** 212–213

Men's Club, The (L. Michaels), **Supp. XVI:** 206, **210–212**

"Men's Sauna" (Huddle), **Supp. XXVI:** 150

"Menstruation at Forty" (Sexton), **Supp. II Part 2:** 686

"Mental Hospital Garden, The" (W. C. Williams), **Retro. Supp. I:** 428

Mental Radio (Sinclair), **Supp. V:** 289

Mentoria; or, The Young Lady's Friend (Rowson), **Supp. XV: 233–234**, 238

"Men We Carry in Our Minds, The" (Sanders), **Supp. XVI:** 273

Men Who Made the Nation, The (Dos Passos), **I:** 485

"Men Who Raised the Dead, The" (Rash), **Supp. XXVII:** 220

Men Without Women (Hemingway), **II:** 249; **Retro. Supp. I:** 170, 176; **Supp. IX:** 202

"Merced" (Rich), **Supp. I Part 2:** 563

"Mercedes" (E. Stoddard), **Supp. XV:** 278

"Mercedes Hospital" (Bishop), **Retro. Supp. II:** 51

"Mercenary, A" (Ozick), **Supp. V:** 267

Mercer, Johnny, **Supp. XXII:** 6

Merchandising (Hwang), **Supp. XXI:** 147

Merchant of Venice, The (Shakespeare), **IV:** 227; **Supp. XIV:** 325

Mercury Theatre, **Retro. Supp. I:** 65

Mercy, Pity, Peace, and Love (Ozick), **Supp. V:** 257, 258

Mercy, The (Levine), **Supp. V:** 194–195

Mercy of a Rude Stream (H. Roth), **Supp. IX:** 231, 234, **235–242**

"Mercy"(P. Benedict), **Supp. XXIII:** 49

Mercy Philbrick's Choice (Jackson), **Retro. Supp. I:** 26, 27, 33

Mercy Street (Sexton), **Supp. II Part 2:** 683, 689

"Mercy"(Thompson), **Supp. XXIII:** 295, 296

Meredith, George, **II:** 175, 186; **Supp. IV Part 1:** 300

Meredith, Mary. *See* Webb, Mary

Meredith, William, **II:** 545; **Retro. Supp. II:** 181

"Merely by Wilderness" (Peacock), **Supp. XIX:** 199

"Merely to Know" (Rich), **Supp. I Part 2:** 554

"Mère Pochette" (Jewett), **II:** 400

"Merger II, The" (Auchincloss), **Supp. IV Part 1:** 34

Meri (Asch), **Supp. XXIII:** 5, 11

"Mericans" (Cisneros), **Supp. VII:** 69

"Merida, 1969" (Matthews), **Supp. IX:** 151

"Meridian" (Clampitt), **Supp. IX: 48–49**

Meridian (Walker), **Supp. III Part 2:** 520, 524, 527, 528, 531–537

Mérimée, Prosper, **II:** 322

Meriwether, James B., **Retro Supp. I:** 77, 91

"Meriwether Connection, The" (Cowley), **Supp. II Part 1:** 142

Merker, Kim K., **Supp. XI:** 261; **Supp. XV:** 75, 77

"Merlin" (Emerson), **II:** 19, 20

Merlin (Robinson), **III:** 522

"Merlin Enthralled" (Wilbur), **Supp. III Part 2:** 544, 554

"Mermother" (A. Finch), **Supp. XVII:** 72

Merril, Judith, **Supp. XVI:** 123

Merrill, Cavafy, Poems, and Dreams (Hadas), **Supp. XXIII: 123–124**

Merrill, Christopher, **Supp. XI:** 329

Merrill, James, **Retro. Supp. I:** 296; **Retro. Supp. II:** 53; **Supp. III Part 1: 317–338; Supp. III Part 2:** 541, 561; **Supp. IX:** 40, 42, 48, 52; **Supp. X:** 73; **Supp. XI:** 123, 131, 249; **Supp. XII:** 44, 254, 255, 256, 261–262, 269–270; **Supp. XIII:** 76, 85; **Supp. XV:** 249, 250, 253; **Supp. XVII:** 123; **Supp. XXIII:** 112, 122, 123; **Supp. XXV:** 222, 227–228; **Supp. XXVI:** 67

Merrill, Mark (pseudonym). *See* Markson, David

Merrill, Robert, **Retro. Supp. II:** 201

Merrill, Ronald, **Supp. IV Part 2:** 521

Merritt, A., **Supp. XXV:** 122

Merritt, Abraham, **Supp. XVII:** 58

Merritt, Theresa, **Supp. VIII:** 332

Merritt, Vernon, **Supp. XXII:** 245

"Merry-Go-Round" (Hughes), **Retro. Supp. I:** 194, 205; **Supp. I Part 1:** 333

Merry-Go-Round, The (Van Vechten), **Supp. II Part 2:** 734, 735

Merry Month of May, The (Jones), **Supp. XI: 227–228**

Merry Widow, The (Lehar), **III:** 183

Merton, Thomas, **III:** 357; **Supp. VIII: 193–212; Supp. XXII:** 83, 90; **Supp. XXIV:** 133

Merwin, W. S., **Supp. III Part 1: 339–360; Supp. III Part 2:** 541; **Supp. IV Part 2:** 620, 623, 626; **Supp. IX:** 152, 155, 290; **Supp. V:** 332; **Supp. XIII:** 274, 277; **Supp. XIX:** 82; **Supp. XV:** 222, 342; **Supp. XXI:** 95; **Supp. XXVI:** 67, 68

Meryman, Richard, **Supp. IV Part 2:** 579, 583

Meshiekhs tsaytn (Times of the Messiah) (Asch), **Supp. XXIII:** 5

Meshugah (Singer), **Retro. Supp. II: 315–316**

Mesic, Michael, **Supp. IV Part 1:** 175

Mesic, Penelope, **Supp. X:** 15

Message in the Bottle, The (Percy), **Supp. III Part 1:** 387–388, 393, 397

"Message in the Bottle, The" (Percy), **Supp. III Part 1:** 388

"Message of Flowers and Fire and Flowers, The" (Brooks), **Supp. III Part 1:** 69

Messengers Will Come No More, The (Fiedler), **Supp. XIII:** 103

Messerli, Douglas, **Supp. XVI:** 293

Messiah (Vidal), **Supp. IV Part 2:** 677, 680, 681–682, 685, 691, 692

"Messiah, The" (Wasserstein), **Supp. XV:** 328

Messiah of Stockholm, The (Ozick), **Supp. V:** 270–271; **Supp. XVII:** 42

Messud, Claire, **Supp. XVIII:** 98

Metamorphic Tradition in Modern Poetry (Quinn), **IV:** 421

Metamorphoses (Golding, trans.), **Supp. XXV:** 226

Metamorphoses (Ovid), **II:** 542–543; **III:** 467, 468; **Supp. XV:** 33; **Supp. XVI:** 20; **Supp. XX: 280; Supp. XXIV:** 132

Metamorphoses (Pound, trans.), **III:** 468–469

"Metamorphosis" (Huddle), **Supp. XXVI:** 151

Metamorphosis, The (Kafka), **IV:** 438; **Retro. Supp. II:** 287–288; **Supp. VIII:** 3; **Supp. XXI:** 89

"Metamorphosis and Survival" (Woodcock), **Supp. XIII:** 33

"Metaphor as Mistake" (Percy), **Supp. III Part 1:** 387–388

"Metaphor for Guatemala, A: The Long Night of White Chickens" (Perera), **Supp. XXV:** 50

Metaphor & Memory: Essays (Ozick), **Supp. V:** 272

Metaphor of Trees and Last Poems (Bronk), **Supp. XXI:** 32

"Metaphors of a Magnifico" (Stevens), **IV:** 92

Metaphysical Club, The (Menand), **Supp. XIV:** 40, 197

"Metaphysical Poets, The" (Eliot), **I:** 527, 586

"Metaphysics" (Ginsberg), **Supp. II Part 1:** 313

Metcalf, Paul, **Supp. XIV:** 96; **Supp. XXIII:** 163, 174

"Meteor, The" (Bradbury), **Supp. IV Part 1:** 102

Methinks the Lady…(Endore), **Supp. XVII:** 61–62

"Metonymy as an Approach to the Real World" (Bronk), **Supp. XXI:** 30

Metress, Christopher P., **Supp. V:** 314

Metrical History of Christianity, The (Taylor), **IV:** 163

"Metrical Regularity" (Lovecraft), **Supp. XXV:** 120

Metropolis, The (Sinclair), **Supp. V:** 285

"Metropolitan Tower, The" (Teasdale), **Supp. XXVII:** 286, 289

"Metterling Lists, The" (Allen), **Supp. XV:** 15

"Metzengerstein" (Poe), **III:** 411, 417

Mew, Charlotte, **Retro. Supp. II:** 247

Mewshaw, Michael, **Supp. V:** 57; **Supp. X:** 82

"Mexican Hands" (Ryan as Quin), **Supp. XVIII:** 227

"Mexico" (R. Lowell), **II:** 553, 554

"Mexico, Age Four" (Salinas), **Supp. XIII:** 315

Mexico City Blues (Kerouac), **Supp. III Part 1:** 225, 229

"Mexico Is a Foreign Country: Five Studies in Naturalism" (Warren), **IV:** 241, 252

"Mexico's Children" (Rodriguez), **Supp. XIV:** 302

Meyer, Carolyn, **Supp. XIX:** 194–195, 197

Meyer, Donald B., **III:** 298

Meyer, Ellen Hope, **Supp. V:** 123

Meyer, Robert, **Supp. XXI:** 23

Meyers, Jeffrey, **Retro. Supp. I:** 124, 138; **Retro. Supp. II:** 191

Meynell, Alice, **Supp. I Part 1:** 220

Mezey, Robert, **Supp. IV Part 1:** 60; **Supp. V:** 180; **Supp. XIII:** 312; **Supp. XV:** 74

Mezzanine, The (Baker), **Supp. XIII: 41–43,** 44, 45, 48, 55

"Mezzo Cammin" (Longfellow), **II:** 490

"Mi Abuelo" (Ríos), **Supp. IV Part 2:** 541

Miami (Didion), **Supp. IV Part 1:** 199, 210

Miami and the Siege of Chicago (Mailer), **Retro. Supp. II:** 206

Miasma (Holding), **Supp. XXII:** 121–122

"Michael" (Wordsworth), **III:** 523

Michael, Magali Cornier, **Supp. XIII:** 32

"Michael Angelo: A Fragment" (Longfellow), **II:** 490, 494, 495, 506; **Retro. Supp. II:** 167

"Michael Egerton" (Price), **Supp. VI:** 257–258, 260

Michael Kohlhaas (Kleist), **Supp. IV Part 1:** 224

Michael O'Halloran (Stratton-Porter), **Supp. XX:** 222

Michaels, Leonard, **Supp. XVI: 201–215**

Michaels, Walter Benn, **Retro. Supp. I:** 115, 369, 379

Michael Scarlett (Cozens), **I:** 358–359, 378

"Michael's Veterans Remember" (Espaillat), **Supp. XXI:** 110

Michaux, Henri, **Supp. XVI:** 288

Michelangelo, **I:** 18; **II:** 11–12; **III:** 124; **Supp. I Part 1:** 363; **Supp. XVII:** 112

Michel-Michot, Paulette, **Supp. XI:** 224–225

Michelson, Albert, **IV:** 27

"Michigan Avenue" (Hecht), **Supp. XXVII:** 85

Mickelsson's Ghosts (Gardner), **Supp. VI:** 63, **73–74**

Mickiewicz, Adam, **Supp. II Part 1:** 299

"Microscope" (Trethewey), **Supp. XXI:** 251

Midair (Conroy), **Supp. XVI:** 63, **71–72**

"Mid-Air" (Conroy), **Supp. XVI:** 69, 71

Mid-American Chants (Anderson), **I:** 109, 114

"Midas" (Winters), **Supp. II Part 2:** 801

"Mid-August at Sourdough Mountain Lookout" (Snyder), **Supp. VIII:** 292–293

Midcentury (Dos Passos), **I:** 474, 475, 478, 490, 492–494; **Supp. I Part 2:** 646

Mid-Century American Poets, **III:** 532

"Mid-Day" (Doolittle), **Supp. I Part 1:** 266–267

"Middle Age" (R. Lowell), **II:** 550

"Middle-Aged, Middle-Class Woman at Midnight, A" (Taggard), **Supp. XXII:** 282–283

"Middleaged Man, The" (Simpson), **Supp. IX:** 274–275

Middle Ages, The (Gurney), **Supp. V:** 96, 105, 108

Middlebrook, Diane Wood, **Supp. IV Part 2:** 444, 451; **Supp. XXVI:** 66

"Middle Daughter, The" (Kingsolver), **Supp. VII:** 209

Middlemarch (G. Eliot), **I:** 457, 459; **II:** 290, 291; **Retro. Supp. I:** 225; **Supp. I Part 1:** 174; **Supp. IX:** 43; **Supp. XI:** 68; **Supp. XII:** 335

Middle of My Tether, The: Familiar Essays (Epstein), **Supp. XIV: 106–107**

"Middle of Nowhere, The" (Wagoner), **Supp. IX:** 327–328

Middle of the Journey, The (Trilling), **Supp. III Part 2:** 495, 504–506

"Middle of the Way" (Kinnell), **Supp. III Part 1:** 242

Middle Passage (C. Johnson), **Supp. VI: 194–196,** 198, 199; **Supp. XIII:** 182

"Middle Passage" (Hayden), **Supp. II Part 1:** 363, 375–376

Middlesex (Eugenides), **Supp. XXIV:** 131, 134–135, **138–142**

"Middle Toe of the Right Foot, The" (Bierce), **I:** 203

Middleton, Thomas, **Retro. Supp. I:** 62

"Middle Way, The"(Hadas), **Supp. XXIII:** 121

Middle Years, The (James), **II:** 337–338; **Retro. Supp. I:** 235

"Middle Years, The" (James), **Retro. Supp. I:** 228, 272

"Midnight" (Dunn), **Supp. XI:** 147

"Midnight Consultations, The" (Freneau), **Supp. II Part 1:** 257

Midnight Cry, A (Mather), **Supp. II Part 2:** 460

"Midnight Gladness" (Levertov), **Supp. III Part 1:** 284–285

Midnight Lantern (Gallagher), **Supp. XXIV:** 167, 171

"Midnight Lantern" (Gallagher), **Supp. XXIV:** 171

"Midnight Magic" (Mason), **Supp. VIII:** 146

Midnight Magic: Selected Stories of Bobbie Ann Mason (Mason), **Supp. VIII:** 148

Midnight Mass (Bowles), **Supp. IV Part 1:** 93

"Midnight Postscript" (F. Wright), **Supp. XVII:** 245, 246

Midnight Queen, The (Lippard), **Supp. XXIII:** 180

"Midnight Show" (Shapiro), **Supp. II Part 2:** 705

"Midpoint" (Updike), **Retro. Supp. I:** 321, 323, 327, 330, 335

Midpoint and Other Poems (Updike), **IV:** 214

"Midrash on Happiness" (Paley), **Supp. VI:** 217

"Midsummer" (Bronk), **Supp. XXI:** 30

"Midsummer in the Blueberry Barrens" (Clampitt), **Supp. IX:** 40–41

"Midsummer Letter" (Carruth), **Supp. XVI:** 47

Midsummer Night's Dream, A (Shakespeare), **Supp. I Part 1:** 369–370; **Supp. X:** 69

Midsummer Night's Sex Comedy, A (film; Allen), **Supp. XV:** 8

"Midwest" (Stafford), **Supp. XI:** 317

"Midwest Poetics" (C. Baxter), **Supp. XVII:** 18

Mieder, Wolfgang, **Supp. XIV:** 126

Mies van der Rohe, Ludwig, **Supp. IV Part 1:** 40

Mighty Aphrodite (film; Allen), **Supp. XV:** 11

"Mighty Fortress, A" (Leopold), **Supp. XIV:** 185

"Mighty Lord, The" (Rowson), **Supp. XV:** 243

"Migration, The" (Tate), **IV:** 130

Mihailovitch, Bata, **Supp. VIII:** 272

Mikado, The (Gilbert and Sullivan), **Supp. XXI:** 151

Miklitsch, Robert, **Supp. IV Part 2:** 628, 629

Mikolowski, Ken and Ann, **Supp. XXIV:** 43

Mila 18 (Uris), **Supp. IV Part 1:** 379; **Supp. XX: 244, 247, 248, 251–252, 253**

Milagro Beanfield War, The (film), **Supp. XIII:** 267

Milagro Beanfield War, The (Nichols), **Supp. XIII:** 253, **265–266**

Milburn, Michael, **Supp. XI:** 239, 242

Milch, David, **Supp. XI:** 348

Mild Day, The (Bronk), **Supp. XXI:** 32

Miles, Barry, **Supp. XII:** 123

Miles, Jack, **Supp. VIII:** 86

Miles, Josephine, **Supp. XIII:** 275

Miles, Julie, **I:** 199

Miles, Kitty, **I:** 199

"Miles of Night, The" (Halliday), **Supp. XIX:** 91

Milestone, Lewis, **Supp. I Part 1:** 281

Milestones (Kramer), **Supp. XXVI:** 26

Miles Wallingford (Cooper). *See Afloat and Ashore* (Cooper)

Milford, Kate, **Supp. XVIII:** 150

Milford, Nancy, **II:** 83; **Supp. IX:** 60

Milhaud, Darius, **Supp. IV Part 1:** 81

Miligate, Michael, **IV:** 123, 130, 132

"Militant Nudes" (Hardwick), **Supp. III Part 1:** 210–211

"Military Parachuting Exercise" (Huddle), **Supp. XXVI:** 150, 153

Milk (film), **Supp. XX: 269**

"Milk Bottles" (Anderson), **I:** 114

"Milk Prose" (Weigl), **Supp. XIX:** 278

Milk Train Doesn't Stop Here Anymore, The (T. Williams), **IV:** 382, 383, 384, 386, 390, 391, 392, 393, 394, 395, 398

Mill, James, **II:** 357

Mill, John Stuart, **III:** 294–295; **Supp. XI:** 196; **Supp. XIV:** 22

Millar, Kenneth. *See* Macdonald, Ross

Millar, Margaret (Margaret Sturm), **Supp. IV Part 2:** 464, 465

Millay, Cora, **III:** 123, 133–134, 135–136

Millay, Edna St. Vincent, **I:** 482; **II:** 530; **III: 122–144; IV:** 433, 436; **Retro. Supp. II:** 48; **Supp. I Part 2:** 707, 714, 726; **Supp. IV Part 1:** 168; **Supp. IV Part 2:** 607; **Supp. IX:** 20; **Supp. V:** 113; **Supp. XIV:** 120, 121, 122, 127; **Supp. XV:** 42, 46, 51, 250, 293, 307; **Supp. XVII:** 69, 75, 96; **Supp. XXII:** 273; **Supp. XXIII:** 164; **Supp. XXVI:** 170, 171; **Supp. XXVII:** 261, 283, 284

Millennium Approaches (Kushner), **Supp. IX:** 141, 142, 145

Miller, Arthur, **I:** 81, 94; **III: 145–169; Supp. IV Part 1:** 359; **Supp. IV Part 2:** 574; **Supp. VIII:** 334; **Supp. XIII:** 127; **Supp. XIV:** 102, 239; **Supp. XVI:** 194

Miller, Mrs. Arthur (Ingeborg Morath), **III:** 162–163

Miller, Mrs. Arthur (Marilyn Monroe), **III:** 161, 162–163

Miller, Mrs. Arthur (Mary Grace Slattery), **III:** 146, 161

Miller, Brown, **Supp. IV Part 1:** 67

Miller, Carol, **Supp. IV Part 1:** 400, 405, 409, 410, 411

Miller, Caroline, **Supp. XXII: 187–201**

Miller, Henry, **I:** 97, 157; **III:** 40, **170–192; IV:** 138; **Retro. Supp. II:** 327; **Supp. I Part 2:** 546; **Supp. V:** 119, 131; **Supp. X:** 183, 185, 187, 194, 195; **Supp. XIII:** 1, 17; **Supp. XXII:** 88, 256, 257, 258; **Supp. XXIII:** 100; **Supp. XXIV:** 52, 281

Miller, Henry (actor), **Supp. XVI:** 182

Miller, Herman, **Supp. I Part 2:** 614, 617

Miller, James E., Jr., **IV:** 352

Miller, Jean Baker, **Supp. XXII:** 18

Miller, Jeffrey, **Supp. IV Part 1:** 95

Miller, J. Hillis, **Supp. IV Part 1:** 387

Miller, Jim Wayne, **Supp. XX: 161–176; Supp. XXIII:** 39

Miller, Joaquin, **I:** 193, 195, 459; **Supp. II Part 1:** 351

Miller, John Duncan, **Supp. I Part 2:** 604

Miller, John E., **Supp. XXII:** 295

Miller, John M., **Supp. XXII:** 214, 218

Miller, Jonathan, **Retro. Supp. II:** 181

Miller, Laura, **Supp. XIII:** 48; **Supp. XIX:** 53, 54, 56; **Supp. XXII:** 239; **Supp. XXV:** 12, 13

Miller, Marilyn, **Supp. XVI:** 187

Miller, Matt, **Supp. XV:** 211

Miller, Matthew, **Supp. XVI:** 47, 51

Miller, Orilla, **Supp. I Part 1:** 48

Miller, Perry, **I:** 546, 547, 549, 550, 560; **IV:** 186; **Supp. I Part 1:** 31, 104; **Supp. I Part 2:** 484; **Supp. IV Part 2:** 422; **Supp. VIII:** 101; **Supp. XXV:** 251

Miller, R. Baxter, **Retro. Supp. I:** 195, 207

Miller, Robert Ellis, **II:** 588

Miller, Ruth, **Supp. X:** 324

Miller, Stuart, **Supp. XVI:** 242

Miller, Sue, **Supp. X:** 77, 85; **Supp. XI:** 190; **Supp. XII: 289–305**

Miller of Old Church, The (Glasgow), **II:** 175, 181

"Miller's Tale" (Chaucer), **III:** 283

Miller Williams and the Poetry of the Particular (Burns), **Supp. XV:** 339

Millett, Kate, **Supp. X:** 193, 196

Millgate, Michael, **Retro. Supp. I:** 91

Mill Hand's Lunch Bucket (Bearden), **Supp. VIII:** 337

Millhauser, Steven, **Supp. XXII:** 49

Millier, Brett C., **Retro. Supp. II:** 39

Milligan, Bryce, **Supp. XIII:** 274, 275, 277

Million Little Pieces, A (Frey), **Supp. XXII:** 95; **Supp. XXIII:** 109; **Supp. XXIV:** 230, 236

Millions of Strange Shadows (Hecht), **Supp. X:** 57, **62–65**

"Million Young Workmen, 1915, A" (Sandburg), **III:** 585

Millroy the Magician (Theroux), **Supp. VIII:** 325

Mills, Alice, **Supp. XIII:** 233

Mills, Benjamin Fay, **III:** 176

Mills, C. Wright, **Supp. I Part 2:** 648, 650

Mills, Florence, **Supp. I Part 1:** 322

Mills, Ralph J., Jr., **III:** 530; **Supp. IV Part 1:** 64; **Supp. XI:** 311

Mills, Tedi López, **Supp. XVI:** 281

Mills of the Kavanaughs, The (R. Lowell), **II:** 542–543, 546, 550; **III:** 508; **Retro. Supp. II:** 178, 179, 188; **Supp. XXIII:** 211

"Mills of the Kavanaughs, The" (R. Lowell), **II:** 542–543

Milne, A. A., **Supp. IX:** 189; **Supp. XXIV:** 132, 133

Milne, A. J. M., **I:** 278

Milosz, Czeslaw, **Supp. III Part 2:** 630; **Supp. VIII:** 20, 22; **Supp. XI:** 267, 312; **Supp. XVII:** 241; **Supp. XX: 165; Supp. XXI:** 132; **Supp. XXII:** 92; **Supp. XXIII:** 134, 140

Miltner, Robert, **Supp. XI:** 142

Milton, Edith, **Supp. VIII:** 79; **Supp. X:** 82

Milton, John, **I:** 6, 138, 273, 587–588; **II:** 11, 15, 113, 130, 411, 540, 542; **III:** 40, 124, 201, 225, 274, 468, 471, 486, 487, 503, 511; **IV:** 50, 82, 126, 137, 155, 157, 241, 279, 347, 422, 461, 494; **Retro. Supp. I:** 60, 67, 127, 360; **Retro. Supp. II:** 161, 295; **Supp. I Part 1:** 124, 150, 370; **Supp. I Part 2:** 412, 422, 491, 501, 522, 622, 722, 724; **Supp. IV Part 2:** 430, 634; **Supp. VIII:** 294; **Supp. X:** 22, 23, 36; **Supp. XII:** 180; **Supp. XIV:** 5, 7; **Supp. XX: 108; Supp. XXIII:** 122; **Supp. XXIV:** 159

Milton, John R., **Supp. IV Part 2:** 503

Milton and His Modern Critics (L. P. Smith), **Supp. XIV:** 347

"Milton by Firelight" (Snyder), **Supp. II Part 1:** 314; **Supp. VIII:** 294

"Miltonic Sonnet, A" (Wilbur), **Supp. III Part 2:** 558

Mimesis (Auerbach), **III:** 453

"Mimnermos and the Motions of Hedonism" (Carson), **Supp. XII: 99–100**

"Mimnermos Interviews, The" (Carson), **Supp. XII: 100–101**

Mims, Edwin, **Supp. I Part 1:** 362, 364, 365, 371

"Mind" (Wilbur), **Supp. III Part 2:** 554

"Mind, The" (Kinnell), **Supp. III Part 1:** 245

Mind Breaths: Poems 1972–1977 (Ginsberg), **Supp. II Part 1:** 326

Mindfield: New and Selected Poems (Corso), **Supp. XII: 136**

"Mind in the Modern World" (Trilling), **Supp. III Part 2:** 512

"Mind Is Shapely, Art Is Shapely" (Ginsberg), **Supp. II Part 1:** 327

Mindlin, Henrique, **Supp. I Part 1:** 92

Mind of My Mind (O. Butler), **Supp. XIII:** 62, 63

Mind of Primitive Man, The (Boas), **Supp. XIV:** 209

Mind-Reader, The (Wilbur), **Supp. III Part 2:** 560–562

"Mind-Reader, The" (Wilbur), **Supp. III Part 2:** 561–562

"Mind's Landscape on an Early Winter Day, The" (Bronk), **Supp. XXI:** 28

"Mind's Own Place, The" (Oppen), **Supp. XXVI:** 227

Mindwheel (Pinsky), **Supp. VI:** 235

Minear, Richard H., **Supp. XVI:** 101, 102

"Mined Country" (Wilbur), **Supp. III Part 2:** 546–548

"Minefields" (Espaillat), **Supp. XXI:** 106

"Mine Own John Berryman" (Levine), **Supp. V:** 179–180

Miner, Bob, **Supp. V:** 23

Miner, Earl, **III:** 466, 479

Miner, Madonne, **Supp. XIII:** 29

Miner, Valerie, **Supp. XXIII:** 295, 296

"Minerva Writes Poems" (Cisneros), **Supp. VII:** 63–64, 66

Mingus, Charles, **Supp. IX:** 152

"Mingus in Diaspora" (Matthews), **Supp. IX:** 166

"Mingus in Shadow" (Matthews), **Supp. IX:** 168–169

Ming Yellow (Marquand), **III:** 56

"Minimal, The" (Roethke), **III:** 531–532

Minimus Poems, The (X. J. Kennedy), **Supp. XV:** 169–170

"Mini-novela: *Rosa y sus espinas*" (Mora), **Supp. XIII:** 218

"Minions of Midas, The" (London), **II:** 474–475

Minister's Charge, The, or The Apprenticeship of Lemuel Barber (Howells), **II:** 285–286, 287

Minister's Wooing, The (Stowe), **II:** 541

"Minister's Wooing, The" (Stowe), **Supp. I Part 2:** 592–595

"Ministration of Our Departed Friends, The" (Stowe), **Supp. I Part 2:** 586–587

Minna and Myself (Bodenheim), **Supp. XXV:** 21

"Minneapolis Poem, The" (Wright), **Supp. III Part 2:** 601–602

Minnesota Grain Show, The (radio, Keillor), **Supp. XVI:** 170

"Minnesota Transcendentalist" (Peseroff), **Supp. IV Part 1:** 71

Minnie, Temple, **II:** 344

Minock, Daniel, **Supp. XXVI:** 187

Minority Report: H. L. Mencken's Notebooks (Mencken), **III:** 112

Minor Pleasures of Life, The (Macaulay), **Supp. XIV:** 348

"Minor Poems" (Eliot), **I:** 579

"Minor Poet" (Hay), **Supp. XIV:** 127

"Minor Topics" (Howells), **II:** 274

Minot, Stephen, **Supp. XXIII:** 290

Minot, Susan, **Supp. VI: 203–215**

"Minotaur Loves His Labyrinth, The" (Simic), **Supp. VIII:** 270, 279, 281

"Minstrel Man" (Hughes), **Supp. I Part 1:** 325

Mint (Nye), **Supp. XIII:** 277

"Minting Time" (Sarton), **Supp. VIII:** 259

Mint Snowball (Nye), **Supp. XIII:** 277–278, **284–285**

"Mint Snowball" (Nye), **Supp. XIII:** 278, 284

"Mint Snowball II" (Nye), **Supp. XIII:** 284, 285

Minty Alley (C. L. R. James), **Supp. XXI:** 159, 161

Mintz, Susannah B., **Supp. XXVI:** 52

Mintzlaff, Dorothy, **Supp. XV:** 153

Minus, Marian, **Supp. XVIII:** 282

Minutes to Go (Corso, Gysin, Beiles and Burroughs), **Supp. XII:** 129

Mi querido Rafa (Hinojosa). *See Dear Rafe* (Hinojosa)

Mirabai: Ecstatic Poems (Hirshfield and Bly, trans.), **Supp. XXIII:** 136

Mirabell: Books of Number (Merrill), **Supp. III Part 1:** 332–334

"Miracle" (Carver), **Supp. III Part 1:** 139–140

Miracle at St. Anna (film, Lee), **Supp. XXVI:** 199

Miracle at St. Anna (McBride), **Supp. XXVI:** 194–199

Miracle at Verdun (Chlumberg), **Supp. XIX:** 242

Miracle Boy and Other Stories (P. Benedict), **Supp. XXIII:** 35, **45–50**

"Miracle Boy"(P. Benedict), **Supp. XXIII:** 45–46, 50

"Miracle for Breakfast, A" (Bishop), **Retro. Supp. II:** 43

Miracle of Catfish, A (L. Brown), **Supp. XXI:** 39–40, 47, **48**

"Miracle of Lava Canyon, The" (Henry), **Supp. II Part 1:** 389, 390

Miracle of Mindfulness, The: A Manual on Meditation (Thich Nhat Hanh), **Supp. V:** 199–200

Mirage (Masters), **Supp. I Part 2:** 459, 470, 471

"Mirages, The" (Hayden), **Supp. II Part 1:** 373

"Miranda" (Buck), **Supp. II Part 1:** 128

Miranda, Carmen, **Supp. XII:** 165

Miranda, Francisco de, **Supp. I Part 2:** 522

"Miranda Over the Valley" (Dubus), **Supp. VII:** 81–83

"Miriam" (Capote), **Supp. III Part 1:** 117, 120, 122

"Miriam" (Whittier), **Supp. I Part 2:** 691, 703

"Miriam Tazewell" (Ransom), **Supp. X:** 58

"Mirror" (Merrill), **Supp. III Part 1:** 322

"Mirror" (Plath), **Retro. Supp. II:** 248–249, 257

"Mirror" (Rash), **Supp. XXVII:** 222

"Mirror, The" (Glück), **Supp. V:** 83

"Mirror, The"(Hadas), **Supp. XXIII:** 116

"Mirroring Evil: Nazi Images/Recent Art" (Epstein), **Supp. XII:** 166

"Mirror of Leopold Leopoldovitch Siegelevsky, The" (Siegel), **Supp. XXII:** 257–258

Mirrors (Creeley), **Supp. IV Part 1:** 156

Mirrors and Windows (Nemerov), **III:** 269, 275–277

Mirrors of Astonishment (Hadas), **Supp. XXIII:** 115–116

"Mirrors of Chartres Street" (Faulkner), **II:** 56

"Mirrors of Tuzun Thune, The" (Howard), **Supp. XXVII:** 123

Mirsky, Norman, **Supp. XX:** 244

Mirvis, Tova, **Supp. XX:** 177–191

Misanthrope, The (Molière; Wilbur, trans.), **Supp. III Part 2:** 552, 560

Miscellaneous Poems (Rowson), **Supp. XV:** 243

Miscellaneous Works of Mr. Philip Freneau, Containing His Essays and Additional Poems (Freneau), **Supp. II Part 1:** 263, 264, 266

Miscellany of American Poetry, A (Untermeyer, ed.), **Supp. XV:** 305, 310

Misérables, Les (Hugo), **II:** 179; **Supp. I Part 1:** 280

Misery (King), **Supp. V:** 140, 141, 142, 147–148, 151, 152

Mises, Ludwig von, **Supp. IV Part 2:** 524

Misfits, The (A. Miller), **III:** 147, 149, 156, 161–162, 163

Misfit: The Strange Life of Frederick Exley (Yardley), **Supp. XXIII:** 97

Mish, Jeanetta Calhoun, **Supp. XXVI:** 112

"Mishōsha, or the Magician and his daughters: A Chippewa Tale"(J. Schoolcraft), **Supp. XXIII:** 234, 235

"Misogamist, The" (Dubus), **Supp. VII:** 86–87

Misread City, The: New Literary Los Angeles (Gioia and Timberg, eds.), **Supp. XV:** 116

Misrepresentations Corrected, and Truth Vindicated, in a Reply to the Rev. Mr. Solomon Williams's Book (Edwards), **I:** 549

Miss Crandall's School for Young Ladies & Little Misses of Color (Nelson and Alexander), **Supp. XVIII:** 171, 175, 181, **185–186**

"Miss Cynthie" (R. Fisher), **Supp. XIX:** 65, 69

Miss Doll, Go Home (Markson), **Supp. XVII:** 138

"Miss Ella" (Z. Fitzgerald), **Supp. IX:** 57, 59, **71–72**

"Miss Emily and the Bibliographer" (Tate), **Supp. II Part 1:** 103

"Miss Furr and Miss Skeene" (Stein), **IV:** 29–30

"Missing Child" (Simic), **Supp. VIII:** 282

"Missing in Action" (Komunyakaa), **Supp. XIII:** 123, 124

Missing/Kissing: Missing Marisa, Kissing Christine (Shanley), **Supp. XIV:** 316

Missing Link (X. J. Kennedy), **Supp. XV:** 165

Missing Link, The (Wells), **Supp. XXVI:** 281

"Missing Poem, The" (Halliday), **Supp. XIX:** 93–94

"Missionary Brings a Young Native to America, A" (H. Johnson), **Supp. XXVI:** 167, 173, 174

"Mission of Jane, The" (Wharton), **Retro. Supp. I:** 367

"Missions, The" (Rodriguez), **Supp. XIV:** 303

Mission to Moscow (film), **Supp. I Part 1:** 281

"Mississippi" (Bass), **Supp. XVI:** 17

"Mississippi" (Faulkner), **Retro. Supp. I:** 77

"Mississippi" (Simpson), **Supp. IX:** 271

"Miss Kate in H-1" (Twain), **IV:** 193

Miss Kelly (Holding), **Supp. XXII:** 133–134

Miss Leonora When Last Seen (Taylor), **Supp. V:** 323

Miss Lonelyhearts (West), **I:** 107; **II:** 436; **III:** 357; **IV:** 287, 288, 290–297, 300, 301, 305, 306; **Retro. Supp. II:** 321, 322, 325, 328, **332–335**

"Miss Lora" (Díaz), **Supp. XXIV:** 86

Miss Mamma Aimee (Caldwell), **I:** 308, 309, 310

"Miss Mary Pask" (Wharton), **IV:** 316; **Retro. Supp. I:** 382

"Miss McEnders" (Chopin), **Retro. Supp. II:** 67

Miss Morissa: Doctor of the Gold Trail (Sandoz), **Supp. XXIV:** 244, **255–256**

"Missoula Softball Tournament" (Hugo), **Supp. VI:** 132

Miss Pinkerton (Rinehart), **Supp. XXV:** 197

Miss Ravenel's Conversion from Secession to Loyalty (De Forest), **IV:** 350

Miss Saigon (musical), **Supp. XXI:** 155

"Miss Tempy's Watchers" (Jewett), **II:** 401; **Retro. Supp. II:** 139

"Miss Terriberry to Wed in Suburbs" (Updike), **Retro. Supp. I:** 335

"Miss Urquhart's Tiara" (Jarman), **Supp. XVII:** 116

Miss Witherspoon (Durang), **Supp. XXIV:** 113, **126**

"Mist, The" (King), **Supp. V:** 144

"Mistaken Charity, A" (Freeman), **Retro. Supp. II:** 138

"Mister Brother" (Cunningham), **Supp. XV:** 68

Misterioso (Sorrentino), **Supp. XXI:** 236, 237

"Mister Toussan" (Ellison), **Retro. Supp. II:** 124–125; **Supp. II Part 1:** 238

"Mistress of Sydenham Plantation, The" (Jewett), **Retro. Supp. II:** 141

Mitcham, Matthew, **Supp. XX:** 264

Mitchell, Burroughs, **Supp. XI:** 218, 222, 227

Mitchell, David, **Supp. XXIV:** 86

Mitchell, Don, **Supp. XXII:** 207, 211, 212

Mitchell, Joan, **Supp. XXIII:** 210

Mitchell, Margaret, **II:** 177; **Supp. XX:** 243; **Supp. XXII:** 195

Mitchell, Pat, **Supp. XXIV:** 35, 42; **Supp. XXVII:** 18, 24

Mitchell, Roger, **Supp. IV Part 1:** 70; **Supp. XV:** 213, 215

Mitchell, Dr. S. Weir, **IV:** 310

Mitchell, Tennessee. *See* Anderson, Mrs. Sherwood (Tennessee Mitchell)

Mitchell, Verner, **Supp. XVIII:** 281, 286

Mitchell, Werner, **Supp. XXVI:** 165, 170, 171–172, 174

Mitchell, Wesley C., **Supp. I Part 2:** 632, 643

"Mitchie-Gawa" (Taggard), **Supp. XXII:** 272

Mitch Miller (Masters), **Supp. I Part 2:** 456, 466, 469–471, 474, 475, 476

Mitchum, Robert, **Supp. IX:** 95, 250

Mitgang, Herbert, **Supp. IV Part 1:** 220, 226, 307; **Supp. VIII:** 124; **Supp. XIX:** 251; **Supp. XX:** 243

Mitla Pass (Uris), **Supp. XX:** 244, 247, **248, 256**

Mixed Company: Collected Short Stories (Shaw), **Supp. XIX:** 251

"Mixed Sequence" (Roethke), **III:** 547

Miyazawa Kenji, **Supp. VIII:** 292

Mizener, Arthur, **II:** 77, 81, 84, 94; **IV:** 132; **Supp. XVIII:** 249

Mizner, Addison, **Supp. XVI:** 191

Mizner, Wilson, **Supp. XVI:** 191, 195

Mladenoff, Nancy, **Supp. X:** 176

"M'liss: An Idyl of Red Mountain" (Harte), **Supp. II Part 1:** 339

"Mnemonic Devices" (Goldbarth), **Supp. XII:** 183

"Mnemosyne" (Hölderlin), **Supp. XXIV:** 152

"Mobile in Back of the Smithsonian, The" (Swenson), **Supp. IV Part 2:** 646

Mobilio, Albert, **Supp. VIII:** 3; **Supp. XIX:** 45; **Supp. XVIII:** 144

Moby Dick (film), **Supp. IV Part 1:** 102, 116

Moby Dick; or, The Whale (Melville), **I:** 106, 354; **II:** 33, 224–225, 236, 539–540; **III:** 28–29, 74, 75, 77, 81, 82, 83–86, 87, 89, 90, 91, 93, 94, 95, 359, 453, 556; **IV:** 57, 199, 201, 202; **Retro. Supp. I:** 160, 220, 243, 244, 248, **249–253,** 254, 256, 257, 335; **Retro. Supp. II:** 121, 186, 275; **Supp. I Part 1:** 249; **Supp. I Part 2:** 579; **Supp. IV Part 2:** 613; **Supp. V:** 281; **Supp. VIII:** 106, 188, 198; **Supp. XXI:** 159; **Supp. XXII:** 81, 268; **Supp. XXIV:** 88

Mock, John, **Supp. XIII:** 174

"Mocking-Bird, The" (Bierce), **I:** 202

"Mock Orange" (Glück), **Supp. V:** 84–85

Modarressi, Mitra, **Supp. IV Part 2:** 657

"Model Father" (Huddle), **Supp. XXVI:** 150

Models of Misrepresentation: On the Fiction of E. L. Doctorow (Morris), **Supp. IV Part 1:** 231

Model World and Other Stories, A (Chabon), **Supp. XI:** 66

Modern American and British Poetry (Untermeyer, ed.), **Supp. XV:** 306

Modern American Poetry (Untermeyer, ed.), **Supp. XV:** 293, 303, 306, 312

Modern American Poets (Aiken, ed.), **Supp. XXVI:** 225

Modern American Verse (Untermeyer, ed.), **Supp. XV:** 301

Modern Brazilian Architecture (Bishop, trans.), **Supp. I Part 1:** 92

Modern British Poetry (Untermeyer, ed.), **Supp. XV:** 305, 308, 312

Modern Fiction Studies, **Supp. V:** 238

Modern Fiction Studies (Haegert), **Supp. XVI:** 69

"Modern Greek for 'Nightmare' Is *Ephialtes,* The" (Stallings), **Supp. XXV:** 233

Modern Instance a Novel, A (Howells), **II:** 275, 279, 282–283, 285

Modern Library, The, **Retro. Supp. I:** 112, 113

Modern Mephistopheles, A (Alcott), **Supp. I Part 1:** 37–38

Modern Poetic Sequence, The (Rosenthal), **Supp. V:** 333

"Modern Poetry" (Crane), **I:** 390

Modern Poetry and the Tradition (Brooks), **Supp. XIV:** 5–7

"Modern Primer: Helpful Hints to Tell Appearances from Truth" (Taubman), **Supp. XXV:** 106

"Modern Race Creeds and Their Fallacies" (Locke), **Supp. XIV:** 210

Modern Rhetoric, with Readings (Brooks and Warren), **Supp. XIV:** 11

"Modern Sorcery" (Simic), **Supp. VIII:** 283

Modern Times (album, Dylan), **Supp. XVIII:** 28, 31, 33

"Modern Times" (Zukofsky), **Supp. III Part 2:** 624

Modern Writer, The (Anderson), **I:** 117

Modersohn, Otto, **Supp. I Part 2:** 573

Modersohn, Mrs. Otto (Paula Becker), **Supp. I Part 2:** 573–574

"Modes of Being" (Levertov), **Supp. III Part 1:** 282

Modest Enquiry into the Nature and Necessity of a Paper-Currency, A (Franklin), **II:** 108–109

"Modest Proposal, A" (Swift), **I:** 295; **Retro. Supp. II:** 287

"Modest Proposal with Feline Feeling, A" (Neugeboren), **Supp. XVI:** 219

"Modest Self-Tribute, A" (Wilson), **IV:** 431, 432

Modigliani, Amedeo, **Supp. XXVI:** 259

Moeller, Philip, **III:** 398, 399

"Moench von Berchtesgaden, Der" (Voss), **I:** 199–200

Moers, Ellen, **Retro. Supp. II:** 99

Moe's Villa and Other Stories (Purdy), **Supp. VII:** 270, 280

Moffat, Juan, **Supp. XX:** 52

Moffet, Penelope, **Supp. XXIV:** 165, 167

Mogen, David, **Supp. IV Part 1:** 106

Mohammed, **I:** 480; **II:** 1

Mohawk (Russo), **Supp. XII:** 326–328

Moir, William Wilmerding, **Supp. V:** 279

Mojo Hand (Phillips), **Supp. XXIII:** 174

Moldaw, Carol, **Supp. XV:** 264; **Supp. XVII:** 127, 130

"Moles" (Oliver), **Supp. VII:** 235

Molesworth, Charles, **Supp. IV Part 1:** 39; **Supp. VIII:** 292, 306; **Supp. XIX:** 121–122

Molière (Jean-Baptiste Poquelin), **III:** 113; **Supp. I Part 2:** 406; **Supp. III Part 2:** 552, 560; **Supp. IV Part 2:** 585; **Supp. V:** 101

"Molino Rojo, El" (Ríos), **Supp. IV Part 2:** 544

Moll Flanders (Defoe), **Supp. V:** 127; **Supp. XIII:** 43

"Molloch in State Street" (Whittier), **Supp. I Part 2:** 687

"Moll Pitcher" (Whittier), **Supp. I Part 2:** 684

"Molly Brant, Iroquois Matron" (Gunn Allen), **Supp. IV Part 1:** 331

"Molly Brant to Willie"(Kenny), **Supp. XXIII:** 153

Molnar, Ferenc, **Supp. XVI:** 187

"Moloch" (H. Miller), **III:** 177

Momaday, N. Scott, **Supp. IV Part 1:** 274, 323, 324, 404; **Supp. IV Part 2:** **479–496,** 504, 557, 562; **Supp. XII:** 209; **Supp. XVIII:** 58

" 'Momentary Stay against Confusion,' A: Frank Conroy's *Stop-Time*" (T. Adams), **Supp. XVI:** 69

Moment of Untruth (Lacy), **Supp. XV:** 206, 207

Moments of the Italian Summer (Wright), **Supp. III Part 2:** 602

Moment to Moment: Poems of a Mountain Recluse (Budbill), **Supp. XIX:** 2, 7, **9–10**

"Momus" (Robinson), **III:** 508

Monaghan, Charles, **Supp. XIX:** 155

Monaghan, Pat, **Supp. XI:** 121

Monaghan, Patricia, **Supp. XVII:** 76, 123, 127, 129

Mona Lisa Overdrive (W. Gibson), **Supp. XVI:** 119, 120, **127–128**

"Mon Ami" (Bourne), **I:** 227

Monday Night (Boyle), **Supp. XXIV:** 54

Monet, Claude, **Retro. Supp. I:** 378

"Monet's 'Waterlilies' " (Hayden), **Supp. II Part 1:** 361–362

Monette, Paul, **Supp. X:** **145–161**

Money (Amis), **Retro. Supp. I:** 278

"Money" (Matthews), **Supp. IX:** 166

"Money" (Nemerov), **III:** 287

Money, Money, Money (Wagoner), **Supp. IX:** 324, **333–334**

Moneyball: The Art of Winning an Unfair Game (M. Lewis), **Supp. XVII:** 210

Moneychangers, The (Sinclair), **Supp. V:** 285

Money Writes! (Sinclair), **Supp. V:** 277

Monica, Saint, **IV:** 140

Monikins, The (Cooper), **I:** 348, 354

Monk, Craig, **Supp. XXIV:** 64

Monk, Thelonious, **Supp. XVIII:** 62

Monk and the Hangman's Daughter, The (Bierce), **I:** 199–200, 209

"Monkey" (Weigl), **Supp. XIX:** 278

Monkey Business (screenplay, Hecht), **Supp. XXVII:** 91, 94

"Monkey Garden, The" (Cisneros), **Supp. VII:** 63

"Monkey Puzzle, The" (Moore), **III:** 194, 207, 211

Monkeys (Minot), **Supp. VI:** 203–205, **206–210**

"Monkeys, The" (Moore), **III:** 201, 202

Monkey Wars, The (Weigl), **Supp. XIX:** 276, 278–280

Monkey Wrench Gang, The (Abbey), **Supp. VIII:** 42; **Supp. XIII:** **9–11,** 16

"Monk of Casal-Maggiore, The" (Longfellow), **II:** 505

"Monocle de Mon Oncle, Le" (Stevens), **IV:** 78, 84; **Retro. Supp. I:** 301; **Supp. III Part 1:** 20; **Supp. X:** 58

"Monody to the Sound of Zithers" (Boyle), **Supp. XXIV:** 63

"Monolog from a Mattress" (Untermeyer), **Supp. XV:** 307

"Monologue for Mothers" (Taggard), **Supp. XXII:** 279

"Mon Plaisir" (July), **Supp. XXIV:** 205–206

Monro, Harold, **III:** 465; **Retro. Supp. I:** 127; **Supp. XV:** 296

Monroe, Harriet, **I:** 235, 384, 390, 393; **III:** 458, 581, 586; **IV:** 74; **Retro. Supp. I:** 58, 131; **Retro. Supp. II:** 82, 83; **Supp. I Part 1:** 256, 257, 258, 262, 263, 267; **Supp. I Part 2:** 374, 387, 388, 464, 610, 611, 613, 614, 615, 616; **Supp. XIV:** 286; **Supp. XV:** 43, 299, 302; **Supp. XXV:** 18; **Supp. XXVII:** 283, 286, 289–290, 297

Monroe, James, **Supp. I Part 2:** 515, 517
Monroe, Lucy, **Retro. Supp. II:** 70
Monroe, Marilyn, **III:** 161, 162–163; **Supp. XXVII:** 95
Monroe's Embassy; or, the Conduct of the Government in Relation to Our Claims to the Navigation of the Mississippi (Brown), **Supp. I Part 1:** 146
Monson, Ander, **Supp. XXIV: 229–242**
"Monsoon Season" (Komunyakaa), **Supp. XIII:** 122
Monsour, Leslie, **Supp. XV:** 125
Monster (graphic novel, Myers), **Supp. XXVII:** 199, 202, 203, 204, 205
"Monster, The" (Crane), **I:** 418
Monster, The, and Other Stories (Crane), **I:** 409
"Monstro" (Díaz), **Supp. XXIV:** 86
Montage of a Dream Deferred (Hughes), **Retro. Supp. I:** 194, **208–209; Supp. I Part 1:** 333, 339–341
Montagu, Ashley, **Supp. I Part 1:** 314
"Montaigne" (Emerson), **II:** 6
Montaigne, Michel de, **II:** 1, 5, 6, 8, 14–15, 16, 535; **III:** 600; **Retro. Supp. I:** 247; **Supp. XIV:** 105; **Supp. XXI:** 111, 205; **Supp. XXVI:** 39
Montale, Eugenio, **Supp. III Part 1:** 320; **Supp. V:** 337–338; **Supp. VIII:** 30; **Supp. XV:** 112
Montalembert, Hughes de, **Supp. XV:** 349
"Montana Memory" (Maclean), **Supp. XIV:** 221
"Montana; or the End of Jean-Jacques Rousseau" (Fiedler), **Supp. XIII: 97–98**
"Montana Ranch Abandoned" (Hugo), **Supp. VI:** 139
"Mont Blanc" (Shelley), **Supp. IX:** 52
Montcalm, Louis Joseph de, **Supp. I Part 2:** 498
Montcalm and Wolfe (Parkman), **Supp. II Part 2:** 596, 609, 610, 611–613
Montemarano, Nicholas, **Supp. XVI:** 227
Montgomery, Benilde, **Supp. XIII:** 202
Montgomery, George, **Supp. XXIII:** 209
Montgomery, Robert, **Supp. I Part 2:** 611; **Supp. IV Part 1:** 130
Month of Sundays, A (Updike), **Retro. Supp. I:** 325, 327, 329, 330, 331, 333, 335
Monti, Luigi, **II:** 504
Montoya, José, **Supp. IV Part 2:** 545
"Montrachet-le-Jardin" (Stevens), **IV:** 82
Mont-Saint-Michel and Chartres (Adams), **I:** 1, 9, 12–14, 18, 19, 21; **Supp. I Part 2:** 417
Montserrat (Hellman), **Supp. I Part 1:** 283–285
Montserrat (Robles), **Supp. I Part 1:** 283–285
"Monument, The" (Bishop), **Supp. I Part 1:** 89
Monument, The (Strand), **Supp. IV Part 2:** 629, 630
"Monument in Utopia, A" (Schnackenberg), **Supp. XV:** 261, 263
"Monument Mountain" (Bryant), **Supp. I Part 1:** 156, 162

"Monument to After-Thought Unveiled, A" (Frost), **Retro. Supp. I:** 124
Moo (Smiley), **Supp. VI:** 292, **303–305**
Moods (Alcott), **Supp. I Part 1:** 33, 34–35, 43
Moody, Anne, **Supp. IV Part 1:** 11
Moody, Richard, **Supp. I Part 1:** 280
Moody, Rick, **Supp. XXI:** 117; **Supp. XXIV:** 131
Moody, Ron, **Supp. XXII:** 49
Moody, William Vaughn, **III:** 507; **IV:** 26
Moody, Mrs. William Vaughn, **I:** 384; **Supp. I Part 2:** 394
Moody-Freeman, Julie, **Supp. XXIII:** 91, 94, 95
"Moon" (A. Finch), **Supp. XVII:** 77
Moon, Henry Lee, **Supp. XVIII:** 281, 285
"Moon and the Night and the Men, The" (Berryman), **I:** 172
"Moon and the Yew Tree, The" (Plath), **Supp. XXVII:** 296
Moon Crossing Bridge (Gallagher), **Supp. XXIV:** 166, 170
"Moon Deluxe" (F. Barthelme), **Supp. XI:** 26, 27, 33, 36
Mooney, Tom, **I:** 505
"Moon-Face" (London), **II:** 475
Moon-Face and Other Stories (London), **II:** 483
"Moon Flock" (Dickey), **Supp. IV Part 1:** 186
Moon for the Misbegotten, A (O'Neill), **III:** 385, 401, 403, 404
Moon in a Mason Jar (Wrigley), **Supp. XVIII: 295–298**
Moon in Its Flight, The (Sorrentino), **Supp. XXI:** 226
"Moon in Its Flight, The" (Sorrentino), **Supp. XXI:** 229
Moon Is a Gong, The (Dos Passos). *See Garbage Man, The* (Dos Passos)
Moon Is Down, The (Steinbeck), **IV:** 51
Moon Lady, The (Tan), **Supp. X:** 289
"Moonlight Alert" (Winters), **Supp. II Part 2:** 801, 811, 815
"Moonlight: Chickens on a Road" (Wrigley), **Supp. XVIII:** 295–296, 297
"Moonlit Night" (Reznikoff), **Supp. XIV:** 285–286
Moon of the Caribbees, The (O'Neill), **III:** 388
Moon Palace (Auster), **Supp. XII:** 22, 27, **30–32**
"Moonshine" (Komunyakaa), **Supp. XIII:** 127, 128
Moons of Jupiter, The (Munro), **Supp. XXVII:** 182, 187–189
"Moons of Jupiter, The" (Munro), **Supp. XXVII:** 188–189
"Moon Solo" (Laforgue), **Supp. XIII:** 346
Moonstone, The (Collins), **Supp. XX:** 236
Moonstruck (screenplay, Shanley), **Supp. XIV:** 315, 316, **321–324**
"Moon upon her fluent Route, The" (Dickinson), **I:** 471

Moony's Kid Don't Cry (T. Williams), **IV:** 381
Moore, Arthur, **Supp. I Part 1:** 49
Moore, C. L., **Supp. XXV:** 122
Moore, Deborah Dash, **Supp. XX: 246**
Moore, Dennis, **Supp. XXVII:** 275
Moore, George, **I:** 103
Moore, Hannah, **Supp. XV:** 231
Moore, Jack B., **Supp. XXV:** 24, 26, 27
Moore, John Milton, **III:** 193
Moore, Julie L., **Supp. XXIII:** 252
Moore, Lorrie, **Supp. VIII:** 145; **Supp. X: 163–180; Supp. XXV:** 142
Moore, Marianne, **I:** 58, 285, 401, 428; **III: 193–217,** 514, 592–593; **IV:** 74, 75, 76, 91, 402; **Retro. Supp. I:** 416, 417; **Retro. Supp. II:** 39, 44, 48, 50, 82, 178, 179, 243, 244; **Supp. I Part 1:** 84, 89, 255, 257; **Supp. I Part 2:** 707; **Supp. II Part 1:** 21; **Supp. III Part 1:** 58, 60, 63; **Supp. III Part 2:** 612, 626, 627; **Supp. IV Part 1:** 242, 246, 257; **Supp. IV Part 2:** 454, 640, 641; **Supp. XIV:** 124, 130; **Supp. XV:** 306, 307; **Supp. XVII:** 131; **Supp. XXI:** 98; **Supp. XXII:** 273–274
Moore, Marie Lorena. *See* Moore, Lorrie
Moore, MariJo, **Supp. XXVI:** 113
Moore, Mary Tyler, **Supp. V:** 107
Moore, Mary Warner, **III:** 193
Moore, Dr. Merrill, **III:** 506
Moore, Steven, **Supp. IV Part 1:** 279, 283, 284, 285, 287; **Supp. XII:** 151; **Supp. XVII:** 230, 231, 232; **Supp. XXII:** 261, 265
Moore, Sturge, **III:** 459
Moore, Thomas, **II:** 296, 299, 303; **Supp. IX:** 104; **Supp. X:** 114; **Supp. XXIII:** 138
Moore, Virginia, **Supp. XV:** 308
Moorehead, Caroline, **Supp. XIV:** 337
Moorepack, Howard, **Supp. XV:** 199
"Moorings" (Hoffman), **Supp. XVIII:** 87
Moos, Malcolm, **III:** 116, 119
"Moose, The" (Bishop), **Retro. Supp. II:** 50; **Supp. I Part 1:** 73, 93, 94, 95; **Supp. IX:** 45, 46
"Moose Wallow, The" (Hayden), **Supp. II Part 1:** 367
"Moowis, The Indian Coquette"(J. Schoolcraft), **Supp. XXIII:** 234
Mooyart-Doubleday, B. M., **Supp. XXVII:** 135
Mop, Moondance, and the Nagasaki Knights (Myers), **Supp. XXVII:** 206
"Moquihuitzin's Answer" (Everwine), **Supp. XV:** 78
Mora, Pat, **Supp. XIII: 213–232**
Moraga, Cherríe, **Supp. XXIII: 193–206**
"Moral Argument Against Calvinism, The" (Channing), **Supp. XXIV: 73–74,** 75
"Moral Bully, The" (Holmes), **Supp. I Part 1:** 302
"Moral Character, the Practice of Law, and Legal Education" (Hall), **Supp. VIII:** 127
"Moral Equivalent for Military Service, A" (Bourne), **I:** 230

"Moral Equivalent of War, The" (James), **II:** 361; **Supp. I Part 1:** 20

"Moral Imperatives for World Order" (Locke), **Supp. XIV:** 207, 213

Moralités Légendaires (Laforgue), **I:** 573

"Morality and Mercy in Vienna" (Pynchon), **Supp. II Part 2:** 620, 624

"Morality of Indian Hating, The" (Momaday), **Supp. IV Part 2:** 484

"Morality of Poetry, The" (Wright), **Supp. III Part 2:** 596–597, 599

Moral Man and Immoral Society (Niebuhr), **III:** 292, 295–297

"Morals Is Her Middle Name" (Hughes), **Supp. I Part 1:** 338

"Morals of Chess, The" (Franklin), **II:** 121

"Moral Substitute for War, A" (Addams), **Supp. I Part 1:** 20

"Moral Theology of Atticus Finch, The" (Shaffer), **Supp. VIII:** 127

"Moral Thought, A" (Freneau), **Supp. II Part 1:** 262

Moran, Thomas, **Supp. IV Part 2:** 603–604

Moran, William L., **Supp. XXIV:** 150–151, 152

Moran of the Lady Letty (Norris), **II:** 264; **III:** 314, 322, 327, 328, 329, 330, 331, 332, 333

Morath, Ingeborg. *See* Miller, Mrs. Arthur (Ingeborg Morath)

Moravec, Paul, **Supp. XIX:** 123

Moravia, Alberto, **I:** 301

More (Crooker), **Supp. XXIII: 60–62**

Moré, Gonzalo, **Supp. X:** 185

More, Henry, **I:** 132

More, Paul Elmer, **I:** 223–224, 247; **Supp. I Part 2:** 423

Moreau, Gustave, **I:** 66

"More Blues and the Abstract Truth" (Wright), **Supp. XV:** 345

More Boners (Abingdon), **Supp. XVI:** 99

More Conversations with Eudora Welty (Prenshaw, ed.), **Retro. Supp. I:** 340, 341, 342, 343, 344, 352, 353, 354

More Dangerous Thoughts (Ryan as Quin), **Supp. XVIII:** 226, **229–230,** 231, 238

More Die of Heartbreak (Bellow), **Retro. Supp. II:** 31, 33, 34

"More Girl Than Boy" (Komunyakaa), **Supp. XIII:** 117

More I Remember More (Brainard), **Supp. XXVII:** 19

"More Light! More Light! (Hecht), **Supp. X:** 60

"More Like an Extension of the Spirit: Clothing in Lyric Poems"(Hadas), **Supp. XXIII:** 124

"Morella" (Poe), **III:** 412; **Retro. Supp. II:** 270

"More Love in the Western World" (Updike), **Retro. Supp. I:** 327–328, 329

"Morels" (W. J. Smith), **Supp. XIII: 336–339**

Moreno, Gary, **Supp. XV:** 5

"More Observations Now" (Conroy), **Supp. XVI:** 75

"More of a Corpse Than a Woman" (Rukeyser), **Supp. VI:** 280

"More Pleasant Adventures" (Ashbery), **Supp. III Part 1:** 1

More Poems to Solve (Swenson), **Supp. IV Part 2:** 640, 642, 648

More Stately Mansions (O'Neill), **III:** 385, 401, 404–405

"More Than Human" (Chabon), **Supp. XI:** 71–72

More Things Change The More They Stay the Same, The (J. W. Miller), **Supp. XX:** 164

More Tish (Rinehart), **Supp. XXV:** 194

More Triva (L. P. Smith), **Supp. XIV:** 339

Morgan, Edmund S., **IV:** 149; **Supp. I Part 1:** 101, 102; **Supp. I Part 2:** 484

Morgan, Edwin, **Supp. IV Part 2:** 688

Morgan, Emanuel. *See* Bynner, Witter

Morgan, Henry, **II:** 432; **IV:** 63; **Supp. XXV:** 255

Morgan, Jack, **Retro. Supp. II:** 142

Morgan, J. P., **I:** 494; **III:** 14, 15

Morgan, Judith, **Supp. XVI:** 103

Morgan, Neil, **Supp. XVI:** 103

Morgan, Robert, **Supp. V:** 5; **Supp. XX: 161, 162**

Morgan, Robin, **Supp. I Part 2:** 569

Morgan, Ted, **Supp. XIV:** 141

Morgan's Passing (Tyler), **Supp. IV Part 2:** 666–667, 668, 669

Morgenstern, Dan, **Supp. XIX:** 159

Morgenthau, Hans, **III:** 291, 309

Morgenthau, Henry, Sr., **Supp. XXIII:** 21, 22, 26, 30

Morgesons, The (E. Stoddard), **Supp. XV:** 270, 273, 274, 278, **279–282,** 283

Morgesons and Other Writings, Published and Unpublished, The (Buell and Zagarell), **Supp. XV:** 269

Moricand, Conrad, **III:** 190

Morison, Samuel Eliot, **Supp. I Part 2: 479–500; Supp. XXII:** 35

Morison, Mrs. Samuel Eliot (Elizabeth Shaw Greene), **Supp. I Part 2:** 483

Morison, Mrs. Samuel Eliot (Priscilla Barton), **Supp. I Part 2:** 493, 496, 497

Morita, Pat, **Supp. XXI:** 146

"Morituri Salutamus" (Longfellow), **II:** 499, 500; **Retro. Supp. II:** 169; **Supp. I Part 2:** 416

"Moriturus" (Millay), **III:** 126, 131–132

Morley, Christopher, **III:** 481, 483, 484; **Supp. I Part 2:** 653; **Supp. IX:** 124

Morley, Edward, **IV:** 27

Morley, Lord John, **I:** 7

Mormon Country (Stegner), **Supp. IV Part 2:** 598, 601–602

"Morning, The" (Updike), **Retro. Supp. I:** 329

"Morning after My Death, The" (Levis), **Supp. XI:** 260, 263–264

"Morning Arrives" (F. Wright), **Supp. XVII:** 244

Morning Face (Stratton-Porter), **Supp. XX: 223**

Morning for Flamingos, A (Burke), **Supp. XIV:** 30, 31, 32

"Morning Glory" (Merrill), **Supp. III Part 1:** 337

Morning Glory, The (R. Bly), **Supp. IV Part 1:** 63–65, 66, 71

"Morning Imagination of Russia, A" (W. C. Williams), **Retro. Supp. I:** 428

Morning in Antibes (Knowles), **Supp. XII:** 249

Morning in the Burned House (Atwood), **Supp. XIII:** 20, 35

Morning Is Near Us, The (Glaspell), **Supp. III Part 1:** 184–185

Morning Noon and Night (Cozzens), **I:** 374, 375, 376, 377, 379, 380

"Morning of the Day They Did It, The" (White), **Supp. I Part 2:** 663

"Morning Prayers" (Harjo), **Supp. XII:** 231

"Morning Roll Call" (Anderson), **I:** 116

"Morning Roudup" (Sorrentino), **Supp. XXI:** 228

"Mornings, I Walk Past the First Cemetery of Athens" (Stallings), **Supp. XXV:** 225

"Morning Shadows" (Skloot), **Supp. XX: 199**

"Mornings in a New House" (Merrill), **Supp. III Part 1:** 327

"Mornings in Ormos"(Hadas), **Supp. XXIII:** 112, 113, 123

Mornings Like This (Dillard), **Supp. VI:** 23, 34

"Morning Song" (Plath), **Retro. Supp. II:** 252; **Supp. XXIII:** 115

Morning Watch, The (Agee), **I:** 25, 39–42

"Morning with Broken Window" (Hogan), **Supp. IV Part 1:** 405

"Moro Like Me" (Goldman), **Supp. XXV:** 51

Morrell, Ottoline, **Retro. Supp. I:** 60

Morris, Bernard E., **Supp. XV:** 154, 169

Morris, Christopher D., **Supp. IV Part 1:** 231, 236

Morris, Gary, **Supp. XXII:** 262

Morris, George Sylvester, **Supp. I Part 2:** 640

Morris, Gouverneur, **Supp. I Part 2:** 512, 517, 518

Morris, Lloyd, **III:** 458

Morris, Robert, **Supp. I Part 2:** 510

Morris, Timothy, **Retro. Supp. I:** 40

Morris, William, **II:** 323, 338, 523; **IV:** 349; **Supp. I Part 1:** 260, 356; **Supp. XI:** 202

Morris, Willie, **Supp. XI:** 216, 231, 234; **Supp. XIX:** 151, 252; **Supp. XXVII:** 269

Morris, Wright, **I:** 305; **III: 218–243,** 558, 572; **IV:** 211

Morrison, Charles Clayton, **III:** 297

Morrison, Jim, **Supp. IV Part 1:** 206

Morrison, Toni, **Retro. Supp. II:** 15, 118; **Supp. III Part 1: 361–381; Supp. IV Part 1:** 2, 13, 14, 250, 253, 257; **Supp. V:** 169, 259; **Supp. VIII:** 213, 214; **Supp. X:** 85, 239, 250, 325; **Supp. XI:** 4, 14, 20, 91; **Supp. XII:** 289, 310; **Supp. XIII:** 60, 185; **Supp. XVI:**

143; **Supp. XVII:** 183; **Supp. XX:** 108; **Supp. XXI:** 172, 243; **Supp. XXII:** 65, 78; **Supp. XXIV:** 183, 184, 185; **Supp. XXV:** 142

Morrison, Tony, **Supp. XXVI:** 14

"Morro Bay" (Jeffers), **Supp. II Part 2:** 422

Morrow, Christopher, **Supp. XXVII:** 216, 225

Morrow, W. C., **I:** 199

Morse, Jedidiah, **Supp. XV:** 243

Morse, Robert, **Supp. XI:** 305

Morse, Samuel F. B., **Supp. I Part 1:** 156

Morse, Samuel French, **Supp. XXI:** 17, 19, 23, 27

Mortal Acts, Mortal Words (Kinnell), **Supp. III Part 1:** 235, 236, 237, 249–254

Mortal Antipathy, A (Holmes), **Supp. I Part 1:** 315–316

"Mortal Enemies" (Humphrey), **Supp. IX:** 109

"Mortal Eternal" (Olds), **Supp. X:** 214

Mortal No, The (Hoffman), **IV:** 113

Mortal Stakes (Parker), **Supp. XIX:** 183–184

Morte D'Arthur, Le (Malory), **Supp. IV Part 1:** 47

Mortmere Stories, The (Isherwood and Upward), **Supp. XIV:** 159

Morton, David, **Supp. IX:** 76

Morton, Jelly Roll, **Supp. X:** 242

Morton, Thomas, **Supp. XXII:** 44, 45, 46

"Mosaic of the Nativity: Serbia, Winter 1993" (Kenyon), **Supp. VII:** 173

Mosby's Memoirs and Other Stories (Bellow), **Retro. Supp. II:** 27

"Moscow, Idaho" (Offutt), **Supp. XIX:** 170

Moscow under Fire (Caldwell), **I:** 296

Moser, Barry, **Supp. XIV:** 223

Moses (Asch), **Supp. XXIII:** 7

Moses (Untermeyer), **Supp. XV: 309**

Moses, Man of the Mountain (Hurston), **Supp. VI:** 149, 158, 160

"Moses on Sinai" (Untermeyer), **Supp. XV:** 300

Mosher, Howard Frank, **Supp. XXII: 203–221**

Moskowitz, Alfred, **Supp. XXI:** 98, 106

Mosle, Sara, **Supp. XI:** 254

Mosley, Walter, **Supp. XIII: 233–252; Supp. XVI:** 143

Mosquito (G. Jones), **Supp. XXIV:** 183, 184, 185, 190, **192–194,** 195

Mosquito Coast, The (film), **Supp. VIII:** 323

Mosquito Coast, The (Theroux), **Supp. VIII:** 321, **322–323**

Mosquitos (Faulkner), **II:** 56; **Retro. Supp. I:** 79, 81

Moss, Howard, **III:** 452; **Supp. IV Part 2:** 642; **Supp. IX:** 39; **Supp. XIII:** 114; **Supp. XV:** 143, 152

Moss, Stanley, **Supp. XI:** 321

Moss, Thylias, **Supp. XI:** 248

Mosses from an Old Manse (Hawthorne), **I:** 562; **II:** 224; **III:** 82, 83; **Retro.**

Supp. I: 157, 248

Moss Mystery, The (Wells), **Supp. XXVI:** 278

"Moss of His Skin" (Sexton), **Supp. II Part 2:** 676

Most, Doug, **Supp. XVIII:** 101

"Most Extraordinary Case, A" (James), **II:** 322; **Retro. Supp. I:** 218

"Most Girl Part of You, The" (Hempel), **Supp. XXI:** 116

Most Likely to Succeed (Dos Passos), **I:** 491

"Most of It, The" (Frost), **Retro. Supp. I:** 121, 125, 129, 139; **Supp. XVIII:** 300

"Most Popular Novels in America, The" (Mabie), **Supp. XVIII:** 257

Motel Chronicles (Shepard), **Supp. III Part 2:** 445

"Mother" (Kooser), **Supp. XIX:** 117, 126, 127

"Mother" (Paley), **Supp. VI: 222–223**

Mother (Schjeldahl), **Supp. XXIV:** 44

"Mother" (Snyder), **Supp. VIII:** 298

Mother (Whistler), **IV:** 369

Mother, The (Buck), **Supp. II Part 1:** 118–119

"Mother and Child #3" (Davison), **Supp. XXVI:** 77

"Mother and Jack and the Rain" (Sexton), **Supp. II Part 2:** 686

"Mother and Son" (Tate), **IV:** 128, 137–138

Mother Country: Britain, the Welfare State and Nuclear Pollution (Robinson), **Supp. XXI:** 211

Mother Courage and Her Children (Brecht), **III:** 160; **Supp. IX:** 140; **Supp. XII:** 249

"Mother Earth: Her Whales" (Snyder), **Supp. VIII:** 302

"Motherhood" (Swenson), **Supp. IV Part 2:** 645

Mother Hubbard (Reed), **Supp. X:** 241

Motherless Brooklyn (Lethem), **Supp. XXII:** 49

Motherless in Brooklyn (Lethem), **Supp. XVIII:** 135, **143–144**

Mother Love (Dove), **Supp. IV Part 1:** 250–251, 254

"Mother Marie Therese" (R. Lowell), **Retro. Supp. II:** 188

Mother Night (Vonnegut), **Supp. II Part 2:** 757, 758, 767, 770, 771

"Mother Rosarine" (Kumin), **Supp. IV Part 2:** 442

"Mothers and Daughters in the Fiction of the New Republic" (Davidson), **Supp. XV:** 238

"Mother's lament for the absence of a child, A"(J. Schoolcraft), **Supp. XXIII:** 236

"Mother Song" (Huddle), **Supp. XXVI:** 151

Mother's Recompense, The (Wharton), **IV:** 321, 324; **Retro. Supp. I:** 382

"Mother's Tale, A" (Agee), **I:** 29–30

"Mother's Things" (Creeley), **Supp. IV Part 1:** 141

"Mother Suite, The"(Crooker), **Supp. XXIII:** 61

"Mother's Voice" (Creeley), **Supp. IV Part 1:** 156

Mother to Daughter, Daughter to Mother (Olsen, ed.), **Supp. XIII:** 295

"Mother Tongue" (Simic), **Supp. VIII:** 283

"Mother to Son" (Hughes), **Retro. Supp. I:** 199, 203; **Supp. I Part 1:** 321–322, 323

Motherwell, Robert, **Supp. XV:** 145; **Supp. XXI:** 125

"Mother Writes to the Murderer, The: A Letter" (Nye), **Supp. XIII:** 276

Moths of the Limberlost (Stratton-Porter), **Supp. XX:** 218

"Motion, The" (Olson), **Supp. II Part 2:** 571

Motion of History, The (Baraka), **Supp. II Part 1:** 55, 56

"Motive for Metaphor, The" (Stevens), **IV:** 89; **Retro. Supp. I:** 310

Motiveless Malignity (Auchincloss), **Supp. IV Part 1:** 31

Motke ganef (Asch), **Supp. XXIII:** 5

Motley, John Lothrop, **Supp. I Part 1:** 299; **Supp. I Part 2:** 479; **Supp. XX: 228, 231**

Motley, Willard, **Supp. XVII: 149–163; Supp. XXIII:** 145

"Motor Car, The" (White), **Supp. I Part 2:** 661

Motor-Flight Through France (Wharton), **I:** 12; **Retro. Supp. I:** 372

Motown and Didi (Myers), **Supp. XXVII:** 204, 211

Mott, Michael, **Supp. VIII:** 204, 208

Motta, Gustavo, **Supp. XXIII:** 125

Mottetti: Poems of Love: The Motets of Eugenio Montale (Montale; Gioia, trans.), **Supp. XV:** 112, **127–128**

Mottke, the Thief (Asch), **Supp. XXIII: 9,** 12

Mottke, the Thief (Asch; tr. Willa and Edwin Muir), **Supp. XXIII:** 5

Mouawad, Nelly, **Supp. XX: 126**

"Mound, The" (Lovecraft and Bishop), **Supp. XXV:** 122

"Mountain, The" (Frost), **Retro. Supp. I:** 121

"Mountain Hermitage, The: Pages from a Japanese Notebook" (Passin), **Supp. XIII:** 337

Mountain Interval (Frost), **II:** 154; **Retro. Supp. I:** 131, 132, 133

"Mountain Lion" (Hogan), **Supp. IV Part 1:** 412

"Mountain Music" essays (Sanders), **Supp. XVI:** 276–277

Mountain on the Desert, The (Richter), **Supp. XVIII:** 216, 219

Mountainous Journey, A (Tuqan), **Supp. XIII:** 278

"Mountains" (Dubus III), **Supp. XXIV:** 101

Mountains, The (Wolfe), **IV:** 461

Mountains and Rivers without End (Snyder), **Supp. VIII:** 295, **305–306**

"Mountains grow unnoticed, The" (Dickinson), **Retro. Supp. I:** 46

Mountains Have Come Closer, The (J. W. Miller), **Supp. XX: 165, 168, 169–170**

Mountains Look Down, The: A History of Chichester, a Company Town in the Catskills (Bennett), **Supp. XXII:** 218

Mountains of California, The (Muir), **Supp. IX:** 183

"Mountain Whippoorwill, The" (Benét), **Supp. XI:** 44–45, 46, 47

"Mount-Joy: or Some Passages Out of the Life of a Castle-Builder" (Irving), **II:** 314

"Mount Venus" (Wright), **Supp. XV:** 346

"Mourners" (Kooser), **Supp. XIX:** 127

"Mourners, The" (Malamud), **Supp. I Part 2:** 431, 435, 436–437

Mourners Below (Purdy), **Supp. VII:** 274, 280

"Mourning and Melancholia" (Freud), **Supp. IV Part 2:** 450; **Supp. XVI:** 161

Mourning Becomes Electra (O'Neill), **III:** 391, 394, 398–400

"Mourning Doves" (Pedersen; Nelson, trans.), **Supp. XVIII:** 180

"Mourning Poem for the Queen of Sunday" (Hayden), **Supp. II Part 1:** 379–380

"Mouse Elegy" (Olds), **Supp. X:** 209

Mouse Is Born, A (Loos), **Supp. XVI:** 193

"Mouse Roulette Wheel, The" (C. Bly), **Supp. XVI:** 34

Moustapha's Eclipse (McKnight), **Supp. XX: 147, 150**

"Mouth of Brass" (Humphrey), **Supp. IX:** 101

Moveable Feast, A (Hemingway), **II:** 257; **Retro. Supp. I:** 108, 171, **186–187**

Movement, The: Documentary of a Struggle for Equality (Student Nonviolent Coordinating Committee), **Supp. IV Part 1:** 369

"Move over Macho, Here Comes Feminismo" (Robbins), **Supp. X:** 272

Movers and Shakers (Sochen), **Supp. XXI:** 1

"Moves, The" (July), **Supp. XXIV:** 205

"Move to California, The" (Stafford), **Supp. XI:** 318, 321

"Movie" (Shapiro), **Supp. II Part 2:** 707

Movie at the End of the World, The (McGrath), **Supp. X:** 127

Moviegoer, The (Percy), **Supp. III Part 1:** 383–385, 387, 389–392, 394, 397

"Movie Magazine, The: A Low 'Slick' " (Percy), **Supp. III Part 1:** 385

Movies (Dixon), **Supp. XII:** 147

Movies About the Movies (Ames), **Supp. XVIII:** 242–243

"Movie Star Peter at the Supper for Street People" (Ferry), **Supp. XXIV:** 153

"Moving Around" (Matthews), **Supp. IX:** 155

"Moving Finger, The" (Wharton), **Retro. Supp. I:** 365

"Moving Inward at Last" (Bly), **Supp. XXI:** 84–85

Moving On (McMurtry), **Supp. V:** 223–224

"Moving On" (Pickering), **Supp. XXI:** 197

Moving Pictures: Memoirs of a Hollywood Prince (Schulberg), **Supp. XVIII:** 242, 243, 254

"Moving Sale" (Stallings), **Supp. XXV:** 228

Moving Target, The (Macdonald), **Supp. IV Part 2:** 462, 463, 467, 470, 471, 473, 474

Moving Target, The (Merwin), **Supp. III Part 1:** 346, 347–348, 352, 357

Mowat, Farley, **Supp. XXVI:** 61

"Mowbray Family, The" (Farrell and Alden), **II:** 45

"Mowing" (Frost), **II:** 169–170; **Retro. Supp. I:** 127, 128

"Moxan's Master" (Bierce), **I:** 206

Moxley, Jennifer, **Supp. XVII:** 70

Moyers, Bill, **Supp. IV Part 1:** 267; **Supp. VIII:** 331; **Supp. XI:** 126, 132; **Supp. XII:** 217; **Supp. XIII:** 274, 276; **Supp. XV:** 212; **Supp. XXIII:** 129, 130, 131, 139

Moynagh, Maureen, **Supp. XXII:** 73

Moynihan, Daniel Patrick, **Retro. Supp. II:** 123; **Supp. VIII:** 241; **Supp. XIX:** 150–151

"Moyshele"(Asch), **Supp. XXIII:** 4

"Mozart" (C. Frost), **Supp. XV:** 94

Mozart, Wolfgang Amadeus, **I:** 479, 588; **IV:** 74, 358; **Supp. IV Part 1:** 284

"Mozart and the Gray Steward" (Wilder), **IV:** 358

Mrabet, Mohammed, **Supp. IV Part 1:** 92, 93

Mr. and Mrs. Baby and Other Stories (Strand), **Supp. IV Part 2:** 631

"Mr. and Mrs. Fix-It" (Lardner), **II:** 431

Mr. Arcularis (Aiken), **I:** 54, 56

"Mr. Big" (Allen), **Supp. XV:** 15

Mr. Bridge (Connell), **Supp. XIV:** 80, 82, 93; **Supp. XXIII:** 302

Mr. Brown Can Moo! Can You? (Geisel), **Supp. XVI:** 104

"Mr. Bruce" (Jewett), **II:** 397; **Retro. Supp. II:** 134, 143

"Mr. Burnshaw and the Statue" (Stevens), **Retro. Supp. I:** 298, 303

"Mr. Carson Death on His Nights Out" (McGrath), **Supp. X:** 118

Mr. Clemens and Mark Twain (Kaplan), **I:** 247–248

"Mr. Coffee and Mr. Fixit" (Carver), **Supp. III Part 1:** 145

"Mr. Cornelius Johnson, Office-Seeker" (Dunbar), **Supp. II Part 1:** 211, 213

"Mr. Costyve Duditch" (Toomer), **Supp. III Part 2:** 486

"Mr. Dajani, Calling from Jericho" (Nye), **Supp. XIII:** 286–287

"Mr. Edwards and the Spider" (R. Lowell), **I:** 544; **II:** 550; **Retro. Supp. II:** 187

Mr. Field's Daughter (Bausch), **Supp. VII:** 47–48, 51–52

"Mr. Flood's Party" (Robinson), **III:** 512

"Mr. Forster's Pageant" (Maxwell), **Supp. VIII:** 172

"Mr. Frost's Chickens" (Oliver), **Supp. VII:** 232–233

Mr. Hodge and Mr. Hazard (Wylie), **Supp. I Part 2:** 708, 709, 714, 721–724

"Mr. Hueffer and the Prose Tradition" (Pound), **III:** 465

Mr. Ives' Christmas (Hijuelos), **Supp. VIII: 85–86**

Mr. Kelso's Lion (Bontemps), **Supp. XXII:** 7

"Mr. Longfellow and His Boy" (Sandburg), **III:** 591

"Mr. Luna and History" (Ríos), **Supp. IV Part 2:** 551

"Mr. Mitochondria" (Stollman), **Supp. XVII:** 50

Mr. Moto Is So Sorry (Marquand), **III:** 57, 58

Mr. Norris Changes Trains (Isherwood), **Supp. XIV:** 161

"Mr. Preble Gets Rid of His Wife" (Thurber), **Supp. I Part 2:** 615

"Mr. Rat"(Thompson), **Supp. XXIII:** 301–302

"Mr. Rolfe" (Wilson), **IV:** 436

Mr. Rutherford's Children (S. and A. Warner), **Supp. XVIII:** 264

"Mrs. Adis" (Kaye-Smith), **Supp. XVIII:** 130–131

Mrs. Albert Grundy: Observations in Philistia (Frederic), **II:** 138–139

Mr. Sammler's Planet (Bellow), **I:** 144, 147, 150, 151, 152, 158; **Retro. Supp. II:** 19, 28, 30

Mrs. Balfame (Atherton), **Supp. XXIV:** 20

"Mrs. Bilingsby's Wine" (Taylor), **Supp. V:** 323

Mrs. Bob Cratchit's Wild Christmas Binge (Durang), **Supp. XXIV:** 113, 125

Mrs. Bridge: A Novel (Connell), **Supp. XIV:** 79, 80, 81, 82, **89–94,** 95; **Supp. XXIII:** 302

"Mrs. Cassidy's Last Year" (Gordon), **Supp. IV Part 1:** 306

"Mrs. Cross and Mrs. Kidd" (Munro), **Supp. XXVII:** 188

Mrs. Dalloway (Woolf), **Supp. IV Part 1:** 299; **Supp. VIII:** 5; **Supp. XV:** 55, 65–66

"Mrs. Dimbleby" (Barnhardt), **Supp. XXVII:** 12

"Mrs. Green" (Huddle), **Supp. XXVI:** 148

"Mr. Shelley Speaking" (Wylie), **Supp. I Part 2:** 719

"Mrs. Jellison" (Hay), **Supp. XIV:** 123

"Mrs. Krikorian" (Olds), **Supp. X:** 211

"Mrs. Maecenas" (Burke), **I:** 271

"Mrs. Mandrill" (Nemerov), **III:** 278

"Mrs. Manstey's View" (Wharton), **Retro. Supp. I:** 362, 363

"Mrs. Mobry's Reason" (Chopin), **Retro. Supp. II:** 61

Mr. Spaceman (R. O. Butler), **Supp. XII:** 62, **74–75**

Mrs. Reynolds (Stein), **IV:** 43

"Mrs. Sen's" (Lahiri), **Supp. XXI: 177–178,** 180–181

Mrs. Stevens Hears the Mermaids Singing (Sarton), **Supp. VIII:** 252–253, **256–257**

Mrs. Ted Bliss (Elkin), **Supp. VI: 56,** 58

"Mrs. Turner Cutting the Grass" (Shields), **Supp. VII:** 319–320

"Mrs. Walpurga" (Rukeyser), **Supp. VI:** 273

"Mr. Thompson's Prodigal" (Harte), **Supp. II Part 1:** 354

"Mr. Trumm's Eyes"(Schott), **Supp. XXIII:** 243

Mr. Vertigo (Auster), **Supp. XII: 34–35,** 36

"Mr. Vonnegut in Sumatra" (Saunders), **Supp. XIX:** 235

"Mr. Whittier" (Scott), **Supp. I Part 2:** 705

Mr. Wilson's War (Dos Passos), **I:** 485

"Mr. Woodriff's Neckties" (Gallagher), **Supp. XXIV:** 175–176

"MS. Found in a Bottle" (Poe), **III:** 411, 416; **Retro. Supp. II:** 274

"Ms. Lot" (Rukeyser), **Supp. VI:** 281

Ms. Magazine, **Supp. V:** 259

Mttron-Hirsch, Sidney, **III:** 484–485

Mu (album, Do Cherry), **Supp. XXVII:** 154

"mu" (Mackey), **Supp. XXVII:** 155, 156

"Muchas Gracias Por Todo" (Nye), **Supp. XIII:** 282–283

"Much Madness is divinest Sense" (Dickinson), **Retro. Supp. I:** 37–38

"Muck-A-Muck" (Harte), **Supp. II Part 1:** 342

"Mud Below, The" (Proulx), **Supp. VII:** 262

Mudge, Alden, **Supp. XIV:** 35

"Mudman"(P. Benedict), **Supp. XXIII:** 47

Mudrick, Marvin, **Retro. Supp. II:** 289

"Mud Season" (Kenyon), **Supp. VII:** 167–168

Mueller, Lisel, **Supp. I Part 1:** 83, 88; **Supp. XIV:** 268

Muggli, Mark, **Supp. IV Part 1:** 207

Muhammad, Elijah, **Supp. I Part 1:** 60

Muir, Edwin, **I:** 527; **II:** 368; **III:** 20; **Supp. XXII:** 166; **Supp. XXIII:** 1; **Supp. XXVI:** 67

Muir, John, **Supp. IX:** 33, **171–188; Supp. VIII:** 296; **Supp. X:** 29; **Supp. XIV:** 177, 178, 181; **Supp. XXVI:** 34, 37, 43

Muir, Willa, **Supp. XXIII:** 1

Muirhead, Deborah, **Supp. XVIII:** 186

Mujica, Barbara, **Supp. VIII:** 89

Mulas, Franco, **Supp. XX: 38**

Mulatto (Hughes), **Retro. Supp. I:** 197, 203; **Supp. I Part 1:** 328, 339

Mulching of America, The (Crews), **Supp. XI:** 107

Muldoon, William, **I:** 500–501

Mule Bone (Hughes and Hurston), **Retro. Supp. I:** 194, 203; **Supp. VI:** 154

Mules and Men (Hurston), **Supp. VI:** 149, 153, 154, 160

Mulford, Prentice, **I:** 193

Mullen, Harryette, **Supp. XXVII: 163–177**

Mullennix, Joel, **Supp. XXIII:** 281

Muller, Kathryn, **Supp. XXVI:** 95

Mulligan, Robert, **Supp. VIII:** 128, 129

Mulligan Stew (Sorrentino), **Supp. XII:** 139; **Supp. XXI:** 233

Mullins, Eustace, **III:** 479

Mullins, Priscilla, **II:** 502–503

"Multiplication of Wool, The" (Sanders), **Supp. XVI:** 268

Multitudes, Multitudes (Clampitt), **Supp. IX:** 39

Mumbo Jumbo (Reed), **Supp. X:** 240, 242, **245–248,** 251

Mumford, Lewis, **I:** 245, 250, 251, 252, 259, 261; **II:** 271, 473–474; **Supp. I Part 2:** 632, 638; **Supp. II Part 2: 471–501**

Mumford, Sophia Wittenberg (Mrs. Lewis Mumford), **Supp. II Part 2:** 474, 475

"Mummers, The" (Di Piero), **Supp. XIX:** 44

Mummy, The (film), **Supp. IV Part 1:** 104; **Supp. XVII:** 57

Mundo y Palabra (Espaillat), **Supp. XXI:** 104

"Mundus et Infans" (Auden), **Supp. II Part 1:** 15

Mundy, Talbot, **Supp. XXVII:** 121

"Munich, 1938" (R. Lowell), **II:** 554

"Munich Mannequins, The" (Plath), **Retro. Supp. II:** 256

"Municipal Report, A" (Henry), **Supp. II Part 1:** 406–407

Muñoz, Manuel, **Supp. XXV: 127–139**

Munro, Alice, **Supp. IX:** 212; **Supp. X:** 290; **Supp. XII:** 289–290, 310; **Supp. XXIII:** 289, 296; **Supp. XXVII: 179–198**

Munsey, Frank, **I:** 501; **Supp. XXVII:** 120

Munson, Gorham, **I:** 252, 388, 432; **Retro. Supp. II:** 77, 78, 79, 82, 83; **Supp. I Part 2:** 454; **Supp. XX: 70, 74**

Münsterberg, Hugo, **Supp. XIV:** 197

Murakami, Haruki, **Supp. XVI:** 124

"Murano" (Doty), **Supp. XI:** 131

Murasaki, Lady, **II:** 577

Muratori, Fred, **Supp. XVI:** 281

Muray, Nicholas, **Supp. I Part 2:** 708

Murchison, Ginger, **Supp. XXV:** 222, 223, 226

Murder, My Sweet (film), **Supp. IV Part 1:** 130

"Murder Comes for the Bishop" (Goldman), **Supp. XXV:** 57

"Murderer Guest, The" (Gordon), **Supp. IV Part 1:** 306

"Murderers" (L. Michaels), **Supp. XVI:** 207–208

"Murderer's Grog" (Howard), **Supp. XXVII:** 121

Murder in Mount Holly (Theroux), **Supp. VIII:** 315–316

Murder in the Cathedral (T. S. Eliot), **I:** 571, 573, 580, 581; **II:** 20; **Retro. Supp. I:** 65; **Retro. Supp. II:** 222

Murder of Lidice, The (Millay), **III:** 140

"Murders in the Rue Morgue, The" (Poe), **III:** 412, 416, 419–420; **Retro. Supp. II:** 271, 272; **Supp. XIX:** 77

Murdoch, Iris, **Supp. VIII:** 167; **Supp. XVIII:** 136,149

Murnau, F. W., **Supp. XV:** 128

Murphy, Brenda, **Supp. XXI:** 6

Murphy, Cullen, **Supp. XXVI:** 61

Murphy, Jacqueline Shea, **Retro. Supp. II:** 143

Murphy, Patrick, **Supp. XIII:** 214

Murphy, Richard, **Retro. Supp. II:** 250; **Supp. XXIII:** 75

Murray, Albert, **Retro. Supp. II:** 119, 120; **Supp. XIX: 147–162**

Murray, Bill, **Supp. XXI:** 51

Murray, Edward, **I:** 229

Murray, G. E., **Supp. X:** 201; **Supp. XI:** 143, 155

Murray, Gilbert, **III:** 468–469

Murray, Jan, **Supp. IV Part 2:** 574

Murray, John, **II:** 304; **III:** 76, 79; **Retro. Supp. I:** 246

Murray, Judith Sargent, **Supp. XV:** 236–237

Murray, Les, **Supp. XIX:** 131

Murray, Margaret A., **Supp. V:** 128

Murrell, John A., **IV:** 265

Mursell, James L., **Supp. I Part 2:** 608

"Muse" (Ammons), **Supp. VII:** 29

"Muse, Postmodern and Homeless, The" (Ozick), **Supp. V:** 272

Muse & Drudge (Mullen), **Supp. XXVII:** 171–172, 176

"Musée des Beaux Arts" (Auden), **Retro. Supp. I:** 430; **Supp. II Part 1:** 14

"Musée des Beaux Arts Revisited" (Collins), **Supp. XXI:** 60

"Muse of Aboutness, The" (Baker), **Supp. XVI:** 288

Muses Are Heard, The (Capote), **Supp. III Part 1:** 126

"Muses of Terrence McNally, The" (Zinman), **Supp. XIII:** 207–208

"Muse's Tragedy, The" (Wharton), **Retro. Supp. I:** 364

Museum (Dove), **Supp. IV Part 1:** 245–247, 248

"Museum" (Hass), **Supp. VI:** 107

Museums and Women (Updike), **Retro. Supp. I:** 321

"Museum Vase" (Francis), **Supp. IX:** 83

"Mushrooms" (Plath), **Retro. Supp. II:** 246; **Supp. I Part 2:** 539

"Music" (Huddle), **Supp. XXVI:** 150

"Music" (Oliver), **Supp. VII:** 236

Music (al-Músíqá) (Gibran), **Supp. XX: 115, 124**

Music After the Great War (Van Vechten), **Supp. II Part 2:** 732

Music and Bad Manners (Van Vechten), **Supp. II Part 2:** 733

Music Appreciation (Skloot), **Supp. XX: 196, 197–201**

"Music for a Farce" (Bowles), **Supp. IV Part 1:** 83

Music for Chameleons (Capote), **Supp. III Part 1:** 120, 125–127, 131, 132

"Music for Museums?" (Van Vechten), **Supp. II Part 2:** 732

"Music for the Movies" (Van Vechten), **Supp. II Part 2:** 733

"Music from Spain" (Welty), **IV:** 272

Music Like Dirt (Bidart), **Supp. XV:** 35

"Music Like Dirt" (Bidart), **Supp. XV:** 35

Music of Chance, The (Auster), **Supp. XII:** 21, 23, **32–33**

"Music of My Own Kind Too, The" (Budbill), **Supp. XIX:** 10

"Music of Prose, The" (Gass), **Supp. VI:** 92

Music of Spain, The (Van Vechten), **Supp. II Part 2:** 734, 735

"Music of the Spheres" (Epstein), **Supp. XII:** 165

"Music School" (B. Kelly), **Supp. XVII:** 124

Music School, The (Updike), **IV:** 214, 215, 219, 226, 227; **Retro. Supp. I:** 320, 328, 329, 330

"Music School, The" (Updike), **Retro. Supp. I:** 326, 329, 335

"Music Swims Back to Me" (Sexton), **Supp. II Part 2:** 673

Muske, Carol, **Supp. IV Part 2:** 453–454

"Mussel Hunter at Rock Harbor" (Plath), **Supp. I Part 2:** 529, 537

Musset, Alfred de, **I:** 474; **II:** 543

Mussolini, Benito, **III:** 115, 473, 608; **IV:** 372, 373; **Supp. I Part 1:** 281, 282; **Supp. I Part 2:** 618; **Supp. V:** 290; **Supp. XVI:** 191

"Mustafa Ferrari" (X. J. Kennedy), **Supp. XV:** 170–171

Mustich, James, **Supp. XXI:** 52

"Must the Novelist Crusade?" (Welty), **IV:** 280

"Mutability of Literature, The" (Irving), **II:** 308

"Mutation of the Spirit" (Corso), **Supp. XII:** 132, 133

Mute, The (McCullers), **II:** 586

Mutilated, The (T. Williams), **IV:** 382, 386, 393

Mutiny of the Elsinore, The (London), **II:** 467

"Muttsy" (Hurston), **Supp. XVIII:** 279; **Supp. XXVI:** 164

Muyumba, Walton, **Supp. XIX:** 158

"My Adventures as a Social Poet" (Hughes), **Retro. Supp. I:** 194, 207

"My Alba" (Ginsberg), **Supp. II Part 1:** 320, 321

My Alexandria (Doty), **Supp. XI:** 119, 120, 121, **123–125,** 130

"My Amendment" (Saunders), **Supp. XIX:** 232

My Amputations (Major), **Supp. XXII:** 174, **175–176**

My Ántonia (Cather), **I:** 321–322; **Retro. Supp. I:** 1, 3, 4, **11–13,** 14, 17, 18, 22; **Supp. IV Part 2:** 608; **Supp. XVI:** 226

"My Appearance" (Wallace), **Supp. X:** 306–307

My Argument with the Gestapo: A Macaronic Journal (Merton), **Supp. VIII:** 207; **Supp. XV:** 344

"My Arkansas" (Angelou), **Supp. IV Part 1:** 15

"My Aunt" (Holmes), **Supp. I Part 1:** 302, 310

"My Beginnings" (Simpson), **Supp. IX:** 273

"My Bird Problem" (Franzen), **Supp. XX:** 94

My Black Horse (Gallagher), **Supp. XXIV:** 170

"My Bodyguard" (Notley), **Supp. XXII:** 230

My Bondage and My Freedom (Douglass), **Supp. III Part 1:** 155, 173

"My Bones Here Are Waiting for Yours" (Vaz), **Supp. XXVI:** 265–266

My Brother (Kincaid), **Supp. VII:** 191–193

"My Brother Paul" (Dreiser), **Retro. Supp. II:** 94

"My Brothers the Silent" (Merwin), **Supp. III Part 1:** 349–350

"My Brother's Work" (Dunn), **Supp. XI:** 147

"My Brother Takes a Hammer to the Mirror" (F. Wright), **Supp. XVII:** 244

"My Butterfly" (Frost), **II:** 151; **Retro. Supp. I:** 124

"My Children, and a Prayer for Us" (Ortiz), **Supp. IV Part 2:** 507

My Children! My Africa! (Fugard), **Supp. XXIV:** 267

"My College Sex Group" (Peacock), **Supp. XIX:** 199

"My Coney Island Uncle" (Swados), **Supp. XIX:** 267–268

"My Confession" (McCarthy), **II:** 562

"My Confessional Sestina" (Gioia), **Supp. XV:** 123

"My Corner" (Major), **Supp. XXII:** 184

My Country and My People (Yutang), **Supp. X:** 291

"My Country Tish of Thee" (Rinehart), **Supp. XXV:** 194

"My Country 'Tis of Thee" (Reznikoff), **Supp. III Part 2:** 616

"My Daughter Considers Her Body" (Skloot), **Supp. XX: 197–198, 200**

My Days of Anger (Farrell), **II:** 34, 35–36, 43

"My Dear Niece" (Boyce), **Supp. XXI:** 10

"My Dear Republican Mother" (C. Bly), **Supp. XVI:** 31–32

My Death My Life by Pier Paolo Pasolini (Acker), **Supp. XII:** 7

My Dog Stupid (Fante), **Supp. XI:** 160, **170–171**

My Dog Tulip (Ackerley), **Supp. XX: 237**

"My Ear-Rings" (J. Schoolcraft), **Supp. XXIII:** 226

My Emily Dickinson (Howe), **Retro. Supp. I:** 33, 43; **Supp. IV Part 2:** 430–431

"My English" (Alvarez), **Supp. VII:** 2

Myers, Christopher, **Supp. XXVII:** 211

Myers, John Bernard, **Supp. XXIII:** 210, 219

Myers, Linda A., **Supp. IV Part 1:** 10

Myers, Walter Dean, **Supp. XXVII: 199–214**

Myerson, Julie, **Supp. XXVII:** 278

"My Extended Family" (Theroux), **Supp. VIII:** 311

My Face for the World to See (Hayes), **Supp. XXVI:** 139, 141–142

"My Father" (Biss), **Supp. XXVI:** 47

"My Father" (Budbill), **Supp. XIX:** 5

"My Father" (L. Michaels), **Supp. XVI:** 214

"My Father" (Sterne), **IV:** 466

"My Father at Eighty-Five" (R. Bly), **Supp. IV Part 1:** 73

"My Father Is a Simple Man" (Salinas), **Supp. XIII:** 324

"My Father Is with Me" (Budbill), **Supp. XIX:** 15

"My Father: October 1942" (Stafford), **Supp. XI:** 323

My Father Photographed with Friends (Bronk), **Supp. XXI:** 26–27, **Supp. XXI:** 31

"My Father Photographed with Friends" (Bronk), **Supp. XXI:** 23, 27

"My Fathers Came From Kentucky" (Lindsay), **Supp. I Part 2:** 395

"My Father's Employment" (Schott), **Supp. XXIII:** 247

"My Father's Friends" (Maxwell), **Supp. VIII:** 171

"My Father's Ghost" (Wagoner), **Supp. IX:** 330

"My Father's God" (Fante), **Supp. XI:** 160, 174

My Father's House (film), **Supp. XXVII:** 141

"My Father's House" (L.-Y. Lee), **Supp. XV:** 225

"My Father's Love Letters" (Gallagher), **Supp. XXIV:** 171–172

"My Father's Love Letters" (Komunyakaa), **Supp. XIII:** 127

"My Father Speaks to me from the Dead" (Olds), **Supp. X:** 210

"My Father's Telescope" (Dove), **Supp. IV Part 1:** 246, 248

"My Father with Cigarette Twelve Years Before the Nazis Could Break His Heart" (Levine), **Supp. V:** 194

"My Favorite Murder" (Bierce), **I:** 205

My Favorite Plant: Writers and Gardeners on the Plants They Love (Kincaid), **Supp. VII:** 193–194

My Favorites in Suspense (Hitchcock, ed.), **Supp. XXII:** 119

"My Fifty-Plus Years Celebrate Spring" (Salinas), **Supp. XIII:** 327

"My First Book" (Harte), **Supp. II Part 1:** 343

My First Summer in the Sierra (Muir), **Supp. IX:** 172, 173, **178–181,** 183, 185; **Supp. XIV:** 177

"My Flamboyant Grandson" (Saunders), **Supp. XIX:** 231–232

"My Fountain Pen" (McClatchy), **Supp. XII:** 254, 260

My Friend, Henry Miller (Perlès), **III:** 189

My Friend, Julia Lathrop (Addams), **Supp. I Part 1:** 25

"My Friend, Walt Whitman" (Oliver), **Supp. VII:** 245

"My Garden Acquaintance" (J. R. Lowell), **Supp. I Part 2:** 420

My Garden \[Book\]: (Kincaid), **Supp. VII:** 193–194

"My Good-bye" (Weigl), **Supp. XIX:** 288

"My Good Man" (Gansworth), **Supp. XXVI:** 114

"My Grandfather" (R. Lowell), **II:** 554

"My Grandmother's Love Letters" (H. Crane), **Retro. Supp. II:** 78

My Grandparents Were Married for Sixty-five Years (Schott), **Supp. XXIII:** 240–241

"My Grandson, Home at Last" (Angelou), **Supp. IV Part 1:** 13

My Green Hills of Jamaica (McKay), **Supp. X:** 132, 142

"My Gun" (Gallagher), **Supp. XXIV:** 175

My Guru and His Disciple (Isherwood), **Supp. XIV:** 157, 164, 172

"My Heart" (Collins), **Supp. XXI:** 58

My Heart's in the Highlands (Saroyan), **Supp. IV Part 1:** 83

"My High School Reunion" (Kingston), **Supp. V:** 169

My Hollywood (Simpson), **Supp. XXVII:** 242–244

"My House New-Painted" (Bronk), **Supp. XXI:** 30

"My Hunt for King Sebastião" (Vaz), **Supp. XXVI:** 260

"My Ideal Home" (Stratton-Porter), **Supp. XX: 222**

"My Indigo" (L.-Y. Lee), **Supp. XV:** 214

My Kind of Place: Travel Stories from a Woman Who's Been Everywhere (Orlean), **Supp. XXV:** 160, 164–165

"My Kinsman, Major Molineux" (Hawthorne), **II:** 228, 229, 237–239, 243; **Retro. Supp. I:** 153–154, 158, 160, 161; **Retro. Supp. II:** 181, 187; **Supp. XVI:** 157

My Kinsman, Major Molineux (R. Lowell), **II:** 545–546

"My Last Afternoon with Uncle Devereux Winslow" (R. Lowell), **II:** 547–548; **Retro. Supp. II:** 189

"My Last Drive" (Hardy), **Supp. VIII:** 32

"My Last Duchess" (R. Browning), **Supp. XV:** 121; **Supp. XXV:** 229; **Supp. XXVII:** 218

Myles, Eileen, **Supp. XXIV:** 45

"My Life" (Strand), **Supp. IV Part 2:** 627

My Life, Starring Dara Falcon (Beattie), **Supp. V:** 31, 34–35

My Life a Loaded Gun: Dickinson, Plath, Rich, and Female Creativity (Bennett), **Retro. Supp. I:** 29

My Life and Hard Times (Thurber), **Supp. I Part 2:** 607, 609

My Life and Loves in Greenwich Village (attr. Bodenheim), **Supp. XXV:** 30

My Life as a Man (P. Roth), **Retro. Supp. II:** 281, 286, 289; **Supp. III Part 2:** 401, 404, 405, 417–418

"My Life as a P.I.G., or the True Adventures of Smokey the Cop" (Abbey), **Supp. XIII:** 3

"My life closed twice before its close" (Dickinson), **Retro. Supp. I:** 38

"My Life had stood a Loaded Gun" (Dickinson), **Retro. Supp. I:** 42, 43, 45, 46; **Supp. IV Part 2:** 430

My Life of Absurdity (C. Himes), **Supp. XVI:** 145

"My Life with Medicine" (Nye), **Supp. XIII:** 282

"My Life with *Playboy*" (Plimpton), **Supp. XVI:** 246

"My Life with R. H. Macy" (Jackson), **Supp. IX:** 118

"My Little Utopia" (Simic), **Supp. VIII:** 283

My Lives and How I Lost Them (Cullen), **Supp. IV Part 1:** 173

"My Lord Bag of Rice" (C. Bly), **Supp. XVI:** 40

My Lord Bag of Rice: New and Selected Stories (C. Bly), **Supp. XVI:** 41

"My Lost City" (Fitzgerald), **Retro. Supp. I:** 102

"My Lost Youth" (Longfellow), **II:** 487, 499; **Retro. Supp. II:** 168

My Love Affair with America: The Cautionary Tale of a Cheerful Conservative (Podhoretz), **Supp. VIII:** 232, 233, 237, **244–246**

"My Lover Has Dirty Fingernails" (Updike), **Retro. Supp. I:** 332, 333

"My lover is tall and handsome"(J. Schoolcraft), **Supp. XXIII:** 235

"My Lucy Friend Who Smells Like Corn" (Cisneros), **Supp. VII:** 68–69

"My Mammogram" (McClatchy), **Supp. XII:** 263–264

"My Man Bovanne" (Bambara), **Supp. XI:** 2

"My Mariner" (Larcom), **Supp. XIII:** 147

My Mark Twain (Howells), **II:** 276

"My Metamorphosis" (Harte), **Supp. II Part 1:** 339

My Mistress's Sparrow Is Dead (Eugenides, ed.), **Supp. XXIV:** 135

"My Moby Dick" (Humphrey), **Supp. IX:** 95

"My Monkey" (Nelson), **Supp. XVIII:** 178

"My Moral Life" (Halliday), **Supp. XIX:** 89

My Mortal Enemy (Cather), **I:** 327–328; **Retro. Supp. I:** 16–17; **Supp. I Part 2:** 719

"My Mother" (Biss), **Supp. XXVI:** 47

My Mother, My Father and Me (Hellman), **Supp. I Part 1:** 290–291

"My Mother and My Sisters" (Ortiz), **Supp. IV Part 2:** 499

My Mother: Demonology (Acker), **Supp. XII:** 6

"My Mother Is Speaking from the Desert" (Gordon), **Supp. IV Part 1:** 309, 314

"My Mother Remembers That She Was Beautiful" (Gallagher), **Supp. XXIV:** 169

"My Mother's Goofy Song" (Fante), **Supp. XI:** 164

"My Mother's Memoirs, My Father's Lie, and Other True Stories" (Banks), **Supp. V:** 15

"My Mother's Nipples" (Hass), **Supp. VI:** 109

"My Mother's Story" (Kunitz), **Supp. III Part 1:** 259

"My Mother's Voice" (Very), **Supp. XXV:** 244

"My Mother"(Taylor), **Supp. XXIII:** 231

"My Mother Then and Now" (Wasserstein), **Supp. XV:** 327

"My Mother with Purse the Summer They Murdered the Spanish Poet" (Levine), **Supp. V:** 194

My Movie Business: A Memoir (Irving), **Supp. VI:** 164

"My Name" (Cisneros), **Supp. VII:** 60

"My Negro Problem—And Ours" (Podhoretz), **Supp. VIII: 234–236**

"My Neighborhood"(Dybek), **Supp. XXIII:** 69

"My New Diet" (Karr), **Supp. XI:** 241

My Next Bride (Boyle), **Supp. XXIV: 53, 59**

"My Number" (Collins), **Supp. XXI:** 64

"My Old Man" (Hemingway), **II:** 263

My Other Life (Theroux), **Supp. VIII:** 310, 324

"My Own Story" (E. Stoddard), **Supp. XV:** 273, 279, 283

My Own True Name: New and Selected Poems for Young Adults, 1984–1999 (Mora), **Supp. XIII:** 222

"My Papa's Waltz" (Roehke), **Supp. XXVII:** 250

"My Parents Have Come Home Laughing" (Jarman), **Supp. XVII:** 113

"My Passion for Ferries" (Whitman), **IV:** 350

"My People" (Hughes), **Retro. Supp. I:** 197; **Supp. I Part 1:** 321–322, 323

"My Philosophy" (Allen), **Supp. XV:** 15

"My Playmate" (Whittier), **Supp. I Part 2:** 699–700

"My Priests" (Monette), **Supp. X:** 159

"My Public" (Rinehart), **Supp. XXV:** 201

Myra Breckinridge (Vidal), **Supp. IV Part 2:** 677, 685–686, 689, 691

"My Race" (H. Johnson), **Supp. XXVI:** 163

"My Raptor" (A. Finch), **Supp. XVII:** 72

"My Recollections of S. B. Fairchild" (Jackson), **Supp. IX:** 118–119

"My Religion" (Carson), **Supp. XII: 105–106**

Myrer, Anton, **Supp. XXV:** 145

"My Road to Hell Was Paved" (Patchett), **Supp. XII:** 310–311

Myron (Vidal), **Supp. IV Part 2:** 677, 685, 686, 691

"My Roomy" (Lardner), **II:** 420, 421, 428, 430

"My Sad Self" (Ginsberg), **Supp. II Part 1:** 320

My San Francisco (Atherton), **Supp. XXIV:** 27

My Secret History (Theroux), **Supp. VIII:** 310, 324

"Myself" (Audubon), **Supp. XVI:** 1–2, 5, 12

Myself Painting (Major), **Supp. XXII:** **184–185**

"My Shoes" (Simic), **Supp. VIII:** 275

"My Side of the Matter" (Capote), **Supp. III Part 1:** 114, 115

My Silk Purse and Yours: The Publishing Scene and American Literary Art (Garrett), **Supp. VII:** 111; **Supp. X:** 7

My Sister Eileen (McKenney), **IV:** 288; **Retro. Supp. II:** 321

My Sister's Hand in Mine: The Collected Works of Jane Bowles, **Supp. IV Part 1:** 82–83

"My Son" (Strand), **Supp. IV Part 2:** 629

My Son, John (film), **Supp. I Part 1:** 67

"My Son, the Murderer" (Malamud), **Supp. I Part 2:** 437

My Son Is a Splendid Driver (Inge), **Supp. XXV:** 93, 95, 107

"My Son the Man" (Olds), **Supp. X:** 212

"My Speech to the Graduates" (Allen), **Supp. XV:** 16

"Mysteries of Caesar, The" (Hecht), **Supp. X:** 73

"Mysteries of Eleusis, The" (Hardwick), **Supp. III Part 1:** 195

Mysteries of Paris, The (Sue), **Supp. XXIII:** 182

Mysteries of Pittsburgh, The (Chabon), **Supp. XI:** 65, 68, **69–71; Supp. XIX:** 135

Mysteries of Small Houses (Notley), **Supp. XXII:** 223, 224, 226, 234–235

"Mysterious Case of R, The" (Conroy), **Supp. XVI:** 72

Mysterious Stranger, The (Twain), **IV:** 190–191, 210

Mystery, A (Shields). *See Swann* (Shields)

"Mystery, The" (Dunbar), **Supp. II Part 1:** 199, 210

"Mystery, The" (Glück), **Supp. V:** 91

"Mystery, The" (Teasdale), **Supp. XXVII:** 293

Mystery and Manners (O'Connor), **Retro. Supp. II:** 230

"'Mystery Boy' Looks for Kin in Nashville" (Hayden), **Supp. II Part 1:** 366, 372

"Mystery of Coincidence, The" (Conroy), **Supp. XVI:** 74

"Mystery of Heroism, A" (Crane), **I:** 414

"Mystery of Marie Rogêt, The" (Poe), **III:** 413, 419; **Retro. Supp. II:** 271

"Mystic" (Plath), **Retro. Supp. II:** 257; **Supp. I Part 2:** 539, 541

"Mystical Poet, A" (Bogan), **Retro. Supp. I:** 36

"Mystic of Sex, The—A First Look at D. H. Lawrence" (Nin), **Supp. X:** 188

"Mystic Vision in 'The Marshes of Glynn'" (Warfel), **Supp. I Part 1:** 366, 373

"Mystification" (Poe), **III:** 425

"My Story" (Monroe), **Supp. XXVII:** 95

"My Strange New Poetry" (Halliday), **Supp. XIX:** 88, 94

My Study Windows (J. R. Lowell), **Supp. I Part 2:** 407

"My Teacher" (Conroy), **Supp. XVI:** 75

"Myth" (Rukeyser), **Supp. VI:** 281–282

"Myth" (Trethewey), **Supp. XXI:** 245, 255, 256

"Myth" (Hadas), **Supp. XXIII:** 119

"Mythmaker" (Trethewey), **Supp. XXI:** 243

Myth of American Manhood, The (Kriegel, ed.), **Supp. XXIV:** 214

Myth of Sisyphus, The (Camus), **I:** 294; **Supp. XIII:** 165

"Myth of the Happy Worker, The" (Swados), **Supp. XIX:** 265

"Myth of the Isolated Artist, The" (Oates), **Supp. II Part 2:** 520

Myth of the Machine, The (Mumford), **Supp. II Part 2:** 476, 478, 482, 483, 493, 497

"Myth of the Powerful Worker, The" (Swados), **Supp. XIX:** 265

Mythology and the Romantic Tradition in English Poetry (Bush), **Supp. I Part 1:** 268

Myths and Texts (Snyder), **Supp. VIII:** **295–296**

"Myths of Bears, The" (Bass), **Supp. XVI:** 19, 20

"My *Tocaya*" (Cisneros), **Supp. VII:** 69

My Uncle Dudley (Morris), **I:** 305; **III:** 219–220

"My Uncle's Favorite Coffee Shop" (Nye), **Supp. XIII:** 283

"My Unopened Life" (Gallagher), **Supp. XXIV:** 171

"My Weariness of Epic Proportions" (Simic), **Supp. VIII:** 276

My Wicked Wicked Ways (Cisneros), **Supp. VII:** 58, 64–68, 71

"My Wicked Wicked Ways" (Cisneros), **Supp. VII:** 58, 64–66

My Wisdom (Thompson), **Supp. XXIII:** **291–293**

"My Word-house" (Mora), **Supp. XIII:** 219, 225

My Works and Days (Mumford), **Supp. II Part 2:** 475, 477, 481

"My World and My Critics" (Stratton-Porter), **Supp. XX:** **220**

My World and Welcome to It (Thurber), **Supp. I Part 2:** 610

N

Nabokov, Peter, **Supp. IV Part 2:** 490

Nabokov, Véra, **Retro. Supp. I:** 266, 270

Nabokov, Vladimir, **I:** 135; **III:** **244–266,** 283, 286; **Retro. Supp. I:** **263–281,** 317, 335; **Supp. I Part 1:** 196; **Supp. II Part 1:** 2; **Supp. IV Part 1:** 135; **Supp. IX:** 152, 212, 261; **Supp. V:** 127, 237, 251, 252, 253; **Supp. VIII:** 105, 133, 138; **Supp. X:** 283; **Supp. XI:** 66; **Supp. XII:** 310; **Supp. XIII:** 46, 52; **Supp. XVI:** 148, 294; **Supp. XVIII:** 98, 102; **Supp. XXII:** 263; **Supp. XXIV:** 133

Nabokov's Dozen (Nabokov), **Retro. Supp. I:** 266

Nabokov's Garden: A Guide to Ada (Mason), **Supp. VIII:** 138

Naca, Kristin, **Supp. XIII:** 133

Nadeau, Robert, **Supp. X:** 261, 270

Nadel, Alan, **Supp. IV Part 1:** 209

Naimy, Mikhail, **Supp. XX:** **116, 119, 120**

Naipaul, V. S., **Supp. IV Part 1:** 297; **Supp. VIII:** 314; **Supp. X:** 131; **Supp. XIV:** 111; **Supp. XX:** 87; **Supp. XXI:** 170; **Supp. XXII:** 240, 241, 242, 246, 253

Naison, Mark, **Supp. XVIII:** 231

Naked and the Dead, The (Mailer), **I:** 477; **III:** 26, 27, 28–30, 31, 33, 35, 36, 44; **Retro. Supp. II:** **197–199; Supp. IV Part 1:** 381; **Supp. XI:** 218; **Supp. XIX:** 248; **Supp. XX:** **248; Supp. XXI:** 277

Naked Author (di Donato), **Supp. XX:** 45

Naked Babies (Quindlen and Kelsh), **Supp. XVII:** 167, 179

Naked in Garden Hills (Crews), **Supp. XI:** 102, **110**

Naked Lunch (Burroughs), **Supp. III Part 1:** 92–95, 97–105; **Supp. IV Part 1:** 90

"Naked Nude" (Malamud), **Supp. I Part 2:** 450

Naked on Roller Skates (Bodenheim), **Supp. XXV:** 27

Naked Poetry (Berg and Mezey, eds.), **Supp. IV Part 1:** 60

Naked Poetry (Levine), **Supp. V:** 180

Naked Revenge (film), **Supp. XVII:** 141

Nall, Gus, **Supp. XXII:** 172, 184

Namedropping: Mostly Literary Memoirs (Coover), **Supp. V:** 40

"Name in the Papers" (Hughes), **Supp. I Part 1:** 330

Name Is Archer, The (Macdonald, under Millar), **Supp. IV Part 2:** 466

"Name Is Burroughs, The" (Burroughs), **Supp. III Part 1:** 93

Name Is Fogarty, The: Private Papers on Public Matters (Farrell), **II:** 49

"Names" (Carruth), **Supp. XVI:** 54, 56

"Names, The" (Collins), **Supp. XXI:** 54, 61–62

Names, The (DeLillo), **Supp. VI:** 3, 10, 13, 14

Names, The (Momaday), **Supp. IV Part 2:** 479, 480, 483, 486, 487, 488, 489

Namesake, The (Lahiri), **Supp. XXI:** 176, 184, **186–188**

Names and Faces of Heroes, The (Price), **Supp. VI:** 258, 260

Names of the Dead, The (O'Nan), **Supp. XXV:** 142, 143–144, 149, 151

Names of the Lost, The (Levine), **Supp. V:** 177–178, 179, 187–188

"Naming for Love" (Carruth), **Supp. XVI:** 48

"Naming Myself" (Kingsolver), **Supp. VII:** 208

"Naming of Names, The" (Sanders), **Supp. XVI:** 268

Naming of the Beasts, The (Stern). *See Rejoicings: Selected Poems, 1966–*

1972 (Stern)

Naming the Unseen (Ray), **Supp. XVIII:** 192, **193–195**

"Naming the Unseen" (Ray), **Supp. XVIII:** 203

Nana (Zola), **III:** 321

Nance, Kevin, **Supp. XXVI:** 58; **Supp. XXVII:** 268

"Nancy Culpepper" (Mason), **Supp. VIII:** 141

Nancy Drew stories, **Supp. VIII:** 133, 135, 137, 142

"Nancy Knapp" (Masters), **Supp. I Part 2:** 461

"Naola Beauty Academy, New Orleans, 1943" (Trethewey), **Supp. XXI:** 246

"Naomi Counting Time"(Thompson), **Supp. XXIII:** 293

"Naomi Shihab Nye: U.S. Mideast-History a Harbinger of 9-11?" (Nye), **Supp. XIII:** 286

"Naomi Trimmer" (X. J. Kennedy), **Supp. XV:** 170

"Nap, The" (Banks), **Supp. V:** 7

"Napoleon" (Emerson), **II:** 6

Napoleon I, **I:** 6, 7, 8, 474; **II:** 5, 309, 315, 321, 523; **Supp. I Part 1:** 153; **Supp. I Part 2:** 518, 519

Napolitano, Louise, **Supp. XX: 35, 45, 46–47**

Narcissa and Other Fables (Auchincloss), **Supp. IV Part 1:** 21, 34

"Narcissus as Narcissus" (Tate), **IV:** 124

"Narcissus Leaves the Pool" (Epstein), **Supp. XIV:** 110

Narcissus Leaves the Pool: Familiar Essays (Epstein), **Supp. XIV:** 110

Nardal, Paulette, **Supp. X:** 139

Nardi, Marcia, **Retro. Supp. I:** 426, 427

"Narragansett Boulevard" (Halliday), **Supp. XIX:** 91

Narration (Stein), **IV:** 27, 30, 32, 33, 36

Narrative of a Four Months' Residence among the Natives of a Valley of the Marquesas Islands (Melville), **III:** 76

Narrative of Arthur Gordon Pym, The (Poe), **III:** 412, 416; **Retro. Supp. II:** 265, **273–275; Supp. XI:** 293

"Narrative of Arthur Gordon Pym, The" (Poe), **Supp. XXII:** 58

Narrative of the Life of Frederick Douglass, an American Slave, Written by Himself (Douglass), **Supp. III Part 1:** 154–159, 162, 165; **Supp. IV Part 1:** 13; **Supp. VIII:** 202

"Narrativity Scenes" (Wright), **Supp. XV:** 345

Narrenschiff, Das (Brant), **III:** 447

"Narrow Fellow in the Grass, A" (Dickinson), **Retro. Supp. I:** 30, 37

Narrow Heart, A: Portrait of a Woman (Gordon), **II:** 197, 217

Narrow Rooms (Purdy), **Supp. VII:** 274

Narrows, The (Connelly), **Supp. XXI:** 71, **76**

Nasby, Petroleum, **Supp. XVIII:** 1

Nash, Noreen, **Supp. XXII:** 256

Nash, Ogden, **Supp. XXI:** 51; **Supp. XXIV:** 45

Nash, Roderick, **Supp. IX:** 185; **Supp. XIV:** 191–192

Nash, Susan Smith, **Supp. XVI:** 274

Nash, Thomas, **Supp. III Part 1:** 387–388

Nashe, Thomas, **I:** 358; **Supp. XVII:** 232

Nashville (film), **Supp. IX:** 143

"Nashville Gone to Ashes" (Hempel), **Supp. XXI:** 115, 118, **120–121**

Nashville Skyline (album, Dylan), **Supp. XVIII:** 27

Nason, Elias, **Supp. XV:** 242

Nasser, Gamal Abdel, **IV:** 490

Nasty Bits (Silver), **Supp. XXIV:** 265

Natalie Mann (Toomer), **Supp. III Part 2:** 484–486

Nathan, Amy, **Supp. XXVII:** 200

Nathan, George Jean, **II:** 91; **III:** 103, 104, 106, 107; **IV:** 432; **Supp. IV Part 1:** 343; **Supp. IX:** 56–57; **Supp. XIII:** 161; **Supp. XXII:** 23; **Supp. XXVII:** 86

"Nathanael West" (Herbst), **Retro. Supp. II:** 325

Nathanael West: The Art of His Life (Martin), **Retro. Supp. II:** 325

Nathan Coulter (Berry), **Supp. X:** 24, 33

National Dream, The: Building the Impossible Railway (Findley and Whitehead), **Supp. XX:** 51

"Nationalist, The" (Anderson), **I:** 115

"Nation Is Like Ourselves, The" (Baraka), **Supp. II Part 1:** 53

"Native, The" (Olds), **Supp. X:** 215

"Native American Attitudes to the Environment" (Momaday), **Supp. IV Part 2:** 481, 491

Native American Renaissance (Lincoln), **Supp. IV Part 2:** 507

Native American Testimony (Nabokov, ed.), **Supp. IV Part 2:** 490

"Native Blessing" (Ray), **Supp. XVIII:** 202

Native Guard (Trethewey), **Supp. XXI:** 243, 244, 247, **254–257**

"Native Guard" (Trethewey), **Supp. XXI:** 256

"Native Hill, A" (Berry), **Supp. X:** 21

Native in a Strange Land: Trials & Tremors (Coleman), **Supp. XI: 84–85,** 87

Native of Winby and Other Tales, A (Jewett), **II:** 396; **Retro. Supp. II:** 138

"Natives Don't Cry" (Boyle), **Supp. XXIV:** 57–58

Native Son (Wright), **IV:** 476, 477, 478, 479, 481, 482–484, 485, 487, 488, 491, 495; **Retro. Supp. II:** 107, 116; **Supp. I Part 1:** 51, 64, 67, 337; **Supp. II Part 1:** 170, 235–236; **Supp. IX:** 306; **Supp. XIV:** 73; **Supp. XVII:** 155; **Supp. XVIII:** 283, 286; **Supp. XXI:** 169

"Native Trees" (Merwin), **Supp. III Part 1:** 355

Natorp, Paul, **Supp. XIV:** 198

Natural, The (Malamud), **II:** 424, 425; **Retro. Supp. II:** 288; **Supp. I Part 2:** 438–441, 443; **Supp. XXVI:** 180

"*Natural, The:* Malamud's World Ceres" (Wasserman), **Supp. I Part 2:** 439

Natural Affection (Inge), **Supp. XXV:** 95, 103, 104–105, 106

"Natural History" (Olds), **Supp. X:** 210

"Natural History Note" (Hay), **Supp. XIV:** 124, 130

"Natural History of Some Poems, A" (Harrison), **Supp. VIII:** 53

"Natural History of the Dead" (Hemingway), **II:** 206; **Retro. Supp. I:** 176

Natural Laws of Good Luck, The (Graf), **Supp. XXVI:** 46

"Naturally Superior School, A" (Knowles), **Supp. XII:** 235, 240–241

"Natural Method of Mental Philosophy" (Emerson), **II:** 14

"Natural Resources" (Rich), **Supp. I Part 2:** 575

Natural Selection (F. Barthelme), **Supp. XI:** 2, 28, 32, 33

Nature (Emerson), **I:** 463; **II:** 1, 8, 12, 16; **IV:** 171, 172–173; **Supp. XXIV:** 75, 79; **Supp. XXV:** 241

"Nature" (Emerson), **Retro. Supp. I:** 250; **Supp. I Part 2:** 383; **Supp. III Part 1:** 387; **Supp. IX:** 178

"Nature" (Very), **Supp. XXV:** 242

"Nature, Inc." (Lewis), **II:** 441

Nature and Destiny of Man, The (Niebuhr), **III:** 292, 303–306, 310

"Nature and Life" (Emerson), **II:** 19

"Nature and New America Painting"(O'Hara), **Supp. XXIII:** 212

"Nature and Nurture: When It Comes to Twins, Sometimes It's Hard to Tell the Two Apart" (Bausch), **Supp. VII:** 40

Nature and Purpose of the Universe, The (Durang), **Supp. XXIV: 115–116**

"Nature-Metaphors" (Lanier), **Supp. I Part 1:** 352

Nature Morte (Brodsky), **Supp. VIII:** 25

Nature of Evil, The (James), **II:** 343

Nature of Generosity, The (Kittredge), **Supp. XXVI:** 186, 187–188, 189

Nature of Peace, The (Veblen), **Supp. I Part 2:** 642

Nature of Things, The (Lucretius; Stallings, trans.), **Supp. XXV:** 221, 226–227

Nature of Things, The (television show), **Supp. XX: 51**

Nature of True Virtue, The (Edwards), **I:** 549, 557–558, 559

Nature of Yearning, The (Huddle), **Supp. XXVI:** 149–150

Nature: Poems Old and New (Swenson), **Supp. IV Part 2:** 652

Nature's Economy: A History of Ecological Ideas (Worster), **Supp. IX:** 19

Nature's Way (Wouk), **Supp. XXV:** 253

Naumburg, Margaret, **Supp. XX: 68, 74–75**

Nausea (Sartre), **Supp. VIII:** 7

"Navajo Blanket, A" (Swenson), **Supp. IV Part 2:** 649

Navarette, Don Martín de, **II:** 310

Navarro, Ramon, **Supp. IV Part 1:** 206

Navigator, The (film), **I:** 31

Navratilova, Martina, **Supp. XX: 264**

Naylor, Gloria, **Supp. VIII: 213–230; Supp. XX: 108**

Naylor, Paul Kenneth, **Supp. IV Part 2:** 420

Nazarene, The (Asch), **Supp. XXIII:** 2, 3, 4, 6, 9, **12–13,** 14, 15, 16

Nazarene, The: or, The Last of the Washingtons (Lippard), **Supp. XXIII:** 183, 184, 187, 190

Nazimova, **III:** 399

Neal, Darlin', **Supp. XXI:** 41

Neal, Larry, **Retro. Supp. II:** 112, 128; **Supp. X:** 324, 328

Neal, Lawrence P., **Supp. II Part 1:** 53

Neal, Patricia, **Supp. I Part 1:** 286; **Supp. IV Part 2:** 524; **Supp. V:** 223

Neale, Walter, **I:** 192, 208

"Near Damascus" (Di Piero), **Supp. XIX:** 43

Nearer the Moon: From "A Journal of Love," the Unexpurgated Diary of Anaïs Nin, 1937–1939, **Supp. X:** 184, 185

Nearing, Helen and Scott, **Supp. XXVI:** 35

Near-Johannesburg Boy and Other Poems, The (Brooks), **Supp. III Part 1:** 86

Near Klamath (Carver), **Supp. III Part 1:** 137

"Near Perigord" (Pound), **Retro. Supp. I:** 289, 290

"Near Spring" (Pickering), **Supp. XXI:** 198

Near the Ocean (R. Lowell), **II:** 543, 550, 551–553, 554, 555; **Retro. Supp. II:** 182, 186, 189–190

"Near View of the High Sierra, A" (Muir), **Supp. IX:** 183

Nebeker, Helen, **Supp. IX:** 122

"Nebraska Blizzard" (F. Wright), **Supp. XVII:** 247

Necessary Angel, The (Stevens), **IV:** 76, 79, 89, 90

Necessities of Life: Poems, 1962–1965 (Rich), **Supp. I Part 2:** 553, 555

"Necessity of Blacks' Writing Fiction About the South, The" (Andrews), **Supp. XXVI:** 1, 13

"Necessity of Lemons, The"(Schott), **Supp. XXIII:** 247, 248

Nechayev, Sergey, **Supp. XXI:** 164

Neck Deep and Other Predicaments (Monson), **Supp. XXIV:** 230, **234– 236,** 241

"Necrological" (Ransom), **III:** 486–489, 490, 492

Ned Christie's War (Conley), **Supp. V:** 232

"Need for a Cultural Base to Civil Rites & Bpower Mooments, The" (Baraka), **Supp. II Part 1:** 48

"Need for Christian Preaching, The" (Buechner), **Supp. XII:** 49

Needful Things (King), **Supp. V:** 139, 146

"Needle" (Simic), **Supp. VIII:** 275

"Needle Trade" (Reznikoff), **Supp. XIV:** 277, 289

"Need of Being Versed in Country Things, The" (Frost), **II:** 154; **Retro.**

Supp. I: 133, 135

"Need to Say It, The" (Hampl), **Supp. XXII:** 94

Neel, Philippe, **Supp. XIV:** 338

Neelakantappa, Tara, **Supp. XV:** 104–105

Neeley, Barbara, **Supp. XVI:** 143

"Negative Capability" (Komunyakaa), **Supp. XIII:** 131

Negligible Tales (Bierce), **I:** 209

"Negotiating the Darkness, Fortified by Poets' Strength" (Karr), **Supp. XI:** 254; **Supp. XIII:** 285

Negotiating with the Dead (Atwood), **Supp. XIII:** 20, 35

Negritude movement, **Supp. X:** 131, 139

"Negro" (Hughes), **Supp. I Part 1:** 321– 322

Negro, The (Du Bois), **Supp. II Part 1:** 178, 179, 185

Negro, The: The Southerner's Problem (Page), **Supp. II Part 1:** 168

Negro and His Music, The (Locke), **Supp. XIV:** 202

"Negro-Art Hokum, The" (Schuyler), **Supp. XXVI:** 167

"Negro Artisan, The" (Du Bois), **Supp. II Part 1:** 166

"Negro Artist and the Racial Mountain, The" (Hughes), **Retro. Supp. I:** 200, 207; **Supp. I Part 1:** 323, 325; **Supp. IV Part 1:** 169

Negro Art: Past and Present (Locke), **Supp. XIV:** 202

"Negro Assays the Negro Mood, A" (Baldwin), **Supp. I Part 1:** 52

"Negro Citizen, The" (Du Bois), **Supp. II Part 1:** 179

"Negro Dancers" (Hughes), **Retro. Supp. I:** 199; **Supp. I Part 1:** 324

"Negroes" (Bodenheim), **Supp. XXV:** 22

Negroes in America, The (McKay), **Supp. X:** 132, 136

"Negroes of Farmville, Virginia, The: A Social Study" (Du Bois), **Supp. II Part 1:** 166

Negro Family, The: The Case for National Action (Moynihan), **Retro. Supp. II:** 123

"Negro Farmer, The" (Du Bois), **Supp. II Part 1:** 167

"Negro Fight, The" (column, C. L. R. James), **Supp. XXI:** 169

"Negro Ghetto" (Hughes), **Supp. I Part 1:** 331

Negro in America, The (Locke), **Supp. XIV:** 208

Negro in American Civilization, The (Du Bois), **Supp. II Part 1:** 179

Negro in American Culture, The (Locke and Butcher), **Supp. XIV:** 202–203

Negro in Art, The: A Pictorial Record of the Negro Artist and of the Negro Theme in Art (Locke), **Supp. XIV:** 202

"Negro in Large Cities, The" (Du Bois), **Supp. II Part 1:** 169

"Negro in Literature and Art, The" (Du Bois), **Supp. II Part 1:** 174

Negro in New York, The (Ellison), **Supp. II Part 1:** 230

"Negro in the Black Belt, The: Some Social Sketches" (Du Bois), **Supp. II Part 1:** 166

Negro in the Caribbean, The (Williams), **Supp. XXI:** 166

"Negro in the Three Americas, The" (Locke), **Supp. XIV:** 211

"Negro in the Well, The" (Caldwell), **I:** 309

"Negro Love Song, A" (Dunbar), **Supp. II Part 1:** 204

"Negro Martyrs Are Needed" (C. Himes), **Supp. XVI:** 138

Negro Mother, The (Hughes), **Supp. I Part 1:** 328

Negro Mother and Other Dramatic Recitations, The (Hughes), **Retro. Supp. I:** 203

Negro Novel in America, The (Bone), **Supp. IX:** 318–319; **Supp. XVIII:** 285

Negro Publication Society of America, **Retro. Supp. I:** 205

"Negro Renaissance, The: Jean Toomer and the Harlem of the 1920s" (Bontemps), **Supp. IX:** 306

"Negro Schoolmaster in the New South, A" (Du Bois), **Supp. II Part 1:** 168

"Negro's Contribution to American Culture, The" (Locke), **Supp. XIV:** 210, 211

"Negro Sermon, A: Simon Legree" (Lindsay), **Supp. I Part 2:** 393

"Negro Sings of Rivers, The" (Hughes), **Supp. IV Part 1:** 16

"Negro Speaks of Rivers, The" (Hughes), **Retro. Supp. I:** 199; **Supp. I Part 1:** 321

"Negro Spirituals, The (Locke), **Supp. XIV:** 201

"Negro Takes Stock, The" (Du Bois), **Supp. II Part 1:** 180

"Negro Theatre, The" (Van Vechten), **Supp. II Part 2:** 735

"Negro Voter Sizes Up Taft, A" (Hurston), **Supp. VI:** 160

"Negro Writer and His Roots, The: Toward a New Romanticism" (Hansberry), **Supp. IV Part 1:** 364

"Negro Youth Speaks" (Locke), **Supp. XIV:** 201

"Nehemias Americanus" (Mather), **Supp. II Part 2:** 453

Nehru, Jawaharlal, **IV:** 490

"Neighbor" (Hugo), **Supp. VI:** 135–136

"Neighborhood Drunk"(Dybek), **Supp. XXIII:** 71

"Neighbors" (Carver), **Supp. III Part 1:** 135, 139, 141; **Supp. XI:** 153

"Neighbors" (Hogan), **Supp. IV Part 1:** 405

"Neighbors, The" (Hay), **Supp. XIV:** 126

"Neighbour Rosicky" (Cather), **I:** 331– 332

Neil Simon (R. K. Johnson), **Supp. IV Part 2:** 573

"Neil Simon's Jewish-Style Comedies" (Walden), **Supp. IV Part 2:** 584, 591

"Neil Simon: Toward Act III?" (Walden), **Supp. IV Part 2:** 591

Neilson, Heather, **Supp. IV Part 2:** 681
Neiman, Gilbert, **Supp. XV:** 140
"Neither Out Far Nor In Deep" (Frost), **I:** 303; **Retro. Supp. I:** 121, 138
"Nellie Clark" (Masters), **Supp. I Part 2:** 461
Nelson, Alice Dunbar, **Supp. XVII:** 75
Nelson, Cary, **Supp. XVIII:** 226, 227, 230, 231; **Supp. XXII:** 271
Nelson, Ernest, **I:** 388
Nelson, Howard, **Supp. IV Part 1:** 66, 68; **Supp. XIX:** 3; **Supp. XXI:** 95
Nelson, Lord Horatio, **II:** 524
Nelson, Lynn (pseudonym). *See* Nelson, Marilyn
Nelson, Marilyn, **Supp. XVII:** 74, 112; **Supp. XVIII: 171–188**
Nelson, Shirley, **Supp. XII:** 293
Nelson, Steve, **Supp. XVIII:** 226
Nelson Algren (Cox and Chatterton), **Supp. IX:** 11–12
Nelson Algren: A Life on the Wild Side (Drew), **Supp. IX:** 2
Nemerov, David, **II:** 268
Nemerov, Howard, **III: 267–289; IV:** 137, 140; **Supp. III Part 2:** 541; **Supp. IV Part 2:** 455, 650; **Supp. IX:** 114
"Nemesis" (Lovecraft), **Supp. XXV:** 119
Nemesis (P. Roth), **Supp. XXIV:** 214
Nemiroff, Robert Barron, **Supp. IV Part 1:** 360, 361, 365, 369, 370, 374
Neoconservative Criticism: Norman Podhoretz, Kenneth S. Lynn, and Joseph Epstein (Winchell), **Supp. VIII:** 241; **Supp. XIV:** 103
"Neo-Formalism: A Dangerous Nostalgia" (Sadoff), **Supp. XXI:** 100
"Neo-Hoodoo Manifesto, The" (Reed), **Supp. X:** 242
Neon Bible, The (Toole), **Supp. XXVI:** 239, 241, 242, 246–250, 253
Neon Rain, The (Burke), **Supp. XIV:** 22, 24, 26–27, 28–29, 30
Neon Vernacular (Komunyakaa), **Supp. XIII:** 121, **127–128,** 131
Neon Wilderness, The (Algren), **Supp. IX:** 3, 4
Neo-Slave Narratives (Rushdy), **Supp. X:** 250
Nepantla: Essays from the Land in the Middle (Mora), **Supp. XIII:** 213, **219–221,** 227
Nephew, The (Purdy), **Supp. VII:** 271, 273, 282
"Nereids of Seriphos, The" (Clampitt), **Supp. IX:** 41
Nericcio, William, **Supp. XIV:** 304–305
Neruda, Pablo, **Supp. I Part 1:** 89; **Supp. IV Part 2:** 537; **Supp. IX:** 157, 271; **Supp. V:** 332; **Supp. VIII:** 272, 274; **Supp. X:** 112; **Supp. XI:** 191; **Supp. XII:** 217; **Supp. XIII:** 114, 315, 323; **Supp. XXI:** 61, 100; **Supp. XXIV:** 170
"Nerves" (Huddle), **Supp. XXVI:** 149
Nesbit, Edith, **Supp. VIII:** 171
Nesbit, Lynn, **Supp. XXIII:** 100
Nesbitt, Robin, **Supp. VIII:** 89

Nessmuk (George Washington Sears), **Supp. XIX:** 10
Nesting Ground, The (Wagoner), **Supp. IX:** 324, **325–326**
Nest of Ninnies, A (Ashbery and Schuyler), **Supp. III Part 1:** 3; **Supp. XV:** 178
"Nests"(Le Sueur), **Supp. XXIII:** 165
Net of Cobwebs (Holding), **Supp. XXII:** 126, **129–130,** 134
Net of Magic: Wonders and Deceptions in India (Siegel), **Supp. XXII:** 262
Nets to Catch the Wind (Wylie), **Supp. I Part 2:** 709, 710–712, 714
Nettleton, Asahel, **I:** 458
"Net to Snare the Moonlight, A" (Lindsay), **Supp. I Part 2:** 387
Neubauer, Carol E., **Supp. IV Part 1:** 9
Neugeboren, Jacob Mordecai. *See* Neugeboren, Jay
Neugeboren, Jay, **Supp. XVI: 217–231**
Neugroschel, Joachim, **Supp. IX:** 138
Neuhaus, Richard John, **Supp. VIII:** 245; **Supp. XIX:** 144
Neumann, Erich, **Supp. I Part 2:** 567; **Supp. IV Part 1:** 68, 69
Neuromancer (W. Gibson), **Supp. XII:** 15; **Supp. XVI:** 117, 119–120, 122, 124, **125–126,** 127, 129, 131
Neurotica: Jewish Writers on Sex (Bukiet, ed.), **Supp. XVII:** 48
"Neurotic America and the Sex Impulse" (Dreiser), **Retro. Supp. II:** 105
Neutra, Richard, **Supp. XVI:** 192
"Never Been" (Huddle), **Supp. XXVI:** 150
"Never Bet the Devil Your Head" (Poe), **III:** 425; **Retro. Supp. II:** 273
Never Come Morning (Algren), **Supp. IX:** 3, **7–9**
Never in a Hurry: Essays on People and Places (Nye), **Supp. XIII:** 273, **280–282,** 286
"Never Marry a Mexican" (Cisneros), **Supp. VII:** 70
"Never Room with a Couple" (Hughes), **Supp. I Part 1:** 330
"Nevertheless" (Moore), **III:** 214
Nevils, René Pol, **Supp. XXVI:** 241, 242, 246
Nevins, Allan, **I:** 253; **Supp. I Part 2:** 486, 493
"Nevsky Prospekt" (Olds), **Supp. X:** 205
New Adam, The (Untermeyer), **Supp. XV:** 304, 305
New Addresses (Koch), **Supp. XV:** 177, 184
"New Age of the Rhetoricians, The" (Cowley), **Supp. II Part 1:** 135
New American Cyclopedia, **Supp. XVIII:** 4
New American Literature, The (Pattee), **II:** 456
New American Novel of Manners, The (Klinkowitz), **Supp. XI:** 347
"New American Ode, The" (Wright), **Supp. XV:** 346
New American Poetry (Allen, ed.), **Supp. XXVI:** 223

New American Poetry, 1945–1960, The (Allen, ed.), **Supp. VIII:** 291, 292; **Supp. XIII:** 112; **Supp. XXIII:** 215–216
New American Poetry, The (Allen, ed.), **Supp. XXVII:** 25
"New American Writer, A" (W. C. Williams), **Retro. Supp. II:** 335
New and Collected Poems (Reed), **Supp. X:** 241
New and Collected Poems (Wilbur), **Supp. III Part 2:** 562–564
New and Selected Poems (Nemerov), **III:** 269, 275, 277–279
New and Selected Poems (Oliver), **Supp. VII:** 240–241, 245
New and Selected Poems (W. J. Smith), **Supp. XIII:** 332
New and Selected Poems (Wagoner), **Supp. IX: 326–327**
New and Selected Poems, 1958–1998 (Sorrentino), **Supp. XXI:** 229
New and Selected Poems: 1974–1994 (Dunn), **Supp. XI: 151–152**
New and Selected Things Taking Place (Swenson), **Supp. IV Part 2:** 648–650, 651
"New Aristocracy, The" (Atherton), **Supp. XXIV:** 24
"New Art Gallery Society, The" (Wolfe), **Supp. III Part 2:** 580
Newberger, Julee, **Supp. XVIII:** 168
"New Birth, The" (Very), **Supp. XXV:** 246, 247, 248
New Black Poetry, The (Major, ed.), **Supp. XXII:** 172, 174, 176, 180
New Bridge, The (Levin), **Supp. XXVII:** 133
"New Capitalist Tool, The" (Wasserstein), **Supp. XV:** 328
New Collected Poems (Oppen), **Supp. XXVI:** 224
Newcomb, Ralph, **Supp. XIII:** 12
Newcomb, Robert, **II:** 111
New Conscience and an Ancient Evil, A (Addams), **Supp. I Part 1:** 14–15, 16
"New Conservatism in American Poetry, The" (Wakoski), **Supp. XVII:** 112
"New Conservatives, The: Intellectuals in Retreat" (Epstein), **Supp. XIV:** 103
New Critical Essays on H. P. Lovecraft (Simmons, ed.), **Supp. XXV:** 123
New Criticism, The (Ransom), **III:** 497–498, 499, 501
"New Day, A" (Levine), **Supp. V:** 182
Newdick, Robert Spangler, **Retro. Supp. I:** 138
Newdick's Season of Frost (Newdick), **Retro. Supp. I:** 138
New Dictionary of Quotations, A (Mencken), **III:** 111
New Directions Anthology in Prose and Poetry (Laughlin, ed.), **Supp. XVI:** 284
"New Directions in Poetry" (D. Locke), **Supp. IX:** 273
"New Dog, The: Variations on a Text by Jules Laforgue" (C. Frost), **Supp. XV:** 98
Newell, Henry, **IV:** 193

"New England" (R. Lowell), **II:** 536

"New England" (Robinson), **III:** 510, 524

"New England Bachelor, A" (Eberhart), **I:** 539

"New Englander, The" (Anderson), **I:** 114

New England Girlhood, A (Larcom), **Supp. XIII:** 137, 142, 143, 144, **147–154**

New England Gothic Literature (Ringel), **Supp. XXII:** 205

New England: Indian Summer (Brooks), **I:** 253, 256

New England Local Color Literature (Donovan), **Retro. Supp. II:** 138

"New England Sabbath-Day Chace, The" (Freneau), **Supp. II Part 1:** 273

New-England Tale, A (Sedgwick), **I:** 341

New England Tragedies, The (Longfellow), **II:** 490, 505, 506; **Retro. Supp. II:** 165, 167

New English Canaan (Morton), **Supp. XXII:** 45

New Era in American Poetry, The (Untermeyer, ed.), **Supp. XV:** 301, 303, 306

Newer Ideals of Peace (Addams), **Supp. I Part 1:** 11–12, 15, 16–17, 19, 20–21

"New Experience in Millinery, A" (Stratton-Porter), **Supp. XX:** 216

New Feminist Criticism, The: Essays on Women, Literature, and Theory (Showalter), **Supp. X:** 97

New Fire: To Put Things Right Again (Moraga), **Supp. XXIII:** 197

"New Folsom Prison" (Matthews), **Supp. IX:** 165

New Formalism, The: A Critical Introduction (McPhillips), **Supp. XV:** 250, 251, 252, 264

Newfound (J. W. Miller), **Supp. XX:** 163, **166, 170–172**

New Found Land: Fourteen Poems (MacLeish), **III:** 12–13

"New Hampshire" (Frost), **Supp. XXVI:** 78

"New Hampshire, February" (Eberhart), **I:** 536

New Hampshire: A Poem with Notes and Grace Notes (Frost), **II:** 154–155; **Retro. Supp. I:** 132, 133, 135

New Hard-Boiled Writers (Panek), **Supp. XIV:** 27

"New Home" (Richter), **Supp. XVIII:** 209

Newhouse, Seth, **Supp. XXVI:** 87, 89, 90

New Industrial State, The (Galbraith), **Supp. I Part 2:** 648

"New Journalism, The" (Wolfe), **Supp. III Part 2:** 571

New Journalism, The (Wolfe and E. W. Johnson, eds.), **Supp. III Part 2:** 570, 579–581, 583, 586; **Supp. XXIV:** 282; **Supp. XXVII:** 38

New Left, The: The Anti-Industrial Revolution (Rand), **Supp. IV Part 2:** 527

"New Letters from Thomas Jefferson" (Stafford), **Supp. XI:** 324

New Letters on the Air: Contemporary Writers on Radio, **Supp. X:** 165, 169, 173

"New Life" (Glück), **Supp. V:** 90

New Life, A (Malamud), **Supp. I Part 2:** 429–466

"New Life, The" (Bynner), **Supp. XV:** 44

"New Life, The"(Schott), **Supp. XXIII:** 242

"New Life at Kyerefaso" (Sutherland), **Supp. IV Part 1:** 9

"New Light on Veblen" (Dorfman), **Supp. I Part 2:** 650

"New Man, A" (E. P. Jones), **Supp. XXII:** 144

Newman, Charles, **Supp. I Part 2:** 527, 546–548

Newman, Edwin, **Supp. IV Part 2:** 526

Newman, Frances, **Supp. XXII:** 198

Newman, Judie, **Supp. IV Part 1:** 304, 305

Newman, Paul, **Supp. IV Part 2:** 473, 474

New Man, The (Merton), **Supp. VIII:** 208

"New Mecca, The" (Saunders), **Supp. XIX:** 235, 236

"New Medea, The" (Howells), **II:** 282

New Mexico trilogy (Nichols), **Supp. XIII:** 269

New Morning (album, Dylan), **Supp. XVIII:** 27, 33

"New Mother" (Olds), **Supp. X:** 206

"New Mothers, The" (Shields), **Supp. VII:** 310

New Music (Price), **Supp. VI:** 264, 265

"New Mutants, The" (Fiedler), **Supp. XIII:** 104

"New Name for Some Old Ways of Thinking, A" (James), **II:** 353

New Native American Novel, The: Works in Progress (Bartlett), **Supp. IV Part 1:** 335

"New Natural History, A" (Thurber), **Supp. I Part 2:** 619

New Negro, The (Locke), **Supp. XIX:** 69

"New Negro, The" (Locke), **Supp. XIV:** 201

New Negro, The (Locke, ed.), **Supp. II Part 1:** 176; **Supp. IX:** 309; **Supp. X:** 137; **Supp. XXII:** 8

New Negro, The: An Interpretation (Locke, ed.), **Retro. Supp. I:** 199; **Supp. IV Part 1:** 170; **Supp. XIV:** 195, 201–202

New Negro for a New Century, A (Washington, Wood, and Williams), **Supp. XIV:** 201

New New Journalism, The (R. Boynton), **Supp. XVII:** 209

"New Nomads, The" (E. Hoffman), **Supp. XVI:** 161

"New Orleans" (Carruth), **Supp. XVI:** 50

New Orleans Sketches (Faulkner), **Retro. Supp. I:** 80

New Path to the Waterfall, A (Carver), **Supp. III Part 1:** 138–140, 147, 149; **Supp. XXIV:** 172

"New Poem, The" (Wright), **Supp. V:** 339, 340

"New Poems" (MacLeish), **III:** 19

"New Poems" (Oliver), **Supp. VII:** 240

New Poems 1960 (Bynner), **Supp. XV:** 51

New Poems: 1980–88 (Haines), **Supp. XII: 209–210**

New Poetry, The (Monroe and Henderson, eds.), **Supp. I Part 2:** 387

"New Poetry Handbook, The" (Strand), **Supp. IV Part 2:** 626

New Poetry of Mexico (Strand, trans.), **Supp. IV Part 2:** 630

New Poets of England and America (Hall, Pack, and Simpson, eds.), **Supp. IV Part 2:** 621

"Newport of Anchuria" (Henry), **Supp. II Part 1:** 409

New Princeton Encyclopedia of Poetry and Poetics (Preminger and Brogan, eds.), **Supp. XV:** 250

"*New Republic* Moves Uptown, The" (Cowley), **Supp. II Part 1:** 142

"New Rose Hotel" (W. Gibson), **Supp. XVI:** 120, 122, 124

"News, The" (McClatchy), **Supp. XII:** 269

News Crew (Cruisers) series (Myers), **Supp. XXVII:** 212

"New Season" (Levine), **Supp. V:** 188

New Seeds of Contemplation (Merton), **Supp. VIII:** 200, 208

News from the Glacier: Selected Poems 1960–1980 (Haines), **Supp. XII:** 207, 208–209

"News Item" (Parker), **Supp. IX:** 190

News of a Kidnapping (García Márquez), **Supp. XXV:** 57

"New Song, A" (Hughes), **Retro. Supp. I:** 202; **Supp. I Part 1:** 328, 331–332

"New Song"(Kenny), **Supp. XXIII:** 156

Newson-Horst, Adele, **Supp. XXIII:** 95

"New South, The" (Lanier), **Supp. I Part 1:** 352, 354, 370

New Southern Girl, The: Female Adolescence in the Works of 12 Women Authors (Town), **Supp. XVIII:** 195

Newspaper Days, 1899–1906 (Mencken), **III:** 100, 102, 120

"New Spirit, The" (Ashbery), **Supp. III Part 1:** 14, 15

New Spoon River, The (Masters), **Supp. I Part 2:** 461–465, 473

New Star Chamber and Other Essays, The (Masters), **Supp. I Part 2:** 455–456, 459

New Tales of the Vampires (Rice), **Supp. VII:** 290

New Tenant, The (Ionesco), **Supp. XXIV:** 113

New Testament, **I:** 303, 457, 458; **II:** 167; **III:** 305; **IV:** 114, 134, 152; **Retro. Supp. I:** 58, 140, 360; **Supp. I Part 1:** 104, 106; **Supp. I Part 2:** 516; **Supp. XVII:** 155; **Supp. XXIII:** 13. *See also* names of New Testament books

New Testament, A (Anderson), **I:** 101, 114

"New Theory of Thorstein Veblen, A" (Galbraith), **Supp. I Part 2:** 650

Newton, Benjamin Franklin, **I:** 454

Newton, Huey P., **Supp. I Part 1:** 66; **Supp. IV Part 1:** 206; **Supp. XXVII:** 168

Newton, Isaac, **I:** 132, 557; **II:** 6, 103, 348–349; **III:** 428; **IV:** 18, 149

Newton, Maud, **Supp. XXIII:** 290

Newton, Sarah Emily, **Supp. XV:** 234

"New-Wave Format, A" (Mason), **Supp. VIII:** 141, 143, 147

New West of Edward Abbey, The (Ronald), **Supp. XIII:** 4

"New Wife" (Halliday), **Supp. XIX:** 89

New Wolves, The: The Return of the Mexican Wolf to the American Southwest (Bass), **Supp. XVI:** 26–27

New Woman's Survival Sourcebook, The (Rennie and Grimstead, eds.), **Supp. I Part 2:** 569

New World, The (Bronk), **Supp. XXI:** 25–26, 31

New World, The (Bynner), **Supp. XV:** 41, 42

"New World, The" (Very), **Supp. XXV:** 248

New World, The: Tales (Banks), **Supp. V:** 8, 9, 10

New World Naked, A (Mariani), **Retro. Supp. I:** 419

New Worlds of Literature (Beaty and Hunter, eds.), **Supp. IV Part 1:** 331

New World Writing (Updike), **IV:** 217

"New Year, The" (Very), **Supp. XXV:** 240, 244

New Year Letter (Auden), **Supp. II Part 1:** 14, 16

"New Year's Day" (Wharton), **Retro. Supp. I:** 381

"New Year's Eve" (Schwartz), **Supp. II Part 2:** 640, 656–657

New Year's Eve/1929 (Farrell), **II:** 43

"New Year's Eve 1968" (R. Lowell), **II:** 554

New Year's Eve: A Play (W. Frank), **Supp. XX:** 75

"New Year's Gift, The" (Stowe), **Supp. I Part 2:** 587

"New Year Two Thousand, The" (Weigl), **Supp. XIX:** 287–288

"New York" (Capote), **Supp. III Part 1:** 122

"New York" (Moore), **III:** 196, 198, 202, 206

"New York 1965" (Bowles), **Supp. IV Part 1:** 94

New York: A Serendipiter's Journey (Talese), **Supp. XVII:** 202, 203

"New York Breeze" (Halliday), **Supp. XIX:** 85

New York City Arts Project, **Supp. III Part 2:** 618

"New York City in 1979"(Acker), **Supp. XII:** 5

New York Edition, **Retro. Supp. I:** 235

"New York Edition" (James), **II:** 336, 337

"New York Gold Conspiracy, The" (Adams), **I:** 4

New York Hat, The (film; Griffith), **Supp. XVI:** 183

New York Intellectuals, **Supp. VIII:** 93

"New York Intellectuals, The" (Howe), **Supp. VI:** 120

"New York Is a City of Things Unnoticed" (Talese), **Supp. XVII:** 202, 209

New York: Its Upper Ten and Lower Million (Lippard), **Supp. XXIII:** 180, 183, 184

New York Jew (Kazin), **Supp. VIII:** 95, **97–100**

New York Madness (Bodenheim), **Supp. XXV:** 28

"New York Theater: Isn't It Romantic" (Wasserstein), **Supp. XV:** 320

New York Trilogy, The (Auster), **Supp. XII:** 21, **24–28**

Next (McNally), **Supp. XIII:** 197

"Next in Line, The" (Bradbury), **Supp. IV Part 1:** 102

"Next Rodeo, The" (Kittredge), **Supp. XXVI:** 185–186

Next Rodeo, The: New and Selected Essays (Kittredge), **Supp. XXVI:** 185–186

Next Room of the Dream, The (Nemerov), **III:** 269, 275, 278, 279–280, 284

"Next Time I Crossed the Line into Oklahoma, The" (Wright), **Supp. XV:** 345

Next-to-Last Things: New Poems and Essays (Kunitz), **Supp. III Part 1:** 257–259, 261, 262, 265, 266, 268

"'Next to Reading Matter' " (Henry), **Supp. II Part 1:** 399

Nexus (H. Miller), **III:** 170, 187, 188, 189

Nguyen, Bich Minh, **Supp. XXVI: 207–222**

Niatum, Duane, **Supp. IV Part 1:** 331; **Supp. IV Part 2:** 505

Nice and Noir (Schwartz), **Supp. XIV:** 23

"Nice Girl" (Nelson), **Supp. XVIII:** 178

Nice Jewish Boy, The (P. Roth), **Supp. III Part 2:** 412

"Nice Part f Town, A" (Hayes), **Supp. XXVI:** 144

Nicholas II, Tsar, **Supp. I Part 2:** 447

"Nicholas in the Park" (Halliday), **Supp. XIX:** 88

Nicholls, Peter, **Supp. XIX:** 232; **Supp. XXVI:** 228, 232

Nichols, Charles, **Retro. Supp. I:** 194

Nichols, Dudley, **Supp. XVIII:** 247

Nichols, John Treadwell, **Supp. XIII: 253–272**

Nichols, Luther, **Supp. X:** 265

Nichols, Mike, **Supp. IV Part 1:** 234; **Supp. IV Part 2:** 577

Nicholson, Colin, **Supp. VIII:** 129

Nicholson, Harold, **Supp. XIV:** 163

Nicholson, Jack, **Supp. V:** 26; **Supp. VIII:** 45; **Supp. XI:** 308

Nicholson, John, **Supp. XVI:** 293

Nick Adams Stories, The (Hemingway), **II:** 258; **Retro. Supp. I:** 174

"Nick and the Candlestick" (Plath), **Supp. I Part 2:** 544

Nickel and Dimed: On (Not) Getting By in America (Ehrenreich), **Supp. XVII:** 210

Nickel Eclipse: Iroquois Moon (Gansworth), **Supp. XXVI:** 110

Nickel Mountain: A Pastoral Novel (Gardner), **Supp. VI:** 63, 64, 68, **69**

Nickerson, Catherine Ross, **Supp. XXV:** 192, 200, 202

"Nicodemus" (Keillor), **Supp. XVI:** 167

Nicoll, Allardyce, **III:** 400

Nicoloff, Philip, **II:** 7

Niebuhr, Gustav, **III:** 292

Niebuhr, H. Richard, **I:** 494

Niebuhr, Lydia, **III:** 292

Niebuhr, Reinhold, **III: 290–313; Supp. I Part 2:** 654; **Supp. XX:** 79

Niedecker, Lorine, **Supp. III Part 2:** 616, 623; **Supp. XIV:** 287; **Supp. XXIII:** 174

Nielsen, Ed, **Supp. IX:** 254

Nielson, Dorothy, **Supp. I Part 2:** 659

Nietzsche, Friedrich Wilhelm, **I:** 227, 283, 383, 389, 396, 397, 402, 509; **II:** 7, 20, 27, 42, 90, 145, 262, 462, 463, 577, 583, 585; **III:** 102–103, 113, 156, 176; **IV:** 286, 491; **Supp. I Part 1:** 254, 299, 320; **Supp. I Part 2:** 646; **Supp. IV Part 1:** 104, 105–106, 107, 110, 284; **Supp. IV Part 2:** 519; **Supp. V:** 277, 280; **Supp. VIII:** 11, 181, 189; **Supp. X:** 48; **Supp. XII:** 98; **Supp. XIV:** 339; **Supp. XX:** 117; **Supp. XXVII:** 34

Nieves, Felipe, **Supp. XVIII:** 90

Niflis, N. Michael, **Supp. IV Part 1:** 175

Niger, S. *See* Charney, Samuel

Nigger Heaven (Van Vechten), **Supp. II Part 2:** 739, 744–746; **Supp. XIX:** 76; **Supp. XVIII:** 123, 127

"Nigger Jeff" (Dreiser), **Retro. Supp. II:** 97

Nigger of the "Narcissus," The (Conrad), **II:** 91; **Retro. Supp. I:** 106; **Supp. XVIII:** 224; **Supp. XXIV:** 286

"NIGGY THE HO" (Baraka), **Supp. II Part 1:** 54

"Night" (H. Johnson), **Supp. XXVI:** 173

"Night" (Huddle), **Supp. XXVI:** 155

"Night, Death, Mississippi" (Hayden), **Supp. II Part 1:** 369

'*Night, Mother* (Norman), **Supp. VIII:** 141

"Night above the Avenue" (Merwin), **Supp. III Part 1:** 355

"Night among the Horses, A" (Barnes), **Supp. III Part 1:** 33–34, 39, 44

"Night and the Madman" (Gibran), **Supp. XX:** 118

Night at the Movies, A, or, You Must Remember This: Fictions (Coover), **Supp. V:** 50–51

"Night at the Opera, A" (Matthews), **Supp. IX:** 167

"Night before the Sentence Is Carried Out, The" (Wright), **Supp. XV:** 341

"Nightbird" (Komunyakaa), **Supp. XIII:** 132

Night-Blooming Cereus, The (Hayden), **Supp. II Part 1:** 367, 373

"Night-Blooming Cereus, The" (Hayden), **Supp. II Part 1:** 367

Night-Born, The (London), **II:** 467

"Nightbreak" (Rich), **Supp. I Part 2:** 556

"Nightclub" (Collins), **Supp. XXI:** 60

Night Country, The (O'Nan), **Supp. XXV:** 141, 148–149, 150

Night Dance (Price), **Supp. VI:** 264

"Night Dances, The" (Plath), **Supp. I Part 2:** 544

"Night Dream, The" (MacLeish), **III:** 15

"Nightfall" (Teasdale), **Supp. XXVII:** 293

"Night Ferry" (Doty), **Supp. XI:** 124

"Nightfishing" (Schnackenberg), **Supp. XV:** 254

"Nighthawks"(Dybek), **Supp. XXIII:** 73, 74

"Night I Met Little Floyd, The" (Wright), **Supp. XV:** 345–346

Night in Acadie, A (Chopin), **Retro. Supp. II: 66–67,** 73; **Supp. I Part 1:** 200, 219, 220, 224

"Night in Acadie, A" (Chopin), **Retro. Supp. II:** 66

"Night in June, A" (W. C. Williams), **Retro. Supp. I:** 424

"Night in New Arabia, A" (Henry), **Supp. II Part 1:** 402

Night in Question, The: Stories (Wolff), **Supp. VII:** 342–344

"Night Journey" (Roethke), **Supp. III Part 1:** 260

"Night Letter to the Reader" (Collins), **Supp. XXI:** 55

Night Light (Justice), **Supp. VII:** 126–127

"Nightmare" (Kumin), **Supp. IV Part 2:** 442

Nightmare Factory, The (Kumin), **Supp. IV Part 2:** 444–447, 451

"Nightmare Factory, The" (Kumin), **Supp. IV Part 2:** 445, 453

Nightmare on Main Street (Poe), **Retro. Supp. II:** 262

"Nightmare" poems (Benét), **Supp. XI:** 46, 58

"Night Mirror" (L.-Y. Lee), **Supp. XV:** 225

Night Music (Odets), **Supp. II Part 2:** 541, 543, 544

"Night of First Snow" (R. Bly), **Supp. IV Part 1:** 71

Night of January 16th (Rand), **Supp. IV Part 2:** 527

Night of the Iguana, The (T. Williams), **IV:** 382, 383, 384, 385, 386, 387, 388, 391, 392, 393, 394, 395, 397, 398

"Night of the Iguana, The" (T. Williams), **IV:** 384

"Night of the Living Beanfield: How an Unsuccessful Cult Novel Became an Unsuccessful Cult Film in Only Fourteen Years, Eleven Nervous Breakdowns, and $20 Million" (Nichols), **Supp. XIII:** 267

Night Passage (Parker), **Supp. XIX:** 185–186

Night Rider (Warren), **IV:** 243, 246–247

Nights (Doolittle), **Supp. I Part 1:** 270, 271

Nights and Days (Merrill), **Supp. III Part 1:** 319, 320, 322–325

"Nights and Days" (Rich), **Supp. I Part 2:** 574

"Night's for Cryin,' The" (C. Himes), **Supp. XVI:** 137

"Night Shift" (Plath), **Supp. I Part 2:** 538

"Nightshine Beyond Memory, A: Ten More Years with Ray" (Gallagher), **Supp. XXIV:** 167, 172

Night-Side (Oates), **Supp. II Part 2:** 522

"Night-Side" (Oates), **Supp. II Part 2:** 523

Night-Side, The (Skloot), **Supp. XX: 193, 196, 205, 208**

Nights in the Gardens of Brooklyn (Swados), **Supp. XIX: 261–264**

"Nights in the Gardens of Brooklyn" (Swados), **Supp. XIX:** 261

"Night Sketches: Beneath an Umbrella" (Hawthorne), **II:** 235–237, 238, 239, 242; **Supp. XXI:** 201

"Night Sport" (Hoffman), **Supp. XVIII:** 86, 87

"Night-Sweat" (R. Lowell), **II:** 554

"Night-Talk" (Ellison), **Retro. Supp. II:** 126; **Supp. II Part 1:** 248

Night the New Jesus Fell to Earth, The (Rash), **Supp. XXVII:** 216–217, 227

Night Thoughts (Young), **III:** 415

"Night-Time River Road, A" (Ferry), **Supp. XXIV:** 150

Night Traveler, The (Oliver), **Supp. VII:** 233

"Night Watch" (Gioia), **Supp. XV:** 117

"Night Watch, The" (Wright), **Supp. V:** 339

"Night We All Had Grippe, The" (Jackson), **Supp. IX:** 118

Nightwood (Barnes), **Supp. III Part 1:** 31, 32, 35–37, 39–43

Night World and the Word Night, The (F. Wright), **Supp. XVII:** 240, 244–245

"Nihilist as Hero, The" (R. Lowell), **II:** 554; **Retro. Supp. II:** 190

Nijinsky, Vaslav, **Supp. XV:** 28–29

Nikolai Gogol (Nabokov), **Retro. Supp. I:** 266

"Nilda" (Díaz), **Supp. XXIV:** 92

Niles, Thomas, **Retro. Supp. I:** 35

Niles, Thomas, Jr., **Supp. I Part 1:** 39

Nilsson, Christine, **Supp. I Part 1:** 355

Nilsson, Harry, **Supp. XI:** 309

Nilsson, Jenny Lind, **Supp. XVI:** 177

Nimitz, Chester, **Supp. I Part 2:** 491

"Nimram" (Gardner), **Supp. VI:** 73

Nims, John Frederick, **III:** 527; **Supp. XVII:** 112

Nin, Anaïs, **III:** 182, 184, 190; **Supp. III Part 1:** 43; **Supp. IV Part 2:** 680; **Supp. X:** 181–200; **Supp. XIX:** 134

"9" (Oliver), **Supp. VII:** 244

"9 Failures of the Imagination" (Lethem), **Supp. XVIII:** 148

"Nine-Ball" (Offutt), **Supp. XIX:** 166, 167

Nine Dragons (Connelly), **Supp. XXI: 74, 79–80**

"Nine from Eight" (Lanier), **Supp. I Part 1:** 352–354

Nine Gates: Entering the Mind of Poetry (Hirshfield), **Supp. XXIII:** 136, 137

Nine Headed Dragon River: Zen Journals 1969–1982 (Matthiessen), **Supp. V:** 199

Nine Horses (Collins), **Supp. XXI:** 55, 60, 61, 62, 65

"Nine Horses" (Collins), **Supp. XXI:** 61

Ninemile Wolves,The (Bass), **Supp. XVI:** 24–25, 26

"Nine Nectarines" (Moore), **III:** 203, 209, 215

Nine Plays (Reznikoff), **Supp. XIV:** 288

"Nine Poems for the Unborn Child" (Rukeyser), **Supp. VI:** 280–281, 284

Nine Stories (Nabokov), **Retro. Supp. I:** 266

Nine Stories (Salinger), **III:** 552, 558–564

"19 Hadley Street" (Schnackenberg), **Supp. XV:** 253

19 Necromancers from Now (Reed), **Supp. X:** 240

19 Varieties of Gazelle (Nye), **Supp. XIII:** 275, **286–288**

"19 Varieties of Gazelle" (Nye), **Supp. XIII:** 286

1984 (Orwell), **Supp. XIII:** 29; **Supp. XVIII:** 137, 138

"1953 Dodge Coronet" (Huddle), **Supp. XXVI:** 151

"1940" (Stafford), **Supp. XI:** 328–329

"1945–1985: Poem for the Anniversary" (Oliver), **Supp. VII:** 237

"1941" (Stone), **Supp. XXVII:** 253

1919 (Dos Passos), **I:** 482, 485–486, 487, 489, 490, 492

"1975" (Wright), **Supp. V:** 341

"1973"(Hirshfield), **Supp. XXIII:** 130

"1910" (Mora), **Supp. XIII:** 215

Nineteenth-Century Minor Poets (Auden), **Supp. XXV:** 237

"1938" (Komunyakaa), **Supp. XIII:** 114

1939 (Boyle), **Supp. XXIV:** 62

"1939" (Taylor), **Supp. V:** 316

1933 (Levine), **Supp. V:** 185–187

"1933" (Levine), **Supp. V:** 188

"Nineteenth New York, The" (Doctorow), **Supp. IV Part 1:** 232

"1929" (Auden), **Supp. II Part 1:** 6

"1926" (Kees), **Supp. XV:** 135

"93990" (Saunders), **Supp. XIX:** 233

"90 North" (Jarrell), **II:** 370, 371

90 Trees (Zukofsky), **Supp. III Part 2:** 631

95 Poems (Cummings), **I:** 430, 433, 435, 439, 446, 447

"91 Revere Street" (R. Lowell), **II:** 547; **Retro. Supp. II:** 188; **Supp. XI:** 240

Ninety Percent of Everything (Lethem, Kelly and Kessel), **Supp. XVIII:** 145

"92 Days" (L. Brown), **Supp. XXI:** 44–45

"Nine Years Later" (Brodsky), **Supp. VIII:** 32

Ninth Avenue (Bodenheim), **Supp. XXV:** 24–25

"Nirvana" (Lanier), **Supp. I Part 1:** 352

Nirvana Blues, The (Nichols), **Supp. XIII:** 266, 267

Nishikigi (play), **III:** 466

Niven, David, **Supp. XI:** 307

Nixon (film), **Supp. XIV:** 48

Nixon, Richard M., **I:** 376; **III:** 38, 46; **Supp. I Part 1:** 294, 295; **Supp. V:** 45, 46, 51; **Supp. XII:** 14; **Supp. XIV:** 306

"NJ Transit" (Komunyakaa), **Supp. XIII:** 132

Nketia, J. H., **Supp. IV Part 1:** 10

Nketsia, Nana, **Supp. IV Part 1:** 2, 10

Nkize, Julius, **Supp. IV Part 1:** 361

Nkrumah, Kwame, **I:** 490, 494; **Supp. IV Part 1:** 361; **Supp. X:** 135

Nkrumah and the Ghana Revolution (C. L. R. James), **Supp. XXI:** 159, 171–172

NO (Major), **Supp. XXII:** 174

"Noah" (Biss), **Supp. XXVI:** 48

Noailles, Anna de, **IV:** 328

Noa Noa (Gauguin), **I:** 34

Nobel Lecture (Singer), **Retro. Supp. II:** 300

"No Better Than a 'Withered Daffodil' " (Moore), **III:** 216

Noble, David W., **Supp. I Part 2:** 650

Noble, Marianne, **Supp. XVIII:** 267

"Noble Rider and the Sound of Words, The" (Stevens), **Retro. Supp. I:** 299

Noble Savage, The (Coover), **Supp. V:** 40

"No Bobolink reverse His Singing" (Dickinson), **Retro. Supp. I:** 45

Nobodaddy (MacLeish), **III:** 5–6, 8, 10, 11, 18, 19, 20

"Nobodaddy" (W. Blake), **Supp. XVII:** 245

"Nobody in Hollywood" (Bausch), **Supp. VII:** 54

Nobody Knows My Name (Baldwin), **Supp. XIII:** 111

"Nobody Knows My Name" (Baldwin), **Retro. Supp. II:** 8; **Supp. I Part 1:** 52

Nobody Knows My Name: More Notes of a Native Son (Baldwin), **Retro. Supp. II:** 6, 8; **Supp. I Part 1:** 47, 52, 55

"Nobody knows this little Rose" (Dickinson), **Retro. Supp. I:** 30

"Nobody Said Anything" (Carver), **Supp. III Part 1:** 141

"Nobody's Business" (Lahiri), **Supp. XXI:** 183

Nobody's Fool (Russo), **Supp. XII:** 326, **331–335,** 340

"No Change of Place" (Auden), **Supp. II Part 1:** 5

"Noche Triste, La" (Frost), **Retro. Supp. I:** 123

Nock, Albert Jay, **I:** 245; **Supp. IV Part 2:** 521, 524

"No Coward Soul Is Mine" (Brontë), **I:** 458

"No Crime in the Mountains" (Chandler), **Supp. IV Part 1:** 129

"Nocturne" (Komunyakaa), **Supp. XIII:** 126

"Nocturne" (MacLeish), **III:** 8

"Nocturne at Bethesda" (Bontemps), **Supp. XXII:** 3, 8

"Nocturne in a Deserted Brickyard" (Sandburg), **III:** 586

Nocturne of Remembered Spring (Aiken), **I:** 50

Nod House (Mackey), **Supp. XXVII:** 156

No Direction Home (documentary film, Scorsese), **Supp. XVIII:** 22, 23, 29

No Direction Home (Shelton), **Supp. XVIII:** 21

No Door (Wolfe), **IV:** 451–452, 456

"No Door" (Wolfe), **IV:** 456

"No End" (Huddle), **Supp. XXVI:** 151

"No Epitaph" (Carson), **Supp. XII:** 111

No Exit (Sartre), **I:** 82, 130; **Supp. XIV:** 320

No Exit (Sartre; Bowles, trans.), **Supp. IV Part 1:** 84

No Gifts from Chance (Benstock), **Retro. Supp. I:** 361

"No-Good Blues" (Komunyakaa), **Supp. XIII:** 130

No Hero (Marquand), **III:** 57

No Heroes: A Memoir of Coming Home (Offutt), **Supp. XIX:** 163, **172–174,** 175

No! In Thunder (Fiedler), **Supp. XIII:** 101

"Noir" (Stallings), **Supp. XXV:** 232

"Noiseless Patient Spider" (Whitman), **III:** 555; **IV:** 348; **Supp. IV Part 1:** 325

Noises Off (Frayn), **Supp. IV Part 2:** 582

Noi vivi. See We the Living (film)

"No Jury Would Convict" (Shaw), **Supp. XIX:** 245

"No Lamp Has Ever Shown Us Where to Look" (MacLeish), **III:** 9

Nolan, Sidney, **Retro. Supp. II:** 189

No Laughing Matter (Heller and Vogel), **Supp. IV Part 1:** 384, 389

No Love Lost, a Romance of Travel (Howells), **II:** 277

Nomad (Ali), **Supp. XXIV:** 15

Nomad's Land (Rinehart), **Supp. XXV:** 195

No Man Is an Island (Merton), **Supp. VIII:** 207

"No Man's Land" (Biss), **Supp. XXVI:** 47, 56

"No More This Home" (Taggard), **Supp. XXII:** 277, 280

No Mother to Guide Her (Loos), **Supp. XVI:** 194

No Name in the Street (Baldwin), **Retro. Supp. II:** 13, 14; **Supp. I Part 1:** 47, 48, 52, 65–66, 67

No Nature: New and Selected Poems (Snyder), **Supp. VIII: 305**

Nonconformist's Memorial, The (Howe), **Supp. IV Part 2:** 434, 435–436

Nonconformity (Algren), **Supp. IX:** 15

None but the Lonely Heart (film), **Supp. II Part 2:** 546

Nones (Auden), **Supp. II Part 1:** 21

"Nones" (Auden), **Supp. II Part 1:** 22–23

None Shall Look Back (Gordon), **II:** 205–207, 208

"No No, Bad Daddy" (Nelson), **Supp. XVIII:** 177, 178

"Non-Tenured" (Halliday), **Supp. XIX:** 90, 91

Nonverbal Communication: Notes on the Visual Perception of Human Relations (Kees and Ruesch), **Supp. XV:** 147

"Noon" (Bryant), **Supp. I Part 1:** 157

No One Belongs Here More Than You (July), **Supp. XXIV:** 199, **200–207**

"No One Remembers" (Levine), **Supp. V:** 187

"Noon Walk on the Asylum Lawn" (Sexton), **Supp. II Part 2:** 673

"Noon Wine" (Porter), **III:** 436, 437–438, 442, 446

"No Pain Whatsoever" (Yates), **Supp. XI:** 341

"No Place for You, My Love" (Welty), **IV:** 278, 279; **Retro. Supp. I:** 353

No Plays of Japan, The (Waley), **III:** 466

No Pockets in a Shroud (McCoy), **Supp. XIII:** 166–168, 171, 172, 173, 174

"No Poem So Fine" (Francis), **Supp. IX:** 83

Norcross, Frances, **I:** 456, 462

Norcross, Louise, **I:** 456, 462

Nordfeldt, B. J. O., **Supp. XXI:** 6

Nordfeldt, Margaret, **Supp. XXI:** 6

Nordyke, Lewis, **Supp. XIII:** 5

No Relief (Dixon), **Supp. XII:** 139, **142–143**

No Resting Place (Humphrey), **Supp. IX:** 94, **106–108**

Norfolk Poems, The (Carruth), **Supp. XVI:** 47, 48

Norma (Bellini), **IV:** 309

Norma Ashe (Glaspell), **Supp. III Part 1:** 175, 186–187

"Normal Life, A"(Thompson), **Supp. XXIII:** 300

"Normal Motor Adjustments" (Stein and Solomons), **IV:** 26

Norman, Charles, **III:** 479

Norman, Gurney, **Supp. X:** 24; **Supp. XXIII:** 42

Norman, Jessye, **Supp. XX:** 110

Norman, Marsha, **Supp. VIII:** 141; **Supp. XXI:** 145; **Supp. XXIV:** 124

Norman Mailer (Poirier), **Retro. Supp. II:** 207–208

Norman Mailer: Modern Critical Views (Bloom), **Retro. Supp. II:** 205

Norman Mailer Revisited (Merrill), **Retro. Supp. II:** 201

Norna; or, The Witch's Curse (Alcott), **Supp. I Part 1:** 33

Norris, Charles, **III:** 320; **Retro. Supp. I:** 100; **Supp. XVIII:** 226

Norris, Frank, **I:** 211, 355, 500, 506, 517, 518, 519; **II:** 89, 264, 276, 289, 307; **III:** 227, **314–336,** 596; **IV:** 29; **Retro. Supp. I:** 100, 325; **Retro. Supp. II:** 96, 101; **Supp. III Part 2:** 412; **Supp. IX:** 14, 15; **Supp. VIII:** 101, 102; **Supp. XV:** 115

"North" (Budbill), **Supp. XIX:** 7–8

"North" (Hugo), **Supp. VI:** 135

North, Milou (pseudonym), **Supp. IV Part 1:** 260. *See also* Dorris, Michael; Erdrich, Louise

North, Sir Thomas, **IV:** 370

"North American Sequence" (Roethke), **I:** 171–172, 183; **III:** 529, 545, 547, 548

"North Beach" (Snyder), **Supp. VIII:** 289

North Country: A Personal Journey Through the Borderland (Mosher), **Supp. XXII: 203–204,** 206, 212, **217–218**

"North Country Sketches" (McClatchy), **Supp. XII:** 256

"Northeast Playground" (Paley), **Supp. VI:** 226–227, 229

Northern Borders (Mosher), **Supp. XXII:** 203, 204, 206, 207, 208, 209, **213–214**

Northern Lights (O'Brien), **Supp. V:** 237, 239, 241–244, 250

"Northern Motive" (Levine), **Supp. V:** 195

Northfield Poems (Ammons), **Supp. VII:** 29

"Northhanger Ridge" (Wright), **Supp. V:** 335, 340

"North Haven" (Bishop), **Retro. Supp. II:** 50

"North Labrador" (Crane), **I:** 386

North of Boston (Frost), **II:** 152, 153–154, 527; **Retro. Supp. I:** 121, 125, 127, **128–130,** 131; **Supp. I Part 1:** 263; **Supp. XIII:** 146

North of Jamaica (Simpson), **Supp. IV Part 2:** 448; **Supp. IX:** 275, 276

North of the Danube (Caldwell), **I:** 288, 290, 293, 294, 309, 310

North: Poems of Home (Kenny), **Supp. XXIII: 147–148**

Northrup, Cyrus, **Supp. I Part 1:** 350

North Sea (Jarman), **Supp. XVII:** 110, 113

"North Sea Undertaker's Complaint, The" (R. Lowell), **II:** 550

North & South (Bishop), **Retro. Supp. II: 41–43; Supp. I Part 1:** 72, 84, 85, 89

North Star, The (Hellman), **Supp. I Part 1:** 281

Northup, Solomon, **Supp. XIV:** 32

"Northwest Writers at Work" (Baker), **Supp. XXIV:** 178

"North Winter" (Carruth), **Supp. XVI:** 53

Norton, Charles Eliot, **I:** 223, 568; **II:** 279, 322–323, 338; **Retro. Supp. I:** 371; **Retro. Supp. II:** 135; **Supp. I Part 1:** 103; **Supp. I Part 2:** 406, 479

Norton, Jody, **Supp. VIII:** 297

Norton, John, **Supp. I Part 1:** 99, 110, 112, 114

Norton Anthology of African American Literature, The (H. L. Gates and McKay, eds.), **Supp. X:** 325; **Supp. XX: 105**

Norton Anthology of American Literature, **Supp. X:** 325; **Supp. XV:** 270

Norton Anthology of Literature by Women (Gilbert and Gubar, eds.), **Supp. XV:** 270

Norton Anthology of Modern Poetry, The, **Supp. XI:** 259; **Supp. XV:** 258; **Supp. XXIV:** 35, 39

Norton Anthology of Poetry, The, **Supp. XVIII:** 20

Norton Anthology of Short Fiction, The, **Supp. IX:** 4

Norton Book of Personal Essays, The, **Supp. XIV:** 105

Norton Lectures, **Retro. Supp. I:** 65

Norwood, Vera, **Supp. IX:** 24

No Safe Harbour (Porter), **III:** 447

Nosferatu: An Opera Libretto (Gioia), **Supp. XV:** 112, **128**

"Nosferatu's Serenade" (Gioia), **Supp. XV:** 128

No Siege Is Absolute (Char; version of F. Wright), **Supp. XVII:** 244

"No Snake" (A. Finch), **Supp. XVII:** 72

"No Speak English" (Cisneros), **Supp. VII:** 63

"Nostalgia" (Collins), **Supp. XXI:** 57

"Nostalgia" (Saunders), **Supp. XIX:** 235

Nostalgia for 70 (J. W. Miller), **Supp. XX: 165**

"Nostalgia of the Lakefronts" (Justice), **Supp. VII:** 118, 119, 120

"Nostalgic Mood" (Farrell), **II:** 45

No Star Is Lost (Farrell), **II:** 34, 35, 44

Nostrandt, Jeanne, **Supp. XVIII:** 80–81

Nostromo (Conrad), **II:** 600; **IV:** 245

"Nosty Fright, A" (Swenson), **Supp. IV Part 2:** 651

"Not" (Huddle), **Supp. XXVI:** 157

Not about Nightingales (T. Williams), **IV:** 381

"Not a Sparrow" (Gallagher), **Supp. XXIV:** 171

Not: A Trio (Huddle), **Supp. XXVI:** 150, 156–157

"Not a Womb in the House" (Quindlen), **Supp. XVII:** 166, 171

"(Not) Born in he U.S.A." (Gansworth), **Supp. XXVI:** 111

Not Coming to Be Barked At (Kooser), **Supp. XIX:** 116, **120**

Not Dancing (Dunn), **Supp. XI:** 143, **148**

"Note about *Iconographs*, A" (Swenson), **Supp. IV Part 2:** 646

Notebook (R. Lowell), **Retro. Supp. II:** 186, 190; **Supp. V:** 343

Notebook 1967–68 (R. Lowell), **II:** 553–555; **Retro. Supp. II:** 182, 186, 190

Notebook of Malte Laurids Brigge, The (Rilke), **III:** 571

Notebooks (Fitzgerald), **Retro. Supp. I:** 110

Notebooks of Captain George, The (Renoir), **Supp. XXII:** 257

No Telephone to Heaven (Cliff), **Supp. XXII:** 66, 69, 71–72

"Note on Abraham Lincoln" (Vidal), **Supp. IV Part 2:** 688

"Note on Commercial Theatre" (Hughes), **Retro. Supp. I:** 207

"Note on Ezra Pound, A" (Eliot), **Retro. Supp. I:** 290

"Note on Lanier's Music, A" (P. Graham), **Supp. I Part 1:** 373

Note on Literary Criticism, A (Farrell), **II:** 26, 49

"Note on Poetry, A" (Doolittle), **Supp. I Part 1:** 254, 267–268

"Note on Realism, A" (Anderson), **I:** 110

"Note on the Limits of 'History' and the Limits of 'Criticism,' A" (Brooks), **Supp. XIV:** 11

"Note on the Poetry of Love, A" (Untermeyer), **Supp. XV:** 304

"Note on the Truth of the Tales, A" (Vollmann), **Supp. XVII:** 230

"Notes" (Dove), **Supp. IV Part 1:** 246

"Notes for a Moving Picture: The House" (Agee), **I:** 33, 34

"Notes for an Autobiography" (Van Vechten), **Supp. II Part 2:** 749

"Notes for a Novel About the End of the World" (Percy), **Supp. III Part 1:** 393

"Notes for a Preface" (Sandburg), **III:** 591, 596–597

"NOTES FOR A SPEECH" (Baraka), **Supp. II Part 1:** 33

Notes for the Green Box (Duchamp), **Supp. IV Part 2:** 423

Notes for the Two-Dollar Window: Portraits from an American Neighborhood (Kriegel), **Supp. XXIV: 223–224**

Notes from a Bottle Found on the Beach at Carmel (Connell), **Supp. XIV:** 80, 87, 96, 97

Notes from a Sea Diary: Hemingway All the Way (Algren), **Supp. IX:** 16

Notes from No Man's Land (Biss), **Supp. XXVI:** 45, 46, 47, 48, 50, 53, 55–57

"Notes from the Childhood and Girlhood" (Brooks), **Supp. III Part 1:** 77

"Notes from the River" (Stern), **Supp. IX:** 285, 287, 294, 295

Notes from Underground (Dostoevsky), **III:** 571; **IV:** 485; **Retro. Supp. II:** 121

Notes Left Behind: Last and Selected Poems (Hayford), **Supp. XXII:** 218

"Notes of a Faculty Wife" (Jackson), **Supp. IX:** 126

"Notes of a Native Daughter" (Didion), **Supp. IV Part 1:** 196, 197, 200, 201

Notes of a Native Son (Baldwin), **Retro. Supp. II:** 1, 2, 3, 5, 6; **Supp. I Part 1:** 50, 52, 54; **Supp. IV Part 1:** 163

"Notes of a Native Son" (Baldwin), **Supp. I Part 1:** 50, 54

Notes of a Son and Brother (James), **II:** 337; **Retro. Supp. I:** 235

"Notes on a Departure" (Trilling), **Supp. III Part 2:** 498

"Notes on Babbitt and More" (Wilson), **IV:** 435

"Notes on 'Camp'" (Sontag), **Supp. III Part 2:** 455–456; **Supp. XIV:** 167

Notes on Democracy (Mencken), **III:** 104, 107–108, 109, 116, 119

Notes on Dialectics (C. L. R. James), **Supp. XXI:** 169

"Notes on Free Verse" (Dobyns), **Supp. XIII:** 77

"Notes on 'Layover' " (Hass), **Supp. VI:** 109

"Notes on Memory and Enthusiasm" (Di Piero), **Supp. XIX:** 42

Notes on Novelists (James), **II:** 336, 337; **Retro. Supp. I:** 235

"Notes on Nukes, Nookie, and Neo-Romanticism" (Robbins), **Supp. X:** 272

"Notes on Poetry" (Eberhart), **I:** 524, 527–528, 529

"Notes on Teaching"(Hadas), **Supp. XXIII:** 122

"Notes on the Craft of Poetry" (Strand), **Supp. IV Part 2:** 626

"Notes on the Decline of Outrage" (Dickey), **Supp. IV Part 1:** 181

"Notes on the New Formalism" (Gioia), **Supp. XV:** 113, 114–115

"Notes on the Novel-as-Autobiography" (P. Bailey), **Supp. XVI:** 69

"Notes on 'The Poetry of Everday Life' " (Notley), **Supp. XXII:** 232

Notes on the State of Virginia (1781–1782) (Jefferson), **Supp. XIV:** 191

"Notes on Writing Weird Fiction" (Lovecraft), **Supp. XXV:** 120–121

"Notes to Be Left in a Cornerstone" (Benét), **Supp. XI:** 46, 58

"Notes toward a Supreme Fiction" (Stevens), **IV:** 87–89; **Retro. Supp. I:** 300, 306, **306–309,** 311; **Supp. I Part 1:** 80

"Notes towards a Poem That Can Never Be Written" (Atwood), **Supp. XIII:** 34–35

"Not Exactly for Talia" (Halliday), **Supp. XIX:** 94

"Not Forgotten" (Davison), **Supp. XXVI:** 70

No Thanks (Cummings), **I:** 430, 431, 432, 436, 437, 441, 443, 446

Not Heaven: A Novel in the Form of Prelude, Variations, and Theme (W. Frank), **Supp. XX:** 80

"Nothing" (C. Frost), **Supp. XV:** 94

"Nothing Big" (Komunyakaa), **Supp. XIII:** 121

Nothing Can Make Me Do This (Huddle), **Supp. XXVI:** 147, 151–152, 158–159

Nothing Ever Breaks Except the Heart (Boyle), **Supp. XXIV:** 59

Nothing for Tigers (Carruth), **Supp. XVI:** 47, 48, 50

"Nothing Gold Can Stay" (Frost), **Retro. Supp. I:** 133

Nothing Gold Can Stay (Rash), **Supp. XXVII:** 215, 224, 229–230

"Nothing in Heaven Functions as It Ought" (X. J. Kennedy), **Supp. XV:** 158–159

Nothing Makes You Free: Writings by Descendants of Jewish Holocaust Survivors (Bukiet, ed.), **Supp. XVII:** 39–40, 48–49

"Nothing Missing" (O'Hara), **III:** 369

Nothing Personal (Baldwin), **Supp. I Part 1:** 58, 60

Nothing Sacred (film), **Supp. XVIII:** 243

Nothing Sacred (screenplay, Hecht), **Supp. XXVII:** 83, 91, 93

"Nothing Song, The" (Snodgrass), **Supp. VI:** 326

"Nothing Stays Put" (Clampitt), **Supp. IX:** 42

"Nothing Sudden" (Davison), **Supp. XXVI:** 76

Nothing to Write Home About (Brainard), **Supp. XXVII:** 20, 28

"Nothing Will Yield" (Nemerov), **III:** 279

No Third Path (Kosinski), **Supp. VII:** 215

"Not Ideas About the Thing but the Thing Itself" (Stevens), **IV:** 87

"No Time" (Collins), **Supp. XXI:** 61

Notions of the Americans: Picked up by a Travelling Bachelor (Cooper), **I:** 343–345, 346

"Not-Knowing" (Barthelme), **Supp. IV Part 1:** 48

"Not Leaving the House" (Snyder), **Supp. VIII:** 300

Notley, Alice, **Supp. XXII: 223–238;** **Supp. XXIII:** 221; **Supp. XXIV:** 35, 37, 39, 41, 43, 45

"'Not Marble nor the Gilded Monument' " (MacLeish), **III:** 12

Not Mine to Finish: Poems, 1928–1934 (Taggard), **Supp. XXII:** 280

"Not My Bones" (Nelson), **Supp. XVIII:** 183

Not Now But Now (M. F. K. Fisher), **Supp. XVII:** 86, 90

Notorious (screenplay, Hecht), **Supp. XXVII:** 83, 91, 93

"Not Quite Social" (Frost), **II:** 156

"Not Sappho, Sacco" (Rukeyser), **Supp. VI:** 277

"Not Sixteen" (Anderson), **I:** 114

"Not Slightly" (Stein), **IV:** 44

Not So Deep as a Well (Parker), **Supp. IX:** 192

"Not Somewhere Else, but Here" (Rich), **Supp. I Part 2:** 552, 573

Not-So-Simple Neil Simon (McGovern), **Supp. IV Part 2:** 573

Not So Simple: The "Simple" Stories by Langston Hughes (Harper), **Retro. Supp. I:** 194, 209

"Not the Point" (Cameron), **Supp. XII:** 83

"Not They Who Soar" (Dunbar), **Supp. II Part 1:** 199

Not This Pig (Levine), **Supp. V:** 178, 181, 182–183

"Not to Be Satan nor to Deal with Him" (Bronk), **Supp. XXI:** 32

Not to Eat; Not for Love (Weller), **III:** 322

Not Wanted on the Voyage (Findley), **Supp. XX: 50, 56–57,** 59

Not Without Laughter (Hughes), **Retro. Supp. I:** 197, 198, 201; **Supp. I Part 1:** 328, 332; **Supp. XIX:** 73, 154

Nouvelle Héloïse, La (Rousseau), **Supp. XV:** 232

Nova Express (Burroughs), **Supp. III Part 1:** 93, 103, 104; **Supp. XVIII:** 137

Novel, The (Bulwer), **Retro. Supp. II:** 58

Novel, The: An Alternative History (Moore), **Supp. XXII:** 261

"Novel as a Function of American Democracy, The" (Ellison), **Retro. Supp. II:** 124

"Novel Démeublé, The" (Cather), **Retro. Supp. I:** 15

Novel History: Historians and Novelists Confront America's Past (and Each Other) (Carnes), **Supp. X:** 14

"Novelists of 2007" (Halliday), **Supp. XIX:** 90

Novella (Goethe; Bogan and Mayer, trans.), **Supp. III Part 1:** 63

Novellas and Other Writings (Wharton), **Retro. Supp. I:** 360

"Novel of the Thirties, A" (Trilling), **Supp. III Part 2:** 499

Novels and Other Writings (Bercovitch), **Retro. Supp. II:** 325

Novels and Tales of Henry James, The (James), **Retro. Supp. I:** 232

"Novel-Writing and Novel-Reading" (Howells), **II:** 276, 290

"November" (Larcom), **Supp. XIII:** 143

"November Cotton Flower" (Toomer), **Supp. IX:** 312

November Twenty Six Nineteen Sixty Three (Berry), **Supp. X:** 24

"Novices" (Moore), **III:** 200–201, 202, 213

Novick, Peter, **Supp. XVI:** 154–155

"Novogodnee" ("New Year's Greetings") (Tsvetayeva), **Supp. VIII:** 30

"Novotny's Pain" (P. Roth), **Supp. III Part 2:** 403

"No Voyage" (Oliver), **Supp. VII:** 231

No Voyage and Other Poems (Oliver), **Supp. VII:** 230–231, 232

Now and Another Time (Hearon), **Supp. VIII:** 58, **61–62**

Now and Then (Buechner), **Supp. XII:** 49, 53

"Now and Then, America" (Mora), **Supp. XIII:** 217

"Nowhere" (J. Scott), **Supp. XVII:** 189

Nowhere Is a Place: Travels in Patagonia (Theroux and Chatwin), **Supp. VIII:** 322

"Now I Am Married" (Gordon), **Supp. IV Part 1:** 299

"Now I Lay Me" (Hemingway), **II:** 249; **Retro. Supp. I:** 175

"Now I Lay Me" (Olds), **Supp. X:** 208

"Now Is the Air Made of Chiming Balls" (Eberhart), **I:** 523

Now Is Your Time! The African American Struggle for Freedom (Myers), **Supp. XXVII:** 209

"No Word" (Kunitz), **Supp. III Part 1:** 263

"No Worst" (Nelson), **Supp. XVIII:** 177, 178

Now Sheba Sings the Song (Angelou), **Supp. IV Part 1:** 16

"Now That We Live" (Kenyon), **Supp. VII:** 165

"Now the Servant's Name Was Malchus" (Wilder), **IV:** 358

"Now We Know" (O'Hara), **III:** 368–369
NOW with Bill Moyers (television), **Supp. XIII:** 286
Noyes, Alfred, **IV:** 434
Nuamah, Grace, **Supp. IV Part 1:** 10
"Nuances of a Theme by Williams" (Stevens), **Retro. Supp. I:** 422
Nuclear Age, The (O'Brien), **Supp. V:** 238, 243, 244, 246–248, 249, 251
"Nuclear Arms and Morality" (Sanders), **Supp. XVI:** 266
"Nude at a Dressing Table" (Peacock), **Supp. XIX:** 204
Nude Croquet (Fiedler), **Supp. XIII:** 103
"Nude Descendig a Staircase" (X. J. Kennedy), **Supp. XV:** 168
Nude Descending a Staircase (Duchamp), **IV:** 408; **Retro. Supp. I:** 416; **Supp. XXII:** 162
Nude Descending a Staircase (X. J. Kennedy), **Supp. XV:** 153, **154–157**
Nugent, Bruce, **Retro. Supp. I:** 200
Nugent, Elliot, **Supp. I Part 2:** 606, 611, 613
Nuggets and Dust (Bierce), **I:** 195
"Nullipara" (Olds), **Supp. X:** 209
Number One (Dos Passos), **I:** 489
"Numbers" (Skloot), **Supp. XX: 196, 207**
"Numbers, Letters" (Baraka), **Supp. II Part 1:** 50
"Numbers Trouble" (Stallings), **Supp. XXV:** 224
Nunc Dimittis (Brodsky), **Supp. VIII:** 25–26, 28
"Nun No More, A" (Fante), **Supp. XI:** 160
"Nun's Priest's Tale" (Chaucer), **III:** 492
Nunzio, Nanzia, **IV:** 89
Nuptial Flight, The (Masters), **Supp. I Part 2:** 460, 471
"Nuptials" (Tate), **IV:** 122
Nursery Rhymes from Mother Stone (Stone), **Supp. XXVII:** 257
"Nurse Whitman" (Olds), **Supp. X:** 203
Nurture (Kumin), **Supp. IV Part 2:** 453–454, 455
Nussbaum, Emily, **Supp. XI:** 143
Nussbaum, Felicity A., **Supp. X:** 189
Nutcracker, The (Tchaikovsky), **Retro. Supp. I:** 196
"Nux Postcoenatica" (Holmes), **Supp. I Part 1:** 303
Nyberg, Björn, **Supp. XXVII:** 128
Nyce, James M., **Retro. Supp. I:** 380
Nye, Naomi Shihab, **Supp. XI:** 316; **Supp. XIII: 273–290; Supp. XXIII:** 253; **Supp. XXVII:** 166
Nyerere, Julius, **Supp. X:** 135
"Nympholepsy" (Faulkner), **Retro. Supp. I:** 81
Nymphs of the Valley ('Ará'is al-Murúj) (Gibran), **Supp. XX: 115, 124, 125**

O

"Ö" (Dove), **Supp. IV Part 1:** 245
Oak and Ivy (Dunbar), **Supp. II Part 1:** 98
"Oak Bluffs" column (D. West), **Supp. XVIII:** 286

Oak Openings, The (Cooper), **I:** 354, 355
Oandasan, Bill, **Supp. IV Part 2:** 499
Oasis, The (McCarthy), **II:** 566–568
Oates, Joyce Carol, **Supp. II Part 2: 503–527; Supp. IV Part 1:** 205; **Supp. IV Part 2:** 447, 689; **Supp. V:** 323; **Supp. XI:** 239; **Supp. XII:** 343; **Supp. XIII:** 306; **Supp. XIV:** 26, 109; **Supp. XXIII:** 35; **Supp. XXV:** 86, 123; **Supp. XXVI:** 126
"Oath, The" (Tate), **IV:** 127
Obbligati (Hecht), **Supp. X:** 57
Ober, Harold, **Retro. Supp. I:** 101, 103, 105, 110, 113
Oberndorf, Clarence P., **Supp. I Part 1:** 315
Obey, André, **IV:** 356, 375
"Obit" (R. Lowell), **II:** 554
"Obituaries" (Collins), **Supp. XXI:** 65
"Obituary Writer, The" (Davison), **Supp. XXVI:** 72
"Objective Value of a Social Settlement, The" (Addams), **Supp. I Part 1:** 4
"Objective Woman, The" (Jong), **Supp. V:** 119
Objectivist Anthology, An, **Supp. XIV:** 287
"Objectivist Ethics, The" (Rand), **Supp. IV Part 2:** 530–532
"Objectivists" Anthology, An (Zukofsky), **Supp. III Part 2:** 613, 615
Objectivist's Anthology, An (Zukofsky, ed.), **Supp. XXVI:** 226
Object Lessons (Quindlen), **Supp. XVII: 173–174**
"Objects" (Wilbur), **Supp. III Part 2:** 545–547
Oblique Prayers (Levertov), **Supp. III Part 1:** 283
"Oblivion" (Justice), **Supp. VII:** 121
Oblivion Seekers, The (Eberhardt), **Supp. IV Part 1:** 92
"Oblong Box, The" (Poe), **III:** 416
"Obnoxious Truth, The" (Notley), **Supp. XXII:** 234
Obregon, Maurice, **Supp. I Part 2:** 488
O'Briant, Don, **Supp. X:** 8
O'Brien, Edward, **Supp. XV:** 140
O'Brien, Edward J., **I:** 289; **III:** 56; **Supp. XIX:** 256; **Supp. XVIII:** 227; **Supp. XX: 34**
O'Brien, Edwin, **Supp. XVIII:** 208
O'Brien, Fitzjames, **I:** 211
O'Brien, Geoffrey, **Supp. IV Part 2:** 471, 473
O'Brien, Joe, **Supp. XXI:** 5, 6
O'Brien, John, **Supp. V:** 48, 49; **Supp. X:** 239, 244; **Supp. XXI:** 228, 229, 233
O'Brien, Tim, **Supp. V: 237–255; Supp. XI:** 234; **Supp. XVII:** 14; **Supp. XXI:** 122; **Supp. XXV:** 142, 143, 153
"Obscene Poem, An" (Creeley), **Supp. IV Part 1:** 150
Obscure Destinies (Cather), **I:** 331–332; **Retro. Supp. I:** 19
"Observation Relative to the Intentions of the Original Founders of the Academy in Philadelphia" (Franklin), **II:** 114
"Observations" (Dillard), **Supp. VI:** 34

Observations (Moore), **III:** 194, 195–196, 197, 199, 203, 205, 215
"Observations Now" (Conroy), **Supp. XVI:** 75
Observations: Photographs by Richard Avedon: Comments by Truman Capote, **Supp. III Part 1:** 125–126
Obsession, The (Levin), **Supp. XXVII:** 133, 136, 138, 143, 147
Obsession with Anne Frank, An: Meyer Levin and the Diary (Graver), **Supp. XXVII:** 136, 137
Obuchowski, Mary DeJong, **Supp. XX: 222**
O Canada: An American's Notes on Canadian Culture (Wilson), **IV:** 429–430
"O Carib Isle!" (Crane), **I:** 400–401
O'Casey, Sean, **III:** 145; **Supp. IV Part 1:** 359, 361, 364
"Occidentals" (Ford), **Supp. V:** 71–72
Occom, Samuel, **Supp. XX: 288**
"Occultation of Orion, The" (Longfellow), **Retro. Supp. II:** 168
"Occurrence at Owl Creek Bridge, An" (Bierce), **I:** 200–201; **II:** 264; **Supp. XXV:** 26
"Ocean 1212-W" (Plath), **Supp. I Part 2:** 528
"Ocean of Words" (Jin), **Supp. XVIII:** 94
Ocean of Words: Army Stories (Jin), **Supp. XVIII:** 89, 92, **93–94**
O'Connell, Nicholas, **Supp. IX:** 323, 325, 334
O'Connell, Shaun, **Supp. XXI:** 231
O'Connor, Edward F., Jr., **III:** 337
O'Connor, Flannery, **I:** 113, 190, 211, 298; **II:** 606; **III: 337–360; IV:** 4, 217, 282; **Retro. Supp. II:** 179, **219–239,** 272, 324; **Supp. I Part 1:** 290; **Supp. III Part 1:** 146; **Supp. V:** 59, 337; **Supp. VIII:** 13, 14, 158; **Supp. X:** 1, 26, 69, 228, 290; **Supp. XI:** 104; **Supp. XIII:** 294; **Supp. XIV:** 93; **Supp. XIX:** 166, 209, 223; **Supp. XV:** 338; **Supp. XVI:** 219; **Supp. XVII:** 43, 114; **Supp. XVIII:** 156, 161, 194; **Supp. XXI:** 197; **Supp. XXIII:** 289; **Supp. XXV:** 142; **Supp. XXVI:** 152, 252; **Supp. XXVII:** 11, 216, 218, 230, 267, 276
O'Connor, Frank, **III:** 158; **Retro. Supp. II:** 242; **Supp. I Part 2:** 531; **Supp. VIII:** 151, 157, 165, 167, 171; **Supp. XV:** 74
O'Connor, Philip F., **Supp. XXIII:** 290
O'Connor, Richard, **II:** 467
O'Connor, T. P., **II:** 129
O'Connor, William, **IV:** 346; **Retro. Supp. I:** 392, 407
O'Connor, William Van, **III:** 479; **Supp. I Part 1:** 195
O'Crowley, Peggy, **Supp. XXVII:** 201
"Octascope" (Beattie), **Supp. V:** 27, 28
"Octaves" (Robinson), **Supp. III Part 2:** 593
"Octet" (Wallace), **Supp. X:** 309
October (Isherwood), **Supp. XIV:** 157, 164

"October" (Oliver), **Supp. VII:** 241

"October" (Swenson), **Supp. IV Part 2:** 649

"October, 1866" (Bryant), **Supp. I Part 1:** 169

"October 1913" (McCarriston), **Supp. XIV:** 266

"October and November" (R. Lowell), **II:** 554

"October in the Railroad Earth" (Kerouac), **Supp. III Part 1:** 225, 227, 229

October Light (Gardner), **Supp. VI:** 63, **69–71,** 72

"October Maples, Portland" (Wilbur), **Supp. III Part 2:** 556

October Palace, The (Hirshfield), **Supp. XXIII:** 131

October Sky (film), **Supp. XXVII:** 101, 103, 106

"October: With Rain" (W. V. Davis), **Supp. XXI:** 94

"Octopus, An" (Moore), **III:** 202, 207–208, 214

"Octopus, The" (Merrill), **Supp. III Part 1:** 321

Octopus, The (Norris), **I:** 518; **III:** 314, 316, 322–326, 327, 331–333, 334, 335

"O Daedalus, Fly Away Home" (Hayden), **Supp. II Part 1:** 377–378

"OD and Hepatitis Railroad or Bust, The" (Boyle), **Supp. VIII:** 1

Odd Couple, The (1985 version, Simon), **Supp. IV Part 2:** 580

Odd Couple, The (film), **Supp. IV Part 2:** 589

Odd Couple, The (Simon), **Supp. IV Part 2:** 575, 579–580, 585, 586; **Supp. XVII:** 8

Odd Jobs (Updike), **Retro. Supp. I:** 334

Odd Mercy (Stern), **Supp. IX: 298–299**

Odd Number (Sorrentino), **Supp. XXI:** 236

"Odds, The" (Hecht), **Supp. X:** 64–65

Odds, The (O'Nan), **Supp. XXV:** 150, 151–152

"Odds, The" (Salinas), **Supp. XIII:** 321

"Ode" (Emerson), **II:** 13

"Ode" (Sobin), **Supp. XVI:** 284–285

"Ode" (X. J. Kennedy), **Supp. XV:** 160

"Ode (Intimations of Immortality)" (Matthews), **Supp. IX:** 162

"Ode for Memorial Day" (Dunbar), **Supp. II Part 1:** 199

"Ode for the American Dead in Asia" (McGrath), **Supp. X:** 119

"Ode: For the Budding of Islands" (Sobin), **Supp. XVI:** 287

"Ode Inscribed to W. H. Channing" (Emerson), **Supp. XIV:** 46

"Ode: Intimations of Immortality" (Wordsworth), **Supp. I Part 2:** 729; **Supp. III Part 1:** 12; **Supp. XIV:** 8

"Ode in Time of Crisis" (Taggard), **Supp. XXII:** 271

Odell, Margaretta Matilda, **Supp. XX: 278, 284, 288**

"Ode: My 24th Year" (Ginsberg), **Supp. II Part 1:** 312

"Ode on a Grecian Urn" (Keats), **I:** 284; **III:** 472; **Supp. XII:** 113; **Supp. XIV:** 8, 9–10; **Supp. XV:** 100; **Supp. XXI:** 64

"Ode on Human Destinies" (Jeffers), **Supp. II Part 2:** 419

"Ode on Indolence" (Keats), **Supp. XII:** 113

"Ode on Melancholy" (Keats), **Retro. Supp. I:** 301

Ode Recited at the Harvard Commemoration (J. R. Lowell), **Supp. I Part 2:** 416–418, 424

"Ode Recited at the Harvard Commemoration" (R. Lowell), **II:** 551

Odes (Horace), **Supp. XXIV:** 153

Odes (O'Hara), **Supp. XXIII:** 216

"Ode: Salute to the French Negro Poets"(O'Hara), **Supp. XXIII:** 216

"Ode Secrète" (Valéry), **III:** 609

"Odes of Estrangement" (Sobin), **Supp. XVI:** 289

Odes of Horace, The (Ferry, trans.), **Supp. XXIV: 153–156**

"Odes to Natural Processes" (Updike), **Retro. Supp. I:** 323

"Ode: The Capris" (Halliday), **Supp. XIX:** 88

"Ode to a Nightingale" (Keats), **II:** 368; **Retro. Supp. II:** 261; **Supp. IX:** 52

"Ode to Autumn" (Masters), **Supp. I Part 2:** 458

"Ode to Cervantes" (Salinas), **Supp. XIII:** 324

"Ode to Coit Tower" (Corso), **Supp. XII:** 122

"Ode to Ethiopia" (Dunbar), **Supp. II Part 1:** 199, 207, 208, 209

"Ode to Fear" (Tate), **IV:** 128

Ode to Harvard and Other Poems, An (Bynner), **Supp. XV:** 41, 44

"Ode to Joy"(O'Hara), **Supp. XXIII:** 208, 216

"Ode to Meaning" (Pinsky), **Supp. VI: 249–250,** 251

"Ode to Michael Goldberg ('s Birth and Other Births)"(O'Hara), **Supp. XXIII:** 209, 216, 218

"Ode to Night" (Masters), **Supp. I Part 2:** 458

"Ode to Our Young Pro-Consuls of the Air" (Tate), **IV:** 135

"Ode to the Austrian Socialists" (Benét), **Supp. XI:** 46, 58

"Ode to the Confederate Dead" (Tate), **II:** 551; **IV:** 124, 133, 137; **Supp. X:** 52

"Ode to the Johns Hopkins University" (Lanier), **Supp. I Part 1:** 370

"Ode to the Maggot" (Komunyakaa), **Supp. XIII:** 130

"Ode to the Mexican Experience" (Salinas), **Supp. XIII:** 316–317

"Ode to the Virginian Voyage" (Drayton), **IV:** 135

"Ode to the West Wind" (Shelley), **Retro. Supp. I:** 308; **Supp. I Part 2:** 728; **Supp. IX:** 52; **Supp. XII:** 117; **Supp. XIV:** 271–272; **Supp. XV:** 221

"Ode to Walt Whitman" (Benét), **Supp. XI:** 52

"Ode to Willem de Kooning"(O'Hara), **Supp. XXIII:** 208, 216

Odets, Clifford, **Supp. I Part 1:** 277, 295; **Supp. I Part 2:** 679; **Supp. II Part 2: 529–554; Supp. IV Part 2:** 587; **Supp. V:** 109; **Supp. VIII:** 96; **Supp. XVIII:** 238; **Supp. XX: 34; Supp. XXVII:** 134

Odier, Daniel, **Supp. III Part 1:** 97

"Odi et Amo" (Catullus), **Supp. XV:** 27, 32, 35

"Odom"(P. Benedict), **Supp. XXIII:** 41

O'Donnell, George Marion, **II:** 67

O'Donnell, Mary King, **Supp. XVIII:** 232

O'Donnell, Thomas F., **II:** 131

"Odor of Verbena" (Faulkner), **II:** 66

O'Doul, Lefty, **II:** 425

Odysseus (Homer), **Supp. XXVI:** 79

"Odysseus to Telemachus" (Brodsky), **Supp. VIII:** 25

Odyssey (Bryant, trans.), **Supp. I Part 1:** 158

Odyssey (Homer), **III:** 14, 470; **Retro. Supp. I:** 286, 290; **Retro. Supp. II:** 121; **Supp. I Part 1:** 185; **Supp. IV Part 2:** 631; **Supp. IX:** 211; **Supp. X:** 114; **Supp. XIV:** 191; **Supp. XVII:** 117; **Supp. XXI:** 36

"Odyssey of a Wop, The" (Fante), **Supp. XI:** 164, 165

Oedipus Rex (Sophocles), **I:** 137; **III:** 145, 151, 152, 332; **Supp. I Part 2:** 428

Oedipus Tyrannus (Sophocles), **II:** 203; **Supp. XV:** 265

Oehlschlaeger, Fritz, **Supp. IX:** 123

Oelze, Richard, **Supp. XXII:** 167

"Of Alexander Crummell" (Du Bois), **Supp. II Part 1:** 170

O'Faoláin, Seán, **Supp. II Part 1:** 101

Of a World That Is No More (Singer), **IV:** 16

Of Being Numerous (Oppen), **Supp. XXVI:** 223, 230, 233–234, 237

"Of Being Numerous" (Oppen), **Supp. XXVI:** 232, 233–234, 236

"Of Booker T. Washington and Others" (Du Bois), **Supp. II Part 1:** 168

"Of Bright & Blue Birds & the Gala Sun" (Stevens), **IV:** 93

"Of Christian Heroism" (Ozick), **Supp. V:** 272

"Of Dying Beauty" (Zukofsky), **Supp. III Part 2:** 610

"Of Epiphanies and Poets" (Phillips), **Supp. XX: 221**

"Of 'Father and Son' " (Kunitz), **Supp. III Part 1:** 262

Offenbach, Jacques, **II:** 427

"Offering for Mr. Bluehart, An" (Wright), **Supp. III Part 2:** 596, 601

"Offerings" (Mason), **Supp. VIII:** 141

"Offertory" (Hempel), **Supp. XXI: 126–127**

Office, The (Asch), **Supp. XXVI:** 18–20, 21, 25

"Office, The" (Munro), **Supp. XXVII:** 183–184

Official Entry Blank (Kooser), **Supp. XIX:** 116, **117–118**

"Official Entry Form" (Kooser), **Supp. XIX:** 117

"Official Piety" (Whittier), **Supp. I Part 2:** 687

Off Keck Road (Simpson), **Supp. XXVII:** 240–242

"Offloading for Mrs. Schwartz" (Saunders), **Supp. XIX:** 225–226

"Of Freemasons, Kings, and Constitutions" (P. N. Warren), **Supp. XX: 273**

"Off-Shore Pirates, The" (Fitzgerald), **II:** 88

Off the Beaten Path (Proulx), **Supp. VII:** 261

Off the Beaten Path: Stories of Place, **Supp. XVI:** 22

"Off the Cuff" (Simpson), **Supp. IX:** 278

"Off the Highway" (Wolfert), **Supp. XXI:** 265

Off the Map (Levine), **Supp. V:** 178

Offut, Chris, **Supp. XIX: 163–176**

Offutt, Chris, **Supp. XXVII:** 217

Of Gravity and Angels (Hirshfield), **Supp. XXIII:** 131

O'Flaherty, George, **Supp. I Part 1:** 202, 205–206

O'Flaherty, Kate. *See* Chopin, Kate

O'Flaherty, Thomas, **Supp. I Part 1:** 202, 203–204, 205

O'Flaherty, Thomas, Jr., **Supp. I Part 1:** 202

"Of Maids and Other Muses" (Alvarez), **Supp. VII:** 11

"Of Margaret" (Ransom), **III:** 491

Of Mice and Men (Steinbeck), **IV:** 51, 57–58

"Of Modern Poetry" (Stevens), **IV:** 92

Of No Country I Know: New and Selected Poems and Translations (Ferry), **Supp. XXIV: 157**

Of Plymouth Plantation (Bradford), **Retro. Supp. II:** 161, 162; **Supp. XXII:** 33, **35–47**

Of Plymouth Plantation (Morison, ed.), **Supp. I Part 2:** 494

"Ofrenda for Lobo" (Mora), **Supp. XIII:** 224

"Often" (Kenyon), **Supp. VII:** 171

"Often, in Dreams, He Moved through a City" (Dobyns), **Supp. XIII:** 90

"Of the Coming of John" (Du Bois), **Supp. II Part 1:** 170

"Of the Culture of White Folk" (Du Bois), **Supp. II Part 1:** 175

Of the Farm (Updike), **IV:** 214, 217, 223–225, 233; **Retro. Supp. I:** 318, 329, 332

"Of the Four-Winged Cherubim as Signature" (Sobin), **Supp. XVI:** 287

"Of 'The Frill' " (McCarriston), **Supp. XIV:** 274

"Of the Passing of the First-Born" (Du Bois), **Supp. II Part 1:** 170

"Of the Sorrow Songs" (Du Bois), **Supp. II Part 1:** 170

"Of the Wings of Atlanta" (Du Bois), **Supp. II Part 1:** 170

Of This Time, Of This Place (Trilling), **Supp. III Part 2:** 498, 504

Of Time and the River (Wolfe), **IV:** 450, 451, 452, 455, 456, 457, 458, 459, 462, 464–465, 467, 468, 469

Of Woman Born: Motherhood as Experience and Institution (Rich), **Supp. I Part 2:** 554, 567–569

Of Women and Their Elegance (Mailer), **Retro. Supp. II:** 209

Ogden, Archie, **Supp. XIII:** 174

Ogden, Henry, **II:** 298

Ogden, Uzal, **Supp. I Part 2:** 516

Ogle, Connie, **Supp. XXIII:** 300, 301

"Oh, Atonement" (Weigl), **Supp. XIX:** 287

"Oh, Fairest of the Rural Maids" (Bryant), **Supp. I Part 1:** 169

"Oh, Immobility, Death's Vast Associate" (Dobyns), **Supp. XIII:** 89

"Oh, Joseph, I'm So Tired" (Yates), **Supp. XI:** 348

Oh, the Places You'll Go! (Geisel), **Supp. XVI:** 111

Oh, the Thinks You can Think! (Geisel), **Supp. XVI:** 111

"O'Halloran's Luck" (Benét), **Supp. XI:** 47

O'Hara, Frank, **Supp. XII:** 121; **Supp. XIX:** 81, 85; **Supp. XV:** 93, 176, 177, 178, 179–180, 182, 186, 187, 215–216; **Supp. XXII:** 226, 236; **Supp. XXIII: 207–222; Supp. XXIV:** 33, 34, 36, 42, 43, 44; **Supp. XXVII:** 19, 22, 23

O'Hara, J. D., **Supp. IV Part 1:** 43; **Supp. V:** 22; **Supp. XVI:** 221; **Supp. XXI:** 228

O'Hara, John, **I:** 375, 495; **II:** 444, 459; **III:** 66, **361–384; IV:** 59; **Retro. Supp. I:** 99, 112; **Supp. I Part 1:** 196; **Supp. II Part 1:** 109; **Supp. IV Part 1:** 31, 383; **Supp. IV Part 2:** 678; **Supp. IX:** 208; **Supp. V:** 95; **Supp. VIII:** 151, 156; **Supp. XIX:** 209

O'Hara, John Myers, **Supp. XXVII:** 285, 289

O'Hara's Choice (Uris), **Supp. XX: 247, 256–257**

"O Heaven born muse! inspire my humble lay" (Very), **Supp. XXV:** 239

O'Hehir, Andrew, **Supp. XII:** 280

O. Henry Biography (C. A. Smith), **Supp. II Part 1:** 395

"Ohio Pagan, An" (Anderson), **I:** 112, 113

Ohio trilogy (Richter), **Supp. XVIII:** 212–215

Oh Mercy (album, Dylan), **Supp. XVIII:** 28, 33

Oh Say Can You Say? (Geisel), **Supp. XVI:** 111

Oil! (Sinclair), **Supp. V:** 276, 277–279, 282, 288, 289

Oil Notes (Bass), **Supp. XVI:** 17

"Oil Painting of the Artist as the Artist" (MacLeish), **III:** 14

"O-jib-way Maid, The"(J. Schoolcraft), **Supp. XXIII:** 235

O'Keeffe, Georgia, **Supp. IX:** 62, 66; **Supp. XX:** 75

"Oklahoma" (Levis), **Supp. XI:** 267

Oklahoma's Poor Rich Indians: An Orgy of Graft and Exploitation of the Five Civilized Tribes—Legalized Robbery (Zitkala-Ša, Sniffen, and Fabens), **Supp. XXV:** 283

Oktenberg, Adrian, **Supp. XVII:** 76; **Supp. XXI:** 253; **Supp. XXIII:** 133

"Old, Old, Old, Old Andrew Jackson" (Lindsay), **Supp. I Part 2:** 398

"Old Amusement Park, An" (Moore), **III:** 216

"Old Angel Midnight" (Kerouac), **Supp. III Part 1:** 229–230

"Old Apple Dealer, The" (Hawthorne), **II:** 227, 233–235, 237, 238

"Old Apple-Tree, The" (Dunbar), **Supp. II Part 1:** 198

"Old Army Game, The" (Garrett), **Supp. VII:** 100–101

"Old Aunt Peggy" (Chopin), **Retro. Supp. II:** 64

"Old Barn at the Bottom of the Fogs, The" (Frost), **Retro. Supp. I:** 138

Old Battle-Ax, The (Holding), **Supp. XXII: 128–129**

Old Beauty and Others, The (Cather), **I:** 331

"Old Boys, Old Girls" (E. P. Jones), **Supp. XXII:** 151

Old Bruin: Commodore Matthew C. Perry, 1794–1858 (Morison), **Supp. I Part 2:** 494–495

Old Bunch, The (Levin), **Supp. XXVII:** 134, 139, 143

"Old Cracked Tune, An" (Kunitz), **Supp. III Part 1:** 264

Old Curiosity Shop, The (Dickens), **I:** 458; **Supp. I Part 2:** 409

"Old Enemy, The" (Teasdale), **Supp. XXVII:** 296

Oldest Killed Lake in North America, The (Carruth), **Supp. XVI:** 51

"Oldest Man, The" (M. F. K. Fisher), **Supp. XVII:** 91

"Old Farmer, The" (Jeffers), **Supp. II Part 2:** 418

Old-Fashioned Girl, An (Alcott), **Supp. I Part 1:** 29, 41, 42

"Old Father Morris" (Stowe), **Supp. I Part 2:** 586

Old Favorites and New Fancies for 1909 (Wells), **Supp. XXVI:** 275

"Old Flame, The" (R. Lowell), **II:** 550

"Old Florist" (Roethke), **III:** 531

"Old Folsom Prison" (Matthews), **Supp. IX:** 165

Old Forest, The (Taylor), **Supp. V:** 320, 321, 326, 327

"Old Forest, The" (Taylor), **Supp. V:** 313, 321, 323, 326

Old Forest and Other Stories (Taylor), **Supp. V:** 326

Old Friends and New (Jewett), **II:** 402; **Retro. Supp. II:** 137, 140

Old Glory, The (R. Lowell), **II:** 543, 545–546, 555; **Retro. Supp. II:** 188

Old Helmet, The (S. and A. Warner), **Supp. XVIII:** 267

"Old Homestead, The" (Dunbar), **Supp. II Part 1:** 198

"Old House" (Espaillat), **Supp. XXI:** 112, 113

Old Indian Legends (Zitkala-Ša), **Supp. XXV:** 275, 278, 285

"Old Iron" (Nye), **Supp. XIII:** 276

"Old Ironsides" (Holmes), **Supp. I Part 1:** 302

Old Jules (Sandoz), **Supp. XXIV:** 243, 244, **245–246,** 249, 251, 255, 257

"Old Lady We Saw, An" (Shields), **Supp. VII:** 310–311

"Old Love" (Singer), **Retro. Supp. II:** 307

"Old McGrath Place, The" (McGrath), **Supp. X:** 114

"Old Maid, The" (Wharton), **Retro. Supp. I:** 381, 382

"Old Man" (Faulkner), **II:** 68, 69

Old Man and the Sea, The (Hemingway), **II:** 250, 256–257, 258, 265; **III:** 40; **Retro. Supp. I:** 180, **185,** 186

"Old Man Drunk" (Wright), **Supp. III Part 2:** 595

"Old Man Feeding Hens" (Francis), **Supp. IX:** 78

"Old Man on the Hospital Porch" (Ríos), **Supp. IV Part 2:** 546–547

Old Man Rubbing His Eyes (R. Bly), **Supp. IV Part 1:** 65

"Old Manse, The" (Hawthorne), **II:** 224

"Old Man's Winter Night, An" (Frost), **Retro. Supp. I:** 126, 131

Old Man Who Love Cheese, The (Keillor), **Supp. XVI:** 177

"Old Man with a Dog" (Wright), **Supp. XV:** 346

Old Marriage and New (Kooser), **Supp. XIX: 120–121**

"Old Meeting House, The" (Stowe), **Supp. I Part 2:** 586

"Old Memory, An" (Dunbar), **Supp. II Part 1:** 198

"Old Men, Old Horses" (P. N. Warren as Kilina), **Supp. XX: 262**

"Old Men, The" (McCarthy), **II:** 566

"Old Men Pitching Horseshoes" (X. J. Kennedy), **Supp. XV:** 166

Old Money (Wasserstein), **Supp. XV: 333–334**

"Old Morgue, The" (Prose), **Supp. XVI:** 250

Old Morning Program, The (radio show, Keillor). *See Prairie Home Companion, A* (radio show, Keillor)

"Old Mortality" (Porter), **III:** 436, 438–441, 442, 445, 446

"Old Mrs. Harris" (Cather), **I:** 332; **Retro. Supp. I:** 19

Old Neighborhood, The (Mamet), **Supp. XIV:** 240, 241, 242, 249–250, 251, 252, 254

Old New York (Wharton), **IV:** 322; **Retro. Supp. I:** 381

"Ol' Doc Hyar" (Campbell), **Supp. II Part 1:** 202

"Old of the Moon" (Offutt), **Supp. XIX:** 165, 166

Old One-Two, The (Gurney), **Supp. V:** 98

"Old Order, The" (Porter), **III:** 443, 444–445, 451

"Old Osawatomie" (Sandburg), **III:** 584

Old Patagonia Express, The: By Train through the Americas (Theroux), **Supp. VIII:** 322

"Old People" (Ferry), **Supp. XXIV:** 162

"Old People, The" (Faulkner), **II:** 71–72

"Old Photograph" (Davison), **Supp. XXVI:** 72

"Old Photograph, An" (Kooser), **Supp. XIX:** 121

"Old Poet Moves to a New Apartment 14 Times, The" (Zukofsky), **Supp. III Part 2:** 628

Old Possum's Book of Practical Cats (T. S. Eliot), **Supp. XIII:** 228, 344

"Old Red" (Gordon), **II:** 199, 200, 203

Old Red and Other Stories (Gordon), **II:** 157

Old Régime in Canada, The (Parkman), **Supp. II Part 2:** 600, 607, 608–609, 612

Old Religion, The (Mamet), **Supp. XIV:** 253

Olds, Sharon, **Supp. X: 201–217; Supp. XI:** 139, 142, 244; **Supp. XII:** 229; **Supp. XIV:** 265; **Supp. XVII:** 114, 240; **Supp. XXI:** 249

"Old Saws" (Garrett), **Supp. VII:** 96–97

Old South, The: "A Summer Tragedy" and Other Stories (Bontemps), **Supp. XXII:** 7

"Old Stories" (Skloot), **Supp. XX: 200**

Old Testament, **I:** 109, 181, 300, 328, 401, 410, 419, 431, 457, 458; **II:** 166, 167, 219; **III:** 270, 272, 348, 390, 396; **IV:** 41, 114, 152, 309; **Retro. Supp. I:** 122, 140, 249, 311, 360; **Retro. Supp. II:** 299; **Supp. I Part 1:** 60, 104, 106, 151; **Supp. I Part 2:** 427, 515, 516; **Supp. IX:** 14. *See also* names of Old Testament books

"Old Things, The" (James), **Retro. Supp. I:** 229

"Old Times on the Mississippi" (Twain), **IV:** 199

Oldtown Folks (Stowe), **Supp. I Part 2:** 587, 596–598

"Old Town of Berwick, The" (Jewett), **Retro. Supp. II:** 132

"Old Trails" (Robinson), **III:** 513, 517

"Old Tyrannies" (Bourne), **I:** 233

"Old West" (Bausch), **Supp. VII:** 48

"Old Whorehouse, An" (Oliver), **Supp. VII:** 235

"Old Woman" (Pinsky), **Supp. VI:** 238

"Old Woman of Beare, The" (X. J. Kennedy), **Supp. XV:** 156

"Old Word, The" (Simic), **Supp. VIII:** 282

"Old-World Landowners" (Gogol), **Supp. XV:** 262

Oldys, Francis. *See* Chalmers, George

Oleanna (Mamet), **Supp. XIV:** 239, 241, 245, 248, 250

Olendorf, Donna, **Supp. IV Part 1:** 196

"Olga Poems, The" (Levertov), **Supp. III Part 1:** 279–281

"Olive Groves of Thasos, The" (Clampitt), **Supp. IX: 51–52**

Olive Kitteridge (Strout), **Supp. XXIII:** 273, 275, **280–284,** 285

Oliver, Bill, **Supp. VIII:** 138

Oliver, Douglas, **Supp. XXII:** 225, 226, 233, 235

Oliver, Mary, **Supp. VII: 229–248; Supp. X:** 31; **Supp. XVI:** 39; **Supp. XVII:** 111, 240; **Supp. XXIII:** 51

Oliver, Sydney, **I:** 409

Oliver Goldsmith: A Biography (Irving), **II:** 315

Oliver Twist (Dickens), **I:** 354; **Supp. IV Part 2:** 464

Olives (Stallings), **Supp. XXV:** 221, 223, 224, 233–234

"Olivia" (Salinas), **Supp. XIII:** 316

"Olivier Bergmann" (Halliday), **Supp. XIX:** 93–94

Olivieri, David (pseudonym), **Retro. Supp. I:** 361. *See also* Wharton, Edith

Ollive, Samuel, **Supp. I Part 2:** 503

Olmsted, Frederick Law, **Supp. I Part 1:** 355

Olor de la memoria, El/The Scent of Memory (Espaillat), **Supp. XXI:** 104

Olsen, Lance, **Supp. IV Part 1:** 54; **Supp. IV Part 2:** 623

Olsen, Tillie, **Supp. V:** 114, 220; **Supp. XIII: 291–309; Supp. XVI:** 83, 90

Olshan, Joseph, **Supp. XIX:** 52

Olson, Charles, **Retro. Supp. I:** 209; **Supp. II Part 1:** 30, 328; **Supp. II Part 2: 555–587; Supp. III Part 1:** 9, 271; **Supp. III Part 2:** 542, 624; **Supp. IV Part 1:** 139, 144, 146, 153, 154, 322; **Supp. IV Part 2:** 420, 421, 423, 426; **Supp. VIII:** 290, 291; **Supp. XII:** 2, 198; **Supp. XIII:** 104; **Supp. XIV:** 96; **Supp. XV:** 177; **Supp. XXI:** 19, 21, 23; **Supp. XXIV:** 42; **Supp. XXVII:** 160

Olson, Clarence, **Supp. XX: 84, 85, 86**

Olson, Ray, **Supp. XVII:** 111, 112, 119

Olson, Tillie, **Supp. XXVII:** 256

"Ol' Tunes, The" (Dunbar), **Supp. II Part 1:** 197

"O Lull Me, Lull Me" (Roethke), **III:** 536–537

O'Malley, Anne, **Supp. XXII:** 56

Omar Khayyam, **Supp. I Part 1:** 363

O'Meally, Robert, **Retro. Supp. II:** 112

Omega the Unknown (comic book series), **Supp. XVIII:** 149

"Omen" (Komunyakaa), **Supp. XIII:** 126, 127

Omensetter's Luck (Gass), **Supp. VI: 80–82,** 87

Omeros (Walcott), **Supp. XV:** 264

"Ominous Baby, An" (Crane), **I:** 411

Ommateum, with Doxology (Ammons), **Supp. VII:** 24–26, 27, 28, 36

Omni-Americans, The: New Perspectives on Black Experience and American

Culture (Murray), **Supp. XIX:** 147, **149–151, 154**

"Omnibus Jaunts and Drivers" (Whitman), **IV:** 350

Omoo: A Narrative of Adventures in the South Seas (Melville), **III:** 76–77, 79, 84; **Retro. Supp. I:** 247

O My Land, My Friends (H. Crane), **Retro. Supp. II:** 76

"On Abrigador Hill" (Nelson), **Supp. XVIII:** 183

"On a Certain Condescension in Foreigners" (J. R. Lowell), **Supp. I Part 2:** 419

"On a Certain Engagement South of Seoul" (Carruth), **Supp. XVI:** 47

"On a Child Who Lived One Minute" (X. J. Kennedy), **Supp. XV:** 152, 155

"On Acquiring Riches" (Banks), **Supp. V:** 5

On a Darkling Plain (Stegner), **Supp. IV Part 2:** 598, 607

On a Fire on the Moon (Mailer), **Retro. Supp. II:** 206

"On a Hill Far Away" (Dillard), **Supp. VI:** 28

"On a Honey Bee, Drinking from a Glass and Drowned Therein" (Freneau), **Supp. II Part 1:** 273

"On a Monument to a Pigeon" (Leopold), **Supp. XIV:** 187–188

"On a Mountainside" (Wagoner), **Supp. IX:** 332

O'Nan, Stewart, **Supp. XI:** 348; **Supp. XXV: 141–155**

"On a New Novel" (Ellis), **Supp. XXVII:** 78

"On an Old Photograph of My Son" (Carver), **Supp. III Part 1:** 140

"Onan's Soliloquy" (X. J. Kennedy), **Supp. XV:** 165

"On Antiphon Island" (Mackey), **Supp. XXVII:** 156

"On a Proposed Trip South" (W. C. Williams), **Retro. Supp. I:** 413

"On a Scale of 1 to 10: Life Writing and Lyrical Pain" (Mintz), **Supp. XXVI:** 52–53

Onassis, Jacqueline Kennedy, **Supp. XVIII:** 287

"On a Tree Fallen across the Road" (Frost), **Retro. Supp. I:** 134

"On a View of Pasadena from the Hills" (Winters), **Supp. II Part 2:** 795, 796–799, 814

"On a Visit to a Halfway House after a Long Absence" (Salinas), **Supp. XIII:** 325

"On a Windy Night" (Dixon), **Supp. XII:** 155

On Becoming a Novelist (Gardner), **Supp. VI:** 64

"On Being an American" (Toomer), **Supp. III Part 2:** 479

"On Being Asked to Write a Poem against the War in Vietnam" (Carruth), **Supp. XVI:** 55–56

"On Being a Woman" (Parker), **Supp. IX:** 201

On Being Blue (Gass), **Supp. VI:** 77, 78, 86, 94; **Supp. XIV:** 305

"On Being Brought from Africa to America" (Wheatley), **Supp. XX: 280–281, 286–287**

"On Being Too Inhibited" (Hay), **Supp. XIV:** 130

"On Being Unable to Read" (Cornell), **Supp. XX: 94–95**

On Beyond Zebra! (Geisel), **Supp. XVI:** 105

"On Burroughs' Work" (Ginsberg), **Supp. II Part 1:** 320

Once (Walker), **Supp. III Part 2:** 519, 522, 530

Once at Antietam (Gaddis), **Supp. IV Part 1:** 285

"Once by the Pacific" (Frost), **II:** 155; **Retro. Supp. I:** 122, 137

Once in a Blue Moon (film), **Supp. XXVII:** 90

"Once More, the Round" (Roethke), **III:** 529

Once More around the Block: Familiar Essays (Epstein), **Supp. XIV: 107**

"Once More to the Lake" (White), **Supp. I Part 2:** 658, 668, 673–675

"On Certain Political Measures Proposed to Their Consideration" (Barlow), **Supp. II Part 1:** 82

"Once There Was Light" (Kenyon), **Supp. VII:** 171–172

Once Upon a Time in Atlanta (Andrews), **Supp. XXVI:** 3, 11

"On *Credo Ut Intelligam*" (Bronk), **Supp. XXI:** 31

Ondaatje, Michael, **Supp. IV Part 1:** 252

"On Dining Alone" (M. F. K. Fisher), **Supp. XVII:** 83

On Distant Ground (R. O. Butler), **Supp. XII:** 62, **66–68,** 69, 74

"On Divers Geometries" (Bronk), **Supp. XXI:** 31

"On Dreams"(Hadas), **Supp. XXIII:** 117

"One, The" (Weigl), **Supp. XIX:** 282–283

"1 January 1965" (Brodsky), **Supp. VIII:** 23–24

O'Neale, Sondra, **Supp. IV Part 1:** 2

"One A.M. with Voices" (X. J. Kennedy), **Supp. XV:** 157

"One Arm" (T. Williams), **IV:** 383

One Arm, and Other Stories (T. Williams), **IV:** 383

"One Art" (Bell), **Supp. X:** 2

One Art (Bishop), **Retro. Supp. II:** 51

"One Art" (Bishop), **Retro. Supp. II:** 50; **Supp. I Part 1:** 72, 73, 82, 93, 94–95, 96; **Supp. XV:** 126; **Supp. XXI:** 58; **Supp. XXIII:** 117; **Supp. XXV:** 222

"One Art: The Poetry of Elizabeth Bishop, 1971–1976" (Schwartz), **Supp. I Part 1:** 81

One Big Self: Prisoners of Louisiana (Wright and Luster), **Supp. XV:** 337, 344, 350, **351–353**

"One Blessing had I than the rest" (Dickinson), **Retro. Supp. I:** 45

"One Body" (Hass), **Supp. VI:** 106

One Boy's Boston, 1887–1901 (Morison), **Supp. I Part 2:** 494

"One Coat of Paint" (Ashbery), **Supp. III Part 1:** 26

"One Dash-Horses" (Crane), **I:** 416

One Day (Morris), **III:** 233–236

One Day, When I Was Lost (Baldwin), **Retro. Supp. II:** 13; **Supp. I Part 1:** 48, 66, 67

"One Dead Friend" (Kumin), **Supp. IV Part 2:** 441

One Destiny: An Epistle to the Christians (Asch), **Supp. XXIII:** 2, 7

"One Down" (Goodman), **Supp. XXVI:** 122–123

One Fish Two Fish Red Fish Blue Fish (Geisel), **Supp. XVI:** 108

One Flesh (Major), **Supp. XXII: 183–184**

One Flew Over the Cuckoo's Nest (Kesey), **III:** 558

One Flew Over the Cuckoo's Nest (Kesey), **Supp. XXIII:** 100

One Foot in Eden (Rash), **Supp. XXVII:** 222–223, 226

"One for the Road" (Swados), **Supp. XIX:** 259

One for the Rose (Levine), **Supp. V:** 178, 179, 181, 187, 189–191

"One for the Rose" (Levine), **Supp. V:** 181, 190

"One Friday Morning" (Hughes), **Supp. I Part 1:** 330

"One Holy Night" (Cisneros), **Supp. VII:** 69–70

"One Home" (Stafford), **Supp. XI:** 321

100 Faces of Death, The, Part IV (Boyle), **Supp. VIII:** 16

100 Great Poets of the English Language (Gioia, ed.), **Supp. XXI:** 99

100 Years of Negro Freedom (Bontemps), **Supp. XXII:** 6

145 Street: Short Stories (Myers), **Supp. XXVII:** 210, 211

$106,000 Blood Money (Hammett), **Supp. IV Part 1:** 345

"$106,000 Blood Money" (Hammett), **Supp. IV Part 1:** 345, 346

One Hundred Days in Europe (Holmes), **Supp. I Part 1:** 317

180 More: Extraordinary Poems for Every Day (Collins, ed.), **Supp. XXI:** 54

158-Pound Marriage, The (Irving), **Supp. VI:** 163, 164, **167–170**

O'Neil, Elizabeth Murrie, **Retro. Supp. I:** 427

O'Neill, Brendan, **Supp. XII:** 286

O'Neill, Eugene, **I:** 66, 71, 81, 94, 393, 445; **II:** 278, 391, 427, 585; **III:** 151, 165, **385–408; IV:** 61, 383; **Retro. Supp. II:** 82, 104; **Supp. III Part 1:** 177–180, 189; **Supp. IV Part 1:** 359; **Supp. V Part 2:** 587, 607; **Supp. V:** 277; **Supp. VIII:** 332, 334; **Supp. XIV:** 239, 320, 328; **Supp. XVI:** 193; **Supp. XVII:** 96, 99–100, 103, 105, 107; **Supp. XX: 69; Supp. XXI:** 6, 13; **Supp. XXII:** 17, 18, 22, 28; **Supp. XXV:** 19

O'Neill, Oona, **Supp. XXII:** 25, 26
"One Is a Wanderer" (Thurber), **Supp. I Part 2:** 616
One Is the Sun (P. N. Warren), **Supp. XX: 269–270**
One L (Turow), **Supp. XVII: 214,** 215, 217
"One Last Look at the Adige: Verona in the Rain" (Wright), **Supp. III Part 2:** 603
One Life (Rukeyser), **Supp. VI:** 273, 281, 283
One Life at a Time, Please (Abbey), **Supp. XIII:** 13
One Man in His Time (Glasgow), **II:** 178, 184
"One Man's Fortunes" (Dunbar), **Supp. II Part 1:** 211, 212–213
One Man's Initiation (Dos Passos), **I:** 476–477, 479, 488
One Man's Meat (White), **Supp. I Part 2:** 654, 669, 676
"One Man's Meat" (White), **Supp. I Part 2:** 655
One Matchless Time: A Life of William Faulkner (Parini), **Supp. XXII:** 205
"One Moment on Top of the Earth" (Nye), **Supp. XIII:** 282
One More July: A Football Dialogue with Bill Curry (Plimpton), **Supp. XVI:** 243
"One More"(Kenny), **Supp. XXIII:** 156
"One More Song" (Lindsay), **Supp. I Part 2:** 400–401
"One More Thing" (Carver), **Supp. III Part 1:** 138, 144
"One More Time" (Gordon), **II:** 200
One Nation (Stegner), **Supp. IV Part 2:** 599, 608
"One-Night Homecoming" (X. J. Kennedy), **Supp. XV:** 167
"ONE NIGHT STAND" (Baraka), **Supp. II Part 1:** 32
"One of Our Conquerors" (Bourne), **I:** 223
One of Ours (Cather), **I:** 322–323; **Retro. Supp. I:** 1, 3, **13–15,** 20
One of the Dangerous Trades (Davison), **Supp. XXVI:** 61, 67–68
"One of the Missing" (Bierce), **I:** 201–202
"One of the Rooming Houses of Heaven" (Doty), **Supp. XI:** 131
"One of the Smallest" (Stern), **Supp. IX:** 299–300
"One of Us" (Fante), **Supp. XI:** 165
Oneóta: or, The Red Race of America (H. Schoolcraft), **Supp. XXIII:** 232
"One Out of Twelve: Writers Who Are Women in Our Century" (Olsen), **Supp. XIII:** 294
"One Part Humor, 2 Parts Whining" (Kakutani), **Supp. XI:** 38
"One Person" (Wylie), **Supp. I Part 2:** 709, 724–727
"One Reel Tragedy" (Stone), **Supp. XXVII:** 254
"One Sister have I in our house" (Dickinson), **Retro. Supp. I:** 34

165 Meeting House Lane (Notley), **Supp. XXII:** 224, 225, 226
"One Song, The" (Strand), **Supp. IV Part 2:** 619
"One Summer in Spain" (Coover), **Supp. V:** 40
One That Got Away, The (Everett), **Supp. XVIII:** 54
1000 Airplanes on the Roof (Glass, Hwang, and Sirlin), **Supp. XXI:** 147
1001 Afternoons in Chicago (Hecht), **Supp. XXVII:** 83, 85, 88
One Thousand Avant-Garde Plays (Koch), **Supp. XV:** 187
"One Thousandth, The" (Weigl), **Supp. XIX:** 288
One Time, One Place: Mississippi in the Depression, a Snapshot Album (Welty), **Retro. Supp. I:** 339, 343, 344
1 x 1 (One Times One) (Cummings), **I:** 430, 436, 438–439, 441, 446, 447, 448
"One Touch of Nature" (McCarthy), **II:** 580
One Train (Koch), **Supp. XV:** 177, 184
"One Trip Abroad" (Fitzgerald), **II:** 95
One True Thing (film), **Supp. XVII:** 176
One True Thing (Quindlen), **Supp. XVIII:** 166, **174–176**
"One Way" (Creeley), **Supp. IV Part 1:** 150–151
One Way or Another (Cameron), **Supp. XII:** 81
One-Way Ticket (Hughes), **Retro. Supp. I:** 206, 207, 208; **Supp. I Part 1:** 333–334
One Way to Heaven (Cullen), **Supp. IV Part 1:** 170, 172
One Way to Reconstruct the Scene (W. V. Davis), **Supp. XXI:** 83, **88–91**
"One Way to Reconstruct the Scene" (W. V. Davis), **Supp. XXI: 88–89,** 90, 91, 92, **93**
One Way to Spell Man (Stegner), **Supp. IV Part 2:** 595, 598, 601, 609
"One Way to Spell Man" (Stegner), **Supp. IV Part 2:** 601
One Whose Eyes Open When You Close Your Eyes, The (F. Wright), **Supp. XVII:** 240, 243
"One Who Skins Cats, The" (Gunn Allen), **Supp. IV Part 1:** 331
One Who Walked Alone (Price), **Supp. XXVII:** 117
"One Who Went Forth to Feel Fear" (Grimms), **Supp. X:** 86
"One Winter I Devise a Plan of My Own" (Ríos), **Supp. IV Part 2:** 549
One Winter Night in August (X. J. Kennedy), **Supp. XV:** 154, 162
One World at a Time (Kooser), **Supp. XIX:** 116, **122–123**
One Writer's Beginnings (Welty), **Retro. Supp. I:** 339, 340, 341, 343, 344, 355–356
"One Year" (Olds), **Supp. X:** 210
On Fire (L. Brown), **Supp. XXI:** 41, **48–49**
On Fire (Silver), **Supp. XXIV:** 264
"On First Looking Into Chapman's Homer" (Keats), **Supp. XXI:** 64;

Supp. XXV: 226
"On First Looking Out through Juan de la Cosa's Eyes" (Olson), **Supp. II Part 2:** 565, 566, 570, 579
"On First Opening *The Lyric Year*" (W. C. Williams), **Retro. Supp. I:** 414
"On Freedom's Ground" (Wilbur), **Supp. III Part 2:** 562
On Glory's Course (Purdy), **Supp. VII:** 275–276, 279, 280
On Grief and Reason (Brodsky), **Supp. VIII:** 31–32
"On Hearing a Symphony of Beethoven" (Millay), **III:** 132–133
"On Hearing the Airlines Will Use a Psychological Profile to Catch Potential Skyjackers" (Dunn), **Supp. XI:** 144–145
On Human Finery (Bell), **Supp. I Part 2:** 636
"On *Imagerie*: Esther Williams, 1944" (Sobin), **Supp. XVI:** 294
"On Imagination" (Wheatley), **Supp. XX: 281**
"On Imminence: An Essay" (Sobin), **Supp. XVI:** 291
On Immunity: An Inoculation (Biss), **Supp. XXVI:** 45, 57–58, 59
"Onionskin" (Goodman), **Supp. XXVI:** 121, 125
"On Ithaka" (Davison), **Supp. XXVI:** 79
On Kingdom Mountain (Mosher), **Supp. XXII:** 203, 205, 206, 207, 208, 209, 212, 214, **216**
Onkl Mozes (Uncle Moses) (Asch), **Supp. XXIII:** 5
"On leaving my children John and Jane at School, in the Atlantic states, and preparing to return to the interior"(J. Schoolcraft), **Supp. XXIII:** 227, 228, 232, 233, 235, 236
On Liberty (Mill), **Supp. XI:** 196
"On Looking Alone at a Place" (M. F. K. Fisher), **Supp. XVII:** 91
"On Looking at a Copy of Alice Meynell's Poems, Given Me, Years Ago, by a Friend" (A. Lowell), **II:** 527–528
"On Lookout Mountain" (Hayden), **Supp. II Part 1:** 380
Only a Few of Us Left (Marquand), **III:** 55
"Only Animal, The" (F. Wright), **Supp. XVII:** 245
"Only a Pawn in Their Game" (song, Dylan), **Supp. XVIII:** 24
Only as Far as Brooklyn (Kenny), **Supp. XXIII: 148–151,** 152
"Only Bar in Dixon, The" (Hugo), **Supp. VI:** 140, 141
Only Dangerous Thing, The (Di Piero), **Supp. XIX: 37–38**
Only Dark Spot in the Sky, The (Dove), **Supp. IV Part 1:** 244
"Only Good Indian, The" (Humphrey), **Supp. IX:** 101
"Only Goodness" (Lahiri), **Supp. XXI:** 186, 188
Only in America (Golden), **Supp. VIII:** 244

"Only in the Dream" (Eberhart), **I:** 523

"Only Path to Tomorrow, The" (Rand), **Supp. IV Part 2:** 524

"Only Professional Player of the Toy Piano, Margaret Leng Tan, The" (Biss), **Supp. XXVI:** 51

"Only Rose, The" (Jewett), **II:** 408

"Only Son of the Doctor, The" (Gordon), **Supp. IV Part 1:** 305, 306

"Only the Cat Escapes", **Supp. XII:** 150–151

"Only the Dead Know Brooklyn" (Wolfe), **IV:** 451

Only the Little Bone (Huddle), **Supp. XXVI:** 152–153

"Only the Little Bone" (Huddle), **Supp. XXVI:** 151, 153

"Only When I Am Quiet and Do Not Speak"(Hirshfield), **Supp. XXIII:** 133

Only When I Laugh (Simon), **Supp. IV Part 2:** 575

Only World, The (Hull), **Supp. XXI:** 129, **138–141**

On Man and Manhood (Kriegel), **Supp. XXIV: 224–225**

"On Manhood, Disease, and the Authentic Self" (Kriegel), **Supp. XXIV:** 215

"On Meditation"(J. Schoolcraft), **Supp. XXIII:** 229

"On Meeting My Father in a Bar for the First Time" (Gansworth), **Supp. XXVI:** 110

"On Messrs. Hussey and Coffin" (Wheatley), **Supp. XX: 280**

On Moral Fiction (Gardner), **Supp. VI:** 61, **71,** 72, 73

"On Morality" (Didion), **Supp. IV Part 1:** 196

"On Mt. Philo in November" (Di Piero), **Supp. XIX:** 37, 39

"On Murder Considered as One of the Fine Arts" (De Quincey), **Supp. XXVI:** 283

"On My Own" (Levine), **Supp. V:** 181, 189–190

"On My Own Work" (Wilbur), **Supp. III Part 2:** 541–542

On Native Grounds: An Interpretation of Modern American Prose Literature (Kazin), **I:** 517; **Supp. I Part 2:** 650; **Supp. VIII:** 93, 96–97, 98, **100–102**

"On Not Being a Dove" (Updike), **Retro. Supp. I:** 323

"On Open Form" (Merwin), **Supp. III Part 1:** 347–348, 353

On Photography (Sontag), **Supp. III Part 2:** 451, 458, 462–465

"On Poetry"(Hadas), **Supp. XXIII:** 115, 116

"On Political Poetry" (R. Bly), **Supp. IV Part 1:** 61

On Politics: A Carnival of Buncombe (Moos, ed.), **III:** 116

"On Pretentiousness" (Kushner), **Supp. IX:** 131–132

"On Quitting a Little College" (Stafford), **Supp. XI:** 321

"On Reading Eckerman's Conversations with Goethe" (Masters), **Supp. I Part 2:** 458

On Reading Shakespeare (L. P. Smith), **Supp. XIV:** 345–346

"On Reading to Oneself" (Gass), **Supp. VI:** 88, 89

"On Recollection" (Wheatley), **Supp. XX:** 287

On Revolution (Arendt), **Retro. Supp. I:** 87

On Second Thought (Kenny), **Supp. XXIII:** 144

"On Seeing Larry Rivers's *Washington Crossing the Delaware* at the Museum of Modern Art" (O'Hara), **Supp. XV:** 186; **Supp. XXIII:** 208, 214

"On Seeing Red" (Walker), **Supp. III Part 2:** 527

"On Social Plays" (A. Miller), **III:** 147, 148, 159

Onstad, Katrina, **Supp. XXIV:** 209

"On Steinbeck's Story 'Flight' " (Stegner), **Supp. IV Part 2:** 596

"On Style" (Sontag), **Supp. III Part 2:** 456–459, 465–466

"On Suicide" (Hay), **Supp. XIV:** 130, 132

"On Teaching the Young Laurel to Shoot" (Bynner), **Supp. XV:** 50

"On the Antler" (Proulx), **Supp. VII:** 252–253

"On the Avenue" (Espaillat), **Supp. XXI:** 112

On the Banks of Plum Creek (L. I. Wilder), **Supp. XXII:** 294, 299

"On the Banks of the Wabash" (Paul Dresser), **Retro. Supp. II:** 94

"On the Beach, at Night" (Whitman), **IV:** 348

"On the Bosom of This Grave and Wasted Land I Will Lay My Head" (Ray), **Supp. XVIII:** 189

On the Boundary (Tillich), **Retro. Supp. I:** 326

"On the Building of Springfield" (Lindsay), **Supp. I Part 2:** 381

"On the Coast of Maine" (Hayden), **Supp. II Part 1:** 381

On the Contrary: Articles of Belief (McCarthy), **II:** 559, 562

"On the Death of a Friend's Child" (J. R. Lowell), **Supp. I Part 2:** 409

"On the Death of Cardinal Tisserant" (Bronk), **Supp. XXI:** 32

"On the Death of General Wooster" (Wheatley), **Supp. XX:** 287

"On the Death of Rev. Mr. George Whitefield—1770" (Wheatley), **Supp. XX: 280,Supp. XX: 282–283**

"On the Death of Senator Thomas J. Walsh" (Winters), **Supp. II Part 2:** 802, 806

"On the Death of Yeats" (Bogan), **Supp. III Part 1:** 59

"On the Death of Zhukov" (Brodsky), **Supp. VIII:** 27

"On the Disadvantages of Central Heating" (Clampitt), **Supp. IX:** 41, 47, 52

"On the Doric Rock, Lake Superior"(J. Schoolcraft), **Supp. XXIII:** 232

On the Drumhead: A Selection from the Writing of Mike Quin (Carlisle, ed.), **Supp. XVIII:** 223, 226

"On the Edge" (Levine), **Supp. V:** 181–182

On the Edge and Over (Levine), **Supp. V:** 178, 180–182, 186

On the Edge of the Great Rift: Three Novels of Africa (Theroux), **Supp. VIII:** 316

"On the Edge of Visible Light"(Schott), **Supp. XXIII:** 242

"On the Eve of the Feast of the Immaculate Conception, 1942" (R. Lowell), **II:** 538; **Retro. Supp. II:** 185

"On the Eyes of an SS Officer" (Wilbur), **Supp. III Part 2:** 548

"On the Failure of Meaning in the Absence of Objective Analogs" (Bronk), **Supp. XXI:** 31

"On the Fall of General Earl Cornwallis" (Freneau), **Supp. II Part 1:** 261

"On the Folly of Writing Poetry" (Freneau), **Supp. II Part 1:** 263

On the Frontier (Auden and Isherwood), **Supp. II Part 1:** 13; **Supp. XIV:** 163

On the Great Atlantic Rainway: Selected Poems, 1950–1988 (Koch), **Supp. XV:** 177

"On the History of Poetry" (Halliday), **Supp. XIX:** 88, 89

"On the Hysterical Playground" (Watman), **Supp. XX:** 93

"On the Island" (Stern), **Supp. IX:** 290

"On the Late Eclipse" (Bryant), **Supp. I Part 1:** 152

On the Laws of the Poetic Art (Hecht), **Supp. X:** 58

On the Line (Swados), **Supp. XIX: 258–260**

"On the Line" (Swados), **Supp. XIX:** 259

"On the Marginal Way" (Wilbur), **Supp. III Part 2:** 558, 559

On the Mesa (Nichols), **Supp. XIII:** 268

"On the Moon and Matriarchal Consciousness" (Neumann), **Supp. IV Part 1:** 68

"On the Morning after the Sixties" (Didion), **Supp. IV Part 1:** 205, 206

On the Motion and Immobility of Douve (Bonnefoy; Kinnell, trans.), **Supp. III Part 1:** 235

"On the Mullica"(Schott), **Supp. XXIII:** 253

"On the Murder of Lieutenant José del Castillo by the Falangist Bravo Martinez, July 12, 1936" (Levine), **Supp. V:** 187

"On the Night of a Friend's Wedding" (Robinson), **III:** 524

"On the Occasion of a Poem: Richard Hugo" (Wright), **Supp. III Part 2:** 596

On the Occasion of My Last Afternoon (Gibbons), **Supp. X:** 46, **50–53**

On the Origin of Species (Darwin), **Supp. XIV:** 192

"On the Parapet" (Tanner), **Retro. Supp. II:** 205

"On the Platform" (Nemerov), **III:** 287

On the Poetry of Philip Levine: Stranger to Nothing (Levis), **Supp. XI:** 257

"On the Pottlecombe Cornice" (Sturgis), **Supp. XX: 233, 240**

"On the Powers of the Human Under-standing" (Freneau), **Supp. II Part 1:** 274

On the Prejudices, Predilections, and Firm Beliefs of William Faulkner (Brooks), **Supp. XIV:** 13

"On the Pulse of Morning" (Angelou), **Supp. IV Part 1:** 15–17

"On the Railway Platform" (Jarrell), **II:** 370

"On the Rainy River" (O'Brien), **Supp. V:** 250

On the Rebound: A Story and Nine Poems (Purdy), **Supp. VII:** 276–277

"On the Religion of Nature" (Freneau), **Supp. II Part 1:** 275

"On the River" (Dunbar), **Supp. II Part 1:** 193

"On the River" (Levine), **Supp. V:** 193

On the River Styx and Other Stories (Matthiessen), **Supp. V:** 212

On the Road (Kerouac), **Retro. Supp. I:** 102; **Supp. III Part 1:** 92, 218, 222–224, 226, 230–231; **Supp. V:** 336; **Supp. X:** 269; **Supp. XIII:** 275; **Supp. XIV:** 138, 150; **Supp. XV:** 221; **Supp. XVIII:** 20, 138; **Supp. XXI:** 53; **Supp. XXIV:** 281; **Supp. XXVI:** 26, 252

"On the Road Home" (Stevens), **Retro. Supp. I:** 306

On the Road with the Archangel (Buechner), **Supp. XII:** 54

"On the Rope" (Richard), **Supp. XIX:** 211–212

"On the Run" (Boyle), **Supp. XXIV:** 52

On These I Stand: An Anthology of the Best Poems of Countee Cullen (Cullen), **Supp. IV Part 1:** 173

"On the Skeleton of a Hound" (Wright), **Supp. III Part 2:** 593

"On the Staten Island Ferry"(Kenny), **Supp. XXIII:** 154

"On the Street" (Peacock), **Supp. XIX:** 199

"On the Street: Monument" (Gunn Allen), **Supp. IV Part 1:** 326

"On the Subway" (Olds), **Supp. X:** 207

"On the System of Policy Hitherto Pursued by Their Government" (Barlow), **Supp. II Part 1:** 82

"On the Teaching of Modern Literature" (Trilling), **Supp. III Part 2:** 509–510

"On the Uniformity and Perfection of Nature" (Freneau), **Supp. II Part 1:** 275

"On the Universality and Other Attributes of the God of Nature" (Freneau), **Supp. II Part 1:** 275

"On the Use of Trisyllabic Feet in Iambic Verse" (Bryant), **Supp. I Part 1:** 156

On the Verge: Emerging Poets (Ellis and Lease, eds.), **Supp. XXI:** 246

On the Waterfront (film, Kazan), **Supp. XVIII:** 250–251, 252, 253

"On the Way" (Stone), **Supp. XXVII:** 251, 253

"On the Way Home" (L. I. Wilder), **Supp. XXII:** 292

On the Way to the Island (Ferry), **Supp. XXIV:** 147, **148–149,** 150

"On the Way to the San Remo"(O'Hara), **Supp. XXIII:** 212, 219

On the Way toward a Phenomenological Psychology: The Psychology of William James (Linschoten), **II:** 362

"On the Way to Work" (Dunn), **Supp. XI:** 149–150

"On the Wide Heath" (Millay), **III:** 130

"On the Writing of Novels" (Buck), **Supp. II Part 1:** 121

On the Yard (Braly), **Supp. XVIII:** 147

On This Island (Auden), **Supp. II Part 1:** 11

On This Side of the River (Ferry), **Supp. XXIV:** **161–162**

"On Time" (O'Hara), **III:** 369–370

"Ontological Episode of the Asylum" (Carruth), **Supp. XVI:** 48, 50

"Ontology of the Sentence, The" (Gass), **Supp. VI:** 77

"On Top" (Leopold), **Supp. XIV:** 188

"On Top" (Snyder), **Supp. VIII:** 304

"On Translating Akhmatova" (Kunitz), **Supp. III Part 1:** 268

"On Turning Ten" (Collins), **Supp. XXI:** 64

"On Visiting a Borrowed Country House in Arcadia" (Stallings), **Supp. XXV:** 233–234

"On Waking to Old Debts" (Keillor), **Supp. XVI:** 167

On William Stafford: The Worth of Local Things (Andrews, ed.), **Supp. XI:** 311, 312, 317, 321, 324, 326

On Writers and Writing (O'Nan, ed.), **Supp. XXV:** 152–153

"On Writing" (Carver), **Supp. III Part 1:** 142–143

"On Writing" (Nin), **Supp. X:** 182

On Your Own (Gallagher), **Supp. XXIV:** 166

Opatoshu, Joseph, **IV:** 9

"Open Boat, The" (Crane), **I:** 408, 415, 416–417, 423; **Retro. Supp. I:** 325; **Supp. XIV:** 51

Open Boat and Other Stories (Crane), **I:** 408

Open Door, The (Skloot), **Supp. XX:** **194, 196, 208**

Open Heart: A Patient's Story of Life-Saving Medicine and Life-Giving Friendship (Neugeboren), **Supp. XVI:** 217, **229–230**

Open House (Roethke), **III:** 529–530, 540

"Open House" (Roethke), **III:** 529

"Opening, An" (Swenson), **Supp. IV Part 2:** 639

Opening of the Field, The (Duncan), **Supp. III Part 2:** 625

Opening the Hand (Merwin), **Supp. III Part 1:** 341, 353, 355

"Open Letter" (Roethke), **III:** 532, 534

"Open Letter to Surrealists Everywhere, An" (H. Miller), **III:** 184

Open Meeting, The (Gurney), **Supp. V:** 98

Open Net (Plimpton), **Supp. XVI:** 241

"Open Road, The" (Dreiser), **II:** 44

Open Sea, The (Masters), **Supp. I Part 2:** 471

Open Season: Sporting Adventures (Humphrey), **Supp. IX:** 95

"Open Secret" (Nelson), **Supp. XVIII:** 185

Open Secrets (Munro), **Supp. XXVII:** 190, 191–192

"Open Secrets" (Munro), **Supp. XXVII:** 191–192

"Open the Gates" (Kunitz), **Supp. III Part 1:** 264–265, 267

"Opera Company, The" (Merrill), **Supp. III Part 1:** 326

Operating Instructions: A Journal of My Son's First Year (Lamott), **Supp. XX:** **136–137, 142**

"Operation, The" (Sanders), **Supp. XVI:** 266

"Operation, The" (Sexton), **Supp. II Part 2:** 675, 679

Operation Shylock: A Confession (P. Roth), **Retro. Supp. II:** 279, 280, 291

Operation Sidewinder (Shepard), **Supp. III Part 2:** 434–435, 439, 446–447

Operations in North African Waters (Morison), **Supp. I Part 2:** 490

Operation Wandering Soul (Powers), **Supp. IX:** 212, **217–219**

Opffer, Emil, **Retro. Supp. II:** 80

"Opinion" (Du Bois), **Supp. II Part 1:** 173

Opinionator, The (Bierce), **I:** 209

Opinions of Oliver Allston (Brooks), **I:** 254, 255, 256

O Pioneers! (Cather), **I:** 314, 317–319, 320; **Retro. Supp. I:** 1, 5, 6, **7–9,** 10, 13, 20; **Retro. Supp. II:** 136

Oppen, George, **IV:** 415; **Supp. III Part 2:** 614, 615, 616, 626, 628; **Supp. XIV:** 285, 286, 287; **Supp. XVI:** 282, 283; **Supp. XVII:** 243; **Supp. XXI:** 19,**Supp. XXI:** 29, 23; **Supp. XXIII:** 165–166, 168; **Supp. XXVI:** **223–238**

Oppen, Mary, **Supp. XXVI:** 225

Oppenheim, James, **I:** 106, 109, 239, 245; **Supp. XV:** 294, 296, 298, 299, 301, 302, 307, 313; **Supp. XX:** **68**

Oppenheimer, J. Robert, **I:** 137, 492

Oppenheimer, Judy, **Supp. IX:** 115, 116, 118, 120, 126

"Opportunity for American Fiction, An" (Howells), **Supp. I Part 2:** 645–646

Opposing Self, The (Trilling), **Supp. III Part 2:** 506–507

"Opposition" (Lanier), **Supp. I Part 1:** 368, 373

Oprah's Roots: An African American Lives Special (television production), **Supp. XX:** 99

Opticks: A Poem in Seven Sections (Goldbarth), **Supp. XII:** 177, **178**

Optimist's Daughter, The (Welty), **IV:** 261, 280; **Retro. Supp. I:** 339, 355

"Optimist's Daughter, The" (Welty), **IV:** 280–281

Options (O. Henry), **Supp. II Part 1:** 410

Opus Posthumous (Stevens), **IV:** 76, 78

Opus Posthumous (W. Stevens), **Supp. XVII:** 241

Oracle at Stoneleigh Court, The (Taylor), **Supp. V:** 328

Orage, Alfred, **III:** 473

"O/Rain-in-the-Face"(Kenny), **Supp. XXIII:** 156

"Oral History" (Goodman), **Supp. XXVI:** 118, 119

Orange, Max (pseudonym). *See* Heller, Joseph

Orange Fish, The (Shields), **Supp. VII:** 318, 320, 323, 328

Orangery, The (Sorrentino), **Supp. XXI:** 228

Oranges (exhibition, Hartigan), **Supp. XXIII:** 210

Oranges (McPhee), **Supp. III Part 1:** 298–299, 301, 309

Oranges: 12 Pastorals (O'Hara), **Supp. XXIII:** 210

"Oranging of America, The" (Apple), **Supp. XVII:** 3–4, 6

Oranging of America and Other Short Stories, The (Apple), **Supp. XVII:** 1–2, **3–4,** 7, 8

Oration Delivered at Washington, July Fourth, 1809 (Barlow), **Supp. II Part 1:** 80, 83

Orations and Addresses (Bryant), **Supp. I Part 1:** 158

Orators, The (Auden), **Supp. II Part 1:** 6, 7, 11, 18–19

Orbach, Jerry, **Supp. XXIII:** 103

Orb Weaver, The (Francis), **Supp. IX:** **81–82**

"Orchard" (Doolittle), **Supp. I Part 1:** 263–264, 265, 266

"Orchard" (Eberhart), **I:** 539

Orchard, The (B. Kelly), **Supp. XVII:** 123, 127, **130–133**

"Orchard, The" (B. Kelly), **Supp. XVII:** 133

Orchard Keeper, The (McCarthy), **Supp. VIII:** **175–176**

Orchestra (Davies), **III:** 541

"Orchid Fever" (Orlean), **Supp. XXV:** 160

"Orchids" (Roethke), **III:** 530–531

Orchid Thief, The: A True Story of Beauty and Obsession (Orlean), **Supp. XXV:** 160, 161–162

"Or Consider Prometheus" (Clampitt), **Supp. IX:** 44

Ordeal of Mansart, The (Du Bois), **Supp. II Part 1:** 185–186

Ordeal of Mark Twain, The (Brooks), **I:** 240, 247, 248; **II:** 482

Ordering the Façade: Photography and Contemporary Southern Women's Writing (Henninger), **Supp. XXI:** 253

"Order of Insects" (Gass), **Supp. VI:** 83

Order Out of Chaos (McPherson), **Supp. IV Part 1:** 2, 12

"Orders" (Duncan), **Supp. XXVII:** 160

"Ordinary Afternoon in Charlottesville, An" (Wright), **Supp. V:** 344

"Ordinary Days" (Dunn), **Supp. XI:** 151

"Ordinary Evening in New Haven, An" (Stevens), **IV:** 91–92; **Retro. Supp. I:** 297, 300, 311, 312

Ordinary Heroes (Turow), **Supp. XVII: 221–222,** 223

Ordinary Life (Crooker), **Supp. XXIII: 56**

Ordinary Love (Smiley), **Supp. VI:** 292, **299–300**

Ordinary Love; and Good Will: Two Novellas (Smiley), **Supp. VI:** 292, **299–300**

Ordinary Miracles (Jong), **Supp. V:** 115, 130–131

Ordinary Seaman, The (Goldman), **Supp. XXV:** 49, 50, 53–54

"Ordinary Time: Virginia Woolf and Thucydides on War" (Carson), **Supp. XII:** 111

"Ordinary Women, The" (Stevens), **IV:** 81

Ordinary Words (Stone), **Supp. XXVII:** 257, 262

Ordways, The (Humphrey), **Supp. IX:** 95, **98–100,** 109; **Supp. XV:** 353

"Oread" (Doolittle), **II:** 520–521; **Supp. I Part 1:** 265–266

Oregon Message, An (Stafford), **Supp. XI: 328–329**

Oregon Trail, The (Parkman), **II:** 312; **Supp. II Part 2:** 592, 595–596, 598, 606

Oresteia (Aeschylus), **Supp. IX:** 103

"Orestes at Tauris" (Jarrell), **II:** 376, 377

Orfalea, Gregory, **Supp. XIII:** 278

Orfeo ed Euridice (Gluck), **II:** 210, 211

Orff, Carl, **Supp. X:** 63

"Organizer's Wife, The" (Bambara), **Supp. XI:** 8–9

"Organmeister: Hasse After Marienkirche" (Bierds), **Supp. XVII:** 34

"Orgy" (Rukeyser), **Supp. VI:** 280

Orgy, The (Rukeyser), **Supp. VI:** 274, 283

"Orgy of Southerness, An" (Pickering), **Supp. XXI:** 203

"Oriental Rug"(Balakian), **Supp. XXIII:** 23, 24–25

"Orientation of Hope, The" (Locke), **Supp. XIV:** 212–213

Orient Express (Dos Passos), **I:** 480

"Orient Express, The" (Jarrell), **II:** 382, 383–384

Origen, Adamantius, **IV:** 153

"Origin" (Harjo), **Supp. XII:** 219

Original Child Bomb: Points for Meditation to Be Scratched on the Walls of a Cave (Merton), **Supp. VIII:** 203

Original Essays on the Poetry of Anne Sexton (George), **Supp. IV Part 2:** 450

"Original Follies Girl, The" (Z. Fitzgerald), **Supp. IX:** 71

Original Light (Goldbarth), **Supp. XII:** 181, **183–184,** 188

Original Love (Peacock), **Supp. XIX: 199–201,** 206

Original of Laura, The (Nabokov), **Retro. Supp. I:** 266

"Original Sin" (Jeffers), **Supp. II Part 2:** 426

"Original Sin" (Vaz), **Supp. XXVI:** 259–260

"Original Sin" (Warren), **IV:** 245

"Original Story" (Gansworth), **Supp. XXVI:** 114

Origin: Hawaii (Taggard), **Supp. XXII:** 272, 284

"Origin of Extermination in the Imagination, The" (Gass), **Supp. VI:** 89

Origin of Species (Darwin), **Supp. XXVII:** 34

Origin of Species, The (Darwin), **II:** 173, 462; **Supp. XVI:** 13

Origin of the Brunists, The (Coover), **Supp. V:** 39, 41, 52

"Origin of the Miscodeed, or the Maid of Taquimenon"(J. Schoolcraft), **Supp. XXIII:** 235

"Origin of the Robin, The"(J. Schoolcraft), **Supp. XXIII:** 234, 235

"Origins and History of Consciousness" (Rich), **Supp. I Part 2:** 570

"Origins of a Nonfiction Writer" (Talese), **Supp. XVII:** 208

"Origins of a Poem" (Levertov), **Supp. III Part 1:** 273

"Origins of the Beat Generation, The" (Kerouac), **Supp. III Part 1:** 231

Origo, Iris, **IV:** 328

"O'Riley's Late-Bloomed Little Son" (X. J. Kennedy), **Supp. XV:** 159

"Orion" (Rich), **Supp. I Part 2:** 557

O'Riordan, Conal Holmes O'Connell, **III:** 465

Orlacs Hände (film, Weine), **Supp. XVII:** 58

Orlando (V. Woolf), **Supp. XVII:** 86

Orlando (Woolf), **Supp. I Part 2:** 718; **Supp. VIII:** 263; **Supp. XII:** 9

Orlando Furioso (Ariosto), **Supp. XV:** 175

Orlean, Susan, **Supp. XXV: 157–167**

Orlik, Emil, **Supp. XXIII:** 6

Orloff, Chana, **Supp. XXIII:** 6

Orlovsky, Peter, **Supp. XII:** 121, 126; **Supp. XIV:** 150; **Supp. XVIII:** 27

Ormonde, Czenzi, **Supp. IV Part 1:** 132

Ormond; or, The Secret Witness (Brown), **Supp. I Part 1:** 133–137

Ornament and Crime (Loos), **Supp. XVI:** 187

Orne, Sarah. *See* Jewett, Sarah Orne

Ornithological Biography; or, An Account of the Habits of the Birds of the United States of America, and Interspersed with Delineations of American Scenery and Manners (Audubon), **7–10; Supp. XVI:**13

"Ornithology" (Hull), **Supp. XXI:** 138–139

Ornitz, Samuel, **Supp. IX:** 227; **Supp. XIII:** 166

Ornstein, Leo, **Supp. XX: 75**

O'Rourke, Meghan, **Supp. XXV:** 10

O'Rourke, William, **Supp. XXII:** 213

Orphan Angel, The (Wylie), **Supp. I Part 2:** 707, 709, 714, 717, 719–721, 722, 724

Orphan's Tale, An (Neugeboren), **Supp. XVI:** 222, 223

Orpheus (film), **Supp. XXVII:** 80

Orpheus (Rukeyser), **Supp. VI:** 273

"Orpheus" (Winters), **Supp. II Part 2:** 801

"Orpheus, Eurydice, Hermes" (Rilke), **Supp. VIII:** 31, 32

"Orpheus (1)" (Atwood), **Supp. XIII:** 35

"Orpheus (2)" (Atwood), **Supp. XIII:** 35

"Orpheus Alone" (Strand), **Supp. IV Part 2:** 632

Orpheus Descending (T. Williams), **IV:** 380, 381, 382, 385, 386, 387, 389, 391–392, 395, 396, 398

Orr, David, **Supp. XXI:** 62

Orr, Peter, **Supp. I Part 2:** 538, 540, 543

Orse, Brian, **Supp. XX: 264**

Ortega y Gasset, José, **I:** 218, 222; **Supp. IV Part 2:** 521; **Supp. XXIII:** 165

Ortiz, Simon J., **Supp. IV Part 1:** 319, 404; **Supp. IV Part 2: 497–515,** 557; **Supp. XII:** 217, 218

"Ortlieb's Uptown Taproom" (Di Piero), **Supp. XIX:** 46, 47

Orton, Joe, **Supp. XXIV:** 113, 126, 263

O'Ruddy, The (Crane), **I:** 409, 424

Orwell, George, **I:** 489; **II:** 454, 580; **Supp. I Part 2:** 523, 620; **Supp. II Part 1:** 143; **Supp. IV Part 1:** 236; **Supp. V:** 250; **Supp. VIII:** 241; **Supp. XIV:** 112, 158; **Supp. XVII:** 228, 229; **Supp. XVIII:** 137, 138; **Supp. XX:** 86

Osborn, Dwight, **III:** 218–219, 223

"Osborn Look, The" (Morris), **III:** 221

Osgood, Frances, **Supp. XVII:** 75

Osgood, J. R., **II:** 283

O'Shea, Kitty, **II:** 137

O'Shea, Milo, **Supp. XI:** 308

"Oshkikwe's Baby" (traditional Chippewa story), **Supp. IV Part 1:** 333

Oshogay, Delia, **Supp. IV Part 1:** 333

Ossana, Diana, **Supp. V:** 230–231, 232

Ossian, **Supp. I Part 2:** 491

Ossip, Kathleen, **Supp. X:** 201

"Osso Bucco" (Collins), **Supp. XXI:** 60

Ostanovka v Pustyne (A halt in the wilderness) (Brodsky), **Supp. VIII:** 21

Oster, Judith, **Supp. XVI:** 151

Ostriker, Alicia, **Supp. I Part 2:** 540; **Supp. IV Part 2:** 439, 447, 449; **Supp. X:** 207, 208; **Supp. XI:** 143; **Supp. XV:** 251; **Supp. XXVII:** 261

Ostrom, Hans, **Retro. Supp. I:** 195

Oswald, Lee Harvey, **III:** 234, 235

Oswald II (DeLillo), **Supp. VI:** 16

Oswald's Tale (Mailer), **Retro. Supp. II:** 212–213

"Otagamiad, The"(J. Schoolcraft), **Supp. XXIII:** 223

O Taste and See (Levertov), **Supp. III Part 1:** 278–279, 281

Othello (Shakespeare), **I:** 284–285

"Other, The" (Sexton), **Supp. II Part 2:** 692

Other America, The (Harrington), **I:** 306

"Other American Renaissance, The" (Tompkins), **Supp. XVIII:** 258

Other Destinies: Understanding the American Indian Novel (Owens), **Supp. IV Part 1:** 404

otherelectricities.com, **Supp. XXIV:** 240–241

Other Electricities: Stories (Monson), **Supp. XXIV:** 230, **231–234,** 235–236, 238, 241

"Other Frost, The" (Jarrell), **Retro. Supp. I:** 121

"Other Gods, The" (Lovecraft), **Supp. XXV:** 114

Other Gods: An American Legend (Buck), **Supp. II Part 1:** 123, 130–131

Other House, The (James), **Retro. Supp. I:** 229

"Other League of Nations, The" (Ríos), **Supp. IV Part 2:** 552

"Other Margaret, The" (Trilling), **Supp. III Part 2:** 504–505

"Other Miller, The" (Wolff), **Supp. VII:** 343–344

"Other Mothers" (Paley), **Supp. VI:** 225

"Other Night at Columbia, The" (Trilling), **Supp. XII:** 126

"Other People's Secrets" (Hampl), **Supp. XXII:** 94

"Other Robert Frost, The" (Jarrell), **Retro. Supp. I:** 135

Others (Shields), **Supp. VII:** 310

Other Side, The (Gordon), **Supp. IV Part 1:** 299, 306, 307–309, 310–311

Other Side, The/El Otro Lado (Alvarez), **Supp. VII:** 9–12

"Other Side, The"(Hadas), **Supp. XXIII:** 120

Other Side of the River, The (Wright), **Supp. V:** 332–333, 342

"Other Side of the River, The" (Wright), **Supp. V:** 335

"Other Tradition, The" (Ashbery), **Supp. III Part 1:** 15, 18

"Other Two, The" (Wharton), **Retro. Supp. I:** 367

Other Voices, Other Rooms (Capote), **Supp. III Part 1:** 113–118, 121, 123–124

"Other Wanderer, The" (Gibran), **Supp. XX: 124**

"Other War, The" (Cowley), **Supp. II Part 1:** 144

"Otherwise" (Kenyon), **Supp. VII:** 172, 174

Otherwise: New and Selected Poems (Kenyon), **Supp. VII:** 167, 172–174

Otherwise Than Being; or, Beyond Essence (Lévinas), **Supp. XVI:** 290, 291

"Other Woman, The" (Anderson), **I:** 114

"Other World, The" (Wrigley), **Supp. XVIII:** 307

Other Worlds Than This (Hadas), **Supp. XXIII:** 118, **124–125**

Otho the Great: A Tragedy in Five Acts (Keats), **Supp. XII:** 113

Otis, Harrison Gray, **Supp. I Part 2:** 479–481, 483, 486, 488

Otis, James, **III:** 577; **Supp. I Part 2:** 486; **Supp. XV:** 229

O to Be a Dragon (Moore), **III:** 215

"Otravida, Otravez" (Díaz), **Supp. XXIV:** 93

Ott, Bill, **Supp. XXVI:** 187

"Ottawa Valley, The" (Munro), **Supp. XXVII:** 185–186

Otto, Rudolf, **Supp. XVII:** 243

"Ouija" (McClatchy), **Supp. XII:** 269–270

Oupensky, Peter, **Supp. XIV:** 188

Our America (Michaels), **Retro. Supp. I:** 379

Our America (W. Frank), **I:** 229; **Supp. IX:** 308; **Supp. XX: 69–70, 75**

Our American Humorists (Masson), **Supp. XXVI:** 275

Our Aperture (Monson), **Supp. XXIV:** 230, 239

"Our Assistant's Column" (Twain), **IV:** 193

"Our Bourgeois Literature" (Sinclair), **Supp. V:** 281

Our Brains and What Ails Them (Gilman), **Supp. XI:** 207

Our Century (Wilder), **IV:** 374

"Our Christmas Party" (E. Stoddard), **Supp. XV:** 273, 278

Our Country (Strong), **Supp. XIV:** 64

"Our Countrymen in Chains!" (Whittier), **Supp. I Part 2:** 688

"Our Cultural Humility" (Bourne), **I:** 223, 228

Our Depleted Society (Seymour), **Supp. XIII:** 264

"Our Dust" (Wright), **Supp. XV:** 345, 346

"Our Eyes" (Davison), **Supp. XXVI:** 78

"Our Father Who Drowns the Birds" (Kingsolver), **Supp. VII:** 208–209

"Our First House" (Kingston), **Supp. V:** 169

Our Gang (P. Roth), **Retro. Supp. II:** 287; **Supp. III Part 2:** 414; **Supp. IV Part 1:** 388

"Our Good Day" (Cisneros), **Supp. VII:** 60

Our Ground Time Here Will Be Brief (Kumin), **Supp. IV Part 2:** 450–452

Our House in the Last World (Hijuelos), **Supp. VIII:** 73, **76–79,** 87, 88

"Our Lady" (A. Finch), **Supp. XVII:** 77

"*Our Lady of the Annunciation*/Nuestra Señora de Anunciación" (Mora), **Supp. XIII:** 217, 224, 228

"Our Lady of the Artichokes" (Vaz), **Supp. XXVI:** 265

Our Lady of the Artichokes and Other Portuguese-American Stories (Vaz), **Supp. XXVI:** 264–268

"Our Lady of Troy" (MacLeish), **III:** 3, 20

"Our Limitations" (Holmes), **Supp. I Part 1:** 314

"Our Martyred Soldiers" (Dunbar), **Supp. II Part 1:** 193

"Our Master" (Whittier), **Supp. I Part 2:** 704

"Our Mother Pocahontas" (Lindsay), **Supp. I Part 2:** 393

Our Mr. Wrenn: The Romantic Adventures of a Gentle Man (Lewis), **II:** 441

Our National Parks (Muir), **Supp. IX:** 181, 184

Our New York: A Personal Vision in Words and Photographs (Kazin),

Supp. VIII: 106–107
Our Nig (Wilson), **Supp. XX: 105**
"Our Old Aunt Who Is Now in a Retirement Home" (Shields), **Supp. VII: 310**
Our Old Home: A Series of English Sketches (Hawthorne), II: 225; **Retro. Supp. I: 163**
"Our Own Movie Queen" (Z. Fitzgerald), **Supp. IX: 71**
"Our River Now" (L.-Y. Lee), **Supp. XV: 224, 225**
Our Selves (Bronk), **Supp. XXI: 32**
Ourselves to Know (O'Hara), III: 362, 365
Our Sister Killjoy: or, Reflections from a Black-Eyed Squint (Aidoo), **Supp. XXII: 68**
"Our Story Begins" (Wolff), **Supp. VII: 345**
"Our Sweating Selves" (Di Piero), **Supp. XIX: 36**
Our Town (Wilder), IV: 357, 364, 365, 366, 368–369
"Our Unplanned Cities" (Bourne), I: 229, 230
Our Wonder World, **Retro. Supp. I: 341**
Ouspensky, P. D., I: 383; **Supp. XX: 116**
"Out" (Harjo), **Supp. XII: 219**
"'Out, Out'" (Frost), **Retro. Supp. I: 131**
"Outcast" (McKay), **Supp. X: 135**
"Outcasts of Poker Flats, The" (Harte), **Supp. II Part 1: 345, 347–348**
Outcroppings (Harte), **Supp. II Part 1: 343**
Out Cry (T. Williams), IV: 383, 393
Outcry, The (James), **Retro. Supp. I: 235**
"Outdoor Shower" (Olds), **Supp. X: 214**
Outer Banks (Siddons), **Supp. XXII: 239**
Outerbridge Reach (Stone), **Supp. V: 306–308**
Outer Dark (McCarthy), **Supp. VIII: 176–177**
Outermost Dream, The: Essays and Reviews (Maxwell), **Supp. VIII: 171–172**
Outermost House, The (Beston), **Supp. XXVI: 31, 34, 37–43**
"Outing, The" (Baldwin), **Supp. I Part 1: 63**
"Outlantish" (Mackey), **Supp. XXVII: 154–155**
Outlaw Journalist (McKeen), **Supp. XXIV: 279, 288**
"Out Like a Lamb" (Dubus), **Supp. VII: 91**
"Outline of an Autobiography" (Toomer), **Supp. III Part 2: 478**
"Outline Toward a Theory of the Mine Versus the Mind and the Harvard Outline" (Monson), **Supp. XXIV: 235**
Outlyer and Ghazals (Harrison), **Supp. VIII: 41**
"Out of Business" (Mora), **Supp. XIII: 217**
Out of Eden: Essays on Modern Art (Di Piero), **Supp. XIX: 41, 42**
"Out of My Deeper Heart" (Gibran), **Supp. XX: 118**

Out of My League (Plimpton), **Supp. XVI: 233, 239**
"Out of Nowhere into Nothing" (Anderson), I: 113
"Out of Season" (Hemingway), II: 263
"Out of the Cradle Endlessly Rocking" (Whitman), IV: 342, 343–345, 346, 351; **Retro. Supp. I: 404, 406**
"Out of the Deeps" (E. Stoddard), **Supp. XV: 286**
"Out of the Hospital and Under the Bar" (Ellison), **Retro. Supp. II: 118–119; Supp. II Part 1: 246**
"Out of the Rainbow End" (Sandburg), III: 594–595
"Out of the Sea, Early" (Swenson), **Supp. IV Part 2: 645**
"Out of the Snow" (Dubus), **Supp. VII: 91**
Out of the Stars (Purdy), **Supp. VII: 281–282**
"Out of the Woods" (Offutt), **Supp. XIX: 169–170**
Out of the Woods: Stories (Offutt), **Supp. XIX: 163, 167, 169–172, 175**
"Out of Your Nakedness, Out of My Nakedness" (Hadas), **Supp. XXIII: 125**
"Outrageous" (Pickering), **Supp. XXI: 202**
Outre-Mer: A Pilgrimage beyond the Sea (Longfellow), II: 313, 491; **Retro. Supp. II: 155, 165**
"Outside" (Stafford), **Supp. XI: 318**
Outside, The (Glaspell), **Supp. III Part 1: 179, 187**
"Outside In" (Pickering), **Supp. XXI: 197**
Outsider, The (Wright), IV: 478, 481, 488, 491–494, 495
Outside Shot, The (Myers), **Supp. XXVII: 205, 206**
Outside World, The (Mirvis), **Supp. XX: 177, 178, 185–190**
Out Went the Candle (Swados), **Supp. XIX: 257**
Out West (Shanley), **Supp. XIV: 317**
"Out with the Old" (Yates), **Supp. XI: 342**
"Ouzo for Robin" (Merrill), **Supp. III Part 1: 326**
"Oval Portrait, The" (Poe), III: 412, 415; **Retro. Supp. II: 270**
"Oven Bird, The" (Frost), **Retro. Supp. I: 131; Supp. XI: 153; Supp. XIX: 15**
"Over 2,000 Illustrations and a Complete Concordance" (Bishop), **Retro. Supp. II: 45; Supp. I Part 1: 90–91**
"Over by the River" (Maxwell), **Supp. VIII: 169, 170**
"Overcoat, The" (Gogol), **Supp. XXII: 59**
"Overgrown Pasture, The" (A. Lowell), II: 523
"Overheard through the Walls of the Invisible City" (Bidart), **Supp. XV: 32**
"Over Kansas" (Ginsberg), **Supp. II Part 1: 320**
Overland to the Islands (Levertov), **Supp. III Part 1: 275, 276**

Overlook, The (Connelly), **Supp. XXI: 78**
"Overlooking Lake Champlain" (Di Piero), **Supp. XIX: 47**
"Overnight Pass" (X. J. Kennedy), **Supp. XV: 168**
Overreachers, The (Talese), **Supp. XVII: 202**
"Over-Soul, The" (Emerson), II: 7
Over the Blue Mountain (Richter), **Supp. XVIII: 220**
"Over the Edge"(Hadas), **Supp. XXIII: 115**
"Over the Hill" (Dubus), **Supp. VII: 76, 79–80**
Overtime (Gurney), **Supp. V: 104**
Overton, Grant, **Supp. XXV: 200**
"Overwhelming Question, An" (Taylor), **Supp. V: 323**
Ovid, I: 62; II: 542–543; III: 457, 467, 468, 470; **Retro. Supp. I: 63; Supp. IV Part 2: 634; Supp. XII: 264**
"Ovid in Exile" (Di Piero), **Supp. XIX: 44**
"Ovid's Farewell" (McClatchy), **Supp. XII: 257–258**
Owen, David, II: 34
Owen, Maureen, **Supp. IV Part 2: 423**
Owen, Wilfred, II: 367, 372; III: 524; **Supp. X: 146; Supp. XIX: 17; Supp. XVII: 245; Supp. XVIII: 92; Supp. XXVII: 295**
Owens, Hamilton, III: 99, 109
Owens, Louis, **Supp. IV Part 1: 404**
"O Where Are You Going?" (Auden), **Supp. X: 116**
"Owl, The" (Wrigley), **Supp. XVIII: 297–298, 301**
Owl in the Attic, The (Thurber), **Supp. I Part 2: 614**
Owl in the Mask of the Dreamer, The: Collected Poems (Haines), **Supp. XII: 211**
"Owl in the Sarcophagus, The" (Stevens), **Retro. Supp. I: 300**
Owl's Clover (Stevens), **Retro. Supp. I: 298, 303–304**
"Owl's Clover" (Stevens), IV: 75
Owl's Insomnia, Poems by Rafael Alberti, The (Strand, trans.), **Supp. IV Part 2: 630**
Owl Spirit Dwelling (Gallagher), **Supp. XXIV: 170**
Owlstone Crown, The (X. J. Kennedy), **Supp. XV: 162, 164**
"Owl Who Was God, The" (Thurber), **Supp. I Part 2: 610**
Owning It All (Kittredge), **Supp. XXVI: 184, 187**
Owning Jolene (Hearon), **Supp. VIII: 66–67**
"Owning the Masters" (Nelson), **Supp. XVIII: 171**
Oxford Anthology of American Literature, The, III: 197; **Supp. I Part 1: 254**
Oxford Book of American Verse (Matthiessen, ed.), **Retro. Supp. I: 40**
Oxford Book of Children's Verse in America, The (Hall, ed.), **Supp. XIV: 126**

Oxford Companion to African American Literature, The (Andrews et al., eds), **Supp. XXVI:** 166

Oxford Companion to Twentieth-Century Poetry (Hamilton, ed.), **Supp. XVII:** 243

Oxford History of the American People, The (Morison), **Supp. I Part 2:** 495–496

Oxford History of the United States, 1783–1917, The (Morison), **Supp. I Part 2:** 483–484

"Oxford Town" (song, Dylan), **Supp. XVIII:** 24

Oxherding Tale (C. Johnson), **Supp. VI:** 190–192, 193, 194, 196

Oxley, William, **Supp. XV:** 125

"O Yes" (Olsen), **Supp. XIII:** 294, 298, **299–300,** 301

"O Youth and Beauty!" (Cheever), **Retro. Supp. I:** 335

"Oysters" (Sexton), **Supp. II Part 2:** 692

"Ozark Odes" (Wright), **Supp. XV:** 346

Ozick, Cynthia, **Supp. V: 257–274;** **Supp. VIII:** 141; **Supp. X:** 192; **Supp. XVII:** 42, 43, 49, 50

O-Zone (Theroux), **Supp. VIII:** 323–324

P

Pace, Patricia, **Supp. XI:** 245

Pacernik, Gary, **Supp. IX:** 287, 291

Pacific and Other Stories, The (Helprin), **Supp. XXV:** 84, 85

"Pacific Distances" (Didion), **Supp. IV Part 1:** 211

"Pacific Village" (M. F. K. Fisher), **Supp. XVII:** 83

"Pacifist War Song" (Lovecraft), **Supp. XXV:** 119

Pack, Robert, **Supp. IV Part 2:** 621

"Packed Dirt, Churchgoing, a Dying Cat, a Traded Cat" (Updike), **IV:** 219

Packer, Nancy Huddleston, **Supp. XXIII:** 290

"Packing Mother's Things" (C. Frost), **Supp. XV:** 97

Pack of Lies (Sorrentino), **Supp. XXI:** 236, 237

Paco's Story (Heinemann), **Supp. XXII:** 103, **109–114,** 115

Paddock, Joe, **Supp. XVI:** 36

Paddock, Nancy, **Supp. XVI:** 36

Padel, Ruth, **Supp. XII:** 107

Padgett, Ron, **Supp. XV:** 190; **Supp. XXIII:** 218, 221; **Supp. XXIV:** 33, 34, 35, 37, 38, 39, 41, 42, 43, 44; **Supp. XXVII:** 18, 19, 20, 22, 24, 26, 28, 29

Padmore, Dorothy, **Supp. XXI:** 166

Padmore, George, **Supp. XXI:** 166

"Paesano with a Trowel" *(Time),* **Supp. XX: 46**

Pafko at the Wall (DeLillo), **Supp. VI:** 4

"Paganini and the Powers of Darkness" (Skloot), **Supp. XX: 201**

"Pagan Prayer" (Cullen), **Supp. IV Part 1:** 170

"Pagan Rabbi, The" (Ozick), **Supp. V:** 262, 264, 265; **Supp. XVII:** 43

Pagan Rabbi and Other Stories, The (Ozick), **Supp. V:** 260, 261, 263–265

Pagan Spain (Wright), **IV:** 478, 488, 495

Page, Geraldine, **Supp. XV:** 7

Page, Kirby, **III:** 297

Page, Myra, **Supp. XXIII:** 166

"Page, The" (Huddle), **Supp. XXVI:** 155

Page, Thomas Nelson, **II:** 174, 176, 194; **Supp. XIV:** 61; **Supp. XXII:** 193

Page, Walter Hines, **II:** 174, 175; **Supp. I Part 1:** 370

Page, William, **Supp. XVIII:** 2, 11

Pages from a Cold Island (Exley), **Supp. XXIII:** 97, **103–106,** 108

"Pages from Cold Point" (Bowles), **Supp. IV Part 1:** 85, 86, 87

Paid on Both Sides: A Charade (Auden), **Supp. II Part 1:** 6, 18–19

Paige, Satchel, **Supp. I Part 1:** 234

Paige, T. D. D., **III:** 475

"Pail, The" (R. Bly), **Supp. XXI:** 85

Pain, Joseph, **Supp. I Part 2:** 502

Paine, Albert Bigelow, **I:** 249

Paine, Thomas, **I:** 490; **II:** 117, 302; **III:** 17, 148, 219; **Retro. Supp. I:** 390; **Supp. I Part 1:** 231; **Supp. I Part 2: 501–525; Supp. XI:** 55

"Pain has an Element of Blank" (Dickinson), **Retro. Supp. I:** 44

"Pain Scale, The" (Biss), **Supp. XXVI:** 51–53

"Painstaking Historian, The" (Skloot), **Supp. XX: 205–206**

"Paint and Powder" (Z. Fitzgerald), **Supp. IX:** 71

Painted Bird, The (Kosinski), **Supp. VII:** 215–217, 219–221, 222, 227

Painted Desert (F. Barthelme), **Supp. XI:** 28–29, 32

Painted Dresses (Hearon), **Supp. VIII: 63**

"Painted Head" (Ransom), **III:** 491, 494; **Supp. II Part 1:** 103, 314

Painted Turtle: Woman with Guitar (Major), **Supp. XXII: 178–180,** 182

Painted Word, The (Wolfe), **Supp. III Part 2:** 580–581, 584; **Supp. XV:** 143

Painter, Pamela, **Supp. XXIII:** 295

"Painter, The" (Ashbery), **Supp. III Part 1:** 5–6, 13

Painter Dreaming in the Scholar's House, The (Nemerov), **III:** 269

"Painters" (Rukeyser), **Supp. VI:** 281

"Painting a Mountain Stream" (Nemerov), **III:** 275

"Pair a Spurs" (Proulx), **Supp. VII:** 263–264

"Pair of Bright Blue Eyes, A" (Taylor), **Supp. V:** 321

"Pair of Glasses, A" (Gallagher), **Supp. XXIV:** 174, 176

Paisan (film, Rossellini), **Supp. XXVI:** 134

"Pajamas" (Olds), **Supp. X:** 206

Pakula, Alan, **Supp. XIII:** 264

Palace at 4 A.M. (Giacometti), **Supp. VIII:** 169

Palahniuk, Chuck, **Supp. XXI:** 116

"Palantine, The" (Whittier), **Supp. I Part 2:** 694, 696

Palatella, John, **Retro. Supp. II:** 48; **Supp. XXIV:** 39

"Palatski Man, The"(Dybek), **Supp. XXIII:** 70

Pale Fire (Nabokov), **III:** 244, 246, 252, 263–265; **Retro. Supp. I:** 264, 265, 266, 270, 271, 272, 276, 278, 335; **Supp. V:** 251, 253; **Supp. XXII:** 260

"Pale Horse, Pale Rider" (Porter), **III:** 436, 437, 441–442, 445, 446, 449

Pale Horse, Pale Rider: Three Short Novels (Porter), **III:** 433, 436–442; **Supp. VIII:** 157

"Pale Pink Roast, The" (Paley), **Supp. VI:** 217

"Pale Rider" (B. Kelly), **Supp. XVII:** 132–133

Paley, Grace, **Supp. IX:** 212; **Supp. VI: 217–233; Supp. X:** 79, 164; **Supp. XII:** 309; **Supp. XXI:** 118; **Supp. XXII:** 172

Paley, William, **II:** 9

Palgrave, Francis Turner, **Retro. Supp. I:** 124; **Supp. XIV:** 340

Palgrave's Golden Treasury (Palgrave), **IV:** 405

Palimpsest (Doolittle), **Supp. I Part 1:** 259, 268, 269, 270–271

Palimpsest (Vidal), **Supp. X:** 186

"Palingenesis" (Longfellow), **II:** 498

Pal Joey (O'Hara), **III:** 361, 367–368

"Pal Joey" stories (O'Hara), **III:** 361

Pallbearers Envying the One Who Rides (Dobyns), **Supp. XIII:** 89

Palm, Edward Frederick, **Supp. XXII:** 103

"Palm, The" (Merwin), **Supp. III Part 1:** 355

Palmer, Charles, **II:** 111

Palmer, Elihu, **Supp. I Part 2:** 520

Palmer, George Herbert, **Supp. XIV:** 197

Palmer, Michael, **Supp. IV Part 2:** 421; **Supp. XVI:** 284; **Supp. XVII:** 240

Palmer, Samuel, **Supp. XV:** 81

Palmerston, Lord, **I:** 15

Palm-of-the-Hand-Stories (Kawabata), **Supp. XV:** 186

"Palm Wine" (McKnight), **Supp. XX: 155**

"Palo Alto: The Marshes" (Hass), **Supp. VI:** 100

Palpable God, A: Thirty Stories Translated from the Bible with an Essay on the Origins and Life of Narrative (Price), **Supp. VI:** 262, 267

Palubinskas, Helen, **Supp. X:** 292

Palumbo, Carmine, **Supp. XXVI:** 241

Pamela (Richardson), **Supp. V:** 127; **Supp. XX: 236; Supp. XXII:** 120

Pamela's First Musical (Wasserstein), **Supp. XV:** 333

Panache de bouquets (Komunyakaa; Cadieux, trans.), **Supp. XIII:** 127

Pan-African movement, **Supp. II Part 1:** 172, 175

Pancake, Breece D'J, **Supp. XXIII:** 35

Pandaemonium (Epstein), **Supp. XII:** 161, **172–173**

"Pandora" (Adams), **I:** 5

Pandora: New Tales of Vampires (Rice), **Supp. VII:** 295
Panek, LeRoy, **Supp. XIV:** 27
"Pangolin, The" (Moore), **III:** 210
Panic: A Play in Verse (MacLeish), **III:** 2, 20
Panic in Needle Park (film), **Supp. IV Part 1:** 198
Pankey, Eric, **Supp. XIX:** 44
Pantagruel (Rabelais), **II:** 112
"Pantaloon in Black" (Faulkner), **II:** 71
"Panther, The: A Bedtime Story"(P. Benedict), **Supp. XXIII:** 40
Panther and the Lash, The (Hughes), **Retro. Supp. I:** 204, 211; **Supp. I Part 1:** 342–344, 345–346
"Panthers, The" (Southern), **Supp. XI:** 295
"Panties and the Buddha" (Peacock), **Supp. XIX:** 199
"Pan *versus* Moses" (Ozick), **Supp. V:** 262
"Paolo Castelnuovo" (Everwine), **Supp. XV:** 83–84
"Papa and Mama Dance, The" (Sexton), **Supp. II Part 2:** 688
"Papago II"(Kenny), **Supp. XXIII:** 149–150
"Papago I"(Kenny), **Supp. XXIII:** 149–150
"Papa Who Wakes Up Tired in the Dark" (Cisneros), **Supp. VII:** 62
Pape, Greg, **Supp. V:** 180; **Supp. XIII:** 312; **Supp. XV:** 73
Paper Boy (Huddle), **Supp. XXVI:** 148, 150, 151
"Paper Covers Rock"(Thompson), **Supp. XXIII:** 291
Paper Doll (Parker), **Supp. XIX:** 184
"Paper Dolls Cut Out of a Newspaper" (Simic), **Supp. VIII:** 282
"Paper House, The" (Mailer), **III:** 42–43
Paper Lion (film, March), **Supp. XVI:** 242
Paper Lion: Confessions of a Last-String Quarterback (Plimpton), **Supp. XVI: 242–243**
Papernick, Jon, **Supp. XVII:** 50
Papers on Literature and Art (Fuller), **Supp. II Part 1:** 292, 299
Papini, Giovanni, **Supp. XVI:** 195; **Supp. XXII:** 159, 161, 163
Papp, Joseph, **Supp. IV Part 1:** 234; **Supp. XXI:** 145
"Paprika Johnson" (Barnes), **Supp. III Part 1:** 33
"Par" (Bausch), **Supp. VII:** 54
"Parable from a Christian" (Notley), **Supp. XXII:** 235
"Parable in the Later Novels of Henry James" (Ozick), **Supp. V:** 257
"Parable of the Gift" (Glück), **Supp. V:** 89
"Parable of the Hostages" (Glück), **Supp. V:** 89
"Parable of the King" (Glück), **Supp. V:** 89
Parable of the Sower (O. Butler), **Supp. XIII: 66–67, 69**

Parable of the Talents (O. Butler), **Supp. XIII:** 61,**Supp. XIII:** 66, **67–69**
"Parable of the Trellis" (Glück), **Supp. V:** 89
Parachutes & Kisses (Jong), **Supp. V:** 115, 123, 125–126, 129
Paracritical Hinge: Essays, Talks, Notes, Interviews (Mackey), **Supp. XXVII:** 159, 160–161
"Paradelle for Susan" (Collins), **Supp. XXI:** 58
"Parade of Painters" (Swenson), **Supp. IV Part 2:** 645
"Paradigm, The" (Tate), **IV:** 128
Paradine Case, The (screenplay, Hecht), **Supp. XXVII:** 93
Paradise (Barthelme), **Supp. IV Part 1:** 52
"Paradise" (Caputo), **Supp. XIX:** 26–27
"Paradise" (Doty), **Supp. XI:** 123
Paradise, Piece by Piece (Peacock), **Supp. XIX:** 193, 194–195, 195–196, **201–202**
Paradise Lost (Milton), **I:** 137; **II:** 168, 549; **IV:** 126; **Supp. XII:** 173, 297; **Supp. XV:** 181; **Supp. XX:** 280
Paradise Lost (Odets), **Supp. II Part 2:** 530, 531, 538–539, 550
Paradise Now (Living Theater), **Supp. XXIV:** 116
"Paradise of Bachelors and the Tartarus of Maids, The" (Melville), **III:** 91
Paradise of Bombs, The (Sanders), **Supp. XVI:** 265, 272–273
Paradise Park (Goodman), **Supp. XXVI:** 126–128
Paradise Poems (Stern), **Supp. IX: 293–294, 295**
Paradiso (Dante), **Supp. IX:** 50
"Paradoxes and Oxymorons" (Ashbery), **Supp. III Part 1:** 23–24
Paradox of Progressive Thought, The (Noble), **Supp. I Part 2:** 650
Paragon, The (Knowles), **Supp. XII:** 249
"Paragraphs" (Carruth), **Supp. XVI:** 52–53
"Parameters" (Dunn), **Supp. XI:** 154
"Para Mi Tataranieto El Astropionero" (Espaillat), **Supp. XXI:** 104
"Paraphrase" (Crane), **I:** 391–392, 393
"Pardon, The" (Wilbur), **Supp. III Part 2:** 544, 550
Paredes, Américo, **Supp. XIII:** 225; **Supp. XIX:** 97, 98, 100
Paredes, Raymund A., **Supp. XIII:** 320, 321
"Parentage" (Stafford), **Supp. XI:** 321, 322
Parentheses: An Autobiographical Journey (Neugeboren), **Supp. XVI:** 217, 218, 219, 221, 226
"Parents" (F. Barthelme), **Supp. XI:** 34
"Parents Taking Shape" (Karr), **Supp. XI:** 243
"Parents' Weekend: Camp Kenwood" (Kenyon), **Supp. VII:** 169
Pareto, Vilfredo, **II:** 577
Paretsky, Sara, **Supp. IV Part 2:** 462; **Supp. XIV:** 26; **Supp. XXV: 169–187**

Parini, Jay, **Supp. X:** 17; **Supp. XIX:** 120, 129; **Supp. XX: 243; Supp. XXI:** 192; **Supp. XXII:** 205; **Supp. XXV:** 251
"Paris" (Collins), **Supp. XXI:** 60
"Paris" (Stern), **Supp. IX:** 300
"Paris, 7 A.M." (Bishop), **Retro. Supp. II:** 41, 42; **Supp. I Part 1:** 85, 89
Paris, Bob, **Supp. XX:** 264
Paris, Paris (Shaw), **Supp. XIX:** 240
Paris France (Stein), **IV:** 45
Park, Ed, **Supp. XXII:** 255
Park, Robert, **IV:** 475
"Park Bench" (Hughes), **Supp. I Part 1:** 331–332
Park City (Beattie), **Supp. V:** 24, 35–36
"Park City" (Beattie), **Supp. V:** 35
Parker, Arthur C., **Supp. XXVI:** 87, 88
Parker, Charlie, **Supp. I Part 1:** 59; **Supp. X:** 240, 242, 246; **Supp. XIII:** 129
Parker, Dorothy, **Retro. Supp. II:** 327; **Supp. IV Part 1:** 353; **Supp. IX:** 62, 114, **189–206; Supp. X:** 164; **Supp. XI:** 28; **Supp. XVIII:** 242, 246, 252; **Supp. XXVI:** 275; **Supp. XXVII:** 283, 284
Parker, Emily, **Supp. XVIII:** 102
Parker, Idella, **Supp. X:** 232, 234–235
Parker, James, **Supp. XXVI:** 84
Parker, Joan, **Supp. XIX:** 187
Parker, Lonnae O'Neal, **Supp. XXIII:** 276
Parker, Muriel, **Supp. IX:** 232
Parker, Patricia, **Supp. XV:** 242
Parker, Robert B., **Supp. IV Part 1:** 135, 136; **Supp. XIX: 177–192**
Parker, Robert Dale, **Supp. XXIII:** 223, 228, 229
Parker, Theodore, **Supp. I Part 1:** 38; **Supp. I Part 2:** 518; **Supp. XXIV:** 70
Parker, Thomas, **Supp. I Part 1:** 102
"Parker's Back" (O'Connor), **III:** 348, 352, 358
"Parkersburg" (Halliday), **Supp. XIX:** 92
Parkes, Henry Bamford, **Supp. I Part 2:** 617
Park-Fuller, Linda, **Supp. XIII:** 297
Parkman, Francis, **II:** 278, 310, 312; **IV:** 179, 309; **Supp. I Part 2:** 420, 479, 481–482, 486, 487, 493, 498; **Supp. II Part 2: 589–616**
Parkman Reader, The (Morison, ed.), **Supp. I Part 2:** 494
Parks, Gordon, Sr., **Supp. XI:** 17
Parks, Larry, **Supp. I Part 1:** 295
Parks, Rosa, **Supp. I Part 1:** 342
"Park Street Cemetery, The" (R. Lowell), **II:** 537, 538
Par le Détroit (cantata) (Bowles), **Supp. IV Part 1:** 82
Parliament of Fowls, The (Chaucer), **III:** 492
Parmenides (Plato), **II:** 10
Parmenter, Jon, **Supp. XXVI:** 85
Parnassus (Emerson), **II:** 8, 18
Parnell, Charles Stewart, **II:** 129, 137
Parole (film), **Supp. XIII:** 166
Parole Fixer (film), **Supp. XIII:** 170

Parrington, Vernon Louis, **I:** 254, 517, 561; **III:** 335, 606; **IV:** 173; **Supp. I Part 2:** 484, 640

Parrish, Dillwyn, **Supp. XVII:** 83–84, 90

Parrish, Robert, **Supp. XI:** 307

"Parrot, The" (Merrill), **Supp. III Part 1:** 320

"Parsley" (Dove), **Supp. IV Part 1:** 245, 246

Parson, Annie, **Supp. I Part 2:** 655

Parsons, Elsie Clews, **I:** 231, 235

Parsons, Ian, **Supp. IX:** 95

Parsons, Louella, **Supp. XII:** 173

Parsons, Talcott, **Supp. I Part 2:** 648

Parsons, Theophilus, **II:** 396, 504; **Retro. Supp. II:** 134; **Supp. I Part 1:** 155

"Parthian Shot, The" (Hammett), **Supp. IV Part 1:** 343

Partial Glossary, A (Bronk), **Supp. XXI:** 26

Partial Payments: Essays on Writers and Their Lives (Epstein), **Supp. XIV:** 111

Partial Portraits (James), **II:** 336

"Partial Relief" (Halliday), **Supp. XIX:** 91

Partial Truth (Nelson), **Supp. XVIII:** **175–176,** 178

"Particulars" (Pickering), **Supp. XXI:** 197

Parties (Van Vechten), **Supp. II Part 2:** 739, 747–749

"Parting" (Kunitz), **Supp. III Part 1:** 263

"Parting Gift" (Wylie), **Supp. I Part 2:** 714

"Parting Glass, The" (Freneau), **Supp. II Part 1:** 273

"Partings" (Hogan), **Supp. IV Part 1:** 413

Partington, Blanche, **I:** 199

Partisans (Matthiessen), **Supp. V:** 201

"Partner, The" (Roethke), **III:** 541–542

Partners, The (Auchincloss), **Supp. IV Part 1:** 31, 34

Partners in Crime: A Rafe Buenrostro Mystery (Hinojosa), **Supp. XIX:** 107–108

"Part of a Letter" (Wilbur), **Supp. III Part 2:** 551

Part of a Long Story: Eugene O'Neill as a Young Man in Love (Boulton), **Supp. XXII:** 18, 21, 27–30

Part of Speech, A (Brodsky), **Supp. VIII:** 22

"Part of the Bee's Body Embedded in the Flesh, The" (C. Frost), **Supp. XV:** 105, 107

"Part of the Story" (Dobyns), **Supp. XIII:** 79

Part of Vermont, A (Taggard), **Supp. XXII:** 284

Parton, Sara, **Retro. Supp. I:** 246

Partridge, Jeffrey F., **Supp. XV:** 219

Partridge, John, **II:** 110, 111

"Parts of a Journal" (Gordon), **Supp. IV Part 1:** 310

Parts of a World (Stevens), **Retro. Supp. I:** **305–306,** 307, 309, 313

"Parturition" (Loy), **Supp. XXII:** 159, 160–161

"Party, The" (Dunbar), **Supp. II Part 1:** 198, 205–206

"Party, The" (Taylor), **Supp. V:** 315

Party at Jack's, The (Wolfe), **IV:** 451–452, 469

"Party Down at the Square, A" (Ellison), **Retro. Supp. II:** 124

Party of Five (television series), **Supp. XIX:** 222

"Party Poem" (Huddle), **Supp. XXVI:** 149

Pascal, Blaise, **II:** 8, 159; **III:** 292, 301, 304, 428; **Retro. Supp. I:** 326, 330

"Paskudnyak" (Pilcer), **Supp. XVII:** 50

"Pass, The" (Neugeboren), **Supp. XVI:** 225

"Passage" (Crane), **I:** 391

"Passage in the Life of Mr. John Oakhurst, A" (Harte), **Supp. II Part 1:** 353–354

Passage in the Night, A (Asch), **Supp. XXIII:** 7

"Passages" (Duncan), **Supp. XVI:** 287

"Passages for Puritans" (Davison), **Supp. XXVI:** 62

"Passages from a Relinquished Work" (Hawthorne), **Retro. Supp. I:** 150

Passages toward the Dark (McGrath), **Supp. X:** 126, 127

"Passage to India" (Whitman), **IV:** 348

Passage to India, A (Forster), **II:** 600; **Supp. XVIII:** 143

Passaro, Vince, **Supp. X:** 167, 302, 309, 310

"Passenger, The" (Brockmeier), **Supp. XXII:** 52

"Passenger Pigeons" (Jeffers), **Supp. II Part 2:** 437

Passin, Herbert, **Supp. XIII:** 337

Passing (Larsen), **Supp. XVIII:** 119, 123, **127–130**

"Passing Beauty" (C. Frost), **Supp. XV:** 97

"Passing of Grandison, The" (Chesnutt), **Supp. XIV:** 62, **66–69**

"Passing of Sister Barsett, The" (Jewett), **Retro. Supp. II:** 138–139, 143

"Passing Ports and Crossing Walks" (Gansworth), **Supp. XXVI:** 114

"Passing Show, The" (Bierce), **I:** 208

"Passing Through" (Kunitz), **Supp. III Part 1:** 265

"Passion, The" (Barnes), **Supp. III Part 1:** 36

"Passion, The" (Merwin), **Supp. III Part 1:** 343

Passionate, Accurate Story, The: Making Your Heart's Truth into Literature (C. Bly), **Supp. XVI:** **41–42**

Passionate Pilgrim, A (James), **II:** 324; **Retro. Supp. I:** 219

"Passionate Pilgrim, A" (James), **II:** 322, 323–324; **Retro. Supp. I:** 218

Passion Play (Kosinski), **Supp. VII:** 215, 225–226

Passions of Uxport, The (Kumin), **Supp. IV Part 2:** 444

Pass It On (Hadas), **Supp. XXIII:** 115, 123

"Pass It On, I" (Hadas), **Supp. XXIII:** 115

"Pass It On, II" (Hadas), **Supp. XXIII:** 115

"Passive Resistance" (McKay), **Supp. X:** 133

Passport to the War (Kunitz), **Supp. III Part 1:** 261–264

Passwords (Stafford), **Supp. XI:** **329–330**

"Past, The" (Bryant), **Supp. I Part 1:** 157, 170

"Past, The" (Kinnell), **Supp. III Part 1:** 235, 253–254

"Past, The" (Kinnell), **Supp. III Part 1:** 254

Past and Present (Carlyle), **Supp. I Part 2:** 410

Pasternak, Boris, **II:** 544; **Supp. XXIII:** 209

"Pastiches et Pistaches" (Van Vechten), **Supp. II Part 2:** 732

"Past Is the Present, The" (Moore), **III:** 199–200

"Pastoral" (Carver), **Supp. III Part 1:** 137, 146

"Pastoral" (Dove), **Supp. IV Part 1:** 249

"Pastoral" (Trethewey), **Supp. XXI:** 257

"Pastoral Hat, A" (Stevens), **IV:** 91

Pastoralia (Saunders), **Supp. XIX:** **227–229**

"Pastoralia" (Saunders), **Supp. XIX:** 227, 229

"Pastor Dowe at Tacaté" (Bowles), **Supp. IV Part 1:** 87

Pastorela (ballet) (Kirstein), **Supp. IV Part 1:** 83

Pastorius, Francis Daniel, **Supp. I Part 2:** 700

"Pasture Poems" (Kumin), **Supp. IV Part 2:** 446

Pastures of Heaven, The (Steinbeck), **IV:** 51

Patch, Jerry, **Supp. XVIII:** 38

Patchen, Kenneth, **Supp. III Part 2:** 625

Patchett, Ann, **Supp. XII:** **307–324**

Patchwork Planet (Lethem), **Supp. XVIII:** 150

Pater, Walter, **I:** 51, 272, 476; **II:** 27, 338; **III:** 604; **IV:** 74; **Retro. Supp. I:** 56, 79; **Retro. Supp. II:** 326; **Supp. I Part 2:** 552; **Supp. IX:** 66

Paterna (Mather), **Supp. II Part 2:** 451

Paternostro, Silvana, **Supp. XXV:** 55, 58

"Paterson" (Ginsberg), **Supp. II Part 1:** 314–315, 321, 329

Paterson (W. C. Williams), **I:** 62, 446; **IV:** 418–423; **Retro. Supp. I:** 209, 284, 413, 419, 421, **424–428,** 428, 429, 430; **Retro. Supp. II:** 321, 328; **Supp. II Part 2:** 557, 564, 625; **Supp. VIII:** 275, 305; **Supp. XIV:** 96; **Supp. XV:** 264, 349

Paterson, Book Five (W. C. Williams), **IV:** 422–423

Paterson, Book One (W. C. Williams), **IV:** 421–422

Paterson, Isabel, **Supp. IV Part 2:** 524

Paterson, Part Three (W. C. Williams), **IV:** 420–421

Pat Garrett and Billy the Kid (film, Peckinpah), **Supp. XVIII:** 27

"Path, The" (Bryant), **Supp. I Part 1:** 169

Pathfinder, The (Cooper), **I:** 349, 350, 355

Pat Hobby Stories, The (Fitzgerald), **Retro. Supp. I:** 114

"Pathos of Low Life, The" (Hapgood), **Supp. XVII:** 103

"Patience of a Saint, The" (Humphrey), **Supp. IX:** 106

Patience Sparhawk and Her Times (Atherton), **Supp. XXIV:** 18, 20, 22, 27

Patient 002 (Skloot), **Supp. XX: 194, 208**

Patinkin, Mandy, **Supp. IV Part 1:** 236

Paton, Alan, **Supp. VIII:** 126

Patria Mia (Pound), **III:** 460–461; **Retro. Supp. I:** 284

"Patria Mia" (Pound), **Retro. Supp. I:** 284

"Patriarch, The" (Alvares), **Supp. V:** 11

"Patrick Kavanagh at First Light" (Skloot), **Supp. XX: 204**

Patrimony: A True Story (P. Roth), **Retro. Supp. II:** 279, 280, 291; **Supp. III Part 2:** 427

Patriot, The (Buck), **Supp. II Part 1:** 122–123

Patriot, The (Connell), **Supp. XIV:** 94–95

Patriot Act (Gansworth), **Supp. XXVI:** 114

Patriotic Gore: Studies in the Literature of the American Civil War (Wilson), **III:** 588; **IV:** 430, 438, 443, 445–445, 446; **Supp. VIII:** 100

"Patriotic Thing, The" (Ryan as Quin), **Supp. XVIII:** 229

"Patriots, The/Los Patriotas" (Kingsolver), **Supp. VII:** 209

Patrol (Myers), **Supp. XXVII:** 208

Patron Saint of Liars, The (Patchett), **Supp. XII:** 307, 310, **311–314,** 317

Pattee, Fred L., **II:** 456

Patten, Gilbert, **II:** 423

Patten, Simon, **Supp. I Part 2:** 640

Patternmaster (O. Butler), **Supp. XIII:** 61, 62, 63

Patternmaster Series (O. Butler), **Supp. XIII: 62–63**

Pattern Recognition (W. Gibson), **Supp. XVI:** 124, **130–131**

"Patterns" (A. Lowell), **II:** 524

Patterson, Floyd, **III:** 38

Patterson, Margot, **Supp. XXII:** 85

Patterson, William M., **Supp. I Part 1:** 265

Patton, General George, **III:** 575; **Supp. I Part 2:** 664

Patton, Venetra K., **Supp. XXVI:** 166

"Patty-Cake, Patty-Cake...A Memoir" (Apple), **Supp. XVII:** 7

Patty Fairfield series (Wells), **Supp. XXVI:** 276

Paul, Saint, **I:** 365; **II:** 15, 494; **IV:** 122, 154, 164, 335; **Retro. Supp. I:** 247; **Supp. I Part 1:** 188

Paul, Sherman, **I:** 244; **IV:** 179

"Paula Becker to Clara Westhoff" (Rich), **Supp. I Part 2:** 573–574

"Paula Gunn Allen" (Ruppert), **Supp. IV Part 1:** 321

Paul Ardenheim, the Monk of Wissahikon (Lippard), **Supp. XXIII:** 178, 186, 187, 189, 190

Paul Bowles: Romantic Savage (Caponi), **Supp. IV Part 1:** 95

Paulding, James Kirke, **I:** 344; **II:** 298, 299, 303; **Supp. I Part 1:** 157

Pauley, Jane, **Supp. XXI:** 39

Paul Jones (Hapgood), **Supp. XVII:** 100–101

Paul Marchand, F.M.C. (Chesnutt), **Supp. XIV:** 76

"Paul Monette: The Brink of Summer's End" (film), **Supp. X:** 152

"Paul Revere" (Longfellow), **II:** 489, 501

"Paul Revere's Ride" (Longfellow), **Retro. Supp. II:** 163

"Paul's Case" (Cather), **I:** 314–315; **Retro. Supp. I:** 3, 5

Paulsen, Friedrich, **III:** 600

"Pauper Witch of Grafton, The" (Frost), **Retro. Supp. II:** 42

"Pause by the Water, A" (Merwin), **Supp. III Part 1:** 354

"Pavane for the Nursery, A" (W. J. Smith), **Supp. XIII:** 335

"Pavement, The" (Olson), **Supp. II Part 2:** 571

Pavese, Cesare, **Supp. XXI:** 132

Pavic, Milorad, **Supp. XXII:** 265

Pavilion of Women (Buck), **Supp. II Part 1:** 125–126

"Pawnbroker, The" (Kumin), **Supp. IV Part 2:** 442, 443–444, 451

Pawnbroker, The (Wallant), **Supp. XVI:** 220

Pay Day (Asch), **Supp. XXVI:** 19, 21–23

"Paying Dues" (Bass), **Supp. XVI:** 16

Payne, Daniel, **Supp. V:** 202; **Supp. XXVI:** 33, 35, 37, 40

Payne, John Howard, **II:** 309

Payne Tom, **Supp. XXII:** 266

Paz, Octavio, **Supp. III Part 2:** 630; **Supp. VIII:** 272; **Supp. XI:** 191; **Supp. XIII:** 223

P. D. Kimerakov (Epstein), **Supp. XII:** 160, **162**

Peabody, Elizabeth Palmer, **Retro. Supp. I:** 155–156, 225; **Supp. XXIV:** 75; **Supp. XXV:** 242, 246, 250

Peabody, Francis G., **III:** 293; **Supp. I Part 1:** 5

Peabody, Josephine Preston, **III:** 507; **Supp. XX: 115**

Peaceable Kingdom, The (Prose), **Supp. XVI:** 256–257

Peace and Bread in Time of War (Addams), **Supp. I Part 1:** 21, 22–23

"Peace Between Black and White in the United States" (Locke), **Supp. XIV:** 205

Peace Breaks Out (Knowles), **Supp. XII:** 249

"Peacemaker" (Kenny), **Supp. XXIII:** 151

"Peace March, The" (Simpson), **Supp. IX:** 279

"Peace of Cities, The" (Wilbur), **Supp. III Part 2:** 545

"Peace of Mind" (Boyle), **Supp. XX: 19**

"Peaches" (Davison), **Supp. XXVI:** 77

"Peaches—Six in a Tin Box, Sarajevo" (Cisneros), **Supp. VII:** 67

Peachtree Road (Siddons), **Supp. XXII:** 239, 240, 242, **246–247, 248–251,** 252

Peaco, Ed, **Supp. XXIV:** 221

Peacock, Doug, **Supp. VIII:** 38; **Supp. XIII:** 12

Peacock, Gibson, **Supp. I Part 1:** 360

Peacock, Molly, **Supp. XIX: 193–207;** **Supp. XVII:** 74

"Peacock, The" (Merrill), **Supp. III Part 1:** 320

"Peacock, The" (Mosher), **Supp. XXII:** 211

Peacock, Thomas Love, **Supp. I Part 1:** 307; **Supp. VIII:** 125

"Peacock Room, The" (Hayden), **Supp. II Part 1:** 374–375

"Peacocks of Avignon, The" (Swados), **Supp. XIX:** 263

Pearce, Richard, **Supp. IX:** 254

Pearce, Roy Harvey, **II:** 244; **Supp. I Part 1:** 111, 114; **Supp. I Part 2:** 475

"Pearl" (Kooser), **Supp. XIX:** 127–128

Pearl, The (Steinbeck), **IV:** 51, 62–63

Pearlman, Daniel, **III:** 479

Pearlman, Mickey, **Supp. XIII:** 293, 306

Pearl of Orr's Island, The (Stowe), **Supp. I Part 2:** 592–593, 595

"Pearls" (A. Finch), **Supp. XVII:** 72

Pears, Peter, **II:** 586; **Supp. IV Part 1:** 84

Pearson, Drew, **Supp. XIV:** 126

Pearson, Norman Holmes, **Supp. I Part 1:** 259, 260, 273

Pearson, Tom, **Supp. XXVI:** 113

"Pear Tree" (C. Frost), **Supp. XV:** 105

"Peasants' Way O' Thinkin' " (McKay), **Supp. X:** 133

Pease, Donald E., **Supp. IV Part 2:** 687

"Peboan and Seegwun (Winter and Spring): A Chippewa Allegory" (J. Schoolcraft), **Supp. XXIII:** 235

Peck, Gregory, **Supp. VIII:** 128, 129; **Supp. XII:** 160, 173

Peckinpah, Sam, **Supp. XI:** 306; **Supp. XVIII:** 27

"Peck of Gold, A" (Frost), **II:** 155

Peculiar Treasures: A Biblical Who's Who (Buechner), **Supp. XII:** 53

Pedagogy of the Oppressed (Freire), **Supp. XXV:** 133

"Pedal Point" (Francis), **Supp. IX:** 87

Pedersen, Inge, **Supp. XVIII:** 179

"Pedersen Kid, The" (Gass), **Supp. VI:** 83

"Pedigree, The" (Creeley), **Supp. IV Part 1:** 150

Peebles, Melvin Van, **Supp. XI:** 17; **Supp. XVI:** 144

"Peed Onk" (Moore). *See* "People Like That Are the Only People Here: Canonical Babbling in Peed Onk" (Moore)

"Peeler, The" (O'Connor), **Retro. Supp. II:** 225

"Peeper, The" (Davison), **Supp. XXVI:** 69

Peich, Michael, **Supp. XV:** 113, 117; **Supp. XXV:** 222

Peikoff, Leonard, **Supp. IV Part 2:** 520, 526, 529

Peirce, Charles Sanders, **II:** 20, 352–353; **III:** 599; **Supp. I Part 2:** 640; **Supp. III Part 2:** 626

Pelagius, **III:** 295

"Pelican, The" (Merrill), **Supp. III Part 1:** 320

"Pelican, The" (Wharton), **IV:** 310; **Retro. Supp. I:** 364

Pellacchia, Michael, **Supp. XIII:** 16

Pelley, Denise, **Supp. XIX:** 205

Pelonero, Michael, **Supp. XXIII:** 125

Peltier, Leonard, **Supp. V:** 212

"Pemberton's Bride" (Rash), **Supp. XXVII:** 225

"Penance"(Dybek), **Supp. XXIII:** 69

"Pen and Paper and a Breath of Air" (Oliver), **Supp. VII:** 245

Pence, Amy, **Supp. XV:** 211, 223

"Pencil, The" (Chandler), **Supp. IV Part 1:** 135

Pencillings by the Way (Willis), **II:** 313; **Supp. XVIII:** 12

"Pencils" (Sandburg), **III:** 592

Pendleton, Devon, **Supp. XVIII:** 151

"Pendulum" (Bradbury and Hasse), **Supp. IV Part 1:** 102

"Penelope's Song" (Glück), **Supp. V:** 89

Penelope: The Story of the Half-Scalped Woman (Schott), **Supp. XXIII:** 240, **244–245**

Penhally (Gordon), **II:** 197, 199, 201–203, 204

"Penis" (McClatchy), **Supp. XII:** 266–267

Penitent, The (di Donato), **Supp. XX: 44, 45**

Penitent, The (Singer), **Retro. Supp. II: 309–310,** 313

Penland, Nell Bates, **Supp. XXII:** 188

Penn, Robert, **I:** 489

Penn, Sean, **Supp. XI:** 107

Penn, Thomas, **II:** 118

Penn, William, **Supp. I Part 2:** 683

Penna, Sandro, **Supp. XIX:** 34

Pennebaker, D. A., **Supp. XVIII:** 19, 26

"Pennsylvania Pilgrim, The" (Whittier), **Supp. I Part 2:** 700

"Pennsylvania Planter, The" (Freneau), **Supp. II Part 1:** 268

Penny, Rob, **Supp. VIII:** 330

"Penny, The" (D. West), **Supp. XVIII:** 283–284

Penrod (Tarkington), **III:** 223

"Penseroso, Il" (Milton), **Supp. XIV:** 8

Pensieri (Leopardi; Di Piero, trans.), **Supp. XIX:** 34

"Pensive Hours"(J. Schoolcraft), **Supp. XXIII:** 230–231

Pentagon of Power, The (Mumford), **Supp. II Part 2:** 498

Pentimento (Hellman), **Supp. I Part 1:** 280, 292–294, 296; **Supp. IV Part 1:** 12; **Supp. VIII:** 243; **Supp. XXVII:** 137

"Peonies at Dusk" (Kenyon), **Supp. VII:** 171

People, The (Glaspell), **Supp. III Part 1:** 179

People, Yes, The (Sandburg), **III:** 575, 589, 590, 591

"PEOPLE BURNING, THE" (Baraka), **Supp. II Part 1:** 49

"People in Hell Just Want a Drink of Water" (Proulx), **Supp. VII:** 263

"People Like That Are the Only People Here: Canonical Babbling in Peed Onk" (Moore), **Supp. X:** 168, **178–179**

People Live Here: Selected Poems 1949–1983 (Simpson), **Supp. IX:** 269, 277

"People Next Door, The" (Simpson), **Supp. IX:** 279

People of the Abyss, The (London), **II:** 465–466

"People on the Roller Coaster, The" (Hardwick), **Supp. III Part 1:** 196

People Shall Continue, The (Ortiz), **Supp. IV Part 2:** 510

People's History of the United States, A (Zinn), **Supp. XXIV:** 87

"People's Surroundings" (Moore), **III:** 201, 202, 203

"People v. Abe Lathan, Colored, The" (Caldwell), **I:** 309

"Peppermint Lounge Revisited, The" (Wolfe), **Supp. III Part 2:** 571

Peppis, Paul, **Supp. XXII:** 160

Pepys, Samuel, **Supp. I Part 2:** 653

"Perchance to Dream" (Franzen), **Supp. XX: 90, 93**

Perchance to Dream: Robert B. Parker's Sequel to Raymond Chandler's "Big Sleep" (Parker), *Supp. XIX:* 189

"Perch'io non spero di tornar giammai" (Cavalcanti), **Supp. III Part 2:** 623

Perch of the Devil (Atherton), **Supp. XXIV:** 24, 29

Percy, Thomas, **Supp. XIV:** 2

Percy, Walker, **Supp. III Part 1: 383–400; Supp. IV Part 1:** 297; **Supp. V:** 334; **Supp. X:** 42; **Supp. XIV:** 21; **Supp. XIX:** 209; **Supp. XXVI:** 253

Percy, William, **Supp. V:** 334

Percy, William Alexander, **Retro. Supp. I:** 341; **Supp. XXII:** 193

Peregrin, Tony, **Supp. XV:** 69

"Peregrine" (Wylie), **Supp. I Part 2:** 712–713, 714

Perelman, Bob, **Supp. XII:** 23

Perelman, S. J., **IV:** 286; **Retro. Supp. I:** 342; **Retro. Supp. II:** 321, 322, 325, 326, 327, 336; **Supp. IV Part 1:** 353; **Supp. XI:** 66

Perera, Victor, **Supp. XXV:** 50, 52

Perestroika (Kushner), **Supp. IX:** 141, 142, 145

Péret, Benjamin, **Supp. VIII:** 272

Peretz, Isaac Leib, **IV:** 1, 3; **Retro. Supp. II:** 299; **Supp. XXIII:** 4, 7, 8–9

Pérez Galdós, Benito, **II:** 275

Perfect Analysis Given by a Parrot, A (T. Williams), **IV:** 395

"Perfect Couple, The" (Nelson), **Supp. XVIII:** 173

"Perfect Day for Bananafish, A" (Salinger), **III:** 563–564, 571

Perfect Fiction, The (Sorrentino), **Supp. XXI:** 228

Perfect Ganesh, A (McNally), **Supp. XIII: 202–203,** 208, 209

"Perfect Gerbil, The: Reading Barthelme's 'The School' " (Saunders), **Supp. XIX:** 235

"Perfection" (Helprin), **Supp. XXV:** 80

"Perfect Knight, The" (Chandler), **Supp. IV Part 1:** 120

Perfect Mother, The (Schott), **Supp. XXIII: 241–242**

Perfect Party, The (Gurney), **Supp. V:** 100, 105, 106–107

"Perfect Things" (F. Barthelme), **Supp. XI:** 30, 33–34

Perfidy (Hecht), **Supp. XXVII:** 95

"Performance, The" (Dickey), **Supp. IV Part 1:** 178–179, 181

"Perfume" (Mora), **Supp. XIII:** 218

"Perhaps the World Ends Here" (Harjo), **Supp. XII:** 228, 231

Perhaps Women (Anderson), **I:** 114

Pericles (Shakespeare), **I:** 585; **Supp. III Part 2:** 624, 627, 629

Perillo, Lucia, **Supp. XXVI:** 68

"Period Metaphor" (Bronk), **Supp. XXI:** 33

Period of Adjustment (T. Williams), **IV:** 382, 386, 387, 388, 389, 390, 392, 393, 394, 397

"Period Pieces from the Mid-Thirties" (Agee), **I:** 28

"Peripheral Vision" (Davison), **Supp. XXVI:** 69–70

"Periphery" (Ammons), **Supp. VII:** 28

Perkins, David, **Supp. I Part 2:** 459, 475; **Supp. XV:** 185

Perkins, Maxwell, **I:** 252, 289, 290; **II:** 87, 93, 95, 252; **IV:** 452, 455, 457, 458, 461, 462, 463, 469; **Retro. Supp. I:** 101, 105, 108, 109, 110, 113, 114, 178; **Supp. IX:** 57, 58, 60, 232; **Supp. X:** 219, 224, 225, 229, 230, 233; **Supp. XI:** 218, 227

Perlès, Alfred, **III:** 177, 183, 187, 189

Perloff, Marjorie, **Supp. I Part 2:** 539, 542; **Supp. IV Part 1:** 68; **Supp. IV Part 2:** 420, 424, 432; **Supp. XXII:** 161, 271; **Supp. XXIII:** 210, 220

Permanence and Change (Burke), **I:** 274

Permanent Errors (Price), **Supp. VI:** 261

"Permanent Traits of the English National Genius" (Emerson), **II:** 18

Permit Me Voyage (Agee), **I:** 25, 27

"Perosa Canavese" (Everwine), **Supp. XV:** 84

Perrault, Charles, **IV:** 266; **Supp. I Part 2:** 622

Perrin, Noel, **Supp. XVI:** 34; **Supp. XXII:** 205, 207, 211, 218

Perrins, Carol. *See* Frost, Carol

Perrota, Tom, **Supp. XXVII:** 5

Perry, Anne, **Supp. V:** 335

Perry, Bliss, **I:** 243

Perry, Donna, **Supp. IV Part 1:** 322, 327, 335

Perry, Edgar A., **III:** 410

Perry, Keith Ronald, **Supp. XXI:** 42

Perry, Lincoln, **Supp. V:** 24, 33

Perry, Matthew C., **Supp. I Part 2:** 494–495

Perry, Pam, **Supp. XXVI:** 12

Perry, Patsy Brewington, **Supp. I Part 1:** 66

Perry, Phyllis Alesia, **Supp. XVIII:** 96

Perry, Ralph Barton, **I:** 224; **II:** 356, 362, 364; **Supp. XIV:** 197

Perry, Dr. William, **II:** 395, 396

Perse, St.-John, **III:** 12, 13, 14, 17; **Supp. III Part 1:** 14; **Supp. IV Part 1:** 82; **Supp. XIII:** 344; **Supp. XV:** 178

"Persephone in Hell" (Dove), **Supp. IV Part 1:** 250, 251

"Persephone"(Le Sueur), **Supp. XXIII:** 162, 165, **170–171**

"Persephone to Psyche" (Stallings), **Supp. XXV:** 234

"Persephone Writes a Letter to Her Mother" (Stallings), **Supp. XXV:** 228

"Persimmons" (L.-Y. Lee), **Supp. XV:** 211, 213

"Persistence of Desire, The" (Updike), **IV:** 222–223, 228

"Persistence of Poetry, The" (Bynner), **Supp. XV:** 49

"Persistences" (Hecht), **Supp. X: 68–69**

Person, Place, and Thing (Shapiro), **Supp. II Part 2:** 702, 705

Personae of Ezra Pound (Pound), **III:** 458

Personae: The Collected Poems (Pound), **Retro. Supp. I:** 285, 286; **Supp. I Part 1:** 255; **Supp. XVII:** 32

"Personal" (Stern), **Supp. IX:** 299

"Personal and Occasional Pieces" (Welty), **Retro. Supp. I:** 355

"Personal and the Individual, The" (L. Michaels), **Supp. XVI:** 201

Personal Injuries (Turow), **Supp. XVII: 219–220,** 221, 223

"Personalities" (column, Briggs), **Supp. XVIII:** 15

Personal Narrative (Edwards), **I:** 545, 552, 553, 561, 562; **Supp. I Part 2:** 700

"Personal Poem #9" (Berrigan), **Supp. XXIV:** 34, 35

"Personal Poem"(O'Hara), **Supp. XXIII:** 219

Personal Recollection of Joan of Arc (Twain), **IV:** 208

Personals (Bontemps), **Supp. XXII:** 7, 8

"Personals" (Didion), **Supp. IV Part 1:** 200

"Personism" (O'Hara), **Supp. XV:** 181

"Personism: A Manifesto" (O'Hara), **Supp. XXIII:** 212, 215; **Supp. XXIV:** 43

Persons and Places (Santayana), **III:** 615

Persons in Hiding (film), **Supp. XIII:** 170

Persons in Hiding (Hoover), **Supp. XIII:** 170

Person Sitting in Darkness, A (Twain), **IV:** 208

"Persons Who Interest Us" (*Harper's Bazaar),* **Supp. XXV:** 277–278

"Perspective" (Francis), **Supp. IX:** 78

"Perspective: Anniversary D-Day" (Karr), **Supp. XI:** 241

Perspectives by Incongruity (Burke), **I:** 284–285

"Perspectives: Is It Out of Control?" (Gleason), **Supp. IX:** 16

Perspectives on Cormac McCarthy (Arnold and Luce, eds.), **Supp. VIII:** 189

Persse, Dudley Jocelyn, **Supp. XX: 232**

Pertes et Fracas (McCoy), **Supp. XIII:** 175

"Peruvian Child" (Mora), **Supp. XIII:** 218

Peseroff, Joyce, **Supp. IV Part 1:** 71

Pesetsky, Bette, **Supp. XXIV:** 173

"Pestilence" (Nelson), **Supp. XVIII:** 186

Pest Maiden, The (Schott), **Supp. XXIII: 245–246**

"Peter" (Cather), **Retro. Supp. I:** 4

"Peter" (Moore), **III:** 210, 212

Peter, Saint, **III:** 341, 346; **IV:** 86, 294

Peterkin, Julia, **Supp. I Part 1:** 328; **Supp. XXII:** 12, 189

"Peter Klaus" (German tale), **II:** 306

Peter Pan (Barrie), **Supp. XV:** 319

"Peter Parley" works (Goodrich), **Supp. I Part 1:** 38

"Peter Pendulum" (Poe), **III:** 425

"Peter Quince at the Clavier" (Stevens), **IV:** 81, 82

Peter Rabbit tales, **Retro. Supp. I:** 335

Peters, Cora, **Supp. I Part 2:** 468

Peters, Jacqueline, **Supp. XII:** 225

Peters, Margot, **Supp. VIII:** 252

Peters, Robert, **Supp. XIII:** 114

Peters, S. H. (pseudonym). *See* Henry, O.

Peters, Timothy, **Supp. XI:** 39

"Peter's Avocado" (Rodriguez), **Supp. XIV:** 308–309

Petersen, David, **Supp. XIII:** 2

Petersen, Donald, **Supp. V:** 180; **Supp. XV:** 74, 92

Peterson, Dorothy, **Supp. XVIII:** 131, 132

Peterson, George, **Supp. XXII:** 250

Peterson, Houston, **I:** 60

Peterson, Roger Tory, **Supp. V:** 202

Peterson, Virgilia, **Supp. IV Part 1:** 30

Peter Whiffle: His Life and Works (Van Vechten), **Supp. II Part 2:** 728–729, 731, 735, 738–741, 749

"Petey and Yotsee and Mario" (H. Roth), **Supp. IX:** 234

"Petition, A" (Winters), **Supp. II Part 2:** 785

"Pet Milk"(Dybek), **Supp. XXIII:** 74

"'Pet Negro' System, The" (Hurston), **Supp. VI:** 159

"Petra and Its Surroundings" (Frost), **Retro. Supp. I:** 124

Petrarch, **I:** 176; **II:** 590; **III:** 4

"Petrarch, Shakespeare, and the Blues" (C. Frost), **Supp. XV:** 92, 104, 105

"Petrified Man" (Welty), **IV:** 262; **Retro. Supp. I:** 345, 351

"Petrified Man, The" (Twain), **IV:** 195

"Petrified Woman, The" (Gordon), **II:** 199

Petronius, **III:** 174, 179

Petry, Ann, **Supp. VIII:** 214; **Supp. XI:** 6, 85; **Supp. XVIII:** 286

Pet Sematary (King), **Supp. V:** 138, 143, 152

Pettengill, Claire C., **Supp. XXV:** 40

Pettengill, Richard, **Supp. VIII:** 341, 345, 348

Pettingell, Phoebe, **Supp. XV:** 251, 256–257, 262

Pettis, Joyce, **Supp. XI:** 276, 277, 278, 281

Pettis, Olive G., **Supp. XXIII:** 189

Petty, Jill, **Supp. XXI:** 244, 248, 249, 250

Pfaelzer, Jean, **Supp. XVI:** 88, 90

Pfaff, Timothy, **Supp. V:** 166

Pfeil, Fred, **Supp. XIV:** 36

Pfister, Karin, **IV:** 467, 475

Phaedo (Plato), **II:** 10

Phaedra (Lowell and Barzun, trans.), **II:** 543–544

"Phantasia for Elvira Shatayev" (Rich), **Supp. I Part 2:** 570

Phantasms of War (A. Lowell), **II:** 512

"Phantom of the Movie Palace, The" (Coover), **Supp. V:** 50–51

Phantom Ship, The (Marryat), **Supp. XVII:** 55

"Pharaoh, The" (Kenyon), **Supp. VII:** 172

"Pharmacy"(Strout), **Supp. XXIII:** 281

Pharr, Mary, **Supp. V:** 147

"Phases" (E. Stoddard), **Supp. XV:** 273

"Phases" (Stevens), **Retro. Supp. I:** 299

Phases of an Inferior Planet (Glasgow), **II:** 174–175

"Pheasant, The" (Carver), **Supp. III Part 1:** 146

Phelan, Alice, **Supp. XXII:** 193

Pheloung, Grant, **Supp. XI:** 39

Phelps, Donald, **Supp. XXIII:** 174

Phelps, Elizabeth Stuart, **Retro. Supp. II:** 146; **Supp. XIII:** 141; **Supp. XVI:** 80

Phelps, Teresa Godwin, **Supp. VIII:** 128

Phelps, William Lyon "Billy", **Supp. XX: 68, 75, 220**

"Phenomena and Laws of Race Contacts, The" (Locke), **Supp. XIV:** 210

Phenomenal Fauna, A (Wells), **Supp. XXVI:** 275

"Phenomenology of Anger, The" (Rich), **Supp. I Part 2:** 562–563, 571

Phenomenology of Moral Experience, The (Mandelbaum), **I:** 61

"Phenomenology of *On Moral Fiction*" (C. Johnson), **Supp. VI:** 188

Phidias, **Supp. I Part 2:** 482

Philadelphia Fire (Wideman), **Supp. X:** 320, 334

Philadelphia Negro, The (Du Bois), **Supp. II Part 1:** 158, 163–164, 166

Philbrick, Thomas, **I:** 343

"Philemon and Baucis"(Hadas), **Supp. XXIII:** 114

"Phil in the Marketplace" (Lethem), **Supp. XVIII:** 148

Philip, Jim, **Supp. XII:** 136

Philip, Maxwell, **Supp. XXI:** 160

Philip, Prince, **Supp. X:** 108

"Philip of Pokanoket" (Irving), **II:** 303

Philippians (biblical book), **IV:** 154

"Philippine Conquest, The" (Masters), **Supp. I Part 2:** 456

"Philip Roth Reconsidered" (Howe), **Retro. Supp. II:** 286

"Philistinism and the Negro Writer" (Baraka), **Supp. II Part 1:** 39, 44

Phillips, Adam, **Supp. XII:** 97–98

Phillips, Anne K., **Supp. XX:** **221**

Phillips, Carl, **Supp. XXI:** 246

Phillips, David Graham, **II:** 444; **Retro. Supp. II:** 101

Phillips, Gene D., **Supp. XI:** 306

Phillips, Jayne Anne, **Supp. XIV:** 21

Phillips, J. J., **Supp. XXIII:** 174

Phillips, J. O. C., **Supp. I Part 1:** 19

Phillips, Robert, **Supp. XIII:** 335, 344

Phillips, Wendell, **Supp. I Part 1:** 103; **Supp. I Part 2:** 524

Phillips, Willard, **Supp. I Part 1:** 154, 155

Phillips, William, **Supp. VIII:** 156

Phillips, William L., **I:** 106

"Philly Babylon" (Di Piero), **Supp. XIX:** 46

"Philoctetes"(Hadas), **Supp. XXIII:** 115

"Philoctetes: The Wound and the Bow" (Wilson), **Supp. XXIV:** 217

"Philosopher, The" (Farrell), **II:** 45

Philosopher of the Forest (pseudonym). *See* Freneau, Philip

Philosophes classiques, Les (Taine), **III:** 323

"Philosophical Cobbler, The" (Sanders), **Supp. XVI:** 268

"Philosophical Concepts and Practical Results" (James), **II:** 352

"Philosophical Investigation of Metaphor, A" (Gass), **Supp. VI:** 79

Philosophical Transactions (Watson), **II:** 114

"Philosophy, Or Something Like That" (P. Roth), **Supp. III Part 2:** 403

"Philosophy and Its Critics" (James), **II:** 360

"Philosophy and the Form of Fiction" (Gass), **Supp. VI:** 85

"Philosophy for People" (Emerson), **II:** 14

"Philosophy in Warm Weather" (Kenyon), **Supp. VII:** 168

"Philosophy Lesson" (Levine), **Supp. V:** 195

Philosophy of Alain Locke, The: Harlem Renaissance and Beyond (Harris, ed.), **Supp. XIV:** 196, 211–212

"Philosophy of Composition, The" (Poe), **III:** 416, 421; **Retro. Supp. II:** 266, 267, 271; **Supp. XXV:** 120, 121

Philosophy of Friedrich Nietzsche, The (Mencken), **III:** 102–103

"Philosophy of Handicap, A" (Bourne), **I:** 216, 218

"Philosophy of History" (Emerson), **II:** 11–12

Philosophy of Literary Form, The (Burke), **I:** 275, 281, 283, 291

Philosophy of the Human Mind, The (Stewart), **II:** 8

Philosophy: Who Needs It (Rand), **Supp. IV Part 2:** 517, 518, 527, 533

Philoxenes, **Supp. VIII:** 201

"Phineas" (Knowles), **Supp. XII:** 238–240

Phineas: Six Stories (Knowles), **Supp. XII:** 249

"Phocion" (R. Lowell), **II:** 536

Phoebe Light (Notley), **Supp. XXII:** 227

Phoenix and the Turtle, The (Shakespeare), **I:** 284

"Phoenix Lyrics" (Schwartz), **Supp. II Part 2:** 665

"Phoenix on the Sword, The" (Howard), **Supp. XXVII:** 117, 124–125

"Phone Booths, The" (Jarman), **Supp. XVII:** 112–113

"Phony War Films" (Jones), **Supp. XI:** 217, 232

"Photograph: Carlisle Indian School (1879–1918)"(Kenny), **Supp. XXIII:** 156

"Photograph: Migrant Worker, Parlier, California, 1967" (Levis), **Supp. XI:** 272

"Photograph of a Bawd Drinking Raleigh Rye" (Trethewey), **Supp. XXI:** 254

"Photograph of a Child on a Vermont Hillside" (Kenyon), **Supp. VII:** 168

"Photograph of My Mother as a Young Girl" (Gioia), **Supp. XV:** 119

"Photograph of the Girl" (Olds), **Supp. X:** 205

"Photograph of the Unmade Bed" (Rich), **Supp. I Part 2:** 558

Photographs (Welty), **Retro. Supp. I:** 343

"Photographs, The" (Barthelme), **Supp. IV Part 1:** 53

"Photography" (Levine), **Supp. V:** 194

Phyrrho, **Retro. Supp. I:** 247

"Physical Universe" (Simpson), **Supp. IX:** 278

"Physicist We Know, A" (Shields), **Supp. VII:** 310

"Physics and Cosmology in the Fiction of Tom Robbins" (Nadeau), **Supp. X:** 270

Physiologie du goût (Brillat-Savarin), **Supp. XVII:** 82, 86

Physiology of Taste, The; or, Meditations on Transcendent Gastronomy (Brillat-Savarin; M. F. K. Fisher, trans.), **Supp. XVII:** 86, 87, 91

"Physiology of Versification, The: Harmonies of Organic and Animal Life" (Holmes), **Supp. I Part 1:** 311

Physique de l'Amour (Gourmont), **III:** 467–468

Piaf, Edith, **Supp. IV Part 2:** 549

Piaget, Jean, **Supp. XIII:** 75

"Piano" (Lawrence), **Supp. XV:** 254

"Piano Fingers" (Mason), **Supp. VIII:** 146

Piano Lesson, The (Bearden), **Supp. VIII:** 342

Piano Lesson, The (Wilson), **Supp. VIII:** **342–345**

Piano Man's Daughter, The (Findley), **Supp. XX:** **59–61**

"Piano Player, The"(Strout), **Supp. XXIII:** 283, 285

Piatt, James, **Supp. I Part 2:** 420

Piatt, John J., **II:** 273

Piazza, Ben, **Supp. XIII:** 163

Piazza, Paul, **Supp. XIV:** 157, 160, 171

"Piazza de Spagna, Early Morning" (Wilbur), **Supp. III Part 2:** 553

Piazza Tales (Melville), **III:** 91

Picabia, Francis, **Retro. Supp. I:** 416; **Retro. Supp. II:** 331; **Supp. XXII:** 162

Picasso (Stein), **IV:** 28, 32, 45

Picasso, Pablo, **I:** 429, 432, 440, 442, 445; **II:** 602; **III:** 197, 201, 470; **IV:** 26, 31, 32, 46, 87, 407, 436; **Retro. Supp. I:** 55, 63; **Supp. IV Part 1:** 81; **Supp. IX:** 66

Piccione, Anthony, **Supp. XV:** 212

"Piccola Comedia" (Wilbur), **Supp. III Part 2:** 561

Pickard, Samuel T., **Supp. I Part 2:** 682

Picked-Up Pieces (Updike), **Retro. Supp. I:** 320, 322, 323, 335

Picker, Lauren, **Supp. VIII:** 78, 83

Picker, Tobias, **Supp. XII:** 253

Pickering, Sam, **Supp. XXI:** **191–207**

Pickford, Mary, **Retro. Supp. I:** 325; **Supp. I Part 2:** 391

"Picking and Choosing" (Moore), **III:** 205

"Pickman's Model" (Lovecraft), **Supp. XXV:** 113, 114

Picnic (film), **Supp. XXV:** 95

Picnic (Inge), **Supp. XXV:** 93, 95, 97–99

"Picnic" (Peacock), **Supp. XIX:** 206

Picnic, Lightning (Collins), **Supp. XXI:** 54, 60

"Picnic, Lightning" (Collins), **Supp. XXI:** 64–65

Picnic Cantata (music) (Bowles), **Supp. IV Part 1:** 89

"Picnic Remembered" (Warren), **IV:** 240

Pictorial History of the Negro in America, A (Hughes), **Supp. I Part 1:** 345

"Picture" (Huddle), **Supp. XXVI:** 150

"Picture, The" (Olson), **Supp. II Part 2:** 574

Picture Bride (Son), **Supp. X:** 292

"Picture I Want, The" (Olds), **Supp. X:** 209

Picture of Dorian Gray, The (Wilde), **Supp. IX:** 105

"Picture of Little J. A. in a Prospect of Flowers, A" (Ashbery), **Supp. III Part 1:** 3

Picture Palace (Theroux), **Supp. VIII:** 322

"Pictures" (Pickering), **Supp. XXI:** 197

"Pictures at an Extermination" (Epstein), **Supp. XII:** 161

"Pictures from an Expedition" (Duffy), **Supp. IV Part 1:** 207

Pictures from an Institution (Jarrell), **II:** 367, 385

Pictures from Brueghel (W. C. Williams), **Retro. Supp. I:** 429–431

"Pictures from Brueghel" (W. C. Williams), **Retro. Supp. I:** 419

"Pictures of Columbus, the Genoese, The" (Freneau), **Supp. II Part 1:** 258

Pictures of Fidelman: An Exhibition (Malamud), **Supp. I Part 2:** 450–451

"Pictures of the Artist" (Malamud), **Supp. I Part 2:** 450

Pictures of the Floating World (A. Lowell), **II:** 521, 524–525; **Supp. XXVII:** 295

Pictures of Travel (Heine), **II:** 281

Picturesque America; or, the Land We Live In (Bryant, ed.), **Supp. I Part 1:** 158

"Picturesque Ghetto, The" (Hapgood), **Supp. XVII:** 101

"Picturesque: San Cristóbal de las Casas" (Mora), **Supp. XIII:** 218

Picture This (Heller), **Supp. IV Part 1:** 386, 388, 390–391

Picturing Will (Beattie), **Supp. V:** 29, 31–32, 34

"Pie" (X. J. Kennedy), **Supp. XV:** 170

"Piece, A" (Creeley), **Supp. IV Part 1:** 155, 156

"Piece of Moon, A" (Hogan), **Supp. IV Part 1:** 407

Piece of My Heart, A (Ford), **Supp. V:** 57, 58–61, 62

Piece of My Mind, A: Reflections at Sixty (Wilson), **IV:** 426, 430, 438, 441

"Piece of News, A" (Welty), **IV:** 263; **Retro. Supp. I:** 345, 346

Pieces (Creeley), **Supp. IV Part 1:** 155

Pieces and Pontifications (Mailer), **Retro. Supp. II:** 209–210

Pieces of the Frame (McPhee), **Supp. III Part 1:** 293

"Pie of the Month"(Thompson), **Supp. XXIII:** 300

Pierce, Franklin, **II:** 225, 226, 227; **III:** 88; **Retro. Supp. I:** 150, 163, 164, 165

Pierce, Frederick, **Retro. Supp. I:** 136

Piercy, Josephine K., **Supp. I Part 1:** 103

"Pierian Handsprings" (column, Untermeyer), **Supp. XV:** 294

Pierpont, Claudia Roth, **Supp. X:** 192, 193, 196

Pierre et Jean (Maupassant), **I:** 421

Pierre: or The Ambiguities (Melville), **III:** 86–88, 89; **IV:** 194; **Retro. Supp. I:** 249, 253–254, 256; **Supp. I Part 2:** 579

Pierrepont, Sarah. *See* Edwards, Sarah

Pierrot qui pleure et Pierrot qui rit (Rostand), **II:** 515

Pierson, George W, **Supp. XXII:** 289

Pig Cookies (Ríos), **Supp. IV Part 2:** 537, 550, 552–554

Pigeon Feathers (Updike), **IV:** 214, 218, 219, 221–223, 226

"Pigeon Feathers" (Updike), **Retro. Supp. I:** 318, 322, 323

"Pigeons" (Rilke), **II:** 544

"Pigeons, The" (Espaillat), **Supp. XXI:** 98

"Pigeons from Hell" (Howard), **Supp. XXVII:** 116, 119–120

"Pigeon Woman" (Swenson), **Supp. IV Part 2:** 644

"Pig Helmet and the Wall of Life"(P. Benedict), **Supp. XXIII:** 48–49

Pigs in Heaven (Kingsolver), **Supp. VII:** 197, 199, 209–210

Pike County Ballads, The (Hay), **Supp. I Part 1:** 352

Piket, Vincent, **Supp. IV Part 1:** 24

Pilar San-Mallafre, Maria del, **Supp. V:** 40

Pilcer, Sonya, **Supp. XVII:** 50

Pilgrim (Findley), **Supp. XX: 61–62**

"Pilgrim" (Freneau), **Supp. I Part 1:** 125

"Pilgrimage" (Ray), **Supp. XVIII:** 193

"Pilgrimage" (Sontag), **Supp. III Part 2:** 454–455

"Pilgrimage" (Trethewey), **Supp. XXI:** 255

"Pilgrimage, The" (Maxwell), **Supp. VIII:** 169, 171

Pilgrimage of Festus, The (Aiken), **I:** 50, 55, 57

Pilgrimage of Henry James, The (Brooks), **I:** 240, 248, 250; **IV:** 433

Pilgrim at Tinker Creek (Dillard), **Supp. VI:** 22, 23–26, 28, 29, **30–31,** 34; **Supp. XVIII:** 189

"Pilgrim Makers" (R. Lowell), **II:** 541

Pilgrim's Harbor (Skloot), **Supp. XX: 196, 207**

Pilgrim's Progress (Bunyan), **I:** 92; **II:** 15, 168, 572; **Supp. I Part 1:** 32, 38; **Supp. I Part 2:** 599

Pili's Wall (Levine), **Supp. V:** 178, 183–184

"Pillar of Fire" (Bradbury), **Supp. IV Part 1:** 113–114

Pillars of Hercules, The: A Grand Tour of the Mediterranean (Theroux), **Supp. VIII:** 325

"Pillow" (L.-Y. Lee), **Supp. XV:** 224

Pilot, The (Cooper), **I:** 335, 337, 339, 342–343, 350

"Pilot from the Carrier, A" (Jarrell), **II:** 374

"Pilots, Man Your Planes" (Jarrell), **II:** 374–375

"Pilots, The" (Levertov), **Supp. III Part 1:** 282

Pilsudski, Joseph, **Supp. XXIII:** 6

"Pimp's Revenge, A" (Malamud), **Supp. I Part 2:** 435, 450, 451

Pinball (Kosinski), **Supp. VII:** 215, 226

Pinchot, Gifford, **Supp. IX:** 184; **Supp. XIV:** 178

Pindar, **I:** 381; **II:** 543; **III:** 610

"Pine" (Dickey), **Supp. IV Part 1:** 183

Pine Barrens, The (McPhee), **Supp. III Part 1:** 298–301, 309

"Pineys, The" (Stern), **Supp. IX:** 288, 296

Pinget, Robert, **Supp. V:** 39

Pinhook: Finding Wholeness in a Fragmented Land (Ray), **Supp. XVIII:** 189, 192, 202–204

"Pink Dog" (Bishop), **Retro. Supp. II:** 48

"Pink Dress, The" (Boulton), **Supp. XXII:** 19

Pinker, James B., **I:** 409; **Retro. Supp. I:** 231

Pinkerton, Jan, **Supp. V:** 323–324

"Pink Moon—The Pond" (Oliver), **Supp. VII:** 234

Pinktoes (C. Himes), **Supp. XVI: 142**

Pinocchio in Venice (Coover), **Supp. V:** 40, 51

Pinsker, Sanford, **Retro. Supp. II:** 23; **Supp. IX:** 293, 327; **Supp. V:** 272; **Supp. XI:** 251, 254, 317

Pinsky, Robert, **Retro. Supp. II:** 50; **Supp. IX:** 155, 158; **Supp. VI: 235–251; Supp. XIII:** 277, 285; **Supp. XXI:** 243; **Supp. XXIII:** 111, 124

Pinter, Harold, **I:** 71; **Supp. XIII:** 20, 196; **Supp. XIV:** 239; **Supp. XVI:** 207

Pinto, Ferdinand Mendes (pseudonym). *See* Briggs, Charles Frederick

Pinto and Sons (Epstein), **Supp. XII:** 170, **171–172**

Pinto letters (Briggs), **Supp. XVIII:** 3, **12–13**

"Pinup" (Collins), **Supp. XXI:** 59

"Pioneer Girl" (L. I. Wilder), **Supp. XXII:** 290, 293, 294, 295

Pioneer Girl (Nguyen), **Supp. XXVI:** 216–220

Pioneers, The (Cooper), **I:** 336, 337, 339, 340–341, 342, 348; **II:** 313

Pioneers of France in the New World (Parkman), **Supp. III Part 2:** 599, 602

"Pioneers! O Pioneers!" (Whitman), **Retro. Supp. I:** 8

"Pioneer's Vision, The" (Larcom), **Supp. XIII:** 140

Pious and Secular America (Niebuhr), **III:** 308

Pipe Night (O'Hara), **III:** 361, 368

Piper, Dan, **Supp. IX:** 65

Pipers at the Gates of Dawn: The Wisdom of Children's Literature (Cott), **Supp. XVI:** 104

"Piper's Rocks" (Olson), **Supp. IV Part 1:** 153

"Pipistrelles" (B. Kelly), **Supp. XVII:** 129–130

Pipkin, Charles W., **Supp. XIV:** 3

Pippa Passes (Browning), **IV:** 128

Piquion, René, **Supp. I Part 1:** 346

Pirandello, Luigi, **Supp. IV Part 2:** 576, 588

Piranesi, Giovanni Battista, **Supp. XV:** 258

Pirate, The (Robbins), **Supp. XII:** 6

Pirate, The (Scott), **I:** 339

Pirates of Penzance, The (Gilbert and Sullivan), **IV:** 386

Pisan Cantos, The (Pound), **III:** 476; **Retro. Supp. I:** 140, 283, 285, 293; **Supp. III Part 1:** 63; **Supp. V:** 331, 337; **Supp. XIV:** 11; **Supp. XV:** 351

Pisarev, Dimitri, **Supp. XXI:** 164

Piscator, Erwin, **IV:** 394

"Pissaro: Tropical Impressions"(Kenny), **Supp. XXIII:** 146

Pissarro, Camille, **I:** 478

"Pissing off the Back of the Boat into the Nevernais Canal" (Matthews), **Supp. IX:** 160–161

Pistol, The (Jones), **Supp. XI:** 219, **223–224,** 227, 234

"Pistol Politics" (Howard), **Supp. XXVII:** 128

Pit, The (Norris), **III:** 314, 322, 326–327, 333, 334

"Pit, The" (Roethke), **III:** 538

"Pit and the Pendulum, The" (Poe), **III:** 413, 416; **Retro. Supp. II:** 264, 269–270, 273

"Pitcher" (Francis), **Supp. IX:** 82

"Pitcher, The" (Dubus), **Supp. VII:** 87

Pitchford, Nicola, **Supp. XII:** 13

"Pits, The" (D. Graham), **Supp. XI:** 252, 254

Pitt, William, **Supp. I Part 2:** 510, 518

Pitts, Rebecca, **Supp. XXII:** 280, 281

"Pittsburgh" (Carruth), **Supp. XVI:** 58

"Pity" (Huddle), **Supp. XXVI:** 151

"Pity Me" (Wylie), **Supp. I Part 2:** 729

Pity the Monsters (Williamson), **Retro. Supp. II:** 185

Pius II, Pope, **III:** 472

Pius IX, Pope, **II:** 79

"Piute Creek" (Snyder), **Supp. VIII:** 293

Pixley, Frank, **I:** 196

Pizer, Donald, **III:** 321; **Retro. Supp. II:** 100, 199

"Place" (Hoffman), **Supp. XVIII:** 86

"Place at the Outskirts" (Simic), **Supp. VIII:** 282

Place Called Estherville, A (Caldwell), **I:** 297, 307

Place Called Freedom, A (Sanders), **Supp. XVI:** 269

Place for My Head, A (Hoffman), **Supp. XVIII:** 76

"Place in Fiction" (Welty), **IV:** 260, 279

Place of Dead Roads, The (Burroughs), **Supp. III Part 1:** 196

Place of Love, The (Shapiro), **Supp. II Part 2:** 702, 706

"Place of Poetry, The" (Stevens), **Retro. Supp. I:** 304

Place of Science in Modern Civilization and Other Essays, The (Veblen), **Supp. I Part 2:** 629, 642

"Place of Trumpets, The" (B. Kelly), **Supp. XVII:** 127

Place on Earth, A (Berry), **Supp. X:** 33–34, 36

Places Left Unfinished at the Time of Creation (Santos), **Supp. XIII:** 274

"Places to Look for Your Mind" (Moore), **Supp. X:** 174–175

"Place They'd Never Seen, A: The Theater" (Wasserstein), **Supp. XV:** 332

"Place to Live, A" (Levertov), **Supp. III Part 1:** 281

"Place to Stand, A" (Price), **Supp. VI:** 258

Place to Stand, A (Wagoner), **Supp. IX:** 324

"Place (Any Place) to Transcend All Places, A" (W. C. Williams), **Retro. Supp. I:** 422

"Place Where My Poems Are Coming From, The"(Crooker), **Supp. XXIII:** 64

Placi, Carlo, **IV:** 328

Plagemann, Catherine, **Supp. XVII:** 91

"Plagiarist, The" (Singer), **IV:** 19

Plagued by the Nightingale (Boyle), **Supp. XXIV:** 51–52, 53, 56

Plague of Dreamers, A (Stern), **Supp. XX:** 178

Plainest Narrative, The (Bronk), **Supp. XXI:** 31

"Plain Language from Truthful James" (Harte). *See* "Heathen Chinee, The"

"Plain Sense of Things, The" (Stevens), **Retro. Supp. I:** 298, 299, 307, 312

"Plain Song" (Carruth), **Supp. XVI:** 54

Plain Song (Harrison), **Supp. VIII:** 38–39

"Plain Song" (Kooser), **Supp. XIX:** 120

"Plain Song for Comadre, A" (Wilbur), **Supp. III Part 2:** 554

"Plain Talk". *See Common Sense* (Paine)

Plaint of a Rose, The (Sandburg), **III:** 579

Plain Truth: Or, Serious Considerations on the Present State of the City of Philadelphia, and Province of Pennsylvania (Franklin), **II:** 117–119

Plainwater: Essays and Poetry (Carson), **Supp. XII:** 97, 99–104

Plan B (C. Himes), **Supp. XVI:** 143, 144

Plan B: Further Thoughts on Faith (Lamott), **Supp. XX:** 142–143

"Planchette" (London), **II:** 475–476

"Planetarium" (Rich), **Supp. I Part 2:** 557

Planet News: 1961–1967 (Ginsberg), **Supp. II Part 1:** 321

Planet Waves (album, Dylan), **Supp. XVIII:** 27

"Plantation a beginning, a" (Olson), **Supp. II Part 2:** 573

Plant Dreaming Deep (Sarton), **Supp. VIII:** 250, 263

Plante, David, **Supp. IV Part 1:** 310

Planting a Sequoia (Gioia), **Supp. XV:** 117

"Planting a Sequoia" (Gioia), **Supp. XV:** 111, 112, 117, 121–122

"Plants Fed On By Fawns" (B. Kelly), **Supp. XVII:** 133

Plarr, Victor, **III:** 459, 477

Plath, James, **Retro. Supp. I:** 334; **Supp. XXIII:** 73, 74, 80

Plath, Sylvia, **Retro. Supp. II:** 181, 241–260; **Supp. I Part 2:** 526–549, 554, 571; **Supp. III Part 2:** 543, 561; **Supp. IV Part 2:** 439; **Supp. V:** 79, 81, 113, 117, 118, 119, 344; **Supp. X:** 201, 202, 203, 215; **Supp. XI:** 146, 240, 241, 317; **Supp. XII:** 217, 308; **Supp. XIII:** 35, 76, 312; **Supp. XIV:** 269; **Supp. XV:** 123, 148, 184, 252, 253, 340; **Supp. XVII:** 239; **Supp. XXI:** 58; **Supp. XXII:** 30, 92, 93; **Supp. XXIII:** 63, 64, 112, 113, 254; **Supp. XXV:** 222; **Supp. XXVI:** 45, 64, 67, 68, 77; **Supp. XXVII:** 261, 296

Plath, Warren, **Supp. I Part 2:** 528

Plato, **I:** 224, 279, 383, 389, 485, 523; **II:** 5, 8, 10, 15, 233, 346, 391–392, 591; **III:** 115, 480, 600, 606, 609, 619–620; **IV:** 74, 140, 333, 363, 364; **Retro. Supp. I:** 247; **Retro. Supp. II:** 31; **Supp. I Part 2:** 595, 631; **Supp. IV Part 1:** 391; **Supp. IV Part 2:** 526; **Supp. X:** 78

"Plato" (Emerson), **II:** 6

"Platonic Relationship, A" (Beattie), **Supp. V:** 22

Platonic Scripts (Justice), **Supp. VII:** 115

Platonov, Dmitri, **Supp. VIII:** 30

Platt, Anthony M., **Supp. I Part 1:** 13–14

Platt, Edward, **Supp. XXIII:** 97

Platte River (Bass), **Supp. XVI:** 19

"Platte River" (Bass), **Supp. XVI:** 20

"Plausible Man" (Davison), **Supp. XXVI:** 71

Plausible Prejudices: Essays on American Writing (Epstein), **Supp. XIV:** 111

Plautus, Titus Maccius, **IV:** 155; **Supp. III Part 2:** 630

"Play, A" (Brainard), **Supp. XXVII:** 18

Play and Other Stories, The (Dixon), **Supp. XII:** 148, 149

Playback (Chandler), **Supp. IV Part 1:** 134–135; **Supp. XVIII:** 138

Playback (script) (Chandler), **Supp. IV Part 1:** 131

"Play Ball!" (Francis), **Supp. IX:** 89

Playboy of the Western World, The (Synge), **Supp. III Part 1:** 34

Play Days (Jewett), **Retro. Supp. II:** 135

Play Days: A Book of Stories for Children (Jewett), **II:** 401–402

Player Piano (Vonnegut), **Supp. II Part 2:** 756, 757, 760–765

Players (DeLillo), **Supp. VI:** 3, 6, 8, 14

"Players, The" (W. J. Smith), **Supp. XIII:** 340, 343

"Playground, The" (Bradbury), **Supp. IV Part 1:** 104

"Playing" (Huddle), **Supp. XXVI:** 151, 154

Playing at Stillness (Espaillat), **Supp. XXI:** 112

Playing in the Dark (Morrison), **Retro. Supp. II:** 118; **Supp. XIII:** 185–186

"Playing the Bawd at Twenty" (Skloot), **Supp. XX:** 204–205

Play in Poetry (Untermeyer), **Supp. XV:** 310

"Playin with Punjab" (Bambara), **Supp. XI:** 6

Play It Again Sam (Allen), **Supp. XV:** 2, 3, 14

Play It as It Lays (Didion), **Supp. IV Part 1:** 198, 201–203, 203, 211

Play It as It Lays (film), **Supp. IV Part 1:** 198

"Plays and Operas Too" (Whitman), **IV:** 350

Plays of Negro Life: A Source-Book of Native American Drama (Locke and Gregory), **Supp. XIV:** 202

Plays: Winesburg and Others (Anderson), **I:** 113

"Playthings" (Komunyakaa), **Supp. XIII:** 126

"Playtime: Danish Fun" (Larsen), **Supp. XVIII:** 120, 122–123

"Playtime: Three Scandinavian Stories" (Larsen), **Supp. XVIII:** 122–123

Playwright's Voice, The (Savran), **Supp. XIII:** 209; **Supp. XV:** 321; **Supp. XXIV:** 263

Plaza Suite (Simon), **Supp. IV Part 2:** 575, 581–582, 583, 589

"Pleaders, The" (Davison), **Supp. XXVI:** 71

Pleading Guilty (Turow), **Supp. XVII:** 218, 219

"Plea for Captain Brown, A" (Thoreau), **IV:** 185

"Plea of a Plebeian" (H. Johnson), **Supp. XXVI:** 173

"Please" (Komunyakaa), **Supp. XIII:** 122

"Please Don't Kill Anything" (A. Miller), **III:** 161

"Please Don't Take My Sunshine Away" (Conroy), **Supp. XVI:** 69

"Pleasure" (Very), **Supp. XXV:** 242, 244

Pleasure Dome (Frankenberg), **I:** 436

Pleasure Dome (Komunyakaa), **Supp. XIII:** 113, 121, **131–133**

Pleasure of Hope, The (Emerson), **II:** 8

"Pleasure of Ruins, The" (McClatchy), **Supp. XII:** 256

"Pleasures of Formal Poetry, The" (Bogan), **Supp. III Part 1:** 51

"Pleasures of Peace, The" (Koch), **Supp. XV:** 180

"Plea to the Protestant Churches, A" (Brooks), **Supp. XIV:** 4

Plimpton, George, **Supp. IV Part 1:** 386; **Supp. IX:** 256; **Supp. V:** 201; **Supp. VIII:** 82, 157; **Supp. XI:** 294; **Supp. XIV:** 82; **Supp. XVI: 233–248**

Pliny the Elder, **Supp. XVI:** 292

Pliny the Younger, **II:** 113

"Ploesti Isn't Long Island" (Zinberg), **Supp. XV:** 195

"Plot against the Giant, The" (Stevens), **IV:** 81

Plotinus, **Supp. XV:** 33; **Supp. XVI:** 291

Plough and the Stars, The (O'Casey), **III:** 159

"Ploughing on Sunday" (Stevens), **IV:** 74

Plowing the Dark (Powers), **Supp. IX:** 212–213, **221–224**

Plum Bun (Fauset), **Supp. XIX:** 73; **Supp. XVIII:** 127

Plumed Serpent, The (Lawrence), **Supp. XV:** 46

"Plumet Basilisk, The" (Moore), **III:** 203, 208, 215

Plumly, Stanley, **Supp. IV Part 2:** 625

Plummer, Amanda, **Supp. IV Part 1:** 236

Plunder (serial movie), **Supp. IV Part 2:** 464

Plunket, Robert, **Supp. XV:** 68

Plunkett, Edward (Lord Dunsany), **Supp. XXV:** 113

"Plunkville Patriot" (O'Henry), **Supp. II Part 1:** 389

"Pluralism and Ideological Peace" (Locke), **Supp. XIV:** 202, 212

"Pluralism and Intellectual Democracy" (Locke), **Supp. XIV:** 202, 208, 212

Pluralistic Universe, A (James), **II:** 342, 348, 357–358

Plutarch, **II:** 5, 8, 16, 555; **Retro. Supp. I:** 360; **Supp. XVI:** 292

Plymell, Charles, **Supp. XIV:** 149

Plymell, Pam, **Supp. XIV:** 149

Pnin (Nabokov), **III:** 246; **Retro. Supp. I:** 263, 265, 266, 275, 335

"Po' Boy Blues" (Hughes), **Supp. I Part 1:** 327

Pocahontas, **I:** 4; **II:** 296; **III:** 584

"Pocahontas to Her English Husband, John Rolfe" (Gunn Allen), **Supp. IV Part 1:** 331

"Pocketbook and Sauerkraut" (Di Piero), **Supp. XIX:** 35, 36, 41, 42, 45

"Pocketknives" (Rash), **Supp. XXVII:** 222

"Pocket Poem" (Kooser), **Supp. XIX:** 128

Podhoretz, Norman, **IV:** 441; **Retro. Supp. II:** 323; **Supp. IV Part 2:** 382; **Supp. IX:** 3; **Supp. VIII:** 93, **231–247**; **Supp. XIV:** 103; **Supp. XXV:** 253, 268

Podnieks, Elizabeth, **Supp. X:** 189, 190, 191, 192

"Pod of the Milkweed" (Frost), **Retro. Supp. I:** 141

Podulka, Fran, **Supp. XXVI:** 6

Poe (screenplay, O'Nan), **Supp. XXV:** 154

Poe, Edgar Allan, **I:** 48, 53, 103, 190, 194, 200, 210, 211, 261, 340, 459; **II:** 74, 77, 194, 255, 273, 295, 308, 311, 313, 421, 475, 482, 530, 595; **III:** 259, **409–432**, 485, 507, 593; **IV:** 123, 129, 133, 141, 187, 261, 345, 350, 432, 438, 439, 453; **Retro. Supp. I:** 41, 273, 365, 421; **Retro. Supp. II:** 102, 104, 160, 164, 220, **261–277**, 322; **Supp. I Part 1:** 36, 309; **Supp. I Part 2:** 376, 384, 385, 388, 393, 405, 413, 421, 474, 682; **Supp. II Part 1:** 385, 410; **Supp. III Part 2:** 544, 549–550; **Supp. IV Part 1:** 80, 81, 101, 128, 341, 349; **Supp. IV Part 2:** 464, 469; **Supp. IX:** 115; **Supp. VIII:** 105; **Supp. X:** 42, 78; **Supp. XI:** 85, 293; **Supp. XIII:** 100, 111; **Supp. XVI:** 294; **Supp. XVIII:** 3, 11; **Supp. XX: 74;** **Supp. XXIII:** 161, 164, 169, 177, 178; **Supp. XXIV:** 54; **Supp. XXV:** 111, 119; **Supp. XXVII:** 84

Poe, Edgar Allen, **Supp. XV:** 275; **Supp. XXI:** 51; **Supp. XXVI:** 282

Poe Abroad: Influence, Reputation, Affinities (Vines), **Retro. Supp. II:** 261

"Poe-et's Nightmare, The" (Lovecraft), **Supp. XXV:** 119

"Poem" (Bishop), **Retro. Supp. II:** 40; **Supp. I Part 1:** 73, 76–79, 82, 95

"Poem" (Harrison), **Supp. VIII:** 38

"Poem" (Justice), **Supp. VII:** 125

"Poem" (Kunitz), **Supp. III Part 1:** 263

"Poem" (Notley), **Supp. XXII:** 228–229

"Poem" (O'Hara), **Supp. XIX:** 85

"Poem" (Wright), **Supp. III Part 2:** 590

"Poem, the Snow, Jane Goodall, the Vase of Daffodils, The" (Huddle), **Supp. XXVI:** 150

"Poem About Black Power, A" (Boyle), **Supp. XXIV:** 64

"Poem About George Doty in the Death House, A" (Wright), **Supp. III Part 2:** 594–595, 597–598

"Poem about People" (Pinsky), **Supp. VI: 240–241,** 244, 248

"Poem as Mask, The" (Rukeyser), **Supp. VI:** 281, 285

"Poem as Time Machine, The" (Gallagher), **Supp. XXIV:** 172

"Poem Beginning 'The' " (Zukofsky), **Supp. III Part 2:** 610, 611, 614

"Poem Catching Up with an Idea" (Carruth), **Supp. XVI:** 56

"Poem for a Birthday" (Plath), **Supp. I Part 2:** 539

"POEM FOR ANNA RUSS AND FANNY JONES, A" (Baraka), **Supp. II Part 1:** 58

"Poem for Black Hearts, A" (Baraka), **Supp. II Part 1:** 50

"POEM FOR DEEP THINKERS, A" (Baraka), **Supp. II Part 1:** 55

"Poem for D. H. Lawrence" (Creeley), **Supp. IV Part 1:** 141

"Poem for Don Cherry" (Mackey), **Supp. XXVII:** 154

"Poem for Dorothy, A" (Merwin), **Supp. III Part 1:** 342

"Poem for Hemingway and W. C. Williams" (Carver), **Supp. III Part 1:** 147

"Poem for my Son" (Kumin), **Supp. IV Part 2:** 442

"Poem for People Who Are Understandably Too Busy to Read Poetry" (Dunn), **Supp. XI:** 147

"Poem for Someone Killed in Spain, A" (Jarrell), **II:** 371

"Poem for the Blue Heron, A" (Oliver), **Supp. VII:** 235–236

"Poem for Two Voices" (Everwine), **Supp. XV:** 89

"Poem For Willie Best, A" (Baraka), **Supp. II Part 1:** 36

"Poem in Prose" (Bogan), **Supp. III Part 1:** 58

"Poem in the Park, The" (Davison), **Supp. XXVI:** 74

"Poem in Which I Refuse Contemplation" (Dove), **Supp. IV Part 1:** 249

"Poem Is a Walk, A" (Ammons), **Supp. VII:** 36

"Poem Like a Grenade, A" (Haines), **Supp. XII:** 204

"Poem of Flight, The" (Levine), **Supp. V:** 189

"Poem of Liberation, The" (Stern), **Supp. IX:** 292

Poem of the Cid (Merwin, trans.), **Supp. III Part 1:** 347

"Poem of the Forgotten" (Haines), **Supp. XII:** 202–203

"Poem (V (F) W)" (O'Hara), **Supp. XXIII:** 219

"Poem on a Line by Anne Sexton, 'We Are All Writing God's Poem' " (Crooker), **Supp. XXIII:** 59

"Poem on the Memorable Victory Obtained by the Gallant Captain Paul Jones" (Freneau), **Supp. II Part 1:** 261

"Poem out of Childhood" (Rukeyser), **Supp. VI:** 272, 277

Poem-Paintings (O'Hara and Bluhm), **Supp. XXIII:** 217

"Poem Read at the Dinner Given to the Author by the Medical Profession" (Holmes), **Supp. I Part 1:** 310–311

Poems (Auden), **Supp. II Part 1:** 6

Poems (Berryman), **I:** 170

Poems (Bryant), **II:** 311; **Supp. I Part 1:** 155, 157

Poems (Cummings), **I:** 430, 447

Poems (E. Stoddard), **Supp. XV:** 274

Poems (Eliot), **I:** 580, 588; **IV:** 122; **Retro. Supp. I:** 59, 291

Poems (Emerson), **II:** 7, 8, 12–13, 17

Poems (Holmes), **Supp. I Part 1:** 303

Poems (J. R. Lowell), **Supp. I Part 2:** 405

Poems (Koch), **Supp. XV:** 179

Poems (Moore), **III:** 194, 205, 215

Poems (Poe), **III:** 411

Poems (Reznikoff), **Supp. XIV:** 282, 283, 284, 285

Poems (Tate), **IV:** 121

Poems (W. C. Williams), **Retro. Supp. I:** 412–413, 416, 424

Poems (W. J. Smith), **Supp. XIII:** 332

Poems (Williams), **Supp. XXIV:** 35

Poems (Winters), **Supp. II Part 2:** 809, 810

Poems (Wordsworth), **I:** 468

Poems, 1909–1925 (Eliot), **Retro. Supp. I:** 64

Poems, 1924–1933 (MacLeish), **III:** 7, 15

Poems, 1943–1956 (Wilbur), **Supp. III Part 2:** 554

Poems, 1953–58 (W. Stone), **Supp. XXVII:** 254

Poems, The (Freneau), **Supp. II Part 1:** 263

Poems 1918–1975 : The Complete Poems of Charles Reznikoff (Cooney, ed.), **Supp. XIV:** 289

Poems 1940–1953 (Shapiro), **Supp. II Part 2:** 703, 711

Poems 1947–1954 (Kees), **Supp. XV:** 147

Poems: 1947–1957 (W. J. Smith), **Supp. XIII:** 333

Poems 1957–1967 (Dickey), **Supp. IV Part 1:** 178, 181

Poems about God (Ransom), **III:** 484, 486, 491; **IV:** 121

"Poems about Painting" (Snodgrass), **Supp. VI:** 316

Poems and Essays (Ransom), **III:** 486, 490, 492

Poems and New Poems (Bogan), **Supp. III Part 1:** 60–62

"Poems and Places" (Haines), **Supp. XII:** 203

Poems and Poetry of Europe, The (Longfellow, ed.), **Retro. Supp. II:** 155

Poems by Emily Dickinson (Todd and Higginson, eds.), **I:** 469, 470; **Retro. Supp. I:** 35, 39

Poems by Emily Dickinson, Second Series (Todd and Higginson, eds.), **I:** 454;

Retro. Supp. I: 35

Poems by Emily Dickinson, The (Bianchi and Hampson, eds.), **Retro. Supp. I:** 35

Poems by Emily Dickinson, Third Series (Todd, ed.), **Retro. Supp. I:** 35

Poems by James Russell Lowell, Second Series (J. R. Lowell), **Supp. I Part 2:** 406, 409

Poems by Sidney Lanier, (Lanier), **Supp. I Part 1:** 364

Poems from Black Africa (Hughes, ed.), **Supp. I Part 1:** 344

"Poems I Have Lost, The" (Ortiz), **Supp. IV Part 2:** 507

Poems: North & South–A Cold Spring, (Bishop), **Supp. I Part 1:** 83, 89

Poems of a Jew (Shapiro), **Supp. II Part 2:** 703, 712–713

"Poems of a Mountain Recluse" (Budbill), **Supp. XIX:** 9, 10

Poems of Anna Akhmatova, The (Kunitz and Hayward, trans.), **Supp. III Part 1:** 269

Poems of Emily Dickinson, The (Bianchi and Hampson, eds.), **Retro. Supp. I:** 35

Poems of Emily Dickinson, The (T. H. Johnson, ed.), **I:** 470

Poems of François Villon (Kinnell, trans.), **Supp. III Part 1:** 235, 243, 249

"Poems of Our Climate, The" (Stevens), **Retro. Supp. I:** 313

Poems of Peter Davison, The (Davison), **Supp. XXVI:** 66, 78

Poems of Philip Freneau, Written Chiefly during the Late War (Freneau), **Supp. II Part 1:** 261

Poems of Places (Longfellow, ed.), **II:** 490; **Retro. Supp. II:** 155; **Supp. I Part 1:** 368

Poems of Stanley Kunitz, The (Kunitz), **Supp. III Part 1:** 258, 263, 264, 266, 268

"Poems of These States" (Ginsberg), **Supp. II Part 1:** 323, 325

Poems of Two Friends (Howells and Piatt), **II:** 273, 277

"POEM SOME PEOPLE WILL HAVE TO UNDERSTAND, A" (Baraka), **Supp. II Part 1:** 49

Poems on Slavery (Longfellow), **II:** 489; **Retro. Supp. II:** 157, 168; **Supp. I Part 2:** 406

Poems on Various Subjects (Rowson), **Supp. XV:** 232

Poems on Various Subjects, Religious and Moral (Wheatley), **Supp. XX: 277, 282, 284, 285, 289**

Poem Spoken at the Public Commencement at Yale College, in New Haven; September 1, 1781, A (Barlow), **Supp. II Part 1:** 67–68, 74, 75

Poems Retrieved (O'Hara), **Supp. XXIII:** 220

Poems to Solve (Swenson), **Supp. IV Part 2:** 642

Poems Written and Published during the American Revolutionary War (Freneau), **Supp. II Part 1:** 273, 274

Poems Written between the Years 1768 and 1794 (Freneau), **Supp. II Part 1:** 269

"Poem That Took the Place of a Mountain" (Olson), **Supp. II Part 2:** 582

"Poem to My First Lover" (Olds), **Supp. X:** 206

"Poem to the Reader" (Olds), **Supp. X:** 213

"Poem with No Ending, A" (Levine), **Supp. V:** 186, 190

"Poem You Asked For, The" (Levis), **Supp. XI:** 259–260

Poe Poe Poe Poe Poe Poe Poe (Hoffman), **Retro. Supp. II:** 265

Poesía Náhuatl, **Supp. XV:** 77

Poésies 1917–1920 (Cocteau), **Retro. Supp. I:** 82

"Poesis: A Conceit" (Sobin), **Supp. XVI:** 288

"Poet" (Taggard), **Supp. XXII:** 284

Poet, The (Connelly), **Supp. XXI: 71,** 78

"Poet, The" (Dunbar), **Supp. II Part 1:** 207, 209–210

"Poet, The" (Emerson), **II:** 13, 19, 20, 170

"Poet, The" (Ortiz), **Supp. IV Part 2:** 505

"Poet and His Book, The" (Millay), **III:** 126, 138

"Poet and His Public, The" (Jarrell), **Supp. I Part 1:** 96

"Poet and His Song, The" (Dunbar), **Supp. II Part 1:** 199

"Poet and the Person, The" (Kinard), **Supp. XIV:** 127

"Poet and the Queen, The" (Shaw), **Supp. XIX:** 241

"Poet and the World, The" (Cowley), **Supp. II Part 1:** 145

"Poet as Anti-Specialist, The" (Swenson), **Supp. IV Part 2:** 638, 643

"Poet as *Curandera*" (Mora), **Supp. XIII:** 214, 220

"Poet as Hero, The: Keats in His Letters" (Trilling), **Supp. III Part 2:** 506–507

"Poet as Religious Moralist, The" (Larson), **Supp. XI:** 328

"Poet at Seven, The" (Rimbaud), **II:** 545

Poet at the Breakfast-Table, The (Holmes), **Supp. I Part 1:** 313–314

"Poète contumace, Le" (Corbiere), **II:** 384–385

"Poet for President, A" (Mora), **Supp. XIII:** 220–221

Poetic Achievement of Ezra Pound, The (Alexander), **Retro. Supp. I:** 293

Poetic Diction: A Study in Meaning (Barfield), **III:** 274, 279

"Poetic Principle, The" (Poe), **III:** 421, 426; **Retro. Supp. II:** 266

"Poetics" (Ammons), **Supp. VII:** 29–30

Poetics (Aristotle), **III:** 422; **Supp. XI:** 249; **Supp. XIII:** 75; **Supp. XIV:** 243; **Supp. XV:** 265

Poetics of Space, The (Bachelard), **Supp. XIII:** 225; **Supp. XVI:** 292

"Poetics of the Periphery: Literary Experimentalism in Kathy Acker's *In*

Memoriam to Identity" (Acker), Supp. XII: 17

"Poetics of the Physical World, The" (Kinnell), **Supp. III Part 1:** 239

"Poetics of Tourette Syndrome, The: Language, Neurobiology, and Poetry" (Schleifer), **Supp. XVIII:** 144

Poet in the World, The (Levertov), **Supp. III Part 1:** 271, 273, 278, 282

"Poet or the Growth of a Lit'ry Figure" (White), **Supp. I Part 2:** 676

Poetry (Barber), **Supp. IV Part 2:** 550

"Poetry" (Moore), **III:** 204–205, 215

"Poetry" (Nye), **Supp. XIII:** 282

"Poetry" (Wrigley), **Supp. XVIII:** 301–302

"Poetry, Community and Climax" (Snyder), **Supp. VIII:** 290

"Poetry, Pleasure, and the Hedonist Reader" (Collins), **Supp. XXI:** 54

"Poetry: A Metrical Essay" (Holmes), **Supp. I Part 1:** 310

"Poetry and Belief in Thomas Hardy" (Schwartz), **Supp. II Part 2:** 666

Poetry and Criticism (Nemerov, ed.), **III:** 269

"Poetry and Drama" (Eliot), **I:** 588

Poetry and Fiction: Essays (Nemerov), **III:** 269, 281

"Poetry and Place" (Berry), **Supp. X:** 22, 28, 31, 32

Poetry and Poets (A. Lowell), **II:** 512

"Poetry and Religion" (Jarman), **Supp. XVII:** 111

Poetry and the Age (Jarrell), **IV:** 352; **Retro. Supp. I:** 121; **Supp. II Part 1:** 135

"Poetry and the Primitive: Notes on Poetry as an Ecological Survival Technique" (Snyder), **Supp. VIII:** 291, 292, 299, 300

"Poetry and the Public World" (MacLeish), **III:** 11

Poetry and the World (Pinsky), **Supp. VI:** 236, 239, 244, 247

Poetry and Truth (Olson), **Supp. II Part 2:** 583

"Poetry and Uncertainty" (Hirshfield), **Supp. XXIII:** 137

"Poetry As a Way of Life" (Bishop interview), **Retro. Supp. II:** 53

"Poetry as Survival" (Harrison), **Supp. VIII:** 45

"Poetry Baron, The" (Gallagher), **Supp. XXIV:** 166, 177

"Poetry Failure" (Halliday), **Supp. XIX:** 92

Poetry for Students (Taibl), **Supp. XV:** 255

"Poetry for the Advanced" (Baraka), **Supp. II Part 1:** 58

"Poetry Friendship on Earth" (Halliday), **Supp. XIX:** 90, 91

Poetry Handbook, A (Oliver), **Supp. VII:** 229, 245

Poetry Home Repair Manual, The (Kooser), **Supp. XIX:** 116, 128

Poetry in Motion (film), **Supp. XXIV:** 33

Poetry in Motion: 100 Poems from the Subways and Buses (Peacock, ed.),

Supp. XIX: 195

"Poetry in Translation: Literary Imperialism or, Defending the Musk Ox" (Gallagher), **Supp. XXIV:** 172

"Poetry of Barbarism, The" (Santayana), **IV:** 353

Poetry of Chaucer, The (Gardner), **Supp. VI:** 63

Poetry of Meditation, The (Martz), **IV:** 151; **Supp. I Part 1:** 107

Poetry of Mourning: The Modern Elegy from Hardy to Heaney (Ramazani), **Supp. IV Part 2:** 450

Poetry of Stephen Crane, The (Hoffman), **I:** 405

Poetry of the Negro, 1746–1949, The (Hughes and Bontemps), **Supp. I Part 1:** 345; **Supp. XXII:** 11

Poetry 180: A Turning Back to Poetry (Collins, ed.), **Supp. XXI:** 54

Poetry Reading against the Vietnam War, A (Bly and Ray, eds.), **Supp. IV Part 1:** 61, 63

"Poetry Workshop, The" (column, Kumin), **Supp. XX: 164**

"Poetry Wreck, The" (Shapiro), **Supp. II Part 2:** 717

Poetry Wreck, The: Selected Essays (Shapiro), **Supp. II Part 2:** 703, 704, 717

"Poets" (X. J. Kennedy), **Supp. XV:** 158

Poet's Alphabet, A: Reflections on the Literary Art and Vocation (Bogan), **Supp. III Part 1:** 55, 64

Poets and Poetry of America (Griswold), **Supp. XV:** 277; **Supp. XXV:** 250

Poet's Choice (Engle and Langland, eds.), **III:** 277, 542

Poet's Guide to Poetry, A (Kinzie), **Supp. XXIII:** 124

"Poet's Husband Engages in Gourmet Cooking, The" (Espaillat), **Supp. XXI:** 99

Poets of the Old Testament, The (Gordon), **III:** 199

Poets of Today (Hall, ed.), **Supp. XXVII:** 253, 256

Poets of Today (Wheelock, ed.), **Supp. IV Part 2:** 639

Poets on Poetry (Nemerov, ed.), **III:** 269

"Poet's Tact, and a Necessary Tactlessness, The" (C. Frost), **Supp. XV:** 94–95

"Poet's View, A" (Levertov), **Supp. III Part 1:** 284

"Poet's Voice, The" (Oliver), **Supp. VII:** 245

"Poets with History and Poets Without History" (Tsvetaeva), **Supp. XXIII:** 168

"Poet Turns on Himself, The" (Dickey), **Supp. IV Part 1:** 177, 181, 185

Poganuc People (Stowe), **Supp. I Part 2:** 581, 596, 599–600

Pogo (comic strip), **Supp. XI:** 105

Pohl, R. D., **Supp. XXVI:** 102

Pohrt, Tom, **Supp. XIX:** 123

Poincaré, Raymond, **IV:** 320

"Point, The" (Hayden), **Supp. II Part 1:** 373

"Point at Issue!, A" (Chopin), **Retro. Supp. II:** 61; **Supp. I Part 1:** 208

"Point of Age, A" (Berryman), **I:** 173

Point of No Return (Marquand), **III:** 56, 59–60, 65, 67, 69

Point Reyes Poems (R. Bly), **Supp. IV Part 1:** 71

"Points" (Hoffman), **Supp. XVIII:** 86

Points for a Compass Rose (Connell), **Supp. XIV:** 79, 80, 96

"Point Shirley" (Plath), **Supp. I Part 2:** 529, 538

Points in Time (Bowles), **Supp. IV Part 1:** 93

"Points West" (column), **Supp. IV Part 1:** 198

Poirier, Richard, **I:** 136, 239; **III:** 34; **Retro. Supp. I:** 134; **Retro. Supp. II:** 207–208; **Supp. I Part 2:** 660, 665; **Supp. IV Part 2:** 690

"Poison Oak" (Huddle), **Supp. XXVI:** 148, 152

Poison Pen (Garrett), **Supp. VII:** 111

Poisonwood Bible, The (Kingsolver), **Supp. VII:** 197–198, 202, 210–213

Poitier, Sidney, **Supp. IV Part 1:** 360, 362

Pokerface (Collins), **Supp. XXI:** 53

"Polack Reverie" (Halliday), **Supp. XIX:** 88

Polanco, Richard, **Supp. XX: 260**

"Polar Bear" (Heller), **Supp. IV Part 1:** 383

"Polar Bears and Others" (Boyle), **Supp. XXIV:** 57

"Polar Seas and Sir John Franklin, The" (Briggs), **Supp. XVIII:** 14

Pole, Rupert, **Supp. X:** 185

"Pole Star" (MacLeish), **III:** 16

Po Li, **Supp. I Part 1:** 262

Police (Baraka), **Supp. II Part 1:** 47

"Police" (Corso), **Supp. XII:** 117, 127

"Police Court Saturday Morning" (X. J. Kennedy), **Supp. XV:** 170

"Police Dreams" (Bausch), **Supp. VII:** 47

Politian (Poe), **III:** 412

"Political and Practical Conceptions of Race, The" (Locke), **Supp. XIV:** 209–210

Political Essays (J. R. Lowell), **Supp. I Part 2:** 407

Political Fable, A (Coover), **Supp. V:** 44, 46, 47, 49, 51

"Political Fables" (Mather), **Supp. II Part 2:** 450

"Political Interests" (Stevens), **Retro. Supp. I:** 295

"Political Litany, A" (Freneau), **Supp. II Part 1:** 257

"Political Migrations: A Family Story" (Mallon), **Supp. XIX:** 141–142

"Political Pastoral" (Frost), **Retro. Supp. I:** 139

"Political Poem" (Baraka), **Supp. II Part 1:** 36

Politics (Acker), **Supp. XII:** 3, 4

Politics (Macdonald), **I:** 233–234

"Politics" (Paley), **Supp. VI:** 217

"Politics, Structure, and Poetic Development" (McCombs), **Supp. XIII:** 33

"Politics and the English Language" (Orwell), **Retro. Supp. II:** 287; **Supp. I Part 2:** 620

Politics and the Novel (Howe), **Supp. VI:** 113

"Politics and the Personal Lyric in the Poetry of Joy Harjo and C. D. Wright" (Goodman), **Supp. XV:** 344

"Politics of Ethnic Authorship, The: Li-Young Lee, Emerson, and Whitman at the Banquet Table" (Partridge), **Supp. XV:** 219

"Politics of Silence, The" (Monette), **Supp. X:** 148

Polito, Robert, **Supp. XVIII:** 33; **Supp. XXIV:** 234; **Supp. XXVI:** 55

Politt, Katha, **Supp. XII:** 159

Poliziano (Angelo Ambrogini), **Supp. XXIV:** 152

Polk, James, **Supp. XIII:** 20

Polk, James K., **I:** 17; **II:** 433–434

Pollack, Sydney, **Supp. XIII:** 159

"Pollen" (Nye), **Supp. XIII:** 284

Pollitt, Katha, **Supp. X:** 186, 191, 193; **Supp. XVI:** 39

Pollock, Jackson, **IV:** 411, 420; **Supp. XIX:** 33; **Supp. XV:** 145, 177, 178; **Supp. XXIII:** 208, 210, 211

"Polly" (Chopin), **Retro. Supp. II:** 72

Polo, Marco, **III:** 395

Polonsky, Abraham, **Supp. XXI:** 261, 275

Polybius, **Supp. I Part 2:** 491

"Polydore" (Chopin), **Retro. Supp. II:** 66

"Pomegranate" (Glück), **Supp. V:** 82

"Pomegranate Seed" (Wharton), **IV:** 316; **Retro. Supp. I:** 382

Ponce de Leon, Luis, **III:** 391

"Pond, The" (Nemerov), **III:** 272

"Pond at Dusk, The" (Kenyon), **Supp. VII:** 168

Ponder Heart, The (Welty), **IV:** 261, 274–275, 281; **Retro. Supp. I:** 351–352

"Ponderosa Pine" (Huncke), **Supp. XIV:** 146

Ponsot, Margaret, **Supp. XVII:** 241

"Pony" (Sanders), **Supp. XVI:** 277

"Pony Car" (P. Benedict), **Supp. XXIII:** 47

Poodle Springs (Parker and Chandler), **Supp. IV Part 1:** 135; **Supp. XIX:** 189

Poodle Springs Story, The (Chandler), **Supp. IV Part 1:** 135

"Pool, The" (Doolittle), **Supp. I Part 1:** 264–265

Poole, Ernest, **II:** 444

"Pool Lights" (F. Barthelme), **Supp. XI:** 25, 26–27, 36

"Pool Room in the Lions Club" (Merwin), **Supp. III Part 1:** 346

"Poolside" (Skloot), **Supp. XX: 202–203**

"Poor Black Fellow" (Hughes), **Retro. Supp. I:** 204

"Poor Bustard, The" (Corso), **Supp. XII:** 134

"Poor but Happy" (Mamet), **Supp. XIV:** 252, 253

"Poor Dead Feet of My First Husband, The" (Schott), **Supp. XXIII:** 241

Poore, Charles, **III:** 364; **Supp. XIX:** 257, 264; **Supp. XX: 38**

Poor Fool (Caldwell), **I:** 291, 292, 308

Poorhouse Fair, The (Updike), **IV:** 214, 228–229, 232; **Retro. Supp. I:** 317, 320

"Poor Joanna" (Jewett), **II:** 394

"Poor Man's Pudding and Rich Man's Crumbs" (Melville), **III:** 89–90

"Poor Richard" (James), **II:** 322

Poor Richard's Almanac for 1733 (Franklin), **II:** 108, 110

Poor Richard's Almanac for 1739 (Franklin), **II:** 112

Poor Richard's Almanac for 1758 (Franklin), **II:** 101

Poor Richard's Almanac (undated) (Franklin), **II:** 112

Poor White (Anderson), **I:** 110–111

"Poor Working Girl" (Z. Fitzgerald), **Supp. IX:** 71

Popa, Vasko, **Supp. VIII:** 272

Pope, Alexander, **I:** 198, 204; **II:** 17, 114; **III:** 263, 267, 288, 517; **IV:** 145; **Retro. Supp. I:** 335; **Supp. I Part 1:** 150, 152, 310; **Supp. I Part 2:** 407, 422, 516, 714; **Supp. II Part 1:** 70, 71; **Supp. X:** 32, 36; **Supp. XII:** 260; **Supp. XV:** 258; **Supp. XX: 280; Supp. XXV:** 119; **Supp. XXVI:** 284

Pope, James, **Supp. XXII:** 196

Pope-Hennessy, James, **Supp. XIV:** 348

"Pope's Penis, The" (Olds), **Supp. X:** 207

"Poplar, Sycamore" (Wilbur), **Supp. III Part 2:** 549

Popo and Fifina: Children of Haiti (Hughes and Bontemps), **Retro. Supp. I:** 203; **Supp. XXII:** 4, 10, 12

"Poppies" (Oliver), **Supp. VII:** 240

"Poppies in July" (Plath), **Supp. I Part 2:** 544

"Poppies in July" (Crooker), **Supp. XXIII:** 61

"Poppies in October" (Plath), **Supp. I Part 2:** 544

"Poppycock" (Francis), **Supp. IX:** 87

"Poppy Juice" (Taggard), **Supp. XXII:** 276

"Poppy Seed" (A. Lowell), **II:** 523

"Popular Art and the Cultural Tradition" (C. L. R. James), **Supp. XXI:** 170

Popular Book, The: A History of America's Literary Taste (Hart), **Supp. XVIII:** 257, 258

Popular Culture (Goldbarth), **Supp. XII: 186**

Popular History of the United States (Gay), **Supp. I Part 1:** 158

Popular Problems (album, Cohen), **Supp. XXVII:** 63

"Popular Songs" (Ashbery), **Supp. III Part 1:** 6

"Populist Manifesto" (Ferlinghetti), **Supp. VIII:** 290

"Porcelain Bowl" (Glück), **Supp. V:** 83

Porcher, Frances, **Retro. Supp. II:** 71

Porco, Mike, **Supp. XVIII:** 24

"Porcupine, The" (Kinnell), **Supp. III Part 1:** 244

Porcupine's Kiss, The (Dobyns), **Supp. XIII: 89–90**

"Por esas coases que pasan" (Hinojosa), **Supp. XIX:** 101

Porgy and Bess (film), **Supp. I Part 1:** 66

Porgy and Bess (play), **Supp. IV Part 1:** 6

"Porn Bought my Football" (Offutt), **Supp. XIX:** 163

"Porphyria's Lover" (Browning), **II:** 522

Portable Beat Reader, The (Charters, ed.), **Supp. XIV:** 152

Portable Blake, The (Kazin, ed.), **Supp. VIII:** 103

Portable Faulkner, The (Cowley, ed.), **II:** 57, 59; **Retro. Supp. I:** 73

Portable Kisses: Love Poems (Gallagher), **Supp. XXIV:** 170

Portable Paul and Jane Bowles, The (Dillon), **Supp. IV Part 1:** 95

Portable Veblen, The (Veblen), **Supp. I Part 2:** 630, 650

"Porte-Cochere" (Taylor), **Supp. V:** 320

"Porter" (Hughes), **Supp. I Part 1:** 327

"Porter" (Nelson), **Supp. XVIII:** 175

Porter, Bern, **III:** 171

Porter, Cole, **Supp. IX:** 189

Porter, Eliot, **Supp. IV Part 2:** 599

Porter, Fairfield, **Supp. XV:** 178; **Supp. XXIII:** 209, 211, 212; **Supp. XXIV:** 41; **Supp. XXVII:** 21

Porter, Herman W., **Supp. I Part 1:** 49

Porter, Horace, **Retro. Supp. II:** 4, 127

Porter, Jacob, **Supp. I Part 1:** 153

Porter, Katherine Anne, **I:** 97, 385; **II:** 194, 606; **III: 433–455,** 482; **IV:** 26, 138, 246, 261, 279, 280, 282; **Retro. Supp. I:** 354; **Retro. Supp. II:** 233, 235; **Supp. IV Part 1:** 31, 310; **Supp. IX:** 93, 94, 95, 98, 128; **Supp. V:** 225; **Supp. VIII:** 156, 157; **Supp. X:** 50; **Supp. XIII:** 294; **Supp. XIV:** 3; **Supp. XV:** 338; **Supp. XXIV:** 52; **Supp. XXVI:** 23

Porter, Nicodemus, **Supp. XXVI:** 87

Porter, Noah, **Supp. I Part 2:** 640

Porter, William Sydney. *See* Henry, O.

"Porter Paints a Picture" (O'Hara), **Supp. XXIII:** 212

Porteus, Beilby, **Supp. I Part 1:** 150

Portis, Rowe, **Supp. XXVI:** 147

"Portland Going Out, The" (Merwin), **Supp. III Part 1:** 345

Portnoy's Complaint (P. Roth), **Retro. Supp. II: 282–286,** 291; **Supp. III Part 2:** 401, 404, 405, 407, 412–414, 426; **Supp. V:** 119, 122; **Supp. XI:** 140; **Supp. XVII:** 8, 43; **Supp. XX: 177; Supp. XXVII:** 142

Port of Saints (Burroughs), **Supp. III Part 1:** 106

"Portrait" (Dixon), **Supp. XII:** 154

"Portrait, A" (Parker), **Supp. IX:** 192–193

"Portrait, The" (Kunitz), **Supp. III Part 1:** 263

"Portrait, The" (Wharton), **Retro. Supp. I:** 364

"Portrait d'une Femme" (Pound), **Retro. Supp. I:** 288

Portrait in Brownstone (Auchincloss), **Supp. IV Part 1:** 21, 23, 27, 31

"Portrait in Georgia" (Toomer), **Supp. IX:** 314

"Portrait in Greys, A" (W. C. Williams), **Retro. Supp. I:** 416

"Portrait of a Girl in Glass" (T. Williams), **IV:** 383

"Portrait of a Jewelry Drummer" (Untermeyer), **Supp. XV:** 299–300

"Portrait of a Lady" (Eliot), **I:** 569, 570, 571, 584; **III:** 4; **Retro. Supp. I:** 55, 56, 62

Portrait of a Lady, The (James), **I:** 10, 258, 461–462, 464; **II:** 323, 325, 327, 328–329, 334; **Retro. Supp. I:** 215, 216, 217, 219, 220, 223, **224–225,** 232, 233, 381

"Portrait of an Artist" (P. Roth), **Supp. III Part 2:** 412

Portrait of an Eye: Three Novels (Acker), **Supp. XII:** 6, **7–9**

"Portrait of an Invisible Man" (Auster), **Supp. XII:** 21

"Portrait of a Supreme Court Judge" (Untermeyer), **Supp. XV:** 299

Portrait of Bascom Hawkes, A (Wolfe), **IV:** 451–452, 456

Portrait of Edith Wharton (Lubbock), **Retro. Supp. I:** 366

Portrait of Logan Pearsall Smith, Drawn from His Letters and Diaries, A (Russell, ed.), **Supp. XIV:** 349

Portrait of Picasso as a Young Man (Mailer), **Retro. Supp. II:** 213

"Portrait of the Artist as an Old Man, A" (Humphrey), **Supp. IX:** 109

Portrait of the Artist as a Young Man, A (Joyce), **I:** 475–476; **III:** 471, 561; **Retro. Supp. I:** 127; **Retro. Supp. II:** 4, 331; **Supp. IX:** 236; **Supp. XIII:** 53, 95

"Portrait of the Artist with Hart Crane" (Wright), **Supp. V:** 342

"Portrait of the Great White Hunter Foxhunting in the Absence of Big Game" (Major), **Supp. XXII:** 183

"Portrait of the Intellectual as a Yale Man" (McCarthy), **II:** 563, 564–565

"Portrait of the Reader with a Bowl of Cereal, A" (Collins), **Supp. XXI:** 55

"Portrait of the Self . . . , A" (Sobin), **Supp. XVI:** 288

Portraits and Elegies (Schnackenberg), **Supp. XV:** 249, **253–256**

"Portraits of Grief" *(New York Times),* **Supp. XIX:** 142

"Port Town" (Hughes), **Retro. Supp. I:** 199

Portuguese Voyages to America in the Fifteenth Century (Morison), **Supp. I Part 2:** 488

"Po' Sandy" (Chesnutt), **Supp. XIV:** 60

Poseidon Adventure, The (film), **Supp. XII:** 321

Poseidon Adventure, The (Gallico), **Supp. XVI:** 238

"Poseidon and Company" (Carver), **Supp. III Part 1:** 137

"Positive Obsession" (O. Butler), **Supp. XIII:** 70

Poss, Stanley, **Supp. XIV:** 166

Possession (Byatt), **Supp. XXI:** 147

"Possessions" (H. Crane), **I:** 392–393; **Retro. Supp. II:** 78

Possible World, A (Koch), **Supp. XV:** 184

Postal Inspector (film), **Supp. XIII:** 166

"Postcard from Greece" (Stallings), **Supp. XXV:** 229, 231

Postcards (Proulx), **Supp. VII:** 249, 256–258, 262

"Postcard to Send to Sumer, A" (Bronk), **Supp. XXI:** 31

"Postcolonialism and Autobiography" (Skinner and Waller), **Supp. XXII:** 78

"Postcolonial Tale, A" (Harjo), **Supp. XII:** 227

"Posthumous Letter to Gilbert White" (Auden), **Supp. II Part 1:** 26

"Post-Larkin Triste" (Karr), **Supp. XI:** 242–243

Postlethwaite, Diana, **Supp. XII:** 317–318; **Supp. XVI:** 176

"Postlude" (W. C. Williams), **Retro. Supp. I:** 415

Postman, Neil, **Supp. XI:** 275

Postman Always Rings Twice, The (Cain), **Supp. XIII:** 165–166

Postman Always Rings Twice, The (film), **Supp. XIV:** 241

"Postmaster and the Clerk, The" (Budbill), **Supp. XIX:** 9

"Postmortem Guide, A" (Dunn), **Supp. XI:** 155

Post Oaks and Sand Roughs (Howard), **Supp. XXVII:** 116

Postrel, Virginia, **Supp. XIV:** 298, 311

"Postscript" (Du Bois), **Supp. II Part 1:** 173

"Postscript" (Nye), **Supp. XIII:** 287

Postsouthern Sense of Place, The (Bone), **Supp. XXII:** 247

"Potato" (Wilbur), **Supp. III Part 2:** 545

"Potatoes' Dance, The" (Lindsay), **Supp. I Part 2:** 394

Pot of Earth, The (MacLeish), **III:** 5, 6–8, 10, 12, 18

Potok, Chaim, **Supp. XXVI:** 124

"Pot Roast" (Strand), **Supp. IV Part 2:** 629

Potshot (Parker), **Supp. XIX:** 185

Pot Shots at Poetry (Francis), **Supp. IX:** **83–84**

Potter, Beatrix, **Supp. I Part 2:** 656; **Supp. XVI:** 100

Potter, Stephen, **IV:** 430

Potter's House, The (Stegner), **Supp. IV Part 2:** 598, 606

Poulenc, Francis, **Supp. IV Part 1:** 81

Poulin, Al, Jr., **Supp. IX:** 272; **Supp. XI:** 259

Pound, Ezra, **I:** 49, 58, 60, 66, 68, 69, 105, 236, 243, 256, 384, 403, 428, 429, 475, 476, 482, 487, 521, 578; **II:** 26, 55, 168, 263, 316, 371, 376, 513, 517, 520, 526, 528, 529, 530; **III:** 2, 5, 8, 9, 13–14, 17, 174, 194, 196, 278, 430, 453, **456–479,** 492, 504, 511, 523, 524, 527, 575–576, 586, 590; **IV:** 27, 28, 407, 415, 416, 433, 446; **Retro. Supp. I:** 51, 52, 55, 58, 59, 63, 82, 89, 127, 140, 171, 177, 178, 198, 216, **283–294,** 298, 299, 359, 411, 412, 413, 414, 417, 418, 419, 420, 423, 426, 427, 430, 431; **Retro. Supp. II:** 178, 183, 189, 326; **Supp. I Part 1:** 253, 255–258, 261–268, 272, 274; **Supp. I Part 2:** 387, 721; **Supp. II Part 1:** 1, 8, 20, 30, 91, 136; **Supp. III Part 1:** 48, 63, 64, 73, 105, 146, 225, 271; **Supp. III Part 2:** 542, **609–617,** 619, 620, 622, 625, 626, 628, 631; **Supp. IV Part 1:** 153, 314; **Supp. IX:** 291; **Supp. V:** 331, 338, 340, 343, 345; **Supp. VIII:** 39, 105, 195, 205, 271, 290, 291, 292, 303; **Supp. X:** 24, 36, 112, 120, 122; **Supp. XII:** 97; **Supp. XIV:** 11, 55, 83, 272, 284, 286, 287, 347; **Supp. XIX:** 42; **Supp. XV:** 20, 42, 43, 51, 93, 161, 181, 297, 298, 299, 301, 302, 306; **Supp. XVI:** 47, 282; **Supp. XVII:** 111, 226–227; **Supp. XXI:** 33; **Supp. XXII:** 165; **Supp. XXIII:** 26, 166, 174; **Supp. XXIV:** 37; **Supp. XXVI:** 143, 144, 224, 226; **Supp. XXVII:** 261, 284, 287, 288

Pound, Louise, **Retro. Supp. I:** 4; **Supp. XV:** 137

Pound, T. S., **I:** 428

"Pound Reweighed" (Cowley), **Supp. II Part 1:** 143

Powell, Anthony, **Supp. XIX:** 131; **Supp. XVIII:** 136, 146

Powell, Betty, **Retro. Supp. II:** 140

Powell, D. A., **Supp. XXIII:** 221

Powell, Dawn, **Supp. IV Part 2:** 678, 682; **Supp. XIX:** 143

Powell, Dick, **Supp. IX:** 250

Powell, John Wesley, **Supp. IV Part 2:** 598, 604, 611

Powell, Lawrence Clark, **III:** 189

Powell, Margaret K., **Supp. XXIV:** 170

Powell, William, **Supp. IV Part 1:** 355

"Power" (Corso), **Supp. XII:** 117, 126, 127, **128**

"Power" (Emerson), **II:** 2, 3

"Power" (Rich), **Supp. I Part 2:** 569

Power, Samantha, **Supp. XXIII:** 25, 26, 27

"Power and Light" (Dickey), **Supp. IV Part 1:** 182

Power and the Glory, The (Greene), **III:** 556

"Powerhouse" (Welty), **Retro. Supp. I:** 343, 346

"Power Never Dominion" (Rukeyser), **Supp. VI:** 281

"Power of Fancy, The" (Freneau), **Supp. II Part 1:** 255

Power of Myth, The (Campbell), **Supp. IX:** 245

"Power of Prayer, The" (Lanier), **Supp. I Part 1:** 357

"Power of Stories, The" (Sanders), **Supp. XVI:** 278

"Power of Suggestion" (Auchincloss), **Supp. IV Part 1:** 33

Power of Sympathy, The (W. H. Brown), **Supp. II Part 1:** 74; **Supp. XXV:** 38

Power Politics (Atwood), **Supp. XIII:** 20, 33–34, 35

Powers, Catherine A., **Supp. XXII:** 217

Powers, J. F., **Supp. V:** 319; **Supp. XVII:** 43

Powers, Kim, **Supp. VIII:** 329, 340

Powers, Richard, **Supp. IX: 207–225; Supp. XVII:** 183; **Supp. XX:** 93; **Supp. XXII:** 49; **Supp. XXIV:** 131

Powers of Attorney (Auchincloss), **Supp. IV Part 1:** 31, 32, 33

"Powers of Darkness" (Wharton), **Retro. Supp. I:** 379

Powless, Peter, **Supp. XXVI:** 87

Powys, John Cowper, **Supp. I Part 2:** 454, 476; **Supp. IX:** 135

Poynton, Jerome, **Supp. XIV:** 147, 150

Pozorski, Aimee L., **Supp. XXII:** 160, 166

Practical Agitation (Chapman), **Supp. XIV:** 41

"Practical Application in This Life, by Men as Social and Intellectual Beings, of the Certainty of a Future State, The" (Very), **Supp. XXV:** 240

Practical Criticism: A Study of Literary Judgment (Richards), **Supp. XIV:** 3, 16

Practical Magic (film), **Supp. X:** 80

Practical Magic (Hoffman), **Supp. X:** 78, 82, **88–89**

"Practical Methods of Meditation, The" (Dawson), **IV:** 151

Practical Navigator, The (Bowditch), **Supp. I Part 2:** 482

Practice of Perspective, The (Dubreuil), **Supp. IV Part 2:** 425

Practice of Reading, The (Donoghue), **Supp. VIII:** 189

Pragmatism (W. James), **Supp. XXVII:** 33

Pragmatism: A New Name for Some Old Ways of Thinking (James), **II:** 352

"Pragmatism's Conception of Truth" (James), **Supp. XIV:** 40

Prague Orgy, The (P. Roth), **Retro. Supp. II:** 280

"Praire, The" (Clampitt), **Supp. IX:** 42

"Prairie" (Sandburg), **III:** 583, 584

Prairie, The (Cooper), **I:** 339, 342

"Prairie Birthday" (Leopold), **Supp. XIV:** 185

Prairie Home Companion, A (Keillor, radio program), **Supp. XIII:** 274; **Supp. XVI:** 169–171, 173–178

Prairie Home Morning Show, A (Keillor, radio program), **Supp. XVI:** 171

"Prairie Life, A Citizen Speaks" (Dunn), **Supp. XI:** 145

"Prairies, The" (Bryant), **Supp. I Part 1:** 157, 162, 163, 166

Praise (Hass), **Supp. VI:** 104–105, 106

"Praise for an Urn" (Crane), **I:** 388

"Praise for Sick Women" (Snyder), **Supp. VIII:** 294

"Praise in Summer" (Wilbur), **Supp. III Part 2:** 546–548, 560, 562

"Praise of a Palmtree" (Levertov), **Supp. III Part 1:** 284

"Praise of the Committee" (Rukeyser), **Supp. VI:** 278

"Praises, The" (Goldbarth), **Supp. XII:** 185

"Praises, The" (Olson), **Supp. II Part 2:** 558, 560, 563, 564

Praises and Dispraises (Des Pres), **Supp. X:** 120

Praisesong for the Widow (Marshall), **Supp. IV Part 1:** 14; **Supp. XI:** 18, 276, 278, **284–286**, 287; **Supp. XX: 154**

"Praise to the End!" (Roethke), **III:** 529, 532, 539

Prajadhipok, King of Siam, **I:** 522

Prater Violet (Isherwood), **Supp. XIV: 164–166,** 169–170, 171

Pratt, Anna (Anna Alcott), **Supp. I Part 1:** 33

Pratt, Louis H., **Retro. Supp. II:** 6

Pratt, Mary Louise, **Retro. Supp. II:** 48

Pratt, Parley, **Supp. IV Part 2:** 603

"Prattler" (newspaper column), **I:** 207

"Prattler, The" (Bierce), **I:** 196

"Prayer" (Gioia), **Supp. XV:** 117

"Prayer" (Olds), **Supp. X:** 204

"Prayer" (Peacock), **Supp. XIX:** 198, 199, 200

"Prayer" (Toomer), **Supp. IX:** 318

"Prayer, A" (Kushner), **Supp. IX: 134**

"Prayer for Columbus" (Whitman), **IV:** 348

"Prayer for My Daughter" (Yeats), **II:** 598

"Prayer for My Grandfather to Our Lady, A" (R. Lowell), **II:** 541–542

"Prayer for my Son" (C. Frost), **Supp. XV:** 98–99

"Prayer for Our Daughters" (Jarman), **Supp. XVII:** 120

Prayer for Owen Meany, A (Irving), **Supp. VI:** 164, 165, 166, **175–176**

"PRAYER FOR SAVING" (Baraka), **Supp. II Part 1:** 52–53

Prayer for the Dying, A (O'Nan), **Supp. XXV:** 141, 142, 144, 145–146, 148

"Prayer in Spring, A" (Frost), **II:** 153, 164

"Prayer Meeting" (Di Piero), **Supp. XIX:** 46, 47

"Prayer on All Saint's Day" (Cowley), **Supp. II Part 1:** 138, 153

Prayers for Dark People (Du Bois), **Supp. II Part 1:** 186

"Prayer to Hermes" (Creeley), **Supp. IV Part 1:** 156, 157

"Prayer to Masks" (Senghor), **Supp. IV Part 1:** 16

"Prayer to the Child of Prague" (Salinas), **Supp. XIII:** 327

"Prayer to the Good Poet" (Wright), **Supp. III Part 2:** 603

"Prayer to the Pacific" (Silko), **Supp. IV Part 2:** 560

"Prayer to the Verb" (Davison), **Supp. XXVI:** 79

Praying Wrong (Davison), **Supp. XXVI:** 66, 76–77

"Pray without Ceasing" (Emerson), **II:** 9–10

Praz, Mario, **IV:** 430

"Preacher, The" (Whittier), **Supp. I Part 2:** 698–699

Preacher and the Slave, The (Stegner), **Supp. IV Part 2:** 599, 608, 609

"Preacher Is Called to Testify for the Accused, The" (Rash), **Supp. XXVII:** 219

"Preacher Who Takes Up Serpents Laments the Presence of Skeptics in His Church, A" (Rash), **Supp. XXVII:** 219

Precaution (Cooper), **I:** 337, 339

"Precautions"(Karyotakis, trans. Hadas), **Supp. XXIII:** 125

"Preconceptions of Economic Science, The" (Veblen), **Supp. I Part 2:** 634

Predecessors, Et Cetera (Clampitt), **Supp. IX:** 37

"Predicament, A" (Poe), **Retro. Supp. II:** 273

Predilections (Moore), **III:** 194

Prefaces and Prejudices (Mencken), **III:** 99, 104, 106, 119

Preface to a Twenty Volume Suicide Note. . . . (Baraka), **Supp. II Part 1:** 31, 33–34, 51, 61

"Preference" (Wylie), **Supp. I Part 2:** 713

"Prejudice against the Past, The" (Moore), **IV:** 91

Prejudices (Mencken), **Supp. I Part 2:** 630

Prejudices: A Selection (Farrell, ed.), **III:** 116

Prejudices: First Series (Mencken), **III:** 105

"Preliminary Remarks on the Poetry in the First Person" (Wright), **Supp. XV:** 339

Prell (exhibition, Brainard), **Supp. XXVII:** 21

Prelude, A: Landscapes, Characters and Conversations from the Earlier Years of My Life (Wilson), **IV:** 426, 427, 430, 434, 445

Prelude, The (Wordsworth), **III:** 528; **IV:** 331, 343; **Supp. I Part 2:** 416, 676; **Supp. XI:** 248

Prelude and Liebestod (McNally), **Supp. XIII:** 201

"Preludes" (Eliot), **I:** 573, 576, 577; **Retro. Supp. I:** 55; **Supp. IV Part 2:** 436

Preludes for Memnon (Aiken), **I:** 59, 65

Preludes from Memnon (Aiken), **Supp. X:** 50

"Prelude to an Evening" (Ransom), **III:** 491, 492–493

Prelude to Darkness (Salinas), **Supp. XIII:** 311, **318–319,** 320

"Prelude to the Present" (Mumford), **Supp. II Part 2:** 471

"Premature Burial, The" (Poe), **III:** 415, 416, 418; **Retro. Supp. II:** 270

"Premeditations"(Schott), **Supp. XXIII:** 247

Preminger, Otto, **Supp. IX:** 3, 9; **Supp. XX:** 246–247

"Premonition" (Hay), **Supp. XIV:** 122

"Premonitions of the Bread Line" (Komunyakaa), **Supp. XIII:** 114, 115

Prenshaw, Peggy Whitman, **Supp. X:** 229

"Preparations" (Silko), **Supp. IV Part 2:** 560

Preparatory Meditations (Taylor), **IV:** 145, 148, 149, 150, 152, 153, 154–155, 164, 165

"Prepare" (Carruth), **Supp. XVI:** 59

Prepositions: The Collected Critical Essays of Louis Zukofsky (Zukofsky), **Supp. III Part 2:** 630

Prescott, Anne, **Supp. IV Part 1:** 299

Prescott, Orville, **Supp. IV Part 2:** 680; **Supp. XI:** 340; **Supp. XXIII:** 13

Prescott, Peter, **Supp. X:** 83

Prescott, Peter S., **Supp. XVI:** 212

Prescott, William, **Retro. Supp. I:** 123

Prescott, William Hickling, **II:** 9, 310, 313–314; **IV:** 309; **Supp. I Part 2:** 414, 479, 493, 494

"Prescription of Painful Ends" (Jeffers), **Supp. II Part 2:** 424

"Presence, The" (Gordon), **II:** 199, 200

"Presence, The" (Kumin), **Supp. IV Part 2:** 445, 455

Presence and Desire: Essays on Gender, Sexuality, Performance (Dolan), **Supp. XV:** 327

"Presence of Others, The" (Kenyon), **Supp. VII:** 164

Presences (Taylor), **Supp. V:** 325

"Present Age, The" (Emerson), **II:** 11–12

Present Danger, The: Do We Have the Will to Reverse the Decline of American Power? (Podhoretz), **Supp. VIII:** 241

"Present for the Boy, A" (Swados), **Supp. XIX:** 259

Present for Young Ladies, A (Rowson), **Supp. XV:** 245

"Present Hour" (Sandburg), **III:** 593–594

Presenting Walter Dean Myers (Bishop), **Supp. XXVII:** 203

Present Philosophical Tendencies (Perry), **I:** 224

"Present State of Ethical Philosophy, The" (Emerson), **II:** 9

"Present State of Poetry, The" (Schwartz), **Supp. II Part 2:** 666

"Preservation of Innocence" (Baldwin), **Supp. I Part 1:** 51

"Preserving Wildness" (Berry), **Supp. X:** 28, 29, 32

"President and Other Intellectuals, The" (Kazin), **Supp. VIII:** 104

Presidential Papers, The (Mailer), **III:** 35, 37–38, 42, 45; **Retro. Supp. II:** 203, 204, 206

"Presidents" (Merwin), **Supp. III Part 1:** 351

Presnell, Robert, Sr., **Supp. XIII:** 166

Pressley, Nelson, **Supp. XVIII:** 37–38

"PRES SPOKE IN A LANGUAGE" (Baraka), **Supp. II Part 1:** 60

"Presto Manifesto" (Stallings), **Supp. XXV:** 227

Presumed Innocent (Turow), 217; **Supp. XVII:** 214–216, 223

Pretending to Be Asleep (Davison), **Supp. XXVI:** 65, 71–72

"Pretext, The" (Wharton), **Retro. Supp. I:** 371

Pretty Baby (film), **Supp. XXI:** 252

Pretty Boy Floyd (McMurtry), **Supp. V:** 231

"Pretty Girl, The" (Dubus), **Supp. VII:** 87–88

"Pretty Mouth and Green My Eyes" (Salinger), **III:** 560

"Previous Condition" (Baldwin), **Supp. I Part 1:** 51, 55, 63

"Previous Tenant, The" (Simpson), **Supp. IX:** 278–279

Prevost, Verbie Lovorn, **Supp. XXI:** 45

Priaulx, Allan, **Supp. XI:** 228

Price, Alan, **Retro. Supp. I:** 377

Price, E. Hoffman, **Supp. XXV:** 114

Price, Novalyne, **Supp. XXVII:** 117

Price, Reynolds, **Supp. IX:** 256, 257; **Supp. VI:** 253–270

Price, Richard, **II:** 9; **Supp. I Part 2:** 522; **Supp. XX:** 85

Price, The (A. Miller), **III:** 165–166

"Price Is Right, The" (Skloot), **Supp. XX:** 198–199

"Price of Poetry, The" (Biss), **Supp. XXVI:** 48

"Price of the Harness, The" (Crane), **I:** 414

Pricksongs & Descants; Fictions (Coover), **Supp. V:** 39, 42, 43, 49, 50

"Pride" (Hughes), **Supp. I Part 1:** 331

Pride and Prejudice (Austen), **II:** 290; **Supp. XXVI:** 117–118

Prideaux, Tom, **Supp. IV Part 2:** 574, 590

"Priesthood, The" (Winters), **Supp. II Part 2:** 786

Priestly, Joseph, **Supp. I Part 2:** 522

Primary Colors, The (A. Theroux), **Supp. VIII:** 312

"Primary Ground, A" (Rich), **Supp. I Part 2:** 563

"Prime" (Auden), **Supp. II Part 1:** 22

"Primer Class" (Bishop), **Retro. Supp. II:** 38, 51

Primer for Blacks (Brooks), **Supp. III Part 1:** 85

Primer for Combat (Boyle), **Supp. XXIV:** 62

"Primer for the Nuclear Age" (Dove), **Supp. IV Part 1:** 246

Primer mensaje a la América Hispana (W. Frank), **Supp. XX:** 76

Primer of Ignorance, A (Blackmur), **Supp. II Part 1:** 91

Prime-Stevenson, Edward Irenaeus, **Supp. XX:** 235

Primitive (Oppen), **Supp. XXVI:** 237

Primitive, The (C. Himes), **Supp. XVI:** 139, **141–142**

"Primitive Black Man, The" (Du Bois), **Supp. II Part 1:** 176

"Primitive Like an Orb, A" (Stevens), **IV:** 89; **Retro. Supp. I:** 309

Primitive People (Prose), **Supp. XVI:** 255, 256, 257

"Primitive Singing" (Lindsay), **Supp. I Part 2:** 389–390

Primitivism and Decadence (Winters), **Supp. II Part 2:** 786, 803–807, 812

Primrose, Archibald Philip, **Supp. XX:** 230

Prince, F. T., **Supp. XXIV:** 45

Prince, Richard, **Supp. XII:** 4

"Prince, The" (Jarrell), **II:** 379

"Prince, The" (Winters), **Supp. II Part 2:** 802

Prince and the Pauper, The (Twain), **IV:** 200–201, 206

Prince Hagen (Sinclair), **Supp. V:** 280

Prince of a Fellow, A (Hearon), **Supp. VIII:** 58, **62–63**

Princess, The (Tennyson), **Supp. I Part 2:** 410

Princess and the Goblins, The (Macdonald), **Supp. XIII:** 75

Princess Casamassima, The (James), **II:** 276, 291; **IV:** 202; **Retro. Supp. I:** 216, 221, 222, 225, **226–227**

"Princess Casamassima, The" (Trilling), **Supp. III Part 2:** 502, 503

Princess of Arcady, A (Henry), **Retro. Supp. II:** 97

"Principles" (Du Bois), **Supp. II Part 1:** 172

Principles of Literary Criticism (Richards), **I:** 274; **Supp. I Part 1:** 264; **Supp. XIV:** 3

Principles of Psychology, The (James), **II:** 321, 350–352, 353, 354, 357, 362, 363–364; **IV:** 28, 29, 32, 37

Principles of Psychology, The (W. James), **Supp. XVII:** 97

Principles of Zoölogy (Agassiz), **Supp. I Part 1:** 312

Prior, Sir James, **II:** 315

Prior, Matthew, **II:** 111; **III:** 521

"Prison, The" (Malamud), **Supp. I Part 2:** 431, 437

"Prisoned Love" (Boyce), **Supp. XXI:** 9

"Prisoner of Ours, The" (Weigl), **Supp. XIX:** 288

Prisoner of Second Avenue, The (Simon), **Supp. IV Part 2:** 583, 584

Prisoner of Sex, The (Mailer), **III:** 46; **Retro. Supp. II:** 206

Prisoner of Zenda, The (film), **Supp. I Part 2:** 615

Prisoner's Dilemma (Powers), **Supp. IX:** 212, **214–216,** 221

Prison Memoirs of an Anarchist (A. Berkman), **Supp. XVII:** 103–104

Pritchard, William, **Supp. XVI:** 71

Pritchard, William H., **Retro. Supp. I:** 131, 141; **Supp. IV Part 1:** 285; **Supp. IV Part 2:** 642; **Supp. XI:** 326

Pritchett, V. S., **II:** 587; **Supp. II Part 1:** 143; **Supp. VIII:** 171; **Supp. XIII:** 168

Pritikin, Renny, **Supp. XXIV:** 40

"Privatation and Publication" (Cowley), **Supp. II Part 1:** 149

Private Contentment (Price), **Supp. VI:** 263

"Private History of a Campaign That Failed" (Twain), **IV:** 195

Private I, The: Privacy in a Public World (Peacock, ed.), **Supp. XIX:** 193, 203

Private Life of Axie Reed, The (Knowles), **Supp. XII:** 249

Private Line (Major), **Supp. XXII:** 174

"Private Man Confronts His Vulgarities at Dawn, A" (Dunn), **Supp. XI:** 146

Private Memoirs and Confessions of a Justified Sinner, The (Hogg), **Supp. IX:** 276

"Private Property and the Common Wealth" (Berry), **Supp. X:** 25

Private Snafu series (Geisel), **Supp. XVI:** 102

"Private Theatricals" (Howells), **II:** 280

Private Women, Public Stage: Literary Domesticity in Nineteenth-Century America (Kelley), **Supp. XVIII:** 257

"Privilege" (Munro), **Supp. XXVII:** 186, 187

Privilege, The (Kumin), **Supp. IV Part 2:** 442–444, 451

Prize Stories 1918 : The O. Henry Awards, **Supp. XVI:** 16

"Probe" (Ryan as Quin), **Supp. XVIII:** 229

"Probing the Dark" (Komunyakaa), **Supp. XIII:** 131

"Problem from Hell, A": America and the Age of Genocide (Power), **Supp. XXIII:** 25, 27–28

"Problem from Milton, A" (Wilbur), **Supp. III Part 2:** 550

"Problem of Anxiety, The" (Koch), **Supp. XV:** 183

"Problem of Being, The" (James), **II:** 360

Problem of Classification in the Theory of Value, The (Locke), **Supp. XIV:** 199

"Problem of Evil into Cocoon" (Taggard), **Supp. XXII:** 284

"Problem of Housing the Negro, The" (Du Bois), **Supp. II Part 1:** 168

"Problem of the Religious Novel, The" (Isherwood), **Supp. XIV:** 172

Problems and Other Stories (Updike), **Retro. Supp. I:** 322, 329

Problems of Dostoevsky's Poetics (Bakhtin), **Supp. XXII:** 259

"Problem Solving" (Goldbarth), **Supp. XII:** 185

Procedures for Underground (Atwood), **Supp. XIII:** 33

"Procedures for Underground" (Atwood), **Supp. XIII:** 33

Process (Boyle), **Supp. XXIV:** 51

Procession, The (al-Mawákib) (Gibran), **Supp. XX: 116, 124**

Processional (Lawson), **I:** 479

"Procession at Candlemas, A" (Clampitt), **Supp. IX:** 41

"Proclamation" (Saunders), **Supp. XIX:** 235

Proclus, **Retro. Supp. I:** 247

"Prodigal" (Ammons), **Supp. VII:** 29

"Prodigal" (Hoffman), **Supp. XVIII:** 86

"Prodigal, The" (Bishop), **Supp. I Part 1:** 90, 92

Prodigal Parents, The (Lewis), **II:** 454–455

"Prodigy" (Simic), **Supp. VIII:** 278

Producers, The (film, M. Brooks), **Supp. XVII:** 45

"Proem" (Crane), **I:** 397

"Proem, The: By the Carpenter" (O. Henry), **Supp. II Part 1:** 409

"Professions for Women" (Woolf), **Supp. XIII:** 305

"Professor" (Hughes), **Supp. I Part 1:** 330

"Professor, The" (Bourne), **I:** 223

Professor at the Breakfast Table, The (Holmes), **Supp. I Part 1:** 313, 316

"Professor Clark's Economics" (Veblen), **Supp. I Part 2:** 634

Professor of Desire, The (P. Roth), **Retro. Supp. II:** 288; **Supp. III Part 2:** 403, 418–420

Professor's House, The (Cather), **I:** 325–336; **Retro. Supp. I:** 16

"Professor Veblen" (Mencken), **Supp. I Part 2:** 630

Proffer, Carl R., **Supp. VIII:** 22

Profile Makers, The (Bierds), **Supp. XVII:** 29, **30–32,** 33

"Profile of the Tenderloin Street Prostitute, A" (Vollmann), **Supp. XVII:** 230

Profits of Religion, The (Sinclair), **Supp. V:** 276

"Prognosis" (Warren), **IV:** 245

"Progress" (F. Wright), **Supp. XVII:** 247

Progress of Love, The (Munro), **Supp. XXVII:** 189

"Progress of Love, The" (Munro), **Supp. XXVII:** 189

"Progress Report" (Simic), **Supp. VIII:** 278

"Project for a Trip to China" (Sontag), **Supp. II Part 2:** 454, 469

"Project for *The Ambassadors*" (James), **Retro. Supp. I:** 229

"Projection" (Nemerov), **III:** 275

"Projective Verse" (Olson), **Supp. III Part 1:** 30; **Supp. III Part 2:** 555, 556, 557, 624; **Supp. IV Part 1:** 139, 153; **Supp. VIII:** 290

"Projector, The" (Baker), **Supp. XIII:** 53, 55

Prokofiev, Sergey Sergeyevich, **Supp. IV Part 1:** 81

"Prolegomena, Section 1" (Pound), **Supp. III Part 2:** 615–616

"Prolegomena, Section 2" (Pound), **Supp. III Part 2:** 616

"Prolegomenon to a Biography of Mailer" (Lucid), **Retro. Supp. II:** 195

Proletarian Literature in the United States (Hicks), **Supp. I Part 2: 609–610; Supp. XXVI:** 134

"Prologue" (MacLeish), **III:** 8, 14

Prologue, for Full Chorus of Mixed Voices and Orchestra (Taggard and Schuman), **Supp. XXII:** 283

"Prologue to a Life" (D. West), **Supp. XVIII:** 280

"Prologue to Our Time" (Mumford), **Supp. III Part 2:** 473

"Prometheus" (Longfellow), **II:** 494

Prometheus Bound (R. Lowell), **II:** 543, 544, 545, 555

Promise, The (Buck), **Supp. II Part 1:** 124

"Promise, The" (Olds), **Supp. X:** 213

"Promise and Fulfillment" (D. West), **Supp. XVIII:** 278

Promised Land (Parker), **Supp. XIX:** 183, 184, 190

Promised Land, The (M. Antin), **Supp. IX:** 227; **Supp. XVI:** 148, 149; **Supp. XX: 1, 2, 3, 4–9,** 11

Promised Land, The (Porter), **III:** 447

"Promised Land, The" (R. Fisher), **Supp. XIX:** 72

Promised Lands (Sontag), **Supp. III Part 2:** 452

Promise of American Life, The (Croly), **I:** 229

"Promise of Blue Horses, The" (Harjo), **Supp. XII:** 228

Promise of Rest, The (Price), **Supp. VI:** 262, 266

Promises (Warren), **Supp. XIV:** 15

Promises, Promises (musical), **Supp. IV Part 2:** 575

Promises: Poems 1954–1956 (Warren), **IV:** 244–245, 249, 252

"Promise This When You Be Dying" (Dickinson), **Retro. Supp. I:** 44, 46

"Pronoun Variations"(Hadas), **Supp. XXIII:** 120

Pronzini, Bill, **Supp. XXVI:** 277, 278, 282

Proof, The (Winters), **Supp. II Part 2:** 786, 791, 792–794

"Proofreader, The" (Huddle), **Supp. XXVI:** 151, 152

Proofs and Theories: Essays on Poetry (Glück), **Supp. V:** 77, 79, 92; **Supp. XIV:** 269

"Propaganda of History, The" (Du Bois), **Supp. II Part 1:** 182

Propertius, Sextus, **III:** 467; **Retro. Supp. II:** 187; **Supp. XII:** 2

Property Of: A Novel (Hoffman), **Supp. X:** 77, 79, **80–82**

"Property of Loss" (W. V. Davis), **Supp. XXI:** 95

"Prophecy of Samuel Sewall, The" (Whittier), **Supp. I Part 2:** 699

Prophet, The (Asch), **Supp. XXIII:** 7

Prophet, The (Gibran), **Supp. XX: 113, 115, 119–121, 126**

"Prophet, The" (Notley), **Supp. XXII:** 229

"Prophet, The" (Very), **Supp. XXV:** 248–249

"Prophet and the Child, The" (Gibran), **Supp. XX: 123**

Propheteers, The (Apple), **Supp. XVII:** 6–7

"Prophetic Pictures, The" (Hawthorne), **II:** 227

"Proportion" (A. Lowell) ?/ ?/, **II:** 525

"Proposal" (Carver), **Supp. III Part 1:** 149

Proposals Relating to the Education of Youth in Pensilvania (Franklin), **II:** 113

"Proposed New Version of the Bible" (Franklin), **II:** 110

Prose, Francine, **Supp. XII:** 333; **Supp. XIX:** 209; **Supp. XVI: 249–264; Supp. XXIII:** 300; **Supp. XXVI:** 121, 130

"Prose for Departure" (Merrill), **Supp. III Part 1:** 336

Prose Pieces (Bynner), **Supp. XV:** 52

"Prose Poem as an Evolving Form, The" (R. Bly), **Supp. IV Part 1:** 64

"Proserpina and the Devil" (Wilder), **IV:** 358

"Prosody" (Espaillat), **Supp. XXI:** 102

"Prosody" (Shapiro), **Supp. II Part 2:** 710

Prospect before Us, The (Dos Passos), **I:** 491

"Prospective Immigrants Please Note" (Rich), **Supp. I Part 2:** 555

Prospect of Peace, The (Barlow), **Supp. II Part 1:** 67, 68, 75

Prospects of Literature, The (L. P. Smith), **Supp. XIV:** 343

Prospects on the Rubicon (Paine), **Supp. I Part 2:** 510–511

Prospectus of a National Institution, to Be Established in the United States (Barlow), **Supp. II Part 1:** 80, 82

Prospice (Browning), **IV:** 366

"Protestant Easter" (Sexton), **Supp. II Part 2:** 684

"Prothalamion" (Schwartz), **Supp. II Part 2:** 649, 652

"Prothalamion" (Spenser), **Retro. Supp. I:** 62

Proud, Robert, **Supp. I Part 1:** 125

"Proud Farmer, The" (Lindsay), **Supp. I Part 2:** 381

Proud Flesh (Humphrey), **Supp. IX:** 94, 95, 96, **102–103,** 104, 105, 109

"Proud Flesh" (Warren), **IV:** 243

Proud Highway, The (Thompson), **Supp. XXIV:** 283

Proud Lady (Boyce), **Supp. XXI:** 7, 12

"Proud Lady" (Wylie), **Supp. I Part 2:** 711–712

Proulx, Annie, **Supp. VII: 249–267; Supp. XXIV:** 245, 251; **Supp. XXVI:** 186

Proust, Marcel, **I:** 89, 319, 327, 377, 461; **II:** 377, 514, 606; **III:** 174, 181, 184, 244–245, 259, 471; **IV:** 32, 201, 237, 301, 312, 328, 359, 428, 431, 434, 439, 443, 466, 467; **Retro. Supp. I:** 75, 89, 169, 335; **Supp. III Part 1:** 10, 12, 14, 15; **Supp. IV Part 2:** 600; **Supp. IX:** 211; **Supp. VIII:** 103; **Supp. X:** 193, 194; **Supp. XII:** 289; **Supp. XIV:** 24, 83, 95; **Supp. XVI:** 295; **Supp. XXI:** 231; **Supp. XXIII:** 122

Proverbs, **Supp. X:** 45

"Proverbs" (Jarman), **Supp. XVII:** 118

"Providence" (Komunyakaa), **Supp. XIII:** 132

"Provident Woman, A" (Boyce), **Supp. XXI:** 10

"Provincetown Postcards" (F. Wright), **Supp. XVII:** 244

"Provincia deserta" (Pound), **Retro. Supp. I:** 289

"Provisional Remarks on Being / A Poet / of Arkansas" (Wright), **Supp. XV:** 337

"Prue" (Munro), **Supp. XXVII:** 188

Pruette, Lorine, **Supp. IV Part 2:** 522

Prufrock and Other Observations (Eliot), **I:** 569–570, 571, 573, 574, 576–577, 583, 584, 585; **Retro. Supp. I:** 59, 62

"Prufrock's Perivigilium" (T. S. Eliot), **Retro. Supp. I:** 57

Pryor, Richard, **Supp. XIII:** 343

Pryse, Marjorie, **Retro. Supp. II:** 139, 146; **Supp. XXV:** 285

"Psalm" (Ginsberg), **Supp. II Part 1:** 312

"Psalm" (Oppen), **Supp. XXVI:** 232–233, 235

"Psalm" (Simic), **Supp. VIII:** 282

"Psalm, A, or Supplication for mercy, and confession of Sin, addressed to the Author of Life, in the Odjibway-Alqonquin tongue"(J. Schoolcraft), **Supp. XXIII:** 232

"Psalm and Lament" (Justice), **Supp. VII:** 116, 117–118, 120–122, 124

"Psalm for Pinhook" (Ray), **Supp. XVIII:** 202

"Psalm Jew, The"(Asch). *See Salvation* (Asch)

"Psalm of Life, A" (Longfellow), **II:** 489, 496; **Retro. Supp. II:** 164, 168, 169; **Supp. I Part 2:** 409

"Psalm of the West" (Lanier), **Supp. I Part 1:** 362, 364

"Psalm: Our Fathers" (Merwin), **Supp. III Part 1:** 350

Psalms (biblical book), **I:** 83; **II:** 168, 232; **Retro. Supp. I:** 62; **Supp. I Part 1:** 125

Psalms, Hymns, and Spiritual Songs of the Rev. Isaac Watts, The (Worcester, ed.), **I:** 458

Psychiatric Novels of Oliver Wendell Holmes, The (Oberndorf), **Supp. I Part 1:** 315

"Psychology and Form" (Burke), **I:** 270

Psychology: Briefer Course (James), **II:** 351–352

Psychology of Art (Malraux), **IV:** 434

Psychology of Insanity, The (Hart), **I:** 241–242, 248–250

Psychopathia Sexualis (Shanley), **Supp. XIV:** 316, **329**

Psychophysiks (Fechner), **II:** 358

Pterodactyls (Silver), **Supp. XXIV: 268–270**

Ptomaine Street (Wells), **Supp. XXVI:** 275

"Pu-239" (Kalfus), **Supp. XVII:** 50

"Publication is the Auction" (Dickinson), **Retro. Supp. I:** 31

"Public Bath, The" (Snyder), **Supp. VIII:** 298

Public Burning, The (Coover), **Supp. IV Part 1:** 388; **Supp. V:** 44, 45, 46–47, 48, 51, 52; **Supp. XVII:** 6

"Public Burning of Julius and Ethel Rosenberg, The: An Historical Romance" (Coover), **Supp. V:** 44

"Public Figure" (Hay), **Supp. XIV:** 124

"Public Garden, The" (R. Lowell), **II:** 550

Public Good (Paine), **Supp. I Part 2:** 509–510

Public Poetry of Robert Lowell, The (Cosgrave), **Retro. Supp. II:** 185

"Public & Private" (column, Quindlen), **Supp. XVII:** 165, 167, 169–170

Public Speech: Poems (MacLeish), **III:** 15–16

Public Spirit (Savage), **II:** 111

"Public Woman, A" (Cliff), **Supp. XXII:** 76

Puccini, Giacomo, **Supp. XXI:** 150, 151

"Puck" (Monette), **Supp. X:** 157–158

Pudd'nhead Wilson (Twain), **I:** 197

"Pudd'nhead Wilson's Calendar" (Twain), **I:** 197

"Pueblo Revolt, The" (Sando), **Supp. IV Part 2:** 510

Puella (Dickey), **Supp. IV Part 1:** 178, 185

Pulitzer, Alfred, **Retro. Supp. I:** 257

Pull Down Vanity (Fiedler), **Supp. XIII:** 103

Pullman, George, **Supp. I Part 1:** 9

"Pullman Car Hiawatha" (Wilder), **IV:** 365–366

Pull My Daisy (film), **Supp. XII:** 126–127

"Pulp Cutters' Nativity, A" (Budbill), **Supp. XIX:** 9

"Pulpit and the Pew, The" (Holmes), **Supp. I Part 1:** 302

"Pulse-Beats and Pen-Strokes" (Sandburg), **III:** 579

"Pump, The" (Humphrey), **Supp. IX:** 101

Pump House Gang, The (Wolfe), **Supp. III Part 2:** 575, 578, 580, 581

Punch, Brothers, Punch and Other Sketches (Twain), **IV:** 200

Punch: The Immortal Liar, Documents in His History (Aiken), **I:** 57, 61

Punishment Without Vengeance (Vega; Merwin, trans.), **Supp. III Part 1:** 341, 347

"Pupil" (F. Barthelme), **Supp. XI:** 26

"Pupil, The" (H. James), **Supp. XX: 233**

"Pupil, The" (James), **II:** 331; **Retro. Supp. I:** 217, 219, 228

"Purchase" (Banks), **Supp. V:** 6

"Purchase of Some Golf Clubs, A" (O'Hara), **III:** 369

"Purdah" (Plath), **Supp. I Part 2:** 602

Purdy, Charles, **Supp. VIII:** 330

Purdy, James, **Supp. VII: 269–285**

Purdy, John Lloyd, **Supp. XXVI:** 101, 103, 105, 111

Purdy, Theodore, **Supp. VIII:** 153

Pure (C. Frost), **Supp. XV:** 93, **101–102,** 104, 106

"Pure" (C. Frost), **Supp. XV:** 101–102

"Pure and the Good, The: On Baseball and Backpaking" (Maclean), **Supp. XIV:** 222

"Pure Good of Theory, The" (Stevens), **Retro. Supp. I:** 310

Purgatorio (Dante), **III:** 182

"Purim Parade" (Espaillat), **Supp. XXI:** 108

Puritan Family (Morgan), **Supp. I Part 1:** 101

"Puritanical Pleasures" (Hardwick), **Supp. III Part 1:** 213–214

Puritan Origins of the American Self, The (Bercovitch), **Supp. I Part 1:** 99

Puritan Pronaos, The: Studies in the Intellectual Life of New England in the Seventeenth Century (Morison), **Supp. I Part 2:** 485

"Puritan Realism: *The Wide, Wide World* and *Robinson Crusoe*" (Kim), **Supp. XVIII:** 267

Puritans, The (P. Miller), **Supp. VIII:** 101

"Puritan's Ballad, The" (Wylie), **Supp. I Part 2:** 723

"Purloined Letter, The" (Poe), **Retro. Supp. II:** 271, 272

Purple Cane Road (Burke), **Supp. XIV:** 32, 33

Purple Decades, The (Wolfe), **Supp. III Part 2:** 584

"Purple Hat, The" (Welty), **IV:** 264

Purple Rose of Cairo, The (film; Allen), **Supp. XV:** 1, **9–10,** 12, 14

Purser, John T., **Supp. XIV:** 4

"Pursuit of Happiness" (Simpson), **Supp. IX:** 279

"Pursuit of Happiness, The" (Ashbery), **Supp. III Part 1:** 23

Pursuit of the Prodigal, The (Auchincloss), **Supp. IV Part 1:** 25

Pushcart at the Curb, A (Dos Passos), **I:** 478, 479

"Pushcart Man" (Hughes), **Supp. I Part 1:** 330

Pushcart Prize, XIII, The (Ford), **Supp. V:** 58

Pushcart Prize VII, The (Hendeson, ed.), **Supp. XVII:** 16

Pushcart Prize XIV, The (Henderson, ed.), **Supp. XVII:** 18

Pushcart Prize XX, The (Henderson, ed.), **Supp. XVII:** 20

"Pushing 100" (Mora), **Supp. XIII:** 215

Pushkin, Aleksander, **III:** 246, 261, 262; **Retro. Supp. I:** 266, 269; **Supp. XVI:** 188

Pussy, King of the Pirates (Acker), **Supp. XII:** 6–7

"Pussycat and the Expert Plumber Who Was a Man, The" (A. Miller), **III:** 146–147

Pussycat Fever (Acker), **Supp. XII:** 6

Putnam, George Haven, **Supp. XVIII:** 257, 260

Putnam, George P., **II:** 314; **Supp. XVIII:** 3–4, 14, 260

Putnam, Phelps, **I:** 288

Putnam, Samuel, **II:** 26; **III:** 479; **Supp. III Part 2:** 615

"Put Off the Wedding Five Times and Nobody Comes to It" (Sandburg), **III:** 586–587

Puttenham, George, **Supp. I Part 1:** 113

Puttermesser Papers, The (Ozick), **Supp. V:** 269

"Putting a Burden Down" (Peacock), **Supp. XIX:** 199

Putting It Together (Sondheim), **Supp. XXIV:** 124

"Putting on *Visit to a Small Planet*" (Vidal), **Supp. IV Part 2:** 683

Put Yourself in My Shoes (Carver), **Supp. III Part 1:** 139

"Put Yourself in My Shoes" (Carver), **Supp. III Part 1:** 139, 141

Putzi, Jennifer, **Supp. XV:** 284

Puzo, Mario, **Supp. IV Part 1:** 390

"Puzzle of Modern Society, The" (Kazin), **Supp. VIII:** 103

Pygmalion (Shaw), **Supp. XII:** 14

Pyle, Ernie, **III:** 148; **Supp. V:** 240; **Supp. XVII:** 61

Pylon (Faulkner), **II:** 64–65, 73; **Retro. Supp. I:** 84, 85

Pynchon, Thomas, **III:** 258; **Retro. Supp. I:** 278; **Retro. Supp. II:** 279, 324; **Supp. II Part 2:** 557, **617–638; Supp. III Part 1:** 217; **Supp. IV Part 1:** 53, 279; **Supp. IV Part 2:** 570; **Supp. IX:** 207, 208, 212; **Supp. V:** 40, 44, 52; **Supp. VIII:** 14; **Supp. X:** 260, 301, 302; **Supp. XI:** 103; **Supp. XII:** 289; **Supp. XIV:** 49, 53, 54, 96; **Supp. XIX:** 223; **Supp. XVI:** 123, 128; **Supp. XVII:** 183, 225, 232, 236; **Supp. XX: 21, 83, 87; Supp. XXIII:** 42, 101; **Supp. XXVII:** 183

Pyne, John, **Supp. XXI:** 7

Pyne, Mary, **Supp. XXI:** 7

Pyrah, Gill, **Supp. V:** 126

"Pyramid Club, The" (Doctorow), **Supp. IV Part 1:** 234

Pyrlaeus, Johann Christopher, **Supp. XXVI:** 86

"Pyrography" (Ashbery), **Supp. III Part 1:** 18

Pythagoras, **I:** 332

Pythagorean Silence (Howe), **Supp. IV Part 2:** 426, 428–429

Q

QBVII (television movie), **Supp. XX:** 247

QBVII (Uris), **Supp. XX:** 244, 247, 248, 251, **253–254**

"Qebehseneuf" (Goldbarth), **Supp. XII:** 186

"Quadroons, The" (Child), **Supp. XVIII:** 124

"Quai d'Orléans" (Bishop), **Supp. I Part 1:** 89

"Quail for Mr. Forester" (Humphrey), **Supp. IX:** 94

"Quail in Autumn" (W. J. Smith), **Supp. XIII:** 334–335, 339

Quaker City, The: or, The Monks of Monk Hall (Lippard), **Supp. XXIII:** 177, 178–179, **180–183,** 184, 187, 188–189, 190

"Quaker Graveyard in Nantucket, The" (R. Lowell), **II:** 54, 550; **Retro. Supp. II:** 178, 186–187

"Quake Theory" (Olds), **Supp. X:** 203

Qualey, Carlton C., **Supp. I Part 2:** 650

Quality of Hurt, The (C. Himes), **Supp. XVI:** 137, 145

"Quality of Wine" (Carruth), **Supp. XVI:** 59

"Quality Time" (Kingsolver), **Supp. VII:** 203

"Quandary" (F. Wright), **Supp. XVII:** 244

Quang-Ngau-chè, **III:** 473

Quarles, Francis, **I:** 178, 179

"Quarrel" (Taggard), **Supp. XXII:** 276

Quarry, The (Chesnutt), **Supp. XIV:** 76

"Quarry, The" (Nemerov), **III:** 272

Quarry, The: New Poems (Eberhart), **I:** 532, 539

Quartermain, Peter, **Supp. IV Part 2:** 423, 434

Quatermain, Peter, **Supp. XXII:** 163

"Quaternions, The" (Bradstreet), **Supp. I Part 1:** 104–106, 114, 122

"Quatrains for Ishi" (Komunyakaa), **Supp. XIII:** 129

Quatuor pour la fin du temps (Messiaen), **Supp. XXVII:** 152

Queechy (S. Warner as Wetherell), **Supp. XVIII:** 257, **264–266**

Queen Christmas (Wells), **Supp. XXVI:** 275

"Queen Elizabeth and the Blind Girl or Music for the Dead Children" (B. Kelly), **Supp. XVII:** 124, 125

Queen of Outer Space (film), **Supp. XXVII:** 94

"Queen of the Black Coast" (Howard), **Supp. XXVII:** 125

"Queen of the Blues" (Brooks), **Supp. III Part 1:** 75

Queen of the Damned, The (Rice), **Supp. VII:** 290, 292–293, 297, 299

Queen of the Mob (film), **Supp. XIII:** 170

"Queens of France" (Wilder), **IV:** 365

"Queen's Twin, The" (Jewett), **Retro. Supp. II:** 138

Queen's Twin, The, and Other Stories (Jewett), **Retro. Supp. II:** 140

Queen Victoria (Strachey), **Supp. I Part 2:** 485, 494; **Supp. XIV:** 342

Queer (Burroughs), **Supp. III Part 1:** 93–102

"Queer Aztlán"(Moraga), **Supp. XXIII:** 201

"Queer Beer" (Hansberry), **Supp. IV Part 1:** 374

"Quelques considérations sur la méthode subjective" (James), **II:** 345–346

"Quest, The" (Gibran), **Supp. XX: 124**

"Question" (Swenson), **Supp. IV Part 2:** 640

"Question and Answer" (Hughes), **Retro. Supp. I:** 211

"Questioning Faces" (Frost), **Retro. Supp. I:** 141

"Question Mark in the Circle, The" (Stegner), **Supp. IV Part 2:** 597

"Questionnaire, The" (Snodgrass), **Supp. VI:** 318

"Question of Fidelity, A" (Beauvoir), **Supp. IX:** 4

"Question of Loneliness, A" (Swados), **Supp. XIX:** 262

"Question of Our Speech, The" (Ozick), **Supp. V:** 272

"Question of Simone de Beauvoir, The" (Algren), **Supp. IX:** 4

Questions About Angels (Collins), **Supp. XXI:** 54, 58, 59, 60, 64

Questions for Ecclesiastes (Jarman), **Supp. XVII:** 109, 110, **118–119**

"Questions of Geography" (Hollander), **Supp. I Part 1:** 96

"Questions of Swimming, 1935" (Davison), **Supp. XXVI:** 76

Questions of Travel (Bishop), **Retro. Supp. II:** 46–48; **Supp. I Part 1:** 72, 83, 92, 94

"Questions of Travel" (Bishop), **Retro. Supp. II:** 47

"Questions to Tourists Stopped by a Pineapple Field" (Merwin), **Supp. III Part 1:** 355

"Questions without Answers" (T. Williams), **IV:** 384

"Quest of the Purple-Fringed, The" (Frost), **Retro. Supp. I:** 139

Quest of the Silver Fleece, The (Du Bois), **Supp. II Part 1:** 176–178

Quevedo y Villegas, Francisco Gómez, **Retro. Supp. I:** 423

Quickly: A Column for Slow Readers (Mailer), **Retro. Supp. II:** 202

Quicksand (Larsen), **Supp. XVIII:** 119, 121, 122, **124–127**

Quicksand and Passing (Larsen; McDowell, ed.), **Supp. XVIII:** 125

"Quies," (Pound), **Retro. Supp. I:** 413

Quiet American, The (Greene), **Supp. XIX:** 29

"Quiet and clear" (Kooser), **Supp. XIX:** 125

Quiet City (Shaw), **Supp. XIX:** 244

Quiet Days in Clichy (H. Miller), **III:** 170, 178, 183–184, 187

"Quiet Desperation" (Simpson), **Supp. IX:** 277–278

"Quiet Hour" (Huddle), **Supp. XXVI:** 149–150

"Quiet Light, A" (Skloot), **Supp. XX: 203**

"Quiet of the Mind" (Nye), **Supp. XIII:** 284

"Quiet Woman, The" (Taggard), **Supp. XXII:** 274

"QUILLA" (Trethewey), **Supp. XXI:** 246

"Quilting" (D. West), **Supp. XVIII:** 283

Quin, Mike (pseudonym). *See* Ryan, Paul William

Quincy, Edmund, **Supp. XVIII:** 4

Quindlen, Anna, **Supp. XVI:** 108; **Supp. XVII:** 165–181

Quinlan, Kathleen, **Supp. X:** 80

Quinn, Anthony, **Supp. XXI:** 46

Quinn, John, **III:** 471

Quinn, Paul, **Supp. V:** 71

Quinn, Sister M. Bernetta, **III:** 479; **IV:** 421

Quinn, Vincent, **I:** 386, 401, 402; **Supp. I Part 1:** 270

"Quinnapoxet" (Kunitz), **Supp. III Part 1:** 263

Quinn's Book (W. Kennedy), **Supp. VII:** 133, 148–150, 153

Quintero, José, **III:** 403

Quintilian, **IV:** 123

Quinzaine for This Yule, A (Pound), **Retro. Supp. I:** 285

Quite Contrary: The Mary and Newt Story (Dixon), **Supp. XII: 144,** 153

Quitting Time (Kriegel), **Supp. XXIV: 225–227**

Quod Erat Demonstrandum (Stein), **IV:** 34

Quo Vadis? (Sienkiewicz), **Supp. IV Part 2:** 518; **Supp. XVI:** 182

R

Raab, Max, **Supp. XI:** 309

Raban, Jonathan, **Supp. XXV:** 208, 217

"Rabbi, The" (Hayden), **Supp. II Part 1:** 363, 369

Rabbit, Run (Updike), **IV:** 214, 223, 230–234; **Retro. Supp. I:** 320, 325, 326, 327, 331, 333, 335; **Supp. XI:** 140; **Supp. XII:** 298; **Supp. XVI:** 220

"Rabbit, The" (Barnes), **Supp. III Part 1:** 34

Rabbit at Rest (Updike), **Retro. Supp. I:** 334

Rabbit Dance (Gansworth), **Supp. XXVI:** 114

Rabbit Factory, The (L. Brown), **Supp. XXI:** 40, **47–48**

"*Rabbit Factory, The:* Escaping the Isolation of the Cage" (Gaughran), **Supp. XXI:** 47–48

Rabbit Is Rich (Updike), **Retro. Supp. I:** 334; **Supp. XXVI:** 142

Rabbit novels (Updike), **Supp. V:** 269

Rabbit Redux (Updike), **IV:** 214; **Retro. Supp. I:** 332, 333

Rabbit's Umbrella, The (Plimpton), **Supp. XVI:** 244

"Rabbits Who Caused All the Trouble, The" (Thurber), **Supp. I Part 2:** 610

Rabe, David, **Supp. XXIV:** 117; **Supp. XXV:** 153

Rabelais, and His World (Bakhtin), **Retro. Supp. II:** 273

Rabelais, François, **I:** 130; **II:** 111, 112, 302, 535; **III:** 77, 78, 174, 182; **IV:** 68; **Supp. I Part 2:** 461

Rabelais and His World (Bakhtin), **Supp. X:** 120

Rabinbach, Anson, **Supp. XII:** 166

Rabinowitz, Dorothy, **Supp. XXVII:** 134

Rabinowitz, Paula, **Supp. V:** 161

"Race" (Emerson), **II:** 6

"Race, Privilege, and the Politics of (Re)Writing History: An Analysis of the Novels of Michelle Cliff" (Edmondson), **Supp. XXII:** 70

"Race Contacts and Inter-Racial Relations" (Locke), **Supp. XIV:** 211

"Race Contacts and Inter-Racial Relations: A Study in the Theory and Practice of Race" (lectures, Locke), **Supp. XIV:** 199, 209

Race Contacts and Interracial Relations: Lectures on the Theory and Practice of Race (Locke, Stewart, ed.), **Supp. XIV:** 196, **209–210**

"'RACE LINE' IS A PRODUCT OF CAPITALISM, THE" (Baraka), **Supp. II Part 1:** 61

"Race of Life, The" (Thurber), **Supp. I Part 2:** 614

"Race Problems and Modern Society" (Toomer), **Supp. III Part 2:** 486

Race Questions, Provincialism, and Other American Problems (Royce), **Supp. XIV:** 199

"Race Riot, Tulsa, 1921" (Olds), **Supp. X:** 205

Race Rock (Matthiessen), **Supp. V:** 201

"Races, The" (R. Lowell), **II:** 554

"Rachel" (D. West), **Supp. XVIII:** 289

Rachel Carson: Witness for Nature (Lear), **Supp. IX:** 19

Rachel River (film, Smolan), **Supp. XVI:** 36

"Racial Progress and Race Adjustment" (Locke), **Supp. XIV:** 210

Racine, Jean Baptiste, **II:** 543, 573; **III:** 145, 151, 152, 160; **IV:** 317, 368, 370; **Supp. I Part 2:** 716

Radcliffe, Ann, **Supp. XX: 108**

Radiance (Crooker), **Supp. XXIII: 57–58**

"Radical" (Moore), **III:** 211

"Radical Chic" (Wolfe), **Supp. III Part 2:** 577–578, 584, 585

Radical Chic & Mau-mauing the Flak Catchers (Wolfe), **Supp. III Part 2:** 577–578

Radical Empiricism of William James, The (Wild), **II:** 362, 363–364

Radicalism in America, The (Lasch), **I:** 259

"Radical Jewish Humanism: The Vision of E. L. Doctorow" (Clayton), **Supp. IV Part 1:** 238

"Radically Condensed History of Postindustrial Life, A" (Wallace), **Supp. X:** 309

Radical's America, A (Swados), **Supp. XIX: 264–265**

Radinovsky, Lisa, **Supp. XV:** 284, 285

"Radio" (O'Hara), **III:** 369

Radio Days (film; Allen), **Supp. XV:** 9

"Radio Pope" (Goldbarth), **Supp. XII:** 188, 192

Raditzer (Matthiessen), **Supp. V:** 201

Radkin, Paul, **Supp. I Part 2:** 539

"Rafaela Who Drinks Coconut & Papaya Juice on Tuesdays" (Cisneros), **Supp. VII:** 63

Rafelson, Bob, **Supp. XIV:** 241

Raffalovich, Marc-André, **Supp. XIV:** 335

Rafferty, Terence, **Supp. XX: 87, 92**

"Raft, The" (Lindsay), **Supp. I Part 2:** 393

Rag and Bone Shop of the Heart, The: Poems for Men (Bly, Hillman, and Meade, eds.), **Supp. IV Part 1:** 67

Rage in Harlem (C. Himes). *See For Love of Imabelle* (C. Himes)

Rage to Live, A (O'Hara), **III:** 361

Raglan, Lord, **I:** 135

Rago, Henry, **Supp. III Part 2:** 624, 628, 629

"Rag Rug"(Hadas), **Supp. XXIII:** 118

Ragtime (Doctorow), **Retro. Supp. II:** 108; **Supp. IV Part 1:** 217, 222–224, 231, 232, 233, 234, 237, 238; **Supp. V:** 45; **Supp. XXIV:** 227

"Ragtime" (Doctorow), **Supp. IV Part 1:** 234

Ragtime (film), **Supp. IV Part 1:** 236

Ragtime (musical, McNally), **Supp. XIII:** 207

Rahab (W. Frank), **Supp. XX: 71–72, 76**

Rahaim, Liz, **Supp. XVII:** 2

Rahv, Philip, **Retro. Supp. I:** 112; **Supp. II Part 1:** 136; **Supp. IX:** 8; **Supp. VIII:** 96; **Supp. XIV:** 3; **Supp. XV:** 140; **Supp. XXVII:** 134

"Raid" (Hughes), **Retro. Supp. I:** 208

Raids on the Unspeakable (Merton), **Supp. VIII:** 201, 208

Raikin, Judith, **Supp. XXII:** 66

Rail, DeWayne, **Supp. XIII:** 312

"Rain, the Rez, and Other Things, The" (Gansworth), **Supp. XXVI:** 111

Rain and Other Fictions (Kenny), **Supp. XXIII:** 157

"Rain and the Rhinoceros" (Merton), **Supp. VIII:** 201

Rainbow, The (Lawrence), **III:** 27

"Rainbows" (Marquand), **III:** 56

Rainbow Stories, The (Vollmann), **Supp. XVII:** 226, 227, 230, 231, 233

Rainbow Tulip, The (Mora), **Supp. XIII:** 221

"Rain Country" (Haines), **Supp. XII:** 210

"Rain-Dream, A" (Bryant), **Supp. I Part 1:** 164

Raine, Kathleen, **I:** 522, 527

"Rain Falling Now, The" (Dunn), **Supp. XI:** 147

"Rain Flooding Your Campfire" (Gallagher), **Supp. XXIV:** 177

"Rain in the Heart" (Taylor), **Supp. V:** 317, 319

Rain in the Trees, The (Merwin), **Supp. III Part 1:** 340, 342, 345, 349, 354–356

"Rainmaker, The" (Humphrey), **Supp. IX:** 101

Raintree County (Lockridge), **Supp. XIX:** 263

Rainwater, Catherine, **Supp. V:** 272

"Rainy Day" (Longfellow), **II:** 498

"Rainy Day, The" (Buck), **Supp. II Part 1:** 127

"Rainy Mountain Cemetery" (Momaday), **Supp. IV Part 2:** 486

Rainy Mountain Christmas Doll (painting) (Momaday), **Supp. IV Part 2:** 493

"Rainy Season: Sub-Tropics" (Bishop), **Supp. I Part 1:** 93

"Rainy Sunday" (Espaillat), **Supp. XXI:** 106

Raised in Captivity (Silver), **Supp. XXIV: 271**

"Raise High the Roof Beam, Carpenters" (Salinger), **III:** 567–569, 571

Raise High the Roof Beam, Carpenters; and Seymour: An Introduction (Salinger), **III:** 552, 567–571, 572

Raise Race Rays Raze: Essays Since 1965 (Baraka), **Supp. II Part 1:** 47, 52, 55

Raisin (musical), **Supp. IV Part 1:** 374

Raising Demons (Jackson), **Supp. IX: 125–126**

Raising the Dead (Rash), **Supp. XXVII:** 220–221, 222

Raisin in the Sun, A (film: Columbia Pictures), **Supp. IV Part 1:** 360, 367

Raisin in the Sun, A (Hansberry), **Supp. IV Part 1:** 359, 360, 361, 362–364; **Supp. VIII:** 343

Raisin in the Sun, A (television film: American Playhouse), **Supp. IV Part 1:** 367, 374

Raisin in the Sun, A (unproduced screenplay) (Hansberry), **Supp. IV Part 1:** 360

Rajan, R., **I:** 390

"Rake, The" (Mamet), **Supp. XIV:** 240

Rake's Progress, The (opera), **Supp. II Part 1:** 24

Rakosi, Carl, **Supp. III Part 2:** 614, 615, 616, 617, 618, 621, 629; **Supp. XIV:** 286, 287

Ralegh, Sir Walter, **Supp. I Part 1:** 98

Raleigh, John Henry, **IV:** 366

Ralph, Brett, **Supp. XVII:** 245

Ramakrishna, Sri, **III:** 567

Ramakrishna and His Disciples (Isherwood), **Supp. XIV:** 164

Ramazani, Jahan, **Supp. IV Part 2:** 450

"Ramble of Aphasia, A" (O. Henry), **Supp. II Part 1:** 410

Ramey, Phillip, **Supp. IV Part 1:** 94

Ramírez, Juan, **Supp. XXIII:** 203

Ramona (Jackson), **Supp. XXIV:** 27

Rampersad, Arnold, **Retro. Supp. I:** 196, 200, 201, 204; **Supp. IV Part 1:** 244, 250

Rampling, Anne, **Supp. VII:** 201. *See also* Rice, Anne

Rampling, Charlotte, **Supp. IX:** 253

Ramsey, Priscilla R., **Supp. IV Part 1:** 15

Ramsey, Roger, **Supp. XVI:** 69

Ramsey, William, **Supp. XVIII:** 66

Ramus, Petrus, **Supp. I Part 1:** 104

Rancière, Jacques, **Supp. XXVI:** 18, 135, 136, 141

Rand, Ayn, **Supp. I Part 1:** 294; **Supp. IV Part 2: 517–535**

Randall, Jarrell, 1914–1965 (Lowell, Taylor, and Warren, eds.), **II:** 368, 385

Randall, John H., **III:** 605

Randolph, John, **I:** 5–6

Randolph, Ladette, **Supp. XXIII:** 274

"Randolphs of the Redwoods, The" (Atherton), **Supp. XXIV:** 18

"Range-Finding" (Frost), **Retro. Supp. I:** 131

Range of the Possible (T. Marshall), **Supp. XVII:** 36

Rangoon (F. Barthelme), **Supp. XI:** 25

Rangus, Eric, **Supp. XXI:** 244, 254

Rank, Otto, **I:** 135; **Supp. IX:** 105; **Supp. X:** 183, 185, 193

Ranke, Leopold von, **Supp. I Part 2:** 492

Rankin, Daniel, **Retro. Supp. II:** 57, 72; **Supp. I Part 1:** 200, 203, 225

Rankin, Tom, **Supp. XXI:** 36

Rankine, Annette, **Supp. XX: 69**

Ranlett, William H., **Supp. XVIII:** 3

Ransohoff, Martin, **Supp. XI:** 305, 306

Ransom, John Crowe, **I:** 265, 301; **II:** 34, 367, 385, 389, 536–537, 542; **III:** 454, **480–502,** 549; **IV:** 121, 122, 123, 124, 125, 127, 134, 140, 141, 236, 237, 433; **Retro. Supp. I:** 90; **Retro. Supp. II:** 176, 177, 178, 183, 220, 228, 246; **Supp. I Part 1:** 80, 361; **Supp. I Part 2:** 423; **Supp. II Part 1:** 90, 91, 136, 137, 139, 318; **Supp. II Part 2:** 639; **Supp. III Part 1:** 318; **Supp. III Part 2:** 542, 591; **Supp. IV Part 1:** 217; **Supp. V:** 315, 331, 337; **Supp. X:** 25, 56, 58; **Supp. XIV:** 1; **Supp. XIX:** 123; **Supp. XXIII:** 145

Ransome, Arthur, **Supp. XXV:** 205

"Rape" (Coleman), **Supp. XI:** 89–90

"Rape, The" (Baraka), **Supp. II Part 1:** 40

Rape of Bunny Stuntz, The (Gurney), **Supp. V:** 109

"Rape of Philomel, The" (Shapiro), **Supp. II Part 2:** 720

"Rape of the Lock, The" (Pope), **Supp. XIV:** 8

Rapf, Joanna, **Supp. XVIII:** 251

Raphael, **I:** 15; **III:** 505, 521, 524; **Supp. I Part 1:** 363

"Rapist" (Dunn), **Supp. XI:** 144

Rap on Race, A (Baldwin and Mead), **Supp. I Part 1:** 66

Rapoport, Nessa, **Supp. XXVI:** 124

"Rappaccini's Daughter" (Hawthorne), **II:** 229

"Rapture of the Deep" (Hempel), **Supp. XXI: 123**

"Rapunzel" (Sexton), **Supp. II Part 2:** 691

Rare & Endangered Species: A Novella & Short Stories (Bausch), **Supp. VII:** 51, 54

"Raree Show" (MacLeish), **III:** 9

Rascoe, Burton, **III:** 106, 115

Rash, Ron, **Supp. XXVII: 215–231**

Raskin, Jonah, **Supp. XV:** 116

Raskin, Saul, **Supp. XXIII:** 6

"Raskolnikov" (Simic), **Supp. VIII:** 282

Rasmussen, Douglas, **Supp. IV Part 2:** 528, 530

Rasmussen, Halfdan, **Supp. XVIII:** 180

"Raspberries" (Rash), **Supp. XXVII:** 222

Rasporich, Beverly, **Supp. XXVII:** 180, 182

Rasselas (S. Johnson), **Supp. XI:** 209

Rathmann, Andrew, **Supp. XV:** 34

Ratiner, Steven, **Supp. XXIII:** 134

"Rat in the Engine" (Espaillat), **Supp. XXI:** 106

"Ration" (Baraka), **Supp. II Part 1:** 50

"Rationale of Verse, The" (Poe), **III:** 427–428; **Retro. Supp. II:** 266

Ratner, Rochelle, **Supp. XV:** 105; **Supp. XXIV:** 168; **Supp. XXVI:** 160

Ratner's Star (DeLillo), **Supp. VI:** 1, 2, 3, 4, 10, 12, 14; **Supp. XVIII:** 140

"Rat of Faith, The" (Levine), **Supp. V:** 192

"Rats in the Walls, The" (Lovecraft), **Supp. XXV:** 109, 112

Rattigan, Terence, **III:** 152

Raugh, Joseph, **Supp. I Part 1:** 286

Rauh, Ida, **Supp. XXI:** 6

Rauschenberg, Robert, **Supp. XV:** 187

Rauschenbusch, Walter, **III:** 293; **Supp. I Part 1:** 7

Ravelstein (Bellow), **Retro. Supp. II:** 19, **33–34**

Raven, Simon, **Supp. XII:** 241

Raven, The (film, Friedlander), **Supp. XVII:** 58

"Raven, The" (Poe), **III:** 413, 421–422, 426; **Retro. Supp. II:** 265, 266–267; **Supp. XVII:** 58

Raven, The, and Other Poems (Poe), **III:** 413

Ravenal, Shannon, **Supp. IV Part 1:** 93

"Raven Days, The" (Lanier), **Supp. I Part 1:** 351

Ravenel, Shannon, **Supp. XXI:** 39

Ravenna, Michael. *See* Welty, Eudora

"Ravens at Deer Creek" (Wrigley), **Supp. XVIII:** 299–300, 306

Raven's Road (Gunn Allen), **Supp. IV Part 1:** 330, 335

Raver, Anne, **Supp. XVIII:** 191

Ravetch, Irving, **Supp. XXV:** 102

"Ravine, The" (Carruth), **Supp. XVI:** 53

Ravits, Martha, **Supp. XXI:** 215

Raw Heaven (Peacock), **Supp. XIX: 196–197**

Rawlings, Marjorie Kinnan, **Supp. X: 219–237; Supp. XVIII:** 194–195

Rawlins, C. L., **Supp. XVII:** 72, 73

Ray, David, **Supp. IV Part 1:** 61

Ray, Janisse, **Supp. XVIII: 189–206**

Ray, Jeanne Wilkinson, **Supp. XII:** 308, 310

Ray, John, **II:** 111, 112

Ray, Man, **IV:** 404; **Retro. Supp. I:** 416; **Supp. XII:** 124; **Supp. XXIII:** 6

Ray, Nicholas, **Supp. XVIII:** 253

Ray Bradbury Theatre, The (television show), **Supp. IV Part 1:** 103

Raymond, Henry J., **Supp. XVIII:** 4

"Raymond and Ann" (Budbill), **Supp. XIX:** 9

"Raymond Andrews as Griot" (Collins), **Supp. XXVI:** 13

Raymond Carver: A Writer's Life (Sklenicka), **Supp. XXIV:** 166

"Raymond Carver: The Kindest Cut" (Wood), **Supp. XXIV:** 166

"Razor's Edge, The" (Wasserstein), **Supp. XV:** 328

Reactionary Essays on Poetry and Ideas (Tate), **Supp. II Part 1:** 106, 146

Read, Deborah, **II:** 122

Read, Forrest, **III:** 478

Read, Herbert, **I:** 523; **II:** 372–373, 377–378; **Retro. Supp. I:** 54; **Supp. III Part 1:** 273; **Supp. III Part 2:** 624, 626

Read, William A., **Supp. XIV:** 4

Reade, Charles, **Supp. I Part 2:** 580

Reader, Constant. *See* Parker, Dorothy

Reader, Dennis J., **Supp. I Part 2:** 454

"Reader, The" (F. Wright), **Supp. XVII:** 246

Reader's Block (Markson), **Supp. XVII: 143–145,** 146

Reader's Encyclopedia, The: An Encyclopedia of World Literature and the Arts (W. Benét), **Supp. XI:** 44

Reader's Guide to William Gaddis's The Recognitions, A (Moore), **Supp. IV Part 1:** 283

Reader's Map of Arkansas (Wright), **Supp. XV:** 348

"Reader's Tale, A" (Doty), **Supp. XI:** 119, 120, 128, 129

"Reading" (Auden), **Supp. VIII:** 155

"Reading, The" (Di Piero), **Supp. XIX:** 41

"Reading, Writing, Region" (J. W. Miller), **Supp. XX: 165**

"Reading an Anthology of Chinese Poems of the Sung Dynasty, I Pause to Admire the Length and Clarity of Their Titles" (Collins), **Supp. XXI:** 56

"Reading at Forty" (Pickering), **Supp. XXI:** 196

"Reading Group Guide", **Supp. XI:** 244–245

"Reading Lao Tzu Again in the New Year" (Wright), **Supp. V:** 343

"Reading Late of the Death of Keats" (Kenyon), **Supp. VII:** 169

"Reading Myself" (R. Lowell), **II:** 555

Reading Myself and Others (P. Roth), **Retro. Supp. II:** 282; **Supp. V:** 45

"Reading *Ode to the West Wind* 25 Years Later" (McCarriston), **Supp. XIV:** 271–272

"Reading of the Psalm, The" (Francis), **Supp. IX:** 79

"Reading Ovid" (Di Piero), **Supp. XIX:** 44

"Reading Philosophy at Night" (Simic), **Supp. VIII:** 272

Reading Rilke: Reflections on the Problems of Translation (Gass), **Supp. VI:** 92, **93–94**

"Reading Rorty and Paul Celan One Morning in Early June" (Wright), **Supp. V:** 343

"Reading Sarcophagi: An Essay" (Sobin), **Supp. XVI:** 290

"Readings of History" (Rich), **Supp. I Part 2:** 554

"Reading the Russians" (Stone), **Supp. XXVII:** 251–252

"Reading the Signs, Empowering the Eye" (Bambara), **Supp. XI:** 17–18

Reading the Spirit (Eberhart), **I:** 525, 527, 530

Ready, Richard M., **Supp. XIX:** 154

"Ready Or Not" (Baraka), **Supp. II Part 1:** 50

Reagan, Ronald, **Supp. IV Part 1:** 224–225

"Real Bowery, The" (Hapgood), **Supp. XVII:** 103

"Real Class" (Vidal), **Supp. IV Part 1:** 35

Real Cool Killers, The (C. Himes), **Supp. XVI:** 143

Real Dope, The (Lardner), **II:** 422–423

"Real Estate" (Moore), **Supp. X:** 178

"Real Gone Guy, A" (McGrath), **Supp. X:** 117

"Real Horatio Alger Story, The" (Cowley), **Supp. II Part 1:** 143

"Realities" (MacLeish), **III:** 4

"Reality in America" (Trilling), **Supp. III Part 2:** 495, 502

"Reality! Reality! What Is It?" (Eberhart), **I:** 536

Reality Sandwiches, 1953–60 (Ginsberg), **Supp. II Part 1:** 315, 320

"Reality U.S.A." (Halliday), **Supp. XIX:** 89

Real Life of Sebastian Knight, The (Nabokov), **III:** 246; **Retro. Supp. I:** 266, 269, 270, 274

"Really Good Jazz Piano, A" (Yates), **Supp. XI:** 342

"Real Movie, with Stars, The" (Hull), **Supp. XXI:** 136

Real Presence: A Novel (Bausch), **Supp. VII:** 42–43, 50

"Real Revolution Is Love, The" (Harjo), **Supp. XII:** 224, 225–226

"Real Surrounding, The: On Canaletto's Venice" (Bronk), **Supp. XXI:** 32

"Real Thing, The" (H. James), **Retro. Supp. I:** 228; **Retro. Supp. II:** 223

"Real Two-Party System" (Vidal), **Supp. IV Part 2:** 679

Real West Marginal Way, The (Hugo), **Supp. VI:** 132, 134; **Supp. XVIII:** 299

"Real World around Us, The" (Carson), **Supp. IX:** 21

Reaper Essays, The (Jarman and McDowell), **Supp. IX:** 270; **Supp. XVII:** 110–111

"*Reaper* Interviews Jean Doh and Sean Dough, The" (Jarman and McDowell), **Supp. XVII:** 110

"Reapers" (Toomer), **Supp. III Part 2:** 481; **Supp. IX:** 312

Reason and Other Women (Notley), **Supp. XXII:** 224, 227, 235, 236, 237

"Reason and Race: A Review of the Literature of the Negro for 1946" (Locke), **Supp. XIV:** 206

"Reason for Moving, A" (Strand), **Supp. IV Part 2:** 624

"Reason for Stories, The: Toward a Moral Fiction" (Stone), **Supp. V:** 298, 300

Reasons for Moving (Strand), **Supp. IV Part 2:** 624–626, 626

"Reasons for Music" (MacLeish), **III:** 19

"Reasons of the Body" (Sanders), **Supp. XVI:** 274

Reasons to Live (Hempel), **Supp. XXI:** 115, 117, 118, **119–122**

Rebecca (du Maurier), **Supp. XIX:** 57–58; **Supp. XXII:** 120

Rebecca, or, The Fille de Chambre (Rowson), **Supp. XV:** 229, **235–236,** 238

Rebecca Harding Davis Reader, A (Pfaelzer, ed.), **Supp. XVI:** 88, 90

Rebel Angels: Twenty-five Poets of the New Formalism (Jarman and Mason, eds.), **Supp. XV:** 251; **Supp. XVII:** 109, 110, 112, 121

"Rebellion" (R. Lowell), **Retro. Supp. II:** 187

Rebel Powers (Bausch), **Supp. VII:** 41, 45–46, 49–51

Rebel without a Cause (film), **Supp. XII:** 9

"Rebirth" (McKnight), **Supp. XX: 147, 157**

"Rebirth of God and the Death of Man, The " (Fiedler), **Supp. XIII:** 108

Rebolledo, Tey Diana, **Supp. XIII:** 214

Reb Shloyme nogid: A poeme fun yidishn leben (Shloyme the wealthy: A poem of Jewish life)(Asch), **Supp. XXIII:** 4, 5

Recapitulation (Stegner), **Supp. IV Part 2:** 598, 600, 612–613

"Recapitulation, The" (Eberhart), **I:** 522

"Recapitulations" (Shapiro), **Supp. II Part 2:** 701, 702, 708, 710–711

"Receding Horizons" (Lethem and Scholtz), **Supp. XVIII:** 145

"Recencies in Poetry" (Zukofsky), **Supp. III Part 2:** 615

Recent Killing, A (Baraka), **Supp. II Part 1:** 55

"Recent Negro Fiction" (Ellison), **Supp. II Part 1:** 233, 235

"Recessional" (A. Finch), **Supp. XVII:** 70–71

"Recital, The" (Ashbery), **Supp. III Part 1:** 14

"Recitative" (H. Crane), **I:** 390; **Retro. Supp. II:** 78

Reckless Eyeballing (Reed), **Supp. X:** 241

Reckless Moment, The (film), **Supp. XXII:** 120, 131, 132

Recognitions, The (Gaddis), **Supp. IV Part 1:** 279, 280–285, 286, 287, 288, 289, 291, 292, 294; **Supp. XX: 91; Supp. XXIV:** 140

"Recollection and Perhaps a Tribute, A" (Espaillat), **Supp. XXI:** 103–104

Recollections (R. H. Stoddard), **Supp. XV:** 271

Recollections of Logan Pearsall Smith: The Story of a Friendship (Gathorne-Hardy), **Supp. XIV:** 344

"Reconciliation" (Whitman), **IV:** 347

"Reconstructed but Unregenerate" (Ransom), **III:** 496

"Reconstruction and Its Benefits" (Du Bois), **Supp. II Part 1:** 171

Recovering (Sarton), **Supp. VIII:** 264

Recovering the U.S. Hispanic Literary Heritage (Paredes), **Supp. XIII:** 320

"Recovery" (Dove), **Supp. IV Part 1:** 248

Re-Creation Story (Gansworth), **Supp. XXVI:** 113–114

Rector of Justin, The (Auchincloss), **Supp. IV Part 1:** 21, 23, 27–30, 36

"Recurrent Dream" (Nelson), **Supp. XVIII:** 176

Recyclopedia: Trimmings, S*PeRM**K*T, and Muse & Drudge (Mullen), **Supp. XXVII:** 171, 174–175

"RED AUTUMN" (Baraka), **Supp. II Part 1:** 55

Red Badge of Courage, The (S. Crane), **I:** 201, 207, 212, 405, 406, 407, 408, 412–416, 419, 421, 422, 423, 477, 506; **II:** 264; **III:** 317; **IV:** 350; **Retro. Supp. II:** 108; **Supp. IV Part 1:** 380; **Supp. XIV:** 51; **Supp. XVII:** 228; **Supp. XVIII:** 75; **Supp. XXI:** 277; **Supp. XXVII:** 207

"Redbirds" (C. Frost), **Supp. XV:** 99

"Red Bow, The" (Saunders), **Supp. XIX:** 232–233, 234

"Redbreast in Tampa" (Lanier), **Supp. I Part 1:** 364

"Red Brocade" (Nye), **Supp. XIII:** 288

Redburn: His First Voyage (Melville), **III:** 79–80, 84; **Retro. Supp. I:** 245, 247–248, 249; **Supp. XVIII:** 6

Red Calico (Miller and Bowden), **Supp. XXII:** 188

"Red Carpet for Shelley, A" (Wylie), **Supp. I Part 2:** 724

Red Channels (Harnett), **Supp. XV:** 198

"Red Clowns" (Cisneros), **Supp. VII:** 63

Red Coal, The (Stern), **Supp. IX: 291–292**

Red Coat, The (Shanley), **Supp. XIV:** 316–317

"Red Cords" (Lamott), **Supp. XX: 142**

"Red"(Crooker), **Supp. XXIII:** 63

"Red Cross" (Hughes), **Retro. Supp. I:** 205

Red Cross (Shepard), **Supp. III Part 2:** 440, 446

Red Death, A (Mosley), **Supp. XIII:** 237, 239, 240

"Red Deer" (C. Frost), **Supp. XV:** 101

Redding, Josephine, **Supp. XXI:** 2

Redding, Saunders, **Supp. I Part 1:** 332, 333

Reddings, J. Saunders, **Supp. IV Part 1:** 164

Red Dust (Levine), **Supp. V:** 178, 183–184, 188

"Red Dust" (Levine), **Supp. V:** 184

"Redemption" (Gardner), **Supp. VI:** 72

Redemption (Uris), **Supp. XX: 244, 246, 247, 248, 254, 255**

"Red Ensign, The" (Gallagher), **Supp. XXIV:** 175, 176

"Redeployment" (Nemerov), **III:** 267, 272

Redfield, Robert, **IV:** 475

Redford, Robert, **Supp. IX:** 253, 259; **Supp. XIII:** 267; **Supp. XIV:** 223

Redgrave, Lynn, **Supp. V:** 107

Red Harvest (Hammett), **Supp. IV Part 1:** 346–348, 348; **Supp. IV Part 2:** 468; **Supp. XXI:** 272

"Red Hat, The"(Hadas), **Supp. XXIII:** 111, 113, 118, 119, 124, 128

Red-Headed Woman (film), **Retro. Supp. I:** 110; **Supp. XVI:** 191

Red Helmet (Hickam), **Supp. XXVII:** 110–111

"Red Horse Wind over Albuquerque" (Harjo), **Supp. XII:** 219

Red Hot Vacuum, The (Solotaroff), **Retro. Supp. II:** 281

Rediscovery of America, The (W. Frank), **Supp. XX: 75**

Rediscovery of Man, The (W. Frank), **Supp. XX: 67–68, 80**

"Red Leaves" (Faulkner), **II:** 72

"Red Meat: What Difference Did Stesichoros Make?" (Carson), **Supp. XII:** 107

"Red Nails" (Howard), **Supp. XXVII:** 126

"Red Pawn" (Rand), **Supp. IV Part 2:** 520

Red Pony, The (Steinbeck), **IV:** 50, 51, 58, 70

Redrawing the Boundaries (Fisher), **Retro. Supp. I:** 39

Red Robins, The (Koch), **Supp. XV:** 185–186, 187

Red Roses for Bronze (Doolittle), **Supp. I Part 1:** 253, 268, 271

Red Rover, The (Cooper), **I:** 342–343, 355

Red Ryder (comic books), **Supp. XXVII:** 23

"Red Rydler and His Dog" (O'Hara and Brainard), **Supp. XXVII:** 23

Reds (Beatty), **Supp. XXIV:** 227

"Red Shadows" (Howard), **Supp. XXVII:** 122

"Red Shift" (Berrigan), **Supp. XXIV:** 46

"Red Silk Stockings" (Hughes), **Retro. Supp. I:** 200

Redskins, The (Cooper), **I:** 351, 353

Red Sox and Bluefish: And Other Things That Make New England New England (Orlean), **Supp. XXV:** 159

"Red Sox Nation, North" (Mosher), **Supp. XXII:** 209

"Red Star, Winter Orbit" (W. Gibson and B. Sterling), **Supp. XVI:** 123

Red Suitcase (Nye), **Supp. XIII:** 277, 278, 287

Red the Fiend (Sorrentino), **Supp. XXI:** 227, 231, 237

Red Wallflower, A (S. Warner), **Supp. XVIII:** 260

"Red Wheelbarrow, The" (W. C. Williams), **IV:** 411–412; **Retro. Supp. I:** 419, 430

"Red Wind" (Chandler), **Supp. IV Part 1:** 122

"Red Wing Church, The" (Kooser), **Supp. XIX:** 119

"Redwings" (Wright), **Supp. III Part 2:** 603

Reed, Edward Bliss, **Supp. XV:** 297, 298, 300

Reed, Ishmael, **Retro. Supp. II:** 111, 324–325; **Supp. II Part 1:** 34; **Supp. X: 239–257,** 331; **Supp. XIII:** 181, 182; **Supp. XVI:** 143; **Supp. XX: 107; Supp. XXII:** 172; **Supp. XXVII:** 167

Reed, J. D., **Supp. XVI:** 174

Reed, John, **I:** 48, 476, 483; **Supp. X:** 136; **Supp. XV:** 295, 299; **Supp. XVII:** 96, 99, 100; **Supp. XVIII:** 225; **Supp. XXI:** 6, 12; **Supp. XXII:** 274, 275; **Supp. XXIII:** 161, 162

Reed, Lou, **Retro. Supp. II:** 266

"Reedbeds of the Hackensack, The" (Clampitt), **Supp. IX:** 41

"Reed of Pan, A" (McCullers), **II:** 585

Reedy, Billy, **Retro. Supp. II:** 65, 67, 71, 73

Reedy, William Marion, **Supp. I Part 2:** 456, 461, 465; **Supp. XXVII:** 287

Reef, The (Wharton), **IV:** 317–318, 322; **Retro. Supp. I:** 372, **373–374**

Reena and Other Stories (Marshall), **Supp. XI:** 275, 277, 278

Reese, Debbie, **Supp. XXVI:** 108–109

"Reese in Evening Shadow" (Skloot), **Supp. XX: 204**

Reeve, F. D., **Supp. XV:** 344, 349

Reeve's Tale (Chaucer), **I:** 131

"Refiguring the Postcolonial Imagination: Tropes of Visuality in Writing by Rhys, Kincaid, and Cliff" (Emery), **Supp. XXII:** 73

Refiner's Fire: The Life and Adventures of Marshall Pearl, a Foundling (Helprin), **Supp. XXV:** 83, 85–86

"Reflection from Anita Loos" (Empson), **Supp. XVI:** 190

"Reflections" (Carruth), **Supp. XVI:** 54

"Reflections" (Komunyakaa), **Supp. XIII:** 117

Reflections at Fifty and Other Essays (Farrell), **II:** 49

"Reflections by a Fire" (Sarton), **Supp. VIII:** 259

Reflections in a Golden Eye (McCullers), **II:** 586, 588, 593–596, 604; **IV:** 384, 396

Reflections of a Jacobite (Auchincloss), **Supp. IV Part 1:** 31

Reflections on a Gift of Watermelon Pickle (Dunning), **Supp. XIV:** 126

Reflections on Poetry and Poetics (Nemerov), **III:** 269

"Reflections on the Constitution of Nature" (Freneau), **Supp. II Part 1:** 274

"Reflections on the Death of the Reader" (Morris), **III:** 237

Reflections on the End of an Era (Niebuhr), **III:** 297–298

"Reflections on the Life and Death of Lord Clive" (Paine), **Supp. I Part 2:** 505

Reflections on the Revolution in France (Burke), **Supp. I Part 2:** 511, 512

Reflections: Thinking Part I (Arendt), **Supp. I Part 2:** 570

"Reflex Action and Theism" (James), **II:** 345, 363

Reflex and Bone Structure (Major), **Supp. XXII: 174–175**

"Refrains/Remains/Reminders" (Goldbarth), **Supp. XII:** 180–181, 181

"Refuge" (Kingsolver), **Supp. VII:** 208

"Refuge" (Teasdale), **Supp. XXVII:** 291

"Refuge, A" (Goldbarth), **Supp. XII:** 190

Refugee Children: Theory, Research, and Services (Ahearn and Athey, eds.), **Supp. XI:** 184

"Refugees, The" (Jarrell), **II:** 371

"Refusal" (C. Frost), **Supp. XV:** 102

"Refusal to Publish Fifth Book" (Halliday), **Supp. XIX:** 94

"Regalia" (H. Johnson), **Supp. XXVI:** 172

Regarding Wave (Snyder), **Supp. VIII: 299–300**

Regina (Epstein), **Supp. XII: 170–171**

"Regional Literature of the South" (Rawlings), **Supp. X:** 228

"Regional Writer, The" (O'Connor), **Retro. Supp. II:** 223, 225

Régnier, Henri de, **II:** 528–529

Regular Guy, A (Simpson), **Supp. XXVII:** 239–240

Regulators, The (King), **Supp. V:** 141

Rehder, Robert, **Supp. IV Part 1:** 69

Rehearsing Absence (Espaillat), **Supp. XXI:** 99

Reich, Tova, **Supp. XVI:** 158

Reichel, Hans, **III:** 183

Reichl, Ruth, **Supp. X:** 79, 85

Reid, B. L., **II:** 41, 47

Reid, Forrest, **Supp. XX: 235**

Reid, Thomas, **II:** 9; **Supp. I Part 1:** 151

Reign of Snakes (Wrigley), **Supp. XVIII:** 293, **302–306**

"Reign of Snakes" (Wrigley), **Supp. XVIII:** 302–304

Reign of Wonder, The (Tanner), **I:** 260

Rein, Yevgeny, **Supp. VIII:** 22

Reinagle, Alexander, **Supp. XV:** 238, 240

"Reincarnation" (Dickey), **Supp. IV Part 1:** 181–182

Reine des pommes, La (C. Himes). *See For Love of Imabelle* (C. Himes)

Reiner, Carl, **Supp. IV Part 2:** 591

Reinfeld, Linda, **Supp. IV Part 2:** 421

Reinhardt, Max, **Supp. XV:** 307

Reinventing the Enemy's Language: Contemporary Native Women's Writing of North America (Bird and Harjo, eds.), **Supp. XII:** 216, 217

Reisman, Jerry, **Supp. III Part 2:** 618

Reiter, Amy, **Supp. XIX:** 54, 56

Reitlinger, Gerald, **Supp. XII:** 161

Reivers, The: A Reminiscence (Faulkner), **I:** 305; **II:** 57, 73; **Retro. Supp. I:** 74, 82, 91

"Rejoicings" (Stern), **Supp. IX:** 289–290

Rejoicings: Selected Poems, 1966–1972 (Stern), **Supp. IX: 289–290**

Relation of My Imprisonment, The (Banks), **Supp. V:** 8, 12–13

"Relations" (Biss), **Supp. XXVI:** 56

"Relations between Poetry and Painting, The" (Stevens), **Retro. Supp. I:** 312

Relations of the Alabama-Georgia Dialect to the Provincial Dialects of Great Britain, The (Brooks), **Supp. XIV:** 3

Relative Stranger, A (C. Baxter), **Supp. XVII:** 19, 22

"Relativity of Beauty, The" (Rawlings), **Supp. X:** 226

Relearning the Alphabet (Levertov), **Supp. III Part 1:** 280, 281

"Release" (C. Baxter), **Supp. XVII:** 15

"Release, The" (MacLeish), **III:** 16

Reles, Abe ("Kid Twist"), **Supp. IV Part 1:** 382

"Relevance of an Impossible Ethical Ideal, The" (Niebuhr), **III:** 298

"Religion" (Dunbar), **Supp. II Part 1:** 199

"Religion" (Emerson), **II:** 6

Religion of Nature Delineated, The (Wollaston), **II:** 108

"Religious Instruction" (Peacock), **Supp. XIX:** 200, 201

Religious Rebel, A: The Letters of "H. W. S." (Mrs. Pearsall Smith) (L. P. Smith), **Supp. XIV:** 349

"Reluctance" (Frost), **II:** 153

Reluctantly: Autobiographical Essays (Carruth), **Supp. XVI:** 45–46, 50

Remains (Snodgrass), **Supp. VI:** 311, **313–314**

"Remains, The" (Strand), **Supp. IV Part 2:** 627

"Remains of Princess Kaiulani's Garden, The" (Vaz), **Supp. XXVI:** 262–263

"Remarks on Color" (Wright), **Supp. XV:** 346

"Remarks on National Literature" (Channing), **Supp. XXIV: 76–77**

"Remarks on Spencer's *Definition of Mind as Correspondence*" (James), **II:** 345

Remarque, Erich Maria, **Retro. Supp. I:** 113; **Supp. IV Part 1:** 380

Rembrandt, **II:** 536; **IV:** 310; **Supp. IV Part 1:** 390, 391

"Rembrandt, The" (Wharton), **IV:** 310

"Rembrandt's Hat" (Malamud), **Supp. I Part 2:** 435, 437

Rembrandt Takes a Walk (Strand), **Supp. IV Part 2:** 631

"Rembrandt to Rembrandt" (Robinson), **III:** 521–522

Remembered Earth, The: An Anthology of Contemporary Native American Literature (Hobson, ed.), **Supp. IV Part 1:** 321

Remembered Yesterdays (R. U. Johnson), **Supp. IX:** 184

"Remembering" (Angelou), **Supp. IV Part 1:** 15

"Remembering Allen Tate" (Cowley), **Supp. II Part 1:** 153

"Remembering Barthes" (Sontag), **Supp. III Part 2:** 451, 471

"Remembering Guston" (Kunitz), **Supp. III Part 1:** 257

"Remembering James Laughlin" (Karr), **Supp. XI:** 242

Remembering Laughter (Stegner), **Supp. IV Part 2:** 598, 606, 607, 608, 611, 614

"Remembering Lobo" (Mora), **Supp. XIII:** 220, 227

"Remembering My Father" (Berry), **Supp. X:** 23

"Remembering My Parents Remembering the Books They Read" (Espaillat), **Supp. XXI:** 107

"Remembering that Island" (McGrath), **Supp. X:** 116

"Remembering the Children of Auschwitz" (McGrath), **Supp. X:** 127

"Remembering the Lost World" (Jarrell), **II:** 388

"Remembering the Sixties" (Simpson), **Supp. IX:** 279

Remember Me to Tom (T. Williams), **IV:** 379–380

"Remember Not" (H. Johnson), **Supp. XXVI:** 166

"Remember the Moon Survives" (Kingsolver), **Supp. VII:** 209

Remember to Remember (H. Miller), **III:** 186

"Remembrance, A" (Gioia), **Supp. XV:** 112

Remembrance of Things Past (Proust), **Supp. IV Part 2:** 600; **Supp. XII:** 9; **Supp. XIII:** 44

Remembrance Rock (Sandburg), **III:** 590

Reminiscence, A (Ashbery), **Supp. III Part 1:** 2

Remnick, David, **Supp. XVI:** 246

"Remora" (Merrill), **Supp. III Part 1:** 326

"Removal" (White), **Supp. I Part 2:** 664–665

"Removal, The" (Merwin), **Supp. III Part 1:** 350, 351

"Removal Service Request" (Halliday), **Supp. XIX:** 90

Removed from Time (Matthews and Feeney), **Supp. IX:** 154

Remsen, Ira, **Supp. I Part 1:** 369

"Rémy de Gourmont, A Distinction" (Pound), **III:** 467

"Renaissance" (Carruth), **Supp. XVI:** 56

Renaissance in the South (Bradbury), **I:** 288–289

Renaldo and Clara (film, Dylan and Shepard), **Supp. XVIII:** 21, 28, 31

"Renaming the Kings" (Levine), **Supp. V:** 184

Renan, Ernest, **Supp. XX:** 122

Renan, Joseph Ernest, **II:** 86; **IV:** 440, 444

Renard, Jules, **IV:** 79

"Renascence" (Millay), **III:** 123, 125–126, 128; **Supp. XV:** 42

Renault, Mary, **Supp. IV Part 2:** 685

"Rendezvous, The" (Kumin), **Supp. IV Part 2:** 455

René, Norman, **Supp. X:** 146, 152

Renée (anonymous author), **Supp. XVI:** 64, 66

"Renegade, The" (Jackson), **Supp. IX:** 120

Renewal of Life series (Mumford), **Supp. II Part 2:** 476, 479, 481, 482, 485, 495, 497

"Reno Hill ... Little Bighorn"(Kenny), **Supp. XXIII:** 155

Renoir, Jean, **Supp. XII:** 259; **Supp. XXII:** 256

Renouvrier, Charles, **II:** 344–345, 346

"Renunciation" (Banks), **Supp. V:** 10

Renza, Louis A., **Retro. Supp. II:** 142

"Repair" (Peacock), **Supp. XIX:** 204

"Repeating Dream" (Gander), **Supp. XV:** 340

Repent in Haste (Marquand), **III:** 59

Reperusals and Re-Collections (L. P. Smith), **Supp. XIV:** 346–347

"Repetitive Heart, The: Eleven Poems in Imitation of the Fugue Form" (Schwartz), **Supp. II Part 2:** 645–646

"Replacing Regionalism" (Murphy), **Retro. Supp. II:** 143

Replansky, Naomi, **Supp. X:** 119

Replenishing Jessica (Bodenheim), **Supp. XXV:** 24, 25

"Reply to Mr. Wordsworth" (MacLeish), **III:** 19

"Report, A" (Jin), **Supp. XVIII:** 93

Reporter, The (Levin), **Supp. XXVII:** 139

"Report from a Forest Logged by the Weyhaeuser Company" (Wagoner), **Supp. IX:** 328

"Report from North Vietnam" (Paley), **Supp. VI:** 227

Report from Part One (Brooks), **Supp. III Part 1:** 70, 72, 80, 82–85

Report from Part Two (Brooks), **Supp. III Part 1:** 87

Report on a Game Survey of the North Central States (Leopold), **Supp. XIV:** 182

"Report on the Barnhouse Effect" (Vonnegut), **Supp. II Part 2:** 756

"Report to an Academy, A" (Kafka), **Supp. XX:** 18

"Report to Crazy Horse" (Stafford), **Supp. XI:** 324–325

"Repose of Rivers" (H. Crane), **I:** 393; **Retro. Supp. II:** 78, 81

"Repossession of a Heritage, The" (Zagarell), **Supp. XV:** 270, 281

Repp, John, **Supp. XXIII:** 302

"Representation and the War for Reality" (Gass), **Supp. VI:** 88

"Representative Indian, The" *(Outlook),* **Supp. XXV:** 277, 278

Representative Men (Emerson), **II:** 1, 5–6, 8

"Representing Far Places" (Stafford), **Supp. XI:** 321

Repression and Recovery (Nelson), **Supp. XVIII:** 226

"REPRISE OF ONE OF A. G.'S BEST POEMS" (Baraka), **Supp. II Part 1:** 59

"RepRoach" (Stallings), **Supp. XXV:** 230–231

"Reproducing Ourselves Is All Very Well" (E. Hoffman), **Supp. XVI:** 155

Republic (Plato), **I:** 485

"Republican Manifesto, A" (Paine), **Supp. I Part 2:** 511

"Republican Mother, The: Woman and the Enlightenment—An American Perspective" (Kerber), **Supp. XXV:** 44

Republic of Love, The (Shields), **Supp. VII:** 323–324, 326, 327

"Requa" (Olsen), **Supp. XIII:** 294, **302–303**, 304

Requa, Kenneth A., **Supp. I Part 1:** 107

"Requa I" (Olsen). *See* "Requa" (Olsen)

"Request for Offering" (Eberhart), **I:** 526

"Requiem" (Akhmatova), **Supp. VIII:** 20

"Requiem" (LaBastille), **Supp. X:** 105

Requiem for a Nun (Faulkner), **II:** 57, 72–73

Requiem for Harlem (H. Roth), **Supp. IX:** 235, 236, **240–242**

"Rescue, The" (Updike), **IV:** 214

Rescued Year, The (Stafford), **Supp. XI:** **321–322**

"Rescued Year, The" (Stafford), **Supp. XI:** 322, 323

"Rescue with Yul Brynner" (Moore), **III:** 215

"Rescuing Moon"(P. Benedict), **Supp. XXIII:** 40

"Resemblance" (Bishop), **Supp. I Part 1:** 86

"Resemblance" (Ferry), **Supp. XXIV:** 161

"Resemblance between a Violin Case and a Coffin, A" (T. Williams), **IV:** 378–379

"Reservations" (Taylor), **Supp. V:** 323

"Reserved Memorials" (Mather), **Supp. II Part 2:** 446, 449

"Resignación" (Espaillat), **Supp. XXI:** 104

"Resignation"(J. Schoolcraft), **Supp. XXIII:** 228, 229–230

"Resistance to Civil Government" (Thoreau), **Supp. X:** 27, 28

Resist Much, Obey Little (Berry), **Supp. XIII:** 2

Resolution (Parker), **Supp. XIX:** 187

"Resolution" (Rash), *Supp. XXVII:* 221

"Resolution and Independence" (Wordsworth), **Supp. XV:** 346

"Resonance" (Stone), **Supp. XXVII:** 253

"Resort" (Hampl), **Supp. XXII:** 86–87

Resort and Other Poems (Hampl), **Supp. XXII:** 83, 86–87

Resources of Hope (R. Williams), **Supp. IX:** 146

"Respectable Place, A" (O'Hara), **III:** 369

"Respectable Woman, A" (Chopin), **Retro. Supp. II:** 66

"Respite" (Pedersen; Nelson, trans.), **Supp. XVIII:** 180

Responses (Wilbur), **Supp. III Part 2:** 541

"Response to a Rumor that the Oldest Whorehouse in Wheeling, West Virginia, Has Been Condemned" (Wright), **Supp. III Part 2:** 602

"Rest Cure" (Boyle), **Supp. XXIV:** 57

Restif de La Bretonne, Nicolas, **III:** 175

"Rest of Life, The" (Gordon), **Supp. IV Part 1:** 311

Rest of Life, The: Three Novellas (Gordon), **Supp. IV Part 1:** 310–312

Rest of My Life, The (Wells), **Supp. XXVI:** 271, 283

Rest of the Way, The (McClatchy), **Supp. XII:** 255, **258–259**

Restoration comedy, **Supp. I Part 2:** 617

Restorers, The (Di Piero), **Supp. XIX:** 42–43, 44

"Restorers, The" (Di Piero), **Supp. XIX:** 43

"Restraint" (F. Barthelme), **Supp. XI:** 26

"Result" (Emerson), **II:** 6

"Résumé" (Parker), **Supp. IX:** 189

"Resurrecting Methuselah" (E. P. Jones), **Supp. XXII:** 151

Resurrection (Della Francesca), **Supp. XV:** 262

"Resurrection" (Harjo), **Supp. XII:** 224

"Resurrection" (Jin), **Supp. XVIII:** 94–95

Resurrection, The (Gardner), **Supp. VI:** 61, 63, **64–65,** 68, 69, 73, 74

"Resurrection, The" (Very), **Supp. XXV:** 247–248

"Retort" (Hay), **Supp. XIV:** 133

Retour amont (Char; Sobin, trans.), **Supp. XVI:** 282

Retrieval System, The (Kumin), **Supp. IV Part 2:** 449, 451, 452

"Retrievers in Translation" (Doty), **Supp. XI:** 132

"Retroduction to American History" (Tate), **IV:** 129

"Retrospects and Prospects" (Lanier), **Supp. I Part 1:** 352

"Return" (Corso), **Supp. XII:** 135

"Return" (Creeley), **Supp. IV Part 1:** 141, 145

"Return" (MacLeish), **III:** 12

"Return" (Oppen), **Supp. XXVI:** 231

"Return, The" (Bidart), **Supp. XV:** 32–33

"Return, The" (Bontemps), **Supp. XXII:** 3, 8

"Return, The" (Pound), **Retro. Supp. I:** 288

"Return, The" (Ray), **Supp. XVIII:** 194

"Return, The" (Roethke), **III:** 533

"Return, The: Orihuela, 1965" (Levine), **Supp. V:** 194

"Return: An Elegy, The" (Warren), **IV:** 239

"Return: Buffalo" (Hogan), **Supp. IV Part 1:** 411

"Returning" (Komunyakaa), **Supp. XIII:** 122

"Returning a Lost Child" (Glück), **Supp. V:** 81

"Returning from the Enemy" (Harjo), **Supp. XII:** 229–230

"Returning the Borrowed Road" (Komunyakaa), **Supp. XIII:** 113, 133

"Return of Alcibiade, The" (Chopin), **Retro. Supp. II:** 58, 64

Return of Ansel Gibbs, The (Buechner), **III:** 310; **Supp. XII: 48**

"Return of Eros to Academe, The" (Bukiet), **Supp. XVII:** 47

"Return of Spring" (Winters), **Supp. II Part 2:** 791

Return of the Native, The (Hardy), **II:** 184–185, 186

Return of the Vanishing American, The (Fiedler), **Supp. XIII:** 103

Return to a Place Lit by a Glass of Milk (Simic), **Supp. VIII:** 274, 276, 283

"Return to Lavinia" (Caldwell), **I:** 310

"Return to Thin Air: The Everest Disaster Ten Years Later" (*Outside*), **Supp. XVIII:** 113

Return to Zion, The (Asch), **Supp. XXIII:** 5

Reuben (Wideman), **Supp. X:** 320

Reuben and Rachel; or, Tales of Old Times (Rowson), **Supp. XV: 240–241**

Reunion (Mamet), **Supp. XIV:** 240, 247, 254

"Reunion in Brooklyn" (H. Miller), **III:** 175, 184

"Reunion Joke, The" (Huddle), **Supp. XXVI:** 156

Reuther brothers, **I:** 493

"Reveille" (Kingsolver), **Supp. VII:** 208

"Reveille" (Untermeyer), **Supp. XV:** 300

"Reveille, The" (Harte), **Supp. II Part 1:** 342–343

Revelation (biblical book), **II:** 541; **IV:** 104, 153, 154; **Supp. I Part 1:** 105, 273

"Revelation" (O'Connor), **III:** 349, 353–354; **Retro. Supp. II:** 237

"Revelation" (Warren), **III:** 490

Revenge (Harrison), **Supp. VIII:** 39, 45

"Revenge of Hamish, The" (Lanier), **Supp. I Part 1:** 365

"Revenge of Hannah Kemhuff, The" (Walker), **Supp. III Part 2:** 521

"Revenge of Rain-in-the-Face, The" (Longfellow), **Retro. Supp. II:** 170

"Reverberation"(Kenny), **Supp. XXIII:** 155

Reverberator, The (James), **Retro. Supp. I:** 227

"Reverdure" (Berry), **Supp. X:** 22

Reverdy, Pierre, **Supp. XV:** 178, 182; **Supp. XXIII:** 208

"Reverend Father Gilhooley" (Farrell), **II:** 45

Reverse Transcription (Kushner), **Supp. IX:** 138

Reversible Errors (Turow), **Supp. XVII: 220–221**

"Rev. Freemont Deadman" (Masters), **Supp. I Part 2:** 463

Reviewer's ABC, A (Aiken), **I:** 58

Review of Contemporary Fiction, 1990 (Tabbi, ed.), **Supp. XVII:** 143

"Revolt, against the Crepuscular Spirit in Modern Poetry" (Pound), **Retro. Supp. I:** 286

"Revolution" (C. L. R. James), **Supp. XXI:** 160

"Revolution" (Taggard), **Supp. XXII:** 275

"Revolutionary Answer to the Negro Problem in the USA, The" (statement, C. L. R. James), **Supp. XXI:** 169

Revolutionary Petunias (Walker), **Supp. III Part 2:** 520, 522, 530

Revolutionary Road (Yates), **Supp. XI:** 334, **335–340**

"Revolutionary Symbolism in America" (Burke), **I:** 272

"Revolutionary Theatre, The" (Baraka), **Supp. II Part 1:** 42

Revolution in Taste, A: Studies of Dylan Thomas, Allen Ginsberg, Sylvia Plath, and Robert Lowell (Simpson), **Supp. IX:** 276

"Revolution in the Revolution in the Revolution" (Snyder), **Supp. VIII:** 300

Revon, Marcel, **II:** 525

"Rewaking, The" (W. C. Williams), **Retro. Supp. I:** 430

"Rewrite" (Dunn), **Supp. XI:** 147

"Rewriting Tradition in the Digital Era: The Vision of Eric Gansworth" (Purdy), **Supp. XXVI:** 105

Rexroth, Kenneth, **II:** 526; **Supp. II Part 1:** 307; **Supp. II Part 2:** 436; **Supp. III Part 2:** 625, 626; **Supp. IV Part 1:** 145–146; **Supp. VIII:** 289; **Supp. XIII:** 75; **Supp. XIV:** 287; **Supp. XV:** 140, 141, 146; **Supp. XXII:** 168

Reynolds, Ann (pseudonym). *See* Bly, Carol

Reynolds, Clay, **Supp. XI:** 254

Reynolds, David, **Supp. XV:** 269; **Supp. XXIII:** 187

Reynolds, Sir Joshua, **Supp. I Part 2:** 716

Reynolds, Quentin, **IV:** 286

Reza, Yasmina, **Supp. XXI:** 148

Rezanov (Atherton), **Supp. XXIV:** 23

Reznikoff, Charles, **IV:** 415; **Retro. Supp. I:** 422; **Supp. III Part 2:** 615, 616, 617, 628; **Supp. XIV: 277–296; Supp. XXIII:** 174; **Supp. XXIV:** 36, 45; **Supp. XXVI:** 226

"Rhapsodist, The" (Brown), **Supp. I Part 1:** 125–126

"Rhapsody on a Windy Night" (Eliot), **Retro. Supp. I:** 55

Rhetoric of Motives, A (Burke), **I:** 272, 275, 278, 279

Rhetoric of Religion, The (Burke), **I:** 275, 279

"Rhobert" (Toomer), **Supp. IX:** 316–317

"Rhode Show" (Mallon), **Supp. XIX:** 137–138

"Rhododendrons" (Levis), **Supp. XI:** 260, 263

Rhubarb Show, The (radio, Keillor), **Supp. XVI:** 178

"Rhyme of Sir Christopher, The" (Longfellow), **II:** 501

Rhymes to Be Traded for Bread (Lindsay), **Supp. I Part 2:** 380, 381–382

Rhys, Ernest, **III:** 458

Rhys, Jean, **Supp. III Part 1:** 42, 43; **Supp. XVIII:** 131

"Rhythm" (Stone), **Supp. XXVII:** 249–250

"Rhythm & Blues" (Baraka), **Supp. II Part 1:** 37–38

Rhythms (Reznikoff), **Supp. XIV:** 279, 282, 283

Rhythms II (Reznikoff), **Supp. XIV:** 282, 283, 284

Ribalow, Harold, **Supp. IX:** 236; **Supp. XXVII:** 133

Ribbentrop, Joachim von, **IV:** 249

Ribicoff, Abraham, **Supp. IX:** 33

Ribot, Théodule Armand, **Supp. XX: 238**

Ricardo, David, **Supp. I Part 2:** 628, 634

Rice, Allen Thorndike, **Retro. Supp. I:** 362

Rice, Anne, **Supp. VII: 287–306**

Rice, Elmer, **I:** 479; **III:** 145, 160–161

Rice, Mrs. Grantland, **II:** 435

Rice, Philip Blair, **IV:** 141

Rice, Stan, **Supp. XII:** 2
Rice, Tim, **Supp. XXI:** 148
Rice, Tom, **Supp. XIV:** 125
Rich, Adrienne, **Retro. Supp. I:** 8, 36, 42, 47, 404; **Retro. Supp. II:** 43, 191, 245; **Supp. I Part 2:** 546–547, **550–578; Supp. III Part 1:** 84, 354; **Supp. III Part 2:** 541, 599; **Supp. IV Part 1:** 257, 325; **Supp. V:** 82; **Supp. VIII:** 272; **Supp. XII:** 217, 229, 255; **Supp. XIII:** 294; **Supp. XIV:** 126, 129; **Supp. XIX:** 83, 193; **Supp. XV:** 176, 252; **Supp. XVII:** 32, 74; **Supp. XXII:** 65, 66; **Supp. XXV:** 3; **Supp. XXVI:** 45, 68; **Supp. XXVII:** 165
Rich, Arnold, **Supp. I Part 2:** 552
Rich, Frank, **Supp. IV Part 2:** 585, 586; **Supp. V:** 106; **Supp. XXI:** 146; **Supp. XXIV:** 121, 124
Richard, Mark, **Supp. XIX: 209–222**
Richard Cory (Gurney), **Supp. V:** 99–100, 105
"Richard Hunt's 'Arachne' " (Hayden), **Supp. II Part 1:** 374
Richard II (Shakespeare), **Supp. XVII:** 244
Richard III (Shakespeare), **Supp. I Part 2:** 422
Richards, Bertrand F., **Supp. XX: 217–218**
Richards, Constance S., **Supp. XXII:** 73
Richards, David, **Supp. IV Part 2:** 576; **Supp. XXIV:** 266, 269
Richards, Grant, **I:** 515
Richards, I. A., **I:** 26, 273–274, 279, 522; **III:** 498; **IV:** 92; **Supp. I Part 1:** 264, 265; **Supp. I Part 2:** 647; **Supp. XXVI:** 63
Richards, Ivor Armonstrong, **Supp. XIV:** 2–3, 16
Richards, Keith, **Supp. XXVII:** 40, 41, 45
Richards, Laura E., **II:** 396; **III:** 505–506, 507
Richards, Leonard, **Supp. XIV:** 48
Richards, Lloyd, **Supp. IV Part 1:** 362; **Supp. VIII:** 331
Richards, Rosalind, **III:** 506
Richards, Tad, **Supp. XVII:** 77
Richardson, Alan, **III:** 295
Richardson, Charles, **Supp. XVIII:** 14, 15
Richardson, Dorothy, **I:** 53; **II:** 320; **Supp. III Part 1:** 65
Richardson, Helen Patges, **Retro. Supp. II:** 95
Richardson, Henry Hobson, **I:** 3, 10
Richardson, Maurice, **Supp. XII:** 241
Richardson, Samuel, **I:** 134; **II:** 104, 111, 322; **Supp. IX:** 128; **Supp. V:** 127; **Supp. XV:** 232; **Supp. XX: 236**
Richardson, Tony, **Supp. XI:** 305, 306
"Richard Wright and Recent Negro Fiction" (Ellison), **Retro. Supp. II:** 116
"Richard Wright's Blues" (Ellison), **Retro. Supp. II:** 117, 124
"Richard Yates: A Requiem" (Lawrence), **Supp. XI:** 335
"Rich Boy, The" (Fitzgerald), **II:** 94; **Retro. Supp. I:** 98, 108

Richer, the Poorer, The: Sketches and Reminiscences (D. West), **Supp. XVIII:** 277, 289
"Riches" (Bausch), **Supp. VII:** 54
"Riches" (Teasdale), **Supp. XXVII:** 290
Richey, Elinor, **Supp. XXIV:** 30
Richler, Mordecai, **Supp. XI:** 294, 297
Rich Man, Poor Man (miniseries), **Supp. XIX:** 252
Rich Man, Poor Man (Shaw), **Supp. XIX:** 251–252
Richman, Robert, **Supp. XI:** 249; **Supp. XV:** 120–121, 251
Richman, Shira, **Supp. XXIV:** 167
Richmond (Masters), **Supp. I Part 2:** 471
Richmond, M. A., **Supp. XX: 277, 279, 282, 286, 289, 290**
Rich Relations (Hwang), **Supp. XXI:** 146–147
Richter, Conrad, **Supp. X:** 103; **Supp. XVIII: 207–222**
Richter, Jean Paul, **II:** 489, 492; **Supp. XVI:** 182
Rick Bass (Weltzien), **Supp. XVI:** 20
Rickman, Clio, **Supp. I Part 2:** 519
Ricks, Christopher, **Retro. Supp. I:** 56; **Supp. XVIII:** 20, 30, 32
Riddel, Joseph N., **IV:** 95
"Riddle, The" (Hay), **Supp. XIV:** 130
"Ride in an Omnibus, A" (Briggs), **Supp. XVIII:** 9, 16
Rideout, Walter B., **Supp. XXVI:** 28
"Riders to the Blood-Red Wrath" (Brooks), **Supp. III Part 1:** 82–83
Riders to the Sea (Synge), **III:** 157
Ridge, Lola, **Supp. IX:** 308; **Supp. XV:** 307; **Supp. XXIV:** 49, 52; **Supp. XXVI:** 23
Riding, Alan, **Supp. XVI:** 294
Riding, Laura, **I:** 437
"Riding Out at Evening" (McCarriston), **Supp. XIV:** 262–263
Riding the Iron Rooster: By Train through China (Theroux), **Supp. VIII:** 324
Ridley, Clifford, **Supp. XXIV:** 282
Riesenberg, Felix, **I:** 360, 361
Riesman, David, **Supp. I Part 2:** 649, 650
"Rif, to Music, The" (Bowles), **Supp. IV Part 1:** 89
Riffs & Reciprocities (Dunn), **Supp. XI: 154–155**
Rifkin, Libby, **Supp. XXIV:** 39, 44
Rifles, The (Vollmann), **Supp. XVII:** 226, 233
Riggs, Marlon, **Supp. XI:** 19
Right Distance, The (Pickering), **Supp. XXI:** 196–197
Right Madness on Skye, The (Hugo), **Supp. VI:** 145–147
Rights of Man (Paine), **Supp. I Part 2:** 508, 511, 512–514, 516, 519, 523
"Rights of Woman" (Rowson), **Supp. XV:** 243
"Rights of Women, The" (Brown). *See Alcuin: A Dialogue* (Brown)
Right Stuff, The (Wolfe), **Supp. III Part 2:** 581–584
Right Thoughts in Sad Hours (Mather), **IV:** 144

Rigney, Barbara Hill, **Supp. VIII:** 215
"Rigorists" (Moore), **III:** 198
Rihani, Ameen, **Supp. XX: 115**
Rihoku, **Supp. XXII:** 228
Riis, Jacob A., **I:** 293; **Supp. I Part 1:** 13; **Supp. XVII:** 101, 106
Riley, Glenda, **Supp. XXIV:** 252
Riley, James Whitcomb, **I:** 205; **Supp. II Part 1:** 192, 193, 196, 197
Rilke, Rainer Maria, **I:** 445, 523; **II:** 367, 381, 382–383, 389, 543, 544; **III:** 552, 558, 563, 571, 572; **IV:** 380, 443; **Retro. Supp. II:** 20, 187; **Supp. I Part 1:** 264; **Supp. I Part 2:** 573; **Supp. III Part 1:** 239, 242, 246, 283, 319–320; **Supp. IV Part 1:** 284; **Supp. V:** 208, 343; **Supp. VIII:** 30, 40; **Supp. X:** 164; **Supp. XI:** 126; **Supp. XIII:** 74, 88; **Supp. XV:** 93, 212, 222, **Supp. XV:** 223, 225; **Supp. XVI:** 292; **Supp. XVII:** 244; **Supp. XXII:** 89, 90, 94; **Supp. XXIII:** 207; **Supp. XXIV:** 37, 38, 152, 162; **Supp. XXVI:** 259
Rilke on Love and Other Difficulties (Rilke), **Supp. X:** 164
"Rilke's Growth as a Poet" (Dobyns), **Supp. XIII:** 77
"Rimbaud" (Kerouac), **Supp. III Part 1:** 232
Rimbaud, Arthur, **I:** 381, 383, 389, 391, 526; **II:** 528, 543, 545; **III:** 23, 174, 189; **IV:** 286, 380, 443; **Retro. Supp. I:** 56; **Retro. Supp. II:** 187, 326; **Supp. III Part 1:** 14, 195; **Supp. IV Part 2:** 624; **Supp. VIII:** 39, 40; **Supp. XII:** 1, 16, 128, 255; **Supp. XIII:** 284; **Supp. XIV:** 338; **Supp. XVIII:** 23, 33; **Supp. XXI:** 225, 233; **Supp. XXIII:** 207; **Supp. XXIV:** 39, 40
Rindge, Debora, **Supp. XXI:** 246
Rinehart, Mary Roberts, **Supp. XXV: 189–203; Supp. XXVI:** 276, 281, 282
Rinehart, Stanley, **III:** 36
Ring, Frances Kroll, **Supp. IX:** 63, 64
Ring and the Book, The (Browning), **Supp. I Part 2:** 416, 468
Ring cycle (Wagner), **Supp. IV Part 1:** 392
Ringe, Donald, **I:** 339, 343; **Retro. Supp. II:** 270
Ringel, Faye, **Supp. XXII:** 205, 207
"Ringing" (Bierds), **Supp. XVII:** 28
"Ringing the Bells" (Sexton), **Supp. II Part 2:** 672, 687
Ringle, Ken, **Supp. X:** 15
Ring of Heaven: Poems (Hongo), **Supp. X:** 292
Rink, The (musical, McNally), **Supp. XIII:** 207
Rin Tin Tin: The Life and the Legend (Orlean), **Supp. XXV:** 160, 165–166
Rio Lobo (film), **Supp. XVI:** 246
Ríos, Alberto Alvaro, **Supp. IV Part 2: 537–556**
"Riot" (Brooks), **Supp. III Part 1:** 71, 84–85
Riot (Myers), **Supp. XXVII:** 208
Ripening (Le Sueur), **Supp. XXIII:** 165

Ripley, Ezra, **II:** 8; **IV:** 172

Rip-off Red, Girl Detective (Acker), **Supp. XII:** 3–4

Ripostes (Pound), **Retro. Supp. I:** 287–288, 413

Ripostes of Ezra Pound, The, Whereunto Are Appended the Complete Poetical Works of T. E. Hulme, with Prefatory Note (Pound), **III:** 458, 464, 465

Riprap (Snyder), **Supp. VIII: 292–294,** 295

"Riprap" (Snyder), **Supp. VIII:** 293–294

"Rip Van Winkle" (Irving), **II:** 304–306; **Supp. I Part 1:** 185

Rischin, Moses, **Supp. XVII:** 101, 103, 106

Risco-Lozado, Eliezar, **Supp. XIII:** 313

Rise and Shine (Quindlen), **Supp. XVII:** 179

Rise of David Levinsky, The (Cahan), **Supp. IX:** 227; **Supp. XIII:** 106; **Supp. XXVI:** 123

Rise of Silas Lapham, The (Howells), **II:** 275, 279, 283–285; **IV:** 202; **Retro. Supp. II:** 93, 101

"Rise of the Middle Class" (Banks), **Supp. V:** 10

Rising and Falling (Matthews), **Supp. IX:** 154, **160**

"Rising Daughter, The" (Olds), **Supp. X:** 204

Rising from the Plains (McPhee), **Supp. III Part 1:** 309–310

Rising Glory of America, The (Brackenridge and Freneau), **Supp. I Part 1:** 124; **Supp. II Part 1:** 67, 253, 256, 263

"Rising of the Storm, The" (Dunbar), **Supp. II Part 1:** 199

Rising Sun in the Pacific, The (Morison), **Supp. I Part 2:** 490

Rising Up and Rising Down (Vollmann), **Supp. XVII:** 225, 226, **229–230,** 232, 233, 235–236

Risk Pool, The (Russo), **Supp. XII: 328–331**

Ristovic, Aleksandar, **Supp. VIII:** 272

"Rita Dove: Identity Markers" (Vendler), **Supp. IV Part 1:** 247, 257

Ritchey, John, **Supp. XIV:** 122

Ritchie, Anne Thackeray, **Supp. XX: 231, 233**

"Rite of Passage" (Olds), **Supp. X:** 206

"Rites and Ceremonies" (Hecht), **Supp. X:** 61

Rites and Witnesses: A Comedy (Hinojosa), **Supp. XIX: 106–107**

"Rites of Spring, The" (Morris), **III:** 223

Ritivoi, Andreea Deciu, **Supp. XVI:** 148

Ritschl, Albrecht, **III:** 309, 604

Ritsos, Yannis, **Supp. X:** 112

"Ritsos and the Metaphysical Moment" (Dobyns), **Supp. XIII:** 78

Rittenhouse, David, **Supp. I Part 2:** 507

Rittenhouse, Jessie, **Supp. XV:** 295; **Supp. XXVII:** 286, 288, 289, 297

"Ritual, The" (Jarman), **Supp. XVII:** 114

"Ritual and Renewal: Keres Traditions in the Short Fiction of Leslie Silko" (Ruoff), **Supp. IV Part 2:** 559

Ritz, The (film), **Supp. XIII:** 206

Ritz, The (McNally), **Supp. XIII:** 198

"Rival, The" (Plath), **Retro. Supp. II:** 254

Riven Rock (Boyle), **Supp. VIII:** 5–6; **Supp. XX: 25–26**

"River" (Ammons), **Supp. VII:** 28

"River, The" (O'Connor), **III:** 344, 352, 353, 354, 356; **Retro. Supp. II:** 229, 231–232

Rivera, Tomás, **Supp. XIII:** 216, 221; **Supp. XIX:** 97, 102

Riverbed (Wagoner), **Supp. IX: 327–328**

"River Driftwood" (Jewett), **Retro. Supp. II:** 132, 133, 147

"River Jordan, The" (DeLillo), **Supp. VI:** 3, 4

River King, The (Hoffman), **Supp. X:** 78, 85, 90, **91–92**

"River Merchant's Wife: A Letter, The" (Pound), **III:** 463

"River Now, The" (Hugo), **Supp. VI:** 144

River of Forgetfulness, The (Hadas), **Supp. XXIII: 120**

"River of Rivers in Connecticut, The" (Stevens), **Retro. Supp. I:** 313

River of the Mother of God and Other Essays by Aldo Leopold, The (Leopold), **Supp. XIV:** 179

"River"(O'Hara), **Supp. XXIII:** 212

"River Profile" (Auden), **Supp. II Part 1:** 26

"River Road" (Kunitz), **Supp. III Part 1:** 260

River Runs Through It, A (film), **Supp. XXVI:** 184

"River Runs Through It, A" (Maclean), **Supp. XIV:** 222–223, **223–229,** 233, 234, 235; **Supp. XVI:** 98

River Runs Through It and Other Stories, A (Maclean), **Supp. XIV:** 221, 223

Rivers, Allison, **Supp. XXIII:** 51

Rivers, Larry, **Supp. III Part 1:** 3; **Supp. XV:** 177, 178, 186; **Supp. XXIII:** 209, 210, 211, 212, 215, 216, 217, 220

Rivers and Mountains (Ashbery), **Supp. III Part 1:** 10, 26

Riverside Drive (Simpson), **Supp. IX: 275–276**

Riverside Poetry (Auden, Moore, and Shapiro, eds.), **Supp. XXI:** 98

Rivers to the Sea (Teasdale), **Supp. XV:** 295; **Supp. XXVII:** 283, 286, 289, 290, 294

"River"(Strout), **Supp. XXIII:** 283

River Styx, Ohio, and Other Poems, The (Oliver), **Supp. VII:** 231, 232

"River That Is East, The" (Kinnell), **Supp. III Part 1:** 241–242

"River"(theater performance, Strout), **Supp. XXIII:** 281

"River Towns" (Masters), **Supp. I Part 2:** 473

Rives, Amélie, **II:** 194

Rivière, Jacques, **Retro. Supp. I:** 63

"Rivington's Last Will and Testament" (Freneau), **Supp. II Part 1:** 261

"Rivulet, The" (Bryant), **Supp. I Part 1:** 155, 162

Rix, Alice, **I:** 199

RL's Dream (Mosley), **Supp. XIII:** 234, **244–245,** 249

Roach, Max, **Supp. X:** 239

"Road, Roadsides, and the Disparate Frames of a Sequence" (Sobin), **Supp. XVI:** 288

"Road, The" (H. Johnson), **Supp. XXVI:** 164

Road, The (McCarthy), **Supp. XXII:** 49

Road, The: In Search of America (Asch), **Supp. XXVI:** 17, 21, 23, 25, 26–28

Road Between, The (Farrell), **II:** 29, 38, 39–40

"Road Between Here and There, The" (Kinnell), **Supp. III Part 1:** 254

"Road Home, The" (Hammett), **Supp. IV Part 1:** 343

Road Home, The (Harrison), **Supp. VIII:** 37, 45, 48, **49–50,** 53

Road Is Before Us, The (Boulton), **Supp. XXII:** 17, 25–26

Roadless Yaak, The: Reflections and Observations about One of Our Last Great Wild Places (Bass, ed.), **Supp. XVI:** 23

"Road Not Taken, The" (R. Frost), **II:** 154; **Retro. Supp. I:** 131; **Supp. XI:** 150; **Supp. XV:** 127

"Roadside Flowers" (Collins), **Supp. XXI:** 61

Roadside Poems for Summer Travellers (Larcom, ed.), **Supp. XIII:** 142

"Roadside Resurrection, A" (L. Brown), **Supp. XXI:** 40, 42

Roads of Destiny (O. Henry), **Supp. II Part 1:** 410

Road through the Wall, The (Jackson), **Supp. IX:** 115, 118, 120, 123–124

"Road to Avignon, The" (A. Lowell), **II:** 516

"Road to Hell, The" (Fante), **Supp. XI:** 160

Road to Los Angeles, The (Fante), **Supp. XI:** 160, 166, 167, **168,** 172

Road to Many a Wonder, The (Wagoner), **Supp. IX:** 327, **336**

Road to the Temple, The (Glaspell), **Supp. III Part 1:** 175, 182, 186; **Supp. XXI:** 6

Road to Wellville, The (Boyle), **Supp. VIII:** 6–8; **Supp. XX:** 24–25, 26, 28

Road to Xanadu, The (Lowes), **IV:** 453

"Road Warrior" (Pickering), **Supp. XXI:** 204

"Roan Stallion" (Jeffers), **Supp. II Part 2:** 428–429

"Roast-beef" (Stein), **IV:** 43

Roast Leviatham (Untermeyer), **Supp. XV:** 307

"Roast Possum" (Dove), **Supp. IV Part 1:** 247, 248

Robards, Jason, Jr., **III:** 163, 403

Robb, Christina, **Supp. XV:** 251

Robbe-Grillet, Alain, **I:** 123; **IV:** 95; **Supp. IV Part 1:** 42; **Supp. V:** 47, 48; **Supp. XXIII:** 213

Robber Bride, The (Atwood), **Supp. XIII: 30–31**

Robber Bridegroom, The (Welty), **IV:** 261, 266–268, 271, 274; **Retro. Supp. I:** 347

Robbins, Amy Moorman, **Supp. XXVII:** 170

Robbins, Harold, **Supp. XII:** 6

Robbins, Henry, **Supp. IV Part 1:** 198, 201, 210, 211

Robbins, Katherine Robinson, **Supp. X:** 264

Robbins, Thomas, **Supp. XV:** 271

Robbins, Tom, **Supp. IV Part 1:** 227; **Supp. VIII:** 14; **Supp. X: 259–288; Supp. XIII:** 11

"Robe, The" (Douglas), **IV:** 434

Robert Bly (Sugg), **Supp. IV Part 1:** 68

"Robert Bly" (W. V. Davis), **Supp. IV Part 1:** 70

"Robert Bly and the Trouble with America" (Mitchell), **Supp. IV Part 1:** 70

Robert Bly: An Introduction to the Poetry (Nelson), **Supp. IV Part 1:** 66

Robert Bly: The Poet and His Critics (W. V. Davis), **Supp. IV Part 1:** 63; **Supp. XXI:** 84, **85–86,** 87, 95

Robert Coover: The Universal Fiction-making Process (Gordon), **Supp. V:** 46

Robert Creeley (Ford), **Supp. IV Part 1:** 140

Robert Creeley and the Genius of the American Common Place (Clark), **Supp. IV Part 1:** 140

Robert Creeley's Poetry: A Critical Introduction (Edelberg), **Supp. IV Part 1:** 155

Robert E. Howard: Selected Poems (Coffman, ed.), **Supp. XXVII:** 118

Robert Frost (Meyers), **Retro. Supp. I:** 138

Robert Lowell (Meyers), **Retro. Supp. II:** 191

Robert Lowell and the Sublime (Hart), **Retro. Supp. II:** 187

Robert Lowell's Shifting Colors (Doreski), **Retro. Supp. II:** 185

Robert Lowell: The First Twenty years (Staples), **Retro. Supp. II:** 187

Roberts, Carol, **Supp. XX: 53**

Roberts, David, **Supp. XVIII:** 106

Roberts, Diane, **Supp. X:** 15; **Supp. XXVII:** 2

Roberts, J. M., **IV:** 454

Roberts, Leo, **II:** 449

Roberts, Margaret, **II:** 449; **IV:** 453, 454

Roberts, Matthew, **Retro. Supp. II:** 324

Roberts, Meade, **IV:** 383

Roberts, Michael, **I:** 527, 536

Roberts, Richard, **III:** 297

Roberts, Victoria, **Supp. XIX:** 205

Roberts, Wally, **Supp. XI:** 119, 120, 126

Roberts, William, **Supp. XI:** 343

Roberts Brothers, **Retro. Supp. I:** 31, 35

Robertson, David, **Supp. VIII:** 305

Robertson, D. B., **III:** 311

Robertson, Lisa, **Supp. XXII:** 155

Robertson, Nan, **Supp. IV Part 1:** 300

Robertson, William, **II:** 8

Robert the Devil (Merwin, trans.), **Supp. III Part 1:** 341, 346

Robeson, Paul, **III:** 392; **Supp. IV Part 1:** 360, 361; **Supp. X:** 137; **Supp. XIX:** 66; **Supp. XXI:** 167

Robeson, Susan L., **Supp. XVIII:** 268

Robespierre, Maximilien, **Supp. I Part 2:** 514, 515, 517

"Robinson" (Kees), **Supp. XV:** 143–144

Robinson, Christopher L., **Supp. XII:** 13, 14

Robinson, David, **Supp. XXIV:** 70, 71, 78–79

Robinson, Dean, **III:** 506

Robinson, Edward, **III:** 505

Robinson, Edward G., **Supp. XI:** 306

Robinson, Edwin Arlington, **I:** 480; **II:** 388, 391, 529, 542; **III:** 5, **503–526,** 576; **Supp. I Part 2:** 699; **Supp. II Part 1:** 191; **Supp. III Part 1:** 63, 75; **Supp. III Part 2:** 592, 593; **Supp. IX:** 77, 266, 276, 308; **Supp. XIX:** 123; **Supp. XV:** 256, 299, 300, 301, 306; **Supp. XVII:** 69; **Supp. XXVII:** 283

Robinson, Forrest G., **Supp. IV Part 2:** 597, 601, 604

Robinson, Herman, **III:** 506–507

Robinson, H. M., **IV:** 369, 370

Robinson, Jackie, **Supp. I Part 1:** 338

Robinson, James Harvey, **I:** 214; **Supp. I Part 2:** 492

Robinson, James K., **Supp. IX:** 328

Robinson, Margaret G., **Supp. IV Part 2:** 597, 601, 604

Robinson, Marilynne, **Supp. XXI: 209–224; Supp. XXII:** 50; **Supp. XXVI:** 45, 187

Robinson, Mary, **Supp. XI:** 26

Robinson, Rowland E., **Supp. XIX:** 6

Robinson, Roxana, **Supp. XXV:** 60

Robinson, Sugar Ray, **Supp. IV Part 1:** 167

Robinson, Ted, **Supp. XIII:** 166

Robinson Crusoe (Defoe), **II:** 159; **III:** 113, 423; **IV:** 369; **Retro. Supp. II:** 274; **Supp. I Part 2:** 714; **Supp. IV Part 2:** 502

Robison, Mary, **Supp. V:** 22; **Supp. XXI:** 115, 116, 118

Roblès, Emmanuel, **Supp. I Part 1:** 283

"Robstown" (Salinas), **Supp. XIII:** 315

Rochefort, Christina, **Supp. XVI:** 143

Rochefoucauld, Louis Alexandre, **Supp. I Part 2:** 510

Rochman, Hazel, **Supp. XXVII:** 204

"Rock" (Nye), **Supp. XIII:** 287

Rock (Wagoner), **Supp. IX:** 324, **334,** 335

Rock, Catherine, **Supp. XII:** 17

Rock, The (Eliot), **Retro. Supp. I:** 65

Rock, The (Stevens), **Retro. Supp. I:** 309, 312

"Rock, The" (Stevens), **Retro. Supp. I:** 312

Rockaway (Shanley), **Supp. XIV:** 315

"Rock Climbers, The" (Francis), **Supp. IX:** 82

Rock-Drill (Pound), **Retro. Supp. I:** 293

Rockefeller, John D., **I:** 273; **III:** 580; **Supp. I Part 2:** 486; **Supp. V:** 286;

Supp. XXIII: 26

Rockefeller, Nelson, **III:** 14, 15

Rocket Boys (Hickam), **Supp. XXVII:** 101, 103–106

Rocket Boys (musical), **Supp. XXVII:** 103

Rockets and Rodeos and Other American Spectacles (Mallon), **Supp. XIX:** 137

Rocket to the Moon (Odets), **Supp. II Part 2:** 541–543, 544

Rock Garden, The (Shepard), **Supp. III Part 2:** 432, 447

"Rocking Horse Winner, The" (Lawrence), **Supp. I Part 1:** 329

Rocking the Boat (Vidal), **Supp. IV Part 2:** 683

"Rockpile, The" (Baldwin), **Supp. I Part 1:** 63

Rock Springs (Ford), **Supp. V:** 57, 58–59, 68–69

Rockwell, John, **Supp. XXVII:** 45, 46

Rocky Mountains, The: or, Scenes, Incidents, and Adventures in the Far West; Digested from the Journal of Captain E. L. E Bonneville, of the Army of the United States, and Illustrated from Various Other Sources (Irving), **II:** 312

Rodden, John, **Supp. XVI:** 63, 69, 72

Roddenberry, Gene, **Supp. XXII:** 60

Rodefer, Stephen, **Supp. XXIV:** 38

Roderick, David, **Supp. XV:** 223

Roderick Hudson (James), **II:** 284, 290, 324, 326, 328; **Retro. Supp. I:** 219, **220–221,** 221, 226; **Supp. IX:** 142

Rodgers, Richard, **III:** 361

Rodgers, Ronald, **Supp. IV Part 2:** 503

Rodker, John, **III:** 470

Rodman, Selden, **Supp. I Part 1:** 83; **Supp. X:** 115

Rodney, Walter, **Supp. XXI:** 171

"Rodrigo Returns to the Land and Linen Celebrates" (Cisneros), **Supp. VII:** 68

Rodríguez, Diane, **Supp. XXIII:** 203

Rodriguez, Randy A., **Supp. XII:** 312

Rodriguez, Richard, **Supp. XIV: 297–313**

Roethke, Charles, **III:** 531

Roethke, Theodore, **I:** 167, 171–172, 183, 254, 285, 521; **III:** 273, **527–550; IV:** 138, 402; **Retro. Supp. II:** 178, 181, 246; **Supp. I Part 2:** 539; **Supp. III Part 1:** 47, 54, 56, 239, 253, 260–261, 350; **Supp. IV Part 2:** 626; **Supp. IX:** 323; **Supp. XV:** 140, 145, 212; **Supp. XVIII:** 90; **Supp. XX: 199; Supp. XXIII:** 19; **Supp. XXIV:** 165, 171; **Supp. XXVII:** 250

"Roger Malvin's Burial" (Hawthorne), **II:** 243; **Retro. Supp. I:** 153

Rogers, Michael, **Supp. X:** 265, 266

Rogers, Pattiann, **Supp. XVIII:** 189

Rogers, Samuel, **II:** 303; **Supp. I Part 1:** 157

Rogers, Will, **I:** 261; **IV:** 388

Roger's Version (Updike), **Retro. Supp. I:** 325, 327, 330

Roget, Peter Mark, **Supp. I Part 1:** 312

"Rogue River Jet-Board Trip, Gold Beach, Oregon, July 4, 1977" (Carver), **Supp. III Part 1:** 140

"Rogue's Gallery" (McCarthy), **II:** 563

Rohr, Richard, **Supp. XX: 143**
Roiphe, Katie, **Supp. XXV:** 10
Roland de La Platière, Jean Marie, **II:** 554
Rolando Hinojosa and the American Dream (Glover), **Supp. XIX:** 112
Rolando Hinojosa: A Reader's Guide (Zilles), **Supp. XIX:** 112
Rolando Hinojosa Reader, The (Saldívar, ed.), **Supp. XIX:** 112
Rôle du Nègre dans la culture des Amériques, La (Locke), **Supp. XIV:** 202
"Role of a Lifetime, The" (Skloot), **Supp. XX: 203**
"Role of Society in the Artist, The" (Ammons), **Supp. VII:** 34
Rolfe, Alfred, **IV:** 427
Rolfe, Frederick, **Supp. XX: 235**
"Roll, Jordan, Roll" (spiritual), **Supp. IV Part 1:** 16
Rolland, Romain, **Supp. XX: 70**
"Roll Call" (Hoffman), **Supp. XVIII:** 86
"Roll Call" (Komunyakaa), **Supp. XIII:** 123
Rolle, Esther, **Supp. IV Part 1:** 367
Rollin, Charles, **II:** 113
Rolling Stones (O. Henry), **Supp. II Part 1:** 410
Rolling Thunder Logbook (Shepard), **Supp. III Part 2:** 433
Rolling Thunder Logbook, The (Shepard), **Supp. XVIII:** 31
"Rolling Up" (Simpson), **Supp. IX:** 265, 274, 280
Rollins, Howard E., Jr., **Supp. IV Part 1:** 236
Rollins, Hyder E., **Supp. IV Part 1:** 168
Rollins, Sonny, **Supp. V:** 195
"Rollo" tales (Abbott), **Supp. I Part 1:** 38
"Roma I" (Wright), **Supp. V:** 338
"Roma II" (Wright), **Supp. V:** 338
Romains, Jules, **I:** 227
Román, David, **Supp. XIII:** 208
Romance, A (Weigl), **Supp. XIX: 277–278**
"Romance, A" (Weigl), **Supp. XIX:** 278
"Romance and a Reading List" (Fitzgerald), **Retro. Supp. I:** 101
Romance of a Plain Man, The (Glasgow), **II:** 175, 180–181
"Romance of Certain Old Clothes, The" (James), **II:** 322; **Retro. Supp. I:** 218
Romance Reader, The (Abraham), **Supp. XXIV:** 1–2, 3, **4–7**
"Roman Elegies" (Brodsky), **Supp. VIII:** 29
"Roman Fever" (Wharton), **Retro. Supp. I:** 382
"Roman Fountain" (Bogan), **Supp. III Part 1:** 56
"*Romanitas* of Gore Vidal, The" (Tatum), **Supp. IV Part 2:** 684
Romaniuk, Zbigniew, **Supp. XVI:** 154
Romano, John, **Supp. XV:** 253
"Roman Sarcophagus, A" (R. Lowell), **II:** 544
Roman Spring of Mrs. Stone, The (T. Williams), **IV:** 383, 385

"Romantic, The" (Bogan), **Supp. III Part 1:** 50
Romantic Comedians, The (Glasgow), **II:** 175, 186, 190, 194
Romantic Education, A (Hampl), **Supp. XXII:** 82, 83, **87–90**, 91
Romantic Egoists, The (Auchincloss), **Supp. IV Part 1:** 25
Romantic Egotist, The (Fitzgerald), **II:** 82
"Romantic Egotist, The" (Fitzgerald), **Retro. Supp. I:** 100
"Romanticism and Classicism" (Hulme), **III:** 196
"Romanticism Comes Home" (Shapiro), **Supp. II Part 2:** 713
Romantic Manifesto, The: A Philosophy of Literature (Rand), **Supp. IV Part 2:** 521, 523, 527, 529–530
"Romantic Regionalism of Harper Lee, The" (Erisman), **Supp. VIII:** 126
Romantics, The (Rinehart), **Supp. XXV:** 196
"Rome" (W. C. Williams), **Retro. Supp. I:** 420
Rome Brothers, **Retro. Supp. I:** 393
Romeo and Juliet (Shakespeare), **Supp. V:** 252; **Supp. VIII:** 223
Romola (G. Eliot), **II:** 291; **IV:** 311
Romulus: A New Comedy (Vidal), **Supp. IV Part 2:** 683
Romulus der Grosse (Dürrenmatt), **Supp. IV Part 2:** 683
Ronald, Ann, **Supp. XIII:** 4, 5, 6, 7, 9, 11
"Rondel for a September Day" (White), **Supp. I Part 2:** 676
"Ron Narrative Reconstructions, The" (Coleman), **Supp. XI:** 83
"Ron Padgett's Visual Imagination" (Notley), **Supp. XXII:** 224
Ron Rash Reader, The (Rash; Wilhelm, ed.), **Supp. XXVII:** 215
Ronsard, Pierre de, **Supp. X:** 65; **Supp. XV:** 165
Rood, John, **IV:** 261
"Roof, the Steeple, and the People, The" (Ellison), **Retro. Supp. II:** 118, 126; **Supp. II Part 1:** 248
"Room" (Levertov), **Supp. III Part 1:** 282
Roomates (film, P. Yates), **Supp. XVII:** 8, 9
Roomates: My Grandfather's Story (Apple), **Supp. XVII:** 2, **7–9**
"Room at the Heart of Things, A" (Merrill), **Supp. III Part 1:** 337
Room Called Remember, A: Uncollected Pieces (Buechner), **Supp. XII:** 53
"Roomful of Hovings, A" (McPhee), **Supp. III Part 1:** 291, 294
Room of One's Own, A (Woolf), **Supp. IX:** 19; **Supp. V:** 127; **Supp. XIII:** 305
Room Rented by a Single Woman (Wright), **Supp. XV:** 340–341
"Rooms" (Collins), **Supp. XXI:** 61
Room Temperature (Baker), **Supp. XIII:** 41, **43–45**, 48, 50
Room to Swing (Lacy), **Supp. XV:** 202, 203, 205, 207

"Room Upstairs, The" (Gioia), **Supp. XV:** 120–121, 124
Roosevelt, Eleanor, **IV:** 371; **Supp. IV Part 2:** 679; **Supp. XXVII:** 137
Roosevelt, Franklin, **Supp. V:** 290
Roosevelt, Franklin Delano, **I:** 482, 485, 490; **II:** 553, 575; **III:** 2, 18, 69, 110, 297, 321, 376, 476, 580, 581; **Supp. I Part 2:** 488, 489, 490, 491, 645, 654, 655
Roosevelt, Kermit, **III:** 508
Roosevelt, Theodore, **I:** 14, 62; **II:** 130; **III:** 508; **IV:** 321; **Retro. Supp. I:** 377; **Supp. I Part 1:** 1, 21; **Supp. I Part 2:** 455, 456, 502, 707; **Supp. IX:** 184; **Supp. V:** 280, 282; **Supp. XIX:** 29; **Supp. XX:** 221; **Supp. XXIII:** 26
Roosevelt After Inauguration And Other Atrocities (Burroughs), **Supp. III Part 1:** 98
"Roosevelt Chair, The" (Skloot), **Supp. XX: 205**
"Roosters" (Bishop), **Retro. Supp. II:** 39, 43, 250; **Supp. I Part 1:** 89
Root, Abiah, **I:** 456
Root, Elihu, **Supp. IV Part 1:** 33
Root, Simeon, **I:** 548
Root, Timothy, **I:** 548
Rootabaga Stories (Sandburg), **III:** 583, 587
"Rootedness: The Ancestor as Foundation" (Morrison), **Supp. III Part 1:** 361
"Roots" (Halliday), **Supp. XIX:** 88
Roots in the Soil (film), **Supp. IV Part 1:** 83
"Rope" (Porter), **III:** 451
Rope (screenplay, Hecht), **Supp. XXVII:** 93
Rope, The (O'Neill), **III:** 388
Ropemakers of Plymouth, The (Morison), **Supp. I Part 2:** 494
"Ropes" (Nye), **Supp. XIII:** 276
"Rope's End, The" (Nemerov), **III:** 282
Roquelaure, A. N., **Supp. VII:** 301. *See also* Rice, Anne
Rorem, Ned, **Supp. IV Part 1:** 79, 84; **Supp. XXIII:** 217
Rorschach Test (F. Wright), **Supp. XVII:** 240, 245
Rorty, James, **Supp. XXII:** 276, 277
"Rosa" (Ozick), **Supp. V:** 271
Rosa, Rodrigo Rey, **Supp. IV Part 1:** 92
Rosaldo, Renato, **Supp. IV Part 2:** 544
"Rosalia" (Simic), **Supp. VIII:** 278
Roscoe, Will, **Supp. IV Part 1:** 330
"Roscoe in Hell" (McKnight), **Supp. XX: 151**
"Rose" (Dubus), **Supp. VII:** 88
Rose (L.-Y. Lee), **Supp. XV:** 211, **212–215**, 218
Rose, Alice, Sister, **III:** 348
Rose, Charlie, **Supp. XIX:** 26, 30; **Supp. XXVII:** 270
Rose, Lloyd, **Supp. XXIV:** 267
Rose, Mickey, **Supp. XV:** 3
Rose, Philip, **Supp. IV Part 1:** 362
"Rose, The" (Roethke), **III:** 537
"Rose, The" (W. C. Williams), **Retro. Supp. I:** 419

Rose, Where Did You Get That Red?: Teaching Great Poetry to Children (Koch), **Supp. XV:** 189

"Rose for Emily, A" (Faulkner), **II:** 72; **Supp. IX:** 96; **Supp. XX: 179; Supp. XXIV:** 136

Rose-Hued Cities (P. N. Warren), **Supp. XX: 261**

Rose in Bloom (Alcott), **Supp. I Part 1:** 42

"Rose-Johnny" (Kingsolver), **Supp. VII:** 203

Rose Madder (King), **Supp. V:** 141, 148, 150, 152

"Rose-Morals" (Lanier), **Supp. I Part 1:** 364

Rosen, Jody, **Supp. XXVII:** 46

Rosen, Jonathan, **Supp. XVII:** 50; **Supp. XX: 179**

Rosen, Kenneth, **Supp. IV Part 2:** 499, 505, 513

Rosen, Norma, **Supp. XVII:** 49, 50

Rosenbaum, Alissa Zinovievna. *See* Rand, Ayn

Rosenbaum, Thane, **Supp. XVII:** 48

Rosenberg, Bernard, **Supp. I Part 2:** 650

Rosenberg, Harold, **Supp. XIX:** 159; **Supp. XV:** 143; **Supp. XXIII:** 211

Rosenberg, Isaac, **Supp. XXVII:** 295

Rosenberg, Julia, **Supp. XVIII:** 136

Rosenberg, Julius and Ethel, **Supp. I Part 1:** 295; **Supp. I Part 2:** 532; **Supp. V:** 45

Rosenberg, Liz, **Supp. XV:** 251

Rosenberg, Shlomo, **Supp. XXIII:** 6

Rosenbloom, Joel, **Supp. IV Part 2:** 527

Rosenblum, Martin, **Supp. XXVI:** 236

Rosenfeld, Alvin H., **Supp. I Part 1:** 120

Rosenfeld, Isaac, **Supp. XII:** 160

Rosenfeld, Paul, **I:** 116, 117, 231, 245

Rosenfelt, Deborah, **Supp. XIII:** 296, 304

Rosenfield, Isaac, **IV:** 3

Rosengarten, Theodore, **Supp. XVIII:** 183

Rosenthal, Ira, **Supp. XIV:** 146–147

Rosenthal, Lois, **Supp. VIII:** 258

Rosenthal, M. L., **II:** 550; **III:** 276, 479; **Supp. V:** 333

Rosenthal, Peggy, **Supp. XVII:** 119

Rose of Wissahikon, The (Lippard), **Supp. XXIII:** 178

"Rose Pogonias" (Frost), **Retro. Supp. I:** 127

"Rose Red and Snow White" (Grimms), **Supp. X:** 82

"Rose Room" (Sorrentino), **Supp. XXI:** 228

"Roses" (Conroy), **Supp. XVI:** 72

"Roses" (Dove), **Supp. IV Part 1:** 246

"Roses and Skulls" (Goldbarth), **Supp. XII:** 192

"Roses for Lubbock" (Nye), **Supp. XIII:** 281

"Roses Only" (Moore), **III:** 195, 198, 200, 202, 215

Rose Tattoo, The (T. Williams), **IV:** 382, 383, 387, 388, 389, 392–393, 394, 397, 398

Rose Theatre (Sorrentino), **Supp. XXI:** 236

"Rosewood, Ohio" (Matthews), **Supp. IX:** 160

Rosie (Lamott), **Supp. XX: 133–134**

"Rosie Baby" (Huddle), **Supp. XXVI:** 147, 152

Rosiebelle Lee Wildcat Tennessee (Andrews), **Supp. XXVI:** 6–7

Rosinante to the Road Again (Dos Passos), **I:** 478

Roskies, David, **Supp. XVII:** 39, 44, 49–50

Roskolenko, Harry, **Supp. XV:** 179

Rosmersholm (Ibsen), **III:** 152

Rosmond, Babette, **II:** 432

Ross, Eleanor. *See* Taylor, Eleanor Ross

Ross, Harold, **Supp. I Part 1:** 174; **Supp. I Part 2:** 607, 617, 653, 654, 655, 660; **Supp. IX:** 190; **Supp. VIII:** 151, 170

Ross, Herbert, **Supp. XV:** 2

Ross, Jean, **Supp. XXI:** 144, 146

Ross, John F., **II:** 110

Ross, Lillilan, **Retro. Supp. II:** 198

Ross, Mary, **Supp. XXII:** 195

Ross, Mitchell S., **Supp. IV Part 2:** 692; **Supp. X:** 260

Ross, Robert, **Supp. XXIV:** 167

Rossen, Robert, **Supp. XI:** 306

Rosset, Barney, **III:** 171

Rossetti, Christina, **Supp. XIV:** 128; **Supp. XXVII:** 284

Rossetti, Dante Gabriel, **I:** 433; **II:** 323; **Retro. Supp. I:** 128, 286; **Supp. I Part 2:** 552; **Supp. XXII:** 156

Rossetti, William Michael, **Retro. Supp. I:** 407

Rossi, Umberto, **Supp. XVIII:** 137, 138–139

Rossini, Clare, **Supp. XVII:** 111

Rosskam, Edwin, **IV:** 477

Ross Macdonald (Bruccoli), **Supp. IV Part 2:** 468, 470

Rostand, Edmond, **II:** 515; **Supp. IV Part 2:** 518

Rosten, Leo, **Supp. XVII:** 9

Rosy Crucifixion, The (H. Miller), **III:** 170, 187, 188–189, 190

Rote Walker, The (Jarman), **Supp. XVII:** 110, **113–115**

Roth, Henry, **Supp. IV Part 1:** 314; **Supp. IX: 227–243; Supp. VIII:** 233; **Supp. XIII:** 106; **Supp. XXVII:** 134

Roth, Philip, **I:** 144, 161; **II:** 591; **Retro. Supp. II:** 22, **279–297; Supp. I Part 1:** 186, 192; **Supp. I Part 2:** 431, 441, 443; **Supp. II Part 1:** 99; **Supp. III Part 2: 401–429; Supp. IV Part 1:** 236, 379, 388; **Supp. IX:** 227; **Supp. V:** 45, 119, 122, 257, 258; **Supp. VIII:** 88, 236, 245; **Supp. XI:** 64, 68, 99, 140; **Supp. XII:** 190, 310; **Supp. XIV:** 79, 93, 111, 112; **Supp. XVI:** 206; **Supp. XVII:** 43, 48, 183; **Supp. XVIII:** 89; **Supp. XXI:** 234; **Supp. XXII:** 268; **Supp. XXVI:** 119, 123; **Supp. XXVII:** 142

Roth, Rita, **Supp. XVI:** 112

Roth, William, **Supp. XV:** 142

Rothenberg, Jerome, **Supp. VIII:** 292; **Supp. XII:** 3; **Supp. XXIV:** 37

Rothermere, Lady Mary, **Retro. Supp. I:** 63

Rothko, Mark, **Supp. XV:** 144

Rothstein, Mervyn, **Supp. VIII:** 142

"Rouen, France"(Kenny), **Supp. XXIII:** 152

"Rouge High" (Hughes), **Supp. I Part 1:** 330

Rougemont, Denis de, **II:** 586; **IV:** 216; **Retro. Supp. I:** 328, 329, 330, 331

Rough Edges (Skloot), **Supp. XX: 196**

Roughing It (Twain), **II:** 312; **IV:** 195, 197, 198

Roughing It in the Bush (Shields), **Supp. VII:** 313

"Rough Outline" (Simic), **Supp. VIII:** 276

"Rough-Skinned Newt, The"(Schott), **Supp. XXIII:** 253–254

Rough South of Larry Brown, The (film, Hawkins), **Supp. XXI:** 39

Rougon-Macquart, Les (Zola), **II:** 175–176

Roumain, Jacques, **Retro. Supp. I:** 202; **Supp. IV Part 1:** 360, 367

"Round, The" (Kunitz), **Supp. III Part 1:** 268

"Roundelay Between Two Shepherdesses, A" (Notley), **Supp. XXII:** 229

"Round Trip" (Dunn), **Supp. XI:** 148–149

Round Up (Lardner), **II:** 426, 430, 431

Rountree, Owen (pseud.). *See* Kittredge, William; Krauzer, Steven M.

Rourke, Constance, **I:** 258; **IV:** 339, 352

Rourke, Milton, **Retro. Supp. II:** 89

Rousseau, Jean-Jacques, **I:** 226; **II:** 8, 343; **III:** 170, 178, 259; **IV:** 80, 173, 440; **Supp. I Part 1:** 126; **Supp. I Part 2:** 637, 659; **Supp. IV Part 1:** 171; **Supp. XI:** 245; **Supp. XVI:** 292; **Supp. XXI:** 83; **Supp. XXVI:** 38–39

Roussel, Raymond, **Supp. III Part 1:** 6, 7, 10, 15, 16, 21; **Supp. XV:** 182

"Route 302" (Halliday), **Supp. XIX:** 93

"Routes" (Everwine), **Supp. XV:** 82

"Route Six" (Kunitz), **Supp. III Part 1:** 258

Route Two (Erdrich and Dorris), **Supp. IV Part 1:** 260

"Routine Things Around the House, The" (Dunn), **Supp. XI:** 148

Rover Boys (Winfield), **III:** 146

Rovit, Earl, **IV:** 102

Rowan, Carl T., **Supp. XIV:** 306

Rowe, Anne E., **Supp. X:** 223

Rowe, John Carlos, **Retro. Supp. I:** 216

Rowe, Kenneth Thorpe, **Supp. XXIII:** 258

Rowell, Charles, **Supp. XXI:** 250, 254, 255; **Supp. XXIV:** 184

"Rowing" (Sexton), **Supp. II Part 2:** 696

"Rowing Endeth, The" (Sexton), **Supp. II Part 2:** 696

Rowlandson, Mary, **Supp. IV Part 2:** 430, 431

Rowling, J. K., **Supp. XXV:** 70

"Rows of Cold Trees, The" (Winters), **Supp. II Part 2:** 790–791, 800

Rowson, Susanna, **Supp. I Part 1:** 128; **Supp. XV: 229–248**

Roxanna Slade (Price), **Supp. VI:** 267

Roxie Hart (Watkins), **Supp. XVI:** 188

Royal Family, The (Vollmann), **Supp. XVII:** 226, 230, 233

"Royal Palm" (Crane), **I:** 401

Royce, Josiah, **I:** 443; **III:** 303, 600; **IV:** 26; **Retro. Supp. I:** 57; **Supp. XIV:** 197, 199; **Supp. XVII:** 97

"Roy McInnes" (Budbill), **Supp. XIX:** 6–7

"Roy Spivey" (July), **Supp. XXIV:** 210

Royster, Sarah Elmira, **III:** 410, 429

Royte, Elizabeth, **Supp. XV:** 59

Różewicz, Tadeusz, **Supp. X:** 60

R. S. Thomas: Poetry and Theology (W. V. Davis), **Supp. XXI: 86–87**

Ruas, Charles, **Supp. IV Part 1:** 383

Ruback, Max, **Supp. XXIII:** 290

Rubáiyát (Khayyám), **I:** 568

Rubáiyát of Omar Khayyam (Fitzgerald), **Supp. I Part 2:** 416; **Supp. III Part 2:** 610; **Supp. XV:** 156; **Supp. XXVII:** 262

"Rubber Life" (Prose), **Supp. XVI:** 256

Rubel, Nora L., **Supp. XXIV:** 7

Rub from Snub, A (Swanwick), **Supp. XV:** 237

"Rubicon" (Cliff), **Supp. XXII:** 76

Rubin, Louis, **Supp. I Part 2:** 672, 673, 679; **Supp. X:** 42

Rubin, Louis D., Jr., **IV:** 116, 462–463

Rubin, Stan, **Supp. XIV:** 307, 310

Rubin, Stan Sanvel, **Supp. IV Part 1:** 242, 245, 252

Rubins, Josh, **Supp. XX: 89**

"Ruby Brown" (Hughes), **Supp. I Part 1:** 327

"Ruby Daggett" (Eberhart), **I:** 539

Rucker, Rudy, **Supp. X:** 302

Rudd, Hughes, **Supp. XII:** 141

"Rude Awakening, A" (Chopin), **Retro. Supp. II:** 64

Rudens (Plautus), **Supp. III Part 2:** 630

Ruderman, Judith, **Supp. IV Part 1:** 380

Rudge, Olga, **Supp. V:** 338

Rudikoff, Sonya, **Supp. XIV:** 113

Rudman, Mark, **Supp. XXIII:** 124; **Supp. XXIV:** 153

Rueckert, William, **I:** 264

Ruesch, Jurgen, **Supp. XV:** 147

Rugby Chapel (Arnold), **Supp. I Part 2:** 416

"Rugby Road" (Garrett), **Supp. VII:** 100

Rugge, John, **Supp. XXII:** 218

Ruining the New Road (Matthews), **Supp. IX:** 154, **155–157**

"Ruins of Italica, The" (Bryant, trans.), **Supp. I Part 1:** 166

Rukeyser, Muriel, **Retro. Supp. II:** 48; **Supp. VI: 271–289; Supp. XV:** 349; **Supp. XVII:** 74

"Rule of Phase Applied to History, The" (Adams), **I:** 19

Rule of the Bone (Banks), **Supp. V:** 16

Rulers of Kings (Atherton), **Supp. XXIV:** 23

"Rules by Which a Great Empire May Be Reduced to a Small One" (Franklin), **II:** 120

Rules For the Dance: A Handbook for Reading and Writing Metrical Verse (Oliver), **Supp. VII:** 229, 247

Rules of Attraction, The (Ellis), **Supp. XXVII:** 68, 70–71, 74, 76

Rules of the Game, The (film), **Supp. XII:** 259

Rulfo, Juan, **Supp. IV Part 2:** 549

Rumba (film, Gering), **Supp. XVII:** 57

Rumbaut, Rubén, **Supp. XI:** 184

Rum Diary, The (Thompson), **Supp. XXIV:** 281, **283–286,** 293

Rümelin-Oesterlen, Natalie, **Supp. XX: 235**

Rumens, Carol, **Supp. XI:** 14; **Supp. XVI:** 212

Rumi, **Supp. XX: 117**

"Rumination of Rivers, The" (Bronk), **Supp. XXI:** 32

Rumkowski, Chaim, **Supp. XII:** 168

Rummel, Mary Kay, **Supp. XIII:** 280

"Rumor and a Ladder" (Bowles), **Supp. IV Part 1:** 93

Rumor of War, A (Caputo), **Supp. XIX: 17–21, 25,** 30

Rumors (Simon), **Supp. IV Part 2:** 582–583, 591

Rumpelstiltskin (Gardner), **Supp. VI:** 72

"Rumpelstiltskin" (Grimm), **IV:** 266

"Rumpelstiltskin" (Sexton), **Supp. II Part 2:** 690

Run, Sheep, Run (Bodenheim), **Supp. XXV:** 27

"Runagate Runagate" (Hayden), **Supp. II Part 1:** 377

Runaway (Munro), **Supp. XXVII:** 190, 193–194

"Runes" (Nemerov), **III:** 267, 277–278

Run Man Run (C. Himes), **Supp. XVI:** 142, 143

"Runner, The" (Grossman), **Supp. XIX:** 83

"Running" (Wilbur), **Supp. III Part 2:** 558–559

"RUNNING-AWAY"(Strout), **Supp. XXIII:** 274

Running Dog (DeLillo), **Supp. VI:** 3, 6, 8, 14

"Running in Church" (A. Finch), **Supp. XVII:** 72

"Running the Table" Conroy), **Supp. XVI:** 75

"Run of Bad Luck, A" (Proulx), **Supp. VII:** 253–254

Run of Jacks, A (Hugo), **Supp. VI:** 131, 133, 134, 135, 136

Run River (Didion), **Supp. IV Part 1:** 197, 199–200, 201

Ruoff, A. LaVonne Brown, **Supp. IV Part 1:** 324, 327; **Supp. IV Part 2:** 559

Rupert, Jim, **Supp. XII:** 215

Ruppert, James, **Supp. IV Part 1:** 321

Rural Hours (Cooper), **Supp. XIII:** 152

"Rural Route" (Wright), **Supp. V:** 340

"Rural South, The" (Du Bois), **Supp. II Part 1:** 174

Rush, Benjamin, **Supp. I Part 2:** 505, 507

Rushdie, Salman, **Supp. IV Part 1:** 234, 297

Rushdy, Ashraf, **Supp. X:** 250

Rushing, Jimmy, **Retro. Supp. II:** 113

Rusk, Dean, **II:** 579

Ruskin, John, **II:** 323, 338; **IV:** 349; **Retro. Supp. I:** 56, 360; **Supp. I Part 1:** 2, 10, 87, 349; **Supp. I Part 2:** 410

Rusnak, Karl, **Supp. XVIII:** 149

Russell, Ada Dwyer, **II:** 513, 527

Russell, Bertrand, **II:** 27; **III:** 605, 606; **Retro. Supp. I:** 57, 58, 59, 60; **Supp. I Part 2:** 522; **Supp. V:** 290; **Supp. XII:** 45; **Supp. XIV:** 337

Russell, Diarmuid, **Retro. Supp. I:** 342, 345, 346–347, 349–350

Russell, George, **Retro. Supp. I:** 342

Russell, Herb, **Supp. I Part 2:** 465–466

Russell, John, **Supp. XIV:** 344, 347, 348; **Supp. XXVII:** 22

Russell, Peter, **III:** 479

Russell, Richard, **Supp. XI:** 102

Russell, Robert, **Supp. XX: 195**

Russell, Sue, **Supp. IV Part 2:** 653

Russello, Gerald, **Supp. XXIV:** 159

Russert, Margaret, **Supp. XVIII:** 62

Russert, Tim, **Supp. XII:** 272

Russia at War (Caldwell), **I:** 296

"Russia Between Myth and Reality: From *Meri* to *Three Cities*"(Krutikov), **Supp. XXIII:** 11

Russian Journal, A (Steinbeck), **IV:** 52, 63

Russo, Richard, **Supp. XI:** 349; **Supp. XII: 325–344; Supp. XXIII:** 302

"Rusty Autumn" (Swenson), **Supp. IV Part 2:** 640

Rutabaga-Roo: I've Got a Song and It's for You (Nye, album), **Supp. XIII:** 274

Ruth (biblical book), **Supp. I Part 2:** 516

Ruth, George Herman ("Babe"), **II:** 423; **Supp. I Part 2:** 438, 440

Rutheiser, Charles, **Supp. XXII:** 244

Ruth Hall (Fern), **Supp. V:** 122

Ruthven, K. K., **Supp. XXII:** 261

Rutkowska, Malgorzata, **Supp. XXII:** 208

Rutledge, Ann, **III:** 588; **Supp. I Part 2:** 471

Ruwe, Donelle R., **Supp. XII:** 215

Ryan, Alan, **Supp. XXVI:** 5

Ryan, Katy, **Supp. XXI:** 215

Ryan, Kay, **Supp. XXI:** 20; **Supp. XXV:** 222

Ryan, Maureen, **Supp. XXI:** 215

Ryan, Paul William, **Supp. XVIII: 223–239; Supp. XXI:** 264–265

Ryder (Barnes), **Supp. III Part 1:** 31, 36–38, 42, 43

"Ryder" (Rukeyser), **Supp. VI:** 273, 283

"Ry¿kan Says" (Budbill), **Supp. XIX:** 11

Ryle, Herbert Edward, **Supp. XX: 230**

Rymer, Thomas, **IV:** 122

S

S. (Updike), **Retro. Supp. I:** 330, 331, 332, 333

S-1 (Baraka), **Supp. II Part 1:** 55, 57

Saadi, **II:** 19

Saar, Doreen Alvarez, **Supp. XV:** 237

Sabbatai Zevi (Asch), **Supp. XXIII:** 12

"Sabbath, The" (Stowe), **Supp. I Part 2:** 587

"Sabbath Mom" (White), **Supp. I Part 2:** 671–672

Sabbaths (Berry), **Supp. X:** 31

Sabbath's Theater (P. Roth), **Retro. Supp. II:** 279, 288

"Sabbatical, The" (Stallings), **Supp. XXV:** 234

"Sabbioneta to Parma" (Di Piero), **Supp. XIX:** 36–37

Sabines, Jaime, **Supp. V:** 178

Sabol, Cathy, **Supp. XXVI:** 160

"Sabotage" (Baraka), **Supp. II Part 1:** 49, 53

"Saboteur" (Jin), **Supp. XVIII:** 97

Sacco, Nicola, **I:** 482, 486, 490, 494; **II:** 38–39, 426; **III:** 139–140; **Supp. I Part 2:** 446; **Supp. IX:** 199; **Supp. V:** 288–289; **Supp. XXII:** 277

Sachs, Hanns, **Supp. I Part 1:** 259; **Supp. X:** 186

Sack Full of Old Quarrels, A (Weigl), **Supp. XIX:** 277

"Sacks" (Carver), **Supp. III Part 1:** 143–144

Sacks, Oliver, **Supp. XVIII:** 143

Sacks, Peter, **Supp. IV Part 2:** 450

Sackville-West, Vita, **Supp. VIII:** 263

"Sacrament of Divorce, The" (Patchett), **Supp. XII:** 309

"Sacrament of Self: Catholic Roots of Contemporary Memoir" (lecture, Hampl), **Supp. XXII:** 81

"Sacraments" (Dubus), **Supp. VII:** 91

Sacred and Profane Memories (Van Vechten), **Supp. II Part 2:** 735, 749

"Sacred Chant for the Return of Black Spirit and Power" (Baraka), **Supp. II Part 1:** 51

"Sacred Factory, The" (Toomer), **Supp. IX:** 320

Sacred Fount, The (James), **II:** 332–333; **Retro. Supp. I:** 219, 228, 232

"Sacred Heart" (Egan), **Supp. XIX:** 52

"Sacred Hoop, The: A Contemporary Perspective" (Gunn Allen), **Supp. IV Part 1:** 324

Sacred Hoop, The: Recovering the Feminine in American Indian Traditions (Gunn Allen), **Supp. IV Part 1:** 319, 320, 322, 324, 325, 328–330, 331, 333, 334

Sacred Journey, The (Buechner), **Supp. XII:** 42, 53

"Sacred Thing, The" (Ryan as Quin), **Supp. XVIII:** 227

Sacred Wood, The (Eliot), **IV:** 431; **Retro. Supp. I:** 59, 60; **Supp. I Part 1:** 268; **Supp. II Part 1:** 136, 146

Sacrifice, The (Bidart), **Supp. XV:** 22, 27–30, 35

"Sacrifice, The" (Bidart), **Supp. XV:** 29

"Sacrifice, The" (Oates), **Supp. II Part 2:** 523

Sacrilege of Alan Kent, The (Caldwell), **I:** 291–292

"Sad Brazil" (Hardwick), **Supp. III Part 1:** 210

Sad Days of Light (Balakian), **Supp. XXIII:** 20

"Sad Dust Glories" (Ginsberg), **Supp. II Part 1:** 376

Sad Dust Glories: Poems Written Work Summer in Sierra Woods (Ginsberg), **Supp. II Part 1:** 326

Sade, Marquis de, **III:** 259; **IV:** 437, 442; **Supp. XII:** 1, 14–15

Sad-Faced Boy (Bontemps), **Supp. XXII:** 5, 12

Sad Flower in the Sand, A (film), **Supp. XI:** 173

Sad Heart at the Supermarket, A (Jarrell), **II:** 386

"Sadie" (Matthiessen), **Supp. V:** 201

"Sadie and Maud" (Brooks), **Supp. XVIII:** 175

Sadness and Happiness (Pinsky), **Supp. VI:** 235, **237–241**

"Sadness of Brothers, The" (Kinnell), **Supp. III Part 1:** 237, 251

"Sadness of Days, The" (Salinas), **Supp. XIII:** 325

Sadness of Days, The: Selected and New Poems (Salinas), **Supp. XIII:** 311, **324–326**

"Sadness of Lemons, The" (Levine), **Supp. V:** 184

Sadoff, Ira, **Supp. XVII:** 241; **Supp. XXI:** 100

"Sad Rite" (Karr), **Supp. XI:** 243

"Sad Strains of a Gay Waltz" (Stevens), **Retro. Supp. I:** 302

"Safe" (Gordon), **Supp. IV Part 1:** 299, 306

"Safe in their Alabaster Chambers" (Dickinson), **Retro. Supp. I:** 30

Safer, Morley, **Supp. XIX:** 25

"Safe Subjects" (Komunyakaa), **Supp. XIII:** 118

Safety Features (Monson), **Supp. XXIV:** 230

"Safeway" (F. Barthelme), **Supp. XI:** 26, 27, 36

Saffin, John, **Supp. I Part 1:** 115

Saffy, Edna, **Supp. X:** 227

Sagan, Miriam, **Supp. XXIII:** 133

"Saga of an American Ranch" (P. N. Warren), **Supp. XX:** 261

"Saga of Arturo Bandini" (Fante), **Supp. XI:** 159, **166–169**

"Saga of King Olaf, The" (Longfellow), **II:** 489, 505; **Retro. Supp. II:** 154, 155, 164

"Sage of Stupidity and Wonder, The" (Goldbarth), **Supp. XII:** 191

Sahl, Mort, **II:** 435–436

"Sah Sin" (Gallagher), *Supp.* XXIV: 171

"Said" (Dixon), **Supp. XII:** 149–150

Said, Edward, **Supp. XXI:** 153

"Sailing after Lunch" (Stevens), **IV:** 73

Sailing Alone Around the Room: New and Selected Poems (Collins), **Supp. XXI:** 54, 56, 62

Sailing Alone Around the World (Slocum), **Supp. XXV:** 205, 206, 208, 213–216, 218

"Sailing Home from Rapallo" (R. Lowell), **Retro. Supp. II:** 189

Sailing through China (Theroux), **Supp. VIII:** 323

"Sailing to Byzantium" (Yeats), **III:** 263; **Supp. VIII:** 30; **Supp. X:** 74; **Supp. XI:** 281

"Sail Made of Rags, The" (Nye), **Supp. XIII:** 277

"Sailor off the Bremen" (Shaw), **Supp. XIX:** 247

"Sailor's Grudge" (Howard), **Supp. XXVII:** 124

"Sailors Lost at Sea" (Shields), **Supp. VII:** 318

"St Anne/Santa Ana" (Mora), **Supp. XIII:** 229

"Saint Anthony of Padua/San Antonio de Padua" (Mora), **Supp. XIII:** 228

"St. Augustine and the Bullfights" (Porter), **III:** 454

Sainte-Beuve, Charles Augustin, **IV:** 432

St. Elmo (Wilson), **Retro. Supp. I:** 351–352

"Saint Emmanuel the Good, Martyr" (Unamuno; Everwine, trans.), **Supp. XV:** 79

Sainte Vierge, La (Picabia), **Retro. Supp. II:** 331

Saint-Exupéry, Antoine de, **Supp. IX:** 247

"St. Francis Einstein of the Daffodils" (W. C. Williams), **IV:** 409–411

Saint-Gaudens, Augustus, **I:** 18, 228; **II:** 551

Saint-Gaudens, Homer, **Supp. XV:** 41

"St. George, the Dragon, and the Virgin" (R. Bly), **Supp. IV Part 1:** 73

St. George and the Godfather (Mailer), **III:** 46; **Retro. Supp. II:** 206, 208

Saint Jack (Theroux), **Supp. VIII:** 319

St. John, David, **Supp. V:** 180; **Supp. XI:** 270, 272; **Supp. XIII:** 312

St. John, Edward B., **Supp. IV Part 2:** 490

St. John, James Hector. *See* Crèvecoeur, Michel-Guillaume Jean de

"Saint John and the Back-Ache" (Stevens), **Retro. Supp. I:** 310

Saint Judas (Wright), **Supp. III Part 2:** **595–599**

"Saint Judas" (Wright), **Supp. III Part 2:** 598–599

St. Louis Woman (Bontemps and Cullen), **Supp. IV Part 1:** 170

St. Mawr (Lawrence), **II:** 595

Saint Maybe (Tyler), **Supp. IV Part 2:** 670–671

"Saint Nicholas" (Moore), **III:** 215

"Saint"(O'Hara), **Supp. XXIII:** 219

St. Petersburg (Biely), **Supp. XII:** 13

Saint-Phalle, Niki de, **Supp. XV:** 187

"St. Roach" (Rukeyser), **Supp. VI:** 286

"Saint Robert" (Dacey), **Supp. IV Part 1:** 70

Saints at the River (Rash), **Supp. XXVII:** 222, 223–224, 226

Saintsbury, George, **IV:** 440; **Supp. XV:** 181

Saints' Everlasting Rest, The (Baxter), **III:** 199; **IV:** 151, 153

Saint-Simon, Claude Henri, **Supp. I Part 2:** 648

"St. Thomas Aquinas" (Simic), **Supp. VIII:** 281

Saks, Gene, **Supp. IV Part 2:** 577, 588

Salamun, Tomaz, **Supp. VIII:** 272

Salazar, Dixie, **Supp. V:** 180; **Supp. XV:** 73

Saldívar, José David, **Supp. IV Part 2:** 544, 545; **Supp. XIX:** 110, 112–113

Sale, Richard, **Supp. IV Part 1:** 379

Sale, Roger, **Supp. V:** 244

Saleh, Dennis, **Supp. V:** 182, 186

"Salem" (R. Lowell), **II:** 550

Salemi, Joseph, **Supp. IV Part 1:** 284

Salem's Lot (King), **Supp. V:** 139, 144, 146, 151

"Sale of the Hessians, The" (Franklin), **II: 120**

Salick, Roydan, **Supp. XXIII:** 93, 94

Salinas, Luis Omar, **Supp. IV Part 2:** 545; **Supp. V:** 180; **Supp. XIII:** 311–330; **Supp. XV:** 73

"Salinas Is on His Way" (Salinas), **Supp. XIII:** 317

"Salinas Sends Messengers to the Stars" (Salinas), **Supp. XIII:** 317

"Salinas Summering at the Caspian and Thinking of Hamlet" (Salinas), **Supp. XIII:** 320

"Salinas Wakes Early and Goes to the Park to Lecture Sparrows" (Salinas), **Supp. XIII:** 320

Salinger, Doris, **III:** 551

Salinger, J. D., **II:** 255; **III: 551–574; IV:** 190, 216, 217; **Retro. Supp. I:** 102, 116, 335; **Supp. IV Part 2:** 502; **Supp. V:** 23, 119; **Supp. VIII:** 151; **Supp. XI:** 2, 66; **Supp. XIV:** 93; **Supp. XXIII:** 100; **Supp. XXVI:** 119

Salisbury, Harrison, **Supp. I Part 2:** 664

Salle, David, **Supp. XII:** 4

Salley, Columbus, **Supp. XIV:** 195

"Sally" (Cisneros), **Supp. VII:** 63

"Sally's Choice" (E. Stoddard), **Supp. XV:** 282

Salmagundi; or, The Whim-Whams and Opinions of Launcelot Langstaff Esq., and Others (Irving), **II:** 299, 300, 304

Salmon, Edward G., **Supp. XVIII:** 258

Salome (Strauss), **IV:** 316

Salon (online magazine), **Supp. VIII:** 310; **Supp. X:** 202

"Salt"(Crooker), **Supp. XXIII:** 62

Salt Eaters, The (Bambara), **Supp. XI:** 1, 12–14

Salt Ecstasies, The (White), **Supp. XI:** 123

Salter, James, **Supp. IX: 245–263; Supp. XIX:** 252; **Supp. XVI:** 237, 247

Salter, Mary Jo, **Supp. IV Part 2:** 653; **Supp. IX:** 37, 292; **Supp. XV:** 251, 253; **Supp. XVII:** 112; **Supp. XXIII:** 112

Salter, Sarah, **Supp. XXVI:** 57

Salt Garden, The (Nemerov), **III:** 269, 272–275, 277

"Salt Garden, The" (Nemerov), **III:** 267–268

Salting the Ocean (Nye, ed.), **Supp. XIII:** 280

Salt Lesson, The (C. Frost), **Supp. XV:** 92, 96

"Salt Lesson, The" (C. Frost), **Supp. XV:** 99

"Salts and Oils" (Levine), **Supp. V:** 190

Salt to the Devil (film, Dmytryk), **Supp. XX:** 41

Saltzman, Arthur, **Supp. XIII:** 48

Saltzman, Harry, **Supp. XI:** 307

"Salut au Monde!" (Whitman), **Retro. Supp. I:** 387, 396, 400

"Salute" (MacLeish), **III:** 13

Salute (Shaw), **Supp. XIX:** 244

"Salute to Mister Yates, A" (Dubus), **Supp. XI:** 347, 349

Salute to Spring (Le Sueur), **Supp. XXIII:** 164, 165, 166, 172

Salvador (Didion), **Supp. IV Part 1:** 198, 207–208, 210

"Salvage" (Clampitt), **Supp. IX:** 41

"Salvage" (Rinehart), **Supp. XXV:** 194

Salvation (Asch), **Supp. XXIII:** 3, 4, **12,** 13, 15

Salvos: An Informal Book About Books and Plays (W. Frank), **Supp. XX:** 75

Samain, Albert, **II:** 528

Same Door, The (Updike), **IV:** 214, 219, 226; **Retro. Supp. I:** 320

"Same in Blues" (Hughes), **Retro. Supp. I:** 208

"Same Kiss After Many Years, The" (Gallagher), **Supp. XXIV:** 169

Same River Twice, The (Offutt), **Supp. XIX:** 163, 164, **167–168,** 175

"Samhain" (A. Finch), **Supp. XVII:** 72

Sam Lawson's Oldtown Fireside Stories (Stowe), **Supp. I Part 2:** 587, 596, 598–599

Sam Patch, the High, Wide & Handsome Jumper (Bontemps and Conroy), **Supp. XXII:** 5, 11

"Sa'm Pèdi" (Bell), **Supp. X:** 17

"Sampler, A" (MacLeish), **III:** 4

Sampoli, Maria, **Supp. V:** 338

Sampson, Edward, **Supp. I Part 2:** 664, 673

Sampson, Martin, **Supp. I Part 2:** 652

"Sam's Dad" (Lamott), **Supp. XX: 142–143**

Sam's Legacy (Neugeboren), **Supp. XVI:** 221, 222

Samson Agonistes (Milton), **III:** 274

"Samson and Delilah" (Masters), **Supp. I Part 2:** 459

Samuel, Maurice, **Supp. XXIII:** 1, 7

Samuel de Champlain: Father of New France (Morison), **Supp. I Part 2:** 496–497

Samuels, Charles Thomas, **Retro. Supp. I:** 334

"Samuel Sewall" (Hecht), **Supp. X:** 58

"Samwheel" (Lamott), **Supp. XX: 144–145**

Sanborn, Franklin B., **IV:** 171, 172, 178

Sanborn, Kate, **Supp. XIII:** 152

Sanborn, Sara, **Supp. XIV:** 113

Sanchez, Carol Anne, **Supp. IV Part 1:** 335

Sanchez, Carol Lee, **Supp. IV Part 2:** 499, 557

Sanchez, Sonia, **Supp. II Part 1:** 34; **Supp. XXVII:** 167

Sánchez Beras, César, **Supp. XXI:** 100, 104

Sanctified Church, The (Hurston), **Supp. VI:** 150

"Sanction of the Victims, The" (Rand), **Supp. IV Part 2:** 528

Sanctuary (Faulkner), **II:** 57, 61–63, 72, 73, 74, 174; **Retro. Supp. I:** 73, 84, 86–87, 87; **Supp. I Part 2:** 614; **Supp. XII:** 16

"Sanctuary" (Larsen), **Supp. XVIII:** 119, 130–131

Sanctuary (Wharton), **IV:** 311

"Sanctuary" (Wylie), **Supp. I Part 2:** 711

"Sanctuary, The" (Nemerov), **III:** 272, 274

"Sanctuary, The" (Teasdale), **Supp. XXVII:** 294

Sanctuary V (Schulberg), **Supp. XVIII:** 254

"Sanctus" (Nelson), **Supp. XVIII:** 183

Sand, George, **II:** 322; **Retro. Supp. I:** 235, 372; **Supp. XV:** 275

"Sandalphon" (Longfellow), **II:** 498

Sand and Foam: A Book of Aphorisms (Gibran), **Supp. XX: 115, 121–122**

Sandbox, The (Albee), **I:** 74–75, 89

Sandburg, Carl, **I:** 103, 109, 384, 421; **II:** 529; **III:** 3, 20, **575–598; Retro. Supp. I:** 133, 194; **Supp. I Part 1:** 257, 320; **Supp. I Part 2:** 387, 389, 454, 461, 653; **Supp. III Part 1:** 63, 71, 73, 75; **Supp. IV Part 1:** 169; **Supp. IV Part 2:** 502; **Supp. IX:** 1, 15, 308; **Supp. XIII:** 274, 277; **Supp. XV:** 293, 299, 300, 301, 302, 306; **Supp. XXII:** 275; **Supp. XXIII:** 161, 165; **Supp. XXV:** 18; **Supp. XXVII:** 83

Sandburg, Mrs. Carl (Lillian Steichen), **III:** 580

Sandburg, Helga, **III:** 583

Sandburg, Janet, **III:** 583, 584

Sandburg, Margaret, **III:** 583, 584

Sand County Almanac and Sketches Here and There, A (Leopold), **Supp. XIV:** 177, 178, **182–192**

"Sand Creek, Colorado"(Kenny), **Supp. XXIII:** 155

"Sand Dabs" (Oliver), **Supp. VII:** 245

"Sand Dunes" (Frost), **Retro. Supp. I:** 137; **Retro. Supp. II:** 41

Sander, August, **Supp. IX:** 211

Sanders, Mark, **Supp. XIX:** 119, 121

Sanders, Scott Russell, **Supp. XVI: 265–280**

Sandlin, Tim, **Supp. XXII:** 114

"Sandman, The" (Barthelme), **Supp. IV Part 1:** 47

Sandman's Dust (Bukiet), **Supp. XVII:** 40, 41

Sando, Joe S., **Supp. IV Part 2:** 510

Sandoe, James, **Supp. IV Part 1:** 131; **Supp. IV Part 2:** 470

Sandoval, Chela, **Supp. XXIII:** 204

Sandoz, Mari, **Supp. XV:** 141; **Supp. XXIII:** 146; **Supp. XXIV: 243–261**

Sandperl, Ira, **Supp. VIII:** 200

"Sand-Quarry and Moving Figures" (Rukeyser), **Supp. VI:** 271, 278

Sand Rivers (Matthiessen), **Supp. V:** 203

"Sand Roses, The" (Hogan), **Supp. IV Part 1:** 401

Sands, Diana, **Supp. IV Part 1:** 362

Sands, Robert, **Supp. I Part 1:** 156, 157

"Sands at Seventy" (Whitman), **IV:** 348

"Sandstone Farmhouse, A" (Updike), **Retro. Supp. I:** 318

Sandy Bottom Orchestra,The (Keillor and Nilsson), **Supp. XVI:** 177

Sanford, John, **IV:** 286, 287

San Francisco (film), **Supp. XVI:** 181, 192

"San Francisco" (Hempel), **Supp. XXI:** 118

"San Francisco Blues" (Kerouac), **Supp. III Part 1:** 225

Sangamon County Peace Advocate, The (Lindsay), **Supp. I Part 2:** 379

Sanger, Margaret, **Supp. I Part 1:** 19; **Supp. XXI:** 6; **Supp. XXIII:** 161

Sankofa (film), **Supp. XX: 154**

Sansom, William, **IV:** 279

Sans Soleil (film), **Supp. IV Part 2:** 436

"Santa" (Sexton), **Supp. II Part 2:** 693

Santa Claus: A Morality (Cummings), **I:** 430, 441

"Santa Fe, New Mexico"(Kenny), **Supp. XXIII:** 150

"Santa Fé Trail, The" (Lindsay), **Supp. I Part 2:** 389

"Santa Lucia" (Hass), **Supp. VI:** 105–106

"Santa Lucia II" (Hass), **Supp. VI:** 105–106

Santayana, George, **I:** 222, 224, 236, 243, 253, 460; **II:** 20, 542; **III:** 64, **599–622; IV:** 26, 339, 351, 353, 441; **Retro. Supp. I:** 55, 57, 67, 295; **Retro. Supp. II:** 179; **Supp. I Part 2:** 428; **Supp. II Part 1:** 107; **Supp. X:** 58; **Supp. XIV:** 199, 335, 340, 342; **Supp. XVI:** 189; **Supp. XVII:** 97, 106; **Supp. XX: 228, 229, 231**

Santiago, Esmeralda, **Supp. XI:** 177

"Santorini: Stopping the Leak" (Merrill), **Supp. III Part 1:** 336

Santos, John Phillip, **Supp. XIII:** 274

Santos, Sherod, **Supp. VIII:** 270

Saphier, William, **Supp. XXV:** 19, 20

Sapir, Edward, **Supp. VIII:** 295; **Supp. XVI:** 283

"Sapphics for Patience" (A. Finch), **Supp. XVII:** 72

Sapphira and the Slave Girl (Cather), **I:** 331; **Retro. Supp. I:** 2, **19–20**

Sappho, **II:** 544; **III:** 142; **Supp. I Part 1:** 261, 269; **Supp. I Part 2:** 458; **Supp. XII:** 98, 99; **Supp. XVII:** 74; **Supp. XXV:** 222; **Supp. XXVII:** 171, 283, 288

"Sappho" (Wright), **Supp. III Part 2:** 595, 604

"Sappho, Keats"(Hadas), **Supp. XXIII:** 113

"Sara" (song, Dylan), **Supp. XVIII:** 28

"Sarah" (Schwartz), **Supp. II Part 2:** 663

Sarah; or, The Exemplary Wife (Rowson), **Supp. XV:** 242

"Saratoga" mysteries (Dobyns), **Supp. XIII:** 79–80

Sardonic Arm, The (Bodenheim), **Supp. XXV:** 22, 23

Sargent, John Singer, **II:** 337, 338; **Supp. XX:** 231

Sarlós, Robert K., **Supp. XXI:** 7, 12, 13

Saroyan, Aram, **Supp. XV:** 182

Saroyan, William, **III:** 146–147; **IV:** 393; **Supp. I Part 2:** 679; **Supp. IV Part 1:** 83; **Supp. IV Part 2:** 502; **Supp. XIII:** 280; **Supp. XXIII:** 20; **Supp. XXV:** 29

Sarris, Greg, **Supp. IV Part 1:** 329, 330

Sarton, George, **Supp. VIII:** 249

Sarton, May, **Supp. III Part 1:** 62, 63; **Supp. VIII: 249–268; Supp. XIII:** 296; **Supp. XVII:** 71

Sartoris (Faulkner), **II:** 55, 56–57, 58, 62; **Retro. Supp. I:** 77, 81, 82, 83, 88

Sartor Resartus (Carlyle), **II:** 26; **III:** 82

Sartre, Jean-Paul, **I:** 82, 494; **II:** 57, 244; **III:** 51, 204, 292, 453, 619; **IV:** 6, 223, 236, 477, 487, 493; **Retro. Supp. I:** 73; **Supp. I Part 1:** 51; **Supp. IV Part 1:** 42, 84; **Supp. IX:** 4; **Supp. VIII:** 11; **Supp. XIII:** 74, 171; **Supp. XIV:** 24; **Supp. XVII:** 137; **Supp. XXIV:** 281

Sassone, Ralph, **Supp. X:** 171

Sassoon, Siegfried, **II:** 367; **Supp. XIX:** 18; **Supp. XV:** 308; **Supp. XXVII:** 295

Satan in Goray (Singer), **IV:** 1, 6–7, 12; **Retro. Supp. II:** 303, **304–305**

Satan Says (Olds), **Supp. X:** 201, 202, **202–204,** 215

"Satan Says" (Olds), **Supp. X:** 202; **Supp. XVII:** 114

Satanstoe (Cooper), **I:** 351–352, 355

"Sather Gate Illumination" (Ginsberg), **Supp. II Part 1:** 329

"Satire as a Way of Seeing" (Dos Passos), **III:** 172

Satires of Persius, The (Merwin, trans.), **Supp. III Part 1:** 347

Satirical Rogue on Poetry, The (Francis). *See Pot Shots at Poetry* (Francis)

Satori in Paris (Kerouac), **Supp. III Part 1:** 231

"Saturday" (Salinas), **Supp. XIII:** 315

"Saturday Matinee" (Trethewey), **Supp. XXI:** 251

Saturday Night (Orlean), **Supp. XXV:** 159, 161

Saturday Night at the War (Shanley), **Supp. XIV:** 315

"Saturday Rain" (Kees), **Supp. XV:** 136

"Saturday Route, The" (Wolfe), **Supp. III Part 2:** 580

Satyagraha (Gandhi), **IV:** 185

"Satyr's Heart, The" (B. Kelly), **Supp. XVII:** 132

Saucedo, José Guadalupe, **Supp. XXIII:** 197

Saudade (Vaz), **Supp. XXVI:** 256–258, 263

Saul and Patsy (C. Baxter), **Supp. XVII:** 22–23

"Saul and Patsy" (C. Baxter), **Supp. XVII:** 17

"Saul and Patsy Are Getting Comfortable in Michigan" (C. Baxter), **Supp. XVII:** 22

"Saul and Patsy Are in Labor" (C. Baxter), **Supp. XVII:** 20, 22

"Saul and Patsy Are Pregnant" (C. Baxter), **Supp. XVII:** 22

Saunders, George, **Supp. XIX: 223–237; Supp. XXII:** 49; **Supp. XXIV:** 199

Saunders, Richard, **II:** 110

Savage, Augusta, **Retro. Supp. II:** 115

Savage, James, **II:** 111

Savage, Tom, **Supp. XXIV:** 45

Savage Holiday (Wright), **IV:** 478, 488

Savage in Limbo: A Concert Play (Shanley), **Supp. XIV:** 315, **319–321,** 323, 324

Savage Love (Shepard and Chaikin), **Supp. III Part 2:** 433

Savage Place, A (Parker), **Supp. XIX:** 185

Savage Sword of Conan, The (comic), **Supp. XXVII:** 129

Savage Wilds (Reed), **Supp. X:** 241

Save Me, Joe Louis (Bell), **Supp. X:** 7, 10, **11–12**

Save Me the Waltz (Z. Fitzgerald), **II:** 95; **Retro. Supp. I:** 110; **Supp. IX:** 58, 59, 65, **66–68**

"Save One for Mainz" (Huddle), **Supp. XXVI:** 150, 153

Savers, Michael, **Supp. XI:** 307

Saving Lives (Goldbarth), **Supp. XII:** 192

Saving Private Ryan (film), **Supp. V:** 249; **Supp. XI:** 234

Savings (Hogan), **Supp. IV Part 1:** 397, 404, 405, 406, 410

Saving Sebastian (Taylor), **Supp. XXIII:** 57

Savo, Jimmy, **I:** 440

Savran, David, **Supp. IX:** 145; **Supp. XIII:** 209; **Supp. XV:** 321; **Supp. XXIV:** 263, 264

"Sawdust" (Offutt), **Supp. XIX:** 164

Sawyer-Lauçanno, Christopher, **Supp. IV Part 1:** 95

Saxon, Lyle, **Retro. Supp. I:** 80

"Saxophone" (Di Piero), **Supp. XIX:** 38

"Sax's and Selves" (Halliday), **Supp. XIX:** 88

"Say All" (Ray), **Supp. XVIII:** 193

Say and Seal (S. and A. Warner), **Supp. XVIII:** 258, 266

Saye and Sele, Lord, **Supp. I Part 1:** 98

Sayer, Mandy, **Supp. XIII:** 118

Sayers, Dorothy, **Supp. IV Part 1:** 341; **Supp. IV Part 2:** 464

Sayers, Valerie, **Supp. XI:** 253; **Supp. XVIII:** 99

"Say Good-bye" (Weigl), **Supp. XIX:** 288

Say Her Name (Goldman), **Supp. XXV:** 50, 59–62

"Sayings/For Luck" (Goldbarth), **Supp. XII:** 176

"Saying What Needs To Be Said" (Skloot), **Supp. XX:** 201

Say! Is This the U.S.A.? (Caldwell), **I:** 293, 294–295, 304, 309, 310

Saylor, Bruce, **Supp. XII:** 253

Sayre, Joel, **Supp. XIII:** 166

Sayre, Nora, **Supp. XII:** 119

Sayre, Zelda, **Retro. Supp. I:** 101, 102–103, 104, 105, 108, 109, 110, 113, 114. *See also* Fitzgerald, Zelda (Zelda Sayre)

"Say Yes" (Wolff), **Supp. VII:** 344

"Say You Love Me" (Peacock), **Supp. XIX:** 198

Scafe, Suzanne, **Supp. XXIII:** 94, 95

"Scale" (Halliday), **Supp. XIX:** 92

"Scales of the Eyes, The" (Nemerov), **III:** 272, 273, 277

Scalpel (McCoy), **Supp. XIII: 174–175**

Scalpel (screen treatment, McCoy), **Supp. XIII:** 174

Scandalabra (Zelda Fitzgerald), **Supp. IX:** 60, 61, 65, 67, **68–70**

"Scandal Detectives, The" (Fitzgerald), **II:** 80–81; **Retro. Supp. I:** 99

Scarberry-García, Susan, **Supp. IV Part 2:** 486

Scarborough, Dorothy, **Supp. XVIII:** 279–280

Scarecrow, The (Connelly), **Supp. XXI:** 71, 74, 78, **79**

"Scarecrow, The" (Farrell), **II:** 45

"Scarf, A" (Shields), **Supp. VII:** 328

Scarface (screenplay, Hecht), **Supp. XXVII:** 83, 91, 92–93

Scarlet Cabinet, The (Notley), **Supp. XXII:** 233

"Scarlet Citadel, The" (Howard), **Supp. XXVII:** 125, 126

Scarlet Letter, The (Hawthorne), **II:** 63, 223, 224, 231, 233, 239–240, 241, 243, 244, 255, 264, 286, 290, 291, 550; **Retro. Supp. I:** 63, 145, 147, 152, **157–159**, 160, 163, 165, 220, 248, 330, 335; **Retro. Supp. II:** 100; **Supp. I Part 1:** 38; **Supp. II Part 1:** 386; **Supp. VIII:** 108, 198; **Supp. XII:** 11; **Supp. XVII:** 143; **Supp. XX:** 178, 183; **Supp. XXII:** 147

"Scarlet Letter Aleph, The" (Mirvis), **Supp. XX:** 183

Scarlet Plague, The (London), **II:** 467

Scarlet Sister Mary (Peterkin), **Supp. XXII:** 189

Scar Lover (Crews), **Supp. XI:** 103, 107, **114–115**

"Scarred Girl, The" (Dickey), **Supp. IV Part 1:** 180

Scates, Maxine, **Supp. XIV:** 264, 265, 274

"Scenario" (H. Miller), **III:** 184

"Scene" (Howells), **II:** 274

"Scene in Jerusalem, A" (Stowe), **Supp. I Part 2:** 587

"Scenes" (Shields), **Supp. VII:** 318

Scènes d'Anabase (chamber music) (Bowles), **Supp. IV Part 1:** 82

"Scenes from a Documentary History of Mississippi" (Trethewey), **Supp. XXI:** 255–256

Scenes from American Life (Gurney), **Supp. V:** 95, 96, 105, 108

Scenes from Another Life (McClatchy), **Supp. XII: 255–256**

"Scenes from Childhood" (W. V. Davis), **Supp. XXI:** 95

"Scenes of Childhood" (Merrill), **Supp. III Part 1:** 322, 323, 327

"Scented Herbage of My Breast" (Whitman), **IV:** 342–343

"Scent of a Woman's Ink" (Prose), **Supp. XVI:** 259

"Scent of Unbought Flowers, The" (Ríos), **Supp. IV Part 2:** 547

Scepticisms (Aiken), **I:** 58

Scève, Maurice, **Supp. III Part 1:** 11

Schad, Christian, **Supp. IV Part 1:** 247

Schafer, Benjamin G., **Supp. XIV:** 144

Schafer, William, **Supp. XIX:** 164, 172

Schaller, George, **Supp. V:** 208, 210–211

Schapiro, Meyer, **II:** 30

Scharmann, Hermann Balthazar, **Supp. XII:** 41

Scharper, Alice, **Supp. XXII:** 175

Scharper, Diane, **Supp. XXIII:** 134

Schary, Dore, **Supp. IV Part 1:** 365; **Supp. XIII:** 163

Schatz, Tom, **Supp. XVIII:** 242

Schaum, Melita, **Supp. XXII:** 166

Schaumbergh, Count de, **II:** 120

Schechner, Richard, **Supp. XXIV:** 116

Scheele, Roy, **Supp. XVI:** 54; **Supp. XXI:** 103

Scheeman, George, **Supp. XXII:** 230

Scheffauer, G. H., **I:** 199

"Scheherazade" (Ashbery), **Supp. III Part 1:** 18

"Scheherazade Is Nailed and Mailed in Five Days" (Stone), **Supp. XXVII:** 257

Scheick, William, **Supp. V:** 272

Schelberg, Budd, **Supp. XVIII: 241–256**

Scheler, Max, **I:** 58

Schelling, Friedrich, **Supp. I Part 2:** 422

Schenck, Joseph, **Supp. XVI:** 186

Schenk, Margaret, **I:** 199

Scheponik, Peter, **Supp. X:** 210

Scherer, Loline, **Supp. XIII:** 161

"Scherzo"(Hadas), **Supp. XXIII:** 113

Schevill, James, **I:** 116

Schickel, Richard, **Supp. XV:** 1

Schifano, Mario, **Supp. XXIII:** 217

Schifino, Martin, **Supp. XXVI:** 145

Schilder, Paul, **Supp. I Part 2:** 622

Schildkraut, Rudolph, **Supp. XXIII:** 8

Schiller, Andrew, **II:** 20

Schiller, Frederick, **Supp. V:** 290

Schiller, Johann Christoph Friedrich von, **I:** 224; **Supp. IV Part 2:** 519; **Supp. XVI:** 292

Schiller, Lawrence, **Retro. Supp. II:** 208, 212, 214

Schimmel, Harold, **Supp. V:** 336

"Schizoid Nature of the Implied Author in Twentieth-Century American Ethnic Novels, The" (Nelson), **Supp. XVIII:** 172

Schjeldahl, Peter, **Supp. XXIV:** 44; **Supp. XXVII:** 23

Schlegel, Augustus Wilhelm, **III:** 422, 424

Schlegell, David von, **Supp. IV Part 2:** 423

Schleiermacher, Friedrich, **III:** 290–291, 309

Schleifer, Ronald, **Supp. XVIII:** 144

Schlepping Through the Alps (S. Apple), **Supp. XVII:** 8

Schlesinger, Arthur, Jr., **III:** 291, 297–298, 309

Schleuning, Neala, **Supp. XXIII:** 165

Schmidt, Jon Zlotnik, **Supp. IV Part 1:** 2

Schmidt, Kaspar. *See* Stirner, Max

Schmidt, Michael, **Supp. X:** 55

Schmitt, Carl, **I:** 386–387

Schmitz, Neil, **Supp. X:** 243

Schnackenberg, Gjertrud, **Supp. XV: 249–268**

Schneeman, George, **Supp. XXIV:** 41

Schneider, Alan, **I:** 87

Schneider, Dean, **Supp. XXVII:** 208

Schneider, Louis, **Supp. I Part 2:** 650

Schneider, Romy, **Supp. IV Part 2:** 549

Schneider, Steven, **Supp. IX:** 271, 274

Schnellock, Emil, **III:** 177

Schneour, Zalman, **IV:** 11

"Schnetzer Day" (Halliday), **Supp. XIX:** 93

Schnitzler, Arthur, **Supp. XV:** 307; **Supp. XVI:** 187

Schoen, Carol, **Supp. XXVII:** 297

Schoerke, Meg, **Supp. XVII:** 110

"Scholar Gypsy, The" (Arnold), **II:** 541

"Scholastic and Bedside Teaching" (Holmes), **Supp. I Part 1:** 305

Schöler, Bo, **Supp. IV Part 1:** 399, 400, 403, 407, 409; **Supp. IV Part 2:** 499

Scholes, Robert, **Supp. V:** 40, 42

Scholtz, Carter, **Supp. XVIII:** 144

Schomburg, Arthur, **Supp. X:** 134; **Supp. XXII:** 6

Schomburg Library of Nineteenth-Century Black Women Writers (H. L. Gates, ed.), **Supp. XX: 105**

Schönberg, Claude-Michel, **Supp. XXI:** 155

Schoolboy Howlers (Abingdon), **Supp. XVI:** 99

Schoolcraft, Henry Rowe, **II:** 503; **Retro. Supp. II:** 160; **Supp. XXIII:** 223, 227, 228, 232, 233–234

Schoolcraft, Jane Johnston (Bamewawagezhikaquay), **Supp. XXIII: 223–238**

"School Days of an Indian Girl, The" (Zitkala-Ša), **Supp. XXV:** 272

"School Daze" (Bambara), **Supp. XI:** 19

School Daze (film), **Supp. XI:** 19, 20

"Schoolhouse" (Levis), **Supp. XI:** 258

"School of Giorgione, The" (Pater), **I:** 51

School of Udhra (Mackey), **Supp. XXVII:** 154–155

"School Play, The" (Merrill), **Supp. III Part 1:** 336

"Schooner Fairchild's Class" (Benét), **Supp. XI:** 55

Schopenhauer, Arthur, **III:** 600, 604; **IV:** 7; **Retro. Supp. I:** 256; **Retro. Supp. II:** 94; **Supp. I Part 1:** 320; **Supp. I Part 2:** 457; **Supp. X:** 187; **Supp. XVI:** 184

Schorer, Mark, **II:** 28; **III:** 71; **Retro. Supp. I:** 115; **Supp. IV Part 1:** 197, 203, 211; **Supp. XVI:** 206

Schott, Penelope Scambly, **Supp. XXIII: 239–256**

Schott, Webster, **Supp. IX:** 257

Schøtt-Khristensen, Lene, **Supp. XXVI:** 124, 125

Schotts, Jeffrey, **Supp. XII:** 193

Schrader, Mary von. *See* Jarrell, Mrs. Randall (Mary von Schrader)

Schreiber, Jan, **Supp. XXI:** 105, 111

Schreiner, Olive, **I:** 419; **Supp. XI:** 203

"Schreuderspitze, The" (Helprin), **Supp. XXV:** 85

Schroeder, Eric James, **Supp. V:** 238, 244

Schubert, Bernard L., **Supp. XVII:** 58

Schubert, David, **Supp. XXIV:** 45

Schubert, Franz Peter, **Supp. I Part 1:** 363

Schubnell, Matthias, **Supp. IV Part 2:** 486

Schudel, Matt, **Supp. XXII:** 205, 214

Schuessler, Jennifer, **Supp. XXVI:** 126

Schulberg, Budd, **II:** 98; **Retro. Supp. I:** 113; **Supp. XIII:** 170; **Supp. XV:** 194; **Supp. XXVII:** 142

Schulberg, Stuart, **Supp. XVIII:** 254

Schulman, Grace, **Supp. XXIII:** 58

Schulman, Tom, **Supp. XXI:** 193, 194

Schultz, David E., **Supp. XXVII:** 128

Schulz, Bruno, **Supp. IV Part 2:** 623; **Supp. XVII:** 41

Schuman, William, **Supp. XII:** 253; **Supp. XXII:** 283

Schumann, Dr. Alanson Tucker, **III:** 505

Schuster, Edgar H., **Supp. VIII:** 126

Schuyler, George S., **III:** 110; **Supp. XIX:** 78; **Supp. XVI:** 142; **Supp. XXVI:** 167

Schuyler, James, **Supp. XV:** 177, 178; **Supp. XXIII:** 207, 212, 215, 217; **Supp. XXIV:** 33; **Supp. XXVII:** 21, 23, 24, 26, 28

Schuyler, William, **Supp. I Part 1:** 211

"Schuylkill, The" (Halliday), **Supp. XIX:** 92

Schwartz, Delmore, **I:** 67, 168, 188, 288; **IV:** 128, 129, 437; **Retro. Supp. II:** 29, 178; **Supp. II Part 1:** 102, 109; **Supp. II Part 2: 639–668; Supp. IX:** 299; **Supp. VIII:** 98; **Supp. XIII:** 320; **Supp. XIV:** 3; **Supp. XIX:** 257; **Supp. XV:** 184

Schwartz, Leonard, **Supp. XVI:** 289

Schwartz, Lloyd, **Supp. I Part 1:** 81; **Supp. XXIV:** 160

Schwartz, Marilyn, **Supp. XII:** 126, 128, 130, 132

Schwartz, Meryl F., **Supp. XXII:** 65, 66

Schwartz, Richard B., **Supp. XIV:** 23, 27

Schwarz, A. B. Christa, **Supp. XIX:** 77, 79

Schwed, Peter, **Supp. XXII:** 119

Schweitzer, Albert, **Supp. IV Part 1:** 373

Schweitzer, Harold, **Supp. X:** 210

Schwerdt, Lisa M., **Supp. XIV:** 155, 171

Schwitters, Kurt, **III:** 197; **Retro. Supp. II:** 322, 331, 336; **Supp. IV Part 1:** 79

"Science" (Jeffers), **Supp. II Part 2:** 426

Science and Health with Key to the Scriptures (Eddy), **I:** 383

"Science Favorable to Virtue" (Freneau), **Supp. II Part 1:** 274

Science of English Verse, The (Lanier), **Supp. I Part 1:** 368, 369

"Science of the Night, The" (Kunitz), **Supp. III Part 1:** 258, 265

"Sci-Fi Floater Genius" (Halliday), **Supp. XIX:** 91

Sciolino, Martina, **Supp. XII:** 9

"Scissors" (C. Baxter), **Supp. XVII:** 19

Scofield, Sandra, **Supp. XXI:** 119

Scooter tetralogy (Murray). *See Magic Keys, The* (Murray); *Seven League Boots, The* (Murray); *Spyglass Tree, The* (Murray); *Train Whistle Guitar* (Murray)

Scopes, John T., **III:** 105, 495

"Scorched Face, The" (Hammett), **Supp. IV Part 1:** 344

"Scorn" (C. Frost), **Supp. XV:** 105

"Scorpion, The" (Bowles), **Supp. IV Part 1:** 84, 86

Scorpions (Myers), **Supp. XXVII:** 203, 204, 205

Scorsese, Martin, **Supp. IV Part 1:** 356; **Supp. XVIII:** 22

"Scotland" (Huddle), **Supp. XXVI:** 155

Scott, Anne Firor, **Supp. I Part 1:** 19

Scott, A. O., **Supp. X:** 301, 302; **Supp. XII:** 343

Scott, Duncan C., **Supp. XXVI:** 87

Scott, Evelyn, **Retro. Supp. I:** 73; **Supp. XXII:** 198

Scott, Gavin, **Supp. XXII:** 218

Scott, George C., **III:** 165–166; **Supp. XI:** 304

Scott, George Lewis, **Supp. I Part 2:** 503, 504

Scott, Hazel, **Supp. XXII:** 12

Scott, Herbert, **Supp. V:** 180

Scott, Howard, **Supp. I Part 2:** 645

Scott, Joanna, **Supp. XVII: 183–197**

Scott, Lizabeth, **Supp. IV Part 2:** 524

Scott, Lynn Orilla, **Retro. Supp. II:** 12

Scott, Mark, **Retro. Supp. I:** 127

Scott, Mary Ellen, **Supp. XXVI:** 235

Scott, Nathan A., Jr., **II:** 27

Scott, Paul, **Supp. IV Part 2:** 690

Scott, Ridley, **Supp. XIII:** 268

Scott, Walter, **Supp. XVI:** 7, 13

Scott, Sir Walter, **I:** 204, 339, 341, 343, 354; **II:** 8, 17, 18, 217, 296, 301, 303, 304, 308; **III:** 415, 482; **IV:** 204, 453; **Retro. Supp. I:** 99; **Supp. I Part 2:** 579, 580, 685, 692; **Supp. IV Part 2:** 690; **Supp. IX:** 175; **Supp. X:** 51, 114

Scott, Whitney, **Supp. XXVI:** 49

Scott, Winfield Townley, **II:** 512; **Supp. I Part 2:** 705; **Supp. XV:** 51

Scottsboro boys, **I:** 505; **Supp. I Part 1:** 330

Scottsboro Limited (Hughes), **Retro. Supp. I:** 203; **Supp. I Part 1:** 328, 330–331, 332

Scoundrel, The (film), **Supp. XXVII:** 90

Scoundrel Time (Hellman), **Supp. I Part 1:** 294–297; **Supp. IV Part 1:** 12; **Supp. VIII:** 243

Scrambled Eggs Super! (Geisel), **Supp. XVI:** 105

Scrambled Eggs & Whiskey: Poems, 1991–1995 (Carruth), **Supp. XVI:** 47

Scratch (MacLeish), **III:** 22–23

"Scratch Music" (Wright), **Supp. XV:** 343

"Scream, The" (R. Lowell), **II:** 550

"Screamer, The" (Coleman), **Supp. XI: 92–93**

"Screamers, The" (Baraka), **Supp. II Part 1:** 38

"Screech Owl" (Huddle), **Supp. XXVI:** 151

"Screen Guide for Americans" (Rand), **Supp. IV Part 2:** 524

"Screen Memory" (Cliff), **Supp. XXII:** 75

"Screeno" (Schwartz), **Supp. II Part 2:** 660

Screens, The (Genet), **Supp. XII:** 12

Screen Sirens Scream! (Parla and Mitchell), **Supp. XXII:** 256

Scribblers on the Roof: Contemporary American Jewish Fiction (Bukiet and Roskies, eds.), **Supp. XVII:** 39, 49–50

Scripts for the Pageant (Merrill), **Supp. III Part 1:** 332, 333, 335

Scrolls from the Dead Sea, The (Wilson), **IV:** 429

Scruggs, Earl, **Supp. V:** 335

Scudder, Horace Elisha, **II:** 400, 401; **Retro. Supp. II:** 67; **Supp. I Part 1:** 220; **Supp. I Part 2:** 410, 414

Scully, James, **Supp. XII:** 131

"Sculpting the Whistle" (Ríos), **Supp. IV Part 2:** 549

"Sculptor" (Plath), **Supp. I Part 2:** 538

"Sculptor's Funeral, The" (Cather), **I:** 315–316; **Retro. Supp. I:** 5, 6; **Supp. XV:** 40

Scum (Singer), **Retro. Supp. II:** 316–317

Scupoli, Lorenzo, **IV:** 156

"Scythe Song" (Lang), **Retro. Supp. I:** 128

Sea and the Mirror, The: A Commentary on Shakespeare's "The Tempest" (Auden), *Supp. II Part 1:* 2, 18

Sea around Us, The (Carson), **Supp. IX:** 19, 23–25

Sea around Us, The (film), **Supp. IX:** 25

Sea Birds Are Still Alive, The (Bambara), **Supp. XI:** 1, 4, 7–12

"Sea Birds Are Still Alive, The" (Bambara), **Supp. XI:** 8

"Sea-Blue and Blood-Red" (A. Lowell), **II:** 524

Seabrook, John, **Supp. VIII:** 157

"Sea Burial from the Cruiser Reve" (Eberhart), **I:** 532–533

Seabury, David, **Supp. I Part 2:** 608

"Sea Calm" (Hughes), **Retro. Supp. I:** 199

"Sea Chanty" (Corso), **Supp. XII:** 118

"Sea Dream, A" (Whitter), **Supp. I Part 2:** 699

"Seafarer, The" (Pound, trans.), **Retro. Supp. I:** 287

Seagall, Harry, **Supp. XIII:** 166

Sea Garden (Doolittle), **Supp. I Part 1:** 257, 259, 266, 269, 272; **Supp. XXVII:** 288

Seager, Allan, **IV:** 305

Seagull on the Step, The (Boyle), **Supp. XXIV:** 60, 62

"Seagulls and Children" (C. Frost), **Supp. XV:** 95

Sea Lady, The (Boyce), **Supp. XXI:** 8, 13

"Sea Lily" (Doolittle), **Supp. I Part 1:** 266

Sea Lions, The (Cooper), **I:** 354, 355

Sealts, Merton M., Jr., **Retro. Supp. I:** 257

Seaman, Benjamin, **Supp. XXIII:** 69–70, 72

Seaman, Donna, **Supp. VIII:** 86; **Supp. X:** 1, 4, 12, 16, 213; **Supp. XIX:** 53, 55, 57, 58, 59, 60, 61; **Supp. XV:** 65; **Supp. XVIII:** 102; **Supp. XXI:** 236; **Supp. XXII:** 266; **Supp. XXIII:** 71, 74, 134, 135, 298; **Supp. XXIV:** 167, 171; **Supp. XXVI:** 150–151, 158

"Seamy Side, The"(Hadas), **Supp. XXIII:** 119

"Séance, The" (Singer), **IV:** 20

Séance and Other Stories, The (Singer), **IV:** 19–21

"Sea Oak" (Saunders), **Supp. XIX:** 228, 229, 231

Sea of Cortez (Steinbeck), **IV:** 52, 54, 62, 69

Sea of Grass, The (film), **Supp. XVIII:** 211

Sea of Grass, The (Richter), **Supp. XVIII: 210–211,** 215–216, 217, 220

"Sea Pieces" (Melville), **III:** 93

Searchers, The (film, Ford), **Supp. XVIII:** 57, 58, 135–136, 141

Searches and Seizures (Elkin), **Supp. VI: 49**

"Search for Southern Identity, The" (Woodward), **Retro. Supp. I:** 75; **Supp. XXII:** 194

Search for the King, A: A Twelfth-Century Legend (Vidal), **Supp. IV Part 2:** 681

Searching for Caleb (Tyler), **Supp. IV Part 2:** 663–665, 671

"Searching for Poetry: Real *vs.* Fake" (B. Miller), **Supp. IV Part 1:** 67

Searching for Survivors (Banks), **Supp. V:** 7

"Searching for Survivors (I)" (Banks), **Supp. V:** 8

"Searching for Survivors (II)" (Banks), **Supp. V:** 7, 8

Searching for the Ox (Simpson), **Supp. IX:** 266, **274–275**

"Searching for the Ox" (Simpson), **Supp. IX:** 275, 280

"Searching in the Britannia Tavern" (Wagoner), **Supp. IX:** 327

Searching Wing, The, (Hellman), **Supp. I Part 1:** 277, 278, 281–282, 283, 292, 297

Search-Light. *See* Frank, Waldo

"Search Party, The" (Matthews), **Supp. IX: 156**

Searle, Ronald, **Supp. I Part 2:** 604, 605

Sea Road to the Indies (Hart), **Supp. XIV:** 97

"Seascape" (Bishop), **Retro. Supp. II:** 42–43

Seascape: Needle's Eye (Oppen), **Supp. XXVI:** 236–237

"Sea's Green Sameness, The" (Updike), **IV:** 217

Seaside and the Fireside, The (Longfellow), **II:** 489; **Retro. Supp. II:** 159, 168

"Season, The" (Stone), **Supp. XXVII:** 250–251

Season in Hell, A (Rimbaud), **III:** 189

Seasons, The (Thomson), **II:** 304; **Supp. I Part 1:** 151

Seasons' Difference, The (Buechner), **Supp. XII:** 47

Seasons of Celebration (Merton), **Supp. VIII:** 199, 208

Seasons of the Heart: In Quest of Faith (Kinard, comp.), **Supp. XIV:** 127

"Seasons of the Soul" (Tate), **IV:** 136–140

Seasons on Earth (Koch), **Supp. XV: 183–184**

"Sea Surface Full of Clouds" (Stevens), **IV:** 82

"Sea Tides" (Hoffman), **Supp. XVIII:** 87

"Sea Treader" (Hoffman), **Supp. XVIII:** 87

"Sea Unicorns and Land Unicorns" (Moore), **III:** 202–203

Seaver, Edwin, **Supp. XXV:** 28

Seaver, Richard, **Supp. XI:** 301

"Seaweed" (Longfellow), **II:** 498

Sea-Wolf, The (London), **II:** 264, 466, 472–473

Sebald, W. G., **Supp. XIV:** 96; **Supp. XXI:** 92

Sebold, Alice, **Supp. XXII:** 55

Seckler, David, **Supp. I Part 2:** 650

"2nd Air Force" (Jarrell), **II:** 375

Second American Revolution and Other Essays (1976–1982), The (Vidal), **Supp. IV Part 2:** 679, 687, 688

Secondary Colors, The (A. Theroux), **Supp. VIII:** 312

Second Avenue (O'Hara), **Supp. XXIII:** 216

"Second Avenue"(O'Hara), **Supp. XXIII:** 208, 211, 218

Second Blush, The (Peacock), **Supp. XIX:** 197, **205–206**

Second Chance (Auchincloss), **Supp. IV Part 1:** 33

"Second Chances" (Hugo), **Supp. VI:** 144, 145

Second Coming, The (Percy), **Supp. III Part 1:** 383, 384, 387, 388, 396–397

"Second Coming, The" (Yeats), **III:** 294; **Retro. Supp. I:** 290, 311; **Supp. VIII:** 24; **Supp. XIX:** 85; **Supp. XVI:** 159

Second Decade, The. See Stephen King, The Second Decade: "Danse Macabre" to "The Dark Half" (Magistrale)

Second Dune, The (Hearon), **Supp. VIII:** 58, **59–60**

Second Flowering, A: Works and Days of the Lost Generation (Cowley), **Retro. Supp. II:** 77; **Supp. II Part 1:** 135, 141, 143, 144, 147, 149

Second Growth (Stegner), **Supp. IV Part 2:** 599, 608

Second-Hand Coat: Poems New and Selected (Stone), **Supp. XXVII:** 250, 257, 262

"Second Hour of the Night, The" (Bidart), **Supp. XV:** 32, **33–34**

Second Marriage (F. Barthelme), **Supp. XI:** 32, 33

"Second Marriage" (McCarriston), **Supp. XIV:** 262

"Second Mortgage" (Shaw), **Supp. XIX:** 245–246

Second Nature (Hoffman), **Supp. X:** 88, 89

"Second Nesting" (Davison), **Supp. XXVI:** 77

Seconds, The (Bierds), **Supp. XVII: 33–34**

Second Set, The (Komunyakaa and Feinstein, eds.), **Supp. XIII:** 125

Second Sex, The (Beauvoir), **Supp. IV Part 1:** 360

"Second Sight" (Mosher), **Supp. XXII:** 214

Second Stone, The (Fiedler), **Supp. XIII:** 102

"Second Swimming, The" (Boyle), **Supp. VIII:** 13, 14

Second Tree from the Corner (White), **Supp. I Part 2:** 654

"Second Tree from the Corner" (White), **Supp. I Part 2:** 651

Second Twenty Years at Hull-House, The: September 1909 to September 1929, with a Record of a Growing World Consciousness (Addams), **Supp. I Part 1:** 24–25

Second Voyage of Columbus, The (Morison), **Supp. I Part 2:** 488

Second Words, (Atwood), **Supp. XIII:** 35

Second World, The (Blackmur), **Supp. II Part 1:** 91

Secret, The (E. Hoffman), **Supp. XVI:** 151, **155–158,** 161

"Secret, The" (Levine), **Supp. V:** 195

Secret Agent, The (Conrad), **Supp. IV Part 1:** 341

Secret Agent X-9 (Hammett), **Supp. IV Part 1:** 355

"Secret Courts of Men's Hearts, The: Code and Law in Harper Lee's *To Kill a Mockingbird*" (C. D. Johnson), **Supp. VIII:** 126

Secret Dog, The (Cameron), **Supp. XII:** 83–84

Secret Garden, The (Burnett), **Supp. I Part 1:** 44

"Secret Garden, The" (Hoffman), **Supp. XVIII:** 86

"Secret Gladness, A" (C. Frost), **Supp. XV:** 91

Secret Historie (J. Smith), **I:** 131

Secret History, The (Tartt), **Supp. XXVII:** 267, 268, 269, 270–273

Secret History of the Dividing Line (Howe), **Supp. IV Part 2:** 424, 425–426

"Secret Integration, The" (Pynchon), **Supp. II Part 2:** 624

"Secret Life of Musical Instruments, The" (Wright), **Supp. XV:** 343

"Secret Life of Walter Mitty, The" (Thurber), **Supp. I Part 2:** 623; **Supp. XVI:** 233

"Secret Lion, The" (Ríos), **Supp. IV Part 2:** 543, 544

"Secret Nature of the Mechanical Rabbit, The"(P. Benedict), **Supp. XXIII:** 49

"Secret Ocean, The" (Jarman), **Supp. XVII:** 120

Secret of Poetry, The: Essays (Jarman), **Supp. XVII:** 110, 111, 120

"Secret of the Russian Ballet, The" (Van Vechten), **Supp. II Part 2:** 732

"Secret Profession, The" (Stone), **Supp. XXVII:** 258–259

"Secret Prune" (Ríos), **Supp. IV Part 2:** 549

Secret River, The (Rawlings), **Supp. X:** 233

Secrets and Surprises (Beattie), **Supp. V:** 23, 27, 29

Secrets from the Center of the World (Harjo), **Supp. XII: 223–224**

"Secret Sharer, The" (J. Conrad), **Supp. IX:** 105; **Supp. XVI:** 158; **Supp. XXV:** 217

"Secret Society, A" (Nemerov), **III:** 282

Secrets of the Heart (Gibran), **Supp. XX: 116**

"Secrets of the Summer, The" (Ellis), **Supp. XXVII:** 75

Secrets of the Universe: Scenes from the Journey Home (Sanders), **Supp. XVI:** 273–274

"Secular" (Trethewey), **Supp. XXI:** 249

Secular Journal of Thomas Merton, The, **Supp. VIII:** 206

"Security" (Boyle), **Supp. XXIV:** 58

"Security" (Stafford), **Supp. XI:** 329

"Security"(Strout), **Supp. XXIII:** 283

Sedaris, David, **Supp. XXIII:** 289

Sedges, John (pseudonym). *See* Buck, Pearl S.

Sedgwick, Catherine Maria, **I:** 341; **Supp. I Part 1:** 155, 157

Sedgwick, Christina. *See* Marquand, Mrs. John P. (Christina Sedgwick)

Sedgwick, Ellery, **I:** 217, 229, 231; **III:** 54–55

Sedgwick, Eve, **Supp. XX: 267**

Sedgwick, Henry, **Supp. I Part 1:** 156

Sedgwick, Robert, **Supp. I Part 1:** 156

Sedore, Timothy, **Supp. XIV:** 312

"Seduction and Betrayal" (Hardwick), **Supp. III Part 1:** 207

Seduction and Betrayal: Women and Literature (Hardwick), **Supp. III Part 1:**

194, 204, 206–208, 212, 213; **Supp. XIV:** 89

See, Carolyn, **Supp. XXII:** 206, 217

Seed, David, **Supp. IV Part 1:** 391

"Seed Eaters, The" (Francis), **Supp. IX:** 82

"Seed Leaves" (Wilbur), **Supp. III Part 2:** 558

"Seeds" (Anderson), **I:** 106, 114

Seeds of Contemplation (Merton), **Supp. VIII:** 199, 200, 207, 208

Seeds of Destruction (Merton), **Supp. VIII:** 202, 203, 204, 208

"Seeing Red" (column, Ryan as Quin), **Supp. XVIII:** 226

Seeing through the Sun (Hogan), **Supp. IV Part 1:** 397, 400, 401–402, 402, 413

"See in the Midst of Fair Leaves" (Moore), **III:** 215

"Seekers, The" (McGrath), **Supp. X:** 117

"Seeking a Vision of Truth, Guided by a Higher Power" (Burke), **Supp. XIV:** 21, 23

"See(k)ing the Self: Mirrors and Mirroring in Bicultural Texts" (Oster), **Supp. XVI:** 151

"Seele im Raum" (Jarrell), **II:** 382–383

"Seele im Raum" (Rilke), **II:** 382–383

"See Naples and Die" (Hecht), **Supp. X:** 69, 70

"Seen from the 'L' " (Barnes), **Supp. III Part 1:** 33

"See the Moon?" (Barthelme), **Supp. IV Part 1:** 42, 49–50, 50

Sefarim, Mendele Mokher, **Supp. XXIII:** 4

Seferis, George, **Supp. XXV:** 225

Segal, D. (pseudonym). *See* Singer, Isaac Bashevis

Segal, George, **Supp. XI:** 343

Segal, Lore, **Supp. XVI:** 203

Segregation: The Inner Conflict in the South (Warren), **IV:** 237, 238, 246, 252

"*Se: Hegel's Absolute and Heidegger's Ereignis*" (Agamben), **Supp. XVI:** 289

Seidel, Frederick, **I:** 185

Seidman, Hugh, **Supp. XXI:** 228

Seize the Day (Bellow), **I:** 144, 147, 148, 150, 151, 152, 153, 155, 158, 162; **Retro. Supp. II:** 19, **23–24,** 27, 32, 34; **Supp. I Part 2:** 428

Selby, Hubert, **Supp. III Part 1:** 125

Selby, Hubert, Jr., **Supp. XXI:** 227

Selby, John, **Retro. Supp. II:** 221, 222

Selden, John, **Supp. XIV:** 344

Seldes, Gilbert, **II:** 437, 445; **Retro. Supp. I:** 108

Selected Criticism: Prose, Poetry (Bogan), **Supp. III Part 1:** 64

Selected Essays (Eliot), **I:** 572

Selected Essays and Reviews (Carruth), **Supp. XVI:** 46

Selected Journals and Other Writings (Audubon), **Supp. XVI:** 10, 12, 13

Selected Letters (Bynner), **Supp. XV:** 52

Selected Letters (Oppen), **Supp. XXVI:** 228

Selected Letters (W. C. Williams), **Retro. Supp. I:** 430

Selected Letters, 1940–1956 (Kerouac), **Supp. XIV:** 137, 144

Selected Letters of Robert Frost (Thompson, ed.), **Retro. Supp. I:** 125

Selected Levis, The (Levis), **Supp. XI:** 257, 272

Selected Plays (O'Hara), **Supp. XXIII:** 216

Selected Poems (A. Lowell), **II:** 512, 516

Selected Poems (Aiken), **I:** 69

Selected Poems (Ashbery), **Supp. III Part 1:** 25–26

Selected Poems (Berrigan), **Supp. XXIV:** 37

Selected Poems (Bodenheim), **Supp. XXV:** 29

Selected Poems (Brodsky), **Supp. VIII:** 22

Selected Poems (Brooks), **Supp. III Part 1:** 82–83

Selected Poems (Bynner), **Supp. XV:** 51, 52

Selected Poems (Corso), **Supp. XII:** 129

Selected Poems (Dove), **Supp. IV Part 1:** 241, 243, 250

Selected Poems (Frost), **Retro. Supp. I:** 133, 136

Selected Poems (Guillevic; Levertov, trans.), **Supp. III Part 1:** 283

Selected Poems (Hayden), **Supp. II Part 1:** 363, 364, 367

Selected Poems (Hughes), **Retro. Supp. I:** 202; **Supp. I Part 1:** 341, 345, 346

Selected Poems (Hugo), **Supp. VI:** 143

Selected Poems (Jarrell), **II:** 367, 370, 371, 374, 377, 379, 380, 381, 382, 384

Selected Poems (Justice), **Supp. VII:** 115

Selected Poems (Kinnell), **Supp. III Part 1:** 235, 253

Selected Poems (Levine, 1984), **Supp. V:** 178, 179

Selected Poems (Merton), **Supp. VIII:** 207, 208

Selected Poems (Moore), **III:** 193, 194, 205–206, 208, 215

Selected Poems (Notley), **Supp. XXII:** 234

Selected Poems (O'Hara; Allen, ed.), **Supp. XXIII:** 220

Selected Poems (O'Hara; Ford, ed.), **Supp. XXIII:** 220

Selected Poems (Pound), **Retro. Supp. I:** 289, 291

Selected Poems (R. Bly), **Supp. IV Part 1:** 60, 62, 65, 66, 68, 69–71

Selected Poems (R. Lowell), **Retro. Supp. II:** 184, 186, 188, 190

Selected Poems (Ransom), **III:** 490, 492

Selected Poems (Reznikoff), **Supp. XIV:** 288

Selected Poems (Rukeyser), **Supp. VI:** 274

Selected Poems (Sexton), **Supp. IV Part 2:** 449

Selected Poems (Sorrentino), **Supp. XXI:** 226

Selected Poems (Strand), **Supp. IV Part 2:** 630

Selected Poems, 1923–1943 (Warren), **IV:** 241–242, 243

Selected Poems, 1928–1958 (Kunitz), **Supp. III Part 1:** 261, 263–265
Selected Poems, 1938–1988 (McGrath), **Supp. X:** 127
Selected Poems, 1958–1980 (Sorrentino), **Supp. XXI:** 228
Selected Poems, 1963–1983 (Simic), **Supp. VIII:** 275
Selected Poems 1936–1965 (Eberhart), **I:** 541
Selected Poems: 1957–1987 (Snodgrass), **Supp. VI:** 314–315, 323, 324
Selected Poems 1965–1975 (Atwood), **Supp. XIII:** 32–34
Selected Poems: 1975–2005 (Skloot), **Supp. XX:** 196
Selected Poems II: Poems Selected and New, 1976–1986 (Atwood), **Supp. XIII:** 20, 34–35
Selected Poems of Ezra Pound (Pound), **Supp. V:** 336
Selected Poems of Gabriela Mistral (Hughes, trans.), **Supp. I Part 1:** 345
Selected Poems of Stanley Kunitz, The, **Supp. XXVI:** 64
Selected Poetry of Amiri Baraka/LeRoi Jones (Baraka), **Supp. II Part 1:** 58
Selected Poetry of Hayden Carruth, The (Carruth), **Supp. XVI:** 53
Selected Stories (Dubus), **Supp. VII:** 88–89
Selected Stories of Richard Bausch, The (Bausch), **Supp. VII:** 42
Selected Translations (Snodgrass), **Supp. VI:** 318, 324, **325–326**
Selected Verse of Margaret Haskins Durber, The (Keillor), **Supp. XVI:** 171
Selected Witter Bynner, The, **Supp. XV:** 52
Selected Works of Djuna Barnes, The (Barnes), **Supp. III Part 1:** 44
Selected Writings (Brainard), **Supp. XXVII:** 20
Selected Writings 1950–1990 (Howe), **Supp. VI:** 116–117, 118, 120
Selected Writings of John Jay Chapman, The (Barzun), **Supp. XIV:** 54
Select Epigrams from the Greek Anthology (Mackail), **Supp. I Part 2:** 461
"Selecting a Reader" (Kooser), **Supp. XIX:** 119–120
"Selene Afterwards" (MacLeish), **III:** 8
"Self" (James), **II:** 351
Self, William, **Supp. XXII:** 172
Self and the Dramas of History, The (Niebuhr), **III:** 308
"Self-Appraisal" (Davison), **Supp. XXVI:** 68
Self-Consciousness (Updike), **Retro. Supp. I:** 318, 319, 320, 322, 323, 324
"Self-Culture" (Channing), **Supp. XXIV:** **78–79**
"Self-Exposed, The" (X. J. Kennedy), **Supp. XV:** 159
Self-Help: Stories (Moore), **Supp. X:** 163, 166, **167–169**, 174, 175
"Self-Importance" (Halliday), **Supp. XIX:** 90
Self-Interviews (Dickey), **Supp. IV Part 1:** 179

"Self-Made Man, A" (Crane), **I:** 420
"Self Pity" (C. Frost), **Supp. XV:** 93, 94, 101, 102, 104
Self Portrait (album, Dylan), **Supp. XVIII:** 27
Self-Portrait (Brainard and Waldman), **Supp. XXVII:** 23–24
"Self-Portrait" (Creeley), **Supp. IV Part 1:** 156
"Self-Portrait" (Davison), **Supp. XXVI:** 68
"Self-Portrait" (Mumford), **Supp. II Part 2:** 471
"(Self) Portrait" (Trethewey), **Supp. XXI:** 253
"Self-Portrait" (Wylie), **Supp. I Part 2:** 729
"Self Portrait at Fifty-three" (Weigl), **Supp. XIX:** 288
Self-Portrait: Ceaselessly into the Past (Millar, ed. Sipper), **Supp. IV Part 2:** 464, 469, 472, 475
"Self-Portrait in a Convex Mirror" (Ashbery), **Supp. III Part 1:** 5, 7, 9, 16–19, 22, 24, 26
"Self-Portrait on a Christmas Night" (Brainard), **Supp. XXVII:** 24–25
"Self-Portrait with 1911 NY Yankees Cap" (Skloot), **Supp. XX:** 202
"Self-Reliance" (Emerson), **II:** 7, 15, 17; **Retro. Supp. I:** 159; **Retro. Supp. II:** 155; **Supp. X:** 42, 45
Selfwolf (Halliday), **Supp. XIX:** 81, **89–91,** 93
Sélincourt, Ernest de, **Supp. I Part 2:** 676
Selinger, Eric, **Supp. XVI:** 47
Selinger, Eric Murphy, **Supp. XI:** 248
Sell, Henry, **Supp. XVI:** 188
Sellers, Isaiah, **IV:** 194–195
Sellers, Peter, **Supp. XI:** 301, 304, 306, 307, 309
Sellers, William, **IV:** 208
Seltzer, Mark, **Retro. Supp. I:** 227
Selznick, David O., **Retro. Supp. I:** 105, 113; **Supp. IV Part 1:** 353; **Supp. XVIII:** 242; **Supp. XXII:** 195
Semi, Allen (pseudonym). *See* Larsen, Nella
"Semi-Lunatics of Kilmuir, The" (Hugo), **Supp. VI:** 145
"Semiotics/The Doctor's Doll" (Goldbarth), **Supp. XII:** 183–184
Semmelweiss, Ignaz, **Supp. I Part 1:** 304
Senancour, Étienne Divert de, **I:** 241
Senator North (Atherton), **Supp. XXIV:** 22
Sendak, Maurice, **Supp. IX:** 207, 208, 213, 214; **Supp. XVI:** 110
Seneca, **II:** 14–15; **III:** 77
Senghor, Leopold Sédar, **Supp. IV Part 1:** 16; **Supp. X:** 132, 139
Senier, Siobhan, **Supp. IV Part 1:** 330
"Senility" (Anderson), **I:** 114
Senior, Olive, **Supp. XXIII:** 94
"Senior Partner's Ethics, The" (Auchincloss), **Supp. IV Part 1:** 33
Senlin: A Biography (Aiken), **I:** 48, 49, 50, 52, 56, 57, 64
Sennett, Dorothy, **Supp. XVI:** 43

Sennett, Mack, **III:** 442
"Señora X No More" (Mora), **Supp. XIII:** 218
"Señor Ong and Señor Ha" (Bowles), **Supp. IV Part 1:** 87
Señor Presidente, El (Asturias), **Supp. XXIV:** 89
"Señor X" (Muñoz), **Supp. XXV:** 135
Sensational Designs: The Cultural Work of American Fiction, 1790–1860 (Tompkins), **Supp. XVIII:** 258–259
Sense and Sensibility (Austen), **Supp. XXVI:** 130, 212
Sense of Beauty, The (Santayana), **III:** 600
Sense of Life in the Modern Novel, The (Mizener), **IV:** 132
"Sense of Shelter, A" (Updike), **Retro. Supp. I:** 318
"Sense of the Meeting, The" (Conroy), **Supp. XVI:** 72
Sense of the Past, The (James), **II:** 337–338
"Sense of the Past, The" (Trilling), **Supp. III Part 2:** 503
"Sense of the Present, The" (Hardwick), **Supp. III Part 1:** 210
"Sense of the Sleight-of-Hand Man, The" (Stevens), **IV:** 93
"Sense of Where You Are, A" (McPhee), **Supp. III Part 1:** 291, 296–298
"Sensibility! O La!" (Roethke), **III:** 536
"Sensible Emptiness, A" (Kramer), **Supp. IV Part 1:** 61, 66
Sensualists, The (Hecht), **Supp. XXVII:** 96
"Sensuality Plunging Barefoot Into Thorns" (Cisneros), **Supp. VII:** 68
"Sentence" (Barthelme), **Supp. IV Part 1:** 47
Sent for You Yesterday (Wideman), **Supp. X:** 320, 321
Sentimental Education (Flaubert), **Supp. XXVII:** 2
"Sentimental Education, A" (Banks), **Supp. V:** 10
"Sentimental Journey" (Oates), **Supp. II Part 2:** 522, 523
"Sentimental Journey, A" (Anderson), **I:** 114
"Sentimental Journey, A" (Sterne), **Supp. I Part 2:** 714
"Sentimental Journeys" (Didion), **Supp. IV Part 1:** 211
Sentimental Journey through France and Italy, A (Sterne), **Supp. XV:** 232
"Sentiment of Rationality, The" (James), **II:** 346–347
"Separated Father" (Halliday), **Supp. XIX:** 92, 93
Separate Flights (Dubus), **Supp. VII:** 78–83
"Separate Flights" (Dubus), **Supp. VII:** 83
Separate Peace, A (Knowles), **Supp. IV Part 2:** 679; **Supp. XII: 241–249**
Separate Way (Reznikoff), **Supp. XIV:** 280
"Separating" (Updike), **Retro. Supp. I:** 321

"Separation, The" (Kunitz), **Supp. III Part 1:** 263

"Sepia High Stepper" (Hayden), **Supp. II Part 1:** 379

Septagon (Levin), **Supp. XXVII:** 139

September (film; Allen), **Supp. XV:** 11

"September" (Komunyakaa), **Supp. XIII:** 130

"September" (Pickering), **Supp. XXI:** 198

"September 1, 1939" (Auden), **Supp. II Part 1:** 13; **Supp. IV Part 1:** 225; **Supp. VIII:** 30, 32; **Supp. XV:** 117–118

September 11, 2001: American Writers Respond (Heyen), **Supp. XIII:** 285

"September's Book" (Notley), **Supp. XXII:** 229

September Song (Humphrey), **Supp. IX:** 101, 102, **108–109**

"September Twelfth, 2001" (X. J. Kennedy), **Supp. XV:** 171

Septet for the End of Time (Mackey), **Supp. XXVII:** 152

"Sept Vieillards, Les" (Millay, trans.), **III:** 142

Sequel to Drum-Taps (Whitman), **Retro. Supp. I:** 406

"Sequence, Sometimes Metaphysical" (Roethke), **III:** 547, 548

Sequence of Seven Plays with a Drawing by Ron Slaughter, A (Nemerov), **III:** 269

Sequoya, Jana, **Supp. IV Part 1:** 334

Seraglio, The (Merrill), **Supp. III Part 1:** 331

Seraphita (Balzac), **I:** 499

Seraph on the Suwanee (Hurston), **Supp. VI:** 149, 159–160

Serena (film), **Supp. XXVII:** 222

Serena (Rash), **Supp. XXVII:** 222, 224–225, 226

Serenissima: A Novel of Venice (Jong). *See Shylock's Daughter: A Novel of Love in Venice (Serenissima)* (Jong)

Sergeant, Elizabeth Shepley, **I:** 231, 236, 312, 319, 323, 328

Sergeant Bilko (television show), **Supp. IV Part 2:** 575

Sergi, Paula, **Supp. XXI:** 246

"Serious Talk, A" (Carver), **Supp. III Part 1:** 138, 144

Serly, Tibor, **Supp. III Part 2:** 617, 619

"Sermon, Now Encrypted" (Monson), **Supp. XXIV:** 239–240

"Sermon by Doctor Pep" (Bellow), **I:** 151

Sermones (Horace), **II:** 154

"Sermon for Our Maturity" (Baraka), **Supp. II Part 1:** 53

"Sermon in the Cotton Field" (Nelson), **Supp. XVIII:** 177

"Sermon in the Depths, The" (Hecht), **Supp. XXVII:** 86

Sermons and Soda Water (O'Hara), **III:** 362, 364, 371–373, 382

"Sermons on the Warpland" (Brooks), **Supp. III Part 1:** 84

"Serpent in the Wilderness, The" (Masters), **Supp. I Part 2:** 458

"Servant of History, A" (Rash), **Supp. XXVII:** 229

Servant of the Bones (Rice), **Supp. VII:** 298, 302

"Servant to Servants, A" (Frost), **Retro. Supp. I:** 125, 128; **Supp. X:** 66

Serve It Forth (M. F. K. Fisher), **Supp. XVII:** 83, 86, 87, 89, 92

Service, Robert W., **Supp. XXI:** 51; **Supp. XXII:** 203

Seshachari, Neila, **Supp. V:** 22

"Session, The" (Adams), **I:** 5

"Sestina" (Bishop), **Supp. I Part 1:** 73, 88

Set-angya, **Supp. IV Part 2:** 493

Seth, Vikram, **Supp. XVII:** 117

Seth's Brother's Wife (Frederic), **II:** 131–132, 137, 144

Sethuraman, Ramchandran, **Supp. XXII:** 73

Setouchi, Jakuch\[omacron\], **Supp. XXIV:** 166

Set This House on Fire (Styron), **IV:** 98, 99, 105, 107–113, 114, 115, 117

Setting Free the Bears (Irving), **Supp. VI:** 163, **166–167,** 169–170

Setting the Tone (Rorem), **Supp. IV Part 1:** 79

Settle, Mary Lee, **Supp. IX:** 96

Settlement Horizon, The: A National Estimate (Woods and Kennedy), **Supp. I Part 1:** 19

Settlers, The (Levin), **Supp. XXVII:** 134, 143, 146

"Settling the Colonel's Hash" (McCarthy), **II:** 559, 562

Setzer, Helen, **Supp. IV Part 1:** 217

"Seurat's Sunday Afternoon along the Seine" (Schwartz), **Supp. II Part 2:** 663–665

Sevag, Aris, **Supp. XXIII:** 28, 29

7 Years from Somehwere (Levine), **Supp. V:** 178, 181, 188–189

Seven against Thebes (Aeschylus; Bacon and Hecht, trans.), **Supp. X:** 57

Seven Ages of Man, The (Wilder), **IV:** 357, 374–375

Seven Deadly Sins, The (Wilder), **IV:** 357, 374–375

Seven Descents of Myrtle, The (T. Williams), **IV:** 382

"Seven Fat Brides, The" (P. Abraham), **Supp. XVII:** 50

Seven Guitars (Wilson), **Supp. VIII:** 331, **348–351**

Seven Lady Godivas, The (Geisel), **Supp. XVI:** 100, 103

Seven League Boots, The (Murray), **Supp. XIX: 156–157**

Seven-League Crutches, The (Jarrell), **II:** 367, 372, 381, 382, 383–384, 389

Seven Mountains of Thomas Merton, The (Mott), **Supp. VIII:** 208

Seven-Ounce Man, The (Harrison), **Supp. VIII:** 51

"Seven Places of the Mind" (Didion), **Supp. IV Part 1:** 200, 210

Seven Plays (Shepard), **Supp. III Part 2:** 434

"Seven Selves, The" (Gibran), **Supp. XX: 118**

"Seven Sentences" (Dybek), **Supp. XXIII:** 74

"Seven Stanzas at Easter" (Updike), **IV:** 215

Seven Storey Mountain, The (Merton), **Supp. VIII:** 193, 195, 198, 200, 207, 208

Seventeen (Berrigan and Padgett), **Supp. XXIV:** 41

Seventh Beggar, The (Abraham), **Supp. XXIV:** 2, 3, **9–12,** 13, 14

Seventh Heaven (Hoffman), **Supp. X:** 87, 89

"Seventh of March" (Webster), **Supp. I Part 2:** 687

"7000 Romaine, Los Angeles 38" (Didion), **Supp. IV Part 1:** 200

"Seventh Street" (Toomer), **Supp. IX:** 316

Seven Types of Ambiguity (Empson), **II:** 536; **IV:** 431

77 Dream Songs (Berryman), **I:** 168, 169, 170, 171, 174, 175, 183–188

73 Poems (Cummings), **I:** 430, 431, 446, 447, 448

Seven Valleys and the Four Valleys, The (Bahá'u'lláh), **Supp. XX: 121**

"Several Short Questions About Crumbs" (Schott), **Supp. XXIII:** 249

Sevier, Jack, **IV:** 378

Sévigné, Madame de, **IV:** 361

Sewall, Richard, **Retro. Supp. I:** 25

Sewall, Samuel, **IV:** 145, 146, 147, 149, 154, 164; **Supp. I Part 1:** 100, 110

Sewell, Elizabeth, **Supp. XIII:** 344

"Sex" (Carruth), **Supp. XVI:** 58

Sex, Economy, Freedom and Community (Berry), **Supp. X:** 30, 36

"Sex Camp" (Mamet), **Supp. XIV:** 240

Sex Castle, The (Lacy), **Supp. XV:** 206

Sex & Character (Weininger), **Retro. Supp. I:** 416

"Sext" (Auden), **Supp. II Part 1:** 22

Sexton, Anne, **Retro. Supp. II:** 245; **Supp. I Part 2:** 538, 543, 546; **Supp. II Part 2: 669–700; Supp. III Part 2:** 599; **Supp. IV Part 1:** 245; **Supp. IV Part 2:** 439, 440–441, 442, 444, 447, 449, 451, 620; **Supp. V:** 113, 118, 124; **Supp. X:** 201, 202, 213; **Supp. XI:** 146, 240, 317; **Supp. XII:** 217, 253, 254, 256, 260, 261; **Supp. XIII:** 35, 76, 294, 312; **Supp. XIV:** 125, 126, 132, 269; **Supp. XIX:** 82, 203; **Supp. XV:** 123, 252, 340; **Supp. XVII:** 239; **Supp. XX:** 199; **Supp. XXVI:** 68; **Supp. XXVII:** 261

Sexual Behavior in the American Male (Kinsey), **Supp. XIII:** 96–97

Sexual Perversity in Chicago (Mamet), **Supp. XIV:** 239, 240, 246–247, 249

"Sexual Revolution, The" (Dunn), **Supp. XI:** 142

Sexus (H. Miller), **III:** 170, 171, 184, 187, 188

"Sex Without Love" (Olds), **Supp. X:** 206

"Sexy" (Lahiri), **Supp. XXI:** 183–184

Seyersted, Per E., **Retro. Supp. II:** 65; **Supp. I Part 1:** 201, 204, 211, 216, 225; **Supp. IV Part 2:** 558

Seyfried, Robin, **Supp. IX:** 324

Seymour, Corey, **Supp. XXIV:** 280

Seymour, Miranda, **Supp. VIII:** 167

"Seymour: An Introduction" (Salinger), **III:** 569–571, 572

Sgt. Pepper column (Christgau), **Supp. XXVII:** 42–44

"Shack" (L. Brown), **Supp. XXI:** 49

Shacochis, Bob, **Supp. VIII:** 80

"Shadow" (Creeley), **Supp. IV Part 1:** 158

"Shadow, The" (A. Lowell), **II:** 522

Shadow and Act (Ellison), **Retro. Supp. II:** 119; **Supp. II Part 1:** 245–246

"Shadow and Shade" (Tate), **IV:** 128

"Shadow and the Flesh, The" (London), **II:** 475

"Shadow A Parable" (Poe), **III:** 417–418

Shadow Country (Gunn Allen), **Supp. IV Part 1:** 322, 324, 325–326

"Shadow Kingdom, The" (Howard), **Supp. XXVII:** 122–123, 127

Shadow-Line, The (Conrad), **Supp. XXV:** 217

Shadow Man, The (Gordon), **Supp. IV Part 1:** 297, 298, 299, 312–314, 315

Shadow of a Dream, The, a Story (Howells), **II:** 285, 286, 290

Shadow of a Man (Moraga), **Supp. XXIII:** 195, 197, **199–203**

Shadow of Heaven (Hayes), **Supp. XXVI:** 137–139

"Shadow of the Crime, The: A Word from the Author" (Mailer), **Retro. Supp. II:** 214

"Shadow of the Vulture, The" (Howard), **Supp. XXVII:** 120–121

Shadow on the Dial, The (Bierce), **I:** 208, 209

"Shadow out of Time, The" (Lovecraft), **Supp. XXV:** 111

Shadow over Innsmouth, The (Lovecraft), **Supp. XXV:** 111, 117–118, 120, 121

"Shadow Passing" (Merwin), **Supp. III Part 1:** 355

Shadowplay (C. Baxter), **Supp. XVII:** 15, 19–20

Shadows (Gardner), **Supp. VI:** 74

Shadows and Fog (film; Allen), **Supp. XV:** 11

Shadows Burning (Di Piero), **Supp. XIX:** 42, 43–44

Shadows by the Hudson (Singer), **IV:** 1

Shadows of Africa (Matthiessen), **Supp. V:** 203

"Shadows of Zamboula" (Howard), **Supp. XXVII:** 125–126

Shadows on the Hudson (Singer), **Retro. Supp. II: 311–313**

Shadows on the Rock (Cather), **I:** 314, 330–331, 332; **Retro. Supp. I:** 18

"Shadows over Lovecraft: Reactionary Fantasy and Immigrant Eugenics" (Lovett-Graff), **Supp. XXV:** 123

Shadow Train (Ashbery), **Supp. III Part 1:** 23–24, 26

"Shad-Time" (Wilbur), **Supp. III Part 2:** 563

Shaffer, Thomas L., **Supp. VIII:** 127, 128

Shaft (Parks; film), **Supp. XI:** 17

Shaftesbury, Earl of, **I:** 559

Shahid, Irfan, **Supp. XX: 113, 127**

Shahn, Ben, **Supp. X:** 24

Shakedown for Murder (Lacy), **Supp. XV:** 203

Shakelford, Dean, **Supp. VIII:** 129

Shaker, Why Don't You Sing? (Angelou), **Supp. IV Part 1:** 16

Shakespear, Mrs. Olivia, **III:** 457; **Supp. I Part 1:** 257

"Shakespeare" (Emerson), **II:** 6

"Shakespeare" (Very), **Supp. XXV:** 244

Shakespeare, William, **I:** 103, 271, 272, 284–285, 358, 378, 433, 441, 458, 461, 573, 585, 586; **II:** 5, 8, 11, 18, 72, 273, 297, 302, 309, 320, 411, 494, 577, 590; **III:** 3, 11, 12, 82, 83, 91, 124, 130, 134, 145, 153, 159, 183, 210, 263, 286, 468, 473, 492, 503, 511, 567, 575–576, 577, 610, 612, 613, 615; **IV:** 11, 50, 66, 127, 132, 156, 309, 313, 362, 368, 370, 373, 453; **Retro. Supp. I:** 43, 64, 91, 248; **Retro. Supp. II:** 114, 299; **Supp. I Part 1:** 79, 150, 262, 310, 356, 363, 365, 368, 369, 370; **Supp. I Part 2:** 397, 421, 422, 470, 494, 622, 716, 720; **Supp. II Part 2:** 624, 626; **Supp. IV Part 1:** 31, 83, 87, 243; **Supp. IV Part 2:** 430, 463, 519, 688; **Supp. IX:** 14, 133; **Supp. V:** 252, 280, 303; **Supp. VIII:** 160, 164; **Supp. X:** 42, 62, 65, 78; **Supp. XII:** 54–57, 277, 281; **Supp. XIII:** 111, 115, 233; **Supp. XIV:** 97, 120, 225, 245, 306; **Supp. XV:** 92; **Supp. XVIII:** 278; **Supp. XXII:** 206; **Supp. XXIV:** 33, 34, 40, 87, 159

Shakespeare and His Forerunners (Lanier), **Supp. I Part 1:** 369

Shakespeare in Harlem (Hughes), **Retro. Supp. I:** 194, 202, 205, 206, 207, 208; **Supp. I Part 1:** 333, 334, 345

Shalit, Gene, **Supp. VIII:** 73

Shalit, Wendy, **Supp. XX: 179, 182, 186**

Shall We Gather at the River (Wright), **Supp. III Part 2:** 601–602; **Supp. XVII:** 241

"Shame" (Oates), **Supp. II Part 2:** 520

"Shame" (Wilbur), **Supp. III Part 2:** 556

"Shame and Forgetting in the Information Age" (C. Baxter), **Supp. XVII:** 21

"Shameful Affair, A" (Chopin), **Retro. Supp. II:** 61

Shamela (Fielding), **Supp. V:** 127

"Shampoo, The" (Bishop), **Retro. Supp. II:** 46; **Supp. I Part 1:** 92

Shange, Ntozake, **Supp. VIII:** 214; **Supp. XVII:** 70; **Supp. XVIII:** 172; **Supp. XXI:** 172

Shank, Randy, **Supp. X:** 252

Shankaracharya, **III:** 567

Shanley, John Patrick, **Supp. XIV: 315–332**

Shannon, Sandra, **Supp. VIII:** 333, 348

"Shape of Flesh and Bone, The" (MacLeish), **III:** 18–19

Shape of Me and Other Stuff, The (Geisel), **Supp. XVI:** 111

Shape of the Journey, The (Harrison), **Supp. VIII:** 53

Shapes of Clay (Bierce), **I:** 208, 209

Shaping Joy, A: Studies in the Writer's Craft (Brooks), **Supp. XIV:** 13

Shapiro, Alan, **Supp. XXIV:** 157

Shapiro, Charles, **Supp. XIX:** 257, 259–260

Shapiro, David, **Supp. XII:** 175, 185; **Supp. XXIV:** 34

Shapiro, Dorothy, **IV:** 380

Shapiro, Edward S., **Supp. XXV:** 253

Shapiro, Karl, **I:** 430, 521; **II:** 350; **III:** 527; **Supp. II Part 2: 701–724; Supp. III Part 2:** 623; **Supp. IV Part 2:** 645; **Supp. X:** 116; **Supp. XI:** 315; **Supp. XIX:** 117, 118, 119; **Supp. XXI:** 98; **Supp. XXV:** 30

Shapiro, Laura, **Supp. IX:** 120; **Supp. XX: 87, 89**

Share, Don, **Supp. XXVII:** 152

"Shared Patio, The" (July), **Supp. XXIV:** 201, 202

Sharif, Omar, **Supp. IX:** 253

"Sharing" (Huddle), **Supp. XXVI:** 153

"Shark Meat" (Snyder), **Supp. VIII:** 300

Shatayev, Elvira, **Supp. I Part 2:** 570

Shaviro, Steven, **Supp. VIII:** 189

Shaw, Chris, **Supp. XXIII:** 155–156

Shaw, Colonel Robert Gould, **II:** 551

Shaw, Elizabeth. *See* Melville, Mrs. Herman (Elizabeth Shaw)

Shaw, George Bernard, **I:** 226; **II:** 82, 271, 276, 581; **III:** 69, 102, 113, 145, 155, 161, 162, 163, 373, 409; **IV:** 27, 64, 397, 432, 440; **Retro. Supp. I:** 100, 228; **Supp. IV Part 1:** 36; **Supp. IV Part 2:** 585, 683; **Supp. IX:** 68, 308; **Supp. V:** 243–244, 290; **Supp. XI:** 202; **Supp. XII:** 94; **Supp. XIV:** 343; **Supp. XVII:** 100; **Supp. XXIV:** 33, 34

Shaw, Irwin, **IV:** 381; **Supp. IV Part 1:** 383; **Supp. IX:** 251; **Supp. XI:** 221, 229, 231; **Supp. XIX: 239–254**

Shaw, Joseph Thompson ("Cap"), **Supp. IV Part 1:** 121, 345, 351; **Supp. XIII:** 161

Shaw, Judge Lemuel, **III:** 77, 88, 91

Shaw, Lytle, **Supp. XXIII:** 208; **Supp. XXIV:** 44

Shaw, Peter, **Supp. XVI:** 70

Shaw, Robert B., **Supp. XXIII:** 112

Shaw, Sarah Bryant, **Supp. I Part 1:** 169

Shaw, Wilbur, Jr., **Supp. XIII:** 162

Shawl, The (Mamet), **Supp. XIV:** 245

Shawl, The (Ozick), **Supp. V:** 257, 260, 271

"Shawl, The" (Ozick), **Supp. V:** 271–272

Shawl and Prarie du Chien, The: Two Plays (Mamet), **Supp. XIV:** 243–244

Shawn, William, **Supp. VIII:** 151, 170

"Shawshank Redemption, The" (King), **Supp. V:** 148

She (Haggard), **III:** 189

Shea, Renee, **Supp. XXIII:** 85, 86, 90, 95
Sheaffer, Louis, **Supp. XXI:** 6
Shearer, Flora, **I:** 199
"Sheaves, The" (Robinson), **III:** 510, 524
"She Came and Went" (J. R. Lowell), **Supp. I Part 2:** 409
"She Devil" (Howard), **Supp. XXVII:** 121
"She-Devil" (Nelson), **Supp. XVIII:** 178
She-Devil Circus (Nelson), **Supp. XVIII:** 176, **178**
Sheed, Wilfrid, **IV:** 230; **Supp. XI:** 233; **Supp. XXI:** 233
Sheeler, Charles, **IV:** 409; **Retro. Supp. I:** 430
"Sheep Child" (B. Kelly), **Supp. XVII:** 131–132
"Sheep Child, The" (Dickey), **Supp. XVII:** 131–132
Sheeper (Rosenthal), **Supp. XIV:** 147
"Shee-Show" (Rash), **Supp. XXVII:** 220
Sheffer, Jonathan, **Supp. IV Part 1:** 95
She Had Some Horses (Harjo), **Supp. XII:** 220–223, 231
"She Had Some Horses" (Harjo), **Supp. XII:** 215, 222
"Shell, The" (Humphrey), **Supp. IX:** 94
Shelley, Mary, **Supp. XX:** 108
Shelley, Percy Bysshe, **I:** 18, 68, 381, 476, 522, 577; **II:** 331, 516, 535, 540; **III:** 412, 426, 469; **IV:** 139; **Retro. Supp. I:** 308, 360; **Supp. I Part 1:** 79, 311, 349; **Supp. I Part 2:** 709, 718, 719, 720, 721, 722, 724, 728; **Supp. IV Part 1:** 235; **Supp. IX:** 51; **Supp. V:** 258, 280; **Supp. XII:** 117, 132, 136–137, 263; **Supp. XIV:** 271–272; **Supp. XV:** 92, 175, 182; **Supp. XX:** 115; **Supp. XXI:** 131
Shellow, Sadie Myers, **Supp. I Part 2:** 608
Shelnut, Blevin, **Supp. XXV:** 36
"Shelter" (C. Baxter), **Supp. XVII:** 19
"Shelter" (Doty), **Supp. XI:** 132
Sheltered Life, The (Glasgow), **II:** 174, 175, 179, 186, 187–188
Sheltering Sky, The (Bowles), **Supp. IV Part 1:** 82, 84, 85–86, 87
Sheltering Sky, The (film), **Supp. IV Part 1:** 94, 95
Shelton, Frank, **Supp. IV Part 2:** 658
Shelton, Richard, **Supp. XI:** 133; **Supp. XIII:** 7
Shelton, Robert, **Supp. XVIII:** 20, 21, 22, 23, 24, 25, 26
Shelton, Mrs. Sarah. *See* Royster, Sarah Elmira
"Shelton Laurel" (Rash), **Supp. XXVII:** 221
Shenandoah (Schwartz), **Supp. II Part 2:** 640, 651–652
"Shenandoah" (Shapiro), **Supp. II Part 2:** 704
Shepard, Alice, **IV:** 287
Shepard, Gregory, **Supp. XXII:** 119
Shepard, Harvey, **Supp. XVII:** 240
Shepard, Jim, **Supp. XXI:** 115
Shepard, Odell, **II:** 508; **Supp. I Part 2:** 418

Shepard, Richard F., **Supp. XXIV:** 216
Shepard, Sam, **Supp. III Part 2:** 431–450; **Supp. XVIII:** 21, 28, 31; **Supp. XXI:** 144, 145
Shepard, Thomas, **I:** 554; **IV:** 158
"Shepherd of Resumed Desire, The" (Wright), **Supp. XV:** 349
Sheppard Lee (Bird), **III:** 423
"She Remembers the Future" (Harjo), **Supp. XII:** 222
Sheridan, Richard Brinsley, **Retro. Supp. I:** 127
Sherlock, William, **IV:** 152
Sherman, Joe, **Supp. XXII:** 205
Sherman, Sarah Way, **Retro. Supp. II:** 145
Sherman, Stuart Pratt, **I:** 222, 246–247; **Supp. I Part 2:** 423
Sherman, Susan, **Supp. VIII:** 265
Sherman, Tom, **IV:** 446
Sherman, William T., **IV:** 445, 446
Sherry, Denver William, **Supp. XXII:** 190
Sherwood, Robert, **II:** 435; **Supp. IX:** 190
Sherwood Anderson & Other Famous Creoles (Faulkner), **I:** 117; **II:** 56
Sherwood Anderson Reader, The (Anderson), **I:** 114, 116
Sherwood Anderson's Memoirs (Anderson), **I:** 98, 101, 102, 103, 108, 112, 116
Sherwood Anderson's Notebook (Anderson), **I:** 108, 115, 117
She's Having a Baby (film, Hughes), **Supp. XXVII:** 5
"She Sings" (Taggard), **Supp. XXII:** 272
She Stoops to Conquer (Goldsmith), **II:** 514
Shestov, Lev, **Supp. VIII:** 20, 24
Shetley, Vernon, **Supp. IX:** 292; **Supp. XI:** 123
"She Wept, She Railed" (Kunitz), **Supp. III Part 1:** 265
"Shiddah and Kuziba" (Singer), **IV:** 13, 15
Shidyak, Paris al-, **Supp. XX:** 117
Shield of Achilles, The (Auden), **Supp. II Part 1:** 21
"Shield of Achilles, The" (Auden), **Supp. II Part 1:** 21, 25
Shields, Carol, **Supp. VII:** 307–330
Shields, John C., **Supp. XX:** 279, 280, 281, 286
Shifting Landscape: A Composite, 1925–1987 (H. Roth), **Supp. IX:** 233–235
Shifts of Being (Eberhart), **I:** 525
Shigematsu, Soiko, **Supp. III Part 1:** 353
Shihab, Aziz, **Supp. XIII:** 273
Shih-hsiang Chen, **Supp. VIII:** 303
Shiksa Goddess; or, How I Spent My Forties (Wasserstein), **Supp. XV:** 319, 320, 325, 332, 333
Shilling, Jane, **Supp. XXVII:** 276
"Shiloh" (Mason), **Supp. VIII:** 140
Shiloh and Other Stories (Mason), **Supp. VIII:** 133, **139–141**, 143, 145
Shilts, Randy, **Supp. X:** 145

Shimmering Verge, The (one-woman show, Peacock), **Supp. XIX:** 194, **204–205**
Shining, The (King), **Supp. V:** 139, 140, 141, 143–144, 146, 149, 151, 152
"Shining Ones, The" (P. N. Warren), **Supp. XX:** 272
Shining Victory (film, Rapper), **Supp. XVII:** 60
Shinn, Everett, **Retro. Supp. II:** 103
Shi Pei Pu, **Supp. XXI:** 152, 153, 154
"Ship in a Bottle"(Strout), **Supp. XXIII:** 283
"Ship of Death" (Lawrence), **Supp. I Part 2:** 728
Ship of Fools (Porter), **III:** 433, 447, 453, 454; **IV:** 138
Shipping News, The (Proulx), **Supp. VII:** 249, 258–259
"Ships" (O. Henry), **Supp. II Part 1:** 409
Ships Going into the Blue: Essays and Notes on Poetry (Simpson), **Supp. IX:** 275
Ship to America, A (Singer), **IV:** 1
"Shipwreck, The" (Merwin), **Supp. III Part 1:** 346
Shirley, John, **Supp. XVI:** 123, 128
"Shirt" (Pinsky), **Supp. VI:** **236–237**, 239, 240, 241, 245, 247
"Shirt Poem, The" (Stern), **Supp. IX:** 292
"Shirts, The" (Gallagher), **Supp. XXIV:** 169
"Shirts of a Single Color" (Ryan), **Supp. XVIII:** 227
"Shiva and Parvati Hiding in the Rain" (Pinsky), **Supp. VI:** 244
Shively, Charley, **Retro. Supp. I:** 391; **Supp. XII:** 181, 182
Shnayerson, Michael, **Supp. XIX:** 248
Shneidman, Edwin, **Supp. XXVI:** 246
"Shock of Good Poetry, The"(Hirshfield), **Supp. XXIII:** 136
Shock of Recognition, The (Wilson), **II:** 530
Shock of the New, The (Hughes), **Supp. X:** 73
Shoe Bird, The (Welty), **IV:** 261; **Retro. Supp. I:** 353
Shoemaker of Dreams (Ferragammo), **Supp. XVI:** 192
"Shoes" (O. Henry), **Supp. II Part 1:** 409
"Shoes of Wandering, The" (Kinnell), **Supp. III Part 1:** 248
Sholem Asch: Zayn levn un zayne verk (Sholem Asch: His life and his work), **Supp. XXIII:** 6
Sholl, Betsy, **Supp. XXI:** 129, 131
Shooter (Myers), **Supp. XXVII:** 203, 204
"Shooters, Inc." (Didion), **Supp. IV Part 1:** 207, 211
"Shooting, The" (Dubus), **Supp. VII:** 84, 85
"Shooting Niagara; and After?" (Carlyle), **Retro. Supp. I:** 408
"Shooting of the Red Eagle" (Zitkala-Ša), **Supp. XXV:** 275
"Shooting Script" (Rich), **Supp. I Part 2:** 558; **Supp. IV Part 1:** 257

Shooting Star, A (Stegner), **Supp. IV Part 2:** 599, 608–609

"Shooting the Works" (Di Piero), **Supp. XIX:** 41–42

Shooting the Works: On Poetry and Pictures (Di Piero), **Supp. XIX:** 41–42

"Shooting Whales" (Strand), **Supp. IV Part 2:** 630

"Shopgirls" (F. Barthelme), **Supp. XI:** 26, 27, 33, 36

Shopping for Joe (O'Hara and Steven Rivers), **Supp. XXIII:** 217

"Shopping with Bob Berwick" (Halliday), **Supp. XIX:** 88

Shop Talk (P. Roth), **Retro. Supp. II:** 282

Shoptaw, John, **Supp. IV Part 1:** 247

Shore Acres (Herne), **Supp. II Part 1:** 198

Shorebirds of North America, The (Matthiessen), **Supp. V:** 204

"Shore House, The" (Jewett), **II:** 397

Shore Leave (Wakeman), **Supp. IX:** 247

"Shoreline Horses" (Ríos), **Supp. IV Part 2:** 553

"Shoreline Life" (Skloot), **Supp. XX:** 201

Shores of Light, The: A Literary Chronicle of the Twenties and Thirties (Wilson), **IV:** 432, 433

Shorey, Paul, **III:** 606

Short Account of the Destruction of the Indies, A (Las Casas), **Supp. XXIV:** 87

Short and the Long of It, The (Kenny), **Supp. XXIII:** 155–156

Short Cuts (film, Altman), **Supp. IX:** 143; **Supp. XXIV:** 166, 172, 178

"Short End, The" (Hecht), **Supp. X:** 65

"Shorter View, The" (X. J. Kennedy), **Supp. XV:** 160, 168

Short Fiction of Norman Mailer, The (Mailer), **Retro. Supp. II:** 205

"Short Flight, The" (Huddle), **Supp. XXVI:** 156

Short Friday and Other Stories (Singer), **IV:** 14–16

Short Girls (Nguyen), **Supp. XXVI:** 212–216

Short Guide to a Happy Life, A (Quindlen), **Supp. XVII:** 167, 179

"Short Happy Life of Francis Macomber, The" (Hemingway), **II:** 250, 263–264; **Retro. Supp. I:** 182; **Supp. IV Part 1:** 48; **Supp. IX:** 106

Short Night, The (Turner), **Supp. XV:** 201

Short Novels of Thomas Wolfe, The (Wolfe), **IV:** 456

Short Poems (Berryman), **I:** 170

"SHORT SPEECH TO MY FRIENDS" (Baraka), **Supp. II Part 1:** 35

Short Stories (Rawlings), **Supp. X:** 224

Short Stories: Five Decades (Shaw), **Supp. XIX:** 252–253

"Short Story, The" (Welty), **IV:** 279

Short Story Masterpieces, **Supp. IX:** 4

Short Studies of American Authors (Higginson), **I:** 455

"Short-timer's Calendar" (Komunyakaa), **Supp. XIII:** 125

"Short Weight" (Davison), **Supp. XXVI:** 75

Shosha (Singer), **Retro. Supp. II:** 313–314

Shostak, Debra, **Supp. XXIV:** 136

Shostakovich, Dimitri, **IV:** 75; **Supp. VIII:** 21

"Shotgun Wedding" (Stone), **Supp. XXVII:** 253

Shot of Love (album, Dylan), **Supp. XVIII:** 28

"Shots" (Ozick), **Supp. V:** 268

Shotts, Jeffrey, **Supp. XV:** 103, 104

"Should Wizard Hit Mommy?" (Updike), **IV:** 221, 222, 224; **Retro. Supp. I:** 335

Shoup, Barbara, **Supp. XV:** 55, 59, 62, 69

"Shoveling Snow with Buddha" (Collins), **Supp. XXI:** 60

"Shovel Man, The" (Sandburg), **III:** 553

Showalter, Elaine, **Retro. Supp. I:** 368; **Supp. IV Part 2:** 440, 441, 444; **Supp. X:** 97; **Supp. XVI:** 80, 92; **Supp. XX:** 274; **Supp. XXIV:** 28

"Shower of Gold" (Welty), **IV:** 271–272

Show World (Barnhardt), **Supp. XXVII:** 1, 7–9

Shreve, Porter, **Supp. XXVI:** 209

Shribman, David M., **Supp. XXII:** 205, 218

"Shrike and the Chipmunks, The" (Thurber), **Supp. I Part 2:** 617

Shrimp Girl (Hogarth), **Supp. XII:** 44

"Shrine and the Burning Wheel, The" (Jarman), **Supp. XVII:** 116

"Shrine with Flowers" (Di Piero), **Supp. XIX:** 43, 44

"Shriveled Meditation" (X. J. Kennedy), **Supp. XV:** 170

Shropshire Lad, A (Housman), **Supp. XV:** 41

"Shrouded Stranger, The" (Ginsberg), **Supp. II Part 1:** 312

"Shroud of Color, The" (Cullen), **Supp. IV Part 1:** 166, 168, 170, 171

Shrunken Head of Pancho Villa, The (Valdez), **Supp. XXIII:** 203

Shtetl (film; Marzynski), **Supp. XVI:** 153

Shtetl: The Life and Death of a Small Town and the World of Polish Jews (E. Hoffman), **Supp. XVI:** 152, 153–155

Shue, Elizabeth, **Supp. XXIII:** 276

Shuffle (L. Michaels), **Supp. XVI:** 202, 203, 213

Shuffle Along (musical), **Supp. I Part 1:** 322; **Supp. X:** 136

Shulman, Polly, **Supp. XXVI:** 158

Shultz, George, **Supp. IV Part 1:** 234

Shuman, R. Baird, **Supp. XXV:** 96

Shurr, William, **Retro. Supp. I:** 43

Shuster, Joel, **Supp. XI:** 67

Shusterman, Richard, **Retro. Supp. I:** 53

"Shut a Final Door" (Capote), **Supp. III Part 1:** 117, 120, 124

Shut Up, He Explained (Lardner), **II:** 432

Shylock's Daughter: A Novel of Love in Venice (Serenissima) (Jong), **Supp. V:** 115, 127, 128–129

Siamanto (Atom Yarjanian), **Supp. XXIII:** 28

"Siasconset: How It Arose and What It Is" (Briggs), **Supp. XVIII:** 9

Siberian Village, The (Dove), **Supp. IV Part 1:** 255, 256

Sibley, Celestine, **Supp. XXII:** 194, 199

Sibley, Mulford Q., **Supp. I Part 2:** 524

"Sibling Mysteries" (Rich), **Supp. I Part 2:** 574

Siblings (Quindlen and Kelsh), **Supp. XVII:** 167, 179

Siblings in Paradise (or Moscow when It Sizzles) (Silver), **Supp. XXIV:** 265

Sibon, Marcelle, **IV:** 288

"Sicilian Emigrant's Song" (W. C. Williams), **Retro. Supp. I:** 413

Sicilian Miniatures (Sobin), **Supp. XVI:** 288

"Sick Wife, The" (Kenyon), **Supp. VII:** 173, 174

" 'Sic transit gloria mundi' " (Dickinson), **Retro. Supp. I:** 30

Sid Caesar Show (television show), **Supp. IV Part 2:** 575

Siddons, Anne Rivers, **Supp. XXII:** 239–254

Siddons, Sarah, **II:** 298

Side Effects (Allen), **Supp. XV:** 3, 14, 15–16

"Side Effects of Lucille, The" (Huddle), **Supp. XXVI:** 155–156

Side of Paradise, This (Fitgerald), **Supp. IX:** 56

"Sidewalk, The" (Biss), **Supp. XXVI:** 48

Sidnee Poet Heroical, The (Baraka), **Supp. II Part 1:** 55

Sidney, Algernon, **II:** 114

Sidney, Mary, **Supp. I Part 1:** 98

Sidney, Philip, **II:** 470; **Supp. I Part 1:** 98, 111, 117–118, 122; **Supp. I Part 2:** 658; **Supp. II Part 1:** 104–105; **Supp. V:** 250; **Supp. XII:** 264; **Supp. XIV:** 128

Sidney, Sylvia, **Supp. I Part 1:** 67

Sidney Lanier: A Bibliographical and Critical Study (Starke), **Supp. I Part 1:** 371

Sidney Lanier: A Biographical and Critical Study (Starke), **Supp. I Part 1:** 371

Siebert, Kathy, **Supp. XX:** 84

Siege (Shaw), **Supp. XIX:** 244

Siegel, Barry, **Supp. XIV:** 82

Siegel, Ben, **Supp. XXIII:** 3, 4, 10, 11, 12, 14, 16

Siegel, Catherine, **Supp. XII:** 126

Siegel, Jerry, **Supp. XI:** 67

Siegel, Lee, **Supp. XXII:** 255–269; **Supp. XXV:** 56

"Siege of London, The" (James), **Retro. Supp. I:** 227

Siegle, Robert, **Supp. XII:** 8

Sienkiewicz, Henryk, **Supp. IV Part 2:** 518; **Supp. XVI:** 182

"Sierra Kid" (Levine), **Supp. V:** 180–181

Sigal, Clancy, **Supp. XXI:** 44; **Supp. XXIII:** 166; **Supp. XXVI:** 26

Sigg, Eric, **Retro. Supp. I:** 53

"Sight" (Merwin), **Supp. III Part 1:** 356

Sighted Singer, The (Halliday), **Supp. XIX:** 82, 86–87

"Sight in Camp in the Daybreak Gray and Dim, A" (Whitman), **II:** 373

Sights and Spectacles (McCarthy), **II:** 562

"Sights from a Steeple" (Hawthorne), **Retro. Supp. I:** 62; **Supp. XXI:** 201

Sights Unseen (Gibbons), **Supp. X:** **49–50**

Sight Unseen and the Confession (Rinehart), **Supp. XXV:** 195, 200

"Signals" (Carver), **Supp. III Part 1:** 143

"Signature for Tempo" (MacLeish), **III:** 8–9

"Signed Confession of Crimes against the State" (Merton), **Supp. VIII:** 201

Signifying Monkey, The (Hughes), **Retro. Supp. I:** 195

Signifying Monkey, The: A Theory of Afro-American Literary Criticism (H. L. Gates), **Supp. X:** 243; **Supp. XX:** **99, 106–107**

"Signing, The (Dixon), **Supp. XII:** **146**

Sign in Sidney Brustein's Window, The (Hansberry), **Supp. IV Part 1:** 359, 365, 369, 370–372

"Sign in the Sky, A: Dating the League of the Haudenosaunee" (Mann and Fields), **Supp. XXVI:** 86

Sign of Jonas, The (Merton), **Supp. VIII:** 194–195, 195, 197, 200, 206, 207

"Sign of Saturn, The" (Olds), **Supp. X:** 206

"Signs" (Rash), **Supp. XXVII:** 219

"Signs, Oakvale, Mississippi, 1941" (Trethewey), **Supp. XXI:** 248–249

Signs and Wonders (Bukiet), **Supp. XVII:** **45–46**

Sigourney, Lydia, **Supp. I Part 2:** 684

Sikora, Malgorzata, **Retro. Supp. II:** 324

Silas Marner (G. Eliot), **II:** 26

Silberg, Richard, **Supp. XV:** 116

Silberman, James, **Supp. XXIV:** 288

"Silence" (Moore), **III:** 212

"Silence" (Munro), **Supp. XXVII:** 193–194

"Silence" (Poe), **III:** 416

"Silence" (Sanders), **Supp. XVI:** 278

"Silence, A" (Clampitt), **Supp. IX:** 53

"Silence—A Fable" (Poe), **III:** 416

Silence and Metaphor (Bronk), **Supp. XXI:** 31, 32

"Silence Before Harvest, The" (Merwin), **Supp. III Part 1:** 352

Silence Dogood Papers, The (Franklin), **II:** 106–107

Silence in the Snowy Fields (R. Bly), **Supp. IV Part 1:** 60–61, 62, 63, 65, 66, 72; **Supp. XXI:** 84, 85

Silence of History, The (Farrell), **II:** 46–47

Silence of the Lambs, The (T. Harris), **Supp. XXI:** 78

Silence Opens, A (Clampitt), **Supp. IX:** 53

Silences (Olsen), **Supp. XIII:** 293, 294, 295, 296, **304–306**

"Silences: When Writers Don't Write" (Olsen), **Supp. XIII:** 294

Silencing the Past: Power and the Production of History (Trouillot), **Supp. X:** 14

"Silent in America" (Levine), **Supp. V:** 183

Silent Life, The (Merton), **Supp. VIII:** 208

Silent Partner, The (Odets), **Supp. II Part 2:** 539

"Silent Piano, The" (Davison), **Supp. XXVI:** 78

"Silent Poem" (Francis), **Supp. IX:** 86

"Silent Season of a Hero, The" (Talese), **Supp. XVII:** 203–204

"Silent Slain, The" (MacLeish), **III:** 9

"Silent Snow, Secret Snow" (Aiken), **I:** 52

Silent Spring (Carson), **Supp. IX:** 19, 24, **31–34**; **Supp. V:** 202; **Supp. XIV:** 177; **Supp. XVI:** 36; **Supp. XVIII:** 189

Silhouettes of American Life (R. H. Davis), **Supp. XVI:** 85

"Silken Tent, The" (Frost), **Retro. Supp. I:** 138–139; **Supp. IV Part 2:** 448

Silko, Leslie Marmon, **Supp. IV Part 1:** 274, 319, 325, 333–334, 335, 404; **Supp. IV Part 2:** 499, 505, **557–572**; **Supp. V:** 169; **Supp. XI:** 18; **Supp. XII:** 217; **Supp. XVIII:** 58; **Supp. XXVI:** 102

Silliman, Ron, **Supp. IV Part 2:** 426; **Supp. V:** 344; **Supp. XVII:** 70, 77

Silliman's Blog (R. Silliman), **Supp. XVII:** 70

Silman, Roberta, **Supp. X:** 6

Silver, Nicky, **Supp. XXIV:** 128, **263–277**

Silver, Sam, **Supp. XXVII:** 36

Silverblatt, Michael, **Supp. XV:** 224

"Silver Crown, The" (Malamud), **Supp. I Part 2:** 434–435, 437; **Supp. V:** 266

"Silver Dish, The" (Bellow), **Retro. Supp. II:** 30

"Silver Filigree" (Wylie), **Supp. I Part 2:** 707

"Silver Key, The" (Lovecraft), **Supp. XXV:** 114

"Silver Lake" (B. Kelly), **Supp. XVII:** 130

Silverman, Joseph, **Supp. XXIII:** 8

Silvers, Phil, **Supp. IV Part 2:** 574

Silverthorne, Elizabeth, **Supp. X:** 220, 221, 222, 226, 234

"Silver To Have and to Hurl" (Didion), **Supp. IV Part 1:** 197

Simic, Charles, **Supp. V:** 5, 332; **Supp. VIII:** 39, **269–287**; **Supp. XI:** 317; **Supp. XIX:** 277, 282; **Supp. XV:** 179, 185

"Similar Cases" (Gilman), **Supp. XI:** 200, 202

Similitudes, from the Ocean and Prairie (Larcom), **Supp. XIII:** 141

Simmel, Georg, **Supp. I Part 2:** 644; **Supp. XVII:** 98

Simmons, Charles, **Supp. XI:** 230

Simmons, David, **Supp. XXV:** 123

Simmons, Maggie, **Retro. Supp. II:** 21

Simms, Michael, **Supp. XII:** 184

Simms, William Gilmore, **I:** 211

Simon, Greg, **Supp. XXIV:** 166

Simon, John, **Supp. IV Part 2:** 691

Simon, Neil, **Supp. IV Part 2:** 573–594; **Supp. XVII:** 8

Simone, Nina, **Supp. XXI:** 243

"Simone Weil's Passion Mysticism: The Paradox of Chronic Pain and the Transformation of the Cross" (Helsel), **Supp. XXVI:** 53

"Simon Gerty" (Wylie), **Supp. I Part 2:** 713

Simonides, **Supp. XII:** 110–111

"Simon Ortiz" (Gingerich), **Supp. IV Part 2:** 510

Simon Ortiz (Wiget), **Supp. IV Part 2:** 509

Simonson, Lee, **III:** 396; **Supp. XXI:** 6

"Simple" (Peacock), **Supp. XIX:** 200

"Simple Art of Murder, The" (Chandler), **Supp. IV Part 1:** 121, 341

"Simple Autumnal" (Bogan), **Supp. III Part 1:** 52–53

Simple Heart (Flaubert), **I:** 504

Simple Honorable Man, A (Richter), **Supp. XVIII:** 208, 218, **219**, 220

"Simple Purchase, A" (Peacock), **Supp. XIX:** 199

Simple Speaks his Mind (Hughes), **Retro. Supp. I:** 209; **Supp. I Part 1:** 337

Simple Stakes a Claim (Hughes), **Retro. Supp. I:** 209; **Supp. I Part 1:** 337

Simple's Uncle Sam (Hughes), **Retro. Supp. I:** 209; **Supp. I Part 1:** 337

Simple Takes a Wife (Hughes), **Retro. Supp. I:** 209; **Supp. I Part 1:** 337

Simple Truth, The (Hardwick), **Supp. III Part 1:** 199, 200, 208

Simple Truth, The (Levine), **Supp. V:** 178, 179, 193–194

"Simple Widsom, The" (Skloot), **Supp. XX:** **207**

"Simplicity" (Sanders), **Supp. XVI:** 276

Simplicity (Stone), **Supp. XXVII:** 257, 262

Simply, Trixi, **Supp. XXV:** 2

Simply Heavenly (Hughes), **Retro. Supp. I:** 209; **Supp. I Part 1:** 338, 339

Simpson, Louis, **Supp. III Part 2:** 541; **Supp. IV Part 2:** 448, 621; **Supp. IX:** **265–283**, 290; **Supp. VIII:** 39, 279; **Supp. XI:** 317; **Supp. XII:** 130; **Supp. XIII:** 337

Simpson, Mona, **Supp. XVI:** 206; **Supp. XXVII:** 180, **233–237**

"Sin" (C. Frost), **Supp. XV:** 96

Sinatra, Frank, **Supp. IX:** 3; **Supp. X:** 119; **Supp. XI:** 213

"Since Death Brushed Past Me" (Teasdale), **Supp. XXVII:** 297

Sincere Convert, The (Shepard), **IV:** 158

Sincerely, Willis Wayde (Marquand), **III:** 61, 63, 66, 67–68, 69

Sincerity (Rowson), **Supp. XV:** 242

Sincerity and Authenticity (Trilling), **Supp. III Part 2:** 510–512

"Sincerity and Objectification: With Special Reference to the Work of Charles Reznikoff" (Zukofsky), **Supp. XIV:** 286

Sinclair, Mary Craig (Mary Craig Kimbrough), **Supp. V:** 275, 286, 287

Sinclair, Upton, **II:** 34, 440, 444, 451; **III:** 580; **Retro. Supp. II:** 95; **Supp. V: 275–293; Supp. VIII:** 11

Sinclair Lewis: An American Life (Schorer), **II:** 459

"Sine Qua Non" (Stallings), **Supp. XXV:** 232

"Singapore" (Oliver), **Supp. VII:** 239, 240

Singer, Bennett L., **Supp. IV Part 1:** 330

Singer, Beth, **Supp. XIV:** 203

Singer, Isaac Bashevis, **I:** 144; **IV: 1–24; Retro. Supp. II:** 22, **299–320; Supp. IX:** 114; **Supp. XVIII:** 215, 220; **Supp. XXI:** 106; **Supp. XXII:** 258

Singer, Israel Joshua, **IV:** 2, 16, 17; **Retro. Supp. II:** 302; **Supp. XVII:** 41

Singer, Joshua, **IV:** 4

Singer, Rabbi Pinchos Menachem, **IV:** 16

Singin' and Swingin' and Gettin' Merry Like Christmas (Angelou), **Supp. IV Part 1:** 2, 5, 6–7, 9, 13, 14

"Singing & Doubling Together" (Ammons), **Supp. VII:** 34–35

Singing Jailbirds (Sinclair), **Supp. V:** 277

"Singing the Black Mother" (Lupton), **Supp. IV Part 1:** 7

Single Hound, The (Sarton), **Supp. VIII:** 251, 265

Single Hound, The: Poems of a Lifetime (Dickinson; Bianchi, ed.), **Retro. Supp. I:** 35

Single Man, A (Isherwood), **Supp. XIV:** 157, 164, **169–170,** 171

"Single Sonnet" (Bogan), **Supp. III Part 1:** 56–58

Singley, Carol, **Retro. Supp. I:** 373

Singular Family, A: Rosacoke and Her Kin (Price), **Supp. VI: 258–259,** 260

"Singular First Person, The" (Sanders), **Supp. XVI:** 274

Singularities (Howe), **Supp. IV Part 2:** 431

Sin in Their Blood (Lacy), **Supp. XV:** 200

"Sinister Adolescents, The" (Dos Passos), **I:** 493

Sinister Street (Mackenzie), **II:** 82

Sinking of Clay City, The (Wrigley), **Supp. XVIII: 294–295**

Sinners in the Hands of an Angry God (Edwards), **I:** 546, 552–553, 559, 562; **Supp. XXIV:** 72

Sinning with Annie, and Other Stories (Theroux), **Supp. VIII:** 318

"Sins of Kalamazoo, The" (Sandburg), **III:** 586

Sintram and His Companions (La Motte-Fouqué), **III:** 78

"Siope" (Poe), **III:** 411

"Sioux Woman's Love for Her Grandchild, A" (Zitkala-Ša), **Supp. XXV:** 281

"Sipapu: A Cultural Perspective" (Gunn Allen), **Supp. IV Part 1:** 323

Sipchen, Bob, **Supp. X:** 145

Sipper, Ralph B., **Supp. IV Part 2:** 475

"Sire" (Cisneros), **Supp. VII:** 62–63, 64

"Siren and Signal" (Zukofsky), **Supp. III Part 2:** 611, 612

Sirens of Titan, The (Vonnegut), **Supp. II Part 2:** 757, 758, 760, 765–767

"Sir Galahad" (Tennyson), **Supp. I Part 2:** 410

Sirin, V. (pseudonym), **Retro. Supp. I:** 266. *See also* Nabokov, Vladimir

Sirlin, Jerome, **Supp. XXI:** 147

Sir Vadia's Shadow: A Friendship across Five Continents (Theroux), **Supp. VIII:** 309, 314, 321, 325

"Sir William's Reply to Molly"(Kenny), **Supp. XXIII:** 153

"Sis" (F. Barthelme), **Supp. XI:** 26

"S is for Sad" (M. F. K. Fisher), **Supp. XVII:** 86

Sisley, Alfred, **I:** 478

Sissman, L. E., **Supp. X:** 69; **Supp. XXVI:** 68, 74

"Sister" (Hughes), **Retro. Supp. I:** 208

"Sister" (Lamott), **Supp. XX:** 142

"Sister, The" (July), **Supp. XXIV:** 202

Sister Age (M. F. K. Fisher), **Supp. XVII:** 88, 91

Sister Carrie (Dreiser), **I:** 482, 497, 499, 500, 501–502, 503–504, 505, 506, 515, 519; **III:** 327; **IV:** 208; **Retro. Supp. I:** 376; **Retro. Supp. II:** 93, **96–99;** **Supp. XVIII:** 76, 243; **Supp. XXIII:** 165; **Supp. XXV:** 129

Sister Mary Ignatius Explains It All for You (Durang), **Supp. XXIV:** 114, **119–120**

"Sister of the Minotaur" (Stevens), **IV:** 89; **Supp. IX:** 332

"Sisters" (Boulton), **Supp. XXII:** 20

"Sisters" (Nelson), **Supp. XVIII:** 176

"Sisters, The" (Whittier), **Supp. I Part 2:** 696

Sister's Choice (Showalter), **Retro. Supp. I:** 368

Sisters-in-Law, The (Atherton), **Supp. XXIV:** 25

Sisters of the Earth: Women's Prose and Poetry About Nature (Anderson, ed.), **Supp. XVIII:** 189

Sisters Rosensweig, The (Wasserstein), **Supp. XV:** 320, **328–330**

"Sisyphus" (Kumin), **Supp. IV Part 2:** 443, 444, 451

"Sitalkas" (Doolittle), **Supp. I Part 1:** 266

"Sites of Memory" (Cliff), **Supp. XXII:** 69, 74

Sitney, P. Adams, **Supp. XII:** 2

Sitting Bull, **Supp. IV Part 2:** 492

"Sitting in a Rocking Chair Going Blind" (Komunyakaa), **Supp. XIII:** 114

Sitting In: Selected Writings on Jazz, Blues, and Related Topics (Carruth), **Supp. XVI:** 46

"Sitting Up Late with My Father, 1977" (F. Wright), **Supp. XVII:** 247

Sitti's Secrets (Nye), **Supp. XIII:** 278

Situation Normal (A. Miller), **III:** 148, 149, 156, 164

Situation of Poetry, The: Contemporary Poetry and Its Traditions (Pinsky), **Supp. VI: 237–238,** 239, 241, 242

Sitwell, Edith, **IV:** 77; **Supp. I Part 1:** 271

6 A.M. (Bodenheim), **Supp. XXV:** 27

"Six Brothers" (Cisneros), **Supp. VII:** 67

Six Characters in Search of an Author (Pirandello), **Supp. IV Part 2:** 576

"Six Days: Some Rememberings" (Paley), **Supp. VI:** 226

"65290" (Leopold), **Supp. XIV:** 184–185

Six French Poets (A. Lowell), **II:** 528–529

"Six in All" (Bierds), **Supp. XVII:** 31

Six Lips (Schott), **Supp. XXIII:** 251–252

"Six Persons" (Baraka), **Supp. II Part 1:** 53

Six Sections from Mountains and Rivers without End (Snyder), **Supp. VIII:** 305

"Sixteen Months" (Sandburg), **III:** 584

1601, or Conversation as It Was by the Fireside in the Time of the Tudors (Twain), **IV:** 201

"Sixth-Month Song in the Foothills" (Snyder), **Supp. VIII:** 297

Sixties, The (magazine) (R. Bly), **Supp. IV Part 1:** 60; **Supp. IX:** 271

"Sixty" (Dunn), **Supp. XI:** 155

"Sixty Acres" (Carver), **Supp. III Part 1:** 141

"64 Elmgrove" (Halliday), **Supp. XIX:** 88

"69 Hidebound Opinions, Propositions, and Several Asides from a Manila Folder concerning the Stuff of Poetry" (Wright), **Supp. XV:** 344–345

Sixty Seconds (Bodenheim), **Supp. XXV:** 26

Sixty Stories (Barthelme), **Supp. IV Part 1:** 41, 42, 44, 47, 49, 50

63: Dream Palace (Purdy), **Supp. VII:** 270–271

"Six Variations" (Levertov), **Supp. III Part 1:** 277–278

"Six-Year-Old Boy" (Olds), **Supp. X:** 206

"Six Years Later" (Brodsky), **Supp. VIII:** 26, 28

"Size and Sheer Will" (Olds), **Supp. X:** 206

Size of Thoughts, The: Essays and Other Lumber (Baker), **Supp. XIII: 52–53,** 55, 56

Sizwe Bansi Is Dead (Fugard), **Supp. VIII:** 330

Sjöwall, Maj, **Supp. XX:** 87

"Skagway" (Haines), **Supp. XII:** 206

"Skaters, The" (Ashbery), **Supp. III Part 1:** 10, 12, 13, 18, 25

"Skaters, The" (Jarrell), **II:** 368–369

Skau, Michael, **Supp. XII:** 129, 130, 132, 134

Skeeters Kirby (Masters), **Supp. I Part 2:** 459, 470, 471

Skeleton at the Feast, The (Wells), **Supp. XXVI:** 278, 282

Skeleton Crew (King), **Supp. V:** 144

"Skeleton in Armor, The" (Longfellow), **Retro. Supp. II:** 168

"Skeleton's Cave, The" (Bryant), **Supp. I Part 1:** 157

Skelton, John, **III:** 521

Skepticisms (Aiken), **Supp. XV:** 298, 302
Sketch Book of Geoffrey Crayon, Gent., The (Irving), **II:** 295, 303, 304–308, 309, 311, 491; **Supp. I Part 1:** 155
Sketches of Art (Jameson), **Retro. Supp. II:** 58
Sketches of Eighteenth Century America (Crèvecoeur), **Supp. I Part 1:** 233, 240–241, 250, 251
"Sketches of Female Biography" (Rowson), **Supp. XV:** 245
Sketches of Switzerland (Cooper), **I:** 346
Sketches Old and New (Twain), **IV:** 198
"Sketch for a Job-Application Blank" (Harrison), **Supp. VIII:** 38
"Sketch"(Kenny), **Supp. XXIII:** 155
Sketch of Old England, by a New England Man (Paulding), **I:** 344
Skibell, Joseph, **Supp. XVII:** 48
"Skier and the Mountain, The" (Eberhart), **I:** 528–529
"Skiing by Moonlight" (Davison), **Supp. XXVI:** 74
"Skin-Boats: 1830, The" (Bierds), **Supp. XVII:** 28
Skinker, Mary Scott, **Supp. IX:** 20
Skinner, Ewart, **Supp. XXII:** 78
Skinny Island (Auchincloss), **Supp. IV Part 1:** 33
Skinny Legs and All (Robbins), **Supp. X:** 267, 273, **276–279**
Skin of Our Teeth, The (Wilder), **IV:** 357, 358, 369–372; **Supp. IV Part 2:** 586; **Supp. XX: 50**
"Skins" (Wright), **Supp. V:** 340
Skins and Bones: Poems 1979–1987 (Gunn Allen), **Supp. IV Part 1:** 321, 331
"Skipper Ireson's Ride" (Whittier), **Supp. I Part 2:** 691, 693–694
"Skirmish at Sartoris" (Faulkner), **II:** 67
"Skirt" (Halliday), **Supp. XIX:** 90
Skirts and Slacks (Di Piero), **Supp. XIX:** 35, 36, 38, 45–47
Sklenicka, Carol, **Supp. XXIV:** 166
Skloot, Floyd, **Supp. XX: 193–209**
Skotheim, Robert Allen, **Supp. XVII:** 104
Skow, John, **Supp. V:** 213; **Supp. XVI:** 174
Skube, Michael, **Supp. XVIII:** 96
"Skunk Cabbage" (Bronk), **Supp. XXI:** 31
"Skunk Cabbage" (Oliver), **Supp. VII:** 235, 236
"Skunk Hour" (R. Lowell), **II:** 548–550; **Retro. Supp. II:** 188, 189; **Supp. XIV:** 269; **Supp. XX: 203**
Skurnick, Lizzie, **Supp. XXVI:** 49
Sky, The Stars, The Wilderness, The (Bass), **Supp. XVI:** 19, 20
Sky Changes, The (Sorrentino), **Supp. XXI:** 228, 230, 231; **Supp. XXVI:** 26
"Sky Dance" (Leopold), **Supp. XIV:** 186
"Sky Line" (Taylor), **Supp. V:** 316
"Sky Line, The" (Mumford), **Supp. II Part 2:** 475
Sky of Stone (Hickam), **Supp. XXVII:** 101, 106, 108–110
"Skyscraper" (Sandburg), **III:** 581–582

Sky's the Limit, The: A Defense of the Earth (Nichols), **Supp. XIII:** 268
"Sky Valley Rider" (Wright), **Supp. V:** 335, 340
Sky-Walk; or the Man Unknown to Himself (Brown), **Supp. I Part 1:** 127–128
Slam! (Myers), **Supp. XXVII:** 201, 202, 206
"Slang in America" (Whitman), **IV:** 348
Slappy Hooper, the Wonderful Sign Painter (Bontemps and Conroy), **Supp. XXII:** 5, 11
Slapstick (Vonnegut), **Supp. II Part 2:** 753, 754, 778
Slapstick Tragedy (T. Williams), **IV:** 382, 393
Slate, Lane, **Supp. IX:** 251, 253
Slattery, Mary Grace. *See* Miller, Mrs. Arthur (Mary Grace Slattery)
Slattery's Hurricane (Wouk), **Supp. XXV:** 257, 262–263
"Slaughterer, The" (Singer), **IV:** 19
Slaughterhouse-Five (Vonnegut), **Supp. II Part 2:** 755, 758–759, 760, 770, 772–776; **Supp. V:** 41, 244; **Supp. XIX:** 235
Slaughter Rule, The (film; Alex and Andrew Smith), **Supp. XIX:** 174
Slave, The (Baraka), **Supp. II Part 1:** 42, 44, 56
Slave, The: A Novel (Singer), **IV:** 13; **Retro. Supp. II: 305–307**
"Slave Canal" (Ray), **Supp. XVIII:** 193
"Slave Coffle" (Angelou), **Supp. IV Part 1:** 16
"Slave of the Sky" (P. N. Warren), **Supp. XX: 261**
"Slave on the Block" (Hughes), **Supp. I Part 1:** 329
Slave Power, The: The Free North and Southern Domination, 1780–1860 (Richards), **Supp. XIV:** 48
"Slave Quarters" (Dickey), **Supp. IV Part 1:** 181
Slavery (Channing), **Supp. XXIV:** 77–78
"Slave's Dream, The" (Longfellow), **Supp. I Part 2:** 409
Slave Ship: A Historical Pageant (Baraka), **Supp. II Part 1:** 47–49, 53, 56–57
"Slave-Ships, The" (Whittier), **Supp. I Part 2:** 687–688
Slaves in Algiers; or, A Struggle for Freedom (Rowson), **Supp. XV:** 236–237
"Slave Trade, The: View from the Middle Passage" (Major), **Supp. XXII:** 182
Slavs! Thinking about the Longstanding Problems of Virtue and Happiness (Kushner), **Supp. IX:** 146
Sledge, Eugene, **Supp. V:** 250
Sleek for the Long Flight (Matthews), **Supp. IX:** 154, 155, **157–158**
Sleep (Dixon), **Supp. XII:** 154
"Sleep, The" (Strand), **Supp. IV Part 2:** 627
Sleeper (film; Allen), **Supp. XV:** 5
"Sleeper, The" (Poe), **III:** 411
"Sleeper 1, The" (Hay), **Supp. XIV:** 132–133

"Sleeper 2, The" (Hay), **Supp. XIV:** 132–133
"Sleepers, The" (Whitman), **IV:** 336
"Sleepers in Jaipur" (Kenyon), **Supp. VII:** 172
Sleepers in Moon-Crowned Valleys (Purdy), **Supp. VII:** 274, 275
Sleepers Joining Hands (R. Bly), **Supp. XXI:** 85
"Sleepers Joining Hands" (R. Bly), **Supp. IV Part 1:** 63, 73
Sleeping Beauty (Macdonald), **Supp. IV Part 2:** 474, 475
Sleeping Beauty, The (Carruth), **Supp. XVI:** 53, 57–58
"Sleeping Beauty IV" (Stone), **Supp. XXVII:** 263
"Sleeping Beauty Syndrome, The: The New Agony of Single Men" (Wasserstein), **Supp. XV:** 328
Sleeping Dogs (Wells), **Supp. XXVI:** 280–281
Sleeping Fires (Atherton), **Supp. XXIV:** 25
"Sleeping Fury, The" (Bogan), **Supp. III Part 1:** 58
Sleeping Fury, The: Poems (Bogan), **Supp. III Part 1:** 55–58
Sleeping Gypsy and Other Poems, The (Garrett), **Supp. VII:** 96–98
Sleeping in the Forest (Oliver), **Supp. VII:** 233
"Sleeping in the Forest" (Oliver), **Supp. VII:** 233–234
Sleeping in the Woods (Wagoner), **Supp. IX:** 328
Sleeping on Fists (Ríos), **Supp. IV Part 2:** 540
Sleeping on the Wing: An Anthology of Modern Poetry (Koch and Farrell, eds.), **Supp. XV:** 187–188
"Sleeping on the Wing"(O'Hara), **Supp. XXIII:** 214
"Sleeping Standing Up" (Bishop), **Supp. I Part 1:** 85, 89, 93
"Sleeping with Animals" (Kumin), **Supp. IV Part 2:** 454
Sleeping with One Eye Open (Strand), **Supp. IV Part 2:** 621–624, 623, 628
Sleeping with the Dictionary (Mullen), **Supp. XXVII:** 173–174, 176
Sleep in Thunder (Lacy), **Supp. XV:** 206
"Sleepless, The" (L.-Y. Lee), **Supp. XV:** 224
"Sleepless at Crown Point" (Wilbur), **Supp. III Part 2:** 561
Sleepless Nights (Hardwick), **Supp. III Part 1:** 193, 208–211
"Sleepless Nights" (Nelson), **Supp. XVIII:** 174
"Sleep-Walkers, The" (Gibran), **Supp. XX: 118**
Sleepy Lagoon Mystery, The (Endore), **Supp. XVII:** 60
"Sleepy People" (Lethem), **Supp. XVIII:** 140
Sleigh, Tom, **Supp. XIX:** 38, 40
Sleight, Ken, **Supp. XIII:** 12
Slick, Sam (pseudonym). *See* Haliburton, Thomas Chandler

"Slick Gonna Learn" (Ellison), **Retro. Supp. II:** 116; **Supp. II Part 1:** 237–238

"Slight Rebellion off Madison" (Salinger), **III:** 553

"Slight Sound at Evening, A" (White), **Supp. I Part 2:** 672

"Slim Graves Show, The" (Keillor), **Supp. XVI:** 172

"Slim Greer" series (Hayden), **Supp. II Part 1:** 369

"Slim in Hell" (Hayden), **Supp. II Part 1:** 369

"Slim Man Canyon" (Silko), **Supp. IV Part 2:** 560

"Slip, Shift, and Speed Up: The Influence of Robinson Jeffers's Narrative Syntax" (Jarman), **Supp. XVII:** 111, 112

"Slippery Fingers" (Hammett), **Supp. IV Part 1:** 343

Slipping-Down Life, A (Tyler), **Supp. IV Part 2:** 660–661

Sloan, Jacob, **IV:** 3, 6

Sloan, John, **I:** 254; **IV:** 411; **Retro. Supp. II:** 103; **Supp. XXII:** 277

Sloane, John, **Supp. XV:** 295

"Slob" (Farrell), **II:** 25, 28, 31

Slocum, Joshua, **Supp. I Part 2:** 497; **Supp. XXV:** 205–219

Slogum House (Sandoz), **Supp. XXIV:** 244, **251–252,** 255

Slonim, Véra. *See* Nabokov, Véra

Slopen, Beverly, **Supp. XX:** 59

Slouching towards Bethlehem (Didion), **Supp. IV Part 1:** 196, 197, 200–201, 202, 206, 210

Slovic, Scott, **Supp. XVI:** 277

"Slow Child with a Book of Birds" (Levis), **Supp. XI:** 268

"Slow Dance with Icarus" (Monson), **Supp. XXIV:** 240

Slow Dancing Through Ether: A Fine Binding Project (Monson and Ingmundson), **Supp. XXIV:** 230, 234

"Slow Down for Poetry" (Strand), **Supp. IV Part 2:** 620

Slow Music (Taggard), **Supp. XXII:** 284

"Slow Pacific Swell, The" (Winters), **Supp. II Part 2:** 790, 793, 795, 796, 799

Slow Parade (Kees), **Supp. XV:** 137

Slow Train Coming (album, Dylan), **Supp. XVIII:** 28

Slow Transparency (Hadas), **Supp. XXIII:** 113–114

Slow Vision (Bodenheim), **Supp. XXV:** 28

"Slum Church" (Espaillat), **Supp. XXI:** 110–111

"Slumgullions" (Olsen), **Supp. IV Part 1:** 54

Slumgullion Stew: An Edward Abbey Reader (Abbey), **Supp. XIII:** 4

Slung, Michelle, **Supp. XX:** 87

"S & M" (Komunyakaa), **Supp. XIII:** 114

"Small" (C. Frost), **Supp. XV:** 102

Small, Albion, **Supp. I Part 1:** 5

"Small, Good Thing, A" (Carver), **Supp. III Part 1:** 145, 147

Small, Miriam Rossiter, **Supp. I Part 1:** 319

Small Boy and Others, A (James), **II:** 337, 547; **Retro. Supp. I:** 235

"Small but Urgent Request to the Unknowable" (Karr), **Supp. XI:** 243

Small Ceremonies (Shields), **Supp. VII:** 312–315, 320

Small Craft Warnings (T. Williams), **IV:** 382, 383, 384, 385, 386, 387, 392, 393, 396, 398

"Small Degrees" (Brockmeier), **Supp. XXII:** 52, 59

"Small Fry" (Peacock), **Supp. XIX:** 206

Small Place, A (Kincaid), **Supp. VII:** 186–187, 188, 191

"Small Rain, The" (Pynchon), **Supp. II Part 2:** 620

Small Room, The (Sarton), **Supp. VIII:** 252, **255–256**

Smalls, Bob, **II:** 128

"Small Song for Andrew" (Weigl), **Supp. XIX:** 280

Small Time Crooks (film; Allen), **Supp. XV:** 11

Small Town, A (Hearon), **Supp. VIII:** **65–66**

"Small Vases from Hebron, The" (Nye), **Supp. XIII:** 283

"Small Vision, The" (Goldbarth), **Supp. XII:** 180

"Small Voice from the Wings" (Everwine), **Supp. XV:** 76

"Small Wire" (Sexton), **Supp. II Part 2:** 696

Small Worlds (A. Hoffman), **Supp. XVII:** 44

Smardz, Zofia, **Supp. XVI:** 155

Smart, Christopher, **III:** 534; **Supp. I Part 2:** 539; **Supp. IV Part 2:** 626

Smart, Joyce H., **Supp. XI:** 169

"Smart Cookie, A" (Cisneros), **Supp. VII:** 64

"Smash"(Thompson), **Supp. XXIII:** 301, 302

"Smashup" (Thurber), **Supp. I Part 2:** 616

Smedly, Agnes, **Supp. XIII:** 295

"Smell of a God, The" (Peacock), **Supp. XIX:** 199

"Smelt Fishing" (Hayden), **Supp. II Part 1:** 367

"Smile of the Bathers, The" (Kees), **Supp. XV:** 145

"Smile on the Face of a Kouros, The" (Bronk), **Supp. XXI:** 31

"Smiles" (Dunn), **Supp. XI:** 151

Smiles, Samuel, **Supp. X:** 167

Smiley, Jane, **Supp. VI: 291–309; Supp. XII:** 73, 297; **Supp. XIII:** 127; **Supp. XIX:** 54

Smith, Adam, **II:** 9; **Supp. I Part 2:** 633, 634, 639; **Supp. XVII:** 235

Smith, Amanda, **Supp. XXVII:** 211

Smith, Annick, **Supp. XIV:** 223; **Supp. XXVI:** 183, 186, 188

Smith, Barbara, **Supp. XXIII:** 194

Smith, Benjamin, **IV:** 148

Smith, Bernard, **I:** 260

Smith, Bessie, **Retro. Supp. I:** 343; **Supp. VIII:** 330; **Supp. XIX:** 147

Smith, Betty, **Supp. XXIII: 257–271**

Smith, Charlie, **Supp. X:** 177

Smith, Clark Ashton, **Supp. XXV:** 111; **Supp. XXVII:** 117

Smith, Dale, **Supp. XV:** 136, 138, 139

Smith, Dave, **Supp. V:** 333; **Supp. XI:** 152; **Supp. XII:** 178, 198; **Supp. XIX:** 277, 282

Smith, David, **Supp. XIII:** 246, 247

Smith, David Nichol, **Supp. XIV:** 2

Smith, Dinitia, **Supp. VIII:** 74, 82, 83; **Supp. XVIII:** 162; **Supp. XXIV:** 2–3

Smith, Elihu Hubbard, **Supp. I Part 1:** 126, 127, 130

Smith, Ernest J., **Supp. XXIII:** 111, 113, 117

Smith, George Adam, **III:** 199

Smith, Hannah Whitall, **Supp. XIV:** 333, 334, 338

Smith, Harrison, **II:** 61

Smith, Henry Justin, **Supp. XXVII:** 85

Smith, Henry Nash, **IV:** 210; **Supp. I Part 1:** 233

Smith, Herbert F., **Supp. I Part 2:** 423

Smith, Iain Crichton, **Supp. XVIII:** 196

Smith, James, **II:** 111

Smith, Jedediah Strong, **Supp. IV Part 2:** 602

Smith, Jerome, **Supp. IV Part 1:** 369

Smith, Joe, **Supp. IV Part 2:** 584

Smith, John, **I:** 4, 131; **II:** 296

Smith, John Allyn, **I:** 168

Smith, Johnston (pseudonym). *See* Crane, Stephen

Smith, Katherine Capshaw, **Supp. XXII:** 10, 13–14

Smith, Kellogg, **Supp. I Part 2:** 660

Smith, Lamar, **II:** 585

Smith, Mrs. Lamar (Marguerite Walters), **II:** 585, 587

Smith, Lane, **Supp. XIX:** 231

Smith, Larry David, **Supp. XVIII:** 22

Smith, Lee, **Supp. XII:** 311; **Supp. XVIII:** 195; **Supp. XXII:** 206, 213

Smith, Lillian, **Supp. XXII:** 67

Smith, Logan Pearsall, **Supp. XIV: 333–351**

Smith, Lula Carson. *See* McCullers, Carson

Smith, Mark, **Supp. XVIII:** 155

Smith, Martha Nell, **Retro. Supp. I:** 33, 43, 46, 47

Smith, Mary Rozet, **Supp. I Part 1:** 5, 22

Smith, Oliver, **II:** 586

Smith, Patricia Clark, **Supp. IV Part 1:** 397, 398, 402, 406, 408, 410; **Supp. IV Part 2:** 509; **Supp. XII:** 218

Smith, Patrick, **Supp. VIII:** 40, 41

Smith, Patti, **Supp. XII:** 136; **Supp. XIV:** 151

Smith, Porter, **III:** 572

Smith, Red, **II:** 417, 424

Smith, Robert McClure, **Supp. XV:** 270

Smith, Robert Pearsall, **Supp. XIV:** 333

Smith, Sarah A., **Supp. XVIII:** 99

Smith, Seba, **Supp. I Part 2:** 411

Smith, Sidonie, **Supp. IV Part 1:** 11; **Supp. XXII:** 70

Smith, Stevie, **Supp. V:** 84

Smith, Sydney, **II:** 295; **Supp. XIV:** 112

Smith, Thorne, **Supp. IX:** 194

Smith, Valerie, **Supp. XXII:** 146

Smith, Wallace, **Supp. XXVII:** 88

Smith, Wendy, **Supp. XII:** 330, 335; **Supp. XVIII:** 89, 92

Smith, Wilford Bascom "Pitchfork", **Supp. XIII:** 168

Smith, William, **II:** 114

Smith, William Gardner, **Supp. XVI:** 142–143

Smith, William Jay, **Supp. XIII: 331–350**

Smitherman, Geneva, **Supp. XXVI:** 13

"Smoke" (Di Piero), **Supp. XIX:** 38

Smoke (film), **Supp. XII:** 21

"Smoke" (Huddle), **Supp. XXVI:** 149

Smoke and Steel (Sandburg), **III:** 585–587, 592

Smoke Dancing (Gansworth), **Supp. XXVI:** 104–105

"Smokehouse" (Offutt), **Supp. XIX:** 166, 167

"Smokers" (Wolff), **Supp. VII:** 340–341

Smokey Bites the Dust (film, C. Griffith), **Supp. XVII:** 9

Smoking Mountain, The: Stories of Postwar Germany (Boyle), **Supp. XXIV:** 61

"Smoking My Prayers" (Ortiz), **Supp. IV Part 2:** 503

"Smoking Room, The" (Jackson), **Supp. IX:** 116

"Smoky Gold" (Leopold), **Supp. XIV:** 186

Smolan, Sandy, **Supp. XVI:** 36

Smollett, Tobias G., **I:** 134, 339, 343; **II:** 304–305; **III:** 61; **Supp. XVIII:** 7; **Supp. XXV:** 258

Smooding, Robert, **Supp. XXIII:** 294

Smuggler's Bible, A (McElroy), **Supp. IV Part 1:** 285

Smuggler's Handbook, The (Goldbarth), **Supp. XII:** 181, 183

Smugglers of Lost Soul's Rock, The (Gardner), **Supp. VI: 70**

Smyth, Albert Henry, **II:** 123

Smyth, Jacqui, **Supp. XXI:** 215

"Snack Firm Maps New Chip Push" (Keillor), **Supp. XVI:** 168, 169

"Snail, The" (Hay), **Supp. XIV:** 124

"Snake, The" (Berry), **Supp. X:** 31

"Snake, The" (Crane), **I:** 420

"Snakecharmer" (Plath), **Supp. I Part 2:** 538

"Snakes, Mongooses" (Moore), **III:** 207

"Snakeskin" (Kooser), **Supp. XIX:** 123

"Snakes of September, The" (Kunitz), **Supp. III Part 1:** 258

"Snapshot of 15th S.W., A" (Hugo), **Supp. VI:** 141

"Snapshot Rediscovered, A" (X. J. Kennedy), **Supp. XV:** 170

"Snapshots in an Album" (Espaillat), **Supp. XXI:** 111

"Snapshots of a Daughter-in-Law" (Rich), **Supp. I Part 2:** 553–554

Snapshots of a Daughter-in-Law: Poems, 1954–1962 (Rich), **Supp. I Part 2:** 550–551, 553–554; **Supp. XII:** 255

Snaring the Flightless Birds (Bierds), **Supp. XVII:** 26

Sneetches and Other Stories, The (Geisel), **Supp. XVI:** 109

"Sneeze, The" (Chekhov), **Supp. IV Part 2:** 585

Snell, Ebenezer, **Supp. I Part 1:** 151

Snell, Thomas, **Supp. I Part 1:** 153

Sniffen, Matthew, **Supp. XXV:** 283

"Snob, The" (Boulton), **Supp. XXII:** 23

"Snob, The" (Shapiro), **Supp. II Part 2:** 705

Snobbery: The America Version (Epstein), **Supp. XIV:** 102, 114–115

Snodgrass, Kathleen, **Supp. XVI:** 42

Snodgrass, W. D., **I:** 400; **Retro. Supp. II:** 179; **Supp. III Part 2:** 541; **Supp. V:** 337; **Supp. VI: 311–328**; **Supp. XI:** 141, 315; **Supp. XIII:** 312; **Supp. XV:** 92, 153; **Supp. XVII:** 239

"Snow" (C. Baxter), **Supp. XVII:** 19

"Snow" (Frost), **Retro. Supp. I:** 133

"Snow" (Haines), **Supp. XII:** 212

"Snow" (Sexton), **Supp. II Part 2:** 696

"Snow" (W. V. Davis), **Supp. XXI:** 89, 90, 93

Snow, C. P., **Supp. I Part 2:** 536

Snow, Dean, **Supp. XXVI:** 86

Snow, Hank, **Supp. V:** 335

Snow Angels (film), **Supp. XXV:** 153–154

Snow Angels (O'Nan), **Supp. XXV:** 142, 143, 150

Snow Ball, The (Gurney), **Supp. V:** 99

"Snow-Bound" (Whittier), **Supp. I Part 2:** 700–703

"Snow Bound at Eagle's" (Harte), **Supp. II Part 1:** 356

"Snowflakes" (Longfellow), **II:** 498

"Snow Goose, The" (Gallico), **Supp. XVI:** 238

Snow-Image and Other Twice Told Tales, The (Hawthorne), **II:** 237; **Retro. Supp. I:** 160

"Snowing in Greenwich Village" (Updike), **IV:** 226; **Retro. Supp. I:** 321

"Snow in New York" (Swenson), **Supp. IV Part 2:** 644

Snow Leopard, The (Matthiessen), **Supp. V:** 199, 207–211

"Snow Man, The" (Stevens), **IV:** 82–83; **Retro. Supp. I:** 299, 300, 302, 306, 307, 312; **Supp. XXI:** 60

"Snowmass Cycle, The" (Dunn), **Supp. XI:** 152

Snow: Meditations of a Cautious Man in Winter (Banks), **Supp. V:** 6

Snow Poems, The (Ammons), **Supp. VII:** 32–34

Snowshoe Trek to Otter River (Budbill), **Supp. XIX:** 11

Snow's Music, The (Skloot), **Supp. XX: 196, 204–205**

"Snows of Kilimanjaro, The" (Hemingway), **II:** 78, 257, 263, 264; **Retro. Supp. I:** 98, 182; **Supp. XII:** 249

"Snows of Studiofiftyfour, The" (Plimpton), **Supp. XVI:** 245

"Snow Songs" (Snodgrass), **Supp. VI:** 324

"Snowstorm, The" (Oates), **Supp. II Part 2:** 523

"Snowstorm as It Affects the American Farmer, A" (Crèvecoeur), **Supp. I Part 1:** 251

Snow White (Barthelme), **Supp. IV Part 1:** 40, 47, 48–49, 50, 52; **Supp. V:** 39

"Snowy Egret" (Weigl), **Supp. XIX:** 280–281

"Snowy Mountain Song, A" (Ortiz), **Supp. IV Part 2:** 506

Snyder, Gary, **Supp. III Part 1:** 350; **Supp. IV Part 2:** 502; **Supp. V:** 168–169; **Supp. VIII:** 39, **289–307**; **Supp. XVI:** 283; **Supp. XXII:** 276

Snyder, Mike, **Supp. XIV:** 36

Soak the Rich (film), **Supp. XXVII:** 90

"So-and-So Reclining on Her Couch" (Stevens), **IV:** 90

"Soapland" (Thurber), **Supp. I Part 2:** 619

Soares, Lota de Macedo, **Retro. Supp. II:** 44; **Supp. I Part 1:** 89, 94

"Sobbin' Women, The" (Benét), **Supp. XI:** 47

Sobin, Gustaf, **Supp. XVI: 281–298**

Sochen, June, **Supp. XXI:** 1

Social Ethics (Gilman), **Supp. XI:** 207

"Social Function of the Story Teller, The" (lecture, Murray), **Supp. XIX:** 153

"Socialism and the Negro" (McKay), **Supp. X:** 135

"Socialism of the Skin, A (Liberation, Honey!)" (Kushner), **Supp. IX:** 135

Social Thought in America: The Revolt against Formalism (White), **Supp. I Part 2:** 648, 650

"Society, Morality, and the Novel" (Ellison), **Retro. Supp. II:** 118, 123–124

"Society of Eros" (Kittredge), **Supp. XXVI:** 178, 184

"Sociological Habit Patterns in Linguistic Transmogrification" (Cowley), **Supp. II Part 1:** 143

"Sociological Poet, A" (Bourne), **I:** 228

Socrates, **I:** 136, 265; **II:** 8–9, 105, 106; **III:** 281, 419, 606; **Supp. I Part 2:** 458; **Supp. XII:** 98

Socrates Fortlow stories (Mosley), **Supp. XIII: 242–243**

So Forth (Brodsky), **Supp. VIII:** 32–33

"So Forth" (Brodsky), **Supp. VIII:** 33

"Soft Flame" (Skloot), **Supp. XX: 203**

"Soft-Hearted Sioux, The" (Zitkala-Ša), **Supp. XXV:** 274, 282

Soft Machine, The (Burroughs), **Supp. III Part 1:** 93, 103, 104

"Soft Mask" (Karr), **Supp. XI:** 243

Soft Side, The (James), **II:** 335; **Retro. Supp. I:** 229

"Soft Spring Night in Shillington, A" (Updike), **Retro. Supp. I:** 318, 319

"Soft Wood" (R. Lowell), **II:** 550–551

"So Help Me" (Algren), **Supp. IX:** 2

Soil and Survival: Land Stewardship and the Future of American Agriculture (C. Bly, J. Paddock and N. Paddock), **Supp. XVI:** 36–37

"Soirée in Hollywood" (H. Miller), **III:** 186

Sojourner, The (Rawlings), **Supp. X:** 233–234

"Sojourn in a Whale" (Moore), **III:** 211, 213

"Sojourns" (Didion), **Supp. IV Part 1:** 205

Sokolow, Jayme, **Supp. XIX:** 134

Solanus, Jane, **Supp. XVI:** 293

Solar Lottery (Dick), **Supp. XVIII:** 138

Solar Storms (Hogan), **Supp. IV Part 1:** 397, 410, 414–415

"Soldier, The" (Frost), **II:** 155

"Soldier Asleep at the Tomb" (Schnackenberg), **Supp. XV:** 262–263

Soldier Blue (film), **Supp. X:** 124

"Soldier of Fortune" (Wright), **Supp. XV:** 341

Soldier of the Great War, A (Helprin), **Supp. XXV:** 83–84, 86–87

"Soldier's Home" (Hemingway), **Retro. Supp. I:** 189

Soldier's Joy (Bell), **Supp. X:** 7, **7–8,** 10, 11; **Supp. XXIII:** 43

Soldiers of the Storm (film), **Supp. XIII:** 163

Soldiers' Pay (Faulkner), **I:** 117; **II:** 56, 68; **Retro. Supp. I:** 80, 81

"Soldier's Testament, The" (Mumford), **Supp. II Part 2:** 473

"Soliloquy: Man Talking to a Mirror" (Komunyakaa), **Supp. XIII:** 116–117

"Solipsism" (Monson), **Supp. XXIV:** 230

"Solitary, The" (Teasdale), **Supp. XXVII:** 296

"Solitary Confinement" (X. J. Kennedy), **Supp. XV:** 157

"Solitary Pond, The" (Updike), **Retro. Supp. I:** 323

So Little Time (Marquand), **III:** 55, 59, 65, 67, 69

"Solitude" (Maupassant), **Supp. I Part 1:** 223

Solnit, Rebecca, **Supp. XXVI:** 45

Solo Faces (Salter), **Supp. IX: 259–260**

Solomon, Andy, **Supp. X:** 11

Solomon, Carl, **Supp. XIV:** 143, 150

Solomon, Charles, **Supp. VIII:** 82

Solomon, Deborah, **Supp. XXI:** 245

Solomon, Henry, Jr., **Supp. I Part 2:** 490

Solomons, Leon, **IV:** 26

"So Long, Marianne" (Cohen), **Supp. XXVII:** 51, 60

So Long, See You Tomorrow (Maxwell), **Supp. VIII:** 156, 160, 162, **167–169; Supp. XVII:** 23

"So Long Ago" (Bausch), **Supp. VII:** 41–42

Solotaroff, Robert, **Retro. Supp. II:** 203

Solotaroff, Theodore, **III:** 452–453; **Retro. Supp. II:** 281; **Supp. I Part 2:** 440, 445; **Supp. X:** 79; **Supp. XI:** 340; **Supp. XII:** 291; **Supp. XIX:** 268; **Supp. XXVI:** 118

Solstice (Di Piero), **Supp. XIX:** 36

"Solstice" (Jeffers), **Supp. II Part 2:** 433, 435

"Solstice, The" (Merwin), **Supp. III Part 1:** 356

"Solus Rex" (Nabokov), **Retro. Supp. I:** 274

Solution, The (Stone), **Supp. XXVII:** 257

"Solutions" (McCarthy), **II:** 578

"Solving the Puzzle" (Dunn), **Supp. XI:** 152

Solzhenitsyn, Alexandr, **Retro. Supp. I:** 278; **Supp. VIII:** 241

"Some Afternoon" (Creeley), **Supp. IV Part 1:** 150–151

Some American People (Caldwell), **I:** 292, 294, 295, 296, 304, 309

"Some Ashes Drifting above Piedra, California" (Levis), **Supp. XI:** 264–265

"Some Aspects of the Grotesque in Southern Fiction" (O'Connor), **Retro. Supp. II:** 223, 224

"Some Birds on a Dun Field" (Bronk), **Supp. XXI:** 27

"Somebody Always Grabs the Purple" (H. Roth), **Supp. IX:** 234

Somebody Else, Somewhere Else: The Raymond Andrews Story (film, Freeman), **Supp. XXVI:** 11

Somebody in Boots (Algren), **Supp. IX:** 3, **5–7,** 12

Somebody's Darling (McMurtry), **Supp. V:** 225

Some Came Running (film), **Supp. XI:** 213

Some Came Running (Jones), **Supp. XI:** 214, 215, 220, **222–223,** 226, 227, 232

Some Can Whistle (McMurtry), **Supp. V:** 229

"Some Children of the Goddess" (Mailer), **Retro. Supp. II:** 204

Someday, Maybe (Stafford), **Supp. XI: 323–325; Supp. XIII:** 281

Some Drawings and Some Notes to Myself (Brainard), **Supp. XXVII:** 20

"Some Dreamers of the Golden Dream" (Didion), **Supp. IV Part 1:** 200

"Some Esoteric Aspects of the League of the Iroquois" (Hewitt), **Supp. XXVI:** 96

Some Faces in the Crowd (Schulberg), **Supp. XVIII:** 252

"Some Foreign Letters" (Sexton), **Supp. II Part 2:** 674

"Some General Instructions" (Koch), **Supp. XV:** 182

"Some Good News" (Olson), **Supp. II Part 2:** 575, 576, 577

"Some Grass along a Ditch Bank" (Levis), **Supp. XI:** 266

"Some Greek Writings" (Corso), **Supp. XII:** 130

Some Honorable Men: Political Conventions, 1960–1972 (Mailer), **Retro. Supp. II:** 208

Some Imagist Poets (A. Lowell), **III:** 511, 518, 520; **Supp. I Part 1:** 257, 261

"Some keep the Sabbath going to Church" (Dickinson), **Retro. Supp. I:** 30; **Supp. XVIII:** 301

"Some Laughed" (L. Michaels), **Supp. XVI:** 207

"Some Like Indians Endure" (Gunn Allen), **Supp. IV Part 1:** 330

"Some Like Them Cold" (Lardner), **II:** 427–428, 430, 431; **Supp. IX:** 202

"Some Lines from Whitman" (Jarrell), **IV:** 352

"Some Matters Concerning the Occupant" (Keillor), **Supp. XVI:** 167

"Some Musicians Play Chamber Music for Us" (Bronk), **Supp. XXI:** 27–28

"Some Negatives: X. at the Chateau" (Merrill), **Supp. III Part 1:** 322

"Some Neglected Points in the Theory of Socialism" (Veblen), **Supp. I Part 2:** 635

"Some Notes for an Autobiographical Lecture" (Trilling), **Supp. III Part 2:** 493, 497, 500

"Some Notes on French Poetry" (R. Bly), **Supp. IV Part 1:** 61

"Some Notes on Miss L." (West), **IV:** 290–291, 295; **Retro. Supp. II:** 322

"Some Notes on Organic Form" (Levertov), **Supp. III Part 1:** 272, 279

"Some Notes on Teaching: Probably Spoken" (Paley), **Supp. VI:** 225

"Some Notes on the Gazer Within" (Levis), **Supp. XI:** 270

"Some Notes on Violence" (West), **IV:** 304; **Retro. Supp. II:** 322, 323

"Some Observations Now" (Conroy), **Supp. XVI:** 75

Some Observations of a Stranger at Zuni in the Later Part of the Century (Major), **Supp. XXII:** 179–180

"Some Observations of a Stranger at Zuni in the Later Part of the Century" (Major), **Supp. XXII:** 179

Some of the Dharma (Kerouac), **Supp. III Part 1:** 225

"Some of Us Have Fewer" (Monson), **Supp. XXIV:** 240

"Someone Is Buried" (Salinas), **Supp. XIII:** 324

"Someone Puts a Pineapple Together" (Stevens), **IV:** 90–91

"Someone's Blood" (Dove), **Supp. IV Part 1:** 245

"Someone Talking" (Harjo), **Supp. XII:** 219–220

"Someone Talking to Himself" (Wilbur), **Supp. III Part 2:** 557

"Someone to Watch Over Me" (Stern), **Supp. IX:** 300

Someone to Watch Over Me: Stories (Bausch), **Supp. VII:** 53

Some People, Places, & Things That Will Not Appear in My Next Novel (Cheever), **Supp. I Part 1:** 184–185

"Some Poets' Criticism and the Age" (Yenser), **Supp. XV:** 113–114

Some Problems of Philosophy: A Beginning of an Introduction to Philosophy (James), **II:** 360–361

"Some Questions You Might Ask" (Oliver), **Supp. VII:** 238–239

"Some Remarks on Humor" (White), **Supp. I Part 2:** 672

"Some Remarks on Rhythm" (Roethke), **III:** 548–549

Somers, Fred, **I:** 196

Somerville, Jane, **Supp. IX:** 289, 296–297

"Some Secrets" (Stern), **Supp. IX:** 286, 287, 288, 289, 295

Some Sort of Epic Grandeur (Bruccoli), **Retro. Supp. I:** 115, 359

"Something" (Oliver), **Supp. VII:** 236

Something Happened (Heller), **Supp. IV Part 1:** 383, 386–388, 389, 392

"Something Happened: The Imaginary, the Symbolic, and the Discourse of the Family" (Mellard), **Supp. IV Part 1:** 387

Something in Common (Hughes), **Supp. I Part 1:** 329–330

Something Inside: Conversations with Gay Fiction Writers (Gambone), **Supp. XII:** 81

Something I've Been Meaning to Tell You (Munro), **Supp. XXVII:** 182, 184–185

"Something Matters but We Don't " (Bronk), **Supp. XXI:** 32

"Something Might Be Gaining" (Mosher), **Supp. XXII:** 209

"Something New" (Stern), **Supp. IX:** 290

"Something Rich and Strange" (Rash), **Supp. XXVII:** 223–224

Some Things (Berrigan, Padgett, and Brainard), **Supp. XXIV:** 41

Something Said (Sorrentino), **Supp. XXI:** 226, 227, 229, 235

"Something's Going to Happen" (Zinberg), **Supp. XV:** 196

"Something Spurious from the Mindinao Deep" (Stegner), **Supp. IV Part 2:** 605

"Something That Needs Nothing" (July), **Supp. XXIV:** 203

"Something to Believe In" (Pitts), **Supp. XXII:** 280

Something to Declare (Alvarez), **Supp. VII:** 1, 2, 11, 17–19

Something to Remember Me By (Bellow), **Retro. Supp. II:** 32

"Something to Remember Me By" (Bellow), **Retro. Supp. II:** 32

"Something Wicked" (O'Nan), **Supp. XXV:** 148

Something Wicked This Way Comes (Bradbury), **Supp. IV Part 1:** 101, 110–111; **Supp. XXV:** 148

"Something Wild . . ." (T. Williams), **IV:** 381

"Some Thoughts" (McNally), **Supp. XIII:** 207

"Some Thoughts on the Line" (Oliver), **Supp. VII:** 238

"Sometimes, Reading" (Stafford), **Supp. XI:** 314

"Sometimes It Just Happens That Way, That's All" (Hinojosa), **Supp. XIX:** 101

"Sometimes I Wonder" (Hughes), **Supp. I Part 1:** 337

Sometimes Mysteriously (Salinas), **Supp. XIII:** 311, **326–328**

"Sometimes Mysteriously" (Salinas), **Supp. XIII:** 328

Some Trees (Ashbery), **Supp. III Part 1:** 3–7, 12

"Some Trees" (Ashbery), **Supp. III Part 1:** 2

"Some Truths About American Readers" (Atherton), **Supp. XXIV:** 24, 27

"Some Views on the Reading and Writing of Short Stories" (Welty), **Retro. Supp. I:** 351

"Somewhere" (Nemerov), **III:** 279–280

"Somewhere Else" (Paley), **Supp. VI:** 227

"Somewhere in Africa" (Sexton), **Supp. II Part 2:** 684–685

Somewhere in the Darkness (Myers), **Supp. XXVII:** 203–204

"Somewhere Is Such a Kingdom" (Ransom), **III:** 492

"Somewhere near Phu Bai" (Komunyakaa), **Supp. XIII:** 123–124

Some Words (Bronk), **Supp. XXI:** 32

"Some Words with a Mummy" (Poe), **III:** 425

"Some Yips and Barks in the Dark" (Snyder), **Supp. VIII:** 291

Sommers, Michael, **Supp. IV Part 2:** 581

Sommers, William, **I:** 387, 388

"Somnambulisma" (Stevens), **Retro. Supp. I:** 310

"So Much Summer" (Dickinson), **Retro. Supp. I:** 26, 44, 45

"So Much the Worse for Boston" (Lindsay), **Supp. I Part 2:** 398

"So Much Water So Close to Home" (Carver), **Supp. III Part 1:** 143, 146

Son, Cathy, **Supp. X:** 292

"Son, The" (Dove), **Supp. IV Part 1:** 245

"Son and Father" (Pickering), **Supp. XXI:** 197

"Sonata" (Schnackenberg), **Supp. XV:** 259

"Sonata for the Invisible" (Harjo), **Supp. XII:** 228

Sonata for Two Pianos (Bowles), **Supp. IV Part 1:** 83

Son at the Front, A (Wharton), **II:** 183; **IV:** 320; **Retro. Supp. I:** 378

Sondheim, Stephen, **Supp. XII:** 260; **Supp. XVI:** 194

Son Excellence Eugène Rougon (Zola), **III:** 322

Son from Sleep, A (Hadas), **Supp. XXIII:** **114–115**

Song (B. Kelly), **Supp. XVII:** 123, **127–130**

"Song" (B. Kelly), **Supp. XVII:** 127

"Song" (Bogan), **Supp. III Part 1:** 57

"Song" (Bryant). *See* "Hunter of the West, The"

"Song" (Dunbar), **Supp. II Part 1:** 199

"Song" (Espaillat), **Supp. XXI:** 106–107

"Song" (Ginsberg), **Supp. II Part 1:** 317

"Song" (Kenyon), **Supp. VII:** 169

"Song" (Rich), **Supp. I Part 2:** 560

"Song" (Wylie), **Supp. I Part 2:** 729

"Song, A" (Creeley), **Supp. IV Part 1:** 145

"Song, The" (Gioia), **Supp. XV:** 117

"Song, The" (Very), **Supp. XXV:** 242

Song and Idea (Eberhart), **I:** 526, 529, 533, 539

"Song: Enlightenment" (X. J. Kennedy), **Supp. XV:** 169

"Song for a Lover Killed in Battle"(J. Schoolcraft), **Supp. XXIII:** 235

Song for Anninho (G. Jones), **Supp. XXIV:** 185, 195

Song for My Father, A: A Play in Two Acts (Budbill), **Supp. XIX:** 3, **15–16**

"Song for Myself and the Deer to Return On" (Harjo), **Supp. XII:** 225

"Song for My Sixtieth Year" (Carruth), **Supp. XVI:** 54

"Song for Occupations, A" (Whitman), **Retro. Supp. I:** 394

"Song for Simeon, A" (Eliot), **Retro. Supp. I:** 64

"Song for the Coming of Smallpox" (Wagoner), **Supp. IX:** 329, 330

"Song for the End of Time" (Gioia), **Supp. XV:** 126–127

"Song for the First People" (Wagoner), **Supp. IX:** 328

"Song for the Last Act" (Bogan), **Supp. III Part 1:** 64

"Song for the Middle of the Night, A" (Wright), **Supp. III Part 2:** 594

"Song for the Rainy Season" (Bishop), **Supp. I Part 1:** 93–94, 96

"Song for the Romeos, A" (Stern), **Supp. IX:** 296

"Song for Woody" (song, Dylan), **Supp. XVIII:** 24

"Song from a Courtyard Window" (Gioia), **Supp. XV:** 119

"Song III" (Taggard), **Supp. XXII:** 284

"Song in the Front Yard, A" (Brooks), **Supp. XVIII:** 181

"Songline of Dawn" (Harjo), **Supp. XII:** 229

"Song: Love in Whose Rich Honor" (Rukeyser), **Supp. VI:** 285

"Song: Now That She Is Here" (Carruth), **Supp. XVI:** 59

"Song of Absinthe Granny, The" (Stone), **Supp. XXVII:** 263

"Song of Advent, A" (Winters), **Supp. II Part 2:** 789

"Song of a Man Who Rushed at the Enemy" (Wagoner), **Supp. IX:** 329, 330

"Song of Courage, A" (Masters), **Supp. I Part 2:** 458

Song of God, The: Bhagavad-Gita (Isherwood and Prabhavananda, trans.), **Supp. XIV:** 156, 157, 164

Song of Hiawatha, The (Longfellow), **II:** 501, 503–504; **Retro. Supp. II:** 155, **159–161**, 162, 163; **Supp. XXIII:** 223, 234–235

"Song of Innocence, A" (Ellison), **Retro. Supp. II:** 126; **Supp. II Part 1:** 248

"Song of My Fiftieth Birthday, The" (Lindsay), **Supp. I Part 2:** 399

"Song of Myself" (Whitman), **II:** 544; **III:** 572, 584, 595; **IV:** 333, 334, 337–339, 340, 341, 342, 344, 348, 349, 351, 405; **Retro. Supp. I:** 388, 389, 395–399, 400; **Supp. IX:** 131, 136, 143, 328, 331; **Supp. V:** 122; **Supp. XIV:** 139; **Supp. XVIII:** 194, 304; **Supp. XXII:** 81

Song of Napalm (Weigl), **Supp. XIX:** 278–282

"Song of Napalm" (Weigl), **Supp. XIX:** 276–277

Song of Russia (film), **Supp. I Part 1:** 281, 294; **Supp. XVII:** 60–61

"Song of Self" (Huncke), **Supp. XIV:** 138–139, 145

Song of Solomon (biblical book), **III:** 118; **IV:** 150

Song of Solomon (Morrison), **Supp. III Part 1:** 364, 368, 369, 372, 379; **Supp. XVIII:** 55

Song of Songs (biblical book), **II:** 538; **IV:** 153–154; **Supp. XV:** 221

"Song of the Adoumboulou: 3" (Mackey), **Supp. XXVII:** 157

"Song of the Adoumboulou: 6" (Mackey), **Supp. XXVII:** 157

"Song of the Adoumboulou: 7" (Mackey), **Supp. XXVII:** 157

"Song of the Andoumboulou" (Mackey), **Supp. XXVII:** 153–154, 155, 156

"Song of the Andoumboulou: 1" (Mackey), **Supp. XXVII:** 153–154

"Song of the Andoumboulou: 8" (Mackey), **Supp. XXVII:** 154

"Song of the Andoumboulou: 16" (Mackey), **Supp. XXVII:** 155

"Song of the Andoumboulou: 26" (Mackey), **Supp. XXVII:** 155

"Song of the Answerer" (Whitman), **Retro. Supp. I:** 393, 399

Song of the Cardinal, The (Stratton-Porter), **Supp. XX: 217, 218,** 219

"Song of the Chattahoochee, The" (Lanier), **Supp. I Part 1:** 365, 368

"Song of the Degrees, A" (Pound), **III:** 466

"Song of the Drunkard" (Ferry), **Supp. XXIV:** 153, 162

"Song of the Dryads" (Taggard), **Supp. XXII:** 272

"Song of the Exposition" (Whitman), **IV:** 332

"Song of the Gavilan" (Leopold), **Supp. XIV:** 189

"Song of the Gourd" (Wright), **Supp. XV:** 348–349

"Song of the Greek Amazon" (Bryant), **Supp. I Part 1:** 168

Song of the Lark, The (Cather), **I:** 312, 319–321, 323; **Retro. Supp. I:** 1, 3, 7, **9–11,** 13, 19, 20

"Song of the Okogis, or Frog in Spring"(J. Schoolcraft), **Supp. XXIII:** 232, 233, 235

"Song of the Open Road" (McGrath), **Supp. X:** 127

"Song of the Open Road" (Whitman), **IV:** 340–341; **Retro. Supp. I:** 400; **Supp. IX:** 265

"Song of the Redwood Tree" (Whitman), **IV:** 348

"Song of the Scullery" (McCarriston), **Supp. XIV:** 272

"Song of the Sky Loom" (traditional Tewa poem), **Supp. IV Part 1:** 325

"Song of the Son" (Toomer), **Supp. III Part 2:** 482–483; **Supp. IX:** 313

"Song of the Sower, The" (Bryant), **Supp. I Part 1:** 169

"Song of the Stars" (Bryant), **Supp. I Part 1:** 163

"Song of the Swamp-Robin, The" (Frederic), **II:** 138

"Song of the Vermonters, The" (Whittier), **Supp. I Part 2:** 692

"Song of Three Smiles" (Merwin), **Supp. III Part 1:** 344

"Song of Wandering Aengus, The" (Yeats), **IV:** 271; **Retro. Supp. I:** 342, 350

"Song of Welcome" (Brodsky), **Supp. VIII:** 32

"Song on Captain Barney's Victory" (Freneau), **Supp. II Part 1:** 261

"Song/Poetry and Language-Expression and Perception" (Ortiz), **Supp. IV Part 2:** 500, 508

"Song Rehearsal, The" (Stallings), **Supp. XXV:** 233

"Song: 'Rough Winds Do Shake the Darling Buds of May' " (Simpson), **Supp. IX:** 268

Songs (Boyce), **Supp. XXI:** 9

Songs and Satires (Masters), **Supp. I Part 2:** 465–466

Songs and Sonnets (L. P. Smith), **Supp. XIV:** 341

Songs and Sonnets (Masters), **Supp. I Part 2:** 455, 459, 461, 466

"Songs for a Colored Singer" (Bishop), **Supp. I Part 1:** 80, 85

Songs for a Summer's Day (A Sonnet Cycle) (MacLeish), **III:** 3

Songs for Eve (MacLeish), **III:** 3, 19

"Songs for Eve" (MacLeish), **III:** 19

"Songs for My Father" (Komunyakaa), **Supp. XIII:** 128

Songs for the Missing (O'Nan), **Supp. XXV:** 143, 148, 150

Songs for the Unborn Second Baby (Notley), **Supp. XXII:** 228

"Songs for Two Seasons" (C. Frost), **Supp. XV:** 95–96

Songs from a Room (album, Cohen), **Supp. XXVII:** 54

Songs from This Earth on Turtle's Back: Contemporary American Indian Poetry (Bruchac, ed.), **Supp. IV Part 1:** 320, 328

"Songs of a Housewife" (Rawlings), **Supp. X:** 221–222

"Songs of Billy Bathgate, The" (Doctorow), **Supp. IV Part 1:** 230

Songs of Innocence (Blake), **Supp. I Part 2:** 708

Songs of Jamaica (McKay), **Supp. X:** 131, 133

Songs of Leonard Cohen (album, Cohen), **Supp. XXVII:** 54, 59

Songs of Love and Hate (album, Cohen), **Supp. XXVII:** 54

"Songs of Maximus, The" (Olson), **Supp. II Part 2:** 567

"Songs of Parting" (Whitman), **IV:** 348

Songs of the Doomed (Thompson), **Supp. XXIV:** 283

Songs of the North: A Sigurd Olson Reader (Mosher, ed.), **Supp. XXII:** 218

Songs of the Sierras (J. Miller), **I:** 459

Songs of Three Centuries (Whittier and Larcom, eds.), **Supp. XIII:** 142

"Song to David" (Smart), **III:** 534

"Song to No Music, A" (Brodsky), **Supp. VIII:** 26

"Song V" (Taggard), **Supp. XXII:** 284

Song Yet Sung (McBride), **Supp. XXVI:** 194, 199–201, 204

Soniat, Katherine, **Supp. XXI:** 245

Sonneschein, Rosa, **Retro. Supp. II:** 65

"Sonnet" (Rukeyser), **Supp. VI:** 284

"Sonnet, A" (Very), **Supp. XXV:** 242

"Sonnet Crown for Two Voices" (Bierds), **Supp. XVII:** 35

"Sonnet"(J. Schoolcraft), **Supp. XXIII:** 229

"Sonnet of Good Cheer, A" (Howard), **Supp. XXVII:** 118–119

"Sonnets" (Carruth), **Supp. XVI:** 56

Sonnets, The (Berrigan), **Supp. XXII:** 224; **Supp. XXIV:** 33, 34, 35, 37, 38–41, 45

Sonnets to Duse and Other Poems (Teasdale), **Supp. XXVII:** 287

Sonnets to Orpheus (Rilke), **Supp. XV:** 222; **Supp. XXIV:** 38

"Sonnet to a Negro in Harlem" (H. Johnson), **Supp. XXVI:** 166, 167–170

"Sonnet-To Zante" (Poe), **III:** 421

"Sonnet XV" (Berrigan), **Supp. XXIV:** 38–39, 44

"Sonny's Blues" (Baldwin), **Retro. Supp. II:** 7, 8, 10, 14; **Supp. I Part 1:** 58–59, 63, 67; **Supp. XI:** 288; **Supp. XXVII:** 201

Son of Laughter, The: A Novel (Buechner), **Supp. XII:** 54

Son of Perdition, The (Cozzens), **I:** 359–360, 377, 378, 379

Son of the Circus, A (Irving), **Supp. VI:** 165, 166, **176–179**

Son of the Gamblin' Man: The Youth of an Artist (Sandoz), **Supp. XXIV:** 244, **256–257**

"Son of the Gods, A" (Bierce), **I:** 202

Son of the Morning (Oates), **Supp. II Part 2:** 518, 519, 520–522

Son of the Morning Star: Custer and the Little Bighorn (Connell), **Supp. XIV:** 80, 82, 97

"Son of the Romanovs, A" (Simpson), **Supp. IX:** 273–274

"Son of the White Wolf" (Howard), **Supp. XXVII:** 121

Son of the Wolf, The (London), **II:** 465, 469

"Son of the Wolfman" (Chabon), **Supp. XI:** 76

"Sonrisas" (Mora), **Supp. XIII:** 216, 219

Sons (Buck), **Supp. II Part 1:** 117–118

"Sons" (Teasdale), **Supp. XXVII:** 295

Sons and Lovers (Lawrence), **III:** 27

Sons of Kai, The: The Story the Indian Told (Beston), **Supp. XXVI:** 33

Sontag, Kate, **Supp. XV:** 104

Sontag, Susan, **IV:** 13, 14; **Retro. Supp. II:** 279; **Supp. I Part 2:** 423; **Supp. III Part 2: 451–473; Supp. VIII:** 75; **Supp. XIV:** 14, 15, 95–96, 167; **Supp. XVI:** 201, 204, 206; **Supp. XX: 205; Supp. XXI:** 243; **Supp. XXVI:** 45

"Soon" (Munro), **Supp. XXVII:** 193, 194

"Soonest Mended" (Ashbery), **Supp. III Part 1:** 1, 13

"Sootfall and Fallout" (White), **Supp. I Part 2:** 671

Sophisticates, The (Atherton), **Supp. XXIV:** 20, 25

Sophocles, **I:** 274; **II:** 291, 385, 577; **III:** 145, 151, 152, 153, 159, 398, 476, 478, 609, 613; **IV:** 291, 363, 368, 370; **Supp. I Part 1:** 153, 284; **Supp. I Part 2:** 491; **Supp. V:** 97; **Supp. VIII:** 332; **Supp. XV:** 265, 266

"Sophronsiba" (Bourne), **I:** 221

Sorayam, Aram, **Supp. XXII:** 25

Sorby, Angela, **Supp. XXIII:** 132

Sorcerer's Apprentice, The: Tales and Conjurations (C. Johnson), **Supp. VI: 192–193,** 194

"Sorcerer's Eye, The" (Nemerov), **III:** 283

Sordello (Browning), **III:** 467, 469, 470

"Sordid? Good God!" (Williams), **Retro. Supp. II:** 334

So Red the Rose (Young), **Supp. XXII:** 190, 193

"Sorghum" (Mason), **Supp. VIII:** 146

Sorkin, Adam, **Supp. XXIV:** 178

Sorokin, Pitirim, **Supp. I Part 2:** 679

Sorrentino, Christopher, **Supp. XVIII:** 148

Sorrentino, Gilbert, **Retro. Supp. I:** 426; **Supp. IV Part 1:** 286; **Supp. XII:** 139; **Supp. XXI: 225–241; Supp. XXII:** 261; **Supp. XXVI:** 26; **Supp. XXVII:** 18

Sorrento (Notley), **Supp. XXII:** 231

"Sorrow" (Komunyakaa), **Supp. XIII:** 119

Sorrow Dance, The (Levertov), **Supp. III Part 1:** 279–280, 283

"Sorrowful Guest, A" (Jewett), **Retro. Supp. II:** 137

Sorrows of Fat City, The: A Selection of Literary Essays and Reviews (Garrett), **Supp. VII:** 111

Sorrows of Young Werther, The (Goethe), **Supp. XI:** 169; **Supp. XX: 234, 236**

Sorrows of Young Werther, The (Goethe; Bogan and Mayer, trans.), **Supp. III Part 1:** 63

"Sorry Fugu" (Boyle), **Supp. XX:** 19

"Sorting Facts; or, Nineteen Ways of Looking at Marker" (Howe), **Supp. IV Part 2:** 434, 436

"Sort of Song, A" (W. C. Williams), **Supp. XVII:** 243

"S O S" (Baraka), **Supp. II Part 1:** 50

"So Sassafras" (Olson), **Supp. II Part 2:** 574

"So There" (Creeley), **Supp. IV Part 1:** 157

"So This Is Nebraska" (Kooser), **Supp. XIX:** 120

Sotirov, Vasil, **Supp. IX:** 152

Soto, Gary, **Supp. IV Part 2:** 545; **Supp. V:** 180; **Supp. XI:** 270; **Supp. XIII:** 313, 315, 316, 320, 323; **Supp. XV:** 73; **Supp. XXV:** 130

"Soto Thinking of the Ocean" (Salinas), **Supp. XIII:** 321

"Sotto Voce" (Kunitz), **Supp. III Part 1:** 265

Sot-Weed Factor, The (Barth), **I:** 122, 123, 125, 129, 130, 131–134, 135; **Supp. XXII:** 259

"Soul" (Ferry), **Supp. XXIV:** 162

Soul, The (Brooks), **I:** 244

Soul and Body of John Brown, The (Rukeyser), **Supp. VI:** 273

Soul Barnacles: Ten More Years with Ray (Gallagher; Simon, ed.), **Supp. XXIV:** 166, 167, 171, 172

Soul Clap Hands and Sing (Marshall), **Supp. XI:** 276, 278, **280–282**

Soul Expeditions (Singer). *See* Shosha (Singer)

Soul Gone Home (Hughes), **Retro. Supp. I:** 203; **Supp. I Part 1:** 328

"Soul inside the Sentence, The" (Gass), **Supp. VI:** 88

Soul Is Here for Its Own Joy, The (Bly, ed.), **Supp. IV Part 1:** 74

Soul of Man under Socialism, The (Wilde), **Supp. IX:** 134–135

"Soul of Spain, The \[In the manner of Gertrude Stein\]" (Hemingway), **Supp. XX: 74**

Soul of the Far East, The (P. Lowell), **II:** 513

"Soul on Bench" (Halliday), **Supp. XIX:** 91

Soul on Ice (Cleaver), **Retro. Supp. II:** 12, 13

"Souls Belated" (Wharton), **Retro. Supp. I:** 364

"Soul selects her own Society, The" (Dickinson), **Retro. Supp. I:** 37

Souls of Black Folk, The (Du Bois), **Supp. II Part 1:** 33, 40, 160, 168–170, 176, 183; **Supp. IV Part 1:** 164; **Supp. IX:** 305, 306; **Supp. X:** 133; **Supp. XIII:** 185, 238, 243

Souls of Black Folk, The (Du Bois), **Supp. XX: 102**

"Sound, The" (Olds), **Supp. X:** 214

Sound and Beauty (Hwang), **Supp. XXI:** 146

"Sound and Fury" (O. Henry), **Supp. II Part 1:** 402

Sound and the Fury, The (Faulkner), **I:** 480; **II:** 55, 57, 58–60, 73; **III:** 237; **IV:** 100, 101, 104; **Retro. Supp. I:** 73, 75, 77, 82, **83–84,** 86, 88, 89, 90, 91, 92; **Supp. IX:** 103; **Supp. VIII:** 215; **Supp. X:** 44; **Supp. XII:** 33; **Supp. XIV:** 12; **Supp. XVII:** 138; **Supp. XVIII:** 84; **Supp. XXVII:** 11

"Sound Bites" (Alvarez), **Supp. VII:** 11

Sound I Listened For, The (Francis), **Supp. IX: 78–79,** 87

"Soundless Trumpet, The" (Antin), **Supp. XX:** 12

"Sound Mind, Sound Body" (R. Lowell), **II:** 554

Sound of a Voice, The (Hwang), **Supp. XXI:** 146

"Sound of Distant Thunder, A" (Elkin), **Supp. VI: 42–43,** 44

"Sound of Light, The" (Merwin), **Supp. III Part 1:** 356

Sound of Mountain Water, The (Stegner), **Supp. IV Part 2:** 595, 596, 598, 600, 608

"Sound of Talking" (Purdy), **Supp. VII:** 270

Sounds of Poetry (television special, Moyers), **Supp. XXIII:** 139

Sounds of Poetry, The (Pinsky), **Supp. VI:** 236, 247, 248; **Supp. XXIII:** 124

Sound the Stars Make Rushing Through the Sky, The: The Writings of Jane Johnston Schoolcraft (Parker, ed.), **Supp. XXIII:** 223–224, 227, 228

Soupault, Philippe, **IV:** 288, 404; **Retro. Supp. II:** 85, 321, 324

Source (Doty), **Supp. XI:** 121, **134–137**

"Source" (Doty), **Supp. XI:** 136

"Source, The" (Olds), **Supp. X:** 211

"Source, The" (Porter), **III:** 443

Source of Light, The (Price), **Supp. VI: 262,** 266

"Sources of Soviet Conduct, The" (Kennan), **Supp. VIII:** 241

Sour Grapes (W. C. Williams), **Retro. Supp. I:** 418

"Sour Grapes"(Moraga), **Supp. XXIII:** 202

"Sourwood Nocturne" (Skloot), **Supp. XX: 202**

"South" (Levis), **Supp. XI:** 266

"South" (Trethewey), **Supp. XXI:** 247, 256

"South, The" (Hughes), **Supp. I Part 1:** 321

South American Journey (W. Frank), **Supp. XX:** 79

"Southampton Variations"(O'Hara), **Supp. XXIII:** 212

"Southbound on the Freeway" (Swenson), **Supp. IV Part 2:** 643

South Dakota Guidebook, The (C. Baxter), **Supp. XVII:** 15

Southern, Terry, **Supp. IV Part 1:** 379; **Supp. V:** 40, 201; **Supp. XI: 293–310; Supp. XVI:** 230

Southern Cross, The (Wright), **Supp. V:** 332, 342

"Southern Cross, The" (Wright), **Supp. V:** 338

"Southerner's Problem, The" (Du Bois), **Supp. II Part 1:** 168

"Southern Girl" (Zelda Fitzgerald), **Supp. IX:** 71

"Southern Gothic" (Trethewey), **Supp. XXI:** 256

"Southern History" (Trethewey), **Supp. XXI:** 256, 257

"Southern Mode of the Imagination, A" (Tate), **IV:** 120

"Southern Road, A" (H. Johnson), **Supp. XXVI:** 165, 167, 172, 174

"Southern Romantic, A" (Tate), **Supp. I Part 1:** 373

"Southern Sojourn, A" (Hoffman), **Supp. XVIII:** 87

Southern Terry, **Supp. XIV:** 82

Southern Writers: A New Biographical Dictionary (Flora, Vogel, and Giemza, eds.), **Supp. XXVI:** 148

Southey, Robert, **II:** 304, 502; **Supp. I Part 1:** 154; **Supp. XXIV:** 74

"South Lingers On, The" (R. Fisher), **Supp. XIX:** 69–70

South Moon Under (Rawlings), **Supp. X:** 225–226, 229, 233

South Pacific Affair (Lacy), **Supp. XV:** 206

Southpaw, The (Harris), **II:** 424–425

"South Sangamon" (Cisneros), **Supp. VII:** 66

"South State Street: Chicago" (Bodenheim), **Supp. XXV:** 22

South to a Very Old Place (Murray), **Supp. XIX: 151–153**

Southwell, Robert, **IV:** 151

Southwestern Homelands (Kittredge), **Supp. XXVI:** 188

Southwick, Marcia, **Supp. XI:** 259

Southworth, E. D. E. N, **Retro. Supp. I:** 246

Souvenir of the Ancient World, Selected Poems of Carlos Drummond de Andrade (Strand, trans.), **Supp. IV Part 2:** 630

Sovereign Bones: New Native American Writing (Gansworth, ed.), **Supp. XXVI:** 113

"Sow" (Plath), **Supp. I Part 2:** 537

"Sowing and Reaping in *Furors Die*" (Nostrandt), **Supp. XVIII:** 80–81

Soyinka, Wole, **Supp. XX:** 100

"Space" (Brockmeier), **Supp. XXII:** 51

Space between Our Footsteps, The: Poems and Paintings from the Middle East (Nye, ed.), **Supp. XIII:** 280

"Space Quale, The" (James), **II:** 349

"Spaces Between, The" (Kingsolver), **Supp. VII:** 209

"Spaceships Have Landed" (Munro), **Supp. XXVII:** 191

"Space Where Sex Should Be, The: Toward a Definition of the Black Literary Tradition" (Nelson), **Supp. XVIII:** 172

Spack, Ruth, **Supp. XXV:** 278

Spackman, Peter, **Supp. XVI:** 221

Spacks, Patricia, **Supp. XVI:** 251

"Spain" (Auden), **Supp. II Part 1:** 12–13, 14

"Spain in Fifty-Ninth Street" (White), **Supp. I Part 2:** 677

Spanier, Sandra, **Supp. XXIV:** 51, 64

"Spanish-American War Play" (Crane), **I:** 422

Spanish Ballads (Merwin, trans.), **Supp. III Part 1:** 347

Spanish Bayonet (Benét), **Supp. XI:** 45, 47

Spanish Earth, The (film), **Retro. Supp. I:** 184

Spanish Love (Rinehart), **Supp. XXV:** 195

Spanish Papers and Other Miscellanies (Irving), **II:** 314

"Spanish Revolution, The" (Bryant), **Supp. I Part 1:** 153, 168

Spanish Student, The (Longfellow), **II:** 489, 506; **Retro. Supp. II:** 165

"Spanish Winter" (Egan), **Supp. XIX:** 52

Spanking the Maid (Coover), **Supp. V:** 47, 48, 49, 52

Spare Change (Parker), **Supp. XIX:** 186–187

Spargo, John, **Supp. I Part 1:** 13

"Spark, The" (Wharton), **Retro. Supp. I:** 381

"Sparkles from the Wheel" (Whitman), **IV:** 348

Sparks, Debra, **Supp. X:** 177

Sparks, Jared, **Supp. I Part 1:** 156; **Supp. XXIV:** 71

"Sparrow" (Berry), **Supp. X:** 31

Sparrow, Henry, **III:** 587

Sparrow, Mrs. Henry, **III:** 587

"Sparrow's Gate, The" (B. Kelly), **Supp. XVII:** 133

Spaulding, William, **Supp. XVI:** 106

"Spawning Run, The" (Humphrey), **Supp. IX:** 95

"Speak, Gay Memory" (Kirp), **Supp. XI:** 129

"Speak, Hoyt-Schermerhorn" (Lethem), **Supp. XVIII:** 148

Speak, Memory (Nabokov), **III:** 247–250, 252; **Retro. Supp. I:** 264, 265, 266, 267, 268, 277; **Supp. XVI:** 148

Speak, Memory (V. Nabakov), **Supp. XVII:** 47

Speaking and Language (Shapiro), **Supp. II Part 2:** 721

Speaking for Nature: How Literary Naturalists from Henry Thoreau to Rachel Carson Have Shaped America (Brooks), **Supp. IX:** 31

Speaking for Ourselves: American Ethnic Writing (Faderman and Bradshaw, eds.), **Supp. XIII:** 313

Speaking of Accidents (Everwine), **Supp. XV:** 75, 88

"Speaking of Accidents" (Everwine), **Supp. XV:** 88–89

"Speaking of Counterweights" (White), **Supp. I Part 2:** 669

Speaking of Literature and Society (Trilling), **Supp. III Part 2:** 494, 496, 499

"Speaking of Love" (Gioia), **Supp. XV:** 124–125

Speaking of Race, Speaking of Sex: Hate Speech, Civil Rights, and Civil Liberties (H. L. Gates, Griffin, Lively, and Strossen), **Supp. XX:** 111

Speaking on Stage (Kolin and Kullman, eds.), **Supp. IX:** 145

Speaking on Stage: Interviews with Contemporary American Playwrights (Balakian), **Supp. XV:** 327

"Speaking Passions" (Kitchen), **Supp. XV:** 215

Speak of the Devil (Holding), **Supp. XXII: 127**

Speak What We Feel (Not What We Ought to Say): Reflections on Literature and Faith (Buechner), **Supp. XII:** 57

Spear, Roberta, **Supp. V:** 180; **Supp. XV:** 73

"Spear and Fang" (Howard), **Supp. XXVII:** 116

"Special Kind of Fantasy, A: James Dickey on the Razor's Edge" (Niflis), **Supp. IV Part 1:** 175

"Special Pleading" (Lanier), **Supp. I Part 1:** 364

"Special Problems in Teaching Leslie Marmon Silko's *Ceremony*" (Gunn Allen), **Supp. IV Part 1:** 333

Special Providence, A (Yates), **Supp. XI:** 342, **344–345**

"Special Time, a Special School, A" (Knowles), **Supp. XII:** 236

Special View of History, The (Olson), **Supp. II Part 2:** 566, 569, 572

Specimen Days (Whitman), **IV:** 338, 347, 348, 350; **Retro. Supp. I:** 408

Specimens of the American Poets, **Supp. I Part 1:** 155

"Speckled Trout" (Rash), **Supp. XXVII:** 222

"Spectacles, The" (Poe), **III:** 425

Spectator Bird, The (Stegner), **Supp. IV Part 2:** 599, 604, 606, 611–612

Spector, Herman, **Supp. XXV:** 26; **Supp. XXVI:** 143

Spector, Robert, **Supp. XIII:** 87

Spectra: A Book of Poetic Experiments (Bynner and Ficke), **Supp. XV:** 43

"Spectre Bridegroom, The" (Irving), **II:** 304

"Spectre Pig, The" (Holmes), **Supp. I Part 1:** 302

"Speculating Woman" (X. J. Kennedy), **Supp. XV:** 168

"Speech Sounds" (O. Butler), **Supp. XIII:** 61, **70**

"Speech to a Crowd" (MacLeish), **III:** 16

"Speech to the Detractors" (MacLeish), **III:** 16

"Speech to the Young" (Brooks), **Supp. III Part 1:** 79, 86

"Speech to Those Who Say Comrade" (MacLeish), **III:** 16

Speedboat (Adler), **Supp. X:** 171

Speed of Darkness, The (Rukeyser), **Supp. VI:** 274, 281

Speed Queen, The (O'Nan), **Supp. XXV:** 142, 144

Speed-the-Plow (Mamet), **Supp. XIV:** 241, 246, 249, 250, 251

"Speedy Gonzales Was the Fastest Mouse in Mexico" (P. N. Warren as Kilina), **Supp. XX: 262**

Speilberg, Steven, **Supp. XI:** 234

Speirs, Logan, **Supp. XIX:** 282

"Spell" (Francis), **Supp. IX:** 87

"Spell, The" (Peacock), **Supp. XIX:** 198, 200

Spellbound (screenplay, Hecht), **Supp. XXVII:** 93

"Spell for the Manufacture & Use of a Magic Carpet" (Hull), **Supp. XXI:** 132–133, 139, 141

Spelling Dictionary, A (Rowson), **Supp. XV:** 244

Spence, Thomas, **Supp. I Part 2:** 518

Spence + Lila (Mason), **Supp. VIII:** 133, **143–145**

Spencer, Edward, **Supp. I Part 1:** 357, 360

Spencer, Elizabeth, **Supp. XXVII:** 13

Spencer, Herbert, **I:** 515; **II:** 345, 462–463, 480, 483, 536; **III:** 102, 315; **IV:** 135; **Retro. Supp. II:** 60, 65, 93, 98; **Supp. I Part 1:** 368; **Supp. I Part 2:** 635; **Supp. XXVII:** 126

Spencer, Sharon, **Supp. X:** 185, 186, 195, 196

Spencer, Theodore, **I:** 433; **Supp. III Part 1:** 2

Spender, Natasha, **Supp. IV Part 1:** 119, 127, 134

Spender, Stephen, **II:** 371; **III:** 504, 527; **Retro. Supp. I:** 216; **Retro. Supp. II:** 243, 244; **Supp. I Part 2:** 536; **Supp. II Part 1:** 11; **Supp. IV Part 1:** 82, 134; **Supp. IV Part 2:** 440; **Supp. X:** 116

Spengler, Oswald, **I:** 255, 270; **II:** 7, 577; **III:** 172, 176; **Retro. Supp. II:** 324; **Supp. I Part 2:** 647

Spens, Sir Patrick, **Supp. I Part 2:** 404

Spenser, Edmund, **I:** 62; **III:** 77, 78, 89; **IV:** 155, 453; **Retro. Supp. I:** 62; **Supp. I Part 1:** 98, 152, 369; **Supp. I Part 2:** 422, 719; **Supp. XXIV:** 159

"Spenser's Ireland" (Moore), **III:** 211, 212

"Spermaceti Papers"(Lippard), **Supp. XXIII:** 178

S*PeRM**K*T (Mullen), **Supp. XXVII:** 169, 170–171

Sperry, Margaret, **Supp. IV Part 1:** 169

Spheres of Existence (C. L. R. James), **Supp. XXI:** 172

Sphere: The Form of a Motion (Ammons), **Supp. VII:** 24, 32, 33, 35, 36

"Sphinx" (Hayden), **Supp. II Part 1:** 373

Spice-Box of Earth, The (Cohen), **Supp. XXVII:** 54

"Spiced Plums" (Ríos), **Supp. IV Part 2:** 553

Spickard, Paul, **Supp. XXI:** 149

"Spider and the Ghost of the Fly, The" (Lindsay), **Supp. I Part 2:** 375

Spider Bay (Van Vechten), **Supp. II Part 2:** 746

"Spider Heart, The" (Peacock), **Supp. XIX:** 200

"Spiders" (Schwartz), **Supp. II Part 2:** 665

Spider's House, The (Bowles), **Supp. IV Part 1:** 87–89, 90, 91

Spider Woman's Granddaughters: Traditional Tales and Contemporary Writing by Native American Women (Gunn Allen, ed.), **Supp. IV Part 1:** 320, 326, 332–333; **Supp. IV Part 2:** 567

Spiegel, Sam, **Supp. XVIII:** 251, 252

Spiegelman, Art, **Supp. XVII:** 48

Spiegelman, Willard, **Supp. XI:** 126

Spielberg, Steven, **Supp. XXI:** 154

Spillane, Mickey, **Supp. IV Part 2:** 469, 472; **Supp. XV:** 200; **Supp. XVIII:** 236, 237

"Spillcorn" (Rash), **Supp. XXVII:** 222

Spiller, Robert E., **I:** 241; **Supp. I Part 1:** 104

Spillers, Hortense, **Supp. XX:** **109**

"Spillikins: Gregor Mendel at the Table" (Bierds), **Supp. XVII:** 34–35

Spillville (Hampl), **Supp. XXII:** 98

Spillway (Barnes), **Supp. III Part 1:** 44

Spingarn, Amy, **Supp. I Part 1:** 325, 326

Spingarn, Joel, **I:** 266; **Supp. I Part 1:** 325

Spinoza, Baruch, **I:** 493; **II:** 590, 593; **III:** 600; **IV:** 5, 7, 11, 12, 17; **Retro. Supp. II:** 300; **Supp. I Part 1:** 274; **Supp. I Part 2:** 643; **Supp. XVI:** 184

"Spinoza of Market Street, The" (Singer), **IV:** 12–13; **Retro. Supp. II:** 307

"Spinster" (Plath), **Supp. I Part 2:** 536

"Spinster's Tale, A" (Taylor), **Supp. V:** 314–315, 316–317, 319, 323

Spiral of Memory, The: The Interviews (Coltelli, ed.), **Supp. XII:** 215

Spires, Elizabeth, **Supp. X:** 8

"Spire Song" (Bowles), **Supp. IV Part 1:** 80

Spirit and Flame: An Anthology of African American Poetry (Gilyard, ed.), **Supp. XXI:** 246

Spirit and the Flesh, The: Sexual Diversity in American Indian Culture (W. L. Williams), **Supp. IV Part 1:** 330

"Spirit Birth" (Cullen), **Supp. IV Part 1:** 168

Spirit Brides (Gibran). *See Nymphs in the Valley*

Spirit in Man, The (Jung), **Supp. IV Part 1:** 68

"Spirit in Me, The" (Hoffman), **Supp. XVIII:** 87

"Spirit Made Visible" (art exhibit), **Supp. XXII:** 180

Spirit of Culver (West), **IV:** 287

Spirit of Labor, The (Hapgood), **Supp. XVII:** 96, 99, 101–102; **Supp. XXI:** 4

Spirit of Romance, The (Pound), **III:** 470; **Retro. Supp. I:** 286

Spirit of the Ghetto, The: Studies of the Jewish Quarter of New York (Hapgood), **Supp. XVII:** 96, 101, 103, 106

Spirit of Youth and the City Streets, The (Addams), **Supp. I Part 1:** 6–7, 12–13, 16, 17, 19

"Spirits" (Bausch), **Supp. VII:** 46–47

Spirits, and Other Stories (Bausch), **Supp. VII:** 46–47, 54

"Spirit Says, You Are Nothing, The" (Levis), **Supp. XI:** 265–266

Spirits Rebellious (al-Arwá&hudot; al-Mutamarrida) (Gibran), **Supp. XX:** **115, 124, 125**

Spiritual Adventures (Symons), **Supp. XX:** **239**

Spiritual Conflict, The (Scupoli), **IV:** 156

Spiritual Exercises, The (Loyola), **IV:** 151; **Supp. XI:** 162

"Spiritual Manifestation, A" (Whittier), **Supp. I Part 2:** 699

"Spirituals and Neo-Spirituals" (Hurston), **Supp. VI:** 152–153

Spits, Ellen Handler, **Supp. XII:** 166

"Spitzbergen Tales" (Crane), **I:** 409, 415, 423

Spitzer, Philip, **Supp. XIV:** 21

Splay Anthem (Mackey), **Supp. XXVII:** 152, 155–156, 159

"Spleen" (Eliot), **I:** 569, 573–574

Spleen de Paris, Le (Baudelaire), **Supp. XIV:** 337

Splendid Drunken Twenties, The (Van Vechten), **Supp. II Part 2:** 739–744

Splendide-Hôtel (Sorrentino), **Supp. XXI:** 233

Splendid Table, The (radio show), **Supp. XXIII:** 138

Splendor in the Grass (screenplay, Inge), **Supp. XXV:** 93, 95, 102–103, 104

"Splinters" (Bukiet), **Supp. XVII:** 47

"Split Infinitive" (Pickering), **Supp. XXI:** 204

"Splitting an Order" (Kooser), **Supp. XIX:** 128–129

"Splittings" (Rich), **Supp. I Part 2:** 570–571

"Splitting Wood at Six Above" (Kumin), **Supp. IV Part 2:** 449

Spofford, Harriet Prescott, **Supp. XIII:** 143

Spoils of Poynton, The (James), **I:** 463; **Retro. Supp. I:** 229–230

Spoken Page, The (Nye), **Supp. XIII:** 274

"Spokes" (Auster), **Supp. XII:** 23

Spokesmen (Whipple), **II:** 456

Spook Sonata, The (Strindberg), **III:** 387, 392

Spooky Art, The: A Book about Writing (Mailer), **Retro. Supp. II:** 214

"Spoon, The" (Simic), **Supp. VIII:** 275

Spoon River Anthology (Masters), **I:** 106; **III:** 579; **Supp. I Part 2:** 454, 455, 456, 460–465, 466, 467, 471, 472, 473, 476; **Supp. IX:** 306; **Supp. XIV:** 282–283; **Supp. XIX:** 121; **Supp. XXII:** 282; **Supp. XXVII:** 211, 290

Sport and a Pastime, A (Salter), **Supp. IX:** 254–257; **Supp. XVI:** 237

Sporting Club, The (McGuane), **Supp. VIII:** 43

Sport of the Gods, The (Dunbar), **Supp. II Part 1:** 193, 200, 207, 214–217

Sports Illustrated Training with Weights (Parker and Marsh), **Supp. XIX:** 187

"Sportsman Born and Bred, A" (Plimpton), **Supp. XVI:** 241

Sportsman's Sketches, A (Turgenev), **I:** 106; **IV:** 277

Sportswriter, The (Ford), **Supp. V:** 57, 58, 62–67

"Spotted Horses" (Faulkner), **IV:** 260

Sprague, Morteza, **Retro. Supp. II:** 115

Spratling, William, **II:** 56; **Retro. Supp. I:** 80

Sprawl trilogy (W. Gibson), **Supp. XVI:** 117, 122, 124

"Spray, The" (Lethem), **Supp. XVIII:** 148

"Spray Paint King, The" (Dove), **Supp. IV Part 1:** 252–253

Spreading Fires (Knowles), **Supp. XII:** 249

Sprigge, Elizabeth, **IV:** 31

"Spring" (Kooser), **Supp. XIX:** 126

"Spring" (Millay), **III:** 126

"Spring" (Mora), **Supp. XIII:** 217

"Spring 1967" (Carruth), **Supp. XVI:** 55

Spring and All (W. C. Williams), **Retro. Supp. I:** 412, 418, **418–420,** 427, 430, 431

"Spring and All" (W. C. Williams), **Retro. Supp. I:** 419

Spring Awakening (Wedeking, trans. Franzen), **Supp. XX:** 85

"Spring Break-Up" (Carruth), **Supp. XVI:** 56

"Spring Bulletin" (Allen), **Supp. XV:** 15

Springer's Progress (Markson), **Supp. XVII:** **141–142,** 143, 146

"Spring Evening" (Farrell), **II:** 45

"Spring Evening" (Kenyon), **Supp. VII:** 173

"Springfield Magical" (Lindsay), **Supp. I Part 2:** 379

Spring in New Hampshire and Other Poems (McKay), **Supp. X:** 131, 135

"Spring in the Naugatuck Valley" (Teasdale), **Supp. XXVII:** 294

"Spring Lizards" (Rash), **Supp. XXVII:** 219

"Spring Notes from Robin Hill" (Carruth), **Supp. XVI:** 48

"Spring Pastoral" (Wylie), **Supp. I Part 2:** 707

"Spring Pools" (Frost), **II:** 155; **Retro. Supp. I:** 137

"Spring Snow" (Matthews), **Supp. IX:** 160

"SPRING SONG" (Baraka), **Supp. II Part 1:** 60

Springsteen, Bruce, **Supp. VIII:** 143

"Spring Strains" (W. C. Williams), **Retro. Supp. I:** 416

Spring Tides (Morison), **Supp. I Part 2:** 494

Springtime and Harvest (Sinclair), **Supp. V:** 280

"Springtime for You" (Halliday), **Supp. XIX:** 87

"Spring Torrents" (Teasdale), **Supp. XXVII:** 293

Spruance, Raymond, **Supp. I Part 2:** 479, 491

"Spruce Has No Taproot, The" (Clampitt), **Supp. IX:** 41–42

"Spunk" (Hurston), **Supp. VI:** 150, 151–152

Spunk: The Selected Stories (Hurston), **Supp. VI:** 150

Spurr, David, **Supp. XV:** 183

Spy, The (Cooper), **I:** 335, 336, 337, 339, 340; **Supp. I Part 1:** 155

"Spy, The" (Francis), **Supp. IX:** 81

Spy, The (Freneau), **Supp. II Part 1:** 260

Spyglass Tree, The (Murray), **Supp. XIX:** **155–156**

Spy in the House of Love, A (Nin), **Supp. X:** 186

Squanto, **Supp. I Part 2:** 486

"Square Business" (Baraka), **Supp. II Part 1:** 49

Square Root of Wonderful, The (McCullers), **II:** 587–588

"Squash in Blossom" (Francis), **Supp. IX:** 81

"Squatter on Company Land, The" (Hugo), **Supp. VI:** 133

"Squatter's Children" (Bishop), **Retro. Supp. II:** 47

"Squeak, Memory" (Bukiet), **Supp. XVII:** 47

Squeeze Play (Auster), **Supp. XII:** 21

Squires, Radcliffe, **IV:** 127; **Supp. XV:** 118

Squirrels (Mamet), **Supp. XIV:** 240

S.S. Gliencairn (O'Neill), **III:** 387, 388, 405

S.S. San Pedro (Cozzens), **I:** 360–362, 370, 378, 379

"Ssshh" (Olds), **Supp. X:** 215

"Stacking the Straw" (Clampitt), **Supp. IX:** 41

Stade, George, **Supp. IV Part 1:** 286

Staël, Madame de, **II:** 298

"Staff of Life, The" (H. Miller), **III:** 187

Stafford, Jean, **II:** 537; **Retro. Supp. II:** 177; **Supp. V:** 316

Stafford, William, **Supp. IV Part 1:** 72; **Supp. IV Part 2:** 642; **Supp. IX:** 273; **Supp. XI:** **311–332; Supp. XIII:** 76, 274, 276, 277, 281, 283; **Supp. XIV:** 119, 123; **Supp. XX:** 161; **Supp. XXI:** 246

"Stage All Blood, The" (MacLeish), **III:** 18

"Staggerlee Wonders" (Baldwin), **Retro. Supp. II:** 15

Stained White Radiance, A (Burke), **Supp. XIV:** 28, 31

Stalin, Joseph, **I:** 261, 490; **II:** 39, 40, 49, 564; **III:** 30, 298; **IV:** 372; **Supp. V:** 290; **Supp. XXI:** 164, 165, 167

"Stalking" (J. W. Miller), **Supp. XX:** 167

"Stalking the Billion-Footed Beast: A Literary Manifesto for the New Social Novel" (Wolfe), **Supp. III Part 2:** 586

Stallings, A. E., **Supp. XXIII:** 111, 124; **Supp. XXV:** **221–236**

Stallings, H. A., **Supp. XXII:** 194

Stallman, R. W., **I:** 405

Stamberg, Susan, **Supp. IV Part 1:** 201; **Supp. XII:** 193

Stamford, Anne Marie, **Supp. XII:** 162

Stanard, Mrs. Jane, **III:** 410, 413

Stand, The (King), **Supp. V:** 139, 140–141, 144–146, 148, 152

"Standard of Liberty, The" (Rowson), **Supp. XV:** 243

"Standard of Living, The" (Parker), **Supp. IX:** **198–199**

Stander, Lionel, **Supp. I Part 1:** 289

"Standing and the Waiting, The" (M. F. K. Fisher), **Supp. XVII:** 83

Standing by Words (Berry), **Supp. X:** 22, 27, 28, 31, 32, 33, 35

Standing Fast (Swados), **Supp. XIX:** **268–269**

"Standing Fast: Fox into Hedgehog" (Davison), **Supp. XXVI:** 72

"Standing Halfway Home" (Wagoner), **Supp. IX:** 324

"Standing Humbly Before Nature" (Gerber), **Supp. XXVI:** 187

"Standing In" (Caputo), **Supp. XIX:** 26

Standing Still and Walking in New York (O'Hara), **Supp. XXIII:** 220

Stand in the Mountains, A (Taylor), **Supp. V:** 324

Standish, Burt L. (pseudonym). *See* Patten, Gilbert

Standish, Miles, **I:** 471; **II:** 502–503

Standley, Fred L., **Retro. Supp. II:** 6

Stand Still Like the Hummingbird (H. Miller), **III:** 184

"Stand Up" (Salinas), **Supp. XIII:** 315

Stand with Me Here (Francis), **Supp. IX:** 76

Stanford, Ann, **Retro. Supp. I:** 41; **Supp. I Part 1:** 99, 100, 102, 103, 106, 108, 109, 113, 117; **Supp. IV Part 2:** 637

Stanford, Charles Villiers, **Supp. XX:** **228**

Stanford, Donald E., **II:** 217

Stanford, Frank, **Supp. XV:** 338, 339, 341, 342–343, 343, 345, 348, 350

Stanford, Ginny (Crouch), **Supp. XV:** 339

Stanford, Leland, **I:** 196, 198

Stanislavsky, Konstantin, **Supp. XIV:** 240, 243

Stanley, Jodee, **Supp. XIX:** 52

Stanley, Marion Cummings, **Supp. XXVII:** 288

"Stanley Kunitz" (Oliver), **Supp. VII:** 237

Stansell, Christine, **Supp. XVII:** 106; **Supp. XXI:** 4

Stanton, Frank L., **Supp. II Part 1:** 192

Stanton, Robert J., **Supp. IV Part 2:** 681

"Stanzas, Written in 1815 before going to hear my Father read religious services" (J. Schoolcraft), **Supp. XXIII:** 229

"Stanzas from the Grande Chartreuse" (Arnold), **Supp. I Part 2:** 417

Stanzas in Meditation (Stein), **Supp. III Part 1:** 13

Staples, Hugh, **Retro. Supp. II:** 187

Star, Alexander, **Supp. X:** 310

Starbuck, George, **Retro. Supp. II:** 53, 245; **Supp. I Part 2:** 538; **Supp. IV Part 2:** 440; **Supp. XIII:** 76; **Supp. XXVI:** 68

Star Child (Gunn Allen), **Supp. IV Part 1:** 324

"Star Dust" (Wrigley), **Supp. XVIII:** 296

Stardust Lounge, The (Digges), **Supp. XXIII:** 57

Stardust Memories (film; Allen), **Supp. XV:** 1, 4, **8,** 9, 13

"Stare, The" (Updike), **Retro. Supp. I:** 329

"Starfish, The" (R. Bly), **Supp. IV Part 1:** 72

"Staring at the Sea on the Day of the Death of Another" (Swenson), **Supp. IV Part 2:** 652

Star Is Born, A (film), **Supp. IV Part 1:** 198; **Supp. IX:** 198; **Supp. XVIII:** 242, 243

Stark, David, **Supp. XII:** 202

Stark, Heidi, **Supp. XXIII:** 228, 233

"Stark Boughs on the Family Tree" (Oliver), **Supp. VII:** 232

Starke, Aubrey Harrison, **Supp. I Part 1:** 350, 352, 356, 360, 362, 365, 370, 371

Starkey, David, **Supp. XII:** 180, 181

Star Ledger (Hull), **Supp. XXI:** 129, **136–138**

"Star Ledger" (Hull), **Supp. XXI:** 136

"Starlight" (Levine), **Supp. V:** 188

"Starlight Scope Myopia" (Komunyakaa), **Supp. XIII:** 123, 124

Starlight Wonder Book, The (Beston), **Supp. XXVI:** 33

Starna, William A., **Supp. XXVI:** 85, 86

Starnino, Carmine, **Supp. XVII:** 74

"Star of the Nativity" (Brodsky), **Supp. VIII:** 33

Starr, Ellen Gates, **Supp. I Part 1:** 4, 5, 11

Starr, Jean. *See* Untermeyer, Jean Starr

Starr, Kevin, **Supp. XXIV:** 17, 22

Starr, Ringo, **Supp. XI:** 309

Star Rover, The (London), **II:** 467

"Starry Night, The" (Sexton), **Supp. II Part 2:** 681

"Stars" (Frost), **II:** 153

Stars, the Snow, the Fire, The: Twenty-five Years in the Northern Wilderness (Haines), **Supp. XII: 199–201,** 206, 209

Star Shines over Mt. Morris Park, A (H. Roth), **Supp. IX:** 227, 236, **236–237**

"Stars of the Summer Night" (Longfellow), **II:** 493

"Stars over Harlem" (Hughes), **Retro. Supp. I:** 207

"Star-Spangled" (García), **Supp. XI:** 177, 178

Star-Spangled Girl, The (Simon), **Supp. IV Part 2:** 579

"Star-Splitter, The" (Frost), **Retro. Supp. I:** 123, 133

Stars Principal (McClatchy), **Supp. XII: 256–258**

"Start Again Somewhere" (Gallagher), **Supp. XXIV:** 169

"Star That Would Not Shine, The" (C. L. R. James), **Supp. XXI:** 160

"Starting from Paumanok" (Whitman), **IV:** 333

Starting from Troy (Hadas), **Supp. XXIII:** 113

Starting Out in the Thirties (Kazin), **Supp. VIII: 95–97; Supp. XXIV:** 223

Starting Over (Spencer), **Supp. XXVII:** 13

Star Trek television series, **Supp. XXII:** 60

"Starved Lovers" (MacLeish), **III:** 19

Starved Rock (Masters), **Supp. I Part 2:** 465

"Starving Again" (Moore), **Supp. X:** 163, 172, 175

"Starving"(Strout), **Supp. XXIII:** 283, 285

"Star Watcher, The" (Davison), **Supp. XXVI:** 69

"State, The" (Bourne), **I:** 233

State and Main (Mamet), **Supp. XIV:** 241

"Statement of Principles" (Ransom), **III:** 496

"Statement of Randolph Carter, The" (Lovecraft), **Supp. XXV:** 114, 123

"Statement: Phillipa Allen" (Rukeyser), **Supp. VI:** 283–284

"Statements on Poetics" (Snyder), **Supp. VIII:** 291, 292

"Statement with Rhymes" (Kees), **Supp. XV:** 139

"State of the Art, The" (Elkin), **Supp. VI:** 52

"State of the Arts, The" (Wasserstein), **Supp. XV:** 332

State of the Nation (Dos Passos), **I:** 489

"State of the Union" (Vidal), **Supp. IV Part 2:** 678

State Versus Elinor Norton, The (Rinehart), **Supp. XXV:** 197, 200

Static Element, The: Selected Poems of Natan Zach (Everwine, trans.), **Supp. XV:** 73, 75, **85–88**

"Statue, The" (Berryman), **I:** 173

"Statue and Birds" (Bogan), **Supp. III Part 1:** 50

"Statue of an Unkown Soldier, The" (Kooser), **Supp. XIX:** 124

"Statues, The" (Schwartz), **Supp. II Part 2:** 654, 659

"Status Rerum" (Pound), **Supp. I Part 1:** 257

Stavans, Ilan, **Supp. XI:** 190

"Stave Church" (W. V. Davis), **Supp. XXI:** 93, 94

"Staying Afloat"(Strout), **Supp. XXIII:** 274

"Staying Alive" (Levertov), **Supp. III Part 1:** 281

Staying Alive (Wagoner), **Supp. IX:** 324, **326**

"Staying at Ed's Place" (Swenson), **Supp. IV Part 2:** 648

Staying Put : Making a Home in a Restless World (Sanders), **Supp. XVI:** 274–275

Stay Me, Oh Comfort Me: Journals and Stories, 1933–1941 (M. F. K. Fisher), **Supp. XVII:** 92

Stayton, Richard, **Supp. IX:** 133

Steadman, Goodman, **IV:** 147

Steadman, Ralph, **Supp. XXIV:** 288

"Steak" (Snyder), **Supp. VIII:** 301

Steal Away: Selected and New Poems (Wright), **Supp. XV:** 337, 340, 348, 350–351

Stealing Beauty (Minot), **Supp. VI:** 205

Stealing Buddha's Dinner (Nguyen), **Supp. XXVI:** 208, 209–212, 217, 218, 219–220

Stealing Glimpses (McQuade), **Supp. IX:** 151

Stealing the Language: The Emergence of Women's Poetry in America (Ostriker), **Supp. XV:** 251

"Stealing the Thunder: Future Visions for American Indian Women, Tribes, and Literary Studies" (Gunn Allen), **Supp. IV Part 1:** 331

"Steam Shovel Cut" (Masters), **Supp. I Part 2:** 468

Stearns, Harold, **I:** 245; **Supp. XVII:** 106

Stedman, Edmund Clarence, **Supp. I Part 1:** 372; **Supp. II Part 1:** 192; **Supp. XV:** 115, 269, 273, 274, 282, 286

Steel, Sharon, **Supp. XIX:** 61

Steele, Lloyd, **Supp. XXV:** 96

Steele, Margaret, **Supp. XXI:** 5

Steele, Max, **Supp. XIV:** 82

Steele, Sir Richard, **I:** 378; **II:** 105, 107, 300; **III:** 430

Steele, Timothy, **Supp. XV:** 251; **Supp. XVII:** 112; **Supp. XXIII:** 111

Steele, Wilbur Daniel, **Supp. XXI:** 5

"Steel Mills: South Chicago" (Bodenheim), **Supp. XXV:** 22

Steelwork (Sorrentino), **Supp. XXI:** 227, 230, 231, 232

Steenburgen, Mary, **Supp. IV Part 1:** 236

Steeple Bush (Frost), **II:** 155; **Retro. Supp. I:** 140; **Retro. Supp. II:** 42

"Steeple-Jack, The" (Moore), **III:** 212, 213, 215

"Steerage" (Goldbarth), **Supp. XII:** 187

Steers, Nina, **Retro. Supp. II:** 25

Stefans, Brian Kim, **Supp. XXII:** 226

Steffens, Lincoln, **II:** 577; **III:** 580; **Retro. Supp. I:** 202; **Retro. Supp. II:** 101; **Supp. I Part 1:** 7; **Supp. XVII:** 98, 101, 106–107; **Supp. XXI:** 2, 3, 5, 7, 10; **Supp. XXIII:** 162

Stegner, Page, **IV:** 114, 116; **Supp. IV Part 2:** 599

Stegner, Wallace, **Supp. IV Part 2: 595–618; Supp. V:** 220, 224, 296; **Supp. X:** 23, 24; **Supp. XIV:** 82, 193, 230, 233; **Supp. XVIII:** 192; **Supp. XXII:** 204, 205, 208

"Stegner's Short Fiction" (Ahearn), **Supp. IV Part 2:** 604

Steichen, Edward, **III:** 580, 594–595

Steichen, Lillian. *See* Sandburg, Mrs. Carl (Lillian Steichen)

Steiger, Rod, **Supp. VIII:** 269; **Supp. XI:** 305

Stein, Edith, **Supp. XXII:** 92–93, 167

Stein, Gertrude, **I:** 103, 105, 476; **II:** 56, 251, 252, 257, 260, 262–263, 264, 289; **III:** 71, 454, 471–472, 600; **IV: 24–48,** 368, 375, 404, 415, 443, 477; **Retro. Supp. I:** 108, 170, 176, 177, 186, 418, 422; **Retro. Supp. II:** 85, 207, 326, 331; **Supp. I Part 1:** 292; **Supp. III Part 1:** 13, 37, 225, 226; **Supp. III Part 2:** 626; **Supp. IV Part 1:** 11, 79, 80, 81, 322; **Supp. IV Part 2:** 468; **Supp. IX:** 55, 57, 62, 66; **Supp. V:** 53; **Supp. XII:** 1, 139; **Supp. XIV:** 336; **Supp. XVI:** 187; **Supp.**

XVII: 98, 105, 107; **Supp. XVIII:** 148; **Supp. XXI:** 7, 33; **Supp. XXII:** 158, 159; **Supp. XXIII:** 166, 207; **Supp. XXVII:** 26

Stein, Howard, **Supp. XXIV:** 116

Stein, Jean, **Supp. XVI:** 245

Stein, Karen F., **Supp. XIII:** 29, 30

Stein, Leo, **IV:** 26; **Supp. XIV:** 336; **Supp. XV:** 298

Stein, Lorin, **Supp. XII:** 254; **Supp. XVIII:** 137, 139

Steinbeck, John, **I:** 107, 288, 301, 378, 495, 519; **II:** 272; **III:** 382, 453, 454, 589; **IV: 49–72; Retro. Supp. II:** 19, 196; **Supp. IV Part 1:** 102, 225; **Supp. IV Part 2:** 502; **Supp. IX:** 33, 171; **Supp. V:** 290, 291; **Supp. VIII:** 10; **Supp. XI:** 169; **Supp. XIII:** 1, 17; **Supp. XIV:** 21, 181; **Supp. XIX:** 3; **Supp. XVII:** 228; **Supp. XVIII:** 90, 102, 254

Steinbeck, Olive Hamilton, **IV:** 51

Steinberg, Saul, **Supp. VIII:** 272

Steinberg, Sybil, **Supp. XVII:** 165, 166; **Supp. XXIII:** 241; **Supp. XXVI:** 258

Steinem, Gloria, **Supp. IV Part 1:** 203; **Supp. XXIII:** 104, 105, 106

Steiner, George, **Retro. Supp. I:** 327; **Supp. IV Part 1:** 286; **Supp. XVI:** 230

Steiner, Michael, **Supp. XXII:** 205

Steiner, Nancy, **Supp. I Part 2:** 529

Steiner, Stan, **Supp. IV Part 2:** 505

Steinfels, Margaret, **Supp. XVII:** 170

Steinhoff, Eirik, **Supp. XVI:** 290

Steinman, Michael, **Supp. VIII:** 172

Steinmetz, Charles P., **Supp. XXIII:** 161

Steinmetz, Charles Proteus, **I:** 483

Steinway Quintet Plus Four, The (Epstein), **Supp. XII:** 159, **162–166**

Stekel, Wilhelm, **III:** 554

Stella (Goethe), **Supp. IX:** 133, 138

Stella (Kushner), **Supp. IX:** 133

Stella, Joseph, **I:** 387

"Stellaria" (Francis), **Supp. IX:** 83

Stelligery and Other Essays (Wendell), **Supp. I Part 2:** 414

St. Elmo (Evans), **Supp. XXII:** 120

Stendhal, **I:** 316; **III:** 465, 467; **Supp. I Part 1:** 293; **Supp. I Part 2:** 445

Stepanchev, Stephen, **Supp. XI:** 312

Stephen, Leslie, **IV:** 440

Stephen, Sir Leslie, **IV:** 440; **Supp. I Part 1:** 306

Stephen, Saint, **II:** 539; **IV:** 228

Stephen Crane (Berryman), **I:** 169–170, 405

Stephen King, The Second Decade: "Danse Macabre" to "The Dark Half" (Magistrale), *Supp. V:* 138, 146, 151

Stephen King: The Art of Darkness (Winter), **Supp. V:** 144

Stephens, Jack, **Supp. X:** 11, 14, 15, 17

Stephens, James, **Supp. XIX:** 204

Stephens, Uriah, **Supp. XXIII:** 187

Stephenson, Gregory, **Supp. XII:** 120, 123

Stephenson, Neal, **Supp. XXII:** 49

"Stepping Out" (Dunn), **Supp. XI:** 140, 141

Stepping Outside (Gallagher), **Supp. XXIV:** 165, 167

Steps (Kosinski), **Supp. VII:** 215, 221–222, 225

"Steps" (Nye), **Supp. XIII:** 288

Steps to the Temple (Crashaw), **IV:** 145

"Steps Toward Poverty and Death" (R. Bly), **Supp. IV Part 1:** 60

Stepto, Robert B., **Retro. Supp. II:** 116, 120, 123

Sterile Cuckoo, The (Nichols), **Supp. XIII:** 258, **259–263,** 264

Sterling, Bruce, **Supp. XVI:** 118, 121, 123, 124, 128–129

Sterling, George, **I:** 199, 207, 208, 209; **II:** 440; **Supp. V:** 286; **Supp. XXII:** 276, 277

Sterling, Phillip, **Supp. XXIII:** 102

Stern, Bernhard J., **Supp. XIV:** 202, 213

Stern, Daniel, **Supp. VIII:** 238

Stern, Frederick C., **Supp. X:** 114, 115, 117

Stern, Gerald, **Supp. IX: 285–303; Supp. XI:** 139, 267; **Supp. XV:** 211, 212

Stern, Madeleine B., **Supp. I Part 1:** 35

Stern, Maurice, **IV:** 285

Stern, Philip Van Doren, **Supp. XIII:** 164

Stern, Richard, **Retro. Supp. II:** 291

Stern, Richard G., **Retro. Supp. II:** 204

Stern, Steven, **Supp. XVII:** 42, 48, 49; **Supp. XX:** 178

"Sterne" (Schwartz), **Supp. II Part 2:** 663

Sterne, Laurence, **II:** 302, 304–305, 308; **III:** 454; **IV:** 68, 211, 465; **Supp. I Part 2:** 714; **Supp. IV Part 1:** 299; **Supp. V:** 127; **Supp. X:** 324; **Supp. XV:** 232

Sterritt, David, **Supp. IV Part 2:** 574

Stetson, Caleb, **IV:** 178

Stetson, Charles Walter, **Supp. XI:** 195, 196, 197, 202, 204, 209

Steve Nelson, American Radical (Nelson), **Supp. XVIII:** 226

Stevens, Frances Simpson, **Supp. XXII:** 159, 162

Stevens, Hampton, **Supp. XXVII:** 45

Stevens, James, **Supp. XXIII:** 152

Stevens, Wallace, **I:** 60, 61, 266, 273, 462, 521, 528, 540–541; **II:** 56, 57, 530, 552, 556; **III:** 19, 23, 194, 216, 270–271, 272, 278, 279, 281, 453, 463, 493, 509, 521, 523, 600, 605, 613, 614; **IV: 73–96,** 140, 141, 332, 402, 415; **Retro. Supp. I:** 67, 89, 193, 284, 288, **295–315,** 335, 403, 411, 416, 417, 422; **Retro. Supp. II:** 40, 44, 326; **Supp. I Part 1:** 80, 82, 257; **Supp. II Part 1:** 9, 18; **Supp. III Part 1:** 2, 3, 12, 20, 48, 239, 318, 319, 344; **Supp. III Part 2:** 611; **Supp. IV Part 1:** 72, 393; **Supp. IV Part 2:** 619, 620, 621, 634; **Supp. IX:** 41; **Supp. V:** 337; **Supp. VIII:** 21, 102, 195, 271, 292; **Supp. X:** 58; **Supp. XI:** 123, 191, 312; **Supp. XIII:** 44, 45; **Supp. XIX:** 7, 40, 86, 87; **Supp. XV:** 39, 41, 92, 115, 250, 261, 298, 302, 306, 307; **Supp. XVI:** 64, 158, 202, 210, 288; **Supp. XVII:** 36, 42, 110,

129, 130, 240, 241; **Supp. XXI:** 19, 28, 60, 133; **Supp. XXII:** 162; **Supp. XXIII:** 53, 57, 65; **Supp. XXIV:** 41, 45; **Supp. XXVI:** 67; **Supp. XXVII:** 261

Stevens, Mrs. Wallace (Elsie Kachel), **IV:** 75

"Stevens and the Idea of the Hero" (Bromwich), **Retro. Supp. I:** 305

Stevens and the Interpersonal (Halliday), **Supp. XIX: 85–86**

Stevenson, Adlai, **II:** 49; **III:** 581

Stevenson, Anne, **Supp. XV:** 121; **Supp. XVII:** 74; **Supp. XXVI:** 66

Stevenson, Burton E., **Supp. XIV:** 120

Stevenson, David, **Supp. XI:** 230

Stevenson, Ellen Borden, **Supp. XXV:** 30

Stevenson, Robert Louis, **I:** 2, 53; **II:** 283, 290, 311, 338; **III:** 328; **IV:** 183–184, 186, 187; **Retro. Supp. I:** 224, 228; **Supp. I Part 1:** 49; **Supp. II Part 1:** 404–405; **Supp. IV Part 1:** 298, 314; **Supp. VIII:** 125; **Supp. XIII:** 75; **Supp. XIV:** 40; **Supp. XVII:** 69; **Supp. XXI:** 204

Stevick, Robert D., **III:** 509

Stewart, Dugald, **II:** 8, 9; **Supp. I Part 1:** 151, 159; **Supp. I Part 2:** 422

Stewart, Elinore Pruitt, **Supp. XXVI:** 183

Stewart, George, **Supp. XVIII:** 138

Stewart, Jeffrey C., **Supp. XIV:** 196, 209, 210

Stewart, Randall, **II:** 244; **Supp. XX: 164**

Stewart, Robert E., **Supp. XI:** 216

"St. Francis of Assisi" (Di Piero), **Supp. XIX:** 43

Stickeen (Muir), **Supp. IX:** 182

Sticks and Bones (Rabe), **Supp. XXIV:** 117

"Sticks and Stones" (L. Michaels), **Supp. XVI:** 205

Sticks and Stones (Mumford), **Supp. II Part 2:** 475, 483, 487–488

Sticks & Stones (Matthews), **Supp. IX:** 154, 155, 157, 158

Stieglitz, Alfred, **Retro. Supp. I:** 416; **Retro. Supp. II:** 103; **Supp. VIII:** 98; **Supp. XVII:** 96; **Supp. XX: 74, 75**

"Stigmata" (Oates), **Supp. II Part 2:** 520

Stiles, Ezra, **II:** 108, 122; **IV:** 144, 146, 148; **Supp. XXIV:** 68

Still, James, **Supp. XX: 163; Supp. XXVII:** 217

Still, William Grant, **Retro. Supp. I:** 203

Still Alice (Genova), **Supp. XXIII:** 127

"Stillborn" (Plath), **Supp. I Part 2:** 544

"Still Here" (Hughes), **Retro. Supp. I:** 211

"Still Just Writing" (Tyler), **Supp. IV Part 2:** 658

"Still Life" (Hecht), **Supp. X:** 68

"Still Life" (Malamud), **Supp. I Part 2:** 450

Still Life (Pickering), **Supp. XXI:** 198

"Still Life" (Pickering), **Supp. XXI:** 198

"Still Life" (Sandburg), **III:** 584

"Still Life" (Vaz), **Supp. XXVI:** 261

"Still Life: Moonlight Striking up on a Chess-Board" (A. Lowell), **II:** 528

"Still Life Or" (Creeley), **Supp. IV Part 1:** 141, 150, 158

Still Life with Oysters and Lemon (Doty), **Supp. XI:** 119, 121, **133–134**

Still Life with Woodpecker (Robbins), **Supp. X:** 260, **271–274**, 282

"Still Moment, A" (Welty), **IV:** 265; **Retro. Supp. I:** 347

Stillness (Gardner), **Supp. VI:** 74

"Stillness in the Air" (Dickinson), **Supp. XV:** 261

Stillness of Dancing, The (Bierds), **Supp. XVII:** 27–28

"Still Small Voices, The" (Fante), **Supp. XI:** 164

Still Such (Salter), **Supp. IX:** 246

"Still the Place Where Creation Does Some Work on Itself" (W. V. Davis), **Supp. IV Part 1:** 68

Stimpson, Catharine R., **Supp. IV Part 2:** 686

Stimson, Eleanor Kenyon. *See* Brooks, Mrs. Van Wyck

"Stimulants, Poultices, Goads" (Wright), **Supp. XV:** 349

"Stings" (Plath), **Retro. Supp. II:** 255; **Supp. I Part 2:** 541

"Stirling Street September" (Baraka), **Supp. II Part 1:** 51

Stirner, Max, **II:** 27

"Stirrup-Cup, The" (Lanier), **Supp. I Part 1:** 364

Stitt, Peter, **Supp. IV Part 1:** 68; **Supp. IV Part 2:** 628; **Supp. IX:** 152, 163, 291, 299; **Supp. XI:** 311, 317; **Supp. XIII:** 87; **Supp. XIX:** 121; **Supp. XV:** 98, 99

Stivers, Valerie, **Supp. X:** 311

St. John, David, **Supp. XV:** 73, 253

St. Louis Woman (Bontemps and Cullen), **Supp. XXII:** 6

St. Mark, Tyler, **Supp. XX: 260**

Stock, Noel, **III:** 479

Stockbroker, the Bitter Young Man, and the Beautiful Girl, The (Hayes), **Supp. XXVI:** 143

Stockton, Frank R., **I:** 201

Stoddard, Charles Warren, **I:** 193, 195, 196; **Supp. II Part 1:** 192, 341, 351

Stoddard, Elizabeth, **II:** 275; **Supp. XV: 269–291**

Stoddard, Richard, **Supp. I Part 1:** 372

Stoddard, Richard Henry, **Supp. XV:** 269, 271, 272, 273, 274, 278, 279, 286

Stoddard, Solomon, **I:** 545, 548; **IV:** 145, 148

Stoffman, Judy, **Supp. XVIII:** 97

Stoic, The (Dreiser), **I:** 497, 502, 508, 516; **Retro. Supp. II:** 95, 96, 101, 108

Stoker, Bram, **Supp. XXVI:** 58

Stokes, Geoffrey, **Supp. XV:** 256

Stokes, Olivia Egleston Phelps, **Supp. XVIII:** 261

"Stolen Calf, The" (Dunbar), **Supp. II Part 1:** 196

Stolen Jew, The (Neugeboren), **Supp. XVI:** 222–224, 225

Stolen Legacy of Anne Frank, The: Meyer Levin, Lillian Hellman, and the Staging of the Diary (Melnick), **Supp.**

XXVII: 137–138

Stolen Past, A (Knowles), **Supp. XII:** 249

Stolen Words: Forays into the Origins and Ravages of Plagiarism (Mallon), **Supp. XIX: 134–135**

Stollman, Aryeh Lev, **Supp. XVII:** 49; **Supp. XXIV:** 2, 8, 10–11

Stolmar, Thomas, **Supp. XVIII:** 138

"Stoma" (Barnhardt), **Supp. XXVII:** 12

Stomping the Blues (Murray), **Supp. XIX:** 158–159

"Stone" (Ozick), **Supp. XVII:** 50

Stone, Edward, **III:** 479

Stone, Herbert S., **Supp. XXI:** 2

Stone, I. F., **Supp. XIV:** 3

Stone, Irving, **II:** 463, 466, 467

Stone, Oliver, **Supp. XIV:** 48, 316

Stone, Phil, **II:** 55

Stone, Richard, **Supp. XIV:** 54

Stone, Robert, **Supp. V: 295–312; Supp. X:** 1; **Supp. XIX:** 54

Stone, Rosetta (pseudonym). *See* Geisel, Theodor Seuss (Dr. Seuss)

Stone, Ruth, **Supp. XXVII: 249–265**

Stone, Wilmer, **Supp. I Part 1:** 49

Stone and the Shell, The (Hay), **Supp. XIV:** 122, 123, 127, 130

"Stone Bear, The" (Haines), **Supp. XII:** 206–207, 212

"Stone City" (Proulx), **Supp. VII:** 251–253

Stone Country (Sanders), **Supp. XVI:** 271–272

Stone Diaries, The (Shields), **Supp. VII:** 307, 315, 324–326, 327

"Stone Dreams" (Kingsolver), **Supp. VII:** 203

Stone Harp, The (Haines), **Supp. XII: 204**, 205, 206, 207

Stonemason, The (McCarthy), **Supp. VIII:** 175, 187

"Stones" (Hoffman), **Supp. XVIII:** 86

"Stones" (Kumin), **Supp. IV Part 2:** 447

Stones (lithograph series, O'Hara and Rivers), **Supp. XXIII:** 217

"Stones, The" (Plath), **Supp. I Part 2:** 535, 539

"Stones in My Passway, Hellhounds on My Trail" (Boyle), **Supp. VIII:** 15

Stones of Florence, The (McCarthy), **II:** 562

"Stone Walls" (Sarton), **Supp. VIII:** 259

"Stop" (Wilbur), **Supp. III Part 2:** 556

Stop-Loss (screenplay, Richard), **Supp. XIX:** 222

"Stop Me If You've Heard This One" (Lardner), **II:** 433

Stopover: Tokyo (Marquand), **III:** 53, 57, 61, 70

Stoppard, Tom, **Retro. Supp. I:** 189

Stopping by Home (Huddle), **Supp. XXVI:** 149

"Stopping by Woods" (Frost), **II:** 154

"Stopping by Woods on a Snowy Evening" (Frost), **Retro. Supp. I:** 129, 133, 134, 135, 139

"Stopping the Bullies" (Myers and Carillo), **Supp. XXVII:** 204

Stopping Westward (Richards), **II:** 396

"Stop Player. Joke No. 4" (Gaddis), **Supp. IV Part 1:** 280

Stop-Time (Conroy), **Supp. XVI: 63–71**, 72, 75, 76–77

"Store, The" (E. P. Jones), **Supp. XXII:** 144–145

Store, The (Stribling), **Supp. VIII:** 126; **Supp. XXII:** 195

"*Store* and *Mockingbird:* Two Pulitzer Novels about Alabama" (Going), **Supp. VIII:** 126

Store of a Million Items, The (Cliff), **Supp. XXII:** 67, 74, 75

"Store of a Million Items, The" (Cliff), **Supp. XXII:** 75

Storer, Edward, **Supp. I Part 1:** 261, 262

Stories, Fables and Other Diversions (Nemerov), **III:** 268–269, 285

Stories: Elizabeth Stoddard, **Supp. XV:** 270

"Stories for Sale" (Kolba), **Supp. XVIII:** 257

Stories for the Sixties (Yates, ed.), **Supp. XI:** 343

Stories from Our Living Past (Prose), **Supp. XVI:** 251

Stories from the Italian Poets (Hunt), **Supp. XV:** 175

Stories from the Old Testament Retold (L. P. Smith), **Supp. XIV:** 342

Stories from World Literature, **Supp. IX:** 4

"Stories in the Snow" (Leopold), **Supp. XIV:** 183

Stories into Film (Kittredge and Krauzer), **Supp. XXVI:** 182

Stories of an Imaginary Childhood (Bukiet), **Supp. XVII:** 41–44, 45

Stories of F. Scott Fitzgerald, The (Cowley, ed.), **Retro. Supp. I:** 115

Stories of F. Scott Fitzgerald, The (Fitzgerald), **II:** 94

Stories of Modern America, **Supp. IX:** 4

Stories of Stephen Dixon, The (Dixon), **Supp. XII:** 152

Stories of the American Experience (Kriegel and Lass, eds.), **Supp. XXIV:** 214

Stories of the Spanish Civil War (Hemingway), **II:** 258

Stories Revived (James), **II:** 322

Stories that Could Be True (Stafford), **Supp. XI:** 325–327

Stories Toto Told Me (Rolfe), **Supp. XX: 235**

Storm, The (Buechner), **Supp. XII: 54–57**

"Storm, The" (Chopin), **Retro. Supp. II:** 60, 68; **Supp. I Part 1:** 218, 224

Storm, The (al-'Awásif) (Gibran), **Supp. XX:** 116, 124, 125

"Storm Fear" (Frost), **II:** 153; **Retro. Supp. I:** 127

"Storm Ship, The" (Irving), **II:** 309

"Storm Warnings" (Kingsolver), **Supp. VII:** 207–208

"Stormy Weather" (Ellison), **Supp. II Part 1:** 233

"Story" (Everwine), **Supp. XV:** 89

"Story, A" (Jarrell), **II:** 371

Story, Julian, **Supp. XX: 232**

Story, Richard David, **Supp. IV Part 2:** 575, 588

Story, William Wetmore, **Supp. XX:** 228

"Story about Chicken Soup, A" (Simpson), **Supp. IX:** 272–273

"Story about the Anteater, The" (Benét), **Supp. XI:** 53

"Story About the Body, A" (Hass), **Supp. VI: 107–108**

Story Behind the Story, The (Turchi and Barrett, eds.), **Supp. XXVII:** 1, 12

"Story for Teddy, A" (Swados), **Supp. XIX:** 266–267

Story for Teddy, A—and Others (Swados), **Supp. XIX: 266–268**

"Story Hearer, The" (Paley), **Supp. VI:** 230, 231

"Story Hour" (Hay), **Supp. XIV:** 124

"Story Hour" (Jarman), **Supp. XVII:** 116

Story Hour: A Second Look at Cinderella, Bluebeard, and Company (Hay), **Supp. XIV:** 119, 124, 125, 132, 133

Story of a Country Town, The (Howe), **I:** 106

Story of a Lover, The (Hapgood), **Supp. XVII:** 99, 100, 104; **Supp. XXI:** 3, 5, 7

"Story of America, The: A Tribalography" (Howe), **Supp. XXVI:** 84

Story of a Million Years, The (Huddle), **Supp. XXVI:** 147, 152, 157–158

Story of an American Family, The: Letters of the Hapgood Family, 1648–1917 (Boyce), **Supp. XVII:** 97; **Supp. XXI:** 9, 14

"Story of an Hour, The" (Chopin), **Retro. Supp. II:** 72; **Supp. I Part 1:** 212–213, 216

Story of a Novel, The (Wolfe), **IV:** 456, 458

"Story of a Proverb, The" (Lanier), **Supp. I Part 1:** 365

"Story of a Proverb, The: A Fairy Tale for Grown People" (Lanier), **Supp. I Part 1:** 365

Story of a Story and Other Stories, The: A Novel (Dixon), **Supp. XII:** 155

Story of a Wonder Man, The (Lardner), **II:** 433–434

"Story of a Year, The" (James), **Retro. Supp. I:** 218

Story of George Washington Carver, The (Bontemps), **Supp. XXII:** 13

Story of G.I. Joe, The (film, Wellman), **Supp. XVII:** 61, 62

"Story of Gus, The" (A. Miller), **III:** 147–148

"Story of How a Wall Stands, A" (Ortiz), **Supp. IV Part 2:** 499, 507

Story of Mist, The (Dybek), **Supp. XXIII: 74–75,** 78

"Story of Mist, The"(Dybek), **Supp. XXIII:** 74–75

Story of Mount Desert Island, Maine, The (Morison), **Supp. I Part 2:** 494

Story of My Boyhood and Youth, The (Muir), **Supp. IX:** 172–174, 176

Story of My Father, The: A Memoir (Miller), **Supp. XII:** 301

Story of O, The (Réage), **Supp. XII:** 9, 10

Story of Our Lives, The (Strand), **Supp. IV Part 2:** 620, 628–629, 629

"Story of Poppy Van Buster, The" (Briggs), **Supp. XVIII:** 8

Story of the Negro (Bontemps), **Supp. XXII:** 6, 12–13

Story of the Normans, The, Told Chiefly in Relation to Their Conquest of England (Jewett), **II:** 406

Story of the Telegraph, The (Briggs, and Maverick), **Supp. XVIII:** 4

"Story of Toby, The" (Melville), **III:** 76

"Story of To-day, A" (Davis). See also Margret Howth

"Story of To-day, A" (R. H. Davis), **Supp. XVI:** 88, 89

Story of Utopias, The (Mumford), **Supp. II Part 2:** 475, 483–486, 495

Story of Wine in California, The (M. F. K. Fisher), **Supp. XVII:** 88

Story on Page One, The (Odets), **Supp. II Part 2:** 546

Storyteller (Silko), **Supp. IV Part 2:** 558, 559, 560, 561, **566–570**

"Storyteller" (Silko), **Supp. IV Part 2:** 569

"Storyteller: Grandmother Spider's Web" (Danielson), **Supp. IV Part 2:** 569

"Storyteller's Notebook, A" (Carver), **Supp. III Part 1:** 142–143

Story Teller's Story, A: The Tale of an American Writer's Journey through His Own Imaginative World and through the World of Facts . . . (Anderson), **I:** 98, 101, 114, 117

"Story That Could Be True, A" (Stafford), **Supp. XI:** 326

Stothard, Peter, **Supp. XXV:** 221

"Stout Gentleman, The" (Irving), **II:** 309

Stover at Yale (Johnson), **III:** 321

Stowe, Calvin, **IV:** 445; **Supp. I Part 2:** 587, 588, 590, 596, 597

Stowe, Charles, **Supp. I Part 2:** 581, 582

Stowe, Eliza, **Supp. I Part 2:** 587

Stowe, Harriet Beecher, **II:** 274, 399, 403, 541; **Retro. Supp. I:** 34, 246; **Retro. Supp. II:** 4, 138, 156; **Supp. I Part 1:** 30, 206, 301; **Supp. I Part 2: 579–601; Supp. III Part 1:** 154, 168, 171; **Supp. IX:** 33; **Supp. X:** 223, 246, 249, 250; **Supp. XI:** 193; **Supp. XIII:** 141, 295; **Supp. XV:** 278; **Supp. XVI:** 82, 85

Stowe, Samuel Charles, **Supp. I Part 2:** 587

Stowe, William, **Supp. IV Part 1:** 129

Strachey, Lytton, **I:** 5; **IV:** 436; **Retro. Supp. I:** 59; **Supp. I Part 2:** 485, 494; **Supp. XIV:** 342; **Supp. XVI:** 191

"Stradivari" (Bierds), **Supp. XVII:** 28

Straight Cut (Bell), **Supp. X:** 5, **6–7,** 10

Straight Man (Russo), **Supp. XII: 335–339,** 340

Straits: Poems (Koch), **Supp. XV:** 184

Strand, Mark, **Supp. IV Part 2: 619–636; Supp. IX:** 155; **Supp. V:** 92, 332, 337, 338, 343; **Supp. XI:** 139, 145; **Supp. XII:** 254; **Supp. XIII:** 76; **Supp. XV:** 74; **Supp. XXIV:** 165

Strand, Paul, **Supp. VIII:** 272

Strandberg, Victor, **Supp. V:** 273

Strange, Sharan, **Supp. XXI:** 246

"Strange Beautiful Woman, A" (Nelson), **Supp. XVIII:** 173

Strange Bedfellows (Woods), **Supp. XXI:** 70

Strange Case of Dr. Jekyll and Mr. Hyde, The (Stevenson), **II:** 290

Strange Children, The (Gordon), **II:** 196, 197, 199, 211–213

Strange Commonplace, A (Sorrentino), **Supp. XXI:** 232, 237, 238

Strange Crime in Bermuda, The (Holding), **Supp. XXII: 124–125,** 127, 129

Strange Fire (Bukiet), **Supp. XVII: 46**

"Strange Fruit" (Harjo), **Supp. XII:** 224, 225

"Strange Fruit" (song), **Supp. I Part 1:** 80; **Supp. XVIII:** 228

Strange Interlude (O'Neill), **III:** 391, 397–398; **IV:** 61; **Supp. XXII:** 24

Stranger, The (Camus), **I:** 53, 292; **Supp. VIII:** 11; **Supp. XV:** 352

"Stranger, The" (Rich), **Supp. I Part 2:** 555, 560

"Stranger, The" (Salinger), **III:** 552–553

Strange Relation (Hadas), **Supp. XXIII:** 111, 113, 120, **127**

"Stranger in My Own Life, A: Alienation in American Indian Poetry and Prose" (Gunn Allen), **Supp. IV Part 1:** 322

Stranger in the Kingdom, A (Mosher), **Supp. XXII:** 204, 205, 206, 207, 208, 209, **212–213**

"Stranger in the Village" (Baldwin), **Retro. Supp. II:** 3; **Supp. I Part 1:** 54; **Supp. IV Part 1:** 10

"Stranger in Town" (Hughes), **Supp. I Part 1:** 334

Stranger Music (Cohen), **Supp. XXVII:** 54

"Strangers" (Howe), **Supp. VI:** 120

Strangers: A Book of Poems (Ferry), **Supp. XXIV: 149–150**

Strangers and Wayfarers (Jewett), **Retro. Supp. II:** 138

"Strangers from the Horizon" (Merwin), **Supp. III Part 1:** 356

"Stranger's Gift, The" (Very), **Supp. XXV:** 242

Strangers on a Train (Highsmith), **Supp. IV Part 1:** 132

Strangers on a Train (screenplay, Hecht), **Supp. XXVII:** 93

"Strange Story, A" (Taylor), **Supp. V:** 323

"Strange Story, A" (Wylie), **Supp. I Part 2:** 723

Strange Things (Atwood), **Supp. XIII:** 35

Strange Victory (Teasdale), **Supp. XXVII:** 284, 296–297

"Strato in Plaster" (Merrill), **Supp. III Part 1:** 328

Stratton-Porter, Gene, **Supp. XX:** 211–225

Straub, Peter, **Supp. XXV:** 145

Straus, Ralph, **Supp. XIII:** 168

Straus, Roger, **Supp. VIII:** 82; **Supp. XV:** 59

Strauss, Harold, **Supp. XV:** 137

Strauss, Helen, **Supp. XXIII:** 258

Strauss, Johann, **I:** 66

Strauss, Richard, **IV:** 316

Strauss, Robert, **Supp. XI:** 141, 142

Stravinsky (De Schloezer), **III:** 474

Stravinsky, Igor, **Retro. Supp. I:** 378; **Supp. IV Part 1:** 81; **Supp. XI:** 133; **Supp. XV:** 265

"Stravinsky's Three Pieces 'Grotesques,' for String Quartet" (A. Lowell), **II:** 523

Straw, The (O'Neill), **III:** 390

"Strawberry Milkshake" (Halliday), **Supp. XIX:** 92, 94

"Stray Document, A" (Pound), **II:** 517

"Strays" (Richard), **Supp. XIX:** 210–211, 220

Streaks of the Tulip, The: Selected Criticism (W. J. Smith), **Supp. XIII:** 333, 334, 344, **347–348**

Streamline Your Mind (Mursell), **Supp. I Part 2:** 608

Strecker, Trey, **Supp. XXI:** 238

"Street, Cloud" (Ríos), **Supp. IV Part 2:** 549

Street, The (Petry), **Supp. XVIII:** 286

Streetcar Named Desire, A (T. Williams), **IV:** 382, 383, 385, 386, 387, 389–390, 395, 398; **Supp. IV Part 1:** 359

Street in Bronzeville, A (Brooks), **Retro. Supp. I:** 208; **Supp. III Part 1:** 74–78

"Street Moths" (X. J. Kennedy), **Supp. XV:** 170

"Street Musicians" (Ashbery), **Supp. III Part 1:** 18

"Street of Crocodiles" (Hull), **Supp. XXI:** 130

"Street off Sunset, A" (Jarrell), **II:** 387

Street of Seven Stars, The (Rinehart), **Supp. XXV:** 193

"Streets" (Dixon), **Supp. XII: 145–146**

Streets in Their Own Ink (Dybek), **Supp. XXIII:** 78

Streets in the Moon (MacLeish), **III:** 5, 8–11, 15, 19

Streets of Laredo (McMurtry), **Supp. V:** 230

"Streets of Laredo" (screenplay) (McMurtry and Ossana), **Supp. V:** 226, 230

Streets of Night (Dos Passos), **I:** 478, 479–480, 481, 488

Streitfield, David, **Supp. XIII:** 234; **Supp. XVI:** 63

Strength of Fields, The (Dickey), **Supp. IV Part 1:** 178

"Strength of Fields, The" (Dickey), **Supp. IV Part 1:** 176, 184–185

"Strength of Gideon, The" (Dunbar), **Supp. II Part 1:** 212

Strength of Gideon and Other Stories, The (Dunbar), **Supp. II Part 1:** 211, 212

"Strenuous Artistry" (Zagarell), **Supp. XV:** 281

Strether, Lambert, **II:** 313

"Stretto" (Davison), **Supp. XXVI:** 77

Stribling, T. S., **Supp. VIII:** 126

Strickland, Barbara, **Supp. XIX:** 102

Strickland, Joe (pseudonym). *See* Arnold, George W.

"Strictly Bucolic" (Simic), **Supp. VIII:** 278

Strictly Business (O. Henry), **Supp. II Part 1:** 410

"Strike, The" (Olsen), **Supp. XIII:** 292, 297

Strike at Shane's, The (Skloot), **Supp. XX:** 216

"Strikers" (Untermeyer), **Supp. XV:** 296

Strindberg, August, **I:** 78; **III:** 145, 165, 387, 390, 391, 392, 393; **IV:** 17; **Supp. XVII:** 100; **Supp. XXII:** 23

"String, The" (Dickey), **Supp. IV Part 1:** 179

String Light (Wright), **Supp. XV: 345–346**

"String Quartet, The" (Weigl), **Supp. XIX:** 278

"Strivings of the Negro People" (Du Bois), **Supp. II Part 1:** 167

Stroby, W. C., **Supp. XIV:** 26

Strohbach, Hermann, **Supp. XI:** 242

"Stroke of Good Fortune, A" (O'Connor), **III:** 344; **Retro. Supp. II:** 229, 232

Strom, Stephen, **Supp. XII:** 223

Strong, Anna Louise, **Supp. XVIII:** 238; **Supp. XXIII:** 166

Strong, George Templeton, **IV:** 321

Strong, Josiah, **Supp. XIV:** 64

"Strong Draughts of Their Refreshing Minds" (Dickinson), **Retro. Supp. I:** 46

Stronghold, The (Levin), **Supp. XXVII:** 143, 145–146

Strong Motion (Franzen), **Supp. XX: 85, 88–89, 92, 95**

Strong Opinions (Nabokov), **Retro. Supp. I:** 263, 266, 270, 276

"Strong Room of the House, The" (Bronk), **Supp. XXI:** 32

"Strong Women" (Dorman), **Supp. XI:** 240

Strout, Elizabeth, **Supp. X:** 86; **Supp. XXIII: 273–287**

Structure of Nations and Empires, The (Niebuhr), **III:** 292, 308

"Structure of Rime, The" (Duncan), **Supp. XVI:** 287

Structuring the Void (Klinkowitz), **Supp. XXI:** 233

Struggle, The (film; Griffith), **Supp. XVI:** 191

"Strumpet Song" (Plath), **Retro. Supp. II:** 246; **Supp. I Part 2:** 536

Strunk, William, **Supp. I Part 2:** 652, 662, 670, 671, 672

Strunsky, Anna, **II:** 465

"Strut for Roethke, A" (Berryman), **I:** 188

Strychacz, Thomas F., **Supp. XVI:** 69–70

Stuart, Dabney, **Supp. XVIII:** 79

Stuart, Gilbert, **I:** 16

Stuart, J. E. B., **III:** 56

Stuart, Jesse, **Supp. XX: 162–163, 165**

Stuart, Michael, **Supp. XV:** 140

Stuart Little (White), **Supp. I Part 2:** 655–658

"Stubborn Kisses" (Gallagher), **Supp. XXIV:** 170

Stuckey, W. J., **Supp. XXII:** 191–192

"Student, The" (Moore), **III:** 212, 215

"Student of Clouds" (Collins), **Supp. XXI:** 60

"Student of Salmanaca, The" (Irving), **II:** 309

"Student's Wife, The" (Carver), **Supp. III Part 1:** 141

Studies in American Indian Literature: Critical Essays and Course Designs (Gunn Allen), **Supp. IV Part 1:** 324, 333

Studies in Classic American Literature (Lawrence), **II:** 102; **III:** 33; **IV:** 333; **Retro. Supp. I:** 421

Studies in Short Fiction (Edmonds), **Supp. XXIII:** 291

Studies in Short Fiction (Malin), **Supp. XVI:** 71

Studies in the Psychology of Sex (Ellis), **Supp. XX: 235**

"Studs" (Farrell), **II:** 25, 28, 31

Studs Lonigan: A Trilogy (Farrell), **II:** 25, 26, 27, 31–34, 37, 38, 41–42

"Study in Orange and White" (Collins), **Supp. XXI:** 60

"Study of Images" (Stevens), **IV:** 79

"Study of Lanier's Poems, A" (Kent), **Supp. I Part 1:** 373

Study of Milton's Prosody (Bridges), **II:** 537

"Study of the Negro Problems, The" (Du Bois), **Supp. II Part 1:** 165

Stuewe, Paul, **Supp. IV Part 1:** 68

Stuhlmann, Gunther, **Supp. X:** 182, 184, 185, 187

Stull, William L., **Supp. XXIV:** 177

Stultifera Navis (Brant), **III:** 447

"Stumps" (Davison), **Supp. XXVI:** 72

Sturak, John Thomas, **Supp. XIII:** 162, 163, 165, 168

Sturgeon, Theodore, **Supp. XVIII:** 145

Sturgis, George, **III:** 600

Sturgis, Howard, **IV:** 319; **Retro. Supp. I:** 367, 373

Sturgis, Howard Overing, **Supp. XX: 227–242**

Sturgis, Julian Russell, **Supp. XX: 228, 233, 238**

Sturgis, Susan, **III:** 600

Sturm, Margaret. *See* Millar, Margaret

Stuttaford, Genevieve, **Supp. IX:** 279

Stuyvesant, Peter, **II:** 301

"Style" (Nemerov), **III:** 275

Styles of Radical Will (Sontag), **Supp. III Part 2:** 451, 459, 460–463

"Stylist, The" (Egan), **Supp. XIX:** 51, 52

Styne, Jule, **Supp. XVI:** 193

Styron, William, **III:** 40; **IV:** 4, **97–119,** 216; **Supp. IX:** 208; **Supp. V:** 201; **Supp. X:** 15–16, 250; **Supp. XI:** 229, 231, 343; **Supp. XIV:** 82; **Supp. XVI:** 235–236; **Supp. XXIII:** 107, 109

Suares, J. C., **Supp. IV Part 1:** 234

Suarez, Ernest, **Supp. IV Part 1:** 175; **Supp. V:** 180

Suarez, Ray, **Supp. XXI:** 243

"Sub, The" (Dixon), **Supp. XII:** 146

Subjection of Women, The (Mill), **Supp. XI:** 196, 203

"Subjective Necessity for Social Settlements" (Addams), **Supp. I Part 1:** 4

"Subject of Childhood, A" (Paley), **Supp. VI:** 221; **Supp. XXI:** 118

"Submarginalia" (Howe), **Supp. IV Part 2:** 422

Substance and Shadow (James), **II:** 344

"Subterranean Homesick Blues" (song, Dylan), **Supp. XVIII:** 25

Subterraneans, The (Kerouac), **Supp. III Part 1:** 225, 227–231

"Subtitle" (Kees), **Supp. XV:** 139

Subtreasury of American Humor, A (White and White), **Supp. I Part 2:** 668

"Suburban Culture, Imaginative Wonder: The Fiction of Frederick Barthelme" (Brinkmeyer), **Supp. XI:** 38

Suburban Sketches (Howells), **II:** 274, 277

"Subversive Element, The" (Ryan as Quin), **Supp. XVIII:** 230

"Subverted Flower, The" (Frost), **Retro. Supp. I:** 139

"Subway, The" (Tate), **IV:** 128

"Subway Singer, The" (Clampitt), **Supp. IX:** 45

"Success" (Mora), **Supp. XIII:** 217

Successful Love and Other Stories (Schwartz), **Supp. II Part 2:** 661, 665

Successful Women (Taves), **Supp. XXV:** 198

Succession, The: A Novel of Elizabeth and James (Garrett), **Supp. VII:** 104–107, 108

"Success is counted sweetest" (Dickinson), **Retro. Supp. I:** 30, 31–32, 38; **Supp. XV:** 126

Success Stories (Banks), **Supp. V:** 14–15

"Success Story" (Banks), **Supp. V:** 15

"Such Counsels You Gave to Me" (Jeffers), **Supp. II Part 2:** 433

Such Silence (Milburn), **Supp. XI:** 242

"Such Things Happen Only in Books" (Wilder), **IV:** 365

Such Was the Season (Major), **Supp. XXII: 177–178,** 179, 182

"Sudden Journey" (Gallagher), **Supp. XXIV:** 169

Suddenly, Last Summer (film) (Vidal), **Supp. IV Part 2:** 683

Suddenly Last Summer (T. Williams), **I:** 73; **IV:** 382, 383, 385, 386, 387, 389, 390, 391, 392, 395–396, 397, 398

Suder (Everett), **Supp. XVIII: 54–55**

Sudermann, Hermann, **I:** 66

Sue, Eugène, **Supp. XXIII:** 182

Sugg, Richard P., **Supp. IV Part 1:** 68

"Suggestion from a Friend" (Kenyon), **Supp. VII:** 171

"Suicide" (Barnes), **Supp. III Part 1:** 33

"Suicide off Egg Rock" (Plath), **Supp. I Part 2:** 529, 538

Suicides and Jazzers (Carruth), **Supp. XVI:** 46

"Suicide's Note" (Hughes), **Retro. Supp. I:** 199

"Suitable Surroundings, The" (Bierce), **I:** 203

"Suitcase, The" (Ozick), **Supp. V:** 262, 264

"Suite for Augustus, A" (Dove), **Supp. IV Part 1:** 245

"Suite for Emily" (Hull), **Supp. XXI:** 139–140

"Suite for Lord Timothy Dexter" (Rukeyser), **Supp. VI:** 283, 285

"Suite from the Firebird" (Stravinsky), **Supp. XI:** 133

"Suitor, The" (Kenyon), **Supp. VII:** 164–165

Sukarno, **IV:** 490

Sukenick, Ronald, **Supp. V:** 39, 44, 46; **Supp. XII:** 139

Sula (Morrison), **Supp. III Part 1:** 362, 364, 367, 368, 379; **Supp. VIII:** 219

Sullivan, Andrew, **Supp. IX:** 135

Sullivan, Arthur, **Supp. XX: 228**

Sullivan, Frank, **Supp. IX:** 201

Sullivan, Harry Stack, **I:** 59

Sullivan, Jack, **Supp. X:** 86; **Supp. XII:** 331

Sullivan, Noel, **Retro. Supp. I:** 202; **Supp. I Part 1:** 329, 333

Sullivan, Patrick, **Supp. XXVI:** 158

Sullivan, Richard, **Supp. VIII:** 124

Sullivan, Walter, **Supp. VIII:** 168

"Sullivan County Sketches" (Crane), **I:** 407, 421

"Sumach and Goldenrod: An American Idyll" (Mumford), **Supp. II Part 2:** 475

Suma Genji (Play), **III:** 466

Sumerian Vistas (Ammons), **Supp. VII:** 34, 35

"Summa Lyrica" (Grossman), **Supp. XIX:** 86

"Summer" (Emerson), **II:** 10

Summer (Gioia), **Supp. XV:** 117

"Summer" (R. Lowell), **II:** 554

Summer (Wharton), **IV:** 317; **Retro. Supp. I:** 360, 367, 374, **378–379,** 382; **Supp. XXIII:** 275, 281

Summer, Bob, **Supp. X:** 1, 5, 6, 42

Summer and Smoke (T. Williams), **IV:** 382, 384, 385, 386, 387, 395, 397, 398; **Supp. IV Part 1:** 84

Summer Anniversaries, The (Justice), **Supp. VII:** 115, 117

Summer Blue (Skloot), **Supp. XX: 196, 207–208**

Summer Brave (Inge), **Supp. XXV:** 99

"Summer Commentary, A" (Winters), **Supp. II Part 2:** 808

"Summer Day" (O'Hara), **III:** 369

"Summer Days, The" (Oliver), **Supp. VII:** 239

"Summer Evening" (Boyle), **Supp. XXIV:** 61

"Summer Lake" (Huddle), **Supp. XXVI:** 150

Summer Lake: New and Selected Poems (Huddle), **Supp. XXVI:** 150

"Summer Love Overheated" (Díaz), **Supp. XXIV:** 89

"Summer Matures" (H. Johnson), **Supp. XXVI:** 174

Summer Never Ends (W. Frank), **Supp. XX: 78**

"Summer Night" (Hughes), **Supp. I Part 1:** 325

"Summer Night, A" (Auden), **Supp. II Part 1:** 8

"Summer Night—Broadway" (Untermeyer), **Supp. XV:** 296

"Summer Noon: 1941" (Winters), **Supp. II Part 2:** 811

"Summer of '82" (Merwin), **Supp. III Part 1:** 355–356

Summer on the Lakes in 1843 (Fuller), **Supp. II Part 1:** 279, 295–296

"Summer People" (Hemingway), **II:** 258–259

"Summer People, The" (Jackson), **Supp. IX:** 120

"Summer People, The" (Merrill), **Supp. III Part 1:** 325–326

"Summer Perdu" (Halliday), **Supp. XIX:** 89

"Summer Planning" (Halliday), **Supp. XIX:** 92

"Summer Ramble, A" (Bryant), **Supp. I Part 1:** 162, 164

Summers, Claude J., **Supp. IV Part 2:** 680–681; **Supp. XIV:** 161, 169

Summers, Robert, **Supp. IX:** 289

"Summer School" (Davison), **Supp. XXVI:** 69

"Summer Solstice, New York City" (Olds), **Supp. X:** 207

"Summer's Reading, A" (Malamud), **Supp. I Part 2:** 430–431, 442

"Summer Storm" (Gioia), **Supp. XV:** 127

"Summer Storm" (Simpson), **Supp. IX:** 268

"'Summertime and the Living . . .'" (Hayden), **Supp. II Part 1:** 363, 366

Summertime Island (Caldwell), **I:** 307–308

"Summer Tragedy" (Bontemps), **Supp. XXII:** 9

"Summer: West Side" (Updike), **Retro. Supp. I:** 320

"Summer with Tu Fu, A" (Carruth), **Supp. XVI:** 55, 58

"Summit Beach, 1921" (Dove), **Supp. IV Part 1:** 249

Summoning of Stones, A (Hecht), **Supp. X:** 57, 58, **58–59**

"Summons" (Gansworth), **Supp. XXVI:** 114

"Summons" (Untermeyer), **Supp. XV:** 296

Summons to Memphis, A (Taylor), **Supp. V:** 313, 314, 327

Summons to the Free, A (Benét), **Supp. XI:** 47

Sumner, Charles, **I:** 3, 15; **Supp. I Part 2:** 685, 687

Sumner, John, **Retro. Supp. II:** 95

Sumner, John B., **I:** 511

Sumner, William Graham, **III:** 102, 108; **Supp. I Part 2:** 640

"Sumptuous Destination" (Wilbur), **Supp. III Part 2:** 553

"Sun" (Moore), **III:** 215

"Sun" (Swenson), **Supp. IV Part 2:** 640

"Sun, Sea, and Sand" (Marquand), **III:** 60

Sun Also Rises, The (Hemingway), **I:** 107; **II:** 68, 90, 249, 251–252, 260, 600; **III:** 36; **IV:** 35, 297; **Retro. Supp. I:** 171, **177–180**, 181, 189; **Supp. I Part 2:** 614; **Supp. XIII:** 263; **Supp. XVIII:** 74; **Supp. XXVII:** 87

"Sun and Moon" (Kenyon), **Supp. VII:** 168

"Sun and the Still-born Stars, The" (Southern), **Supp. XI:** 295

Sun at Midnight (Soseki; Merwin and Shigematsu, trans.), **Supp. III Part 1:** 353

"Sun Crosses Heaven from West to East Bringing Samson Back to the Womb, The" (R. Bly), **Supp. IV Part 1:** 73

Sun Dance Land (Hanson), **Supp. XXV:** 280

Sun Dance Opera, The (Zitkala-Ša and Hanson), **Supp. XXV:** 279–280

"Sun Dance Shield" (Momaday), **Supp. IV Part 2:** 491

Sunday, Billy, **II:** 449

"Sunday Afternoon" (Munro), **Supp. XXVII:** 194

"Sunday Afternoons" (Komunyakaa), **Supp. XIII:** 127

Sunday after the War (H. Miller), **III:** 184

"Sunday at Home" (Hawthorne), **II:** 231–232

"Sunday Evening at Middlefork Creek Pentecostal Church" (Rash), **Supp. XXVII:** 219

"Sunday Following Mother's Day. The" (E. P. Jones), **Supp. XXII:** 145

"Sunday Morning" (Stevens), **II:** 552; **III:** 278, 463, 509; **IV:** 92–93; **Retro. Supp. I:** 296, 300, 301, 304, 307, 313; **Supp. XIX:** 40; **Supp. XV:** 120; **Supp. XVI:** 210; **Supp. XVII:** 42; **Supp. XXI:** 28, 133; **Supp. XXIII:** 57

"Sunday Morning Apples" (Crane), **I:** 387

"Sunday Morning Prophecy" (Hughes), **Supp. I Part 1:** 334

"Sunday Morning with the Sensational Nightingales" (Collins), **Supp. XXI:** 60

"Sundays" (B. Kelly), **Supp. XVII:** 124–125

"Sundays" (Salter), **Supp. IX:** 257

"Sundays, They Sleep Late" (Rukeyser), **Supp. VI:** 278

"Sundays of Satin-Legs Smith, The" (Brooks), **Supp. III Part 1:** 74, 75

"Sundays Visiting" (Ríos), **Supp. IV Part 2:** 541

Sundial, The (Jackson), **Supp. IX:** 126–127

Sundog (Harrison), **Supp. VIII: 46–48**

Sun Dogs (R. O. Butler), **Supp. XII: 64–65**

Sun Do Move, The (Hughes), **Supp. I Part 1:** 339

Sundquist, Eric, **Supp. XIV:** 66, 71

"Sunfish" (C. Frost), **Supp. XV:** 100–101, 102

"Sunflower Sutra" (Ginsberg), **Supp. II Part 1:** 317, 321; **Supp. XV:** 215

Sung Sex (Elmslie), **Supp. XXVII:** 20

Sunlight Dialogues, The (Gardner), **Supp. VI:** 63, **68,** 69, 70

"Sunlight Is Imagination" (Wilbur), **Supp. III Part 2:** 549

"Sunny Ridge, The" (Halliday), **Supp. XIX:** 92

Sun Out: Selected Poems, 1952–1954 (Koch), **Supp. XV:** 179

"Sunrise" (Lanier), **Supp. I Part 1:** 370

"Sunrise and the Bomb" (Halliday), **Supp. XIX:** 84, 85, 92

Sunrise over Fallujah (Myers), **Supp. XXVII:** 207

"Sunrise runs for Both, The" (Dickinson), **Retro. Supp. I:** 45

Sunrise with Seamonsters: Travels and Discoveries, 1964–1984 (Theroux), **Supp. VIII:** 311, 313, 323, 325

"Sun Rising" (Donne), **Supp. VIII:** 164

"Sunset" (Ransom), **III:** 484

"Sunset from Omaha Hotel Window" (Sandburg), **III:** 584

Sunset Gun (Parker), **Supp. IX:** 192

Sunset Limited (Burke), **Supp. XIV:** 32, 33

Sunset Limited (Harrison), **Supp. VIII:** 51

"Sunset Maker, The" (Justice), **Supp. VII:** 123

Sunset Maker, The: Poems, Stories, a Memoir (Justice), **Supp. VII:** 116, 118, 119, 123–124

Sunshine Boys, The (film), **Supp. IV Part 2:** 589

Sunshine Boys, The (Simon), **Supp. IV Part 2:** 575, 584–585

"Sunthin' in the Pastoral Line" (J. R. Lowell), **Supp. I Part 2:** 415–416

Sun to Sun (Hurston), **Supp. VI:** 154

Sun Tracks (Ortiz), **Supp. IV Part 2:** 499, 500

Sun Under Wood (Hass), **Supp. VI:** 103, 108–109

"Superb Lily, The" (Pinsky), **Supp. VI:** 250

"Super Goat Man" (Lethem), **Supp. XVIII:** 148

"Superman Comes to the Supermarket" (Mailer), **Retro. Supp. II:** 204

"Supermarket in California, A" (Ginsberg), **Supp. XI:** 135

"Supernatural Horror in Literature" (Lovecraft), **Supp. XXV:** 120

"Supernatural Love" (Schnackenberg), **Supp. XV:** 257, 259–260

Supernatural Love: Poems 1976–1992 (Schnackenberg), **Supp. XV:** 253, 256, 260, 263

Suplee, Curt, **Supp. XVI:** 202

"Supper After the Last, The" (Kinnell), **Supp. III Part 1:** 239

"Supposedly Fun Thing I'll Never Do Again, A" (Wallace), **Supp. X:** 315

Supposedly Fun Thing I'll Never Do Again, A: Essays and Arguments (Wallace), **Supp. X: 314–316**

Suppressed Desires (Glaspell and Cook), **Supp. III Part 1:** 178; **Supp. XXI:** 6

Suppression of the African Slave Trade to the United States of America, 1638–1870 (Du Bois), **Supp. II Part 1:** 157, 162

Supreme Fiction, The (Stevens), **Supp. XVI:** 158

"Supremes, The" (Jarman), **Supp. XVII:** 115

Sure Hand of God, The (Caldwell), **I:** 297, 302

Sure Signs: New and Selected Poems (Kooser), **Supp. XIX:** 116, 117, **121–122**

"Surety and Fidelity Claims" (Stevens), **Retro. Supp. I:** 296, 309

Surface of Earth, The (Price), **Supp. VI:** 261–262

"Surfaces" (Ammons), **Supp. VII:** 36

Surfaces and Masks (Major), **Supp. XXII:** 180

Surfacing (Atwood), **Supp. XIII:** 20, 21, **22–23,** 24, 33, 35

"Surgeon at 2 A.M." (Plath), **Supp. I Part 2:** 545

Summer Knowledge (Schwartz), **Supp. II Part 2:** 662, 665

"Surprise" (Kenyon), **Supp. VII:** 173

Surprised by Sin: The Reader in Paradise Lost (Fish), **Supp. XIV:** 15

Surreal South (eds. P. Benedict and L. Benedict), **Supp. XXIII:** 35

"Surround, The Imagining Herself as the Environment,/She Speaks to James Wright at Sundow" (Dickey), **Supp. IV Part 1:** 185

"Surrounded by Weasels" (Gray and Gallagher), **Supp. XXIV:** 178

"Survey of Literature" (Ransom), **III:** 480

"Survey of the Literature, A" (Saunders), **Supp. XIX:** 235

"Surveyor, The" (H. Roth), **Supp. IX:** 233, 234

Survival (Atwood), **Supp. XIII:** 20, 22, 35

"Survival, Infantry" (Oppen), **Supp. XXVI:** 232

"Survival as Tao, Beginning at 5:00 A.M." (Carruth), **Supp. XVI:** 56

Survival of the Bark Canoe, The (McPhee), **Supp. III Part 1:** 301, 302, 308, 313

Survival This Way: Interviews with American Indian Poets (Bruchac), **Supp. IV Part 2:** 506

"Surviving Love" (Berryman), **I:** 173

Survivor (O. Butler), **Supp. XIII:** 62, 63

Susan and Anna Warner (Foster), **Supp. XVIII:** 265

Susan and God (film; Cukor), **Supp. XVI:** 192

Susanna Moodie: Voice and Vision (Shields), **Supp. VII:** 313

Susan Warner ("Elizabeth Wetherell") (A. Warner), **Supp. XVIII:** 259, 260

Suspect in Poetry, The (Dickey), **Supp. IV Part 1:** 177

"Sustained by Fiction" (Hoffman), **Supp. X:** 90, 92

"Susto" (Ríos), **Supp. IV Part 2:** 553

Sutherland, Donald, **IV:** 38, 44; **Supp. IX:** 254

Sutherland, Efua, **Supp. IV Part 1:** 9, 16

Sutherland, Zena, **Supp. XXVII:** 202

Sutherland-Smith, James, **Supp. X:** 211, 212

Sut Lovingood (Harris), **II:** 70; **Supp. XXII:** 193

Sutton, Roger, **Supp. X:** 266; **Supp. XXVII:** 212

Sutton, Walter, **III:** 479

"Sutton Pie Safe, The"(P. Benedict), **Supp. XXIII:** 36

Suttree (McCarthy), **Supp. VIII:** 178–180, 189

Suvero, Mark di, **Supp. IX:** 251

"Suzanne" (Cohen), **Supp. XXVII:** 51, 54, 59

Svevo, Italo, **Supp. XIV:** 112

Swados, Harvey, **Supp. XI:** 222; **Supp. XIX: 255–271**

Swales, Martin, **Supp. XIX:** 183

Swallow, Alan, **Supp. X:** 112, 115, 116, 120, 123

Swallow Barn (J. P. Kennedy), **II:** 313

Swallow Barn (Kennedy), **Supp. XXII:** 193

Swallow the Lake (Major), **Supp. XXII:** 174

"Swamp Boy" (Bass), **Supp. XVI:** 20

Swan, Barbara, **Supp. IV Part 2:** 447

Swan, Jon, **Supp. IV Part 1:** 176

Swan Lake (Helprin), **Supp. XXV:** 83, 87

Swan Lake (Tchaikovsky), **Supp. IX:** 51

Swan Lake Trilogy (Helprin), **Supp. XXV:** 81, 84, 87

"Swan Legs" (Stern), **Supp. IX:** 299

Swann (Shields), **Supp. VII:** 315, 318–323, 326

Swann, Brian, **Supp. IV Part 2:** 500

Swanson, Gloria, **II:** 429

Swanson, Stevenson, **Supp. XIV:** 111

Swan Song (Hecht and MacArthur), **Supp. XXVII:** 90

Swanton, John Reed, **Supp. VIII:** 295

Swan Watch (Schulberg), **Supp. XVIII:** 254

Swanwick, John, **Supp. XV:** 237

Swanwick, Michael, **Supp. XVI:** 128

"Swarm, The" (Plath), **Retro. Supp. II:** 255

"Sway" (Simpson), **Supp. IX:** 276

Sweat (Hurston), **Supp. VI:** 152

Swedenborg, Emanuel, **II:** 5, 10, 321, 342, 343–344, 396

Sweeney Agonistes (Eliot), **I:** 580; **Retro. Supp. I:** 64, 65; **Retro. Supp. II:** 247

"Sweeney Among the Nightingales" (Eliot), **III:** 4

"Sweeper, The" (Kooser), **Supp. XIX:** 125

Sweet, Blanche, **Supp. I Part 2:** 391

Sweet, Timothy, **Supp. IV Part 1:** 330

Sweet and Lowdown (film; Allen), **Supp. XV:** 11

Sweet and Sour (O'Hara), **III:** 361

"Sweet Armageddon" (Hoffman), **Supp. XVIII:** 85, 86

Sweet Bird of Youth (T. Williams), **IV:** 382, 383, 385, 386, 387, 388, 389, 390, 391, 392, 395, 396, 398; **Supp. IV Part 1:** 84, 89

Sweet Charity (musical), **Supp. IV Part 2:** 575

Sweet Flypaper of Life, The (Hughes), **Supp. I Part 1:** 335–336

"Sweetgrass"(Kenny), **Supp. XXIII:** 148

"Sweetheart" (Notley), **Supp. XXII:** 231

"Sweetheart of the Song Tra Bong, The" (O'Brien), **Supp. V:** 243, 249

"Sweethearts" (Ford), **Supp. V:** 69

Sweet Hereafter, The (Banks), **Supp. V:** 15–16

Sweet Illusions (Myers), **Supp. XXVII:** 208–209

Sweet Lorain (Weigl), **Supp. XIX:** 282

Sweet Machine (Doty), **Supp. XI:** 121, **131–132,** 135

Sweet Science, The (Liebling), **Supp. XXVII:** 46–47

Sweet Sue (Gurney), **Supp. V:** 105, 107–108

Sweet Sweetback's Baadasss Song (Peebles; film), **Supp. XI:** 17

Sweet Thursday (Steinbeck), **IV:** 50, 52, 64–65

Sweet Will (Levine), **Supp. V:** 178, 187, 189, 190

"Sweet Will" (Levine), **Supp. V:** 190

"Sweet Willy"(J. Schoolcraft), **Supp. XXIII:** 226, 231

"Sweet Words on Race" (Hughes), **Retro. Supp. I:** 211

Sweezy, Paul, **Supp. I Part 2:** 645

"Swell-Looking Girl, A" (Caldwell), **I:** 310

Swenson, May, **Retro. Supp. II:** 44; **Supp. IV Part 2: 637–655; Supp. XIX:** 123; **Supp. XXVI:** 66, 67

Swetman, Glenn R., **Supp. XXI:** 91

"Swift" (Schwartz), **Supp. II Part 2:** 663

Swift, Jonathan, **I:** 125, 194, 209, 441; **II:** 110, 302, 304–305, 577; **III:** 113; **IV:** 68; **Retro. Supp. I:** 66; **Supp. I Part 2:** 406, 523, 603, 656, 665, 708, 714; **Supp. IV Part 1:** 51; **Supp. IV Part 2:** 692; **Supp. XI:** 105, 209; **Supp. XII:** 276; **Supp. XV:** 258; **Supp. XVI:** 110; **Supp. XVIII:** 2, 12; **Supp. XXV:** 87

"Swimmer" (Francis), **Supp. IX:** 82

"Swimmer" (Skloot), **Supp. XX: 199, 200**

"Swimmer, The" (Cheever), **Supp. I Part 1:** 185, 187

"Swimmer, The" (Glück), **Supp. V:** 82

"Swimmers" (Untermeyer), **Supp. XV:** 300

"Swimmers, The" (Fitzgerald), **Retro. Supp. I:** 110, 111

"Swimmers, The" (Tate), **IV:** 136

"Swimming" (Harjo), **Supp. XII:** 218

Swimming Pool, The (Rinehart), **Supp. XXV:** 189, 198, 200, 202

"Swimming Pool, The"(Strout), **Supp. XXIII:** 284

"Swim Team, The" (July), **Supp. XXIV:** 201

Swinburne, Algernon C., **I:** 50, 384, 568; **II:** 3, 4, 129, 400, 524; **IV:** 135; **Retro. Supp. I:** 100; **Supp. I Part 1:** 79; **Supp. I Part 2:** 422, 552; **Supp. XIV:** 120, 344

"Swinburne as Poet" (Eliot), **I:** 576

Swinger of Birches, A: A Portrait of Robert Frost (Cox), **Retro. Supp. I:** 132

"Swinging an Arc Before Him As He Goes" (Espaillat), **Supp. XXI:** 108

"Swinging on a Birch-Tree" (Larcom), **Supp. XIII:** 147

Swiss, Tom, **Supp. XIX:** 40

Switch, The (Dixon), **Supp. XII:** 141

Swope, D. B., **Supp. IX:** 95

Sword Blades and Poppy Seed (A. Lowell), **II:** 518, 520, 522, 532

Sword of God, The: Jeanne D'Arc (Endore), **Supp. XVII:** 55

Sybil (Auchincloss), **Supp. IV Part 1:** 25

Sybil and Chryssa (S. and A. Warner), **Supp. XVIII:** 264

"Sycamore" (Stern), **Supp. IX:** 294

"Sycamore, The" (Moore), **III:** 216

"Sycamores, The" (Whittier), **Supp. I Part 2:** 699

Sylvester, Johnny, **Supp. I Part 2:** 438

Sylvester, Joshua, **I:** 178, 179; **II:** 18; **III:** 157; **Supp. I Part 1:** 98, 104, 114, 116

Sylvia (Gurney), **Supp. V:** 105

"Sylvia" (L. Michaels), **Supp. XVI:** 202, 213

"Sylvia" (Larcom), **Supp. XIII:** 144

"Sylvia" (Stern), **Supp. IX:** 297

Sylvia: A Fictional Memoir (L. Michaels), **Supp. XVI:** 202, 213

Sylvia Plath: Method and Madness (Butscher), **Supp. I Part 2:** 526

Sylvia Plath: Poetry and Existence (Holbrook), **Supp. I Part 2:** 526–527

"Sylvia's Death" (Sexton), **Supp. II Part 2:** 671, 684, 685

"Symbol and Image in the Shorter Poems of Herman Melville" (Dickey), **Supp. IV Part 1:** 176

Symbolist Movement in Literature, The (Symons), **I:** 50, 569; **Retro. Supp. I:** 55

Symonds, John Addington, **I:** 241, 242, 251, 259; **IV:** 334; **Supp. XIV:** 329, 335; **Supp. XX:** 230

Symons, Arthur, **I:** 50, 569; **Retro. Supp. I:** 55; **Supp. XX: 239; Supp. XXVII:** 287

Symons, Julian, **Supp. IV Part 1:** 343, 351

"Sympathy" (Dunbar), **Supp. IV Part 1:** 15

Sympathy of Souls, A (Goldbarth), **Supp. XII:** 175, 176, **186–187**

"Symphony, The" (Lanier), **Supp. I Part 1:** 352, 360–361, 364; **Supp. I Part 2:** 416

Symposium (Plato), **Retro. Supp. II:** 31; **Supp. IV Part 1:** 391

Symposium: To Kill a Mockingbird (Alabama Law Review), **Supp. VIII:** 127, 128

Symptoms and Madness (Major), **Supp. XXII:** 174

Symptoms of Being 35 (Lardner), **II:** 434

Synanon (Endore), **Supp. XVII:** 65

Synanon (film, Quine), **Supp. XVII:** 65

Synanon City (Endore), **Supp. XVII:** 65

Syncopated Cakewalk, The (Major), **Supp. XXII:** 174

Synge, John Millington, **I:** 434; **III:** 591–592; **Supp. III Part 1:** 34; **Supp. VIII:** 155

Synthetic Philosophy (Spencer), **II:** 462–463

"Syringa" (Ashbery), **Supp. III Part 1:** 19–21, 25

"Syrinx" (Clampitt), **Supp. IX:** 53

"Syrinx" (Merrill), **Supp. III Part 1:** 328

Syrkin, Marie, **Supp. XIV:** 279, 288, 291; **Supp. XXVII:** 133–134

"System, The" (Ashbery), **Supp. III Part 1:** 14, 15, 18, 21–22

System of Dante's Hell, The (Baraka), **Supp. II Part 1:** 39–41, 55

"System of Dante's Inferno, The" (Baraka), **Supp. II Part 1:** 40

"System of Doctor Tarr and Professor Fether, The" (Poe), **III:** 419, 425

System of General Geography, A (Brown), **Supp. I Part 1:** 146

Szaylay, Michael, **Supp. XXI:** 267

Sze, Mai-mai, **Supp. X:** 291

Szentgyorgyi, Tom, **Supp. IX:** 135, 136, 140, 141–142

Szilagyi, Anca, **Supp. XXVI:** 218

Szukalski, Stanislaus, **Supp. XXV:** 19, 23

Szulc, Tad, **Supp. XVI:** 154

Szumskyj, Benjamin, **Supp. XXVII:** 128

Szwarc, Marek, **Supp. XXVII:** 140

Szymborka, Wislawa, **Supp. XI:** 267

Szymborska, Wislawa, **Supp. XVIII:** 29

T

"T-2 Tanker Blues" (Snyder), **Supp. VIII:** 294

Tabios, Eileen, **Supp. XV:** 214, 225, 226

"Table of Delectable Contents, The" (Simic), **Supp. VIII:** 276

Tabloid Dreams (R. O. Butler), **Supp. XII:** 70–72, 74

Tacey Cromwell (Richter), **Supp. XVIII:** 211, 215, 217

Tacitus, Cornelius, **I:** 485; **II:** 113

Tadic, Novica, **Supp. VIII:** 272

Taft (Patchett), **Supp. XII:** 307, 312, 314–317

"Tag" (Hughes), **Supp. I Part 1:** 341

Taggard, Genevieve, **IV:** 436; **Supp. XXII: 271–287; Supp. XXVI:** 144

Taggart, John, **Supp. IV Part 2:** 421

Tagore, Rabindranath, **I:** 383; **Supp. XX:** 117

"Taibele and Her Demon" (Singer), **Retro. Supp. II:** 307

Taibl, Erika, **Supp. XV:** 255

"Tailor Shop, The" (H. Miller), **III:** 175

"Tails" (Dixon), **Supp. XII:** 154

Taine, Hippolyte, **I:** 503; **II:** 271; **III:** 323; **IV:** 440, 444

"Tain't So" (Hughes), **Supp. I Part 1:** 330

"Taipei Tangle" (Halliday), **Supp. XIX:** 91

Takasago (play), **III:** 466

Takazauckas, Albert, **Supp. XXIII:** 203

Take Away the Darkness (Bynner), **Supp. XV:** 51

Take Heart (Peacock), **Supp. XIX: 197–199,** 206

Take Me Back: A Novel (Bausch), **Supp. VII:** 41, 43–45, 46, 49

"Take My Saddle from the Wall: A Valediction" (McMurtry), **Supp. V:** 219

"'Take No for an Answer'" (Didion), **Supp. IV Part 1:** 203

"Take Pity" (Malamud), **Supp. I Part 2:** 427, 428, 435, 436, 437

"Takers, The" (Olds), **Supp. X:** 205

"Take the I Out" (Olds), **Supp. X:** 213

Take the Money and Run (film; Allen), **Supp. XV: 3–4,** 6

"Taking a Stitch in a Dead Man's Arm" (Vaz), **Supp. XXVI:** 264

"Taking Away the Name of a Nephew" (Ríos), **Supp. IV Part 2:** 545–546

Taking Care of Mrs. Carroll (Monette), **Supp. X:** 153

Taking Care: Thoughts on Storytelling and Belief (Kittredge), **Supp. XXVI:** 181, 182, 183, 185

"Taking of Captain Ball, The" (Jewett), **Retro. Supp. II:** 134

"Taking Off Emily Dickinson's Clothes" (Collins), **Supp. XXI:** 59, 60

"Taking Out the Lawn Chairs" (Karr), **Supp. XI:** 241

"Taking the Bypass" (J. Epstein), **Supp. XIV:** 110; **Supp. XVI:** 230

"Taking the Forest" (Howe), **Supp. IV Part 2:** 433

"Taking the Lambs to Market" (Kumin), **Supp. IV Part 2:** 455

Talbot, Daniel, **Supp. XIX:** 264

"Tale, A" (Bogan), **Supp. III Part 1:** 50, 51

Taleb-Khyar, Mohamed, **Supp. IV Part 1:** 242, 243, 244, 247, 257

Talented Mr. Ripley, The (Highsmith), **Supp. XXII:** 119

"Tale of Jerusalem, A" (Poe), **III:** 411

Tale of Possessors Self-Dispossessed, A (O'Neill), **III:** 404

Tale of the Body Thief, The (Rice), **Supp. VII:** 290, 293–294, 297

Tale of Two Cities, A (film), **Supp. I Part 1:** 67

"Tale of Two Liars, A" (Singer), **IV:** 12

Tales (Baraka), **Supp. II Part 1:** 39, 55

Tales (Poe), **III:** 413

Tales and Stories for Black Folks (Bambara, ed.), **Supp. XI:** 1

Tales before Midnight (Benét), **Supp. XI:** 46, 53, 57

Talese, Gay, **Supp. XVI:** 273; **Supp. XVII: 199–211; Supp. XXIV:** 282

Tales of a Traveller (Irving), **II:** 309–310

Tales of a Wayside Inn (Longfellow), **II:** 489, 490, 501, 502, 504–505; **Retro. Supp. II:** 154, **162–165**

Tales of Glauber-Spa (Bryant, ed.), **Supp. I Part 1:** 157

Tales of H. P. Lovecraft (Oates, ed.), **Supp. XXV:** 123

Tales of Manhattan (Auchincloss), **Supp. IV Part 1:** 23

Tales of Men and Ghosts (Wharton), **IV:** 315; **Retro. Supp. I:** 372

Tales of My People (Asch), **Supp. XXIII:** 7

Tales of Rhoda, The (Rice), **Supp. VII:** 288

Tales of Soldiers and Civilians (Bierce), **I:** 200–203, 204, 206, 208, 212

Tales of the Argonauts (Harte), **Supp. II Part 1:** 337, 348, 351

Tales of the Fish Patrol (London), **II:** 465

Tales of the Grotesque and Arabesque (Poe), **II:** 273; **III:** 412, 415; **Retro. Supp. II:** 270

Tales of the Jazz Age (Fitzgerald), **II:** 88; **Retro. Supp. I:** 105; **Supp. IX:** 57

Tales You Won't Believe (Stratton-Porter), **Supp. XX:** 217

Taliaferro, Frances, **Supp. XXII:** 210

"Talisman, A" (Moore), **III:** 195–196

Talisman, The (King), **Supp. V:** 140, 144, 152

"Talkin Bout Sonny" (Bambara), **Supp. XI:** 6–7

"Talking" (Merwin), **Supp. III Part 1:** 354

Talking All Morning (R. Bly), **Supp. IV Part 1:** 59, 60, 61, 62, 64, 65

Talking Dirty to the Gods (Komunyakaa), **Supp. XIII: 130–131**

Talking History (television program), **Supp. XXI:** 172

"Talking Horse" (Malamud), **Supp. I Part 2:** 435

Talking Soft Dutch (McCarriston), **Supp. XIV: 260–263,** 266, 270, 271

"Talking to Barr Creek" (Wagoner), **Supp. IX:** 328

"Talking to Sheep" (Sexton), **Supp. II Part 2:** 695

Talking to the Sun: An Illustrated Anthology of Poems for Young People (Koch and Farrell, eds.), **Supp. XV:** 188

"Talking Water" (Taggard), **Supp. XXII:** 276

"Talk of Heroes" (C. Bly), **Supp. XVI:** 34

"Talk of the Town" (*The New Yorker* column), **IV:** 215; **Supp. IV Part 1:** 53, 54

"Talk on Guadalcanal" (Wolfert), **Supp. XXI:** 264

Talk Talk (Boyle), **Supp. XX:** 24

"Talk with the Yellow Kid, A" (Bellow), **I:** 151

Tallent, Elizabeth, **Supp. IV Part 2:** 570

Tallman, Warren, **Supp. IV Part 1:** 154

TallMountain, Mary, **Supp. IV Part 1:** 324–325

Talma, Louise, **IV:** 357

Talmadge, Constance, **Supp. XVI:** 186, 187, 196

Talmadge, Norma, **Supp. XVI:** 186, 187, 196

Talmadge Girls, The (Loos), **Supp. XVI:** 186, 196

Talmey, Allene, **Supp. IV Part 1:** 197; **Supp. XIII:** 172

Talmud, **IV:** 8, 17

Taltos: Lives of the Mayfair Witches (Rice), **Supp. VII:** 299–300

"Tamar" (Jeffers), **Supp. II Part 2:** 427–428, 436

Tamar and Other Poems (Jeffers), **Supp. II Part 2:** 416, 419

"Tambourine Life" (Berrigan), **Supp. XXIV:** 42

Tambourines to Glory (Hughes), **Supp. I Part 1:** 338–339

"Tame Indians" (Jewett), **Retro. Supp. II:** 141

"Tamerlane" (Poe), **III:** 426

Tamerlane and Other Poems (Poe), **III:** 410

"Tammany Man, The" (Hapgood), **Supp. XVII:** 103

"Tam O'Shanter" (Burns), **II:** 306

Tamsen Donner: A Woman's Journey (Whitman), **Supp. XXI:** 246

Tan, Amy, **Supp. X: 289–300**

Tangential Views (Bierce), **I:** 209

"Tangier 1975" (Bowles), **Supp. IV Part 1:** 94

Tanguay, Pablo, **Supp. XXIII:** 299

"Tankas" (McClatchy), **Supp. XII:** 266

Tanner, Laura E., **Supp. X:** 209; **Supp. XXI:** 217

Tanner, Obour, **Supp. XX: 281, 288**

Tanner, Tony, **I:** 260, 261; **Retro. Supp. II:** 205; **Supp. IV Part 1:** 285; **Supp. XVI:** 65, 69

Tannhäuser (Wagner), **I:** 315

"Tan Ta Ra, Cries Mars...," (Wagoner), **Supp. IX:** 325

Tao of Physics, The (Capra), **Supp. X:** 261

Tao Teh Ching (Bynner, trans.), **Supp. XV:** 46, 47

Tapahonso, Luci, **Supp. IV Part 1:** 404; **Supp. IV Part 2:** 499, 508

Tape for the Turn of the Year (Ammons), **Supp. VII:** 31–33, 35

"Tapestry" (Ashbery), **Supp. III Part 1:** 22–23

"Tapestry" (E. P. Jones), **Supp. XXII:** 152

Tapestry Room Murder, The (Wells), **Supp. XXVI:** 282

"Tapiama" (Bowles), **Supp. IV Part 1:** 89–90

"Tapiola" (W. C. Williams), **Retro. Supp. I:** 429

Tappan, Arthur, **Supp. I Part 2:** 588

Tapping the White Cane of Solitude (F. Wright), **Supp. XVII:** 243

Taps at Reveille (Fitzgerald), **II:** 94, 96; **Retro. Supp. I:** 113

Taradash, Daniel, **Supp. XXV:** 95

Tar: A Midwest Childhood (Anderson), **I:** 98, 115; **II:** 27

Tarantino, Quentin, **Supp. IV Part 1:** 356

Tarantula (Dylan), **Supp. XVIII:** 21, 29, **31–32**

Tar Baby (Morrison), **Supp. III Part 1:** 364, 369–372, 379; **Supp. IV Part 1:** 13

Tarbell, Ida, **III:** 322, 580; **Retro. Supp. II:** 101

"Target Practice" (Offutt), **Supp. XIX:** 171

"Target Study" (Baraka), **Supp. II Part 1:** 49–50, 54

Tarkington, Booth, **II:** 444; **III:** 70; **Retro. Supp. I:** 100; **Supp. XV:** 41

Tarnawsky, Yuriy (George) Orest, **Supp. XX:** 259

Tarpon (film), **Supp. VIII:** 42

Tarr, Rodger L., **Supp. X:** 222, 224, 226

Tárrega, Francisco, **Supp. XXI:** 100

Tartt, Donna, **Supp. XVIII:** 135; **Supp. XXVII:** 67, **267–281**

Tartuffe (Molière; Wilbur, trans.), **Supp. III Part 2:** 560

Tarumba, Selected Poems of Jaime Sabines (Levine and Trejo, trans.), **Supp. V:** 178

Tarzan Finds a Son (film, Weismuller), **Supp. XX:** 18

"Tarzan Is an Expatriate" (Theroux), **Supp. VIII:** 313

Tasis, Juan de, **Supp. XXI:** 104

Task, The (Cowper), **II:** 304

Tasker Street (Halliday), **Supp. XIX:** 82, **87–89**

Tasso, Torquato, **I:** 276

Taste of Palestine, A: Menus and Memories (Shihab), **Supp. XIII:** 273

Tate, Alan, **Supp. XV:** 141

Tate, Allen, **I:** 48, 49, 50, 67, 69, 381, 382, 386, 390, 396, 397, 399, 402, 441, 468; **II:** 197–198, 367, 536, 537, 542, 551, 554; **III:** 424, 428, 454, 482, 483, 485, 493, 495, 496, 497, 499, 500, 517; **IV: 120–143**, 236, 237, 433; **Retro. Supp. I:** 37, 41, 90; **Retro. Supp. II:** 77, 79, 82, 83, 89, 176, 178, 179; **Supp. I Part 1:** 364, 371; **Supp. I Part 2:** 423; **Supp. II Part 1:** 90–91, 96, 98, 103–104, 136, 139, 144, 150, 151, 318; **Supp. II Part 2:** 643; **Supp. III Part 2:** 542; **Supp. V:** 315, 331; **Supp. X:** 1, 52; **Supp. XIV:** 2; **Supp. XXI:** 256; **Supp. XXII:** 277

Tate, Mrs. Allen (Caroline Gordon). *See* Gordon, Caroline

Tate, Mrs. Allen (Helen Heinz), **IV:** 127

Tate, Mrs. Allen (Isabella Gardner), **IV:** 127

Tate, Benjamin Lewis Bogan, **IV:** 127

Tate, Greg, **Supp. XIII:** 233, 237

Tate, James, **Supp. V:** 92, 338; **Supp. VIII:** 39, 279; **Supp. XV:** 250; **Supp. XVII:** 242

Tate, John Allen, **IV:** 127

Tate, Michael Paul, **IV:** 127

Tate, Nancy, **II:** 197

Tatonetti, Lisa, **Supp. XXIII:** 149–150

Tattooed Countess, The (Van Vechten), **I:** 295; **Supp. II Part 2:** 726–728, 738, 742

Tattooed Feet (Nye), **Supp. XIII:** 274

"Tattoos" (McClatchy), **Supp. XII:** 266–267, 268

"Tattoos" (Wright), **Supp. V:** 335, 340

Tatum, Anna, **I:** 516

Tatum, James, **Supp. IV Part 2:** 684

Taubman, Howard, **Supp. XXV:** 106

Taupin, René, **II:** 528, 529; **Supp. III Part 2:** 614, 615, 617, 621

Tavano, John, **Supp. XXI:** 99

Taves, Isabella, **Supp. XXV:** 198

Tawney, Richard Henry, **Supp. I Part 2:** 481

Taylor, Ann, **Supp. XXIII:** 231

Taylor, Bayard, **II:** 275; **Supp. I Part 1:** 350, 361, 362, 365, 366, 372; **Supp. XV:** 269

Taylor, Chuck, **Supp. XXIII:** 57

Taylor, Cora. *See* Howarth, Cora

Taylor, Deems, **III:** 138

Taylor, Edward, **III:** 493; **IV: 144–166**; **Supp. I Part 1:** 98; **Supp. I Part 2:** 375, 386, 546

Taylor, Mrs. Edward (Elizabeth Fitch), **IV:** 147, 165

Taylor, Mrs. Edward (Ruth Wyllys), **IV:** 148

Taylor, Eleanor Ross, **Supp. V:** 317, 318

Taylor, Elizabeth, **II:** 588

Taylor, Frank, **III:** 81

Taylor, Frederick Winslow, **Supp. I Part 2:** 644

Taylor, Graham, **Supp. I Part 1:** 5

Taylor, Henry, **Retro. Supp. I:** 212; **Supp. XI:** 317; **Supp. XIII:** 333

Taylor, Henry W., **IV:** 144

Taylor, Jeremy, **II:** 11; **III:** 487; **Supp. I Part 1:** 349; **Supp. XII:** 45; **Supp. XIV:** 344, 345

Taylor, John, **IV:** 149

Taylor, Katherine, **Supp. VIII:** 251

Taylor, Kezia, **IV:** 148

Taylor, Nathaniel W., **Supp. I Part 2:** 580

Taylor, Paul, **I:** 293

Taylor, Peter, **Retro. Supp. II:** 179; **Supp. V: 313–329; Supp. XIV:** 3

Taylor, Raynor, **Supp. XV:** 238

Taylor, Richard, **IV:** 146

Taylor, Robert, **Supp. I Part 1:** 294; **Supp. XV:** 135, 138; **Supp. XVI:** 277

Taylor, Samuel A., **Supp. XX:** 253

Taylor, Stephan, **Supp. XVI:** 203

Taylor, Thomas, **II:** 10

Taylor, William, **IV:** 145–146

Taylor, Zachary, **I:** 3; **II:** 433–434

Tchelitchew, Peter, **II:** 586

Tea and Sympathy (Anderson), **Supp. I Part 1:** 277; **Supp. V:** 108

"Tea at the Palaz of Hoon" (Stevens), **Retro. Supp. I:** 300, 302, 306

"Teacher's Pet" (Thurber), **Supp. I Part 2:** 605–606

"Teaching and Story Telling" (Maclean), **Supp. XIV:** 234

Teaching a Stone to Talk: Expeditions and Encounters (Dillard), **Supp. VI:** 23, 26, 28, 32, 33, 34–35

"Teaching Emily Dickenson"(Hadas), **Supp. XXIII:** 115

"Teaching Hanh the Blues" (Weigl), **Supp. XIX:** 287

Teachings of Don B., The (Barthelme), **Supp. IV Part 1:** 53

Teachout, Terry, **Supp. XIX:** 137

Teale, Edwin Way, **Supp. XIII:** 7

Teall, Dorothy, **I:** 221

"Team Blue/Team Square: Revisiting the Lyric and the Narrative" (Biss and Zapruder), **Supp. XXVI:** 54–55

"Team Players" (Biss), **Supp. XXVI:** 46

Team Team Team (film), **Supp. IX:** 251

"Tea on the Mountain" (Bowles), **Supp. IV Part 1:** 90

"Tea Party, The" (MacLeish), **III:** 11

Tear and a Smile, A (Dam'a wa Ibtisáma) (Gibran), **Supp. XX: 116, 118, 124**

Teare, Brian, **Supp. XXII:** 236

"Tears, Idle Tears" (Lord Tennyson), **Supp. XIV:** 8

"Tears of the Pilgrims, The" (McClatchy), **Supp. XII:** 256

Teasdale, Sara, **Retro. Supp. I:** 133; **Supp. I Part 2:** 393, 707; **Supp. XIV:** 127; **Supp. XV:** 295, 297, 301, 305, 307, 308; **Supp. XVII:** 69, 75; **Supp. XXVII: 283–298**

"Tease" (Swados), **Supp. XIX:** 267

Tebeaux, Elizabeth, **Supp. IX:** 109

"Technical Manifesto of Futurist Literature" (Marinetti), **Supp. XXII:** 161

Technics and Civilization (Mumford), **Supp. I Part 2:** 638; **Supp. II Part 2:** 479, 493, 497

Technics and Human Development (Mumford), **Supp. I Part 2:** 638; **Supp. II Part 2:** 497

Technique of the Mystery Story, The (Wells), **Supp. XXVI:** 277, 280, 281–282

"Technology, The" (Egan), **Supp. XIX:** 61

"Teddy" (Salinger), **III:** 561–563, 571

"Te Deum" (Reznikoff), **Supp. XIV:** 281

Tedlock, Dennis, **Supp. IV Part 2:** 509

"Teeth Mother Naked at Last, The" (R. Bly), **Supp. IV Part 1:** 63, 68, 73

Teggart, Richard, **Supp. I Part 2:** 650

Tegnér, Esaias, **Retro. Supp. II:** 155

Teilhard de Chardin, Pierre, **Supp. I Part 1:** 314

Tekonwatonti/Molly Brant (Kenny), **Supp. XXIII:** 143, 147, 151, **152–153,** 154

"Telegraphs from a Distracted Sibyl" (Mullen), **Supp. XXVII:** 166, 176

Telephone, The (film), **Supp. XI:** 309

"Telephone Call, A" (Parker), **Supp. IX:** 202–203

"Telephone Number of the Muse, The" (Justice), **Supp. VII:** 124–125

Telephone Poles and Other Poems (Updike), **IV:** 214, 215

"Television" (Beattie), **Supp. V:** 33

Teller, Edward, **I:** 137

"Tell Him About Brother John" (Muñoz), **Supp. XXV:** 136

"Telling" (Ortiz), **Supp. IV Part 2:** 509

"Telling It in Black and White: The Importance of the Africanist Presence in *To Kill a Mockingbird*" (Baecker), **Supp. VIII:** 128

Telling Secrets (Buechner), **Supp. XII:** 53–54

Telling Stories (Didion), **Supp. IV Part 1:** 197

"Telling Stories" (Didion), **Supp. IV Part 1:** 197

"Telling the Bees" (Whittier), **Supp. I Part 2:** 694–695

Telling the Little Secrets (J. Burstein), **Supp. XVII:** 44

Telling the Truth: The Gospel as Tragedy, Comedy, and Fairy Tale (Buechner), **Supp. XII:** 53

"Tell Me" (Hughes), **Supp. VIII:** 213

"Tell Me, Sir, ... What Is 'Black' Literature?" (H. L. Gates), **Supp. XX: 108**

Tell Me, Tell Me (Moore), **III:** 215

Tell Me Again (Notley), **Supp. XXII:** 224, 230–231

Tell Me Again How the White Heron Rises and Flies across the Nacreous River at Twilight toward the Distant Islands (Carruth), **Supp. XVI:** 56

Tell Me a Riddle (film), **Supp. XIII:** 295

Tell Me a Riddle (Olsen), **Supp. XIII:** 294, 296, **298–302,** 303, 305

"Tell Me a Riddle" (Olsen), **Supp. XIII:** 294, 297, 298, **300–302,** 305

"Tell Me a Story" (McDermott), **Supp. XVIII:** 177

Tell Me How Long the Train's Been Gone (Baldwin), **Retro. Supp. II:** 9, **11–12,** 14; **Supp. I Part 1:** 48, 52, 63–65, 67

"Tell Me My Fortune" (Epstein), **Supp. XII:** 163

Tell Me True: Memoir, History, and Writing a Life (Hampl and May, eds.), **Supp. XXII:** 81–82, 84, **94–95**

Tell Me Your Answer True (Sexton), **Supp. II Part 2:** 683

Tell My Horse (Hurston), **Supp. VI:** 149, 156, 158

"Tell-Tale Heart, The" (Poe), **III:** 413, 414–415, 416; **Retro. Supp. II:** 267, 269, 270; **Supp. XXV:** 112

"Tell the Women We're Going" (Carver), **Supp. III Part 1:** 138, 144

"Telluride Blues—A Hatchet Job" (Abbey), **Supp. XIII:** 10

Telushkin, Dvorah, **Retro. Supp. II:** 317

Temblor (Howe), **Supp. IV Part 2:** 431

Temperamental People (Rinehart), **Supp. XXV:** 196

Tempering of Eugene O'Neill, The (D. Alexander), **Supp. XVII:** 99

"Temper of Steel, The" (Jones), **Supp. XI:** 218

Tempers, The (W. C. Williams), **Retro. Supp. I:** 413–414, 415, 416, 424

Tempest, The (Shakespeare), **I:** 394; **II:** 12; **III:** 40, 61, 263; **Retro. Supp. I:** 61; **Supp. IV Part 2:** 463; **Supp. V:** 302–303; **Supp. XII:** 54–57; **Supp. XV:** 255, 256

Temple, Minnie, **II:** 323

Temple, The (Herbert), **IV:** 145, 153

Temple, William, **III:** 303

Temple House (E. Stoddard), **Supp. XV:** 273, **284–286**

Temple of My Familiar, The (Walker), **Supp. III Part 2:** 521, 527, 529, 535, 537; **Supp. IV Part 1:** 14

"Temple of the Holy Ghost, A" (O'Connor), **III:** 344, 352; **Retro. Supp. II:** 232

Templin, Charlotte, **Supp. V:** 116

Temporary Shelter (Gordon), **Supp. IV Part 1:** 299, 305–307

"Temporary Shelter" (Gordon), **Supp. IV Part 1:** 306

Temptation Game, The (Gardner), **Supp. VI:** 72

Temptation of Don Volpi, The (Hayes), **Supp. XXVI:** 135, 137

"Temptation of St. Anthony, The" (Barthelme), **Supp. IV Part 1:** 47

Temptations, The, **Supp. X:** 242

"10 Best Weathers of 1983, The" (Notley), **Supp. XXII:** 224

"10 Things I Do Every Day" (Berrigan), **Supp. XXII:** 224; **Supp. XXIV:** 41

"Tenancy, A" (Merrill), **Supp. III Part 1:** 322, 323

"Tenant" (Hoffman), **Supp. XVIII:** 86

Tenants, The (Malamud), **Supp. I Part 2:** 448–450

"Ten Best Issues of Comic Books, The" (Notley), **Supp. XXII:** 224

Ten Commandments (McClatchy), **Supp. XII:** 262–265

Ten Days That Shook the World (Reed), **II:** 577; **Supp. X:** 136; **Supp. XVIII:** 225

Tendencies in Modern American Poetry (A. Lowell), **II:** 529

"Tender, Hilarious Reminiscences of Life in Mythical Lake Wobegon" (MacDougall), **Supp. XVI:** 174

Tender Buttons (G. Stein), **I:** 103, 105; **IV:** 27, 42–43; **Retro. Supp. II:** 331; **Supp. XV:** 347; **Supp. XXVII:** 169

"Tenderfoot" (Haines), **Supp. XII:** 209

Tender Is the Night (Fitzgerald), **I:** 375; **II:** 79, 84, 91, 95–96, 97, 98, 420; **Retro. Supp. I:** 105, 108, 109, **110–112,** 114; **Supp. IX:** 59, 60, 61; **Supp. XV:** 197; **Supp. XXI:** 11

"Tenderloin" (Crane), **I:** 408

"Tenderly" (Dobyns), **Supp. XIII:** 86–87

"Tender Man, A" (Bambara), **Supp. XI:** 9–10

"Tenderness" (Dunn), **Supp. XI:** 149, 150

"Tender Offer, The" (Auchincloss), **Supp. IV Part 1:** 34

"Tender Organizations, The" (C. Bly), **Supp. XVI:** 40, 42

"Tenebrae" (Komunyakaa), **Supp. XIII:** 132

Tenenbaum, Joseph, **Supp. XX:** 253

"Ten Forty-Four" (Kingsolver), **Supp. VII:** 208

Ten Indians (Bell), **Supp. X:** 7, **12**

Ten Introductions: A Collection of Modern Verse (Taggard and Fitts, ed.), **Supp. XXII:** 281

Tennant, Agnieszka, **Supp. XX:** 140

"Ten Neglected American Writers Who Deserve to Be Better Known" (Cantor), **Supp. IV Part 1:** 285

Tennent, Gilbert, **I:** 546

Tennessee Day in St. Louis (Taylor), **Supp. V:** 324

"Tennessee's Partner" (Harte), **Supp. II Part 1:** 345, 348–350

"Tennis" (Pinsky), **Supp. VI:** 241, 242

Tennis Court Oath, The (Ashbery), **Supp. III Part 1:** 7, 9, 12, 14, 26

Ten North Frederick (O'Hara), **III:** 361

Tennyson, Alfred, Lord, **I:** 587–588; **II:** 18, 82, 273, 338, 404, 439, 604; **III:** 5, 409, 469, 485, 511, 521, 523; **Retro. Supp. I:** 100, 325; **Retro. Supp. II:** 135; **Supp. I Part 1:** 349, 356; **Supp. I Part 2:** 410, 416, 552; **Supp. IX:** 19; **Supp. X:** 157; **Supp. XIII:** 111; **Supp. XIV:** 40, 120; **Supp. XV:** 275; **Supp. XVIII:** 78; **Supp. XXVII:** 261

"Tenochtitlan" (Bronk), **Supp. XXI:** 31

"Ten O'Clock News" (Ortiz), **Supp. IV Part 2:** 503–504

"Te-Non-An-At-Che"(Kenny), **Supp. XXIII:** 151

Tenorman (Huddle), **Supp. XXVI:** 150, 151, 153, 156, 159

Ten Poems (Dove), **Supp. IV Part 1:** 244

Ten Poems of Francis Ponge Translated by Robert Bly and Ten Poems of Robert Bly Inspired by the Poems by Francis Ponge (R. Bly), **Supp. IV Part 1:** 71

"Tension in Poetry" (Tate), **IV:** 128, 129, 135

Tenth Muse, The (Bradstreet), **Supp. I Part 1:** 102, 103, 114

10,000 Days of Thunder: A History of the Vietnam War (Caputo), **Supp. XIX:** 29

Tenting Tonight (Rinehart), **Supp. XXV:** 195

"Tent on the Beach, The" (Whittier), **Supp. I Part 2:** 703

"Ten True Things" (July), **Supp. XXIV:** 205

"Teodoro Luna Confesses after Years to His Brother, Anselmo the Priest, Who Is Required to Understand, But Who Understands Anyway, More Than People Think" (Ríos), **Supp. IV Part 2:** 552

Teodoro Luna's Two Kisses (Ríos), **Supp. IV Part 2:** 550–552, 553

"Tepeyac" (Cisneros), **Supp. VII:** 69

"Terce" (Auden), **Supp. II Part 1:** 22

Terence, **IV:** 155, 363; **Supp. I Part 2:** 405

Terkel, Studs, **Supp. IV Part 1:** 364

"Term" (Merwin), **Supp. III Part 1:** 356–357

"Terminal Days at Beverly Farms" (R. Lowell), **Retro. Supp. II:** 189

Terminating, or Sonnet LXXV, or "Lass Meine Schmerzen nicht verloren sein, or Ambivalence" (Kushner), Supp. IX: 132

Terminations (James), **Retro. Supp. I:** 229

"Terminus" (Emerson), **II:** 13, 19

"Terminus" (Wharton), **Retro. Supp. I:** 371

"Terms in Which I Think of Reality, The" (Ginsberg), **Supp. II Part 1:** 311

Terms of Endearment (film), **Supp. V:** 226

Terms of Endearment (McMurtry), **Supp. V:** 224–225

"Terrace, The" (Wilbur), **Supp. III Part 2:** 550

Terrarium (Sanders), **Supp. XVI:** 270

"Terrence McNally" (Bryer), **Supp. XIII:** 200

"Terrence McNally" (Di Gaetani), **Supp. XIII:** 200

Terrence McNally: A Casebook (Zinman), **Supp. XIII:** 209

"Terrestrial Cuckoo"(O'Hara), **Supp. XXIII:** 210

"Terrible Peacock, The" (Barnes), **Supp. III Part 1:** 33

Terrible Threes, The (Reed), **Supp. X:** 241, 253

Terrible Twos, The (Reed), **Supp. X:** 241, **252–253**

"Terrific Mother" (Moore), **Supp. X:** 178

Territory Ahead, The (Morris), **III:** 228–229, 236

Terrorism (Wright), **Supp. XV:** 341, 342

"Terrorism" (Wright), **Supp. XV:** 341

"Terrors of the Amazon" (Grossman), **Supp. XXV:** 66

Terry, Edward A., **II:** 128, 129

Terry, Rose, **Supp. I Part 2:** 420

Tertium Organum (Ouspensky), **I:** 383; **Supp. XX:** **116**

Terzian, Peter, **Supp. XXV:** 12, 13

Tess of the d'Ubervilles (Hardy), **II:** 181; **Retro. Supp. II:** 100

"Testament" (Berry), **Supp. X:** 36

"Testament" (Carruth), **Supp. XVI:** 59

"Testament (Or, Homage to Walt Whitman)" (Jong), **Supp. V:** 130

"Testament of Flood" (Warren), **IV:** 253

Testament of François Villon, The (Pound, opera), **Retro. Supp. I:** 287

"Testament: Vermeer in December" (Bierds), **Supp. XVII:** 33

"Testimonia on the Question of Stesichoros' Blinding by Helen" (Carson), **Supp. XII:** 107

"Testimonies of a Roasted Chicken" (Jarman), **Supp. XVII:** 120

"Testimony" (Komunyakaa), **Supp. XIII:** 129

"Testimony of James Apthorp, The" (Kees), **Supp. XV:** 146

Testimony: The United States (1885–1890): Recitative (Reznikoff), **Supp. XIV:** 279, 280, 281, 285, **289–291**

Testimony: The United States (1891–1900): Recitative (Reznikoff), **Supp. XIV:** 291

Testing-Tree, The (Kunitz), **Supp. III Part 1:** 260, 263, 264, 267, 268

"Testing-Tree, The" (Kunitz), **Supp. III Part 1:** 269

Test of Poetry, A (Zukofsky), **Supp. III Part 2:** 618, 622

Teuton, Christopher, **Supp. XXVI:** 102, 110, 111

"Teutonic Scholar" (X. J. Kennedy), **Supp. XV:** 161

"Texas Moon, and Elsewhere, The" (McMurtry), **Supp. V:** 225

Texas Poets in Concert: A Quartet (Gwynn, ed.), **Supp. XIII:** 277

Texas Summer (Southern), **Supp. XI:** 309

Texasville (McMurtry), **Supp. V:** 228, 233

Thacher, Molly Day, **IV:** 381

Thacker, Robert, **Supp. XXVII:** 180, 182

Thackeray, William Makepeace, **I:** 194, 354; **II:** 182, 271, 282, 288, 316, 321, 322; **III:** 64, 70; **IV:** 326; **Retro. Supp. I:** 218; **Supp. I Part 1:** 307; **Supp. I Part 2:** 421, 495, 579; **Supp. IV Part 1:** 297; **Supp. IX:** 200; **Supp. XI:** 277; **Supp. XIV:** 306; **Supp. XX:** **228**

Thaddeus, Janice Farrar, **Supp. IV Part 1:** 299

"Thailand" (Barthelme), **Supp. IV Part 1:** 41

Thalberg, Irving, **Retro. Supp. I:** 109, 110, 114; **Supp. XVI:** 191, 192

Thales, **I:** 480–481

Thalia Trilogy (McMurtry), **Supp. V:** 220–223, 234

Tham, Claire, **Supp. VIII:** 79

"Thanatopsis" (Bryant), **Supp. I Part 1:** 150, 154, 155, 170

Thanatos Syndrome, The (Percy), **Supp. III Part 1:** 385, 397–399

"Thanks Can Be Named to Death" (Peacock), **Supp. XIX:** 199

"Thanksgiving" (Davison), **Supp. XXVI:** 74

"Thanksgiving" (Glück), **Supp. V:** 83

"Thanksgiving, A" (Auden), **Supp. II Part 1:** 26

"Thanksgiving for a Habitat" (Auden), **Supp. II Part 1:** 24

Thanksgivings (Traherne), **Supp. XVI:** 288

"Thanksgiving Spirit" (Farrell), **II:** 45

Thanksgiving Visitor, The (Capote), **Supp. III Part 1:** 116, 118, 119

"Thank You, Esther Forbes" (Saunders), **Supp. XIX:** 235

Thank You, Fog (Auden), **Supp. II Part 1:** 24

"Thank You, Lord" (Angelou), **Supp. IV Part 1:** 15

Thank You, Mr. Moto (Marquand), **III:** 57, 58

Thank You and Other Poems (Koch), **Supp. XV:** 180–181

"Thank You in Arabic" (Nye), **Supp. XIII:** 273, 281

"Thar's More in the Man Than Thar Is in the Land" (Lanier), **Supp. I Part 1:** 352–353, 359–360

That Affair Next Door (Green), **Supp. XXVI:** 277

"That Evening Sun" (Faulkner), **II:** 72; **Retro. Supp. I:** 75, 83

That Horse (Hogan), **Supp. IV Part 1:** 397, 404, 405

"That House, This Room" (W. V. Davis), **Supp. XXI:** 90

"That I Had the Wings" (Ellison), **Supp. II Part 1:** 238

That Night (McDermott), **Supp. XVIII:** 155, **158–160,** 162, 163, 166

"That's the Place Indians Talk About" (Ortiz), **Supp. IV Part 2:** 511

That Tantalus (Bronk), **Supp. XXI:** 31

"That the Soul May Wax Plump" (Swenson), **Supp. IV Part 2:** 650

"That the Universe Is Chrysalid" (Sobin), **Supp. XVI:** 284

"That Tree" (Porter), **III:** 434–435, 446, 451

That Was the Week That Was (television program), **Supp. XIV:** 125

"That Winter" (Stone), **Supp. XXVII:** 253

"That Year" (Olds), **Supp. X:** 203

"Thaw" (C. Frost), **Supp. XV:** 93, 104, 105

Thaxter, Celia, **Retro. Supp. II:** 136, 147; **Supp. XIII:** 143, 153

Thayer, Abbott, **I:** 231

Thayer, Scofield, **I:** 231; **Retro. Supp. I:** 58

Thayer and Eldridge, **Retro. Supp. I:** 403

"Theater" (Toomer), **Supp. IX:** 309, 317–318

"Theater Chronicle" (McCarthy), **II:** 562

"Theater Problems? Call Dr. Chekhov" (Wasserstein), **Supp. XV:** 320

Theatricals (James), **Retro. Supp. I:** 228

The Blacker the Berry: A Novel of Negro Life (Thurman), **Supp. XIX:** 73; **Supp. XVIII:** 281

"Theft" (Porter), **III:** 434, 435

Theft, A (Bellow), **Retro. Supp. II:** 31–32, 34

The Harder They Fall (Schulberg), **Supp. XVIII:** 247, 253

The Harder They Fall: Celebrities Tell Their Real-Life Stories of Addiction and Recovery (F. Wright), **Supp. XVII:** 240

Their Dogs Came with Them (Viramontes), **Supp. XXV:** 130, 138

Their Eyes Were Watching God (Hurston), **Supp. VI:** 149, 152, 156–157; **Supp. XX: 107**

Their Heads Are Green and Their Hands Are Blue: Scenes from the Non-Christian World (Bowles), **Supp. IV Part 1:** 89

"Their Losses" (Taylor), **Supp. V:** 320

"Their Name is Macaroni" (Boyle), **Supp. XXIV:** 61

"Their Sleep" (W. V. Davis), **Supp. XXI:** 93

Their Wedding Journey (Howells), **II:** 277–278; **Retro. Supp. I:** 334

them (Oates), **Supp. II Part 2:** 503, 511–514

Theme Is Freedom, The (Dos Passos), **I:** 488–489, 492, 494

Theme Time Radio Hour (radio show, Dylan), **Supp. XVIII:** 28

"Theme with Variations" (Agee), **I:** 27

"Then" (Barthelme), **Supp. IV Part 1:** 48

"Then as Now" (Cliff), **Supp. XXII:** 76

"The Night Rhonda Ferguson Was Killed" (E. P. Jones), **Supp. XXII:** 144

"Then It All Came Down" (Capote), **Supp. III Part 1:** 125, 131

Theocritus, **II:** 169; **Retro. Supp. I:** 286; **Supp. XXIV:** 156

Theodore Roethke's Far Fields: The Evolution of His Poetry (Balakian), **Supp. XXIII:** 19

"Theodore the Poet" (Masters), **Supp. I Part 2:** 461

Theological Position, A (Coover), **Supp. V:** 44

Theophrastus, **I:** 58

"Theoretical and Scientific Conceptions of Race, The" (Locke), **Supp. XIV:** 209

"Theoretical Subject(s) of *This Bridge Called My Back,* The"(Alarcón), **Supp. XXIII:** 204–205

"Theories of Time and Space" (Trethewey), **Supp. XXI:** 255

"Theory" (Huddle), **Supp. XXVI:** 149

Theory and Practice of Rivers and Other Poems, The (Harrison), **Supp. VIII:** 47, 49

Theory of Business Enterprise, The (Veblen), **Supp. I Part 2:** 638, 641, 644

Theory of Flight (Rukeyser), **Supp. VI:** 272, 275, **277–278,** 284

"Theory of Flight" (Rukeyser), **Supp. VI:** 277–278

Theory of Moral Sentiments, The (A. Smith), **Supp. I Part 2:** 634

Theory of the Leisure Class, The (Veblen), **I:** 475–476; **Supp. I Part 2:** 629, 633, 641, 645; **Supp. IV Part 1:** 22

"There" (Taylor), **Supp. V:** 323

"There Are No Such Trees in Alpine California" (Haines), **Supp. XII:** 207

"There Goes (Varoom! Varoom!) That Kandy-Kolored Tangerine-Flake Streamline Baby" (Wolfe), **Supp. III Part 2:** 569–571

"There Have Been Changes" (Pickering), **Supp. XXI:** 202–203

"There Is a Lesson" (Olsen), **Supp. XIII:** 292, 297

"There is a Man" (Espaillat), **Supp. XXI:** 108–109

"There Is Only One of Everything" (Atwood), **Supp. XIII:** 34

There Is Something Out There (McNally). *See And Things That Go Bump in the Night* (McNally)

"There Must Be" (Peacock), **Supp. XIX:** 199

"There's a certain Slant of light" (Dickinson), **Retro. Supp. I:** 38

There's a Wocket in My Pocket! (Geisel), **Supp. XVI:** 111

Thérèse de Lisieux, Saint, **Supp. VIII:** 195

"There She Is She Is Taking Her Bath" (Anderson), **I:** 113, 114

"There Was a Child Went Forth" (Whitman), **IV:** 348; **Supp. XXVI:** 230

"There Was a Man, There Was a Woman" (Cisneros), **Supp. VII:** 70

"There Was an Old Woman She Had So Many Children She Didn't Know What to Do" (Cisneros), **Supp. VII:** 60

"There Was a Youth Whose Name Was Thomas Granger" (Olson), **Supp. II Part 2:** 558, 560, 563

There Were Giants in the Land (Benét), **Supp. XI:** 50

"There Will Come Soft Rains" (Teasdale), **Supp. XXVII:** 295

There You Are (Simpson), **Supp. IX: 279–280**

"There You Are" (Simpson), **Supp. IX:** 279

"Thermopylae" (Clampitt), **Supp. IX:** 43

Theroux, Alexander, **Supp. VIII:** 312

Theroux, Marcel, **Supp. VIII:** 325

Theroux, Paul, **Supp. V:** 122; **Supp. VIII: 309–327**

"These Are My People" (Hayden), **Supp. II Part 1:** 365

These Are My Same Hands (Schott), **Supp. XXIII:** 241, 242

"These are the days when Birds come back" (Dickinson), **Retro. Supp. I:** 30

"These Days" (Davison), **Supp. XXVI:** 79

"These Days" (Olds), **Supp. X:** 215

"These Flames and Generosities of the Heart: Emily Dickinson and the Illogic of Sumptuary Values" (Howe), **Supp. IV Part 2:** 431

"These Hands" (Brockmeier), **Supp. XXII:** 51, 52, 53

These Happy Golden Years (L. I. Wilder), **Supp. XXII:** 294, 297, 299

These Low Grounds (Turpin), **Supp. XVIII:** 283

"These Nerves" (Biss), **Supp. XXVI:** 50–51

"These saw Visions" (Dickinson), **Retro. Supp. I:** 46

These Thirteen (Faulkner), **II:** 72

These Three (film), **Supp. I Part 1:** 281

These Times (Untermeyer), **Supp. XV: 299–300,** 303

"These Times" (Untermeyer), **Supp. XV:** 300

"Thessalonica: A Roman Story" (Brown), **Supp. I Part 1:** 133

Thévenaz, Paul, **Supp. XV:** 42

Thew, Harvey, **Supp. XIII:** 166

"They Ain't the Men They Used To Be" (Farrell), **II:** 45

"They Burned the Books" (Benét), **Supp. XI:** 46

They Came Like Swallows (Maxwell), **Supp. VIII: 155–159,** 168, 169

"They Can't Turn Back" (Baldwin), **Supp. I Part 1:** 52

They Do Not: The Letters of a Non-Professional Lady Arranged for Public Consumption (Clements), **Supp. XVI:** 190

They Feed They Lion (Levine), **Supp. V:** 178, 179, 181, 184–185, 186

"They Feed They Lion" (Levine), **Supp. V:** 188

"They Lion Grow" (Levine), **Supp. V:** 184–185

"They're Not Your Husband" (Carver), **Supp. III Part 1:** 141, 143

They're Playing Our Song (musical), **Supp. IV Part 2:** 589

They Seek a City (Bontemps and Conroy), **Supp. XXII:** 5, 11

They Shall Inherit the Laughter (Jones), **Supp. XI:** 217, 218, 232

"They Shall Not Die" (Ryan as Quin), **Supp. XVIII:** 228–229

They Shoot Horses (film), **Supp. XIII:** 159

They Shoot Horses, Don't They? (McCoy), **Supp. XIII:** 159, **164–166,** 168, 171, 172, 174; **Supp. XXV:** 26

"They Sing, They Sing" (Roethke), **III:** 544

They Stooped to Folly (Glasgow), **II:** 175, 186–187

They Were Expendable (film), **Supp. XVIII:** 247

"They Weren't Going to Die" (Boyle), **Supp. XXIV:** 61

They Whisper (R. O. Butler), **Supp. XII: 72–73**

They Who Knock at Our Gates: A Complete Gospel of Immigration (Antin), **Supp. XX: 2–3, 10–11,** 12

"Thick and Thin"(Hadas), **Supp. XXIII:** 119

Thidwick the Big-Hearted Moose (Geisel), **Supp. XVI:** 104

Thief's Journal, The (Genet), **Supp. XXIV:** 210

"Thief's Philosophy of Life, The" (Hapgood), **Supp. XVII:** 103

"Thief's Wife, The" (B. Kelly), **Supp. XVII:** 125–126

"Thieves" (Yates), **Supp. XI:** 349

Thieves of Paradise (Komunyakaa), **Supp. XIII:** 113, **128–130,** 132

"Thimble, The" (Kenyon), **Supp. VII:** 164

"Thing and Its Relations, The" (James), **II:** 357

"Things" (Haines), **Supp. XII:** 207

"Things" (Kenyon), **Supp. VII:** 169

"Things, The" (Kinnell), **Supp. III Part 1:** 246

Things As They Are (Stein), **IV:** 34, 37, 40

"Things Can Be Named to Death" (Peacock), **Supp. XIX:** 199

"Things Don't Stop" (Nye), **Supp. XIII:** 287

Things Gone and Things Still Here (Bowles), **Supp. IV Part 1:** 91

"Things of August" (Stevens), **Retro. Supp. I:** 309

Things of This World (Wilbur), **Supp. III Part 2:** 552–555

Things That Fall from the Sky (Brockmeier), **Supp. XXII: 50–53**

"Things That Fall from the Sky" (Brockmeier), **Supp. XXII:** 51, 53

Things Themselves: Essays and Scenes (Price), **Supp. VI:** 261

Things They Carried, The (T. O'Brien), **Supp. V:** 238, 239, 240, 243, 248–250; **Supp. XVII:** 14; **Supp. XXI:** 122

"Things to Do in New York City" (Berrigan), **Supp. XXII:** 224

Things We Don't Understand and Definitely Are Not Going to Talk About (performance piece, July), **Supp. XXIV:** 200

"Thing That Killed My Father Off, The" (Carver), **Supp. III Part 1:** 143

Thingy World!: or, How We Got to Where We Are: A Satire in One Act (Budbill), **Supp. XIX: 13–14**

"Think about It" (Conroy), **Supp. XVI:** 75

Think Back on Us . . . (Cowley), **Supp. II Part 1:** 139, 140, 142

Think Fast, Mr. Moto (Marquand), **III:** 57, 58

"Thinking about Barbara Deming" (Paley), **Supp. VI:** 227

"Thinking about Being Called Simple by a Critic" (Stafford), **Supp. XI:** 328

Thinking about the Longstanding Problems of Virtue and Happiness: Essays, a Play, Two Poems, and a Prayer (Kushner), **Supp. IX:** 131, 134, 135

"Thinking about the Past" (Justice), **Supp. VII:** 123–124

"Thinking about Western Thinking" (Didion), **Supp. IV Part 1:** 204, 206

"'Thinking against Oneself': Reflections on Cioran" (Sontag), **Supp. III Part 2:** 459–460

"Thinking Back Through Our Mothers: Traditions in Canadian Women's Writing" (Shields), **Supp. VII:** 307–308

"Thinking for Berky" (Stafford), **Supp. XI:** 320

"Thinking in Subversion" (Gansworth), **Supp. XXVI:** 114

"Thinking like a Mountain" (Leopold), **Supp. XIV:** 188, 189

"Thinking of the Lost World" (Jarrell), **II:** 338–389

Thinking Out Loud (Quindlen), **Supp. XVII:** 167, **169–170**

Thin Man, The (film), **Supp. IV Part 1:** 342, 355

Thin Man, The (Hammett), **Supp. IV Part 1:** 354–355

"Thinnest Shadow, The" (Ashbery), **Supp. III Part 1:** 5

"Thin People, The" (Plath), **Supp. I Part 2:** 538, 547

Thin Red Line, The (film; Malick), **Supp. V:** 249; **Supp. XV:** 351

Thin Red Line, The (Jones), **Supp. XI:** 219, **224–225,** 229, 231, 232, 233, 234

"Thin Strips" (Sandburg), **III:** 587

"Third and Final Continent, The" (Lahiri), **Supp. XXI: 178–180**

"Third Avenue in Sunlight" (Hecht), **Supp. X:** 61

"Third Body, A" (R. Bly), **Supp. IV Part 1:** 71

Third Circle, The (Norris), **III:** 327

"Third Expedition, The" (Bradbury), **Supp. IV Part 1:** 103, 106

Third Generation, The (C. Himes), **Supp. XVI:** 135, **140–141**

Third Life of Grange Copeland, The (Walker), **Supp. III Part 2:** 520, 527–536

Third Mind, The (Burroughs), **Supp. XII:** 3

"Third Myth, The" (Muñoz), **Supp. XXV:** 134

Third Rose, The (Brinnin), **IV:** 26

"Third Sermon on the Warpland, The" (Brooks), **Supp. III Part 1:** 85

"Third Thing That Killed My Father Off, The" (Carver), **Supp. III Part 1:** 144

Third Violet, The (Crane), **I:** 408, 417–418

Thirlwall, John C., **Retro. Supp. I:** 430

"Thirst: Introduction to Kinds of Water" (Carson), **Supp. XII: 103**

"13, 1977, 21" (Lethem), **Supp. XVIII:** 148

13 by Shanley (Shanley), **Supp. XIV:** 316

13 Seconds: A Look Back at the Kent State Shootings (Caputo), **Supp. XIX:** 29

Thirteen Hands: A Play in Two Acts (Shields), **Supp. VII:** 322–323

Thirteen O'Clock (Benét), **Supp. XI:** 46

Thirteen Other Stories (Purdy), **Supp. VII:** 278

Thirteen Stories and Thirteen Epitaphs (Vollmann), **Supp. XVII:** 226

"Thirteenth and Pennsylvania" (Stafford), **Supp. XI:** 324

Thirteenth Month, The (Pedersen; Nelson, trans.), **Supp. XVIII:** 179–180

"Thirteen Ways of Looking at a Blackbird" (Stevens), **IV:** 94; **Supp. IX:** 47; **Supp. XVII:** 130; **Supp. XXIII:** 253

"Thirteen Ways of Looking at a Blackbird" (W. Stevens), **Supp. XX:** 110

Thirteen Ways of Looking at a Black Man (H. L. Gates), **Supp. XX: 102, 110**

30/6 (poetry chapbook), **Supp. V:** 5, 6

"30. Meditation. 2. Cor. 5.17. He Is a New Creature" (Taylor), **IV:** 144

30: Pieces of a Novel (Dixon), **Supp. XII:** 152, **153–154**

"Thirty Bob a Week" (Davidson), **Retro. Supp. I:** 55

"Thirty Delft Tiles" (Doty), **Supp. XI:** 131

"35/10" (Olds), **Supp. X:** 206

"35,000 Feet—The Lanterns" (Goldbarth), **Supp. XII:** 182

31 Letters and 13 Dreams (Hugo), **Supp. VI:** 141–144

Thirty Poems (Bryant), **Supp. I Part 1:** 157, 158

Thirty-Six Poems (Warren), **IV:** 236, 239, 240

"33" (Alvarez), **Supp. VII:** 4

"3275" (Monette), **Supp. X:** 148, 159

Thirty Years (Marquand), **III:** 56, 60–61

Thirty Years of Treason (Bentley), **Supp. I Part 1:** 297

This, My Letter (Hay), **Supp. XIV:** 121, 122, 129, 131

"This, That & the Other" (Nemerov), **III:** 269

This Body Is Made of Camphor and Gopherwood (R. Bly), **Supp. IV Part 1:** 63–65, 66, 71; **Supp. XXI:** 85

This Boy's Life: A Memoir (T. Wolff), **Supp. VII:** 334–339, 340, 343; **Supp. XI:** 246, 247; **Supp. XXV:** 208

This Bridge Called My Back: Writings by Radical Women of Color (Moraga and Anzaldúa, eds.), **Supp. XXIII:** 193, 194, 196, **204–205**

"This Bright Dream" (Benét), **Supp. XI:** 55

This Coffin Has No Handles (McGrath), **Supp. X:** 117

"This Configuration" (Ashbery), **Supp. III Part 1:** 22

"This Corruptible" (Wylie), **Supp. I Part 2:** 727, 729

"This Crazy Wickedness, Little Nests of Light" (Notley), **Supp. XXII:** 228

"This Crutch That I Love" (Nye), **Supp. XIII:** 288

"This Gentile World" (H. Miller), **III:** 177

"This Hand" (Wylie), **Supp. I Part 2:** 713

"This Hour" (Olds), **Supp. X:** 212

"This House I Cannot Leave" (Kingsolver), **Supp. VII:** 208

This Hunger (Nin), **Supp. X:** 185

This in Which (Oppen), **Supp. XXVI:** 225, 230, 232–233, 234

"This Is a Photograph of Me" (Atwood), **Supp. XIII:** 33

"This Is a Poem, Good Afternoon" (Keillor), **Supp. XVI:** 167

"This Is a Young World" (Howard), **Supp. XXVII:** 118

"This Is for You" (Cohen), **Supp. XXVII:** 60

This Is How You Lose Her (Díaz), **Supp. XXIV:** 83, 84, 86, 88, **92–93**

"This Is It" (Stern), **Supp. IX:** 290

"This Is Just to Say" (W. C. Williams), **Supp. XI:** 328

This Is My God: The Jewish Way of Life (Wouk), **Supp. XXV:** 253, 255–256, 263, 268

"This Is My Heart" (Harjo), **Supp. XII:** 230

This Is Not a Novel (Markson), **Supp. XVII:** 145–146

"This Is Not Who We Are" (Nye), **Supp. XIII:** 285, 286

This Is Our Time: Secular Cantata No. 1, Mixed Voice Chorus and Orchestra (Taggard, Schuman and Weissleder), **Supp. XXII:** 283

"This Is Us, Excellent" (Richard), **Supp. XIX:** 212

"This Is What I Said" (Salinas), **Supp. XIII:** 322

This Journey (Wright), **Supp. III Part 2:** 605–606

"This Lime-Tree Bower My Prison" (Coleridge), **Supp. XXI:** 52, 55

This Man and This Woman (Farrell), **II:** 42

"This Monkey, My Back" (Boyle), **Supp. XX: 17**

"This Morning" (Huddle), **Supp. XXVI:** 151

"This Morning" (Kenyon), **Supp. VII:** 164

"This Morning, This Evening, So Soon" (Baldwin), **Supp. I Part 1:** 63

"This Morning Again It Was in the Dusty Pines" (Oliver), **Supp. VII:** 240

This Music Crept by Me upon the Waters (MacLeish), **III:** 21

"This New England: Newport, Vermont" (Mosher), **Supp. XXII:** 209

This Old House (J. Davison), **Supp. XXVI:** 65

This People Israel: The Meaning of Jewish Existence (Baeck), **Supp. V:** 260

"This Person" (July), **Supp. XXIV:** 202

"This Personal Maze Is Not the Prize" (Selinger), **Supp. XI:** 248

"This Place in the Ways" (Rukeyser), **Supp. VI:** 273–274

This Property Is Condemned (T. Williams), **IV:** 378

This Proud Heart (Buck), **Supp. II Part 1:** 119–120

This Same Sky: A Collection of Poems from around the World (Nye, ed.), **Supp. XIII:** 280

"This Sandwich Has No Mayonnaise" (Salinger), **III:** 552–553

"This Shape We're In" (Lethem), **Supp. XVIII:** 145

"This Shape We're In" (Lethem), **Supp. XVIII:** 148

This Side of Paradise (Fitzgerald), **I:** 358; **II:** 77, 80, 81, 82–83, 84, 85–87, 88; **Retro. Supp. I:** 99–100, **101–102,** 103, 105, 106, 110, 111; **Supp. XVIII:** 248

This Singing World: An Anthology of Modern Poetry for Young People (Untermeyer, ed.), **Supp. XV:** 306

This Strange Joy: Selected Poems of Sandro Penna (Di Perio, trans.), **Supp. XIX:** 34

This Stubborn Self: Texas Autobiographies (Almon), **Supp. XIII:** 288

"This They Took with Them" (Boyle), **Supp. XXIV:** 61

This Thing Don't Lead to Heaven (Crews), **Supp. XI: 112**

This Time: New and Selected Poems (Stern), **Supp. IX:** 290–291, **299**

"Thistle Seed in the Wind" (Francis), **Supp. IX:** 81

"Thistles in Sweden, The" (Maxwell), **Supp. VIII:** 169

"This Tokyo" (Snyder), **Supp. VIII:** 298

This Tree Will Be Here for a Thousand Years (R. Bly), **Supp. IV Part 1:** 65–66, 71, 72

This Tree Will Be Here for a Thousand Years (revised edition) (R. Bly), **Supp. IV Part 1:** 66

This Very Earth (Caldwell), **I:** 297, 302

This Waiting for Love (Mitchell, ed.), **Supp. XXVI:** 165, 173

This Wheel's on Fire: Levon Helm and the Story of the Band (Helm), **Supp. XVIII:** 26

This Woman (di Donato), **Supp. XX: 33, 41–42, 46**

Thoens, Karen, **Supp. V:** 147

Thomas, Brandon, **II:** 138

Thomas, Dave, **Supp. XXVI:** 18

Thomas, Debra, **Supp. XIII:** 114

Thomas, D. M., **Supp. VIII:** 5

Thomas, Dylan, **I:** 49, 64, 382, 432, 526, 533; **III:** 21, 521, 528, 532, 534; **IV:** 89, 93, 136; **Supp. I Part 1:** 263; **Supp. III Part 1:** 42, 47; **Supp. IX:** 114; **Supp. V:** 344; **Supp. VIII:** 21; **Supp. X:** 115; **Supp. XV:** 74; **Supp. XVII:** 135; **Supp. XX: 199, 204; Supp. XXIV:** 54; **Supp. XXVII:** 222

Thomas, Edna Lewis, **Supp. XVIII:** 281

Thomas, Edward, **II:** 154; **Retro. Supp. I:** 127, 131, 132; **Supp. I Part 1:** 263; **Supp. II Part 1:** 4

Thomas, Jacob ("Jake"), **Supp. XXVI:** 83

Thomas, James, **Supp. XVI:** 268

Thomas, Joseph, **Supp. XVIII:** 183

Thomas, J. Parnell, **Supp. I Part 1:** 286; **Supp. XV:** 198

Thomas, June, **Supp. XXV:** 2, 3

Thomas, Lewis, **Retro. Supp. I:** 323

Thomas, Lorenzo, **Supp. XXIV:** 37; **Supp. XXVII:** 166, 167

Thomas, Louisa, **Supp. XXIII:** 280, 283

Thomas, Rob, **Supp. XVIII:** 100, 101

Thomas, R. S., **Supp. XXI:** 83, 86–87, 93, 95, 96

Thomas, William I., **Supp. I Part 2:** 641

Thomas-a-Kempis, **Retro. Supp. I:** 247

Thomas and Beulah (Dove), **Supp. IV Part 1:** 242, 247–248, 249; **Supp. XVIII:** 174; **Supp. XXI:** 249

Thomas Aquinas (Saint), **I:** 13, 14, 265, 267; **III:** 270; **Retro. Supp. II:** 222; **Supp. IV Part 2:** 526

"Thomas at the Wheel" (Dove), **Supp. IV Part 1:** 248

"Thomas Eakins and the Photograph of a Man in Motion" (Major), **Supp. XXII:** 183

"Thomas Eakins' Delaware River Paintings" (Major), **Supp. XXII:** 183

"Thomas McGrath: Words for a Vanished Age" (Vinz), **Supp. X:** 117

Thomas Merton on Peace, **Supp. VIII:** 208

Thomas Merton Studies Center, The, **Supp. VIII:** 208

Thompson, Barbara, **Supp. V:** 322

Thompson, Caroline, **Supp. XXIII:** 291

Thompson, Cy, **I:** 538

Thompson, Daniel, **Supp. XXIII:** 174

Thompson, Dorothy, **II:** 449–450, 451, 453; **Supp. XV:** 307

Thompson, Edward, **Supp. XXI:** 172

Thompson, E. P., **Supp. X:** 112, 117

Thompson, Francis, **Retro. Supp. I:** 55

Thompson, Frank, **II:** 20

Thompson, George, **Supp. I Part 2:** 686; **Supp. XXIII:** 182

Thompson, Hunter S., **Supp. VIII:** 42; **Supp. XI:** 105; **Supp. XIII:** 1, 17; **Supp. XVII:** 95, 102, 228; **Supp. XXIV: 279–294**

Thompson, James R., **Supp. IV Part 1:** 217

Thompson, Jean, **Supp. XXIII: 289–305**

Thompson, John, **Supp. V:** 323; **Supp. XXI:** 151

Thompson, Juliet, **Supp. XX:** 117

Thompson, Lawrance, **II:** 508

Thompson, Lawrance Roger, **Retro. Supp. I:** 138, 141

Thompson, Lisa B., **Supp. XXIII:** 202

Thompson, Morton, **Supp. XIII:** 170

Thompson, Theresa, **Supp. V:** 141

Thompson, William T., **Supp. I Part 2:** 411

Thomson, James, **II:** 304; **Supp. I Part 1:** 150, 151; **Supp. XXIV:** 159

Thomson, Virgil, **IV:** 45; **Supp. IV Part 1:** 81, 83, 84, 173; **Supp. XVI:** 195

"Thoreau" (J. R. Lowell), **Supp. I Part 2:** 420, 422

Thoreau, Henry David, **I:** 98, 104, 228, 236, 257, 258, 261, 305, 433; **II:** 7, 8, 13, 17, 101, 159, 224, 273–274, 295, 312–313, 321, 457–458, 540, 546–547; **III:** 171, 174, 186–187, 189, 208, 214–215, 453, 454, 507, 577; **IV: 167–189,** 191, 341; **Retro. Supp. I:** 51, 62, 122; **Retro. Supp. II:** 13, 96, 142, 158; **Supp. I Part 1:** 29, 34, 116, 188, 299, 358; **Supp. I Part 2:** 383, 400, 420, 421, 507, 540, 579, 580, 655, 659, 660, 664, 678; **Supp. III Part 1:** 340, 353; **Supp. IV Part 1:** 236, 392, 416; **Supp. IV Part 2:** 420, 430, 433, 439, 447; **Supp. IX:** 25, 90, 171; **Supp. V:** 200, 208; **Supp. VIII:** 40, 42, 103, 105, 198, 201, 204, 205, 292, 303; **Supp. X:** 21, 27, 28–29, 101, 102; **Supp. XI:** 155; **Supp. XIII:** 1, 17; **Supp. XIV:** 40, 54, 106, 177, 181; **Supp. XVIII:** 4; **Supp. XX: 116, 221; Supp. XXI:** 203, 217; **Supp. XXII:** 206; **Supp. XXIII:** 174; **Supp. XXVI:** 31, 34, 37

Thoreau, John, **IV:** 171, 182

Thoreau, Mrs. John, **IV:** 172

"Thoreau's Hound: On Hiddenness" (Hirshfield), **Supp. XXIII:** 137

"Thorn, The" (Gordon), **Supp. IV Part 1:** 314

Thorne, Francis, **Supp. XII:** 253

"Thorn Merchant, The" (Komunyakaa), **Supp. XIII:** 119–120

Thornton, Billy Bob, **Supp. VIII:** 175

Thornton, Lionel, **III:** 291

"Thorofare" (Minot), **Supp. VI: 209–210**

"Thorow" (Howe), **Supp. IV Part 2:** 419, 420, 421, 431, 433–434

Thorp, Willard, **Supp. XIII:** 101

Thorslev, Peter L., Jr., **I:** 524

Thorstein Veblen (Dowd), **Supp. I Part 2:** 650

Thorstein Veblen (Qualey, ed.), **Supp. I Part 2:** 650

Thorstein Veblen: A Chapter in American Economic Thought (Teggart), **Supp. I Part 2:** 650

Thorstein Veblen: A Critical Interpretation (Riesman), **Supp. I Part 2:** 649, 650

Thorstein Veblen: A Critical Reappraisal (Dowd, ed.), **Supp. I Part 2:** 650

Thorstein Veblen and His America (Dorfman), **Supp. I Part 2:** 631, 650

Thorstein Veblen and the Institutionalists: A Study in the Social Philosophy of Economics (Seckler), **Supp. I Part 2:** 650

"Those before Us" (R. Lowell), **II:** 550

"Those Being Eaten by America" (R. Bly), **Supp. IV Part 1:** 62

Those Bones Are Not My Child (Bambara), **Supp. XI:** 1, 14, **20–22**

Those Extraordinary Twins (Twain), **IV:** 205–206

"Those Graves in Rome" (Levis), **Supp. XI:** 266

"Those of Us Who Think We Know" (Dunn), **Supp. XI:** 146

Those That Be in Bondage (Webber), **Supp. XXI:** 160

"Those Times . . ." (Sexton), **Supp. II Part 2:** 670, 684

"Those Various Scalpels" (Moore), **III:** 202

"Those Were the Days" (Levine), **Supp. V:** 190

"Those Who Don't" (Cisneros), **Supp. VII:** 60

"Those Who Love" (Teasdale), **Supp. XXVII:** 296

"Those Who Thunder" (Hogan), **Supp. IV Part 1:** 406

"Thought, A" (Sarton), **Supp. VIII:** 262

Thought and Character of William James (Perry), **II:** 362

Thoughtbook of Francis Scott Key Fitzgerald (Fitzgerald), **Retro. Supp. I:** 99

"Thought Experiment" (Saunders), **Supp. XIX:** 235

"Thoughtful Roisterer Declines the Gambit, The" (Hecht), **Supp. X:** 63

"Thought of Heaven, The" (Stern), **Supp. IX:** 297

"Thoughts after Lambeth" (Eliot), **I:** 587; **Retro. Supp. I:** 324

Thoughts and Reflections (Lord Halifax), **II:** 111

Thoughts in Solitude (Merton), **Supp. VIII:** 207

"Thoughts on Being Bibliographed" (Wilson), **IV:** 435

"Thoughts on the Establishment of a Mint in the United States" (Paine), **Supp. I Part 2:** 512

"Thoughts on the Gifts of Art" (Kenyon), **Supp. VII:** 167

Thousand Acres, A (Smiley), **Supp. VI:** 292, **301–303**

"Thousand and Second Night, The" (Merrill), **Supp. III Part 1:** 324

"Thousand Dollar Vagrant, The" (Olsen), **Supp. XIII:** 292, 297

"Thousand Faces of Danny Torrance, The" (Figliola), **Supp. V:** 143

"Thousand Genuflections, A" (McCarriston), **Supp. XIV:** 266

Thousand-Mile Walk to the Gulf, A (Muir), **Supp. IX: 177–178**

Thousand Plateaus, A (Deleuze and Guattari), **Supp. XXV:** 123

"Thou Shalt Not Steal" (McClatchy), **Supp. XII:** 264

"Thread, The" (Merwin), **Supp. III Part 1:** 351

Three (film), **Supp. IX:** 253

3-3-8 (Marquand), **III:** 58

"3 A.M. Kitchen: My Father Talking" (Gallagher), **Supp. XXIV:** 169

"Three Academic Pieces" (Stevens), **IV:** 90

"Three Agee Wards, The" (Morris), **III:** 220–221

"Three American Singers" (Cather), **Retro. Supp. I:** 10

"Three Around the Old Gentleman" (Berryman), **I:** 188

"Three Avilas, The" (Jeffers), **Supp. II Part 2:** 418

"Three Black Women Writers" (C. L. R. James), **Supp. XXI:** 172

Three Books of Song (Longfellow), **II:** 490

"Three Bushes" (Yeats), **Supp. I Part 1:** 80

Three Cantos (Pound), **Retro. Supp. I:** 290

Three Centuries of Harvard (Morison), **Supp. I Part 2:** 485

Three Changes (Silver), **Supp. XXIV:** 275

Three Circles of Light (di Donato), **Supp. XX: 33, 42–43, 44, 46**

Three Cities: A Trilogy (Asch), **Supp. XXIII:** 1, 5, **10–12**

Three Comrades (Remarque), **Retro. Supp. I:** 113

"Three Corollaries of Cultural Relativism" (Locke), **Supp. XIV:** 202

"Three-Day Blow, The" (Hemingway), **II:** 248

Three Essays on America (Brooks), **I:** 246

Three Farmers on Their Way to a Dance (Powers), **Supp. IX:** 211–212, **213–214**, 222

"Three Fates, The" (Benét), **Supp. XI:** 48–49, 50

"Three Generations of Secrets" (A. Finch), **Supp. XVII:** 73

"Three Gifts, The" (Gibran), **Supp. XX: 124**

Three Gospels (Price), **Supp. VI:** 267

365 Days (Boyle), **Supp. XXIV:** 50, 60

"Three Kings, The: Hemingway, Faulkner, and Fitzgerald" (Ford), **Supp. V:** 59

Three Lives (Auchincloss), **Supp. IV Part 1:** 25

Three Lives (Stein), **I:** 103; **IV:** 26, 27, 31, 35, 37–41, 42, 45, 46; **Supp. IX:** 306; **Supp. XXIII:** 166

"THREE MOVEMENTS AND A CODA" (Baraka), **Supp. II Part 1:** 50

Three One Act Plays (Riverside Drive, Old Saybrook, and *Central Park West)* (Allen), **Supp. XV:** 3

Three on the Tower: The Lives and Works of Ezra Pound, T. S. Eliot, and William Carlos Williams (Simpson), **Supp. IX:** 276

Three Papers on Fiction (Welty), **IV:** 261

Three-Penny Opera (Brecht), **I:** 301; **Supp. XIV:** 162

"Three Percent Own All the Wealth" (Ryan as Quin), **Supp. XVIII:** 231–232

Three Philosophical Poets (Santayana), **III:** 610–612

"Three Pigs in Five Days" (Prose), **Supp. XVI:** 257, 258

"Three Players of a Summer Game" (T. Williams), **IV:** 383

Three Poems (Ashbery), **Supp. III Part 1:** 2, 3, 14, 15, 18, 24–26

"Three Poems for my Daughter" (Di Piero), **Supp. XIX:** 40

"Three Pokes of a Thistle" (Nye), **Supp. XIII:** 281

Three Prophets of Religious Liberalism (Wright), **Supp. XXIV:** 71

Three Roads, The (Macdonald, under Millar), **Supp. IV Part 2:** 466, 467

Three Short Plays with Long Titles (Silver and Ann), **Supp. XXIV:** 264

"Three Silences of Molinos, The" (Longfellow), **Retro. Supp. II:** 169

Three Sisters, The (Chekhov), **Supp. XV:** 323

"Three Sisters, The" (Cisneros), **Supp. VII:** 64

Three Soldiers (Dos Passos), **I:** 477–478, 480, 482, 488, 493–494; **Supp. XXI:** 277

"Three Songs at the End of Summer" (Kenyon), **Supp. VII:** 169–170

"Three Steps to the Graveyard" (Wright), **Supp. III Part 2:** 593, 596

Three Stories and Ten Poems (Hemingway), **II:** 68, 263; **Supp. XVII:** 105

Three Tall Women (Albee), **Supp. XXIV:** 270

Three Taverns, The (Robinson), **III:** 510

"Three Taverns, The" (Robinson), **III:** 521, 522

Three Tenant Families (Agee), **I:** 37–38

Three Tenors, One Vehicle: A Book of Songs (X. J. Kennedy, Camp, and Waldrop), **Supp. XV:** 165

"Three Types of Poetry" (Tate), **IV:** 131

"Three Vagabonds of Trinidad" (Harte), **Supp. II Part 1:** 338

"Three Waterfalls, The" (Lanier), **Supp. I Part 1:** 350

"Three-Way Mirror" (Brooks), **Supp. III Part 1:** 69–70

Three Weeks in Spring (Parker and Parker), **Supp. XIX:** 187

"Three Women" (Plath), **Supp. I Part 2:** 539, 541, 544, 545, 546

Three Young Poets (Swallow, ed.), **Supp. X:** 116

Threnody (Emerson), **Supp. I Part 2:** 416

"Threnody" (Emerson), **II:** 7

"Threnody for a Brown Girl" (Cullen), **Supp. IV Part 1:** 166

"Threshing-Floor, The" (Baldwin), **Supp. I Part 1:** 50

"Threshing Wheat" (Huddle), **Supp. XXVI:** 148

Threshold (film), **Supp. IX:** 254

"Threshold" (Goldbarth), **Supp. XII:** 175

Threshold (Jackson), **Supp. IX:** 117

Thriller (television show), **Supp. XXVII:** 119

"Throat" (Goldbarth), **Supp. XII:** 177–178

Throne of Labdacus, The (Schnackenberg), **Supp. XV:** 260, **263–266**

Thrones (Pound), **Retro. Supp. I:** 293

Through Dooms of Love (Kumin), **Supp. IV Part 2:** 444

Through Glacier Park in 1915 (Rinehart), **Supp. XXV:** 195

"Through the Black Curtain" (Kingston), **Supp. V:** 169

Through the Forest: New and Selected Poems, 1977–1987 (Wagoner), **Supp. IX:** 330–331

"Through the Gates of the Silver Key" (Lovecraft and Price), **Supp. XXV:** 114, 123

"Through the Hills of Spain" (Salinas), **Supp. XIII:** 315

"Through the Hole in the Mundane Millstone" (West), **Retro. Supp. II:** 321, 322

Through the Ivory Gate (Dove), **Supp. IV Part 1:** 242, 243, 251, 252, 253–254, 254

"Through the Kitchen Window, Chiapas" (Nye), **Supp. XIII:** 277

Through the Safety Net (C. Baxter), **Supp. XVII:** 17, 22

"Through the Smoke Hole" (Snyder), **Supp. VIII:** 299

Throw Like a Girl (Thompson), **Supp. XXIII:** 299–300

"Throw Like a Girl"(Thompson), **Supp. XXIII:** 299, 300

"Thrush Relinquished, The" (Grossman), **Supp. XIX:** 83

Thucydides, **II:** 418; **IV:** 50; **Supp. I Part 2:** 488, 489, 492; **Supp. IV Part 1:** 391; **Supp. XIII:** 233

Thunderbolt and Lightfoot (film), **Supp. X:** 126

"Thunder from a Cloudless Sky" (Mosher), **Supp. XXII:** 209

"Thunderhead" (MacLeish), **III:** 19

Thurber, James, **I:** 487; **II:** 432; **IV:** 396; **Supp. I Part 2: 602–627,** 653, 654, 668, 672, 673, 679; **Supp. II Part 1:** 143; **Supp. IV Part 1:** 349; **Supp. IX:** 118; **Supp. XIV:** 104; **Supp. XVI:** 167; **Supp. XVII:** 4

Thurber, Mrs. James (Althea Adams), **Supp. I Part 2:** 613, 615, 617

Thurber, Mrs. James (Helen Muriel Wismer), **Supp. I Part 2:** 613, 617, 618

Thurber, Robert, **Supp. I Part 2:** 613, 617

Thurber, Rosemary, **Supp. I Part 2:** 616

Thurber, William, **Supp. I Part 2:** 602

Thurber Album, The (Thurber), **Supp. I Part 2:** 611, 619

Thurber Carnival, The (Thurber), **Supp. I Part 2:** 620; **Supp. XIV:** 104

Thurman, Judith, **Supp. IV Part 1:** 309; **Supp. XXV:** 2

Thurman, Wallace, **Retro. Supp. I:** 200; **Supp. I Part 1:** 325, 326, 328, 332; **Supp. IV Part 1:** 164; **Supp. X:** 136, 139; **Supp. XIX:** 78; **Supp. XVI:** 135; **Supp. XVIII:** 279, 281; **Supp. XXII:** 2

"Thursday" (Millay), **III:** 129

"Thurso's Landing" (Jeffers), **Supp. II Part 2:** 433

"Thus Do I Refute Gioia" (Junker), **Supp. XV:** 116

"Thus Far by Faith" (Nelson), **Supp. XVIII:** 177

Thus Spake Zarathustra (Nietzsche), **II:** 463; **Supp. IV Part 1:** 110; **Supp. IV Part 2:** 519

Thwaite, Lady Alicia. See Rawlings, Marjorie Kinnan

"Thyme" (Stallings), **Supp. XXV:** 232–233

Thy Neighbor's Wife (Talese), **Supp. XVII:** 204, 205–206, 207, 208, 210

"Tiara" (Doty), **Supp. XI:** 122

"Tibetan Time" (Prose), **Supp. XVI:** 255

Ticket for a Seamstitch, A (Harris), **II:** 424–425

Tickets for a Prayer Wheel (Dillard), **Supp. VI:** 22, 34

Ticket That Exploded, The (Burroughs), **Supp. III Part 1:** 93, 103, 104

Tickless Time (Glaspell), **Supp. III Part 1:** 179

Ticknor, George, **II:** 488; **Supp. I Part 1:** 313

Ticknor, William, **Supp. XVIII:** 258

"Ti Démon" (Chopin), **Supp. I Part 1:** 225

Tide of Time, The (Masters), **Supp. I Part 2:** 471

"Tide of Voices" (Hull), **Supp. XXI:** 132, 133–134, 136

"Tide Rises, the Tide Falls, The" (Longfellow), **I:** 498

"Tides" (Hoffman), **Supp. XVIII:** 86

Tidewater Blood (Hoffman), **Supp. XVIII: 82–83**

Tidyman, Ernest, **Supp. V:** 226

Tietjens, Eunice, **Supp. XV:** 47, 297; **Supp. XXVII:** 286

"Tiger" (Blake), **Supp. I Part 1:** 80; **Supp. VIII:** 26

Tiger (Bynner), **Supp. XV:** 42, 50

"Tiger, The" (Buechner), **Supp. XII:** 48

Tiger in the House, The (Van Vechten), **Supp. II Part 2:** 736

Tiger Joy (Benét), **Supp. XI:** 45

Tiger-Lilies (Lanier), **Supp. I Part 1:** 350–351, 357, 360, 371

Tiger Who Wore White Gloves, The: or, What You Are, You Are (Brooks), **Supp. III Part 1:** 86

Till, Emmett, **Supp. I Part 1:** 61

Till, Eric, **Supp. XXIII:** 103

Tillich, Paul, **II:** 244; **III:** 291, 292, 303, 309; **IV:** 226; **Retro. Supp. I:** 325, 326, 327; **Supp. V:** 267; **Supp. XIII:** 74, 91

Tillie Olsen: A Study of the Short Fiction (Frye), **Supp. XIII:** 292, 296, 298, 299, 302

Tillman, Lynne, **Supp. XII:** 4

Tillotson, John, **II:** 114

Tillotson, Kristen, **Supp. XVII:** 23

Tillstrom, Burr, **Supp. XIV:** 125

Till the Day I Die (Odets), **Supp. II Part 2:** 530, 533–536, 552

Tilton, Eleanor, **Supp. I Part 1:** 317

Tilton, Theodore, **Supp. XVIII:** 4

Timaeus (Plato), **II:** 10; **III:** 609

Tim: A Story of School Life (Sturgis), **Supp. XX: 227,** 230, 232, **233–235**

Timber (Jonson), **II:** 16

Timberg, Scott, **Supp. XV:** 116

"Timberwolf" (Halliday), **Supp. XIX:** 91

Timbuktu (Auster), **Supp. XII:** 34, **35–36**

"Time" (Matthews), **Supp. IX: 165–166**

"Time" (Merrill), **Supp. III Part 1:** 325

"Time" (Very), **Supp. XXV:** 249

"Time and Again" (Sanders), **Supp. XVI:** 269

Time and a Place, A (Humphrey), **Supp. IX:** 95, 98, **100–102**

"Time and Distance Overcome" (Biss), **Supp. XXVI:** 55–56

"Time and the Garden" (Winters), **Supp. II Part 2:** 801, 809

"Time and the Liturgy" (Merton), **Supp. VIII:** 199

Time and the River (Edgell), **Supp. XXIII:** 84, 85, **91–93**

Time and Tide: A Walk through Nantucket (Conroy), **Supp. XVI:** 63, 71, **76–77**

"Time Exposure" (C. Baxter), **Supp. XVII:** 20–21

Time Exposures, by Search-Light (W. Frank), **Supp. XX: 75**

Time in the Rock (Aiken), **I:** 65

Time Is Noon, The (Buck), **Supp. II Part 1:** 129, 130–131

Time & Money (Matthews), **Supp. IX:** 155, **165–167**

"Time of Death, A" (Munro), **Supp. XXVII:** 180

"Time of Friendship, The" (Bowles), **Supp. IV Part 1:** 90–91

"Time of Her Time, The" (Mailer), **III:** 37, 45; **Retro. Supp. II:** 200

Time of Our Time, The (Mailer), **Retro. Supp. II:** 213–214

Time of the Assassins, The: A Study of Rimbaud (H. Miller), **III:** 189

"Time of the Missile" (Oppen), **Supp. XXVI:** 232

Time Out of Mind (album, Dylan), **Supp. XVIII:** 28

"Time Past" (Morris), **III:** 232

"Time Present" (Morris), **III:** 232

"Times" (Beattie), **Supp. V:** 31

"Times, The" (Emerson), **II:** 11–12

Times Are Never So Bad, The (Dubus), **Supp. VII:** 87–88

Time's Arrow (Amis), **Retro. Supp. I:** 278

"Time Shall Not Die" (Chandler), **Supp. IV Part 1:** 120

Times of Melville and Whitman, The (Brooks), **I:** 257

"Times They Are A-Changin', The" (album, Dylan), **Supp. XVIII:** 20, 25

"Times They Are A-Changin,' The" (song, Dylan), **Supp. XVIII:** 30

"Timesweep" (Sandburg), **III:** 595–596

Time to Act, A (MacLeish), **III:** 3

Time to Be Born, A (Powell), **Supp. XIX:** 143

Time to Go (Dixon), **Supp. XII:** 147

Time to Kill (film), **Supp. IV Part 1:** 130

Time to Speak, A (MacLeish), **III:** 3

Time Will Darken It (Maxwell), **Supp. VIII:** 159, **162–164,** 169

"Timing of Sin, The" (Dubus), **Supp. VII:** 91

Tim O'Brien (Herzog), **Supp. V:** 239

Timoleon (Melville), **III:** 93; **Retro. Supp. I:** 257

Timothy Dexter Revisited (Marquand), **III:** 55, 62, 63

Timothy Findley: Stories from a Life (Roberts), **Supp. XX: 53**

Timrod, Henry, **Supp. XVIII:** 31, 33

Tin Can, The (W. J. Smith), **Supp. XIII:** 334, **Supp. XIII:** 336, 337

"Tin Can, The" (W. J. Smith), **Supp. XIII: 337–339**

Tin Can Tree, The (Tyler), **Supp. IV Part 2:** 659–660

Tinguely, Jean, **Supp. XV:** 187

Tinker, Chauncey Brewster, **Supp. XIV:** 12

"Tinseled Bucks: A Historical Study of Indian Homosexuality" (Kenny), **Supp. XXIII:** 149

Tintern Abbey (Wordsworth), **Supp. I Part 2:** 673, 675

Tiny Alice (Albee), **I:** 81–86, 87, 88, 94

"Tiny Closet, The" (Inge), **Supp. XXV:** 105–106

"Tiny Mummies! The True Story of the Ruler of 43rd Street's Land of the Walking Dead" (Wolfe), **Supp. III Part 2:** 573, 574

Tip on a Dead Jockey and Other Stories (Shaw), **Supp. XIX:** 251

"Tip-Top Club, The" (Keillor), **Supp. XVI:** 172

"Tired" (Hughes), **Supp. I Part 1:** 331

"Tired and Unhappy, You Think of Houses" (Schwartz), **Supp. II Part 2:** 649

"Tiresias" (Garrett), **Supp. VII:** 96–97

'Tis (McCourt), **Supp. XII:** 271, **279–286**

Tisch (Dixon), **Supp. XII:** 141, **155–156**

" 'Tis Finished" (Very), **Supp. XXV:** 249

Tish (Rinehart), **Supp. XXV:** 194

Tish Marches On (Rinehart), **Supp. XXV:** 194

Tish Plays the Game (Rinehart), **Supp. XXV:** 194

Titan, The (Dreiser), **I:** 497, 501, 507–508, 509, 510; **Retro. Supp. II:** 94, 101, 102

Titanic Operas (Dickinson Electronic Archives), **Supp. XXVII:** 261

Titian, **Supp. I Part 2:** 397, 714

"Tito's Goodbye" (García), **Supp. XI:** 190

"To a Bird, Seen Under My Window in the Garden" (J. Schoolcraft), **Supp. XXIII:** 230

To a Blossoming Pear Tree (Wright), **Supp. III Part 2:** 602–605

"To a Blossoming Pear Tree" (Wright), **Supp. III Part 2:** 604

"To Abolish Children" (Shapiro), **Supp. II Part 2:** 717

To Abolish Children and Other Essays (Shapiro), **Supp. II Part 2:** 703

"To a Calvinist in Bali" (Millay), **Supp. XXVI:** 170

"To a Caty-Did, the Precursor of Winter" (Freneau), **Supp. II Part 1:** 274–275

"To a Chameleon" (Moore), **III:** 195, 196, 215

"To a Conscript of 1940" (Read), **II:** 372–373, 377–378

"To a Contemporary Bunk Shooter" (Sandburg), **III:** 582

"To a Cough in the Street at Midnight" (Wylie), **Supp. I Part 2:** 727, 729–730

"To a Defeated Savior" (Wright), **Supp. III Part 2:** 593–594, 596

"To a Face in the Crowd" (Warren), **IV:** 239

"To a Fish Head Found on the Beach near Malaga" (Levine), **Supp. V:** 185

"To a Friend" (Nemerov), **III:** 272

"To a Friend" (O'Hara), **Supp. XXIII:** 212

"To a Friend Whose Work Has Come to Triumph" (Sexton), **Supp. II Part 2:** 683

To a God Unknown (Steinbeck), **I:** 107; **IV:** 51, 59–60, 67

"To a Greek Marble" (Aldington), **Supp. I Part 1:** 257

"To a Locomotive in Winter" (Whitman), **IV:** 348

"To a Mad Friend" (Davison), **Supp. XXVI:** 69

"To a Military Rifle" (Winters), **Supp. II Part 2:** 810, 811, 815

"To a Mouse" (Burns), **Supp. IX:** 173

"To an American Workman Dying of Starvation" (Taggard), **Supp. XXII:** 282

"To an Athlete Dying Young" (Houseman), **Supp. XVII:** 121

"To a Negro Jazz Band in a Parisian Cabaret" (Hughes), **Supp. I Part 1:** 325

"To an Old Philosopher in Rome" (Stevens), **III:** 605; **Retro. Supp. I:** 312

"To an Old Poet in Peru" (Ginsberg), **Supp. II Part 1:** 322

"To a Now-Type Poet" (X. J. Kennedy), **Supp. XV:** 161

"To Answer Your Question" (Jarman), **Supp. XVII:** 114–115

"To Any Would-Be Terrorists" (Nye), **Supp. XIII:** 285, 286

"To a Picture of Eleonora Duse" (Teasdale), **Supp. XXVII:** 287

"To a Poet" (Rich), **Supp. I Part 2:** 571; **Supp. XIX:** 83

"To a Prize Bird" (Moore), **III:** 215

"To a Republican, with Mr. Paine's Rights of Man" (Freneau), **Supp. II Part 1:** 267

"To a Revolutionary Girl" (Bodenheim), **Supp. XXV:** 28

"To a Shade" (Yeats), **III:** 18

"To a Skylark" (Shelley), **Supp. I Part 2:** 720; **Supp. X:** 31

"Toast to Harlem, A" (Hughes), **Supp. I Part 1:** 338

"To Aunt Rose" (Ginsberg), **Supp. II Part 1:** 320

"To Autumn" (Keats), **Supp. IX:** 50

"To a Waterfowl" (Bryant), **Supp. I Part 1:** 154, 155, 162, 171

"To a Young Poet" (X. J. Kennedy), **Supp. XV:** 161

"To a Young Writer" (Stegner), **Supp. X:** 24

"Tobacco" (Rash), **Supp. XXVII:** 218

Tobacco Road (Caldwell), **I:** 288, 289, 290, 295–296, 297, 298, 302, 307, 309, 310; **IV:** 198; **Supp. XXII:** 196

"To Be a Monstrous Clever Fellow" (Fante), **Supp. XI:** 167

"To Become Music or Break" (Jauss), **Supp. XXI:** 133

To Bedlam and Part Way Back (Sexton), **Retro. Supp. II:** 245; **Supp. II Part 2:** 672–678; **Supp. IV Part 2:** 441; **Supp. XI:** 317

"To Beethoven" (Lanier), **Supp. I Part 1:** 364

To Begin Again: Stories and Memoirs, 1908–1929 (M. F. K. Fisher), **Supp. XVII:** 92

Tobey, Mark, **Supp. X:** 264

To Be Young, Gifted, and Black: Lorraine Hansberry in Her Own Words (Nemiroff), **Supp. IV Part 1:** 372, 374

"To Big Mary from an Ex-Catholic" (Mora), **Supp. XIII:** 217, 224, 228

Tobin, Jacqueline L., **Supp. XXVI:** 200

"Tobin's Palm" (O. Henry), **Supp. II Part 1:** 408; **Supp. XV:** 40

Tobit (apocryphal book), **I:** 89

"To Build a Fire" (London), **II:** 468

Toby Tyler: or, Ten Weeks with a Circus (Otis), **III:** 577

"To Change in a Good Way" (Ortiz), **Supp. IV Part 2:** 511

"To Charlotte Cushman" (Lanier), **Supp. I Part 1:** 364

"To Cole, the Painter, Departing for Europe" (Bryant), **Supp. I Part 1:** 157, 161

Tocqueville, Alexis de, **III:** 261; **IV:** 349; **Retro. Supp. I:** 235; **Supp. I Part 1:** 137; **Supp. I Part 2:** 659, 660; **Supp. II Part 1:** 281, 282, 284; **Supp. XIV:** 306, 312

"To Crispin O'Conner" (Freneau), **Supp. II Part 1:** 268

"To Da-Duh, In Memoriam" (Marshall), **Supp. XI:** 276

"TODAY" (Baraka), **Supp. II Part 1:** 55

"Today" (Ginsberg), **Supp. II Part 1:** 328

"Today Is a Good Day To Die" (Bell), **Supp. X:** 7

"Today" (O'Hara), **Supp. XXIII:** 210–211

"Today Will Be a Quiet Day" (Hempel), **Supp. XXI:** 117, **Supp. XXI:** 118

Todd, Mabel Loomis, **I:** 454, 470; **Retro. Supp. I:** 33, 34, 35, 39, 47

"To Death" (Levertov), **Supp. III Part 1:** 274

"To Delmore Schwartz" (R. Lowell), **II:** 547; **Retro. Supp. II:** 188

"to disembark" (Brooks), **Supp. III Part 1:** 86

"To Dorothy on Her Exclusion from The Guinness Book of Records" (X. J. Kennedy), **Supp. XV:** 166

"To Dream of Bears" (Gallagher), **Supp. XXIV:** 176

"To Dr. Thomas Shearer" (Lanier), **Supp. I Part 1:** 370

"To Earthward" (Frost), **II:** 154

"To Edward John Moreton Drax Plunkett, Eighteenth Baron Dunsany" (Lovecraft), **Supp. XXV:** 113

"To Edwin V. McKenzie" (Winters), **Supp. II Part 2:** 801

"To Eleonora Duse" (A. Lowell), **II:** 528

"To Elizabeth Ward Perkins" (A. Lowell), **II:** 516

"To Elsie" (W. C. Williams), **Retro. Supp. I:** 419

"To Emily Dickinson" (H. Crane), **Retro. Supp. II:** 76

"To E. T." (Frost), **Retro. Supp. I:** 132

To Feel These Things (L. Michaels), **Supp. XVI:** 205, 213–214

"To Feel These Things" (L. Michaels), **Supp. XVI:** 214

Toffler, Alvin, **Supp. IV Part 2:** 517

"To Fill" (Moore), **Supp. X:** 168, 169

"To Gabriela, a Young Writer" (Mora), **Supp. XIII:** 220

"To George May" (Bodenheim), **Supp. XXV:** 25

To Have and Have Not (film), **Supp. XV:** 347

To Have and Have Not (Hemingway), **I:** 31; **II:** 253–254, 264; **Retro. Supp. I:** 182, **183,** 187

"To Helen" (Poe), **III:** 410, 411, 427; **Retro. Supp. II:** 102

"To Hell With Dying" (Walker), **Supp. III Part 2:** 523

"To His Coy Mistress" (Marvell), **Supp. XXIII:** 62

"To His Excellency General Washington" (Wheatley), **Supp. XX: 289**

"To His Father" (Jeffers), **Supp. II Part 2:** 415

Toilet, The (Baraka), **Supp. II Part 1:** 37, 40–42

"To James Russell Lowell" (Holmes), **Supp. I Part 1:** 311

To Jerusalem and Back (Bellow), **Retro. Supp. II:** 29

"To Jesus on His Birthday" (Millay), **III:** 136–137

"To John Keats" (A. Lowell), **II:** 516

"To Judge Faolain, Dead Long Enough: A Summons" (McCarriston), **Supp. XIV:** 264–265

"To Justify My Singing" (Wright), **Supp. III Part 2:** 590

"To Kill a Deer" (C. Frost), **Supp. XV:** 102

To Kill a Mockingbird (film), **Supp. VIII:** 128–129

To Kill a Mockingbird (Lee), **Supp. VIII: 113–129; Supp. XIX:** 142; **Supp. XVI:** 259; **Supp. XXVII:** 13

"*To Kill a Mockingbird:* Harper Lee's Tragic Vision" (Dave), **Supp. VIII:** 126

To Kill a Mockingbird: Threatening Boundaries (C. D. Johnson), **Supp. VIII:** 126

Toklas, Alice B., **IV:** 27; **Supp. IV Part 1:** 81, 91; **Supp. XVI:** 187

"Tokyo Story" (Wasserstein), **Supp. XV:** 328

"To Larry Rivers" (O'Hara), **Supp. XXIII:** 212

"To Light" (Hogan), **Supp. IV Part 1:** 402

"To Ligurinus" (Horace; Ferry, trans.), **Supp. XXIV:** 155

"To Ligurinus" (Horace; Howard, trans.), **Supp. XXIV:** 155

"To Live and Diet" (Wasserstein), **Supp. XV:** 328

Tolkien, J. R. R., **Supp. V:** 140

Tolkin, Michael, **Supp. XI:** 160

Toller, Ernst, **I:** 479

"To Lose the Earth" (Sexton), **Supp. II Part 2:** 684, 685

Tolson, Melvin, **Retro. Supp. I:** 208, 209, 210

Tolstoy, Leo, **I:** 6, 7, 58, 103, 312, 376; **II:** 191–192, 205, 271, 272, 275, 276, 281, 285, 286, 320, 407, 542, 559, 570, 579, 606; **III:** 37, 45, 61, 323, 467, 572; **IV:** 17, 21, 170, 285; **Retro. Supp. I:** 91, 225; **Retro. Supp. II:** 299; **Supp. I Part 1:** 2, 3, 6, 20; **Supp. IV Part 1:** 392; **Supp. IX:** 246; **Supp. V:** 277, 323; **Supp. XI:** 68; **Supp. XII:** 310, 322; **Supp. XIV:** 87, 97, 98; **Supp. XIX:** 241; **Supp. XXIII:** 4, 11, 275; **Supp. XXIV:** 132; **Supp. XXV:** 142

"To Lu Chi" (Nemerov), **III:** 275

"To Lydia" (Horace; Ferry, trans.), **Supp. XXIV:** 154

"To Lydia" (Horace; McHugh, trans.), **Supp. XXIV:** 154

Tom (Cummings), **I:** 430

"Tom" (Oliver), **Supp. VII:** 232

"To M." (Teasdale), **Supp. XXVII:** 297

"Tom, Tom, the Piper's Son" (Ransom), **Supp. X:** 58

"To M, with a Rose" (Lanier), **Supp. I Part 1:** 364

To Make a Prairie (Kumin), **Supp. IV Part 2:** 440, 441

"To Make Words Disappear" (Simpson), **Supp. IX:** 265–266

Tomás and the Library Lady (Mora), **Supp. XIII:** 216, 221

"Tomatoes" (Francis), **Supp. IX:** 82

"Tom Ball's Barn" (Kooser), **Supp. XIX:** 119

"Tom Brown at Fisk" (Du Bois), **Supp. II Part 1:** 160

Tom Brown's School Days (Hughes), **Supp. I Part 2:** 406

"Tomb Stone" (Dickey), **Supp. IV Part 1:** 185

"Tombstone Blues" (song, Dylan), **Supp. XVIII:** 30

Tomcat in Love (O'Brien), **Supp. V:** 238, 240, 243, 252–254

"Tomcat's Wife, The" (C. Bly), **Supp. XVI:** 40

Tomcat's Wife and Other Stories, The (C. Bly), **Supp. XVI:** 40–41

"Tom Fool at Jamaica" (Moore), **III:** 215

To Mix with Time (Swenson), **Supp. IV Part 2:** 637, 643–645, 645

Tom Jones (Fielding), **I:** 131; **Supp. V:** 127

Tomlinson, Charles, **Supp. XVI:** 284

Tommy Gallagher's Crusade (Farrell), **II:** 44

Tommyknockers, The (King), **Supp. V:** 139, 144

"Tommy's Burglar" (Henry), **Supp. II Part 1:** 399, 401

"Tommy Stames" (Budbill), **Supp. XIX:** 8

Tomo Cheeki (pseudonym). *See* Freneau, Philip

Tomorrow Is Another Day (E. P. Jones), **Supp. XXII:** 252

Tomorrow is Another Day (film, Feist), **Supp. XVII:** 62

"Tomorrow the Moon" (Dos Passos), **I:** 493

Tomorrow Will Be Better (B. Smith), **Supp. XXIII:** 258, 264–267

"Tom Outland's Story" (Cather), **I:** 325–326

Tompkins, Jane, **Supp. XVI:** 89; **Supp. XVIII:** 258, 259, 263

Tompson, Benjamin, **Supp. I Part 1:** 110, 111

"Tom-Rock Through Eels" (Hempel), **Supp. XXI:** 116, 118, 123–124

Tom Sawyer (Twain). *See Adventures of Tom Sawyer, The* (Twain)

Tom Sawyer Abroad (Twain), **II:** 482; **IV:** 19, 204

Tom Sawyer Detective (Twain), **IV:** 204

Tom Sawyer (musical) (Gurney), **Supp. V:** 96

"Tom's Husband" (Jewett), **Retro. Supp. II:** 132, 141

Tom Swift (Stratemeyer), **III:** 146

Tom-Walker, The (Sandoz), **Supp. XXIV:** 244, **253**, 253–255

"Tom Wolfe's Guide to Etiquette" (Wolfe), **Supp. III Part 2:** 578

"To My Brother Killed: Haumont Wood: October, 1918" (Bogan), **Supp. III Part 1:** 58

"To My Class, on Certain Fruits and Flowers Sent Me in Sickness" (Lanier), **Supp. I Part 1:** 370

"To my ever beloved & lamented son William Henry"(J. Schoolcraft), **Supp. XXIII:** 226, 231

"To My Father's Ghost" (Everwine), **Supp. XV:** 76

"To My Ghost Reflected in the Auxvasse River" (Levis), **Supp. XI:** 265

"To My Greek" (Merrill), **Supp. III Part 1:** 326

"To My Mother" (Berry), **Supp. X:** 23

"To My Sister—Ernestine Kealoha Taggard, 1900–1943" (Taggard), **Supp. XXII:** 284

"To My Small Son, at the Photographer's" (Hay), **Supp. XIV:** 121

"To My Small Son, on Certain Occasions" (Hay), **Supp. XIV:** 121

"To My Students" (Taggard), **Supp. XXII:** 280

"To Name is to Possess" (Kincaid), **Supp. VII:** 194

Tone, Aileen, **I:** 21–22

"Tongue Is, The" (Komunyakaa), **Supp. XIII:** 113

"Tongue of the Jews" (Bukiet), **Supp. XVII:** 47

Tongues (Shepard and Chaikin), **Supp. III Part 2:** 433

Tongues of Angels, The (Price), **Supp. VI:** 265

Tongues Untied (Riggs; film), **Supp. XI:** 19, 20

"Tonight" (R. Lowell), **II:** 538

"Tonight Is Part of the Struggle"(Le Sueur), **Supp. XXIII: 172**

Tonight Is the Night of the Prom (Jarman), **Supp. XVII:** 110, **112–113**

"Tonight Is the Night of the Prom" (Jarman), **Supp. XVII:** 113

Tonkin, Boyd, **Supp. XXVII:** 270

Tony Kushner in Conversation (Vorlicky, ed.), **Supp. IX:** 132

"Too Anxious for Rivers" (Frost), **II:** 162

"Too Blue" (Hughes), **Retro. Supp. I:** 207

"Too Damn Close: Thresholds and Their Maintenance in Rick Bass's Work" (Kerridge), **Supp. XVI:** 26

"Too Early" (Leopold), **Supp. XIV:** 186

"Too Early Spring" (Benét), **Supp. XI:** 53

"Too Far from Home" (Bowles), **Supp. IV Part 1:** 94–95

Too Far from Home: Selected Writings of Paul Bowles (Halpern, ed.), **Supp. IV Part 1:** 94, 95

Too Far to Go: The Maples Stories (Updike), **Retro. Supp. I:** 321

"Too Good To Be True": The Life and Art of Leslie Fiedler (Winchell), **Supp.**

XIII: 94, 98, 99, 101

Toohey, John Peter, **Supp. IX:** 190

Toolan, David, **Supp. IV Part 1:** 308

Too Late (Dixon), **Supp. XII:** 143–144

"Too Late" (Pickering), **Supp. XXI:** 197

"Too-Late Born, The" (Hemingway), **III:** 9

Toole, John Kennedy, **Supp. XIV:** 21; **Supp. XXVI: 239–254**

"Toolless" (Pickering), **Supp. XXI:** 204

Too Many Bottles (Holding), **Supp. XXII:** 126, **134–135**

"Too Many Friends" (video, Ellis), **Supp. XXVII:** 80

Toomer, Jean, **Retro. Supp. II:** 79; **Supp. I Part 1:** 325, 332; **Supp. III Part 2: 475–491**; **Supp. IV Part 1:** 16, 164, 168; **Supp. IX: 305–322**; **Supp. XIII:** 305; **Supp. XVIII:** 122; **Supp. XX:** 73; **Supp. XXII:** 6

Toomer, Nathan Eugene Pinchback. *See* Toomer, Jean

Too Much Happiness (Munro), **Supp. XXVII:** 195

"Too Much Happiness" (Munro), **Supp. XXVII:** 195

Too Much Johnson (film), **Supp. IV Part 1:** 83

"To One Who Said Me Nay" (Cullen), **Supp. IV Part 1:** 166

"Tooth, The" (Jackson), **Supp. IX:** 122

Tooth and Claw (Boyle), **Supp. XX:** 20

Tooth of Crime, The (Shepard), **Supp. III Part 2:** 432, 441–445, 447

"Too Young" (O'Hara), **III:** 369

Topaz (film), **Supp. XX:** 253

Topaz (Uris), **Supp. XX:** 247, 248, 253

"Top Israeli Official Hints at 'Shared' Jerusalem" (Nye), **Supp. XIII:** 287

"To P. L., 1916–1937" (Levine), **Supp. V:** 185

"To Please a Shadow" (Brodsky), **Supp. VIII:** 30

"Top of the Food Chain" (Boyle), **Supp. XX:** 20

"Top of the Hill" (Jewett), **II:** 406

"Topography" (Olds), **Supp. X:** 208

Topography and Other Poems (Stone), **Supp. XXVII:** 256, 262

Topper (T. Smith), **Supp. IX:** 194

To Praise the Music (Bronk), **Supp. XXI:** 31, 32

To Quito and Back (Hecht), **Supp. XXVII:** 89

Torah, **IV:** 19

"Torch Songs" (Wrigley), **Supp. XVIII:** 296

Torday, Daniel, **Supp. XXII:** 151

"To Reach Japan" (Munro), **Supp. XXVII:** 195

"Toronto, More or Less, in Fifteen Years" (Gansworth), **Supp. XXVI:** 110

Torpedo 8: The Story of Swede Larsen's Bomber Squadron (Wolfert), **Supp. XXI:** 267

Torpedo Junction (Hickam), **Supp. XXVII:** 103, 111

"Torquemada" (Bukiet), **Supp. XVII:** 44

"Torquemada" (Longfellow), **II:** 505; **Retro. Supp. II:** 164

Torrence, Ridgely, **III:** 507
Torrent and the Night Before, The (Robinson), **III:** 504
Torrents of Spring, The (Hemingway), **I:** 117; **II:** 250–251
Torres, Ben Fong, **Supp. XXVI:** 209
Torres, Héctor A., **Supp. XIII:** 225
Torres, Louis, **Supp. IV Part 2:** 529, 530
Torres-Saillant, Silvio, **Supp. XXI:** 104, 105, 108, 109
Torsney, Cheryl, **Retro. Supp. I:** 224
Tortilla Curtain, The (Boyle), **Supp. VIII: 9–10; Supp. XX: 28–29**
Tortilla Flat (Steinbeck), **IV:** 50, 51, 61, 64
Tortilla Flats (Steinbeck), **Supp. XX: 28**
Tortured Skins, and Other Fictions (Kenny), **Supp. XXIII:** 150, 156, 157
Tory Lover, The (Jewett), **II:** 406; **Retro. Supp. II:** 144–145
"Toscana" (Dixon), **Supp. XII:** 154
"To Sestius" (Horace; Ferry, trans.), **Supp. XXIV:** 155
"To Sestius" (Horace; Lasdun, trans.), **Supp. XXIV:** 154
"To Sir Toby" (Freneau), **Supp. II Part 1:** 269
"To Sophy, Expectant" (Mumford), **Supp. II Part 2:** 475
"To Speak of Woe That Is in Marriage" (R. Lowell), **II:** 550
"To Statecraft Embalmed" (Moore), **III:** 197
To Stay Alive (Levertov), **Supp. III Part 1:** 280–282
"Total Eclipse" (Dillard), **Supp. VI:** 28
"Total Eclipse of the Moon"(Crooker), **Supp. XXIII:** 55
Total Immersion (Goodman), **Supp. XXVI:** 118–121, 125
"Total Immersion" (Goodman), **Supp. XXVI:** 120
Total Recall (Paretsky), **Supp. XXV:** 172, 180, 181, 183–184
Toth, Emily, **Retro. Supp. II:** 71
Toth, Susan Allan, **Retro. Supp. II:** 138
"To the Americans of the United States" (Freneau), **Supp. II Part 1:** 271
"To the Apennines" (Bryant), **Supp. I Part 1:** 157, 164
"To the Bleeding Hearts Association of American Novelists" (Nemerov), **III:** 281
"To the Botequim & Back" (Bishop), **Retro. Supp. II:** 51
To the Bright and Shining Sun (Burke), **Supp. XIV:** 22, 25
"To the Citizens of the United States" (Paine), **Supp. I Part 2:** 519–520
"To the Dandelion" (J. R. Lowell), **Supp. I Part 2:** 424
"To the End" (Haines), **Supp. XII:** 212–213
To the Ends of the Earth: The Selected Travels of Paul Theroux, **Supp. VIII:** 324
"To the Fabulous Constellation" (Ferry), **Supp. XXIV:** 148–149
"To the Film Industry in Crisis"(O'Hara), **Supp. XXIII:** 214

To the Finland Station: A Study in the Writing and Acting of History (Wilson), **IV:** 429, 436, 443–444, 446
"To the Governor & Legislature of Massachusetts" (Nemerov), **III:** 287
To the Green Man (Jarman), **Supp. XVII:** 110, 120–121
"To the Harbormaster" (O'Hara), **Supp. XXIII:** 208, 212, 214; **Supp. XXIV:** 42
To the Holy Spirit (Winters), **Supp. II Part 2:** 810
"To the Keeper of the King's Water Works" (Freneau), **Supp. II Part 1:** 269
"To the Lacedemonians" (Tate), **IV:** 134
"To the Laodiceans" (Jarrell), **Retro. Supp. I:** 121, 140
To the Lighthouse (Woolf), **I:** 309; **II:** 600; **Retro. Supp. II:** 337; **Supp. VIII:** 155
"To the Man on Trail" (London), **II:** 466
"To the Memory of the Brave Americans Under General Greene" (Freneau), **Supp. II Part 1:** 262, 274
"To the Miscodeed"(J. Schoolcraft), **Supp. XXIII:** 230
"To the Muse" (Wright), **Supp. III Part 2:** 601
"To the Natural World: at 37" (Taggard), **Supp. XXII:** 279–280
"To the Nazi Leaders" (Hay), **Supp. XIV:** 121
"To the New World" (Jarrell), **II:** 371
"To the One of Fictive Music" (Stevens), **IV:** 89; **Retro. Supp. I:** 297, 300
"To the One Upstairs" (Simic), **Supp. VIII:** 283
"To the Peoples of the World" (Du Bois), **Supp. II Part 1:** 172
"To the Pine Tree on first seeing it on returning from Europe"(J. Schoolcraft), **Supp. XXIII:** 225, 228, 232–233
To the Place of Trumpets (B. Kelly), 132; **Supp. XVII: 123–127**
"To the Pliocene Skull" (Harte), **Supp. II Part 1:** 343–344
"To the Powers of Darkness" (Taggard), **Supp. XXII:** 279, 280
"To the Powers of Desolation" (Taggard), **Supp. XXII:** 280
"To the pure all things are pure" (Very), **Supp. XXV:** 242, 248
"To the Queen of Heaven" (Taggard), **Supp. XXII:** 280
"To the Reader" (Baudelaire), **II:** 544–545
"To The Reader" (Jarman), **Supp. XVII:** 115
"To the Reader" (Levertov), **Supp. III Part 1:** 277
"To the Republic" (Horace; Ferry, trans.), **Supp. XXIV:** 154
"To the Right Honourable William, Earl of Dartmouth" (Wheatley), **Supp. XX: 278, 284, 287–288**
"To the River Arve" (Bryant), **Supp. I Part 1:** 163

"To the Snake" (Levertov), **Supp. III Part 1:** 277
"To the Stone-Cutters" (Jeffers), **Supp. II Part 2:** 420
"To the Unseeable Animal" (Berry), **Supp. X:** 31
"To the Western World" (Simpson), **Supp. IX:** 269, 270
To the White Sea (Dickey), **Supp. IV Part 1:** 186, 190–191
"To the Young Who Want to Die" (Brooks), **Supp. III Part 1:** 85–86
"To Tlaoc of the Rain" (Everwine), **Supp. XV:** 77
"To Train a Writer" (Bierce), **I:** 199
"Touch, The" (Sexton), **Supp. II Part 2:** 687
Touch and Go (M. F. K. Fisher and D. Parrish), **Supp. XVII:** 84
"Touching the Tree" (Merwin), **Supp. III Part 1:** 355
Touching the World (Eakin), **Supp. VIII:** 167
Touch of Danger, A (Jones), **Supp. XI:** 226, **228–229**
Touch of the Poet, A (O'Neill), **III:** 385, 401, 404
Touchstone, The (Wharton), **Retro. Supp. I:** 365
Touchstone Anthology of Contemporary Nonfiction, The: Work from 1970 to the Present (Williford and Martone, eds.), **Supp. XXVI:** 53
"Touch-up Man" (Komunyakaa), **Supp. XIII:** 119
Tough Guys Don't Dance (Mailer), **Retro. Supp. II:** 211
"Tough People" (Offutt), **Supp. XIX:** 170–171
Toulet, Paul Jean, **IV:** 79
Tour (McNally), **Supp. XIII:** 197
"Tour 5" (Hayden), **Supp. II Part 1:** 381
To Urania (Brodsky), **Supp. VIII:** 22, 28–29
Tourgée, Albion W., **Supp. XIV:** 63
"Tour Guide" (Komunyakaa), **Supp. XIII:** 114
"Tourist Death" (MacLeish), **III:** 12
Tourmaline (J. Scott), **Supp. XVII: 192–194,** 195
Tour of Duty (Dos Passos), **I:** 489
"Tour of the Labyrinth" (Stallings), **Supp. XXV:** 229
Touron the Prairies, A (Irving), **II:** 312–313
Toussaint L'Ouverture, **Supp. XXI:** 166
Toussaint L'Ouverture (C. L. R. James), **Supp. XXI:** 167
Tovey, Donald Francis, **Supp. XIV:** 336
"To Virgil" (Horace; Ferry, trans.), **Supp. XXIV:** 155
"To Virgil" (Horace; Wright, trans.), **Supp. XXIV:** 155
To Walk a Crooked Mile (McGrath), **Supp. X:** 117
Toward a New Synthesis (Begiebing), **Retro. Supp. II:** 210
"Toward an Understanding of the Public Life" (Davison), **Supp. XXVI:** 73

"Toward Nightfall" (Simic), **Supp. VIII:** 277

Towards a Better Life (Burke), **I:** 270

"Towards a Chicano Poetics: The Making of the Chicano Subject, 1969–1982" (Saldívar), **Supp. IV Part 2:** 544

Towards an Enduring Peace (Bourne), **I:** 232

"Towards Morning" (Pedersen; Nelson, trans.), **Supp. XVIII:** 180

Toward the Blanched Alphabets (Sobin), **Supp. XVI:** 290

Toward the Gulf (Masters), **Supp. I Part 2:** 465–466

"Toward the Solstice" (Rich), **Supp. I Part 2:** 575–576

Toward Wholeness in Paule Marshall's Fiction (Pettis), **Supp. XI:** 276

"Tower" (Merwin), **Supp. III Part 1:** 343

"Tower Beyond Tragedy, The" (Jeffers), **Supp. II Part 2:** 429–430

Tower of Ivory (Atherton), **Supp. XXIV:** 21, 23

Tower of Ivory (MacLeish), **III:** 3–4

"Tower of Song" (Cohen), **Supp. XXVII:** 52

"Tower of the Elephant, The" (Howard), **Supp. XXVII:** 117, 125

Towers, Robert, **Supp. IX:** 259; **Supp. XVI:** 211; **Supp. XXV:** 86

"To What Red Hell" (C. Himes), **Supp. XVI:** 137

"To Whistler, American" (Pound), **III:** 465–466

"To Wine" (Bogan), **Supp. III Part 1:** 57, 58

Towle, Tony, **Supp. XXIII:** 221; **Supp. XXVII:** 23

Town, Caren J., **Supp. XVIII:** 195, 199

Town, The (Faulkner), **II:** 57, 73; **Retro. Supp. I:** 74, 82

Town, The (Richter), **Supp. XVIII:** 207, **214–215,** 217

Town and the City, The (Kerouac), **Supp. III Part 1:** 222–224; **Supp. XIV:** 143

"Town Crier" (Bierce), **I:** 193, 194, 195, 196

"Town Crier Exclusive, Confessions of a Princess Manqué: 'How Royals Found Me "Unsuitable" to Marry Their Larry' " (Elkin), **Supp. VI:** 56

Town Down the River, The (Robinson), **III:** 508

"Town Dump, The" (Nemerov), **III:** 272, 275, 281

Towne, Robert, **Supp. XI:** 159, 172, 174

"Townhouse Interior with Cat" (Clampitt), **Supp. IX:** 40

Townie (Dubus III), **Supp. XXIV:** 98, **108–111**

"Townies" (Dubus), **Supp. VII:** 86

Town in the Forest, The: Life Story of Richmond, New Hampshire (Boyce; Faust, ed.), **Supp. XXI:** 8

"Town of the Sound of a Twig Breaking" (Carson), **Supp. XII: 102**

"Town Poor, The" (Jewett), **Retro. Supp. II:** 138, 139, 143

Townsend, Alison, **Supp. XIII:** 222; **Supp. XXIII:** 132, 139

Townsend, Ann, **Supp. V:** 77

Townsend, Jim, **Supp. XXII:** 243

"Towns in Colour" (A. Lowell), **II:** 523–524

Townsman, The (Sedges), **Supp. II Part 1:** 124–125

Town Smokes (P. Benedict), **Supp. XXIII: 35–39**

"Town Smokes" (P. Benedict), **Supp. XXIII:** 37

"To World War Two" (Koch), **Supp. XV:** 184

Toys in a Field (Komunyakaa), **Supp. XIII: 121–122**

"Toys in a Field" (Komunyakaa), **Supp. XIII:** 122

Toys in the Attic (Hellman), **Supp. I Part 1:** 289–290

Toyter mentsh, Der (The dead man) (Asch), **Supp. XXIII:** 9

Tracer (F. Barthelme), **Supp. XI:** 31–32, 33

Traces of Thomas Hariot, The (Rukeyser), **Supp. VI:** 273, 274, 283

"Tracing Life with a Finger" (Caldwell), **I:** 291

Tracker (Wagoner), **Supp. IX:** 329, **336–337**

"Tracking" (Wagoner), **Supp. IX:** 329

"Track Meet, The" (Schwartz), **Supp. II Part 2:** 665

Tracks (Erdrich), **Supp. IV Part 1:** 259, 262–263, 269, 272, 273–274, 274, 275

"Track-Workers" (Bodenheim), **Supp. XXV:** 22

"Tract" (W. C. Williams), **Retro. Supp. I:** 414

"Tract against Communism, A" (Twelve Southerners), **IV:** 125, 237

Tractatus (Wittgenstein), **Supp. XVII:** 143

Tracy, Benjamin, **Supp. XVIII:** 4

Tracy, D. H., **Supp. XVIII:** 178

Tracy, Lee, **IV:** 287, 288

Tracy, Steven, **Retro. Supp. I:** 195

"Trade, The" (Levine), **Supp. V:** 193

Trading Twelves (Callahan and Murray, eds.), **Retro. Supp. II:** 119

Trading Twelves: The Selected Letters of Ralph Ellison and Albert Murray (Murray and Callahan, eds.), **Supp. XIX:** 148, 158

Traditional History of the Confederacy of the Six Nations (Scott), **Supp. XXVI:** 87

" 'Traditional' Marriage: A Secular Affair" (P. N. Warren), **Supp. XX:** 273

"Tradition and Industrialization" (Wright), **IV:** 489–490

"Tradition and Mythology: Signatures of Landscape in Chicana Poetry" (Rebolledo), **Supp. XIII:** 214

"Tradition and the Individual Talent" (Eliot), **I:** 441, 574, 585; **Retro. Supp. I:** 59, 286

Tragedies, Life and Letters of James Gates Percival (Swinburne), **Supp. I Part 2:** 422

Tragedy of Bees, A (P. N. Warren), **Supp. XX: 261**

"Tragedy of Bees, A" (P. N. Warren), **Supp. XX: 272**

Tragedy of Don Ippolito, The (Howells), **II:** 279

"Tragedy of Error, A" (James), **II:** 322; **Retro. Supp. I:** 218

Tragedy of Pudd'nhead Wilson, The (Twain), **IV:** 206–207

Tragic America (Dreiser), **Retro. Supp. II:** 95

"Tragic Dialogue" (Wylie), **Supp. I Part 2:** 724

Tragic Ground (Caldwell), **I:** 297, 306

Tragic Muse, The (James), **Retro. Supp. I:** 227

Traherne, Thomas, **IV:** 151; **Supp. III Part 1:** 14; **Supp. V:** 208; **Supp. XV:** 212; **Supp. XVI:** 282, 288, 295

"Trail, The" (W. J. Smith), **Supp. XIII:** 342

Trailerpark (Banks), **Supp. V:** 12

"Trailing Arbutus, The" (Whittier), **Supp. I Part 2:** 691

Trail of the Lonesome Pine, The (Fox), **Supp. XIII:** 166

"Train, The" (O'Connor), **Retro. Supp. II:** 225

"Train Dreams" (Berrigan), **Supp. XXIV:** 45

"Train Ride" (Berrigan), **Supp. XXIV:** 42, 43–44

"Train Rising Out of the Sea" (Ashbery), **Supp. III Part 1:** 22

"Trains" (Banks), **Supp. V:** 8

"Train Tune" (Bogan), **Supp. III Part 1:** 64

Train Whistle Guitar (Murray), **Supp. XIX: 153–155,** 157

Traitor, The (Wouk), **Supp. XXV:** 256, 259

"Traits of Indian Character" (Irving), **II:** 303

Trakl, Georg, **Supp. XVII:** 241

Tramp Abroad, A (Twain), **IV:** 200

Tramping With a Poet in the Rockies (S. Graham), **Supp. I Part 2:** 397

Tramp's Excuse, The (Lindsay), **Supp. I Part 2:** 379, 380, 382

Tran, Sharon, **Supp. XXVI:** 216, 218

"Trance, The" (Taggard), **Supp. XXII:** 280

"Transaction" (Cliff), **Supp. XXII:** 75

"Transatlantic" (Toomer), **Supp. III Part 2:** 486

Transatlantic Sketches (James), **II:** 324; **Retro. Supp. I:** 219

"Transcendental Etude" (Rich), **Supp. I Part 2:** 576

"Transcontinental Highway" (Cowley), **Supp. II Part 1:** 141

"Transducer" (Ammons), **Supp. VII:** 28

"Transfiguration" (Jarman), **Supp. XVII:** 118, 119

"Transfigured Bird" (Merrill), **Supp. III Part 1:** 320–321

"Transformations" (Harjo), **Supp. XII:** 226

Transformations (Sexton), **Supp. II Part 2:** 689–691; **Supp. IV Part 2:** 447; **Supp. XIV:** 125

Transforming Madness: New Lives for People Living with Mental Illness (Neugeboren), **Supp. XVI:** 229

"Transit" (Conroy), **Supp. XVI:** 72

Transit to Narcissus, A (Mailer), **Retro. Supp. II:** 196

"Translation" (Espaillat), **Supp. XXI:** 107

"Translation and Transposition" (Carne-Ross), **Supp. I Part 1:** 268–269

"Translation of a Fragment of Simonides" (Bryant), **Supp. I Part 1:** 153, 155

"Translations" (Rich), **Supp. I Part 2:** 563

Translations of Ezra Pound, The (Kenner, ed.), **III:** 463

Translations of the Gospel Back into Tongues (Wright), **Supp. XV: 342–343,** 346

"Translator's Task, The"(Benjamin), **Supp. XXIII:** 28

"Trans-National America" (Bourne), **I:** 229, 230

"Transparency" (X. J. Kennedy), **Supp. XV:** 159–160

"Transparent Itineraries: 1983" (Sobin), **Supp. XVI:** 287

"Transparent Itineraries: 1984" (Sobin), **Supp. XVI:** 287

"Transparent Itineraries: 1992" (Sobin), **Supp. XVI:** 289

"Transparent Itineraries" poems (Sobin), **Supp. XVI:** 290

Transparent Man, The (Hecht), **Supp. X:** 57, **69–71**

"Transparent Man, The" (Hecht), **Supp. X: 69–70**

Transparent Things (Nabokov), **Retro. Supp. I:** 266, 270, 277

"Transport" (Simic), **Supp. VIII:** 282

Transport to Summer (Stevens), **IV:** 76, 93; **Retro. Supp. I:** 309–312

Tranströmer, Thomas, **Supp. IV Part 2:** 648

"Traps for the Unwary" (Bourne), **I:** 235

Trash Trilogy (McMurtry), **Supp. V:** 225–226, 231

Traub, James, **Supp. XXIV:** 221, 222

Traubel, Horace, **IV:** 350

"Travel: After a Death" (Kenyon), **Supp. VII:** 169

Travel Alarm (Nye), **Supp. XIII:** 277

"Traveled World, The" (Pickering), **Supp. XXI:** 203

"Traveler, The" (Haines), **Supp. XII:** 203–204, 210

"Traveler, The" (Stegner), **Supp. IV Part 2:** 605

Traveler at Forty, A (Dreiser), **I:** 515

Traveler from Altruria, a Romance A, (Howells), **II:** 285, 287

Traveler's Tree, The: New and Selected Poems (W. J. Smith), **Supp. XIII:** 332, 347

"Traveling" (Paley), **Supp. VI:** 230

"Traveling Light" (Wagoner), **Supp. IX:** 329

Traveling Mercies: Some Thoughts on Faith (Lamott), **Supp. XX: 132, 140–142**

"Traveling Onion, The" (Nye), **Supp. XIII:** 276

Traveling through the Dark (Stafford), **Supp. XI:** 311, 316, **318–321**

"Traveling through the Dark" (Stafford), **Supp. XI:** 318–320, 321, 323, 329

Travelling in Amherst: A Poet's Journal, 1931–1954, **Supp. IX: 88–89**

Travelling Standing Still: Poems, 1918–1928 (Taggard), **Supp. XXII:** 278

Travelling Thirds, The (Atherton), **Supp. XXIV:** 23

Travels in Alaska (Muir), **Supp. IX:** 182, 185–186

"Travels in Georgia" (McPhee), **Supp. III Part 1:** 293–294

"Travels in North America" (Kees), **Supp. XV:** 133–134

Travels in the Congo (Gide), **III:** 210

"Travels in the South" (Ortiz), **Supp. IV Part 2:** 506

Travels with Charley (Steinbeck), **IV:** 52

"Travel Writing: Why I Bother" (Theroux), **Supp. VIII:** 310

Travis, Merle, **Supp. V:** 335

Travisano, Thomas, **Retro. Supp. II:** 40

Treadway, Jessica, **Supp. XXIII:** 280

Treasure Hunt (Buechner), **Supp. XII:** 52

Treasure Island (Stevenson), **Supp. X:** 230

Treasure of the Humble, The (Maeterlinck), **Supp. XX: 116**

"Treasure of the Redwoods, A" (Harte), **Supp. II Part 1:** 337

Treasury of Art Masterpieces, A: From the Renaissance to the Present Day (Craven), **Supp. XII:** 44

Treasury of English Aphorisms, A (L. P. Smith), **Supp. XIV:** 344

Treasury of English Prose, A (L. P. Smith, ed.), **Supp. XIV:** 341

Treasury of the Theatre, A (Gassner), **Supp. I Part 1:** 292

Treasury of Yiddish Stories, A (Howe and Greenberg, eds.), **Supp. I Part 2:** 432; **Supp. XXIII:** 7

Treat 'Em Rough (Lardner), **II:** 422–423

Treatise Concerning Religious Affections (Edwards), **I:** 547, 552, 554, 555, 557, 558, 560, 562

Treatise Concerning the Lord's Supper (Doolittle), **IV:** 150

"Treatise on Poetry" (Milosz), **Supp. VIII:** 20

Treatise on Right and Wrong, A (Mencken), **III:** 110, 119

"Treatise on Tales of Horror, A" (Wilson), **IV:** 438

Treatise on the Gods, A (Mencken), **III:** 108–109, 119

"Treatment" (Wright), **Supp. XV:** 343

Trece poetas del mundo azteca (León-Portilla), **Supp. XV:** 77

Tre Croce (Tozzi), **Supp. III Part 2:** 616

"Tree, a Rock, a Cloud, A" (McCullers), **II:** 587

"Tree, The" (Pound), **Retro. Supp. I:** 286; **Supp. I Part 1:** 255

"Tree, The" (Stone), **Supp. XXVII:** 250

"Tree, the Bird, The" (Roethke), **III:** 548

"Tree at My Window" (Frost), **II:** 155

Tree Grows in Brooklyn, A (B. Smith), **Supp. XVII:** 9; **Supp. XXIII:** 257, **259–264,** 265, 271

Tree Grows in Brooklyn, A (film; Kazan), **Supp. XVI:** 193

"Tree House at Night, The" (Dickey), **Supp. IV Part 1:** 179

"Tree House"(Thompson), **Supp. XXIII:** 301

Tree Is Older Than You Are, The (Nye, ed.), **Supp. XIII:** 280

"Tree of Laughing Bells, The" (Lindsay), **Supp. I Part 2:** 376

"Tree of Life, The" (Swados), **Supp. XIX:** 268

"Tree of Night, A" (Capote), **Supp. III Part 1:** 114, 120

Tree of Night and Other Stories, A (Capote), **Supp. III Part 1:** 114

"Trees, The" (Rich), **Supp. I Part 2:** 555

Trees, The (Richter), **Supp. XVIII: 212–213,** 220

"Trees at Night" (H. Johnson), **Supp. XXVI:** 174

"Trees Listening to Bach" (Merrill), **Supp. III Part 1:** 336

Tree Tall Woman (Mullen), **Supp. XXVII:** 166–167, 169, 170, 172, 174, 176

Tree That Came to Stay, The (Quindlen), **Supp. XVII:** 167

Tree Where Man Was Born, The (Matthiessen), **Supp. V:** 199, 203, 204

Trejo, Ernesto, **Supp. V:** 178, 180; **Supp. XIII:** 313, 316; **Supp. XV:** 73

Trelawny, Edward John, **Supp. I Part 2:** 721

"Trellis for R., A" (Swenson), **Supp. IV Part 2:** 647

Tremblay, Bill, **Supp. XIII:** 112

Tremble (Wright), **Supp. XV: 348–349**

"Trespass" (Frost), **Retro. Supp. I:** 139

Trespassing (Pickering), **Supp. XXI:** 202

"Trespassing" (Pickering), **Supp. XXI:** 202

Trethewey, Eric, **Supp. XXI:** 243, 244

Trethewey, Natasha, **Supp. XXI: 243–259**

"Tretitoli, Where the Bomb Group Was" (Hugo), **Supp. VI:** 138

Trevelyan, Robert C., **Supp. XIV:** 334

Trevor-Roper, Hugh, **Supp. XIV:** 348

Trial, The (Kafka), **IV:** 113; **Retro. Supp. II:** 20

"Trial, The" (Rukeyser), **Supp. VI:** 278

"Trial by Existence, The" (Frost), **II:** 166

"Trial for Arson, The"(Hadas), **Supp. XXIII:** 114

Trial of a Poet, The (Shapiro), **Supp. II Part 2:** 710

Trial of the Hawk, The: A Comedy of the Seriousness of Life (Lewis), **II:** 441

"Trial path, The" (Zitkala-Ša), **Supp. XXV:** 274–275, 282

Trials of the Human Heart (Rowson), **Supp. XV:** 237, 239

Tribal Secrets: Recovering American Indian Intellectual Traditions

(Warrior), **Supp. IV Part 1:** 329

"Tribute" (A. Finch), **Supp. XVII:** 72, 73–74

"Tribute, A" (Easton), **Supp. IV Part 2:** 461

"Tribute, The" (Doolittle), **Supp. I Part 1:** 267

"Tribute (To My Mother)" (Cullen), **Supp. IV Part 1:** 166

Tribute to Freud (Doolittle), **Supp. I Part 1:** 253, 254, 258, 259, 260, 268

Tribute to the Angels (Doolittle), **Supp. I Part 1:** 272

"Trick on the World, A" (Ríos), **Supp. IV Part 2:** 553

"Tricks" (Olds), **Supp. X:** 203–204

"Trick Scenery" (F. Barthelme), **Supp. XI:** 26

Trifler, The (Masters), **Supp. I Part 2:** 459–460

Trifles (Glaspell), **Supp. III Part 1:** 175, 178, 179, 182, 186, 187; **Supp. X:** 46; **Supp. XXI:** 12

Trifonov, Iurii V., **Retro. Supp. I:** 278

Triggering Town, The: Lectures and Essays on Poetry and Writing (Hugo), **Supp. VI:** 133, 140

Trilling, Diana, **II:** 587, 600; **Supp. I Part 1:** 297; **Supp. XII:** 126; **Supp. XXI:** 271, 275

Trilling, Lionel, **I:** 48; **II:** 579; **III:** 308, 310, 319, 327; **IV:** 201, 211; **Retro. Supp. I:** 19, 97, 121, 216, 227; **Supp. III Part 2: 493–515; Supp. IX:** 266, 287; **Supp. V:** 259; **Supp. VIII:** 93, 98, 190, 231, 236, 243; **Supp. XIII:** 100–101; **Supp. XIV:** 280, 288–289; **Supp. XV:** 20, 140, 152

Trilogy (Doolittle), **Supp. I Part 1:** 271, 272

Trilogy of Desire (Dreiser), **I:** 497, 508; **Retro. Supp. II:** 94, 96, **101–102**

Trimberger, Ellen Kay, **Supp. XVII:** 96, 106; **Supp. XXI:** 12

Trimmed Lamp, The (O. Henry), **Supp. II Part 1:** 410

Trimmings (Mullen), **Supp. XXVII:** 169–170, 171

"Trinc" (McGrath), **Supp. X:** 127

Trinity (Uris), **Supp. XX: 243, 244, 245, 246, 247, 248, 253, 254–255**

Trio (Baker), **Supp. I Part 1:** 277

Trio (Saroyan), **Supp. XXII:** 25

"Triolets for Triolet" (Nelson), **Supp. XVIII:** 179

"Trip" (F. Barthelme), *Supp. XI:* 26

Triple Thinkers, The: Ten Essays on Literature (Wilson), **IV:** 428, 431; **Supp. II Part 1:** 146

"Triplex" (Doolittle), **Supp. I Part 1:** 271

Tripmaster Monkey: His Fake Book (Kingston), **Supp. V:** 157, 158, 169, 170–173

Trippings in Authorland (Forrester), **Supp. XVIII:** 13

Trippings of Tom Pepper, The (Briggs), **Supp. XVIII:** 3, **13–14**

"Trip to Hanoi" (Sontag), **Supp. III Part 2:** 460–462

Trip to Parnassus, A; or, The Judgement of Apollo on Dramatic Authors and Performers (Rowson), **Supp. XV: 232–233**

"Triptych" (Eberhart), **I:** 522, 539

Tristam Shandy (Sterne), **Supp. XXII:** 267

Tristan and Iseult, **Retro. Supp. I:** 328, 329, 330, 331

Tristessa (Kerouac), **Supp. III Part 1:** 225, 227, 229

Tristram (Robinson), **III:** 521, 522, 523

Tristram Shandy (Sterne), **I:** 299; **IV:** 465–466; **Supp. V:** 127; **Supp. XVIII:** 60

"Triumph" (C. L. R. James), **Supp. XXI:** 160

"Triumphal March" (Eliot), **I:** 580; **III:** 17; **Retro. Supp. I:** 64

Triumph of Achilles, The (Glück), **Supp. V:** 79, 84–86, 92

"Triumph of a Modern, The, or, Send for the Lawyer" (Anderson), **I:** 113, 114

"Triumph of the Egg, The" (Anderson), **I:** 113

Triumph of the Egg, The: A Book of Impressions from American Life in Tales and Poems (Anderson), **I:** 112, 114

Triumph of the Spider Monkey, The (Oates), **Supp. II Part 2:** 522

Triumphs of the Reformed Religion in America (Mather), **Supp. II Part 2:** 453

Trivial Breath (Wylie), **Supp. I Part 2:** 709, 722–724

Trivia; or, the Art of Walking the Streets of London (Gay), **Supp. XIV:** 337

Trivia: Printed from the Papers of Anthony Woodhouse, Esq. (L. P. Smith), **Supp. XIV:** 336, **337–340**

"Trivia Tea" (Skloot), **Supp. XX:** 205

Trocchi, Alexander, **Supp. XI:** 294, 295, 301

Troilus and Criseyde (Chaucer), **Retro. Supp. I:** 426

Trois contes (Flaubert), **IV:** 31, 37

Trojan Horse, The: A Play (MacLeish), **III:** 21

"Trojan Women, The" (Maxwell), **Supp. VIII:** 169

Troll Garden, The (Cather), **I:** 313, 314–316, 322; **Retro. Supp. I:** 5, 6, 8, 14

"Trolling for Blues" (Wilbur), **Supp. III Part 2:** 563–564

Trollope, Anthony, **I:** 10, 375; **II:** 192, 237; **III:** 51, 70, 281, 382; **Retro. Supp. I:** 361

Tromly, Albert Edmund, **Supp. I Part 2:** 403

Trombold, John, **Supp. XVIII:** 111

"Trompe L'Oeil" (Collins), **Supp. XXI:** 60

"Troop Train" (Shapiro), **Supp. II Part 2:** 707

"Tropes of the Text" (Gass), **Supp. VI:** 88

Tropic of Cancer (H. Miller), **III:** 170, 171, 174, 177, 178–180, 181, 182, 183, 187, 190; **Supp. V:** 119; **Supp.**

X: 187; **Supp. XXII:** 230, 257

Tropic of Capricorn (H. Miller), **III:** 170, 176–177, 178, 182, 183, 184, 187, 188–189, 190

"Tropic of Cuba" (di Donato), **Supp. XX: 45**

Trotsky, Leon, **I:** 366; **II:** 562, 564; **IV:** 429; **Supp. XXI:** 161, 164, 165, 167, 168

Trotter, W., **I:** 249

"Trouble at the Home Office" (Huddle), **Supp. XXVI:** 156

Troubled Air, The (Shaw), **Supp. XIX: 249–250**

Troubled Island (opera; Hughes and Still), **Retro. Supp. I:** 203

Troubled Lovers in History (Goldbarth), **Supp. XII:** 176, **192–193**

Trouble Follows Me (Macdonald, under Millar), **Supp. IV Part 2:** 466

Trouble in July (Caldwell), **I:** 297, 304–305, 306, 309

Trouble Island (Hughes), **Supp. I Part 1:** 328

"Trouble of Marcie Flint, The" (Cheever), **Supp. I Part 1:** 186

Trouble with Francis, The: An Autobiography (Francis), **Supp. IX:** 76, 77, 82, **84–85**

Trouble with God, The (Francis), **Supp. IX:** 88

"Trouble with Poetry, The" (Collins), **Supp. XXI:** 57

Trouble with Poetry and Other Poems, The (Collins), **Supp. XXI:** 55, 57, 62

"Trouble with the Stars and Stripes" (Nye), **Supp. XIII:** 277

Trouillot, Michel-Rolphe, **Supp. X:** 14–15

Troupe, Quincy, **Retro. Supp. II:** 15, 111; **Supp. X:** 242

"Trout" (Hugo), **Supp. VI:** 135

Trout Fishing in America (Brautigan), **Supp. VIII:** 43

"Trouvée" (Bishop), **Retro. Supp. II:** 49

Troy (film), **Supp. XX: 273**

"Truce" (Taggard), **Supp. XXII:** 276–277

"Truce of the Bishop, The" (Frederic), **II:** 139–140

"Truck Stop: Minnesota" (Dunn), **Supp. XI:** 145–146

Trudeau, Garry, **Supp. XXIV:** 283

True Account, The: A Novel of the Lewis & Clark & Kinneson Expeditions (Mosher), **Supp. XXII:** 206, 207, 208, **214–215**

True and False: Heresy and Common Sense for the Actor (Mamet), **Supp. XIV:** 241, 243

True Blood (television series), **Supp. XIX:** 174

Trueblood, Valerie, **Supp. XIII:** 306

True Confessions (Dunne), **Supp. IV Part 1:** 198

True Confessions (film), **Supp. IV Part 1:** 198

"True Crime" (Gansworth), **Supp. XXVI:** 114

"True Feeling Leaves No Memory" (Davison), **Supp. XXVI:** 69

Trueheart, Charles, **Supp. XXI:** 238

True History of the Conquest of New Spain, The (Castillo), **III:** 13

True Intellectual System of the Universe, The (Cuddleworth), **II:** 10

"True Love" (Olds), **Supp. X:** 212

Trueman, Matthew (pseudonym). *See* Lowell, James Russell

"True Morality" (Bell), **Supp. X:** 13

"True Romance" (Everett), **Supp. XVIII:** 65

Truesdale, C. W., **Supp. XXI:** 246

True Stories (Atwood), **Supp. XIII:** 34–35

"True Stories" (Atwood), **Supp. XIII:** 34

"True Stories of Bitches" (Mamet), **Supp. XIV:** 246, 252

"Truest Sport, The: Jousting with Sam and Charlie" (Wolfe), **Supp. III Part 2:** 581–582

"True Vine" (Wylie), **Supp. I Part 2:** 723

True West (Shepard), **Supp. III Part 2:** 433, 441, 445, 447, 448

Truman, Harry, **III:** 3

Truman Capote: In Which Various Friends, Enemies, Acquaintances, and Detractors Recall His Turbulent Career (Plimpton), **Supp. XVI:**245

Truman Show, The (film), **Supp. XVI:** 271

Trumbo, Dalton, **Supp. I Part 1:** 295; **Supp. XIII:** 6; **Supp. XVII:** 63; **Supp. XX:** 246; **Supp. XXI:** 45

Trumbull, John, **Supp. II Part 1:** 65, 69, 70, 268

Trump, Donald, **Supp. IV Part 1:** 393

Trumpener, Katie, **Retro. Supp. I:** 380

"Trumpet Player" (Hughes), **Supp. I Part 1:** 333

"Trumpet Player, 1963" (Halliday), **Supp. XIX:** 92

Trumpet Shall Sound, The (Wilder), **IV:** 356

Trumpet Unblown, The (Hoffman), **Supp. XVIII:** 71, **74–75**

Trunk Music (Connelly), **Supp. XXI:** 72, 75

"Truro Bear, The" (Oliver), **Supp. VII:** 234

Truscott, Lucian K., **Supp. IV Part 2:** 683

Trust (Ozick), **Supp. V:** 257–258, 259, 260–263, 270, 272

Trust Me (Updike), **Retro. Supp. I:** 322

"Trusty, The" (Rash), **Supp. XXVII:** 229–230

"Trust Yourself" (Emerson), **II:** 10

"Truth" (Emerson), **II:** 6

"Truth, The" (Halliday), **Supp. XIX:** 87, 88, 94

"Truth, The" (Jarrell), **II:** 381–382

Truth About Celia, The (Brockmeier), **Supp. XXII:** 53–55

"Truth about God, The" (Carson), **Supp. XII:** 105–106

"Truth be told" (Trethewey), **Supp. XXI:** 255, 256

"Truthful James" (Harte), **IV:** 196

"Truth Is, The" (Hogan), **Supp. IV Part 1:** 401–402

"Truth Is Forced, The" (Swenson), **Supp. IV Part 2:** 652

"Truth of the Matter, The" (Nemerov), **III:** 270

Truth Serum (Cooper), **Supp. XI:** 129

"Truth the Dead Know, The" (Sexton), **Supp. II Part 2:** 681

"Trying to Evangelize a Cut Flower" (Peacock), **Supp. XIX:** 199

Trying to Find Chinatown (Hwang), **Supp. XXI:** 147

Trying to Save Piggy Sneed (Irving), **Supp. VI:** 19–165

"Trying to Talk with a Man" (Rich), **Supp. I Part 2:** 559

"Tryptich I" (Bell), **Supp. X:** 7

"Tryst, The" (Wharton), **Retro. Supp. I:** 378

"Try the Girl" (Chandler), **Supp. IV Part 1:** 125

Try! Try! (O'Hara), **Supp. XXIII:** 209, 210, 216

"Ts'ai Chih" (Pound), **III:** 466

T. S. Eliot and American Philosophy (Jain), **Retro. Supp. I:** 58

T. S. Eliot's Silent Voices (Mayer), **Retro. Supp. I:** 58

Tsuji, Shizuo, **Supp. XVII:** 90

Tsurikgekumen (The return) (Asch), **Supp. XXIII:** 5

Tsvetaeva, Marina, **Supp. VIII:** 30; **Supp. XXIII:** 168

"Tuberoses" (E. Stoddard), **Supp. XV:** 282

Tubert, Susana, **Supp. XXIII:** 203

Tuck, James A., **Supp. XXVI:** 83

Tucker, Benjamin R., **Supp. XXI:** 9

Tuckerman, Frederick Goddard, **IV:** 144; **Supp. XXV:** 241

Tucker's People (Wolfert), **Supp. XXI:** 261, 262, 263, 267, **267–275,** 278

"Tuesday, November 5th, 1940" (Benét), **Supp. XI:** 46, 52

"Tuesday April 25th 1966" (Olson), **Supp. II Part 2:** 585

"Tuesday Night at the Savoy Ballroom" (Komunyakaa), **Supp. XIII:** 132

Tuffield, Aviva, **Supp. XVI:** 147, 148

"Tuft of Flowers, The" (Frost), **II:** 153; **Retro. Supp. I:** 126, 127

Tufts, James Hayden, **Supp. I Part 2:** 632

Tu Fu, **II:** 526; **Supp. XV:** 47

Tu Fu (Ayscough), **II:** 527

Tugwell, Rexford Guy, **Supp. I Part 2:** 645

"Tulip" (Hammett), **Supp. IV Part 1:** 356

"Tulip Man, The" (McCarriston), **Supp. XIV:** 261

"Tulips" (Nye), **Supp. XIII:** 281

"Tulips" (Plath), **Retro. Supp. II:** 252–253; **Supp. I Part 2:** 540, 542, 544

"Tulips" (Snodgrass), **Supp. VI:** 325

Tulips and Chimneys (Cummings), **I:** 436, 437, 440, 445, 447

"Tulips"(Strout), **Supp. XXIII:** 283, 285

"Tulips"(theater performance, Strout), **Supp. XXIII:** 281

Tully, Jim, **III:** 103, 109

Tumble Home (Hempel), **Supp. XXI:** 115, **124–125**

"Tumble Home" (Hempel), **Supp. XXI:** 115, 116, **124–125,** 126

Tumble Tower (Modarressi and Tyler), **Supp. IV Part 2:** 657

"Tuned in Late One Night" (Stafford), **Supp. XI:** 327–328

Tunnel, The (Gass), **Supp. V:** 44; **Supp. VI:** **89–91,** 94

"Tunnel, The" (Strand), **Supp. IV Part 2:** 622

"Tunnels" (Komunyakaa), **Supp. XIII:** 123

Tunnel Vision (Paretsky), **Supp. XXV:** 173–174, 177, 178, 181

Tuon, Bunkong, **Supp. XXVI:** 211, 220

Tuqan, Fadwa, **Supp. XIII:** 278

Tura, Cosimo, **III:** 474–475

Turandot and Other Poems (Ashbery), **Supp. III Part 1:** 3

Turco, Lewis, **Supp. XV:** 118

Turgenev, Ivan Sergeevich, **I:** 106; **II:** 263, 271, 275, 280, 281, 288, 319, 320, 324–325, 338, 407; **III:** 461; **IV:** 17, 277; **Retro. Supp. I:** 215, 222; **Supp. VIII:** 167

Turgot, Anne Robert Jacques, **II:** 103; **Supp. I Part 1:** 250

"Turkey and Bones and Eating and We Liked It" (Stein), **IV:** 44

"Turkey Season, The" (Munro), **Supp. XXVII:** 188

Turman, Glynn, **Supp. IV Part 1:** 362

Turnbull, Dr. George, **II:** 113

Turnbull, Lawrence, **Supp. I Part 1:** 352

"Turned" (Gilman), **Supp. XI:** 207

Turner, Addie, **IV:** 123

Turner, Darwin, **Supp. I Part 1:** 339; **Supp. IV Part 1:** 165

Turner, Frederick Jackson, **Supp. I Part 2:** 480, 481, 632, 640; **Supp. IV Part 2:** 596

Turner, Guinevere, **Supp. XXVII:** 68

Turner, Nat, **IV:** 113–114, 115, 116, 117

Turner, Patricia A., **Supp. XIII:** 237; **Supp. XX:** 110

Turner, Russell. *See* Lacy, Ed

Turner, Victor, **Supp. IV Part 1:** 304

"Turning Away Variations on Estrangement" (Dickey), **Supp. IV Part 1:** 183

Turning Point, The (McCoy), **Supp. XIII:** 175

"Turning Thirty, I Contemplate Students Bicycling Home" (Dove), **Supp. IV Part 1:** 250

Turning Wind, A (Rukeyser), **Supp. VI:** 272–273, 279–280

Turn in the South, A (Naipaul), **Supp. XXII:** 240

Turn of the Screw, The (H. James), **Retro. Supp. I:** 219, 231; **Supp. IV Part 2:** 682

"Turn of the Screw, The" (H. James), **II:** 331–332; **Retro. Supp. I:** 228, 229, 231, 232; **Supp. XVII:** 143

Turns and Movies and Other Tales in Verse (Aiken), **I:** 65

"Turn with the Sun, A" (Knowles), **Supp. XII:** 237–238

"Turn Your Radio On" (J. W. Miller), **Supp. XX: 169**

Turow, Scott, **Supp. V:** 220; **Supp. XVII: 213–224**

"Turpentine" (Gallagher), **Supp. XXIV:** 174, 175, 176

Turpin, E. Walters, **Supp. XVIII:** 283

Turrinus, Lucius Mamilius, **IV:** 373

"Turtle" (Hogan), **Supp. IV Part 1:** 401

Turtle, Swan (Doty), **Supp. XI: 121–122**

"Turtle, Swan" (Doty), **Supp. XI:** 121–122

Turtle Island (Snyder), **Supp. VIII: 300–303**

Turtle Moon (Hoffman), **Supp. X:** 77, **87–88,** 89

"Turtle Shrine near Chittagong, The" (Nye), **Supp. XIII:** 277

Turtotte, James, **Supp. XXIII:** 125

Turturro, John, **Supp. XI:** 174

Tuscan Cities (Howells), **II:** 280

Tuskegee movement, **Supp. II Part 1:** 169, 172

Tuten, Frederic, **Supp. VIII:** 75, 76; **Supp. XIII:** 237, 249

Tuten, James, **Supp. XVIII:** 195

Tuthill, Louisa Cavolne, **Supp. I Part 2:** 684

"Tutored Child, The" (Kunitz), **Supp. III Part 1:** 264

Tuttleton, James W., **Supp. IV Part 1:** 166, 168

"T.V.A." (Agee), **I:** 35

Tvedten, Brother Benet, **Supp. IV Part 2:** 505

"TV Men" (Carson), **Supp. XII: 105, 112**

Twain, Mark, **I:** 57, 103, 107, 109, 190, 192, 193, 195, 197, 203, 209, 245, 246, 247–250, 255, 256, 257, 260, 261, 292, 342, 418, 469, 485; **II:** 70, 140, 259, 262, 266–268, 271, 272, 274–275, 276, 277, 280, 285–286, 287, 288, 289, 301, 304, 306, 307, 312, 415, 432, 434, 436, 446, 457, 467, 475, 476, 482; **III:** 65, 101, 102, 112–113, 114, 220, 347, 357, 409, 453, 454, 504, 507, 554, 558, 572, 575, 576; **IV: 190–213,** 333, 349, 451; **Retro. Supp. I:** 169, 194, 195; **Retro. Supp. II:** 123; **Supp. I Part 1:** 37, 39, 44, 247, 251, 313, 317; **Supp. I Part 2:** 377, 385, 393, 410, 455, 456, 457, 473, 475, 579, 602, 604, 618, 629, 651, 660; **Supp. II Part 1:** 344, 354, 385; **Supp. IV Part 1:** 386, 388; **Supp. IV Part 2:** 463, 468, 603, 607, 693; **Supp. IX:** 14, 171; **Supp. V:** 44, 113, 131; **Supp. VIII:** 40, 189; **Supp. X:** 51, 227; **Supp. XII:** 343; **Supp. XIII:** 1, 17; **Supp. XV:** 41; **Supp. XVI:** 66, 208; **Supp. XVIII:** 1, 9, 13; **Supp. XXI:** 205; **Supp. XXII:** 89, 203, 205, 206; **Supp. XXIII:** 85; **Supp. XXVII:** 84, 218

"Twa Sisters, The" (ballad), **Supp. I Part 2:** 696

Twelfth Night (Shakespeare), **Supp. IV Part 1:** 83; **Supp. IX:** 14; **Supp. XXII:** 229

Twelve (Blok), **Supp. XXVI:** 144

"12 O'Clock News" (Bishop), **Retro. Supp. II:** 48

Twelve Men (Dreiser), **Retro. Supp. II:** 94, 104

Twelve Moons (Oliver), **Supp. VII:** 231, 233–236, 238, 240

Twelve Southerners, **IV:** 125; **Supp. X:** 25

Twelve Years a Slave (Northup), **Supp. XIV:** 32

Twentieth Century (Hecht and MacArthur), **Supp. XXVII:** 90

Twentieth Century Authors, **I:** 376, 527

"Twentieth Century Fiction and the Black Mask of Humanity" (Ellison), **Retro. Supp. II:** 118

Twentieth Century Pleasures (Hass), **Supp. VI:** 103, 106, 109

Twenty Drawings (Gibran), **Supp. XX: 116**

"28" (Levine), **Supp. V:** 187, 191

"Twenty-Four Poems" (Schwartz), **Supp. II Part 2:** 646, 649

"2433 Agnes, First Home, Last House in Missoula" (Hugo), **Supp. VI:** 139–140

"Twenty Hill Hollow" (Muir), **Supp. IX:** 178

Twenty Love Poems and a Song of Despair (Neruda), **Supp. XXIV:** 170

"Twenty Minutes" (Salter), **Supp. IX:** 260

29 Mini-Essays (Brainard), **Supp. XXVII:** 28

"Twenty-One Love Poems" (Rich), **Supp. I Part 2:** 572–573

"Twenty-One Poems" (MacLeish), **III:** 19

Twenty Poems (Haines), **Supp. XII:** 204, **205–206**

Twenty Poems of Anna Akhmatova (Kenyon), **Supp. VII:** 165–166

Twenty Questions: (Posed by Poems) (McClatchy), **Supp. XII:** 254, **259–262**

27 Views of Raleigh (Barnhardt, ed.), **Supp. XXVII:** 12

27 Wagons Full of Cotton and Other One-Act Plays (T. Williams), **IV:** 381, 383

Twenty-seventh City, The (Franzen), **Supp. XX: 83–84,** 84, 85, **86–88,** 88, **89, 91, 92, 95**

Twentysomething Essays by Twentysomething Writers (Kellogg and Quint, eds.), **Supp. XXVI:** 53

Twenty Thousand Leagues under the Sea (Verne), **I:** 480; **Supp. XI:** 63

"Twenty Years Ago" (Lindsay), **Supp. I Part 2:** 384, 399

Twenty Years at Hull-House (Addams), **Supp. I Part 1:** 3, 4, 11, 16

Twersky, David, **Supp. XX:** 244

Twice over Lightly: New York Ten and Now (Hayes and Loos), **Supp. XVI:** 195

Twice-Told Tales (Hawthorne), **I:** 354; **II:** 224; **III:** 412, 421; **Retro. Supp. I:** 154–155, 160

Twichell, Chase, **Supp. V:** 16; **Supp. XVII:** 110, 112

Twilight (Frost), **II:** 151

"Twilight's Last Gleaming" (Burroughs and Elvins), **Supp. III Part 1:** 93, 94, 101

Twilight Sleep (Wharton), **IV:** 320–322, 324–325, 327, 328; **Retro. Supp. I:** 381

"Twin, The" (Olds), **Supp. X:** 207

"Twin Beds in Rome" (Updike), **Retro. Supp. I:** 332

"Twins of Table Mountain, The" (Harte), **Supp. II Part 1:** 355

"Twist, The" (Olson), **Supp. II Part 2:** 570

Twitch and Shout (film), **Supp. XVIII:** 143

Twitchell-Waas, Jeffrey, **Supp. XVIII:** 99; **Supp. XXII:** 163

"Two" (Huddle), **Supp. XXVI:** 150

Two Admirals, The (Cooper), **I:** 350

Two against One (F. Barthelme), **Supp. XI:** 32, 33, 36

"Two and One"(Hadas), **Supp. XXIII:** 114–115

"Two Boys" (Moore), **Supp. X:** 173

"Two Brothers, The" (Jewett), **Retro. Supp. II:** 132

Two-Character Play, The (T. Williams), **IV:** 382, 386, 393, 398

Two Citizens (Wright), **Supp. III Part 2:** 602–604

"Two Deer" (Bass), **Supp. XVI:** 24

"Two Domains, The" (Goldbarth), **Supp. XII:** 192

"Two-Eleven All Around" (Offutt), **Supp. XIX:** 170

"Two Environments, The" (Trilling), **Supp. III Part 2:** 510

"Two-Fisted Self Pity" (Broyard), **Supp. XI:** 348

Two for Texas (Burke), **Supp. XIV:** 25, 34

"Two Friends" (Cather), **I:** 332

"Two Gardens in Linndale" (Robinson), **III:** 508

Two Gentlemen in Bonds (Ransom), **III:** 491–492

Two: Gertrude Stein and Her Brother (Stein), **IV:** 43

"Two Ghosts" (Francis), **Supp. IX:** 87

Two-Gun Bob (Szumskyj), **Supp. XXVII:** 128

"Two Hangovers" (Wright), **Supp. III Part 2:** 596

Two-Headed Poems (Atwood), **Supp. XIII:** 34

Two Hot to Handle (Lacy), **Supp. XV:** 206

Two Hours to Doom (Bryant), **Supp. XI:** 302

"Two Hundred Years in an Hour" (Boyce), **Supp. XXI:** 8

"Two Kitchens in Provence" (M. F. K. Fisher), **Supp. XVII:** 88, 91

"Two Ladies in Retirement" (Taylor), **Supp. V:** 320

Two Letters to the Citizens of the United States, and One to General Washing-

ton (Barlow), **Supp. II Part 1:** 80

Two Little Women on a Holiday (Wells), **Supp. XXVI:** 277

"Two Lives, The" (Hogan), **Supp. IV Part 1:** 400, 402, 403, 406, 411

Two Long Poems (Stern), **Supp. IX:** 296

"Two Look at Two" (Frost), **Supp. XXI:** 26

"Two Lovers and a Beachcomber by the Real Sea" (Plath), **Supp. I Part 2:** 536

"Two Men" (McClatchy)", **Supp. XII:** 269

Two Men (E. Stoddard), **Supp. XV:** 272, 273, **283–284**

Two Men of Sandy Bar (Harte), **Supp. II Part 1:** 354

Twomey, Jay, **Supp. XVII:** 111

"Two Moods of Love" (Cullen), **Supp. IV Part 1:** 166

Two Moons (Mallon), **Supp. XIX:** 132, **138–141**

"Two Morning Monologues" (Bellow), **I:** 150; **Retro. Supp. II:** 20

"Two Nations of Black America, The" *(Frontline),* **Supp. XX:** 99

Two-Ocean War, The (Morison), **Supp. I Part 2:** 491

"Two of Hearts" (Hogan), **Supp. IV Part 1:** 410

"Two on a Party" (T. Williams), **IV:** 388

"Two or Three Things I Dunno About John Cassavetes" (Lethem), **Supp. XVIII:** 148

"Two Pendants: For the Ears" (W. C. Williams), **Retro. Supp. I:** 423

"Two Poems of Going Home" (Dickey), **Supp. IV Part 1:** 182–183

"Two Portraits" (Chopin), **Supp. I Part 1:** 218

"Two Presences, The" (R. Bly), **Supp. IV Part 1:** 65

"Two Rivers" (Stegner), **Supp. IV Part 2:** 605

Tworkov, Jack, **Supp. XII:** 198

"Two Scenes" (Ashbery), **Supp. III Part 1:** 4

Two Serious Ladies (Jane Bowles), **Supp. IV Part 1:** 82

"Two Silences" (Carruth), **Supp. XVI:** 55

"Two Sisters" (Farrell), **II:** 45

Two Sisters: A Memoir in the Form of a Novel (Vidal), **Supp. IV Part 2:** 679

"Two Sisters of Persephone" (Plath), **Retro. Supp. II:** 246

"Two Songs on the Economy of Abundance" (Agee), **I:** 28

Two Sons, The (Boyce), **Supp. XXI:** 7, 13

"Two Tales of Clumsy" (Schnackenberg), **Supp. XV:** 258

"Two Temples, The" (Melville), **III:** 89–90

Two Thousand Seasons (Armah), **Supp. IV Part 1:** 373

Two Towns in Provence (M. F. K. Fisher), **Supp. XVII:** 91

Two Trains Running (Wilson), **Supp. VIII:** 345–348

"Two Tramps in Mudtime" (Frost), **II:** 164; **Retro. Supp. I:** 137; **Supp. IX:** 261

"Two Twilights for William Carlos Williams" (Boyle), **Supp. XXIV:** 63

"Two Views of a Cadaver Room" (Plath), **Supp. I Part 2:** 538

"Two Villages" (Paley), **Supp. VI:** 227

"Two Voices in a Meadow" (Wilbur), **Supp. III Part 2:** 555

Two Weeks in Another Town (Shaw), **Supp. XIX:** 251

"Two Witches" (Frost), **Retro. Supp. I:** 135

"Two Words" (Francis), **Supp. IX:** 81

Two Worlds Walking: A Mixed-Blood Anthology (Glancy and Truesdale, eds.), **Supp. XXI:** 246

Two Years Before the Mast (Dana), **I:** 351; **Supp. XXV:** 208

"Tyger, The" (Blake), **Supp. XVII:** 128

Tyler, Anne, **Supp. IV Part 2: 657–675;** **Supp. V:** 227, 326; **Supp. VIII:** 141; **Supp. X:** 1, 77, 83, 85; **Supp. XII:** 307; **Supp. XVI:** 37; **Supp. XVIII:** 157, 195; **Supp. XXIII:** 298

Tyler, Royall, **I:** 344; **Retro. Supp. I:** 377

Tymms, Ralph, **Supp. IX:** 105

Tyndale, William, **II:** 15

Tyndall, John, **Retro. Supp. II:** 93

Typee: A Peep at Polynesian Life (Melville), **III:** 75–77, 79, 84; **Retro. Supp. I:** 245–246, 249, 252, 256

Types From City Streets (Hapgood), **Supp. XVII:** 103

"Typewriter, The" (D. West), **Supp. XVIII:** 279; **Supp. XXVI:** 164

Typewriter Town (W. J. Smith), **Supp. XIII:** 332

"Typhus" (Simpson), **Supp. IX:** 277

Tyranny of the Normal (Fiedler), **Supp. XIII: 107–108**

"Tyranny of the Normal" (Fiedler), **Supp. XIII:** 107–108

"Tyrant of Syracuse" (MacLeish), **III:** 20

"Tyrian Businesses" (Olson), **Supp. II Part 2:** 567, 568, 569

Tytell, John, **Supp. XIV:** 140

Tzara, Tristan, **Supp. III Part 1:** 104, 105

U

U and I (Baker), **Supp. XIII: 45–47,** 48, 52, 55

Überdie Seelenfrage (Fechner), **II:** 358

Ubik (Dick), **Supp. XVIII:** 136

"*Ubi Sunt* Lament for the Eccentric Museums of My Childhood" (Stallings), **Supp. XXV:** 232

Ubu Roi (Jarry), **Supp. XV:** 178, 186

Ueland, Brenda, **Supp. XVII:** 13

Uhry, Alfred, **Supp. XX: 177**

ukanhavyrfuckinciti back (Phillips), **Supp. XXIII:** 174

Ukrainian Dumy (P. N. Warren as Kilina and Tarnawsky, trans.), **Supp. XX: 261**

"Ulalume" (Poe), **III:** 427; **Retro. Supp. II:** 264, 266

Ulin, David, **Supp. XIII:** 244; **Supp. XVI:** 74

Ullman, Leslie, **Supp. IV Part 2:** 550; **Supp. XVIII:** 175

Ultimate Good Luck, The (Ford), **Supp. V:** 57, 61–62

Ultimate Punishment: A Lawyer's Reflections on Dealing with the Death Penalty (Turow), **Supp. XVII:** 220–221

Ultima Thule (Longfellow), **II:** 490; **Retro. Supp. II:** 169

"Ultima Thule" (Nabokov), **Retro. Supp. I:** 274

Ultramarine (Carver), **Supp. III Part 1:** 137, 138, 147, 148

"Ultrasound" (Stallings), **Supp. XXV:** 225, 233, 234

Ulysses (Joyce), **I:** 395, 475–476, 478, 479, 481; **II:** 42, 264, 542; **III:** 170, 398; **IV:** 103, 418, 428, 455; **Retro. Supp. I:** 59, 63, 290, 291; **Retro. Supp. II:** 121; **Supp. I Part 1:** 57; **Supp. III Part 2:** 618, 619; **Supp. IV Part 1:** 285; **Supp. IV Part 2:** 424; **Supp. IX:** 102; **Supp. V:** 261; **Supp. X:** 114; **Supp. XIII:** 43, 191; **Supp. XV:** 305; **Supp. XVII:** 140, 227; **Supp. XXV:** 65; **Supp. XXVII:** 6, 70

"Ulysses, Order and Myth" (Eliot), **Retro. Supp. I:** 63

"Umbrella, The" (Peacock), **Supp. XIX:** 203–204

Unaccountable Worth of the World, The (Price), **Supp. VI:** 267

Unaccustomed Earth (Lahiri), **Supp. XXI:** 176, **181–183,** 183, 188

"Unaccustomed Earth" (Lahiri), **Supp. XXI:** 186

Unamuno y Jugo, Miguel de, **III:** 310; **Supp. XV:** 79

"Unattached Smile, The" (Crews), **Supp. XI:** 101

"Unbelievable Thing Usually Goes to the Heart of the Story, The: Magic Realism in the Fiction of Rick Bass" (Dwyer), **Supp. XVI:** 16

"Unbeliever, The" (Bishop), **Retro. Supp. II:** 43

"Unborn Song" (Rukeyser), **Supp. VI:** 274

Unbought Spirit: A John Jay Chapman Reader (Stone, ed.), **Supp. XIV:** 54

Uncalled, The (Dunbar), **Supp. II Part 1:** 200, 211, 212

Uncentering the Earth: Copernicus and The Revolutions of the Heavenly Spheres (Vollmann), **Supp. XVII:** 226

Uncertain Certainty, The: Interviews, Essays, and Notes on Poetry (Simic), **Supp. VIII:** 270, 273, 274

Uncertainty and Plenitude: Five Contemporary Poets (Stitt), **Supp. IX:** 299

"Uncle" (Levine), **Supp. V:** 186

"Uncle Adler" (Kooser), **Supp. XIX:** 120

"Uncle Christmas" (Ríos), **Supp. IV Part 2:** 552

"Uncle Jim's Baptist Revival Hymn" (Lanier and Lanier), **Supp. I Part 1:** 353

"Uncle Lot" (Stowe), **Supp. I Part 2:** 585–586

Uncle Moses (Asch), **Supp. XXIII:** 14

"Uncle Moustapha's Eclipse" (McKnight), **Supp. XX:** 148

Uncle Remus Tales (Harris), **Supp. II Part 1:** 201

"Uncle Tomitudes" (Briggs), **Supp. XVIII:** 14

Uncle Tom's Cabin (Stowe), **II:** 291; **Supp. I Part 1:** 49; **Supp. I Part 2:** 410, 579, 582, 589–592; **Supp. II Part 1:** 170; **Supp. III Part 1:** 154, 171; **Supp. IX:** 19; **Supp. X:** 246, 249, 250; **Supp. XIII:** 95; **Supp. XVI:** 82, 85, 88; **Supp. XVIII:** 14

Uncle Tom's Children (Wright), **IV:** 476, 478, 488; **Supp. II Part 1:** 228, 235; **Supp. XVIII:** 283

"Uncle Wiggily in Connecticut" (Salinger), **III:** 559–560, 563

"Unclouded Day, The" (Proulx), **Supp. VII:** 254–255

"Uncommon Visage" (Brodsky), **Supp. VIII:** 31

"Uncommon Woman: An Interview with Wendy Wasserstein" (Cohen), **Supp. XV:** 323

Uncommon Women and Others (Wasserstein), **Supp. XV:** 320–321, **322–323; Supp. XXIV:** 117

Uncompromising Fictions of Cynthia Ozick (Pinsker), **Supp. V:** 272

"Unconscious Came a Beauty" (Swenson), **Supp. IV Part 2:** 646

"Uncreation, The" (Pinsky), **Supp. VI:** 245

"Undead, The" (Wilbur), **Supp. III Part 2:** 556

"Undefeated, The" (Hemingway), **II:** 250; **Retro. Supp. I:** 180

Under a Glass Bell (Nin), **Supp. X:** 186

"Under Ben Bulben" (Yeats), **Supp. V:** 220

Undercliff: Poems 1946–1953 (Eberhart), **I:** 528, 536–537

Under Cover (Goldbarth), **Supp. XII:** 177, 180, 193

Undercover Doctor (film), **Supp. XIII:** 170

"Under Cygnus" (Wilbur), **Supp. III Part 2:** 558

"Under Forty" (Trilling), **Supp. III Part 2:** 494

"Underground" (Hayes), **Supp. XXVI:** 144

Underground, The Story of a People (Tenenbaum), **Supp. XX: 253**

Underground Man, The (film), **Supp. IV Part 2:** 474

Underground Man, The (Macdonald), **Supp. IV Part 2:** 474, 475

Underground Woman, The (Boyle), **Supp. XXIV:** 62

"Under Libra: Weights and Measures" (Merrill), **Supp. III Part 1:** 328

Under Milk Wood (D. Thomas), **III:** 21

"Undersea" (Carson), **Supp. IX:** 21

Understanding Cynthia Ozick (Friedman), **Supp. V:** 273

Understanding Drama (Brooks and Heilman), **Supp. XIV:** 12

Understanding E. L. Doctorow (Fowler), **Supp. IV Part 1:** 226

Understanding Fiction (Brooks and Warren), **IV:** 279; **Supp. XIV:** 11

Understanding Fiction (Brooks and Warren, eds.), **Supp. XIX:** 246

Understanding Flannery O'Connor (Whitt), **Retro. Supp. II:** 226

Understanding Nicholson Baker (Saltzman), **Supp. XIII:** 48

Understanding Poetry: An Anthology for College Students (Brooks and Warren), **IV:** 236; **Retro. Supp. I:** 40, 41; **Supp. XIV:** 4–5

Understanding Robert Bly (W. V. Davis), **Supp. XXI: 84–85,** 88

Understanding Ron Rash (Lang), **Supp. XXVII:** 215–216

"Understandings of Food as Culture" (Dusselier), **Supp. XXVI:** 210

Understanding Tim O'Brien (Kaplan), **Supp. V:** 241

Understanding To Kill a Mockingbird: A Student Casebook to Issues, Sources, and Documents (C. D. Johnson), **Supp. VIII:** 127

Under Stars (Gallagher), **Supp. XXIV:** 166, 167, 168–169, 170

Undertaker's Garland, The (Wilson and Bishop), **IV:** 427

Under Taos Mountain: The Terrible Quarrel of Magpie and Tía (Schott), **Supp. XXIII: 250–251**

Under the Banner of Heaven: A Story of Violent Faith (Krakauer), **Supp. XVIII:** 105, **114–116,** 117

"Under the Cedarcroft Chestnut" (Lanier), **Supp. I Part 1:** 364

Under the Feet of Jesus (Viramontes), **Supp. XXV:** 130

"Under the Harbour Bridge" (Komunyakaa), **Supp. XIII:** 125

"Under the Influence" (Sanders), **Supp. XVI:** 274, 277

"Under the Language Sea" (Davison), **Supp. XXVI:** 79

Under the Lilacs (Alcott), **Supp. I Part 1:** 42–43, 44

"Under the Maud Moon" (Kinnell), **Supp. III Part 1:** 246–247

Under the Mountain Wall: A Chronicle of Two Seasons in the Stone Age (Matthiessen), **Supp. V:** 202

Under the Red Flag (Jin), **Supp. XVIII:** 89, **94–95**

"Under the Roof of Memory" (Davison), **Supp. XXVI:** 78

"Under the Rose" (Pynchon), **Supp. II Part 2:** 620

"Under the Seal of My Widowhood" (Lombard), **Supp. XXVII:** 262

Under the Sea-Wind: A Naturalist's Picture of Ocean Life (Carson), **Supp. IX:** 19, **22–23**

Under the Shadow (Sorrentino), **Supp. XXI:** 236–237

Under the Sign of Saturn (Sontag), **Supp. III Part 2:** 451, 452, 458, 470–471

"Under the Sign of Saturn" (Sontag), **Supp. III Part 2:** 470

"Under the Sky" (Bowles), **Supp. IV Part 1:** 87

"Under the Sun"(Schott), **Supp. XXIII:** 247, 248

" 'Under the Umbrella of Black Civilization': A Conversation with Reginald McKnight" (Ashe), **Supp. XX:** 154

Under the Volcano (M. Lowry), **Supp. XVII:** 135, 139, 140; **Supp. XXVI:** 28

"Under the Willows" (J. R. Lowell), **Supp. I Part 2:** 416

Under the Willows and Other Poems (J. R. Lowell), **Supp. I Part 2:** 424

"Undertow" (Boyce), **Supp. XXI:** 10

"Underwater Spring" (Huddle), **Supp. XXVI:** 153

Underwood, John Curtis, **Supp. XXIV:** 29

Underwood, Wilbur, **Retro. Supp. II:** 79

Underworld (DeLillo), **Supp. VI:** 2, 4–5, 6–7, 8, 9, 10, 11, **13–15; Supp. XI:** 68; **Supp. XX: 91; Supp. XXVII:** 6

Underworld (screenplay, Hecht), **Supp. XXVII:** 83, 90, 91

Underworld, The (Wolfert). *See Tucker's World* (Wolfert)

"Undesirable, The" (Huddle), **Supp. XXVI:** 148, 153

Undine (La Motte-Fouqué), **II:** 212; **III:** 78

Undiscovered Country, The (Howells), **II:** 282

"Undressing, The" (C. Frost), **Supp. XV:** 98

"Undressing the Vanity Dolls" (Vaz), **Supp. XXVI:** 260–261

Uneasy Chair, The (Stegner), **Supp. IV Part 2:** 599

"Unemployed, Disabled, and Insane, The" (Haines), **Supp. XII:** 211–212

Unending Blues (Simic), **Supp. VIII: 278–279**

Unending Dialogue: Voices from an AIDS Poetry Workshop (Hadas, Barber, et al), **Supp. XXIII:** 118, **125–126**

"Unexpected Freedom" (Peacock), **Supp. XIX:** 199

"Unexpressed" (Dunbar), **Supp. II Part 1:** 199

"Unfinished Bronx, The" (Paley), **Supp. VI:** 228

Unfinished Crime, The (Holding), **Supp. XXII:** 120, **123–124,** 135, 136

"Unfinished Poems" (Eliot), **I:** 579

"Unfinished Song" (C. Frost), **Supp. XV:** 97

Unfinished Woman, An (Hellman), **Supp. I Part 1:** 292, 293, 294; **Supp. IV Part 1:** 12, 353–354; **Supp. IX:** 196, 200–201

Unforeseen Wilderness, The: An Essay on Kentucky's Red River Gorge (Berry),

Supp. X: 28, 29, 30, 36

Unforgotten Years (L. P. Smith), **Supp. XIV:** 333, 334, 335, 336, 347

"Unfortunate Coincidence" (Parker), **Supp. IX:** 190

Unframed Originals (Merwin), **Supp. III Part 1:** 341

Ungar, Sanford, **Supp. XI:** 228

Ungaretti, Giuseppe, **Supp. V:** 337

Unguided Tour (Sontag), **Supp. III Part 2:** 452

"Unheimliche, Das" (The Uncanny) (Freud), **Supp. XVI:** 157–158

Unholy Garden (screenplay, Hech and MacArthur), **Supp. XXVII:** 90

Unholy Sonnets (Jarman), **Supp. XVII:** 109, 110, **119–120; Supp. XVIII:** 178

"Unholy Sonnets" (Jarman), **Supp. XVII:** 118, 119–120

"Unidentified Flying Object" (Hayden), **Supp. II Part 1:** 368

"Unifying Principle, The" (Ammons), **Supp. VII:** 28

"Unimportant Man, An" (D. West), **Supp. XVIII:** 280

"Union" (Hughes), **Supp. I Part 1:** 331

"Union" (Stone), **Supp. XXVII:** 254

"Union Square" (Teasdale), **Supp. XXVII:** 286, 289

"Union Street: San Francisco, Summer 1975" (Carver), **Supp. III Part 1:** 138

"Unitarian Christianity" (Channing), **Supp. XXIV: 71–73,** 77

Unitarians and the Universalists, The (Robinson), **Supp. XXIV:** 70

"United"(Kenny), **Supp. XXIII:** 149

United States Army in World War II (Morison), **Supp. I Part 2:** 490

United States Constitution, **I:** 6, 283

United States Essays, 1951–1991 (Vidal), **Supp. IV Part 2:** 678, 687

"United States of Huck, The: Introduction to *Adventures of Huckleberry Finn*" (Saunders), *Supp. XIX:* 235

United States of Poetry, The (television series), **Supp. XIII:** 274

"Unity through Diversity" (Locke), **Supp. XIV:** 212, 213

Universal Baseball Asociation, Inc., J. Henry Waugh, Prop., The (Coover), **Supp. V:** 39, 41–42, 44, 46

Universal Passion (Young), **III:** 111

"Universe of Death, The" (H. Miller), **III:** 184

Universe of Time, A (Anderson), **II:** 27, 28, 45, 46, 48, 49

"Universities" (Emerson), **II:** 6

"Universities: A Mirage? " (Mora), **Supp. XIII:** 219

"University" (Shapiro), **Supp. II Part 2:** 704–705, 717

"University Avenue" (Mora), **Supp. XIII:** 216

"University Days" (Thurber), **Supp. I Part 2:** 605

"University Hospital, Boston" (Oliver), **Supp. VII:** 235

"University's Peril, The" (Taggard), **Supp. XXII:** 273

"Unknowable, The" (Levine), **Supp. V:** 195

"Unknown Girl in the Maternity Ward" (Sexton), **Supp. II Part 2:** 676

"Unknown Love, The" (Chandler), **Supp. IV Part 1:** 120

Unknown Messages (Stone), **Supp. XXVII:** 257

Unknown Rilke, The (Rilke; F. Wright, trans.), **Supp. XVII:** 244

"Unknown War, The" (Sandburg), **III:** 594

Unkown Constellations, The (Swados), **Supp. XIX:** 256

Unleashed (anthology), **Supp. XI:** 132

Unleashed: Poems by Writers' Dogs (Hempel and Shepard, eds.), **Supp. XXI:** 115

"Unlighted Lamps" (Anderson), **I:** 112

Unlit Lamp, The (Holding), **Supp. XXII: 121,** 130

Unloved Wife, The (Alcott), **Supp. I Part 1:** 33

Unmarried Woman, An (film), **Supp. IV Part 1:** 303

"Unnatural Mother, The" (Gilman), **Supp. XI:** 207

"Unnatural State of the Unicorn" (Komunyakaa), **Supp. XIII:** 119

"Unparalleled Adventure of One Hans Pfaall, The" (Poe), **III:** 424

"Unpleasant Profession of Jonathan Hoag, The" (Heinlein), **Supp. XVIII:** 149

Unprecedented Era, The (Goebbels), **III:** 560

"Unprofitable Servant, The" (O. Henry), **Supp. II Part 1:** 403

Unpublished Poems of Emily Dickinson (Bianchi and Hampson, ed.), **Retro. Supp. I:** 35

Unpunished (Gilman), **Supp. XI:** 208

Unraveling Strangeness, The (Weigl), **Supp. XIX: 287–288**

"Unreal City" (Eliot), **Supp. XV:** 218

"Unreality of Modern Realism, The" (Rinehart), **Supp. XXV:** 201

"Unreasoning Heart" (Untermeyer), **Supp. XV:** 309

"Unsaid (Gioia), **Supp. XV:** 129

"Unseen, The" (Pinsky), **Supp. VI:** 243–244

"Unseen, The" (Singer), **Retro. Supp. II:** 307

Unseen Hand, The (Shepard), **Supp. III Part 2:** 439, 445–446

Unselected Poems (Levine), **Supp. V:** 179

Unsettling of America, The: Culture and Agriculture (Berry), **Supp. X:** 22, 26, 29, 32, 33, 35; **Supp. XIV:** 177, 179

Unspeakable Gentleman, The (Marquand), **III:** 53–54, 60, 63

Unspeakable Practices, Unnatural Acts (Barthelme), **Supp. IV Part 1:** 39

"Unspeakable Things Unspoken: The Afro-American Presence in American Literature" (Morrison), **Supp. III Part 1:** 375, 377–379

Unspoken and Other Poems, The (Bremer), **Supp. XXII:** 277

"Untelling, The" (Strand), **Supp. IV Part 2:** 629

Unterecker, John, **I:** 386

Untermeyer, Jean Starr, **II:** 530; **Supp. XV:** 294, 295, 303, 307, 308, 310; **Supp. XXVII:** 286

Untermeyer, Louis, **II:** 516–517, 530, 532; **III:** 268; **Retro. Supp. I:** 124, 133, 136; **Supp. III Part 1:** 2; **Supp. IX:** 76; **Supp. XIV:** 119, 123; **Supp. XV: 293–318; Supp. XXI:** 277; **Supp. XXV:** 21, 23; **Supp. XXVII:** 252, 286, 289

Untimely Papers (Bourne), **I:** 218, 233

"Untitled" (C. Frost), **Supp. XV:** 103

"Untitled Blues" (Komunyakaa), **Supp. XIII:** 117

Unto the Sons (Talese), **Supp. XVII:** 199–200, **206–207,** 208, 209, 210

"Untrustworthy Speaker, The" (Glück), **Supp. V:** 86

"Unused" (Anderson), **I:** 112, 113

Unvanquished, The (Faulkner), **II:** 55, 67–68, 71; **Retro. Supp. I:** 84; **Supp. I Part 2:** 450

"Unvexed Isles, The" (Warren), **IV:** 253

"Unwedded" (Larcom), **Supp. XIII:** 144

"Unweepables, The" (Karr), **Supp. XI:** 243

"Unwelcome Guest, An" (Papernick), **Supp. XVII:** 50

Unwelcome Man, The (W. Frank), **Supp. XX: 70, 76**

Unwelcome Words (Bowles), **Supp. IV Part 1:** 93, 94

"Unwelcome Words" (Bowles), **Supp. IV Part 1:** 94, 95

Unwin, T. Fisher, **Supp. XI:** 202

"Unwithered Garland, The" (Kunitz), **Supp. III Part 1:** 265

Unwobbling Pivot, The (Pound, trans.), **III:** 472

"Unwritten, The" (Merwin), **Supp. III Part 1:** 352

"Unwritten Law" (Glück), **Supp. V:** 91

Up (Sukenick), **Supp. V:** 39

Up Above the World (Bowles), **Supp. IV Part 1:** 82, 91, 92

"Up and Down" (Merrill), **Supp. III Part 1:** 328

Upanishads, **IV:** 183

Up Country: Poems of New England (Kumin), **Supp. IV Part 2:** 446, 447–448, 453

"Update" (Dunn), **Supp. XI:** 150–151

Updike, John, **I:** 54; **III:** 572; **IV: 214–235; Retro. Supp. I:** 116, **317–338; Retro. Supp. II:** 213, 279, 280; **Supp. I Part 1:** 186, 196; **Supp. IV Part 2:** 657; **Supp. IX:** 208; **Supp. X:** 23, 43, 95, 119; **Supp. VIII:** 151, 167, 236; **Supp. XI:** 65, 66, 99, 140; **Supp. XII:** 140, 296, 298, 310; **Supp. XIII:** 45–46, 47, 52; **Supp. XIV:** 79, 93, 111; **Supp. XVI:** 205, 207, 220; **Supp. XX: 17; Supp. XXI:** 116, 226; **Supp. XXIII:** 109

Updike, Mrs. Wesley, **IV:** 218, 220

Up from Slavery (Washington), **Supp. II Part 1:** 169; **Supp. IX:** 19

Upham, Thomas Goggswell, **II:** 487

"Upholsterers, The" (Lardner), **II:** 435

"Up in Michigan" (Hemingway), **II:** 263; **Supp. XIX:** 241

Upjohn, Richard, **IV:** 312

"Upon a Spider Catching a Fly" (Taylor), **IV:** 161

"Upon a Wasp Child with Cold" (Taylor), **IV:** 161

"Upon Meeting Don L. Lee, in a Dream" (Dove), **Supp. IV Part 1:** 244

"Upon My Dear and Loving Husband His Going into England, Jan. 16, 1661" (Bradstreet), **Supp. I Part 1:** 110

"Upon My Mother's Death"(Hadas), **Supp. XXIII:** 118

"Upon Returning to the Country Road" (Lindsay), **Supp. I Part 2:** 382

"Upon the Burning of Our House, July 10th, 1666" (Bradstreet), **Supp. I Part 1:** 107–108, 122

"Upon the Sweeping Flood" (Taylor), **IV:** 161

"Upon Wedlock, and Death of Children" (Taylor), **IV:** 144, 147, 161

"Upon Westminster Bridge" (Wordsworth), **Supp. XXIV:** 148

"Upset, An" (Merrill), **Supp. III Part 1:** 336

Upstairs and Downstairs (Vonnegut), **Supp. II Part 2:** 757

Upstate (Wilson), **IV:** 447

Upton, Lee, **Supp. X:** 209

"Upturned Face" (Crane), **I:** 423

Upward, Allen, **Supp. I Part 1:** 262

Upward, Edward, **Supp. XIV:** 159, 160

"Upward Moon and the Downward Moon, The" (R. Bly), **Supp. IV Part 1:** 71

Urama, Kelechi, **Supp. XXVII:** 202

Urania: A Rhymed Lesson (Holmes), **Supp. I Part 1:** 300

"Urban Convalescence, An" (Merrill), **Supp. III Part 1:** 322–324

"Urban Renewal" (Komunyakaa), **Supp. XIII:** 113

Urban Tumbleweed: Notes from a Tanka Diary (Mullen), **Supp. XXVII:** 175–176

Urdang, Constance, **Supp. XV:** 74

"Urganda and Fatima" (Rowson), **Supp. XV:** 234

Urial Accosta: A Play (Reznikoff), **Supp. XIV:** 282, 288

Urich, Robert, **Supp. V:** 228

"Uriel" (Emerson), **II:** 19

Uris, Leon, **Supp. IV Part 1:** 285, 379; **Supp. XX: 243–258; Supp. XXVII:** 147

Uroff, Margaret D., **Supp. I Part 2:** 542

Ursu, Liliana, **Supp. XXIV:** 178

"Us" (Sexton), **Supp. II Part 2:** 687

U.S. 1 (Rukeyser), **Supp. VI:** 272, 278, 283, 285

U.S.A. (Dos Passos), **I:** 379, 475, 478, 482–488, 489, 490, 491, 492, 493, 494, 495; **Retro. Supp. II:** 197; **Supp. I Part 2:** 646; **Supp. III Part 1:** 104, 105; **Supp. XIV:** 24; **Supp. XXVI:** 23

"U.S.A. School of Writing, The" (Bishop), **Retro. Supp. II:** 43

USA the Movie (film), **Supp. XXVII:** 263

"U.S. Commercial Orchid, The" (Agee), **I:** 35

"Used-Boy Raisers, The" (Paley), **Supp. VI:** 218, 228

"Used Cars on Oahu" (Nye), **Supp. XIII:** 282

"Used Side of the Sofa, The" (Ríos), **Supp. IV Part 2:** 551

Useless Servants, The (Hinojosa), **Supp. XIX:** 98, 103, 104, **109–110**

Use of Fire, The (Price), **Supp. VI:** 265

"Use of Force, The" (W. C. Williams), **Retro. Supp. I:** 424

Use of Poetry and the Use of Criticism, The (Eliot), **Retro. Supp. I:** 65

Uses of Enchantment, The: The Meaning and Importance of Fairy Tales (Bettelheim), **Supp. X:** 77; **Supp. XIV:** 126

"Uses of Hell, The" (E. Hoffman), **Supp. XVI:** 154

"Uses of Hell, The: An Exchange"(Novick, Katz, and Szulc), **Supp. XVI:** 154

Uses of Literacy, The (Hoggart), **Supp. XIV:** 299

Uses of Literature, The (Calvino), **Supp. XXII:** 263

"Uses of Poetry, The" (W. C. Williams), **Retro. Supp. I:** 412

"Uses of the Blues, The" (Baldwin), **Retro. Supp. II:** 8

"Use-Unuse of Us, The" (Bronk), **Supp. XXI:** 32

"USFS 1919: The Ranger, the Cook, and a Hole in the Sky" (Maclean), **Supp. XIV:** 230, 234

Ushant: An Essay (Aiken), **I:** 49, 54, 55, 56, 57

"Usher 11" (Bradbury), **Supp. I Part 2:** 622

U.S.I. (Kramer), **Supp. XXVI:** 26

"Using Parrots to Kill Mockingbirds: Yet Another Racial Prosecution and Wrongful Conviction in Maycomb" (Fair), **Supp. VIII:** 128

USS Constellation: Pride of the American Navy (Myers), **Supp. XXVII:** 208

Ustedes y Nosotros: Nuevo Mensaje a Ibero-América (W. Frank), **Supp. XX: 79**

"Usual Objects"(Schott), **Supp. XXIII:** 248

Usual Star, The (Doolittle), **Supp. I Part 1:** 270

"Usurpation (Other People's Stories)" (Ozick), **Supp. V:** 268, 271

Utopia 14 (Vonnegut), **Supp. II Part 2:** 757

V

V. (Pynchon), **Supp. II Part 2:** 618, 620–622, 627–630; **Supp. IV Part 1:** 279

"Vacation" (Stafford), **Supp. XI:** 321, 322

Vacationland (Monson), **Supp. XXIV:** 230, 231, 234

"Vacation Trip" (Stafford), **Supp. XI:** 322

Vachel Lindsay: A Poet in America (Masters), **Supp. I Part 2:** 473, 474

"Vachel Lindsay: The Midwest as Utopia" (Whitney), **Supp. I Part 2:** 403

"Vachel Lindsay Writes to Floyd Dell" (Tanselle), **Supp. I Part 2:** 403

"Vacillation" (Yeats), **Supp. XV:** 253

Vadim, Roger, **Supp. XI:** 293, 307

"Vag" (Dos Passos), **I:** 487–488

Vagina Monologues, The (Ensler), **Supp. XIX:** 204–205

Vail, Laurence, **Supp. XXIV:** 50

Valdez, Luis, **Supp. XXIII:** 203

"Vale" (Stallings), **Supp. XXV:** 230, 231

Valediction (Parker), **Supp. XIX:** 185

Valentine, Jean, **Supp. V:** 92

Valentine, Saint, **IV:** 396

Valentines (Kooser), **Supp. XIX:** 116, 123, **128–129**

Valentino, Rudolph, **I:** 483

Valéry, Paul, **II:** 543, 544; **III:** 279, 409, 428, 609; **IV:** 79, 91, 92, 428, 443; **Retro. Supp. II:** 187

"Valhalla" (Francis), **Supp. IX:** 77

Valhalla and Other Poems (Francis), **Supp. IX:** 76

Valiant Runaways, The (Atherton), **Supp. XXIV:** 22

Validity in Interpretation (Hirsch), **Supp. XIV:** 15

Valitsky, Ken, **Supp. XII:** 7

Vallejo, César, **Supp. IX:** 271; **Supp. V:** 332; **Supp. XIII:** 114, 315, 323; **Supp. XXI:** 132

Valley, The (Asch), **Supp. XXVI:** 17, 21, 23–26

"Valley, The" (Bass), **Supp. XVI:** 20, 22

Valley, The (Hinojosa), **Supp. XIX:** 97, 99, **100–101**

"Valley Between, The" (Marshall), **Supp. XI:** 278

Valley of Decision, The (Wharton), **IV:** 311, 315; **Retro. Supp. I:** 365–367

"Valley of the Monsters, The" (Peacock), **Supp. XIX:** 198

Valley of the Moon, The (London), **II:** 467, 481

"Valley of Unrest, The" (Poe), **III:** 411

Valli, Alida, **Supp. IV Part 2:** 520

"Valor" (Bausch), **Supp. VII:** 54

Valparaiso (DeLillo), **Supp. VI:** 4, 12

"Value of a Place, The" (Bass), **Supp. XVI:** 18

"Values and Fictions" (Toomer), **Supp. III Part 2:** 485–486

"Values and Imperatives" (Locke), **Supp. XIV:** 199, 202, 212

Values of Veblen, The: A Critical Appraisal (Rosenberg), **Supp. I Part 2:** 650

"Vampire" (Karr), **Supp. XI:** 241

Vampire Armand, The (Rice), **Supp. VII:** 290, 294–295

Vampire Chronicles, The (Rice), **Supp. VII:** 290

Vampire Lestat, The (Rice), **Supp. VII:** 290–292, 298, 299

Van Aalst, Mariska, **Supp. XIX:** 50, 51

Van Arsdale, Sarah, **Supp. XXV:** 4

Van Buren, Martin, **II:** 134, 312; **III:** 473
"Vandals" (Munro), **Supp. XXVII:** 192
Vande Kieft, Ruth M., **IV:** 260
Vanderbilt, Cornelius, **III:** 14
VanDerWerff, Todd, **Supp. XXV:** 75
Van Dine, S. S., **Supp. IV Part 1:** 341; **Supp. XXVI:** 283
Van Doren, Carl, **I:** 252–253, 423; **II:** 103, 111, 112; **Supp. I Part 2:** 474, 486, 707, 709, 717, 718, 727; **Supp. II Part 1:** 395; **Supp. VIII:** 96–97
Van Doren, Mark, **I:** 168; **III:** 4, 23, 589; **Supp. I Part 2:** 604; **Supp. III Part 2:** 626; **Supp. IX:** 266, 268; **Supp. VIII:** 231; **Supp. XV:** 152, 305, 307; **Supp. XXII:** 275
Vandover and the Brute (Norris), **III:** 314, 315, 316, 320–322, 328, 333, 334
Van Duyn, Mona, **Supp. IX:** 269
Van Dyke, Annette, **Supp. IV Part 1:** 327
Van Dyke, Henry, **I:** 223; **II:** 456
Van Gogh, Vincent, **I:** 27; **IV:** 290; **Supp. I Part 2:** 451; **Supp. IV Part 1:** 284; **Supp. XXII:** 171–172
Van Gogh Field and Other Stories, The (Kittredge), **Supp. XXVI:** 181, 182, 184
Van Gogh's Room at Arles (Elkin), **Supp. VI:** 56
"Vanilla Dunk" (Lethem), **Supp. XVIII:** 139
"Vanisher, The" (Whittier), **Supp. I Part 2:** 691
Vanishing of Betty Varian, The (Wells), **Supp. XXVI:** 278
Vanishing Point (Markson), **Supp. XVII:** 135, 137, 138, 145–146
"Vanishing Point, The" (Davison), **Supp. XXVI:** 76
"Vanishing Point: Former City" (Monson), **Supp. XXIV:** 238
"Vanishing Point for Solo Voice" (Monson), **Supp. XXIV:** 239
Vanishing Point: Not a Memoir (Monson), **Supp. XXIV:** 230, **236–239,** 241–242
"Vanishing Point: Panera" (Monson), **Supp. XXIV:** 238
"Vanishing Red, The" (Frost), **Retro. Supp. II:** 47
"Vanity" (B. Diop), **Supp. IV Part 1:** 16
Vanity Fair (Thackeray), **I:** 354; **II:** 91; **III:** 70; **Supp. IX:** 200
"Vanity of All Wordly Things, The" (Bradstreet), **Supp. I Part 1:** 102, 119
Vanity of Duluoz (Kerouac), **Supp. III Part 1:** 221, 222
"Vanity of Existence, The" (Freneau), **Supp. II Part 1:** 262
Van Matre, Lynn, **Supp. V:** 126
Vann, Barbara, **Supp. XV:** 187
Vanquished, The (Faulkner), **I:** 205
"Vanquished, The" (Rash), **Supp. XXVII:** 220
Van Rensselaer, Stephen, **I:** 351
Van Vechten, Carl, **I:** 295; **IV:** 76; **Retro. Supp. I:** 199; **Supp. I Part 1:** 324, 327, 332; **Supp. I Part 2:** 715; **Supp. II Part 2: 725–751; Supp. X:** 247; **Supp. XIX:** 76; **Supp. XVI:** 135; **Supp. XVII:** 96, 97, 101, 104; **Supp.**

XVIII: 123, 131, 132, 279, 280; **Supp. XX: 69; Supp. XXI:** 5, 8; **Supp. XXII:** 5, 158, 160
Van Vliet, Don, **Supp. XXIII:** 174
Vanya and Sonia and Masha and Spike (Durang), **Supp. XXIV: 127–128**
Vanzetti, Bartolomeo, **I:** 482, 486, 490, 494; **II:** 38–39, 426; **III:** 139–140; **Supp. I Part 2:** 446, 610, 611; **Supp. IX:** 199; **Supp. V:** 288–289; **Supp. XXII:** 277
"Vapor Trail Reflected in the Frog Pond" (Kinnell), **Supp. III Part 1:** 242–243
"Vapor Trails" (Snyder), **Supp. VIII:** 298
"Variant Text" (Goodman), **Supp. XXVI:** 118
"Variation: Ode to Fear" (Warren), **IV:** 241
"Variation on a Sentence" (Bogan), **Supp. III Part 1:** 60
"Variation on Gaining a Son" (Dove), **Supp. IV Part 1:** 248
"Variation on Pain" (Dove), **Supp. IV Part 1:** 248
"Variations: The air is sweetest that a thistle guards" (Merrill), **Supp. III Part 1:** 321
"Variations: White Stag, Black Bear" (Merrill), **Supp. III Part 1:** 321
"Varick Street" (Bishop), **Supp. I Part 1:** 90, 92
Varieties of Metaphysical Poetry, The (Eliot), **Retro. Supp. I:** 65
Varieties of Religious Experience, The (William James), **II:** 344, 353, 354, 359–360, 362; **IV:** 28, 291; **Supp. IX:** 19
Variety (film), **Supp. XII:** 7
Variorum (Whitman), **Retro. Supp. I:** 406
Various Antidotes (J. Scott), **Supp. XVII: 188–189**
Various Miracles (Shields), **Supp. VII:** 318–320, 323, 324
"Various Miracles" (Shields), **Supp. VII:** 318–319, 324
Various Poems (Zach), **Supp. XV:** 86
Various Positions (album, Coen), **Supp. XXVII:** 54
"Various Tourists" (Connell), **Supp. XIV:** 79
"Varmint Question, The" (Leopold), **Supp. XIV:** 180–181
Varno, David, **Supp. XIX:** 205
Vasari, Giorgio, **Supp. I Part 2:** 450; **Supp. III Part 1:** 5
Vasquez, Robert, **Supp. V:** 180
Vassall Morton (Parkman), **Supp. II Part 2:** 595, 597–598
Vasse, W. W., **III:** 478
Vaudeville for a Princess (Schwartz), **Supp. II Part 2:** 661–662
"Vaudeville Moment" (Bodenheim), **Supp. XXV:** 22
Vaughan, Henry, **IV:** 151; **Supp. XV:** 251
Vaughn, Robert, **Supp. XI:** 343
Vaughn, Stephanie, **Supp. XXV:** 142
"Vaunting Oak" (Ransom), **III:** 490
Vaz, Katherine, **Supp. XXVI: 255–269**
Vazirani, Reetika, **Supp. XIII:** 133

Veblen (Hobson), **Supp. I Part 2:** 650
Veblen, Andrew, **Supp. I Part 2:** 640
Veblen, Oswald, **Supp. I Part 2:** 640
Veblen, Thorstein, **I:** 104, 283, 475–476, 483, 498, 511; **II:** 27, 272, 276, 287; **Supp. I Part 2: 628–650; Supp. IV Part 1:** 22
Veblen, Mrs. Thorstein (Ellen Rolfe), **Supp. I Part 2:** 641
Veblenism: A New Critique (Dobriansky), **Supp. I Part 2:** 648, 650
"Veblen's Attack on Culture" (Adorno), **Supp. I Part 2:** 650
Vecsey, Christopher, **Supp. XXVI:** 90
Vectors and Smoothable Curves (Bronk), **Supp. XXI: 24–26,** 32
Vedanta for Modern Man (Isherwood, ed.), **Supp. XIV:** 164
Vedanta for the Western World (Isherwood, ed.), **Supp. XIV:** 164
Vedas, **IV:** 183
Vega, Janine Pommy, **Supp. XIV:** 148
Vega, Lope de, **Retro. Supp. I:** 285; **Supp. III Part 1:** 341, 347
Vegetable, The (Fitzgerald), **Retro. Supp. I:** 105; **Supp. IX:** 57
Vegetable, The, or From President to Postman (Fitzgerald), **II:** 91
"Vegetable Love" (Apple), **Supp. XVII:** 4
"Vegetable Love"(Crooker), **Supp. XXIII:** 62
"Vegetable Wisdom" (Halliday), **Supp. XIX:** 88
Veg tsu zikh, Der (The road to one's self) (Asch), **Supp. XXIII:** 5, 11
Veil of Snows, A (Helprin), **Supp. XXV:** 84, 87
Veinberg, Jon, **Supp. V:** 180; **Supp. XIII:** 313; **Supp. XV:** 76–77, 86
Vein of Iron (Glasgow), **II:** 175, 186, 188–189, 191, 192, 194
Vein of Riches, A (Knowles), **Supp. XII:** 249
Vein of Words (J. W. Miller), **Supp. XX: 165**
Velie, Alan R., **Supp. IV Part 2:** 486
Velocities: New and Selected Poems, 1966–1992 (Dobyns), **Supp. XIII:** 86–87, 87, 88
"Velocity" (Collins), **Supp. XXI:** 61
"Velorio" (Cisneros), **Supp. VII:** 66
"Velvet Gentleman, The (Skloot), **Supp. XX: 201**
"Velvet Shoes" (Wylie), **Supp. I Part 2:** 711, 714
Venant, Elizabeth, **Supp. XI:** 343
Vencloca, Thomas, **Supp. VIII:** 29
Vendler, Helen H., **Retro. Supp. I:** 297; **Retro. Supp. II:** 184, 191; **Supp. I Part 1:** 77, 78, 92, 95; **Supp. I Part 2:** 565; **Supp. IV Part 1:** 245, 247, 249, 254, 257; **Supp. IV Part 2:** 448; **Supp. V:** 78, 82, 189, 343; **Supp. XII:** 187, 189; **Supp. XV:** 20, 184
"Venetian Blind, The" (Jarrell), **II:** 382–383
Venetian Glass Nephew, The (Wylie), **Supp. I Part 2:** 707, 709, 714, 717–719, 721, 724

Venetian Life (Howells), **II:** 274, 277, 279
Venetian Vespers, The (Hecht), **Supp. X:** 57, **65–69**
"Venetian Vespers, The" (Hecht), **Supp. X:** 65, **66–67**
Venice Observed (McCarthy), **II:** 562
Ventadorn, Bernard de, **Supp. IV Part 1:** 146
"Ventriloquists' Conversations" (Gentry), **Supp. IV Part 1:** 236
Venturesome Voyages of Captain Voss, The (Voss), **Supp. XXV:** 217
"Venus, Cupid, Folly and Time" (Taylor), **Supp. V:** 322–323
Venus and Adonis (film), **Supp. IV Part 1:** 82
Venus and Don Juan (C. Frost), **Supp. XV:** 93, **102–103,** 104, 107
"Venus and Don Juan" (C. Frost), **Supp. XV:** 103
Venus Blue (Sobin), **Supp. XVI: 293–294,** 294
Venus in Sparta (Auchincloss), **Supp. IV Part 1:** 25
"Venus Pandemos" (Halliday), **Supp. XIX:** 85, 89, 90, 93
"Venus's-flytraps" (Komunyakaa), **Supp. XIII:** 126, 127
"Veracruz" (Hayden), **Supp. II Part 1:** 371, 373
Verducci, Tom, **Supp. XXII:** 209
"Verdun" (Beston), **Supp. XXVI:** 32
Verga, Giovanni, **II:** 271, 275
Verghese, Abraham, **Supp. X:** 160
Verhaeren, Emile, **I:** 476; **II:** 528, 529
Verlaine, Paul, **II:** 529, 543; **III:** 466; **IV:** 79, 80, 86, 286; **Retro. Supp. I:** 56, 62; **Retro. Supp. II:** 326
"Vermeer" (Nemerov), **III:** 275, 278, 280
Vermeer, Jan, **Retro. Supp. I:** 335
"Vermont" (Carruth), **Supp. XVI:** 54
"Vermont" (Huddle), **Supp. XXVI:** 161
Vermont Journal: 1971 (Brainard), **Supp. XXVII:** 27
Vermont Notebook, The (Ashbery), **Supp. III Part 1:** 1
"Vermont Tale, A" (Helprin), **Supp. XXV:** 85
Vermont Writers: A State of Mind (Daley), **Supp. XXII:** 216
"Vernal Ague, The" (Freneau), **Supp. II Part 1:** 258
Verne, Jules, **I:** 480; **Retro. Supp. I:** 270; **Supp. XI:** 63
Vernon, John, **Supp. X:** 15
Verplanck, Gulian C., **Supp. I Part 1:** 155, 156, 157, 158
Verrazano, Giovanni da, **Supp. I Part 2:** 496, 497
Verse (Zawacki), **Supp. VIII:** 272
"Verse for Urania" (Merrill), **Supp. III Part 1:** 329, 330
Verses (Wharton), **Retro. Supp. I:** 362
Verses, Printed for Her Friends (Jewett), **II:** 406
"Verses for Children" (A. Lowell), **II:** 516
"Verses Made at Sea in a Heavy Gale" (Freneau), **Supp. II Part 1:** 262

"Verses on the Death of T. S. Eliot" (Brodsky), **Supp. VIII:** 19
"Version of a Fragment of Simonides" (Bryant), **Supp. I Part 1:** 153, 155
"Vers Libre Epidemic, The" (Lovecraft), **Supp. XXV:** 120
Verulam, Baron. *See* Bacon, Francis
Very, Jones, **III:** 507; **Supp. XXV: 237–252**
"Very Hot Sun in Bermuda, The" (Jackson), **Supp. IX:** 126
Very Old Bones (W. Kennedy), **Supp. VII:** 133, 148, 150–153
"Very Old Man with Enormous Wings, A" (García Márquez), **Supp. XXIV:** 190
Very Persistent Gappers of Frip, The (Saunders), **Supp. XIX:** 229–230
"Very Proper Gander, The" (Thurber), **Supp. I Part 2:** 610
"Very Short Story, A" (Hemingway), **II:** 252; **Retro. Supp. I:** 173
"Vesalius in Zante" (Wharton), **Retro. Supp. I:** 372
Vesey, Denmark, **Supp. I Part 2:** 592
Vesey, Desmond, **Supp. XIV:** 162
"Vespers" (Auden), **Supp. II Part 1:** 23
"Vespers" (Glück), **Supp. V:** 88
"Vespers"(Dybek), **Supp. XXIII:** 78
Vestal Lady on Brattle, The (Corso), **Supp. XII:** 119, **120–121,** 134
Vested Interests and the Common Man, The (Veblen), **Supp. I Part 2:** 642
"Vesuvius at Home" (Rich), **Retro. Supp. I:** 42
"Veteran, The" (Crane), **I:** 413
"Veterans' Cemetery" (Gioia), **Supp. XV:** 117
"Veteran Sirens" (Robinson), **III:** 512, 524
"Veterinarian" (X. J. Kennedy), **Supp. XV:** 168
"Vetiver" (Ashbery), **Supp. III Part 1:** 26
Vetter, Lara, **Supp. XXII:** 166
"Via Dieppe-Newhaven" (H. Miller), **III:** 183
"Via Negativa" (Salter), **Supp. IX:** 257
Vicar of Wakefield, The (Goldsmith), **I:** 216
Vicious Circle, The (film, Wilder), **Supp. XVII:** 62
"Vicissitudes of the Avant-Garde, The" (Gass), **Supp. VI:** 91
Vicky Van (Wells), **Supp. XXVI:** 280
Vico, Giambattista, **Supp. XX: 38**
Victim, The (Bellow), **I:** 144, 145, 147, 149, 150, 151, 152, 153, 155, 156, 158, 159, 164; **IV:** 19; **Retro. Supp. II:** 21, 22, 34
"Victor" (Mumford), **Supp. II Part 2:** 476
Victoria (Rowson), **Supp. XV:** 231
Victorian in the Modern World, A (Hapgood), **Supp. XVII:** 95, 97, 100, 101, 103, 105, 106; **Supp. XXI:** 8
"Victoria's Secret" (Collins), **Supp. XXI:** 58–59
"Victories" (Untermeyer), **Supp. XV:** 300

"Victory at Sea" (television series), **Supp. I Part 2:** 490
"Victory comes late" (Dickinson), **Retro. Supp. I:** 45
"Victory of the Moon, The" (Crane), **I:** 420
Vida, Vendela, **Supp. XIX:** 49, 50, 53, 57, 58, 59, 61, 62
Vidal, Gore, **II:** 587; **IV:** 383; **Supp. IV Part 1:** 22, 35, 92, 95, 198; **Supp. IV Part 2: 677–696;** **Supp. IX:** 96; **Supp. X:** 186, 195; **Supp. XIV:** 156, 170, 338; **Supp. XIX:** 131, 132
Video Poems (Collins), **Supp. XXI:** 53
Viebahn, Fred, **Supp. IV Part 1:** 248
Viera, Joseph M., **Supp. XI:** 178, 186
Viereck, Peter, **Supp. I Part 2:** 403
Viertel, Berthold, **Supp. XIV:** 165
Viertel, Salka, **Supp. XVI:** 192
Viet Journal (Jones), **Supp. XI: 230–231**
Vietnam (McCarthy), **II:** 578–579
"Vietnam in Me, The" (O'Brien), **Supp. V:** 241, 252
Vietnamization of New Jersey, The (Durang), **Supp. XXIV:** 113, **117–118**
Vietnam Reader, The: The Definitive Collection of Fiction and Nonfiction on the War (O'Nan, ed.), **Supp. XXV:** 153
Vie unanime, La (Romains), **I:** 227
"View, The" (Roussel), **Supp. III Part 1:** 15, 16, 21
View from 80, The (Cowley), **Supp. II Part 1:** 141, 144, 153
"View from an Institution" (F. Wright), **Supp. XVII:** 244
View from Castle Rock, The (Munro), **Supp. XXVII:** 194–195
"View from the Backyard" (W. V. Davis), **Supp. XXI:** 96
View from the Bridge, A (A. Miller), **III:** 147, 148, 156, 158, 159–160; **Supp. XXV:** 93
View from the Seventh Layer, The (Brockmeier), **Supp. XXII: 59–61**
"View from the Seventh Layer, The" (Brockmeier), **Supp. XXII:** 61
View of My Own, A: Essays in Literature and Society (Hardwick), **Supp. III Part 1:** 194, 200
"View of the Capital from the Library of Congress" (Bishop), **Retro. Supp. II:** 45
View of the Soil and Climate of the United States, A (Brown, trans.), **Supp. I Part 1:** 146
"View of the Woods, A" (O'Connor), **III:** 349, 351, 358; **Retro. Supp. II:** 237
"Viewpoint" (column, Siddons), **Supp. XXII:** 240, 245
"Views of the Mysterious Hill: The Appearance of Parnassus in American Poetry" (Strand), **Supp. IV Part 2:** 631
"Vigil" (Karr), **Supp. XI:** 241
"Vigil, The" (Dante), **III:** 542
"Vigil at Heiligenkreuz" (W. V. Davis), **Supp. XXI:** 93
"Vigil"(Dybek), **Supp. XXIII:** 78

"Vignette" (Trethewey), **Supp. XXI:** 253, 254

Vigny, Alfred Victor de, **II:** 543

Vildrac, Charles, **Supp. XV:** 50

Vile Bodies (Waugh), **Supp. I Part 2:** 607

Villa, Pancho, **I:** 210; **III:** 584

"Villa dei Pini" (Davison), **Supp. XXVI:** 79

"Village, The" (Huddle), **Supp. XXVI:** 156

"Village Blacksmith, The" (Longfellow), **Retro. Supp. II:** 167, 168; **Supp. I Part 2:** 409

Village Hymns, a Supplement to Dr. Watts's Psalms and Hymns (Nettleton), **I:** 458

"Village Improvement Parade, The" (Lindsay), **Supp. I Part 2:** 388, 389

Village Magazine, The (Lindsay), **Supp. I Part 2:** 379–380, 382

Village Virus, The (Lewis), **II:** 440

"Villanelle at Sundown" (Justice), **Supp. VII:** 119, 122–123

"Villanelle of Change" (Robinson), **III:** 524

Villard, Oswald, **Supp. I Part 1:** 332

"Villa Selene" (Simpson), **Supp. IX:** 279

Villon, François, **II:** 544; **III:** 9, 174, 592; **Retro. Supp. I:** 286; **Supp. I Part 1:** 261; **Supp. III Part 1:** 235, 243, 249, 253; **Supp. III Part 2:** 560; **Supp. IX:** 116

"Villonaud for This Yule" (Pound), **Retro. Supp. I:** 286

Vincent, Steven, **Supp. XXV:** 201

"Vincenzo Tailor" (Di Piero), **Supp. XIX:** 38

Vindication of the Rights of Woman (Wollstonecraft), **Supp. I Part 1:** 126; **Supp. XI:** 203

Viner, Katherine, **Supp. XXVII:** 276

Vines, Lois Davis, **Retro. Supp. II:** 261

"Vineyard of Red Wine, The" (Beston), **Supp. XXVI:** 32

Vintage Book of Amnesia, The (Lethem, ed.), **Supp. XVIII:** 138

"Vintage Thunderbird, A" (Beattie), **Supp. V:** 27

Vinz, Mark, **Supp. X:** 117

Viol de Lucrèce, Le (Obey), **IV:** 356

Violence (Bausch), **Supp. VII:** 48–49, 54

Violent Bear It Away, The (O'Connor), **III:** 339, 345–348, 350, 351, 354, 355, 356, 357; **Retro. Supp. II:** 233, 234–236

Violent Hero, Wilderness Heritage and Urban Reality, The: A Study of the Private Eye in the Novels of Dashiell Hammett, Raymond Chandler and Ross Macdonald (Parker), **Supp. XIX:** 177

"Violent Vet, The" (O'Brien), **Supp. V:** 238

Violin (Rice), **Supp. VII:** 302

Viorst, Judith, **Supp. X:** 153

Viper Run (Karr), **Supp. XI: 248–251**

Viramontes, Helene María, **Supp. XXV:** 130, 133, 138

Virgil, **I:** 312, 322, 587; **II:** 133, 542; **IV:** 137, 359; **Retro. Supp. I:** 135; **Supp.**

I Part 1: 153; **Supp. I Part 2:** 494; **Supp. IV Part 2:** 631

"Virgin and Child with Music and Numbers" (Bronk), **Supp. XXI:** 30

"Virgin and the Dynamo" (Adams), **III:** 396

"Virgin Carrying a Lantern, The" (Stevens), **IV:** 80

Virgin Huntress, The (Holding), **Supp. XXII:** 119, 124, **135–136**

Virginia (Glasgow), **II:** 175, 178, 181–182, 193, 194

"Virginia" (Lindsay), **Supp. I Part 2:** 398

"Virginia Britannia" (Moore), **III:** 198, 208–209

"Virginians Are Coming Again, The" (Lindsay), **Supp. I Part 2:** 399

Virginia Reels (Hoffman), **Supp. XVIII:** 79, 86

Virgin Spain (W. Frank), **Supp. XX: 76**

"Virgins Plus Curtains Minus Dots" (Loy), **Supp. XXII:** 161

Virgin Suicides, The (Eugenides), **Supp. XXIV:** 134, **136–138,** 141, 142

Virgin Time: In Search of the Contemplative Life (Hampl), **Supp. XXII:** 82, 83–84, **90–92**

"Virgin Violeta" (Porter), **III:** 454

"Virility" (Ozick), **Supp. V:** 262, 265

Virtual Light (W. Gibson), **Supp. XVI:** 124, **129,** 130

Virtue of Selfishness, The: A New Concept of Egoism (Rand), **Supp. IV Part 2:** 527, 530–532

"Virtuoso" (Francis), **Supp. IX:** 82

Virtuous Girl, A (Bodenheim), **Supp. XXV:** 27

Virtuous Woman, A (Gibbons), **Supp. X: 44–45,** 46, 50

Visconti, Luchino, **Supp. V:** 51

Viscusi, Robert, **Supp. XX: 46**

Visible Saints: The History of a Puritan Idea (Morgan), **IV:** 149

"Vision, A" (Olds), **Supp. X:** 214

"Vision, A" (Winters), **Supp. II Part 2:** 785, 795

"Vision and Prayer" (D. Thomas), **I:** 432

"Visionary, The" (Poe), **III:** 411

Visionary Farms, The (Eberhart), **I:** 537–539

Visioning, The (Glaspell), **Supp. III Part 1:** 175–177, 180, 187, 188

Vision in Spring (Faulkner), **Retro. Supp. I:** 79

Vision of Columbus (Barlow), **Supp. I Part 1:** 124; **Supp. II Part 1:** 67, 68, 70–75, 77, 79

Vision of Sir Launfal, The (J. R. Lowell), **Supp. I Part 1:** 311; **Supp. I Part 2:** 406, 409, 410

"Vision of the World, A" (Cheever), **Supp. I Part 1:** 182, 192

"Visions and Voices" (Davison), **Supp. XXVI:** 71

"Visions of Budhardin"(Dybek), **Supp. XXIII:** 70–71

Visions of Cody (Kerouac), **Supp. III Part 1:** 225–227

Visions of Gerard (Kerouac), **Supp. III Part 1:** 219–222, 225, 227, 229

"Visions of the Daughters of Albion" (Blake), **III:** 540

"Visit" (Ammons), **Supp. VII:** 28–29

"Visit, The" (Kenyon), **Supp. VII:** 169

"Visitant, The" (Dunn), **Supp. XI:** 147

"*Visitation, The*/La Visitación" (Mora), **Supp. XIII:** 217, 224, 228

"Visitation"(Kenny), **Supp. XXIII:** 157

"Visit Home, A" (Stafford), **Supp. XI:** 318

Visit in 2001, The (musical, McNally), **Supp. XIII:** 207

"Visiting My Own House in Iowa City" (Stern), **Supp. IX:** 300

Visiting Villain, The (Wells), **Supp. XXVI:** 278, 280

"Visit of Charity, A" (Welty), **IV:** 262

"Visit of the Hawk" (Huddle), **Supp. XXVI:** 149

"Visitors" (J. W. Miller), **Supp. XX: 167**

"Visitors" (Salinas), **Supp. XIII:** 318

"Visitors, The/Los Visitantes" (Kingsolver), **Supp. VII:** 208

"Visits to St. Elizabeths" (Bishop), **Retro. Supp. II:** 47

Visit to a Small Planet: A Comedy Akin to Vaudeville (Vidal), **Supp. IV Part 2:** 682–683

"Visit to a Small Planet" (teleplay) (Vidal), **Supp. IV Part 2:** 682

"Visit to Avoyelles, A" (Chopin), **Supp. I Part 1:** 213

"Visit to Manafon, A" (W. V. Davis), **Supp. XXI:** 96

"Vissi d'Arte" (Moore), **Supp. X: 173–174**

Vistas of History (Morison), **Supp. I Part 2:** 492

"Vita" (Stafford), **Supp. XI:** 330

"Vita Brevis" (Hull), **Supp. XXI:** 138

Vital, David, **Supp. XVI:** 160

Vital Provisions (Price), **Supp. VI:** 262–263

"Vitamins" (Carver), **Supp. III Part 1:** 138

Vita Nova (Glück), **Supp. V:** 90–92

Vitruvius, **Supp. XVI:** 292

Vittorio, the Vampire (Rice), **Supp. VII:** 295–296

Viudas (Dorfman), **Supp. IX:** 138

"Vivaldi"(Dybek), **Supp. XXIII:** 68

"Viva Vargas!" (Allen), **Supp. XV:** 15

Viva Villa! (screenplay, Hecht), **Supp. XXVII:** 93

Viviparous Quadrupeds of North America, The (Audubon and Bachman), **Supp. XVI:** 10

Vivisections (Siegel), **Supp. XXII:** 257

Vizenor, Gerald, **Supp. IV Part 1:** 260, 262, 329, 404; **Supp. IV Part 2:** 502

Vladimir Nabokov: The American Years (Nabokov), **Retro. Supp. I:** 275

Vlag, Piet, **Supp. XV:** 295

"Vlemk, the Box Painter" (Gardner), **Supp. VI:** 73

"V-Letter" (Shapiro), **Supp. II Part 2:** 707

V-Letter and Other Poems (Shapiro), **Supp. II Part 2:** 702, 706

"Vocabulary of Dearness" (Nye), **Supp. XIII:** 284

"Vocation" (Stafford), **Supp. XI:** 312, 321

Vocation and a Voice, A (Chopin), **Retro. Supp. II:** 67, 72

"Vocation and a Voice, A" (Chopin), **Retro. Supp. II:** 72; **Supp. I Part 1:** 200, 220, 224, 225

Vogel, David, **Supp. XV:** 88

Vogel, Speed, **Supp. IV Part 1:** 390

"Vogue Vista" (Peacock), **Supp. XIX:** 200

"Voice" (F. Wright), **Supp. XVII:** 245

"Voice" (Notley), **Supp. XXII:** 230

"Voice, The" (Dunn), **Supp. XI:** 152

Voice at the Back Door, The (Spencer), **Supp. XXVII:** 13

Voiced Connections of James Dickey, The (Dickey), **Supp. IV Part 1:** 177

"Voice from the Wilderness" (Ray), **Supp. XVIII:** 202

"Voice from the Woods, A" (Humphrey), **Supp. IX:** 101

"Voice from Under the Table, A" (Wilbur), **Supp. III Part 2:** 553, 554

Voice in the Mountain, A (Davison), **Supp. XXVI:** 65, 73–75, 77

"Voice of God, The" (Very), **Supp. XXV:** 243

Voice of Reason, The: Essays in Objectivist Thought (Rand), **Supp. IV Part 2:** 527, 528, 532

"Voice of Rock, The" (Ginsberg), **Supp. II Part 1:** 313

Voice of the Butterfly, The (Nichols), **Supp. XIII:** 270

Voice of the City, The (O. Henry), **Supp. II Part 1:** 410

"Voice of the Mountain, The" (Crane), **I:** 420

Voice of the Negro (Barber), **Supp. II Part 1:** 168

"Voice of the Past, The" (Skloot), **Supp. XX:** 207

Voice of the People, The (Glasgow), **II:** 175, 176

Voice of the Turtle: American Indian Literature 1900–1970 (Gunn Allen, ed.), **Supp. IV Part 1:** 332, 334

Voices from the Moon (Dubus), **Supp. VII:** 88–89

"Voices from the Other World" (Merrill), **Supp. III Part 1:** 331

Voices in the House (Sedges), **Supp. II Part 1:** 125

Voices of a Summer Day (Shaw), **Supp. XIX:** 251

Voices of the Night (Longfellow), **II:** 489, 493; **Retro. Supp. II:** 154, 157, 168

"Voices of Village Square, The" (Wolfe), **Supp. III Part 2:** 571–572

Voice That Is Great within Us, The (Caruth, ed.), **Supp. XIII:** 112

Void Moon (Connelly), **Supp. XXI:** 73, 74

Voigt, Ellen Bryan, **Supp. XIII:** 76

"Voir Dire" (Monson), **Supp. XXIV:** 237

Voix humaine, La (Cocteau), **Supp. XX:** 236

Volkening, Henry, **Retro. Supp. II:** 117; **Supp. XV:** 142

Vollmann, William T., **Supp. XIV:** 96; **Supp. XVII: 225–237; Supp. XX: 93**

Volney, Constantin François de Chasseboeuf, **Supp. I Part 1:** 146

Voltaire, **I:** 194; **II:** 86, 103, 449; **III:** 420; **IV:** 18; **Retro. Supp. II:** 94; **Supp. I Part 1:** 288–289; **Supp. I Part 2:** 669, 717; **Supp. XV:** 258; **Supp. XX:** 285

Voltaire! Voltaire! (Endore), **Supp. XVII:** 65

Volunteer Poilu, A (Beston), **Supp. XXVI:** 32

Volunteers, The (Rowson and Reinagle), **Supp. XV:** 238

Volynsky, Akim (Chaim Flekser), **Supp. XXIII:** 11

Vonnegut, Kurt, **Retro. Supp. I:** 170; **Supp. II Part 2:** 557, 689, **753–784; Supp. IV Part 1:** 227, 392; **Supp. V:** 40, 42, 237, 244, 296; **Supp. X:** 260; **Supp. XI:** 104; **Supp. XII:** 139, 141; **Supp. XVIII:** 242, 252; **Supp. XXI:** 226; **Supp. XXIII:** 42, 101, 109

Vonnegut, Kurt, Jr., **Supp. XIX:** 223; **Supp. XVII:** 41, 135

"Voracities and Verities" (Moore), **III:** 214

Vore, Nellie, **I:** 199

Vorlicky, Robert, **Supp. IX:** 132, 135, 136, 141, 144, 147

Vorse, Mary Heaton, **Supp. XVII:** 99; **Supp. XX: 76; Supp. XXI:** 5, 6, 9, 13

Vortex, The (Coward), **Supp. XXIV:** 267

"Vorticism" (Pound), **Retro. Supp. I:** 288

Vosjoli, Philippe de, **Supp. XX:** 253

Voss, J. C., **Supp. XXV:** 217

Voss, Ralph E., **Supp. XXV:** 93

Voss, Richard, **I:** 199–200

"Vow, The" (Hecht), **Supp. X:** 64

"Vowels 2" (Baraka), **Supp. II Part 1:** 51

Vow of Conversation, A: Journal, 1964–1965 (Merton), **Supp. VIII:** 206

Vox (Baker), **Supp. XIII: 47–49,** 50, 52, 53

"Voyage" (MacLeish), **III:** 15

Voyage, The (Caputo), **Supp. XIX:** 25, 27–28

"Voyage, The" (Irving), **II:** 304

Voyage, The, and Other Versions of Poems by Baudelaire (R. Lowell), **Retro. Supp. II:** 187

Voyage dans la Haute Pennsylvanie et dans l'état de New-York (Crèvecoeur), **Supp. I Part 1:** 250–251

Voyage of the Beagle (Darwin), **Supp. IX:** 211

Voyage of the Dawn Treader (C. S. Lewis), **Supp. XXV:** 74

Voyage of the Destroyer from New York to Brazil, The (Slocum), **Supp. XXV:** 208, 212–213

Voyage of the Liberdade, The (Slocum), **Supp. XXV:** 208, 210–212

Voyage Out, The (Woolf), **Supp. XV:** 65

"Voyager, The" (Everwine), **Supp. XV:** 75

"Voyages" (H. Crane), **I:** 393–395; **Retro. Supp. II:** 78, 80, 81

"Voyages" (Levine), **Supp. V:** 190

Voyages and Discoveries of the Companions of Columbus (Irving), **II:** 310

Voyage to Pagany, A (W. C. Williams), **IV:** 404; **Retro. Supp. I:** 418–419, **420–421,** 423

Voyaging Portraits (Sobin), **Supp. XVI:** 282, 287

"Voyeur, The" (Gioia), **Supp. XV:** 125

"Voz de America" (column, W. Frank), **Supp. XX:** 80

Voznesensky, Andrei, **II:** 553; **Supp. III Part 1:** 268; **Supp. III Part 2:** 560

Vrbovska, Anca, **Supp. IV Part 2:** 639

V. S. Naipaul: An Introduction to His Work (Theroux), **Supp. VIII:** 314, 318

"V. S. Pritchett's Apprenticeship" (Maxwell), **Supp. VIII:** 172

Vukelich, James, **Supp. XXIII:** 228, 233

"Vulgarity in Literature" (Huxley), **III:** 429–430

"Vultures" (Oliver), **Supp. VII:** 235

"Vultures of Wahpeton" (Howard), **Supp. XXVII:** 126–127

"V. V." (Alcott), **Supp. I Part 1:** 37

W

W (Viva) (Cummings), **I:** 429, 433, 434, 436, 443, 444, 447

Wabash (R. O. Butler), **Supp. XII:** 61, **68–69**

Wade, Grace, **I:** 216

"Wading at Wellfleet" (Bishop), **Retro. Supp. II:** 42, 43; **Supp. I Part 1:** 80, 85, 86

Wadsworth, Charles, **I:** 454, 470; **Retro. Supp. I:** 32, 33

Wage, William, **Supp. XXVI:** 87

Wagenknecht, Edward, **II:** 508; **Supp. I Part 2:** 408, 584; **Supp. IV Part 2:** 681

"Wages of Poetry, The" (Wright), **Supp. XV:** 337

Wagner, Erica, **Supp. XXI:** 117

Wagner, Jean, **Supp. I Part 1:** 341, 346; **Supp. IV Part 1:** 165, 167, 171

Wagner, Karl, **Supp. XXVII:** 128

Wagner, Richard, **I:** 284, 395; **II:** 425; **III:** 396, 507; **Supp. IV Part 1:** 392

Wagner, Robert, **Supp. IX:** 250

"Wagnerians, The" (Auchincloss), **Supp. IV Part 1:** 23

"Wagner Matinee, A" (Cather), **I:** 315–316; **Retro. Supp. I:** 5, 8

Wagoner, David, **Supp. IX: 323–340; Supp. XII:** 178; **Supp. XX: 200**

Wahlöö, Per, **Supp. XX:** 87

Waid, Candace, **Retro. Supp. I:** 360, 372, 373

Waif, The (Longfellow, ed.), **Retro. Supp. II:** 155

"Waif of the Plains, A" (Harte), **Supp. II Part 1:** 354

Wain, John, **Supp. XIV:** 166

"Wait" (Kinnell), **Supp. III Part 1:** 250

"Waiter in a California Vietnamese Restaurant" (Major), **Supp. XXII:** 182

"Waiting" (Dubus), **Supp. VII:** 87

Waiting (Jin), **Supp. XVIII:** 89, **96–97,** 99

"Waiting" (W. C. Williams), **Retro. Supp. I:** 418

"Waiting, The" (L.-Y. Lee), **Supp. XV:** 218

"Waiting, The" (Olds), **Supp. X:** 209

"Waiting between the Trees" (Tan), **Supp. X:** 290

"Waiting by the Gate" (Bryant), **Supp. I Part 1:** 171

Waiting for God (Weil), **I:** 298

Waiting for Godot (Beckett), **I:** 78, 91, 298; **Supp. IV Part 1:** 368–369; **Supp. XXIII:** 213

Waiting for Lefty (Odets), **Supp. I Part 1:** 277; **Supp. II Part 2:** 529, 530–533, 540; **Supp. V:** 109; **Supp. XIX:** 242

Waiting for Sweet Betty (Major), **Supp. XXII:** 183

Waiting for Teddy Williams (Mosher), **Supp. XXII:** 205, 206, 207, 208, 209, **215–216**

Waiting for the End of the World (Bell), **Supp. X:** 4–5, 11

"Waiting for the Ladies" (L. Brown), **Supp. XXI:** 44

Waiting for the Verdict (R. H. Davis), **Supp. XVI:** 85, 89, 90

"Waiting in a Rain Forest" (Wagoner), **Supp. IX:** 329

Waiting in the Wings (Loraga), **Supp. XXIII:** 195

Waiting Room, The (Kees), **Supp. XV:** 133, 148

Waiting to Exhale (McMillan), **Supp. XIII:** 184, 185, **189–190,** 191

"Waiting to Freeze" (Banks), **Supp. V:** 5, 6

Waiting to Freeze: Poems (Banks), **Supp. V:** 6, 8

Waits, Tom, **Supp. VIII:** 12

Wait until Spring, Bandini (Fante), **Supp. XI:** 160, 161, 164, 165, **166–167**

Wait until Spring, Bandini (film), **Supp. XI:** 173

"Wake, The" (Dove), **Supp. IV Part 1:** 250

"Wakefield" (Hawthorne), **Retro. Supp. I:** 154, 159

Wakefield, Dan, **Supp. VIII:** 43; **Supp. XIX:** 257, 258; **Supp. XVI:** 220

Wakefield, Richard, **Supp. IX:** 323

"Wake Island" (Rukeyser), **Supp. VI:** 273

"Wake"(Kenny), **Supp. XXIII:** 155

Wakeman, Frederic, **Supp. IX:** 247

Wake Up and Live! (Brande), **Supp. I Part 2:** 608

"Waking" (C. Frost), **Supp. XV:** 93

Waking (Rash), **Supp. XXVII:** 220, 221–222, 224

Waking, The (Roethke), **III:** 541

"Waking Early Sunday Morning" (R. Lowell), **II:** 552

"Waking Early Sunday Morning" (R. Lowell), **Retro. Supp. II:** 190

"Waking in the Blue" (R. Lowell), **II:** 547; **Retro. Supp. II:** 180

"Waking in the Dark" (Rich), **Supp. I Part 2:** 559

"Waking Up the Rake" (Hogan), **Supp. IV Part 1:** 415–416, 416

Wakoski, Diane, **Supp. V:** 79; **Supp. XII:** 184; **Supp. XV:** 252; **Supp. XVII:** 112; **Supp. XXIII:** 52; **Supp. XXIV:** 37

Walbridge, John, **Supp. XX:** 125

Walcott, Charles C., **II:** 49

Walcott, Derek, **Supp. VIII:** 28; **Supp. X:** 122, 131; **Supp. XV:** 256; **Supp. XXIV:** 86

Walcott, Jersey Joe, **Supp. V:** 182

Wald, Alan, **Supp. XV:** 202; **Supp. XVIII:** 223; **Supp. XXI:** 261, 262, 271, 275–276, 277, 278

Wald, Lillian, **Supp. I Part 1:** 12

Walden (Thoreau), **Supp. XIV:** 177, 227; **Supp. XV:** 275; **Supp. XVIII:** 14, 80, 189; **Supp. XXIV:** 73; **Supp. XXVI:** 34, 41, 43

Walden, Daniel, **Supp. IV Part 2:** 584, 591; **Supp. V:** 272

Walden; or, Life in the Woods (Thoreau), **I:** 219, 305; **II:** 8, 142, 159, 312–313, 458; **IV:** 168, 169, 170, 176, 177–178, 179–182, 183, 187; **Retro. Supp. I:** 62; **Supp. I Part 2:** 579, 655, 664, 672; **Supp. VIII:** 296; **Supp. X:** 27, 101; **Supp. XIII:** 152

Waldman, Anne, **Supp. XIV:** 150; **Supp. XXIII:** 221; **Supp. XXIV:** 33, 41, 45; **Supp. XXVII:** 22, 23, 26

Waldmeir, Joseph, **III:** 45

Waldmeir, Joseph J., **Supp. I Part 2:** 476

Waldo (Theroux), **Supp. VIII:** 313, 314, **314–315**

Waldo Frank: A Study (Munson), **Supp. XX:** 74

Waldron, Jeremy, **Supp. XVII:** 235

Waldron, Nan Turner, **Supp. XXVI:** 37

Waldrop, Keith, **Supp. XV:** 153, 165

Waley, Arthur, **II:** 526; **III:** 466; **Supp. V:** 340

"Walk, A" (Snyder), **Supp. VIII:** 297

Walkabout Year: Twelve Months in Australia (Pickering), **Supp. XXI:** 199, 200

"Walk at Sunset, A" (Bryant), **Supp. I Part 1:** 155

"Walk before Mass, A" (Agee), **I:** 28–29

Walker, Alice, **Retro. Supp. I:** 215; **Supp. I Part 2:** 550; **Supp. III Part 2:** 488, **517–540;** **Supp. IV Part 1:** 14; **Supp. IX:** 306, 311; **Supp. VIII:** 141, 214; **Supp. X:** 85, 228, 252, 325, 330; **Supp. XIII:** 179, 185, 291, 295; **Supp. XVI:** 39; **Supp. XVIII:** 200, 283; **Supp. XX:** 84, 107, 108; **Supp. XXI:** 172; **Supp. XXII:** 172

Walker, Cheryl, **Supp. XI:** 145; **Supp. XXVII:** 284, 296

Walker, David, **Supp. V:** 189; **Supp. XVII:** 246

Walker, Franklin D., **III:** 321

Walker, Gue, **Supp. XII:** 207

Walker, Margaret, **Supp. XVIII:** 282; **Supp. XX:** 106

Walker, Marianne, **Supp. VIII:** 139

Walker, Obadiah, **II:** 113

Walker, Scott, **Supp. XV:** 92

Walker in the City, A (Kazin), **Supp. VIII:** **93–95,** 99

Walk Hard (Blum and Hill), **Supp. XV:** 194

Walk Hard-Talk Loud (Zinberg), **Supp. XV:** 194, 202

"Walking" (Hogan), **Supp. IV Part 1:** 416

"Walking" (Thoreau), **Supp. IV Part 1:** 416; **Supp. IX:** 178

"Walking Along in Winter" (Kenyon), **Supp. VII:** 167

"Walking around the Block with a Three-Year-Old" (Wagoner), **Supp. IX:** 331–332

"Walking at Noon Near the Burlington Depot in Lincoln, Nebraska" (Kooser), **Supp. XIX:** 122

"Walking Backwards into the Future" (R. Williams), **Supp. IX:** 146

Walking Down the Stairs: Selections from Interviews (Kinnell), **Supp. III Part 1:** 235, 249

"Walking Home" (Schnackenberg). *See* "Laughing with One Eye" (Schnackenberg)

"Walking Home at Night" (Ginsberg), **Supp. II Part 1:** 313

"Walking Is Almost Falling" (Peacock), **Supp. XIX:** 196, 197

Walking Light (Dunn), **Supp. XI:** 140, 141, 153

"Walking Man of Rodin, The" (Sandburg), **III:** 583

"Walking Sticks and Paperweights and Water Marks" (Moore), **III:** 215

Walking Tall (Dunn), **Supp. XI:** 140

Walking the Black Cat (Simic), **Supp. VIII:** 280, **282–284**

Walking the Boundaries (Davison), **Supp. XXVI:** 65, 72–73, 74

"Walking the Boundaries" (Davison), **Supp. XXVI:** 73

Walking to Gatlinburg (Mosher), **Supp. XXII:** 204, 205, 206, 207, 208, 209, 215, **216–217**

Walking to Martha's Vineyard (F. Wright), **Supp. XVII:** 240, 241, 245, 246

Walking to Sleep (Wilbur), **Supp. III Part 2:** 557–560

"Walking to Sleep" (Wilbur), **Supp. III Part 2:** 544, 557, 559, 561, 562

"Walking Wounded" (Shaw), **Supp. XIX:** 248

Walkin' the Dog (Mosley), **Supp. XIII:** 242

"Walk in the Moonlight, A" (Anderson), **I:** 114

Walk Me to the Distance (Everett), **Supp. XVIII:** 55–56, 57

Walk on the Wild Side, A (Algren), **Supp. IX:** 3, **12–13,** 14; **Supp. V:** 4

"Walks in Rome" (Merrill), **Supp. III Part 1:** 337

Walk to the River, A (Hoffman), **Supp. XVIII:** 77–78

Walk with Tom Jefferson, A (Levine), **Supp. V:** 179, 187, 190–191

Wall, Cheryl, **Supp. XXVI:** 165, 166

"Wall, The" (Bronk), **Supp. XXI:** 31

"Wall, The" (Brooks), **Supp. III Part 1:** 70, 71, 84

Wall, The (Hersey), **IV:** 4; **Supp. XX: 251**

Wall, The (Rinehart), **Supp. XXV:** 197–198, 200

"Wall, The" (Roethke), **III:** 544

"Wall, The" (Sexton), **Supp. II Part 2:** 696

Wallace, Daniel, **Supp. XXII:** 49

Wallace, David, **Supp. XXI:** 277

Wallace, David Foster, **Retro. Supp. II:** 279; **Supp. X:** 301–318; **Supp. XIX:** 223; **Supp. XVII:** 226; **Supp. XX: 91, 93; Supp. XXII:** 260, 261; **Supp. XXVII:** 6, 79

Wallace, Henry, **I:** 489; **III:** 111, 475; **Supp. I Part 1:** 286; **Supp. I Part 2:** 645

Wallace, Jim, **Supp. XX: 143**

Wallace, Mike, **Supp. IV Part 1:** 364; **Supp. IV Part 2:** 526; **Supp. XX: 102**

Wallace, Paul, **Supp. XXVI:** 90, 96–97

Wallace, Richard, **Supp. XVIII:** 101–102

Wallace Stevens (Kermode), **Retro. Supp. I:** 301

Wallace Stevens: The Poems of our Climate (Bloom), **Retro. Supp. I:** 299

Wallace Stevens: Words Chosen out of Desire (Stevens), **Retro. Supp. I:** 297

Wallach, Eli, **III:** 161

Wallant, Edward Lewis, **Supp. XVI:** 220

Wallas, Graham, **Supp. I Part 2:** 643

"Walled City" (Oates), **Supp. II Part 2:** 524

Wallenstein, Anna. *See* Weinstein, Mrs. Max (Anna Wallenstein)

Waller, Edmund, **III:** 463

Waller, Fats, **IV:** 263

Waller, Nicole, **Supp. XXII:** 78

"Wallet, The" (Rash), **Supp. XXVII:** 222

Walling, William English, **Supp. I Part 2:** 645; **Supp. XV:** 295

"Wall of Paintings, The" (Notley), **Supp. XXII:** 230

Wall of the Sky, the Wall of the Eye, The (Lethem), **Supp. XVIII:** 139

Walls Do Not Fall, The (Doolittle), **Supp. I Part 1:** 271, 272

Walls of Jericho, The (R. Fisher), **Supp. XIX:** 65, 67, 70, **72–77,** 78

"Wall Songs" (Hogan), **Supp. IV Part 1:** 413

Wall Writing (Auster), **Supp. XII:** 23–24

Walpole, Horace, **I:** 203; **Supp. I Part 2:** 410, 714

Walpole, Hugh, **Retro. Supp. I:** 231; **Supp. XX: 232**

Walpole, Robert, **IV:** 145

Walsh, David M., **Supp. XV:** 5

Walsh, Ed, **II:** 424

Walsh, Ernest, **Supp. XXIV:** 50

Walsh, George, **Supp. IV Part 2:** 528

Walsh, Keenan, **Supp. XXVI:** 152

Walsh, Raoul, **Supp. XIII:** 174

Walsh, Richard J., **Supp. II Part 1:** 119, 130

Walsh, William, **Supp. IV Part 1:** 242, 243, 246, 248, 252, 254, 257; **Supp. XXVI:** 4, 9

"Walt, the Wounded" (Di Piero), **Supp. XIX:** 37

"Walt and Will" (Apple), **Supp. XVII:** 6

Walter, Eugene, **Supp. XVI:** 230

Walter, Joyce, **Supp. XV:** 121

Walter, Natasha, **Supp. XXVII:** 275

Walter Benjamin at the Dairy Queen: Reflections at Sixty and Beyond (McMurtry), **Supp. V:** 232

Walters, Barbara, **Supp. XIV:** 125

Walters, Marguerite. *See* Smith, Mrs. Lamar (Marguerite Walters)

"Walter T. Carriman" (O'Hara), **III:** 368

Walton, Izaak, **Supp. I Part 2:** 422

"Walt Whitman" (Kooser), **Supp. XIX:** 118

"Walt Whitman" (Masters), **Supp. I Part 2:** 458

"Walt Whitman at Bear Mountain" (Simpson), **Supp. IX:** 265

Walt Whitman Bathing (Wagoner), **Supp. IX:** 331–332

Walt Whitman Handbook (Allen), **IV:** 352

Walt Whitman Reconsidered (Chase), **IV:** 352

"Waltz, The" (Parker), **Supp. IX:** 204

"Waltzer in the House, The" (Kunitz), **Supp. III Part 1:** 258

Waltzing Matilda (Notley), **Supp. XXII:** 229–230

"Waltzing Matilda" (Notley), **Supp. XXII:** 230

Waltzing the Magpies: A Year in Australia (Pickering), **Supp. XXI:** 199, 200

Walzer, Kevin, **Supp. XII:** 202; **Supp. XV:** 118; **Supp. XVIII:** 174

Wambaugh, Joseph, **Supp. X:** 5; **Supp. XXI:** 67

Wampeters, Foma, & Granfalloons (Vonnegut), **Supp. II Part 2:** 758, 759–760, 776, 779

Wand, David Hsin-fu, **Supp. X:** 292

"Wanderer, The" (W. C. Williams), **Retro. Supp. I:** 414, 421

Wanderer, The: His Parables and His Sayings (Gibran), **Supp. XX: 116, 123–124**

"Wanderers, The" (Welty), **IV:** 273–274

"Wandering Jew, The" (Robinson), **III:** 505, 516–517

Wanderings of Oisin (Yeats), **Supp. I Part 1:** 79

Wang, Dorothy, **Supp. X:** 289

Wang Wei, **Supp. XV:** 47

Waniek, Marilyn Nelson, **Supp. IV Part 1:** 244. *See also* Nelson, Marilyn

Wanking 'Tards (Silver), **Supp. XXIV:** 265

"Wan Lee, the Pagan" (Harte), **Supp. II Part 1:** 351

"Want, The" (Olds), **Supp. X:** 210

Want Bone, The (Pinsky), **Supp. VI:** 236–237, 244–245, 247

"Wanted: An Ontological Critic" (Ransom), **III:** 498

"Wanting to Die" (Sexton), **Supp. II Part 2:** 684, 686; **Supp. XIV:** 132

"Wants" (Paley), **Supp. VI:** 219

Waples, Dorothy, **I:** 348

Wapshot Chronicle, The (Cheever), **Supp. I Part 1:** 174, 177–180, 181, 196

Wapshot Scandal, The (Cheever), **Supp. I Part 1:** 180–184, 187, 191, 196

"War" (Findley), **Supp. XX: 49**

"War" (H. Johnson), **Supp. XXVI:** 173

"War" (Jin), **Supp. XVIII:** 93

"War" (Kingston), **Supp. V:** 169

"War" (Simic), **Supp. VIII:** 282

"War, Response, and Contradiction" (Burke), **I:** 283

"War and Peace" (Sanders), **Supp. XVI:** 277

War and Peace (Tolstoy), **I:** 6, 7; **II:** 191, 205, 291; **IV:** 446; **Supp. V:** 277; **Supp. XI:** 68; **Supp. XIV:** 97; **Supp. XXIII:** 11

War and Remembrance (miniseries), **Supp. XXV:** 265

War and Remembrance (Wouk), **Supp. XX: 243; Supp. XXV:** 253, 254, 257, 258, 264–265

"War and the Small Nations" (Gibran), **Supp. XX: 127**

War and War (F. Barthelme), **Supp. XI:** 25

"War Between Men and Women, The" (Thurber), **Supp. I Part 2:** 615

War Bulletins (Lindsay), **Supp. I Part 2:** 378–379

Ward, Aileen, **II:** 531

Ward, Artemus (pseudonym). *See* Browne, Charles Farrar

Ward, Douglas Turner, **Supp. IV Part 1:** 362

Ward, Geoff, **Supp. XXIII:** 218

Ward, Henry, **Supp. I Part 2:** 588

Ward, Mrs. Humphry, **II:** 338

Ward, Leo R., **Supp. VIII:** 124

Ward, Lester F., **Supp. I Part 2:** 640; **Supp. XI:** 202, 203

Ward, Lynn, **I:** 31

Ward, Nathaniel, **Supp. I Part 1:** 99, 102, 111, 116

Ward, Susan, **Supp. XXIII:** 146

Ward, Theodora, **I:** 470; **Retro. Supp. I:** 28

Ward, William Hayes, **Supp. I Part 1:** 371

"War Debt, A" (Jewett), **Retro. Supp. II:** 138, 141

"War Diary" (Boyce), **Supp. XVII:** 104; **Supp. XXI:** 6

"War Diary, A" (Bourne), **I:** 229

War Dispatches of Stephen Crane, The (Crane), **I:** 422

"Ward Line, The" (Morris), **III:** 220

Ware, Amy, **Supp. XXVI:** 113

Warfel, Harry R., **Supp. I Part 1:** 366

War Games (Morris), **III:** 238

War Goes On, The (Asch), **Supp. XXIII:** 6

"Warhol / Blue Jackie"(Balakian), **Supp. XXIII:** 32

War in Heaven, The (Shepard and Chaikin), **Supp. III Part 2:** 433
War Is Kind (S. Crane), **I:** 409; **III:** 585
"War Is Kind" (S. Crane), **I:** 419; **Supp. XXVI:** 173
Warlock (Harrison), **Supp. VIII:** 45, **46**
Warm as Wool (Sanders), **Supp. XVI:** 269
"Warming" (Trethewey), **Supp. XXI:** 245
Warner, Anna, **Supp. XVIII:** 258–275
Warner, Charles Dudley, **II:** 405; **IV:** 198
Warner, Jack, **Supp. XII:** 160–161; **Supp. XVIII:** 249; **Supp. XXVII:** 92
Warner, John R., **III:** 193
Warner, Oliver, **I:** 548
Warner, Susan, **Retro. Supp. I:** 246; **Supp. XV:** 275; **Supp. XVIII: 257–275**
Warner, Sylvia Townsend, **Supp. VIII:** 151, 155, 164, 171
Warner, W. Lloyd, **III:** 60
Warner Family and the Warner Books, The (Baker), **Supp. XVIII:** 259, 267
"Warning" (Hughes), **Supp. I Part 1:** 343
"Warning" (Pound), **III:** 474
"Warning, A" (Howard), **Supp. XXVII:** 118
"Warning, The" (Creeley), **Supp. IV Part 1:** 150
"Warning, The" (Longfellow), **II:** 498
Warning Hill (Marquand), **III:** 55–56, 60, 68
"War of Eyes, A" (Coleman), **Supp. XI:** 93–94
War of Eyes and Other Stories, A (Coleman), **Supp. XI: 91–92**
War of the Classes (London), **II:** 466
"War of the Wall, The" (Bambara), **Supp. XI:** 15–16
"War of Vaslav Nijinsky, The" (Bidart), **Supp. XV:** 21–22, **27–29**
Warp (Grossman), **Supp. XXV:** 64, 65–66
"War Poems" (Sandburg), **III:** 581
Warren, Austin, **I:** 265, 268, 271; **Supp. I Part 2:** 423
Warren, David, **Supp. XXIV:** 269
Warren, Earl, **III:** 581
Warren, Gabriel, **IV:** 244
Warren, Mercy Otis, **Supp. XV:** 230
Warren, Patricia Nell, **Supp. XX:** 259–276
Warren, Robert Penn, **I:** 190, 211, 517; **II:** 57, 217, 228, 253; **III:** 134, 310, 382–383, 454, 482, 485, 490, 496, 497; **IV:** 121, 122, 123, 125, 126, **236–259**, 261, 262, 279, 340–341, 458; **Retro. Supp. I:** 40, 41, 73, 90; **Retro. Supp. II:** 220, 235; **Supp. I Part 1:** 359, 371; **Supp. I Part 2:** 386, 423; **Supp. II Part 1:** 139; **Supp. III Part 2:** 542; **Supp. IX:** 257; **Supp. V:** 261, 316, 318, 319, 333; **Supp. VIII:** 126, 176; **Supp. X:** 1, 25, 26; **Supp. XI:** 315; **Supp. XII:** 254, 255; **Supp. XIV:** 1, 2, 3, 4, 11, 14, 15; **Supp. XIX:** 246; **Supp. XVIII:** 77, 78–79; **Supp. XXI:** 256; **Supp. XXVI:** 63, 67, 78
Warren, Mrs. Robert Penn (Eleanor Clark), **IV:** 244
Warren, Rosanna, **IV:** 244; **Supp. XIX:** 34; **Supp. XV:** 251, 261, 262, 263

Warren, Vincent, **Supp. XXIII:** 218, 219
Warrington Poems, The (Ríos), **Supp. IV Part 2:** 540
Warrior, Robert Allen, **Supp. IV Part 1:** 329
"Warrior, The" (Gunn Allen), **Supp. IV Part 1:** 326
"Warrior: 5th Grade" (Olds), **Supp. X:** 214
"Warrior Road" (Harjo), **Supp. XII:** 217
"Warrior's Daughter, A" (Zitkala-Ša), **Supp. XXV:** 274, 275, 282
Wars, The (Findley), **Supp. XX:** 53–54
Warsh, Lewis, **Supp. XXIV:** 41
Warshavsky, Isaac (pseudonym). *See* Singer, Isaac Bashevis
Warshow, Robert, **Supp. I Part 1:** 51
Wars I Have Seen (Stein), **IV:** 27, 36, 477
Wartime (Fussell), **Supp. V:** 241
War Trash (Jin), **Supp. XVIII:** 89, **100–101**
"War Widow, The" (Frederic), **II:** 135–136
"Was" (Creeley), **Supp. IV Part 1:** 155
"Was" (Faulkner), **II:** 71
"Wash" (Faulkner), **II:** 72
Wash, Richard, **Supp. XII:** 14
"Washboard Wizard" (Nelson), **Supp. XVIII:** 182
Washburn, Keith, **Supp. XXVI:** 148–149
"Washed in the Rain" (Fante), **Supp. XI:** 165
"Washing of Hands, A" (Kooser), **Supp. XIX:** 115
Washington, Booker T., **Supp. I Part 2:** 393; **Supp. II Part 1:** 157, 160, 167, 168, 171, 225; **Supp. XIV:** 198, 199, 201; **Supp. XVIII:** 121–122
Washington, D.C. (Vidal), **Supp. IV Part 2:** 677, 684, 686–687, 690
"Washington, D.C. Journal" (Brainard), **Supp. XXVII:** 27
Washington, George, **I:** 453; **II:** 313–314; **Supp. I Part 2:** 399, 485, 508, 509, 511, 513, 517, 518, 520, 599
Washington, Mary Helen, **Supp. XVIII:** 119, 284
Washington and His Generals (Lippard), **Supp. XXIII:** 178, **185–186**, 187
Washington Crossing the Delaware (Rivers), **Supp. XV:** 186
Washington Post Book World (Lesser), **Supp. IV Part 2:** 453; **Supp. VIII:** 80, 84, 241; **Supp. X:** 282
Washington Square (James), **II:** 327, 328; **Retro. Supp. I:** 215, 220, **222–223**
"Washington Square, 1946" (Ozick), **Supp. V:** 272
Washington Square Ensemble, The (Bell), **Supp. X:** 1, **3–4**
"Washman"(P. Benedict), **Supp. XXIII:** 40
"Was Lowell an Historical Critic?" (Altick), **Supp. I Part 2:** 423
Wasserman, Earl R., **Supp. I Part 2:** 439, 440
Wasserman, Jakob, **Supp. I Part 2:** 669
Wasserstein, Wendy, **Supp. IV Part 1:** 309; **Supp. XV: 319–336; Supp. XXIV:** 116, 117, 119, 128

Wasson, Ben, **Retro. Supp. I:** 79, 83
"Waste Carpet, The" (Matthews), **Supp. IX: 158–159**
Waste Land, The (T. S. Eliot), **I:** 107, 266, 298, 395, 396, 482, 570–571, 572, 574–575, 577–578, 580, 581, 584, 585, 586, 587; **III:** 6–8, 12, 196, 277–278, 453, 471, 492, 586; **IV:** 122, 123, 124, 140, 418, 419, 420; **Retro. Supp. I:** 51, 60, **60–62**, 63, 64, 66, 210, 290, 291, 299, 311, 420, 427; **Retro. Supp. II:** 85, 121, 190; **Supp. I Part 1:** 272; **Supp. I Part 2:** 439, 455, 614; **Supp. II Part 1:** 4, 5, 11, 96; **Supp. III Part 1:** 9, 10, 41, 63, 105; **Supp. IV Part 1:** 47, 284; **Supp. IX:** 158, 305; **Supp. V:** 338; **Supp. X:** 125; **Supp. XIII:** 341–342, 344, 346; **Supp. XIV:** 6, 284; **Supp. XIX:** 288; **Supp. XV:** 21, 181, 261, 306; **Supp. XVI:** 204; **Supp. XVII:** 140–141, 144, 227; **Supp. XVIII:** 78, 79–80; **Supp. XXIII:** 23, 25, 79, 165; **Supp. XXIV:** 140; **Supp. XXVII:** 287
"Waste Land, The": A Facsimile and Transcript of the Original Drafts Including the Annotations of Ezra Pound (Eliot, ed.), **Retro. Supp. I:** 58
Waste Land and Other Poems, The (T. S. Eliot), **Supp. XV:** 305
Wat, Alexander, **Supp. XVI:** 155, 161
Watch, The (Bass), **Supp. XVI: 16–17**
"Watch, The, —" (Bass), **Supp. XVI:** 17
Watch and Ward (James), **II:** 323; **Retro. Supp. I:** 218, **219**, 220
"Watcher" (Trethewey), **Supp. XXI:** 247
"Watcher, The" (R. Bly), **Supp. IV Part 1:** 71
"Watcher by the Dead, A" (Bierce), **I:** 203
Watchfires (Auchincloss), **Supp. IV Part 1:** 23
"Watching Crow, Looking toward the Manzano Mountains" (Harjo), **Supp. XII:** 219
"Watching the Oregon Whale" (A. Finch), **Supp. XVII:** 77
"Watching the Sunset" (Coleman), **Supp. XI:** 92
"Watching the Vulture at the Road Kill" (Stallings), **Supp. XXV:** 230
Watch on the Rhine (Hellman), **Supp. I Part 1:** 276, 278, 279–281, 283–284; **Supp. IV Part 1:** 83
"Watch Out for Landmines" (Biss), **Supp. XXVI:** 47, 51, 56
"Water" (Emerson), **II:** 19
"Water" (Komunyakaa), **Supp. XIII:** 132
"Water" (R. Lowell), **II:** 550
"Waterbird" (Swenson), **Supp. IV Part 2:** 651
"Water Borders" (Dillard), **Supp. VI:** 27
"Water Buffalo" (Komunyakaa), **Supp. XIII:** 122
"Watercolor of Grantchester Meadows" (Plath), **Supp. I Part 2:** 537
Water Cure, The (Everett), **Supp. XVIII: 64–66**
"Water Drum"(Kenny), **Supp. XXIII:** 144

"Waterfall, The" (Clampitt), **Supp. IX:** 44

Waterfront (Schulberg), **Supp. XVIII: 251–252**

"Water Hose Is on Fire, The" (Simic), **Supp. XV:** 185

Waterhouse, Keith, **Supp. VIII:** 124

"Waterlily Fire" (Rukeyser), **Supp. VI:** 285, 286

Waterlily Fire: Poems 1935–1962 (Rukeyser), **Supp. VI:** 274, 283, 285

Watermark (Brodsky), **Supp. VIII:** 29

Water-Method Man, The (Irving), **Supp. VI:** 163, **167–179,** 180

Water Music (Boyle), **Supp. VIII:** 1, 3–5, 8, 14; **Supp. XX: 20–22**

"Water Music for the Progress of Love in a Life-Raft Down the Sammamish Slough" (Wagoner), **Supp. IX:** 326

"Water People" (Burke), **Supp. XIV:** 21

"Water Picture" (Swenson), **Supp. IV Part 2:** 641

"Water Quilt" (Rash), **Supp. XXVII:** 222

"Water Rising" (Hogan), **Supp. IV Part 1:** 400

Waters, Ethel, **II:** 587

Waters, Frank, **Supp. X:** 124

Waters, Muddy, **Supp. VIII:** 345

Watershed (Everett), **Supp. XVIII: 58–59,** 64

"Watershed" (Kingsolver), **Supp. VII:** 208

"Watershed" (Warren), **IV:** 239

"Watershed, The" (Auden), **Supp. II Part 1:** 5

Waters of Kronos, The (Richter), **Supp. XVIII:** 207, 208, **218–219,** 220

Waters of Siloe, The (Merton), **Supp. VIII:** 196, 208

Waterston, Sam, **Supp. IX:** 253

Water Street (Merrill), **Supp. III Part 1:** 321–323

"Water Walker" (Wilbur), **Supp. III Part 2:** 548, 560

Water-Witch, The (Cooper), **I:** 342–343

"Water Witch"(P. Benedict), **Supp. XXIII:** 38

Waterworks, The (Doctorow), **Supp. IV Part 1:** 218, 222, 223, 231–233, 234

"Water Works, The" (Doctorow), **Supp. IV Part 1:** 234

Watkin, E. I., **Retro. Supp. II:** 187

Watkins, Floyd C., **IV:** 452

Watkins, James T., **I:** 193, 194

Watkins, Maureen, **Supp. XVI:** 188

Watkins, Mel, **Supp. X:** 330; **Supp. XIII:** 246

Watman, Max, **Supp. XX: 92**

Watrous, Peter, **Supp. VIII:** 79

Watson, Brook, **Supp. XX: 284**

Watson, Burton, **Supp. XV:** 47

Watson, James Sibley, Jr., **I:** 261

Watson, Jay, **Supp. XVIII:** 195; **Supp. XXI:** 46

Watson, J. B., **II:** 361

Watson, Julia, **Supp. XXV:** 8

Watson, Richard, **Supp. I Part 2:** 516, 517

Watson, William, **II:** 114

Watsonville: Some Place Not Here (Moraga), **Supp. XXIII:** 195, 196, 202, 203

Watt, Ian, **Supp. VIII:** 4

Watteau, Jean Antoine, **III:** 275; **IV:** 79

Watts, Emily Stipes, **Supp. I Part 1:** 115

Waugh, Arthur, **Supp. XXIV:** 30

Waugh, Evelyn, **I:** 480; **III:** 281; **Supp. I Part 2:** 607; **Supp. IV Part 2:** 688; **Supp. XI:** 305, 306; **Supp. XIX:** 131; **Supp. XXV:** 70

Waugh, Robert H., **Supp. XXV:** 123

"Wave" (Snyder), **Supp. VIII:** 299

Wave, A (Ashbery), **Supp. III Part 1:** 1, 4, 24–26

"Wave, A" (Ashbery), **Supp. III Part 1:** 9, 19, 24–25

"Wave, The" (MacLeish), **III:** 19

"Wave, The" (Untermeyer), **Supp. XV:** 300

Wave Amplitude in the Mona Passage (Schott), **Supp. XXIII: 242–243**

"Wavemaker Falters, The" (Saunders), **Supp. XIX:** 225

"Waxwings" (Francis), **Supp. IX:** 82

Way, The (Steiner and Witt, eds.), **Supp. IV Part 2:** 505

"Way Down, The" (Kunitz), **Supp. III Part 1:** 263

"Way It Is, The" (Ellison), **Supp. II Part 1:** 245

"Way It Is, The" (Jones), **Supp. XI:** 229

Way It Is, The (Stafford), **Supp. XIII:** 274

"Way It Is, The" (Strand), **Supp. IV Part 2:** 627

"Wayland" (Sanders), **Supp. XVI:** 275

Wayne, John, **Supp. IV Part 1:** 200

Way of Chuang-Tzu, The (Merton), **Supp. VIII:** 208

"Way of Exchange in James Dickey's Poetry, The" (Weatherby), **Supp. IV Part 1:** 175

Way of Life According to Laotzu, The (Bynner), **Supp. XV:** 46, 48

Way Out, A (Frost), **Retro. Supp. I:** 133

Wayside Motor Inn, The (Gurney), **Supp. V:** 96, 105, 109

"Ways of Breaking: Lynda Hull's 'Ornithology' " (Jauss), **Supp. XXI:** 139

"Ways of Talking" (Jin), **Supp. XVIII:** 93

Ways of the Hour, The (Cooper), **I:** 354

Ways of White Folks, The (Hughes), **Retro. Supp. I:** 203, 204; **Supp. I Part 1:** 329, 330, 332

Way Some People Die, The (Macdonald), **Supp. IV Part 2:** 470, 471, 472, 474

Way Some People Live, The (Cheever), **Supp. I Part 1:** 175

"Way the Cards Fall, The" (Komunyakaa), **Supp. XIII:** 117

"Way the Luck Runs, The" (Wolfert), **Supp. XXI:** 265

"Way Things Are, The" (Turow, unpub.), **Supp. XVII:** 215, 218

Way to Rainy Mountain, The (Momaday), **Supp. IV Part 2:** 485–486, 487–489, 491, 493

Way to Wealth, The (Franklin), **II:** 101–102, 110; **Supp. XX: 27**

Wayward and the Seeking, The: A Collection of Writings by Jean Toomer (Toomer), **Supp. III Part 2:** 478–481, 484, 487

Wayward Bus, The (Steinbeck), **IV:** 51, 64–65

"Way We Live Now, The" (Sontag), **Supp. III Part 2:** 467–468

"Way You'll Never Be, A" (Hemingway), **II:** 249

"W. D. Sees Himself Animated" (Snodgrass), **Supp. VI:** 327

"W. D. Sits in Kafka's Chair and Is Interrogated Concerning the Assumed Death of Cock Robin" (Snodgrass), **Supp. VI:** 319

"W. D. Tries to Warn Cock Robin" (Snodgrass), **Supp. VI:** 319

"We" (Alexander), **Supp. XVIII:** 185

Weaks, Mary Louise, **Supp. X:** 5

Weales, Gerald, **II:** 602

"Wealth," from *Conduct of Life, The* (Emerson), **II:** 2, 3–4

"Wealth," from *English Traits* (Emerson), **II:** 6

Wealth of Nations, The (A. Smith), **II:** 109

"We Are Looking at You, Agnes" (Caldwell), **I:** 309

We Are Not Afraid (Hickam), **Supp. XXVII:** 99, 100

We Are Not in This Together (Kittredge), **Supp. XXVI:** 182, 183, 184

We Are Still Married: Stories and Letters (Keillor), **Supp. XVI:** 176, 177

"We Are the Crazy Lady and Other Feisty Feminist Fables" (Ozick), **Supp. V:** 259

Weary Blues, The (Hughes), **Retro. Supp. I:** 195, 197, 198, 199, 200, 203, 205; **Supp. I Part 1:** 325

"Weary Blues, The" (Hughes), **Retro. Supp. I:** 198, 199; **Supp. I Part 1:** 324, 325

"Weary Kingdom" (Irving), **Supp. VI:** 163

Weasels and Wisemen: Ethics and Ethnicity in the Work of David Mamet (Kane), **Supp. XIV:** 250

Weather and the Women Treat Me Fair, The (Everett), **Supp. XVIII:** 66

Weatherby, H. L., **Supp. IV Part 1:** 175

Weather Central (Kooser), **Supp. XIX:** 116, **123–125**

"Weathering Out" (Dove), **Supp. IV Part 1:** 248

"Weather Report" (Huddle), **Supp. XXVI:** 152

"Weather Within, The" (M. F. K. Fisher), **Supp. XVII:** 88, 91

Weaver, Harriet, **III:** 471

Weaver, James, **Supp. XVIII:** 72

Weaver, Michael, **Supp. XVIII:** 176, 177

Weaver, Mike, **Retro. Supp. I:** 430

Weaver, Robert, **Supp. XXVII:** 181

Weaver, Will, **Supp. XVI:** 39

"Weaving" (Larcom), **Supp. XIII:** 142, **Supp. XIII:** 144–145, 150, 151

"Web" (Oliver), **Supp. VII:** 236
Web and the Rock, The (Wolfe), **IV:** 451, 455, 457, 459–460, 462, 464, 467, 468
Webb, Beatrice, **Supp. I Part 1:** 5
Webb, Mary, **I:** 226
Webb, Phyllis, **Supp. XX: 56**
Webb, Sidney, **Supp. I Part 1:** 5
Webb, W. P., **Supp. V:** 225
Webber, A. R. F., **Supp. XXI:** 160
Weber, Brom, **I:** 383, 386
Weber, Carl, **Supp. IX:** 133, 138, 141
Weber, Max, **I:** 498; **Supp. I Part 2:** 637, 648
Weber, Sarah, **Supp. I Part 1:** 2
Weberman, A. J., **Supp. XVIII:** 27
Web of Earth, The (Wolfe), **IV:** 451–452, 456, 458, 464, 465
Web of Iniquity, The (Nickerson), **Supp. XXV:** 200
"Web of Life, The" (Nemerov), **III:** 282
Webster, Brenda, **Supp. XVI:** 157, 161
Webster, Daniel, **II:** 5, 9; **Supp. I Part 2:** 659, 687, 689, 690
Webster, John, **I:** 384; **Supp. I Part 2:** 422
Webster, Noah, **Supp. I Part 2:** 660; **Supp. II Part 1:** 77
Wector, Dixon, **II:** 103
Wedding, The (D. West), **Supp. XVIII:** 277, **287–289; Supp. XXVI:** 174
"Wedding, The" (Everwine), **Supp. XV:** 83
"Wedding, The" (Major), **Supp. XXII:** 185
Wedding, The (television miniseries), **Supp. XVIII:** 277, 289
"Wedding Cake" (Nye), **Supp. XIII:** 283
"Wedding Dance, The" (Di Piero), **Supp. XIX:** 47
"Wedding Day" (Boyle), **Supp. XXIV:** 56–57
Wedding Day and Other Stories (Boyle), **Supp. XXIV: 56–57**
"Wedding in Brownsville, A" (Singer), **IV:** 15
Wedding in Hell, A (Simic), **Supp. VIII:** 280, **282**
"Wedding of Henry Markowitz, The" (Goodman), **Supp. XXVI:** 121–122
"Wedding of the Rose and Lotus, The" (Lindsay), **Supp. I Part 2:** 387
"Wedding Supper, The" (Rowson), **Supp. XV:** 243
"Wedding Toast, A" (Wilbur), **Supp. III Part 2:** 561
Wedekind, Frank, **III:** 398; **Supp. XX:** **85; Supp. XXII:** 23
Wedge, The (W. C. Williams), **Retro. Supp. I:** 424
"We Didn't"(Dybek), **Supp. XXIII:** 77–78
"Wednesday at the Waldorf" (Swenson), **Supp. IV Part 2:** 647
We Don't Live Here Anymore (Dubus), **Supp. XXIV:** 97
"We Don't Live Here Anymore" (Dubus), **Supp. VII:** 78–79, 85
"Weed" (McCarriston), **Supp. XIV:** 259, 273

"Weed, The" (Bishop), **Supp. I Part 1:** 80, 88–89
"Weed, The" (Taggard), **Supp. XXII:** 284
"Weeds, The" (McCarthy), **II:** 566
"Weekend" (Beattie), **Supp. V:** 27
"Weekend" (Hempel), **Supp. XXI:** 124
Weekend, The (Cameron), **Supp. XII:** 80, 81, **86–88**
"Weekend at Ellerslie, A" (Wilson), **IV:** 431
Weekend Edition (National Public Radio), **Supp. IX:** 299; **Supp. XVII:** 240, 242
Weekend in Dinlock (Sigal), **Supp. XXIII:** 166
"Week in the Word, A" (Hampl), **Supp. XXII:** 85
Week on the Concord and Merrimack Rivers, A (Thoreau), **IV:** 168, 169, 177, 182–183; **Supp. I Part 2:** 420; **Supp. XIV:** 227
Weeks, Edward, **III:** 64
Weeks, Jerome, **Supp. VIII:** 76
"Weeping Burgher" (Stevens), **IV:** 77
"Weeping Women" (Levertov), **Supp. III Part 1:** 282
We Fished All Night (W. Motley), **Supp. XVII: 155–158,** 159, 160
We Fly Away (Francis), **Supp. IX: 79–80,** 84
" ' We Had Some Good Times Anyway' " (Gansworth), **Supp. XXVI:** 114
We Happy Few (Hinojosa), **Supp. XIX:** 99, **111–112**
We Have Always Lived in the Castle (Jackson), **Supp. IX:** 121, 126, **127–128**
"We Have Our Arts So We Won't Die of Truth" (Bradbury), **Supp. IV Part 1:** 105
We Have Tomorrow (Bontemps), **Supp. XXII:** 6, 12
Weich, Dave, **Supp. XII:** 321; **Supp. XVIII:** 91
Weidman, Jerome, **Supp. XXVII:** 142
"Weighing In" (Espaillat), **Supp. XXI:** 111
"Weight" (Wideman), **Supp. X:** 321
"Weights" (C. Baxter), **Supp. XVII:** 16
Weigl, Bruce, **Supp. VIII:** 269, 274; **Supp. XIX: 273–290; Supp. XV:** 342
Weik, Alexa, **Supp. XXIV:** 64
Weil, Dorothy, **Supp. XV:** 231
Weil, James L., **Supp. XXI:** 23, 31
Weil, Robert, **Supp. IX:** 236
Weil, Simone, **I:** 298; **Supp. XV:** 259; **Supp. XXII:** 93; **Supp. XXVI:** 234
Weiland (C. B. Brown), **Supp. XIII:** 100
Weinauer, Ellen, **Supp. XV:** 270, 284
Weinberger, Eliot, **Supp. IV Part 1:** 66; **Supp. VIII:** 290, 292; **Supp. XVI:** 284
Weinberger, Eric, **Supp. XXII:** 264
Weinfield, Henry, **Supp. XXI:** 24, 28, 33
Weininger, Otto, **Retro. Supp. I:** 416
Weinraub, Judith, **Supp. XXI:** 39
Weinreb, Mindy, **Supp. X:** 24
Weinreich, Regina, **Supp. XIV:** 22
Weinstein, Cindy, **Supp. XVIII:** 261
Weinstein, Hinda, **IV:** 285
Weinstein, Max, **IV:** 285

Weinstein, Mrs. Max (Anna Wallenstein), **IV:** 285, 287
Weinstein, Nathan. *See* West, Nathanael
Weinstein, Selma, **Supp. XXI:** 170
Weir, Sybil, **Supp. XXIV:** 20
Weisheit, Rabbi, **IV:** 76
Weismuller, Johnny, **Supp. X:** 264; **Supp. XX: 18**
Weiss, David, **Supp. XVI:** 55
Weiss, Jane, **Supp. XVIII:** 267, 269
Weiss, Peter, **IV:** 117
Weiss, Theodore, **Supp. IV Part 2:** 440; **Supp. IX:** 96
Weissleder, Paul, **Supp. XXII:** 283
Weist, Dianne, **Supp. X:** 80
Weithas, Art, **Supp. XI:** 231
Welch, Dave, **Supp. XXI:** 118
Welch, Don, **Supp. XIX:** 119
Welch, James, **Supp. IV Part 1:** 404; **Supp. IV Part 2:** 503, 513, 557, 562; **Supp. XXIV:** 257; **Supp. XXVI:** 186, 188
Welch, Lew, **Supp. V:** 170; **Supp. VIII:** 303; **Supp. XXII:** 276
"Welcome from War" (Rukeyser), **Supp. VI:** 286
"Welcome Morning" (Sexton), **Supp. II Part 2:** 696
"Welcome the Wrath" (Kunitz), **Supp. III Part 1:** 261
Welcome to Hard Times (Doctorow), **Supp. IV Part 1:** 218, 219–220, 222, 224, 230, 238
Welcome to Hard Times (film), **Supp. IV Part 1:** 236
"Welcome to New Dork" (Leonard), **Supp. XVIII:** 148
Welcome to Our City (Wolfe), **IV:** 461
Welcome to the Castle (Hayes), **Supp. XXVI:** 144
Welcome to the Monkey House (Vonnegut), **Supp. II Part 2:** 758
Welcome to the Moon (Shanley), **Supp. XIV:** 318
Welcome to the Moon and Other Plays (Shanley), **Supp. XIV:** 315, **316–319**
Weld, Theodore, **Supp. I Part 2:** 587, 588
Weld, Tuesday, **Supp. XI:** 306
Welded (O'Neill), **III:** 390; **Supp. XXII:** 24
"Welfare Worker, Disenchanted, Contemplates Friday Afternoon, The" (Trethewey), **Supp. XXI:** 246
"Well, The" (Momaday), **Supp. IV Part 2:** 483
"Well Dressed Man with a Beard, The" (Stevens), **Retro. Supp. I:** 297
Wellek, René, **I:** 253, 261, 282; **II:** 320; **Supp. XIV:** 12, 14
Weller, George, **III:** 322
Welles, Gideon, **Supp. I Part 2:** 484
Welles, Orson, **IV:** 476; **Supp. I Part 1:** 67; **Supp. IV Part 1:** 82, 83; **Supp. V:** 251; **Supp. VIII:** 46; **Supp. XI:** 169, 307
"Wellfleet Whale, The" (Kunitz), **Supp. III Part 1:** 263, 269
Wellfleet Whale and Companion Poems, The (Kunitz), **Supp. III Part 1:** 263

Wellink, Yvonne, **Supp. XVIII:** 257

Wellman, Flora, **II:** 463–464, 465

Wellman, Rita, **Supp. XXV:** 20

"Well Rising, The" (Stafford), **Supp. XI:** 318

Wells, Carolyn, **Supp. XXVI: 271–287**

Wells, H. G., **I:** 103, 226, 241, 243, 253, 405, 409, 415; **II:** 82, 144, 276, 337, 338, 458; **III:** 456; **IV:** 340, 455; **Retro. Supp. I:** 100, 228, 231; **Supp. XVI:** 190; **Supp. XXI:** 8

Wellspring, The (Olds), **Supp. X: 211–212**

Well Wrought Urn, The: Studies in the Structure of Poetry (Brooks), **Supp. XIV:** 1, **8–9,** 14, 15, 16

Welsh, Mary, **Supp. XIX:** 248. *See also* Hemingway, Mrs. Ernest (Mary Welsh)

Welty, Eudora, **II:** 194, 217, 606; **IV: 260–284; Retro. Supp. I:** 339–358; **Retro. Supp. II:** 235; **Supp. IV Part 2:** 474; **Supp. V:** 59, 315, 336; **Supp. VIII:** 94, 151, 171; **Supp. X:** 42, 290; **Supp. XII:** 310, 322; **Supp. XIV:** 3; **Supp. XV:** 338; **Supp. XXIV:** 223; **Supp. XXVI:** 152; **Supp. XXVII:** 216, 218, 267

Welty, Eurora, **Supp. XIX:** 151

Weltzien, O. Alan, **Supp. XVI:** 20–21, 28

"We miss Her, not because We see—" (Dickinson), **Retro. Supp. I:** 46

We Must Dance My Darlings (Trilling), **Supp. I Part 1:** 297

Wendell, Barrett, **III:** 507; **Supp. I Part 2:** 414; **Supp. XIV:** 197

Wendell, Sarah. *See* Holmes, Mrs. Abiel (Sarah Wendell)

Wendy Wasserstein: A Casebook (Barnett), **Supp. XV:** 323, 330

"Wendy Wasserstein's Three Sisters: Squandered Privilege" (Brewer), **Supp. XV:** 330

Wenner, Jann S., **Supp. XXIV:** 280, 283

Wept of Wish-ton-Wish, The (Cooper), **I:** 339, 342, 350

Werbe, Peter, **Supp. XIII:** 236

"We Real Cool" (Brooks), **Supp. III Part 1:** 80

"We're All Pharaohs When We Die" (Gallagher), **Supp. XXIV:** 170

We're Back! A Dinosaur's Story (screenplay, Shanley), **Supp. XIV:** 316

"We're Friends Again" (O'Hara), **III:** 372–373

"Were the Whole Realm of Nature Mine" (Watts), **I:** 458

Werewolf (M. Sommers), **Supp. XVII:** 55

Were-Wolf, The (C. Housman), **Supp. XVII:** 55

Werewolf of Paris, The (Endore), **Supp. XVII:** 55–56

Werewolves in Their Youth (Chabon), **Supp. XI:** 66, **76–77**

Werlock, Abby, **Supp. XIII:** 293

Werthman, Michael, **Supp. V:** 115

"Wer-Trout, The" (Proulx), **Supp. VII:** 255–256

Wescott, Glenway, **I:** 288; **II:** 85; **III:** 448, 454; **Supp. VIII:** 156; **Supp. XIV:** 342; **Supp. XVI:** 195

"We Shall All Be Born Again But We Shall Not All Be Saved" (Matthews), **Supp. IX:** 162

West, Anthony, **Supp. IV Part 1:** 284

West, Benjamin, **Supp. I Part 2:** 511

West, Dorothy, **Supp. XIII:** 295; **Supp. XIX:** 72; **Supp. XVIII: 277–291; Supp. XXVI:** 164, 173, 174

West, James, **II:** 562

West, Nathanael, **I:** 97, 107, 190, 211, 298; **II:** 436; **III:** 357, 425; **IV: 285–307; Retro. Supp. II: 321–341; Supp. IV Part 1:** 203; **Supp. VIII:** 97; **Supp. XI:** 85, 105, 159, 296; **Supp. XII:** 173, 310; **Supp. XIII:** 106, 170; **Supp. XIX:** 223; **Supp. XVIII:** 251, 253, 254

West, Ray, **Supp. XV:** 142

West, Rebecca, **II:** 412, 445; **Supp. XVI:** 152, 153

Westall, Julia Elizabeth. *See* Wolfe, Mrs. William Oliver (Julia Elizabeth Westall)

"We Stand United" (Benét), **Supp. XI:** 46

"West Authentic, The: Willa Cather" (Stegner), **Supp. IV Part 2:** 608

"West Coast, The: Region with a View" (Stegner), **Supp. IV Part 2:** 608–609

"West Coast Waterfront: End of an Era" (Swados), **Supp. XIX:** 264

Westcott, Edward N., **II:** 102

"Western Association of Writers" (Chopin), **Supp. I Part 1:** 217

"Western Ballad, A" (Ginsberg), **Supp. II Part 1:** 311

Western Borders, The (Howe), **Supp. IV Part 2:** 424–425

Western Canon (Bloom), **Supp. XXV:** 251

Western Canon: The Books and Schools of the Ages (Bloom), **Supp. IX:** 146

Western Lands, The (Burroughs), **Supp. III Part 1:** 106

"Western North Carolina" (Halliday), **Supp. XIX:** 85

Western Star (Benét), **Supp. XI:** 46, 47, 57

"Westland" (C. Baxter), **Supp. XVII:** 18, 19

"West Marginal Way" (Hugo), **Supp. VI:** 131, 135

West of Eden: Writers in Hollywood, 1928–1940 (Fine), **Supp. XVIII:** 248

West of Yesterday, East of Summer: New and Selected Poems, 1973–1993 (Monette), **Supp. X:** 159

West of Your City (Stafford), **Supp. XI:** 316, **317–318,** 321, 322

Weston, Jessie L., **II:** 540; **III:** 12; **Supp. I Part 2:** 438

"West Real" (Ríos), **Supp. IV Part 2:** 539, 540

West-running Brook (Frost), **II:** 155; **Retro. Supp. I:** 136, 137

"West-running Brook" (Frost), **II:** 150, 162–164

"West Wall" (Merwin), **Supp. III Part 1:** 355

"Westward Beach, A" (Jeffers), **Supp. II Part 2:** 418

Westward Ho (Harrison), **Supp. VIII:** 51, **52**

Westward the Course of Empire (Leutze), **Supp. X:** 307

"Westward the Course of Empire Takes Its Way" (Wallace), **Supp. X: 307–308; Supp. XXII:** 260

"West Wind" (Oliver), **Supp. VII:** 246

"West Wind, The" (Bryant), **Supp. I Part 1:** 155

West Wind: Poems and Prose Poems (Oliver), **Supp. VII:** 243, 246–248

"Wet Casements" (Ashbery), **Supp. III Part 1:** 18–20

We the Living (film), **Supp. IV Part 2:** 520

We the Living (Rand), **Supp. IV Part 2:** 520–521

Wetherell, Elizabeth (pseudonym). *See* Warner, Susan

Wet Parade (Sinclair), **Supp. V:** 289

Wetzsteon, Ross, **Supp. XXI:** 12

"We've Adjusted Too Well" (O'Brien), **Supp. V:** 247

Wevill, David, **Retro. Supp. II:** 247, 249

"We Wear the Mask" (Dunbar), **Supp. II Part 1:** 199, 207, 209–210

We Were Heroes: The Journal of Scott Pendleton Collins, a World War II Soldier, Normandy, France, 1944 (Myers), **Supp. XXVII:** 208

We Will Be Citizens: New Essays on Gay and Lesbian Theatre (Fischer, ed.), **Supp. XXIV:** 263

We Will Never Die (Hecht), **Supp. XXVII:** 94

Weybright, Victor, **Supp. XIII:** 172

Weyden, Rogier van der, **Supp. IV Part 1:** 284

Whalen, Marcella, **Supp. I Part 1:** 49

Whalen, Philip, **Supp. VIII:** 289; **Supp. XXII:** 226

Whalen-Bridge, John, **Retro. Supp. II:** 211–212

"Whales off Wales, The" (X. J. Kennedy), **Supp. XV:** 163

"Whales Weep" (Boyle), **Supp. XX:** 19

"Whales Weep Not!" (D. H. Lawrence), **Supp. XVII:** 77

Wharton, Edith, **I:** 12, 375; **II:** 96, 180, 183, 186, 189–190, 193, 283, 338, 444, 451; **III:** 69, 175, 576; **IV:** 8, 53, 58, **308–330; Retro. Supp. I:** 108, 232, **359–385; Supp. IV Part 1:** 23, 31, 35, 36, 80, 81, 310; **Supp. IX:** 57; **Supp. XII:** 308; **Supp. XIV:** 337, 347; **Supp. XVI:** 189; **Supp. XVIII:** 278; **Supp. XX: 227, 229, 232, 239, 240; Supp. XXIII:** 275; **Supp. XXIV:** 29, 64; **Supp. XXV:** 201; **Supp. XXVI:** 145, 276; **Supp. XXVII:** 4

Wharton, Edward Robbins, **IV:** 310, 313–314, 319

"What" (Dunn), **Supp. XI:** 144

What a Kingdom It Was (Kinnell), **Supp. III Part 1:** 235, 238, 239

"What America Would Be Like without Blacks" (Ellison), **Retro. Supp. II:** 123

What Are Masterpieces (Stein), **IV:** 30–31

What Are Years (Moore), **III:** 208–209, 210, 215

"What Are Years?" (Moore), **III:** 211, 213

What a Way to Go (Morris), **III:** 230–232

"What a Wonder among the Instruments Is the Walloping Trombone!" (Carruth), **Supp. XVI:** 51

"What Became of the Flappers?" (Zelda Fitzgerald), **Supp. IX:** 71

"What Can I Tell My Bones?" (Roethke), **III:** 546, 549

What Century? (O'Hara), **Supp. XXIII:** 216

"What Child Is This?" (Jarman), **Supp. XVII:** 113–114, 115

"What Do I Care?" (Teasdale), **Supp. XXVII:** 284

"What Do I Care for Morning" (H. Johnson), **Supp. XXVI:** 173

"What Do We Have Here" (Carson), **Supp. XII:** 101

"What Do We See" (Rukeyser), **Supp. VI:** 282

What Do Women Want? Bread Roses Sex Power (Jong), **Supp. V:** 115, 117, 129, 130

"What Do You Do in San Francisco?" (Carver), **Supp. III Part 1:** 143

What Dreams My Come (Atherton as Frank Lin), **Supp. XXIV:** 28

What D'Ya Know for Sure (Zinberg), **Supp. XV:** 196

Whatever Happened to Gloomy Gus of the Chicago Bears? (Coover), **Supp. V:** 51, 52

Whatever Happened to Jacy Farrow? (Cleveland), **Supp. V:** 222

"What Every Boy Should Know" (Maxwell), **Supp. VIII:** 169

"What Feels Like the World" (Bausch), **Supp. VII:** 46

"What Fort Sumter Did for Me" (E. Stoddard), **Supp. XV:** 282

"What Girls Read" (Salmon), **Supp. XVIII:** 258

"What God Is Like to Him I Serve" (Bradstreet), **Supp. I Part 1:** 106–107

"What Happened Here Before" (Snyder), **Supp. VIII:** 302

"What Happened to Georgia" (Ray), **Supp. XVIII:** 194

What Happens (Herrmann), **Supp. XXII:** 277

What Have I Ever Lost by Dying? (R. Bly), **Supp. IV Part 1:** 71–72

What Have You Lost? (Nye, ed.), **Supp. XIII:** 280

What I Believe (Asch), **Supp. XXIII:** 2

"What I Believe" (Mumford), **Supp. II Part 2:** 479

"What I Call What They Call Onanism" (Goldbarth), **Supp. XII:** 175

What I Did Last Summer (Gurney), **Supp. V:** 96, 100, 107, 108

"What if God" (Olds), **Supp. X:** 208

What I Have Done with Birds: Character Studies of Native American Birds (Stratton-Porter), **Supp. XX:** 218

"What I Have to Defend, What I Can't Bear Losing" (Stern), **Supp. IX:** 286, 287, 288, 298

"What I Knew" (Nelson), **Supp. XVIII:** 178

"What I Know about Being a Playwright" (McNally), **Supp. XIII:** 195, 207

"What I Mean" (Ortiz), **Supp. IV Part 2:** 497

"What Is an Emotion" (James), **II:** 350

What Is Art? (Tolstoy), **I:** 58

"What Is Civilization? Africa's Answer" (Du Bois), **Supp. II Part 1:** 176

"What Is College For?" (Bourne), **I:** 216

"What Is Exploitation?" (Bourne), **I:** 216

What Is Found There: Notebooks on Poetry and Politics (A. Rich), **Supp. XVII:** 74

"What Is It?" (Carver), **Supp. III Part 1:** 139

What Is Man? (Twain), **II:** 434; **IV:** 209

"What Is Poetry" (Ashbery), **Supp. III Part 1:** 19

"What Is Seized" (Moore), **Supp. X:** 164, 168, 169, 172, 175

"What Is the Earth?" (Olds), **Supp. X:** 213

"What Is This Poet" (Stern), **Supp. IX:** 295

What Is To Be Done? (Lenin), **Supp. XXI:** 164

"What I Think" (Hogan), **Supp. IV Part 1:** 406

What Love Comes To: New & Selected Poems (Stone), **Supp. XXVII:** 249, 257, 262

What Maisie Knew (H. James), **II:** 332; **Retro. Supp. I:** 229, **230;** **Supp. XVIII:** 160

What Makes Sammy Run? (NBC broadcast, Schulberg and Schulberg), **Supp. XVIII:** 254

What Makes Sammy Run (Schulberg), **Supp. XXVII:** 142

What Makes Sammy Run? (Schulberg), **Supp. XIII:** 170; **Supp. XVIII:** 241, **244–247,** 248, 249, 253

"What Makes Sammy Run?" (Schulberg), **Supp. XVIII:** 241

What Moon Drove Me to This? (Harjo), **Supp. XII:** **218–220**

"What Must" (MacLeish), **III:** 18

What My Father Believed (Wrigley), **Supp. XVIII:** 298–300

"What My Father Believed" (Wrigley), **Supp. XVIII:** **298–299**

What Price Hollywood? (film), **Supp. XVIII:** 243

Whatsaid Serif (Mackey), **Supp. XXVII:** 155, 156

"What Sally Said" (Cisneros), **Supp. VII:** 63

What Saves Us (Weigl), **Supp. XIX:** 282

"What's Happening in America" (Sontag), **Supp. III Part 2:** 460–461

"What She Couldn't Tell" (Hampl), **Supp. XXII:** 92

"What's in Alaska?" (Carver), **Supp. III Part 1:** 141, 143

"What's in a Name" (H. L. Gates), **Supp. XX:** 101

What's New, Pussycat? (film; Allen), **Supp. XI:** 307; **Supp. XV:** 1, 2, 14

"What's New in American and Canadian Poetry" (R. Bly), **Supp. IV Part 1:** 67

What's O'Clock (A. Lowell), **II:** 511, 527, 528

What's Up, Tiger Lily? (film; Allen), **Supp. XV:** 2, **3**

"What the Arts Need Now" (Baraka), **Supp. II Part 1:** 47

"What the Bed Knows"(Schott), **Supp. XXIII:** 249

"What the Body Can Say" (Trethewey), **Supp. XXI:** 255

"What the Brand New Freeway Won't Go By" (Hugo), **Supp. VI:** 132–133

"What the Gypsies Told My Grandmother While She Was Still a Young Girl" (Simic), **Supp. VIII:** 283

"What the Prose Poem Carries with It" (R. Bly), **Supp. IV Part 1:** 64

"What the Stone Says" (Huddle), **Supp. XXVI:** 151

What They Found: Love on 145th Street (Myers), **Supp. XXVII:** 210–211

"What They Wanted" (Dunn), **Supp. XI:** 151

What Thou Lovest Well (Hugo), **Supp. VI:** 140, 141

"What Thou Lovest Well Remains American" (Hugo), **Supp. VI:** 140, 141

What Time Collects (Farrell), **II:** 46, 47–48

What to Do? (Chernyshevsky), **Retro. Supp. I:** 269

"What to Keep, What to Discard" (Taggard), **Supp. XXII:** 280

"What to the Slave is Your Fourth of July?"(Douglass), **Supp. XXIII:** 167

What Use Are Flowers? (Hansberry), **Supp. IV Part 1:** 359, 368–369, 374

What Was Literature? (Fiedler), **Supp. XIII:** 96–97, **105–106**

What Was Mine (Beattie), **Supp. V:** 33, 35

What Was the Relationship of the Lone Ranger to the Means of Production? (Baraka), **Supp. II Part 1:** 58

"What We Came Through" (Goldbarth), **Supp. XII:** 179–180

"What Were the White Things?" (Hempel), **Supp. XXI:** 126

What We Talk About When We Talk About Love (Carver), **Supp. III Part 1:** 142–146; **Supp. XII:** 139; **Supp. XXIV:** 177

"What Why When How Who" (Pinsky), **Supp. VI:** 244

What Will Suffice: Contemporary American Poets on the Art of Poetry (Buckley and Young, eds.), **Supp. XIII:** 313

What Work Is (Levine), **Supp. V:** 181, 187, 192–193

"What You Hear from Em" (Taylor), **Supp. V:** 314, 320, 324

"What You Live For" (Huddle), **Supp. XXVI:** 150

What You See in the Dark (Muñoz), **Supp. XXV:** 127, 137–139

"What You Want" (O. Henry), **Supp. II Part 1:** 402

"What You Would Do" (Weigl), **Supp. XIX:** 288

Wheatley, Phillis, **Supp. XIII:** 111; **Supp. XVII:** 74–75; **Supp. XX: 106, 277–291**

Whedon, Tony, **Supp. XXI:** 131, 132

"Wheelchairs" (Kriegel), **Supp. XXIV:** 220

Wheeler, David, **Supp. XVI:** 277

Wheeler, John, **II:** 433

Wheeler, Monroe, **Supp. XV:** 295

Wheelock, John Hall, **IV:** 461; **Supp. IX:** 268; **Supp. XIV:** 120; **Supp. XV:** 301; **Supp. XXVII:** 286, 291, 293, 294, 297

Wheel of Life, The (Glasgow), **II:** 176, 178, 179, 183

Wheelwright, Philip, **Supp. XV:** 20

"When" (Olds), **Supp. X:** 207

When Boyhood Dreams Come True (Farrell), **II:** 45

"When Death Came April Twelve 1945" (Sandburg), **III:** 591, 593

"When Death Comes" (Oliver), **Supp. VII:** 241

"When De Co'n Pone's Hot" (Dunbar), **Supp. II Part 1:** 202–203

"When God First Said" (Zach; Everwine trans.), **Supp. XV:** 87

"When Grandma Died—1942" (Shields), **Supp. VII:** 311

"When Howitzers Began" (Carruth), **Supp. XVI:** 55

"When I Buy Pictures" (Moore), **III:** 205

"When I Came from Colchis" (Merwin), **Supp. III Part 1:** 343

"When I Have Fears I May Cease to Be" (Keats), **Supp. XIX:** 92

"When I Left Business for Literature" (Anderson), **I:** 101

"When I Love You" (Peacock), **Supp. XIX:** 199

"When in Rome—Apologia" (Komunyakaa), **Supp. XIII:** 120

"When It Comes" (Olds), **Supp. X:** 213

"When It's Clear and Hot" (Trethewey), **Supp. XXI:** 246

When I Was Alive (Notley), **Supp. XXII:** 228

"When I Was Alive" (Notley), **Supp. XXII:** 229

"When I Was Seventeen" (Kincaid), **Supp. VII:** 181

"When I Was Thirty-Five, You Took My Photograph" (Stone), **Supp. XXVII:** 254

"When I Was Twenty-five" (Talese), **Supp. XVII:** 202

When Knighthood Was in Flower (Major), **III:** 320

"\[When\] Let by rain" (Taylor), **IV:** 160–161

"When Lilacs Last in the Dooryard Bloom'd" (Whitman), **IV:** 347–348, 351; **Retro. Supp. I:** 406; **Supp. IV**

Part 1: 16; **Supp. XV:** 215

"When Malindy Sings" (Dunbar), **Supp. II Part 1:** 200, 204–205

When Peoples Meet: A Study of Race and Culture (Locke and Stern), **Supp. XIV:** 202, 213

When She Was Good (P. Roth), **Retro. Supp. II:** 282, 283, 284; **Supp. III Part 2:** 403, 405, 410–413

"When Sue Wears Red" (Hughes), **Retro. Supp. I:** 195, 204

"When the Acacia Blooms"(Crooker), **Supp. XXIII:** 60

"When the Dead Ask My Father about Me" (Olds), **Supp. X:** 210

"When the Frost Is on the Punkin" (Riley), **Supp. II Part 1:** 202

When the Jack Hollers (Hughes), **Retro. Supp. I:** 203; **Supp. I Part 1:** 328

"When the Last Riders" (Zach; Everwine, trans.), **Supp. XV:** 75, 86

"When the Light Gets Green" (Warren), **IV:** 252

"When the Model Does Not Show" (Major), **Supp. XXII:** 184

"When the Peace Corps Was Young" (Theroux), **Supp. VIII:** 314

When the Sun Tries to Go On (Koch), **Supp. XV:** 185

"When the Sun Tries to Go On" (Koch), **Supp. XV:** 179, 180

"When the World Ended as We Knew It" (Harjo), **Supp. XII:** 231

When Time Was Born (Farrell), **II:** 46, 47

"When We Dead Awaken: Writing as Re-Vision" (Rich), **Supp. I Part 2:** 552–553, 560

"When We Gonna Rise" (Baraka), **Supp. II Part 1:** 48

"When We Have To" (Salinas), **Supp. XIII:** 322–323

"WHEN WE'LL WORSHIP JESUS" (Baraka), **Supp. II Part 1:** 54

"When We Sold the Tent" (Espaillat), **Supp. XXI:** 102

"When we speak of God, is it God we speak of?" (J. Logan), **Supp. XVII:** 113

"When Women Throw Down Bundles: Strong Women Make Strong Nations" (Gunn Allen), **Supp. IV Part 1:** 328

"When You Come into Your Kingdom" (Muñoz), **Supp. XXV:** 136

"'When You Finally See Them': The Unconquered Eye in *To Kill a Mockingbird*" (Champion), **Supp. VIII:** 128

"When You Lie Down, the Sea Stands Up" (Swenson), **Supp. IV Part 2:** 643

"Where Are the People of Color?" (Myers), **Supp. XXVII:** 199

"Where Blue Is Blue" (Richard), **Supp. XIX:** 221

Where Does One Go When There's No Place Left to Go? (Crews), **Supp. XI:** 103

Where Does the Day Go? (Myers), **Supp. XXVII:** 199, 200, 202

"Where Go the Boats" (R. Stevenson), **Supp. XVII:** 69

Where Horizons Go (Espaillat), **Supp. XXI:** 99, 103, 104

"Where I Come from Is Like This" (Gunn Allen), **Supp. IV Part 1:** 319

"Where I'm Calling From" (Carver), **Supp. III Part 1:** 145

Where I'm Calling From: New and Selected Stories (Carver), **Supp. III Part 1:** 138, 148; **Supp. XXIV:** 178

"Where I Ought to Be" (Erdrich), **Supp. IV Part 1:** 265

Where Is My Wandering Boy Tonight? (Wagoner), **Supp. IX:** 335–336

"Where Is the Island?" (Francis), **Supp. IX:** 78

"Where Is the Voice Coming From?" (Welty), **IV:** 280; **Retro. Supp. I:** 355

Where Joy Resides (Isherwood), **Supp. XIV:** 156

"Where Knock Is Open Wide" (Roethke), **III:** 533–535

"Where My Sympathy Lies" (H. Roth), **Supp. IX:** 234

Where's Daddy? (Inge), **Supp. XXV:** 95, 105, 106

Where's My Money? (Shanley), **Supp. XIV:** 316, 328, **330–331**

Where the Bluebird Sings to the Lemonade Springs (Stegner), **Supp. IV Part 2:** 596, 597, 598, 600, 604, 606, 613; **Supp. XXII:** 205

"Where the Bones Move" (W. V. Davis), **Supp. XXI:** 92

Where the Cross Is Made (O'Neill), **III:** 388, 391

Where There's a Will (Rinehart), **Supp. XXV:** 193

Where the Rivers Flow North (Mosher), **Supp. XXII:** 205, 207, 208, **210–212**

"Where the Rivers Flow North" (Mosher), **Supp. XXII:** 204, 206, 207, 208, 209, **210–211**

Where the Sea Used to Be (Bass), **Supp. XVI:** 21

"Where the Sea Used to Be" (Bass), **Supp. XVI:** 20, 21

"*Where the Sea Used to Be:* Rick Bass and the Novel of Ecological Education" (Dixon), **Supp. XVI:** 21

"Where the Soft Air Lives" (Nye), **Supp. XIII:** 275

Where the Twilight Never Ends (Haines), **Supp. XII:** 211

Where the Wild Grape Grows: Selected Writings, 1930–1950 (D. West; Mitchell and Davis, eds.), **Supp. XVIII:** 283, 286

Where the Wild Things Are (Sendak), **Supp. IX:** 207

"Wherever Home Is" (Wright), **Supp. III Part 2:** 605, 606

"Wherever I Am Not" (Huddle), **Supp. XXVI:** 156–157

Where Water Comes Together With Other Water (Carver), **Supp. III Part 1:** 147, 148

"Where We Crashed" (Hugo), **Supp. VI:** 138

"Where We Must Look for Help" (R. Bly), **Supp. XXI:** 84

"Where You Are" (Doty), **Supp. XI:** 131
Where You'll Find Me, and Other Stories (Beattie), **Supp. V:** 30–31
Whicher, Stephen, **II:** 20
"Which Is More Than I Can Say for Some People" (Moore), **Supp. X:** 177, 178
Which Ones Are the Enemy? (Garrett), **Supp. VII:** 98
"Which Theatre Is the Absurd One?" (Albee), **I:** 71
"Which Way to the Future?" (Rehder), **Supp. IV Part 1:** 69
"While Hendrix Played a Solo: 'Burning of the Midnight Lamp' " (Gansworth), **Supp. XXVI:** 112
While I Was Gone (Miller), **Supp. XII:** 290, **301–303**
"While Seated in a Plane" (Swenson), **Supp. IV Part 2:** 645
While the Messiah Tarries (Bukiet), **Supp. XVII:** 43, **46–47**
While We've Still Got Feet (Budbill), **Supp. XIX:** 5, 7, **10–11**, 15
Whilomville Stories (Crane), **I:** 414
"Whip, The" (Robinson), **III:** 513
Whipple, Thomas K., **II:** 456, 458; **IV:** 427
"Whippoorwill, The" (Francis), **Supp. IX:** 90
"Whip-poor-will, The" (Thurber), **Supp. I Part 2:** 616
Whirl Asunder, A (Atherton), **Supp. XXIV:** 22
Whirlpool (film, Preminger), **Supp. XVII:** 62
"Whisperer in Darkness, The" (Lovecraft), **Supp. XXV:** 114
"Whispering Gallery, The" (Komunyakaa), **Supp. XIII:** 132
"Whispering Leaves" (Glasgow), **II:** 190
Whispering to Fool the Wind (Ríos), **Supp. IV Part 2:** 540–541, 544, 545
"Whispers in the Next Room" (Simic), **Supp. VIII:** 278
"Whispers of Heavenly Death" (Whitman), **IV:** 348
"Whispers of Immortality" (Eliot), **Supp. XI:** 242
Whistle (Jones), **Supp. XI:** 219, 224, **231–234**
"Whistle, The" (Franklin), **II:** 121
"Whistle, The" (Komunyakaa), **Supp. XIII:** 111, 126
"Whistle, The" (Welty), **IV:** 262
Whistler, James, **I:** 484; **III:** 461, 465, 466; **IV:** 77, 369
Whistler, James Abbott McNeill, **Supp. XIV:** 335–336
"Whistling Dick's Christmas Stocking" (O. Henry), **Supp. II Part 1:** 390, 392
Whistling in the Dark (Garrett), **Supp. VII:** 111
Whistling in the Dark: True Stories and Other Fables (Garrett), **Supp. VII:** 95
Whitcher, Frances Miriam Berry, **Supp. XIII:** 152
"White" (Simic), **Supp. VIII: 275–276**
White, Barbara, **Retro. Supp. I:** 379
White, Dana, **Supp. XXII:** 251

White, E. B., **Retro. Supp. I:** 335; **Supp. I Part 2:** 602, 607, 608, 612, 619, 620, **651–681; Supp. II Part 1:** 143; **Supp. IX:** 20, 32; **Supp. VIII:** 171; **Supp. XVI:** 167
White, Elizabeth Wade, **Supp. I Part 1:** 100, 103, 111
White, Henry Kirke, **Supp. I Part 1:** 150
White, James L., **Supp. XI:** 123
White, Joel, **Supp. I Part 2:** 654, 678
White, Katharine. (Katharine Sergeant Angell), **Supp. I Part 2:** 610, 653, 655, 656, 669; **Supp. VIII:** 151, 171
White, Lillian, **Supp. I Part 2:** 651
White, Lucia, **I:** 258
White, Maria. *See* Lowell, Mrs. James Russell (Maria White)
White, Morton, **I:** 258; **Supp. I Part 2:** 647, 648, 650
White, Roberta, **Supp. XII:** 293
White, Stanford, **Supp. IV Part 1:** 223
White, Stanley, **Supp. I Part 2:** 651, 655
White, T. H., **III:** 522
White, T. W., **III:** 411, 415
White, Walter, **Supp. I Part 1:** 345; **Supp. XIX:** 73; **Supp. XVIII:** 123, 127
White, William, **Retro. Supp. II:** 326
White, William A., **I:** 252
White Album, The (Didion), **Supp. IV Part 1:** 198, 202, 205–207, 210
"White Album, The" (Didion), **Supp. IV Part 1:** 205, 206
"White Angel" (Cunningham), **Supp. XV:** 59
"White Apache" (Markson), **Supp. XVII:** 136
"White as Snow" (Boyle), **Supp. XXIV:** 58, 59
White Boys (McKnight), **Supp. XX: 155–157**
"White Boys, The" (McKnight), **Supp. XX:** 155–157
White Buildings (H. Crane), **I:** 385, 386, 390–395, 400; **Retro. Supp. II:** 77–78, **80–81**, 82, 83, 85
White Butterfly (Mosley), **Supp. XIII:** 237, 238, 240
White Center (Hugo), **Supp. VI:** 144–145
"White Center" (Hugo), **Supp. VI:** 144, 146
Whited, Stephen, **Supp. XI:** 135
White Deer, The (Thurber), **Supp. I Part 2:** 606
White Doves at Morning (Burke), **Supp. XIV:** 22–23, 32, 35–36
"White Eagle, The" (Chopin), **Retro. Supp. II:** 72
White Fang (London), **II:** 471–472, 481
Whitefield, George, **I:** 546; **Supp. XX: 280**
White-Footed Deer and Other Poems (Bryant), **Supp. I Part 1:** 157
White Goddess, The (Graves), **Supp. IV Part 1:** 280
White-Haired Lover (Shapiro), **Supp. II Part 2:** 703, 717
Whitehead, Alfred North, **III:** 605, 619, 620; **IV:** 88; **Supp. I Part 2:** 554, 647

Whitehead, Mrs. Catherine, **IV:** 116
Whitehead, Colson, **Supp. XIII:** 233, 241
Whitehead, James, **Supp. XV:** 339
Whitehead, Margaret, **IV:** 114, 115, 116
Whitehead, William, **Supp. XX: 50–51,** **53**
White Heat (Walsh), **Supp. XIII:** 174
"White Heron, A" (Jewett), **II:** 409; **Retro. Supp. II:** 17
White Heron and Other Stories, A (Jewett), **II:** 396
White Horses (Hoffman), **Supp. X: 83–85,** 90, 92
"White Horses of Vienna, The" (Boyle), **Supp. XXIV: 59–60**
White Horses of Vienna, The, and Other Stories (Boyle), **Supp. XXIV:** 57, **58–59**
White House Diary, A (Lady Bird Johnson), **Supp. IV Part 1:** 22
White-Jacket; or, The World in a Man-of-War (Melville), **III:** 80, 81, 84, 94; **Retro Supp. I:** 248, 249, 254; **Supp. XVIII:** 7, 9
White Lantern, The (Connell), **Supp. XIV:** 97
"White Lies" (Trethewey), **Supp. XXI:** 244, 246, 251
"White Lights, The" (Robinson), **III:** 524
"White Lilies, The" (Glück), **Supp. V:** 88
White Man, Listen! (Wright), **IV:** 478, 488, 489, 494
White Morning, The (Atherton), **Supp. XXIV:** 24, 29
"White Mulberry Tree, The" (Cather), **I:** 319; **Retro. Supp. I:** 7, 9, 17
White Mule (W. C. Williams), **Retro. Supp. I:** 423
"White Negro, The" (Mailer), **III:** 36–37; **Retro. Supp. II:** 202
"Whiteness of the Whale, The" (Melville), **III:** 84, 86
"White Night" (Oliver), **Supp. VII:** 236
"White Nights" (Auster), **Supp. XII:** 23–24
White Noise (DeLillo), **Supp. VI:** 1, 3–4, 5–7, 10, 11–12, 16; **Supp. XVIII:** 140; **Supp. XX:** 91
White Oxen and Other Stories, The (Burke), **I:** 269, 271
White Paper on Contemporary American Poetry (McClatchy), **Supp. XII:** 253, **259–260**
"White Phosphorous" (Notley), **Supp. XXII:** 232, 233
"White Pine" (Oliver), **Supp. VII:** 244
White Pine: Poems and Prose Poems (Oliver), **Supp. VII:** 243–246
White Poems, The (Crooker), **Supp. XXIII: 54–55**
White Rat (G. Jones), **Supp. XXIV:** 185
White Roots of Peace (Wallace), **Supp. XXVI:** 90, 96–97
White Sail (Sorrentino), **Supp. XXI:** 228
"White Ship, The" (Lovecraft), **Supp. XXV:** 113
"White Silence, The" (London), **II:** 468
"White Silk" (Nye), **Supp. XIII:** 275
"White Snake, The" (Sexton), **Supp. II Part 2:** 691

"White Spot" (Anderson), **I:** 116
"White-Tailed Hornet, The" (Frost), **Retro. Supp. I:** 138
"White Trash Cowboys of *Father and Son,* The" (Bjerre), **Supp. XXI:** 41
"White Trees, Hammer Moon" (Dubus III), **Supp. XXIV:** 101, 104
Whitfield, Raoul, **Supp. IV Part 1:** 345
Whitfield, Stephen J., **Supp. XX: 243, 244**
Whitlock, Brand, **II:** 276
Whitman (Masters), **Supp. I Part 2:** 473, 475, 476
Whitman, George, **IV:** 346, 350
Whitman, Ruth, **Supp. XXI:** 246
Whitman, Sarah Wyman, **Retro. Supp. II:** 136
Whitman, Walt, **I:** 61, 68, 98, 103, 104, 109, 219, 220, 227, 228, 242, 246, 250, 251, 260, 261, 285, 381, 384, 386, 396, 397, 398, 402, 419, 430, 459, 460, 483, 485, 486, 577; **II:** 7, 8, 18, 127, 140, 273–274, 275, 289, 295, 301, 320, 321, 373, 445, 446, 451, 457, 494, 529, 530, 552; **III:** 171, 175, 177, 181–182, 189, 203, 234, 260, 426, 430, 453, 454, 461, 505, 507–508, 511, 528, 548, 552, 555, 559, 567, 572, 576, 577, 579, 584, 585, 595, 606, 609; **IV:** 74, 169, 191, 192, 202, **331–354,** 405, 409, 416, 444, 450–451, 457, 463, 464, 469, 470, 471; **Retro. Supp. I:** 8, 52, 194, 254, 283, 284, 333, **387–410,** 412, 417, 427; **Retro. Supp. II:** 40, 76, 93, 99, 155, 156, 158, 170, 262; **Supp. I Part 1:** 6, 79, 167, 311, 314, 325, 365, 368, 372; **Supp. I Part 2:** 374, 384, 385, 387, 389, 391, 393, 399, 416, 436, 455, 456, 458, 473, 474, 475, 525, 540, 579, 580, 582, 682, 691; **Supp. III Part 1:** 6, 20, 156, 239–241, 253, 340; **Supp. III Part 2:** 596; **Supp. IV Part 1:** 16, 169, 325; **Supp. IV Part 2:** 597, 625; **Supp. IX:** 8, 9, 15, 38, 41, 44, 48, 53, 131, 292, 298, 299, 308, 320; **Supp. V:** 113, 118, 122, 130, 170, 178, 183, 277, 279, 332; **Supp. VIII:** 42, 95, 105, 126, 198, 202, 269; **Supp. X:** 36, 112, 203, 204; **Supp. XI:** 83, 123, 132, 135, 203, 321; **Supp. XII:** 132, 185, 190, 256; **Supp. XIII:** 1, 77, 115, 153, 221, 304, 335; **Supp. XIV:** 89, 312, 334, 335, 338; **Supp. XIX:** 118, 276; **Supp. XV:** 41, 93, 181, 183, 212, 213, 218, 250, 275, 301, 302, 303, 309, 352; **Supp. XVI:** 209; **Supp. XVII:** 42, 71, 112, 133; **Supp. XVIII:** 4, 194, 196, 304; **Supp. XX: 69, 115, 116, 221; Supp. XXI:** 169, 217, 227, 256; **Supp. XXII:** 81, 82, 86, 92; **Supp. XXIII:** 19, 109, 166, 207; **Supp. XXVI:** 227, 230, 233, 234; **Supp. XXVII:** 160
"Whitman Pinch Hits, 1861" (Skloot), **Supp. XX: 203**
"Whitman: The Poet and the Mask" (Cowley), **Supp. II Part 1:** 143
Whitmarsh, Jason, **Supp. VIII:** 283
Whitmer, Peter, **Supp. X:** 264, 265

Whitney, Blair, **Supp. I Part 2:** 403
Whitney, Josiah, **Supp. IX:** 180, 181
Whitt, Margaret Earley, **Retro. Supp. II:** 226
Whittemore, Reed, **III:** 268; **Supp. XI:** 315
Whittier, Elizabeth, **Supp. I Part 2:** 700, 701, 703; **Supp. XIII:** 141, 142
Whittier, John Greenleaf, **I:** 216; **II:** 275; **III:** 52; **Retro. Supp. I:** 54; **Retro. Supp. II:** 155, 163, 169; **Supp. I Part 1:** 168, 299, 313, 317, 372; **Supp. I Part 2:** 420, 602, **682–707; Supp. VIII:** 202, 204; **Supp. XI:** 50; **Supp. XIII:** 140, 145; **Supp. XV:** 246; **Supp. XXIII:** 156
Whittier, Mary, **Supp. I Part 2:** 683
"Whittier Birthday Speech" (Twain), **Supp. I Part 1:** 313
"Who" (Kenyon), **Supp. VII:** 174
"Who" (Sobin), **Supp. XVI:** 284–285
"Who Am I—Who I Am" (Corso), **Supp. XII:** 134
"Who Be Kind To" (Ginsberg), **Supp. II Part 1:** 323
Who Do You Love (Thompson), **Supp. XXIII:** 289, **295–296**
Who Do You Think You Are? (Munro), **Supp. XXVII:** 181, 182, 184, 186–187, 194
"Whoever Was Using This Bed" (Carver), **Supp. III Part 1:** 148
"Whoever You Are Holding Me Now in Hand" (Whitman), **IV:** 342; **Retro. Supp. I:** 52
Who Gathered and Whispered behind Me (Goldbarth), **Supp. XII:** 181, 182
"Who in One Lifetime" (Rukeyser), **Supp. VI:** 276, 279
Who Is the Widow's Muse? (Stone), **Supp. XXVII:** 257, 262
Who Is Witter Bynner? (Kraft), **Supp. XV:** 40, 52
"Who Is Your Mother? Red Roots of White Feminism" (Gunn Allen), **Supp. IV Part 1:** 329
Whole Hog (Wagoner), **Supp. IX:** 337–338
"Whole Mess…Almost, The" (Corso), **Supp. XII:** 135
"Whole Moisty Night, The" (R. Bly), **Supp. IV Part 1:** 69
Whole New Life, A (Price), **Supp. VI:** 265, **266,** 267
"Whole Self, The" (Nye), **Supp. XIII:** 275
"Whole Soul, The" (Levine), **Supp. V:** 192
"Whole Story, The" (Strand), **Supp. IV Part 2:** 622
Whole Town's Talking, The (Loos), **Supp. XVI:** 187
Whole Wide World, The (film), **Supp. XXVII:** 117
"Whole World Knows, The" (Welty), **IV:** 272; **Retro. Supp. I:** 343
Who'll Stop the Rain (film), **Supp. V:** 301
Who Lost an American? (Algren), **Supp. IX: 15–16**

Who Owns America? (symposium), **Supp. XIV:** 4
Who Owns the West? (Kittredge), **Supp. XXVI:** 185
"Who Puts Together" (Hogan), **Supp. IV Part 1:** 403, 405, 412–413
"Whore of Mensa, The" (Allen), **Supp. XV:** 15
Whores for Gloria (Vollmann), **Supp. XVII:** 226, 230
Whorf, Benjamin Lee, **Supp. XVI:** 283
Who's Afraid? (Holding), **Supp. XXII:** 120, **125–126**
Who's Afraid of Virginia Woolf? (Albee), **I:** 71, 77–81, 83, 85, 86, 87, 94; **IV:** 230
Who Shall Be the Sun? Poems Based on the Lore, Legends, and Myths of the Northwest Coast and Plateau Indians (Wagoner), **Supp. IX:** 328, **329–330,** 337
"Whosis Kid, The" (Hammett), **Supp. IV Part 1:** 344
"Who Sit Watch in Daylight" (Wright), **Supp. XV:** 342
"Who's Passing for Who?" (Hughes), **Supp. I Part 1:** 330
"Who Speak on the Page?" (Sanders), **Supp. XVI:** 278
Who We Are: On Being (and Not Being) a Jewish American Writer (Rubin, ed.), **Supp. XXIV:** 3
Who Will Run the Frog Hospital?: A Novel (Moore), **Supp. X:** 163, 165, 169, **175–177**
Who Wrote the Book of Love? (Siegel), **Supp. XXII: 265–267,** 267
Why Are We in Vietnam? (Mailer), **III:** 27, 29, 30, 33, 34–35, 39, 42, 44; **Retro. Supp. II:** 205–206
"Why Bother?" (Franzen). *See* "Perchance to Dream" (Franzen)
"Why China?" (Egan), **Supp. XIX:** 51, 52
"Why Did the Balinese Chicken Cross the Road?" (Walker), **Supp. III Part 2:** 527
"Why Do the Heathens Rage?" (O'Connor), **III:** 351
"Why Do They Prate?" (H. Johnson), **Supp. XXVI:** 174
"Why Do You Write About Russia?" (Simpson), **Supp. IX:** 277
"Why Have We Not More Great Novelists?" (Atherton), **Supp. XXIV:** 24
"Why I Am a Danger to the Public" (Kingsolver), **Supp. VII:** 204
"Why I Am a Pagan" (Zitkala-Ša), **Supp. XXV:** 276–277
Why I Am Not a Christian (Russell), **Supp. I Part 2:** 522
"Why I Am Not a Painter"(O'Hara), **Supp. XXIII:** 208
Why I Came to Judevine (Budbill), **Supp. XIX:** 2, 7–8, 15
"Why I Do Not Wish to Float in Space"(Schott), **Supp. XXIII:** 251
"Why I Entered the Gurdjieff Work" (Toomer), **Supp. III Part 2:** 481

"Why I Like Laurel" (Patchett), **Supp. XII:** 309

"Why I Live at the P.O." (Welty), **IV:** 262; **Retro. Supp. I:** 345

"Why I Make Sam Go to Church" (Lamott), **Supp. XX:** 141

"Why Is American Literature Bourgeois?" (Atherton), **Supp. XXIV:** 24, 28

"Why Is Economics Not an Evolutionary Science?" (Veblen), **Supp. I Part 2:** 634

"Why I Write" (Didion), **Supp. IV Part 1:** 201, 203

"Why I Wrote *Phil:* An Exclusive Essay for Amazon.com" (Saunders), **Supp. XIX:** 230–231

Why Johnny Can't Read: And What You Can Do About It (Flesch), **Supp. XVI:** 105

"Why Negro Women Leave Home" (Brooks), **Supp. III Part 1:** 75

Why Poetry Matters (Parini), **Supp. XIX:** 120, 129

"Why Resign from the Human Race?" (Swados), **Supp. XIX:** 265

"Why the Little Frenchman Wears His Hand in a Sling" (Poe), **III:** 425

Why Torture Is Wrong, and the People Who Love Them (Durang), **Supp. XXIV:** 126–127

"Why We Are Forgiven" (Weigl), **Supp. XIX:** 282–283

Why We Behave Like Microbe Hunters (Thurber), **Supp. I Part 2:** 606

Why We Were in Vietnam (Podhoretz), **Supp. VIII:** 241

"Why Write?" (Updike), **Retro. Supp. I:** 317

"Wichita Vortex Sutra" (Ginsberg), **Supp. II Part 1:** 319, 321, 323–325, 327

Wickenden, Dorothy, **Supp. XXIII:** 291

Wickes, George, **Supp. XIV:** 165

Wickford Point (Marquand), **III:** 50, 58, 64–65, 69

Wicks, Robert Russell, **Supp. XII:** 49

Wide, Wide World, The (S. Warner as Wetherell), **Supp. XV:** 275; **Supp. XVIII:** 257, 260, **262–264,** 265

Wide Blue Yonder (Thompson), **Supp. XXIII:** 289, **296–298**

"Wide Empty Landscape with a Death in the Foreground" (Momaday), **Supp. IV Part 2:** 492

Wideman, Edgar, **Supp. XXV:** 146, 147

Wideman, John Edgar, **Retro. Supp. II:** 123; **Supp. X:** 239, 250, **319–336; Supp. XI:** 245; **Supp. XIII:** 247; **Supp. XVIII:** 89; **Supp. XXI:** 246; **Supp. XXIV:** 183

Widener, Jeff, **Supp. XVIII:** 91

"Wideness" (Pickering), **Supp. XXI:** 203

"Wide Net, The" (Welty), **IV:** 266

Wide Net and Other Stories, The (Welty), **IV:** 261, 264–266, 271; **Retro. Supp. I:** **347–349,** 352, 355

Widening Spell of the Leaves, The (Levis), **Supp. XI:** 258, 259, 261, **268–269,** 271

"Wide Prospect, The" (Jarrell), **II:** 376–377

Wide Sargasso Sea (Rhys), **Supp. XVIII:** 131

"Widespread Enigma Concerning Blue-Star Woman" (Zitkala-Ša), **Supp. XXV:** 282–283

"Widow" (Peacock), **Supp. XIX:** 206

"Widower" (Robison), **Supp. XXI:** 118

Widow for One Year, A (Irving), **Supp. VI:** 165, **179–181**

Widow's Mite (Holding), **Supp. XXII:** **136**

Widows of Thornton, The (Taylor), **Supp. V:** 320, 321

Widow's Story, A (Oates), **Supp. XXV:** 60

"Widow's Wish, The" (Briggs), **Supp. XVIII:** 15

Wieland; or, The Transformation. An American Tale (Brown), **Supp. I Part 1:** 128–132, 133, 137, 140

Wiene, Robert, **Retro. Supp. I:** 268

Wiener, John, **Supp. IV Part 1:** 153

Wieners, John, **Supp. II Part 1:** 32; **Supp. XXIII:** 215

Wiesel, Elie, **Supp. XVII:** 47, 48, 49

Wiest, Dianne, **Supp. XV:** 12

"Wife, Forty-five, Remembers Love, A" (Shields), **Supp. VII:** 310

"Wifebeater, The" (Sexton), **Supp. II Part 2:** 693

"Wife for Dino Rossi, A" (Fante), **Supp. XI:** 165

"Wife of His Youth, The" (Chesnutt), **Supp. XIV: 63–66**

Wife of His Youth and Other Stories of the Color Line, The (Chesnutt), **Supp. XIV:** 62, 63

"Wife of Jesus Speaks, The" (Karr), **Supp. XI:** 250–251

"Wife of Nashville, A" (Taylor), **Supp. V:** 320

"Wife's Story, The" (R. H. Davis), **Supp. XVI:** 85, 91, 92–93

Wife's Story, The (Shields), **Supp. VII:** 316. *See also* Happenstance

"Wife-Wooing" (Updike), **IV:** 226

Wigan, Gareth, **Supp. XI:** 306

Wiget, Andrew, **Supp. IV Part 2:** 509

Wigglesworth, Michael, **IV:** 147, 156; **Supp. I Part 1:** 110, 111

Wilbur, Richard, **III:** 527; **Retro. Supp. II:** 50; **Supp. III Part 1:** 64; **Supp. III Part 2: 541–565; Supp. IV Part 2:** 626, 634, 642; **Supp. V:** 337; **Supp. VIII:** 28; **Supp. X:** 58, 120; **Supp. XII:** 258; **Supp. XIII:** 76, 336; **Supp. XV:** 51, 251, 256; **Supp. XVII:** 26; **Supp. XVIII:** 178; **Supp. XIX: 199; Supp. XXI:** 247; **Supp. XXIV:** 36, 45; **Supp. XXVI:** 64, 68

Wilcocks, Alexander, **Supp. I Part 1:** 125

Wilcox, Ella Wheeler, **Supp. II Part 1:** 197

Wilcox, Kirstin, **Supp. XX: 283, 284, 285**

Wild, John, **II:** 362, 363–364

Wild, Peter, **Supp. V:** 5

Wild, Robert, **IV:** 155

"Wild, The" (Berry), **Supp. X:** 30

Wild 90 (film) (Mailer), **Retro. Supp. II:** 205

Wild and Woolly (film), **Supp. XVI:** 185

"Wild Boar in These Woods: The Influence of Seamus Heaney on the Poetry of Ron Rash" (Boyelston), **Supp. XXVII:** 216

Wild Boy of Aveyron, The (Itard). *See De l'éducation d'un homme sauvage*

Wild Boys, The: A Book of the Dead (Burroughs), **Supp. III Part 1:** 106–107

Wild Card Quilt: Taking A chance on Home (Ray), **Supp. XVIII:** 189, 192, 193, 196, 198, **200–202,** 204

Wilde, Oscar, **I:** 50, 66, 381, 384; **II:** 515; **IV:** 77, 350; **Retro. Supp. I:** 56, 102, 227; **Retro. Supp. II:** 76, 326; **Supp. IV Part 2:** 578, 679, 683; **Supp. IX:** 65, 66, 68, 189, 192; **Supp. V:** 106, 283; **Supp. X:** 148, 151, 188–189; **Supp. XIV:** 324, 334; **Supp. XV:** 350; **Supp. XXIV:** 263

Wilder, Alec, **Supp. XXVII:** 42

Wilder, Amos Parker, **IV:** 356

Wilder, Mrs. Amos Parker (Isabella Thornton Niven), **IV:** 356

Wilder, Billy, **Supp. IV Part 1:** 130; **Supp. XI:** 307

Wilder, Isabel, **IV:** 357, 366, 375

Wilder, Laura Ingalls, **Supp. XXI:** 2; **Supp. XXII: 289–303; Supp. XXVI:** 217

Wilder, Thornton, **I:** 360, 482; **IV: 355–377,** 431; **Retro. Supp. I:** 109, 359; **Supp. I Part 2:** 609; **Supp. IV Part 2:** 586; **Supp. IX:** 140; **Supp. V:** 105; **Supp. XII:** 236–237; **Supp. XX: 50**

"Wilderness" (Leopold), **Supp. XIV:** 190

Wilderness (Parker), **Supp. XIX:** 177, **188–189**

"Wilderness" (Sandburg), **III:** 584, 595

Wilderness (Warren), **IV:** 256

"Wilderness, The" (Merwin), **Supp. III Part 1:** 340, 345

"Wilderness, The" (Robinson), **III:** 524

Wilderness of Vision, The: On the Poetry of John Haines (Bezner and Walzer, eds.), **Supp. XII:** 202

Wilderness Plots: Tales about the Settlement of the American Land (Sanders), **Supp. XVI:** 267–268, 269

"Wilderness Station, A" (Munro), **Supp. XXVII:** 191

"Wilderness"(Thompson), **Supp. XXIII:** 301

Wilderness World of Anne LaBastille, The (LaBastille), **Supp. X: 105,** 106

Wild Flag, The (White), **Supp. I Part 2:** 654

"Wildflower, The" (W. C. Williams), **Retro. Supp. I:** 420

"Wild Flowers" (Caldwell), **I:** 310

"Wildflowers" (Minot), **Supp. VI:** 208

"Wild Geese" (Oliver), **Supp. VII:** 237

"Wild Honey Suckle, The" (Freneau), **Supp. II Part 1:** 253, 264, 266

Wild in the Country (Odets), **Supp. II Part 2:** 546

"Wild in the Woods" (Skloot), **Supp. XX: 206**

Wild Iris, The (Glück), **Supp. V:** 79, 87–89, 91

Wildlife (Ford), **Supp. V:** 57, 69–71

Wildlife in America (Matthiessen), **Supp. V:** 199, 201, 204

"Wildlife in American Culture" (Leopold), **Supp. XIV:** 190, 191

"Wild Light" (Skloot), **Supp. XX: 200**

Wild Man, The (P. N. Warren), **Supp. XX: 260, 270–272**

"Wildness" (Sanders), **Supp. XVI:** 276

Wild Old Wicked Man, The (MacLeish), **III:** 3, 20

Wild Palms, The (Faulkner), **II:** 68–69; **Retro. Supp. I:** 85

"Wild Palms, The" (Faulkner), **II:** 68

"Wild Peaches" (Wylie), **Supp. I Part 2:** 707, 712

Wild Roses of Cape Ann and Other Poems (Larcom), **Supp. XIII:** 142, 147

Wild Seed (O. Butler), **Supp. XIII:** 62, 63

"Wild Swans at Coole, The " (W. B. Yeats), **Supp. XVI:** 48

"Wild Swans at Norfolk, The" (Carruth), **Supp. XVI:** 48

"Wild Thing" (L. Brown), **Supp. XXI:** 44

Wild Thorn (Hoffman), **Supp. XVIII: 84–85**

Wild to the Heart (Bass), **Supp. XVI:** 16

"Wild Turkeys: Dignity of the Damned" (B. Kelly), **Supp. XVII:** 129

"Wildwest" (MacLeish), **III:** 14

Wiley, Catherine, **Supp. XXIII:** 199

Wiley, Craig, **Supp. VIII:** 313

Wilhelm, Randall, **Supp. XXVII:** 215, 224

Wilhelm Meister (Goethe), **II:** 291

Wilkes, John, **Supp. I Part 2:** 503, 519, 522

Wilkie, Curtis, **Supp. V:** 11

Wilkins, Roy, **Supp. I Part 1:** 345

Wilkinson, Alec, **Supp. VIII:** 164, 168, 171

Wilkinson, Marguerite, **Supp. XXVII:** 292–293

Wilkinson, Max, **Supp. IX:** 251

Will, The (Swados), **Supp. XIX: 265–266**

Willard, Nancy, **Supp. XIX:** 138

Willard, Samuel, **IV:** 150

Willard Gibbs (Rukeyser), **Supp. VI:** 273, 283, 284

Willcutts, Tim, **Supp. XVII:** 239, 241, 246

Willett, Ralph, **Supp. XIV:** 27

Willey, Basil, **Retro. Supp. II:** 243

"William Butler Yeats Among the Ghosts" (Skloot), **Supp. XX: 204–205**

William Carlos Williams (Koch), **Retro. Supp. I:** 428

William Carlos Williams: An American Artist (Breslin), **Retro. Supp. I:** 430

William Carlos Williams and Alterity (Ahearn), **Retro. Supp. I:** 415

William Carlos Williams and the Meanings of Measure (Cushman), **Retro. Supp. I:** 430

William Carlos Williams: The American Background (Weaver), **Retro. Supp. I:** 430

William Ellery Channing: An Intellectual Portrait (Edgell), **Supp. XXIV:** 71

William Ellery Channing: Selected Writings (Robinson, ed.), **Supp. XXIV:** 71

William Faulkner: A Critical Study (Howe), **Supp. VI:** 119–120, 125

William Faulkner: Early Prose and Poetry (Faulkner), **Retro. Supp. I:** 80

William Faulkner: First Encounters (Brooks), **Supp. XIV:** 13

"William Faulkner's Legend of the South" (Cowley), **Supp. II Part 1:** 143

"William Faulkner: The Stillness of *Light in August*" (Kazin), *Supp. VIII:* 104

William Faulkner: The Yoknapatawpha Country (Brooks), **Supp. XIV: 12–13,** 16

William Faulkner: Toward Yoknapatawpha and Beyond (Brooks), **Supp. XIV:** 13

"William Humphrey, 73, Writer of Novels about Rural Texas" (Gussow), **Supp. IX:** 93

William Humphrey, Destroyer of Myths (Almon), **Supp. IX:** 93

William Humphrey. Boise State University Western Writers Series (Winchell), **Supp. IX:** 109

"William Humphrey Remembered" (Masters), **Supp. IX:** 96

William Humphrey. Southwestern Series (Lee), **Supp. IX:** 109

William Inge and the Subversion of Gender (J. Johnson), **Supp. XXV:** 98

"William Ireland's Confession" (A. Miller), **III:** 147–148

William James and Phenomenology: A Study of the "Principles of Psychology" (Wilshire), **II:** 362

William Lloyd Garrison (Chapman), **Supp. XIV:** 46–51, 52, 53, 55

William Maxwell Portrait, A: Memories and Appreciations (C. Baxter, Collier, and Hirsch, eds.), **Supp. XVII:** 23

Williams, Annie Laurie, **Supp. IX:** 93

Williams, Blanch Colton, **Supp. XVIII:** 279

Williams, Cecil, **II:** 508

Williams, Charles, **Supp. II Part 1:** 15, 16

Williams, C. K., **Supp. XIII:** 114; **Supp. XVII:** 112

Williams, Cratis, **Supp. XX: 163**

Williams, Dakin, **IV:** 379

Williams, David Reichard, **Supp. XIII:** 162

Williams, Edward, **IV:** 404

Williams, Edwina Dakin, **IV:** 379

Williams, Eric, **Supp. XXI:** 166, 170, 171

Williams, Esther, **Supp. XII:** 165

Williams, Fannie Barrier, **Supp. XIV:** 201

Williams, Garth, **Supp. XXII:** 301

Williams, George, **Supp. V:** 220

Williams, Henry Sylvester, **Supp. XXI:** 166

Williams, Horace, **IV:** 453

Williams, Joan, **Supp. IX:** 95

Williams, John A., **Supp. XVI:** 143

Williams, John Alexander, **Supp. XXIII:** 39

Williams, John Sharp, **IV:** 378

Williams, Jonathan, **Supp. XXII:** 168

Williams, Kenny J., **Supp. XX: 281, 286**

Williams, Lyle, **Supp. XIV:** 22

Williams, Michael, **Supp. V:** 286

Williams, Miller, **Supp. XIV:** 126; **Supp. XV:** 339; **Supp. XVIII:** 177

Williams, Paul, **IV:** 404

Williams, Raymond, **Supp. IX:** 146

Williams, Roger, **Supp. I Part 2:** 699; **Supp. XXIII:** 15

Williams, Rose, **IV:** 379

Williams, Sherley Anne, **Supp. V:** 180

Williams, Solomon, **I:** 549

Williams, Stanley T., **II:** 301, 316; **Supp. I Part 1:** 251

Williams, Stephen, **IV:** 148

Williams, Ted, **IV:** 216; **Supp. IX:** 162

Williams, Ted. C., **Supp. XXVI:** 102

Williams, Tennessee, **I:** 73, 81, 113, 211; **II:** 190, 194; **III:** 145, 147; **IV:** 4, **378–401; Supp. I Part 1:** 290, 291; **Supp. IV Part 1:** 79, 83, 84, 359; **Supp. IV Part 2:** 574, 682; **Supp. IX:** 133; **Supp. XI:** 103; **Supp. XIII:** 331; **Supp. XIV:** 250, 315; **Supp. XVI:** 194; **Supp. XXIV:** 113; **Supp. XXV:** 94, 96, 97

Williams, Terry Tempest, **Supp. XIII:** 16; **Supp. XVIII:** 189

Williams, Walter L., **Supp. IV Part 1:** 330, 331

Williams, William, **IV:** 404, 405

Williams, William Carlos, **I:** 61, 62, 229, 255, 256, 261, 285, 428, 438, 446, 539; **II:** 133, 536, 542, 543, 544, 545; **III:** 194, 196, 198, 214, 269, 409, 453, 457, 458, 464, 465, 591; **IV:** 30, 74, 75, 76, 94, 95, 286, 287, **402–425; Retro. Supp. I:** 51, 52, 62, 209, 284, 285, 288, 296, 298, **411–433; Retro. Supp. II:** 178, 181, 189, 250, 321, 322, 326, 327, 328, 334, 335; **Supp. I Part 1:** 254, 255, 259, 266; **Supp. II Part 1:** 9, 30, 308, 318; **Supp. II Part 2:** 421, 443; **Supp. III Part 1:** 9, 147, 239, 271, 275, 276, 278, 350; **Supp. III Part 2:** 542, 610, 613, 614, 615, 616, 617, 621, 622, 626, 628; **Supp. IV Part 1:** 151, 153, 246, 325; **Supp. IX:** 38, 268, 291; **Supp. V:** 180, 337; **Supp. VIII:** 195, 269, 272, 277, 292; **Supp. X:** 112, 120, 204; **Supp. XI:** 311, 328; **Supp. XII:** 198; **Supp. XIII:** 77, 90, 335; **Supp. XIV:** 280, 284, 285, 293; **Supp. XIX:** 1, 42, 117, 119, 121; **Supp. XV:** 42, 51, 182, 250, 306, 307; **Supp. XVI:** 48, 282; **Supp. XVII:** 36, 113, 227, 243; **Supp. XXI:** 226, 227, 230, 233; **Supp. XXII:** 162, 165, 168, 226, 227, 228; **Supp. XXIII:** 164, 207, 211; **Supp. XXIV:** 39, 41, 52, 63; **Supp. XXV:** 19; **Supp. XXVI:** 78, 143, 224, 226; **Supp. XXVII:** 284

Williams, Mrs. William Carlos (Florence Herman), **IV:** 404

Williams, Wirt, **Supp. XIV:** 24
Williamson, Alan, **Retro. Supp. II:** 185; **Supp. XIX:** 91
Williamson, J. W., **Supp. XX: 164**
William Styron's Nat Turner: Ten Black Writers Respond (Clarke, ed.), **IV:** 115
Williams-Walsh, Mary Ellen, **Supp. IV Part 2:** 611
William the Conqueror, **Supp. I Part 2:** 507
William Wetmore Story and His Friends (James), **Retro. Supp. I:** 235; **Supp. XX: 228**
William Wilson (Gardner), **Supp. VI:** 72
"William Wilson" (Poe), **II:** 475; **III:** 410, 412; **Retro. Supp. II:** 269; **Supp. IX:** 105
"Willie" (Angelou), **Supp. IV Part 1:** 15
Willie Masters' Lonesome Wife (Gass), **Supp. VI:** 77, **84–85, 86–87**
"Willing" (Moore), **Supp. X:** 178
Willingly (Gallagher), **Supp. XXIV:** 166, 168, 169, 170, 176
Willis, Bruce, **Supp. IV Part 1:** 236
Willis, Dail, **Supp. XXIII:** 298
Willis, Gordon, **Supp. XV:** 7
Willis, Mary Hard, **Supp. V:** 290–291
Willis, Meredith, **Supp. XXVI:** 153
Willis, Nathaniel Parker, **II:** 313; **Supp. I Part 2:** 405; **Supp. XVIII:** 12
Willis, Rachel, **Supp. XXVII:** 216
Williwaw (Vidal), **Supp. IV Part 2:** 677, 680, 681
Willow Field, The (Kittredge), **Supp. XXVI:** 184
"Willow Woman" (Francis), **Supp. IX:** 78
Wills, Garry, **Supp. I Part 1:** 294; **Supp. IV Part 1:** 355
Wills, Ridley, **IV:** 122
Wills, Ross B., **Supp. XI:** 169
"Will to Believe, The" (James), **II:** 352; **Supp. XIV:** 50
Will to Believe, The, and Other Essays in Popular Philosophy (James), **II:** 356; **IV:** 28
Will to Change, The: Poems, 1968–1970 (Rich), **Supp. I Part 2:** 551, 557–559
Will to Live On, The: This Is Our Heritage (Wouk), **Supp. XXV:** 257, 266
"Will We Plug Chips into Our Brains?" (W. Gibson), **Supp. XVI:** 117–118
Will You Please Be Quiet, Please? (Carver), **Supp. III Part 1:** 138, 140, 144
"Will You Please Be Quiet, Please?" (Carver), **Supp. III Part 1:** 137, 141
"Will You Tell Me?" (Barthelme), **Supp. IV Part 1:** 42, 47
Wilsdorf, Anne, **Supp. XVI:** 177
Wilsey, Sean, **Supp. XXV:** 1, 8
Wilshire, Bruce, **II:** 362, 364
Wilshire, Gaylord, **Supp. V:** 280
Wilson, Adrian, **Supp. XV:** 147
Wilson, Alexander, **Supp. XVI:** 4, 6
Wilson, Angus, **IV:** 430, 435
Wilson, August, **Supp. VIII: 329–353; Supp. XIX:** 132
Wilson, Augusta Jane Evans, **Retro. Supp. I:** 351

Wilson, Earl, **Supp. X:** 264
Wilson, Edmund, **I:** 67, 185, 236, 247, 260, 434, 482; **II:** 79, 80, 81, 86, 87, 91, 97, 98, 146, 276, 430, 530, 562, 587; **III:** 588; **IV:** 308, 310, **426–449; Retro. Supp. I:** 1, 97, 100, 101, 103, 104, 105, 115, 274; **Retro. Supp. II:** 321, 327, 329; **Supp. I Part 1:** 372; **Supp. I Part 2:** 407, 646, 678, 709; **Supp. II Part 1:** 19, 90, 106, 136, 137, 143; **Supp. III Part 2:** 612; **Supp. IV Part 2:** 693; **Supp. IX:** 55, 65, 190; **Supp. VIII:** 93, 95, 96, 97, 98–99, 100, 101, 103, 105, 162; **Supp. X:** 186; **Supp. XI:** 160; **Supp. XIII:** 170; **Supp. XIV:** 338; **Supp. XV:** 142, 308; **Supp. XVI:** 194; **Supp. XX: 76, 81; Supp. XXII:** 278; **Supp. XXIII:** 104–105, 106; **Supp. XXIV:** 62, 217, 222, 281
Wilson, Edmund (father), **IV:** 441
Wilson, E. O., **Supp. X:** 35
Wilson, Harriet, **Supp. XX: 105**
Wilson, Henry, **Supp. XIV:** 48
Wilson, Reuel, **II:** 562
Wilson, Robert, **Supp. XI:** 144
Wilson, Robley, **Supp. XXIII:** 290
Wilson, Sloan, **Supp. IV Part 1:** 387
Wilson, Thomas, **IV:** 153
Wilson, Tracy, **Supp. XVIII:** 101
Wilson, Victoria, **Supp. X:** 166
Wilson, Woodrow, **I:** 245, 246, 490; **II:** 183, 253; **III:** 105, 581; **Supp. I Part 1:** 21; **Supp. I Part 2:** 474, 643; **Supp. V:** 288
Wilton, David, **IV:** 147
Wiman, Christian, **Supp. XV:** 251, 253, 264; **Supp. XVII:** 74; **Supp. XVIII:** 173, 174
Wimberly, Lowry, **Supp. XV:** 136, 137
"Wimp, The" (Gallagher), **Supp. XXIV:** 174
Wimsatt, William K., **Supp. XIV:** 12
Winch, Terence, **Supp. XXIII:** 291
Winchell, Mark, **Supp. VIII:** 176, 189
Winchell, Mark Royden, **Supp. IX:** 97, 98, 109; **Supp. VIII:** 241; **Supp. XIII:** 94, 98, 99, 101; **Supp. XIV:** 103, 106, 111
Winchell, Walter, **Supp. XXV:** 29
Winckelmann, Johann Joachim, **Supp. XII:** 178
Wind, Sand, and Stars (Saint-Exupéry), **Supp. IX:** 247
Wind Across the Everglades (film, Ray), **Supp. XVIII:** 253
Wind Chrysalid's Rattle (Sobin), **Supp. XVI:** 283
"Windfall" (B. Kelly), **Supp. XVII:** 132
Windflower Home Almanac of Poetry, The (Kooser, ed.), **Supp. XIX:** 119
Windham, Donald, **IV:** 382
"Windhover" (Hopkins), **I:** 397; **II:** 539; **Supp. IX:** 43
Winding Stair and Other Poems, The (Yeats), **Supp. XV:** 253
"Winding Street, The" (Petry), **Supp. XI:** 6
"Window" (Pinsky), **Supp. VI:** 237, 247

"Window, The" (Hull), **Supp. XXI:** 140–141
Window at the White Cat, The (Rinehart), **Supp. XXV:** 192
Windows (Creeley), **Supp. IV Part 1:** 157, 158
"Windows" (Jarrell), **II:** 388, 389
"Window Seat, A" (Goldbarth), **Supp. XII:** 185
Wind Remains, The (opera) (Bowles), **Supp. IV Part 1:** 83
"Winds, The" (Welty), **IV:** 265; **Retro. Supp. I:** 348, 350
"Winds and Clouds over a Funeral" (Jin), **Supp. XVIII:** 94
Winds of War, The (miniseries), **Supp. XXV:** 265
Winds of War, The (Wouk), **Supp. XX: 243; Supp. XXV:** 254, 257, 258
"Wind up Sushi" (Goldbarth), **Supp. XII:** 186–187
Windy City Blues (Paretsky), **Supp. XXV:** 171
"Windy Day at the Reservoir, A" (Beattie), **Supp. V:** 33
Windy McPherson's Son (Anderson), **I:** 101, 102–103, 105, 111
"Wine" (Carver), **Supp. III Part 1:** 138
"Wine Menagerie, The" (H. Crane), **I:** 389, 391; **Retro. Supp. II:** 82
Wine of the Puritans, The: A Study of Present-Day America (Brooks), **I:** 240
"Wine of Wizardry, A" (Sterling), **I:** 208
Winer, Linda, **Supp. IV Part 2:** 580; **Supp. XV:** 332
Winesburg, Ohio: A Group of Tales of Ohio Small Town Life (Anderson), **I:** 97, 102, 103, 104, 105–108; **III:** 112, 113, 114, 116, 224, 579; **Supp. IX:** 306, 308; **Supp. V:** 12; **Supp. XI:** 164; **Supp. XVI:** 17; **Supp. XXII:** 282; **Supp. XXIV:** 281
Winfrey, Oprah, **Supp. XIX:** 194, 204; **Supp. XX: 83, 93**
Wing-and-Wing, The (Cooper), **I:** 350, 355
Winged Seed, The: A Remembrance (L.-Y. Lee), **Supp. XV:** 211, **220–223**
Winged Words: American Indian Writers Speak (Coltelli), **Supp. IV Part 2:** 493, 497
"Wingfield" (Wolff), **Supp. VII:** 341–342
"Wings, The" (Doty), **Supp. XI:** 124
"Wings in the Night" (Howard), **Supp. XXVII:** 122
Wings of the Dove, The (James), **I:** 436; **II:** 320, 323, 333, 334–335; **Retro. Supp. I:** 215, 216, 217, 232, **233–234; Supp. II Part 1:** 94–95; **Supp. IV Part 1:** 349
Winik, Marion, **Supp. XXVI:** 212
Winkelberg (Hecht), **Supp. XXVII:** 95
"Wink of the Zenith, The" (Skloot), **Supp. XX: 207**
Wink of the Zenith, The: The Shaping of a Writer's Life (Skloot), **Supp. XX: 195, 196, 207**
"Winkte" (Kenny), **Supp. XXIII:** 148–149

"Winky" (Saunders), **Supp. XIX:** 228–229, 229

"Winner, The" (Davison), **Supp. XXVI:** 64

Winner Names the Age, The: A Collection of Works by Lillian Smith (Cliff, ed.), **Supp. XXII:** 67

Winner Take Nothing (Hemingway), **II:** 249; **Retro. Supp. I:** 170, 175, 176, 181

"Winnie" (Brooks), **Supp. III Part 1:** 86

Winokur, Maxine. *See* Kumin, Maxine

Winslow, Art, **Supp. XVIII:** 102

Winslow, Devereux, **II:** 547

Winslow, Harriet, **II:** 552–553

Winslow, Ola Elizabeth, **I:** 547

Winslow, Warren, **II:** 540

Winston, Andrew, **Supp. XII:** 189

Winston, Michael R., **Supp. XIV:** 197

Winter, Douglas, **Supp. V:** 144

Winter, Johnny and Edgar, **Supp. V:** 334

Winter, Kate, **Supp. X:** 104

"Winter Branch, A" (Irving), **Supp. VI:** 163

"Winter Burial, A" (Clampitt), **Supp. IX:** 48

Winter Carnival (film), **Retro. Supp. I:** 113

"Winter Concert"(Strout), **Supp. XXIII:** 283

"Winter Daybreak at Vence, A" (Wright), **Supp. III Part 1:** 249–250

Winter Diary, A (Van Doren), **I:** 168

"Winter Dreams" (Fitzgerald), **II:** 80, 94; **Retro. Supp. I:** 108

"Winter Drive, A" (Jewett), **Retro. Supp. II:** 147

"Winter Eden, A" (Frost), **Retro. Supp. I:** 137

"Winter Father, The" (Dubus), **Supp. VII:** 83, 87

Winter Hours: Prose, Prose Poems, and Poems (Oliver), **Supp. VII:** 230, 247

"Winter in Dunbarton" (R. Lowell), **II:** 547; **Retro. Supp. II:** 187

"Wintering" (Plath), **Retro. Supp. II:** 255

"Wintering Over" (Davison), **Supp. XXVI:** 76

Winter Insomnia (Carver), **Supp. III Part 1:** 138

Winter in the Blood (Welch), **Supp. IV Part 2:** 562

"Winter Landscape" (Berryman), **I:** 174; **Retro. Supp. I:** 430

Winter Light (W. V. Davis), **Supp. XXI:** 92, 93

"Winter Light" (W. V. Davis), **Supp. XXI:** 90, 92

Winter Lightning (Nemerov), **III:** 269

Winter Morning Walks: One Hundred Postcards to Jim Harrison (Kooser), **Supp. XIX:** 116, **125–126**

Winter News (Haines), **Supp. XII:** 199, **201–204,** 207–208, 208

"Winter Night, A" (Teasdale), **Supp. XXVII:** 289

Winternitz, Mary. *See* Cheever, Mrs. John (Mary Winternitz)

Winter: Notes from Montana (Bass), **Supp. XVI:** 17–18

Winter of Our Discontent, The (Steinbeck), **IV:** 52, 65–66, 68

"Winter on Earth" (Toomer), **Supp. III Part 2:** 486

"Winter Piece, A" (Bryant), **Supp. I Part 1:** 150, 155

"Winter Rains, Cataluña" (Levine), **Supp. V:** 182

"Winter Remembered" (Ransom), **III:** 492–493

"Winter Roses" (W. V. Davis), **Supp. XXI:** 94

Winterrowd, Prudence, **I:** 217, 224

Winters, Jonathan, **Supp. XI:** 305

Winters, Yvor, **I:** 59, 63, 386, 393, 397, 398, 402, 471; **III:** 194, 498; **IV:** 153; **Retro. Supp. II:** 76, 77, 78, 82, 83, 85, 89; **Supp. I Part 1:** 268; **Supp. II Part 2:** 416, 666, **785–816;** **Supp. IV Part 2:** 480; **Supp. V:** 180, 191–192; **Supp. XIV:** 287; **Supp. XV:** 74, 341; **Supp. XXV:** 250

"Winter Sacrament" (Bronk), **Supp. XXI:** 33

"Winter Scenes" (Bryant). *See* "Winter Piece, A"

Winterset (Anderson), **III:** 159

"Winter Shrub, A" (Bronk), **Supp. XXI:** 28

"Winter Skyline Late" (F. Wright), **Supp. XVII:** 245

"Winter Sleep" (Wylie), **Supp. I Part 2:** 711, 729

Winter's Night (Boyce), **Supp. XXI:** 7, **12–13**

Winter's Tale (film, Goldsman), **Supp. XXV:** 86

Winter's Tale (Helprin), **Supp. XXV:** 79–80, 81, 82, 83, 86

Winter's Tale, The (Shakespeare), **Supp. XIII:** 219

Winter Stars (Levis), **Supp. XI:** 259, **266–268**

"Winter Stars" (Levis), **Supp. XI:** 267–268

"Winter Stars" (Teasdale), **Supp. XXVII:** 295

Winter Stop-Over (Everwine), **Supp. XV:** 74, 76

"Winter Stop-Over" (Everwine), **Supp. XV:** 76

Winter Studies and Summer Rambles in Canada (Jameson), **Supp. XXIII:** 225, 226

"Winter Sunrise" (Davison), **Supp. XXVI:** 69

"Winter Swan" (Bogan), **Supp. III Part 1:** 52

"Winter Thunder" (Sandoz), **Supp. XXIV:** 255

Winter Thunder (X. J. Kennedy), **Supp. XV:** 167

"Winter Thunder" (X. J. Kennedy), **Supp. XV:** 169

"Winter Trees" (Pedersen; Nelson, trans.), **Supp. XVIII:** 180

Winter Trees (Plath), **Retro. Supp. II:** 257; **Supp. I Part 2:** 526, 539, 541; **Supp. XXVII:** 296

"Winter Walk" (W. V. Davis), **Supp. XXI:** 92

"Winter Weather Advisory" (Ashbery), **Supp. III Part 1:** 26

"Winter Wheat" (Hoffman), **Supp. XVIII:** 86, 87

"Winter Wind" (Munro), **Supp. XXVII:** 185

"Winter without Snow, The" (C. Frost), **Supp. XV:** 96, 105–106

"Winter Words" (Levine), **Supp. V:** 192

Winthrop, John, **Supp. I Part 1:** 99, 100, 101, 102, 105; **Supp. I Part 2:** 484, 485

Winthrop Covenant, The (Auchincloss), **Supp. IV Part 1:** 23

"Wires of the Night, The" (Collins), **Supp. XXI:** 64

Wirt, William, **I:** 232

Wirth, Louis, **IV:** 475

Wisconsin Death Trip (Lesy), **Supp. XXV:** 146

Wisconsin Death Trip (Levy), **Supp. XIX:** 102

"Wisdom" (Teasdale), **Supp. XXVII:** 291

"Wisdom Cometh with the Years" (Cullen), **Supp. IV Part 1:** 166

Wisdom of the African World (McKnight, ed.), **Supp. XX: 157–158**

Wisdom of the Desert, The: Sayings from the Desert Fathers of the Fourth Century (Merton), **Supp. VIII:** 201

Wisdom of the Heart, The (H. Miller), **III:** 178, 184

Wise Blood (O'Connor), **III:** 337, 338, 339–343, 344, 345, 346, 350, 354, 356, 357; **Retro. Supp. II:** 219, 221, 222, 223, **225–228**

Wise Men, The (Price), **Supp. VI:** 254

"Wiser Than a God" (Chopin), **Retro. Supp. II:** 61; **Supp. I Part 1:** 208

Wishes, Lies, and Dreams: Teaching Children to Write Poetry (Koch), **Supp. XV:** 176, 189; **Supp. XXVII:** 26

"Wish for a Young Wife" (Roethke), **III:** 548

Wishful Thinking: A Theological ABC (Buechner), **Supp. XII:** 53

Wishing Tree, The: Christopher Isherwood on Mystical Religion (Adjemian, ed.), **Supp. XIV:** 164, 173

"Wish List" (Goodman), **Supp. XXVI:** 119–120

Wish You Were Here (O'Nan), **Supp. XXV:** 142, 147–148, 150, 152

Wismer, Helen Muriel. *See* Thurber, Mrs. James (Helen Muriel Wismer)

Wisse, Ruth, **Supp. XII:** 167, 168

Wister, Owen, **I:** 62; **Retro. Supp. II:** 72; **Supp. XIV:** 39

Wit (Edson), **Supp. XVIII:** 35–36, 37, **38–51**

"Witchbird" (Bambara), **Supp. XI:** 11

"Witch Burning" (Plath), **Supp. I Part 2:** 539

Witchcraft of Salem Village, The (Jackson), **Supp. IX:** 121

"Witch Doctor" (Hayden), **Supp. II Part 1:** 368, 380

Witches of Eastwick, The (Updike), **Retro. Supp. I:** 330, 331

Witch from Castile, The (Asch), **Supp. XXIII:** 6, 10

Witching Hour, The (Rice), **Supp. VII:** 299–300

"Witch of Coös, The" (Frost), **II:** 154–155; **Retro. Supp. I:** 135; **Retro. Supp. II:** 42

"Witch of Owl Mountain Springs, The: An Account of Her Remarkable Powers" (Taylor), **Supp. V:** 328

"Witch of Wenham, The" (Whittier), **Supp. I Part 2:** 694, 696

Witek, Terri, **Supp. XVII:** 117

"With a Little Help from My Friends" (Kushner), **Supp. IX:** 131

With Bold Knife and Fork (M. F. K. Fisher), **Supp. XVII:** 89, 91

"With Che at Kitty Hawk" (Banks), **Supp. V:** 6

"With Che at the Plaza" (Banks), **Supp. V:** 7

"With Che in New Hampshire" (Banks), **Supp. V:** 6

"With Child" (Taggard), **Supp. XXII:** 276, 278

"Withdrawal Symptoms" (Mora), **Supp. XIII:** 216

"Withered Leaf, A—Seen on a Poet's Table" (Very), **Supp. XXV:** 243

"Withered Skins of Berries" (Toomer), **Supp. III Part 2:** 485; **Supp. IX:** 320

Withers, Harry Clay, **Supp. XIII:** 161

Witherspoon, John, **Supp. I Part 2:** 504

With Eyes at the Back of Our Heads (Levertov), **Supp. III Part 1:** 276–277

With Her in Ourland (Gilman), **Supp. XI:** 208–209

With His Pistol in His Hand (Paredes), **Supp. XIII:** 225; **Supp. XIX:** 98

"Within the Words: An Apprenticeship" (Haines), **Supp. XII:** 197

"With Kit, Age 7, at the Beach" (Stafford), **Supp. XI:** 323

With Love to Lesbia (Kenny), **Supp. XXIII:** 145

"With Mercy for the Greedy" (Sexton), **Supp. II Part 2:** 680

With My Trousers Rolled (Epstein), **Supp. XIV:** 101, 105

Without a Hero (Boyle), **Supp. VIII:** 16; **Supp. XX:** 20

Without Feathers (Allen), **Supp. XV:** 3, 14, 15

Without Stopping (Bowles), **Supp. IV Part 1:** 79, 81, 85, 90, 91, 92

"Without Tradition and within Reason: Judge Horton and Atticus Finch in Court" (C. D. Johnson), **Supp. VIII:** 127

With Shuddering Fall (Oates), **Supp. II Part 2:** 504–506

"With the Dog at Sunrise" (Kenyon), **Supp. VII:** 170

With the Empress Dowager of China (Carl), **III:** 475

"With the Horse in the Winter Pasture" (McCarriston), **Supp. XIV:** 262

With the Old Breed: At Peleliu and Okinawa (Sledge), **Supp. V:** 249–250

"With the Violin" (Chopin), **Retro. Supp. II:** 61

"Witness" (Clampitt), **Supp. IX:** 42–43, 45, 46

"Witness" (Dubus), **Supp. VII:** 89

"Witness" (Harjo), **Supp. XII:** 227–228

Witness (McNally), **Supp. XIII:** 197

"Witness" (Nelson), **Supp. XVIII:** 186

"Witness, The" (Porter), **III:** 443–444

"Witness for Poetry, A" (Stafford), **Supp. XI:** 324

"Witness for the Defense" (Hay), **Supp. XIV:** 124

"Witnessing My Father's Will" (Karr), **Supp. XI:** 241

"Witnessing to a Shared World" (Sanders), **Supp. XVI:** 278

Witness to the Times! (McGrath), **Supp. X:** 118

Witness Tree, A (Frost), **II:** 155; **Retro. Supp. I:** 122, 137, 139

Wit's End: Days and Nights of the Algonquin Round Table (Gaines), **Supp. IX:** 190

Wits Recreations (Mennes and Smith), **II:** 111

Witt, Shirley Hill, **Supp. IV Part 2:** 505

Witte, John, **Supp. XX: 200**

Wittels, Anne F., **Supp. XV:** 59

Wittenberg, Judith Bryant, **Retro. Supp. II:** 146

Wittgenstein, Ludwig, **Retro. Supp. I:** 53; **Supp. III Part 2:** 626–627; **Supp. X:** 304; **Supp. XII:** 21; **Supp. XV:** 344, 346

Wittgensteins' Mistress (Markson), **Supp. XVII:** 135, 142, 143, 145

Wittliff, William, **Supp. V:** 227

"Witty War, A" (Simpson), **Supp. IX:** 268

Witz (Cohen), **Supp. XXII:** 268

"Wives and Mistresses" (Hardwick), **Supp. III Part 1:** 211–212

Wizard of Loneliness, The (Nichols), **Supp. XIII:** 259, 263, 264

Wizard of Oz, The (Baum), **Supp. IV Part 1:** 113

Wizard of Oz, The (film), **Supp. X:** 172, 214

Wizard's Tide, The: A Story (Buechner), **Supp. XII:** 54

"WLT (The Edgar Era)" (Keillor), **Supp. XVI:** 172

WLT: A Radio Romance (Keillor), **Supp. XVI:** 176

Wobegon Boy (Keillor), **Supp. XVI:** 177

Wodehouse, P. G., **Supp. IX:** 195; **Supp. XXI:** 204–205

Woiwode, Larry, **Supp. VIII:** 151; **Supp. XVI:** 206

Wojahn, David, **Supp. IX:** 161, 292, 293; **Supp. XXI:** 130, 131, 132, 138, 139, 141

Wolcott, James, **Supp. IX:** 259

Wolf, Christa, **Supp. IV Part 1:** 310, 314

Wolf, Daniel, **Retro. Supp. II:** 202

Wolf, Robert L., **Supp. XXII:** 274, 277, 279, 280

Wolf: A False Memoir (Harrison), **Supp. VIII:** 40, **41–42**, 45

Wolfe, Ben, **IV:** 454

Wolfe, Gregory, **Supp. XIV:** 307

Wolfe, James, **Supp. I Part 2:** 498

Wolfe, Linnie, **Supp. IX:** 176

Wolfe, Mabel, **IV:** 454

Wolfe, Thomas, **I:** 288, 289, 374, 478, 495; **II:** 457; **III:** 40, 108, 278, 334, 482; **IV:** 52, 97, 357, **450–473**; **Retro. Supp. I:** 382; **Supp. I Part 1:** 29; **Supp. IV Part 1:** 101; **Supp. IX:** 229; **Supp. X:** 225; **Supp. XI:** 213, 216, 217, 218; **Supp. XIII:** 17; **Supp. XIV:** 122; **Supp. XVIII:** 78; **Supp. XX: 163**; **Supp. XXVII:** 38

Wolfe, Tom, **Supp. III Part 2: 567–588**; **Supp. IV Part 1:** 35, 198; **Supp. V:** 296; **Supp. X:** 264; **Supp. XI:** 239; **Supp. XV:** 143; **Supp. XVII:** 202; **Supp. XVIII:** 72, 117; **Supp. XXIV:** 282, 283

Wolfe, William Oliver, **IV:** 454

Wolfe, Mrs. William Oliver (Julia Elizabeth Westall), **IV:** 454

"Wolfe Homo Scribens" (Cowley), **Supp. II Part 1:** 144

Wolfert, Ira, **Supp. XXI: 261–279**

Wolfert's Roost (Irving), **II:** 314

Wolff, Cynthia Griffin, **Retro. Supp. I:** 379; **Supp. IV Part 1:** 203

Wolff, Donald, **Supp. XIII:** 316, 317, 326

Wolff, Geoffrey, **Supp. II Part 1:** 97; **Supp. XI:** 239, 245, 246; **Supp. XXII:** 206, 211; **Supp. XXV:** 217

Wolff, Tobias, **Retro. Supp. I:** 190; **Supp. V:** 22; **Supp. VII: 331–346**; **Supp. X:** 1; **Supp. XI:** 26, 239, 245, 246, 247; **Supp. XV:** 223; **Supp. XVI:** 39, 41, 63, 70, 77; **Supp. XXIII:** 289; **Supp. XXV:** 142, 208

"Wolf in the Bed, The"(Hadas), **Supp. XXIII:** 118

Wolfreys, Julian, **Supp. XVIII:** 61

"Wolfshead" (Howard), **Supp. XXVII:** 116, 119

Wolfson, P. J., **Supp. XIII:** 172

"Wolf Town" (Carson), **Supp. XII: 102**

Wolf Willow: A History, a Story, and a Memory of the Last Plains Frontier (Stegner), **Supp. IV Part 2:** 595, 596, 597, 598, 599, 600, 601, 604, 606, 611, 613, 614

Wolitzer, Hilma, **Supp. XV:** 55; **Supp. XXIII:** 108

Wolitzer, Meg, **Supp. XV:** 65

Wolkomir, Richard, **Supp. XXII:** 218

Wollaston, William, **II:** 108

Wollstonecraft, Mary, **Supp. I Part 1:** 126; **Supp. I Part 2:** 512, 554

"Wolves in the Asheville Zoo, The" (Rash), **Supp. XXVII:** 220

"Wolves in the Marsh" (Dubus III), **Supp. XXIV:** 99–100

Womack, Craig, **Supp. XXIII:** 147, 153, 154–155

"Woman" (Bogan), **Supp. X:** 102

"Woman, I Got the Blues" (Komunyakaa), **Supp. XIII:** 117

"Woman, Why Are You Weeping?" (Kenyon), **Supp. VII:** 174–175

"Woman, Young and Old, A" (Paley), **Supp. VI:** 222, 225

Woman Aroused, The (Lacy), **Supp. XV:** 199–200

"Woman at the Pond, The" (Rash), **Supp. XXVII:** 215, 230

Woman at the Washington Zoo, The (Jarrell), **II:** 367, 386, 387, 389

Woman Before an Aquarium (Hampl), **Supp. XXII:** 83, 86, 98

"Woman Before an Aquarium" (Hampl), **Supp. XXII:** 85, 98

"Womand and the Woman's Movement" (Briggs), **Supp. XVIII:** 14

"Woman Dead in Her Forties, A" (Rich), **Supp. I Part 2:** 574–575

Woman Driver, The (Thompson), **Supp. XXIII:** 291, **294–295**

"Woman Enough" (Gallagher), **Supp. XXIV:** 169

"Woman Hanging from the Thirteenth Floor Window, The" (Harjo), **Supp. XII:** 216, 221

"Woman Hollering Creek" (Cisneros), **Supp. VII:** 70

Woman Hollering Creek and Other Stories (Cisneros), **Supp. VII:** 58, 68–70

"Womanhood" (Brooks), **Supp. III Part 1:** 77

"Woman in Rain" (X. J. Kennedy), **Supp. XV:** 168

Woman in the Dark (Hammett), **Supp. IV Part 1:** 343

"Woman in the House, A" (Caldwell), **I:** 310

Woman in the Nineteenth Century (Fuller), **Retro. Supp. I:** 156; **Supp. II Part 1:** 279, 292, 294–296; **Supp. XI:** 197, 203; **Supp. XVIII:** 3, 11

"Woman in the Shoe, The" (Ryan as Quin), **Supp. XVIII:** 231

Woman in White, The (Collins), **Supp. I Part 1:** 35, 36

"Woman Is Talking to Death, A" (Grahn), **Supp. XXIII:** 195

"Womanizer, The" (Ford), **Supp. V:** 71, 72

"Woman Like Yourself, A" (C. Frost), **Supp. XV:** 107

Woman Lit by Fireflies, The (Harrison), **Supp. VIII: 50–51**

"Woman Loses Cookie Bake-Off, Sets Self on Fire" (R. O. Butler), **Supp. XII:** 72

Woman of Andros, The (Wilder), **IV:** 356, 363–364, 367, 368, 374

Woman of Means, A (Taylor), **Supp. V:** 319–320

"Woman of Tomorrow, The" (Atherton), **Supp. XXIV:** 29

Woman on the Edge of Time (Piercy), **Supp. XIII:** 29

Woman on the Porch, The (Gordon), **II:** 199, 209–211

"Woman on the Stair, The" (MacLeish), **III:** 15–16

"Woman's Dream, A" (E. Stoddard), **Supp. XV:** 278

Woman's Fiction: A Guide to Novels By and About Women in America, 1820–1870 (Baym), **Supp. XVIII:** 258

"Woman's Heartlessness" (Thaxter), **Retro. Supp. II:** 147

Woman's Honor (Glaspell), **Supp. III Part 1:** 179

"Woman Singing" (Ortiz), **Supp. IV Part 2:** 513

Woman's Place, A (C. L. R. James and Weinstein), **Supp. XXI:** 170

Woman's Share in Primitive Culture (Mason), **Supp. I Part 1:** 18

"Woman Struck by Car Turns into Nymphomaniac" (R. O. Butler), **Supp. XII:** 72

"Woman's Work" (Alvarez), **Supp. VII:** 4

"Woman Taken in Adultery, A" (Thompson), **Supp. XXIII:** 300

"Woman Uses Glass Eye to Spy on Philandering Husband" (R. O. Butler), **Supp. XII:** 70, 72

Woman Warrior (Kingston), **Supp. IV Part 1:** 12; **Supp. V:** 157, 158, 159, 160–164, 166, 169; **Supp. X:** 291–292; **Supp. XIV:** 162

Woman Warrior, The (Kingston), **Supp. XV:** 220

"Woman Who Believed in Jaguars, The" (Rash), **Supp. XXVII:** 228

Woman Who Fell from the Sky, The (Harjo), **Supp. XII: 226–228**

"Woman Who Fell From the Sky, The" (Iroquois creation story), **Supp. IV Part 1:** 327

Woman Who Owned the Shadows, The (Gunn Allen), **Supp. IV Part 1:** 320, 322, 326, 327–328

"Woman Who Plays Trumpet Is Deported, A" (Cliff), **Supp. XXII:** 74

"Woman Who Prayed, The" (Gallagher), **Supp. XXIV:** 175

"Woman Who Raised Goats, The" (Gallagher), **Supp. XXIV:** 168

"Woman Who Went Backwards, The" (Schott), **Supp. XXIII:** 241

Woman Within, The (Glasgow), **II:** 183, 190–191

"Womanwork" (Gunn Allen), **Supp. IV Part 1:** 326

Women (Bukowski), **Supp. XI:** 172

"Women" (Didion), **Supp. IV Part 1:** 205

"Women" (Swenson), **Supp. IV Part 2:** 647

Women, The (Boyle), **Supp. XX: 24, 26–27**

Women, The (film), **Retro. Supp. I:** 113

Women, The (film; Cukor), **Supp. XVI:** 181, 192

"Women and Children First" (Prose), **Supp. XVI:** 254

Women and Children First: Stories (Prose), **Supp. XVI:** 254

Women and Economics (Gilman), **Supp. I Part 2:** 637; **Supp. V:** 284; **Supp. XI:** 200, **203–204,** 206

"Women and Poetry" (Notley), **Supp. XXII:** 236

Women and Thomas Harrow (Marquand), **III:** 50, 61, 62, 66, 68, 69–70, 71

Women and Vodka (Markson as Merrill, ed.), **Supp. XVII:** 136

Women and Wilderness (LaBastille), **Supp. X:** 97, **102–104**

"Women as They Are" (Rowson), **Supp. XV:** 243

Women at Point Sur, The (Jeffers), **Supp. II Part 2:** 430–431

Women Authors of Our Day in Their Homes (Halsey), **Supp. XXIV:** 20

Women in Love (Lawrence), **III:** 27, 34; **Supp. XXIV:** 58

Women in Praise of the Sacred: 43 Centuries of Spiritual Poetry by Women (Hirshfield, ed.), **Supp. XXIII:** 136, 137

"Women of Auschwitz, The" (Gallagher), **Supp. XXIV:** 171

Women of Belize: Gender and Change in Central America (McClaurin), **Supp. XXIII:** 84

Women of Brewster Place, The: A Novel in Seven Stories (Naylor), **Supp. VIII:** 213, **214–218**

Women of Manhattan: An Upper West Side Story (Shanley), **Supp. XIV:** 315, **326–327**

"Women of My Color" (Coleman), **Supp. XI:** 88–89

Women of Mystery: The Lives and Works of Notable Women Crime Novelists (DuBose), **Supp. XXV:** 199

Women of Trachis (Pound, trans.), **III:** 476

"Women on the Breadlines" (Le Sueur), **Supp. XXIII:** 166, 167

Women on the Wall, The (Stegner), **Supp. IV Part 2:** 599, 605, 606

Women Poets in English (Stanford, ed.), **Retro. Supp. I:** 41

"Women Reformers and American Culture, 1870–1930" (Conway), **Supp. I Part 1:** 19

Women's Barracks (T. Levin), **Supp. XXVII:** 140

"Women's Movement, The" (Didion), **Supp. IV Part 1:** 206

"Women Waiting" (Shields), **Supp. VII:** 320

"Women We Love Whom We Never See Again" (R. Bly), **Supp. IV Part 1:** 66

"Women We Never See Again" (R. Bly), **Supp. IV Part 1:** 66

Women Who Make Our Novels, The (Overton), **Supp. XXV:** 200

Women with Men (Ford), **Supp. V:** 57, 71–72

"Wonder" (Olds), **Supp. X:** 210

Wonder Boys (Chabon), **Supp. XI:** 67, **73–75, Supp. XI:** 78; **Supp. XVI:** 259

Wonder Boys (film), **Supp. XI:** 67

Wonderful O, The (Thurber), **Supp. I Part 2:** 612

"Wonderful Old Gentleman, The" (Parker), **Supp. IX:** 197

"Wonderful Pen, The" (Swenson), **Supp. IV Part 2:** 650

Wonderful Wizard of Oz, The (Baum), **Supp. XXV:** 129

Wonderful Words, Silent Truth: Essays on Poetry and a Memoir (Simic), **Supp. VIII:** 270

Wonder Hat and Other One-Act Plays, The (Hecht and Goodman), **Supp. XXVII:** 89

Wonderland (Oates), **Supp. II Part 2:** 511, 512, 514–515

Wonders Hidden (Sanders), **Supp. XVI:** 269

Wonders of the African World (television series), **Supp. XX:** 99

Wonders of the Invisible World, The (Mather), **Supp. II Part 2:** 456–459, 460, 467

Wonder-Working Providence (E. Johnson), **IV:** 157

Wong, Hertha, **Supp. IV Part 1:** 275

Wong, Jade Snow, **Supp. X:** 291

Wong, Nellie, **Supp. XVII:** 72

Wong, Shawn, **Supp. XV:** 221

Wong, Timothy, **Supp. XVIII:** 94

"Wood" (Nye), **Supp. XIII:** 276

Wood, Audrey, **IV:** 381

Wood, Charles Erskine Scott, **Supp. XV:** 301

Wood, Clement, **Supp. XV:** 298

Wood, Clement Biddle, **Supp. XI:** 307

Wood, Gaby, **Supp. XXIV:** 166

Wood, Harrison, **Supp. XXII:** 283

Wood, Mrs. Henry, **Supp. I Part 1:** 35

Wood, James, **Supp. XIV:** 95–96; **Supp. XIX:** 138

Wood, Mabel, **I:** 199

Wood, Michael, **Supp. IV Part 2:** 691

Wood, Norman Barton, **Supp. XIV:** 201

Wood, Susan, **Supp. XVI:** 123

Woodard, Calvin, **Supp. VIII:** 128

Woodard, Charles L., **Supp. IV Part 2:** 484, 493

Woodard, Deborah, **Supp. XIII:** 114

Woodberry, George Edward, **III:** 508

Woodbridge, Frederick, **I:** 217, 224

Woodbridge, John, **Supp. I Part 1:** 101, 102, 114

Woodbury, Hanni, **Supp. XXVI:** 8, 82, 87, 90, 95

"Wood-Choppers, The" (Chopin), **Retro. Supp. II:** 72

Woodcock, George, **Supp. XIII:** 33

Woodcome, Beth, **Supp. XVII:** 240

"Wood Dove at Sandy Spring, The" (MacLeish), **III:** 19

"Wooden Spring" (Rukeyser), **Supp. VI:** 285

"Wooden Umbrella, The" (Porter), **IV:** 26

Woodhull, Victoria, **Supp. XVIII:** 4

"Woodnotes" (Emerson), **II:** 7, 19

"Wood-Pile, The" (Frost), **Retro. Supp. I:** 128; **Supp. IV Part 2:** 445

Woodrow, James, **Supp. I Part 1:** 349, 366

"Woods, Books, and Truant Officers, The" (Maclean), **Supp. XIV:** 221, 225

Woods, James, **Supp. XXVII:** 277

"Woods, New York, The" (Bronk), **Supp. XXI:** 27

Woods, Paula L., **Supp. XXI:** 70

Woods, Robert A., **Supp. I Part 1:** 19

Woods, The (Mamet), **Supp. XIV:** 241, 254–255

Woodswoman (LaBastille), **Supp. X:** 95, 96–99, 108

Woodswoman III: Book Three of the Woodswoman's Adventures (LaBastille), **Supp. X:** 95, 106–107

"Wood Thrush" (Kenyon), **Supp. VII:** 172

Woodward, C. Vann, **IV:** 114, 470–471; **Retro. Supp. I:** 75, 76; **Supp. XIX:** 152; **Supp. XXII:** 194

"Woof: A Plea of Sorts" (Saunders), **Supp. XIX:** 235

"Wooing the Inanimate" (Brodsky), **Supp. VIII:** 32

Woolcott, Alexander, **Supp. IX:** 197

Wooley, Bryan, **Supp. V:** 225

Woolf, Douglas, **Supp. XXIII:** 174

Woolf, Leonard, **Supp. IX:** 95

Woolf, Virginia, **I:** 53, 79, 112, 309; **II:** 320, 415; **IV:** 59; **Retro. Supp. I:** 59, 75, 170, 215, 291, 359; **Supp. I Part 2:** 553, 714, 718; **Supp. IV Part 1:** 299; **Supp. IX:** 66, 109; **Supp. V:** 127; **Supp. VIII:** 5, 155, 251, 252, 263, 265; **Supp. XI:** 134, 193; **Supp. XII:** 81, 98, 289; **Supp. XIII:** 305; **Supp. XIV:** 341–342, 342, 343, 346, 348; **Supp. XIX:** 134; **Supp. XV:** 55, 65; **Supp. XXIII:** 275; **Supp. XXVII:** 183

Woollcott, Alexander, **IV:** 432; **Retro. Supp. II:** 327; **Supp. I Part 2:** 664; **Supp. IX:** 190, 194

Woolley, Leonard, **Supp. XXIII:** 33

Woollstonecraft, Mary, **Supp. XVI:** 184

"Woolly Mammoth" (X. J. Kennedy), **Supp. XV:** 163–164

Woolman, John, **Supp. VIII:** 202, 204, 205

Woolson, Constance Fenimore, **Retro. Supp. I:** 224, 228

Woolverton, Linda, **Supp. XXI:** 148

Wooster, David, **Supp. XX:** 288

Worcester, Samuel, **I:** 458

Word and Idioms: Studies in the English Language (L. P. Smith), **Supp. XIV:** 343

"Word by Word" (column, Lamott), **Supp. XX:** 140

"Word from the Outer Dark, A" (Howard), **Supp. XXVII:** 118

"Wordless Winter" (Davison), **Supp. XXVI:** 75–76

Word of God and the Word of Man, The (Barth), **Retro. Supp. I:** 327

"Word out of the Sea, A" (Whitman), **IV:** 344

Words (Creeley), **Supp. IV Part 1:** 139, 150–153, 154, 155, 158

"Words" (Creeley), **Supp. IV Part 1:** 152

"Words" (Gioia), **Supp. XV:** 125

"Words" (Merwin), **Supp. III Part 1:** 352

"Words" (Plath), **Supp. I Part 2:** 547

"Words" (Shields), **Supp. VII:** 323

"Words, The" (Wagoner), **Supp. IX:** 326

"Words above a Narrow Entrance" (Wagoner), **Supp. IX:** 325

"Words for a Bike-Racing, Osprey-Chasing Wine-Drunk Squaw Man" (Gunn Allen), **Supp. IV Part 1:** 325

Words for Dr. Y (Sexton), **Supp. II Part 2:** 698

"Words for Hart Crane" (R. Lowell), **I:** 381; **II:** 547; **Retro. Supp. II:** 188

"Words for Love" (Berrigan), **Supp. XXIV:** 35

"Words for Maria" (Merrill), **Supp. III Part 1:** 327

"Words for My Father" (Davison), **Supp. XXVI:** 72

"Words for My Grandmother"(Balakian), **Supp. XXIII:** 19, 20

Words for the Chisel (Taggard), **Supp. XXII:** 276–277

"Words for the Unknown Makers" (Kunitz), **Supp. III Part 1:** 264

Words for the Wind (Roethke), **III:** 529, 533, 541, 543, 545

"Words for the Wind" (Roethke), **III:** 542–543

Words in the Mourning Time (Hayden), **Supp. II Part 1:** 361, 366, 367

"Words in the Mourning Time" (Hayden), **Supp. II Part 1:** 370–371

"Words into Fiction" (Welty), **IV:** 279

"Words into Worlds Won't Go" (Major), **Supp. XXII:** 174

"Words Like Freedom" (Hughes), **Retro. Supp. I:** 207

"Words of a Young Girl" (R. Lowell), **II:** 554

"Words of Prey" (Stallings), **Supp. XXV:** 230

Words under the Words: Selected Poems (Nye), **Supp. XIII:** 277

Wordsworth, Dorothy, **Supp. IX:** 38

Wordsworth, William, **I:** 283, 522, 524, 525, 588; **II:** 7, 11, 17, 18, 97, 169, 273, 303, 304, 532, 549, 552; **III:** 219, 263, 277, 278, 511, 521, 523, 528, 583; **IV:** 120, 331, 343, 453, 465; **Retro. Supp. I:** 121, 196; **Supp. I Part 1:** 150, 151, 154, 161, 163, 312, 313, 349, 365; **Supp. I Part 2:** 375, 409, 416, 422, 607, 621, 622, 673, 674, 675, 676, 677, 710–711, 729; **Supp. II Part 1:** 4; **Supp. III Part 1:** 12, 15, 73, 279; **Supp. IV Part 2:** 597, 601; **Supp. IX:** 38, 41, 265, 274; **Supp. V:** 258; **Supp. VIII:** 273; **Supp. X:** 22, 23, 65, 120; **Supp. XI:** 248, 251, 312; **Supp. XIII:** 214; **Supp. XIV:** 184; **Supp. XIX:** 1; **Supp. XV:** 93, 250; **Supp. XX:** 108, 116; **Supp. XXI:** 131; **Supp. XXIV:** 74, 159

" 'Word Which Made All Clear, The': The Silent Close of *The House of Mirth*" (Benstock), **Supp. XX:** 240

Work (Alcott), **Supp. I Part 1:** 32–33, 42

Work (Dixon), **Supp. XII:** 141, 143

"Work" (Halliday), **Supp. XIX:** 85

"Work" (Huddle), **Supp. XXVI:** 149

"Work" (Oliver), **Supp. VII:** 243

Work and Love (Dunn), **Supp. XI:** 147–148

"Worker" (Coleman), **Supp. XI:** 89

Worker Writers (Le Sueur), **Supp. XXIII:** 165

Working a Passage; or, Life on a Liner (Briggs), **Supp. XVIII:** 2, **9–10**

Working Class Movement in America, The (E. Marx and E. Aveling), **Supp. XVI:** 85

Working Papers: Selected Essays and Reviews (Carruth), **Supp. XVI:** 46

"Working Roots: A Collection of Poetry and Prose" (Trethewey), **Supp. XXI:** 245

"Working the Landscape" (Dunn), **Supp. XI:** 151

Working Through: A Teacher's Journey in the Urban University (Kriegel), **Supp. XXIV: 222–223**

Workin' on the Chain Gang: Shaking Off the Dead Hand of History (Mosley), **Supp. XIII:** 247, 248

Workman, Ross, **Supp. XXVII:** 206, 209–210

"Work Notes '66" (Baraka), **Supp. II Part 1:** 47

Work of Art (Lewis), **II:** 453–454

"Work of Shading, The" (Simic), **Supp. VIII:** 277–278

Work of Stephen Crane, The (Follett, ed.), **I:** 405

"Work on Red Mountain, The" (Harte), **Supp. II Part 1:** 339

Works and Days (Erga Kai Hémerai) (Hesiod; Stallings, trans.), **Supp. XXV:** 221

"Workshop" (Espaillat), **Supp. XXI:** 105

Works of Love, The (Morris), **III:** 223–224, 225, 233

Works of Witter Bynner, The (Kraft, ed.), **Supp. XV:** 52

"World, The" (Bronk), **Supp. XXI:** 32

"World, The" (Simic), **Supp. VIII:** 282

"World, the Flesh, and the Devil, The"(P. Benedict), **Supp. XXIII:** 48

World, the Worldless, The (Bronk), **Supp. XXI: 29–31**

"World, World—" (Oppen), **Supp. XXVI:** 233

World According to Garp, The (Irving), **Supp. VI:** 163, 164, **170–173,** 181

World and Africa, The: An Inquiry into the Part Which Africa Has Played in World History (Du Bois), **Supp. II Part 1:** 184–185

"World and All Its Teeth, The" (Nye), **Supp. XIII:** 282

"World and the Door, The" (O. Henry), **Supp. II Part 1:** 402

"World and the Jug, The" (Ellison), **Retro. Supp. II:** 112, 119, 123

"World as We Know It, The" (Barresi), **Supp. XV:** 100

World Authors 1950–1970, **Supp. XIII:** 102

World Away, A (O'Nan), **Supp. XXV:** 141, 144–145, 149

World Below, The (Miller), **Supp. XII: 303–304**

World Below the Window, The: Poems 1937–1997 (W. J. Smith), **Supp. XIII:** 332, 340, 345

World Doesn't End, The (Simic), **Supp. VIII:** 272, **279–280**

World Elsewhere, A: The Place of Style in American Literature (Poirier), **I:** 239

"World Ends Here, The" (Harjo), **Supp. XII:** 227–228

World Enough and Time (Warren), **IV:** 243, 253–254

World Gone Wrong (album, Dylan), **Supp. XVIII:** 28

"World I Live In, The" (T. Williams), **IV:** 388

World I Never Made, A (Farrell), **II:** 34, 35, 424

World in the Attic, The (Morris), **III:** 222–223, 224

World in the Evening, The (Isherwood), **Supp. XIV:** 157, 164, 165, **166–167,** 170

World Is a Wedding, The (Schwartz), **Supp. II Part 2:** 643, 654–660

"World Is a Wedding, The" (Schwartz), **Supp. II Part 2:** 655–656, 657

"World Is Too Much with Us, The" (Wordsworth), **Supp. I Part 1:** 312

Worldly Hopes (Ammons), **Supp. VII:** 34

Worldly Philosophers, The (Heilbroner), **Supp. I Part 2:** 644, 650

World Made Straight, The (film), **Supp. XXVII:** 222

World Made Straight, The (Rash), **Supp. XXVII:** 222, 224, 228, 229

World of Apples, The (Cheever), **Supp. I Part 1:** 191, 193

World of David Wagoner, The (McFarland), **Supp. IX:** 323

"World of Easy Rawlins, The" (Mosley), **Supp. XIII:** 234, 236

World of Gwendolyn Brooks, The (Brooks), **Supp. III Part 1:** 83, 84

World of H. G. Wells, The (Brooks), **I:** 240, 241, 242

World of Light, A (Skloot), **Supp. XX: 196, 205, 206–207**

"World of Light, A" (Skloot), **Supp. XX: 194, 207**

World of Light, A: Portraits and Celebrations (Sarton), **Supp. III Part 1:** 62; **Supp. VIII:** 249, 253, 262

World of Our Fathers: The Journey of the Eastern European Jews to America and the Life They Found and Made (Howe), **Supp. VI:** 113, 114, 116, 118, 119, **120–125; Supp. XIV:**104; **Supp. XXIII:** 3; **Supp. XXVI:** 220–221

"World of Pure Experience, A" (James), **II:** 356–357

World of Raymond Chandler, The (Spender), **Supp. IV Part 1:** 119

World of Sex, The (H. Miller), **III:** 170, 178, 187

"World of the Perfect Tear, The" (McGrath), **Supp. X:** 116, 118

World of the Ten Thousand Things, The: Selected Poems (Wright), **Supp. V:** 333

"World of Tomorrow, The" (White), **Supp. I Part 2:** 663

World of Washington Irving, The (Brooks), **I:** 256–257

World Over, The (Wharton), **Retro. Supp. I:** 382

World Revolution (C. L. R. James), **Supp. XXI:** 167

"Worlds" (Goldbarth), **Supp. XII:** 183, 189

World's Body, The (Ransom), **III:** 497, 499; **Supp. II Part 1:** 146

World's End (Boyle), **Supp. VIII: 11–12; Supp. XX: 22–23**

World's End and Other Stories (Theroux), **Supp. VIII:** 322

"World's Fair" (Berryman), **I:** 173

World's Fair (Doctorow), **Supp. IV Part 1:** 217, 224, 227–229, 234, 236–237

World's Fair, The (Fitzgerald), **II:** 93

Worlds of Color (Du Bois), **Supp. II Part 1:** 185–186

"Worlds of Color" (Du Bois), **Supp. II Part 1:** 175

World So Wide (Lewis), **II:** 456

"World's Worst Boyfriends, The" (Wasserstein), **Supp. XV:** 328

"World-Telegram" (Berryman), **I:** 173

World to Come, The (D. Horn), **Supp. XVII:** 50

"World Trade Center / Mail runner / '73"(Balakian), **Supp. XXIII:** 32–33

World View on Race and Democracy: A Study Guide in Human Group Relations (Locke), **Supp. XIV:** 205, 206

World within the Word, The (Gass), **Supp. VI:** 77

"World Without Objects Is a Sensible Place, A" (Wilbur), **Supp. III Part 2:** 550

"World Without Rodrigo, The" (Cisneros), **Supp. VII:** 68

"Worm Moon" (Oliver), **Supp. VII:** 234

Wormser, Baron, **Supp. XXIII:** 57

"Worms of the Earth" (Howard), **Supp. XXVII:** 123–124

"Worn Path, A" (Welty), **IV:** 262; **Retro. Supp. I:** 345–346

"Worsening Situation" (Ashbery), **Supp. III Part 1:** 17–18

"Worship" (Emerson), **II:** 2, 4–5

"Worship" (H. Johnson), **Supp. XXVI:** 172

"Worship and Church Bells" (Paine), **Supp. I Part 2:** 521

Worster, Donald, **Supp. IX:** 19

Worthington, Marjorie, **Supp. XII:** 13

Wouk, Herman, **Supp. XX: 243; Supp. XXV: 253–270; Supp. XXVII:** 134, 147

Wouldn't Take Nothing for My Journey Now (Angelou), **Supp. IV Part 1:** 10, 12, 14, 15, 16

"Wound" (Pedersen; Nelson, trans.), **Supp. XVIII:** 180

Wound and the Bow, The: Seven Studies in Literature (Wilson), **IV:** 429; **Supp. XXIV:** 217

Wounded (Everett), **Supp. XVIII:** 54, **64,** 65

Wounds in the Rain (Crane), **I:** 409, 414, 423

Woven Stone (Ortiz), **Supp. IV Part 2:** 501, 514

Woven Stories (Ortiz), **Supp. IV Part 2:** 503

"Wraith, The" (Roethke), **III:** 542

"Wrath of God, The" (Fante), **Supp. XI:** 160, 164

"Wreath for a Bridal" (Plath), **Supp. I Part 2:** 537

"Wreath for Emmet Till, A" (Nelson), **Supp. XVIII:** 177

Wreath for Emmett Till, A (Nelson), **Supp. XVIII:** 171, 173, 175, 181, **183–185**

Wreath for Garibaldi and Other Stories, A (Garrett), **Supp. VII:** 99–101

"Wreath of Women" (Rukeyser), **Supp. VI:** 280

Wreckage (Jin), **Supp. XVIII: 98–99**

Wreckage of Agathon, The (Gardner), **Supp. VI:** 63, **65–66**

Wrecking Crew (Levis), **Supp. XI: 259–260**

Wrecking Yard, The (Benedict), **Supp. XXIII:** 35, **39–41**

"Wrecking Yard, The (P. Benedict), **Supp. XXIII:** 39–40

"Wreck of Rivermouth, The" (Whittier), **Supp. I Part 2:** 694, 696–697

"Wreck of the Deutschland" (Hopkins), **Supp. X:** 61

"Wreck of the Hesperus, The" (Longfellow), **Retro. Supp. II:** 168, 169

Wrestler's Cruel Study, The (Dobyns), **Supp. XIII: 82–83**

"Wrestler with Sharks, A" (Yates), **Supp. XI:** 341

"Wrestling with Augie March" (Kriegel), **Supp. XXIV:** 220

Wright, Bernie, **I:** 191, 193

Wright, C. D. (Carolyn Doris), **Supp. XV: 337–355**

Wright, Charles, **Supp. V:** 92, **331–346; Supp. VIII:** 272; **Supp. XIII:** 114; **Supp. XVII:** 71; **Supp. XXI:** 95, 255; **Supp. XXIV:** 155

Wright, Chauncey, **II:** 344

Wright, Conrad, **Supp. XXIV:** 71, 72

Wright, Farnworth, **Supp. XXVII:** 120, 125

Wright, Frank Lloyd, **I:** 104, 483

Wright, Franz, **Supp. XVII: 239–249**

Wright, George, **III:** 479

Wright, Harold Bell, **II:** 467–468

Wright, Holly, **Supp. VIII:** 272

Wright, James, **I:** 291; **Supp. III Part 1:** 249; **Supp. III Part 2:** 541, **589–607; Supp. IV Part 1:** 60, 70; **Supp. IV Part 2:** 557, 558, 561, 566, 571, 623; **Supp. IX:** 152, 155, 159, 265, 271, 290, 293, 296; **Supp. V:** 332; **Supp. X:** 69, 127; **Supp. XI:** 150; **Supp. XII:** 217; **Supp. XIII:** 76; **Supp. XIX:** 122, 273; **Supp. XV:** 79, 93, 212; **Supp. XVII:** 239, 241, 243, 244; **Supp. XXVI:** 68

Wright, Nathalia, **IV:** 155

Wright, Philip Green, **III:** 578, 579, 580

Wright, Richard, **II:** 586; **IV:** 40, **474–497; Retro. Supp. II:** 4, 111, 116,

120; **Supp. I Part 1:** 51, 52, 64, 332, 337; **Supp. II Part 1:** 17, 40, 221, 228, 235, 250; **Supp. IV Part 1:** 1, 11, 84, 374; **Supp. IX:** 316; **Supp. VIII:** 88; **Supp. X:** 131, 245, 254; **Supp. XI:** 85; **Supp. XII:** 316; **Supp. XIII:** 46, 233; **Supp. XIV:** 73; **Supp. XVI:** 135, 139, 141, 143; **Supp. XVIII:** 277, 282, 286; **Supp. XXI:** 169; **Supp. XXIII:** 166

Wright, Mrs. Richard (Ellen Poplar), **IV:** 476

Wright, Sarah, **Supp. IV Part 1:** 8; **Supp. XIII:** 295

Wright, William, **Retro. Supp. II:** 76, 77

Wrigley, Robert, **Supp. XVIII: 293–308**

"Writer" (Sanders), **Supp. XVI:** 277

"Writer, The" (Wilbur), **Supp. III Part 2:** 561, 562

"Writer and the Jewish Community, The" (Levin), **Supp. XXVII:** 134

"Writer as Alaskan, The" (Haines), **Supp. XII:** 199

Writer in America, The (Brooks), **I:** 253, 254, 257

Writer in America, The (Stegner), **Supp. IV Part 2:** 597, 599, 607

"Writers" (R. Lowell), **II:** 554

Writer's Almanac, The (Keillor, radio program), **Supp. XIII:** 274; **Supp. XVI:** 178; **Supp. XXIII:** 138

Writer's America, A: Landscape in Literature (Kazin), **Supp. VIII:** 106

Writers and Their Craft (Delbanco, ed.), **Supp. XXII:** 204

"Writer's Bed, A" (Mirvis), **Supp. XX: 179**

Writer's Capital, A (Auchincloss), **Supp. IV Part 1:** 21, 23, 24, 31

"Writer's Credo, A" (Abbey), **Supp. XIII:** 1, 17

Writer's Eye, A: Collected Book Reviews (Welty), **Retro. Supp. I:** 339, 354, 356

Writers in America (Schulberg), **Supp. XVIII:** 242, 243, 250, 254

Writers in Revolt (Southern, Seaver, and Trocchi, eds.), **Supp. XI:** 301

Writer's Life, A (Talese), **Supp. XVII:** 208–209, 210

Writer's Notebook, A (Maugham), **Supp. X:** 58

Writers on America (U.S. Department of State, ed.), **Supp. XIII:** 288

Writers on the Left (Aaron), **IV:** 429; **Supp. II Part 1:** 137

Writers on Writing (Prose), **Supp. XVI:** 259

"Writer's Prologue to a Play in Verse" (W. C. Williams), **Retro. Supp. I:** 424

"Writer's Quest for a Parnassus, A" (T. Williams), **IV:** 392

Writers' Workshop (University of Iowa), **Supp. V:** 42

"Writers Workshop, The" (Conroy), **Supp. XVI:** 76

"Writing" (Nemerov), **III:** 275

"Writing About the Universe" (Mosley), **Supp. XIII:** 247

"Writing American Fiction" (P. Roth), **Retro. Supp. II:** 279; **Supp. I Part 1:**

192; **Supp. I Part 2:** 431; **Supp. III Part 2:** 414, 420, 421; **Supp. V:** 45

"Writing and a Life Lived Well" (Patchett), **Supp. XII:** 308

"Writing and Writers: *Disjecta Membra*" (Sorrentino), **Supp. XXI:** 235

Writing a Woman's Life (Heilbrun), **Supp. IX:** 66

"Writing Between Worlds" (Mirvis), **Supp. XX: 177, 178, 179**

Writing Brave and Free: Encouraging Words for People Who Want to Start Writing (Kooser and Cox), **Supp. XIX:** 116, 128

Writing Chicago: Modernism, Ethnography, and the Novel (Cappetti), **Supp. IX:** 4, 8

Writing Creative Nonfiction: The Literature of Reality (Talese and Lounsberry, eds.), **Supp. XVII:** 208

Writing Dylan: The Songs of a Lonesome Traveler (Smith), **Supp. XVIII:** 22

Writing from the Center (Sanders), **Supp. XVI:** 266, 275–276

"Writing from the Inside Out: Style Is Not the Frosting; It's the Cake" (Robbins), **Supp. X:** 266

Writing Habit, The (Huddle), **Supp. XXVI:** 152, 160

"Writing Habit, The" (Huddle), **Supp. XXVI:** 160

"Writing here last autumn of my hopes of seeing a hoopoe" (Updike), **Retro. Supp. I:** 335

Writing Home (Crooker), **Supp. XXIII:** 54

Writing in an Age of Silence (Paretsky), **Supp. XXV:** 169, 181

Writing in Restaurants (Mamet), **Supp. XIV:** 246

"Writing Is Work" (Rinehart), **Supp. XXV:** 198

"Writing Lesson, The" (Gordon), **Supp. IV Part 1:** 306

Writing Life, The (Dillard), **Supp. VI:** 23, 31

"Writing of Apollinaire, The" (Zukofsky), **Supp. III Part 2:** 616, 617

"Writing of *Fearless Jones,* The" (Mosley), **Supp. XIII:** 242

Writing on the Wall, The, and Literary Essays (McCarthy), **II:** 579

Writings to an Unfinished Accompaniment (Merwin), **Supp. III Part 1:** 352

"Writing the Rez: Popular Obsessions in the Works of Eric Gansworth" (de la Paz and Purdy), **Supp. XXVI:** 102, 111

"Writing the Universe-Mind" (Tabios), **Supp. XV:** 225

Writing the World (Stafford), **Supp. XI:** 314

"Writing to Save Our Lives" (Milligan), **Supp. XIII:** 274

Writing Vietnam, Writing Life: Caputo, Heinemann, O'Brien, Butler (Herzog), **Supp. XXII:** 116

Writin' Is Fightin' (Reed), **Supp. X:** 241

"Writ on the Eve of My 32nd Birthday" (Corso), **Supp. XII:** 129–130

"Written History as an Act of Faith" (Beard), **Supp. I Part 2:** 492
"Written on the Land" (J. W. Miller), **Supp. XX: 170**
"Wrong Man, The" (Larsen), **Supp. XVIII:** 124
"Wrong Notes" (S. Kauffmann), **Supp. XVI:** 74
"Wrought Figure" (McCarriston), **Supp. XIV:** 272
Wrozynski, Henryk, **Supp. XXIII:** 64
"Wunderkind" (McCullers), **II:** 585
Wunderlich, Mark, **Supp. XI:** 119, 132
Wundt, Wilhelm, **II:** 345
Wurlitzer, Rudolph, **Supp. XXVI:** 26
Wurster, William Wilson, **Supp. IV Part 1:** 197
WUSA (film), **Supp. V:** 301
Wuthering Heights (E. Brontë), **Supp. V:** 305; **Supp. X:** 89
Wuthering Heights (screenplay, Hecht and MacArthur), **Supp. XXVII:** 90
WWII (Jones), **Supp. XI:** 219, 231
Wyandotté (Cooper), **I:** 350, 355
Wyatt, Robert B., **Supp. V:** 14
Wyatt, Thomas, **Supp. I Part 1:** 369
Wyce, Marion, **Supp. XXVI:** 57
Wycherly Woman, The (Macdonald), **Supp. IV Part 2:** 473
Wych Hazel (S. and A. Warner), **Supp. XVIII:** 267, **268–269**
Wydra, Ewa. *See* Hoffman, Eva
Wyeth, Andrew, **Supp. XIX:** 117
Wyler, William, **Supp. XV:** 195
Wylie, Elinor, **IV:** 436; **Supp. I Part 2: 707–730; Supp. III Part 1:** 2, 63, 318–319; **Supp. XI:** 44; **Supp. XIV:** 127; **Supp. XV:** 307; **Supp. XXVII:** 283, 284
Wylie, Horace, **Supp. I Part 2:** 708, 709
Wylie, Philip, **III:** 223
Wyllys, Ruth. *See* Taylor, Mrs. Edward (Ruth Wyllys)
"Wyoming Valley Tales" (Crane), **I:** 409
Wyzewa, Théodore de, **Supp. XIV:** 336

X

Xaipe (Cummings), **I:** 430, 432–433, 447
Xarque and Other Poems (G. Jones), **Supp. XXIV:** 194
Xenogenesis trilogy (O. Butler), **Supp. XIII: 63–66, 69**
Xenophon, **II:** 105
X Factor, The: A Quest for Excellence" (Plimpton), **Supp. XVI:** 241
X Files (television series), **Supp. XVI:** 125
Xiaojing, Zhou, **Supp. XV:** 214
Xicana Codex of Changing Consciousness, A: Writings, 2000–2010 (Moraga), **Supp. XXIII:** 197
Xingu and Other Stories (Wharton), **IV:** 314, 320; **Retro. Supp. I:** 378
Xionia (Wright), **Supp. V:** 333
XLI Poems (Cummings), **I:** 429, 432, 440, 443
Xu, Wenying, **Supp. XXVI:** 212
"Xuthal of the Dusk" (Howard), **Supp. XXVII:** 126

Y

Yabroff, Jennie, **Supp. XIX:** 50, 58, 61
Yacoubi, Ahmed, **Supp. IV Part 1:** 88, 92, 93
Yage Letters, The (Burroughs), **Supp. III Part 1:** 94, 98, 100
Yagoda, Ben, **Supp. VIII:** 151
Yamamoto, Isoroku, **Supp. I Part 2:** 491
Yancey's War (Hoffman), **Supp. XVIII:** 71, **75–76**
Yankee City (Warner), **III:** 60
Yankee Clipper (ballet) (Kirstein), **Supp. IV Part 1:** 82
Yankee in Canada, A (Thoreau), **IV:** 188
Yankey in London (Tyler), **I:** 344
"Yánnina" (Merrill), **Supp. III Part 1:** 329
"Yanosz Korczak's Last Walk" (Markowick-Olczakova), **Supp. X:** 70
Yarboro, Chelsea Quinn, **Supp. V:** 147
Yarbro-Bejarano, Yvonne, **Supp. XXIII:** 196, 201
Yardley, Jonathan, **Supp. V:** 326; **Supp. XI:** 67; **Supp. XXIII:** 97, 99, 103, 104, 107, 108, 109
"Yard Sale" (Kenyon), **Supp. VII:** 169
Yates, Richard, **Supp. XI: 333–350; Supp. XXIII:** 289; **Supp. XXIV:** 97; **Supp. XXV:** 154
"Year, The" (Sandburg), **III:** 584
Year at the Races, A (Parker and Parker), **Supp. XIX:** 187
Year Before Last (Boyle), **Supp. XXIV: 52–53**
"Year Between, The" (Neugeboren), **Supp. XVI:** 226
Year in Provence, A (Mayle), **Supp. XVI:** 295
Yearling, The (Rawlings), **Supp. X:** 219, **230–231**, 233, 234; **Supp. XXII:** 195
"Year of Grace" (Swados), **Supp. XIX:** 262–263
Year of Happy, A (Goldbarth), **Supp. XII:** 180
Year of Magical Thinking, The (Didion), **Supp. XXV:** 60, 208
"Year of Mourning, The" (Jeffers), **Supp. II Part 2:** 415
Year of Silence, The (Bell), **Supp. X:** 1, **5–6**, 7
"Year of Silence, The" (Brockmeier), **Supp. XXII:** 59
"Year of the Double Spring, The" (Swenson), **Supp. IV Part 2:** 647
Year's Best Fantasy and Horror, 2004, **Supp. XXII:** 55
Year's Best Science Fiction, The (Merril, ed.), **Supp. XVI:** 123
Year's Life, A (J. R. Lowell), **Supp. I Part 2:** 405
"Years of Birth" (Cowley), **Supp. II Part 1:** 149
Years of Conscience: The Muckrakers: An Anthology of Reform Journalism (Swados, ed.), **Supp. XIX:** 264
Years of My Youth (Howells), **II:** 276
"Years of Wonder" (White), **Supp. I Part 2:** 652, 653
"Years Without Understanding, The" (Weigl), **Supp. XIX:** 282–283
Years With Ross, The (Thurber), **Supp. I Part 2:** 619
Year the Lights Came On, The (Kay), **Supp. XXVII:** 104
Year We Left Home, The (Thompson), **Supp. XXIII:** 301, **302–303**
Yeats, Jack, **Supp. XVI:** 190
Yeats, Jack B., **Supp. XX: 201**
Yeats, John Butler, **III:** 458; **Supp. XX: 69**
Yeats, William Butler, **I:** 69, 172, 384, 389, 403, 434, 478, 494, 532; **II:** 168–169, 566, 598; **III:** 4, 5, 8, 18, 19, 20, 23, 29, 40, 205, 249, 269, 270–271, 272, 278, 279, 294, 347, 409, 457, 458–460, 472, 473, 476–477, 521, 523, 524, 527, 528, 533, 540, 541, 542, 543–544, 591–592; **IV:** 89, 93, 121, 126, 136, 140, 271, 394, 404; **Retro. Supp. I:** 59, 66, 127, 141, 270, 283, 285, 286, 288, 290, 311, 342, 350, 378, 413; **Retro. Supp. II:** 185, 331; **Supp. I Part 1:** 79, 80, 254, 257, 262; **Supp. I Part 2:** 388, 389; **Supp. II Part 1:** 1, 4, 9, 20, 26, 361; **Supp. III Part 1:** 59, 63, 236, 238, 253; **Supp. IV Part 1:** 81; **Supp. IV Part 2:** 634; **Supp. IX:** 43, 119; **Supp. V:** 220; **Supp. VIII:** 19, 21, 30, 155, 156, 190, 239, 262, 292; **Supp. X:** 35, 58, 119, 120; **Supp. XI:** 140; **Supp. XII:** 132, 198, 217, 266; **Supp. XIII:** 77, **Supp. XIII:** 87; **Supp. XIV:** 7; **Supp. XV:** 36, 41, 181, 186; **Supp. XVI:** 47–48, 159; **Supp. XVII:** 36; **Supp. XXI:** 61; **Supp. XXVII:** 227, 228
Yee, Amy, **Supp. XVIII:** 93, 94
"Ye Have Your Closes" (Davison), **Supp. XXVI:** 78
Yehuda (Levin), **Supp. XXVII:** 139, 146
Yellin, Jean Fagan, **Supp. XVI:** 88, 89
Yellow Back Radio Broke-Down (Reed), **Supp. X:** 240, 242, **243–245**
"Yellow Dog Café" (Komunyakaa), **Supp. XIII:** 126
Yellow Face (Hwang), **Supp. XXI:** 143, 148, **154–156**
"Yellow Girl" (Caldwell), **I:** 310
Yellow Glove (Nye), **Supp. XIII:** 275, **276–277**
"Yellow Glove" (Nye), **Supp. XIII:** 276
"Yellow Gown, The" (Anderson), **I:** 114
Yellow House on the Corner, The (Dove), **Supp. IV Part 1:** 244, 245, 246, 254
"Yellow Raft, The" (Connell), **Supp. XIV: 85–86**
"Yellow River" (Tate), **IV:** 141
Yellow Room, The (Rinehart), **Supp. XXV:** 198, 200
"Yellowstone, The"(Kenny), **Supp. XXIII:** 155
"Yellow Violet, The" (Bryant), **Supp. I Part 1:** 154, 155
"Yellow Wallpaper, The" (Gilman), **Supp. XI: 198–199**, 207; **Supp. XVI:** 84
"Yellow Woman" (Keres stories), **Supp. IV Part 1:** 327

"Yellow Woman" (Silko), **Supp. IV Part 2:** 567–568

Yelverton, Theresa, **Supp. IX:** 181

Yenser, Stephen, **Supp. X:** 207, 208; **Supp. XV:** 113–114

"Yentl the Yeshiva Boy" (Singer), **IV:** 15, 20

Yerkes, Charles E., **I:** 507, 512

Yerma (opera) (Bowles), **Supp. IV Part 1:** 89

Yertle the Turtle and Other Stories (Geisel), **Supp. XVI:** 109

"Yes" (Stafford), **Supp. XI:** 329

Yes, Mrs. Williams (W. C. Williams), **Retro. Supp. I:** 423

Yes, Yes, No, No (Kushner), **Supp. IX:** 133

"Yes and It's Hopeless" (Ginsberg), **Supp. II Part 1:** 326

"Yes"(Crooker), **Supp. XXIII:** 62

Yesenin, Sergey, **Supp. VIII:** 40

"Yes: I Mean So OK–Love" (Bronk), **Supp. XXI:** 31

"Yes! No!" (Oliver), **Supp. VII:** 243–244

Yesterday and Today: A Comparative Anthology of Poetry (Untermeyer, ed.), **Supp. XV:** 309

Yesterday's Self: Nostalgia and the Immigrant Identity (Ritivoi), **Supp. XVI:** 148

Yesterday Will Make You Cry (C. Himes), **Supp. XVI:** 137

"Yet Another Example of the Porousness of Certain Borders" (Wallace), **Supp. X:** 309

"Yet Do I Marvel" (Cullen), **Supp. IV Part 1:** 165, 169

Yet Other Waters (Farrell), **II:** 29, 38, 39, 40

"Yevtushenko" (Kooser), **Supp. XIX:** 124

Yevtushenko, Yevgeny, **Supp. III Part 1:** 268

Yezzi, David, **Supp. XII:** 193

Yiddish Policemen's Union, The (Chabon), **Supp. XXII:** 49

Yizkor Book, **Supp. XVI:** 154

...y no se lo tragó la tierra (Rivera), **Supp. XIX:** 99, 101

Y no se lo trago la tierra (And the Earth Did Not Cover Him) (Rivera), **Supp. XIII:** 216

¡Yo! (Alvarez), **Supp. VII:** 1, 15–17

"Yogurt of Vasirin Kefirovsky, The" (Apple), **Supp. XVII:** 3, 4

Yohannan, J. D., **II:** 20

"Yoke, The" (Bidart), **Supp. XV:** 33

Yonge, Charlotte, **II:** 174

"Yonnondio" (Whitman), **Supp. XIII:** 304

Yonnondio: From the Thirties (Olsen), **Supp. XIII:** 295, 295, **Supp. XIII:** 292, 296, **303–304,** 305

"Yore" (Nemerov), **III:** 283

York, Jake Adam, **Supp. XXI:** 257

York, Lorraine, **Supp. XX:** 51

"York Beach" (Toomer), **Supp. III Part 2:** 486

Yorke, Dorothy, **Supp. I Part 1:** 258

Yorke, Henry Vincent. *See* Green, Henry

"York Garrison, 1640" (Jewett), **Retro. Supp. II:** 141

Yosemite, The (Muir), **Supp. IX:** 185

"Yosemite Glaciers: Ice Streams of the Great Valley" (Muir), **Supp. IX:** 181

Yoshe Kalb (Singer), **IV:** 2

"You, Andrew Marvell" (MacLeish), **III:** 12–13

"You, Dr. Martin" (Sexton), **Supp. II Part 2:** 673

You, Emperors, and Others: Poems 1957–1960 (Warren), **IV:** 245

"You, Genoese Mariner" (Merwin), **Supp. III Part 1:** 343

"You, Reader" (Collins), **Supp. XXI:** 55

"You, Too, Will Have This Printed Word (World) of Your Own" (Gansworth), **Supp. XXVI:** 114

"You All Know the Story of the Other Woman" (Sexton), **Supp. II Part 2:** 688

"You Are Gorgeous and I'm Coming"(O'Hara), **Supp. XXIII:** 219

You Are Happy (Atwood), **Supp. XIII:** 34

"You Are Happy" (Atwood), **Supp. XIII:** 34

"You Are in Bear Country" (Kumin), **Supp. IV Part 2:** 453, 455

"You Are Not I" (Bowles), **Supp. IV Part 1:** 87

"You Begin" (Atwood), **Supp. XIII:** 34

You Bright and Risen Angels (Vollmann), **Supp. XVII:** 225, 226

"You Bring Out the Mexican in Me" (Cisneros), **Supp. VII:** 71

You Came Along (film), **Supp. IV Part 2:** 524

"You Can Go Home Again" (TallMountain), **Supp. IV Part 1:** 324–325

"You Can Have It" (Levine), **Supp. V:** 188–189

You Can't Go Home Again (Wolfe), **IV:** 450, 451, 454, 456, 460, 462, 468, 469, 470

You Can't Keep a Good Woman Down (Walker), **Supp. III Part 2:** 520, 525, 531

You Can't Pet a Possom (Bontemps), **Supp. XXII:** 4, 12

You Can't Take It with You (Kaufman and Hart), **Supp. XIV:** 327

"You Can't Tell a Man by the Song He Sings" (P. Roth), **Supp. III Part 2:** 406

"You Don't Know What Love Is" (Carver), **Supp. III Part 1:** 147

You Don't Love Me Yet (Lethem), **Supp. XVIII: 149–150**

"You Have Left Your Lotus Pods on the Bus" (Bowles), **Supp. IV Part 1:** 91

You Have Seen Their Faces (Caldwell), **I:** 290, 293–294, 295, 304, 309

You Know Me, Al: A Busher's Letters (Lardner), **Supp. XVI:** 189

You Know Me Al (comic strip), **II:** 423

You Know Me Al (Lardner), **II:** 26, 415, 419, 422, 431

"You Know More Than You Think You Do"(Hadas), **Supp. XXIII:** 124

"You Know What" (Beattie), **Supp. V:** 33

"You Know Who You Are" (Nye), **Supp. XIII:** 275

"You Live Like a God" (Cohen), **Supp. XXVII:** 60

You Might As Well Live: The Life and Times of Dorothy Parker (Keats), **Supp. IX:** 190

"You Must Relax!" (J. Scott), **Supp. XVII:** 189

You Must Revise Your Life (Stafford), **Supp. XI:** 312–313, 313–314, 315

"Young" (Sexton), **Supp. II Part 2:** 680

Young, Al, **Supp. X:** 240; **Supp. XXVI:** 12

Young, Art, **IV:** 436

Young, Barbara, **Supp. XX: 119, 123**

Young, Brigham, **Supp. IV Part 2:** 603

Young, Courtland, **Supp. XXII:** 21

Young, David, **Supp. XIX:** 276

Young, Dianne, **Supp. XXII:** 252

Young, Edward, **II:** 111; **III:** 415, 503

Young, Gary, **Supp. XV:** 88

Young, Hershini Bhana, **Supp. XXIV:** 189

Young, Mary, **Supp. XIII:** 236, 238, 239, 240

Young, Philip, **II:** 306; **Retro. Supp. I:** 172

Young, Stark, **Supp. XXII:** 193

Young Adventure (Benét), **Supp. XI:** 44

"Young America" (Brooks), **Supp. XV:** 298

Youngblood Hawke (film), **Supp. XXV:** 263

Youngblood Hawke (Wouk), **Supp. XXV:** 256, 257, 258, 259, 263

"Young Child and His Pregnant Mother, A" (Schwartz), **Supp. II Part 2:** 650

Young Christian, The (Abbott), **Supp. I Part 1:** 38

"Young Dr. Gosse" (Chopin), **Supp. I Part 1:** 211, 216

Younger Choir, The (anthology), **Supp. XV:** 294

Younger Quire, The (Untermeyer), **Supp. XV:** 294, 297

"Young Folks, The" (Salinger), **III:** 551

Young Folk's Cyclopaedia of Persons and Places (Champlin), **III:** 577

"Young Girl's Lament, A" (Jin), **Supp. XVIII:** 99

"Young Goodman Brown" (Hawthorne), **II:** 229; **Retro. Supp. I:** 151–152, 153, 154; **Supp. XI:** 51; **Supp. XIV:** 48, 50

Young Harvard: First Poems of Witter Bynner (Bynner), **Supp. XV:** 41

Young Hearts Crying (Yates), **Supp. XI:** 348

"Young Housewife, The" (W. C. Williams), **Retro. Supp. I:** 415

Young Immigrants, The (Lardner), **II:** 426

"Young Lady's Friend, The: Verses, Addressed to a Young Lady, on Her Leaving School" (Rowson), **Supp. XV:** 234

Young Landlords (Myers), **Supp. XXVII:** 204

"Young Lions" (E. P. Jones), **Supp. XXII:** 145

Young Lions, The (Shaw), **Supp. XIX:** **248–249**

Young Lonigan: A Boyhood in Chicago Streets (Farrell), **II:** 31, 41

Young Manhood of Studs Lonigan, The (Farrell), **II:** 31, 34

"Young Man on the Go" (column, Siddons), **Supp. XXII:** 244

Young Martin's Promise (Myers), **Supp. XXVII:** 209

Young Men and Fire (Maclean), **Supp. XIV:** 221, **231–233**

Young People's Pride (Benét), **Supp. XI:** 44

Young Poet's Primer (Brooks), **Supp. III Part 1:** 86

Youngren, J. Alan, **Supp. XVI:** 174

"Young Sammy's First Wild Oats" (Santayana), **III:** 607, 615

"Young Sor Juana, The" (Mora), **Supp. XIII:** 218

"Your Arkansas Traveler" (Schulberg), **Supp. XVIII:** 252

"Your Dailiness" (Notley), **Supp. XXII:** 227

"Your Death" (Dove), **Supp. IV Part 1:** 250

"You're History" (Hampl), **Supp. XXII:** 84, 95

You're Only Old Once! (Geisel), **Supp. XVI:** 111

"You're Ugly, Too" (Moore), **Supp. X:** 171

"Your Face on the Dog's Neck" (Sexton), **Supp. II Part 2:** 686

"Your Hand, Your Hand" (Hoffman), **Supp. XVIII:** 79

Your Job in Germany (film, Capra), **Supp. XVI:** 102

Your Job in Japan (film, Capra), **Supp. XVI:** 102

"Your Life" (Stafford), **Supp. XI:** 329

"Your Mother's Eyes" (Kingsolver), **Supp. VII:** 209

"You Take a Train through a Foreign Country" (Dobyns), **Supp. XIII:** 90

"Youth" (Hughes), **Supp. I Part 1:** 321; **Supp. XXII:** 12

"Youth" (Huncke), **Supp. XIV:** 145

Youth and Life (Bourne), **I:** 217–222, 232

Youth and the Bright Medusa (Cather), **I:** 322; **Retro. Supp. I:** 14

"Youthful Religious Experiences" (Corso), **Supp. XII:** 117

Youth of Parnassus, and Other Stories, The (L. P. Smith), **Supp. XIV:** 336

Youth's First Steps in Geography (Rowson), **Supp. XV:** 243

You Touched Me! (Williams and Windham), **IV:** 382, 385, 387, 390, 392–393

"You Touch Me" (X. J. Kennedy), **Supp. XV:** 166

You Went Away (Findley), **Supp. XX:** 49

"You Who Sleep Soundly Through Our Bleakest Hour" (Espaillat), **Supp. XXI:** 110

Yurchenco, Henrietta, **Supp. XVIII:** 20

Yurka, Blanche, **Supp. I Part 1:** 67

Yutang, Adet, **Supp. X:** 291

Yutang, Anor, **Supp. X:** 291

Yutang, Lin, **Supp. X:** 291; **Supp. XVI:** 190

Yutang, Mei-mei, **Supp. X:** 291

Yvernelle: A Legend of Feudal France (Norris), **III:** 314

Y & X (Olson), **Supp. II Part 2:** 556

Z

Zabel, Morton Dauwen, **II:** 431; **III:** 194, 215; **Supp. I Part 2:** 721

Zach, Natan, **Supp. XV:** 75, 82, 85

Zaehner, R. C., **Supp. XXII:** 258

Zagajewski, Adam, **Supp. XVII:** 241

Zagarell, Sandra, **Supp. XV:** 269, 270, 278, 281, 282

Zagarell, Sandra A., **Retro. Supp. II:** 140, 143

"Zagrowsky Tells" (Paley), **Supp. VI:** 229

Zaino, Nick, **Supp. XXII:** 207

Zakrzewska, Marie, **Retro. Supp. II:** 146

Zaleski, Jeff, **Supp. XI:** 143; **Supp. XIX:** 54; **Supp. XXVI:** 158

Zall, Paul, **Supp. XIV:** 156

Zaltzberg, Charlotte, **Supp. IV Part 1:** 374

"Zambesi and Ranee" (Swenson), **Supp. IV Part 2:** 647

Zamir, Israel, **Retro. Supp. II:** 303, 317

Zamora, Bernice, **Supp. IV Part 2:** 545

Zamoyski, Adam, **Supp. XV:** 257

Zangwill, Israel, **I:** 229; **Supp. XX:** 2

Zanita: A Tale of the Yosemite (Yelverton), **Supp. IX:** 181

Zanuck, Darryl F., **Supp. XI:** 170; **Supp. XII:** 165

Zapata, Emiliano, **Supp. XIII:** 324

"Zapatos" (Boyle), **Supp. VIII:** 15

Zapruder, Matthew, **Supp. XVI:** 55; **Supp. XXVI:** 54

Zarathustra, **III:** 602

Zawacki, Andrew, **Supp. VIII:** 272

"Zaydee" (Levine), **Supp. V:** 186

Zebra-Striped Hearse, The (Macdonald), **Supp. IV Part 2:** 473

Zechariah (biblical book), **IV:** 152

Zeidner, Lisa, **Supp. IV Part 2:** 453; **Supp. XXIII:** 297

"Zeitl and Rickel" (Singer), **IV:** 20

Zeke and Ned (McMurtry and Ossana), **Supp. V:** 232

Zeke Proctor, Cherokee Outlaw (Conley), **Supp. V:** 232

Zelazny, Roger, **Supp. XXV:** 73

Zelazo, Suzanne, **Supp. XXII:** 158, 167

Zelda: A Biography (Milford), **Supp. IX:** 60

"Zelda and Scott: The Beautiful and Damned" (National Portrait Gallery exhibit), **Supp. IX:** 65

Zelig (film; Allen), **Supp. XV:** 4, 6, **8–9**

Zeller, Maya Jewell, **Supp. XXIV:** 167

Zen and the Birds of Appetite (Merton), **Supp. VIII:** 205–206, 208

Zend-Avesta (Fechner), **II:** 358

"Zenith: Walker Creek" (Davison), **Supp. XXVI:** 74

Zeno, **Retro. Supp. I:** 247

Zero db and Other Stories (Bell), **Supp. X:** 1, 5, 6

"Zeus over Redeye" (Hayden), **Supp. II Part 1:** 380

Zevi, Sabbatai, **IV:** 6

Ziegfeld, Florenz, **II:** 427–428

Ziegler, Cyd, **Supp. XX:** 273

Ziegler, Heidi, **Supp. XXII:** 260

Ziggurat (Balakian), **Supp. XXIII:** 19, **32–33**

Zigrosser, Carl, **I:** 226, 228, 231

Zigzagger (Muñoz), **Supp. XXV:** 127, 132, 133, 134

"Zigzagger" (Muñoz), **Supp. XXV:** 134

Zilles, Klaus, **Supp. XIX:** 112

Zimmerman, Paul D., **Supp. IV Part 2:** 583, 589, 590

Zimmerman, Robert. *See* Dylan, Bob

Zimmerman, Robert Allen. *See* Dylan, Bob

Zinberg, Leonard S. *See* Lacy, Ed

Zinman, Toby Silverman, **Supp. XIII:** 207–208, 209

Zinn, Howard, **Supp. V:** 289; **Supp. XXIV:** 87

Zinovyev, Grigory, **Supp. XXI:** 167

Zinsser, Hans, **I:** 251, 385

Zip: A Novel of the Left and Right (Apple), **Supp. XVII:** 4–5

Zipes, Jack, **Supp. XIV:** 126

"Zipper, The" (L. Michaels), **Supp. XVI:** 214

Zitkala-Ša (Gertrude Simmons Bonnin), **Supp. XXV:** **271–287**

"Zizi's Lament" (Corso), **Supp. XII:** 123

Zodiac, The (Dickey), **Supp. IV Part 1:** 178, 183–184, 185

"Zog-19: A Scientific Romance"(P. Benedict), **Supp. XXIII:** 49

Zola, Émile, **I:** 211, 411, 474, 500, 502, 518; **II:** 174, 175–176, 182, 194, 275, 276, 281, 282, 319, 325, 337, 338; **III:** 315, 316, 317–318, 319–320, 321, 322, 323, 393, 511, 583; **IV:** 326; **Retro. Supp. I:** 226, 235; **Retro. Supp. II:** 93; **Supp. I Part 1:** 207; **Supp. II Part 1:** 117

Zolotow, Maurice, **III:** 161

"Zone" (Bogan), **Supp. III Part 1:** 60–61

Zone Journals (Wright), **Supp. V:** 332–333, 342–343

"Zooey" (Salinger), **III:** 564–565, 566, 567, 569, 572

"Zoo Revisited" (White), **Supp. I Part 2:** 654

Zoo Story, The (Albee), **I:** 71, 72–74, 75, 77, 84, 93, 94; **III:** 281

Zorach, William, **I:** 260

Zu-Bolton, Ahmos, **Supp. XXVII:** 166, 168

Zuccotti, Susan, **Supp. XVI:** 154

Zuckerman Bound: A Trilogy and Epilogue (P. Roth), **Supp. III Part 2:** 423

Zuckerman Unbound (P. Roth), **Retro. Supp. II:** 283; **Supp. III Part 2:** 421–422

Zueblin, Charles, **Supp. I Part 1:** 5

Zuger, Abigail, **Supp. X:** 160

Zukofsky, Celia (Mrs. Louis), **Supp. III Part 2:** 619–621, 623, 625, 626–629, 631

Zukofsky, Louis, **IV:** 415; **Retro. Supp. I:** 422; **Supp. III Part 2: 619–636;** **Supp. IV Part 1:** 154; **Supp. XIV:** 279, 282, 285, 286–287; **Supp. XXVI:** 224, 226, 227, 229

Zukofsky, Paul, **Supp. III Part 2:** 622, 623–626, 627, 628

Zuleika Dobson (Beerbohm), **Supp. I Part 2:** 714

Zulus (Everett), **Supp. XVIII:** 54, **56–57**

"Zuni Potter: Drawing the Heartline" (Bierds), **Supp. XVII:** 26

Zverev, Aleksei, **Retro. Supp. I:** 278

Zwinger, Ann, **Supp. X:** 29

Zyda, Joan, **Retro. Supp. II:** 52